KW-328-647

R. L. C. Hunter
imrose Cottage
ce of Tilliefoure
Nr. Monymusk, Inverurie
Aberdeenshire AB3 7JB

THE LAW OF CIVIL REMEDIES IN SCOTLAND

THE LAW OF CIVIL REMEDIES IN SCOTLAND

by

DAVID M. WALKER

M.A., LL.B.(Glas.), LL.D.(Lond.), Ph.D., LL.D., Hon.LL.D.(Edin.)

One of Her Majesty's Counsel in Scotland
Of the Middle Temple, Barrister-at-Law
Regius Professor of Law in the
University of Glasgow

Published under the auspices of
THE SCOTTISH UNIVERSITIES LAW INSTITUTE

EDINBURGH
W. GREEN & SON LTD.
1974

First Published 1974

© 1974 The Scottish Universities Law Institute

ISBN 0 414 00563 5

Printed in Great Britain
by The Eastern Press Limited
of London and Reading

PREFACE

THE law of civil remedies does not appear to have previously been regarded as a distinct branch of Scottish private law, nor been examined comprehensively in Scotland, though certain kinds of remedies have previously been the subject of books and many individual kinds of remedies have been discussed in chapters of books dealing primarily with particular branches of substantive law, in relation thereto, and in sections of books dealing with civil procedure. No authority ever appears even to have tried to define or delimit " remedies." The subject has proved difficult to reduce to order and to expound systematically partly by reason of its uncertain scope, and partly because it is very difficult at many points to distinguish questions of remedies from, on the one hand, questions of the substantive rights and duties of parties in particular relationships, and, on the other, questions of procedure, pleading and diligence. Nevertheless the subject has a coherence which makes it well worthy of study and exposition as a whole. It is apparent that sharp divisions cannot be drawn between the rights and duties of parties, the remedies for the infringement of rights and the breach of duties, and the procedure for establishing and enforcing particular remedies, but, because a book on remedies cannot and should not restate all the substantive and procedural law from the standpoint of an aggrieved individual, an attempt has been made severely to limit exposition, on the one hand, of the rights and duties of parties and what constitutes infringement of rights or breach of duty, and, on the other hand, of procedure, practice and diligence. I have accordingly made no attempt to cite fully or discuss the authorities relevant solely or primarily to substantive law or to procedure and diligence. My purpose has been rather to concentrate attention on what remedies are available, the competency of particular remedies in particular circumstances, and the conditions and qualifications applicable to each, and also, in relation to damages, the factors relevant to quantification of damages.

The book deals with, among others, the topics dealt with in my book *The Law of Damages in Scotland*, published in 1955, and includes re-written or very substantially revised versions of much of that book, and it is intended, as well as being a new book of much more extensive coverage, to supersede that book.

I am indebted to the Scottish Universities Law Institute for sponsoring the book, to many colleagues who have stimulated my thoughts, to my wife for her constant patient support, to Mrs. Simpson and Mrs. Buchanan who have laboured to convert my manuscript into typescript, to Mrs. A. M. McLean and Mrs. E. E. Shapiro who prepared the Tables of Cases and of Statutes; to Dr. G. R. Thomson of Messrs. W. Green & Son for his attention to every detail of publication, and to the staff of The Eastern Press for the skill and care which they have devoted to production of the book.

I have tried to take account of all relevant developments in the law down to October 1, 1973.

Department of Private Law,
The University of Glasgow,
Glasgow, G12 8QQ.
October 1, 1973.

D. M. W.

CONTENTS

PART VI

POSSESSORY REMEDIES

PART VII

ENFORCING PERFORMANCE OF DUTIES

PART VIII

SUBSTITUTIONAL REDRESS—DAMAGES

1. Generally

2. Contracts Generally

3. The Particular Contracts

(a) Relative to Personal Relations

8. Statutory Obligations

9. General matters

Part IX

CONSISTORIAL REMEDIES

Part X

ADMIRALTY REMEDIES

Part XI

STATUTORY REMEDIES

Part XII

MISCELLANEOUS REMEDIES

TABLE OF CASES

TABLE OF STATUTES

PART I

INTRODUCTORY

CHAPTER 1

THE SCOPE AND NATURE OF CIVIL REMEDIES

AT the outset of any consideration of the branch of law relating to civil remedies it is necessary to ascertain the general nature of civil remedies and to delimit the scope or area of investigation. The first problem is to consider where civil remedies fit into the general pattern of the divisions and branches of the law of Scotland. Hitherto civil remedies have hardly been regarded as a distinct branch of private law at all, and some remedies, notably dissolution of marriage and damages, have been dealt with chiefly in books on husband and wife, and on contract or delict respectively. It is no doubt convenient to deal with the remedies for breaches of obligations in close connection with the constitution of and the rights and duties attaching to those kinds of obligations, but this approach prevents remedies being looked at as a group. So too some remedies, such as reduction, have in the past been discussed mainly in books on court procedure, giving the impression that remedies are part of procedure, and this also prevents remedies being looked at as a group, in relation to one another, and as a distinct branch of private law.

The classical authorities on Scots law, following the Roman law, divide the subject into law of persons, things and actions,[1] but the last division is treated mainly from the standpoint of the procedure whereby rights may be evidenced, found, and secured. Thus Stair, under the head of actions, having dealt with the jurisdiction of the Court of Session,[2] examines ordinary actions and classifies them [3] as real and personal, principal and accessory actions, and actions declaratory, petitory and possessory, and then [4] deals with the different kinds of declarators, and other actions, and the modes of proof and the decrees following on these processes. Bankton [5] distinguishes actions as perpetual or temporary, civil or criminal, real or personal, *bonae fidei*, *stricti juris* or arbitrary, recuperatory or penal, private or popular, ordinary or extraordinary, and distinguishes ordinary actions into declaratory, petitory, possessory or accessory, then dealing with proof, decrees and execution thereof. Erskine divides actions into real and personal,[6] reipersecutory or penal,[7] principal

[1] Stair, I, 1, 23; Mack. I, 2, 1; Bankt. I, 1, 85; Ersk. I, 2, 1.
[2] IV, 1–2.
[3] IV, 3, 45.
[4] IV, 4–52.
[5] IV, 24, 1.
[6] IV, 1, 10.
[7] IV, 1, 14.

and accessory,[8] and petitory or possessory, dealing thereafter with probation [9] and sentences or decrees.[10]

Bell, in his *Principles*, broke away from the Roman classification, but, having devoted four books to various groups of rights, devoted the fifth to the evidence and enforcement of rights.

In modern times more thorough analysis of legal concepts seems to require and justify modification of rather than complete jettison of the divisions adopted by the Roman lawyers and the Scottish institutional writers. In particular it justifies distinctions between on the one hand the rights and duties attaching to particular relationships and the consequence of their not being implemented, and on the other between the remedies which the legal system may grant, and the procedural forms and machinery whereby those remedies may be sought and, if the court is satisfied, granted. Remedies, in short, can, and should be, studied separately both from the obligations, breaches of which call for remedies, and from the rules of procedure whereby rights and duties are stated and declared, and remedies awarded for infringement of rights and non-implement of duties.

Substantive law and procedure

One of the orthodox divisions of the law, applicable alike to public and private law, to civil, administrative and criminal law,[11] is into substantive law and procedure. It is impossible, however, completely satisfactorily to say how or where the dividing line should be drawn in any of these branches, though it may be easy in many particular cases to say on which side of the line a particular question falls. One view is that substantive law defines the rights and duties which attach to particular legal persons in particular circumstances, and procedure the means whereby those rights are secured and those duties enforced. Another is that substantive law is concerned with the ends which the administration of justice seeks to achieve and the interests which it seeks to recognise and perfect, and procedure with the machinery whereby those ends are sought to be attained. " So far as the administration of justice is concerned with the application of remedies to violated rights, we may say that the substantive law defines the remedy and the right, while the law of procedure defines the modes and conditions of the application of the one to the other." [12]

8 IV, 1, 18.

9 IV, 2.

10 IV, 3.

11 Public law is partly civil, partly administrative and partly criminal; private law is wholly civil in character. The division into public or private is basically into law concerning the state and man, and law concerning man and man; the division into civil, administrative and criminal is basically according to the courts and procedures whereby the principles are applied and secondarily according to the ends sought to be attained by the different bodies of principles and rules.

12 Salmond, *Jurisprudence* (11th ed.) 504.

The difficulty of this division springs in practice chiefly from the uncertain ambit of the term "procedure." Procedure in a narrow and strict sense covers only the rules prescribing how each form of legal claim is initiated, what steps must be taken, and what stages gone through before the court makes a final order in relation to the controversy, granting or refusing the claim. But procedure is connected with the bodies of rules of jurisdiction, and of evidence, the rules, conventions, usages and understandings, which amount to court practice, the skills of written and oral pleading, the rules as to representation in litigation, as to diligence whereby decrees may, if necessary, be enforced, and as to the expenses of litigation. Sometimes, indeed, the term "procedure" is used generally and compendiously to cover all these distinct bodies of knowledge and legal principles, because all are parts of and concerned with the machinery of finding the rights of parties in particular circumstances and enforcing them, if need be, against other parties, and in the antithesis of substantive law and procedure it is normally this wide, but inaccurate, sense of the term "procedure" that is employed. Substantive law is then the whole remaining bodies of the civil, administrative or criminal law, after deduction of all the topics falling under "procedure."

Substantive law and adjective law

To avoid this confusion of uses of the term "procedure" the term "adjective law" is frequently substituted for procedure in its broader, and inaccurate, sense. Adjective law may be defined as the body of principles, rules and practices which exist to enable rights and duties to be found, declared and made effective. It includes jurisdiction, procedure (in the proper, narrower sense of that word), rules of practice, pleading, evidence, representation, legal aid, diligence and expenses.

Adjective law wider than procedure

The distinction between substantive law and procedure coincides with the distinction between substantive law and adjective law only if one understands "procedure" in the very wide and inaccurate sense, including jurisdiction, evidence, diligence, representation and expenses as well as the rules of procedure strictly so called, together with the less formal rules of pleading and practice. If the term "procedure" is restricted to its strict, narrow and correct usage, covering the steps and stages which may, or must, be taken between initiating a claim and obtaining a final decree, adjective law is much wider than procedure.

The place of remedies

If one accepts this division, do remedies, such as claims for implement of an obligation or for damages for non-implement, fall into the category of substantive law or of procedure (in the broad sense) or adjective law? It is submitted that remedies belong primarily to substantive law, not to adjective law, that, for example, the rights to divorce, to stop goods *in transitu*, or to claim damages, belong to the sphere of the rights and duties of parties to the relationship in question rather than to the sphere of legal machinery. " [Counsel] argued that if the law of England affords no remedy, the defence on that ground raises a question of remedy which must always be determined by the law of the country in which action is brought. That appears to me to be a confusion of things which ought to be distinguished. The method by which a right may be enforced is a question of procedure; but whether there is any remedy at all, or in other words, whether there is a right of action, is not a question of procedure, but a question of legal right depending on the existence of an obligation *ex contractu* or *ex delicto*, and the question of obligation must be determined first, before we can consider what the remedy is." [13]

Yet in *Boys* v. *Chaplin* [14] Lord Hodson said: " The nature of the plaintiff's remedy is a matter of procedure to be determined by the *lex fori*. This includes the quantification of damages, but the question arises whether or not the English remedy sought and obtained by the judgment here fits in with the right as fixed by the foreign, that is the Maltese, law. It is argued that . . . questions such as whether loss of earning capacity or pain and suffering are admissible heads of damage are questions of substantive law distinct from mere quantification which is purely a procedural matter.

" The distinction between substance and procedure was clearly stated by Tindal, C.J. in *Huber* v. *Steiner* [15] and by Lord Brougham in *Don* v. *Lippmann*.[16] The latter said: ' The law on this point is well settled in this country, where this distinction is properly taken, that whatever relates to the remedy to be enforced must be determined by the *lex fori*, the law of the country to the tribunals of which the appeal is made '."

It is unfortunately impossible to accept this; as will be seen later only some topics of remedies are determined by the *lex fori*, and it just confuses the issue to equate the distinctions between substance and procedure and that between rights and remedies. " There certainly seems to be some artifice in regarding a man's right to recover damages for pain and suffering as a matter of procedure. To do so, at any rate, goes well beyond the principle, which I entirely accept, that matters of assessment or quantification, including no doubt the manner in which provision is made for future or prospective losses, are for the *lex fori* to determine.

" Yet, unless the claim can be classified as procedure, there seems no basis on the traditional approach for denying the application of the Maltese law. . . . " [17]

[13] *Evans* v. *Stein* (1904) 7 F. 65, 71, *per* Lord Kinnear.
[14] [1971] A.C. 356, 378.
[15] (1835) 2 Bing. N.C. 202.
[16] (1837) 2 S. & McL. 682, 723.
[17] *Boys* v. *Chaplin* [1971] A.C. 356, 393, *per* Lord Wilberforce.

Remedies distinct from procedure

It is important to distinguish the law of remedies from the procedure whereby a particular remedy is sought. Remedies are those judicial awards which entitle a pursuer or petitioner to some right which, at least to some extent, corrects the results of the misconduct of the defender and renders to the pursuer or petitioner what is deemed justly due to him. Procedure, with which must be conjoined pleading and practice, is the body of rules and customs prescribing what steps have to be taken to request and obtain a remedy from the court. The two though connected are quite independent. It would make no difference in remedy if the Rules of the Court of Session, dealing with procedure, were changed so that nullity of marriage were sought by action and damages by petition, or all claims initiated by special case or some new form of initial writ. Nor would it if the stages of litigation were fundamentally altered. Moreover in some cases a legal remedy can be obtained without resorting to a court or its rules of procedure at all.

Remedies and procedure are nevertheless related in that the choice of the remedy sought may determine the procedure to be followed. Some remedies are, by rules of law or procedure or practice, not competent in particular courts. Some remedies have procedural peculiarities not shared by others. For practical reasons remedies and the procedure for obtaining them cannot be entirely separated.

Rights and remedies

Another common antithesis in legal discourse is that of rights and remedies, which is satisfactory so far as it distinguishes between rights, such as to performance of a contract or to freedom from being injured in person or property, and remedies, such as claims to interdict against threatened injury or damages for breach of contract, but unsatisfactory if and in so far as it implies that a claim for a remedy, such as for interdict or damages, is not a legal right, conferred by the rules of the legal system just as much as is a right to have delivery of goods purchased or a right not to be personally injured. Both categories are equally legal rights, there being correlative duties imposed on other persons, and sanctions for non-implement. A buyer has a legal right to have delivery of the goods sold to him, and he also has a legal right, failing delivery, to have specific implement of the contract or to recover damages for non-delivery. A person has in many circumstances a legal right to have precautions taken so that he is not personally injured, and he also has a legal right, if injury results to him from the due precautions not having been taken, to recover damages as compensation for the injuries. Remedies are accordingly not distinct from rights, but kinds of legal rights.

In *Higgins* v. *Ewing's Trs.*[18] Lord Anderson observed that laws for the limitation of actions were of two kinds—" Those which bar the

[18] 1925 S.C. 440, 449.

remedy and those which extinguish the right—and that the latter form of limitation, being substantive of a party's rights, must be given effect to in whatever court the remedy is sought. . . ." The former kind, it is implied, are procedural.

A variant of this same antithesis is that between law and remedy. " The distinction between the law and the remedy is pointed out by Lord Brougham in the case of *Don*[19] . . . where his Lordship said: 'This question mainly arises upon the defence of prescription. Shall the French or the Scottish law of prescription be applied to the case? The law upon the point is now well settled in this country; the distinction is taken between the contract and the remedy. Whatever relates to the nature of the obligation—*ad valorem contractus*—is to be governed by the law of the country where it was made—the *lex loci*; whatever relates to the remedy, by suits to compel performance, or by action for a breach—*ad decisionem litis*—is to be governed by the *lex fori*—the law of the country to whose courts the application is made for performance or for damages'."[20] The last part of this statement is unacceptably wide; if a contract is made in Scotland for performance there, but malperformance requires an action for damages against the party in breach who, for reasons of jurisdiction, is sued in England, it is just not the case that " whatever relates to the remedy " is governed by English law.

Legal rights, primary or antecedent or substantive, and secondary or consequential or remedial

A more satisfactory view is, therefore, to accept that the principles and rules of Scots law establish and confer on persons both primary or antecedent rights, such as to matrimonial fidelity, to the performance of contracts undertaken, to the observance of reasonable care in conduct to avoid injury in dealings with fellow-men, and many others, and also secondary or consequential or remedial rights, implied adjuncts of primary rights, which come into actuality only if and when a primary legal right exists and has been infringed, and only if a claim to the remedy is made, and which confer consequential legal rights, such as to obtain divorce, or damages or such other remedy as may be prescribed by law as competent and is appropriate. Primary or substantive rights and secondary or remedial rights are both equally legal rights existing by virtue of principles and rules of law.[21] But secondary or remedial rights remain in the background, in potentiality only, so long as parties implement their legal obligations and are brought forward into actuality only if there is breach of obligation and a desire for redress.

Distinct from the remedial rights to which a person is entitled on

19 *Don* v. *Lippmann* (1837) 2 S. & McL. 682, 723. The case raised the question whether a bill, drawn and payable in France, was extinguished by the Scottish sexennial prescription when later sued on in Scotland.

20 *Sheaf S.S. Co.* v. *Compania Transmediterranea*, 1930 S.C. 660, 666, *per* L.J.C. Alness.

21 Paton, *Jurisprudence*, Chap. 23.

infringement of some primary right vested in him are the principles and rules determining by what evidence the infringement may or must be proved, the principles and rules laying down the procedure whereby the chosen remedy may be sought and, if the court agrees, granted, the less formal rules of practice and pleading which govern the manner of seeking the remedy, the rules regulating diligence or the means for enforcing a legal remedy granted by a competent court, and ancillary matters such as rights to professional legal representation, to legal aid, and to expenses for outlays necessarily incurred. Even in the spheres of evidence, procedure and diligence, there are many rules which are truly legal rights, such as the privilege against liability for defamation when testifying, and conclusive presumptions of law, the right to appeal against an unsatisfactory decision, the right to do diligence on a decree without liability in damages, and so on.

Position in international private law

In cases raising problems of international private law, however, a distinction drawn is commonly that between substance and procedure, or between right and remedy, apparently on the assumption that the dividing line in each of these antitheses is drawn at the same point, and the principle stated is usually that the substantive rights of the parties must be determined by a system of law chosen by them or by the circumstances of their relationship, the *lex causae*, but that all matters pertaining to procedure must be determined by the *lex fori*, the law of the courts in which the claim for declaration of rights or the grant or redress is made.[22] Among matters pertaining to " procedure " are usually included the nature and extent of the remedy sought. While it seems obvious that a court in any country can grant an applicant only the remedies competent under its own system of law and procedure, and cannot and should not grant either less or more merely because the parties did in some other jurisdiction the things which have given rise to the claim for remedy and because their conduct would have given rise in that jurisdiction to a different claim, it is a misuse of language to call the nature and extent of a legal remedy a matter of procedure, and it would be better simply to say that, for practical reasons, the competence of remedies is regulated by the *lex fori*, as are all matters of adjective law, such as evidence, procedure, pleading and diligence or execution. It might be slightly better to describe the nature and extent of a legal remedy as a matter of adjective law, as that term is wider than procedure, at least in its strict and narrow sense, but it is submitted that this is still a misuse of language. In fact all the neat phrases on the matter proceed on the premiss that the antitheses of substantive law and procedure, substantive law and adjective law, and right and remedy, are synonymous, and imply a division drawn at the same point in each pair, a division moreover which a competent lawyer will know, without much difficulty, where to draw. In fact this is not so.

[22] See further, Chap. 2, *infra.*

No exact correlation between remedies and particular procedures

Moreover, particular kinds of legal remedies cannot be neatly paired with particular kinds of actions or procedure. Some legal remedies, such as self-help or rescission of a contract, do not require resort to court procedure at all. In other cases one form of procedure, such as the petitory action, seeking payment of money, may be appropriate for the recovery of money unpaid and due as a debt, and also for the recovery of damages, which are quite different forms of remedies, competent in different cases. In Scots law there is accordingly no exact correlation between particular remedies and particular procedure or forms of action; Scots law has never had a strict system of forms of action, in which claims for particular remedies have each their own form of procedure.

In every case, assuming that there has been an infringement of a primary right, the first question is of what remedy or remedies is or are legally competent and appropriate in the circumstances, and the second question is of what procedural means must or should be followed to obtain that remedy, failing voluntary satisfaction by the defender of the pursuer's claim for redress.

Civil remedies

The term " civil remedies " is possibly tautologous, as only the civil courts grant remedies. Remedies or remedial rights make up a branch of civil and not of administrative or of criminal law. Criminal courts impose penalties of various kinds for various kinds of conduct but do not seek to grant remedies to persons aggrieved or harmed by the conduct in question. The same conduct may give rise to a criminal prosecution and also to a civil claim for remedy, but each is, and must proceed as, a distinct case under the appropriate rule of procedure. Similarly, administrative officials and tribunals do not, in the strict sense of the term, grant remedies, but grant legal claims or award legal benefits. Furthermore, the same events may give rise both to a claim for a remedy and to a claim for an award or benefit, but again each claim must proceed independently and follow its own course of procedure.

The term " civil remedies " is, however, useful to distinguish civil legal remedies from administrative remedies obtainable by claim to an administrative officer, such as a social security benefit or an award of compensation for criminal injuries, and political remedies obtained by application to and the intervention of a political person, such as a local councillor or an M.P. In the interests of absolute clarity accordingly the title has been adopted for this branch of law and the subject of this book.

The idea of remedy

The word " remedy " is used repeatedly in statutes,[23] books and cases

[23] *e.g.*, Sale of Goods Act 1893, heading to ss. 49 and 51.

but seems to be nowhere comprehensively defined; it is assumed that everyone knows what a legal remedy is.[24] One finds the phrase " remedy of appeal." [25] But the essential idea is redress for a grievance: " In my view the partner has misconceived his remedy. If he has a grievance . . . then in that case his appropriate remedy was. . . . " [26] In *Goulandris Bros.* v. *Goldman* [27] Pearson J. referred to the *Oxford Dictionary*, which defined " remedy " as " legal redress," and Webster's English Dictionary, which defined it as " the legal means to recover a right or to obtain redress for a wrong." These authorities correctly bring out that the essence of remedy is the idea of redress of wrong or of breach of duty.

In *Smart Bros. Ltd.* v. *Ross* [28] it was held that the owners of goods let on hire-purchase, in resuming possession thereof under a new agreement superseding the hire-purchase contract, were exercising a right, and not a remedy, under the hire-purchase contract, but the nature of the distinction was not inquired into. In *Harvey's Trs.* v. *Harvey* [29] reference was made to " remedies unknown to the common law " which were, in that case, declaratory acts and decrees under the Entail Acts.

The difficulty really arises when one has to decide whether certain conduct which a person may pursue is or is not the exercise of or the claim to a legal remedy, or is merely the adoption of a legal procedure. Thus it would probably be disputed by few that securing payment of money owed, or damages in compensation for harm done, or an order stopping an infringement of rights, are legal remedies, but what of multiplepoinding, or petition for sequestration or liquidation, or special case? Are these distinct remedies or merely names for particular kinds of procedure? There is an argument for saying that they are remedies in that they are means for securing money due, or for securing legal exoneration and discharge on certain conditions and thereby securing relief from pressures.

It is clear in principle that remedies and the procedure or legal machinery whereby they are sought are distinct; it does not matter whether damages are sought by action or by petition or by summary application, stated case or other means; these matters relate to the mode of claim, not the remedy itself.

Civil remedies in public law

In Scots law, while civil remedies have been developed in, and are mainly illustrated in the context of, private law disputes, the general principle is that civil remedies are equally applicable in public law as in private law, as between man and man, government department, local

[24] Jacob's *Law Dictionary* defines it as " The action or means given by Law for the recovery of a right; and it is a maxim of Law, that whenever the Law giveth any thing, it gives a remedy for the same."
[25] *Philp* v. *Reid*, 1927 S.C. 224, 230.
[26] *Macdonald* v. *Inverness Mags.*, 1918 S.C. 141, 150 *per* L.P. Strathclyde.
[27] [1957] 3 All E.R. 100, 111.
[28] [1943] A.C. 84.
[29] 1942 S.C. 582, 584.

authority, public corporation or other person or body having special standing and powers. To this principle there are certain exceptions which will be noted in the proper contexts. But it is important that there are few distinct kinds of civil remedies peculiar to public law.

Ubi jus ibi remedium (where there is a right there is a remedy)

This ancient maxim [30] emphasises the correlative nature of primary and remedial rights, and lays down the general principle that if a primary right exists and is infringed the legal system will as a rule give a remedy. This is generally the case but is not invariably so. A primary right for the infringement of which no right of action is recognised is valueless but may nevertheless exist. Does an individual have no right of privacy, no right to be free from interference, eavesdropping and unwelcome publicity, or does he have such a right but no remedy is given for infringement of it, unless on other grounds? Parliamentary privilege and Acts of Indemnity may result in the refusal of a remedy for what was otherwise an actionable wrong.

Furthermore, a remedy is not necessarily given purely because a person complains of having suffered loss or harm. The loss or harm may be *damnum sine injuria* and loss without breach of duty or infringement of right gives no claim. " The infliction of damage on a plaintiff [*sic*] does not in itself give a cause of action. Damage due to the legitimate exercise of a right is not actionable, even if the actor contemplates the damage. It is *damnum absque injuria*. The damage must be attributable to the breach by the defendant of some duty owing to the plaintiff." [31] A right, or duty owed, and infringement thereof are essential for the claim of a remedy.

Furthermore, if a right exists and is infringed, it is not always necessary, to make a remedy competent, that there should have been any consequential harm or loss. Thus in some cases damages will be given on account of the mere breach of obligation and for resulting inconvenience though no actual loss be proved.

Lex semper dabit remedium (The law will always give a remedy)

This maxim similarly lays down a general principle which is generally accepted but not invariable.[32] If there is a substantial grievance, a complaint of infringement of right, the court will be slow to deny the complainer any remedy. But it will not neccessarily give him the remedy he seeks.

30 See generally Broom's *Legal Maxims*; *Ashby* v. *White* (1703) 2 Ld. Raym. 938; *Constantine* v. *Imperial Hotels* [1944] K.B. 693; *Best* v. *Samuel Fox & Co.* [1951] 2 K.B. 639.
It was cited in *Young* v. *Rankin*, 1934 S.C. 499, 515, 516. On the latter page Lord Murray said that the question in that case was whether there was any *jus*, that is to say, *jus actionis*. This seems incorrect. A right to give rise to a remedy need not be a right of action in court. It may also be a right to do something at one's own hand.

31 *Bourhill* v. *Young*, 1942 S.C. (H.L.) 78, 89, *per* Lord Wright.

32 *Young* v. *Rankin*, 1934 S.C. 499, 518.

In *Steven* v. *Broady Norman & Co.*[33] Lord Anderson said: " As every wrong has a remedy, a person wronged is entitled to invoke the aid of the court until he has succeeded in obtaining the remedy which is his due. Put more briefly, a litigant is entitled to sue, and to keep on suing, until he has obtained satisfaction for his wrong."

A court may, and frequently has to, deny a complainer the remedy he seeks, or on the ground he seeks it, or on the evidence with which he supports his claim, but that does not mean that there is no remedy.

Nature of civil remedies

Remedial rights are accordingly legal rights permitted or granted by law to an aggrieved person, so far as possible to set right what another party has failed to do, or has done wrongfully, in breach of a legal right vested in the aggrieved person. They are remedial, not punitive, in purpose, and in consequence attention must be focussed on the complainer and on what harm or loss he alleges he has suffered, not on the nature or wrongness of the defender's conduct.

Common law and statutory remedies

Remedial rights exist both at common law and under statute. Statutory remedies may consist in the application of a common law remedy such as a claim of damages, to circumstances which do not at common law give a claim for damages, such as for some breaches of statutory duty, or in the conferment by statute of a remedial right which does not exist at all by common law, such as to enforce performance of a statutory duty. The latter kind may also require a special course of procedure.

In *Harvey's Trs.* v. *Harvey* [34] the question was raised whether the entitlement of parties to a special case to the fee of a share of heritage [35] could be decided in that special case. Lord Justice-Clerk Cooper observed " Section 47 and section 48 of the Rutherford Act [36] are two of the many provisions of the Entail Acts which introduce remedies unknown to the common law, and the Acts prescribe in detail the procedure to be followed when these new remedies are invoked . . . I am prepared to affirm that, where a party wishes a judgment of the court on the question whether he can invoke a special statutory remedy for which a special procedure with special effects is prescribed, the proper method of testing the matter is to present the appropriate statutory application."

Lord Mackay said [37]: " To my mind this is essentially one of these cases where a statutory new right or remedy is prescribed, coupled with a carefully defined and entirely novel method of enforcement, to which

[33] 1928 S.C. 351, 365.
[34] 1942 S.C. 582, 584.
[35] Under the Entail Amendment (Rutherford) Act 1848, ss. 47–48.
[36] Entail Amendment Act 1848.
[37] p. 587.

I drew attention in the Riot Act case, *Pompa's Trs.* v. *Edinburgh Magistrates*."[38]

Lord Jamieson said[39]: "Now, where an Act provides a remedy and prescribes how such remedy may be made effectual, the procedure so laid down must be complied with."

Statutory remedies for statutory liability

Where statute imposes a duty or liability which did not exist at all at common law, the remedy provided therefor is necessarily a statutory one, though it may take the form of using a common law name and common law form. Thus a statutory duty relative to the construction of window sashes was held to give rise to no civil remedy available to a person allegedly injured in consequence of non-implement of the duty.[40] If special machinery is incorporated in the statute for enforcing compliance with the statutory obligation, the general rule is that performance cannot be enforced in any other manner.[41] The question of the remedy is one of the interpretation of the particular statute and section thereof in every case.[42]

Scope of civil remedies

The scope of the subject of civil remedies can accordingly be described only by saying that it is the branch of the private and civil law concerned with the consequential legal rights which come into existence if and when one party to a legal relationship has been in breach of some legal duty owed by him to the other party and has thereby infringed a right vested in that other party, justifying the latter in expecting performance or implement of what that duty required. A claim for a remedy always implies the existence of a prior legal right, and infringement thereof, or a prior legal duty on the other party and non-implement thereof.

It has been observed that in the older English law the existence of a right depended on the existence of a remedy, on whether there had already been recognised a form of action giving a remedy for the complainer in the circumstances which had arisen, whereas in Scots law the availability of a remedy has always depended on the recognition of the legal right, infringement of which is alleged. This is in fact correct. If there is a legally recognised right, and it has been infringed, there must be a remedy. To some extent the choice of remedy is in the complainer's hands, to some extent it is defined by rules of law. Conversely, if there is no right infringed, there can be no remedy.

Furthermore, if only to keep the discussion within bounds, in considering what civil remedies are recognised by the Scottish courts, and

38 1942 S.C. 119.
39 p. 590.
40 *Pullar* v. *Window Clean Ltd.*, 1956 S.C. 13.
41 *Pasmore* v. *Oswaldtwistle U.D.C.* [1898] A.C. 387, 394; *Cutler* v. *Wandsworth Stadium Ltd.* [1949] A.C. 398, 407.
42 *Cutler, supra.*

may be granted by them, one cannot consider in detail what primary rights are or are not recognised and what interests are or are not protected by the law. The discussion of these topics, *e.g.* whether particular conduct amounts to adultery as a breach of the other spouse's right to sexual fidelity, or whether there is a right to have one's privacy respected, is a matter for other branches of law. The discussion of remedies must proceed on the basis of accepting the primary rights and duties of parties defined by those other branches of the substantive law, the law of persons, contracts, delict, property, trusts, and so on. If one of these branches accepts that there is no right, *e.g.* no right to complain of even malicious harm by competition in trade, that is a matter of that branch of law, not of the branch of law dealing with remedies. But it follows that there will be no remedy, no secondary or consequential remedial right, if there has been no recognised primary or substantive right to be infringed. The possibility of a secondary or consequential remedial right depends on the legally recognised existence of a primary or substantive right, and on its not having been implemented.

Overlapping and conflicting claims

In various circumstances an individual who has suffered harm or loss may also have legal claims which are not claims for a civil remedy as herein defined. Thus he may have a claim against his insurer under a policy of insurance, or a claim for some social security benefit under the National Insurance or National Insurance (Industrial Injuries) Acts, or a claim on the Criminal Injuries Compensation Board for compensation, or a claim on a charitable fund set up to assist such persons as himself, or some other kind of claim. The conditions under which a person may have one or more such claims is discussed in books dealing with these various kinds of claims.[43] None of these claims is a kind of civil remedy, as that term is used in this book. But the existence of these other kinds of claims raises the possibility of overlap or conflict of claims.

The general principle is that a claim for a civil remedy may be made independently, of, without prejudice to, and unprejudiced by, the making of a separate claim on any such ground, or the recovery of any money under any such separate claim. Whether and how far any recovery of money or property by way of civil remedy affects the competency or amount of any award under any such other claim depends on the rules regulating that other claim. Whether and how far any recovery under any such other claim affects the competency or amount of any award of a civil remedy is discussed at the appropriate points hereafter.

[43] See *e.g. Preston and Colinvaux on Insurance*; Ivamy, *General Principles of Insurance Law*; Potter and Stansfield, *National Insurance*; Potter and Stansfield, *National Insurance (Industrial Injuries) Act*; Vester and Cartwright, *Industrial Injuries*. For Criminal Injuries Compensation, see Appendix 2 and *Walker on Delict*, Vol. II, Appx. For Social Security Benefit, see Appendix 3.

The choice of the appropriate remedy

The choice of the legal remedy appropriate for an individual who believes that he has a grievance depends on what kind of loss he has suffered, personal injury, loss of a relative, loss of or damage to property, interference with an economic interest, what kind of remedy he wants, restitution, stopping of the harm, compensation or otherwise, on what is the legal ground of his complaint, *e.g.* whether breach of contract, breach of general duty not to harm, breach of trust, breach of statutory duty, and on knowledge of what legal remedies exist and of the competency in different circumstances of those different kinds of remedies. To advise an aggrieved client accordingly requires a knowledge of what kinds of legal remedies are allowed or may be granted by the Scottish civil courts, in what circumstances each is competent and appropriate, and what conditions affect each. This knowledge is the subject-matter of this book.

The taking of proceedings to obtain a particular remedy may be further limited by questions whether the court, or a particular court, has in the circumstances jurisdiction to grant the remedy sought, whether the complainer has in the circumstances sufficient title and interest to sue for the remedy sought, whether the defender or respondent called is the person truly liable to be ordered by the court to do what is necessary to effect the remedy, whether the complainer can make averments relevant to justify the court in ordering the remedy sought, and whether, in case of dispute as to matters of fact, the complainer can satisfy the court of the facts necessary to found his claim.

The third factor mentioned, the competency of a particular legal remedy in particular circumstances, is the fundamental one, and most of the present book is concerned with the circumstances in which particular remedies are competent or incompetent. The choice of remedy is in fact mainly determined by what is competent in the circumstances. In the particular case of damages or pecuniary compensation the further questions arise where damages are competent, what factors should be included in or excluded from account in fixing the sum to be awarded as damages, and what sum of money is appropriate in the circumstances?

The court frequently holds that it cannot grant the remedy sought; this does not mean that there is no remedy, but only that the remedy actually claimed cannot be granted. Thus a court cannot modify or re-form a contract.[44]

Court's discretion in granting remedy

In general if a person's claim satisfies the requirements he is entitled to his remedy and the court has no discretion to grant or withhold or qualify it. But in some cases the court has discretion.

44 *Steuart's Trs.* v. *Hart* (1875) 3 R. 192; *Pender-Small* v. *Kinloch's Trs.*, 1917 S.C. 307.

"It appears to me that a superior court, having equitable jurisdiction, must also have a discretion, in certain exceptional cases, to withhold from parties applying for it that remedy which, in ordinary circumstances, they would be entitled as a matter of course. In order to justify the exercise of such a discretionary power there must be some very cogent reason for depriving litigants of the ordinary means of enforcing their legal rights. There are, so far as I know, only three decided cases,[45] in which the Court of Session, there being no facts sufficient to raise a plea in bar of the action, have nevertheless denied to the pursuer the remedy to which, in strict law, he was entitled. These authorities seem to establish, if that were necessary, the proposition that the court has the power of declining, upon equitable grounds, to enforce an admittedly legal right; but they also show that the power has been very rarely exercised." [46]

In that case the House of Lords, affirming the Court of Session, held that an order to remove buildings which had been completed pending litigation to interdict their erection would not be granted when the respondents had offered to give open ground in substitution for that wrongfully built on.

Lord Watson further [47] indicated the considerations which moved him to refuse the remedy sought in that case, namely that the respondents in that case had an interest on both sides of the litigation, and that the alternative offer was *res noviter* and had emerged since the interdict was first granted. In the result the House made an order declaratory of the rights of parties instead of an order on the respondents to remove buildings.

Types of civil remedial rights

The major distinction of civil remedial rights is into two categories. Firstly, there are those rights which may be invoked and exercised by a person at his own hand, without need to resort to any court or legal procedure. In some cases a right of this kind exists by bare force of law, such as a right of retention, but in other cases the right must have been applied to the parties' relationship by contract and cannot otherwise be invoked; an instance is an irritancy clause in a contract.[48]

The other, and larger, category comprises those remedial rights which can be granted only by a competent civil court on application being made to it according to its jurisdictional and procedural rules and, so far as necessary, after satisfying it by legal argument and evidence of disputed facts. This category comprises judicial declarations of rights, orders prohibiting breaches of duty, compelling performance of duties, ordering

45 *Macnair* v. *Cathcart* (1795) Mor. 12832; *Sanderson* v. *Geddes* (1874) 1 R. 1198; *Begg* v. *Jack* (1876) 3 R. 35; all explained in *Grahame, infra.*
46 *Grahame* v. *Kirkcaldy Mags.* (1882) 9 R.(H.L.) 91, 92, *per* Lord Watson.
47 At p. 95.
48 Parts II and III (Chaps. 3–7), *infra.*

payment, compensating for loss caused by breach of duty, and various other cases.[49]

In a very broad sense every application made to a civil court may be said to be remedial but in many applications the request to the court is for assistance, guidance, authority or sanction rather than for remedy or redress; it seems stretching the general understanding of " remedy " to say that obtaining the appointment of a judicial factor or a grant of powers to trustees, or a decision in a special case on the interpretation of a will, or the appointment of an executor, is a " remedy."

The older classification of actions was into principal actions, brought to enforce or protect a right, and accessory actions, which are truly judicial steps of procedure incidental to other actions. Principal actions are rescissory, declaratory, petitory or possessory.[50] The chief accessory actions are exhibition of writings, transumpt, proving the tenor, transference and of wakening.[51]

A more satisfactory classification is into proceedings properly remedial and proceedings administrative, executorial or accessory, without regard to whether the proceedings are initiated by action, petition or otherwise. The former includes actions declaratory, rescissory, petitory and possessory, and also actions preventive and competitive and claims peculiar to consistorial and Admiralty jurisdiction. The latter includes under administrative proceedings the cognition of the insane, appointment of factors and trustees, the grant of authority to trustees, entail petitions, adoption of children, many petitions relative to companies and the like.

Under executorial proceedings fall those concerned with the execution of decrees and the doing of diligence, such as adjudication for debt, furthcoming, poinding of the ground, and sequestration, and accessory proceedings, which are normally ancillary to substantive actions, such as proving of the tenor.

[49] Parts IV–X (Chaps. 8–75), *infra*.
[50] Ersk. IV, 1, 18.
[51] Ersk. IV, 1, 52.

CHAPTER 2

PROBLEMS ARISING IN CASES WITH A FOREIGN ELEMENT

CASES in which some material factual element is non-Scottish and which consequently raise a problem of international private law or conflict of laws, may give rise to acute difficulties in relation to remedies. Of the possible systems of law concerned in any particular such case, which determines what remedy may be granted and any conditions or qualifications attaching to the remedy?

One of the most common general statements in books and cases on this topic is that the substantive rights of parties are governed by the *lex causae*, the system of law most appropriate to regulate those rights, which may be a foreign system of law, but that matters of procedure are regulated exclusively by the *lex fori.*[1] In this context " procedure " seems to be used in a wide sense, covering not merely the rules of procedure in court, but actionability, title to sue and liability to defend, the competency of particular courts, evidence, procedure *stricto sensu*, practice and pleading, enforcement, representation, legal aid and expenses, and apparently covering also the remedies competent, conditions qualifying them, and the terms and measures of any remedy granted. Thus reference has been made to " procedural (or adjectival or non-substantive) law." [2] If it means procedure in the narrow sense of the steps of litigation it is undoubtedly true, but wholly unhelpful because it does not deal with remedies.

The difficulty about this general principle lies in delimiting in practice the spheres of substantive law and of adjective law or " procedure," and of deciding whether a particular matter belongs to " procedure " or not, when it is apparent that " procedure " may mean more than the prescribed series of formalities which have to be gone through to present a complaint to a court and obtain a judicial order, which is what is meant in its strict and narrow sense. " Substance " and " procedure " cannot be assigned to clear-cut categories.[3] The " line " between them does not exist to be discovered by logic and analysis, but has to be drawn in accordance with

[1] Story, *Conflict of Laws*, § 556; Westlake, *Private International Law*, § 341; Cheshire, *Private International Law*, 581; Anton, *Private International Law*, 541; Dicey and Morris, *Conflict of Laws*, (8th ed.) 1089; Morris, *The Conflict of Laws*, 455; *British Linen Co.* v. *Drummond* (1830) 10 B. & C. 903; *De la Vega* v. *Vianna* (1830) 1 B. & Ad. 284; *Huber* v. *Steiner* (1835) 2 Bing.N.C. 202; *Don* v. *Lippmann* (1837) 2 S. & McL. 682, 723; *Williamson* v. *Taylor* (1845) 8 D. 156; *Boys* v. *Chaplin* [1971] A.C. 356.

[2] *Boys* v. *Chaplin* [1971] A.C. 356, 394, *per* Lord Pearson.

[3] Cook, *Logical and Legal Basis of Conflict of Laws*, 154 *et seq.*

the convenience of the court and the need to achieve justice.[4] The general principle does not take one far and the individual problems encountered in seeking a remedy where the case involves a non-Scottish element must be examined individually. The drawing of the " line," so far as that is of use, must, in a matter arising before a Scottish court, be determined by Scots law.

The fact is that the general principle does not help at all, and that each issue in a case involving a non-Scottish element must be considered separately. The only useful distinction is between matters determined by the *lex causae*, which may be a foreign system, and matters determined by the *lex fori* (Scots law). If one likes, the former may then be labelled as matters of substance, and the latter as matters of procedure, but to do so is unnecessary and unhelpful.

Jurisdiction over defender

The first question is inevitably: Does the Scottish court appealed to for a remedy have jurisdiction over the defender? A Scottish court must always decide this issue by the *lex fori*, by its own rules of law and practice as to jurisdiction, with reference to the kind of controversy in issue and the kind of remedy sought.[5] What these rules are are stated elsewhere.[6] The fact that some other system of law takes the view that the Scottish courts have or have not jurisdiction is irrelevant. Jurisdiction cannot be assumed or enlarged because by some other system of law, also involved in the case, the Scottish court would have had jurisdiction, or a wider jurisdiction, nor denied because by some other system the Scottish courts would have had no jurisdiction. Related matters, such as whether Scotland is *forum non conveniens*, must also be determined by Scots law.[7]

Subsidiary to this is the secondary jurisdictional problem; does the particular kind of Scottish court actually appealed to have jurisdiction over the proposed defender to grant the kind of remedy sought? Thus even if the Scottish courts have jurisdiction, only the Court of Session, but no sheriff court, has jurisdiction to grant decree of divorce. The secondary jurisdictional problem must be solved by the Scottish courts according to their *lex fori*.

Title to sue

The second practical question is whether the party designated as pursuer or petitioner in a claim for a remedy from a Scottish court has a

[4] *Cf. Boys* v. *Chaplin* [1971] A.C. 356, 394, *per* Lord Pearson: " I do not think there is any exact and authoritative definition of the boundary between substantive law and procedural (or adjectival or non-substantive) law, and the boundary remains to be settled by further decisions in particular cases."

[5] This proposition never seems to have been questioned and always to have been treated as axiomatic. *Cf. Hamlyn* v. *Talisker Distillery* (1894) 21 R. (H.L.) 21 (whether arbitration clause excluded jurisdiction of courts).

[6] Duncan and Dykes, *Principles of Civil Jurisdiction, passim*; Anton, *Private International Law, passim*; Walker, *Principles of Scottish Private Law*, Chap. 11.

[7] *Orr Ewing's Trs.* v. *Orr Ewing* (1885) 13 R. (H.L.) 1.

title to sue, in the circumstances disclosed, for the kind of remedy sought. Title to sue is a facet of the actionability of a claim and must be determined by the system of law which regulates its actionability. As was said in a delict case: " When considering whether the act or omission complained of is ' actionable ' by the *lex loci delicti*, the Scottish courts will not limit the inquiry to the question whether the act or omission is actionable in the abstract, but will extend it to the further question—On whom does the *lex loci delicti* confer a *jus actionis*, and for what? " [8] Thus though a woman may in Scotland sue for damages for being seduced,[9] a woman was held not entitled to sue when the alleged seduction had taken place in England since by English law (*lex loci delicti*) the wrong was at that time actionable only by her parent or employer.[10] She had no title to sue, or alternatively the wrong was not an actionable one, at least not *by her*, by the *lex loci delicti*. Again, since an executrix has a title by English law to sue for pecuniary loss caused to the dependants of a deceased,[11] and for loss caused to his estate by the death,[12] such an executrix would doubtless have had a title to sue in Scotland for these claims where the death had been caused in England, if she brought her action timeously,[13] even though if the cause of action had arisen in Scotland the title to sue would have been vested in the surviving relatives of the deceased,[14] and the executrix could not have claimed for pain caused to the deceased before his death,[15] but only for any pecuniary loss to him between the time of injury and his death,[16] nor for any loss of financial support falling on surviving close relatives.[17]

In what style and name a claimant claims will, however, always be regulated by Scots law as *lex fori*.[18]

Liability to be sued

The third question is: who should be sued? The party properly liable to be sued is the party who, by the system of law properly applicable to the cause, such as the proper law of the contract, or the *lex loci delicti*, was in breach of duty or otherwise legally responsible for the happenings believed to justify a remedy. Thus whether a foreign principal is liable under a contract depends on the proper law of the contract.[19] Whether a party is vicariously liable for a wrong committed outside Scotland depends on whether, and under what conditions, he would be liable by

[8] *McElroy* v. *McAllister*, 1949 S.C. 110, 135, *per* L.P. Cooper.
[9] *e.g. Murray* v. *Fraser*, 1916 S.C. 623.
[10] *Rosses* v. *Bhagvat Sinhjee* (1891) 19 R. 31. In English law all right of action for seduction of a child has now been abolished: Law Reform (Misc. Prov.) Act 1970, s. 5.
[11] Fatal Accidents Acts 1846–1959.
[12] Law Reform (Misc. Prov.) Act 1934.
[13] *McElroy, supra*; see on this point Lord Russell at p. 125.
[14] *Eisten* v. *N. B. Ry.* (1870) 8 M. 980.
[15] *Stewart* v. *L.M.S. Ry.*, 1943 S.C. (H.L.) 19; *Smith* v. *Duncan Stewart & Co.*, 1960 S.C. 329.
[16] *Smith* v. *Duncan Stewart & Co.*, 1961 S.C. 91.
[17] *Stewart, supra.*
[18] *Jones* v. *Somervell's Tr.*, 1907 S.C. 545.
[19] *Girvin, Roper & Co.* v. *Monteith* (1895) 23 R. 129.

the *lex loci delicti.*[20] Whether parties are jointly, or jointly and severally, liable, depends on whether, by the *lex causae,* such liability exists in such circumstances.[21]

Actionability of conduct complained of

The fourth question is whether the conduct complained of is civilly actionable in Scotland, which depends on whether the system of law which determines the substantive rights of the parties in the circumstances recognises what has happened as giving rise to a claim for a civil remedy. That the conduct should also be civilly actionable by Scots law is at least sometimes also required. Thus if by the law of Ruritania selling goods in that country under a false trade description is civilly actionable as a breach of contract, a Scottish importer, deceived thereby, may probably sue for damages in Scotland (assuming that he can found jurisdiction) though he could not do so in a case where his rights were determined solely by Scots law.[22] If such conduct is by Ruritanian law civilly actionable as a delict the Scottish importer probably cannot sue in Scotland because an alleged delict must be actionable both by the *lex loci delicti* and by Scots law,[23] and the conduct is probably not delictual by Scots law.

In cases of breach of contract the rights of parties (including the questions whether there was an enforceable contract, and whether in the circumstances there has been unjustifiable breach) fall to be determined by the proper law of the contract,[24] which may be the *lex loci contractus,* the *lex loci solutionis,* or some other system deemed to be that with which the contract has the most substantial connection.

In cases of delict the conduct complained of must be civilly actionable both by the *lex loci delicti* and by the *lex fori.*[25] If the wrong complained of is not actionable by Scots law it cannot be sued on in a Scottish court merely because it would have founded an action in the *forum delicti.* If it was delictual by Scots law but by the *lex loci delicti* it was legally permissible or justifiable and not civilly actionable, no action is competent in Scotland.[26] Similarly, if by the *lex loci delicti* the conduct gives rise only to a claim for social welfare benefits,[27] or to another special form of remedy, or it has been excused by statute,[28] or any claim has been excluded by contract,[29] or it has been settled by agreement, it is not actionable in

20 *Cf. General S.N. Co.* v. *Guillon* (1843) 11 M. & W. 877; *The Halley* (1868) L.R. 2 P.C. 193.
21 *Cf. Bullock* v. *Caird* (1875) L.R. 10 Q.B. 276.
22 Trade Descriptions Act 1968, s. 35.
23 *McElroy* v. *McAllister,* 1949 S.C. 110.
24 On this see Anton, 185; Cheshire, 215; Dicey and Morris, 767.
25 *McElroy* v. *McAllister,* 1949 S.C. 110.
26 *e.g.* defamatory matter communicated only to the pursuer and not published to anyone else is not actionable by English law. *Cf. The Mary Moxham* (1876) 1 P.D. 107.
27 *Walpole* v. *Canadian Northern Ry.* [1923] A.C. 113; *McMillan* v. *Canadian Northern Ry.* [1923] A.C. 120.
28 *Phillips* v. *Eyre* (1870) L.R. 6 Q.B. 1; *Carr* v. *Fracis Times & Co.* [1902] A.C. 120.
29 *Cf. McKay* v. *Scottish Airways,* 1948 S.C. 254.

the Scottish courts any more than it would be if excused or defeated or settled by Scots law. If it gives rise only to a criminal prosecution and to no civil remedy it may not be actionable in Scotland, and it is not actionable if the conduct were merely a moral wrong by the *lex loci delicti.*[30]

The theory that actionability of a delict should depend on the proper law of the delict *i.e.* the legal system with which the delict has the most substantial connection,[31] has not yet been discussed or adopted in Scotland. In England it has been discussed and criticised as unreliable.[31a] It would certainly lead to bizarre results, such as that a tort in Malta is regulated only by English law if both parties are English and one sues the other in England,[31] but, presumably, regulated by Scots law if the parties are Scottish and the action in Scotland. If Frenchman injured German in Malta, and sued him in Italy, *quid juris*? Can one in any circumstances, that is, disregard the *lex loci delicti* completely?

Qualifications of actionability—prescriptions and limitations

Actionability includes also any inherent qualifications or restrictions on the claimant's right of action, attached thereto by the *lex causae*, such as that the action must be brought within a restricted time, failing which it ceases to be actionable or the cause of action is totally extinguished. Thus in *McElroy* v. *McAllister* [32] one reason for rejecting the pursuer's claim as executrix was that she founded on a right conferred by an English statute, which right had to be enforced by claim brought within one year, and that period had elapsed. This limitation was deemed an inherent qualification of the pursuer's right of action.

A distinction has to be drawn between prescriptions proper, which wholly extinguish a cause of action after the lapse of a stated period, and limitations (though sometimes called prescriptions), which provide that after the lapse of a stated time a cause of action is no longer actionable, though they do not necessarily wholly extinguish the cause of action, or which provide that a cause of action is subject to stated restrictions and qualifications, such as the need to prove absence of good faith, or malice and lack of probable cause, or the need to prove it by specially limited modes of proof, as under the Scottish triennial and other short prescriptions.[33]

A prescription proper depends primarily on the *lex causae*, in that if a right is conferred in particular circumstances by a given system of law, that system must also determine when that right ceases to exist as a ground of action.[34] But this is subject to the overriding rule that the *lex causae*

30 *McElroy*, *supra*, explaining *McLarty* v. *Steele* (1881) 8 R. 435.
31 Advocated by J. H. C. Morris in (1949) 12 M.L.R. 248 in a note on *McElroy* v. *McAllister*, *supra*, and discussed in *Boys* v. *Chaplin* [1971] A.C. 356.
31a *Boys*, *supra*.
32 1949 S.C. 110.
33 *Cf. Huber* v. *Steiner* (1835) 2 Bing.N.C. 203; *Don* v. *Lippmann* (1837) 2 S. & MacL. 682.
34 *Cf. Harris* v. *Quine* (1869) L.R. 4 Q.B. 653; *McElroy*, *supra*.

cannot override or avoid the effect of a prescription applicable by Scots law as *lex fori*, such as the long negative prescription.[35]

A limitation proper is, however, a rule of procedural character in that it must be for the *lex fori* to say when it will decline to enforce a right, and it can hardly refuse to apply its own rule because the right has been acquired under another system. Thus an action claiming damages for personal injury must in Scotland be, in general, brought within three years.[36] If action is brought in Scotland this rule must be applied by the Scottish courts even if by the *lex loci delicti*, which conferred the right of action, action might have been brought within some longer period. In *British Linen Co.* v. *Drummond*[37] the English courts applied the English limitation of six years to an action on a Scottish contract, although it would have been actionable for forty years in Scotland.

A Scottish court must determine whether a provision is truly a prescription or a limitation, which may involve investigation of foreign law, if it is averred that a right under foreign law is subject to such a qualification.[38]

Nature of the remedy

It is clear that the nature of the remedy claimed, and of the remedy which may be granted, is determined in a Scottish litigation by Scots law alone. Hence a pursuer may be entitled by Scots law to other or greater or lesser remedies for the infringement of his rights than he could have claimed if he had sued in other courts. Conversely he cannot obtain from a Scottish court any remedy not competent under Scots law merely because he might have obtained that remedy from another court. What remedies are competent by Scots law and in what circumstances are discussed hereafter.[39] But not everything relating to the remedy is determined by Scots law.

Rights exercisable by party at his own hand

It seems that remedial rights, such as of retention or lien, or of compensation, appear to be exercisable in Scotland according to Scottish rules, whatever the proper law of the transaction giving rise to the claim thereto.[40]

Claims competent

If the general class of remedy, such as a claim for damages, is one competent by Scots law, what kind of claims within that general class

[35] *Low* v. *Low* (1893) 1 S.L.T. 43; *Stirling's Trs.* v. *Legal & General Assce. Socy. Ltd.*, 1957 S.L.T. 73.
[36] Prescription and Limitation (Scotland) Act, 1973, ss. 17–19.
[37] (1830) 10 B. & C. 903.
[38] *Higgins* v. *Ewing's Trs.*, 1925 S.C. 440. *Cf. Westminster Bank* v. *McDonald*, 1955 S.L.T. (Notes) 73.
[39] Chaps. 3–75, *infra*.
[40] *Robertson & Co.'s Tr.* v. *Bairds* (1852) 14 D. 1010.

can be made depends on the *lex causae*. Thus, if by Ruritanian law an employee wrongfully dismissed from an employment regulated by that law can claim for loss of earnings till re-employed and also for hurt to feelings caused by the manner of dismissal, he can claim under both heads in a Scottish court, even though if the employment had been regulated by Scots law, he would have had no claim under the latter head.[41]

Similarly, in *Kremezi* v. *Ridgway*,[42] a case of breach of a promise of marriage made and to be performed in England between an Englishman and a Greek girl, it was held that the English court had jurisdiction and that English law governed the contract and applied also to the question of remedy. Under English law damages were at large, but under Greek law they were limited to the cost of the trousseau and other expenses necessitated by the contract and lost through its breach. There was, however, no real discussion of the ground for holding that English law governed the kind of claims competent, whether as being *lex causae* or *lex fori.*

Again by Scots law a widow may claim from the person who caused her husband's death damages in name of solatium for the pain and grief felt at the loss, damages for the financial support lost by reason of the death, and reimbursement of funeral and other expenses.[43] The claims for solatium and for loss of support, though normally claimed together in a single undivided claim, are independent rights and claims, not merely heads of a single claim of damages.[44] If a widow sues in Scotland in respect of her husband's death caused in England, she cannot make the claim for solatium because that is a kind of claim not recognised by English law, the *lex loci delicti.*[44]

Heads of damages

By " heads of damages " are meant distinct kinds or items of injury or loss which may be considered in assessing damages. Thus injury to feelings, physical pain and suffering, loss of earnings, damage to reputation, financial loss by reason of damage to or destruction of property, expenses and outlays, and so on are all distinct " heads of damages." What heads of damages can be taken into account in a particular case is an aspect of actionability. If the wrongdoer is liable at all by the law of X, that law must also state for what *damna* he is liable. Thus " an act done in England without reasonable care by a defendant which causes the death of a third party is actionable in a suit brought on behalf of a dependant of the deceased if its consequence is pecuniary loss to the dependant. It is not actionable if its consequences is only injury to the health or happiness of a survivor of the deceased. . . . The ' heads of damages,' as distinct from the ' quantification of damages ' sustained under

[41] *Addis* v. *Gramophone Co.* [1909] A.C. 488.
[42] [1949] 1 All E.R. 662.
[43] Chap. 54, *infra.*
[44] *Naftalin* v. *L.M.S. Ry.*, 1933 S.C. 259; *McElroy* v. *McAllister*, 1949 S.C. 110.

each head, are matters of substantive law on which the decider of fact, whether jury or judge, has no discretion to give effect to an idiosyncratic opinion. For what is compendiously called ' assessment of damages ' involves two distinct inquiries. The first is to ascertain what loss or injury of the particular kind or kinds which make the defendant's act ' actionable ' were in fact sustained by the plaintiff as a consequence of the defendant's act. It would be too irrational, even for English law, if this inquiry were conducted by applying any different criteria than those which determine whether the act of the defendant is actionable at all. The second inquiry is to estimate what is the appropriate monetary equivalent of the loss or injury so ascertained. In this inquiry the court cannot do otherwise than form its own idiosyncratic estimate.

" Where because the act of the defendant has been committed abroad, the law to be applied in determining whether the act was actionable at all is the *lex loci delicti*, the first inquiry involved in the assessment of damages is, in my opinion, to be conducted by applying the criteria as to ' heads of damage ' provided by the *lex loci delicti*. . . . " [45]

Diplock L.J. accordingly held that, in the circumstances of the case before him, as under the *lex loci delicti* physical injuries did not give rise to civil liability for pain and suffering, no damages were recoverable under that head of damages, but damages were recoverable under the head of loss of earnings, which loss alone was actionable by the *lex loci delicti.*

On the other hand, in the same case Lord Upjohn thought [46] that

> " the ordinary rule must apply, namely, that even if, contrary to my opinion, the *lex loci delicti* applies to questions of substantive law, all questions of the remedy, both as to its nature and kinds or heads of assessment of pecuniary damage, must be determined in an English action entirely by English principles . . . . The rule that the *lex fori* must be applied to all questions of the remedy is clear and simple and gives rise to no difficulty in its application; it does no injustice, for I cannot see any injustice in claiming damages here of a kind or head which, by some local rule of the *locus delicti*, is denied to the plaintiff. The difficulties of trying to apply some foreign rule about damages would be immense. . . . I would stick to the rule that damages must be awarded in accordance with the *lex fori.*"

The difficulty about the simple rule is that an injured person may thereby be, as he was in *Boys* v. *Chaplin*,[47] much better off financially because he was held able to sue in England and to secure the support of a majority of the court for the view that English law ruled all matters, than if he had had to sue in the *forum delicti*, as he would have had to do if the English court had found itself unable to claim jurisdiction, or in the Ruritanian courts if in the circumstances the wrongdoer had been a Ruritanian and only the Ruritanian courts had had effective jurisdiction.

[45] *Boys* v. *Chaplin* [1968] 2 Q.B. 1, 41, *per* Diplock L.J. dissenting.
[46] pp. 32–33.
[47] *Supra.*

The case of *MacKinnon* v. *Iberia Shipping Co.*[48] is unfortunately a confused authority. A Scot was injured on board a British ship anchored within the territorial waters of the Dominican Republic, and claimed for solatium and patrimonial loss in the Scottish courts. It was held (rightly) that the actionability of the claim depended on its actionability both under the *lex fori* (Scotland) and the *lex loci delicti* (Dominica), but (wrongly) that as solatium was a distinct right peculiar to Scots law nothing could be recovered in respect thereof.

The latter part of the decision is incorrect because while solatium in the context of a claim by a surviving relative of a deceased is a distinct claim,[49] solatium in the context of a claim by a surviving injured party is merely a head of damages, distinct from damages for loss of earnings, corresponding to English " general damages," [50] and if Dominican law recognised as a head of damages in a claim for personal injuries an element for pain and suffering, the pursuer's claim under this head should have been admitted.[51] Whether Dominican law did or did not recognise such a head of damages should have been a matter of averment and proof by the defender, failing which the presumption that foreign law is the same as Scots law unless proved to be different should have led the court to admit the claim for solatium.

In *Boys* v. *Chaplin* [52] one Englishman was injured by the fault of another Englishman on a road in Malta. By Maltese law damages for pain and suffering are not recoverable; by English law they are, under the name of general damages. In an action in the English courts it was held in the Court of Appeal that damages must be assessed by English law, either, as Lord Denning M.R. thought,[53] because English law was the law of the country with which the parties had the most significant connection and that this should be applied both as to the cause of action and as to the measure of damages, or as Lord Upjohn thought,[54] because there was a cause of action in tort actionable in England and the rules of English law must apply not only to procedure but also to substantive law, including the measure of damages which accordingly, like all questions of remedy [*sic*] was governed by the *lex fori*. It is submitted that both *rationes* are unsound. As to that of Lord Denning M.R., the doctrine of a " proper law of the tort," that of the country with which the parties had the most substantial connection, is not the law of England nor of Scotland. As to that of Lord Upjohn, it is not the law that the *lex fori* applies also to questions of substantive law, nor is it the case that all questions of remedy are governed by the *lex fori*. It is difficult to resist

48 1955 S.C. 20.
49 *Kendrick* v. *Burnett* (1897) 25 R. 82; *Naftalin, supra; McElroy, supra*; and see Chap. 54, *infra*.
50 Chap. 53, *infra*.
51 Lord Sorn, at p. 38, noted the difference between the two kinds of solatium, and it is apparent that the mistake arose because the difference was not noted in argument.
52 [1968] 2 Q.B. 1; [1971] A.C. 356.
53 *Ibid.*, at p. 24.
54 *Ibid.*, at p. 32.

the conclusion that both of their Lordships were excessively influenced by the desire to secure the greater award of damages for the plaintiff. Diplock L.J. dissented powerfully,[55] taking the view that the law to be applied in determining whether the conduct was actionable was the *lex loci delicti*, and that this system also provided the criteria as to what heads of damages could be considered, though the valuing of the admissible heads of damages in money must be done by English law and practice. This view is, it is submitted, in accordance with the earlier English and with the Scottish authorities.

On appeal to the House of Lords,[56] the House unanimously, but for very varied reasons, affirmed the majority view of the Court of Appeal.

Lord Hodson [57] considered that actionability and the heads of damages recoverable depended on the proper law of the tort (which he held to be English law) and that damages fell to be assessed by English law. Lord Guest [58] declined to introduce the concept of the " proper law of the tort " but held that though questions as to heads of damages were for the *lex loci delicti*, damages for pain and suffering were merely an element in quantification of the total compensation and therefore to be determined by the *lex fori*. This seems unsound. Lord Donovan [59] was also against the concept of the " proper law of the tort," and ignored any distinction between heads of damages and quantification of damages; the English court could entertain the action and " once it had done so it was right that it should award its own remedies." Lord Wilberforce [60] thought that if there were civil liability for the harm under the foreign law and it were actionable in England that should be enough, and that there was nothing in legal policy to prevent English law applying its own rule. Lord Pearson [61] thought it was right to apply the English substantive law, as being the *lex fori*, and that damages for pain and suffering was a question of substantive law. It is not clear what, if any, *ratio* is yielded by the decision as a whole, but the question of what heads of damages were recoverable under the *lex loci delicti* seems not to have been distinguished from the question of quantification of damages.

Remoteness of injury, remoteness of damage and quantification of damages

In respect of damages it is particularly important to draw the line between matters of substantive right, governed by the *lex causae*, and of adjective law, governed by the *lex fori*. Whether a particular piece of conduct gives rise to a claim of damages is a matter of substantive right, and this includes questions of remoteness of injury,[62] that is, of whether

[55] *Ibid.*, at p. 33.
[56] [1971] A.C. 356.
[57] pp. 373, esp. 378–379.
[58] pp. 380, esp. 381–382.
[59] p. 383.
[60] pp. 384, esp. 392–393.
[61] pp. 393, esp. 394–395.
[62] On this concept, see Walker, *Delict*, Chap. 7, and Chap. 52, *infra*.

the harm was too distantly connected with the alleged breach of duty for the court to be entitled to hold the defender liable for that harm at all. Whether an injury is or is not too remote is a facet of its actionability. Matters of remoteness of damage,[63] that is, of whether, once the breach of duty is admitted or proved, some heads of the loss allegedly sustained must be deemed too remote, or consequential, to entitle the court to make an award in respect thereof, must also be determined by the *lex causae*, because the principle of remoteness of damages operates as a limitation upon the extent of the complainer's right to damages. But matters of quantification of damages,[64] that is, of deciding how much money to award in respect of the admissible heads of loss, is a pure matter of remedy for the *lex fori*. If the Scottish practice is to award about £5,000 for the extent of injuries suffered, it matters not that in a court furth of Scotland the injured person might have got about £10,000 or $50,000. These three factors must be considered more closely.

Remoteness of injury: Existence or not of liability for harm

The plea, sometimes advanced in defence in delict cases, of remoteness of injury,[65] that is, that the harm or loss complained of is so remotely or distantly connected with the conduct alleged to be a breach of duty on the defender's part, that it is not just to saddle the defender with liability therefor at all, even though causal connection between breach and harm might be established, is a facet of the actionability of the conduct in question.[66] For the court to uphold this plea is to hold the defender's conduct entirely non-actionable, and this plea must accordingly be deemed a qualification of or restriction on actionability and determined also by the system of law which determines actionability.

Remoteness of damage: Extent of harm or loss for which claim competent

The principle of remoteness of damage[67] may be invoked to limit the extent of a defender's liability and to exclude liability for some items of claim or heads of loss suffered, on the ground that such heads were consequential on or too remote from the original breach of duty to be justifiably compensable by the defender. This principle operates not as an exclusion of, but only as a qualification or limitation on, the extent of loss caused by an infringement of right which may be taken into account in computing damages, and falls to be determined by the system of law which regulates rights of parties, namely, the *lex causae*. Thus if Y is sued for breach of a contract, the proper law of which is English law, he is liable for only the consequences of the breach foreseeable by him at the time he made the contract, his foresight being determined by what knowledge he

63 On this, see Walker, *Delict*, Chap. 7, and Chap. 52, *infra*.
64 On this, see Chaps. 53–57, *infra*.
65 On this, see further Chap. 52, *infra*.
66 *Cf. Muir* v. *Glasgow Corpn.*, 1943 S.C. (H.L.) 3; *Malcolm* v. *Dickson*, 1951 S.C. 542; *Blaikie* v. *B.T.C.*, 1961 S.C. 44.
67 On this, see further Chaps. 28 (contract), 52 (delict), *infra*.

actually had and what he should have had of the consequences likely to result from a breach of contract in such circumstances.[68] Similarly, if X is injured in England and if by English law the wrongdoer is liable only for the reasonably foreseeable consequences of his negligent conduct [69] and he sues Y in Scotland, the Scottish court must limit Y's liability in that way, though by Scots law a wrongdoer is liable for all the natural and direct consequences of his negligent conduct,[70] which may well be greater than the foreseeable consequences thereof. The principle of remoteness of damage is a limitation on or qualification of the extent of a defender's liability to make reparation. It is concerned not with his liability or freedom from liability but with how far he is liable and for what losses he must pay, not with the existence of liability but with its extent.

In *J. D'Almeida Araujo Lda.* v. *Becker*,[71] a case of breach of contract, the court distinguished between remoteness of damage and quantification of damages, holding that under the former head the court had to determine in respect of what items of loss the plaintiff could recover compensation, and that this was a matter of substance for the *lex causae*, but that under the latter head the court had to determine how much to award in respect of those items of loss for which the defendant was liable, and that this was a matter of adjective law for the *lex fori.*

Quantification of damages

The last question is by what system the damages are to be measured. The general rule is that damages must be assessed in accordance with the *lex fori.*[72] "I would stick to the rule that damages must be awarded in accordance with the *lex fori.* That has the practical advantage that counsel experienced in these matters can give their expert opinion, so helpful and sometimes economical to their clients, and so useful in the speedy administration of justice, on matters of payment into court; if the court was bound to administer some different method of awarding damages, this might be very difficult and nearly impossible." [73]

But assessment of damages falls into two branches, namely, determining what heads of damages are to be taken into account, and, secondly, putting a value on each admissible head of damages in the circumstances, thereby producing a total award. "Questions such as whether loss of earning capacity or pain and suffering are admissible heads of damage must be questions of substantive law. The law relating to damages is partly procedural and partly substantive, the actual quantification under the relevant heads being procedural only." [74]

68 *Hadley* v. *Baxendale* (1854) 9 Ex. 341, 354; *Victoria Laundry* v. *Newman* [1949] 2 K.B. 528; *Koufos* v. *Czarnikow* [1967] 3 All E.R. 686.
69 *Overseas Tankship (U.K.) Ltd.* v. *Morts Dock and Engineering Co.* [1961] A.C. 388.
70 *McKillen* v. *Barclay Curle*, 1967 S.L.T. 48; *McKew* v. *Holland & Hannen & Cubitts (Sc.) Ltd.*, 1969 S.L.T. 101.
71 [1953] 2 Q.B. 329.
72 *Kohnke* v. *Karger* [1951] 2 K.B. 670.
73 *Boys* v. *Chaplin* [1968] 2 Q.B. 1, 33, *per* Lord Upjohn.
74 *Boys* v. *Chaplin* [1971] A.C. 379, *per* Lord Hodson.

The problem of how much money should be assessed, under each admissible claim and head of claim, as fair compensation, must be determined in a Scottish court exclusively by Scottish law and practice. The *forum* can look only to its own *lex fori* and its own practice and experience for guidance on quantum of damages. This includes such considerations as the effect, if any, to be given to recoupment of the loss from other sources, such as inheritance, insurance contracts, social security payments and so on. On the question of an appropriate sum in money the forum must look at its own practice and see what amount is reasonably consistent with awards made for comparable losses in the recent past and in current practice.

In *Boys* v. *Chaplin* [75] Lord Denning M.R. took the view that the law of the country with which the parties had the most significant connection, as the " proper law of the tort " should be applied both in regard to the cause of action and in regard to the measure of damages. But this could result sometimes in a court being compelled to try to assess damages by the standards applied in another jurisdiction, an impossible task. Lord Upjohn held that the rules of English law must apply in relation not only to procedure but also to substantive law, including the measure of damages which like all questions of remedy [*sic*] was governed by the *lex fori*. This view simply ignores the fact that the wrong took place abroad, in a place where nothing could be given for pain and suffering. Diplock L.J., who dissented, considered that the first inquiry involved in the assessment of damages was to be conducted by applying the criteria as to " heads of damages " provided by the *lex loci delicti*. Accordingly, as in that case the *lex loci delicti* gave no right of action for general damages, or damages for pain and suffering, no such damages could be awarded by the English court.

Interest

Liability to pay interest arising by express or implied agreement depends on the proper law of the contract.[76] The same is probably true of interest as damages for delay in payment of money.[77] Interest on damages on the other hand, being regulated by exclusively Scottish statutes, is determined by Scots law as *lex fori*.[78]

Effect of prior proceedings in foreign court

If a pursuer has recovered damages from a defender in previous proceedings he cannot claim further damages, on the ground of their inadequacy or any other ground, the cause of action having become *res judicata*.[79] If he has recovered damages from a defender in previous

[75] [1968] 2 Q.B. 1.
[76] *Cochrane* v. *Gilkison* (1857) 20 D. 213; *Price and Logan* v. *Wise* (1862) 24 D. 491.
[77] *St Patrick Assurance Co.* v. *Brebner* (1829) 8 S. 51.
[78] Chap. 23, *infra*.
[79] *e.g. Balfour* v. *Baird*, 1959 S.C. 64.

proceedings in a foreign court he is probably barred from later proceedings against the same defender in a Scottish court founding on the same cause of action.[80]

But if he has recovered damages from one or more of joint wrongdoers in previous proceedings in a foreign court, that is no bar to later proceedings against another joint wrongdoer in a Scottish court for the same loss, provided that the sum recovered in the previous proceedings is brought into account to avoid double compensation.[81]

Procedure for obtaining the remedy

It is quite clear that procedure, in the narrower sense of the steps having to be taken between complaint and judicial decision, must be determined by the *lex fori*. If a Scottish court accepts jurisdiction in a case (a matter which itself can only be raised by a summons or petition in Scottish form, with defences or answers, averments and pleas, in Scottish form), all questions of pleadings, pleas-in-law, relevancy, debates, hearing by proof or jury trial, and the like can be determined only by Scots law. A Scottish court can never utilise procedural rules other than its own. Hence a pursuer in Scotland may be entitled to trial by jury though he would not if he had sued in another jurisdiction.

Facts to be proved and proof thereof

What facts require to be proved to establish a claim to a remedy depend on the proper law of the claim because these are inseparable from the actionability of the conduct complained of.

Thus in a Scottish action for defamation the pursuer must aver that the defender communicated the statement " maliciously " but he need not lead evidence of actual malice; malice sufficient to sustain the action is implied from the communication of matter of a defamatory character.[82] So too he need neither aver nor prove that the defender published the statement to anyone other than the pursuer himself.[83] But if the alleged defamation took place in Utopia where either or both of these facts need to be proved, either or both will need to be proved in an action in Scotland because they will be necessary constituents of the wrong by the *lex loci delicti.*

In an action in Scotland for breach of a contract, the putative proper law of which is English, the pursuer must, if need be, prove that there was consideration for the promise of performance, because that is a necessary constituent of a contract enforceable by English law.

Evidence

It is equally clear that technical matters of the evidence needed to

80 *Barber* v. *Lamb* (1860) 8 C.B.(N.S.) 95; *Taylor* v. *Hollard* [1902] 1 K.B. 676; *Kohnke* v. *Karger* [1951] 2 K.B. 670.
81 *Kohnke, supra.*
82 *Hulton* v. *Jones* [1910] A.C. 20.
83 *Mackay* v. *McCankie* (1883) 10 R. 537; *Evans* v. *Stein* (1904) 7 F. 65.

establish any disputed fact, and questions of admissibility, competency, relevancy, corroboration and so on, are determined by the *lex fori.*[84] Thus a Scottish court will normally demand corroboration though the *lex causae* might not demand it.

Difficulties may arise in respect of presumptions and burden of proof. A presumption so called may be truly a rule of substantive law masquerading as a rule of evidence, such as the irrebuttable presumption that a child under eight is incapable of committing crime, or be a rebuttable presumption which justifies a decision in the absence of adequate countervailing evidence, such as the presumption that a married woman's husband is the father of her child.

It is submitted that if the *lex causae* involves a presumption of the former kind it must be given effect to as a matter of substantive law, if action is brought in the Scottish courts. On the other hand a presumption of the latter kind attaching under the *lex causae* is evidential only and if the matter arises in a foreign court that court is not bound to apply the presumption, but must apply its *lex fori.*

Questions of burden of proof are important in such matters as contributory negligence. The issue of burden of proof should be determined also by the *lex causae* because if that system of law recognises the right of action it also should define the qualifications on that right, including such matters as whether a complainer has to show himself free from blame, or is to be taken to be free of blame unless the other party proves the contrary.[85] But the Scottish courts have tended to apply their own rules.[86] The matter may also be important if by the *lex causae* a harm has been caused in circumstances of strict liability, *i.e.*, where there is liability if the harm is proved, without proof of fault, but by the *lex fori* harm in such circumstances would demand proof of fault to justify damages.

Proof and interpretation of statutes and documents

The existence and terms of a statute or document on which a party founds must be proved by the *lex fori.*[87]

Its authentication and formal validity must, however, be judged by the system of law by which it is governed, normally that under which it was drawn up. This may require expert evidence as to authentication, sealing, stamping, registration, publication or other formalities requisite for its legal validity.

Once its terms have been established it must moreover be interpreted according to the system of law by which it is governed. Thus if a statute applicable to England only is pleaded in a Scottish case [88] the Scottish

84 *Yeats* v. *Thomson* (1835) 1 S. & MacL. 795; *Don* v. *Lippmann* (1837) 2 S. & MacL. 682, 726; *Bain* v. *Whitehaven Ry.* (1850) 3 H.L.Cas. 1, 19.

85 *Cf. Re Cohn* [1945] 1 Ch. 5.

86 *Robertson* v. *Burdekin* (1843) 6 D. 17; *Mackenzie* v. *Hall* (1854) 17 D. 164; *Strathern* v. *Masterman* (1850) 12 D. 1087; *Girvin, Roper & Co.* v. *Monteith* (1895) 23 R. 129, 131.

87 *Cf. Brown* v. *Thornton* (1837) 6 A. & E. 185.

88 As in *Rosses* v. *Bhagvat Sinhjee* (1891) 19 R. 31; *McElroy* v. *McAllister*, 1949 S.C. 110.

court must ascertain by expert evidence what interpretation the English courts would place on it in the circumstances, and may not try to interpret it for itself by reference to English books and relevant prior English cases or otherwise. A Scottish court cannot assume judicial knowledge of the law, including the interpretation of the statutes and the evaluation of cases interpreting those statutes, of another jurisdiction. But if the statute is common to Scotland and to England the court may reach its own interpretation, and in so doing may, and probably even must, look at interpretations placed on the passage in question in English cases and probably even in English textbooks.[89]

Other matters of foreign, including English, law are matters of fact which have to be established by evidence, and which cannot be determined by judicial knowledge, nor by reading English textbooks and cases, save that opinions in English and other foreign cases may possibly be treated as expert opinions on the foreign law.

In relation to contracts, it has, however, been held in England that the rule that oral evidence is not admissible to supplement, modify or contradict the writing is a rule of evidence which the forum must apply, though the rule that oral evidence is admissible to show that the parties intended to incorporate a condition customarily included in a contract of that particular kind is a rule of interpretation, not of evidence.[90]

Decrees, and currency problems

A Scottish court can grant a decree for a remedy only in accordance with its own law and practice.

Where the decree is for, or includes, an order for, payment of money, this can only be for payment in British money. Hence if the claim is for recovery of a debt incurred abroad, or for damages for the breach of a foreign contract, or for damages for a delict committed abroad where the amount of damages is fixed by the *lex loci delicti*,[91] the decree must be for the sum in British currency required at the rate of exchange ruling at the date of the default,[92] to purchase the amount of foreign currency found payable.[93] In one case it is provided that conversion must be according to the rate of exchange prevailing at the date of judgment, namely, where a foreign judgment expressed in foreign currency is registered in England or Scotland under the Foreign Judgments (Reciprocal Enforcement) Act 1933, s. 2 (3).[94]

Enforcement and diligence

The enforcement of any decree granted is regulated by the *lex fori*,

89 *Cf. Inland Revenue* v. *Glasgow Police Athletic Assocn.*, 1953 S.C. (H.L.) 13.
90 *Korner* v. *Witkowitzer* [1950] 2 K.B. 128.
91 *S.S. Celia* v. *S.S. Volturno* [1921] 2 A.C. 544.
92 *S.S. Celia, supra*, 563.
93 *Manners* v. *Pearson* [1898] 1 Ch. 581, 593.
94 See also *East India Trading Co. Ltd.* v. *Carmel Exporters and Importers Ltd.* [1952] 2 Q.B. 439.

that is, of a Scottish decree by Scots law only, whatever may be the compulsitors open under the *lex causae*.[95]

If the decree is registrable in another jurisdiction,[96] it may, once registered, be enforced in that other jurisdiction by the compulsitors competent by that legal system. Conversely a foreign decree, if registrable [97] and registered in Scotland, is enforceable by Scottish measures. A charge on a decree registered under one of the Acts will not be suspended for merely trivial non-compliance with the Rules of Court.[98]

Conclusion

It would appear that it is wholly unhelpful to say that questions of substantive law are determined by the *lex causae* and matters of procedure by the *lex fori*. This statement does not determine whether matters affecting the remedy sought, or, if they are divisible and distinguishable, which of them, are classified as substantive law and which as adjective law or " procedure." It would appear that some matters affecting remedy are substantive, and some, such as quantification of damages, are adjective. The only useful and necessary decision is whether particular problems should be determined in a Scottish court by Scots law as *lex fori* or by some other system of law which may be deemed involved in some material way. One cannot make that decision on *a priori* categorisation of topics as pertaining to substantive law or to " procedure."

95 *Don* v. *Kealey* (1850) 12 D. 1016; *Elder* v. *Young* (1854) 17 D. 56; *Mackenzie* v. *Hall* (1854) 17 D. 164. *Cf. De la Vega* v. *Vianna* (1830) 1 B. & Ad. 284.

96 *e.g.* under Judgments Extension Act 1868; Inferior Courts Judgments Extension Act 1882; Administration of Justice Act 1920; Foreign Judgments (Reciprocal Enforcement) Act 1933; Maintenance Orders Act 1950.

97 See *e.g. Platt* v. *Platt*, 1958 S.C. 95; *Doohan* v. *N.C.B.*, 1959 S.C. 310.

98 *Medinelli* v. *Malgras*, 1958 S.C. 489.

Part II

REMEDIES NOT REQUIRING RESORT TO COURT

CHAPTER 3

SELF-HELP

SELF-HELP is the generic name for those forms of remedial action which an aggrieved individual may exercise at his own hand, without need to resort to any court or tribunal, and without any express authority in the form of judicial decree or warrant. His authority for his conduct exists only in and must be found in general rules of law.

In view of the undesirability of persons taking the law into their own hands, and of the danger of resulting disputes and even violence, it is clear that the law does not favour resort by persons to self-help, certainly in cases beyond those where it has been recognised as justifiable, and that it should never be advised, nor utilised, lightly or without consideration, nor, where practicable, without prior warning to the wrongdoer, or request to him to desist from or prevent the conduct objected to. The cases where self-help is recognised as permissible are commonly cases where there is no time to resort to court.

Arrest of wrongdoer

A police constable may always apprehend a person if he has a warrant entitling him to do so, and a constable is authorised by numerous statutes to arrest without warrant in particular circumstances. A constable may also, at common law, arrest without warrant, if he sees a crime being committed, or receives credible information that a person is escaping from the place where he committed a crime, or a criminal is found in hiding, or the constable is credibly informed or has good reason to believe that a criminal is in hiding and is about to abscond, or if a suspected individual belongs to a class of persons reputed to live by crime, or who have no fixed residence or known means of honest livelihood, though in no case should there be undue delay in obtaining subsequent formal warrant for the offender's detention. On the other hand, if an individual, even though accused of crime, be a person of respectability and there be no reasonable grounds for supposing that he means to abscond there is nothing to justify apprehension without warrant.[1]

An ordinary citizen may also apprehend a person actually committing a crime, including a crime against himself, or having credible information that the person has committed crime, and detain him until he can be handed over to the police.[2]

[1] *Hume on Crimes*, II, 76; *Peggie* v. *Clark* (1868) 7 M. 89, 93, *per* Lord Deas; see also *Leask* v. *Burt* (1893) 21 R. 32.

[2] *Leask*, *supra*; *Lundie* v. *MacBrayne* (1894) 21 R. 1085; *Somerville* v. *Sutherland* (1899) 2 F. 185.

An ordinary citizen in a position of responsibility, such as that of captain of a ship or aircraft, has limited statutory powers of arrest,[3] and may also arrest a passenger if he deems that necessary for the security of his craft and the safety of the passengers and crew. He will be legally liable only if he has acted maliciously and without probable cause.[4]

Where arrest is effected without a warrant the person apprehended is entitled to know the reason, and the true reason, for the arrest, save that there is no need to explain the reason where he is caught red-handed.[5]

A person, such as a store detective, if he has reasonable grounds for believing that a crime such as theft has been committed, may request the suspected thief to return to the premises, and may detain him there for a reasonable time, as short as is reasonably practicable, but, unless he then releases the suspect, he must inform the police as soon as possible and have him transferred to legal custody as soon as is reasonable practicable.[6]

Restraint of dangerous individual

There seems little doubt that, if a person is acting in a way which appears substantially dangerous to himself or to others, as by reason of drink or mental unbalance, any person may justifiably act to restrain him and to prevent him doing any such harm.[7] Such a person would be legally liable for assault or detention only if he acted quite unnecessarily or unjustifiably,[8] or used excessive force in restraining, or restrained for an unreasonable time, or acted maliciously and without probable cause.

Self-defence

A person assaulted by another may defend himself, provided the force and the means of defence he uses are no greater than are reasonably necessary for his own protection.[9] This extends to both assaults with intent to harm, and technical assaults, such as kissing a girl without her consent. Similarly a person may probably resist an unlawful arrest.[10] What is reasonable force is a question of fact in each case.

If the assaulted person uses excessive force, or a weapon or other means seriously disproportionate to that, if any, with which he was assaulted,[11] or if he persists in using force after the time necessary for his own defence, his conduct may be held to be, not self-defence, but a substantive counter-assault. But the court will not judge too strictly the conduct of one assaulted and put in a position of danger. " If you are attacked with a deadly weapon you can defend yourself with a deadly weapon or with any other weapon which may protect your life. The law

3 *Lundie* v. *MacBrayne* (1894) 21 R. 1085.
4 *Coutts and Park* v. *MacBrayne Ltd.*, 1910 S.C. 386.
5 *Christie* v. *Leachinsky* [1947] A.C. 573.
6 *John Lewis Ltd.* v. *Tims* [1952] A.C. 676.
7 As to emergency admission to mental hospital, see Mental Health (Sc.) Act 1960, s. 31.
8 *Mackenzie* v. *Cluny Hill Hydro Co.*, 1908 S.C. 200.
9 *Hallowell* v. *Niven* (1843) 5 D. 759.
10 *Codd* v. *Cabe* (1876) 1 Ex. D. 352.
11 *Dowie* v. *Douglas*, May 30, 1817, F.C.; (1822) 1 Sh.App. 125.

does not concern itself with niceties in such matters. If you are attacked by a prize-fighter you are not bound to adhere to the Queensberry rules in your defence." [12] It is a question of what was reasonable in the circumstances. In criminal law [13] a belief, on reasonable grounds, even if ultimately held to be erroneous, that the panel was in imminent danger of being killed or seriously wounded, has been held sufficient to justify use of a weapon in self-defence, resulting in the death of the assailant. The same principle should apply in the civil law and a person be held to have done no more than act in self-defence, even if he caused death, if he believed on reasonable grounds that he was in imminent danger of being killed.

Defence of the person of another

There appears to be no express authority in civil law for the proposition that a person may use reasonable force to defend another from attack, but it is submitted that this is the law. It is certainly the law in the context of assault as a crime.[14]

One problem in this context may be of how widely the liberty of defending another extends. It very probably extends to any person whom the defender is under any legal duty to defend and protect, such as parents, spouse or child,[15] but it probably extends also to the defence of any person who appears to be in danger and to need assistance, particularly old persons, women and children, where there can be said to be a moral duty to assist and defend, or to protect from violence.

The kind and extent of force permitted is again a question of what is reasonable in the circumstances.

Defence of one's own property

A person may defend his own property, heritable or moveable,[16] by passive means, such as fences, railings, walls, lights, patrols, guard-dogs,[17] alarm bells and the like, but he may not in general defend it by active means such as electrically charged wires or fences, guns set off by tripwires,[18] man-traps,[19] dogs not under control which attack intruders, nor, still less, by shooting at intruders.[20] It is permissible and not an assault to apprehend a person believed to be poaching.[21]

Stronger measures may be used where an intruder has been disturbed but is apparently deliberately seeking to do damage, or threatening or attempting personal violence to the owner, occupier or possessor of the

12 *Turner* v. *M.G.M. Pictures Ltd.* [1950] 1 All E.R. 449, 471, *per* Lord Oaksey, *obiter.*
13 *Owens* v. *H.M.A.*, 1946 J.C. 119.
14 *H.M.A.* v. *Carson*, 1964 S.L.T. 21.
15 *Cf.* Bell, *Prin.* § 2032; *Leward* v. *Basely* (1695) 1 Ld.Raym. 62.
16 *Cf.* Bell, *Prin.* § 2032.
17 *Cf. Daly* v. *Arrol* (1886) 14 R. 154.
18 But see *Ilott* v. *Wilkes* (1820) 3 B. & Ad. 304.
19 *Cf. Bird* v. *Holbrook* (1828) 4 Bing. 628; *Jordin* v. *Crump* (1841) 8 M. & W. 782.
20 *Cf. H.M.A.* v. *Phipps* (1905) 4 Adam 616.
21 *Bell* v. *Shand* (1870) 7 S.L.R. 267.

property. Force, even in extreme cases to the extent of killing the intruder, may be used in such cases, but always subject to the qualification that it is not substantially greater than was reasonably necessary to defend the property.[22]

In the case of trespass, defence of property by physical ejection is not justifiable in the case of simple trespass, by mere presence on or passage over private property,[23] but trespass combined with actual or threatened damage to property justifies physical ejection,[24] and if a trespasser refuses to comply with a reasonable request to go, he may be forcibly ejected.[25]

Similarly a person who has been permitted to come on to property, but who then refuses to go, or misconducts himself there, or contravenes the implied conditions under which he was entitled to be there, becomes a trespasser and may be requested to go, and, if he does not, be ejected with reasonable and necessary force.[26]

Similarly a proprietor of land may act at his own hand to protect his land against a threatened flood even if the result is to flood his neighbour's lands,[27] though he may not divert flood water already on his land on to the lands of a neighbour.[28]

Defence of the property of another

A person may probably act similarly in the defence of the property of another. This is pretty certainly so where the defender was under any legal duty to preserve or keep safe or guard another's property, as in the case of employees, watchmen, security men, storekeepers and the like. But even in other cases it is in the general public interest that anyone should be entitled to take reasonable steps, *e.g.* to prevent boys breaking windows or smashing property, and should be held justified if he does so, so long always as his protective or preventive measures are not wholly excessive or unreasonable, or such as to amount to substantive crimes or delicts. Thus though it may be permissible to fire guns to scare them away, it goes beyond permitted defence of another's property, intentionally, or recklessly, to discharge firearms at poachers whereby they are injured.[29]

Police may use reasonable force to keep back crowds or prevent them trespassing or doing damage, and such is not actionable.

22 *Oakes* v. *Wood* (1837) 2 M. & W. 791.
23 *Wood* v. *N.B. Ry.* (1899) 2 F. 1.
24 *Bell, supra.*
25 *Wood, supra.*
26 *Highland Ry.* v. *Menzies* (1878) 5 R. 887; *Apthorpe* v. *Edinburgh Tramways* (1882) 10 R. 344; *Scott* v. *G.N.S. Ry.* (1895) 22 R. 287; *MacRaild* v. *N.B. Ry.* (1902) 10 S.L.T. 348; (passengers ejected from trains); *Cf. Wallace* v. *Mooney* (1885) 12 R. 710; *Blasquez* v. *Lothians Racing Club* (1889) 16 R. 893; *Cook* v. *Paxton* (1910) 48 S.L.R. 7 (persons in premises).
27 *Cf. Nield* v. *L.N.W. Ry.* (1874) L.R. 10 Ex. 4; *Maxey Drainage Board* v. *G.N. Ry.* (1912) 106 L.T. 429; *Gerrard* v. *Crowe* [1921] 1 A.C. 395.
28 *Whalley* v. *L. & Y. Ry.* (1884) 13 Q.B.D. 131.
29 *H.M.A.* v. *Phipps* (1905) 4 Adam 616.

Trespass for protection of property

Trespass by a person on another's property is justifiable if reasonably believed to be necessary for the taking of steps against real and imminent danger to the trespasser's property, such as from fire. The justification exists even if the steps taken turn out in the end not to have been necessary in fact. The question is whether there is real and imminent danger such that the acts done were reasonably necessary, such as a reasonable man would do to meet a real danger.[30]

Shooting dogs which are worrying sheep

If dogs or other animals chase or threaten sheep, cattle or similar animals the owner of the sheep or cattle may take effective measures to stop the harm, including shooting the attacking dog. The onus of proof of necessity is on the person shooting, and he must establish that at the time of shooting, the dog was either actually attacking the animals he wished to protect [31] or, if left at large, would renew the attack so that the animals would be left presently subject to real and imminent danger unless renewal was prevented, and also that there was, in fact, no practicable means, other than shooting, of stopping the present attack or preventing such renewal, or that, having regard to all the circumstances in which he found himself, he acted reasonably in regarding the shooting as necessary for the protection of the animals against attack or renewed attack.[32]

If the facts do not justify the shooting the owner of the cattle threatened may be found liable for malicious destruction of the dog.

Poinding straying animals

At common law the owner of lands on to which another's animals have strayed is probably entitled only to chase the animals away, and to seek to recover by action compensation for any harm done, as by way of crops eaten or trampled.

By the Winter Herding Act 1686, possessors of lands are ordained to herd their horses, nolt (*i.e.*, black cattle), sheep, swine and goats the whole year and keep them enclosed at night so that they may not eat or destroy their neighbour's ground, woods, hedges or planting, under a penalty of a half-mark Scots [33] for each animal trespassing, as well as the actual damage to grass or planting.[33a] A neighbour harmed by the animals' trespassing on his lands may detain the animals until the penalty is paid,

[30] *Cope* v. *Sharpe* (No. 2) [1912] 1 K.B. 496, 504, 510.

[31] *Cf. Scott* v. *White* (1886) 2 Guthrie Shf.Ct.Cas. 470; *Bathgate* v. *Black* (1890) 2 Guthrie Shf.Ct.Cas. 469.

[32] *Gott* v. *Measures* [1948] 1 K.B. 234; *Cresswell* v. *Sirl* [1948] 1 K.B. 241. *Cf. Hamps* v. *Darby* [1948] 2 K.B. 311 (homing pigeons eating crops). In *Grant* v. *Barclay Allardice* (1830) 5 Mur. 133, it was said that shooting was justified if the dog were known to be a worrier of sheep and is prowling about or shows hostile intentions to the sheep.

[33] A merk or mark was thirteen shillings and fourpence Scots, or 1s. 1⅓d. sterling, or approximately 6p. A half merk can be taken as 3p. The duration of trespass does not appear to affect the penalty.

[33a] See also *Brown* v. *Lord Advocate*, 1973 S.L.T. 205.

and may also recover the necessary expenses of keeping them, but may not detain them in security of his claim for damages. There is no need for poinding or detention, to found a claim for the penalties, if there is adequate evidence of the trespass.[34] The Act has been held applicable to all cultivated land, both corn and grass,[35] to unenclosed Highland sheep-farms,[36] and to gardens.[37] It matters not that no actual damage can be shown to have been suffered.[38] Animals on the public road are not trespassing on a proprietor's lands.[39]

It is not a prerequisite of recovering the penalty that the animals are detained,[40] but it gives security for payment.[41] Poinding is justifiable only while the animals were actually on the detainer's land, when taken possession of, and not if they had left it before being detained,[42] though if they have been detained on the lands and escape, they may be recaptured and brought back.[43]

The person poinding may not hold the animals for any other purpose, nor attach conditions to releasing them,[44] if he is tendered the penalty and any expense incurred in keeping them.

The poinding will be loosed if tender is made of the penalties and damages due under the Act, and an owner of straying animals is entitled to recover them on tendering what is due.

Damage by game

If a landowner deliberately, or by neglect to keep down the game population, causes or permits an excessive population of game, or of any kind of game, to breed on his land, whence they go and cause damage to the crops or grounds of his neighbour, the latter is entitled to take all legitimate steps to keep them down on his land, but may not without consent enter on the first party's land to attack the breeding-places of the game. Thus he may scare them away, or shoot them while on or over his land.

As between landlord and agricultural tenant, the right to kill game is not carried by a lease, unless expressly,[45] though, if there is no contrary stipulation, the tenant is entitled at common law, by himself or anyone authorised by him, to destroy rabbits on the holding, as an ordinary agricultural operation for the protection of his crops, whether or not there is then any particular crop which requires to be protected.[46]

34 *Pringle* v. *McRae* (1829) 7 S. 352.
35 *Govan* v. *Lang*, Feb. 18, 1794, F.C.
36 *Pringle, supra.*
37 *McArthur* v. *Miller* (1873) 1 R. 248.
38 *Shaw* v. *Ewart*, Mar. 2, 1809, F.C.; *Pringle, supra.*
39 *McArthur* v. *Jones* (1878) 6 R. 41.
40 *Shaw, supra.*
41 *McArthur* v. *Jones* (1878) 6 R. 41.
42 *McArthur, supra*, 43.
43 *Ibid.*
44 *Fraser* v. *Smith* (1899) 1 F. 487.
45 *Welwood* v. *Husband* (1874) 1 R. 507.
46 *Inglis* v. *Moir's Tutors* (1872) 10 M. 204; *Stuart* v. *Murray* (1884) 12 R. (J). 9; *Crawshay* v. *Duncan*, 1915 S.C. (J). 64.

Various statutory provisions give a tenant rights to compensation for game damage.[47]

By the Ground Game Act 1880, s. 1, every occupier of land has, as incident to and inseparable from his occupation of the land, the right to kill and take ground game (*i.e.*, hares and rabbits) thereon, concurrently with any other person entitled to do so on the same land, provided that he does so only [48] by himself or by one other person duly authorised by him in writing, that a person authorised must be a member of his household resident on the land in his occupation,[49] a person in his ordinary service on such land, or any one other person bona fide employed by him for reward in the taking and destruction of ground game,[50] and that every person so authorised must produce his authority on demand by a person having a concurrent right to take and kill the ground game or any one authorised by him in writing to make the demand. Agreements contravening this right are void. Further provision is made for crofters by the Crofters (Sc.) Act 1955, ss. 27 (5), 38 (2) and (3) and Sched. 6.

In respect of ground game accordingly a tenant or other occupier must keep the game population down to a tolerable extent by his own exertions.

Abatement of nuisance

A person may at his own hand abate a nuisance originating on the land of his neighbour if he can do so without trespassing on the neighbour's land. Thus he may, even without notice, cut the branches of trees which overhang his lands, beyond the boundary of the land on which they grow,[51] or cut the roots of trees which have encroached on his lands beneath the surface.[52]

Save in emergency it is not permissible to go on to the neighbour's land to remove the nuisance, unless the complainer has first given his neighbour notice himself to remove the nuisance and adequate opportunity to do so.[53]

Any branches or roots cut belong to the owner of the tree and cannot be removed without his agreement.

Similarly a riparian proprietor may probably at his own hand remove an obstruction in a stream put there by another riparian proprietor.

In cases such as an obstruction on the highway it may be removed only if it is not reasonably possible to circumvent it.[54]

[47] Agricultural Holdings (Sc.) Act 1949, s. 15.

[48] Persons outwith the permitted classes contravene the Day Trespass Act 1832 if they shoot game, even with the occupier's permission: *Niven* v. *Renton* (1888) 15 R. (J.) 42; *Richardson* v. *Maitland* (1897) 24 R. (J.) 32; see also *Calder* v. *Robertson* (1878) 6 R. (J.) 3; *Jack* v. *Nairne* (1887) 14 R. (J.) 20.

[49] See *Stuart* v. *Murray* (1884) 12 R. (J.) 9.

[50] *Bruce* v. *Prosser* (1898) 25 R. (J.) 54.

[51] *Lemmon* v. *Webb* [1895] A.C. 1

[52] *Butler* v. *Standard Telephones Ltd.* [1940] 1 K.B. 399.

[53] *Lemmon, supra.*

[54] *Dimes* v. *Petley* (1850) 15 Q.B. 276. *Cf. Campbell Davys* v. *Lloyd* [1901] 2 Ch. 518.

Abatement of nuisance is a remedy which the law does not favour.[55] If it be done unnecessary damage must be avoided and the least, or less, harmful of alternative modes of abating be adopted, unless that would inflict some wrong on an innocent third party or on the public, and previous notice should be given where possible.[55]

Repossession by an owner of his moveable property

A person who has lent,[56] deposited, or otherwise given possession of some piece of his moveable property to another for a limited time or a temporary purpose may, after the expiry of that time or the termination of the purpose or, at all events, after the lapse of a time reasonable in the circumstances, repossess the property at his own hand. He must be clear that he does not act in breach of contract in so doing, and it is probably reasonable first to request the return of the article before acting. Also the right to repossess does not authorise trespass or breaking into premises to do so. If X lends his car to Y and Y does not return it, X can take it away from in front of Y's house, but may not open Y's garage to take it. If X leaves his car with Y for repair, Y has a lien over the car and X acts wrongfully if he seeks to defeat the lien by removing the car.

At common law hiring and hire-purchase agreements commonly expressly authorise the owner to repossess his property from the hirer without legal process in certain stated circumstances, such as failure for stated periods to pay hire or hire-purchase instalments. Such authority is necessary because the hirer or hire-purchaser is in possession of the goods for the duration of the contract with the owner's consent and, apart from the authority, the latter's only right is to sue for unpaid rental.

In the case of transactions subject to the Hire-Purchase (Sc.) Act 1965, goods are deemed " protected goods " if they satisfy the conditions of section 33, and the lessor on hire-purchase or seller under a conditional sale agreement may not enforce any right to recover possession of protected goods from the hirer or buyer otherwise than by action (s. 34 (1) and (2)). Nothing in this section is to be taken to confer on a lessor or seller any right to recover, otherwise than by action, possession of any goods let on hire-purchase or agreed to be sold under a conditional sale agreement if they are not " protected goods " (s. 34 (3)). But such a right may be stipulated for in the contract if it does not fall within the 1965 Act, or if the goods are not " protected goods." Provisions as to the action for possession are contained in sections 35 to 44. These sections also apply in relation to protected goods where the agreement is a conditional sale agreement within the meaning of the 1965 Act, subject to certain modifications (s. 45).

55 *Lagan Navigation Co.* v. *Lambeg Bleaching Co.* [1927] A.C. 226, 244.

56 In the case of *commodatum* only; if the loan is *mutuum*, the property has passed to the borrower and the borrower's liability is to restore the equivalent, and the lender has probably no right at his own hand to take an equivalent.

Public necessity

Overriding public necessity sometimes entitles a person to do what in normal circumstances would require consent or judicial authority. Thus a shipmaster may jettison cargo if necessary to preserve the safety of the ship. A fireman on duty or a constable may enter and, if necessary, break into any premises or place in which a fire has or is reasonably believed to have broken out, or any premises or place which it is necessary to enter for the purposes of extinguishing a fire or of protecting the premises or place from acts done for fire-fighting purposes, without the consent of the owner or occupier thereof, and may do all such things as he may deem necessary for extinguishing the fire or for protecting from fire, or from acts done as aforesaid, any such premises or place or for rescuing any person or property therein.[57]

[57] Fire Services Act 1947, s. 30 (1).

CHAPTER 4

RESCISSION OF CONTRACT

RESCISSION of contract is the remedy open in certain circumstances to a party to a contract whereby he may decline to hold himself bound, or any longer bound, by the contract, and may refuse to implement all obligations incumbent on him thereby, being himself, of course, thereby disentitled to demand performance from the other contracting party. Where a right to rescind is being utilised, the proper course is to intimate to the other party that the party rescinding holds himself no longer bound by the contract, as from a stated date, and will perform no further. If intimation be not made, and the other party acts further on the basis that the contract is valid and mutually enforceable, and particularly if he incurs obligations or expense on that basis, the party seeking to rescind may be held barred by his failure to intimate.[1] An unexpressed desire or intention to rescind is valueless. The reason for the rescission should, moreover, be stated, as the justification for the rescission may be challenged, and may indeed ultimately be found inadequate, and an intimation of rescission without any reason given may be indistinguishable from a unilateral repudiation of the contract. If the justification for the rescission is challenged as unfounded or inadequate, the party rescinding may seek to reduce the contract, or may plead his intimation of rescission in defence to an action brought against him by the other party in an attempt to enforce the contract.

Rescission of a contract on such a ground as fraud is not adequately effected by notifying other parties than the other contracting party. Thus where the sale of a car was induced by fraud and the car taken away, it was held that the sale was not rescinded by notifying the police.[2]

The date of rescission of a contract is the date when intimation thereof is made, not the date when decree to that effect is pronounced by the court.[3]

Rescission conditional on restitution in integrum

Rescission of a contract is conditional on it being possible for each party to make mutual restitution *in integrum* of any money or property already transferred in pursuance of the contract. If this is no longer in fact possible, rescission is precluded.[4]

[1] *Dunford & Elliot* v. *Macleod* (1902) 4 F. 912, 920; *Sanderson* v. *Armour*, 1921 S.C. 18; affd. 1922 S.C. (H.L.) 117.
[2] *MacLeod* v. *Kerr*, 1965 S.C. 253.
[3] *Westville Shipping Co.* v. *Abram S.S. Co.*, 1923 S.C.(H.L.) 68.
[4] *Western Bank of Scotland* v. *Addie* (1867) 5 M. (H.L.) 80; *Hay* v. *Rafferty* (1899) 2 F. 302; *Gamage* v. *Charlesworth's Tr.*, 1910 S.C. 257, 266; *Boyd & Forrest* v. *G.S.W. Ry.*, 1915 S.C.(H.L.) 20. *Cf. Steuart's Trs.* v. *Hart* (1875) 3 R. 192.

The rule as to restitution *in integrum* must not be applied too literally, and a person held guilty of fraudulent misrepresentation is not entitled, in bar of restitution, to found on dealings with the subjects of contract which he was enabled to carry through by his fraud.[5]

Rescission precluded by third party's acquisition of rights

Rescission is similarly precluded if, before it was intimated to the other party, any third party has, in good faith and for value, acquired rights in property transferred under the contract now sought to be avoided, as where a bona fide purchaser has, for value, bought goods obtained by the seller from a previous seller under a contract voidable for fraudulent misrepresentation, without notice of any defect in the title of the seller to him.[6] It is not precluded if the third party did not obtain the goods in good faith, or did not give fair value for them. Thus if A sells goods to B, the contract being voidable for fraudulent misrepresentation as to B's ability to pay, but before A has rescinded it B resells to C, C acquires a good title provided he has taken in good faith, for value and without notice of B's voidable title, and once C has acquired title, A's right to rescind lapses.[7] If C is an accomplice of B and takes in bad faith, rescission is not excluded.

Equitable character of rescission

" The remedy of rescission and recovery of the property is an equitable remedy, and, though as between seller and buyer a *brevi manu* operation may be effectual, it requires, where other interests are concerned, the interposition of the court. . . . The remedy is an equitable remedy, and the court is bound, I think, to look all round, and to consider whether there are counter equities." [8]

Furthermore, a party who might have been entitled to rescind may be barred from doing so by his own fault, by delay, by neglect to take reasonable business precautions, and the like, particularly where the interests of other creditors are involved and might be prejudiced if rescission were allowed.[9]

Where contract void

Where a purported contract is, on any ground of law, believed by a party to be void, it is a legal nullity, and rescission is theoretically not necessary to terminate duties and liabilities under the contract, but

[5] *Erlanger* v. *New Sombrero Phosphate Co.* (1878) 3 App.Cas. 1218; *Adam* v. *Newbigging* (1888) 13 App.Cas. 308; *Lagunas Nitrate Co.* v. *Lagunas Syndicate* [1899] 2 Ch. 392; *Spence* v. *Crawford*, 1939 S.C.(H.L.) 52.

[6] *Tennent* v. *City of Glasgow Bank* (1879) 6 R. (H.L.) 69; *Gamage* v. *Charlesworth's Tr.*, 1910 S.C. 257, 266. See *e.g. Bonnington Sugar Refining Co. Liqdr.* v. *Thomson's Trs.* (1879) 6 R. (H.L.) 90; *MacLeod* v. *Kerr*, 1965 S.C. 253. *Cf. Phillips* v. *Brooks* [1919] 2 K.B. 243.

[7] *MacLeod, supra.*

[8] *Gamage* v. *Charlesworth's Tr.*, 1910 S.C. 257, 267–8, *per* Lord Johnston.

[9] *Gamage, supra*, 270, *per* Lord Johnston; 272 *per* Lord Salvesen.

intimation of rescission is still desirable, if not indeed necessary, to the other party, to apprise him of the fact that the contract is in fact challenged and going to be disregarded. It may indeed be a matter of dispute whether the contract is truly void in law, or whether facts rendering it void have occurred, or whether on the other hand it is valid,[10] or merely voidable.

Where contract voidable

Rescission is, however, always essential where a contract is merely voidable, as, *ex hypothesi*, such a contract is valid until and unless avoided. If rescission be not intimated the party entitled to do so must go on and perform his part and the other party is entitled to perform his part and claim any payment due. It may again be a difficult question whether the contract is truly voidable or is in fact valid.

Grounds for rescission: where contract induced by misrepresentation or concealment

If error in a substantial or essential respect has been induced in the mind of one contracting party by the misrepresentation or concealment or, in the case of a contract *uberrimae fidei*, non-disclosure by the other contracting party, of any fact material to the contract, the contract is always at least voidable, and may indeed be wholly void, if the error induced was such as completely to exclude true consent to the contract.[11] If the party imposed upon deems it voidable and wishes to avoid it, he must rescind, by intimation to the other party to the contract. Intimation to the police that a car had been obtained by fraudulent misrepresentation as to the buyer's name and credit-worthiness cannot be treated as equivalent to intimated rescission,[12] but intimation to a third party, such as a prospective buyer from the fraudulent person, would suffice.[13] Public intimation, as by advertisement, would probably suffice if it had actually come to the notice of the third party, but not otherwise.

Where contract vitiated by force and fear, facility or undue influence

The right to rescind may be exercised on such other grounds as that the party rescinding contracted by reason of force or fear or when subject to duress,[14] or that the contract was extortionate,[15] or that he contracted

[10] *Cf. Houldsworth* v. *Gordon Cumming*, 1910 S.C.(H.L.) 49; *Mathieson Gee (Ayrshire) Ltd.* v. *Quigley*, 1952 S.C.(H.L.) 38.

[11] *e.g. Morrisson* v. *Robertson*, 1908 S.C. 332; *Gamage* v. *Charlesworth's Tr.*, 1910 S.C. 257.

[12] *MacLeod* v. *Kerr*, 1965 S.C. 253, 257, 259.

[13] *MacLeod*, *supra*, 258, *per* Lord Carmont.

[14] Stair I, 9, 8; Ersk. III, 1, 16; Bell, *Prin.* § 12; *Stuart* v. *Whitefoord* (1677) Mor. 16489; *Priestnell* v. *Hutcheson* (1857) 19 D. 495; *Craig* v. *Paton* (1865) 4 M. 192; *Gelot* v. *Stewart* (1871) 9 M. 957; *McIntosh* v. *Chalmers* (1883) 11 R. 8; *Stewart Bros.* v. *Keddie* (1899) 7 S.L.T. 92. *Cf. Gow* v. *Henry* (1899) 2 F. 48.

[15] This ground probably applies to contracts with money-lenders only: *A.B.* v. *Joel* (1849) 12 D. 188; *McLachlan* v. *Watson* (1874) 11 S.L.R. 549; though inadequacy of consideration may in other cases be evidence of fraud: *Young* v. *Gordon* (1896) 23 R. 419. Under the Moneylenders Acts 1900 and 1927, the court has powers to reopen transactions which are " harsh and unconscionable ": see *Davis* v. *McNally* (1904) 12 S.L.T. 234; *Blumberg* v. *Shand-Harvey* (1908) 16 S.L.T. 4; *Midland Discount Co.* v. *Macdonald*, 1909 S.C. 477; *Howard & Cope* v. *Leckie*, 1909, 2 S.L.T. 444; *Debenham* v. *McCall*, 1923 S.L.T. 365.

when in a state of facility and was circumvented,[16] or was at the time subject to undue influence.[17]

Where performance impossible or frustrated

Rescission may also be utilised on the ground that performance has become impossible in fact,[18] or in law,[19] or that the contract has become frustrated,[20] but not merely because performance has been rendered more difficult or expensive or less profitable or wholly unprofitable.[21]

Intimation of rescission is unnecessary where an event happens which *ipso jure* terminates the obligation, such as the death of a party to a contract involving *delectus personae*.[22] Bankruptcy does not, in general, have this effect.

Rescission on other party's breach of contract

Where two parties have made a valid and enforceable contract and each is bound to do something for the other, it is normally implied that if one party refuses or fails to implement his part, the other is not bound to perform his part.[23] Only exceptionally will one party be held bound to perform though the other is not performing his counterpart.[24] Accordingly where either party refuses, or fails in a material respect, to perform his obligations the other may normally rescind or cancel the contract and claim damages for any loss he may thereby sustain, and is himself released from the obligation to make counter-performance. It is not obligatory to warn the party in breach of intention to cancel [25] but may nevertheless be prudent.

Rescission in case of anticipatory breach

Where one party to a contract clearly indicates, by word or act, at any time before the due date for performance, that he will not perform

16 *Mackay* v. *Campbell*, 1966 S.C. 237; 1967 S.C.(H.L.) 53.

17 *Gray* v. *Binny* (1879) 7 R. 332; *Ross* v. *Gosselin's Exors.*, 1926 S.C. 325; *Forbes* v. *Forbes' Trs.*, 1957 S.C. 325; *Allan* v. *Allan*, 1961 S.C. 200.

18 *Taylor* v. *Caldwell* (1863) 3 B. & S. 826; *Baily* v. *de Crespigny* (1869) L.R. 4 Q.B. 180; *Newington Local Board* v. *Cottingham Local Board* (1879) 12 Ch.D. 725; *Shipton Anderson & Co.* v. *Harrison* [1915] 3 K.B. 676; *London Shipping Co.* v. *The Admiralty*, 1920 S.C. 309; *Stevenson* v. *Maule*, 1920 S.C. 335.

19 *Re Anglo-Russian Merchant Traders and Batt* [1917] 2 K.B. 679; *Stevenson* v. *Cartonnagen Industrie* [1918] A.C. 239.

20 *Horlock* v. *Beal* [1916] 1 A.C. 486; *Tamplin S.S. Co.* v. *Anglo-American Co.* [1916] 2 A.C. 397; *Metropolitan Water Board* v. *Dick Kerr & Co.* [1918] A.C. 119; *Bank Line* v. *Capel* [1919] A.C. 435.

21 *Holliday* v. *Scott* (1830) 8 S. 831; *Duke of Sutherland* v. *Marquis of Stafford* (1892) 19 R. 502; *Summerlee Steel Co.* v. *Caledonian Ry.*, 1909 S.C. 536; *Macmaster* v. *Cox, McEuen & Co.*, 1921 S.C.(H.L.) 24.

22 Partnership Act 1890, s. 33; *Hoey* v. *McEwan & Auld* (1867) 5 M. 814; *Torrance* v. *Traill's Tr.* (1897) 24 R. 837.

23 Stair I, 10, 16; Ersk. III, 3, 86; Bell, *Comm.* II, 92; *Barclay* v. *Anderson Foundry Co.* (1856) 18 D. 1190, 1196; *Johnston* v. *Robertson* (1861) 23 D. 646, 656; *Turnbull* v. *McLean* (1874) 1 R. 730, 738.

24 *Pendrigh's Tr.* v. *Dewar* (1871) 9 M. 1037; *Forrest* v. *Scottish County Investment Co.*, 1916 S.C.(H.L.) 28; *Speirs* v. *Petersen*, 1924 S.C. 428.

25 *Barclay*, *supra*.

when that date arrives, there is said to be an anticipatory breach of contract. Only a clear and distinct refusal to perform when the time comes,[26] or an intimation of inability to do so, or conduct which will disable the party from making performance when the due time comes, such as using up goods sold, or selling to another,[27] can safely be treated as a repudiation. It will not suffice that a party intimates his reluctance to perform, or his doubts as to the likelihood of his ability to do so,[28] and in such cases the other party is not in safety in rescinding the contract, though he may seek explanation or clarification of the situation, or give a warning.

If performance is due at a fixed future date or on the occurrence of a certain event it is not an anticipatory breach or repudiation to be unable at some time before the fixed date to perform, and rescission is unjustifiable; the party bound may yet become able to perform.[29] But in such a case it may be permissible to warn the other party that, unless adequate assurance of due performance is given, the contract will be rescinded.[30]

If, however, performance is due on demand, or on the occurrence of an uncertain event, *e.g.* to supply goods as and when ordered, the party bound must be constantly able to perform, and his inability at any time to perform, even before performance is required to be made, is a repudiation.[31]

A contracting party's insolvency before the date of performance is not such a repudiation as entitles the other party to rescind [32] because the trustee in bankruptcy may take up and perform the contract,[33] though it may justify other remedies such as retention. Still less is feared or threatened insolvency a repudiation.[34] But an employer's bankruptcy is a breach of contract with his employees.[35] Nor would rescission necessarily be justifiable if the other party intimates not refusal or inability to perform but only inability to perform completely, or that performance will be defective in some non-fundamental or even immaterial respect. Such a lesser failure would justify damages only.

Courses available on anticipatory repudiation

Where there is anticipatory breach or repudiation by one party this

26 *Hochster* v. *De la Tour* (1853) 2 E. & B. 678; *Frost* v. *Knight* (1872) L.R. 7 Ex. 111; *Whitehead* v. *Phillips* (1902) 10 S.L.T. 577; see also *Morison* v. *Morison* (1902) 10 S.L.T. 324.

27 *Short* v. *Stone* (1846) 8 Q.B. 358; *Lovelock* v. *Franklyn* (1846) 8 Q.B. 371; *N.B. Ry.* v. *Benhar Coal Co.* (1886) 14 R. 141; *Ross* v. *Macfarlane* (1894) 21 R. 396; *Synge* v. *S.* [1894] 1 Q.B. 466; *Omnium D'Enterprises* v. *Sutherland* [1919] 1 K.B. 618.

28 *Johnstone* v. *Milling* (1886) 16 Q.B.D. 460; *Thornloe* v. *Macdonald* (1892) 29 S.L.R. 409; *cf. Anderson* v. *Hamilton* (1875) 2 R. 355, 367.

29 *Smith* v. *Butler* [1900] 1 Q.B. 694.

30 *Davis* v. *Nisbett* (1861) 10 C.B.(N.S.) 752; *Stickney* v. *Keeble* [1915] A.C. 386. *Cf. Rodger (Builders) Ltd.* v. *Fawdry*, 1950 S.C. 483.

31 *Omnium D'Enterprises* v. *Sutherland* [1919] 1 K.B. 618.

32 *Cf.* Sale of Goods Act 1893, s. 48.

33 *Asphaltic Limestone Co.* v. *Glasgow Corpn.*, 1907 S.C. 463.

34 *Linton* v. *Sutherland* (1889) 17 R. 213.

35 *Hoey* v. *McEwan & Auld* (1867) 5 M. 814, 817; *Day* v. *Tait* (1900) 8 S.L.T. 40; *Laing* v. *Gowans* (1902) 10 S.L.T. 461.

does not by itself terminate the contract but merely puts it in the power of the other party to rescind the contract and claim damages for the loss of the whole contract.[36] A party repudiating cannot insist on the contract being terminated.[37] The other party may accept the repudiation, choose there and then to rescind the contract and he may also claim damages for any loss caused him thereby, and that even though he was not himself then able to perform his part of the contract,[38] and despite the possibility that the repudiating party might, if he had waited, have in fact been able to perform when the due date arrived.[39]

Alternatively, the other party may elect to ignore the repudiation, treat the contract as still subsisting, and, when the due date for performance arrives, demand performance, and claim damages if it is not then duly made.[40] In that event damages will fall to be measured as at the due date for performance, and may be more or less than if the repudiation had been accepted when made, the contract rescinded and damages then claimed.[41] Or, in the case where the performance is for the innocent party to make, he has been said, at least where he can perform without the co-operation of the repudiating party, to be entitled to make performance, even if it is no longer wanted by the repudiating party, and to exact the full contract payment therefor.[42] This view ignores both the obligation to minimise claims arising from breach of contract [43] and the folly of allowing one party to make unwanted performance to the other and charging the full price thereof when in reason and justice he should be allowed to recover only his loss of profit on the transaction which he has now been asked not to perform.

Subsequent offer to fulfil, or excuse for non-fulfilment

If one party definitely repudiates his obligation by refusing to perform or disabling himself from performing, and the other accepts the repudiation and elects to rescind the contract, the repudiating party cannot subsequently offer to tender, or actually tender, performance, whether before or at the contractual date.[44] His right to do so has gone, and the other party may justifiably refuse a subsequent change of mind and tender of performance, save that he may find it reasonable to make a

36 *Johnstone, supra*; *Haggarty & Kelly* v. *Cosmopolitan Ins. Corpn.*, 1913 S.C. 377; *Mohad* v. *Anchor Line*, 1922 S.C. (H.L.) 53; *White & Carter (Councils) Ltd.* v. *McGregor*, 1962 S.C. (H.L.) 1.

37 *Heyman* v. *Darwins, Ltd.* [1942] A.C. 356; *White & Carter (Councils) Ltd., supra.*

38 *Cort* v. *Ambergate Ry.* (1851) 17 Q.B. 127; *British & Benington* v. *Cachar Tea Co.* [1923] A.C. 48.

39 *Avery* v. *Bowden* (1855) 5 E. & B. 714; *Universal Cargo Carriers Corpn.* v. *Citati* [1957] 2 Q.B. 401, 436.

40 *Hochster* v. *De la Tour* (1853) 2 E. & B. 678; *Frost* v. *Knight* (1872) L.R. 7 Ex. 111; *Johnstone* v. *Milling* (1886) 16 Q.B.D. 460.

41 *Howie* v. *Anderson* (1848) 10 D. 355; *cf. Roper* v. *Johnson* (1873) L.R. 8 C.P. 167; *Michael* v. *Hart* [1902] 1 K.B. 482; *Melachrino* v. *Nicholl & Knight* [1920] 1 K.B. 693; *Millett* v. *Van Heek* [1921] 2 K.B. 369.

42 *White & Carter, supra.*

43 Chap. 28, *infra.*

44 *Gilfillan* v. *Cadell and Grant* (1893) 21 R. 269.

fresh contract with the repudiating party in discharge of his obligation to minimise his loss resulting from the breach.[45]

If, on the other hand, the other party does not accept the repudiation and does not rescind the contract, the contract remains in being for all purposes, and the party repudiating may reconsider his repudiation, withdraw it and affirm his willingness to perform, or may simply tender performance at the due date. In this event the other party must accept the performance tendered (assuming that it is due performance in quantity, quality and other respects) and make counter-performance.[46] The anticipatory repudiation, not having been accepted and acted on at the time, cannot be founded on.

Furthermore in this event if any circumstances supervene after the repudiation has been made (but not accepted) which give the party who repudiated a legal excuse for not performing, such as an outbreak of war which makes performance unlawful as being trading with an enemy,[47] the party repudiating may rely on this excuse as justifying his eventual non-performance and as exempting him from liability in damages. Similarly a subsequent frustrating event may excuse his non-performance at the due date.

Threat of non-material breach

Where the breach intimated by anticipation is not total nor in a material respect, but only in some respect not material or fundamental in the circumstances,[48] it is questionable whether the innocent party has the right to rescind. He would not have such a right if non-material breach were made at the due date for performance without prior warning,[49] and it is difficult to see why he should have the right, merely because he has been warned. It is submitted that if the kind of breach threatened is immaterial, the other party does not have the right to rescind, but can only claim damages if the ultimate performance is in fact defective, as threatened.

Breach at due date for performance

If at the due date for performance one party refuses to perform, or fails to perform entirely or in some material respect, the other party again becomes entitled to rescind, *i.e.* to treat the contract as repudiated, and to claim damages on that basis, and is released from his obligations and is not bound to make counter-performance combined with a claim of damages for the loss suffered.[50]

[45] *Payzu* v. *Saunders* [1919] 2 K.B. 581, and see Chap. 28, *infra.*
[46] *Frost* v. *Knight* (1872) L.R. 7 Exch. 111.
[47] *Avery* v. *Bowden* (1856) 6 E. & B. 953.
[48] *e.g.* that some of the goods will be a day or two late, or that the labels on the containers are of the wrong size.
[49] *Infra.*
[50] *Cf.* Sale of Goods Act 1893, s. 11 (2).

Materiality of breach justifying rescission

It is well settled that not every breach of a contract justifies rescission. A breach in a material respect, one which goes to the root of the contract,[51] or is such that a failure to perform it would make the performance of the rest of the contract a different thing from what the other party had stipulated for,[52] justifies rescission, but a breach in an immaterial or non-fundamental respect justifies a claim of damages only, and does not justify rescission.

Whether a particular breach is or is not material is a question of fact. Parties may competently specify in their contract that failure in any stated respect is to be deemed material, but failing such stipulation it is a matter of interpretation in the circumstances whether the breach which has happened could justifiably be deemed material or not.[53] "The general rule is that only a breach of a material term of a contract justifies its rescission. But here the parties have made it a part of their agreement that any breach on the part of the hirer entitles the owner to resume possession of the vehicle." [54]

There is no doubt that a total failure in performance is a material breach justifying rescission.[55] Failure in respect of one or two of a number of stipulations is very much a question of degree, depending on the circumstances of the particular case.[56] In case of defective performance, contractual stipulations as to character, quantity,[57] description,[58] or quality are normally material, but whether or not the right to rescind exists depends on the degree of failure.[59] In case of delay in performance, the materiality of the breach depends not only on the length of the delay, but on the nature of the contract, the nature of the goods, whether they are perishable, of fluctuating price, and so on. In contracts of charter-party delay in shipment,[60] or in the arrival of a ship [61] are commonly material. In contracts for the supply or carriage of goods of fluctuating price, stipulations as to time are prima facie material.[62]

51 *Wade* v. *Waldon,* 1909 S.C. 571, 576; *Forselind* v. *Bechely-Crundall,* 1922 S.C. (H.L.) 173, 192.

52 *Bettini* v. *Gye* (1876) 1 Q.B.D. 183.

53 *Shaw* v. *McDonell* (1786) Mor. 9185; *Birkett, Sperling & Co.* v. *Engholm* (1871) 10 M. 170; *Davie* v. *Stark* (1876) 3 R. 1114; *Grieve* v. *Konig* (1880) 7 R. 521; *London Guarantee Co.* v. *Fearnley* (1880) 5 App.Cas. 911; *Wade, supra,* 576; *Bell Bros. (H.P.) Ltd.* v. *Aitken,* 1939 S.C. 577, 588.

54 *Bell Bros. (H.P.) Ltd.* v. *Aitken,* 1939 S.C. 577, 589, *per* Lord Fleming.

55 *Johannesburg Municipal Council* v. *Stewart,* 1909 S.C.(H.L.) 53.

56 See *e.g. Shaw* v. *McDonell* (1786) Mor. 9185; *Birkett, Sperling & Co.* v. *Engholm* (1871) 10 M. 170; *Davie* v. *Stark* (1876) 3 R. 1114; *Wade* v. *Waldon,* 1909 S.C. 571.

57 *Cf.* Sale of Goods Act 1893, s. 30 (1) and (2).

58 *Cf.* Sale of Goods Act 1893, s. 30 (3).

59 See *e.g. Webster* v. *Cramond Iron Co.* (1875) 2 R. 752; *Scottish Heritable Security Co.* v. *Granger* (1881) 8 R. 459; *Bradley* v. *Dollar* (1886) 13 R. 893; *Webster* v. *Brown* (1892) 19 R. 765; *Hampton* v. *Galloway & Sikes* (1899) 1 F. 501; *McKimmie's Trs.* v. *Armour* (1899) 2 F. 156; *Todd* v. *Bowie* (1902) 4 F. 435.

60 *Bowes* v. *Shand* (1877) 2 App. Cas. 455; *Grieve* v. *Konig* (1800) 7 R. 521; *Shaw Macfarlane & Co.* v. *Waddell,* (1900) 2 F. 1070.

61 *Mackenzie* v. *Liddell* (1883) 10 R. 705; *Dunford & Elliot* v. *Macleod* (1902) 4 F. 912; *Nelson* v. *Dundee East Coast Shipping Co.,* 1907 S.C. 927.

62 *Colvin* v. *Short* (1857) 19 D. 890.

On the other hand delay in payment is not by any means always breach of a material condition of the contract.[63] It may be, but only in rather special circumstances.[64] But a seller is not bound to wait indefinitely for payment and after the lapse of a reasonable time may rescind the contract.[65]

Cases of instalment contracts

Difficult questions may arise in instalment contracts as to whether a breach in respect of one or more instalments amounts to a repudiation of the whole contractual obligation.[66] Apart from the case where each instalment is stated by the contract to be a separate contract,[67] the decision has been said to depend on the ratio quantitatively which the breach bears to the contract as a whole and the degree of probability or improbability that such a breach will be repeated.[68] It has been recognised that the further the parties have proceeded with performance the more difficult it is to infer total repudiation from a breach in respect of one instalment.[69] Repeated defaults justify rescission.[70] By stipulation, or from the nature of the contract, it may be apparent that due performance of every instalment was essential and any lapse fundamental. Equally one party is not bound to put up with repeated defaults, even though each by itself might be trivial.[71] If one defective instalment is accepted subject to a claim of damages for the defect, the defect cannot be treated as a repudiation of the contract or as justifying rescission of the rest of the contract.[72]

Wrong decision to treat as material

If a party treats as material a breach which in the circumstances was truly only immaterial and intimates rescission of the contract on that account, this wrongful and unjustified rescission is itself a fundamental breach of contract which entitles the other party to rescind and claim damages. In *Wade* v. *Weldon*,[73] W. engaged R. to perform at his theatres, subject to the condition, *inter alia*, that artistes must give fourteen days notice and bill matter. R. failed to do so and W. refused to let him appear. In counter-actions for breach of contract, the first Division held that R. was in breach of contract to a non-material extent, but that this did not

63 *Forbes* v. *Campbell* (1885) 12 R. 1065. *Cf.* Sale of Goods Act 1893, s. 10 (1); *Linn* v. *Shields* (1863) 2 M. 88; *Rodger (Builders) Ltd.* v. *Fawdry*, 1950 S.C. 483 (sale of heritage).

64 *Barclay* v. *Anderston Foundry Co.* (1856) 18 D. 1190; *Turnbull* v. *McLean* (1874) 1 R. 730; *Morris* v. *Baron* [1918] A.C. 1.

65 *Black* v. *Dick* (1814) Hume 699.

66 See *e.g. Mersey Steel & Iron Co.* v. *Naylor Benzon & Co.* (1884) 9 App. Cas. 434.

67 *Higgins* v. *Pumpherston Oil Co.* (1893) 20 R. 532.

68 *Maple Flock Co.* v. *Universal Furniture Products Ltd.* [1934] 1 K.B. 148, 157.

69 *Honck* v. *Muller* (1881) 7 Q.B.D. 92; *Cornwall* v. *Henson* [1900] 2 Ch. 298, 304.

70 *Goran Rope and Sailcloth Co.* v. *Weir* (1897) 24 R. 368.

71 *Barr* v. *Waldie* (1893) 21 R. 224; *Dunford & Elliot* v. *Macleod* (1902) 4 F. 912.

72 *Sanderson* v. *Armour*, 1922 S.C. (H.L.) 117.

73 1909 S.C. 571. *Cf. Carswell* v. *Collard* (1893) 20 R.(H.L.) 47.

entitle W. to rescind, by refusing to let him appear. On the other hand W. was in undoubted breach of contract in not allowing R. to play, and this was unjustified, inasmuch as W. had no right to treat R's failure as a breach entitling him to put an end to the contract altogether. R. was therefore allowed a proof as to the damage he had suffered.[73]

Damages combined with rescission

A party who is entitled to, and who does justifiably, rescind a contract, may also claim damages in compensation for any loss he has incurred by reason of the total non-performance of the contract.[74]

Rescission and real rights in property

The exercise of the right to rescind a contract affects future liabilities only, and does not effect a cancellation of real rights in property already acquired by either party under the contract. Thus if the property in goods has passed to the buyer under a contract of sale the property does not revert if the buyer refuses to pay, even though that failure is material and would have entitled the seller to refuse delivery if made earlier.[75] The same is true in a case of sale of heritage, though excambion is exceptional in that if either party is evicted he may recover the lands which he has conveyed.[76] On the other hand where under the contract the party in breach has acquired a right not amounting to a right of property his right may be ended by his material breach; thus a landlord has frequently been held entitled to irritate a tenant's lease where the tenant has failed to remain in possession.[77]

Rescission and independent debts

A material breach of contract justifying rescission by the other party does not exempt the innocent party from liability for debts to the party in breach which accrued previously and independently, though it may entitle him to exercise a right of retention in security of his claim of damages. Thus a landlord is entitled to arrears of rent though in breach to the tenant to an extent which entitles the latter to retain his rent or even rescind the lease,[78] an employee to his wages for past services, though dismissed for fault,[79] and an agent is entitled to commission earned for the period prior to his being in breach of contract with his principal.[80]

[74] *Couston, Thomson & Co.* v. *Chapman* (1872) 10 M.(H.L.) 74; *Davie* v. *Stark* (1876) 3 R. 1114; *Duff* v. *Iron Buildings Co.* (1891) 19 R. 119; *Dunford & Elliot* v. *Macleod* (1902) 4 F. 912; *Johannesburg Municipal Council* v. *Stewart*, 1909 S.C. 860, 877, revd. 1909 S.C.(H.L.) 53. On the measures of damages see Chap. 30 *infra*.

[75] Stair I, 14, 2; Bell, *Comm.* I, 257; *Richmond* v. *Railton* (1854) 16 D. 403; *cf.* Sale of Goods Act 1893, ss. 17, 39.

[76] Stair I, 14, 1; *Home* v. *Ker* (1622) Mor. 3677; *Wards* v. *Balcomie* (1629) Mor. 3678.

[77] *Hamilton* v. *H.* (1845) 8 D. 308; *Edmond* v. *Reid* (1871) 9 M. 782.

[78] *Christie* v. *Wilson*, 1915 S.C. 645.

[79] *Gibson* v. *McNaughton* (1861) 23 D. 358.

[80] *Graham* v. *United Turkey Red Ltd.*, 1922 S.C. 533.

Rescission precluded by counter-performance

Rescission is precluded if the innocent party has already performed all obligations incumbent on him under the contract and only awaits payment by the other. In such a case his sole remedy is to seek to exact payment, by threats, by taking decree and doing diligence, or by petitioning for sequestration or liquidation.

CHAPTER 5

CLAIMS OF RETENTION OR LIEN AND OF COMPENSATION; RIGHT OF STOPPAGE IN TRANSITU

WHERE one party to a contract does not desire to rescind the contract on the ground of the other party's failure, or where the latter's breach is not so material as to justify rescission of the contract,[1] he may have some remedy by withholding performance of the obligations incumbent on him as a compulsitor on the other party to perform, or as security for his claim of damages. This involves exercise of the right of retention, which may in some cases be given effect to by pleading compensation or set off against the other party's claim. The right of stoppage *in transitu* is a right peculiar to sale of goods but essentially similar in nature and purpose to the form of retention known as lien. " Compensation and retention and balancing accounts in bankruptcy are all equitable pleas and are available only when founded on equity." [2]

RETENTION

A claim of retention covers all cases where one party claims a right to withhold performance of some or all of the obligations incumbent on him until those due to him are implemented. It takes three forms, a right of retention on a title of property, a right of retention of money payable until a counter-obligation is implemented, and a right to retain some corporeal moveable property belonging to the debtor but in the creditor's possession until a debt is paid. The last form is commonly called a right of lien.

The basis of all three forms of claim is the general equitable rule of Scots law that reciprocal obligations arising under a mutual contract are the counterparts of each other and that, under suitable circumstances, a party to such a contract will be permitted to withhold performance of his obligations unless and until the other party performs his, or, to put it from the opposite angle, that failure to perform a material part of the contract on the part of one party will disentitle him from demanding performance from the other.[3] Retention is " one of the equitable remedies available generally in respect of mutual contracts containing reciprocal

1 *Cf. Linn* v. *Shields* (1863) 2 M. 88; *Macdonald* v. *Kydd* (1901) 3 F. 923; *Todd* v. *Bowie* (1902) 4 F. 435.

2 *Shepherd's Trs.* v. *Macdonald, Fraser & Co.* (1898) 5 S.L.T. 296.

3 Bell, *Prin.* § 1410; *Stobbs* v. *Hislop*, 1948 S.C. 216, 223, *per* L.P. Cooper, citing Bell, *Prin.* § 71; Rankine, *Leases*, 327; Gloag, *Contract*, 628.

obligations, wherever circumstances permit of resort to it. Its exercise is, however, always controlled by the court and regulated by reference to equitable considerations in the light of the circumstances of each case." [4]

(1) Retention based on right of property

A right of retention exists where a person holds property, heritable or moveable, under a title *ex facie* absolute and unqualified but in fact subject to a personal obligation to transfer it to another, as where an owner has agreed to sell goods but the property has not passed to the buyer, or where he holds heritable property *ex facie* absolutely but subject to an obligation to reconvey. In such circumstances he is not bound to transfer or convey until all claims due to him have been satisfied, and that whether or not the claims have any connection with the obligation under which he is bound to transfer.[5] This form of retention is based on right of property, not on mere possession, and exists even if the creditor does not have actual possession.[6]

Thus in sale of goods at common law the seller could not be required to deliver goods (and delivery was then necessary to pass the right of property) until the price was paid, or any other claim against the buyer satisfied,[7] and the same principle would still apply in a case of sale of heritage. Under the Sale of Goods Act 1893, s. 61, the unpaid seller may still have this common law right of retention if the property has not passed, but section 39 (2) may mean that he has no better right when the property has not passed than when it has. If, however, as normally happens, the property has passed (ss. 17–18) independently of delivery, the seller can exercise only the rights of lien, stoppage *in transitu* and resale conferred by the Act (s. 39), and that only when the whole of the price has not been paid or tendered, or when a bill or other negotiable instrument had been received as conditional payment and the condition not been fulfilled (s. 38).

Similarly where heritage [8] is disponed, or an incorporeal moveable right [9] is conveyed, or a bill of lading transferred or a delivery order transferred and the transfer intimated to the storekeeper,[10] *ex facie* absolutely but truly in security, the transferee holds the property not only for the debt for which it was transferred but also for any subsequent claim against the transferor.[11] The right of retention is, moreover, not excluded

4 *Ibid.* 228, *per* Lord Russell.

5 Bell, *Comm.* I, 724; *Maitland* v. *Cockerell* (1827) 6 S. 109; *Mein* v. *Bogle* (1828) 6 S. 360; *Tierney* v. *Court* (1832) 10 S. 664; *Russell* v. *E. Breadalbane* (1831) 5 W. & S. 256; *Leckie* v. *Leckie* (1854) 17 D. 77.

6 *Melrose* v. *Hastie* (1851) 13 D. 880; *Nelson* v. *Gordon* (1874) 1 R. 1093.

7 *Black* v. *Incorporation of Bakers* (1867) 6 M. 136, 140; see also *Robertson's Tr.* v. *Baird* (1852) 14 D. 1010; *Wyper* v. *Harveys* (1861) 23 D. 606; *Distillers' Co.* v. *Russell's Tr.* (1889) 16 R. 479.

8 *National Bank* v. *Forbes* (1858) 21 D. 79; *Nelson* v. *Gordon* (1874) 1 R. 1093; *National Bank* v. *Union Bank* (1886) 14 R. (H.L.) 1.

9 *Russell* v. *E. Breadalbane* (1831) 5 W. & S. 256; *Colquhoun's Trs.* v. *Diack* (1901) 4 F. 358; *Robertson's Trs.* v. *Riddell*, 1911 S.C. 14.

10 *Hamilton* v. *Western Bank* (1856) 19 D. 152.

11 *Hamilton, supra; Nelson, supra; Hayman* v. *McLintock*, 1907 S.C. 936.

by an undertaking in any back-bond or other deed qualifying the transfer to reconvey on demand [12] or on a particular claim being satisfied.[13] But the transferee cannot ignore a provision in the back-bond that the transfer is to cover debts not exceeding a stated sum only,[14] nor can he retain in security of advances made after receipt of intimation that the transferor's right of reversion has been assigned to a third party in security of other advances.[15]

(2) Retention of money until counter-claim satisfied

Where counter-obligations arise from a single contract, each is dependent and conditional on the other and if performance on one side is not made, or defectively made, the other party may withhold payment until performance is made or his claim for damages for non-performance or defective performance quantified.[16] Thus retention may be exercised of freight where a carrier has delayed goods or damaged them,[17] of storage dues where the storekeeper has damaged the goods,[18] of wages where the employee has failed to perform his duties,[19] of payment where a contractor has delayed to complete his contract,[20] of rent where the landlord has failed to make the premises available to the tenant [21] or to put them into tenantable repair [22] or has caused damage by mineral workings,[23] though not for the landlord's delay in repairing,[24] or his failure to provide a proper water supply,[25] of the price where delivery or performance had not been made at the due time,[26] or within a reasonable time,[27] of the final payment under a building contract until a claim for damages for

12 *Colquhoun's Trs., supra.*

13 *Russell, supra.*

14 *Anderson's Tr.* v. *Somerville & Co.* (1899) 36 S.L.R. 833.

15 *Union Bank* v. *National Bank* (1886) 14 R.(H.L.) 1; *cf. Hopkinson* v. *Rolt* (1861) 9 H.L. Cas. 514; *Deeley* v. *Lloyds Bank* [1912] A.C. 756.

16 Bell, *Prin.* § 71; *Gloag on Contract*, 628; *Macbride* v. *Hamilton* (1875) 2 R. 775, 779.

17 *Taylor* v. *Forbes* (1830) 9 S. 113; *McDonald* v. *Thomson* (1843) 5 D. 719.

18 *Gibson & Stewart* v. *Brown* (1876) 3 R. 328.

19 *Tait* v. *McIntosh* (1841) 13 S.Jur. 280; *Scottish N.E. Ry.* v. *Napier* (1859) 21 D. 700; *Gibson* v. *McNaughton* (1861) 23 D. 358; *Sharp* v. *Rettie* (1884) 11 R. 745. See also *Pegler* v. *Northern Agricultural Implement Co.* (1877) 4 R. 435.

20 *Johnston* v. *Robertson* (1861) 23 D. 646; *Macbride* v. *Hamilton* (1875) 2 R. 775.

21 *Kilmarnock Gas Light Co.* v. *Smith* (1872) 11 M. 58; *Guthrie* v. *Shearer* (1873) 1 R. 181; *Sawers* v. *McConnell* (1874) 1 R. 392; *Critchley* v. *Campbell* (1884) 11 R. 475; *Muir* v. *Macintyres* (1887) 14 R. 470; *Duncan* v. *Brooks* (1894) 21 R. 760; *Dougall* v. *Dunfermline Mags.*, 1908 S.C. 151. *Cf. Brodie* v. *MacLachlan* (1900) 8 S.L.T. 145.

22 *Graham* v. *Gordon* (1843) 5 D. 1207; *Munro* v. *McGeochs* (1888) 16 R. 93; *Sivwright* v. *Lightbourne* (1890) 17 R. 917; *Macdonald* v. *Kydd* (1901) 3 F. 923; *Christie* v. *Birrells*, 1910 S.C. 986; *E. Galloway* v. *McConnell*, 1911 S.C. 846; *Haig* v. *Boswall-Preston*, 1915 S.C. 339; *Fingland & Mitchell* v. *Howie*, 1926 S.C. 319. See also *Christie* v. *Wilson*, 1915 S.C. 645.

23 *Daniel Stewart's Hospital* v. *Waddell* (1890) 17 R. 1077.

24 *Guthrie* v. *Shearer* (1873) 1 R. 181; *Stewart* v. *Campbell* (1889) 16 R. 346; *Christie* v. *Birrells, supra.*

25 *Burns* v. *McNeil* (1898) 5 S.L.T. 289; *Russell* v. *Sime*, 1912, 2 S.L.T. 344; *cf. Christie* v. *Wilson*, 1915 S.C. 645.

26 *Johnston* v. *Robertson* (1861) 23 D. 646.

27 *British Motor Body Co.* v. *Shaw*, 1914 S.C. 922, overruling contrary opinion in *Macbride* v. *Hamilton* (1875) 2 R. 775.

delay in completion was settled,[28] of an executry estate in extinction of a debt due to the executor's solicitor by the deceased,[29] of feuduties so long as the superior's obligation to form streets was unfulfilled,[30] and in other similar cases.

In the particular case of sale of goods the right is unaffected by the Sale of Goods Act 1893; by section 53 (1) a failure to perform a material part of the contract may be set up by the buyer against the seller in diminution of the price.[31]

This plea of retention may be invoked *ope exceptionis* in defence to a claim by the other party for the price.[32]

Exclusion of right of retention

The right of retention may be excluded expressly or by implication in the contract giving rise to the question of retention. Thus a lease may exclude the right to retain rent,[33] though an exclusion clause should be narrowly construed if its terms permit.[34] A sale may doubtless provide for payment whether performance be delayed or not.

Similarly the right may be held inconsistent with relevant statutory provisions, such as the provisions of the Rent Acts regulating possession of a house.[35]

Equitable control of right of retention

Certainly in cases of retention of rent, the courts have had regard to the materiality of the landlord's breach of contract and the probable damage sustained by the tenant in determining whether, and if so how much, rent might be retained.[36]

Liquid debt cannot be retained by reason of illiquid claim arising on another ground

Moreover, a person is not in general entitled to withhold payment of a sum due to another because that other is in default to him on another contract.[37] It will not even suffice to elide this rule that both contracts were within a single course of dealing.[38] Nor can a debt which is liquid and ascertained in terms of money and also due and payable be withheld under a plea of retention in respect of a claim of damages arising out of

[28] *Port Glasgow Mags.* v. *Scottish Construction Co.*, 1960 S.L.T. 319.
[29] *Mitchell* v. *Mackersy* (1905) 8 F. 198.
[30] *Arnott's Trs.* v. *Forbes* (1881) 9 R. 89; see also *Thom* v. *Chalmers* (1886) 13 R. 1026.
[31] *Cf. British Motor Body Co., supra*, 928–929.
[32] *British Motor Body Co., supra.*
[33] *Skene* v. *Cameron*, 1942 S.C. 393.
[34] *Ibid.* 401, *per* Lord Normand.
[35] *Stobbs* v. *Hislop*, 1948 S.C. 216.
[36] *Bowie* v. *Duncan* (1807) Hume 839; *Stobbs* v. *Hislop*, 1948 S.C. 216, 226.
[37] *Scottish N.E. Ry.* v. *Napier* (1859) 21 D. 700; *Smith* v. *S.* (1866) 4 M. 279; *Mackie* v. *Riddell* (1874) 2 R. 115; *Sutherland* v. *Urquhart* (1895) 23 R. 284; *Grewar* v. *Cross* (1904) 12 S.L.T. 84; *Asphaltic Limestone Co.* v. *Glasgow Corpn.*, 1907 S.C. 463.
[38] *Scott* v. *Aitken*, 1950 S.L.T.(Notes) 34; *Fulton Clyde Ltd.* v. *McCallum*, 1960 S.L.T. 253 (point not reported in 1960 S.C. 78).

another contract,[39] or arising on another ground of law.[40] Thus a debt, being the price of a thing sold, could not, it was held, be retained in respect of a claim of damages for delict, namely fraud which had allegedly induced the sale.[41] In such a case, however, decree may be granted for the liquid debt and the action be continued to try the defender's counter-claim.[42]

In exceptional cases, however, retention has been permitted by virtue of an illiquid claim where the latter could be readily and quickly verified, or where, in the court's view, it would be unjust to refuse the claim to retain.[43]

Balancing accounts in bankruptcy

Also, where one party is bankrupt, or at least it is averred that he is insolvent, on the principle of balancing accounts in bankruptcy, the other party may withhold payment of a sum due and payable in respect of a claim against the bankrupt which is contingent, or not yet due, or illiquid, as otherwise he would have to pay in full and seek to recover only a dividend on any sum found due to him.[44] Probably any claim against the bankrupt may justify retention in the case of bankruptcy, unless the claim is so speculative, or dependent on a contingency so remote, that it is impossible to arrive at its present value. " It is practically settled that anyone who has a claim against an insolvent estate is entitled to keep back money which he owes to that estate, and cannot be compelled to pay in full while he only receives a dividend." [45]

(3) Retention of (or lien on) moveables founded on possession

The principle of mutuality of obligations arising from contract also underlies the rule that where, under a contract, one person lawfully obtains possession of the corporeal moveable property of another, that person has a right to retain those moveables until certain counter-claims against the owner of the moveables are satisfied. Under the influence of English law this kind of retention is frequently called a right of lien.[46] Retention " may be described as a right to retain a subject legitimately in one's possession until a debt shall be paid, or an engagement performed, the *jus exigendi* of which is in the possessor." [47] " It is the general rule,

93 Ersk. III, 4, 15; Bell, *Prin.* § 573; *National Exchange Co.* v. *Drew* (1855) 2 Macq. 103; *Scottish N.E. Ry., supra*; *Fulton Clyde Ltd.* v. *McCallum*, 1960 S.C. 78.

40 *Burt* v. *Bell* (1861) 23 D. 13.

41 *Smart* v. *Wilkinson*, 1928 S.C. 383.

42 *Fulton Clyde Ltd., supra.*

43 *Munro* v. *Macdonald's Exors.* (1866) 4 M. 687; *Ross* v. *R.* (1895) 22 R. 461; *Lovie* v. *Baird's Trs.* (1895) 23 R. 1 (on which see *Sutherland* v. *Urquhart* (1895) 23 R. 284); *Henderson* v. *Turnbull*, 1909 S.C. 510; *Booth* v. *Thomson*, 1972 S.L.T. 141. Contrast *McConnell & Reid* v. *Muir* (1906) 14 S.L.T. 79.

44 Bell, *Comm.* II, 122; *Mill* v. *Paul* (1825) 4 S. 219; *Borthwick* v. *Scottish Widows Fund* (1864) 2 M. 595; *Hannay's Tr.* v. *Armstrong* (1877) 4 R.(H.L.) 43; *Scott's Tr.* v. *Scott* (1887) 14 R. 1043; *Taylor's Tr.* v. *Paul* (1888) 15 R. 313; *Ross, supra.*

45 *Ross, supra*, 465, *per* Lord McLaren.

46 *Cf.* generally Bell, *Prin.* § 1410 *et seq.*

47 Bell, *Prin.* § 1410.

apart from any question of custom of trade, or the law affecting any particular class of employment, that the party who has been placed in possession of an article belonging to another that he may do some work upon it is not bound to return it until he is paid for his work." [48] A lien is "a particular instance of the right of retention, which the law for equitable reasons confers on those who have possession of the property or goods of another, to withhold or detain such property or goods from the proprietor till indemnified for labour or money expended on them under any contract, or till payment of any debts due by the proprietor to the possessor; the right in the former case being known as a special lien and in the latter case as a general lien." [49]

Applicable to moveables only

The right of retention or lien can be exercised in respect of corporeal moveables only, not of heritage.[49a] At common law,[50] and normally also by its Articles of Association, a company has a lien over shares held by a shareholder in satisfaction of debts due by the shareholder to the company. In this case the lien is properly over the money paid to the company, represented by the shares, and which would be repayable to the member on liquidation if the company is solvent. The right of lien does not seem to exist in respect of any other kind of incorporeal moveable right.

Over what things exercisable

Lien can probably be founded on possession of any kind of moveable property, certainly over vehicles, ships [51] and articles of commerce, but also over books of account,[52] title deeds,[53] negotiable instruments,[54] stock and share certificates,[55] and domesticated animals. An unpaid seller who has made part delivery of goods sold may exercise his right of lien on the remainder, unless such part delivery was made in such circumstances as to show an agreement to waive the lien.[56]

Services giving rise to right

Any kind of services on or in relation to the goods may justify a right of retention or lien. Thus lien has been exercised by virtue of services

[48] Gloag, *Contract*, 631.
[49] *Grand Empire Theatres Liqdr.* v. *Snodgrass*, 1932 S.C.(H.L.) 73, 76, *per* Lord Macmillan.
[49a] *Turner* v. *T.* (1811) Hume 854; *Castle-Douglas Ry.* v. *Lee* (1859) 22 D. 18.
[50] *Hotchkis* v. *Royal Bank* (1797) Mor. 2673; 3 Pat. 618; *Burns* v. *Lawrie's Trs.* (1840) 2 D. 1348; *Bell's Tr.* v. *Coatbridge Tinplate Co.* (1886) 14 R. 246; *Paul's Tr.* v. *Justice*, 1912 S.C. 1303.
[51] *Barr & Shearer* v. *Cooper* (1875) 2 R.(H.L.) 14; *Ross & Duncan* v. *Baxter* (1885) 13 R. 185.
[52] *Liqdr. of Donaldson & Co.* v. *White & Park*, 1908 S.C. 309.
[53] *Drummond* v. *Muirhead & Guthrie Smith* (1900) 2 F. 585; *Liqdr. of Weir & Wilson* v. *Turnbull & Findlay*, 1911 S.C. 1006.
[54] *Robertson's Tr.* v. *Royal Bank* (1890) 18 R. 12.
[55] *Alston's Tr.* v. *Royal Bank* (1893) 20 R. 887.
[56] Sale of Goods Act 1893, s. 42. *Cf. Mechan* v. *N.E. Ry.*, 1911 S.C. 1348.

as carrier,[57] repairer,[58] storer,[59] bleacher,[60] professional services,[61] and it may be exercised by a seller of goods, as seller,[62] or as agent or custodier for the buyer.[63] If a person obtains possession of goods under a contract for services he may retain them for a debt arising from that employment, even though he may have done no work on the goods themselves but merely used them in connection with the services which he was employed to do.[64]

For what claims competent

A right of retention or lien may be exercised in respect of a claim for payment for the work done on or in relation to the goods retained,[65] or in respect of a claim of damages for a breach of contract by the other party.[66] But if a buyer of goods rejects the goods as being disconform to contract he may not retain them in security of a claim for damages.[67] If he retains, he retains as buyer.

Lien and express contract

The right of retention or lien is conferred by legal implication, particularly in contracts of sale,[68] of *locatio operis faciendi* and *locatio custodiae.* It may also be conferred expressly by the contract under which possession is transferred. It has been defined as a " contract of pledge collateral to another contract of which it is an incident." [69]

The right may also be expressly excluded by contract,[70] but this exclusion will not readily be inferred merely from such a document as a receipt,[71] or an undertaking to grant a discharge when required.[72] It has been held excluded where the hire-purchaser or other limited owner of moveables himself held them under a contract which precluded him from creating any lien over the moveable subject for repairs, even though this limitation was not disclosed to the party claiming the right to retain for money unpaid,[73] on the principle that, as in express pledge, the possessor can give no better title than he has himself acquired from the owner, unless

57 Bell, *Prin.* § 1423–1425.
58 *Ross & Duncan* v. *Baxter* (1885) 13 R. 185; *Garscadden* v. *Ardrossan Dry Dock Co.*, 1910 S.C. 178.
59 *Laurie* v. *Denny's Tr.* (1853) 15 D. 404.
60 *Harper* v. *Faulds* (1791) Bell *Oct. Cas.* 440.
61 *Findlay* v. *Waddell*, 1910 S.C. 670.
62 Sale of Goods Act 1893, s. 41 (1).
63 *Ibid.*, s. 41 (2).
64 *Meikle & Wilson* v. *Pollard* (1880) 8 R. 69; *Robertson* v. *Ross* (1887) 15 R. 67; *Findlay* v. *Waddell*, 1910 S.C. 670.
65 *e.g. Findlay* v. *Waddell*, 1910 S.C. 670.
66 *Moore's Carving Machine Co.* v. *Austin* (1890) 33 S.L.R. 613; *Glendinning* v. *Hope*, 1911 S.C.(H.L.) 73.
67 *Padgett* v. *McNair* (1852) 15 D. 76; *Lupton* v. *Schulze* (1900) 2 F. 1118.
68 Sale of Goods Act 1893, ss. 39 (1) (*a*), 41.
69 *Miller* v. *Hutcheson & Dixon* (1881) 8 R. 489, 492, *per* Lord Young.
70 *Fisher* v. *Smith* (1878) 4 App.Cas. 1. *Cf. Fleming* v. *Smith* (1881) 8 R. 548.
71 *Robertson's Tr.* v. *Royal Bank* (1890) 18 R. 12.
72 *Cf. Colquhoun's Tr.* v. *Diack* (1901) 4 F. 358.
73 *Lamonby* v. *Foulds*, 1928 S.C. 89.

the owner is personally barred from founding on the limited title he has given the possessor.[74]

The claim, though not expressly excluded, may also be held excluded if inconsistent with the express terms of the contract under which the possession was obtained, as where money was deposited with a solicitor for an express purpose, which failed, and the solicitor sought to retain the money in respect of a business account due by the depositor.[75]

Possession essential for lien

For this right of retention or lien to arise it is essential that the person claiming it should have been entrusted with legal possession of the subjects, and not merely have the custody thereof. The distinction is that a possessor holds physically for his own rights and interests, saving only the claim of the absolute owner, whereas the custodier holds physically for and on behalf of the owner or possessor, and may have no right or interest of his own in the subjects at all.[76] Thus an accountant instructed to audit a company's books,[77] a solicitor,[78] the factor on a landed estate,[79] the repairer of a motor vehicle,[80] and a farmer on whose land a potato merchant's potatoes had been pitted [81] have been held to have full possession. On the other hand a servant,[82] a commercial traveller,[83] the manager of a branch business,[84] and the secretary of a company [85] have been held custodiers only, and consequently not entitled to claim a right of retention or lien. An employee, it is thought, has never more than custody of those articles belonging to his employer, which are entrusted to him in the course of, and for the purpose of, doing his work. To claim a lien he must be an independent contractor.

The possession requisite for lien must have been obtained lawfully and not by theft or fraud or accident or mistake,[86] and not when acting in another capacity from that of creditor in the obligation in issue.[87]

Possession under a contract of deposit, or with a specific appropriation inconsistent with the lien claimed will not justify retention.[88]

74 *Mitchell* v. *Heys* (1894) 21 R. 600.
75 *Middlemass* v. *Gibson*, 1910 S.C. 577. *Cf. McGregor* v. *Alley & McLellan* (1887) 14 R. 535.
76 Bell, *Prin.* § 1412.
77 *Findlay* v. *Waddell*, 1910 S.C. 670; *cf. Reid* v. *Galbraith* (1893) 1 S.L.T. 278; *Morrison* v. *Fulwell's Tr.* (1901) 9 S.L.T. 34; *Train & McIntyre* v. *Forbes*, 1925 S.L.T. 286.
78 *Paul* v. *Meikle* (1868) 7 M. 235.
79 *Robertson* v. *Ross* (1887) 15 R. 67; *Macrae* v. *Leith*, 1913 S.C. 901.
80 *Lamonby* v. *Foulds*, 1928 S.C. 89.
81 *Paton's Trs.* v. *Finlayson*, 1923 S.C. 872.
82 *Burns* v. *Bruce* (1799) Hume 29; *Martin* v. *Boyd* (1882) 19 S.L.R. 447.
83 *Dickson* v. *Nicholson* (1855) 17 D. 1011.
84 *Clift* v. *Portobello Pier Co.* (1877) 4 R. 462.
85 *Gladstone* v. *McCallum* (1896) 23 R. 783; *Barnton Hotel Co.* v. *Cook* (1899) 1 F. 1190.
86 Bell, *Prin.* § 1413; *Glendinning's Crs.* v. *Montgomery* (1745) Mor. 2573; *Harper* v. *Faulds* (1791) Bell's Oct.Cas. 440; *Mackenzie* v. *Newall* (1824) 3 S. 206; *Louson* v. *Craik* (1842) 4 D. 1452; *Dickson* v. *Nicholson* (1855) 17 D. 1011; *Shepherd's Trs.* v. *Macdonald, Fraser & Co.* (1898) 5 S.L.T. 296. *Cf. Brown* v. *Marr* (1880) 7 R. 427; *Martinez y Gomez* v. *Allison* (1890) 17 R. 332.
87 *National Bank* v. *White & Park*, 1909 S.C. 1308
88 Stair, I, 13, 9; Bell, *Prin.* § 1414; *Brown* v. *Sommerville* (1844) 6 D. 1267; *Lawrie* v. *Denny's Tr.* (1853) 15 D. 404; *National Bank* v. *Forbes* (1858) 21 D. 79; *Gray's Trs.* v. *Royal Bank* (1895) 23 R. 199; *Middlemas* v. *Gibson*, 1910 S.C. 577.

Possession after debtor's bankruptcy ineffectual

No claim of retention or lien can be founded on possession obtained after the debtor's bankruptcy,[89] or even in the knowledge of his insolvency.[90] Though a lien may be acquired over goods handed over in the ordinary course of business even though bankruptcy supervenes within sixty days,[91] it is thought that no effectual security could be created by deliberately transferring goods as security for a prior debt if bankruptcy supervened within sixty days.[92]

Extent of right of lien—special and general lien

In the normal case Scots law recognises only a special lien, or right to retain the thing in respect of a claim for work done on or in relation thereto only, and not a general lien, or right to retain the thing for any general balance of debt due to the claimant by the owner of the thing.[93] In the normal case, that is, retention or lien is based on the mutuality of obligations arising from one particular transaction, not on the state of accounts between those parties.

Thus it has been recognised that a person, such as a carrier by land or sea,[94] a bleacher,[95] a storekeeper,[96] a ship-carpenter[97] or shipbuilder,[98] given possession of moveables so that he may do something to or with them, is entitled to a special right of retention or lien only. Where a farmer allowed a potato merchant to use his land for the purpose of growing potatoes and the merchant became bankrupt, it was held that the farmer was entitled to a special lien over the potatoes from the time they were lifted and pitted on the land, if not from the time of planting.[99]

Debts covered by special lien

The claim in respect of which the right of retention or lien may be exercised may be a claim for the price of the goods themselves,[1] or of the work done,[2] or a claim for damages for breach of the contract under which possession was obtained.[3] Lien does not cover the expenses incurred in bringing an action for the price or the money due.[4]

89 Bell, *Comm.* II, 89; *Jackson* v. *Fenwick's Tr.* (1899) 6 S.L.T. 319; *Scottish Union and National Ins. Co.* v. *Fairley* (1900) 8 S.L.T. 154.
90 *Dickson* v. *Nicholson* (1855) 17 D. 1011.
91 *Anderson's Tr.* v. *Fleming* (1871) 9 M. 718; *Crockart's Tr.* v. *Hay*, 1913 S.C. 509; contrast *Morton's Tr.* v. *Fifeshire Auction Co.*, 1911, 1 S.L.T. 405.
92 *Anderson's Tr.*, *supra*.
93 Bell, *Prin.* § 1411.
94 Bell, *Prin.* § 1423–1425.
95 *Harper* v. *Faulds* (1791) Bell's Oct. Cas. 440; *Anderson's Tr.* v. *Fleming* (1871) 9 M. 718.
96 *Laurie* v. *Denny's Tr.* (1853) 15 D. 404.
97 *Ross & Duncan* v. *Baxter & Co.* (1885) 13 R. 185; *Garscadden* v. *Ardrossan Dry Dock Co.*, 1910 S.C. 178.
98 *Barr & Shearer* v. *Cooper* (1875) 2 R.(H.L.) 14.
99 *Paton's Trs.* v. *Finlayson*, 1923 S.C. 872.
1 Sale of Goods Act 1893, ss. 39 (1) (*a*); *Paton's Trs.* v. *Finlayson*, 1923 S.C. 872.
2 *Cf. Lamonby* v. *Foulds*, 1928 S.C. 89.
3 *Moore's Carving Machine Co.* v. *Austin* (1890) 33 S.L.R. 613; *Glendinning* v. *Hope*, 1911 S.C. (H.L.) 73.
4 *Garscadden* v. *Ardrossan Dry Dock Co.*, 1910 S.C. 178.

Unpaid seller's lien over goods sold

An unpaid seller of goods [5] still in possession of the goods, notwithstanding that the property in the goods may have passed to the buyer,[6] is entitled to retain possession until payment or tender of the price (a) where the goods have been sold without any stipulation as to credit, (b) where the goods have been sold on credit, but the term of credit has expired, and (c) where the buyer becomes insolvent.[7] The seller may exercise his right of lien notwithstanding that he is in possession of the goods as agent or custodier for the buyer.[8]

The lien is a lien for the price only, and not for charges for keeping the goods, because they are being kept against the buyer's will, and against him, not for him,[9] unless possibly in the case where the seller is holding as custodier for the buyer.

Where an unpaid seller has made part delivery of the goods, he may exercise his right of lien or retention on the remainder, unless such part delivery has been made under such circumstances as to show an agreement to waive the lien or right of retention.[10] The unpaid seller of goods loses his lien or right of retention thereon (a) when he delivers the goods to a carrier or other custodier for the purpose of transmission to the buyer without reserving the right of disposal of the goods, (b) when the buyer or his agent lawfully obtains possession [11] of the goods, and (c) by waiver thereof. The unpaid seller of goods, having a lien or right of retention thereon, does not lose his lien or right of retention by reason only that he has obtained decree for the price of the goods.[12]

Innkeeper's lien

An innkeeper [13] has a lien over the goods of travellers brought to the inn in the ordinary way, as the property of the guest, even though they are not really his, and even though the goods be not of the kind ordinarily brought by travellers for their use on a journey, but not over the known property of a third person, for the expense of keep or entertainment while in his inn on that journey.[14] By the Hotel Proprietors Act 1956, s. 2 (2), an hotel proprietor is not as innkeeper to have any lien on any vehicle or

5 As defined by Sale of Goods Act 1893, s. 38 (1).

6 *Ibid.*, s. 39 (1) (*a*).

7 *Ibid.*, s. 41 (1).

8 *Ibid.*, s. 41 (2).

9 *Somes* v. *British Empire Shipping Co.* (1860) 8 H.L. Cas. 338, 345.

10 *Ibid.*, s. 42; *cf. Mechan* v. *N.E. Ry.*, 1911 S.C. 1348.

11 *Cf. Paton's Trs.* v. *Finlayson*, 1923 S.C. 872, where potatoes grown on the seller's land and still there, though lifted by the buyer, were held still to be in the possession of the seller.

12 *Ibid.*, s. 43.

13 The duties, liabilities and rights which prior to the Hotel Proprietors Act 1956, attached to an innkeeper as such, by s. 1 (1) of that Act and subject to the provisions of that Act attach only to the proprietor of an hotel as defined by s. 1 (3) of that Act and not to any other person.

14 Bell, *Prin.* § 1428.

any property left therein, or any horse or other live animal or its harness or other equipment. His lien appears accordingly now to be limited to a guest's luggage.

The proprietor of premises who is not an hotel proprietor as statutorily defined [15] is not an " innkeeper " within the meaning of the law and does not have an innkeeper's lien. But he probably has at common law a lien over his guests' luggage, animals and vehicles brought on to his premises, for the amount of the guests' outstanding bill.

A livery stable-keeper has a lien at common law.[16]

Carrier's lien

A carrier by land or water, and probably also a carrier by air, has a lien over goods entrusted to him for freight [17] and for average,[18] and in the case of passengers, for their fare, but not without special contract for dead freight [19] nor for wharfage dues.

Lien for average loss

Where a general average loss has been incurred in the course of carriage by sea the shipmaster has a lien over and is entitled to detain the cargo for the cargo-owners' several shares of the average claim.[19a]

Salvor's lien

Persons performing salvage services have a lien over things salved for their salvage reward.[20]

General right of retention or lien

Only exceptionally is the right recognised to retain possession of moveables until all debts due to the claimant by the owner of the moveables are paid, even though the possession were obtained for a special purpose under a contract.[21] This wider right is recognised as an implied term of the contract of employment in the case of certain professions and trades only, probably on the basis of usage of trade or a rule based on such usage.[22]

15 Hotel Proprietors Act 1956, s. 1 (3).

16 Bell, *Prin.* § 1428.

17 Bell, *Prin.* § 1422–1423.

18 Bell, *Prin.* § 1423, 1426.

19 *Maclean & Hope* v. *Fleming* (1871) 9 M.(H.L.) 38; *Gray* v. *Carr* (1871) L.R. 6 Q.B. 522.

19a Bell, *Prin.* § 1426.

20 Bell, *Prin.* § 1427; See also Merchant Shipping Act 1894, s. 562. Salvors also have a maritime hypothec (or lien) for salvage independently of possession.

21 Bell, *Prin.* § 1431; *Harper* v. *Faulds* (1791) Bell's Oct. Cas. 440; *Stevenson* v. *Likly* (1824) 3 S. 291; *Stewart & Fletcher* v. *Macgregor* (1829) 7 S. 622; *Brown* v. *Sommerville* (1840) 6 D. 1267; *Laurie* v. *Denny's Tr.* (1853) 15 D. 404; *Hamilton* v. *Western Bank* (1856) 19 D. 152; *National Bank* v. *Forbes* (1858) 21 D. 79; *Smith* v. *Aikman* (1859) 22 D. 344.

22 Bell, *Comm.* II, 105.

Thus it has been recognised in cases of a solicitor,[23] for his business account and outlays, but not for advances,[24] a banker, for any balance due by the customer,[25] but not over papers held as depositary only,[26] an innkeeper, for the amount of the bill,[27] and a company over a shareholder's shares for debts due by him to the company,[28] but rejected in the cases of accountants [29] and of a factor on landed estate.[30]

It has also been recognised in cases of bleacher,[31] packers [32] and calico printers [33] but refused, on failure of proof of custom of trade, in cases of storekeepers [34] and scourers.[35]

A general lien is recognised also in probably all cases of mercantile agency, without proof of usage in the particular class of agency concerned, over all goods, documents, bills and money belonging to the employer which have come into the agent's possession in the course of the agency.[36] Thus it has been recognised in the case of a mercantile agent or factor for the purchase or sale of goods,[37] a stockbroker,[38] and an auctioneer.[39] The factor's lien extends not only over the goods themselves but over the price of the goods sold by the factor if the price be payable to him and be still unpaid, or if bills for the price are in his hands blank indorsed, or even if he have powers as factor to levy and discharge the debt.[40] It covers the agent's salary or commission, advances made to the principal and any liabilities incurred by him on the principal's behalf.[41] It does not cover, at least as against a principal who is bankrupt, debts to the agent arising on some separate account.[42]

[23] *Richardson* v. *Merry* (1863) 1 M. 940; *Paul* v. *Meikle* (1868) 7 M. 235; *Smith* v. *Jackson* (1871) 10 M. 211; *Palmer* v. *Lee* (1880) 7 R. 651; *Largue* v. *Urquhart* (1883) 10 R. 1229; *Adam & Winchester* v. *White's Tr.* (1884) 11 R. 863; *McIntosh* v. *Chalmers* (1883) 11 R. 8; *Reid, Johnston & Co.* v. *Japp & Yeaman* (1898) 6 S.L.T. 231; *Drummond* v. *Muirhead & Guthrie Smith* (1900) 2 F. 585; *Tawse* v. *Rigg* (1904) 6 F. 544; *Rorie* v. *Stevenson,* 1908 S.C. 559; *Liqdr. of Donaldson & Co.* v. *White & Park,* 1909 S.C. 309; *National Bank* v. *White & Park,* 1909 S.C. 1308; *Liqdr. of Weir & Wilson* v. *Turnbull & Findlay,* 1911 S.C. 1006.

[24] *Christie* v. *Ruxton* (1862) 24 D. 1182; *Wylie's Exrx.* v. *McJannet* (1901) 4 F. 195.

[25] Bell, *Prin.* § 1451; *Robertson's Tr.* v. *Royal Bank* (1890) 18 R. 12; *Alston's Tr.* v. *Royal Bank* (1893) 20 R. 887; contrast *National Bank* v. *Dickie's Tr.* (1895) 22 R. 740.

[26] *Brandao* v. *Burnett* (1846) 12 Cl. & F. 787; *Robertson's Tr.* v. *Royal Bank* (1890) 18 R. 12.

[27] Bell, *Prin.* § 1428.

[28] *Bell's Tr.* v. *Coatbridge Tinplate Co.* (1886) 14 R. 246; *Paul's Tr.* v. *Justice,* 1912 S.C. 1303.

[29] *Fulwell's Tr.* v. *Morrison* (1901) 9 S.L.T. 34; *Findlay* v. *Waddell,* 1910 S.C. 670.

[30] *Macrae* v. *Leith,* 1913 S.C. 901; see also *Robertson* v. *Ross* (1887) 15 R. 67.

[31] Bell, *Comm.* II, 104; *Aberdeen & Smith* v. *Paterson* (1812) Hume 127; *Anderson's Tr.* v. *Fleming* (1871) 9 M. 718.

[32] *Strong* v. *Phillips* (1878) 5 R. 770.

[33] *Mitchell* v. *Heys* (1894) 21 R. 600.

[34] *Laurie* v. *Denny's Tr.* (1853) 15 D. 404.

[35] *Smith* v. *Aikmans* (1859) 22 D. 344.

[36] Bell, *Prin.* § 1445.

[37] Bell, *Comm.* II, 109; *Prin.* § 1445; *Miller* v. *Hutcheson & Dixon* (1881) 8 R. 489; *Crockart's Tr.* v. *Hay,* 1913 S.C. 509.

[38] *Glendinning* v. *Hope,* 1911 S.C.(H.L.) 73.

[39] *Miller, supra*; *Mackenzie* v. *Cormack,* 1950 S.C. 183.

[40] Bell, *Comm.* II, 111; *Mackenzie, supra,* 195.

[41] *Sibbald* v. *Gibson* (1852) 15 D. 217; *Glendinning, supra.*

[42] *Miller* v. *McNair* (1852) 14 D. 955; *Brown* v. *Smith* (1893) 1 S.L.T. 158.

Debts covered by general lien

Where a general right of lien is recognised its range and extent depends on the custom of the particular profession or trade. Thus a solicitor's lien covers his business account,[43] and disbursements,[44] but not cash advances made to the client,[45] nor the account of his Edinburgh agent,[46] nor the account of his English correspondent, at least in cases where he has not paid the account and is not personally liable therefore.[47] Where a solicitor has acted for both parties he may still exercise his right of lien over the title deeds of the property, but not to the prejudice of the creditor in the transaction.[48] Nor can a solicitor who has undertaken to deliver certain writs withhold them under a plea of retention in respect of payment allegedly due by a previous owner of the property disponed.[49]

Debts not covered by general lien

Even where a general right of lien is recognised, because it is founded on an implied term of contract, it covers only debts arising from the exercise of the profession, business or trade in question, and not purely private debts, and is exercisable only over property possession of which has been acquired in the exercise of that profession, business or trade. Hence the solicitor's lien covers professional charges, but not advances of money to the client.[50] Lien cannot be claimed over property obtained by wrongful act[51] or by accident or mistake[52] or otherwise not under contract. A person entitled to a general lien in one capacity may not claim to exercise it over property possession of which he obtained in another capacity; thus a banker has a general lien as banker, but not over property deposited by the customer for safety, in relation to which the banker is a depositary.[53]

Effect of lien

The effect of a lien properly exercised over moveables is to deprive the owner of the use and benefit of the thing until his debt be satisfied or the counterpart of the contract otherwise be performed.[54] It is unaffected by the sale or other disposition of the goods by the owner, and may be exercised against the buyer as much as against the seller.

43 *Paul* v. *Meikle* (1868) 7 M. 235.
44 *Palmer* v. *Lee* (1880) 7 R. 651.
45 *Christie* v. *Ruxton* (1862) 24 D. 1182; *Wylie's Exrx.* v. *McJannet* (1901) 4 F. 195. *Cf. Anderson's Trs.* v. *Fleming* (1871) 9 M. 718.
46 *Largue* v. *Urquhart* (1883) 10 R. 1229.
47 *Grand Empire Theatre Liqdr.* v. *Snodgrass*, 1932 S.C.(H.L.) 73.
48 *Drummond* v. *Muirhead & Guthrie Smith* (1900) 2 F. 585.
49 *Reid, Johnston & Co.* v. *Japp & Yeaman* (1898) 6 S.L.T. 231.
50 *Christie* v. *Ruxton* (1862) 24 D. 1182; *Wylie's Exrx.* v. *McJannet* (1901) 4 F. 195. *Cf. Anderson's Tr.* v. *Fleming* (1871) 9 M. 718.
51 *Shepherd's Tr.* v. *Macdonald, Fraser & Co.* (1898) 5 S.L.T. 296.
52 *Louson* v. *Craik* (1842) 4 D. 1452; *Shepherd's Tr., supra.*
53 *McCall* v. *Black* (1824) 2 Sh.App. 188; *Brandao* v. *Burnett* (1846) 12 Cl. & F. 787; *National Bank* v. *White & Park*, 1909 S.C. 1308.
54 Bell, *Prin.* § 1417.

Loss of lien

A right of retention or lien, whether special or general, is lost if possession is surrendered of the thing over which the right existed.[55] A thing over which a lien subsists may be moved without affecting the lien, so long as possession is not surrendered.[56] Some of the things over which a lien exists may be surrendered without affecting the lien over the others.[57] Possession may also be surrendered but expressly under reservation of the security created by the lien, as where papers are claimed from a solicitor by a trustee in bankruptcy, or the liquidator of a company.[58]

Once possession has been surrendered and lien lost it does not revive if possession be recovered. There is no right to stop *in transitu* to preserve a lien.[59]

Lien is not lost by the death of either the party claiming the lien nor the party liable in the debt giving rise to the claim.[60]

Waiver of lien

A right of lien may always be waived by conduct indicating intention to surrender it. It has been held not to have been waived by taking in payment of the sum due a bill at short date and giving a receipt therefor the bill being discounted but dishonoured at maturity.[61]

Lien subject to control of court

A right of lien is an equitable claim and always subject to the control of the court,[62] and if the amount claimed is consigned the court will, certainly where the debt is disputed, require the article to be surrendered.[63] But if the debt is not disputed the court will not necessarily require surrender of the property merely on an offer of caution.[64] So too if the subject of a lien will deteriorate or become valueless if not sold, it is competent for the court to direct a sale, under reservation of the same preference over the price as existed before the sale over the subject itself.[65] Again a person having a lien over books and papers may be required to surrender them, without prejudice to the preference secured by the claim of lien.[66]

55 Bell, *Prin.* § 1415. *Cf. Johnston* v. *Duncan* (1827) 5 S. 660.
56 *Barr & Shearer* v. *Cooper* (1875) 2 R.(H.L.) 14.
57 *Gray* v. *Graham* (1855) 2 Macq. 435.
58 Bankruptcy (Sc.) Act, 1913, s. 76; Companies Act 1948, s. 268 (3); *Skinner* v. *Henderson* (1865) 3 M. 867; *Adam & Winchester* v. *White's Tr.* (1884) 11 R. 863; *Lochee Sawmills Co.* v. *Stevenson*, 1908 S.C. 559; *Train* v. *McIntyre's J.F.*, 1925 S.L.T. 286; *Miln's J.F.* v. *Spence's Trs.*, 1927 S.C. 425.
59 Bell, *Prin.* § 1416; *Morrison* v. *Fulwell's Tr.* (1901) 9 S.L.T. 34.
60 *Paul* v. *Meikle* (1868) 7 M. 235.
61 *Palmer* v. *Lee* (1880) 7 R. 651.
62 *Ferguson & Stuart* v. *Grant* (1856) 18 D. 536; *Garscadden* v. *Ardrossan Dry Dock Co.*, 1910 S.C. 178.
63 *Craig* v. *Howden* (1856) 18 D. 863; *Garscadden, supra.*
64 *Ferguson & Stuart, supra.*
65 *Parker* v. *Brown* (1878) 5 R. 979.
66 *Reid* v. *Galbraith* (1893) 1 S.L.T. 273; *Liqdr. of Donaldson & Co.* v. *White & Park*, 1908 S.C. 309; *Findlay* v. *Waddell*, 1910 S.C. 670.

Giving effect to lien

A lien, whether special or general, is by itself a right to retain in security only, which may be utilised in defence to a claim for return of the subjects held. It does not automatically give any right to sell or realise the subjects to pay the debt.

A person in right of a lien may, if he is a mercantile agent or factor and probably if he is a banker or stockbroker, and if the subjects over which the lien exists are realisable, sell the subjects to meet his claim.[67] The terms on which property is transferred may, however, permit a right of lien but not permit sale or realisation, at least without further authority.[68] It is very questionable if a tradesman employed to do work on property, such as to repair a car, is entitled to sell it for his repair charges, at least without notice and the authority of the court.[69] An unpaid seller of goods who has exercised his right of lien over goods still in his possession, notwithstanding that the property therein has passed to the buyer,[70] may, subject to the Act, resell the goods and recover damages for any loss occasioned by the original buyer's breach of contract.[71] An innkeeper has a statutory right of sale after six weeks, subject to statutory conditions.[72] Where the subject of a lien would become valueless or greatly deteriorated if it is not converted into money the court may, notwithstanding objections by the holder of the lien, direct a sale under reservation of the same preference over the price as existed before conversion over the subject itself.[73]

Under the Disposal of Uncollected Goods Act 1952, s. 1 (1) and (2), goods deposited for repair or other treatment may be sold by the depositary if the depositor fails both to pay or tender to the depositary his charges in relation to the goods, and to take delivery of the goods or give directions as to their delivery. The right of sale is conditional (s. 1 (3)) on (a) conspicuous display of a notice indicating that the deposit is subject to the Act and that it confers a right of sale after twelve months; (b) the giving of a notice, complying with section 1 (7) of the Act, that the goods are ready for redelivery; (c) after twelve months from the giving of the foregoing notice and not less than 14 days before the sale, the giving of a further notice, complying with section 1 (7), of intention to sell.

The sale must not be in a lot with another depositor's goods, nor otherwise than by public auction. The right to sell is suspended (s. 1 (4)) by a dispute between the parties about payment or redelivery, but a dispute may be treated as determined by notice by depositary to depositor (s. 1 (5)).

[67] Bell, *Comm.* II, 91; *Scott's Tr.* v. *Stewart, Primrose & Co.*, 17 Dec. 1814, F.C.
[68] *Robertson's Tr.* v. *Royal Bank* (1890) 18 R. 12, 20.
[69] *Cf. Gibson & Stewart* v. *Brown* (1876) 3 R. 328.
[70] Sale of Goods Act 1893, ss. 39 (1), 41.
[71] *Ibid.*, s. 48.
[72] Innkeepers Act 1878, s. 1.
[73] *Parker* v. *Brown* (1878) 5 R. 979 (maize stored in grain store).

The Act makes provision also for procedure after sale, and the return of any surplus to the depositor (s. 3).

COMPENSATION

Where two parties have mutual claims, both of which are liquid, *i.e.* due, and ascertained in terms of money,[74] it is competent to claim to set one off against the other and thus reduce the greater and extinguish the lesser.[75] In effect the party more indebted can claim to have to pay only the balance to the party less indebted.

Compensation must be expressly pleaded

Compensation does not operate automatically, and if a debtor has a claim with which to oppose and compensate his creditor's claim, he must table it in defence.[76] If decree passes against him, whether *in foro* or in absence, it is too late to plead compensation, and a counter-action must be brought.[77] Parties having mutual claims may, without action or decree, set off one against the other, though if an agreement to compensate is to extinguish a debt it probably must be in writing.[78]

If, however, compensation is pleaded and sustained, its effect is retrospective to the time when the parties became mutual debtor and creditor, and no interest is due *ex lege* from that date.[79]

Prescription may preclude compensation

It follows that a claim may be extinguished by prescription, even though until the prescriptive period had run, it could have been pleaded in compensation.[80] If the claim is affected by one of the short prescriptions it is not extinguished but, unless or until established by the competent mode of proof in a separate action, it cannot be founded on in defence, because it is no longer liquid or instantly verifiable.[81]

Debts must be liquid

Compensation applies in the ordinary case only between debts which are liquid, *i.e.* the amount of which is ascertained,[82] as by contract or decree, and which are due and payable. Accordingly a party sued cannot, in defence to a claim for a determinate sum presently due and payable,

[74] Bell, *Comm.* II, 122.
[75] Compensation Act 1592; Bell, *Comm.* II, 120; see also *Fowler* v. *Brown*, 1916 S.C. 597.
[76] Ersk. III, 4, 12; Bell, *Comm.* II, 124; *Prin.* § 575. Stair, I, 18, 6, has not been followed.
[77] Stair I, 18, 6; Ersk. III, 4, 19; *Anderson* v. *Schaw* (1739) Mor. 2646; *Paterson's Crs.* v. *McAulay* (1742) Mor. 2646. There is an exception in the case of a claim which has become liquid before the charge on the decree was given or the suspension disposed of, or where the original defender had no opportunity of pleading compensation as a bar to decree. This has been applied to a decree for expenses only: *Fowler* v. *Brown*, 1916 S.C. 579.
[78] *Cowan* v. *Shaw* (1878) 5 R. 680.
[79] *Cleland* v. *Stevenson* (1669) Mor. 2682; *Campbell* v. *Carruthers* (1757) Mor. Tack, Appx. 1.
[80] *Carmichael* v. *C.* (1719) Mor. 2677.
[81] *Baillie* v. *McIntosh* (1753) Mor. 2680; *Galloway* v. *G.* (1799) Mor. 11122.
[82] Bell, *Comm.* II, 122.

plead compensation by a debt not yet payable by the pursuer,[83] nor by a claim for which the pursuer's liability is only contingent,[84] nor by a claim which is disputed,[85] nor by a claim of damages, unless this counter-claim can be constituted and ascertained almost immediately.[86] In this last case it it always a question of circumstances and discretion whether the court is to allow ascertainment, or to require that to be done in a separate process.[86a] It is favourable to the defender's plea that he has already commenced action to constitute his claim,[87] but unfavourable that the claims could long ago have been constituted.[88] Ascertainment will commonly be allowed where the defender in a pecuniary claim has exercised a claim of retention, and where the ascertainment of his illiquid claim of retention is no more than investigating the merits of his defence against the pursuer's claim.

A plea of compensation has been admitted based on a debt due by an association in defence to a claim by the association for contributions to pay its debts,[89] on a claim for maintenance against a widow's claim for *jus relictae*,[90] on a claim under decrees against a claim for arrears of alimentary payments.[91]

A plea of compensation has been refused when based on a claim for meliorations during a lease in defence to a claim for the expense of repairs necessitated by the tenant's neglect,[92] on a claim of debt to, against a claim to a liferent from, a trust,[93] on a claim of expenses against a claim to payment of an alimentary allowance,[94] and on sums due under a decree-arbitral by, against arrears of calls on shares of, a company.[95]

Concursus debiti et crediti

To found a plea of compensation, the parties must be mutual debtor and creditor in the same legal capacities. Thus a person sued for a personal debt cannot plead compensation by virtue of a sum owed to him as executor,[96] or owed to a trust in which he had a beneficial interest,[97] or

[83] Ersk. III, 4, 15; Bell, *supra*; *Grewar* v. *Cross* (1904) 12 S.L.T. 84; *Pegler* v. *Northern Agricultural Implement Co.* (1877) 4 R. 435.
[84] *Paul & Thain* v. *Royal Bank* (1869) 7 M. 361.
[85] *Armour & Melvin* v. *Mitchell*, 1934 S.C. 94.
[86] *Ross* v. *Ross* (1895) 22 R. 461.
[86a] *Logan* v. *Stephen* (1850) 13 D. 262; *Johnston* v. *Robertson* (1861) 23 D. 646; *Stuart* v. *S.* (1869) 7 M. 366; *Lovie* v. *Baird's Trs.* (1895) 23 R. 1; *Sutherland* v. *Urquhart* (1895) 23 R. 284; *Grewar* v. *Cross* (1904) 12 S.L.T. 84; *Henderson* v. *Turnbull*, 1909 S.C. 510.
[87] *Munro* v. *Macdonald's Exors.* (1866) 4 M. 685; *Ross* v. *R.* (1895) 22 R. 461.
[88] *Hamilton* v. *McQueen* (1845) 7 D. 295.
[89] *Shiells* v. *Ferguson, Davidson & Co.* (1876) 4 R. 250.
[90] *Mackenzie* v. *Mackenzie's Trs.* (1873) 11 M. 681; see also *Wick* v. *Wick* (1898) 1 F. 199.
[91] *Drew* v. *Drew* (1870) 9 M. 163.
[92] *Scott's Exors.* v. *Hepburn* (1876) 3 R. 816.
[93] *Cook* v. *Cook's Trs.*, 1911, 2 S.L.T. 64.
[94] *Reid* v. *Bell* (1884) 12 R. 178.
[95] *Cowan* v. *Gowans* (1878) 5 R. 581. *Cf. Cowan* v. *Shaw* (1878) 5 R. 680; *Liqdr. of Property Investment Co. of Scotland* v. *National Bank* (1891) 28 S.L.R. 884; *Liqdr. of Property Investment Co. of Scotland* v. *Aikman* (1891) 28 S.L.R. 955.
[96] *Stuart* v. *S.* (1869) 7 M. 366; *Gray's Trs.* v. *Royal Bank* (1895) 23 R. 199. *Cf. Tait* v. *Wallace* (1894) 2 S.L.T. 136.
[97] *Johnston* v. *J.* (1875) 2 R. 986.

plead a debt due by one in defence to a claim by that one and others jointly and severally,[98] or plead a debt due by one in defence to a claim by another who held a deposit receipt payable to either that one or to himself.[99] A debtor to a firm cannot plead compensation by virtue of a claim against another firm, merely because the partners of the creditor firm are among the partners of the debtor firm.[1] The debtor to an agent may not plead compensation in respect of a debt due to him by the agent.[2]

For the purpose of this rule a deceased and his executor are accounted the same person [3] but, provided six months have expired since the death and no creditor has used diligence against the estate, an executor may compensate a claim due to him as an individual by a claim due by him as executor,[4] though he may not pay himself at once if the estate proves to be insolvent.[5]

Compensation in partnership cases

Complications may arise in partnership cases from the rules that the firm, not the partners, is the creditor in sums due to the firm,[6] but in debts due by the firm, the individual partners are jointly and severally liable for the firm's debts, though subsidiarily to the liability of the firm.[7] Hence if the firm sues for a debt due to it, the debtor cannot plead compensation by virtue of a claim against a partner.[8]

Again if a creditor sues a firm for a debt due to him, any partner can plead compensation by virtue of a claim against the pursuer. This is even clearer if the creditor sues a partner of a now dissolved firm for a debt of that firm. This rule has been justified on the grounds that an assignation of the claim by the partner to the firm may be implied, which makes the firm a party to both claims, or that no assignation is necessary, each partner being a debtor in debts due by his firm.[9]

A partner sued for a debt incurred personally cannot plead compensation by reason of a debt owed by the pursuer to the partner's firm, as the firm and not he is the creditor in the latter debt. But after the firm is dissolved he is a creditor in the latter debt to the extent of his *pro rata* share in the former firm, and to that extent can plead compensation.[10]

Again if a partner sues for a debt owed to him personally, his debtor

98 *Burrell* v. *B's Trs.*, 1916 S.C. 729.
99 *Anderson* v. *N. of S. Bank* (1901) 4 F. 49; *Allan's Exor.* v. *Union Bank*, 1909 S.C. 206.
1 *Mitchell* v. *Canal Basin Foundry Co.* (1869) 7 M. 480.
2 *Lavaggi* v. *Pirie* (1872) 10 M. 312; *Matthews* v. *Auld & Guild* (1873) 1 R. 1224.
3 *Mitchell* v. *Mackersy* (1905) 8 F. 198.
4 Stair III, 8, 73; III, 9, 44; *McDowal's Crs.* v. *McDowal* (1744) Mor. 10007; *Globe Ins. Co.*, v. *Mackenzie* (1849) 11 D. 618, 638; affd. (1850) 7 Bell 296.
5 *Salaman* v. *Sinclair's Tr.*, 1916 S.C. 698.
6 *Heggie* v. *Heggie* (1858) 21 D. 31; *Mitchell* v. *Canal Basin Co.* (1869) 7 M. 480.
7 Partnership Act 1890, s. 9; Bell, *Comm.* II, 553; *Mitchell* v. *Canal Basin Co.*, *supra.*
8 Bell, *supra*; *Morrison* v. *Hunter* (1822) 2 S. 68.
9 *Cf. Raleigh* v. *Hughson & Dobson* (1861) 23 D. 352, where held in the Outer House that the rule operated even where the partner did not consent to assign, but this was doubted in the Inner House.
10 *Oswald's Tr.* v. *Dickson* (1833) 12 S. 156; *Heggie* v. *H.* (1858) 21 D. 31.

may plead compensation by virtue of a claim against the partner's firm, because the partner is jointly and severally liable for the firm's debts, though the firm is primarily liable.[11]

Where one party bankrupt

Where compensation is pleaded by a creditor against a claim by a trustee in bankruptcy, the *concursus debiti et crediti* must have arisen before the debtor's bankruptcy.[12] The creditor accordingly cannot subsequently acquire claims against the bankrupt so as to ground a plea of compensation.[13] But in the case of bankruptcy compensation may be pleaded by virtue of a merely contingent liability, so long as it was incurred before the bankruptcy.[14]

Compensation cannot be pleaded between a claim against the bankrupt, which he incurred before bankruptcy, and a claim belonging to the trustee in sequestration acquired thereafter.[15]

Exclusion of plea of compensation

It is thought that it is competent by agreement expressly to exclude the plea of compensation.

Apart from express exclusion in particular circumstances it may appear that there was an obligation on a creditor not to plead compensation against a claim made by his debtor, as where one agreed to pay an annuity to another and later became creditor under certain decrees for expenses against the other, and it was held that the annuity was alimentary and that the plea of compensation could not be given effect to.[16] Similarly if money is deposited expressly for a particular purpose, which fails, the depository may not retain it under a plea of compensation for an independent claim against the depositor.[17]

Specialties in Crown proceedings

By the Crown Proceedings Act 1947, s. 35 (2) as applied to Scotland by s. 50, a person is not entitled to avail himself of any set-off or counterclaim in any proceedings by the Crown for the recovery of taxes, duties or penalties, or to avail himself in proceedings of any other nature by the Crown of any set-off or counterclaim arising out of a right or claim to repayment in respect of any taxes, duties or penalties; a person is not entitled without the leave of the court to avail himself of any set-off or counterclaim in any proceedings by the Crown if the subject-matter of

11 *Russell* v. *McNab* (1824) 3 S. 63; see also *Mitchell* v. *Canal Basin Co.* (1869) 7 M. 480.
12 *Meldrum's Trs.* v. *Clark* (1826) 5 S. 122.
13 Bell, *Comm.* II, 123; *Cauvin* v. *Robertson* (1783) Mor. 2581.
14 *Hannay & Son's Tr.* v. *Armstrong* (1875) 2 R. 399, esp. 417; affd. (1877) 4 R.(H.L.) 43.
15 *Mill* v. *Paul* (1825) 4 S. 219.
16 *Reid* v. *Bell* (1884) 12 R. 178.
17 Stair I, 18, 6; Ersk. III, 4, 17; Bell, *Prin.* § 574; *Campbell* v. *Little* (1823) 2 S. 484; *Hendry* v. *Grant & Jamieson* (1868) 5 S.L.R. 544; *McGregor* v. *Alley & McLellan* (1887) 14 R. 535; *Middlemas* v. *Gibson*, 1910 S.C. 577.

set-off or counterclaim does not relate to the Government Department on whose behalf the proceedings are brought; and the Crown, in any proceedings against a Government Department, or against the Lord Advocate on behalf of a Government Department is not without the leave of the court entitled to avail itself of any set-off or counterclaim if the subject-matter does not relate to that department.

In *Atlantic Engine Co. (1920) Ltd. in Liquidation* v. *Lord Advocate* [18] it was held that a ministry was entitled to set off overpayments on work done for three ministries against a sum agreed as compensation to the company for requisition of its undertaking during the war.

Stoppage in Transitu

Where one person has sold goods to another and the property in the goods has passed to the buyer the seller, if unpaid for the goods, has, in case of the insolvency of the buyer, a right of stopping the goods *in transitu* after he has parted with possession of them.[19] If the property has not passed to the buyer the unpaid seller has, in addition to his other remedies, a right of withholding delivery similar to and co-extensive with his right of lien and stoppage *in transitu* where the property has passed to the buyer.[20]

The right of stoppage *in transitu* is founded on mercantile practice and borrowed from the custom of merchants.[21] It was first applied to Scotland by the House of Lords in 1790.[22] The principle of the remedy is that the unpaid seller may recover possession of goods sold so long as they are still in the hands of an intermediary and have not got into the hands of the buyer or an agent for him. There is no room for the remedy if delivery is made by the seller himself, or the goods are uplifted by the buyer himself.

The conditions attaching to this remedy are contained in the Sale of Goods Act 1893, ss. 44–46. When the buyer of goods becomes insolvent, the unpaid seller who has parted with the possession of the goods has the right of stopping them *in transitu*, that is to say, he may resume possession of the goods as long as they are in course of transit, and may retain them until payment or tender of the price.[23] Accordingly, for the exercise of this right to be competent goods must have been sold to a buyer,[24] the property in the goods must have passed to the buyer,[25] the goods must

[18] 1955 S.L.T. 17.
[19] Sale of Goods Act 1893, s. 39 (1) (*b*).
[20] *Ibid.* s. 39 (2)
[21] *Kendall* v. *Marshall, Stevens & Co.* (1883) 11 Q.B.D. 356, 368; *Blackburn on Sale*, pp. 204–209.
[22] Bell, *Prin.* § 1307; *Allen, Stewart & Co.* v. *Stein's Creditors* (1709) Mor. 4949; 3 Paton 191.
[23] Sale of Goods Act 1893, s. 44.
[24] Not merely agreed to be sold, nor let on hire or hire-purchase terms.
[25] Under the principles set out in Sale of Goods Act 1893, ss. 16–19.

have passed out of the possession of the seller,[26] the seller must be unpaid,[27] and the buyer must have become insolvent.

The buyer's insolvency

The buyer must be insolvent, that is, if he either has ceased to pay his debts in the ordinary course of business, or cannot pay his debts as they become due, whether he has committed an act of bankruptcy in England and Wales or not, and whether he has become a notour bankrupt or not.[28]

It will not suffice that the seller has thought that the buyer was, or was about to be, insolvent, or that he had received credible information that the buyer was insolvent. If he acts on any such view he does so at his peril.

Duration of transit

This is defined by the Sale of Goods Act 1893, s. 45, as follows:

(1) Goods are deemed to be in course of transit from the time when they are delivered to a carrier by land or water [29] or other custodier for the purpose of transmission to the buyer, until the buyer, or his agent in that behalf, takes delivery of them from such carrier or other custodier.[30]

(2) If the buyer or his agent in that behalf obtains delivery of the goods before their arrival at the appointed destination,[31] the transit is at an end.[32]

(3) If after the arrival of the goods at the appointed destination, the carrier or other custodier acknowledges to the buyer or his agent that he holds the goods on his behalf, and continues in possession of them as custodier for the buyer, or his agent, the transit is at an end, and it is immaterial that a further destination for the goods may have been indicated by the buyer.[33]

(4) If the goods are rejected by the buyer, and the carrier or other custodier continues in possession of them, the transit is not deemed to be at an end, even if the seller has refused to receive them back.[34]

26 If they have not, the unpaid seller may exercise a right of lien over them: 1893 Act, ss. 41–43.

27 As defined by Sale of Goods Act 1893, s. 38.

28 1893 Act, s. 62 (3).

29 The Act does not expressly cover carriage by air, which was unknown at its date; the following words probably cover a carrier by air.

30 See *e.g. Schotsmans* v. *L. & Y. Ry.* (1867) 2 Ch.App. 332; *Coventry* v. *Gladstone* (1868) L.R. 6 Eq. 44; *Ex p. Gibbes* (1875) 1 Ch.D. 101; *Ex p. Watson* (1877) 5 Ch.D. 35; *Ex p. Barrow* (1877) 6 Ch.D. 783; *Ex. p. Rosevear China Clay Co.* (1879) 11 Ch.D. 560; *Kemp* v. *Falk* (1882) 7 App.Cas. 573; *Ex p. Francis* (1887) 4 Morr. 146; *Bethell* v. *Clark* (1888) 20 Q.B.D. 615; *Lyons* v. *Hoffnung* (1890) 15 App.Cas. 391; *Ex p. Hughes* (1892) 9 Morr. 294; *Kemp* v. *Ismay* (1909) 100 L.T. 996; *Mechan* v. *N.E. Ry.*, 1911 S.C. 1348.

31 Defined in *Mechan* v. *N.E. Ry.*, 1911 S.C. 1348, 1357 as " the destination appointed and agreed to by and between the vendor and vendees."

32 *e.g. L.N.W. Ry.* v. *Bartlett* (1861) 7 H. & N. 400.

33 *e.g. Kendall* v. *Marshall, Stewart & Co.* (1883) 11 Q.B.D. 356; *Ex p. Miles* (1885) 15 Q.B.D. 39.

34 *e.g. Bolton* v. *L. & Y. Ry.* (1866) L.R. 1 C.P. 431.

(5) When goods are delivered to a ship chartered by the buyer it is a question depending on the circumstances of the particular case, whether they are in the possession of the master as a carrier, or as agent to the buyer.[35]

(6) Where the carrier or other custodier wrongfully refuses to deliver the goods to the buyer or his agent in that behalf, the transit is deemed to be at an end.[36]

(7) Where part delivery of the goods has been made to the buyer, or his agent in that behalf, the remainder of the goods may be stopped *in transitu*, unless such part delivery has been made under such circumstances as to show an agreement to give up possession of the whole of the goods.[37]

How stoppage in transitu is effected

This is defined by the Sale of Goods Act 1893, s. 46, as follows:

(1) The unpaid seller may exercise his right of stoppage *in transitu* either by taking actual possession of the goods, or by giving notice of his claim to the carrier or other custodier in whose possession the goods are. Such notice may be given either to the person in actual possession of the goods or to his principal. In the latter case the notice, to be effectual, must be given at such time and under such circumstances that the principal, by the exercise of reasonable diligence, may communicate it to his servant or agent in time to prevent a delivery to the buyer.[38]

(2) When notice of stoppage *in transitu* is given by the seller to the carrier, or other custodier in possession of the goods, he must redeliver the goods to, or according to the directions of, the seller. The expenses of such redelivery must be borne by the seller.[39]

If instructions to effect stoppage *in transitu* be given to a carrier but he fails to effect it and delivers the goods to the buyer, the seller's right of stoppage is defeated and the goods are assets in the buyer's sequestration, but the carrier is liable in damages to the seller for the loss sustained by his failure to obey instructions.[40]

Effect of sub-sale or pledge by buyer

Under the Sale of Goods Act 1893, s. 47, an unpaid seller's right of stoppage *in transitu* is not affected by any sale, or other disposition of the goods which the buyer may have made, unless the seller has assented

35 *e.g. Berndtson* v. *Strang* (1867) L.R. 4 Eq. 481; 3 Ch.App. 588; *Ex p. Rosevear China Clay Co.* (1879) 11 Ch.D. 560.

36 *e.g. Bird* v. *Brown* (1850) 4 Exch. 786.

37 *Bolton* v. *L. & Y. Ry.* (1866) L.R. 1 C.P. 431; *Ex p. Cooper* (1879) 11 Ch.D. 68; *Kemp* v. *Falk* (1882) 7 App.Cas. 573; *Mechan* v. *N.E. Ry.*, 1911 S.C. 1348.

38 *Whitehead* v. *Anderson* (1842) 9 M. & W. 518; *Ex p. Watson* (1877) 5 Ch.D. 35; *Kemp* v. *Falk* (1882) 7 App.Cas. 573.

39 *The Tigress* (1863) L.J.P.M. & A. 97; *Booth S.S. Co.* v. *Cargo Fleet Iron Co.* [1916] 2 K.B. 570.

40 *Mechan* v. *N.E. Ry.*, 1911 S.C. 1348.

thereto.[41] Provided that where a document of title to goods has been lawfully transferred to any person as buyer or owner of the goods, and that person transfers the document to a person who takes the document in good faith and for valuable consideration, then, if such last-mentioned transfer was by way of sale the unpaid seller's right of stoppage *in transitu* is defeated, and if such last-mentioned transfer was by way of pledge or other disposition for value, the unpaid seller's right of stoppage *in transitu* can only be exercised subject to the rights of the transferee.[42]

Consequence of valid exercise of right

If a right of stoppage *in transitu* arises and is validly exercised the seller re-acquires actual, or at least constructive, possession of the goods sold, but the sale is not thereby automatically rescinded.[43] The seller may retain the goods and subsequently, if satisfied that he will be paid, again permit the goods to be delivered to the buyer. But where an unpaid seller who has exercised his right of stoppage *in transitu* resells the goods, the buyer acquires a good title thereto as against the original buyer.[44] Where the goods are of a perishable nature, or where the unpaid seller gives notice to the buyer of his intention to resell, and the buyer does not within a reasonable time pay or tender the price, the unpaid seller may resell the goods and recover from the original buyer damages for any loss occasioned by his breach of contract.[45] Where the seller expressly reserves a right of re-sale in case the buyer should make default, and on the buyer making default, resells the goods, the original contract of sale is thereby rescinded, but without prejudice to any claim the seller may have for damages.[46]

The passing of the property to the buyer is not affected by the resale by the seller, who resells as a holder of the goods in security, not as owner. Accordingly, if he should make a profit by the resale, he must account to the buyer for the profit[47]; conversely, if he resells at a loss he has a claim against the buyer for that loss and for any expenses incurred in effecting the stoppage, repossession and resale.[48]

Invalid exercise of right

If a seller invalidly exercises the right of stoppage *in transitu*, as where he is not an unpaid seller, or the buyer is not insolvent, or the goods are not in transit, he commits a breach of contract and is liable to the buyer in damages for non-delivery or for delayed delivery.

41 *e.g. Pearson* v. *Dawson* (1858) E.B. & E. 448; *Woodley* v. *Coventry* (1863) 2 H. & C. 164; *Knights* v. *Wiffen* (1870) L.R. 5 Q.B. 660; *Merchant Banking Co.* v. *Phoenix Bessemer Iron Co.* (1877) 5 Ch.D. 205.
42 *Leask* v. *Scott* (1877) 2 Q.B.D. 376.
43 Sale of Goods Act 1893, s. 48 (1).
44 *Ibid.* s. 48 (2).
45 *Ibid.* s. 48 (3); *Page* v. *Cowasjee* (1866) L.R. 1 P.C. 127; *Lord* v. *Price* (1874) L.R. 9 Ex. 54; *Ex p. Stapleton* (1879) 10 Ch.D. 586. As to whether the seller can, as *negotiorum gestor* or agent of necessity, sell on behalf of the buyer, see *Prager* v. *Blatspiel* [1924] 1 K.B. 566, on which see *Jebara* v. *Ottoman Bank* [1927] 2 K.B. 254, 271.
46 *Ibid.* s. 48 (4); *Lamond* v. *Davall* (1847) 9 Q.B. 1030.
47 *Gallagher* v. *Shilcock* [1949] 2 K.B. 765.
48 1893 Act, s. 48 (3).

PART III

CONTRACTUALLY STIPULATED REMEDIES

CHAPTER 6

IRRITANCY PROVISIONS

AN irritancy clause in a contract is a clause entitling one party to irritate or terminate the contract in the event of specified breaches or misconduct by the other party. Such clauses are common in contracts of feu and of lease, but are not confined to such classes of contracts.[1] An irritancy clause may be legal, *i.e.* one implied into a contract of a particular kind by force of a rule of the general law, or conventional, *i.e.* one agreed upon by parties in a particular case and expressed in their contract.

Legal irritancies—feu-contracts

Legal irritancies are recognised in the case of feu-contracts, for two consecutive years' non-payment of feu-duty,[2] the so-called irritancy *ob non solutum canonem.*[3] If such an irritancy is incurred it cuts down also the rights of sub-vassals.[4] It is no defence in such a case that there is an outstanding question between superior and vassal as to the latter's right to erect certain buildings.[5] The annulling of the vassal's right does not imply nullity of securities granted by him, but unless the security-holders purge the irritancy the superior will recover the fee free of the securities.[6] An irritancy incurred in respect of one feu does not affect another feu from the same superior though contained in one feu-contract.[7]

By analogy with feu-contracts statute has provided for an adjudication being led where two years' ground annual is unpaid.[8]

Legal irritancies—leases

A legal irritancy exists in the case of agricultural leases by virtue of the Act of Sederunt, 14th December, 1756, which provides (s. 4) that if a tenant falls two full years in arrear with his rent the Court of Session or sheriff court may order him to remove, though the irritancy may be purged

1 *e.g. Hannan* v. *Henderson* (1879) 7 R. 380 (partnership).

2 Feuduty Act 1597, c. 250; Bell, *Prin.* § 701. It applied to feu-duties payable in kind: *Hope* v. *Aitken* (1872) 10 M. 347. See also special provision under War Damage to Land (Sc.) Act 1939, s. 4: *Neill's Tr.* v. *Macfarlane's Trs.*, 1952 S.C. 356.

3 So-called by analogy with the civil law contract of *emphyteusis*. As to the finality of decree in a question with third parties see Conveyancing Amendment (Sc.) Act 1938, s. 6 (4).

4 *Sandeman* v. *Scottish Property Investment Co.* (1885) 12 R. (H.L.) 67; *Cassels* v. *Lamb* (1885) 12 R. 722. See also *Nelson's Trs.* v. *Tod* (1901) S.L.T. 369. As to giving intimation of the action to sub-feuars, heritable creditors and others, see Conveyancing Amendment (Sc.) Act 1938, s. 6 (1) (3).

5 *Thom* v. *Chalmers* (1886) 13 R. 1026.

6 Ersk. II, 5, 79; Bell, *Prin.* § 701; *Drummond* v. *Hamilton's Crs.* (1686) Mor. 7235.

7 *Welsh* v. *Jack* (1882) 10 R. 113.

8 Conveyancing (Sc.) Act 1924, s. 23 (*b*).

if payment be made by the tenant at any time before declarator passes.[9] It further provides (s. 5) that if the tenant either falls one full year in arrear [10] with his rent or deserts possession or neglects to cultivate the ground, the sheriff shall ordain him to find caution for the arrears and for the rent of the five succeeding crops, if the lease be expressed to last so long, or for the unexpired duration of the lease if shorter, and on the tenant's failure to do so, shall decern him summarily to remove.[11] In this case payment to account during the proceedings will not discharge the landlord's claim,[12] but consignation of the rent before decree passes purges the irritancy, so that caution cannot be ordered.[13] This remedy is inapplicable to lands within the Small Landholders (Scotland) Act 1911 and even in the case of larger holdings has been largely superseded by the Hypothec Abolition Act 1880, ss. 2 and 3, and the Agricultural Holdings (Scotland) Act 1949, s. 19, which provides for the removal of the tenant of an agricultural holding when six months' rent is due and unpaid.

The irritancy under the Act of Sederunt of 1756 does not apply to urban subjects of let.[14]

Legal irritancies—entails

In the case of land entailed it was originally necessary under the Entail Act 1685 to include in the deed of entail clauses prohibitory of alienation of the lands, charging them for debt and of altering the succession. These clauses had to be clear and pointed in directing the prohibitions, and were fenced with irritant and resolutive clauses, avoiding the act or deed prohibited and resolving the right of him who contravened the prohibition.[15] By the Entail Amendment Act 1848, s. 39, in " new " entails dated on or after 1st August 1848 irritant and resolutive clauses are implied in a clause authorising registration in the Register of Entails, so that irritancy of an entail so registered, in the event of contravention, is now a legal irritancy. By section 43 an entail defective as regards any one prohibition is deemed invalid and ineffectual as regards all prohibitions. If contravention of the entail be committed the remedy is an action of declarator of contravention and irritancy.[16]

Conventional irritancies

A conventional irritancy is a provision inserted by agreement in a contract, providing for termination of the contract in stated circumstances. It may be to any effect which may be agreed on by the parties, and frequently provides for such contingencies as a tenant's physical or mental

[9] Ersk. II, 6, 44.
[10] *Urquhart* v. *McKenzie* (1824) 3 S. 56; *Hamilton* v. *Cuthill* (1831) 9 S. 926.
[11] *Mackenzie* v. *Mackenzie* (1848) 10 D. 1009; *Oliver* v. *Weir's Trs.* (1870) 8 M. 786.
[12] *Marshall* v. *Read* (1803) Hume 569; *Sutherland* v. *McKenzie* (1854) 26 Sc.Jur. 466.
[13] *McDonald* v. *Jardine* (1825) 4 S. 230.
[14] *Wright* v. *Wightman* (1875) 3 R. 68.
[15] Ersk. III, 8, 25; Bell, *Prin.* § 1731.
[16] *Gibson* v. *Gibson* (1869) 7 M. 790; *E. Breadalbane* v. *Jamieson* (1877) 4 R. 667.

incapacity or bankruptcy. A conventional irritancy must be based on a fair and reasonable stipulation, looking to the terms of the contract and the whole circumstances of the case.[17] It may do no more than express what the law would imply in contracts of that particular kind, as when it provides for terminating a lease when rent is unpaid to a stated extent.

It is settled that, though a conventional irritancy provision is to the effect that in stated circumstances the contract is to be null and void, the effect is to render it voidable only and to put it in the power of the party benefited by the clause to bring a declarator of irritancy,[18] and in practice conventional irritancies are frequently stated to avoid the contract at the innocent party's option.

The party in right of the irritancy clause may waive his right [19] or even contract out of it,[20] or be held in the circumstances to have acquiesced in contraventions and accordingly to be barred from enforcing the irritancy.[21]

Only the party in right of the irritancy may invoke it. The other party may not incur the irritancy so as to rid himself of the contract and liability thereunder.[22]

Whether irritancy incurred

Whether an irritancy has been incurred depends on the provisions of the contract and on what has actually happened. Conditions fenced by irritancy provisions have to be construed according to the true intention of the parties.[23] Thus it has been held that an irritancy of a lease in the event of assignation was incurred by the grant of a factory and commission giving unlimited power of management,[24] an irritancy for failure to reside on a farm by living elsewhere but visiting for a few days about twice a month.[25]

Where the irritancy was stated to be incurred if the tenant, in the opinion of the landlord, misconducted himself, it was held that the landlord was not bound to give reasons for his opinion.[26] But where there was no reference to the landlord's opinion the court has dismissed an action for declarator of forfeiture of the lease on the ground that the averments did not disclose anything the court considered sufficient to amount to the forfeiting circumstance.[27]

17 *Hannan* v. *Henderson* (1879) 7 R. 380.
18 *Bidoulac* v. *Sinclair's Tr.* (1889) 17 R. 144.
19 Whether he has done so is a question of fact: *Kinloch* v. *Mansfield* (1836) 14 S. 905.
20 *McVicar* v. *Cochrane & Ker* (1740) Mor. 4180; Bell, *Conveyancing*, I, 625.
21 *Ben Challum Ltd.* v. *Buchanan*, 1955 S.C. 348.
22 *Kinloch*, *supra*; *Bidoulac* v. *Sinclair's Tr.* (1889) 17 R. 144.
23 *Napier* v. *McGavin* (1831) 9 S. 655; *Glasgow Mags.* v. *Hay* (1883) 10 R. 635.
24 *Lyon* v. *Irvine* (1874) 1 R. 512. *Cf. Walker* v. *McKnights* (1886) 13 R. 599 (sequestration equivalent to assignation).
25 *Stuart* v. *Warnocks* (1883) 2 S.L.R. 863.
26 *Guild* v. *McLean* (1897) 25 R. 106. But what if the tenant averred that the landlord was not acting in good faith and had no grounds for his opinion?
27 *Noble* v. *Hart* (1896) 24 R. 174.

A consequential matter relates to waygoing claims which may not apply where the lease is terminated under an irritancy.[28]

Another question which may arise is whether the contract has been terminated by the landlord by virtue of the irritancy or been abandoned by the tenant; only in the latter case can the landlord claim damages for breach of contract.[29] If the landlord has exercised his right to avoid he has no claim for damages for breach.[29]

Enforcement

In considering enforcement questions of hardship are irrelevant [30] and the court will not consider whether one of the parties has made a hard bargain or not.[31] An irritancy clause is enforceable according to its terms.[32] Acquiescence by a landlord in breaches by a tenant does not debar him from enforcing against a later tenant an irritancy provision directed against what the tenant has done,[33] nor is it a defence to a declarator of irritancy that there is an outstanding question between the parties as to the rights of one of them,[34] nor is a party barred from enforcing an irritancy because he has previously waived an option to enforce it.[35]

Unless the circumstances which incur the irritancy are admitted or obvious, enforcement normally requires a declarator that the irritancy has been incurred.[36] This may be followed, if need be, by proceedings to remove a vassal or tenant, and may need to be preceded by a decree against the vassal *ad factum praestandum*, as where the vassal was obliged to build but no time was prescribed for completion of the building.[37] So, too, even a provision that on the tenant's bankruptcy the landlord might resume possession without declarator has been held not to dispense with the need for notice to remove.[38]

In a case of an extraordinary removing of a tenant on the ground of an irritancy incurred, whether a preliminary conclusion declaratory of the incurring of the irritancy is necessary or not is a matter for the discretion of the court, and a declarator is not always essential, nor a removing incompetent in its absence.[39]

In the case of irritancy for non-payment of feu-duty declarator of irritancy is not final until recorded in the Register of Sasines.[40]

28 *M. Breadalbane* v. *Stewart* (1904) 6 F. (H.L.) 23.
29 *Buttercase & Geddie's Tr.* v. *Geddie* (1897) 24 R. 1128. *Cf. Walker's Trs.* v. *Manson* (1886) 13 R. 1198; *Bidoulac* v. *Sinclair's Tr.* (1889) 17 R. 144.
30 *Cf. Sandeman, supra*; *Cassels, supra.*
31 *Moncrieff* v. *Hay* (1842) 5 D. 249, 258; *Glasgow Magistrates* v. *Hay* (1883) 10 R. 635; *cf. Edinburgh Corpn.* v. *Gray*, 1948 S.C. 538; *Young* v. *Oswald*, 1949 S.C. 412.
32 *Hannan* v. *Henderson* (1879) 7 R. 380.
33 *L. Belhaven* v. *Chassels* (1904) 12 S.L.T. 290.
34 *Thom* v. *Chalmers* (1886) 13 R. 1026.
35 *Lurie* v. *Demarco*, 1968 S.L.T. (Notes) 89.
36 Bell, *Prin.* § 701; *e.g. Ardgowan Estates Ltd.* v. *Lawson*, 1948 S.L.T. 186.
37 *Anderson* v. *Valentine*, 1957 S.L.T. 57; 1957 S.L.T. (Notes) 27.
38 *Waugh* v. *More Nisbett* (1882) 19 S.L.R. 427.
39 *D. Argyll* v. *Campbeltown Coal Co.*, 1924 S.C. 844.
40 Conveyancing Acts Amendment Act 1887, s. 4.

Purgation of irritancy—legal irritancy

It is an established rule that a legal irritancy, or a conventional irritancy which merely expresses and repeats what the law implies, even though incurred, may be purged by payment of the arrears of feu-duty or rent or other payment due at any time before decree passes in an action to enforce the irritancy.[41] The court may even delay its interlocutor to give a defender a final opportunity to purge the irritancy.[42] Where the right of the superior or landlord has been transmitted during the period of non-payment purgation is effected by tendering the sum due to the claimant and it need not include sums due to his predecessor in title.[43] An irritancy fencing an obligation *ad factum praestandum* has been held purgeable at any time before decree.[44] The right to purge is an equitable right and the court has considerable discretion as to the terms on which it may allow purgation.[43] Purgation may be allowed without interest on the arrears.[43]

Purgation of irritancy—conventional irritancy

On the other hand a conventional irritancy, once incurred, cannot normally be purged by payment or other performance.[45] Thus purgation has been refused in cases of leases where rent was allowed to fall into arrears,[46] or the tenant was sequestrated,[47] or made an unauthorised assignation,[48] or failed to reside personally on and manage a farm,[49] or failed to erect buildings as he was taken bound to do.[50] Parties, having expressly agreed to the provision, are bound by it. A provision in a lease disentitling the tenant to purge a conventional irritancy has been held valid.[51] In obligations *ad factum praestandum* fenced with a conventional irritancy the irritancy is purgeable at any time before a decree of declarator of irritancy has been extracted [52] or before decree.[53]

The opinion has also been expressed that an irritancy for failure to manage a common grazing as a club stock grazing would have been purgeable before decree.[54]

The court, however, has stated that it retains a residual equitable

41 *Lockhart* v. *Shiells* (1770) Mor. 7244; *Tailors of Aberdeen* v. *Coutts* (1840) 1 Rob. 296, 449; *Duncanson* v. *Giffen* (1878) 15 S.L.R. 356; *Maxwell's Trs.* v. *Bothwell School Board* (1893) 20 R. 958.

42 *Thom* v. *Chalmers* (1886) 13 R. 1026.

43 *Maxwell's Trs., supra.*

44 *Anderson* v. *Valentine*, 1957 S.L.T. 57.

45 Ersk. III, 5, 27; *Lyon* v. *Irvine* (1874) 1 R. 512; *Hannan* v. *Henderson* (1879) 7 R. 380; *Duncanson, supra*; *Chalmer's Tr.* v. *Dick's Tr.*, 1909 S.C. 761; *D. Argyll* v. *Campbeltown Coal Co.*, 1924 S.C. 844; *McDouall's Trs.* v. *MacLeod*, 1949 S.C. 593.

46 *Finlayson* v. *Clayton* (1761) Mor. 7239; *McDouall's Trs.* v. *MacLeod*, 1949 S.C. 593.

47 *Stewart* v. *Watson* (1864) 2 M. 1414; see also *Walker* v. *McKnights* (1886) 13 R. 599.

48 *Lyon* v. *Irvine* (1874) 1 R. 512.

49 *Stuart* v. *Warnocks* (1883) 20 S.L.R. 863; see also *Guild* v. *McLean* (1897) 25 R. 106; *Noble* v. *Hart* (1896) 24 R. 174; *Macnab* v. *Nelson*, 1909 S.C. 1102.

50 *Napier* v. *Spiers' Trs.* (1831) 9 S. 655; *Glasgow Mags.* v. *Hay* (1883) 10 R. 635.

51 *E. Elgin* v. *Whittaker & Street* (1902) 9 S.L.T. 375.

52 *Duncanson* v. *Giffen* (1878) 15 S.L.R. 356.

53 *Anderson* v. *Valentine*, 1957 S.L.T. 57; 1957 S.L.T. (Notes) 27.

54 *Elliot* v. *Mackay* (1935) 24 S.L.C.R. 3.

jurisdiction in exceptional circumstances to permit purgation of an irritancy if the stipulation were of a penal nature,[55] or being misused or used oppressively,[56] notwithstanding an intention apparent from the contract to make it enforceable immediately. But though asserted there appears to be no instance reported of the actual exercise of this power.

Irritancy and other remedies

Irritancy and other remedies are generally alternative and not cumulative. If circumstances giving rise to an irritancy take place the party in right is not bound to enforce the irritancy, but may elect to take his remedy in damages, if damages are otherwise competent and suitable.[57] It is settled also that enforcement of the irritancy of a feu-contract excludes a claim for unpaid arrears of feuduty,[58] and the same applies to ground annuals.[59] In leases an irritancy incurred by bankruptcy precludes a claim of damages for failure to implement the lease,[60] though it may be otherwise if the irritancy depended on something which *per se* necessarily involved a breach of contract, as it did not in these cases.[61]

55 *Hannan* v. *Henderson* (1879) 7 R. 380.
56 *Stewart* v. *Watson* (1864) 2 M. 1414; *McDouall's Trs., supra. Cf. Cassels* v. *Lamb* (1885) 12 R. 722, 777; *Maxwell's Trs.* v. *Bothwell School Board* (1893) 20 R. 958.
57 *Kinloch* v. *Mansfield* (1836) 14 S. 905; *Bidoulac* v. *Sinclair's Tr.* (1889) 17 R. 144.
58 *Edinburgh Mags.* v. *Horsburgh* (1834) 12 S. 593; *Cassels* v. *Lamb* (1885) 12 R. 722, 782; *Buttercase & Geddie's Tr.* v. *Geddie* (1897) 24 R. 1128.
59 *Wingate's Trs.* v. *Wingate* (1892) 29 S.L.R. 406.
60 *Walker's Trs.* v. *Manson* (1886) 13 R. 1198; *Bidoulac, supra*; *Buttercase, supra.*
61 *Cf. Nelson* v. *Dundee East Coast Shipping Co.*, 1907 S.C. 927.

CHAPTER 7

LIQUIDATE DAMAGES AND PENALTY PROVISIONS

PARTICULARLY where parties have embodied a contract in writing they may, and frequently do, make express provision therein for the payment by one party to the other, in the event of breach, of a fixed sum of money, or of a sum to be calculated in a fixed way. Such provisions are often variously described as liquidate damages or as penalty provisions. The term " liquidate damages " connotes damages already liquidated or fixed and ascertained, as distinct from a claim for unliquidate damages, that is, a claim for damages for such loss as may be proved to have been sustained by the breach, where the sum of damages is not ascertained or assessed until the court fixes it and grants decree therefor. Other names are also found for such provisions, such as " minimum payment clause " or " deduction " or " indemnity " or provision for the event of premature termination of the contract.[1] Sometimes such a provision is called pactional damages.

Competency of such provisions

An express provision for stated payments to be made in the event of breach is probably competent in any kind of contract. They are common in contracts for building and engineering works and hire-purchase contracts. Such clauses are traditionally found in bonds for the repayment of money, charterparties, and some other kinds of contracts.

> " The parties to a contract may expressly stipulate not only what will be what I there called their primary obligations and rights under the contract, *i.e.* those which are discharged by performance of the contract, but also what will be their secondary obligations and rights, *i.e.* those which arise on non-performance of any primary obligation by one of the parties to the contract. Of these secondary obligations and rights, the commonest is the obligation of the non-performer to make to the other party and the corresponding right of such other party to claim from the non-performer reparation in money for any loss sustained by the other party which results from the failure of the non-performer to perform his primary obligation. The right of parties to a contract to make such a stipulation is subject, however, to the rule of public policy that the court will not enforce it against the party in breach if it is satisfied that the stipulated sum was not a

[1] *e.g. Page* v. *Sherratt* (1907) 15 S.L.T. 731; *Paterson* v. *S.W.S. Electricity Board*, 1950 S.C. 583.

genuine estimate of the loss likely to be sustained by the party not in breach, but was a sum in excess of such anticipated loss and thus, if exacted, would be in the nature of a penalty or punishment imposed on the contract-breaker. Where the court refuses to enforce a ' penalty clause ' of this nature, the injured party is relegated to his right to claim that lesser measure of damages to which he would have been entitled at common law for the breach actually committed if there had been no penalty clause in the contract." [2]

Enforceability of such provisions

The primary question of enforceability is whether the party alleged to have incurred liability under the provision is in fact in breach of contract or has, for example, justifiably rescinded the contract for breach by the party claiming, or is justifiably pleading frustration of the contract, or has otherwise exercised a right to terminate the contract. Thus in *Campbell Discount Co.* v. *Bridge*,[3] the Court of Appeal held that a hirer had exercised his right to terminate a hire-purchase contract but the House of Lords held that he had broken his contract.

The general principle as to enforceability is that parties may competently provide beforehand for the event of breach and for the damages to be payable in that event, and such a provision will be enforceable according to its terms, at least so long as it bears some reasonable relation to the loss likely to be sustained by reason of the breach, but that one party may not penalise or punish the other.[4] " Perhaps it is somewhat inaccurate to call such sums by the name of penalty, because, properly speaking, a penalty is a punishment, and nothing can be clearer than this, that parties are not entitled to make punishment the subject of agreement. Parties cannot lawfully enter into an agreement that the one party shall be punished at the suit of the other. The rule stated in the old case of *Home* v. *Hepburn* [(1549) Mor. 10,033] is *de practica regni, poenae conventionales non possunt exigi, nisi quatenus interest actores.* It is plain that *poena*—penalty—is used to mean a sum stipulated to be paid in the event of breach of contract, which is the sense in which the word is used in this agreement. The reason assumed for the rule in that case—' *quia sapiunt quendam usuram et inhonestum questum* ' is not quite the ground on which the rule of law proceeds. It is not unlikely that the rule was ascribed to some such principle in the sixteenth century, when the principles of the canon law were in force in this country. But the reason to which I have already referred is rather the true one, namely, that it is not legal to stipulate for punishment." [5]

" The court will generally give effect to the bargain if it be reasonable

2 *Robophone Facilities Ltd.* v. *Blank* [1966] 3 All E.R. 128, 141–142, *per* Diplock L.J., referring to *Koufos* v. *Czarnikow* [1966] 2 Q.B. 695, C.A., affd. [1969] 1 A.C. 350.

3 [1962] A.C. 600.

4 *Robertson* v. *Driver's Trs.* (1881) 8 R. 555.

5 *Craig* v. *McBeath* (1863) 1 M. 1020, 1022, *per* L.J.C. Inglis.

that damages be paid. But if, again the penalty be truly a penalty—that is, a punishment—the court will not allow that, because the law will not let people punish each other. They may contract that the one will be bound to reimburse the other for any loss caused, but not for punishment. Anything beyond compensation, which is a reasonable enough penalty, is punishment, and will not be enforced." [6]

The court has, accordingly, in each case to determine whether a provision for payment by the party in breach is in substance a liquidate damages provision or a penalty provision.

Whether a provision is one rather than the other " depends in the first place on the intention of the parties to be gathered from the contract as a whole. If the intention is to secure performance of the contract by the imposition of a fine or penalty, then the sum specified is a penalty; but if, on the other hand, the intention is to assess the damages for breach of the contract, it is liquidated damages." [7] In discovering intention regard must accordingly be had to the wording of the contract, and to the general intention evidenced by the contract.

It has been observed [8] that a court should not be astute to descry a " penalty clause " in every provision of a contract which stipulates a sum to be payable by one party to the other in the event of a breach by the former.

Relevance of term used

The term used by the parties themselves in describing their own contractual provision is relevant but is not conclusive.[9] " The word ' penalty ' is sometimes used to express liquidate damages, and, again, what is called liquidate damages is really penalty. The court will look into the circumstances of each case, without being influenced by the term used, and having ascertained the truth, will act accordingly." [10] Though provisions have frequently been held to be in substance what they have been called,[11] in some cases provisions described as " liquidate damages " have been held to be truly penalties,[12] and conversely.[13] If the word

[6] *Robertson, supra*, 562, *per* Lord Young.

[7] *Law* v. *Redditch Local Board* [1892] 1 Q.B. 127, 132, *per* Lopes J.

[8] *Robophone Facilities Ltd.* v. *Blank* [1966] 3 All E.R. 128, 142, *per* Diplock L.J. *Cf. Stewart* v. *Carapanayoti* [1962] 1 All E.R. 418.

[9] *Johnston* v. *Robertson* (1861) 23 D. 646, 654, 655.

[10] *Robertson* v. *Driver's Trs.* (1881) 8 R. 555, 562, *per* Lord Young.

[11] *Craig* v. *McBeath* (1863) 1 M. 1020; *Dingwall* v. *Burnett*, 1912 S.C. 1097; *cf. Beattie* v. *Ritchie* (1901) 9 S.L.T. 2; *Page* v. *Sherratt* (1907) 15 S.L.T. 731.

[12] *Kemble* v. *Farran* (1829) 6 Bing. 141; *Re Newman, ex p. Capper* (1876) 4 Ch.D. 724; *Public Works Commr.* v. *Hills* [1906] A.C. 368; *cf. Bridge* v. *Campbell Discount Co.* [1962] A.C. 600.

[13] *Johnston* v. *Robertson* (1861) 23 D. 646 (explained in *Craig, supra*); *Forrest and Barr* v. *Henderson* (1869) 8 M. 187; *Elphinstone* v. *Monkland Iron Co.* (1886) 13 R.(H.L.) 98; *Beattie* v. *Ritchie* (1901) 9 S.L.T. 2; *Steel* v. *Bell* (1900) 3 F. 319; *Clydebank Engineering Co.* v. *Castaneda* (1904) 7 F.(H.L.) 77; *Cameron-Head* v. *Cameron*, 1919 S.C. 627; *Cellulose Acetate Silk Co.* v. *Widnes Foundry* [1933] A.C. 20; *Alder* v. *Moore* [1961] 2 Q.B. 57.

"penalty" is used it throws an onus on the party asserting the contrary to satisfy the court that the payment is not truly penal.[14]

General criteria whether provision is for penalty or for liquidate damages

In *Dunlop Pneumatic Tyre Co. Ltd.* v. *New Garage and Motor Co. Ltd.*,[15] Lord Dunedin summed up the propositions which he thought were deducible from the decisions which were authoritative, as follows:

> "1. Though the parties to a contract who use the words 'penalty' or 'liquidated damages' may prima facie be supposed to mean what they say, yet the expression used is not conclusive. The court must find out whether the payment stipulated is in truth a penalty or liquidated damages. This doctrine may be said to be found *passim* in nearly every case.[16]
>
> 2. The essence of a penalty is a payment of money stipulated as *in terrorem* of the offending party; the essence of liquidated damages is a genuine covenanted pre-estimate of damage (*Clydebank Engineering and Shipbuilding Co.* v. *Don Jose Ramos Yzquierdo y Castaneda* [1905] A.C. 6).[17]
>
> 3. The question whether a sum stipulated is penalty or liquidated damages is a question of construction to be decided upon the terms and inherent circumstances of each particular contract, judged of as at the time of the making of the contract, not as at the time of the breach (*Public Works Commissioner* v. *Hills* [1906] A.C. 368, and *Webster* v. *Bosanquet* [1912] A.C. 394).
>
> 4. To assist this task of construction various tests have been suggested, which if applicable to the case under consideration may prove helpful or even conclusive. Such are:
>
> (a) It will be held to be penalty if the sum stipulated for is extravagant and unconscionable in amount [18] in comparison with the greatest loss that could conceivably be proved to have followed from the breach. (Illustration given by Lord Halsbury in *Clydebank* case.[19])
>
> (b) It will be held to be a penalty if the breach consists only in not paying a sum of money, and the sum stipulated is a sum greater than the sum which ought to have been paid (*Kemble* v. *Farran* (1829) 6 Bing. 141). This, though one of the most ancient instances, is truly a corollary to the last test. Whether it had its historical origin in the doctrine of the common law that when A promised to pay B

14 *Willson* v. *Love* [1896] 1 Q.B 626, 630.

15 [1915] A.C. 79.

16 See also cases cited under previous section.

17 Also (1904) 7 F.(H.L.) 77.

18 This must be judged of with reference to the point of time at which the stipulation is made: *Forrest and Barr* v. *Henderson* (1869) 8 M. 187, 193, approved in *Clydebank* case, *infra*, at p. 82.

19 (1904) 7 F.(H.L.) 77, 78. Lord Halsbury observed there that it is impossible to lay down any abstract rule as to what it may or may not be extravagant or unconscionable to insist upon without reference to the particular facts and circumstances which are established in the individual case. A great deal must depend, he said, upon the nature of the transaction, the thing to be done, the loss likely to accrue, and so forth.

a sum of money on a certain day and did not do so, B could only recover the sum with, in certain cases, interest, but could never recover further damages for non-timeous payment, or whether it was a survival of the time when equity reformed unconscionable bargains merely because they were unconscionable—a subject which much exercised Jessel, M.R. in *Wallis* v. *Smith* (1882) 21 Ch.D. 243—is probably more interesting than material.[20]

(c) There is a presumption (but no more) that it is a penalty when ' a single lump sum is made payable by way of compensation, on the occurrence of one or more or all of several events, some of which may occasion serious and others but trifling damage ' (Lord Watson in *Lord Elphinstone* v. *Monkland Iron and Coal Co.*, 11 App.Cas. 332).[21]

On the other hand:

(d) It is no obstacle to the sum stipulated being a genuine pre-estimate of damage, that the consequences of the breach are such as to make precise pre-estimation almost an impossibility. On the contrary, that is just the situation when it is probable that pre-estimated damage was the true bargain between the parties (*Clydebank* case, Lord Halsbury [22]; *Webster* v. *Bosanquet*, Lord Mersey [23])."

The principles restated in this case have been accepted in later cases and authoritative and superseding earlier decisions inconsistent therewith.[24]

A sum cannot, within one contract, be treated as a penalty for some purposes and as liquidated damages for others, as penal in respect of some breaches but not of others, or conversely. Nor will the court sever the applications of the stipulations. But parties may stipulate separate sums for different kinds of breach,[25] in which case one or more may be held penal and another or others liquidate damages, or may stipulate a sum payable for particular breaches, any others to be redressible by action for unliquidated damages.

Tempus inspiciendum

Circumstances must be considered by reference to the time of making the contract, not the time of breach.[26] It is irrelevant that by reason of changes of prices or values the sum has become inadequate or excessive.

20 This historical excursus is irrelevant in Scotland, whe e the equity jurisdiction has never " reformed " unconscionable bargains.

21 Also (1886) 13 R.(H.L.) 98, 106. See also *Craig* v. *McBeath* (1863) 1 M. 1020, 1022; *Dingwall* v. *Burnett*, 1912 S.C. 1097, 1103–1104; *Ford Motor Co.* v. *Armstrong* (1915) 31 T.L.R. 267; *Bell Bros. (H.P.) Ltd.* v. *Aitken*, 1939 S.C. 577, 588; *Inter-office Telephones Ltd.* v. *Freeman* [1958] 1 Q.B. 190, 194. Conversely where there is a single breach on which the sum is payable it is more likely to be held liquidate damages.

22 (1904) 7 F.(H.L.) 77, 78–79. Lord Halsbury there pointed out that the very reason why parties do in fact agree to such a stipulation is that sometimes the nature of the damage is such that proof of it is complex, difficult and expensive.

23 [1912] A.C. 394, 398.

24 *Cf. Widnes Foundry* v. *Cellulose Acetate Silk Co.* [1931] 2 K.B. 393, 405, *per* Scrutton L.J.

25 *e.g. Imperial Tobacco Co.* v. *Parslay* [1936] 2 All E.R. 515.

26 *Clydebank Engineering Co.* v. *Castaneda* (1904) 7 F.(H.L.) 77, 82, *per* Lord Davey; *Public Works Commissioner* v. *Hills* [1906] A.C. 368, 376, *per* Lord Dunedin; *Dunlop Tyre Co.*, *supra*, 86–87, *per* Lord Dunedin.

Similarly in the *Clydebank* case [27] it was held irrelevant that if the warships had been delivered in time they would have been sunk, whereas by reason of late delivery they survived.

Applicability of liquidate damages or penalty clause

A party has been held debarred from founding on a liquidate damages provision where he had not himself followed the requirements of the clause, which were that if a contractor suspended work the employer might complete the work himself and, in the event, the employer employed another contractor to complete the works.[28] Nor is such a clause enforceable if the event bringing the clause into operation, delay in performance, was caused by the fault of the employer.[29] In each case a claim for damages at common law was still competent.

Where a building contract contained a clause penalising delay and the employer ordered extra work it was held that the onus was on the contractor to show that the delay was due to the actings of the employer and, failing his doing so, the penalty clause was enforceable.[30]

Effect of clause held to be liquidate damages clause

If a provision is held to be one for liquidate damages it is enforceable according to its terms. Proof of the extent of loss or damage actually suffered is unnecessary and indeed incompetent, the purpose of the contractual provision being, at least partly, to exclude need for inquiry into the damage suffered and the need to try to evaluate it in money.[31] It is incompetent to seek to prove that greater damage than pre-estimated was in fact suffered, or on the other side to prove that lesser, or no, damage was suffered.[32] If greater loss than covered by the contractual provision has been suffered the provision does not cease to be for liquidate damages nor become invalid, as a defender may quite properly limit his liability beforehand.[33]

The court has no power to modify a liquidate damages provision,[34] save that it may do so on grounds of equity if the amount stipulated should be wholly exorbitant and unconscionable in the circumstances,[35] and as Lord Davey pointed out in the *Clydebank* case,[36] the fact that a claim is for an exorbitant or unconscionable amount as compared with any

[27] *Supra*, 79–80, *per* L.C. Halsbury.
[28] *British Glanzstoff Mfg. Co.* v. *General Accident, etc. Assce. Corpn.*, 1913 S.C.(H.L.) 1.
[29] *McElroy* v. *Tharsis Sulphur & Copper Co.* (1877) 5 R. 161; revd. on another point (1878) 5 R.(H.L.) 171.
[30] *Steel* v. *Bell* (1900) 3 F. 319.
[31] Bell, *Prin.* § 34.
[32] *Clydebank Engineering Co.* v. *Castaneda* (1904) 7 F.(H.L.) 77, 82; *Diestal* v. *Stevenson* [1906] 2 K.B. 345.
[33] *Cellulose Acetate Silk Co.* v. *Widnes Foundry (1925) Ltd.* [1933] A.C. 20.
[34] *Johnston* v. *Robertson* (1861) 23 D. 646, 653; *Craig* v. *McBeath* (1863) 1 M. 1020, 1022.
[35] *Johnston* v. *Robertson* (1861) 23 D. 646; *Forrest and Barr* v. *Henderson* (1869) 8 M. 187, 193; *Elphinstone* v. *Monkland Iron Co.* (1886) 13 R.(H.L.) 98; *Clydebank Engineering Co.* v. *Castaneda* (1904) 7 F.(H.L.) 77.
[36] *Supra*, 82.

possible damages which could have been contemplated by the parties is a reason for holding it not to be liquidate damages but a penalty.

Parties may not ignore their contractual stipulation, save possibly by agreement to delete that provision from the contract. Hence an innocent party may not, if he finds that the liquidate damages provision would not compensate him adequately, disregard the provision and claim damages at common law.

Effect of clause held to be penalty clause

If a provision is held to be properly a penalty clause, it is not automatically enforceable as such, but may be modified by the court to the amount of the loss actually suffered by the pursuer.[37] The onus is on the defender to set forth grounds for modification of the penalty.[37] If the defender does not ask for modification, the pursuer may claim the full penalty, without alleging that he has suffered damage, or alleging the amount of damage suffered: " I think that the effect of adjecting a penalty for breach of contract is, that the party complaining of the breach is entitled to assume that the damage he has sustained is equal to the amount of the penalty, and that it lies on the defender to allege that the damage has not been so great, and that he is in equity entitled to have the penalty abated, and made to correspond with the amount of the damage. I think this stands on principle and authority." [38] If the pursuer has suffered greater loss than is compensated by the sum in the penalty clause he can recover no more; but he may ignore the penalty clause and sue for damages in the ordinary way, in which case he can recover the whole of his proven loss.[39] If the defender can satisfy the court that the sum stated is a pure penalty, imposed *in poenam*, the court will not give effect to it at all.

Waiver of claim

The innocent party to a contract containing a liquidate damages or penalty provision may waive any claim competent to him thereunder, just as he may waive a claim for unliquidate damages, but it is a question of circumstances whether waiver should be inferred. It has been held that payment of the last instalment of the price and acceptance of the goods did not, in the circumstances before the court, import waiver of rights under a clause entitling the purchaser to a specified sum as damages for late delivery.[40]

[37] Stair I, 10, 14; IV, 18, 3; Bell, *Comm.* I, 699; *Prin.* § 34; *Home* v. *Hepburn* (1549) Mor. 10033; *Arnot* v. *Arnot* (1742) Mor. 10045; *Sibbald* v. *Fletcher* (1758) Mor. 588; *Mackenzie* v. *Craigies*, June 18, 1811, F.C.; *Wright* v. *McGregor* (1826) 4 S. 454; *Watson* v. *Merrilees* (1848) 10 D. 370; *Craig* v. *McBeath* (1863) 1 M. 1020; *Robertson* v. *Driver's Trs.* (1881) 8 R. 555, 559, *per* Lord Lee, Ordinary.

[38] *Craig*, *supra*, 1023, *per* L.J.C. Inglis.

[39] *Hyndman's Trs.* v. *Miller* (1895) 33 S.L.R. 359; *Dingwall* v. *Burnett*, 1912 S.C. 1097; distinguishing *Johnstone's Trs.* v. *Johnstone*, Jan. 19, 1819, F.C.; *Wall* v. *Rederi A/B Luggude* [1915] 3 K.B. 66; approved in *Watts, Watts & Co.* v. *Mitsui* [1917] A.C. 227.

[40] *Clydebank Engineering Co.* v. *Castaneda* (1904) 7 F.(H.L.) 77.

Unenforceability of claim

A provision for payment of a fixed sum for each week of delay in performance has been held unenforceable when part of the delay was caused by the fault of the party complaining, his only remedy being then an action of damages at common law.[41] If a party in breach seeks to establish that a penalty provision is unenforceable on this ground the onus is on him to prove that non-completion was due to the act or omission of the other party.[42]

Penalty does not excuse performance

In many cases provision is made for a penalty " by and attour performance " or " over and above performance," and these words are implied where the court is of the opinion that the sum agreed on for breach of the agreement is so agreed on by way of penalty merely and is not to be treated as liquidate damages.[43] There seems to be no case where such words, when expressed, have been held to be consistent with an intention to fix liquidate damages.[43] Alternatively it can be said that a penalty provision does not permit discharge of the obligation by payment of the penalty.[44] The penalty is one mode of enforcing the obligation and does not give a party in breach the option to get quit of his obligation by paying the penalty.[45] Nor does it deprive the innocent party of the right to invoke any other remedy appropriate.[46]

The only exception appears to be that in the case of an undertaking to be answerable for the performance of an act by a third party, the party bound is released by payment of the penalty.[47]

Breaches outwith liquidate damages provision

If a breach of contract occurs outwith the ambit of the penalty or liquidate damages provision in the contract the provision does not apply thereto and unliquidated damages may be claimed in an action for breach in the usual way. Thus in *A/S Reidar* v. *Arcos* [48] a charterparty contained the usual provision for demurrage as liquidate damages for delay in loading but the charterers delayed so long to load that the date passed after which it was no longer permissible to carry a summer cargo, and it was permissible only to carry a smaller winter cargo. It was held that the demurrage provisions fixed the damages for the detention of the ship, not for the loss resulting from being able to carry only a winter cargo, and unliquidated damages were awarded for the latter loss.

41 *McElroy* v. *Tharsis Sulphur Co.* (1877) 5 R. 161; revd. on another point (1878) 5 R.(H.L.) 171.
42 *Steel* v. *Bell* (1900) 3 F. 319.
43 *Dingwall* v. *Burnett*, 1912 S.C. 1097, 1103.
44 Stair I, 17, 20; Ersk. III, 3, 86; Bell, *Prin.* § 34; *Gold* v. *Houldsworth* (1870) 8 M. 1006.
45 *University of Glasgow* v. *Faculty of Physicians* (1840) 1 Rob. 397, 415; *Curtis* v. *Sandison* (1831) 10 S. 72.
46 *Mackenzie* v. *Craigie*, June 18, 1811, F.C.; affd. (1815) 6 Pat. 117; *Gold, supra*; *Dalrymple* v. *Herdman* (1878) 5 R. 847.
47 *Cochran* v. *Montgomery* (1702) Mor. 10041; *Bairdiner* v. *Drysdale* (1706) Mor. 10043.
48 [1927] 1 K.B. 352.

Particular Cases

Liquidate damages or penalty provisions are more commonly found in some categories of contracts than in others and, having been frequently considered in particular contexts, stipulations tend to be regarded as liquidate damages provisions in some kinds of contracts and as penalty provisions in other kinds of contracts.

(a) *Cases where stipulations usually held to be liquidate damages provisions*

Demurrage

A provision in a charterparty for the loading or unloading of a ship at a specified rate or in a specified time, and for demurrage at a stated rate if loading or unloading takes longer, is in substance a provision for liquidate damages for a particular type of breach of a particular kind of contract.[49] Such provisions have long been held to be enforceable as such and on proof of breach of contract by detention of the ship the agreed sum only is recoverable.[50]

A demurrage provision may, however, be interpreted as imposing a limit on the claims for which liability may arise by delay in loading or unloading. In this case the pursuers must prove the loss actually sustained and if it is less than the amount fixed they can recover the proven loss only; if it is more they can recover up to the fixed limit only.[51]

Building and engineering contracts

Provisions in building and engineering contracts for payments of stated sums for each week or month by which performance is delayed are common and have normally been held to be of the nature of liquidate damages.[52]

Conditions affecting resale

Contractual conditions restricting the right of one party to resell or market goods with a provision for payment if he should contravene have frequently been held to be of the nature of liquidate damages.[53]

Covenants in restraint of trade

A contractual provision restraining an employee's future employment

49 Scrutton on *Charterparties* (17 ed.), 305; *A/S Reidar* v. *Arcos* [1926] 2 K.B. 83; [1927] 1 K.B. 352; *Chandris* v. *Isbrandsten-Moller Co.* [1951] 1 K.B. 240, 249.
50 *Suisse Atlantique Société* v. *N.V. Rotterdamsche Kolen Centrale* [1967] 1 A.C. 361.
51 *Suisse Atlantique, supra, per* Viscount Dilhorne, *obiter.*
52 *e.g. Wallis* v. *Smith* (1882) 21 Ch.D. 243; *Law* v. *Redditch Local Board* [1892] 1 Q.B. 127; *Beattie* v. *Ritchie* (1901) 9 S.L.T. 2; *Clydebank Engineering Co.* v. *Castaneda* (1904) 7 F. (H.L.) 77; *Public Works Commr.* v. *Hills* [1906] A.C. 368 (held penalty); *Cellulose Acetate Silk Co.* v. *Widnes Foundry* [1933] A.C. 20.
53 *e.g. Webster* v. *Bosanquet* [1912] A.C. 394; *Dunlop Tyre Co.* v. *New Garage Co.* [1915] A.C. 79; *Imperial Tobacco Co.* v. *Parslay* [1936] 2 All E.R. 515. Contrast *Ford Motor Co.* v. *Armstrong* (1915) 31 T.L.R. 267.

fenced by a provision for payment has been held liquidate damages,[54] and this has been the usual attitude to such cases in England.

(b) *Cases where stipulations usually held to be penalties*

Bonds to pay money

The traditional wording of a bond to pay money obliges the granter to repay " with one fifth part more in name of liquidate penalty in case of failure " of payment of principal or interest. Such a provision is not enforceable in its terms [55] and the courts have power to modify it so as not to exceed the real and necessary expenses incurred in making the debt effectual.[56] Under such a penalty clause, however, the creditor may give a charge for payment of the principal and penalty and the charge will not be suspended unless tender be made of the expenses actually incurred by the creditor.[57] The penalty clause has been held, failing express provision for interest, to justify recovery of interest,[58] and to cover expenses incurred by the creditor in vindicating his right to subjects conveyed in security along with the bond, both in a question with the debtor [59] and with other bondholders or competing claimants,[60] but not to justify any compensation for inconvenience or loss resulting from delayed payment.[61]

A provision in a bond that in default of punctual payment of interest a higher rate of interest will be demanded is questionably valid,[62] but a provision that if payment be punctually made a lower rate than that specified will be accepted is valid and enforceable.[63] A different legal result in these two cases, merely because of different wording, seems hardly justifiable. In either case it is in effect a provision for discount.

Forfeiture of deposit on sale

Where a contract of sale (whether of heritage or of moveables) provides for payment of a deposit and for forfeiture of that deposit if the buyer does not carry out his purchase, the forfeiture clause is normally enforceable according to its terms.[64] " Where, in a contract of sale, the intending buyer deposits part of the price, he cannot, if he repudiates the contract

54 *Page* v. *Sheratt* (1907) 15 S.L.T. 731.
55 Bell, *Comm.* I, 700; *Nasmyth* v. *Samson* (1785) 3 Pat. 9.
56 Debts Securities (Sc.) Act 1856, s. 5.
57 Bell, *Comm.* I, 701; *Borthwick* v. *L.A.* (1862) 1 M. 94 (explained in *Craig* v. *McBeath* (1863) 1 M. 1020); *Mitchell* v. *Allardyce*, 1915, 2 S.L.T. 398.
58 *Semple* v. *Semple* (1622) Mor. 10033.
59 *Bruce* v. *Scottish Amicable Assce. Socy.*, 1907 S.C. 637. Contrast *Smith* v. *McLean's Crs.* (1800) Mor. Expenses, Appx. 2. The security covers the claim for expenses also: *Bruce*, *supra*.
60 *Allardes* v. *Morison* (1788) Mor. 10052; *Orr* v. *Mackenzie* (1839) 1 D. 1046.
61 *Allan* v. *Young* (1757) Mor. 10047.
62 *Cf. Wallis* v. *Smith* (1882) 21 Ch.D. 243.
63 *Gatty* v. *Maclaine*, 1921 S.C.(H.L.) 1. See also *Paterson* v. *Tod* (1827) 6 S. 1062; *Scott-Chisholme* v. *Brown* (1893) 20 R. 575; *Leeds and Hanley Theatre* v. *Broadbent* [1898] 1 Ch. 343.
64 *Commercial Bank* v. *Beal* (1890) 18 R. 80 (heritage); *Roberts & Cooper* v. *Salvesen*, 1918 S.C. 794 (moveables).

without justification, claim repayment of the deposit. That is upon the ground either that a man who repudiates a contract is not entitled to rescind that contract, or that a man who is in default cannot take advantage of his own default, or that a man who has paid down money as a security for performance of a contract cannot have the money back if he deliberately elects to throw up the contract." [65] Nevertheless it is thought that there could be circumstances where the deposit is so large that to order forfeiture of it all would be a penalty and objectionable as such.[66]

Pactional rent clause

It was formerly the law that a provision in a lease for additional rent of agricultural land in the event of breach of certain conditions of the lease was enforceable according to its terms,[67] but since 1908 [68] this is not so. It is now provided [68] that " notwithstanding any provision in a lease of an agricultural holding making the tenant thereof liable to pay a higher rent or other liquidated damages in the event of a breach or non-fulfilment of any of the terms or conditions in the lease, the landlord shall not be entitled to recover any sum in consequence of any breach or non-fulfilment in excess of the damage actually suffered by him in consequence of the breach or non-fulfilment." A pactional rent provision is, accordingly, assimilated to a penalty at common law.

Minimum payment clauses in hire-purchase contracts

It is commonly provided in hire-purchase contracts that if the hirer is in breach of contract or terminates the contract prematurely he must, if he has not already done so, pay any sums required to make up his payments to a stated minimum sum to compensate the owner for the depreciation on his goods, which can only be rehired or resold as second-hand. In many such cases the question has arisen whether a minimum payment provision was truly a penalty or a liquidate damages provision. In some such cases the provision has been held to be one for a penalty,[69] in others for liquidate damages.[70] But in a case of premature termination rather than a breach, it may be [71] that the clause in question does not imply either liquidate damages or a penalty, but lays down the financial conditions which the hirer must observe in return for the advantage of terminating the contract at his own hand.

In cases subject to the Hire-Purchase (Scotland) Act 1965, if the hirer terminates the agreement by agreement or by notice in writing under

[65] *Roberts & Cooper, supra,* 806, *per* L.P. Strathclyde.
[66] *Cf. Stockloser* v. *Johnson* [1954] 1 Q.B. 476.
[67] *Cf. Mackenzie* v. *Morrison* (1937) 26 S.L.C.R. 10.
[68] Now Agricultural Holdings (Sc.) Act 1949, s. 16.
[69] *e.g. Cooden Engineering Co.* v. *Stanford* [1953] 1 Q.B. 86; *Landom Trust* v. *Hurrell* [1955] 1 All E.R. 839; *Bridge* v. *Campbell Discount Co.* [1962] A.C. 600 (second-hand goods); *U.D.T. (Commercial) Ltd.* v. *Ennis* [1967] 2 All E.R. 345.
[70] *Bell Bros. (H.P.) Ltd.* v. *Aitken,* 1939 S.C. 577; *Re Apex Supply Co. Ltd.* [1942] Ch. 108; *Phonographic Equipment Ltd.* v. *Muslu* [1961] 3 All E.R. 626.
[71] As in *Bell Bros., supra.*

section 27 thereof, he is liable, by section 28, in the case of a hire-purchase agreement, to pay the amount, if any, by which one-half of the hire-purchase price exceeds the total of the sums paid and the sums due, or, in the case of a conditional sale agreement, the amount, if any, by which one-half of the total purchase price exceeds the total of the sums paid and the sums due, or in either case, any lesser amount specified in the agreement. Any provision for additional payment is void (s. 29). There are also restrictions on money claims in certain other circumstances (ss. 43–45).

Penalty clauses in charterparties

A clause in a charterparty such as " penalty for non-performance estimated amount of freight " or " . . . proved damages not exceeding the estimated amount of freight " is frequently found in charterparties, but appears to be practically ineffective. On the one hand, it does not limit the amount of damages which may be claimed; on the other, it does not entitle either party to claim the amount of the penalty for a partial breach of contract.[72] In *Watts, Watts & Co.* v. *Mitsui* [73] Lord Sumner treated it as clearly a penalty clause and immaterial.

[72] *Stroms Bruks A/B* v. *Hutchison* (1904) 6 F. 486; (1905) 7 F.(H.L.) 131; *Wall* v. *Rederiaktiebolaget Luggude* [1915] 3 K.B. 66; *Watts, Watts & Co.* v. *Mitsui* [1917] A.C. 227.
[73] [1917] A.C. 227.

PART IV

JUDICIAL DECLARATION OF RIGHTS

CHAPTER 8

DECLARATOR

" DECLARATORY actions are those, wherein the right of the pursuer is craved to be declared, but nothing is claimed to be done by the defender; but the effect is, that in petitory or possessory actions, the defender is excluded from any defence that might have been proposed in the declaratory action. . . .

The summons on actions declaratory are called declarators; and such actions may be pursued for instructing and clearing any kind of right relating to liberty, dominion, or obligation; but they used not to be raised or insisted on, where there is no competition or pretence of any other right. . . . As declarators may be in all points of right or possession; so, in some cases, they must be before possessory judgments can proceed; as declarators of right of property, or declarators of redemption of wadsets, etc." [1]

" A declaratory action is one in which some right either of property, of servitude, of status, or some other inferior right, is sought to be declared in favour of the pursuer but where nothing is demanded to be paid or performed by the defender." [2]

Generality of right to declarator

" The general rule is, that any right may be ascertained by a declarator." [3] This is illustrated throughout the reports by the enormous variety of rights which persons have in different circumstances sought to have declared.

Decree declares existing right only

A decree of declarator confers no new right on the pursuer, but merely declares authoritatively that he possesses some status or right previously doubted or denied. It is accordingly retrospective to the date when the status or right commenced or the circumstances first arose giving rise to the question, *e.g.* to the date of contracting of a " marriage " now declared null *ab initio*. Declarator is accordingly generally inappropriate where it is sought to effect a change of status or to acquire a new right of any kind.

Alternative conclusions may sometimes be necessary, either declaring the pursuer's status or right or obtaining for him some status or right, as where a pursuer seeks declarator of having been divorced elsewhere, or alternatively seeks divorce now.

1 Stair IV, 3, 47.
2 Ersk. IV, 1, 46.
3 *Barbour* v. *Grierson* (1827) 5 S. 603, 604, *per* Lord Glenlee.

Jurisdiction

The Court of Session has jurisdiction in all declaratory actions. The sheriff court has jurisdiction in declarators, except actions of declarator of marriage or nullity of marriage and actions the direct or main object of which is to determine the personal status of individuals.[4] This may give rise to a question of what a personal status is, and of whether particular conditions amount to " personal status " or not. It has been held that a declarator of paternity was competent in the sheriff court because it did not determine the legitimacy or otherwise of the child.[5]

Title and interest to sue

It is plain on general principles as to title and interest to sue that a party may seek declarator only of some right claimed by him,[6] and only if he has an interest to have that right declared, in that he will be benefited if it is declared and prejudiced if it is not declared.[7] Thus declarator is incompetent if there is no averment of the violation of any civil right involving patrimonial interest entitling the pursuer to redress.[8] A person may not seek declarator of anyone else's rights, nor of any right of his own which is not challenged or doubted.

The right which the pursuer seeks to have declared need not necessarily be immediate. It may be a future[9] or contingent [10] right, so long as all parties interested or who may become interested can be, and are, called.

Where a duty has been imposed on someone by statute, it is a question of interpretation whether an alleged breach of that statutory duty does or does not confer on any individual a title to enforce a provision of the statute or a title to recover damages for harm caused him by breach thereof.[11] Thus it has been held that ownership of a house in a square did not give a title or interest to challenge, by declarator, the right of the local planning authority under statute to grant planning permission for demolition of part of the square and its redevelopment.[12]

Title and interest will normally exist where pursuer and defender stand in the continuing relationship of superior and vassal,[13] or of landlord

4 Sheriff Courts (Sc.) Act 1907, s. 5 (1).

5 *A. B. or C.* v. *D.* (1949) 65 Sh.Ct.Rep. 181.

6 *Baillie* v. *Seton* (1853) 16 D. 216.

7 *Cf. Gifford* v. *Trail* (1829) 7 S. 854; *Lyle* v. *Balfour* (1830) 9 S. 22; *Torrie* v. *D. Athol* (1849) 12 D. 329; *Baillie* v. *Seton* (1853) 16 D. 216; *Bosville* v. *Lord Macdonald*, 1910 S.C. 597; *Orr* v. *Alston*, 1912, 1 S.L.T. 95.

8 *Drennan* v. *Associated Ironmoulders*, 1921 S.C. 151.

9 *Provan* v. *Provan* (1840) 2 D. 298, 300; *Fleming* v. *McLagan* (1879) 6 R. 588.

10 *Mackenzie's Trs.* v. *Mackenzie's Tutors* (1846) 8 D. 964.

11 *Cutler* v. *Wandsworth Stadium Ltd.* [1949] A.C. 398; *Pullar* v. *Window Clean Ltd.*, 1956 S.C. 13.

12 *Simpson* v. *Edinburgh Corpn.*, 1960 S.C. 313.

13 *e.g. Eagle Lodge Ltd.* v. *Keir and Cawder Estates Ltd.*, 1964 S.C. 30; *Howard de Walden Estates Ltd.* v. *Bowmaker Ltd.*, 1965 S.C. 163. See also *Stewart* v. *Bunton* (1878) 5 R. 1108; *E. Zetland* v. *Hislop* (1882) 9 R.(H.L.) 40; *Waddell* v. *Campbell* (1898) 25 R. 456; *Menzies* v. *Caledonian Canal Commrs.* (1900) 2 F. 953; *Forrest* v. *Watson's Hospital* (1907) 8 F. 341; *Macdonald* v. *Douglas*, 1963 S.C. 374. Contrast *e.g. Edinburgh Mags.* v. *Mac-*

and tenant,[14] or otherwise are linked by contract, but exist where the parties are not contractually bound only if the party claiming title and interest to enforce conditions of the contract can establish that he has a *jus quaesitum tertio* under the contract.[15] Title and interest have been held to exist in the cases of building restrictions [15] and of obligations *ad factum praestandum*, such as to form a road or street.[16] Similarly ratepayers of a burgh have title and interest to challenge the magistrates' conduct in incurring certain expenditure.[17]

Contradictors

Particularly in declarators as to the pursuer's rights in a matter of succession, it is essential that all proper contradictors be in court.[18] If they cannot be, the declaratory conclusions are incompetent. " I have never known, and counsel have been unable to produce to us, any action of declarator where the court gave a declarator as to a right without there being a proper contradictor present." [19]

The contradictor called must moreover be a party having a real and genuine interest to deny the pursuer's claim. " It seems to me that the whole argument we have listened to this morning was vitiated by an assumption as to who the contradictor in this case is. The Insurance Company is not the contradictor as in the question of whom the insurance policy belongs to. The contradictor must be found among the ranks of the parties to whom at various times the policy belonged, and depends upon the question of whether these various steps or links of the chain of title are or are not correct. The Insurance Company have no interest whatever, except simply to pay the policy when it becomes a proper claim." [20]

A good test of the propriety of the contradictor called is whether an action of multiplepoinding could have been raised; could the contradictor have been a claimant in such a process? [20] Accordingly trustees whose sole

farlane (1858) 20 D. 156; *Campbell* v. *Clydesdale Bank* (1868) 6 M. 943; *Fraser* v. *Downie* (1877) 4 R. 942; *Johnstone* v. *Walker's Trs.* (1897) 24 R. 1061; where pursuer's interest had ceased.

14 *e.g. Baird* v. *Feuars of Kilsyth* (1878) 6 R. 116.

15 *Hislop* v. *MacRitchie's Trs.* (1881) 8 R.(H.L.) 95; modifying principles stated in *Heriot's Hospital* v. *Cockburn* (1826) 2 W. & S. 293, 302; *Robertson* v. *N.B. Ry. Co.* (1874) 1 R. 1213, 1218; *Dalrymple* v. *Herdman* (1878) 5 R. 847, 854; followed in *Calder* v. *Edinburgh Merchant Co.* (1886) 13 R. 623; *Braid Hills Hotel Co.* v. *Manuel*, 1909 S.C. 120; *Thomson* v. *Mackie* (1903) 11 S.L.T. 562; *Nicolson* v. *Glasgow Blind Asylum*, 1911 S.C. 391; *Eagle Lodge Ltd., supra.*

16 *Fimister* v. *Milne* (1860) 22 D. 1100; *Guthrie* v. *Young* (1871) 9 M. 544; *Charlton* v. *Scott* (1894) 22 R. 109; *cf. Stevenson* v. *Steel Co. of Scotland* (1896) 23 R. 1079; (1899) 1 F.(H.L.) 91.

17 *Ewing* v. *Glasgow Police Commrs.* (1839) McL. & Rob. 847; *Stirling C.C.* v. *Falkirk Mags.*, 1912 S.C. 1281.

18 *Fleming* v. *McLagan* (1879) 6 R. 588; *Barron* v. *Barron* (1881) 19 S.L.R. 275; *Smith* v. *McColl's Trs.*, 1910 S.C. 1121; *Murray* v. *Murray*, 1909, 1 S.L.T. 122; *Allgemeine Deutsche Credit Anstalt* v. *Scottish Amicable Life Assce. Socy.*, 1908 S.C. 33; *Gillespie* v. *Riddell*, 1909 S.C.(H.L.) 3; *Blair* v. *Kerr's Trs.*, 1919, 1 S.L.T. 125.

19 *Allgemeine Deutsche Credit Anstalt, supra*, 38, *per* L.P. Dunedin.

20 *Ibid.*

interest is to pay and be judicially discharged and an insurance company concerned only to pay the policyholder are not proper contradictors.[20]

Positive and negative declarators

A declarator normally takes the form of a positive claim, that the pursuer is of some status or has some legal right.

The opinion has on occasion been expressed [21] that a declarator of a negative, at least without any operative conclusion, was incompetent, but this view has been criticised,[22] and there seems to be no necessary incompetency in a declarator asserting a negative.[22] Moreover, some of the commonest forms of declarator, *e.g.* of nullity of marriage, or of bastardy, are essentially negative in substance, whatever they may be in verbal form, because they seek to declare that the legal position is not as it has appeared to be.

There is a substantial number of decisions where pursuers have sought declarators to a negative effect.

In *Butchart* v. *Prophet* [23] a conclusion was for declarator that the defenders had no right of servitude over certain lands, with one exception. A cross-action sought declarator that the defenders had no exclusive right to certain lands.

In *Tay Ferry Trustees* v. *Edinburgh, Perth and Dundee Ry.*[24] the action was for declarator that the defender had no right to ply for hire with ferry-boats within certain limits.

In *Perth General Station Committee* v. *Ross* [25] a railway company sought to interdict the defender from entering their station to meet travellers, except as permitted by the company. The House of Lords held that the pursuers were entitled to a declaration that, subject to any order or regulation which might thereafter be made, the defender had no right to do so, except with the complainers' leave and under such conditions as they might prescribe, and that in respect thereof it was necessary to dispose of the prayer for interdict. In *Midlothian C.C.* v. *Musselburgh Co-operative Socy.*[26] the local authority sought declarator that the defenders were not entitled to build over the pursuers' sewer. In *Hope* v. *Gemmell* [27] the conclusion was for declarator that an alleged right of way did not exist. In *Norrie* v. *Kirriemuir Magistrates* [28] the action was for declarator that the pursuer held lands free of any public right of way. In *Simpson* v. *Edinburgh Corporation* [29] the action was for declarator that building operations were contrary to the city's development plan and *ultra vires*.

21 *e.g. N.B. Ry. Co.* v. *Birrell's Trs.*, 1918 S.C.(H.L.) 33, 40, *per* Lord Johnston.
22 *Ibid.* 47, *per* Lord Dunedin.
23 (1841) 3 D. 1040.
24 (1851) 14 D. 103.
25 (1897) 24 R.(H.L.) 44.
26 1960 S.C. 177.
27 (1898) 1 F. 74; similarly *M. Bute* v. *McKirdy & McMillan Ltd.*, 1937 S.C. 93.
28 1945 S.C. 302.
29 1960 S.C. 313.

It would appear that whether a declaratory conclusion is framed positively or negatively does not matter; whichever grammatical form can be chosen which is more appropriate to focus the difference of opinion between the parties. In particular where the right in question is one conferred by statute it is frequently convenient to frame the declarator to the effect that the pursuer has, or the defender has not, right to do what is required or permitted by the statute. It will frequently be convenient to combine a negative declarator with an interdict, or other consequential remedy, but this does not seem a requisite of the competency of declarator of a negative.

Declarator decisive, not advisory

> " The function of the court in an action of declarator is to decide the disputed rights of parties and not to advise them as to their future course of action.[30] Therefore the court will refuse to entertain, as being premature, a declarator as to a question which may never arise.[31] Further, ' the court will not give a declarator of right where parties who may be contradictors are not convened or are not at present convenable, for in that case the decree would not be *res judicata* against them and would be mere opinion.' [32] But where a party has an interest to obtain the decision of the court on a question which is ' neither academic or premature, but is both practical and of immediate urgency,' the court will answer the question—See Lord President Normand in *Turner's Trs.* v. *Turner.*[33] If in such circumstances a party is ' excusably uncertain ' as to his rights, an action of declarator can be competently raised in order to avert the consequences of his being compelled to test his rights by experiment.[34] The recent practice of the court is less strict than formerly as to the competency of actions of declarator, and ' the modern tendency appears to be to open the doors wider to such proceedings.' [35]" [36]

It is, however, different where the form of process is a special case for the opinion, or opinion and judgment, of the Court of Session, the decision in which is professedly advisory, as to the interpretation of a settlement or other deed or the application of a rule of law to the case before the court. In *Morton* v. *Gardner* [37] it was held that decree in the form of a declarator could not competently be pronounced in a special case, but there seems force in the dissenting judgment of Lord Kinloch,

30 *E. Galloway* v. *Garlies* (1838) 16 S. 1212; *Harveys* v. *H.'s Trs.* (1860) 22 D. 1310, 1328, *per* L.J.C. Inglis; *Blair* v. *Kerr's Trs.*, 1918, 2 S.L.T. 214; 1919, 1 S.L.T. 125.

31 *Blair, supra.*

32 *Blair*, 1918, 2 S.L.T. at 216, *per* Lord Sands; *Smith* v. *McColl's Trs.*, 1910 S.C. 1121, 1128, *per* L.P. Dunedin.

33 1943 S.C. 389 at p. 398.

34 *Chaplin's Trs.* v. *Hoile* (1890) 18 R. 27, Lord Young at p. 32.

35 *Turner's Trs., supra,* at p. 394, *per* Lord Carmont; *Davidson* v. *D.* (1906) 14 S.L.T. 337; Mackay's *Manual of Practice*, p. 375.

36 *Macnaughton* v. *M.'s Trs.*, 1953 S.C. 387, 389, *per* Lord Guthrie.

37 (1871) 9 M. 548.

who thought that the same opinion as might have been given if the case had been brought in the form of a declarator of irritancy was obtainable by means of a special case.

Court's duty to examine right sought to be declared

Quite apart from any other objections the court must examine carefully the legal right the pursuer in a declarator seeks to have declared. It may hold that there is no such legal right, or no legal right in such terms as contended for by the pursuer.[38] Thus in *Southern Bowling Club Ltd.* v. *Ross* [39] the court declined to declare " that the defenders, or any other officer, constable or member of the police force of the city of Edinburgh, are not entitled to demand entrance to or to enter the pursuer's said premises at pleasure . . . ," taking the view that the police had a right to enter in plain clothes to ascertain if there was illegal trafficking in liquor in the club. As Lord Kincairney observed, the first question was whether the conclusions expressed, or were based on, sound legal propositions. The court must be careful not to declare in the particular case what in the general case is an unsound legal proposition.

Where declarator unnecessary

A declarator may be dismissed as unnecessary where the status or right in question has already been adjudicated on by a competent court and the grant of declarator would not add any force or effect to what has already been done, as where a pursuer has already judicially divorced or been judicially divorced in circumstances where the court's jurisdiction would be recognised,[40] but it cannot be regarded as unnecessary where the right or status has not been adjudicated on judicially.[41] Again it is unnecessary and indeed incompetent when the fact sought to be declared is not disputed.[42]

Where declarator incompetent

The court will not entertain a declarator of an abstract or general proposition of law, such as of the rights and powers of the police, or of the legal relations in general between innkeepers and travellers,[43] but only of the application of a proposition to the case of the pursuer, as where the pursuer has been denied some right inherent in the relationship. " It is not every fact that can be declared or negatived by a declarator. It must be something of a practical kind, leading to patrimonial conclusions, that is sought to be established. . . . " [44] A merely abstract and

[38] *Cf. Henderson* v. *Earl of Minto* (1860) 22 D. 1126.
[39] (1902) 4 F. 405.
[40] *e.g. McKay* v. *Walls*, 1951 S.L.T.(Notes) 6.
[41] *Makouipour* v. *Makouipour*, 1967 S.C. 116.
[42] *Drennan* v. *Associated Ironmoulders*, 1921 S.C. 151.
[43] *Callender's Cable Co.* v. *Glasgow Corpn.* (1900) 2 F. 397, 399, 401; *Southern Bowling Club Ltd.* v. *Ross* (1902) 4 F. 405, 410; *N.B. Ry.* v. *Birrell's Trs.*, 1918 S.C.(H.L.) 33, 47; *Rothfield* v. *N.B. Ry.*, 1920 S.C. 805, 830.
[44] *Officers of State* v. *Alexander* (1866) 4 M. 741, 753, *per* Lord Neaves.

general declarator will not do. Nor will the court grant an absolute declarator if it is clear that it would not apply in all circumstances and contingencies.[45]

Nor will it entertain a declarator of an abstract state of facts when the pursuer cannot show that he has any interest to establish those facts, or that any right of his follows from the declarator.[46]

Nor is declarator competent to declare what is undisputed,[47] nor remote and contingent or conditional rights, but only matters of present and pressing controversy.[48] " Declaratory actions of this kind are designed for the purpose of making that clear which is at present doubtful, and which it is necessary to make clear. They are not intended to establish truisms." [49]

On the other hand it is competent to seek declarator of the defender's statutory duties in relation to the pursuer's circumstances.[50]

Hypothetical questions

The courts do not sit to decide hypothetical questions, and consequently a question which has not arisen or may never arise cannot competently be made the subject of a declarator.[51] It is not always easy to say whether a question is hypothetical. " Our courts have consistently acted on the view that it is their function in the ordinary run of contentious litigation to decide only live, practical questions, and they have no concern with hypothetical, premature or academic questions, nor do they exist to advise litigants as to the policy which they should adopt in the ordering of their affairs. The courts are neither a debating club nor an advisory bureau. Just what is a live practical question is not always easy to decide and must, in the long run, turn on the circumstances of the particular case. I doubt whether any good purpose is to be served by trying to extract any general rule from the decided cases. Each case as it arises must be considered on its merits, and the court must make up its mind as to the reality and immediacy of the issue which the case seeks to raise. Unless the court is satisfied that this is made out, it should sustain the plea of incompetence, as it is only with live and practical issues that the court is concerned." [52]

Vagueness of declarator

A declarator will not be granted, though possibly rather on the ground of irrelevancy than of incompetency, if it is sought in terms too vague, wide, general or otherwise unspecific.[53] The court will not grant a

45 *Southern Bowling Club*, *supra*, 411.
46 *Gifford* v. *Trail* (1829) 7 S. 854; *Lyle* v. *Balfour* (1830) 9 S. 22; *Steuart* v. *E. Seafield* (1871) 8 S.L.R. 335.
47 *Drennan* v. *Associated Ironmoulders*, 1921 S.C. 151.
48 *Edinburgh Mags.* v. *Warrender* (1863) 1 M. 887.
49 *Edinburgh Mags.*, *supra*, 896, *per* Lord Neaves.
50 *Cuthill* v. *Inverkeilor Parish Council*, 1910 S.C. 206.
51 *Morton* v. *Gardner* (1871) 9 M. 548; *Bothwell Parochial Board* v. *Pearson* (1873) 11 M. 399; *Callender's Cable Co.* v. *Glasgow Corpn.* (1900) 2 F. 397.
52 *Macnaughton* v. *Macnaughton's Trs.*, 1953 S.C. 387, 392, *per* L.J.C. Thomson.
53 *Cf. Glasgow Corpn.* v. *Lord Advocate*, 1959 S.C. 203, 235.

declarator which could cover cases not considered by it. " For, if [the pursuer's] crave were for a declarator alone, I do not think that the court would be justified in granting it in the general terms of the crave. I respectfully agree with Lord Jamieson (1948 S.C. at p. 120) that ' There are no averments which would enable the court, after enquiry, to ascertain the amount of the pursuer's indebtedness and the crave appears to be much too vague.' " [54] " It would not be right to grant a declarator in unqualified terms that the appellant is entitled to a reconveyance on repayment of the debt, even if the debt had been specified and even if the sale to [a third party] had not been completed. But here the debt is not specified. . . . " [55]

Declarator in matter of discretion or opinion

Declarator is incompetent of any state of fact which depends on the discretion, choice or opinion of some person as particular cases arise. Thus where manufacturers sought declarator that their product satisfied a corporation by-law, that the defender's master of works had formed an opinion adverse to the pursuer's product, and that their trade has suffered in consequence, the action was dismissed as incompetent.[56] The court could not, and would not, grant a declarator which would have fettered the master of works' exercise of his judgment in future cases and have bound the local Dean of Guild Court.

Declarator generally not competent where other appeal competent

Declarator is also incompetent if there is open to the pursuer and unused or unexhausted a special mode of appeal; that mode of appeal must first be utilised.[57] Thereafter declarator may be competent in some circumstances, though not necessarily always, the special mode of appeal being possibly exclusive. On the other hand declarator may be invoked where there is no mode of appeal competent or appropriate to the circumstances,[58] and if any special statutory procedure is inapplicable in the precise conditions which have arisen.[59] Similarly it has been held incompetent to bring a declarator that the defender was not the heir of a certain deceased person, the proper form of process being a petition for service as heir.[60]

Prematurity of declarator

A declarator is incompetent if it is premature, that is, has been brought

54 *Aberdeen Trades Council* v. *Shipconstructors and Shipwrights Assocn.*, 1949 S.C.(H.L.) 45, 53, *per* Lord Simonds.
55 *Ibid.* 57, *per* Lord Normand.
56 *Callender's Cable and Construction Co.* v. *Glasgow Corpn.* (1900) 2 F. 397.
57 *Denny & Bros.* v. *Board of Trade* (1880) 7 R. 1019; *Caledonian Ry.* v. *Glasgow Corpn.* (1905) 7 F. 1020; *Grubb* v. *Perth Educational Trust* (1907) 15 S.L.T. 492; *Dante* v. *Ayr Assessor*, 1922 S.C. 109.
58 *Hope* v. *Edinburgh Mags.* (1897) 5 S.L.T. 195.
59 *Fraser* v. *McNeill*, 1948 S.C. 517.
60 *Officers of State* v. *Alexander* (1866) 4 M. 741; not discussed on appeal (1868) 6 M. (H.L.) 54.

before the issue on which a decision is being sought really requires to be answered, or while it is still a future or hypothetical problem,[61] and particularly if there may be a change in circumstances which would alter the decision, or if possible contradictors may emerge in the future,[62] or if another, and primary, remedy has not yet been exhausted.[63]

Declarator ab ante

The court will in general not grant declarator as to some future or contingent state of affairs. Thus declarator was refused of the effectual character of a deed, where no question had actually been raised of the validity of the title,[64] of the fact that persons had power to test on provisions made in their favour and that on the death of each without issue the testament would be effectual,[65] of the fact that assignees of a life insurance policy, the insured being still alive, had right to the policy and that the company would be bound, on the policy becoming payable, to pay to them.[66]

But this is not an invariable rule; in a case as to assessment for poor relief it was said that " it may be inexpedient to raise questions by anticipation, and in many of the minor details of assessment and distribution the proper course would be to wait till the wrong were actually done. But if the point in dispute involve large and general principles on which the assessment of a particular rate-payer, or class of rate-payers, ought to be laid on, and if the Board have on former occasions taken what is conceived to be an erroneous view of those principles, I really see neither incompetency nor inexpediency in the party aggrieved resorting to the ordinary remedy of ascertaining and fixing, in the form of declarator, what these principles truly are, and how, consistently with them, the assessment ought to be made." [67] So too: " This peculiar process of declarator, which I have always regarded as the triumph and pride of our judicial system, must be jealously watched. The Court have always checked its abuse, and will not entertain it with regard to speculative questions, which may *de fururo* arise. There must be something precedent. There must be something which would justify a suspension or reduction to precede it. Now we have that here. . . . " [68]

An apprehended dispute or question regarding the validity or priority of almost any legal right may be anticipated and adjudicated upon in a declarator before it actually arises, provided all parties interested, or who

[61] *Fleming* v. *McLagan* (1879) 6 R. 588; *Millar* v. *Millar's Trs.* (1896) 4 S.L.T. 122; *Ayr Mags.* v. *Secretary of State for Scotland*, 1966 S.L.T. 16; *cf. Bothwell Parochial Board* v. *Pearson* (1873) 11 M. 399. Contrast *Falconer Stewart* v. *Wilkie* (1892) 19 R. 630.

[62] *Smith* v. *McColl's Trs.*, 1910 S.C. 1121; *Mair* v. *Kerr's Trs.*, 1919, 1 S.L.T. 125.

[63] *Caledonian Ry.* v. *Glasgow Corpn.* (1905) 7 F. 1020.

[64] *E. Galloway* v. *Garlies* (1838) 16 S. 1213. " I am against telling a party that he will be right if he do this, and wrong if he do that ": Lord Medwyn at p. 1216. *Cf. Murray* v. *M.* (1833) 11 S. 629.

[65] *Harvey* v. *H.'s Trs.* (1860) 22 D. 1310.

[66] *Allgemeine Deutsche Credit Anstalt* v. *Scottish Amicable Life Assce. Socy.*, 1908 S.C. 33.

[67] *Edinburgh & Glasgow Ry.* v. *Meek* (1849) 12 D. 153, 159, *per* Lord Fullerton.

[68] *Ibid.* 162, *per* Lord Jeffrey.

may be interested, can be, and in fact are, duly called.[69] "It is not doubtful that, according to the practice of the court, an apprehended dispute or question regarding the validity or priority of almost any legal right may be anticipated and adjudicated upon in a declarator before it actually arises, provided all parties interested, or who may be interested, can be and in fact are duly called." [70] A party entitled to a postponed and contingent provision under a marriage contract has been held entitled to have his rights ascertained by declarator if the debtor in the obligation questioned their existence or validity.[71]

Again it was held competent for a person holding an estate in liferent under a disposition providing for forfeiture of the liferent if he sold it, to seek *ab ante* declarator of his right to sell without incurring forfeiture.[72]

Again where a right of relief was in danger of being defeated by the running of time under a limitation statute a declarator that the pursuers were entitled to contribution towards any damages or expenses in which they might be found liable was held competent.[73]

It has been observed, *obiter*,[74] that "the modern tendency appears to be to open the doors wider to such proceedings, as will be seen by comparing the case of *Earl of Galloway* v. *Lord Garlies* [75] (in 1838) with *Chaplin's Trustees* v. *Hoile* [76] (in 1890) and with *Davidson* v. *Davidson* [77] (in 1906)," and later,[78] that "if a trust confers upon a beneficiary an immediate right to a payment either of capital or of income, and there is dispute between the beneficiary and the trustees about the amount of the payment, each of the two parties, the beneficiary and the trustees, has a good title and sufficient interest to bring a declarator in order to have the question between them determined. . . . The question what is the amount which the widow is entitled to receive is neither academic nor premature, but is both practical and of immediate urgency."

Conjunction of declaratory with other conclusions

A declaratory conclusion can be combined with, probably, any other kind of conclusion, such as reduction, interdict, *ad factum praestandum*, or damages.

Hence declarator may be prefixed to a conclusion for damages if the existence or extent in the circumstances of the duty alleged to have been breached (and thus justifying damages) is seriously doubted or disputed. Thus it is undoubted law that a person injured by negligence is entitled to damages, and declarator thereof as a preliminary to a claim of damages

69 *Fleming* v. *McLagan* (1879) 6 R. 589.
70 *Ibid.* 598, *per* Lord Young.
71 *Mackenzie's Trs.* v. *Mackenzie's Tutors* (1846) 8 D. 964.
72 *Chaplin's Trs.* v. *Hoile* (1890) 18 R. 27.
73 *Central S.M.T. Co.* v. *Lanarkshire C.C.*, 1949 S.C. 450.
74 *Turner's Trs.* v. *Turner*, 1943 S.C. 389, 394, *per* Lord Carmont.
75 (1838) 16 S. 1212.
76 (1890) 18 R. 27.
77 (1906) 14 S.L.T. 337.
78 1943 S.C. 398, *per* L.P. Normand.

is unnecessary. But, for example, a declarator may competently be brought by a traveller, who desires to establish the existence of the rights of the public as to accommodation in an hotel, against a hotelkeeper who refuses to recognise them, though a declaratory conclusion is not essential in such a case.[79]

Declarator as preliminary to other conclusions

Declarator is necessary as a preliminary to petitory or possessory claims where the right on which the latter claims depend is uncertain as to existence or extent.[80] Thus declarator of irritancy of a lease may be a necessary prelude to an extraordinary removing[81]; where a right is claimed in face of long adverse possession, a declaratory conclusion must precede any possessory conclusion[82]; and an action of reduction of an *ex facie* absolute and onerous deed on the ground that it was truly in trust and gratuitous must, at least as between truster and trustee,[83] have a preliminary declarator of the trust.[84]

But declarator was incompetent when its purpose was admittedly to obtain a decree which might be used as evidence before the Privy Council in support of a claim to be placed on the roll of baronets, and any decree would be otherwise inoperative.[85]

Competency of declarator generally

A declarator is competent to the effect that the pursuer has some legal right which has been doubted or challenged, or is in some doubt, in the circumstances, or that the circumstances in which the pursuer finds himself are such as to entitle him to some legal right or status or position.

The general rule appears to be that declarator is proper and sometimes, indeed, necessary before an action can proceed to enforce a right if the existence or extent of the right is not clear. But if the existence of the right is clear and merely whether it applies in the circumstances or has in the circumstances been infringed, declarator is unnecessary.

Within the limits of a declaratory conclusion stated too widely the court has power to pronounce such declarator as it thinks right in the circumstances,[86] but this does not entitle a pursuer to ask for anything in the hope that the court will give him something.

It has been observed[87] that " a question of liability on one hand, or exemption from liability on the other, to pay a continuing money payment,

79 *Rothfield* v. *N.B. Ry.*, 1920 S.C. 805, 827, *per* L.J.C. Scott Dickson; 838, *per* Lord Ormidale.
80 *Cruickshank* v. *Irving* (1854) 17 D. 286, 289; *D. Argyll* v. *Campbeltown Coal Co.*, 1924 S.C. 844, 852.
81 *D. Argyll*, *supra*.
82 *L. Lovat* v. *Fraser* (1845) 8 D. 316; *Grierson* v. *School Board of Sandsting and Aithsting* (1882) 9 R. 437.
83 *L. Elibank* v. *Hamilton* (1827) 6 S. 69.
84 *Anstruther* v. *Mitchell and Cullen* (1857) 19 D. 674.
85 *Menzies* v. *McKenna*, 1914 S.C. 272.
86 *Assets Co. Ltd.* v. *Ogilvie* (1897) 24 R. 400; *Rothfield* v. *N.B. Ry.*, 1920 S.C. 805, 830.
87 *Hogg* v. *Auchtermuchty Parochial Board* (1880) 7 R. 986.

whether that liability depends on the application of statute law or of common law to the facts of a particular case, may always be raised in a declarator." Thus the legality of an assessment should be tried by declarator rather than by suspension and interdict [88] or special case.[89]

On the other hand declarator of an undisputed fact [90] or of an admitted obligation [91] is incompetent.

Competency of bare declarator

It is sometimes said that only exceptionally is an action competent which concludes for declarator alone. It is customary and convenient to add conclusions for enforcement of the right declared, but there seems no reason in principle why, if a pursuer is confident that the defender will give effect to the pursuer's right, if it once be declared to be his right, he should not rest content with a bare conclusion for declarator, provided always that there is a live issue in dispute and that the pursuer has a legal interest to obtain the declarator sought, and accordingly that there is no necessary incompetence in a bare declarator.[92]

This is certainly no fixed or invariable rule, and an action will not be dismissed on this ground if there is, or still is notwithstanding the disappearance from the action of other conclusions and pleas, a live practical question between the parties.[93] Declarator of right to a heritable office has been entertained by itself.[94] A bare declaration that a contract of sale had been concluded subject to the rules of a certain trade association has been held competent when one of the rules of that association referred all claims of damages for breach of contract to arbitration.[95] A bare declarator that the pursuer was entitled to the benefit of a motor insurance policy in respect of certain claims was not challenged, and was granted.[96]

In *Smart* v. *Bargh* [97] the main conclusion was a declarator of property with no executory conclusion following thereon. The First Division dealt with the action, by consent, on the basis that the absence of an operative decree to effectuate the declarator was of no significance, though observing that if all the objections which might have been raised against the competency of this action had been stated, several additional questions would have had to be answered. A declarator of status does not require any executory conclusions in addition.[98] A police authority has, without objection, sought declarator only as to the Secretary of State's action in appointing a chief constable.[99]

[88] *British Fisheries Socy.* v. *Wick Mags.* (1872) 10 M. 426.
[89] *Bothwell Parochial Board* v. *Pearson* (1873) 11 M. 399.
[90] *Drennan* v. *Associated Ironmoulders*, 1921 S.C. 151.
[91] *Sime* v. *Grimond*, 1920, 1 S.L.T. 270.
[92] See *e.g. Ayr Mags.* v. *Lord Advocate*, 1950 S.C. 102; *McLay* v. *Farrell*, 1950 S.C. 149; *Fife C.C.* v. *Lord Advocate*, 1950 S.C. 314.
[93] *B.O.C.* v. *S.W. Scotland Electricity Board*, 1958 S.C. 53, 63.
[94] *E. Lauderdale* v. *Scrymgeour Wedderburn*, 1910 S.C.(H.L.) 35.
[95] *Stewart* v. *Sillars* (1906) 13 S.L.T. 800.
[96] *Kelly* v. *Cornhill Insurance Co.*, 1964 S.C.(H.L.) 46.
[97] 1949 S.C. 57, 60.
[98] *e.g. Makouipour* v. *Makouipour*, 1967 S.C. 116.
[99] *Kilmarnock Mags.* v. *Secretary of State for Scotland*, 1961 S.C. 350.

It is also uncertain whether the alleged general rule that a bare declarator is incompetent is affected by the Crown Proceedings Act 1947, s. 21, which authorises an order declaratory of the rights of parties in lieu of interdict or specific implement against the Crown.[1]

The real objection to a bare declarator is that if the defender declines to give effect to the right declared to subsist in the pursuer (and a declarator by itself is only moral persuasion), the latter must bring a fresh action, which might require reinvestigation of some of the same facts, and will cause expense and delay.[2] Another possible objection is that the courts do not sit to answer general questions and that no consequential right may flow from a bare declarator.[2]

Declarator to obtain decree cognitionis causa tantum

It is competent to bring a declarator to establish indebtedness only, *cognitionis causa tantum*, without any conclusion for payment.

Thus in *Hope Johnstone* v. *Cornwall* [3] the pursuer successfully sought declarator that the deceased, of whom the defender was executor, had borrowed money from the pursuer, granted a promissory note therefor, and subsequently replaced it by another promissory note, and that the principal and interest were outstanding and that the pursuer had an interest in the means and estate of the deceased for the payment thereof.

Declarator of jurisdiction

It has been held competent for the magistrates of a royal burgh to obtain from the Court of Session a declarator of their jurisdiction under a Crown charter, and it was observed that, before the abolition of heritable jurisdictions, it would have been competent for anyone having such rights to have their extent declared in the event of dispute.[4] In modern practice, where most jurisdiction is statutory, the need for such an action could rarely arise, but it might still be necessary in respect of uncertainties as to the common law jurisdiction of an inferior court.

Declarator as to meaning of a statute

It has been held incompetent by declarator to obtain an abstract decision on the meaning of a public Act of Parliament [5] and has been held incompetent " to declare the meaning of the terms of a public statute." [6] Similarly a declarator was dismissed when the decision was not craved as a step towards obtaining a competent remedy, but was as to the construction of a statute within the jurisdiction of another tribunal

[1] *Griffin* v. *L.A.*, 1950 S.C. 448.
[2] *Cf. Sinclair-Lockhart's Trs.* v. *Central Land Board*, 1950 S.L.T. 283; affd. 1951 S.C. 258.
[3] (1895) 22 R. 314.
[4] *Edinburgh Mags.* v. *Officers of State* (1825) 4 S. 319.
[5] *Balfour* v. *Malcolm* (1842) 1 Bell 163; *cf. Hogg* v. *Parochial Board of Auchtermuchty* (1880) 7 R. 986; *Orr* v. *Alston*, 1912, 1 S.L.T. 95.
[6] *Todd and Higginbotham* v. *Burnet* (1854) 16 D. 794.

exclusively.[7] But in other cases declarators have been granted of what the pursuers might or might not do under particular statutes.[8] The distinction has been drawn between the incompetency of declarator of a proposition already declared in a statute, and the competency of a declarator that such a proposition does or does not apply to a particular concrete subject,[9] or of a declarator of the right of the pursuer and the liability of the defender under the statute.[10]

It is suggested that competency in relation to the meaning of a statute depends on the recognised principles that it is not the function of a court to decide academic disputes, and that a declarator in the abstract is incompetent, but that where there is a live dispute and parties are justifiably doubtful as to what one may or may not do under some statutory provision, declarator is competent. It is difficult to see that the case of declarator is any different from any other form of action under which parties in dispute raise the issue of what one of them may or may not do under a statute. Thus, without challenge to competency, declarator was granted that a local authority was not liable to purchase tax on certain manufacturing activities,[11] that a particular person was not entitled to travel in special cheap-rate tramcars, run in terms of a statute,[12] a church officer's house was occupied by a " charity " within the meaning of a local authority valuation Act,[13] and that a cremation society was a " charity " and entitled to remission of local rates.[14] And it has been observed [15] that a question of liability or of exemption from liability, whether depending on common law or statute, may always be raised in a declarator.

Declarator of meaning of decrees

Declarator is competent of the meaning of a final decree of the Court of Session,[16] but not of the validity of the decree, which should be challenged by reduction.[17] Declarator has been brought that a judgment of the Rota, the supreme Roman Catholic tribunal in matrimonial cases, that a marriage was null under canon law, was a decree *in rem* and valid in Scotland, but was refused.[18] Declarator of the validity of a non-

[7] *Morton* v. *Gardner* (1871) 9 M. 548.

[8] *Macdonell* v. *Caledonian Canal Commrs.* (1830) 8 S. 881; *Tennent* v. *Turner* (1837) 16 S. 192; *Leith Police Commrs.* v. *Campbell* (1866) 5 M. 247; *Hogg, supra*; *Glasgow City and District Ry.* v. *Glasgow Mags.* (1884) 11 R. 1110; *West Highland Ry.* v. *Inverness C.C.* (1904) 6 F. 1052; *Norfor* v. *Aberdeenshire Education Authy.*, 1924 S.C. 590.

[9] *Leith Police Commissioners* v. *Campbell* (1866) 5 M. 251, *per* L.J.C. Inglis; *Steuart* v. *Keith Parochial Board* (1869) 8 M. 26; *British Fisheries Socy.* v. *Wick Mags.* (1872) 10 M. 426.

[10] *Sullivan* v. *Close* (1898) 6 S.L.T. 2.

[11] *Glasgow Corpn.* v. *Lord Advocate*, 1959 S.C. 203.

[12] *Lanarkshire Tramways* v. *McNaughton*, 1924 S.C. 35.

[13] *Belhaven-Westbourne Church* v. *Glasgow Corpn.*, 1965 S.C.(H.L.) 1.

[14] *Scottish Burial Reform and Cremation Socy.* v. *Glasgow Corpn.*, 1967 S.C.(H.L.) 116.

[15] *Hogg* v. *Auchtermuchty Parochial Board* (1880) 7 R. 986.

[16] *Ross* v. *Mackenzie* (1836) 14 S. 845; *Morton, Whitehead & Greig* v. *Smith* (1865) 3 M. 29; *Barstow* v. *Black* (1870) 8 M. 671.

[17] *Ross, supra.*

[18] *Di Rollo* v. *Di Rollo*, 1959 S.C. 75.

Scottish decree or judgment is incompetent; the Scottish courts may decline to recognise or enforce a foreign judgment but cannot say that it is invalid. Still less can Scottish courts declare the meaning of a foreign decree; only the foreign court can explain its own decree, and application must be made to it.

Declarator of illegality

Where a defender is acting in a manner which may be *ultra vires*, the legality of his actings must be tried by declarator rather than by interdict. But the court, it has been observed, " has always, and as I think most properly, been exceedingly chary in entertaining declarators relating to the working out of Acts of Parliament." [19]

In *British Fisheries Society* v. *Wick Magistrates* [20] magistrates imposed a larger assessment than necessary for immediate purposes to accumulate funds for prospective capital works. It was held that the legality of this could not be challenged in a suspension and interdict but might have been by declarator.

Declarator in Particular Cases

Subject to the general principles already mentioned declarator can be sought of any kind of legal right which the pursuer claims to have and which is denied, and which he has an interest to have declared, such as that a decision of the Local Government Board was conclusive that a parish council was bound to afford the pursuer adequate relief and that an offer to maintain her in their poorhouse was not an adequate offer.[21]

Declarators of Personal Status

Declarator is the normal mode of having the court declare that a person has or has not a particular status.

Declarator that person is a subject of Her Majesty

By the Legitimacy Declaration Act 1858, s. 9, any person domiciled in Scotland, or claiming any heritable or moveable property in Scotland, may raise an action of declarator in the Court of Session for the purpose of having it found and declared that he is entitled to be deemed a subject of Her Majesty, and the court has the same power to deal with it as in declarators of legitimacy and of bastardy.

Declarator of sex

It is doubtless competent to bring a declarator that a person is truly of one sex rather than of the other, where this fact has implications in

[19] *Steuart* v. *Parochial Board of Keith* (1869) 8 M. 26, 30, *per* Lord Benholme.
[20] (1872) 10 M. 426.
[21] *Cuthill* v. *Inverkeilor Parish Council*, 1910 S.C. 206.

respect of a " marriage " which that person has purported to enter into,[22] or is relevant to that person's entitlement to some right, *e.g.* in succession, or to that person's freedom from some liability, *e.g.* to compulsory national service.[23]

It is competent at the instance of the person himself, or probably of any other person who has a legal interest, such as one entitled to succeed as a substitute, failing the person whose sex is questioned.

Declarator of paternity

It is competent to seek declarator that one is the child of a designated father, if this is a fact having patrimonial consequences or consequences in relation to status.[24]

Declarator of legitimacy

Declarator is competent of one's own legitimacy,[25] or of the legitimacy of one's own ancestor, at least where entitlement to some right flows from the legitimacy of the ancestry,[26] though probably not if the action is brought merely to expunge a lapse in the family reputation.

Declarator of bastardy

Declarator is competent that a child is in fact a bastard and not the pursuer's legitimate offspring.[27] Such an action has been allowed at the instance of the heir-at-law of the husband of the alleged bastard, claiming to succeed on the failure of a conveyance by the husband to his wife and her heirs, she having predeceased without issue,[28] and a conclusion for declarator of bastardy of a child may be included in an action of divorce.[29]

Declarator of legitimation

Declarator is competent that a child has been legitimated *per subsequens matrimonium*, the matters requiring clarification being the child's parentage on both sides and the fact of the parent's marriage at some time. It may probably be brought by either parent, or by the child claiming to have been legitimated, but cannot be brought after the death of the child who might have been legitimated; posthumous legitimation is not recognised.[30]

22 *Cf. Corbett* v. *Corbett* [1970] 2 All E.R. 33.

23 *Cf. Walsh* v. *Lord Advocate*, 1956 S.C.(H.L.) 126.

24 *Grant* v. *Countess of Seafield*, 1926 S.C. 274, 290. *Cf. A.B. or C.* v. *D.* (1949) 65 Sh.Ct. Rep. 181.

25 *Shedden* v. *Patrick* (1849) 11 D. 1333, (1853) 15 D. 379; *Benson* v. *Benson* (1854) 16 D. 555; *Morley* v. *Jackson* (1888) 16 R. 78; *Grant* v. *Countess of Seafield*, 1926 S.C. 274.

26 *Moncreiff* v. *Lord Moncreiff* (1904) 6 F. 1021; *Bosville* v. *Lord Macdonald*, 1910 S.C. 597.

27 *Rose* v. *Ross* (1827) 5 S. 605; *Imre* v. *Mitchell*, 1958 S.C. 439 (where there was also a conclusion for putting the defender (father) to silence anent the child's paternity).

28 *Smith* v. *Dick* (1869) 8 M. 31.

29 *Brown* v. *Brown*, 1972 S.L.T. 143.

30 *McNeill* v. *McGregor* (1901) 4 F. 123.

Declarator of paternity

It is competent to bring an action for declarator that the defender is the father of the pursuer's illegitimate child,[31] and for aliment.

Affiliation truly declaratory

An action of affiliation and aliment is essentially, under the affiliation head, of a declaratory nature, decree being declaratory of the defender's paternity of the child. It has certain elements of an action to determine status.[32] It is competent to bring a declarator of the paternity of an illegitimate child even though there is no conclusion for aliment.[33]

Putting to silence

An action of, or conclusion for, putting the defender to silence is competent as ancillary to a conclusion for declarator of legitimacy or of bastardy.[34]

Declarator of marriage

Declarator is the proper mode of establishing a marriage which is doubtful or disputed, particularly where entered into by *de presenti* consent,[35] by promise *subsequente copula*,[36] or by cohabitation with habit and repute.[37]

At least in the case of marriage by promise *subsequenta copula* the declarator may be brought by a child of the parties.[38]

Where the marriage was regular, declarator is no doubt the competent mode of establishing it if it be doubted or denied but the evidence of the register of Births, Deaths and Marriages is sufficient [39] unless shown to be erroneous, as by proof of impersonation.

Exceptionally proof of marriage has been allowed incidentally to another action, but such a decision would not be *res judicata* between the

[31] *Macaulay* v. *Hussain*, 1966 S.C. 204.

[32] *Hepburn* v. *Tait* (1874) 1 R. 875, 878; *McDonald* v. *Ross*, 1929 S.C. 240, 248.

[33] *McDonald*, *supra*, 252, 253.

[34] *Imre* v. *Mitchell*, 1958 S.C. 439.

[35] *e.g. Dalrymple* v. *Dalrymple* (1811) 2 Haggard 54; *Walker* v. *Macadam* (1813) 5 Pat. 675; *Leslie* v. *Leslie* (1860) 22 D. 993; *Dysart Peerage Case* (1881) 6 App.Cas. 489; *Imrie* v. *Imrie* (1891) 19 R. 185; *Duran* v. *Duran* (1904) 7 F. 87; *Petrie* v. *Petrie*, 1911 S.C. 360; *Davidson* v. *Davidson*, 1921 S.C. 341; *Courtin* v. *Elder*, 1930 S.C. 68; *Dunn* v. *Dunn's Trs.*, 1930 S.C. 131. Marriage in this mode is not competent after 1st January, 1940: Marriage (Sc.) Act 1939, s. 5.

[36] *e.g. Ross* v. *Macleod* (1861) 23 D. 972; *Longworth* v. *Yelverton* (1867) 5 M.(H.L.) 144; *Morrison* v. *Dobson* (1869) 8 M. 347; *Maloy* v. *Macadam* (1885) 12 R. 431; *Mackie* v. *Mackie*, 1917 S.C. 276; *Lindsay* v. *Lindsay*, 1927 S.C. 395; *N.* v. *C.*, 1933 S.C. 492. Marriage in this mode is not competent after January 1, 1940: Marriage (Sc.) Act 1939, s. 5.

[37] *Hamilton* v. *Hamilton* (1839) 2 D. 89; *Campbell* v. *Campbell* (1867) 5 M.(H.L.) 115; *De Thoren* v. *Wall* (1876) 3 R.(H.L.) 28; *Hendry* v. *L.A.*, 1930 S.C. 1027; *Bairner* v. *Fels*, 1931 S.C. 674; *A.B.* v. *C.D.*, 1957 S.C. 415.

[38] *X.* v. *Y.*, 1921, 1 S.L.T. 79.

[39] Registration of Births, Deaths and Marriages (Sc.) Act 1965, ss. 30–31, 41.

spouses, and the court may always insist on declarator.[40] No third party can obtain a declarator of marriage decree in which would be *res judicata* between the spouses.[41] It is competent, in a petition for declarator of nullity of marriage to include a crave for a finding that the defender (" husband ") was already married to another woman,[42] or in a declarator of marriage to conclude for nullity of a second " marriage " of the defender.[43]

Declarator of marriage can be brought against the heirs of a deceased spouse [44] but it is questionable whether a deceased partner's executor may continue an action commenced by the deceased.[45]

Nullity of marriage

Declarator may be sought of nullity of marriage, either on the ground that the apparent marriage was void *ab initio*,[46] or on the ground that it was voidable and that the petitioner now wishes it declared void.[47] Declarator that a marriage has been void *ab initio* may be brought not only by either spouse, but by any person having a patrimonial interest in the decision,[48] or by the *curator bonis* of an incapax who had gone through a ceremony of marriage,[49] but declarator voiding a merely voidable marriage is personal to the spouses,[50] but competent to either of them,[51] and on the basis of either the defender's, or the pursuer's own, impotency.[51]

A decree of nullity affirms that the " marriage " is and has been null for all purposes [52] and there must be, so far as possible, mutual restitution *in integrum* of property transferred in reliance on the " marriage." [53]

Declarator that previous marriage dissolved

Declarator that a pursuer's previous marriage has been dissolved is unnecessary where that has been done judicially by a court recognised as having jurisdiction, or by a court recognised by the courts of the husband's domicile as having jurisdiction,[54] but is, if not necessary, certainly competent where the marriage has been dissolved non-judicially.[55] Declarator

40 *Lenaghan* v. *Monkland Iron Co.* (1857) 19 D. 975; *Rudland* v. *Gilbert* (1843) 16 Sc.Jur. 97; *Beattie* v. *Baird* (1863) 1 M. 273; *Wright* v. *Sharp* (1880) 7 R. 460; *McDonald* v. *Mackenzie* (1891) 18 R. 502; *Wallace* v. *Fife Coal Co.*, 1909 S.C. 682.

41 *Leslie* v. *L.* (1860) 22 D. 993.

42 *Courtin* v. *Elder*, 1930 S.C. 68.

43 Lothian, *Consistorial Law*, 87.

44 *Leslie* v. *L.* (1860) 22 D. 993; *Mackie* v. *M.*, 1917 S.C. 276; *X.* v. *Y.*, 1921, 1 S.L.T. 79. See also *Lowrie* v. *Mercer* (1840) 2 D. 953; *Forster* v. *F.* (1869) 7 M. 797.

45 *Green* v. *Green or Borthwick* (1896) 24 R. 211.

46 *e.g. MacDougall* v. *Chitnavis*, 1937 S.C. 390; *Long* v. *Long*, 1950 S.L.T. (Notes) 32; *Aldridge* v. *A.*, 1954 S.C. 58; *Prawdzic-Lazarska* v. *P.L.*, 1954 S.C. 98; *A.B.* v. *C.D.*, 1957 S.C. 415 (wife's action); *Orlandi* v. *Castelli*, 1961 S.C. 113.

47 *e.g. G.* v. *G.*, 1924 S.C.(H.L.) 42; *S.G.* v. *W.G.*, 1933 S.C. 728.

48 Fraser, *H. & W.* II, 1244.

49 *Parnell* v. *P.* (1814) 2 Hagg.Consist. 169, 170.

50 Bell, *Prin.* § 1524.

51 *F.* v. *F.*, 1945 S.C. 202; *H.* v. *H.*, 1949 S.C. 587.

52 *A.B.* v. *C.B.'s Trs.* (1907) 15 S.L.T. 108, 908.

53 Stair I, 4, 20; Ersk. I, 6, 43; Fraser, *H. & W.* I, 49; *Wright* v. *Sharp* (1880) 7 R. 460, 464; *Wilkie* v. *W.* (1908) 45 S.L.R. 451.

54 *McKay* v. *Walls*, 1951 S.L.T. (Notes) 6.

55 *Makouipour* v. *Makouipour*, 1967 S.C. 116.

has been entertained of the question whether a decision of the Rota, the supreme Roman Catholic appeal tribunal in matrimonial cases, that a marriage was null under canon law was a decree *in rem* and entitled to recognition by the Scottish courts.[56]

Declarator of freedom and putting to silence

In this case the declarator is to the effect that there has never been a marriage between pursuer and defender, and for decree ordaining the defender to desist from falsely asserting that fact.[57] If the defence is that there has been a marriage that plea can be entertained without need for a separate declarator of marriage, and decree will be *res judicata* on that matter.[58]

Declarator of other quasi-status

Declarator is a competent mode of having determined the pursuer's possession or not of any other quasi-status, provided it has some civil legal consequences, or involves some patrimonial interest[59] such as that the pursuer was " a regular minister " of a stated religious denomination and in consequence exempt from national service.[60] If the question were solely whether or not the pursuer had the status of an ordained clergyman this would seem to be a matter for the ecclesiastical courts. Similarly, where a session-clerk alleged that he had been appointed *ad vitam aut culpam* and had been dismissed, no *culpa* having been alleged against him, it was indicated that his remedy was by declarator, and reduction of the sentence dismissing him, not by action for reparation.[61] A declarator that the pursuer was of sound mind has been allowed in the sheriff court, because it did not relate to status.[62] *Sed quaere.* Similarly declarator is appropriate to determine whether or not a person is a member of a trade union,[63] or is or is not still a member of a religious order.[64]

Proceedings for presumption of death

Proceedings to have it judicially presumed that a person is dead are declaratory in substance, and may be in the form of a declaratory action.[65]

The presumption is that a person, unless known to be dead, continues

[56] *Di Rollo* v. *Di Rollo*, 1959 S.C. 75.
[57] *e.g. A.B.* v. *C.D.* (1901) 8 S.L.T. 406; *Williams* v. *Forsythe*, 1909, 2 S.L.T. 252.
[58] *H.* v. *R.* (1844) 16 Sc.Jur. 576; *Longworth* v. *Yelverton* (1862) 1 M. 161; (1864) 2 M. (H.L.) 49.
[59] *Cf. McMillan* v. *Free Church* (1860) 22 D. 290; (1862) 24 D. 1282; *Forbes* v. *Eden* (1866) 5 M. (H.L.) 36; *Wight* v. *Presbytery of Dunkeld* (1870) 8 M. 921; *Skerret* v. *Oliver* (1896) 23 R. 468.
[60] *Walsh* v. *Lord Advocate*, 1956 S.C.(H.L.) 126; *cf. H.M.A.* v. *Ballantyne* (1859) 3 Irv. 352.
[61] *Goldie* v. *Christie and Petrie* (1868) 6 M. 541; *cf. Mackay and Esslemont* v. *Lord Advocate*, 1937 S.C. 860.
[62] *Mears* v. *Mears*, 1969 S.L.T.(Sh.Ct.) 21.
[63] *Martin* v. *Scottish T. & G.W.U.*, 1952 S.C.(H.L.) 1.
[64] *McDonald* v. *Burns*, 1940 S.C. 376.
[65] *e.g. Greig, infra.*

in life for a substantial time [66]; no precise time is fixed, but scripture states the days of man's age as three score years and ten.[67] Stair mentions eighty or one-hundred years,[68] and statistics and actuarial tables show that the average expectation of life is about seventy-five years.

At common law an action to find and declare that death must be presumed at or about a stated date requires positive evidence sufficient to overcome the presumption of continuing life.[69] It does not require certainty of death to be shown. The court must have regard to the person's age, health and habits of life, the circumstances in which he was last heard from or of, and any factors which might indicate unusual danger to life, such as participation in an Arctic expedition,[70] a singularly chequered career,[71] illness in a notoriously unhealthy climate,[72] setting out on a perilous journey,[73] his known disappearance in a catastrophe, and the general prospects and possibilities affecting the person's survival.

Under the Presumption of Life Limitation (Scotland) Act 1891, if a person has disappeared and has not been heard of for seven years or more, the court may find the fact of disappearance, the date on which the absent person was last known to be alive, and that he died at some specified date or, failing sufficient evidence of death at any definite date, that he is to be presumed to have died seven years after the date on which he was last known to be alive.

Petition under this Act is competent at the instance of anyone entitled to succeed to any estate on the death of the absent person, or entitled to any estate the transmission of which depends on the death of the absentee, or of the fiar of any estate burdened with a liferent in favour of the absentee. An absentee, if he returns, may recover any estate from any person who has acquired title to it under the Act or from his gratuitous alienee, or the price of it if it has been sold, for thirteen years from the date when the title to the estate, if registrable in a public register, was so registered, or in other cases from the date on which possession was taken. Thereafter any right of recovery is excluded. The Act does not apply to claims under policies of insurance.

Decree under the Act may alter the succession to an estate,[74] and beneficiaries may obtain payment of their shares subject to an obligation to repay in the event of the presumption being found to be unjustified.[74]

Dissolution of marriage on ground of presumed death

The Divorce (Scotland) Act 1938, s. 5, provides that a married person who alleges that reasonable grounds exist for supposing that the other

66 Dickson, *Evidence*, § 116.
67 Psalm 90, v. 10.
68 IV. 45, 17.
69 *Greig* v. *Edinburgh Merchant Company*, 1921 S.C. 76.
70 *Fairholme* v. *Fairholme's Trs.* (1858) 20 D. 813.
71 *Bruce* v. *Smith* (1871) 10 M. 130.
72 *Rhind's Trs.* v. *Bell* (1878) 5 R. 527.
73 *Williamson* v. *Williamson* (1886) 14 R. 226.
74 *Barr* v. *Campbell*, 1925 S.C. 317.

party to the marriage is dead may petition the court for dissolution of the marriage on the ground of the presumed death of the other party. The fact that for a period of seven years or upwards the other party has been continually absent from the petitioner and the petitioner has no reason to believe that the other party has been living within that time, is evidence that the other party is dead unless the contrary is proved.

It is a question of fact whether the circumstances indicate wilful desertion by the absentee, justifying divorce,[75] or absence giving rise to a presumption of death.[76]

This provision deals with dissolution of marriage only and not with any other aspect of status, nor with the proprietary rights of, or rights in succession to, the absentee.

Declarators in relation to Contract

Declarator, though frequently competent, is not much used in cases involving contracts, as most disputes are raised by seeking other remedies. But declarator is frequently competent, and sometimes sought, as to the effect that the pursuer was a partner in a firm,[77] that the defenders must comply with the Articles of Association of the company of which they were members,[78] that an agreement was valid and subsisting,[79] that certain provisions of an agreement were null and void,[80] that a contract had been induced by fraud and that the pursuers were entitled to rescind and had rescinded the contract,[81] that defenders had forfeited right to property disponed in security and that the pursuer was free from an obligation to recover it,[82] that on a sound construction of a contract, annual payments fell to be paid under deduction of tax.[83]

Declarators of Proprietary Rights

Declarator of right of property

Declarator is an appropriate mode of having found that certain property standing in the name of another truly belongs to the pursuer,[84] or of having determined whether his title, which is disputable, ambiguous or of undefined boundaries, truly confers on him a proprietary right to particular subjects.[85] Thus in a case of uncertain boundaries the proprietor

[75] 1938 Act, s. 1 (1) (*a*).
[76] *Lench* v. *Lench*, 1945 S.C. 295; *cf. Irvine* v. *Irvine* (1884) 21 S.L.R. 493.
[77] *Munro* v. *Stein*, 1961 S.C. 362.
[78] *Lyle & Scott* v. *Scott's Trs.*, 1959 S.C.(H.L.) 64.
[79] *East Kilbride Development Corpn.* v. *Pollok*, 1953 S.C. 370.
[80] *Duncan* v. *Motherwell Bridge Co.*, 1952 S.C. 131.
[81] *Gamage* v. *Charlesworth's Tr.*, 1910 S.C. 257.
[82] *Gillies* v. *Craigton Garage Co.*, 1935 S.C. 423.
[83] *Allen* v. *Bruce*, 1933 S.C. 253.
[84] *e.g. Johnstone* v. *Dryden* (1890) 18 R. 191; *McCarroll* v. *McKinstery*, 1924 S.C. 396.
[85] *Cruickshank* v. *Irving* (1854) 17 D. 286; see also *D. Argyll* v. *Campbeltown Coal Co.*, 1924 S.C. 844, 852.

was held bound to obtain a declarator of right to property as a preliminary to a claim for interdict against another who proposed to build thereon.[85] But a lesser degree of uncertainty would not necessitate declarator.

A declarator is appropriate to determine whether or not the pursuer has title to any piece of heritage,[86] or to fix the boundaries of a feu,[87] or to determine whether a superior has sole right to minerals.[88]

Declarator of servitude

It is likewise appropriate to assert a claim to a servitude right.[89]

Declarator of lease

It is competent to seek declarator that an agreement constitutes a valid lease of heritable subjects.[90]

Declarator of right of way

Declarator is the appropriate process for establishing the existence of a right of way between two places,[91] or for establishing freedom from a right of way.[92]

Other rights connected with heritage

Among other rights connected with heritage which have been made the subject of declarators have been the right of ferry upon a river,[93] the right to the water in a stream,[94] the right to the water of a river in an unpolluted state, and for interdict against polluting it,[95] the right of a

86 *Steele* v. *Oliver* (1832) 10 S. 858; *Butchart* v. *Prophet* (1841) 3 D. 1040; *Aberdeen Harbour Commrs.* v. *Aberdeen Ry.* (1852) 15 D. 75; *Mushet* v. *Duke of Buccleuch* (1851) 13 D. 713, (1856) 18 D. 322; *Russel's Trs.* (1865) 3 M. 850; *cf. Lightbody* v. *Lawrie* (1855) 17 D. 653; *Denvir* v. *Denvir,* 1969 S.L.T. 301; *cf. Ross* v. *Graesser,* 1962 S.C. 66 (declarator in Land Court).

87 *Campbell* v. *McLaren* (1861) 24 D. 57.

88 *Kerse Estates Ltd.* v. *Welsh,* 1935 S.C. 387.

89 *Steele* v. *Oliver* (1832) 10 S. 858; *Sanderson* v. *Lees & Brown* (1859) 21 D. 1011; *Rattray* v. *Tayport Patent Slip Co.* (1866) 1 S.L.R. 194; *Macfie* v. *Stewart* (1872) 10 M. 408; *Kerr* v. *Brown,* 1939 S.C. 140; *Campbell* v. *Henderson,* 1949 S.C. 172; *Millar* v. *Christie,* 1961 S.C. 1; *Hunter* v. *Fox,* 1964 S.C.(H.L.) 95; *Largs Hydropathic Ltd.* v. *Largs Town Council,* 1967 S.C. 1.

90 *Banff Mags.* v. *Ruthin Castle Ltd.,* 1944 S.C. 36; *Gray* v. *Edinburgh University,* 1962 S.C. 157; *Buchanan* v. *Neill,* 1966 S.L.T.(Sh.Ct.) 62.

91 *Earl of Cassilis* v. *Wigton Mags.* (1750) Mor. 16122; *Tait* v. *Lauderdale* (1827) 5 S. 330; *Cuthbertson* v. *Young* (1851) 13 D. 1308; *Bates & Baring* v. *McQueen* (1853) 15 D. 455; *Anderson* v. *Maxwell* (1855) 17 D. 1072; *East of Fife Ry. Co.* v. *Tulloch* (1859) 32 Sc.Jur. 2; *Ferguson* v. *Hoyle* (1859) 21 D. 430; *Tulloch* v. *Baird* (1859) 21 D. 957; *Elgin Mags.* v. *Robertson* (1862) 24 D. 788; *Wilson* v. *Hagart* (1862) 24 D. 1086; *Hay* v. *Earl of Morton* (1862) 24 D. 116, 1054; 4 M.(H.L.) 53; *Macfarlane* v. *Morrison* (1865) 4 M. 257; *Scott* v. *Drummond* (1866) 4 M. 819; *Jenkins* v. *Murray* (1866) 5 M. 39; *Anderson* v. *Colville* (1868) 6 S.L.R. 24; *Jenkins* v. *Robertson* (1869) 7 M. 739; *Murray* v. *Arbuthnot* (1870) 9 M. 198; *Macfie* v. *Stewart* (1872) 10 M. 408; *Mackintosh* v. *Moir* (1872) 10 M. 517; *Robertson* v. *D. Atholl* (1905) 8 F. 150.

92 *Norrie* v. *Kirriemuir Mags.,* 1945 S.C. 302.

93 *Tay Ferry Trs.* v. *Edinburgh, Perth and Dundee Ry.* (1851) 14 D. 103; *Leslie* v. *Grieve* (1861) 33 Sc.Jur. 318.

94 *Thorburn* v. *Charters* (1841) 4 D. 169; *Brand* v. *Charters* (1842) 4 D. 345; *Lennox* v. *Hurlet & Campsie Alum Co.* (1859) 22 D. 178.

95 *Duke of Buccleuch* v. *Cowan* (1866) 4 M. 475.

landlord of mines as to the maintenance of certain levels,[96] to the free use of a moor for the purpose of holding markets,[97] that building conditions had been contravened,[98] that the pursuers were entitled to extend a building without consent,[99] that buildings contravened conditions in a feu-charter,[1] that the pursuer had exclusive right of property in sand on a farm,[2] that the defenders were bound to maintain the navigable channel of a river [3]; that the defender had no right to fish in a loch [4]; that the defender was bound to reside on a farm.[5]

Declarator of non-entry

A declarator of non-entry was formerly competent where the successor of a vassal had failed to enter with the superior and to pay the casualty due on his succession.[6]

By the Conveyancing (Scotland) Act 1874, s. 4 (4), no lands may thereafter be deemed in non-entry but a superior who would formerly have been entitled to bring a declarator of non-entry may bring an action of declarator and for payment of any casualty exigible at the date of the action, decree in which operates as a decree of declarator of non-entry under the former law but ceases to have effect on the payment of the casualty, without prejudice to the superior's title to the rents due for the period while he is in possession of the lands under such decree, nor to any feu-duties or arrears due or exigible at or prior to the date of such payment, or his rights and remedies for recovering them.

Declarator of tinsel of superiority

A declarator was competent that the superior had forfeited his right of superiority if he failed to infeft his vassal.[7] Now if a subject superior's title is incomplete so as to enable him to enter any heir or disponee of the last vassal, or adjudger or other party deriving right from or through such vassal, the heir, disponee, adjudger or other party may if the reddendo does not exceed £5 per annum petition the Court to ordain the superior to complete his title and grant entry to the petitioner, failing which, unless there is reasonable cause for the delay or refusal, he shall forfeit his superiority and the petitioner will be entitled to hold as vassal of and under the next over superior.[8] If the reddendo exceeds £5, or the heir, etc., elects he may petition for authority to apply for an entry by the

[96] *Earl of Hopetoun* v. *Scots Mining Co.* (1859) 21 D. 218.
[97] *Henderson* v. *Earl of Minto* (1860) 22 D. 1126.
[98] *Howard de Walden Estates Ltd.* v. *Bowmaker Ltd.*, 1965 S.C. 163.
[99] *Eagle Lodge Ltd.* v. *Keir and Cawder Estates Ltd.*, 1964 S.C. 30.
[1] *Ben Challum Ltd.* v. *Buchanan*, 1955 S.C. 348.
[2] *Borthwick-Norton* v. *Gavin Paul & Sons*, 1947 S.C. 659.
[3] *Fleming & Ferguson* v. *Paisley Mags.* 1948 S.C. 547.
[4] *Kilsyth Fish Protection Assocn.* v. *McFarlane*, 1937 S.C. 757.
[5] *Pollok* v. *Whiteford*, 1936 S.C. 402.
[6] *Cf. Earl of Fife's Trs.* v. *Sinclair* (1844) 6 D. 1194.
[7] Stair IV, 7.
[8] Titles to Land Consolidation (Sc.) Act 1868, s. 104.

Crown, or mediate over superior in place of the recusant superior.[9] In such proceedings a superior may by minute relinquish his right of superiority,[10] and he may relinquish it by deed.[11]

Declarator of irritancy of feu

The legal irritancy of holdings of land in feu-farm for non-payment of feu-duty [12] requires declarator that it has been incurred [13] as a prelude to removing the vassal.

In the case of a conventional irritancy of a feu-right [14] declarator is probably necessary only if there is a substantial question as to the legality of the irritancy, or of whether it has been incurred, or if otherwise it seems desirable that the irritancy be first declared before its consequence be sought.[15]

The War Damage to Land (Scotland) Act 1939, s. 4, empowers the sheriff court to grant a declarator of irritancy of a feu or lease where war damage has occurred to land.[16]

Action of declarator and for payment of casualty

Under the Conveyancing (Sc.) Act 1874, s. 4, infeftment by registration of a conveyance in the Register of Sasines implies entry with the superior and accordingly no lands can now be deemed to be in non-entry, but a superior who would formerly have been entitled to sue a declarator of non-entry [17] may bring an action for declarator and for payment of any casualty exigible [18] against the successor of the vassal in the lands, decree in which operates as a declarator of non-entry hitherto did, but has no effect on the payment of such a casualty, and does not prejudice the superior's right to the rents for the period while he is in possession of the lands under such decree, nor to any feuduties or arrears thereof due at or prior to such payment or the remedies competent for recovering the same.

Declarator of irritancy of lease

Where a lease contains a clause providing for irritancy of that lease, whether a legal or a conventional irritancy,[19] it is the general rule that declarator that the irritancy has been incurred should precede the conclusion for ejection in an extraordinary removing, *i.e.* one brought other than at the normal termination of the lease, or at a break in the lease.[20]

9 *Ibid.* s. 105.
10 *Ibid.* s. 107.
11 *Ibid.* s. 110.
12 On this see Chap. 6 *supra.*
13 *D. Argyll* v. *Campbeltown Coal Co.*, 1924 S.C. 844, 850.
14 On this see Chap. 6 *supra.*
15 *e.g. Neill's Tr.* v. *Macfarlane's Trs.*, 1952 S.C. 356.
16 *Cf. Neill's Tr.* v. *Macfarlane's Trs.*, 1952 S.C. 356.
17 See Stair IV, 8.
18 Form in 1874 Act, Sched. B.
19 On irritancies of leases, see generally Chap. 6 *supra.*
20 More, *Notes*, lxxx; Bell, *Leases*, II, 16; *D. Argyll* v. *Campbeltown Coal Co.*, 1924 S.C. 844, 850; *Brodie* v. *Ker* 1952 S.C. 216.

But in the case of irritancy of a lease for non-payment of rent for two successive years enforcement was made competent in the sheriff court by removing without declarator.[21]

It has, however, long been held competent to enforce a conventional irritancy in a lease by removing without declarator,[22] at least unless there is serious question as to the legality of the irritancy, or its having been incurred.[23]

The modern position is that it appears to be a question of convenience, expediency and of circumstances whether a declaratory conclusion is desirable as a preface to the conclusion for removing.[24] There is no inflexible rule based upon legal principle which renders declaratory conclusions necessary. Declarator is desirable, if not indeed necessary, if there is serious question as to the existence or legality of the irritancy,[25] and in such a case the court could dismiss as incompetent an action which does not seek declarator, and there are thought to be many cases of extraordinary removings where declaratory conclusions are both appropriate and expedient.[26] If the title requires investigation or proof, or the validity of the lease is in doubt, preliminary declarator may be highly expedient, but whether it is so in a particular case is one of degree.[27]

Declarator is unnecessary if the facts which bring the irritancy into operation are admitted by the defender or are so simple and notorious that they admit of instant verification.[28]

Declarator of expiry of the legal

Where a creditor has brought an action for adjudication of his debtor's heritage for debt and obtained decree adjudging the heritable rights to him in satisfaction of his claim he obtains not an absolute right but a judicial security only, and the debtor retains a right of redemption.[29] This right of redemption subsists for ten years, a period known as "the legal," *i.e.* the legal period for redemption, and during this period, if the debt be extinguished by payment or by the creditor's receipt of rents, the debt is discharged and the debtor is entitled to recover his lands.

After the expiry of the ten years the creditor may raise an action of declarator of expiry of the legal, in which he calls on the debtor to exercise his right of redemption, failing which it will be judicially declared that the right of redemption is foreclosed. Despite the lapse of ten years the heritage is redeemable until decree in the declarator is pronounced, but thereafter it is wholly excluded.[30]

21 A.S. 14 Dec. 1756; *D. Argyll, supra.*
22 *Gordon* (1805) Mor. Tack, Appx. 11; *Scott* v. *Wotherspoon* (1829) 7 S. 481; *Stewart* v. *Watson* (1864) 2 M. 1414.
23 Mackay, *Manual of Practice*, 78; *D. Argyll, supra*, 851; *Brodie, supra.*
24 *D. Argyll* v. *Campbeltown Coal Co.*, 1924 S.C. 844, 851.
25 Mackay, *Manual*, 78.
26 *D. Argyll, supra.*
27 *D. Argyll, supra*, 852, citing *Cruickshanks* v. *Irving* (1854) 17 D. 286.
28 *Ibid.*
29 *Grindley* v. *Drysdale* (1833) 11 S. 896; *Cochrane* v. *Bogle* (1849) 11 D. 908; affd. (1850) 7 Bell 65.
30 *Govan* v. *G.* (1758) 2 Pat. 27.

The decree enables the creditor to complete an irredeemable title to the subjects adjudged by recording the decree in the appropriate division of the Register of Sasines and possessing in reliance thereon.

If even after decree the creditor has not been paid his due he may still bring an action for the balance,[31] but if the adjudication was restricted to adjudication in security, the adjudger must account for his intromissions with the heritage both before and after the declarator.[32]

If the declarator be obtained in absence, it may be reduced on proof that the debt had really been paid or extinguished within the legal, or on proof that there was material objection to the original adjudication or irregularity therein, or in the action of declarator of expiry of the legal. But the right of reduction will be excluded by the lapse of the long negative prescription.[33] It may also be re-opened as where the debtor was abroad and had been a minor during part of the legal.[34]

Declarator of ownership or possession of moveable property

It is competent to seek declarator that moveable property, such as shares, registered in the name of another, is the property of the pursuer,[35] or that animals on a farm did not fall into the sequestrated estates of the farmer.[36]

Similarly declarator has been sought that the pursuers had the sole right of possession and control of a ship, for delivery of it, and for interdict against the defender interfering with it.[37]

Commercial rights

The entitlement of parties to various commercial proprietary rights may be determined by declarator, though other forms of action are more common. Thus declarator has been sought that the pursuers were entitled to describe and market their products as "Harris Tweed."[38]

Declarators in relation to Trusts and Succession

Declarator of trust

Where a person alleges that property, the title to which appears to be vested absolutely in another person, is truly held by that person not absolutely but in trust only, he may substantiate that only by a declarator of trust.[39] Moreover it is settled law that, at least in a question between

[31] Shand's *Practice of the Court of Session*, 717.

[32] *Walker* v. *Macpherson & Forrester* (1720) Mor. 302.

[33] *Paul* v. *Reid*, Feb. 8, 1814, F.C.

[34] Bell, *Comm.* I 744, citing *Aitken* v. *A.* (1809).

[35] *McCarroll* v. *McKinstery*, 1926 S.C.(H.L.) 1; *Kennedy* v. *Macrae*, 1946 S.C. 118.

[36] *Newbigging* v. *Ritchie's Tr.*, 1930 S.C. 273.

[37] *Azcarate* v. *Iturrizaga*, 1938 S.C. 573.

[38] *Argyllshire Weavers Ltd.* v. *Macaulay*, 1962 S.C. 388.

[39] *Bryson* v. *Chalmers* (1833) 5 Sc.Jur. 401; *Pickard* v. *Pickard*, 1963 S.C. 604.

truster and trustee, the fact of trust can be proved only by the writ or oath of the alleged trustee.[40] The writ need not be probative,[41] nor even need be signed.[42]

Declarator is not necessary where the title deed bears *in gremio* to be a conveyance in trust only, nor where the alleged trustee intervened voluntarily as a *negotiorum gestor*,[43] nor where there is no deed of trust alleged.[44]

Third parties may prove trust *prout de jure*, the Act of 1696 being inapplicable [45] and the trustee may prove *prout de jure* that he holds only as trustee and not absolutely.[46]

Parole evidence is also competent where the allegation is that the relationship was mandate, not trust,[47] or partnership rather than trust,[48] or where it is relevantly averred that there was fraud in the constitution of the title,[49] or where the alleged trustee admits that the title in his name does not represent the true relationship between the pursuer and himself, but that it is subject to qualifications,[50] or where the alleged trustee already stood in some other fiduciary relationship to the truster who was a person under legal disability.[51]

In all cases, if it is admitted or proved that the property is held in trust, the terms and purposes of the trust may be proved by any means.[52]

Declarator is similarly competent to the effect that the pursuers were trustees of a fund and entitled to act as such.[53]

Similarly it is competent to seek declarator that a trust is at an end.[54] A sole surviving trustee has been held entitled to sue a beneficiary for, *inter alia*, declarator that he and his co-trustees (who had resigned and died respectively) were entitled to be discharged.[55]

40 Blank Bonds and Trusts Act 1696, c. 25; *Duggan* v. *Wight* (1797) Mor. 12761; 3 Paton 610; *Mackay* v. *Ambrose* (1829) 7 S. 699; *Lyon* v. *Reid* (1830) 8 S. 789; *Chalmers* v. *C.* (1845) 7 D. 865; *Dunn* v. *Pratt* (1898) 25 R. 461.

41 *Mackay*, *supra*; *Taylor* v. *Crawford* (1833) 12 S. 39; *Macfarlane* v. *Fisher* (1837) 15 S. 978.

42 *Knox* v. *Martin* (1850) 12 D. 719; *Seth* v. *Hain* (1855) 17 D. 1117; *Walker* v. *Buchanan, Kennedy & Co.* (1857) 20 D. 259; *Thomson* v. *Lindsay* (1873) 1 R. 65.

43 *Spruel* v. *Crawford* (1741) Mor. 16201; *Marshall* v. *Lyell* (1859) 21 D. 521.

44 *Gardiner* v. *Cowie* (1897) 4 S.L.T. 256; *Govan New Bowling Green Club* v. *Geddes* (1898) 25 R. 485.

45 *Wink* v. *Speirs* (1867) 6 M. 77, 82; *City of Glasgow Bank* v. *Nicolson's Tr.* (1882) 9 R. 689; *Anderson* v. *Yorston* (1906) 14 S.L.T. 54.

46 *Murdoch* v. *Wylie* (1832) 10 S. 445; *Hastie* v. *Steel* (1886) 13 R. 843.

47 *Mackay* v. *Ambrose* (1829) 7 S. 699; *Horne* v. *Morrison* (1877) 4 R. 937; *Pant Mawr Quarry Co.* v. *Fleming* (1883) 10 R. 457; *Dunn* v. *Pratt* (1898) 25 R. 461; *Anderson* v. *Yorston* (1906) 14 S.L.T. 54; *McConnachie* v. *Geddes*, 1918 S.C. 391; *Galloway* v. *G.*, 1929 S.C. 160.

48 *Forrester* v. *Robson's Trs.* (1875) 2 R. 755; *Laird* v. *Rutherford* (1884) 12 R. 294.

49 *Chalmers* v. *C.* (1845) 7 D. 865; *Walker* v. *Buchanan, Kennedy & Co.* (1857) 20 D. 259; *Marshall* v. *Lyell* (1859) 21 D. 521; *Tennant* v. *T's Trs.* (1868) 6 M. 876.

50 *Fortune* v. *Luke* (1831) 10 S. 115; *Murray* v. *Wright* (1870) 8 M. 722; *Grant's Trs.* v. *Morison* (1875) 2 R. 377; *Grant* v. *Mackenzie* (1899) 1 F. 889.

51 *Anderson* v. *A's Trs.* (1898) 6 S.L.T. 204, approved in *Galloway* v. *G.*, 1929 S.C. 160; but contrast *Newton v. N.*, 1923 S.C. 15.

52 *Grant* v. *Mackenzie* (1899) 1 F. 889; *Livingstone* v. *Allans* (1900) 3 F. 233.

53 *St. Giles Church Vestry* v. *St. Silas Church Trustees*, 1945 S.C. 110.

54 *Rosyth Canadian Fund Trs.*, 1924 S.C. 352.

55 *Dickson's Tr.* v. *Dickson*, 1959 S.L.T.(Notes) 55.

Declarator of rights in succession

Declarator is commonly invoked to determine the nature and extent of the pursuer's rights by way of succession in and to some estate, if those be denied. Thus declarator has been brought that certain deeds were mere instructions to an agent and not testamentary,[56] that a will had been validly executed,[57] that a settlement was the deceased's only valid testamentary writing,[58] that a person had died intestate,[59] that the fee of the residue of an estate had fallen into intestacy,[60] that in certain circumstances the residue would be divided among the pursuers,[61] that the exercise of a power of appointment was null,[62] that a beneficiary was entitled to decline an alimentary liferent bequeathed to him,[63] that parties had validly renounced marriage contract provisions,[64] and that an alimentary provision of a stated sum had been made in the pursuers' favour.[65]

Declarator of right to inherit

It is competent to bring a declarator that one is legatee under a valid testamentary bequest, even after a multiplepoinding, in which some of the claimants were cited but did not appear, had resulted in other persons being preferred as next-of-kin, and that without first reducing the decree of preference in the multiplepoinding, when the claim was essentially to a bequest which was a burden on the succession of the next-of-kin.[66]

Declarators as to wills

It is doubtless competent to bring declarator that a document is truly a will of a particular deceased, and an action has been brought for declarator of the nullity of a settlement found torn in two parts.[67]

Declarator that will holograph

A will which bears *in gremio* to be holograph of the granter thereof was, though unattested, formerly presumed to be truly holograph until the contrary was proved,[68] but otherwise a person founding on the deed as being holograph had to prove it to be in fact holograph, by the evidence of witnesses or *comparatione litterarum.*[69] It was later held, however,

56 *Maclean* v. *Maclean's Trs.* (1861) 23 D. 1099.
57 *Gorrie's Tr.* v. *Stiven's Executrix,* 1952 S.C. 1.
58 *Fisher* v. *Fisher,* 1952 S.C. 347.
59 *Ferguson* v. *Russell's Trs.* 1919 S.C. 80.
60 *Ness* v. *Mills's Trs.,* 1923 S.C. 344; *Swain* v. *Benzie's Trs.,* 1960 S.C. 357.
61 *Macnaughton* v. *Macnaughton's Trs.,* 1961 S.C. 312.
62 *Cunninghame* v. *Cunninghame's Trs.,* 1961 S.C. 32.
63 *Ford* v. *Ford's Trs.,* 1961 S.C. 122.
64 *Douglas-Hamilton* v. *Hamilton's Trs.,* 1961 S.C. 205.
65 *Bailey* v. *McLetchie's Trs.,* 1935 S.C. 95.
66 *Dundee Mags.* v. *Lindsay* (1856) 19 D. 168.
67 *Dow* v. *Dow* (1848) 10 D. 1465.
68 Ersk. III, 2, 22; Dickson, *Evidence,* § 759.
69 *Anderson* v. *Gill* (1858) 20 D.(H.L.) 7; *Cranston* (1890) 17 R. 410; *Frederick* v. *Craig,* 1932 S.L.T. 315.

that such a statement *in gremio* was of no evidential value unless the subscription was admitted or proved to be genuine.[70]

The Commissary Court practice had long been, particularly in unopposed applications, to grant confirmation on the basis of a will purporting to be holograph, as if it were fully probative,[71] and, to settle doubts raised by *Harper* v. *Green*,[70] the Conveyancing Amendment Act 1938, s. 11, provided that any writing of a testamentary character on which confirmation of executors-nominate had, prior to that Act, been granted should be deemed probative. After *Harper* v. *Green*,[70] however, a declarator that an apparently holograph will was truly holograph became more necessary.

The Succession (Sc.) Act 1964, s. 21, enacted that confirmation of an executor to property disposed of in a holograph testamentary disposition should not be granted unless the court were satisfied by evidence consisting at least of an affidavit by each of two persons that the writing and signature of the testamentary disposition were in the writing of the testator. Accordingly in all cases of an unattested holograph will it is necessary to bring a declarator that the will is holograph and satisfy the court at least by the kind and quantity of evidence required by the Act. If the action should be defended further and better evidence would be desirable and probably necessary.

Considering holograph wills as links in title to heritage the Wills Act 1963, s. 5,[72] provided that any testamentary instrument should be treated as probative for the conveyance of heritage in Scotland if confirmation of executors to property disposed of in the instrument had been certified or recorded in Scotland. This was replaced by the Succession (Sc.) Act 1964, s. 32,[73] which provided that any testamentary disposition shall be treated as probative if confirmation of an executor to property disposed of in the disposition had been granted in Scotland, or probate issued elsewhere in respect of property disposed of in the disposition has been certified or resealed in Scotland.

In every case accordingly where a holograph will is not attested a declarator that it is holograph is necessary before confirmation can be granted thereon. If granted, confirmation can issue, and the will is then a probative deed for use as a link in title.

Other cases of declarator

Actions cognitionis causa

An action of constitution *cognitionis causa* is declaratory in nature, because it does not conclude for payment or for anything to be done but only determines what debt was due by a defunct, that it may affect his estate.[74]

70 *Harper* v. *Green*, 1938 S.C. 198.
71 *Cranston, supra.*
72 Effective January 1, 1964.
73 Effective September 10, 1964.
74 Stair, IV, 19.

An action of constitution of a personal debt can be insisted in against the heir of the deceased without calling his executors.[75]

Such a claim may be necessary as a basis for a claim to be confirmed as executor-creditor, and in such an action it is enough to call the deceased's next-of-kin, without calling his trustees.[76]

Declarator in sequestration

Declarator has been sought that a person was entitled to a ranking for a lump sum payment in sequestration in priority to other creditors.[77]

Declarator of competency of diligence

It has been held that a party, in doubt as to the wisdom of doing diligence on a defective bill, might obtain declarator of the competency of his proposed diligence and was not obliged to risk having the diligence suspended or being held liable in damages for executing it.[78]

Declarator in default of other remedy

Declarator has sometimes been resorted to in default of any other apparent form of remedy, such as that an air raid distress fund had failed to administer the fund in terms of the resolution under which it was established, and should be ordained to adjust a scheme for administering their fund accordingly.[79] But declarator is incompetent if merely used as a means of appeal, or rectification of failure to use statutory procedure, where there exists a statutory remedy of appeal. Thus where appeal against the inclusion of the pursuer's name in the local valuation roll had not been made, a declarator of not being a tenant and of non-liability to be rated was held incompetent.[80] Accordingly, where some form of appeal is competent it must be utilised and declarator cannot be invoked to the same effect. Similarly a declarator that sequestration proceedings were void was dismissed since the petitioners could have resorted to an action of reduction or to a petition under the Bankruptcy (Sc.) Act 1913.[81]

Again a declarator has been dismissed as premature where a statutory appeal against the same actings, alleged to be under a misinterpretation of a statute, had been competently lodged, it being indicated that declarator might be proper if the appeal were wrongly dismissed.[82]

Declarator in exercise of nobile officium

The Court of Session may be petitioned, in the exercise of its *nobile officium*, to grant a declarator, but has declined to do so where an ordinary legal remedy was competent.[83]

75 *British Linen Co.* v. *Lord Reay* (1850) 12 D. 949.
76 *Smith's Trs.* v. *Grant* (1862) 24 D. 1142.
77 *Thornton's Extrx.* v. *Angus & Son's Tr.*, 1934 S.C. 279.
78 *Barbour* v. *Grierson* (1827) 5 S. 603.
79 *Fraser* v. *McNeill*, 1948 S.C. 517.
80 *Dante* v. *Assessor for Ayr*, 1922 S.C. 109.
81 *Central Motor Engineering Co.* v. *Gibbs*, 1917 S.C. 490.
82 *Caledonian Ry.* v. *Glasgow Corpn.* (1905) 7 F. 1021.
83 *Central Motor Engineering Co.* v. *Gibbs*, 1917 S.C. 490.

Miscellaneous cases

Declarator has also been invoked in a large number of quite miscellaneous cases, such as that an arbiter was disqualified from acting in a submission,[84] that an entail was invalid,[85] that it was illegal to levy tolls on a road,[86] that defenders were bound by an arbiter's award,[87] that a teacher was entitled to responsibility payment,[88] that the defenders had discriminated unduly against a class of consumers, including the pursuers,[89] that payments by a kirk session were illegal and *ultra vires*,[90] that the Secretary of State was bound to appoint a woman doctor to a post,[91] and that a censure and fine on a club by the Scottish Football Association was contrary to natural justice and illegal.[92]

Declarator by Special Case

The procedure by special case presented for the opinion, or opinion and judgment, of the Court of Session,[93] one whereby the interpretation of wills, trust deeds and similar instruments is frequently determined and the rights of various parties decided, is declaratory in character, in that it finds and declares what the court believes to be the true intention and interpretation of the deed under construction in the circumstances which have happened, but does not order any payment or other action.

Declarator in Public Law

Declarator is a valuable remedy in respect of official acts and omissions, particularly as persons and bodies exercising public functions will commonly act in accordance with what is declared to be the law without further coercion. There are few specialities in or obstacles to the use of declarator in respect of official actings, and declarator has been frequently used. Some examples include: farmers and magistrates in a locality obtaining declarator that turnpike trustees were required to use toll receipts for repairing the roads[94]; tenants and merchants seeking reduction of a decree of the justices ordering a road to be shut up and of declarator that it was a public parish road [95]; commissioners seeking interdict of a resolution alleged to be in breach of a police statute and to have it declared that the defenders were bound to levy a rate for the repair of

84 *Drew* v. *Drew* (1851) 14 D. 212.
85 *Glassford* v. *Borthwick* (1862) 24 D. 1136.
86 *Duke of Athole* v. *Robertson* (1869) 8 M. 304.
87 *Bellshill and Mossend Co-operative Socy. Ltd.* v. *Dalziel Co-operative Socy. Ltd.*, 1960 S.C. (H.L.) 64.
88 *Anderson* v. *Roxburgh C.C.*, 1960 S.C. 287.
89 *B.O.C.* v. *S.S.E.B.*, 1959 S.C. (H.L.) 17.
90 *Moffat* v. *Canonbie Kirk Session*, 1936 S.C. 209.
91 *Adams* v. *Secretary of State for Scotland*, 1958 S.C. 279.
92 *St. Johnstone F.C.* v. *S.F.A.*, 1965 S.L.T. 171.
93 R.C. 265.
94 *Guild* v. *Scott*, Dec. 21, 1809, F.C.
95 *Tait* v. *E. Lauderdale* (1827) 5 S. 330.

streets [96]; a licensee obtaining declarator that the licensing jurisdiction of the county justices of the peace, by whom he had been licensed, had not been transferred to the burgh magistrates by statute [97]; an ice-cream seller obtaining declarator that the conditions which magistrates proposed to attach to the grant of a statutory licence for selling ice-cream were *ultra vires* [98]; ratepayers obtaining declarator that the local authority had no right to levy rates from them to pay for the expenses of the unsuccessful promotion of a provisional order seeking extension of the burgh's boundaries [99]; a police authority obtaining declarator that a public inquiry into a proposed police reorganisation was irregular, *ultra vires* and contrary to natural justice [1]; a police authority seeking declarator that the Secretary of State, in appointing a chief constable was bound to have regard only to certain qualifications [1a]; a local authority seeking declarator that it had power to make an order regulating traffic on a specified road [1b]; a local authority seeking declarator that a reference by another local authority to the Secretary of State was inept and that the dispute was one to be determined by the court [2]; a local authority seeking declarator that a water board's area of supply excluded the burgh as extended [3]; the Crown seeking declarator that it had right to buried treasure[4]; a local authority seeking declarator that a housing association's rents scheme was *ultra vires* and invalid [5]; persons seeking declarator that the Secretary of State was bound to try to secure that a woman was appointed to a particular post, and that such an appointment was practicable [6]; a local authority seeking declarator that certain determinations of the former Central Land Board were *ultra vires* [7]; that builders were entitled to sell without the defenders' consent certain houses subsidised by the defenders [8]; that a local authority was not entitled to require bus operators to obtain a licence from them.[9]

Jurisdiction to grant declarator against Crown

The court has jurisdiction to grant a declarator against the Crown.[10]

By the Crown Proceedings Act 1947, s. 21 (1), as applied to Scotland by section 43 (*a*), where any such relief is sought as might between subjects

[96] *Taylor* v. *Kilmarnock Police Commrs.* (1858) 20 D. 501.
[97] *Tennent* v. *Partick Mags.* (1894) 21 R. 735.
[98] *Rossi* v. *Edinburgh Mags.* (1904) 7 F. (H.L.) 85.
[99] *Stirling C.C.* v. *Falkirk Burgh*, 1912 S.C. 1281.
[1] *Ayr Mags.* v. *Lord Advocate*, 1950 S.C. 102.
[1a] *Kilmarnock Mags.* v. *Secretary of State for Scotland*, 1961 S.C. 350.
[1b] *Fife C.C.* v. *Lord Advocate*, 1950 S.C. 314.
[2] *Lanarkshire C.C.* v. *East Kilbride Town Council*, 1967 S.C. 235.
[3] *Grangemouth* v. *Stirlingshire Water Board*, 1963 S.C. (H.L.) 49.
[4] *Lord Advocate* v. *Aberdeen University*, 1963 S.C. 533.
[5] *Midlothian C.C.* v. *S.S.H.A.*, 1959 S.C. 8.
[6] *Adams* v. *Secretary of State for Scotland*, 1958 S.C. 279 (declarator refused but order to similar effect made).
[7] *Glasgow Corpn.* v. *Central Land Board*, 1956 S.C. (H.L.) 1.
[8] *Western Heritable Investment Co.* v. *Glasgow Corpn.* 1956 S.C. (H.L.) 64.
[9] *S.M.T. Co.* v. *Lanarkshire C.C.*, 1929 S.C. (H.L.) 110.
[10] Crown Proceedings Act 1947, s. 21 (1).

be granted by way of interdict or specific implement the court shall not grant interdict nor make an order for specific implement but may in lieu make an order declaratory of the right of parties. This has been held not to justify the grant of declarator *ad interim*, where that would have required accepting the pursuer's averments *pro veritate*, that such an order would in the circumstances have been hypothetical, and that the 1947 Act did not entitle the court to make a hypothetical declaratory order.[11] In England it has been held that the court has no jurisdiction under section 21 to make interim declarations.[12]

Other limitations on jurisdiction in public law

Particularly important in public law cases is the principle that no declarator may be granted where an alternative remedy exists which, in the view of the court, should be utilised before resort is made to the court, above all where it has been provided that disputes should be dealt with by special tribunal or particular machinery.[13] In some cases, however, particularly where the alternative statutory proceedings would be criminal or penal the court has accepted that it is better to declare in advance what the pursuer may or may not do, than condemn him to take the chance of being penalised if he does what is held to be impermissible.[14] Declarator will the more readily be granted if the matter in dispute is not such as can conveniently be raised or settled by the prescribed statutory procedure.[15]

No declarator where no enforceable right

The court will also decline to grant declarator if the right sought is not one judicially enforceable, but *e.g.* one within the discretion of a minister of the Crown.[16]

[11] *Ayr Town Council* v. *Secy. of State for Scotland*, 1965 S.C. 394; *Robertson* v. *Lord Advocate* (1950) 1965 S.C. 400.

[12] *Underhill* v. *Minister of Food* [1950] 1 All E.R. 591; *International G.E.C. of N.Y. Ltd.* v. *Commrs. of Customs and Excise* [1962] Ch. 784.

[13] *Balfour* v. *Malcolm* (1842) 1 Bell's App. 153; *Caledonian Ry.* v. *Glasgow Corpn.* (1905) 7 F. 1020; *Dante* v. *Ayr Assessor*, 1922 S.C. 107.

[14] *Macdonell* v. *Caledonian Canal Commrs.* (1830) 8 S. 881; *Edinburgh & Glasgow Ry.* v. *Meek* (1849) 12 D. 153; *Hogg* v. *Auchtermuchty Parochial Board* (1880) 7 R. 986; *Glasgow District Ry.* v. *Glasgow Mags.* (1884) 11 R. 1110; *West Highland Ry.* v. *Inverness C.C.* (1904) 6 F. 1052.

[15] *Hope* v. *Edinburgh Mags.* (1897) 5 S.L.T. 195; *Fraser* v. *McNeill*, 1948 S.C. 517.

[16] *Mackie* v. *Lord Advocate* (1898) 25 R. 769; *Smith* v. *Lord Advocate* (1897) 25 R. 112; *Smith* v. *Lord Advocate*, 1932 S.L.T. 374; *Griffin* v. *Lord Advocate*, 1950 S.C. 448. *Cf. Borthwick Parochial Board* v. *Temple Parochial Board* (1891) 18 R. 1190.

CHAPTER 9

REDUCTION

AN action of reduction is in a way the converse of a declarator. " Rights are declared two ways; *affirmativè*, declaring the right itself to be good, and valid, and sufficient to exclude any other right; or *negativè*, by reducing and annulling any pretended right, whereupon action and exception might be founded, in prejudice of the pursuer's right. Both these ways may, and ofttimes use to be joined in the same summons, reducing opposite rights, and declaring the pursuer's own right, which require divers grounds. . . ." [1] It is an action to annul any deed, decree or other writing executed, or any illegal act done, to the prejudice of the pursuer's right.[2]

Reduction and reduction-improbation

Actions of reduction were formerly distinguished into actions of simple reduction and actions of reduction-improbation, the latter being appropriate where forgery was alleged or where the document was an execution by an officer of law, *e.g.* of a diligence.[3] In modern practice it seems that only simple reduction survives and applies in all cases.

Object and forms of reduction

The object of reduction is to have judicially annulled and set aside some deed, decree or other writing, prejudicial to the pursuer's rights and against which he can adduce adequate grounds for its reduction.

Reduction takes two main forms, reduction of deeds or actings and reduction of decrees of court. The former falls into two divisions, reduction of deeds or actings as between private individuals, and reduction of resolutions, decisions, and awards of persons and bodies exercising administrative or quasi-judicial functions. The second of these is, accordingly, in substance the use of reduction as a means of having the court review administrative or quasi-judicial decisions. The latter is, in substance, a form of appeal or challenge of the decision of the court, and is sometimes available where an appeal in ordinary mode is not competent.

REDUCTION OF DEEDS OR WRITINGS

" I do not think it admits of doubt that this Court [the Court of Session] is competent to entertain actions for reduction of any documents or

1 Stair IV, 20, 2.
2 Stair, *supra*; Ersk. IV, 1, 18.
3 Ersk. IV, 1, 18; *McVitie* v. *Barbour* (1838) 16 S. 1185; *Balfour* v. *Robertson* (1839) 1 D. 458; *Reid* v. *Clark*, 1914, 2 S.L.T. 68. See also Stair IV, 20, 3–13 and 22; *McLellan* v. *Graham* (1841) 16 F.C. 1209; *McKinney* v. *His Creditors* (1864) 2 M. 889.

proceedings unless reduction is excluded by the nature of the documents or proceedings themselves, or by statutory enactment." [4]

Reduction is applicable only to deeds and written documents of any kind, which constitute or evidence some legal right. Actings, oral transactions, and conduct not recorded in writing cannot be reduced, though minutes or other records of actings can be reduced.

Necessity for reduction

Reduction is generally necessary of any deed which *ex facie* bars, excludes or discharges a right now claimed by the pursuer, as a preliminary to his enforcing that right. Thus an action on a debenture was held barred until a discharge, endorsed thereon, was reduced.[5] In *Sadler* v. *Webster* [6] a trade incorporation passed an illegal resolution restricting the admission of future members, but subsequently departed from this attitude. In an action of reduction of the minute of the illegal resolution the court held that " the minutes ought now to be reduced, in order that there may be no dubiety regarding your Lordships' opinion as to their essential nullity," even though the illegal resolution had been voluntarily departed from.

In *McGowan* v. *City of Glasgow Friendly Society*,[7] where a member challenged the election of a person as a delegate to the board of management of the society, by way of declarator of his disqualification and of interdict against his acting, it was observed that reduction of the minute appointing the person to be a delegate, desiderated by the sheriff, was not necessary, apparently on the ground that the minute was a mere record of the election not necessary under the Society's rules, and that the disqualification might have arisen after the election. The real remedy was that concluded for in the second place, interdict.

Again, in *Mason's Trs.* v. *Poole & Robinson* [8] one claimant on a fund founded on a decree in absence against a company and another claimant was held entitled to challenge the first claim as having been founded on an *ultra vires* agreement,without the necessity of raising an action of reduction of it.

Reduction was formerly frequently necessary as a preliminary action or conclusion, where an *ex facie* valid and regular deed prevented the pursuer asserting rights by declarator or petitory claim,[9] but it is not always necessary to reduce a deed before obtaining declarator of a contrary or inconsistent right.[10]

The court does not favour the bringing of a reduction if the object

4 *Kerr* v. *Hood*, 1907 S.C. 895, 902, *per* Lord Ardwall.

5 *Niven* v. *Ayr Mags.* (1899) 1 F. 400; *cf. McLean* v. *Hassard* (1902) 10 S.L.T. 107; *McKinlay* v. *Life and Health Assce. Assocn.* (1905) 13 S.L.T. 102.

6 (1893) 21 R. 107.

7 1913 S.C. 991.

8 (1903) 5 F. 789.

9 *Birrell* v. *Dundee Gaol Commrs.* (1856) 29 Sc.Jur. 46; *Rhind* v. *Commercial Bank* (1857) 19 D. 519; (1860) 22 D.(H.L.) 2; *McIntyre* v. *McRaild* (1867) 5 M. 526.

10 *McGowan* v. *City of Glasgow Friendly Socy.*, 1913 S.C. 991; *Dundee General Hospitals* v. *Bell's Trs.*, 1952 S.C.(H.L.) 78, 88.

can be obtained by other means, possibly even unless the main object of the proceedings is the amendment of the deed objected to and the object cannot be attained in any other way.[11]

Challenge by exception, without reduction

A matter of considerable practical importance is whether and in what circumstances one may challenge the validity of a writing or contract, as a defence to an action brought thereon, rather than have to challenge its validity by reduction. " It is quite true that ' exception ' in our older law meant a ' defence,' a defence which did not object to the libel, but assumed the competency and relevancy of the action, and met the substance and merits of the action. But the word ' exception ' has gradually received a larger and more extensive meaning in our law; and when it is said that you may plead an objection *ope exceptionis*, it means that you may do so otherwise than by raising an action." [12] In older cases challenge by reduction or reduction-improbation was frequently demanded.[13] In many cases challenge by exception has been allowed,[14] and an Act of Sederunt of March 20, 1907, provided that where in any action a deed or writing was founded on by either party all objections thereto might be stated and maintained by way of exception without the necessity of bringing a reduction thereof, unless the court considered that the matter would be more conveniently tried in a separate action of reduction. It is therefore now a matter of circumstances and judicial discretion whether to require reduction, or to allow the point to be raised in defence.

In *Oswald* v. *Fairs* [15] it was held that a defence founded on essential error in relation to the contract, induced by fraud, should not have been sustained, in respect that a defence involving reduction of a contract cannot be pleaded *ope exceptionis* unless the pursuer has been given fair notice before the proof of the defence he has to meet.

On the other hand reduction has frequently been insisted on,[16] and may again be insisted on if it does not appear convenient to try both claim and defence together.

Alienations of property by a party insolvent or notour bankrupt, which are voidable at common law or under statute, have long been deemed challengeable by way of exception both in the Court of Session and the sheriff court.[17]

11 *Nivison* v. *Howat* (1883) 11 R. 182; *Smith* v. *Smith's Trs.* (1905) 12 S.L.T. 782; *Kinghorn* v. *Glenyards Fireclay Co.* (1907) 14 S.L.T. 683.

12 *Dickson* v. *Murray* (1866) 4 M. 797, 799, *per* L.J.C. Inglis; see also *Mackenzie* v. *Calder* (1868) 6 M. 833, 834.

13 *e.g. Telfer* v. *Barron* (1844) 7 D. 170; *Williamson* v. *Kennedy* (1857) 19 D. 443.

14 *e.g. Thomson's Trs.* v. *Muir* (1867) 6 M. 145; *Mackenzie* v. *Calder* (1868) 6 M. 833; *Brown's Trs.* v. *Fraser* (1870) 8 M. 820; *Dickson* v. *Carter* (1878) 5 R. 1023.

15 1911 S.C. 257.

16 *Niven* v. *Ayr Mags.* (1899) 1 F. 400; *MacLean* v. *Hassard* (1902) 10 S.L.T. 107; *McKinlay* v. *Life and Health Assce. Assocn.* (1905) 13 S.L.T. 102; See also *Dickson* v. *Carter* (1878) 5 R. 1023; *National Bank* v. *Adamson*, 1932 S.L.T. 492.

17 *Dickson* v. *Murray* (1866) 4 M. 797; *Moroney* v. *Muir* (1869) 6 M. 7; *Mackenzie* v. *Calder* (1868) 6 M. 833; *Thomas* v. *Waddell* (1869) 7 M. 558; *Brown's Trs.* v. *Fraser* (1870) 8 M. 820.

The Sheriff Courts (Scotland) Act 1907 [18] has provided that " when a deed or writing is founded on by any party in a cause, all objections thereto may be stated and maintained by way of exception, without the necessity of bringing a reduction thereof " but this has been held not to apply unless the party objecting could reduce the deed without need for additional declaratory conclusions,[19] nor to apply to a decree *in foro*,[20] nor to apply where the deed challenged was the basis of a party's alleged right of action or defence.[21]

Jurisdiction

Actions of reduction are competent only in the Court of Session,[22] save in so far as the jurisdiction is conferred expressly on another court. " This Court is competent to entertain actions for reduction of any documents or proceedings unless reduction is excluded by the nature of the documents or proceedings themselves, or by statutory enactment." [23]

The sheriff court has no jurisdiction in actions of reduction. The Sheriff Courts (Scotland) Act 1907, s. 5 confers jurisdiction on the sheriff court in, *inter alia*, " actions relating to questions of heritable right or title (except . . . actions of reduction)." A sheriff court action craving for reduction, delivery and payment has, however, been sustained *quoad* the remaining craves where the crave for reduction could be read as containing the grounds of action on which the petitory craves rested.[24] The sheriff court also has jurisdiction to set aside a deed by exception.[25]

It is not sufficient to give the Court of Session jurisdiction that the testator, whose will is sought to be reduced, was a domiciled Scotsman,[26] nor that the defender has a claim on a trust, part of which is heritage in Scotland and held by trustees, of whom he is not one.[27]

The jurisdiction of the Court of Session to review and, if thought right, to reduce decisions of officials acting quasi-judicially may be excluded by statute but only by words which are clear and unambiguous.[28] It is especially difficult to hold that Parliament has delegated to anyone to declare the exclusion of the jurisdiction of the Supreme Court.[28]

Exclusion or limitation of reduction

Particularly in cases of administrative and quasi-judicial functions, and of decisions of certain courts, challenge of the actings in question

18 Sch. I, r. 50.
19 *D. Argyll* v. *Muir*, 1910 S.C. 96.
20 *Leggatt Bros.* v. *Gray*, 1912 S.C. 230.
21 *Donald* v. *Donald*, 1913 S.C. 274.
22 *Dickson* v. *Murray* (1866) 4 M. 797.
23 *Kerr* v. *Hood*, 1907 S.C. 895, 902, *per* Lord Ardwall.
24 *Moroney* v. *Muir* (1869) 6 M. 7.
25 See *Dickson* v. *Murray* (1866) 4 M. 797; *Mackenzie* v. *Calder* (1868) 6 M. 833; *Brown's Trs.* v. *Fraser* (1870) 8 M. 820; *Wilson* v. *Glasgow Tramways Co.* (1878) 5 R. 981; *Nivison* v. *Howat* (1883) 11 R. 182; *Scott* v. *Cook* (1886) 24 S.L.R. 34; *D. Argyll* v. *Muir*, 1910 S.C. 96; *Donald* v. *Donald*, 1913 S.C. 274.
26 *Morrison* v. *Vallance's Trs.* (1906) 14 S.L.T. 372.
27 *Gemmell* v. *Emery* (1905) 13 S.L.T. 490.
28 *Kerr* v. *Hood*, 1907 S.C. 895.

may be excluded on specified grounds, or completely, or otherwise limited. But exclusion or limitation must be effected by clear and unambiguous words in a statute, or must appear by clear implication.[29]

Furthermore cases not within the categories excluded from review by reduction may competently be challenged thereby [29]; excluded categories are not to be extended by analogy, nor otherwise given any wider application than is reasonably necessary.

Pursuer's title and interest to reduce

The pursuer in a reduction must have both title and interest to sue the reduction. Title and interest are connected but distinct. To have title the pursuer must be the person, or among the persons, having a claim against the defender. To have interest he must show that he will be prejudiced in status, patrimony or otherwise if his claim is rejected. It has been observed [30] that there can be no clearer case of title and interest than that of a proprietor of heritage who seeks to challenge a document which purports to place a real burden on his heritable property.

Thus in *Bootland* v. *McFarlane* [31] persons who might have objected to the grant of a public-house licence were held entitled to pursue a reduction of an application for a licence. In many cases next of kin of a deceased have been held to have title to pursue a reduction of a will prejudicial to their claims,[32] and in general a person having right under a deed, or a *ius quaesitum* under it, have title to sue a reduction of other deeds granted in prejudice thereof.[33] A person may have title to sue notwithstanding that he is a partner in a firm which also has title to sue.[34]

A pursuer's title to sue is not excluded by deeds or titles which it is the object of his action to reduce, least of all where he alleges that they were fraudulently concocted to exclude his rights.[35] Thus a person may challenge by reduction a codicil which purports to have excluded him from interest in an estate, if he can make relevant averments to justify his action.

In *Crichton* v. *Crichton's Trs.*[36] the heirs in heritage and in moveables respectively of a deceased, after doubts as to the latter's testamentary capacity had been raised, granted deeds ratifying her settlement and assigning to the mother of the residuary legatee (possibly as tutor for her) their right to reduce the settlement. They later sought to reduce their ratification and assignation, and themselves sought to reduce the settlement. The competency of assigning the right to reduce was not discussed, but it must be questioned whether it is competent to assign a right to reduce, particularly to a person who appears to have had no title to any part of

29 *Kerr* v. *Hood*, 1907 S.C. 895.
30 *Dowell's Ltd.* v. *Heriot's Trust*, 1941 S.C. 13, 24.
31 (1900) 2 F. 1014. Contrast *McDonald* v. *Chambers*, 1956 S.C. 542.
32 *e.g. Gilchrist* v. *Morrison* (1891) 18 R. 599.
33 *McGowan* v. *Robb* (1862) 1 M. 141.
34 *Melville* v. *Cummings*, 1912 S.C. 1185.
35 *Clark* v. *Loudon* (1856) 18 D. 499.
36 (1874) 1 R. 688.

the estate, either under the will or on intestacy. It is submitted that a right to reduce is personal to a person having title and interest, and not an assignable right.

Lack of interest to pursue reduction was successfully pleaded in *Strathmore* v. *Strathmore's Trs.*[37] where an heir excluded by an entail, sought to challenge deeds conflicting with the entail; in *Kerr* v. *Vaughan*,[38] where an heir sought to challenge a deed and, if it were avoided, the estate would have fallen to the next of kin; in *Swanson* v. *Manson*,[39] where one of the next of kin sought to reduce a will, with the effect of setting up a previous will which excluded the next of kin; in *Wright* v. *Buchanan*[40] where an unsuccessful bidder at an auction sale failed to aver that the purchaser was other than a *bona fide* bidder; and in *Agnew* v. *Laughlan*[41] where the husband of a woman now deceased sought to reduce an order now spent and inoperative for her admission to a mental hospital, on the ground that this implied some slur on him.

Want of pecuniary interest will not be too closely examined, if there is a good title to sue and a possible interest exists.[42]

Reduction and patrimonial rights

The court will not set aside by reduction a resolution or decision of a voluntary body except in so far as it affects patrimonial rights. Among such cases are resolutions in conflict with the constitution of a religious body,[43] suspending a member of a club from playing football,[44] and expelling a member from a stud-book society.[45]

The possession of a particular status, meaning the capacity to perform certain functions or hold certain offices, is a thing which the law recognises as a patrimonial interest. Instances are the status of advocate or enrolled solicitor or registered medical practitioner.[46]

Defender's interest

An action for the reduction of an instrument must be brought against the party having an interest in that instrument.[47] Thus a sheriff has been held to have no personal interest in an order which he has made in the proper exercise of his jurisdiction, certainly so long as no damages be claimed for misuse of that jurisdiction, and an action against him for reduction only is incompetent.[47] But it was observed[47] that the sheriff

37 (1829) 8 S. 530, affd. (1831) 5 W. & S. 170.
38 (1829) 8 S. 694, affd. (1831) 5 W. & S. 718.
39 1907 S.C. 426.
40 1917 S.C. 73.
41 1948 S.C. 656.
42 *Swanson* v. *Manson*, 1907 S.C. 426, 429, *per* Lord Ardwall, instancing *Duncan* v. *Duncan* (1892) 20 R. 200.
43 *Skerret* v. *Oliver* (1896) 23 R. 468.
44 *Murdison* v. *Scottish Football Union* (1896) 23 R. 449.
45 *Anderson* v. *Manson*, 1909 S.C. 838.
46 *Forbes* v. *Eden* (1865) 4 M. 143; 5 M.(H.L.) 47; see also *Skerret, supra*, 491.
47 *Mackintosh* v. *Arkley* (1868) 6 M.(H.L.) 141, 146.

would have had an interest if his conduct in pronouncing it had been challenged and it had been sought to make him liable in damages for having so acted judicially.

Competency of bare reduction

An action of reduction without any executory or other conclusions is competent,[48] as if the objectionable deed is out of the way it may be obvious or admitted what must then happen. Thus if a will is reduced the estate must be distributed on the basis of intestacy or of any previous will still standing. Again it is competent to reduce a decree improperly obtained or technically invalid, though there be no other conclusions, if only to clear the records of anything against the pursuer's reputation.[49] And a reduction is in such circumstances probably essential as a preliminary to recovery of any money paid, and to claiming damages for loss following from a decree improperly obtained.[50]

But particularly in the case of a bare reduction with no other conclusions, it is essential that the pursuer show that he has an adequate interest to insist in his action. It will not suffice that it is alleged to be necessary to reduce deeds as preliminary to another action, particularly where the documents are spent and no longer operative.[51] " None of the cases in which (with obvious soundness) reduction has been granted, without any further decree, have been thus resultless. They have led, directly and by their own force, to the establishment of patrimonial right or to immunity from patrimonial claim." [52]

This issue has been complicated by some cases in which a reductive conclusion has been treated as merely ancillary to one for damages, and where, accordingly, the reductive conclusion has been held not to stand if that for damages was abandoned or rejected.[53]

Partial reduction

In general a reduction must be complete and total, but in some cases the courts have allowed a partial reduction. " Partial reduction of a deed may perhaps be competent where it is proposed to reduce a part of a deed which is clearly severable from the rest but it is quite clear that it is beyond the power of a court to make a new bargain for the parties, and, if partial reduction would have that result, it would plainly be incompetent . . ." [54] Partial reduction has been refused where the transaction was one and in-

[48] *Ferguson* v. *Malcolm* (1850) 12 D. 732, 736; *Graham* v. *North British Bank* (1850) 12 D. 907; *Life and Health Assce. Assocn. Ltd.* v. *Yule* (1904) 6 F. 437; *Bruce* v. *British Motor Trading Corpn.*, 1924 S.C. 908, 921; *Agnew* v. *Laughlan*, 1948 S.C. 656.

[49] *Beattie* v. *McLellan* (1844) 6 D. 1088; *Ferguson* v. *Malcolm* (1850) 12 D. 732; *Rachkind* v. *Donald*, 1916 S.C. 751; *Bruce, supra.*

[50] *Bruce, supra*, 925–926.

[51] *Agnew* v. *Laughlan*, 1948 S.C. 656.

[52] *Skerret* v. *Oliver* (1896) 23 R. 468, 491, *per* L.P. Robertson.

[53] *e.g. McMillan* v. *Free Church* (1859) 22 D. 219; (1861) 23 D. 314.

[54] *Anderson* v. *Lambie*, 1954 S.C.(H.L.) 43, 60–61, *per* Lord Reid.

divisible [55] but allowed where it dealt with distinguishable and separable elements.[56] A person may reduce a deed so far as affecting his interest, without concluding for reduction *in toto*,[57] or reduce all offers made at a sale of heritage under articles of roup which were in excess of the upset price and made by persons disentitled from binding at the sale; it was not necessary that the sale be set aside *in toto*.[58]

In *Adams* v. *G.N.S. Ry.*[59] it was held competent and proper to reduce a decree-arbitral *quoad* the excess of the award over the sums claimed by the other party.

In *McLay* v. *McQueen* [60] doubts were expressed of the competency of reducing an ante-nuptial marriage-contract, *quoad excessum*, but no decision needed to be, or was, given on the point. In *Darney* v. *Calder District Committee* [61] glue manufacturers sought to reduce an order from the defenders sanctioning their operations so far as it contained a condition objectionable to them and, they contended, incompetently adjected thereto. The condition was held inseparable from the permission granted, and the court refused reduction.

In some circumstances partial reduction is essential and complete reduction could not be granted. Thus where a son who had a protected succession under his parents' ante-nuptial marriage contract sought to reduce his father's trust disposition and settlement, the court refused reduction on the ground that the later deed contained a number of provisions which were valid notwithstanding the marriage contract.[62] A partial reduction might have been appropriate.

Reduction of voidable and of void deeds

A deed which is merely voidable is *ex hypothesi* good until or unless successfully challenged, and reduction is always necessary in such a case. A deed which, on the other hand, is void is already a nullity and, in theory, need not be, and indeed cannot be, reduced. Nevertheless in the latter case it is frequently necessary to bring a reduction, as a means of having determined whether the deed was truly void or not, and of having judicially affirmed that it was void, despite assertions or appearances to the contrary.[63] In this last class of case, a declarator would serve the same purpose.

55 *White* v. *Forbes* (1890) 17 R. 895; *cf. Shiell* v. *Guthrie's Trs.* (1874) 1 R. 1083; *McLay* v. *McQueen* (1899) 1 F. 804; *Darney* v. *Calder District Cttee.* (1904) 7 F. 239; *McEwen's Trs.* v. *Church of Scotland Trs.*, 1940 S.L.T. 357.

56 *Glasgow Feuing Co.* v. *Watson's Trs.* (1887) 14 R. 610; *Bain* v. *Lady Seafield* (1887) 14 R. 939; *Balls* v. *Macdonald* 1909, 2 S.L.T. 310; *cf. Pender-Small* v. *Kinloch's Trs.*, 1917 S.C. 307.

57 *McConachy* v. *McIndoe* (1853) 16 D. 315; *Martin* v. *Scottish T. & G.W.U.*, 1952 S.C.(H.L.) 1.

58 *Faulds* v. *Corbet* (1859) 21 D. 587.

59 (1889) 16 R. 843; affd. (1890) 18 R.(H.L.) 1.

60 (1899) 1 F. 804, 810, *per* Lord Adam. See also *Carphin* v. *Clapperton* (1867) 5 M. 797; *Watson* v. *Grants Trs.* (1874) 1 R. 882.

61 (1904) 7 F. 239, distinguishing *Macbeth* v. *Ashley* (1874) 1 R.(H.L.) 14.

62 *Smith* v. *Smith's Trs.* (1905) 12 S.L.T. 782.

63 *Cf. Clark* v. *Clark's Trs.*, 1948 S.L.T. (Notes) 58.

Thus in *Drysdale* v. *Nairne* [64] D. brought a reduction of a decree of reduction of a settlement of lands in his favour, and of a disposition by him in favour of another. Having failed on the reduction of the decree, it was held that he had no title to pursue the reduction of the disposition, as he had no title to the lands and the disposition by him was a nullity, proceeding *a non domino*. In *Life and Health Assurance Association* v. *Yule* [65] it was provided in a proposal form for insurance that if there were a misstatement the policy should be void. Y. made a material misstatement in the proposal. The court granted reduction. In *Dowell's, Ltd.* v. *Heriot's Trust* [66] a reduction was brought of a memorandum of agreement for the commutation of casualties into an additional feu-duty on the ground that one party to the agreement had ceased to be proprietors of the subjects and that it was accordingly a nullity. This was held competent and necessary, the agreement being *ex facie* valid.

Reduction of bye-laws as ultra vires

The bye-laws made by any authority statutorily empowered to make bye-laws may be challenged by action of reduction on such grounds as that they are *ultra vires* of the authority,[67] repugnant to the general law of Scotland,[68] uncertain,[69] or unreasonable.[70]

Call for production

The first element in the conclusion of an action for reduction is the call on the defender to produce the deed or writing objected to. If a summons of reduction appears *ex facie* incompetent and irrelevant, the defender will not be appointed to satisfy production.[71] On the other hand an objection to competency and relevancy may be proper to be reserved, and not be one deemed valid against the call for production.[72] The defender may decline to produce the deed only if he objects to the pursuer's title to sue,[73] or founds on a decree of absolviter in a previous reduction as *res judicata*,[74] or asserts an exclusive title to the deed, or has another objection to production. He cannot be required to lodge the document if

64 (1835) 13 S. 348.
65 (1904) 6 F. 437.
66 1941 S.C. 13.
67 *Macbeth* v. *Ashley* (1874) 1 R.(H.L.) 14; *Wilson* v. *Rust* (1896) 23 R.(J.) 56; *Kerr* v. *Auld* (1890) 18 R.(J.) 12; *Auld* v. *Barr* (1897) 25 R.(J.) 13; *Scott* v. *Glasgow Corpn.* (1899) 1 F.(H.L.) 51; *Mackenzie* v. *Somerville* (1900) 3 F.(J.) 4; *Rossi* v. *Edinburgh Mags.* (1904) 7 F.(H.L.) 85; *McGregor* v. *Disselduff*, 1907 S.C.(J.) 21; *McCall* v. *Mitchell*, 1911 S.C.(J.) 1; *McKenna* v. *Sim*, 1916 S.C.(J.) 24; *McElfrish* v. *Barlow*, 1917 J.C. 32; *Blair* v. *Smith*, 1924 J.C. 24; *McAlister* v. *Forth Pilotage Authy.*, 1944 S.L.T. 109.
68 *Barvas School Board* v. *Macgregor* (1891) 18 R. 647; *Kerr* v. *Hood*, 1907 S.C. 895; *Beechgrove Co.* v. *A/S Fjord*, 1916 S.C.(H.L.) 1.
69 *Rutherford* v. *Somerville* (1901) 4 F.(J.) 15; *Dunsmore* v. *Lindsay* (1903) 6 F.(J.) 14.
70 *Kruse* v. *Johnson* [1898] 2 Q.B. 91; *Dunsmore*, *supra*.
71 *Ramsay* v. *Bruce* (1849) 12 D. 243.
72 *Cochran* v. *Dunlop* (1872) 9 S.L.R. 597.
73 *E. Perth* v. *Willoughby d'Eresby's Trs.* (1869) 7 M. 642; (1871) 9 M.(H.L.) 83; *Rixon* v. *Edinburgh Northern Tramways Co.* (1889) 16 R. 653; but see also *United College of St. Andrews* v. *Blyth* (1864) 2 M. 810.
74 *Maule* v. *Maule* (1826) 5 S. 256.

it belongs to a third party. Failure to state a plea of incompetency of the action as a defence against satisfying production does not bar the defender from later stating it as a defence on the merits.[75] The court may order production under reservation of the defender's pleas to competency and relevancy,[76] or subject to conditions,[77] or may, exceptionally, hold production satisfied by production of a copy of the deed concerned.[78] It may require production of a deed though a discharge by the pursuer of all claims under that deed is still unreduced, in an action to reduce both.[79]

The proper person to satisfy the call for production is the person having possession and control of the document in question, such as the sheriff-clerk in an action for reduction of process-caption,[80] the executor in a reduction of a will, the proprietor in a reduction of a conveyance of heritage, the arbiter in a reduction of a decree-arbitral,[81] and so on.

If production is not satisfied the pursuer may move for decree of reduction *contra non producta.*[82] The defender may be given an opportunity to bring an action of proving of the tenor to set up certain lost deeds.[83]

If the defender's preliminary objections to satisfying production are sustained the action comes to an end.

Second reductions and res judicata

The general rule is that if a pursuer brings an action on one ground and fails he is not prevented from seeking the same result on another ground by the principle of *res judicata.* But an exception exists in the case of reductions. If a reduction has been brought and failed, a fresh reduction can be brought on different facts but not on other grounds; it is not competent to bring as many reductions as one can devise pleas in law.[84]

Reduction of Deeds: Kinds of Deeds Reducible

Reduction of ex facie valid deed

A deed which is *ex facie* valid and regular cannot be ignored, or the rights conferred thereunder taken away, save by reduction of that deed, or declarator of trust.[85] "Deeds in themselves regular and complete must receive effect until reduced, and the right thereby validly constituted cut down and taken away in that established form of procedure." [86]

75 *Mackintosh* v. *Arkley* (1868) 6 M.(H.L.) 141.
76 *Cochran* v. *Dunlop* (1872) 9 S.L.R. 597.
77 *Bradley* v. *Walls* (1894) 2 S.L.T. 354.
78 *Law* v. *Law's Trs.* (1903) 11 S.L.T. 155.
79 *Fraser* v. *Macleay* (1882) 9 R. 1036.
80 *Watt* v. *Thomson* (1870) 8 M.(H.L.) 77.
81 *Miller* v. *Oliver & Boyd* (1901) 9 S.L.T. 287.
82 *Miller* v. *Oliver & Boyd* (1901) 9 S.L.T. 287.
83 *Lebrun* v. *Ferguson* (1852) 14 D. 486.
84 *G.S.W. Ry.* v. *Boyd & Forrest,* 1918 S.C.(H.L.) 14, 28, *per* Lord Shaw, explaining Stair IV, 40, 16, and 52, 3.
85 *Anstruther* v. *Mitchell and Cullen* (1857) 19 D. 674.
86 *Ibid.* 680, *per* L.J.C. Hope.

Thus a discharge of a bond or other obligatory instrument requires to be reduced before a claim be made for payment or otherwise under the bond.[87]

The kind of deed or writ is immaterial. There seems to be no decision limiting the categories of deeds which may be challenged by reduction and no kind of deed is exempt. The only apparent exception is *J. and J.* v. *C.'s Tutor*,[88] where it was held that an adoption order could not be reduced. But the order, it was pointed out, was not a contract but a decree affecting the status of the adoptive child and the regularity of the procedure leading up to the decree was not challenged, and adoption proceedings were *sui generis.*

Registration of certain summonses of reduction

A notice of any signeted summons of reduction of any conveyance or deed of or relating to lands may be registered in the General Register of Inhibitions and Adjudications, and no summons of reduction has any effect in rendering the lands litigious except from and after the date of registration of such notice.[89]

Extract decree of reduction to be recorded in Register of Sasines

An extract of the decree of reduction of a deed, decree or instrument recorded in the Register of Sasines, or forming a mid-couple or link of title in a title recorded in that register, shall be recorded in that register, and is not pleadable against a third party who in bona fide onerously acquires right to the land, lease or heritable security contained in the deed reduced prior to an extract being so recorded.[90]

Reduction of Deeds: Grounds for Reduction

"When it is sought to reduce a deed, it is necessary to go behind the deed and discover the real facts. . . . The question is whether the real facts are such that the disposition must be reduced. . . . There is a heavy onus on a party who seeks to reduce a probative deed. . . ." [91]

Reduction on ground of lack of capacity, power or title to grant

A deed granted by one lacking capacity, such as an undertaking by one mentally *incapax*,[92] or lacking legal power to grant that kind of deed,

87 *Niven* v. *Ayr Mags.* (1899) 1 F. 400.
88 1948 S.C. 636.
89 Titles to Land Consolidation (Scotland) Act 1868, s. 159; Conveyancing (Scotland) Act 1924, s. 44.
90 Conveyancing (Scotland) Act 1924, s. 46.
91 *Anderson* v. *Lambie*, 1954 S.C.(H.L.) 43, 62, *per* Lord Reid.
92 *Crichton* v. *Crichton's Trs.* (1874) 1 R. 688; *cf. Morrison* v. *Maclean's Trs.* (1862) 24 D. 625; *Hope* v. *Hope's Trs.* (1896) 23 R. 513.

such as a lease granted by a trustee expressly forbidden by the trust deed to grant leases, or lacking title to grant it, such as a disposition of lands granted by a non-owner, is totally void.

Thus in *Stobie* v. *Smith* [93] a disposition of heritage granted by a person who had been served as heir to the last owner was reduced when the decree of service was reduced, that person having been thereby found to be a *non dominus* and one having no title to grant the disposition.

Reduction on ground of granter's incapacity

If it be alleged that the granter of a deed was at the time physically or mentally *incapax*, reduction is necessary.[94] The incapacity, as by reason of drink, must be such as deprived the granter of capacity to give or withhold consent, or to apply his mind to the transaction in question.[95]

Reduction on ground of inadequate authentication

If the inadequacy of authentication of a deed is *ex facie* apparent, as where it is superscribed, not subscribed,[96] or there is no granter's signature at all,[97] or only one signature of an attesting witness,[98] reduction is unnecessary but is competent.[99] But it is necessary if no defect is apparent and the deed is *ex facie* properly authenticated, because in this case the court cannot disregard the deed unless there is allegation of the defect, the defect is one vitiating the purported authentication, and there is proof of facts supporting the allegation.

A deed *ex facie* regularly executed and probative requires substantial and convincing, even " overpowering," evidence to persuade the court to reject it.[1]

Even where such facts have been established the pursuer may be barred from taking advantage of the latent defect in the deed if the deed was executed with the intention that it be used for a particular purpose and was so used, and innocent third parties have acted in reliance on it.[2]

Thus reduction is competent if it be averred and proved that the instrumentary witnesses neither saw the granter sign nor heard him acknowledge his signature,[3] or that the witnesses, or one of them, did not

93 1921 S.C. 895.
94 *Hamilton* v. *Henderson* (1849) 11 D. 577; *Hope* v. *Hope's Trs.* (1896) 23 R. 513; *Houston* v. *Aitken*, 1912 S.C. 1037.
95 Stair I, 10, 13; Ersk. III, 1, 16; *Johnston* v. *Clark* (1854) 17 D. 228; *Taylor* v. *Provan* (1864) 2 M. 1226; lesser incapacity may suffice if fraud also is averred: *Couston* v. *Miller* (1862) 24 D. 607.
96 *e.g. McLay* v. *Farrell*, 1950 S.C. 149.
97 *e.g. Waterson's Trs.* v. *St. Giles Boys' Club*, 1943 S.C. 369.
98 Ignoring those cases where, by statute, one witness suffices.
99 *Donald* v. *McGregor's Exors.*, 1926 S.L.T. 103.
1 *Smith* v. *Bank of Scotland* (1824) 2 Sh.App. 265; *Baird's Tr.* v. *Murray* (1883) 11 R. 153; *Forrest* v. *Low's Tr.*, 1907 S.C. 1240; *McArthur* v. *McArthur's Exors.*, 1931 S.L.T. 463.
2 *Baird's Tr., supra*; *McLeish* v. *B.L. Bank*, 1911, 2 S.L.T. 168; *Boyd* v. *Shaw*, 1927 S.C. 414. See also *National Bank* v. *Campbell* (1892) 19 R. 885; *Sinclair* v. *Sinclair*, 1949 S.L.T. (Notes) 16; *Smellie's Trs.* v. *Smellie*, 1953 S.L.T.(Notes) 22.
3 *Cumming* v. *Skeoch's Trs.* (1879) 6 R. 540; *Baird's Trs.* v. *Murray* (1883) 11 R. 153; *Young* v. *Paton*, 1910 S.C. 63.

sign until after the death of the granter,[4] or until after an excessive interval.[5]

The courts have long struggled against having to set aside a deed on account of some trivial technicality, and it is questionable if any defect which could be rectified as an " informality of execution " [6] can be made a ground of reduction.

In cases of notarial execution reduction has been granted where it was admitted or proved that the docquet was not holograph of the notary,[7] or the granter's authority not obtained, or the notarial docquet and signature not adhibited before two witnesses, or not in presence of the granter,[8] or that the notary [9] or his business partner [10] was disqualified by interest, such as having been appointed a trustee by the deed executed, or that the notary's signature was not adhibited *unico contextu* with the docquet but before or substantially after it was appended to the deed,[11] or otherwise that the notarial execution has not complied with the Conveyancing (Sc.) Act 1924, s. 18.

Reduction of deed as being ultra vires

A deed which, though *ex facie* regular and valid, was one outwith the powers of the granter to grant may be challenged by reduction.[12] Similarly, a resolution of the board of directors of a company has been sought to be reduced as being *ultra vires.*[13]

Reduction of deed in breach of obligation

A deed, such as a will, can be reduced if framed and executed in breach of a prior undertaking by the granter or agreement inconsistent therewith.[14] The problem of the proof of the alleged agreement may be the most difficult one in such a case, and if the agreement relates to heritage, it must be constituted in writing probative or equivalent thereto, and certainly if the undertaking to benefit by will is gratuitous,[15] or if of an innominate and unusual kind, it must be established by writ or oath.[16]

Similarly missives of sale of heritage and a disposition in implement thereof may both be reduced where the seller had previously entered into an obligation, not discharged or departed from nor rescissible, to sell to another.[17]

4 *Walker* v. *Whitwell*, 1916 S.C.(H.L.) 75, overruling *Tener* v. *Tener's Trs.* (1879) 6 R. 1111.
5 *Frank* v. *Frank* (1795) Mor. 16824; (1809) 5 Pat. 278; *Thomson* v. *Clarkson's Trs.* (1892) 20 R. 59.
6 Conveyancing (Scotland) Act 1874, s. 39.
7 *Henry* v. *Reid* (1871) 9 M. 503.
8 *Kissack* v. *Webster's Trs.* (1894) 2 S.L.T. 172.
9 *Ferrie* v. *Ferrie's Trs.* (1863) 1 M. 291; *Newstead* v. *Dansken*, 1918, 1 S.L.T. 136.
10 *Finlay* v. *Finlay's Trs.*, 1948 S.C. 16; *Gorrie's Tr.* v. *Stiven's Exrx.*, 1952 S.C. 1; *Crawford's Trs.* v. *Glasgow Royal Infirmary*, 1955 S.C. 367.
11 *Hynd's Tr.* v. *Hynd's Trs.*, 1955 S.C.(H.L.) 1.
12 *Viscountess Strathallan* v. *Glenlyon's Trs.* (1837) 15 S. 971.
13 *Anderson* v. *James Sutherland (Peterhead) Ltd.*, 1941 S.C. 203.
14 *Paterson* v. *Paterson* (1893) 20 R. 484. *Cf. McLachlan* v. *Seton's Trs.*, 1937 S.C. 206.
15 *Smith* v. *Oliver*, 1911 S.C. 103.
16 *Edmonston* v. *Edmonston* (1861) 23 D. 995; *Paterson, supra*; *Gray* v. *Johnston*, 1928 S.C. 659; *Fisher* v. *Fisher and Others*, 1952 S.C. 347.
17 *Rodger (Builders) Ltd.* v. *Fawdry*, 1950 S.C. 483.

Reduction on ground of minority and lesion

A contract entered into by a minor, *i.e.* one under 18,[18] formerly one under 21, is voidable and subject to reduction at his instance at any time within four years of his having attained majority (*quadriennium utile*) on proof of his minority at the time and of enorm lesion.[19] Exceptions are recognised in the cases of the minor who is engaged in a business or profession,[20] who represented himself as of full age and was believed on reasonable grounds,[21] or who, after attaining majority and in full knowledge of the facts and of his legal rights, has ratified the transaction.[22] Reduction is not barred by the fact that the court has authorised the transaction.[23]

Enorm lesion is seriously inadequate consideration for the contract, where the consideration the minor got was immoderately disproportionate to what might have been got.[24] It is not necessarily to be determined in the light of facts known to the parties at the time of the contract.[25] The onus of proof of enorm lesion is on the minor,[26] but it is presumed in the cases of gifts, gratuitous surrenders of rights, and cautionary obligations,[27] and presumed in cases of loan to, or sale by and payment of the price to, a minor unless it be shown that the money is still in his hands or has been profitably expended [28]; if he has squandered it, he is lesed.[29] A rather lesser degree of injury will suffice if the minor contracted alone than if with the consent and concurrence of his curator.[30]

Reduction on ground of forgery

A deed, such as a will,[31] if forged, is a nullity but it requires to be reduced if it bears to be testamentary in effect and to be probative or holograph or adopted as holograph. So, too, bonds [32] and discharges thereof may be reduced for forgery.

Reduction on this ground may be barred if the party now challenging has delayed to challenge or, having discovered the deed alleged to be forged, has allowed another to act on the faith of its validity.[33]

18 Age of Majority (Sc.) Act 1969.

19 Stair I, 6, 44; Ersk. I, 7, 34; Bell, *Prin.* § 2098; Fraser, *P. & Ch.* 498; Gloag, 84; *McGuire* v. *Addie & Sons' Collieries*, 1950 S.C. 537.

20 Ersk. I, 7, 38; *McFeetridge* v. *Stewarts & Lloyds, Ltd.*, 1913 S.C. 773; *O'Donnell* v. *Brownieside Coal Co.*, 1934 S.C. 534.

21 *Wilkie* v. *Dunlop* (1874) 12 S. 506.

22 *McGibbon* v. *McGibbon* (1852) 14 D. 605.

23 *Wallace* v. *Wallace*, 8 Mar. 1817, F.C.; *Gillam's Curator* (1908) 15 S.L.T. 1043.

24 *Robertson* v. *Henderson* (1905) 7 F. 776, 785.

25 *McGuire* v. *Addie & Son's Collieries*, 1950 S.C. 537, 540.

26 *Munro* v. *Munro* (1735) *Elchies, voce Minor*, No. 1; *Sutherland* v. *Lady Kinminity* (1737) Mor. 12732; *Williamson* v. *Fraser* (1739) Mor. 8965; *Falconer* v. *Thomson* (1792) Mor. 16380; *Hill* v. *City of Glasgow Bank* (1879) 7 R. 68; *Robertson, supra*; *McFeetridge, supra.*

27 Stair I, 6, 44; Ersk. I, 7, 37.

28 *Harkness* v. *Graham* (1836) 14 S. 1015 (payment of debts); *Stark* v. *Tennent* (1843) 5 D. 542 (maintenance and education).

29 *Harkness* v. *Graham* (1833) 11 S. 760; *Ferguson* v. *Yuill* (1835) 13 S. 886.

30 Ersk. I, 7, 33; *Cooper* v. *Cooper's Trs.* (1885) 12 R. 473.

31 *Jamieson* v. *McQueen* (1839) 2 D. 147; *Hamilton* v. *Henderson* (1849) 11 D. 577; *Irvine* v. *Powrie's Trs.*, 1915 S.C. 1006 (declarator that will not genuine and for reduction thereof).

32 *Muir's Exors.* v. *Craig's Trs.*, 1913 S.C. 349.

33 *McKenzie* v. *B.L. Co.* (1881) 8 R.(H.L.) 8; *Muir's Exors., supra.*

Reduction of contract or deed which incorrectly expresses agreement

Where a contract has been reduced to writing and that writing does not correctly express the agreement which the parties reached, either party may have the contract reduced on proof of its disconformity to the agreement.[34]

Similarly where the contract is not inaccurate but a disposition of heritage or other deed necessary to give effect to the contract does not accurately do so, the disposition, even though recorded in the Register of Sasines, will be reduced, and have to be replaced by a deed which does accurately do so.[35] This is so even though the disposition, once executed, normally supersedes the contract and rules the rights of parties,[36] because the real issue is one of the intention of the parties, nor merely of interpretation.

Similarly reduction was held essential where it was alleged that an insurance company's official had altered the proposal form completed by the pursuer, and that the policy accordingly did not include what the pursuer believed were the agreed terms.[37]

It is doubtless competent to, but unnecessary to, reduce a contract where the mistake in giving effect to the parties' agreement is patent, as where the contract contains a superfluous word " not." Such an apparent mistake may simply be corrected.[38]

Similarly it was held competent to bring a reduction of a recorded agreement under the Workmen's Compensation Act where it was disputed whether any agreement had been reached capable of being recorded.[39]

Reduction on grounds of essential error excluding consent

A reduction may be brought of a contract on the ground of consent thereto having been excluded by essential error in any one or more of the five respects in which error may vitiate a contract,[40] where the error is either common to both parties,[41] or mutual, that is, each party being mistaken as to the other's intention,[42] or is unilateral, *i.e.* exists on the part of one party only, and was induced in him by the representation, innocent, negligent or fraudulent, made by or on behalf of the other contracting party.[43] Damages may be claimed in addition only where

34 *Glasgow Feuing and Building Co.* v. *Watson's Trs.* (1887) 14 R. 610. *Cf. Krupp* v. *Menzies*, 1907 S.C. 903, where plea of disconformity taken in defence.

35 *Anderson* v. *Lambie*, 1954 S.C.(H.L.) 43.

36 *Lee* v. *Alexander* (1883) 10 R.(H.L.) 91; *Edinburgh United Breweries* v. *Molleson* (1894) 21 R.(H.L.) 10.

37 *McKinlay* v. *Life & Health Assce. Assocn.* (1905) 13 S.L.T. 102.

38 Ersk. III, 3, 87; *Glen's Trs.* v. *Lancashire and Yorkshire Ins. Co.* (1906) 8 F. 915; *Anderson, supra* at 59.

39 *Hughes* v. *Thistle Chemical Co.*, 1907 S.C. 607.

40 Bell, *Prin.* § 11; approved *Stewart* v. *Kennedy* (1890) 17 R.(H.L.) 25, 28.

41 *Hamilton* v. *Western Bank* (1861) 23 D. 1033; *Sibson & Kerr* v. *Barcraig Co.* (1896) 24 R. 91, 98. The error probably must relate to the kind of thing in issue, not merely to its value: *Dawson* v. *Muir* (1851) 13 D. 843; or to the extent of injuries: *McGuire* v. *Addie's Collieries*, 1950 S.C. 537.

42 *Stuart* v. *Kennedy* (1885) 13 R. 221.

43 *Edgar* v. *Hector*, 1912 S.C. 348; *Fletcher* v. *Lord Advocate*, 1923 S.C. 27.

the error was induced by fraudulent or by negligent misrepresentations,[44] but not where the misrepresentation was innocent.

Reduction is, it is submitted, not competent where the error is unilateral, *i.e.* exists on the part of one party only, but was not induced by anything said or done by or on behalf of the other contracting party,[45] where, that is, one party has simply made a mistake, and that even though the other party realised that.

A gratuitous unilateral undertaking or discharge may, however, be reduced, if entered into under error in fact, even though the error were uninduced, and probably also even if under error of law.[46]

Error in law, at least as to some matter of general law, is not, at least in the general case, sufficient to justify reduction,[47] but it may be otherwise if the error is as to a matter of law between the parties only, such as the interpretation of a particular deed or contract or will.[48] The court is particularly unwilling to reduce an agreement involving an element of transaction or compromise.[49]

A reduction may similarly be brought of a will on the ground of essential error caused by misrepresentation.[50]

Reduction on ground of misrepresentation

Even if it does not induce essential error so as to exclude consent it is now settled that fraudulent, negligent or innocent misrepresentation made by one party to a contract to the other, as to some matter of fact material to the contract, thereby inducing the contract on the terms on which the parties finally agreed, leaves the contract voidable and subject to reduction on the ground of those misrepresentations. If the misrepresentations were innocently made reduction of the contract is the sole remedy [51]; if the misrepresentations were made fraudulently [52] or negligently [53] damages can also be recovered for the loss caused by the failure of the contract, or damages can be recovered without reduction or rescission of the contract.[54] A party cannot insist on a contract on terms which he induced by misrepresentation. General averments of fraud are insufficient; they must be specific and facts alleged supporting the inference that fraud has been

44 Chap. 29, *infra.*
45 Bell, *Prin.* § 11; *Stewart* v. *Kennedy, supra*; *Bennie's Trs.* v. *Couper* (1890) 17 R. 782; *Royal Bank* v. *Greenshields*, 1914 S.C. 259.
46 *Ross* v. *Mackenzie* (1842) 5 D. 151; *Dickson* v. *Halbert* (1854) 16 D. 586; *Mercer, supra.* Contrast *Wood* v. *N.B. Ry.* (1891) 18 R.(H.L.) 27; *Dornan* v. *Allan* (1900) 3 F. 112.
47 *Munro* v. *Strain* (1874) 1 R. 522; *Kippen* v. *Kippen's Tr.* (1874) 1 R. 1171; *Manclark* v. *Thomson's Tr.*, 1958 S.C. 147.
48 *Mercer* v. *Anstruther's Trs.* (1871) 9 M. 618, 628, 652; affd. on other grounds (1872) 10 M. (H.L.) 39.
49 *Manclark, supra.*
50 *Munro, supra.*
51 *Lees* v. *Tod* (1882) 9 R. 807; *Boyd & Forrest* v. *G.S.W. Ry.*, 1912 S.C.(H.L.) 93; 1915 S.C.(H.L.) 20.
52 *McConechy* v. *McIndoe* (1853) 16 D. 315; *Derry* v. *Peek* (1889) 14 App.Cas. 339; *Spence* v. *Crawford*, 1939 S.C.(H.L.) 52.
53 *Hedley Byrne & Co.* v. *Heller & Partners* [1964] A.C. 465.
54 *Smith* v. *Sim*, 1954 S.C. 357.

committed.[55] Fraud is a personal delict, and averments must be directed against a particular person, not against a firm or corporate body.[56]

Reduction on ground of facility and fraud or circumvention

Both contracts and wills may be challenged on the ground that one party, or the testator, as the case may be, was at the time of contracting or executing in a state of facility, and was circumvented so that he made an arrangement contrary to his own interests. Facility is a state of bodily and/or mental weakness, not amounting to incapacity, which renders the individual more than normally susceptible to advice, guidance or pressure, and liable to be overreached and taken advantage of. It commonly arises from illness or old age.[57]

Circumvention is deceit or fraud,[58] a species of the genus fraud, dishonest impetration.[59] There must be express averments of the means used alleged to amount to circumvention or fraud, at or very least of the type or nature of the fraud of which complaint is made.[60] " The essence of circumvention and facility is that a person practises on the debility of another whose individuality is impaired by infirmity or age, and moulds the inclinations of the latter, to his own profit." [61] It must be clearly averred by what person or persons the deed is alleged to have been impetrated.[62] But it is not necessary to aver distinct instances of practices directed against the facile person.[63] There must be some relation between the facility and the acts employed against the granter.[64]

It must also be relevantly averred that the pursuer suffered lesion by granting the deed now complained of.[65] Lesion is serious loss, as by transferring rights or property for a substantially inadequate consideration, or gratuitously. If substantial lesion is averred, relatively weak averments of circumvention may be compensated for by strong and circumstantial averments of weakness and facility.[66]

There appears to be no difference in the principles applicable to contracts and to wills respectively.

Reduction on ground of undue influence

" The essence of undue influence is that a person, who has assumed

[55] *Cf. Shedden* v. *Patrick* (1852) 14 D. 721; affd. 17 D.(H.L.) 18; *Leslie* v. *Lumsden* (1856) 18 D. 1046; *Hogg* v. *Campbell* (1864) 2 M. 848; *Broatch* v. *Jenkins* (1866) 4 M. 1030; *Boustead* v. *Gardner* (1879) 7 R. 139.

[56] *Thomson* v. *Pattison, Elder & Co.* (1895) 22 R. 432.

[57] *Cf. Clunie* v. *Stirling* (1854) 17 D. 15; *Maclean* v. *Maclean's Trs.* (1861) 23 D. 1099 (trust deed); *Horsburgh* v. *Thomson's Trs.*, 1912 S.C. 267 (will); *Houston* v. *Aitken*, 1912 S.C. 1037; *L.A.* v. *Davidson's J.F.*, 1921, 2 S.L.T. 267 (will); *Mackay* v. *Campbell*, 1966 S.C. 237, 249 (contract).

[58] Stair I, 9, 9; Bell, *Law Dictionary*, s.v. Circumvention.

[59] *McDougal* v. *McDougal's Trs.*, 1931 S.C. 102, 116.

[60] *McDougal, supra.*

[61] *Ross* v. *Gosselin's Exors.*, 1926 S.C. 325, 334, *per* L.P. Clyde.

[62] *Baird* v. *Harvey's Trs.* (1869) 20 D. 1220.

[63] *Clunie* v. *Stirling* (1854) 17 D. 15, 18.

[64] *Morrison* v. *Maclean's Trs.* (1862) 24 D. 625; *Houston* v. *Aitken*, 1912 S.C. 1037.

[65] *Cf. Mackay, supra.*

[66] *Mackay, supra*, 249.

or undertaken a position of quasi-fiduciary responsibility in relation to the affairs of another, allows his own self-interest to deflect the advice or guidance he gives, in his own favour." [67] The pursuer must accordingly show that the defender stood to him in such a relation as parent to child, trustee to beneficiary, spiritual or legal or other adviser to layman, or the like, so that reliance on the defender's influence, guidance and views was natural, probable and almost inevitable, and dissent from his guidance and advice was less likely. It is not necessary to establish error,[68] still less actual fraud, misrepresentation, concealment or biased advice. Nor is bad or wrong advice undue influence but there must be allegations of persuasion, pressure and cajolement. On the other hand a proper and fair explanation of the issues involved, adequate disclosure of relevant information and, particularly, the provision of, or even the fullest readiness to permit access to, independent sources of information and advice go far to rebut any inference of undue influence.[69] Secondly the pursuer must show that in consequence of the influence he has suffered prejudice as by giving some material gratuitous benefit to the person exercising the influence.[70]

In English law a presumption of undue influence arises in certain relationships, which may, however, be rebutted, but in Scots law there is never a presumption, though undue influence may be established in any case.[71]

While undue influence is a ground for bringing a reduction both of contracts and wills, the meaning and effect of the concept may not be the same in both categories of cases.[72]

In respect of contracts it is necessary to show that the defender was in a position to exercise a dominant influence over the pursuer and concealed or altered any material facts, gave partial advice, or did not permit access to independent advice, and in any way gained, or stood to gain, gratuitous benefit or advantage from the transaction. " An onerous contract entered into by a party of full age cannot be reduced on the ground that his consent was the result of undue influence exercised upon him, unless the influence was exerted to the detriment of that party by or on behalf of the other party to the deed in breach of a duty arising out of a fiduciary or quasi-fiduciary relationship." [73] The undue influence must have been exercised by or on behalf of the other party to the agreement and, to be an adequate cause for reduction, the influence must have been exercised in other than genuine devotion to the interests of the person influenced.[74]

67 *Ross* v. *Gosselin's Exors.*, 1926 S.C. 325, 334, *per* L.P. Clyde. *Cf. Smith Cunninghame* v. *Anstruther's Trs.* (1872) 10 M.(H.L.) 39, 47; *Gray* v. *Binny* (1879) 7 R. 332, 342.
68 *Forbes* v. *Forbes's Trs.*, 1957 S.C. 325, 330.
69 *Gray* v. *Binny*, *supra*, 347; *Forbes* v. *Forbes's Trs.*, 1957 S.C. 325, 335; *Allan* v. *Allan*, 1961 S.C. 200.
70 *Gray*, *supra*, 347; *Forbes*, *supra*, 336.
71 Winder " Undue Influence in English and Scots Law " (1940) 56 L.Q.R. 97.
72 *Forrest* v. *Low's Trs.*, 1907 S.C. 1240, 1255; affd. 1909 S.C.(H.L.) 16; *Forbes* v. *Forbes's Trs.*, 1957 S.C. 325, 331.
73 *Forbes*, *supra*, 333, *per* Lord Guthrie.
74 *Ibid.*

In respect of wills the same general requisites apply. The doctrine of undue influence in relation to wills has been said to be confined to cases where the relationship between the two persons is such that the natural and legitimate consequence is influence upon the one side, and trust and confidence upon the other,[75] and a will is reducible if it be established that such a person as a clergyman, medical practitioner, or lawyer has abused his influence and overcome the will of the parishioner or patient or client.[76] If one party writes or prepares the will of another under which he takes a benefit, that circumstance excites the suspicion of the court.[77] But no presumption arises that a person benefited, such as a mistress, has exercised undue influence.[78]

In the particular case of a will prepared by a solicitor and benefiting that solicitor or his close relatives or connections, this is never a proper course of conduct and indeed throws on the solicitor the onus of proving that the settlement in his favour was the free and uninfluenced act of the testator, deliberately entertained and carried through with an entire knowledge of its effect.[79]

Grounds of undue influence, and of facility and circumvention, combined

The grounds of undue influence, and of facility and circumvention, may both be invoked in the circumstances of one case and the action be tried on both grounds together.[80] Where undue influence is exercised on a facile person, the case may be treated as one of facility and circumvention without averment of any special deception.[81]

Reduction on ground of force and fear

A grant of a deed induced by force and fear is void, not merely voidable,[82] but reduction is normally necessary to establish that the obligation was so induced. To amount to force and fear there must have been applied by the one contracting party to the other actual force, or reasonable apprehension of serious physical violence,[83] subjection to arbitrary and illegal imprisonment,[84] imprisonment under illegal diligence,[85] or other similar pressure, and this must have been a major influence on the party's decision to make the contract or will, grant the discharge or otherwise act.

75 *McKechnie* v. *McKechnie's Trs.*, 1908 S.C. 93, 102.
76 *Munro* v. *Strain* (1874) 1 R. 522, 525; *Williams* v. *Philip* (1907) 15 S.L.T. 396; *Forrest* v. *Low's Trs.*, 1909 S.C.(H.L.) 16.
77 *Barry* v. *Butlin* (1838) 2 Moo.P.C. 480, approved in *Forrest, supra.*
78 *McKechnie, supra.*
79 *Grieve* v. *Cunningham* (1869) 8 M. 317, 322; *Weir* v. *Grace* (1899) 2 F. (H.L.) 30, 36; *Forrest* v. *Low's Trs.*, 1909 S.C.(H.L.) 16; *Stewart* v. *MacLaren*, 1920 S.C.(H.L.) 148.
80 *McKechnie* v. *McKechnie's Trs.*, 1908 S.C. 93; *Ross* v. *Gosselin's Exors.*, 1926 S.C. 325.
81 *Ibid.* 335.
82 Dig. IV, 2; Stair I, 9, 8; Ersk. III, 1, 16; Bell, *Prin.* § 12.
83 *E. Orkney* v. *Vinfra* (1606) Mor. 16481; *Tenants of Winton* v. *Bakers of Canongate* (1748) Mor. 16514; *Gelot* v. *Stewart* (1870) 8 M. 649; (1871) 9 M. 957.
84 *Stuart* v. *Whitefoord* (1677) Mor. 16489.
85 *McIntosh* v. *Chalmers* (1883) 11 R. 8.

The pressure may have been exerted not against the contracting party himself, but against a close relative or person in the same interest.[86]

The threats or pressure, and consequent fear, must have been of something illegal or unjustifiable. The threat of legal process or diligence or sequestration may be legitimate, and an obligation undertaken to stave off such a consequence is not reducible,[87] but such a threat is not legitimate if used to secure assent to an unconnected obligation.[88]

Reduction on ground of extortion

It would appear that a reduction cannot be brought merely on averments that a party has paid an excessive or unreasonable price, or has received a wholly inadequate return for what he has done or given, or that a transaction was otherwise unfair.[89] Exceptionally, however, the court has given a remedy where a transaction was obviously grossly extortionate, so much so as to be equivalent to fraud or duress.[90]

The courts have, however, powers under the Moneylenders Act 1927, to reopen a transaction with a moneylender which is harsh and unconscionable, and may set aside, in whole or in part, or revise or alter, any security given or agreement made, relieve the debtor from liability for any sum beyond what the court deems reasonable, order repayment of any amount paid exceeding that sum, and order the moneylender to indemnify the borrower if he has parted with any security given.[91] In judging whether a transaction is harsh and unconscionable, the major factor is the extent of the moneylender's risk in the particular case,[92] and the rate of interest is only an element. The Act provides that interest at a rate exceeding 48 per cent is to be deemed excessive and the transaction harsh and unconscionable unless the contrary is proved.

Reduction of gratuitous alienations and fraudulent preferences

Gratuitous alienations. Where a person has become insolvent, in the sense that his liabilities exceed his assets, any creditor,[93] or the trustee in his resultant sequestration,[94] may reduce any gratuitous alienation, either at common law, or under the Bankruptcy (Sc.) Act 1621, which annuls all alienations by a debtor, without a true, just and necessary cause and

[86] Bell, *Comm.* I, 315; *Prin.* § 12; *McIntosh* v. *Farquharson* (1671) Mor. 16485; *Canison* v. *Marshall* (1764) 6 Pat. 759; *Priestnell* v. *Hutcheson* (1857) 19 D. 495; *Williams* v. *Bayley* (1866) L.R. 1 H.L. 200; *Gow* v. *Henry* (1899) 2 F. 48.

[87] *Murray* v. *Spalding* (1672) Mor. 16487; *Ker* v. *Edgar* (1698) Mor. 16503; *Priestnell* v. *Hutcheson* (1857) 19 D. 495; *Craig* v. *Paton* (1865) 4 M. 192; *Rudman* v. *Jay*, 1908 S.C. 552.

[88] *Nisbet* v. *Stewart* (1708) Mor. 16512; *Arratt* v. *Wilson* (1718) Rob.App. 234; *Fraser* v. *Black*, Dec. 13, 1810, F.C.; *McIntosh* v. *Chalmers* (1883) 11 R. 8.

[89] *A.B.* v. *Joel* (1849) 12 D. 188; *Latta* v. *Park* (1865) 3 M. 508; *McLachlan* v. *Watson* (1874) 11 S.L.R. 549; *Caledonian Ry.* v. *N.B. Ry.* (1881) 8 R.(H.L.) 23.

[90] *Young* v. *Gordon* (1896) 23 R. 419; *Gordon* v. *Stephen* (1902) 9 S.L.T. 307.

[91] 1927 Act, s. 10.

[92] *Davis* v. *McNally* (1904) 12 S.L.T. 234; *Midland Discount Co.* v. *Macdonald*, 1909 S.C. 477; *Howard & Cope* v. *Leckie*, 1909, 2 S.L.T. 444; *Debenham* v. *McCall*, 1923 S.L.T. 365.

[93] *Wink* v. *Speirs* (1867) 6 M. 77.

[94] Bankruptcy (Sc.) Act 1913, s. 9.

without a just price truly paid, to conjunct or confident persons, after the contracting of lawful debts from true creditors.

At common law the onus of proof that the granter was at the time insolvent and the grant gratuitous was on the challenger.

In a reduction brought under the 1621 Act the onus is on the debtor to prove that he was solvent at the time, or that the transaction was onerous.[95] A presumption of insolvency at the date of granting is raised by insolvency at the date of challenge.[96] It is a defence to prove that the alienation was made for a true, just and necessary cause, such as in implement of an obligation undertaken while solvent.[97] The defence has been held to fail in the case of a disposition of moveables to a daughter who had long acted as unpaid housekeeper,[98] or a lease at a low rent.[99]

True, just and necessary cause includes an ante-nuptial marriage provision.[1] A provision by a husband for his wife in an ante-nuptial marriage contract is valid, unless he was at the time insolvent and his prospective wife was aware of the fact.[2]

A provision in a post-nuptial marriage contract may be valid, even though the husband was insolvent at the time, so long as the amount is reasonable and the provision is not to take effect until after the dissolution of the marriage.[3]

Conjunct persons are those closely related to the insolvent by blood or affinity, such as a daughter,[4] son,[5] father,[6] or wife,[7] or intended wife.[8]

Confident persons are those closely connected with the insolvent in business, such as partners, employees, solicitors and the like.[9]

The onus is on the conjunct or confident person to prove the sale a bona fide transaction.[10] If a conjunct or confident person has received property from the insolvent and transferred it to a *bona fide* third party it is not recoverable, but the conjunct or confident person is liable for the value thereof.[11]

Fraudulent preferences. Similarly any transaction which fraudulently prefers or favours a particular creditor is reducible at the instance of creditors, or the trustee in sequestration, or the liquidator of a company, at common law, on the ground of insolvency at its date, or under the

95 *Bolden* v. *Ferguson* (1863) 1 M. 522; *Dawson* v. *Thorburn* (1888) 15 R. 891.
96 *Hodge* v. *Morrisons* (1883) 21 S.L.R. 40.
97 *Pringle's Tr.* v. *Wright* (1903) 5 F. 522.
98 *Dawson* v. *Thorburn* (1888) 15 R. 891.
99 *Gorrie's Trs.* v. *Gorrie* (1890) 17 R. 1051.
1 *McLay* v. *McQueen* (1899) 1 F. 814.
2 *McLay* v. *McQueen* (1899) 1 F. 814; see also *Watson* v. *Grant's Trs.* (1874) 1 R. 882.
3 *Robertson's Tr.* v. *Robertson* (1901) 3 F. 359; see also *McBain* v. *Robertson* (1900) 8 S.L.T. 101.
4 *Hodge* v. *Morrisons* (1883) 21 S.L.R. 40; *Jones' Tr.* v. *J.* (1888) 15 R. 328.
5 *Gorrie's Tr.* v. *Gorrie* (1890) 17 R. 1051.
6 *Williamson* v. *Allan* (1882) 9 R. 859.
7 *Tennant* v. *Miller* (1897) 4 S.L.T. 318.
8 *McLay* v. *McQueen* (1899) 1 F. 814.
9 *Edmond* v. *Grant* (1853) 15 D. 703; *Bank of Scotland* v. *Gardiner* (1907) 15 S.L.T. 229.
10 *N.B. Ry.* v. *White* (1882) 20 S.L.R. 129.
11 1621 Act, *supra*.

Bankruptcy (Sc.) Act 1696, on the ground that it was effected within sixty days before notour bankruptcy supervened.

If the challenge be made at common law it is necessary to prove that the granter was insolvent, and aware of his insolvency,[12] or that the transaction challenged was a disposition of his whole estate and necessarily made him insolvent.[13] Intent to defraud must also be established.[14] Among fraudulent preferences at common law have been a disposition of heritage when insolvent to the person who had lent money to build the heritage,[15] consent to a decree for redelivery of goods sold,[16] an agreement to set aside a stated sum from income to pay certain creditors,[17] a promissory note granted to one creditor.[18] But the category does not extend to a security granted by an insolvent who ultimately became bankrupt, in consideration of advances to be made,[19] nor an assignation to a creditor advancing money to enable an insolvent to pay a composition.[20]

Among transactions struck at by the Act have been a transfer of possession of pawnbroking premises and pledges,[21] a grant of security under an obligation to do so when required,[22] dispositions of heritage in security,[23] an invalidly created security by delivery order,[24] a further security in exchange for an invalid one,[25] a security given to a third party to pay a creditor,[26] an undertaking to pay if an interdict were withdrawn,[27] a simulate sale,[28] a promise to give delivery orders,[29] a debtor's consent to redelivery of goods sold to him,[30] a voluntary trust deed not acceded to by all creditors,[31] a bill granted and paid for a debt not yet prestable.[32]

The Act has been held not to strike at a new security granted in substitution for a prior security,[33] nor where a valid security had been given outwith the sixty days,[34] nor where a proprietor resumed possession of

12 *Macdonald* v. *Logan* (1903) 11 S.L.T. 369.
13 *McDougall's Tr.* v. *Ironside*, 1914 S.C. 186.
14 *Adamson, Howie & Co.* v. *Guild* (1867) 6 M. 347; *Ehrenbacher* v. *Kennedy* (1874) 1 R. 1131; *Macdonald* v. *Logan* (1903) 11 S.L.T. 369.
15 *Wylie, Stewart & Marshall* v. *Jervis*, 1913, 1 S.L.T. 465.
16 *Laurie's Tr.* v. *Beveridge* (1867) 6 M. 85.
17 *Munro* v. *Rothfield*, 1920 S.C.(H.L.) 165.
18 *Bank of Scotland* v. *Faulds* (1870) 7 S.L.R. 619.
19 *McInnes* v. *McCallum* (1901) 9 S.L.T. 215. See also *Renton & Gray's Tr.* v. *Dickison* (1880) 7 R. 951.
20 *Hay* v. *Rafferty* (1899) 2 F. 302.
21 *Paterson's Tr.* v. *Paterson's Trs.* (1891) 19 R. 91.
22 *Gourley* v. *Mackie* (1887) 14 R. 403.
23 *Hill's Tr.* v. *MacGregor* (1901) 8 S.L.T. 484.
24 *Dobell, Beckett & Co.* v. *Neilson* (1904) 7 F. 281.
25 *Price & Pierce* v. *Bank of Scotland*, 1910 S.C. 1095; affd. 1912 S.C.(H.L.) 19.
26 *Tait* v. *Mowat* (1893) 1 S.L.T. 75; *Craig's Tr.* v. *Craig* (1903) 10 S.L.T. 556.
27 *Dods* v. *Welsh* (1904) 12 S.L.T. 110.
28 *Stiven* v. *Scott* (1871) 9 M. 923.
29 *Wright* v. *Mitchell* (1871) 9 M. 516; *Gourley* v. *Hodge* (1875) 2 R. 738; *Rhind's Tr.* v. *Robertson & Baxter* (1891) 18 R. 623.
30 *Laurie's Tr.* v. *Beveridge* (1867) 6 M. 85.
31 *Mackenzie* v. *Calder* (1868) 6 M. 833.
32 *McFarlane* v. *Robb* (1870) 9 M. 370.
33 *Roy's Tr.* v. *Colville & Drysdale* (1903) 5 F. 769.
34 *Moore* v. *Gledden* (1869) 7 M. 1016.

farm stock lent by him,[35] the actual registration within the sixty days of shares pledged earlier.[36]

Exceptions

Transactions which fall outwith the class of fraudulent preferences are payments in cash, transactions in the usual course of trade, and *nova debita*, or transfers for consideration given at the time.[37] Payments in cash include payments by cheque and endorsements and transfers of cheques in the debtor's favour,[38] but not transfers of a bill of exchange not instantly payable, not even if that was the debtor's usual means of payment.[39] But even a payment in cash is reducible if made before the debt was payable and made voluntarily, during insolvency, and the payer being cognisant of his insolvency; neither *animus fraudandi* nor collusion on the part of the payee need be proved. If however it be made when the debt is due it is reducible only if collusion in intent to defraud be established.[40]

Transactions in the usual course of trade have included returning an article sold and delivered but not paid for,[41] a displenishing sale, the auctioneer retaining the price against sums due to him,[42] and retiring a bill before its maturity.[43]

Nova debita have been held to include a cautionary obligation undertaken as a condition of the renewal of a bill,[44] the payment and renewal of heritable loans,[45] a disposition in security to a new cautioner for an existing debt,[46] the indorsation and delivery of a bill of lading for an advance from a bank,[47] the assignation of property in security of new advances and the continuation of old advances,[48] an assignation in security of a debt paid off and then renewed.[49]

Pactum de quota litis

A bargain by an advocate or solicitor to receive, as remuneration for professional services, a share of the subject in dispute is illegal at common law, and under the principle of the Land Purchase Act 1594, and is reducible.[50]

[35] *Torrance* v. *Traill's Trs.* (1897) 24 R. 837.
[36] *Guild* v. *Young* (1884) 22 S.L.R. 520. *Cf. Scottish Provident Institution* v. *Cohen* (1888) 16 R. 112.
[37] Bell, *Comm.* II, 201; *Taylor* v. *Farrie* (1851) 17 D. 639.
[38] *Whatmough's Tr.* v. *B.L. Bank*, 1934 S.C.(H.L.) 51, explaining *Carter* v. *Johnstone* (1886) 13 R. 698, where the contrary was held, as a method unusual in the trade. See also *Anderson's Tr.* v. *Somerville* (1899) 7 S.L.T. 75; *Richmond* v. *United Collieries* (1905) 13 S.L.T. 458; *Craig* v. *Hunter* (1905) 13 S.L.T. 525.
[39] *Nicol* v. *McIntyre* (1882) 9 R. 1097; *Horsburgh* v. *Ramsay* (1885) 12 R. 1171.
[40] *Coutts' Tr.* v. *Webster* (1886) 13 R. 1112; *Whatmough's Tr., supra.*
[41] *Loudon Bros.* v. *Reid & Lauder's Tr.* (1877) 5 R. 293.
[42] *Crockart's Tr.* v. *Hay*, 1913 S.C. 509.
[43] *McLaren's Tr.* v. *National Bank* (1897) 24 R. 920.
[44] *Ferguson* v. *Welsh* (1869) 7 M. 592.
[45] *Renton & Gray's Tr.* v. *Dickison* (1830) 7 R. 951.
[46] *McDougall's Tr.* v. *Gibbon* (1889) 16 R. 740.
[47] *Cowdenbeath Coal Co.* v. *Clydesdale Bank* (1895) 22 R. 682.
[48] *Browne's Trs.* v. *Browne* (1902) 10 S.L.T. 97.
[49] *Robertson's Tr.* v. *Union Bank*, 1917 S.C. 549.
[50] Stair I, 10, 8; Bell, *Prin.* § 36 (2). *Cf. Drysdale* v. *Nairne* (1835) 13 S. 348.

Reduction ex capite lecti

It was formerly a relevant ground for reduction of a testamentary writing that it had been executed on deathbed, when the deceased was labouring under the disease from which he died,[51] but the law of deathbed has been abolished by statute in at least most cases.[52]

Miscellaneous uses of reduction

An action of reduction has been held competent in various other circumstances, such as to obtain cancellation of a commissary clerk's certificate issued on the basis of erroneous information.[53]

Proceedings for revocation of a patent take the form of an action of reduction.[54]

On the other hand an adoption order made by a competent court cannot be reduced on the ground of essential error induced by misrepresentation, or of non-compliance with statutory provisions,[55] or possibly on any grounds at all.

Defences to reduction: (1) interests of third parties

A voidable contract is no longer reducible if a third party has, in good faith, for value and without notice of the defect, acquired a real right of property in the subject-matter of the voidable contract, as where a thing sold under a voidable contract has been resold,[56] or pledged,[57] or land acquired by fraud been resold,[58] or disponed in security.[59] In all cases the third party must have acted in good faith, given fair value, and been ignorant of the circumstances rendering the prior transaction voidable. The same principle applies where a person obtains a merely voidable authority to deal with goods and does so, as by pawning them,[60] but not where he has no authority at all thus to deal with them.[61]

But reduction is not precluded where a third party has acquired a merely personal right following on the voidable contract. Thus if a sale of goods has been induced by fraud it is voidable and reducible notwithstanding an agreement by the purchaser to resell or pledge the goods.[62] The same principle applies in heritage.[63] Similarly, an assignee of a

51 See Bell, *Prin.* § 1786; *e.g. Jamieson* v. *McQueen* (1839) 2 D. 147; *Eason* v. *Eason* (1863) 1 M. 1163; *Thain* v. *Thain* (1891) 18 R. 1196; *Hay* v. *Coutts' Trs.* (1890) 18 R. 244.

52 Reduction *ex capite lecti* Abolition Act 1871.

53 *Baines's Exor.* v. *Clark*, 1957 S.C. 342.

54 Patents Act 1949, s. 103 (2).

55 *J. and J.* v. *C's Tutor*, 1948 S.C. 636.

56 Sale of Goods Act 1893, s. 23. If the first sale were wholly void, the sub-sale is also void, irrespective of the sub-purchaser's good faith: *Morrisson* v. *Robertson*, 1908 S.C. 332.

57 *Price & Pierce* v. *Bank of Scotland*, 1910 S.C. 1095; 1912 S.C.(H.L.) 19.

58 Stair I, 40, 22; *Wilson* v. *Elliott* (1826) 4 S. 429; (1828) 3 W. & S. 60; *Fraser* v. *Hankey* (1847) 9 D. 415.

59 *Williamson* v. *Sharp* (1851) 14 D. 127.

60 *Brown* v. *Marr, Barclay & Co.* (1880) 7 R. 427; *Bryce* v. *Ehrmann* (1905) 7 F. 5.

61 *Mitchell* v. *Heys* (1894) 21 R. 600.

62 *Price & Pierce, supra.*

63 Stair IV, 40, 21; *Neilson* v. *Ireland* (1755) 5 B.S. 828.

personal right in general takes no better right than his assignor had, and his right is reducible if the assignor's right were voidable.

Defences to reduction: (2) restitution in integrum

It is in general a condition of reduction of a voidable contract that mutual *restitutio in integrum* be made, and accordingly, if this cannot be done, reduction is impossible.[64] Thus a contract *locatio operis faciendi* cannot be rescinded once the work thereunder has been done,[65] nor a contract of sale if the goods have been resold [66] or consumed or irreversibly altered.[67]

But reduction is not precluded if in all substantials, though possibly not exactly and literally, restitution is possible, as where any alteration made in goods bought was immaterial,[68] or shares indistinguishable from those sold can be restored.[69] The principle of requiring restitution is not to be interpreted too literally.[70]

If a thing bought, such as an animal, has perished by reason of a defect which, if the animal had not perished, would have rendered the contract voidable, the impossibility of making restitution does not bar reduction of the contract and recovery of the price paid.[71] But if it has perished for some other reason, whether with or without the buyer's fault, it may be that the buyer has no remedy because he cannot make restitution, unless possibly the cause of its perishing amounted to a breach of warranty.

Defences to reduction: (3) personal bar

A party entitled to challenge a contract as voidable may be held personally barred from doing so if the circumstances justify an inference of acquiescence in or approval of the voidable transaction. The right to reduce will be cut off by the long negative prescription,[72] but short of that time, delay and failure to challenge, certainly if the other party is thereby permitted to alter his position on the faith of the validity of his right,[73] may bar an action. Delay is also very relevant if by reason of the lapse of time evidence has been lost, because evidence lost must be assumed favourable to the defender.[74] If on the other hand misrepresentation

64 *Addie* v. *Western Bank* (1867) 5 M.(H.L.) 80; *Houldsworth* v. *City of Glasgow Bank* (1880) 7 R.(H.L.) 53; *Dowell's Ltd.* v. *Heriot's Trust*, 1941 S.C. 13, 22.
65 *Boyd and Forrest* v. *G.S.W. Ry.*, 1915 S.C.(H.L.) 20.
66 *Edinburgh United Breweries* v. *Molleson* (1894) 21 R.(H.L.) 10.
67 *Bald* v. *Scott* (1847) 10 D. 289.
68 *Westville Shipping Co.* v. *Abram Shipping Co.*, 1923 S.C.(H.L.) 68.
69 *Spence* v. *Crawford*, 1939 S.C.(H.L.) 52.
70 *Spence, supra.*
71 *Wright* v. *Blackwood* (1833) 11 S. 722; *Kinnear* v. *Brodie* (1901) 3 F. 540.
72 See also *Mackenzie* v. *Catton's Trs.* (1877) 5 R. 313, 317; *C.B.* v. *A.B.* (1885) 12 R.(H.L.) 36, 40; *Alexander's Trs.* v. *Muir* (1903) 5 F. 406.
73 *Cf. Cuninghame* v. *Boswell* (1868) 6 M. 890; *Robson* v. *Bywater* (1870) 8 M. 757; *Stewart* v. *North* (1893) 20 R. 260; *Chrystal* v. *C.* (1900) 2 F. 373.
74 *Harrison* v. *N. of S. Bank* (1890) 28 S.L.R. 162; *Bain* v. *Assets Co.* (1905) 7 F.(H.L.) 104; *Mackison* v. *Burgh of Dundee*, 1910 S.C.(H.L.) 27; *Lees' Trs.* v. *Duncan*, 1913 S.C.(H.L.) 12; *Miller's Exors.* v. *Miller's Trs.*, 1922 S.C. 150.

inducing the contract has been admitted, delay in pursuing a reduction will not prejudice the pursuer.

The clearest cases of personal bar are where the party entitled to challenge has expressly or impliedly ratified or homologated the transaction. Homologation may be inferred from such conduct as continuing in possession and paying rent though the lease was voidable,[75] or acceptance of rent,[76] or acceptance of money under a contract for dissolution of partnership,[77] or payment of interest on a bond,[78] or reducing a royalty payable under a lease of minerals,[79] or accepting expenses incurred in negotiations for a lease.[80]

Similarly a party has been held barred from seeking on the ground of no jurisdiction to reduce proceedings under which he had submitted to the jurisdiction.[81]

In all cases of alleged personal bar it is probably essential to show that the party seeking to reduce, but alleged to be barred, at all times knew, or at least had full opportunities and means, of knowledge of the facts justifying reduction. A man cannot be held to have delayed seeking a remedy, or to have homologated, if he was justifiably ignorant of the misrepresentation or other relevant facts.

Invalid defences

It is no defence to an action for reduction of a deed on such grounds as fraud or error that the deed, or one to the same effect, was one which the pursuer was in law bound to grant.[82]

Reduction of Administrative or Quasi-judicial Actings

Reduction is applicable not only to deeds in private relations but to documents emanating from official sources containing official decisions, not, however, amounting to decrees of court.

The actings and decisions of any person or body entrusted with administrative functions or quasi-judicial powers may sometimes be challenged by action of reduction, notwithstanding that no appeal in the ordinary sense lies to the courts from the decisions. But reduction is not competent on the merits,[83] because that would be to make the court an appeal tribunal, but only on such grounds as acting in excess of jurisdiction, acting illegally, oppressively or dishonestly, acting in a way disconform to statute, or in breach of the rules of natural justice. Nor is it

75 *Rigg* v. *Durward* (1776) Mor. Fraud, Appx. 2.
76 *Hamilton* v. *Cardross* (1712) Rob.App. 37; *Oliphant* v. *Scott* (1830) 8 S. 985.
77 *Gall* v. *Bird* (1855) 17 D. 1027.
78 *McCalman* v. *McArthur* (1864) 2 M. 678.
79 *L.A.* v. *Wemyss* (1899) 2 F.(H.L.) 1.
80 *Danish Dairy Co.* v. *Gillespie*, 1922 S.C. 656.
81 *Irvine* v. *Hart* (1869) 7 M. 723.
82 *Purdon* v. *Rowat's Trs.* (1856) 19 D. 206, 217.
83 e.g. *Mitchell* v. *Aberdeen Insurance Cttee.*, 1918 S.C. 415.

competent to challenge by reduction an interlocutor of a sheriff, to whom appeal lay against an administrative decision by a local authority, appointing parties to be heard but not disposing of the appeal.[84]

The distinction between administrative and quasi-judicial actings is important. A person entrusted with an administrative function must use his judgment and discretion in reaching a decision, but is under no obligation to hear evidence and may take a decision on his own knowledge and experience. So long as he decides in good faith and within the scope of his jurisdiction, the court cannot examine the merits of his decisions, though the extent of his jurisdiction and competence may be challenged in the courts.[85] On the other hand a person entrusted with a quasi-judicial function must act like a court, informing himself by evidence and giving parties an opportunity to be heard.

At least normally, where any mode of appeal is provided against a decision of an administrative or quasi-judicial body that appeal should be invoked and exhausted instead of reduction or at least before resort is had to action of reduction.[86]

Actings in excess of jurisdiction

If a person or body charged with administrative or quasi-judicial functions acts in excess of jurisdiction any decision reached may be reduced by the court.[87]

> " Whenever any inferior tribunal or any administrative body has exceeded the powers conferred on it by statute to the prejudice of the subject, the jurisdiction of the court to set aside such excess of power as incompetent and illegal is not open to dispute." [88] " It is within the jurisdiction of the Court of Session to keep inferior judicatories and administrative bodies right, in the sense of compelling them to obey those conditions without the fulfilment of which they have no powers whatsoever. It is within the power of the Court of Session to do that, but it is not within the power or function of the Court of Session itself to do work set by the Legislature to be performed by those administrative bodies or inferior judicatories themselves." [89]

This ground of reduction includes the plea that the conduct objected to is *ultra vires*; thus by-laws have been objected to as *ultra vires*.[90]

84 *Roxburgh C.C.* v. *Dalrymple's Trs.* (1894) 21 R. 1063; see also *Milne* v. *Aberdeen District Cttee.* (1900) 2 F. 220.

85 *Glasgow and District Restaurateurs Assocn.* v. *Dollan*, 1941 S.C. 93, 108.

86 *Caledonian Ry.* v. *Glasgow Corpn.* (1905) 7 F. 1020; *Mitchell* v. *Aberdeen Insurance Cttee.*, 1918 S.C. 415.

87 *Ashley* v. *Rothesay Mags.* (1873) 11 M. 708; *Brand* v. *Arbroath Police Commrs.* (1890) 17 R. 790; *Lundie* v. *Falkirk Mags.* (1890) 18 R. 60; *Glasgow and District Restaurateurs' Assocn.* v. *Dollan*, 1941 S.C. 93; *Glasgow Corpn.* v. *Glasgow Churches' Council*, 1944 S.C. 97. *Cf. Crosbie* v. *McMinn* (1866) 4 M. 803; *Mitchell* v. *Aberdeen Mags.* (1893) 20 R. 253.

88 *Moss' Empires* v. *Glasgow Assessor*, 1917 S.C.(H.L.) 1, 6, *per* Lord Kinnear, *cf.* Viscount Haldane at p. 4.

89 *Ibid.* 11, *per* Lord Shaw.

90 *e.g. Scott* v. *Glasgow Corpn.* (1899) 1 F.(H.L.) 51; *Glasgow and District, supra.*

Disconformity to statutory procedure

Where a statutory procedure is prescribed for any quasi-judicial proceedings that procedure must be followed out and a decision is reducible if it follows on a failure to conform to the procedure.[91] Procedural failure includes failure to give notices required,[92] failure of an advisory committee to make proper inquiry as to the pursuer's qualifications.[93]

Thus a reduction was competently but unsuccessfully brought against a presbytery, as local education authority at the time, of their sentence of deposition of a parish schoolmaster on the ground of irregularities in procedure,[94] and a similar reduction of the judgment of a school board, removing a schoolmaster, and of its confirmation by the Board of Education for Scotland, on the ground of their deviation from statutory procedure, also failed.[95] The school board, it was said: "can do nothing except under statutory authority. They can exercise no power whatever, except that which is given to them by this statute; and if they do not conform to the conditions upon which the statute authorises them to exercise that power then they are no longer acting under the statute, and their proceedings would be liable to be set aside as incompetent." [96] "If the duty is statutory this court has jurisdiction to determine whether it has been performed in the way the statute has prescribed; and if it has not, this court has jurisdiction to set it aside." [97]

Similarly a reduction was held competent of certain decisions by a returning officer at a school board election on the validity of the nomination of candidates.[98]

A licensing appeal court's refusal to grant a certificate is not reducible because a ground of objection has been stated on appeal which was not stated in the Licensing Court, as such does not constitute a contravention of any statutory provision.[99]

Actings contrary to natural justice

The main precepts or requirements of natural justice are that a person charged with any misconduct should have fair notice of the conduct charged and a fair opportunity to hear the case made against him, and to prepare and present his defence, that the person or persons deciding the issue should hear both sides, giving them equal opportunities, and that

91 *Brown* v. *Heritors of Kilberry* (1825) 4 S. 174; *Stirling* v. *Hutcheon* (1874) 1 R. 935; *Caledonian Ry.* v. *Glasgow Corpn.* (1905) 7 F. 1020; *McDonald* v. *Lanarkshire Fire Brigade Cttee.*, 1959 S.C. 141; *Palmer* v. *Inverness Hospitals Board*, 1963 S.C. 311.

92 *Moss's Empires Ltd.* v. *Assessor for Glasgow*, 1917 S.C.(H.L.) 1; *McDonald* v. *Lanarkshire Fire Brigade Cttee.*, *supra*.

93 *Hayman* v. *Lord Advocate*, 1951 S.C. 621.

94 *Sutherland* v. *Presbytery of Dornoch* (1850) 13 D. 190.

95 *Macfarlane* v. *Mochrum School Board* (1875) 3 R. 88; *cf. Robb* v. *Logiealmond School Board* (1875) 2 R. 417, 698; *Morrison* v. *Glenshiel School Board* (1875) 2 R. 715.

96 3 R. 98, *per* L.P.Inglis.

97 *Ibid.* 99.

98 *Kerr* v. *Hood*, 1907 S.C. 895.

99 *Sleigh* v. *Fraser*, 1949 S.C. 446. See also *Aldridge* v. *Simpson-Bell*, 1971 S.L.T. 188.

the person or persons deciding should have no personal interest in the result of the dispute and be free from bias.[1]

Thus reduction has been granted of decisions on the grounds that they were contrary to natural justice, as where persons who had not heard all the proceedings took part in the decision,[2] or extraneous persons or representatives of one side only of the controversy were present when the decision was arrived at,[3] or disciplinary proceedings were conducted without compliance with a discipline regulation,[4] or a teacher was dismissed without being given an opportunity to be heard.[5]

It has been questioned whether membership of an association, an object of which was to reduce the number of licensed premises, was enough to disqualify a person from sitting as member of a licensing court.[6]

Error in law other than as to jurisdiction

It is uncertain whether the court can reduce the decision of an administrative or quasi-judicial body on the ground that it has in its decision made an error in law, other than an error as to its jurisdiction, competence and powers.

The justification for allowing reduction for non-jurisdictional error in law is that if it is not permitted tribunals and authorities (which may be composed of non-lawyers) may act within their jurisdiction but by misapplying some relevant rule of law effect grave injustice. Thus if an assessor sets a value of £X on a house that may be wholly wrong, but cannot be challenged save in the Valuation Appeal Committee; but if he set the value of £X on the house in the belief that under the statutes he had in doing so to take account of the owner's income that would be error in law and, it is submitted, the decision would be reducible.

What is error of law?

It is impossible comprehensively to define error of law, but it includes ignorance or disregard or misinterpretation of any rule of statute or common law which may be relevant in the circumstances, failure to comply with any statutory requirements as to notices, publicity, intimation, inquiries and the like, and exercise of a discretion where the limits for the exercise have been misconceived or misunderstood.

Such an error may lead a tribunal or administrative authority to decline to exercise its jurisdiction, or to exercise jurisdiction in cases not properly entrusted to it, but equally may lead the tribunal or authority to exercise its jurisdiction in a mistaken or legally erroneous way. The latter is the category of case which causes difficulty.

[1] On natural justice generally see *Ridge* v. *Baldwin* [1964] A.C. 40. These principles do not necessarily apply to ordinary contracts of employment.
[2] *Goodall* v. *Bilsland*, 1909 S.C. 1152.
[3] *Barrs* v. *British Wool Marketing Board*, 1957 S.C. 72; *Palmer* v. *Inverness Hospitals Board*, 1963 S.C. 311.
[4] *McDonald* v. *Lanarkshire Fire Brigade*, 1959 S.C. 141.
[5] *Malloch* v. *Aberdeen Corpn.*, 1971 S.L.T. 245 (H.L.).
[6] *Goodall, supra.*

The Court of Session may, however, decline to treat as error of law a possible interpretation of a statutory provision relative to a matter within its area of expertise, even though another interpretation is also perfectly possible.

By the Tribunals and Inquiries Act 1971, s. 13, a party to proceedings before certain tribunals, if dissatisfied in point of law with a decision (including any direction or order) of the tribunal may appeal therefrom to the Court of Session or require the tribunal to state and sign a case for the opinion of the Court of Session.[7] Rules of Court may provide for authorising or requiring a tribunal, in the course of proceedings before it, to state a case for the opinion of the Court of Session on any question of law arising in the proceedings.[8] An appeal lies, with leave of the Court of Session or the House of Lords, from any decision of the Court of Session under this section.[9] In certain other cases special provision is made for appeals, as from industrial tribunals to the National Industrial Relations Court.[10]

Where there is provision for appeal in these ways reduction is probably incompetent if resort has not been had to the statutory form of appeal.

In cases where there is no provision for appeal it is not clear whether a remedy by reduction is competent on the ground of alleged error of law not affecting jurisdiction. In *Pryde* v. *Heritors of Ceres*[11] the court ordered cases on the general question whether it was competent to review the determinations of the heritors and kirk-session of a parish with regard to allowances for the poor. A majority of the whole court held that it was so competent and ordained the respondents to reconsider the application and make an addition thereto. Lord Cockburn observed[12]: " I presume, for example, that the court can always interfere to correct error in law. And, under this principle, I include the cases in which the heritors and session refuse to act, or in which, under pretence of performing their duty, they plainly show that they mean to invade it . . . or if they go wrong in law, etc., etc., I have no doubt that they are liable to be controlled by the Supreme Court." In *Macfarlane* v. *Mochrum School Board*[13] a schoolmaster sought to reduce a judgment of the school board removing him from office, and the confirmation thereof by the Board of Education, on the grounds of deviation from statutory procedure and of malice and oppression. The court held that it had jurisdiction to consider the first ground but that the averments on the second ground were not relevant. The boards could exercise no power except that which was given to them by statute; " and if they do not conform to the conditions upon which the statute authorises them to exercise that power then they are no longer

[7] s. 13 (1) as modified by subss. (6) and (9).
[8] s. 13 (2) as modified by subss. (6).
[9] s. 13 (6) (*c*).
[10] Industrial Relations Act 1971, s. 114.
[11] (1843) 5 D. 552.
[12] p. 557.
[13] (1875) 3 R. 88.

acting under the statute, and their proceedings would be liable not to be reviewed but to be set aside as incompetent." [14] " Review, in the proper meaning of the term, is excluded. But, at the same time, if a judgment is contrary to the statute, it can on that ground be quashed or set aside by this court. Deviation from the statute, on the part of a body created by that statute, is matter for the consideration of the Court. . . ." [15]

In *Jeffray* v. *Angus* [16] where a Dean of Guild Court had purported to act under criminal procedure statutes and to convict a person criminally, the court entertained an appeal and Lord Justice Clerk Macdonald observed [17] that that court had, like all inferior courts, "to keep a record to be reviewed by the Supreme Court, unless the keeping of a record was made unnecessary and review excluded by express enactment."

In *Moss' Empires* v. *Glasgow Assessor* [18] the House of Lords held that an action in the Court of Session for reduction of an entry in the valuation roll was competent, when it had been increased without the required statutory notice being given. Lord Haldane observed [19] that " whenever an inferior tribunal has done something contrary to law which may lead to liability or deprivation of rights, then, unless Parliament has stepped in and prevented the Court of Session declaring that to be a nullity and a noxious nullity which is a nullity and a noxious nullity, the Court of Session has power to make a declaration to that effect. That is of the very essence of the power of suspension and reduction." And Lord Kinnear observed [20]: " Now I apprehend that there can be no question at all of the jurisdiction of the Court of Session to entertain an action of that kind. Whenever any inferior tribunal or any administrative body has exceeded the powers conferred upon it by statute to the prejudice of the subject, the jurisdiction of the court to set aside such excess of power as incompetent and illegal is not open to dispute " and later [21] " Now the true objection of the pursuer is that what has been done is in excess of power—it goes beyond any power contained in the Act—and I think it is no answer to say that you cannot find fault with a departure from the provisions of the Act as regards procedure." Similarly Lord Shaw said [22]: " It is within the jurisdiction of the Court of Session to keep inferior judicatories and administrative bodies right, in the sense of compelling them to keep within the limits of their statutory powers or of compelling them to obey those conditions without the fulfilment of which they have no power whatsoever."

Again in *Ross & Coulter* v. *Inland Revenue* [23] Lord Simonds remarked:

[14] p. 98, *per* L.P. Inglis.
[15] p. 103, *per* Lord Ardmillan.
[16] 1909 S.C. 400.
[17] p. 404.
[18] 1917 S.C.(H.L.) 1. The Court of Session (1916 S.C. 366) held by 4:3, reversing the Lord Ordinary, that the action was competent.
[19] p. 4.
[20] p. 6.
[21] p. 8.
[22] p. 11.
[23] 1948 S.C.(H.L.) 1, 35.

" For though, generally, it may be said that a discretion has not been judicially exercised if its statutory basis which rests upon a true construction of the statute has been misconceived, it is convenient in this case to treat as in a separate category the failure of the Commissioners to exercise their discretion properly just because they misinterpreted the statute. A consideration of all the cases leaves me in no doubt that they did misinterpret it." Similarly Lord Morton of Henryton said [24]: " In my view the Special Commissioners have failed to exercise their discretion under proviso (ii) judicially in the present case and in others of the series of cases now under appeal. The reason for this failure is that they have misconstrued the statute in thinking that. . . ."

In *Sinclair-Lockhart's Trs.* v. *Central Land Board* [25] Lord President Cooper accepted that the Board's determination was not appealable in the ordinary way but pointed out that " there are still at least two situations in which the court may interfere—(1) if the exercise of the Board's jurisdiction has not conformed to its statutory basis, and (2) if it has not been exercised judicially. These grounds of challenge may overlap, for a judicial discretion is not judicially exercised if those exercising it have misconceived its nature and limits. . . . If the Board . . . have transgressed their statutory duty as, for example, by valuing ' the wrong thing,' we can interfere by setting their determination aside. . . ."

Contrary authorities

It must be conceded that there are decisions suggesting, but in no case, it is submitted, deciding, that, even if there is an error in law apparent from the decision of the tribunal or authority, the Court of Session may not reduce the decision if it was within the tribunal's jurisdiction.[26] Among these decisions contractual arbitrations must be regarded separately because it is well settled that an arbiter's award is not reducible for error in law.

Whether jurisdictional and non-jurisdictional error distinct

The line between error of law going to jurisdiction and error of law in other respects is a narrow one, and it may be argued that there is no distinction. Thus it may be that though a tribunal had jurisdiction to deal with a case its conduct in dealing with it may be such as to make the decision a nullity. Instances include giving a decision in bad faith, making a decision it had no power to make, failing in the course of an

[24] p. 37.

[25] 1951 S.C. 258, 269. Reference may also be made to *Campbell* v. *Brown* (1829) 3 W. & S. 441; *Edinburgh & Glasgow Ry.* v. *Meek* (1849) 12 D. 153; *Mathewson* v. *Yeaman* (1900) 2 F. 873.

[26] *e.g. Simpson* v. *Harley* (1830) 8 S. 977; *Milne* v. *Aberdeen District Cttee.* (1899) 2 F. 220; *Don Bros., Buist & Co.* v. *Scottish Insurance Commrs.*, 1913 S.C. 607; *Dante* v. *Ayr Assessor*, 1922 S.C. 109; *McEwen's Trs.* v. *Church of Scotland General Trs.*, 1940 S.L.T. 357; *Inland Revenue* v. *Barrs*, 1959 S.C. 273, 280, 301; contrary views at pp. 295, 299; majority view affirmed 1961 S.C.(H.L.) 22 (a very special case indeed).

inquiry to comply with the requirements of natural justice, in perfect good faith misconstruing the provisions giving it power to act, or refusing to take into account something it should have done.[27] To put it another way: if a tribunal has jurisdiction to deal with a matter, has it any jurisdiction to deal with it other than fairly, honestly and with strict regard to the proper intention of the relevant law?

Finality clauses—whether reduction excluded

In many cases of administrative or quasi-judicial proceedings the relevant statute provides that the decision of the tribunal, or of some other person or body such as the sheriff to whom alone appeal is competent, is to be final and not subject to review. The interpretation generally given to such a provision is that it excludes review on the merits, whether by reduction or otherwise,[28] but that reduction remains competent if relevant averments [29] are made of bias,[30] illegal conduct, such as exceeding the jurisdiction,[31] disconformity to statutory procedure,[32] infringement of the rules of natural justice,[33] or otherwise of conduct which fundamentally vitiates the proceedings or amounts to a denial of justice.[34] Any other interpretation would permit a finality clause to excuse all kinds of illegalities and injustices. In one such case [35] it was said: " The present is not a process of review. . . . It is a proceeding brought in the Court for the purpose of setting aside as incompetent and illegal the proceedings of an inferior court, and the jurisdiction of this court to entertain such an action cannot be doubted, notwithstanding the entire prohibition of review of any kind. This is not review, as I said before, but it is the interference of the Supreme Court for the purpose of keeping inferior courts within the bounds of their jurisdiction. . . ." Similarly where a statute provided that a particular matter might be challenged on specified grounds only, and in these cases not by reduction, it was held that reduction was competent when it was based on another ground.[36]

A finality clause may protect the body or tribunal in case of error of law as well as error of fact.[37]

Limitation provisions

Similarly it is thought that a statutory provision that action or complaint must be brought within a limited period of time will always be ineffective if it be relevantly averred that the conduct was vitiated in a

[27] *Anisminic Ltd.* v. *Foreign Compensation Commission* [1969] 2 A.C. 147, 171, *per* Lord Reid.
[28] *e.g. Milne* v. *Aberdeen District Cttee.* (1900) 2 F. 220.
[29] *Milne, supra,* where averments of fraud held not relevant.
[30] *Cf. Goodall* v. *Bilsland,* 1909 S.C. 1152, 1176.
[31] *Ashley* v. *Rothesay Mags.* (1873) 11 M. 708; contrast *Brand* v. *Arbroath Police Commrs.* (1890) 17 R. 790; *Walsh* v. *Pollokshaws Mags.,* 1907 S.C.(H.L.) 1; *cf. Milne, supra,* 230.
[32] *Stirling* v. *Hutcheon* (1874) 1 R. 935.
[33] *e.g.* members of licensing court absent from hearing yet voting: *Goodall, supra.*
[34] *e.g.* corruption: *Walsh, supra,* 3.
[35] *Ashley, supra,* 716, *per* L.P. Inglis.
[36] *Kerr* v. *Hood,* 1907 S.C. 895.
[37] *Milne, supra.*

fundamental respect. In *Mitchell* v. *Aberdeen Insurance Committee* [38] where an action of reduction was held barred by the (now repealed) Public Authorities Protection Act 1893, it was observed [39]: "If the proceedings had been entirely without warrant no doubt this Act would not have been a bar to a reduction. . . ."

Interdict before, or reduction after, proceedings

The question has arisen, in the context of particular statutory procedure, namely whether a veto poll under the Temperance (Scotland) Act 1913 in a burgh whose boundaries had been extended, should be in the form appropriate to a poll in a burgh where a no-licence resolution was in force or to a poll in a burgh in which a poll was to be taken for the first time, whether persons challenging the arrangements made for the poll were entitled to interdict it until the question was decided by the court, or should challenge it by *ex post facto* action of reduction.[40] In the context of the particular statutory provision the Court held that the Act contemplated reduction rather than interdict and decision prior to the poll, but this issue must depend in every case on the interpretation of any relevant provision of the statute in question.

Reduction as a Mode of Review of Decisions of Courts

In some circumstances reduction may be utilised as a mode of review of the decision of a court. The purpose is to effect restitution for the avoidance of injustice.[41] "The right of review by reduction is a common law right which has existed for a very long time, and is a mode of review which cannot be taken away except by statutory enactment." [42] "I think that . . . a reduction is the common law mode of having an error rectified and injustice avoided. . . ." [43] "A right of access to the Court of that cannot be taken away by implication. . . ." [44]

A conclusion for the reduction of an inferior court decree may be combined with further conclusions to elucidate the rights of the parties.[45]

In general, where an interlocutor, decree or other decision of any court may be reviewed by some form of appeal, under whatever name or procedure, reduction is improper and incompetent, and the appropriate form of appeal should be invoked.[46] Pursuers of actions of reduction

[38] 1918 S.C. 415.
[39] p. 437, *per* Lord Salvesen.
[40] *Anderson* v. *Kirkintilloch Mags.*, 1948 S.C. 27.
[41] *Cf. Brown* v. *Graham* (1849) 11 D. 1330.
[42] *Mathewson* v. *Yeaman* (1900) 2 F. 873, 881, *per* Lord Trayner.
[43] *Ibid.* 881, *per* Lord Young.
[44] *Taylor's Trs.* v. *McGavigan* (1896) 23 R. 945, 948, *per* Lord Kincairney, citing *Maclachlan* v. *Rutherford* (1854) 16 D. 937; *Marr* v. *Lindsay* (1881) 8 R. 784.
[45] *Taylor's Trs., supra*, 949.
[46] *Lang* v. *Irvine Presbytery* (1864) 2 M. 823; *Darney* v. *Calder District Cttee.* (1904) 7 F. 239; *Adair* v. *Colvilles*, 1926 S.C.(H.L.) 51, 56; *Philp* v. *Reid*, 1927 S.C. 224.

have sometimes been held barred by not having availed themselves of a statutory power of appeal.[47]

It does not follow that where appeal is excluded or incompetent reduction is competent,[48] but in some cases where a decision cannot be reconsidered by appeal it may be reduced. " Laying aside the case in which review is altogether excluded, I have always understood that while reduction is the appropriate mode of reviewing a final judgment where no other remedy is competent, and in certain cases where another remedy is competent, these other cases must be brought within one or other of the two categories, *viz.*, either, 1st, where the judgment has been extracted, or 2nd, where it is a judgment which falls to be executed without extract." [49]

Decrees of Particular Courts

Judgments of the House of Lords

A decree of the Court of Session may be attacked by reduction notwithstanding that it has been considered and affirmed or altered by the House of Lords on such a ground as that the decree was obtained by fraud on the court.[50] The important point is that the decree challenged is that of the Court of Session, even though it may have been reviewed by the House of Lords and ultimately affirmed or altered in conformity with the opinions expressed in the House. The judgment of the House probably cannot be challenged by way of reduction.

Judgments of the High Court of Justiciary

Judgments of the High Court cannot be examined or set aside by reduction or other civil process.[51] That court is supreme in its own sphere. " We [the judges of the Court of Session] have nothing to do with the matter any more than if this were a complaint that the Court of Justiciary had pronounced a wrong judgment, or had gone out of their way and violated their own form of process, or their Act of Adjournal." [52] The only possible mode of reopening a matter, apart from reference back to the High Court by the Secretary of State for Scotland,[53] would be to present a petition to the *nobile officium* of the High Court but the very clearest and strongest averments would have to be made. Inferior criminal courts may, however, be controlled by the Court of Session.[54]

47 *Baillie* v. *McGibbon* (1845) 8 D. 10; *Crawford* v. *Lennox* (1852) 14 D. 1629.
48 *Scoular* v. *McLaughlan* (1864) 2 M. 955, 960.
49 *Scoular*, *supra*, 962, *per* Lord Deas.
50 *Shedden* v. *Patrick* (1849) 11 D. 1333; (1850) 12 D. 694; (1852) 14 D. 721; (1854) 17 D. (H.L.) 18; 1 Macq. 535; *Longworth* v. *Yelverton* (1862) 1 M. 161; (1863) 2 M.(H.L.) 49; (1864) 3 M. 645; (1868) 7 M. 70.
51 *Strachan* v. *Commrs. of Justiciary* (1684) Mor. 7415.
52 *Stirling* v. *Holm* (1873) 11 M. 480, 487, *per* L.P. Inglis.
53 Criminal Appeal (Sc.) Act 1926, s. 16, amended by Criminal Justice (Sc.) Act 1949, s. 30 (2); *Gallacher* v. *H.M. Advocate*, 1951 J.C. 38, 49 note.
54 *Phillips* v. *Steel* (1847) 9 D. 318.

Decrees of the Court of Session

One of the attributes of a supreme court is that it has power to reduce even its own decrees,[55] and the Court of Session may reduce its own decrees. It has exclusive power to do so.[56]

Jurisdiction to reduce decrees

The Court of Session can reduce a decree of a Scottish court only if it has jurisdiction over the defender on ordinary grounds of jurisdiction. It does not have jurisdiction merely because it, or another Scottish court, granted the decree challenged. Thus where a husband by false evidence of domicile induced the Court of Session to exercise jurisdiction and to grant him a divorce it was held that that court could not subsequently reduce that decree when the husband was not personally subject to its jurisdiction.[57] The court dismissed the arguments that it had jurisdiction on the ground of necessity, or by virtue of any duty to undo the illegal decree which it had been induced to grant. This seems questionable; should the Supreme Court of a country not always accept jurisdiction to rectify errors it, or an inferior court of the country, has been led to make by the party which obtained the decree or order now challenged (as distinct from errors of fact or law it may itself have made)? It seems at least unfortunate that jurisdiction in the reduction should have depended on whether the defender was or was not personally subject to the jurisdiction of the Court of Session. If he had been subject the court would have had jurisdiction and reduction would probably have been granted.[57a]

Reduction or challenge ope exceptionis

A decree, certainly in the cases of a decree in absence and a decree *in foro*, may be challenged by reduction or, unless the court considers the matter would be more conveniently tried in a reduction, set aside *ope exceptionis* in another action.[58] In particular in a multiplepoinding this will frequently be appropriate.[59] A decree in absence, it was held, did not require to be reduced when the agreement which it sought to enforce was *ultra vires* of the other party thereto, and it was consequently *ultra vires* to submit to decree passing in absence.[60]

Though the sheriff court has power to disregard a deed or writing *ope exceptionis*,[61] this does not empower it to set aside its own decrees *ope exceptionis*.[62]

55 *Jarvie's Trs.* v. *Bannatyne*, 1927 S.C. 34, 38.
56 *Innes* v. *Dunbar* (1534) Mor. 7320.
57 *Acutt* v. *Acutt*, 1936 S.C. 386, following *Longworth* v. *Yelverton* (1868) 7 M. 70 (declarator of marriage); *Jack* v. *Jack*, 1940 S.L.T. 122. In *Corbidge* v. *Somerville*, 1913 S.C. 858 (divorce) the issue of jurisdiction was not really discussed.
57a See now Domicile and Matrimonial Proceedings Act 1973, s. 9.
58 *Fischer* v. *Andersen* (1896) 23 R. 395; *Dickson & Walker* v. *Mitchell*, 1910 S.C. 139; *Jack* v. *Jack*, 1940 S.L.T. 122.
59 *Jarvie's Trs.* v. *Bannatyne*, 1927 S.C. 34.
60 *Mason's Trs.* v. *Poole & Robinson* (1903) 5 F. 789.
61 Sheriff Courts (Sc.) Act 1907, Sch. I, r. 50.
62 *Leggat Bros.* v. *Gray*, 1912 S.C. 230.

Title and interest to reduce decree

The person against whom decree has passed has always title and interest to challenge it by reduction. The trustee on the bankrupt estate of a divorced spouse has been held entitled to bring a reduction of the decree of divorce, in a desire to recover certain marriage contract funds which were forfeited by reason of the divorce, though it was observed that a better course would have been to sue the marriage contract trustees and challenge the decree of divorce *ope exceptionis* in that action.[63] It is not at all certain that a creditor has title to reduce a decree determining the status of other persons.[63] A divorced wife has title and interest to sue her now deceased husband's trustees to reduce the decree of divorce, in view of the patrimonial consequences of being divorced.[64] A trustee in an English liquidation has been held to have no interest to reduce a Scottish sequestration of the same debtor when he made no averments of claims against the Scottish estate.[65] A person bringing a reduction in the Scottish courts for his own protection does not thereby submit himself to the jurisdiction of those courts *ex reconventione*.[66]

At least in the case where the original decree was fundamentally invalid, it has been held that the party against whom decree had passed had title and interest to reduce it without qualifying any patrimonial interest to be secured by obtaining decree of reduction, and two judges were of opinion that the party had sufficient patrimonial interest in respect that the decree precluded action for recovery of the money paid and for damages for the wrongous proceedings, and was detrimental to his credit.[67]

Personal bar against challenge of decree

A party may be barred from reducing a decree if he already homologated it, as by implementing it,[68] or by entering into any transaction with the holder of the decree which implies acceptance of it.[69] Reduction is not barred by a debt having been paid by a third party.[70]

Reduction of Court of Session decree *in foro*

A decree granted *in foro* cannot be reduced on the merits, whether on grounds of fact and/or law which the party failed to put forward in the former action, or on grounds of fact and/or law which he did put forward but which were held to be inadequate to prevent decree passing. The first set of grounds would be open to the plea of " competent and omitted,"

63 *Corbidge* v. *Somerville*, 1913 S.C. 858.
64 *Walker* v. *Walker*, 1911 S.C. 163.
65 *Gibson* v. *Munro* (1894) 21 R. 840.
66 *Davis* v. *Cadman* (1897) 24 R. 297; *Macaulay* v. *Hussain*, 1966 S.C. 204.
67 *Bruce* v. *British Motor Trading Corpn.*, 1924 S.C. 908.
68 *Philp* v. *Reid*, 1927 S.C. 224, 230, 234.
69 *Bruce* v. *British Motor Trading Corpn.*, 1924 S.C. 908, 933. See also *Sinclair* v. *Brown* (1835) 13 S. 594; (1837) 15 S. 770; (1841) 3 D. 871; *Barclay* v. *Alexander* (1846) 8 D. 549; *Gillespie* v. *Dods* (1857) 19 D. 475; *Mackenzie* v. *Smith* (1861) 23 D. 1201; *Scott* v. *Handyside's Trs.* (1868) 6 M. 753; *Grieve* v. *Burns* (1871) 9 M. 582.
70 *Beattie* v. *McLellan* (1844) 6 D. 1088, 1096.

unless a relevant case of *res noviter* can be established [71] and the other to the plea of " proponed and repelled " or of *res judicata.*[72] " On the merits " means that the pursuer may establish that the facts and law of the original action did not entitle the pursuer therein to the decree which he obtained.[73]

But such a decree may be challenged on grounds not going to the merits of the decision, such as absence of jurisdiction.[74]

Decree by default

A decree passing by default is a decree *in foro* [75] and may be reduced,[76] and inadvertence has been held a sufficient ground though requiring strong evidence to support it.[77]

Decree of consent

A pursuer has been held disentitled to have reduced a decree bearing to be pronounced of consent, when her counsel had been present at the time and she did not reclaim against it nor make any motion to have it corrected, but merely averred that her counsel did not in fact consent to the decree.[78] But reduction of such a decree might be competent if it could be established that there had not in fact been consent.

Decrees of absolvitor

It has been questioned whether the Court of Session can reduce a decree of absolvitor, at least where there is no petitory or declaratory conclusion combined with the reduction, though it has been observed that if the decree of absolvitor were sought to be reduced on the ground of informality no such conclusions would be necessary.[79] There seems, however, to be no necessary incompetency in reduction of a decree of absolvitor, though to seek to reduce an absolvitor and to re-assert the same claim as previously failed can competently be countered by the plea of *res judicata.*[80]

Decree in absence

Reduction is not competent so long as a defender against whom decree has passed may apply to be reponed. After the reponing days have elapsed a decree in absence may be reduced. It may be reduced where the decree

[71] *Cheape* v. *Lord Advocate* (1871) 9 M. 377; *Stewart* v. *Gelot* (1871) 9 M. 1057.

[72] Ersk. IV, 3, 3; *Cleland* v. *Paterson* (1842) 5 D. 345; *Carmichael* v. *Anstruther* (1866) 4 M. 842.

[73] Maclaren, *Practice*, 693; *J. and J.* v. *C's Tutor*, 1948 S.C. 636.

[74] These grounds are discussed separately, *infra.*

[75] *Forrest* v. *Dunlop* (1875) 3 R. 15.

[76] *Mackenzie* v. *Munro* (1894) 22 R. 45.

[77] *Forrest, supra*, 16.

[78] *Lauder* v. *National Bank*, 1918, 1 S.L.T. 43.

[79] *Ramsay* v. *Bruce* (1849) 12 D. 243.

[80] *Mackintosh's Tr.* v. *Stewart's Trs.* (1906) 8 F. 467.

has been extracted but not implemented,[81] or where it can be put into execution without being extracted,[82] and this seems to be the only case where reduction is competent when the decree has not been extracted.[83] Reduction is not appropriate save where the decree has been put into execution, or where, as in actions of declarator or of interdict, the decree requires nothing to be paid or performed to satisfy it.[84]

Reduction is competent either on the merits, *i.e.* on averment and proof that the facts and law did not entitle the pursuer in the earlier action to decree. In such a case the onus is on the pursuer in the reduction to show that the decree was unwarranted.[85] Alternatively, the decree may be challenged on grounds not going to the merits, such as absence of jurisdiction, or fraud on the court.[86]

The reduction may be brought at any time before the decree has become equivalent to a decree *in foro, i.e.* until sixty days after the expiry of a charge on the decree, or twenty years after the date of a decree on which a charge is not competent, provided in either case that the action was served on the defender personally, or that he entered appearance to defend,[87] or in any other case until forty years from the decree.[88] A decree in absence may also be challenged *ope exceptionis* in an action of multiplepoinding [89] and a decree of divorce in an undefended case challenged *ope exceptionis* in an action for payment of trust funds.[90]

Grounds for reduction of decree in foro

The general principle is that reduction may not be granted on the merits, that is, merely on averments that the interlocutor, decree or other decision was unwarranted on the facts, or granted under an erroneous view of the law, because if that were so a reduction would be in substance merely a further appeal, and would always be available where the ordinary mode of appeal had been neglected or exhausted, or even where no appeal in the ordinary sense was permitted. " Reduction has been the common law remedy for such a case of hardship for which in any civilised country there must be a remedy. . . . I should give no countenance to the notion that we should allow actions of reduction to be substituted for and come in the place of appeals. . . . I think the court would not entertain, and I should not myself be at all prepared to assent to the court entertaining, an action of reduction to serve the purpose of an ordinary appeal. . . ." [1]

81 *McLeod* v. *Collie* (1869) 42 Sc.Jur. 62.
82 *Jack* v. *Umpherston* (1837) 15 S. 833.
83 *Scoular* v. *McLaughlan* (1864) 2 M. 955.
84 Ersk. IV, 3, 8.
85 *Dingwall* v. *Burns* (1871) 9 M. 582; *Bald* v. *Bald,* 1938 S.N. 3.
86 *Graham* v. *Graham* (1881) 9 R. 327; *Walker* v. *Walker,* 1911 S.C. 163; *Corbidge* v. *Somerville,* 1913 S.C. 858, 866. These grounds are discussed separately, *infra.*
87 Court of Session Act 1868, s. 24; *Bald* v. *Bald,* 1938 S.N. 3.
88 *Cf. Philp* v. *Reid,* 1927 S.C. 224, 231.
89 *Jarvie's Trs.* v. *Bannatyne,* 1927 S.C. 34.
90 *Corbidge* v. *Somerville,* 1913 S.C. 858.
1 *Mathewson* v. *Yeaman* (1900) 2 F. 873, 881, *per* Lord Young.

Nor is reduction competent if by choice or oversight appeal was not taken, or not taken timeously,[2] nor if a plea was not taken in the former action.[3]

Grounds for reduction—no jurisdiction

Reduction is in general competent where a court has exercised a jurisdiction which, it is averred, it did not truly possess under its own rules of law and practice, whether that assumption of jurisdiction was *per incuriam*,[4] or was induced by averments and evidence dishonestly made by a party.[5] No doubt a decree granted in excess of jurisdiction is a nullity but until reduced it stands on the books of the court with nothing to indicate that it was unjustifiably granted and may give rise to difficulties if the holder of the decree tries to enforce it.

In a consistorial case it was observed: "But if the Court and the House of Lords were, by the misrepresentation or concealment of parties, led to pronounce judgments which they had not the jurisdiction to pronounce, the party conceiving herself to be injured is not without remedy, for the courts of the country in which the parties are domiciled will not be bound by any judgment of this Court and the House of Lords which these tribunals can be shown to have had no jurisdiction to pronounce."[6] But this does not get over the difficulty that the decree stands in the records.

But before it can reduce a decree the Court of Session must have jurisdiction over the defender in the action of reduction and, if it has not, it cannot competently reduce the decree, even though that decree was one which it had not truly had jurisdiction to grant in the first place.[7] Jurisdiction to reduce cannot, it has been held, be founded merely on the need to undo what the court illegally did by its former judgment. Hence, to set aside a decree of divorce the defender must have been cited when personally present in Scotland.[7] If there is no jurisdiction to reduce the decree it must stand, because no court outwith Scotland can reduce a Scottish decree, though a court outwith Scotland could, if apprised of the facts, treat it as a nullity. This is an unsatisfactory state of the law and it would be only reasonable if the Court of Session asserted a jurisdiction to rectify its own mistake in granting the former decree, on the ground of necessity or of reconvention.

The courts of each country have jurisdiction to liquidate the affairs of debtors within their own jurisdiction and accordingly it was held incompetent to seek to reduce the sequestration of, and the appointment of a trustee on the estates of, a Scottish debtor on the ground that the court

[2] *Philp* v. *Reid*, 1927 S.C. 224.

[3] *Carmichael* v. *Anstruther* (1866) 4 M. 842.

[4] This is error in law on the part of the court. The error in *Bruce* v. *British Motor Trading Corpn.*, 1924 S.C. 908, would appear to be of this kind.

[5] *Longworth* v. *Yelverton* (1868) 7 M. 70; *Corbidge* v. *Somerville*, 1913 S.C. 858; *Acutt* v. *Acutt*, 1936 S.C. 386; *Macaulay* v. *Hussain*, 1966 S.C. 204.

[6] *Longworth* v. *Yelverton* (1868) 7 M. 70, 74, *per* L.P. Inglis.

[7] *Longworth* v. *Yelverton* (1868) 7 M. 70; *Acutt* v. *Acutt*, 1936 S.C. 386, followed in *Jack* v. *Jack*, 1940 S.L.T. 122. See now Domicile and Matrimonial Proceedings Act 1973, s. 9.

had had no jurisdiction by reason of the existence, unknown to all parties, of a prior liquidation of the debtor's estates in England.[8] The existence of bankruptcy proceedings elsewhere may be a ground for refusing a petition for sequestration in Scotland, or for recalling it, but prior sequestration elsewhere does not deprive the court of jurisdiction and, if granted, it is not a nullity.[9]

A reduction of a decree *in foro* on this ground may be incompetent.[10]

Grounds for reduction—defective citation

The plea that a party was not properly cited in an action in which decree passed against him, which decree he now seeks to reduce, goes to jurisdiction, but is a distinct matter. If the party was not properly cited the court cannot exercise jurisdiction over him, unless there have been actings held to have the effect of dispensing with citation or curing defective citation.[11]

Grounds for reduction—fraud on the court

Fraud on the court covers all dishonest misrepresentation to or concealment from the court of any fact which, if known, would have led it to decline to hear the case or to refuse the remedy sought.[12] "There can be no doubt that if a judgment of a Court be obtained by fraud—that is to say, if the person who obtains the judgment, although it be a judgment *in foro*, comes into Court with false representations, which he knows to be false, for the purpose of obtaining his decree upon these false representations, and succeeds in deceiving both his opponents and the Court—that is a relevant ground of reduction."[13] The principle covers collusive agreements and concealment of the fact that a matrimonial offence had been condoned. Thus in an action of reduction of a decree of divorce Lord President Dunedin said[14]: "I have no doubt whatever that, apart from all question of collusion, it would be a good ground of reduction of a decree of divorce if it could be shewn that the party getting the decree had intentionally kept back from the court the fact that there had been condonation, and had also so arranged matters, by keeping away from the witness-box by persuasion the only person who was likely to say much about it, namely, the other spouse, as to make it unlikely that anything that would excite the suspicions of the Judge would appear. . . . When we are asked to set aside that judgment [of the Lord Ordinary], I

8 *Gibson* v. *Munro* (1894) 21 R. 840.

9 *Tennent* v. *Martin & Dunlop* (1879) 6 R. 786; *Fletcher* v. *Anderson* (1883) 10 R. 835.

10 Maclaren, *Practice*, 695.

11 *Cf. Bruce* v. *British Motor Trading Corpn.*, 1924 S.C. 908.

12 *Stewart* v. *Stewart* (1863) 1 M. 449; *Breadalbane* v. *Breadalbane's Trs.* (1868) 6 M. 807, 816; *Graham* v. *Graham* (1881) 9 R. 327; *Walker* v. *Walker*, 1911 S.C. 163; *Acutt* v. *Acutt*, 1936 S.C. 386.

13 *Breadalbane* v. *Breadalbane's Trs.* (1868) 6 M. 807, 816, *per* L.P. Inglis, citing *Shedden* v. *Patrick* (1854) 17 D.(H.L.) 18.

14 *Walker*, *supra*, 169.

think it is absolutely necessary that there should be conclusive proof of the fact that something was concealed from the court. . . ." [15]

It has been said [16] that " if reduction of a decree is to be obtained on the ground of fraud, it can only be where the fraud is something extrinsic to what happened in the former trial, and whether that can be made out is an issue of fact."

Under the head of fraud on the court, perjured evidence or suborning witnesses to commit perjury require consideration. In general a decree cannot be set aside on the ground that perjury was committed by party or witnesses in obtaining it: if the court or jury believed the witnesses it is not open to the disappointed party later to assert that what the witnesses said was deliberately not true.[17] If challenge by reduction were competent on such averments every decision on fact could be challenged, and there would be no end to investigation of the facts. There may be an exception if it has been admitted, or proved independently, as in a prosecution for perjury, that the evidence was deliberately false, because a party should not be allowed to enjoy the benefit of a decree obtained by deliberately false evidence. No doubt a decree cannot be challenged because the court or jury believed what may have been inaccurate evidence but it is regrettable that even the strongest averments of perjury will not, in general, suffice to ground an action of reduction. Moreover, the distinction between giving perjured evidence and intentionally concealing from the court a relevant defence, such as condonation,[18] is very narrow.

Subornation of perjury on the other hand has always been held a relevant ground of reduction, because a party cannot be allowed to benefit by his own fraud.[19] " Subornation of perjury is a plain issue of fact, and can be proved by examining witnesses as to what actually happened. But when it is the evidence of one of the parties himself that is said to be perjured, how are you to proceed to prove that he suborned himself to commit perjury? " [20]

Grounds for reduction—res noviter veniens ad notitian

A reduction of a decree is not competent merely on the basis of averments that the pursuer did not know certain facts when he made his claim or defence in the previous action and that in consequence decree went against him. But it may be if there are relevant averments of *res noviter*.[21]

15 *Walker, supra,* 170.

16 *Mackintosh's Tr.* v. *Stewart's Trs.* (1906) 8 F. 467, 474, *per* L.P. Dunedin.

17 *Forster* v. *Forster* (1871) 9 M. 445; *Lockyer* v. *Ferryman* (1877) 4 R.(H.L.) 32; *Flower* v. *Lloyd* (1878) 10 Ch.D. 327; *Begg* v. *Begg* (1889) 16 R. 550; *Mackintosh's Tr.* v. *Stewart's Trs.* (1906) 8 F. 467; *McCarroll* v. *McKinstery,* 1926 S.C.(H.L.) 1, 6; *Greenwood* v. *Mundle,* 1958 S.L.T.(Notes) 11.

18 *Cf. Walker, supra,* 169–170.

19 *Forster, supra*; *Begg, supra*; *Snodgrass* v. *Hunter* (1899) 2 F. 76; *Mackintosh's Tr., supra*; *Sands* v. *Sands,* 1964 S.L.T. 80.

20 *Mackintosh's Tr., supra,* 474, *per* L.P. Dunedin.

21 Stair IV, 1, 44; Ersk. IV, 3, 3; *Cheape* v. *Lord Advocate* (1871) 9 M. 377, 393; *Stewart* v. *Gelot* (1871) 9 M. 1057.

"Nothing can be *res noviter* that was within the power of the party to discover with ordinary care." [22] *Res noviter* "must refer to some fact which not only was not known, but could not have been known, or that at all events could not, with reasonable care and precaution, have been known before." [23] "But in order to make way for the plea of *res noviter*, it must be shown that the party was excusably ignorant of how matters stood." [24] Matters of law cannot be pleaded as *res noviter* because a party cannot plead ignorance of law; if he does not know the relevant law he should have taken advice and become informed of it. If he has been misadvised he may have a remedy against his adviser. Relevant averments of facts newly discovered and material to the rightness of the decree may found an action of reduction, but the facts must be very clearly *res noviter*, and there must be no fault attributable to the pursuer in not having known, or found, them previously.[25] "There is abundant authority for saying that, where the pursuer relies on *res noviter*, he must not merely aver that something material has newly come to his knowledge, but he must aver it with such circumstantiality as will show that he could not by the exercise of reasonable diligence have known of it in time to have made use of it in the original action. He must give particulars of its discovery and of the circumstances which bear upon the possibility of his having acquired earlier knowledge of it. As reasonable diligence is relative to the person of whom it is required, and to his position and surroundings, it is admissible to take into account what is known of the pursuer and his history in this connexion." [26] But a fact known but forgotten and later remembered is not *res nova*,[27] and the onus of showing why it could not have been produced earlier is a heavy one.[28]

Grounds for reduction—departure from procedure or practice

A decree may be reduced if granted in circumstances amounting to departure from the rules of procedure or the practice of the court, as where a decree by default had been granted and there had not yet been default.[29] This principle might extend to private communication between one party or his representatives and the judge or judges, or to actual corruption of the court.[30]

Mere irregularity in procedure is not a sufficient ground for reduction.[31]

22 *Campbell* v. *Campbell* (1865) 3 M. 501, 504, *per* L.P. McNeill.
23 *Stewart* v. *Gelot* (1871) 9 M. 1057, 1060, *per* L.J.C. Moncreiff.
24 *Ibid.* 1065, *per* Lord Neaves. See also *Barbour* v. *McGauchie* (1828) 7 S. 18; *N.B. Ry.* v. *Brown, Gordon & Co.* (1856) 18 D. 1283; (1857) 19 D. 840; *Longworth* v. *Yelverton* (1865) 3 M. 645; *Cheape, supra*; *Macintosh* v. *Smith* (1878) 6 R. 206.
25 *Stewart, supra.*
26 *McCarroll* v. *McKinstery*, 1926 S.C.(H.L.) 1, 7, *per* Lord Sumner.
27 *Barbour* v. *McGauchie* (1828) 7 S. 18; *Dixon* v. *Graham* (1817) 5 Dow 266; *McWhirter* v. *Guthrie* (1822) 1 S. 354, is contrary but disapproved in *McCarroll, supra*, 10. See also *Coul* v. *Ayr C.C.*, 1909 S.C. 422.
28 *Dumbarton Mags.* v. *Campbell* (1813) 5 Dow 266; *Grahame* v. *Grahame* (1822) 1 W. & S. 353; *McCarroll, supra.*
29 *Hog* v. *Hog* (1837) 15 S. 532.
30 *Stirling* v. *Holm* (1873) 11 M. 480.
31 *Cf. Ritchie* v. *Littlejohn* (1899) 1 F. 1097.

Grounds for reduction—appearance unauthorised

Where a decree passed *in foro* it was held, on averments that appearance by counsel and agent in the process had been unauthorised, that reduction was necessary, and suspension incompetent.[32]

Grounds for reduction—mistakes

Reduction has sometimes been allowed to rectify mistakes in decrees. Thus reduction has been granted where decree had been granted for a sum brought out by wrong calculation and the wrong figure had not been acquiesced in,[33] and where the interlocutor did not conform to the court's judgment.[34]

Grounds for reduction—inherent nullity

Reduction is competent if in some other respect the proceedings leading to the decree were inherently null.[35] But informality in some respect does not amount to inherent nullity.[35]

Evidence in support of reduction

The court will always look for clear and cogent evidence before setting aside a decree. In a reduction of a decree of divorce it has been held that it was competent to look at the evidence in the original divorce action.[36]

A reduction of a decree of divorce, or probably of any consistorial decree or one affecting status, is itself a consistorial action and one affecting status, and accordingly no decree can be pronounced in absence, but only if the grounds of reduction are substantiated by evidence.[37]

Reduction of decrees and suspension of decrees

The general rule has been stated [38] to be, that where suspension of an extracted decree is competent, reduction is not. The argument that suspension and reduction are coordinate remedies, and that if one is available the other is also, has been expressly disapproved.[39] But while not always both competent, in some circumstances reduction and suspension may both be competent, as in the case of an extracted decree.[40]

Decrees of interdict

Once decree of perpetual interdict has become final it can be set aside

[32] *Hamilton* v. *Marshall*, Nov. 25, 1813, F.C. *Cf. Riach* v. *Wallace* (1899) 2 F. 149.
[33] *Brown* v. *Graham* (1849) 11 D. 1330.
[34] *Mathewson* v. *Yeaman* (1900) 2 F. 873.
[35] *Munro* v. *Rose* (1855) 18 D. 292, 295.
[36] *Stewart* v. *Stewart* (1863) 1 M. 449.
[37] *Acutt* v. *Acutt*, 1935 S.C. 525.
[38] *Martin* v. *Barclay* (1844) 6 D. 1136, approved by Lord Ardmillan in *Scoular* v. *McLaughlan* (1864) 2 M. 955, 963.
[39] *Scoular*, *supra*, 960, 963.
[40] *Scoular*, *supra*, 960; *McLeod* v. *Collie* (1869) 7 S.L.R. 64.

normally only by reduction. In *Bowie*,[41] however, the court, in granting an unopposed petition to the *nobile officium* to do something inconsistent with a decree of perpetual interdict granted a century earlier, made no reference to the fact that the petitioners had taken no steps to have the decree of perpetual interdict reduced. It raises the question whether averments of necessity, or at least strong expediency, in changed circumstances when the proposed action aroused no opposition would justify reduction, and the decision implies an affirmative answer.

Jury verdict

A reduction of a jury verdict, and of the interlocutor applying the verdict, is competent, though not merely on allegations that the party seeking to reduce had not appeared at the jury trial, had been unable to find money to pay for the trial, and had not had notice of the trial.[42]

Settlements and compromises authorised by court

Where any dispute has been settled or compromised and the court has approved it or interponed authority to it, the agreement and the court's relative interlocutor may both be reduced if it is established that the underlying basis of the settlement was misstated or did not justify the settlement made,[43] or there was concealment or non-disclosure.[44]

Exclusion of reduction

" The right of review by reduction is a common law right which has existed for a very long time, and is a mode of review which cannot be taken away except by statutory enactment." [45] The right to challenge a decision by reduction may be excluded by statute, but this must be done clearly and expressly, and will not readily be held to have been done by implication.[46] Moreover, where statute provides that the proceedings of an inferior court or of a statutory body are to be final, this provision is normally read as applicable exclusively to procedure which is *intra vires* and regular, and does not affect the power to reduce fundamental nullities.[47] " Proceedings such as are here complained of . . . would not be an irregularity in the execution of the Act . . . but would be a proceeding fundamentally illegal—oppression under the name of the Act, but without any warrant under, or foundation in the Act—to which, therefore, reduction is the appropriate remedy." [48]

41 1967 S.C. 36.
42 *Gilchrist* v. *Gilchrist* (1844) 7 D. 214.
43 *Assets Co. Ltd.* v. *Bain's Trs.* (1904) 6 F. 692; reversed on another ground (1905) 7 F.(H.L.) 104.
44 *Assets Co. Ltd.* v. *Phillips' Trs.* (1904) 6 F. 754; reversed on another ground (1905) 7 F. (H.L.) 104.
45 *Mathewson* v. *Yeaman* (1900) 2 F. 873, 881, *per* Lord Young.
46 *Marr* v. *Lindsay* (1881) 8 R. 784, 785; *Mathewson* v. *Yeaman* (1900) 2 F. 873, 880.
47 *Manson* v. *Smith* (1861) 3 M. 492; *Breadalbane* v. *Breadalbane's Trs.* (1868) 6 M. 807, 817, 819; *Walsh* v. *Pollokshaws Mags*, 1907 S.C.(H.L.) 1; *Goodall* v. *Bilsland*, 1909 S.C. 1152; *Moss' Empires* v. *Glasgow Assessor*, 1917 S.C.(H.L.) 1.
48 *Ferguson* v. *Malcolm* (1850) 12 D. 732, 734, *per* L.J.C. Hope.

Finality clauses—whether reduction excluded

Statute may provide that no appeal from or review of decisions of a particular court shall be competent, or that they shall be competent only on defined grounds. The principle deducible from cases dealing with attempts by reduction to review decisions in some such cases has been stated [49] to be: " That where the judgment or conviction complained of amounts to an excess of power, the court will give redress, if there be no remedy provided in the special Act; but where what is complained of is only irregularity of procedure [50] or error in judgment, review will be excluded."

Lands Valuation Appeal Court

The Lands Valuation Appeal Court is a supreme court in its own sphere and its decisions cannot be reviewed by reduction or otherwise in the Court of Session.[51] But the conduct of a local valuation appeal committee or an assessor is subject to the reductive jurisdiction of the Court of Session if it, or he, has acted *ultra vires* or in a manner not authorised by statute or contrary to natural justice.

Teind Court

The Teind Court is supreme in its own sphere and its decisions cannot be reduced by the Court of Session.[52] The Teind Court itself may entertain an action of reduction of, and it was held that it could actually reduce one of its own decrees, approving a report by a sub-commission for the valuation of teinds and interponing authority thereto, on the ground that the decree was disconform to the sub-commissioners' report and contained a fundamental error.[53] In other cases reduction seems to be competent only on the ground of fraud or other ground independent of the merits.[54]

A reduction of a decision of a sheriff and, on appeal, the Lord Ordinary on Teinds, under the Ecclesiastical Buildings and Glebes Act 1868, under which Act the latter's decision was final, was held incompetent when there was neither an excess of jurisdiction nor a refusal to exercise it: " before we could set aside the decisions of the sheriff and the Lord Ordinary, it would require to be shown not only that these judges had erred on the merits but that they had done something not warranted by their powers, in other words, something *ultra vires*, or, as I observe it is otherwise put, that they had refused to exercise their jurisdiction." [55]

49 *Riach* v. *Wallace* (1899) 2 F. 149, 151 *per* Lord Kincairney, citing *Cumming* v. *Spencer* (1868) 6 M. 156; *Pringle* v. *Robertson* (1887) 14 R. 474; *McLean* v. *McKenzie* (1895) 3 S.L.T. 142.

50 *e.g. Crombie* v. *McEwan* (1861) 23 D. 333; *Lennon* v. *Tully* (1879) 8 R. 1253; *Gray* v. *Smart* (1892) 19 R. 692.

51 *Stirling* v. *Holm* (1873) 11 M. 480; *Abercromby* v. *Badenoch* (1909) 47 S.L.R. 18; see also *Moss' Empires* v. *Glasgow Assessor*, 1917 S.C.(H.L.) 1, 7.

52 *Moss' Empires, supra*, 7.

53 *McNeill's Trs.* v. *Campbell* (1872) 11 M. 211.

54 *Abercromby* v. *Erskine* (1800) Mor. *voce* Teinds, Appx. 8.

55 *Earl of Camperdown* v. *Auchterarder Presbytery* (1902) 5 F. 61.

Courts of the Church of Scotland

Within their proper sphere courts of the Church of Scotland are supreme but their decisions are subject to reduction if there is excess of jurisdiction or essential illegality.[56]

Courts-martial

Appeal lies under certain conditions to the Courts-Martial Appeal Court and to the House of Lords but reduction is probably competent in the event of illegality or injustice falling outwith the scope of appeal.

Inferior courts

The Court of Session may reduce the decisions of inferior civil courts which act illegally or improperly. This action of reduction " is a proceeding brought in the court for the purpose of setting aside as incompetent and illegal the proceedings of an inferior court, and the jurisdiction of this Court to entertain such an action cannot be doubted, notwithstanding the entire prohibition of review of any kind. This is not review, as I said before, but it is the interference of the Supreme Court for the purpose of keeping inferior courts within the bounds of their jurisdiction." [57]

" It is within the jurisdiction of the Court of Session to keep inferior judicatories and administrative bodies right in the sense of compelling them to keep within the limits of their statutory powers or of compelling them to obey those conditions without the fulfilment of which they have no powers whatsoever." [58]

The Court of Session may accordingly reduce decrees of the sheriff court in its civil capacity (excluding the Sheriff Small Debt Court).

A sheriff court decree cannot be set aside *ope exceptionis* in a sheriff court action under the rule which permits that court to consider objections by way of exception without the necessity for reduction.[59]

Reduction is not an alternative to appeal, and is not competent if the pursuer can avail himself, or should have availed himself, of some form of appeal.[60]

Decrees of the sheriff court

The general rule is that the judgment of an inferior court cannot be brought under review by reduction until the decree has been extracted.[61]

A decree in absence of the sheriff court may be reduced by the Court of Session in the same circumstances as a decree in absence of the Court of Session itself.[62]

56 *Brown* v. *Heritors of Kilbery* (1825) 3 S. 480; on appeal, as *Campbell* v. *Brown* (1829) 3 W. & S. 441, 448; *Lang* v. *Irvine Presbytery* (1864) 2 M. 823; *Gray* v. *Anderson* (1893) 20 R. 941.

57 *Ashley* v. *Rothesay Mags.* (1873) 11 M. 708, 716, *per* L.P. Inglis.

58 *Moss' Empires* v. *Glasgow Assessor*, 1917 S.C.(H.L.) 1, 11, *per* Lord Shaw.

59 *Leggat Bros.* v. *Gray*, 1912 S.C. 230.

60 *Tough's Tr.* v. *Edinburgh Parish Council*, 1918 S.C. 107.

61 *Scoular* v. *McLaughlan* (1864) 2 M. 955, 960.

62 *McLachlan* v. *Rutherford* (1856) 16 D. 937. The sheriff may (Sheriff Courts (Sc.) Act 1907, r. 27) repone a defender at any time before implement of the decree.

A decree *in foro*, if it has been extracted [63] or cannot be extracted [64] may be reviewed by way of reduction. If it can be, but has not been, extracted, it cannot be reviewed unless reduction should be the only competent remedy.[65]

It may also be reduced on the ground of incompetency of the proceedings, or irregularity,[66] or fraud on the court,[67] or such a miscarriage of justice as renders the proceedings fundamentally null.[68]

A decree by default may be reduced, but caution for expenses may be demanded.[69] A decree cannot be reduced merely because it had been allowed by mistake to pass.[70]

At common law reduction was a competent process by which to submit to review a sheriff court decree of removing [71]; and this has not been affected by statute which substituted suspension for advocation as the normal mode of review.[72]

A decree of court is not a " deed or writing " capable of being set aside in the sheriff court by exception, under the statutory power to do so.[73]

Unextracted decrees

Where an interlocutor or decree is extractable but has not been extracted reduction is in general incompetent.[74] " The general rule is that the judgment of an inferior court cannot be brought under review by reduction until the decree has been extracted." [75] " The general rule is that a judgment not extracted, or not tantamount to an extracted decree, cannot be brought under review by reduction, unless in circumstances where there is no other remedy available." [76]

There are, however, certain exceptional cases, " as where, by reason of the nature of the proceeding, the judgment or deliverance, though final, is not extractable, but may be put into immediate execution without extract, or where the judgment is a final decree of absolvitor, and in circumstances in which neither advocation nor suspension is available." [77] Examples are where a warrant of imprisonment granted by justices could

63 *Watt Bros.* v. *Foyn* (1879) 7 R. 126; *Weir* v. *Tudhope* (1892) 19 R. 858; *Taylor's Trs.* v. *McGavigan* (1896) 23 R. 945; *Mathewson* v. *Yeaman* (1900) 2 F. 873.
64 *Holmes* v. *Tassie* (1828) 6 S. 394; *cf. Jack* v. *Umpherston* (1837) 15 S. 833.
65 *Scoular* v. *McLaughlan* (1864) 2 M. 955, 961.
66 *Macdonald* v. *McKessack* (1888) 16 R. 168; *Mackenzie* v. *Munro* (1894) 22 R. 45; *cf. Brennan* v. *Central S. M. T. Co.*, 1947 S.N. 7.
67 *Adair* v. *Colvilles*, 1926 S.C.(H.L.) 51, 56.
68 *Adair, supra. Cf. Tough's Tr.* v. *Edinburgh Parish Council*, 1918 S.C. 107, 115.
69 *Campbell* v. *McCance*, 1929 S.L.T. 26.
70 *Stewart* v. *Lothians Construction (Edinburgh) Ltd.*, 1972 S.L.T.(Notes) 75.
71 *Johnstone* v. *Dickson* (1831) 9 S. 452; *Hog* v. *Hog* (1837) 15 S. 532; *McDonald* v. *Sinclair* (1843) 5 D. 1253; *McDougall* v. *Galt* (1863) 1 M. 1012; *Taylor's Trs.* v. *McGavigan* (1896) 23 R. 945; *Mathewson* v. *Yeaman* (1900) 2 F. 873; *Graham, supra.*
72 *Graham* v. *Stirling*, 1922 S.C. 90.
73 Sheriff Courts (Sc.) Act 1907, Sch. I, r. 50; *Neil* v. *McNair* (1901) 3 F. (J.) 85; *Leggat Bros.* v. *Gray*, 1912 S.C. 230.
74 *Buchanan* v. *Lumsden* (1837) 15 S. 958; *Broom* v. *Anderson* (1837) 15 S. 977; *Coutts* v. *Keith's Exors.* (1843) 6 D. 125; *Scoular* v. *McLaughlan* (1864) 2 M. 955. *Cf. Macrae's Trs.* v. *Lord Lyon*, 1927 S.L.T. 285.
75 *Scoular, supra*, 960, *per* L.P. McNeill.
76 *Ibid.* 961, *per* L.P. McNeill.
77 *Ibid.* 962, *per* L.P. McNeill.

be put into execution without being extracted,[78] or the decree was one for absolvitor with expenses which could not be advocated because of the smallness of the sum involved.[79]

Non-extractable decree

Where a decree is of a kind which cannot be extracted reduction thereof is competent.[80]

Award of sequestration

Reduction of an award of sequestration is competent,[81] but only in very exceptional and special circumstances, and where recall under the Bankruptcy Act is not open.[82] Goudy suggests that, when recall has become incompetent, owing to lapse of time, reduction might be brought on such a ground as that the award had been obtained by forgery or gross fraud,[83] or if in awarding sequestration the judge had disregarded the Act of Parliament either intentionally or by inadvertence, as by awarding sequestration without having before him any evidence of citation of the defender.[84]

In respect of subsequent proceedings in sequestration a reduction of a sheriff's interlocutor is probably competent if the proceedings were fundamentally null.[85]

Decrees of the Sheriff Small Debt Court

By the Small Debt (Scotland) Act 1837, s. 30, no small debt decree shall be subject to reduction, advocation, suspension or appeal, or any other form of review or stay of execution, either on account of any omission or irregularity or informality in the citation or proceedings,[86] or on the merits, or on any ground or reason whatever, but (s. 31) appeal may be taken to the High Court of Justiciary, but only if founded on corruption or malice and oppression on the part of the sheriff,[87] or on such deviations in point of form from the statutory enactments as the court shall think took place wilfully, or prevented substantial justice from being done, or on incompetency,[88] including defect of jurisdiction of the sheriff. But where the

78 *Jack* v. *Umpherston* (1837) 15 S. 833, quoted in *Scoular, supra*, 961.
79 Example quoted in *Scoular, supra*, 961.
80 *Holmes* v. *Tassie* (1826) 6 S. 394; *Jack* v. *Umpherston* (1837) 15 S. 833; *Taylor's Trs.* v. *McGavigan* (1896) 23 R. 945, 948.
81 *Gibson* v. *Munro* (1894) 21 R. 840; *Whitlie* v. *Gibb* (1898) 25 R. 412; *Central Motor Engineering Co.* v. *Gibbs*, 1917 S.C. 490; *Central Motor Engineering Co.* v. *Galbraith*, 1918 S.C. 755.
82 *Central Motor Eng. Co.* v. *Galbraith*, 1918 S.C. 755, 769. *Cf. Reid* v. *Somerville & Co.* (1889) 16 R. 751.
83 *Bankruptcy*, 3rd ed., 164 (4th ed., 147) approved in 1918 S.C. 755, 770; *cf. Whitlie, supra.*
84 *Central Motor Co.*, 1918 S.C. 755, 770.
85 *Tough's Tr.* v. *Edinburgh Parish Council*, 1918 S.C. 107.
86 *Cf. Lennon* v. *Tully* (1879) 6 R. 1253; *Robertson* v. *Pringle* (1887) 14 R. 474; *Quinn* v. *Walker*, 1940 S.L.T. 172.
87 *Scottish N.E. Ry.* v. *Matthews* (1866) 5 Irv. 237; *McKenzie* v. *McPhee* (1889) 2 White 188; *Henderson* v. *National Telephone Co.*, 1909 S.C.(J.) 46; *Robson* v. *Menzies*, 1913 S.C.(J.) 90; *McCulloch* v. *McLaughlin*, 1930 J.C. 8.
88 Said in *Murchie* v. *Fairbairn* (1863) 1 M. 800, 802, to cover any incompetency.

purpose is not to review a decision, but to annul vitiated proceedings, reduction is competent, as on the ground of fundamental nullity of the proceedings,[89] or of irregularities after decree.[90] These provisions have been repealed with effect from the time when small debt proceedings are replaced by summary causes.[91]

Decrees of the J.P. Small Debt Court

Under the Justices of the Peace Small Debt (Scotland) Act 1825, s. 14, a decree of the justices in the exercise of their Small Debt jurisdiction is not subject to advocation, suspension, appeal or other stay of execution, nor liable to be " set aside nor altered in an action of reduction before the Court of Session, on any other ground except that of malice and oppression on the part of the justices,[91a] nor shall any such action of reduction be at all competent after the expiration of one year from the date of the decree of the justices." The pursuer must (s. 15) find sufficient caution for such expenses as may be awarded against him.

Thus a reduction on the ground of want of jurisdiction has been dismissed.[91b]

Decisions of sheriff in administrative capacity

Such decisions may be reduced if there has been serious disconformity to statutory procedure [92] or excessive use of power,[93] or refusal to exercise jurisdiction in a matter plainly committed to the sheriff.[93] They cannot be reviewed on the merits by action of reduction.

A decree of service as heir in heritage to a person deceased, obtained under the law as to completion of title to heritage in force prior to the Succession (Scotland) Act 1964 is reducible within twenty years of its granting [94] if obtained unjustifiably, whether deliberately or inadvertently.[95] The onus of proof is on the pursuer in the reduction and is discharged by proving that the service proceeded on insufficient evidence.[96]

The Crown has title and interest to sue a reduction of a service on which a person claimed to have right to peerages and other honours granted by the Crown.[96]

Confirmation of executors

A decree of confirmation of a petitioner as executor may be reduced

89 *Manson* v. *Smith* (1871) 9 M. 492; *cf. Cruickshank* v. *Gow* (1888) 15 R. 326; *Spalding* v. *Valentine* (1883) 10 R. 1092; *Brown* v. *Rodger* (1884) 12 R. 340.
90 *Murchie, supra.*
91 Sheriff Courts (Scotland) Act 1971, s. 35.
91a *Cf.* similar phrase in relation to decrees of Sheriff Small Debt Court, *supra.*
91b *Scoular* v. *McLaughlan* (1864) 2 M. 955.
92 *Leith Police Commrs.* v. *Campbell* (1866) 5 M. 247; *Anderson* v. *Widnell* (1868) 7 M. 81; *L.A.* v. *Perth Police Commrs.* (1869) 8 M. 244; *Stirling* v. *Hutcheon* (1874) 1 R. 935; *Caledonian Ry.* v. *Glasgow Corpn.* (1905) 7 F. 1020.
93 *Milne* v. *Aberdeen District Cttee.* (1899) 2 F. 220, 230.
94 Reduction Act 1617, c. 13.
95 *Stobie* v. *Smith,* 1921 S.C. 894.
96 *Alexander* v. *Officers of State* (1868) 6 M.(H.L.) 54.

on the grounds of essential invalidity, such as that the person confirmed was not truly one of the next of kin of the deceased.[97] An executor can have reduced a certificate of the grant of probate in England when it has been found to have been granted in error.[98]

Fiars courts

The courts held for the purposes of striking the prices of grain victual for a county are administrative rather than judicial bodies, and reduction of their verdicts has several times been held competent,[3] but not merely on averments that their verdict was contrary to the evidence.[4]

Court of the Lord Lyon

This court is not supreme in its judicial capacity in its own sphere, since appeal lies to the Court of Session and House of Lords,[5] but it is thought that illegality, such as excess of jurisdiction,[6] could be challenged by reduction in the Court of Session. But the Court of Session will never interfere by way of reduction with a coat of arms granted by Lyon in his ministerial capacity, unless the complainer can aver and show that he is entitled to the coat of which he complains.[7]

Dean of Guild Court

The Dean of Guild Court is a court of civil jurisdiction [8] and, quite apart from any right of appeal,[9] the Court of Session can probably reduce any illegal warrant or actings of the court.

Licensing courts

The decisions of licensing courts may be reduced by the Court of Session on the ground of excess of jurisdiction,[10] or if the hearing were in the circumstances contrary to natural justice.[11]

Arbitrations

A submission to arbitration is reducible, and is a necessary preliminary to bringing an action or otherwise acting inconsistently with the submission, but it is not a sufficient ground for reduction that the named

97 *Dowie* v. *Barclay* (1871) 9 M. 726.
98 *Baines's Exor.* v. *Clark*, 1957 S.C. 342.
3 *Lewars* v. *Earl of Haddington* (1725) Mor. 7464; *Knox* v. *Law* (1771) Mor. 4420; *cf. Horne* v. *Swinton*, Feb. 7, 1806, F.C.
4 *Ritchie* v. *Littlejohn* (1899) 1 F. 1097.
5 *Stewart Mackenzie* v. *Fraser Mackenzie*, 1922 S.C.(H.L.) 39.
6 *Cf. Royal College of Surgeons* v. *Royal College of Physicians*, 1911 S.C. 1054; *Macrae's Trs.* v. *Lord Lyon*, 1927 S.L.T. 285.
7 *McDonell* v. *McDonald* (1825) 4 S. 371; *Stewart Mackenzie, supra*, 44, 46–47.
8 *Fraser* v. *Downie* (1901) 3 F. 881; *Jeffray* v. *Angus*, 1909 S.C. 400.
9 For which see now Building (Scotland) Act 1959, s. 16.
10 *Ashley* v. *Rothesay Mags.* (1873) 11 M. 708; *Lundie* v. *Falkirk Mags.* (1890) 18 R. 60; *Walsh* v. *Pollokshaws Mags.*, 1907 S.C.(H.L.) 1; *Glasgow and District Hotelkeepers' Assocn.* v. *Dollan*, 1941 S.C. 93.
11 *Goodall* v. *Bilsland*, 1909 S.C. 1152 (and see also *Goodall* v. *Shaw*, 1913 S.C. 630); *McGeehen* v. *Knox*, 1913 S.C. 688; *Baillie* v. *Wilson*, 1917 S.C. 55.

arbiter has received an appointment which might tend to bias him, such as a full-time post with one of the parties; such is not a legal disqualification.[12]

Reduction of decrees-arbitral

A decree arbitral is reducible if the arbiter had an interest in the case not disclosed to the party challenging the award and such as would have justified a judge in declining jurisdiction,[13] or if the arbiter has proceeded *ultra fines compromissi* and dealt with a matter not submitted to him,[14] or has not dealt with the whole matters submitted to him,[15] or has mistaken the point in issue.

By the Act of Regulations 1695 it is provided that a decree-arbitral is not reducible save on the grounds of corruption, bribery or falsehood.

Accordingly a doubtful decision on relevancy,[16] or an error in law,[17] is not a ground of reduction. An infringement of the principles of natural justice, such as not hearing one party, will also justify reduction.[18]

Arbiters' awards

These are reducible [19] but on limited grounds only. The competent grounds are (i) that the arbiter was disqualified from acting by personal interest not known to the party challenging at the time of the reference, including the holding of shares in a company which is a party to the dispute [20]; (ii) that the arbiter has acted *ultra fines compromissi,* in which case the whole award is reducible unless the part *ultra vires* is severable [21]; (iii) that the arbiter has mistaken the point in issue, or has not exhausted the matters referred to him [22]; (iv) under the Act of Regulations 1695, on the ground of corruption, bribery or falsehood, categories which do not extend to or include error in law [23]; and probably (v) that the arbiter has been guilty of a fundamental denial of natural justice; as by refusing to hear one party.[24] In an action of reduction the court may take into account the arbiter's note.[25]

These limitations do not apply to an agreement for the redemption of Workmen's Compensation payments though these are declared enforceable as a decree arbitral.[26]

12 *Phipps* v. *Edinburgh and Glasgow Ry.* (1843) 5 D. 1025.
13 *Maule* v. *Maule,* Mar. 4, 1817, F.C.; *Edinburgh Mags.* v. *Lownie* (1903) 5 F. 711; *Sellar* v. *Highland Ry.,* 1919 S.C.(H.L.) 18.
14 *Miller* v. *Oliver & Boyd* (1903) 6 F. 77.
15 *Cf. Pollich* v. *Heatley,* 1910 S.C. 469; *Donald* v. *Shiell's Exrx.,* 1937 S.C. 52.
16 *Brown* v. *Assoc. Fireclay Companies,* 1937 S.C.(H.L.) 42.
17 *Adams* v. *G.N.S. Ry.* (1890) 18 R.(H.L.) 1.
18 *Holmes Oil Co.* v. *Pumpherston Oil Co.* (1891) 18 R.(H.L.) 52; *Black* v. *Williams,* 1923 S.C. 510; *Islay Estates Co.* v. *McCormick,* 1937 S.N. 28.
19 *e.g. Miller* v. *Oliver & Boyd* (1904) 6 F. 77; *Black* v. *Williams,* 1924 S.C.(H.L.) 22; *Donald* v. *Shiell's Executrix,* 1937 S.C. 52.
20 *Dimes* v. *Grand Junction Canal Co.* (1852) 3 H.L.Cas. 759; *Edinburgh Mags.* v. *Lownie* (1903) 5 F. 711; *Sellar* v. *Highland Ry.,* 1919 S.C.(H.L.) 18.
21 *Miller, supra.*
22 *Pollich* v. *Heatley,* 1910 S.C. 469; *Donald* v. *Shiell's Exrx.,* 1937 S.C. 52.
23 *Adams* v. *G.N.S. Ry.* (1890) 18 R.(H.L.) 1.
24 *Holmes Oil Co.* v. *Pumpherston Oil Co.* (1891) 18 R.(H.L.) 52; *Black, supra.*
25 *Farrans* v. *Roxburgh C.C.,* 1970 S.L.T. 334.
26 *McGuire* v. *Addie's Collieries Ltd.,* 1950 S.C. 537.

Judicial references

When parties agree judicially to refer a matter to the decision of a named person, the referee's award may be objected to and opened up by the court, or may be reduced by the court, but only on such grounds as may be relied on under the Act of Regulations of 1695 in relation to arbitrations.[27] The referee's report cannot be challenged on the merits, or on mistaken view of the facts or of the law, but only if *ultra vires* or *ultra fines compromissi*, or if his award is objectionable on the ground of corruption. It is not necessary for the objector to prove his case *ex facie* of the award itself, but he must at least make a relevant statement indicative of *ultra vires* actings or corruption.[28]

Illegal warrants

Reduction is a competent mode of obtaining review of irregular proceedings such as execution of a charge and poinding,[29] or under an application for incarceration of an alleged debtor as being *in meditatione fugae*, and that even though the debtor had granted a bond *de judicio sisti* in order to avoid imprisonment,[30] and probably of an order to detain a person as of unsound mind.[31]

Warrant irregularly granted by sheriff

Reduction may be granted of a warrant, such as a warrant for summary ejection, granted by a sheriff, when there had been no prior default justifying the granting of the warrant and it was therefore irregularly granted.[32]

Letters of horning

It is competent to reduce letters of horning and adjudication following thereon.[33]

[27] *Mackenzie* v. *Girvan* (1841) 3 D. 318; *Watmore* v. *Burns* (1841) 4 D. 150; *Rogerson* v. *Rogerson* (1885) 12 R. 583.
[28] *Rogerson, supra*, 587.
[29] *Beattie* v. *McLellan* (1844) 6 D. 1088.
[30] *Irvine* v. *Hart* (1869) 7 M. 723.
[31] *Cf. Agnew* v. *Laughlan*, 1948 S.C. 656.
[32] *Macdonald* v. *Mackessack* (1888) 16 R. 168.
[33] *Smyth* v. *Walker* (1867) 5 M. 552.

PART V

PREVENTION OF INFRINGEMENT OF RIGHTS

CHAPTER 10

SUSPENSION

"SUSPENSION, as the name insinuates, signifieth a stopping of execution, and that either for a time, till such and such things occur and be done, as shall be decerned by decreet of suspension, or by stopping the execution for ever." [1] "A suspension is an action, at the instance of the suspender, against any party that hath obtained decreet, or hath obtained letters for charging the suspender to pay or perform any thing for which he is charged, and whereupon he may be denounced rebel, whereby his escheat would fall to the King, or his liferent escheat to his superior, or whereby his person may be taken by caption and incarcerated, or his goods or sums may be poinded, or his lands may be apprised upon decreets for poinding the ground, or adjudged for these, or for personal debts." [2]

"Suspension is that form of law, by which the effect of a sentence condemnatory, that hath not received execution, is stayed or put off till the cause be again considered." [3] "Where there is no decree there may be a suspension, though not in the strict acceptation of that word; for suspension is a process authorised by law, for putting a stop not only to the execution of iniquitous decrees, but to all encroachments either on property or possession, and, in general, to every unlawful proceeding. Thus a building, or the exercise of any illegal power which one assumes to himself, is a proper subject of suspension. . . ." [4]

"Suspension is the process whereby the injury of rights is prevented, as distinguished from the remedies where such injury has been accomplished. Its object is to stay or arrest some act or proceeding complained of, and to retain matters in their present position until the rights of parties can be determined by a final judgment." [5]

Suspension, if granted, has the effect of stopping the proceedings objected to, but it does not have any future effect against continuance or repetition. Such an effect requires interdict to be conjoined with suspension.

Uses of suspension

Suspension may be resorted to in two main categories of cases, to

[1] Stair IV, 52, 2.
[2] *Ibid.* IV, 52, 8.
[3] Ersk. IV, 3, 8.
[4] Ersk. IV, 3, 20.
[5] Mackay, *Manual of Practice*, 420.

stay the use of legal diligence, and as a means of review of certain decisions of courts.

It is incompetent as a mode of complaining of the election of a local authority official, after he has been sworn in and acted for some time,[6] or to try whether a party had right to the office of constabulary of an ancient priory,[7] or to decide an issue between the trustees of a mortification,[8] or to try the legality of an assessment larger than necessary for annual outlays, in order to accumulate funds for a capital project.[9]

It has been questioned whether a suspension was an appropriate mode of trying a question of the liability of property for rates.[10]

Combined claims

A crave for suspension may be combined with one for liberation, where it is desired to secure the suspender's release from civil imprisonment, or with one for interdict where it is desired also to prevent the other party continuing with or repeating the diligence threatened or done, as where a charge on a decree has been served and has expired and poinding has followed but a sale has not yet been executed, or with one for liberation and for interdict, where an expired charge has been followed by both imprisonment and poinding.

Jurisdiction

The Court of Session has privative jurisdiction to suspend proceedings complained of, unless the amount does not exceed £50.[11]

The Court of Session may also suspend charges or threatened charges which are wholly unwarranted, even though the sum involved is within the privative jurisdiction of the sheriff court.[12]

The sheriff court of the defender's domicile has jurisdiction to suspend charges or threatened charges on decrees of that court or decrees of registration proceeding on bonds, bills, contracts or other obligations registered in the Books of Council and Session, Sheriff Court Books, or other competent records, where the debt, exclusive of interest and expenses, does not exceed £50.[13]

6 *Glasgow Magistrates* v. *Abbey* (1825) 4 S. 266.
7 *Lord Lovat* v. *Fraser* (1845) 8 D. 316.
8 *Lanark Mags.* v. *Wyllie* (1852) 24 Sc.Jur. 536.
9 *British Fisheries Socy.* v. *Wick Mags.* (1872) 10 M. 426.
10 *Tod* v. *Mitchell* (1858) 20 D. 445.
11 Sheriff Courts (Scotland) Act 1907, s. 5; *Bryson* v. *Belhaven Engineering Co.* (1908) 15 S.L.T. 1043; *Maule* v. *Page* (1909) 47 S.L.R. 110; *Duke of Argyll* v. *Muir*, 1910 S.C. 96; *Pagan & Osborne* v. *Haig*, 1910 S.C. 341; *Stevenson* v. *Sharpe*, 1910 S.C. 580; *Aitchison* v. *McDonald*, 1911 S.C. 174; *Abrahams* v. *Campbell*, 1911 S.C. 353; *Brown and Critchley* v. *Decorative Art Journals Ltd.*, 1922 S.C. 192.
12 *Pagan & Osborne* v. *Haig*, 1910 S.C. 341; *Aitchison* v. *McDonald*, 1911 S.C. 174.
13 Sheriff Courts (Scotland) Act 1907, s. 5 (5), and Sch. I, rules 123–125, amended by Sheriff Courts (Scotland) Act 1913. It is questionable whether this provision gives a sheriff power to review his own decree. The provision does not in terms apply to decrees but only to charges: *Brown & Critchley*, *supra*.

No court may suspend diligence following on a decree of the Small Debt Court,[14] unless the proceedings were fundamentally null.[15]

Title to suspend

A person actually threatened by a charge or other step of diligence always has title and interest to suspend.[16] A person has no title, it has been held, to seek in his own name to suspend diligence affecting goods which he alleged belonged to his son,[17] nor has an assignee title after granting a retrocession, notwithstanding the existence of a back letter saying that it was to be operative only in a certain event which had not happened.[18]

Procedure

Suspension was formerly appropriated procedurally to the Bill Chamber, originally initiated by Bill of Suspension which, if passed, was warrant for expeding letters of suspension under the signet, and from 1838 by Note of Suspension. In modern practice suspension is sought by petition, which by the authority of a Lord Ordinary is intimated and to which answers may be lodged. Interim orders such as for interim sist of execution, interim liberation or interim interdict may be granted, with or without caution, consignation or other condition as the Lord Ordinary may see fit.[19]

A caveat may be lodged by the party liable to have his actings suspended. If this has been done intimation of the petition is made to him so that he may object.

An interim sist stops the running of the days of charge,[20] poinding,[21] removing[22] or imprisonment[23] but not arrestment, inhibition or adjudication[24] nor, provided notour bankruptcy has been constituted, sequestration.[25] When recalled the days of charge run as if uninterrupted.[26] It also gives the suspender an opportunity to find a cautioner or the money to consign. If diligence is done notwithstanding a sist, it is a contempt of court.[27]

Once granted it subsists until the cause is heard and if granted without

14 *Wilson* v. *Scott* (1890) 18 R. 233; *Beveridge* v. *Macfarlane* (1906) 14 S.L.T. 169.
15 *Manson* v. *Smith* (1871) 9 M. 492; *Aitchison* v. *McDonald*, 1911 S.C. 174.
16 *Aitchison* v. *McDonald*, 1911 S.C. 174.
17 *McLaren* v. *Ramsay* (1834) 12 S. 515.
18 *McDonald* v. *Houston* (1860) 22 D. 674.
19 R.C. 234–237.
20 *Laird* v. *Scott*, 1913, 2 S.L.T. 409.
21 *Stewart* v. *Stewart* (1751) Mor. 10535; *Keltie* v. *Wilson* (1828) 7 S. 208.
22 *Tait* v. *Gordon* (1828) 6 S. 1056.
23 *Keltie, supra.*
24 *Miller* v. *Wilson* (1749) Mor. 15148; *Henderson* v. *Smith* (1750) Mor. 6563; *Matheson* v. *Simpson* (1822) 1 S. 542; *Clyne* v. *Murray* (1831) 9 S. 338; Graham Stewart on *Diligence*, 755.
25 *Train* v. *Steven* (1904) 7 F. 47.
26 *Clark* v. *Monteith* (1885) 12 R. 939.
27 *Tait, supra*; *Keltie, supra.*

caution and continued on caution, it subsists during the fourteen days allowed for finding caution.[28]

Interim liberation or interim interdict subsists, provided any conditions attaching to the grant are satisfied, until the case is finally disposed of.[29]

If interim sist of execution or interim liberation is granted on caution, caution must be found before the time for lodging Answers begins to run, and if caution is not found the Petition may be refused.

Suspension on caution

The court may make it a condition of proceeding to an investigation of the grounds alleged for suspension that the suspender finds caution. " The common rule is, that the suspension cannot pass the signet, till either consignation or sufficient caution be found, that what shall be decerned shall be paid or performed." [30] The older practice seems to have been to demand caution or consignation in all cases, but in modern practice it is a question for the discretion of the court. In older cases neither caution nor consignation was demanded where a bill had been obtained by a creditor from a bankrupt as the price of his consent to a discharge on composition contract,[31] where forgery was apparent,[32] where there was manifest abuse of legal process,[33] and when it was admitted that not all of the sum in a bond had been advanced,[34] or the charger, on reference to his oath, swore that he had received payment but not in extinction of the debt charged on.[35]

> " In a suspension the complainer undertakes to find caution, if the court thinks it right not to allow the suspension to be proceeded with unless caution be found—that is, caution that the intending charger shall not be in a worse position than he is at the time of the finding of the caution by not being able at once to charge on his decree." [36]

Caution is found by one or more cautioners entering into a bond of caution.[37] The obligation in the bond of caution is that the suspender will pay the sums charged on, if the court finds that he ought to do so, and that payment shall be made of whatever sum the Lords shall modify in name of damages, and expenses [38] in case of wrongous suspending.

The cautioner is taken bound equally with the suspender to pay or

28 *Cassells* v. *Sillers*, 1910, 2 S.L.T. 447.
29 *Clippens Oil Co. Ltd.* v. *Edinburgh & District Water Trs.* (1906) 8 F. 731, 749; *Home Drummond* v. *McLachlan*, 1908 S.C. 12.
30 Stair IV, 52, 24. Letters of suspension do not now pass the signet.
31 *Thomson* v. *Robertson* (1825) 4 S. 139.
32 *Ross* v. *Millar* (1831) 10 S. 95.
33 *Gordon* v. *Baird* (1856) 28 Sc.Jur. 682.
34 *Hamilton* v. *Paul* (1829) 7 S. 479.
35 *Thomson* v. *Wyld* (1840) 3 D. 150.
36 *Stewart* v. *Forbes* (1897) 24 R. 1112, 1115, *per* L.J.C. Macdonald.
37 Form in *Juridical Styles*, 3rd ed., III, 471.
38 *i.e.* the expenses of process, not damages for injury caused by the use of suspension: Mackay, *Manual of Practice*, 427. See also *Buchanan* v. *Douglas* (1853) 15 D. 365.

perform to the charger or to any other person to whom payment or performance shall be decerned to be made by the decree in the cause.

The cautioner's signature must be attested and the attestor is bound as cautioner for the cautioner, and liable as fully as the cautioner himself but subsidiarily. A certificate must be appended by a justice of the peace that cautioner and attestor are both habit and repute responsible for the obligations therein contained. The bond covers the expenses of litigation and, in the case of suspension and interdict, damages for wrongous interdict.[39]

The bond of caution contains the usual clause consenting to registration in the Books of Council and Session.

In modern practice the bond of caution is extended by or under the direction of the Deputy Principal Clerk of Session and shall contain the necessary clauses adapted to the requirements of the Rules of Court. The Deputy Principal Clerk must consider the sufficiency of the caution offered when the bond of caution is tendered,[40] and may request information if this appears to be called for. The charger may state objections to the caution by letter addressed to the Deputy Principal Clerk, who must take the objections and any further information he may have called for into consideration in deciding as to the sufficiency of the caution, or he may refer the matter for decision by the court. If he decides the issue himself any party aggrieved by his decision may bring the matter before the court by motion.[41]

If the cautioner has been sequestrated or become notour bankrupt, or executed a trust deed for creditors, or called a meeting of creditors, or died unrepresented, the charger may present a note to the court, praying the court to order new caution to be found, and the court shall pronounce such order thereon as the justice of the case shall require.[42]

Caution shall be taken not only for obedience to the charge, but also for refunding to the charger such expenses as the court may modify at the discussing of the suspension.[43]

The charger has no responsibility for ensuring that the bond of caution is signed by all cautioners, so that if caution has to be found by two cautioners and the signature of one is forged, the other is not freed from liability, even though he had signed on the faith of its being also validly subscribed by the other cautioner.[44]

The cautioner in a suspension has never been entitled to demand that the suspender be sued first (benefit of discussion),[45] nor entitled to be released under the septennial prescription of cautionary obligations. He is presumed to be represented by the suspender and cannot appear

39 *Buchanan* v. *Douglas* (1851) 13 D. 547; *Knox* v. *Paterson* (1861) 23 D. 1263.
40 The court has not been in the habit of questioning the discretion of the Clerk in judging the sufficiency of caution: *Gow* v. *Napier* (1832) 10 S. 812.
41 R.C. 238 (*a*)–(*e*). See also Stair IV, 52, 10; IV, 53, 24.
42 R.C. 238 (*f*).
43 R.C. 239.
44 *Simpson* v. *Fleming* (1860) 22 D. 679, 683.
45 Ersk. III, 3, 72; *Strachan* v. *Forbes* (1714) Mor. 3583.

for himself, unless he alleges fraud and collusion. If the suspender abandons the suspension, the cautioner may carry it on,[46] failing which he is liable in the same way as the principal. The cautioner and attestor are parties to the cause and may without finding caution appear for their own interest.[47]

It is desirable, if the suspender fails to proceed, or is prevented, *e.g.* by death or bankruptcy, from proceeding, for the charger to intimate the fact to the cautioner, before proceeding to take decree against him, in case the cautioner has any other ground of defence.[48]

The cautioner is freed from liability by any extraordinary step taken by the suspender without his consent, such as a judicial reference,[49] or by an application by the charger for new caution; the charger may proceed and take decree against the cautioner, or against the suspender for failure to find new caution.[50]

If the suspender's grounds of suspension are rejected decree passes against the suspender, finding the charge orderly proceeded, and allowing diligence to proceed. If the charger requires to enforce the decree against the cautioner, he charges directly on the decree and the bond of caution, although the cautioner is not named therein, without need for further constitution.[51] The extent of the cautioner's liability depends on the terms in which he is bound. He may be liable in payment of the charger's expenses though the liability of the suspender may be limited.[52]

Juratory caution

If a suspender cannot find a sufficient cautioner, he may offer juratory caution, that is, what the suspender swears is all that, in the circumstances, he can offer.[53] He must offer a disposition and assignation of his estate and depone as to his assets of every kind.

In modern practice, when the Lord Ordinary appoints the petition for suspension to be answered, he must name a commissioner to take the petitioner's deposition, and the petitioner must intimate to the opposite party to attend at the time and place fixed by the commissioner so that he may cross-interrogate him as to his assets. If he acknowledges any assets he must condescend thereon and depone that he has no other assets, and lodge with the Deputy Principal Clerk the bond of caution, a full inventory of his subjects and effects of every kind, and an enactment that he will not dilapidate or dispose of or uplift any debts due to him,

46 *Eadie* v. *Smith* (1833) 11 S. 421.
47 *Henderson* v. *Young* (1828) 7 S. 142; *Stewart* v. *Hickman* (1843) 6 D. 151; *Potter* v *Bartholomew* (1847) 10 D. 97, 100, 108; *Addison* v. *Brown*, 1910, 1 S.L.T. 185.
48 *Stewart* v. *Hickman* (1843) 6 D. 151.
49 *Stewart*, *supra*; *Potter* v. *Bartholomew* (1847) 10 D. 97.
50 *Eadie*, *supra*.
51 *Potter*, *supra*, 101–102; *Simpson* v. *Fleming* (1860) 22 D. 679.
52 *Stewart* v. *Forbes* (1897) 24 R. 1112.
53 Stair IV, 52, 26; Ersk. IV, 3, 19. For examples under older law see *Marshall* v. *Grant* (1860) 22 D. 926; *McGregor* v. *Lord Strathallan* (1862) 24 D. 1006; *Logan* v. *Weir* (1870) 8 M. 1009.

without the respondent's consent or the authority of the judge, till the petition be discussed and there be an opportunity of doing diligence for any expenses that may ultimately be found due by him. The petitioner must also lodge the vouchers of debts due to him and the title deeds of any heritage belonging to him and, if so required, grant a special disposition to the respondent of any heritable subjects and an assignation of all debts or other rights due to him for the respondent's further security, to remain in the hands of the Deputy Principal Clerk till the petition be discussed. Till all lodgment is made it is not necessary for the other party to give in his answers to the petition.[54]

Suspension on consignation

The court may similarly permit suspension only on consignation being made, and this has the same effect as finding caution and is in general alternative thereto. Consignation is effected by lodging the sum charged for in bank on deposit receipt in the joint names of the charger and suspender but subject to the orders of the court, the deposit receipt being lodged with the Accountant of Court. According as the case is ultimately decided, warrant should be granted to uplift the consigned sum with accrued interest.[55]

In certain cases, by statute or custom, consignation was formerly required, notwithstanding an offer of full caution. The only surviving instance appears to be under the Bank Notes (Scotland) Act 1765, s. 5.

Consignation is usually required only of the amount charged for, and not also for expenses.[56]

Failure to find caution or to consign

If an order has been made for caution or consignation, and caution has not been found or consignation made within the time allowed, the Clerk must issue a certificate of no caution or consignation, and the petition must be refused and any interim sist recalled.[57]

The suspender may, notwithstanding the certificate of no caution, move the court to recall the certificate, and allow caution now to be found or consignation made, and the court may recall the certificate.[58]

SUSPENSION OF DILIGENCE

Suspension is competent where there is a threat to do diligence on a decree or registered bill or bond, or diligence is actually done, except in the case of diligence following on a decree of the Small Debt Court, where suspension of diligence is incompetent equally with suspension of

54 R.C. 240.
55 *Field* v. *Watt's Trs.* (1865) 3 M. 609.
56 *Peddie* v. *Davidson* (1856) 18 D. 1306.
57 *Cf. Purdie* v. *Bryson* (1861) 24 D. 85.
58 *Andrew* v. *Colquhoun* (1853) 15 D. 482.

the decree itself.[59] Even in such a case it may be competent to have diligence suspended where the grounds of suspension do not touch the validity of the decree itself, as where the decree is admitted but a receipt produced for the sum in the decree and the expenses decerned for,[60] or facts have emerged since the decree which make it contrary to justice and the true meaning of the decree to enforce it.[61]

In the ordinary case a party in right of a decree may do diligence thereon, but it is competent to seek by suspension to have diligence on the decree stayed, on the ground that it would be an unreasonable hardship on the defender.[62] The right to do diligence is not affected, nor is it by itself a ground for suspension, that the party bound by the decree has presented a petition of appeal to the House of Lords.[62]

Suspension of decrees

A petition for suspension may be brought to hold up the operation of an interlocutor or decree or warrant [62a] granted by a court, unless suspension is, in particular circumstances, excluded by statute.[63] Thus suspension of a decree of the Small Debt Court is excluded by statute [64] unless there is a defect so serious that the proceedings are null *ab initio*.[65]

But in general a decree may be suspended. " If a man has got a decree for a sum which he claims, that decree may be suspended, though nothing is done on it." [66] Suspension of an unextracted decree is competent.[67]

Though a decree in absence stands unrecalled it is competent in a subsequent suspension and interdict to review the decree on its merits.[68]

Grounds for suspending a decree include lack of jurisdiction over the defender,[69] that the debt has been paid or discharged,[70] and serious defect in form such as failure to cite the defender,[71] or citation at a wrong place,[72] though if there is jurisdiction mere irregularity in citation does not amount to fundamental nullity.[72] It is not generally competent to

[59] *Wilson* v. *Scott* (1890) 18 R. 233; *Christie* v. *Hoseason* (1898) 6 S.L.T. 123; *Crawford* v. *Copland & Lye* (1901) 9 S.L.T. 76; *Beveridge* v. *Macfarlane* (1906) 14 S.L.T. 169. But see *Samuel* v. *Mackenzie & Bell* (1876) 4 R. 187.
[60] *Wilson, supra*, 236.
[61] *Wilson, supra*, 237.
[62] *Glasgow and Londonderry S.P. Co.* v. *Clyde Shipping Co.* (1859) 22 D. 2.
[62a] *e.g.* warrant for civil imprisonment: *McWilliams* v. *McWilliams*, 1963 S.C. 259.
[63] *Bryson* v. *Belhaven Engineering, Ltd.* (1908) 15 S.L.T. 1043 (sheriff court decree in absence for less than £50).
[64] Small Debt (Scotland) Act 1837, s. 30; *Graham* v. *Mackay* (1845) 7 D. 515; *Turnbull* v. *Russell* (1851) 14 D. 45; *Lennon* v. *Tully* (1879) 6 R. 1253; *Robertson* v. *Pringle* (1887) 14 R. 474; *Wilson* v. *Scott* (1890) 18 R. 233; see also *Glass* v. *Laughlin* (1876) 4 R. 108.
[65] *Manson* v. *Smith* (1871) 9 M. 492.
[66] *Watson* v. *Merrilees* (1848) 10 D. 370, 372, *per* Lord Mackenzie.
[67] *Paul* v. *Henderson* (1867) 5 M. 1120.
[68] *Macdonald* v. *Denoon*, 1929 S.C. 172.
[69] *Cf. Graham* v. *Mackay* (1845) 7 D. 515; *Wilson* v. *Scott* (1890) 18 R. 233, 235; *Brown & Critchley* v. *Decorative Art Journals Co.*, 1922 S.C. 192.
[70] *Cf. Turnbull* v. *Russell* (1851) 14 D. 45.
[71] *Cf. Lennon* v. *Tully* (1879) 6 R. 1253.
[72] *Brown & Critchley, supra.*

suspend a decree *in foro* on an averment that appearance by counsel and agent in the process had not been authorised; the suspender must, it was stated, proceed by reduction,[73] though suspension was once granted on caution, on averments that the suspender was not a party to the process and had never authorised appearance on his behalf.[74]

Suspension of a final decree *in foro* has been refused, when brought on grounds which might have been urged before the decree was pronounced.[75]

Suspension of threatened diligence

Where a decree has been obtained, even though not extracted,[76] or a bond containing a clause of registration for execution has been registered and an extract obtained, or the protest of a bill of exchange been registered and an extract obtained, a suspension is competent to stop any diligence.[77] A charge need not have actually been given but it will suffice that one had been threatened and the threat has not been withdrawn.[78] The threatened charge will be suspended if in the circumstances it was unwarranted. Thus it is not competent to protest and do summary diligence on a cheque, and accordingly a threat of charge based thereon is incompetent.[79] Withdrawal must be express, and a merely verbal disclaimer of intent to proceed will not suffice to bar a suspension.[80] If a charge, or threat of a charge, has been withdrawn, suspension is not competent even though the withdrawal was not accompanied by an offer of expenses.[81] Moreover unless the withdrawal has been made and intimated to the suspender before he presents his petition, the suspender may proceed unless his expenses are paid.[82]

Similarly it has been held that suspension was competent where there was a threat to charge for poor-rate assessment, and the sum demanded was alleged to be an over-charge.[83]

The provision in the Small Debt Act excluding suspension does not exclude suspension where the proceedings are fundamentally null.[84]

Suspension of charge on decree, bond or bill

Where a charge has actually followed on a decree [85] or an extract registered bond or a protested bill of exchange, it may be suspended.

73 *Hamilton* v. *Marshall*, Nov. 25, 1813, F.C.; *Young & List* v. *McHardie* (1862) 24 D. 587.
74 *Dewar* v. *Reid* (1832) 11 S. 193.
75 *Kerr* v. *James* (1866) 1 S.L.R. 119.
76 *Paul* v. *Henderson* (1867) 5 M. 1120.
77 *Lowson* v. *Reid* (1861) 23 D. 1089, 1094.
78 Ersk. IV, 3, 20; *Templeton* v. *Templeton* (1837) 16 S. 100; *Watson* v. *Merrilees* (1848) 10 D. 370; *Paul, supra*; *Manson* v. *Smith* (1871) 9 M. 492; *Mackay* v. *Parish Council of Resolis* (1899) 1 F. 521; *Glickman* v. *Linda*, 1950 S.C. 18.
79 *Glickman, supra.*
80 *Templeton, supra.*
81 *Douglas* v. *Brand & Brown* (1853) 15 D. 283.
82 *McAulay* v. *Brown* (1833) 11 S. 411; *Henderson* v. *Plenderleath* (1850) 12 D. 1076; see also *Douglas, supra.*
83 *Steuart* v. *Keith Parochial Board* (1869) 8 M. 26.
84 *Manson* v. *Smith* (1871) 9 M. 492.
85 Including a decree for expenses: *McCarroll* v. *McKinstery*, 1923 S.C. 94.

Suspension may be granted on a technical point, because precision is important in diligence.[86] But suspension of a charge and its warrant is not a competent mode of reviewing a decree on its merits.[87]

In a suspension of a charge on an extract protested bill of exchange, the onus is on the charger, the bill being improbative, to prove that the signatures on the bill purporting to be those of the complainer were in fact adhibited by him.[88] The reverse is the rule in the case of a probative deed.[89] In such a suspension it is not competent to investigate the preliminaries leading up to the agreement in respect of which the bill was accepted,[90] nor whether an obligant was truly a party or a cautioner.[91]

It is not competent to suspend a charge on a foreign judgment registered in Scotland, though notice of registration had not been given as required by the Rules of Court, when the suspender had failed to oppose the petition for registration, and had appeared to seek to suspend it,[92] nor, in such a case to entertain any question as to the merits of the case, though such matters may be raised with the foreign court which granted the decree.[93]

It is competent to suspend a charge to the extent of any sums admitted not to be due, and to find it orderly proceeded as to the balance.[94]

Suspension to prevent immediate execution of a charge on a decree for expenses is rare but competent.[95]

Suspension of a charge on a sheriff court decree of adherence and aliment is competent on averments that the party charged had expressed genuine willingness to adhere.[96]

Grounds for suspension of threatened or executed charge

Grounds for suspension have been partial or total payment, or satisfaction of the decree,[1] or tender of the sum due and, if it is refused, consignation of it in bank, or the arising of any circumstances after the date of the decree which have wholly or partially extinguished the debt [2]; that the sum charged for was excessive, to the extent of the excess [3]; defect in the extract [4]; defect in the charge [5]; irregularity of the charge [6];

86 *Mitchell* v. *St. Mungo Lodge of Ancient Shepherds*, 1916 S.C. 689.
87 *Smith* v. *Kirkwood* (1897) 24 R. 872.
88 *Anderson* v. *Gill* (1858) 3 Macq. 180; *McIntyre* v. *National Bank of Scotland*, 1910 S.C. 150, explaining *Gellatly* v. *Jones* (1851) 13 D. 961.
89 *Ferrie* v. *Ferrie's Trs.* (1863) 1 M. 291.
90 *McAllister* v. *McGallagley*, 1911 S.C. 112.
91 *Scott* v. *Davidson*, 1914 S.C. 791.
92 *Medinelli* v. *Malgras*, 1958 S.C. 489.
93 *Wotherspoon* v. *Connolly* (1871) 9 M. 510.
94 *Haughhead Coal Co.* v. *Gallocher* (1903) 11 S.L.T. 156.
95 *McCarroll* v. *McKinstery*, 1923 S.C. 94, 98.
96 *Brown* v. *Brown*, 1970 S.L.T.(Notes) 79.
1 *Smith* v. *Kirkwood* (1897) 24 R. 872.
2 Stair I, 18, 4; Ersk. III, 4, 5; *Paul* v. *Henderson* (1867) 5 M. 1120.
3 *Davidson* v. *Dunbar* (1821) 1 S. 43; *Ledingham* v. *Mackenzie* (1824) 3 S. 113; *McMartin* v. *Forbes* (1824) 3 S. 275; *Richan* v. *Hill* (1832) 11 S. 237; *Dick* v. *Murison* (1845) 8 D. 1; *Wilson* v. *Stronach* (1862) 24 D. 271; *Haughhead Coal Co.* v. *Gallacher* (1903) 11 S.L.T. 156.
4 *Graham Stewart on Diligence*, 279.
5 *Ibid.* 291; *Paul, supra*, 1126; *Dunbar* v. *Mitchell*, 1928 S.L.T. 225.
6 *Mackay* v. *Parish Council of Resolis* (1899) 1 F. 521 (charge bearing to be "on pain of imprisonment").

fundamental nullity of the proceedings,[7] or forgery of the bond or bill charged on.[8] A charge will be suspended if it is unjustifiable even if procedurally regular.[9]

In a very special case it was held competent to suspend charges on decrees for expenses when the suspender was pursuing a reduction of those and other related decrees as having been obtained by fraud.[10] A charge on a bill accepted by a minor cannot be suspended on the ground of minority and lesion; reduction is the remedy.[11] It is incompetent to suspend a charge for judicial expenses, the merits of the case not being brought under review.[12]

It is incompetent in a suspension to consider questions of the debtor's liability which appear *ex facie* of the documents or can be readily verified, but not all objections can be examined, without a separate investigation.[13]

Suspension of warrant to imprison

Warrant to imprison, as for wilful refusal to pay aliment, may be suspended. It is desirable, if not necessary, also to suspend the charge on which the warrant of imprisonment proceeds, and this is essential if the suspender seeks to challenge the sum unpaid and for which the charge has been served.[14] A decree for reimbursement of sums expended in alimenting a bastard, obtained in an action raised after the legal duty of providing aliment had ceased is not a decree for " sums decerned for aliment " within the meaning of the Debtors (Scotland) Act 1880, on which imprisonment can follow.[15]

Suspension of warrant to search

Suspension may be brought to challenge the legality of a warrant granted to search premises and seize documents,[16] but must be supported by relevant averments of illegality in the grant or use of the warrant.

Suspension of calls on contributories

By the Companies Act 1948, s. 275, (1) where an order has been made for winding up a company by the court, the court may grant decree against contributories for payment of the sums certified by the liquidator to be due by them, with interest, " to the same effect as if they had severally consented to registration for execution, on a charge of six days, of a legal obligation to pay those calls and interest. (2) Any such decree may

7 *Manson* v. *Smith* (1871) 9 M. 492.
8 *Paterson* v. *Sparrow* (1821) 1 S. 223; *Golder* v. *Deans* (1826) 5 S. 161; *Wylie* v. *Brand* (1836) 14 S. 553.
9 *Parkinson* v. *Bowen*, 1951 S.L.T. 393.
10 *McCarroll* v. *McKinstery*, 1923 S.C. 94.
11 *Waddle* v. *Gibson*, 18 Jan. 1827, F.C.
12 *Simpson* v. *Young* (1852) 24 Sc.Jur. 588; *cf. Findlay* v. *Duncan* (1854) 16 D. 938.
13 *Dick's Trs.* v. *Hannah* (1870) 8 S.L.R. 137.
14 *Glenday* v. *Johnston* (1905) 8 F. 24; *McWilliams* v. *McWilliams*, 1963 S.C. 259.
15 *Glenday, supra.*
16 *Paterson* v. *Macpherson*, 1924 J.C. 38.

be extracted immediately and no suspension thereof shall be competent, except on caution, or consignation, unless with special leave of the court."

Though suspension is the appropriate and proper remedy, it is probably not the only one and does not exclude a reclaiming motion.[17]

Suspension in case of competition of diligence

Suspension is the appropriate remedy if a debtor's reason for not satisfying a decree which he has been charged to satisfy is that his funds due to the creditor have been arrested by a third party.[18] This principle probably extends to all cases where there are good grounds for not paying the charging creditor.[19]

Suspension and liberation

Suspension and liberation is the appropriate remedy where there has been irregularity in proceedings justifying suspension, and the complainer was imprisoned in consequence of non-compliance.[20] A suspension and liberation may be brought despite the refusal of an earlier petition for suspension alone.[21]

It will now be uncommon because imprisonment for civil debt is now incompetent, except in cases of failure to pay rates and assessments, taxes (death duties and purchase tax only),[22] fines or penalties due to the Crown,[23] wilful refusal to pay aliment,[24] or failure to find caution in an application for law burrows.[25] A decree does not cease to be a decree for aliment because it includes sums for inlying expenses and expenses of process.[26]

It is also competent where an order has been made committing a person to a mental hospital as being of unsound mind,[27] and where a person has been committed to prison for contempt of court in civil proceedings.[28] In the latter category of case the bill may be brought in the Court of Session [29] or in the High Court of Justiciary.[30]

17 *Cumpstie* v. *Waterston*, 1933 S.C. 1 (under Companies Act 1929, s. 222).
18 *Mitchell* v. *Strachan* (1871) 8 M. 154; *Ferguson* v. *Bothwell* (1881) 9 R. 687; *Caw, Prentice, Clapperton & Co.* v. *Creighton & Co.* (1898) 25 R. 518.
19 *Ferguson, supra.*
20 *e.g. Wilson* v. *Stronach* (1862) 24 D. 271; *Shiell* v. *Mossman* (1872) 10 M. 58.
21 *Barr* v. *Wotherspoon* (1850) 13 D. 305.
22 Crown Proceedings Act 1947, s. 49.
23 Debtors (Sc.) Act 1880, s. 4.
24 See *McWilliams* v. *McWilliams*, 1963 S.C. 259.
25 Civil Imprisonment (Sc.) Act 1882. Since this Act suspension of a decree of law burrows is incompetent; it can be reviewed only by stated case under the Summary Jurisdiction Act 1954: *Mackenzie* v. *Maclennan*, 1916 S.C. 617.
26 *Cheyne* v. *McGungle* (1860) 22 D. 1490.
27 *Campbell* v. *Herron*, 1948 J.C. 127 (bill brought in High Court).
28 *Graham* v. *Robert Younger Ltd.*, 1955 J.C. 28 (bill brought in High Court).
29 *Graham, supra*, 33, referring to *Caledonian Ry.* v. *Hamilton* (1850) 7 Bell 272; *Henderson* v. *Maclellan* (1874) 1 R. 920; *Stark's Trs.* v. *Duncan* (1906) 8 F. 429; *Maclachlan* v. *Bruce*, 1912 S.C. 440.
30 *MacLeod* v. *Speirs* (1884) 11 R.(J.) 26; *Graham, supra*, 33.

Suspension and interdict

Suspension and interdict must be conjoined where the complainer wishes to have held up some decree or diligence, and also to prevent any threatened further steps against him thereunder.

Combined suspension and interdict has been founded on such defects as defect in the conduct of a poinding preliminary to a sale,[31] excessive poinding,[32] delay in reporting poinding to the sheriff,[33] delay in obtaining warrant to sell,[34] defect in the warrant to sell,[35] inadequate notice of the sale,[36] the fact that goods poinded are not the debtor's property or are subject to rights precluding poinding.[37]

Combined suspension and interdict is usually sought as a remedy for diligence proceeding upon a warrant for the collection of rates, even where diligence has only been threatened,[38] though suspension alone is sufficient in the case of threatened or attempted diligence for recovery of national taxation.[39]

Second petitions

When a petition for suspension is refused in respect that caution has not been found or consignation not made, or on any ground not on the merits, or when the petition has been appointed to the adjustment roll and a certificate of no caution or consignation, or of failure to implement any conditions, has been issued, it is competent, on payment of previous expenses, to present a second petition.[40] In older cases a second suspension has been permitted, on a change of circumstances,[41] or on the withdrawal of the first one,[42] or if sufficiently different not to be a mere repetition of the first,[43] and the court has refused a suspension where the facts were scantily stated, reserving to the suspender to put in a new bill of suspension with a fuller narrative.[44]

A third suspension has even been found.[45]

SUSPENSION AS A MODE OF REVIEW

Although a process of suspension is *ex sua natura* a process for sisting diligence it may also be used as one for reviewing certain decrees of

31 *Sangster* v. *Burness* (1857) 20 D. 355.
32 *McKinnon* v. *Hamilton* (1866) 4 M. 852; *Le Conte* v. *Douglas & Richardson* (1880) 8 R. 175.
33 *Sampson* v. *McCubbin* (1822) 1 S. 407; *Lyle* v. *Greig* (1827) 5 S. 845; *Miller* v. *Stewart* (1834) 13 S. 483.
34 *Henderson* v. *Grant* (1896) 23 R. 659.
35 *Kewlay* v. *Andrew* (1843) 5 D. 860; *McVicar* v. *Kerr* (1857) 19 D. 948; *McKinnon, supra.*
36 *McNeill* v. *McMurchy* (1841) 3 D. 554.
37 *Smith* v. *Flowerdew* (1842) 5 D. 335; *Anderson* v. *Buchanan* (1848) 11 D. 270; *McDonald* v. *Urquhart* (1852) 15 D. 191.
38 *Glasgow Ry. Co.* v. *Abbey Parish, Paisley, Parochial Board* (1850) 13 D. 304; *Leys* v. *Riddell* (1851) 13 D. 630; *Neil* v. *Hamilton* (1864) 2 M. 1081.
39 *Renfrew & Brown* v. *Glasgow Mags.* (1861) 23 D. 505; *Borthwick* v. *L.A.* (1862) 1 M. 94.
40 R.C. 243.
41 *Wallace* v. *Grant* (1825) 3 S. 539; *Allan, infra*; *Barr* v. *Wotherspoon* (1850) 13 D. 305.
42 *Taylor* v. *Glasgow, Paisley & Ardrossan Canal Co.* (1852) 15 D. 14.
43 *Allan* v. *Wilkie Bros.* (1854) 16 D. 917.
44 *Wylie* v. *Brand* (1836) 14 S. 553.
45 *Wallace, supra*; *Stewart* v. *Ferguson* (1841) 3 D. 668.

court. Though, apart from various modes of appeal, reduction is the primary mode of obtaining review of a decree, it does not follow that, because reduction is competent, suspension is excluded.[46]

Decrees of Court of Session

The Court of Session may suspend certain of its own decrees. But where in the Court of Session a judgment has been pronounced by a Lord Ordinary, the normal mode of having that reviewed is by reclaiming motion and the court will not sanction review by suspension where the party desiring review has neglected to use the ordinary and, indeed, statutory form for obtaining such review.[47]

It is incompetent to suspend a Court of Session decree *in foro*[48] (including a decree by default[49]), but diligence proceeding upon a decree *in foro* may be suspended, on the ground that the debt has been paid or consigned since the decree, or that the diligence has been irregular.[50]

Suspension of decrees in absence

By the Court of Session (No. 1) Act 1838, s. 5, a party may bring a suspension of any decree in absence pronounced in the Court of Session, at any time before it has been implemented, or become final, or become equal to a decree *in foro*.[51] Suspension is competent of decrees on which a charge is competent[52] and also of decrees on which no charge could follow.[53] The ambit of this includes a decree in absence obtained in an undefended action of divorce,[54] and a decree in absence in a reduction,[55] and it is not restricted to decrees in absence of such a character that a charge could follow thereon.[56]

Where decree passed in absence and a suspension was brought and the defender was allowed to lodge defences, but failed to do so and decree was again granted, it was held that the second decree was not in absence, but *in foro* and that suspension was incompetent.[57]

Suspension is incompetent where a decree has been implemented or

[46] *Scoular* v. *McLaughlan* (1864) 2 M. 955; *Cunningham* v. *Cunningham*, 1928 S.C. 790.

[47] *Lumsdaine* v. *Australian Co.* (1834) 13 S. 215; *Maule* v. *Tainsh* (1878) 6 R. 44; *Lamb* v. *Thompson* (1901) 4 F. 88, 92.

[48] *Irvine* v. *Valentine* (1793) 3 Pat. 287; *Stewart* v. *Leslie*, 10 Dec. 1811, F.C.; *Hamilton* v. *Marshall* (1815) Hume 497; *Scott* v. *King* (1831) 10 S. 67; *Munro* v. *Rose* (1854) 16 D. 476; *Lowson* v. *Cooper* (1861) 23 D. 1089; *Young* v. *List and McHardie* (1862) 24 D. 587; *Macpherson* v. *Graham* (1863) 1 M. 973; *McCarroll* v. *McKinstery*, 1923 S.C. 94, 98; *Greenwood* v. *Mundle*, 1957 S.L.T.(Notes) 15.

[49] *Lumsdaine* v. *Australian Co.* (1834) 13 S. 215; *Macpherson* v. *Grant* (1863) 1 M. 973; *Maule* v. *Tainsh* (1878) 6 R. 44.

[50] Stair I, 18, 4; Ersk. III, 4, 5; *Paul* v. *Henderson* (1867) 5 M. 1121.

[51] Court of Session Act 1868, ss. 23–24. In other cases a decree does not become final for forty years.

[52] *Lowson* v. *Cooper* (1861) 23 D. 1089.

[53] *Lowson*, *supra*; *Grant & Sillars* v. *Marshall* (1863) 1 M. 1167; *Newton* v. *Couper* (1865) 3 M. 573; *Cunningham* v. *Cunningham*, 1928 S.C. 790.

[54] *Cunningham* v. *Cunningham*, 1928 S.C. 790.

[55] *Grant & Sillars* v. *Marshall* (1863) 1 M. 1167; *cf.* *Newton* v. *Couper* (1865) 3 M. 573.

[56] *Lowson* v. *Cooper or Reid* (1861) 23 D. 1089.

[57] *Munro* v. *Rose* (1854) 16 D. 476.

acquiesced in,[58] of a decree of absolvitor,[59] or of a decree for expenses following on absolvitor.[60]

It is also incompetent on the allegation that the suspender was unaware of legal proceedings carried on in his name.[61]

Suspension by Court of Session of sheriff court decrees

In general the Court of Session may suspend decrees of the sheriff court. " Suspension is a mode of obtaining review of an inferior court judgment of very ancient standing, and was distinctly recognised as being so in the Act of 1838.[62] It is as competent now as it was then." [63] " There are three modes of review of inferior court decrees—appeal, suspension and reduction. The only limitation is that if the party has already appealed, and failed in the Supreme Court, whether on the merits or by default, he cannot fall back on another mode of review, viz. suspension. It must be observed that if suspension is adopted the complainer may have to find caution, which acts as a check upon litigants who prefer to resort to that process instead of appeal. It is clear from the case of *Watt* [64] and others which have been referred to,[65] as well as from the treatises of Shand and Dove Wilson, that suspension is a competent mode of reviewing the decrees of inferior courts. The cases of *Maule* [66] and *Lumsdaine* [67] were cases of Supreme Court judgments, where a different rule applies." [68]

Thus it has been used to examine the competency of an action of removing from one subject following on a notice to quit applicable also to other premises.[69]

Suspension in the Court of Session is incompetent if the sum in the decree brings the case within the privative jurisdiction of the sheriff court.[70]

It is not competent to set aside by suspension a sheriff court decree on the ground that it has been obtained by fraud, the proper remedy being reduction.[71]

It is similarly competent for the Court of Session to suspend a charge on a sheriff court decree.[72]

58 *Macintosh* v. *Robertson* (1830) 9 S. 75; *Ewing* v. *Cheape* (1835) 13 S. 515; *Wotherspoon* v. *Winning* (1849) 11 D. 371; *McDougall* v. *Galt* (1863) 1 M. 1012.
59 *Danish Asiatic Co.* v. *E. Morton* (1741) Elchies, Suspension, 5.
60 *Scott* v. *King* (1831) 10 S. 67; *Whyte* v. *Vallance* (1835) 13 S. 470; *Simpson* v. *Young* (1852) 14 D. 990; *Findlay* v. *Reid's Trs.* (1854) 16 D. 938; *Young* v. *List and McHardie* (1862) 24 D. 587; *McDougall* v. *Galt* (1863) 1 M. 1012; *cf. Douglas* v. *Samuel* (1828) 6 S. 461; *Miller* v. *Miller* (1829) 7 S. 617; *Menzies* v. *Caldwell* (1834) 12 S. 772.
61 *Hamilton* v. *Marshall*, Nov. 25, 1813, F.C.; *Cowan* v. *Farnie* (1836) 14 S. 634; *Young, supra.*
62 Court of Session (No. 1) Act 1838, s. 4.
63 *Lamb* v. *Thompson* (1901) 4 F. 88, 92, *per* Lord Trayner.
64 *Watt Bros.* v. *Foyn* (1879) 7 R. 126.
65 *e.g. Wilson* v. *Bartholomew* (1860) 22 D. 1410; *Smith* v. *Kirkwood* (1897) 24 R. 872.
66 *Maule* v. *Tainsh* (1878) 6 R. 44.
67 *Lumsdaine* v. *Australian Co.* (1834) 13 S. 215.
68 *Lamb, supra*, 92, *per* Lord Moncreiff.
69 *Falconer* v. *Chisholm's Trs.*, 1925 S.L.T. 222.
70 *Brown & Critchley* v. *Decorative Art Journals Co.*, 1922 S.C. 192.
71 *Smith* v. *Kirkwood* (1897) 24 R. 872.
72 *Lamb, supra*; *Brown* v. *Brown*, 1970 S.L.T.(Notes) 79.

It is incompetent for the Court of Session to review by suspension a decree of law burrows of the sheriff court, by reason of the Civil Imprisonment Act 1882; the only mode of review is by stated case under the Summary Jurisdiction Act 1954.[73]

It is incompetent to bring a suspension of a decree of absolvitor pronounced *in foro* in the sheriff court,[74] or of a decree for expenses following on or accompanying a decree of absolvitor pronounced *in foro* in that court, on grounds involving the merits of the decree of absolvitor,[74] but the decree for expenses might be suspended, challenging it on grounds not involving the merits of the decree of absolvitor.[74]

Suspension by sheriff court of sheriff court decrees

The sheriff court of the defender's domicile [75] itself may [76] suspend charges or threatened charges on decrees of court granted by the sheriff or on decrees of registration proceeding on bonds, bills, contracts, or other obligations registered in the sheriff court books, or the Books of Council and Session, or any others competent, or on letters of horning following on such decrees, where the debt exclusive of interest and expenses does not exceed £50. To this extent suspension is excluded from the Court of Session,[77] save that where there was fundamental nullity, as where the defender was not subject to the jurisdiction of the sheriff court,[78] or a charge proceeded on a decree not granted against the person charged,[79] the Court of Session has held that it had jurisdiction, even though the sums involved were under £50.

Suspension is incompetent where appeal is still competent,[80] but is competent where the period for appeal has expired,[81] or where extract has been issued,[82] or where ordinary appeal is excluded but suspension is not excluded.[83]

Suspension of a decree *in foro* is incompetent.[84]

It is also incompetent where appeal has been taken to the Court of Session and has failed,[85] or not been insisted in.[86]

73 *Mackenzie* v. *Maclennan*, 1916 S.C. 617.
74 *McGregor* v. *Lord Strathallan* (1862) 1 M. 1002.
75 *Brown & Critchley* v. *Decorative Art Journals Co. Ltd.*, 1922 S.C. 192.
76 Sheriff Courts (Sc.) Act 1907, ss. 5, 7, rr. 123–125, amd. 1913 Act. See also *Pettie* v. *Broadbent Finance (Leeds)* 1970 S.L.T.(Sh.Ct.) 70.
77 *Bryson* v. *Belhaven Engineering, Ltd.* (1908) 15 S.L.T. 1043; *Dickson & Walker* v. *Mitchell*, 1910 S.C. 139; *Brown & Critchley, supra.* On whether a claim exceeds £50 see *Maule* v. *Page* (1909) 47 S.L.R. 110; *Pagan & Osborne* v. *Haig*, 1910 S.C. 341; *D. Argyll* v. *Muir*, 1910 S.C. 96; *Stevenson* v. *Sharpe*, 1910 S.C. 580; *Aitchison* v. *McDonald*, 1911 S.C. 174; *Abrahams* v. *Campbell*, 1911 S.C. 353; *Brown & Critchley, supra.*
78 *Pagan & Osborne, supra*; *Brown & Critchley, supra.*
79 *Aitchison* v. *McDonald*, 1911 S.C. 174.
80 Mackay, *Practice*, 482.
81 Mackay, *Manual*, 615.
82 *Turner* v. *Gray* (1824) 3 S. 235.
83 As under Court of Session Act 1825, s. 44; see *Paul* v. *Henderson* (1867) 5 M. 1120; *Fletcher* v. *Davidson* (1874) 2 R. 71; *Campbell's Trs.* v. *O'Neill*, 1911 S.C. 188; *Macdonald* v. *Denoon*, 1928 S.L.T. 439.
84 *Lamont* v. *Hall*, 1964 S.L.T.(Sh.Ct.) 25.
85 *Watt Bros.* v. *Foyn* (1879) 7 R. 126; *Mackenzie* v. *N.B. Ry. Co.* (1879) 17 S.L.R. 129; *Lamb* v. *Thomson* (1901) 4 F. 88.
86 *Watt Bros., supra.*

If the value of the cause does not exceed the privative jurisdiction of the sheriff court appeal to the Court of Session in a suspension is incompetent.[87]

If the suspension has proceeded as a summary cause appeal to the Court of Session in the suspension is incompetent save under the conditions applicable to appeals in summary causes.[88]

Decrees in absence

A suspension of a decree in absence is unnecessary so long as the decree has not been implemented because till then the defender may apply to be reponed, and the lodging and intimation of a reponing note operates a sist of diligence.[89] A decree in absence may be suspended on the ground of essential nullity,[90] or on the ground that the debt has been paid or satisfied,[91] or on the ground of irregularities in the proceedings subsequent to the date of decree.[92]

Suspension of removings

By the Court of Session (Judicature) Act 1825, s. 44, and the Court of Session Act 1868, s. 78, if a tenant has been ordained to remove by decree of an inferior court, the only mode of application for review open to him is by way of suspension.[1] This covers an extraordinary removing,[2] and a "summary ejection," *i.e.* summary removing.[3] The reason may be that removings demand despatch.[3a] In such a suspension it is not competent to amend the terms of the decree granted in the inferior court, if disconform to the breach of contract alleged to have warranted the removing. Hence where the lease provided for removing by stages and the decree was for instant removing, the court had to suspend the decree.[4] Nor is it competent to seek to prove by parole that an *ex facie* regular charge to remove is false.[5] Suspension is applicable also to statutory small tenants.[5a]

The statutory restriction does not apply to an interlocutory judgment allowing proof in an action of removing, against which appeal is competent.[6]

87 *Wilsons & Clyde Coal Co.* v. *Cairnduff*, 1911 S.C. 647.
88 *Summerlea Iron Co.* v. *Duff*, 1920 S.C. 291.
89 Sheriff Courts (Sc.) Act 1907, rr. 27–33.
90 *Aitchison* v. *McDonald*, 1911 S.C. 174; *Christie Bros.* v. *Remington Typewriting Co.*, 1912, 1 S.L.T. 123.
91 *Samuel* v. *Mackenzie & Bell* (1876) 4 R. 187.
92 *Gray* v. *Smart* (1892) 19 R. 692.
1 *Roy* v. *Wemyss* (1840) 2 D. 1345; *Lyon* v. *Irvine* (1873) 1 R. 512; *Fletcher* v. *Davidson* (1874) 2 R. 71; *Barbour* v. *Chalmers* (1891) 18 R. 610, 614; *Campbell's Trs.* v. *O'Neill*, 1911 S.C. 188; *Hendry* v. *Walker*, 1924 S.C. 757; *Robertson* v. *Thorburn*, 1927 S.L.T. 562; *Kemp* v. *Ballachulish Estate Co.*, 1933 S.C. 478; *Mackay* v. *Menzies*, 1937 S.C. 691.
2 *Lyon*, *supra*.
3 *Campbell's Trs.*, *supra*; *Kemp*, *supra*.
3a Rankine, *Leases*, 589.
4 *Lyon*, *supra*.
5 *Dun* v. *Craig*, Mar. 11, 1824, F.C.
5a *Cheyne* v. *Paterson*, 1929 S.C. 119.
6 *Stirling* v. *Graham*, 1920 S.C. 4.

A decree for summary ejection of persons possessing without any title, *vi, clam aut precario*, such as squatters, is, however, open to appeal in the ordinary way.[7]

The limitation of review of removings to suspension does not, however, exclude review by way of action of reduction.[8]

Decree of Sheriff Small Debt Court

Review by suspension of a decree pronounced in the Sheriff Small Debt Court is incompetent,[9] save that a suspension may be brought in case of inherent nullity [10] or essential illegality in subsequent procedure.[11]

Decree of J.P. Small Debt Court

Decrees of the J.P. Small Debt Court are not subject to any suspension, appeal or other stay of execution, excepting only in the case of consignation, as provided (s. 8) for the purpose of a rehearing before the justices.[12] This seems to imply that, if consignation of the sum decerned for be made in the hands of the clerk at any time before the days of charge elapse, suspension is competent.

Other courts

Suspension may be sought where an inferior court clearly exceeds its jurisdiction or powers,[13] or where the proceedings are vitiated by fundamental injustice,[14] even though the appellate jurisdiction of the Court of Session is excluded. It has, however, been held incompetent to suspend a decree on the ground of fraud; this required a reduction.[14]

Administrative and quasi judicial tribunals

Suspension may be competent as a means of having reviewed the decisions of administrative or quasi-judicial tribunals from which no appeal lies. The Tribunals and Inquiries Act 1971, s. 14 (2), provides that " any provision in an Act passed before August 1, 1958, that any order or determination shall not be called into question in any court, or any provision in such an Act which by similar words excludes any jurisdiction which the Court of Session would otherwise have to entertain *an application for reduction or suspension* of any order or determination, or otherwise to consider the validity of any order or determination, shall not have effect so as to prevent the exercise of any such jurisdiction." This implies that suspension at least may be competent in

7 *Clark* v. *Clarkes* (1890) 17 R. 1064; *Barbour* v. *Chalmers & Co.* (1891) 18 R. 610; *Robb* v. *Brearton* (1895) 22 R. 885; *Campbell's Trs., supra*, 192–193.

8 *Graham* v. *Stirling*, 1922 S.C. 90.

9 Small Debt (Sc.) Act 1837, ss. 30–31; *Crombie* v. *McEwan* (1871) 23 D. 333.

10 *Manson* v. *Smith* (1871) 9 M. 492.

11 *Shiell* v. *Mossman* (1872) 10 M. 58; *Brown* v. *Rodger* (1884) 12 R. 340; *Gray* v. *Smart* (1892) 19 R. 692.

12 Justices of the Peace Small Debts (Sc.) Act 1825, s. 14.

13 *Lindsay* v. *Barr* (1826) 3 S. 748; *Bruce* v. *Irvine* (1835) 13 S. 437; *Campbell* v. *Brown* (1829) 3 W. & S. 441; *Miller* v. *McCallum* (1840) 3 D. 65; Maclaren, *Bill Chamber Practice*, 86.

14 *Smith* v. *Kirkwood* (1897) 24 R. 872.

some cases. But the use of the remedy for such a purpose does not appear to be illustrated by case-law.

If the function of a sheriff in deciding on medical evidence whether or not to commit a person to a mental hospital as being of unsound mind be regarded as quasi-judicial (and it is " not strictly comparable either to his ordinary civil jurisdiction or indeed to his criminal jurisdiction"[15]), a bill of suspension and liberation has been entertained.[16] It was observed that " our function in criminal matters extends, in proper and necessary cases, to interfering where the liberty of the subject in any degree at all is taken away or infringed by an order of any court, albeit there is no court of review set up by these statutes. But this interference is allowable only . . . if that liberty has been taken away or affected by excess of jurisdiction or some gross abuse of the power conferred by statute upon the sheriff. The existence of our power depends on defect of power below or on one of these errors of procedure which go to the vitals and fundamentals of a case. In no other view . . . do we seem to possess a general power of review in the ordinary acceptation." [17] It is proper to observe that a plea to the competency of this bill of suspension was tabled in the answers, but was not insisted in at the hearing.[18] The case can accordingly hardly be treated as an authority sustaining the competency of reviewing a quasi-judicial decision by suspension, though if it had been utterly incompetent the High Court would hardly have ignored the point.

If suspension is competent it is submitted that it does not allow review of the decision challenged on its merits, but review only on such grounds as excess of jurisdiction, fundamental irregularity, unjudicial conduct or other objection nullifying the determination.

Bills of suspension in criminal cases

The bill of suspension utilised as a mode of review in certain summary criminal cases appears to be truly a civil remedy used in criminal cases. The form of a bill of suspension is civil, with its crave, condescendence and pleas-in-law, service on the prosecutor, his answers and pleas-in-law and the possibility of inquiry into the facts. Its function is parallel to that of the petition to suspend a civil decree and its consequences. Not least, it is not a competent mode of reviewing the justification for the summary court's decision or of challenging a conviction on the merits, whether on the evidence or the law applicable,[19] but is a mode of challenging the propriety or legality of the proceedings. It is competent, and the proper mode of challenge, where there are allegations

15 *Campbell* v. *Herron*, 1948 J.C. 127, 130, *per* L.J.C. Thomson.
16 *Campbell, supra* (petition to High Court of Justiciary).
17 *Ibid.* 133–134, *per* Lord Mackay.
18 *Ibid.* 130.
19 *O'Hare* v. *Mill*, 1938 J.C. 4; *Keanie* v. *Laird*, 1943 J.C. 73; *Fairley* v. *Muir*, 1951 J.C. 56; *Farquhar* v. *Burrell*, 1955 J.C. 66; *McShane* v. *Paton*, 1922 J.C. 26, is a special case.

of radical defect amounting to fundamental nullity,[20] irrelevant complaint,[21] excess of or refusal to exercise jurisdiction,[22] total inadequacy of evidence to prove charge,[23] gross irregularity in proceedings,[24] oppressive prosecution,[25] conviction for contravention of an *ultra vires* by-law,[26] oppressive conduct of presiding magistrate,[27] oppressive or incompetent sentence,[28] where the conviction is vitiated in some material aspect,[29] or there is other disregard of the requirements of justice.[30] Suspension will not be granted where there is a trivial irregularity,[31] or no such prima facie case of oppression as justifies inquiry.[32] The High Court has an inherent power to entertain a suspension where there is fundamental nullity even though review be expressly excluded [33] or other mode of review be provided.[34]

It is unsuitable, if not indeed incompetent, by suspension to try to exclude certain matters from evidence in a criminal trial yet to be held, the admissibility of the evidence being a matter for the trial judge.[35]

The summary method of setting aside a conviction in the summary criminal courts [36] does not apply to a bill of suspension.[37]

The right to bring a bill of suspension may be barred by mora and acquiescence, as by partial payment of a fine and subsequent delay to challenge the conviction.[38]

It cannot be used to enable an accused, who had refrained from putting before the court at his trial matters relevant to his mental condition, subsequently to disclose them when appealing against conviction and

20 *Collins* v. *Lang* (1887) 15 R.(J.) 7; *Hutchison* v. *Stevenson* (1902) 4 F.(J.) 69; *Morison* v. *Peters*, 1909 S.C.(J.) 58; *McGregor* v. *MacDonald*, 1952 J.C. 4.

21 *Owens* v. *Calderwood* (1869) 7 M. 556; *Walker* v. *Rodger* (1885) 12 R.(J.) 32; *Gladstone* v. *Stevenson* (1902) 4 F.(J.) 66; *Adams* v. *McKenna* (1906) 5 Adam 106; *Smith* v. *Semphill*, 1911 S.C.(J.) 30.

22 *Caledonian Ry.* v. *Fleming* (1869) 7 M. 554; *Muckersie* v. *McDougall* (1874) 2 R.(J.) 12; *McPherson* v. *Boyd* (1907) 5 Adam 247.

23 *Lockwood* v. *Walker*, 1910 S.C.(J.) 3.

24 *Jamieson* v. *Wilson* (1901) 3 F.(J.) 90; *Leavack* v. *Macleod*, 1913 S.C.(J.) 51; *Aitken* v. *Wood*, 1921 J.C. 84.

25 *Mackenzie* v. *McPhee* (1889) 16 R.(J.) 53; *Paton* v. *Wood* (1899) 1 F.(J.) 38; *Kelly* v. *Mitchell*, 1907 S.C.(J.) 52.

26 *McGregor* v. *Disselduff*, 1907 S.C.(J.) 21.

27 *Harper* v. *Neilson* (1898) 1 F.(J.) 1.

28 *Macleod* v. *Mackenzie* (1901) 4 F.(J.) 13; *Stewart* v. *Cormack*, 1941 J.C. 73, 77; *Young* v. *Brown*, 1960 J.C. 77.

29 *Clarkson* (1871) 2 Coup. 125; *Connell* v. *Mitchell*, 1913 S.C.(J.) 13.

30 *Cf. Kelly* v. *Mitchell*, 1907 S.C.(J.) 52; *Ewart* v. *Strathern*, 1924 J.C. 45.

31 *Taylor* v. *Tarras* (1901) 3 F.(J.) 39; *Ross* v. *Boyd* (1903) 5 F.(J.) 64; *McAtee* v. *Hogg* (1903) 5 F.(J.) 67.

32 *Nardini* v. *Walker* (1903) 5 F.(J.) 69.

33 *McKenzie* v. *McPhee* (1889) 16 R.(J.) 53; *Craig* v. *Tarras* (1897) 24 R.(J.) 88; *Massey* v. *Lamb* (1906) 8 F.(J.) 88.

34 *Schulze* v. *Steel* (1890) 17 R.(J.) 47.

35 *Paterson* v. *Macpherson*, 1924 J.C. 38.

36 Summary Jurisdiction (Scotland) Act 1908, s. 73 (now Summary Jurisdiction (Scotland) Act 1954, s. 72).

37 *Jensen* v. *Wilson*, 1912 S.C.(J.) 3; *Loudon* v. *Torrance*, 1916 S.C.(J.) 42.

38 *McLure* v. *Douglas* (1872) 2 Coup. 177; *Macfarlan* v. *Fishmongers of London* (1904) 6 F.(J.) 60; *cf. Deans* v. *Mitchell* (1901) 4 F.(J.) 1.

sentence,[39] and is unsuitable for dealing with an issue of the admissibility of certain evidence.[40]

It may also be used to challenge a sentence of imprisonment fo contempt of court committed by breach of an undertaking given in the course of criminal proceedings [41] though in such a case an appeal could also be taken to the Court of Session.[42]

Where the accused has been sentenced to imprisonment the appropriate form of bill is for suspension and liberation.[43] It is also appropriate where there has been committal to a mental hospital.[44]

39 *Farquhar* v. *Burrell*, 1955 J.C. 66.
40 *Fairley* v. *Muir*, 1951 J.C. 56.
41 *McLeod* v. *Speirs* (1884) 5 Coup. 387; 11 R.(J.) 26; *Graham* v. *Robert Younger Ltd.*, 1955 J.C. 28.
42 *Maclachlan* v. *Bruce*, 1912 S.C. 440; *Graham, supra*, 33.
43 *Galloway* v. *Adair*, 1947 J.C. 7.
44 *Campbell* v. *Herron*, 1948 J.C. 127 (where a plea to the competency of the Bill was not insisted in).

CHAPTER 11

INTERDICT

SUSPENSION, or supension and interdict, has also been utilised as a remedy of wider application than merely to stop wrongful diligence or threats of diligence.[1] " Where there is no decree, there may be a suspension though not in the strict acceptation of that word; for suspension is a process authorised by law, for putting a stop not only to the execution of iniquitous decrees, but to all encroachment either on property or possession and, in general, to every unlawful proceeding, *tit. ff. De nov. oper. nunc.* Thus a building, or the exercise of any illegal power which one assumes to himself, is a proper subject of suspension. . . . "[2]

The older practice was to initiate procedure by a bill craving letters of suspension and interdict. If the bill were granted letters of suspension were granted narrating and repeating any interim interdict granted. In 1838 procedure by bill of suspension and interdict was abolished and procedure by note, presented in the Bill Chamber, was introduced. The form of note was regulated by the Schedule to the Act of Sederunt of December 21, 1838. In 1936 following on the abolition of the Bill Chamber the modern procedure was introduced of presenting a petition for suspension and interdict in the Outer House.

In older practice interdict is normally found conjoined with suspension, and a note of suspension and interdict was brought to stop a wrong in progress and prevent its continuation or repetition but latterly, apart from proper cases of suspension and interdict in respect of diligence,[3] though nominally the remedy sought was suspension and interdict, the emphasis has been on the element of interdict, or order to desist from repeating or from perpetrating an infringement of right, and more recently, save in cases where it is desired to stop conduct in progress as well as to prevent continuance or repetition,[4] interdict alone is concluded for.[5] Indeed interdict is now deemed competent to stop wrongs in progress as well as wrongs apprehended, and the element of suspension is being forgotten.

This use of interdict seems to derive little if anything from the interdicts of the Roman law and may indeed rather derive from the interdict of the canon law, which was a prohibition on the performance of ecclesiastical rites. The Roman law interdicts have contributed more to the use of interdict as a means of regulating possession.[6]

[1] Chap. 10, *supra*.
[2] Ersk. IV, 3, 20.
[3] See Chap. 10, *supra*.
[4] *e.g. Neville* v. *Inverness Mags.*, 1942 S.C. 461; *McCormick* v. *Lord Advocate*, 1953 S.C. 396; *Trapp* v. *Aberdeenshire C.C.*, 1960 S.C. 302.
[5] *e.g. Exchange Telegraph Co.* v. *White*, 1961 S.L.T. 104; *Pease* v. *Pease*, 1967 S.C. 112.
[6] Chap. 12, *infra*.

Interdict generally

" Interdict is a remedy, by decree of court, either against a wrong in course of being done, or against an apprehended violation of a party's rights, only to be awarded on evidence of the wrong, or on reasonable grounds of apprehension that such violation is intended." [7] " The remedy of judicial interdict is a most important one, for it proceeds on the principle that prevention is better than cure, and that in many cases it is more expedient to prevent a wrong from being done than merely to attempt to give subsequent redress. But interdict is never granted as a matter of course and ought not to be applied for or granted without strong, or, at least, reasonable grounds." [8]

" It is essential to keep in view the very peculiar nature of a process of interdict, which differs materially from every other civil suit, and may not inaptly be termed quasi-criminal. If the party interdicted fails in any particular to observe the interdict he is liable to be brought to the bar, and subjected summarily to censure, fine and imprisonment, or any of these punishments, as well as to be mulcted in expenses. An interdict is thus of the nature of an extraordinary remedy, not to be given except for urgent reasons, and even then not as a matter of right, but only in the exercise of a sound judicial discretion. If granted at all it must be in terms so plain that he who runs may read. The responsibility of making it so lies upon the party asking the interdict, and the Court is not called upon to relieve him of that responsibility. He may be allowed to amend his prayer, but if interdict cannot be granted in accordance with the original or amended prayer it cannot be granted at all." [9]

" Interdict is a preventive proceeding, and by its very nature it may competently be invoked in suitable circumstances to restrain the commission in the future of a violation of rights not yet committed but only reasonably apprehended." [10]

" The essence of a case for interdict is that either there is a wrong being actually committed, or that a wrong is apprehended." [11] " Interdicts are granted by this and other courts of law when appreciable wrong to a man, whether in his property or other rights is threatened." [12] " The court is not in the habit of granting the remedy of interdict unless a wrong has been done or is apprehended." [13] " Broadly speaking, interdict is granted against a wrong which is in the course of being committed or where there is reasonable

[7] *Hay's Trs.* v. *Young* (1877) 4 R. 398, 401, *per* Lord Ormidale, quoting sheriff-substitute; quoted by Lord Blades in *Inverurie Mags.* v. *Sorrie*, 1956 S.C. 175, 184–185.
[8] *Ibid.* 402, *per* Lord Gifford.
[9] *Kelso School Board* v. *Hunter* (1874) 2 R. 228.
[10] *Gavin* v. *Ayrshire County Council*, 1950 S.C. 197, 207, *per* L.P. Cooper.
[11] *Hay's Trs.*, *supra*, 402, *per* Lord Gifford.
[12] *Winans* v. *Macrae* (1885) 12 R. 1051, 1063, *per* Lord Young.
[13] *Earl of Crawford* v. *Paton*, 1911 S.C. 1017, 1028, *per* Lord Salvesen.

ground for apprehending that a wrong is intended to be committed." [14] " A decree of permanent interdict is an order prohibiting a defender from doing an illegal act." [15]

It is sometimes stated [16] that in the Court of Session interdict is never concluded for alone, but only combined with another conclusion, most commonly with suspension. This is not so and interdict may be concluded for alone,[17] or combined with any other conclusion appropriate in the circumstances. The Rules of Court, 1965, refer [18] to petitions for suspension, suspension and interdict, and suspension and liberation, and also provide [19] that a conclusion for interim interdict may be included in the conclusions of any cause initiated by summons, in which case a separate petition for suspension and interdict is unnecessary. Though the phrase " suspension and interdict " seems normally to be used in the Court of Session [20] at least until recently, it is submitted that the words " suspension and " are pleonastic and meaningless, and appropriate only in those cases where there is an actual wrong, such as an unwarranted charge, to be suspended, as well as a threatened future wrong against which interdict is to be sought.[21] In the Sheriff Court interdict may be craved by itself.[22] Moreover even in the Court of Session where there is another conclusion the interdict conclusion simply seeks " interdict," [23] and it is plain that the phrase " suspension and interdict " should be confined to cases where the complainer seeks both to suspend some illegality and to interdict future or further steps, and in the context of the present chapter interdict alone is in issue, and it merely causes confusion to have to use the meaningless phrase " *suspension and* interdict," unless one is also concluding for declarator or payment or damages or some other remedy as well.

Interdict quasi-criminal in character

Interdict has been said [24] to be a quasi-criminal proceeding, as being one which may be attended with highly penal consequences in the event of breach.

" It is essential to keep in view the very peculiar nature of a process of interdict, which differs materially from every other civil suit, and

[14] *Inverurie Mags.* v. *Sorrie*, 1956 S.C. 175, 179, *per* L.J.C. Thomson.
[15] *Ibid.* 181, *per* Lord Patrick.
[16] Green's *Encyclopaedia,* VIII, s. 782; Thomson and Middleton, *Manual of Court of Session Procedure.*
[17] *Exchange Telegraph Co.* v. *White*, 1961 S.L.T. 104.
[18] R.C. 234–247.
[19] R.C. 79.
[20] *e.g.* in *Ben Nevis Distillery Co.* v. *N.B. Aluminium Co.*, 1948 S.C. 592.
[21] These cases are dealt with in Chap. 10, *supra.*
[22] *Inverurie Mags.* v. *Sorrie*, 1956 S.C. 175.
[23] In *Exchange Telegraph Co.* v. *Giulianotti*, 1959 S.C. 19, the two main conclusions were simply " For interdict. . . ."
[24] *Henderson* v. *Maclellan* (1874) 1 R. 920, 924; *Laing's Sewing Machine Co.* v. *Norrie* (1877) 5 R 29, 31, but see 33.

may not inaptly be termed quasi-criminal. If the party interdicted fails in any particular to observe the interdict he is liable to be brought to the bar, and subjected summarily to censure, fine and imprisonment, or any of these punishments, as well as to be mulcted in expenses. An interdict is thus of the nature of an extraordinary remedy, not to be given except for urgent reasons, and even then not as a matter of right, but only in the exercise of a sound judicial discretion." [25]

But this is probably the only respect in which it partakes of a criminal character and in the normal case it is purely civil.

Interdict and statutory penalty

Where a new offence has been created by statute and fenced with a penalty, that is presumed to be the sole sanction and a person contravening is not also liable to be interdicted from committing the offence. In *Institute of Patent Agents* v. *Lockwood* [26] it was held that a person, not registered as such, who practised as a patent-agent, rendered himself liable to the penalty for so doing but not to interdict at the instance of registered patent-agents. In *Magistrates of Buckhaven and Methil* v. *Wemyss Coal Co.*[27] the local authority was held to have no title to seek interdict against the defenders discharging refuse on the foreshore within the burgh when that conduct was a statutory offence with a penalty attached. " It has long been settled in Scotland that a statutory body which is set up to enforce a system of statutory regulations, or to establish and enforce a system of regulation by bye-laws of its own, has no power to resort to the common law process of interdict for the purpose of enforcing such regulations or bye-laws when the statute provides penalties for their breach and authorises recovery of such penalties. To protect a private right from invasion or abuse is one thing; to enforce conformity to a public regulation is another. The remedy of interdict is appropriate in the first case, but not in the second." [28]

Interdict or statutory appeal

In some circumstances a person aggrieved and wishing to stop proposed action by another may have to consider whether to seek interdict at common law or some special statutory form of appeal against the proposal. It is probably the general rule that where a special statutory appeal is competent it should be utilised before, or instead of, interdict.[29]

[25] *Kelso School Board* v. *Hunter* (1874) 2 R. 228, 232, *per* Lord Deas.
[26] (1894) 21 R.(H.L.) 61, 68, 69.
[27] 1932 S.C. 201.
[28] *Mags. of Buckhaven*, *supra*, 211–212, *per* L.P. Clyde, citing *Tay District Fishery Board* v. *Robertson* (1887) 15 R. 40; *cf. Kelso School Board* v. *Hunter* (1874) 2 R. 228; *Kelso Mags.* v. *Alexander*, 1939 S.C. 78.
[29] *Cf. Cumming* v. *Inverness Mags.*, 1953 S.C. 1.

Jurisdiction

Both the Court of Session and the sheriff court have jurisdiction to grant interdict but may normally do so only in respect of contraventions of right done or threatened within the court's area of jurisdiction and, because of the need in case of non-implement to enforce the decree by fine or imprisonment of the party in breach, against persons present within that jurisdiction.[30] The jurisdiction extends to foreigners.[31] A person resident outwith the jurisdiction is amenable to the jurisdiction if he has voluntarily submitted to it.[32]

If a sheriff grants interdict the party interdicted may appeal but cannot have the Court of Session recall the sheriff's interdict pending the appeal, though he may ask the sheriff to suspend operation of the interdict pending the appeal.[33]

As the sheriff's duties in the diligence of poinding are primarily ministerial he may entertain a crave for interdict against carrying out the sale of poinded goods under a warrant granted by himself.[34]

It has been held incompetent to seek to challenge by suspension and interdict a notice issued under statutory powers calling up the complainers for National Service when objection could have been taken in proceedings for enforcement by the military authorities in a court of summary criminal jurisdiction.[35]

The courts have no jurisdiction to enquire whether a governmental act, such as causing a royal proclamation in particular terms to be published, is or is not conform to law, and a petition to interdict such an act is accordingly incompetent.[36]

Complainer's title to sue

The complainer must show both title and interest [37] to sue for the protection of his right from infringement. But " it requires little interest to give a title to complain of what is unlawful." [38]

" To justify the interposition of the Court in granting an interdict, the party applying for it must show a legal title to the subject, of which his use and enjoyment and right of possession are alleged to be unlawfully interfered with; and, further, he must show either that there has been plain invasion of his property by a party having no right or title whatever in or to the subject or its use; or, as against a party pleading a competing

30 *Kermick* v. *Watson* (1871) 9 M. 984; *Waygood* v. *Bennie* (1885) 12 R. 651; *Toni Tyres Ltd.* v. *Palmer Tyre Ltd.* (1905) 7 F. 477.

31 *Toni Tyres Ltd., supra.*

32 *White* v. *Spottiswoode* (1846) 8 D. 952; *Longmuir* v. *Longmuir* (1850) 12 D. 926; *Gill* v. *Cutler* (1895) 23 R. 371.

33 *Trainer* v. *Renfrewshire Upper District Committee*, 1907 S.C. 1117.

34 *Jack* v. *Waddell's Trs.*, 1918 S.C. 73.

35 *Green* v. *Lord Advocate*, 1918 S.C. 667.

36 *McCormick* v. *Lord Advocate*, 1953 S.C. 396.

37 On interest see *Cowan* v. *Millar* (1895) 22 R. 833, 838; *Wishaw Burgh Commrs.* v. *Cleland Co-operative Socy. Ltd.* (1899) 2 F.58; *Ballachulish Slate Quarries Ltd.* v. *Grant* (1903) 5 F. 1105.

38 *Milne* v. *Leslie* (1888) 15 R. 460, 469, *per* Lord Rutherfurd Clark.

title, that he has had possession (in virtue of his title) for at least seven years prior to that attempt to innovate on it of which he complains, when he will be entitled to interdict *uti possidetis*." [39] It is not essential that his title be complete at the time of petition,[40] but interest alone will not suffice.[41] Title may be based on ownership of property prejudiced by the defender's actings, or on contract, or as being in right of a fiduciary duty.[42] A superior has been held entitled to protect the subject of a feuright by interdict without the vassal's consent,[43] a landlord to interdict a nuisance complained of by the tenant,[44] and a tenant to interdict pollution of a stream running through his landlord's, and his, lands.[45] "So far as an interdict against trespass is concerned, the title required by the law of Scotland as a foundation for interdict, in the absence of a competing title, is any lawful title which *ex facie* applies to the subject encroached upon." [46]

Where two or more parties have a common interest they may complain together to protect that interest, but not to protect separate rights elsewhere.[47]

A landlord may have a title but has no interest to interdict an alleged trespasser who has the tenant's permission to cross the ground in question.[48]

Magistrates acting under the Burgh Police Act 1892 have no title to vindicate by interdict rights over the foreshore, which are subject to the rights of the Crown and of the proprietor of the foreshore.[49]

A petition at the instance of the Lord Advocate in the public interest may be competent in a case of persistent defiance of a statutory regulation.[49]

A board set up under statute, with statutory powers and remedies, has no title to sue at common law for interdict.[50]

If a pursuer or petitioner for interdict loses his title to sue during the course of the action, as where he ceased to belong to the body whose misconduct he challenged, the proceedings must be dismissed.[51]

It is not generally competent for a private person to seek to vindicate a general public right,[52] and individual ratepayers have no title to challenge

[39] *Colquhoun* v. *Paton* (1859) 21 D. 996, 1001, *per* Lord Cowan.

[40] *Cranston & Elliot* v. *Dobson* (1899) 2 F. 271; *Mackay* v. *Mackay*, 1914 S.C. 900.

[41] *Anstruther* v. *E. Fife Ry. Co.* (1852) 1 Macq. 98; *Graham* v. *Warnock*, 1926 S.N. 1; *Nicol* v. *Dundee Harbour Trs.*, 1915 S.C.(H.L.) 7, 12, where observed that a rival trader has an interest but not a title.

[42] *Nicol*, *supra*, 12–14, *per* Lord Dunedin, giving many examples.

[43] *M. Breadalbane* v. *Campbell* (1851) 13 D. 647.

[44] *McEwen* v. *Steedman & McAlister*, 1912 S.C. 156; 1913 S.C. 761.

[45] *Jolly* v. *Brown* (1826) 6 S. 872; *Arthur* v. *Aird*, 1907 S.C. 1170; *Fleming* v. *Gemmill*, 1908 S.C. 340.

[46] *L.M.S. Ry.* v. *McDonald*, 1924 S.C. 835, 840, *per* L.P. Clyde.

[47] *Arthur* v. *Aird*, 1907 S.C. 1170; *cf. Kincaid Smith* v. *Cameron* (1900) 2 F. 1179.

[48] *Steuart* v. *Stephen* (1877) 4 R. 873; *cf. Gould* v. *McCorquodale* (1869) 8 M. 165.

[49] *Buckhaven and Methil Mags.* v. *Wemyss Coal Co.*, 1932 S.C. 201.

[50] *Tay District Fishery Board* v. *Robertson* (1887) 15 R. 40.

[51] *Donaghy* v. *Rollo*, 1964 S.C. 278; contrast *Spowart* v. *T. & G.W.U.*, 1926 S.L.T. 245. *Cf. Innes* v. *Partridge* (1825) 4 S. 761.

[52] *McCormick* v. *Lord Advocate*, 1953 S.C. 396; *cf. Milne* v. *Leslie* (1888) 15 R. 460.

maladministration of a burgh's common good,[53] but individual ratepayers have been held entitled to interdict their local authority from imposing an illegal assessment,[54] an individual patrimonial interest being enough to entitle a pursuer to object to the imposition of an illegal tax,[55] and an individual ratepayer held entitled to challenge the local authority's infringement of the customary rights of all in open ground.[56]

If pursuers have a common interest in a subject, such as the fishing in a stream on which the estates of both verge, they may petition jointly for interdict to protect that interest, but otherwise may not do so.[57] Thus two proprietors cannot obtain joint interdict against trespassing on either estate.[58]

A single *pro indiviso* proprietor is entitled to interdict an outsider who is troubling him in the possession of the property held *pro indiviso*.[59]

If the complainer's title is not clear the proper remedy is declarator and interdict,[60] though in some cases the court has allowed a matter of title to be determined incidentally in a suspension and interdict.[61]

A corporate body has title to sue for the protection of its corporate name and the interests of members in their membership, certainly where patrimonial interests are involved.[62]

There is nothing comparable in Scots law to relator proceedings in English law whereby the Attorney-General may, at the instigation of an aggrieved individual, apply in the public interest to restrain unlawful conduct by an individual or public authority. The absence of comparable procedure has on occasion been pointed out.[63] The Lord Advocate would, of course, be the proper petitioner if the interests of the Crown, or Parliament or the public as a whole were endangered.[64]

Defender

The actual alleged wrongdoer is the proper defender.[65] Interdict is " only granted against any person on the ground of acts done by him

53 Ersk. I, 4, 23; *Mollison* v. *Inverurie Mags.*, Dec. 14, 1820, F.C.; *Grahame* v. *Kirkcaldy Mags.* (1881) 9 R.(H.L.) 91, 96; *Conn* v. *Renfrew Corpn.* (1906) 8 F. 905.

54 *Stirling C.C.* v. *Falkirk Mags.*, 1912 S.C. 1281; *Farquhar & Gill* v. *Aberdeen Mags.*, 1912 S.C. 1294.

55 *Ewing* v. *Glasgow Police Commrs.* (1836) 15 S. 389; (1839) MacL. & R. 847.

56 *Grahame, supra.*

57 *Forbes* v. *Leys, Mason & Co.* (1824) 2 S. 515; *Duke of Buccleuch* v. *Cowan* (1864) 2 M. 653; *Arthur* v. *Aird*, 1907 S.C. 1170.

58 *Arthur, supra*, 1173.

59 *Warrand* v. *Watson* (1905) 8 F. 253, 261.

60 *Lovat* v. *Fraser* (1845) 8 D. 316; *Cruickshank* v. *Irving* (1854) 17 D. 286; *Scott* v. *McDowall* (1857) 19 D. 769; *Green* v. *Shepherd* (1866) 4 M. 1028; *Grierson* v. *Sandsting School Board* (1882) 9 R. 437; *Cronin* v. *Sutherland* (1899) 2 F. 217.

61 *E. Fife* v. *Banff Mags.* (1829) 8 S. 137; *Edinburgh Ministers* v. *Edinburgh Mags.* (1836) 16 S. 400; *Colquhoun* v. *Paton* (1853) 16 D. 206; (1859) 21 D. 996; *E. Stair* v. *Austin* (1881) 8 R. 683; *Thurlow* v. *Tait* (1893) 1 S.L.T. 62.

62 *Accountants in Edinburgh* v. *Corporation of Accountants Ltd.* (1893) 20 R. 750.

63 *Nicol* v. *Dundee Harbour Trs.*, 1915 S.C.(H.L.) 7, 10, 17. See further *Buckhaven and Methil Mags.* v. *Wemyss Coal Co.*, 1932 S.C. 201, 213–214.

64 *Buckhaven, supra.*

65 *Stirling Crawfurd* v. *C.N. Trs.* (1881) 8 R. 826.

constituting an infringement or menace of the rights sought to be protected . . . [It is] a purely personal remedy directed against the person who is said in the action to have violated the pursuer's rights."[66] Accordingly interdict is not competent against a defender merely because he is the successor of one who infringed the pursuer's rights. An interdict cannot be granted against a person not called as defender or respondent, and for that reason a third party cannot generally claim to be sisted as a party, even though he alleges an interest.[67] In particular circumstances he may, however, be allowed to sist himself and to be heard.[68] Once a wrong justifying interdict has been committed the person responsible is liable and the proper respondent, and not anyone else who has succeeded to his position.[69]

Misnomer of the defender invalidates the interdict.[70]

The court has expressed the view that it is inexpedient or unjust to interdict one defender but not another, on the ground that the court has no jurisdiction over him, when both are equally involved in the conduct sought to be interdicted.[71]

The courts may not grant an interdict against the Crown but where, in proceedings against the Crown, such relief is sought as might between private persons be granted by way of interdict the court may in lieu make an order declaratory of the rights of the parties.[72] It has been held that this does not entitle the court to make a hypothetical declaratory order.[73] An interim declaratory order is not possible.[74]

An interdict is not competent against a foreign sovereign state, unless it submits to the jurisdiction or actively invokes the jurisdiction on its own behalf.[75]

It is competent to seek interdict against the police but not against their doing anything which they have legal right to do, such as sending officers in plain clothes to ascertain whether the law was being broken in certain premises,[76] still less against doing anything which they have a duty to do.

There is no rule that if a corporation acts *ultra vires* only the Crown

[66] *Bankier Distillery* v. *Young's Collieries* (1899) 2 F. 89, 90, *per* L.P. Balfour.

[67] *Laing's Sewing Machine Co.* v. *Norrie* (1877) 5 R. 29; *Weir* v. *Denny* (1894) 1 S.L.T. 451. Contrast *Gill* v. *Cutler* (1895) 23 R. 371; *Gas Power Co.* v. *Power Gas Corpn.*, 1911 S.C 27.

[68] *Gas Power Co., supra.*

[69] *Bankier Distillery* v. *Young's Collieries* (1899) 2 F. 89.

[70] *Overseas League* v. *Taylor*, 1951 S.C. 105.

[71] *California Redwood Co. Liqdrs.* v. *Walker* (1886) 13 R. 810; contrast *Pacific Coast Mining Co. Liqdrs.* v. *Walker* (1886) 13 R. 816.

[72] Crown Proceedings Act 1947, s. 21 (1) (*a*), as applied to Scotland by s. 43 (*a*); *cf. McCormick* v. *Lord Advocate*, 1953 S.C. 396.

[73] *Ayr Mags.* v. *Secretary of State for Scotland*, 1965 S.C. 394.

[74] *Underhill* v. *Ministry of Food* [1950] 1 All E.R. 591; *International G.E.C. of New York* v. *Customs and Excise Commrs.* [1962] Ch. 784.

[75] *The Cristina* [1938] A.C. 485; *Republic of Spain* v. *National Bank*, 1939 S.C. 413.

[76] *Southern Bowling Club Ltd.* v. *Ross* (1902) 4 F. 405; *cf. Shepherd* v. *Menzies* (1900) 2 F. 443.

can complain, unless the act complained of has a direct injurious effect on some patrimonial interest of the complainer.[77]

It is not competent to seek interdict against persons who have not infringed the pursuer's rights, and who have no apparent intention of doing so, merely on the ground that they are officers or managers of a body to which the actual alleged infringer belongs, unless possibly it were averred that they had instructed, permitted, caused or otherwise been parties to the alleged infringement.[78]

Equitable jurisdiction

In deciding whether to grant or refuse interdict the court exercises an equitable jurisdiction, so that it is never bound to grant or refuse interdict [79] and it may refuse even when the petitioner has shown good ground in law for the grant, particularly where some public interest is involved [80] and even though the inconvenience or loss to the defender will be greater than that caused by the complainer by its refusal of interdict.[81] Thus interdict has been refused against one who had trespassed unintentionally and in good faith.[82] Again a complainer who has built up a business by perpetrating frauds on the public as to the qualities of his products cannot obtain interdict to protect his trade name.[83]

In building cases " There is an equitable power vested in the Court in virtue of which, when the exact restoration of things to their former condition is either impossible or would be attended with unreasonable loss and expense, quite disproportionate to the advantage which it would give to the successful party, the court can award an equivalent—in other words—they can say upon what equitable conditions the building should be allowed to remain where it is, although it has been placed there without legal right." [84]

In the exercise of this equitable discretion the court may, in an application for interdict, make a declaratory finding, and suspend the operation of that finding pending the progress of remedial measures, in cases where

77 *Nicol* v. *Dundee Harbour Trs.*, 1915 S.C.(H.L.) 7, 15, citing *Ewing* v. *Glasgow Police Commrs.* (1839) McL. & Rob. 847; *Rodgers* v. *Tailors of Edinburgh* (1843) 5 D. 295; *Baird* v. *Dundee Mags.* (1865) 4 M. 69; *Sanderson* v. *Lees* (1860) 22 D. 24; *Grahame* v. *Kirkcaldy Mags.* (1882) 9 R.(H.L.) 91; *Leith Dock Commrs.* v. *Leith Mags.* (1899) 1 F. (H.L.) 65.

78 *Shepherd, supra.*

79 *Kelso School Board* v. *Hunter* (1874) 2 R. 228; *White* v. *Dickson* (1881) 8 R. 896, 901; *Ben Nevis Distillery Co.* v. *N.B. Aluminium Co.*, 1948 S.C. 592, 598; *Inverurie Mags.* v. *Sorrie*, 1956 S.C. 175.

80 *e.g.* in *Ben Nevis Distillery Co.* v. *N.B. Aluminium Co.*, 1948 S.C. 592, though damage was proved the court refused to grant interdict because of the public interest at that time in keeping the aluminium works in production.

81 *Grahame* v. *Kirkcaldy Mags.* (1882) 9 R.(H.L.) 91; *Bank of Scotland* v. *Stewart* (1891) 18 R. 957; *Glen* v. *West Highland Ry.* (1895) 2 S.L.T. 489; *Clippens Oil Co.* v. *Edinburgh & District Water Trs.* (1897) 25 R. 370.

82 *Hay's Trs.* v. *Young* (1877) 4 R. 398.

83 *Leather Cloth Co. Ltd.* v. *American Leather Cloth Co.* (1865) 11 H.L.C. 523; *Perry* v. *Truefitt* (1843) 6 Beav. 66; *Holloway* v. *Holloway* (1850) 13 Beav. 209; *Pidding* v. *How* (1856) 8 Sim. 477; *Bile Bean Mfg. Co.* v. *Davidson* (1906) 8 F. 1181.

84 *Jack* v. *Begg* (1875) 3 R. 35, 43, *per* Lord Gifford, citing *Sanderson* v. *Geddes* (1874) 1 R. 1198.

either the grant of immediate interdict would be attended with consequences to the rights of the respondent as injurious, or possibly more so, than the wrong that was complained of, or because the effect of an immediate interdict would be to cause some great and immediate public inconvenience.[85]

Need for precision

The prayer of a petition for interdict or the terms of a conclusion therefor, must be precise, clear and definite, so that if granted it is clear to the defender what he must not do, and what kinds of conduct will be contraventions.[86] " It would be unfair to the defender to grant any interdict against him without specifying precisely what it is he is prohibited from doing, so that he may know, and know exactly, what he may do without incurring the penalties which attach to breach of interdict." [87] " The interdict as granted offends against the fundamental and salutary rule that an interdict ought not to be expressed in language which is of doubtful meaning. A respondent is entitled to know exactly what it is that he must abstain from doing." [88] If the prayer is too general it is not competent to refer to the statement of facts annexed to ascertain its precise application.[89] " The essence of a case for interdict is that either there is a wrong being actually committed, or that a wrong is apprehended. There must be reasonable grounds for fearing that the respondent in a petition such as this will do the act which he is to be interdicted from doing. The Court is not to be asked without any cause shown to interdict and prohibit all the world from doing anything contrary to law. It will presume that the law will be obeyed unless it is shown that an infraction is seriously threatened, or on good ground apprehended." [90] If the prayer is not, or cannot be made, precise, interdict cannot be granted.[91] An interdict echoing a statutory provision is not competent; it must be directed against some specific act alleged to be in contravention of the statute.[92] Nor can an interdict be granted save against the respondent called.[93]

Similarly " it is the custom in Scotland to prescribe in the decree with particularity both what is permitted and what is prohibited." [94] If this cannot be done, interdict cannot be granted.[95]

85 *Clippens Oil Co.* v. *Edinburgh & District Water Trs.* (1898) 25 R. 373, 383, approved in *Ben Nevis Distillery Co.* v. *North British Aluminium Co.*, 1948 S.C. 592, 598.
86 *Kelso School Board* v. *Hunter* (1874) 2 R. 228, 232, 235; *Cairns* v. *Lee* (1892) 20 R. 16; *Earl of Crawford* v. *Paton*, 1911 S.C. 1017, 1026.
87 *Perth General Station Committee* v. *Ross* (1896) 23 R. 885, 894, *per* Lord Trayner.
88 *B.T.H. Co.* v. *Charlesworth Peebles & Co.*, 1922 S.C. 680, 685, *per* Lord Skerrington.
89 *Cairns, supra.*
90 *Hay's Trs.* v. *Young* (1877) 4 R. 398, 402, *per* Lord Gifford.
91 *Kelso School Board* v. *Hunter* (1874) 2 R. 228; *Cairns* v. *Lee* (1892) 20 R. 16; *Perth General Station Cttee.* v. *Ross* (1896) 23 R. 885; 24 R.(H.L.) 44.
92 *Fleming* v. *Liddesdale District Cttee.* (1897) 24 R. 281.
93 *Laing's Sewing Machine Co.* v. *Norrie* (1877) 5 R. 29.
94 *Pirie* v. *Earl of Kintore* (1906) 8 F.(H.L.) 16, 18, *per* L.C. Halsbury.
95 *Robertson* v. *Wright* (1885) 13 R. 174.

De minimis principle

The court will not grant interdict against infringement of rights where the infringement is negligible in extent,[1] or there have been only a few petty instances of infringement,[2] particularly where it holds it not proved that the defender had failed to take reasonable precautions to prevent the infringement complained of,[3] or the infringement has been inadvertent rather than deliberate.[4] " Interdicts are granted by this and other courts of law where appreciable wrong to a man, whether in his property or in his other rights, is threatened. Here there was no appreciable wrong." [5]

Mistake, good faith, etc.

Interdict will not normally be granted against a person who has infringed another's rights by mistake,[6] in good faith,[7] in the belief that he had permission,[8] or accidentally rather than deliberately.[9]

Negative interdict

An interdict is in its nature a prohibitory order, in effect saying, " Thou shalt not . . . " A negative interdict is in effect an order that the party interdicted shall do something, the form in effect being, " Thou shall not refrain from, or refuse to. . . " It has been said that " however the claim may be disguised, the substance of it is that we are asked to interdict the arbiter from not hearing the pursuer's witnesses—to grant a negative interdict. That has never been done, and I presume your Lordships will not now be disposed to create such a precedent." [10] A negative interdict would be in effect a decree akin to a *mandamus* or a decree for specific implement, and accordingly would seem to be normally incompetent.

Interim and perpetual interdict

In any action initiated by summons the pursuer may include a conclusion for interim interdict and may move the court, before the summons is called or after calling but before defences are lodged, to grant interim interdict.[11]

Similarly when a petition for suspension and interdict is presented an application may be made for interim interdict, and the court may make an interim order, or further interim order, or vary an interim order, with or

1 *Winans* v. *Macrae* (1885) 12 R. 1051; *Robertson* v. *Wright* (1885) 13 R. 174.
2 *Thomson* v. *Robertson* (1888) 15 R. 880.
3 *Robertson, supra.*
4 *Bass, Ratcliff & Gretton Ltd.* v. *Laidlaw* (1886) 13 R. 898.
5 *Winans, supra*, 1063, *per* Lord Young (the wrong was the trespass by a lamb on to a deer forest of 200,000 acres).
6 *Bass, Ratcliff & Gretton* v. *Laidlaw* (1908) 16 S.L.T. 660.
7 *Hay's Trs.* v. *Young* (1877) 4 R. 398.
8 *Steuart* v. *Stephen* (1877) 4 R. 873.
9 *Thomson* v. *Robertson* (1888) 15 R. 880.
10 *Wemyss* v. *Ardrossan Harbour Co.* (1893) 20 R. 500, 505, *per* Lord McLaren.
11 R.C. 79.

without caution, consignation, or other conditions, or make an interim interdict already granted perpetual.[12] Interim interdict is appropriate where the action, if not stopped at once, may do irretrievable harm.[13] Relevancy of averment is not a sufficient ground for granting interim interdict.[14]

If the Lord Ordinary reserves the question of interim interdict until answers to the petition have been lodged and considered, this is not a refusal of interim interdict, and cannot be reclaimed against as a refusal.[15]

The grant or refusal of interim interdict is a matter for the discretion of the Lord Ordinary.[16] "The question upon which the granting or refusal of interim interdict depends is simply the question on which side the balance of convenience with regard to the interim regulation of the actings of the parties (pending a decision on the merits of the dispute between them) lies. But it is essential to the decision of that question that one should understand what the nature of the dispute is."[17] "In determining that matter it is the practice of the Court to consider where the balance of convenience lies."[18] In that case[17] it was held that interim interdict might be granted notwithstanding a plea that interdict was incompetent, and that a question of its competency might ultimately arise for decision. Where the action is based on misleading representations the court will not, unless under very exceptional circumstances, grant interim interdict, except against the particular representation complained of, or any other representation which was a mere paraphrase or a colourable variation of the statement complained of.[19]

A distinction has been drawn between cases where the complainer's right certainly exists, and he is therefore entitled to immediate interim interdict against the party injuring him, and cases where he is not entitled to do so until he has established his right by action. The former class includes rights of patent or of copyright where the right is presumed unless the infringer can successfully challenge the pursuer's right.[20] The latter class includes cases where the pursuer undertakes to prove his right, and the defender's fraudulent invasion of it, as a preliminary to his obtaining interdict, and for this purpose it matters not whether the pursuer establishes his right by declarator or by action of damages.[20]

The effect of interim interdict is to prohibit immediately the conduct complained of, without prejudice to any motion by the defender for the recall of the interim interdict pending the hearing, or to the ultimate grant or refusal of perpetual interdict. If interim interdict is granted it

12 R.C. 236.
13 *Innes* v. *Innes* (1829) 7 S. 762; *Trapp* v. *Aberdeenshire C.C.*, 1960 S.C. 302; *Pease* v. *Pease*, 1967 S.C. 112.
14 *Rankin* v. *McLachlan* (1864) 3 M. 128.
15 *Gauldie* v. *Arbroath Mags.*, 1936 S.C. 861.
16 *Hay* v. *Hay*, 1968 S.C. 179, 184.
17 *Scottish Milk Marketing Board* v. *Paris*, 1935 S.C. 287, 296, *per* L.P. Clyde.
18 *Ibid.* 302, *per* Lord Fleming; *cf. Trapp* v. *Aberdeenshire Education Authy.*, 1960 S.C. 302.
19 *Henderson* v. *Munro* (1905) 7 F. 636, 639–640.
20 *Green* v. *Shepherd* (1866) 4 M. 1028.

subsists until recalled,[21] or the petition is finally disposed of by the court.[22] It may be recalled if adequate justification be shown for the conduct complained of,[23] particularly if the continuance of the conduct will not cause irretrievable harm.

Interim interdict is incompetent against a wrong already completed,[24] and has been refused where the complainer had unduly delayed in seeking it.[25]

It may be granted before inquiry as to the facts, particularly where there has been a previous instance of the same wrong,[26] or the facts are *prima facie* identical with facts already decided,[27] or there is a strong *prima facie* case,[28] or after inquiry, and in the latter case even notwithstanding a report as to remedial operations, or a further report that the harm no longer existed.[29]

The court is hesitant to grant interim interdict against the proceedings of a public body acting in the public interest,[30] but may do so where there are powerful considerations of justice at stake.[31]

Where the real issue is not decided in proceedings for interim interdict, leave is required to appeal against the grant or refusal of it to the House of Lords.[32]

When interdict effective

The final decree prohibitory in a suspension and interdict draws back to the date of the application, and strikes against everything done by the respondent after that date, whether or not there has been an interim interdict. *Pendente lite nihil innovandum* is the rule, and whatever a party chooses to do after the matter is litigious he does at his own risk, and it may be ordered to be undone.[33]

Works completed pending interdict case

If works have been completed while a petition for interdict was in court but the works have been found to constitute a contravention of the petitioner's rights the court may require them to be removed.[34] In such a case " the question does not appear to me to depend on a consideration of the balance of inconvenience or loss which would result to the parties

21 *Home Drummond* v. *McLachlan*, 1908 S.C. 12.
22 *Clippens Oil Co.* v. *Edinburgh & District Water Trs.* (1906) 8 F. 731; affd. 1907 S.C.(H.L.) 9.
23 *Crawford* v. *Paisley Mags.* (1870) 8 M. 693.
24 *Glen* v. *Caledonian Ry.* (1868) 6 M. 797.
25 *Ayala* v. *Dowell* (1893) 1 S.L.T. 374.
26 *Duke of Buccleuch* v. *Brown* (1873) 1 R. 85.
27 *Free Church* v. *Johnston* (1905) 7 F. 517.
28 *Incandescent Gas Light Co.* v. *McCulloch* (1897) 5 S.L.T. 180.
29 *Fraser's Trs.* v. *Cran* (1877) 4 R. 794.
30 *Bell* v. *Secretary of State for Scotland*, 1933 S.L.T. 519; *Alexander & Sons* v. *Traffic Commissioners*, 1936 S.N. 38; *cf. Scottish Milk Marketing Board* v. *Paris*, 1935 S.C. 287.
31 *Lockhart* v. *Irving*, 1936 S.L.T. 567; *Innes* v. *Burgh of Kirkcaldy*, 1963 S.L.T. 325.
32 *Adelphi Hotel (Glasgow) Ltd.* v. *Walker*, 1960 S.C. 182.
33 *Grahame* v. *Kirkcaldy Mags.* (1882) 9 R.(H.L.) 91, 94, 97.
34 *Jack* v. *Begg* (1875) 3 R. 35, 43; *Grahame* v. *Kirkcaldy Mags.* (1882) 9 R.(H.L.) 91, 94.

respectively . . . such as we would have to deal with in a question of the granting or refusing of an interim interdict. The operations in question have been found by a final judgment of this court to be illegal . . . it is the case of a clear interference by the respondents with the private property and rights of the complainers. In these circumstances, it appears to me that the respondents must shew some cogent reasons why the complainers should not be permitted now to vindicate their established rights and have the encroachment on their property put an end to." [35]

Caution

Interdict, particularly interim interdict, may in the discretion of the court be granted only if caution be found for loss caused by stopping the actings of the respondent,[36] or refused only if caution be found for loss caused by the continuance of the respondent's actings.[37]

Interdict granted on caution is not operative until caution be found, and accordingly a person cannot claim damages for wrongful interdict unless the interdict granted had been rendered effectual by the finding of caution.[38]

Interdict competent only against wrong

It is competent to interdict only what is a legal wrong and infringement of the complainer's rights. It is not competent against something which is merely unwelcome, unpleasant or harmful if it is legally permissible or authorised by statute or common law.[39] " It is quite a competent mode of proceeding to ask for interdict against any one obstructing a party in the exercise of an undoubted right or the discharge of a clear duty. But I apprehend that to justify such a course the right or the duty must be very clear. We are not to try doubtful questions in a process of interdict. That must be done in a different form." [40] " Interdict is not a remedy to be had for the asking; it involves penal consequences in case of breach; and it will only be given upon clear averment and proof of actual or definitely apprehended invasion of a legal right." [41] Thus interdict will not normally be granted against taking decree, or doing diligence, or petitioning for sequestration, or the like legal action, but only if in such cases there had been a specific undertaking not to take the step in question. It has been held incompetent to interdict a tenant from making use of

[35] *Clippens Oil Co. Ltd.* v. *Edinburgh & District Water Trs.* (1897) 25 R. 370, 382, *per* Lord Adam.

[36] *e.g. Curtis* v. *Sandison* (1831) 10 S. 72; *Finnie* v. *G.S.W. Ry.* (1856) 18 D. 325; *Williams* v. *Fairbairn* (1899) 1 F. 944.

[37] *Johnston* v. *Dumfriesshire Road Trs.* (1867) 5 M. 1127; *Fergusson-Buchanan* v. *Dunbarton C.C.*, 1924 S.C. 42.

[38] *Wilson* v. *Gilchrist* (1900) 2 F. 391.

[39] *West* v. *Aberdeen Harbour Commrs.* (1876) 4 R. 207; *Don* v. *N.B. Ry.* (1878) 5 R. 972; *Gillespie* v. *Lucas & Aird* (1893) 20 R. 1035; *Shepherd* v. *Menzies* (1900) 2 F. 443; *Southern Bowling Club* v. *Ross* (1902) 4 F. 405.

[40] *Kelso School Board* v. *Hunter* (1874) 2 R. 228, 230, *per* L.P. Inglis.

[41] *Earl of Crawford* v. *Paton*, 1911 S.C. 1017, 1026, *per* Lord Dundas; *cf.* Lord Salvesen at p. 1028.

subjects let to him, on the allegation that he is notour bankrupt.[42] Nor is it competent against the mere assertion of a contrary or conflicting right without action which infringes the complainer's rights.[43]

Interdict is also not appropriate for ascertaining and adjusting the rights of adjoining proprietors in a canal and regulating the complainer's use of his rights.[44] So too it has been refused where there was no evidence of actual or apprehended invasion of a legal right.[45]

Interdict is not competent against performance of an imperative statutory duty,[46] nor against doing anything authorised by statute,[47] nor in a case of a contravention of a statute which has a penalty provided.[48] But it is competent where a result has been authorised by statute but the means of achieving the result cause harm and it is not established that all reasonable steps have been taken to obviate the harm.[49]

Nor is it competent where the effect would be to insist on a state of affairs which the court could not secure or maintain by decree of specific implement.[50]

It is not a ground for refusing to enforce an established right by interdict that the granting of interdict will cause inconvenience or pecuniary loss to the person interdicted out of all proportion to the loss which would result to the other party from refusing interdict.[51]

Wrong must be threatened or continuing one

Interdict is inappropriate and incompetent against a wrong completed,[52] or one done once and for all. It is appropriate only against a wrong threatened, or in progress, or done but likely to be repeated or otherwise continuing.[53] " To support an application for interdict the complainer has to establish such action on the part of the respondents as will justify a reasonable apprehension that they are going to interfere with his rights." [54]

Prematurity of interdict

Interdict will not be granted against a person merely because he may at some future time contravene the petitioner's rights, but only if there is evidence of an immediate threat or likelihood or intention to do so.[55]

42 *Wauchope* v. *Stevens* (1826) 4 S. 766.
43 *Warrand* v. *Watson* (1905) 8 F. 253; *Inverurie Mags.* v. *Sorrie*, 1956 S.C. 175.
44 *Ligerwood* v. *Lanarkshire and Dumbartonshire Ry.* (1903) 11 S.L.T. 55.
45 *Earl of Crawford* v. *Paton*, 1911 S.C. 1017.
46 *Thomson* v. *Thomson & Co.* (1902) 4 F. 930.
47 *Gillespie* v. *Lucas & Aird* (1893) 20 R. 1035, 1039; *Ogston* v. *Aberdeen Tramways o.* (1896) 24 R.(H.L.) 8, 12; *Shepherd* v. *Menzies* (1900) 2 F. 443.
48 *Buckhaven and Methil Mags.* v. *Wemyss Coal Co.*, 1932 S.C. 201.
49 *Gillespie* v. *Lucas & Aird* (1893) 20 R. 1035.
50 *Murray* v. *Dunbarton C.C.*, 1935 S.L.T. 239.
51 *Bank of Scotland* v. *Stewart* (1891) 18 R. 957, 971.
52 *Glen* v. *Caledonian Ry.* (1868) 6 M. 797; *Begg* v. *Jack* (1874) 1 R. 366; *Caledonian Ry.* v. *G.S.W. Ry.* (1903) 11 S.L.T. 510; *Edgar* v. *City of Glasgow Friendly Socy.*, 1914, 2 S.L.T. 408. See also *Grahame* v. *Kirkcaldy Mags.* (1882) 9 R.(H.L.) 91; *Place* v. *West Highland Ry.* (1895) 2 S.L.T. 487.
53 *Farquhar & Gill* v. *Aberdeen Mags.*, 1912 S.C. 1294; *cf. Toni Tyres Ltd.* v. *Palmer Tyre Ltd.* (1905) 7 F. 477.
54 *Warrand* v. *Watson* (1906) 8 F. 1098, 1100, *per* Lord McLaren.
55 *Caledonian Ry.* v. *Glasgow Mags.* (1897) 25 R. 74.

Interdict against the Crown

By the Crown Proceedings Act 1947, s. 21 (1) (*a*) where in any proceedings against the Crown any such relief is sought as might in proceedings between subjects be granted by way of interdict the court shall not grant an interdict but may in lieu make an order declaratory of the rights of the parties. By s. 21 (2) the court shall not in any civil proceedings grant any interdict or make any order against an officer of the Crown if the effect of granting the interdict or making the order would be to give any relief against the Crown which could not have been obtained in proceedings against the Crown. The assumption is that the Crown and its officers will give effect to any declaration of rights made by the court. In consequence the proper form of action is declarator. There is however, no provision for interim declarator in lieu of interim interdict.[56]

This provision limits the powers of the court as compared with the pre-1947 position.[57]

Misuse of delegated legislative power

It may be possible by interdict to challenge, as being *ultra vires*, the exercise of delegated legislative power, where the delegation is to a person or body other than a minister of the Crown, department of state or other person or body acting on behalf of the Crown. In *Glasgow Insurance Committee* v. *Scottish Insurance Commissioners*[58] regulations made by the defenders under statutory powers were challenged by interdict, but the petition was dismissed on the ground that the regulations could not be challenged as being *ultra vires* provided they dealt with matters within the scope of the relevant part of the Act, but could be set aside only by the Parliamentary procedure provided. But if no provision were made for the laying of the regulations before Parliament, would interdict not be competent, and if it were not, would the result not be that the delegate had in fact unfettered legislative powers?

Abuses of power by public authorities

Interdict may be a competent remedy where an individual's rights are threatened by illegal official action or abuse of power by an administrative authority. Thus it may be invoked where a statutory body is alleged to be acting *ultra vires*[59]: " in all matters regarding their jurisdiction they are, of course, allowed to exercise those powers according to that judgment and discretion; but in all cases where they exceed those powers they are

56 *Ayr Town Council* v. *Secretary of State for Scotland*, 1965 S.C. 394; *cf. Robertson* v. *L.A.* (1950), 1965 S.C. 400; *Underhill* v. *Ministry of Food* [1950] 1 All E.R. 591; *International G.E.C. of N.Y.* v. *Commrs. of Customs and Excise* [1962] Ch. 784.

57 *e.g. Bell* v. *Secretary of State for Scotland*, 1933 S.L.T. 519.

58 1915 S.C. 504. In *Institute of Patent Agents* v. *Lockwood* (1894) 21 R.(H.L.) 61, 70, Lord Morris expressed the view that a court could consider whether regulations were *intra vires* or *ultra vires*, and that they do not receive any *imprimatur* from having been laid before both Houses of Parliament.

59 *Campbell* v. *Leith Police Commrs.* (1870) 8 M.(H.L.) 31.

immediately arrested by interdict or by injunction, as the case may be, . . . it not being a sufficient answer on their part to say, ' you will have your remedy at law if the powers are exceeded.' But the courts will hold a strict hand over those to whom the legislature has entrusted such powers, in order to take care that no injury is done by the extravagant assertion of them." [60] There are many instances of the exercise of authority being challenged as *ultra vires*.[61]

Though conduct be *intra vires* interdict may be invoked to restrain it if the body exercising the power is failing to exercise reasonable care in so doing and is in consequence injuring the pursuer in some way,[62] unless the body has authority to act in the way it is doing irrespective of harmful consequences, or the particular operations are directly sanctioned. So too if the inevitable result of the proposed operations will be an infringement of a statutory provision designed to protect public health interdict is competent.[63]

Exercise of administrative discretion

In *Pollok School* v. *Glasgow Town Clerk*,[64] the proprietors of a private school sought by interdict to challenge the proposal by the local authority to requisition its premises for use as housing. The court held [65] that the discretion conferred on the respondent by statutory instrument included a discretion to decide whether the supply of houses was a purpose within the ambit of the Regulation, and that its exercise could not be reviewed by the court except on the ground of bad faith. The allegation of bad faith was not persisted in,[66] and it was held that there having been a valid exercise of the discretion it could not be challenged.[67] The only loopholes appear accordingly to be (1) if the discretion is exercised outwith the powers of the administrative official or agency, and (2) if the discretion is exercised in bad faith.

Similarly in *Brown* v. *Kirkcudbright Magistrates* [68] where a landowner sought to interdict the local authority from entering on his lands for the construction of a sewer, Lord Adam observed [69] that it was not the sheriff's function to inquire whether the sewer was necessary or whether it might be made to follow some other course, but only to consider whether the proposal was statutorily authorised or on the other hand infringed the petitioners' rights.

[60] *Ibid.* 38, *per* L.C. Hatherley.

[61] *e.g. Hope* v. *Edinburgh Mags.* (1897) 5 S.L.T. 195; *Grieve* v. *Edinburgh & District Water Trs.*, 1918 S.C. 700; *Adams* v. *Secretary of State for Scotland*, 1958 S.C. 279.

[62] *Gillespie* v. *Lucas & Aird* (1893) 20 R. 1035; *cf. Geddis* v. *Proprs. of Bann Reservoir* (1878) 3 App.Cas. 430, 456; *Metropolitan Asylum Board* v. *Hill* (1881) 6 App.Cas. 193.

[63] *Gavin* v. *Ayrshire County Council*, 1950 S.C. 197.

[64] 1946 S.C. 373; 1947 S.C. 605.

[65] 1946 S.C. 373.

[66] 1947 S.C. 605, 620.

[67] 1947 S.C. 605.

[68] (1905) 8 F. 77.

[69] p. 88.

Acquisition of statutory powers

The court has declined by interdict to prevent a public company from going to Parliament for statutory powers, one judge observing that the court had no power to interdict such an application.[70] This seems an overstatement, but a refusal to interfere may be only prudent, leaving it to Parliament to decide whether to grant or refuse the powers sought. Moreover in *Russell* v. *Hamilton Magistrates* [71] where the local authority had promoted a provisional order which was clearly *ultra vires* of the Act authorising applications for provisional orders, the court interdicted the holding of a public inquiry into the draft order.

Interdict excluded by special form of appeal

It is a general principle that interdict at common law against any kind of public authority is not competent if there is any special statutory or other form of appeal competent against the use of power objected to.[72]

In relation to the administration of justice

The court will not generally interdict a person from taking any legal step which he is prima facie entitled to do, such as serving a summons or otherwise initiating a legal claim, or making a complaint to the police or procurator-fiscal which may result in a criminal prosecution. Such conduct is not normally an actionable wrong, and normally therefore cannot be interdicted. But no doubt interdict might be granted against a legally unjustifiable proposal or attempt to initiate legal proceedings, such as a threat to sue for a sum of money notwithstanding a prior undertaking not to do so.

The court will not interfere by way of interdict to prevent the publication of a report of proceedings in an open court of justice, British or foreign, including letters produced in evidence and read, unless it is alleged that the report is unfair.[73] " If this is a fair and accurate report of proceedings in a court of competent jurisdiction, reported for a legitimate purpose, I do not see that it is possible to entertain the application for interdict." [74] " In the general case it is undoubtedly law that, where it is proposed to publish a report of proceedings in a court of justice, that report being a fair and accurate report, the court should not interfere to restrain the publication. If any person can show that he has been injured by the publication, and that the publication was made maliciously for the purpose of injuring him, he must maintain his claim to damages in another action." [75]

[70] *Wedderburn* v. *Scottish Central Ry.* (1848) 10 D. 1317.

[71] (1897) 25 R. 350; contrast *Ayr Mags.* v. *Secretary of State for Scotland*, 1965 S.C. 394.

[72] *Anderson* v. *Kirkintilloch Mags.*, 1948 S.C. 27; *Fife County Council* v. *Railway Executive*, 1951 S.C. 499; *Cumming* v. *Inverness Mags.*, 1953 S.C. 1.

[73] *Riddell* v. *Clydesdale Horse Socy.* (1885) 12 R. 976; see also *Newton* v. *Fleming* (1848) 6 Bell 175.

[74] *Riddell*, *supra*, 983, *per* L.P. Inglis.

[75] *Riddell*, *supra*, 984, *per* Lord Shand.

Interdict of legal proceedings

Prima facie the use of interdict to restrain legal proceedings is limited; parties should not in general be hindered from having their disputes adjudicated on. But there are exceptional cases.

An interdict is competent at common law, if the court has jurisdiction, to restrain parties from proceeding in actions elsewhere with reference to matters which are *sub judice* in Scotland. If there is jurisdiction, interdict may be granted against proceeding with an action abroad, as in the New York courts.[76]

Under the Companies Act 1948, s. 226, at any time after the presentation of a winding-up petition and before a winding-up order has been made, the company or any creditor or contributory may (a) where any action or proceeding against the company is pending in the High Court or Court of Appeal in England or Northern Ireland, apply to the court in which the action or proceeding is pending for a stay of proceedings therein; and (b) where any other action or proceeding is pending against the company apply to the court having jurisdiction to wind up the company to restrain further proceedings in the action or proceeding; and the court to which application is so made may, as the case may be, stay or restrain the proceedings accordingly on such terms as it thinks fit.

By section 231, when a winding-up order has been made or a provisional liquidator has been appointed, no action or proceeding shall be proceeded with or commenced against the company except by leave of the court and subject to such terms as the court may impose.[77]

Interdict against diligence

It is competent to obtain interdict against proceeding with, or proceeding further with, diligence if this is unwarranted or the prior procedure has been in any material way irregular.[78]

Interdict against arbitration

Where an arbitration or similar adjudication is pending an interdict may be granted if there are grounds for believing that the arbiter has no urisdiction.[79] The court will not always, however, regard this as desirable, and it will not interdict an arbitration in progress unless it is established that the claim is, in whole or in part, clearly ill-founded, or that the arbiter is being asked to exercise powers which he does not have.[80]

Interdict in personal relations

Interdict is competent against a minor, who required but did not have

[76] *California Redwood Co.* v. *Merchant Banking Co. of London* (1886) 13 R. 1202.

[77] *Cf. California Redwood Co.* v. *Walker* (1886) 13 R. 810; *Pacific Coast Mining Co.* v. *Walker* (1886) 13 R. 816.

[78] *Cf. Brady* v. *Napier*, 1944 S.C. 18.

[79] *G.S.W. Ry.* v. *Caledonian Ry.* (1871) 44 Sc.Jur. 29; *McCoard* v. *Glasgow Corpn.*, 1935 S.L.T. 117.

[80] *Dumbarton Water Works Commrs.* v. *Blantyre* (1884) 12 R. 115 (statutory arbitration); *G.S.W. Ry.* v. *Caledonian Ry.* (1871) 44 Sc.Jur. 29 (contractual arbitration).

parental consent to do so, from marrying in Scotland [81] and against a registrar performing such a ceremony of marriage,[81] and also against the defender in a divorce action making away with estate alleged to belong to him, and from which a capital payment is being claimed if divorce is granted.[82]

Interdict in relation to partnerships

Interdict is competent by one partner against another to prevent detriment to the partnership business and assets.[83]

Interdict in relation to companies

A company may be interdicted by a member from attempting to do anything which is *ultra vires*, or from passing resolutions oppressive of the rights of the minority shareholders,[84] or from dealing at a meeting with an incompetent resolution.[85]

When a company has passed an *ex facie* valid special resolution for voluntary winding up it is questionable whether it is competent to interdict a person from acting as liquidator.[86]

Interdict against breach of undertaking

Interdict is competent against threatened or actual breach of a unilateral undertaking, and the meaning and effect of the undertaking may be determined in the interdict process.[87]

Interdict against breach of contract

Where a party to a contract has undertaken a negative obligation to refrain from some conduct, and threatens to do, or actually does, what he should not do, or should not have done, the other party is entitled as a general rule to interdict against the contravening conduct. Accordingly a condition in restraint of trade in a contract, provided it is not void on the ground of unreasonableness as between the parties or having regard to the public interest,[88] is enforceable by interdict.[89] The unreasonableness of the restriction, and its consequent nullity, is a defence commonly adduced in proceedings for interdict.

81 *Pease* v. *Pease*, 1967 S.C. 112 (interim interdict granted); refused in *Hoy* v. *Hoy*, 1968 S.C. 179.

82 Succession (Scotland) Act 1964, s. 27 (1); *Johnstone* v. *Johnstone*, 1967 S.C. 143.

83 *Smith* v. *Smith* (1892) 20 R. 27.

84 *Adelphi Hotel (Glasgow) Ltd.* v. *Walker*, 1960 S.C. 182.

85 *Ball* v. *Metal Industries Ltd.*, 1957 S.C. 315.

86 *Howling's Trs.* v. *Smith* (1905) 7 F. 390.

87 *Dumfriesshire Education Authy.* v. *Wright*, 1926 S.L.T. 217.

88 On this issue, see *Gloag on Contract* (2nd ed.) 569; *Nordenfelt* v. *Maxim-Nordenfelt Guns and Ammunition Co.* [1894] A.C. 535; *Dumbarton Steamboat Co.* v. *MacFarlane* (1899) 1 F. 993.

89 *e.g. Stewart* v. *S.* (1899) 1 F. 1158; *Williams* v. *Fairbairn* (1899) 1 F. 944; *Ballachulish Slate Quarries* v. *Grant* (1903) 5 F. 1105; *Vettese* v. *Vettese*, 1951 S.L.T.(Notes) 61; *B.M.T.A.* v. *Gray*, 1951 S.C. 586.

Similarly, interdict has been said to be competent to a tenant where the landlord has undertaken not to use his other property in a competing business.[90] But such an undertaking may not be binding on a third party or an assignee from him.[91]

A negative stipulation may be implied in a contract.[92]

Interdict is again the appropriate remedy for an infringement of building restrictions, which may be coupled with an order for the removal of the infringing structures.[93] If the buildings have been completed the latter order alone is competent,[94] and even that will not be made if the consequent loss falling on the defender would be grossly disproportionate to the pursuer's interest.[95] If the buildings were completed without protest or proceedings for interdict there may be held to be such acquiescence as will bar a decree for removal of the building, though not an action for damages.[96]

Interdict will not, however, necessarily be granted against conduct inconsistent with a contract though not contrary to any actual stipulation thereof; thus a contractor was refused interdict at the end of a contract against the other party's employing another contractor and rebuilding the work.[97]

Interdict against delict

Interdict is also a competent remedy against the threatened commission of, the actual commission of, so long as it is still in progress, or the resumption or continuation of, any kind of delictual conduct. Interdict is " the appropriate remedy to prevent an apprehended wrong, even if no similar wrong has actually been committed." [98]

Apprehended wrong

To justify a grant of interdict, " a process of law, which was intended for protection," [1] there must be reasonable apprehension of the commission, or repetition, of a wrong. " It is everyday practice that . . . a threatened encroachment [may be] prevented by means of an interdict. There is no better ground for granting interdict than that an encroachment has been threatened . . . " [2] The fact that a person alleges a legal right to do something does not justify interdicting him. " The process of interdict

[90] *Campbell* v. *Watt* (1795) Hume 788; *Davie* v. *Stark* (1876) 3 R. 1114.
[91] *Mackenzie* v. *Imlay's Trs.*, 1912 S.C. 685.
[92] *Addison* v. *Brown* (1907) 15 S.L.T. 674.
[93] *Campbell* v. *Clydesdale Banking Co.* (1868) 6 M. 943, 949; *Grahame* v. *Kirkcaldy Mags.* (1882) 9 R.(H.L.) 91, 95.
[94] *Naismith* v. *Cairnduff* (1876) 3 R. 863.
[95] *Grahame*, *supra*; *Davidson* v. *Macpherson* (1889) 30 S.L.R. 2.
[96] *Shand* v. *Henderson* (1814) 2 Dow 579; *Forbes* v. *Inverurie Picture House Ltd.* (1937) 53 Sh.Ct.Rep. 43.
[97] *Miller* v. *Lochgelly U.P. Church* (1867) 5 S.L.R. 79.
[98] *Wilson* v. *Shepherd*, 1913 S.C. 300, 305–306, *per* Lord Salvesen.
[1] *Hay's Trs.*, *supra*, 401, *per* L.J.C. Moncreiff.
[2] *Macleod* v. *Davidson* (1886) 14 R. 92, 94, *per* L.J.C. Moncreiff.

is not directed against the statement of claims but is intended to prevent people from translating words into deeds. If they so conduct themselves as to lead to reasonable apprehension that they will take action in purported exercise of the right claimed, interdict follows. It is reasonable apprehension that there is an intention to go on the lands . . . that matters. It is the threat to trespass, not the threat to litigate, that leads to interdict."[3] Permanent interdict " is granted only if there is a reasonable apprehension that the defender may do the illegal act. Good evidence of that apprehension in the normal case is the fact that there has been recent wrongdoing of the same kind by the defender, but the threat of wrongdoing may be proved although there has been no wrongdoing in the past. . . . A claim of competing right advanced by the defender in an action of interdict, unaccompanied by evidence of past illegal actings or of intentions on his part to act upon that claim even though it prove unsound, does not amount to a threat of illegal action such as to justify a permanent interdict. To claim to have a right which competes with another's claim is not a wrong. A wrong is only threatened and permanent interdict only justified if the evidence justifies the inference that the defender may act in derogation of the pursuer's rights, whether his own claim be right or wrong." [4]

But where there have been recent illegal actings and the defender in addition maintains a claim to be entitled to do so, and the court has no assurance that there will not be such actings again in the future, interdict will follow.[5]

Contingency of wrong

Interdict is not, however, appropriate against a merely contingent injury which might never arise.[6] " Interdict is granted to prevent immediate and impending wrong. It cannot be asked for the protection of such a contingent right as we have in the present case. . . . To prevent the defender in the meantime from using his property in the manner dictated by common sense and by legitimate interest, merely because, in some remote future, the well might fail, is a step in the way of vindication of contingent rights that I know no precedent for." [7]

> " Interdict is a preventive proceeding and by its very nature it may competently be invoked in suitable circumstances to restrain the commission in the future of a violation of rights not yet committed but only reasonably apprehended. That is the general rule. But, when the subject of an application for interdict is an anticipated nuisance, the rule requires to be formulated with greater precision. There are certain operations or works which are ' ticketed by law

[3] *Inverurie Mags.* v. *Sorrie*, 1956 S.C. 175, 179–180, *per* L.J.C. Thomson. So too *Warrand* v. *Watson* (1906) 8 F. 253, 1098.

[4] *Inverurie Mags.*, *supra*, 181, *per* Lord Patrick.

[5] *Macleod* v. *Davidson* (1887) 14 R. 92, explained in *Inverurie Mags.*, *supra.*

[6] *Hood* v. *Traill* (1884) 12 R. 362.

[7] *Hood*, *supra*, 373, *per* Lord Fraser.

as nuisances . . . because the law holds that they cannot be carried on without constituting a nuisance'—*Kirkwood's Trs.* v. *Leith*,[8] Lord President Inglis at p. 259; and in the case of such inherently objectionable and 'notorious' works or operations, it is competent to apply for interdict against the construction of the works or the performance of the operations *ab ante* and without waiting for the inevitable nuisance to materialise. Even in the case of nuisances of this notorious description, the interdict, if granted, may be limited in scope so as to admit of care and contrivance to obviate the nuisance—*Trotter* v. *Farnie*[9]; *Pedie* v. *Swinton*.[10] But, where the subject of complaint does not fall within this extreme category but consists of works which, when completed and brought into use, may or may not at some future time create a nuisance, it by no means follows that their construction can be interdicted out of hand. In such cases apprehension will not normally be equated to realisation unless it is made to appear that the creation of a nuisance is in a practical sense a necessary and virtually inevitable consequence of the construction of the proposed works or the performance of the projected operation. In *Steel* v. *Gourock Police Commissioners*,[11] Lord President Inglis, in dismissing an application for interdict against the construction of a drainage scheme in circumstances closely resembling the present, said (at p. 958): 'If it could be demonstrated, or if it were relevantly stated, that the operations of the Commissioners would *necessarily* have the effect of causing a nuisance, there might be a question for our consideration.' This formulation of the rule seems to me to be specially appropriate to a case like the present in which the applicant for interdict is not left without a remedy if the works are allowed to proceed, but is assured of a statutory right to compensation from a local authority with power to rate, and is also free, if and when any nuisance materialises, to invoke all her common law or statutory rights and remedies." [12]

Wrong in progress

Interdict is competent against a wrong in progress, but not against one completed, or even practically completed.[13]

Accordingly application for interdict must be made promptly and interdict is incompetent after the event. Moreover wrongs, though completed, if liable to be resumed or repeated, may be interdicted,[14] but

8 (1889) 16 R. 255.
9 (1831) 5 W. & S. 649; (1832) 10 S. 423.
10 (1839) McL. & Rob. 1018.
11 (1872) 10 M. 954.
12 *Gavin* v. *Ayrshire County Council*, 1950 S.C. 197, 207–208, *per* L.P. Cooper.
13 *Dick* v. *Thom* (1829) 8 S. 232; *Hoyle* v. *Shaws Water Co.* (1854) 17 D. 83; *McCubbin* v. *Venning* (1859) 22 D. 164; *Lawson's Trs.* v. *Cramond* (1863) 3 M. 53; *Begg* v. *Jack* (1874) 1 R. 366.
14 *Dickson* v. *Dickie* (1863) 1 M. 1157; *Farquhar & Gill* v. *Aberdeen Mags.*, 1912 S.C. 1294.

if of a continuing character and acquiesced in for a substantial period may not entitle to interdict.[15]

The wrong may be any kind of conduct which amounts to a continuing or repeated delict, including a continuing inducement to a third party to act in breach of contract with the pursuer.[16]

Forms of wrong justifying interdict

The kinds of wrong may be very varied; they include deliberate and legally unjustifiable inducement of breach of contract,[17] appointment of a successor to the petitioner while the legality of his dismissal was still subject to enquiry,[18] infringement of a registered design,[19] interference with the alveus of a river.[20]

In relation to trade unions

Interdict is competent against an alleged conspiracy to injure,[21] and proposed misapplication by trustees of branch funds.[22]

In relation to companies

Interdict is competent against the inclusion in the agenda of an extraordinary general meeting of a resolution which could not competently be put at that meeting,[23] and to prevent a liquidator dividing the surplus assets among shareholders, in a voluntary winding-up, without making provision against the pursuer's future or contingent claim on the assets.[24]

In relation to heritage

Interdict is competent against trespass,[25] nuisance,[26] interference with a billposting hoarding,[27] infringement of a right of ferry,[28] interference with the free passage of fish in a river,[29] against infringement of fishing

15 *Dunoon Presbytery* v. *Campbell* (1844) 6 D. 1262; *Blackburn* v. *Finlay* (1848) 10 D. 590; *Hoyle, supra*; *Harvie* v. *Robertson* (1903) 5 F. 338, 344, 346.

16 *Exchange Telegraph Co.* v. *Giulianotti*, 1959 S.C. 19.

17 *B.M.T.A.* v. *Gray*, 1951 S.C. 587; *Exchange Telegraph Co.* v. *Giulianotti*, 1959 S.C. 19.

18 *Trapp* v. *Aberdeenshire C.C.*, 1960 S.C. 302.

19 *Harvey* v. *Secure Fittings Ltd.*, 1966 S.L.T. 121.

20 *Gay* v. *Malloch*, 1959 S.C. 110.

21 *Crofter Co.* v. *Veitch*, 1942 S.C.(H.L.) 1.

22 *A.S.R.S.* v. *Motherwell Branch* (1880) 7 R. 867.

23 *Ball* v. *Metal Industries Ltd.*, 1957 S.C. 315.

24 *Elphinstone* v. *Monkland Iron Co.* (1886) 13 R.(H.L.) 98.

25 *Macleod* v. *Davidson* (1886) 14 R. 92; *Merry & Cuninghame* v. *Aitken* (1895) 22 R. 247; *Arthur* v. *Aird*, 1907 S.C. 1170; *Inverurie Mags.* v. *Sorrie*, 1956 S.C. 175; see also *Robertson* v. *Wright* (1885) 13 R. 174; *Macleay* v. *Macdonald*, 1928 S.C. 776; 1929 S.C. 371; *Millar* v. *McRobbie*, 1949 S.C. 1.

26 *Dowie* v. *Oliphant*, Dec. 11, 1813, F.C.; *Trotter* v. *Farnie* (1830) 9 S. 144; *Shotts Iron Co.* v. *Inglis* (1882) 9 R.(H.L.) 78; *Hislop* v. *Fleming* (1882) 10 R. 426; *Gillespie* v. *Lucas & Aird* (1893) 20 R. 1035; *Ogston* v. *Aberdeen Tramway Co.* (1896) 24 R.(H.L.) 8; *Kincaid Smith* v. *Cameron* (1900) 2 F. 1179; *Fleming* v. *Gemmill*, 1908 S.C. 340; *McEwan* v. *Steedman & McAlister*, 1912 S.C. 156; *Ben Nevis Distillery* v. *North British Aluminium Co.*, 1948 S.C. 592.

27 *David Allen & Sons* v. *Dundee & District Billposting Co. Ltd.*, 1912 S.C. 970.

28 *L.M.S. Ry.* v. *McDonald*, 1924 S.C. 835.

29 *Pirie* v. *Earl of Kintore* (1906) 8 F. 12.

rights in a tidal river,[30] against interference with the alveus of a river,[30] against infringement of the right of exclusive occupation of the family pew in a parish church,[31] against working coal in a way which would interfere with the pursuers' rights to work other minerals,[32] against continued occupation of a croft to possession of which the defender had never been entitled,[33] damage by engineering operations,[34] the unjustified removal of a gravestone,[35] the unauthorised obstruction of a common entrance,[36] building in defiance of a servitude of prospect,[37] contravening building restrictions in the title,[38] encroachment on the pursuer's lands[39] and selling refreshments on the foreshore.[40]

Interdict against what is a reasonable and natural use of property requires to be supported by the plainest expression of contract and obligation, such as conditions restrictive of use, there being, moreover, a presumption against restrictions on normal and beneficial use of land.[41]

Interdict has also been granted against a creditor selling heritable property when his statement of the debtor's indebtedness was not admitted or liquidated and required investigation.[42]

In relation to moveable property

Interdict has been competently sought to stop alleged invasion of the pursuer's proprietary right in corporeal moveables,[43] but refused in respect of notes made by a professional searcher of records, these being the searcher's own property.[44]

In relation to industrial and intellectual property

Interdict is competent in cases of infringement of copyright,[45] passing-off goods,[46] infringement of patent,[47] or of trade-mark,[48] or of trade name,[49] acting in prejudice of the goodwill of a business sold, by canvassing

30 *Duke of Buccleuch* v. *Smith*, 1911 S.C. 409; *Gilbertson* v. *Mackenzie* (1878) 5 R. 610; *Duke of Buccleuch* v. *Kean* (1890) 17 R. 829; *Gay* v. *Malloch*, 1959 S.C. 110.
31 *Paterson* v. *Brown*, 1913 S.C. 292.
32 *Shawsrigg Fireclay Co.* v. *Larkhall Collieries* (1903) 5 F. 1131.
33 *Colquhoun* v. *Mackenzie* (1894) 22 R. 23.
34 *Gillespie* v. *Lucas & Aird* (1893) 20 R. 1035.
35 *Wright* v. *Wright* (1881) 9 R. 15.
36 *Stewart, Pott & Co.* v. *Brown Bros. & Co.* (1878) 6 R. 35.
37 *Largs Hydropathic Ltd.* v. *Largs Town Council*, 1967 S.C. 1.
38 *Howard de Walden Estates Ltd.* v. *Bowmaker*, 1965 S.C. 163.
39 *Gauldie* v. *Arbroath Mags.*, 1936 S.C. 861.
40 *Marquess of Ailsa* v. *Monteforte*, 1937 S.C. 805.
41 *Hood* v. *Traill* (1884) 12 R. 362, 370–371.
42 *Lucas* v. *Gardner* (1876) 4 R. 195.
43 *Wilson* v. *Shepherd*, 1913 S.C. 300; *Leitch* v. *Leydon*, 1931 S.C.(H.L.) 1.
44 *Earl of Crawford* v. *Paton*, 1911 S.C. 1017.
45 *Leslie* v. *Young & Sons* (1894) 21 R.(H.L.) 57; *Harpers Ltd.* v. *Barry, Henry & Co.* (1892) 20 R. 133; see also *Earl of Crawford* v. *Paton*, 1911 S.C. 1017.
46 *Coca-Cola Co.* v. *Struthers*, 1968 S.C. 214; *Haig* v. *Forth Blending Co.*, 1954 S.C. 35.
47 *Harvie* v. *Ross* (1886) 14 R. 71; *Gill* v. *Cutler* (1895) 23 R. 371; *Toni Tyres Ltd.* v. *Palmer Tyre Ltd.* (1905) 7 F. 477.
48 *Woolley* v. *Morrison* (1904) 6 F. 451; *Coca-Cola Co.* v. *Struthers*, 1968 S.C. 214.
49 *G.N.S. Ry.* v. *Mann* (1892) 19 R. 1035; *Bayer* v. *Baird* (1898) 25 R. 1142; *Cellular Clothing Co. Ltd.* v. *Maxton & Murray* (1899) 1 F.(H.L.) 29; *Argyllshire Weavers Ltd.* v. *Macaulay*, 1962 S.C. 388; *Coca-Cola Co.*, *supra*.

former customers,[50] publishing information in breach of duty of confidentiality,[51] displaying a misleading hotel sign,[52] using the trade name attached to premises sold to the complainer [53] and publishing the substance of a university professor's course of lectures.[54]

Interdict has, however, been refused against the professed publication of a private correspondence, for reasons which are not apparent, as prima facie that is an infringement of copyright.[55]

In relation to other incorporeal rights

Interdict is competent to prevent the use by a person not entitled to it of any professional designation or initials indicative thereof.[56]

In relation to trustees

Interdict is competent to restrain trustees from paying trust income to other than the person authorised by the court to receive it.[57]

In relation to bankruptcy

It is competent to interdict a trustee in bankruptcy from paying away the estate,[58] but not to interdict him from paying a dividend as and when he was bound to do under the Bankruptcy Act.[59]

In relation to diligence

It is competent to interdict sale following on a poinding alleged not to have been executed legally.[60]

In relation to arbitrations

It is competent to interdict an arbitration from being commenced or carried through [61] but the court is reluctant to do so. The court will not interfere with the action of an arbiter *ex facie* well appointed, unless it is perfectly plain that he has no such power as that which he is called on to exercise.[62] " It is not to be assumed that they [arbiters] will exceed their jurisdiction, or act otherwise than as they ought; and dealing as we are here with objections, . . . to an arbitration which is prima facie regular,

50 *Dumbarton Steamboat Co.* v. *MacFarlane* (1899) 1 F. 993.
51 *Brown's Trs.* v. *Hay* (1898) 25 R. 1112.
52 *Crawford's Trs.* v. *Lennox* (1896) 23 R. 747.
53 *G.N.S. Ry.* v. *Mann* (1892) 19 R. 1035; *Cowan* v. *Miller* (1895) 22 R. 833.
54 *Caird* v. *Sime* (1887) 14 R.(H.L.) 37.
55 *White* v. *Dickson* (1881) 8 R. 896.
56 *Accountants in Edinburgh* v. *Corporation of Accountants Ltd.* (1893) 20 R. 750.
57 *Edgar* v. *Fisher's Trs.* (1893) 21 R. 59; sequel, 21 R. 1076.
58 *Scobie* v. *Hill's Tr.* (1870) 8 M. 161; distinguished in *Hodge* v. *Wishart*, 1912 S.C. 1012.
59 *Thomson* v. *Thomson & Co.* (1902) 4 F. 930.
60 *Brady* v. *Napier*, 1944 S.C. 18.
61 *Fraser* v. *Wright* (1838) 12 S. 1049; *Drew* v. *Drew* (1855) 2 Macq. 1; *Young* v. *Arnott* (1857) 19 D. 1000; *Pearson* v. *Oswald* (1859) 21 D. 419; *G.S.W. Ry.* v. *Caledonian Ry.* (1871) 44 Sc.Jur. 29; *Wemyss* v. *Ardrossan Harbour Board* (1893) 20 R. 500.
62 *Dumbarton Water Commrs.* v. *Blantyre* (1884) 12 R. 115; *Glasgow, Yoker and Clydebank Ry.* v. *Lidgerwood* (1895) 23 R. 195.

I do not think an interdict would be justified. It may be for the court to interfere when the arbiter has either failed to exercise, or has exceeded his jurisdiction." [63] Thus the court has refused to interdict an arbiter from dealing with a claim part of which was beyond his powers to decide when he had merely allowed a proof and had done nothing to warrant the inference that in deciding the claim he would exceed his jurisdiction.[64] But if the claim made related to a matter *ultra vires* of the arbiter that would be a proper case for stopping the arbitration.[65]

It is also an unusual step to interfere with the progress of an arbitration on an *ex facie* valid claim, though interdict might be granted where there is a good answer to the claim which can be instantly verified, such as a statutory provision providing a special way of disposing of claims. The more usual course, where there is a possibility that an arbiter may be invited to decide questions beyond his statutory powers, is to leave such anticipated questions to be determined after the arbitration is closed.[66] " We can only interfere with the decrees of arbiters by way of reduction when we have a final decree, and can only restrain them from proceeding when the proceedings are outwith the reference. . . . If a party thinks he has sustained an injustice during arbitration proceedings, and means to found on the proceedings in an action of reduction or other form of relief, he should be careful to give the arbiter every opportunity of retracing his steps and allowing what he has originally denied." [67]

The court, on the other hand, has granted interdict against further proceedings before an arbiter where one party had mistaken their remedy in applying to the arbiter in that there could be no dispute as to the meaning of the words in the contract alleged to have been contravened. The interdict should have been against the other party not implementing the contract.[68]

Suspending execution of decree

If decree is granted interdicting a defender's conduct and he appeals he may seek to have execution of the decree deferred. The pursuer is entitled to interim execution pending the outcome of the appeal, but the court may, for the avoidance of hardship, supersede extract for a period.[69]

Interdict deferred to permit remedial measures

Particularly in cases of nuisance and pollution the court may, even though it finds facts justifying interdict proved, defer interdict to enable the defender to have an opportunity of trying to effect a remedy, and for

[63] *Licences Ins. Corpn. Ltd.* v. *Shearer*, 1907 S.C. 10, 15, *per* Lord Kyllachy.
[64] *Bennets* v. *Bennet* (1903) 5 F. 376; *Moore* v. *McCosh* (1903) 5 F. 946.
[65] *Bennets, supra*, 381; *cf. Pearson, supra*; *G.S.W. Ry., supra*.
[66] *Glasgow, Yoker and Clydebank Ry.* v. *Lidgerwood* (1895) 23 R. 195.
[67] *Wemyss* v. *Ardrossan Harbour Co.* (1893) 20 R. 500, 505, *per* Lord McLaren.
[68] *Greenock Parochial Board* v. *Coghill* (1878) 5 R. 732.
[69] *Ballachulish Slate Quarries Co. Ltd.* v. *Grant* (1903) 5 F. 1105, 1117.

that purpose may decline *in hoc statu* to make the interdict perpetual, or may continue the cause.[70] The court may remit to persons of skill to assist it in devising remedial measures or framing regulations which will prevent encroachment by the one party on the rights of the other.[71] But where pollution has been proved, that is prima facie ground for interdict, and the pursuer is entitled to interdict even if remedial measures have been put in train and, unless the defender is prepared to submit to an interdict, the remedial works must be tested over a substantial period by a neutral authority.[72]

Under the Court of Session Act 1868, s. 79, where appeal has been taken to the Court of Session against, *inter alia*, an interdict granted in the sheriff court, the defender may move in the sheriff court that the interdict be suspended until the appeal has been decided.[73] It is incompetent in such circumstances to have the Court of Session recall the interdict granted in the sheriff court.

Where interdict prohibited by statute

By the Copyright Act 1956, s. 17 (4), in an action for infringement of copyright in respect of the construction of a building,[74] no interdict or other order shall be made (a) after the construction of the building has been begun, so as to prevent it from being completed, or (b) so as to require the building, in so far as it has been constructed, to be demolished. This exception applies only to actions founded on infringement of copyright in the design, not on any other ground of law.

Enforcement and change of circumstances

After interdict has been obtained change of circumstances may affect the enforceability of the interdict. Thus when a patentee alters his patent by disclaimer he cannot thereafter enforce an interdict obtained on the patent before alteration, as the amended patent may be liable to objections not applicable to the former patent.[75] Similarly if after interdict is obtained a party ceases to have an interest in the contract or property in relation to which it was obtained he can no longer enforce the interdict.[76]

After perpetual interdict has been granted it is competent for the court, in the exercise of the *nobile officium,* if satisfied that it is necessary or at least highly expedient to do so in view of changed circumstances, to allow actings in conflict with the interdict, without reducing the interdict.[77]

[70] *Duke of Buccleuch* v. *Cowan* (1873) 11 M. 675; *Fraser's Trs.* v. *Cran* (1877) 4 R. 794; (1877) 5 R. 290; (1879) 6 R. 451; *Fleming* v. *Gemmill,* 1908 S.C. 340, 349, 350.

[71] *Earl of Kintore* v. *Pirie* (1906) 8 F. 1058, 1068; affd. 8 F.(H.L.) 16.

[72] *Seafield* v. *Kemp* (1899) 1 F. 402, 411, *per* L.O. Kyllachy.

[73] *Trainer* v. *Renfrewshire Upper District Cttee.,* 1907 S.C. 1117.

[74] *i.e.* infringing the architect's, or his client's (see s. 4), copyright in a work of architecture, which is an " artistic work " under the Copyright Act 1956, s. 3 (1) (*b*).

[75] *Dudgeon* v. *Thomson* (1877) 4 R.(H.L.) 88.

[76] *Berlitz School* v. *Duchene* (1903) 6 F. 181.

[77] *Bowie,* 1968 S.C. 36.

Breach of interdict

A failure by any party to obtemper an interdict is a serious matter, and any such party is liable to judicial censure, fine and imprisonment.[78] Breach of interdict is not properly described as a contempt of court; it is a challenge to the supremacy of the law and therefore punishable.[79] Nor is it a criminal proceeding, but a method by which the court protects its own authority from contempt.[80] There can be no breach by a person not named in the interdict.[81] The court will have regard to the motives of the party complained against [82] and will normally take a lenient view of a breach committed by inadvertence,[83] though it is no defence to have acted in the belief that interdict had been granted incompetently.[84] An intention to commit breach of interdict is not punishable.[85]

The matter is brought before the court by petition and complaint, which is invalidated by misnomer of the respondent.[86] A complaint for breach of interdict is not a criminal proceeding.[87] If the fact of breach is not admitted it may be necessary to have a proof.[88] The standard of proof of breach is proof beyond reasonable doubt.[89] If the respondent is ordained to present himself in court for censure and does not appear, warrant for his apprehension may be granted.[90] The complainer may competently state that he does not insist on the respondent being summoned before the court.[91]

It will be served on the party interdicted on such inducíae as the court deems proper, normally eight days.[92] The party interdicted may be punished by judicial censure or fine or imprisonment,[93] and the court may order removal of offending objects at the defender's expense, but the court may, if a proper apology be tendered to the court and an adequate undertaking be given to comply in future with its orders, remit the remainder of the sentence.[94] A sentence of imprisonment on petition and

78 *Lord Gray* v. *Petrie* (1849) 11 D. 1021; *Kelso School Board* v. *Hunter* (1874) 2 R. 228; *Earl of Galloway* v. *Nixon* (1877) 5 R. 28; *Johnson* v. *Grant*, 1923 S.C. 789; *Macleay* v. *Macdonald*, 1928 S.C. 776. On the crime of deforcing a messenger-at-arms instructed to serve a note of suspension and interdict on persons against whom it was directed, see *H.M.A.* v. *McLean* (1886) 14 R.(J.) 1.

79 *Johnson, supra*, 790.

80 *Stark's Trs.* v. *Duncan* (1906) 8 F. 429, 434.

81 *Pattison* v. *Fitzgerald* (1823) 2 S. 536.

82 *Hamilton* v. *Caledonian Ry.* (1850) 7 Bell 272.

83 *Keltie* v. *Wilson* (1828) 7 S. 208; *Taylor* v. *Kilgour* (1844) 17 Sc.Jur. 89.

84 *Duke of Argyll* v. *McArthur* (1861) 23 D. 1236.

85 *Hunter* v. *Wilson* (1848) 10 D. 893.

86 *Overseas League* v. *Taylor*, 1951 S.C. 105.

87 *Christie Miller* v. *Bain* (1879) 6 R. 1215.

88 *Mackenzie* v. *Dingwall Mags.* (1831) 5 W. & S. 351; (1839) 1 D. 487; *Ramage* v. *Steel* (1843) 6 D. 146; *Harvie* v. *Ross* (1886) 14 R. 71.

89 *Entectic Welding Alloys Co. Ltd.* v. *Whitting*, 1969 S.L.T.(Notes) 79.

90 *Duke of Athole* v. *Robertson* (1872) 10 M. 298; *Welsbach Incandescent Gas Light Co.* v. *McMann* (1901) 4 F. 395.

91 *Walker* v. *Junor* (1903) 5 F. 1035.

92 *Costa* v. *Costa*, 1929 S.N. 62.

93 *e.g. Macleod's Trs.* v. *Macpherson* (1883) 10 R. 792; *Mackenzie* v. *Coulthart* (1889) 16 R. 1127.

94 *Johnson* v. *Grant*, 1923 S.C. 789.

complaint for breach of interdict is the sentence of the court that pronounces it, and no application with regard to it can be dealt with except by that court.[95] A sentence of fine or imprisonment for breach of interdict may competently be pronounced in the defender's absence [96] where the interdict had been broken, though not wilfully. The court in one case imposed no penalty.[97]

In proceedings for breach of interdict it is incompetent for the defender to challenge the merits of the grant of the interdict. " Persons are not entitled to disobey an order made by the court, and then to claim to show that the court ought not to have made the order." [98] Similarly in a petition and complaint for breach of interdict against infringement of a patent, it has been held that the defender cannot challenge the validity of the patent.[99]

If an appeal has been lodged in the breach of interdict proceedings interim liberation should be granted.[1]

A judgment of a sheriff, imposing a sentence of fine or imprisonment for breach of interdict granted in the sheriff court can be appealed to the Court of Session,[2] or from the Court of Session to the House of Lords.[3]

More than one petition and complaint may be brought if there is repetition of the breach.[4]

A party who has entered appearance in a case cannot plead ignorance of the fact that interim interdict has been granted or continued, and such alleged ignorance is no defence to a petition and complaint.[5]

Declarator and interdict

Where there is any doubt or dispute about the complainer's right, it is convenient to have that settled by declarator, and to combine with it an interdict against the infringement being done or threatened. Moreover, what is in effect a declaratory finding as to the rights of the pursuer may be pronounced in a process of interdict although interdict is refused.[6] But this is not essential. " It may be, and often is, competent and expedient to determine in a note of suspension and interdict questions of right or of title which might properly be made the subject of an action of declarator. On the other hand, the court may, and frequently does, refuse to do more in a note of suspension and interdict than make interim regulations until

[95] *Johnson, supra*, 790.
[96] *Stark's Trs.* v. *Duncan* (1906) 8 F. 429; see also *Walker* v. *Junor* (1903) 5 F. 1035.
[97] *Fraser's Trs.* v. *Cran* (1879) 6 R. 451.
[98] *Stark's Trs., supra*, 433–434.
[99] *Harvie* v. *Ross* (1886) 14 R. 71.
[1] *Johnson* v. *Grant*, 1923 S.C. 789; *Macleay* v. *Macdonald*, 1928 S.C. 776; 1929 S.C. 371.
[2] *Henderson* v. *Maclellan* (1874) 1 R. 920; *Stark's Trs.* v. *Duncan* (1906) 8 F. 429; *Maclachlan* v. *Bruce*, 1912 S.C. 440; *Macleay, supra.*
[3] *Caledonian Ry.* v. *Hamilton* (1850) 7 Bell 272.
[4] *Walker* v. *Junor* (1903) 5 F. 1035.
[5] *Henderson* v. *Maclellan* (1874) 1 R. 920; but see *Anderson* v. *Moncrieff*, 1966 S.L.T.(Sh.Ct.) 28.
[6] *Perth General Station Committee* v. *Ross* (1897) 24 R.(H.L.) 44; *Stirling C.C.* v. *Falkirk Mags.*, 1912 S.C. 1281; *Farquhar & Gill* v. *Aberdeen Mags.*, 1912 S.C. 1294; *Wilson* v. *Shepherd*, 1913 S.C. 300, 306; see also *Fraser's Trs.* v. *Cran* (1879) 6 R. 451, 453.

the question of right or title can be determined in an appropriate action." [7] Equally a declaratory finding may be made and suspended pending the progress of remedial measures.[8] All cases where this has been done are cases where either the granting of immediate interdict would be attended with consequences to the rights of the respondent as injurious, or possibly more so, than the wrong that was complained of; or because the effect of an immediate interdict would be to cause some great and immediate public inconvenience. It is also a condition of the exercise of this equitable power that the party subject to the interdict should offer immediate remedial measures with the view of obviating the necessity for interdict passing against him.[9]

Damages or declarator in lieu of interdict

It is competent to conclude for interdict or alternatively, failing interdict, for damages, and this is appropriate where there may be doubt whether in the circumstances the court will grant interdict.

It is not, however, open to a court to decline to grant interdict, where interdict alone has been sought, and to give damages in lieu, but it is competent to decline to grant interdict and in lieu to grant a declarator that the defender has no right to do what he has sought to do.[10] The court may further suspend the operation of the declaratory finding pending the progress of measures to remedy the ground of complaint. The power to suspend has been said [11] to exist in two categories of cases, where either the granting of the immediate interdict would be attended with consequences to the rights of the respondents as injurious, or possibly more so, than the wrong that was complained of; or because the effect of an immediate interdict would be to cause some great and immediate public inconvenience.

Notwithstanding a grant of perpetual interdict persons interdicted or their successors in title may petition the court, in the exercise of its *nobile officium*, to permit them to do some of the things forbidden by the interdict, and if the court is satisfied that it is necessary or at least highly expedient to permit the doing of the forbidden things it may so permit, certainly in the absence of opposition. It is not necessary, at least where the permission relates only to part of the conduct interdicted, to reduce the decree of perpetual interdict.[12]

Interdict and damages combined

Interdict and damages are frequently combined so as to recover compensation for harm done and prevent harm threatened. Examples are

7 *Toni Tyres Ltd.* v. *Palmer Tyre Ltd.* (1905) 7 F. 477, 483, *per* Lord Low.
8 *Clippens Oil Co. Ltd.* v. *Edinburgh & District Water Trs.* (1897) 25 R. 370, 383, *per* Lord McLaren.
9 *Clippens Oil Co., supra*, 383–384, approved in *Ben Nevis Distillery* v. *British Aluminium Co.*, 1948 S.C. 592, 598.
10 *Perth General Station Cttee.* v. *Ross* (1897) 24 R.(H.L.) 44.
11 *Clippens Oil Co.* v. *Edinburgh & District Water Trs.* (1897) 25 R. 370.
12 *Bowie*, 1967 S.C. 36.

encroachment on land,[13] pollution of a river,[14] damage to requisitioned property,[15] converting a shop into a house,[16] interfering with an advertisement hoarding,[17] breach of a restricted condition in a lease,[18] publishing a libellous circular,[19] nuisance[20] and infringement of copyright,[21] patent[22] or trade-name.[23]

Wrongful use of interdict

The wrongful obtaining and use of interdict by a complainer may be a civil wrong actionable by the respondent. " A wrongful interdict does not of itself entitle the man who is placed under the interdict to have damages. He must show that there has been an invasion of his legal right and resultant civil wrong done to him." [24] If it invaded no legal right, as where it prevented the erection by the parties of a sawmill on a site where they had no legal right to erect it, it gives no right to damages.[25] To put it another way, parties cannot get damages for being interdicted from what they had no right to do.[26] Damages are given not for the mere pronouncement of interdict but for the being stopped from doing the thing that they might do, as defined in the light of the true rights of parties.[27] To show that the defenders were trying to cripple the pursuers of set purpose has nothing to do with the interdict being wrongful.[28] Even if interdict was irregularly obtained, if the respondent did not, by the operation of the interdict, suffer any invasion of legal right, he has no claim for damages.[29]

In the case of interim interdict, which is normally sought and granted on *ex parte* statements, prima facie it is sought *periculo petentis* and a recall shows that it was wrongful.[30] Where interim interdict is improperly obtained, no distinction can be drawn between cases based on positive false statements and cases where it is obtained by the suppression or non-disclosure of facts necessary to enable the judge to determine the

13 *Menzies* v. *Duff* (1827) 5 S. 884.
14 *Bankier Distillery Co.* v. *Young* (1892) 19 R. 1083; (1893) 20 R.(H.L.) 76; (1899) 2 F. 89; *Fleming* v. *Gemmill*, 1908 S.C. 340.
15 *Demetriades* v. *Glasgow Corpn.* [1951] W.N. 108.
16 *Moore* v. *Munro* (1896) 4 S.L.T. 172.
17 *Allen* v. *Dundee Billposting Co.*, 1912 S.C. 970.
18 *Randall* v. *Summers*, 1919 S.C. 396.
19 *British Legal Life Assce. Co.* v. *Pearl Legal Life Assce. Co.* (1887) 14 R. 818.
20 *Chalmers* v. *Dixon* (1876) 3 R. 461; *Barony Board* v. *Cadder Board* (1883) 10 R. 510.
21 *Birn* v. *Keene* [1918] 2 Ch. 281.
22 *e.g. B.T.H.* v. *Charlesworth Peebles & Co.*, 1923 S.C. 599.
23 *Singer* v. *Kimball & Morton* (1873) 11 M. 267; *Thomson* v. *Dailly* (1897) 24 R. 1173; *Bayer* v. *Baird* (1898) 25 R. 1142.
24 *Macdonald* v. *Lord Blythswood*, 1914 S.C. 930, 933, *per* L.P. Strathclyde.
25 *Ibid.*
26 *Jack* v. *Begg* (1875) 3 R. 35.
27 *Clippens Oil Co. Ltd.* v. *Edinburgh & District Water Trs.* (1906) 8 F. 731, 751.
28 *Ibid.* 752.
29 *Aird* v. *Tarbert School Board*, 1907 S.C. 305.
30 *Wolthekker* v. *Northern Agricultural Co.* (1863) 1 M. 211; *Glasgow City & District Ry.* v. *Glasgow Coal Exchange* (1885) 12 R. 1287; *Fife* v. *Orr* (1895) 23 R. 8; *Clippens Oil Co.* v. *Edinburgh & District Water Trs.* (1906) 8 F. 731, 751; *Aird* v. *Tarbert School Board*, 1907 S.C. 305, 310.

expediency of granting interim interdict.[31] In the case of perpetual interdict on the other hand, granted after hearing or at least after having given the respondent full opportunity to appear and answer the petitioner's allegations, neither ultimate refusal, nor recall after change of circumstances, establishes that any grant was wrongful.

In the case both of interim and of perpetual interdict so long as the interdict stands unrecalled it cannot be challenged as wrongful. That argument can be pursued only by way of appeal against the grant of the interdict.

An interdict may be wrongful in part only, as where it puts an unjustifiable restraint on the respondent's actings. In such a case, even if the excessive restraint has resulted from a misapprehension by the petitioner of the extent to which he is entitled to have protection for his rights and the extent to which he is entitled to restrict the respondent's actings, the petitioner is " liable in damages for whatever loss was sustained by the [respondent] in consequence of the interdict being in excess of what it ought to have been." [32]

If interdict has been wrongfully granted damages are recoverable only for pecuniary loss caused thereby, and not for hurt to feelings or reputation resulting from being interdicted.[33]

As a general rule an averment that the defender in obtaining the interdict was motivated by malice and lacked probable cause for his acting is not necessary. " An interdict is not granted as a matter of right. It is only granted on cause shown, that is, on a consideration and in respect of the representations of the party applying for it. If, therefore, it turns out that these representations are erroneous or that, for any other reason, the interdict was ill-founded and ought not to have been applied for, it is only reasonable and just that the party obtaining it should answer for the injurious consequences, without it being necessary in an action of damages to aver, and in the issue to charge, malice and want of probable cause." [34] In particular interim interdict is frequently granted on the faith of *ex parte* statements, and accordingly *periculo petentis.*[35]

[31] *Fife, supra,* 11.

[32] *Clippens Oil Co. Ltd.* v. *Edinburgh & District Water Trs.,* 1907 S.C.(H.L.) 9, 11, *per* L.C. Loreburn.

[33] *Clippens Oil Co., supra*; *Aird* v. *Tarbert School Board,* 1907 S.C. 305; *cf. Addis* v. *Gramophone Co.* [1909] A.C. 488.

[34] *Kennedy* v. *Fort William Police Commrs.* (1877) 5 R. 302, 306, *per* Lord Ormidale, following *Wolthekker* v. *Northern Agricultural Co.* (1863) 1 M. 211; *Robinson* v. *N.B. Ry.* (1864) 2 M. 84.

[35] *Kennedy, supra,* 307, citing *Miller* v. *Hunter* (1865) 3 M. 740.

PART VI

POSSESSORY REMEDIES

CHAPTER 12

SECURING OF RIGHTS OF POSSESSION

THE securing of rights of possession arises in the contexts of both corporeal heritable and corporeal moveable property, and in each case both in relation to a person having possession and seeking to protect it against a threatened or attempted dispossession, and in relation to a person claiming to recover possession against an actual possessor, who may have had a legitimate right to possess, or never have had any right to possess, but who in either case delays or refuses to yield possession in response to a claim.

In possessory actions no question is for decision as to title of ownership, but only as to who has right to the actual possession and control and use of the subject in question. A question as to title is a separate matter and to be decided by other process.

What is possession

In relation to heritable property possession is the right to occupy, use, take the fruits of, and exclude others from, a distinguishable piece of ground or other subject of heritable proprietary right.

In relation to moveable property possession is the right to hold, use, take the profits of, and exclude others from the use of, a distinguishable object or other subject of moveable proprietary right.

HERITABLE PROPERTY

Jurisdiction

At common law jurisdiction in questions of possession of heritage belongs to the sheriff. The Sheriff Courts (Scotland) Act 1907, s. 5, provides that the sheriff's jurisdiction includes

> "(4) Actions relating to questions of heritable right or title (except actions of adjudication save in so far as now competent and actions of reduction) including all actions of declarator of irritancy and removing, whether at the instance of a superior against a vassal or of a landlord against a tenant. . . .
>
> Provided that actions relating to questions of heritable right or title, including irritancy and removing, . . . shall, if raised in the sheriff court, be raised in the sheriff court of the jurisdiction and district where the property forming the subject in dispute is situated, and all parties against whom any such action may be brought shall in such action be subject to that jurisdiction: Provided also that it shall be competent for either party at the closing of the record or

within six days thereafter to require the cause to be remitted to the Court of Session in the case of actions—

(*a*) Relating to questions of heritable right and title where the value of the subject in dispute exceeds fifty pounds by the year or one thousand pounds in value: . . ."

Title and interest to sue

Title to sue depends on having a title to the property in question which prima facie includes as one of its elements a right of possession. The title may be that of an owner, heir of entail in possession, liferenter or tenant. A *pro indiviso* proprietor has a possessory action against an outsider who is troubling him in the possession of the property held *pro indiviso*.[1]

THREATENED DISPOSSESSION

A person having actual possession of some piece of corporeal heritable property may by interdict seek to maintain the existing state of possession and resist any threatened or attempted dispossession. This use of interdict appears to be derived from the Roman law interdicts. The principle is that established possession will be protected unless the defender shows a title better than that of the possessor seeking interdict against him. "To justify the interposition of the court in granting an interdict, the party applying for it must show a legal title to the subject, of which his use and enjoyment and right of possession are alleged to be unlawfully interfered with; and, further, he must show either that there has been plain invasion of his property by a party having no right or title whatever in or to the subject or its use or as against a party pleading competing title, that he has had possession, in virtue of his title, for at least seven years prior to that attempt to innovate on it, of which he complains, when he will be entitled to interdict *uti possidetis*." [2]

To entitle him to interdict he must show some prima facie legal title giving him an exclusive right of possession. This may be infeftment as feudal proprietor,[3] or as long leaseholder,[4] or tenant under a lease of ordinary duration,[5] but any title which, even if not expressly including the subjects in dispute, is at least prima facie applicable thereto,[6] will suffice.

The possession in question may be the actual occupation and use of lands or buildings, or the use of a road across another's farm,[7] or a right

1 *Warrand* v. *Watson* (1905) 8 F. 253, 261, 263.

2 *Colquhoun* v. *Paton* (1859) 21 D. 996, 1001, *per* Lord Cowan; *cf. St. Andrews Ladies Golf Club* v. *Denham* (1887) 14 R. 686.

3 *e.g. Colquhoun, supra*; *Marquess of Ailsa* v. *Monteforte*, 1937 S.C. 805.

4 *e.g. McDonald* v. *Dempster* (1871) 10 M. 94.

5 *e.g. Young* v. *Cunningham* (1839) 8 S. 959; *Anderson* v. *McCallum* (1857) 20 D. 2; *Begbie* v. *France* (1857) 20 D. 81; *Calder* v. *Adam* (1870) 8 M. 645, 647; *Galloway* v. *Cowden* (1885) 12 R. 578.

6 *Liston* v. *Galloway* (1835) 14 S. 97.

7 *Galloway, supra*; *Calder* v. *Adam* (1870) 8 M. 645.

of access to premises,[8] or the use of a public footpath,[9] or the enjoyment of a servitude right attaching to lands owned or occupied.[10]

Duration and quality of possession requisite to obtain protection

To be entitled to a judgment affirming his right to possess a petitioner for interdict must alternatively show that he has possessed the heritage, or the right in relation thereto which is in question, for a period of seven years continuously,[11] and that such possession has been open, peaceful and exercised as a matter of right, rather than by contract or permission, or obtained stealthily, or violently or fraudulently[12] or otherwise unlawfully.[13] It must have been exercised *nec vi, nec clam, nec precario.* " It is not every sort of possession that would be enough, and any possession proved might be rebutted or explained away. It might on investigation be shown to have been a precarious possession, or to have arisen from compact, or accident which might negative the idea that there was a public road." [14] Where land is let " as possessed by " a previous tenant, that previous tenant's possession can be counted towards the seven years.[15]

As against a person who puts forward no competing title to the land but claims only the rights of a member of the public a petitioner for interdict need prove only possession and not necessarily full ownership.[16]

Where the complainer's possession has not lasted for seven years continuously, he cannot rely on possession as giving him a title to interdict dispossession but must aver ownership.

A fortiori where the respondent in the interdict proceedings establishes that the right claimed by the petitioner, such as exclusive possession of a road, has on the contrary been used by the public for at least seven years, interdict must be refused.[17] In resisting such an application it is questionable if any title be required; if the defence be that the right is a public one the only title required is that the respondent is a member of the public.[18]

Even where, however, the public has enjoyed the use of a public footpath across lands without gates for more than seven years, the proprietor may erect swing wicket gates across the path, so long as not of an obstructive character, and interference with such gates may be interdicted.[19] The same is true of a servitude right of way.[20]

8 *McDonald, supra*; *Millar* v. *Christie*, 1961 S.C. 1.
9 *McKerron* v. *Gordon* (1876) 3 R. 429.
10 *Crichton* v. *Turnbull*, 1946 S.C. 52; *Hunter* v. *Fox*, 1964 S.C.(H.L.) 95.
11 *Colquhoun, supra*; *Calder* v. *Adam* (1870) 8 M. 645.
12 *Brown's Trs.* v. *Fraser* (1870) 8 M. 820.
13 *Shearer* v. *Hamilton* (1871) 9 M. 456; *McKerron* v. *Gordon* (1876) 3 R. 429.
14 *Calder, supra*, 648, *per* Lord Neaves.
15 *Galloway, supra.*
16 *Mather* v. *Alexander*, 1926 S.C. 139; *cf. Irvine* v. *Robertson* (1872) 11 M. 298.
17 *Calder, supra.*
18 *Calder, supra*, 648.
19 *Sutherland* v. *Thomson* (1876) 3 R. 485.
20 *Wood* v. *Robertson*, 9 March 1809, F.C., discussed in *Sutherland, supra.*

Mode of dispossession

The interference with, or inversion of, possession may be by the threat of, or the actual, seizing occupation of the lands or buildings, or erecting buildings on lands,[21] or by putting a barrier across an access,[22] or insisting on using a private pier the gate of which was locked,[23] or by any kind of trespass on or over lands,[24] or encroachment under the surface of lands, or gathering seaware *ex adverso* of the pursuer's lands [25] or carrying away sand from the seashore.[26]

If dispossession has taken the form of actual occupation of part of the complainer's lands his remedy is not interdict but ejection.[27]

Regulation of possession

Where no question of heritable right arises, but it is admitted or undisputed, but yet the parties are at issue as to the mode in which they may use the right in question, the court may regulate the use and possession, as by permitting a stated number of wicket gates to be erected on a footpath, permitting use of the path, yet preventing cattle straying.[28]

Limits to possessory judgment

A possessory judgment determines only the right to possess and does not settle any question of right or title of ownership, absolute or limited. It may be granted in a case where neither party has, nor can acquire a title of ownership, the ground belonging to the Crown.[29]

If, however, a party obtains a possessory judgment, he is entitled to be considered a bona fide possessor, and to retain possession until his title is challenged on its merits.

Possession of servitude rights

A person having title to a dominant tenement,[30] the possessor of which is entitled to a servitude right over a servient tenement, such as a right of way over it, may vindicate his right to possess and use that servitude right by interdict against any act by the owner of the servient tenement, or by a third party, which infringes his right, such as the shutting up of the way over which there is a servitude right to pass.[31] A question may arise

21 *Irvine* v. *Robertson* (1873) 11 M. 298.
22 *McDonald, supra*; *cf. Millar* v. *Christie*, 1961 S.C. 1.
23 *Colquhoun, supra.*
24 Including unauthorised golfing by a non-member: *St. Andrews Ladies Golf Club* v. *Denham* (1887) 14 R. 686; selling ice-cream on the foreshore: *Marquess of Ailsa* v. *Monteforte*, 1937 S.C. 805; but not merely an assertion of a claim which, if executed, might have been trespass: *Warrand* v. *Watson* (1905) 8 F. 253; *Inverurie Magistrates* v. *Sorrie*, 1956 S.C. 175.
25 *Fullerton* v. *Baillie* (1697) Mor. 13524; *L. Saltoun* v. *Park* (1857) 20 D. 89.
26 *Macalister* v. *Campbell* (1837) 15 S. 490.
27 *Mather* v. *Alexander*, 1926 S.C. 139, 149.
28 *Sutherland, supra.*
29 *Irvine* v. *Robertson* (1873) 11 M. 298.
30 On title to vindicate a servitude right, see *Calder* v. *Adam* (1870) 8 M. 645, 648.
31 *Wood* v. *Robertson*, March 9, 1809, F.C., discussed in *Sutherland* v. *Thomson* (1876) 7 R. 485.

whether the right of passage is enjoyed by virtue of servitude right or *vi, clam aut precario*, and the right claimed can be vindicated only if enjoyed by right rather than in any illegal way or by toleration or contract.

RECOVERY OF POSSESSION

Where the issue is of the recovery of possession of heritage from one in actual possession a distinction has to be taken between an actual possessor who has never had any legal right or title to the possession which in fact he enjoys, such as a squatter, and an actual possessor who obtained possession by some legal right or title, such as of tenancy, but whose title, it is alleged, has now terminated, though he has delayed or refused to yield possession.

Possessor never having had right to possess

Where a possessor has never had legal right to possess, such as a squatter,[32] he may be ousted by an action of ejection.[33] " It is well settled that an action of ejection is only competent if the defender's possession of the subjects is violent, fraudulent or precarious." [34] Ejection is a substantive action, not ancillary to any other proceeding,[35] and if he is successful the pursuer gets a warrant for summary ejection of the defender.[36] It is the lineal successor of the older intrusion, and of the still older novel dissasine.[37] At common law it belongs to the jurisdiction of the sheriff. " A warrant for summary ejection is not granted unless it is prima facie plain that the occupier is one who has and can pretend no title to the occupation challenged." [38] Indeed " I do not doubt that there are cases in which an owner is entitled to turn out a wrongdoer *brevi manu* without legal process. If, in my absence, a stranger takes possession of my house, he may be ejected for force. He cannot be allowed to say your house is my castle, and I will remain in it until you establish your right to dispossess me by an action of removing." [39] Ejection can be brought only by a pursuer who can aver and prove that he has a title to possess and who wishes the defender ejected so that he may himself again possess the subjects.[40] He must show that the defender's occupation is precarious,

[32] A squatter also commits a criminal contravention of the Trespass (Sc.) Act 1865, s. 3: *Paterson* v. *Robertson*, 1944 J.C. 166.

[33] Rankine on *Leases*, 594; *Hally* v. *Lang* (1867) 5 M. 951; *Scottish Property Investment Socy.* v. *Horne* (1881) 8 R. 737; *Gibson* v. *Gibson* (1899) 36 S.L.R. 522; *Dunbar's Trs.* v. *Bruce* (1900) 3 F. 137; *Sinclair* v. *Tod*, 1907 S.C. 1038; *Walker* v. *Kerr*, 1917 S.C. 107; *Lowe* v. *Gardiner*, 1921 S.C. 211; *Scottish Supply Assocn.* v. *Mackie*, 1921 S.C. 882; *Mather* v. *Alexander*, 1926 S.C. 139.

[34] *White* v. *Stevenson*, 1956 S.C. 84, 89, *per* L.P. Clyde, citing *Lowe*, *supra*.

[35] In particular it is distinguishable from the warrant of ejection which follows on decree in an action of removing.

[36] *Cf. Campbell's Trs.* v. *O'Neill*, 1911 S.C. 188, 192, 194, *per* Lord Johnston.

[37] *Price* v. *Watson*, 1951 S.C. 359, 363.

[38] *Dunbar's Trs.* v. *Bruce* (1900) 3 F. 137, 145, *per* Lord Trayner.

[39] *Macdonald* v. *Watson* (1883) 10 R. 1079, 1081, *per* Lord McLaren.

[40] Hope, *Major Pract.*, VI, 15; Stair I, 9, 26; *Craig* v. *Inchbreckie* (1573) Mor. 7175; *Mather* v. *Alexander*, 1926 S.C. 139; *Price*, *supra*.

that is, possession *vi, clam aut precario.*[41] Proceedings by way of ejection are not made incompetent by the fact that a question of law is involved.[42]

Where an owner of heritage has been sequestrated his whole rights in the heritage vest in the trustee and so long as the sequestration lasts he has no right of any kind to possess or occupy the heritage and is liable to an action of ejection. He is reduced to the position of a squatter.[43] On the other hand a person who has obtained possession of heritage as purchaser does not become a merely precarious possessor if the seller, even justifiably, rescinds the contract of sale, and ejection is then incompetent.[44]

A *pro indiviso* proprietor is entitled to bring an action of ejection against an outsider who is disturbing his possession of the property,[45] but while it is not certain that one *pro indiviso* proprietor can never eject another from the joint or common property the normal remedy will be an action of division and sale.[46]

If the defender has any title to occupy the premises an action of ejection is not competent and an action of removing should be brought.[47] But it is not a good defence to an action for removing that the defender had no title to occupy and that accordingly an action of removing was not the proper form of action.[48] By statute [49] a proprietor in personal occupation of subjects disponed in security who has made default in payment of principal or interest is deemed to be an occupant without a title and he can be evicted by action of ejection [50] but this is not applicable in the case of security by disposition *ex facie* absolutely with back letter.[51] That statute [49] does not entitle a heritable creditor to require his debtor, before defending an action for ejection, to find caution for violent profits.[52]

Possessor whose title has terminated

Where a possessor has had a legal right to possess but that has terminated, the appropriate remedy is an action of removing. The prime case of such a possessor is a tenant. It must be remembered that, in the absence of notice of termination by one party to the other, the relationship of landlord and tenant is, notwithstanding the arrival of the contractual date of termination of the lease, continued by the principle of tacit relocation for a further year, if originally entered into for a year or longer, and for the same period again, if originally entered into for a shorter

41 *Hally* v. *Lang* (1867) 5 M. 951, 954; *Lowe, supra*; *Cairns* v. *Innes*, 1942 S.C. 164, 171.
42 *Whyte* v. *Haddington School Board* (1874) 1 R. 1124; *Cairns* v. *Innes*, 1942 S.C. 164.
43 *White* v. *Stevenson*, 1956 S.C. 84.
44 *Lowe, supra.*
45 *Warrand* v. *Watson* (1905) 8 F. 253.
46 *Price* v. *Watson*, 1951 S.C. 359.
47 *Lowe* v. *Gardiner*, 1921 S.C. 211; *Cook* v. *Wylie*, 1963 S.L.T.(Sh.Ct.) 29.
48 *Breadalbane* v. *Cameron*, 1923 S.L.T.(Sh.Ct.) 6; *E. Eglinton* v. *McLuckie*, 1944 S.L.T.(Sh. Ct.) 21.
49 Heritable Securities (Scotland) Act 1894, s. 5.
50 *Cf. Inglis' Trs.* v. *Macpherson*, 1910 S.C. 46.
51 *Scottish Property Investment Socy.* v. *Horne* (1881) 8 R. 737.
52 *Inglis' Trs., supra.*

period.[53] But as tacit relocation rests on implied consent, it is excluded by arrangements for a new lease on other terms, though not yet completed in probative form,[54] and by conduct inconsistent with tacit relocation, such as remaining in possession notwithstanding an intimation by the landlord of increased rent,[55] or intimation by the tenant of intent to remove at the term.[56]

An ineffectual notice to remove does not exclude tacit relocation,[57] and a notice to quit, not followed up or insisted in, may be held to have been departed from, in which case a new lease by tacit relocation may be inferred.[58]

Tacit relocation does not apply to those kinds of leases where, by common understanding, the let is seasonal only, such as of furnished houses, grass parks, fishings or shootings, and in these cases the let terminates, without notice, on the expiry date.[59]

Land exceeding two acres

Where land exceeding two acres in extent, not falling within the definition of an agricultural holding, is held under a probative lease specifying a term of endurance, and whether such lease contains an obligation on the tenant to remove without warning or not, the lease or an extract thereof from the books of a court of record has the same force and effect as an extract decree of removing obtained in an ordinary action and, along with authority in writing from the lessor or one in his right, is sufficient warrant to any sheriff officer to eject the persons in possession at the expiry of the lease. Prior notice must have been given, in the case of leases for three years and upwards, between one and two years before the termination, and in the case of leases from year to year (including lands occupied by tacit relocation) or for any other period less than three years, not less than six months before the termination, failing which the lease is renewed by tacit relocation for another year and thereafter from year to year. Removal by virtue of this section is not competent after six weeks from the date of the ish last in date. These provisions do not apply to subjects let for any period less than a year.[60]

Where a tenant in possession of lands exceeding two acres in extent, with or without a written lease, has granted a letter of removal, holograph or attested by one witness, such letter of removal has the same force and effect as an extract decree of removing and is sufficient warrant for

53 Stair II, 9, 23; Rankine, *Leases*, 598.
54 *Buchanan* v. *Harris & Sheldon* (1900) 2 F. 935.
55 *Macfarlane* v. *Mitchell* (1900) 2 F. 901.
56 *Tod* v. *Fraser* (1889) 17 R. 226.
57 *Gates* v. *Blair*, 1923 S.C. 430.
58 *Taylor* v. *E. Moray* (1892) 19 R. 399.
59 *Macharg* (1805) Mor. Removing, Appx. 4.
60 Sheriff Courts (Sc.) Act 1907, s. 34. The provisions as to notice do not apply to any stipulations in a lease entitling the landlord to resume land for building, planting, feuing, or other purposes.

ejection. If dated and signed within twelve months before the ish, notice by either party is unnecessary.[61]

In these cases no process of removing or ejection is necessary and the tenant may be ejected without decree of court, but if there is serious dispute between parties, proceedings for removing are preferable and are competent.

Where lands exceeding two acres in extent are occupied by a tenant without a written lease, and the tenant has given no letter of removal, the lease terminates on written notice [62] being given by either party to the other not less than six months before the end of the tenancy, which notice entitles the proprietor, if the tenant does not remove, to obtain a summary warrant of ejection against the tenant and everyone deriving right from him.[63] This summary warrant of ejection is probably the same as the warrant for summary ejection provided for by the 1907 Act, s. 37. It is sought by initial writ craving warrant summarily to eject, and proceeds as an ordinary action, and is in substance an action of removing.[64]

Agricultural holdings

The removal provisions of the Sheriff Courts (Sc.) Act 1907 apply to agricultural holdings, as defined by the Agricultural Holdings (Sc.) Act 1949, ss. 1 and 93, subject to the provisions of the 1949 Act.[65] Notice of intention to terminate the tenancy must be given between one and two years before the termination.

The notice to quit does not have effect if within one month the tenant serves a counter-notice requiring the application of section 25 (1) of the 1949 Act, unless the Land Court consents to the operation of the notice. In certain cases section 25 (1) does not apply [66] and consent must be withheld unless the Land Court is satisfied of one or other of certain stated conditions.[67]

Houses or land not exceeding two acres

Where houses, with or without land attached, not exceeding two acres in extent, lands not exceeding two acres in extent let without houses, mills, fishings, shootings, and other heritable subjects (excepting land exceeding two acres in extent) are let for a year or more, forty days' notice of termination must be given in writing by or on behalf of either party to the other,[68] which notice does not warrant summary ejection from the subjects let to a tenant, but entitles the proprietor to apply to the sheriff

61 *Ibid.* s. 35.
62 *Ibid.* Sched. I, Form H.
63 *Ibid.* s. 36.
64 *Cf. Campbell's Trs.* v. *O'Neill*, 1911 S.C. 188.
65 Agricultural Holdings (Sc.) Act 1949, s. 24.
66 *Ibid.* s. 25 (2), amd. Agriculture Act 1958, Sched.
67 *Ibid.* s. 26 (1), amd. Agriculture Act 1958, Sched.
68 On the notice and its service, see Sheriff Courts (Sc.) Act 1907, Sched. I, rr. 110–114, and Form J.

for a warrant for summary ejection in common form [69] against the tenant, and everyone deriving right from him.[70]

If the defender, having been thus judicially ordained to do so, fails to remove, the pursuer may then apply for warrant to eject the defender.[71]

Summary removings—subjects let for less than a year

Where houses or other heritable subjects are let for a shorter period than a year any person by law authorised may present to the sheriff a summary application for removing, decree in which shall have the force and effect of a decree of removing and warrant of ejection. Application is made on an official printed form of Summary Removing Petition and Complaint, and the proceedings are conducted summarily, save that if the defender has found caution for violent profits, or if such caution has been dispensed with, he may give in written answers, in which case the action proceeds as an ordinary action for removing.[72] Notice of removal must be given and in the absence of express stipulation, the period of notice must be one-third of the duration of the let, if for not exceeding four months, and forty days if it exceeds four months.[73] The form of notice of removal is Form J of the Sheriff Courts (Scotland) Act 1907, Sched. I.

Small dwelling-houses

In the case of small dwelling-houses in burghs and urban districts, as statutorily defined,[74] all lets, except those for less than a month, shall terminate and are terminable at noon on the 28th of a month, or, if that day is a Sunday, on the following day, and all lets for a shorter period terminate and are terminable at noon on a Monday.[75] Notice to terminate on the day on which a payment of rent falls due may be given by either party in accordance with the Sheriff Courts (Scotland) Act 1907, but shall expire at noon on the day on which that payment of rent falls due, unless that day is not a lawful date for the termination of a let under the Act, in which case it shall expire at noon on the lawful date next following the said day. If, however, the let be for more than three months, the notice shall be forty days before the rent-day or next lawful date, and if the let be for three months or less, the notice must be one third of the said period, so, however, that in no case shall the notice be less than twenty-eight days.[76] Notwithstanding the foregoing provisions, if the occupier of a small dwelling-house is at any time in arrear with his rent for not less than seven

[69] Explained in *Campbell's Trs.* v. *O'Neill*, 1911 S.C. 188, 195, as truly meaning an order to remove.

[70] Sheriff Courts (Sc.) Act 1907, s. 37.

[71] 1907 Act, Sched. I, Forms K and L.

[72] Sheriff Courts (Sc.) Act 1907, Sched. I, rr. 121, 122.

[73] Sheriff Courts (Sc.) Act 1907, s. 38.

[74] House Letting and Rating (Sc.) Act 1911, amended by House Letting and Rating (Sc.) Act 1920, and Rent Restriction Act 1920, ss. 16, 18.

[75] 1911 Act, s. 3.

[76] 1911 Act, s. 4, amended by Rent Act 1971, s. 131 and Sched. 18.

days, the owner may give him notice to terminate the let on the expiry of twenty-eight days from the date of the notice, and the production of a certificate signed by or on behalf of the owner that the occupier is in arrear with rent for not less than seven days is prima facie evidence thereof in any process to follow thereon.[77]

If any occupier fails to remove from a small dwelling-house on the expiration of notice to terminate the let in terms of the 1911 Act, the owner may make to the sheriff or burgh police court a summary application for removing, decree whereon shall have the full force and effect of a decree of removing and warrant of ejection. No delay beyond forty-eight hours may be granted by the sheriff or magistrate to the occupier unless on cause shown, or on caution for, or consignation of, the rent due being found or made. The cause shown for delay must be stated in the order granting delay.[78]

Forms of extract decrees of ejection, or absolvitor or dismissal, have been provided.[79] If decree of ejection is granted it is to be not sooner than at 12 noon on a specified date.[79] If decree in absence is granted the sheriff may give directions for the preservation of the defender's goods and effects.[80] But if within three days the defender shall satisfy the sheriff that there was reasonable excuse for his non-appearance, the sheriff may rehear the cause, and, if decree has been granted and not implemented, may recall the decree upon such conditions as to expenses and otherwise as the sheriff shall deem reasonable.[80]

The decision in such a case is not subject to review,[81] but this may not exclude review by suspension on the plea that the let was truly one for a year or longer.[82] If written answers have been lodged and the case dealt with as an ordinary action of removing, it may be reviewed in the ordinary way.[83]

Right of tenant to remain as statutory tenant

Removal from dwelling-houses is subject to the right of the tenant, if his tenancy is a protected tenancy within the Rent (Scotland) Act 1971, s. 1, to claim the protection of that Act and to remain in possession as a statutory tenant.[84] A court may not make an order for possession of a dwelling-house which is let on a protected tenancy or subject to a statutory tenancy unless the court considers it reasonable to make such an order and either the court is satisfied that suitable alternative accommodation is or will be available for the tenant or the case falls within one of the cases specified in Schedule 3, Part I, of the 1971 Act.[85]

77 *Ibid.* s. 5, amended by Rent Act 1971, s. 135 and Sched 18.
78 *Ibid.* s. 6.
79 A.S. Feb. 3, 1933, s. 7 and Sched. F.
80 1907 Act, Sched. I, r. 117.
81 Sheriff Courts (Sc.) Act 1907, Sched. I, r. 119.
82 *Robertson* v. *Thorburn*, 1927 S.L.T. 562.
83 1907 Act, Sched. I, rr. 121, 122.
84 1971 Act, ss. 3–5 and Sched. I.
85 *Ibid.* s. 10; *cf. Barclay* v. *Hannah*, 1947 S.C. 245, 248; *Turner* v. *Keiller*, 1950 S.C. 43.

If the court order removal of a tenant under section 10, nothing in the order affects the right of a sub-tenant to whom the dwelling-house or part of it has been lawfully let before the commencement of the proceedings to retain possession by virtue of the Act.[86]

Person with limited personal right to possess

Where a person has had a limited personal right to occupy and possess, not amounting to a real right in the land, such as the right of a licensee, such as a monthly holiday tenant or a lodger or a camper, but his right has terminated by lapse of the time for which it was granted, or, if no time were specified, by request to remove, the appropriate remedy is probably an action of ejection, possession being precarious, at the will of the owners. In these cases there is no place for the principle of the tenancy or licence being extended by tacit relocation. The same applies where a person had a personal right exercisable only against the granter and not against his singular successor.[87]

An employee who has the occupation of a house under his contract of employment as part of the remuneration for his services ceases to have a title to possess when he gives up the employment or he is dismissed, whether justifiably or wrongfully, and he must remove on being given a reasonable time to do so. He cannot recover damages from his employer if the latter removes him and his possessions without a warrant.[88] In such a case a summary application for removing would be competent [89] but not strictly necessary.

Security of tenure of tenants of furnished houses

The tenant of a furnished dwelling-house has a limited security of tenure under the Rent (Scotland) Act 1971, ss. 92–95.

EXTRAORDINARY REMOVINGS

An extraordinary removing is one brought at other than the contractually stipulated date of termination of the lease. It is competent (1) at common law, where two years' rent of lands is unpaid [90]; (2) at common law, if a tenant falls one full year into arrears or deserts possession or neglects to cultivate his lands, the court may ordain him to find security for the arrears and for the rent of the five following crops, or during the currency of the lease if less than five years, and on the tenant's failure to do so, shall decree him to remove summarily as if his lease had expired and he had

86 *Ibid.* s. 17.

87 *Mann* v. *Houston*, 1957 S.L.T. 89; *Wallace* v. *Simmers*, 1960 S.C. 255.

88 *Sinclair* v. *Tod*, 1907 S.C. 1038. *Cf. Cairns* v. *Innes*, 1942 S.C. 164. In an action for damages for ejection without warrant a possessor must set forth his title to possess: *Macdonald* v. *Duchess of Leeds* (1860) 22 D. 1075; *Macdonald* v. *Watson* (1883) 10 R. 1079.

89 *Sinclair*, *supra*, 1044; *cf. Dunbar's Trs.* v. *Bruce* (1900) 3 F. 137, where held on the facts that the employee was a tenant.

90 Ersk. II, 6, 44; A.S. Dec. 14, 1756.

been warned to remove [90]; (3) where six months' rent of an agricultural holding is due and unpaid, when the landlord is entitled to raise an action of removing in the sheriff court, concluding for the tenant's removal from the holding at the term of Whitsunday or Martinmas next ensuing after the action is raised, and the sheriff may, unless the arrears of rent then due are paid or caution is found to his satisfaction for them, and for one year's rent further, decern the tenant to remove, and may eject him at the said term in like manner as if the lease were determined and the tenant had been legally warned to remove [91]; (4) where the tenant of a small dwelling-house is in arrears with his rent for not less than seven days, notice to terminate the let twenty-eight days after the date of the notice may be given [92]; (5) where a vassal or tenant has incurred a legal or conventional irritancy of his feu-charter or lease and, in the case of a legal irritancy, has failed to purge it before decree.[93]

In all cases the appropriate form of action is an ordinary action of removing. It is a question of circumstances and convenience whether in the case of an irritancy it is necessary to combine a declarator that the irritancy has been incurred with the crave for removing.[94]

Appeal in removings and ejections

In actions of removing there is no appeal to the Court of Session [95] but a suspension may be brought before the decree is extracted.[96] Suspension is incompetent after a decree has been implemented or executed [97] and the only remedy is by way of reduction of the decree.[98] A decree of summary ejection may be appealed to the Court of Session.[99]

Caution for violent profits

Violent profits are penal damages incurred by one who takes or keeps possession without a legal title; and in actions of removing or summary ejection a defender must find caution for them at giving in his defences unless he instantly verify a defence excluding the action, such as possession in good faith.[1] They are the profits of possession after the occupier should have removed. In any defended action of removing from subjects let for a year or longer the sheriff may order the defender to find caution

91 Agricultural Holdings (Sc.) Act 1949, s. 19 (1). On the outgoing tenant's rights, see s. 19 (2).
92 House Letting and Rating (Sc.) Act 1911, s. 5, amended by Rent (Sc.) Act 1971, s. 131.
93 On irritancies and their purgation, see Chap. 6, *supra*.
94 *Duke of Argyll* v. *Campbeltown Coal Co.*, 1924 S.C. 844.
95 Court of Session Act 1825, s. 44; Court of Session Act 1868, ss. 64–65; *McNair* v. *Blantyre's Tutors* (1833) 11 S. 935; *Roy* v. *Earl of Wemyss* (1840) 2 D. 1345; *Fletcher* v. *Davidson* (1874) 2 R. 71; *Ross* v. *Brims* (1878) 15 S.L.R. 438.
96 *Graham* v. *Gordon* (1843) 5 D. 1207; *Ballantyne* v. *Brechin* (1893) 1 S.L.T. 306.
97 *McDougall* v. *Galt* (1863) 1 M. 1012.
98 *Hog* v. *Hog* (1837) 15 S. 532.
99 *Clarke* v. *Clarkes* (1890) 17 R. 1064; *Barbour* v. *Chalmers* (1891) 18 R. 610; *Robb* v. *Brearton* (1895) 22 R. 885; *Hutchison* v. *Alexander* (1904) 6 F. 532.
1 Stair II, 9, 44; IV, 29, 2; Ersk. II, 6, 54; Bell, *Prin.* § 1268C; *Oliver* v. *Weir's Trs.* (1870) 8 M. 786; *Houldsworth* v. *Brand's Trs.* (1877) 4 R. 369.

for violent profits.[1a] In actions for summary removing also caution may be ordered [2] and also in an action of ejection of squatters,[2a] but cannot be ordered in an action of ejection [3] by a heritable creditor of his debtor. It is competent in industrial subjects as well as subjects let for habitation.[3a] It is competent in the case of ejection of a precarious occupier.[3b] Caution is security for the rent which would otherwise be recoverable. The amount of violent profits is all the profits which the pursuer could have made by the property if he had been in possession, together with any damage done to the subjects by the defender,[4] or, by custom, double the rent of houses in burghs.[5] A defender may be found liable for violent profits even though he was not obliged to find caution.

The pursuer may after appearance has been entered for the defender move that the defender be ordained to find caution. Caution is found by lodging in process a bond of caution acceptable to the court and to the pursuer for the sum fixed by the court. If an order for caution be made and not implemented, decree of removal may at once be granted.

Violent profits fell under the triennial prescription.[6]

The obligation to pay violent profits is elided by good faith, and can arise only from the time when good faith ceases and the defender is aware that he has no title.[7]

Moveable Property

In relation to moveable property also one has to consider the protection of possession from threatened dispossession, and the recovery of possession from one who has no title to possess, or whose title to possess has expired.

Threatened dispossession

Interdict is competent against a threat to dispossess, as the taking of corporeal moveables without the possessor's consent would be, civilly, a spuilzie and, criminally, possibly theft. Any lawful title of possession would suffice to justify interdict, including possession as owner, borrower, depositary, pledgee, hirer, hire-purchaser, agent or factor for an owner, unpaid seller still retaining possession under his right of lien until payment or tender of the price,[8] unpaid seller who has resumed possession under

[1a] Sheriff Courts (Sc.) Act 1907, Sched. I, r. 110.
[2] *Ibid.* r. 121.
[2a] *Glasgow Lock Hospital* v. *Ashcroft*, 1949 S.L.T.(Sh.Ct.) 58; *Fife C.C.* v. *Hatten*, 1950 S.L.T.(Sh.Ct.) 13.
[3] *Inglis' Trs.* v. *Macpherson*, 1910 S.C. 46.
[3a] *Jute Industries Ltd.* v. *Wilson & Graham Ltd.*, 1955 S.L.T.(Sh.Ct.) 46.
[3b] *Cheshire* v. *Irvine*, 1963 S.L.T.(Sh.Ct.) 28.
[4] *Gardner* v. *Beresford's Trs.* (1877) 4 R. 1091.
[5] Bell, *supra*; *Macdonald* v. *Macdonald* (1906) 22 Sh.Ct.Rep. 11.
[6] Ersk. III, 7, 16.
[7] As to when good faith ceases see *Houldsworth* v. *Brand's Trs.* (1876) 3 R. 304. *Cf. Duke of Gordon* v. *Innes* (1830) 4 W. & S. 305; *Carnegy* v. *Scott* (1830) 4 W. & S. 431; *Howard* v. *Muir* (1870) 8 S.L.R. 6.
[8] Sale of Goods Act 1893, s. 41 (1).

his right of stoppage *in transitu*,[9] carrier, warehouseman or other custodier. But interdict will not be granted against a threatened dispossession by a person having a title to possess superior to that of the possessor. Thus a borrower or hirer will not be protected in his possession against one who asserts that he is owner and that the borrower's or hirer's title has ended.

Recovery of Possession

In relation to moveable property also the distinction must be drawn between recovering possession from a person who has possession without ever having had any title thereto, and from a person who originally obtained possession lawfully, but whose title to possess has been terminated or has expired.

Possessor without title to possess

A person lawfully entitled to possession of any corporeal moveables, such as an owner, borrower, pledgee, depositary, hire-purchaser,[10] hirer, carrier or onerous custodier is probably entitled at his own hand to take or retake goods unjustifiably in the possession of another, or removed from his possession by another, so long as he can do so without trespass on the other's lands or assault or other physical violence. If he cannot do so, or if there is dispute as to the actual possessor's title to possess, he must bring an action for delivery on the basis of restitution, normally with an alternative conclusion, failing restitution, for damages on the basis of spuilzie. If goods have been misdelivered to a person, he should hand them over, or a claim for delivery will lie against him. Again, if a thief is still in possession of stolen goods he must make restitution of them [11]; if he has got rid of possession, he is liable in damages as reparation for the value of the goods taken.[12]

Where goods have been stolen or otherwise dishonestly acquired a *vitium reale* taints the goods so that no person acquiring the goods by subsequent transmission, even in good faith, is entitled to keep them against a claim by the true owner.[13]

Where, however, the actual possessor, C, possesses in good faith, as where he has purchased from an intermediary, B, who acquired the goods from the pursuer, A, now claiming possession, his (C's) title to possess depends on the validity of the transaction under which he acquired possession and on the title of the intermediary to the goods. Thus if the intermediary acquired the goods under a sale which was wholly null by reason of the seller's essential error as to the buyer's identity, induced by the latter's misrepresentations, the intermediary had no title to resell and

9 Sale of Goods Act 1893, s. 44.
10 *McArthur* v. *O'Donnell*, 1969 S.L.T.(Sh.Ct.) 24.
11 *Dalhanna Knitwear Co.* v. *Mohammed Ali*, 1967 S.L.T.(Sh.Ct.) 74.
12 *Gorebridge Co-operative Socy.* v. *Turnbull*, 1952 S.L.T.(Sh.Ct.) 91.
13 *International Banking Corpn.* v. *Ferguson, Shaw & Co.*, 1910 S.C. 182; *Macdonald* v. *Provan (of Scotland St.)*, 1960 S.L.T. 231.

can pass no right of property in the goods, and the actual possessor must restore the goods to the original owner.[14] The same would follow if the intermediary had stolen the goods. If, on the other hand, the intermediary acquired the goods under a sale which was voidable by the seller for misrepresentation, and resells before the first sale had been avoided, he thereby passes a good title to the goods to the ultimate possessor, provided the latter took in good faith, for value, and without notice of any vitiation in the first sale.[15]

In the special case, however, of money, bank notes and negotiable instruments the third party possessor has a good title, notwithstanding any defect in the title of the intermediary, provided he (the third party) took the money or other negotiable instrument in good faith, for value and without notice of any defect in the intermediary's title. But if he had notice of the defect in the intermediary's title that defect vitiates his title to possess and he is liable to make restitution. Hence a bona fide taker of money or negotiable instruments from a thief is not liable to restore the things taken or their value to the original owner.[16]

Recovery of possession of stolen property

Where goods have been stolen and are in the possession of a third party they may be ordered to be delivered up to the owner on such terms as a magistrate thinks fit, though no such order shall prevent any broker or dealer from recovering possession of such goods by action at law from the person into whose possession they may have come by the magistrate's order, the action to be commenced within three months of the order.[17] In a case under a generally similar provision of a Glasgow Police Act[18] it was held that the magistrate should have awarded possession only, subject to all legal claims competent against the person to whom the goods were delivered.

Possessor whose title has terminated

In this case the possessor initially obtained possession (but not ownership) with the consent of the true owner, as under a contract of loan, deposit, pledge, hiring, carriage, or onerous custody, but his entitlement to possess has terminated and he should have restored the goods, as where the period of loan or hiring has terminated. Whether it has so expired depends on the terms of the particular contract under which he obtained possession. If no period was fixed for the temporary possession the contract must be terminated by notice and a request made for delivery at or by a stated time. If the transaction were one, such as pledge or onerous custody, under which money is due to the temporary possessor,

[14] *Morrisson* v. *Robertson*, 1908 S.C. 332; *cf. Cundy* v. *Lindsay* (1878) 3 App.Cas. 459.
[15] *MacLeod* v. *Kerr*, 1965 S.C. 253.
[16] *Gorebridge Co-operative Socy., supra.*
[17] Burgh Police (Scotland) Act 1892, s. 413.
[18] *Robertson* v. *Burns*, 1943 J.C. 1.

payment or tender of all sums due to him is a condition precedent of a valid claim for redelivery.

In such a case if redelivery be not made the true owner may retake possession of the goods at his own hand if he can do so without trespass on the possessor's property, assault on his person or other wrongful conduct. Thus a bicycle lent to and left by the borrower at his back door may be retaken by the true owner. But if the true owner cannot recover possession without trespass he must bring an action for delivery, normally with an alternative conclusion, failing delivery, for payment of the fair value of the thing in question.

Delivery of moveables

An action *ad factum praestandum*, concluding for delivery, is appropriate where the defender is alleged to be in possession of moveables, possession of which should have been ceded to the pursuer, and the pursuer claims delivery to himself.[19] The duty to deliver may arise from wrongful withholding, as of goods abstracted or stolen,[19] or from withholding goods obtained under a contract, such as goods taken on hire or hire-purchase.[20]

As in the case of other decrees of specific implement [21] the sanction for non-implement of the decree is imprisonment.[22]

Defences

The possessor may be entitled to rely on one or more of various defences, as that the contractual conditions for making redelivery have not been satisfied, or that the possessor has a claim of lien over the goods, or that the owner has not paid or tendered any charges due in respect of the possession.

Entitlement to possession under sale

When a sale of goods has been concluded, the property in the goods passes, independently of delivery, at the time when the parties intend it to be transferred, which has to be ascertained by regard to the terms of the contract, the conduct of the parties, and the circumstances of the case.[23] Failing other indications of intention the parties' intention is determined by rules [24] of which the most important is that the property in specific goods in a deliverable state passes when the contract is made, whether payment or delivery or both be postponed or not.[25] Where this

19 *Henry* v. *Morrison* (1881) 8 R. 692; see also *Singer Mfg. Co.* v. *Jessiman* (1881) 8 R. 695.
20 *e.g. Rudman* v. *Jay*, 1908 S.C. 552.
21 See Chap. 13, *infra*.
22 *Rudman, supra.*
23 Sale of Goods Act 1893, s. 17.
24 *Ibid.* s. 18.
25 *Ibid.* s. 18, r. 1.

rule applies the buyer is entitled to possession (unless delivery be contractually delayed) and may demand delivery, or bring an action claiming delivery, or claim damages for non-delivery [26] subject always to implementing any duty to make payment by a fixed date, or before or on delivery.

But the unpaid seller,[27] so long as in possession of the goods, though the property therein has passed to the buyer, may exercise a right to retain them, or to stop them *in transitu* to the buyer,[28] and, if in the circumstances the property in the goods has not passed to the buyer, a right to withhold delivery coextensive with his right of retention or lien.[29]

Entitlement to possession of goods let on hire or hire-purchase

Where goods are let on hire or hire-purchase the contract frequently provides that on default in payments of rent, the hirer is to be deemed no longer in possession with the owner's consent, in which case he must surrender possession on demand. But such a provision does not authorise forcible entry into his premises to remove the hired article, nor assault on or intimidation of the hirer. If he refuses to surrender possession the only course is an action for delivery, or alternatively for payment of the full value of the thing wrongfully retained.[30]

The possessor on hire or hire-purchase may have an excuse for not yielding possession, if the thing hired has perished without his fault, the onus of proof of which would be on the possessor.[31]

Protected goods in hire-purchase and conditional sale

Under the Hire-Purchase (Scotland) Act 1965, goods covered by the Act [32] and acquired under a hire-purchase or conditional sale agreement [33] are deemed " protected goods " if let under a hire-purchase agreement, or agreed to be sold under a conditional sale agreement, if one-third of the hire-purchase price or total purchase price has been paid or tendered, and the hirer or buyer has not terminated the agreement by virtue of any right vested in him.[34] The owner or seller of protected goods may not enforce any right to recover possession otherwise than by action. If he does so, the agreement terminates, the hirer or buyer is released from all liability and is entitled to recover all sums paid, and any guarantor may recover all sums paid.[35]

In an action brought to recover possession the court has power,[36] on

26 *Ibid.* s. 51.
27 Defined, *ibid.* s. 38.
28 *Ibid.* s. 39 (1); see also as to lien ss. 41–43, and as to stoppage *in transitu*, ss. 44–46.
29 *Ibid.* s. 39 (2).
30 *Rudman* v. *Jay*, 1908 S.C. 552.
31 *McLean* v. *Warnock* (1883) 10 R. 1052.
32 1965 Act, ss. 2–4.
33 As defined by 1965 Act, s. 1.
34 1965 Act, s. 33.
35 *Ibid.* s. 34.
36 *Ibid.* ss. 35 and 45.

the application of the owner, to make such orders as it thinks just for protecting the goods from damage or depreciation, including orders restricting or prohibiting the use of the goods or giving directions as to their custody. The court has power, without prejudice to any other power, to make an order for specific delivery of all the goods to the owner or seller, or to make such an order and postpone its operation subject to conditions as to payment,[37] or to make an order for specific delivery of part of the goods to the owner or seller and the transfer to the hirer or purchaser of the owner's title to the remainder.[38]

After the owner or seller has begun an action to which section 35 applies, he may not take any step to enforce payment of any sum due under the agreement, or under any relative guarantee, except by claiming that sum in that action.[39]

Where the owner or seller has brought an action to recover possession of protected goods and the court has made an order but it has not been complied with, or there has been failure to comply with any condition of the postponement, or with any term of the agreement as varied by the court, or the hirer or purchaser has wrongfully disposed of the goods, and the owner or seller has not recovered possession of all the goods which were directed to be delivered to him, the owner or seller may apply to the court, which may revoke the previous order or order payment of a sum determined under this section of the Act.[40]

37 For circumstances in which a postponed order may be made see s. 36; for its effect, see ss. 38 and 45 (3); for further powers, see s. 39.

38 For restrictions on orders transferring owner's title see s. 37; for provisions supplementary to ss. 35 to 39, see s. 40.

39 1965 Act, s. 41.

40 *Ibid.* s. 42. Provision is also made in ss. 43–44 for monetary claims under a minimum payment provision or after an order for specific delivery of goods. S. 46 provides for the recovery of possession and money claims after the death of the hirer or buyer.

PART VII

ENFORCING PERFORMANCE OF DUTIES

CHAPTER 13

DECREES AD FACTUM PRAESTANDUM

A DECREE *ad factum praestandum* is a judicial order to do or perform some act, other than to pay money, which the defender should have done in implement of a legal duty incumbent on him, whether by statute, common law or by contractual undertaking, or an order to undo some act which the defender should not have done but did in breach of a legal duty incumbent on him. If the duty is to pay money, then the remedy is, in general, an action for payment.

The duty to do or not to do may have become incumbent on the defender by force of statute, or of general law, or under a contractual obligation.

Jurisdiction

Both the Court of Session and the Sheriff Court have jurisdiction to order implement of duties not implemented, subject to certain statutory exceptions. In order to decide whether an action craving an order *ad factum praestandum* is within the privative jurisdiction of the Sheriff Court it is competent to consider not only the crave but the averments.[1]

Need for precision in conclusion

In an action with a conclusion *ad factum praestandum* it is essential, apart from any other requisites, that the precise act which the pursuer calls on the court to order the defender to do should be stated precisely, clearly, in detail and unambiguously.

In a case relating to an alleged obligation to maintain a navigable channel Lord President Cooper observed[2]: " When the pursuers use in their conclusion the word ' navigable,' they must surely indicate by what the channel is to be navigated, for a specification of the beam and length of the ships to be accommodated is just as important for determining the dimensions of the channel and the radius of the curves as the draught. These are not idle questions. An answer is indispensable to the remedy sought. . . ."

Decree must be specific

> " In pronouncing decree *ad factum praestandum* the Court has to bear in mind the consequence and sanctions of such a decree. Failure to implement such a decree exposes the defender to the penalty of

1 *General Guarantee Corpn.* v. *Alexander*, 1918 S.C. 662.
2 *Fleming & Ferguson* v. *Paisley Magistrates*, 1948 S.C. 547, 558.

imprisonment which it is in the power of the pursuer to put in force. I therefore think that in the case of decrees which may be thus enforced, or which expose a defender to penal consequences, it is right that the Court should so express the decree that the defender shall be in no doubt regarding the obligation he has to discharge. To take an illustration, if a person who has been interdicted commits a breach of interdict, he is liable to prosecution and imprisonment, and accordingly, the Court always frames its interlocutor in these cases so that there shall be no vagueness, and that the person who has been interdicted shall be in no doubt as to the measure of his liability. It appears to me that the same reasoning applies to such a decree as is here in question, and I cannot acquiesce in the demand of the pursuer to pronounce a decree for implement of the obligation 'forthwith.' Such a decree would be appropriate in the case of a single act, such as the delivery of a writ, which is completed instantly on its commencement; but it is not so in the case of the building of a house, which must be a long operation, and requires a tract of time for its execution, even where the greatest despatch is used." [3]

"This Court will not pronounce a decree *ad factum praestandum* except in terms of such precision as will leave the defenders in no doubt as to the exact obligation to be discharged by them (*Middleton* v. *Leslie* [4]; *McArthur* v. *Lawson*,[5] Lord President Inglis at p. 1136). The same principle of course applies to a declarator preliminary to a decree of specific performance." [6]

The pursuer of an action *ad factum praestandum* is interested, and it is his duty, to obtain a decree plainly specifying what is to be done.[7]

"It is impossible for us with propriety to pronounce any decree *ad factum praestandum* which is not absolutely precise in every particular, both as to time and as to place. . . ." [8]

The decree must, in fairness and reason, give the defender a reasonable time in which to do what is necessary to obey it, but delay in implement does not justify the court in suspending a charge to do so.[9]

Sanction for non-implement

The primary sanction for non-implement of a court's order *ad factum praestandum* is imprisonment of the party in breach until he satisfies the court of his willingness to obtemper its orders. The imprisonment is not a penalty. It is " only an invocation of the power inherent in every civil court to ordain performance of acts within its jurisdiction, and in default

[3] *Middleton* v. *Leslie* (1892) 19 R. 801, 802, *per* L.P. Robertson.
[4] (1892) 19 R. 801.
[5] (1877) 4 R. 1134.
[6] *Fleming & Ferguson* v. *Paisley Magistrates*, 1948 S.C. 547, 557, *per* L.P. Cooper.
[7] *Marshall* v. *Callander Hydro Ltd.* (1896) 24 R. 33.
[8] *Munro* v. *Balnagowan Estates Co. Liqr.*, 1949 S.C. 49, 55, *per* L.P. Cooper
[9] *McKellar* v. *Dallas's Ltd.*, 1928 S.C. 503.

to commit the defaulter to prison. A criminal prosecution is of an entirely different nature." [10]

The apprehension and imprisonment of a person under a decree *ad factum praestandum* are saved from the general abolition of imprisonment for debt by the Debtors (Scotland) Act 1880, s. 4,[11] and the qualifications on imprisonment as a penalty for crime, such as restrictions on imprisonment of first offenders, do not apply.[12] The procedure is regulated by the Personal Diligence Act 1838, s. 11, and in the case of Small Debt actions, by the Small Debt (Scotland) Acts 1837–89.[13]

Decrees Ordering Performance of Statutory Duties

Prima facie the sanction for non-implement of a statutory duty is criminal prosecution, and it is indeed commonly provided expressly that prosecution in prescribed form and liability to certain penalties is the sanction. In some cases where non-implement has resulted in personal injuries it has been held that an action of damages at the instance of the injured person is also competent.[14]

Under the Mines and Quarries Act 1954, s. 146, an inspector may require a remedy for an immediate or apprehended danger, and a contravention is, by section 152, an offence, unless (s. 157) it was impracticable to avoid or prevent the contravention.

Under the Factories Act 1961, s. 157, where the occupier or owner of a factory is convicted of an offence under that Act, the court may, in addition to or instead of inflicting a fine, order him to take such steps as may be specified for remedying the matters in respect of which the contravention occurred, subject to fine for continuing non-compliance.[15]

General power to order performance of statutory duty

By the Court of Session Act 1868, s. 91, it is lawful for the court " upon application by summary petition . . . to order the specific performance of any statutory duty under such conditions and penalties (including fine and imprisonment where consistent with the statute) in the event of the order not being implemented, as to the Court shall seem proper."

This provision has been little invoked and is little illustrated by case law. Such an order is roughly equivalent to the English mandamus [16]

10 *Wilson* v. *McKellar* (1896) 24 R. 254.
11 *Cf. Mackenzie* v. *Balerno Paper Mill Co.* (1883) 10 R. 1147, 1151.
12 *Cf. Wilson* v. *McKellar* (1896) 24 R. 254.
13 *Stewart* v. *McDougall*, 1908 S.C. 315; *Rudman* v. *Jay*, 1908 S.C. 552.
14 For discussion of this see Chap. 64, *infra*.
15 On procedure and penalties see *Perdikou* v. *Glasgow Corpn.*, 1951 J.C. 149.
16 A relic of mandamus may survive in what is left of the jurisdiction of the former Scottish Court of Exchequer: see *Lord Advocate* v. *Edinburgh Commissioners of Supply* (1861) 23 D. 933.

and the pursuer must state in precise terms the order sought from the court.[17]

For an order under this section to be competent it is clear that there must be in force a statute, or order or instrument having the force of statute, imposing a duty, and not merely conferring a power,[18] on the defender sued, and that the defender has refused or failed or delayed unreasonably to implement it. If there is no duty to the effect alleged, or it is one not incumbent on the defender, or there has been no delay or failure to implement it, there is no place for an order of specific performance.[19] The statute may be public general,[20] or local and personal.[21] An order under the section is not precluded by the existence of an alternative remedy.[22]

It seems implied that a petition may be brought only by a person to whom the statutory duty was owed and who is prejudiced by its non-implement. A duty may be owed to the community as a whole, or only to other members of the community.

It is questionable whether petition under the section lies against the Crown or a Department of State.[23] It may lie against a court or judge. It certainly lies against a local authority,[24] a quasi-judicial body such as a local valuation appeal committee,[25] a society regulated by statute,[26] and against a private person such as an employer who is subject to a statutory duty.

It has been invoked successfully to have a local authority required to construct sewers, as they were required to do by the Burgh Police Act 1892.[27]

It would seem an appropriate mode of compelling performance of *e.g.* a statutory duty to make provision for safety, health or welfare of employees, at the instance of an employee, independently of the powers of the factory inspectorate to prosecute for contravention, and of the right of an employee to claim damages if he is injured by failure to make the necessary provision. Title to sue would be confined to persons having an interest, particularly employees. Outsiders could not sue. It is questionable if a trade union could.

It is hard to resist the conclusion that this remedy is insufficiently well known, and not sufficiently employed.

[17] *Carlton Hotel Co.* v. *Lord Advocate*, 1921 S.C. 237; see also *Smith* v. *Lord Advocate*, 1932 S.L.T. 374.
[18] *Cf. Fleming & Ferguson Ltd.* v. *Paisley Magistrates*, 1948 S.C. 547.
[19] *Carlton Hotel Co.* v. *Lord Advocate*, 1921 S.C. 237.
[20] *Langlands* v. *Manson*, 1962 S.C. 493.
[21] *Adamson* v. *Edinburgh Street Tramways Co.* (1872) 10 M. 533 (Edinburgh private Act).
[22] *Docherty* v. *Burgh of Monifieth*, 1971 S.L.T. 13; contrast *Annan* v. *Leith Licensing Authority* (1901) 9 S.L.T. 63.
[23] *Carlton Hotel Co., supra*; see also *Smith* v. *Lord Advocate*, 1932 S.L.T. 374.
[24] *Docherty* v. *Burgh of Monifieth*, 1971 S.L.T. 13.
[25] *Macandrew, Petr.*, 1925 S.L.T. 78; *Langlands* v. *Manson*, 1962 S.C. 493.
[26] *Sons of Temperance Friendly Society*, 1926 S.C. 418.
[27] *Docherty, supra.*

At the same time it is clear that the court would not enter into the details of performance of a statutory duty [28]; whether one mode of performance or another is employed is very much a matter of discretion, and considerations of cost, practicability and the like have to be considered; the court will not order a defender *how to* perform his statutory duty.

In the sheriff court the 1868 Act is inapplicable but there is a reported instance [29] of a sheriff court action in which the craves were for declarator that the defenders had refused or neglected to obey a statutory provision and to ordain them to obey the said provisions in stated ways. The action was not challenged on competency but failed on other grounds. In another case [30] the pursuers craved the court to ordain the defender to produce a full return of pigs sold by him so that the pursuers might under statutory powers levy a rate due on such sales. The action was treated as competent but failed, the transactions not falling within the scope of the levy.

Special powers to order performance of particular statutory duties

Apart from the foregoing general power particular statutes empower the court to order particular kinds of action to comply with statutory duties imposed thereby.

Under the Employers and Workmen Act 1875, s. 6, the sheriff may make an order directing an apprentice to perform his duties under the indenture of apprenticeship, on pain of imprisonment.[31] In view of changed conditions a century later these provisions are pretty certainly unenforceable, though the legal power exists.

The Public Health (Scotland) Act 1897 empowers a local authority to require the author of a nuisance to remove it, and if he does not do so, to petition the sheriff or any magistrate or justice who may decern its removal or discontinuance, subject to penalty. The order for removal or otherwise must be clear, precise and specific if it is to be enforceable. From this order there is, in general, no appeal; in particular, the proceedings being essentially civil and not criminal, appeal to the High Court by stated case is incompetent.[32]

The Factories Act 1961, s. 157, empowers the court to order a factory-occupier or owner to remedy the matters in respect of which a statutory contravention has occurred. The order must specify the steps to be taken to remedy the matters in question.[33]

Where statute has provided a particular course of procedure, with its own sanctions, it is incompetent to seek at common law an order to implement a duty imposed by the statute. In *Kelso Magistrates* v. *Alexander* [34] the pursuers, in the exercise of statutory powers relative to

28 *Cf. Guthrie* v. *Miller* (1827) 5 S. 711; *Docherty, supra.*
29 *Hardie* v. *Walker*, 1948 S.C. 674.
30 *Edinburgh Magistrates* v. *Cowper*, 1936 S.C.(H.L.) 67.
31 *Cf. McDermott* v. *Ramsay* (1876) 4 R. 217.
32 *Wright* v. *Kennedy*, 1946 J.C. 142.
33 *Perdikou* v. *Glasgow Corpn.*, 1951 J.C. 149.
34 1939 S.C. 78.

housing, required the defender to demolish certain buildings; the defender lodged a statutory appeal, promising to make certain improvements, and the court recalled the authority's order and ordained the defender to execute the improvements. She failed to do so and the authority brought a common law action in the sheriff court for an order *ad factum praestandum*. This was held incompetent. The statutory code of procedure alone had to be applied and followed.

Decrees to Compel Performance of Common Law Non-contractual Duties

Many common law non-contractual duties of a personal character, such as to adhere to, aliment, and be faithful to one's spouse, will not be ordered to be implemented, as the only sanction for refusal to implement would be imprisonment,[35] and both compulsory implement and imprisonment for failure to implement would be impossible and unsatisfactory and profitless to the aggrieved spouse.

Inferior judges and public officers

The Court of Session, as supreme civil court of Scotland, has an inherent jurisdiction to compel inferior courts and judges and public officers to do their duties.

> " There is no doubt whatever that whenever an inferior judge, no matter of what kind, fails to perform his duty, or transgresses his duty, either by going beyond his jurisdiction, or failing to exercise his jurisdiction when called upon to do so by a party entitled to come before him, there is a remedy in this court, and the inferior judge, if it turns out that he is wrong, may be ordered by this court to go on and perform his duty, and if he fails to do so he will be liable to imprisonment as upon a decree *ad factum praestandum*. The same rule applies to a variety of other public officers, such as statutory trustees and commissioners, who are under an obligation to exercise their functions for the benefit of the parties for whose benefit these functions are entrusted to them, and if they capriciously and without just cause refuse to perform their duty they will be ordained to do so by decree of this court and failing their performance will, in like manner, be committed to prison. Now all this belongs to the Court of Session as the Supreme Civil Court of this country in the exercise of what is called, very properly, its supereminent jurisdiction. It is not of very much consequence to determine whether it is in the exercise of its high equitable jurisdiction, or in the performance of what is sometimes called its *nobile officium*." [36]

[35] For an exception see Civil Imprisonment (Scotland) Act 1882, s. 4; *McWilliams* v. *McWilliams*, 1963 S.C. 259.

[36] *Forbes* v. *Underwood* (1886) 13 R. 465, 467–468, *per* L.P. Inglis.

Similarly an arbiter who has accepted a submission may be ordered by the court to execute and issue a decree arbitral.[37] The court will, of course, consider any reasons adduced for the arbiter not proceeding and may hold them sufficient, but if there is no adequate reason he may be ordained to proceed under penalty of imprisonment.[38] It is incompetent to ask the court to ordain a statutory arbiter to state a case on proposed questions of law.[39]

Where the police have illegally taken photographs or finger-print impressions of the pursuer, he is entitled to an order for the delivery up or destruction of the photographs and impressions.[40]

Domestic relations

An action for delivery of a child by one parent to the other is competent. " An order for delivery is an application for a decree *ad factum praestandum*, and, as such, is an order made in this Court in only the last resort, if the other orders prescribing custody or degree of access are not listened to. And such an order, as asked, is enforceable by personal diligence." [41]

Heritable property

Where an innovation has been made on heritable property which infringes the right of another the court may order the innovation to be removed. Thus the court may be asked to order the removal of a haleing or fishing stance constructed in the bed of a river to the prejudice of the rights of other riparian proprietors,[42] or to order the removal of a wall which encroached on the pursuer's property.[43]

Where one party has erected a building on ground on which he has not right to build, such as ground not belonging to him, the court may order the building to be removed. But it has been held [44] that the court may, instead of ordering removal of the building, ordain that other ground be made over in compensation or that otherwise equitable compensation be made.

Statutory restriction in respect of buildings

By the Copyright Act 1956, s. 17 (4), in an action for infringement of copyright in respect of the construction of a building,[45] no interdict or other order shall be made (a) after the construction of the building has

37 *Marshall* v. *Edinburgh & Glasgow Ry.* (1853) 15 D. 603.
38 *Forbes*, *supra*, 469.
39 *Forsyth-Grant* v. *Salmon*, 1961 S.C. 54.
40 *Adamson* v. *Martin*, 1916 S.C. 319, distinguished in *Adair* v. *McGarry*, 1933 J.C. 72.
41 *Brown* v. *Brown*, 1948 S.C. 5, 11, *per* Lord Mackay.
42 *Gay* v. *Malloch*, 1959 S.C. 110; *cf. Anderson* v. *Robertson*, 1958 S.C. 367.
43 *Brown* v. *Baty*, 1957 S.C. 351 (where question of acquiescence in the encroachment discussed).
44 *Grahame* v. *Kirkcaldy Mags.* (1882) 9 R.(H.L.) 91, citing *Macnair* v. *Cathcart* (1802) Mor. 12832; *Sanderson* v. *Geddes* (1874) 1 R. 1198; *Jack* v. *Begg* (1875) 3 R. 35.
45 *i.e.* infringing the architect's, or his client's (see s. 4), copyright in a work of architecture, which is an " artistic work " under the Copyright Act 1956, s. 3 (1) (*b*).

been begun, so as to prevent it from being completed, or (b) so as to require the building, in so far as it has been constructed, to be demolished. This exception applies only to actions founded on infringement of copyright in the design, not on any other ground of law.

Property held by another

Where one person holds the property of another and that other, or his representative, desires delivery of the property, resort is necessary to an action for delivery. In exceptional circumstances, where the Court considers that imprisonment would be inexpedient or ineffective in securing the property, the Court may grant warrant to messengers-at-arms to search for and take the property, if necessary, opening lockfast places in the process.[46]

Interference with diligence

Under the Personal Diligence Act 1838, s. 30, if any person unlawfully intromits with or carries off effects which have been poinded under that Act, he is liable on summary complaint [47] to be imprisoned until he restore the effects or pays double the appraised value.

Decrees of Specific Implement of Contracts

It is frequently open to a party to a contract to request the court to ordain the other party specifically to implement his contract and to perform what he undertook to do, to obtain, that is a decree *ad factum praestandum*, rather than merely compensation for non-implement. Scots law, as compared with English, favours a claim for specific implement [48] and there is a presumption in Scots law that an obligation is enforceable by such a decree unless there be ground in equity for refusing it.[49] If such a decree be considered inappropriate in the circumstances the court may award damages in lieu, as compensation for the non-implement. Indeed Lord President Inglis observed [50]:

> " A contract which cannot be enforced by specific implement, in so far as regards its form and substance, is no contract at all, and cannot form the ground of an action of damages. There are cases of contracts which give ground for actions of damages, though not of implement, but that is not from defect of form but from considerations outside of the written instrument. For example the Court will not decree

[46] *Ferguson's C.B.* (1905) 7 F. 898.

[47] The summary complaint is a civil process, not a criminal one, and does not require the consent of the procurator-fiscal: *Wilson* v. *McKellar* (1896) 24 R. 254.

[48] *Stewart* v. *Kennedy* (1890) 17 R.(H.L.) 1, 5, 9, 11.

[49] *Beardmore* v. *Barry*, 1928 S.C. 101, 108, 113, 115; affd. 1928 S.C.(H.L.) 47; *cf.* Stair I, 17, 16; Bell, *Prin.* § 29; Gloag, *Contract*, 592; *Seaforth Trs.* v. *Macaulay* (1844) 7 D. 180; *Rollo's Trs.* v. *Rollo*, 1940 S.C. 578, 584; *White & Carter (Councils) Ltd.* v. *McGregor*, 1962 S.C.(H.L.) 1, 20.

[50] *McArthur* v. *Lawson* (1877) 4 R. 1134, 1136.

implement of a contract which the party cannot possibly perform because that would be to condemn the party to perpetual imprisonment—'*Loca facti imprestabilis subest damnum et interesse.*' There are other cases. An engagement to marry or to enter into a partnership will not be enforced, not because of defect in the termini of the contract, but because it would be inequitable or contrary to policy to enforce specific implement. But a contract, in order to found an action, must be complete, and as much so to found an action of damages as an action of specific implement."

Crave must be definite and specific

For a decree of specific implement to be competent it is essential that the claim for the decree be precisely framed and specify exactly what the defender must do to comply with the decree,[51] and the decree must be one which can be obeyed by some specific act done on the part of the defender.[52] A decree in vague or indefinite terms is unenforceable [53] If the contract itself is vague or indefinite it may be void, or at least not have indicated the defender's duty of implement with such precision as to make it reasonable to make an order against him that he implement it. It must be clear what he should have done before the court will order him to do it. Hence implement of a continuing operation, such as cultivating lands let, will not be ordered.[54] Nor will specific implement be decreed until the time of implement has arrived, even though there has been a prior refusal to perform.[55] A claim that the court ordain performance "forthwith" is appropriate only in the case of a single act; if what is required must take some time to perform, such as to build a house, a stated period of time should be assigned.[56]

Where specific implement appropriate

Specific implement has been held appropriate in the following cases:

In relation to heritage: to grant a disposition of lands sold, the price being tendered,[57] to accept a disposition and pay the price,[58] to execute a formal lease in terms of a draft,[59] to give possession of lands let,[60] to enter into possession of lands let and to pay the rent,[61] to furnish a shop and keep it heated and aired,[62] to erect buildings in terms of a feu-contract,[63]

[51] *Robertson* v. *Cockburn* (1875) 3 R. 21; *Middleton* v. *Leslie* (1892) 19 R. 801.
[52] *Hendry* v. *Marshall* (1878) 5 R. 687, 690.
[53] *Robertson, supra*; *Hendry, supra.*
[54] *Hendry, supra.*
[55] *Harvey* v. *Smith* (1904) 6 F. 511.
[56] *Middleton, supra.*
[57] *Corbett* v. *Robertson* (1872) 10 M. 329; *Petrie* v. *Forsyth* (1874) 2 R. 214; *Stewart* v. *Kennedy* (1890) 17 R.(H.L.) 1; *Mackay* v. *Campbell*, 1966 S.C. 237; 1967 S.C.(H.L.) 53.
[58] *Harvey* v. *Smith* (1904) 6 F. 511 (where action failed: contract not binding).
[59] *Wight* v. *Newton*, 1911 S.C. 762.
[60] *Seaforth Trustees* v. *Macaulay* (1844) 7 D. 180.
[61] *Erskine* v. *Glendinning* (1871) 9 M. 656; *Robertson* v. *Cockburn* (1875) 3 R. 21.
[62] *Whitelaw* v. *Fulton* (1871) 10 M. 27.
[63] *Middleton* v. *Leslie* (1892) 19 R. 801; *McKellar* v. *Dallas's Ltd.*, 1928 S.C. 503.

to rebuild buildings in terms of a feu-contract,[64] to maintain a bridge so as to leave a stated clearance above a road,[65] to construct a railway crossing.[66]

In *Hendry* v. *Marshall* [67] where a landlord registered a lease under a clause of registration contained therein and charged the tenant to implement the whole conditions of the lease, the charge was held incompetent as being too general, as it would be impossible for anyone receiving it to understand what the landlord proposed to enforce by means of the charge. A decree of court, or on registration, must be one which could be obeyed by some specific act done on the part of the defender.

In *Hay* v. *Aberdeen Corporation* [68] the pursuer sought declarator that the defenders were bound to implement an agreement by accepting from him a disposition of certain heritable rights, and for decree ordaining them to accept a disposition in such terms. The court refused decree, holding that a disposition in the terms proposed was inept, but did not discuss the competency of the crave, which seems questionable. Can the court force a defender to accept a disposition? If the disposition offered is valid and a good tender of performance of the contract the defender would be liable for damages if he refused to accept it, but would a court ever compel him to accept it, and, if so, how?

In relation to moveables: It is competent to grant specific implement of a mixed contract for the sale of heritage and of moveables.[69] In respect of contracts relative to moveables alone specific implement is competent of a contract to purchase a specific thing or article, when the obligation to deliver will be enforced,[70] and particularly where the thing is unique or possesses qualities not possessed by alternatives or has a *pretium affectionis*,[71] or to deliver certain goods in exchange for other goods.[72] It is not normally appropriate for generic goods, where other goods can be obtained from an alternative supplier and damages for non-delivery is normally an adequate remedy.[73]

Delivery has been sought of goods delivered to the defenders by a third party under contract with the pursuers, who alleged that they had not been paid and wished to recover the goods.[74]

Decree *ad factum praestandum* may also be necessary to effect a remedy

64 *Marshall* v. *Callander Hydro Co.* (1896) 23 R.(H.L.) 55; sequels 24 R. 33, 713. See also *Clark* v. *Glasgow Life Assce. Co.* (1850) 12 D. 1047; revd. (1854) 1 Macq. 668.
65 *Lanarkshire C.C.* v. *N.C.B.*, 1948 S.C. 698.
66 *Summerlee and Mossend Iron Co.* v. *Caledonian Ry.*, 1909 S.C. 536; 1911 S.C. 458.
67 (1878) 5 R. 687.
68 1909 S.C. 554.
69 *Mackay* v. *Campbell*, 1966 S.C. 237; 1967 S.C.(H.L.) 53.
70 *Sutherland* v. *Montrose Shipbuilding Co.* (1860) 22 D. 665, 671; *Purves* v. *Brock* (1867) 5 M. 1003; Sale of Goods Act 1893, s. 52; *Behnke* v. *Bede Shipping Co.* [1927] 1 K.B. 649; *Munro* v. *Balnagowan Estates Co.*, 1949 S.C. 49. See also *Aurdal* v. *Estrella*, 1916 S.C. 882.
71 *Union Electric Co.* v. *Holman*, 1913 S.C. 954.
72 *Widenmeyer* v. *Burn, Stewart & Co.*, 1967 S.C. 85.
73 Sale of Goods Act 1893, s. 51.
74 *Graham* v. *Glenrothes Development Corpn.*, 1967 S.C. 284; *cf. Bell Bros. (H. P.) Ltd.* v. *Reynolds*, 1945 S.C. 213.

when a contract has been terminated, such as to recover goods let on hire-purchase to a person who has terminated the agreement but not returned the goods,[75] or to give a remedy when the defender delays or refuses to deliver goods as he should do.[76]

In cases falling within the Hire-Purchase (Scotland) Act 1965, if one-third of the hire-purchase price or total sale price (under a conditional sale agreement) has been paid or tendered by or on behalf of the hirer or buyer and the hirer or buyer has not terminated the agreement, the goods are " protected goods " and may be recovered only by action.[77] In such an action the court may make an order for delivery of all of the goods, or postpone its operation, or order delivery of part of the goods.[78] In the event of non-compliance with such an order the court may on application revoke the order and order payment of money representing the price of the unrecovered goods.[79]

In relation to incorporeal rights: In the case of incorporeal rights evidenced by documents such as share certificates, implement of a contract may be sought by an action for delivery of share certificates.[80] Where by the articles of association of a private company shareholders had first to offer shares for sale to the company, the court has ordained shareholders to implement the relevant article.[81]

In relation to rights in security: When property of any kind is conveyed in security of a loan or advance of money or of an obligation to be performed, there is an implied obligation on the lender to reconvey the subjects of security when the loan has been repaid or the other obligation performed. This obligation may be enforced by action for delivery and for the execution of any deed necessary to re-vest the security subjects in the borrower.[82]

In relation to succession: A person may validly contract to make a will, create a trust or otherwise deal with his or her estate by way of succession, but it is doubtful if the court would order specific implement of such a contract.[83] It is doubtful, moreover, whether the court will enforce an obligation to exercise a power of testamentary disposal conferred by a third party.[84]

In relation to granting deeds: Where the conclusion for implement requires the defender to execute some deed, such as a disposition of lands, it is competent to include an alternative conclusion to authorise the Clerk of Court to execute the necessary deed on behalf of the defender, failing

75 *e.g. Rudman* v. *Jay*, 1908 S.C. 552; *General Guarantee Corpn.* v. *Alexander*, 1918 S.C. 663; *English* v. *Donnelly*, 1958 S.C. 494.

76 *e.g. Garscadden* v. *Ardrossan Dry Dock Co.*, 1909 S.C. 179.

77 Hire-Purchase (Scotland) Act 1965, ss. 33–34, 45.

78 *Ibid.* ss. 35–41, 45.

79 *Ibid.* ss. 42, 45.

80 *Robb* v. *Gow Bros. & Gemmell* (1905) 8 F. 90.

81 *Lyle & Scott* v. *Scott's Trs.*, 1959 S.C.(H.L.) 64.

82 *e.g. Nelson* v. *National Bank*, 1936 S.C. 570 (shares).

83 *Paterson* v. *Paterson* (1893) 20 R. 484; *Rollo's Trs.* v. *Rollo*, 1940 S.C. 578, 580.

84 *Rollo's Trs., supra.* See also *Campbell's Trs.* v. *Adamson*, 1936 S.C.(H.L.) 31.

implement by him.[85] Alternatively a separate application could be made to the *nobile officium* to grant such authority,[86] though this course might not be appropriate in the case of a trustee who declines to sign a document relating to the trust property.[87]

In relation to arbitrations: An arbiter who has accepted a submission may be compelled by the court to execute and issue a decree arbitral.[88]

Where parties have executed a minute of reference of certain matters to arbitration, and the two arbiters have differed, one party may bring an action to have them ordained to execute a minute of devolution on the oversman.[89] Only the Court of Session has jurisdiction to do so.[90]

Where specific implement inappropriate

Specific implement is generally an inappropriate remedy [91] where the subject-matter of contract does not possess any unique or special qualities, so that the loss of it can adequately be compensated in money,[92] where compliance or enforced performance is impossible,[93] where the compulsory performance would involve an intimate relationship, as of marriage [94] or service [95] or agency or partnership,[96] where the performance of the contract would require supervision by the court,[97] where exceptional hardship would be caused,[98] where it would be inequitable or contrary to public policy to enforce implement,[1] where the court could not enforce its order against the defender,[1a] and generally where the court decides in its discretion that damages are quite appropriate and sufficient in the circumstances.[2]

Can the court order a defender to accept unwanted performance of a contract if the pursuer seeks to thrust such performance on him? If the performance involves the co-operation or participation of the defender it

85 *Mackay* v. *Campbell*, 1966 S.C. 237; 1967 S.C.(H.L.) 53.

86 *Whyte* v. *Whyte*, 1919, 2 S.L.T. 85; *Wallace's C.B.* v. *Wallace*, 1924 S.C. 212; *Pennell's Tr.*, 1928 S.C. 605; *Lennox*, 1950 S.C. 546; *Boag*, 1967 S.C. 322.

87 *Pennell's Tr., supra.*

88 *Marshall* v. *Edinburgh & Glasgow Ry.* (1853) 15 D. 603.

89 *Sinclair* v. *Fraser* (1884) 11 R. 1139; *Forbes* v. *Underwood* (1886) 13 R. 465.

90 *Forbes, supra.*

91 See also Gloag, *Contract*, 655; *White & Carter (Councils) Ltd.* v. *McGregor*, 1960 S.C. 276, 283 (revd. on other grounds, 1962 S.C.(H.L.) 1).

92 *Union Electric Co.* v. *Holman*, 1913 S.C. 954, 958.

93 *McArthur* v. *Lawson* (1877) 4 R. 1134, 1136; *Sinclair* v. *Caithness Flagstone Co.* (1898) 25 R. 703; *Rudman* v. *Jay*, 1908 S.C. 552; *Bell Bros. (H.P.) Ltd.* v. *Reynolds*, 1945 S.C. 213, 216; *cf. McKellar* v. *Dallas's Ltd.*, 1928 S.C. 503.

94 *McArthur, supra.*

95 *McArthur, supra*; *Rose St. Foundry Co.* v. *Lewis*, 1917 S.C. 341; *cf. Murray* v. *Dunbarton C.C.*, 1935 S.L.T. 239.

96 *McArthur, supra*; *Pert* v. *Bruce*, 1937 S.L.T. 475; *cf. Skerret* v. *Oliver* (1896) 23 R. 468.

97 *Wheatley* v. *Westminster Coal Co.* (1869) L.R. 9 Eq. 538; *Ryan* v. *Mutual Tontine Assocn.* [1893] 1 Ch. 116.

98 *Grahame* v. *Kirkcaldy Mags.* (1882) 9 R. (H.L.) 91; *Davidson* v. *Macpherson* (1889) 30 S.L.R. 2; *Wilson* v. *Pottinger*, 1908 S.C. 580. Sentimental value of the subjects to the defender will not suffice; *Mackay* v. *Campbell*, 1966 S.C. 237.

1 *McArthur, supra.*

1a *Gall* v. *Loyal Glenbogie Lodge of Oddfellows* (1900) 2 F. 1187; contrast *Collins* v. *Barrowfield United Oddfellows*, 1915 S.C. 190; see also *Ponder* v. *Ponder*, 1932 S.C. 233.

2 *Moore* v. *Paterson* (1881) 8 R. 337; *Davidson, supra*; *Stewart* v. *Kennedy* (1890) 17 R.(H.L.) 1, 10; *Wilson, supra*; *Aurdal* v. *Estrella*, 1916 S.C. 882.

probably cannot, but in *White & Carter (Councils) Ltd.* v. *McGregor* [3] the House of Lords in effect held that this was competent where such co-operation was not necessary, by holding that an advertising contractor might, despite a repudiation of the contract on the day it was made, insist on displaying advertisements and on recovering the price therefor, instead of merely damages for loss of profit by reason of the repudiation of the contract. This decision seems to place undue reliance on the principle that repudiation by one party does not terminate the contract, and inadequate reliance on the duty of minimisation of loss to the party in breach. The decision could probably not have been the same if the contract had been *e.g.* to paint the inside of the defender's premises, because that would have required his co-operation. Should the decision depend on whether co-operation is needed or not?

Statutory restriction in employment contracts

By the Industrial Relations Act 1971, s. 128 (1) no court shall by way of an order for specific implement of a contract of employment, or an interdict restraining a breach or threatened breach of such a contract, compel an employee to do any work or to attend at any place for the purpose of doing any work, and (3) no court shall, by granting an interdict restraining an employee from working in accordance with a lawful contract of employment, compel him to take part in a strike or in any irregular industrial action short of a strike.

Implement not to be enforced indirectly

In a case where the court will not grant decree of specific implement, it will not normally grant another remedy such as interdict which would have the same effect. Thus in *Murray* v. *Dunbarton County Council* [4] the court held that it would not grant interdict against the local authority transferring a teacher to another school since it would not have granted an order on the local authority ordaining it to continue to employ the teacher in his existing post. The two remedies, though different in form, would have had the same effect.

Payment of money

Where what is due is merely a payment of money the normal remedy is to sue for the sum due, with interest, rather than to seek specific implement.[5] Moreover, the sanction of imprisonment for non-payment of money has, in general, been abolished [6] but the sanction for failure to

[3] 1962 S.C.(H.L.) 1; see comments in 78 L.Q.R. 263; 25 M.L.R. 364.

[4] 1935 S.L.T. 239.

[5] *Cf. White & Carter (Councils) Ltd.* v. *McGregor*, 1962 S.C.(H.L.) 1, 16: "The present case is one in which specific implement could not be decreed, since the only obligation of the respondent under the contract was to pay a sum of money for services to be rendered by the appellants."

[6] Debtors (Sc.) Act 1880, s. 4, amd. Crown Proceedings Act 1947, s. 49.

implement an order of court is imprisonment and the court is not disposed to order implement where the consequence of failure would be what it could not otherwise order. Hence implement *eo nomine* will not normally be granted of an obligation to pay money.

By statute, however, specific implement is competent of a contract to take up and pay for debentures in a company,[7] and such a decree has been granted in a case of an undertaking to subscribe for shares.[8] An order is also competent requiring a party to consign money in court, which is a decree *ad factum praestandum* and enforceable by imprisonment.[9]

Alternative conclusion for damages

In view of the court's discretion whether to grant or to refuse specific implement it is normal and prudent if concluding for specific implement to include an alternative conclusion for damages.[10] Furthermore a conclusion is frequently tabled for damages in the event of failure in performance; in this case the conclusion for damages is subsidiary to that for implement, and if the conclusion for implement is not insisted in, or is rejected by the court, the claim for damages falls with it, as being conditional on decree for implement being granted and not implemented.[11] The inclusion of such an alternative conclusion does not amount to an election to accept damages if implement be not made; it is still open to the pursuer to try to enforce implement.[12]

Where it is reasonably practicable for a pursuer to implement a contract himself, he may be authorised to do so and to recover the cost of performance from the defender,[13] such a decree being an essential prerequisite to recovering the cost of performing himself.[14]

Where there is a contract for the sale of a specific thing and that thing perishes without the fault of either party before the time for delivery, the contract is avoided and the buyer is entitled neither to implement, nor to damages in lieu.[15]

Measure of damages recoverable in lieu of implement

The measure of damages recoverable depends largely on the kind of contract implement of which has not been made, and on the loss sustained thereby. Thus in the case of failure to convey heritable property the proper measure of damages would appear to be any excess price necessarily paid to secure a reasonably suitable and equivalent alternative

[7] Companies Act 1948, s. 92.
[8] *Beardmore* v. *Barry*, 1928 S.C. 101; affd. 1928 S.C.(H.L.) 47.
[9] *Mackenzie* v. *Balerno Paper Mill Co.* (1883) 10 R. 1147.
[10] Bell, *Prin.* § 29; *Union Electric Co.* v. *Holman*, 1913 S.C. 954. Such may be added by amendment: *Summerlee Iron Co. Ltd.* v. *Caledonian Ry.*, 1911 S.C. 458.
[11] *Harvey* v. *Smith* (1904) 6 F. 511; see also *Skerret* v. *Oliver* (1896) 23 R. 468.
[12] *McKellar* v. *Dallas's Ltd.*, 1928 S.C. 503.
[13] *Davidson* v. *Macpherson* (1889) 30 S.L.R. 2.
[14] *Northern Lighthouse Commrs.* v. *Edmonston* (1908) 16 S.L.T. 439.
[15] *Leitch* v. *Edinburgh Ice Co.* (1900) 2 F. 904; Sale of Goods Act 1893, s. 7.

property,[16] something for inconvenience in having had to find it and for not having had it for a time,[17] and for expenses fruitlessly incurred on the faith of the contract not implemented.

In the case of non-performance of an obligation to do something the appropriate measure of damages would appear to be the cost of executing the obligation at one's own hand. Thus if a defender bound himself to rebuild and failed to do so, the cost of rebuilding appears to be the proper measure of damages.[18]

Adjudication in implement

In the particular case of an obligation to convey land which the person bound has delayed or refused to implement the remedy takes the form of an action for adjudication in implement, decree in which is a judicial conveyance of title.[19] The obligation may arise from promise or contract, or from the terms of a will or trust deed.

Adjudication in implement originated in the *nobile officium* of the Court of Session and was in use before the Act of 1672 introduced adjudication of lands for debt in place of the former apprising. It has been defined [20] as " a form of legal diligence by which the want of a complete voluntary title to land or other heritage is judicially supplied to those who hold a disposition or other conveyance without a precept or procuratory, or who hold an obligation entitling them to demand a full conveyance of any particular subject."

Title to sue and to defend

Title is vested in a party who by virtue of missives of sale and having himself complied with, or being ready and willing to comply with, any obligations incumbent on him, such as to pay the price, is entitled to have conveyed to him certain lands or heritages.

The action may be directed against the obligee in the obligation to convey, or if he be dead, against his heir,[21] or if no heir can be ascertained, against the Crown as *ultimus haeres.*[22]

When action competent

The action is competent where there is in existence a valid and enforceable contract for the transfer by one party to another of land or heritage and the owner fails or refuses to grant the necessary conveyance. The

[16] *Cf.* conclusions in *Rodgers* v. *Fawdry*, 1950 S.C. 483; see also *Harvey* v. *Smith* (1904) 6 F. 511, 517 (point considered in Outer House only).

[17] *Cf. Bailey* v. *Bullock* (1950) 66 T.L.R. (Pt. 2) 791.

[18] *Marshall* v. *Callander Hydro Co.* (1895) 22 R. 954; 23 R.(H.L.) 55; *Rankine* v. *Logie Den Land Co.* (1902) 4 F. 1074.

[19] Stair III, 2, 45; IV, 51, 9; Ersk. II, 12, 47; Bell, *Prin.* § 835.

[20] Bell, *Comm.* I, 783.

[21] *Monteith* v. *Ingels* (1869) 7 M. 523.

[22] *Cf. Cunningham's Exor.* v. *Millar's Heirs* (1902) 10 S.L.T. 109.

lands or heritage may have been agreed to be transferred outright, or in security.[23]

The action has also been utilised to complete a valid progress of titles where a previous transfer to the pursuer had been questionable,[24] and has been said to be the proper way for the executor and general disponee of the purchaser of a house to make up title after the death of all parties and when the heirs of the granter could not be found and the Crown must be assumed to be *ultimus haeres*.[25]

Effect of decree

The effect of a decree is laid down as being equivalent to and having the effect of a conveyance in ordinary form of the lands therein contained granted in favour of the adjudger by the ancestor of such apparent heir, or the owner or proprietor in trust or otherwise, and whether in life or deceased, of the lands adjudged, or by the seller of the lands sold, although in nonage or of unsound mind.[26]

Completion of adjudger's title

An adjudger may complete title by infeftment on the decree or by using it, for the purpose of infeftment, as an assignation or as one of a series of assignations of an unrecorded conveyance, as the case may be.[27]

In the event of competition between parties bringing actions for adjudication in implement, the title first completed by registration in the Register of Sasines is the preferable, even though it proceeded on a decree later in date than the other decree.

23 *Macgregor* v. *Macdonald* (1843) 5 D. 888.
24 *Stewart* v. *Tennant* (1868) 5 S.L.R. 684.
25 *Cunningham's Exor.* v. *Millar's Heirs* (1902) 10 S.L.T. 109.
26 Titles to Land Consolidation (Scotland) Act 1868, s. 62, as substituted by Conveyancing (Scotland) Act 1874, s. 62.
27 *Ibid.*

CHAPTER 14

CLAIMS FOR RESTITUTION

A CLAIM for restitution arises where the law deems it just and equitable that one party should make some payment or transfer some thing to another because, if he is not required to do so, he will reap an unjustified benefit at the expense of the other, infringing the principle *nemo ex aliena jactura locupletior fieri debet.*

The claim is based not on promise or contract, nor on any implied undertaking or agreement to pay, but solely on equity, on the unfairness and unreasonableness of allowing one person to reap the benefit of another's outlay or effort without liability to restore the balance.

This claim takes several distinct forms in different circumstances, namely, the claim for restitution of moveables, the claim for repetition or recovery of money, the claim for recompense for expenses incurred, the claim for compensation for expense incurred when acting as a volunteer (*negotiorum gestor*), the claim for reward for salvage services, and the claim for general average contribution.

RESTITUTION OF PROPERTY

An obligation to make restitution of goods arises where a person is in actual possession of goods legally possessed by another, whether as owner or not, without his consent or legal justification, and the person truly entitled to possession may by action for delivery claim restitution or delivery of them from the person having actual custody.[1] There is no obligation to make restitution if and so long as the custodier holds with the legal possessor's consent, as under contract of loan or pledge or deposit, of hire or hire-purchase or for work thereon or for custody, but an obligation arises in these cases under the contract to restore on request or if and when the contract is terminated. Nor is there any obligation to make restitution if the custodier holds without consent but with legal justification, as in the exercise of a right of lien, or under a decree or warrant of court.

But the obligation does exist in such cases as where goods have been misdelivered to the wrong consignee,[2] or have been found, the true owner or possessor being unknown,[3] or have been stolen and come into the hands

[1] Stair I, 7; Ersk. III, 1, 10; Bell, *Prin.* § 526.
[2] Ersk., *supra*; Bell, *Prin.* § 530; *Pride* v. *St. Anne's Bleaching Co.* (1838) 16 S. 1376; *cf. Webster* v. *Thomson* (1830) 8 S. 528.
[3] *Cf. Lawson* v. *Heatly*, 1962 S.L.T. 53.

of the person now possessing them,[4] or been transferred for a purpose which has failed or been abandoned.[5]

In the case of misdelivery, the recipient discharges his obligation if he returns the goods to the carrier to be delivered properly or returned to the consignor. He may, but need not, seek out the proper consignee and make delivery himself.

In the case of finding, the obligation to make restitution is adequately discharged by handing over the goods to the police, who may in stated circumstances award the goods to the finder or sell them.[6]

In the case of theft, quite apart from any criminal consequences, if the true possessor can identify the thief, he has a claim against him for restitution of the stolen property, failing which, for its value.[7]

In all cases the person truly entitled to possession may call on the actual possessor to deliver to him and, if need be, bring an action for delivery against such possessor. Frequently, however, he will not know who is actually in possession.

If a person, such as a warehouseman or other temporary custodier having lawful possession of goods not his own, parts with possession unjustifiably as by lending or selling the goods to a third party, the true owner can recover the goods from the third party, who is bound to make restitution. The true owner is entitled to follow the goods and demand restitution, into whosesoever hands the goods may come.[8]

Damages failing restitution

If the goods cannot be specifically restored, as where they have been used or consumed or spoiled or resold to another, or the custodier refuses to restore them, a claim lies for damages, as compensation for wrongful retention, failing restitution. The measure of damages is the fair value of the goods not restored,[9] together with compensation for any natural consequences of not having or recovering them.

In *International Banking Corpn.* v. *Ferguson, Shaw & Sons*[10] oil belonging to C, lawfully held by B, was sold by B *in bona fide* to A; A took delivery and used the oil in manufacturing a new commodity, such that the oil could not be separated or restored to its original condition; it was held that C was entitled, failing restitution of the oil, to recover the value of the oil from A. A doubtless had a claim for relief against B for the price paid.

In *Gorebridge Co-operative Socy.* v. *Turnbull*,[11] T broke into G's premises and stole goods and money. It was held that the proper remedy

[4] *Cf. Robertson* v. *Burns*, 1943 J.C. 1.
[5] Ersk., *supra.*
[6] Burgh Police (Sc.) Act 1892, s. 412; Lost Property (Sc.) Act 1965.
[7] Bell, *Prin.* § 527; *Gorebridge Co-operative Socy.* v. *Turnbull*, 1952 S.L.T. (Sh.Ct.) 91.
[8] *International Banking Corpn.* v. *Ferguson, Shaw & Sons*, 1910 S.C. 182, 191–192.
[9] *Pride, supra.*
[10] 1910 S.C. 182.
[11] 1952 S.L.T.(Sh.Ct.) 91; 68 Sh.Ct.Rep. 236.

would have been a claim for restitution against the present possessor of the goods, failing which a claim against the thief for reparation for the loss caused. Similarly a claim lies against a resetter for the value of goods reset and not recovered by the owner.[12]

Goods rightfully possessed but wrongfully passed to third party

Where a party having lawful possession of another's goods, wrongfully, whether mistakenly or deliberately wrongfully, gives or sells them to a third party, the first question is as to his title to give or sell. In general a mere possessor has no title to give or sell, and can confer no valid title of ownership on the third party by so doing. But exceptionally a possessor may do so and confer a valid title on the third party.[13]

If the possessor has transferred the goods in circumstances giving the third party a valid title of ownership,[14] the true owner cannot recover the goods from the new owner, but can only claim damages from the possessor for the loss, to the extent of the fair value of the goods of which he has been deprived, measured, prima facie, by the price which the new owner paid for the goods.

If on the other hand the possessor has transferred the goods in circumstances conferring no title on the third party, as where a hire-purchaser purports to sell the hired goods,[15] the true owner can claim restitution from the third party, leaving it to the third party to recover the " price " from the possessor who had tried to sell, if indeed he can be found. If for any reason the true owner cannot recover the goods from the third party, he can recover their fair value from the third party, who in this case also has his right of relief against the intermediate possessor *quantum valeat.*

Goods wrongfully possessed and wrongfully transmitted to third party

Where goods belonging to one party are wrongfully in the custody of a second, *e.g.* having been stolen, and he transfers them to a third party, the first party may recover them from the third so long as they exist *in forma specifica*, whether or not the third party knew of any defect in the second party's title to transfer. Thus if A obtains goods from B by theft, or under a contract which is void, *e.g.* for misrepresentation as to the identity of B,[16] and resells to C, the right of property has not passed to B and A can recover the goods from C, leaving C to recover, if he can, from B what he paid for the goods.[17] If, however, B's obtaining from A was under a contract not void but merely voidable, *e.g.* for misrepresentation of B's

12 *Dalhanna Knitwear Co.* v. *Mohammed Ali*, 1967 S.L.T.(Sh.Ct.) 74.
13 The circumstances where the possessor can do so are set out in Walker, *Principles of Scottish Private Law*, Chap. 95.
14 *e.g.* sale by hire-purchaser of a motor vehicle to a private purchaser who takes in good faith and without notice of the hire-purchase agreement, under Hire-Purchase Act 1964, ss.27–29, as amended by Hire-Purchase (Scotland) Act 1965.
15 Except in circumstances falling within the foregoing note.
16 *Morrisson* v. *Robertson*, 1908 S.C. 332.
17 Bell, *Comm.* I, 299; *Prin.* § 527.

credit-worthiness,[18] the right of property has passed to B and, unless the contract is avoided before he resells, he may validly do so and pass a good title to C, in which case A cannot recover the goods from C. It probably does not matter if C knew that B's title was under a voidable contract with A, because a voidable contract is valid until and unless avoided, and it may never be avoided.

An exception arises in the case of money, banknotes and negotiable instruments, to which *vitium reale* does not attach by reason of any defect in the mode of their acquisition, so that, while the actual thief should make restitution, and is liable to an action demanding restitution, a third party to whom he transfers property of these kinds acquires a title free from the defect attaching to the thief's title, provided that he takes in good faith, for value and without notice of the defect in the thief's title, and is not liable to make restitution.[19] But if the third party is, in criminal terminology, a resetter, and does not take in good faith, or for value, or without notice of the defect in title, the third party has no title and is liable to make restitution.

If in such a case the goods have been used or perished the final possessor is liable for their value.[20] Alternatively the true possessor may sue the intermediate party who has passed on the goods but can recover damages only, measured by the profit that party made by the transaction.[21]

Repetition of Money

A person who has paid money may recover it under a claim of *condictio indebiti*, enforced by action for payment, and the payee is obliged to repay it, if it has been paid under mistake of fact,[22] such as double payment, or overpayment, or payment to the wrong person, or under mistake of law affecting the parties only, such as the legal interpretation of a contract [23] or will,[24] but not if under mistake or ignorance as to some general rule of law.[25] It is not, however, recoverable if the payment proceeded on a natural obligation, though one not legally enforceable,[26] or was paid in the knowledge that it was not legally exigible, as by way of gift, reward,

18 *MacLeod* v. *Kerr*, 1965 S.C. 253.

19 Bell, *Prin.* § 528; *Scott* v. *Kilmarnock Bank*, Feb. 27, 1812, F.C.; *Gorebridge Co-operative Socy., supra.*

20 *Faulds* v. *Townsend* (1861) 23 D. 437; *Oliver & Boyd* v. *Marr Typefounding Co.* (1901) 9 S.L.T. 170.

21 *Scot* v. *Low* (1704) Mor. 9123; *Walker* v. *Spence & Carfrae* (1765) Mor. 12802; *Faulds, supra*, 439.

22 Stair, I, 7, 9; Ersk. III, 3, 54; Bell, *Prin.* § 531, 534.

23 *British Hydro Carbon Chemicals* v. *B.T.C.*, 1961 S.L.T. 280.

24 *Armour* v. *Glasgow Royal Infirmary*, 1909 S.C. 916; *cf. Ministry of Health* v. *Simpson* [1951] A.C. 251.

25 *Wilson* v. *Sinclair* (1830) 4 W. & S. 398; *Dixon* v. *Monkland Canal Co.* (1831) 5 W. & S. 445; *Young* v. *Campbell* (1851) 14 D. 63; *Dickson* v. *Halbert* (1854) 16 D. 586; *Bremner* v. *Taylor* (1866) 3 S.L.R. 24; *Baird's Trs.* v. *Baird* (1877) 4 R. 1005; *Agnew* v. *Ferguson* (1903) 5 F. 879; *Oswald* v. *Kirkcaldy Mags.*, 1919 S.C. 147; *Glasgow Corpn.* v. *Lord Advocate*, 1959 S.C. 203. *Contra*, Ersk., *supra.*

26 Ersk., *supra*; Bell, *Prin.* § 532.

compromise or *ex gratia* payment,[27] nor if paid in implement of a legal decree, unless the decree be also reduced.

It is recoverable all the more if the error were one induced in the payer's mind by misrepresentations made to him by the payee, and if those misrepresentations were made negligently or fraudulently the payer may also recover damages for any loss caused him by the transaction. If the misrepresentation were made negligently or fraudulently by a third party, the payment is recoverable from the payee, and damages may be recovered from the misrepresentor.[28]

It is also recoverable under a claim of *condictio causa data, causa non secuta* if paid for a consideration which has failed,[29] as where a contract has been frustrated.[30]

In general only the payer, and not anyone claiming to be the proper payee, can claim repetition.[31]

Recompense

A claim for recompense arises where the claimant has incurred outlays, expenses or other financial loss and another party has gained thereby, there being no intention to donate to or confer a gratuitous benefit on him.[32] Error is essential to a successful claim of recompense.[33] Where competent the claim is made by way of action for payment. It is not competent where the claimant has incurred outlays and expense for his own purposes or needs and the other incidentally gains some benefit therefrom, the claimant not having sustained any loss,[34] nor where the defender has not benefited from the expenditure,[35] nor where the claimant expended money in the belief that it would ultimately be for his own benefit, a belief which turned out to be disappointed.[36]

In particular a claim on the basis of recompense is not competent if the remuneration of the claimant is regulated by contract. So long as the contract stands he cannot obtain more return for his work than the contract provides by claiming under the principle of recompense.[37] If, however, the contract is set aside, any work done before then can only and must be rewarded on the basis of recompense. Similarly if the con-

27 Ersk. III, 3, 54; Bell, *Prin.* § 533; see also *Seamen of Dundee* v. *Cockerill* (1869) 8 M. 278.

28 *e.g. Thin & Sinclair* v. *Arrol* (1896) 24 R. 198; see also *Campbell* v. *Clason* (1838) 1 D. 270.

29 Dig. 12, 4; Code 4, 6; Stair, I, 7, 7; Bankt. I, 8, 23; Ersk. III, 1, 10; Bell, *Prin.* § 530; *Watson* v. *Shankland* (1872) 10 M. 142; 11 M.(H.L.) 51.

30 *Davis & Primrose* v. *Clyde Shipbuilding Co.*, 1917, 1 S.L.T. 297; *Cantiere San Rocco* v. *Clyde Shipbuilding Co.*, 1923 S.C.(H.L.) 105.

31 *Armour, supra*, where an exception was recognised.

32 Stair, I, 8, 6; Ersk. III, 1, 11; Bell, *Prin.* § 438.

33 *Rankin* v. *Wither* (1886) 13 R. 903, 908.

34 *Burns* v. *McLellan's Crs.* (1735) Mor. 13402; *Stewart* v. *Stewart* (1878) 6 R. 145; *Yellowlees* v. *Alexander* (1882) 9 R. 765; *Ruabon S.S. Co.* v. *London Assurance Co.* [1900] A.C. 6; *Edinburgh Tramways Co.* v. *Courtenay*, 1909 S.C. 99; *cf. Exchange Telegraph Co.* v. *Giulianotti*, 1958 S.C. 19.

35 *Buchanan* v. *Stewart* (1874) 2 R. 78.

36 *Rankin* v. *Wither* (1886) 13 R. 903.

37 *Boyd and Forrest* v. *G.S.W. Ry.*, 1915 S.C.(H.L.) 20.

tract is so departed from by consent that it cannot fairly be held still to regulate the relations of parties a claim on recompense is competent.[38] So, too, if the contract is unenforceable for purely technical legal reasons recompense is competent.[39] A claim based on recompense may also be brought where the undertaking to pay for the goods or services is one requiring proof by writ or oath and neither method of proof is available.[40] But it is not competent where a contracting party has done more or better than he was required to do by the contract, and the excess is not separable, nor capable of being rejected.[41]

Improvements to land

A claim for recompense does, however, lie where one by mistake builds on another's land and the other claims the buildings,[42] though not where the builder has built in *mala fide* or in the knowledge that his title to the site was defective.[43] But no claim normally arises for improvements made by a temporary owner, such as a liferenter or tenant, it being presumed that he made them for his own benefit.[44] Some exceptions to this last principle have been allowed on proof of local custom, or long-settled understanding.[45]

Other cases

A claim for recompense also arises where a pupil or person of unsound mind or one incapacitated by drink obtains necessaries from a supplier thereof,[46] and where a person managed property in the reasonable belief that it belonged to him.[47]

Basis for computing recompense

If a claim for recompense is competent the basis for computing the sum due may be either *quantum meruit*, *i.e.* such sum as the services have justified, or *quantum lucratus*, *i.e.* such sum as the claimant has lost and the defender gained.

38 *e.g.* excess goods supplied and accepted: Sale of Goods Act 1893, s. 30.

39 *Cuthbertson* v. *Lowes* (1870) 8 M. 1073.

40 *Bell* v. *Bell* (1841) 3 D. 1201; *Hamilton* v. *Lochrane* (1899) 1 F. 478 (on which see *Gilchrist* v. *Whyte*, 1907 S.C. 984); *Mackay* v. *Rodger* (1907) 15 S.L.T. 42; *cf. Newton* v. *Newton*, 1925 S.C. 715; *Gray* v. *Johnston*, 1928 S.C. 659.

41 *Scott* v. *Marshall* (1847) 10 D. 226; *Grant* v. *Macleod* (1856) 19 D. 127; *Tharsis Sulphur Co.* v. *McElroy* (1878) 5 R.(H.L.) 171.

42 *Binning* v. *Brotherstone* (1676) Mor. 13401; *York Buildings Co.* v. *Mackenzie* (1793) Mor. 13367; 3 Paton 378 and 579; *Selkirk Mags.* v. *Clapperton* (1830) 9 S. 9; *Stewart* v. *Stewart* (1878) 6 R. 145, 149; *Edinburgh Life Assce. Co.* v. *Balderston*, 1909, 2 S.L.T. 323; *Newton* v. *Newton*, 1925 S.C. 715.

43 Ersk. III, 1, 11; Bell, *Prin.* § 538; *Barbour* v. *Halliday* (1840) 2 D. 1279; *D. Hamilton* v. *Johnston* (1877) 14 S.L.R. 298; *Waugh* v. *Nisbett* (1882) 19 S.L.R. 427; Stair I, 8, 6, is erroneous on this point, and *Steuart's Trs.* v. *Hart* (1875) 3 R. 192, *Yellowlees* v. *Alexander* (1882) 9 R. 765 must be treated as cases special on their facts.

44 *Reedie* v. *Yeaman* (1875) 12 S.L.R. 625; *Morrison* v. *Allan* (1896) 13 R. 1156; *Morgan* v. *Morgan's Factor*, 1922 S.L.T. 247 (liferenters); Ersk. III, 1, 11; Bell, *Prin.* § 1255; *Scott's Exors.* v. *Hepburn* (1876) 3 R. 816; *Walker* v. *McKnight* (1886) 13 R. 599 (tenants).

45 *McTavish* v. *Fraser's Trs.* (1790) Hume 546; *McIntosh* v. *Ogilvy* (1806) Hume 822; *Officer* v. *Nicolson* (1807) Hume 827.

46 Sale of Goods Act 1893, s. 2.

47 *Anderson* v. *Anderson* (1869) 8 M. 157.

NEGOTIORUM GESTIO

Where one party, voluntarily, without express legal authority, and without being under any antecedent legal duty to do so, reasonably undertakes the management of the affairs of another who is absent, or incapacitated, or otherwise temporarily disabled or prevented from managing them himself, the party acting has a claim against the other for recompense of outlays and expenses and for an indemnity against obligations reasonably undertaken.[48]

The party acting, the *negotiorum gestor*, must show that his intervention, though not legally justified, was reasonable in the circumstances and justified by some kind of emergency. Mere officious intervention, however well-intentioned, is not justified and the intervener has no claim, save possibly on the basis of recompense for benefit conferred.[49]

Intervention has been regarded as justifiable where a person, without legal title, managed property belonging to one who was absent,[50] or of a relative who became mentally incapax,[51] where a person managed property for pupils or minors,[52] where a person acted in place of an absent executor,[53] where a person managed a business during the imprisonment of the owner,[54] where a person shipped goods otherwise about to fall into the hands of revolutionaries.[55]

Gestor's claims

Where intervention is justified the *negotiorum gestor* has a claim for reimbursement of expenditure and outlays made, whether or not that can be shown to have been beneficial to the other party,[56] and accordingly wider than a claim for recompense. He has no claim for remuneration for his services, which are wholly gratuitous.

The gestor, by acting, renders himself liable to claims arising out of what he does, as for the employment of professional services or tradesmen, but has a right of relief against the party for whom he acts, and is entitled to be indemnified against any liabilities incurred in the course of the *gestio*. But parties employed by the gestor may alternatively claim directly from the party for whom the gestor was acting.[57]

Liability of gestor

Where a person has justifiably undertaken to act as gestor he may not discontinue acting until the business for which he intervened has been

48 Dig. III, 5; Code, II, 18; Stair I, 8, 3; Ersk. III, 3, 52; Bell, *Prin.* § 540.
49 Ersk. III, 3, 53; *Wallace* v. *Braid* (1900) 2 F. 754.
50 *Smith's Reps.* v. *E. Winton* (1714) Mor. 9275.
51 *Graham* v. *Ker* (1757) Mor. 3529; 2 Paton 13; *Fernie* v. *Robertson* (1871) 9 M. 437; *Dunbar* v. *Wilson & Dunlop's Tr.* (1887) 15 R. 210.
52 *Paterson* v. *Greig* (1862) 24 D. 1370; *Fulton* v. *Fulton* (1864) 2 M. 893.
53 *Bannatine's Trs.* v. *Cuninghame* (1872) 10 M. 319.
54 *Gemmell* v. *Annandale* (1899) 36 S.L.R. 658.
55 *Kolbin* v. *Kinnear*, 1931 S.C.(H.L.) 128.
56 Dig. III, 5, 10 and 22; Stair I, 8, 3.
57 *Fernie* v. *Robertson* (1871) 9 M. 437; *Dunbar* v. *Wilson & Dunlop's Tr.* (1887) 15 R. 210.

completed, or the other party has returned or reacquired capacity to look after his or her affairs, or the gestor has been superseded by a legally appointed representative, such as a judicial factor.[58] If he does discontinue acting he will be liable for any loss caused to the other party by his conduct.

Similarly while a gestor is acting as such he must take reasonable care and use reasonable diligence such as a prudent man would take in relation to his own interests, and he will be liable for loss attributable to failure to exercise such care or to take reasonable precautions against loss or harm.[59]

Negotiorum gestio and agency of necessity

The principles of *negotiorum gestio* cover also cases falling under the similar and narrower principle of agency of necessity. The latter principle, possibly confined to carriers of goods,[60] is to the affect that a person such as a ship's captain, entrusted with goods for carriage, may, if circumstances arise necessitating his action,[61] if there is no means of salving the goods,[62] and if communication with and the obtaining of authority from the consignors is impossible,[63] assume authority, as agent, to dispose of the goods.[64] If the conditions are satisfied the carrier as agent is entitled to credit for expenses incurred and is not liable for non-delivery, but must account for the balance of the sale price to the consignors.

If the conditions are not satisfied the carrier is liable in damages [65] and the purchaser from him obtains no title to the goods,[66] even though the agent took what he believed to be, and what turned out to be, the best course.

Other Claims

Claims for salvage and for recovery of general average contributions are in their nature claims for restitution, but historically are derived from the general maritime law rather than the Roman law and jurisdictionally and procedurally belong to Admiralty remedies rather than common law remedies. They are accordingly dealt with under the latter heading.[67]

58 Bell, *Prin.* § 541.
59 Bell, *supra*; *Kolbin* v. *Kinnear*, 1930 S.C. 724, 746, 757; 1931 S.C.(H.L.) 128, 139.
60 *Jebara* v. *Ottoman Bank* [1927] 2 K.B. 254.
61 *Springer* v. *G.W. Ry.* [1921] 1 K.B. 257.
62 *Atlantic Mutual Ins. Co.* v. *Huth* (1880) 16 Ch.D. 474.
63 *Australasian S.N. Co.* v. *Morse* (1872) L.R. 4 P.C. 222; *Acatos* v. *Burns* (1878) 3 Ex.D. 282; *Springer* v. *G.W. Ry.* [1921] 1 K.B. 257.
64 Bell, *Comm.* I, 584; *Prin.* § 450; Carver, *Carriage by Sea* (11th ed.) 631; Scrutton, *Charterparties* (17th ed.) 256.
65 *Springer* v. *G.W. Ry.* [1921] 1 K.B. 257.
66 *Atlantic Mutual Ins. Co.* v. *Huth* (1880) 16 Ch.D. 474.
67 Chap. 63, *infra*.

CHAPTER 15

PAYMENT OF DEBT

A CLAIM for payment of a debt arises in many circumstances, from a common law obligation, such as to aliment, a contractual obligation, as where one party has promised money to another but has delayed or refused to pay it, or for the recovery of money lent, for the price of land or goods let on hire, for the instalments due under hire-purchase, credit-sale or conditional sale, for the salary or wages of service, the freight for carriage, the fee for custody, and other instances of contract, from an obligation of restitution such as to make recompense or compensate a *negotiorum gestor*, from a statutory obligation, such as to pay rates or taxes, from an obligation under a trust to pay a beneficiary, from a legal obligation under the rules of succession or under a will, and so on. In every case there is a duty to pay, which has not been implemented and which can be enforced by action for payment.

A claim for payment of debt is competent only for payment of an ascertained sum, which sum can be justified as being due under some principle of liability. If the pursuer does not know how much is due to him the proper action is one for count, reckoning and payment.[1] If his claim is for such compensation as the court deems proper his claim is for damages, not for debt.[1a]

Whether claim of debt appropriate

Whether a claim for debt or some other claim is proper in particular circumstances may depend on the true interpretation of a contract. In *Muirhead & Turnbull* v. *Dickson*[2] M contracted with D who, having obtained and paid instalments on, a piano, then defaulted. M sued for redelivery, contending that the contract was one of hiring. It was held that D had rightly understood that the transaction was sale with instalment payments, that the property in the piano had passed to D thereunder, and that M's proper remedy was accordingly a claim for the balance of the price. Similar problems may arise as between loan, sale, credit-sale, conditional sale, hire-purchase and hiring.

Similarly an alleged beneficiary's claim for payment of a legacy or other right under succession may raise a question of the interpretation of a will or trust deed, to decide his entitlement and consequently the amount of his share, rather than a simple question of enforcing payment.

[1] For this see Chap. 17, *infra*.
[1a] Chap. 24, *infra*.
[2] (1905) 7 F. 686.

Where contract repudiated by party bound to pay

It is said to be the law that where one party to a contract repudiates it before the due date for performance, and even before any steps had been taken to make, or prepare to make, performance, or any outlay has been incurred with a view to performance, the other party may, certainly where there is an express provision to this effect in the contract, at once sue for the full contract price, tendering in return due performance of the contract, even though this be now unwanted.[3] If this principle is right it must be confined to cases where the unwanted performance can be made without the co-operation of, and free from possible prevention by, the party in breach; it cannot apply where the party in breach has to give access to his premises, or otherwise co-operate, before performance could be made. The other party cannot compel co-operation. Also it ignores the principle that the innocent party to a breach of contract must take reasonable steps to minimise the loss and his resultant claim against the other.[4] The decision [3] must be regarded as a decision on the terms of the particular contract; otherwise it is highly questionable and a claim for loss of the anticipated profit on the transaction seems to be all that should have been allowed. It carries too far the rule that the innocent party cannot be compelled to accept an anticipatory repudiation; that rule merely entitles him to disregard it prior to the due date of performance but not when that time comes to thrust unwanted performance on the other party and cause him extra loss thereby.

A similar decision is more understandable where the contract was for a correspondence course of instruction in return for a fixed sum, payable by instalments, and the student discontinued the course half-way through and declined to complete the payments, and he was held liable to pay the whole balance of the payments.[5] In this case partial performance had been made and accepted, and preparations for completing the performance had doubtless been made. The instructor, in short, had had to do his bit of the work. Moreover, neither performance nor payment was apportionable into stages or distinct bits; both were indivisible units. It might have been otherwise if the contract had been for a first and a second year course, with distinct fees for each, and the breach had taken place at the end of the first year. Also in view of Scots law's favour for the principle of the unity of a contract it is quite reasonable to order payment of the full price when performance had been required, and had been made to the extent of about half of the total demandable.

Duty to minimise claim

The decision in *White & Carter* v. *McGregor* [6] may also raise a doubt

[3] *White & Carter (Councils) Ltd.* v. *McGregor*, 1962 S.C.(H.L.) 1, by a bare majority reversing Second Division, and overruling *Langford* v. *Dutch*, 1952 S.C. 15. See also 78 L.Q.R. 263; [1962] C.L.J. 213; 25 M.L.R. 364.

[4] On this see Chap. 28, *infra*.

[5] *International Correspondence Schools Ltd.* v. *Irving*, 1915 S.C. 28; *cf. International Correspondence Schools Ltd.* v. *Ayres* (1912) 28 T.L.R. 408.

[6] 1962 S.C.(H.L.) 1.

whether the principle, well settled in claims for unliquidated damages,[7] that the claiming pursuer must take reasonable steps to minimise the loss caused by the breach of contract and to mitigate his claim against the party in breach, has any application in claims for debt. In other words, if B incurs a contractual debt to A, as distinct from a liability in damages to A, is A under any duty to take reasonable steps to minimise his claim, as by cancelling his preparations for performance or by reselling unaccepted goods elsewhere? In *White & Carter's* case [6] Lord Morton [8] considered that the pursuers' only claim was for damages and that they were bound to take steps to minimise their loss, and Lord Keith [9] stated generally that " the party complaining of the breach also has a duty to minimise the damage he has suffered which is a further reason for saying that, after the date of breach, he cannot continue to carry on his part of an executory contract," and later [10] that to allow a party to make unwanted performance " cuts across the rule that where one party is in breach of contract the other must take steps to minimise the loss sustained by the breach." The majority, however, though not laying down expressly that the duty to minimise loss has no place in a claim for a debt, namely, the contract price, imply this by their insistence that the innocent party is not deprived of any rights by the guilty party's breach, nor bound to modify the contract, but is entitled to exact payment of what the other party has bound himself to pay.

This decision apart, all considerations of reason point to the rule requiring reasonable steps to be taken to minimise loss and the claim against the party in breach being a rule applicable to a claim for debt as much as to a claim for damages. On the facts of *White & Carter* [11] the pursuers should have recovered only their estimated loss of profit. If a pursuer elects to ignore an anticipatory repudiation of contract and goes on to make an unwanted performance, he cannot (at least in some cases, such as *White & Carter*) be prevented, but he should not be allowed to increase his claim, and the defender's loss, thereby, particularly when his insistence cannot increase his profit or otherwise benefit him. A person engaged for employment and then told he is not required is not entitled to sit back for the duration of the employment and claim the lost wages. His claim is for damages for the breach and it will amount to the full loss of wages only if he has tried to, but cannot, obtain reasonably comparable employment.[12] A seller of goods, where the buyer has repudiated the contract before delivery by saying that he does not want the goods, can sometimes claim the price [13] but normally only damages for non-

7 Chap. 28, *infra*.
8 p. 16.
9 p. 21.
10 p. 24.
11 *Supra*.
12 *Cf. White & Carter, supra*, 22, *per* Lord Keith, citing *Hochster* v. *de la Tour* (1853) 2 E. & B. 678 and *Ross* v. *McFarlane* (1894) 21 R. 396.
13 Sale of Goods Act 1893, s. 49.

acceptance.[14] Where the property has passed, he may sue for either. In either case, it is thought, he must take reasonable steps to find another purchaser; if he cannot find one his claim is for the price, or damages equivalent thereto; if he can his claim is for damages, representing the loss on the resale.[15]

Modes of satisfying claim of debt

Failing contrary agreement, the onus is on the debtor to seek out his creditor and tender payment, without demand, at the creditor's ordinary place of business,[16] within business hours, or at his residence at a reasonable time.

Failing contrary agreement the creditor is entitled to have, and the debtor bound to make, payment in money of legal tender.[17] Bank of England notes are legal tender in England and Wales and such notes of denominations of less than £5 are legal tender in Scotland.[18] Scottish bank notes are not legal tender anywhere, but are merely promissory notes. Gold coins, though no longer issued, are legal tender to any amount.[19] Silver coins of denominations not less than 10p. are legal tender up to £10, of denominations of less than 10p. up to £5, and bronze coins up to 20p.[20]

Where a bill or cheque is agreed to be accepted it operates as payment subject to resolutive condition only, and if it is not honoured by the bank the debt revives.[21]

The creditor is not obliged, unless he has agreed to do so, to accept payment by instalments, and should decline any tender of a sum " to account " or as an instalment, failing which he may be held to have agreed to accept such a mode of payment. Still less should he accept a sum less than the full sum due, not expressly stated to be a partial payment, as acceptance might raise an inference of acceptance of it as in full satisfaction.

Contracts of employment: the Truck Acts

The Truck Acts 1831–1940 apply to the employment of workmen, as defined by the Employers and Workmen Act 1875, s. 1.[22] They provide that the wages of such an employee shall be payable in the current coin of the realm only and not otherwise, and a contract is illegal, null and void, if providing that the whole or any part of the wages are payable in

14 *Ibid.* s. 50.
15 *Ibid.* s. 50 (2).
16 *Haughhead Coal Co.* v. *Gallacher* (1903) 11 S.L.T. 156.
17 *Fessard* v. *Mugnier* (1868) 18 C.B.(N.S.) 286.
18 Currency and Bank Notes Act 1954, s. 1 (2).
19 Coinage Act 1870, s. 4.
20 Decimal Currency Act 1969, s. 1. For coinage superseded in 1971 see Coinage Act 1946, s. 1; Decimal Currency Act 1969, s. 1.
21 *Leggat Bros.* v. *Gray*, 1908 S.C. 67.
22 Definition in Truck Amendment Act 1887, s. 2.

any other manner [23] or providing directly or indirectly respecting the place where, or the manner in which, or the person or persons with whom, the whole or any part of the wages due or to become due shall be laid out or expended.[24] Similar provisions are contained in the Hosiery Manufacture (Wages) Act 1874, while the Payment of Wages in Public Houses Prohibition Act 1883 prohibits, with exceptions, the payment of wages in licensed premises.

Payment in bank notes, or bank drafts payable on demand, is permissible, with the workman's consent.[25]

By the Payment of Wages Act 1960, however, it is lawful, if an employee requests his employer to pay his wages in a way specified in the request and authorised by the Act, for payment to be made by any of (a) payment into an account at a bank; (b) payment by postal order; (c) payment by money order; (d) payment by cheque.[26] A request may subsequently be cancelled.[27]

Creditor's right of action

If the debtor does not tender payment in full by the due date for payment, or where no date is fixed, after a reasonable time, the creditor may without further demand bring an action for payment and, though he must stop proceedings if payment is tendered, is entitled to tender not only of the debt but of the expenses of process necessitated by the delay in tender.[28]

Proof of discharge of debt

The general rule is *unumquodque eodem modo dissolvitur quo colligatur.* A debt incurred under an oral transaction may be proved by any evidence to have been paid.[29] Thus a ready money transaction may be proved to have been settled, even though delivery and payment were not coincident in time,[30] but not if there were a substantial interval between delivery and payment or if the sale was on credit.[31]

Where the debt arises under a contract, but there is no document constituting the debt, if the contract were written, proof of the payment of money becoming due thereunder must be by writ or oath of the creditor,[32] unless probably the termly payment were less than £100 Scots.[33]

[23] Truck Act 1831, s. 1.
[24] *Ibid.* s. 2.
[25] *Ibid.* s. 8.
[26] s. 1.
[27] s. 3.
[28] *Pollock* v. *Goodwin's Trs.* (1898) 25 R. 1051.
[29] Ersk. IV, 2, 13; *Newlands* v. *McKinlay* (1885) 13 R. 353.
[30] *McDonald* v. *Callender* (1786) Mor. 12366.
[31] *Tod* v. *Flockhart* (1799) Hume 498; *Shaw* v. *Wright* (1877) 5 R. 245; *Kilpatrick* v. *Dunlop*, 1909, 2 S.L.T. 307; *Young* v. *Thomson*, 1909 S.C. 529.
[32] Stair I, 43, 4; Ersk. IV, 2, 21; Dickson, *Evidence*, § 610; Rankine, *Leases*, 319.
[33] *E. Lauderdale* v. *Tenants of Swinton* (1662) Mor. 12362; *Brown* v. *Mason* (1856) 19 D. 137.

Where the debt, whatever its amount, is constituted by a document of debt, such as a bill, bond or I.O.U., proof of payment is restricted to the writ or oath of the creditor.[34] In the case of bills this is still the rule, notwithstanding section 100 of the Bills of Exchange Act 1882, which provides that any fact relating to a bill, cheque or promissory note, which is relevant to any question of liability thereon, may be proved by parole evidence.[35] Apparently an allegation of payment is not a " fact relevant to liability "; *sed quaere*?

Receipt

The document founded on as the creditor's receipt need not be probative,[36] nor in any particular form. It may be a separate document, or be endorsed on or attached to any document evidencing the debt. If for over £2 it formerly had to bear a 2d stamp, which had to be cancelled, failing which it was not admissible in evidence.[37] A cheque for the sum due drawn by the debtor and indorsed by the creditor is presumed to have been given and accepted in payment, but the creditor may overcome this presumption.[38] A cheque, whether indorsed or not, which appears to have been paid by the banker on whom it is drawn is evidence of the receipt by the payee of the sum payable by the cheque.[39]

A written receipt contained in a formal probative deed cannot be rebutted save by the writ or oath of the granter thereof, unless there are relevant averments of fraud.[40] A written but informal receipt, however, may be challenged and disproved by proof by the creditor of non-payment, which proof may be parole.[41] Thus a receipt granted for payment by cheque may be challenged by proof that the cheque was dishonoured.[42]

Presumptions of payment

In certain cases a presumption arises that debts have been paid. There is a presumption of law that counsel's fees have been paid [43]; accordingly, they cannot be sued for save that if the solicitor has been paid, counsel may sue the solicitor,[44] and counsel has been allowed to sue for a " pension " granted him by a town council.[45] Similarly Fellows of the Royal College of Physicians, if prohibited by bye-law of their College from suing for their fees, are presumed to have been paid.[46]

[34] *Patrick* v. *Watt* (1859) 21 D. 637; *Thiem's Trs.* v. *Collie* (1899) 1 F. 764; *Robertson* v. *Thomson* (1900) 3 F. 5; *Bishop* v. *Bryce*, 1910 S.C. 426.

[35] *Robertson* v. *Thomson* (1900) 3 F. 5; *Nicol's Trs.* v. *Sutherland*, 1951 S.C.(H.L.) 21.

[36] *Mitchell* v. *Berwick* (1845) 7 D. 382; *McLaren* v. *Howie* (1869) 8 M. 106; *cf. Paterson* v. *Paterson* (1897) 25 R. 144.

[37] Stamp Act 1891, ss. 8, 14, 101–103, and Sched. I.

[38] *Nicoll* v. *Reid* (1878) 6 R. 216; *Robb* v. *Robb's Trs.* (1884) 11 R. 881.

[39] Cheques Act 1957, s. 3.

[40] *Gordon* v. *Trotter* (1833) 11 S. 696; *Swan* v. *Baird* (1836) 15 S. 251; *Grant's Trs.* v. *Morison* (1875) 2 R. 377. On fraud see *Kirkwood* v. *Bryce* (1871) 8 S.L.R. 435.

[41] *Henry* v. *Miller* (1884) 11 R. 713.

[42] *Cf. Duke of Buccleuch* v. *McTurk* (1845) 7 D. 927, where, in view of the special circumstances of the case, proof by writ or oath was demanded.

[43] *Batchelor* v. *Pattison and Mackersy* (1876) 3 R. 914, 918.

[44] *Ogilvie* v. *Simpson* (1837) 15 S. 746; *Cullen* v. *Buchanan* (1862) 24 D. 1132.

[45] *McKenzie* v. *Town of Burntisland* (1728) Mor. 11421.

[46] Medical Act 1956, s. 27.

A rebuttable presumption of fact arises in the case of hotel and inn bills that, if the guest is allowed to depart, his bill has been paid.[47] Under the principle *apocha trium annorum* the production of receipts for the last three consecutive payments of termly payments such as feu-duty, rent, interest or an annuity, raise a presumption that all prior instalments have been duly paid.[48] The presumption does not arise from a receipt for the sum due at several terms,[49] nor does a receipt by a singular successor in lands, or an assignee of a bond or debt, raise any presumption that all sums due to his predecessor in title have been discharged.[50] If such a receipt discharges only that term's payment the presumption can probably be rebutted by any evidence,[51] but if it bears to discharge all sums previously due it may require rebuttal by writ or oath.[52]

Under the principle *chirographum apud debitorem repertum praesumitur solutum*, if a document of debt is in the possession of the debtor, even though *ex facie* undischarged, a rebuttable presumption arises that it has been paid. But the creditor may prove, by any evidence, that its possession must be otherwise explained and that payment has not been made.[53]

Similarly if a creditor is unable to produce a document of debt there arises a rebuttable presumption that the debt has been paid and the document destroyed. If it appears that the creditor destroyed the document the presumption is that he received payment or has discharged or waived the debt, but if he alleges that he has lost it, or destroyed it accidentally, he may, on giving clear proof of its terms and of the *casus amissionis*,[54] re-establish the document by an action of proving of the tenor.

Claim of debt in contract of sale of goods: Unpaid seller's claim for price

The seller of goods, within the meaning of the Sale of Goods Act 1893, is deemed to be an unpaid seller (a) when the whole of the price has not been paid or tendered; (b) when a bill of exchange or other negotiable instrument has been received as conditional payment, and the condition on which it was received has not been fulfilled by reason of the dishonour of the instrument or otherwise.[55] The price may be fixed by the contract, or be left to be fixed in manner thereby agreed, or may be determined by the course of dealing between the parties. If not thereby determined the buyer must pay a reasonable price, which is a question of fact dependent on the circumstances of each particular case.[56]

47 *Barnet* v. *Colvil* (1840) 2 D. 337.
48 Stair I, 18, 2; IV, 40, 35; Ersk. III, 4, 10; Bell, *Prin.* § 567; Dickson, *Evid.* § 177.
49 Dickson, *supra.*
50 *Master of Corstorphine* v. *Tenants* (1636) Mor. 11396.
51 *Cameron* v. *Panton's Trs.* (1891) 18 R. 728; *Stenhouse* v. *Stenhouse's Trs.* (1899) 36 S.L.R. 637.
52 *Hunter* v. *Lord Kinnaird's Trs.* (1829) 7 S. 548.
53 *Edwards* v. *Fyfe* (1823) 2 S. 431; *Knox* v. *Crawford* (1862) 24 D. 1088; *Henry* v. *Miller* (1884) 11 R. 713.
54 *Winchester* v. *Smith* (1863) 1 M. 685; *Walker* v. *Nisbet*, 1915 S.C. 639.
55 Sale of Goods Act 1893, s. 38 (1).
56 *Ibid.* s. 8.

Apart from rights against the goods themselves [57] the unpaid seller has an action for the price. By section 49 " (1) where, under a contract of sale, the property in the goods has passed to the buyer, and the buyer wrongfully neglects or refuses to pay for the goods according to the terms of the contract, the seller may maintain an action against him for the price of the goods." The price is payable if the property has passed and the goods been delivered, or at least the seller is able, willing and ready to deliver the goods, because delivery of the goods and payment of the price are concurrent conditions.[58] The neglect or refusal to pay must be wrongful. Thus it is not wrongful for the buyer to neglect or refuse to pay if the sale was made on credit, or payment is dependent on an unsatisfied condition,[59] or the price has been retained in the exercise of a right of retention,[60] *e.g.* against a claim of damages for defective quality or delayed delivery.

Neglect or refusal to pay *according to the terms of the contract* implies that if the buyer tries to pay in any other way than that agreed, it need not be accepted and action is competent. Thus an offer of payment to account, or an instalment of the price, or an article in lieu of money, or a post-dated cheque need not, and should not, be accepted. There may be an express or implied agreement to accept payment by bill or cheque, but failing that, it is the duty of the debtor to pay in legal tender.

If there is agreement to accept payment by a bill payable at a future date and such a bill is not given when payment is due, the seller's remedy is a claim of damages for breach of the agreement to give a bill [61]; he may sue for the price only when the date comes on which the bill would have matured, as only then is the money due.

If there is agreement to accept payment by a bill or cheque and one is given it is deemed payment subject to a resolutive condition, and if it is dishonoured, the debt revives and the seller may sue for payment of the price, or on the dishonoured bill or cheque.[62] But a bill or cheque may be taken as absolute payment in which case only the latter claim is competent if it be not honoured.

> Section 49 (2): " Where under a contract of sale, the price is payable on a day certain irrespective of delivery, and the buyer wrongfully neglects or refuses to pay such price, the seller may maintain an action for the price, although the property in the goods has not passed, and the goods have not been appropriated to the contract."

A " day certain " has been defined as " a time specified in the contract not depending on a future or contingent event." [63] In this case the

[57] 1893 Act, ss. 39–48.

[58] 1893 Act, s. 28.

[59] *e.g. Calcutta Co.* v. *De Mattos* (1863) 32 L.J.Q.B. 322.

[60] *Cf. British Motor Body Co.* v. *Shaw*, 1914 S.C. 922.

[61] *Paul* v. *Dod* (1846) 2 C.B. 800; as to measure of damages see *Gordon* v. *Whitehouse* (1856) 18 C.B. 747.

[62] *Davis* v. *Reilly* [1898] 1 Q.B. 1.

[63] *Merchant Shipping Co.* v. *Armitage* (1873) L.R. 9 Q.B. 99; *Shell-Mex Ltd.* v. *Elton Cop Dyeing Co.* (1928) 34 Com.Cas. 39.

seller may sue for the price although the property in the goods has not passed and the goods have not been appropriated to the contract. The buyer must, however, *wrongfully* neglect or refuse to pay on the day certain fixed for payment. He does not " wrongfully " neglect or refuse if he has ascertained, or possibly even if he has good reason to believe, that the seller will not be able to deliver the goods when the date for delivery arrives, nor probably if the seller has discontinued business or become insolvent.

> Section 49 (3): " Nothing in this section shall prejudice the right of the seller in Scotland to recover interest on the price from the date of tender of the goods, or from the date on which the price was payable, as the case may be."

The seller's right to recover interest on the price is discussed in Chapter 23.

Claim of debt in contract for sale of land

The rule is that the price is payable, in exchange for a valid duly executed disposition of the lands sold, on the date fixed for settlement, or, if entry takes place before settlement, on that date, failing which interest will run on it till settlement. In practice the risk of non-payment and the running of interest are avoided by the payer lodging the price on deposit-receipt in the joint names of the buyer and seller, the deposit-receipt being endorsed by the buyer and handed to the seller at settlement. The seller is entitled to the interest accruing on the deposit-receipt.[64]

In the case of land, non-payment of the price on the date of entry, or on a stipulated date, is not a justification, save possibly in special circumstances, for rescinding the contract, nor for delivering an ultimatum threatening rescission failing payment within a stated limited time.[65] It may be otherwise if payment on a stipulated date is made an essential condition of the contract, or if serious doubts have arisen as to the buyer's capacity to pay.[66] If on or after entry the buyer, on being called on and offered a valid disposition, unjustifiably delays or refuses to tender payment he may be sued for the price with interest, or, after fair warning to him, the sale may be rescinded and damages claimed for the loss of bargain.

[64] *Cf. Grandison's Trs.* v. *Jardine* (1895) 22 R. 925; *Prestwick Cinema Co.* v. *Gardiner*, 1951 S.C. 98.
[65] *Rodger (Builders) Ltd.* v. *Fawdry*, 1950 S.C. 483, 492.
[66] *Black* v. *Dick* (1814) Hume 699; *Burns* v. *Garscadden* (1901) 8 S.L.T. 321.

CHAPTER 16

ACTION OF CONSTITUTION

AN action of constitution is brought to have determined judicially a liability to pay and the amount payable, without demanding payment. The common form of a decree for constitution includes a declarator that the debt is due and a decree for payment. A decree for payment is in fact in itself a decree of constitution.[1] An action for damages seeks constitution of the claim and also payment. Constitution is rarely sought alone, but usually along with payment or adjudication. If a claim is made against a solvent debtor a decree of constitution of the debt as presently due is as good to support a charge for payment as is a decree for payment *eo nomine*.[2]

The cases where a decree of constitution only is proper include cases where the debtor has died and no executors have been appointed, or they have declined to confirm,[3] or they are outwith the jurisdiction, to have it found that the debt is a lawful one and still resting-owing, or where he has been sequestrated and a trustee been appointed on his estate, who is not personally liable to any of the creditors and who can at most admit the creditor's claim to a ranking,[1] or where there is no executor and the deceased's next of kin are not *lucrati* by the succession, in which case an action of constitution against the *haereditas jacens* is competent.[4] Where an executor has been confirmed creditors are entitled not merely to a decree *cognitionis causa tantum*, but to a decree of constitution *qua* executor.[5] Where an executry estate is small and the amount of claims uncertain and the existence of the alleged debt is at all doubtful an executor is entitled to protect himself and the estate by requiring formal constitution.[6]

In *Forrest* v. *Forrest* [7] a creditor of the deceased Forrest sued the latter's widow and children as his next of kin or executors or as otherwise representing him concluding for payment of a bill of exchange. It was observed that if the next of kin, being charged, renounced the succession, decree *cognitionis causa* would be pronounced in favour of the pursuer; if they were not charged and were therefore under no obligation to renounce the next question would be, whether they had intromitted with the estate or done anything actively or passively to render themselves liable

1 *Thomson & Co.* v. *Friese-Greene's Tr.*, 1944 S.C. 336, 341.
2 *Thomson, supra*, 345.
3 *Davidson* v. *Clark* (1867) 6 M. 151.
4 *Smith* v. *Tasker*, 1955 S.L.T. 347.
5 *Crawfurd* v. *Cook* (1833) 11 S. 406.
6 *McGann* v. *McGann's Trs.* (1883) 11 R. 249.
7 (1863) 1 M. 806. See also *Ferrier* v. *Crockart*, 1937 S.L.T. 205; *Stevens* v. *Thomson*, 1971 S.L.T. 136.

for his obligations. If not, they were entitled to be assoilzied, but the pursuer would still be entitled to his remedy, if he restricted his demand to a claim for a decree *cognitionis causa tantum*. It was also observed that an alternative remedy, such as to petition for appointment as executor-creditor, might be open.

A creditor who seeks a decree *cognitionis causa tantum* should call as defenders all the known heirs of an intestate deceased.[8]

In *Crichton's Tr.* v. *Stewart*,[9] S sued the trustee on the sequestrated estate of a bankrupt, restricting the conclusion to one for constitution only of the debt and for interest. It was held that such a decree did not warrant a charge for payment against the trustee, not being a decree against the trustee personally. The debtor being insolvent and his estates sequestrated, a decree of constitution afforded no warrant for payment.

An action of constitution for an illiquid claim is also necessary before it can be used to compensate a liquid claim, and for this purpose an action on a liquid claim has been sisted or its disposal deferred.[10]

It is competent to sue a trustee, who has distributed the whole trust estate and been discharged by the beneficiaries, to constitute a claim against the trust estate and to obtain a decree of constitution which affects him solely as trustee and not personally as an alternative to a decree for count, reckoning and payment.[11]

" A person is entitled to bring an action of constitution against the representatives of his debtor, for the purpose of establishing the liability of his (the debtor's) executry estate for a money claim even if he (the pursuer) may be unable to obtain a decree for payment against these representatives. The fact of a testamentary trustee having resigned, or executed the trust, does not, in my judgment, deprive a creditor of this right, although other remedies, such as confirmation as executor creditor, may possibly be open to him." [12]

If a party is sued for reparation for delict and wishes to claim relief from another party as being the party truly to blame, or as being also to blame, " it is essential that the primary liability be constituted, by joint and several decree, or by some equivalent instrument constituting the debt, and not be arrived at by compromise of the pursuer's claim or in any similar way." [13]

The pursuing creditor must himself pay the expenses of an action of constitution [14] unless his claim is opposed, in which event he may claim expenses in the usual way.

8 *Smith* v. *Tasker*, 1955 S.L.T. 347.

9 (1866) 4 M. 689, explained in *Thomson, supra*; *cf. Sutherland* v. *Fraser* (1826) 5 S. 116.

10 *Munro* v. *Macdonald's Exors.* (1866) 4 M. 687.

11 *Assets Co. Ltd.* v. *Falla's Trs.* (1894) 22 R. 178.

12 *Assets Co. Ltd.* v. *Bain's Trs.* (1904) 6 F. 692, 704; revd. on other grounds (1905) 7 F.(H.L.) 105.

13 *N.C.B.* v. *Thomson*, 1959 S.C. 353. (Since this decision the introduction of third-party procedure may facilitate having the party alleged to be truly to blame before the court.)

14 *Earl of Rosslyn* v. *Lawson* (1872) 9 S.L.R. 291; *Mason* (1904) 12 S.L.T. 82.

CHAPTER 17

COUNT, RECKONING AND PAYMENT

A CLAIM for count, reckoning and payment is appropriate where there is a right to demand and a liability to render an account, where the pursuer believes that money is due to him and he wishes to exact payment but he cannot state precisely how much is due, and accordingly in the first place calls on the defender to count and reckon, or account for his intromissions, and to pay the balance found justly due. The main conclusions are for the production of accounts, and for payment of a sum stated as the balance, or such other sums as may be ascertained to be the true balance. It is a mixture of an action *ad factum praestandum*, to produce accounts, with an action for payment.[1] To cover the possibility that the defender will not be able to account, there is always an alternative conclusion, failing an accounting, for payment of a random sum, stated as the highest sum which could reasonably be due by the defender. Accounting is normally called for down to the date of citation, at which date the balance is ascertained, and interest is allowable from that date only. But it is competent to conclude for a continuous accounting down to the date of decree. This requires a special conclusion, or the consent of parties.[2]

The claim is accordingly appropriate against persons who have been legitimately intromitting with funds which, or the income of which, should be or have been transferred to the pursuer. Thus it lies against executors,[3] trustees,[4] a trustee in bankruptcy, after the bankrupt has been discharged,[5] and against another partner,[6] and anyone acting in the capacity of an agent.[7]

It lies also against the representatives of persons, such as trustees, now deceased, resigned, or discharged, who should during their period of intromission, have accounted for their intromissions.[8] Where a trustee has resigned and been discharged, the discharge must be reduced before he or his representatives can be called on to account.[9] The liability of trustees or their representatives to account is not elided by the lapse of the long

[1] *Hutcheson & Co.'s Administrator* v. *Taylor's Exrx.*, 1931 S.C. 484, 492.
[2] *Wauchope* v. *N.B. Ry.* (1860) 23 D. 191; *Wallace* v. *Henderson* (1875) 2 R. 999, 1001.
[3] *e.g. Hutcheson & Co.'s Administrator* v. *Taylor's Exrx.*, 1931 S.C. 484; *Polland* v. *Sturrock's Exor.*, 1952 S.C. 535; *Ventisei* v. *Ventisei's Exors.*, 1966 S.C. 21.
[4] *e.g. Clarke* v. *Clarke's Trs.*, 1925 S.C. 693; *Hastie's J.F.* v. *Morham's Exors.*, 1951 S.C. 668; *Tennent's J.F.* v. *Tennent*, 1954 S.C. 215; *Smith* v. *Cotton's Trs.*, 1956 S.C. 338; *Young* v. *Young's Trs.*, 1957 S.C. 318.
[5] *Goudy on Bankruptcy*, 364; *Wallace on Bankruptcy*, 180; *White* v. *Stevenson*, 1956 S.C. 84, 90.
[6] *Smith* v. *Barclay*, 1962 S.C. 1.
[7] *Unigate Foods* v. *Scottish Milk Marketing Board*, 1972 S.L.T. 137.
[8] *e.g. Barns* v. *Barn's Trs.* (1857) 19 D. 626; *Hastie's J.F.*, *supra.*
[9] *Hastie's J.F.*, *supra.*

negative prescription.[10] It is not competent against a judicial factor for the purpose of overhauling his accounts when he has annually presented accounts to which the Accountant of Court has not objected.[11]

Title to sue

Title to sue is restricted to those persons who have financial interest in the accuracy and honesty of the intromissions by the defenders, to such as the beneficiaries of a trust, the beneficiaries under the will of, or heirs on intestacy of, a deceased person, or persons who are otherwise creditors of the fund in question.

Outsiders, third parties to the relations in question, have no title to call for accounting any more than they have to exact payment.

Prerequisites of claim

The pursuer must also satisfy the court that any prerequisites to his claiming an accounting have been satisfied. In *Smith* v. *Cotton's Trs.*[12] the defenders had power to hold shares in a company and were directed, if they decided to sell them, to offer them first to the pursuer at a stated price. The company went into voluntary liquidation and the pursuer claimed from the defenders an accounting for and payment of the difference between the sum received by the defenders for the shares and the maximum price he would have had to pay if they had decided to sell and had offered him the shares. It was held that the contingency dependent on which his right to the shares depended had not arisen, and that no right to accounting and payment had emerged.

Liability to account

A liability to account is owed by every person who pays and receives or otherwise intromits with money truly belonging in whole or in part to another, by such persons as agents of every kind,[13] mandataries, partners, executors, trustees and judicial factors, trustees in bankruptcy and the like. An executor is, however, accountable for his intromissions as such and for the actings of the deceased, whom he represents, as an individual, but not as executor or universal legatee of another.[14] " A relevant action of accounting only emerges where it is alleged that the defender has, either by himself or by his agents, intromitted with estate to which the pursuer has right or in which he is interested. An order pronounced on a defender who has had no intromissions to produce an account of them would only be a futile proceeding." [15]

10 *Barns, supra*; *Hastie's J.F., supra*; Prescription and Limitation (Sc.) Act, 1973, Sch. 3 (e).
11 *Cormack* v. *Simpson's J.F.*, 1960 S.L.T. 197.
12 1956 S.C. 338.
13 *Unigate Food* v. *Scottish Milk Marketing Board*, 1972 S.L.T. 137.
14 *Hutcheson & Co.'s Administrator* v. *Taylor's Exrx.*, 1931 S.C. 484, 492.
15 *Ibid., per* Lord Morison.

It arises also in the case of persons who by breach of duty to the pursuer have obtained moneys justly due to the pursuer. Thus a pursuer may demand damages or an accounting for profits from one who has infringed his copyright,[16] patent,[17] or plant breeders' right.[18]

Form of accounting requisite

Ideally an accounting should take the form of a proper itemised account, periodically audited by a competent person and docqueted as correct and adequately vouched, or supported by bank books, record of and receipts for payments made, record of moneys received, and all other relevant vouchers, but it is almost a basic hypothesis of this form of action that such an account has not been, or cannot be, prepared, or that it is inadequate, defective, or includes items disputed or not vouched. But a strictly formal and correct accounting is not indispensable.

> " In an action of count, reckoning and payment what matters is the account of the intromissions put in by the defender, and not the books or invoices or accounts or whatever they may be, which are simply the raw materials on the basis of which the account of the intromissions is made up . . . it is not the presence or absence of the books that is the vital thing but the presentation of an account of intromissions, and there may be ways and means of producing an account of the intromissions apart from the papers which have gone amissing. In these circumstances it seems to me that the proper course is to give the defender an opportunity to produce what account he can of his intromissions, an account which of course can be disputed and controverted by the pursuer in the usual way." [19]

The real question is how much, if any sum, the defender justly owes the pursuer, not whether the books were properly kept.

If there is dispute as to the method of accounting or as to details, such as allowances for bad debts, or apportionment between capital and income, a remit may be made to an accountant to examine and report on the method used.

If the pursuer objects to the accounts lodged he must make specific, not vague general, objections.[20]

Decree for payment under alternative conclusions

Decree for payment of the sum claimed alternatively to payment, or for some part of that sum, is a last resort, appropriate only where the defender has, after adequate warning and opportunity to do so, utterly failed to account or to account at all adequately for his intromissions.

16 Copyright Act 1956, s. 17 (1).
17 Patents Act 1949, s. 60.
18 Plant Varieties and Seeds Act 1964, s. 4 (1).
19 *Smith* v. *Barclay*, 1962 S.C. 1, 9, *per* L.J.C. Thomson.
20 *Guthrie* v. *McKimmie's Trs.*, 1952 S.L.T.(Sh.Ct.) 49.

Decree deferred

Where there was a contingent tax liability outstanding the court has declined to grant decree but ordered that the sum in issue be consigned.[21]

Compromise

An action of accounting may be compromised; if a trustee or judicial factor or a trust estate proposes to compromise the question must be considered whether such compromise is or is not at variance with the terms and purposes of the trust,[22] so as to require the authority of the court.[23]

[21] *Dunlop* v. *Dunlop*, 1959 S.L.T.(Notes) 5.
[22] Trusts (Sc.) Act 1921, s. 4 (1).
[23] *Tennent's J.F.* v. *Tennent*, 1954 S.C. 215; see also *Young* v. *Young's Trs.*, 1957 S.C. 318, which shows that a decree based on a compromise may found a plea of *res judicata*.

CHAPTER 18

PETITION FOR SEQUESTRATION OR LIQUIDATION

A CREDITOR who petitions for the sequestration of his debtor, as a means, usually the ultimate means, of securing payment of at least part of his debt, uses " a remedy which the law gives absolutely and without qualification. Any person is entitled to apply for the sequestration of a debtor who is indebted to him to a certain extent and who has, within a certain period previously, been made notour bankrupt . . . there is clearly a distinction between [diligence] and an application to the court for sequestration. A petition for sequestration is, I think, an action, and though where it is granted it has the force of diligence (and that of the strongest kind) that does not take away from the petition its nature as an action." [1] " The petition for sequestration is an action in the first instance, and privileged as such, although it may ultimately take the shape of a diligence." [2] " I agree with your Lordships in holding that an application for sequestration of a debtor's estates, though it results in diligence of a sweeping nature, is a judicial proceeding." [3]

Jurisdiction to sequestrate

Sequestration may be awarded by the Court of Session or by the sheriff of any county in which the debtor has resided or carried on business for the year preceding the date of the petition, or in the case of a deceased debtor for the year preceding the date of his death; Provided (1) that no sequestration shall be awarded by any court after production of evidence that a sequestration has been awarded in another court, and is still undischarged; (2) that, where a prior petition for sequestration is in dependence before any court, the court to which a subsequent petition has been presented may remit such subsequent petition to the court in which the prior petition is in dependence.[4] Where sequestration is awarded by the sheriffs of two counties the later is to be remitted to the county which earlier awarded sequestration. Where both or all are of the same date the Court of Session shall remit to such sheriff court as it deems expedient.[5] After appeal to, or award of sequestration by, the Court of Session, no proceedings may be taken under order of the sheriff, except for the preservation of the estate.[6] After sequestration has been awarded it may be

[1] *Kinnes* v. *Adam* (1882) 9 R. 698, 702, *per* L.P. Inglis.
[2] *Ibid.* 703, *per* Lord Deas.
[3] *Ibid.* 703, *per* Lord Shand.
[4] Bankruptcy (Sc.) Act 1913, s. 16.
[5] *Ibid.* s. 17.
[6] *Ibid.* s. 18.

brought before the Court of Session by appeal and that Court may transfer the sequestration to another sheriff court.[7]

Competency of petition

The court may [8] award sequestration of the estates of a person (1) in the case of a living debtor subject to the jurisdiction of the supreme courts of Scotland (a) on his own petition, with the concurrence of a creditor or creditors whose debt or debts together amount to not less than £50, whether such debts are liquid or illiquid, provided they are not contingent [9]; (b) on the petition of a creditor or creditors, qualified as above, provided the debtor be notour bankrupt as defined by ss. 5–7 of the Act,[10] and have within a year before the date of the presentation of the petition resided or had a dwelling house or place of business in Scotland,[11] or otherwise, in the case of company [12] being notour bankrupt, if it has within such time carried on business in Scotland, and any partner have so resided or had a dwelling house or if the company have had a place of business in Scotland; (2) in the case of a deceased debtor who at the date of his death was subject to the jurisdiction of the supreme courts of Scotland (a) on the petition of a mandatary to whom he had granted a mandate to apply for sequestration; (b) on the petitition of a creditor or creditors qualified as above.[13]

Petitions for sequestration of a living debtor without his concurrence are competent only within four months of the date of his notour bankruptcy; petitions for sequestration of the estates of a deceased debtor at the instance of a creditor may be presented at any time after the debtor's death, but no sequestration shall be awarded until the expiry of six months from the death, unless he was at the time of his death notour bankrupt, or unless his successors concur in the petition or renounce the succession, in which cases sequestration shall be awarded forthwith; and in all other cases [14] falling under the 1913 Act petition is competent at any time, and sequestration may follow.[15]

Petition, vouchers and oath

The procedure is initiated by petition, the petitioning or concurring creditor producing also the accounts and vouchers of the debt [16] and an

[7] *Ibid.* s 19.
[8] *Ibid.* s. 11.
[9] *Forbes* v. *Whyte* (1890) 18 R. 182; *Stuart & Stuart* v. *Macleod* (1891) 19 R. 223; contrast *Strathdee* v. *Paterson*, 1913, 1 S.L.T. 498.
[10] *Fleming* v. *Yeaman* (1884) 9 App.Cas. 966; *Neil's Tr.* v. *B.L. Bank* (1898) 6 S.L.T. 227; *Baillie & Son* (1899) 6 S.L.T. 324; *Arrol* v. *Christie* (1901) 4 F. 262; *Laird* v. *Scott*, 1913, 2 S.L.T. 409.
[11] *Gairdner* v. *Macarthur*, 1918, 2 S.L.T. 123.
[12] Including bodies corporate, politic or collegiate, and partnerships: 1913 Act, s. 2.
[13] *Ibid.* ss. 11–12.
[14] *i.e.* petitions by the debtor with concurrence, or by a mandatary for a deceased debtor.
[15] *Ibid.* s. 13.
[16] *Ibid.* s. 20; see *Simpson* v. *Myles* (1881) 9 R. 104; as to ambiguous affidavit and voucher see *Clark* v. *Thom* (1884) 11 R. 469; a decree in absence is a sufficient voucher: *Aitken* v. *Kyd* (1890) 28 S.L.R. 115.

oath taken before a judge ordinary, magistrate, J.P., notary public, or a commissioner for oaths to the verity of the debt, stating what other persons, if any, besides the bankrupt are liable for the debt or any part thereof,[17] and specifying any security which he holds over the estate of the bankrupt or of other obligants, and deponing that he holds no other obligants or securities than those specified or that he holds no other person than the bankrupt so bound, and no security.[18] All that the Act requires is that the creditor shall swear that the debt is resting-owing.[19] The affidavit is invalid if the creditor is not put on oath.[19] Sequestration may be recalled if the account produced is wholly lacking in specification.[20] An award of sequestration may be reduced but will not be reduced if the debtor's averments can be investigated in the sequestration process.[21]

Award of sequestration

If a petition is presented by, or with the concurrence of, the debtor, or if dead, of his successor, or if his successor shall renounce the succession, the Lord Ordinary or sheriff shall forthwith award sequestration.[22] If the petition is not by or with the concurrence of the debtor, or he does not appear at the diet of appearance and show cause why sequestration cannot competently be awarded or pay his debts, the court shall award sequestration.[23] The deliverance awarding sequestration is not subject to review but a debtor may within 40 days petition for recall of sequestration.[24] No petition for recall is competent after 40 days, save in stated circumstances.[25] Subsequent procedure is regulated by the statute.

Effect of sequestration

The issue of an Act and Warrant in favour of the trustee appointed on the sequestrated estate [26] transfers to and vests in him or any succeeding trustee, for behoof of the creditors, absolutely and irredeemably, as at the date of the sequestration, with all right, title and interest, the whole property of the debtor, both heritable and moveable, together with real estate in England, Ireland or any of Her Majesty's dominions, and any non-vested contingent right of succession or interest in property conceived in favour of the bankrupt under a will or trust.[27] Property acquired after sequestration also falls under it.[28]

17 *Fraser* (1897) 5 S.L.T. 29.
18 *Ibid.* s. 21. As to oath by a creditor outside Great Britain or Ireland, see s. 22, and as to deceased debtor, see s. 23. As to oath by creditor who is a corporation, partnership, person under age or incapable, see s. 24 and *Dow & Co.* v. *Union Bank* (1875) 2 R. 459.
19 *Blair* v. *N.B. and Mercantile Ins. Co.* (1889) 16 R. 947; (1890) 17 R.(H.L.) 76.
20 *Riddell* v. *Galbraith* (1896) 24 R. 51; contrast *Gillon* v. *Caesar* (1882) 10 R. 59.
21 *Whitlie* v. *Gibb* (1898) 25 R. 412.
22 *Ibid.* s. 28.
23 *Ibid.* s. 29.
24 *Ibid.* s. 30.
25 *Ibid.* s. 31.
26 Under 1913 Act, s. 70.
27 *Ibid.* s. 97.
28 *Ibid.* s. 98.

Enforcement of creditor's claim

A creditor whose debtor's estates have been sequestrated must make his claim, if he has not done so at the stage of petitioning for sequestration, by way of lodging a claim, supported by the accounts and vouchers necessary to prove the debt, and by an oath to the same effect and taken in the same manner as if petitioning for sequestration,[29] at the meeting of creditors called to appoint the trustee.[30] To entitle a creditor to participate in the first dividend [31] he must produce his claim and oath at least two months before payment of the first dividend, or one month before if payment has been accelerated,[32] and at least two months before the time for payment of any subsequent dividend.[33] The trustee may require further evidence in support of a claim [34] and must within the 14 days before the time for payment of a dividend, examine the oaths and grounds of debt and in writing reject or admit them,[35] or require further evidence in support thereof, and make up a list of creditors entitled to payment of a dividend,[36] and intimate his decision to each creditor. A creditor dissatisfied may appeal to the court.[37] A trustee is not entitled to sustain claims which have prescribed merely on being satisfied that they are just debts, without having legal evidence to elide prescription.[38] A claim for future aliment is not a contingent debt merely because it contains elements incapable of valuation.[39]

PETITION FOR LIQUIDATION OF A COMPANY

A creditor may similarly, in the last resort, where his claim is against a company, petition for liquidation of the company as a means of securing payment of at least part of his claim. "A winding-up order is, in my opinion, a perfectly proper remedy for enforcing payment of a just debt." [40] It is incompetent to sequestrate under the Bankruptcy Act a company registered under the Companies Acts.[41]

Jurisdiction

Jurisdiction to wind up a company registered in Scotland is vested in the Court of Session, or, if the paid up share capital does not exceed

29 *Ibid.* ss. 45–62.
30 *Ibid.* s. 63.
31 Payable six months after sequestration: *ibid.* s. 126.
32 Under s. 130.
33 *Ibid.* s. 119.
34 See *Oliver* v. *Wallace* (1869) 7 M. 407; *Purvis* v. *Dowie* (1869) 7 M. 764.
35 *Ritchie* v. *Balgarnie* (1875) 2 R. 297.
36 *Ibid.* s. 123.
37 *Ibid.* s. 124.
38 *Marshall* v. *Smith* (1871) 9 S.L.R. 42.
39 *Matthew* v. *Matthew's Tr.* (1907) 16 S.L.T. 326; contrast *Downs* v. *Wilson's Tr.* (1886) 13 R. 1101.
40 *Speirs* v. *Central Building Co. Ltd.*, 1911 S.C. 330, 334, *per* Lord Mackenzie; *cf. Re Amalgamated Properties of Rhodesia Ltd.* [1917] 2 Ch. 115.
41 *Standard Property Investment Co.* v. *Dunblane Hydropathic Co.* (1884) 12 R. 328.

£10,000, the sheriff court of the sheriffdom in which the registered office of the company is situated. Petitions may be remitted from one court to the other.[42] Jurisdiction to wind up a company registered in England is vested in the High Court and in certain county courts.[43]

Competency of petition

A company may be wound up by the court if, *inter alia*, it is unable to pay its debts,[44] as statutorily defined,[45] or if the court is of opinion that it is just and equitable that the company should be wound up,[46] or if there is subsisting a floating charge over property comprised in the company's property and undertaking, and the court is satisfied that the security of the creditor entitled to the benefit of the floating charge is in jeopardy, as statutorily defined.[47] If there is a bona fide dispute as to liability the court may dismiss the petition on consignation [48] or may sist the petition to enable the petitioner to constitute his debt.[49]

Petitioners

Petition may be presented by the company, or by any creditor or creditors (including any contingent or prospective creditor or creditors), contributory or contributories, or by all or any of those parties, together or separately.[50] The court will be slow to refuse a creditor's petition, unless it is clear that there are no assets from which he can be paid.[51] The court may dismiss the petition, adjourn it conditionally or unconditionally, make any interim order, or any other order that it thinks fit, but shall not refuse to make a winding-up order on the ground only that the assets of the company have been mortgaged to an amount equal to or in excess of those assets or that the company has no assets.[52] An order made shall operate in favour of all the creditors and of all the contributories of the company as if made on the joint petition of a creditor and of a contributory.[53]

Effect of making winding-up order

The winding up is deemed to commence at the time of the presentation of the petition for winding up,[54] save that, if a resolution had previously been passed by the company for voluntary winding up, it is deemed to

42 Companies Act 1948, ss. 220–221.
43 *Ibid.* ss. 218–219.
44 *Ibid.* s. 222 (*e*); *Stephen* v. *Scottish Banking Co.* (1884) 31 S.L.R. 764; *Cowan* v. *Scottish Publishing Co.* (1892) 19 R. 437.
45 *Ibid.* s. 223; *cf. Speirs* v. *Central Building Co. Ltd.*, 1911 S.C. 330.
46 *Ibid.* s. 222 (*f*).
47 Companies (Floating Charges and Receivers) (Scotland) Act 1972, s. 4.
48 *Cuninghame* v. *Walkinshaw Oil Co.* (1886) 14 R. 87; *Pollok* v. *Gaeta Mining Co.*, 1907 S.C 182.
49 *Landauer* v. *Alexander*, 1919 S.C. 492.
50 Companies Act 1948, s. 224.
51 *Gardner* v. *Link* (1894) 21 R. 967. On absence of assets, see s. 225 (1).
52 *Ibid.* s. 225 (1).
53 *Ibid.* s. 232.
54 *Liqdr. of Property Investment Co. of Scotland* v. *National Bank* (1891) 28 S.L.R. 884.

have commenced at the time of the passing of the resolution and all proceedings taken in the voluntary winding up are deemed to have been validly taken unless the court thinks fit to direct otherwise on proof of fraud or mistake.[55] Any disposition of the property of the company, including incorporeal rights, and any transfer of shares or alteration in the status of the members of the company made thereafter, are void unless the court otherwise orders.[56] Attachment or sequestration of the effects of a company registered in England, or of the effects in England of a company registered in Scotland, made thereafter, is void.[57] When a winding-up order has been made or a provisional liquidator has been appointed, no action or proceeding may be commenced or proceeded with against the company except by leave of the court and subject to such terms as it may impose.[58]

Effect of winding up on antecedent transactions

Any transaction done by or against the company within six months before winding up which, if done by an individual within six months before petition for his sequestration, would be deemed in his bankruptcy an alienation or preference voidable by statute or at common law on the ground of insolvency or notour bankruptcy, is deemed a fraudulent preference and is accordingly invalid, and any conveyance by a company of all its property to trustees for the benefit of all its creditors is void for all purposes.[59]

Effect of prior diligences

Winding up is equivalent to an arrestment in execution and decree of furthcoming and to an executed or completed poinding, and no arrestment or poinding executed on or after the sixtieth day prior to that date is effectual, and the funds or effects or the proceeds of those effects, if sold, are to be made forthcoming to the liquidator, but an arrester or poinder thus deprived of the benefit of his diligence is to have preference for his expenses bona fide incurred. It is also equivalent to an adjudication of the heritable estates of the company, subject to preferable rights and securities and the right to poind the ground, but no poinding of the ground not carried into execution by sale sixty days before winding up is available in any question with the liquidator. The provisions of the Bankruptcy (Scotland) Act 1913, ss. 108–113 and 116 apply to the realisation of heritable estates affected by such heritable rights and securities as aforesaid, subject to verbal adaptations.[60]

[55] *Ibid.* s. 229.
[56] *Ibid.* s. 227.
[57] *Ibid.* s. 228.
[58] *Ibid.* s. 231.
[59] *Ibid.* s. 320.
[60] *Ibid.* s. 327; *cf.* Bankruptcy (Sc.) Act 1913, ss. 103–104.

Vesting of company's property in liquidator

In Scotland if and so long as there is no liquidator, all the company's property is deemed to be in the custody of the court. If a liquidator or provisional liquidator has been appointed, he must take into his custody or under his control all the property and incorporeal rights to which the company is or appears to be entitled.[61] The court may direct that all or part of the property of the company or held by trustees on its behalf shall vest in the liquidator, and it shall thereupon vest accordingly, and the liquidator may, after giving such indemnity, if any, as the court may direct, bring or defend in his official name any action or other legal proceeding which relates to that property or which it is necessary to bring or defend for the purpose of effectually winding up the company and recovering its property.[62]

In a winding up by the court in Scotland the liquidator has the same powers as the trustee on a bankrupt estate.[63]

Proof and ranking of claims against company

In every winding up (subject, in the case of insolvent companies, to the application in accordance with the provisions of the 1948 Act of the law of bankruptcy) all debts payable on a contingency, and all claims against the company, present or future, certain or contingent, ascertained or sounding only in damages, shall be admissible to proof against the company, a just estimate being made, so far as possible, of the value of such debts or claims as may be subject to any contingency or sound only in damages, or for some other reason do not bear a certain value.[64]

The provisions of sections 45 to 62, 96 and 105 of the Bankruptcy (Scotland) Act 1913, relating respectively to voting and ranking for payment of dividends, and to the reckoning of majorities and the interruption of prescription, apply, so far as consistent with the 1948 Act as they apply in the sequestration of a bankrupt's estate, subject to verbal adaptation,[65] provided that the holder of a debenture secured by a floating charge is now required to value and deduct the security for the purpose of voting at meetings of creditors of the company.[66]

A creditor accordingly must lodge with the liquidator his claim, supported by accounts and vouchers necessary to prove his debt, and an oath to the effect and taken in the manner required by the Bankruptcy (Scotland) Act 1913, ss. 21 to 24. The court may fix a time or times within which creditors are to prove their debts or claims or to be excluded from the benefit of any distribution made before those debts are proved.[67]

61 *Ibid.* s. 243.
62 *Ibid.* s. 244.
63 *Ibid.* s. 245 (5).
64 1948 Act, s. 316.
65 *Ibid.* s. 318.
66 Companies (Floating Charges and Receivers) (Scotland) Act 1972, s. 11 (6).
67 1948 Act, s. 264.

A creditor dissatisfied with the decision of the liquidator on a question of ranking or preference may appeal to the court.[68]

Appeal lies from any order or decision made in a winding up by the court in the same way as in the exercise of its ordinary jurisdiction by the court.[69]

Voluntary winding up

A company may also be wound up voluntarily if, *inter alia*, it resolves [70] that it cannot by reason of its liabilities continue its business, and that it is advisable to wind up. It may be a members' voluntary winding up,[71] or a creditors' voluntary winding up.[72] The rules as to claims, proof and ranking are the same as in a winding up by the court. But it is incompetent to try to attach to a voluntary winding up the incidents of a judicial winding up.[73] A claim of damages against the company should be constituted in the usual way and not determined by the court incidentally to the liquidation.[74] A creditor in a future or contingent claim may have the liquidator judicially interpelled from dividing surplus assets without making provision for his claims.[75]

Winding up subject to supervision of the court

When a company has passed a resolution for voluntary winding up, the court may make an order that it shall continue but subject to the supervision of the court.[76] A single creditor is not entitled as a matter of right to a supervision order without allegations that other creditors are securing preferable rights or that the management of the company has been improper.[77] But a majority of creditors will secure a supervision order against a minority.[78] The rules as to claims, proof and ranking are the same as in a winding up by the court.

68 1948 Act, s. 245 (5); *cf.* Bankruptcy (Sc.) Act 1913, s. 124. But see *MacLellan* v. *Liqr. of British Patent Buoy Co.*, 1909, 2 S.L.T. 408.
69 1948 Act, s. 277.
70 As to validity of resolution, see *Wilson* v. *McGenn* (1876) 3 R. 474; *Sdenard* v. *Gardner* (1876) 3 R. 577; *Howling's Trs.* v. *Smith* (1905) 7 F. 390.
71 1948 Act, ss. 278–291, 301–310, 316–327.
72 *Ibid.* ss. 278–283, 292–300, 301–310, 316–327.
73 *Clark* v. *Wilson* (1878) 5 R. 867.
74 *Crawford* v. *McCulloch*, 1909 S.C. 1063.
75 *Elphinstone* v. *Monkland Iron Co.* (1886) 13 R.(H.L.) 98; *Collins' Trs.* v. *Borland*, 1907 S.C. 1287.
76 1948 Act, ss. 311–315, 316–327.
77 *Macquisten* v. *Adam, Sons & Co.* (1896) 23 R. 910; *Crawford* v. *Cowper* (1902) 4 F. 849; *Bouboulis* v. *Mann, Macneal & Co.*, 1926 S.C. 637.
78 *Gardner* v. *Hughes* (1883) 10 R. 1138; *Pattison's Ltd.* v. *Kinnear* (1899) 1 F. 551; *Elsmie* v. *Tomatin Spey Distillery Co.* (1906) 8 F. 434.

CHAPTER 19

LANDLORD'S SEQUESTRATION FOR RENT

BY legal implication a landlord has a right of hypothec, or right in security without possession, over moveables brought by his tenant on to the premises let, in security of the rent of the land and buildings, and this right is enforced, if necessary, by a process of sequestration for rent.[1] This is a species of action *in rem*, though applicable to personal estate, a real action or real diligence.[2] It has been described as " an ordinary . . . remedy . . . obtained as a matter of right." [3] By the so-called Hypothec Abolition (Scotland) Act 1880, the right was abolished as regards land exceeding two acres in extent, let for agriculture or pasture. It remains competent in the case of urban subjects [4] and holdings of land not exceeding two acres.

Titles to enforce right

A landlord certainly has title to bring an action for sequestration for rent. Where a tenant has power to sublet and has done so, the tenant may use the process of sequestration for rent against his sub-tenant. Joint proprietors may sue jointly, or each may bring a separate action for his own share of the rent.[5] A liferenter may invoke the remedy.[6] So also may a disponee, whether outright or *ex facie* outright but truly in security,[7] an assignee of the landlord's rights,[8] as may a heritable creditor in possession under a decree of maills and duties.[9] A bare assignation of rents may not entitle the assignee to sequestrate.[10]

Proceedings for sequestration for rent are not affected by the tenant having been sequestrated as notour bankrupt,[11] and are not rendered incompetent or wrongful by the fact that the tenant has an illiquid counterclaim of damages against the landlord.[12]

Jurisdiction

Only the sheriff court of the district where the subjects of let are situated

[1] Stair I, 13, 15; Ersk. II, 6, 60; Bell, *Prin.* § 1244.
[2] *Duncan* v. *Lodijenski* (1904) 6 F. 408, 411.
[3] *Jack* v. *Black*, 1911 S.C. 691, 696, *per* Lord Johnston.
[4] *Clark* v. *Keirs* (1888) 15 R. 458.
[5] *Stewart* v. *Wand* (1842) 4 D. 622.
[6] Rankine on *Leases* (3rd ed.) 369; *Zuill* v. *Buchanan* (1833) 11 S. 682.
[7] *Scottish Heritable Securities Co.* v. *Allan Campbell & Co.* (1876) 3 R. 333.
[8] *Guthrie & McConnachy* v. *Smith* (1880) 8 R. 107; *Duncan* v. *Smith* (1904) 20 Sh.Ct.Rep. 161.
[9] *Stewart*, *supra*; *Forsyth* v. *Aird* (1853) 16 D. 197; *MacRosty* v. *Phillips* (1897) 13 Sh.Ct.Rep. 274; (1898) 14 Sh.Ct.Rep. 69.
[10] Bell, *Prin.* § 1243; *Bannatyne* v. *Finlayson* (1824) 2 S. 625.
[11] *Hardie* v. *Adamson* (1922) 39 Sh.Ct.Rep. 229.
[12] *McLaughlan* v. *Reilly* (1892) 20 R. 41; *Alexander* v. *Campbell's Trs.* (1903) 5 F. 634.

has jurisdiction.[13] The jurisdiction may be exercised in the ordinary court or in the Summary (formerly Small Debt) Court. It does not matter whether one of the parties is resident there or not.[14]

Competency

The right exists for the recovery of rent only and not even for the charge for occupation under what is not a lease,[15] nor for the recovery of rates where the tenant pays a combined sum for rent and rates.

Where the right is available it must be exercised in respect of each year's rent within three months after the last term of payment.[16] There is no security for earlier arrears. The landlord may sequestrate in security of rent still payable, particularly if the tenant is *vergens ad inopiam*, or is displenishing the premises of let, or during the three months after the last term, sequestrate both for the last term's rent and in security of the rent for the term then current.

The right to sequestrate is unaffected by proceedings under the Bankruptcy (Scotland) Act 1913.[17]

Property subject to or exempt from hypothec

The security right extends to all *invecta et illata*, or moveables brought on to or into the subjects of let, including furniture and plenishing, bedding and clothing, books, paintings, jewellery, vehicles, animals, raw materials, goods sold to a customer but left in the seller's shop,[18] a vending machine in a shop,[19] and goods which were there at some time within the period during which the rent accrued.[20]

At common law there were exempt clothing, so far as not excessive for the needs of tenant and family,[21] business books, bills and documents of debt, and papers generally,[22] but probably not tools of trade.[23]

By the House-Letting and Rating (Scotland) Act 1911, s. 10, all bedding material as well as tools and implements of trade used or to be used by the occupier of a small dwelling-house [24] or any member of his family, as the

[13] There appears to be no express statutory exclusion of the jurisdiction of the Court of Session but the action is always brought in the sheriff court: see *Duncan* v. *Lodijenski* (1904) 6 F. 408, 410.

[14] *Duncan*, *supra*.

[15] *Auld* v. *Baird* (1827) 5 S. 246; *Catterns* v. *Tennent* (1834) 1 S. & McL. 694, 717; *Clark* v. *Stewart* (1872) 10 S.L.R. 152; *Heritable Securities Inv. Co.* v. *Wingate* (1880) 7 R. 1094; *Glen* v. *Roy* (1882) 10 R. 239.

[16] Stair I, 13, 15; IV, 25; Ersk. II, 6, 62; Bell, *Comm.* II, 33; *Prin.* § 1240.

[17] 1913 Act, s. 115.

[18] *Ryan* v. *Little*, 1910 S.C. 219: The Sale of Goods Act 1893, by s. 61 (5) does not prejudice the landlord's hypothec or right of sequestration for rent.

[19] *Ditchburn* v. *Dundee Corpn.*, 1971 S.L.T. 218.

[20] *Thomson* v. *Barclay* (1883) 10 R. 694; *Donald* v. *Leitch* (1886) 13 R. 790; *Sawers* v. *Kinnair* (1897) 25 R. 45.

[21] Bell, *Comm.* II, 29; *Prin.* § 1276; *Callander* v. *Campbell* (1703) Mor. 6244.

[22] Bell, *Prin.*, *supra*; *Trowsdale's Trs.* v. *Forcett Ry. Co.* (1870) 9 M. 88.

[23] Graham Stewart on *Diligence*, 466, criticising *Moore* v. *McKean* (1895) 11 Sh.Ct.Rep. 231; *Wright* v. *Kemp* (1896) 12 Sh.Ct.Rep. 180.

[24] The Act applies to " small dwelling-houses " as defined in s. 1 thereof by reference to yearly rent or value in the valuation roll, of £10 or under if the population of the burgh or special

means of his, her or their livelihood, which are in the dwelling-house, and also such further furniture and plenishing in a small dwelling-house as the occupier may select to the value, according to the sheriff officer's inventory, of ten pounds, shall be wholly exempt from the right of hypothec of the owner. In houses falling outwith that Act articles of the enumerated kinds are not protected from sequestration.

Goods in the premises belonging to third parties, held on hire or hire-purchase by the tenant, fall under the hypothec,[25] though possibly not if hired for a temporary purpose only,[26] but goods merely lent to or deposited with him do not necessarily do so,[27] and goods belonging to members of the tenant's family, lodgers, and friends temporarily resident do not.[28] Goods of third parties in a warehouse, cellar or inn are not subject to hypothec, whether there on pledge or deposit, for manufacture, sale or *in transitu*.[29] Goods held by a tenant on sale or return probably fall under hypothec.[30]

The landlord has been held entitled to assume that *invecta et illata* belong to the tenant and to sequestrate and inventory everything on the premises.[31] In so far as goods to which hypothec does not extend are included in the inventory the owner thereof should appear and seek to have them withdrawn.[32]

Until sequestration is effected goods can be freely sold or otherwise dealt with by the tenant,[33] and even after sequestration goods which are the tenant's stock in trade may be sold and dealt with; if the landlord wishes to prevent this he must obtain judicial warrant to have the premises closed and the goods removed.[34]

Warrant to carry back

If the landlord fears that articles subject to hypothec are going to be removed from the subjects so as to defeat his right, he may interdict the removal.[35] If articles subject to hypothec have been removed before sequestration has been granted the landlord may, by minute endorsed on

district is less than 20,000; £15 or under if 20,000 to 50,000, and £21 or under if the population is 50,000 or upwards, but excluding dwelling-houses let with land or with a shop, workshop, stable or byre. Population is determined by the Census of 1911. The monetary values were raised by 25 per cent. by the Increase of Rent and Mortgage Interest (Restrictions) Act 1920, ss. 16 and 18.

25 Bell, *Comm.* II, 31; *Prin.* § 1276; *Wauchope* v. *Gall* (1805) Hume, 227; *Stewart* v. *Bell*, May 31, 1814, F.C.; *Penson* v. *Robertson*, June 6, 1820, F.C.; *Nelmes* v. *Ewing* (1883) 11 R. 193; *Bell* v. *Andrews* (1885) 12 R. 961; *Ditchburn* v. *Dundee Corpn.*, 1971 S.L.T. 218.

26 *Adam* v. *Sutherland* (1863) 2 M. 6.

27 Contrast *Wilson* v. *Spankie*, Nov. 12, 1814, F.C.; *Bell* v. *Andrews*, *supra*; with *Cowan* v. *Perry* (1804) Bell, *Comm.* II, 31; *Gow & Shepherd & Anderson* (1808) Hume, 517; *Adam* v. *Sutherland*, *supra*.

28 Bell, *supra*.

29 Bell, *Prin.*, *supra*; *Pulsometer Eng. Co.* v. *Gracie* (1887) 14 R. 316.

30 *Macdonald* v. *Westren* (1888) 15 R. 988; *cf.* *Brown* v. *Marr* (1880) 7 R. 427.

31 *Adam*, *supra*.

32 *McKechnie* v. *D. Montrose* (1853) 15 D. 623; *Lindsay* v. *E. Wemyss* (1872) 10 M. 708.

33 Bell, *Comm.* II, 31.

34 Bell, *Prin.* § 1276; More, Notes, 83, Rankine, *Leases*, 405.

35 *Preston* v. *Gregor* (1845) 7 D. 942.

the initial writ or lodged separately, obtain warrant to have them brought back to the premises, there to be sequestrated and inventoried.[36] This is an extraordinary remedy.[37] Warrant may, exceptionally, be granted *de plano* or, and, preferably, the minute may be intimated to the tenant and to any third party involved and a short opportunity given him or them to explain their conduct before warrant is granted.[38] The intimation should be such notice as will give the tenant an opportunity of appearing to explain his action, and to oppose the application, and, if necessary, to find security.[39] A warrant without notice is one to be granted only with great care, and after deliberation and a full statement of the circumstances which are said to make it necessary.[40] Warrant is justifiable only if the articles were still subject to the landlord's hypothec. Thus moveables removed from a house between 15th May and 28th May [41] have never been in the premises for the purposes of rent accruing after Whitsunday.[42] But where sequestration was applied for between 15th and 28th May in respect of rent due in advance on 15th May and not then paid it was held competent.[43] A pursuer who acts on a warrant obtained without intimation to the defender acts at his own risk and is liable in damages if the step was taken unjustifiably.[44]

If the goods have been removed by a purchaser or a poinding creditor warrant to carry back suffices and an action for restitution of the goods or payment of their value is unnecessary.[45] If they have been sold by auction and the auctioneer holds the price, he may be required to consign it.[46] If they have been transferred to other rented premises and thus fallen under the hypothec of another landlord they may still be brought back.[47]

Procedure

The initial writ in a process of landlord's sequestration usually craves warrant to sequestrate for payment of rent due and unpaid, and/or in security of rent to become due, with interest from the term of payment, and expenses, warrant to sell the sequestrated goods and to pay the pursuer from the proceeds, decree against the defender for any balance due, an order to replenish the subjects let if insufficient effects are left

36 *McLellan* v. *Graham* (1841) 16 F.C. 1209; *McKechnie* v. *D. Montrose* (1853) 15 D. 623; *Brown* v. *Halley* (1895) 3 S.L.T. 22.
37 *Jack* v. *Black*, 1911 S.C. 691, 696, *per* Lord Johnston.
38 *Johnston* v. *Young* (1890) 18 R.(J.) 6; *Gray* v. *Weir* (1891) 19 R. 25; *McLaughlan* v. *Reilly* (1892) 20 R. 41; *Shearer* v. *Nicoll*, 1935 S.L.T. 313.
39 *Jack*, *supra*, 697.
40 *Johnston*, *supra*, approved in *Jack*, *supra*.
41 The term day under the Removal Terms (Scotland) Act 1881.
42 *Thomson* v. *Barclay* (1883) 10 R. 694; *Sawers* v. *Kinnair* (1897) 25 R. 45; *McQueen* v. *Armstrong* (1908) 24 Sh.Ct.Rep. 377.
43 *Henderson* v. *Huzzard* (1934) 50 Sh.Ct.Rep. 300.
44 *Johnston*, *supra*; *Gray* v. *Weir* (1891) 19 R. 25; *McLaughlan*, *supra*; *Jack* v. *Black*, 1911 S.C. 691.
45 *Cooper* v. *Bone* (1823) 2 S. 511.
46 *Middleton* v. *Macbeth* (1894) 11 Sh.Ct.Rep. 9; *Menzies* v. *Templeton* (1895) 12 Sh.Ct.Rep. 323.
47 *Christie* v. *Macpherson*, Dec. 14, 1814, F.C.

thereon after the sequestration and, failing that, warrant to eject the defender and to relet the premises. Unless a caveat has been lodged the sheriff normally by his first deliverance sequestrates the tenant's effects and grants warrant to inventory and secure them.[48] All warrants to sequestrate, inventory, sell, eject or relet are deemed to include authority, if need be, to open shut and lockfast places for the purpose of carrying such warrants into execution.[48]

A sheriff officer then proceeds to the premises and in presence of a witness makes an inventory of articles therein subject to hypothec. It is not necessary to appraise the items in the inventory.[49] The inventory may be returned annexed to the initial writ with the sheriff officer's execution of service, or there may be a separate inventory specifying the articles. A copy of the inventory should be left with the tenant or an inmate of the house. The inventory is conclusive as to what articles have been sequestrated.[50]

Defences

If the tenant opposes the necessity of sequestration, as where he claims to exercise a right of retention of rent, he must lodge defences in the usual way. The petition may be dismissed if the landlord has been in material breach of the conditions of let, as by not giving the tenant full possession of the subjects [51] or otherwise.[52] If any breach is less material caution or consignation may be ordered.[53] If the tenant has justifiably abandoned the premises as uninhabitable, the landlord cannot sequestrate for rent for the period during which the premises were not occupied.[54]

The sequestration must be recalled if it is illegal, or incompetent, or if the rent is consigned or caution found for payment of it.

Effect of sequestration

Sequestration does not affect the right of property in the goods inventoried, but merely identifies them and transfers them notionally into the custody of the court.[55] Accordingly a tenant who interferes with articles sequestrated is liable to fine or imprisonment for breach of sequestration. A third party who knowingly participates in a breach of sequestration is liable to the same penalties, and also liable to the landlord for the appraised value of the articles removed, or, it may be, for the whole amount of rent due by the tenant.[56] He may alternatively petition the sheriff to have the goods restored to him.[57]

48 Sheriff Courts (Sc.) Act 1907, Sched. I, r. 105. By r. 7, such a warrant must be signed by the sheriff personally.
49 *Lochgilphead Town Council* v. *McIntyre* (1940) 59 Sh.Ct.Rep. 178.
50 *Horsburgh* v. *Morton* (1825) 3 S. 596.
51 *Kilmarnock Gas Light Co.* v. *Smith* (1872) 11 M. 58; *Tennent's Trs.* v. *Maxwell* (1880) 17 S.L.R. 463.
52 *Guthrie* v. *Shearer* (1873) 1 R. 181.
53 *Gray* v. *Renton* (1840) 3 D. 203.
54 *Campbell* v. *Boswall* (1839) 1 D. 1023.
55 Bell, *Prin.* § 1244.
56 *Jack* v. *McCaig* (1880) 7 R. 465.
57 *Jack, supra*, 467.

Breach of sequestration

Breach of sequestration is a defiance of the authority of the court and any interference with or dealing with articles sequestrated may be made the subject of an application to the court, narrating the circumstances and craving the court to ordain the defender to appear and to restore the articles or find caution for or consign the rent. It also craves the imposition of a fine on the defender and, failing payment of the fine, imprisonment, and accordingly requires the concurrence of the procurator-fiscal.

If the defender does not appear, it is presumed that his breach of sequestration is wilful and warrant to imprison may be granted. If, however, he tenders some reasonable excuse and satisfies the court that his breach was not wilful, the penalty may be waived.[58]

It is not a branch of sequestration to continue to use the articles.[59]

Warrant of sale

Once the term of payment of the rent due has passed [60] without payment or consignation the sheriff may grant warrant to sell so much of the sequestrated effects as will satisfy the pursuer's claim for rent, interest and expenses. If sequestration was granted in security the case is normally continued until the date for payment. If it was granted both for payment and in security the sheriff may appoint a fit person to take charge of the sequestrated effects, or may require the tenant to find caution that they shall be made forthcoming.[61]

The sheriff may order the sequestrated effects to be sold at the sight of an officer of court or other person named.[62] Until warrant of sale is granted it is competent to apply for interdict against the sale, but it is incompetent thereafter.[63]

The sale must not be conducted without regard to the interests of the tenant, and if it is, a claim of damages lies.[64] The sequestrated effects must be sold to the extent necessary to satisfy the landlord's claim and for his expenses, and not materially more.[65]

When a sale follows, it must be reported within fourteen days and the pursuer must lodge the roup rolls or certified copies thereof and a state of the debt.[66] The auditor taxes the accounts, the sheriff approves the sale, the debt and expenses are paid to the landlord and the balance is paid to the tenant.

58 *Laing* v. *Harper* (1829) 7 S. 335; *Kippen* v. *Oppenheim* (1846) 8 D. 957.

59 *McGlashan* v. *D. Athole*, June 29, 1819, F.C.; *Miller* v. *Paterson* (1831) 9 S. 792; *Gordon* v. *Suttie* (1836) 14 S. 954. See also *Gordon* v. *Fiddler* (1823) 2 S. 486.

60 *Dow* v. *Hay* (1784) Mor. 6202; *Wells* v. *Proudfoot* (1800) Hume 225.

61 Sheriff Courts (Sc.) Act 1907, Sched. I, r. 109.

62 *Ibid.* r. 106.

63 *Lindsay* v. *E. Wemyss* (1872) 10 M. 708.

64 *Robertson* v. *Galbraith* (1857) 19 D. 1016.

65 *Cargill* v. *Baxter* (1829) 7 S. 662; *Galloway* v. *McPherson* (1830) 8 S. 539; *Robertson, supra.*

66 *Ibid.* r. 107.

In the interlocutor approving the report of sale, or by separate interlocutor, the sheriff may give decree against the defender for any balance remaining due.[67]

Third party's rights in goods sequestrated

A third party, such as the owner of goods held on loan or hire or hire-purchase or credit-sale terms by the tenant, may have an interest, even a right of property, in the subjects being sequestrated. A sheriff officer making an inventory is entitled to proceed on the basis that all subjects in the premises let are the property of the tenant, and to inventory them accordingly. He is not bound to give any effect to a mere oral intimation by the tenant or another person, such as a lodger, that goods belong to him. The proper course for a third party is to intervene in the process by minute, intimate his interest and ask the court to exclude the articles in question from the sale,[68] or if warrant to sell has been granted, to bring a suspension, or to petition for interdict of the sale *quoad* the items claimed, narrating his title to the articles in question,[69] or to go to the judge of the roup and ask that the article in dispute should not be put up until the other articles have been sold.[70] If the third party does not intervene in such a way he cannot complain if his property is sold. The creditor is entitled to go on selling until his debt is fully covered. If intimation, even informal, be made that particular items are claimed by third parties as their property, it seems prudent to reserve them to a late stage of the sale so that, if possible, items sold are all the undisputed property of the debtor himself.[70]

Registration

All sequestrations for rent must be registered in the Register of Sequestrations prescribed by the Hypothec Amendment (Scotland) Act 1867, s. 7.[71]

Superior's sequestration for feuduty

A superior has a hypothec, similar to but preferable to the landlord's hypothec for rent, for his feuduties over the *invecta et illata* in urban subjects and holdings not exceeding two acres.[72]

67 *Ibid.* r. 108.
68 *Lindsay* v. *E. Wemyss* (1872) 10 M. 708; *Hoare* v. *Mackay* (1905) 13 S.L.T. 588; *McIntosh* v. *Potts* (1905) 7 F. 765; *Ryan* v. *Little*, 1910 S.C. 219; *Boni* v. *McIver* (1933) 49 Sh.Ct.Rep. 191.
69 *Jack* v. *Waddell's Trs.*, 1918 S.C. 73.
70 *McIntosh, supra*, 768. See also *Ditchburn* v. *Dundee Corpn.*, 1971 S.L.T. 218.
71 Amended by S.R. & O. 1933, No. 48.
72 Stair II, 4, 7; Ersk. II, 6, 63; Bell, *Comm.* II, 26; *Prin.* § 698; *Stormonth* v. *Andersons* (1675) Mor. 10514; *Yuille* v. *Lawrie & Douglas* (1823) 2 S. 140.

CHAPTER 20

POINDING OF THE GROUND

POINDING of the ground [1] is "a combination of a real petitory action and a real diligence" [2] and is quite different in nature and effect from personal poinding.[2] It has also been said to be the "diligence by which the creditor in a *debitum fundi* . . . can attach the moveables on the ground in so far as these belong to or are available to his debtor or his successor in the lands, but that only so long as they remain thereon and have not been transferred to a *bona fide* purchaser or carried off under completed diligence." [3] The legal position is that the creditor in a *debitum fundi* has a kind of floating charge over the moveables on the ground affected which he can make effective at any time by serving a summons of poinding of the ground and thereby attaching the actual moveables then on the ground.[4] The creditor is not trying to acquire a preference but is rather asking for declarator of a right which he already has.[5] A heritable creditor in raising an action of poinding of the ground does not seek to acquire a preference, but merely to give effect to a preference already existing,[6] and the action may proceed though the summons is served after the commencement of sequestration [7] or winding up.[6] But in competition with the trustee in the debtor's sequestration the poinding of the ground is available only for the current term's feuduty and one year's arrears,[8] but this restriction does not apply against the trustee in an English bankruptcy.[9]

Jurisdiction

The action is competent both in the Court of Session and in the Sheriff Court.[10]

Title and interest to sue

The action is competent only to a real creditor holding a *debitum fundi* over lands.[11] The proper title is infeftment in the subjects, but a pursuer

[1] See generally Stair II, 5, 8; III, 2, 13; IV, 23 and 47; Bankt. II, 5, 7 and 20; Ersk. II, 8, 33; IV, 1, 11; Bell, *Comm.* I, 724; II, 56; *Prin.* § 699, 914, 922, 2285; Ross, *Lect.* II, 392; *Graham Stewart on Diligence*, 491.

[2] *Royal Bank* v. *Bain* (1877) 4 R. 985, 989, *per* Lord Deas, who outlines the history of the remedy. See also *Bell* v. *Cadell* (1831) 10 S. 100; *Campbell's Trs.* v. *Paul* (1835) 13 S. 237; *Campbell* v. *Turner & Son's Trs.* (1910) 48 S.L.R. 193.

[3] *Graham Stewart on Diligence*, 493.

[4] *Royal Bank*, *supra*; *Traill's Trs.* v. *Free Church*, 1915 S.C. 655, 666, 671.

[5] *Lyons* v. *Anderson* (1880) 8 R. 24, 25.

[6] *Athole Hydropathic Co. Liqdr.* v. *Scottish Provincial Assce. Co.* (1868) 13 R. 818.

[7] *Dick's Tr.* v. *Whyte's Tr.* (1879) 6 R. 586; *Campbell* v. *Edinburgh Parish Council*, 1911 S.C. 280.

[8] *Campbell*, *supra.*

[9] *Scottish Union and National Ins. Co.* v. *James* (1886) 13 R. 928.

[10] Ross, *Lect.* II, 454; *Comm.*, II, 57; *Prin.* § 2285.

[11] Ersk. IV, 1, 11; Bell, *Prin.* § 2285.

may sue if he has a personal title connecting himself with the infeftment constituting the *debitum fundi*, such as being the executor of the superior, or the executor or assignee of a heritable creditor duly infeft.[12]

It is accordingly competent to a superior for feuduties,[13] though not, after he has sold the superiority, for the recovery of arrears,[14] to the creditor in a real burden secured over land,[15] the creditor in a ground annual,[16] the creditor in a bond and disposition in security,[17] or a standard security, a creditor who has obtained a decree of maills and duties,[18] and an assignee in security of a liferent of heritage.[19]

It is not competent to a proprietor against his own tenants,[20] nor to a heritable creditor holding lands under an *ex facie* absolute disposition qualified by a back letter,[21] nor to a creditor under a bond and assignation in security of a registered long lease,[22] nor to a proper liferenter in possession,[23] nor to an adjudger in possession.[24]

Distinct parties having separate securities over the same land do not have sufficient community of interest to entitle them to join in one action.[25]

The pursuer must either be infeft or be able to connect himself with an infeftment, as being the executor,[26] or assignee.[27] A case always regarded as exceptional in the disposition of land under burden of a debt in favour of a third party, where the latter can poind the ground though not infeft.[28] It is sufficient that the title is prima facie good.[29] A pursuer uninfeft at the date of citation cannot create his title by subsequently taking infeftment,[30] and he loses his title to the remedy if before citation he has become uninfeft, even though reserving a right to arrears due.[31]

12 *Waugh* v. *Jamieson* (1676) Mor. 5453; *Tweedie* v. *Beattie* (1836) 14 S. 337; *Marquess of Ailsa* v. *Jeffrey* (1859) 21 D. 492, 503.

13 Stair IV, 23, 5; Bankt. II, 5, 20; Ersk. IV, 1, 11; Bell, *Prin.* § 2285; *Morrison's Trs.* v. *Webster* (1878) 5 R. 800; *Stewart* v. *Gibson's Tr.* (1880) 8 R. 270.

14 *Scottish Heritages Co.* v. *N.B. Property Investment Co.* (1885) 12 R. 550, but questioned in *Maxwell's Trs.* v. *Bothwell School Board* (1893) 20 R. 958.

15 Ersk. IV, 1, 11; Bell, *Comm.* I, 732; *Prin.* § 922, 2285; *A.* v. *B.* (n.d.) Mor. 10550; *Wilson* v. *Fraser* (1822) 1 S. 292; 2 Sh.App. 162; *Anstruther* v. *Anstruther* (1838) 16 S. 1132; *Stewart, supra.*

16 *Bell's Trs.* v. *Copeland* (1896) 23 R. 650.

17 Ersk. IV, 1, 11; Bell, *Prin.* § 914, 2285; *Thomson* v. *Scoular* (1882) 9 R. 430; *Urquhart* v. *Macleod's Tr.* (1883) 10 R. 991.

18 *Henderson* v. *Wallace* (1896) 23 R. 634.

19 *Scottish Union and National Ins. Co.* v. *James* (1886) 13 R. 928; *cf. Scottish Heritable Security Co.* v. *Allan Campbell & Co.* (1876) 3 R. 333.

20 Ersk. II, 5, 42; IV, 1, 11.

21 *Scottish Heritable Security Co.* v. *Allan Campbell & Co.* (1876) 3 R. 333; *Scottish Union and National Ins. Co., supra*; see also *Henderson* v. *Wallace* (1875) 2 R. 272, 276.

22 *Luke* v. *Wallace* (1896) 23 R. 634.

23 Ersk. IV, 1, 11; Ross, *Lect.* II, 431.

24 *Henderson* v. *Wallace* (1875) 2 R. 272.

25 *Douglas* v. *Tait* (1884) 12 R. 10.

26 *Waugh* v. *Jamieson* (1676) Mor. 5453; *Andrews* v. *Laurie* (1849) 12 D. 344; *Marquess of Ailsa* v. *Jeffrey* (1859) 21 D. 492.

27 *Tweedie* v. *Beattie* (1836) 14 S. 337.

28 Ross, *Lect.* II, 436; *Wilson* v. *Fraser* (1822) 2 Sh.App. 162.

29 *Cf. Borthwick* v. *E. Crawford* (1676) 2 B.S. 199; *Anstruther* v. *Anstruther* (1838) 16 S. 1132; *Marquess of Ailsa* v. *Jeffrey, supra.*

30 *Hardie* v. *Horn* (1888) 4 S.L.R. 409.

31 *Scottish Heritages Co., supra.*

Defender

The action should be directed against the debtor as proprietor or vassal of the lands and, if there be any, the tenants or possessors of the lands. Each must be called in his proper character.[32] If the proprietor has died his apparent heir should be called for his interest, but it is unnecessary to constitute the debt against him. If the lands have been sold the purchaser should be called for his interest. A heritable creditor has title to defend [33] and other security holders over the same subjects should be called as defenders for their interest.[34]

It has been held competent against a firm, although the ground and buildings affected by the bond and disposition in security were feudally vested in two of the partners as individuals [35] or as trustees for their firm.[36]

The action is incompetent against an occupier who is not liable for rent, even though he be bound to pay for his occupancy.[37]

In an action by postponed bondholders first bondholders are entitled to appear and insist on having their preference reserved on the face of the decree, but they are liable for the expenses of their appearance.[38] A proprietor cannot object to decree passing in absence against his tenants.[39]

Competency

The action is competent, as stated, only to the holder of a *debitum fundi*, and at the time the action is raised the debt payable from the heritage must be actually due, or the debtor must be averred to be *vergens ad inopiam*, or other justification must be alleged.[40] Action is competent for a payment current but not yet due, but payment cannot be demanded until the stipulated term arrives.[41] A creditor under a bond may bring an action for principal, arrears of interest, and interest currently becoming due. In such a case the action has the effect of converting the arrears into a principal sum carrying interest, itself secured as *debitum fundi*.

It is directed against the vassal or proprietor [42] or against him and the tenants or possessors of the subjects,[43] and the conclusions vary according as the defender is in possession, or as he possesses mediately through tenants. It seeks warrant to poind and distrain all moveable goods and effects poindable or distrainable which are or shall happen to be upon the grounds of the lands and others described and contained in the subjects,

32 *Brown* v. *Scott* (1859) 22 D. 273; *Scottish Heritages Co., supra.*
33 *Scottish Heritages Co., supra.*
34 *Scottish Heritages Co., supra*; *Young's Tr.* v. *Hill's Tr.* (1893) 1 S.L.T. 357.
35 *Mackenzie's Trs.* v. *Smith* (1883) 20 S.L.R. 351.
36 *Kelly's Tr.* v. *Moncreiff's Tr.*, 1920 S.C. 461.
37 *Brown* v. *Scott* (1859) 22 D. 273.
38 *Young's Trs.* v. *Hill's Tr.* (1893) 1 S.L.T. 357.
39 *Buchan* v. *Scott* (1829) 7 S. 296.
40 *Stewart* v. *Gibson's Trs.* (1880) 8 R. 270.
41 *Stewart, supra.*
42 R.C. Form 1 (27a).
43 R.C. Form 2 (27b).

and for payment thereof to the pursuer to the amount due, including, where appropriate, as in a bond in common form, liquidate penalty and termly failures. The only personal conclusion is for expenses.

In the sheriff court the crave is for warrant to poind and the decree is authority for the poinding.[44]

Poinding of the ground in relation to sequestration

The Act and Warrant of confirmation in favour of the trustee in the sequestration vests in him the whole property of the debtor, " subject always to such preferable securities as existed at the date of the sequestration, and are not null and reducible, and the creditors' right to poind the ground." [45] A creditor may accordingly poind the ground, notwithstanding the sequestration of the debtor. But no poinding of the ground which has not been carried into execution by sale of the effects sixty days before the date of the sequestration, shall be available in any question with the trustee, except to the extent of the interest on the debt for the current half-yearly term, and for the arrears of interest for one year immediately before that. Poinding of the ground may be executed after sequestration but is available, in competition with the trustee, to that limited extent only.[46]

But the restriction of the heritable creditor's right does not apply to the creditors of the bankrupt's ancestor, and it has been held that a poinding of the ground executed by a heritable creditor of an ancestor after sequestration of the estates of the heir in possession was effectual to attach moveables thereon belonging to the bankrupt as if there had been no sequestration.[47] Whether the creditors of the ancestor are personal or secured creditors on the heritable estate they are to stand just exactly in the same position as they would have done if the estate had not been vested in the way here provided in the trustee in the sequestration.[48] The Act and Warrant in favour of the trustee is provided to operate in favour of the ancestor's creditors as a complete diligence, probably to the effect of vesting the trustee with the general estate of the ancestor for behoof of the ancestor's creditors generally, and to no other effect, so that the moveables in question are not carried by the statute to the trustee for behoof of the ancestor's creditors.[49]

Procedure and effect

Service of the summons on the defender attaches the effects of the defender, and in appropriate cases, of his tenants, on the subjects affected, and this has the effect of interpelling the defender, or his tenants, or anyone on his or their behalf, or anyone with knowledge of the action, from

[44] *Kennedy* v. *Ramsay's Trs.* (1852) 14 D. 513.
[45] Bankruptcy (Sc.) Act 1913, s. 97 (1) and (2).
[46] *Ibid.* s. 114.
[47] *Ibid.* s. 97 (2). *Millar's Trs.* v. *Millar & Son's Tr.* (1886) 13 R. 543.
[48] *Millar's Trs., supra,* 549, *per* L.P. Inglis.
[49] *Millar's Trs., supra,* 550, *per* Lord Shand.

dealing with them.[50] It attaches only moveables actually then on the ground, and not moveable property of the defender but then elsewhere,[50] even though brought on to the ground subsequently,[51] or moveables removed from the ground prior to service of the summons, even if to prevent their being attached.[52] If the removal were done wrongfully to defeat the creditor's diligence, he may have a remedy in damages against the person removing the goods.[53] It attaches also only such moveables as are the property of the debtor, or his tenant, or occupier, and not the property of third parties.[54] Hence the goods of a lender or lessor to him are not attached, nor those of any stranger who has no connection with the lands,[55] but the mere fact that a third party's moveables have been erroneously included in the execution of a poinding of the ground does not entitle him to claim damages from the poinding creditor.[56]

Citation of a tenant is not equivalent to an intimation of an assignation to the rents contained in the bond, so as to interpel the tenant from paying to the landlord future rents as they fall due.[57]

Assignability of preferential right

The preferential right over the moveables created by serving a summons in an action of poinding of the ground may be assigned to another creditor. Thus where a first bondholder acquired a preference over the moveables by serving such a summons and obtained payment by selling the heritage, and assigned his preference to the second bondholder, it was held, in a question between the trustee on the debtor's sequestrated estates and the second bondholder, that the first bondholder was bound so far as possible to take payment from the moveables or to assign his preference to the second bondholder and as he has taken payment from the heritage the second bondholder had right to his preference over the moveables.[58]

Decree and execution

Decree in the action in the Court of Session is merely a warning of intention to, and a warrant to, apply for letters of poinding. In the Sheriff Court decree itself is direct authority for poinding.[59]

In an action by second bondholders it has been held that the first

[50] *Campbell's Trs.* v. *Paul* (1835) 13 S. 237; *Barstow* v. *Mowbray* (1852) 18 D. 846; *Lyons* v. *Anderson* (1880) 8 R. 24; *Thomson* v. *Scoular* (1882) 9 R. 430; *Traill's Trs., infra.*
[51] *Thomson, supra.*
[52] *Urquhart* v. *Macleod's Trs.* (1883) 10 R. 991; *Traill's Trs.* v. *Free Church,* 1915 S.C. 655.
[53] *Urquhart, supra.*
[54] Ersk. IV, 1, 13; Bell, *Comm.* II, 57; *Brown* v. *Scott* (1860) 22 D. 273; *Thomson, supra*; *Kelly's Tr.* v. *Moncreiff's Tr.,* 1920 S.C. 461.
[55] *Collet* v. *Master of Balmerinoch* (1679) Mor. 10550; *Campbell's Trs.* v. *Paul* (1835) 13 S. 237; *Kelly's Tr.* v. *Moncreiff's Tr.,* 1920 S.C. 461, 466.
[56] *Nelmes* v. *Gillies* (1883) 10 R. 890.
[57] *Royal Bank* v. *Dixon* (1868) 6 M. 995.
[58] *Nicol's Tr.* v. *Hill* (1889) 16 R. 416.
[59] *Kennedy* v. *Ramsay's Trs.* (1852) 14 D. 513.

bondholders were entitled to appear and to insist on having their preference reserved on the face of the decree, on payment of the expenses of their appearance.[60]

Charge

No charge is necessary on the extract decree as preliminary to poinding and sale, unless there is decree for expenses, because there is no personal conclusion in the summons.[61]

Poinding

In a Court of Session action decree is warrant for obtaining letters of poinding under the Signet, which are obtained on application to the Petition Department of the offices of the Court, and grant authority to poind the moveables on the ground conform to the decree.[62] In a sheriff court action the extract decree is itself warrant to poind without any separate precept from the sheriff.[63] But poinding cannot proceed till fifteen days after decree, as being the time within which the debtor may satisfy the decree or have it suspended, or in the sheriff court, seven days.[64] Poinding under a decree of poinding of the ground, unlike personal poinding, may be executed although the original debtor has died, or the lands have been transferred to a singular successor, or the tenants have changed; there is no need to reconstitute the debt, or transfer it, against the heir or successor, because there are no personal conclusions in the action, but it is directed against the moveables on the lands only.[65]

The poinding proceeds in the same way as in a personal poinding.

The goods attachable by poinding include all corporeal moveables on the ground which belong to the debtor, to the extent of the full sum due. Goods which are the joint property of the debtor and of another may not be poinded for the debt of one.[66] It attaches only goods actually on the ground at the time of serving the summons.[67] Moveables belonging to the debtor on another, though adjacent, property are not attached.[68] If the debtor has sold the subjects, moveables on the ground belonging to the purchaser or his tenants may be attached.

Poinding attaches also the moveables belonging to tenants in actual possession of the subjects, but only to the extent of any arrears of rent due

[60] *Young's Trs.* v. *Hill's Tr.* (1893) 1 S.L.T. 357.
[61] Ersk. IV, 1, 12; Bell, *Prin.* § 2285.
[62] Ross, *Lect.* II, 453; Bell, *Comm.* II, 57; *Prin.* § 2285.
[63] *Kennedy* v. *Ramsay's Trs.* (1852) 14 D. 513.
[64] Stair, IV, 23, 17; Bankt., II, 5, 7; Ross, *Lect.* II, 436; Bell, *Comm.* II, 57; *Prin.* § 2285.
[65] Stair, IV, 23, 14; Bankt., *supra*; Ersk., IV, 1, 13; Bell, *supra*; *Forrester* (1612) Mor. 10543; *Keir* v. *Hepburn* (1624) Mor. 10544; *Watson* v. *Reid* (1628) Mor. 10545; *Adamson* v. *Balmerinoch* (1662) Mor. 10547; *Crighton* v. *E. Nithsdale* (1695) 4 B.S. 262.
[66] *Fleming* v. *Twaddle* (1828) 7 S. 92; *Byng* v. *Campbell* (1894) 21 R. 1096; *Glen* v. *Cameron* (1896) 3 S.L.T. 231.
[67] *Urquhart* v. *McLeod's Tr.* (1883) 10 R. 991.
[68] Stair, IV, 23, 20; *Stewarts* v. *Home* (1629) Mor. 10545.

by them and of rent due for the current term, even though the date for payment has not arrived.[69]

Moveables belonging to third parties, though on the ground, cannot be attached by poinding. This covers goods hired by tenants [70] or in a tenant's possession by virtue of contract,[71] or deposited in cellars rented from a tenant.[72] Goods sold by a debtor or tenant to a third party but undelivered will normally be unattachable, the property having passed to the purchaser.[73] Goods brought by the debtor on to the ground after the service of the summons are not attachable.[74]

Effect of poinding

As in the case of personal poinding effected after decree and charge, the poinding of goods notionally puts the goods in the charge of the court and a person interfering with or carrying off the poinded effects is liable for contempt of court.[75] At common law the poinder may sue the intromitter for damages, which may amount to the whole value of his debt.[76] The debtor may still use poinded goods if this is necessary, *e.g.* for preservation of live-stock, whether poinded or not. The debtor has a title to sell to a third party and a third party who purchases in good faith is not an intromitter or liable for contempt of court,[77] but the debtor is acting in defiance of the prohibition implied in the poinding. If the purchaser becomes aware of the circumstances he must not pay the price to the debtor but hold it subject to the poinding creditor's claim.[78] If he has paid the price in good faith he is discharged but the debtor must account for it.

Execution of poinding

When poinding has been effected the officer must complete an execution stating the date, warrant for the poinding, names of the creditor and debtor, the amount of the debt,[79] and stating the place, the effects poinded, the names and designations of the valuators, the person in whose hands the goods were left, and the delivery of the schedule of poinding to the possessor.[80] It should be subscribed on each page by the officer and the two valuators as witnesses to the poinding.

[69] Stair II, 5, 9; IV, 23, 14–20; Ersk. II, 8, 33; Ross, *Lect.* II, 437; Bell, *Comm.* II, 56; *L. Pitfoddels* (1674) Mor. 10548; *Fotheringham* v. *L. Balmerinoch* (1676) Mor. 10549; *Collet* v. *L. Balmerinoch* (1679) Mor. 10550; *Lovett's Tr.* v. *Wilson* (1896) 3 S.L.T. 423.

[70] *Nelmes* v. *Gillies* (1883) 10 R. 890.

[71] Ersk. IV, 1, 13; Bell, *Comm.* II, 57; *Collet, supra*; *Brown* v. *Scott* (1859) 22 D. 273.

[72] *Collet, supra.*

[73] Sale of Goods Act 1893, ss. 17–18.

[74] *Thomson* v. *Scoular* (1882) 9 R. 430.

[75] Personal Diligence Act 1838, s. 30; *Brown* v. *Stephenson* (1849) 11 D. 1083; *Jaffrey* v. *Duncan* (1852) 14 D. 442; *Wilson* v. *McKeller* (1896) 24 R. 254.

[76] *Arnot* v. *Dowie* (1863) 2 M. 119.

[77] *Henderson* v. *Grant* (1896) 23 R. 659, 667.

[78] *Turner* v. *Mitchell & Rae* (1884) 2 Guthrie Sel.Sh.Ct.Cas. 152.

[79] Omission to do so is fatal: *Sangster* v. *Burness* (1857) 20 D. 355.

[80] Personal Diligence Act 1838, s. 25; see also *Renfrew & Brown* v. *Glasgow Mags.* (1861) 23 D. 505.

Report of poinding

Within eight days, unless cause can be shown why report could not be made earlier, the poinding must be reported to the court.[81] When this has been done the sheriff may give orders, if he deems it necessary, for the security of the goods poinded or, if they include perishables, order immediate sale.

Sale

The sheriff may on the application of the creditor grant warrant to sell the poinded goods by public roup when, where, by whom, and with such public notice of the sale, as he may specify as expedient.[82] Application must be made without unreasonable delay and the diligence may be held to have fallen if there has been delay.[83] The sale may be not less than eight nor more than twenty days after publication of the notice of sale.[84] A copy of the warrant of sale must be served on the debtor and, if he be a different person, on the actual holder of the poinded effects, at least six days before the date of sale, save in the case of perishables.[85] In granting warrant the sheriff's function is ministerial only, and the only objections he may consider are as to the liability of particular articles to be poinded and sold, the ownership of the poinded articles,[86] and patent objections to the regularity of the diligence. At the sale the poinded goods are offered for sale at the appraised value and must be sold if this is offered, but cannot be sold for less.[87] The poinder, or any other creditor, may purchase.[88] If no purchaser offers at least the appraised sum, the judge of the roup must deliver so much of the goods as, at their appraised value, satisfy the debt, interest and expenses, to the poinding creditor.[89]

The judge of the roup must, within eight days after the sale or delivery of the goods to the creditor, report it to the sheriff and, where goods have been sold, lodge the roup rolls or certified copies thereof, and an account of the sum arising from and of the expenses of the sale, which sum the sheriff may order to be lodged with the sheriff clerk.[90] Where there are no other claimants than the poinding creditor and any conjoined with him, the sheriff must have the expenses taxed by the auditor of court and the amount available for the creditor found. The sheriff then approves of the report and orders payment to the creditors of the balance so far as neces-

[81] Personal Diligence Act 1838, s. 25; *Sampson* v. *McCubbin* (1822) 1 S. 381; *Lyle* v. *Greig* (1827) 5 S. 785; *Munro* v. *Hogg* (1830) 9 S. 171; *Miller* v. *Stewart* (1835) 13 S. 483.

[82] Personal Diligence Act 1838, s. 26. See also *Kewly* v. *Andrew* (1843) 5 D. 860; *McVicar* v. *Kerr* (1857) 19 D. 948; *McKinnon* v. *Hamilton* (1866) 4 M. 852.

[83] *Scoullar* v. *Campbell* (1824) 3 S. 50; *Henderson* v. *Grant* (1896) 23 R. 659.

[84] *McNeill* v. *McMurchy, Ralston & Co.* (1841) 3 D. 554.

[85] 1838 Act, s. 26; *Lochhead* v. *Graham* (1883) 11 R. 201.

[86] *Mitchell* v. *Cuddie* (1822) 1 S. 461; *Clark* v. *Clark* (1824) 3 S. 96.

[87] 1838 Act, s. 27.

[88] *Ibid.* s. 29.

[89] *Ibid.* s. 27.

[90] *Ibid.* s. 28.

sary to pay their debts with interest and expenses.[90] If there is any surplus it is paid to the debtor; if there is any deficit the sheriff reserves further execution under the diligence for recovery thereof. The sheriff clerk must maintain a register of poindings and show the report to any interested person on payment of 5p.[90]

CHAPTER 21

MAILLS AND DUTIES

MAILLS and duties is an ancient term for rents, maills signifying money payments and duties personal services,[1] and any action to enforce payment of rents was formerly called an action of maills and duties, and such was accordingly competent to anyone entitled to be in possession of lands or to enter into possession thereof. The action is now considered unnecessary and indeed incompetent to any proprietor in actual possession of lands. It is now competent only in the case of a heritable creditor who has an assignation of the rents, express or implied, along with the disposition to him of the lands in security,[2] and who thus has a right in security over the rents due from tenants, and seeks to enforce, as against and in preference to the proprietor, his right to exact payment from the tenants. "It is only an incumbrancer that requires to use a process of maills and duties in order to give him a title, in a question with the tenant, to uplift the rents." [3] It is incompetent to a proprietor in possession.[2]

The action is not intended to establish a right to the rents, but merely to enable the pursuer to enforce payment to himself and to prevent the tenants making payment to anyone else.[4]

If there are no tenants and no rents, the action is incompetent.[5]

Jurisdiction

The action may be brought in the Court of Session, if the amount sued for exceeds £50,[6] or in the sheriff court of the county in which the lands lie,[7] or if the amount of rent does not exceed £5 and the title is not disputed, in the J.P. Small Debt Court.[8]

Title to sue

Title to sue extends to heritable creditors under a bond and disposition in security who have not entered into possession, the holder of a bond and disposition in security who subsequently held, subject to the liferent of another, an *ex facie* absolute disposition of the same lands,[9] the holder of

1 Ross, *Lect.* II, 235.
2 *Smith's Trs.* v. *Chalmers* (1890) 17 R. 1088, 1090, *per* Lord McLaren.
3 *Scottish Heritable Security Co.* v. *Allan Campbell & Co.* (1876) 3 R. 333, 340, *per* L.P. Inglis.
4 *Home* v. *Tenants of Kello* (1666) 1 B.S. 522; *Forsyth* v. *Aird* (1853) 16 D. 197; *Chambers's J.F.* v. *Vertue* (1893) 20 R. 257.
5 *Smith's Tr., supra.*
6 For form of conclusion, see R.C. Appx., Form 2, No. 26.
7 For form of summons, see Heritable Securities (Scotland) Act 1894, Sched. A, as modified by Sheriff Courts (Scotland) Acts 1907 and 1913.
8 Justice of the Peace Small Debt (Scotland) Act 1825, ss. 2, 25.
9 *Crichton's Trs.* v. *Clarke*, 1909, 1 S.L.T. 467.

a ground annual having, under his contract, a disposition of the lands in security and an assignation of the rents,[10] and, doubtless, the creditor in a modern standard security. The bond must be valid and not one which has prescribed.[11]

A proprietor in common who has granted a heritable security over his *pro indiviso* share of the property may bring an action for the defender's proportion of the rents, if his co-proprietors and the tenants do not object.[12]

A proprietor has no title to sue, nor has a creditor holding an *ex facie* absolute title to the lands,[13] nor a creditor who has already taken possession in exercise of his right in security,[14] nor a creditor in a reserved real burden,[15] nor a superior for feu-duties.[16]

Defenders

Prior to the Heritable Securities Act 1894, the action was directed against the proprietor, in effect, called merely for his interest [17] and not necessarily called,[18] and all the tenants as actual possessors of the lands; the decree was ineffective against any tenants not called,[19] but, so long as all the tenants in possession at the time of raising the action were called, the decree could be enforced without further intimation against any person acquiring right as tenant thereafter.[20] It could not competently be raised against a proprietor who was himself in possession, because there were no rents.[19] A *pro indiviso* proprietor in common may be sued, the other *pro indiviso* proprietors being called also for their interest.[21]

Under the 1894 Act, s. 3, the tenants in actual possession of the heritage need not be called as defenders, but notice given to them in the form of Schedule B to the Act interpels them from making payment of rent to the proprietor, just as if they had been called as defenders.

Competency

There must be one or more tenants holding leases from the debtor and liable to pay him rent, because the form of action [22] asks for a finding that the creditor has right to the rents of the subjects, or so much of them as will satisfy his claim. Hence the action is incompetent against a debtor in sole personal occupation,[23] or if the only persons holding from him are not tenants but *e.g.* service occupiers.

10 *Somerville* v. *Johnston* (1899) 1 F. 726.
11 *Marr's Exrx.* v. *Marr's Trs.*, 1936 S.C. 64.
12 *Schaw* v. *Black* (1889) 16 R. 336.
13 *Scottish Heritable Security Co., supra.*
14 *Ibid.*
15 *M. Tweeddale's Trs.* v. *E. Haddington* (1880) 7 R. 620, 631.
16 *Prudential Assce. Co.* v. *Cheyne* (1884) 11 R. 871; *Nelson's Trs.* v. *Todd* (1896) 23 R. 1000.
17 *Schaw* v. *Black* (1889) 16 R. 336; *Robertson's Trs.* v. *Gardner* (1889) 16 R. 705.
18 *Haliburton* v. *Tenants of Carse* (1702) Mor. 2232.
19 *Smith's Trs.* v. *Chalmers* (1890) 17 R. 1088.
20 *Robertson's Trs., supra.*
21 *Schaw, supra.*
22 Heritable Securities (Sc.) Act 1894, s. 3 and Sched. A.
23 *Smith's Trs.* v. *Chalmers* (1890) 17 R. 1088.

The debtor must be in arrears with payments of interest under his bond or have failed to repay the capital, having been called on to do so. If the debtor is not yet in default in payment the action is incompetent.[24]

A heritable creditor may still bring the action and collect the rents in preference to a judicial factor appointed to manage the debtor's estates [25] or to a trustee appointed on the debtor's sequestrated estates.[26]

Effect of clause of assignation of rents

In the standard form of bond and disposition in security the clause of assignation of rents entitled the creditor on default in payment to enter into possession of the lands disponed in security and to uplift the rents thereof and to make necessary repairs, subject to accounting to the debtor for the balance of rents actually recovered beyond what is necessary for payment of principal, interest, penalties and expenses.[27] But infeftment under the bond did not interpel the tenants from paying rent to the debtor, which could only be done by individual intimation to all the tenants,[28] or appearance in an action of multiplepoinding claiming the rents,[29] or raising an action of maills and duties.[30] And the creditor cannot under such a clause enter into possession without an action of maills and duties.[31] The legality of stipulations entitling the creditor to enter into possession without judicial proceedings and draw the rents was very doubtful.[32]

Under the modern standard security [33] an assignation of rents is neither expressed nor implied. But under Standard Condition 10 [34] the creditor may, inter alia, enter into possession of the security subjects and receive or recover feu-duties, ground annuals, or the rents of the subjects or any part thereof.

Effect of raising the action

Under the Heritable Securities (Scotland) Act 1894 a creditor may bring the action without calling the tenants as defenders. On notice of the raising of the action being given to them by registered letter, they are interpelled from paying the rents due by them, just as if called as defenders in the action.[35]

Any person interested may take proceedings to interpel the creditor

24 *Gibson* v. *Blair*, 1918 S.C. 353.
25 *Ferguson* v. *Murray* (1853) 15 D. 682.
26 Conveyancing Act 1874, s. 55 (repealed), restoring common law.
27 Titles to Land Consolidation (Scotland) Act 1868, s. 119.
28 Ersk. III, 5, 4; *Forsyth* v. *Aird* (1853) 16 D. 197; *Neils* v. *Lyle* (1863) 2 M. 168.
29 *Wylie* v. *Heritable Securities Investment Assocn.* (1871) 10 M. 253; *Budge* v. *Brown's Trs.* (1872) 10 M. 958; *Stevenson* v. *Dawson* (1896) 23 R. 496.
30 Heritable Securities (Sc.) Act 1894, s. 3.
31 *Blair* v. *Galloway* (1853) 16 D. 291; *McFarlane* v. *Campbell* (1857) 19 D. 623; *Neils* v. *Lyle*, *supra*; *Wylie*, *supra*.
32 *McFarlane*, *supra*; *Wylie*, *supra*.
33 Conveyancing and Feudal Reform (Sc.) Act 1970, ss. 9–1
34 *Ibid.* s. 11 and Sched. 3, para. 10.
35 s. 3 and Sched. B.

from entering into possession of the lands disponed in security or collecting the rents thereof.[36]

Effect of decree

Decree gives the pursuer the means of entering into possession and drawing the rents. On intimation of the decree obtained being made to the tenants by registered letter they must make payment of the rents due by them respectively in the same manner and under the like legal compulsitors as if decerned for and a charge given in an action for maills and duties under the law and practice then existing, and payment made shall be a complete exoneration and discharge to the tenants: But no decree affects the right of the tenants to refuse payment of the rents on any grounds not affecting the title of the creditor or the right of any prior creditor to enter into possession, and nothing in the section prevents an action of maills and duties from being raised in the form previously in use, or deprive a creditor of any existing right of entering into possession without having recourse to an action of maills and duties.[37] The creditor may obtain a warrant for summary ejection of a person occupying without title [38] and a proprietor in personal occupation is by statute equated to a tenant at will and may be summarily removed.[39] He may probably remove tenants under the Act of Sederunt 1756, and a creditor under a bond which authorised him to output and input tenants has been held entitled to decree of summary removal against a tenant without having raised an action of maills and duties.[40] Such a decree is competent against a party in possession in a capacity similar to that of a tenant at will under no obligation to pay rent.[41]

Decree also gives the pursuer the rights to draw the rents and also to use the remedies of a landlord against the tenants, such as to charge them to pay, or use arrestment and poinding, or utilise landlord's sequestration.[42] Without such a decree he might intimate to the tenants the assignation of rents to him in the bond and enforce payment by petitory action.[43]

Decree does not destroy the proprietary right of the defender but only encumbers his title. He retains his right of redemption until he surrenders it, or it is extinguished by proceedings for foreclosure.[44]

But the creditor in possession may let the lands held in security, or part thereof, for not longer than seven years,[45] or, under the warrant of the sheriff and subject to conditions, for longer.[46]

36 *Ibid.* s. 4.
37 Heritable Securities (Scotland) Act 1894, s. 3 and Sched. C.
38 *Hutchison* v. *Alexander* (1904) 6 F. 532.
39 Heritable Securities (Scotland) Act 1894. s. 5.
40 *Forsyth* v. *Aird* (1853) 16 D. 197.
41 *Blair* v. *Galloway* (1853) 16 D. 291.
42 *Railton* v. *Muirhead* (1834) 12 S. 757; *Hood* v. *Martin's Creditors* (1835) 13 S. 923; *Robertson's Trs.* v. *Gardner* (1889) 16 R. 705; *MacRosty* v. *Phillips* (1898) 14 S.L.R. 69.
43 *Neils* v. *Lyle* (1863) 2 M. 168; Titles to Land Consolidation (Sc.) Act 1868, s. 119; Conveyancing (Sc.) Act 1924, s. 25.
44 Heritable Securities (Sc.) Act 1894, s. 8.
45 *Ibid.* s. 6.
46 *Ibid.* s. 7.

A creditor in possession is in the position of a judicial assignee of the proprietor's rights and if the proprietor was in breach of a fundamental condition of a lease to a tenant, the tenant may retain rent as against the creditor just as he could have done against the proprietor.[47]

Decree does not give the creditor any kind of right over the tenant's moveables, save that if he enters into possession he is held to stand in the shoes of the landlord and thus is able to utilise landlord's sequestration.[48]

Creditor's liability to account

A heritable creditor who has taken possession and is drawing the rents under a decree of maills and duties must account for his intromissions. He stands in the place of the debtor in questions with superior, local authority and third parties generally.[49] He must pay feu-duty, rates, expenses of management, insurance and repairs,[50] and apply the balance to reduction of his debt, or pay the interest due thereon to himself and the balance of rents to the proprietor.

47 *Marshall's Trs.* v. *Banks*, 1934 S.C. 405.
48 *Robertson's Trs.* v. *Gardner* (1889) 16 R. 705.
49 *City of Glasgow Bank* v. *Nicolson's Trs.* (1882) 9 R. 689.
50 Titles to Land Consolidation (Sc.) Act 1868, s. 119; Conveyancing (Sc.) Act 1924, s. 25; *City of Glasgow Bank, supra.*

CHAPTER 22

REMEDIES OF SECURED CREDITORS

A PERSON who is creditor in an obligation undertaken by another person to pay money or perform something has the remedies of action for payment or *ad factum praestandum*, as may be appropriate in the circumstances, to compel performance of the personal obligation. If the creditor has in addition a right in security over heritage created by standard security,[1] or over heritable and/or moveable property created by floating charge, he has further remedies.

STANDARD SECURITY OVER HERITAGE

A standard security may be granted over any estate or interest in land, other than an entailed estate or any interest therein, which is capable of being owned or held as a separate interest and to which a title may be recorded in the Register of Sasines, and is now the only competent mode of creating heritable security.[2] It is constituted by deed in the form of Form A or Form B of Schedule 2 to the 1970 Act. Where a standard security is duly recorded it operates to vest the interest over which it is granted in the grantee as a security for the performance of the contract to which the security relates.[3] Every standard security is subject to the standard conditions set out in Schedule 3 of the 1970 Act, except in so far as these conditions can be, and have been, modified in the particular case.[4] These include creditor's remedies on default by the debtor. Where the debtor is in default,[5] the creditor may,[6] without prejudice to his exercising any other remedy arising from the contract to which the standard security relates or to which he is entitled by law, exercise, in accordance with the provisions of Part II of the 1970 Act (ss. 9–32) and of any other enactment applying to standard securities,[7] such of the following remedies as he may consider appropriate, namely: to sell the security subjects or any part thereof [8]; to enter into possession of the security subjects and to receive or

[1] For the import of the personal obligation to pay contained in a standard security in conformity with Form A of Sched. 2 of the Conveyancing and Feudal Reform (Sc.) Act 1970, see s. 10 of that Act.

[2] Conveyancing and Feudal Reform (Scotland) Act 1970, s. 10. The former modes of constituting heritable security now apply only to entailed estate and to certain loans by local authorities under the Small Dwellings Acquisition (Scotland) Acts 1899 to 1923, which may be by bond and disposition in security but not by disposition *ex facie* absolute qualified by back-letter.

[3] 1970 Act, s. 11 (1).

[4] 1970 Act, s. 11 (2)–(4), amended by Redemption of Standard Securities (Sc.) Act 1971.

[5] Defined, standard condition 9.

[6] 1970 Act, s. 20, and standard condition 10.

[7] Including the Redemption of Standard Securities (Sc.) Act 1971.

[8] s. 20 (2) and standard condition 10 (2). Detailed procedure in ss. 19–27.

recover feu-duties, ground annuals or, as the case may be, the rents of the subjects or any part thereof[9]; where he has entered into possession as aforesaid, to let the security subjects or any part thereof; or to apply to the court for a decree of foreclosure.[10]

For the purposes of these provisions the court is the sheriff having jurisdiction over any part of the security subjects, whatever their value.[11]

REMEDIES OF CREDITOR SECURED BY FLOATING CHARGE OVER HERITAGE AND/OR MOVEABLES

An incorporated company (whether a company within the meaning of the Companies Act 1948 or not),[12] or a society registered under the Industrial and Provident Societies Acts,[13] may, for the purpose of securing any debt or other obligation (including a cautionary obligation) incurred or to be incurred by, or binding upon, the company or any other person, create in favour of the creditor a floating charge over all or any part of the property (including uncalled capital) which may from time to time be comprised in its property and undertaking.[14] A floating charge created by a company, on the commencement of the winding up of the company, subject to sections 106A and 322 of the Companies Act 1948, attaches to the property then comprised in the company's property and undertaking, or, as the case may be, in part of that property and undertaking, but subject to the rights of any person who (a) has effectually executed diligence on the property or any part of it; or (b) holds a fixed security [15] over the property or any part of it ranking in priority to the floating charge; or (c) holds over the property or any part of it another floating charge so ranking, and, subject as aforesaid, the provisions of the Companies Act 1948 relating to winding up, except section 327 (1) (*c*) thereof, have effect as if the charge were a fixed security over the property to which it has attached in respect of the principal of the debt or obligation to which it relates and interest due or to become due thereon; provided that nothing is to prejudice the operation of section 319 (5) of the 1948 Act. Subject to the 1948 Act, s. 322, interest accrues until payment of the sum due under the floating charge is made.[16]

The Act provides for the mode of creation of a floating charge,[17] its alteration,[18] its effect in relation to heritable property,[19] and the extension

[9] s. 20 (3)–(5) and standard condition 10 (3)–(6).
[10] Standard condition 10 (7). Detailed procedure in 1970 Act, s. 28, as amended by 1971 Act.
[11] 1970 Act, s. 29.
[12] Companies (Floating Charges and Receivers) (Scotland) Act 1972, s. 1 (1), replacing Companies (Floating Charges) (Scotland) Act 1961.
[13] Industrial and Provident Societies Act 1967, Part II and Sched., amended by Companies (Floating Charges and Receivers) (Scotland) Act 1972, s. 10.
[14] 1972 Act, s. 1 (1).
[15] Defined 1972 Act, s. 31 (1).
[16] 1972 Act, s. 1 (2)–(4). *Cf. National Commercial Bank* v. *Telford, Grier Mackay & Co., Liqdrs.*, 1969 S.L.T. 306.
[17] 1972 Act, s. 2.
[18] 1972 Act, s. 7.
[19] 1972 Act, s. 3.

of the power of the court to wind up a company to include the case where there is subsisting a floating charge over property comprised in the company's property and undertaking, and the court is satisfied that the creditor's security is in jeopardy, which is deemed to be the case if the court is satisfied that events have occurred or are about to occur which render it unreasonable in the interests of the creditor that the company should retain power to dispose of the property which is subject to the floating charge.[20]

Provision is made for the ranking of floating charges[21] and the registration of charges with the Registrar of Companies and by the company itself.[22]

Enforcement by creditor in floating charge of remedy by liquidation

If a creditor in a floating charge satisfies the court having jurisdiction to wind up the company that his security is in jeopardy he may petition for the winding up of the company.[23] If a winding-up order is made the creditor ranks against the company's assets as a secured creditor, the ranking of secured creditors *inter se* being determined by section 5.

Enforcement by creditor in floating charge by appointment of a receiver

Alternatively, the holder of a floating charge,[24] or the court, on the application of such a person,[25] may appoint a receiver of such part of the property of the company as is subject to the charge. A receiver must be a natural person, not being an undischarged bankrupt.

Circumstances justifying appointment

A receiver may be appointed by the holder of the floating charge on the occurrence of any event which, by the provisions of the instrument creating the charge, entitles the holder of the charge to make the appointment and, in so far as not otherwise provided for therein, on the occurrence of any of the following events, namely—

(*a*) the expiry of a period of twenty-one days after the making of a demand for payment of the whole or any part of the principal sum secured by the charge, without payment having been made;

(*b*) the expiry of a period of two months during the whole of which interest due and payable under the charge has been in arrears;

(*c*) the making of an order or the passing of a resolution to wind up the company;

20 1972 Act, s. 4.
21 1972 Act, s. 5.
22 1972 Act, s. 6, adding new Part IIIA (ss. 106A–106K) to Companies Act 1948. See also *Archibald Campbell, Hope & King*, 1967 S.C. 21; *Amalgamated Securities Ltd.*, 1967 S.C. 56; *Scottish Homes Investment Co. Ltd.*, 1968 S.C. 244, all decided under 1961 Act.
23 1972 Act, s. 4.
24 1972 Act, s. 11 (1).
25 1972 Act, s. 11 (2).

(*d*) the appointment of a receiver by virtue of any other floating charge created by the company.[26]

A receiver may be appointed by the court on the occurrence of any event which, by the provisions of the instrument creating the floating charge, entitles the holder of the charge to make that appointment and, in so far as not otherwise provided for therein, on the occurrence of any of the following events, namely—

(*a*) where the court, on the application of the holder of the charge, pronounces itself satisfied that the position of the holder of the charge is likely to be prejudiced if no such appointment is made;

(*b*) any of the events referred to in section 12 (1), paras. (*a*) to (*c*).[27]

Mode of appointment

Appointment by the holder of a floating charge is by means of a validly executed instrument in writing, a certified copy whereof is to be delivered by or on behalf of the person making the appointment to the Registrar of Companies for registration within seven days of its execution and to be accompanied by a notice in the prescribed form. The receiver is regarded as appointed on the date of the execution of the instrument of his appointment. On his appointment the floating charge, subject to sections 106A and 322 of the Companies Act 1948, attaches to the property then subject to the charge; and such attachment shall have effect as if the charge were a fixed security over the property to which it has attached.[28]

Application for the appointment of a receiver by the court is made by petition to the court, served on the company. The court may make the appointment on such terms as to caution as the court may think fit, and a copy of the court's interlocutor is to be delivered by or on behalf of the petitioner to the Registrar of Companies for registration, accompanied by a notice in the prescribed form, within seven days of the date of the interlocutor or such longer period as the court may allow. The receiver is regarded as appointed on the date of his appointment by the court. On his appointment the floating charge by virtue of which he was appointed attaches to the property then subject to the charge; and such attachment has effect as if the charge were a fixed security over the property to which it has attached.[29]

Notification of appointment

Where a receiver has been appointed notification must be made on the company's stationery that a receiver has been appointed,[30] and notice must be given to the company and various information transmitted to and by him.[31]

[26] 1972 Act, s. 12 (1).
[27] 1972 Act, s. 12 (2).
[28] 1972 Act, s. 13. The section provides for execution of the instrument.
[29] 1972 Act, s. 14.
[30] 1972 Act, s. 24.
[31] 1972 Act, ss. 25–27.

Powers of receiver

Subject to the rights of any person who has effectually executed diligence on all or any part of the property of the company prior to the appointment of the receiver, and subject to the rights of any person who holds over all or any part of the property of the company a fixed security or floating charge having priority over, or ranking *pari passu* with, the floating charge by virtue of which the receiver was appointed, a receiver has, in relation to such part of the property of the company as is attached by the floating charge by virtue of which he was appointed the powers, if any, given to him by the instrument creating the charge and, in addition, the following powers, in so far as they are not inconsistent with any provision in that instrument, namely—

(*a*) power to take possession of, collect and get in the property from the company or a liquidator thereof or any other person, and for that purpose to take such proceedings as may seem to him expedient;

(*b*) power to sell, feu, hire out or otherwise dispose of the property by public roup or private bargain and with or without advertisement;

(*c*) power to borrow money and grant security therefor over the property;

(*d*) power to appoint a solicitor or accountant or other professionally qualified person to assist him in the performance of his functions;

(*e*) power to apply to the court for directions in connection with the performance of his functions;

(*f*) power to bring or defend any action or other legal proceedings in the name and on behalf of the company;

(*g*) power to refer to arbitration all questions affecting the company;

(*h*) power to effect and maintain insurances in respect of the business and property of the company;

(*i*) power to use the company's seal;

(*j*) power to do all acts and to execute in the name and on behalf of the company any deed, receipt or other document;

(*k*) power to draw, accept, make and endorse any bill of exchange or promissory note in the name and on behalf of the company;

(*l*) power to appoint any agent to do any business which he is unable to do himself or which can more conveniently be done by an agent and power to employ and discharge servants;

(*m*) power to have carried out to the best advantage any work on the property of the company and in general to do all such other things as may be necessary for the realisation of the property;

(*n*) power to make any payment which is necessary or incidental to the performance of his functions;

(*o*) power to carry on the business of the company so far as he thinks it desirable to do so;

(*p*) power to grant any lease of the property, and to input and output tenants, and to take on lease any property required or convenient for the business of the company;

(*q*) power to rank and claim in the bankruptcy, insolvency, sequestration or liquidation of any person or company indebted to the company and to receive dividends, and to accede to trust deeds for creditors of any such person;

(*r*) power to present or defend a petition for the winding up of the company; and

(*s*) power to do all other things incidental to the exercise of the power mentioned in this subsection.[32]

A person transacting with a receiver is not concerned to inquire whether any event has happened to authorise the receiver to act.[33]

A receiver or manager of an English company which owns property in Scotland has the same powers in relation thereto as he has in relation to the English property, so far as these powers are not inconsistent with Scots law.[34]

Precedence among receivers

Where two or more floating charges subsist over all or any part of the property of the company, a receiver may be appointed under the Act by virtue of each such charge, but a receiver appointed by, or on the application of, the holder of a floating charge having priority of ranking over any other floating charge by virtue of which a receiver has been appointed has the statutory powers of a receiver to the exclusion of any other receiver.[35] Where two or more floating charges rank with one another equally, and two or more receivers have been appointed by virtue thereof, the receivers so appointed are deemed to have been appointed as joint receivers.[36] Receivers appointed, or deemed to have been appointed, as joint receivers act jointly unless the instrument of appointment or respective instruments of appointment otherwise provide.[37] The powers of a receiver appointed by, or on the application of, the holder of a floating charge are suspended by, and as from the date of, the appointment of a receiver by, or on the application of, the holder of a floating charge having priority of ranking over that charge to such extent as may be necessary to enable the latter receiver to exercise his powers under section 15; and any powers so suspended take effect again when the floating charge having priority of ranking ceases to attach to the property then subject to the

[32] 1972 Act, s. 15 (1) and (2).
[33] 1972 Act, s. 15 (3).
[34] 1972 Act, s. 15 (4).
[35] 1972 Act, s. 16 (1).
[36] 1972 Act, s. 16 (2).
[37] 1972 Act, s. 16 (3).

charge, whether the cessation is by virtue of section 22 (6) of the Act or otherwise.[38] The suspension of the power of a receiver under section 16 (4) does not have the effect of requiring him to release any part of the property (including any letters or documents) of the company from his control until he receives from the receiver superseding him a valid indemnity (subject to the limit of the value of such part of the property of the company as is subject to the charge by virtue of which he was appointed) in respect of any expenses, charges and liabilities he may have incurred in the performance of his functions as receiver.[39] Nor does the suspension of his powers cause the floating charge to cease to attach to the property to which it attached by section 13 (7) or 14 (7) of the Act.[40] Nothing in section 16 prevents the same receiver being appointed by virtue of two or more floating charges.[41]

The receiver's agency and liability for contracts

A receiver is deemed to be the agent of the company in relation to such of its property as is attached by the floating charge by virtue of which he was appointed. Subject thereto, a receiver (including one whose powers are subsequently suspended under section 16) is personally liable on any contract entered into by him in the performance of his functions, except in so far as the contract otherwise provides. A receiver who is personally liable is entitled to be indemnified out of the property in respect of which he was appointed. Any contract entered into by or on behalf of the company prior to the appointment of a receiver, subject to the terms thereof, continues in force notwithstanding that appointment, but the receiver does not by virtue only of his appointment incur any personal liability on any such contract. Any contract entered into by a receiver in the performance of his functions, subject to the terms thereof, continues in force although the powers of the receiver are subsequently suspended under section 16 of the Act.[42]

Receiver's remuneration

This is fixed by agreement or by the auditor of the Court of Session.[43]

Preferential payments

Where a receiver is appointed and the company is not then in course of being wound up, certain debts are to be paid out of any assets coming to the hands of the receiver in priority to any claim for principal or interest by the holder of the following charge by virtue of which he was appointed. These debts are those (a) which in every winding up are, under Part V of

[38] 1972 Act, s. 16 (4).
[39] 1972 Act, s. 16 (5).
[40] 1972 Act, s. 16 (6).
[41] 1972 Act, s. 16 (7).
[42] 1972 Act, s. 17.
[43] 1972 Act, s. 18.

the Companies Act 1948, to be paid in priority to all other debts; and (b) which, by the end of six months after advertisement by the receiver for claims in the *Edinburgh Gazette* and in a newspaper circulating in the district where the company carries on business, either (i) have been intimated to him, or (ii) have become known to him. In the application of Part V of the 1948 Act, section 319 is to be construed as if the provision for payment of accrued holiday remuneration were a provision for payment of such remuneration becoming payable on the termination of employment before or by the effect of the appointment of the receiver. Periods of time mentioned in Part V are to be reckoned from the date of the appointment of the receiver under section 13 (6) or 14 (6) of the 1972 Act. Any payments made under this section are to be recouped as far as may be out of the assets of the company available for payment of ordinary creditors.[44]

Distribution of monies

The receiver is to pay monies received by him to the holder of the floating charge by virtue of which he was appointed in or towards satisfaction of the debt secured by the floating charge, subject, however, to s. 21 of the 1972 Act and to the rights of (a) the holder of any fixed security which is over property subject to the floating charge and which ranks prior to, or *pari passu* with, it; (b) all persons who have effectually executed diligence on any part of the property of the company which is subject to the charge by virtue of which the receiver was appointed; (c) creditors in respect of all liabilities, charges and expenses incurred by or on behalf of the receiver; (d) the receiver in respect of his liabilities, expenses and remuneration; and (e) the preferential creditors entitled to payment under section 19 of the 1972 Act.[45]

Any balance of monies remaining after the foregoing provisions and those of section 21 of the 1972 Act have been satisfied are to be paid in accordance with their respective rights and interests to the following persons, as the case may require, namely—(a) any other receiver; (b) the holder of a fixed security which is over property subject to the floating charge; (c) the company or its liquidator, as the case may be.[46]

Where any question arises as to the person entitled to a payment under the foregoing provisions of section 20, or where a receipt or a discharge of a security cannot be obtained in respect of any such payment, the receiver has to consign the amount of such payment in any joint stock bank of issue in Scotland in name of the Accountant of Court for behoof of the person or persons entitled thereto.[47]

[44] 1972 Act, s. 19. This corresponds generally to Companies Act 1948, s. 94, in respect of English companies.

[45] 1972 Act, s. 20 (1).

[46] 1972 Act, s. 20 (2).

[47] 1972 Act, s. 20 (3).

Disposal of interests in property

Where the receiver sells or dispones of, or is desirous of selling or disposing of, any property or interest in property of the company which is subject to the floating charge by virtue of which the receiver was appointed and which is (a) subject to any security or interest of, or burden or encumbrance in favour of, a creditor the ranking of which is prior to, *pari passu* with, or postponed to the floating charge; or (b) property or an interest in property affected or attached by effectual diligence executed by any person; and the receiver is unable to obtain the consent of such creditor or, as the case may be, such person to such a sale or disposal, the receiver may apply to the court for authority to sell or dispose of the property or interest in property free of such security, interest, burden, encumbrance or diligence. On such application to the court, the court may, if it thinks fit, authorise the sale or disposal of the property or interest in question free of such security, interest, burden, encumbrance or diligence, and such authorisation may be on such terms or conditions as the court thinks fit: provided that such authorisation shall not be given where a fixed security over the property or interest in question which ranks prior to the floating charge has not been met or provided for in full. Where any sale or disposal is effected in accordance with the authorisation of the court the receiver must grant to the purchaser or disponee an appropriate document of transfer or conveyance of the property or interest in question, and that document has the effect, or, where recording, intimation or registration of that document is a legal requirement for completion of title to the property or interest, then that recording, intimation or registration has the effect of (a) disencumbering the property or interest of the security, interest, burden or encumbrance affecting it; and (b) freeing the property or interest from the diligence executed upon it. Nothing in these provisions prejudices the right of any creditor of the company to rank for his debt in the winding up of the company.[48]

Cessation of receiver's appointment

A receiver appointed by the holder of a floating charge under section 11 (1) may resign on giving one month's notice. A receiver appointed by the court under section 11 (2) may resign only with the authority of the court and on such terms and conditions, if any, as may be laid down by the court. A receiver may, on application to the court by the holder of a floating charge by virtue of which he was appointed, be removed by the court on cause shown. When a receiver ceases to act as such he is entitled to be indemnified out of the property which is subject to the floating charge by virtue of which he was appointed in respect of any expenses, charges or other liabilities he may have incurred in the performance of his functions as receiver. When a receiver ceases to act as such otherwise than by death and when a receiver is removed by the court, the holder of the floating

[48] 1972 Act, s. 21.

charge by virtue of which he was appointed must, within seven days of the cessation or removal give the Registrar of Companies notice to that effect. If by the expiry of a month following the removal of a receiver or his ceasing to act as such no other receiver has been appointed, the floating charge by virtue of which the receiver was appointed (a) thereupon ceases to attach to the property then subject to the charge; and (b) again subsists as a floating charge.[49]

Powers of court

A holder of a floating charge by virtue of which a receiver was appointed may apply to the court for directions in any matter arising in connection with the performance by the receiver of his functions.[50] Where a floating charge by virtue of which a person is purported to have been appointed receiver is discovered to be invalid, the court may, if it thinks fit, in whole or in part relieve that person from personal liability in respect of anything done or omitted to be done which, had he been validly appointed, would have been properly done or omitted; and the court may, if it thinks fit, make the person by whom the invalid appointment was made personally liable in respect of anything done or omitted to be done to the extent to which the person purported to have been appointed receiver has been relieved of personal liability.[51]

Agricultural Charges

A society registered in Scotland under the Industrial and Provident Societies Acts, having for its principal object the provision and sale of agricultural requisites to its members or the sale, either after a process of manufacture or otherwise, of agricultural produce purchased from its members, may create by instrument in writing in favour of a bank a charge on the stocks of merchandise from time to time belonging to it and in its possession in pursuance of its objects as security for sums advanced or to be advanced to it or paid or to be paid on its behalf under any guarantee by the bank and interest, commission and charges thereon. It may be in such form and made on such conditions as the parties thereto may agree, and cautioners may be parties thereto.[52] *Inter se*, such charges have priority according to dates of registration.[53]

Such a charge may, on the happening of any event specified in the instrument creating the charge as an event authorising such enforcement, be enforced by sequestration and sale of such property in the same manner

[49] 1972 Act, s. 22.
[50] 1972 Act, s. 23 (1).
[51] 1972 Act, s. 23 (2).
[52] Agricultural Credits (Scotland) Act 1929, ss. 5 and 9. As to registration of such charges, see s. 8.
[53] *Ibid.* s. 7.

as in the case of landlord's hypothec.[54] It is, however, postponed to the claims of superior and landlord.[55]

Securities over Moveables

Security by pledge of moveables

When moveables are pledged with a creditor as security for repayment of advances made, the creditor has no power of sale unless such power is obtained on summary application to the sheriff.[56] In cases within the Pawnbrokers Acts 1872–1960, pledges are redeemable within six months and seven days; thereafter if pawned for £2 or less the pledge becomes the pawnbroker's property [57]; if pawned for over £2 a pledge remained redeemable until sold by the pawnbroker by public auction, at which the pawnbroker may himself bid and purchase.[58]

Security by hypothec over moveables

Cases where a creditor has security by legal hypothec over moveables, without possession, include the cases of the superior, who has a hypothec over the vassal's moveables in security of his feuduty,[59] and the landlord, who has a hypothec over the tenant's moveables in security of his rent.[60] Both are enforceable by the process of sequestration for feuduty or rent.[61]

Maritime hypothecs

A maritime hypothec (usually called a maritime lien) is recognised in the cases of a ship's master for his wages and disbursements properly made on account of the ship,[62] of members of the crew for their wages,[63] of a salvor for his salvage reward,[64] of another vessel for a claim for collision damage,[65] of owners of goods for damage done by improper stowage,[66] or for average loss.[67] Enforcement is by constituting the debt by action *in rem* against the ship herself and by petitioning the court to declare the lien and to order judicial sale of the ship in satisfaction thereof.[68] It is competent if suing *in personam* to arrest the ship on the dependence of the action.[69]

54 For this, see Chap. 19.
55 *Ibid.* s. 6.
56 Stair I, 13, 11; Ersk. III, 1, 33; Bell, *Prin.* § 207.
57 Pawnbrokers Act 1872, s. 17, as amended by Pawnbrokers Act 1960.
58 *Ibid.* ss. 18–19.
59 Bell, *Comm.* II, 260.
60 Ersk. II, 6, 56; Bell, *Comm.* II, 27; *Prin.* §§ 1234, 1275, 1887.
61 Chap. 19, *supra.*
62 M.S.A. 1894, s. 167 (2); *McConnachie*, 1914 S.C. 853.
63 M.S.A. 1894, s. 156.
64 *Duncan* v. *Dundee, Perth & London Shipping Co.* (1878) 5 R. 742; *Hatton* v. *A/S Durban Hansen*, 1919 S.C. 154.
65 *Currie* v. *McKnight* (1896) 24 R.(H.L.) 1; *Clan Line* v. *E. Douglas Steamship Co.*, 1913 S.C. 967; *Dorie S.S. Co.*, 1923 S.C. 593.
66 Bell, *Comm.* II, 38; *Prin.* § 1399.
67 Bell, *Comm.* II, 39; *Prin.* § 1401.
68 *Clan Line, supra*; see also *Clydesdale Bank* v. *Walker & Bain*, 1926 S.C. 72.
69 *Clan Line, supra.*

Bonds of bottomry and respondentia

Each of these kinds of bonds creates security over, in the first case, the ship herself, and in the second the ship's cargo, without possession thereof. Enforcement of the bond is in the first case by arrestment of the ship and petition for her judicial sale,[70] and in the second by the bondholder arresting the cargo and, if need be, obtaining judicial authority to sell it.

Security over ships by mortgage

Security over a ship without possession may be obtained by obtaining a mortgage under the Merchant Shipping Act 1894, ss. 31–38, which is postponed to a bond of bottomry or a maritime lien, but preferred to all other creditors.[71] This confers power to sell the ship (s. 35).

Security over aircraft by mortgage

Security over an aircraft without possession may be obtained by obtaining a mortgage under the Mortgaging of Aircraft Order 1972.[72] Such a mortgage must be registered in a Register of Aircraft Mortgages kept by the Civil Aviation Authority.

Securities over Incorporeal Rights

Security by assignation of incorporeal rights

An incorporeal right, such as an insurance policy, shares in a company, a copyright, and the like, if capable of being assigned at all, may be assigned in security by assignation, which may or may not bear to be in security, and in the latter case may have the true nature of the transaction explained by back-letter. The assignation must be intimated to the insurance company, company or other party against whom the debtor had a claim. An arrangement for pledge of shares may not permit reconveyance of any until the whole advance has been repaid.[73]

In what circumstances the assignee is entitled to retain the rights assigned free from any reversionary claim by the assignor depends on the terms of the contract under which the assignation was effected. If the assignation is *ex facie absolute* qualified by a separate obligation to reconvey on repayment, the assignee, if not repaid at the due time or on request, probably has a power to retain for his own behoof or to realise,[74]

70 *Lucovitch, Petr.* (1885) 12 R. 1090.

71 *The Staffordshire* (1872) L.R. 4 P.C. 194; *The Arbonne* (1925) 33 Ll.L.R. 141; see also *Clydesdale Bank Ltd.* v. *Walker & Bain*, 1926 S.C. 72.

72 S.I. 1972 No. 1268, made under Civil Aviation Act 1968, s. 16.

73 *Coats* v. *Union Bank of Scotland*, 1929 S.C.(H.L.) 114. See also *Crerar* v. *Bank of Scotland*, 1922 S.C.(H.L.) 137.

74 *Cf. Baillie* v. *Drew* (1884) 12 R. 199; *Duncan* v. *Mitchell* (1893) 21 R. 37 (*ex facie* absolute dispositions of heritage). He may sell without notice to the debtor: *Aberdeen Trades Council* v. *Shipconstructors and Shipwrights Assocn.*, 1949 S.C.(H.L.) 45.

but if the assignation bears to be in security the assignor's reversionary right subsists until cut off by the running of the long negative prescription, or until power of sale is obtained from the court and exercised.[75] In exercising a power of sale the creditor has a duty to have regard to the debtor's reversionary interest.[76]

[75] *Cf.* Bell, *Prin.* § 207; *Murray* v. *Smith* (1899) 6 S.L.T. 357.
[76] *Nelson* v. *National Bank*, 1936 S.C. 570.

CHAPTER 23

INTEREST

A CLAIM for interest is the normal remedy for loss caused by delay in the payment of money due, whereby the creditor does not gain the ordinary legal profits of money, or loses by having to replace it from another source.[1] " The most obvious ground of claim for interest is breach of engagement, in consequence of which the person who is to receive money suffers a loss, or fails to procure an expected and possible gain. Other grounds of a claim for interest arise from positive statute, or from contract, express or implied." [2]

In general, damages cannot be claimed for non-payment or delay in payment of money, but only the sum due with interest thereon.[3] But where the circumstances are such that there is a special loss foreseeable at the time of the contract as a consequence of non-payment, such a loss may be recoverable in damages.[4] Breach of contract in respect of failure to pay or delay in payment gives rise to a claim for interest without inquiry as to actual damage suffered, as distinct from proper damages where the amount must be assessed with regard to the circumstances of the case and the loss suffered. In pecuniary obligations there is not necessarily any particular injury or damage to the creditor, but his loss consists in not gaining the ordinary profits of money, which is properly compensated by an award of interest.[5]

Circumstances where interest is due

It is very difficult to bring under general principles or heads the cases where interest is due. Erskine [6] distinguished only cases where it is due *ex lege* and *ex pacto*. Bell [7] could formulate only a list of circumstances in which it was due.

In *Blair's Trustees* v. *Payne* [8] Lord Craighill said:

> " Nothing can be considered less amenable to a settled general principle than our law upon a creditor's right to interest. Interest upon bills and notes is settled by statute [9]; that on bonds by express contract [10]; that on loans by legal implication.[10] But when this has

1 Bell, *Comm.* I, 691; *Prin.* § 32.
2 *Ibid.* 690.
3 *Roissard de Bellet* v. *Scott's Trs.* (1897) 24 R. 861.
4 *Trans Trust* v. *Danubian Trading Co.* [1952] 1 All E.R. 970, 977–978.
5 Bell, *Comm.* I, 691.
6 III, 3, 76.
7 *Comm.* I, 691.
8 (1884) 12 R. 104, 108.
9 But it must be express: *Forbes* v. *Welsh and Forbes* (1894) 21 R. 630.
10 *Garthland's Trs.* v. *McDowall*, May 26, 1820, F.C.

been said, almost all that has been fixed is presented. We must bear in mind that every liquid debt past due does not bear interest. Feu-duties,[11] ground-annuals,[12] and rents [13] are cases in point where payment of interest has not been made a matter of express obligation. But what of other debts, mercantile accounts, law agents' business accounts, accounts for services of any description? The most that can be said is that where there is anything in the course of dealing or in the custom of trade which suggests that, if the debt should not be paid at a particular period, interest will run, that will be allowed, otherwise not.

A demand for payment more or less urgent seems to me, apart from contract, to be a condition precedent to liability for interest. Commonsense itself suggests that a man who pays whenever payment is asked pays in good time."

In the same case, Lord Fraser said [14]:

" Claims for interest cannot be brought under any general rule. They are said to arise *ex lege*, or *ex pacto*, or *ex mora*. With regard to interest due *ex pacto* the case is quite clear. It is lawful to stipulate for interest, and now that the usury laws are abolished any amount of interest may be agreed upon and exacted. It is when the claim is founded, not on paction, but on some rule of law, that the difficulty arises. Interest is due *ex lege* in various cases by statute; and it is in virtue of statutory enactment that it is claimable in Scotland upon bills of exchange and promissory notes,[15] and there are other instances in which the claim has statutory sanction. Interest is also due by law upon money lent; and it was so found although there was no stipulation for interest,[16] and the demand for it was only made thirty-four years after the loan was made, and when the lender and borrower were both dead.[17] But it is not correct to say that interest is claimable on all debts, either from the date when the account was closed or from the date that it was rendered. It is sometimes said that interest is due as damages for the undue detention of money when a debt clearly ascertained remains unpaid. By those lawyers who hold this opinion interest is considered incident legally to every debt certain in amount and payable at a certain time. This is plainly not good law. There are many illustrations to the contrary. No debt can be more certain in amount or certain as to the time of payment than feuduties or ground-annuals and yet it has been determined

11 *Maxwell's Trs.* v. *Bothwell School Board* (1893) 20 R. 958.
12 *Moncrieff* v. *Lord Dundas* (1835) 14 S. 61.
13 *Advocate-General* v. *Sinclair's Trs.* (1855) 17 D. 290.
14 *Ibid.* 109.
15 From the date of presentment or maturity: Bills of Exchange Act 1681; Inland Bills Act 1696; Bills of Exchange Act 1882, ss. 9, 57.
16 *Garthland's Trs.* v. *McDowall*, May 26, 1820, F.C.
17 *Cunninghame* v. *Boswell* (1868) 6 M. 890.

> frequently that interest is not due upon arrears of these. . . .[18] According to the principle of these decisions, interest would not be claimable upon rents unless expressly stipulated for; and for this latter proposition (which has not been expressly decided) there are judicial dicta of high authority.[19] The ground of these decisions simply was, that parties having stipulated for the payment of a specific sum without stipulating for interest on non-payment, it was not intended that interest in such circumstances should be claimed. The cases of bills and loans of money, in regard to which interest is due though not stipulated for, rest on special grounds. Interest is due on bills by virtue of statute. And the law implies an obligation to pay interest on loans arising from the very nature of the contract. The mere fact therefore of delay in payment after payment could have been, or has been, demanded, will not necessarily ground a claim for interest, and consequently there must be distinctions made, consequent upon the nature of the debt due and upon the reasons of the non-payment of it. Lord Westbury, in the case of *Carmichael*,[20] expresses himself as follows: 'Interest can be demanded only in virtue of a contract express or implied, or by virtue of the principal sum of money having been wrongfully withheld and not paid on the day when it ought to have been paid.' According to this opinion, the mere non-payment of money was not sufficient. It must be 'wrongfully' withheld." [21]

Again it has been said that "interest is only due where there is either a contract to pay interest, or a duty to invest, or in respect of *morata solutio*," [22] and that "It seems to be established that, by Scots law, a pursuer may recover interest by way of damages when he is deprived of an interest-bearing security or a profit-producing chattel, but otherwise, speaking generally, he will only recover interest, apart from contract, by virtue of a principal sum having been wrongfully withheld and not paid on the day when it ought to have been paid." [23]

Interest on foreign transactions

The liability to pay interest and the rate payable in respect of a debt is determined by the proper law of the contract under which the debt is incurred.[24] Interest payable by way of damages for the detention of

18 *Napier* v. *Spiers' Trs.* (1831) 9 S. 655; *Wallace* v. *Eglinton* (1835) 13 S. 564; *Wallace* v. *Crawfurd's Exors.* (1838) 1 D. 162; *Maxwell's Trs.* v. *Bothwell School Board* (1893) 20 R. 958.

19 *Advocate-General* v. *Sinclair's Trs.* (1855) 17 D. 290.

20 *Carmichael* v. *Caledonian Ry.* (1870) 8 M.(H.L.) 119, 131, approved by Lord Young in *Durie's Trs.* v. *Ayton* (1894) 22 R. 34, 38 and adopted by Lord Shaw in *Greenock Harbour Trs.* v. *G.S.W.R.*, 1919 S.C.(H.L.) 49. But Gloag (*Contract*, 2nd ed., p. 681, n. 3) submits the principle in this case was rather recompense.

21 On "wrongful" withholding, see *Roger* v. *J. & P. Cochrane & Co.*, 1910 S.C. 1.

22 *Ross* v. *Ross* (1896) 23 R. 802, 805, *per* Lord McLaren.

23 *Kolbin* v. *Kinnear*, 1931 S.C.(H.L.) 128, 137.

24 Dicey and Morris, *Conflict of Laws*, 8th ed., p. 846; Maclaren's *Practice*, 306; *Wilkinson* v. *Monies* (1821) 1 S. 90; *Gillow* v. *Burgess* (1824) 3 S. 45; *Evans* v. *Buchan* (1845) 8 D. 296; *Parker* v. *Royal Exch. Assce.* (1846) 8 D. 365; *Fergusson* v. *Fyffe* (1841) 8 Cl. & Fin. 121, 140; *Graham* v. *Keble* (1820) 2 Bli. 126. *Cf. Price and Logan* v. *Wise* (1861) 24 D. 491.

money, and not as a matter of express or implied contract, is generally governed by the *lex fori*.[25]

Interest Due by Statute

Interest due ex lege by express provision

Interest is due by express legal provision on bills of exchange [26] and promissory notes [27] from their date in case of non-acceptance, or from the date of falling due if accepted but not paid.[28] If a bill bears no terms of payment, or is payable on demand, no interest can be exacted till demand be made, which must appear by a notarial protestation,[29] or by citation in an action for payment.[30]

Interest is due at 3 per cent. on arrears of income tax assessed under Schedule D and surtax.[31]

It is also due at 3 per cent. on sums payable as estate duty,[32] with certain exceptions.

Compulsory purchase of lands

Where entry is made on lands compulsorily acquired before payment of compensation, interest is due on the compensation at rates fixed from time to time by statutory instrument.[33]

Interest on damages

In certain cases interest may, or must, be awarded under statute on sums decerned for as damages. This is dealt with at the end of this chapter.

Interest Due at Common Law

In many cases interest is deemed due by common law, liability to pay interest being held implied by the nature of the transaction.

Interest due by implied stipulation

Interest may be due by presumed paction. Thus a promise to pay interest already due implies an undertaking for interest so long as the debt is unpaid.[34]

> " By implied contract interest is due: (1) where one has levied moneys belonging to another, which bore interest in the hands of the former debtor. As, for example, if one who is due £100 assign to his

[25] Dicey and Morris, 848.
[26] Bills of Exchange Act 1681; Inland Bills Act 1696.
[27] Bills of Exchange Act 1772, s. 36.
[28] Ersk. III, 3, 77; Bell, *Comm.* I, 692; see also Bills of Exchange Act 1882, ss. 9, 57.
[29] Ersk., *supra*.
[30] Ersk. III, 3, 80.
[31] Income Tax Act 1952, s. 495.
[32] Finance Act 1970, s. 30; 1971, s. 62. The rate has varied at different times in the past. The Treasury now has power to vary the rate of interest by statutory instrument.
[33] Land Compensation (Scotland) Act 1963, s. 40.
[34] Ersk. III, 3, 82.

creditor a bond for £200, and the creditor uplift the whole sum, he is held bound, without any express stipulation, to pay interest for what he shall so have received.[35] So, an executor levying debts due to the deceased, which bore interest in the hands of the original debtor,[36] is held liable for interest if he have taken up the money without necessity, or at all events, from the time at which he ought to have distributed the fund. (2) Interest is, by implied contract, due on a marriage portion; for it is intended to contribute forthwith to the wife's subsistence, or the expense of the marriage. (3) On the ground also of implied contract, mandate, or as his factor or agent, in consequence of his mandate, or as his factor or agent, is held entitled to full reimbursement of interest, as well as of the principal sum advanced.[37] (4) The doctrine is gradually extending, so as to recognise a claim of interest in all cases of loan and debt in which one enjoys the use of money belonging to another.[38] (5) An agreement to pay the past interest is also held to imply an obligation for future interest [39]; and where it has been the course of dealing between the parties to pay interest, an adherence to that course is implied. (6) By implied contract, interest is due on the price or value of any property to the use and benefit of which the buyer enters, to the deprivation of the seller, and this without any regard to breach of contract or mora, but as the counterpart or consideration for the enjoyment of the fruits and profits.[40] (7) On the same principle, where money has been used, and interest saved, or profit made by the use, the person reaping the benefit is presumed to have agreed to pay interest for the use.[41] (8) A trustee or factor, who has money belonging to his principal in his hand, is liable either for full interest, or at least for bank interest, partly from implied contract, partly on the ground of neglect.[42] And judicial factors are liable for interest upon such rents as they shall recover, or ought to have recovered.[43] (9) All money obligations, taken to one in liferent and another in fee, imply interest as the sole liferent profit derivable from money so lent.[44]"[45]

Interest is also due when money is paid on account of another; thus a mandatary is entitled to reimbursement with interest from the time of the advance.[46]

35 *Irving* v. *Gordon* (1710) Mor. 553; see also *Erskine* v. *Lauderdale* (1736) Mor. 554.
36 *Arbuthnot* v. *Arbuthnot* (1758) Mor. 539.
37 Ersk. III, 3, 80.
38 *Garthland's Trs.* v. *McDowall*, May 26, 1820, F.C.
39 *Hume* v. *Seaton* (1669) Mor. 486; see also *Carnegie* v. *Durham* (1676) Mor. 484.
40 *Durie* v. *Ramsay* (1624) Mor. 542; *Clunie & Stirling* v. *Ogilvie* (1626) Mor. 543; *Stirling* v. *Panter* (1627) Mor. 3728; *Balnagown* v. *McKenzie* (1663) Mor. 545; *Wallace* v. *Oswald* (1825) 3 S. 525.
41 *Hardie* v. *Cauvin* (1823) 2 S. 213.
42 *Campbell* v. *Rose* (1752) Mor. 516; *Elphinston* v. *Keiths* (1790) Mor. 4067.
43 *Cranstoun* v. *Scott* (1826) 5 S. 62.
44 Ersk. III, 3, 79.
45 Bell, *Comm.* I, 692–693.
46 Ersk. III, 3, 80.

Interest on contract price

Where it is necessary to sue for the price due under a contract interest can be claimed from the date when the money should have been paid. In various cases problems have arisen as to the date from which interest should run. Thus in *Union Canal Co.* v. *Carmichael* [47] possession of land was given under an agreement to pay for the value of stone in it, as soon as it should be discovered. It was held that interest was due only from the time the stone was found and its quantity ascertained. In *Forrest and Barr* v. *Henderson* [48] a contract provided for payment by a bill at four months when the machinery was accepted. It was not accepted for nearly four years but in an action for the price the jury gave interest from four months after it began to be used, and the court declined to disturb the verdict.

Sale of goods

In the particular case of sale of goods the Sale of Goods Act 1893, s. 49 (3), provides that nothing in the Act is to prejudice the right of the seller in Scotland to recover interest on the price from the date of tender of the goods, or from the date on which the price was payable. It is established that a seller can always sue for the price and interest from the date when the money should have been paid on the basis of an implied breach of contract.[49] But if the seller recovers the price, interest and the expenses of process, he cannot also recover extra-judicial expenses by way of damages.[50]

Sale of land

Interest runs on the price of land sold from the date of entry [51] if settlement is delayed, and even though the seller may not be in a position to give a clear title.[52] Liability for interest on the buyer's part may be avoided by lodging the purchase price in bank on deposit receipt in the joint names of the buyer and seller or their respective agents; on settlement of the transaction the buyer delivers the deposit receipt endorsed and the seller uplifts the money deposited together with interest accrued at deposit receipt rate.[53] It does not matter which party has been responsible for the delay.[54] Where the price was payable by instalments it was held that interest ran only on the instalments in arrears.[55]

The general rule is also applicable to sales by virtue of compulsory powers.[56]

[47] (1842) 1 Bell 316.
[48] (1869) 8 M. 187.
[49] Bell, *Comm.* I, 692; *Prin.* § 32.
[50] *McDowall* v. *Stewart* (1871) 10 M. 193.
[51] *Stewart* v. *E. of Cassillis*, Dec. 21, 1811, F.C.; *Wallace* v. *Oswald* (1825) 3 S. 525.
[52] Ersk. III, 3, 79; Bell, *Comm.* I, 693; Bell, *Conveyancing*, II, 724; *Wallace, supra*; *Spiers* v. *Ardrossan Canal Co.* (1827) 5 S. 764; *Dickson* v. *Munro* (1855) 17 D. 524; *West Highland Ry.* v. *Place* (1894) 21 R. 576; *Greenock Harbour Trs.* v. *G.S.W. Ry.*, 1909 S.C.(H.L.) 49.
[53] *Prestwick Cinema Co.* v. *Gardiner*, 1951 S.C. 98.
[54] *Ibid.*
[55] *Baird's Trs.* v. *Baird* (1877) 4 R. 1005.
[56] *West Highland Ry.* v. *Place* (1894) 21 R. 576; *Greenock Harbour Trs., supra*; see also *Carmichael* v. *Caledonian Ry.* (1870) 8 M.(H.L.) 119; *Burke* v. *Burke* (1904) 12 S.L.T. 180.

The rate of interest customarily allowed from entry till payment or consignation in bank has usually been 5 per cent.,[57] but this is not a rule.[58] In *Traill* v. *Connon* [59] 4 per cent. was allowed for a period while the validity of the title was in dispute, the question in issue being one of great difficulty. In *Greenock Harbour Trs.* v. *Glasgow and South-Western Ry.*[60] 3½ per cent. was allowed. But where the rate chargeable on bank overdraft is higher there is no reason why a corresponding rate should not be demanded of a dilatory purchaser.

Accounts for services rendered

Similarly the general rule is that interest is due on an account for services rendered, such as that of a solicitor for professional services or of a tradesman for work done.[61] But it is not due merely because an account has been rendered, unless an action has been raised to secure payment or intimation has been made that interest will be claimed in the event of non-payment.[62] Erskine's view [63] was that a year's credit was allowed on an ordinary open account and this has been applied in the case of a solicitor's business account,[64] but was disapproved as a general rule in *Blair's Trs.*[61]

In the case of a solicitor interest after a year from the date of the last item in the account has been allowed [65] and in some circumstances on outlays as well as fees.[66] It has been allowed too on cash lent by them from the date of the advance.[67] Delay may preclude him from claiming interest.[68] The question is one of circumstances in every case and there is no fixed rule. Where a solicitor inmixed a client's funds with his own, the client was held entitled to interest at 5 per cent.[69] Compound interest has been disallowed on cash advances made by an agent to his client,[70] but in an earlier case simple interest was allowed.[71]

In *McLelland* v. *Redfearn* [72] interest was allowed at 4 per cent. on an

57 *Grandison's Trs.* v. *Jardine* (1895) 22 R. 925.

58 *Prestwick Cinema Co.* v. *Gardiner*, 1949 S.C. 645, 650, quoting *Kearon* v. *Thomson's Trs.*, 1947 S.C. 287.

59 (1877) 5 R. 25.

60 1909 S.C.(H.L.) 49.

61 *Blair's Trs.* v. *Payne* (1884) 12 R. 104; *Bunten* v. *Hart* (1902) 9 S.L.T. 476; *Somervell's Trs.* v. *Edinburgh Life Assce. Co.*, 1911 S.C. 1069. *Cf. Cardno and Darling* v. *Steuart* (1869) 7 M. 1026.

62 *Somervell, supra.*

63 Ersk. III, 3, 80.

64 *Henry* v. *Sutherland*, Feb. 13, 1801, F.C.; *Young* v. *Baillie* (1830) 8 S. 624; *Walls* v. *Spiers* (1865) 3 M. 536.

65 Bell, *Comm.* I, 648; *Henry* v. *Sutherland*, Feb. 13, 1801, F.C.; *Young* v. *Baillie* (1830) 8 S. 624; *Bremner* v. *Mabon* (1837) 16 S. 217; *Walls* v. *Spiers, supra*; *Graham's Exors.* v. *Fletcher's Exors.* (1870) 9 M. 298.

66 *Barclay* v. *Barclay* (1850) 22 Sc.Jur. 354; *Blair's Trs., supra.*

67 *Young, supra.*

68 *Napier* v. *Balfour* (1835) 13 S. 853 (twenty-six years); *Bremner* v. *Mabon* (1837) 16 S. 217 (twenty years); *Forman* v. *Home* (1844) 6 D. 1189.

69 *Jopp* v. *Johnston's Trs.* (1905) 13 S.L.T. 522.

70 *McLelland* v. *Redfearn* (1844) 7 D. 179; *Munro's Trs.* v. *Murray* (1871) 9 S.L.R. 174; *Bunten* v. *Hart* (1902) 9 S.L.T. 476.

71 *Graham's Exors.* v. *Fletcher's Exors.* (1870) 9 M. 298.

72 (1844) 7 D. 179.

agent's accounts from the last article till citation and thereafter at 5 per cent. till payment, but compound interest was refused. Where the agent had delayed to render his account for several years despite repeated requests, he was held entitled to interest on outlays only.[73]

It has been held that a law agent has no exceptional privilege entitling him to compound interest when a business account is not rendered annually.[74] In *Forman* v. *Home* [75] an agent rendered an account for nine years' services with the words " ex. int." after the total due. The sum was paid and five years later a further account included an item for interest; it was held that the agent was not entitled to charge interest, as he had abandoned his claim and was not entitled to compound interest in any event.

In *Somervell's Tr.* v. *Edinburgh Life Assce. Co.*[76] law-agents claimed interest on professional charges for work done on the employment of the trustee on a bankrupt estate. There were three separate accounts for one of which action had been raised against the trustee; the second had been submitted with the warning that interest would be claimed and had received the approval of the commissioners in the sequestration; the third account had merely been rendered. It was held that interest was due on the first from the date of citation in the action and on the second from the date on which it was passed by the commissioners, but that it was not due on the third. It was also observed that in special circumstances interest might be due even on an open account as, for example, possibly in the case where goods were sold expressly for cash payments, but without any definite claim for interest. Lord Salvesen said [77]: " It is a wholesome general rule that interest will not be allowed on open accounts until there has been either a judicial demand made for payment, or an intimation that after a certain date interest will be charged on that account if not paid by that date. That is in accordance with general custom and practice, both as regards traders' accounts and as regards lawyers' accounts."

A tradesman has been held not entitled to charge interest on a current account, which is rendered periodically, from each date when it is rendered. The question whether he is entitled to interest from the date of last rendering was left undecided.[78]

Rate of interest on accounts

Where the court allows interest on a solicitor's account the rate has usually been 5 per cent.[79] The rule has frequently been adopted in practice of stating interest at 5 per cent. on outlays and 3 per cent. on professional charges; the interest on outlays is calculated from the dates when

73 *Bremner* v. *Mabon* (1837) 16 S. 213; *Napier* v. *Balfour* (1835) 13 S. 853.
74 *Munro's Trs.* v. *Murray and Ferrier* (1871) 9 S.L.R. 174.
75 (1844) 6 D. 1189.
76 1911 S.C. 1069, foll. *Blair's Trs.* v. *Payne* (1884) 12 R. 104.
77 *Supra*, at p. 1071.
78 *Cardno and Darling* v. *Steuart* (1869) 7 M. 1026.
79 *Graham's Exors.* v. *Fletcher's Exors.* (1870) 9 M. 298; *Walls* v. *Spiers* (1865) 3 M. 536.

the disbursements were made and that on professional charges is reckoned only after giving a year's credit.[80]

Condictio indebiti

When repayment falls to be made of money paid in error, interest is also due [81] unless there is ground in equity for holding that interest was not meant to be demanded.[82] So 3 per cent. was allowed in a repetition of surplus teinds,[83] and interest on overpayment of poor rates made pending settlement of the principle of assessment,[81] 4 per cent. on income tax which fell to be repaid to an insurance society,[84] but interest has been refused where the sums were paid not only erroneously but negligently,[85] and only bank interest was allowed where a levy imposed illegally by a statutory body had to be repaid.[86] In the old case of *Duncan* v. *Bruce* [87] it was said that as a general rule the highest legal rate was due on repayment of money but it is conceived that this rule must yield to circumstances and is not fixed. In *Mills* v. *Brown's Trs.*[88] trustees illegally though in bona fide appointed one of their number salaried manager of a business which was part of the trust estate; he was held liable to repay the sums received by him but not liable in interest thereon.

Advances

Advances of money carry interest: this includes arrears of sums advanced towards aliment of children [89]; advances made by a law-agent [90] though this does not extend to ordinary judicial outlays,[91] or by a judicial factor.[92] " A cash advance is a loan of money, and loans of money as a matter of legal implication, where the contrary is not stipulated, bear interest as if there had been an express provision to this effect." [93] Outlays made by a law-agent which are considered as advances on which the agent can claim interest include advances incurred for the repair of property, payments for premiums of insurance, payments of debts due, counsel's and accountant's fees, stamps and such like.[94] He may not charge compound interest on his cash advances.[95]

80 Begg on *Law Agents*, 135.
81 *Glasgow Gas Light Co.* v. *Barony Parochial Board of Glasgow* (1868) 6 M. 406 (rate not stated): *cf. Greig* v. *Edinburgh Mags.* (2½ per cent. on arrears of poor rates).
82 Bell, *Prin.* § 32; *Durie's Trs.* v. *Ayton* (1894) 22 R. 34.
83 *Gwydyr* v. *Lord Advocate* (1894) 2 S.L.T. 280.
84 *Scottish Widows Fund* v. *Inland Revenue*, 1909 S.C. 1372.
85 *Cromartie* v. *Lord Advocate* (1871) 9 M. 988 (surplus teinds).
86 *Haddon's Exx.* v. *Scottish Milk Marketing Board*, 1938 S.C. 168.
87 (1836) 14 S. 583.
88 (1901) 3 F. 1012.
89 *Hill* v. *Gilroy* (1821) 1 S. 33.
90 *Findlay, Bannatyne & Co.'s Assignee* v. *Donaldson* (1864) 2 M.(H.L.) 86; *Graham's Exors.* v. *Fletcher's Exors.* (1870) 9 M. 298; *Blair's Trs.* v. *Payne* (1884) 12 R. 104; *Bunten* v. *Hart* (1902) 9 S.L.T. 476.
91 *Macpherson* v. *Tytler* (1853) 15 D. 706 (judicial expenses); *Barclay* v. *Barclay* (1850) 22 Sc.Jur. 354 (printing outlays).
92 *Scott* v. *Handyside's Trs.* (1868) 6 M. 753.
93 *Blair's Trs., supra*, 108, *per* Lord Craighill, citing Bell, *Prin.* § 32.
94 *Blair's Trs., supra*, 109, *per* Lord Fraser; *Graham's Exors., supra.*
95 *Bunten* v. *Hart* (1902) 9 S.L.T. 476.

A judicial factor has been held entitled to charge interest at 5 per cent. on advances made by him.[96] Again an allottee of shares in a company who was found entitled to restore them as having been issued *ultra vires* was held to be a creditor and entitled to repayment of the price with interest at 4 per cent.[97] In *Galashiels Provident Building Socy.* v. *Newlands*[98] it was held that granting a heritable bond to a building society did not supersede the latter's rule relative to advances, and hence that a discharge of bond and interest did not discharge an obligation under the rules to pay 10 per cent. on arrears of interest on advances.

In partnership, unless express provision is made to the contrary a partner is entitled to interest upon any advances he has made to the firm beyond the amount of capital he has agreed to subscribe.[99]

A cautioner is entitled to interest on any payments he may have made on behalf of the principal debtor.[1] Interest is likewise due by or to a commercial agent on a balance in his hands or resting owing to him.[2]

Loan of money

As a general rule the law implies that interest shall be paid upon a loan of money[3] even though there was no stipulation for interest,[4] but that implication may be displaced by the circumstances of the case.[5] Relationship of the parties,[5] absence of demands for interest over a long period,[6] the acknowledgment that the money was to be repaid at a later unspecified time[7] and an instruction to use the money "as if it were your own"[8] tend to displace the implication. Even where the demand for interest was not made till thirty-four years after the loan was made and both borrower and lender were dead, decree for interest was granted,[9] it being held that as there was a written acknowledgment of the loan the plea of mora and taciturnity could not apply. Moreover, if a promissory note is granted for an advance of money on loan the surrender of the note and the grant of a new one does not discharge the claim for interest on the loan.[10] Where money is paid on an obligation to repay it on the occur-

96 *Dundee Suburban Ry.* (1902) 9 S.L.T. 464; *Scott, supra.*

97 *Waverley Hydropathic Co.* v. *Barrowman* (1895) 23 R. 136.

98 (1893) 20 R. 821; but compare *N.B. Bldg. Socy.* v. *McLellan* (1887) 14 R. 827.

99 Partnership Act 1890, s. 24, r. 3. *Cf. Ewing & Co.* v. *Ewing* (1882) 10 R.(H.L.) 1; *McArthur* v. *Scott* (1898) 6 S.L.T. 162 (dissolution).

1 Ersk. III, 3, 78; Bell, *Prin.* § 32; Bell, *Comm.* I, 696.

2 Bell, *Comm.* I, 693; *Findlay, Bannatyne & Co.'s Assignee* v. *Donaldson* (1864) 2 M.(H.L.) 86.

3 *Blair's Trs.* v. *Payne* (1884) 12 R. 104, 110, *per* Lord Fraser. As to the rates a moneylender may exact, see Moneylenders Act 1927, s. 10 (1).

4 *Garthland's Trs.* v. *McDowall*, May 26, 1820, F.C. But interest does not run on the sum in an IOU, unless expressly stipulated for, but only from the date of citation: *Winestone* v. *Wolifson*, 1954 S.C. 77.

5 *Christie* v. *Matheson* (1871) 10 M. 9; *Smellie's Exrx.* v. *Smellie*, 1933 S.C. 725; *cf. Shaw's Trs.* v. *Shaw* (1870) 8 M. 419; *Williamson* v. *Williamson's Trs.*, 1948 S.L.T.(Notes) 72.

6 *Thiem's Trs.* v. *Collie* (1898) 1 F. 764 (11 years); *Smellie's Exrx., supra* (18 years).

7 *Smellie's Exrx., supra.*

8 *Christie* v. *Matheson* (1871) 10 M. 9.

9 *Cuninghame* v. *Boswell* (1868) 6 M. 890.

10 *Hope Johnstone* v. *Cornwall* (1895) 22 R. 314.

rence of a certain event, interest is due from the date of payment.[11] Where a loan has been made on the understanding that repayment would not be demanded until the borrower's circumstances improved, interest was held not to be due until the date of citation.[12] In the *Glasgow* case [11] Lord President Inglis said that " a party receiving payment of money, reserving the question of his title to receive it, is surely bound to repay it with interest, when he is found to be in the wrong. There can be no clearer case of interest being due than that " though it might be otherwise in the case of a party receiving payment in good faith, believing it to be his own.[13]

Bell states further [14] that: " interest is due in all cases where money is lent or where the use of it is taken or retained; unless from the circumstances of the case there is ground in equity to hold that interest was not meant to be demanded."

A creditor who received a large payment in a multiplepoinding on account of a supposed preference in a bond which was reduced, was held bound to repay the excess with 5 per cent. interest.[15] Lord Mackenzie said that the highest legal rate was due as a general rule on repetition of money.

For cases of interest on improvement expenditure, see the undernoted cases.[16]

Bonds and obligations to pay

Interest is due on all bonds and obligations for the payment of money on a precise day, if that day should pass without payment,[17] though this does not extend to feuduties or ground-annuals. If no precise term be fixed, and the date of payment is in the option of the creditor, a judicial or notarial demand will raise a claim of interest from that date onward.[18] If a bond contains no stipulation for interest, it appears to be a question of circumstances whether the creditor may exact any and it will only be allowed if grounds can be shown for presuming that to have been the intention of the parties.[19] The interest on a personal bond accrues *de die in diem* and in the absence of contrary stipulation will be payable by equal portions at Whitsunday and Martinmas in each year.[20] The rate of interest should be specified in the bond,[21] and Lord Low suggested that a bond for a sum with interest but without specifying the rate was not a

11 *Glasgow Gas-Light Co.* v. *Barony Parish* (1868) 6 M. 406.
12 *Forbes* v. *Forbes* (1869) 8 M. 35.
13 *Glasgow Gas-Light Co.* v. *Barony Parish* (1868) 6 M. 406, 413–414; *Haddon's Exrx.* v. *Scottish Milk Marketing Board*, 1938 S.C. 168.
14 *Comm.* I, 692.
15 *Duncan* v. *Bruce* (1836) 14 S. 583.
16 *Sinclair* v. *McBeath* (1868) 7 M. 273; *Shepherd's Exors.* v. *Mackenzie*, 1913 S.C. 144.
17 Bell, *Comm.* I, 691.
18 *Ibid.*; *Watt* v. *Burnett's Trs.* (1839) 2 D. 132; *Smellie's Exrx.* v. *Smellie*, 1938 S.C. 725.
19 *Cunninghame* v. *Cunninghame* (1821) 1 S. 231. As to a bond with a condition referring to the market rate of interest, see *Field* v. *Watt's Trs.* (1863) 2 M. 33.
20 Bell's *Lectures on Conveyancing*, I, 257.
21 See Titles to Land Consolidation (Scotland) Act 1868, Sched. FF.

valid security for the interest.[22] A stipulation for " legal interest " in a bond is usually held to mean 5 per cent.[23]

If a debt is not yet constituted as liquid, or one on which interest is not originally due, the claim to interest will lie from the date of citation [24] or of decree constituting the debt,[25] though an exception was admitted in one case which was a claim of aliment for an illegitimate child when the father was abroad.[26]

It is competent for a bond to stipulate for payment of a certain high rate of interest on the bond, which is qualified by a back-letter to the effect that so long as the interest is duly paid a lower rate will be accepted. Such an agreement is strictly construed,[27] and a delay of seven days is not " punctual payment." [28] Alternatively the bond may itself declare that if the stipulated interest is not paid within a certain period after the specified terms, then a higher rate of interest will be exigible from the debtor who has granted the bond, but this is objectionable as a penalty [29] and unenforceable in its terms.[30] The penalty clause in a bond will not authorise the charging of interest on interest,[31] though it will extend to cover interest on interest paid by a cautioner for the debtor.[32] Where a debtor in a bond consigned the money pending delivery to him of a valid discharge, he was held liable for no more than bank interest.[33]

Among other obligations interest has been held due on arrears of aliment for a bastard.[34]

Claims in bankruptcy

A claimant on the sequestrated estates of a bankrupt may claim in respect of the accumulated amount of principal and interest due him down to the date of sequestration, but not for interest which accrues thereafter.[35] Apart from contrary agreement, interest is calculated at 5 per cent. but clear usage of trade will regulate both the term and the rate of interest.[36] If there is any balance of estate after payment of all claims admitted to

22 *Forbes* v. *Welsh* (1894) 21 R. 630; *Alston* v. *Nellfield Co.*, 1915 S.C. 912.
23 Bell's *Lectures*, I, 256. See Rate of Interest, *infra*.
24 *Gillow* v. *Burgess* (1824) 3 S. 45.
25 *Wallace* v. *Geddes* (1821) 1 Sh.App. 42.
26 *Hill* v. *Gilroy* (1821) 1 S. 33.
27 *Gatty* v. *Maclaine*, 1921 S.C.(H.L.) 1 (" punctual payment "), following *Leeds and Hanley Theatre of Varieties* v. *Broadbent* [1898] 1 Ch. 343 (" punctually ") and disapproving Lord McLaren in *Scott-Chisholme* v. *Brown* (1893) 20 R. 575; *Kennedy* v. *Begg, Kennedy & Elder*, 1954 S.L.T.(Sh.Ct.) 103.
28 *Gatty*, *supra*.
29 Craigie, *Moveable Rights*, 204, is in error in saying this is possible.
30 *Nasmyth* v. *Samson* (1785) 3 Paton 9.
31 *McNeil* v. *McNeil* (1826) 4 S. 620; revd. (1830) 4 W. & S. 455.
32 *Inglis* v. *Renny* (1825) 4 S. 113.
33 *Grant* v. *Thomson* (1835) 13 S. 878.
34 *Pott* v. *Pott* (1833) 12 S. 183.
35 Bankruptcy (Scotland) Act 1913, s. 48; *Love* v. *Anderson* (1846) 8 D. 1016; *Paterson* v. *Lumsden* (1846) 19 Sc.Jur. 144. As to calculation of interest on a moneylender's loan in bankruptcy proceedings, see Moneylenders Act 1927, s. 9 (1).
36 Bankruptcy (Scotland) Act 1913, s. 48. See also *Crawford* v. *Bertram*, May 15, 1812, F.C.

ranking, the creditor may claim out of the residue the full amount of interest in terms of law.[37] This interest probably falls to be distributed in the same way as ordinary dividends, and creditors should probably count former dividends against interest accrued on their initial claims.[38] Postponed creditors are possibly entitled to a dividend in preference to any such payments of interest.[39]

Advances to trust beneficiaries

A beneficiary or legatee is liable in 5 per cent. interest and accumulations on advances made to him beyond the value of his due share in the trust estate.[40] It has been questioned whether an advance made during a father's lifetime and the interest thereon falls to be deducted from legitim,[41] but in *Gilmour's Trs.* v. *Gilmour* [42] it was held that in the absence of evidence of a contrary intention by the parent, interest on a parental advance need not be added to the capital sum, when the advance falls to be brought into collation by the child's claiming legitim. When trustees made advances to beneficiaries authorised by the testator simple interest was held due.[43] On the other hand *ultra vires* annual allowances or advances were made to beneficiaries in *Baird's Trs.* v. *Duncanson*,[44] and it was held that the *ultra vires* advances with interest at the rate which the rest of the trust fund was yielding fell to be imputed to the beneficiaries' respective eventual share of residue. In *Smith's Trs.* v. *Sellar* [45] it was held on consideration of the trust settlement that advances by the truster to a son-in-law fell to be imputed to the share of residue falling to the latter's children but without interest.

Statutory prior rights and legal rights in succession

On the death of a person intestate, a surviving spouse is entitled to, *inter alia*, £4,000 or £8,000 out of the intestate estate, according as there are, or are not, surviving issue, with interest at 4 per cent. from the date of death till payment.[46]

The surviving spouse has also a claim to *jus relicti vel relictae* out of the net moveable estate after deduction of any claims to statutory prior rights under sections 8 and 9.[47] At common law the claim is treated as a claim of debt against the estate bearing interest *a morte*.

In *Reid* v. *Reid's Trs.*[48] a widow claimed *jus relictae* after a delay caused

37 *Ibid.*
38 *Wilson's Trs.* v. *Watson* (1900) 2 F. 761.
39 *Goudy on Bankruptcy* (4th ed.), 331.
40 *Plaine* v. *Thomson* (1836) 15 S. 194.
41 *Johnston* v. *Cochran* (1829) 7 S. 226. See Bell's *Prin.* § 1588.
42 1922 S.C. 753.
43 *Mathew's Trs.* v. *Mathew* (1905) 13 S.L.T. 470.
44 (1892) 19 R. 1045.
45 (1894) 21 R. 633.
46 Succession (Sc.) Act 1964, s. 9, amended Succession (Sc.) Act, 1973, s. 1.
47 *Ibid.* s. 10 (2).
48 1927 S.L.T. 18.

neither by her fault nor that of the trustees, and was held entitled to a sum under that head together with all revenue accrued and interest on the revenue invested.

Legitim is claimable from the deceased's estate by any surviving issue of the deceased.[49] It is a debt due by the deceased's moveable estate to his issue and therefore *ex lege* carries interest from the date of death till payment.[50] It has even been held that a daughter entitled to legitim was entitled to interest from the date of her father's death, although no claim had been made for about twenty years thereafter.[51] Interest runs even though no charge of *mora* can be brought against the trustees.[52] Where a parent has made advances to a child which fall to be brought into collation by the child's claiming legitim, interest need not be added to the capital sum of the advance from the date when it was made in the absence of evidence of a contrary intention on the parent's part.[53] Where there is justification for delay in payment a lesser rate is usually allowed and full interest only from the time when the legitim was properly payable.[54]

The rate of interest was formerly firmly established as 5 per cent. where an executor delayed to pay without justifiable excuse,[55] but exceptions were not infrequently made in unusual circumstances. In *Ross* v. *Ross*[56] Lord McLaren observed that there was no statutory rate of interest and no rule obliging the court to award 5 per cent. in perpetuity, and suggested that the court had power to reduce the rate usually awarded in the event of a permanent fall in the rate of interest obtainable in the country, reserved his opinion on the question of the rate permissible where the right to legitim could be immediately determined, but where the claim was allowed to lie over without fault on either side. In that case the claim was delayed for thirteen years after the father's death but election could not have been made earlier, and the executrix was found liable in interest only at 4 per cent. as the rate which the money would have earned under prudent administration and which it had admittedly earned. Similarly in *McCall's Trs.* v. *McCall's C.B.*[57] a delay of twelve years took place and interest was awarded at the rate earned by the trust, as also in *Grant* v. *Grant's Trs.*,[58] where the delay was eight years. In

49 Succession (Sc.) Act, ss. 10 (2) and 11.

50 *McMurray* v. *McMurray's Trs.* (1852) 14 D. 1048; *Ross* v. *Ross* (1896) 23 R. 802; *Henderson* v. *Henderson's Trs.*, 1916, 2 S.L.T. 292; *Duncan* v. *Crichton's Trs.*, 1917 S.C. 728. *Cf.* also cases on *communio bonorum*: *Smith* v. *Barlas* (1857) 19 D. 267; *Hardie* v. *Kay's Trs.* (1823) 2 S. 213; *Kennedy* v. *Bell* (1866) 1 S.L.R. 105.

51 *Sime* v. *Balfour*, March 1, 1804, F.C.; affd. (1811) 5 Paton 525.

52 *Kearon* v. *Thomson's Trs.*, 1949 S.C. 287.

53 *Gilmour's Trs.* v. *Gilmour*, 1922 S.C. 753.

54 *Ross*, *supra*; *Gilchrist* v. *Gilchrist's Trs.* (1889) 16 R. 1118; *Smith's Trs.* v. *Smith*, 1912, 1 S.L.T. 484; *Kearon*, *supra*.

55 *McMurray* v. *McMurray's Trs.* (1852) 14 D. 1048; *Gilchrist* v. *Gilchrist's Trs.* (1889) 16 R. 1118, *per* Lord Fraser; *Bishop's Trs.* v. *Bishop* (1894) 21 R. 728; *Reid* v. *Reid's Trs.*, 1927 S.L.T. 18.

56 (1896) 23 R. 802. See also the Lord Ordinary's note. Four per cent. was given. *Cf.* *Smith's Trs.* v. *Smith*, 1912, 1 S.L.T. 484.

57 (1901) 3 F. 1065. Lord Moncreiff suggested 3 per cent. as enough.

58 (1898) 25 R. 948. See Lord Young's observation on the rate at p. 950.

Smith's Trs. v. *Smith* [59] several years elapsed before the child's claim to legitim was made and a litigation caused further delay. Interest at trust rate was allowed till the date of claim and at 5 per cent. thereafter. Four per cent. was allowed in *Mason* v. *Mitchell*,[60] and 5 per cent. refused in *Davidson* v. *Mackenzie*,[61] while in *Kearon* v. *Thomson's Trs.*[62] 3 per cent. was allowed when there had been no unavoidable delay. It was made plain that " legal interest " was not fixed at 5 per cent. but the appropriate rate was a question of circumstances, one of which, and often the determining one, being the rate actually earned by the trust or executry estate.[63] In the absence of special cause, 5 per cent., however, remains the recognised rate for penal interest exacted against a debtor who has fraudulently withheld punctual payment of a debt. The court's conclusion was that the rate of interest should be determined by reference to the rate earned by the estate under prudent administration, the rate at which the recipient might prudently have invested the money had it been available to him for that purpose at the date of death, and the rates generally ruling on government and trustee securities generally. Opinion was reserved on cases complicated by deferred election, impropriety of conduct, or where consignation had been made of a disputed sum.

In *Wick* v. *Wick* [64] a delay of seventeen years ensued but the pursuer's claim was held not to be barred; interest was, however, refused.

Legacies

Legacies differ somewhat from legal rights in that they do not constitute a debt due *ex lege* from the deceased's estate but are rather gifts payable from the residue of the estate. As between executor and legatee they rank as debts though postponed thereto. Nevertheless the rights which accrue to a legatee as appearing on the face of the will are enhanced by natural accessions to the subject matter thereof,[65] and hence a legacy of a specific security carries with it the interest accruing thereon *a morte testatoris,* even though the period of payment or delivery has been postponed, provided that the right vested at the testator's death.[66]

Unless expressly excluded by the terms of the will interest is therefore due on a legacy. The former rule was that it was payable at all events from twelve months after the testator's death.[67]

In several cases interest has been held to run from a period after the testator's death when such a time appears reasonable for payment: in such

59 1912, 1 S.L.T. 484.
60 (1895) 3 S.L.T. 3.
61 (1898) 6 S.L.T. 25.
62 1949 S.C. 287. *Cf. Gloag on Contract,* 683; *Menzies on Trustees,* § 1107.
63 *Ibid.* 296.
64 (1898) 1 F. 199.
65 *McLaren on Wills,* § 1053; *Cunninghame* v. *Vassall* (1871) 10 M. 49.
66 *Ibid.* § 1060; *Glasgow's Trs.* v. *Glasgow* (1830) 9 S. 87; *Paterson* v. *Macnaughton* (1838) 1 D. 241; *Duff's Trs.* v. *Societies of Scripture Readers* (1862) 24 D. 552.
67 *McAllister* v. *McAllister* (1827) 5 S. 862 (4 per cent. allowed); *Stevenson* v. *Macintyre* (1826) 4 S. 776; *Inglis' Trs.* v. *Breen* (1891) 18 R. 487, *per* Lord McLaren.

cases, however, the ratio appears to be *morata solutio.* For instance, legacies were directed to be paid on conversion of the estate and after the expiry of a liferent: it was held that interest ran from one year after the testator's death as this was a reasonable time to allow for conversion and the liferent did not prevent conversion being effected.[68] In *Ogilvie's Legatees* v. *Hamilton* [69] legacies were payable from the proceeds of the sale of land, the trustees having a discretion as to the time of sale. It was held that interest ran from the first term after three years from the testator's death, which was allowed as a reasonable period within which to have sold the lands. McLaren [70] was of the view that this case should not be treated as a precedent, pointing out that it has subsequently been decided that the right to beneficial enjoyment emerges one year after the testator's death in the absence of any express direction as to time. Where a sum due to a testatrix, on which interest had never either been demanded or paid was specially bequeathed by her, the legatee was held entitled to the accumulations on the assumption that interest was payable on the debt, *i.e.* in effect to compound interest.[71]

The modern practice is, however, to hold interest due from the date of death of the testator,[72] or from the period at which the funds become productive.[73] Apart from questions of delay, a legacy will bear interest from the date of payment, if such a date is expressly or impliedly mentioned, on the principle that legacies bear interest like any other money debt from the date when they are due and payable,[74] which will normally be the date of death, so that interest will run *a morte testatoris.*[75]

While this may be stated as a general rule it cannot be taken as universal.[76] So interest has been limited to what the estate was earning when the legatee delayed to claim for three years, and no interest was allowed when the estate was insolvent for a long period and no asset was realisable to meet the legacies nor was there any interest-bearing subject.[77]

In *Waddell's Trs.* v. *Crawford* [78] Lord Justice-Clerk Alness was disposed to put the question as being one of circumstances, and held that there was no inflexible rule of law compelling the court in all circumstances to allow interest on a legacy *a morte testatoris.* Similarly in *Ewing* v. *Mathieson* [79] it became possible at the end of a liferent to pay the balance of outstanding legacies, and interest was refused as the capital had not been in the hands of the executors as an interest-bearing subject; and in *Inglis's*

68 *Young's Trs.* v. *Young* (1869) 6 S.L.R. 456 (4 per cent. allowed).
69 (1833) 12 S. 189.
70 § 1059, referring to §§ 1865 *et seq.*
71 *Cunninghame* v. *Vassall* (1871) 10 M. 49.
72 McLaren, § 1059; *Kirkpatrick* v. *Bedford* (1878) 6 R.(H.L.) 4; *McLean's Trs.* v. *McLean* (1891) 18 R. 892; *Duff's Trs.* v. *Scripture Readers* (1862) 24 D. 552.
73 *Waddell's Trs.* v. *Crawford*, 1926 S.C. 654.
74 *May's Trs.* v. *Paul* (1900) 2 F. 657, 660, *per* Lord Trayner.
75 *Duff's Trs., supra*; *Macalister's Trs.* v. *Macalister* (1836) 15 S. 170; *May's Trs., supra*; Bell, *Prin.*, § 1885; *Kirkpatrick* v. *Bedford* (1878) 6 R.(H.L.) 4.
76 *Waddell's Trs., supra, per* L.J.C. Alness, at 663.
77 *Waddell's Trs., supra.*
78 1926 S.C. 654, 664, quoting *Ross* v. *Ross* (1896) 23 R. 802.
79 (1904) 41 S.L.R. 594.

Trs. v. *Breen*,[80] where payment of a legacy was postponed for several years owing to the beneficiary's delay to elect between legal rights and conventional provisions, the legatee was held entitled only to the rate actually received down to the date of her election and it was observed that there was no general rule that the rate was 5 per cent. where the trustees were not in *mora.* When a testator advances sums to his children prior to his death, directing that these are to be deducted from their shares of his trust estate, it has been held that no interest is to be reckoned on the advances,[81] though it is otherwise where the advances were made by trustees.[82]

Where a sum was due to a testatrix, on which interest had never been demanded or paid, and she bequeathed this sum specially, the legatee was held entitled to the accumulations, on the presumption that interest was payable on the debt.[83] In *Young's Trs.* v. *Young* [84] a truster directed his trustees to realise his estate and pay certain legacies on the death of his wife who had a liferent. It was held that as the conversion might have taken place in her lifetime and as vesting was *a morte*, interest at 4 per cent. ran from a year after the trustee's death, as being a reasonable period for conversion. Where a legatee entitled to two legacies ultimately held to be cumulative received payment of one and granted a full discharge of all claims against the trustees, and, 20 years later claimed the second legacy, it was undecided whether she was entitled to interest on the second legacy.[85] Where a truster gave his trustees discretion as to the times of sale of lands for payment of legacies which were declared not payable till after such a sale and several years elapsed, three years were allowed as a reasonable period for executing the sale and interest ran on the special legacies from the first term thereafter.[86] Postponement of the period of payment will not prevent interest running from the first term after the testator's death when the legacy vested *a morte.*[87] When a legacy was left on condition that the legatee paid interest on it to a third party, 3½ per cent. was allowed.[88] Where a specific legacy of a substantial sum was set apart for younger children, interest arising thereon before the fund was payable was held to accresce to capital.[89] It was observed in *Waddell's Trs.* v. *Crawford*,[90] where a beneficiary claimed interest on a legacy in respect of a long delay in distributing the estate, that there was no absolute rule to the effect that the rate of legal interest should be 5 per cent., the rate being in every case a question for the discretion of the court in the particular circumstances.

80 (1891) 18 R. 487. Contrast *Paterson* v. *Danson* (1897) 5 S.L.T. 64 (5 per cent. where several years' delay).

81 *Smith's Trs.* v. *Sellar* (1894) 21 R. 633; *cf. Johnston* v. *Cochran* (1829) 7 S. 226.

82 *Mathew's Trs.* v. *Mathew* (1905) 13 S.L.T. 470.

83 *Cunninghame* v. *Vassall* (1871) 10 M. 49.

84 (1869) 6 S.L.R. 456.

85 *Burn* v. *Fairholme* (1840) 12 Sc.Jur. 387.

86 *Ogilvie's Legatees* v. *Hamilton* (1833) 12 S. 189.

87 *Johns* v. *Munro's Trs.* (1833) 12 S. 146.

88 *Crawfurd* v. *Ballantine's Trs.* (1833) 6 Sc.Jur. 71.

89 *Glasgow's Trs.* v. *Glasgow* (1830) 9 S. 87.

90 1926 S.C. 654.

The clearest case for exacting interest is where there is *morata solutio*[91] or wrongful withholding of the legacy by the executors.[92] Thus trustees were held liable in interest at 4 per cent. when they were found personally liable for the sale of certain stock and for the resultant loss to the trust estate.[93]

Rate of interest on legacies

There is nowadays no inflexible rule of law requiring the court to award 5 per cent. interest on an unpaid legacy,[94] and lesser rates have frequently been awarded, such as 4 per cent.,[95] 3½ per cent.,[96] and 3 per cent.,[97] or no interest at all where the estate was for long insolvent and unproductive,[98] or the rate actually received by the trustees on the trust investments.[99] The rate is a matter to be decided having regard to the circumstances of the case[1] and regard must be had to the general rates of interest available at the time.[2] Hence it would appear that 5 per cent. will now be held in reserve as a penal rate exigible only when the executors have wrongfully delayed to pay or have withheld the legacy unjustifiably.[3]

In the general case compound interest is not due.[4]

Difficulties may arise in cases where legacies are payable at a fixed future date or on the occurrence of an event and the cases are not readily reconcilable. In *McLean's Trs.* v. *McLean*[5] legacies were held on the terms of the will to carry interest *a morte testatoris*, while in *Playfair's Trs.* v. *Hunter*[6] a direction to hold till a certain date was held not to carry interest, which fell into residue. In this latter case, however, vesting was postponed and in the former only payment was postponed and there was power to use the income for the beneficiary.

From what date interest due

Bell[7] gives the following rules for the commencement of interest:

1. Where there is an express agreement concerning the commencement of interest, it rules the case. 2. Otherwise, in the general case, interest runs from the stipulated day of payment. 3. Where the day of payment is

91 *Ewing* v. *Mathieson* (1904) 41 S.L.R. 594, 596, *per* Lord Stormonth-Darling; *Inglis' Trs.* v. *Breen* (1891) 18 R. 487; *Carmichael* v. *Caledonian Ry.* (1870) 8 M.(H.L.) 119, 131; *Ross* v. *Ross* (1896) 23 R. 802; *Kearon* v. *Thomson's Trs.*, 1949 S.C. 287.

92 *Miller's Exors.* v. *Miller's Trs.*, 1922 S.C. 150.

93 *Hardie's Trs.* v. *Graham* (1896) 3 S.L.T. 277.

94 *Inglis' Trs.* v. *Breen* (1891) 18 R. 487; *Campbell's Exor.* v. *Campbell's Trs.* (1898) 25 R. 687; *Grant* v. *Grant's Trs.* (1898) 25 R. 948.

95 *McInnes* v. *McAllister* (1827) 5 S. 862; *Young's Trs.* v. *Young* (1869) 6 S.L.R. 456; *Ross* v. *Ross* (1896) 23 R. 802; *May's Trs.* v. *Paul* (1900) 2 F. 657.

96 *Crawfurd* v. *Ballantine's Trs.* (1833) 6 Sc.Jur. 71.

97 *Campbell's Exor., supra.*

98 *Waddell's Trs.* v. *Crawford*, 1926 S.C. 654.

99 *Inglis' Trs.* v. *Breen* (1891) 18 R. 487.

1 *Waddell's Trs., supra.*

2 *Cf. Kearon* v. *Thomson's Trs.*, 1949 S.C. 287, a legitim case.

3 McLaren, § 1063; *Inglis' Trs., supra.*

4 McLaren, § 1064. *Cf. Gunn* v. *Gordon's Trs.* (1854) 16 D. 1027.

5 (1891) 18 R. 892.

6 (1890) 17 R. 1241.

7 *Comm.* I, 694.

optional, interest runs only from the day ascertained by the act declaring the option. So, in bills payable at sight, or so many days after it, the presentment regulates the running of interest; and this is fixed either by a date adjected to the acceptance or by a protest. Or where there is no evidence of the date of presentment, but only of the presentment having taken place, it will be held as of a date as early [8] as circumstances render probable. So, a bill payable on demand will bear interest from the protest [9] or citation in an action.[10] 4. Interest runs upon arrears of cess from the expiration of six months after the term of payment.[11] 5. Interest runs on money advanced by mandatories, etc., from the date of advance.[12] The court, by one decision, refused to extend this rule to law agents [13]; and by a later decision found a law agent entitled to interest after a year from the date of the last article.[14] 6. The price of property bears interest from the time the benefit of possession accrues to the purchaser, the price being a surrogatum for the subject; and while the rents are accruing to the purchaser, the running of interest is not stopped by any attachment or by want of sufficient titles: it can be stopped only by consignation.[15] 7. It is a frequent stipulation in contracts of partnership, that on the death or bankruptcy of a partner his interest in the stock shall be ascertained as at the date of the last balance; but for the conveniency of the company, and to prevent confusion from a sudden demand, the sum due is made payable at a future term and sometimes by instalments [16]; and it has been doubted whether interest runs during the time between the date of the balance and the stipulated term of payment. According to the general rule, by which the money becomes the surrogatum of the share of company stock, which is a fund bearing profit, it would appear that, unless where the usage of trade or practice of the parties has made an exception, interest would be due.[17] 8. Interest on merchant's accounts of furnishings begins on the expiration of the accustomed credit; or if there be no special custom to regulate it, from the date of citation when the money should have been paid. 9. Interest at the legal rate begins to run on sums lent on bottomry from the termination of the voyage. 10. Sums due by underwriters on policies of insurance have been found to bear interest from the time when the loss should have been settled.[18]

Interest from date prior to citation

Interest may be claimed from a date prior to citation in cases where

[8] *Kinloch* v. *Mercer's Reps.* (1748) M. 477.
[9] Ersk. III, 3, 77.
[10] *Moncreiff* v. *Moncreiff* (1752) M. 481.
[11] Act 1686, c. 2.
[12] See *supra*.
[13] *Muirhead* v. *Town of Haddington* (1750) M. 532.
[14] *Henry* v. *Sutherland* (1801) M. App. Annualrent No. 1. See also *Young* v. *Baillie* (1830) 8 S. 624.
[15] See also *infra*.
[16] *Cf. Ewing & Co.* v. *Ewing* (1882) 10 R.(H.L.) 1; *McArthur* v. *Scott* (1898) 6 S.L.T. 162.
[17] *Findlay, Bannatyne & Co.'s Assignee* v. *Donaldson* (1864) 2 M.(H.L.) 87.
[18] *Crawford and Stark* v. *Bertram*, May 15, 1812, F.C. See Arnould on *Marine Insurance*, § 1284.

interest runs *ex lege* by statute, as in the case of bills of exchange and promissory notes, from the date of presentment or maturity.[19] Interest may also be due *ex pacto* [20] and from the date specified interest will run.[21] In cases of loan interest runs from the date of the loan even though there is no stipulation for interest,[22] unless it is apparent that interest was not intended to be charged,[23] and similarly on cash advances.[24]

Interest from the date of citation

Interest from the date of citation in the action raised to recover the sum due is usually concluded for where the debt is not liquid,[25] or where interest on the principal sum has not been provided for or in cases where the principal sum is not due to be paid either by agreement or by custom of trade at any particular time.[26] A debt arising from a contract will bear interest at latest from the date of citation.[27] In actions of damages for breach of contract a statement of the law has been put forward that interest on the sum of damages is not, as a rule, due until the damages have been ascertained, but that rule does not necessarily apply to all cases.[28] Ordinary professional accounts and tradesmen's business accounts carry interest from the date of citation so long as there is no custom of trade or agreement to the contrary, or any written intimation which would make the defender *in mora* prior to the raising of the action.[29] A cautioner suing to recover relief against his principal is entitled to interest from the date of citation.[30]

Termination of interest

Bell gives the following guidance as to the termination of interest [31]: The natural rule is that interest shall continue to run till the day of payment. But there are exceptions in respect that the claim against a proper [32] cautioner is limited to seven years,[33] unless his obligation is renewed, and in bankruptcy, the fund in the trustee's hands bears, at most, bank interest from the time when the debtor's transactions are stopped.

19 *Wauchope* v. *N.B. Ry.*, (1863) 2 M. 326. Bills of Exchange Act 1882, ss. 5, 57.
20 *Forbes* v. *Welsh & Forbes* (1894) 21 R. 630.
21 *Linlithgow Oil Co.* v. *N.B. Ry.* (1904) 12 S.L.T. 421.
22 *Garthland's Trs.* v. *McDowall*, May 25, 1820, F.C.; *Cuninghame* v. *Boswell* (1868) 6 M. 890.
23 *Christie* v. *Matheson* (1871) 10 M. 9.
24 *Findlay, Bannatyne & Co.'s Assignee* v. *Donaldson* (1864) 2 M.(H.L.) 86; *Graham's Executors* v. *Fletcher's Executors* (1870) 9 M. 298; *Blair's Trs.* v. *Payne* (1884) 12 R. 104.
25 *Wallace* v. *Geddes* (1821) 1 Shaw's App. 42.
26 *Blair's Trs.* v. *Payne* (1884) 12 R. 104.
27 *Napier* v. *Gordon* (1831) 5 W. & S. 745; *Somervell's Tr.* v. *Edinburgh Life Assurance Co.*, 1911 S.C. 1069, 1071, *per* Lord Salvesen; in *London, Chatham & Dover Ry. Co.* v. *S.E. Ry.* [1893] A.C. 429, 443, Lord Shand contrasts English and Scots law.
28 *Denholm* v. *London & Edinburgh Shipping Co.* (1865) 3 M. 815; *Martin* v. *Robertson, Ferguson & Co.* (1872) 10 M. 949; *Dunn* v. *Anderston Foundry Co.* (1894) 21 R. 880.
29 *Blair's Trs., supra*; *Somervell's Tr., supra.*
30 *Drummond & Co.* v. *Croom* (1824) 2 S. 608.
31 *Comm.* I, 694.
32 *Ross* v. *Craigie* (1729) M. 11,014; *Douglas, Heron & Co.* v. *Riddick* (1792) M. 11,032. See Craigie's *Moveable Conveyancing*, pp. 221–225.
33 Cautioners Act 1695, c. 5 (now replaced by Prescription and Limitation (Scotland) Act, 1973, s. 6); *Molleson* v. *Hutchison* (1892) 19 R. 581: see also *Stocks* v. *McLagan* (1890) 17 R. 1122.

Rate of interest generally

Despite the frequency of the term "legal interest,"[34] there has been held to be no legal rate.[35] Where the phrase occurred in an assignation, 5 per cent. was allowed,[36] and this is the figure usually connected with the term,[37] but no sanctity attaches to that figure.[38] When the price of heritage is consigned in bank pending settlement of the purchase, in the joint names of seller and purchaser, only the rate of bank interest allowed on the deposit receipt is due,[39] but legal interest is due from entry till such consignation.[40] Where a trustee unnecessarily and without justification withheld payment from the beneficiaries and deposited the money in bank at 2 per cent., he was observed to be getting off lightly, being held liable only for 4 per cent. and not 5 per cent.[41] But the rate is not rigidly fixed for any case and the court has a discretion, having regard to the circumstances of the case and the rates being currently earned on first-class investments.[42] Five per cent. remains the customary rate for circumstances of a penal character[43] where there has been unjustifiable delay in payment, but where there has not been any such reprehensible conduct a lesser rate is now allowed. In exceptional circumstances the court may find that no interest at all is due in a case where it normally is payable.[44]

The fact is that the court will today have regard to the rate of interest which good securities have been earning during the period in question, the safety and security of the funds, the degree of delay or reprehensible conduct causing the non-payment and any particular circumstances of the case which justifies special consideration.

Accordingly lesser rates have been fixed in some cases: where trustees left trust funds for nineteen years on deposit-receipt earning $2\frac{3}{8}$ per cent. and avoided expense on investments and safe investments were earning over 3 per cent., the trustees were debited with interest at 3 per cent.[45] In *Ross* v. *Ross*[46] a claim for legitim which could not have been made earlier was held to carry 4 per cent., the rate which the trust funds had earned. In *Bishop's Trs.* v. *Bishop*,[47] interest on legitim was allowed at 5 per cent.,

34 On the term see *Innerpeffray Mortification* v. *Drummond* (1894) 2 S.L.T. 45, and *Kearon*, *infra*.

35 *Greenock Harbour Trs.* v. *G.S.W. Ry.*, 1909 S.C. 1438; 1909 S.C.(H.L.) 49; *Inglis's Trs.* v. *Breen* (1891) 18 R. 487; *Grant* v. *Grant's Trs.* (1898) 25 R. 948; *Ross* v. *Ross* (1896) 23 R. 802; *Waddell's Trs.* v. *Crawford*, 1926 S.C. 654; *Kearon* v. *Thomson's Exors.*, 1949 S.C. 287.

36 *Christie's Factor* v. *Hardie* (1899) 1 F. 703.

37 *Smith* v. *Barlas* (1857) 19 D. 267.

38 *Kearon* v. *Thomson's Exors.*, 1949 S.C. 287; *Prestwick Cinema Co.* v. *Gardiner*, 1949 S.C. 645; 1951 S.C. 98.

39 *Grandison's Trs.* v. *Jardine* (1895) 22 R. 925.

40 *Prestwick Cinema Co.* v. *Gardiner*, 1951 S.C. 98.

41 *Darling* v. *Adamson* (1834) 12 S. 598.

42 *Ross*, *supra*.

43 But even this is not invariable: *Lees's Trs.* v. *Dun*, 1913 S.C.(H.L.) 12.

44 *Waddell's Trs.* v. *Crawford*, 1926 S.C. 654. *Cf. Ross*, *supra*, and *McCall's Trs.* v. *McCall's C.B.* (1901) 3 F. 1065.

45 *Melville* v. *Noble's Trs.* (1896) 24 R. 243.

46 (1896) 23 R. 802.

47 (1894) 21 R. 728.

the question being treated as determined by the rule established by *McMurray.*[48] This view would not now be followed.

Compound interest

Compound interest is only exceptionally allowed [49] and, apart from express agreement, is only normally allowed as a penalty for the breach of duties of trust, or in a case where the holder of a fund is under an obligation to invest and accumulate.[50] The most notable general exception is the case of the terms on which banks lend money, *e.g.*, by cash-credit bond where the interest is yearly or half-yearly added to the principal and thereafter itself bears interest.[51] In *Douglas* v. *Douglas's Trs.*[52] Lord Justice-Clerk Patton stated the general rule as follows: " A claim for compound interest with annual rests is a demand which can only be maintained either in the case of a fixed usage in commercial dealings [53] or where there has been an abuse in the party trusted with funds and violating his trust." [54] It was also allowed in a number of older cases,[55] and may still competently be given by decree of the House of Lords on the interest included in judicial accumulations.[56] In the case of current accounts between principal and agent the annual balance is accumulated and bears interest.[57]

Advances by a factor on a trust estate bear accumulated interest,[58] but there is no accumulation of interest in the case of ordinary loans,[59] though interest due *ex lege* or *ex facto* and unpaid at the date of citation may be accumulated with the principal and interest claimed on the whole sum from citation till payment,[60] nor is compound interest due on cash advances by a solicitor,[61] nor on a lawyer's account not rendered annually.[62]

Where a party claiming a share of a fund had been allowed the benefit of accumulation of interest on a general settlement as to the balance of a

48 (1852) 14 D. 1048.
49 Bell, *Prin.* § 32; Ersk. III, 3, 81; Bell, *Comm.* I, 695; *Graham's Exors.* v. *Fletcher's Exors.* (1870) 9 M. 298; *Douglas* v. *Douglas's Trs.* (1867) 5 M. 827, 836; *Clyde Navigation Trs.* v. *Kelvin Shipping Co.*, 1927 S.C. 622, 658. As to moneylenders, see Moneylenders Act 1927, s. 7.
50 *Grahame* v. *Frier* (1824) 2 S. 606; *Montgomerie* v. *Wauchope* (1822) 1 S. 453; *Campbell* v. *Keith* (1840) 2 D. 1367; *Cranstoun* v. *Scott* (1826) 5 S. 62.
51 *Reddie* v. *Williamson* (1863) 1 M. 228; *Gilmour* v. *Bank of Scotland* (1880) 7 R. 734; *Commercial Bank* v. *Pattison's Trs.* (1891) 18 R. 476; *Cruickshank* v. *B.L. Co.* (1834) 13 S. 91.
52 (1867) 5 M. 827.
53 *Cf. Findlay, Bannatyne & Co.'s Assignee* v. *Donaldson* (1864) 2 M.(H.L.) 86; *Boswell* v. *Montgomerie* (1836) 14 S. 554; *Blair* v. *Russell* (1829) 8 S. 72.
54 *Cf. Jolly* v. *McNeill* (1830) 4 W. & S. 455; *Napier* v. *Gordon* (1831) 5 W. & S. 745; *Maclean* v. *Campbell* (1856) 18 D. 609; *Hamilton* v. *Marshall*, Feb. 25, 1813, F.C.
55 *Duke of Queensberry* v. *Tait* (1826) 5 S. 189; *Graham* v. *Keble* (1820) 6 Paton 616; *Palmer* v. *Glass's Trs.* (1835) 13 S. 308; *Fyffe* v. *Ferguson* (1838) 16 S. 1038; 2 Rob. 267; *Lambe* v. *Ritchie* (1837) 16 S. 219; *Campbell* v. *Keith* (1840) 2 D. 1367.
56 Court of Session Act 1808, s. 19; *Napier* v. *Gordon, supra.*
57 *Duke of Queensberry, supra.*
58 *Hall* v. *Jerdon*, Nov. 23, 1813, F.C.; *Scott* v. *Handyside's Trs.* (1868) 6 M. 753.
59 *McNeill* v. *McNeill* (1826) 4 S. 620; (1830) 4 W. & S. 455; *Jolly* v. *McNeill* (1829) 7 S. 666.
60 *Napier* v. *Gordon* (1831) 5 W. & S. 745; *Maclean* v. *Campbell* (1856) 18 D. 609; *Douglas* v. *Douglas's Trs.* (1867) 5 M. 827.
61 *Bunten* v. *Hart* (1902) 9 S.L.T. 476.
62 *Munro's Trs.* v. *Murray & Ferrier* (1871) 9 S.L.R. 174.

claim which remained due, she was held also liable to have accumulations charged against her as to prior advances made to herself.[63] Compound interest has been sustained when acquiesced in for a long period of years in a series of accounts between brothers.[64]

In *Maclean* v. *Campbell*[65] it was affirmed that accumulation is a penal demand only to be given effect to in circumstances which justify it except in the case of persons having a fiduciary character, or in commercial dealings. A *curator bonis* who retained his ward's funds in his own hands has been held liable in compound interest at 5 per cent. on annual balances.[66] A bank's claim to compound interest has been repelled as being inapplicable to the liquidation arrangement to which the bank had acceded.[67] As a general rule compound interest will be refused to solicitors,[68] even on cash advances[69] with an occasional exception where the advances have been such as are usually made by bankers.[70]

In *Clyde Navigation Trs.* v. *Kelvin Shipping Co.*,[71] the pursuers were found entitled to recover the cost of removing a vessel sunk in the fairway of the River Clyde with interest, but interest was disallowed on a further portion of the claim, being itself interest on expenditure in connection with certain of the pursuer's operations, as amounting to the recovery of compound interest.

Interest on decrees

The rate of interest deemed to be included in or exigible under a decree or extract in the Court of Session is fixed by Act of Sederunt.[71a] In the sheriff court the interest included in a decree or extract decree was deemed to be 5 per cent. unless otherwise stated,[71b] but the Court of Session may now, by Act of Sederunt, amend that and substitute the rate specified in the Act of Sederunt.[71c]

The House of Lords may order the payment of interest, simple or compound, by any of the parties to an appeal, as it thinks meet.[71d] If an appeal to the Lords is dismissed for want of prosecution the respondents may apply to the Court of Session, which may order interest, simple or compound, to be paid to the respondents.[71e]

When a charge on an extract decree has expired it is competent to

[63] *Baillie's Trs.* v. *Stewart* (1834) 12 S. 285.
[64] *Boswell* v. *Montgomerie* (1836) 14 S. 554.
[65] (1856) 18 D. 609, approved in *Douglas* (1867) 5 M. 827.
[66] *Blair* v. *Murray* (1843) 5 D. 1315; *Buchanan* v. *Mackersey* (1847) 9 D. 700. See also *Campbell* v. *E. of Galloway*, Mar. 9, 1802, F.C.; *Hamilton* v. *Marshall*, Feb. 25, 1813, F.C.
[67] *Gourlay* v. *Clydesdale Bank* (1899) 7 S.L.T. 77.
[68] *Forman* v. *Home* (1844) 6 D. 1189; *McLelland* v. *Redfearn* (1844) 7 D. 179.
[69] *Graham's Exors.* v. *Fletcher's Exors.* (1870) 9 M. 298.
[70] *Macdonald* v. *Macdonald* (1856) 18 D. 630.
[71] 1927 S.C. 622.
[71a] A.S. (Rules of Court Amendment No. 5) 1969 (S.I. 1969 No. 1819) (7 per cent.).
[71b] Sheriff Courts (Scotland) Extracts Act 1892, s. 9.
[71c] Administration of Justice (Scotland) Act 1972, s. 4.
[71d] Court of Session Act 1808, s. 19.
[71e] *Ibid.* s. 20.

register it, and this has the effect of accumulating the debt and interest into a capital sum on which interest thereafter becomes due.[71f]

Liability of trustees for interest

Trustees who can be charged with unreasonable delay in the distribution or investment of the funds committed to their charge are liable in payment of legal interest for the time during which the money is unnecessarily retained, on the ordinary principle that every liquid debt carries interest from the time of payment if that payment is unduly withheld. Furthermore, if there be a positive breach of trust, as by using the trust funds for other than trust purposes, the trustees will be liable for such accumulation of interest as the fund would have yielded if it had been properly invested.[72]

If a trustee be chargeable with unreasonable delay in accounting to the trust beneficiaries for any funds in his hands after the period of distribution has arrived, he is liable to be charged with interest from the period when the beneficiary should have been put into possession, even though the property has been unproductive from its situation or nature of investment.[73] He is also liable in interest to creditors of the trust estate in the event of failure to settle punctually with them,[74] although it appears from older cases that interest on debts is not exigible until one year after the testator's death, which time is allowed as a reasonable interval for the collection and realisation of the trust assets.[75]

Trustees are liable to penal interest where money is by breach of trust employed in business or for the advantage or convenience of the trustee; it infers liability for the profits actually made on the principle that the whole produce of the fund is to be restored, as if the investment had been made for the benefit of the trust.[76] Trust funds must be maintained separate from those of the trustee, even though their security be not endangered.[77] If the trustee retains the money instead of investing it in his business or so deals with it that the profit thereon cannot be exactly ascertained, the court may either charge the trustee with the highest legal rate of interest, or with compound interest at a lower rate, normally 4 per cent.[78] So, too, a *curator bonis* retaining his ward's funds in his own hands has been held liable in compound interest at 5 per cent. on annual balances.[79] Where gratuitous trustees made an illegal investment of the trust

[71f] Debtors (Scotland) Act 1838, ss. 5, 10.

[72] *McLaren on Wills*, § 2254.

[73] McLaren, § 2255; *Elphinstone* v. *Keith* (1790) M. 4067; *Lynedoch* v. *Ouchterlony* (1832) 11 S. 60 (4 per cent.).

[74] *Graham* v. *McNab* (1822) 2 S. 22; *Arbuthnott* v. *Arbuthnott* (1758) M. 539.

[75] *Elphinstone*, *supra*; *Cranstoun* v. *Scott* (1826) 5 S. 62.

[76] McLaren, § 2257; *Roxburghe* v. *Swinton* (1824) 2 Sh.App. 18; *Cochrane* v. *Black* (1857) 19 D. 1019; *Laird* v. *Laird* (1858) 20 D. 973.

[77] *Wellwood's Trs.* v. *Boswell* (1856) 19 D. 187.

[78] *Plaine* v. *Thomson* (1836) 15 S. 194; *Fortune's Trs.* v. *Gillies* (1839) 2 D. 59 (4 per cent.); *Wellwood's Trs.* v. *Boswell* (1856) 19 D. 187 (4 per cent.); *Campbell* v. *Keith* (1840) 2 D. 1367.

[79] *Blair* v. *Murray* (1843) 5 D. 1315; *Buchanan* v. *Mackersey* (1847) 9 D. 700.

funds in redeeming feu duties, they were liable, although acting in bona fide, to account for interest from the date of investment, such as might have been obtained on the proper security, but were entitled to set off the feu duties saved.[80]

Trustees who improperly paid away trust funds without making or attempting to make profit for themselves were held liable to 3 per cent. interest on the sum paid away, that being the average rate of trust interest.[81] Where a trustee lost a sum of trust money by negligence, his representatives had to refund with interest at 3½ per cent.,[82] and again loss by unauthorised investments had to be repaid with interest at 3 per cent., as being the net average yield of good trust investments over a series of years.[83]

Where a trustee retained funds uninvested he was charged with 4 per cent. interest and it was observed that penal interest is exacted in such a case in a question with the fiar because of the risk the latter runs in the loss of good security but that this does not apply equally in a question with a liferenter.[84] Where funds were allowed to remain for fifteen years uninvested in the hands of the trust solicitors, the trustees were held liable for the full rate of 5 per cent.[85] Where trust funds were sold without authority interest was allowed at 4 per cent. from the date of the sale.[86] A trustee illegally but in bona fide appointed salaried manager of part of the trust estate was not liable in interest on the repetition of sums received by him.[87] Where trustees raised an action of multiplepoinding and delayed improperly to condescend on the fund *in medio* they were held liable for interest.[88]

Liability of executors for interest

Executors who failed to keep a separate bank account for their executry estate have been held liable for interest at 4 per cent. on their intromissions.[89] In another case simple interest at 5 per cent. was allowed against the representatives of a deceased executor who had retained funds on deposit receipt.[90] In a case of partial intestacy the executor-dative has been held liable to the trustees under the partial trust disposition and settlement for interest at 3 per cent. on the sum assigned to the trustees from the date of death till payment.[91]

Liability of judicial factors for interest

A judicial factor must lodge in bank in a separate account or on

80 *Pollexfen* v. *Stewart* (1841) 4 D. 224.
81 *Heritable Securities Investment Assocn.* v. *Miller's Trs.* (1893) 20 R. 675.
82 *Lees' Trs.* v. *Dun,* 1913 S.C.(H.L.) 12.
83 *Melville* v. *Noble's Trs.* (1896) 24 R. 243.
84 *Graham's Tr.* v. *Graham* (1870) 8 S.L.R. 107.
85 *Bryson* v. *Bryson's Trs.* (1907) 14 S.L.T. 750.
86 *Hardie's Trs.* v. *Graham* (1896) 3 S.L.T. 277.
87 *Mills* v. *Brown's Trs.* (1901) 3 F. 1012.
88 *Graham* v. *McNab's Trs.* (1822) 2 S. 22; *Williamson* v. *Suttie* (1843) 15 Sc.Jur. 637.
89 *Malcolm's Exors.* v. *Malcolm* (1869) 8 M. 272.
90 *Miller's Exx.* v. *Miller's Trs.,* 1922 S.C. 150.
91 *Campbell's Exor.* v. *Campbell's Trs.* (1898) 25 R. 687.

deposit in his own name as judicial factor all money in his hands. If he retains more than £50 belonging to the estate for more that ten days he is liable to be charged at the rate of 20 per cent. on the excess above that amount for any period beyond ten days, which sum is payable to the estate; he is further liable to be dismissed from his office and to be allowed no claim for commission unless the money has been kept from innocent causes. In the case of sheriff court factories the limit is £25.[92] The accountant of court may investigate bank books in this connection.[93] So a factor has been held liable at common law for money retained at 3 per cent. and at 5 per cent. on such sums as he should have invested from the time he could reasonably have done so,[94] while tutors and curators,[95] factors,[96] agents,[97] and other parties in fiduciary relations [98] who have retained money for which they should have accounted or invested have been held liable in compound interest from the date of default, but this liability has been limited to simple interest at average trust rate in special circumstances.[99]

A factor has been held entitled to interest on advances he has made.[1]

Liability of trustees in bankruptcy for interest

Trustees in bankruptcy are similarly penalised for failure to lodge in bank all sums which they receive in their official capacity. If a trustee retains more than £50 belonging to the bankrupt's estate in his hands for more than ten days, he is liable to pay interest thereon at the rate of 20 per cent. on the excess over £50 for such time as the money is in his hands beyond ten days.[2] The authority of the Commissioners in the sequestration is no defence,[3] but the penalty will not apply to payments made by the trustee unless in *mala fide*.[4] The provisions also apply to the fund set apart for the payment of dividends, and it is no excuse that the money has been drawn to pay dividends and not collected.[5] The trustee is further liable to be dismissed from his office unless the money has been kept from innocent causes, without any claim for remuneration, and is also liable in expenses.[6] He is not liable for penal interest after such dismissal but only

92 Judicial Factors Act 1849, s. 5; A.S. 1849, s. 5; *Acct. of Court* (1852) 1 Stu. 441; *Macdonald* (1854) 16 D. 1023; *Maxwell* (1862) 24 D. 1181. As to duty of banks to accumulate principal and interest on accounts of money lodged by judicial factors, tutors and curators, see 1849 Act, s. 37.

93 *Ibid.* s. 33.

94 *Lady Montgomerie* v. *Wauchope* (1822) 1 S. 491. Older cases in *Irons on Judicial Factors*, 79.

95 *Hamilton* v. *Marshall*, Feb. 25, 1813, F.C.; *Ralston* v. *Eaton* (1826) 4 S. 421; *Lambe* v. *Ritchie* (1837) 16 S. 219; *Blair* v. *Murray* (1843) 5 D. 1315.

96 *Graham* v. *Freer* (1824) 2 S. 606.

97 *Lady Montgomerie, supra*; *Wellwood's Trs.* v. *Boswell* (1856) 19 D. 187.

98 *Plaine* v. *Thomson* (1836) 15 S. 194.

99 *Morrison* v. *Dryden* (1890) 17 R. 704.

1 *Scott* v. *Handyside's Trs.* (1868) 6 M. 753; *Dundee Suburban Ry.* (1902) 9 S.L.T. 464.

2 Bankruptcy Act 1913, s. 79. As to dividends, s. 121.

3 *Black* v. *Kennedy* (1824) 3 S. 261.

4 *Ferrier* v. *Berry* (1835) 13 S. 1081; *Maben* v. *Perkins* (1837) 15 S. 1087.

5 *Acct. in Bankruptcy* v. *Freyd's Tr.* (1864) 2 M. 1293.

6 B. A. 1913, s. 79. *Cf.* s. 158. *Acct. in Bankruptcy* v. *Peacock's Tr.* (1867) 6 M. 158.

in simple interest on the accumulated sum.[7] Where a trustee had failed to deposit a sum to meet dividends on a disputed claim, he was held liable in interest on the sum from the time when he had the means of depositing it, but not in interest accumulated annually.[8]

Liability of solicitors for interest

The rate of interest chargeable against solicitors in respect of sums belonging to clients retained in their hands is a question of circumstances in each case and no fixed rule can be given.[9] Where the agent was under no obligation to pay the money over or to invest it bank interest only was charged,[10] as also where the delay was caused by the client,[11] but where the delay was the agent's fault a rate intermediate between bank and penal interest has been allowed.[12] Where trust funds were not invested during a period of dispute 4 per cent. was held sufficient.[13] But if there is no reason for delay in investment an agent will be liable to 5 per cent. interest [14] or possibly compound interest at 4 per cent. as a penal rate,[15] and if money is improperly and unjustifiably retained, the agent will be liable for penal interest and probably with annual accumulations.[16] It appears too that an agent, even if entitled to retain funds, is bound to pay compound interest thereon.[17] Where an agent realised stock and put the proceeds on deposit receipt in his own name he was held liable for 5 per cent. interest, as he should have invested the money or banked it separately in his client's name.[18] A client has also been found entitled to interest at 3 per cent. on periodical balances of cash in the hands of her solicitor where the solicitor had kept the money on deposit in his own name and should have invested it or at least banked it in the client's name.[19]

Interest Due under Express Contract

It is always lawful to stipulate for interest at such rate as may be agreed, as in a bond to repay money lent,[20] and in general such a stipulation is enforceable according to its terms. There is no objection to a provision

[7] *Johnstone* v. *Johnstone* (1826) 4 S. 487.
[8] *Houston* v. *Duncan* (1841) 4 D. 80, 1220.
[9] Begg on *Law-Agents*, 137.
[10] *McKenzie* v. *Campbell*, Dec. 19, 1818, F.C.
[11] *Shirras* v. *Black* (1824) 3 S. 183.
[12] *Robarts* v. *Court* (1835) 13 S. 877; (1838) 3 S. & McL. 317.
[13] *Fortune's Trs.* v. *Gibson Craig* (1839) 2 D. 59 explaining *Lady Montgomery* v. *Wauchope* (1822) 1 S. 453.
[14] *Fortune's Trs., supra. Brown's Trs.* v. *Brown* (1830) 4 W. & S. 28. See *Robarts, supra.*
[15] *Wellwood's Trs.* v. *Hill* (1856) 19 D. 187; *Malcolm's Exors.* v. *Malcolm* (1869) 8 M. 272. *Cf. Graham* v. *Freer* (1824) 2 S. 606; *Lambe* v. *Ritchie* (1837) 16 S. 219.
[16] *Fortune's Trs., supra, per* Lord Glenlee; *Blair* v. *Murray* (1843) 5 D. 1315; *Buchanan* v. *Mackersey* (1847) 9 D. 700. *Cf. Tyrrell* v. *Bank of London* (1862) 31 L.J.Ch. 369.
[17] *Duke of Queensberry's Exors.* v. *Tait* (1822) 1 S. 428; (1826) 5 S. 180. *Cf. Graham* v. *Freer* (1824) 2 S. 606; Bell's *Lectures on Conveyancing* I, 259.
[18] *Jopp* v. *Johnston's Trs.* (1905) 13 S.L.T. 522.
[19] *Ibid.* See also *Mills J. F.* (1904) 12 S.L.T. 444.
[20] Ersk. III, 3, 75, 81; Bell, *Comm.* I, 692.

that if payment be punctually made a lower rate of interest than that agreed will be accepted.[21]

Under the Moneylenders Act 1900, s. 1, the court may reopen a transaction with a moneylender, as defined in the Act, if, *inter alia*, the interest charged in respect of the sum actually lent is excessive, and the transaction is harsh and unconscionable,[22] unless the contrary is proved, if the rate exceeds 48 per cent. In such cases the court may set aside, in whole or in part, or revise or alter any security given or agreement made, or relieve the debtor from liability for any sum more than the court, having regard to the risk and all the circumstances, may adjudge to be reasonable, or order repayment of any amount paid in excess of such sum.

The Moneylenders Act 1927, s. 9, limits the rate of interest which may be claimed by a moneylender claiming in his debtor's bankruptcy to 5 per cent., without prejudice to recovering out of the estate, after all debts have been paid in full, any higher rate of interest to which he may be entitled.

Interest Not Due Save by Express Contract

There are, however, many cases where there is no implied undertaking to pay interest and liability must be founded on express contract, such as on arrears of feuduties,[23] though it has been questioned whether interest might not run on feuduties after an extra-judicial demand has been made for payment [24] and it is competent to stipulate for interest on arrears. Interest has been allowed on arrears from the date of citation in an action for their recovery.[25]

Interest is not impliedly due on arrears of ground-annuals.[26]

Interest has, however, been held due on a grassum or duplicand,[27] though only at a reduced rate in view of the delay in claiming, and " legal interest " from the date of the summons in an action for declarator and for payment of a casualty of non-entry.[28]

Teind and stipend

It has been doubted whether interest ran on teinds [29] and it has been refused on a claim for arrears.[30]

Though sometimes disallowed in the circumstances [31] interest has

21 *Gatty* v. *Maclaine*, 1921 S.C.(H.L.) 1.

22 On the interpretation of this phrase see *Davis* v. *McNally* (1904) 12 S.L.T. 234; *Midland Discount Co.* v. *Macdonald*, 1909 S.C. 477; *Howard & Cope* v. *Leckie*, 1909, 2 S.L.T. 444; *Debenham* v. *McCall*, 1923 S.L.T. 365.

23 *Napier* v. *Spiers' Trs.* (1831) 9 S. 655, 658; *Wallace* v. *Eglinton* (1835) 13 S. 564; *Moncrieff* v. *Dundas* (1835) 14 S. 61; *Tweeddale's Trs.* v. *Haddington* (1880) 7 R. 620; *Blair's Trs.* v. *Payne* (1884) 12 R. 104; *cf. Maxwell's Trs.* v. *Bothwell School Board* (1893) 20 R. 958.

24 *Tweeddale's Trs.*, *supra*, 643.

25 *Tweeddale* v. *Aytoun* (1842) 4 D. 862; *Pollok* v. *Edinburgh Mags.* (1862) 24 D. 371.

26 *Moncrieff* v. *Dundas* (1835) 14 S. 61; *Blair's Trs.*, *supra*.

27 *Murdoch* v. *Caledonian Ry.* (1906) 14 S.L.T. 527; affd. 15 S.L.T. 453.

28 *Stewart* v. *Murdoch and Rodger* (1882) 19 S.L.R. 649.

29 *Drummond* v. *Montgomerie* (1842) 5 D. 277.

30 *Glasgow University* v. *Pollok* (1868) 6 M. 878.

31 *Glasgow University*, *supra*; *E. Rosslyn* v. *E. Strathmore's Trs.* (1843) 6 D. 90.

several times been found due on arrears of stipend [32] or augmented stipend.[33]

Rent

The balance of authority supports the view that interest is not impliedly due on arrears of rent.[34] An exception is admitted in an action for payment of arrears when interest runs from the date of citation,[35] and legal interest has been allowed where a tenant delayed to pay rent admittedly due.[36]

Rates

Apart from statutory provisions for recovery of interest it is thought that interest may be claimed in an action for recovery of unpaid rates. Interest has been allowed pending the decision of a question of liability,[37] and on the repetition of overpayments.[38]

Demurrage

Interest does not run on a claim for demurrage.[39]

Payments under insurance policy

It is uncertain whether interest runs on payments due under an insurance policy.[40] The rule in England is that interest does not run as a matter of course [41] but may be awarded, if the court thinks fit, for the wrongful retention of money which should have been paid.[42] Payment of interest may be regulated by a special condition in the policy.[43]

Interest on Damages

At common law interest ran *ex lege* on an award of damages, or from the date of the interlocutor applying a jury's verdict awarding damages, because only from either of these dates were damages a liquid and ascertained sum and due and payable.[44] If an appeal has been reasonably

[32] *Drummond* v. *Montgomerie* (1842) 5 D. 277; *Adv. Gen.* v. *Sinclair's Trs.* (1855) 17 D. 290; *Preston* v. *Edinburgh Mags.* (1870) 8 M. 502; *Haldane* v. *Ogilvy* (1871) 10 M. 62; *Peters* v. *Greenock Mags.* (1894) 21 R. 886.

[33] *Anderson* v. *Urquhart*, Jan. 31, 1805, F.C.; *Dawson* v. *Pringle*, June 15, 1805, F.C.

[34] *Moncrieff* v. *Dundas* (1835) 14 S. 61; *Adv. Gen.* v. *Sinclair's Trs.* (1855) 17 D. 290; *Stirling and Dunfermline Ry.* v. *Edinburgh and Glasgow Ry.* (1857) 19 D. 598; *Blair's Trs.* v. *Payne* (1884) 12 R. 104.

[35] *Tweeddale* v. *Aytoun* (1842) 4 D. 862, 863; *Pollok* v. *Edinburgh Mags.* (1862) 24 D. 371.

[36] *Moir* v. *Graham* (1821) 1 S. 16.

[37] *Greig* v. *Edinburgh Mags.* (1879) 6 R. 801.

[38] *Glasgow Gas Light Co.* v. *Barony Parish* (1868) 6 M. 406; see also *Durie's Trs.* v. *Aytoun* (1894) 22 R. 34.

[39] *Pollich* v. *Heatly*, 1910 S.C. 469, 478.

[40] Bell, *Comm.* I, 691; *Crawford* v. *Bertram*, May 15, 1812, F.C.

[41] *Webster* v. *British Empire Mutual Life Assce. Co.* (1880) 15 Ch.D. 169, 174.

[42] *Webster*, *supra*.

[43] *e.g. Fitton* v. *Accidental Death Insurance Co.* (1864) 17 C.B.(N.S.) 122.

[44] *Flensburg Steam Shipping Co.* v. *Seligmann* (1871) 9 M. 1011; *Martin* v. *Robertson, Ferguson & Co.* (1872) 10 M. 949; *Macrae* v. *Reed and Mallik Ltd.*, 1961 S.C. 68.

taken, interest is normally allowed only from the affirmation of the verdict for the pursuer.[45] But the Inner House and the House of Lords had, and have, power to award damages from an earlier date if, but for unnecessary delay, the verdict might have been applied from that earlier date.[46] It has been observed that the House of Lords has an unlimited discretion in the matter of interest.[47] Accordingly, the standard practice at common law was to conclude for damages " with interest from the date of the decree to follow hereon until payment."

The Interest on Damages (Scotland) Acts 1958 [48] and 1971, now provide that:

> " 1 (1) [49] Where a court pronounces an interlocutor decerning for payment by any person of a sum of money as damages, the interlocutor may include decree for payment by that person of interest, at such rate or rates as may be specified in the interlocutor, on the whole or any part of that sum for the whole or any part of the period between the date when the right of action arose and the date of the interlocutor.
>
> (1A) [49] Where a court pronounces an interlocutor decerning for payment of a sum which consists of or includes damages or solatium in respect of personal injuries sustained by the pursuer or any other person, then (without prejudice to the exercise of the power conferred by subsection (1) of this section in relation to any part of that sum which does not represent such damages or solatium) the court shall exercise that power so as to include in that sum interest on those damages and on that solatium or on such part of each as the court considers appropriate, unless the court is satisfied that there are reasons special to the case why no interest should be given in respect thereof.
>
> (1B) [50] For the avoidance of doubt, it is hereby declared that where, in any action in which it is competent for the court to award interest under this Act, a tender made in the course of the action, the tender shall, unless otherwise stated therein, be in full satisfaction of any claim to interest thereunder by any person in whose favour the

[45] *Hurlet and Campsie Alum Co.* v. *Earl of Glasgow* (1850) 13 D. 370; *Taylor, supra*; *Roger* v. *Cochrane*, 1910 S.C. 1, 3; *McGovern* v. *Nimmo*, 1938 S.C.(H.L.) 18, 29; *McCormack* v. *N.C.B.*, 1957 S.C. 277.

[46] *Lenaghan* v. *Monkland Iron Co.* (1858) 20 D. 848; *Taylor* v. *Macfarlane* (1868) 40 Sc.Jur. 332; *Flensburg, supra*; *Martin, supra*; *Clancy* v. *Dixon's Ironworks Ltd.*, 1955 S.C. 17; *McCormack* v. *N.C.B., supra.*

[47] Court of Session Act 1808, s. 19; *Roger, supra*; *McGovern, supra*; *Green* v. *Brown & Gracie Ltd.*, 1960 S.L.T.(Notes) 43.

[48] Passed in implement of the Law Reform Committee for Scotland's Third Report (Cmnd. 141, 1957). It empowered the court to give interest from the date of citation. The 1971 Act extends the power to an earlier date, the date when the right of action arose. Where a pursuer concluded for interest from the date of citation, it was held that he could not after trial recover interest from an earlier date: *Cassidy* v. *Petit*, 1972 S.L.T.(Notes) 59. But where the pursuer had not concluded for it interest should be awarded, it was held, from the date of the accident: *Andrew* v. *Scottish Omnibuses*, 1972 S.L.T.(Notes) 72.

[49] New subs. (1) substituted by 1971 Act, s. 1 (1) for that in 1958 Act, s. 1 (1).

[50] New subsection added by 1971 Act, s. 1 (1).

tender is made; and in considering in any such action whether an award is equal to or greater than an amount tendered in the action, the court shall take account of the amount of any interest awarded under this Act, or such part of that interest as the court considers appropriate.

(2) [51] Nothing in this section shall—

(*a*) authorise the granting of interest upon interest, or

(*b*) prejudice any other power of the court as to the granting of interest, or

(*c*) affect the running of any interest which apart from this section would run by virtue of any enactment or rule of law."

Commentary

The ground of action for the claim for damages is irrelevant. The 1958 Act has been applied to personal injury cases,[52] wrongful death cases,[53] property damage cases [54] and breach of contract cases.[55]

Under section 1 (1), as substituted, a court now has power to award interest from the date when the right of action arose down to the date of the interlocutor.

The date when the right of action arose is the date when breach of contract took place, or delict was committed, or the other circumstances giving rise to the claim happened. In the case of anticipatory breach of contract a right of action arises if the defender intimates before the due date for performance that he cannot or will not perform when the due date for performance arrives and the pursuer elects to accept that intimation as a breach there and then, though he may decline to do so and await the due date for performance, in which case a right of action arises if performance is not made when that date has arrived. In the ordinary case of breach of contract at the date for performance a right of action arises if the defender does not properly perform his obligations at the due time. In the case of delict a right of action arises when all the necessary elements of delict, namely, breach of duty to the pursuer, causal connection, and resultant harm to the pursuer, have happened. There is no right of action until harm has been caused, even though the breach of duty took place some time earlier.[56] But a right of action may be complete though the pursuer has not appreciated that he has suffered and is still suffering loss and damage.[57]

It is plain from the wording that the court must consider the elements

[51] Subs. 1 (2) of the 1958 Act is unamended by the 1971 Act.

[52] *Macrae* v. *Reed and Mallik*, 1961 S.C. 68.

[53] *Killah* v. *Aberdeen Milk Marketing Board*, 1961 S.L.T. 232; *Webster* v. *Simpson's Motors*, 1967 S.L.T.(Notes) 36.

[54] *Fraser* v. *J. Morton Wilson Ltd.*, 1966 S.L.T. 22.

[55] *Dempster* v. *Motherwell Bridge & Engineering Co.*, 1964 S.C. 308; *Macrae, supra*, 73, 76; Lord Strachan's reservation (*Macrae, supra*, 86) relates not to whether the Act applies to breach of contract cases but as to how it should be applied.

[56] *Watson* v. *Fram Reinforced Concrete Co.*, 1960 S.C.(H.L.) 92.

[57] *Cartledge* v. *Jopling* [1963] A.C. 758.

of its total award and the prevailing rate of interest, and may award interest at different rates on different parts of the award. Also it may award interest only on part of the award, and for part only of the period to the date of the interlocutor. In *Macrae* v. *Reed and Mallik Ltd.*[58] the Second Division held that the discretion conferred by section 1 (1) had to be exercised on a selective and discriminating basis, and that a Lord Ordinary's exercise of his discretion was open to review in the same way as any other part of his interlocutor. It was not merely a matter of deciding to award or refuse interest from the date of citation (or, now, from the date when the cause of action arose) but of considering on which elements of a total award to award interest, and it stressed that interest from a date prior to a Lord Ordinary's interlocutor or the date of application of a jury verdict could never be justified on loss which the pursuer had not yet sustained at the date of the proof or trial,[59] and pointed out that an award for future loss had no existence or quantum until the award was made. It also held that interest from a date earlier than the decree could be allowed only on damages awarded for loss suffered before the date of decree where such loss could be definitely ascertained and for that reason that interest on solatium could never run from a date earlier than the decree, though on both points the Lord Justice-Clerk had a different opinion. Under the 1971 Act it has been held that there was no indication that the power was to be exercised in any way different from the manner in which the courts had exercised their power under the 1958 Act.[60]

Examples of the discriminating approach include *Killah* v. *Aberdeen Milk Marketing Board*[61] (interest from citation till date when verdict applied), *Fraser* v. *J. Morton Wilson Ltd.*[62] (interest given on damages for property damage, but refused on damages for loss of profits) and *Webster* v. *Simpson's Motors*[63] (interest given on sum for loss of support, refused on sum for solatium).

In *Killah* v. *Aberdeen Milk Marketing Board*,[64] a claim by a widow and children, it was held that though a tender, including an admission of liability, had been lodged, this was not an acknowledgment of a debt amounting to the sum in the tender, that interest should be awarded on the sums awarded for loss of support from the date of death till the trial, restricted to 4 per cent. because three-fifths of these sums related to the period prior to the date of citation, and interest at 4 per cent. thereon from the date of citation until the date on which the verdict would in the normal course have been applied. Furthermore, since a motion for a new

58 1961 S.C. 68 (decided on s. 1 (1) of 1958 Act).

59 This will cover in an injuries case, solatium for future pain and suffering and loss of faculties, and future loss of earnings, and in a wrongful death case, solatium for future grief and loss of financial support for the future.

60 *Smith* v. *Middleton*, 1972 S.L.T.(Notes) 3.

61 1961 S.L.T. 232.

62 1966 S.L.T. 22.

63 1967 S.L.T.(Notes) 36.

64 1961 S.L.T. 232.

trial had been lodged and then withdrawn and that this had delayed payment, interest at 5 per cent. was allowed on all the sums from the date when the verdict would normally have been applied until the date of actual payments. The trial judge did not award interest on either solatium or loss of support for the future, nor on the award of solatium for grief already suffered.

Where in one case damages were agreed before the action was raised, interest at 5 per cent. from the date of citation was allowed.[65]

Case of personal injury or death

Under section 1 (1A), which applies only to awards of or including damages or solatium in respect of personal injuries sustained by the pursuer or any other person,[66] the court is obliged to exercise its power to award interest on the damages and solatium as it considers appropriate, unless the court is satisfied that there are reasons special to the case why no interest should be given in respect thereof. This provision initially gave rise to difficulties by reason of the practice of juries to make lump sum awards, not discriminating between solatium and patrimonial loss or loss of support, and seemed to necessitate allowing proofs rather than jury trials in such cases. Finally, after divergent opinions had been expressed in various cases,[67] the Second Division ruled [68] that where it is not possible to split the damages awarded into their component parts, interest would have to be awarded on the whole sum, although it must include elements on which it would not be appropriate to award interest. Rough justice might be achieved by counterbalancing the larger award on which interest was awarded by a reduction in the rate of interest or of the period for which it was awarded or both. In that case the total damages were agreed by joint minute and the jury's sole task was to determine liability and the degree of contributory negligence.

Subsequently, however, in *Macdonald* v. *Glasgow Corpn.*,[69] the First Division allowed a jury trial and ruled that the jury should be instructed if they found for the pursuer, to find separate sums of damages for loss of earnings to date, future loss of earnings, solatium to date, and solatium for the future, thus giving the presiding judge the materials on which to base his awards of interest. It seems to follow that a similar course should be adopted in cases of claims by surviving relatives, and it would

[65] *Bell's Sports Centre (Perth)* v. *William Briggs & Sons*, 1971 S.L.T.(Notes) 48.

[66] The last four words make the provision applicable to a claim by a tutor or judicial factor for injuries sustained by his ward, and probably to claims by an executor for injuries sustained by the deceased whom he represents, and by one or more entitled surviving relatives for loss sustained by reason of the death of a relative. " Personal injuries " are defined (1971 Act, s. 1 (3), substituting new subsection (2) for that in section 3 of 1958 Act) as " including any disease and any impairment of a person's physical or mental condition."

[67] *McFadyen* v. *Crudens*, 1972 S.L.T.(Notes) 11 and 62; *Crowe* v. *Stewart*, 1972 S.L.T.(Notes) 12; *McMahon* v. *Coats*, 1972 S.L.T.(Notes) 16; *Cooper* v. *Pat Munro (Alness) Ltd.*, 1972 S.L.T.(Notes) 20.

[68] *Ross* v. *British Railways Board*, 1972 S.L.T. 174.

[69] 1973 S.L.T.(Notes) 2.

follow that argument on interest on the motion for application of the jury's verdict will normally be necessary.

From the reported examples of the exercise of the power few conclusions can yet be drawn:

There is power to award interest from a date prior to decree only where the pursuer's loss had been incurred and could be quantified prior to decree, *e.g.* on past loss of wages, or solatium for suffering prior to that date.[70]

Interest has been given at 6 per cent. on two-thirds of solatium for a fractured leg.[71]

Interest has been awarded on past loss of wages at 5 per cent. from the date of citation only,[72] and at 3 per cent. on past loss of earnings from the accident to decree.[71]

Pre-decree interest has been refused on a widow's award for loss of future support.[73] Pre-decree interest on solatium for future suffering can probably never be justified.[74]

Special reasons for refusing interest

The court may, however, decline to exercise the power under section 1 (1A) if it " is satisfied that there are reasons special to the case why no interest should be given " on damages and solatium. It is clear that the reasons must be connected with the circumstances of the particular case, but it is difficult to predict what may or may not be special reasons. A suitable case for refusal might be one where there had been some abuse of process or where the pursuer, having disclaimed any intention to claim, had served a summons at the last possible moment and after evidence had been lost to the defender.

Awarding or withholding interest function of court

In the case of awards made by a jury, it is thought that, as hitherto, the awarding or withholding of interest is a function of the judge who applies the verdict. The difficulty in such a case is that unless the jury is instructed to, and does, return a verdict showing how much it awards under various heads, the judge applying the verdict is left in the dark and must speculate.[75] The truth is that jury trial is unsuitable as a means of fixing the awards.

Cases where tender lodged

The effect of section 1 (1B) is to put the onus on the parties to consider

70 *Macrae* v. *Reed & Mallik Ltd.*, 1961 S.C. 68.

71 *Ward* v. *Tarmac Civil Engineering*, 1972 S.L.T.(Notes) 52.

72 *Picken* v. *J. Stuart & Co. (Contractors)*, 1972 S.L.T.(Notes) 12; *cf. Ross* v. *British Railways Board*, 1972 S.L.T. 174.

73 *Killah* v. *Aberdeen Milk Marketing Board*, 1961 S.L.T. 232; *McCuaig* v. *Redpath Dorman Long*, 1972 S.L.T.(Notes) 42; *cf. Macrae* v. *Reed & Mallik Ltd.*, 1961 S.C. 68 (where it was indicated that this could never be justified).

74 *Macrae*, *supra*.

75 *Cf. Macrae*, *supra*, where the jury assessed damages at £12,000 to cover all heads of claim.

the interest element in making a tender and in deciding whether or not to accept it. A tender is prima facie of the sum offered as damages with interest thereon, presumably down to the date of tender, but it is clearly competent to render a sum of damages only, and, if the tender is accepted, to ask the court to fix the interest.

When considering whether a pursuer who has gone to proof or trial has beaten a sum tendered or not the court has to take into account interest awarded under the Act, or such part of it as the court considers appropriate. Thus if the defender tenders £1,000 and the pursuer goes to trial and is awarded £900 and £150 interest he is deemed to have beaten the tender. The last phrase in section 1 (1B) seems to be intended to take account of the case where a tender is not accepted but the pursuer goes to trial and may have to compare an award with a tender made months previously. Thus if a defender tendered £1,000 (including interest) and the pursuer, months later, was awarded £900 damages and £150 interest he would not be deemed to have beaten the tender if £100 of the interest had accrued between the date of the tender and the date of the award.

Other provisions

" 1 (2) [76] Nothing in this section shall—

(*a*) authorise the granting of interest upon interest, or

(*b*) prejudice any other power of the court as to the granting of interest, or

(*c*) affect the running of any interest which apart from this section would run by virtue of any enactment or rule of law."

Interest upon interest or compound interest is rarely if ever justifiable. It is thought that the purpose of head (*a*) is to ensure that *e.g.* a money-lender's claim for payment of money advanced and unpaid interest is not to rank as a claim of damages carrying interest on the whole sum. Heads (*b*) and (*c*) preserve the common law and other statutory powers of the courts to award interest.

Interest between date of interlocutor and payment

The provisions of the Acts deal only with interest down to the date of the interlocutor. But clearly courts may continue at common law to decree interest from the date of the interlocutor until actual payment, as being money wrongfully withheld.[77] Interest on the principal sum of damages and expenses runs *ex lege* from the date of decree.[78]

It has been held that interest could not competently be granted on an award of damages after the final decree had been pronounced.[79]

[76] 1958 Act, unamended by 1971 Act.
[77] *Cf. Killah* v. *Aberdeen Milk Marketing Board*, 1961 S.L.T. 232.
[78] *Dalmahoy and Wood* v. *Brechin Mags.* (1859) 21 D. 210; *McCormack* v. *N.C.B.*, 1957 S.C. 277.
[79] *Hendren* v. *Scottish Construction Co.*, 1967 S.L.T.(Notes) 21.

Appeals from sheriff court

"2.[80] Section thirty-one of the Sheriff Courts (Scotland) Act 1907 (which among other things specifies the grounds on which an interlocutor of a sheriff entering judgment under that section may be appealed to the Court of Session) shall have effect as if after head (4) there were inserted the following head—

"(5) That no grant of interest on the damages (if any) has been included in the interlocutor or that any such grant so included is inadequate or is excessive" and as if there were added at the end of the section the words "and upon any such appeal so far as based on the ground specified in head (5) of this section the court may make such order as to it seems just having regard to the provisions of the Interest on Damages (Scotland) Acts 1958 and 1971."

The wrongful granting or refusal of interest is accordingly a ground of appeal.

Interest after final decree

Interest cannot competently be granted on an award of damages after final decree.[81]

INTEREST ON JUDICIAL EXPENSES

A sum decerned for as expenses of process bears interest from the date of final decree.[82] It has been allowed where interim decree for expenses had been granted, extracted and charged upon.[83] Exceptionally, in special circumstances, interest has sometimes been given on expenses prior to decree.[84] In later cases [85] a distinction was drawn between a solicitor's cash advances, on which interest was allowed, and business charges for professional work and judicial expenses and outlays, on which no interest is recoverable.

In a petition to apply the judgment of the House of Lords in a case the court gave decree for expenses and for interest from the date at which the original petition praying for decree for expenses was presented to the court.[86] It has also been held that a party to a House of Lords appeal seeking interim execution of a decree for expenses is not entitled to interest on them.[87]

80 1958 Act, with words at end "having regard to . . . 1971" added by 1971 Act, s. 1 (2).

81 *Hendren* v. *Scottish Construction Co.*, 1967 S.L.T.(Notes) 21.

82 *Dykes* v. *Cullen* (1852) 24 Sc.Jur. 616; *Caledonian and Dunbartonshire Ry.* v. *Lockhart* (1858) 20 D. 390; *Dalmahoy and Wood* v. *Brechin Mags.* (1859) 21 D. 210; *McCormack* v. *N.C.B.*, 1957 S.C. 277, 278.

83 *Wallace* v. *Henderson* (1876) 4 R. 264.

84 See *Warner* v. *Cunninghame*, May 29, 1813, F.C., as explained in *McDowall* v. *McDowall* (1821) 1 S. 200; *Groat* v. *Sinclair*, May 15, 1819, F.C.; *Pearse* v. *MacDonell* (1825) 2 S. 603; *Earl of Fife* v. *Duff* (1827) 5 S. 524.

85 *Barclay* v. *Barclay* (1850) 22 Sc.Jur. 354; *Macpherson* v. *Tytler* (1853) 15 D. 706; *Blair's Trs.* v. *Payne* (1884) 12 R. 104.

86 *Whitehead and Morton* v. *Cullen* (1861) 24 D. 86.

87 *Dunlop* v. *Speir* (1825) 4 S. 179.

Where the Lords have ordered an unsuccessful respondent to repay expenses for which the appellant was held liable in the Court of Session, interest cannot be demanded unless the House so orders,[88] or the bond of caution says so.[89] If, however, the respondent is successful the Court of Session may allow interest.[90]

[88] Court of Session Act 1808, s. 19; *Fenton* v. *Livingstone* (1859) 22 D. 17; *Ewart* v. *Latta* (1865) 3 M. 1167; *Fleming* v. *Howden* (1868) 7 M. 79; *Young* v. *Hermand Oil Co.* (1892) 19 R. 867; *Roger* v. *J. & P. Cochrane*, 1910 S.C. 1.

[89] *Fleming, supra.*

[90] Court of Session Act 1808, s. 20.

PART VIII

SUBSTITUTIONAL REDRESS

CHAPTER 24

DAMAGES IN GENERAL

SUBSTITUTIONAL redress is the judicial remedy of ordering a payment of money in substitution or compensation for something lost by reason of another party's breach of duty to the claimant. This kind of remedy, by an award of pecuniary compensation, is the commonest kind of legal remedy, and the one of widest application. It is called damages. The term damage is used of the loss, physical or financial, sustained by a person, the term damages of the pecuniary compensation for that loss. The law of damages is mainly a matter of common law as worked out by practice and the decisions of the courts. Only in particular respects does statute intervene, and then rather to impose qualifications of common law rules in particular cases than to lay down general principles.

Definition of damages

Damages may be defined as the sum of money payable under the order of a competent judicial tribunal by one juristic person to another in compensation for the prejudice suffered by the latter in consequence of the breach by the former of a duty to or right of obligation vested in the latter person.

Mayne, the leading English text-writer on the subject, originally [1] defined damages as the pecuniary satisfaction obtainable by success in an action. This definition is sufficiently wide to cover practically every case of the recovery of money by process of law and is consequently much wider than the generally accepted legal meaning of the term " damages." If, however, parties to a contract agree beforehand on a sum to be payable by whichever of them should fail to fulfil his due part of their agreement, the sum may or may not be a form of damages.[2] In the rewritten version of that book [3] damages are defined as the pecuniary compensation obtainable by success in an action, for a wrong which is either a tort or a breach of contract. This covers most but not all cases, because breaches of obligations of other kinds may also give rise to claims of damages.

Other definitions are:—

Damages are the pecuniary reparation due for loss or injury sustained by one person through the fault of another.[4]

[1] *Mayne on Damages*, 11th ed., 1.
[2] Chap. 7, *supra*.
[3] *McGregor on Damages*, 13th ed., 3.
[4] Bell, *Law Dictionary*, *s.v.* " Damages."

Damages are the sum of money which a person wronged is entitled to receive from the wrongdoer as compensation for the wrong.[5]

Damages constitute the pecuniary compensation or satisfaction which a plaintiff can recover by process of law in respect of injury sustained through the act or default of a defendant, or of persons for whose acts a certain defendant may be liable.[6]

Damages may be defined as the pecuniary compensation which the law awards to a person for the injury he has sustained by reason of the act or default of another, whether that act or default is a breach of contract or a tort; or, put more shortly, damages are the recompense given by process of law to a person for the wrong that another has done him.[7]

" Damages " to an English lawyer imports this idea, that the sums payable by way of damages are sums which fall to be paid by reason of some breach of duty or obligation, whether that duty or obligation is imposed by contract, by the general law, or legislation.[8]

In all cases of civil injury and of breach of contract the declared object of awarding damages is to give compensation for pecuniary loss.[9]

With reference to contract, the American *Restatement*[10] defines damages as a sum of money awarded as compensation for injury caused by a breach of contract; with reference to tort,[11] as a sum of money awarded to a person injured by the tort of another.

The definition of damages adopted herein goes some distance to define the scope of the subsequent chapters which are limited to those circumstances where the payment of money falls to be made in compensation for a breach of civil obligation.[12]

Although one set of circumstances may give rise to both civil and criminal liability to pay money, money payable in satisfaction of criminal liability is not damages but a fine, not compensatory but punitive.

The problems in an action of damages

The practical questions which arise in an action to recover a sum of money by way of damages in contract or delict comprise two separate but closely related problems, apart from any question of liability. The problem of liability or no liability is always the preliminary question, and if there is held to be no liability no problems about damages arise. Whether

5 Gahan, *Damages*, 1.

6 *Arnold on Damages and Compensation*, 2nd ed., 1.

7 Halsbury's *Laws of England* (3rd ed.), XI, s. 383, approved in *Jabbour* v. *Israel Property Custodian* [1954] 1 All E.R. 145, 150.

8 *Hall Bros.* v. *Young* [1939] 1 K.B. 748, 756, *per* Greene M.R., accepted as appropriate in Scotland also: *Hamilton* v. *B.T.C.*, 1957 S.C. 300, 304.

9 *Sedgwick on Measure of Damages*, s. 30.

10 *Contracts*, s. 326.

11 *Torts*, ss. 902–908.

12 *Dixon* v. *Calcraft* [1892] 1 Q.B. 458. The word " compensation " is not ordinarily used as equivalent to " damages ": *ibid*. 463. But " compensation " payable by directors for untrue statements in a company prospectus (Companies Act 1948, s. 43) is identical in quantum and mode of ascertainment with damages: *Clark* v. *Urquhart* [1930] A.C. 28, 56, 57.

there is or is not any liability in a particular case is, however, a problem of the substantive law of contract or of delict, as the case may be, and not a problem of damages at all.

In the first place, if it be found that the pursuer is entitled to compensation from the defender for an established breach of legal obligation, it is necessary to determine what heads of the loss alleged to have been sustained by him in consequence thereof may properly be included in the claim for damages, and what must be excluded as inadmissible, irrelevant, or as too remote consequences of the initial wrongful act or omission to justify an award of damages to compensate the claimant for the occurrence to him of these items of loss.

Secondly, having determined the admissible elements or heads of claim, it remains to quantify the damages in money by assessing how much pecuniary compensation is fairly exigible from the defender in respect of those admissible heads, having regard to aggravating and mitigating factors and the considerations proper to the particular kind of case before the court, and, in the case of claims *ex delicto*, having regard to the amount of money generally considered reasonable and proper according to the current practice of the court for cases of the kind in question. In claims of the last kind amounts within certain limits are conventionally accepted as reasonable and the propriety of an award is judged largely by reference to that standard. " Although there is no fixed and unalterable standard [of damages] the courts have been making these assessments over many years, and I think that they do form some guide to the kind of figure which is appropriate to the facts of any particular case." [13]

Pecuniary and non-pecuniary losses

A basic distinction, whatever the legal ground for the claim of damages, is between pecuniary losses, where the loss caused by the defender's breach of duty was an immediate and actual pecuniary loss, such as loss of profit where a sub-sale is cancelled, or loss of earnings where a man is prevented from working by injury, and non-pecuniary losses, where the loss caused by the defender's breach of duty was immediately and actually not pecuniary, such as trouble and inconvenience, hurt feelings, physical injury or shock, grief and the like. The former kind of loss may be accurately measured in money and fully and completely compensated by an award of pecuniary damages. The latter kind cannot be accurately measured at all, in money or otherwise, and compensation by an award of pecuniary damages is only and always a solace.

Liquidate and unliquidate damages

Damages are unliquidate when they are not fixed beforehand by statutory provision or prior agreement of parties, but are " at large " and determinable at the proof or trial of the action in the discretion of the

[13] *Bird* v. *Cocking* [1951] 2 T.L.R. 1260, 1263, *per* Birkett L.J.

court or jury. Liquidate damages, on the other hand, are a sum fixed by a statute as recoverable in certain circumstances,[14] or a sum assessed by the parties themselves and contractually agreed to be paid as damages by the party in default in certain specified circumstances so as to avoid the necessity of inquiry into and proof of the damage actually sustained.[15] The basis of this is that the parties have estimated the loss which will be caused by the breach of contract, that payment of the specified sum is part of the bargain between them,[16] and hence that the court when granting decree for that sum is maintaining performance of the contract according to the intention of the parties.[17]

Damages and contractual penalty

In general, damages must be contrasted with penalty not only in respect that the object of an award of damages is compensatory while that of the imposition of a penalty is punitive, but also because parties may competently stipulate beforehand that a certain sum shall be payable in the event of a breach of contract by the party in breach to the other, and such a provision will be given effect to by the courts only provided it is designed to be a genuine pre-estimate of the damages likely to be suffered by the breach of contract, and not a penal provision *in terrorem* of the breaker of the contract designed to enforce due performance, as the law will not permit persons to inflict penalties on one another. If such a provision is interpreted to be penal it falls.[18]

Dicta in older cases [19] to the effect that damages are partly imposed *in poenam* and that, if the negligence were gross, the penalty ought to be great cannot now be supported.[20]

Damages and statutory penalty

Damages are distinguishable in purpose, legal basis, mode of assessment and mode of recovery from statutory penalties imposed to punish non-compliance with a statutory requirement. In some cases, however, both statutory penalty and common law damages are exigible, but by different claimants under different procedures.[21]

Damages and statutory compensation

Damages are distinguishable from compensation payable under statute for loss caused by such events as compulsory sale of property, not so much in purpose, as because the justification for the payment is not a breach of obligation and because the mode of claim is not a common law

14 *e.g.*, Bills of Exchange Act 1882, s. 57 (1).
15 Chap. 7, *supra*.
16 *Commercial Bank* v. *Beal* (1890) 18 R. 80.
17 *Wallis*, note 44, *infra*.
18 Chap. 7, *supra*.
19 *e.g.*, *Morton* v. *Edinburgh and Glasgow Ry.* (1845) 8 D. 288; *Auld* v. *Shairp* (1874) 2 R. 191, 196.
20 *Black* v. *N.B. Ry.*, 1908 S.C. 444, 453.
21 Chap. 59, *infra*.

action, and the mode of assessment of the sum due is not quantification by a judge or jury.[22]

Damages and expenses

Damages are also distinguishable from the expenses of making good some damage, harm or loss, sometimes made recoverable by statute from the person responsible for the damage, harm or loss. Such a liability is not a liability in damages.[23]

Requisites of an award of damages

An award of damages may be made only by order of a competent judicial tribunal. A sum paid by one party to another by agreement to compromise a claim or in settlement of an action is not properly an award of damages, though its function is identical and the considerations governing the choice of an appropriate sum are the same as in an award of damages, so that, in practice, such sums can be, and are commonly, looked upon as damages.

An award of damages must be unconditional [24] and payable in a lump sum [25] in money of British legal tender.[26] An award of periodical payments such as an annuity is incompetent.[25] The amount awarded cannot be varied after the case has been finally disposed of, unless by legislation or agreement, and a further action to recover damages for the same wrong is incompetent, even for a loss emerging subsequent to the first action.[27]

Currency of damages

The Scottish courts can only give a decree for damages expressed in British currency [28] and hence, when decree is granted for a sum of money which will be actually payable in another currency, the amount must be expressed in British currency and converted. In cases of breach of contract the rate of exchange to be taken is that prevailing at the date of the breach and not at the date of decree.[29] In cases of delict, where the

[22] See also *Dixon* v. *Calcraft* [1892] 1 Q.B. 458, 463; *cf. Smith* v. *Brown* (1871) L.R. 6 Q.B. 729, 732.

[23] *e.g., The Stonedale No.* 1 [1954] P. 338, 356, 364, modified on another point by Merchant Shipping (Liability of Shipowners and Others) Act 1958, s. 2.

[24] *Banbury* v. *Bank of Montreal* [1918] A.C. 626, 668, 700, 716.

[25] *Fournier* v. *C.N. Ry.* [1927] A.C. 167.

[26] *S.S. Celia* v. *S.S. Volturno* [1921] 2 A.C. 544, 549, 555, 560; *Re United Railways of Havana* [1961] A.C. 1007.

[27] *Stevenson* v. *Pontifex and Wood* (1887) 15 R. 125; *Delaney* v. *Stirling* (1893) 20 R. 506; *Steven* v. *Broady Norman & Co.*, 1928 S.C. 351; *Balfour* v. *Baird*, 1959 S.C. 64. But this does not apply to instalment contracts nor to continuing wrongs, such as subsidence, where each fresh subsidence is a fresh ground of action: *D. Abercorn* v. *Merry and Cunningham*, 1909 S.C. 750.

[28] *Manners* v. *Pearson* [1898] 1 Ch. 581, 587; *Barry* v. *Van Den Heek* [1920] 2 K.B. 709, 712; *Di Ferdinando* v. *Simon, Smits & Co.* [1920] 3 K.B. 409, 412; *Re Chesterman's Trusts* [1923] 2 Ch. 466, 489.

[29] *Manners, supra*; *Di Ferdinando, supra*; *Barry, supra*; *Lebeaupin* v. *Crispin* [1920] 2 K.B. 714; *Re British American Continental Bank Ltd.* [1922] 2 Ch. 575; [1923] 1 Ch. 276; *Peyrae* v. *Wilkinson* [1924] 2 K.B. 166, 167; *Ottoman Bank* v. *Chakarian* [1930] A.C. 277; *Ottoman Bank of Nicosia* v. *Chakarian* [1938] A.C. 260; see also *Ottoman Bank* v. *Menni* [1939] 4 All E.R. 9; *E. I. Trading Co.* v. *Carmel Exporters* [1952] 1 All E.R. 1053.

damage is fixed as at a particular date, the same rule applies, and the date for conversion into sterling is the date of the delict,[30] even though it may take time to discover all the consequences of the wrong and to determine the full extent of the damage, and probably even if the damages were prospective or continuing.[31]

The same applies to non-payment of a debt where the date of breach is established by the default in making payment on the due date,[32] and also to a bill of exchange, in which case the material time is the date of maturity.[33]

A creditor will normally expect and can, indeed, be compelled to accept the currency of the foreign country where payment is to be made [34] if there is an exchange there whereby the rate of exchange can be calculated [35]; but difficulties arise when the currency of the country of payment is changed, and the question then is a matter of the interpretation of the contract [36]; it may provide against such a contingency.[37]

Objects of an award of damages

The object of an award of damages is compensation: the underlying principle has often been described as *restitutio in integrum*.[38] Damages are, therefore, not a form of punishment of a wrongdoing defender.[39] The sum of money awarded as damages is in theory the amount which will restore the pursuer to as good a position as he would have been in if his contract had been duly performed,[40] or if the wrong which caused him

30 *S.S. Celia* v. *S.S. Volturno* [1921] 2 A.C. 544; *Re British American Continental Bank Ltd.* [1922] 2 Ch. 589; *Madeleine Vionnet et Cie* v. *Wills* [1940] 1 K.B. 72; see also *Graumann* v. *Treitel* [1940] 2 All E.R. 188, and *The Baarn* [1933] P. 251, expld. *The Baarn* (*No.* 2) [1934] P. 171; *Cummings* v. *London Bullion Co.* [1952] 1 All E.R. 383; *E. I. Trading Co.* v. *Carmel Exporters* [1952] 1 All E.R. 1053. But see Carriage by Air Act 1961, Sch. I, art. 22 (5), for a special rule.

31 *S.S. Celia, supra*, at 553.

32 *Uliendahl* v. *Pankhurst* (1923) 39 T.L.R. 628; *Peyrae* v. *Wilkinson* [1924] 2 K.B. 166; *Ottoman Bank* v. *Menni* [1939] 4 All E.R. 9; *Madeleine Vionnet et Cie* v. *Wills* [1940] 1 K.B. 72; *Graumann* v. *Treitel* [1940] 2 All E.R. 188; *E. I. Trading Co.* v. *Carmel Exporters* [1952] 1 All E.R. 1053.

33 *Khoury* v. *Khayat* [1943] A.C. 507.

34 *Ottoman Bank of Nicosia* v. *Chakarian* [1930] A.C. 277; *Ottoman Bank of Nicosia* v. *Descalapoulos* [1934] A.C. 354; *Ottoman Bank of Haifa* v. *Chakarian* [1938] A.C. 260.

35 *Marrache* v. *Ashton* [1943] A.C. 311.

36 *Ottoman Bank* v. *Menni* [1939] 4 All E.R. 9; *cf. Cummings* v. *London Bullion Co.* [1952] 1 All E.R. 383.

37 *Feist* v. *Société Intercommunal Belge* [1934] A.C. 161. *Cf. New Brunswick Ry.* v. *British and French Trust Corporation* [1939] A.C. 1, and *de Bueger* v. *Ballantyne* [1938] A.C. 452.

38 *Dunlop* v. *Higgins* (1848) 6 Bell 195, 211; *The Columbus* (1849) 3 W.Rob. 158; *The Argentino* (1888) 13 P.D. 191, 196, 200, 201; see also *Hobbs* v. *L. & S. W. Ry.* (1875) L.R. 10 Q.B. 111, 121; *Watson Laidlaw* v. *Pott, Cassels and Williamson*, 1914 S.C.(H.L.) 18, 29; *H.M.S. London* [1914] P. 72, 78; *Boyd and Forrest* v. *G.S.W. Ry.*, 1915 S.C.(H.L.) 20, 28; *Liesbosch* v. *Edison* [1933] A.C. 449, 464; but see *Admiralty Commrs.* v. *S.S. Valeria* [1922] 2 A.C. 242, 248.

39 *Addis* v. *Gramophone Co.* [1909] A.C. 488.

40 Ersk. III, 3, 86; *Robinson* v. *Harman* (1848) 1 Exch. 850, 855; *Lock* v. *Furze* (1866) L.R. 1 C.P. 441, 450, 453; *The Columbus* (1849) 3 W.Rob. 158; *France* v. *Gaudet* (1871) L.R. 6 Q.B. 199; *Bain* v. *Fothergill* (1874) L.R. 7 H.L. 158, 207; *Houldsworth* v. *Brand's Trs.* (1877) 4 R. 369, 374, 375; *The Argentino, supra*, 197; *Chaplin* v. *Hicks* [1911] 2 K.B. 786, 794, approved in *Duke of Portland* v. *Wood's Trs.*, 1926 S.C. 640, 645; affd. 1927 S.C.(H.L.) 1; *Wertheim* v. *Chicoutimi Pulp Co.* [1911] A.C. 301; *British Westinghouse Co.* v. *Underground Ry.* [1912] A.C. 673, 689; *Watts* v. *Mitsui* [1917] A.C. 227, 241; *Abrahams* v. *Reiach* [1922]

loss had not been committed by the defender.[41] The fundamental rule is that the pursuer is to be compensated for his loss measured in money.[42]

In many cases, however, particularly of delict, the object cannot be attained with any accuracy, and the principle of restitution remains largely theoretical.[43] In most cases of breach of contract the damage actually suffered can be assessed in money with some accuracy, though even there the damages awarded are frequently not really commensurate with the full loss and injury suffered; thus in the case of the non-payment of money, the only measure of damages normally allowed is interest on the principal sum in addition thereto, although the damage sustained in consequence of the non-payment may be very substantial.[44]

In cases of delict, it may be possible to assess damages more or less accurately in the case of injury to property, but in the case of personal injuries no amount of monetary payment can be full or adequate compensation to the injured party, and frequently the consequences of the initial wrong far exceed the amount of compensation which can be given.[45] Many quite imponderable factors have to be taken into account.

> " In the case of damages in general there is one principle which does underlie the assessment. It is what may be called that of restoration. The idea is to restore the person who has sustained injury and loss to the condition in which he would have been had he not so sustained it. In the cases of financial loss, injury to trade, and the like, caused either by breach of contract or by tort, the loss is capable of correct appreciation in stated figures. In a second class of cases, restoration being in point of fact difficult—as in the case of loss of reputation, or impossible—as in the case of loss of life, faculty or limb—the task of restoration under the name of compensation calls into play inference, conjecture and the like. And this is necessarily accompanied by those deficiencies which attach to the conversion into money of certain elements which are very real, which go to make up the happiness and usefulness of life, but which were never so converted or measured. The restoration by way of compensation is therefore accomplished to a large extent by the exercise of a sound

1 K.B. 477, 480; *Banco de Portugal* v. *Waterlow* [1932] A.C. 452, 474; *A/B Karlshamns Oljefabriker* v. *Monarch S.S. Co.*, 1949 S.C.(H.L.) 1, 18, 20; *Victoria Laundry* v. *Newman* [1949] 2 K.B. 528; *Spencer* v. *Macmillan's Trs.*, 1958 S.C. 300, 303, 315; *Koufos* v. *Czarnikow* [1969] 1 A.C. 350, 420.

41 *Phillips* v. *L.S.W. Ry.* (1879) 5 Q.B.D. 78, 87; *Livingstone* v. *Rawyards Coal Co.* (1880) 7 R. (H.L.) 1, 7; *The City of Peking* (1890) 15 App.Cas. 438; *The Mediana* [1900] A.C. 113, 119; *Liesbosch* v. *Edison* [1933] A.C. 449, 463; *Pomphrey* v. *Cuthbertson*, 1951 S.C. 147, 152, 161, 162; *Cruikshank* v. *Shiels*, 1951 S.C. 741, 753; *British Transport Commission* v. *Gourley* [1956] A.C. 185, 197; *cf.* also *Hutchison* v. *Davidson*, 1945 S.C. 395; Bell, *Prin.* § 553 speaks of the pursuer being " indemnified." *Cf.* Ersk. III, 1, 14.

42 *Hutchison* v. *Davidson*, 1945 S.C. 395, 413, *per* Lord President Normand.

43 *Admiralty Commrs.* v. *S.S. Valeria, supra. Cf. Phillips, supra.* Bell, *Prin.* § 545 (2).

44 Bell, *Prin.* § 33 (1); *Fletcher* v. *Tayleur* (1855) 17 C.B. 21, 29; *British Columbia Sawmill Co.* v. *Nettleship* (1868) L.R. 3 C.P. 499, 506. See also *Wallis* v. *Smith* (1882) 21 Ch.D. 243, 257, *per* Jessel M.R.

45 *Armstrong* v. *S.E. Ry.* (1847) 11 Jur. 758, 760; *Rowley* v. *L.N.W. Ry.* (1873) L.R. 8 Ex. 221, 230; *Phillips* v. *L.S.W. Ry.* (1879) 5 Q.B.D. 78; *Johnston* v. *G.W. Ry.* [1904] 2 K.B. 250; *Admiralty Commrs.* v. *S.S. Valeria* [1922] 2 A.C. 242, 248; *The Edison* [1933] A.C. 449.

imagination and the practice of the broad axe. It is in such cases, whether the result has been attained by the verdict of a jury or the finding of a single judge, that the greatest weight attaches to the decision of the court of first instance." [46]

Object common to contract and delict

It appears that the general object of an award of damages is the same in both contract and delict, namely, the payment of a sum which, so far as money can compensate, will give the wronged party compensation,[47] and it is only in the working-out of this principle that differences arise. Particularly in cases of delict the idea of punishment has to be eschewed. So juries have been charged in these terms: "You are not here to revenge the injury or to punish the wrongdoer but to administer reparation to the injured." [48] "Give what is fair and just and reasonable. You are not to punish or revenge: you are merely to compensate." [49] "It is not your duty to inflict punishment, but merely to fix a moderate sum in name of compensation for an injury." [50] But the court must so regulate the assessment of the award that, while it seeks to give effect to the principle of compensating the claimant for all the direct and natural consequences of the wrongful act, it will neither enrich nor impoverish him beyond the position in which he would have been if the wrongful act had not occurred.[51]

Limitations on principle

The principle of seeking to make restitution is limited by three other principles, firstly the principle that compensation will not be ordered for harm or loss not caused by the initial breach of duty, secondly, the principle that compensation will not be given for harm or loss deemed to be too remote from the initial breach of duty to be fairly chargeable against the party in breach, and thirdly, the principle that the innocent party must take reasonable steps to minimise the loss sustained and to mitigate damages.[52]

Damages a general rule

The obligation to pay damages in the event of a breach of contract is one implied as a general rule of law, and it can only be excluded by an

[46] *Watson, Laidlaw & Co.* v. *Pott, Cassels & Williamson*, 1914 S.C.(H.L.) 18, 29, *per* Lord Shaw.

[47] *Wertheim* v. *Chicoutimi Pulp Co.* [1911] A.C. 301 (contract); *Admiralty Commrs.* v. *S.S. Susquehanna* [1926] A.C. 655, 661, *per* Lord Dunedin; *Livingstone* v. *Rawyards Coal Co.* (1880) 7 R.(H.L.) 1, 7 (delict); *Watts* v. *Mitsui* [1917] A.C. 227, 241; *Hutchison* v. *Davidson*, 1945 S.C. 395, 404; *Pomphrey* v. *Cuthbertson*, 1951 S.C. 147, 161, 162.

[48] *Gibson* v. *Anderson* (1846) 9 D. 1, 6, *per* Ld. Pres. Boyle (wrongful imprisonment).

[49] *Tucker* v. *Aitchison* (1846) 9 D. 21, 23, *per* Ld. Pres. Boyle (breach of promise).

[50] *Muckarsie* v. *Dixon* (1848) 11 D. 4, 5, *per* Ld. Pres. Boyle (assault).

[51] *Hutchison*, *supra*, at p. 408.

[52] Chap. 28, *infra*.

express term in the contract.[53] "It would require express language in any contract to indicate any intention of negativing a right to damages for the breach of an obligation imposed by it." [54] So, too, the duty to make compensation for a delict is implied by law and may only be limited or excluded by binding statutory provision or express agreement, as where a traveller's ticket contains conditions limiting or excluding his right to damages.[55] The instances where such limitations have been held to arise are noted subsequently, but failing any such clear exclusion, a claim of damages arises as a general rule on the breach of the primary obligation between the parties. "If they have bound themselves to do something and fail to do it they will be liable in damages, however honestly or innocently they have been mistaken or misadvised as to what their obligation was." [56] Again, "the only answer to a claim of damages for the defender's failure to perform his contract would have been that there was absolutely no chance of the pursuer benefiting by the performance of the obligation which the defender undertook." [57]

Damages for breach of contract and for delict

In each case damages are being sought as compensation for breach of legal obligation which has resulted in loss measurable in terms of money, and some cases have suggested that the principles applicable to both classes of cases should be, or are, the same.[58] It is now clear [59] that this is not so because "in the case of contract two parties, usually with some knowledge of one another, deliberately undertake mutual duties. They have the opportunity to define clearly in respect of what they shall and shall not be liable. The law has to say what shall be the boundaries of their liability where this is not expressed, defining that boundary in relation to what has been expressed and implied. In tort two persons, usually unknown to one another, find that the acts or utterances of one have collided with the rights of the other, and the court has to define what is the liability for the ensuing damage, whether it shall be shared, and how far it extends. If one tries to find a concept of damages which will fit both these different problems there is a danger of distorting the rules to accommodate one or the other and of producing a rule that is satisfactory for neither. The problems certainly have one thing in common. In both the use of words with differing shades of meaning in the various cases makes it hard to discern with exactitude where the boundaries lie." [60]

53 *Wallis* v. *Pratt* [1910] 2 K.B. 1003, 1016; revd. [1911] A.C. 394; and see *Beck* v. *Szymanowski* [1924] A.C. 43. *Cf. Hood* v. *Anchor Line*, 1918 S.C.(H.L.) 143. *Cf. Restatement of Contracts*, s. 327.
54 *Wallis* v. *Pratt, supra.*
55 *e.g. Mackay* v. *Scottish Airways*, 1948 S.C. 254.
56 *Houldsworth* v. *Brand's Trs.* (1876) 3 R. 304, 319, *per* Lord Gifford.
57 *Stiven* v. *Watson* (1874) 1 R. 412, 416. *Quaere*, what about nominal damages? See *infra.*
58 See *e.g. The Notting Hill* (1884) 9 P.D. 105, 113; *Addis* v. *Gramophone Co.* [1909] A.C. 488, 497; *H.M.S. London* [1914] P. 72, 77; *The Susquehanna* [1926] A.C. 655, 661.
59 *Koufos* v. *Czarnikow* [1969] 1 A.C. 350.
60 *Ibid. per* Lord Pearce; see also Lord Upjohn at p. 424.

Pursuer's position to be regarded

It likewise follows from the proposition that damages are designed to afford compensation to an injured party and not to punish a wrongdoer,[61] that it is the pursuer's and not the defender's position which has to be regarded. Hence, in general, it is not relevant to consider the means and position of the defender, nor any advantage which he may have derived from the breach of obligation complained of, when estimating the amount of damages to be awarded.[62] Nor does it matter whether he be rich or poor, liable to be reduced to bankruptcy by having to pay damages, or entitled to full indemnity by insurance; the court must look at the damage suffered by the pursuer which has to be repaired and assess the damages with reference to the loss. It is as a rule irrelevant that the defender acted maliciously[63] or with gross carelessness.[64]

Date at which damages assessed

Damages have to be assessed with regard to the position of the injured party at the time when the loss or damage was suffered, which is normally the date of the breach of contract,[65] or of the delict,[66] though in the case of delict developments after the initial delict casting light on the probable duration, extent and gravity of the loss must be taken into account.[67]

Difficulty of assessing damages

It is apparent that while the underlying principle of damages is *restitutio in integrum*, it is probably never possible to effect this completely by a monetary award and, in many cases, any pecuniary compensation is inadequate and can in no sense effect proper restoration of the previous state of affairs. In most cases, too, the assessment and quantification of damages is difficult, and no approximation to absolute accuracy can be sought nor, indeed, should it be too strenuously attempted. In *The Mediana*[68] Lord Chancellor Halsbury said: "The whole region of inquiry into damages is one of extreme difficulty. You very often cannot even lay down any principle upon which you can give damages; nevertheless, it is remitted to the jury, or those who stand in the place of the jury, to consider what compensation shall be given in money for what is a wrongful act. Take the most familiar and ordinary case: how is anybody to measure pain and suffering in moneys counted? Nobody can suggest that you can by any arithmetical calculation establish what is the exact

61 *Addis* v. *Gramophone Co.* [1909] A.C. 488, 494.

62 *Somerville* v. *Thomson* (1896) 23 R. 576; *Keyse* v. *Keyse* (1886) 11 P.D. 100.

63 *Clippens Oil Co.* v. *Edinburgh Water Trs.*, 1907 S.C.(H.L.) 9, 15.

64 *Black* v. *N.B. Ry.*, 1908 S.C. 444.

65 *Di Ferdinando* v. *Simon, Smits & Co.* [1920] 3 K.B. 409; *Madeleine Vionnet et Cie* v. *Wills* [1940] 1 K.B. 72; see also *Slater* v. *Hoyle & Smith* [1920] 2 K.B. 11; *Campbell Mostyn (Provisions) Ltd.* v. *Barnett Trading Co.* [1954] 1 Lloyds Rep. 65.

66 *S.S. Celia* v. *S.S. Volturno* [1921] 2 A.C. 544; *Philips* v. *Ward* [1956] 1 All E.R. 874.

67 *Bishop* v. *Cunard White Star Co.* [1950] P. 240; *Carslogie S.S. Co.* v. *Royal Norwegian Govt.* [1952] A.C. 292.

68 [1900] A.C. 113, 116.

amount of money which would represent such a thing as the pain and suffering which a person has undergone by reason of an accident . . . nevertheless the law recognises that as a topic upon which damages can be given." So, too, Lindley L.J.,[69] " It must be remembered that the rules as to damages can in the nature of things only be approximately just, and that they have to be worked out, not by mathematicians, but by juries "; and Lord Haldane,[70] " In some of the cases there are expressions as to the principles governing the measure of general damages which at first sight seem difficult to harmonise. The apparent discrepancies are, however, mainly due to the varying nature of the particular questions submitted for decision. The quantum of damage is a question of fact, and the only guidance the law can give is to lay down general principles which afford at times but scanty assistance in dealing with particular cases. The judges who give guidance to juries in these cases have necessarily to look at their special character, and to mould for the purposes of different kinds of claim, the expression of the general principles which apply to them, and this is apt to give rise to an appearance of ambiguity." Or again [71]: " Many, varied and complex are the types of vessels and the modes of employment in which their owners may use them. Hence, the difficulties constantly felt in defining rules as to the measure of damages. I think it impossible to lay down any universal formula."

Where ascertainment difficult or impossible

It is, however, no reason for refusing an award of damages,[72] or for making an only nominal award,[73] that it is difficult to estimate the injury or loss suffered, or to assess the damages properly payable therefor with any certainty or accuracy.[74] At least in England, if some damage has been sustained but ascertainment is impossible, nominal damages only are recoverable,[75] and this is probably the law of Scotland also in cases of contract,[76] and possibly in delict, except negligence.[77]

The facts that there are no absolutely binding rules for the quantification of damages, and that the circumstances of every case have to be considered separately, involve that quantification is practically always difficult, and in such cases as personal injury the assessment of monetary

69 *Rodocanachi* v. *Milburn* (1886) 18 Q.B.D. 67, 78.

70 *British Westinghouse* v. *Underground Rys.* [1912] A.C. 673, 688. *Cf. The Susquehanna* [1925] P. 196, 210.

71 *Liesbosch* v. *Edison* [1933] A.C. 449, 464. See also *A/B Karlshamns Oljefabriker* v. *Monarch S.S. Co.*, 1949 S.C.(H.L.) 1 at 21, 28.

72 *Hall* v. *Ross* (1813) 1 Dow. 201; *Chaplin* v. *Hicks* [1911] 2 K.B. 786.

73 *Ungar* v. *Sugg* (1891) 8 R.P.C. 385; *Hillas* v. *Arcos* (1932) 147 L.T. 503.

74 *Hall, supra*; *Simpson* v. *L.N.W. Ry.* (1876) 1 Q.B.D. 274; *Ungar, supra*; *Chaplin, supra*; *Bovet* v. *Walter* (1917) 62 S.J. 104. The loss, must, however, be a reasonable probability and not a merely speculative possibility: *Barnett* v. *Cohen* [1921] 2 K.B. 461. *Cf. Bourne* v. *Lothians Racing Syndicate*, 1951 S.L.T.(Notes) 37.

75 *Erie Gas Co.* v. *Carroll* [1911] A.C. 105; *Weld-Blundell* v. *Stephens* [1920] A.C. 956.

76 *Webster* v. *Cramond Iron Co.* (1875) 2 R. 752, 754; *Murray* v. *Marr* (1892) 20 R. 119, 124.

77 See further, *infra*.

compensation for physical loss and suffering is really impossible, but is only resorted to as the only possible alleviation of and compensation for the wrong.

It also follows from these considerations that no guidance can be given *a priori* on what sums may properly be sought as damages in any given circumstances, nor what sums should reasonably be awarded. Some guidance in general terms may, however, be derived from certain prior decisions and general deductions may be drawn from consideration of the trend of decisions in particular kinds of cases, particularly where any decision on quantum of damages has been adequately considered by an appellate court. But there can, in general, be no question of following precedent on questions purely of quantum of damages as distinct from principle.

Though difficulty of assessment is not a reason for refusing damages, damages will be refused if they are purely speculative and such that the court cannot be sure they would not have been incurred just as much if there had been no breach of obligation [78]; and damages must be refused if it be shown that even due fulfilment of the contract would not have prevented the loss.[79]

Rules of damages

It has been observed that " the whole region of inquiry into damages is one of extreme difficulty," [80] and this difficulty is enhanced by the fact that probably no rules can be laid down which are universally binding for any class of cases. The measure of damages, though not controlled by rigid rules, is not to be ascertained by caprice, but only by application of the proper principle, which is the principle of *restitutio in integrum*.[81] The measure of damages is always very much a question of fact in the circumstances of each case,[82] yet by no means entirely so, in that principles of very general application may be derived from the decisions on a particular topic: but in probably no case are there any rules for the quantification of damages which are imperatively binding on the court, with the exception of those few cases where statute sets limits to or otherwise imposes restrictions on the free quantification of damages. Nor is it even practicable to derive much assistance from decided cases, as the courts have set their faces against deducing any formulae which can be applied in cases of loss or injury. Within the framework of a few general principles every case must be considered on its own merits. In cases of contract this

78 *The Parana* (1877) 2 P.D. 118: on this case see further *Dunn* v. *Bucknall Bros.* [1902] 2 K.B. 614; *Koufos* v. *Czarnikow* [1969] 1 A.C. 350. *Cf. Sapwell* v. *Bass* [1910] 2 K.B. 486.

79 *Millar's Trs.* v. *Polson* (1897) 24 R. 1038; *Coldman* v. *Hill* [1919] 1 K.B. 443.

80 *The Mediana* [1900] A.C. 113, 116, *per* Lord Halsbury.

81 *Hutchison* v. *Davidson*, 1945 S.C. 395, 410; *Admiralty Commrs.* v. *S.S. Susquehanna* [1926] A.C. 655, 661.

82 *A/B Karlshamns Oljefabriker* v. *Monarch S.S. Co.*, 1949 S.C.(H.L.) 1, 28; *British Westinghouse* v. *Underground Rys.* [1912] A.C. 673, 688.

is even more so, as no two cases are more than generally similar in circumstances. In reparation, the variable factors are so numerous that no rules could possibly be applied to all cases.

Hence, while there are numerous references to " rules " of damages, there are, in truth, no such things. The quantum of damage is a question of fact,[83] and it is impossible to lay down any universal formula [84] so that the dominant and, indeed, the only rule of law is the principle of *restitutio in integrum*, and subsidiary rules can only be justified if they give effect to that rule.[85] Consequently, there are expressions of principles governing the measure of damages in various cases which seem difficult to harmonise, but such apparent discrepancies are mainly due to the varying nature of the questions for decision by the court.[86] The only conclusions which can be drawn, therefore, are principles of general but not universal validity for particular types of cases derived from judicial decisions which cannot be treated as binding rules and must, occasionally, be departed from to give effect to the overriding general rule of fair compensation. " The owner of an article which has been damaged through the fault of another is entitled to reparation for the wrongful act, and for all the natural and direct consequences of the wrongful act. He is entitled to *restitutio in integrum*. To give effect to that general principle of law certain rules have been evolved in practice." [87]

" I do not doubt the wisdom of the judges who . . . have laid down rules or principles for the guidance of those whose duty it is, as judges or jurymen, to assess damages. When those rules or principles are applied, however, it is essential to remember . . . that in the end, what has to be decided is a question of fact, and, therefore, a question proper for a jury. Circumstances are so infinitely various that, however carefully general rules are framed, they must be construed with some liberality, and not too rigidly applied. It was necessary to lay down principles lest juries should be persuaded to do injustice by imposing an undue, or perhaps an inadequate, liability on a defendant. The court must be careful, however, to see that the principles laid down are never so narrowly interpreted as to prevent a jury, or judge of fact, from doing justice between the parties." [88] " Though an excellent attempt was made in *Hadley* v. *Baxendale* [89] to lay down a rule on the subject, it will be found that the rule is not capable of meeting all cases; and when the matter comes to be further considered, it will probably turn out that there is no such thing as a rule, as to the legal measure of damages, applicable in all cases." [90]

83 *A/B Karlshamns Oljefabriker* v. *Monarch S.S. Co.*, 1949 S.C.(H.L.) 1, 20, 28. It is a jury question: *Hutchison* v. *Davidson*, 1945 S.C. 395, 407.
84 *Liesbosch* v. *Edison* [1933] A.C. 449, 464.
85 *Ibid.* 463.
86 *British Westinghouse* v. *Underground Rys.* [1912] A.C. 673, 688.
87 *Pomphrey* v. *Cuthbertson*, 1951 S.C. 147, 161, *per* Lord Jamieson. The rules are rules of practice not binding rules of law. *Cf.* Lord Mackay, *ibid.*, at pp. 156–159.
88 *A/B Karlshamns Oljefabriker* v. *Monarch S.S. Co.*, 1949 S.C.(H.L.) 1, 28.
89 (1854) 9 Ex. 341, 354.
90 *Gee* v. *Lancs & Yorks Ry.* (1860) 6 H. & N. 211, 221.

In *Duke of Portland* v. *Wood's Trs.*[91] Lord President Clyde said that Scots law was probably less favourably inclined than English law to the formulation of judge-made rules for the assessment of damages, and pointed out that the true value might only be found after applying more measures of damages than one and checking one result with another. Lord Sands and Lord Ashmore expressed similar opinions. Similarly, in *Hutchison* v. *Davidson*,[92] where a house was destroyed by fire, regard was had both to the cost of replacement and to the depreciation in selling value in quantifying damages.

Nevertheless, " the measure of damages ought never to be governed by mere rules of practice, nor can such rules override the principles of the law on this subject." [93] The principle is *restitutio in integrum*, but it falls to be worked out in various ways.[94] So, too, in *Pomphrey* v. *Cuthbertson*,[95] it was pointed out that there were no rigid or limiting rules as to measure of damages, and that all methods of arriving fairly at chargeable sums were open for consideration, albeit some methods were so obviously fair in the ordinary cases that a court would be surprised if they were departed from, but they could not be stated higher than as methods in familiar use, and not as rules.

Varieties of damages

Several varieties of damages have been distinguished. The first is nominal damages, which is a phrase signifying that the court has negatived anything amounting to real damage, but is affirming by a nominal award of damages that there is an infraction of a legal right, which, though it gives the pursuer no right to any substantial damages at all, yet gives him a right to the verdict in respect that his legal right has been infringed.[96] The amount awarded as such is consequently small, and in practice, in view of the probable effect on expenses, actions are not brought in Scotland purely for nominal damages, though an award of nominal damages may be made where breach of right has been proved but substantial loss has not been established.[97] In England, a claim for nominal damages is sometimes made to vindicate the right alleged to be infringed [98]: in Scotland a process of declarator would frequently be more appropriate.

91 1926 S.C. 640, 651, citing Stair I, 17, 16. See also his tracing at pp. 649–650 of the connection between older Scottish rules and the rules of *Hadley* v. *Baxendale*.

92 1945 S.C. 395.

93 *Admiralty Commrs.* v. *S.S. Chekiang* [1926] A.C. 637, 643, *per* Lord Sumner; *cf. Liesbosch* v. *Edison* [1933] A.C. 449.

94 *Hutchison* v. *Davidson*, 1945 S.C. 395, 410.

95 1951 S.C. 147, 156.

96 *The Mediana* [1900] A.C. 113, 116; *Teacher* v. *Calder* (1898) 25 R. 661, 672; *Webster* v. *Cramond Iron Co.* (1875) 2 R. 752; *cf. Restatement of Contracts*, s. 328.

97 *Morton* v. *Barclay* (1824) 3 Mur. 401; *Bradley* v. *Menley*, 1913 S.C. 923, 926. An action for nominal damages as such, if competent at all in Scotland, could be brought only in the Small Debt Court. A declarator is usually the proper form of establishing a disputed right. There seem to be no pure cases of nominal damages in Scots law, *i.e.*, claims simply for nominal damages.

98 *Embrey* v. *Owen* (1851) 6 Ex. 353; *Northam* v. *Hurley* (1853) 1 E. & B. 665.

The second variety of damages is generally designated contemptuous, where the amount awarded is derisory, such as a penny, and indicates that the court has formed a very low opinion of the worth of the pursuer's legal claim, or considers that his conduct has been ungentlemanly, morally unjustifiable, or such as to give little or no moral basis for his claim though it be sound in law. The effect of such a verdict on the question of expenses cannot be ignored. This variety of damages is most commonly and probably exclusively found in actions founded in delict, particularly such as defamation, breach of promise or seduction, where in effect the court or jury indicates by such an award that the pursuer deserved the treatment of which he complains, or at least has little real basis for his claim.[99]

The most normal award of damages is, however, the variety characterised as ordinary or substantial or compensatory, where the award is intended to represent fair and adequate compensation for the loss, damage or injury sustained by the pursuer. Such an award signifies that the court has found that a real breach of obligation has taken place resulting in some actual and substantial loss to the pursuer for which he is entitled to substantial and theoretically equivalent compensation.[1] The amount actually awarded represents a genuine though often unsatisfactory, and, at times, lamentably defective attempt to fix a sum of money which will achieve, so far as possible, the aim of restoration. The fact that the compensation must be in money inevitably renders it an inadequate compensation. Parties are entitled to make an estimate of the damages likely to flow from the breach and payable in such an event; if such is a genuine pre-estimate it will bind the court,[2] or they may lawfully contract that, whatever damage be suffered, the party in breach shall not be liable to pay more than a specified amount,[3] but such an agreement will only bind the parties to it, and a third party with a title to sue could recover damages on ordinary principles.[4] Equally damages may be prohibited or restricted by statute in certain cases.[5]

The last variety of damages distinguishable is described as exemplary, punitive or vindictive, where the court is said to assess damages at a high figure to express indignation at the enormity of the offence, or to punish the defender's misbehaviour; this is to some extent the counterpart of contemptuous damages, in this case increasing the sum by having regard to the moral quality of the wrong complained of. This variety of damages is, however, wholly unknown today in the law of Scotland, though competent in England,[6] and Scottish courts may not express displeasure

99 *Sproll* v. *Walker* (1900) 2 F. 73 (¼d.); *Bradley* v. *Menley*, 1913 S.C. 923 (6d.); *Madden* v. *Glasgow Corpn.*, 1923 S.C. 102 (¼d.); *Thain* v. *Thain* [1948] C.L.Y. 4185 (¼d.).

1 *Cf. Restatement of Contracts*, s. 329.

2 Chap. 7, *supra*.

3 *Cellulose Acetate Co.* v. *Widnes Foundry* [1933] A.C. 20.

4 *Nunan* v. *S. Ry.* [1924] 1 K.B. 223.

5 *e.g.*, Carriage of Goods by Sea Act 1924, Sched., Art. III, para. 8.

6 *Rookes* v. *Barnard* [1964] A.C. 1129; *Broome* v. *Cassell* [1971] 2 All E.R. 187.

by enhancing the damages.[7] It is certainly not found in cases of contract.[8] In delict there is no authority for any distinction between " damages " and " exemplary damages " in Scots law: the idea of reparation excludes this. The basis of exemplary damages is probably malice, and hence the doctrine can never apply where the defender is not the actual wrongdoer but only vicariously liable.[9] It must, however, be conceded that there are recorded awards of damages in Scottish cases which appear to go beyond proper compensation. This enhancement of the sum awarded is, however, to be distinguished from questions of aggravation when the amount of damages ordinarily recoverable is increased in consequence of the seriousness of the injury complained of and the loss suffered, as in the case of particularly gross defamation, or particularly severe loss or injury. Cases of this kind are just cases of substantial damage where elements of particularly serious loss are present.

General and special damages

The distinction between general and special damages is more commonly found in English authorities than in Scottish, and the terms are there used with various meanings. One usage distinguishes between damages for loss arising naturally and damages for loss arising only in special circumstances unforeseen by the defendant unless brought to his notice.[10] Another distinction is between such damages as may be awarded in accordance with the judgment of the reasonable man, and such damages as are given in respect of any consequences reasonably and probably arising from the breach of duty complained of.[11] Another again is the distinction between damages which may be awarded on general evidence of the loss, and damages which are exceptional in character and must be claimed specially and proved strictly.[12] Another again flows from the rule that some torts, *e.g.* slander, are actionable only on proof of special damage, so that assumed hurt to feelings will not suffice, and special, *i.e.* actual, proven material loss.[13] In Scotland the distinction is not so rigidly or clearly drawn, and the same names are sometimes applied to the distinction between direct and consequential damages. In *Ströms Bruks A/B*

[7] *Addis* v. *Gramophone Co.* [1909] A.C. 488; *Black* v. *North British Ry.*, 1908 S.C. 444, 453; *cf. Hyslop* v. *Staig* (1816) 1 Mur. 24; *Tucker* v. *Aitchison* (1846) 9 D. 21; *cf. Berry* v. *Da Costa* (1866) L.R. 1 C.P. 331, 334; *Hamlin* v. *G.N. Ry.* (1856) 1 H. & N. 408, 411. *Contra, Morton* v. *Edinburgh & Glasgow Ry.* (1845) 8 D. 288.

[8] *Addis, supra, cf. Restatement of Contracts*, s. 342.

[9] *Black, supra*, at pp. 453–454, *per* Ld. Pres. Dunedin.

[10] *A/B Karlshamns Oljefabriker* v. *Monarch S.S. Co.*, 1949 S.C.(H.L.) 1, 19–20, *per* Lord Wright.

[11] *Prehn* v. *Royal Bank of Liverpool* (1870) L.R. 5 Ex. 92.

[12] *Ashby* v. *White* (1703) 2 Ld. Raym. 938; *Marzetti* v. *Williams* (1830) 1 B. & Ad. 415; *Aerial Advertising Co* v. *Batchelors Peas Ltd.* [1938] 2 All E.R. 788; *Perera* v. *Vandiyar* [1953] 1 All E.R. 1109 (contract); *Hiort* v. *L.N.W. Ry.* (1879) 4 Ex.D. 188; *The Mediana* [1900] A.C. 113. See also *McLaurin* v. *N.B. Ry.* (1892) 19 R. 346; *Ströms Bruks A/B* v. *Hutchison* (1905) 7 F.(H.L.) 131, 135; *Admiralty Commrs.* v. *S.S. Susquehanna* [1926] A.C. 655, 661; *Hutchison* v. *Davidson*, 1945 S.C. 395; *B.T.C.* v. *Gourley* [1956] A.C. 185, 206.

[13] *Finlay* v. *Chirney* (1888) 20 Q.B.D. 494; *Ratcliffe* v. *Evans* [1892] 2 Q.B. 524; *Neville* v. *London Express Newspaper Ltd.* [1919] A.C. 368. *Cf.* also *Restatement of Torts*, s. 904.

v. *Hutchison* [14] Lord Macnaghten said: " 'General damages' . . . are such as the law will presume to be the direct, natural, or probable consequence of the act complained of. 'Special damages,' on the other hand, are such as the law will not infer from the nature of the act. They do not follow in ordinary course. They are exceptional in their character and they must be claimed specially and proved strictly." [15] Again, in *A/B Karlshamns Oljefabriker* v. *Monarch S.S. Co.*,[16] Lord Wright equated the distinction between general and special damages to the distinction between damages arising naturally and in the ordinary course of events, and damages arising where there were special and extraordinary circumstances beyond the reasonable prevision of the parties. Put thus, the distinction is no more than that between ordinary and consequential damages.[17]

It is always necessary in Scotland to make averments of loss actually suffered and to conclude for a specified sum of money in name of damages to justify more than a nominal award of general damages. If there is no averment of loss the action is liable, in the cases of negligence and trespass where actual damage is of the essence of the claim, to be rejected as irrelevant: moreover, if in other cases breach of obligation be averred but no loss be disclosed, the claim is probably incompetent in other than the Sheriff Court as not *ex facie* disclosing matter on which an award of more than £50 could reasonably be made. Special damage such as pecuniary loss and outlays must be specified. While the distinction in the English senses of the terms must be borne in mind when studying English authorities, the distinction in that sense is largely foreign to Scots law,[18] and the alternative senses, as equivalent to direct and consequential damage, are the only ones really significant.

Damages assessed once and for all

It is a general rule in both breach of contract and delict cases that the damages which arise from one and the same cause of action [19] must all be assessed and recovered in one action.[20] The pursuer may bring only one action and must recover damages for all his loss, past, present and future, certain and contingent, direct and consequential, and that either in delict or breach of contract.[20] So, too, where several pursuers have the same right of action in respect of one injury, they must all concur in the one action.[21] If, however, two or more separate causes of action arise

14 (1905) 7 F.(H.L.) 131, 135.

15 *Cf. Kerr* v. *Earl of Orkney* (1857) 20 D. 298, 303. In *Aarons* v. *Fraser*, 1934 S.C. 137, and *Buchanan & Carswell* v. *Eugene*, 1936 S.C. 160, 180 a distinction on the English lines was taken. *Cf. Brown's Trs.* v. *Hay* (1898) 25 R. 1112, 1119; *Hutchison, supra*; *Pomphrey* v. *Cuthbertson*, 1951 S.C. 147, 159, 162.

16 1949 S.C.(H.L.) 1, 19–20.

17 This distinction is considered more fully in Chap. 28, *infra*.

18 It was used in this sense in *Hutchison* v. *Davidson*, 1945 S.C. 395.

19 *Gibbs* v. *Cruickshank* (1873) L.R. 8 C.P. 454.

20 *Stevenson* v. *Pontifex and Wood* (1887) 15 R. 125; *Brunsden* v. *Humphrey* (1884) 14 Q.B.D. 141; *Darley Main Colliery* v. *Mitchell* (1886) 11 App.Cas. 127; *Rowntree* v. *Allen* (1935) 41 Com.Cas. 90 (where contract assigned).

21 *Darling* v. *Gray* (1892) 19 R.(H.L.) 31; *Pollok* v. *Workman* (1900) 2 F. 354; *Kinnaird* v. *McLean*, 1942 S.C. 448.

even though from the same initial wrong, such as personal injury and damage to property, two actions would be competent.[22] A second action cannot be brought in respect of the same cause of action as a previous action because that cause has become *res judicata*,[23] even though great loss may subsequently accrue, and however substantial or unexpected it may be.[24] But parties may competently settle an action on the basis that if damages turn out to be greater than anticipated the right to sue is unimpaired.[25] Excusable ignorance of the extent of loss originally suffered may, however, permit a further action.[26] Also, where there is a continuing cause of action arising from the continuance or repetition of wrongs of the same kind, such as subsidences of land by reason of mineral workings, actions may be brought when and as often as damage takes place.[27]

It follows that, unless the cause of action be a continuing one, the pursuer must recover prospective damages in his one and only action. Prospective damages are properly recoverable in such cases as the breach of a continuing contract,[28] or personal injuries with continuing loss or permanent disability.[29] But it has been held competent to recover damages for the past breach of a continuing contract, under reservation of claims for damages in the event of failure to implement in the unexpired period, and then to sue for damages in respect of the later breach.[30] Where there is a continuing cause of action, as from the repetition or continuance of a series of wrongs of the same type in the same circumstances, a fresh action may be brought in respect of each fresh incident and hence prospective damages are not recoverable but only damages up to the date of the quantification in the action.[31]

In *Stevenson* v. *Pontifex and Wood*,[32] Lord President Inglis said:

> "... I am of opinion that a single act amounting either to a delict or a breach of contract cannot be made the ground of two or more actions, for the purpose of recovering damages arising within different periods but caused by the same act. On the contrary, I hold the true rule of practice based on sound principle to be, that though the delict or breach of contract be of such a nature that it will necessarily be followed by injurious consequences in the future, and though it may for this reason be impossible to ascertain with precise accuracy at the date of the action or of the verdict the amount of loss which will

22 *Brunsden, supra.*
23 *Brunsden, supra*; *Darley Main Colliery, supra*; *Macdougall* v. *Knight* (1890) 25 Q.B.D. 1; *Furness Withy* v. *Hall* (1909) 25 T.L.R. 233; *Conquer* v. *Boot* [1928] 2 K.B. 336.
24 *Darley Main Colliery Co.* v. *Mitchell* (1886) 11 App.Cas. 127, 144.
25 *Lee* v. *Lancs. & Yorks. Ry.* (1871) 6 Ch.App. 527, 534.
26 *D. Abercorn* v. *Merry & Cunninghame*, 1909 S.C. 750.
27 *Darley Main Colliery* v. *Mitchell* (1886) 11 App.Cas. 127; see also *Cameron-Head* v. *Cameron*, 1919 S.C. 627.
28 *Emery* v. *Wells* [1906] A.C. 515; *Dominion Coal Co.* v. *Dominion Iron Co.* [1909] A.C. 293.
29 *Infra*, Chap. 53.
30 *Jackson* v. *Cowie* (1872) 9 S.L.R. 617.
31 *Hole* v. *Chard Union* [1894] 1 Ch. 293; *Wheeler* v. *Keble* [1920] 1 Ch. 57. See also *Cameron-Head* v. *Cameron*, 1919 S.C. 627.
32 (1887) 15 R. 125, 129.

result, yet the whole damage must be recovered in one action because there is but one cause of action. The most familiar illustration of this rule is to be found in actions for injury to the person, in which the practice is invariable.

" Where the breach of contract or delict complained of consists not of one but of a series of acts the rule is different. Thus, if one contracts to deliver a certain quantity of goods during each month in the ensuing year, and fails to perform in the first or second month, that is in itself a distinct breach of contract, and if the purchaser sues for damages for that breach, he cannot in the same action claim for an apprehended breach in subsequent months, for the obligant may perform his contract for the future, and if he fails in any subsequent month, that is a fresh breach of contract, for which a separate action will lie.

" So also an operation *in suo* which creates a nuisance to one's neighbour may be followed by long continued loss and damage to that neighbour, and yet it may not be necessary to recover the whole damage in one action; because he who commits a nuisance is under a constant legal obligation to abate it, and so long as he fails in performing that legal obligation he is every day committing a fresh nuisance."

Damnum absque injuria

One person is not necessarily entitled to exact damages from another merely because he has suffered loss by reason of that person's actings. It may be a case of *damnum sine* (or *absque*) *injuria*. In this phrase, and the converse *injuria absque damno*, the words " damage " and " injury " follow the strict usage of the civil law. So used " injury " is limited to actionable wrong, while damage means loss or harm occurring in fact, whether actionable or not. If A is damaged by the action of B, A nevertheless has no remedy against B, if B's act is lawful in itself and is carried out without employing unlawful means. In such a case A has to endure *damnum absque injuria*.[33] To justify an award of damages there must always have been an infringement of a right vested in the first party which obtains the protection of the law,[34] that is, the breach of some legal duty owed him in the circumstances by the person from whom he seeks compensation. " Damage due to the legitimate exercise of a right is not actionable, even if the actor contemplates the damage. It is *damnum absque injuria*. The damage must be attributable to the breach by the defendant of some duty owing to the plaintiff." [35] Hence, the use of a

[33] *Crofter Co.* v. *Veitch*, 1942 S.C.(H.L.) 1, 7–8, *per* Ld. Ch. Simon.

[34] *Mogul S.S. Co.* v. *McGregor* [1892] A.C. 25; *Allen* v. *Flood* [1898] A.C. 1; *S. C. W. S.* v. *Glasgow Fleshers* (1898) 35 S.L.R. 645; *Quinn* v. *Leathem* [1901] A.C. 495; *Sorrell* v. *Smith* [1925] A.C. 700; *Crofter Co.* v. *Veitch*, 1942 S.C.(H.L.) 1; *Ware and de Freville* v. *M. T. Assocn.* [1921] 3 K.B. 40; *Hardie* v. *Chilton* [1928] 2 K.B. 300; *Thorne* v. *M. T. Assocn.* [1937] A.C. 797; *Greyvensteyn* v. *Hattingh* [1911] A.C. 355.

[35] *Bourhill* v. *Young*, 1942 S.C.(H.L.) 78, 89, *per* Lord Wright.

trade-name is protected by the law and damages will be given for infringement thereof,[36] but a house-name is not so protected and even proof of inconvenience and actual loss will not found an action of damages without malicious intention.[37] So, too, a trader is not entitled to legal protection against ordinary trade competition and he cannot complain of the operations of competitors unless they amount to an actionable conspiracy.[38]

Again, an owner of heritable property may use his land to the prejudice of any other person without incurring any liability to him, if in the circumstances he owed that other no duty to refrain from such actings.[39] An accountant does not owe a duty of care to any third party who acts in reliance on his accounts and so is not liable if loss results to the third party consequent on reliance on inaccurate accounts,[40] but he does owe a duty to a third party whom he knows to be likely to rely thereon.[41]

So, too, a shipowner who ran excursion trips on a navigable river was held to have no title *qua* shipowner to interdict a statutory body which proposed to use a ship for the same purpose, although this would have been a contravention of the statute.[42] A landlord is not liable in damages for injury to his tenant's credit if he raises an action for payment of rent or for sequestration as soon as the term of payment is past; he is within his rights [43]; to disentitle a pursuer from taking decree in absence, any tender made by the defender must include expenses. Failing such, he is not liable in damages for taking decree in absence.[44] Dismissal from a religious community in alleged breach of a vow is not a breach of contract for which a claim of damages will lie,[45] and a similar conclusion is arrived at where loss is sustained consequent on the act of a person with whom one is not in direct contractual or fiduciary relations and whom, therefore, one cannot sue either in contract or delict.

It has also been held that a trader was not entitled to recover damages even if he had suffered loss by the actings of a defender who had been guilty of no unlawful act in having a trade name registered in respect of American imported flour, although in fact this name had been previously used in America by the pursuers.[46] It was suggested, too, in *Muir* v. *Robbie*,[47] that for a father to procure the breach by his son of a promise of marriage was not an actionable wrong. This view received support from

[36] *Kinnell* v. *Ballantine*, 1910 S.C. 246.
[37] *Johnston* v. *Orr-Ewing* (1882) 7 App.Cas. 219; *Day* v. *Brownrigg* (1878) 10 Ch.D. 294; *Street* v. *Union Bank of Spain* (1885) 30 Ch.D. 156.
[38] *Quinn* v. *Leathem*, *supra*; *Sorrell* v. *Smith*, *supra*; see also *B. M. T. A.* v. *Salvadori* [1949] Ch. 556; *B. M. T. A.* v. *Gilbert* [1951] 2 All E.R. 641.
[39] *Mayor of Bradford* v. *Pickles* [1895] A.C. 587; *Chasemore* v. *Richards* (1859) 7 H.L.C. 349.
[40] *Candler* v. *Crane, Christmas & Co.* [1951] 2 K.B. 164.
[41] *Hedley, Byrne & Co.* v. *Heller & Partners* [1965] A.C. 465.
[42] *Nicol* v. *Dundee Harbour Trs.*, 1915 S.C.(H.L.) 7.
[43] *Pollock* v. *Goodwin's Trs.* (1898) 25 R. 1051. See also *Oswald* v. *Graeme* (1851) 13 D. 1229; *Alexander* v. *Campbell's Trs.* (1903) 5 F. 634.
[44] *Pollock* v. *Goodwin's Trs.*, *supra*.
[45] *Mulcahy* v. *Herbert* (1898) 25 R. 1136.
[46] *Reid* v. *Thompson* (1905) 13 S.L.T. 32; 22 R.P.C. 376.
[47] (1898) 6 S.L.T. 244.

Findlay v. *Blaylock*,[48] where it was held that an action of this kind was irrelevant in the absence of averment of malicious or improper motives actuating the father's act. Without such averments the wrong is *damnum absque injuria* as parental duty extends to preventing a child from contracting an improvident marriage. The foundation of these decisions is that the father's act is not the commission of a wrong but the discharge of a parental duty, and this differentiates the cases from other and more ordinary cases of actions of damages for inducing breach of contract.[49] It has been observed, moreover, that in the case of wrongful interdict, damages are not given for the mere pronouncement thereof but for the being stopped from doing what otherwise might be done.[50]

Other instances of *damnum absque injuria* are loss arising from acting in reliance on a telegram negligently misdelivered,[51] loss resulting from innocent misrepresentation,[52] loss arising from breach of a statutory duty for which the statutory penalty is exclusive,[53] and loss caused by defamatory statements made on a privileged occasion. These cases serve to emphasise the importance of the element of wrongful act in breach of obligation in questions of damages, and it is only if, in the circumstances, such is present that damages can be awarded.[54]

It is well established that the reasonable exercise of imperative statutory powers without negligence will not ground a claim of damages even though resulting in loss.[55] Workmen who strike and thereby subject their employer to loss are not necessarily liable therefor: their act is prima facie legal and it is *damnum absque injuria*.[56]

Moreover, a person suffering *damnum* can, in general, only recover damages if the *injuria* is also done to himself, and not if inflicted on another.[57] In delict there are certain exceptional cases where a person may recover for a wrong done to a near relative and only indirectly a wrong to himself. Damage resulting from a breach of contract falling on a party who is neither a party to the contract nor a *tertius* with a *jus quaesitum*

48 1937 S.C. 21; *cf. Crofter Co.* v. *Veitch*, 1942 S.C.(H.L.) 1, 8.

49 *e.g., Quinn* v. *Leathem* [1901] A.C. 495; *Sorrell* v. *Smith* [1925] A.C. 700; *Couper* v. *Macfarlane* (1879) 6 R. 683.

50 *Clippens Oil Co.* v. *Edin. & Dist. Water Trs.* (1906) 8 F. 731, 751, *per* Ld. Pres. Dunedin.

51 *Dickson* v. *Reuter's Telegram Co.* (1877) 3 C.P.D. 1.

52 *Derry* v. *Peek* (1889) 14 App.Cas. 337.

53 *Pasmore* v. *Oswaldtwistle U.D.C.* [1898] A.C. 387; *Phillips* v. *Britannia Laundry Co.* [1923] 2 K.B. 832.

54 *Johnston* v. *Commercial Bank* (1858) 20 D. 790; *Wallace* v. *Henderson* (1867) 5 M. 270; as to delict, see also *Chasemore* v. *Richards* (1859) 7 H.L.Cas. 349; *Mayor of Bradford* v. *Pickles* [1895] A.C. 587, 597; *Blair* v. *Findlay* (1870) 9 M. 204; *Filshill* v. *Campbell* (1887) 14 R. 592; *Murdoch* v. *Wallace* (1881) 8 R. 855.

55 *Vaughan* v. *Taff Vale Ry.* (1860) 5 H. & N. 679; *Mersey Docks and Harbour Commrs.* v. *Gibbs* (1866) L.R. 1 H.L. 93, 112; *Jones* v. *Festiniog Ry.* (1868) L.R. 3 Q.B. 733; *National Telephone Co.* v. *Baker* [1893] 2 Ch. 186; *Port-Glasgow & Newark Sailcloth Co.* v. *Caledonian Ry.* (1893) 20 R.(H.L.) 35, esp. at 41.

56 Fraser, *Master and Servant*, 424. *Cf.* Trade Union Acts 1871 to 1965; Industrial Relations Act 1971.

57 *Le Lièvre* v. *Gould* [1893] 1 Q.B. 491; *Donoghue* v. *Stevenson*, 1932 S.C.(H.L.) 31.

thereunder gives him no ground for a claim of damages laid in contract.[58] Nevertheless, it has been held in England that while *damnum absque injuria* will not itself ground an action, it may be a sufficient ground for damages where a claim is based on some other independent cause of action.[59]

Under this head may be included those cases where a plea in defence that there is no *jus quaesitum tertio* has been upheld. If a person employs a qualified solicitor to do something for the benefit of a third party and there is no communication between the solicitor and the third party, and then, through the negligence of the solicitor in transacting some piece of business, the intended benefit to the third party be lost, the latter cannot recover any damages from the solicitor for the loss sustained.[60] So, too, a beneficiary losing money through an imprudent investment of trust funds by trustees, consequent on faulty advice by their solicitor, cannot sue him,[61] nor can a sub-purchaser sue a supplier for damages for delay in supply when there is no *jus quaesitum tertio* linking two separate contracts, and the latter's contract is only with the principal purchaser.[62]

Injuria absque damno

It would seem consistent with legal logic to say that every act or omission which is wrongful as being in breach of obligation will necessarily be followed by an award of at least nominal damages, that is, that the fact that no identifiable loss has been sustained will not necessarily wholly absolve the defender if his breach of obligation be proved.[63] This is the established position in English law,[64] but it is not clear in Scots law that the occurrence of a legal wrong will always give a right to some damages, though those damages may only be nominal where no distinct loss can be proved.[65] If such be accepted as the general attitude of Scots law also, it is not unqualified and must be taken subject to exceptions. "A breach of contract, or wrongful act, is no doubt an *injuria*, but it may be *injuria sine damno*, and *damnum* is an essential factor to any claim of damages." [66]

In the case of contract, it has been said [67] that a breach of contract, even in respect of time, entitles the party wronged to claim nominal damages, but the award actually made in that case,[67] was more than

58 *Earl* v. *Lubbock* [1905] 1 K.B. 253, C.A. *Cf. Phillips* v. *Britannia Laundry* [1923] 2 K.B. 832; *Cavalier* v. *Pope* [1906] A.C. 428; *Cameron* v. *Young*, 1908 S.C.(H.L.) 7; *Anglo-Algerian S.S. Co.* v. *Houlder Line* [1908] 1 K.B. 659; *Peek* v. *Gurney* (1873) L.R. 6 H.L. 377.

59 *Griffith* v. *Richard Clay* [1912] 2 Ch. 291.

60 *Robertson* v. *Fleming* (1861) 4 Macq. 167, citing Bell, *Prin.* § 154, Bell, *Comm.* I, 461.

61 *Raes* v. *Meek* (1888) 15 R. 1033; affd. on this point (1889) 16 R.(H.L.) 31.

62 *Blumer* v. *Scott* (1874) 1 R. 379; see also *Campbell* v. *Morrison* (1891) 19 R. 282; *Tully* v. *Ingram* (1891) 19 R. 65.

63 *Morton* v. *Barclay* (1824) 3 Mur. 401.

64 *Ashby* v. *White* (1703) 2 Ld. Raym. 938; *The Mediana* [1900] A.C. 113.

65 *Cf. Leitch* v. *Leydon*, 1931 S.C.(H.L.) 1, on the applicability of English principles to Scotland.

66 *Aarons* v. *Fraser*, 1934 S.C. 137, 143.

67 *Webster* v. *Cramond Iron Co.* (1875) 2 R. 752 (£10 awarded): *cf. Murray* v. *Marr* (1892) 20 R. 119, 124; *Salvesen* v. *Rederi A/B Nordstjernan* (1905) 7 F.(H.L.) 101; *Aarons* v. *Fraser*, 1934 S.C. 137.

nominal and there appears to have been an element of recognition of the undoubted trouble and inconvenience which must have been caused by the delay.[67] Similarly, in *Murray* v. *Marr*,[68] it was said that a failure to fulfil a contract had not been justified and hence the court " must award some damages." No actual damage beyond annoyance and inconvenience was shown and the award was commensurate with these elements.[69] It does, however, seem to be the rule that a breach of contract justifies nominal damages, even though no actual loss be proved.

It is clear, however, in the case of delict that the rule of damages following as a necessary consequence from proof of a wrongful act, whether or not there be loss, is not unqualified in Scotland despite dicta apparently to the contrary effect.[70] In the case of innocent trespass by simple entry on land without damage to or destruction of game or property, no damages can be recovered without proof of actual injury or loss.[71] Again, no damages are recoverable for wrongful interdict if no loss has been suffered by the pursuer. A claim of damages will not lie merely for the pronouncement of interdict but only for the loss involved in being prevented from doing what the person might otherwise do.[72] Again, where a landlord illegally resumed possession of land let to a tenant, but the latter recovered possession and reaped a crop sown by the interim tenant so that he sustained no actual loss, he was held not entitled to damages.[73] In cases of negligence proof of some loss is an essential of the action, and failure to prove any loss flowing from the defender's acts results in there being no liability at all in damages.[74] The same is true in cases falling under the more stringent liability of the principle in *Rylands* v. *Fletcher* [75] and its Scottish counterpart.

The general rule is that a relevant averment of an invasion or infringement of legal rights is a ground of action, but there must be inquiry to determine whether loss has been sustained,[76] and the pursuer is not entitled to any award unless he establishes some loss.[77] But some damage,

[68] (1893) 20 R. 119, 124 (£25 awarded). *Cf. Brown's Trs.* v. *Hay* (1898) 25 R. 1112, 1119.

[69] It should be noted that in *A/B Karlshamns Oljefabriker* v. *Monarch S.S.*, 1949 S.C.(H.L.) 1 the defenders' unsuccessful contention was for only nominal damages, not for no damages at all, the breach of contract being admitted.

[70] *e.g.*, *Bradley* v. *Menley & James*, 1913 S.C. 923, 926: " The jury cannot find a verdict for the pursuer—where the claim is for damages—without finding some damages due." The action was for slander (where some damage is presumed) and nominal damages of 6d. were awarded on each of three issues.

[71] Rankine on *Landownership*, 4th ed., 140. *Graham* v. *Duke of Hamilton* (1868) 6 M. 965; *Hay's Trs.* v. *Young* (1877) 4 R. 398; *Ld. Advocate* v. *Glengarnock Iron and Steel Co.*, 1909, 1 S.L.T. 15. *Contra* in England.

[72] *Clippens Oil Co.* v. *Edinburgh Water Trs.* (1906) 8 F. 731. See also *Bell* v. *Simpson* (1867) 5 M. 298; *Jack* v. *Begg* (1875) 3 R. 35; *Aird* v. *Tarbert School Board*, 1907 S.C. 305, approving *Bostock* v. *Ramsay Urban Council* [1900] 2 Q.B. 616.

[73] *Waugh* v. *More Nisbett* (1882) 19 S.L.R. 427.

[74] *Millar's Trs.* v. *Polson* (1897) 24 R. 1038; *Irving* v. *Burns*, 1915 S.C. 260; *Randall* v. *Summers*, 1919 S.C. 396; *cf. Rankin* v. *Waddell*, 1949 S.C. 555: see also *Cameron* v. *Camerons* (1820) 2 Mur. 235.

[75] (1868) L.R. 3 H.L. 330.

[76] *Cassidy* v. *Connochie*, 1907 S.C. 1112 (slander); *cf. Walker* v. *Robertson* (1821) 2 Mur. 519; *Hamilton* v. *Hope* (1827) 4 Mur. 253.

[77] *Cameron* v. *Camerons* (1820) 2 Mur. 235; *Collins* v. *Hamilton* (1837) 15 S. 895; *Rankin*, *supra*.

at least to feelings, is presumed from the nature of some legal wrongs, wrongs of the nature of an *actio injuriarum*, particularly slander, even where no actual loss is established.[78] " But if a slander has been uttered the pursuer is prima facie entitled to some damages or, at all events, to an apology." [79] Several awards of nominal damages have in fact been recorded in actions *ex delicto*.[80] On the whole, accordingly, while the authorities are not wholly consistent, it seems that the Scottish rule is that in wrongs based originally on the *actio injuriarum*, at least a nominal award is necessary if the wrong be established, though no actual loss be proved, but that in wrongs based originally on the *actio legis Aquiliae* no award is justifiable unless some actual loss be proved and nominal damages are not justified merely by a breach of duty without resulting loss.

Cases where there is wrong but no damages due

To the general principle that any failure in the performance of a due obligation results in an award of damages against the person responsible, there is at least one fairly general exception, in that, as a general rule, no damages can be exacted for a delay or failure to pay money.[81] In pecuniary obligations an award of interest is usually [82] the only form of damages due.[83] But to this general exception there is in turn at least one exception where the ordinary rule applies, for it has been held that a customer who has a current account with a bank is entitled to have his cheques honoured up to the amount of his credit balance, and a bank which, having funds at his credit, dishonours his cheque is liable to him in damages. The distinction is that the bank is thereby not just failing to pay money due, but by implication unjustifiably casting aspersions on the customer's financial soundness, and injury to his financial reputation falls to be considered in assessing damages, as that must be held to have been within the reasonable contemplation of the parties to the contract as a natural consequence of its breach.[84] No proof of diminished credit is necessary to justify substantial damages, but only proof that the dishonour was unjustified. Similarly, in *Wilson* v. *United Counties Bank*,[85] where a bank

[78] *Mackay* v. *McCankie* (1883) 10 R. 537; *Stuart* v. *Moss* (1885) 13 R. 299; *cf. Outram* v. *Reid* (1852) 14 D. 577; *Kennedy* v. *Baillie* (1855) 18 D. 138.

[79] *Cassidy, supra*, 1116.

[80] *Cleland* v. *Mack* (1829) 5 Mur. 70 (slander, —1s.); *Edwards* v. *Parochial Board of Kinloss* (1891) 18 R. 867 (*ultra vires* demolition of house by local authority, —£10); *Sproll* v. *Walker* (1900) 2 F. 73 (slander, —¼d.); *Bradley* v. *Menley and James*, 1913 S.C. 923 (slander, —6d. on each of three issues); *Madden* v. *Glasgow Corpn.*, 1923 S.C. 102 (personal injuries, —¼d.). The award in *Madden* was clearly perverse and the case is not authoritative on this point.

[81] Ersk. III, 3, 86; Gloag, 680; *Roissard* v. *Scott's Trs.* (1897) 24 R. 861; *cf.* Bell, *Comm.* I, 690; *Carmichael* v. *Caledonian Ry.* (1870) 8 M.(H.L.) 119, 131; *Blair's Trs.* v. *Payne* (1884) 12 R. 104.

[82] The rule may not be invariable: see *Trans Trust S. P. R. L.* v. *Danubian Trading Co.* [1952] 2 Q.B. 297.

[83] Bell, *Prin.* § 32; see further Chap. 23, *supra*.

[84] *King* v. *British Linen Co.* (1899) 1 F. 928 (account £161: cheque for £38 dishonoured, —£100 damages).

[85] [1920] A.C. 102. *Cf.* also *Rolin* v. *Steward* (1854) 14 C.B. 595; *Marzetti* v. *Williams* (1830) 1 B. & Ad. 415; *Larios* v. *Gurety* (1873) L.R. 5 P.C. 346; *Forman* v. *Bank of England* (1902) 18 T.L.R. 339.

negligently mismanaged a customer's business into bankruptcy, £7,500 damages were awarded, though no special damage was proved as to credit or reputation, as well as a sum to compensate for loss to the estate.

It should be observed that section 57 of the Bills of Exchange Act 1882 appears to lay down a statutory rule for the measure of damages due on the dishonour of a bill (which, by section 73 of that Act, includes a cheque), and this rule is not readily to be reconciled with these decisions.

It has further been suggested,[86] that a second possible case in which damages proper might be exigible for the delay or failure to pay money is where it is proved that the debtor was aware, at the time of entering into the contract from which the debt resulted, that his failure to make payment on the due date would necessarily result in exceptional loss to the creditor. There were no such averments in the case of *Roissard* v. *Scott's Trs.*,[87] where damages were claimed on averments that the pursuer had been compelled to realise property at a loss owing to the failure of the defender to make timeous payments to the pursuer of money due to him. The action which was laid in delict, not contract, was dismissed as irrelevant, Lord Kincairney observing that: " The damage due for delay in payment of money is nothing but interest. That rule seems to hold whether the claim is rested on breach of contract or delict." On the other hand, in *Mansfield* v. *Campbell*,[88] A sold an estate to B, who became bound to make payments at certain terms; A then gave notice to C, who was a heritable creditor, that his bond would be repaid on a stipulated date. B failed to make any payments until more than a year later, so that A was unable to pay off the bond, whereupon C sued A successfully for damages for the loss thereby sustained by him, and B was in turn held liable to relieve A of the damages he had had to pay C.

Again, in *Trans Trust S.P.R.L.* v. *Danubian Trading Co.*,[89] Romer L.J. was not prepared to subscribe to the view that in no case could damages be recovered for the non-payment of money. He thought that in certain circumstances such damages might well be recoverable " provided the loss occasioned to the plaintiff by the defendant's default was reasonably within the contemplation of the parties when the bargain between them was made."

The position is therefore probably that, as a general but not universal rule, the only damages for the non-payment of money are interest.

Statutory limitations on claims of damages

Statutes in some cases impose limitations on the amount of damages which can be recovered in particular circumstances. The main instances are:

[86] Gloag, 680.
[87] (1897) 24 R. 861.
[88] (1836) 14 S. 585; 11 Fac. 510. See also *Gilchrist* v. *Whyte*, 1907 S.C. 984; Gloag, p. 680, note 7.
[89] [1952] 2 Q.B. 297.

Carriers Act 1830, amended 1865 and Railways Act 1921 (limitation of liability of carrier by road or rail for loss of certain enumerated goods);

Civil Aviation Act 1949, s. 42 (limitation of liability for damage caused by aircraft);

Hotel Proprietors Act 1956, s. 2 (limitation of liability of hotel proprietor for certain losses of guest's property);

Merchant Shipping Act 1894, s. 503, amended by Merchant Shipping (Liability of Shipowners and Others) Act 1958 (limitation of liability for loss of life or personal injury, or loss of or damage to goods);

Railways Act 1921, s. 56 (limitation of liability for animals and goods: as to sea transit, see Regulation of Railways Act 1868, s. 14).

CHAPTER 25

EXCLUSION OR LIMITATION OF LIABILITY IN DAMAGES BY CONTRACT

PARTIES may in general quite freely by contract exclude completely their liability in damages for breaches of stated kinds of a contract between them, or for any kind of breach of their contract at all, or limit any liability which may arise to a stated sum or to a sum computed in a stated way. They may similarly by contract exclude or limit liability for harm caused by delict, though this, naturally, is only possible where the claim founded on delict arises in circumstances where the parties have been brought by contract into a relationship, such as of carrier and passenger, where a duty of care is owed by the one to the other, and impossible where there has been no pre-existing contractual relationship, such as driver and pedestrian, and the duty of care is owed solely by virtue of the general principle of duty of care for one's neighbour and has arisen only very shortly before it was breached.

Statutory prohibitions on exclusion clauses

In certain cases, however, statute expressly prohibits the inclusion in contracts of clauses designed to limit or exclude liability, and in these cases a clause is necessarily ineffective.[1]

Whether clause provides for liquidate damages or limitation

A question may arise whether a clause stating a sum payable as damages in the event of certain breach is a provision for liquidate damages, or a provision limiting the amount of damages recoverable.[2] This is a question of interpretation.[3] The difference in result is that if the clause is a liquidate damages provision, the agreed sum is recoverable on proof of breach without proof of the extent of loss, whereas if the clause is a limitation provision, breach and extent of loss must be proved and if the loss proved

[1] Companies Act 1948, s. 205 (provision protecting officers of company); Law Reform (Personal Injuries) Act 1948, s. 1 (3) (provision excluding or limiting liability of employer for personal injuries caused by fellow employee); Road Traffic Act 1960, s. 151 (restriction of liability for death of or injury to passengers in public service vehicles); Carriage by Air Act 1961, Sched. I, Art. 23 (provisions relieving carrier by air of liability); Building Societies Act 1962, s. 92 (provisions protecting officers from liability); Transport Act 1962, s. 43 (prohibition on British Rail carrying passengers on terms purporting to exclude or limit liability); Carriage of Goods by Sea Act 1971, Sched., Art. III (8); Carriage by Railway Act 1972, Sched., Art. 10 (limitation of railway carrier's liability); Road Traffic Act 1972, s. 148 (certain exceptions in policies of insurance).

[2] *e.g. Cellulose Acetate Silk Co.* v. *Widnes Foundry* [1933] A.C. 20.

[3] *Cf. Suisse Atlantique* v. *N.V. Rotterdamsche Kolen Centrale* [1967] 1 A.C. 361, 420, *per* Lord Upjohn.

is less than the limit fixed, damages for the proven loss only can be recovered, but if the loss proved is greater than the limit, the limited sum only can be recovered. The common clause in charterparties " Penalty for non-performance of this agreement proved damages, not exceeding estimated amount of freight " has been held to be a penalty and not a limitation of liability.[4]

Whether document contractual or not

Terms of contract cannot be imported by something which no reasonable person would regard as being a contractual document, but which would normally be regarded only as a receipt,[5] or a ticket to obtain entry,[6] or a means of identification, such as a cloakroom ticket, or a pass to enter certain premises.[7] In a travel ticket, on the other hand, there is almost a presumption that the traveller knew that there would be conditions.[8]

Whether exemption or limitation a term of contract

The next question is whether the exception or limitation clause has truly been made a term of the contract between the parties. No difficulty arises where the party alleged to have surrendered his rights has signed a contractual document, in which case he is bound by the conditions, whether or not he has read them,[9] and even if the document were signed by his agent [10] or if he cannot read [11] or understand the conditions.[12] He is bound by his signature. He might be able to challenge the conditions if he could relevantly aver fraud or possibly even innocent misrepresentation.[13]

More difficult questions arise where one party has sought by notice,[14] or by a statement on, or referred to in,[15] the unsigned contractual document, to import an exclusion condition. In such cases the question is whether the one party has done what is reasonably sufficient to bring the terms of the exclusion provision, or at very least the existence thereof

4 *Wall* v. *Rederiaktiebolaget Luggude* [1915] 3 K.B. 66; *Watts, Watts & Co.* v. *Mitsui* [1917] A.C. 227.

5 *Chapelton* v. *Barry U.D.C.* [1940] 1 K.B. 532; *Thornton* v. *Shoe Lane Parking Ltd.* [1971] 2 Q.B. 163.

6 *Skrine* v. *Gould* (1912) 29 T.L.R. 19; *Taylor* v. *Glasgow Corpn.*, 1952 S.C. 440.

7 *Henson* v. *L.N.E. Ry.* [1947] 1 All E.R. 653.

8 *Coyle* v. *L.M.S. Ry.*, 1930 S.L.T. 349; *Gray* v. *L.N.E. Ry.*, 1930 S.C. 989.

9 *Parker* v. *S.E. Ry.* (1877) 2 C.P.D. 416, 421; *Hood* v. *Anchor Line*, 1918 S.C.(H.L.) 143; *L'Estrange* v. *Graucob* [1934] 2 K.B. 394. *Cf. C.P. Ry.* v. *Parent* [1917] A.C. 195.

10 *Grand Trunk Ry. of Canada* v. *Robinson* [1915] A.C. 740.

11 *Thompson* v. *L.M.S. Ry.* [1930] 1 K.B. 41.

12 *Parker* v. *S.E. Ry.* (1877) 2 C.P.D. 416, 423.

13 *Cf. Curtis* v. *Chemical Cleaning Co.* [1951] 1 K.B. 805.

14 *McCutcheon* v. *MacBrayne*, 1964 S.C.(H.L.) 28. *Cf. Oakbank Oil Co.* v. *Love and Stewart*, 1918 S.C.(H.L.) 54. A notice may be a mere warning and not a contractual term at all: *Jude* v. *Edinburgh Corpn.*, 1943 S.C. 399, 402.

15 *Stirling* v. *L.S.W. Ry.* (1895) 12 T.L.R. 69; *Nunan* v. *S. Ry.* [1924] 1 K.B. 223; *Gray* v. *L.N.E. Ry.*, 1930 S.C. 989; *Thompson* v. *L.M.S. Ry.* [1930] 1 K.B. 41; see also *Penton* v. *S. Ry.* [1931] 2 K.B. 103. But where the reference was obscured by a date stamp the limitation was held not to apply: *Sugar* v. *L.M.S. Ry.* [1941] 1 All E.R. 172. Where tickets were in a book, it was held enough to print the conditions inside the book: *Zunz* v. *S.E. Ry.* (1869) L.R. 4 Q.B. 539; *Burke* v. *S.E. Ry.* (1875) 5 C.P.D. 1.

and where the full terms can be seen, to the notice of the other contracting party.[16] The onus is on the party seeking to rely on the exclusion provision. In such a case the question for the court has been said [17] to be: "If the person receiving the ticket did not see or know that there was any writing on the ticket, he is not bound by the conditions [18]; if he knew that there was writing and knew or believed that the writing contained conditions, then he is bound by the conditions [19]; if he knew that there was writing on the ticket but did not know or believe that the writing contained conditions, nevertheless he would be bound, if the delivering of the ticket to him in such a manner that he could see there was writing upon it was, in the opinion of the jury, reasonable notice that the writing contained conditions." Among facts relevant to reasonable notice or lack of it are the size of type in which the exclusion clause is printed, the place of the clause or reference thereto on the document, and the presence or absence of means likely to draw attention to the condition.[20]

In the case of free passes, reduced rate tickets, excursion tickets and the like a passenger may be more readily held to have known, or held that he should have known, of an exclusion or limitation of liability.[21]

Time of importation of exclusion clause

The purported exclusion or limitation clause must be brought to the other party's notice before or at the time of contracting.[22] Thus the limitation provided by the Hotel Proprietors Act 1956, cannot be made a term of the contract by a notice in the guest's bedroom, the contract having already been made.[23] Save by agreement a term cannot be added to the contract subsequently.[24]

Exemption imported by course of dealing

If two parties have made a series of similar contracts, each containing certain conditions, and then they make another without expressly referring to these conditions, these conditions ought to be implied into the later contract if the course of dealing was consistent, and indicates that the

16 *Parker* v. *S.E. Ry.* (1877) 2 C.P.D. 416.
17 *Parker* v. *S.E. Ry.* (1877) 2 C.P.D. 416; approved *Hood* v. *Anchor Line*, 1918 S.C.(H.L.) 143, *per* Lord Dunedin. See also *Richardson* v. *Rowntree* [1894] A.C. 217.
18 *Henderson* v. *Stevenson* (1875) 2 R.(H.L.) 71.
19 *Harris* v. *G.W. Ry.* (1876) 1 Q.B.D. 515; *Gray*, *supra*.
20 See *e.g.* *Grieve* v. *Turbine Steamers* (1903) 11 S.L.T. 379; *Hooper* v. *Furness Ry.* (1907) 23 T.L.R. 451; *Cooke* v. *Wilson* (1915) 85 L.J.K.B. 888; *Williamson* v. *N. of S.S.N. Co.*, 1916 S.C. 534; *Hood* v. *Anchor Line*, 1918 S.C.(H.L.) 143; *Lewis* v. *Laird Line*, 1925 S.L.T. 316; *Morris* v. *Laird Line*, 1925 S.L.T. 321.
21 *McCawley* v. *Furness Ry.* (1872) L.R. 8 Q.B. 57; *Gallin* v. *L.N.W. Ry.* (1875) L.R. 10 Q.B. 212; *Hall* v. *N.E. Ry.* (1875) L.R. 10 Q.B. 437; *Duckworth* v. *L. & Y. Ry.* (1901) 84 L.T. 774; *Hearn* v. *S. Ry.* (1925) 41 T.L.R. 305; *Coyle* v. *L.M.S. Ry.*, 1930 S.L.T. 349; *Penton* v. *S. Ry.* [1931] 2 K.B. 103; *Sugar* v. *L.M.S. Ry.* [1941] 1 All E.R. 172.
22 *Olley* v. *Marlborough Court Ltd.* [1949] 1 K.B. 532; *Spurling* v. *Bradshaw* [1956] 2 All E.R. 12; *Burnett & Westminster Bank* [1966] 1 Q.B. 742.
23 *Huntly* v. *Bedford Hotel Co.* (1891) 7 T.L.R. 641; *Olley* v. *Marlborough Court* [1949] 1 K.B. 532.
24 *McCutcheon* v. *MacBrayne*, 1964 S.C.(H.L.) 28.

party affected must have known of, and must be taken to have agreed to, the particular term or condition in issue, namely, the exclusion or limitation of liability. The previous dealings must be such as to prove knowledge of the term in question, and assent to it. If the course of dealing is not consistent it cannot give rise to any implication.[25]

Whether exemption clauses need be reasonable

The question whether the court, faced by an exemption clause in the most extreme terms, could disregard it as being unreasonable, has arisen,[26] but there is no authority for such a power being exercised.[27]

Whether exemption or limitation applicable

The next problem is whether the exemption or limitation clause applies to the circumstances and the kind of breach of duty which have arisen. This depends in every case on the wording of the relevant clause and on what has happened.

Clauses of this kind fall to be construed strictly [28] and *contra proferentem*,[29] and if not expressed clearly and unambiguously they are liable to be disregarded.[30] So far as possible an exception clause will be construed as exempting only from strict liability, as for breach of warranty, and not from negligence as well.[31] But negligence need not be expressly mentioned in the clause if the general tenor of the clause [32] or other words [33] indicate that the intention was to exempt from liability for negligent harm.

If, however, a clause is clear it is no objection that it seeks to exclude liability for all grounds of claim,[34] nor that it exclude claims not only by the contracting party but that of a relative whose claim is founded upon the contracting party's having a claim.[35]

Extent of protection conferred

The protection extended by an exemption or limitation clause covers

25 *Ibid.*
26 *e.g. Parker* v. *S.E. Ry.* (1877) 2 C.P.D. 416, 428; *Thompson* v. *L.M.S. Ry.* [1930] 1 K.B. 44, 56; *McKay* v. *Scottish Airways*, 1948 S.C. 254, 263; *Lee* v. *Railway Executive* [1949] 2 All E.R. 581, 584.
27 *Cf. Grand Trunk Ry. of Canada* v. *Robinson* [1915] A.C. 740, 747; *Tamplin* v. *Anglo-Mexican Petroleum Products Co.* [1916] 2 A.C. 397, 404; *British Movietonews* v. *London and District Cinemas* [1952] A.C. 166, 183.
28 *e.g.* " preventing delivery " means rendering delivery impossible, not merely difficult; *Charlesworth* v. *Watson* [1906] A.C. 14; *Tennants* v. *Wilson* [1917] A.C. 495, 518; *Re Comptoir Commercial Anversois and Power* [1920] 1 K.B. 868.
29 *Horsley* v. *Baxter* (1893) 20 R. 333; *Van Til Hartman* v. *Thomson*, 1931 S.N. 30; *White* v. *Warwick* [1953] 2 All E.R. 1021.
30 *Rutter* v. *Palmer* [1922] 2 K.B. 87, 92; *Alison* v. *Wallsend Slipway Co.* (1927) 43 T.L.R. 323; *White* v. *Warwick* [1953] 2 All E.R. 1021.
31 *Alderslade* v. *Hendon Laundry* [1945] K.B. 189.
32 *Alderslade, supra.*
33 *M.S. & L. Ry.* v. *Brown* (1883) 8 App.Cas. 703; *Pyman S.S. Co.* v. *Hull & Barnsley Ry.* [1914] 2 K.B. 788; *Travers* v. *Cooper* [1915] 1 K.B. 73; *Reynolds* v. *Boston Deep Sea Fishing Co.* (1921) 38 T.L.R. 22, 429.
34 *Beaumont Thomas* v. *Blue Star Line* [1939] 2 All E.R. 127 (" all risks whatever of the passage "); *McKay* v. *Scottish Airways*, 1948 S.C. 254.
35 *McKay, supra.*

the contracting party only, and not third parties, such as his employees,[36] unless the latter are also made parties to the contract, or he is agent for them.

Failure of exception or limitation clause

It has frequently been held that where there has been a fundamental breach of contract by the party entitled to rely on the exception clause, or a breach of a fundamental term of the contract, the party guilty of breach cannot rely on the exception provisions, or, alternatively, it has been said that exempting clauses, no matter how widely they are drawn, only avail a party when he is carrying out the contract in its essential respects.[37] There is, however, no rule of law that a clause exempting from or limiting liability is nullified by a fundamental breach of contract or breach of a fundamental term.[38] In each case the terms and scope of the exempting clause have to be considered, and also the contract as a whole. It may be that it appears from construction of the contract as a whole that the exception clause continues in effect notwithstanding a breach of a kind which would justify the innocent party in rescinding the contract, or it may be that the exception clause is not intended to apply to and continue in effect after such a breach, in which case the party in breach is unable to rely on the exceptions clause.[39] Prima facie there is a rule of construction that an exception or exclusion clause should be construed as not applying to a situation created by a fundamental breach of contract.[40]

The question has frequently arisen where, despite a fundamental breach which would have justified rescission, the innocent party has elected to affirm the contract but to claim damages; if he has elected to rescind, the exception clause falls with the rest of the rescinded contract.[41] In other cases it has arisen where the fundamental breach has not been discovered till the contract has been completed, when the innocent party can no longer rescind, but can only claim damages.

[36] *Adler* v. *Dickson* [1955] 1 Q.B. 158; *Scrutton* v. *Midland Silicones Ltd.* [1962] A.C. 446. *Cf. Genys* v. *Matthews* [1965] 3 All E.R. 24; *Gore* v. *Van der Lann* [1967] 2 Q.B. 31.

[37] *Lilley* v. *Doubleday* (1881) 7 Q.B.D. 510; *Mallet* v. *G.E. Ry.* [1899] 1 Q.B. 309; *Thorley* v. *Orchis S.S. Co.* [1907] 1 K.B. 660; *Gunyon* v. *S.E. & C. Ry. Co.'s Cttee.* [1915] 2 K.B. 370; *Gibaud* v. *G.E. Ry.* [1921] 2 K.B. 426; *Stag Line Ltd.* v. *Foscolo Mango* [1932] A.C. 328; *Bontex Knitting Works Ltd.* v. *St. John's Garage* [1944] 1 All E.R. 381n.; *Alexander* v. *Railway Executive* [1951] 2 K.B. 882; *Smeaton Handscomb* v. *Sassoon I. Setty & Co.* [1953] 2 All E.R. 1471; *Karsales (Harrow) Ltd.* v. *Wallis* [1956] 2 All E.R. 866; *Yeoman Credit* v. *Apps* [1962] 2 Q.B. 508; *Sze Hai Tong Bank Ltd.* v. *Rambler Cycle Co.* [1959] A.C. 576; *Astley Industrial Trust Ltd.* v. *Grimley* [1963] 2 All E.R. 33; *Charterhouse Credit Co.* v. *Tolly* [1963] 2 Q.B. 683; *U.G.S. Finance Ltd.* v. *National Mortgage Bank of Greece* [1964] 1 Lloyd's Rep. 446; *Mechans Ltd.* v. *Highland Marine Charters Ltd.*, 1964 S.C. 48.

[38] On the difference between these phrases, see *Suisse Atlantique*, *infra*, especially Lord Upjohn.

[39] *Wallis* v. *Pratt & Haynes* [1911] A.C. 394; *Pollock* v. *Macrae*, 1922 S.C.(H.L.) 192; *Suisse Atlantique Société d'Armement Maritime* v. *N.V. Rotterdamsche Kolen Centrale* [1967] 1 A.C. 361. See also 87 L.Q.R. 515; 28 C.L.J. 221.

[40] *U.G.S. Finance Ltd.*, *supra*; *Suisse Atlantique*, *supra*.

[41] *Suisse Atlantique*, *supra*.

Any clause intended to give exemption from the normal legal consequences of breach, particularly fundamental breach, must be expressed in clear and unambiguous terms,[42] and it must be quite apparent that such is its purpose and intention. There is a strong, though rebuttable, presumption that, in inserting a clause of exclusion or limitation in their contract, the parties are not contemplating breaches of fundamental terms and that such clauses do not apply to relieve a party from the consequences of such a breach even where the contract continues in force.[43]

[42] *The Cap Palos* [1921] P. 458; *Cunard S.S. Co.* v. *Buerger* [1927] A.C. 1; *L.N.W. Ry.* v *Neilson* [1922] 2 A.C. 263; *Suisse Atlantique, supra.*

[43] *Suisse Atlantique, supra, per* Lord Upjohn.

Chapter 26

THE RELEVANCE OF TAXATION TO DAMAGES

Income Tax

Until recently taxation was regarded as irrelevant in the quantification of an award of damages. But in *British Transport Commission* v. *Gourley*,[1] a case of damages for personal injuries, the House of Lords held that in the calculation of the plaintiff's damages for loss of earnings, past and future, account had to be taken of the unified income tax which would have been payable if the earnings had been received as such. The damages had to be, in brief, a surrogatum for net or taxed earnings or " take-home " earnings rather than gross, untaxed or notional earnings. The justification for the decision was that the incidence of taxation was universal, a matter of general law, and not a factor too remote to be taken into account. Though the case was a tort case, concerned with personal injuries, several of their Lordships stated that they were dealing with a principle applicable also to wrongful dismissal.[2] There is no doubt that the principle applies to Scots law also,[3] and it probably applies to all claims of damages, provided the two conditions requisite for the application of the *Gourley* principle are satisfied, namely (1) that the sum of money for the loss of which the damages are being given would have been subject to income tax if received in the ordinary way and not as damages, and (2) that the sum awarded as damages would not itself be subject to tax. Both conditions must be satisfied before deduction in respect of tax is competent, but if both are satisfied deduction must be made. " For the application of the principle of those two cases [4] there appear to be two requisites. First, what is claimed by the injured party must be a payment which is in effect a surrogatum for earnings which would have been subject to tax, and second that the Inland Revenue are not in use to exact tax from the surrogatum." [5]

It is one of the difficulties of the principle that where a deduction is made by the court from damages on account of income tax, the sum deducted is not paid to the Inland Revenue, and in fact the principle benefits the defender and his insurers, who have to pay a lesser sum in damages.

[1] [1956] A.C. 185, approving *McDaid* v. *Clyde Navigation Trs.*, 1946 S.C. 462, overruling *Jordan* v. *Limmer Co.* [1946] K.B. 356; *Blackwood* v. *Andre*, 1947 S.C. 333; *Billingham* v. *Hughes* [1949] 1 K.B. 643 (all personal injury cases) and *Fairholme* v. *Firth & Brown* (1933) 49 T.L.R. 470 (wrongful dismissal).

[2] *Ibid.* 210, *per* Lord Goddard, Lords Somervell and Radcliffe concurring.

[3] The decision was considered by both the English and Scottish Law Reform Committees (Reports, Cmnd. 501, 1958, and Cmnd. 635, 1959, respectively). Both recommended no change in the law, at least for the time being. See also *Spencer* v. *Macmillan's Trs.*, 1958 S.C. 300; *Stewart* v. *Glentaggart Ltd.*, 1963 S.C. 300, 305.

[4] *B.T.C.* v. *Gourley*, *supra*, and *West Suffolk C.C.* v. *Rought* [1957] A.C. 403.

[5] *Spencer*, *supra*, 315, *per* L.J.C. Thomson.

Furthermore as the Inland Revenue is not a party to such an award of damages a decision to make a deduction would not be *res judicata* in a question with the Revenue and could not prevent it making a demand for tax from the award if it were so disposed.[6]

Condition (1)—The sum lost would have been taxable

If the sum of money, compensation for the loss of which is being made by the award of damages, would have been subject to income tax either by deduction at source or by subsequent assessment, if it had been received in the normal course, a deduction from the award may have to be made in recognition of the fact that the sum would have been taxed. This will apply to awards for loss of earnings or profits, but not to awards for pain and suffering, damage to reputation, property damage, or other loss of a "capital" rather than an "income" nature. It will apply to damages for loss of profits from the use of a capital asset, but not to damages for the loss of the capital asset itself. In *West Suffolk C.C.* v. *Rought*[7] a deduction was made from statutory compensation for loss of profits resulting from compulsory acquisition of the company's premises, there being an undertaking from the Inland Revenue that the company would not be taxed on the compensation. In *Spencer* v. *Macmillan's Trs.*,[8] an action of damages for breach of a contract to sell to the partner the whole issued share capital of a limited company, the damages claimed being the difference between the contract price and the sum which would have been the value of the company at the date of breach, the Second Division held that the tax element fell to be excluded from consideration, since it was not possible to say that failure to deliver the share transfers necessarily involved any loss of profits. The damages were for loss of a capital asset. The *Gourley* principle did not apply as condition (1) was not satisfied.

Condition (2)—the award itself would not be taxable

This condition is complicated, because it is not the case that sums awarded as damages are never subject to income tax. Damages awarded based on an estimate of profits lost by reason of the defender's detention of a ship,[9] compensation for the premature termination of an agency agreement,[10] and interest awarded as damages[11] have all been held taxable. Whether an award is taxable or not depends on the nature of the loss for which it is compensation and on the terms of relevant taxing legislation. It is clear that damages for a non-pecuniary loss, such as the loss of a limb or the smashing of a car, are of a capital rather than an income character and will not be taxable, But damages awarded as com-

6 *Cf. Spencer, supra*, 317, 324.
7 [1957] A.C. 403.
8 1958 S.C. 300.
9 *Burmah S.S. Co.* v. *Inland Revenue*, 1931 S.C. 156.
10 *Kelsall Parsons & Co.* v. *Inland Revenue*, 1938 S.C. 238.
11 *Riches* v. *Westminster Bank* [1947] A.C. 390.

pensation for loss of business or trading profits should be shown in the pursuer's profit and loss account and are taxable.

Income tax in breach of contract cases

The *Gourley* principle has been applied to cases of wrongful dismissal from employment,[12] though now complicated by the rule [13] that the first £5,000 of a sum paid in such a case is exempt but, *quoad ultra*, money so paid is taxable. In *Bold* v. *Brough, Nicolson and Hall* [14] the trial judge in effect applied the *Gourley* principle to the first £5,000, but not to the excess, in a very complicated way. In *Stewart* v. *Glentaggart* [15] the Lord Ordinary (Hunter) held that damages should be assessed by ascertaining the net amount which would have been received by the employee after estimating the tax which he would have paid, if there had been no breach of his contract of employment, and that then the sum should be ascertained, after taking into account his liability to tax under the Finance Act 1960 [13] which would leave the employee with that amount. This seems to achieve the legally correct result in a way as simple as the subject admits of, and therefore to be preferable.

In such cases as damages for loss caused by non-delivery of goods carried, where the basic measure of damages is the value of the goods at the due time and place of delivery, or damages for loss caused by delayed delivery, where the basic measure of damages is the diminution in the value of the goods by reason of the delay, or damages for loss caused by non-acceptance or non-delivery of goods sold or bought, where the basic measure of damages is the extra cost of selling off the goods elsewhere or obtaining them from another source, if the goods were stock-in-trade of the claimant of the damages, the damages will be a trading receipt and therefore taxable, so that the second condition will not be satisfied and no tax will fall to be deducted from the award of damages.[16] If on the other hand the goods were capital assets of the claimant the damages will not be a trading receipt and therefore not taxable so that the first condition will not be satisfied, and again no tax will fall to be deducted from the award of damages.[17]

It seems to be undeniable that damages paid as compensation for breach of a charter-party,[18] for premature termination of an agency,[19] for lost trading profits [20] and the like, should go into the pursuer's profits for the year and be taxed accordingly. In such cases condition (2) would not be satisfied and no tax should be deducted from the court's award.

12 *Beach* v. *Reed Corrugated Cases* [1956] 2 All E.R. 652; *Phipps* v. *Orthodox Unit Trusts* [1958] 1 Q.B. 314; *Shindler* v. *Northern Raincoat Co.* [1960] 2 All E.R. 239; *Parsons* v. *B.N.M. Laboratories* [1964] 1 Q.B. 95.

13 Finance Act 1960, ss. 37–38, now Income and Corporation Taxes Act 1970, ss. 187–188.

14 [1963] 3 All E.R. 849.

15 1963 S.C. 300. See now *Lyndale Fashion Mfrs* v. *Rich* [1973] 1 All E.R. 33.

16 *Cf. Sommerfelds* v. *Freeman* [1967] 2 All E.R. 143.

17 *Cf. Spencer* v. *Macmillan's Trs.*, 1958 S.C. 300 (sale of company).

18 *Burmah S.S. Co.* v. *Inland Revenue*, 1931 S.C. 156.

19 *Kelsall Parsons & Co.* v. *Inland Revenue*, 1938 S.C. 238.

20 *Burmah S.S. Co.*, *supra*; *Diamond* v. *Campbell Jones* [1961] Ch. 22.

Income tax in delict cases—injuries and death

In personal injury cases a distinction has to be drawn between compensation for " capital " losses, such as pain suffered, limbs lost, bodily functions impaired, duration of life lost and the like, compensated by solatium, and " income " losses, such as earnings lost down to the date of trial, and future estimated loss of earnings. The latter kinds of losses only are of sums which would have been taxed if earned and from which, therefore, a deduction in respect of tax must be made, provided that condition (2) is satisfied and that the damages award is not taxable in the hands of the pursuer. No deduction should be made for tax from compensation for any of the former kinds of losses, nor from any part of the award which is reimbursement of expenses incurred, or provision for expenses to be incurred, in treatment or coping with disability. The simplest way of taking account of the tax factor is to compute compensation for " income " losses by reference to net (taxed) earnings, not gross earnings, to base it, that is, on " take-home " pay.

In cases of claims arising from the wrongful death of a relative the distinction must similarly be drawn between the award of solatium for pain and grief felt at the death, and the award in compensation for loss of financial support. The financial support alone would have been taxed if it had been earned by the now deceased, and deductions must be made from the gross sum calculated as being support lost, or alternatively loss of support must be calculated on the basis of the deceased's net (taxed) earnings, not his gross earnings. Furthermore, account has to be taken of the fact that the sum awarded for loss of support should be invested and will earn interest but that tax will be payable on that interest. No deduction should be made from the award for solatium, nor from any award for funeral expenses. Again, the simplest way to take proper account of tax is to calculate loss of support by reference to the deceased's net (taxed) earnings, not to gross earnings. It does not matter whether loss of support is treated as loss of future earnings, or loss of future earning capacity, because in either case earnings would be taxed.

Income tax on interest on damages

By the Income and Corporation Taxes Act 1970, s. 375A,[21] tax is not due from any interest on damages or solatium in respect of personal injuries sustained by a pursuer or by any other person, decree for payment of which is included in any interlocutor by virtue of s. 1 of the Interest on Damages (Scotland) Act 1958.[22] This provision does not appear to cover any interest on damages awarded at common law, from the date of the decree. It is submitted that, whether any part of the capital of a damages award be taxable in the recipient's hands or not, the interest awarded from the date of the decree is a taxable receipt of the pursuer, but the tax factor

21 Added by Finance Act 1971, s. 19.
22 Now amended by Interest on Damages (Scotland) Act 1971. See Chap. 23, *supra*.

should be ignored by the court, conditions (1) and (2) for the application of the *Gourley* principle not being satisfied. In *The Norseman* [23] interest awarded on damages for ship collision damage was held to be " interest on money " within the meaning of the Income Tax Act 1952, ss. 169–170 (now Income and Corporation Taxes Act 1970, ss. 52–53), and to be subject to deduction of tax at the basic rate by the defendants, they being bound to account for it to the Revenue.

Income tax in other delict cases

In defamation cases tax should be ignored in so far as an award of damages is compensation for hurt feelings or injury to honour or reputation, but in so far as it is compensation for loss of profits, damage to business, goodwill and the like, some deduction should be made under the *Gourley* principle. In *Lewis* v. *Daily Telegraph* [24] a distinction was drawn between an individual being defamed, and a company, it being observed that a company cannot be injured in its feelings, but only in its pocket, and that injury by loss of income or damage to goodwill affects it only by actual or anticipated diminution in profits.

In cases of economic loss, as by loss caused by cutting off power, damages will be a surrogatum for profits lost, and must be accounted for to tax, so that the damages should not be reduced to take account of tax.

In cases of damage to or destruction of moveable property, such as damage to or loss of a ship, the loss is a capital one and the damages would not be reducible.[25] But a claim for loss of profits, by reason of detention for repairs, would be a receipt in the pursuer's accounts and taxable.[26] And damage to or loss of moveables which are part of the pursuer's stock-in-trade, *e.g.* cars in the hands of a car-dealer, would justify damages as surrogatum for profits in trade.

In the case of damage to or loss of heritable property the damages are prima facie to compensate a capital loss,[27] but may include an element for loss of profits of use, which will be taxable in the pursuer's hands.[28]

Practical difficulties in taking account of tax

Where under the principle of *B.T.C.* v. *Gourley* [29] account has to be taken in quantifying damages of income tax liability, the practical difficulties may be considerable. In that case the House of Lords made clear that exact computation was not required, and mathematical accuracy was

[23] [1957] P. 224.
[24] [1964] A.C. 234.
[25] *Burmah S.S. Co.* v. *Inland Revenue*, 1931 S.C. 156, 159–160.
[26] *Burmah S.S. Co., supra*; *Pryce* v. *Elwood* (1964) 108 Sol.Jo. 583; *Morahan* v. *Archer and Belfast Corpn.* [1957] N.I. 61.
[27] *Cf. Glenboig Union Fireclay Co.* v. *Inland Revenue*, 1922 S.C.(H.L.) 112 (land rendered unavailable for use); *London & Thames Haven Oil Wharves* v. *Attwooll* [1967] Ch. 772 (damage to wharf).
[28] *London & Thames, supra.*
[29] [1956] A.C. 185.

impossible. As damages can be only a fair compensation, based on a fair estimate of the relevant factors, the account to be taken of tax should be a fair estimate and not an inspector's assessment.

Account must be taken of tax at the rate applicable to the pursuer's case at the time of assessment of damages, ignoring the facts that the rates may be altered and liability increased or diminished by changes in reliefs and allowances.

Whether account should be taken, in cases of damages for loss continuing into the future, of future possibilities which would affect tax such as marriage, birth of children, and the like, and in all cases of such factors as increase or diminution of unearned income or other sources of income, is more doubtful. There are dicta favouring the view that little regard should be had to such factors,[30] though regard can be had to declared intentions which would affect the pursuer's liability to tax.[31]

It is obvious that a sum of damages reducible for tax must be regarded as spread over the period of time for which it is intended to compensate the pursuer and not be treated as if it were income of the year of award. It is not clear, however, in a case where an injured person has income other than that for the loss of which damages are being given, whether the income lost and being replaced should be regarded as the first slice or the last slice of the pursuer's total income, a decision which would affect the rate at which tax falls to be deducted.[32] There is much to be said for taking the average rate of tax applicable over all the pursuer's income,[33] and some authority for treating the lost income as the first slice,[34] particularly if the income lost was the income of his primary occupation.

Capital Gains Tax

To infer liability to capital gains tax there must be a chargeable gain accruing to a person on the disposal of " assets," [35] which term includes all forms of property.[36] There is a disposal of assets

> " where any capital sum is derived from assets notwithstanding that no asset is acquired by the person paying the capital sum, and this subsection applies in particular to—
>
> (*a*) capital sums received by way of compensation for any kind of damage or injury to assets or for the loss, destruction or dissipation of assets, or for any depreciation or risk of depreciation of an asset,

30 *B.T.C.* v. *Gourley*, *supra*, 209; *Beach* v. *Reed Corrugated Cases* [1956] 2 All E.R. 652, 658.

31 *Beach*, *supra*.

32 *e.g.* if a man earning £5,000 p.a. and having £10,000 p.a. income from another business interest is injured so that he is incapacitated from earning, is his loss of £5,000 p.a. to be treated as £1–£5,000 of his total earnings or £10,001–£15,000, the former slice being taxed at 30 per cent. and the latter slice at 60 and 65 per cent?

33 *Cf. Re Houghton Main Colliery Co.* [1956] 3 All E.R. 300.

34 *Bold* v. *Brough, Nicholson and Hall* [1963] 3 All E.R. 849. *Cf.* exemption of first £5,000 from tax under Income and Corporation Taxes Act 1970, ss. 187–188.

35 Finance Act 1965, s. 19.

36 *Ibid.* s. 22 (1).

(*b*) capital sums received under a policy of insurance of the risk of any kind of damage or injury to, or the loss or depreciation of assets,

(*c*) capital sums received in return for forfeiture or surrender of rights, or for refraining from exercising rights, and

(*d*) capital sums received as consideration for use or exploitation of assets." [37]

The breadth of this provision is such that prima facie every damages award is a disposal giving rise to a chargeable gain.

Losses accruing on the disposal of an asset are to be computed in the same way as gains and may be set off against gains.[38] Having regard to the principle that damages are compensation for loss, this will in many cases result in there being no capital gain and no liability. If a car or ship is destroyed or damaged there is a loss to the extent of its pre-accident value or the diminution therein, and if damages are awarded measured by its pre-accident value, or the diminution therein, there will be no capital gain.

In some cases of damages for breach of contract there may be a capital gain. If one person sells and the buyer fails to accept, and the market price has fallen below the contract price, damages should be only nominal but, unless the seller is a dealer and the damages go into his trading receipts, it may be a capital gain.

If one person buys and the seller fails to deliver, and the market price has risen, damages should be the extra cost required to obtain the goods from another source and if for any reason the extra cost does not have to be expended, there may be a capital gain.

Interaction with income tax

There is excluded from consideration for a disposal of assets any money or money's worth charged to income tax or corporation tax.[39] Hence any award of damages which falls to be treated as a trading receipt, being chargeable to income or corporation tax, is not chargeable to capital gains tax. In respect of damages for wrongful dismissal, the first £5,000 is exempted from income tax and also from capital gains tax [40]; the balance is subject to income tax.

Exemptions

There is, however, exempted from liability " sums obtained by way of compensation or damages for any wrong or injury suffered by an individual in his person or in his profession or vocation." [41] This would appear to cover damages for personal injury or for defamation affecting

[37] *Ibid.* s. 22 (3).
[38] *Ibid.* ss. 19 (4) and 23.
[39] *Ibid.* Sch. 6, para. 2 (1).
[40] *Ibid.* Sch. 6, paras. 2 (1) and 21 (2).
[41] *Ibid.* s. 27 (8).

a person in his profession or vocation, and probably covers both solatium for pain and suffering, loss of faculties and other losses, and compensation for past and future loss of earnings. It is questionable, however, whether it covers awards of damages to surviving relatives for the loss resulting from the death of a relative, and it clearly does not cover awards of damages for economic losses or damage to property of any kind. In these cases absence of liability to tax must depend, not on exemption, but on there being an allowable loss to balance the money received, or on the money being chargeable to income or corporation tax rather than to capital gains tax. This raises the question whether hurt to a surviving relative's feelings and prospective loss of financial support are " property." It is submitted that the rights of action on these grounds are " property " which is " disposed of " when action is brought and exchanged for their fair value in money. If this argument is accepted there would be no chargeable gain where a relative recovers damages, and the argument could apply also to other kinds of awards of damages also.

Treatment of capital gains tax in making damages award

There is no authority, as there is in the case of income tax,[42] for saying that a court in awarding damages must have regard to the possible incidence of capital gains tax, and in no case does it appear that the two conditions for the application of the *Gourley* [42] rule will be satisfied.

Estate Duty

Estate duty is a levy payable on property passing, or deemed to pass, on death of which the deceased was then competent to dispose.[43] It is thought that, where damages are awarded to a living pursuer, there is no liability to estate duty and that the court can take no account of the fact that if the recipient dies without having given the award away a sufficient time before his death a large part of it may be taken as estate duty, nor of the effect the award may have on any other person's inheritance from the recipient of the damages.

Where a claim of damages is made by an executor, continuing a claim vested in the deceased whom he represents, any sum awarded will fall into the deceased's estate and may be subject to estate duty, but that fact has not hitherto been taken into account by the court in awarding damages. A claim by surviving relatives of a deceased for solatium and patrimonial loss resulting to them from the death is not a claim ever vested in the deceased, nor exigible by his executor, and any sums awarded are not part of his estate but belong to the pursuers.

42 *B.T.C.* v. *Gourley* [1956] A.C. 185.
43 Finance Act 1894, Part I, as amended.

Chapter 27

GENERAL PRINCIPLES OF DAMAGES IN CONTRACT

General

It is of little assistance in determining the general principles to be applied in ascertaining what damages are properly due on the occurrence of a breach of contract to say that they should be such a sum of money as will put the wronged party into the same position as he would have been in if the contract had in fact been duly performed,[1] because this is rather an ideal which is seldom if ever attainable, and such a statement gives no real assistance towards determining the tests to be applied in the assessment or quantification of damages.[2] It has been pointed out repeatedly that the rules as to damages can, in the nature of things, only be approximately just,[3] and in particular there are three general limitations imposed by the law in respect of the extent to which the defender may be found liable for the consequences of his breach of contract. These limitations are considered separately.[4]

Former Scottish rule

The course formerly followed in Scotland in arriving at an assessment of the damages due for breach of contract was to take " either the highest price which might have been got for the goods at any time after the day of sale, or the average value between the stipulated day of delivery and the date of the action " [5]; but Professor Bell adds: " the fair criterion seems to be that of the English practice—namely, the price at which the buyer could procure the goods in market at the stipulated time of delivery."

In the early nineteenth century a conflict of opinion was visible as to the true measure of damages: it was repeatedly laid down in older cases that there was no absolute rule in Scotland of taking the market price at which undelivered goods could be bought in to give the measure of

[1] *Robinson* v. *Harman* (1848) 1 Ex. 850, 855; *Lock* v. *Furze* (1866) L.R. 1 C.P. 441; *France* v. *Gaudet* (1871) L.R. 6 Q.B. 199; *Bain* v. *Fothergill* (1874) L.R. 7 H.L. 158; *Houldsworth* v. *Brand's Trs.* (1877) 4 R. 369, 374, 375; *Livingstone* v. *Rawyards Coal Co.* (1880) 7 R.(H.L.) 1; *Wertheim* v. *Chicoutimi Pulp Co.* [1911] A.C. 301, 307; *Chaplin* v. *Hicks* [1911] 2 K.B. 786; *Abrahams* v. *Reiach* [1922] 1 K.B. 477, 480; *Banco de Portugal* v. *Waterlow* [1932] A.C. 452, 457; *Sunley* v. *Cunard White Star* [1940] 1 K.B. 740, 745; *Victoria Laundry* v. *Newman* [1949] 2 K.B. 528, 539.

[2] *Cf. Banco de Portugal* v. *Waterlow* [1932] A.C. 452, 475, *per* Viscount Sankey.

[3] *Rodocanachi* v. *Milburn* (1886) 18 Q.B.D. 67, 78; see also *Hobbs* v. *L.S.W. Ry.* (1875) L.R. 10 Q.B. 111; *The Mediana* [1900] A.C. 113; *Boyd and Forrest* v. *G.S.W. Ry.*, 1915 S.C. (H.L.) 20, 28, *per* Lord Atkinson; *Liesbosch* v. *Edison* [1933] A.C. 449, 460, *per* Lord Wright.

[4] *Infra*, Chap. 28.

[5] Bell, *Prin.* § 33 (2) citing older cases.

damages, and that in every case the whole circumstances were to be looked at to give the pursuer fair compensation for his loss.[6] In *Watt* v. *Mitchell* [6] the court declined to accept the rule of the difference between the contract and market prices as providing the measure of damages in a case of a seller's failure to supply goods which were readily obtainable in the open market, holding that each case must be regarded in its own circumstances, and that there was no fixed rule as to the time at which the difference in the price of goods should be taken for the purpose of estimating the damage sustained.

In *Dunlop* v. *Higgins*,[7] Lord Chancellor Cottenham stated that the jury were entitled by the law of Scotland to look into all the circumstances of the case for the purpose of measuring the damages. This statement is contrary to the modern practice of the courts, to the provisions of the Sale of Goods Act 1893, and has since been rejected by the House of Lords,[8] who indicated that today there is no difference in this matter between the law of Scotland and that of England. It is submitted that there remains an element of validity in these statements of the law in respect that the modern rule of damages is not a binding rule exclusive of all other considerations. Sections 50 (3) and 51 (3) of the Sale of Goods Act 1893, incorporating the modern practice for ascertaining the quantum of damages in cases of sale of goods, only state it as a prima facie rule, and in modern cases regard may be had to other relevant considerations.[9] Bell [10] pointed out that a court is not to be tied down by a hard-and-fast rule to give as damages for a seller's breach of contract only the difference between the contract price and the market value at the date of the breach, but is bound to consider all the facts proved. But in the ordinary case, and if there is no evidence of other loss, the obvious and natural measure of damages is the difference rule.

Emergence of the modern principle of reasonable contemplation

The basis of the modern rule of Scottish law is probably to be found in Pothier.[11] He founded on the theory of reasonable contemplation, and expressed the principle as being that " the debtor is only liable for the damages and interest which might have been contemplated at the time of the contract; for to such alone the debtor can be considered as having intended to submit." [12]

6 Stair I, 17, 16. *Watt* v. *Mitchell* (1839) 1 D. 1157 (citing *Paterson* v. *Keith*, Feb. 28, 1745, Elchies.); *Howie* v. *Anderson* (1848) 10 D. 355; *Higgins* v. *Dunlop* (1847) 9 D. 1407: affd. 6 Bell's App. 195; 1 H.L.C. 381; *Baird* v. *Reilly* (1856) 18 D. 734; *Garrow* v. *Forbes* (1866) 2 S.L.R. 203. See also *Dickson* v. *Henderson* (1849) 12 D. 306, and *Warin & Craven* v. *Forrester* (1876) 4 R. 190; 4 R.(H.L.) 75.

7 (1847) 9 D. 1407; affd. (1848) 6 Bell's App. 195, 1 H.L.Cas. 381.

8 *Stroms Bruks Aktie Bolag* v. *Hutchison* (1904) 6 F. 486; revd. (1905) 7 F.(H.L.) 131, 133.

9 *e.g.* in *Banco de Portugal* v. *Waterlow* [1932] A.C. 452 a bank's desire to maintain its own credit was admitted as an element magnifying the damages otherwise due.

10 *Prin.* § 33 (2).

11 *Traité des Obligations*, Part I, c. 2, Art. III, ss. 159–172; Evans's trans. (1806) I, 90.

12 See also *Traité du Vente*, s. 73; Bell, *Comm.* I, 479, notes.

In 1821 M. P. Brown [13] stated the general principle of damages with special reference to the law of sale as being that " the vendor is liable merely for such loss as it can be presumed that the parties contemplated at the time of the contract, as likely to arise from the non-delivery of the thing sold; and that, in the ordinary case, they are presumed to have contemplated merely that loss which related to the thing sold itself, and might result directly from the vendee not receiving it, but not that further loss which is extrinsic to the thing sold and arises remotely and indirectly," and he cites the Roman law [14] and Erskine.[15] But, he continues, " when it appears from the terms of the contract that remote and indirect damage has actually been in the contemplation of the parties, and that the vendor has either expressly or tacitly charged himself with such damage in case of his failing to deliver, he will be made liable accordingly." [16]

Shaw in 1847 [17] laid down the rules as follows: " In obligations not pecuniary, damage is due in respect of the loss sustained on the thing itself (*propter rem ipsam non habitam* [18]); or foreseen, or naturally in the contemplation of the parties [19]; but not collateral or consequential damage, unless either such damage has, by special stipulation of the parties, been brought into view; or unless it be a loss on the thing itself, as by a rise or fall of markets; or unless the failure to fulfil the engagement be fraudulent or wilful."

So too Professor Bell [20] laid down the law as being that a disappointed buyer's claim is " for such damage only as at the time of the contract was foreseen as a necessary consequence of the failure to deliver the article . . . but the general principles will also extend to that sort of damage which, although not strictly attaching to the article sold, is by stipulation, or by necessary consequence at the time of the sale, placed in view of the parties, as foreseen effects of the non-performance of the contract; and as dangers from which, expressly or tacitly, the seller is by faithful performance to save the buyer."

The rules in Hadley v. Baxendale

In 1854 the question of damages came before the Court of Exchequer in England in the case of *Hadley* v. *Baxendale*,[21] a breach of contract of carriage by delayed delivery, raising the question of whether the whole of the profit lost by reason of the delay was recoverable, and there the court (Parke (later Lord Wensleydale), Alderson and Martin BB.), after serious

13 *The Law of Sale*, Edinburgh, 1821, pp. 211 *et seq.*
14 Dig. xix, 1.
15 III, 3, 75 and 86.
16 *Ibid.* 219.
17 Patrick Shaw, *Treatise on the Law of Obligations and Contracts*, p. 217.
18 *London and Leith Shipping Co.* v. *Duffus* (1841) 3 D. 929.
19 *Strachan and Gavin* v. *Paton* (1824) 3 S. 184.
20 *Comm.* I, 478–479.
21 (1854) 9 Exch. 341, 354, *per* Alderson B. In *Victoria Laundry* v. *Newman* [1949] 2 K.B. 528, 537, it was pointed out that the headnote to *Hadley* v. *Baxendale* was misleading in so far as it stated that the carrier was told that the mill was stopped and of the need for immediate delivery of the shaft.

consideration,[22] laid down the rule in the following terms: "Now we think the proper rule in such a case is this: where the two parties have made a contract which one of them has broken, the damages which the other party ought to receive in respect of such breach of contract should be either such as may fairly and reasonably be considered as either arising naturally, *i.e.*, according to the usual course of things, from such breach of contract itself, or such as may reasonably be supposed to have been in the contemplation of both parties, at the time they made the contract, as the probable result of the breach of it." [23] This statement is then in entire accordance with the earlier writings in Scotland if not with some earlier Scottish decisions and it has since been adopted completely [24] and followed repeatedly in Scotland so that earlier and inconsistent decisions must now be considered of no authority.

Alderson B. then continued: " Now if the special circumstances under which the contract was actually made were communicated by the plaintiffs to the defendant, and thus known to both parties, the damages resulting from the breach of such a contract which they would reasonably contemplate would be the amount of injury which would ordinarily follow from a breach of contract under these special circumstances so known and communicated.[25] But on the other hand if these special circumstances were wholly unknown to the party breaking the contract he at the most could only be supposed to have had in his contemplation the amount of injury which would arise generally, and in the great multitude of cases, not affected by any special circumstances, from such a breach of contract. For had the special circumstances been known, the parties might have specially provided for the breach of contract by special terms as to the damages in that case, and of this advantage it would be very unjust to deprive them. The above principles are those by which we think the jury ought to be guided in estimating the damages arising out of any breach of contract." [26]

Effect of this judgment

This statement of principle does two things: it defines generally the proper quantum of damages in the ordinary case of breach of contract as being " such as may fairly and reasonably be considered either arising

[22] *Cf.* Pollock C.B. in *Wilson* v. *Newport Dock Co.* (1866) 35 L.J.Ex. 97, 103.

[23] On the elements which led to this judgment, see Washington, " Damages in Contract at Common Law " (1932) 48 L.Q.R. 102. See also F. E. Smith (1900) 16 L.Q.R. 276.

[24] *e.g.* Bell, *Prin.*, 10th ed., § 33 (2): *Warin and Craven* v. *Forrester* (1877) 4 R.(H.L.) 75; *A/B Karlshamns Oljefabriker* v. *Monarch S.S. Co.*, 1949 S.C.(H.L.) 1.

[25] Esher M.R. in *Hammond* v. *Bussey* (1887) 20 Q.B.D. 79, 88 considered this sentence as rather an exemplification of the second branch of the rule than a part of it.

[26] In some older English cases the rules of *Hadley* were treated as being three, but modern practice regularly treats them as being two, relating respectively to " damages arising in the usual course " and " damages in the contemplation of both parties," or to normal and abnormal loss, or as two branches of one rule. This rule has likewise been fully accepted in Scotland, *e.g. Mackenzie* v. *Liddell* (1883) 10 R. 705; *Keddie, Gordon & Co.* v. *N.B. Ry.* (1887) 14 R. 233; *Duff* v. *Iron Buildings Co.* (1891) 19 R. 199; *Millar* v. *Bellvale Chemical Co.* (1898) 1 F. 297; *Den of Ogil* v. *Caledonian Ry.* (1902) 5 F. 99; *Buchanan and Carswell* v. *Eugene*, 1936 S.C. 160, 180; *A/B Karlshamns Oljefabriker* v. *Monarch S.S. Co.*, 1949 S.C.(H.L.) 1.

naturally, *i.e.*, according to the usual course of things . . . or such as may reasonably be supposed to have been in contemplation " at the time of the contract. Though vague, this is as general a statement as can properly be made on the quantum of damages in contract and goes further to define the proper measure of damages than a mere statement that compensation is to be effected, or the party restored *in integrum*. " In short, the damages are to be what would be the natural consequence of a breach under circumstances which both parties were aware of and contemplated as the foundation of their dealing at the time of the contract." [27] Secondly and more particularly, as in the earlier Scottish pronouncements, this statement distinguishes natural or direct damage from remote or abnormal or consequential damage, and thereby provides the broad criterion of remoteness of damage in contract.[28] The judgment has been acted on repeatedly [29] and recognised in the House of Lords.[30]

While regularly spoken of as " rules " of damages it should not be forgotten that this statement of the law is truly only a broad principle of general application and not a binding rule.[31] There are circumstances where neither branch of the rule is held to be applicable,[32] and the virtual adoption of the rule in the Sale of Goods Act 1893 [33] states it as only a prima facie rule.

Other statements of principle to the same effect can be multiplied. Thus in *Cory* v. *Thames Ironworks Co.*[34] Blackburn J. said: " The measure of damages when a party has not fulfilled his contract is what might be reasonably expected in the ordinary course of things to flow from the non-fulfilment of the contract, not more than that, but what might be reasonably expected to flow from the non-fulfilment of the contract in the ordinary state of things, and to be the natural consequences of it."

Principle restated

In *Victoria Laundry* v. *Newman* [35] the Court of Appeal restated the fundamental principle of *Hadley* [36] in the light of subsequent decisions as follows:

> " (1) It is well settled that the governing purpose of damages is to put the party whose rights have been violated in the same position, so far as money can do so, as if his rights had been observed: *Wertheim* v. *Chicoutimi Pulp Co.*[37] This purpose, if relentlessly pursued, would

[27] Bell, *Prin.* § 33 (2).
[28] On this topic, see further Chap. 28, *infra.*
[29] *Hammond* v. *Bussey* (1887) 20 Q.B.D. 79, 87, *per* Lord Esher M.R.
[30] *Watts* v. *Mitsui* [1917] A.C. 227, 241; *Clayton* v. *Oliver* [1930] A.C. 209, 221; *Banco de Portugal* v. *Waterlow* [1932] A.C. 452, 474; *A/B Karlshamns Oljefabriker* v. *Monarch S.S. Co.*, 1949 S.C.(H.L.) 1; *Koufos* v. *Czarnikow* [1969] 1 A.C. 350.
[31] *Gee* v. *L. & Y. Ry.* (1860) 6 H. & N. 211, 221, *per* Wilde B.
[32] *Collins* v. *Howard* [1949] 2 All E.R. 324: see 65 L.Q.R. 140.
[33] ss. 50–51.
[34] (1868) L.R. 3 Q.B. 181, 190.
[35] [1949] 2 K.B. 528, 539.
[36] (1854) 9 Exch. 341, 354.
[37] [1911] A.C. 301.

provide him with a complete indemnity for all loss *de facto* resulting from a particular breach, however improbable, however unpredictable. This, in contract at least, is recognised as too harsh a rule. Hence,

"(2) In cases of breach of contract the aggrieved party is only entitled to recover such part of the loss actually resulting as was at the time of the contract reasonably foreseeable as liable to result from the breach.[38]

"(3) What was at that time reasonably so foreseeable [39] depends on the knowledge then possessed by the parties or, at all events, by the party who later commits the breach.

"(4) For this purpose knowledge 'possessed' is of two kinds; one imputed, the other actual. Everyone, as a reasonable person, is taken to know the 'ordinary course of things' and consequently what loss is liable to result from a breach of contract in that ordinary course. This is the subject-matter of the 'first rule' in *Hadley* v. *Baxendale*.[36] But to this knowledge which a contract-breaker is assumed to possess, whether he actually possesses it or not, there may have to be added in a particular case knowledge which he actually possesses, of special circumstances outside the 'ordinary course of things,' of such a kind that a breach in those special circumstances would be liable to cause more loss. Such a case attracts the operation of the 'second rule' so as to make additional loss also recoverable.

"(5) In order to make the contract-breaker liable under either rule it is not necessary that he should actually have asked himself what loss is liable to result from a breach. As has often been pointed out, parties at the time of contracting contemplate not the breach of contract, but its performance. It suffices that, if he had considered the question, he would as a reasonable man have concluded that the loss in question was liable to result [40] (see certain observations of Lord du Parcq in the recent case of *A/B Karlshamns Oljefabriker* v. *Monarch S.S. Co.*[41]).

"(6) Nor, finally to make a particular loss recoverable, need it be proved that upon a given state of knowledge, the defendant could, as a reasonable man, foresee that a breach must necessarily result in that loss. It is enough if he could foresee it was likely so to result. It is indeed enough, to borrow from language of Lord du Parcq in the same case [41] at page [30], if the loss (or some factor without which it would not have occurred) is a 'serious possibility' or a 'real danger.' For short, we have used the word 'liable' to result. Possibly the colloquialism 'on the cards' indicates the shade of meaning with some approach to accuracy."

[38] Loss which "may fairly and reasonably be considered as arising in the usual course of things" is necessarily within reasonable foresight or imputed knowledge.

[39] This phrase was criticised by Lord Reid in *Koufos* v. *Czarnikow* [1969] 1 A.C. 350 as confusing measure of damages in contract with measure of damages in tort.

[40] Lord Reid criticised this phrase in *Koufos* v. *Czarnikow* [1969] 1 A.C. 350 as being very vague.

[41] 1949 S.C.(H.L.) 1.

In *Koufos* v. *Czarnikow* [42] the House of Lords criticised some phrases in this reformulation of the principle. " It has never been held to be sufficient in contract that the loss was foreseeable as ' a serious possibility ' or ' a real danger ' or as being ' on the cards.' " [43] " It is clear that on the one hand the test of foreseeability as laid down in the case of tort is not the test for breach of contract; nor on the other hand must the loser establish that the loss was a near certainty, or an odds-on probability. I am content to adopt as the test a 'real danger' or a 'serious possibility.' " [44] On the other hand Lord Morris [45] deprecated reliance on any particular words and regarded the judgment in the *Victoria Laundry* case as a most valuable analysis of the rule, while Lord Hodson [46] did not find it possible to improve on the phrase " liable to result," and Lord Pearce [47] thought the expressions used in the *Victoria Laundry* case were right, save for the phrase " on the cards."

The American *Restatement of Contracts* [48] draws a similar distinction. It provides: " In awarding damages compensation is given for only those injuries that the defendant had reason to foresee as a probable result of his breach when the contract was made. If the injury is one that follows the breach in the usual course of events, there is sufficient reason for the defendant to foresee it; otherwise, it must be shown specifically that the defendant had reason to know the facts and to foresee the injury."

In this country also the view was taken long ago [49] that there was only one rule: " The damages for breach of contract are such damages as a reasonable man sharing the knowledge of both contracting parties would have apprehended at the time the contract was made as likely to spring proximately from its breach. . . . *Hadley's* case bases the liability to pay damages for breach of contract on the knowledge, actual or constructive, which the party making default had of the probable consequences of his breach."

In considering the principle more closely it is, however, convenient to separate consideration of normal damage resulting in the usual course of things, which must be held to be within contemplation, from abnormal damage which is within the reasonable man's contemplation only if he knows of the conditions which may give rise to it. This distinction is commonly spoken of as the first and second rules, or branches of the rule, of *Hadley* v. *Baxendale.*

Criticism of the rule

The rule of *Hadley* v. *Baxendale* [50] and the distinction drawn therein

42 [1969] 1 A.C. 350.
43 Lord Reid at p. 390.
44 Lord Upjohn at p. 425.
45 p. 399.
46 p. 411.
47 p. 415.
48 s. 330.
49 F. E. Smith in (1900) 16 L.Q.R. 277–278, 286–287.
50 (1854) 9 Exch. 341, 354.

between ordinary and consequential damages has not escaped verbal criticism. The words used were "damages . . . arising naturally . . . from such breach of contract itself."[51] In *Smith* v. *Green*[52] "natural" was objected to and it was said that "normal or likely or probable of occurrence in the ordinary course of things would perhaps be the more correct expression." Again it has been objected that there is no uniformity in the naturalness of consequence[53] or that the phrase means no more than that the damages must not be too remote.[54] It is true that one consequence of the same act may be natural in one set of circumstances and another in another: but this is true of every alternative word also. It has also been said[55] that "arising naturally" is not helpful as everything which happens does so naturally. This criticism seems to confuse naturally, *i.e.* in the course of events determined by Nature, with naturally, meaning "as a rule" or "what one would expect," which latter view is supported by Alderson B.'s gloss, "*i.e.* according to the usual course of things. . . ."

Various other phrases have been suggested such as "immediately flowing out of the breach of contract . . . immediately connected with it,"[56] "direct and immediate consequence,"[57] "necessary consequence,"[58] "probable consequence,"[59] "natural and direct consequences,"[60] "direct and natural consequences,"[61] "naturally and directly flowing,"[62] "loss directly and naturally resulting,"[63] and many more,[64] some of which are more appropriate to questions of damages *ex delicto* than *ex contractu.*

Directness does not really provide any better criterion as it is equally incapable of more precise definition and variable in differing circumstances.[65] The test of probability is likewise not exclusive though it may be useful where a series of physical phenomena have to be investigated.[66]

The latest authorities[67] rely solely on the test of damages within reasonable contemplation and reasonably likely loss. It may, however, be helpful to apply other tests subsidiarily to assist in determining whether a

51 See the phrase explained in terms of the foresight of reasonable men by Lord du Parcq in *A/B Karlshamns Oljefabriker* v. *Monarch S.S. Co.*, 1949 S.C.(H.L.) 1, 29.

52 (1866) 1 C.P.D. 92.

53 Smith in (1900) 16 L.Q.R. at 280.

54 *Gloag on Contract*, 690.

55 *Weld-Blundell* v. *Stephens* [1920] A.C. 956, 983.

56 *Hobbs* v. *L.S.W. Ry.* (1875) L.R. 10 Q.B. 111.

57 *Lancs. & Yorks. Ry.* v. *Gidlow* (1875) L.R. 7 H.L. 517.

58 *McMahon* v. *Field* (1881) 7 Q.B.D. 591.

59 *Ibid.*

60 *Admiralty Commrs.* v. *S.S. Susquehanna* [1926] A.C. 655, 661.

61 *Saint Line* v. *Richardson* [1940] 2 K.B. 99.

62 *A/B Karlshamns Oljefabriker* v. *Monarch S.S. Co.*, 1949 S.C.(H.L.) 1, 13, 18.

63 Sale of Goods Act 1893, ss. 50, 51, 53.

64 See list in *H.M.S. London* [1914] P. 72, 77.

65 A difficult case, if directness be adopted as the test, is *Seton* v. *Paterson* (1880) 8 R. 236, where a very consequential death was said to be direct. The decision is however patently perverse and contrary to the evidence; *cf.* also *Isitt* v. *Railway Passengers' Assce. Co.* (1889) 22 Q.B.D. 504.

66 *Weld-Blundell* v. *Stephens* [1920] A.C. 956, 983.

67 *Victoria Laundry* v. *Newman* [1949] 2 K.B. 528, 539; *Koufos* v. *Czarnikow* [1969] 1 A.C. 350.

particular loss was reasonably foreseeable or not. Thus in the *Monarch S.S. Co.* case,[62] Lord Wright said [68] " the question . . . must always be what reasonable business men must be taken to have contemplated as the natural or probable result if the contract was broken."

General rule of nominal damages

Having then determined that in the general case a defender guilty of a breach of contract is liable for the loss which should reasonably have been contemplated by him at the time of the contract as liable to result in the known circumstances from his breach, the question arises whether damages necessarily follow once a breach of contract is established even if no further actual loss be proved. There is little absolutely clear Scottish authority on this point as business men do not bring actions merely for nominal damages amounting to a pound or so in the event of a breach of contract without resulting loss, and such an action could in any event only be brought in the Sheriff Court. This is, however, consonant with the proposition that some damages are recoverable for any breach of a legal obligation, which is established law in England.[69] Dicta in *Webster* v. *Cramond Iron Co.*[70] suggest that it is the law of Scotland too that an award of at least nominal damages necessarily follows from the establishment of a breach of contract.[71] In *Fife Coal Co.* v. *MacBain* [72] some miners went on strike and the owners sued them each for 5s. damages for breach of contract of service, but some actual loss must have been sustained by the miners' refusal to work so that the claim was not purely in respect of the mere breach.

In Scotland this proposition was accepted for contract in *Webster* v. *Cramond Iron Co.*,[73] though rather more hesitantly, but the rule is so obviously sound and consonant with principle that it should prevail despite having been disregarded on occasion. In that case Webster purchased certain pipes for his mill from the defenders. The latter delivered them late, which caused Webster a certain amount of trouble and inconvenience though no actual pecuniary loss. The First Division nevertheless held that he was entitled to £10 damages. Lord President Inglis said: " But the question remains, what is to be the verdict, for we are here in the position of a jury? The contract and the breach of it are established. That leads

68 At p. 21.

69 *Marzetti* v. *Williams* (1830) 1 B. & Ad. 415, 423; *Valpy* v. *Oakley* (1851) 16 Q.B. 941; *Griffiths* v. *Perry* (1859) 1 E. & E. 680; *The Mediana* [1900] A.C. 113. See also American *Restatement of Contracts*, s. 328.

70 (1875) 2 R. 752. *Cf. Murray* v. *Marr* (1892) 20 R. 119, 124, 127; *Teacher* v. *Calder* (1898) 25 R. 661; *Brown's Trs.* v. *Hay* (1898) 25 R. 1112, 1119. See too *Stephenson* v. *Duncan* (1937) 53 Sh.Ct.Rep. 269, where £5 was awarded where no loss or damage was found proved.

71 But on the facts there must have been some general inconvenience to the pursuer arising from the breach.

72 (1935) 52 Sh.Ct.Rep. 84.

73 (1875) 2 R. 752, 754. See also *Seaton Brick & Tile Co.* v. *Mitchell* (1900) 2 F. 550, 554; *Buchanan & Carswell* v. *Eugene*, 1936 S.C. 160.

of necessity to an award of damages. It is impossible to say that a contract can be broken even in respect of time without the party being entitled to claim damages—at the lowest, nominal damages. In directing a jury I should have stated that principle, and told them that if they were satisfied that the pursuers were not put to any serious inconvenience they might give them the smallest imaginable sum, but if they thought that, though no specific damage had been proved, the pursuers had been put to serious inconvenience and trouble, then their duty was to give something more substantial. This latter view occurs to me as the one which is applicable here. The correspondence shows that this affair caused considerable annoyance and trouble to the pursuers, and I propose to fix the damages at £10." Again in *Murray* v. *Marr* [74] it was said: " there has been here a failure to fulfil a contract, and that the defender has not justified that failure and that therefore the pursuer is entitled to succeed and that we must award him a sum of damages." No serious damage was proved and the award was £25.[75]

In *Teacher* v. *Calder*,[76] Teacher invested £15,000 for a time on loan in Calder's business on condition that Calder should keep an equivalent sum in the business. Calder withdrew his money, whereupon Teacher sued on the breach of contract but led no evidence of the amount of any loss sustained, and in the Outer House the action was dismissed on the finding that though breach of contract had been proved, no actual damages had resulted. On appeal, however, it was held that the pursuer was entitled in any event to at least nominal damages, and these the court moderately estimated at £250. Lord President Robertson observed [77]: " Even if no substantial damage had been proved, the mere fact of the breach of contract entitles the pursuer to damages, even were they merely nominal—*Webster* v. *Cramond Iron Co.*"

In *Aarons & Co.* v. *Fraser*,[78] a gratuitous depositary wrongfully retained goods for three months and thereafter tendered delivery to the owner. No special damage was proved although the owner had been caused trouble and inconvenience. It was held that he had suffered damage which was not entirely illusory and was entitled to a sum for the wrongous retention which the court fixed at £10.[79] The principles laid down in *Webster* [80] and *The Mediana* [81] were both approved. Though the latter case was founded on negligence, it contains an obiter dictum, stating the law as to nominal damages, which seems equally applicable to contract. " Nominal damages," Lord Chancellor Halsbury said, " is a technical phrase which

74 (1892) 20 R. 119, 124. Lord Trayner at p. 127 refers to the annoyance and inconvenience caused.
75 *Cf.* also *Houldsworth* v. *Brand's Trs.* (1876) 3 R. 304, 319, *per* Lord Gifford, *obiter*.
76 (1898) 25 R. 661; altered (1899) 1 F.(H.L.) 39.
77 25 R. at 672.
78 1934 S.C. 137.
79 In all these cases the award was more than strictly nominal damages and included an element for trouble and inconvenience.
80 (1875) 2 R. 752.
81 [1900] A.C. 113.

means that you have negatived anything like real damage, but that you are affirming by your nominal damages that there is an infraction of a legal right which, though it gives you no right to any real damages at all, yet gives you a right to the verdict or judgment because your legal right has been infringed. But the term ' nominal damages ' does not mean small damages. The extent to which a person has a right to recover what is called by the compendious phrase 'damages,' but may also be represented as compensation for the use of something that belongs to him, depends upon a variety of circumstances, and it certainly does not in the smallest degree suggest that because they are small they are necessarily nominal damages." [82]

By an extension of this principle it has been held in England that where a breach of contract has taken place, and the innocent party has taken steps to mitigate the damages due, as he is bound to do,[83] and has in fact, owing to a turn of the market or other good fortune, sustained no loss at all, or even made a profit he is still entitled to nominal damages in respect of the fact of the breach of contract. So in *Erie County Gas Co.* v. *Carroll* [84] the defendants in breach of contract failed to supply the plaintiffs with gas to enable them to drive their quarry machinery. The plaintiffs thereupon acquired gas leases for themselves and erected works to operate the gas wells and supplied themselves and sold the leases and works at a substantial profit when the defendants resumed supply. They were therefore held entitled only to nominal damages.

Anomalous cases

This principle of awarding nominal damages for a breach without resulting loss has not always been followed in Scotland. In *Waugh* v. *More Nisbett* [85] a landlord illegally resumed possession of a tenant's land. The tenant was later found entitled to possession and reaped a crop which had been sown by the interim tenant with the authority of the landlord. It appeared from the proof that the tenant had suffered no damage but had in fact gained by the crop reaped, and it was held that he was not entitled to damages for illegal deprivation of possession. Gloag [86] thought this might probably be explained on the ground that the possibility of nominal damages was not suggested. Alternatively it may be that the profit derived from the crop which he had not sown was tacitly ascribed to the head of damages and set off to extinguish it. In *Seaton Brick & Tile Co.* v. *Mitchell*,[87] the court may have been influenced to award more than

[82] *Cf.* also the defender's unsuccessful attempts in *Mackenzie* v. *Liddell* (1883) 10 R. 705; *Stroms Bruks A/B* v. *Hutchison* (1904) 6 F. 486; revd. (1905) 7 F.(H.L.) 131; and *A/B Karlshamns Oljefabriker* v. *Monarch S.S. Co.*, 1949 S.C.(H.L.) 1, to have the damages limited to nominal damages only. They did not contend for no damages at all.

[83] *Vide, infra*, Chap. 28.

[84] [1911] A.C. 105; *cf. Staniforth* v. *Lyall* (1830) 7 Bing. 169; *Wertheim* v. *Chicoutimi Pulp Co.* [1911] A.C. 301; *Weir* v. *Dobell* [1916] 1 K.B. 722.

[85] (1882) 19 S.L.R. 427.

[86] *Contract*, 2nd ed., 684.

[87] (1900) 2 F. 550, 554–555, *per* Lord Trayner (£40 awarded).

nominal damages by the considerations that the pursuer had been forced into court by the defender's denial of the breach of contract and consequently that some loss must have been incurred. But, on the contrary, if there is no difference between the contract price and the current market price, damages cannot be more than nominal.[88]

In *Irving* v. *Burns* [89] a tradesman averred that he had made a contract with the secretary of a limited company and done work thereunder, but that the contract did not, as it purported, bind the company and that the company had no assets. The tradesman sued the secretary for damages for breach of warranty of authority and the action was dismissed on the ground that the company could not in any event have paid anything and therefore no loss had resulted to the pursuer from the breach. Here again an award of at least nominal damages does not appear to have been suggested, possibly on the ground that the pursuer had himself averred that the company had no assets, and hence he could have been in no better position even had the contract bound the company nor could he have recovered even an award of nominal damages. Yet on principle such an award would have seemed appropriate, however nugatory the decree might have been.

In *Hawick Heritable Investment Bank* v. *Huggan* [90] the pursuer obtained a public-house licence in name of the defender, who had agreed to indorse the certificate when called on to do so, with a view to its transfer to a new tenant, as part of an arrangement whereby he was relieved of the obligations of the lease. He refused to implement this obligation. The indorsation or lack of it had no statutory effect, but licensing courts commonly accepted it as proof that the existing holder assented to a new application, although this could have been established in other ways. The landlord's action of damages for breach of contract was held irrelevant when he could show no resulting loss. In the Outer House the Lord Ordinary held that the pursuer had been deprived of a facility for which he had expressly stipulated and which would have made it easier and probably less expensive to obtain a transfer of the licence. Gloag's conclusion [91] was that an award of nominal damages would have been proper.[92]

Motive as affecting damages

With an exception in the anomalous case of breach of promise of marriage,[93] the motive of a party in breach of contract cannot be considered in computing the damages recoverable for breach of contract nor

[88] *Warin & Craven* v. *Forrester* (1876) 4 R. 190; (1877) 4 R.(H.L.) 75; *Ashmore & Son* v. *Cox & Co.* [1899] 1 Q.B. 436.
[89] 1915 S.C. 260.
[90] (1902) 5 F. 75.
[91] *Contract*, p. 684.
[92] But see *Dominion Bank* v. *Bank of Scotland* (1889) 16 R. 1081, 1095; *Stiven* v. *Watson* (1874) 1 R. 412; *Gillespie* v. *McLinnachie & Ellis* (1894) 2 S.L.T. 291.
[93] *Cf. Findlay* v. *Blaylock*, 1937 S.C. 21.

can any injurious circumstances which do not follow from the breach of contract itself.[94] The exception may be attributed to the fact that while breach of promise is in name and form a breach of contract, it partakes in nature and consequences much more of delict that contract and accordingly motive becomes a material consideration, as it is generally in reparation. In *Brown* v. *Magistrates of Edinburgh* [95] an action of damages, for dismissal in breach of a contract of employment or otherwise wrongfully, was dismissed and it was observed that an allegation that malice had actuated the dismissal was irrelevant when the dismissal was not a wrong or breach of contract; an act which does not amount to a legal injury could not be actionable because it was done with a bad motive. Malicious motive is likewise irrelevant as a ground for damages beyond the actual loss if the dismissal was unjustified. It is otherwise in cases of delict where malicious motive is regularly a material element in the constitution of the wrong.

The first rule of Hadley v. Baxendale considered

This rule lays down that effect is to be given to the general principle of putting the pursuer in as good a position as he would have been in if the contract had been performed by awarding him such damages or pecuniary compensation as "may fairly and reasonably be considered as arising naturally, *i.e.*, according to the usual course of things," [96] from the breach of contract; or "such part of the loss actually resulting as was at the time of the contract reasonably foreseeable as liable to result from the breach" [97] having regard to the extent of knowledge which must be imputed to a reasonable person; or "such damage only as at the time of the contract was foreseen as a necessary consequence of the failure." [98]

Contracts vary infinitely in nature and terms and it is only possible to indicate by reference to typical kinds of contracts what consequences have been held to arise "in the ordinary course of things" or to be reasonably probable or such as "might be reasonably expected in the ordinary course of things to flow from the non-fulfilment of the contract." [99] The operation of the principle in relation to particular kinds of contracts is exemplified in the chapters on the various kinds of contracts.

If some loss was natural and probable in the circumstances, it matters not that the actual loss was not foreseen, or unexpected, or improbable, as where grain was sold for cattle food into which lead had penetrated, in consequence of eating which the cattle died. The supplier was held liable for the loss of the cattle. "For anything which amounts to a breach of contract, whether foreseen or unforeseen, the party who breaks the contract is responsible. If those consequences result solely from the act in

[94] *Addis* v. *Gramophone Co.* [1909] A.C. 488.
[95] 1907 S.C. 256. *Cf. Addis, supra*; *Allen* v. *Flood* [1898] A.C. 1.
[96] *Hadley* v. *Baxendale* (1854) 9 Exch. 341, 354.
[97] *Victoria Laundry* v. *Newman* [1949] 2 K.B. 528, 539.
[98] Bell, *Comm.* I, 478.
[99] *Cory* v. *Thames Ironworks Co.* (1868) L.R. 3 Q.B. 181, 190.

question, and are the usual state of things, they are the ordinary and usual consequences of that act, and the defendants are liable." [1] A wrongdoer is liable for all damages causally resulting from the injurious consequences of his breach of contract even if these consequences should not have been foreseen by him. Although the resulting damages are payable only so far as naturally resulting from the injury which has been the consequence of the breach of contract and so as having been within anticipation, liability for the breach itself generally renders the wrongdoer liable for all its injurious consequences even if these be unforeseen.

Examples—Sale of goods

In the ordinary case of a contract for the sale and purchase of an ascertained commodity, breach may take place by the buyer's default in failing to accept delivery of the goods when tendered to him on the due date. The natural result of this breach, and what ensues in the usual course of things, is that the seller is left in possession of the goods which were the subject of the contract of sale, and has not the price which he had confidently expected to receive from the buyer. He can most readily put himself in the position he would have been in if the contract had been duly performed by selling the goods to a third party for the best price he can get and charging the defaulting buyer with any diminution in price received. He thereby is restored *in integrum* by disposing of his goods and obtaining the contract price partially from the alternative buyer as the price of the goods and as to the balance from the defaulting buyer in damages. Hence in a case of a buyer's default, the seller's damages which follow in the ordinary course of things are the difference between the original contract price and the price obtained from a purchaser in the market who takes the goods off his hands. This has been adopted as the prima facie measure of damages in such a case by the Sale of Goods Act 1893.[2]

The converse is where the seller is in default by failing to deliver. What naturally happens then is that the buyer has the money but not the goods, and his loss in the usual course is the value of the goods which are the subject of sale, less the price he would have had to pay to obtain them. He may effect restitution *in integrum* by going into the market and purchasing the desired goods from an alternative source of supply and then charging the defaulting seller with any excess over the contracted amount which he has to pay to obtain these alternative goods. Thus the measure of damages is prima facie the difference between the contract price and the market price.[3]

It will be seen therefore that the ordinary or normal damage which may be expected to follow in usual course of things from the default of one

[1] *Wilson* v. *Dunville* (1879) 6 L.R.Ir. 210, 217, *per* Palles C.B.; approved *A/B Karlshamns Oljefabriker* v. *Monarch S.S. Co.*, 1947 S.C. 179, 195–196, *per* Lord Moncrieff. *Cf. Randall* v. *Newsom* (1877) 2 Q.B.D. 102, 105.

[2] s. 50 (2) and (3); see *Warin & Craven* v. *Forrester* (1876) 4 R. 190; affd. 4 R.(H.L.) 75.

[3] Rule adopted by Sale of Goods Act 1893, s. 51 (2) and (3); *cf. Duff* v. *Iron Buildings Co.* (1891) 19 R. 199; Bell, *Comm.* I, 478. On the whole topic, see further Chap. 43.

party or other to the contract of sale is measured by the difference between the contract price and the market price of the subject of contract as at the day appointed for the implement of the contract.[4] "The market value is taken because it is presumed to be the true value of the goods to the purchaser. In the case of non-delivery, where the purchaser does not get the goods he purchased, it is assumed that these would be worth to him, if he had them, what they would fetch in the open market; and that, if he wanted to get others in their stead, he could obtain them in that market at that price."[5] If there is no available market for the particular kind of goods in question, the value must be otherwise estimated; so, for example, if the buyer has himself agreed to resell the goods, their resale price may be taken as representing their value, in which case the seller who defaults will be required to pay the difference between the contract price and the resale price even though he may have had no notice of the sub-contract.[6] In the case of a defaulting buyer the seller's damages will be the whole commercial loss.

Examples—Carriage

The second typical case is where a carrier of goods either delays or entirely fails to make delivery of goods consigned in his charge.[7] If the failure is merely in point of time, *i.e.*, one of delay, as distinct from complete failure to deliver at all, the damage which the consignee is presumed to have suffered as the natural consequence of the carrier's delay in the usual course of things is any diminution in market price which has taken place between the contractual date of delivery and the date when delivery is in fact made.[8] The damages which will be payable as compensation will accordingly be this difference, which will take account of such factors as a seasonal fall in the market, or the loss of the season for the particular kind of goods.[9] Where the goods are obviously for use, the loss will be measured by the loss of profit which could reasonably have been made by their use.[10]

In the case where the carrier not merely delays but fails to deliver the goods at all to the consignee, the loss which the latter has sustained owing to the carrier's default is equivalent in the normal course of things to the value of the goods to him, excluding the freight which he would have had to pay on their safe delivery into his hands.[11] The value of the goods falls to be taken at their market value, and any particular value those goods

[4] See Sale of Goods Act 1893, ss. 50 (3) and 51 (3); Chap. 43, *infra*.
[5] *Wertheim* v. *Chicoutimi Pulp Co.* [1911] A.C. 301, 307.
[6] *Stroud* v. *Austin* (1883) Cab. & El. 119; *Patrick* v. *Russo-British Grain Co.* [1927] 2 K.B. 535.
[7] See generally Chap. 45, *infra*, and the distinction drawn by Lord Dunedin in *Williams Bros.* v. *Agius* [1914] A.C. 510.
[8] *Collard* v. *S.E. Ry.* (1861) 7 H. & N. 79; *Margetson* v. *Glynn* [1892] 1 Q.B. 337.
[9] *Wilson* v. *Lancashire & Yorks. Ry.* (1861) 9 C.B.(N.S.) 632; *Schulze* v. *G.E. Ry.* (1887) 19 Q.B.D. 30; *Koufos* v. *Czarnikow* [1969] 1 A.C. 350.
[10] *Victoria Laundry* v. *Newman* [1949] 2 K.B. 528.
[11] *Rodocanachi* v. *Milburn* (1886) 18 Q.B.D. 67, 76.

may have had to the particular consignee must be ignored as not being a loss which would follow in the ordinary course of things from the carrier's breach of contract.[12] This sum of damages effects *restitutio in integrum* by giving the consignee the sum of money which it will cost him to obtain equivalent goods from an alternative source of supply.[13] If there is no market for those particular goods their value at the time and place of due delivery must be arrived at by reference to a contract for resale [14] or by taking into consideration the cost price to the consignee of the lost goods, the cost of transport and freight charges and also the reasonable profit which a normal person in the ordinary course of business might be considered as likely to make.[15]

Examples—Manufacture

When the breach of contract consists in the supply by a manufacturer of goods for use, such as machinery, which after due trial are found to be deficient in certain qualities and inadequate for their task, the loss sustained by the user in consequence of the failure is measured in the ordinary course of events by the amount necessarily expended to make the goods fit for their task,[16] or, if this cannot be done, to replace them with others which will perform the same task with efficiency equal to that which the defaulting goods should have exhibited, or the amount by which the value is diminished by the breach of contract.[17] The measure of damages will therefore be (a) the cost of repair, or (b) the capital cost of replacement, making allowance in this case for any break-up or scrap value the unsatisfactory machine may realise,[18] or (c) the profit lost by reason of the defective performance. A claim cannot be made both for the capital cost and for loss of profits.[19] Allowance must also be made for any extra benefit to the user from scrapping the machinery and replacing it by new if in fact the new is more economical or efficient than the old could have been, even if it had been up to specification in all respects and had functioned correctly.[20] Once again no allowance can normally be made in computing the damages for any dire consequences which are the result of the failure to supply or the supply of faulty machinery, such as the buyer's default on a sub-contract, as such are not likely to be held the natural and probable consequence of the manufacturer's initial failure for which he is liable in damages,[21] but are too remote to be covered by the first rule in *Hadley* v. *Baxendale*.[22]

[12] *The Arpad* [1934] P. 189.
[13] *Rodocanachi, supra*; *Williams* v. *Agius* [1914] A.C. 510.
[14] *France* v. *Gaudet* (1871) L.R. 6 Q.B. 199; but see *The Arpad, supra.*
[15] *O'Hanlan* v. *G.W. Ry.* (1865) 6 B. & S. 484; *Ströms Bruks A/B* v. *Hutchison* (1905) 7 F. (H.L.) 131.
[16] *Munro* v. *Bennett*, 1911 S.C. 337; *cf. Mags. of Montrose* v. *Forsyth* (1834) 12 S. 429; *London, etc., Shipping Co.* v. *Duffus* (1841) 3 D. 929.
[17] *Gillespie* v. *Howden* (1885) 12 R. 800.
[18] *Cf. Restatement of Contracts*, s. 346.
[19] *Cullinane* v. *British " Rema " Mfg. Co.* [1954] 1 Q.B. 292.
[20] *British Westinghouse Electric Co.* v. *London Underground Rys.* [1912] A.C. 673.
[21] *Cf. Hydraulic Engineering Co.* v. *McHaffie* (1878) 4 Q.B.D. 670.
[22] (1854) 9 Exch. 341.

It must be kept in mind that knowledge may sometimes have to be imputed to a party in breach of contract of certain possible consequences as being the direct and natural consequences of such breach, even though he did not have actual knowledge of these possible consequences, provided they were such as an intelligent and reasonable man in his position must be taken to have had in mind if he had applied his mind to the question at all.[23] Consequences which fall under this head of reasonably imputed knowledge come under the first rather than the second rule of *Hadley* v. *Baxendale*[22]: on the other hand consequences coming under the second rule of that case require actual knowledge.[24]

Further examples

A few examples will show further what have been held to be injurious consequences following naturally and within the reasonable contemplation of the parties: damage to crops by bad weather consequent on the non-delivery at the contractual date of a threshing machine[25]; the liability to make reparation to the relatives of a workman killed in consequence of the failure of machinery supplied by defendant to plaintiff and not reasonably fit for the contractual purpose[26]; loss of custom consequent on a carrier's failure to bring supplies to the plaintiff[27]; loss of trade and a fine resulting from the supply of meat unfit for human consumption[28]; the cost of obtaining advances from a third party when the defendants wrongly failed to accept the plaintiff's drafts[29]; loss sustained by detention of a vessel by reason of improper repairs[30]; loss of premises by fire in consequence of an unauthorised sublet to a turpentine distiller[31]; loss by horses catching cold in consequence of the defendant's failure to provide stabling as he had contracted to do[32]; damage resulting from the appearance of the defender's name in a " Black List," the pursuer having taken decree in absence in breach of an agreement not to do so[33]; where cloth was damaged in transit, had to be repacked and hence was rejected as delivered too late, the carriers were liable for loss of value by losing the market[34]; the difference between actual earnings and expected earnings when a ship was delivered late and freights had fallen[35]; the cost of transhipment when a ship was delayed through unseaworthiness so that war

23 *e.g. Mackenzie* v. *Liddell* (1883) 10 R. 705.

24 *Victoria Laundry* v. *Newman* [1949] 2 K.B. 528.

25 *Smeed* v. *Foord* (1859) 1 E. & E. 602.

26 *Mowbray* v. *Merryweather* [1895] 2 Q.B. 640.

27 *Lancs. & Yorks. Ry.* v. *Gidlow* (1875) L.R. 7 H.L. 517.

28 *Cointat* v. *Myham* [1913] 2 K.B. 220.

29 *Prehn* v. *Royal Bank of Liverpool* (1870) L.R. 5 Ex. 92.

30 *Wilson* v. *General Iron Screw Co.* (1877) 47 L.J.Q.B. 239.

31 *Lepla* v. *Rogers* [1893] 1 Q.B. 31.

32 *McMahon* v. *Field* (1881) 7 Q.B.D. 591.

33 *Gibson* v. *Anderson* (1897) 24 R. 556; *cf. Rarity* v. *Stubbs* (1893) 1 S.L.T. 74; *Gray* v. *Macintosh* (1906) 14 S.L.T. 403.

34 *Keddie, Gordon & Co.* v. *N.B. Ry.* (1886) 14 R. 233; *cf. Finlay* v. *N.B. Ry.* (1870) 8 M. 959.

35 *Fletcher* v. *Tayleur* (1855) 17 C.B. 21; *Collard* v. *Carswell* (1892) 19 R. 987; (1893) 20 R. (H.L.) 47.

intervened and she was prevented from completing her voyage [36]; estimated loss of profits of a firm of launderers when a boiler they had bought was damaged and installation delayed [37]; the loss of profit sustained by sellers in consequence of the buyers' failure to open a confirmed credit [38]; but not loss incurred by selling shares to provide money for a contract, and then having to reinvest at a higher price, the contract having been repudiated.[39]

Indirect consequences

General statements of the principle of damages subsequent to *Hadley* v. *Baxendale* frequently added the requirement of " directness " to " naturalness " in their formulation.[40] It is questionable whether in the modern reliance on reasonable contemplation it makes any material difference because reasonable contemplation would normally cover both direct and natural consequences. In certain older cases, however, direct and indirect have been taken as the test.[41] In *Hobbs* v. *L.S.W. Ry.*,[42] Cockburn C.J. having stated a rule of reasonable contemplation went on to desiderate something immediately connected with the breach of contract and " not merely connected with it through a series of causes intervening between the immediate consequence of the breach of contract and the damage or injury. . . ." Blackburn J. also thought that " a person is to recover in the case of a breach of contract the damages directly proceeding from that breach of contract. . . ."

This test of directness and indirectness has been applied in some other cases,[43] more particularly with reference to causation of the loss, and it would follow from adopting this test that a loss occasioned by causes independently of the breach of contract is not recoverable. The general adoption of this test to exclude remote consequences would, however, conflict with certain decisions and clearly may conflict with the rule of reasonable foresight in respect that an indirect cause of loss may well be reasonably foreseeable. Thus in the *Monarch S.S. Co.* case [44] the breach of contract consisted in the supply of an unseaworthy ship which resulted directly in delay. What caused the loss sued for was the outbreak of war which was not a direct consequence of the breach but only a circumstance such that it would not have operated to cause loss if there had not been the precedent unseaworthiness and delay. On the other hand, in the circumstances, this was within reasonable contemplation.

36 *A/B Karlshamns Oljefabriker* v. *Monarch S.S. Co.*, 1949 S.C.(H.L.) 1.
37 *Victoria Laundry* v. *Newman* [1949] 2 K.B. 528.
38 *Trans Trust S.P.R.L.* v. *Danubian Trading Co.* [1952] 1 All E.R. 970.
39 *Collins* v. *Howard* [1949] 2 All E.R. 324.
40 *Weld-Blundell* v. *Stephens* [1920] A.C. 956, 983.
41 In *Howie* v. *Anderson* (1848) 10 D. 355, 357 Lord Justice-Clerk Hope spoke of " special loss, being the direct, and not the remote, consequence of the breach of bargain. . . ." *Cf.* also the antithesis in *Saint Line* v. *Richardson* [1940] 2 K.B. 99.
42 (1875) L.R. 10 Q.B. 111, 117.
43 *Hoey* v. *Felton* (1861) 11 C.B.(N.S.) 142; *Burton* v. *Pinkerton* (1867) L.R. 2 Ex. 340; *Baird* v. *Banff District Lunacy Board*, 1914, 1 S.L.T. 284, 287. The test is important in cases of delict.
44 1947 S.C. 179 at 196; affd. 1949 S.C.(H.L.) 1.

Lord Moncrieff, however, gave the ratio of his judgment [44] as being that a wrongdoer is liable for all damages causally resulting from the injurious consequences of his breach of contract even if these consequences should not have been foreseen by him. " An efficient cause . . . does not become remote merely because its operation was unexpected." [45] So, too, if a breach of contract is one of two causes, which operate together and with equal efficacy to cause the loss, damages fall to be awarded.[46]

This indicates that the rule of reasonable foresight is the complete and proper expression of the rule of damages and that the test of directness, though it may in many cases lead to the same result, can only be regarded as subsidiary.

Damages a question of law or fact

Dicta in various English cases are directed to the question whether the reasonably foreseeable consequences of a breach of contract in the ordinary course is a question of fact or of law. In the sense in which the antithesis of fact and law corresponds to the different functions of judge and jury the question is of no consequence in Scots law as cases of breach of contract are tried by a judge or sheriff without a jury.[47] In the other sense in which the terms involve a rule to be applied as a matter of law as opposed to a prima facie principle to be applied if circumstances justify, it is submitted that the principle of giving the reasonable foreseeable damages is a question of fact in that the court has to and does consider the circumstances of each case and is not bound to apply any given measure of damages. But the courts have, as a matter of practice, practically considered themselves bound by decisions as to whether or not a particular element of damages is recoverable. In *Chaplin* v. *Hicks* [48] it was pointed out that in such an ordinary case as a breach of contract of sale by non-delivery where a market existed in which alternative goods could be obtained, the rule of damages to be applied was quite fixed, though in other cases the matter was at large.

Dicta of the House of Lords also indicate that damages is a question of fact to be determined in the circumstances and not by the application of a rule of law. " The quantum of damage is a question of fact, and the only guidance the law can give is to lay down general principles which afford at times but scanty assistance in dealing with particular cases." [49] " Circumstances are so infinitely various that, however carefully general rules

45 *Ibid.* at p. 195.

46 *Heskell* v. *Continental Express* [1950] 1 All E.R. 1033.

47 In *Howie* v. *Anderson* (1848) 10 D. 355, a case of breach of contract of sale of shares tried by a jury, Lord Justice-Clerk Hope said at p. 358 that the rule for estimating the amount of damages in contract was a question of law for the court, but that the judge must always tell the jury the principle they were to adopt.

48 [1911] 2 K.B. 786, 792, 795.

49 *British Westinghouse* v. *Underground Rys.* [1912] A.C. 688, *per* Viscount Haldane.

are framed, they must be construed with some liberality and not too rigidly applied."[50] Similarly, the question whether certain consequences are or are not too remote is a question of fact.[51]

50 *A/B Karlshamns Oljefabriker* v. *Monarch S.S. Co.*, 1949 S.C.(H.L.) 1, 28, *per* Lord du Parcq.
51 *Ibid.* 20, *per* Lord Wright.

CHAPTER 28

LIMITATIONS ON RIGHT TO DAMAGES FOR BREACH OF CONTRACT

WHILE the basic principle is that a party injured by a breach of contract may recover such damages as may fairly and reasonably be considered as arising naturally from the breach of contract itself, this is subject to three limitations or qualifications, namely that the loss must have been caused by the breach of contract and not by some other factor, that the loss must not be too remote from the breach in the sense of being beyond the contemplation of the party in breach, and that the innocent party should have taken reasonable steps to mitigate or minimise the loss resulting from the breach. These limitations require separate consideration.

THE LOSS MUST HAVE BEEN CAUSED BY THE BREACH

To recover damages for a loss following on a breach of contract the pursuer must prove that the loss was directly caused by and entirely or at least mainly attributable to that breach. If the loss were entirely or mainly caused by some other factor he cannot recover damages therefor from the party in breach. In some cases, frequently under the inaccurate rubric of " remoteness," the question has arisen whether the loss in question was attributable to the breach or not.

In the context of breach of contract problems as to the direct causal connection between breach and loss or absence thereof do not normally cause much difficulty, but a few cases raise difficulties.

The first and most peculiar of those cases which require notice is *Seton* v. *Paterson*.[1] A horse was hired for riding and ridden at a gallop in a grass field. In consequence thereof it went lame and was found to have split its pastern bone. Six weeks later, when almost recovered, it died from inflammation of the bowels and the owner sued the hirer for the value. It was held by a bare majority and, so far as appears from the report, in flat contradiction of the evidence, that the death was attributable to the want of exercise consequent upon the injury and hence, the galloping being a departure from the conditions of hiring, that the hirer was liable. The decision is " very remarkable " [2] but, if accepted as to causation and liability, the damages awarded were such as arose naturally from the breach. No true question of remoteness of damage was raised.

In *Wilson* v. *Carmichael* [3] the pursuer ordered a variety of cabbage seed

[1] (1880) 8 R. 236.
[2] *Gloag on Contract*, 2nd ed., 691.
[3] (1894) 21 R. 732. *Cf. Taylor* v. *Sharp* (1868) 6 S.L.R. 95.

from the defender, sowed it and sold plants to customers before discovering that the seed was disconform to contract. It was proved that a skilled gardener would have discovered the disconformity before the subsales. The pursuer was held entitled to damages in respect that, as a direct and natural consequence of the defender's breach of contract, his ground had been occupied by an unremunerative crop, but not entitled to damages for loss of business with his customers, or for claims of damages made by them against him, because " the proximate cause of the mistake of the customers' getting late instead of early plants was the omission of the pursuer or his son to notice that the plants which he sold to his customers were late cabbages, and this was not a natural consequence of the defenders' breach of contract." [4] Alternatively it might be said that the pursuers' own fault was a fresh supervening cause. In any event the question was causation and not truly of remoteness of damage.

In *Millar* v. *Bellvale Chemical Co.*,[5] a golf ball manufacturer supplied balls to a wholesaler which were disconform to contract. Damages were recovered in respect of loss of profits on balls actually sold to the wholesaler and rejected by him, and a sum for prospective loss of profit. The question was raised whether he was entitled to damages for injury to his trade from loss of reputation but not decided, Lord Trayner, however, indicating that the damages given covered the direct consequence of the breach, which might reasonably have been in the contemplation of the parties when the contract was made.

In *Baird* v. *Banff District Lunacy Board*,[6] the matron of an asylum gave up her employment and claimed damages from the defenders for their breach of contract. She further claimed damages for loss of permanent employment, of pension rights, and for wages and board wages for a period. These items were held to be too remote as not reasonably within the contemplation of the parties and not sufficiently closely connected causally with the breach. In any event those losses arose from the pursuer's own act in quitting the employment. The Lord Ordinary (Dewar) on the question of directness and remoteness of causation quoted with approval the general rule laid down by Cockburn C.J., in *Hobbs* v. *L.S.W. Ry.*[7] " To entitle a person to damages by reason of a breach of contract the injury for which compensation is asked should be one that may be fairly taken to have been contemplated by the parties as the possible result of the breach of contract. Therefore you must have something immediately flowing out of the breach of contract complained of, something immediately connected with it, and not merely connected with it through a series of causes intervening between the immediate consequence of the breach of contract and the damage or injury complained of." In that case the plaintiff and his wife were in consequence of the defendants'

4 *Ibid.* 734, *per* Lord President Robertson.
5 (1898) 1 F. 297.
6 1914, 1 S.L.T. 284.
7 (1875) L.R. 10 Q.B. 111, 117. See further *McMahon* v. *Field* (1881) 7 Q.B.D. 591 and *cf.* also *Burton* v. *Pinkerton* (1867) L.R. 2 Ex. 340; *Atkins* v. *Hutton* (1910) 103 L.T.513.

breach of contract deposited at the wrong station at midnight and had to walk four to five miles home in the rain. The wife caught cold and incurred expenses for medical attention. Damages were allowed for the inconvenience but not for the illness and its results which were too remote from the breach of contract to justify damages as naturally resulting from it. Cockburn C.J. explained later [8]: " It is not the necessary consequence, it is not even the probable consequence of a person being put down at an improper place, and having to walk home that he should sustain either personal injury or catch a cold." [9]

Accordingly, despite the rubrics these cases raised questions of directness of causation and the relationship and connection between the breach of contract and the loss, and do not impinge on the principles of remoteness which depend on the test of the contemplation of the reasonable man. They are all in fact cases illustrating the first branch of *Hadley* v. *Baxendale* and the question is not whether they are natural consequences of the breach or remote consequences not contemplated without notice but whether they are sufficiently directly related in point of causation to be classed as " naturally resulting from the breach of contract."

In *A/B Karlshamns Oljefabriker* v. *Monarch S.S. Co.*[10] Lord Moncrieff said: " As soon as the injury has been sufficiently related to the breach of contract as an effect (probable or improbable) of the breach and liability has equally and in either case been affirmed, the expectation of the party in breach becomes of the highest relevance for the assessing of the damages. . . . Liability depends on cause and effect alone, and is independent of probability; the measure of liability depends on cause and effect but is further dependent (apart from a special engagement) on the presumed expectation of the debtor." Moreover, the fact that loss is caused by two equally co-operating causes does not prevent damages being given for breach of contract, if the breach was one of the two.[11]

There would, however, appear to be nothing to prevent the parties by sufficient disclosure of circumstances or express agreement from bringing even possible indirect consequences of breach within their contemplation, so that damages would be recoverable therefor if the contemplated result followed.

Loss caused by intervention of third party

Where, following on a breach of contract by the defender, the actings of a third party have intervened, the presumption probably is that the defender is still liable for the loss, certainly where the intervention is the

8 *Ibid.* 119.

9 Blackburn J. at p. 121 contrasted lack of reasonable care in transit causing the passenger to break a leg, which is a direct consequence. See also Lord Moncrieff in *A/B Karlshamns Oljefabriker* v. *Monarch S.S. Co.*, 1947 S.C. 179, 195.

10 1947 S.C. 179, 196; (affd. 1949 S.C.(H.L.) 1) quoting *Wilson* v. *Dunville* (1879) 6 L.R.Ir. 210.

11 *Heskell* v. *Continental Express* [1950] 1 All E.R. 1033.

kind of thing which is likely to happen,[12] but he is less likely to be held liable where the intervening act is unforeseeable, unlikely or purely coincidental.[13] In *Weld-Blundell* v. *Stephens* [14] W employed S to investigate a company and gave him a letter containing statements defamatory of officers of the company. They saw the letter and recovered damages from W, who sought to recover the damages and costs incurred from S. It was held that he could recover nominal damages only since, though S had been careless, the main fault had been the plaintiff's own in writing the letter. But such carelessness was a kind of thing quite likely to happen, and not at all unforeseeable.

Loss caused by intervening external event

If an external event supervenes on a breach of contract, the party in breach is relieved only if the event was wholly independent of the contract. Thus in *A/B Karlshamns Oljefabriker* v. *Monarch S.S. Co.*[15] the shipowners were in breach in providing a defective ship. It was accordingly so delayed that war broke out and it was diverted to another port and the cargo had to be transhipped. The shipowners were held liable but it would have been otherwise if the ship had been overwhelmed by a typhoon.

Loss in consequence of pursuer's own actings

Where the proximate cause of the loss is some act of the party who incurred that loss, the loss will then be too remote to be reasonably ascribed to the breach of contract of the defender. So in *Stephen* v. *Swayne* [16] a ship was slipped for repairs and on completion was detained in security in view of the failure of the owners to pay the account for repairs. The repairers then claimed additional damages in the shape of slip-dues for the period the vessel was detained, and loss of profits in respect of their business being interfered with thereby. Interest was held recoverable as damages for non-payment of the account, but the additional items were disallowed. This principle may be taken as the counterpart of the obligation to mitigate damages, that just as a pursuer who has a claim of damages must take reasonable steps to minimise that claim, so too he may not and must not do anything which will enhance the claim. In any event a party exercising a right of retention may not profit therefrom though he may recover necessary expenses of safe custody.

So too if a carrier delays goods in transit he will not be held responsible for damages which would not have occurred if the goods had been properly packed and fit for the journey.[17] A plaintiff *en route* for Australia was

12 *De la Bere* v. *Pearson* [1908] 1 K.B. 280; *London Joint Stock Bank* v. *Macmillan* [1918] A.C. 777; *Stansbie* v. *Troman* [1948] 2 K.B. 48.
13 *Cf. Pounder* v. *N.E. Ry.* [1892] 1 Q.B. 385; *Cobb* v. *G.W. Ry.* [1894] A.C. 419.
14 [1920] A.C. 956.
15 1949 S.C.(H.L.) 1, distinguishing *Associated Portland Cement* v. *Houlder* (1917) 86 L.J.K.B. 1495.
16 (1861) 24 D. 158; *cf. Anglo-Algerian S.S. Co.* v. *Houlder Line* [1908] 1 K.B. 659.
17 *Baldwin* v. *L.C. & D. Ry.* (1882) 9 Q.B.D. 582. *Cf. Keddie Gordon* v. *N.B. Ry.* (1886) 14 R. 233.

delayed by being wrongfully put off the ship by error of the shipping company. He was offered a passage in another ship almost immediately but delayed his departure to attend the action and claimed as damages the expenses of his detention. It was held that he could not recover this as damages as the delay had been his own action.[18] Again where a traveller was wrongfully removed from a train and claimed damages for the loss of a pair of race-glasses left in the carriage, it was held that he could not recover therefor since the loss was found to be his own fault.[19]

On a similar principle may be explained those cases where a breach of contract having taken place, loss is sustained of which the proximate cause is the party's own wrongful or negligent act. No damages can be recovered in such a case even though the breach of contract was an essential pre-requisite to the damaging consequences and possibly furnished the opportunity or inducement to the wrongful act.[20] So in *Scouller* v. *Robertson* [21] where the question actually arose in a case of servitude, S was entitled to pass waste water into R's sewer; the amount of water S greatly increased quite wrongfully by erecting a distillery, and R, to protect his property from the overflow, built an embankment whereby A's property was damaged. A recovered damages from R, which R was held unable to recover from S, as such damages were consequential and arose from R's and not S's wrongful act.

So too where a firm supplied ropes for use as slings in unloading ships, without warranting that they were reasonably fit for that purpose, and the ropes broke while in use so that a workman was injured, the sum of damages which he was awarded against the employers could not be recovered by them from the makers of the ropes. Lord President Dunedin pointed out that even if there had been a warranty of reasonable fitness, the damages would still have been irrecoverable. The principle was that the proximate cause was the employers' negligence in failing to inspect the ropes, even though the prior breach of contract was a condition precedent to the occurrence of accident.[22] This case is contrary to and doubted the dicta in *Mowbray* v. *Merryweather* [23] in England, in which the defendant supplied the plaintiff with chains for use in discharging cargo, one of which broke and injured a workman. The compensation obtained by the workman was held recoverable from the defendant as a natural and not too remote consequence of his breach of contract. The cases are really distinguishable. In *Wood* the proximate cause of the accident was the negligence of stevedores in failing to inspect the rope supplied by the ship-owners. In *Mowbray* the chain was part of the permanent fittings of the ship with which the stevedores could not interfere, and it was warranted

18 *Ansett* v. *Marshall* (1853) 22 L.J.Q.B. 118.
19 *Glover* v. *L. & S.W. Ry.* (1867) L.R. 3 Q.B. 25.
20 *British Stamp Machine Co.* v. *Haynes* [1921] 1 K.B. 377.
21 (1829) 7 S. 344.
22 *Wood* v. *Mackay* (1906) 8 F. 625.
23 [1895] 2 Q.B. 640. See also *Vogan* v. *Oulton* (1899) 15 T.L.R. 33; 16 T.L.R. 37; *Scott* v. *Foley* (1899) 16 T.L.R. 55.

reasonably fit for its purpose, and there was no duty of inspection on the stevedores.

But in *Baxter* v. *Boswell*,[24] which was not cited in *Wood*,[22] Lord Kincairney held relevant a claim for relief in respect of a sum of damages paid to the widow of a person killed, repelling the contention that the proximate cause of the death was the negligence of the pursuers and that they were consequently not entitled to recover. This decision is inconsistent with the later decision of the First Division in *Wood*.[22] Moreover in such cases the employer may be in the difficult position that if he settles the claim founded on delict, he cannot recover the sum, as it is an ultroneous payment, while if he pays after being found guilty of negligence, that may be held to be the true cause and he then cannot recover either.[25]

In *Clippens Oil Co.* v. *Edinburgh Water Trs.*[26] a company was interdicted from mining in their main seam and closed their works to their own great loss. When the interdict was recalled they claimed the total loss consequent on the closure of the works but were held entitled only to a smaller sum as they had failed to take steps to minimise the damages and further loss was due to their own action in closing the works when that was not absolutely necessary. Similarly in *Quinn* v. *Burch Brothers (Builders) Ltd.*[27] the defendants, in breach of contract, failed to provide a stepladder; he used a trestle, which slipped and he sustained injury. It was held that the breach of contract provided the occasion for the plaintiff's injury but the real cause was his own voluntary act in using the trestle. Accordingly the damage was not a natural and probable consequence of the breach of contract and the defendants were not liable for the plaintiff's injury.

Co-operating causes of loss

Where a loss has been caused by two or more equally co-operating causes, one of which is the defender's breach of contract, that is sufficient to render the defender liable for the loss.[28]

The Loss Must Not be Too Remote

The second general limitation on the recovery of damages for breach of contract is that the loss for which the claim is made must not be too remote from the breach of contract. This is a limitation on the extent of the losses for which the defender, if in breach, will be liable. It is obvious that a breach of contract having once taken place the possible consequences are almost unlimited and may be very disastrous and have the most drastic consequences for the party damnified and disappointed by the breach.

24 (1899) 6 S.L.T. 278.
25 *Gardiner* v. *Mann* (1894) 22 R. 100. *Cf. Kiddle* v. *Lovett* (1886) 16 Q.B.D. 605.
26 1907 S.C.(H.L.) 9.
27 [1966] 2 Q.B. 370.
28 *Heskell* v. *Continental Express Ltd.* [1950] 1 All E.R. 1033, 1047.

But it is neither just nor feasible to make a wrongdoer automatically or always responsible for all the consequences in the series set in motion by his original wrongful act. The law, it has been said, " cannot take account of everything that follows a wrongful act; it regards some subsequent matters as outside the scope of its selection, because ' it were infinite for the law to judge the cause of causes ' or consequence of consequences. Thus the loss of a ship by collision, due to the other ship's sole fault, may force the shipowner into bankruptcy and that again may involve his family in suffering, loss of education or opportunities in life, but no such loss could be recovered from the wrongdoer. In the varied web of affairs, the law must abstract some consequences as relevant, not perhaps on grounds of pure logic but simply for practical reasons." [29]

Hence the distinction has been drawn between natural, ordinary or direct loss or damage resulting from the breach of contract, which can be taken into consideration in assessing damages, and indirect, remote or consequential loss or damage which must generally be ignored in assessing damages. So Erskine says [30] that " no damage which is remote or indirect ought to enter into the computation." This statement, while true, goes no distance to determining a test by which one may segregate ordinary from remote damage. The consequences of the breach of contract, direct or remote, must always be connected with the breach to the extent that they would not have followed if the breach had not taken place. If they would have followed, even if the contract had been completely performed, then they can hardly be said with any accuracy to be consequences at all of the breach of contract.

This fundamental criterion for distinguishing between ordinary or direct and remote or consequential damages was drawn clearly in the distinction between the so-called first and second rules or branches of the rule of *Hadley* v. *Baxendale*.[31] The first rule or branch of that case, as has been seen, relates to ordinary damage, defined as " such as might fairly and reasonably be considered as arising naturally, *i.e.*, according to the usual course of things, from the breach of contract itself." The second rule or branch relates to damage such as " may reasonably be supposed to have been in the contemplation of both parties at the time of making the contract as the probable result of the breach of it," and the decision whether a given consequence of a particular breach falls under the first or the second rule or branch determines whether or not that consequence is too remote in the circumstances.[32] Whether it falls under the first or second rule or branch is a question of fact in the circumstances

29 Lord Wright in *Liesbosch Dredger* v. *Edison* [1933] A.C. 449, 460, quoting Bacon, Max. Leg. 1.

30 *Inst*. III, 3, 86.

31 (1854) 9 Ex. 341, 354.

32 The rules of *Hadley* v. *Baxendale* will be found quoted repeatedly in Scottish cases on the subject and, particularly since the statutory adoption of the rules in the Sale of Goods Act 1893, they undoubtedly express Scots law as well as English.

of each case.[33] Bell [34] stated the principle as to the effect that indemnification for loss extended to " that sort of damage which, though not strictly attaching to the article sold, is, by stipulation or by necessary consequence at the time of the sale, placed in view of the parties as foreseen effects of the non-performance of the contract; and as dangers from which, expressly or tacitly, the seller is by faithful performance to save the buyer."

The distinction was restated in *Victoria Laundry* v. *Newman* [35] in the form that the aggrieved party is entitled to recover " such part of his loss actually resulting as was at the time of the contract reasonably foreseeable as liable to result from the breach." What is reasonably foreseeable depends on the knowledge possessed by the parties, or at all events, by the party who later commits the breach. The knowledge possessed is of two kinds, one imputed, the other actual. " Everyone as a reasonable person, is taken to know the ' ordinary course of things ' and consequently what loss is liable to result from a breach of contract in the ordinary course. . . . But to this knowledge which a contract-breaker is assumed to possess, whether he actually possesses it or not, there may have to be added in a particular case knowledge which he actually possesses, of special circumstances, outside the ' ordinary course of things ' of such a kind that a breach in those special circumstances would be liable to cause more loss." The distinction can be put negatively in the form that any loss which would not arise in the ordinary course of things is too remote unless the party in breach had actual knowledge of the possibility of that loss. " A party who breaks his contract is liable for those consequences which a reasonable man, possessing the knowledge which the party had at the time of contracting, would have anticipated." [36]

The latest reconsideration of the criterion for determining whether certain loss is or is not too remote is the decision of the House of Lords in *Koufos* v. *Czarnikow*,[37] where the headnote [38] reads: " *Held*, that the sole rule as to the measure of damages for any kind of breach of any kind of contract was that the aggrieved party was entitled to recover such part of the damage actually caused by the breach as the defaulting party should reasonably have contemplated would flow from the breach; that since prices in a commodity market were liable to fluctuate, shipowners should reasonably contemplate that (*per* Lord Reid) it was not unlikely; (*per* Lord Morris of Borth-y-Gest) the result was liable to be or at least the result was not unlikely to be; (*per* Lord Hodson) the result was liable to be; (*per* Lord Pearce and Lord Upjohn) there was a serious possibility or real danger that, if their ships delayed their voyage, the value of marketable goods on board their ships would decline."

[33] *A/B Karlshamns Oljefabriker* v. *Monarch S.S. Co.*, 1949 S.C.(H.L.) 1.
[34] *Comm.* I, 479.
[35] [1949] 2 K.B. 528, 539.
[36] *Gloag on Contract*, 697.
[37] [1969] 1 A.C. 350.
[38] Said in *Vacwell Engineering Co.* v. *B.D.H. Chemicals* [1969] 3 All E.R. 1681, 1696, to be a convenient summary of the result of the opinions of their Lordships.

Test of reasonable contemplation

The distinction drawn in *Hadley* v. *Baxendale* has been described [39] as between "damages arising naturally (which means in the ordinary course of things) and cases where there were special and extraordinary circumstances beyond the reasonable prevision of the parties: in the latter event it is laid down that the special facts must be communicated by and between the parties . . . the latter are such that, if they are not communicated, it would not be fair or reasonable to hold the defendant responsible for losses which he could not be taken to contemplate as likely to result from his breach of contract." "The question whether damage is remote or 'natural' and direct, can in general only be decided on a review of the circumstances of each special case." [40] "The question in a case like the present must always be what reasonable business men must be taken to have contemplated as the natural or probable result if the contract was broken." [41] Again "damages arise 'according to the usual course of things' if, in the circumstances existing at the date of the contract, both parties to it, supposing them to have considered the probable effects of a breach of the contract, with due regard to events which might reasonably be expected to occur, must be assumed as reasonable men to have foreseen such damage as a serious possibility." [42]

The test for distinguishing ordinary damages from remote or consequential damages is accordingly that of the contemplation of the defender: would he, with the knowledge he possessed at the time of contracting, have contemplated as a serious possibility the item of damage in issue?

Whether bare knowledge adequate to infer liability

Doubts have been expressed whether the mere fact of knowledge brought home to the defender or communication to him of the special circumstances of a particular case is by itself sufficient to impose on the defender the liability to pay damages for the full consequences of failure to implement his contract, unless he were informed expressly or impliedly that he would be held liable for those uttermost consequences, and indeed unless he assented to undertake this extra liability. In *Horne* v. *Midland Ry.*,[43] Blackburn J. went so far as to say, "In order that the notice [of special circumstances] may have any effect it must be given under such circumstances as that an actual contract arises on the part of the defendant to bear the exceptional loss." In this case and in *Gee* v. *Lancashire and Yorkshire Ry.*,[44] opinions were expressed to the effect that a carrier might be justified in refusing to take over goods for carriage in circumstances where specially onerous liability would attach to him in case of failure by

39 *A/B Karlshamns Oljefabriker* v. *Monarch S.S. Co.*, 1949 S.C.(H.L.) 1, 19, *per* Lord Wright.
40 *Ibid.* 20.
41 *Ibid.* 21.
42 *Ibid.* 29, *per* Lord du Parcq.
43 (1873) L.R. 8 C.P. 131. See also Kelly C.B. (p. 136), and Lush J. (p. 145).
44 (1860) 6 H. & N. 211.

delay, unless the consignor paid an extra charge. This view may, however, conflict with the principle that a common carrier must accept all goods offered, and the rules which in certain cases now regulate the rates which may be charged for carriage of goods.

In *British Columbia Sawmill* v. *Nettleship* [45] the defendants were entrusted with cases of machinery consigned to Vancouver, one of which was lost in transit. Willes J. stated the requirement as being that where knowledge of special circumstances is relied on as enhancing the damage recoverable that knowledge must have been brought home to the defendant at the time of the contract, and in such circumstances that the defendant impliedly undertook to bear any special loss referable to a breach in those special circumstances. This requires almost acceptance of the contract with a condition of liability for exceptional loss attached. "The mere fact of knowledge cannot increase the liability. The knowledge must be brought home to the party sought to be charged, under such circumstances that he must know that the person he contracts with reasonably believes that he accepts the contract with the special condition attached to it. Knowledge on the part of the carrier is only important if it forms part of the contract. It may be that the knowledge is acquired casually from a stranger, the person to whom the goods belong not knowing or caring whether he had such knowledge or not. Knowledge, in effect, can only be evidence of fraud, or of an understanding by both parties that the contract is based upon the circumstances which are communicated."

It may be doubted whether this requirement of implied acceptance of the condition adjected to the contract could apply outside cases of carriage where standard charges are fixed, as in cases where there is no restriction the contracting party is usually free to charge a higher rate for the contract in consideration of the acceptance of the more onerous responsibility,[46] and may be taken to have accepted the condition of additional liability if he does not do so, so long as the communication of knowledge is so full and clear as to justify this inference. But where the defender has no option to refuse the contract, nor is at liberty to demand extra remuneration therefor, the fact of acceptance of the contract after notice or knowledge of the special circumstances is not a fact from which acceptance of liability for consequential damages is readily to be inferred.

Extent of disclosure required

The leading Scottish case on this branch of law is *Den of Ogil Co.* v. *Caledonian Ry.*[47] The steamship *Den of Ogil* broke a piston and was detained at Plymouth until a replacement dispatched from the owners via the defender's railway system should arrive. The railway company was

[45] (1868) L.R. 3 C.P. 499, 509, approved *Victoria Laundry* v. *Newman* [1949] 2 K.B. 528, 538. See also *Elbinger A./G.* v. *Armstrong* (1874) L.R. 9 Q.B. 473; *Grébert-Borgnis* v. *Nugent* (1885) 15 Q.B.D. 85.

[46] *Cf. Den of Ogil Co.* v. *Caledonian Ry.* (1902) 5 F. 99, where a higher charge was made.

[47] (1902) 5 F. 99. See also *Keddie, Gordon & Co.* v. *N.B. Ry.* (1886) 14 R. 233.

informed that delay in delivery of the replacement involved the detention of the ship, and the casting was to go by passenger train, at a special rate, but the company was not informed of the size of the ship and the large crew necessarily kept idle. A delay of several days did in fact occur through the fault of the defenders and the shipowners sued the railway company for damages which included a sum for outlays and loss of profits caused by the detention. It was held that the defenders were liable for part of the outlays, but not for the loss of profits. The latter head of claim was repelled as not having been sufficiently brought to the notice of the railway company, though it was observed that the owners would have had a strong claim for the whole of their outlays if the notice to the railway company had been specific as to the size of the ship and as to its having a cargo and crew on board ready to sail on a trading voyage. It was held on the one hand that the defenders were " affected with notice " that the transit was urgent, and that the effect of non-punctual fulfilment would be the delay of the steamer, but on the other hand they were not informed that the ship was so large or had such a big crew nor that the piston was an essential part of the ship's machinery, and the full loss of profit was accordingly disallowed.[48]

This seems a logical corollary of the rule that liability only extends to actual knowledge of extraordinary facts. Compare with this *Wilson* v. *General Iron Screw Co.*,[49] where owners of a ship claimed damages for the loss sustained by detention of their vessel by reason of previous improper repairs to it having to be put right. It was held that detention of the vessel was a probable and natural result of the defendant's earlier breach in respect of the supply of defective machinery. Though no evidence was given that the vessel could actually have been employed and been earning, the consequences were held not to be too remote and damages amounting to the full loss of earnings for the period of detention were given. Again in *Cory* v. *Thames Ironworks Co.*[50] the non-disclosure of the peculiar use contemplated by the plaintiff made the full measure of damages irrecoverable.[51]

Time of disclosure

If any disclosure of special circumstances falls to be made so as to bring consequences which would not arise naturally or in the ordinary course of things within the reasonable contemplation of the other party it must be made before or at the time the contract is entered into and not afterwards.[52] The test of remoteness is whether the loss was " at the time of the contract reasonably foreseeable as liable to result from the breach." [53]

48 On the question how far general notice is sufficient, see further *Horne* v. *Midland Ry.* (1873) L.R. 8 C.P. 131.
49 (1878) 47 L.J.Q.B. 239.
50 (1868) L.R. 3 Q.B. 181.
51 On the extent of disclosure of sub-contracts, see p. 464, *infra*.
52 *Hydraulic Engineering Co.* v. *McHaffie* (1878) 4 Q.B.D. 670, 676. *Cf. Gee* v. *L. & Y. Ry.* (1860) 6 H. & N. 211.
53 *Victoria Laundry* v. *Newman* [1949] 2 K.B. 528.

Cases where consequential damages not recoverable

Many cases illustrate the proposition that remote or consequential damages not within the contemplation of the parties when the contract was entered into and not reasonably foreseeable by the defender, having regard to his knowledge in the circumstances, are irrecoverable. So where a mill-shaft was sent for repair without disclosing that the mill was stopped for lack of it, the carriers who delayed it in transit were not liable for the loss of profits which resulted from the mill standing idle [54]; where a railway company delayed to deliver raw cotton not knowing that the plaintiffs' mill was idle for lack of the material and not contemplating that it had no reserve stocks, loss of profits and wages were not recoverable [55]; where a railway company so delayed to deliver a consignment of boots, in ignorance of the very high price payable for the boots which were in fact a special order for the French Army, and the consignee rejected them, they were held liable for loss at market value only and not at the high contractual price [56]; where the defendants sent a parcel of goods to their representative without disclosing the object of the dispatch, it was held that damages for loss of sale due to delay were not recoverable [57]; where a commercial traveller delivered samples to a carrier without further disclosure and was unemployed and incurred expenditure in consequence of their delay, these damages were held irrecoverable [58]; where a seaman left his ship on the grounds that the voyage had become illegal and involved greater danger than he had contracted for and was imprisoned on shore as a deserter, it was held that damages for imprisonment were a consequence too remote from the defendant's breach in taking part in warlike activities to be recoverable in damages [59]; where an unintelligible cipher message was entrusted to the defendants for transmission to America and was not sent so that plaintiffs lost commission on an order to which the message related, only nominal damages were recoverable as the defendants could not have foreseen the full possible loss [60]; where it was not disclosed that the loss of a particular part of a consignment would render the whole valueless, damages beyond the cost of replacing that item were refused [61]; where a sub-contract unknown to the carrier was breached in consequence of his delay.[62]

Several cases illustrate the application of the principles of remoteness to contracts for manufacture and construction. For instance where the

54 *Hadley* v. *Baxendale* (1854) 9 Exch. 341, as explained in *Victoria Laundry* v. *Newman* [1949] 2 K.B. 528.
55 *Gee* v. *Lancs. & Yorks. Ry.* (1860) 6 H. & N. 211; *cf. Le Peintur* v. *S.E. Ry.* (1860) 2 L.T. (N.S.) 170.
56 *Horne* v. *Midland Ry.* (1873) L.R. 8 C.P. 131; see also *Schulze* v. *G.E. Ry.* (1887) 19 Q.B.D. 30.
57 *G.W. Ry.* v. *Redmayne* (1866) L.R. 1 C.P. 329; see also *Hales* v. *L.N.W. Ry.* (1863) 4 B. & S. 66; *Hawes* v. *S.E. Ry.* (1884) 54 L.J.Q.B. 174.
58 *Woodger* v. *G.W. Ry.* (1867) L.R. 2 C.P. 318.
59 *Burton* v. *Pinkerton* (1867) L.R. 2 Ex. 340.
60 *Sanders* v. *Stuart* (1876) 1 C.P.D. 326.
61 *British Columbia Sawmill Co.* v. *Nettleship* (1868) L.R. 3 C.P. 499.
62 *Walton* v. *Fothergill* (1835) 7 C. & P. 392.

plaintiff had contracted to repair a steam threshing-machine by a given date, and to effect this sub-contracted with the defendant to make a new fire-box, the defendant delayed in doing so, so that the plaintiff was unable to perform the principal contract and was found liable in damages for his breach. These damages, it was held, he could not recover from the defendant as they were not the ordinary consequence of the breach, and the possible consequences of the defendant's failure on the principal contract had not been communicated to him so as to bring it within his reasonable contemplation when he entered into the contract.[63] In *Smeed* v. *Foord*[64] the defendant contracted to deliver a threshing-machine to the farmer plaintiff within three weeks, knowing that it was the farmer's practice to thresh in the field. On account of delay the farmer had to carry home the crop and stack it, where it was damaged by rain, so that when the machine was finally delivered and the crop threshed it had to be dried and then sold for a lower price, as the price had fallen during the delay. The defendant was held liable for the expense of stacking, for loss from deterioration by rain, and for the expense of drying it, but not for the fall in market price. The former three items were, whereas the loss was not, a matter within reasonable contemplation. In *Foaminol Laboratories Ltd.* v. *British Artid Plastics Ltd.*,[65] the plaintiffs ordered from the defendants containers for cosmetics, few of which were in fact delivered. It was held that the loss of co-operation of the editresses of certain ladies' journals who had agreed to assist in boosting the sales of the new product was not in the contemplation of the parties and hence too remote to be considered in quantifying damages.

In *Trans Trust S.P.R.L.* v. *Danubian Trading Co.*[66] sellers sold steel to buyers who made a contract for resale, having agreed that a confirmed credit would be opened forthwith. The buyers were unable to do so and the sellers sued for breach of contract. It was held that as they were aware that the sellers could not obtain the goods from their suppliers unless the credit was opened the sellers were entitled to their loss of profit on the contract as a foreseeable consequence of the breach, but, as the buyers were not aware that the sellers' suppliers also depended on the credit to obtain the goods, a loss by them and a possible right of recovery against the sellers were not within the contemplation of the parties but were too remote, and the sellers were accordingly not entitled to a declaration of right to indemnity against any damages payable by them to their suppliers. It was further observed that loss due to impecuniosity was not necessarily too remote[67] if the loss might reasonably be supposed to be in the contemplation of the parties.

63 *Portman* v. *Middleton* (1858) 4 C.B.(N.S.) 322. Contrast *Hydraulic Engineering Co.* v. *McHaffie* (1878) 4 Q.B.D. 670.

64 (1859) 1 E. & E. 602.

65 [1941] 2 All E.R. 393.

66 [1952] 1 All E.R. 970.

67 For a case where it was held to be too remote, see *Liesbosch* v. *Edison* [1933] A.C. 449.

Again it has been held that though in the commercial world at September 1949 the devaluation of the pound sterling was a serious possibility, loss accruing in consequence of payment being delayed so as to have to be made in devalued pounds was not recoverable as it was not a reasonably foreseeable consequence.[68]

Cases where consequential damages recoverable

There are likewise many illustrations of the general principle that consequential damages are recoverable if in the circumstances of the case it is accepted by the court that the defender had such knowledge that he could reasonably have foreseen those consequences as liable to result from his breach of contract.

In *Mackenzie* v. *Liddell*[69] a tug was hired to fulfil a salvage contract, but by the tug-owner's default arrived too late to take part in the operations. It was held that that contract sufficiently disclosed that it was hired for salvage duties and that the loss of high salvage rewards must have been contemplated, and hence substantial damages were awarded. In *Robertson* v. *Connolly*[70] the defender put a glandered horse in the field where he was pasturing the pursuer's horse, and the latter in ignorance put the horse in his stable so that two other horses were infected and died; the defender was held liable for the value of all three horses as a natural and probable consequence of the defender's breach of contract.

In *Grébert-Borgnis* v. *Nugent*[71] defendants contracted to supply to plaintiffs goods known to be required to enable the latter to execute a contract with a third party. The defendants failed to deliver and, there being no market, the third party recovered damages from the plaintiffs, who were in turn held entitled to recover this amount and also their loss of profit on the transaction as damages.[72]

Where a newspaper offered to give financial advice and in response to a request recommended as a stockbroker a man who was an undischarged bankrupt and not a member of the Stock Exchange and he embezzled the plaintiffs' money, it was held that there was a breach of contract and the plaintiffs' whole loss flowed directly from that breach.[73]

Where the defendants contracted to supply wheels and axles to the plaintiffs, who had disclosed that they were under contract to deliver wagons but had not mentioned that this had to be done by a fixed date under a penalty for failure, the defendants, on delaying delivery, were held liable for substantial damages amounting to the total penalties,

[68] *Mehmet Dogan Bey* v. *G. G. Abdeni & Co.* [1951] 2 K.B. 405.

[69] (1883) 10 R. 705. *Cf. Den of Ogil Co.* v. *Caledonian Ry.* (1902) 5 F. 99.

[70] (1851) 13 D. 779; (1852) 14 D. 315; *cf. Smith* v. *Green* (1875) 1 C.P.D. 92 (cow infecting other cows: breach of warranty that it was free from disease); *Mullett* v. *Mason* (1866) L.R. 1 C.P. 559 (cow infecting other cows; fraudulent representation that free from disease); *Hill* v. *Balls* (1857) 2 H. & N. 299 (glandered horse); *Ward* v. *Hobbs* (1878) 3 Q.B.D. 150; affd. 4 App.Cas. 13 (pigs); *Waddington* v. *Buchan Poultry Products Ltd.*, 1963 S.L.T. 168.

[71] (1885) 15 Q.B.D. 85.

[72] *Cf. Hammond* v. *Bussey* (1887) 20 Q.B.D. 79.

[73] *De La Bere* v. *Pearson* [1908] 1 K.B. 280.

though the plaintiffs were not as a matter of law entitled to recover the amount of the penalties.[74]

In *Hydraulic Engineering Co.* v. *McHaffie* [75] the plaintiffs had contracted to make a pile-driver for a third party, and in turn contracted with the defendant to make a particular part of that machine, informing him that the whole machine was required by the third party at the end of August. The defendant did not deliver his part till the end of September, whereupon the third party refused to accept the machine. It was held that the plaintiffs were entitled to recover damages representing the loss of profit on the contract and the fruitless expenditure on the rest of the machine, as it was quite useless and unsaleable. The defendant, it was proved, knew and must have contemplated that his failure would cause the failure of the whole contract. He was therefore liable for the full damages which failure of the whole contract necessarily entailed.

In *Strachan and Gavin* v. *Paton* [76] the defender was employed to repair a ship in the knowledge that she was intended for whale-fishing, and he exceeded the contract time for repairs, so that the ship in consequence lost the whaling season. He was hence held liable for the average profit which her voyage should have produced.

A manufacturer is, however, credited with the ordinary knowledge of a reasonable person in his line of business and he will be assumed to know that profit will be lost by loss of time if he supplies defective machinery which cannot be renewed without loss of time. So where iron stills were supplied to a chemical company and warranted fit for a known special purpose and were proved to be unfit therefor, it was held that the damages due for breach of warranty included the cost of substitute goods and also a sum representing the loss of time to the purchaser and the loss of profits which that involved.[77]

In *Patrick* v. *Russo-British Grain Export Co.*[78] wheat was bought and before delivery resold at a profit: the sellers knew that the purchase was for resale; they delayed to deliver and, there being no market at the due date of delivery, were found liable for the full difference between the contract price and the resale price.

Where defendants contracted to carry gas coal to the plaintiffs in the knowledge that it was to be used for manufacturing gas and by-products and by mistake delivered steam coal, it was held that, there being no market, the plaintiffs acted reasonably in using the steam coal and were entitled to recover the loss of value of the gas coal for the purpose of making gas and by-products.[79]

[74] *Elbinger A/G* v. *Armstrong* (1874) L.R. 9 Q.B. 473.
[75] (1878) 4 Q.B.D. 670; *cf. Borries* v. *Hutchinson* (1865) 18 C.B.(N.S.) 445.
[76] (1828) 3 W. & Sh. 19; *cf.* late delivery of a new vessel whereby she lost a season's trade; *Fletcher* v. *Tayleur* (1855) 17 C.B. 21; and *cf. Ex. p. Cambrian S. P. Co.* (1868) L.R. 4 Ch. 112.
[77] *Fleming* v. *Airdrie Iron Co.* (1882) 9 R. 473.
[78] [1927] 2 K.B. 535.
[79] *Monte Video Gas Co.* v. *Clan Line Steamers* (1921) 37 T.L.R. 866.

Where a railway company ran trains intended to suit a particular market and were in the circumstances liable for damages for delay, the damages were held to be not such as would have arisen from a delay in the ordinary course of events but for the loss which arose from missing that particular market.[80] The company were held to have sufficient notice of special circumstances by the fact of running the train for that market and this implied acceptance of the responsibility for the consequences of loss of market. But where a particular train is habitually used, without being a special run to catch a market, it is probably a question of the circumstances of the case whether or not the railway authorities could be held liable. In *Macdonald* v. *Highland Ry.*[81] goods marked " perishable " were left behind while non-perishables were forwarded by the defenders. It was held that as the nature of the goods was disclosed, that laid on the carriers the obligation to give them a preference as they customarily did and they were held liable in damages for failure to do this.

The relevance of the extent of loss

In *Vacwell Engineering Co.* v. *B.D.H. Chemicals Ltd.*,[82] chemicals were sold in glass ampoules for use in a manufacturing process. Neither party knew that the chemical exploded violently on contact with water. When two scientists were handling ampoules prior to use in the process an explosion occurred, killing one and causing extensive damage to premises. It was held that an explosion of a minor kind was foreseeable as a result of the defendants' breach of contract in not warning of an unusual hazard in use, and that though an explosion of the magnitude which occurred was not reasonably foreseeable, it was the direct result of the defendants' failure to give adequate warning, and accordingly the damage was not too remote to be recoverable. The court held that it could not find that because the damage to property was much greater than could have been reasonably foreseeable, it was too remote to be recoverable in law.

It appears accordingly that if consequential harm should have been contemplated and if there is liability therefor, the liability is for the harm actually caused and it matters not that the nature or extent of that harm would not have been contemplated.

Sub-contracts

A party who breaks his contract may as a reasonable man have to anticipate the possibility that the goods he has failed to supply or deliver may have been required to fulfil a sub-contract between the other party to his contract and a third party. Such knowledge and foresight is of the

80 *Anderson* v. *N.B. Ry.* (1875) 2 R. 443. See also *Simpson* v. *L.N.W. Ry.* (1876) 1 Q.B.D. 274. *Candy* v. *Midland Ry.* (1878) 38 L.T.(N.S.) 226; similarly at sea; *Dunn* v. *Bucknall Bros.* [1902] 2 K.B. 614; *Bates* v. *Cameron* (1855) 18 D. 186.

81 (1873) 11 M. 614, 615.

82 [1969] 3 All E.R. 1681.

kind which may have to be imputed to him by law. The grounds for the imputation may vary but they are strongest where the disappointed party is a dealer in the kind of goods in question in the contract and is probably not buying for his own consumption. Consequently the party in breach must be taken to foresee that his failure will in all probability force the other party to obtain alternative supplies elsewhere or to become himself liable for breach of the sub-contract. Hence he will be liable for loss of profit on the sub-contract and for any damages payable for failure thereunder even though he may not have had actual knowledge of the sub-contract, so long as the damages and loss of profit are normal and not exceptional.[83] A sub-contract on ordinary terms is therefore frequently a matter of ordinary rather than remote or consequential damages.

Much depends on what knowledge can reasonably be imputed to the parties in the circumstances. Thus it was said in *Duff* v. *Iron Buildings Co.*,[84] where loss of profit on sub-contracts was held recoverable: "It could not be supposed that the pursuers would want 108 pioneer huts for their personal use and the defenders had constituted the pursuers their sole agents for sale within the colony." In *Koufos* v. *Czarnikow* [85] it was pointed out that a carrier could not be expected to know so much about a trade as the consignee of the goods.

But in default of express information a contracting party can only be presumed to know that breach of a sub-contract is a possible consequence of his failure and he will not be held liable for more than the ordinary consequences thereof. He cannot be held to anticipate that the sub-contract will contain any exceptional terms and any sub-contract on unusual or exceptional terms will fall under the rule of consequential damages requiring express or actual knowledge in the party as a condition precedent to full liability.

Thus a party is not liable to the full extent for resultant breach of a sub-contract containing a penalty provision in case of failure,[86] or of a sub-contract on exceptionally profitable terms,[87] though he is liable where the circumstances of the sub-contract are known.[88]

Loss on a sub-contract may therefore be either ordinary and natural or remote and consequential damage depending on the circumstances of the case. Furthermore the extent of disclosure required may vary in different kinds of cases: for it has been pointed out [89] that a carrier commonly knows less than a seller about the purposes for which a buyer or consignee requires the goods or about other special circumstances which may cause

83 *Keddie, Gordon & Co.* v. *N.B. Ry.* (1886) 14 R. 233; *Ströms Bruks A/B* v. *Hutchison* (1904) 6 F. 486; revd. (1905) 7 F.(H.L.) 131; *Victoria Laundry* v. *Newman* [1949] 2 K.B. 528.
84 (1891) 19 R. 199, 205.
85 [1969] 1 A.C. 350.
86 *Borries* v. *Hutchinson* (1865) 18 C.B.(N.S.) 445; *Elbinger A.G.* v. *Armstrong* (1874) L.R. 9 Q.B. 473.
87 *Horne* v. *Midland Ry.* (1873) L.R. 8 C.P. 131; *Duff* v. *Iron Buildings Co.* (1891) 19 R. 199. *Cf. Dunlop* v. *McKellar*, May 31, 1815, F.C.
88 *Grébert-Borgnis* v. *Nugent* (1885) 15 Q.B.D. 85.
89 *Victoria Laundry* v. *Newman* [1949] 2 K.B. 528, 536.

exceptional loss. In consequence the same sub-contract might well require greater disclosure to affect a carrier with full liability than to affect a seller.

Exceptional use contemplated

Where parties have not in contemplation the same ultimate use for the article to be supplied, the defender can only be held liable for consequences with reference to whatever use he had in contemplation at the time of contracting, which in the absence of further information than a reasonable man's foresight supplies, will necessarily be the natural, ordinary and obvious use. That is, if a man contracts to supply an article, he will only be liable for his failure to the extent he would if it were put to its ordinary use, even though the other party has actually sustained loss to a greater amount. In *Cory* v. *Thames Ironworks* [90] the defendants agreed to sell and deliver to the plaintiffs within a certain time the hull of a floating boom derrick, but in fact were six months late in doing so. The plaintiffs' purpose was novel and not disclosed to the defendants—the latter thinking the hull was to be used as a coal store, while the former in fact intended to and did use it to tranship coal direct from colliers into barges. The plaintiffs accordingly suffered greater loss by the defendants' delay than they would if the hull had been put to the normal use. It was held that the plaintiffs were entitled only to the damages which followed in the normal course, and the excess of loss sustained in consequence of the special use they had in mind was something which they could not reasonably be held to have contemplated as a result of their delay in performing their contract.

Supervening contingency

Damages are generally too remote in so far as they depend on a contingency superadded to the breach complained of, so that proof of breach of contract will not justify an award of substantial damages if those damages depended not only on the breach but in addition on some uncertain element, unless that element is expressly made known to the defender as a possible cause of greater loss than would naturally result. Thus a carrier who delays delivery of a competition model is not liable in damages for loss of the prize, but only for damages for delay and in respect of the value of the labour and materials employed in making the model [91]; damages for loss of profits expected to arise from service of the plaintiff's mare by the defender's stallion have been held too remote [92]; loss of business due to delay on a journey is likewise too remote.[93] Even if the contingency is brought to the defender's notice the loss therefrom might still be sustained even though he had performed his contract.

[90] (1868) L.R. 3 Q.B. 181, 187. See also *Bridge* v. *Wain* (1816) 1 Stark. 504; *Ex p. Cambrian Steam Packet Co.* (1868) L.R. 4 Ch. 112, 117; *Kimber* v. *Willett* [1947] K.B. 570.

[91] *Watson* v. *Ambergate Ry.* (1857) 15 Jur. 448.

[92] *Sapwell* v. *Bass* [1910] 2 K.B. 486.

[93] *Cf.* loss of possible situation by false imprisonment: *Hoey* v. *Felton* (1861) 11 C.B.(N.S.) 142; and loss of promotion: *Boyce* v. *Bayliffe* (1807) 1 Camp. 58, quoting Lord Alvanley: *cf.* also such loss of promotion as a consequence of an accident, *Armstrong* v. *Paterson*, 1935 S.C. 464.

This principle is probably subject to the modification that where the contingency amounts to a substantial chance and is known to the defender he will be liable to a substantial extent. Such is the case of a defendant's breach of contract whereby the other party was prevented from taking part in a competition in which there was a mathematically substantial chance of winning a prize.[94]

THE INNOCENT PARTY MUST SEEK TO MINIMISE THE LOSS

General nature of the obligation

When a wrongful act is done, whether a breach of contract or a delict or other breach of obligation, the extent of the damage it causes may be reduced or minimised by prudent action on the part of the innocent party. It would moreover be unreasonable to allow an innocent party to remain idle and allow the uttermost consequences of a breach of duty to occur and then to seek to recover the full damage sustained from the party in breach. So he is bound to take all reasonable steps to minimise the consequences of the other party's wrongful act, and can only recover such damages as fairly represent the loss which the adoption of reasonable preventive measures could not avert.[1] He is bound to act not only in his own interest but in that of the party in breach.[2] " A contracting party is not entitled to proceed so as to cause unnecessary loss to the other party without any resulting benefit to himself." [3] A party is not entitled to recover damages if the breach of contract has been caused by his own initial wrongful act, or is due to his own neglect.[4]

Hence in the ordinary case of breach of contract of sale a disappointed seller is bound to take immediate steps to dispose of his goods in the market at the best price he can obtain and he is only entitled to recover as damages the difference between the contract price and the market price at the time of the breach. If he delays so that the market price falls he will not be entitled to recover the extra loss as it was avoidable by prompt action, and conversely in the case of a disappointed buyer.[5] So too if owing to delay the goods are utterly ruined he will not be entitled to recover the full

94 *Chaplin* v. *Hicks* [1911] 2 K.B. 786. Contrast *Bourne* v. *Lothians Racing Syndicate*, 1951 S.L.T.(Notes) 37.

1 *Gloag on Contract*, 2nd ed., 688; *Harries* v. *Edmonds* (1845) 1 C. & K. 686 (charterparty); *Frost* v. *Knight* (1872) L.R. 7 Ex. 111 (promise of marriage); *Brown* v. *Muller*, *ibid.*, 319 (sale of goods—fluctuating market); *Dunkirk Colliery Co.* v. *Lever* (1879) 41 L.T. 633 (coal); *Erie Gas Co.* v. *Carroll* [1911] A.C. 105; *British Westinghouse Co.* v. *Underground Ry.* [1912] A.C. 673, 689; *Jamal* v. *Moolla, Dawood & Co.* [1916] 1 A.C. 175 (shares); *Cazalet* v. *Morris*, 1916 S.C. 952; *Credito Italiano* v. *Swiss Bankverein* (1916) 114 L.T. 776 (money); *Hill* v. *Showell* (1918) 87 L.J.K.B. 1106 (H.L.) (raw materials); *British Automatic Co.* v. *Haynes* [1921] 1 K.B. 377 (hire of machines); *Houndsditch Warehouse Co.* v. *Waltex* [1944] K.B. 579; *Pomphrey* v. *Cuthbertson*, 1951 S.C. 147 (delict).

2 *Smailes* v. *Hans Dessen & Co.* (1905) 94 L.T. 492; 95 L.T. 809.

3 *Dunford & Elliot* v. *Macleod* (1902) 4 F. 912, 920, *per* Lord McLaren.

4 *Jamal* v. *Moolla, Dawood & Co.* [1916] 1 A.C. 175.

5 *Warin & Craven* v. *Forrester* (1876) 4 R. 190, 193; affd. (1877) 4 R.(H.L.) 75; *Duff & Co.* v. *Iron and Steel Fencing Co.* (1891) 19 R. 199, 204; *Ireland* v. *Merryton Coal Co.* (1894) 21 R. 989.

value. If, however, there is no available market for the goods in question the full value will be recoverable.

In the case where perishable goods are sent in a state which justifies their rejection by the purchaser, he is entitled and probably bound to sell them at once rather than return them to the seller, as such a course will mitigate the damages due and return of the goods would result in total loss.[6] The only difficulty in such a course lies in the question whether the purchaser's action is justifiable in the circumstances of the case, which is a question of fact in each case.[7]

An employee dismissed from his place is likewise bound to take reasonable steps to obtain alternative employment and he can only recover the full amount of loss sustained by not doing so if he can show that no other suitable and comparable employment was reasonably obtainable by him. The Lord Justice-Clerk (Macdonald) said [8]: " The pursuer was of course not entitled to sit idle and make no effort to obtain suitable employment. He must fairly and reasonably exert himself to earn his living and can only come against the defender for the loss he sustains from inability to secure a position as good as that which was agreed upon with the defender."

Lord President Inglis explained the law fully in *Warin & Craven* v. *Forrester*.[9] In that case the purchasers of sugar repudiated the contract and the sellers delayed for three months before reselling during which time the market price fell. " A seller's right to charge against a buyer a loss upon a resale of goods cannot be properly exercised by a resale occurring three months after the breach of contract. That would be a very loose and inexpedient proceeding to sanction, and I am not aware that any such privilege of delay has been admitted. A seller is certainly not entitled to speculate either for himself or for any other party. He is not entitled to consider his own interest.[10] He must resell whatever the state of the market, and it is only if he immediately does so that he can charge the difference between the contract and the market price against the buyer. What was done here in January should have been done in November. . . . The true estimate must therefore be the difference between the contract price and what the goods would have brought if sold in November. Whatever loss has arisen by the postponement of the sale till January must be deducted from the sum of damages found due to the pursuers."

In *Frost* v. *Knight* [11] Cockburn C.J. phrased the principle as follows: " In assessing the damages for breach of performance, a jury will of course take into account whatever the plaintiff has done, or has had the means of doing, and, as a prudent man, ought in reason to have done, whereby his loss has been, or would have been diminished."

6 *Pommer & Thomsen* v. *Mowat* (1906) 14 S.L.T. 373.
7 *Payzu* v. *Saunders* [1919] 2 K.B. 581.
8 *Ross* v. *Macfarlane* (1894) 21 R. 396, 406. See too *Brace* v. *Calder* [1895] 2 Q.B. 253.
9 (1876) 4 R. 190, 193; affd. (1877) 4 R.(H.L.) 75.
10 *Cf. Smailes* v. *Dessen* (1905) 94 L.T. 492, *per* Channell J.
11 (1872) L.R. 7 Ex. 111, 115.

In *Admiralty Commrs.* v. *S.S. Chekiang* [12] Lord Sumner said: " The object of that principle [of minimising damages] is to prevent a tort sufferer from recovering for damage, which is really self-inflicted, because with reasonable effort he could have avoided it. This does not extend to investing the tortfeasor with a right to call on him to do things which do not follow from the collision, in order to diminish liability for the wrong." " A man may not increase damages by unreasonable conduct. He is bound to act not only in his own interest, but in the interests of the party who would have to pay the damages and he must therefore keep them down, so far as it is reasonable and proper, by acting reasonably in the matter." [13]

Application of the obligation

The obligation is applicable generally to cases of breach of contract; in cases of sale it applies where the article supplied is disconform to warranty and must be replaced,[14] where the seller fails to supply and an alternative purchase must be made from another source of supply,[15] or where a buyer fails to accept and the goods must be sold off elsewhere,[16] where there is a breach of warranty [17] or fraudulent misrepresentation,[18] or where reasonable care in inspection would have averted subsequent loss.[19] The rule is applicable to sale of shares in a company and a seller retaining the shares after a breach of the contract by the buyer cannot recover from the buyer any further loss if the market falls after the date of the breach when he should have sold at the best obtainable price (nor is he liable to have the damages reduced if the market rises).[20] It applies also to contracts of employment and it has been given effect to where a dismissed employee had been offered other employment [21]: in such a case he is bound to take reasonable steps to look for and to take, if he can find it, employment reasonably suitable to his qualifications and experience; and to cases of hiring where the articles should be relet to another party.[22]

In contracts of carriage it has been held that the pursuer who was complaining of delay in the delivery of goods should have given notice to the defender, the carrier, of the undue detention.[23] A shipowner has been held entitled to delay a voyage and deviate to obtain cargo so as to minimise

12 [1926] A.C. 637, 646.
13 *Smailes* v. *Hans Dessen & Co.* (1905) 94 L.T. 492, *per* Channell J.; affd. (1906) 95 L.T. 809.
14 *British Westinghouse Co.* v. *Underground Rys.* [1912] A.C. 673.
15 *Roper* v. *Johnson* (1873) L.R. 8 C.P. 167.
16 *Warin & Craven* v. *Forrester* (1876) 4 R. 190; *Tredegar Iron & Coal Co.* v. *Hawthorn* (1902) 18 T.L.R. 716; *British Automatic Co.* v. *Haynes* [1921] 1 K.B. 377.
17 *Sopers* v. *Johnston* [1944] 2 All E.R. 42, 586.
18 *Jewelowski* v. *Propp* [1944] K.B. 510.
19 *Carter* v. *Campbell* (1885) 12 R. 1075; *Wilson* v. *Carmichael* (1894) 21 R. 732.
20 *Jamal* v. *Moolla, Dawood* [1916] 1 A.C. 175.
21 *Hoey* v. *McEwan and Auld* (1867) 5 M. 814; *Ross* v. *Macfarlane* (1894) 21 R. 396; *Brace* v. *Calder* [1895] 2 Q.B. 253; *Simon* v. *Pawson* (1933) 38 Com.Cas. 151. See also *Clayton-Greene* v. *De Courville* (1920) 36 T.L.R. 790 (actor).
22 *British Stamp Machine Co.* v. *Haynes* [1921] 1 K.B. 377.
23 *Dobson* v. *Edin. & Glasgow Ry.* (1861) 33 Sc.Jur. 443; *cf. Wilson* v. *Hicks* (1857) 26 L.J.Ex. 242.

the damage arising from a charterer's failure to load a full cargo.[24] Again where before the expiry of the lay-days a charterer who had failed to provide a cargo offered the captain another cargo at a lesser freight saying that the difference would be made up, but this the captain refused it was held that he was not bound to accept the offer, but if the contract had been broken by no cargo being loaded during the lay-days, the captain should have taken a cargo at the most he could get to reduce the damages so far as possible.[25] In *Wilson* v. *Hicks* [26] the captain took his ship to each loading port named, no cargo was supplied and he was requested to go back to one of them or elsewhere in hopes of obtaining a cargo, which he declined to do: it was held that if the jury deemed his conduct unreasonable they might diminish the damages recoverable.

In *White & Carter (Councils) Ltd.* v. *McGregor*,[27] where the defender repudiated a contract before the pursuers had done anything towards performance they were nevertheless held entitled to make unwanted performance and recover the full cost, though they could have caused the defender much less loss by suing only for their loss of profit on the contract. The case can be explained either on the basis that it was a claim of debt and that no obligation to minimise exists in such a case, or on the basis that the pursuers could not be compelled to accept repudiation of the contract, even though, without benefit to themselves, they were thereby being allowed to maximise the loss to the defender. The decision is very unsatisfactory for this reason.

Extent of obligation

The obligation to mitigate or minimise damages is not absolute in extent. The innocent party is only bound to take reasonable steps and to act in the interests of both himself and the party in breach [28] and the other party cannot challenge his failure to make extraordinary efforts, nor will a party be penalised because he has failed to take the best possible course or all possible steps to minimise damages. In *Gunter* v. *Lauritzen* [29] a Danish merchant contracted to supply hay and straw for resale; the goods on delivery were rejected as disconform to warranty. The buyer claimed as damages the full loss of profit on the sub-sale, proving that there was no market for such goods at the time and place of delivery. The seller averred that the buyer could have obtained the goods in three lots from private sellers at different places in this country. It was held that even if this were possible the buyer was under no duty to make extraordinary exertions to supply himself with goods elsewhere and the full loss of profit on the sub-sale was awarded as damages. The question of reasonableness

[24] *Wallems* v. *Muller* [1927] 2 K.B. 99.
[25] *Harries* v. *Edmonds* (1845) 1 Car. & K. 686.
[26] (1857) 26 L.J.Ex. 242. See also *Weir* v. *Dobell* [1916] 1 K.B. 722; *Dunford & Elliott* v. *Macleod* (1902) 4 F. 912.
[27] 1962 S.C.(H.L.) 1.
[28] *Smailes* v. *Dessen* (1905) 94 L.T. 492.
[29] (1894) 31 S.L.R. 359.

is one of fact in each case.[30] In *Henderson* v. *Turnbull* [31] the charterer of a ship had failed to provide a full cargo and a claim for dead freight was made. Lord Ardwall observed [32] that it was " vain to say that the captain was bound to incur trouble, expense and delay in going about . . . and endeavouring to make up a cargo." In particular, scrutiny of the conduct of the pursuer is being made *ex post facto* and should accordingly not be too rigid.

It is settled that a pursuer need not destroy or injure his own property or rights just to mitigate damages. So a charterer who had lost the use of the vessel chartered due to its requisition by the Government was not bound to give notice to terminate the charterparty, though this course would have reduced his claim of damages, as he would thereby have lost the benefit of having the right to the use of the vessel on the termination of the period of requisition.[33]

Nor is he bound to adopt a course which will mitigate damages if this would be harmful to the commercial credit or business reputation of the pursuer. In *Banco de Portugal* v. *Waterlow* [34] the defendants, printers of bank-notes for the plaintiffs, handed over to a third party in breach of contract and in the mistaken belief that he had authority to obtain them, a large quantity of notes which the third party fraudulently put into circulation. The plaintiffs on discovering this fraud withdrew the whole issue of notes and exchanged all those in circulation for a fresh issue of good notes. It was pleaded that the damages awarded were excessive as the Bank could have ascertained quickly the means of distinguishing good notes from bad and that it was not in the usual course of things for a Bank to pay forged notes. The majority of the House of Lords however held that the Bank was entitled for the sake of their financial reputation and the national credit to honour the forged notes and redeem them even though that enhanced the damages suffered. Hence the larger sum was recoverable. A further reason was to avoid damage to innocent third parties. In *Finlay* v. *Kwik Hoo Tong* [35] it was held that a firm will not be bound to mitigate damages if that will get them a bad name in their trade or ruin their commercial reputation, as by enforcing sub-contracts which were legally enforceable though the plaintiffs knew that the goods were not in fact in conformity with what they had contracted to supply to the sub-purchasers. To do so would " violate the standard of morality which would attach to an English firm of standing. . . .[36] A seller who has committed a breach of contract cannot, in my opinion, compel his buyer who has not broken his contract to take action to minimise the damage of

30 *Payzu* v. *Saunders* [1919] 2 K.B. 581. *Cf. Pomphrey* v. *Cuthbertson*, 1951 S.C. 147.
31 1909 S.C. 510.
32 *Ibid.* 520.
33 *Elliott Steam Tug Co.* v. *Shipping Controller* [1922] 1 K.B. 127, 140, *per* Scrutton L.J. *Cf. Weir* v. *Dobell* [1916] 1 K.B. 722.
34 [1932] A.C. 452, especially *per* Sankey L.C. at 471, and in C.A. (1931) 47 T.L.R. 359 at 361, *per* Scrutton L.J.
35 [1929] 1 K.B. 400.
36 The firm was in fact Scottish.

claiming from another money to which he knows he is not entitled—a proceeding which will ruin his credit in the business world." [37] "A person is not obliged to minimise damages on behalf of another who has broken his contract, if by doing so he would have injured his commercial reputation by getting a bad name in the trade." [38]

Further a pursuer is not bound to do anything outside the ordinary course of his business,[39] nor to compromise a claim,[40] nor to spend money to minimise the damages.[41] In *Lesters Leather Co.* v. *Home and Overseas Brokers Ltd.*,[42] the plaintiffs bought snake-skins which were rejected when found not to be merchantable. They sued for damages for non-delivery and recovered the price and £2,000 for loss of profit. The defendants appealed, contending that the plaintiffs should have mitigated their damages by buying skins available in India. It was held that the buyers were under no duty to send to India with a view to obtaining goods 8 or 9 months after the delivery date of the original contract. But some benefit was allowed to the sellers because on the evidence they might have bought in India, but that was all that the seller could expect as there was no available market in Britain. The familiar concept of " available market " is a useful touchstone and prima facie it would appear that a disappointed party is not bound to go far if at all beyond the " market " in the quest for alternative means of supply or disposal. In *Sopers of Harrow Ltd.* v. *Johnston* [43] the defendants sold to the plaintiffs, retailers of food, a quantity of a beverage which was misdescribed and in breach of statutory warranty of quality. In an action for breach by misdescription and breach of warranty the defendants contended that the plaintiffs could have minimised their damages by adding the deficient sugar, by attaching a fresh label to the bottles and by reselling the goods to an offeror inspired by the defendants. It was held that they were not required to take any such steps, as they were not in the circumstances reasonable steps. In *Pilkington* v. *Wood* [44] a solicitor negligently failed to secure a good title to the purchaser of a house. It was held in an action against him that the purchaser was under no duty to have first sued the seller under the covenant for title [45] as it was no part of his duty to embark on a complicated litigation to protect the solicitor from the consequences of his own negligence.

No duty prior to breach

The duty to act so as to minimise or mitigate damages only arises when the wrongful act or breach of obligation has been committed. Hence

37 *Ibid.* at p. 410, *per* Scrutton L.J.
38 *Ibid.* at p. 418, *per* Sankey L.J. *Cf. Banco de Portugal* v. *Waterlow* [1932] A.C. 452.
39 *Dunkirk Colliery Co.* v. *Lever* (1878) 9 Ch.D. 20; *British Westinghouse* v. *Underground Ry.* [1912] A.C. 673, 689.
40 *Biggin* v. *Permanite* [1951] 1 K.B. 422; revd. in part [1951] 2 K.B. 314.
41 *Jewelowski* v. *Propp* [1944] 1 K.B. 510; *Henderson* v. *Turnbull*, 1909 S.C. 510, 520.
42 (1948) 64 T.L.R. 569.
43 [1944] 2 All E.R. 42; affd. *ibid.* 586.
44 [1953] 1 Ch. 770.
45 *Scoticé* warrandice.

in case of anticipatory breach, where repudiation of a contract is intimated before the due date for performance has arrived, the duty to mitigate damages does not arise until and unless the repudiation has been accepted and the breach becomes effective, or if it is not accepted, until the due date for performance arrives without due performance being tendered.[46]

If anticipatory breach be made but not accepted by the other party, no obligation to take steps to minimise the loss becomes incumbent until the due date for performance arrives and due performance is not then made, when the breach of contract becomes effective and the measure of damages is quantified by reference to prices ruling on that date.

If the contract is repudiated by anticipation and the other party treats the repudiation as a present breach and brings his action without waiting for the contractual date of performance, he must in the usual way take reasonable steps to mitigate his loss.[47] A question may arise as to the proper measure of damages, whether they must be assessed by reference to the forward market prices and rates quoted for the contractual date of performance at the date the breach is accepted, or by reference to the spot rates or prices as existing at the due date of performance. If the market is working properly there would be no difference in the two rates. In *Brown* v. *Muller* [48] damages were quantified at the date for performance and it was said that the plaintiff was not bound to accept the forward prices ruling at the date the breach was intimated. The same occurred in *Roper* v. *Johnson* [49] but it was said that, if it were reasonable the plaintiff should mitigate his damages by determining them by the prices at the date of the breach. In *Roth* v. *Taysen* [50] it was held that the plaintiff, if he had acted reasonably, would have fixed his damages by prices at the date of breach and could only claim them on that basis. Hence it would appear that the party claiming damages must quantify them on whatever basis results in a lesser amount being claimed. In *Melachrino* v. *Nickoll and Knight* [51] it was decided that, if the seller can show that the buyer acted unreasonably in not buying in against him at once, the damages will have to be quantified by reference to the market price at the date on which the buyer had a reasonable opportunity and ought to have gone into the market to mitigate the damages. Hence where the buyer did not in fact buy in at the date of breach and the price had fallen below the contract price by the date of performance, he was not allowed to claim damages measured by what he would have sustained if he had bought at the date of breach, and only nominal damages were awarded. The true rule was laid down [52] as being

46 *Wilson* v. *Hicks* (1857) 26 L.J.Ex. 242; *Brown* v. *Muller* (1872) L.R. 7 Ex. 319; *Hudson* v. *Hill* (1874) 43 L.J.C.P. 273; *Roth* v. *Taysen* (1896) 12 T.L.R. 211; *Tredegar Co.* v. *Hawthorn* (1902) 18 T.L.R. 716; *Michael* v. *Hart* [1902] 1 K.B. 482; *Payzu* v. *Saunders* [1919] 2 K.B. 581; *Melachrino* v. *Nickoll* [1920] 1 K.B. 693; *Millett* v. *Van Heek* [1921] 2 K.B. 369.

47 *Roth* v. *Taysen* (1896) 12 T.L.R. 211.

48 (1872) L.R. 7 Ex. 319.

49 (1873) L.R. 8 C.P. 167.

50 (1896) 12 T.L.R. 211 approved in *Nickoll* v. *Ashton* [1900] 2 Q.B. 298.

51 [1920] 1 K.B. 693.

52 [1920] 1 K.B. at 699 *per* Bailhache J.

that " where there is anticipatory breach by a seller to deliver goods for which there is a market at a fixed date the buyer without buying against the seller may bring his action at once, but that if he does so his damages must be assessed with reference to the market price of the goods at the time when they ought to have been delivered under the contract. If the action comes to trial before the contractual date for delivery has arrived the court must arrive at that price as best it can.

" To this rule there is one exception for the benefit of the defaulting seller—namely, that if he can show that the buyer acted unreasonably in not buying against him the date to be taken is the date at which the buyer ought to have gone into the market to mitigate damages."

It would appear then from these cases that in the case of an anticipatory breach, accepted as discharging the contract, the party claiming damages must assess them by reference either to the forward market rates for the date of performance quoted at the date of breach, or to the spot rates or prices as existing at the due date of performance, whichever is the lesser.

So, too, the captain, owner or charterer of a vessel is not bound to accept any offer inconsistent with his subsisting charterparty before there has been a final breach thereof by the other party and accepted by him,[53] and an owner cannot claim damages for detention of the ship, if that were avoidable by a reasonable course.[54]

Failure to mitigate

If it is sought to prove that due diligence was not shown by the pursuer in efforts to mitigate the loss sustained in consequence of the defender's breach of contract, the onus of proof will rest on the party in breach as he will be complaining that the damages claimed are greater than need have been incurred, and it is primarily in his interests that the mitigation should be as complete as possible, or that any substantial failure to minimise the consequences should be brought home to the pursuer.[55] But it is established that the court will not judge the pursuer's actings too strictly and will not fault him for any or every slight error of judgment. In particular they will not reduce the damages merely because the defender can show in the light of subsequent knowledge that the pursuer's action was not the very best he might have taken in the circumstances, or that some alternative course of action might or would have been preferable. This has been repeatedly affirmed in the highest courts. In *Clippens Oil Co.* v. *Edinburgh Water Trs.*,[56] Lord Collins said: " I think the wrongdoer is not entitled to criticise the course honestly taken by the injured person on the advice of his experts even though it should appear by the light of after

[53] *Harries* v. *Edmonds* (1845) 1 C. & K. 686; *Hudson* v. *Hill* (1874) 43 L.J.C.P. 273.

[54] *Hick* v. *Rodocanachi* [1891] 2 Q.B. 626, 632; *The Arne* [1904] P. 154; *cf. Carlberg* v. *Wemyss Coal Co.*, 1915 S.C. 616; *Weir* v. *Dobell* [1916] 1 K.B. 722. See also *Wallems Rederi A/S* v. *Muller* [1927] 2 K.B. 99.

[55] *Roper* v. *Johnson* (1873) L.R. 8 C.P. 167; *Melachrino* v. *Nickoll* [1920] 1 K.B. 693; *Finlay* v. *Kwik Hoo Tong* [1929] 1 K.B. 400.

[56] 1907 S.C.(H.L.) 9, 14.

events that another course might have saved loss." [57] So, too, in the *Banco de Portugal* case,[58] Lord Macmillan said: "Where the sufferer from a breach of contract finds himself in consequence of that breach placed in a position of embarrassment the measures which he may be drawn to adopt in order to extricate himself ought not to be weighed in nice scales at the instance of the party whose breach of contract has occasioned the difficulty."

In *Connal, Cotton & Co.* v. *Fisher Renwick & Co.*[59] a shipowner broke his contract to carry goods to Montreal. The shipper alleged that owing to the lateness of the season and the closure of the St. Lawrence by ice he could not procure another steamer to Montreal but had to send his goods by a more circuitous route at greater cost. The shipowners pleaded in reply to a claim for damages amounting to the difference between the contract rate and the carriage actually paid, that the shipper was bound to justify conveyance by a means so much more costly. It was held that the onus was on the shipowner to show that the mode of conveyance adopted was more expensive than was reasonably necessary and that he was liable on failing to show this.

A buyer's failure to inspect the goods timeously may result in some item of loss being incurred which would have been avoidable by reasonable inspection and, if this is so, loss so far as avoidable by such inspection will not be included in the damages recoverable.[60]

If, however, reasonable steps have not in fact been taken to mitigate damages, then the sum awarded cannot exceed the sum which would have been due, had the loss been minimised.[61]

Excessive expenditure

It would appear moreover that a party who adopts a more expensive course than necessary for the restoration of his position cannot recover from the wrongdoing party any more than the cost of the reasonably necessary steps adopted in the normal manner. This appears from the case of *The Admiralty* v. *Aberdeen Steam Trawling Co. Ltd.*,[62] where a naval vessel, damaged in a collision for which the other ship was entirely to blame, was taken to Chatham for repairs. It was proved that the cost of docking at Chatham was greater than it would have been elsewhere and that the charge for the use of the dock was more than would have been charged at other docks where the repairs might reasonably have been carried out. It was therefore held that the pursuers were only entitled to recover under both heads the cost incurred in ordinary circumstances and usually paid for such repairs and not the full amount charged them in

57 *Cf.* in delict the "agony" rule: *The Bywell Castle* (1879) 4 P.D. 219.
58 [1932] A.C. 452, 506.
59 (1883) 10 R. 824.
60 *Carter* v. *Campbell* (1885) 12 R. 1075; *Wilson* v. *Carmichael* (1894) 21 R. 732.
61 *Wilson* v. *Hicks* (1857) 26 L.J.Ex. 242. *Cf. Houndsditch Warehouse Co.* v. *Waltex* [1944] K.B. 579; *Blythswood Motors* v. *Raeside*, 1966 S.L.T.(Sh.Ct.) 13.
62 1910 S.C. 553: *cf.* also *Pomphrey* v. *Cuthbertson*, 1951 S.C. 147.

consequence of the particular course of action adopted by the pursuers. Or as Lord Patrick expressed it in *Pomphrey* v. *Cuthbertson* [63]: "The party aggrieved must take all reasonable steps to mitigate the resulting loss. He is not entitled to adopt a method of restoring himself to a position equivalent to that which he occupied before the casualty if there is another and cheaper method of effecting such restoration."

Compromise offers

It has been held moreover in England that a disappointed buyer in the case of the breach of a contract of sale by the seller may have to accept an offer made by the seller by way of compromise, with a view to mitigating damages, such as to take the defective goods off the buyer's hands. In *Houndsditch Warehouse Co.* v. *Waltex* [64] the plaintiffs bought goods and later, alleging they were disconform to sample, sued for damages for breach of contract. The defendants offered to take back all the goods which were still in the same condition as delivered and refund the price. The plaintiffs refused; it was held that the offer was genuine and not a tactical manoeuvre to dispose of the action and that the plaintiffs had acted unreasonably in refusing it without obtaining a definition of its precise terms. If it were made outside the action and without prejudice to the rights of parties (as was found to be the case) the plaintiffs should have accepted it in mitigation of damages. On the other hand, if it were an offer to compromise part of the claim, the plaintiffs were under no obligation to accept it. It will, therefore, be a question of circumstances in each case depending on what is the nature of any offer made.

Similar questions may arise where an offer is made to perform the contract though on different terms, and it has been held that if a reasonable man would have accepted the offer, failure to do so may result in a reduction of the sum to be awarded on the ground of failure to mitigate the full claim of damages.[65] In *Hudson* v. *Hill* [66] charterers were unable to load a vessel and offered within the lay-days to provide a cargo if she would go to an island ninety miles off. It was held that the master was not bound to accept such an offer as he might reasonably believe it would amount to repudiating the original charter.

Increased loss

If a pursuer, reasonably and in bona fide, takes proper steps to mitigate damages and in the events which happen the injury he sustains is thereby increased, he is still entitled to recover the extra loss sustained, for he is not required to show perfect knowledge or exercise impossible foresight.[67]

[63] 1951 S.C. 147 at p. 162.
[64] [1944] K.B. 579. *Cf. Harries* v. *Edmonds* (1845) 1 C. & K. 686; *Wilson* v. *Hicks* (1857) 26 L.J.Ex. 242 (both charterparties); and *Biggin* v. *Permanite* [1951] 1 K.B. 422: revd. in part [1951] 2 K.B. 314.
[65] *Ross* v. *McFarlane* (1894) 21 R. 396.
[66] (1874) 43 L.J.C.P. 273.
[67] *Hales* v. *L.N.W. Ry.* (1863) 4 B. & S. 66; *Jones* v. *Watney* (1912) 28 T.L.R. 399; *cf. Bloor* v. *Liverpool Derricking Co.* [1936] 3 All E.R. 394.

Similarly a pursuer claiming damages in respect of personal injuries is entitled to claim for the cost of remedial treatment reasonably and bona fide, though fruitlessly or even mistakenly, incurred.[68] But if the medical treatment were so negligent as to be actionable, the results thereof would probably not be recoverable, as being *novus actus interveniens* and too remote.

Recovery of expenses

If the pursuer incurs expense and makes outlays in connection with alternative arrangements reasonably made in an effort to mitigate damages he may recover these sums from the party in breach of contract.[69] Where, however, the pursuer in the course of reasonable attempts to mitigate his damages and make alternative arrangements secures greater benefit to himself, as by getting goods better than the original contract would have provided him,[70] or making greater profit than the frustrated venture would have brought,[71] these elements must be taken into consideration and set off against the claim of damages. If the innocent party actually profits by the breach, he is only entitled to nominal damages.[72]

In *Cazalet* v. *Morris* [73] charterers were unable to discharge a ship within the lay-days owing to a shortage of railway wagons and the shipowners completed the discharge of the cargo into lighters from which it was transferred to railway wagons as these became available. It was held that the shipowners were entitled to take such a step on their own responsibility and their action had materially reduced the period during which the vessel would otherwise have been on demurrage, and consequently that they were entitled to recover the outlay on the lighters from the charterers to the extent of the demurrage claim thereby saved.

Allowance for benefits

Furthermore if any action reasonably taken by a pursuer to mitigate damages should result to his advantage, such fact must be taken into consideration to offset the damages recoverable.[74] So in *British Westinghouse Electric Co.* v. *Underground Electric Railways* [75] the appellants provided machinery which failed to satisfy the contractual requirements with respect to economy and steam consumption. After some period of unsatisfactory working the respondents replaced the machines with others which, it was proved, would have been more efficient and economical than

68 *Rubens* v. *Walker*, 1946 S.C. 215.

69 *Staniforth* v. *Lyall* (1830) 7 Bing. 169; *Erie Gas Co.* v. *Carroll* [1911] A.C. 105; *British Westinghouse Co.* v. *Underground Rys. Ltd.* [1912] A.C. 673; *Banco de Portugal* v. *Waterlow* [1932] A.C. 452, 506.

70 *British Westinghouse, supra.*

71 *Staniforth, supra.*

72 *Ibid.*

73 1916 S.C. 952, 963.

74 This is the case even though it would have been no breach of the duty to mitigate not to take the action in question: *Staniforth* v. *Lyall* (1830) 7 Bing. 169; *Erie County Gas Co.* v. *Carroll* [1911] A.C. 105; *Wertheim* v. *Chicoutimi Pulp Co.* [1911] A.C. 301.

75 [1912] A.C. 673.

the original machines, even if these had complied with the contract specification, and that it would have been to the pecuniary advantage of the respondents to have replaced the machines at their own cost independently of the failure. The respondents were found entitled to damages in respect of the period during which they used the inefficient machines and to the cost of the replacement machines but under deduction of a sum representing the benefit obtained by their replacement by more efficient machines. Viscount Haldane said that the plaintiff was not under any obligation to take any step which a reasonable and prudent man would not ordinarily take in the course of his business. " But when in the course of his business he has taken action arising out of the transaction, which action has diminished his loss, the effect in actual diminution of the loss he has suffered may be taken into account even though there was no duty on him to act." [76] . . . " Provided the course taken to protect himself by the plaintiff in such an action was one which a reasonable and prudent person might in the ordinary course of business properly have taken, and in fact did take whether bound to or not, a jury or an arbitrator may properly look at the whole of the facts and ascertain the result in estimating the quantum of damage." [77]

From such a case must be distinguished such cases as *Bradburn* v. *G.W. Ry.*[78] where it was held that a sum recovered under an insurance policy by a person seeking damages for personal injury due to negligence should not be considered, as this advantage was derived from a wholly separate contract, independent of the relations between the parties to the action of negligence; as regards the latter it is *res inter alios acta.* Similarly, in *Morison & Milne* v. *Bartolomeo and Massa,*[79] a ship collision case, the jury found for the pursuers and awarded damages, and added to the verdict the remark that the pursuers had already received a sum under a policy of insurance. It was held that the pursuers were entitled to decree for the full amount of the damages, without deduction of the insurance money. Insurance benefits are accordingly collateral and cannot be used in mitigation of damages.[80]

A defender may also prove in mitigation of damages that the pursuer was in consequence of the defender's breach of contract enabled to execute other contracts, the profit from which is to be taken into account to balance the loss on the contract with the defender.[81] But for this argument to be

[76] *British Westinghouse, supra,* at p. 689; *Re Vic Mill* [1913] 1 Ch. 465, 473; *Payzu* v. *Saunders* [1919] 2 K.B. 581, 586; *Houndsditch Warehouse Co.* v. *Waltex* [1944] K.B. 579; *Demby Hamilton* v. *Barden* [1949] 1 All E.R. 435.

[77] *British Westinghouse, supra,* at p. 690; *cf. Erie Gas Co.* v. *Carroll* [1911] A.C. 105 and *Wertheim* v. *Chicoutimi Pulp Co.* [1911] A.C. 301.

[78] (1875) L.R. 10 Ex. 1. See also *Jebsen* v. *E. & W. India Dock Co.* (1875) L.R. 10 C.P. 300; *British Westinghouse, supra*; *Banco de Portugal* v. *Waterlow* [1932] A.C. 452, 473; *Yates* v. *Whyte* (1838) 4 Bing.N.C. 272; *Simpson* v. *Thomson* (1877) 3 App.Cas. 285; *Shearman* v. *Folland* [1950] 2 K.B. 43.

[79] (1867) 5 M. 848.

[80] *Port-Glasgow and Newark Sailcloth Co.* v. *Caledonian Ry.* (1892) 19 R. 608.

[81] *Hill* v. *Showell* (1918) 87 L.J.K.B. 1106 (H.L.). *Cf. Tyne Tug and Steamboat Federation Co. Ltd.* (1917) 142 L.T.J. 239 (where losses and gains on different instalments had to be balanced and set off); *Collard* v. *Carswell* (1892) 19 R. 987.

successful it must be shown by the defender that the alternative contracts could only have been executed in consequence of and dependent on the failure of the prime contracts: if the pursuer can show that he would still have executed the extra work even if the contract in question had not been breached the argument fails and no deduction falls to be made.[82] Exceptionally it may even be shown by the defender that the alternative was more profitable in which case only nominal damages can be recovered for the original breach.[83]

A defender may also show that the subject-matter of the contract is worth less by reason of some misconduct or breach of obligation by the pursuer.[84]

Inability to mitigate

In the *Liesbosch* case [85] it was held that damages recoverable could not be increased because the financial embarrassment of the plaintiffs prevented their taking action in mitigation by obtaining a replacement vessel. Their financial position was a collateral matter not resulting from the wrong and not imputable to the defendants. If however damage sustained is truly a consequence of the wrongful act and the pursuer is thereby unable through lack of funds to minimise the damages he is not in breach of the obligation to act reasonably. The wrongdoer must take the pursuer as he finds him and cannot complain if he is not in a position to mitigate damages.[86] So too in *British Stamp Machine Co.* v. *Haynes* [87] the defendant was in breach of an agreement to take two machines on hire and these the plaintiffs made no attempt to relet during the whole period of hire. They were held entitled as damages to hire only for the time the plaintiffs would reasonably require to relet the machines to another, and the fact that they always kept a stock of machines was a special circumstance not in the contemplation of both parties and consequently too remote.

82 *Hill, supra. Cf. Mackenzie* v. *Liddell* (1883) 10 R. 705.
83 *Staniforth* v. *Lyall* (1830) 7 Bing. 169.
84 *Allen* v. *Cameron* (1833) 1 Cr. & M. 832; *Street* v. *Blay* (1831) 2 B. & Ad. 456; *Poulton* v. *Lattimore* (1829) 9 B. & C. 259.
85 *Liesbosch Dredger* v. *S.S. Edison* [1933] A.C. 449, 460.
86 *Ibid.* 461; *Clippens Oil Co.* v. *Edinburgh and Dist. Water Trs.*, 1907 S.C.(H.L.) 9, 14, *per* Lord Collins.
87 [1921] 1 K.B. 377.

CHAPTER 29

CLAIMS ARISING OUT OF THE FORMATION OF CONTRACTS

THE negotiations and transactions leading up to the conclusion of a contract sometimes give rise to claims for damages.

Offers open for specified time

The inclusion in an offer to contract of a clause that the offer shall be open to acceptance for a specified period or up till a certain time may have the effect of intimating exclusion of any acceptances received after the closing date.[1] In general, however, such a clause stating that an offer is open for a certain time amounts to an enforceable promise to keep the offer open for that time, and the offeror will be bound contractually by an acceptance given within the specified period.[2] It follows, too, that the offeror will be liable in damages for failure to keep the offer open for that period, on the ground that the promise constitutes a binding and enforceable obligation. In *Littlejohn* v. *Hadwen*,[3] an offer to sell heritage was phrased so as to give the pursuer the option for ten days; it was withdrawn within that time and subsequently, but within the ten-day period, the pursuer accepted, and maintained that a valid contract was concluded. The Lord Ordinary (Fraser) was of the opinion that an offer in that form was not revocable and that the pursuer had the right to accept within the ten days, whether the offer were withdrawn or not. Such an offer was in fact an obligation inferring legal consequences if anyone chose to accept it within the period.

The measure of the damages recoverable in such a case is nowhere laid down. On principle, it is suggested that a suitable measure would be the difference between the price at which the offer was accepted and the price which the disappointed would-be purchaser requires to pay to obtain a substitute from an alternative source of supply. But in the case of an offer for the sale of heritage, difficult questions may arise as the buyer normally has, in view of the *pretium affectionis* attaching to heritage, the right to sue for specific implement of the contract of sale, or only alternatively for damages.[4] The difficulty of assessment in such a case would

[1] *Heys* v. *Kimball and Morton* (1890) 17 R. 381, *per* Ld. Pres. Inglis.

[2] Bell, *Prin.* § 72; Bankton, I, 11; More's Notes to Stair, 58; Brodie's Supplement to Stair, 906; *Marshall* v. *Blackwood*, 1747, Elchies, *voce* Sale, No. 6 and notes; *Thomson* v. *James* (1855) 18 D. 1, 11, 18.

[3] (1822) 20 S.L.R. 5 (O.H.).

[4] *Cf.* also the facts in *Dickinson* v. *Dodds* (1876) 2 Ch.D. 463, where D offered to B a house for sale at £800, the offer to be open for two days. D sold to A within that time, and the plaintiff (B) accepted also within the time limit. In Scotland he would have been entitled to damages. In England he failed, as he was held to know of the prior acceptance, and the promise to keep the offer open was unenforceable for lack of consideration. See *Pollock on Contract*, 13th ed., 24, who considers the matter on principle.

make such damages somewhat conjectural, but difficulty of assessment is *per se* no ground for refusing a claim of damages.[5]

In the same way an undertaking to keep an offer open until the occurrence of a certain event is binding, even though the offeree should not be bound to accept. So in *Graham & Co.* v. *Pollock* [6] Pollock sold tobacco to Graham subject to the condition that Graham should inspect a book with particulars of the consignment before deciding whether or not to adhere to the bargain. Pollock resold to a third party before this and it was held that Graham was entitled to damages as Pollock was bound to sell to Graham until and unless he made his election not to buy after having inspected the shipping book. The rule of differences would again appear or be the appropriate measure of damages in such a case.

Where a fixed time is specified for acceptance of an offer, it is sufficient compliance with this condition if the acceptance is dispatched before the time-limit expires, even though it should not be received by the offeror until afterwards.[7]

Illegal contracts

While the fundamental characteristic of illegal contracts is that *ex turpi causa non oritur actio*, some such contracts are totally ineffective in law but not others. A contract declared by statute or common law to be void is totally ineffective. In *Bowmakers* v. *Barnet* [8] it was laid down that no claim founded on an illegal contract will be enforced by the court but this rule is not universal. Knowledge of the parties may be material in cases where a contract *ex facie* lawful is intended to be put by the other party to an illegal use. So if A hires a car to B in ignorance of B's intention to use it in connection with house-breaking, he can probably recover damages for injury to the car [9]; it is otherwise if he knows of the illegal purpose,[10] and B cannot recover damages for A's failure to supply the car.[11] The defence of ignorance is of limited scope, confined by the maxim *ignorantia juris haud excusat* and the fact that circumstances may

[5] *Chaplin* v. *Hicks* [1911] 2 K.B. 786.

[6] (1763) Mor. 14198. Observe that a contract of this kind with one party not bound is neither a sale nor an agreement to sell under the Sale of Goods Act 1893, s. 25, or the Factors Act 1889, s. 8: see *Helby* v. *Matthews* [1895] A.C. 471.

[7] *Jacobson* v. *Underwood* (1894) 21 R. 654; *Bruner* v. *Moore* [1904] 1 Ch. 305. See also *Dunlop* v. *Higgins* (1847) 9 D. 1407; affd. (1848) 6 Bell's App. 195 (acceptance delayed in post), and *Household Fire Insurance Co.* v. *Grant* (1879) 4 Ex.D. 216 (application for company shares never received). But compare with this *Mason* v. *Benhar Coal Co.* (1882) 9 R. 883, *per* Lord Shand at p. 890.

[8] [1945] K.B. 65. *Cf. Parkinson* v. *College of Ambulance* [1925] 2 K.B. 1.

[9] *Millward* v. *Littlewood* (1850) 5 Ex. 775; *Spiers* v. *Hunt* [1908] 1 K.B. 720. But see *Siveyer* v. *Allison* [1935] 2 K.B. 403.

[10] *Jennings* v. *Throgmorton* (1825) Ry. & M. 251; *Appleton* v. *Campbell* (1826) 2 C. & P. 347; *Pearce* v. *Brooks* (1866) L.R. 1 Ex. 213; *Upfill* v. *Wright* [1911] 1 K.B. 506 (lettings for immoral purposes). See also *Cowan* v. *Milbourn* (1867) L.R. 2 Ex. 230.

[11] *Berg* v. *Sadler and Moore* [1937] 2 K.B. 158.

be taken to affect the party with constructive knowledge.[12] Where both parties know of the illegality neither party can sue on the contract.[13]

When under a contract of employment deductions were made from wages in contravention of the Truck Acts it was held that the whole contract was on that account void *ab initio* and accordingly the employers could not enforce a counterclaim of damages for breach of contract.[14]

When, however, the contract is illegal but not wholly ineffective damages may be recoverable for a breach. Certainly where the illegal element is separable from another legal element, the taint of illegality and hence the prohibition of enforcement measures only extends so far as the contract is illegal.[15]

Where a contract is such that it may be performed in either a legal or an illegal manner, it will be presumed that the legal manner will be adopted and hence a claim of damages will be competent unless it is proved that the intention was to perform it in the illegal manner.[16]

Contracts entered into under error

When a contract is vitiated by error affecting the intention of either or both parties to it, it is conceived that a claim of damages will never lie so long as the error is uninduced by one of the parties, but only if the error is induced by misrepresentation.[17]

Contracts induced by misrepresentation

When one party enters into a contract under error which is induced by the misrepresentations of the other party damages are sometimes recoverable. A misrepresentation [18] consists in an untrue statement of fact [19] or of the speaker's view of the law [20] made by one party to the other, before or at the time of contracting, relating to some present fact or past event connected with the subject of the contract which is a material cause in inducing the concluding of the contract on the terms on which it is actually entered upon.[21] It may be effected either innocently, negligently, or fraudulently, and the distinction is highly material on the topic of damages. Innocent misrepresentation involves honest but mistaken

12 *Cf. Taylor* v. *Barnett* [1953] 1 W.L.R. 562.

13 *Scott* v. *Brown, Doering, McNab & Co.* [1892] 2 Q.B. 724; *Gordon* v. *Metropolitan Police Commr.* [1910] 2 K.B. 1080. *Cf. Hamilton* v. *Waring*, May 21, 1816, F.C.; *Stewart* v. *Gibson* (1860) 1 Rob.App. 260; *Jackson, Stansfield & Sons* v. *Butterworth* (1948) 64 T.L.R 481; *Bostel Bros.* v. *Hurlock* [1949] 1 K.B. 74; *Boissevain* v. *Weil* [1949] 1 K.B. 482; *Jamieson* v. *Watt's Trustee*, 1950 S.C. 265; *Howden* v. *Irving* (1950) 66 Shf.Ct.Rep. 107. See also *Howell* v. *Falmouth Boat Construction Co.* [1951] A.C. 837.

14 *Duncan* v. *Motherwell Bridge and Engineering Co.*, 1952 S.C. 131, 146, 157, 159.

15 *Re Prudential Assurance Co.'s Trust Deed* [1934] Ch. 338.

16 *Waugh* v. *Morris* (1873) L.R. 8 Q.B. 202; *Hindley* v. *General Fibre Co.* [1940] 2 K.B. 517.

17 On error generally see *Gloag on Contract*, Chap. XXVI; Walker, *Principles*, Chap. 33.

18 See generally *Gloag on Contract*, Chap. XXVII.

19 *Edgington* v. *Fitzmaurice* (1885) 29 Ch.D. 459; *Anderson* v. *Pacific Insce. Co.* (1872) L.R. 7 C.P. 65; *Re Ambrose Mining Co.* (1880) 14 Ch.D. 390; *Angus* v. *Clifford* [1891] 2 Ch. 449, 470.

20 *Rashdall* v. *Ford* (1866) L.R. 2 Eq. 750; *Hirschfield* v. *L.B. & S.C. Ry.* (1876) 2 Q.B.D. 1.

21 *Behn* v. *Burness* (1863) 3 B. & S. 751; *Heilbut, Symons & Co.* v. *Buckleton* [1913] A.C. 30, 36.

belief misleading the other party [22]; negligent misrepresentation involves a failure to take the care in inquiry due in the circumstances and a consequent misleading of the other party [23]; fraudulent misrepresentation involves wilful and conscious falsehood designed to deceive.[24] " Fraud is proved when it is shown that a false representation has been made knowingly, or without belief in its truth, or recklessly, careless whether it be true or false." [25] In general, while rescission of a contract induced by material misrepresentation is competent in any case, it is only exceptionally in the case of innocent but generally in the case of negligent or fraudulent misrepresentation that damages are recoverable.[26] Negligent or fraudulent misrepresentation, that is, renders the contract voidable [27] and is also a ground of action *ex delicto* for damages for the negligence or deceit involved. But till the contract is avoided it remains valid and binding and third parties may acquire enforceable rights and interests.

A representation is distinct from a warranty, which the maker undertakes will be exactly and literally accurate, as in a representation the undertaking is only that there is no substantial untruth.[28]

Exclusion of liability for misrepresentation

An express term in the contract may exclude liability for misrepresentation, as in the case of *Boyd & Forrest* v. *G.S.W. Ry.*,[29] and if the misrepresentation in question is interpreted as falling within the scope of the clause, action for rescission of the contract on that ground will be barred. But probably such a clause could not on grounds of public policy be pleaded as a defence to relevant averments of fraudulent misrepresentation. " It is a sound principle . . . that the terms of a contract . . . cannot be founded on as a protection against fraud of either contracting party. It could not be so . . . even although the contract were expressed in such a particular." [30]

Innocent misrepresentation

A contract is accordingly reducible on the ground of innocent misrepresentation whether or not that misrepresentation produced such error in the mind of the representee as to preclude any real consent on his part. But unless exceptionally, damages cannot be claimed for innocent

22 *Angus* v. *Clifford* [1891] 2 Ch. 449; *Low* v. *Bouverie* [1891] 3 Ch. 82; *Le Lievre* v. *Gould* [1893] 1 Q.B. 491; *Boyd and Forrest* v. *G.S.W. Ry.*, 1912 S.C.(H.L.) 93.
23 *Hedley Byrne & Co.* v. *Heller & Partners* [1964] A.C. 465.
24 *Cf.* Bell, *Prin.* § 13. " Fraud is a machination or contrivance to deceive."
25 *Derry* v. *Peek* (1889) 14 App.Cas. 337, 374, *per* Lord Herschell.
26 *Heilbut, Symons & Co.* v. *Buckleton* [1913] A.C. 30; *Barnes* v. *Cadogan Developments Ltd.* [1930] 1 Ch. 479.
27 *Western Bank* v. *Addie* (1867) 5 M.(H.L.) 80.
28 *Brownlie* v. *Miller* (1880) 7 R.(H.L.) 66; *Pennsylvania S.S. Co.* v. *Compagnie Nationale de Navigation* [1936] 2 All E.R. 1167.
29 1915 S.C.(H.L.) 20, 35–36; *cf. Arnison* v. *Smith* (1889) 41 Ch.D. 348; *Pearson* v. *Dublin Corpn.* [1907] A.C. 351; *Hedley Byrne & Co., supra.*
30 *Boyd and Forrest, supra, per* Lord Shaw. See also *Pearson, supra.*

misrepresentation.[31] In *Gilchester Properties* v. *Gomm* [32] the seller of a house innocently misrepresented that the rents derived from leases were higher than they were in fact. It was held that the buyer could not demand specific performance of the contract with an abatement of the purchase price in respect that such an abatement would be in effect to give damages for an innocent misrepresentation. So too in *Boyd and Forrest* v. *G.S.W. Ry.*, the claim for *quantum meruit* or damages for extra work consequent on an innocent misrepresentation was virtually an award of damages and hence refused on appeal.[33]

The exceptional cases where damages may be recovered for innocent misrepresentation are:—

(i) where the representation is a warranty;
(ii) in cases of breach of warranty of authority;
(iii) under the Companies Acts.

Representation and warranty

It is frequently a matter of importance and difficulty to distinguish between a representation inducing the contract but which is not intended by the parties to be incorporated into and form a term of the contract, sometimes called a mere representation, and, on the other hand, one which does so constitute a term of the contract, forming an undertaking or warranty for the truth of which the party making the representation is liable, and on which depends the validity of the contract as a source of legal obligation. When one party makes an untrue representation to the other though not fraudulently, that may constitute a ground for reducing the contract but not for an award of damages as that party is neither in breach of contract nor guilty of the delict of fraud.[34] If, however, that representation is to be construed as a warranty that the facts are truly as represented, the untruth of the representation constitutes a breach of a term of the contract for which damages may be claimed,[35] thus constituting an exception to the general rule that no damages will lie for an innocent misrepresentation.

It is probably generally true that a statement inducing the contract, as to a matter collateral to the subject of the contract rather than to the subject itself is only a representation,[36] though any statement may be expressly made a warranty for the accuracy of which the party pledges himself, as in life insurance contracts.[37] Under the Sale of Goods Act,[38]

31 *Redgrave* v. *Hurd* (1881) 20 Ch.D. 1; *Harrison* v. *Knowles and Foster* [1918] 1 K.B. 608, 610, *per* Scrutton L.J.; *Gilchester Properties Ltd.* v. *Gomm* [1948] 1 All E.R. 493; *Manners* v. *Whitehead* (1898) 1 F. 171; *Brownlie* v. *Miller* (1878) 5 R. 1076; affd. (1880) 7 R.(H.L.) 66; *Dunnett* v. *Mitchell* (1887) 15 R. 131; *Boyd and Forrest* v. *G.S.W. Ry.*, 1912 S.C.(H.L.) 93.

32 [1948] 1 All E.R. 493, applying *Heilbut, Symons & Co.* v. *Buckleton* [1913] A.C. 30.

33 1915 S.C.(H.L.) 20.

34 *Manners* v. *Whitehead* (1898) 1 F. 171.

35 *Heilbut, Symons & Co.* v. *Buckleton* [1913] A.C. 30; *Lawrence* v. *Hull* (1924) 41 T.L.R. 75.

36 *Stewart* v. *Kennedy* (1890) 17 R.(H.L.) 25; *Menzies* v. *Menzies* (1893) 20 R.(H.L.) 108; *Hart* v. *Fraser*, 1907 S.C. 50.

37 *Thomson* v. *Weems* (1884) 11 R.(H.L.) 48.

38 s. 13.

a statement relating to the existing state of the subject-matter of the contract, where the contract is a sale by description, or by sample and description, is a warranty by the seller and not a representation. The question is not determined by the use of writing [39] or any form of words.[40] But a representation as to credit must be evidenced in writing [41] whether the parties intended the representation complained of to be a warranty or not.[42] Otherwise it is a question to be determined on the whole evidence available in the case. Breach of warranty will not necessarily entitle the party to rescind the whole contract if the breach is not in a vital particular, but this leaves the right to damages unaffected. Moreover when a representation is construed as a warranty, the untruth of the statement itself gives a ground of action, whereas if the representation amounts to a fraudulent misrepresentation, all the constituent elements of fraud require to be proved to entitle the pursuer to an award of damages.[43]

Measure of damages

Where an untrue representation inducing the contract is held to have been intended as a warranty damages are recoverable for all loss directly and naturally resulting from such breach of contract. Such would amount in the ordinary case to the difference between the consideration which the party gave for the contract and the amount he would have given had he been informed that the warranted item of information was otherwise, or alternatively what he would have given to enter upon the same contract at the same time with another party but without the offending warranty.

Misrepresentation of authority

A further exception to the general rule that an action of damages will not lie against a person who honestly makes a misrepresentation which misleads another and thereby induces a contract, or possibly an independent principle,[44] is found in the case where an agent assumes an authority which he does not possess.[45] The principle of this has been expressed as being that " the obligation arising in such a case is well expressed by saying that a person professing to contract as agent for another, impliedly, if not expressly, undertakes to or promises to the person who enters into such contract, upon the faith of the professed agent being duly author-

39 *Brownlie* v. *Miller* (1880) 7 R.(H.L.) 66, 81; *Behn* v. *Burness* (1863) 3 B. & S. 751, 754.

40 *Brownlie* v. *Miller, supra*; *Stucley* v. *Baily* (1862) 1 H. & C. 405, 417. See also *Barnard* v. *Faber* [1893] 1 Q.B. 340, 343.

41 Mercantile Law Amendment Act 1856, s. 6; *Clydesdale Bank* v. *Paton* (1896) 23 R.(H.L.) 22, 27, 31.

42 *Hyslop* v. *Shirlaw* (1905) 7 F. 875, 881; *Scott* v. *Steele* (1857) 20 D. 253; *Robeson* v. *Waugh* (1874) 2 R. 63; *Rough* v. *Moir* (1875) 2 R. 529; *Robey* v. *Stein* (1900) 3 F. 278; *Paul* v. *Glasgow Corpn.* (1900) 3 F. 119; *Heilbut, Symons & Co.* v. *Buckleton* [1913] A.C. 30; *Hopkins* v. *Tanqueray* (1854) 15 C.B. 130; *Stucley* v. *Baily* (1862) 1 H. & C. 405, 416.

43 *Le Lievre* v. *Gould* [1893] 1 Q.B. 491; *Anderson* v. *Fitzgerald* (1853) 4 H.L.C. 484.

44 *Starkey* v. *Bank of England* [1903] A.C. 114; *Dickson* v. *Reuter's Telegram Co.* (1877) 3 C.P.D. 1.

45 *Firbanks' Exors.* v. *Humphreys* (1886) 18 Q.B.D. 54.

ised, that the authority he professes to have does in point of fact exist." [46] By a legal fiction he is presumed to have authority to contract so is liable for breach of contract if he has in fact no authority and cannot implement his contract.[47] So where the defendant signed a lease as agent for another from whom he had no authority to do so, though both parties believed he had, he was liable in damages,[46] or where auctioneers, after a selling race, sold a mare to the pursuer under the erroneous belief that they were commissioned to do so and the mare was reclaimed by the owner, they were liable in damages,[48] or where a broker instructed to apply for shares in one particular company, applied by mistake for shares in another company with a similar name,[49] or where directors issued debentures in excess of statutory limits,[45] or where, without the agent's knowledge, actual authority has expired by the death or insanity of his principal.[50]

The doctrine is not confined to contracts but extends to every business transaction wherein one party is induced to enter by a representation that the person with whom he is dealing has authority from some other person.[51] This case of course falls to be distinguished from the case where the agent possesses no authority to act as such; yet if he nevertheless represents to the contrary and consequently causes loss to the party with whom he contracts he is liable to be sued in delict for his fraud.[52, 53]

Measure of damages

The amount of damages for which an agent, who has assumed authority when in fact he had none and misrepresented his position, may be held liable is in general what the pursuer lost by losing that particular contract [54] or by reliance on the deception.[55] Where he has mistakenly entered upon a contract he will be liable to the party who contracts upon the faith of his representations, for any loss which may have been occasioned by and which results naturally and directly from acting in reliance on his representation [56]; so, too, where a person professing to have authority as agent induces another to act in a matter of business on the faith of his having that authority.[57] When he represents that he has authority to bind his principal to a contract, he will be liable for the loss

46 *Collen* v. *Wright* (1859) 8 E. & B. 647, 657, approved in *Anderson* v. *Croall* (1903) 6 F. 153, *per* Lord Stormonth-Darling.
47 Bell, *Comm.* I, 543n.; Pothier, *Obligations*, § 75; Gloag, 155.
48 *Anderson* v. *Croall, supra.*
49 *Re National Coffee Palace Co.* (1883) 24 Ch.D. 367.
50 *Yonge* v. *Toynbee* [1910] 1 K.B. 215.
51 *Firbanks* v. *Humphreys* (1886) 18 Q.B.D. 54; *Starkey* v. *Bank of England* [1903] A.C. 114; *cf. British-Russian Gazette* v. *Associated Newspapers* [1933] 2 K.B. 616.
52 *Polhill* v. *Walter* (1832) 3 B. & Ad. 114.
53 *Lewis* v. *Nicholson* (1852) 18 Q.B. 503.
54 *Meek* v. *Wendt* (1888) 21 Q.B.D. 126.
55 *Edwards* v. *Porter* [1923] 2 K.B. 538.
56 *Collen* v. *Wright* (1857) 7 E. & B. 301; affd. 8 E. & B. 647. But where the principal is insolvent the damages will possibly be nil: *Richardson* v. *Williamson* (1871) L.R. 6 Q.B. 276, 279, *per* Blackburn J.; *Weeks* v. *Propert* (1873) L.R. 8 C.P. 439.
57 *Starkey* v. *Bank of England* [1903] A.C. 114. See also *British-Russian Gazette* v. *Assoc. Newspapers* [1933] 2 K.B. 616.

of profit which the third party would have made if the representation had been true and the contract duly performed. So in *Anderson* v. *Croall* [58] the purchaser was held entitled to recover the difference between the price he had paid and the ascertained value of the horse, as representing the loss of the bargain, and an element for the trouble and outlay to which he was put before the action was raised. The net sum paid for the mare was, of course, recoverable on handing her back to the true owner. Lord Stormonth-Darling expressed the question as being " what would the pursuer here have gained if the contract had been made with authority, and, therefore, been enforceable? " [59]

Where an agent applied without authority for shares for a principal in a company which went into liquidation it was held that the damages for which he was liable were to be measured by taking the benefit which the company would have obtained if the principal had been actually bound to take the shares and the solvency of the alleged principal and the chance of the company's allotting those shares to other parties were matters relevant for consideration.[60] The principle of considering what benefit would have been gained if the contract had been enforceable was applied again in *Irving* v. *Burns* [61] where an agent contracted ostensibly on behalf of a company and the other party claimed damages from him for his breach of contract on finding that the company was not bound by the contract; the action was however dismissed as irrelevant as the pursuer's pleadings were that the company had no assets, and in consequence he had suffered no loss from the fact that the company was not bound and could not have benefited even if the authority had been valid and the contract completed. It would appear on principle that an award of nominal damages would have been appropriate in this case, but does not appear to have been suggested to the court,[62] though in this respect the decision is contrary to the general rule that any infringement of a right sounds in damages.[63]

The damages may include the cost of any legal proceedings undertaken unsuccessfully against the supposed principal to enforce performance of the contract or exact damages for its breach, provided the expenditure on such litigation was reasonably incurred, as where the professed agent was made aware of the litigation and either expressly sanctioned it, as by lodging defences or assisting in the defence, or impliedly sanctioned it, as by permitting it to go on and not disavowing his purported authority. In *Collen* v. *Wright* [64] an agent, in the belief that he had proper authority,

[58] (1903) 6 F. 153. Gloag's criticism (p. 157) is that the purchaser had only lost the chance of buying a horse which was not for sale. But had he not lost a horse at that price and also incurred expense and trouble in a fruitless purchase? As far as he was concerned, the horse was for sale and he lost a bargain, for which compensation must be made.

[59] *Anderson* v. *Croall, supra*, at p. 156. So too in *Godwin* v. *Francis* (1870) L.R. 5 C.P. 295, 306 (sale of estate).

[60] *Re National Coffee Palace Co.* (1883) 24 Ch.D. 367.

[61] 1915 S.C. 260.

[62] *Gloag on Contract*, 684.

[63] *Webster* v. *Cramond Iron Co.* (1875) 2 R. 752.

[64] *Collen* v. *Wright* (1857) 7 E. & B. 301; affd. 8 E. & B. 647.

let a farm to Collen on terms not authorised by the owner, who consequently refused to execute the lease or to give possession and defended a suit for specific performance: this action was intimated to the agent, who was held on the facts to have persisted in his assertion of authority and was consequently found liable in the expenses of the unsuccessful action, as well as for outlays on the farm incurred on the faith of the validity of the lease. So, too, where an architect ordered stone for a church, though without authority to do so from the body for whom he professed to act, and maintained his assertion of authority to the end, he was held liable to the mason with whom he had purported to contract, for the price of the stone and for the expenses of the latter's fruitless action for the price against the church committee.[65]

The agent persisted in assertions of his authority in *Hughes* v. *Graeme* [66] where a broker, acting for both parties, purported to sell wool on terms which the sellers later repudiated as unauthorised. The buyer was held entitled to recover from the broker, although the latter was his agent too, (a) damages for the loss of the bargain, (b) expenses paid to the successful sellers incurred in defending successfully an action by the buyer for specific performance and for an injunction against the sale of the wool elsewhere, and (c) the buyer's own taxed expenses of the action.

Principle of damages in cases of breach of warranty of authority

The representation by an agent that he possesses the authority from his principal to make the contract into which he purports to enter amounts to a warranty of its existence,[67] and carries an implied promise of indemnity to a person who acts upon the assumption that such authority in fact exists, against all loss which arises naturally and directly from the absence of such authority. In consequence such an agent is justifiably held liable for all loss which is incurred by the third party who acts to his detriment on the faith of the agreement into which the purported agent bears to lead him. The third party to whom the representation of authority is made, and who acts upon it, is entitled to believe that it is true and to act upon it as such. It follows that all loss which accrues to him from the falsity of the representation is properly chargeable against the agent who made it, if he must be taken to have intended that it should be acted upon.[68] But where the loss would have accrued to the pursuer whether or not the representation were justified, it cannot be held to be the consequence, either direct or indirect, of the false statement. So where a plaintiff unsuccessfully resisted an action of ejection brought against him by the

65 *Randall* v. *Trimen* (1856) 18 C.B. 786. See also *Hughes* v. *Graeme* (1864) 33 L.J.Q.B. 335; *Starkey* v. *Bank of England* [1902] 1 Ch. 665; affd. [1903] A.C. 114; *Yonge* v. *Toynbee* [1910] 1 K.B. 215; *Spedding* v. *Nevell* (1869) L.R. 4 C.P. 212; and see *Simmons* v. *Patchett* (1857) 7 E. & B. 568; *Godwin* v. *Francis* (1870) L.R. 5 C.P. 295; *Re National Coffee Palace Co.* (1883) 24 Ch.D. 367; followed in *Meek* v. *Wendt* (1888) 21 Q.B.D. 126.

66 (1864) 33 L.J.Q.B. 335.

67 *Salvesen* v. *Rederi A/B Nordstjernan* (1905) 7 F.(H.L.) 101, 102, *per* Ld. Davey.

68 *Firbank's Exors.* v. *Humphreys* (1886) 18 Q.B.D. 54, 60, *per* Esher M.R.; *Oliver* v. *Bank of England* [1902] 1 Ch. 610; affd. *sub. nom. Starkey* v. *Bank of England* [1903] A.C. 114.

owners of a property of which he had purported to take a verbal lease for seven years through an unauthorised agent of the owners, it was held that he could not recover his expenses from the agent, as his defence was bad in any case, amounting to averments of a verbal lease for a term of years which really only conferred a tenancy at will, and the lack of authority of the agent had not affected that or been the cause of his loss.[69] So, too, where the directors of a public company executed an agreement in a form which, in terms of the firm's articles, did not bind the company, the directors were held personally liable but not liable in respect of certain proceedings for injunction, as there was no representation by them that they had the authority of the company to assign its property as they had purported to do.[70]

In *Richardson* v. *Dunn* [71] the plaintiff had been negotiating for the purchase of a business and instructed Dunn to ascertain from the seller the profits, in reliance on which he purchased the business, Dunn having fraudulently represented that they were other than they were shown him to be. Richardson unsuccessfully sued the seller and her man of business, and then recovered from Dunn his loss, but the costs of the prior unsuccessful action were disallowed, as not being a natural consequence of Dunn's representation.

In *Salvesen* v. *Rederi Aktiebolaget Nordstjernan* [72] it was held by the House of Lords that, where an agent mistakenly represented to his principal that he had concluded a contract with a third party on the principal's behalf, he was liable to the principal for the expenses incurred by the latter's actings, proceeding on the belief that the contract had in fact been completed, but not liable (altering on this point the decision of the Second Division) for the loss of profit which the principal would have made on that same basis, in respect that he was not acting and had not represented himself to be acting for the third party. He could not be liable for breach of warranty to the person who granted the authority and knew its extent, as that party must, if anyone, have known the true extent and limits of his authority. In any event the latter loss was only a remote consequence, and to justify recovery there must be real loss or actual damage and not merely a probable or possible one.[73] In *Johnston* [73] a principal was induced by his agent's negligence to enter into a transaction, and it was held that he might recover the amount actually lost and compensation for loss of time, but not profits which might otherwise have been made by employing the time and money otherwise and not in that transaction.

69 *Pow* v. *Davis* (1861) 1 B. & S. 220.

70 *McCollin* v. *Gilpin* (1880) 5 Q.B.D. 390. *Cf. Richardson* v. *Williamson* (1871) L.R. 6 Q.B. 276; form sufficient but purpose *ultra vires* of company.

71 (1860) 8 C.B.(N.S.) 655.

72 (1905) F.(H.L.) 101; *cf. Cassaboglou* v. *Gibb* (1886) 11 Q.B.D. 797.

73 *Johnston* v. *Braham & Campbell* [1917] 1 K.B. 586.

Limits to doctrine of implied warranty

There are certain limitations to the rule that, when an agent purports to enter into an agreement on behalf of his principal, he impliedly warrants that he has the requisite authority to enter into that contract so as validly to bind his principal, with the consequent liability for failure. Obviously, if the other contracting party was aware of any limitations on the agent's authority, he is not entitled to contract with him on the chance that the latter's principal will ratify the agreement,[74] nor probably if he had reasonable cause to believe, despite the agent's affirmations to the contrary, that he did not in fact possess the necessary authority. The representation relied on must generally be one of fact and not of law to render an agent liable for breach of implied warranty of authority. So if an agent submits a written document of authority to the party with whom he seeks to contract and that party, after consideration, deems it adequate and duly enters into a contract with the agent on the faith of its authority, he cannot subsequently sue the agent if the latter's authority is repudiated and the construction of the document of authority is held not to cover the agent's actings in respect of that particular contract.[75]

Again where, at an auction sale, the auctioneer mistakenly sold an article below the advertised reserve price, he was held not to have warranted his authority to do so and was not liable to the purchaser [76]; and where a shipbroker contracted by telegraphic authority, this was held on proof of custom of trade not to warrant that his interpretation of the telegram was correct, and consequently he was not held liable when it was found that he was mistaken.[77] In *Dunn* v. *Macdonald* [78] it was held that a party who makes a contract expressly on behalf of the Crown cannot be held liable on the ground that he has warranted that he has authority to make it. The presumption is that a Crown official acting in his public capacity does so within the limits of his constitutional authority.[79] The principle that an agent warrants his authority does not apply in the case of a Department of State.[80] It is undecided whether there is anything in the Crown Proceedings Act 1947 to alter this rule.[81]

Directors as agents of company

Cases of breach of implied warranty frequently involve company directors. In the contemplation of the law, directors are agents of the company which they represent, and are consequently amenable to the

74 *Halbot* v. *Lens* [1901] 1 Ch. 344.
75 *Beattie* v. *Lord Ebury* (1872) L.R. 7 Ch. 777, 800, *per* Mellish L.J.; affd. (1874) L.R. 7 H.L. 102.
76 *McManus* v. *Fortescue* [1907] 2 K.B. 1.
77 *Lilly* v. *Smales* [1892] 1 Q.B. 456. See also *Suart* v. *Haigh* (1893) 9 T.L.R. 488 (H.L.).
78 [1897] 1 Q.B. 555; *cf. Riach* v. *Lord Advocate*, 1932 S.C. 138.
79 *Dunn* v. *Macdonald, supra*; *Commercial Cable Co.* v. *Government of Newfoundland* [1916] 2 A.C. 610; *cf. Robertson* v. *Minister of Pensions* [1949] 1 K.B. 227.
80 *Kenny* v. *Cosgrove* [1926] Ir.R. 517.
81 See *Howell* v. *Falmouth Boat Construction Co.* [1951] A.C. 837; *Att.-Gen. for Ceylon* v. *Silva* [1953] A.C. 461, 479.

general law of principal and agent.[82] They are therefore not personally liable on contracts which they make on behalf of the company and purporting to bind it, unless it appears that they undertook personal responsibility.[83] As agents they are not liable on contracts which purport to bind the company, and only the company is liable; if they have not authority, they are still not personally liable on the contract,[82] though they may be liable to an action for breach of implied warranty of authority.[84] They may of course bind themselves personally, and it depends on the circumstances of each case and particularly on the terms of the contract in question whether they have done so.[85]

When directors purport to contract on behalf of their company and *ex facie* of the contract bind the company to do something which it has no power to do, under the honest though mistaken impression that their contract is *intra vires* of the company, then the representation is probably one of law only, as the means of discovering the powers of the company are open to all by inspection of the firm's articles of association, and in consequence the directors will not be personally liable.[86] But if the act of a director contracting on behalf of the company can be interpreted as involving a representation of fact to the effect that he is really vested with authority to bind the company, and if his action is in fact *ultra vires*, he may be personally liable, as for example by issuing debentures in excess of the company's borrowing powers; he is then held to have represented in fact that the directors had authority to issue them and will be personally liable to parties to whom they are issued.[87]

Other exceptional cases where damages recoverable

There are certain other exceptional cases where damages may be recovered in respect of an innocent misrepresentation. Sections 38 and 43 of the Companies Act 1948, prescribe the matters to be stated and the reports to be set out in every prospectus issued by or on behalf of a company, and the civil liability to make compensation to persons deceived by misstatements in the prospectus. This liability is treated further elsewhere.[88] To succeed in such an action, the pursuer must not only show that he has sustained damage, but also that he would not have become a shareholder in the company if he had known of the contracts undisclosed in the prospectus.[89]

[82] *Ferguson* v. *Wilson* (1867) L.R. 2 Ch.App. 77.

[83] *Lindus* v. *Melrose*, 3 H. & N. 177; *McCollin* v. *Gilpin* (1880) 5 Q.B.D. 390.

[84] *Collen* v. *Wright* (1857) 7 E. & B. 307; affd., 8 E. & B. 647; *Coventry's Case* [1891] 1 Ch. 202; *Ferguson* v. *Wilson, supra.*

[85] See *Gadd* v. *Houghton* (1866) L.R. 1 Ex. 357; *Aggs* v. *Nicholson* (1856) 1 H. & N. 165; *McCollin* v. *Gilpin* (1880) 5 Q.B.D. 390.

[86] *Beattie* v. *Lord Ebury* (1874) L.R. 7 H.L. 102; *Rashdall* v. *Ford* (1866) L.R. 2 Eq. 750; *Mahony* v. *East Holyford Mining Co.* (1875) L.R. 7 H.L. 869.

[87] *Chapleo* v. *Brunswick Building Socy.* (1881) 6 Q.B.D. 696; *Firbank's Exors.* v. *Humphreys* (1886) 18 Q.B.D. 54; *West London Commercial Bank* v. *Kitson* (1884) 13 Q.B.D. 360.

[88] *Vide*, Chap. 36, *infra*.

[89] *Macleay* v. *Tait* [1906] A.C. 24.

Distinction of damages and indemnity

While the general rule is that a contract induced by innocent misrepresentation is voidable at the instance of the person deceived but no damages may be claimed, claims not unlike those to damages may arise. Reduction of the contract can in general only be effected on condition that the other party is restored to the position in which he was before the contract was made [90] and reduction may be precluded if *restitutio in integrum* is impossible for some reason. "There ought to be a giving back and a taking back on both sides." [91] This involves restoration of any benefits actually received under the contract, such as property, money, shares or land, by each party to the other, and secondly the pursuer must be indemnified by the payment of monetary compensation in respect of all burdens undertaken by him under the contract which would otherwise have been incumbent on the defender, in so far as these have not been discharged, or the pursuer may become liable for their implement in the future. These must also be taken back in the only way possible to permit the full attainment of the restoration of the *status quo ante contractum*.[92] A distinction however falls to be drawn between damages and indemnity in view of the fundamental rule that damages cannot be recovered for an innocent misrepresentation. The pursuer is not entitled to an indemnity against every obligation which he may have incurred as a result of the contract, nor to have the *status quo* restored *in toto*; there would otherwise be no difference between indemnity and damages.

In *Newbigging* v. *Adam* [93] Bowen L.J. made this distinction:—"I should not like to lay down the proposition that a person is to be restored to the position which he held before the misrepresentation was made, nor that the person injured must be indemnified against loss which arises out of the contract, unless you place on the words 'out of the contract' the limited and special meaning which I have endeavoured to shadow forth. Loss arising out of the contract is a term which would be too wide. It would embrace damages at common law, because damages at common law are only given upon the supposition that they are damages which would naturally and reasonably follow from the injury done."

The indemnity, then, is confined to those obligations which are necessarily created by the contract in question, and not against all those obligations which have arisen under or out of or as a result of the contract, only those burdens which are incumbent on the pursuer as a necessary and inevitable result of the position he took up under the contract. In *Newbigging* v. *Adam*,[94] one partner obtained the dissolution of his partnership with two other persons on the ground of innocent misrepresentation and

[90] *Boyd and Forrest* v. *G.S.W. Ry.*, 1915 S.C.(H.L.) 20.

[91] *Newbigging* v. *Adam* (1886) 34 Ch.D. 582, 595, *per* Bowen L.J.

[92] But the doctrine of *restitutio in integrum* must not be applied too literally: *Spence* v. *Crawford*, 1939 S.C.(H.L.) 52.

[93] (1886) 34 Ch.D. 582, 594.

[94] (1886) 34 Ch.D. 582; affd. *sub nom. Adam* v. *Newbigging* (1888) 13 App.Cas. 308.

it was held that he was entitled to an indemnity against the personal liability for debts of the partnership contracted while he was a member of the firm. This was a proper subject for indemnity in that his position as a partner was created by the contract and the burden of liability for firm debts was the inevitable and entirely automatic legal consequence of this position. The distinction was further illustrated in *Whittington* v. *Seale-Hayne* [95] where the plaintiffs entered into a lease on the faith of an innocent misrepresentation, not imported into the lease, that the premises were sanitary. In fact they were not and the plaintiffs sustained loss by the death of their prize poultry, illness, and the necessity of renewing the drains. They were held entitled to rescind the contract with a right to indemnity to the extent of rates and repairs only. Other claims for the loss of their poultry, loss of profit on sales, loss of season, removal and medical expenses were disallowed as being in substance a claim of damages. The former items were necessary and inevitable consequences of the lease, but the latter were not, as the contract neither created nor rendered inevitable any obligation to carry on poultry-farming. A party is not entitled in the name of restitution to recover expenses incidentally incurred through reliance on the contract, as that would be in effect to award damages where no wrong has been committed to justify such an award.

The remedies moreover for innocent misrepresentation are restricted to reduction of the contract and the recovery of payments made under it. A party cannot maintain the contract on the terms which would have been arrived at if no misrepresentation had been made; he may affirm the contract, or reduce it altogether, if disadvantageous to him.[96]

Negligent misrepresentation

Damages are probably recoverable where the representor should, in the circumstances, have taken care before making his representation, and has not done so, or not taken care adequate to the circumstances, and has thereby misrepresented to and misled the other party.[97] The damages would represent the loss caused by reliance on the misrepresentation.

Fraudulent misrepresentation

The main class of cases where damages may be recovered when a contract has been induced by misrepresentation comprises those cases where the misrepresentation in question has been made fraudulently. If damages are sought to be recovered as well as the contract rescinded specific averment and proof of actual fraud are essential [98] and the persons whose actings are averred to be fraudulent must be particularised.[99]

[95] (1900) 16 T.L.R. 181.
[96] *Wishart* v. *Howatson* (1897) 5 S.L.T. 84; *cf. Manners* v. *Whitehead* (1898) 1 F. 171.
[97] *Hedley Byrne & Co.* v. *Heller & Partners* [1964] A.C. 465.
[98] *Kisch* v. *Central Ry. of Venezuela* (1865) 12 L.T. 295; affd. (1867) L.R. 2 H.L. 99.
[99] *Thomson* v. *Pattison, Elder & Co.* (1895) 22 R. 432; *Houston Ltd.* v. *Metal Industries (Salvage) Ltd.*, 1953 S.L.T.(Notes) 73.

Fraudulent is distinguished from innocent misrepresentation by the element of wilful deception. It must be shown that the defender knew that the representations he made were untrue or that he had no honest belief in their truth, or that he made them recklessly without knowing or caring whether they were true or not and thereby induced the pursuer to act on the faith of the untrue representation.[1] Absence of honest belief is essential to constitute fraud, and gross carelessness may indicate this[2] or neglect to inquire when this was possible.[3]

If there is honest belief in the truth of the representations, even though it be unfounded, there is no fraud.[4] Carelessness in making a statement is not fraud even when third parties may act in reliance on it as, in general,[5] the maker of a statement owes no duty of care to third persons.[6]

Nor do silence or non-disclosure constitute misrepresentation in the general case, but only exceptionally, in cases where there is a duty to disclose all relevant information, as in contracts *uberrimae fidei*, in cases of fiduciary relations, and if the silence distorts a positive representation, but positive concealment may well be fraudulent.[7] Knowledge of the falseness of the representations must be brought home to justify averments of fraud as bona fides is a valid defence to an action of damages[8] though not to a claim for rescission.[9] Alternatively, if the party making the representation does not know that his statement is untrue, but yet does not believe it to be true and it is in fact untrue, he will also be liable.[10] On the other hand if he does not know that his representation is true, but believes it to be so, or has reasonable grounds for doing so, he will not be liable, even though his belief should be mistaken.[11] Absence of reasonable grounds for the belief does not by itself constitute fraud, but it is to be

1 *Lees* v. *Todd* (1882) 9 R. 807, overruling earlier contrary cases; *Smith* v. *Chadwick* (1884) 9 App.Cas. 187, 195; *Derry* v. *Peek* (1889) 14 App.Cas. 337; *Wilkinson* v. *Downton* [1897] 2 Q.B. 57; *Nocton* v. *Lord Ashburton* [1914] A.C. 932; *Robinson* v. *National Bank of Scotland*, 1916 S.C.(H.L.) 154.

2 *Derry, supra*, 369; *Western Bank* v. *Addie* (1867) 5 M.(H.L.) 80.

3 *Derry, supra*, 376; *Brownlie* v. *Miller* (1880) 7 R.(H.L.) 66, 81.

4 *Derry* v. *Peek* (1889) 14 App.Cas. 337; *Lees* v. *Todd* (1882) 9 R. 807; *Boyd and Forrest* v. *G.S.W. Ry.*, 1912 S.C.(H.L.) 93.

5 *e.g.* directors, *Derry* v. *Peek, supra*; but see now Companies Act 1948, s. 38; directors' annual reports, *Lees, supra*; directors declaring a dividend, *Dovey* v. *Cory* [1901] A.C. 477; accountants, *Candler* v. *Crane, Christmas & Co.* [1951] 2 K.B. 164; trustee and beneficiary, *Low* v. *Bouverie* [1891] 3 Ch. 82; banker as to customer's credit, *Robinson* v. *National Bank*, 1916 S.C.(H.L.) 154; but see *Hedley Byrne & Co.* v. *Heller & Partners* [1964] A.C. 465; (as to investments see *Banbury* v. *Bank of Montreal* [1918] A.C. 626); telegraph company sending telegram, *Dickson* v. *Reuters* (1877) 3 C.P.D. 1; statement for intending partner, *Manners* v. *Whitehead* (1898) 1 F. 171; surveyor or architect granting certificate, *Le Lievre, infra*. Suggested exceptions are a manager's annual report, *Lees, supra*; and a doctor's report to the Procurator-Fiscal, *Urquhart* v. *Grigor* (1864) 3 M. 283.

6 *Le Lievre* v. *Gould* [1893] 1 Q.B. 491, 502; *Candler* v. *Crane, Christmas & Co.* [1951] 2 K.B. 164. See also Morison, " Liability in Negligence for False Statements " (1951) 67 L.Q.R. 212; Seavey, " Candler *v.* Crane, Christmas & Co." (1951) 67 L.Q.R. 466.

7 *Gloag on Contract*, 457–462.

8 *Campbell* v. *Boswall* (1841) 3 D. 639; *Derry* v. *Peek* (1889) 14 App.Cas. 337; *Manners* v. *Whitehead* (1898) 1 F. 171.

9 *Ferguson* v. *Wilson* (1904) 12 S.L.T. 117.

10 *Smith* v. *Chadwick* (1884) 9 App.Cas. 187, 203; *Taylor* v. *Ashton* (1843) 11 M. & W. 415; *Evans* v. *Edmonds* (1853) 13 C.B. 786.

11 *Lees* v. *Todd* (1882) 9 R. 807; *Boyd and Forrest* v. *G.S.W. Ry.*, 1912 S.C.(H.L.) 93.

regarded as an element in considering whether the representation was made bona fide or not.[12]

Misrepresentation by third party

A claim of damages may be made in respect of fraudulent misrepresentation against, not the other contracting party, but a third party, if that third party were the author of the fraud inducing the contract. In *Thin & Sinclair* v. *Arrol*[13] T made advances to B on the strength of information (averred to be fraudulent) obtained from A. It was observed that the pursuer was not entitled to be relieved of his contract by the third party, who had induced it, as neither T nor the court could make a contract between A and B, but he might only recover damages, and on the facts fraudulent misrepresentation was not established. The damages sued for in that case amounted to the whole sum advanced (which would have relieved the pursuers entirely of their obligation) but it was admitted that no actual loss had been sustained, and the court observed that the only remedy would have been the recovery of damages for the loss resulting directly or naturally from the fraud.[14]

Misrepresentation by a third party to the contract would probably have the effect of invalidating the contract in at least two cases, namely, if it were so material as to induce essential error, in which case the contract is void, or if the representation were such that its truth was made a warranty of the contract.[15] It is submitted that in such cases no damages are recoverable *ex contractu* but the parties may recover any payments made.

Alternative or cumulative remedies

The twin remedies for fraud, namely, rescission of the contract and an award of damages, are cumulative rather than alternative.[16] The pursuer may therefore have the contract reduced as a whole unless parts of the contract are distinct and separable,[17] and also recover damages. He may also have the contract rescinded without damages, or claim damages for the fraud, the contract standing unrescinded.[18]

Again it has been held that it is impossible to rescind a contract of

[12] *Derry* v. *Peek*, *supra*, at pp. 369, 375.

[13] (1896) 24 R. 198. *Cf. Campbell* v. *Clason* (1838) 1 D. 270, revd. (1845) 17 Sc.Jur. 500 (H.L.).

[14] Such a case is an example of an action of damages for fraud purely *ex delicto* and independent of the contract. Moreover, as the misrepresentation was made by a third party to the contract it can have no invalidating effect on the contract, which is not reducible: *Karberg's Case* [1892] 3 Ch.1. But misrepresentations of an agent have the same effect as if made by the principal: *New Brunswick Ry.* v. *Conybeare* (1862) 9 H.L.C. 711, 726; *Weir* v. *Bell* (1878) 3 Ex.D. 238, 245; but not where an agent innocently makes a statement which the principal knew to be false: *Armstrong* v. *Strain* [1952] 1 K.B. 232.

[15] *e.g. Karberg's Case* [1892] 3 Ch. 1.

[16] *Newbigging* v. *Adam* (1886) 34 Ch.D. 582, 592.

[17] *Smyth* v. *Muir* (1891) 19 R. 81, 89, *per* Lord Kinnear; *United Shoe Machinery Co.* v. *Brunet* [1909] A.C. 330; *David* v. *Sabin* [1893] 1 Ch. 523.

[18] *Smith* v. *Sim*, 1954 S.C. 357. See also *Campbell* v. *Blair* (1897) 5 S.L.T. 28; but see *Bryson* v. *Bryson*, 1916, 1 S.L.T. 361, where no distinction was taken between fraud and breach of contract. *Cf. Laing* v. *Nixon* (1866) 4 M. 710; *Dobbie* v. *Duncanson* (1872) 10 M. 810; *Brownlie* v. *Miller* (1880) 7 R.(H.L.) 66, 79.

copartnery on the ground of fraudulent misrepresentation if there are some of the partners who desire the contract to stand and against whom no fraud is alleged. The only possible remedy is damages and not reduction and that directed personally against the delinquent partners.[19]

In the ordinary case the contract may have to stand unreduced if *restitutio in integrum* [20] is impossible, as that is an essential prerequisite of reduction, as where a thing purchased on the faith of fraudulent misstatements has been used or destroyed so that restoration is impossible. In such a case where things are no longer *in statu quo* an action of damages is clearly competent.[21] It is also conceivable that a party should wish to affirm the contract and yet seek damages for the fraud perpetrated on him, as where the contract is reasonably satisfactory despite the fraud which induced it.

Where a party contracts for work, induced by another party's fraud which is not discovered until the work is completed, he may sue that other party for damages for fraud without reducing the contract.[22]

The competency of such an action of damages without rescission of the contract is very doubtful in the case where a contract is made with a principal by a fraud for which an agent was really responsible. In *Houldsworth* [23] Lord President Inglis said in general terms that he was not aware of any remedy in such a case except or at least without rescission.[24] On appeal, however, this dictum was doubted by Lord Blackburn.[25] If, however, the contract has been performed, so that reduction is impossible, the principal may yet be sued for damages for the fraud of the agent.[26]

In the case of a person purchasing shares in a company an action for reduction of the contract to take shares may only be raised while the company is still a going concern [27] and under statutory conditions.[28] He may recover the amount paid for the shares but this is not as damages, but as part of restitution *in integrum* or alternatively on the basis of the rule that the company cannot keep money obtained through the fraud of its agents. If reduction of the agreement to take shares is precluded in the circumstances of the case, there is no remedy against the company. It was held in *Houldsworth* [25] that so long as a man remained a partner in a company he could have no action of damages against it. There were averments of fraud on the part of the directors inducing the pursuer to take shares, and he sued for the price paid for them and also for damages to cover the loss sustained and to be sustained by calls in the liquidation,

19 *Rose* v. *McDonald* (1899) 7 S.L.T. 288.
20 This is not to be interpreted too literally: *Spence* v. *Crawford*, 1939 S.C.(H.L.) 52.
21 *Gloag on Contract*, 480, quoting *Houldsworth* v. *City of Glasgow Bank* (1879) 6 R. 1164; affd. (1880) 7 R.(H.L.) 53, *per* Lord Shand, 6 R. at 1168. See too Bell, *Comm.* I, 262, and Gloag's comments thereon, p. 479.
22 *Boyd and Forrest* v. *G.S.W. Ry.*, 1915 S.C.(H.L.) 20, 28, *per* Lord Atkinson.
23 (1879) 6 R. 1164.
24 At p. 1168.
25 (1880) 7 R.(H.L.) 53 at 64.
26 *Boyd and Forrest* v. *G.S.W. Ry.*, 1911 S.C. 33; revd. 1912 S.C.(H.L.) 93.
27 *Oakes* v. *Turquand* (1867) L.R. 2 H.L. 325.
28 *Palmer on Companies*, 21st ed., 455 *et seq.*; *Gloag on Contract*, 539, 544.

or alternatively for a decree ordaining the defenders to relieve him of such calls. Lord Chancellor Cairns explained the principle of the decision as being that a party agreeing to take shares contracts with the other shareholders that the assets shall be applied to meet existing and future liabilities, and that these liabilities do not include damages due to any of the shareholders for his having been fraudulently induced to take shares.[29] Gloag explains this as being an action really directed against one's fellow shareholders.[30]

Actionable damage

Only damage in the sense of patrimonial loss can be considered for the purpose of quantifying damages. Mental disturbance unaccompanied by physical upset and the loss of social benefits or advantages to which no pecuniary value can be attached cannot be considered.[31]

Furthermore, to be actionable, patrimonial damage sustained must be shown to be the natural and probable consequence of the misrepresentation being believed and acted upon. Consequences not the natural and direct consequence of the misrepresentation are too remote.[32] If it is not shown that the damage is the direct consequence of acting on the faith of the misrepresentation the loss is similarly too remote.[33] These are questions of law for the court.[34]

Among the kinds of damage which have been held actionable are the loss arising out of the contract entered into induced by and in reliance on the misrepresentation, loss of profits,[35] loss of property,[36] and expenses [37] though it has been held that the expenses incurred to reverse the consequences of a misrepresentation on the discovery of its falsity are too remote damage to be allowable.[38]

The measure of damages for which an agent is responsible in consequence of his misrepresentations is the loss which the principal actually sustains thereby, but not including anticipated profit which might have accrued to the principal if the representation had been true.[39]

29 7 R.(H.L.) 53, 55. See further *Burgess's Case* (1880) 15 Ch.D. 507.

30 *Contract*, 481.

31 *Cf. Chamberlain* v. *Boyd* (1883) 11 Q.B.D. 407 (loss of election to club is not actual damage).

32 See Chap. 52, *infra*.

33 *Collins* v. *Cave* (1860) 6 H. & N. 131; *Dashwood* v. *Jermyn* (1879) 12 Ch.D. 776; *Ajello* v. *Worsley* [1898] 1 Ch. 274; *Barry* v. *Croskey* (1861) 2 J. & H. 1; *Peek* v. *Gurney* (1873) L.R. 6 H.L. 377, 412; *Angus* v. *Clifford* [1891] 2 Ch. 449, 481. Not too remote were *Barley* v. *Walford* (1846) 9 Q.B. 197; *Mullett* v. *Mason* (1866) L.R. 1 C.P. 559; *Wilkinson* v. *Downton* [1897] 2 Q.B. 57, 59; *Janvier* v. *Sweeny* [1919] 2 K.B. 316.

34 *Clydesdale Bank* v. *Paton* (1896) 23 R.(H.L.) 22; *Tallerman* v. *Dowsing Radiant Heat Co.* [1900] 1 Ch. 1; *Stevens* v. *Hoare* (1904) 20 T.L.R. 407.

35 *Barley* v. *Walford* (1846) 9 Q.B. 197.

36 *Mullett* v. *Mason* (1866) L.R. 1 C.P. 559 (loss of cows infected by purchased cow).

37 *Barley, supra*; *Milne* v. *Marwood* (1855) 15 C.B. 778; *Richardson* v. *Silvester* (1873) L.R. 9 Q.B. 34; *Pritty* v. *Child* (1902) 71 L.J.K.B. 512.

38 *Hyde* v. *Bulmer* (1868) 18 L.T. 293.

39 *Salvesen* v. *Rederi A/B Nordstjernan* (1905) 7 F.(H.L.) 101; *Johnston* v. *Braham and Campbell* [1917] 1 K.B. 586.

Measure of damages for fraudulent misrepresentation

When a contract has been induced by fraudulent misrepresentation, the quantum of damages will be the amount which is proper compensation for the loss directly or naturally resulting from the fraud.[40] Where the loss is doubtful it has been held in England that nominal damages may be awarded.[41] The damages will normally amount to but are not confined to the difference between the price paid or consideration given for the contract and the price which would have been paid if the truth had been stated, *i.e.* in the absence of the offending misrepresentation [42]; alternatively it may be stated as the difference between the actual or true value of the property and the sum the pursuer was induced to give for it.[43] Where the article is destroyed or damaged while in the pursuer's possession, he can only recover the difference between the value which the article was misrepresented to have and the real value at the time of the purchase.[44] Where a cattle dealer fraudulently misrepresented that a cow was free from disease and the purchaser put it in a byre with other cows which caught the disease, the purchaser was held entitled to the value of all six cows.[45]

Where a promoting company sold to a theatre company with misrepresentations the measure of damages was held to be the difference in value between the consideration paid by the theatre company and the actual value at the date of the purchase of the properties which it acquired.[46] Again in *Waddell* v. *Blockey* [47] the defendant fraudulently represented that rupee paper which he had been instructed to buy for the plaintiff belonged to third parties whereas it was really his own, and thus sold it to the plaintiff and the value of rupee paper declined, but the plaintiff held on to the rupee paper and finally sold it at heavy loss, it was held that the proper measure of damages was not the amount of loss ultimately sustained but the difference between the price paid for the rupee paper and the price which he would have received if he had resold it in the market forthwith after purchasing and before the decline had taken effect. He was not entitled to damages so far as consequent on keeping the rupee paper while the price was tumbling. Bramwell L.J.[48] instanced the case of an animal sold with a fraudulent warranty where the damages would be the difference between the purchase price and the price at which it might have been sold.

40 *Thin & Sinclair* v. *Arrol* (1896) 24 R. 198, 206, *per* L.P. Robertson.
41 *Cracknell* v. *Davy* (1858) 1 F. & F. 57.
42 *Davidson* v. *Tulloch* (1860) 22 D.(H.L.) 7.
43 *Pearson* v. *Wheeler* (1825) Ry. & M. 303; *Hamer* v. *James* (1886) 2 T.L.R. 852; *Arnison* v. *Smith* (1889) 41 Ch.D. 348; *Duncan* v. *Scaife* (1888) 4 T.L.R. 716. Contrast *Baxter* v. *Gapp & Co.* [1939] 2 K.B. 271.
44 *Twycross* v. *Grant* (1877) 2 C.P.D. 469.
45 *Mullett* v. *Mason* (1866) L.R. 1 C.P. 559. *Cf. Smith* v. *Green* (1875) 1 C.P.D. 92, warranty but no fraud, and contrast *Hill* v. *Balls* (1857) 2 H. & N. 299; *Ward* v. *Hobbs* (1878) 3 Q.B.D. 150; 14 App.Cas. 13.
46 *Re Leeds and Hanley Theatre of Varieties Ltd.* [1902] 2 Ch. 809.
47 (1879) 4 Q.B.D. 678.
48 (1879) 4 Q.B.D. 678, 681.

The date of ascertainment of values for the purposes of damages is the date of purchase. " If a man is induced by misrepresentation to buy an article and while it is in his possession it becomes destroyed or damaged, he can only recover the difference between the value represented and the real value at the time he bought it.[49] Thus in company cases, where false representations have induced a man to take shares, the proper measure of damages is to take the difference between the price paid for the shares and their actual value at the time of allotment, which value falls to be ascertained not only by the market value but by regard to subsequent events including the results of the winding up if the company has been liquidated.[50] The actual value at the date of allotment is not necessarily the market price as that may have been inflated by the same misrepresentation, but it is the real value of the assets behind them.

If a purchaser has resold goods at a profit he cannot obtain any damages, even though he has not succeeded in obtaining the profit he might reasonably have expected if the representations had been true. Damages extend also to injury which is the direct and natural result of the misrepresentation: so that where a cow was fraudulently misrepresented sound and infected other animals, the seller was held liable for the value of all the animals.[51]

In *McConnel* v. *Wright* [52] the measure of damages was said to be, at highest, the whole extent of the loss measured by the money formerly in the plaintiff's pocket and now in the other party's pocket; but, in so far as the plaintiff had got an equivalent for his money that loss is diminished and he is not damaged: in so far as they fell short of being an equivalent he is damaged. Only if the subjects purchased are quite worthless is he entitled to recover the whole sum paid as consideration for the transfer, and benefits received under the contract must be taken into consideration.

Company cases

Where shares have been taken up under a misrepresentation, the measure of damages is the difference between the price paid for the shares and their real value at the date of the purchase, but the real value is not necessarily the price for which the shares would sell on the market; it may be ascertained by the light of subsequent events which show that the company was originally worthless.[53]

In *Peek* v. *Derry* [54] where the plaintiff was induced to take shares on the faith of the defendant's misrepresentations [55] Cotton L.J. said, " The damage to be recovered by the plaintiff is the loss which he sustained by

49 *Twycross* v. *Grant* (1877) 2 C.P.D. 469; *cf. Waddell* v. *Blockey* (1879) 4 Q.B.D. 678.
50 *Arkwright* v. *Newbold* (1880) 17 Ch.D. 301; *Arnison* v. *Smith* (1889) 41 Ch.D. 348, 363; *Shaw* v. *Holland* [1900] 2 Ch. 305; *Cackett* v. *Keswick* [1902] 2 Ch. 456.
51 *Mullett* v. *Mason* (1866) L.R. 1 C.P. 559.
52 [1903] 1 Ch. 546.
53 *Peek* v. *Derry* (1887) 37 Ch.D. 541; see also *Henderson* v. *Lacon* (1867) L.R. 5 Eq. 249.
54 (1887) 37 Ch.D. 541, 591. Revd. on another ground (1889) 14 App.Cas. 337.
55 Held at this stage (C.A.) to be fraudulent; finally held (H.L.) not to be fraudulent: the reversal does not invalidate the opinions on damages.

acting on the representations of the defendants. That action was taking the shares. Before he was induced to buy the shares, he had the £4,000 in his pocket. The day when the shares were allotted to him, which was the consequence of his action, he paid over that £4,000, and he got the shares; and the loss sustained by him in consequence of his acting on the representations of the defendants was having the shares, instead of having in his pocket the £4,000. The loss, therefore, must be the difference between his £4,000 and the then value of the shares.

" Now, it must not be taken that the value of the shares must be what they would have sold for in the market, because that might not show the real value at all. I do not know whether there was any market in this case, but the market might have been affected by the representations which were made by the defendants, which induced the plaintiff to act, and which might have induced others to act. Neither can the plaintiff get the benefit of any loss or depreciation in the shares which was occasioned by subsequent acts. . . . And of course a plaintiff cannot aggravate the damages by acting unreasonably, . . . But I think it is . . . in accordance with principle that the real value, and not the market value, is to be ascertained immediately after the day when the shares were allotted to the plaintiff." [56]

Where the directors of a company were induced by one of themselves by fraudulent misrepresentation to make an advance on what proved to be inadequate security the measure of damages was held to be the difference between the money advanced and the value of the debenture at the date of issue.[57] Where a shareholder applied for shares on the faith of a prospectus which failed to specify statutory particulars, the director responsible was held liable to refund the sum paid for the shares, despite a clause in the prospectus holding applicants to have waived claims against the company for not complying more fully with the requirements of the Companies Act.[58] Where allotments of shares were made *ultra vires* to directors, it was held that the measure of damages was the value when they were so allotted.[59] Where a man purchased shares under a forged transfer, he was held entitled to recover from the company as damages for the loss of the shares their value at the time the company first refused to recognise him as a shareholder, with interest.[60]

Minimisation of damages

The principle of requiring a pursuer to take reasonable steps to minimise damages applies to damages for fraudulent misrepresentation as in other cases. Where a plaintiff was induced thereby to advance money on a debenture and the company went into liquidation, and the plaintiff

[56] Citing *Davidson* v. *Tulloch* (1860) 3 Macq. 783, 790.
[57] *Exploring Land Co.* v. *Kolckmann* (1905) 94 L.T. 234.
[58] *Watts* v. *Bucknall* [1903] 1 Ch. 766.
[59] *Shaw* v. *Holland* [1900] 2 Ch. 305.
[60] *Re Bahia and San Francisco Ry.* (1868) L.R. 3 Q.B. 584; *cf. Karberg's Case* [1892] 3 Ch. 1; *Re Ottos Kopje Diamond Mines* [1893] 1 Ch. 618.

bought the company's assets and then sold them at a profit, it was held that this profit should not be deducted from the claim for loss on the debenture, as while the plaintiff's duty was to minimise his damages, he was under no obligation to have spent money in doing so.[61] A plaintiff fraudulently induced to purchase rupee paper was disentitled from recovering full damages when they were partially due to his having retained the rupee paper for some time while the market price was falling.[62]

Limits of liability

The person who has made a fraudulent misrepresentation is liable in the general case only to the person to whom that representation was addressed, and not to any third party who accidentally comes to hear the representation and incurs loss by acting on the faith thereof. So it has been held that a liquidator of a company could not found on the fact that one shareholder had fraudulently induced another person to take over his shares so as to reduce the transaction and put the original shareholder on the list of contributories in the winding up.[63] Representations as to the credit of a certain party may subject to liability a person to whom that representation has been made, or to his principal if he is known to be acting as an agent, but does not extend to third parties to whom the misrepresentation may be repeated.[64] So too a sale, induced by fraudulent misrepresentation, could not be reduced by a sub-purchaser who had, without any misrepresentation at all affecting the sub-sale, paid an inflated price in consequence thereof.[65] In that case neither buyer nor sub-purchaser had a title to sue, the buyer having disposed of the property and the sub-purchaser being disentitled to challenge the principal transaction. But where misrepresentations were made in a sale and repeated in a sub-sale, it was held that on reduction of the sub-sale, the original purchaser's title to sue for reduction of the principal sale revived.[66] It is probable that in such a case the original purchaser would have a right of relief against the original seller for any damages recovered by the sub-purchaser. But where a person is induced by fraudulent statements on the part of another to contract with a third party, he is not entitled to be relieved of his contract by the other but only to recover damages from that other for the loss naturally and directly resulting from his fraud.[67] Exceptionally, however, a man may be liable for fraud to a person other than him to whom the misleading statement was made on the ground that he must be held to contemplate the possibility or even the likelihood of his

[61] *Jewelowski* v. *Propp* [1944] 1 K.B. 510.
[62] *Waddell* v. *Blockey* (1879) 4 Q.B.D. 678.
[63] *Re Discoverers' Finance Corpn.* [1910] 1 Ch. 207, 312; *McLintock* v. *Campbell*, 1916 S.C. 966.
[64] Bell, *Comm.* I, 392; *Stewart* v. *Scott* (1803) Hume 91; *Salton* v. *Clydesdale Bank* (1898) 1 F. 110; *Hockey* v. *Clydesdale Bank* (1898) 1 F. 119.
[65] *Edinburgh United Breweries* v. *Molleson* (1893) 20 R. 581; affd. (1894) 21 R.(H.L.) 10.
[66] *Westville Shipping Co.* v. *Abram Shipping Co.*, 1922 S.C. 571; affd. 1923 S.C.(H.L.) 68. *Cf. Blumer* v. *Scott* (1874) 1 R. 379; *Mags. of Arbroath* v. *Strachan's Trs.* (1842) 4 D. 538.
[67] *Thin and Sinclair* v. *Arrol* (1896) 24 R. 198; *Brown* v. *Stewart* (1898) 1 F. 316, 323, *per* Lord Kinnear. See, too, *Macfarlane, Strang & Co.* v. *Bank of Scotland* (1903) 11 S.L.T. 199.

statements being acted on by persons other than the receiver of the misrepresentation. So in *Langridge* v. *Levy*[68] the seller of a gun was held liable in damages to the son of the purchaser when it burst and caused injury, he having fraudulently represented that it was a sound gun. It was held that the seller must in the circumstances be held to have contemplated that persons other than the purchaser would act in reliance on his statement. Similarly a banker will be presumed to know that inquiries made by another bank as to the credit of a customer are made on behalf of someone for whom the second bank is acting.[69] If of course a misrepresentation is addressed to the general public, as in the case of a fraudulent prospectus for a company, it may be founded on by any member of the public who is misled by it and incurs loss by acting on the faith of it,[70] but not by subsequent purchasers of the shares,[71] unless the fraud by the company is continued after the purchaser is entered in the register.[72]

Remoteness

In accordance with the general principle the pursuer in an action based on fraudulent misrepresentation cannot recover damages if they are too remote and do not follow as the direct and natural consequence of the defender's actings.[73] Thus it has been held that expenses incurred in rectifying the consequences of a misrepresentation on its discovery are too remote to be given.[74] Again where directors issued balance sheets in which the company assets were over-valued, damages arising from the improper continuance of the business were held to be too remote.[75]

Where a cattle dealer sold a cow fraudulently representing that it was free from disease and the buyer placed it with five other cows, which also caught the disease and died, he was held entitled to recover as damages the value of all six cows.[76] The costs of a prior action against the seller of a business, who had not personally made the fraudulent representation, were refused as not in the circumstances a natural and proximate consequence of an intermediary's misrepresentation, but a sum for loss of time was not too remote.[77]

68 (1837) 2 M. & W. 519. *Cf. Donoghue* v. *Stevenson*, 1932 S.C.(H.L.) 31.
69 *Gloag on Contract*, 483; *Robinson* v. *National Bank*, 1916 S.C. 46; affd. 1916 S.C.(H.L.) 154.
70 *Lees* v. *Todd* (1882) 9 R. 807.
71 *Peek* v. *Gurney* (1873) L.R. 6 H.L. 377.
72 *Andrews* v. *Mockford* [1896] 1 Q.B. 372 (fraud in prospectus, and also later in published telegrams to sustain price of shares).
73 *Corbett* v. *Brown* (1832) 5 C. & P. 363; *Green* v. *Button* (1835) 2 C.M. & R. 707; *Mullett* v. *Mason* (1866) L.R. 1 C.P. 559; *Peek* v. *Gurney* (1873) L.R. 6 H.L. 377; *Angus* v. *Clifford* [1891] 2 Ch. 449; *Collins* v. *Cave* (1860) 6 H. & N. 131.
74 *Hyde* v. *Bulmer* (1868) 18 L.T. 293.
75 *Re Kingston Cotton Mill Co.* [1896] 1 Ch. 331, 349.
76 *Mullett* v. *Mason* (1866) L.R. 1 C.P. 559.
77 *Richardson* v. *Dunn* (1860) 8 C.B.(N.S.) 655. *Cf. Johnston* v. *Braham and Campbell* [1917] 1 K.B. 586.

CHAPTER 30

DAMAGES FOR BREACH OF CONTRACT

General

Damages are in general due from the party who fails in any particular respect to make due performance of all or any part of the obligations undertaken by him in a valid and subsisting legal contract. There are to this rule exceptions in those cases where an excuse for non-performance is adduced which is legally satisfactory. This has the effect of releasing the party from the liability to make performance or to pay damages in compensation for that failure. The parties may also competently agree to waive a breach. The American *Restatement* [1] defines breach of contract as the non-performance of any contractual duty of immediate performance, and it may be total or partial, by failure to perform acts promised, by prevention or hindrance, or by repudiation.

Title to sue for breach of contract

As a general rule, apart from cases of agency, a person is liable for breach of contract only to the other party to the contract. If failure in his contractual duties causes loss he is not liable to any third party with whom he had no contract and on whom the loss has happened to light.[2] There may be liability on the ground of the breach of a duty of care owed to that third party and from the fact that his failure to perform his contractual obligations was in the circumstances a breach of that duty and amounted to negligence or delict,[3] but such liability to the third party does not arise *ex contractu*, and attempts made to import liability on any such principle as *jus quaesitum tertio* have been unsuccessful. The principle of *jus quaesitum*,[4] where it applies, will permit the *tertius* to sue for non-performance of the contract intended for his benefit, but has been said not to entitle him to claim damages for misfeasance or faulty performance.[5] The reason for this has been explained as being that the real foundation of the title of the *tertius* to sue on a contract is that the debtor in the contract has agreed to be liable to him, and it is not to be presumed that the debtor in a contract has agreed to be liable to a *tertius* in respect of his defective performance. So it has been held that the liability of a law agent for loss caused by his negligence or failure to exhibit due professional

1 *Contracts*, s. 312.
2 *Blumer* v. *Scott* (1874) 1 R. 379.
3 *e.g. Donoghue* v. *Stevenson*, 1932 S.C.(H.L.) 31; *Langridge* v. *Levy* (1837) 2 M. & W. 519; *Longmeid* v. *Holliday* (1857) 6 Ex. 761; *cf. Duke* v. *Jackson*, 1921 S.C. 362, criticised in *Wilson* v. *Rickett Cockerell & Co.* [1954] 1 All E.R. 868.
4 On the whole doctrine of *jus quaesitum tertio*, see *Gloag on Contract*, 234 *et seq.*
5 *Gloag on Contract*, 239.

skill and care, which liability must necessarily rest on breach of contract, is only to the person who employed him, directly or indirectly, and to no one else. Examples of this are the failure to intimate or register a bond and assignation in security of a lease entered into for the benefit of cautioners.[6] By the agent's failure, the cautioners had no preference on the bankruptcy of their principal. A jury awarded the cautioners damages but the House of Lords ordered a new trial with a declaration that the issue whether or not the agent had been employed by the authority of the pursuers should have been raised. The Lord Chancellor (Campbell) laid down that the liability of a law agent was in such circumstances confined to the person who employed him, and thus established a rule which had been in doubt in prior cases.[7] The modern cases [8] show that a law agent does not owe a general duty, but is only liable for professional negligence within the bounds of his contract of employment, unlike a medical practitioner who owes a duty of care to his patient and is liable to him for lack of professional skill independently of the consideration of who employed him.[9] Privity of contract is not necessarily determined by ascertaining who pays the professional fee, as where an agent is employed to carry through a transaction in which several parties are interested but no other agent is instructed for other parties; in such a case the inference will readily be drawn that he is acting for all parties even though his fees may be recoverable from one only, and he will be liable in damages for professional negligence even though the person on whom the loss falls should not be the one who pays his account.[10]

An assignee of a contract has a title to sue for damages for defective performance,[11] but it is necessary to aver the assignee's title and the damage incurred by the cedent.[12] The assignee may sue in his own name or sist himself in an action commenced by his cedent.[13]

Personal injury claims ex contractu

If personal injury accrues to any person as a result of the negligent or defective performance of a contract, such as a passenger injured in consequence of the mishandling of a vehicle, any action for damages, if based on the contract, may only be at the instance of the other party to the contract. So when ship carpenters who were under contract with a firm of shipbuilders laid a gangway from the dockside to the ship and an

[6] *Robertson* v. *Fleming* (1861) 4 Macq. 167.

[7] *Goldie* v. *Macdonald* (1757) M. 3527; *Goldie* v. *Goldie* (1842) 4 D. 1489.

[8] *Robertson* v. *Fleming, supra*; *Williamson* v. *Begg* (1887) 14 R. 720; *Raes* v. *Meek* (1888) 15 R. 1033; affd. (1889) 16 R.(H.L.) 31; *Tully* v. *Ingram* (1891) 19 R. 65. See also *McKnight* v. *Lanark District Council* (1899) 7 S.L.T. 47.

[9] *Edgar* v. *Lamont*, 1914 S.C. 277.

[10] *Lang* v. *Struthers* (1827) 2 W. & S. 563; explained in *Robertson* v. *Fleming* (1861) 4 Macq. 167; *Williamson* v. *Begg* (1887) 14 R. 720.

[11] Stair III, 1, 13; Ersk. III, 5, 2; Bell, *Prin.* § 1459; *Gloag on Contract*, 2nd ed., 413; *International Fibre Syndicate* v. *Dawson* (1901) 3 F.(H.L.) 32.

[12] *Levett* v. *L.N.W. Ry.* (1866) 2 S.L.R. 206.

[13] *Fraser* v. *Duguid* (1838) 16 S. 1130.

engineer fell off the gangway, which was defective, and sustained injuries for which he claimed damages, it was held that no question of delict was involved and the injured workman had no title to sue, as he could not rest any claim on the ground that the defective gangway involved a breach of the carpenters' contract with the shipbuilders.[14] Similarly a liability of a landlord for the defective condition of his property which causes injury rests on the breach of an express or implied contract to keep the premises in proper repair and this exists only *vis-à-vis* the other party to the contract of let; so that, while a tenant may sue for damages for injury sustained in consequence of a defect, other persons, such as the tenant's wife and family, or visitors, or lodgers, have no title to sue an action founded on breach of contract.[15] Their title must be founded on breach of non-contractual legal duty to them.[16]

Sub-contracts

The rule of privity of contract which in general permits only a party to the contract to sue thereon extends to debar a third party linked to one of the contracting parties by a sub-contract. So in one case shipbuilders sold an unfinished ship and undertook to complete the fitting of the engines through a named firm of engineers. They sub-contracted with the named engineers informing them of the sale of the ship. The engineers delayed to deliver the engines and the builders and the purchaser of the ship sued for damages for delay. The action at the instance of the purchaser was dismissed on the ground that he was not a party to the contract for the engines and had no *jus quaesitum*.[17] The purchaser was only entitled to sue the shipbuilders, with whom he had a contractual bond, and the latter were entitled to sue the engineers and reclaim any damages recovered from them by the purchaser.[18]

In some similar circumstances, however, the rule of *Donoghue* v. *Stevenson* [19] may permit the injured party to sue the original wrong-doer but such an action is based on negligence and subject to the limitations inherent in the *ratio* of *Donoghue*.

Negligence arising out of contract

Similarly it frequently happens that when two parties are brought into contractual relations, the misconduct of one in performing his part of the contract causes loss, injury or damage to a third party, but in cases where a contracting party has been found liable to such a third party the liability rests on delict and not on breach of contract. A party to a contract is not absolved by his duty to fulfil the contract from any other legal duty existing

14 *Campbell* v. *Morison* (1891) 19 R. 282.
15 *Cameron* v. *Young*, 1907 S.C. 475; affd. 1908 S.C.(H.L.) 7; *Cavalier* v. *Pope* [1906] A.C. 428; *Bottomley* v. *Bannister* [1932] 1 K.B. 458; *Otto* v. *Bolton* [1936] 2 K.B. 46.
16 Occupiers' Liability (Scotland) Act 1960, s. 3.
17 *Blumer* v. *Scott & Sons* (1874) 1 R. 379.
18 On this see, further, Chap. 51, *infra*.
19 1932 S.C.(H.L.) 31.

independently, such as that to take reasonable care that other persons who come in proximity to him are not injured or prejudiced.[20] Such a duty to have due regard for the interests of other persons exists independently of contract and neither it nor the consequent liability to make reparation for damage rests on the foundation of the contract. The question accordingly in such a case comes to be not one of the existence or otherwise of a contract which confers a title to sue or whether the third party can sue on a contract to which he is not a party, but of the existence and breach of a legal duty on which any injured person can found in pursuing an action founded in delict or negligence. The distinction was drawn by Lord President Robertson in *Cramb* v. *Caledonian Ry.*,[21] where bags of sugar became impregnated with arsenic from liquid weedkiller which leaked from a case placed beside it in a railway company's van. Persons who subsequently purchased the sugar died of poisoning and claims were made against the railway company (who had been ignorant of the dangerous nature of the other goods). The claim was repelled. " It is necessary again," the Lord President said," to emphasise the fact that the action against them [the railway company] is brought by persons entirely unconnected with them by contract, and of whom they had no knowledge. We are not considering, and we have no occasion and no means to determine, whether the railway company duly fulfilled the obligations incumbent on them as carriers of the bags of sugar. In the present action fault must be brought home to the railway company in the omission to perform some duty which they owed to all the world." That is, the action must be laid in delict and founded on a breach of a general duty of care and not on any breach of the contract of carriage which only existed between the railway company and the consignor of the goods.

Insolvency or bankruptcy

Insolvency does not, as a general rule, terminate contractual relations between the insolvent and another party.[89] Hence insolvency *per se* is not a breach of contract, nor does it prevent the insolvent entering into contracts,[90] unless the insolvency is notorious and indicates an intention to abandon the estate to creditors, when it becomes a fraud to contract thereafter.[91] The fact of insolvency may, however, be material in entitling the other party to exercise a right of retention, which if wrongly used will give a claim of damages.[92] If an insolvent buyer has given the seller such

[20] *Donoghue* v. *Stevenson*, 1932 S.C.(H.L.) 31.
[21] (1892) 19 R. 1054, 1059.
[89] Bell, *Comm.* I, 264; Goudy on *Bankruptcy* (4th ed.), 20; *Grant* v. *Grant* (1748) M. 949; *Richmond* v. *Railton* (1854) 16 D. 403; *Weir* v. *Buchanan* (1876) 4 R. 8; *Ehrenbacher* v. *Kennedy* (1874) 1 R. 1131.
[90] Bell, Goudy, *ut supra*; *Grant, supra*; *Richmond, supra*; *Morton* v. *Abercromby* (1858) 20 D. 362.
[91] Bell, *Comm.* I, 266; Goudy, 20–21; *Schuurmans* v. *Goldie* (1828) 6 S. 1110; *Crawford* v. *Black* (1829) 8 S. 158; *Watt* v. *Findlay* (1846) 8 D. 529; *Richmond, supra*; *Morton, supra*; *Hutton* v. *Fleming* (1871) 9 M. 718.
[92] Bell, *Comm.* II, 154; see Chap. 5, *supra*; *The Constantia* (1807) 6 Rob.Adm. 321; *McNair* v. *Don* (1932) 48 Sh.Ct.Rep. 99.

notice of his state of affairs as amounts to a declaration of inability or unwillingness to pay the price,[93] the seller may treat this as a repudiation of the contract and claim damages unless the trustee within a reasonable time elects to complete the contract by payment in cash.[94]

Sequestration

Sequestration by itself does not necessarily constitute a breach of a contract between the bankrupt and another party, nor does it amount to a repudiation of the contract. The whole property of the bankrupt becomes vested in the trustee, but it is established that the trustee is not bound to take up such of the bankrupt's contracts as are of an onerous character. They may be disclaimed, when the other party will normally be entitled to a ranking on the estate in respect of his claim of damages for breach of contract,[95] or the contracts may be adopted and carried through for the benefit of the estate.[96] Where goods are deliverable in instalments, the trustee of a bankrupt purchaser may not adopt the contract and claim further deliveries in implement thereof without paying for the goods delivered prior to the bankruptcy.[97] A trustee in bankruptcy is not bound to take up the bankrupt's contracts and implement them, but may do so and will be liable in damages if he does not and the contract is not one which the bankrupt himself can carry out.[1] Where the contract is personal and involves *delectus personae* it cannot be taken up at all by the trustee,[2] but the bankrupt may proceed with the contract and perform it and the benefit will go to the estate.[3] If he does not go on with such a contract the other party will be entitled to damages.[3]

If however the contract is pecuniary or patrimonial, the trustee can in most cases at least take it up for the benefit of the estate,[4] but the intention to do so must be declared within a reasonable time in the circumstances.[5] A trustee is not bound to take up contracts of the bankrupts of an onerous or speculative character, though in the case of repudiation a claim for damages will lie at the instance of the aggrieved person.[6] In any event the trustee's decision must be made within a reasonable time.[7]

In leases, bankruptcy of a tenant does not put an end to the lease unless

93 *Re Phoenix Bessemer Steel Co.* (1876) 4 Ch.D. 108.
94 *Ex p. Chalmers* (1873) L.R. 8 Ch. 289.
95 *Kirkland* v. *Cadell* (1838) 16 S. 860; *cf. Ex p. Stapleton* (1879) 10 Ch.D. 586.
96 *Asphaltic Limestone Co.* v. *Glasgow Corpn.*, 1907 S.C. 463.
97 *Ex p. Chalmers* (1873) L.R. 8 Ch. 289.
1 *Anderson* v. *Hamilton* (1875) 2 R. 355; *Kirkland* v. *Cadell* (1838) 16 S. 860; Goudy (4th ed.), 282; *Bidoulac* v. *Sinclair's Tr.* (1889) 17 R. 144.
2 *Caldwell* v. *Hamilton*, 1919 S.C.(H.L.) 100, 104; *cf. Gibson* v. *Carruthers* (1841) 8 M. & W. 321.
3 Bell, *Comm.* II, 413; *Kirkland* v. *Cadell, supra.*
4 *Anderson* v. *Hamilton* (1875) 2 R. 355; *Asphaltic Limestone* v. *Glasgow Corpn.*, 1907 S.C. 463.
5 *Anderson* v. *Hamilton, supra.*
6 Bell, *Comm.* II, 413; *Anderson* v. *Hamilton, supra*; *Cuthill* v. *Jeffrey*, Nov. 21, 1818, F.C.; *Kirkland* v. *Gibson* (1831) 9 S. 596; affd. (1833) 6 W. & S. 340; *Kirkland* v. *Cadell, supra*; *Shead* v. *Cox* (1835) 13 S. 280.
7 *Anderson* v. *Hamilton, supra.*

there is provision in the lease to that effect,[8] with an exception in cases where the lease is held by a partnership, in which case the lease is avoided as the partnership comes to an end and there is no longer a tenant.[9] But the bankruptcy of one joint tenant does not have the effect of avoiding the lease, where there is no partnership, and so long as one remains solvent an irritancy clause founded on bankruptcy does not apply.[10] Where a tenant becomes bankrupt and the trustee refuses to adopt the lease, the landlord may rank in the bankruptcy in respect of his claim of damages.[11] The lease will pass to the trustee, unless expressly excluded.[12] He will thereby become personally liable for the tenant's obligations, including arrears of rent.[13] In the *Ebbw Vale Steel Co.* case,[11] Lord President Robertson laid down the measure of damages for the case where a trustee declined to take up an unexpired lease and consequently became liable in damages to the landlord for damage accruing to the estate from the tenant's failure to fulfil his contract. " In assessing the damages," he said, " regard must be had to the fact that while the landlord loses the stipulated rent, he on the other hand regains access to the use of the subject of the lease, and can draw whatever profit it may yield, either in his own possession or in the form of rent from a new tenant. It is quite clear for example that, if on the trustee's declining to take up the lease, the subject was let to a solvent tenant at the same rent, the damages would be nominal; or if it were let, after fair trial, at a reduced rent, the damages would be the amount of the difference between the two rents capitalised as for a present payment. On the other hand, if it be the case that the subject can only be worked at a loss, and therefore cannot be either let or worked to profit by the landlord himself, then there is nothing to set against the claim for the amount of the rents which would have been paid each year till the end of the lease, and which owing to the bankruptcy will no longer be paid. . . . The matter is more complicated where, as in the instance before us, the tenant is bound for a term of years, but with a power of terminating his lease upon his doing certain things. Here the question is what are the probabilities that the tenant, if he had remained solvent, would have done these things and thus terminated his obligation to pay the stipulated rent, and at what period would he have done so? According as these chances are appraised by the tribunal considering the claim of damages, may the unexpired term of say 20 years be treated for practical purposes as no more than 15 or 5. Obviously the calculation of any contingency cannot pretend to exactitude, and must necessarily be conjectural; but this constitutes no objection to the system and furnishes no alternative to it."

[8] Bell, *Comm.* I, 76; *Fraser* v. *Robertson* (1881) 8 R. 347; *Bidoulac* v. *Sinclair's Tr.* (1889) 17 R. 144.

[9] Partnership Act 1890, s. 33; *Walker* v. *McKnight* (1886) 13 R. 599.

[10] *Young* v. *Gerard* (1843) 6 D. 347; *Buttercase & Geddie's Tr.* v. *Geddie* (1897) 24 R. 1128.

[11] Bell, *Comm.* II, 343; *Ebbw Vale Steel Co.* v. *Wood's Tr.* (1898) 25 R. 439, 446, *per* Ld. Pres. Robertson.

[12] Stair II, 9, 26; Bell, *Prin.* § 1216.

[13] *Gibson* v. *Kirkland* (1833) 6 W. & S. 340; Rankine on *Leases* (3rd ed.), 698.

In the case of building contracts, if the trustee does not take up the contract on the bankrupt's failure, the employer may claim damages for breach of contract and to use the plant and materials on the site, though allowing an abatement *quantum meruit* in respect of the work already done by the builder.[14]

A contract of service is not determined by the employer's bankruptcy as it would be by his death; the employee is not, however, bound to continue in the employment and the bankruptcy constitutes a breach of the contract of employment for which a claim of damages may be made.[15] If an employee stays on and the business is being continued by a trustee or liquidator, a new contract of service may be inferred.[16] Such a claim by an employee being for damages and not wages is not entitled to any preferential ranking.[17]

An agent's bankruptcy will revoke the authority given him, but it is undecided whether any claim of damages accrues to the principal in the case of an agency for a fixed term.[18] On principle it would appear that such a claim should lie.

The bankruptcy of either party does not rescind a contract of sale, but the buyer's bankruptcy gives the seller the right to withhold delivery or stop the goods *in transitu*, or resell, unless payment of the price is made or tendered.[19]

If a trustee in a sequestration does adopt a contract he can only enforce fulfilment of provisions conceived in favour of the bankrupt if he can implement those incumbent on him,[20] but he may adopt one contract with a second party and repudiate another with the same party.[21] The trustee by adopting a contract renders himself personally liable thereunder.[22]

Prevention of performance

Where one party to a contract is able and willing to make due performance and the act or default of the other party prevents his so doing in terms of the contract, he is discharged from further liability under the contract and is not liable to a claim of damages for non-performance.[23] The preventing party is himself in breach. So too if the action of one party renders it impossible for the other to satisfy some condition precedent to performance, the contract is held to have been performed.[24] Similarly

14 *Kerr* v. *Dundee Gas Co.* (1861) 23 D. 343.

15 *Puncheon* v. *Haig's Tr.* (1790) Mor. 13990; *Hoey* v. *McEwan & Auld* (1867) 5 M. 814, 817; *Day* v. *Tait* (1900) 8 S.L.T. 40; *Laing* v. *Gowans* (1902) 10 S.L.T. 461; *Chapman's Case* (1866) L.R. 1 Eq. 346; *McDowall's Case* (1886) 32 Ch.D. 366.

16 *Gloag on Contract*, 363, n. 7.

17 *Day* v. *Tait*, *supra*.

18 Bell, *Comm.* I, 525.

19 Sale of Goods Act 1893, ss. 41–48.

20 *Mitchell's Tr.* v. *Galloway's Trs.* (1903) 5 F. 612.

21 *Asphaltic Limestone Co.* v. *Glasgow Corpn.*, 1907 S.C. 463.

22 *Mackessack* v. *Molleson* (1886) 13 R. 445; *Sturrock* v. *Robertson's Trs.*, 1913 S.C. 582.

23 *Jones* v. *St. John's College, Oxford* (1870) L.R. 6 Q.B. 115; *Dodd* v. *Churton* [1897] 1 Q.B. 562; *Ross* v. *McFarlane* (1894) 21 R. 396.

24 *Mackay* v. *Dick* (1881) 8 R.(H.L.) 37; Bell, *Prin.* § 50.

a party cannot be sued for non-performance until and unless any condition precedent within the other's sphere of responsibility has been performed, such as obtaining a licence,[25] nor if he declines to perform, the other party having already abandoned the project for which the work was instructed.[26] In much the same way a principal may be liable in damages to his agent if he should by default prevent him earning commission on the work on which he was employed.[27] To do any act which would render the other party liable to an action at the instance of a third party if he did tender performance will excuse non-performance and not give rise to any liability in damages.[28] If performance be prevented by any subsequent agreement between the parties when the party suing on the breach could reasonably have foreseen that such would be the result, no claim of damages for breach will lie.[29] In an action on breach of contract the defender may not found on prior negligence of the pursuer's unless the pursuer owed a duty to the defender.[30]

Breach by the other party

It is not always an excuse for the non-performance by one party that the other party to the contract is in breach of the contract. This is not necessarily quite the same as to say that a party in breach of contract cannot himself sue on that contract. It depends on the distinction between material breaches which go to the root of the contract and discharge the contract, absolving the other party from any liability to perform, and those non-material breaches which are breaches sufficient to justify a claim of damages but which do not discharge the contract in respect that they do not render further performance or completion of the contract entirely purposeless.[31]

This distinction has also been made to depend, at least in England, on the vague and confusing distinction between dependent and independent promises. In the case of independent promises one party's liability to perform subsists even though the other party fails to perform, and in such a case one party may sue for breach even though he is himself in breach of an independent promise.[32] Moreover neither party may claim that the contract is discharged so as to relieve him from liability to make further performance. In the case of dependent promises one party cannot sue unless he can show that he has performed or is ready to perform his side

[25] *Gallini* v. *Laborie* (1793) 5 T.R. 242; *Mackay, supra,* but *cf. McCormick* v. *Dalrymple* (1904) 12 S.L.T. 85.

[26] *Planché* v. *Colburn* (1831) 8 Bing. 14; *Ross* v. *McFarlane* (1894) 21 R. 396.

[27] *Macoun* v. *Erskine* [1901] 2 K.B. 493; *Re Finlay* [1913] 1 Ch. 565; *Christoforides* v. *Terry* [1924] A.C. 566; *Trollope* v. *Martyn* [1934] 2 K.B. 436; *Trollope* v. *Caplan* [1936] 2 K.B. 382; but see *Luxor* v. *Cooper* [1941] A.C. 108.

[28] *European Mail Co.* v. *R.M.S.P. Co.* (1861) 30 L.J.C.P. 247; *Omnium d'Enterprises* v. *Sutherland* [1919] 1 K.B. 618; *Guy-Pell* v. *Foster* [1930] 2 Ch. 169.

[29] *Dodd* v. *Churton* [1897] 1 Q.B. 562.

[30] *Vaile* v. *Hobson* (1933) 149 L.T. 283.

[31] *Wade* v. *Waldon,* 1909 S.C. 571.

[32] *Huntoon Co.* v. *Kolynos* [1930] 1 Ch. 528.

of the agreement, and breach by the one party discharges the liability of the other. The criterion of dependency or independency is one of intention.[32] The Scottish authorities favour the principle of mutuality in contracts [33] and hence tend to hold that mutual promises are dependent *inter se*, and the test is more usually one of materiality rather than intention although the latter test may enter in also.

The position then is that a party himself in material breach of contract cannot sue the other party for the latter's breach as the first breach has discharged the contract, but a party himself in non-material breach (which gives a claim of damages but does not discharge the contract) may sue for non-performance despite his own breach. Hence the other party's breach is only an excuse for non-performance if it is so material as to discharge the contract. In *Wade* v. *Waldon* [34] Wade made an inessential breach of contract on March 2. Waldon wrongly treated it on March 13 as terminating the contract, refused to allow Wade to perform, though he was willing, and Wade sued him for damages for breach. Waldon then sued Wade for damages for breach. The court allowed a proof of damage in Wade's action and dismissed Waldon's action. The earlier inessential breach by Wade left the contract standing till terminated by Waldon's essential breach. But Waldon was barred by his own essential breach from insisting in the claim for damages against Wade.

But parties may competently agree that any particular matters shall between them be essential or conditions precedent and effect must be given to such an agreement.[35]

Anticipatory breach of contract

Anticipatory breach of contract is made when either party, before the due date for performance, intimates expressly to the other that he refuses to implement the obligations he has undertaken, or takes such action as impliedly indicates the same intention and effectively debars him from making due implement of his contractual duties.[22] It has been pointed out that the expression is unfortunate in that, properly speaking, no actual breach by non-performance in any particular can be made until the time for performance has arrived,[23] but the true position is that the one party has repudiated a promise of future performance which is presently binding on him. " His breach is a breach of a presently binding promise, not an anticipatory breach of an act to be done in the future." [24] The party thus repudiating is in default in renouncing a promise binding on him from the time of contracting till that of performance. Hence if such repudiation

33 Ersk. III, 3, 86.
34 1909 S.C. 571.
35 *Bettini* v. *Gye* (1875) 1 Q.B.D. 183; *London Guarantee Co.* v. *Fearnley* (1880) 5 App.Cas. 911.
22 *Synge* v. *Synge* [1894] 1 Q.B. 466; *Hochster* v. *De la Tour* (1853) 2 E. & B. 678; *Martin* v. *Stout* [1925] A.C. 359; *cf. Restatement of Contracts*, s. 318.
23 *Frost* v. *Knight* (1872) L.R. 7 Exch. 111, 114.
24 *Bradley* v. *Newsom* [1919] A.C. 16, 53, *per* Lord Wrenbury.

be made the party not in breach is entitled to treat this action as a repudiation of the contract and to put into effect at once the remedies which are appropriate to the particular contract breached but which would not in the ordinary way have been available to him until the due date for performance had arrived without performance being given.[25] The party who has repudiated is liable for breach now in that he has repudiated a promise presently binding on him, and he remains liable for non-performance if he stands obstinate and does not tender performance on the appointed day.

What amounts to repudiation

Not every communication between parties constitutes a repudiation of the contract. Expressions of doubt of ability to perform at the due date, or of unwillingness, do not amount to repudiation. There must be a definite refusal to perform, an expression of intention to break the contract, or acts of such a nature as to lead a reasonable person to the conclusion that the other party will not be able to perform his part.[26] It may also take the form of any action by which a party voluntarily puts it out of his power to perform the contract when the time for performance arrives; such may be treated as equivalent to an immediate refusal to perform and therefore as a repudiation of the contract.[27] If the obligation is one prestable on demand, the obligant must in general keep himself ready to perform, and any act which excludes performance, even though it may be not irremediable, will amount to a repudiation of the contract.[28] But, on the other hand, if a definite date be assigned for performance, it is sufficient if the obligant be able to perform at that time, and prior inability is of no effect, and the sale of unascertained goods or shares is not avoided by the fact that at some time prior to the date of performance the seller does not possess the requisite goods for performance.

Nor will every intermediate setback which is remediable prior to the date of the performance, such as the refusal of a third party's necessary consent, justify immediate repudiation.[29] But persistent failure or refusal to secure such consent will justify repudiation before the date of performance unless an assurance of completion is forthcoming within a reasonable time [30] and a party will not be justified in reselling something which he believes is already sold just because the other party to the prior contract disputes its validity, as such does not amount to a refusal to implement it nor does it decide the validity of the prior contract, which the seller must

[25] *Cf. White & Carter (Councils) Ltd.* v. *McGregor,* 1962 S.C.(H.L.) 1, overruling *Langford* v. *Dutch,* 1952 S.C. 15.

[26] *Forslind* v. *Bechely-Crundall,* 1922 S.C.(H.L.) 173, 190, *per* Lord Dunedin; *Freeth* v. *Burr* (1874) L.R. 9 C.P. 208; *Johnstone* v. *Milling* (1886) 16 Q.B.D. 460; *Shaffer* v. *Findlay, Durham & Brodie* [1953] 1 W.L.R. 106; *White & Carter (Councils) Ltd.* v. *McGregor,* 1962 S.C.(H.L.) 1.

[27] *N.B. Ry.* v. *Benhar Coal Co.* (1886) 14 R. 141.

[28] *Lovelock* v. *Franklyn* (1846) 8 Q.B. 371; *Synge* v. *Synge* [1894] 1 Q.B. 466; *Omnium D'Enterprises* v. *Sutherland* [1919] 1 K.B. 618.

[29] *Smith* v. *Butler* [1900] 1 Q.B. 694.

[30] *Davis* v. *Nisbett* (1861) 10 C.B.(N.S.) 752; *Stickney* v. *Keeble* [1915] A.C. 386.

remain in a position to implement.[31] It is not a repudiation of a contract for a local authority to make a by-law which incidentally results in rendering the contract commercially impossible, as they cannot be bound by the existence of the contract not to make such a by-law.[32]

To amount to a repudiation the refusal to perform the contract must be distinct and unqualified and must be treated as a breach by the innocent party who would have been entitled to insist upon performance.[33] It is not enough to justify an assumption of repudiation that a declaration of incapacity to perform has been made,[34] or a statement that the party had no means to enable him to meet the cost of his obligation,[35] or a threat of refusal to perform failing a revisal of certain conditions of price,[36] nor is the insolvency of a party the equivalent of a refusal to perform a contract, though it may give rise to other precautionary remedies, such as lien or stoppage *in transitu.*[37]

Alternatively, when the repudiation is indicated implicitly rather than expressly, it must be evidenced by some such act done by the other party as puts it outwith that party's power to perform the contract when the time for performance arrives or such as would lead a reasonable person to the conclusion that he does not intend to fulfil his part of the contract.[38] The innocent party may then treat that as equivalent to an immediate refusal to perform and so as a repudiation of the contract.[39] But before this line of action can be adopted it is probably essential that the other party's act should have finally and irretrievably rendered performance by him at a future date practically impossible. While it is a question of circumstances in each case, the facts must be such that a reasonable man would draw the inference of intention to repudiate the contract.[40] So to hire a driver and sell one's car before he arrives would not be such a breach, as another car could be readily acquired. But to marry one lady during the subsistence of a promise to marry another is a sufficient implied refusal to amount to breach as the chance of being able to offer performance at the due date is practically impossible.[41]

It is not open to a party who is under a contractual obligation to

31 *Harvey* v. *Smith* (1904) 6 F. 511, *per* Lord Kinnear; *Stickney* v. *Keeble, supra.*
32 *Cory & Son* v. *London Corporation* [1951] 2 K.B. 476.
33 *Reid* v. *Hoskins* (1855) 4 E. & B. 979; *Avery* v. *Bowden* (1855) 5 E. & B. 714; 6 E. & B. 963; *Danube Ry.* v. *Xenos* (1862) 11 C.B.(N.S.) 152; 13 C.B.(N.S.) 825; *Bartholomew* v. *Markwick* (1864) 15 C.B.(N.S.) 711; *Inchbald* v. *W. Neilgherry Coffee Co.* (1864) 17 C.B.(N.S.) 733; *Mersey Steel & Iron Co.* v. *Naylor* (1884) 9 App.Cas. 434; *Dominion Coal Co.* v. *Dominion Steel & Iron Co.* [1909] A.C. 293; *Omnium D'Enterprises* v. *Sutherland* [1919] 1 K.B. 618; *Millett* v. *Van Heek* [1921] 2 K.B. 369.
34 *Barrick* v. *Buba* (1857) 2 C.B.(N.S.) 563.
35 *Johnstone* v. *Milling* (1886) 16 Q.B.D. 460.
36 *Thornloe* v. *Macdonald* (1892) 29 S.L.R. 409.
37 Sale of Goods Act 1893, s. 48 (1).
38 *Forslind* v. *Bechely-Crundall,* 1922 S.C.(H.L.) 173; *Shaffer* v. *Findlay Durham & Brodie* [1953] 1 W.L.R. 106.
39 *N.B. Ry.* v. *Benhar Coal Co.* (1886) 14 R. 141.
40 *Carswell* v. *Collard* (1892) 19 R. 987; affd. (1893) 20 R.(H.L.) 47; *Forslind* v. *Bechely-Crundall,* 1922 S.C.(H.L.) 173; *Mersey Steel & Iron Co.* v. *Naylor* (1884) 9 App.Cas. 434, 438, *per* Lord Selborne.
41 *Short* v. *Stone* (1846) 8 Q.B. 358.

another to rid himself of it or limit his liability under it by repudiating and insisting that such repudiation be accepted and damages calculated thereon. The other party is entitled to reject the intimation, to refuse to rescind the contract and to await the date of performance and then sue for damages calculated on the loss sustained by him as at that date.

In such a case, when rescission is not effected by the innocent party at the earlier date and damages calculated as at that time, the party who intimated repudiation may reconsider his decision and make due performance at the proper time.[42] In such a case the contract remains in full force and effect as regards both parties, and the party who has offered earlier to repudiate may complete the contract or take advantage of any later circumstances favourable to him, such as a change of market price which lessens the damages due if he fails to perform on the appointed day after all, or circumstances which justify him in declining to fulfil the contract or even in finding the other party in breach and obtaining damages therefor. So in *Avery* v. *Bowden* [43] a person who had chartered a ship to load at a Russian port, intimated to the master within the running-days that he could not furnish a cargo, and advised the ship to sail. This repudiation of the contract was refused. Within the running-days war broke out, which excused the charterer from his obligation to furnish a cargo, by virtue of the prohibition on trading with enemy subjects, and was a valid defence to the shipper's claim for breach of contract. It has been held however that a promise of marriage is broken by marriage with a third party, and all conditions precedent connected with the contract to marry lapse thereby, so that even if the marriage be dissolved by death or otherwise before the conditions would have been satisfied, the original contract has been broken.[44]

Courses open to innocent party

The innocent party in such circumstances has the option of accepting the repudiation by the other party and availing himself at once of the remedies open to him, even although the time for performance has not arrived and there has therefore been no actual breach, or he may ignore the repudiation and wait until the time for performance arrives before setting in train proceedings for remedy. There is no obligation to wait and see if the other party will reconsider his refusal and make implement after all, for the innocent party is entitled not only to ultimate performance on the due date, but to an expectation of performance in the meantime, and the disappointment of this expectation amounts to a breach of the contract.[45] It is not necessary to entitle a party to accept an anticipatory repudiation that he was not himself ready to perform his part of the contract. So where a

[42] *Frost* v. *Knight* (1872) L.R. 7 Ex. 111.
[43] (1856) 6 E. & B. 953.
[44] *Short* v. *Stone* (1846) 8 Q.B. 358; *Caines* v. *Smith* (1846) 15 M. & W. 189.
[45] *Martin* v. *Stout* [1925] A.C. 359, 363; *White & Carter (Councils) Ltd.* v. *McGregor*, 1962 S.C.(H.L.) 1.

railway company intimated before the time of delivery that railway chairs which they had ordered would not be accepted, the manufacturer was held entitled to his claim of damages despite the fact that the chairs had not been manufactured and could not have been supplied then.[46]

And it would appear on principle that the same would apply even if the innocent party could not possibly have fulfilled his part of the contract and was even on the point of making default himself. Such a state of affairs will of course be material in arriving at the assessment of damages, in respect that he will only be entitled to recompense for the loss and outlays and nothing can be claimed for work not done.

Where refusal to perform accepted

It is clear that if a distinct refusal to perform be made, the other party may accept this as a repudiation of the contract, and in that case a subsequent offer by the other party is too late, even if made within the time originally fixed for performance or within a reasonable time. So when objection was taken to the title to heritage and an undertaking to remedy it was not given within a period assigned, the other party was entitled to resile from the bargain and a subsequent offer to clear the title came too late.[47] In such a case the innocent party accepting the repudiation must take reasonable steps to minimise the damage due to the breach and act reasonably in the circumstances.[48]

It is also well established that when an anticipatory breach of contract has taken place the innocent party may take action at once and need not wait until the due date for performance merely to ascertain the damages. So where a person married within the period in which he had promised to marry another, the other was entitled to sue at once,[49] and when a servant received intimation that his services were not required a month before his appointment commenced, an immediate action was competent.[50]

Measure of damages in case of anticipatory breach

The measure of damages exigible for breach of contract may be materially affected by the decision to accept or not to accept an intimation by the other party of his intention to repudiate the contract. Where the prior intimation of refusal is duly made by the one party and accepted by the other, the contract is rescinded as at the date of the acceptance, and damages are exigible, quantified as at that date, and not as at the due date of performance, which may be still in the future.

Where the prior intimation is refused, the damages fall to be calculated

[46] *Cort* v. *Ambergate Ry.* (1851) 17 Q.B. 127; *British & Beningtons* v. *N.W. Cachar Tea Co.* [1923] A.C. 48.

[47] *Gilfillan* v. *Cadell and Grant* (1893) 21 R. 269; see too *Martin* v. *Stout* [1925] A.C. 359.

[48] *Roth* v. *Taysen* (1896) 12 T.L.R. 211.

[49] *Whitehead* v. *Phillips* (1902) 10 S.L.T. 577; *Frost* v. *Knight* (1872) L.R. 7 Ex. 111. See *Morison* v. *Morison* (1902) 10 S.L.T. 324.

[50] *Hochster* v. *De la Tour* (1853) 2 E. & B. 678.

with reference to the market price ruling at the due date of delivery.[51] The difference in damages which these alternative courses of action may bring out may be material, as in the case of a subject of sale with a fluctuating price. Neither party will be allowed to profit or lose from any such fluctuation by choosing a date at which damages are to be fixed, but the market rate ruling at the date when repudiation becomes effective, by acceptance of the repudiation and repurchase elsewhere, or by non-performance, decides the question.[52] So if repudiation be intimated but not accepted and performance later be not made, the damages, being the difference between the contract price and the market price at the date of performance, will not be enhanced by the fact that the price has been higher in the interval.[52] If over that period the price has risen the disappointed buyer will receive that much more in his award of damages, and conversely if the price has fallen. If the price has fallen below the contract price, *semble*, the buyer is entitled to nominal damages for the breach.[53]

If there is no fixed time for delivery the measure of damages will be the difference between the contract price and the market price at the time of refusal to deliver; the time may be fixed by reference to an event such as the arrival of a certain ship at a port.[54]

When a buyer accepts an anticipatory refusal to deliver as final he may at once go into the market and buy in against the seller, charging the latter in the claim of damages with the difference between what he has paid and the contract price; but if, however, he does not choose to buy, the measure of damages will be the difference between the contract price and the price ruling at the date when the contract should have been performed, except in the case where the seller can show that the buyer has acted unreasonably in not mitigating his damages by buying the goods.[54]

In *Howie* v. *Anderson* [71] Howie bought railway stock from Anderson to be delivered on January 8 following. The latter intimated repudiation of the contract on October 31 which Howie refused to accept and it was held that the true measure of damages for failure to implement the obligation was the difference between the purchase-money and the selling price of the stock, as at January 8, when the shares were to have been delivered, and not as at October 31 when the seller intimated his withdrawal from the bargain. It was pointed out that in the absence of acceptance, the contract was not brought to an end on October 31 as one party cannot unilaterally terminate a contract. " The very intimation was a wrongful act—the commencement of the wrong which was consummated by the actual failure of delivery. . . . The bargain continued to subsist as

51 *Howie* v. *Anderson* (1848) 10 D. 355.
52 *Michael* v. *Hart* [1902] 1 K.B. 482 (C.A.).
53 *Michael* v. *Hart* [1902] 1 K.B. 482, 492–493; *Melachrino* v. *Nickoll and Knight* [1920] 1 K.B. 693.
54 *Melachrino, supra*; *Millett* v. *Van Heek* [1921] 2 K.B. 369.
71 (1848) 10 D. 355, referring to *Watt* v. *Mitchell* (1839) 1 D. 1157.

a binding contract to be fulfilled at the proper time by the defender, after his intimation . . . exactly as if that intimation had not been made. It was still a current binding obligation, imposing on the defender the same duty of precise and punctual performance; and it was in no degree broken in any sense which can affect the interests of the pursuer to demand compensation if not fulfilled on the stipulated day." [72]

It has been held by the Court of Appeal in England that the rule prescribed in section 51 (3) of the Sale of Goods Act 1893, does not apply to anticipatory breach. In any event that only bears to be a prima facie rule, to ascertain the measure of damages, where there is an available market for the goods in question, by taking the difference between the contract price and the market price at the due time of delivery, or if no time was fixed, at the time of refusal to deliver.[73]

If a purchaser accepts an intimation of repudiation of the contract by the seller and claims damages immediately on the repudiation, the damages fall to be assessed with reference to the market price of the goods at the time when they ought to have been delivered under the contract. "If the action comes to trial before the contractual date for delivery has arrived, the court must arrive at the price as best it can. . . . If [the seller] can show that the buyer acted unreasonably in not buying against him the date to be taken is the date when the buyer ought to have gone into the market to mitigate damages." [74]

The court is not, however, bound to a rigid application of rules but must judge whether the action of the parties is reasonable in the circumstances. So in *Dunkirk Colliery* v. *Lever*,[75] where the contract was for the sale of coal by weekly deliveries, the buyer wrongfully repudiated shortly after the commencement of the contract and the sellers spent several weeks attempting to dissuade the buyer before accepting his repudiation. By this time there was no available market and they only with great difficulty sold to a new purchaser. It was held that their conduct had been reasonable despite the lapse of time and that they were entitled to the full amount of the difference in prices as damages.

On the other hand where charterers of a ship were in breach of their obligation to supply cargo, but offered the master of the ship a choice of three other ports, with the guarantee of a good cargo and payment of all extra charges incurred, it was held that damages fell to be substantially reduced when the master refused to go elsewhere but waited at the port designated till the contracted date and claimed full damages, on the ground that he had not done what was reasonable in the circumstances.[76] So, too, it has been held unreasonable to refuse an offer by the sellers to take back

[72] *Ibid., per* L.J.C. Hope, at 358.
[73] *Millett* v. *Van Heek & Co.* [1921] 2 K.B. 369.
[74] *Melachrino, supra, per* Bailhache J.
[75] (1878) 9 Ch.D. 20, affd. (1880) 43 L.T. 706.
[76] *Wilson* v. *Hicks* (1857) 26 L.J.Ex. 262.

unsatisfactory goods so as to mitigate damages, and damages were accordingly reduced.[77]

Remote consequences

In *Howie* v. *Anderson* [78] it was remarked that if the pursuer could have shown any special loss, being the direct and not the remote consequence of the breach of bargain which he had sustained, owing to the wrongful act of the defender, over and above the loss of the subject of the contract, it might have been competent to include that in the claim. So if the agreement contemplated at the time of the sale that the purchaser was buying for resale he can recover in his damages the loss of profit he would have made on that resale as well as any expenses or damages he may be required to pay by failure to fulfil that subsequent contract.[79] And in any event the loss on any sub-contract may be evidential of the damage directly sustained in cases when there is no market for the goods at the place of delivery.[80]

Breach at due time for performance

Breach of contract taking place at the due date for performance may occur in several ways, by tendering performance defective in quality, or defective in quantity by short delivery or excess delivery, or defective by not being tendered till after the due time, or defective in respect of performance not being tendered at all. More than one of these may occur in any one contract and there may also be a failure in any other respect to implement any of the obligations undertaken in the contract. In each case the failure will give rise to a claim of damages, and if it is so material as to go to the root of the contract will justify rescission of the contract altogether with a claim of damages on that basis.[81] These varieties of breach are fully considered and illustrated in later chapters under the separate heads applicable to particular classes of contracts. Certain general considerations are considered here.

Unless excused by circumstances, performance necessary to discharge a contract must be in strict accordance with its terms and anything else is a breach of contract.[82] So a contract for insurance of a ship was held breached by failure to keep the ship insured for three days though the ship had been delivered by the underwriters and the policy was later executed accordingly.[83]

[77] *Houndsditch Warehouse Co.* v. *Waltex* [1944] K.B. 579.
[78] (1848) 10 D. 355.
[79] *Grébert-Borgnis* v. *Nugent* (1885) 15 Q.B.D. 85, 90; *Re Bourgeois and Wilson Holgate & Co.* (1921) 25 Com.Cas. 260; *Patrick* v. *Russo-British Grain Export Co.* [1927] 2 K.B. 535.
[80] *Elbinger Actien-Gesellschaft* v. *Armstrong* (1874) L.R. 9 Q.B. 473; *Stroud* v. *Austin* (1883) 1 Cab. & E. 119.
[81] *Wade* v. *Waldon*, 1909 S.C. 571.
[82] *Thomas* v. *Harrowing S.S. Co.* [1915] A.C. 58; *Brandt & Co.* v. *Morris* [1917] 2 K.B. 784.
[83] *Parry* v. *Great Ship Co.* (1863) 4 B. & S. 556.

Essential or inessential breach

A breach, of whatever form it takes, entitles the innocent party to maintain an action for damages: it does not, however, always or necessarily discharge the contract and absolve the parties from further performance of their obligations thereunder.[84] Breach of a stipulation which does not go to the root of the contract does not entitle the party pleading the breach to declare the contract at an end though it entitles him to claim damages: only essential breach does that.[85] It is of course competent for parties to stipulate that some matters, however trivial they may be, shall between them form conditions precedent, the breach of which will entitle the innocent party to declare the contract at an end and also claim damages,[86] but otherwise it is for the court to say, looking to the nature and importance of the stipulation in question, whether it goes to the essence of the contract or not.[87] In *Wade*,[84] failure by a music-hall artiste to give fourteen days' notice of bill-matter was held not to justify rescission, but only damages: in *Birkett, Sperling & Co.* v. *Engholm* [88] failure to provide an adequate policy in a c.i.f. contract was sufficiently material to justify rescission, as was the conduct of an agent in taking a secret commission and acting for trade rivals.[89]

Alternatively a breach of contract may be said to discharge the contract only if its effect is to render it purposeless for the innocent party to proceed further with performance, as when the party in breach shows an intention no longer to be bound by the contract [91] or breaks a stipulation so essential to the continuance of the contractual tie that the very foundation of the contract is destroyed.[92] It is material to note that if the contract is discharged by the breach the innocent party is not only entitled to recover damages from the defaulting party but is relieved of the obligations he had himself undertaken under the contract. The quantum of damages will also be affected; in the one case the party in breach will only be liable for damages in respect of the breach of one or two possibly trifling elements in the contract, in the other he will be liable for the damages flowing from the complete failure of the contract. Where the party aggrieved by the breach has already paid any part of the price or other consideration for the contract, he is entitled to recover this on the breach taking place, whether or not damage has been suffered, and in addition to any claim of damages he may make.[93]

84 *Wade* v. *Waldon*, 1909 S.C. 571.
85 *Wade, supra*; *Wallis* v. *Pratt and Haynes* [1910] 2 K.B. 1003, 1012.
86 *e.g. Standard Life Assce. Co.* v. *Weems* (1884) 11 R.(H.L.) 48; *Dawsons Ltd.* v. *Bonnin*, 1922 S.C.(H.L.) 156; *Provincial Assce. Co.* v. *Morgan* [1933] A.C. 240; *cf. Guy-Pell* v. *Foster* [1930] 2 Ch. 169, 187.
87 *Wade, supra*; *London Guarantie Co.* (1880) L.R. 5 App.Cas. 911; *Bettini* v. *Gye* (1875) L.R. 1 Q.B.D. 183; *Bentsen* v. *Taylor* [1893] 2 Q.B. 274, 280; *Re Rubel Bronze & Metal Co. and Vos* [1918] 1 K.B. 315, 321; *Guy-Pell* v. *Foster* [1930] 2 Ch. 169, 187; *Forslind* v. *Bechely-Crundall*, 1922 S.C.(H.L.) 173, 190.
88 (1872) 10 M. 170.
89 *Graham* v. *United Turkey Red Co.*, 1922 S.C. 533.
91 *Freeth* v. *Burr* (1874) L.R. 9 C.P. 208, 213.
92 *Mersey Steel & Iron Co.* v. *Naylor* (1884) 9 App.Cas. 434, 443.
93 *Aird and Coghill* v. *Pullan and Adams* (1904) 7 F. 258.

Effect of distinction on claims of damages

The distinction of materiality between those breaches of contract which amount to a repudiation of the contract and justify the other party in declaring it at an end and those minor breaches which do not so go to the root of the contract as to justify rescission, has an effect on the amount of damages recoverable. If the breach is sufficiently material to justify rescission of the contract the party in breach is liable for all the natural and direct consequences of the failure of the whole contract. On the other hand if the breach is only of a minor stipulation of the contract the damages due will be only such as compensate the innocent party for the prejudice suffered by that breach. Furthermore, if one party alleges that the other is in breach of a material stipulation and purports to rescind the contract and claim damages on that account, and is then found not to have been justified in rescinding the contract, that party will then become liable to the other for breach of contract. Thus, in *Wade* v. *Waldon* [94] a comedian was in breach of his contract with a theatre manager, and the latter treated it as a material breach and attempted to rescind the contract as well as claiming damages. It was held that he was not entitled to the rescission but only to the damages, and the comedian in turn was entitled to damages from him for wrongfully purporting to rescind and not allowing him to play.[95] Where the breach is material and the injured party elects to rescind the contract he is entitled whether the breach was actual or anticipatory to recover damages for the loss of the contract as a whole, and even though the breach though essential be merely partial.[96] Regard must be had in measuring the damages not only to the particular breach but to the fact that the contract has been completely determined. A partial breach which leads to rescission amounts in effect to a constructive and anticipatory abandonment of the entire contract and damages are to be ascertained accordingly.[97]

Operation of essential breach

The occurrence of an essential breach, while entitling the innocent party to declare the contract at an end and claim damages on that basis, does not however *automatically* terminate the contract except probably in the case where the breach is so essential as to frustrate the contract by rendering further performance by the defaulting party impossible, *e.g.*, where a ship-owner breaks contract by scuttling the ship.[98] More usually the contract is

[94] 1909 S.C. 571.
[95] *Cf. Carswell* v. *Collard* (1893) 20 R.(H.L.) 47.
[96] *Laird* v. *Pim* (1841) 7 M. & W. 474, 478; *Hochster* v. *De la Tour* (1853) 2 E. & B. 678; *Frost* v. *Knight* (1872) L.R. 7 Ex. 111; *Noble* v. *Edwardes* (1877) 5 Ch.D. 378; *Lodder* v. *Slowey* [1904] A.C. 442, 453; *General Billposting Co.* v. *Atkinson* [1909] A.C. 118; *Dominion Coal Co.* v. *Dominion Iron & Steel Co.* [1909] A.C. 293; *Mayson* v. *Clouet* [1924] A.C. 980; *Hirji Mulji* v. *Cheong Yue S.S. Co.* [1926] A.C. 497; *Wood Brick Co.* v. *Ferris* [1935] 1 K.B. 613; [1935] 2 K.B. 198; *Joseph Constantine S.S. Line* v. *Imperial Smelting Corp.* [1942] A.C. 154, 171.
[97] *Salmond and Williams on Contract*, 562.
[98] *Constantine Line* v. *Imperial Smelting Corpn.* [1942] A.C. 154, 191, *per* Lord Wright.

only rendered voidable so that it is in the option of the innocent party to rescind and claim damages for the loss of the contract as a whole [99] or to affirm the contract and claim damages for the breach.[1]

If in the period between essential breach and election to treat the contract as rescinded or subsisting subject to the claim for damages some event happens which dissolves the contract, such as supervening impossibility of performance, the right of rescission is lost but the claim of damages for the breach still subsists.[2]

These conditions apply where the breach is essential but in respect of part of the contract, but in such a case regard must be had not only to the particular partial breach but to the fact that this breach has involved the failure of the whole contract. The instance has been put that if a building contract is broken by the failure of the building contractor to proceed with the work in due time, so that the building owner is entitled to rescind the contract and does so, he is entitled to recover damages, not merely for the loss so suffered by the delay up to the date of the rescission, but also for the loss suffered by him through the total non-performance of the contract, although the time for complete performance may not have arrived at the date of rescission. " In other words, a partial breach which leads to rescission amounts in effect to a constructive and anticipatory abandonment of the entire contract, and in an action for damages the plaintiff's compensation is determined accordingly. In such an action for damages the plaintiff may, of course, include his loss in respect of any acts of performance which he himself may have done before rescission; and conversely, he must reduce his claim by the amount of any benefit received by him through acts of performance done by the other party." [3]

Notice of rescission on occurrence of essential breach

A party who wishes to exercise his right to rescind a contract and claim damages on the ground of the breach of a material stipulation in the contract is not bound to intimate the fact to the other contracting party but it is advisable to do so, as if no such intimation be made and the other party is led to act upon the assumption that the contract still stands, as where he incurs expense or use of material and labour, the innocent party may find his right to rejection barred. The reason is that a contracting party is not entitled so to act as to cause unnecessary loss to the other party without any resulting benefit to himself [4] just as he must take reasonable steps to

[99] *Lodder* v. *Slowey* [1904] A.C. 442, 453; *General Billposting Co.* v. *Atkinson* [1909] A.C. 118; *Dominion Coal Co.* v. *Dominion Iron Co.* [1909] A.C. 293, 311; *Mayson* v. *Clouet* [1924] A.C. 980; *Hirji Mulji* v. *Cheong Yue* [1926] A.C. 497, 510; *Harold Wood* v. *Ferris* [1935] 2 K.B. 198; *Joseph Constantine S.S. Line* v. *Imperial Smelting Co.* [1942] A.C. 154, 171, 187.

[1] *Bentsen* v. *Taylor* [1893] 2 Q.B. 274; *Mayson* v. *Clouet* [1924] A.C. 980, 985; *Hindley* v. *General Fibre Co.* [1940] 2 K.B. 517, 553.

[2] *Avery* v. *Bowden* (1856) 6 E. & B. 953.

[3] *Salmond and Williams on Contract*, 562.

[4] *Dunford and Elliot* v. *Macleod* (1902) 4 F. 912, 920, *per* Lord McLaren; *Sandersen* v. *Armour*, 1921 S.C. 18; 1922 S.C.(H.L.) 117, *per* L.P. Clyde; *Bentsen* v. *Taylor* [1893] 2 Q.B. 274.

minimise the amount of damages he claims.[5] This will apply particularly if an innocent third party be affected.

Hence in *Dunford & Elliot* v. *Macleod*,[6] where a shipbroker had contracted to supply vessels to convey iron-ore in about equal monthly instalments from September to December and supplied no ships till late October, it was held that the charterer was entitled to rescind the contract on the ground of undue delay, but that, having previously written accepting these vessels, which arrived at the end of October, in part implement of the contract, he could not refuse to load them when they arrived and a counter-claim of damages for refusal to load was sustained. Where goods have not been paid for, however, it seems unnecessary to intimate rescission of the contract as a prelude to refusing further supplies.[7]

Partial failure in performance of the contract

It has already been stated that breach of contract does not always justify rescission but that it is a question of degree and the materiality of the condition breached whether such a remedy is appropriate in addition to a claim of damages. A minor breach of a condition which is part of the contract but not an essential stipulation going to the root of the contract will justify only a claim of damages.[8] It depends whether breach of a particular stipulated condition of the contract would make the performance of the rest of the contract a materially different thing from what the other party had stipulated for, or whether it merely partially affects it in a way which may be adequately compensated by damages.[9]

It is open to parties to specify in their contract that certain conditions shall be material, breach of which will justify rescission, and they may competently bring the most minor and unimportant conditions within that category. In the absence of any such provision it is however a question of construction of the contract and for the court to determine whether a particular stipulation is material for this purpose, looking to the intention of the parties so far as that is discoverable. No more conclusive criterion can be given for the question whether any given partial breach may be treated, failing express provision in the contract, as justifying rescission and damages, or damages alone, than that it is a question of materiality. Of course a total failure or refusal to perform undoubtedly justifies the innocent party in declaring the contract at an end.[10] Beyond that the question can only be illustrated.[11]

[5] Chap. 28, *supra*.
[6] *Supra*, note 4.
[7] *Barclay* v. *Anderston Foundry Co.* (1856) 18 D. 119.
[8] *Wade* v. *Waldon*, 1909 S.C. 571; *Forslind* v. *Bechely-Crundall*, 1922 S.C.(H.L.) 173; *Re Rubel Bronze Co.* [1918] 1 K.B. 315.
[9] *Bettini* v. *Gye* (1876) 1 Q.B.D. 183.
[10] *Johannesburg Municipal Council* v. *Stewart & Co.*, 1909 S.C. 860; 1909 S.C.(H.L.) 53.
[11] See *Wade* v. *Waldon*, 1909 S.C. 571 (theatre artiste); *Poussard* v. *Spiers* (1876) 1 Q.B.D. 410 (actress); *Davie* v. *Stark* (1876) 3 R. 1114 (lease); *Shaw* v. *McDonell* (1786) M. 9185 (book); *Birkett Sperling & Co.* v. *Engholm* (1871) 10 M. 170 (sale); *Reidar* v. *Arcos* [1927] 1 K.B. 352 (charterparty).

Partial breach may be treated broadly under the heads of failure in point of time, *i.e.*, delayed performance, and failure in quantity or quality, *i.e.* defective performance.

Materiality of time of performance

It depends on the nature and terms of the contract in question whether a failure in respect of time of performance is the breach of a material stipulation of the contract or not. Where the price of the goods is liable to vary from day to day, as in contracts for supply or carriage of goods, it would appear prima facie that stipulations as to time of performance are of the essence of the contract. In contracts for the sale of goods time of performance is prima facie of the essence of the contract.[12] So it has been held, where sugar was to be shipped from a foreign port with a stipulation that shipment was to be made " during August next," that failure to ship a material part of the consignment during August entitled the purchaser to repudiate the contract.[13] It was indicated in that case that the pursuers had lost by not getting their sugar shipped in August, though no positive evidence was given of this. The buyer's failure to provide a ship on the date agreed for delivery of coals was held to justify the seller's repudiation of any obligation to deliver.[14] When the price is fluctuating delivery of goods or warrants for goods is material and tender a day late will not satisfy the contract.[15] In charterparties statements that the ship will be at a place on a given day,[16] or that she will be ready to receive cargo on a certain day,[17] or that she will sail by a certain day,[18] are usually material stipulations, though failure therein from perils excepted in the charter may protect from damages but not the right of rescission.[19] Also material is a provision as to date of arrival.[20]

It is always open to the parties to make the time of performance an express stipulation of the contract, in which case time will clearly be held to be of the essence of the contract. Otherwise the matter must depend on their implied intention and on the general circumstances of the case whether the court will regard the time of performance as essential and so material as to justify repudiation.[21]

When one party engages to do something, performance of which depends entirely on himself, and the contract makes no express stipulation as to the time of performance, there will be implied an understanding to

12 *Bowes* v. *Shand* (1877) 2 App.Cas. 455; *Reuter* v. *Sala* (1879) 4 C.P.D. 239; *Sharp* v. *Christmas* (1892) 8 T.L.R. 687; *Hartley* v. *Hymans* [1920] 3 K.B. 475; *Rickards* v. *Oppenhaim* [1950] 1 K.B. 616. Contrast *Paton* v. *Payne* (1897) 35 S.L.R. 112 (printing machine).

13 *Grieve, Son & Co.* v. *Konig & Co.* (1880) 7 R. 521, 524, *per* Lord Shand. See too, *Bowes* v. *Shand* (1877) 2 App.Cas. 455.

14 *Shaw & Co.* v. *Waddell & Son* (1900) 2 F. 1070.

15 *Colvin* v. *Short* (1857) 19 D. 890.

16 *Corkling* v. *Massey* (1873) L.R. 8 C.P. 395.

17 *Oliver* v. *Fielden* (1849) 4 Ex. 135; *Seeger* v. *Duthie* (1860) 8 C.B.(N.S.) 45.

18 *Bentsen* v. *Taylor* [1893] 2 Q.B. 274.

19 *Smith* v. *Dart* (1884) 14 Q.B.D. 105.

20 *Dunford & Elliot* v. *Macleod* (1902) 4 F. 912; *Mackenzie* v. *Liddell* (1883) 10 R. 705; *Nelson* v. *Dundee Shipping Co.*, 1907 S.C. 927.

21 *Cf. Macbride* v. *Hamilton* (1875) 2 R. 775.

perform within what is, having regard to all the circumstances of the case, a reasonable time [22]; the phrase " discharged with all dispatch according to the custom of the port " in a charterparty was held to mean that the charterer was bound to discharge within a reasonable time, having regard to every impediment arising out of the custom or practice of the particular port, which the charterer could not have overcome by the use of reasonable diligence.[23]

Such phrases as " directly," [24] " forthwith," [25] or " as soon as possible," [26] imply greater expedition than merely performance within a reasonable time, and require active avoidance of delay and due diligence to obviate hindrance so as to perform within such a time as is reasonably considered sufficient for a person with the necessary appliances to execute the contract. A word or phrase of time may also be construed by reference to the context of the contract. So where goods were sold to be delivered forthwith, and the price was to be payable within fourteen days of the contract, it was held to be obvious that the parties' intention was that delivery should be made within the same fourteen days.[27]

In contracts for the sale of goods prima facie " month " means a calendar month,[28] and the same holds for bills of exchange, cheques and promissory notes.[29] By the common law of Scotland a month probably means a calendar month [30]; in England a lunar month,[31] with many exceptions.

The interpretation of " day " in contracts, particularly charterparties, has frequently caused dispute, for though general rules can be given, each case depends very much on its own particular wording. In the absence of a custom of the port,[32] days mean consecutive calendar days of twenty-four hours commencing at midnight, and include Sundays and holidays.[33] Part of a day counts as a whole day.[34]

In contracts for the sale of land it is established, at least in England,

22 *Postlethwaite* v. *Freeland* (1880) 5 App.Cas. 599; *Castlegate Shipping Co.* v. *Dempsey* [1892] 1 Q.B. 854; *Hick* v. *Raymond* [1893] A.C. 22; *Carlton Steamship Co.* v. *Castle Mail Packet Co.* [1898] A.C. 486; *Lyle Shipping Co.* v. *Cardiff Corpn.* [1900] 2 Q.B. 638; *Hulthen* v. *Stewart* [1903] A.C. 389; *Barque Quilpué Ltd.* v. *Brown* [1904] 2 K.B. 264.

23 *Postlethwaite* v. *Freeland, supra.*

24 *Duncan* v. *Topham* (1849) 8 C.B. 225; *Verlest* v. *M.U. Insurance Co.* [1925] 2 K.B. 137.

25 *Roberts* v. *Brett* (1865) 11 H.L.C. 337; *Hudson* v. *Hill* (1874) 43 L.J.C.P. 273; *Middleton* v. *Leslie* (1892) 19 R. 801; *Pollock* v. *N.B. Ry.* (1900) 3 F. 727; *Larsen* v. *Hart* (1900) 2 F.(J.) 54; *Brown* v. *Mags. of Bonnyrigg*, 1936 S.C. 258.

26 *Hydraulic Engineering Co.* v. *McHaffie* (1879) 4 Q.B.D. 670; *Attwood* v. *Emery* (1856) 1 C.B.(N.S.) 110.

27 *Staunton* v. *Wood* (1851) 16 Q.B. 638.

28 Sale of Goods Act 1893, s. 10 (2).

29 Bills of Exchange Act 1882, s. 14 (4). As to calculation of a calendar month, see *Migotti* v. *Colville* (1879) 4 C.P.D. 233, 236, *per* Brett L.J.

30 *Farquharson* v. *Whyte* (1886) 13 R.(J.) 29.

31 *Phipps & Co.* v. *Rogers* [1925] 1 K.B. 14. For trade meaning of " month " see *Bissell* v. *Beard* (1873) 28 L.T. 740.

32 *Nielsen* v. *Wait* (1885) 16 Q.B.D. 67; *Cornfoot* v. *Royal Exchange Assurance* [1903] 2 K.B. 363; [1904] 1 K.B. 40.

33 *The Katy* [1895] P. 56.

34 *Commercial S.S. Coy.* v. *Boulton* (1875) L.R. 10 Q.B. 346.

that the time of completion is not of the essence of the contract,[35] and the reasoning seems equally applicable in Scotland.[36]

Even, however, in mercantile contracts, it is only a presumption that time is of the essence of the contract and delay breach of a material term. There is no absolute rule that a short delay in delivery or acceptance of goods will justify repudiation of the contract. A party should act reasonably and wait for a time which is reasonable in the circumstances of the case before intimating the rescission of the contract.[37] But if the market for goods is liable to sudden and substantial fluctuations in demand and price, or if there seemed reasonable ground for apprehension that the party in delay was not in fact going to fulfil his contract at all, then a lesser delay will justify repudiation of the contract.[38]

In contracts of employment such as for the execution of engineering projects which extend over a substantial period of time, failure to complete a particular part of the work within the time fixed will not in general justify rejection, but only a claim of damages for the delay.[39] So, too, a tenant cannot throw up a lease because the landlord has not completed certain repairs within the stipulated time.[40] But in cases of this kind it must be a question of degree of the materiality, and rejection and rescission of the contract is possible when the delay becomes unreasonable.

Damages for delay

In all these cases, however, independently of rescission of the contract, a claim of damages is competent for failure to perform the contractual obligation at the specified time or within a reasonable time.[41] Such will amount normally to the difference, if any, between the value of the goods at the time when they should have been delivered and that ruling at the time when they were delivered.[42] In addition, damages will be recoverable for such natural and direct consequences as should reasonably have been within the contemplation of the parties when they made the contract. But in carriage by sea, this may not be applicable if the voyage is an ocean one of uncertain duration and if the parties cannot be taken to have contracted with any reasonable expectation as to the length of transit or the state of the market,[43] and in such a case the cargo-owner can only recover damages in the form of interest on the value of the goods during the delay.[44]

Materiality of time of payment

It is only in very special cases that the time of payment is treated as a

35 *Stickney* v. *Keeble* [1915] A.C. 386; *Steedman* v. *Drinkle* [1916] 1 A.C. 275.
36 *Rodger (Builders)* v. *Fawdry*, 1950 S.C. 483.
37 *Carswell* v. *Collard* (1892) 19 R. 987; affd. (1893) 20 R.(H.L.) 47.
38 *Cf. Shaw* v. *Waddell* (1900) 2 F. 1070.
39 *Macbride* v. *Hamilton* (1875) 2 R. 775, and see *Paton* v. *Payne* (1897) 35 S.L.R. 112. But see *Hydraulic Engineering Co.* v. *McHaffie* (1878) 4 Q.B.D. 670.
40 *Todd* v. *Bowie* (1902) 4 F. 435; *McKimmie's Trs.* v. *Armour* (1899) 2 F. 156.
41 *Webster* v. *Cramond Iron Co.* (1875) 2 R. 752.
42 *Williams* v. *Agius* [1914] A.C. 510, 522.
43 *The Parana* (1877) 2 P.D. 118; *cf. Dunn* v. *Bicknall Bros.* [1902] 2 K.B. 614.
44 *Cf. British Columbia Sawmill Co.* v. *Nettleship* (1868) L.R. 3 C.P. 499.

material condition of the contract, though it may always expressly be made so.[45] The Sale of Goods Act 1893,[46] enacts as a general rule that unless a different intention appears from the terms of the contract, stipulations as to time of payment are not deemed to be of the essence of a contract of sale. Even prior to the Act this view was upheld in *Linn* v. *Shields*,[47] where stacks of corn were sold to be delivered as required, and it was held that failure to pay for each stack as delivered was not so material as to justify repudiation of the contract.[48]

The seller is, however, only required to wait a reasonable time for payment and not indefinitely, and if a reasonable time has elapsed without tender of payment, he is entitled to obtain a decree annulling the sale.[49] Under the Sale of Goods Act [50] the seller's remedy is an action for the price where the property has passed, or though it has not, where the price was payable on a day certain, irrespective of delivery.[51] Failure to pay an instalment of money is not, prima facie, an essential breach justifying the rescission of the contract.[52]

Nevertheless, exceptionally, stipulations as to the time of payment have been held to be material in several cases: as where an instalment contract provided for payment by bills at certain specified dates. These were dishonoured and though it was ultimately arranged that debentures should be taken for them, it was held that the suppliers were entitled to repudiate the contract.[53] But the party in breach in that case was known to be an undischarged bankrupt, and the peculiar arrangements for payment were designed to transmit payments from sub-purchasers to the sellers. In *Payzu* v. *Saunders* [54] an inference of intended repudiation drawn from failure to make punctual payment for the first instalment of a contract was held to be unjustified, and the defendants, who had sought to rescind, were found liable in damages for breach of contract. In *Turnbull* v. *McLean* [55] it was held that refusal to pay for one instalment on a ground which, if justified, would have justified refusal of future payments, constituted a breach of a material condition which rendered the contract voidable at the instance of the other party.

Again, when a dispute in a contract of sale was settled on the basis that the purchaser should have three months to pay for what he had received, and an option to require delivery of the remainder, the House of Lords were of the opinion that payment within the three months was a condition precedent to the exercise of the option to the remainder.[56]

45 *Gatty* v. *Maclaine*, 1921 S.C.(H.L.) 1.
46 s. 10 (1).
47 (1863) 2 M. 88.
48 *Cf. Martindale* v. *Smith* (1841) 1 Q.B. 389. See also *Mersey Steel Co.* v. *Naylor* (1884) 9 App.Cas. 434, 444.
49 *Black* v. *Dick* (1814) Hume 699.
50 s. 49 (1).
51 s. 49 (2).
52 *Mersey Steel & Iron Co., supra.*
53 *Barclay* v. *Anderston Foundry Co.* (1856) 18 D. 1190.
54 [1919] 2 K.B. 581.
55 (1874) 1 R. 730.
56 *Morris* v. *Baron* [1918] A.C. 1.

In other contracts the time of payment is not usually of the essence of the contract.[57]

Materiality of defective performance

When a contract is performed timeously but the quality or character of performance is not of the contractual standard, it is a question of fact in each case whether the degree of failure is so material as to justify rescission of the contract in addition to damages for the breach. Under the Sale of Goods Act 1893,[58] the buyer may reject the goods for a material defect and repudiate the contract or retain them and claim damages.[59] In the case of machinery it appears that a remediable defect is not so material as to justify rescission, and the proper remedy is to have the defect put right at the supplier's expense,[60] that is, in effect to exact damages for defective quality equivalent to the cost of repairs. This question has frequently arisen in the case of leases, and there are many narrow distinctions of fact whether failure in particular circumstances to maintain subjects in a tenantable condition is so material as to justify repudiation of the lease.[61]

Total failure in performance

When breach of contract is made by total non-performance there is no doubt that this may be treated as a repudiation of the contract, entitling the innocent party to declare the contract at an end and also to recover damages.[62] It is hard to conceive of circumstances in which a party would decline to treat a complete failure or refusal to perform as giving ground for rescinding the contract. In such a case the appropriate measure of damages is the whole loss caused directly and naturally by the non-performance of the contract. What this will amount to, and how it is to be quantified in different cases, is a question of circumstances which can only be dealt with under the various kinds of contracts, but it will regularly include the loss of profit on the whole transaction and any expenditure rendered fruitless thereby.[63]

Breach of instalment contracts

The difficulty of deciding whether any particular breach of a term of a contract is sufficiently material to imply repudiation of the whole contract, and to entitle the other party to treat the contract as repudiated is particularly apparent in cases of instalment contracts. To some extent the answer will depend on whether the contract is to be interpreted as a single contract

57 *e.g. Burns* v. *Gascadden* (1900) 8 S.L.T. 321; *Rodger (Builders) Ltd.* v. *Fawdry*, 1950 S.C. 483 (sale of heritage).
58 s. 11 (2). See further Chap. 43, *infra*.
59 *Webster* v. *Cramond Iron Co.* (1875) 2 R. 752; *Bradley* v. *Dollar* (1886) 13 R. 893.
60 *Morrison & Mason* v. *Clarkson* (1898) 25 R. 427, 437.
61 See further, Chap. 47, *infra*.
62 *Johannesburg Municipal Council* v. *Stewart & Co.*, 1909 S.C.(H.L.) 53.
63 *Hydraulic Engineering Co.* v. *McHaffie* (1878) 4 Q.B.D. 670.

to be performed on a number of occasions or over a period, or consists of a number of separate contracts, to be performed at different periods, each to be treated as a contract on its own, and linked by no more than the identity of the parties to the several contracts. An instalment contract may be expressly declared to be a series of separate contracts,[64] in which case a breach of contract in respect of one instalment can have no effect on the others, but damages in respect of that breach fall to be calculated in the same way as if that instalment were a single contract separate from all the others. The point again arises that repudiation of the whole contract for failure in one instalment may, if it be unfounded, lead to liability for damages instead of a claim of damages.[65] The same follows if repudiation is tardy and causes unnecessary loss to the other party.[66]

The tendency of Scottish authority is to hold that, in the absence of reasonable indication to the contrary, an instalment contract is a single entity, and the provision for instalment delivery and, it may be, payment is merely a matter of arrangement for the mutual convenience of the parties.[67] Furthermore, in many cases, the size of the contract and the quantities involved are such that delivery other than by instalments would be all but physically impossible.[68] In such cases the difficulty of estimating the weight to be attached to a breach of contract in respect of one instalment is greater than in the previous case. The Court of Appeal indicated in *Maple Flock* v. *Universal Furniture Products Ltd.*,[69] that the principal considerations are not the subjective mental state of the party in default but the ratio quantitatively which the breach bears to the contract as a whole, and, secondly, the degree of probability or improbability that such a breach will be repeated. This indicates that a first default might justify repudiation of the contract,[70] while a failure at the end might not.[71] It has also been recognised that it is more difficult to infer that a breach represents a complete repudiation of liability under the contract, the further the parties have proceeded in the due performance of that contract [72]; so that it will be practically impossible, as well as contrary to reason, to treat a failure in a final or nearly final consignment as a sufficient ground for repudiation of the contract as a whole. Damages in respect of the failure in that consignment only would reasonably be obtainable. Moreover, parties must always act reasonably, and it may well not be

64 *Higgins* v. *Pumpherston Oil Co.* (1893) 20 R. 532; *Handyside* v. *Harris* (1900) 19 Sh.Ct.Rep. 201.

65 *Cornwall* v. *Henson* [1900] 2 Ch. 298 (lease of land held not justified by delay in last instalment of purchase price, and purchaser entitled to damages as seller unable to give possession of subjects sold).

66 *Dunford & Elliot* v. *Macleod* (1902) 4 F. 912.

67 *e.g. Somerville* v. *B. F. Goodrich Co.* (1904) 12 S.L.T. 188. So too in England, *Honck* v. *Muller* (1881) 7 Q.B.D. 89; *Mersey Steel & Iron Co.* v. *Naylor* (1884) 9 App.Cas. 434; *Maple Flock Co.* v. *Universal Furniture Products* [1934] 1 K.B. 148.

68 *e.g. Tancred Arrol & Co.* v. *Steel Co. of Scotland* (1890) 17 R.(H.L.) 31; contract for 30,000 tons of steel.

69 [1934] 1 K.B. 148, 157 (C.A.).

70 *Honck* v. *Muller* (1881) 7 Q.B.D. 92.

71 *Cornwall* v. *Henson* [1900] 2 Ch. 298 (instalment payment for land).

72 *Cornwall* v. *Henson* [1900] 2 Ch. 298, 304 (C.A.), *per* Collins L.J.

reasonable to repudiate such a contract at any stage without reasonable warning to the other party who is in breach.

In *Freeth* v. *Burr* [73] it was laid down that " the real matter for consideration is whether the acts or conduct of the one do or do not amount to an intimation of an intention to abandon and altogether refuse performance of the contract. . . . The true question is whether the acts and conduct of the party evince an intention no longer to be bound by the contract."

Prima facie, failure to pay an instalment of money is not an essential breach going to the root of the contract.[74]

Lord McLaren indicated in *Govan Rope and Sailcloth Co.* v. *Weir*,[75] that repudiation would not normally be justified by failure in one instalment by reason of defective performance, though persistence in this would justify complete rescission. But where one instalment of a contract of sale of goods is accepted, despite allegations that it is defective, subject to a claim of damages for its defective state, the purchaser may not treat this as amounting to a repudiation of the contract which would justify his refusal of further instalments.[76]

Moreover, where payment is made by instalments and constructive partial delivery and appropriation of the goods takes place with each instalment of payment, the purchaser is not barred from claiming damages for breach of contract, if it appears finally that such has taken place, notwithstanding his having taken possession of the subjects.[77]

Time with reference to which damages calculated

Damages cannot be awarded in respect of any loss or damage which occurred prior to the pursuer's acquisition of his right of action. There can be, that is, no damages retrospective beyond that date. With regard to damage suffered after the cause of action has accrued, as only one action may be brought in respect of each cause of action,[78] it follows that all damage suffered or liable to be suffered must be recovered at once, all damage suffered between the accrual of the cause of action and the date of assessment by the court, damage expected to follow after that date, and contingent damage likely or liable to follow in the future, so long as these may be reasonably anticipated and are not too remote or merely speculative. Where, however, the initial breach of duty results in a continuing

[73] (1874) L.R. 9 C.P. 208, 213. *Cf. Mersey Steel & Iron Co.* v. *Naylor* (1884) 9 App.Cas. 434, explained in *Rhymney Ry.* v. *Brecon Ry.* (1900) 69 L.J.Ch. 813; *Barclay* v. *Anderston Foundry Co.* (1856) 18 D. 1190; *Turnbull* v. *McLean* (1874) 1 R. 730; *Ireland* v. *Merryton Coal Co.* (1894) 21 R. 989; *Veit* v. *Ireland* (1896) 33 S.L.R. 526; *Barr* v. *Waldie* (1893) 21 R. 224; *Dunford & Elliot* v. *Macleod* (1902) 4 F. 912.

[74] *Mersey Steel & Iron Co., supra*, 439, 444; *cf.* Sale of Goods Act 1893, s. 10 (1); *Somerville* v. *B. F. Goodrich Co.* (1904) 12 S.L.T. 188.

[75] (1897) 24 R. 368, 373.

[76] *Sanderson* v. *Armour*, 1921 S.C. 18; affd. 1922 S.C.(H.L.) 117.

[77] *Spencer* v. *Dobie* (1879) 7 R. 396.

[78] *Stevenson* v. *Pontifex and Wood* (1887) 15 R. 125; *Rowntree* v. *Allen*, 41 Com.Cas. 90.

cause of action,[79] damages fall to be calculated only down to the date of assessment, as the pursuer may sue for and recover damages from time to time as fresh damage is suffered. If the same incident gives rise to distinct causes of action, the pursuer may sue in respect of these separately and recover damages calculated with reference to each cause independently, as, for example, personal injury and damage to property both arising from the same accident.[80]

The question of future loss arises most commonly in actions *ex delicto*, but it may arise in actions founded on breach of contract also. Certain or even probable future loss may certainly be considered.[81] If the future loss is contingent, as any estimate of future loss necessarily is to some extent, a reasonable estimate must be made on the best available information and a future contingency is not necessarily incapable of quantification because it depends on the will of a third party.[82] But future damages cannot be recovered if they are not the natural and probable result of the initial wrongs and, hence, too remote to be considered, nor if any future damage could be made the occasion of a fresh action, as in cases of continuing nuisance.

Alternative ways of performance

When a person is bound by contract to do one or other of two things, and does neither, the damages recoverable will be compensation only for the loss sustained by failure to perform the lesser of the alternatives, and not the more beneficial to the other party.[83] Similarly, where a contract may be performed in more than one alternative way, the other party is not liable for electing to perform it in the way least burdensome to himself, so long as it is not an unreasonable or uncontemplated way.[84] So long as the way adopted is within the permitted limits of the contract he is entitled to adopt that course and it is good performance of his contract.[85]

The existence of alternative ways of performance within the limits of the contract may obviate the plea that performance is precluded by impossibility or frustration, for if one of the alternative ways of performance remains open, it must be adopted so as to perform the contract.[86] Examples of this are: one only of alternative voyages contemplated in a charterparty precluded by war or legislation [87]; right to export cut off but

[79] Defined by Lindley L.J. in *Hole* v. *Chard Union* [1894] 1 Ch. 293 as " a cause of action which arises from the repetition of acts or omissions of the same kind as that for which the action was brought."

[80] *Brunsden* v. *Humphrey* (1884) 14 Q.B.D. 141; 11 App.Cas. 144; *Serrao* v. *Noel* (1885) 15 Q.B.D. 549; *Macdougall* v. *Knight* (1890) 25 Q.B.D. 1.

[81] *Richardson* v. *Mellish* (1824) 2 Bing. 229.

[82] *Chaplin* v. *Hicks* [1911] 2 K.B. 786.

[83] *Robinson* v. *Robinson* (1857) 1 De G.M. & G. 247, 257, *per* Lord Cranworth; *Deverill* v. *Burnell* (1873) L.R. 8 C.P. 475, 480; *Weir* v. *Dobell* [1916] 1 K.B. 722; *Kaye S. N. Co.* v. *Barnett* (1932) 48 T.L.R. 440; *Withers* v. *General Theatre Corpn.* [1933] 2 K.B. 536.

[84] *Abrahams* v. *Reiach* [1922] 1 K.B. 477.

[85] *Cf.* also *West Stockton Iron Co.* v. *Neilson and Maxwell* (1880) 7 R. 1055; *Johnson and Reay* v. *Nicoll* (1881) 8 R. 437 (delegated performance).

[86] *Barkworth* v. *Young* (1856) 26 L.J.Ch. 153.

[87] *Scottish Navigation Co.* v. *Souter* [1917] 1 K.B. 222; *Anglo-Northern Trading Co.* v. *Emlyn Jones and Williams* [1918] 1 K.B. 372.

other ways of disposal open to the buyers, the sellers not knowing that export had been intended [88]; detention of a ship at a port owing to strikes when she might have gone to other ports specified in the charterparty [89]; performance by book-transfer possible though by physical delivery impossible [90]; breach of a contract of agency when the defendant's factory was burned, though he could still have performed by purchasing the goods for his agent to sell [91]; exercise of option to load one of several permissible cargoes prevented but still possible to take alternative [92]; or opting for one port of delivery when another was affected by the prohibition on trading with the enemy.[93]

It is, however, a question of intention of the parties and their contract, whether a party is bound, when one alternative becomes impossible, to perform the other alternative or is discharged altogether.[94] A party is probably only bound to perform the alternative if it was one contemplated by the parties as reasonable men.[95] The choice is with the debtor in the obligation, and probably he may elect at any time up to the time for performance.[96] It has been held that partial performance of one alternative amounts to final election which is to be performed.[97] To allow the date of performance of one alternative to pass without performance is an election to perform the other.[98]

If a selected alternative becomes impossible of fulfilment, the case is the same as if the contract had been originally to perform that only.[99] If the impossibility of performing one alternative be due to the act of that party,[1] or of a stranger,[2] then he must perform the other, but he is discharged if it is due to the obligee.[3]

Where the obligation prestable is not truly alternative, as where a party becomes bound to do something or pay a penalty in case of failure, the debtor in the obligation cannot elect to pay the penalty and thereby rid himself of further obligation.[4] A truly alternative course, such as a break in a lease, will be open to both parties equally.[5]

88 *McMaster* v. *Cox, McEuen & Co.*, 1921 S.C.(H.L.) 24.
89 *Brown* v. *Turner, Brightman & Co.* [1912] A.C. 12.
90 *Smith, Coney & Barrett* v. *Becker, Grey & Co.* [1916] 2 Ch. 86.
91 *Turner* v. *Goldsmith* [1891] 1 Q.B. 544.
92 *Bunge y Born* v. *Brightman* [1925] A.C. 799.
93 *Hindley* v. *General Fibre Co.* [1940] 2 K.B. 517. See further *Stevens* v. *Webb* (1835) 7 C. & P. 60; *Wharton* v. *King* (1831) 2 B. & Ad. 528.
94 *Anderson* v. *Commercial Union Assce. Co.* (1885) 2 T.L.R. 191, *per* Bowen L.J.
95 Gloag, 720; *Anstruther* v. *Pittenweem Mags.*, 1742, Elchies Notes, Alternative, No. 1; *Christie* v. *Wilson*, 1915 S.C. 645; *Reed* v. *Kilburn Co-op Socy.* (1875) L.R. 10 Q.B. 264.
96 Bankton, I, 23, 83; *contra*, *Brown* v. *Royal Insurance Co.* (1859) 1 E. & E. 853.
97 *Collector of Taxation* v. *English* (1675) 2 B.S. 180; *Town of Edinburgh* v. *Gairden* (1694) 4 B.S. 157.
98 *Reed* v. *Kilburn Co-op Socy.* (1875) L.R. 10 Q.B. 264.
99 *Brown* v. *Royal Insce. Co.* (1859) 1 E. & E. 853.
1 *McIlquham* v. *Taylor* [1895] 1 Ch. 53.
2 *Basket* v. *Basket* (1677) 2 Mod. 200.
3 *Basket*, *supra*.
4 Stair I, 17, 20; Ersk. III, 3, 86; Bell, *Prin.* § 34; *University of Glasgow* v. *Faculty of Physicians* (1840) 1 Rob. 397, 415; *Curtis* v. *Sandison* (1831) 10 S. 72; *National Prov. Bank* v. *Marshall* (1888) 40 Ch.D. 112; *Gold* v. *Houldsworth* (1870) 8 M. 1006.
5 *Grant* v. *Sinclair* (1861) 23 D. 796.

CHAPTER 31

ELEMENTS AND MEASURE OF DAMAGES FOR BREACH OF CONTRACT

General

This chapter attempts to list the more important and common items or heads of claim which may normally be recovered when damages are awarded for breach of contract and to ascertain the standard of calculation by which damages are assessed. The principles of remoteness discussed in a previous chapter may frequently operate on the facts of a particular case to exclude consideration of some items for which the pursuer may claim, or to render certain items inadmissible in the circumstances, but this chapter is confined to the discussion of heads of claim which are admissible or inadmissible not only on grounds of remoteness but on grounds of relevancy. The question is principally—for what kinds of damage can a pursuer recover compensation? There are some elements which may in all probability never enter into the computation of damages. This subject is also considered more particularly in subsequent chapters with particular reference to the kinds of contracts discussed therein which illustrate the working of the principle of *restitutio in integrum* by awarding damages.

No fixed rules determining the measure of damages can be laid down though in each type of case certain relevant considerations have to be kept in mind,[1] and the proper elements for consideration and the measure of damages is a matter to be deduced from decisions. In the commoner classes of cases the measure and elements to be considered are conventionally stereotyped but this does not obviate consideration of the special circumstances of each case. All methods of arriving fairly at the sum properly chargeable on the defender as damages are competent but in the ordinary and simple cases some methods are so obviously fair and so available that the court will not readily depart from them,[2] but it is erroneous to regard any so-called rules as being rigid or limiting.[3] Moreover " the measures employed to estimate the money value of anything (including the damage flowing from a breach of contract) are not to be confounded with the value which it is sought to estimate; and the true value may only be found after employing more measures than one—in

[1] *Admiralty Commrs.* v. *S.S. Susquehanna* [1926] A.C. 655, 661, *per* Lord Dunedin; *The Edison* [1932] P. 52, 61.
[2] *Hutchison* v. *Davidson*, 1945 S.C. 395, 405.
[3] *Pomphrey* v. *Cuthbertson*, 1951 S.C. 147.

themselves all legitimate, but none of them necessarily conclusive by itself —and checking one result with another." [4]

Forms of breaches of contract

Breaches of contract can in general all be reduced to one or another of the three forms, namely, delayed performance, defective performance, and total non-performance. The losses which follow from each of these differ in nature and, accordingly, in appropriate compensation.

Elements to be disregarded in assessing damages—Means and position of defender

In the ordinary case of breach of contract it is clearly irrelevant to have any regard to the means of the defender or his position in life, and his consequent ability to satisfy any decree which may be pronounced against him without serious loss or ruin to himself. This follows from the proposition that an award of damages is intended as compensation to the pursuer for harm or loss caused him, and compensation so far as possible to the extent to which he has been damnified by the defender's wrongful action.[5] It has therefore no relation to the latter's means and in most cases of contract inquiry would be out of the question even were it admissible. It is similarly inadmissible to lead evidence of the defender's means in an action founded on negligence.[6] In *Keyse* v. *Keyse*,[7] an action of divorce where damages were being claimed from the co-respondent, it was stated that his means had nothing to do with the question of what damages he should pay, and the only question was what loss the petitioner had sustained. In cases of breach of promise of marriage there is an apparent exception but the true inquiry is not as to the means of the defender, but to show what position the pursuer has lost by not obtaining the promised match and this is only admitted as being the only real way to quantify the pursuer's loss.[8] The exception is consequently more apparent than real. In such cases it is essential to have averments and evidence of the defender's means.[9] The pursuer's loss is greater if she would have gained by the marriage and enjoyed wealth and position,[10] as well as acquiring valuable contingent rights, such as to *jus relictae*. A diligence for the recovery of business books to prove the defender's financial position has been refused [11] in such a case and conflicting dicta were expressed as to the desirability of this. In subsequent cases however such a diligence has

4 *Duke of Portland* v. *Wood's Tr.*, 1926 S.C. 640, 651, *per* Ld. Pres. Clyde.
5 The question which sometimes arises whether a particular defender is " worth suing " is a matter of practice, not law, and has no relevance to his liability or the extent to which he may be found liable in damages.
6 *Black* v. *N.B. Ry.*, 1908 S.C. 444, 448.
7 (1886) 11 P.D. 100.
8 *Somerville* v. *Thomson* (1896) 23 R. 576.
9 *Smith* v. *Woodfine* (1857) 1 C.B.(N.S.) 660; *A.* v. *B.* (1875) 12 S.L.R. 621.
10 *Berry* v. *Da Costa* (1866) L.R. 1 C.P. 331.
11 *Somerville* v. *Thomson* (1896) 23 R. 576.

been granted.[12] In *Smith* v. *Woodfine*,[9] Willes J. quoted with approval Sedgwick on *Damages*[13] where that writer says:—" In this action, although in form *ex contractu*, yet it being impossible from the nature of the case to fix any rate or measure of damages, the jury are allowed to take into their consideration all the circumstances; and provided their conduct is not marked by prejudice, passion or corruption, they are permitted to exercise an absolute discretion over the amount of compensation." Even in such a case there is no Scottish authority for allowing a pursuer exemplary damages.[14]

Injury to feelings

In actions based on contract incidental injury to the defender's feelings in respect of the mere fact or the manner of the breach of contract or in respect of any consequential trouble or on the ground that a servant dismissed was attached to the place[15] is not an admissible element in the assessment of the measure of damages. In *Campbell* v. *McLauchlan*[16] a servant pursuing an action for damages for wrongful dismissal claimed in his damages a sum for board-wages and a further sum of £50 for injury to feelings. Lord Kyllachy hesitatingly allowed the full sum to be scheduled in the issue and left it to be decided at the trial whether the pursuer could recover this sum. It is submitted that the hesitation was well founded.

This decision is, moreover, contrary to the later case of *Addis* v. *Gramophone Co.*[17] in the House of Lords, where it was held that a servant who had been wrongfully dismissed could claim damages only for the wages he would have earned if the contract had been performed and that nothing could be added to this sum because the dismissal was abrupt or insulting in manner or because of the fact that the dismissal would make it more difficult to obtain fresh employment. Lord Shaw considered the law of Scotland on the matter[18] and disapproved Lord Fraser's statement of the law,[19] holding that it was truly as now stated above. He pointed out further that if the employer's manner of dismissal contained charges amounting to slander, damages would be recoverable in respect thereof as a separate delict, but it could not be looked at otherwise so as to enhance the damages due from the employer in respect of the breach of contract involved in the dismissal.[20] The two questions could competently be

12 *Brodie* v. *McGregor* (1900) 8 S.L.T. 200 (O.H.); *Stroyan* v. *McWhirter* (1901) 9 S.L.T. 242 (O.H.).
13 7th ed., II, 449.
14 *Cf. Black* v. *N.B. Ry.*, 1908 S.C. 444; contrast in England, *Butterworth* v. *Butterworth* [1920] P. 126. *Cf.* also *Clayton* v. *Oliver* [1930] A.C. 209, 220.
15 *Beckham* v. *Drake* (1849) 2 H.L.C. 607, *per* Erle C.J.
16 (1896) 4 S.L.T. 143 (O.H.).
17 [1909] A.C. 488, 491, distinguished in *Diesen* v. *Samson*, 1971 S.L.T.(Sh.Ct.) 49. See also *Jarvis* v. *Swans Tours Ltd.* [1973] 1 All E.R. 71.
18 p. 502.
19 *Master and Servant*, 2nd ed., 135; 3rd ed., 163.
20 *Addis*, *supra*, at p. 503.

raised in the same action, but with two separate conclusions for the two separate amounts of damages claimed in respect of the two distinct grounds of claim.[21] Lord Loreburn (with the concurrence of four of his brethren) stated that considerations of the manner of dismissal had never been allowed to influence damages in that kind of case.[22] In *Baker* v. *Denkera Ashanti Mining Corporation Ltd.*,[23] damages were claimed for admitted wrongful dismissal, and it was held that the defendants could not be made liable for more damages simply because they had not a good reason for dismissing the plaintiff. In *Clayton* v. *Oliver* [24] it was observed that vindictive or exemplary damages in tort find no place in contract nor accordingly can injury to feelings or vanity be regarded. In *Beckham* v. *Drake* [25] it was laid down that a dismissed servant could not recover heavier damages because of any *pretium affectionis* or because he had felt attached to the place he had lost. In *Groom* v. *Crocker* [26] loss of reputation as a careful driver and injury to feelings in consequence were disregarded; in *Bailey* v. *Bullock* [27] annoyance and distress and loss of social prestige by not getting possession of one's own house were ignored.

In the case of breach of promise of marriage, however, injury to the feelings of the innocent party is an admissible element and damages are given not only for loss of the match and for expenses but as solatium for the injury inflicted on the sensibilities of the pursuer.[28] But this action though nominally contractual is in fact more delictual in nature and the measure of damages partakes accordingly of the character of the delictual damages. Such a case has been described as being " based on the hypothesis of a broken contract, yet it is attended with some of the consequences of a personal wrong." [29] Similarly the quantum of damages is liable to be enhanced if there were also seduction as the element of solatium bulks more largely in the award in these circumstances.[30]

Again damages have been allowed for hurt feelings resulting from breach of contract where the hurt feelings were sustained not by the fact or the manner of the breach but were the loss sustained. A professional photographer failed to attend the pursuer's wedding to take photographs so that she had none, and was upset thereby. Damages were awarded, the principle of *Addis* being distinguished.[31]

21 *Mollison* v. *Baillie* (1885) 22 S.L.R. 595.

22 *Addis*, *supra*, at p. 491, disagreeing with and practically overruling *Maw* v. *Jones* (1890) 25 Q.B.D. 107, where possible injury to character from dismissal was admitted. It was distinguished in *Baker* v. *Denkera Ashanti Corpn.* (1903) 20 T.L.R. 37. *Cf. Re Rubel Bronze Co. and Vos* [1918] 1 K.B. 315.

23 *Supra.*

24 [1930] A.C. 209, 220.

25 (1849) 2 H.L.Cas. 579, 607.

26 [1939] 1 K.B. 194.

27 [1950] 2 All E.R. 1167.

28 *Hogg* v. *Gow*, May 27, 1812, F.C.; Bell, *Prin.* § 1508.

29 *Finlay* v. *Chirney* (1888) 20 Q.B.D. 494, 504, *per* Bowen L.J.

30 *Cathcart* v. *Brown* (1905) 7 F. 951.

31 *Diesen* v. *Samson*, 1971 S.L.T.(Sh.Ct.) 49.

Injury to reputation or credit

A breach of contract may readily lead to incidental injury to the personal reputation or credit of the pursuer. This is, however, generally an irrelevant item in a claim of damages. Thus in *Addis* v. *Gramophone Co.*[32] this was held irrelevant in a case of dismissal from service. But business reputation may be otherwise; in *Millar* v. *Bellvale Chemical Co.*[33] the question whether injury to business reputation consequent on a breach of contract was a sufficiently direct result thereof to justify an award of damages was left undecided. But in *Cointat* v. *Myham*[34] such a consequence was held to be sufficiently direct to be included.

In *Cameron* v. *Fletcher*[35] a servant was wrongfully dismissed and claimed wages and solatium but was held entitled only to damages for the breach but exceeding the amount of loss of wages in respect that in the circumstances he must have sustained some injury: the claim to solatium was not mentioned in judgment.

Profit made by party in breach

From the fundamental proposition that damages are intended as compensation for loss suffered by the breach, it follows that it is irrelevant to consider what profit may have been made by the party who is in breach of contract from his own breach. But the extent of any such profit may be utilised to evidence the profit which would have accrued to the innocent party by proper fulfilment of the contract, that is, to quantify his loss, though it is open to the party in breach to show that the innocent party could not have made any such profit. In *Watson, Laidlaw & Co.* v. *Pott, Cassels & Williamson*,[36] which was an action for damages by a patentee in respect of the sale of articles which infringed his patent, it was held that prima facie the measure of damages was the profit which the pursuer would have made, had he effected himself the sales made by the rival firm in breach of patent, but that such an amount of damages was liable to diminution if and to the extent to which it could be proved by the defender that the pursuer could not in fact have effected those sales. Regard must be had to the nature of the trade in question, the area in which it was carried on, the amount of competition to be faced and the business energy and acumen of the defender. Lords Dundas and Salvesen added opinions to the effect that there might be circumstances in which a pursuer may also fairly claim, as an item of damages, that he has been compelled, owing to the defenders' illegal competition, to sell some of his patented articles at a lower price than he had formerly done.

[32] [1909] A.C. 488.
[33] (1898) 1 F. 297; *cf. Dempster* v. *Wallace* (1833) 12 S. 548.
[34] [1913] 2 K.B. 220; *cf. Marcus* v. *Myers* (1895) 11 T.L.R. 327; *Bostock* v. *Nicholson* [1904] 1 K.B. 725.
[35] (1872) 10 M. 301.
[36] 1913 S.C. 762; affd. 1914 S.C.(H.L.) 18.

In *United Horse-Shoe and Nail Co. Ltd.* v. *Stewart & Co.*[37] Lord Kinnear as Lord Ordinary in the Court of Session (whose interlocutor was restored on appeal to the House of Lords) thought the reduction of price relevant. Lord Macnaghten in the Lords, however, thought it inadmissible in the circumstances as not the natural or direct result of the infringement of the patent, on the ground that if the pursuers believed in their case, it was not a reasonable course on their part to reduce the prices of the articles so as to injure their own trade, and they seemed to have done so, prompted by the desire to provide for the contingency of failure in their action. A substantial sum was however allowed on this account in *Meters Ltd.* v. *Metropolitan Gas Meters Ltd.*[38] The question is probably truly one of fact in each case.

It is however competent for a defender, in mitigation of damages, to lead evidence to the effect that the pursuers, claiming damages for breach of contract to deliver raw materials whereby they were prevented from executing certain orders which they had obtained, were in consequence enabled to execute other orders whereby they made profits which might be taken into consideration in reduction of the damages sustained by the breach of contract.[39]

But where breach took place of a contract made with several persons jointly for the quick discharge of a ship, and some of the plaintiffs had in consequence made profits they would not otherwise have made, it was held that the amount of damages could not be reduced by the profits so made by some of the plaintiffs individually.[40]

Damage due to pursuer's own actings

When the true cause of some head of loss is not the default of the defender but some voluntary act of the pursuer or of his agent or servant for whom he is responsible, then the pursuer cannot recover damages in respect of that head of claim. His act breaks the chain of causation initiated by the defender's wrong. In *Ansett* v. *Marshall*[44] the plaintiff was detained by the defendant's fault and missed his ship but could have gone a week later instead of which he stayed several months to prosecute his claim of damages. Living expenses during this delay were accordingly refused *qua* damages, though allowable *qua* costs if it were right that he should have been kept back as a necessary witness. Similarly when a ship was damaged in collision the damages were limited to the loss sustained thereby and did not cover loss incurred when the master refused assistance and failed to display ordinary skill to save the vessel.[45] Other instances

[37] (1887) 14 R. 266; reversed 15 R.(H.L.) 45; 13 App.Cas. 401.
[38] (1911) 27 R.P.C. 721; 28 R.P.C. 157.
[39] *Hill* v. *Showell* (1918) 87 L.J.K.B. 1106.
[40] *Jebsen* v. *E. & W. India Dock Co.* (1875) L.R. 10 C.P. 300.
[44] (1853) 22 L.J.Q.B. 118.
[45] *The Flying Fish* (1865) 34 L.J.Adm. 113, P.C.

are delay to goods in transit due to their being improperly packed in the first place.[46]

It is not, however, every act by the pursuer which breaks the chain of causation so as to render further damage irrecoverable: damage may still be recoverable if due initially to the defender's default, though the particular damage would not have occurred but for the pursuer's act, so long as that act was in the ordinary course of things and, at least generally, not blameworthy, and the same may be true of the act of a third party.[47]

In much the same way a pursuer cannot recover damages for breach of contract if the proximate cause of the liability to pay damages was his own negligence, and that even though the breach of contract was a condition precedent to the negligence or provided the opportunity or inducement for it. So if one party supplies faulty goods to another in breach of contract and the second party incurs liability to a third party by reason of his own negligence supervening on that fault, the second party can have no claim for indemnification against the first party in respect of that liability.[48]

Damage due to pursuer's failure to mitigate

It is the duty of a pursuer injured by breach of contract to take reasonable steps to minimise or mitigate the damage which results from the breach of contract.[49] If and in so far as he fails to exert reasonable diligence to do so his loss results from his own failure and not from the defender's original breach and hence is irrecoverable. It may equally be regarded as irrecoverable as being remote and consequential damage.[50] A defender cannot found on his own failure to minimise as breaking the chain of causation though he may found on the pursuer's failure to do so.

Necessity or cost of legal proceedings

No regard can generally be had in assessing damages to the loss of time, worry and trouble connected with the fact of having to take legal proceedings to enforce performance or to recover damages as compensation for the breach of contract. If he has to take legal proceedings for damages, the pursuer may recover the expenses of process in the usual way, subject to the discretion of the court, but no more. Moreover, if he sues for substantial damages and only proves the breach of contract but no

46 *Baldwin* v. *L.C. & D. Ry.* (1882) 9 Q.B.D. 582; *cf.* also *Tucker* v. *Linger* (1882) 21 Ch.D. 18; *Summers* v. *Salford Corpn.* [1943] A.C. 283.

47 *Summers* v. *Salford Corpn.* [1943] A.C. 283; *The Oropesa* [1943] P. 32; *cf. The Gusty and the Daniel M.* [1940] P. 159.

48 *Wood* v. *Mackay* (1906) 8 F. 625, doubting *Mowbray* v. *Merryweather* [1895] 2 Q.B. 640, on which see also *Buchanan and Carswell* v. *Eugene*, 1936 S.C. 160. *Cf.* also *Baxter* v. *Boswell* (1899) 6 S.L.T. 278.

49 Chap. 28, *supra*.

50 *Wilson* v. *Hicks* (1857) 26 L.J.Ex. 242; *Frost* v. *Knight* (1872) L.R. 7 Ex. 111, 114; *Roper* v. *Johnson* (1873) L.R. 8 C.P. 167, 181; *The Blenheim* (1885) 10 P.D. 167; *Nickoll and Knight* v. *Ashton* [1900] 2 Q.B. 298; [1901] 2 K.B. 106; *Payzu* v. *Saunders* (1919) 35 T.L.R. 657; *cf. Le Blanche* v. *L.N.W. Ry.* (1876) 1 C.P.D. 286; *Lodge Holes Coal Co.* v. *Wednesbury Corpn.* [1908] A.C. 323, 326; *Credito Italiano* v. *Swiss Bankverein* (1916) 85 L.J.K.B. 1477, 1480.

actual damage, or only illusory damage, he is likely to be refused expenses.[51] In England it has been pointed out in similar circumstances that where a pursuer recovers only nominal damages, he is not usually entitled to expenses unless the action was brought for only nominal damages as a vindication of his infringed right.[52]

Similarly, inconvenience amounting merely to annoyance is not a good head of damages,[53] but otherwise, if the convenience has amounted to actual pecuniary loss.[54] In *Seaton Brick and Tile Co.* v. *Mitchell*,[55] an unsuccessful defender's persistence in litigating and disputing his liability led to an award of £40 in respect of loss, trouble and extrajudicial expenses, and also full expenses.

Motive

The motive for any breach of contract as a general rule is quite irrelevant and does not affect the measure of damages.[56] It is conceived that in all cases of breach of contract, malicious, violent, or fraudulent motive is irrelevant, though it may be otherwise if a claim be made *ex delicto* from the same facts. Similarly, though fraud may give rise to a claim *ex delicto*, a pursuer cannot, so far as his action depends on contract, enhance his damages by showing fraudulent motive.[57] This question seems most likely to arise in contracts of service and also in cases of breach of promise of marriage. Breach of promise of marriage is an apparent exception arising from its truly delictual nature, and hence malicious motive may probably be considered in such a case.[58]

Generally admissible heads of claim—extra cost of securing performance

Where a contract is performed late, or defectively, or not at all, the basic measure of damages is the difference between the value of the performance, if any, tendered, and the performance which should have been tendered. If performance is late the aggrieved party may have had to buy in from elsewhere at greater cost, but at very least will have had inconvenience and possible loss of use or loss of business.[58a] If performance is defective he may have to buy in from elsewhere, or to rectify the defects, or to accept something less valuable than he should have received.[58b] If performance is not made at all he suffers loss of use by not

51 *Cf.* MacLaren on *Expenses*, pp. 28–29.

52 *Anglo-Cyprian Trade Agencies* v. *Paphos Wine Industries* [1951] 1 All E.R. 873.

53 *Hamlin* v. *G.N. Ry.* (1856) 1 H. & N. 408, 411; *Bostock* v. *Nicholson* [1904] 1 K.B. 725; *cf. Fletcher* v. *Tayleur* (1855) 17 C.B. 21, 29; *Marcus* v. *Myers* (1895) 11 T.L.R. 327; *Addis* v. *Gramophone Co.* [1909] A.C. 488.

54 *Webster* v. *Cramond Iron Co.* (1875) 2 R. 752; *Christie* v. *Wilson*, 1915 S.C. 645.

55 (1900) 2 F. 550, 554.

56 *Berry* v. *Da Costa* (1866) L.R. 1 C.P. 331, 334; *Addis* v. *Gramophone Co.* [1909] A.C. 488; *Clayton* v. *Oliver* [1930] A.C. 209, 220, *per* Ld. Ch. Buckmaster; *cf. Baker* v. *Denkera Ashanti Corpn.* (1903) 20 T.L.R. 37.

57 *Sikes* v. *Wild* (1863) 1 B. & S. 587, 594; *Engel* v. *Fitch* (1869) L.R. 3 Q.B. 327; *Bain* v. *Fothergill* (1874) L.R. 7 H.L. 158, 206; *Brown* v. *Edinburgh Mags.*, 1907 S.C. 256.

58 *Cf. Findlay* v. *Blaylock*, 1937 S.C. 21.

58a *e.g. Victoria Laundry* v. *Newman* [1949] 2 K.B. 528.

58b *e.g.* Sale of Goods Act 1893, s. 53 (3).

having what he should have had, or may have to pay more for securing performance from another source.[58c]

Damages for loss of business or profits

The cases on damages for loss of profits are not always readily to be reconciled.[59] The clearest cases are those where there has been a failure or delay to supply or deliver to the pursuer what is obviously a profit-making item of the pursuer's assets or stock or equipment, the want of which must obviously prevent him from doing the profitable business which he might otherwise reasonably have been expected to do, utilising that item of stock.[60] So where a ship was delivered by her builders late, and too late for the most profitable passenger season in her trade, a fact which, in the circumstances, the defendants must be taken to have known and foreseen, they were held liable for the difference between the profits earned and the profits which could have been earned if the vessel had been promptly delivered, as damages for late delivery.[61] Where the repair of a steamship was delayed beyond the contractual period, it was held that the damages would be the net profit which the owners might have obtained by chartering the vessel if one had been delivered at the due date of completion of the repairs.[62] Much the same is the case where a vessel is built deficient in carrying capacity.[63] So too where a boiler required for a laundry was delivered late.[63a]

A second category is where goods have been sold for resale, at least in cases where there was no alternative market for the goods. Such loss may be estimated by reference to the cost of replacement goods,[64] or an estimate of the profit which would have been made.[65] In *Munro* v. *Bennet*[66] a purchaser of machinery whose goods were rejected by a sub-purchaser on account of defects existing therein due to the fault of the seller, recovered in respect of loss of profit on the transaction, as being a natural consequence of the original seller's failure. On the other hand, in *Wilson* v. *Carmichael*,[67] loss of profit on a resale was not an admissible item as the loss was due to the purchaser's own fault and not to the original seller's failure, in that due diligence and inspection by the purchaser would have disclosed the defect much earlier.

58c *e.g. A/B Karlshamns Oljefabriker* v. *Monarch S.S. Co.*, 1949 S.C.(H.L.) 1.

59 See generally *Victoria Laundry* v. *Newman* [1949] 2 K.B. 528, 536.

60 *Cf.* deprivation of use of a ship due to collision: *Liesbosch* v. *Edison* [1933] A.C. 559; *The Philadelphia* [1917] P. 101.

61 *Fletcher* v. *Tayleur* (1855) 17 C.B. 21.

62 *Re Trent and Humber Co., ex p. Cambrian Steam Packet Co.* (1868) L.R. 6 Eq. 396; affd. (1868) L.R. 4 Ch. 112. See also *The Argentino* (1888) 14 App.Cas. 519; *Steam Herring Fleet* v. *Richards* (1901) 17 T.L.R. 731. *Cf. Mitsui* v. *Watts* [1916] 2 K.B. 826; [1917] A.C. 227.

63 *Gillespie* v. *Howden* (1885) 12 R. 800; *Australian Steamship Proprietary* v. *Lewis*, 47 Ll.L.R. 132.

63a *Victoria Laundry* v. *Newman* [1949] 2 K.B. 528.

64 *Hinde* v. *Liddell* (1875) L.R. 10 Q.B. 265.

65 *Leavey* v. *Hirst* [1944] K.B. 24.

66 1911 S.C. 337.

67 (1894) 21 R. 732.

In *Mackenzie* v. *Liddell* [68] a party who had a contract to salve a ship chartered a tug which, due to the shipowner's breach of contract, arrived too late to execute the contract of salvage. It was held that the charterer could recover from the tugowners the profit he had lost on the salvage contract, and further, that it must have been contemplated that the contract was one of salvage with consequently high rewards, and hence the party in breach was liable on that basis. In *Gunter* v. *Lauritzen* [69] a merchant who had contracted to supply a cargo of hay and straw, subcontracted therefor and then, on delivery, had to reject the goods tendered as being disconform to warranty. Loss of profit on his principal contract was allowed in his claim of damages, without deduction in respect of his ability to obtain supplies from elsewhere, as this course would have entailed extraordinary exertions on his part.

In *Duff* v. *Iron Buildings Co.*,[70] manufacturers of iron huts contracted with merchants in South Africa for the supply of huts for resale there. Earlier consignments were sold at a profit but later ones rejected as disconform to contract. The merchants claimed damages from the manufacturers and were allowed a reasonable allowance for loss of profits, the ordinary rule of taking the difference between the contract price and the market price being inapplicable in the circumstances as there was no market for the goods in question and they could not be sold.[71] Moreover, this ordinary rule presumes, as Lord McLaren pointed out, that a purchaser for resale will not lose his profit on the adventure but will buy in the market and make the same profit as he would have under the contract, but partly from the sub-purchaser and partly from the defaulting seller in the form of damages. Advertising, travelling expenses, and outlays in connection with sales were also allowed.

In *Smeed* v. *Foord* [72] a farmer contracted for the purchase of a threshing machine and on non-delivery did not hire another owing to repeated promises of delivery. In consequence his corn was much damaged by rain. The loss of profit on sale was held to have arisen naturally and in the usual course from this breach of contract, and hence was recoverable. In *Borries* v. *Hutchinson* [73] H had contracted to deliver caustic soda to B for resale abroad. Part was never delivered and part delivered late, and there was no alternative source of supply; hence B was found entitled to his loss of profit measured by the price which he would have obtained on resale less the cost of delivery.

In *Teacher* v. *Calder* [74] a partner in violation of agreement reduced his capital in the business below the agreed minimum: the aggrieved partner

[68] (1883) 10 R. 705.
[69] (1894) 31 S.L.R. 359.
[70] (1891) 19 R. 199.
[71] *Cf. Grébert-Borgnis* v. *Nugent* (1885) 15 Q.B.D. 85; *Borries* v. *Hutchinson* (1865) 18 C.B.(N.S.) 445; *Patrick* v. *Russo-British Grain Co.* [1927] 2 K.B. 535.
[72] (1859) 1 E. & E. 602.
[73] (1865) 18 C.B.(N.S.) 445.
[74] (1899) 1 F.(H.L.) 39.

was held entitled to damages assessed not by computation of profits made by the diverted capital but by calculation of the extra profits which might have been made had it been employed in the business and not been withdrawn.

Damages for loss of profits or business have also been held admissible where there has been failure or delay in delivery of an essential part of a profit-earning piece of machinery, such as a ship's propeller,[75] or a ship's engines,[76] or a laundry boiler [77]; breach of an agreement to grant a lease in the knowledge that the tenant intended to carry on business in the subjects,[78] failure to insert a tradesman's advertisement,[79] detention of a ship for replacement of machinery faultily constructed by defendant,[80] failure by mineral tenants to remove in terms of the lease,[81] the supply of unfit meat which had to be condemned and involved the consignee in liability for a fine,[82] though not where steel was not timeously delivered to a barge-builder,[83] nor in a case of the supply of defective golf balls to a wholesaler.[84] In *Lancashire and Yorkshire Ry.* v. *Gidelow*,[85] loss of customers was held to be a direct and immediate consequence of the carrier's failure to carry coal for the merchant.

It has been held that it is competent for a pursuer with a view to the estimation of damages to show his loss of profits by the average profits of other persons in the same trade during the same period though in a different part of the country.[86]

An intermediate category of cases exists where damages for loss of business profits has often been awarded, and that is where ordinary mercantile goods have been sold to a merchant with knowledge by the seller that they were required for resale. This is particularly so where there is no available market where the purchaser could buy similar goods against the contract in the event of the seller's default. So in *Borries* v. *Hutchinson*,[87] a contract required summer delivery. Part of the consignment was not delivered till the autumn and part not at all. The plaintiff recovered the increased cost of freight and insurance on the late delivery and loss of profit on the rest. In *Hydraulic Engineering Co.* v. *McHaffie* [88] the defendant's failure to deliver part of a machine which the plaintiff was, to his knowledge, making for a third party, caused the loss of the whole contract by the third party's rejection thereof. The plaintiff accordingly

75 *Wilson* v. *General Iron Screw Co.* (1878) 47 L.J.Q.B. 23.
76 *Saint Line* v. *Richardson* [1940] 2 K.B. 99.
77 *Victoria Laundry* v. *Newman* [1949] 2 K.B. 528.
78 *Jaques* v. *Millar* (1877) 6 Ch.D. 153; overruled on another point *Marshall* v. *Berridge* (1881) 19 Ch.D. 233.
79 *Marcus* v. *Myers* (1895) 11 T.L.R. 327.
80 *Wilson* v. *General Iron Screw Co., supra.*
81 *Houldsworth* v. *Brand's Trs.* (1877) 4 R. 369.
82 *Cointat* v. *Myham* [1913] 2 K.B. 220.
83 *Watson* v. *Gray* (1900) 16 T.L.R. 308.
84 *Millar* v. *Bellvale Chemical Co.* (1898) 1 F. 297.
85 (1875) L.R. 7 H.L. 517; *cf. Millar, supra.*
86 *Watson* v. *Kidston & Co.* (1839) 1 D. 1254. See also *Bell* v. *Leighton* (1819) 2 Mur. 74.
87 (1865) 18 C.B.(N.S.) 445.
88 (1878) 4 Q.B.D. 670.

recovered, as well as the cost of making the machine, the profit he would have made on the sale. Other similar cases include the failure to deliver goods in terms of a contract known to be substantially the same as a sub-contract.[89]

Loss of profits rarely given

On the other hand in ordinary cases of carriage or the sale of goods for which there is a market readily available the courts are slow to allow loss of profits as a separate element in damages. This is particularly so where, as in the ordinary course, there is an available market where a disappointed buyer may obtain supplies or a disappointed seller dispose of his stock.[90] Furthermore, a carrier commonly knows less than a seller about the circumstances and the purposes for which the buyer or consignee requires the goods, or of any circumstances which may cause exceptional loss if due delivery be not made.[91] In the case of a carrier, where there is no market, a resale price is only evidence of value and that value has to be determined by all available evidence.[92]

In *Dunlop* v. *Higgins*[93] damages were awarded assessed at the difference between the contract price and the market price, and also loss of profit. This reasoning gives the pursuer his profit twice over, as ordinary profits are allowed for in contract price.[94] In cases of sale there is not generally liability for further loss of profits, such as a purchaser might have made on a resale, even though his intention was, to the knowledge of both parties, to resell.[95]

In any case, loss of profit may be excluded if the profit is due to special circumstances outwith the knowledge of the other party, in accordance with the rules of remoteness,[96] and this applies particularly where the profits lost are unduly large.[97]

Loss of market

A consideration closely related to loss of profits is loss of market. A person may reasonably be taken to appreciate that the demand for certain commodities fluctuates with the seasons, the weather, the trend of fashion and the occurrence of social, sporting and other seasonal events. So furs are more saleable in autumn than spring and conversely with sports

89 *Grébert-Borgnis* v. *Nugent* (1885) 15 Q.B.D. 85.
90 *Vide infra*, Chap. 43.
91 *Hadley* v. *Baxendale* (1854) 9 Ex. 341; *Gee* v. *Lancs. & Yorks. Ry.* (1860) 6 H. & N. 211 (mill stopped for lack of raw material); *Hales* v. *L.N.W. Ry.* (1863) 4 B. & S. 66; *Woodger* v. *G.W. Ry.* (1867) L.R. 2 C.P. 318; *British Columbia Sawmill Co.* v. *Nettleship* (1868) L.R. 3 C.P. 499; *Watson* v. *Gray* (1900) 16 T.L.R. 308; *Heskell* v. *Continental Express* [1950] 1 All E.R. 1033.
92 *The Arpad* [1934] P. 189; *cf. Williams* v. *Agius* [1914] A.C. 510; *Slater* v. *Hoyle* [1920] 2 K.B. 11.
93 (1848) 6 Bell's App. 195, 211: the case is no longer authoritative.
94 *Cf. Duff* v. *Iron Buildings Co.* (1891) 19 R. 199, *per* Lord McLaren.
95 *Williams* v. *Reynolds* (1865) 6 B. & S. 495; *Thol* v. *Henderson* (1881) 8 Q.B.D. 457.
96 *Supra*, Chap. 28. On loss of contingent profits, see *The Bodlewell* [1907] P. 286.
97 *e.g. Horne* v. *Midland Ry.* (1873) L.R. 8 C.P. 131.

equipment. A short delay may result in difficulty or even impossibility in effecting anticipated business. In *Wilson* v. *Lancs. & Yorks. Ry.*[98] cloth in transit to cap manufacturers was delayed so long that the season was gone before the articles ordered could be made up. Damages were awarded based not on loss of profits but for the loss of season, namely the diminished value of the cloth by reason of delivery at the end of the season. So too in *Collard* v. *South Eastern Ry.*[99] a fall in market value between the due date of delivery and the actual date was held recoverable from a carrier even though the fall was accidental, as this element was not severable from the element of loss due to the carrier's negligent handling of the goods whereby they were delayed. Again in *Bates* v. *Cameron*[1] fancy muslins were delayed in transit to America and missed the spring season: hence the consignees would have been entitled to their loss of profit had they proved it, but this not having been proved, the carriers were liable for the invoice price of the goods, and were entitled to dispose of the goods as best they could. In *Schulze* v. *G.E. Ry.*[2] samples were delivered to the defendants to be forwarded to the plaintiffs but were delayed until the season at which they could have been utilised for procuring orders had passed and they had consequently become valueless. The plaintiff could not have procured similar samples in the market, and it was held that he was entitled to recover as damages the value to him of the samples at the time when they should have been delivered.

Where, however, a cargo-owner sustained damage by loss of market in consequence of delay occasioned by a collision at sea, such damage is too remote to be recovered by him in an action of delict against the shipowner.[3]

It was formerly held that no certainty attached to long ocean voyages, so that when a voyage was protracted beyond the contractual period and in the interval the market price of the goods shipped had fallen, damages for loss of market were not recoverable.[4] In *Dunn* v. *Bucknall Bros.*[5] and *Koufos* v. *Czarnikow*[5a] this view was disapproved in view of the greater certainty with which long ocean voyages are now regularly accomplished.

In *Govan Rope and Sail Co.* v. *Weir*,[6] a quantity of a special quality of rope was ordered and not all taken up by the customer. The manufacturer sued for loss of profits and he was held entitled to the difference between the contract price and the cost of raw material plus the cost of manufacture.

In *Keddie Gordon & Co.* v. *N.B. Ry.*[7] the pursuers made a special parcel of goods for an urgent order and consigned them by the defenders' railway. Owing to the defenders' negligence the parcel was damaged, had

98 (1861) 9 C.B.(N.S.) 632.
99 (1861) 7 H. & N. 79.
1 (1855) 18 D. 186.
2 (1887) 19 Q.B.D. 30.
3 *The Notting Hill* (1884) 9 P.D. 105.
4 *The Parana* (1877) 2 P.D. 118; *The Notting Hill, supra.*
5 [1902] 2 K.B. 614. *Cf. Ströms Bruks A/B* v. *Hutchison* (1905) 7 F.(H.L.) 131.
5a [1969] 1 A.C. 350.
6 (1897) 24 R. 368.
7 (1886) 14 R. 233.

to be repacked, and was refused and returned by the consignee and finally sold at considerable loss by the pursuers who recovered damages for the loss of market, namely the difference between invoice price and the price actually obtained, along with certain expenses.

Again it has been held in England that if a vendor of real property is unable to give a good title thereto, the intending purchaser is not entitled to damages for the loss of the bargain.[8]

Loss of profits refused

In *Williams* v. *Reynolds* [9] it was held that the loss of profit on a resale of goods could not be taken into account in quantifying the seller's liability for damages for non-delivery, even though the original contract of sale was one for " forward delivery " and the resale had actually been made before the breach of the original contract, and also though, in the circumstances, purchases were normally made for resale. Such a loss was neither natural nor in the contemplation of parties.

Loss of profits was again refused in *Sanders* v. *Stuart*,[10] where the plaintiff gave the defendant a message, unintelligible because of being in cypher, for transmission to America. By the defendant's omission to send it, the plaintiff lost commission on an order to which the message related. It was held that only nominal damages could be awarded as the defendant was ignorant of the subject-matter of the message and hence the loss of the order was not in his contemplation.

Again, loss of profits was refused in *Gee* v. *Lancashire and Yorkshire Ry.*,[11] where cotton was delayed in transit. It was not revealed till the time of transit and delay that the plaintiff's mill was stopped for lack of the cotton, so that neither loss of profits nor wages were found due, as this fact had not been disclosed, and the loss arose partly from the fact that plaintiffs had no cotton to go on with. In *Holden* v. *Bostock*,[12] where brewers had sent out poisoned beer, the defendants having supplied bad ingredients, no damages for general loss of business were given. In *British Columbia Sawmill* v. *Nettleship* [13] a shipowner was held not to be liable for loss of profits through stoppage of a mill while awaiting replacement of machinery lost by the defendant, but only for the cost of replacement, carriage to the plaintiffs, and interest, as he was ignorant of the nature and purpose of the goods carried, and did not know that the whole mill was stopped for lack of the part lost.

Damages can be recovered for loss of profits only to the extent that there is a basis for estimating their amount with reasonable certainty, failing which interest alone on the value of the property may be awarded.[14]

8 *Bain* v. *Fothergill* (1874) L.R. 7 H.L. 158.
9 (1865) 6 B. & S. 495.
10 (1876) 1 C.P.D. 326.
11 (1860) 6 H. & N. 211.
12 (1902) 18 T.L.R. 317.
13 (1868) L.R. 3 C.P. 499. See further *Archer* v. *Williams* (1846) 2 C. & K. 26; *Skinner* v. *City of London Marine Insce. Corpn.* (1885) 14 Q.B.D. 882; *Hanslip* v. *Padwick* (1850) 5 Ex. 615.
14 *Restatement of Contracts*, s. 331.

Loss of profits too remote

Loss of profits has also been refused when it is a consequence of, but one legally too remote from, the original breach. So where a passenger was injured in stepping out of a train, damages for loss of time and profits were refused.[15] Likewise in an action for damages for injuries sustained in a railway accident, damages for loss of profits on contracts which might have been entered into by the plaintiff have been held irrecoverable.[16] Where delay in transit has caused stoppage of businesses or profit-making undertakings, loss of profits are too remote unless brought within the defender's contemplation.[17] Where the loss of profits depends on a contingency such that they are too remote, they are irrecoverable. Examples are: failure of stallion to serve a mare whereby a valuable foal was probably lost[18]; injury in a railway accident to a person who might have concluded valuable contracts.[19] Loss of profit on a sub-contract is not recoverable unless the liability to indemnify was in contemplation at the time of the original contract.[20]

Mitigation of loss of profits by alternative profits

In *Hill* v. *Showell*,[21] an action of damages for breach of a contract to deliver raw material, it was shown that the plaintiffs had been prevented from executing orders which they had obtained, but it was shown that they had, in consequence, been enabled to execute other orders and made profits thereon, and this, it was held, might be taken into consideration in reduction of the damages sustained by the defendant's breach of contract. But where only some of joint plaintiffs had individually profited on a substituted contract, it was held that the damages for the breach of the main contract could not be reduced by the profits so made.[22] Again, in *Mackenzie* v. *Liddell*,[23] a tug was chartered to assist in performing a salvage contract, but arrived too late to execute the contract. The charterer sued the tug-owner for loss of profit on the salvage contract, he having received only £50, as against £600 if the tug had been there and he had effected the salvage. The tug-owner was held liable for £250, having regard to the fact that the charterers had obtained a new, though not equally advantageous, contract to tow and repair the stranded vessel.[24]

15 *Theobald* v. *Railway Passengers' Assce. Co.* (1854) 10 Ex. 45.
16 *Priestley* v. *Maclean* (1860) 2 F. & F. 288.
17 *Hadley* v. *Baxendale* (1854) 9 Ex. 341; *Gee* v. *Lancs. & Yorks. Ry.* (1860) 6 H. & N. 211; *Den of Ogil Co.* v. *Caledonian Ry.* (1902) 5 F. 99.
18 *Sapwell* v. *Bass* [1910] 2 K.B. 486.
19 *Priestley* v. *Maclean* (1860) 2 F. & F. 288; *cf. Theobald, supra.*
20 *Horne* v. *Midland Ry.* (1873) L.R. 8 C.P. 131; *Schulze* v. *G.E. Ry.* (1887) 19 Q.B.D. 30.
21 (1918) 87 L.J.K.B. 1106, H.L.
22 *Jebsen* v. *E. & W. India Dock Co.* (1875) L.R. 10 C.P. 300.
23 (1883) 10 R. 705.
24 *Quaere*, would he not have probably obtained this contract even if the tug-owner had not been in breach? An alternative contract is truly one which could only be made in the event of the breach of the first. This seems to be a case of a subsequent contract, which should not normally be brought in in mitigation of damages. *Cf. Re Vic Mill Ltd.* [1913] 1 Ch. 183.

Duplication of loss of profits

It is clearly inadmissible on principle to give damages for loss of profits in circumstances where loss of profits is covered by some other head of claim or included in some method of computing damages. Thus, if goods are bought, to the knowledge of the seller, for the purpose of fulfilling a sub-contract, and no market exists for the goods, the buyer may recover as damages the difference between the contract price and the sub-sale price.[25] This measure of damages makes allowance for loss of profits as it presumes that the buyer was reselling at a profit to the sub-purchaser. Hence, in such a case, it is improper to recover loss of profits as a separate head of claim. If, however, the sub-sale were not known to the seller, the price at which the sub-sale was made is, in the absence of a market, relevant to the measure of damages as tending to show the value of the goods at the date appointed for delivery,[26] and the excess over the contract price may be awarded [27] under the head of loss of profits on the transaction.

Similarly, in a case of delay in transit,[28] it was held that the measure of damage was the price at which the goods were obtainable in the market, if any, at the time and place at which they should have been delivered, and that, if not so obtainable, the damages must be ascertained by adding cost price, expenses of carriage and reasonable profit.

Lord McLaren pointed out in *Duff* v. *Iron Buildings Co.*,[29] that in the ordinary case of sale the rule usually applied of giving the difference between the contract price and the market price at the time when the breach of contract is ascertained, " presupposes that a purchaser for resale is not to lose his profit on the adventure, because, if he acts upon the rule, that is, if he supplies himself with goods at the market price of the day, he is able to make the same profit on the substituted goods that he would have made on the goods to be supplied under the contract, only his profit is paid to him in two portions, so much by the sub-vendee, and the balance by the seller who is liable in damages." In short, his resale price includes the element of normal profits. The older view suggested in *Dunlop* v. *Higgins*,[30] that loss of profit might be awarded separately, cannot be sustained.[31]

Cost of alternative contract

In the ordinary case when a breach of contract has taken place and the aggrieved party can achieve his purpose by making an alternative contract

[25] *Patrick* v. *Russo-British Grain Co.* [1927] 2 K.B. 535; *Hall* v. *Pim* (1928) 33 Com.Cas. 324. *Cf. Pommer and Thomson* v. *Mowat* (1906) 14 S.L.T. 373; *Guild's Tr.* v. *Edinburgh United Breweries*, 1909, 1 S.L.T. 468.

[26] *Grébert-Borgnis* v. *Nugent* (1885) 15 Q.B.D. 85, 89; *Stroud* v. *Austin* (1883) Cab. & E. 119; *Engell* v. *Fitch* (1869) L.R. 4 Q.B. 659.

[27] *Leavey* v. *Hirst* [1944] K.B. 24; *Household Machines Ltd.* v. *Cosmos Exporters Ltd.* [1946] 2 All E.R. 622.

[28] *O'Hanlon* v. *G.W. Ry.* (1863) 6 B. & S. 484.

[29] (1891) 19 R. 199, 204.

[30] (1848) 6 Bell's App. 195.

[31] The case was rejected by the House of Lords in *Ströms Bruks A/B* v. *Hutchison* (1905) 7 F.(H.L.) 131.

with a third party, his proper course is to do so and he will be entitled to recover as damages from the party in breach of contract any excess cost or loss imposed on him thereby.[32] So in the ordinary case of sale of goods, it is beyond doubt that the duty of the disappointed party is to go into the market and buy or sell as the case may be, charging the defaulting buyer or seller with the loss incurred on the sale or the extra cost required to obtain an equivalent supply. Thus, Tindal C.J. said [33]: " Where a contract to deliver goods at a certain price is broken, the proper measure of damages in general is the difference between the contract price and the market price of such goods at the time when the contract is broken, because the purchaser having the money in his hands, may go into the market and buy. So, if a contract to accept and pay for goods is broken, the same rule may be properly applied, for the seller may take his goods into the market and obtain the current price for them." This is the substance of the provisions of the Sale of Goods Act 1893, ss. 50 (3) and 51 (3).[34]

So, too, Bell says [35] that if a buyer has been obliged to supply himself elsewhere, a claim of damages will lie for the price paid in order to satisfy that demand.[36] This rule has been applied in England, even where loss to the full extent of the difference has not been sustained by reason of an intervening resale by the buyer at an intermediate price.[37] The principle of this is, that the defaulting seller is neither to be damnified by a sub-contract at an exceptional price unknown to him, nor to be benefited by a sub-contract causing less than normal loss.

Similarly, in cases of carriage, work and service and other cases, the loss or extra cost caused by having to enter into an alternative contract in order to have the original purpose achieved is recoverable in the shape of damages.[38]

Loss of sub-contract

When a party fails to implement a contract to supply or carry goods in terms of his contract, he must frequently, from his knowledge of the nature of the goods, and is held in law to, anticipate the possibility that the goods are required not for use or consumption by the consignee but in satisfaction of a sub-contract previously entered into whereby the consignee may already have disposed of the goods, and that, in consequence, a failure on the part of the supplier or carrier will compel the other party to obtain the goods, if he can, from any other readily available source, or otherwise to pay damages for failure to implement his own

[32] *Cf. Duff* v. *Iron Buildings Co.* (1891) 19 R. 199.
[33] *Barrow* v. *Arnaud* (1846) 8 Q.B. 604, 609.
[34] See also full discussion, Chap. 43, *infra*.
[35] Comm., I, 480.
[36] Citing *Taylor* v. *Morrison*, June 17, 1809, F.C.
[37] *Williams* v. *Agius* [1914] A.C. 510.
[38] *e.g. Ströms Bruks A/B* v. *Hutchison* (1905) 7 F.(H.L.) 131; *McWilliam* v. *Fletcher* (1905) 13 S.L.T. 455; *Seaton Brick and Tile Co.* v. *Mitchell* (1900) 2 F. 550.

sub-contract.[39] This consideration will apply particularly where the article in question is of the nature of raw material to be worked on by the consignee, or parts of a larger undertaking, or goods are consigned to a wholesaler. So a party in default will be found liable for damages incurred by the other party by default on that sub-contract, or for excess price paid in buying in from elsewhere in satisfaction of it, and for any loss of profit on the sub-contract, provided that (in the absence of special notice) neither damages nor profit were exceptional. This rule is a corollary of the general principle that the ordinary damages for failure to supply goods should be assessed at the difference between the price payable in terms of the contract, and the price at which they are obtainable from an alternative source at the time of failure, or if no such other means of supply be available, their value as at the place and time fixed for delivery. Assuming that there are no exceptional provisions in the contract, the amount payable as damages for failure in a sub-contract is evidence of such difference in price or value.

So, unless a pursuer in an action of damages has limited his claim on the pleadings to the actual loss sustained on his sub-contract, it would appear that it would be no gain to the defender to prove that on account of a variation between the terms of the original contract and the sub-contract, the breach of the sub-contract was not a direct result of the breach of the other contract.[40]

In *Ströms Bruks Aktie Bolag* v. *Hutchison*,[41] A contracted with B to supply a ship for the carriage of wood pulp from Sweden to Cardiff, and he failed to do so. No alternative transport was available. The charterer, B, had previously contracted to sell the wood pulp to be delivered on a particular date to C. Owing to A's failure, B failed to implement his contract and C bought in from elsewhere and recovered the excess price from B. B then sued A for this sum. In the Court of Session A succeeded by showing that he might have kept to the terms of his contract and yet delivered too late for B to implement his contract with C, and so he was held liable only for a small amount in respect of trouble and inconvenience occasioned to B. On appeal, this decision was reversed, the House of Lords holding that, even if it were assumed that A's failure were not necessarily the direct cause of B's failure to implement his sub-contract with C, B was still entitled to recover from A the cost of replacing the goods at their place of destination at the time when they ought to have arrived, less the value of the goods in Sweden, and the amount of the freight and insurance,[42] that is the difference between the cost to him of wood pulp delivered at Cardiff and the cost of obtaining it there, as he was entitled to buy in from elsewhere as soon as he discovered that the original goods could not be delivered in terms of the contract.

39 *Ströms Bruks A/B* v. *Hutchison* (1905) 7 F.(H.L.) 131, 133, *per* Lord Macnaghten.
40 *Gloag on Contract*, 697–698.
41 (1904) 6 F. 486; revd. 7 F.(H.L.) 131; disapproving *Dunlop* v. *Higgins* (1848) 1 Bell's App. 197.
42 *Per* Lord Davey at p. 137.

In *Keddie Gordon & Co.* v. *N.B. Ry.*,[43] goods were delivered to a railway company addressed to a shipping agent who was to forward them to Germany. The latter found that the covering had been torn and damaged in transit and returned them to the sender to be repacked. The consequent delay in final delivery caused the customer in Germany to reject the goods when finally tendered. The railway company were held liable in damages for the loss of market by the delay in respect that it had been occasioned by the negligence of their servants handling the packages in transit, and this was assessed at the difference between the contract price and the price at which the goods were subsequently disposed of elsewhere, plus certain expenses occasioned by the need to sell off elsewhere.

If, however, a buyer or consignee has at the time of the contract entered into a sub-contract, its actual terms, so far as affecting the principal contract, are special circumstances of which notice must be given for damages to be recoverable in respect thereof.[44] Thus, where A contracted to sell 144 bags of coffee to B, who thereupon contracted to sell 174 bags to C, and A defaulted, he was held liable to pay B loss of profit on 144 bags only, the loss on the remaining 30 being consequential.[45] This applies in particular to cases where the terms are in any way exceptional.

Consequently, a party in breach of contract is not liable where the sub-contract contained provision for a penalty,[46] or was at an exceptionally high price,[47] or would make exceptional profits.[48] He is only liable to the same extent as he would have been in the ordinary case.

Irreplaceable goods

In the case where goods are not duly forthcoming by a default of the supplier or carrier, and yet cannot be replaced from an alternative source of supply for want of a market, their value, and hence the measure of damages, must be established otherwise than by reference to market value. If there has been a contract to resell them, that contract price may be taken as evidence of value,[49] but if a substantial time has elapsed that contract may be of little evidential value.[50] If there has been no such contract the value may be taken as the purchase price together with the cost of transport and an element of normal profits, or the price at the nearest available

[43] (1886) 14 R. 233.
[44] *Hydraulic Engineering Co.* v. *McHaffie* (1878) 4 Q.B.D. 670; *Portman* v. *Middleton* (1858) 4 C.B.(N.S.) 322.
[45] *Dunlop* v. *McKellar*, May 31, 1815, F.C.
[46] *Elbinger A.G.* v. *Armstrong* (1874) L.R. 9 Q.B. 473; *Sawdon* v. *Andrew* (1874) 30 L.T. 23; *Grébert-Borgnis* v. *Nugent* (1885) 15 Q.B.D. 85.
[47] *Horne* v. *Midland Ry.* (1872) L.R. 7 C.P. 583.
[48] *Cory* v. *Thames Ironworks* (1868) L.R. 3 Q.B. 181.
[49] *Borries* v. *Hutchinson* (1865) 18 C.B.(N.S.) 445; *Engell* v. *Fitch* (1869) L.R. 4 Q.B. 659; *Godwin* v. *Francis* (1870) L.R. 5 C.P. 295; *France* v. *Gaudet* (1871) L.R. 6 Q.B. 199, expld. *The Arpad* [1934] P. 189; *Stroud* v. *Austin* (1883) Cab. & E. 119; *Grébert-Borgnis* v. *Nugent* (1885) 15 Q.B.D. 85, 89; *McNeill* v. *Richards* [1899] 1 Ir.R. 79; *Ströms Bruks A/B* v. *Hutchison* (1905) 7 F.(H.L.) 131; *Patrick* v. *Russo-British Co.* [1927] 2 K.B. 535; *cf.* *Mitsui* v. *Watts* [1917] A.C. 227.
[50] *The Arpad* [1934] P. 189.

market or at the ultimate destination, with allowance for the cost of carriage.[51] Alternatively, without reference to any sub-contract, the proper measure of damages is the profits which the purchaser would have made if the contract had been carried out.[52]

In *Marshall* v. *Nicoll*,[53] where goods were specially made to specification and were not purchasable in the open market, default was made in supplying the goods. It was held that, nevertheless, there was an " available market " within the meaning of the Sale of Goods Act 1893,[54] and the pursuers were awarded as damages the difference between the contract price and the price current at the time of the refusal to deliver, or possibly the sum calculated on the basis of what the goods would have been worth to the purchasers if they had been delivered.

In *Hinde* v. *Liddell* [55] the defendant informed the plaintiff before the due date of delivery of the goods that he would be unable to fulfil his contract by the time specified, whereupon the plaintiff, to fulfil his sub-contract for shipment abroad, bought elsewhere a better quality of article, being all that he could get, at a higher price and thereby implemented his sub-contract but received only the price contracted for. It was held that, as there was no market for the article of the quality contracted for, the measure of damages was the difference between the value at the time of breach and the contract price with the defendant.

Expenses and outlays

Where a breach of contract has taken place so that the innocent party is compelled to make alternative arrangements to supply himself, he will be entitled to recover from the party in breach a reasonable sum in respect of expenses and outlays genuinely and bona fide necessarily incurred in making those arrangements, or otherwise necessitated by the breach of contract. So, in *Duff* v. *Iron Buildings Co.*,[56] pursuers were found entitled to an allowance for advertising and travelling incurred on the faith of the fulfilment of the contract and rendered unremunerative by the breach.

Expenses incurred fruitlessly on the faith of a contract which fails completely of performance are similarly recoverable. So, in *Hydraulic Engineering Co.* v. *McHaffie*,[57] expenditure on making parts of a machine was rendered nugatory by the failure of a sub-contractor to deliver an essential part which resulted in the rejection of the whole machine, and this was held recoverable from the sub-contractor; in *Herring* v. *Tomlin* [58] expenses on journeys in connection with an intended partnership were recoverable when the agreement to enter into partnership was breached.

51 *O'Hanlon* v. *G.W. Ry.* (1865) 6 B. & S. 484; *Wertheim* v. *Chicoutimi Pulp Co.* [1911] A.C. 301.
52 *Leavey* v. *Hirst* [1944] K.B. 24; *cf. Gunter* v. *Lauritzen* (1894) 1 S.L.T. 435.
53 1919 S.C.(H.L.) 129.
54 s. 51 (3).
55 (1875) L.R. 10 Q.B. 265, following *Borries* v. *Hutchinson* (1865) 18 C.B.(N.S.) 445.
56 (1891) 19 R. 199.
57 (1878) 4 Q.B.D. 670.
58 (1854) 23 L.T.(O.S.) 92.

Similarly, wages paid to workmen kept idle or unprofitably employed in consequence of the defender's failure may be recoverable if within the defender's contemplation, but in the instances where the point has been discussed this head of claim has been too remote in the circumstances.[59] The reasonable expenses of searching for missing goods may be recovered,[60] but not the cost of transferring goods to a more favourable market for resale.[61] Where bankers failed to honour bills as they had agreed to, the notarial and telegraphic expenses of making alternative arrangements were allowed.[62]

Other cases where expenses have been held recoverable are the expense of stacking grain due to failure to deliver a threshing machine,[63] the expense of advertising that goods sent out had been discovered to be poisonous so as to minimise any possible harm or loss of business,[64] of hiring to finish a journey improperly terminated,[65] though hiring a special train is normally unreasonable,[66] or of delay overnight in a hotel awaiting completion of the contract of carriage.[67] In such cases the loss of business appointments by reason of the delay is normally too remote,[68] but damages are recoverable if the carrier had notice that such loss would result.[69] Expenses have also been recovered in respect of the detention of a ship due to improper repairs.[70]

Expenses have been refused as a head of damages where they were incurred before the plaintiff had ascertained whether or not the defendant could complete a provisional contract.[71] They were held to have been imprudently and excessively incurred.

A party prejudiced by a breach of contract is obliged to take reasonable steps to mitigate his loss,[72] and expenses reasonably and legitimately incurred in an effort to avoid or mitigate inconvenience or loss arising from the defender's breach of contract are recoverable.[73] If such expenditure results on balance in advantage to the pursuer beyond what due per-

59 *Hadley* v. *Baxendale* (1854) 9 Ex. 341; *Gee* v. *Lancs. & Yorks. Ry.* (1860) 6 H. & N. 211; *Den of Ogil* v. *Caledonian Ry.* (1902) 5 F. 99.

60 *Hales* v. *L.N.W. Ry.* (1863) 4 B. & S. 66; *Woodger* v. *G.W. Ry.* (1867) L.R. 2 C.P. 318; *Candy* v. *Midland Ry.* (1878) 38 L.T. 226.

61 *Black* v. *Baxendale* (1847) 1 Ex. 410.

62 *Prehn* v. *Royal Bank of Liverpool* (1870) L.R. 5 Ex. 92.

63 *Smeed* v. *Foord* (1859) 1 E. & E. 602.

64 *Holden* v. *Bostock* (1902) 18 T.L.R. 317.

65 *G.N. Ry.* v. *Hawcroft* (1852) 21 L.J.Q.B. 178; *Cranston* v. *Marshall* (1850) 5 Ex. 395; *Hamlin* v. *G.N. Ry.* (1856) 1 H. & N. 408.

66 *Le Blanche* v. *L.N.W. Ry.* (1876) 1 C.P.D. 286; *G.W. Ry.* v. *Lowenfeld* (1892) 8 T.L.R. 230; held reasonable in *Buckmaster* v. *G.E. Ry.* (1870) 23 L.T. 471.

67 *Hamlin* v. *G.N. Ry.* (1856) 1 H. & N. 408.

68 *Buckmaster, supra*; *cf. Cooke* v. *Midland Ry.* (1892) 57 J.P. 388.

69 *Buckmaster, supra.*

70 *Wilson* v. *General Iron Screw Co.* (1877) 47 L.J.Q.B. 239.

71 *Hanslip* v. *Padwick* (1850) 5 Ex. 685.

72 Chap. 28, *supra.*

73 *Hamlin* v. *G.N. Ry.* (1856) 1 H. & N. 408; *Hinde* v. *Liddell* (1875) L.R. 10 Q.B. 265, 268; *cf. Le Blanche* v. *L.N.W. Ry.* (1876) 1 C.P.D. 286; *Millen* v. *Brash* (1881) 8 Q.B.D. 35; *Grosvenor Hotel* v. *Hamilton* [1894] 2 Q.B. 836; *Erie Gas Co.* v. *Carroll* [1911] A.C. 105.

formance of the contract would have brought him the gain and loss must be set off against each other.[74]

Again, where goods have not been delivered, and substitute goods are obtained at greater cost, the additional expense is recoverable,[75] but if no additional expenses had been incurred or the pursuer were no worse off, only nominal damages could be awarded.[76]

The fact of breach does not entitle the innocent party to incur expenditure wildly in the hope that he will be able to recover it all from the party in breach of contract. Increased cost is recoverable if what he does is fair and reasonable in the circumstances, and any advantage or profit secured thereby must be set against the loss incurred. So where machinery was supplied and shown to be unsatisfactory and not conform to contract, and then consequently had to be replaced by new machinery of a more efficient kind, the purchaser was held entitled to recover the price of the new machinery, but on proof that the new was more satisfactory and efficient than the other would have been, even if it had been conform to contract specification, an allowance was made for the advantage the purchasers had obtained by installing the new machines, as their benefit was not entirely to be ascribed to the deficiency of the machine originally supplied, but was partly due to the intrinsic superiority of the new.[77]

Where a train missed a connection and a passenger, to avoid being stranded, took a special train to his destination, it was held that, even assuming the railway company had guaranteed the connection, they were not liable for such an expense, as it was done merely to avoid the tedium of waiting for a later train, and the question was whether in these particular circumstances an ordinary and reasonable man would have incurred that expense if he had known that he had no recourse.[78] But, obviously, there may be circumstances where such a course would be reasonable and each case must be judged on its own facts. The modern counterparts would be chartering a special plane, or hiring a private car. Mayne suggested that it would be justifiable in the case of a physician going to a patient, or a barrister to a case.[79] A passenger may charge a railway company which has failed to convey him to his destination to which he has paid the fare, with his hotel bill and the cost of a special conveyance if this is reasonable in the circumstances of the case.[80]

Ascertainment of value by reference to market

The commonest basis for estimating damages is by reference to market price. If there is a market for the goods in question regard must be had

[74] *British Westinghouse* v. *Underground Ry.* [1912] A.C. 673; *cf. Erie Gas Co.* v. *Carroll*, *supra.*
[75] *Hinde* v. *Liddell* (1875) L.R. 10 Q.B. 265, 268.
[76] *Erie Gas Co.* v. *Carroll* [1911] A.C. 105; *cf. British Westinghouse* v. *Underground Ry.* [1912] A.C. 673.
[77] *British Westinghouse Co.* v. *Underground Rys.* [1912] A.C. 673.
[78] *Le Blanche* v. *L.N.W. Ry.* (1876) 1 C.P.D. 286.
[79] *Mayne on Damages* (11th ed.), 17.
[80] *Hamlin* v. *G.N. Ry.* (1856) 1 H. & N. 408.

to the market value at the date of the breach of contract, and sub-contracts cannot be regarded either to enhance or diminish damages, unless they were within the contemplation of both parties. Market does not necessarily involve a market in the sense of a single place to which buyers and sellers of the commodity in question congregate, or the existence of a large class of suppliers. It is sufficient for a " market " for the purposes of the law of damages that more than one competing quotation for the sale or purchase of the goods or services in question can be obtained, so that there is something which may be called a current price.[81] In *Dunkirk Colliery Co.* v. *Lever*,[82] James L.J. defined a market as " that when the defendant refused to take . . . the plaintiffs might have sent it in wagons somewhere else where they could sell it . . . that is to say, that there was a fair market where they could have found a purchaser either by themselves or through some agent at some particular place."

The conception of market is important in damages as it is regularly taken as the best criterion of the value of the goods or services in question, and this is the starting point for the computation of damages. If, however, no current market value can be arrived at, the value must be ascertained in other ways.

Sub-contracts as evidence of value

A sub-contract is not normally to be taken as providing an appropriate means of measuring the damage following from a breach of contract unless the sub-contract was within the contemplation of both parties.[83] The proper measure of damages is to be ascertained by reference to the market value at the date of the breach. But if there is no market for the goods in question at the date of breach sub-contracts may be referred to as evidencing the value, and the sub-contract nearest in date to the date of breach is most likely to give a true picture of the true value of the goods.[84] But even in such a case, a sub-contract may have to be ignored if its circumstances are so peculiar as not to subject the other party to liability without knowledge of the special circumstances.[85] Sub-contracts far removed in time from the date of the breach of contract will necessarily be neglected in considering the measure of damages.[86]

Liability under sub-contract

The question whether or not a disappointed party can recover as part of his damages for breach of contract any liability he has incurred to a third party under a sub-contract, depends fundamentally on the question whether or not that liability was too remote, that is, whether it was a

81 *Marshall* v. *Nicoll*, 1919 S.C. 244; affd. 1919 S.C.(H.L.) 129.
82 (1878) L.R. 9 Ch.D. 20, 25.
83 *Finlay* v. *Kwik Hoo Tong* [1929] 1 K.B. 400; *France* v. *Gaudet* (1871) L.R. 6 Q.B. 199.
84 *The Arpad* [1934] P. 189; *Grébert-Borgnis* v. *Nugent* (1881) 15 Q.B.D. 85, 89.
85 *Horne* v. *Midland Ry.* (1873) L.R. 8 C.P. 131.
86 *Rodocanachi* v. *Milburn* (1884) 18 Q.B.D. 67, 76; *The Arpad, supra.*

consequence within the contemplation of the parties or not when they made their contract. In *Elbinger Actien-Gesellschaft* v. *Armstrong*,[87] the defendant contracted to supply wheels and axles known to be for export in satisfaction of another contract, though the date for delivery thereunder was not specified nor the fact that the plaintiffs were liable to penalties for failure. Delay ensued and the plaintiffs had to pay certain penalties amounting to £100, and this they sought to recover from the defendant in an action for delay; they were held entitled to this sum not as a matter of right, but as a reasonable estimate of the damages consequent on the delay.

In *Grébert-Borgnis* v. *Nugent* [88] the defendants contracted to supply certain goods to the plaintiff. The defendants knew that, except as to price, the contract was substantially the same as a contract between the plaintiff and a third party, and was made in fulfilment of that contract. On the defendant's breach the third party recovered damages from the plaintiff for breach of the second contract. It was held that the plaintiff could recover as damages from the defendant his loss of profit on the second contract, and also damages in respect of the liability to the third party.

In *Biggin* v. *Permanite* [89] plaintiffs ordered from the defendants (who obtained from third parties) an adhesive substance for supply to the Dutch Government, who supplied it to sub-contractors. The adhesive supplied was unsatisfactory and the Dutch Government claimed damages from the plaintiffs and this claim was settled. The plaintiffs then claimed this amount from the defendants and the defendants claimed the same amount from the third parties. It was held that, though the amount paid in settlement of the Dutch Government's claim was not conclusive as between plaintiff and defendant as the upper limit of that liability, yet such amount should be taken as the measure of damages if, having regard to the facts and the evidence, the amount was reasonable.

Expenses of litigation with third parties

If it is reasonable in the whole circumstances of the case, the expenses of a litigation with a third party incurred consequent upon the breach of contract may be recovered from the party in breach of contract as one of the ordinary and natural consequences of that breach of contract.[90] If, however, the litigation is unreasonable, it will fall to be considered an extraordinary and too remote consequence of the breach of contract. Accordingly, a party who has defaulted on one contract in consequence of another's failure in a sub-contract cannot defend the action if he knows, or reasonably should have known, that he has no ground for resisting the claim against him, and then expect to recover the expenses of his unsuccessful defence from the party in default on the sub-contract. Such expendi-

87 (1874) L.R. 9 Q.B. 473.
88 (1885) 15 Q.B.D. 85: see also *Sawdon* v. *Andrew* (1874) 30 L.T. 23.
89 [1951] 2 K.B. 314.
90 *Restatement of Contracts*, s. 334.

ture is not reasonable in the circumstances, nor is it a consequence which flows naturally from the initial breach of the sub-contract.[91] Conversely, the expenses of reasonable defence and negotiations are recoverable, where such a course is justifiable, from the party primarily responsible, as where there are reasonable grounds for belief that a defence is sound.[92] The party originally in default will be liable if his conduct gives the defender reasonable ground for believing that there is a maintainable defence to an action on the principal contract.

In *Dougall* v. *Magistrates of Dunfermline*,[93] the pursuer sought to interdict habitual trespassers on the farm which he leased from the defenders; they alleged a right of passage derived from the defenders; he had first asked the defenders to stop the trespassing but they neither justified it nor interfered. The interdict was refused, the trespassers establishing their right, and the pursuer was found liable in expenses which he then recovered, as well as his own expenses in the action, from the defenders on the grounds that they had been reasonably incurred in defending his title; the defenders were also liable for breach of the warrandice against eviction in the lease. A distinction was taken, however, between such expenses and expenses incurred by a purchaser or tenant in resisting an unsuccessful or unjustified attempt at eviction by a third party. The seller or lessor is not liable therefor as he cannot guarantee that attempted eviction will not be made.[94]

In *Munro* v. *Bennet* [95] M contracted to supply to a local authority a pump capable of certain specified work, and ordered one from B to fulfil the order. After installation complaints were made and though B alleged that he had put the pump in order the local authority rejected it. M sued for the price on B's assurance that the pump was conform to contract and settled the action on discovering that this was not so. It was held that M might recover from B the expenses of the unsuccessful action, on the ground that in the circumstances attempted recovery of the price was reasonable, and the expenses thereof flowed directly from B's breach of contract. Again, in *Agius* v. *Great Western Colliery*,[96] A contracted with G to supply coal expressly for shipment by N. G delayed to supply so that N sued A, who intimated the claim to G and defended the action. This was held reasonable and A was entitled to recover from G the costs reasonably incurred in defending the action.

91 *Barkley* v. *Simpson* (1897) 24 R. 346; *The Wallsend* [1907] P. 302.

92 *Hammond* v. *Bussey* (1887) 20 Q.B.D. 79; *Agius* v. *G.W. Colliery Co.* [1899] 1 Q.B. 413; *Rederi A/B Nordstjernan* v. *Salvesen* (1903) 6 F. 64; revd. (1905) 7 F.(H.L.) 101; *Dougall* v. *Mags. of Dunfermline*, 1908 S.C. 151; *Munro* v. *Bennet*, 1911 S.C. 337; *Kasler* v. *Slavonski* [1928] 1 K.B. 78 (sequel—*Slavonski* v. *La Pelleterie de Roubaix* (1928) 137 L.T. 645); *Parker* v. *Oloxo* [1937] 3 All E.R. 524.

93 1908 S.C. 151; *cf. Child* v. *Stenning* (1879) 11 Ch.D. 82.

94 *Inglis* v. *Anstruther* (1771) Mor. 16633; *Stephen* v. *Lord Advocate* (1878) 6 R. 282; *Straiton Estate Co.* v. *Stephens* (1880) 8 R. 299.

95 1911 S.C. 337.

96 [1899] 1 Q.B. 413.

In *Hammond* v. *Bussey*[97] H purchased from B coal for resale to steamers: the steamship owners claimed against H for the bad quality of the coal. H defended the action but B would not co-operate beyond supplying certificates which tended to show that the coal was of the requisite quality. H was found liable in damages, and on being found to have acted reasonably in defending the action recovered from B the damages paid and his costs. The decision was rested on the general rule of remoteness of damage rather than any express or implied contract of indemnity.

It is clear then that expenses incurred in litigation are not necessarily too remote, and that remoteness depends on the reasonableness or unreasonableness in the circumstances of incurring the expenses.

It is, however, quite incompetent to attempt to recover by separate action extra-judicial expenses incurred in connection with one action, but which have not been allowed in that action.[98] When a party has in an appeal to the House of Lords obtained a reversal of a judgment pronounced against him in the Court of Session, he cannot competently claim in an action of damages as an item of loss sustained by him, his expenses in the appeal which, in accordance with the practice of the House of Lords, had not been awarded to him.[99]

Recovery of expenses is frequently connected with claims of relief or for damages in respect of liability in damages to third parties, and many of the cases considered under those heads also illustrate the recovery of expenses paid incidentally to a prior claim of damages.

It would appear that expenses connected with defending a criminal prosecution may be recovered in the same way so long as they are in the circumstances the natural and probable consequence of the defender's breach of contract, and apparently so long as the pursuer has not been fined for any personal fault.[1]

Claims of relief

A claim of relief properly arises only between joint delinquents or between parties one of whom is bound expressly or impliedly to indemnify the other.[2] Frequently, however, claims are made under that name, sometimes alternatively to a claim of damages *ex contractu* for the recovery by a party who has had to pay damages, of that sum from another party who is averred to be truly liable for those damages. A claim of relief is properly competent only when the original and subsequent claims are at least to some extent commensurate as regards quantum of damages and founded on the same kind of liability.[3] Examples of this

[97] (1887) 20 Q.B.D. 79.

[98] *McDowell* v. *Stewart* (1871) 10 M. 193; *Mushets* v. *Mackenzie Bros.* (1899) 1 F. 756.

[99] *Heddle* v. *Baikie* (1846) 10 D. 376.

[1] *Cointat* v. *Myham* [1913] 2 K.B. 220; revd. (1914) 30 T.L.R. 282.

[2] *e.g. Eliott's Trs.* v. *Eliott* (1894) 21 R. 858.

[3] *Caledonian Ry.* v. *Colt* (1860) 3 Macq. 833, 848; *Ovington* v. *McVicar* (1864) 2 M. 1066, 1073.

are a builder's employer recovering from the builder sums of damages he had had to pay adjoining proprietors for damage to their property caused by the builder's unskilful performance of his work under his contract with the employer [4]; a proprietor, who had been found liable for damage to the house below by flooding, recovering from the plumber whose defective work had caused the flooding both the damages paid and expenses [5]; but a proprietor was not entitled to indemnity from engineers against a claim made by tenants whose property had been damaged by the engineers' faulty work, when liability to the tenants had been neither established nor admitted.[6] In *Clarke* v. *Scott* [7] a shipowner partially insured his vessel; while under charter it caused damage by collision; the owner settled the claim, recovered the insurance and sued the charterer for the balance. It was held that he had no right of relief as he was not liable for the charterer's fault and he had settled the claim voluntarily without notice to the charterer.

The distinction between a proper action of relief and one of damages for breach of contract is narrow, and there is no necessary antithesis between them.[8] In either case, the damages fall to be tested by *Hadley* v. *Baxendale*, but in the former case the pursuer must show that the defenders were the primary obligants and could have been sued direct by the third party who has already recovered damages from the present pursuer.[9]

In *Household Machines* v. *Cosmos Exporters*,[10] H contracted with C to supply goods known to be for resale to exporters; H failed to deliver and C declined to pay for earlier consignments; H then sued for the price and C counterclaimed for damages for non-delivery and for a declaration of indemnity. C was held entitled to damages for breach of contract based on that loss of profit, and to a declaration of indemnity in respect of such damages as might be found to be due to a subsequent purchaser, as a result of H's default on the original contract.

A contract may provide expressly for indemnity or relief,[10a] and in such a case it is a question of the interpretation of the contract whether there exists a good claim for relief. In *L.N.E. Ry.* v. *Furness Shipbuilding Co.*[11] L employed F to reconstruct a bridge, and F was to indemnify L against all claims for injuries caused " in connection with the works." Two workmen having been injured by the open door of a train which was due to the negligence of a servant of L, actions were brought for damages against L and settled for reasonable sums. It was held that there was sufficient connection with the works to enable L to recover, and the clause

4 *Pollock* v. *Wilkie* (1856) 18 D. 1311.
5 *McIntyre* v. *Gallacher* (1883) 11 R. 64, where Lord Young said that he could not treat the action as one of relief.
6 *Duncan's Trs.* v. *Steven* (1897) 24 R. 880.
7 (1896) 23 R. 442.
8 *Buchanan & Carswell* v. *Eugene*, 1936 S.C. 160, 181.
9 *Ibid.*, 182.
10 [1947] K.B. 217.
10a *e.g. Hamilton* v. *Anderson*, 1953 S.C. 129.
11 (1933) 49 T.L.R. 21; affd. (H.L.) 50 T.L.R. 257.

was not limited to defaults of F. In *Boyle* v. *Morton*,[12] M sold goods to B, M agreeing to indemnify B from " any legal action " in connection with the use of the goods, which were thought possibly to infringe a patent. K sued B successfully for infringement and B was held entitled to indemnity against M not only for the costs of the adverse judgment but was held entitled to have refused to lend their name for an appeal except on conditions.

Recovery of damages paid to third party

It is quite competent to seek to recover in an action of damages for breach of contract the damages already paid by the pursuer to some third party, provided always that the ordinary rules of remoteness are satisfied, *i.e.*, that the payment of those damages was a direct and natural consequence of the initial breach of contract by the defender. If the liability to pay damages was too remote a consequence then it will normally be irrecoverable.[13] In such cases damages paid *ex delicto* may be recoverable from a defender *ex contractu*. Thus in *Buchanan & Carswell* v. *Eugene* [13] P recovered damages from B for personal injury caused by the defective condition of B's machine; B sued E for a sum of damages representing the damages paid, expenses paid, and his own expenses of defending P's action, alleging breach of warranty of fitness of the machine supplied by E. Proof before answer was allowed on the basis that this was an action of damages: it was undecided whether it was competently laid as an action of relief. For a claim of relief payment must have been made under a legal obligation to do so. Thus in *Gardiner* v. *Main* [14] G contracted with W to do mason work on a building and M with W to do the joiner work and erect the masons' scaffolds. A scaffold fell, injuring some of G's workmen who sued G for damages. G intimated the actions to M and then settled the claims and sued M for the sums paid and his expenses, averring that he was not liable to make those payments. It was held that the payments were voluntary payments and also that there was no privity of contract between G and M so as to make M liable to G for any breach of his contract. Equally an action of relief was rejected as irrelevant when the pursuer did not aver that he was or had been found liable, but the claim had only been intimated.[15]

In *Ovington* v. *McVicar* [16] an employer settled extra-judicially a claim by the relatives of a workman killed by the failure of a chain in the works. The employer sought relief against the makers of the chain. The claim was held irrelevant as the two claims were not commensurate nor founded on the same kind of liability.

12 (1903) 5 F. 416: the amount of damages due to K had not been ascertained at the date of the action and B reserved his claim against M in respect of those damages and further costs. See also *Howard* v. *Lovegrove* (1871) L.R. 6 Ex. 43.

13 *Buchanan & Carswell* v. *Eugene*, 1936 S.C. 160, 180–181.

14 (1894) 22 R. 100.

15 *Duncan's Trs.* v. *Steven* (1897) 24 R. 880.

16 (1864) 2 M. 1066. See also *Weems* v. *Mathieson* (1862) 4 Macq. 215.

In *Baxter* v. *Boswell*[17] the defender furnished the pursuer with a clamp securing an elevator chain. In consequence of a failure of this a man was killed and his widow recovered damages from the pursuer who now sought to recover from the defender the damages and expenses paid in the first action and his own expenses in defending it. Lord Kincairney held these claims relevant as not too remote and as naturally flowing from the breach of contract (following *Mowbray* v. *Merryweather*[18]). It is submitted that this decision does not give full effect to the argument put to the judge that, as the pursuer had been found liable in the previous action for fault and negligence on his own part causing the accident, recovery was impossible and the claim irrelevant, and the decision is inconsistent with *Wood* v. *Mackay*[19] where such an argument was successful.

In *Wood* v. *Mackay*[20] a workman was injured by the breaking of a rope used in unloading a vessel. He recovered damages from his employers for negligence in failing to inspect the sling. The employers sued the shipowners to recover the amount of damages. It was found that it was the shipowners' duty to supply ropes to the satisfaction of the employers and the defect would have been easily ascertained on inspection. Hence the sole fault was that of the employers in failing to inspect the rope and they had no claim for relief. The Lord President pointed out that even if there had been a warranty the damages would not have been recoverable. In *Buchanan*[21] this was treated as a proper action of relief and the claim was excluded by the rule in *Hadley* v. *Baxendale*. The very similar case of *Mowbray* v. *Merryweather*[22] was commented on: in that case the facts were identical except that the shipowner had agreed to supply all necessary gear reasonably fit for unloading and what broke was a link of the chain on a ship's crane, the defect being one discoverable by inspection. The employers settled the action for a reasonable sum and recovered it from the shipowners: this seems explicable only on the basis that the shipowners warranted the chain and that the chain was part of the ship's fittings which the employers had no right or duty to inspect.

In *Mors-le-Blanch* v. *Wilson*[23] the charterer of a ship recovered from the consignee of goods, whose delay had rendered the charterer liable to the shipowner in damages, those damages, and also the expenses of the defence, which were held reasonable in the circumstances of the case. In *Hammond* v. *Bussey*,[24] H purchased from B coal for the disclosed purpose

[17] (1899) 6 S.L.T. 278.

[18] [1895] 2 Q.B. 640. *Cf. Kiddle* v. *Lovett* (1885) 16 Q.B.D. 605.

[19] (1906) 8 F. 625.

[20] *Ibid.*

[21] *Supra.*

[22] [1895] 2 Q.B. 640. See the two cases explained in *Buchanan & Carswell* v. *Eugene*, 1936 S.C. 160, 182. See also *Campbell* v. *Morrison* (1891) 19 R. 282.

[23] (1873) L.R. 8 C.P. 227, 233. But see Fry L.J. on this case in *Hammond* v. *Bussey* (1887) 20 Q.B.D. 79, 101.

[24] *Supra.* See also *Scott* v. *Foley* (1899) 16 T.L.R. 55; *G.W. Ry* v. *Fisher* [1905] 1 Ch. 316; *The Solway Prince* (1914) 31 T.L.R. 56; *Grébert-Borgnis* v. *Nugent* (1885) 15 Q.B.D. 85.

of resale to ships. The shipowners claimed damages from H for the faulty quality of the coal. H defended the action and B provided evidence that the coal was of the contract quality: it was found, however, not to be reasonably fit for its purpose and H was found liable in damages, which he sought to recover together with his costs from B. It was found that his defence in the prior action was reasonable in the circumstances and he was found entitled to recover the sum of damages and costs from B. The Court of Appeal affirmed the judgment, holding that the consequences were reasonably foreseeable within the rule of *Hadley* v. *Baxendale*. A chain of successive purchasers was involved in *Pinnock Bros.* v. *Lewis & Peat*,[25] where the party originally at fault was found liable for damages and costs recovered by subsequent purchasers. But where the use made of the goods was not in the contemplation of the defenders at the time of sale they will not be liable for any damages the pursuers may have to pay in consequence of deficiency on a sub-sale.[26] This principle has been applied to many cases of damages such as for skin disease from the dye in a fur collar,[27] faulty repair of a motor-vehicle,[28] unsatisfactory coal supplied to a merchant causing breach of a contract for resale to ship-owners,[29] faulty laying of roadway which involved a tramways company in liability for damages,[30] one carrier employing another who damaged the goods in transit,[31] unfit sacks supplied for unloading a ship,[32] blocking up a right of way resulting in liability in damages therefor,[33] ship repairers employing an engineer who did faulty work,[34] a trustee primarily liable for breach of trust indemnifying his co-trustee's expenses,[35] defective adhesive resold through a chain of buyers,[36] damages paid to a new tenant for failure to give possession due to the previous tenant having remained in possession,[37] damages paid to a third party for innocent infringement of his trade mark by compliance with the defendant's instructions in his contract,[38] and selling a picture with a warranty, the same as that with which it was bought but wrong.[39]

25 [1922] 1 K.B. 690. In such a case it seems to be essential that the contracts should all be the same if the same measure of damages is to apply through the chain: *Dexters* v. *Hill Crest Oil Co.* [1926] 1 K.B. 348.

26 *Bostock* v. *Nicholson* [1904] 1 K.B. 725. (Sulphuric acid used to make brewing sugar.)

27 *Bennett* v. *Kreeger* (1925) 41 T.L.R. 609.

28 *Britannia Laundry* v. *Thornycroft* (1925) 94 L.J.K.B. 858; 95 L.J.K.B. 237.

29 *Agius* v. *G.W. Colliery Co.* [1899] 1 Q.B. 413.

30 *Fisher* v. *Val de Travers Asphalte Co.* (1876) 1 C.P.D. 511.

31 *Baxendale* v. *L.C. & D. Ry.* (1874) L.R. 10 Ex. 35.

32 *Vogan* v. *Oulton* (1899) 81 L.T. 435.

33 *G.W. Ry.* v. *Fisher* [1905] 1 Ch. 316. See also *Assicurazioni Generali* v. *Empress Assurance Corpn. Ltd.* [1907] 2 K.B. 814; *Nevill's Dock Co.* v. *Maatschappij S.S. Bestevaer, Rotterdam* (1913) 108 L.T. 568.

34 *Prince of Wales Dry Dock Co.* v. *Fownes* (1904) 90 L.T. 527.

35 *The Millwall* [1905] P. 155.

36 *Biggin* v. *Permanite Ltd.* [1951] 2 K.B. 314.

37 *Bramley* v. *Chesterton* (1857) 2 C.B.(N.S.) 592.

38 *Dixon* v. *Fawcus* (1861) 3 E. & E. 537.

39 *Pennell* v. *Woodburn* (1835) 7 C. & P. 117. See also *Ronneberg* v. *Falkland Islands Co.* (1864) 17 C.B.(N.S.) 1; *Walton* v. *Fothergill* (1835) 7 C. & P. 392; *Portman* v. *Middleton* (1858) 4 C.B.(N.S.) 322; *Richardson* v. *Dunn* (1860) 8 C.B.(N.S.) 655.

Notice to person ultimately responsible

It is normally necessary where one party is thus sued for a breach of contract consequential on a previous breach to intimate the action to the party responsible for the prior breach and therefore *ex facie* ultimately responsible for the whole course of events. If no notice is given to the party ultimately liable the defence is in danger of being held unreasonable and the cost thereof irrecoverable, because the third party had no opportunity of saying whether or not the action should be defended.[40]

Where notice has been given and no reply is received it has been said that the silence may be taken as authority to defend the action.[41]

Where action settled

When a claim is made on one party and settled by him and he then seeks to recover that sum from the person whose prior default subjected him to liability under the sub-contract, the amount paid in that settlement is the upper limit of the amount recoverable but is not conclusive of the extent of such liability. If, however, having regard to the facts and the evidence, that amount of settlement was proper and reasonable it should be taken as the measure of damages.[42] If, however, such an action is settled when there was really no liability, the money paid in settlement is not recoverable as damages.[43]

Where a prior action arises *ex delicto* the pursuer may be in the dilemma that if he settles that action, it is a voluntary payment and hence irrecoverable, and if he defends and is found liable, the payment is irrecoverable because he has been found liable for fault.

Where action defended

A question of the utmost materiality in these cases is whether the defence undertaken in the prior action has been reasonable or not, so as to entitle or disentitle the pursuer to recover the expenses from the party primarily to blame. This is clearly a question of fact depending on the circumstances of each individual case as to which no general principles can confidently be laid down. If, however, the defence is undertaken with the express or implied assent of the party primarily in breach, or proceeds to any material extent on evidence supplied or volunteered by that party,[44] it is conceived that that party virtually becomes *dominus litis* and will be responsible for all ordinary expenses of litigation whether the defence be reasonable or not. In the absence of such assent or assistance it is suggested that if the defence is prepared and conducted by solicitors and counsel

40 *The Wallsend* [1907] P. 302. *Cf. Boyle* v. *Morton* (1903) 5 F. 416.
41 *Rolph* v. *Crouch* (1867) L.R. 3 Ex. 44.
42 *Biggin* v. *Permanite Ltd.* [1951] 2 K.B. 314.
43 *Kiddle* v. *Lovett* (1885) 16 Q.B.D. 605.
44 *Hammond* v. *Bussey* (1887) 20 Q.B.D. 79.

of ordinary professional experience and competence, who, in full possession of the facts, advise that the defence be insisted in, the court will be slow to find that the defence was unreasonable even though it should be unsuccessful. If the defence is unfounded in law and persisted in on the defender's instructions, in face of doubts and protests from legal advisers, that would generally, it is thought, be held unreasonable and not subjecting the party in breach to the expenses thereof. In *Baxendale* v. *L.C. & D. Ry.*,[45] the Court of Exchequer Chamber, reversing the Court of Exchequer, held that when the defender had persisted in an unstateable defence, despite repeated tenders of advice that it was unsound in law, he could not recover the expenses from the party in breach in a subsequent action, as it was not a reasonable defence and the expenses incurred were consequently not a proximate consequence of the original breach of contract.

This case was followed in *Fisher* v. *Val de Travers Asphalte Co.*,[46] where a tramway company employed F to lay a tramway: F employed V whose work was so bad that H was injured and sued the tramway company for damages for personal injury. F defended the action, V standing aloof, and settled it: he then sued V to recover the damages and costs paid in the settlement and his own costs. The settlement was found reasonable but the items of costs were held not to be recoverable, Brett J. holding that the costs, however reasonably incurred, were not a sufficiently direct consequence of the initial breach of contract, though the damages paid were admittedly the direct and natural consequence of the breach of contract. This decision is, however, contrary to principle as it must be contemplated that litigation necessarily involves expenses, even if the prior action is not defended at all: even if settled before a summons is served certain legal expenses will be incurred, and it seems verging on casuistry to distinguish the damages payable as direct consequences, and the legal expenses inseparable therefrom as remote consequences of the original failure.[47] Considering that F's settlement of the action was found reasonable it is little short of incomprehensible why his reasonable expenses of negotiating the settlement were refused.

In *Dougall* v. *Mags. of Dunfermline* [48] the defenders let a farm to the pursuer reserving right to themselves or persons with their authority to fish in a boundary stream, and with a grant of absolute warrandice. The tenant found persons habitually trespassing without authority, but who alleged they did so by virtue of a fishing right. He requested the defenders to take steps to prevent the trespass; this was ignored and he then unsuccessfully sought interdict. He was held entitled to an abatement of rent in respect of partial eviction by the establishment of a public right of fishing in the stream, and entitled to recover the expenses for which he had

[45] (1874) L.R. 10 Ex. 35.
[46] (1876) 1 C.P.D. 511.
[47] But see the same judge's (by then Esher M.R.'s) doubt in *Hammond* v. *Bussey* (1887) 20 Q.B.D. 79, 92, of the rightness of his reason in this case.
[48] 1908 S.C. 151.

been found liable and his own expenses in the interdict action, as in the circumstances, and in view of the defenders' attitude in neither justifying the trespass nor intervening to prevent it, this action to defend his rights was reasonable.

Appeals

In *Vogan* v. *Oulton* [49] O hired to V sacks for unloading a ship. They were not reasonably fit for that purpose and in consequence a man was injured and recovered damages from V. V's appeal was dismissed and it was held that he could not recover the expenses of the appeal from O, though he could recover the damages and other expenses. Sub-contractors who were liable to the plaintiffs for injuries sustained in consequence of their negligence were not liable for the costs of their principal's unsuccessful appeal to which they did not consent.[50]

Loss measured by waste of time and effort

In the case of goods supplied for a purpose rendered fruitless by the breach the loss sustained by the pursuer in consequence thereof has sometimes been estimated by reference to the time and effort wasted by reason of the breach of contract. So where the wrong kind of cabbage-seed was supplied, damages were quantified by reference to the unprofitable occupation of the pursuer's land and waste of his labour.[51]

Where a contract to manufacture and supply goods has been broken the manufacturer's claim of damages will amount to the profit he has lost on the transaction as compensation for the time and effort wasted in the work. In *Cort* v. *Ambergate Ry.*[52] a supplier was instructed to discontinue supply, and was held entitled to recover the difference between the contract price and the cost of production, regard being had to a sum required to be paid to a sub-contractor to release him from the sub-contract, and to the supply of material fruitlessly ordered and the expenses of building a special foundry for production of the goods ordered. Similarly in *Hydraulic Engineering Co.* v. *McHaffie* [53] a person under contract to make a machine sub-contracted for a part of it. The sub-contractor defaulted, whereby the principal contract was lost. The plaintiff was held entitled to the expense incurred in making the machine and to the loss of profit on the principal contract. Again in *Watson* v. *Ambergate Ry.*[54] a model was so delayed in transit as to miss the competition for which it had been made and the damages were the value of the work and materials thrown away on the construction.

49 (1899) 81 L.T. 435.

50 *Maxwell* v. *Brit. Thomson-Houston Co.* [1904] 2 K.B. 342. See also *Shepheard* v. *Bray* [1906] 2 Ch. 235 and *Boyle* v. *Morton* (1903) 5 F. 416, as to whether an agreement to indemnify imports consent to an appeal.

51 *Wilson* v. *Carmichael* (1894) 21 R. 732. *Cf. Randall* v. *Newson* (1877) 2 Q.B.D. 102, and *Waters* v. *Towers* (1853) 8 Ex. 401.

52 (1851) 17 Q.B. 127.

53 (1878) 4 Q.B.D. 670.

54 (1851) 15 Jur. 448.

Loss of value for use

Things purchased for use and not for resale or further treatment, as by manufacture, cannot be valued for the purposes of damages except by reference to the use for which the thing was intended, and the diminution in its use-value by not being supplied conform to specification or being defective or inadequate. So where a ship was duly supplied but turned out to be deficient in cargo-carrying capacity, it was held that the proper measure of damages was the difference in earning power, the diminution being imputable to the deficiency.[55] Similarly, the late delivery of a ship subjected the builder to damages measured by the difference between what she should have earned if delivered at the proper time and her actual earnings on her first trip, the freights having suffered a seasonal fall and delay having caused the vessel to miss the most profitable season.[56] Where a ship was built with excessive draught and a deficiency in dead-weight capacity, regard was to be had in estimating damages to the probable cost of reducing the excess draught and to the probable loss of net freight, both having regard to the estimated life of the vessel, and allowing for such contingencies as her loss, sale, or lack of employment.[57]

Where the subjects in question are totally destroyed the loss of value amounts to their whole value: so where a warehouseman stored goods in breach of contract at another place than that specified, where they were destroyed by fire, the owner was held entitled to the full value as damages.[58]

Cost of repairing defective performance

Where a contract has not been fully performed or has been defectively performed, it does not follow that the cost of doing what is necessary to achieve proper performance is the true measure of damages. In *Wigsell* v. *School for the Indigent Blind* [59] the defendants had failed to build a wall round their property as they had covenanted to do. It appeared that the value of the adjacent land was not decreased by anything like the amount it would have cost to build the wall. Hence the true measure of damages was the difference between W's present position and his position if the contract had been performed, *i.e.*, the diminution in value of the adjacent land due to the non-performance, and not what it would cost to build the wall.

These considerations appear applicable particularly to cases of failure to implement certain of the prestations in a feu-contract. In *Rankine* v. *Logie Den Land Co.*[60] ground was feued with a condition that the disponee

55 *Gillespie* v. *Howden* (1885) 12 R. 800. In *Walker, Henderson & Co.* v. *Hutchinson* (1885) 22 S.L.R. 903, a similar case, it was said that the damages ought to be estimated by deducting from the total price a sum proportional to the difference between the actual and stipulated capacity.

56 *Fletcher* v. *Tayleur* (1855) 17 C.B. 21; *Collard* v. *Carswell* (1893) 20 R.(H.L.) 47.

57 *Australian Steamship Proprietary* v. *Lewis*, 47 Ll.L.R. 132.

58 *Lilley* v. *Doubleday* (1881) 7 Q.B.D. 570: see also cases of Deposit. *Cf. The Mediana* [1900] A.C. 113.

59 (1882) 8 Q.B.D. 357.

60 (1902) 4 F. 1074.

and his heirs and assignees should erect buildings of a certain value; it was held that so long as the condition was not implemented, each successive vassal was liable for damages for non-implement, jointly and severally, failing implement by the present vassal. The quantum of damages was not discussed: as the buildings had not been started the whole cost of erection would probably be the correct measure, but had they been erected but inadequate the rule of *Wigsell* would appear applicable.

In such cases as machinery and ships it is clear that the cost of modification is not the full extent of the damages. Thus where a machine was disconform to contract the measure of damages was stated as the difference between the value of the machine actually supplied and the value it would have had to the purchasers if it had been in all respects conform to contract.[61] Where a ship had a deficient carrying capacity damages were measured as the difference between her expected and actual earning power.[62] In short the measure of damages is the loss sustained, not the cost of repair.[63] But if the defect is so great that complete replacement has to be effected the cost of doing so is the basic measure of damages.[64]

Loss of opportunities

When it can be shown to have been in the contemplation of the parties that the whole or part of the benefit which one party will derive from the contract consists in the opportunity of enhancing his reputation,[65] winning a prize [66] or acquiring other benefits apart from direct remuneration, the failure by the other party to give a reasonable opportunity for the acquisition of such benefit will be a breach of contract sounding in damages for loss of opportunity. The possibility may in the particular circumstances be held to be too remote to be admissible, or dependent on too many contingencies to be calculable.[67] While accurate assessment of the chances cannot be looked for, the chance must always be at least reasonable before it can be considered under the head of loss of opportunity. Quite substantial damages may be recovered where the chance is moderately promising.[68]

This head of claim is particularly applicable to persons such as actors and actresses, and refusal, in breach of contract, to allow such a person to appear justifies an award of damages when it can be shown that it was within the reasonable contemplation of both parties that the chance of establishing or enhancing a reputation existed.[69] In *Pell* v. *Shearman* [70]

61 *Electric Construction Co.* v. *Hurry & Young* (1897) 24 R. 312, 325.
62 *Gillespie* v. *Howden* (1885) 12 R. 800; *cf. Australian Steamship Pty.* v. *Lewis*, 47 Ll.L.R. 132.
63 Compare further cases on damage to heritable property.
64 *British Westinghouse* v. *Underground Rys.* [1912] A.C. 673.
65 p. 568, *infra*.
66 p. 567, *infra*.
67 *Sapwell* v. *Bass* [1910] 2 K.B. 486; *cf. Watson* v. *Ambergate Ry.* (1851) 15 Jur. 448.
68 *Chaplin* v. *Hicks* [1911] 2 K.B. 786.
69 *Fechter* v. *Montgomery* (1863) 33 Beav. 22; *Bunning* v. *Lyric Theatre* (1894) 71 L.T. 396; *Marbé* v. *Edwardes* [1928] 1 K.B. 269; *Clayton* v. *Oliver* [1930] A.C. 209, overruling *Turpin* v. *Victoria Palace* [1918] 2 K.B. 539; *Withers* v. *General Theatre Corpn.* [1933] 2 K.B. 536.
70 (1855) 10 Ex. 766.

the defendants contracted in certain circumstances to sink a pit and make a substantial payment if a marketable seam of coal should be found. On their failure to implement their obligations, the plaintiff proved that marketable coal might have been found, and hence it was held that substantial damages were due for the loss of the opportunity of finding marketable coal and the true measure of damages was the amount lost in consequence of being deprived of that opportunity.

Similarly where the performance of the contract would give the other party the opportunity of earning commission, damages will be given for failure to give due and reasonable employment which will afford these opportunities [71]; so too where the remuneration is by piece-rates, work must be given,[72] or by royalties on a book, a reasonable publication must be made,[73] and in cases of failure damages will be assessed on these bases.

Loss of prize or reward

In *Chaplin* v. *Hicks* [74] the Court of Appeal upheld an award of £100 damages to a plaintiff who, having reached the final of a beauty competition, was denied reasonable opportunity of being interviewed in accordance with the rules and consequently lost a chance of a prize of which she had at least a reasonable chance. The contingency that she would not have won anything was not exclusive of all chance and the fact that damages were difficult but not incapable of assessment could not deprive her of a claim. The chance of winning was in the circumstances not too remote either, the plaintiff being one of fifty from whom twelve winners were to be selected.[75] It is suggested that a different decision would apply in the earlier stages of such a competition where the contingency of winning is both more remote and almost incalculable. Thus it has been held in an action on negligence [76] for injury to a racehorse, that no regard could be had in assessing damages to the possibility that it might have won substantial prize money in subsequent races that season, such being incalculable and dependent on many factors apart from the animal's physical fitness, with which alone the negligence had interfered. Similarly in *Sapwell* v. *Bass* [77] a contract to have a stallion serve a mare was breached. Damages for loss of the expected profit from the sale of the foals was too remote to be recoverable, as depending entirely on incalculable contingencies, and hence only nominal damages could be awarded.

In *Watson* v. *Ambergate Ry.*[78] a prize was offered for a model of certain machinery. The plaintiff's entry was delayed and arrived too late, but

[71] *Turner* v. *Goldsmith* [1891] 1 Q.B. 844.
[72] *Devonald* v. *Rosser* [1906] 2 K.B. 728.
[73] *Abrahams* v. *Reiach* [1922] 1 K.B. 477.
[74] [1911] 2 K.B. 786.
[75] Similarly in *Richardson* v. *Mellish* (1824) 2 Bing. 229, an award of damages was made where a contingency was " almost a certainty."
[76] *Bourne* v. *Lothians Racing Syndicate Ltd.*, 1951 S.L.T.(Notes) 37.
[77] [1910] 2 K.B. 486; *cf. Bunting* v. *Tory* (1947) 64 T.L.R. 353.
[78] (1851) 15 Jur. 448; *cf.* also *Boyce* v. *Bayliffe* (1807) 1 Camp. 58; *Hoey* v. *Felton* (1861) 11 C.B.(N.S.) 142; *Burton* v. *Pinkerton* (1867) L.R. 2 Ex. 340.

the defendants did not know of the competition. Doubts were expressed whether the value of the prize could be included in the quantum of damages, it is submitted, rightly, but the point did not call for decision.

Loss of income or remuneration

In an action for wrongful dismissal a pursuer is entitled to recover the wages in respect of the period of employment unexpired as well as wages already accrued,[79] but regard must be had to the consideration whether he had or reasonably could have obtained other occupation.[80] This question is treated at length under the head of Employment.[81]

There can, however, be no claim for commission which the employee might have gained if the employment had continued, so long as the master was not obliged expressly or impliedly to continue the business.[82] In the case, however, where there is employment with an opportunity of making incidental profit, damages may include an estimated amount in respect of the value of the opportunities of profit open to the employee.[83]

Loss of publicity

In *Clayton* v. *Oliver* [84] the respondent objected to the part assigned to him in a play and sued for breach of contract. It was held competent, having regard to the character of the contract, to give him damages for loss of publicity on the basis that damages must be such as may be supposed to have been in contemplation and that it was contemplated that to be billed and advertised was a valuable right. Though necessarily speculative in amount, enhancing a reputation is not too remote to be contemplated. The jury's award of £1,000 was said to be extravagant (for a six weeks' run of the play) but was not interfered with. Damage to an already existing reputation cannot, however, be considered.[85]

Similar considerations apply to authors [86] and writers of scripts and lyrics for films,[87] but not to an impresario.[88]

So too, where an advertisement was wrongfully discontinued by a newspaper and loss of business ensued for which no other explanation could be given, the advertisement being the only one of its kind in that paper, it was held that the loss of business arose from the loss of publicity and was not

[79] *Goodman* v. *Pocock* (1850) 15 Q.B. 576; *Hochster* v. *De la Tour* (1853) 2 E. & B. 678; *Frost* v. *Knight* (1872) L.R. 7 Ex. 111; *Brace* v. *Calder* [1895] 2 Q.B. 253.
[80] *Reid* v. *Explosives Co.* (1887) 19 Q.B.D. 264; *Brace, supra.*
[81] Chap. 33, *infra.*
[82] *Re English and Scottish Marine Insce. Co.* (1870) 5 Ch.App. 737; *Turner* v. *Goldsmith* [1891] 1 Q.B. 544; *Re Newman Ltd.* [1916] 2 Ch. 309.
[83] *Inchbald* v. *Western Neilgherry Co.* (1864) 34 L.J.C.P. 15.
[84] [1930] A.C. 209, followed in *Withers* v. *General Theatre Corpn.* [1933] 2 K.B. 536. Also *Marbé* v. *Edwardes* [1928] 1 K.B. 269; *Re Golomb & Porter's Arbitration* (1931) 144 L.T. 583; *Bunning* v. *Lyric Theatre* (1894) 71 L.T. 396.
[85] *Withers* v. *General Theatre Corpn.* [1933] 2 K.B. 536, dissenting from *Marbé* v. *Edwardes, supra.*
[86] *Tolnay* v. *Criterion Film Productions, Ltd.* [1937] 2 All E.R. 1625 (screenplay).
[87] *Miller* v. *Cecil Film, Ltd.* [1937] 2 All E.R. 464 (screen credit for song).
[88] *Fielding* v. *Moiseiwitsch* (1946) 62 T.L.R. 265.

too remote as it must have been in the contemplation of the parties, and hence that the damages were to be measured by the diminution in business and not merely by the cost of the advertisement.[89]

Loss of appointment

In *Simon* v. *Pawson & Leafs*[90] girls at a school were instructed to obtain certain uniforms and that the plaintiff alone could supply them; the plaintiff was also informed of this and of the date by which the clothes had to be supplied but she was not formally appointed, nor was any duration of appointment fixed. She ordered materials from the defendants, disclosing the date by which they were required. On account of delay by the defendants and defects in garments supplied, the plaintiff's appointment was cancelled and she claimed damages from the defendants for the loss thereof. It was held that damages for loss of appointment were not in the contemplation of both parties and so were too remote, and also that the loss of appointment was not due to the defendants' breach by failing to supply but to the plaintiff's own failure to obtain the material timeously elsewhere.

Similarly, where a plaintiff alleged that he would have obtained a situation but for the defendant's false imprisonment of him, that was held too remote.[91] So too, in *Armstrong* v. *Paterson*,[92] an action for personal injuries, an averment of loss by having to postpone sitting a promotion examination was classed as " highly speculative."

Loss of reputation or goodwill

In general loss of reputation is a matter for which damages can only be claimed in cases of defamation. It may be however that such could result from a breach of contract. So where cosmetic manufacturers enlisted the assistance of beauty editresses of newspapers in advertising a product, and breach of contract caused a failure of the promised product, it was held on the facts of the case that damages could not be recovered for loss of the future co-operation of the editresses, that is, in effect for loss of reputation in their eyes and their goodwill, though the claim might be a good one otherwise as " loss of reputation caused by breach of contract is not sufficient to preclude the plaintiffs from recovering in respect of that pecuniary loss." [93]

Further where a breach of contract of advertising was made in a manner detrimental to the other party's credit and reputation damages were recoverable for the resultant pecuniary loss, though not directly for any damage to reputation.[94]

89 *Marcus* v. *Myers* (1895) 11 T.L.R. 327.
90 (1933) 148 L.T. 154; 38 Com.Cas. 151.
91 *Hoey* v. *Felton* (1861) 11 C.B.(N.S.) 142. *Cf. Burton* v. *Pinkerton* (1867) L.R. 2 Ex. 340; *Boyce* v. *Bayliffe* (1807) 1 Camp. 58, example given from Lord Alvanley.
92 1935 S.C. 464.
93 *Foaminol* v. *British Plastics* [1941] 2 All E.R. 393, 400.
94 *Aerial Advertising Co.* v. *Batchelor's Peas, Ltd.* [1938] 2 All E.R. 788.

Akin to this is loss of commercial goodwill. In *Bostock* v. *Nicholson* [95] the defendants contracted to sell suphuric acid commercially free from arsenic for an unknown purpose. The acid supplied was not commercially free from arsenic so that brewing sugar made therewith was faulty and made poisonous beer in consequence of which the plaintiffs had to pay damages to the brewers. It was held that damages were not recoverable for the loss of goodwill.

In *Cointat* v. *Myham* [96] the defendants sold to the plaintiff, a butcher, meat unfit for human food. The meat was seized and destroyed and the plaintiff convicted and fined. In an action against the defendants for breach of warranty he recovered the amount of the fine and costs, and damages for loss of trade. But in *Millar* v. *Bellvale Chemical Co.*,[97] where defective goods were supplied to a wholesaler, it was questioned whether the pursuer was entitled to damages for injury to his trade from loss of reputation. The determination in each case whether this element of damages is recoverable really depends on whether it is considered to be natural and probable or not in the circumstances.[98]

Damages for inconvenience

A breach of contract generally causes trouble and inconvenience and a measure of dislocation of business, although the party whose contract has been broken may not have sustained any actual loss,[99] or may even have made a profit by a fortunate variation of the market price of his commodity. In such a case nominal damages would be of no avail, as a pursuer who averred but did not prove any actual loss would probably be found liable in expenses. While there is no legal measure for the damages sustained by commercial disruption, it has been recognised in the case of commercial contracts that an award of damages is due. In *McWilliam & Son* v. *Fletcher* [1] a shipowner failed, in breach of his contract, to provide a ship, and the charterer had to secure another at a higher rate: it was held that the charterer was entitled to damages measured by the difference of freight, and also for such further items of loss as he could prove that he fairly incurred as arising in the ordinary course of his business out of the shipowners' breach, and also to damages for inconvenience, trouble, and annoyance. Similarly in *Webster* v. *Cramond Iron Co.*,[2] where delay in delivery of iron pipes caused no specific pecuniary loss, it was held that the pursuers were entitled to moderate damages for the trouble and inconvenience they were put to before they could obtain fulfilment of the

95 [1904] 1 K.B. 725. See also *Holden* v. *Bostock* (1902) 18 T.L.R. 317.

96 [1913] 2 K.B. 220. But see *Leslie* v. *Reliable Advertising Agency* [1915] 1 K.B. 652; *Proops* v. *Chaplin* (1920) 37 T.L.R. 112.

97 (1898) 1 F. 297; *cf. Wilson* v. *Carmichael* (1894) 21 R. 732.

98 *Cf.* Lord Chelmsford in *L. & Y. Ry.* v. *Gidlow* (1875) L.R. 7 H.L. 517.

99 *Webster* v. *Cramond Iron Co.* (1875) 2 R. 752.

1 (1905) 13 S.L.T. 455. See also *Webster* v. *Cramond Iron Co.* (1875) 2 R. 752; *Ströms Bruks Aktie Bolag* v. *Hutchison* (1904) 6 F. 486, revd. on other grounds (1905) 7 F.(H.L.) 131.

2 (1875) 2 R. 752.

contract, and these, including an element of purely nominal damage in respect of the fact of the breach of contract, were assessed at £50.

In *Hobbs* v. *L.S.W. Ry.*[3] a railway company, in breach of contract, set down a man and his wife and family at a wrong station at night, whence they had to walk home several miles in the rain, and substantial damages were awarded for the inconvenience caused, though not for the wife's resulting illness.

If however inconvenience caused to a party is not substantial, and only really amounts to vexation, petty annoyance and trouble, incapable of being assessed in money and not sounding in pecuniary loss, this head of claim cannot be pressed, as every breach involves some measure of inconvenience.[4] The maxim *de minimis non curat lex* applies.

In *Bailey* v. *Bullock*[5] the plaintiff instructed solicitors to take steps to recover for him possession of his house but possession was substantially delayed by the solicitors' breach of duty and for a time he had to live in uncomfortable and unsuitable accommodation. It was held that his claim was properly founded in contract, and that he could recover damages for the inconvenience and discomfort which he had suffered resulting directly from the defendants' breach of contract, but not in respect of annoyance and mental distress, nor in respect that he and his wife had not thought it possible to have another child. Special damages in respect of the cost of storing furniture were allowed but the expenses of an illness consequent on the inconvenience and discomfort were too remote. A claim on similar lines is appropriate where a landlord fails to keep premises in wind-and-water-tight condition.[6] The decision has been followed in a case where a travel agency booked inferior accommodation so that the plaintiff's holiday was spoilt.[7]

This principle does not extend to the case where legal proceedings have to be taken in consequence of the breach of contract and it is well settled that the only damages recoverable in respect thereof are the taxed expenses of process.

Damage from use of article

A person must be reasonably presumed to have in contemplation without special notice to him the fact that an article which he undertakes to supply is intended for use by the party contracting for the supply or purchase, and he will therefore be held liable for any loss directly resulting from his failure in respect of the quality of the article making it unfit for

[3] (1875) L.R. 10 Q.B. 111. But on this see *McMahon* v. *Field* (1881) 7 Q.B.D. 594. See further *Cooke* v. *Midland Ry.* (1892) 57 J.P. 388; *Atkins* v. *Hutton* (1910) 103 L.T. 574; *Grosvenor Hotel* v. *Hamilton* [1894] 2 Q.B. 836; *cf. Burton* v. *Pinkerton* (1867) L.R. 2 Ex. 340.

[4] *Hamlin* v. *G.N. Ry.* (1856) 1 H. & N. 408.

[5] [1950] 2 All E.R. 1167; £300 awarded.

[6] *Hart* v. *Rogers* [1916] 1 K.B. 646; *Hewitt* v. *Rowlands* (1924) 93 L.J.K.B. 1080: see also *Green* v. *Eales* (1841) 2 Q.B. 225.

[7] *Stedman* v. *Swan's Tours* (1951) 95 S.J. 727. See also *Tolman* v. *Dyson* [1952] C.P.L. 745.

its ordinary and normal use. This may amount to a claim alternatively for breach of contract or for delict should the defective article cause actual damage or physical injury to the person or property of the consignee when put to its ordinary use. Despite the fact that any injury so resulting may have no relation to the value of the article and may exceed it to an indefinite extent, such consequences must normally be held to have been within the contemplation of the supplier, and damages will accordingly be recoverable from him should such consequences ensue. But it would appear that he will not be liable for any such loss resulting from an unusual use of the article, or one for which it was not intended, in the absence of special notice, on the ground that such is outside the reasonable contemplation of a supplier.[8]

The provisions of section 14 of the Sale of Goods Act 1893 must be borne in mind in this connection, and reference should be made to the detailed discussion of these provisions,[9] and to the decisions on reasonably contemplated use of various articles and foods. A landlord is held liable for injury to a tenant's health which arises from the defective state of the house, as where a tenant sustained injury by falling down the stair owing to an upright of the railing, which he had grasped, giving way.[10] In *Fitzpatrick* v. *Barr*[11] a householder injured by an explosion of household coal recovered damages for breach of the implied warranty of fitness for the purpose for which the coal was bought, under section 14 (1) and (2) of the Sale of Goods Act 1893. This case was distinguished from the similar circumstances of *Duke* v. *Jackson*,[12] where the Act did not apply as no defect in the fitness of the goods supplied was averred, the explosion being caused in that case by an extrinsic article (a detonator) which had no place in the contract of sale: this ratio is unsatisfactory; an alternative claim founded on negligence was, however, more successful in this case.

Physical injury resulting from breach of contract was held too remote in *Hobbs* v. *L.S.W. Ry.*,[13] where the plaintiff's wife, put down at the wrong station, had to walk home in the rain and caught cold. This was doubted in *McMahon* v. *Field*,[14] where the plaintiff hired stabling accommodation from the defendant for twelve horses. The latter, in breach of contract, let the same stabling to a third party who arrived and turned the plaintiff's horses out without their rugs so that some of them caught cold before fresh stabling could be found. It was held that the loss in value by the damage to the health of the animals was recoverable as a probable consequence of the breach of contract.

8 *Cf. Cory* v. *Thames Ironworks* (1868) L.R. 3 Q.B. 181; *Macfarlane* v. *Taylor* (1867) 6 M. (H.L.) 1.

9 Chap. 43, *infra*.

10 *Dickie* v. *Amicable Property Investment Co.*, 1911 S.C. 1079.

11 1948 S.L.T.(Sh.Ct.) 5. *Cf. Nicholson* v. *N.C.B.*, 1952 S.L.T.(Sh.Ct.) 44; *Lusk* v. *Barclay*, 1953 S.L.T.(Sh.Ct.) 23.

12 1921 S.C. 362. *Cf. Preist* v. *Last* [1903] 2 K.B. 148; *Jackson* v. *Watson* [1909] 2 K.B. 193; *Wilson* v. *Rickett, Cockerell & Co.* [1954] 1 Q.B. 598.

13 (1875) L.R. 10 Q.B. 111.

14 (1881) 7 Q.B.D. 591.

Damages where loss uncertain

A party in breach of his contract may competently and relevantly attempt to establish, as a defence to a claim for substantial damages, that even complete performance on his part would not have averted the loss sustained by the pursuer. In that event the onus of such proof will be on the defender. So when one trustee embezzled the trust funds, his co-trustee successfully proponed, in defence to an action of damages for lack of reasonable care in the performance of his duties as trustee, the plea that, in the circumstances of the case and of the defaulting trustee, no amount of care on his part would have preserved the trust funds intact.[15] For such a defence to be successful it must be shown, not just that the defender's full performance of his due obligations might not or even probably would not have averted the pursuer's loss but that in the circumstances of the case it certainly would and could not have averted the loss. In other words, it must be more than a possibility or even probability, and in such cases the defender will still be held liable,[16] but before he can be found liable it must be shown that the loss sustained by the pursuer was certain and consequential on the defender's failure.

A defender may likewise also relevantly prove in defence that the right which would have been secured by his due fulfilment of the contract must necessarily have been valueless, so that there would be no loss. So in *McLean* v. *Grant* [17] a law agent was employed to carry out an adjudication and made two errors, each fatal to the validity and force of his purported diligence. Only the second error could be held in the circumstances to be lack of reasonable professional skill. It was held that, while damages might be claimed by the client for this error, none were due, as that error could only have caused the loss of a diligence already invalid by the prior error for which in the circumstances he could not be held responsible, the point being still at that time a matter of judicial dispute. It is conceived that such a plea can generally only result in a mitigation of damages, as it involves an admission of failure to fulfil an obligation incumbent on the defender and such will entitle the pursuer to nominal damages. This conclusion could only be avoided in *McLean* [17] on the basis that the prior error was not one for which the defender could be found liable in damages. Had the second mistake been the only one it is thought that some damages would have followed.

Damages where loss contingent

Damages are exigible for a breach of contract notwithstanding that the loss incurred thereby depends in part on some contingency or un-

15 *Millar's Trs.* v. *Polson* (1897) 24 R. 1038; *Coldman* v. *Hill* [1919] 1 K.B. 443; *Hobday* v. *Peters* (1860) 28 Beav. 603.

16 Chap. 28, *supra*.

17 (1805) M.App. *voce* Reparation, No. 2; Nov. 15, 1805, F.C., and Bell, Comm. I, 490. See also *Hawick Herit. Inv. Bank* v. *Huggan* (1902) 5 F. 75; *Bank of Scotland* v. *Dominion Bk.* (1889) 16 R. 1081; affd. (1891) 18 R.(H.L.) 21.

certainty. So it has been said [18] that the only answer to a claim of damages for the defender's failure to perform his contract would have been to show that there was absolutely no chance of the pursuer benefiting by the performance of the obligation which the defender undertook. But if the contingency is very substantial and indeed likely it may operate to make the claim of damages somewhat speculative. In *Stiven* [18] A delayed to deliver to S yarn sold to him but agreed that tow should be held by W for behoof of A till the yarn should be delivered. W failed to intimate the delivery order to the railway company so that the property did not pass, A himself removed the tow and went bankrupt, and it was held that the defence that no damage had been sustained could not be upheld as it was not certain that the agreement would have been reduced as a fraudulent preference. The possession of the tow by W *might* have caused the delivery of the overdue yarn. So too in *Davidson* v. *Mackenzie* [19] opinions were expressed that the plea in defence that an inhibition was already null by reason of prior defects was not a relevant defence to an action against the Keeper of the Registers for damages for the loss of the debt by failing to record the inhibition " in respect of the impracticability of ascertaining that if such duty had been performed, any other objections to the diligence would have been successful, or would ever have been urged or persisted in." [20]

Other instances of this principle are the liability of patent agents for failure to renew a patent notwithstanding their averment that it would have been open to challenge on the ground of prior user (because this depended on the speculative chance of some party challenging the patent successfully) [21]; or where a charterer was found entitled to damages when the ship should have been sent to load at a port in the Black Sea but could not pass the Dardanelles owing to the war of 1914, as he would have been able to insure against war risks if the ship had arrived, even though there was in fact no proof that he would have considered the heavy premium worthwhile [22]; or where a solicitor lost a client's money by failing to complete a security and was held liable although even if the security had been properly completed it would have been challengeable as granted within sixty days of bankruptcy (but successful challenge was only a contingency).

It has been held that where a vessel running at a loss to establish a new trade was put out of employment, it was impossible to include as an item of loss the contingent profit which it was hoped thereafter to earn.[23] In other cases the contingency has been more substantial and been taken

18 *Stiven* v. *Watson* (1874) 1 R. 412, 416.

19 (1856) 18 D. 226.

20 *Ibid.*, 253, *per* Lord Curriehill. *Cf. Chatto* v. *Marshall*, Jan. 17, 1811, F.C., and *McMillan* v. *Gray*, Mar. 2, 1820, F.C.

21 *Turnbull* v. *Cruickshank & Fairweather* (1905) 7 F. 791.

22 *Watts* v. *Mitsui* [1917] A.C. 227.

23 *The Bodlewell* [1907] P. 286; *cf. The Anselma de Larrinaga* (1913) 29 T.L.R. 587; *Main* v. *Leask*, 1910 S.C. 772.

account of. In *Ebbw Vale Steel Co.* v. *Wood's Tr.*[24] lessees of a coalfield subleased it on certain conditions, one of which entitled the subtenants to surrender the sublease. The subtenants having been sequestrated the lessee claimed in the sequestration for damages on the basis of the unexpired years of the sublease. It was held that in computing the damages an allowance must be made for the contingency that the subtenants would have surrendered the sublease. It was no objection that calculation of the contingency could not pretend to exactitude.

Again damages are too remote where they depend upon a contingency supervening on the act complained of, so that where a carrier delayed delivery of a model intended for a prize competition, no damages could be awarded in respect of the loss of the prize,[25] though damages were recoverable in respect of the labour and materials fruitlessly employed,[26] or where a person injured by assault was prevented thereby from applying for a post, the loss thereof did not sound in damages.[27]

However, where a contingency of loss resulting amounts to " almost a certainty " damages are recoverable.[28] From the defender's angle, if he is to escape liability by pleading that the loss was contingent he must show that the contingency was very substantial if not certain to deprive the pursuer of benefit or avoid his loss.[29]

Speculative loss

Speculative loss is such as may or may not and is not certain to be suffered and which therefore cannot be estimated.

In *The Parana* [30] it was held in a case of carriage of goods by sea that damages for loss of market were irrecoverable as being too speculative. The decision, however, proceeded at least partly on the basis that carriage by sea was very uncertain, but, as was later pointed out,[31] such voyages are nowadays accomplished with considerable certainty. It remains true, however, that if a particular loss be speculative, damages cannot be awarded in respect thereof, or at least not to the full extent. Even where the quantification of damages is difficult any loss considered must be based on reasonable probability and not on mere speculative possibility.[32] So no award could be made in respect of the loss of contracts which might have been entered into by the plaintiff had he not been injured in a railway accident.[33] Again, where land was sold and was found to be subject to building restrictions it was said that the damages had to be limited to its

24 (1898) 25 R. 439.
25 *Watson* v. *Ambergate Ry.* (1851) 15 Jur. 448.
26 *Jameson* v. *Midland Ry.* (1884) 50 L.T. 428.
27 *Hoey* v. *Felton* (1861) 11 C.B.(N.S.) 142.
28 *Richardson* v. *Mellish* (1824) 2 Bing. 229.
29 *Cf. Stiven* v. *Watson* (1874) 1 R. 412.
30 (1877) 2 P.D. 118. So too, in *The Notting Hill* (1884) 9 P.D. 105, and *cf. Den of Ogil* v. *Caledonian Ry.* (1902) 5 F. 99.
31 *Dunn* v. *Bucknell Bros.* [1902] 2 K.B. 614, 616; *Koufos* v. *Czarnikow* [1969] 1 A.C. 350.
32 *Barnett* v. *Cohen* [1921] 2 K.B. 461.
33 *Priestley* v. *Maclean* (1860) 2 F. & F. 288.

fair value at the time of the sale, and more could not be awarded in respect of the prevention of the buyer's full enjoyment of the subjects. The cases on damages for loss of the chance to win a prize afford further illustrations of speculative loss.[34]

Again where a pedigree bull was bought without disclosure that it was for breeding and certain wrong particulars relative to it shown in the catalogue were not discovered till three years later it was held that the damages must be limited to the difference between the value of the bull at the time of delivery and the value it would have had if the catalogue had been accurate, and did not extend to the difference between the value of the bull's progeny and the value they would have had if the catalogue had been accurate.[35]

Prospective damages

As all the damage arising from one delict or breach of contract must be recovered in one action [36] prospective damages may be recovered where future loss can be reasonably anticipated,[37] as for the breach of an annual contract which provides that the purchaser shall ultimately buy all the existing material in the seller's possession,[38] or on the wrongful discontinuance of an advertisement causing loss of business.[39] So, too, where a ship was built with excess draught and deficient in cargo-carrying capacity, damages were awarded on the basis of the probable cost of rectifying the excess draught and the probable loss of net freight for the estimated life of the vessel, with an allowance for such contingencies as her loss, sale or lack of employment.[40]

In *Re Vic Mill Co. Ltd.*,[41] a company went into liquidation before the delivery of certain machines ordered by them. Machines manufactured but not delivered were altered and sold elsewhere, and the measure of damages for them was the whole loss of profit and not merely the loss of resale plus the cost of alterations, there being no available market, and in respect of machines not yet built the damages were the full amount of prospective profits lost by the non-fulfilment of the contract, it not being proved that the makers' works would not have been big enough to enable them to perform their contract in addition to other contracts actually performed.[42]

34 *Supra*, p. 567.

35 *Bunting* v. *Tory* (1947) 64 T.L.R. 353. *Cf. Sapwell* v. *Bass* [1910] 2 K.B. 486; *Bourne* v. *Lothians Racing Syndicate*, 1951 S.L.T.(Notes) 37.

36 *Stevenson* v. *Pontifex and Wood* (1887) 15 R. 125.

37 *Richardson* v. *Mellish* (1824) 2 Bing. 229; *Chaplin* v. *Hicks* [1911] 2 K.B. 786; *Barnett* v. *Cohen* [1921] 2 K.B. 461.

38 *Emery* v. *Wells* [1906] A.C. 515. *Cf. Dominion Coal Co.* v. *Dominion Iron and Steel Co.* [1909] A.C. 293; *Millar* v. *Bellvale Chemical Co.* (1898) 1 F. 297.

39 *Marcus* v. *Myers* (1895) 11 T.L.R. 327.

40 *Australian Steamship Pty.* v. *Lewis*, 47 Ll.L.R. 132.

41 [1913] 1 Ch. 465.

42 But for this, a question of alternative profits in mitigation might have arisen.

An unforeseen future happening will not permit a fresh action [43] and difficulty of assessment does not justify merely nominal damages.[44] This principle is commonly applied in cases of damages *ex delicto* where prospective damages for future loss are regularly given.

In the case of continuing damage sustained in consequence of a continuing wrong, such as subsidence of buildings, it is, however, permissible to bring further actions in respect of further subsidences,[45] and it was pointed out in *Stevenson* [46] that the rule of recovering all damage in one action would not apply to such a case as where a breach of contract was a continuing act, nor to a contract for delivery by instalments, because in such a case one consignment might be defective or delivered late, thereby giving rise to a claim for damages though not necessarily to any right to rescind the contract *quoad* the future, and future consignments might be correct or defective.

Ascertainment difficult or impossible

The fact that the ascertainment of the measure of damages is a matter of difficulty is no ground for the court not awarding damages.[47] So where the respondent let fishing stations to the appellant and then erected a dock whereby the fishing was injured, the Court of Session decided that some damage had been sustained but pronounced against the claim of damages on the ground that the degree of injury could not be exactly ascertained. The House of Lords reversed this judgment, holding that where damage was admitted or proved some compensation was due.[48] So, too, where the plaintiff was deprived of her chance of a prize in a beauty competition by the defendant's breach of contract, the fact that the damages could not be assessed with precision did not relieve the defendant from the liability to pay damages.[49]

On the other hand, purely speculative damages are not recoverable [50]: the distinction is that in such cases it is doubtful whether any loss has been sustained, while in cases of the former kind loss has clearly been sustained and it is only the quantification which is doubtful or difficult. Nor can the party in breach complain in such a case that the damages are too great, as he must suffer from the impossibility of accurately ascertaining the amount of damage.[51] This is, however, subject to the qualification that the damages must have some reasonable relation to an estimate of the loss

43 *Darley Main Co.* v. *Mitchell* (1886) 11 App.Cas. 127; *Furness Withy Co.* v. *Hall* (1909) 25 T.L.R. 233.
44 *Hall* v. *Ross* (1813) 1 Dow. 201; *Ungar* v. *Sugg* (1891) 8 R.P.C. 385; *Chaplin, supra.*
45 *Backhouse* v. *Bonomi* (1861) 9 H.L.Cas. 503; *Darley Main Colliery* v. *Mitchell* (1886) 11 App.Cas. 127; *West Leigh Co.* v. *Tunnicliffe* [1908] A.C. 27; *Duke of Abercorn* v. *Merry and Cunningham*, 1909 S.C. 750.
46 (1887) 15 R. 125.
47 *Bovet* v. *Walter* (1917) 62 S.J. 104.
48 *Hall* v. *Ross* (1813) 1 Dow. 201.
49 *Chaplin* v. *Hicks* [1911] 2 K.B. 786. See also *Ungar* v. *Sugg* (1892) 9 R.P.C. 114; *Leavey* v. *Hirst* [1944] K.B. 24.
50 *The Parana* (1877) 2 P.D. 118.
51 *Duke of Leeds* v. *Amherst* (1855) 20 Beav. 239.

suffered, though it goes rather far to say that no damages can be recovered which are incapable of being specifically stated and appreciated with certainty or which depend merely on the feelings or inclination of the jury.[52]

Fines and penalties

These may be recovered if not too remote from the breach of contract. When a meat-salesman sold meat which was, unknown to him, unfit for human consumption and which had to be destroyed, he recovered damages for breach of warranty in respect of the goods, for loss of trade, and also in respect of the fine and costs imposed on him in respect of his conviction for having bad meat on the premises.[53] All these matters were taken to be such as might reasonably have been in the contemplation of the parties as a natural and probable consequence of the breach. But in *Leslie* v. *Reliable Advertising Agency* [54] the plaintiff was convicted under the Moneylenders Act 1900, of knowingly sending a circular to an infant without reasonable grounds for belief that he was of full age: through the negligence of the defendants who sent them out, a circular was sent to a minor. The claim for indemnification was refused as the plaintiff had been convicted of not himself having reasonable grounds for belief that the addressee was over twenty-one, *i.e.*, in respect of his personal fault, and the contract with the defendants did not give such reasonable grounds. Again in *Proops* v. *Chaplin* [55] the plaintiff had been prosecuted but not fined and sued the suppliers for breach of warranty in respect of the goods and recovered the costs of defending the criminal prosecution.

It is suggested that a material test, apart from the consideration whether it was a natural and probable consequence in the circumstances that the pursuer should be prosecuted, is whether any personal fault is to be attributed to him.[55a] Hence his knowledge, actual or imputed, or lack of reasonable care is a material element, and if he had no reasonable opportunity of intermediate examination of the goods, or is otherwise personally innocent, it is submitted that he should be indemnified by the original supplier who was in breach of contract.[56]

Breach of agreement in settlement of dispute

Where parties come to an agreement in settlement of certain pre-existing disputes, that agreement supersedes those disputes, so that in the

52 *Hamlin* v. *G.N. Ry.* (1856) 1 H. & N. 408.

53 *Cointat* v. *Myham* [1913] 2 K.B. 220; revd. (1914) 30 T.L.R. 282, *contra Fitzgerald* v. *Leonard*, 32 L.R.Ir. 675. In *Crage* v. *Fry* (1903) 67 J.P. 240, the amount of fine was not recovered.

54 [1915] 1 K.B. 652.

55 (1920) 37 T.L.R. 112.

55a *Cf. Burrows* v. *Rhodes* [1899] 1 Q.B. 816.

56 *Cf.* what would have happened on the facts of *Donoghue* v. *Stevenson* if instead of an action by the consumer there had been initiated criminal proceedings against the supplier. It is suggested that the intermediate supplier would have had recourse against Stevenson for the amount of any fine or penalty.

event of breach, damages must be calculated with reference to the loss caused by the breach of the agreement and not by reference to any loss by the previous causes of dispute. In *London and Northern Trading Co.* v. *Arcos* [57] an agreement was come to in settlement of disputes arising out of contracts between the parties, but this agreement in turn was breached; it was held that damages followed, such as naturally flowed from the breach, namely the amount which the defendants had agreed to pay plaintiffs, and that the contract and market prices did not affect the measure of damages. In effect in such a case the original contract is replaced by novation and only the substituted contract may be considered.

[57] (1931) 41 Ll.L.R. 150.

CHAPTER 32

CONTRACTS OF MANDATE AND AGENCY

THE contract of mandate is that whereby one empowers another to transact any business on his behalf without reward therefor.[1]

MANDANT'S CLAIMS

The mandatary is bound by acceptance of the mandate to execute the instructions given him, to account for his intromissions, and to restore anything entrusted to him for the performance of the mandate. He will be liable in damages for breach of contract in any of these respects, the liability being measured by the loss sustained by reason of his failure.

Even though the mandatary's undertaking was gratuitous he owes, by acceptance of the mandate, a duty to show reasonable skill and diligence and to take reasonable care in the performance of the mandate.[1a] In these respects the standard is somewhat lower than would be demanded of a paid agent, but the gratuitous mandatary must still be reasonably skilled, diligent and careful, like other gratuitous agents such as the depositary.[1b] A mandatary will accordingly be liable in damages for loss caused by his substantial lack of skill, diligence or care.[1c]

MANDATARY'S CLAIMS

A mandatary has no claim for reward, but has a claim to be relieved from obligations undertaken and to be reimbursed for expenses and outlays. Nor has he a claim if the mandate be revoked, because he has no right to have it continued for any specified time.

AGENCY

The circumstances in which an agent acting on behalf of a principal may sue or be sued for damages in respect of transactions with a third party in which he has acted as agent belong properly to the authorities on the law of contract rather than of the law of damages. Such cases, involving relations with third parties outside the relationship of principal and agent, present no specialties so far as concerns the manner of assessing damages or quantum thereof.[2] As between the principal and his agent,

[1] Stair I, 12, 1; Ersk. III, 3, 31; Bell, *Prin.* § 216–9.

[1a] *Stiven* v. *Watson* (1874) 1 R. 412, 416.

[1b] Bell, *Prin.* § 218; *cf. Kay* v. *Simpson* (1801) Hume 328; *Grierson* v. *Muir* (1802) Hume 329; *McDonald* v. *McDonald* (1807) Hume 344.

[1c] *Stiven, supra.*

[2] On these cases see generally *Gloag on Contract*, Chap. 8; *Bowstead on Agency*, Chaps. VIII–IX.

however,[2a] claims of damages may also arise, which do not concern any third party but spring from a failure on one or other part in the performance of the contract of agency.

PRINCIPAL'S CLAIMS

An agent who violates his duties to his principal by exceeding his authority [3] or by misconduct or negligence,[4] or failure to execute his mandate [5] or to perform his true function as an agent,[6] is responsible to and bound to indemnify his principal. It does not matter whether the loss or damage be caused directly to the principal, or indirectly, through his having to make compensation to third parties to satisfy his liability to them incurred by the agent on his behalf. The loss or damage need not be directly or immediately caused by the act which is done or which is omitted to be done. It will be sufficient if it be fairly attributable to it, as a natural result.[7] But it will not be sufficient if it be merely a remote consequence or an accidental mischief. It must be a real loss or actual damage and not merely a probable or possible one.[8] Where the breach of duty is clear it will be presumed that nominal damage has been sustained,[9] though if performance could not have benefited the principal, and consequently non-performance cannot have caused injury, the action will fail.

The loss for which the principal claims compensation must be traceable to the acts or omissions of the agent, though these need not be the proximate cause.[11] If the real cause of the loss is a failure on the principal's part to minimise resulting damage, he will not be entitled to recover from the agent.

Where an agent enters into a contract which he was not authorised to make, the principal is bound to implement the contract to the best of his ability and recover his loss thereon from the agent.[12] If an agent has entered into a contract in excess of his authority and has been held bound to relieve the principal of the contract, he is vested with all the rights of action such as for reduction or damages which would have been competent to the principal against the other party to the contract.[13]

Quantum of damages

The measure of damages in accordance with general principles extends

[2a] As to the duties of principal and agent towards each other, see generally *Bowstead on Agency*, Chaps. V–VII; American *Restatement of Agency*, Chaps. XIII–XIV.
[3] *Fay* v. *Miller* [1941] 1 Ch. 360; *C.P. Ry.* v. *Lockhart* [1942] A.C. 591.
[4] *Columbus* v. *Clowes* [1903] 1 K.B. 244; *Williams's Trs.* v. *Macandrew and Jenkins*, 1960 S.L.T. 246; *cf. Pringle of Scotland* v. *Continental Express* [1962] 2 Lloyd's Rep. 80.
[5] *Wright* v. *Baird* (1868) 6 S.L.R. 95; *cf. Turnbull* v. *Cruickshank and Fairweather* (1905) 7 F. 791.
[6] *Keppel* v. *Wheeler* [1927] 1 K.B. 577.
[7] *Cf. Barkley* v. *Simpson* (1897) 24 R. 346; *Lilley* v. *Doubleday* (1881) 7 Q.B.D. 510.
[8] *Johnston* v. *Braham and Campbell* [1917] 1 K.B. 586. *Cf. Salvesen* v. *Rederi A/B Nordstjernan* (1905) 7 F.(H.L.) 101.
[9] *Van Wart* v. *Woolley* (1830) Mood. & M. 520.
[11] *Gilmour* v. *Clark* (1853) 15 D. 478.
[12] *Barkley* v. *Simpson* (1897) 24 R. 346.
[13] *Milne* v. *Ritchie* (1882) 10 R. 365.

to indemnification for all the actual loss sustained,[14] which is the natural and probable consequence of the agent's breach of contract,[15] or which was within the contemplation of parties when the contract was made.[16] The most usual items will be outlays and loss of value or profits actually sustained,[17] but not anticipated profits which might have been made.[18] In many cases the extent of loss sustained may be accurately assessed and such is recoverable so as to effect restitution *in integrum*.[19] In *Mainwaring* v. *Brandon* [20] an agent bought an inferior quality of goods and the eventual buyer recovered damages from the principal in respect thereof; the principal recovered this sum and the costs from the agent as being his loss, and not merely the difference in value between the proper and inferior quality of goods. So where an agent fails to buy, the proper measure is the value of the goods, not the value of the money given to the agent to do the buying.[21]

If a principal delays unduly whereby his loss is aggravated, his damages may be restricted to what they would have been if he had acted promptly and cut his loss.[22] Where the agent's default has resulted in the principal's liability to make reparation to a third party, the principal is entitled to relief against the agent to that extent.[23]

Similarly, when the agent negligently fails to conclude an enforceable contract, the principal is liable for the expenses involved in trying to enforce it as well as for the loss sustained,[24] for the amount recoverable under an insurance not effected,[25] the value of goods lost by failure to collect the price.[26] When an agent wrongfully abandoned his agency, he was held liable for loss of business consequential on the injury to the principal's credit, and for loss from the suspension of the business.[27] Where an agent knowingly deposited goods in an improper place and fire accidentally destroyed them he was held liable.[28] And when an agent's barge deviated and was lost by storm, the agent was held liable.[29] In neither case can the wrongdoer seek to qualify his wrong, by stating the possibility of the same loss, even had his wrongful act not been done.

14 *Smith* v. *Price* (1862) 2 F. & F. 748; *Neilson* v. *James* (1882) 9 Q.B.D. 546; unless the loss is not a legal loss; *Cohen* v. *Kittell* (1889) 22 Q.B.D. 680; *Cheshire* v. *Vaughan Bros.* [1920] 3 K.B. 240.

15 *Mainwaring*, n. 20, *infra*; *cf. Re United Service Co., Johnson's Claim* (1871) 6 Ch.App. 212.

16 *Boyd* v. *Fitt* (1864) 11 L.T. 280.

17 *Cheshire* v. *Vaughan Bros.* [1920] 3 K.B. 240.

18 *Salvesen* v. *Rederi A/B Nordstjernan* (1905) 7 F.(H.L.) 101; *Cassaboglou, infra*; *Johnston* v. *Braham and Campbell* [1917] 1 K.B. 586.

19 Ersk. III, 1, 14; *Hamilton* v. *Dundas* (1710) M. 3153; *Mason* v. *Thom* (1787) M. 3535; *Watt* v. *Adamson* (1828) 7 S. 177; *Allan* v. *Mansfield* (1834) 12 S. 329.

20 (1818) 8 Taunt. 202. So too *Cassaboglou* v. *Gibb* (1883) 11 Q.B.D. 797.

21 *Ehrensperger* v. *Anderson* (1848) 3 Exch. 148.

22 *Waddell* v. *Blockey* (1879) 4 Q.B.D. 678.

23 *Smith* v. *Grant* (1858) 20 D. 1077; *Baxter* v. *Gapp* [1939] 2 K.B. 27.

24 *Sivewright* v. *Richardson* (1852) 19 L.T.(o.s.) 10.

25 *Smith* v. *Price* (1862) 2 F. & F. 748; *cf. Maydew* v. *Forrester* (1814) 5 Taunt. 615.

26 *Stearine* v. *Heintzmann* (1864) 17 C.B.(N.S.) 56.

27 *Boyd* v. *Fitt* (1864) 11 L.T. 280.

28 *Caffrey* v. *Darby* (1801) 6 Ves. 496; *cf. Lilley* v. *Doubleday* (1881) 7 Q.B.D. 510; *Royal Exchange Shipping Co.* v. *Dixon* (1886) 12 App.Cas. 11.

29 *Davis* v. *Garrett* (1830) 6 Bing. 716.

The consequences for which damages are recoverable are restricted to those which result naturally and directly and proximately from the agent's breach of contract. In *Cassaboglou* v. *Gibb* [30] an agent was instructed to buy and ship a particular kind of opium but actually sent opium of an inferior kind. It was held that the difference between the price paid and the market value of the opium ordered (which was claimed) was the measure of damages properly applicable to the relation of buyer and seller, and that the true measure applicable to that of principal and agent was the repayment of money expended in buying the inferior article never ordered together with incidental expenses and damages recovered from the principal by a dissatisfied sub-purchaser.

Damages in respect of loss of profits have, however, been refused where they are only prospective. Where an agent made an incorrect statement which induced the principal to contract for the purchase of the goodwill of a public-house, he was held liable for the loss on resale of the goodwill, a sum for personal loss and inconvenience, but the costs of an unsuccessful prior action against the seller were refused as not the natural and proximate result of the agent's actings.[31]

Similarly in *Salvesen* v. *Rederi A/B Nordstjernan* [32] where an agent who was employed to conduct negotiations on behalf of his principals stated incorrectly that he had concluded a contract on their behalf, the measure of damages was restricted to the loss actually sustained in consequence of his misrepresentation and made no allowance for profits which the principals might have made had the representation been true. But the defenders had failed to take steps to minimise their loss.

Again it was held in *Johnston* v. *Braham & Campbell* [33] that a principal, induced to enter into an unsuccessful adventure by his agent's negligence, may recover from the agent the amount he has actually lost, together with compensation for loss of time. But nothing can be added in respect of the profits he might have made if he had had at his disposal the money sunk in the adventure which has miscarried.

In *Lewcock* v. *Bromley* [34] an agent employed to find a purchaser for a house signed a contract without authority, and the purchaser who had brought an action for specific performance was held entitled to nominal damages against the agent. Again in *Keppel* v. *Wheeler* [35] agents employed to sell land accepted an offer subject to contract but neglected to inform the principal of a better offer received before a final contract had been concluded. They were held liable for not disclosing the later offer, the amount of damages being the difference between the actual sale price and the price which would have been obtained if the later offer had been

30 (1882) 9 Q.B.D. 220; (1883) 11 Q.B.D. 797; approved *Salvesen* v. *Rederi A/B Nordstjernan* (1905) 7 F.(H.L.) 101.
31 *Richardson* v. *Dunn* (1860) 8 C.B.(N.S.) 655.
32 (1905) 7 F.(H.L.) 101.
33 [1917] 1 K.B. 586.
34 (1920) 37 T.L.R. 48.
35 [1927] 1 K.B. 577.

accepted: in the circumstances the agents were held still entitled to commission.

Principal's right to interest

An agent is not in general liable to pay interest to his principal on sums of money recovered on his behalf, in the absence of an express or implied contract to do so. But it is otherwise if there has been some default,[36] such as dealing with the money in breach of duty, or failing to pay it over at the principal's request,[37] or using the money in his own business,[38] or failing to invest.[39] Interest is payable in cases of fraud,[40] and on bribes [41] and secret profits.[42]

Interest, if due, runs from the date of failure or refusal to pay over the sum due.[43] The rate is a matter for the court but in view of the element of breach of duty the full penal rate would probably be allowed.[44]

AGENT'S CLAIMS

The claims of the agent against his principal are for remuneration, reimbursement and indemnification.

The commonest case of action by agent against the principal is for recovery of the salary or commission,[45] or other remuneration expressly or impliedly due to him for his services, provided he has at least substantially [46] performed what he agreed to do,[47] or, in the absence of any contract, for a payment *quantum meruit* in respect thereof.[48] Any such claim does not properly fall within the scope of damages. An agent does not necessarily lose his right to remuneration by failure of the transaction [49] or lack of benefit to the principal,[50] nor through having made a bona fide mistake even though it amounts to a breach of duty.[51]

36 *Webster* v. *British Empire Mutual Co.* (1880) 15 Ch.D. 169.
37 *Edgell* v. *Day* (1865) L.R. 1 C.P. 80; *Harsant* v. *Blaine* (1887) 56 L.J.Q.B. 511.
38 *Rogers* v. *Boehm* (1798) 2 Esp. 702.
39 *Browne* v. *Southouse* (1790) 3 Bro.C.C. 107.
40 *Hardwicke* v. *Vernon* (1808) 14 Ves. 504.
41 *Boston Deep Sea Fishing Co.* v. *Ansell* (1888) 39 Ch.D. 339, 371.
42 *Nant-y-glo and Blaina Ironworks Co.* v. *Grave* (1878) 12 Ch.D. 738.
43 *Harsant* v. *Blaine, Macdonald & Co.* (1887) 56 L.J.Q.B. 511; *Barclay* v. *Harris* (1915) 85 L.J.K.B. 115.
44 *Boston, supra* (5 per cent.); *Nant-y-glo, supra* (4 per cent.).
45 The terms of each contract must be looked at in the light of its own material circumstances: *Luxor (Eastbourne)* v. *Cooper* [1941] A.C. 108.
46 *Rimmer* v. *Knowles* (1874) 30 L.T. 496; *Keppel* v. *Wheeler* [1927] 1 K.B. 577. *Cf. Robertson* v. *Burrell* (1899) 6 S.L.T. 368; *Burchell* v. *Gowrie* [1910] A.C. 614; *Walker, Fraser and Steele* v. *Fraser's Trs.*, 1910 S.C. 222; *Gibb* v. *Bennett* (1906) 14 S.L.T. 64.
47 *Bull* v. *Price* (1831) 7 Bing. 237; *Martin* v. *Perry and Daw* [1931] W.N. 101.
48 Bell, *Prin.* § 226; *Kennedy* v. *Glass* (1890) 17 R. 1085; *Bryant* v. *Flight* (1839) 5 M. & W. 114; *Manson* v. *Baillie* (1855) 2 Macq. 80; *Williamson* v. *Hine* [1891] 1 Ch. 390. For an exceptional case, see *Dinesmann* v. *Mair*, 1912, 1 S.L.T. 217.
49 *Fuller* v. *Eames* (1892) 8 T.L.R. 278; *Passingham* v. *King* (1898) 14 T.L.R. 392; *Vulcan Car Agency* v. *Fiat Motors, Ltd.* (1915) 32 T.L.R. 73; *Menzies, Bruce-Low & Thomson* v. *McLennan* (1895) 22 R. 299.
50 *Green* v. *Lucas* (1875) 33 L.T. 584; *Moir* v. *Marten* (1891) 7 T.L.R. 330.
51 *Nitedals Taendstikfabrik* v. *Bruster* [1906] 2 Ch. 671; *Keppel* v. *Wheeler* [1927] 1 K.B. 577; *Harrods, Ltd.* v. *Lemon* (1931) 47 T.L.R. 248.

It is an implied condition that a contract of agency may be brought to an end if the principal's business is discontinued [52] without liability in damages but if the contract contains an obligation to employ the agent for a period,[53] or to execute the orders which he may be able to secure,[54] there may be an implied obligation not voluntarily to discontinue the business and a consequential liability in damages if it is so discontinued or the agency otherwise prematurely terminated.

An agent also has a claim if his engagement is terminated prematurely or unreasonably so as to prevent him earning the commission or remuneration expected and contracted for.[55] In *Dowling* [55] an agent engaged for a year was dismissed after four months and was held entitled to the balance of his salary for the year, but not to anything in respect of the bonus commission on sales as this was too speculative, and there was nothing to show that he would have obtained sufficient orders to entitle him to commission. Again where agents secured a purchaser for heritage and a conditional agreement was come to, the seller, having then sold to a third party, was held liable to the agents for having prevented them from earning their commission, and the agents were entitled to recover damages measured by the commission which they would have earned if the contract of sale which they had procured had been completed.[56]

Quantum of damages

The measure of damages will be the loss sustained by the agent as a natural and probable consequence of his principal's breach of contract, and, where he has done all he could have, this will amount to the full amount he would have earned if the principal had duly executed his contract and completed the transaction.[57] Where the agent has not done everything which would entitle him to remuneration, but has only been prevented by some act or default of the principal from being able to earn the remuneration to which he would have been entitled in terms of the contract of agency, the proper measure of damages will be the amount of money which the agent might reasonably have earned as remuneration in accordance with the conditions and duration of the agency agreement.[58]

It depends in every case upon the terms of the contract between principal and agent,[59] or upon the usages of the particular trade in ques-

52 *Patmore* v. *Cannon* (1892) 19 R. 1004; *S.S.* " *State of California* " *Co.* v. *Moore* (1895) 22 R. 562; *Rhodes* v. *Forwood* (1876) 1 App.Cas. 256; *French* v. *Leeston Shipping Co.* [1922] 1 A.C. 451; *London, etc. Shipping Co.* v. *Ferguson* (1850) 13 D. 51.

53 *Turner* v. *Goldsmith* [1891] 1 Q.B. 544; *Dowling* v. *Henderson* (1890) 17 R. 921.

54 *Reigate* v. *Union Mfg. Co.* [1918] 1 K.B. 592.

55 *Dowling* v. *Henderson* (1890) 17 R. 921; *Lothian* v. *Jenolite*, 1970 S.L.T. 31.

56 *Dudley Bros.* v. *Barnet*, 1937 S.C. 632. Contrast *Bentall, Horsley & Baldry* v. *Vicary* [1931] 1 K.B. 253. *Cf. Trollope* v. *Martin* [1934] 2 K.B. 436, approved in *Luxor (Eastbourne)* v. *Cooper* [1941] A.C. 108; *Nelson* v. *Rolfe* [1950] 1 K.B. 139.

57 *Harris* v. *Petherick* (1878) 39 L.T. 543; *Roberts* v. *Barnard* (1884) 1 C. & E. 336; *Prickett* v. *Badger* (1856) 1 C.B.(N.S.) 296; *Dudley Bros.* v. *Barnet*, 1937 S.C. 632.

58 *Lazarus* v. *Cairn Line* (1912) 106 L.T. 378; *Reigate* v. *Union Mfg. Co.* [1918] 1 K.B. 592.

59 *Simpson* v. *Lamb* (1856) 17 C.B. 603; *cf. Turner* v. *Goldsmith* [1891] 1 Q.B. 544; *Brace* v. *Calder* [1895] 2 Q.B. 253.

tion,[60] whether a particular act or omission by the principal which disentitles the agent from earning commission is, in fact, such a wrongful breach of contract as to entitle the agent to recover damages.

Agent's claim for reimbursement and indemnification

The agent is entitled to be indemnified by the principal for all liabilities and obligations necessarily incurred by the agent in the execution of his duties.[61] But there is an implied term to indemnify the agent only when he acts according to his instructions,[62] and the implication may be excluded by special agreement or custom of trade [63] or the express terms of the contract.[64] The right is unaffected by the fact that the payment in respect of which the agent seeks indemnity could not be enforced against the principal.[65]

Extent of right to indemnity

The right to indemnity covers any direct losses actually sustained by the agent,[66] such as exceptional expenditure incurred in consequence of the principal's concealment of a material fact,[67] or his failure to provide credits,[68] to payment of an award of damages to a third party in consequence of the principal's refusal to implement a contract duly and rightly entered into by the agent on his behalf,[69] the cost of legal proceedings on the principal's behalf,[70] relief in respect of loss incurred by delay in payment and resale of the goods,[71] loss incurred in consequence of acting on untrue representations by the principal as to his means [72] and being forced to sell goods at a loss.[73]

It extends to liabilities incurred by the agent, even though they may never be enforced against him,[74] though not to the mere possibility of a future claim,[75] and to liabilities incurred under a bona fide mistake of judgment.[76] It does not extend to losses incurred by robbery or shipwreck,

60 *Simpson, supra.*

61 *Brittain* v. *Lloyd* (1845) 14 M. & W. 762; *Walker* v. *Somerville* (1837) 16 S. 217; *Ex p. Bishop* (1880) 15 Ch.D. 400; *Frixione* v. *Tagliaferro* (1856) 10 Moo.P.C. 175.

62 *Westropp* v. *Solomon* (1849) 8 C.B. 345.

63 *Dinesmann* v. *Mair*, 1912, 1 S.L.T. 217.

64 *Morris* v. *Cleasby* (1816) 4 M. & S. 566 (*del credere* agent).

65 *Brittain* v. *Lloyd* (1845) 14 M. & W. 762; *Adams* v. *Morgan* [1924] 1 K.B. 751.

66 Bell, *Prin.* § 226. It includes payments paid to preserve trade reputation: *Finlay* v. *Kwik Hoo Tong* [1929] 1 K.B. 400.

67 *Mackenzie* v. *Blakeney* (1879) 6 R. 1329.

68 *Blackett* v. *Aronson*, 52 Ll.L.R. 288.

69 *Glassford* v. *Brown* (1830) 9 S. 105; *McBraire* v. *Hamiltons* (1826) 2 W. & S. 66; *Stevenson* v. *Duncan* (1842) 5 D. 167; *Lacey* v. *Hill* (1874) L.R. 18 Eq. 182; *Warlow* v. *Harrison* (1858) 1 E. & E. 295, 309; *Brittain* v. *Lloyd* (1845) 14 M. & W. 762.

70 *Alison* v. *Smart* (1840) 15 F.C. 703.

71 *Drummond* v. *Cairns* (1852) 14 D. 611; *cf. Haig* v. *Hannay* (1813) 1 Dow 259.

72 *Risk* v. *Auld & Guild* (1881) 8 R. 729.

73 *Auchie* v. *Burns* (1822) 1 S. 538.

74 *Lacey* v. *Hill* (1874) L.R. 18 Eq. 182.

75 *Dyson* v. *Peat* [1917] 1 Ch. 99.

76 *Broom* v. *Hall* (1859) 7 C.B.(N.S.) 503; *Pettman* v. *Keble* (1850) 9 C.B. 701.

unless the course of duty exposed the agent to these in particular degree,[77] nor to liabilities incurred in consequence of default,[78] or breach of duty,[79] or unlawful transactions,[80] or transactions outwith the scope of his employment and not ratified.[81] The agency must have been the cause and not just the occasion for the loss in question.[82] There can be no claim for indemnity in respect of illegal acts,[83] but if the principal affirms the transaction in the knowledge of the true situation he is bound to complete it.[84] So, too, money paid in pursuance of an illegal contract to which the money had not been applied cannot be recovered.[85]

Remoteness

Some elements may, however, have to be excluded from the claim for indemnity on the ground of remoteness. So in one case an agent abroad drew bills on his principal for advances made on the principal's directions; the principal was solvent but the bills were returned dishonoured and the agent's credit was damaged. It was questioned but not determined whether damages in respect thereof were not consequential.[86]

The right may be enforced by action against the principal or by an exercise of the agent's right of retention.[87]

77 Stair I, 12, 10.
78 *Duncan* v. *Hill* (1873) L.R. 8 Ex. 242; *Frixione* v. *Tagliaferro* (1856) 10 Moo.P.C. 175.
79 *Thomas* v. *Atherton* (1878) 10 Ch.D. 185; *Ellis* v. *Pond* [1898] 1 Q.B. 426.
80 *Josephs* v. *Pebrer* (1825) 3 B. & C. 639; unless the agent was ignorant of the fact, *Cory* v. *Lambton* (1916) 86 L.J.K.B. 401. See too *Smith* v. *Lindo* (1858) 5 C.B.(N.S.) 587.
81 *Bowlby* v. *Bell* (1846) 3 C.B. 284.
82 Story, *Agency*, § 341; *Duncan* v. *Hill* (1873) L.R. 8 Ex. 242.
83 *Read* v. *Anderson* (1884) 13 Q.B.D. 779; *Perry* v. *Barnett* (1885) 15 Q.B.D. 388.
84 *Loring* v. *Davis* (1886) 32 Ch.D. 625; *Harrods* v. *Lemon* [1931] 2 K.B. 157.
85 *Parker* v. *Mason* [1940] 2 K.B. 590.
86 *Dempster* v. *Wallace* (1833) 12 S. 548.
87 *Sibbald* v. *Gibson* (1852) 15 D. 217; *Gairdner* v *Milne* (1858) 20 D. 565.

CHAPTER 33

CONTRACTS OF SERVICE OR EMPLOYMENT

UNDER a contract of service or employment one party undertakes, in return for salary or wages, to work for the other as he may be instructed and directed to do. The contract is regulated not only by common law but by the Industrial Relations Act 1971 and the Contracts of Employment Act 1972, and in subsidiary matters by various other statutes. The Code of Industrial Practice issued under the authority of the Industrial Relations Act 1971 also lays down rules of persuasive effect, though not mandatory. In many cases resort to the legal remedies competent may be avoided by making known a complaint or grievance and on the other side redressing it.

By the Industrial Relations Act 1971, s. 113, there is power to confer on industrial tribunals jurisdiction to deal with claims of damages for breach, by any party to it, of any contract of employment or of any term of such a contract, other than damages in respect of personal injuries or death.[1]

Under the Employers and Workmen Act 1875, s. 3,[2] the sheriff may, in any dispute between employer and workman [3] (including a seaman [3]) arising out of or incidental to their relation as such, (1) adjust and set off the one against the other all such claims on the part either of the employer or of the workman, arising out of or incidental to the relation between them, as the court may find to be subsisting, whether such claims are liquidated or unliquidated, and are for wages, damages or otherwise; and (2) may rescind the contract between them on such terms as to the apportionment of wages and other sums due thereunder, and as to the payment of wages or damages, or other sums due, as he thinks just. It is questionable whether the latter power entitles the sheriff to override arbitration clauses or awards under contracts of service which have already terminated.[4]

EMPLOYEE'S CLAIMS

The employee is always entitled to claim damages for any breach by the employer of a condition, express or implied, of the contract of employment, and where the breach is in some fundamental respect he may in addition leave the employment.

[1] For general principles as to assessment of compensation in proceedings before the Industrial Court or an industrial tribunal under the 1971 Act, see s. 116.
[2] Amended by Industrial Relations Act 1971.
[3] Defined, s. 10.
[4] *Wilson* v. *Glasgow Tramways Co.* (1878) 5 R. 981.

Acceptance of employee

Having engaged an employee an employer is liable in damages if he does not take him into the employment.[5] Failure to do so is equivalent to unjustified dismissal at the due date of commencement of the employment. The damages will be the earnings due down to the first date at which the employee could lawfully have been dismissed.

Provision of work

There is no general duty to provide work,[6] but only in cases where opportunity to work is essential, to enable the employee to practise his skill,[7] to give him the opportunity to develop his reputation,[8] and where the earnings depend in whole or in part on the work done, *i.e.* are based on piecework or commission.[9]

Provision of food and lodging

In cases where it is customary [10] or there is an express obligation to do so, an employer is liable if he does not provide food and accommodation, or either is not of the kind or quality reasonably adequate in the circumstances.

Provision of care and medical aid

In older cases there was held to be no duty to provide medical aid,[11] but more modern authority indicates that, particularly in the case of employees living on the premises, the employer must obtain medical aid in case of need.[12] In particular cases there is a statutory duty to make such provision.[13]

Payment of salary or wages

It is a clear breach of duty to refuse or fail to pay salary or wages at the rate agreed upon or fixed by statute, negotiating machinery or otherwise. Unless the contract provides otherwise the duty to pay continues during sickness of normal duration.[14] The remedy for non-payment is, however, action for payment with interest, rather than action for damages.[15]

[5] Bell, *Prin.* § 182; *Collier* v. *Sunday Referee Publishing Co.* [1940] 2 K.B. 647; *Cameron* v. *Lord Advocate*, 1952 S.C. 165. If the refusal anticipates the due time of commencement the employee can claim for anticipatory breach: *Hochster* v. *De la Tour* (1853) 2 E. & B. 678; *Frost* v. *Knight* (1872) L.R. 7 Ex. 111; *Johnstone* v. *Milling* (1886) 16 Q.B.D. 460.
[6] *Turner* v. *Sawdon* [1901] 2 K.B. 653; *Konski* v. *Peet* [1915] 1 Ch. 530.
[7] *Collier* v. *Sunday Referee Publishing Co.* [1940] 2 K.B. 647.
[8] *Cf. Clayton* v. *Oliver* [1930] A.C. 209.
[9] Bell, *Prin.* § 192; *Cowdenbeath Coal Co.* v. *Drylie* (1886) 3 Sh.Ct.Rep.1; *Turner* v. *Goldsmith* [1891] 1 Q.B. 544; *Devonald* v. *Rosser* [1906] 2 K.B. 728.
[10] Bankt. I, 2, 55; Bell, *Prin.* § 182.
[11] *Mitchell* v. *Adam* (1874) 1 Guthrie Sh.Ct.Cas. 361.
[12] *Jeffrey* v. *Donald* (1901) 9 S.L.T. 199; *McKeating* v. *Frame*, 1921 S.C. 382.
[13] Mines and Quarries Act 1954, ss. 91, 92, 115; Factories Act 1961, s. 11.
[14] *Morrison* v. *Bell* [1939] 2 K.B. 187; *Orman* v. *Saville Sportswear Ltd.* [1960] 3 All E.R. 105; *cf. Petrie* v. *MacFisheries Ltd.* [1940] 1 K.B. 258.
[15] *Davies* v. *City of Glasgow Friendly Society*, 1935 S.C. 224; *Eunson* v. *Johnson & Greig*, 1940 S.C. 49; *Paul* v. *Colvilles Ltd.*, 1947 S.C. 67.

Wrongful dismissal

At common law an employee dismissed without legal justification is entitled to claim damages, measured *prima facie* by the amount he would have earned if the employment had continued to the time when it could first lawfully have been terminated,[16] less any amount which the employee, in pursuance of the obligation on him to minimise his loss,[17] has earned from alternative employment down to that date, or with reasonable diligence could have earned.[18] If there is no prospect of obtaining suitable employment damages must be calculated prospectively, in rather the same way as in a case of personal injuries.[19] What the employee would have earned depends on his contractual salary or wage, and includes bonus,[20] rent free accommodation,[21] and any perquisites of the job, such as tips,[22] and also benefits under pension schemes.[23] If part of the remuneration was by commission allowance must be made for this.[24]

If part of the remuneration was contingent on the will of the employer, consideration must be directed to the questions whether the employee had any legal entitlement to that kind of remuneration and, if not, to the probability that he would have obtained any benefit of the kind in question.[25]

It is now settled that the calculation of damages must take into account the tax which would have been payable if the money had been received as earnings rather than as damages.[26] It has also been held [27] that unemployment benefit and redundancy payment [27a] received by a plaintiff fell to be deducted from damages for loss of earnings.

Deduction has to be made of earnings from employment taken in lieu of that lost,[28] but not from employment which might have been taken in addition to that lost, such as evening work, and of earnings from alternative employment which reasonably could have been obtained.[29] A dismissed employee is not obliged or expected, in mitigation of damages, to accept employment at a substantially lower grade or in an entirely different

16 *Cameron* v. *Fletcher* (1872) 10 M. 301; *Moffat* v. *Boothby* (1884) 11 R. 501.
17 Chap. 28, *supra.*
18 *Beckham* v. *Drake* (1849) 2 H.L.C. 579, 607.
19 *Cf. Edwards* v. *S.O.G.A.T.* [1970] 3 All E.R. 689.
20 *Lake* v. *Campbell* (1862) 5 L.T. 582; but see *Lavarack* v. *Woods of Colchester* [1967] 1 Q.B. 278.
21 *Re English Joint Stock Bank, Yelland's Case* (1867) L.R. 4 Eq. 350.
22 *Manubens* v. *Leon* [1919] 1 K.B. 208.
23 *Bold* v. *Brough, Nicholson & Hall* [1963] 3 All E.R. 849.
24 *Devonald* v. *Rosser* [1906] 2 K.B. 728; *Addis* v. *Gramophone Co.* [1909] A.C. 488; *Re Rubel Bronze & Metal Co. and Vos* [1918] 1 K.B. 315; *Reigate* v. *Union Mfg. Co.* [1918] 1 K.B. 592.
25 See *e.g. Beach* v. *Reeds Corrugated Cases* [1966] 2 All E.R. 652; *Bold, supra*; *Lavarack, supra.*
26 *B.T.C.* v. *Gourley* [1956] A.C. 185; *Stewart* v. *Glentaggart Ltd.*, 1963 S.C. 300; *Lyndale Fashion Mfrs.* v. *Rich* [1973] 1 All E.R. 33; Chap. 26, *supra.*
27 *Parsons* v. *B.N.M. Laboratories* [1964] 1 Q.B. 95.
27a *Stocks* v. *Magna Merchants* [1973] 2 All E.R. 329.
28 *e.g. Reid* v. *Explosives Co.* (1887) 19 Q.B.D. 264.
29 *e.g. Brace* v. *Calder* [1895] 2 Q.B. 253.

capacity [30]; the question is one of reasonableness,[31] and it may be reasonable to accept re-employment by the defender, particularly if the dismissal had been a technical one.[32]

Injury to feelings and reputation

No account can be taken of the hurt to feelings or reputation by the manner of the dismissal, unless the facts amount to actionable defamation and, if they do, they give rise to a separate claim and not to an aggravating factor in the claim for wrongful dismissal.[33]

Loss of publicity

Where the contract of employment was intended to enhance the pursuer's reputation by publicity, as by allowing the pursuer to appear as an actor or performer, the element of loss of publicity has been recognised as admissible.[34] For the loss of the opportunity to play in public and so enhancing or maintaining his reputation he is entitled to damages, but not to damages for injury to an existing reputation as an actor.[35] This principle has been applied to actors,[36] the author of a screen play,[37] and probably extends to all persons offering literary or artistic work to the public. It has been held inapplicable to such cases as a company director,[38] the chief sub-editor of a newspaper,[39] a local authority surveyor [40] and an impresario.[41]

Unfair dismissal

An employee, save in certain kinds of employments, also has a statutory right not to be unfairly dismissed,[42] the onus of proof of fair dismissal being on the employer and the reason having to be one statutorily prescribed.[43] If a complaint of unfair dismissal is made to an industrial tribunal and it finds that the complaint is well-founded it may recommend that the employee be re-engaged, stating the terms on which it considers that it would be reasonable for him to be so re-engaged. Otherwise, or if the recommendation is not complied with, it awards compensation.[44] If the applicant unreasonably refuses to comply with the recommendation the

30 *Ross* v. *Pender* (1874) 1 R. 352; *Jackson* v. *Hayes* [1938] 4 All E.R. 587; *Yetton* v. *Eastwoods Froy* [1966] 3 All E.R. 353; *Edwards* v. *S.O.G.A.T.* [1970] 3 All E.R. 689.
31 *Cf. Shindler* v. *Northern Raincoat Co.* [1960] 2 All E.R. 239.
32 *Brace*, *supra* (dismissal by dissolution of partnership which employed him).
33 *Addis* v. *Gramophone Co.* [1909] A.C. 488; *Withers* v. *General Theatre Corpn.* [1933] 2 K.B. 536. See also *Campbell* v. *McLachlan* (1896) 4 S.L.T. 143.
34 *Bunning* v. *Lyric Theatre* (1894) 71 L.T. 396; *Marbé* v. *Edwardes* [1928] 1 K.B. 269; *Clayton* v. *Oliver* [1930] A.C. 269.
35 *Withers* v. *General Theatre Corpn.* [1933] 2 K.B. 536, 554.
36 *Marbé*, *supra*; *Clayton*, *supra*.
37 *Tolnay* v. *Criterion Films* [1936] 2 All E.R. 1625.
38 *Re Gollomb* (1931) 144 L.T. 583.
39 *Collier* v. *Sunday Referee Publishing Co.* [1940] 2 K.B. 647.
40 *Moss* v. *Chesham U.D.C.* (1945) 172 L.T. 301.
41 *Fielding* v. *Moiseiwitsch* (1946) 62 T.L.R. 265.
42 Industrial Relations Act 1971, ss. 22–23, 27.
43 *Ibid.* s. 24.
44 *Ibid.* s. 106.

tribunal must reduce the compensation. The amount of compensation must be just and equitable,[45] subject to the principle that, as at common law, the applicant must mitigate his damages.

Redundancy

Under the Redundancy Payments Act 1965, an employee is entitled to a redundancy payment, subject to certain qualifying conditions, if he has been dismissed by reason of redundancy [46] or is laid off or kept on short time to specified extents and has given notice in writing to his employer indicating his intention to claim a redundancy payment.[47] An employee who leaves voluntarily is not entitled to benefit.

The purpose of redundancy payments is to compensate workers for loss of security, possible loss of earnings and fringe benefits, and the uncertainty and anxiety of change of job, and these factors may be present even if a man gets a new job immediately.[48]

Claims for redundancy payments are determined by industrial tribunals; they are not claims of damages and there may be no breach of contract on the employer's part, or only a breach of a technical kind, as where an employing partnership is dissolved. The amount of payment is according to a scale.[49]

Loss of property

There is not in all cases an implied term that the employer will take care of the belongings of the employee while he is at work,[50] but this may be implied in particular cases.

Testimonial or " character "

An employer is bound if requested by the employee or a third party, such as an employment agency or prospective new employer, to furnish a testimonial or report on the employee's qualities. He may be liable in damages for failing to do so, or for defaming the employee therein, if malice be proved,[51] or liable to a third party who suffers loss by acting in reliance on it.[52]

Personal injuries or death

An employer owes numerous duties, both at common law and under statute, to take care in various circumstances for the safety of the employee. Breach of any such duty is normally treated as a delict rather than as a

45 *Ibid.* s. 116 (1); *S.C.W.S.* v. *Lloyd* [1973] I.C.R. 137.
46 1965 Act, s. 1 (1) (*a*), (2) and 3.
47 *Ibid.* ss. 1 (1) (*b*), 6 and 7. See generally, Grunfeld, *Law of Redundancy*.
48 *Wynes* v. *Southrepps Hall Broiler Farm Ltd.* [1968] I.T.R. 407.
49 Sched. I.
50 *Deyong* v. *Shenburn* [1946] K.B. 227; *Edwards* v. *West Herts Group Hospital Management Cttee* [1957] 1 All E.R. 541.
51 *Anderson* v. *Wishart* (1818) 1 Mur. 429.
52 *Anderson, supra*; *cf. Mushets* v. *Mackenzie* (1899) 1 F. 756.

breach of an implied or statutory term of the contract of employment.[53] The factors relevant to damages are entirely those applicable to a claim arising *ex delicto*.[54]

EMPLOYER'S CLAIMS

If the employee is in breach of contract the employer may claim damages for the loss resulting to him therefrom. If the breach is in an essential or fundamental respect he may summarily dismiss the employee from the employment.

Failure to enter on employment

If a person fails to take up an appointment and to enter on the duties of a post at the agreed date, the employer may be justified in dismissing him and may in any event claim damages for loss resulting from his non-appearance. Prima facie this would be the cost of paying for a replacement.[55]

Continuance in employment

Similarly an employee must continue in the employment until it is terminated in a lawful manner, and abandonment of the employment without justification is a breach inferring liability in damages for loss.[56]

Disclosure of personal defects

An employee is apparently not always bound voluntarily to disclose matters of his own previous history.[57] But he may be so bound where the failure involves his own safety at work and the safety of fellow-employees,[58] or where the work contemplated involves risk of the kind of trouble which has previously afflicted the employee.[59]

Obedience to orders

An employee should obey lawful orders and instructions on matters within the scope of and relative to the employment,[60] and refusal or failure to do so may justify immediate dismissal,[61] though it may be reasonable to give a warning in the first place rather than resort at once to dismissal.

53 In *Matthews* v. *Kuwait Bechtel Corpn.* [1959] 2 Q.B. 57, the English Court of Appeal held that an employee might sue for damages for personal injury on the ground of breach of contract.

54 See Chaps. 51–54, *infra*.

55 *N.C.B.* v. *Galley* [1958] 1 All E.R. 91.

56 *McKenzie* v. *Sheffield Cutlery Service*, 1950 S.L.T.(Sh.Ct.) 81.

57 *Fletcher* v. *Krell* (1872) 42 L.J.Q.B. 55 (governess concealing having been divorced); *Hands* v. *Simpson, Fawcett & Co.* (1928) 44 T.L.R. 295 (previous conviction for drunken driving); *Walker* v. *Greenock Hospitals Board*, 1951 S.C. 464 (doctor previously dismissed from post).

58 *Cork* v. *Kirby, Maclean Ltd.* [1952] 2 All E.R. 402 (undisclosed liability to fits).

59 *e.g.* can a man previously convicted of embezzlement take a job as a cashier without disclosing his conviction? *Cf. Balmer* v. *Hayes*, 1950 S.C. 477 (bus driver not disclosing susceptibility to fits).

60 *Moffat* v. *Boothby* (1884) 11 R. 501.

61 *Silvie* v. *Stewart* (1830) 8 S. 1010; *McKellar* v. *Macfarlane* (1852) 15 D. 246; *A.* v. *B.* (1853) 16 D. 269; *Thomson* v. *Stewart* (1888) 15 R. 806; *Pepper* v. *Webb* [1969] 2 All E.R. 216.

Moral conduct

In the case of employees resident in the employer's household immoral or scandalous conduct, particularly if connected with another member of the household,[62] is a breach of duty. Dishonesty by any employee justifies dismissal.[63] Serious or repeated drunkenness may have the same consequence.[64] Insolent behaviour may also justify dismissal.[65]

Refusal or failure to do work

Where an employee unjustifiably refuses or fails to do some work which was assigned to him to do, damages are due, measured prima facie by the cost of obtaining another person to do the work.[66] To this may have to be added damages compensating for loss within the contemplation of the defender consequential on this default, such as loss of output,[67] stoppage of production, or expenses fruitlessly incurred on the faith of the defender's willingness to work.[68]

An employee is not, however, bound to do work of a kind other than that for which he was engaged, nor to work in a lower grade, even without loss of earnings,[69] nor to work at a place far removed from that contemplated by the contract.[70]

Defective work

An employee impliedly warrants that he has reasonable competence in the profession, craft or trade which he professes, and that he will exercise reasonable ability, skill and care in doing the work assigned to him.[71] He is therefore liable if he damages the employer's equipment, tools or machinery, or ruins or damages raw materials entrusted to him for processing, or does so badly work undertaken by his employer for a third party that the third party rejects it, claims damages or otherwise.

Under the Hosiery Manufacture (Wages) Act 1874, s. 1, deductions from wages are competent for bad and disputed workmanship. Under the Truck Act 1896, ss. 1–3, the imposition of fines on workmen within the Act depends on there being a contract between employer and employee, and notices must be displayed giving information about the possible fines.[72] Deductions for bad or negligent work or injury to materials or other property belonging to the employer may not be made unless (*a*)

62 *Cf. Atkin* v. *Acton* (1830) 4 C. & P. 208; *Matheson* v. *Mackinnon* (1832) 10 S. 825.
63 Bell, *Prin.* § 178.
64 *Edwards* v. *Mackie* (1848) 11 D. 67; *McKellar, supra.*
65 *Scott* v. *McMurdo* (1869) 6 S.L.R. 301.
66 *Richards* v. *Hayward* (1841) 2 M. & G. 574; *Bowes & Partners* v. *Press* [1894] 1 Q.B. 202; *N.C.B.* v. *Galley* [1958] 1 All E.R. 91.
67 *Ebbw Vale Steel Co.* v. *Tew* (1935) 79 Sol.Jo. 593; *N.C.B., supra.*
68 *Anglia Television* v. *Reed* [1972] 1 Q.B. 60.
69 *Ross* v. *Pender* (1874) 1 R. 352; *Moffat* v. *Boothby* (1884) 11 R. 501.
70 *O'Brien* v. *Associated Fire Alarms Ltd.* [1969] 1 All E.R. 93.
71 Ersk. III, 3, 16; Bell, *Comm.* I, 488; *Prin.* § 148–150, 154; *Hinshaw* v. *Adam* (1870) 8 M. 933; *Dickson* v. *Hygienic Institute*, 1910 S.C. 352; *Free Church* v. *MacKnight's Trs.*, 1916 S.C. 349. *Cf. Superlux* v. *Plaisted* [1958] C.L.Y. 195.
72 *Cf. Squire* v. *Bayer* [1901] 2 K.B. 299.

the terms on which such deductions are to be made are contained in a notice displayed at places open to the workmen in such a position that it may easily be seen, read and copied or the contract is in writing signed by the workman [73]; (*b*) the deduction or payment does not exceed the actual or estimated damage or loss occasioned by the workman or by some person over whom the workman has control, or for whom the workman has, by the contract, agreed to be responsible, and (*c*) the amount of the deduction or payment is fair and reasonable having regard to all the circumstances of the case. All deductions or payments must be made in pursuance of the contract and the workman must be supplied with particulars in writing on each occasion when a deduction or payment is made showing the acts of omission of which the employer complains and the amount to be deducted or paid.[74]

Actings contrary to good faith of employment

It is an implied term of employment that an employee will not allow conflict between his personal interests or those of others and those of his employer or act inconsistently with the good faith of the employment.[75] This duty may be breached by using the employer's materials for the benefit of another,[76] taking information for use by himself later or by a subsequent employer,[77] revealing or using information when working on secret processes,[78] soliciting custom for himself or a prospective new employer,[79] disclosing confidential knowledge to another,[80] working in his spare time for a competitor,[81] undertaking to work for a client of the employer,[82] or borrowing money from the till without the employer's knowledge.[83] Such conduct has been held to justify immediate dismissal and damages for loss sustained.

This principle does not prevent a man carrying away from employment increased knowledge, skill and ability, as such are almost inevitable consequences of being employed and inseparable from the individual.

Breach may justify interdict and, where there has been identifiable loss, damages measured by the loss sustained.

This principle covers honesty in accounting for money or other property passing through the employee's hands. Inability to do so will normally justify dismissal but will also justify a claim for the loss sustained by

[73] *Cf. Williams* v. *North Navigation Collieries* [1906] A.C. 136.

[74] As to the recovery of sums paid contrary to the Act see s. 5. See also *Pritchard* v. *James Clay Ltd.* [1926] 1 K.B. 238; *Riversdale Mill Co.* v. *Hait* [1928] 1 K.B. 176; *Bird* v. *British Celanese Ltd.* [1945] K.B. 336.

[75] *Pearce* v. *Foster* (1886) 17 Q.B.D. 536; *Boston Deep Sea Fishing Co.* v. *Ansell* (1888) 39 Ch.D. 339.

[76] *Lamb* v. *Evans* [1893] 1 Ch. 218.

[77] *Merryweather* v. *Moore* [1892] 2 Ch. 518.

[78] *Amber Size & Chemical Co.* v. *Menzel* [1913] 2 Ch. 239.

[79] *Wessex Dairies Ltd.* v. *Smith* [1935] 2 K.B. 80; *Sanders* v. *Parry* [1967] 2 All E.R. 803.

[80] *Robb* v. *Green* (1895) 2 Q.B.D. 315; *Liverpool Victoria Friendly Socy.* v. *Houston* (1900) 3 F. 42; *Bents Brewery Co. Ltd.* v. *Hogan* [1945] 2 All E.R. 570.

[81] *Hivac* v. *Park Royal Scientific Instruments Ltd.* [1946] Ch. 169.

[82] *Sanders* v. *Parry* [1967] 2 All E.R. 803.

[83] *Sinclair* v. *Neighbour* [1966] 3 All E.R. 988.

the dishonesty or negligence. Similarly secret benefits made " on the side " must be accounted for.[84]

Accounting for property received in charge

An employee must also be able to account for all property placed in his charge, or received by him on account of his employer, and will be liable for the value of all he cannot satisfactorily account for.[85]

Conduct inferring legal liability on employer to third parties

If an employee acts in such a way as to cause loss or injury to a third party, for which the third party recovers damages from the employer, as being vicariously liable for the fault of the employee, the employer has a claim of damages or for relief against the employee, measured by the sum the employer has had to pay together with expenses of process reasonably incurred in the action at the instance of the third party.[86]

Claims after employee has left employment

An employer is entitled to protection from competition by a former employee who has left his employment only if such competition is contrary to a valid and enforceable contract restraining the employee's liberty of action.[87] Such a contract or condition falls if the employee was wrongfully dismissed [88] or the employer's business sold to another.[89]

If a restrictive covenant or contract is enforceable breach may be prevented or ended by interdict, even though provision was made for liquidate damages, or the pursuer may elect which remedy to pursue.[90] There would appear to be no reason why, if contravention had been taking place for some time, damages should not be claimed in compensation for loss shown to have been sustained, as well as interdict for the future.

[84] *Graham* v. *United Turkey Red Co.*, 1922 S.C. 533; *Reading* v. *A.G.* [1951] A.C. 507.
[85] *Cf. Superlux* v. *Plaisted* [1958] C.L.Y. 195.
[86] *Lister* v. *Romford Ice Co.* [1957] A.C. 555; distinguished in *Harvey* v. *O'Dell* [1958] 2 Q.B. 78. See also *Jones* v. *Manchester Corpn.* [1952] 2 Q.B. 852.
[87] On such contracts and contractual conditions see generally Gloag on *Contract* (2nd ed.), 569 *et seq.*; Pollock on *Contract* (13th ed.), 332; Cheshire and Fifoot on *Contract* (8th ed.), 357.
[88] *General Billposting Co.* v. *Atkinson* [1909] A.C. 118.
[89] *Berlitz School* v. *Duchene* (1903) 6 F. 181.
[90] *General Accident Assce. Corpn.* v. *Noel* [1902] 1 K.B. 377.

CHAPTER 34

CONTRACTS FOR SERVICES

IN contracts for services, *locatio operis faciendi*, the contract is for the rendering of services with a view to bringing about a particular result. The employer does not have any power of control in detail over the execution of the work, relying on the skill, knowledge and experience of the person employed. He pays not a salary or wage to the person employed but a fee for the performance of the task entrusted to him and has no exclusive claim to the attention of the person employed for any particular time, unless this be expressly contracted for.

Such contracts cover a great variety of circumstances, from the employment of professional men, such as physicians,[1] surgeons,[1] para-medical persons, dentists, veterinary surgeons, solicitors, accountants, architects, engineers, and the like, to contracts with builders, engineering firms of many kinds, shipbuilders and the like. Exceptionally, by long-standing custom, counsel act under a mandate, not a contract for services, and are not liable for breach of contract, nor, probably, for delict.[2]

PROFESSIONAL SERVICES

Whether there has been a breach of contract in a particular case depends on the terms of the particular contract and on those terms implied into it by general law. It is an implied term in every case that a person or firm employed to perform services will possess the knowledge and exhibit the standard of skill and care to be expected of reasonably skilled and competent practitioners of the profession or business in question. Hence a practitioner of a profession will be liable in damages for failure to possess that standard of knowledge, or to show that standard of skill or care, but not for error of judgment, nor mistaken exercise of discretion, nor difference of opinion.[3] What the standards are is a question of fact, to be judged on the evidence of persons of experience and skill in the same profession. Deviation from the course of ordinary professional practice is not negligent unless there is a practice, it was not adopted, and the course

[1] Under the National Health Service the patient does not normally employ the physician or surgeon but uses a public service, and accordingly can have no claim based on breach of contract.

[2] *Purves* v. *Landell* (1845) 12 Cl. & Fin. 91; *Swinfen* v. *Lord Chelmsford* (1860) 5 H. & N. 890; *Batchelor* v. *Pattison & Mackersy* (1876) 3 R. 914; *Rondel* v. *Worsley* [1967] 1 All E.R. 993.

[3] Bell, *Prin.* § 153–154; *Lanphier* v. *Phipos* (1831) 8 C. & P. 475; *Jenkins* v. *Betham* (1855) 15 C.B. 168; *Harmer* v. *Cornelius* (1858) 5 C.B.(N.S.) 236; *Rich* v. *Pierpont* (1862) 3 F. & F. 35; *R.* v. *Bateman* (1925) 41 T.L.R. 557; *Crawford* v. *Campbell* [1948] C.L.Y. 4600; *Hunter* v. *Hanley*, 1955 S.C. 200 (doctors); *Hart* v. *Frame* (1839) McL. & Rob. 595; *Purves* v. *Landell* (1845) 4 Bell 46; *Cooke* v. *Falconer's Reps.* (1850) 13 D. 157; *Hamilton* v. *Emslie* (1868) 7 M. 173; *Blair* v. *Assets Co.* (1896) 23 R.(H.L.) 36 (solicitors).

adopted was one which no professional man of ordinary skill and acting with ordinary care would have taken.

To whom duty owed

Professional persons always owe duties under contract to those who employ them, but may also owe duties *ex lege*, more widely, to persons whom they should reasonably have contemplated as likely to be injured in some way by their failure to take due care. The owing of duties more widely is most commonly illustrated in cases of physicians and surgeons but applies also in some cases to accountants,[3a] bankers,[3b] surveyors,[3c] valuers [3c] and analysts,[3c] solicitors,[3d] and generally to all persons who engage in a calling which requires special knowledge and skill. Independently of contract there may be circumstances where information is given or where advice is given which establish a relationship which creates a duty not only to be honest but also to be careful.[3e] " If, in a sphere in which a person is so placed that others could reasonably rely on his judgment or his skill or on his ability to make careful inquiry, a person takes it on himself to give information or advice to, or allows his information or advice to be passed on to another person who, as he knows or should know, will place reliance on it, then a duty of care will arise." [4] But the duty must have been owed to the person actually suffering loss and claiming for it; that person must have been contemplated by the professional person as likely to be injured if due care was not taken. Loss suffered by a person outwith the ambit of the duty is not a delict giving him a right of action. Thus a scientist or expert, or the author of a legal textbook, is not liable to his readers for careless statements in his published work. He publishes his work simply to give information, and not with any particular transaction in mind. When, however, a scientist or an expert makes an investigation and report for the very purpose of a particular transaction, he is under a duty of care in respect of that transaction.[4a] An architect who neglects customary and necessary standards and designs an edifice which collapses is liable *ex contractu* to his client and also *ex delicto* to the injured occupants of the building. A solicitor is liable *ex contractu* to his client and *ex delicto* to anyone to or for whom he knows his client is obtaining advice, but not to someone to whom his client ultroneously passes on the advice; no duty is owed to this third party. A professional

[3a] *Candler* v. *Crane, Christmas & Co.* [1951] 2 K.B. 164, as modified by *Hedley Byrne & Co.*, *infra.*

[3b] *Robinson* v. *National Bank*, 1916 S.C.(H.L.) 154; *Banbury* v. *Bank of Montreal* [1918] A.C. 626; *Woods* v. *Martins Bank* [1959] 1 Q.B. 55; *Hedley Byrne & Co.* v. *Heller & Partners* [1964] A.C. 465.

[3c] Cases instanced by Denning L.J. in *Candler*, *supra*, based on *Le Lievre* v. *Gould* [1893] 1 Q.B. 491; *Cann* v. *Willson* (1888) 39 Ch.D. 39; *Old Gate Estates* v. *Toplis and Harding and Russell* [1939] 3 All E.R. 209.

[3d] *Nocton* v. *Lord Ashburton* [1914] A.C. 932.

[3e] *Hedley Byrne*, *supra.*

[4] *Ibid.* 503, *per* Lord Morris.

[4a] *Candler*, *supra*, 183, *per* Denning L.J.

person owes a duty of care though giving advice gratuitously and without contract.[4b] Since *Hedley Byrne & Co.* v. *Heller & Partners* [4c] the older view that some professional men owed duties *ex contractu* only cannot be supported. It is, however, the case that some classes of professional men, such as doctors, more frequently owe duties of care *ex lege* than do such as solicitors.

A duty of care is also owed *ex lege* in fiduciary relationships, such as those of parent and child, guardian and ward, trustee and beneficiary, and solicitor and client, and in those cases too, independently of contract, one party may be liable to the other for failure to take reasonable care in advising or guiding action.

Measure of damages

If a claim is founded on breach of contract the appropriate measure of damages is the contractual one, namely the sum required to restore the clients to the position they would have been in if the practitioner had properly and skilfully performed the duties incumbent on him.[5] Examples are liability to pay the client the whole sum receivable if the agent had not neglected to lead an adjudication,[6] for the loss the client sustained in consequence of a sale not taking effect,[7] for the expenses, loss, and damages incurred by the client to a third party in consequence of the agent's blunder,[8] for the full amount of a debt lost by the agent's failure to use diligence to recover it,[9] for the full sum in a decree which, with the process, the agent lost,[10] for the amount in a bill when an undischarged bankrupt was accepted as a cautioner, in a suspension of a charge thereon, together with the expenses of the suspension,[11] for the loss arising through delay to get a valid title to heritage,[12] for the inconvenience and discomfort of having to live with relatives for two years in consequence of bungled proceedings to recover possession of a house,[13] for the excessive price paid for property when the solicitor failed to inform the purchaser that building plans had not been approved,[14] for the whole price of a property to which there was no valid title, the agent being entitled to a conveyance of the property,[15] for the whole sum lost in consequence of taking an invalid

4b *Cf. Shiells* v. *Blackburne* (1789) 1 Hy.Bl. 158, 162; *Banbury* v. *Bank of Montreal* [1918] A.C. 626, 689.

4c [1964] A.C. 465.

5 Ersk. III, 1, 14; *Hamilton* v. *Dundas* (1710) Mor. 3153; *Groom* v. *Crocker* [1939] 1 K.B. 194; *Lake* v. *Bushby* [1949] 2 All E.R. 964.

6 *Mason* v. *Thom* (1787) Mor. 3535.

7 *Allan* v. *Mansfield* (1834) 12 S. 329.

8 *Wood* v. *Fullerton* (1710) Mor. 13960; *Fraser's Trs.* v. *Falconer* (1830) 5 Mur. 299; *Frame* v. *Campbell* (1836) 14 S. 914; affd. (1839) McL. & Rob. 595; *Smith* v. *Grant* (1858) 20 D. 1077.

9 *Garden and Donaldson* v. *Pilmore and Lindsay* (1710) Mor. 3519; *Chatto* v. *Marshall*, Jan. 17, 1811, F.C.; *Slater* v. *Henderson & Scott* (1822) 1 S. 241; *Graham* v. *Hunter's Trs.* (1831) 9 S. 543; *McFarlane's Exors.* v. *Ferguson* (1835) 13 S. 477.

10 *McMillan* v. *Gray*, March 2, 1820, F.C.

11 *Brown* v. *Wemyss and Walker* (1829) 7 S. 626.

12 *Brown* v. *Cheyne* (1831) 9 S. 573; (1833) 11 S. 497.

13 *Bailey* v. *Bullock* (1950) 66 T.L.R. (Pt. 2) 791.

14 *Lake* v. *Bushby* [1949] 2 All E.R. 964.

15 *Donald's Trs.* v. *Yeats* (1839) 1 D. 1249; see also *Hunter* v. *Fleming* (1829) 8 S. 234.

security,[16] for the whole sum lent on inadequate security, in exchange for an assignation,[17] for the amount of prior burdens undisclosed,[18] for the deficiency on a bad security as well as for arrears of interest,[19] for the loss to a person's estate by failing to advise him of the right to secure the property by disentail,[20] for the loss due to failure to make a war damage claim,[21] for expenditure thrown away by failure to disclose information.[21a]

Where an action for a debt has been lost by the agent's negligence, the amount of the debt is not necessarily the measure of damages,[22] and it is doubtful if the proper measure is the full amount of the debt in the case of the negligent loss of a claim against a bankrupt estate,[23] though it is not necessarily restricted to the dividend the estate would have yielded.[24] Where an action for damages was lost because the solicitor delayed to raise an action until the period of limitation had expired, the measure of damages was held to be the value of the lost chance to recover damages.[24a]

It is a defence that the debt was discharged [25] or that no debt was due,[26] but not that nothing would have been recovered [27] or that a prior error had already vitiated the proceedings.[28]

Measure of damages—delict

If the action is founded on delict caused by breach of a duty owed *ex lege* the measure of damages is that required to restore the pursuer to the position he would have been in if the harm had not been done him. If the loss has taken the form of financial loss this is measured by the loss sustained.[29]

If the loss has taken the form of personal injuries or death the damages fall to be measured in the same way as in other cases of delict causing loss of these kinds.[30]

16 *Lillie* v. *Macdonald* (1819) 1 Bligh 315, expl. *Campbell* v. *Clason* (1838) 1 D. 270; see also *McLeod* v. *Macdonald* (1835) 13 S. 287; *Stuart* v. *Miller* (1840) 3 D. 255; *Ronaldson* v. *Drummond and Reid* (1881) 8 R. 767.

17 *Graham* v. *Hunter's Trs.* (1831) 9 S. 543; *Haldane* v. *Donaldson* (1840) 1 Rob.App. 226.

18 *Campbell* v. *Clason* (1840) 2 D. 1113.

19 *Pretty* v. *Fowke* (1889) 3 T.L.R. 845.

20 *Otter* v. *Church, Adams, Tatham & Co.* [1953] 1 W.L.R. 156.

21 *O'Rourke* v. *Wood* [1952] C.P.L. 264.

21a *Williams's Trs.* v. *Macandrew and Jenkins*, 1960 S.L.T. 246.

22 *Urquhart* v. *Grigor* (1857) 19 D. 853.

23 *Pentland* v. *Wight* (1833) 11 S. 804; *Brown* v. *McKie* (1852) 14 D. 358.

24 *Lizar's Children* v. *Dickie's Reps.* (1760) Mor. 3532; *Chatto* v. *Marshall*, Jan. 17, 1811, F.C.; *McMillan* v. *Gray*, March 2, 1820, F.C.

24a *Yeoman* v. *Ferries*, 1967 S.C. 255.

25 *Wallace* v. *Donald* (1825) 3 S. 433.

26 *Murray* v. *Taylor* (1828) 6 S. 802; *Davidson* v. *Mackenzie* (1856) 19 D. 253; see also *Robertson* v. *Ogilvie* (1834) 12 S. 580; *Sinclair* v. *Wilson* (1830) 4 W. & S. 398.

27 *Chatto* v. *Marshall*, Jan. 17, 1811, F.C.; *McMillan, supra*; *McFarlane's Exors.* (1835) 13 S. 477.

28 *McLean* v. *Grant*, Nov. 15, 1805, F.C.; *Davidson* v. *Mackenzie* (1856) 19 D. 226.

29 In *Candler* v. *Crane, Christmas & Co.* [1951] 2 K.B. 164, Denning L.J., who was in favour of giving the plaintiff a remedy, would have awarded £2,000, the sum lost by reliance on the misstatement.

30 Chaps. 53–54, *infra*.

Contracts for Execution of Work

The same general principles apply to contracts for the execution of work, such as building contracts, shipbuilding contracts, contracts for construction or repair of any kind of machinery and the like.

The primary mutual rights and duties are to pay the contract price and to complete the work in accordance with the terms of the contract, failing which a claim of damages will lie. It is implied that work shall be done in a good and workmanlike manner.[9]

The contractor's claim will be for the contract price, together with interest for any delay in payment, or for a sum *quantum meruit*, calculated by reference to the value of the work done, if the price has not been fixed. Extras can only be recovered for by a claim *quantum meruit*.[10] Deviations from the original contract are only recoverable if the employer knew or was informed of extra cost involved.[11] If the employer fails to perform some condition precedent to the commencement of the work, the contractor may throw up the contract at once and claim damages for the breach.[12] A breach in lesser degree will justify only a claim of damages,[13] or possibly a claim *quantum meruit* instead of for the price.[14] The nearer a contract is to completion the less likely it is that a breach amounts to a repudiation of the contract.[15]

The measure of damages recoverable by the employer for breach of such a contract is regulated by the general principles of damages *ex contractu* and the prima facie measure will be the discrepancy in value between the work as it should have been when done and as it actually is,[16] measured usually by the cost of making the work conform to the contract,[17] or the profit lost on account of the deficiency.[18] It is always a question of degree and materiality in the circumstances whether any particular breach on either side will justify rescission of the contract or a claim of damages only.[19]

Provision is frequently made for liquidate damages for non-completion of the work,[20] but the recovery of penalties or liquidate damages may be

9 *Pearce* v. *Tucker* (1862) 3 F. & F. 136.

10 But see *Taverner* v. *Glamorgan C.C.* (1941) 57 T.L.R. 243.

11 *Lovelock* v. *King* (1831) 1 M. & Rob. 60.

12 *Holme* v. *Guppy* (1838) 3 M. & W. 387; *cf. Cort* v. *Ambergate Ry.* (1851) 17 Q.B. 127.

13 *Roberts* v. *Bury Commissioners* (1870) L.R. 5 C.P. 310; *Lawson* v. *Wallasey Local Board* (1882) 11 Q.B.D. 229; *Macintosh* v. *Midland Counties Ry.* (1845) 14 M. & W. 548.

14 *Bush* v. *Whitehaven Port Trs.* (1888) 52 J.P. 392; *cf. Smellie* v. *Caledonian Ry.* (1916) 53 S.L.R. 336.

15 *Cornwall* v. *Henson* [1900] 2 Ch. 298, 303.

16 *Mondel* v. *Steel* (1841) 8 M. & W. 858.

17 *Mertens* v. *Home Freeholds, Ltd.* [1921] 2 K.B. 526; *Ramsay* v. *Brand* (1898) 25 R. 1212. See also *Forrest* v. *Scottish County Investment Co.*, 1915 S.C. 115.

18 *Fletcher* v. *Tayleur* (1855) 17 C.B. 21; *Gillespie* v. *Howden* (1885) 12 R. 800.

19 *Hosking* v. *Pahang Corporation* (1891) 8 T.L.R. 125; *cf. Mersey Steel and Iron Co.* v. *Naylor, Benzon & Co.* (1884) 9 App.Cas. 423; *Rhymney Ry.* v. *Brecon Ry.* (1900) 69 L.J.Ch. 813; *Wade* v. *Waldon*, 1909 S.C. 571.

20 *Johnston* v. *Robertson* (1861) 23 D. 646 (builder); *Clydebank Engineering Co.* v. *Castaneda* (1904) 7 F.(H.L.) 77 (shipbuilding); *Ranger* v. *G.W. Ry.* (1854) 5 H.L.Cas. 72; *Re Newman* (1876) 4 Ch.D. 724; *cf. Public Works Commissioners* v. *Hills* [1906] A.C. 368.

barred by failure to deduct from payments at the proper time.[21] If a contractor proceeds with work despite the breach by the employer of a condition precedent, he may be relieved from a provision for liquidate damages and may still have a claim of damages.[22]

Where work not duly completed

Where a contract for building has not been completed, the employer who has instructed the work will be entitled to recover damages from the builder for his breach of contract, unless he has accepted the incomplete work,[23] and even though he has paid the contract price.[24] The measure of damages in such a case will normally be the difference between the cost or contract price of the works as contracted for and the cost of completing the works conform to the contract specification,[25] with an allowance for the loss of profits or rents or business earnings incurred in consequence of the breach of contract,[26] *i.e.* lost by not having the building or works, as in the ordinary case some such loss must be contemplated,[27] though beyond that any exceptional loss must be shown to have been in the contemplation of both parties as a reasonably foreseeable consequence.[28] In some cases the loss of interest on the cost of the contract works, and of the land on which they are built, is the measure of damages.[29] If the employers have justifiably refused to accept they may refuse to pay and also recover for any damage they have sustained.[30]

The recovery of consequential damages depends on the nature of the transaction and the object and uses for which the structure was designed if known to the builder.[31]

If completion has not been made timeously, the damages will include an element for deprivation of use of the buildings between the contractual date of completion and the actual date thereof.[32]

[21] *Mackintosh* v. *G.W. Ry.* (1865) 4 Giff. 683; *Laidlaw* v. *Hastings Pier Co.* (1874) Hudson's *Building Contracts*, II, 13. See also *Felton* v. *Wharrie* (1906), Hudson, II, 398.

[22] *Dodd* v. *Churton* [1897] 1 Q.B. 562; *cf. Duncanson* v. *Scottish County Investment Co.* (1915) 52 S.L.R. 790.

[23] *Cf. Gillespie* v. *Howden* (1885) 12 R. 800; where acceptance was subject to reservation of a claim of damages.

[24] *Davis* v. *Hedges* (1871) L.R. 6 Q.B. 687; *Newton Abbot Development Co.* v. *Stockman* (1931) 47 T.L.R. 616.

[25] *Thornton* v. *Place* (1832) 1 Moo. & R. 218; *Portman* v. *Middleton* (1858) 4 C.B.(N.S.) 322; *Elbinger Actien-Gesellschaft* v. *Armstrong* (1874) L.R. 9 Q.B. 473; *Welch, Perrin & Co.* v. *Anderson* (1891) 61 L.J.Q.B. 167; *Gillespie* v. *Howden* (1885) 12 R. 800; *Merten* v. *Home Freeholds* [1921] 2 K.B. 526. *Cf.* also *Ramsay* v. *Brand* (1898) 25 R. 1212; *Steel* v. *Young*, 1907 S.C. 360.

[26] *Fletcher* v. *Tayleur* (1855) 25 L.J.C.P. 65; *Waters* v. *Towers* (1853) 8 Ex. 401; *Hydraulic Engineering Co.* v. *McHaffie* (1878) 4 Q.B.D. 670; *Cory* v. *Thames Ironworks Co.* (1868) L.R. 3 Q.B. 181; *Re Trent and Humber Co.* (1868) 4 Ch.App. 112; *Gillespie, supra*; *Erie County Gas Co.* v. *Carroll* [1911] A.C. 105.

[27] *Victoria Laundry* v. *Newman* [1949] 2 K.B. 528.

[28] *Hadley* v. *Baxendale* (1854) 9 Ex. 341; *Victoria Laundry, supra*. *Cf. Cory* v. *Thames Ironworks Co.* (1868) L.R. 3 Q.B. 181.

[29] *Wilson* v. *General Iron Screw Co.* (1877) 47 L.J.Q.B. 239; *cf. Smith* v. *Johnson* (1899) 15 T.L.R. 179.

[30] *Waters* v. *Towers* (1853) 8 Ex. 401.

[31] *Birch* v. *Clifford* (1891) 8 T.L.R. 103.

[32] *Wilson* v. *General Iron Screw Co.* (1877) 47 L.J.Q.B. 239; *Macbride* v. *Hamilton* (1875) 2 R. 775; *British Motor Body Co.* v. *Shaw*, 1914 S.C. 922.

Forfeiture clauses

Building contracts commonly include a power to the employer to determine the contract, or to take over the works and complete them himself on the occurrence of certain events,[33] such as failure to begin the work,[34] or to proceed satisfactorily,[35] or to comply with instructions,[36] or to complete in time,[37] to leave unfinished [38] or not to comply with specification.[39] This right may be made conditional on any event [40] and, if exercised, must be in an unqualified manner.[41] Independently of any such contractual power, the employer retains his common law power to rescind the contract if the contractor evinces the intention not to be bound by it.[42]

A forfeiture clause is commonly buttressed by provisions for liquidate damages or penalty: even without any such provision damages are due for the contractor's failure to perform his contract.[43]

Wrongful forfeiture

If power under a forfeiture clause be wrongfully exercised [44] or exceeded [45] the contractor may treat the contract as rescinded and recover *quantum meruit* [46] or sue for damages for the employer's breach of contract. An employer who forfeits wrongfully may not justify his action by reference to a subsequent event which would have justified it.[47] The measure of damages for a wrongful forfeiture is such sum as would put the contractor in as nearly as possible the same position as if he had been allowed to complete the contract without interruption.[48]

Work completed but defective

The position in the event of complete but defective performance of the contract is complicated by the fact that breach in an immaterial particular may not readily be remediable, if at all, though it may have little or no effect on the value, stability, or amenity of the building. Conversely a material deviation from contract and specification may be readily remediable, *e.g.*, substitution of one kind of slates for another. The particular

[33] Examples in Hudson on *Building Contracts*, 7th ed., 404.
[34] *Mohan* v. *Dundalk Ry.* (1880) 6 L.R.Ir. 477.
[35] *Stradhard* v. *Lee* (1863) 32 L.J.Q.B. 75.
[36] *Hunt* v. *S.E. Ry.* (1875) 45 L.J.Q.B. 87.
[37] *Tooth* v. *Hallett* (1869) L.R. 4 Ch. 242.
[38] *Ex p. Newitt* (1881) 16 Ch.D. 522.
[39] *Stevens* v. *Taylor* (1860) 2 F. & F. 419.
[40] *Davies* v. *Swansea Corpn.* (1853) 22 L.J.Ex. 297.
[41] *Drew* v. *Josolyne* (1887) 18 Q.B.D. 590.
[42] *Mersey Steel and Iron Co.* v. *Naylor* (1884) 9 App.Cas. 434; *Cork Corpn.* v. *Rooney* (1881) 7 L.R.Ir. 191.
[43] *Lowther* v. *Heaver* (1889) 41 Ch.D. 248; *Marshall* v. *Macintosh* (1898) 78 L.T. 750.
[44] *Felton* v. *Wharrie* (1906) Hudson on *Building Contracts*, 4th ed., II, 398.
[45] *Lodder* v. *Slowey* [1904] A.C. 442; *Roberts* v. *Bury Commrs.* (1870) L.R. 5 C.P. 310.
[46] *Lodder* v. *Slowey* [1904] A.C. 442.
[47] *Re Walker* (1884) 26 Ch.D. 510.
[48] *Ranger* v. *G.W. Ry.* (1854) 5 H.L.Cas. 72. See also *Woods* v. *Russell* (1822) 5 B. & Ald. 942; *Smith* v. *Howden Union* (1890) Hudson, 4th ed., II, 156.

kind of contract and the nature, extent and effect of the breach are therefore worthy of consideration. Lord President Robertson pointed out in *Ramsay* v. *Brand* [49] that a builder " has no right to disregard a specification altogether, or to modify it as by supplying one material in place of another; and neither in the case of total departure nor in the case of a partial deviation from the specification will it avail to prove that what has been done is as good as what was promised. Accordingly the rule is, that if the builder chooses to depart from his contract he loses his right to sue for the contract price. But further, losing the right to sue for the contract price, he does not acquire the right to sue for *quantum meruit*, the other party never having agreed to pay according to its value for work which *ex hypothesi* he never ordered. In the application of this rule it suffers a modification which in no way invades the principle. A building contract by specification necessarily includes minute particulars, and the law is not so pedantic as to deny action for the contract price on account of any and every omission or deviation. It gives effect to the principle by deducting from the contract price whatever sum is required to complete the work in exact compliance with the contract." This must, however, be taken subject to the general rule that failure justifying rescission of the whole contract must be material and the materiality must be judged at the end of the day when the building is completed.

In *Ramsay* v. *Brand* [50] the contract was a lump sum one for building a cottage according to plan and specification. Certain defects were alleged, remediable for an expenditure of £40, and the court held the defects matters of detail justifying that amount being deducted from the price as damages but not calling for rescission of the contract or justifying refusal of the finished building.

In *Steel* v. *Young* [51] the defect was such that the building would have had to be taken down and rebuilt to bring it within the specification, although the difference in value as erected was trifling. The defect was held material and the party who ordered the work was entitled to reject, though the builder had a claim based on recompense for the value of what he had done on the building which was in fact kept by the employer. In fact the difference in value and sufficiency of the building was negligible or at least insubstantial, so that the defender was not seriously prejudiced, but the deviation was held to be material and irremediable and not a matter of detail. The builder consequently could not claim the price but only a sum in recompense. In *Forrest* v. *Scottish County Investment Co.*[52] irremediable

49 (1898) 25 R. 1212; 35 S.L.R. 927.

50 (1898) 25 R. 1212; 35 S.L.R. 927. See also *Thornton* v. *Place* (1832) 1 Moo. & R. 218; *Portman* v. *Middleton* (1858) 4 C.B.(N.S.) 322; *Elbinger Actien-Gesellschaft* v. *Armstrong* (1874) L.R. 9 Q.B. 473; *Welch, Perrin & Co.* v. *Anderson & Co.* (1891) 61 L.J.Q.B. 167. In *McMorran* v. *Morrison & Co.* (1906) 14 S.L.T. 578 (O.H.), minor but irremediable defects did not bar an action for the contract price, but a counterclaim of damages in respect of the defects was allowed.

51 1907 S.C. 360, doubted in *Forrest* v. *Scottish County Investment Co.*, 1915 S.C. 115; affd. 1916 S.C.(H.L.) 28, *per* Lord Parmoor.

52 *Ut supra*. The case was ultimately decided on the footing that the architect had sanctioned the alterations with authority.

departures from specification were made, though the difference in the value of the building was negligible. Lord Parmoor thought that in a measure and value contract, exact compliance with specification was not an essential for an action for the price.

Again, where defective mortar was supplied so that the building had to be taken down, the builder was held entitled to recover the cost of demolition and rebuilding as well as damages for loss of ground rent.[53]

In *Speirs* v. *Petersen* [54] a builder was in breach of implied conditions of work in failing to provide precautions against damp. This was held not to be so material as to prevent him suing for the price, under deduction of the amount necessary to rectify his faulty work. Similarly in *Dakin* v. *Lee* [55] defects and omissions which amounted only to negligent performance of the contract allowed the builders to recover the price, less the sum required to make the work accord with specification.

The basis of a claim of damages for defective performance appears accordingly to be, provided the defects are remediable, the difference in value between the work as it is and as it should have been.[56]

In general the contractor alone is liable to third parties for injuries done to [57] or prejudice suffered by them in consequence of the operations, but the employer will be liable if the work is dangerous or necessarily injurious to third parties.[58]

As regards liability for injury to the employer, it has been held in England that a builder who builds a house for sale is under no duty either to a future purchaser or to persons who come to live in the house to ensure that it is well constructed and safe.[59]

Engineering construction

The ordinary rules of damages as discussed above apply to works of engineering construction. Examples are the installation of a defective hot-water apparatus, where a deduction from the price was made [60]; the non-repair timeously of a machine, where the cost of obtaining parts elsewhere was recovered but not damages paid to an eventual purchaser, the latter contract being undisclosed [61]; increased expenditure incurred in consequence of failure to give timeous possession of the site for works,[62] loss caused by insufficiency in machinery manifested within the period of

53 *Smith* v. *Johnson* (1899) 15 T.L.R. 179.
54 1924 S.C. 428.
55 [1916] 1 K.B. 566.
56 *Mondel* v. *Steel* (1841) 8 M. & W. 858; *Forrest* v. *Scottish County Investment Co.*, 1916 S.C.(H.L.) 28; *Speirs, supra.*
57 *Blake* v. *Woolf* [1898] 2 Q.B. 426; *Holliday* v. *National Telephone Co.* [1899] 2 Q.B. 392.
58 *Rylands* v. *Fletcher* (1868) L.R. 3 H.L. 330; *Dalton* v. *Angus* (1881) 6 App.Cas. 740; *Hardaker* v. *Idle D.C.* [1896] 1 Q.B. 335; *Stewart* v. *Adams*, 1920 S.C. 129.
59 *Otto* v. *Bolton* [1936] 2 K.B. 46; see also *Bottomley* v. *Bannister* [1932] 1 K.B. 458.
60 *Cutler* v. *Close* (1832) 5 C. & P. 337.
61 *Portman* v. *Middleton* (1858) 27 L.J.C.P. 231. *Cf. Hydraulic Engineering Co.* v. *McHaffie* (1878) 4 Q.B.D. 670.
62 *Bush* v. *Whitehaven Trs.*, Hudson's *Building Contracts*, 4th ed., II, 130; *cf. Mackay* v. *Leven Police Commrs.* (1893) 20 R. 1093.

guarantee,[63] the cost of removing defective water-pipes and consequent inconvenience.[64]

Construction and repair of vehicles and ships

General principles again regulate damages in these cases [65]: examples are the loss of profits given where a ship was delivered late and lost a profitable season,[66] or was deficient in carrying capacity [67]; the penalties to which a company was subjected by the defendant's failure to supply wheels and axles timeously [68]; damages for an unauthorised modification in design which made a vessel inconvenient and indeed dangerous [65]; damages for detention of a ship and inability to use her owing to the failure to execute repairs in a workmanlike manner [69]; loss of profits and wages paid to idle crews when fishing boats were late in building and delivery [70]; depreciation in value owing to injuries sustained before delivery [71]; increased cost of building due to late delivery of steel.[72]

Payment of the price of machinery does not preclude a claim of damages, if the defects could not have been discovered prior to the payment; and *de recenti* repairs are evidential of original insufficiency of the work.[73] Where a vessel is paid for by instalments while building, the purchaser is not barred from claiming damages for non-delivery at the contractual date by acceptance at a later date.[74] [75]

Claims by contractors against employers

Breach of contract by the employer may be material and going to the root of the contract in which case if it takes place before the works have been commenced, the contractor is not bound to go on with the works and may recover as his damages the amount of profit he would have made if he had been allowed to complete the contract,[76] or, if the work has been partially performed, the cost of the work done and materials supplied so far as the work has been already completed, or alternatively for damages for breach of the contract.[77]

63 *London, etc., Shipping Co.* v. *Duffus* (1841) 3 D. 929.
64 *McDonald* v. *Mackie* (1831) 5 W. & Sh. 462.
65 *e.g. Burrell* v. *Russell* (1900) 2 F.(H.L.) 80.
66 *Fletcher* v. *Tayleur* (1855) 25 L.J.C.P. 65; *Steam Herring Fleet* v. *Richards* (1901) 17 T.L.R. 731; see also *Clydebank Engineering Co.* v. *Castaneda* (1904) 7 F.(H.L.) 77; as to cars, see *British Motor Body Co.* v. *Shaw*, 1914 S.C. 922.
67 *Walker, Henderson & Co.* v. *Hutchison* (1885) 22 S.L.R. 903; *Gillespie* v. *Howden* (1885) 12 R. 800.
68 *Elbinger A/G* v. *Armstrong* (1874) L.R. 9 Q.B. 473.
69 *Wilson* v. *General Iron Screw Co.* (1877) 47 L.J.Q.B. 239; *Strachan* v. *Gavin and Paton* (1828) 3 W. & Sh. 19.
70 *Steam Herring Fleet* v. *Richards* (1901) 17 T.L.R. 731.
71 *Savory, Young & Co.* v. *Priestman* (1886) 2 T.L.R. 467.
72 *Watson* v. *Gray* (1900) 16 T.L.R. 308.
73 *Napier* v. *Campbell* (1841) 3 D. 879.
74 *Sutherland* v. *Montrose Shipbuilding Co.* (1860) 22 D. 665.
75 See also *Phillips* v. *Britannia Hygienic Laundry Co.* [1923] 1 K.B. 539; *Herschtal* v. *Stewart & Ardern* [1940] 1 K.B. 155; *Malfroot* v. *Noxal* (1934) 51 T.L.R. 551.
76 *Cf. Inchbald* v. *Western Neilgherry Coffee Co.* (1864) 17 C.B.(N.S.) 733.
77 *Lodder* v. *Slowey* [1904] A C. 442, 451, 453.

If the breach does not go to the root of the contract and the contractor goes on with the works, he will be entitled to recover for the loss and expense caused by the employer's default, as by delay in giving possession of the site,[78] and that even although an extension of time for completion has been allowed in consequence of the delay.[79]

A claim may also have to be made for loss of use of plant kept idle [80] or liability incurred to sub-contractors in consequence of the breach.[81]

Provision for liquidate damages or penalty

Such provisions are common in building and engineering contracts to ensure punctual performance. The principles of interpretation to be applied to considering them are discussed elsewhere.[82] Such a provision may cease to be enforceable if there is no date from which the clause is to run,[83] or if the claim for it has been waived.[84] In the absence of express provision, a claim for liquidate damages cannot be made, if the employer has justifiably exercised a power to forfeit the contract,[85] but if there is provision therefor, liquidate damages may be exigible down to final completion of the works.[86]

If the employer's right to liquidate damages has gone, he cannot recover unliquidate damages unless the contractor fails to complete within a reasonable time.[87] If a reasonable time be exceeded the employer would probably be entitled to recover unliquidate damages.

78 *Lawson* v. *Wallasey Local Board* (1883) 48 L.T. 507; *cf. Mackay* v. *Leven Police Commrs.* (1893) 20 R. 1093.

79 *Re Trollope & Sons* (1913) 1 Hudson's *Building Contracts*, 4th ed., 849.

80 *Cf. The Greta Holme* [1897] A.C. 596; *The Mediana* [1900] A.C. 113; *The Marpessa* [1906] P. 95.

81 *Sawdon* v. *Andrew* (1874) 30 L.T. 23. The latter head may raise questions of remoteness and the extent of the employer's knowledge is material.

82 Chap. 7, *supra*. See also *Johnston* v. *Robertson* (1861) 23 D. 646.

83 *Dodd* v. *Churton* [1897] 1 Q.B. 562.

84 *Macintosh* v. *G.W. Ry.* (1865) 11 Jur.(N.S.) 681; *Laidlaw* v. *Hastings Pier Committee* (1874) 2 Hudson's *Building Contracts*, 4th ed., 13. See, too, *Steel* v. *Bell* (1900) 38 S.L.R. 217.

85 *Re Morrish* (1882) 22 Ch.D. 410.

86 *Re Yeadon Waterworks Co.* (1895) 72 L.T. 538.

87 *Ford* v. *Cotesworth* (1870) L.R. 5 Q.B. 544; *Tyers* v. *Rosedale and Ferryhill Iron Co.* (1875) L.R. 10 Ex. 195.

CHAPTER 35

CONTRACTS OF PARTNERSHIP

THE relationship of partnership may give rise to many claims by a prospective partner or partners against the firm, and conversely, or by partners *inter se*.

Agreement to enter into partnership

An agreement to enter into partnership is subject to the ordinary principles of contract and, if a partner establishes that his agreement was induced by misrepresentation, innocent,[1] negligent or fraudulent,[2] he may, on making restitution of any benefit acquired under the agreement, rescind the contract,[3] claim repayment of any money paid into the firm, indemnity against any liabilities incurred,[3a] and, in the case of negligent or fraudulent misrepresentation, also claim damages for loss sustained in consequence of being induced to enter into the relationship under misapprehension.[4]

Failure to enter into partnership

If a person, having undertaken to do so, fails without adequate justification, to enter into a partnership, the other partner or partners are entitled to damages for any loss sustained.[5] Discovery of misrepresentations having induced the agreement would be a justification. It has been held not to be a defence that the defendant had discovered that the other was an unsuitable person with whom to be associated in partnership,[6] but this rule cannot be absolute. If a solicitor or doctor discovers that one with whom he was about to enter into partnership was unqualified would that not be a defence? If one partner agrees to bring in a person as a new partner, even unknown to the other existing partners, and they decline to accept him, the third party has a claim for breach of the agreement.[7] Similarly if one partner agrees with his partner that on his death a specified person shall become partner in his place and that person declines to become a partner, the other partners have a right of action for breach of contract.[8] Where action lies the measure of damages is the loss sustained.

[1] *Redgrave* v. *Hurd* (1881) 20 Ch.D. 1; *Adam* v. *Newbigging* (1888) 13 App.Cas. 308.
[2] *Cf. Spence* v. *Crawford*, 1939 S.C.(H.L.) 52.
[3] *Redgrave, supra*; *Adam, supra*; *Spence, supra*.
[3a] *Rawlins* v. *Wickham* (1858) 3 DeG. & J. 304; see also Partnership Act 1890, s. 41.
[4] *McConnel* v. *Wright* [1903] 1 Ch. 546.
[5] *Walker* v. *Harris* (1793) 1 Anst. 245; *Gale* v. *Leckie* (1817) 2 Stark. 107; *Figes* v. *Cutler* (1822) 3 Stark. 139.
[6] *Andrews* v. *Garstin* (1861) 10 C.B.(N.S.) 444.
[7] *McNeill* v. *Reid* (1832) 9 Bing. 68.
[8] *Downs* v. *Collins* (1848) 6 Hare 418.

Withdrawal of capital

A partner who in breach of contract withdraws from the firm capital which he was bound to leave in, is liable in damages for loss occurring in consequence.[9] The appropriate measure of damages has been held to be the extra profits which might have been earned by the employment in the business of the capital diverted by the withdrawal.[9]

Liability for causing firm loss

Every partner is an agent of the firm and his other partners for the purpose of the business of the partnership.[10] A partner who as such agent enters into a transaction detrimental to the firm is accordingly liable to his partners for the loss sustained thereby.[11] So, too, every partner is jointly and severally liable with the other partners for the debts and obligations of the firm incurred while he is a partner.[12] This implies a right of relief against the partner personally in fault in incurring the obligation.[13] Similarly if one partner in the ordinary course of the firm's business, by wrongful act or omission, causes loss or injury to a third party, the firm is liable therefor to the same extent as the partner.[14] The partner's liability in such a case is joint and several [15] and each accordingly has a right of action against the erring partner for indemnity to the extent of the liability incurred.[16] Innocent partners are liable for misrepresentations of one of their partners in matters connected with the ordinary business of the firm.[17]

Where a partner acting within the scope of his apparent authority or a firm in the course of its business receives money or property of a third person, and it is misapplied by one or more of the partners while in the custody of the firm, the firm is liable to make good the loss,[18] but liability of the partners is joint and several [19] which implies that the innocent partners have a claim of relief against the partner actually in default for their share of the loss.[20]

If, however, one partner by negligence causes injury to another partner, the firm is not vicariously liable for, nor are the other partners jointly and severally liable along with, the individual partner in fault; he alone is personally liable.[21]

9 *Teacher* v. *Calder* (1899) 1 F.(H.L.) 39.
10 Partnership Act 1890, s. 5.
11 *Cf. Lloyd* v. *Grace, Smith & Co.* [1912] A.C. 716.
12 1890 Act, s. 9.
13 *Cf. Mair* v. *Wood*, 1948 S.C. 83.
14 1890 Act, s. 10; *cf. Blyth* v. *Fladgate* [1891] 1 Ch. 337; *Hamlyn* v. *Houston* [1903] 1 K.B. 81.
15 1890 Act, s. 12.
16 Law Reform (Misc. Prov.) (Scotland) Act 1940, s. 3. *Cf. Lister* v. *Romford Ice Co.* [1957] A.C. 555.
17 *Rapp* v. *Latham* (1819) 2 B. & Ald. 795.
18 1890 Act, s. 11; *De Ribeyre* v. *Barclay* (1857) 23 Beav. 107; *Re Collie, ex parte Adamson* (1878) 8 Ch.D. 807; contrast *New Mining and Exploring Syndicate Ltd.* v. *Chalmers*, 1912 S.C. 126.
19 1890 Act, s. 12.
20 Law Reform (Misc. Prov.) (Scotland) Act 1940, s. 3.
21 *Mair* v. *Wood*, 1948 S.C. 83.

Actings contrary to good faith

A partner may not act in a way contrary to the good faith of the partnership, as by carrying on for his own benefit a business competing with that carried on by the firm.[22] If he is found to be doing so he may be held liable in damages for the loss caused thereby,[23] of which the profits made by the competing business would be an indication; also relevant would be a calculation of the extra profit which might have been made if the partner had not operated in competition.[24]

Care and diligence

A partner owes a duty to his fellow partners to exercise care and diligence in the business of the partnership. The standard of that duty may be lower than the duty expected of a partner in relation to third parties, and be measured by the diligence which he would show in his own affairs.[25] Such failure gives rise to a claim against the delinquent partner by his co-partners for the loss caused to the partnership or to their interests as partners.[26]

Change in firm as regards third parties

A change in the composition of a firm, by the retiral of a partner, or the admission of a new partner, may constitute a breach of contract with a third party, for which there will be liability in damages.[27] This will apply only where the contract is in absolute terms,[27] or where there is some element of *delectus personae*, so that the reconstitution of the firm makes a material and not merely formal difference to the contract. If the change is involuntary, as by the death of a partner, it is not a breach of contract.[28] Bankruptcy is, however, a breach of contract, even though arising innocently, as from recession in trade.[29]

Admission of new partners

If it is provided that a partner may nominate a person to succeed to his share on his retirement or death the firm is obliged to admit his nominee or be liable in damages,[30] but will not be ordained to admit him as a partner, nor will the court compel the nominee to enter into the partnership.[31]

[22] 1890 Act, s. 30.
[23] *Cf. Dean* v. *Macdowell* (1878) 8 Ch.D. 345.
[24] *Cf. Teacher* v. *Calder* (1899) 1 F.(H.L.) 39.
[25] *Mair* v. *Wood*, 1948 S.C. 83, 90.
[26] *Mair, supra*, 91.
[27] *Brace* v. *Calder* [1895] 2 Q.B. 253.
[28] *Hoey* v. *MacEwan and Auld* (1867) 5 M. 814.
[29] *Hoey, supra*, 817.
[30] *McNeill* v. *Reid* (1832) 9 Bing. 68; *Byrne* v. *Reid* [1902] 2 Ch. 735.
[31] *Downs* v. *Collins* (1848) 6 Hare 418; *Lancaster* v. *Allsop* (1887) 57 L.T. 53.

Unjustified withdrawal

If a partner withdraws from a firm before a time when he might legitimately have done so, or without giving any notice required in the circumstances,[32] he is liable in damages for any loss caused by his withdrawal.[33]

[32] See 1890 Act, s. 32.
[33] *Cf. Teacher* v. *Calder* (1899) 1 F.(H.L.) 39.

CHAPTER 36

CONTRACTS RELATIVE TO COMPANIES

THIS chapter deals only with claims of damages by shareholders against the company, or its promoters or directors, or by the company against its promoters or directors, arising out of the relationships between promoters, directors, shareholders and the company, and not with claims by or against companies, against or at the instance of outsiders. The former are, and the latter are not, affected by these relationships and by certain provisions of the Companies Acts.

Formation of company

A promoter guilty of fraud towards the nascent company is liable to it in damages measured by the difference between the price paid by the company and the actual value of the property sold it at the date of sale,[1] or by the difference between the value of the property which the company would have acquired if the representations made had been accurate and the real value of the property at the time of purchase,[2] though the promoter may apparently show in mitigation of damages that the value even as represented was less than the sum paid.[3]

Misrepresentation in company prospectus

A person deceived by misrepresentation in a company prospectus is entitled at common law to rescind his contract to take shares, recover money paid in respect thereof, and, if the misrepresentation were made negligently or fraudulently,[3a] to recover damages. Rescission is conditional on ability to make restitution; if that is impossible rescission is impossible.[3b] A shareholder cannot, so long as he remains a member of the company, claim damages from it for a fraud which induced his membership [4] and if rescission of the contract to take shares should be impossible,[5] he can only claim damages against those directors personally responsible for the fraud.[6] In judging whether a statement was believed true or not the court must have regard to the sense in which a representation was understood, albeit erroneously, by the person making it.[6a]

1 *Erlanger* v. *New Sombrero Phosphate Co.* (1878) 3 App.Cas. 1218; *Gluckstein* v. *Barnes* [1900] A.C. 240; *Re Leeds and Hanley Theatre of Varieties* [1902] 2 Ch. 809.
2 *Twycross* v. *Grant* (1877) 2 C.P.D. 469, 544; *Arkwright* v. *Newbold* (1881) 17 Ch.D. 301; *Peek* v. *Derry* (1887) 37 Ch.D. 541; *Broome* v. *Speak* [1903] 1 Ch. 586.
3 *McConnel* v. *Wright* [1903] 1 Ch. 546.
3a As to what is fraud, see *Derry* v. *Peek* (1889) 14 App.Cas. 337.
3b *Houldsworth* v. *City of Glasgow Bank* (1880) 7 R.(H.L.) 53.
4 *Houldsworth, supra.*
5 *Addie* v. *Western Bank* (1867) 5 M.(H.L.) 80; *Houldsworth, supra.*
6 *Addie, supra.*
6a *Lees* v. *Tod* (1882) 9 R. 807, 854; *Derry* v. *Peek, supra*; *Angus* v. *Clifford* [1891] 2 Ch. 449; *Akerhielm* v. *de Mare* [1959] A.C. 789.

The proper measure of damages, which must be shown to be the actual loss to the pursuer himself,[7] is the loss sustained by acting on the false representations, namely, the difference between what he paid for the shares and what they were worth when allotted to him.[8] What they were worth is not necessarily their market value at that time, but their fair real value immediately after the day of allotment has to be ascertained [9]; there might be no market value or it might have been affected by the same misrepresentations, nor is the pursuer's claim to be affected by any subsequent loss or depreciation in the shares due to subsequent acts, nor again can they be increased if he has acted unreasonably.[10]

Statutory remedy

The action at common law has been largely superseded by the statutory remedy given originally under the Directors' Liability Act 1890, and now embodied in the Companies Act 1948, s. 43.[11] Under this (a) every director at the time of the issue of the prospectus; (b) every person who has authorised himself to be named and is so named therein as a director or as having agreed to become a director; (c) every promoter; and (d) every person who has authorised the issue of the prospectus; but not (e) an expert whose consent is requisite to the issue of the prospectus, except in so far as concerns statements purporting to be made by him, are liable [12] to pay compensation to all persons who subscribe [13] for any shares or debentures on the faith of the prospectus for loss they may have sustained by reason of any untrue statement therein. Liability depends on misstatement, irrespective of whether innocent, negligent or fraudulent.[14] Liability is cumulative with and not in substitution for the common law of fraud, though damages may not be recovered twice over.[14a] Damage occasioned by the misstatement must be proved [15] and the compensation is to be estimated by reference to the loss sustained and not as a penalty.[16] Under this section there is no claim against the company but only against the persons responsible, nor has the company a remedy thereunder against its promoters, though a claim under the section may be combined with a claim for rescission and the recovery of monies paid.[17]

The measure of compensation is the difference between the price paid

7 *Hyde* v. *Bulmer* (1868) 18 L.T. 293.
8 *Davidson* v. *Tulloch* (1860) 3 Macq. 783; *Arkwright* v. *Newbold* (1881) 17 Ch.D. 301, 312; *Peek* v. *Derry* (1887) 37 Ch.D. 541, 593 (revd. on another point (1889) 14 App.Cas. 337); *Arnison* v. *Smith* (1889) 41 Ch.D. 348, 363; *McConnel* v. *Wright* [1903] 1 Ch. 546; *cf.* *Twycross* v. *Grant* (1877) 2 C.P.D. 469; *Cackett* v. *Keswick* [1902] 2 Ch. 456.
9 *Peek* v. *Derry, supra*; *Davidson* v. *Hamilton* (1904) 12 S.L.T. 353.
10 *Peek, supra.*
11 For effect of the change, see *Geipel* v. *Peach* [1917] 2 Ch. 108, 114.
12 For defences open, see s. 43 (2) and (3).
13 *Peek* v. *Gurney* (1873) L.R. 6 H.L. 377; *Arnison* v. *Smith* (1889) 41 Ch.D. 348.
14 *Cackett* v. *Keswick* [1902] 2 Ch. 456; *Nash* v. *Calthorpe* [1905] 2 Ch. 237; *Macleay* v. *Tait* [1906] A.C. 24.
14a *Aaron's Reefs* v. *Twiss* [1896] A.C. 273.
15 *Shepheard* v. *Broome* [1904] A.C. 342; *Nash* v. *Calthorpe* [1905] 2 Ch. 237; *Macleay, supra.*
16 *Thomson* v. *Clanmorris* [1900] 1 Ch. 718, 726.
17 *Frankenburg* v. *Great Horseless Carriage Co.* [1900] 1 Q.B. 504.

for the shares or debentures and their real value at the date of allotment.[18] It is accordingly the same as the measure of damages in an action for fraud.[19] The statement must be untrue [20] but whether or not it was made fraudulently is immaterial,[21] but if true when the pursuer subscribed, the action is excluded, even though untrue when made.[22]

Failure to allot or take shares

The court has jurisdiction to order specific implement of the contract by an individual to take shares or by a company to allot shares.[23] The exercise of this jurisdiction is, however, a matter of judical discretion [24] and, in any event, if at the time of the action all the shares have been allotted, the only remedy available will be an award of damages.[25] The proper measure of damages, it is suggested, in the case of the company, for failure to take, will be the amount, if any, by which the value of the shares has fallen since the date of allotment; in the case of the individual, for failure to allot, the amount paid for the shares together with any rise in value since the due date of allotment. Where an order was made on the company to make specific performance, the only damages recoverable by the shareholder were the equivalent of the dividends at the rates declared by the company between the date when the shares should have been allotted and the date of actual allotment, with interest till payment.[26]

A person who without authority agrees to take shares on behalf of another is liable in damages for breach of warranty of authority, the measure of which is the amount which the company has lost by losing the contract to take shares.[27] Where the shares have become unsaleable this amounts to the nominal value of the shares.[27]

A company may give an option to a person to take all or any of its shares and this option may be exercised after winding up has commenced.[28] If the liquidator refuses to issue the shares, the measure of damages recoverable by the party in right of the option is the amount which he, as the holder of fully-paid shares, would have received as his share of assets, less the amount which he was due to pay for them.[28]

[18] *Davidson* v. *Tulloch* (1860) 3 Macq. 783; *Peek* v. *Derry* (1887) 37 Ch.D. 541, at p. 591; *Smith* v. *Moncrieff* (1894) 2 S.L.T. 140; *Broome* v. *Speak* [1903] 1 Ch. 586; affd. [1904] A.C. 342; *McConnel* v. *Wright* [1903] 1 Ch. 546 (but see *Clark*, *infra*, at p. 68); *Stevens* v. *Hoare* (1904) 20 T.L.R. 407; *Davidson* v. *Hamilton* (1904) 12 S.L.T. 353.

[19] *Clark* v. *Urquhart* [1930] A.C. 28.

[20] See 1948 Act, s. 46; *Broome, supra*; misleading statements are untrue even if not untrue in the sense of those who publish them: *Greenwood* v. *Leather Shod Wheel Co.* [1900] 1 Ch. 421; the material meaning is that conveyed: *Drincqbier* v. *Wood* [1899] 1 Ch. 393; *Greenwood, supra.*

[21] *Shepheard* v. *Broome* [1904] A.C. 342; *cf. Clark, supra.*

[22] *Ship* v. *Crosskill* (1870) L.R. 10 Eq. 73; *cf. McConnel, supra.*

[23] *Oriental Inland S.N. Co.* v. *Briggs* (1861) 31 L.J.Ch. 241; *Odessa Tramways Co.* v. *Mendel* (1878) 8 Ch.D. 235; *Beardmore* v. *Barry*, 1928 S.C. 101. As to debentures, see s. 92.

[24] *Beardmore, supra*; delay may disentitle a company: *Nicol's Case* (1885) 29 Ch.D. 421.

[25] *Ferguson* v. *Wilson* (1866) 2 Ch.App. 77.

[26] *Sri Lanka Omnibus Co.* v. *Perera* [1951] 2 T.L.R. 1184.

[27] *Re National Coffee Palace Co.* (1883) 24 Ch.D. 367.

[28] *Hirsch & Co.* v. *Burns* (1897) 77 L.T. 377 (H.L.).

Rectification of the register

The register of members may be rectified by the court if the name of any person is, without sufficient cause,[29] entered in or omitted from the register, or if default or unnecessary delay takes place in entering on the register the fact that any person has ceased to be a member,[30] or if it is necessary to enable the members of the company to have a fair and reasonable exercise of their rights.[31] The jurisdiction is discretionary.[32] If the court orders rectification of the register (but not if it refuses) the company may be ordered to pay damages [33] measured by the value of the shares at the time of the refusal to register.[34] Misrepresentation has sometimes been taken as a ground for an application to rectify the register.[35]

Transfer of shares

Unless directors have a discretion to refuse transferees of shares,[35a] the company will be liable in damages for the wrongful refusal to register a transferee.[36] Nominal damages only were given in the case cited but the transfer did not set out the true consideration and the company had no notice of a special agreement between seller and buyer. A company may, however, refuse to register a transfer inadequately stamped,[37] and frequently the articles give directors powers to refuse transfer in all or in certain cases. The proper measure of damages for a wrongful refusal to register a transfer of shares is the difference between the price of the shares when the transferee ultimately gets them and what he would have got for them if his transfer had been registered in due time, and he had realised them prudently as soon as he could do so after that time, yet at the same time without undue haste; regard must be had to the number of shares comprised in the transfer and the prices ruling at the time when it should have been registered and also all other surrounding circumstances.[38] Where a company delayed registration of a transfer on the ground of indebtedness to the company which was found not to exist, the transferor recovered nominal damages.[39]

Where directors have power under the articles [40] to refuse to register

[29] *Elliott* v. *Mackie*, 1935 S.C. 81.

[30] 1948 Act, s. 116 (1); *cf. Shepherd's Trs.* v. *Shepherd*, 1950 S.C.(H.L.) 60.

[31] *Burns* v. *Siemens Bros. Ltd.* [1919] 1 Ch. 225.

[32] *Ex p. Shaw* (1877) 2 Q.B.D. 463; *Re Kimberley Diamond Co.* (1888) 59 L.T. 579.

[33] *Re Ottos Kopje Diamond Mines Ltd.* [1893] 1 Ch. 618; *Skinner* v. *City of London Marine Insurance Corpn.* (1885) 14 Q.B.D. 882.

[34] *Re Ottos, supra.*

[35] *Blakiston* v. *London & Scottish Banking Co.* (1894) 21 R. 417; *Scottish Petroleum Co.* (1883) 23 Ch.D. 413; *Chambers* v. *Edinburgh & Glasgow Bread Co.* (1891) 18 R. 1039; *secus, Blaikie* v. *Coats* (1893) 21 R. 150; see also *Scottish Amalgamated Silks* v. *Macalister*, 1930 S.N. 121.

[35a] As in *Lyle & Scott* v. *Scott's Trs.*, 1959 S.C.(H.L.) 64.

[36] *Skinner* v. *City of London Marine Insurance Co.* (1885) 14 Q.B.D. 882.

[37] *Maynard* v. *Consolidated Kent Collieries* [1903] 2 K.B. 121.

[38] *Hooper* v. *Herts* [1906] 1 Ch. 549.

[39] *Skinner* v. *City of London Marine Insce. Corpn.* (1885) 14 Q.B.D. 882.

[40] *Cf.* 1948 Act, Sched. I, Table A, cl. 24.

transfers, either generally [41] or in certain cases [42] they are not bound to give reasons for their refusal and the court will presume that the discretion has been exercised in bona fide.[43] The power is, however, discretionary and fiduciary and on evidence that it has been exercised improperly, the court will intervene and may make an order for rectification of the register. Where the directors may exercise their power on several grounds, they must state on which ground they act unless excused by the articles.[44] If reasons are given the court may overrule the decision if the directors have acted on a wrong principle.[45]

Forged transfers

Companies are empowered by the Forged Transfers Acts 1891 and 1892 to make compensation by cash payments out of their funds for any loss arising from a transfer of their shares or stock in pursuance of a forged transfer or of a transfer under a forged power of attorney.[46] A company making compensation under these Acts for any loss arising from forgery, has the same right or remedy against the person liable for the loss as the person compensated would have had.[47] While the company must restore the original owner of the shares to the position he was in before the transfer was registered,[48] it is entitled to be indemnified by the person putting forward the forged transfer though acting innocently or without negligence.[49] Where a forged transfer has been registered, the transferee cannot compel the company to accept him as the owner of the shares.[50]

When a forgery is discovered the name of the transferee may be removed from the register, but he or a bona fide purchaser from him may recover damages from the company for loss sustained thereby.[51] The measure of damages for a bona fide transferee who thereby loses his shares is the value of the shares at the time of the company's refusal to register him or of their removal of his name from the register.[52]

Forfeiture of shares

The articles of a company generally contain provisions for the for-

[41] *Stevenson* v. *Wilson*, 1907 S.C. 445; *Cassel* v. *Inglis* [1916] 2 Ch. 211; *Weinberger* v. *Inglis* [1919] A.C. 606.
[42] *Coalport China Co.* [1895] 2 Ch. 404. The onus is on the person alleging that the refusal is wrongful: *Hannans King Mining Co.* (1898) 14 T.L.R. 314. See, too, *Stewart* v. *Keiller* (1902) 4 F. 657.
[43] *Berry* v. *Tottenham Hotspur F.C.* [1936] 3 All E.R. 554; *Re Smith and Fawcett Ltd.* [1942] Ch. 304.
[44] *Berry, supra.*
[45] *Skinner, supra.*
[46] Forged Transfers Act 1891, s. 1 (1), as explained by 1892 Act, s. 2.
[47] *Ibid.*, s. 1 (5).
[48] *Barton* v. *N. Staffordshire Ry.* (1888) 38 Ch.D. 458; *Sloman* v. *Bank of England* (1845) 14 Sim. 475.
[49] *Starkey* v. *Bank of England* [1903] A.C. 114; *Sheffield* v. *Barclay* [1905] A.C. 392; *Bank of England* v. *Cutler* [1908] 2 K.B. 208.
[50] *Simm* v. *Anglo-American Telegraph Co.* (1879) 5 Q.B.D. 188.
[51] *Re Bahia Co.* (1868) L.R. 3 Q.B. 595; *Balkis Consolidated Co.* v. *Tomkinson* [1893] A.C. 396; *Bloomenthal* v. *Ford* [1897] A.C. 156.
[52] *Re Ottos Kopje Diamond Mines* [1893] 1 Ch. 618; *Re Bahia, supra.*

feiture of shares for non-payment of calls or instalments.[53] Such a power is not inherent in a company [54] but only exists under the articles.[55] When given, directors exercising it do so in a fiduciary capacity, so collusion [56] and irregularity in its exercise, even slight, is fatal.[57] A clause as to forfeiture may be invalid if it is contrary to the policy of the law or infringes the shareholders' legal rights.[58] A shareholder whose shares have been irregularly forfeited can sue the company for damages, or rank for a claim of damages in a winding up.[59] The prima facie measure of damages is the value of the shares irregularly forfeited as at the date of forfeiture. If the directors are empowered to annul the forfeiture, they may only do so and reinstate the holder as a shareholder with his consent.[60]

Liability for fraud and delict

Directors are personally liable for frauds,[61] false reports,[62] and other delicts on the principle that a man is none the less liable because he was acting as agent of another,[63] and it makes no difference that the company is also liable therefor.[64] All the directors are each liable for the whole damage done with a right of relief, where all have concurred in authorising or instructing the wrongful act, but a director cannot be held responsible for a fraud of his fellow-directors unless he has authorised it expressly or impliedly,[65] but he may be, if he takes no steps to prevent a colleague's breach of trust.[66] Directors are not personally liable for the company's delicts unless they expressly directed the acts complained of, and even if they are the only shareholders.[67]

Liability of directors to company for negligence

A director will be liable in damages if he performs his duties negligently. So long as he acts honestly he cannot be made liable in damages unless

53 *Cf.* Table A, clauses 33–39.

54 *Clarke* v. *Hart* (1858) 6 H.L.C. 633.

55 *Dawkins* v. *Antrobus* (1881) 17 Ch.D. 615; *Allen* v. *Gold Reefs of West Africa* [1900] 1 Ch. 656.

56 *Spackman* v. *Evans* (1878) L.R. 3 H.L. 171.

57 *Garden Gully Co.* v. *McLister* (1876) 1 App.Cas. 39; *Johnson* v. *Lyttle's Iron Agency* (1877) 5 Ch.D. 687.

58 *Hope* v. *International Financial Socy.* (1876) 4 Ch.D. 327.

59 *Re New Chile Gold Co.* (1890) 45 Ch.D. 598.

60 *Larkworthy's Case* [1903] 1 Ch. 711.

61 *Supra*, p. 612.

62 *Scott* v. *Dixon* (1859) 29 L.J.Ex. 62n.

63 *Cullen* v. *Thompson's Trs.* (1862) 4 Macq. 424.

64 *Houldsworth* v. *City of Glasgow Bank* (1880) 7 R.(H.L.) 53; *National Exchange Co.* v. *Drew* (1855) 2 Macq. 103; *New Brunswick Ry.* v. *Conybeare* (1862) 9 H.L.C. 711; *Barwick* v. *English Joint Stock Bank* (1866) L.R. 2 Ex. 259.

65 *Cargill* v. *Bower* (1878) 10 Ch.D. 502. See also *Land Credit Co. of Ireland* v. *Fermoy* (1870) L.R. 5 Ch.App. 763; *Re Denham & Co.* (1883) 25 Ch.D. 752; *Dovey* v. *Cory* [1901] A.C. 477; *Prefontaine* v. *Grenier* [1907] A.C. 101; *Western Bank* v. *Bairds* (1862) 34 Sc.Jur. 435.

66 *Re Lands Allotment Co.* [1894] 1 Ch. 616.

67 *Rainham Chemical Works* v. *Belvedere Fish Guano Co.* [1921] 2 A.C. 465; *Performing Right Socy.* v. *Ciryl Theatrical Syndicate* [1924] 1 K.B. 1; *B.T.H. Co.* v. *Sterling Accessories Ltd.* [1924] 2 Ch. 33.

guilty of culpable negligence in a business sense.[68] In addition to acting honestly he must exercise some degree of both skill and diligence. He need not exhibit in the performance of his duties a greater degree of skill than may reasonably be expected from a person of his knowledge and experience and directors are not liable for mere errors of judgment.[69] A director need not attend all board meetings, though he ought to attend whenever in the circumstances he is reasonably able to do so.[70] Further, in the absence of ground for suspicion and having regard to the exigencies of the business, he is justified in trusting officials to perform honestly the duties which properly may be left to them.[71] Directors have a wide discretion and are not liable to be accused of negligence when acting honestly within it.[72] In judging of negligence the court will look at the character of the business, the number of directors, their ordinary course of management and practice and the whole circumstances of the case.[73]

Directors' breach of trust or misfeasance

Under these heads also a director may be personally liable, as for loss arising from wilful default or fraud, or culpable neglect of duty, or *ultra vires* actings.[74] All directors concerned are liable jointly and severally.[75] They are liable thereunder for applying the company's funds to *ultra vires* objects,[76] even though honestly but yet in error [77] or in ignorance of the misapplication.[78]

Measure of damages for directors' breach of trust

Where a company was fraudulently induced by a director to advance money to him on inadequate debenture security, the quantum of damages for that director's breach of duty was held to be the difference between the amount of money advanced and the value of the property obtained or the money realised therefrom, and this measure of damages is applicable whether the action be for fraudulent misrepresentation or for breach of

68 *Re City Equitable Fire Insce. Co.* [1925] Ch. 407. See also *Re Forest of Dean Co.* (1878) 10 Ch.D. 450; *Turquand* v. *Marshall* (1869) L.R. 4 Ch.App. 376; *Overend Gurney & Co.* v. *Gibb* (1872) L.R. 5 H.L. 480; *Lagunas Nitrate Co.* v. *Lagunas Syndicate* [1899] 2 Ch. 392; *Re National Bank of Wales* [1899] 2 Ch. 629; *Dovey* v. *Cory* [1901] A.C. 477.

69 *Marzetti's Case* (1880) 28 W.R. 541.

70 *Perry's Case* (1876) 34 L.T. 716.

71 *Addie* v. *Western Bank* (1865) 3 M. 899, 901; *Lees* v. *Tod* (1882) 9 R. 807; *Dovey* v. *Cory* [1901] A.C. 477.

72 *e.g. Re Liverpool Household Stores* (1890) 59 L.J.Ch. 616; *Re Forest of Dean Co.* (1878) 10 Ch.D. 450.

73 *Dovey* v. *Cory* [1901] A.C. 477; *Re City Equitable Fire Insce. Co.* [1925] Ch. 407.

74 *Tulloch* v. *Davidson* (1858) 3 Macq. 783; *Western Bank* v. *Douglas* (1860) 23 D. 447; *Western Bank* v. *Baird's Trs.* (1866) 4 M. 1071; (1872) 11 M. 96; *Caledonian Heritable Security Co.* v. *Curror's Trs.* (1882) 9 R. 1115.

75 *Ashurst* v. *Mason* (1875) L.R. 20 Eq. 225; *Brenes* v. *Downie*, 1914 S.C. 97; *Re London and S. Western Canal Co.* [1911] 1 Ch. 346. See also *Walsh* v. *Bardsley* (1931) 47 T.L.R. 564.

76 *Hirsche* v. *Sims* [1894] A.C. 654.

77 *Cullerne* v. *London Permanent Bldg. Socy.* (1890) 25 Q.B.D. 485; *Re Liverpool Household Stores Asscn.* (1890) 59 L.J.Ch. 616.

78 *Re National Funds Assce. Co.* (1878) 10 Ch.D. 118; *Joint Stock Discount Co.* v. *Brown* (1869) L.R. 8 Eq. 381.

duty.[79] Where one director applied company's funds to an *ultra vires* object it was held that he could not recover contribution from another who had assented to its misuse by signing the cheque where the money had been applied for the sole benefit of the director who claimed the contribution.[80] Contribution can be claimed, however, from the estate of a deceased fellow-director.[81]

Effect of exemption clauses in Articles of Association

It is not now competent to include in a company's Articles of Association a clause which will entirely protect directors from liability to the company.[82] Such clauses were formerly usual and were effective against " wilful default " [83] though not in the case of " act or default." [84] Section 205 of the Companies Act 1948 now renders void any such provision in the articles or by contract, which is designed to exempt any officer of the company (which includes a director) or auditor employed by the company from, or to indemnify him against, any liability which by virtue of any rule of law would otherwise attach to him in respect of any negligence, default, breach of duty or breach of trust. There are saving clauses for actings done while such an exemption was in force and for the right of a company to indemnify any officer or auditor from any liability incurred in defending proceedings, civil or criminal, in which judgment is given in his favour, or in which he is acquitted, or in connection with an application under section 448 of the Act.[85]

Statutory relief

Provision is made under section 448 of the Companies Act 1948 for the court relieving directors or other officers of a company in the case of proceedings for negligence, default, breach of duty or breach of trust. In such a case if it appears to the court that the officer is or may be liable but has acted " honestly and reasonably, and that, having regard to all the circumstances of the case, including the circumstances of his appointment, he ought fairly to be excused " the court may relieve him wholly or partly. To come within the scope of the section it is necessary to show not only that the director acted reasonably and honestly but in addition that he ought fairly to be excused.[86] The section has been held applicable

79 *Exploring Land & Min. Co.* v. *Kolckmann* (1906) 94 L.T. 234, 239, *per* Vaughan Williams L.J.
80 *Walsh* v. *Bardsley* (1931) 47 T.L.R. 564.
81 *Shepheard* v. *Bray* [1907] 2 Ch. 571.
82 As to construction, see *Tomlinson* v. *Liquidators of Scottish Amalgamated Silks*, 1935 S.C.(H.L.) 1.
83 *Re Brazilian Rubber Estates Ltd.* [1911] 1 Ch. 425; *Re City Equitable Fire Insurance Co.* [1925] Ch. 407; see also *Wilson* v. *Guthrie, Smith & Co.* (1894) 2 S.L.T. 338.
84 *Re City of London Insurance Co.* (1925) 41 T.L.R. 521.
85 *Vide infra, sub.* " statutory relief."
86 *Cf. National Trustee Co. of Australasia* v. *General Finance Co.* [1905] A.C. 373; *Re Smith, Smith* v. *Thompson* (1902) 71 L.J.Ch. 411; *Re Turner, Barker* v. *Ivimey* [1897] 1 Ch. 536; *Re Second Dulwich Building Socy.* (1899) 68 L.J.Ch. 196; *Re Grindey, Clews* v. *Grindey* [1898] 2 Ch. 593; *Perrins* v. *Bellamy* [1899] 1 Ch. 797; *Re Lord de Clifford* [1900] 2 Ch. 707; *Re City Equitable Fire Insce. Co.* [1925] 1 Ch. 407; *Selangor United Rubber Estates* v. *Cradock* [1968] 2 All E.R. 1073; *Re Duomatic Ltd.* [1969] 2 Ch. 365.

to *ultra vires* acts as where directors acted upon counsel's opinion that their acting was *intra vires*.[87]

Furthermore an officer may apply to the court for relief if he has reason to apprehend that a claim will or may be made against him in respect of such negligence and default and the court may relieve him as if the proceedings had been brought.

Other officers of company

Managers, secretaries and other officers are similarly placed to directors with regard to proceedings for negligence, default, breach of trust or breach of duty, and indemnity and relief in respect thereof.[88] Thus a secretary may not make a secret profit,[89] and a general manager is liable in damages if he commits such a breach of duty as causes a loss to the company.[90]

Liability in winding up

It is provided by section 332 of the 1948 Act that if it appears that any business of the company had been carried on with intent to defraud creditors,[91] persons knowingly parties to the carrying on of the business in that manner are to be personally liable and the court may so declare them, without limitation of liability, for all or any of the debts or liabilities of the company. The court's order must be for a definite amount, not necessarily limited to the extent of debts of the creditors defrauded by the actings in question.[92] The provision does not, however, create any new rights in any creditor.[93]

Under section 333 of the Act of 1948, if it appears in the course of winding up a company that a promoter, past or present director, manager, liquidator or other officer of the company is accountable for money or liable for misfeasance or breach of trust the court may examine his conduct and compel restoration of the money or property or part thereof, with interest at such rate as the court thinks just, or may order contribution of such sum by way of compensation as the court thinks just. It is the liquidator's duty to proceed under this section and the section has been invoked in such cases as the diversion of funds to objects not sanctioned by the memorandum,[94] the payment of dividends out of capital,[95] making

87 *Re Claridge's Patent Asphalte Co.* [1921] 1 Ch. 543.

88 Companies Act 1948, ss. 205, 448.

89 *McKay's Case* (1875) 2 Ch.D. 1; *cf. Boston Deep Sea Fishing Co.* v. *Ansell* (1888) 39 Ch.D. 339 (manager).

90 *Leeds Estate Building Co.* v. *Shepherd* (1887) 36 Ch.D. 787.

91 *Re Leitch Bros.* [1932] 2 Ch. 71; [1933] 1 Ch. 261; *Re Patrick and Lyon* [1933] Ch. 786.

92 *Re Leitch Bros.* [1932] 2 Ch. 71.

93 *Re Leitch Bros.* [1933] 1 Ch. 261.

94 *Cullerne* v. *London Building Socy.* (1890) 25 Q.B.D. 485; *Re Liverpool Household Stores* (1890) 59 L.J.Ch. 616; *Joint Stock Discount Co.* v. *Brown* (1869) L.R. 8 Eq. 381; *Hardy* v. *Metropolitan Land Co.* (1872) L.R. 7 Ch. 427; *Coats* v. *Crossland* (1904) 20 T.L.R. 800.

95 *Re National Funds Assce. Co.* (1872) 10 Ch.D. 118; *Flitcroft's Case* (1882) 21 Ch.D. 519; *Re Sharpe* [1892] 1 Ch. 154; *Moxham* v. *Grant* [1900] 1 Q.B. 88.

secret profits,[96] selling the director's own property to the company,[97] and neglect of duty by auditors.[97a]

The action is a personal one against the officer himself and does not apply as against his executors, at least in England.[98] The court's jurisdiction is discretionary [99] and it ceases to exist when the company is dissolved.[1]

96 *Hay's Case* (1875) L.R. 10 Ch. 593; *Carling's Case* (1875) 1 Ch.D. 115; *Pearson's Case* (1877) 5 Ch.D. 336.

97 *Re Cape Breton Co.* (1885) 29 Ch.D. 795.

97a *Re Thomas Gerrard & Son* [1968] Ch. 455.

98 *Felton's Exors. Case* (1865) L.R. 1 Eq. 219; *Re British Guardian Life Assce. Co.* (1880) 14 Ch.D. 335.

99 *Re Sunlight Gas Lamp Co.* (1900) 16 T.L.R. 535; *Re Home and Colonial Insce. Co.* [1930] 1 Ch. 102.

1 *Pulsford* v. *Devenish* [1903] 2 Ch. 625.

CHAPTER 37

CONTRACTS OF CAUTIONRY

IN entering into a cautionary obligation a party undertakes that, if another person primarily responsible for payment of a sum or performance of an obligation fails to implement his undertaking, the cautioner will do so.

Claims between debtor and cautioner

As between debtor and cautioner, the debtor may have a claim if a person, having undertaken to act as his cautioner, subsequently without justification goes back on his undertaking before having committed himself to the creditor, and if the debtor sustains any loss in consequence. The cautioner will have a claim of damages if he is induced by negligent or fraudulent misrepresentation in any material respect on the debtor's part to undertake the obligation, though as the obligation is with the creditor he will not be able to rescind that contract unless the misrepresentation were made by the creditor.[1] The creditor is not bound to disclose the full nature or extent of the debtor's liability to him as a proposed cautioner, it being for the latter to make his own inquiries.[2] But if he does so, it must be a fair and honest disclosure, and failure to make such a disclosure will release the cautioner and give him a claim for any loss sustained. And a creditor has been held bound to disclose to cautioners that the principal debtor had defaulted previously.[3]

The cautioner has no claim of damages against the principal debtor if he is called on to pay the creditor, because that is precisely the obligation which he undertook, but he has a claim for relief against the principal debtor for all he has paid.[4]

Claims between creditor and cautioner

If on the primary debtor's default the creditor makes a claim on the cautioner the claim is one for payment or performance, not for damages. The cautioner has probably not impliedly undertaken to be solvent and able to satisfy the creditor's contingent claim, so that he is not in breach or liable in damages if he is himself unable to satisfy the creditor's claim.[5] That is the creditor's misfortune.

[1] Bell, *Prin.* § 251; *French* v. *Cameron* (1893) 20 R. 966; *Wallace's Factor* v. *McKissock* (1898) 25 R. 642. *Cf. Young* v. *Clydesdale Bank Ltd.* (1889) 17 R. 231; *Thin & Sinclair* v. *Arrol* (1896) 24 R. 198.

[2] *Young, supra.*

[3] *Smith* v. *Bank of Scotland* (1829) 7 S. 244; *Railton* v. *Matthews* (1844) 3 Bell 56; *French, supra.*

[4] Bell, *Prin.* § 255.

[5] *Cf. Calder & Co.* v. *Cruikshank's Tr.* (1889) 17 R. 74 where debtor and cautioner both sequestrated.

CHAPTER 38

CONTRACTS OF INSURANCE

INSURANCE is a contract to indemnify against possible or probable loss, in consideration of a sum or premium paid, or held to be paid.[1] The contract is one *uberrimae fidei* and may be rescinded by the insurer not only for misrepresentation, fraudulent or innocent, but for non-disclosure of any fact which should have been considered relevant for the consideration of a prudent insurer, or for inaccurate answer to any question in the proposal for insurance, the accuracy of which was warranted.[2] If the contract is found to be voidable only after a claim has been satisfied, the insurer can probably recover it under the principle of repetition.

A breach of a stipulation which is not a condition of the policy does not affect the validity of the policy or the insurer's liability,[3] but does give a claim of damages.[4]

Claim under policy

In the event of a loss occurring from any of the kinds of risks insured against the claim which the insured may make is a claim for implement of the policy, not a claim for damages. This claim is quite distinct from and without prejudice to any claim of damages which the assured may have against a third party for having caused the loss, and such a claim is unaffected by his being insured.[5] If the insurer pays he is subrogated to the insured's rights and has the same right as the insured had to sue any wrongdoer who caused the loss and recover damages from him, or to recover from the insured any damages paid to him.[6]

Failure or refusal to pay claim

An unjustified failure or refusal to satisfy a claim brought under a policy is a breach of contract justifying an award of damages, the loss being measured by the sum which should properly have been paid as fair and reasonable indemnity under the policy for the loss sustained.[7]

1 Bell, *Prin.* § 457.
2 *Standard Life Assoc. Co.* v. *Weems* (1884) 11 R.(H.L.) 51.
3 *Ballantine* v. *Employer's Insurance Co.* (1893) 21 R. 305.
4 *London Guarantee Co.* v. *Fearnley* (1880) 5 App.Cas. 911; *Re Coleman's Depositories Ltd. and Life and Health Assce. Association* [1907] 2 K.B. 798.
5 *Port Glasgow & Newark Sailcloth Co.* v. *Caledonian Ry.* (1893) 20 R.(H.L.) 35.
6 *Simpson* v. *Thompson* (1877) 5 R.(H.L.) 40.
7 *Cf. Ballantine, supra.*

CHAPTER 39

CONTRACTS TO PAY MONEY EVIDENCED BY BONDS, BILLS OR CHEQUES

WHERE one party has promised orally to pay money, or has undertaken, by granting a personal bond or promissory note or accepting a bill of exchange, to do so, and has failed to do so, he is in breach of contract, and is liable to an action for payment, and for interest for failure to pay as undertaken.

Oral undertaking to pay

An oral undertaking to pay, which, if gratuitous, must be proved by the defender's writ or admission on oath,[1] justifies a demand for payment, with interest in the event of delay.

Personal bond

A personal bond commonly binds the granter to pay, or repay, the stated sum "with one fifth part more of liquidate penalty in case of failure" and, so long as the principal sum is outstanding, interest at a stated rate. It is settled that such a penalty provision covers only the actual expenses of obtaining payment and any loss and damage incurred by the creditor by reason of the debtor's default.[1a] If a fixed period has been agreed upon neither can the creditor demand payment nor can the debtor insist on payment before the due date.[1b]

Promissory note

A promissory note is an unconditional promise in writing made by one person to another signed by the maker, engaging to pay, on demand or at a fixed or determinable future time, a sum certain in money, to, or to the order of, a specified person or to bearer.[2] The provisions of the Bills of Exchange Act 1882 apply with exceptions and necessary modifications to promissory notes.[2a] A note may be expressly made payable with interest in which case, unless it provides otherwise, interest runs from the date of the bill, and if the bill is undated from the issue thereof.[2b]

Accordingly if a promissory note is dishonoured by non-payment on

[1] *Millar* v. *Tremamondo* (1771) Mor. 12395; *Smith* v. *Oliver*, 1911 S.C. 103.

[1a] See *e.g. Gordon* v. *Maitland* (1761) Mor. 10050; *Young* v. *Sinclair* (1796) Mor. 10053; *Orr* v. *Mackenzie* (1839) 1 D. 1046; *Bruce* v. *Scottish Amicable Life Assurance Socy.*, 1907 S.C. 637.

[1b] *Ashburton* v. *Escombe* (1892) 20 R. 187.

[2] Bills of Exchange Act 1882, s. 83 (1).

[2a] *Ibid.* s. 89.

[2b] *Ibid.* s. 9 (3).

demand or at the fixed or determinate future time stated therein as the time for payment an immediate right of recourse against the maker arises. The measure of damages is provided by section 57 of the Act,[2c] made applicable to notes by section 89(2) thereof.

Bills of exchange

"A bill of exchange is an unconditional order in writing, addressed by one person to another, signed by the person giving it, requiring the person to whom it is addressed to pay on demand or at a fixed or determinable future time a sum certain in money to or to the order of a specified person, or to bearer." [2d] The effect of drawing a bill payable to a third person is a contract by the drawer to pay the payee (the third person), if the acceptor does not. The effect of acceptance by the person to whom the bill is addressed is a contract to pay the payee. The effect of indorsing is a contract to pay the immediate or any succeeding payee if the acceptor defaults.

Measure of damages

Under the Bills of Exchange Act 1882 statutory provision is made as to the measure of damages recoverable against the parties to a dishonoured bill. Section 57 lays down as follows:

> " Where a bill is dishonoured,[3] the measure of damages, which shall be deemed to be liquidate damages, shall be as follows:—
>
> (1) The holder may recover from any party liable on the bill, and the drawer who has been compelled to pay the bill may recover from the acceptor, and an indorser who has been compelled to pay the bill may recover from the acceptor or from the drawer, or from a prior indorser [3a]—
>
> (*a*) The amount of the bill:
>
> (*b*) Interest thereon from the time of presentment for payment if the bill is payable on demand,[4] and from the maturity of the bill in any other case [5] :
>
> (*c*) The expenses of noting, or when protest is necessary,[6] and the protest has been extended, the expenses of protest.
>
> (2) In the case of a bill which has been dishonoured abroad,[7] in lieu of the above damages, the holder may recover from the drawer or an indorser, and the drawer or an indorser who has been compelled to pay the bill may recover from any party

[2c] Quoted *infra*.
[2d] Bills of Exchange Act 1882, s. 3 (1).
[3] As to non-acceptance, see s. 43; non-payment, s. 47.
[3a] See *McCall Ltd.* v. *Hargreaves* [1932] 2 K.B. 423.
[4] *Re East of England Banking Co.* (1868) L.R. 4 Ch. 14.
[5] *Laing* v. *Stone* (1828) 2 M. & Ry. 562.
[6] In the case of a foreign bill only.
[7] The holder of such a bill has no option to claim under subs. 1, *supra*: *Re Commercial Bank of S. Australia* (1887) 36 Ch.D. 522.

liable to him, the amount of the re-exchange [8] with interest thereon until the time of payment.[9]

(3) Where by this Act interest may be recovered as damages, such interest may, if justice require it, be withheld wholly or in part,[10] and where a bill is expressed to be payable with interest at a given rate, interest as damages may or may not be given at the same rate as interest proper." [11]

By section 89 these provisions apply with the necessary modifications to promissory notes.[12] Under section 73 the provisions of the Act applicable to a bill of exchange payable on demand apply to a cheque. Despite this section it has been held that substantial damages are recoverable from a bank failing to honour a customer's cheque, though no actual proof of resulting injury to the latter's credit is necessary.[13]

Damages in cases of banker and customer

When a cheque is presented to a banker for payment and is dishonoured, the banker is liable to the customer in damages [14] if he had sufficient funds in his hands to meet the cheque, unless the funds were paid into the credit too late for the banker to have been able with reasonable diligence to discover the state of the account.[15] In England it has been held that the damages will be only nominal [16] unless special damage be proved [17] or unless the customer is a trader.[17] In England, however, it has also been laid down that the jury should give moderate damages as reasonable compensation for the injury the plaintiff must have sustained from his cheque having been dishonoured,[18] and substantial damages may still be awarded even if the dishonoured cheque is paid the following day.[19] A banker has been held liable when, although the cash balance was against the customer, he held securities and in a previous course of dealing of the same nature cheques had been paid.[20]

Interest

Where interest is expressly provided for in the bill it runs, unless the instrument provides otherwise, from the date of the bill or, if undated,

8 Explained in *Byles on Bills*, 20th ed., 335–336.
9 *Re Commercial Bank of S. Australia* (1887) 36 Ch.D. 522, 538.
10 See *Webster* v. *British Empire Co.* (1880) 15 Ch.D. 169, 175.
11 4 per cent. given: *Re Commercial Bank, supra*; *Keene* (1857) 3 C.B.(N.S.) 144; *Riches* v. *Westminster Bank, Ltd.* [1943] 2 All E.R. 725.
12 *Hope Johnstone* v. *Cornwall* (1895) 22 R. 314.
13 *King* v. *British Linen Co.* (1899) 1 F. 928; *Wilson* v. *United Counties Bank* [1920] A.C. 102; *Rolin* v. *Steward* (1854) 14 C.B. 595.
14 *Marzetti* v. *Williams* (1830) 1 B. & Ad. 415; *Gray* v. *Johnston* (1868) L.R. 3 H.L. 1, 14; *Greenwood* v. *Martins Bank* [1933] A.C. 51.
15 *Whitaker* v. *Bank of England* (1835) 1 C.M. & R. 744, 749.
16 *Gibbons* v. *Westminster Bank* (1939) 55 T.L.R. 888; *Marzetti, supra.*
17 *Gibbons, supra. Cf. Davidson* v. *Barclays Bank* [1940] 1 All E.R. 316.
18 *Rolin* v. *Steward* (1854) 14 C.B. 595, 599; verdict for £500 modified by court. But not if the cheque is payable to self: *Kinlan* v. *Ulster Bank* [1928] Ir.R. 171.
19 *Fleming* v. *Bank of New Zealand* [1900] A.C. 577.
20 *Cumming* v. *Shand* (1860) 29 L.J.Ex. 129.

from its issue,[20a] and is recoverable as interest, and not as damages, and every drawer or indorser is liable to pay that interest at the rate specified, as it is an integral part of the debt contracted to be paid and recoverable as such.[21] It does not matter where subsequent indorsements of the bill have been made. If, however, interest is expressly reserved in the bill but no rate is specified the rule is probably that the rate falls to be determined by the *lex loci contractus*, unless it can be shown that another law such as the *lex loci solutionis* was in contemplation. If the bill is expressed to be payable with interest, it runs from the date of the bill or, if undated, from the issue thereof.[22]

It has been held that the renewal of promissory notes given in security of a loan does not discharge the claim for interest from the date of the loan.[23]

Where interest is not payable by the terms of the bill, it is of the nature of damages and due under section 57 (3). Interest on the principal sum in the bill is then the normal form of damages for the dishonour of a bill [24]: independently of this the bill may have been expressed as to be payable with interest.[25] The distinction between the two kinds of interest is material from the point of view of calculating the precise sum due. The true principle would appear to be that interest payable in terms of the bill down to the date of payment or maturity falls to be added to the principal sum before addition of the interest due as liquidate damages for dishonour in terms of section 57, thereby in effect allowing interest upon interest.[26] If this is not the true interpretation and interest as damages is to be calculated on the original principal sum, there is no provision under the Act for the recovery of the contractual interest.

Interest payable as damages runs, in terms of section 57 (1) (*b*), from the time of presentment for payment if payable on demand, or from the date of maturity otherwise.[27] Interest as damages runs till final decree.[28]

If a bill be drawn payable by instalments and the whole balance to become due on the failure of any instalment, it has been held that the interest is to be calculated upon the whole amount which remains due after the failure rather than upon the individual instalments at the time when they would otherwise have become payable.[29]

By section 57 (3) interest as damages is subject to the discretionary control of the court and may be withheld.

20a 1882 Act, s. 9 (3).
21 *Hudson* v. *Fossett* (1844) 13 L.J.C.P. 141.
22 1882 Act, s. 9 (3).
23 *Hope Johnstone, supra.*
24 *Ex p. Williams* (1813) 1 Rose 399; *Du Belloix* v. *Waterpark* (1822) 1 Dow. & Ry. 16.
25 Bills of Exchange Act 1882, s. 9 (3); *Roffey* v. *Greenwell* (1839) 10 A. & E. 222. This is merely declaratory of common law.
26 *Cf. Watkins* v. *Morgan* (1834) 6 C. & P. 661; *Hudson* v. *Fossett* (1844) 13 L.J.C.P. 141.
27 *Upton* v. *Ferrers* (1801) 5 Ves. 801.
28 *Robinson* v. *Bland* (1760) 2 Burr. 1077, 1088. Interest and expenses were due in Scotland under the Act, 1681, c. 20.
29 *Blake* v. *Lawrence* (1802) 4 Esp. 147.

Rate of interest

The rate of interest to be awarded as damages will, in the absence of contrary provision, be calculated at the rate customary in the place according to whose laws the bill is payable. In England bills and notes bear interest at 5 per cent.[30] and it is conceived that the rule in Scotland is the same but a lesser rate has been given.[31] Otherwise it falls to be determined as a question of fact what is the current rate according to the *lex loci solutionis.* It has been held that a higher rate than Scottish legal interest is allowed on bills payable in a foreign country where " legal interest " is at a higher rate than 5 per cent.[32]

Re-exchange

Re-exchange is the measure of damage sustained by the holder of a dishonoured bill, drawn in one country on a person in another, and is payable in addition to the amount of the bill.[33]

It is the damage accruing from the dishonour of the bill in a foreign country and the necessity of having recourse back on the place of drawing. The existence and amount of it depend on the rate of exchange between the two countries. It may arise in two ways: by a redraft or bill drawn at sight by the payee from the place of payment back upon the drawer, or one of the indorsers for the amount which will yield what he should have got for the dishonoured bill; or by the accumulation of the exchange of the several countries through which the bill may have been negotiated.[34] By section 57 (2) the amount of re-exchange with interest is the alternative measure of damages applicable to the case of a bill dishonoured abroad. The rule has been laid down [35] that the drawer must answer for all the direct damage accruing from the dishonour of his bill: it matters not how many hands the bill has passed through nor how much accumulation of exchange charges has taken place: the drawer, by making himself liable for the acceptor, makes himself liable for the acceptor's default also,[36] and the same rule applies to an indorser.[37] There is some doubt as to an acceptor: he is generally held liable by the law of England,[38] though there are contrary authorities. There is no Scottish decision; Bell's *Principles,* § 342, states that the acceptor is not liable but the *Commentaries* are uncertain.[39]

30 *Upton* v. *Ferrers* (1801) 5 Ves. 803; *Ward* v. *Morrison* (1842) Car. & M. 368.
31 *Re Commercial Bank of S. Australia* (1887) 36 Ch.D. 522; *Riches* v. *Westminster Bank* [1943] 2 All E.R. 725.
32 *Fyffe* v. *Fergusson* (1838) 16 S. 1038; (1841) 2 Rob.App. 267.
33 *Willans* v. *Ayers* (1877) 3 App.Cas. 133.
34 Bell, *Comm.* I, 430. See also Byles on *Bills,* 22nd ed., 335; *cf. Strickland* v. *Neilson* (1869) 7 M. 400.
35 Bell, *supra.*
36 *Mellish* v. *Simeon* (1794) 2 H.Bl. 378.
37 *Auriol* v. *Thomas* (1787) 2 T.R. 52; 1882 Act, s. 57.
38 *Francis* v. *Rucker* (1768) Amb. 671; *Walker* v. *Hamilton* (1860) 1 De G.F. & J. 602; *Re General S. American Co.* (1876) 7 Ch.D. 637.
39 See the authorities for and against collected in Bell, *Comm.* I, 431, note 7.

As well as the actual amount of the bill and interest thereon from the date of protest, re-exchange necessarily includes the expenses of protest, of bank commission, of the stamp if a redraft is drawn on the original drawer, the cost of travelling to obtain payment and postages when these are necessarily incurred,[40] but not the costs of a protest for better security,[41] nor, where the claim is on the bill itself and not by way of re-exchange, the banker's commission, costs of brokerage, stamp, or postages.[42]

Re-exchange otherwise than under the Act

Although by the terms of section 57 (2) the provisions as to re-exchange are only applicable to bills dishonoured abroad, it has been held in England that where a bill has been drawn abroad payable in England and when the drawer was liable, by the law of the country where it was drawn, to pay to the holder damages for re-exchange if the bill is not paid by the acceptor, the drawer could recover from the acceptor any re-exchange paid: if the drawer has not paid it, he can rank in the bankruptcy of the acceptor in respect of the contingent liability for re-exchange charges.[43] Exceptionally banker's commission, brokerage, and postage have been disallowed as items in re-exchange.[44] Where the holder of a bill is liable to re-exchange his remedy against other parties to the bill who are liable to indemnify him is always under section 57 (2) and not section 57 (1).[45]

Expenses other than those allowed under section 57 (1) or (2) are probably not recoverable unless there is a special contract to pay them.[46] In *Prehn* v. *Royal Bank of Liverpool* [47] an action was brought while bills were still current for refusing to honour acceptances of the plaintiff's drafts, and banker's commission and telegraphic expenses were allowed as damages flowing naturally from the defendant's breach of contract, but it would have been otherwise if the action had been brought on the acceptances themselves, though these expenses would probably have been recoverable if the defendants had been liable for re-exchange.

Conflict of laws

The provisions of the Act governing cases of conflict of laws are contained in section 72. This section is not, however, exhaustive and has been adversely criticised by some authorities. It is sometimes stated that the place at which any party to a bill undertakes that he will pay it determines the system of law which will govern his liability,[48] and hence the amount of interest payable by him as damages in the event of default.[49]

[40] *Re Commercial Bank of S. Australia* (1887) 36 Ch.D. 522, 528.
[41] *Re English Bank of River Plate* [1893] 2 Ch. 438, 445.
[42] *Banque Populaire de Bienne* v. *Cavé* (1895) 1 Com.Cas. 67.
[43] *Re Gillespie, ex p. Robarts* (1886) 18 Q.B.D. 286.
[44] *Banque Populaire de Bienne* v. *Cavé* (1895) 1 Com.Cas. 67.
[45] *Re Commercial Bank of South Australia* (1887) 36 Ch.D. 522.
[46] *Banque Populaire de Bienne* v. *Cavé* (1895) 1 Com.Cas. 67.
[47] (1870) L.R. 5 Ex. 92, 97.
[48] See *Bank Polski* v. *Mulder* [1942] 1 K.B. 497.
[49] Byles, 22nd ed., 321; Chalmers, 13th ed., 189.

So in *Cooper* v. *Waldegrave* [50] a bill was drawn, indorsed and accepted in France but payable in England: it was held in an action against the acceptor that he was liable for interest at the rate specified by English law. Had the action been against the drawer on the acceptor's default, the liability to interest would have been at the rate ruling in France. This question is material in the case where a bill is drawn in one country and indorsed in another, whether the liability of an indorser is to be ascertained according to the law of the initial country or origin or that of the indorser's country.[51] The balance of English authority is in favour of the latter.[52]

The question of choice of law with regard to the measure of damages is not, however, expressly dealt with in the Bills of Exchange Act but the courts have generally treated the measure of damages recoverable under a bill of exchange or a note as a matter of substantive law.[53] The damages recoverable from a party to a bill or note are accordingly determined by the proper law of the contract made by that party.[54] Hence the rate of interest which a drawer must pay to a drawee in the event of dishonour is determined by the law governing the contract between drawer and payee, and not by the law governing the acceptance.[55] It is a matter of doubt whether for these purposes the proper law of the contract is the *lex loci contractus* or the *lex loci solutionis*, probably the latter.[56]

A party to a bill who pays damages under the law governing his liability may recover indemnity in damages from another party to the bill so far as the law governing their contract allows him to do so, which may include the amount of damages already paid by the claimant under the law regulating his own liability.

Measure of damages

It may be that the law applicable to a party in default on a bill is the law of the place at which he has undertaken that he will pay, which is generally, unless in the case of an acceptor, the place where he made the contract. An indorser might in consequence be liable for a higher rate of interest than he could recover elsewhere from the drawer,[57] or the drawer for a higher rate than he could recover from the acceptor.

50 (1840) 2 Beav. 282. See also *Allen* v. *Kemble* (1848) 6 Moo.P.C. 314, 321; *Gibbs* v. *Fremont* (1853) 9 Ex. 25.

51 *Gibbs, supra.*

52 *Cooper, supra*; *Allen, supra*; see also *Hirschfeld* v. *Smith* (1866) L.R. 1 C.P. 340; *Level* v. *Tucker* (1867) 8 B. & S. 830.

53 Dicey and Morris on *Conflict of Laws*, 8th ed., 841.

54 *Re Gillespie, ex p. Robarts* (1886) 18 Q.B.D. 286, 292; *Re Commercial Bank of S. Australia* (1887) 36 Ch.D. 522, 525; Chalmers' *Bills of Exchange Act, 1882*, 11th ed., p. 238.

55 *Allen* v. *Kemble* (1848) 6 Moo.P.C. 314; *Gibbs* v. *Fremont* (1853) 9 Ex. 25.

56 Dicey and Morris, 842, quoting *Gibbs, supra*; Chalmers, 238.

57 Story on *Conflict of Laws*, 8th ed., s. 314, quoted in Byles, 22nd ed., 321. See *Allen* v. *Kemble* (1848) 6 Moo.P.C. 314; *Gibbs* v. *Fremont* (1853) 9 Ex. 25.

CHAPTER 40

CONTRACTS OF LOAN, DEPOSIT, CUSTODY AND PLEDGE

COMMODATUM—PROPER LOAN

THE first kind of loan, *commodatum*, is the proper loan of goods, such as a vehicle or a book, for use.[1] The property in the goods rests with the lender, the borrower being obliged to restore the particular thing lent at the end of the agreed period of loan, or on demand, or after a reasonable time.

Lender's claim

While he has the goods on loan the borrower is liable in damages for loss, whether accidental or negligent, while using the goods in any way exceeding the terms, express or implied, of the loan,[2] but not for ordinary wear and tear,[3] damage by third parties,[4] or inevitable accidents, if occurring within the scope of the use contemplated in the loan.[5] If the thing cannot be returned as it was, fair wear and tear excepted, the onus is on the borrower to show that he exercised all reasonable care, failing which he must pay damages, measured by the diminution in value, if the thing be damaged,[6] or its full pre-loan value if it be lost altogether or rendered useless.[7] He is also liable in damages for delaying to return the thing borrowed at the expiry of the agreed period, or after a request to return it, or in any event after a reasonable time for the contemplated use has elapsed, which may be measured by the reasonable cost of hiring a replacement if such were necessary or, if not, by a nominal sum for the inconvenience of not having the thing lent.

Borrower's claim

The lender will be liable to the borrower for loss, injury or damage caused to him by known defect in the thing lent,[8] so long as occurring in connection with the use for which the thing was lent,[9] or a use subsequently authorised by the lender, but not for loss caused by unknown defect, nor

[1] Bell, *Comm.* I, 275; *Prin.* §§ 194–199; Walker, *Prin.* Chap. 38.
[2] *Bain* v. *Strang* (1888) 16 R. 186; *Douglas* v. *Colvill* (1905) 13 S.L.T. 665.
[3] *Blakemore* v. *Bristol and Exeter Ry.* (1858) 8 E. & B. 1035, 1051.
[4] *Claridge* v. *S. Staffs Tramways Co.* [1892] 1 Q.B. 422.
[5] *Colville* v. *Fleming* (1693) 1 Fount. 712; *Buchanan* v. *Baillie* (1696) 1 Fount. 712.
[6] *Bain, supra*; *cf. Sutherland* v. *Hutton* (1896) 23 R. 718; *Bullen* v. *Swan Electric Co.* (1906) 22 T.L.R. 276; *Wiehe* v. *Dennis Bros.* (1913) 24 T.L.R. 250.
[7] *Douglas, supra.*
[8] *MacCarthy* v. *Young* (1861) 6 H. & N. 329; *Coughlin* v. *Gillison* [1899] 1 Q.B. 145.
[9] *Blakemore, supra*; *Coughlin, supra.*

for loss occurring in connection with or caused by unauthorised or improper use, as where something lent breaks under an excessive load.

MUTUUM—IMPROPER LOAN

In the second kind of loan, *mutuum*,[10] loan for consumption, as of bread or petrol, the property in the subject lent passes to the borrower, whose obligation is to return an equal quantity of the same kind and quality of thing, without regard to market value, at the agreed time, or on demand, or after a reasonable time.[11]

Lender's claim

The property in the thing lent passes to the borrower and any loss or damage falls on the borrower but he must nevertheless replace what he has borrowed.[12] If the equivalent of the subject of loan is not returned at the due time or after a reasonable time, the primary remedy is an action for delivery, with an alternative conclusion for damages, representing the value of the thing which should have been given in return.

Borrower's claim

The borrower probably has a claim for loss, injury or damage caused him by the borrowed thing if the lender knew, or should have known, that it was dangerous, provided the thing is used for a purpose contemplated in the borrowing, but not if he used it for an uncontemplated purpose.

The commonest case of mutuum is loan of money, in which case interest is due *ex lege* from the date of the loan [13] unless there is ground in equity for holding that interest was not intended to be payable.[14] Interest is frequently due by express stipulation. If there is default in repayment the remedy is an action for payment of principal and unpaid interest, with interest thereon until paid.

DEPOSIT

In case of gratuitous deposit,[15] the depositary must provide a safe place of custody [16] and take reasonable care to prevent damage to or loss of the goods while in his charge.[17] A rather lower standard of care is demanded in the case of gratuitous deposit than of onerous custody.[18]

10 Stair I, 11, 5; Ersk. III, 1, 18; Bell, *Prin.* §§ 200–202.
11 *Anderson* v. *Crompton* (1870) 9 M. 122, 126.
12 Bell, *Prin.* § 201.
13 *Cunninghame* v. *Boswell* (1868) 8 M. 890.
14 Bell, *Comm.* I, 691; *Prin.* § 32.
15 Stair I, 13, 1; Ersk. III, 1, 26; Bell, *Comm.* I, 277; *Prin.* §§ 210–215.
16 *Searle* v. *Laverick* (1874) L.R. 9 Q.B. 122; *Smith* v. *Cook* (1876) 1 Q.B.D. 79; *McLean* v. *Warnock* (1883) 10 R. 1052.
17 Bell, *Prin.* § 212; *Allen & Pointer* v. *Williamson* (1870) 7 S.L.R. 214; *Gibson & Stewart* v. *Brown* (1876) 3 R. 328; *Snodgrass* v. *Ritchie & Lamberton* (1890) 17 R. 712; *Ballingall* v. *Dundee Ice Co.*, 1924 S.C. 238, 243.
18 Stair I, 13, 2; *Coggs* v. *Bernard* (1703) 2 Ld. Raym. 909; *Ronneberg* v. *Falkland Islands Co.* (1864) **17** C.B. (N.S.) 1; *Giblin* v. *McMullen* (1868) L.R. 2 P.C. 317.

Depositor's claim

If the goods are lost, destroyed or damaged while in the depositary's custody he is liable only if he has failed to take the care of the property which a prudent man would have taken of his own.[19] He is not liable for loss or damage caused by the acts of third parties,[20] unless there were gross negligence on his part.[21] The measure of damages is the diminution in value of the thing, or its total value if it be wholly destroyed.

Depositary's claim

If the goods deposited cause harm or injury to the depositary or his property,[22] or to the property of another deposited in the same place,[23] as by leaking or taking fire, the depositor is prima facie liable for the damage done.

Involuntary deposit

The finder of lost property [24] who takes it into his care constitutes himself an involuntary depositary, and is liable to the true owner in all the obligations thereof,[25] though a rather lesser standard of care may be expected from him than from a voluntary depositary. He may probably also be regarded as a *negotiorum gestor*.[26]

LOCATIO CUSTODIAE

The contract of custody for reward [27] covers cases of express deposit for reward, as of warehousing goods, storing furniture, and leaving articles in a left-luggage office; and also all cases where, under a contract *locatio operis faciendi*, goods are necessarily left with the contractor that work may be done on them, in which case the contract implies a *locatio custodiae* as an inherent element thereof.[28]

Owner's claim

A custodier for reward must use due care and diligence, such as a careful and vigilant man would use in the custody of his own goods in similar circumstances,[29] and greater care than is demanded of a gratuitous depositary. He is liable for deliberate or negligent loss or damage, but

19 *McLean, supra.*
20 *Giblin, supra.*
21 *Giblin, supra.*
22 *Ibid.*
23 *Sutherland* v. *Hutton* (1896) 23 R. 718.
24 See Burgh Police (Sc.) Act 1893, s. 412; Lost Property (Sc.) Act 1965, s. 1.
25 *Newman* v. *Bourne & Hollingsworth* (1915) 31 T.L.R. 209. *Cf. Clayton* v. *Le Roy* [1911] 2 K.B. 1031.
26 *Cf.* Chap. 50, *infra.*
27 Walker, *Prin.* Chap. 45.
28 *Sinclair* v. *Juner*, 1952 S.C. 35; *cf. XYZ* v. *Kennedy* (1946) 62 Sh.Ct.Rep. 117.
29 Bell, *Prin.* § 155; *Coggs* v. *Bernard* (1703) 2 Ld.Raym. 909; *Sinclair* v. *Juner*, 1952 S.C. 35.

not for harm attributable to inevitable accident [30] or to acts of third parties or their servants.[31] He must take reasonable care to see that the storage premises are fit [32] and free from patent danger to the goods,[33] and that the goods are kept properly,[34] inspected periodically,[35] protected against unexpected dangers,[36] recovered if stolen,[37] and the depositor's interest maintained against adverse claims.[38] A depositary is not entitled to sub-contract the care; if he does he remains liable for loss or damage, without recourse against the sub-contractor.

If loss or damage takes place the onus is on the custodier to disprove lack of due care, precautions and diligence [39] though he is not bound to prove the precise cause of the damage.[40] He is not liable for inevitable accident, but fire is not always an inevitable accident,[41] nor for act of the Queen's enemies, or the owner's own fault.[41] He is, of course, liable for the default or negligence of his agents or servants when acting within the scope of their authority or employment.[42]

If there is liability the custodier is liable for the diminution in the value of goods damaged or the full value of goods lost or ruined.[43]

Contracts for custody commonly limit or exclude liability or impose limitations or qualifications on recovery of damages. Questions may arise of whether such conditions have been validly incorporated in the contract.[44]

Any such limitation of liability may not be binding if the custodier is in material breach of contract as by keeping the goods in a place other than the agreed one,[45] or by allowing a person not producing the contractual receipt to have access to the goods.[46]

Strict liability of innkeepers

Under the praetorian edict *nautae, caupones, stabularii* [47] innkeepers

30 *McDonell* v. *Ettles*, Dec. 15, 1809, F.C.; *Searle* v. *Laverick* (1874) L.R. 9 Q.B. 122; *Sutherland* v. *Hutton* (1896) 23 R. 718.
31 *Mintz* v. *Silverton* (1920) 36 T.L.R. 399; contrast *Williams* v. *Curzon Syndicate Ltd.* (1919) 35 T.L.R. 399; *Sanderson* v. *Collins* (1904) 1 K.B. 628; *Central Motors* v. *Cessnock Garage Co.*, 1925 S.C. 796.
32 *Searle*, *supra*; *Brabant* v. *King* [1895] A.C. 632; *Turner* v. *Stallibrass* [1898] 1 Q.B. 56.
33 *Smith* v. *Cook* (1875) 1 Q.B.D. 79; *McLean* v. *Warnock* (1883) 10 R. 1052; *Sutherland* v. *Hutton* (1896) 23 R. 718.
34 *Quiggin* v. *Duff* (1836) 1 M. & W. 174, 180.
35 *Snodgrass* v. *Ritchie* (1890) 17 R. 712.
36 *Brabant*, *supra*, but *cf. Searle*, *supra.*
37 *Coldman* v. *Hill* [1919] 1 K.B. 443.
38 *Ranson* v. *Platt* [1911] 2 K.B. 291.
39 *Reeve* v. *Palmer* (1858) 5 C.B.(N.S.) 84; *Phipps* v. *New Claridge's Hotel* (1905) 22 T.L.R. 49; *Travers* v. *Cooper* [1915] 1 K.B. 73; *Coldman* v. *Hill* [1919] 1 K.B. 443; *Sinclair* v. *Juner*, 1952 S.C. 35; *cf. Wilson* v. *Orr* (1880) 7 R. 266; *McLean* v. *Warnock* (1883) 10 R. 1052; *Mustard* v. *Paterson*, 1923 S.C. 142, 156.
40 *Bullen* v. *Swan Electric Co.* (1907) 23 T.L.R. 258.
41 *Mustard*, *supra*; *Sinclair*, *supra*.
42 *Central Motors* v. *Cessnock Garage Co.*, 1925 S.C. 796.
43 *Cf. Mustard*, *supra*.
44 See *e.g. Van Toll* v. *S.E. Ry.* (1862) 12 C.B.(N.S.) 75; *Parker* v. *S.E. Ry.* (1877) 2 C.P.D. 416; *Harris* v. *G.W. Ry.* (1876) 1 Q.B.D. 515, 532.
45 *Edwards* v. *Newland* [1950] 1 All E.R. 1072; *cf. Lilley* v. *Doubleday* (1881) 7 Q.B.D. 510.
46 *Alexander* v. *Railway Executive* [1951] 2 K.B. 882.
47 Dig. IV, 9, 1; see Mackintosh (1891) 3 J.R. 306.

were at common law strictly liable for the loss of goods brought to their premises by travellers, but not for damage thereto, in which case negligence had to be proved.[48]

The innkeeper was accordingly liable, without proof of negligence or the cause of loss, for the property of guests, unless the loss were due to act of God,[49] such as accidental fire,[50] act of the Queen's enemies,[51] or the personal negligence of the guest.[52] The onus of evading liability is on the defender.[53] Liability extended to cars left in the car park, despite a notice purporting to exempt the innkeeper,[54] but not if merely allowed to be parked outside.[55]

Liability of hotel proprietors

Under the Hotel Proprietors Act 1956 [56] only a hotel as defined by the Act [57] is an inn, and the rights and liabilities of an innkeeper attach to the proprietor of such a hotel and not to any other person.[58] A hotel proprietor is under the same liability, if any, to make good to any guest any damage to property brought to the hotel as to make good the loss thereof.[59] A hotel proprietor is strictly liable to make good loss of or damage to property only where (a) at the time of the loss or damage sleeping accommodation had been engaged for the traveller; and (b) the loss or damage occurred during the period between the midnight immediately preceding and the midnight immediately following the period for which the traveller was a guest at the hotel.[60] He is not strictly liable to make good any loss of or damage to any vehicle or any property left therein, or any horse or other live animal or its harness or equipment.[61] If the hotel proprietor is strictly liable, his liability to any one guest is not to exceed £50 in respect of any one article or £100 in all, except where (a) the property was stolen, lost or damaged through the default, neglect [62] or wilful act [63] of the proprietor or some servant of his;

48 *Butler* v. *Quilter* (1900) 17 T.L.R. 158; *Winkworth* v. *Raven* [1931] 1 K.B. 652.
49 *Mustard* v. *Paterson*, 1923 S.C. 143, 148; *cf. Nugent* v. *Smith* (1875) 1 C.P.D. 19; (1876) 1 C.P.D. 423.
50 *McDonell* v. *Ettles*, Dec. 15, 1809, F.C.; explained in *Sinclair* v. *Juner*, 1952 S.C. 35.
51 *Mustard, supra.*
52 It is doubtful whether personal custody of the goods makes the guest liable: *Richmond* v. *Smith* (1828) 8 B. & C. 9.
53 *Mustard, supra.*
54 *Williams* v. *Linnitt* [1951] 2 K.B. 565. *Cf. Aria* v. *Bridge House Hotel* (1927) 137 L.T. 299; *Davies* v. *Clarke* (1952) 103 L.T. 141.
55 *Watson* v. *People's Refreshment Assocn.* [1952] 1 K.B. 318; *Gresham* v. *Lyon* [1954] 2 All E.R. 786.
56 Replacing Innkeepers Liability Act 1863.
57 s. 1 (3).
58 s. 1 (1); this certainly excludes edictal liability of the keepers of restaurants or boarding houses; whether it abolishes the edictal liability of a livery stable-keeper is uncertain.
59 s. 1 (2).
60 s. 2 (1).
61 s. 2 (2).
62 *Bonham-Carter* v. *Hyde Park Hotel Ltd.* (1948) 64 T.L.R. 177.
63 See *Squire* v. *Wheeler* (1867) 16 L.T. 93; *Behrens* v. *Grenville Hotel (Bude) Ltd.* (1925) 69 S.J. 346; "wilful" qualifies "act" only: *Bellville* v. *Palatine Hotel Co.* (1944) 171 L.T. 363.

or (b) the property was deposited by or on behalf of the guest expressly for safe custody[64] with the proprietor or some servant of his authorised, or appearing to be authorised for the purpose, and, if so required by the proprietor or that servant, in a container fastened or sealed by the depositor; or (c) at a time after the guest had arrived at the hotel, either the property in question was offered for deposit as aforesaid and the proprietor or his servant refused to receive it, or the guest or some other guest acting on his behalf wished so to offer the property in question but through the default of the proprietor or a servant of his, was unable to do so.[65]

The proprietor is not entitled to the protection of section 2 (3) unless at the time when the property in question was brought to the hotel, a copy of the notice in the Schedule to the Act printed in plain type was conspicuously displayed in a place where it could conveniently be read by guests at or near the reception office or desk or, where there is no reception office or desk, at or near the main entrance to the hotel.[66] If the notice is not displayed the hotel proprietor is strictly liable under the Edict without qualification or limitation of value.[67] The Act is without prejudice to any other liability incurred by him with respect to property, so that it does not affect liability for loss or damage proven to have been caused intentionally or negligently, nor liability undertaken or limited or excluded by contract.

Liability of livery stable keepers[68]

The same strict liability as applied to innkeepers extended at common law to the keepers of livery stables,[69] but this liability has not been extended to a modern garage-keeper.[70] Whether it still applies, even to stable-keepers proper, is doubtful.[71] Whether it does or not, if there is injury to a horse, the onus of disproof of lack of care is on the stable-keeper,[72] and his liability, if it exists, is for the diminution in value of the animal.[73]

PLEDGE

Pledge requires the actual, or constructive, or symbolical, delivery of goods, or means of exclusive control thereof, or of a document of title symbolising the goods, to a pledgee to be held by as security.[74] So long

[64] *O'Connor* v. *Grand International Hotel Co.* [1898] L.R. 2 Q.B.(Ir.) 92; *Whitehouse* v. *Pickett*, 1908 S.C.(H.L.) 31. The proprietor must be told that the deposit is for safe custody.

[65] s. 2 (3).

[66] s. 2 (3), proviso. *Cf. Shacklock* v. *Ethorpe* (1939) 55 T.L.R. 895.

[67] *Spice* v. *Bacon* (1877) 2 Ex.D. 463; see also *Carey* v. *Long's Hotel Co.* (1890) 7 T.L.R. 213; *Huntley* v. *Bedford Hotel Co.* (1891) 7 T.L.R. 641; *Hodgson* v. *Ford* (1892) 8 T.L.R. 722.

[68] Stair I, 9, 5; I, 13, 2; Bankt. I, 17, 1; Ersk. III, 1, 28; Bell, *Comm.* I, 498; *Prin.* § 236.

[69] Whether attached to an inn or not: *Mustard* v. *Paterson*, 1923 S.C. 142.

[70] *Central Motors* v. *Cessnock Garage Co.*, 1925 S.C. 796.

[71] See Hotel Proprietors Act 1956, s. 1 (1).

[72] *Mustard, supra.*

[73] *Mustard, supra.*

[74] Stair I, 13, 11; Ersk. III, 1, 33; Bell, *Comm.* I, 258; *Prin.* §§ 203–209.

as they are in the creditor's possession, he must take ordinary reasonable care of them.[75]

Pledgor's claim

When the purpose of the pledge has been served, the pledgee must restore the things pledged with all natural fruits thereof. He is liable for the value of the pledge if the thing were lost by negligence, or if he otherwise cannot restore the pledge, or it has been damaged while in his custody.

Pledgee's claim

The pledgee has a claim for any harm or loss caused to him or his property by the goods while held in pledge by him, measured by the extent of harm or loss done.

[75] Bell, *Prin.* § 206.

CHAPTER 41

CONTRACTS OF HIRING OF GOODS

THE contract of hiring is one whereby one party, the lessor, transfers to another, the hirer, the temporary possession and right of use of some moveable property in return for a consideration called the rent or hire, for a determinate time, and for purposes expressed or implied in the contract.[1]

Claims by hirer

The lessor must put the hirer in possession of the thing hired at the due date and time, and will be liable in damages for delay.[2] If the subject be specific and be destroyed beforehand without fault the contract is frustrated.[3] If the subject of hiring be generic he is not released and is liable for breach.[4]

The thing let must also be of the kind, quality and capacity contracted for and if there is material discrepancy between contract and actuality the hirer may rescind the contract and claim damages, or if the discrepancy be less material, claim damages in compensation for the inconvenience and excess cost of doing what he wished to do with, for example, a machine of lesser capacity or one more expensive to run.

The lessor must also allow the hirer the reasonable and proper use of the thing and he is liable for failing to maintain him in possession and use of it.

The hirer, however, has no claim if his use is interfered with by the wrongful or negligent acts of third parties, though in such a case replacement of the thing hired or an abatement from the contractual hire must be allowed.[5] He may recover damages from the third party if he is wrongfully dispossessed, though he must account to the lessor for anything recovered in excess of his own loss.[6]

The lessor is also bound to take reasonable care that any article let is reasonably fit for the normal purpose of hire, or for any particular purpose disclosed by the hirer,[7] but he does not give any warranty of its fitness or of absence of latent defect.[8] He will therefore be held liable in damages for loss or damage caused by any defect known to, or which should

[1] See generally Ersk. III, 1, 18; Bell, *Comm.* I, 481; *Prin.* § 137.
[2] *Cf. Mackenzie* v. *Liddell* (1883) 10 R. 705.
[3] *Cf. Taylor* v. *Caldwell* (1863) 3 B. & S. 826; *Muir* v. *McIntyre* (1887) 14 R. 470.
[4] *Taylor, supra.*
[5] Bell, *Prin.* § 141; *Muir* v. *McIntyre* (1887) 14 R. 470.
[6] *The Winkfield* [1902] P. 42.
[7] Ersk. III, 3, 15; *Wilson* v. *Norris*, Mar. 10, 1810, F.C.; *Oliver* v. *Saddler*, 1929 S.C.(H.L.) 94.
[8] Bell, *Prin.* § 141; *Wood* v. *Mackay* (1906) 8 F. 625, 637.

reasonably have been known to or suspected by him,[9] and which renders the thing let unfit for its purpose, but was not disclosed to the hirer.[10] He is also liable for loss caused by the thing breaking down in normal use unless he can show that the breakdown was not attributable to any lack of care on his part.[11]

Claims by lessor

The lessor has a claim of damages if the hirer fails to take delivery of the thing hired at the due date, measured by the loss of rent.

He also has a claim of damages if loss or damage is caused to the thing let by misuse, excessive use,[12] or use for a purpose forbidden or not contemplated,[13] as by jumping [14] or galloping [15] a horse hired for riding only, and for harm caused by failure by the hirer to take the same reasonable care of the thing hired as a prudent man would take of his own property.[16] But the hirer is not liable for fair wear and tear, injury by *damnum fatale*,[17] negligence of a third party,[18] or delict of another, even though a servant.[19] The hirer is presumed responsible [20] and the onus of proof that the cause of damage is not within his responsibility is on him,[21] but he need prove only that he took reasonable care and need not prove the exact cause of the damage.

He further has a claim of damages if the thing hired be not returned by the time of expiry of the hiring or, if no date be fixed, by a time fixed which gives reasonable notice. The damages may include loss of another hire, or damages paid for breach of a subsequent hiring contract.

9 *Lyon* v. *Lamb* (1838) 16 S. 1188; *Fowler* v. *Lock* (1872) L.R. 7 C.P. 272; *Hyman* v. *Nye* (1881) 6 Q.B.D. 685; *Oliver* v. *Saddler*, 1928 S.C. 608, 615; revd. 1929 S.C.(H.L.) 94, 101.

10 *Blakemore* v. *Bristol and Exeter Ry.* (1858) 8 E. & B. 1051; *Coughlin* v. *Gillison* [1899] 1 Q.B. 145; *Reed* v. *Dean* [1949] 1 K.B. 188; *cf. Clarke* v. *Army & Navy Stores* [1903] 1 K.B. 155; *Wilson* v. *Wordie* (1905) 7 F. 929.

11 Bell, *Comm.* I, 482; *Johnston* v. *Rankin* (1687) Mor. 10080; *Readhead* v. *Midland Ry.* (1867) L.R. 2 Q.B. 412; *Francis* v. *Cockrell* (1870) L.R. 5 Q.B. 501.

12 *Pullars* v. *Walker* (1858) 20 D. 1238.

13 Bell, *Prin.* § 144; *Campbell* v. *Kennedy* (1828) 6 S. 806.

14 *Burnard* v. *Haggis* (1863) 14 C.B.(N.S.) 45.

15 *Gardner* v. *McDonald* (1792) Hume 299; *Seton* v. *Paterson* (1880) 8 R. 236.

16 Bell, *Comm.* I, 483; Beven, *Negligence*, 967, 970; notes to *Coggs* v. *Bernard*, 1 Sm.L.C. 191; *Handford* v. *Palmer* (1820) 2 B. & B. 359; *Campbell* v. *Kennedy* (1828) 6 S. 806; *Giblin* v. *McMullen* (1868) L.R. 2 P.C. 317; *McLean* v. *Warnock* (1883) 10 R. 1052; *Tilling* v. *Balmain* (1892) 8 T.L.R. 517; *Brice* v. *Christiani* (1928) 44 T.L.R. 335.

17 *Taylor* v. *Caldwell* (1863) 3 B. & S. 826, 838.

18 *Tilling* v. *Balmain* (1892) 8 T.L.R. 517.

19 *Trotter* v. *Buchanan* (1688) Mor. 10080; *Smith* v. *Melvin* (1845) 8 D. 264; *Walker* v. *British Guarantee Assocn.* (1852) 18 A. & E. 277; *cf. Cheshire* v. *Bailey* [1905] 1 K.B. 237; see also *Coupé Co.* v. *Maddick* [1891] 2 Q.B. 413; *Central Motors Co.* v. *Cessnock Garage Co.*, 1925 S.C. 796.

20 *Wilson* v. *Orr* (1879) 7 R. 266.

21 *Binny* v. *Veaux* (1679) Mor. 10079; *Robertson* v. *Ogle*, June 23, 1809, F.C.; *Marquis* v. *Ritchie* (1823) 2 S. 386; *Pyper* v. *Thomson* (1843) 5 D. 498; *Moes, Moliere & Co.* v. *Leith Shipping Co.* (1867) 5 M. 988; *Hinshaw* v. *Adam* (1870) 8 M. 933; *Wilson, supra*; *Bain* v. *Strang* (1888) 16 R. 186; *Copland* v. *Brogan*, 1916 S.C. 277; *Mustard* v. *Paterson*, 1923 S.C. 142.

CHAPTER 42

CONTRACTS OF BARTER OF GOODS

THE rules as to barter are determined by the principles regulating sale of goods at common law, not by the Sale of Goods Act 1893.[1] The kinds of breach of contract which may arise are failure by one party to deliver the thing which is the counterpart of the other party's transfer of goods, or delay to do so, or delivery of a thing which is defective.

If there is total failure to deliver the counterpart article the party aggrieved may rescind the contract, demanding redelivery of what he has himself delivered, or claim damages, measured by the market value of the thing which should have been delivered to him. The risk of loss passes when the goods are actually transferred, or appropriated to the contract.[1a]

If there is delay in delivering the counterpart a claim of damages lies for loss caused by the delay and for the inconvenience of not having the counterpart article at the time it should have been delivered.

If there is delivery of a counterpart article which is defective the principle of sale at common law will apply, namely that, if there is a latent defect, the goods may be rejected, and specific goods bartered by description may be rejected even when they have been seen and examined, if they turn out to be different in kind from those described, and the difference was not apparent on inspection,[2] but they may not be accepted and a claim made for pecuniary compensation for the defect in quality or quantity.[3]

[1] Stair I, 14, 1; Ersk. III, 3, 4 and 13; Bell, *Prin.* § 92 (3). *Cf. Urquhart* v. *Wylie*, 1953 S.L.T.(Sh.Ct.) 87.

[1a] *Widenmeyer* v. *Burn, Stewart & Co.*, 1967 S.C. 85.

[2] *Cf.* Bell, *Prin.* § 97; *Jaffé* v. *Ritchie* (1860) 23 D. 242; *Carter* v. *Campbell* (1885) 12 R. 1075.

[3] *McCormick* v. *Rittmeyer* (1869) 7 M. 854.

CHAPTER 43

CONTRACTS OF SALE OF GOODS

General

Damages are recoverable in several distinct sets of circumstances arising out of the contract of sale of goods. The law on this matter has been largely codified by the Sale of Goods Act 1893, which makes statutory provision for the damages recoverable in certain cases. The provisions of the Act are not obligatory on the parties and may be varied or excluded by express agreement to that effect or by a course of dealing, or by binding usage but in the absence of such agreement the Act will be held to apply.[1] It applies to the sale of all corporeal moveables [2] except money [3]; it has no application to sales of heritage. It may also extend to contracts for work which involve supplying materials, *e.g.* false teeth,[4] or mechanical parts.[5] While in several respects the Act innovated upon the pre-existing common law of Scotland, the provisions as to damages are largely declaratory of accepted principles and existing law and practice.

If the provisions of the Act should be excluded by unequivocal agreement, the former common law rules will be applicable [6] and the ordinary principles of damages in contract. Furthermore the rules contained in Part V of the Act,[7] relating to actions for breach of the contract, are all subject to the proviso contained in section 54 that nothing in the Act shall affect the right of the buyer or the seller to recover interest or special damages in any case where by law interest or special damages may be recoverable, or to recover money paid where the consideration for the payment of it has failed, *i.e.* the *condictio causa data causa non secuta.*[8]

The circumstances in which breach of a contract for the sale of goods gives rise to a claim of damages are broadly threefold. The buyer may fail to take delivery of goods sold to him and give the seller a claim for the price or for damages for breach of contract; the seller may fail to deliver goods which he has sold to the buyer; or the seller may deliver goods disconform to contract in one of a number of respects. Claims of damages may be made under each of these heads and must be examined separately.

1 s. 55, as substituted by Supply of Goods (Implied Terms) Act 1973, s. 4.
2 As to incorporeal moveable rights, see Chap. 49, *infra*.
3 s. 62 (1); on what are " goods " see also Benjamin on *Sale*, 8th ed., 171 *et seq.*
4 *Samuels* v. *Davis* [1943] K.B. 526.
5 *Myers* v. *Brent Cross Service Co.* [1934] 1 K.B. 46.
6 See M. P. Brown on *Sale*, 1821; Brown on *The Sale of Goods Act*, 2nd ed., 1911.
7 ss. 49 to 54.
8 *Cf. Cantiere San Rocco* v. *Clyde Shipbuilding Co.*, 1923 S.C.(H.L.) 105.

SELLER'S CLAIMS

Remedies of the seller

The remedies open to the seller are prescribed by sections 49 and 50 of the Act. A distinction must be drawn between cases where the property in the goods sold has passed to the buyer and cases where it has not so passed.[9] In addition, if the goods have not yet passed into the buyer's possession, the seller has certain remedies against the goods themselves.[10]

Where property has passed and goods accepted [10a]

In this case the seller's remedy is not damages but an action for the price under section 49 (1), and possibly also for interest under section 49 (3).

Section 49 provides:

> " (1) Where, under a contract of sale, the property in the goods has passed to the buyer, and the buyer wrongfully [11] neglects or refuses to pay for the goods according to the terms of the contract, the seller may maintain an action against him for the price of the goods.
>
> [Subs. (2) is omitted].
>
> (3) Nothing in this section shall prejudice the right of the seller in Scotland to recover interest on the price from the date of tender of the goods, or from the date on which the price was payable, as the case may be." [12]

Unless the right to rescind the contract failing payment has been expressly reserved [13] delay or failure to pay the price does not entitle the seller to rescind the contract and demand redelivery of the goods,[14] although if the contract was induced by fraud the seller may reduce the contract and recover the goods in a question with the buyer or the trustee in his sequestration. It is adequate proof of fraud if it be shown that the buyer purchased the goods without any intention of paying for them.[15] Nor does the fact of the buyer's bankruptcy entitle the seller to rescind the contract, as the trustee may adopt and perform the contract.

If it be part of the contract that payment is to be made by bill of exchange, this payment is conditional on the bill being honoured when it matures. If not, the seller may sue on it or on the original contract. He is still an unpaid seller and may avail himself of remedies against the goods. If the bill is not given as agreed the seller may claim damages for

[9] On where the property has passed see 1893 Act, ss. 17–19.

[10] ss. 38 *et seq.* See Benjamin on *Sale*, 8th ed., 834 *et seq.*

[10a] As to what is " acceptance " see s. 35 and *Mechan* v. *Bow McLachlan & Co.*, 1910 S.C. 758.

[11] This saves the cases where the buyer is claiming for breach of warranty, or where payment has been made to depend on a specific contingency; *cf. Calcutta Co.* v. *De Mattos* (1863) 32 L.J.Q.B. 322.

[12] This provision is merely declaratory of Scots common law: see Bell, *Prin.* § 32; *Comm.* I, 692; Brown on *Sale of Goods Act*, 2nd ed., 372; *McDowall* v. *Stewart* (1871) 10 M. 193.

[13] As in *Lamond* v. *Davall* (1847) 9 Q.B. 1030.

[14] *Muirhead and Turnbull* v. *Dickson* (1905) 7 F. 686. But as to instalment contracts see *Turnbull* v. *McLean* (1874) 1 R. 730; *Angus* v. *Scott*, 1916, 2 S.L.T. 181.

[15] *Gamage* v. *Charlesworth's Tr.*, 1910 S.C. 257.

the breach of contract, but may not sue for the price until the time when the bill would have matured, provided such a period of credit was contemplated.[16]

It is not a relevant defence to an action for the price of goods that they were bought to satisfy a subsale and the subpurchaser has intimated a claim against the buyer for delay in delivery or defective quality. Such a claim cannot be investigated in the same process.[17]

Time of payment

The Act provides in section 10:

"(1) Unless a different intention appears from the terms of the contract [17a] stipulations as to time of payment are not deemed to be of the essence of a contract of sale. Whether any other stipulation as to time is of the essence of the contract or not depends on the terms of the contract." In several cases time of payment has been held to be of the essence of the contract [17b] and in a case of continuing contract for monthly deliveries of coal and monthly payments it was held that the time of payment was as much of the essence of the contract as payment itself.[17c]

Where property has passed and goods not accepted

In these circumstances the seller may either bring an action for the price under section 49 (1) and (3), or claim damages for non-acceptance under section 50.

Section 50 enacts:

> "(1) Where the buyer wrongfully neglects or refuses to accept and pay for the goods, the seller may maintain an action against him for damages for non-acceptance.
>
> (2) The measure of damages is the estimated loss directly and naturally resulting, in the ordinary course of events, from the buyer's breach of contract.
>
> (3) Where there is an available market for the goods in question the measure of damages is prima facie to be ascertained by the difference between the contract price and the market or current price at the time or times [18] when the goods ought to have been accepted,[19] or, if no time was fixed for acceptance, then at the time of the refusal to accept." [20]

16 *Mussen* v. *Price* (1803) 4 East 147.

17 *Dorman Long & Co.* v. *Harrower* (1899) 1 F. 1109; *Brush Electrical Co.* v. *Scott Stirling & Co.* (1907) 14 S.L.T. 751.

17a *Cf. Gatty* v. *Maclaine*, 1921 S.C.(H.L.) 1.

17b *Young* v. *Dunn* (1785) Mor. 14191; *Hill* v. *Buchanans* (1785) Mor. 14200; affd. (1786) 3 Pat. 47; *Brodie* v. *Todd*, May 25, 1814, F.C.; *cf. Colvin* v. *Short* (1857) 19 D. 890.

17c *Turnbull* v. *McLean* (1874) 1 R. 730, 738.

18 *Cf. Brown* v. *Muller* (1872) L.R. 7 Ex. 319; *Roper* v. *Johnson* (1873) L.R. 8 C.P. 167.

19 *Warin and Craven* v. *Forrester* (1877) 4 R. 190; affd. *ibid.* (H.L.) 75. If the date of performance has been postponed, damages fall to be calculated at the latest date which would have been a due performance: *Hickman* v. *Haynes* (1875) L.R. 10 C.P. 598; *Ashmore* v. *Cox* [1899] 1 Q.B. 436.

20 *Philpotts* v. *Evans* (1839) 5 M. & W. 475. As to delivery in a reasonable time, see *Millett* v. *Van Heek* [1921] 2 K.B. 369.

If the seller claims the price under section 49, he must be still ready to hand over the goods; if he claims damages under section 50 he need not, but may, and, if the circumstances made it prudent so to do to minimise damages, must resell the goods.

In the case of c.i.f. and f.o.b. contracts where the buyers refuse the goods, the sellers cannot claim the price but can claim only damages under section 50.[21] So too if the seller resells under a contractual or the statutory power of resale [22] he may claim damages only. If at the date of resale the property were vested in the buyer, the seller must probably account to him for any profit on the resale.[23] To sue for damages involves acceptance of the buyer's repudiation of the contract.[24]

In the case of breach of an instalment contract by refusal to accept one instalment the seller can sue for the price of that instalment and for damages in respect of future instalments not yet due.[25]

Where property has not passed

In this case, save for one exception, a claim of damages under section 50 is the only remedy. The exceptional case is in cases where a claim for the price is competent under section 49 (2). It provides:

> " (2) Where, under a contract of sale, the price is payable on a day certain [26] irrespective of delivery, and the buyer wrongfully neglects or refuses to pay such price, the seller may maintain an action for the price, although the property in the goods has not passed, and the goods have not been appropriated to the contract."

This section is applicable to an instalment contract if the price of each instalment is payable separately on a fixed day irrespective of delivery.[27] Even though no delivery can be made, as where the property has perished after the contract was made, if the property and risk had passed and the price was payable on a day certain, the seller may recover the full price.[28]

Where the property has not passed, the seller is still owner of the goods and is entitled to resell them immediately [29] and preferably under a warrant from the sheriff.[30]

Apart from the exceptional case covered by section 49 (2) the seller's

21 *Shell-Mex Ltd.* v. *Elton Cop Dyeing Co.* (1928) 34 Com.Cas. 39; *Stein, Forbes & Co.* v. *County Tailoring Co.* (1916) 86 L.J.K.B. 448.

22 Act, s. 48 (3) and (4).

23 *Gallagher* v. *Shilcock* [1949] 2 K.B. 765.

24 *Cf. Colley* v. *Overseas Exporters* [1921] 3 K.B. 302.

25 *Acton Hall Colliery Co.* v. *Taylor* (1896) 3 S.L.T. 239; *Goven Rope Co.* v. *Weir* (1897) 24 R. 368; *Ashmore* v. *Cox* [1899] 1 Q.B. 436.

26 Not an indefinite date: *Merchant Shipping Co.* v. *Armitage* (1873) L.R. 9 Q.B. 99; *Stein* v. *County Tailoring Co.* (1916) 86 L.J.K.B. 448; *Colley* v. *Overseas Exporters* [1921] 3 K.B. 302; *Napier* v. *Dexters* (1926) 26 Ll.L.R. 62.

27 *Workman, Clark & Co.* v. *Lloyd Brazileno* [1908] 1 K.B. 968; *Shell-Mex* v. *Elton Co.* (1928) 34 Com.Cas. 39.

28 *Alexander* v. *Gardner* (1835) 1 Bing.N.C. 671.

29 If he delays he must take any loss or gain in market price: *Warin and Craven* v. *Forrester* (1877) 4 R.(H.L.) 75; *Jamal* v. *Moolla, Dawood* [1916] 1 A.C. 175.

30 Bell, *Prin.* § 128.

claim is not for the full price of the goods but for the damage he sustained by the non-acceptance,[31] assessed in accordance with section 50 (2), of which the prima facie measure is laid down by section 50 (3). This is merely declaratory of the previous presumptive rule.[32] When it is not applicable the damages fall to be assessed under the wider rule of section 50 (2) which is substantially declaratory of the first branch of *Hadley* v. *Baxendale*.[33] The seller's right to recover consequential damages is preserved by section 54, which provides:

> " Nothing in this Act shall affect the right of the buyer or the seller to recover interest or special damages in any case where by law interest or special damages may be recoverable, or to recover money paid where the consideration for the payment of it has failed."

The rules of remoteness of damage developed under *Hadley* v. *Baxendale* apply.[34]

The measure of damages prescribed by the Act may be varied by the parties, if this intention is clearly expressed, or the damages may be fixed by the contract.[35]

Available market

If there is an available market for the goods the damages are to be assessed by reference to the market price.[36] A market is " somewhere else where they could sell it." [37] The question whether there is an available market for particular goods and a market or current price is a question of fact.[38] Even when goods are not kept in stock and are not purchasable in the open market but were specially made to specification, it may be held that there was a market or current price for the purpose of assessing damages.[39] A distant place may be considered an available market, allowance being made for the cost of carriage.[40] The seller must act reasonably and mitigate his damages so far as reasonably possible.[41] If the difference between the contract and market prices favours the seller, or if there be no difference, nominal damages are due.[42]

[31] *Laird* v. *Pim* (1841) 7 M. & W. 474, 478.
[32] *e.g. Barrow* v. *Arnaud* (1846) 8 Q.B. 604: see also *Valpy* v. *Oakley* (1851) 16 Q.B. 941; *Griffiths* v. *Perry* (1859) 1 E. & E. 680.
[33] (1854) 9 Ex. 341. See, *e.g. Trans Trust S.P.R.L.* v. *Danubian Trading Co.* [1952] 1 All E.R. 970.
[34] *Trans Trust S.P.R.L., supra.*
[35] *Diestal* v. *Stevenson* [1906] 2 K.B. 345.
[36] s. 50 (3).
[37] *Dunkirk Colliery Co.* v. *Lever* (1878) 9 Ch.D. 20, 25; affd. (1880) 43 L.T. 706; criticised but followed in *Thompson* v. *Robinson (Gunmakers)* [1955] Ch. 177 and *Charter* v. *Sullivan* [1957] 2 Q.B. 117; see also *Wertheim* v. *Chicoutimi Pulp Co.* [1911] A.C. 301.
[38] *Marshall* v. *Nicoll*, 1919 S.C.(H.L.) 129, 130.
[39] *Marshall* v. *Nicoll*, 1919 S.C. 244.
[40] *Wertheim, supra.*
[41] *Brown* v. *Muller* (1872) 7 Ex. 319, 322; *Roper* v. *Johnson* (1873) 8 C.P. 167.
[42] *Valpy* v. *Oakley* (1851) 16 Q.B. 941; *Griffiths* v. *Perry* (1859) 1 E. & E. 680; *Charter* v. *Sullivan* [1957] 2 Q.B. 117.

No available market

If there is no available market the right to damages is not affected, but quantum falls to be computed in accordance with the ordinary principle, as laid down in section 50 (2),[43] which normally only differs from the prima facie rule of section 50 (3) in that the difference to be ascertained is that between the contract price and the value of the goods which should have been accepted. As this falls to be arrived at by means other than the market level, the price at which the goods were in fact resold by the seller is valuable presumptive evidence of that value,[44] or if the goods are not resaleable to anyone, the cost of the article and the loss of profit is the measure.[45] The seller is probably allowed greater latitude than in the case of an available market as to his course of action, and he may have regard to trade practice, and the standing and quality of an alternative purchaser, but always within the limits of acting reasonably, having regard to the interests of both parties. If no loss has been sustained or if even a profit has been made, the damages will be nominal.[46] If a sub-contract has been made on ordinary terms, the loss of profit on it may be used as an indication of value.[47] Where the goods had not been produced at the date of breach the seller was entitled to the normal seller's profit.[48]

Date of breach

The date at which the market price or other value is to be taken for the assessment of damages is laid down as the " time or times when the goods ought to have been accepted," *i.e.* the contractual date of delivery, or if no time was fixed for acceptance, at the time of the refusal to accept. The damages fall to be assessed at that date, whether or not the seller does resell the goods. A time may be fixed even though a day certain has not been specified.[49] Damages payable in foreign currency must be such a sum in British money as would produce that sum of foreign currency at the rate of exchange current at the date of default.[50] If the seller does not resell, the measure of damages will not be affected by subsequent fluctuation of the market price. While the seller is bound to take reasonable steps to obtain the best price he can and minimise the buyer's loss, he is not obliged on that account to delay resale, and even if he does and the market price rises, the buyer is not entitled to benefit from that, nor conversely is he to be prejudiced by a fall in market price, his liability being

[43] *Marshall* v. *Nicoll*, 1919 S.C.(H.L.) 129, 131, *per* Lord Shaw. See too Lord McLaren in *Duff* v. *Iron Fencing Co.* (1891) 19 R. 199, 204. As to proof of current market price, see *Whealler* v. *Methuen* (1843) 5 D. 402, 1221.

[44] See, *e.g. Stroud* v. *Austin* (1883) Cab. & E. 119, a case of non-delivery.

[45] *Re Vic Mill* [1913] 1 Ch. 465; *Swift* v. *Board of Trade* [1925] A.C. 520.

[46] *Erie County Gas Co.* v. *Carroll* [1911] A.C. 105, 117.

[47] *Patrick* v. *Russo-British Grain Export Co.* [1927] 2 K.B. 535.

[48] *Cort* v. *Ambergate Ry.* (1851) 17 Q.B. 127; *Silkstone Coal Co.* v. *Joint Stock Coal Co.* (1877) 35 L.T. 668; *Re Vic Mill Ltd., supra*. *Cf. Hill* v. *Showell* (1918) 87 L.J.K.B. 1106.

[49] *Philpotts* v. *Evans* (1839) 5 M. & W. 475. *Cf. Sharpe* v. *Nosawa* [1917] 2 K.B. 814.

[50] *Barry* v. *Van Den Hurk* [1920] 2 K.B. 709; *Lebeaupin* v. *Crispin* [1920] 2 K.B. 714; *Di Ferdinando* v. *Simon, Smits & Co.* [1920] 3 K.B. 409; *cf. S.S. Celia* v. *S.S. Volturno* [1921] 2 A.C. 544.

quantified once and for all at the date of breach.[51] In the case of anticipatory breach of contract [52] the date for assessment of damages depends on whether the intimation of repudiation be accepted, in which case damages are to be assessed as at the date of such acceptance,[53] or whether the intimation be rejected, in which case damages are to be assessed at the due date for performance if acceptance of the goods be not then taken.[54] The seller need not accept a buyer's repudiation, even though it appear that the buyer will not be able to perform the contract at the date fixed.[55] If he acts reasonably he will not be prejudiced though he does not accept the repudiation at once but seeks to persuade the buyer to accept.[56] Where the times of delivery are indefinite and in the option of the buyer, it seems that he is bound to take the whole quantity at reasonable times and damages will be assessed with reference to the market price at what was in the circumstances a reasonable date for delivery of the residue.[57] But it will be otherwise if the offer is merely to supply such amounts as may from time to time be requested. Then there is no obligation to take any particular quantity and there is no breach in not taking more.[58]

Buyer's insolvency

The buyer's insolvency [59] is not *per se* a breach of the contract as the trustee may elect to continue the contract,[60] and must be given an opportunity to do so, and so must a sub-purchaser, it seems,[61] but if the seller has so intimated his insolvency as to amount to a repudiation of the contract,[62] the seller may treat it as such and resell and claim in the sequestration for his damages.[63] If the purchaser becomes insolvent in a case of instalment delivery, the purchaser's trustee can only adopt the contract on paying for prior deliveries.[64]

51 *Jamal* v. *Moolla, Dawood* [1916] 1 A.C. 175.

52 On this, see Chap. 30, *supra*; *Frost* v. *Knight* (1872) L.R. 7 Ex. 111; *Roth* v. *Taysen* (1896) 12 T.L.R. 211; *Mersey Steel Co.* v. *Naylor* (1884) 9 App.Cas. 434; *Dominion Coal Co.* v. *Dominion Iron Co.* [1909] A.C. 293.

53 *Roth* v. *Taysen* (1896) 12 T.L.R. 211; *Melachrino* v. *Nickoll* [1920] 1 K.B. 693; *Millett* v. *Van Heek* [1921] 2 K.B. 369; *Payzu* v. *Saunders* [1919] 2 K.B. 581.

54 *Boorman* v. *Nash* (1829) 9 B. & C. 145; *Philpotts* v. *Evans* (1839) 5 M. & W. 475; *Michael* v. *Hart* [1902] 1 K.B. 482; *Braithwaite* v. *Foreign Hardwood Co.* [1905] 2 K.B. 543.

55 *Tredegar Iron & Coal Co.* v. *Hawthorn* (1902) 18 T.L.R. 716.

56 *Dunkirk Colliery* v. *Lever* (1878) 9 Ch.D. 20; affd. (1880) 43 L.T. 706; see too *British & Beningtons* v. *North-western Cachar Co.* [1923] A.C. 48.

57 *Chapman* v. *Lerin* (1879) 4 Can.S.C.R. 349.

58 *G.N. Ry.* v. *Witham* (1873) L.R. 9 C.P. 16.

59 *Tolhurst* v. *Assoc. Portland Cement Co.* [1903] A.C. 414 (voluntary liquidation); *cf. Asphaltic Co.* v. *Glasgow Corpn.*, 1907 S.C. 463; *Goudy on Bankruptcy*, 4th ed., 20, 368.

60 Goudy, 282 *et seq.*; *Anderson* v. *Hamilton* (1875) 2 R. 355.

61 *Ex p. Stapleton* (1879) 10 Ch.D. 586.

62 *Re Phoenix Bessemer Steel Co.* (1876) 4 Ch.D. 108. Mere notice of insolvency is not enough: *Mess* v. *Duffus* (1901) 6 Com.Cas. 165.

63 Goudy, 282 *et seq.*; *Kirkland* v. *Cadell* (1838) 16 S. 860; *Bidoulac* v. *Sinclair's Tr.* (1889) 17 R. 144; *cf. Bertram* v. *Guild* (1880) 7 R. 1122; *Ex p. Chalmers* (1873) L.R. 8 Ch. 289; *Ex p. Stapleton, supra.*

64 *Ex p. Chalmers, supra.*

Seller's claim for loss caused by delay in acceptance

Section 37 provides:

"When the seller is ready and willing to deliver the goods, and requests the buyer to take delivery, and the buyer does not within a reasonable time after such request take delivery of the goods, he is liable to the seller for any loss occasioned by his neglect or refusal to take delivery, and also for a reasonable charge for the care and custody of the goods. Provided that nothing in this section shall affect the rights of the seller where the neglect or refusal of the buyer to take delivery amounts to a repudiation of the contract."

It appears from the reference to "care and custody" that this section contemplates only cases where the property has passed and only delivery remains to be made. The claim is not for non-acceptance but for failure to take actual possession. It is founded on *Greaves* v. *Ashlin.*[65] The question of what is a reasonable time in the circumstances of the case is a question of fact.[66] It has been held that a contract providing for delivery of specific goods "as required" precludes an action for delay, as the time is indefinite and in the buyer's option and this supplants the ordinary rule of reasonable time.[67] The appropriate action in such a case, if the delay is considered wholly unreasonable, is to offer delivery or inquire whether the buyer intends to take delivery of the goods, and the seller may repudiate the contract if the buyer does not request delivery within a reasonable time after such inquiry.[68] If both parties are in default as to giving and taking delivery, neither can claim damages from the other.[69]

BUYER'S CLAIMS

Remedies of the buyer—damages for non-delivery

The remedy open to the disappointed buyer on the failure by the seller to make delivery is to recover damages for non-delivery.

Section 51 of the Act provides:

"(1) Where the seller wrongfully neglects or refuses to deliver the goods to the buyer, the buyer may maintain an action against the seller for damages for non-delivery.

(2) The measure of damages is the estimated loss directly and naturally resulting, in the ordinary course of events, from the seller's breach of contract.

(3) Where there is an available market for the goods in question the measure of damages is prima facie to be ascertained by the difference

[65] (1813) 3 Camp. 426. *Cf. M. P. Brown on Sale*, 354.
[66] Act, s. 56.
[67] *Jones* v. *Gibbons* (1853) 8 Ex. 920. *Cf.* also *G.N. Ry.* v. *Harrison* (1852) 12 C.B. 576.
[68] *Ross* v. *Shaw* [1917] 2 Ir.R. K.B. 367.
[69] *Forrestt* v. *Aramayo* (1900) 83 L.T.R. 335.

between the contract price and the market or current price of the goods at the time or times when they ought to have been delivered, or, if no time was fixed,[70] then at the time of the refusal to deliver.[71] "

These provisions in favour of the buyer correspond to the seller's remedy against the buyer for non-acceptance under section 50, and the general characteristics of the remedy are the same in each case. As in the case of damages for non-acceptance the prima facie rule of subsection (3) is a presumptive rule [72] forming a branch of the more general rule of subsection (2) which is itself founded on the first rule of *Hadley* v. *Baxendale.*[73] This section is applicable (a) where no delivery at all is made of the goods sold, and also (b) where goods are tendered to the buyer which are completely disconform to the contract, so that the buyer properly rejects them, unless other goods which correspond with the description of goods sold are appropriated to the contract before the due date of delivery.[74] Damages fall to be ascertained as at the date of failure to deliver and are not altered by subsequent changes in circumstances.[75] If there is no difference between contract price and market price, nominal damages may be given.[76]

The section applies to *wrongful* refusal to deliver, so that there may be circumstances where the seller may have a good answer to the buyer's claim for non-implement of the contract. In *Shaw, Macfarlane & Co.* v. *Waddell,*[77] it was held that the time of delivery was of the essence of the contract, that the pursuers were themselves in breach by failing to take delivery timeously and hence that the defenders were justified in repudiating the contract. In those circumstances the refusal to deliver was not " wrongful."

The section may apply to a case of delay in delivery if the date of delivery formed part of the description of the goods,[78] but normally delay in delivery has to be distinguished from complete non-delivery and a different measure of damages applies [79]; in non-delivery damages are the difference between the contract price and the market price; in late delivery damages are the difference between the contract price and their value when delivered, or otherwise, the loss due to the delay.[80]

70 A time may be fixed by reference to an event though the time of its happening be uncertain. *Melachrino* v. *Nickoll* [1920] 1 K.B. 693. As to reasonable time see *Millett* v. *Van Heek* [1921] 2 K.B. 369.

71 The last words do not apply to an anticipatory breach in which case damages require to be assessed under s. 51 (2); *Millett* v. *Van Heek* [1921] 2 K.B. 369.

72 *Wertheim* v. *Chicoutimi Pulp Co.* [1911] A.C. 301, 307.

73 (1854) 9 Ex. 341.

74 *Borrowman* v. *Free* (1878) 4 Q.B.D. 500.

75 *Di Ferdinando* v. *Simon Smits & Co.* [1920] 3 K.B. 409; *Lebeaupin* v. *Crispin* [1920] 2 K.B. 714.

76 *Valpy* v. *Oakley* (1851) 16 Q.B. 941; *Erie Gas Co.* v. *Carroll* [1911] A.C. 105.

77 (1900) 2 F. 1070.

78 *Taylor* v. *Bank of Athens* (1922) 27 Com.Cas. 142.

79 *Williams* v. *Agius* [1914] A.C. 510.

80 *Wertheim* v. *Chicoutimi Pulp Co.* [1911] A.C. 301, explained *Williams, supra*; *Borries* v. *Hutchinson* (1865) 18 C.B.(N.S.) 455.

The fact that the buyer has already paid the price without making any reservation of his right to damages in the event of non-delivery does not import any waiver of his right to damages.[81] It has been held, however,[82] that where goods had been paid for but not delivered, the damages should be measured by the difference between the contract price and the market price at the date of the trial, as the buyer had no funds to buy similar goods in the market in replacement. But he is not entitled to the highest price attained in the interval between the non-delivery and the trial, because it cannot be presumed that he would have resold and got the advantage of that price.[83] Extraneous circumstances, such as contracts with third parties, do not come into consideration in quantifying damages between buyer and seller.[84]

Measure of damages—where there is a market

It is convenient first to consider cases which fall within the prima facie rule of section 51 (3), that is, where there is an available market for the goods which the seller has wrongfully failed to deliver. The rule of measuring the damages by the difference between the contract price and the market price was applied both in England [85] and Scotland [86] at common law prior to the Act as well as since.[87] Thus in *Marshall* v. *Nicoll* [88] the pursuers sued the defenders for failure to implement contracts for the supply of steel sheets. The contract price was £6,693; on the date of delivery the market price for such a quantity was held to have been £10,168: the difference, or £3,475 was awarded as damages.

The existence or non-existence of a market is a question of fact and it is immaterial that it is limited and not regular or fixed.[89] If there be no market at the place of delivery the price ruling at the nearest place or in a controlling market may be taken, or the price at a place known according to the course of dealing between the parties to be the destination of the goods, making allowance for the cost of carriage.[90] It does not

[81] *Clydebank Engineering Co.* v. *Castaneda* (1904) 7 F.(H.L.) 77.

[82] *Elliott* v. *Hughes* (1863) 3 F. & F. 387; see *Startup* v. *Cortazzi* (1835) 3 C.M. & R. 165. *Cf. Shepherd* v. *Johnson* (1802) 2 East 211; *Downes* v. *Back* (1816) 1 Stark. 318.

[83] *McArthur* v. *Seaforth* (1810) 2 Taunt. 257: see also *Michael* v. *Hart* [1901] 2 K.B. 867.

[84] *Rodocanachi* v. *Milburn* (1886) 18 Q.B.D. 67.

[85] *Leigh* v. *Paterson* (1818) 8 Taunt. 540; *Gainsford* v. *Carroll* (1824) 2 B. & C. 624; *Shaw* v. *Holland* (1846) 15 M. & W. 136; *Valpy* v. *Oakley* (1851) 16 Q.B. 941; *Peterson* v. *Eyre* (1853) 13 C.B. 353; *Griffiths* v. *Perry* (1859) 1 E. & E. 680; *Chinery* v. *Viall* (1860) 5 H. & N. 288; *Josling* v. *Irvine* (1861) 6 H. & N. 512; *Elbinger A/G* v. *Armstrong* (1874) L.R. 9 Q.B. 473, 476; *Hinde* v. *Liddell* (1875) L.R. 10 Q.B. 265; *Hickman* v. *Haynes* (1875) L.R. 10 C.P. 598.

[86] *Paterson* v. *Keith*, 1745 Elchies, Dam. & Int. 2; *Robinson* v. *McCulloch*, Dec. 23, 1808, F.C., *per* Lord Pres. Blair; *Anderson* v. *Goddard*, Feb. 21, 1809, F.C.; *Duff* v. *Iron Buildings Co.* (1891) 19 R. 199. Older Scottish cases contrary to the modern rule must now be considered as unsound: see *Ströms Bruks A/B* v. *Hutchison* (1905) 7 F.(H.L.) 131, 133, *per* Lord Macnaghten.

[87] *Ashmore* v. *Cox* [1899] 1 Q.B. 436; *Wertheim* v. *Chicoutimi Pulp Co.* [1911] A.C. 301; *Williams* v. *Agius* [1914] A.C. 510. *Cf. Ireland* v. *Merryton Coal Co.* (1894) 21 R. 989 (instalments).

[88] 1919 S.C.(H.L.) 129.

[89] *Marshall* v. *Nicoll*, 1919 S.C.(H.L.) 129.

[90] *Wertheim* v. *Chicoutimi Pulp Co.* [1911] A.C. 301; *Macaulay* v. *Horgan* [1925] 2 Ir.R. 1.

matter what factors of supply and demand or other causes influence the price at that market.[91]

Prima facie rule inapplicable

Exceptionally, however, other than the prima facie measure of damages may be awarded where there is a market. In *Ogle* v. *Earl Vane*[92] the defendant, owing to an accident to his furnaces, failed to make delivery of iron according to contract: the plaintiff, at the defendant's request, delayed to buy other iron in replacement. Hence the plaintiff was held entitled to recover damages in the end at the greatly increased market price which had risen during the delay, because his delay had been made at the other party's request.

In *Tyers* v. *Rosedale Iron Co.*[93] the defendants had contracted to make monthly deliveries and withheld some at the request of the plaintiffs. The latter in the last month demanded the whole outstanding amount and claimed for non-delivery when more than the monthly quota was not forthcoming. It was held that the defendants were not justified in refusing to deliver the whole residue and that the damages should be measured by reference to the market price at the date of refusal to deliver in the last month.

Again in *Trans Trust S. P. R. L.* v. *Danubian Trading Co.*[94] buyers were in breach of contract by failing to open a confirmed credit so that the sellers could not obtain the goods from their suppliers. At all material times the market value of the goods was higher than the contract price so that if the prima facie measure of damages under the Act were applied the seller would have got only nominal damages. In fact the seller was allowed his loss of profit on the contract because the loss was such as might reasonably be expected to be in the contemplation of the parties as likely to flow from the breach of the buyer's obligation.

Anticipatory breach by seller

In accordance with the principle of *Frost* v. *Knight*[95] a buyer who is informed beforehand that the seller cannot or will not perform his contract when the time comes may either accept the repudiation and sue at once, or he may decline to accept as a breach of the contract the seller's repudiation. In the former case he must act reasonably to mitigate the damages[95] and go into the market if a favourable opportunity offers, in which case the damages will be calculated by reference to the market price at the date of repurchase. He may be bound to accept a reasonable offer made by the

[91] *Joslin* v. *Irvine* (1861) 6 H. & N. 512, 517.

[92] (1868) L.R. 3 Q.B. 272; followed in *Hickman* v. *Haynes* (1875) L.R. 10 C.P. 598; distinguished in *Ex p. Llansamlet Tin Plate Co.* (1873) L.R. 16 Eq. 155.

[93] (1875) L.R. 8 Ex. 305; L.R. 10 Ex. 195.

[94] [1952] 1 All E.R. 970.

[95] (1871) L.R. 7 Ex. 111. *Cf. Wilson* v. *Hicks* (1857) 26 L.J.Ex. 242; *Melachrino* v. *Nickoll* [1920] 1 K.B. 693; *Millett* v. *Van Heek* [1920] 3 K.B. 535; affirmed [1921] 2 K.B. 369.

seller.[96] If he lets the opportunity go by, the seller can claim to have the damages quantified by reference to a date when a fresh contract might and should have been made.[97] In the latter case he is not compelled to mitigate his loss as soon as possible, but if the market is rising can await the due date of performance.[98] The damages will then be calculated by reference to the market price on the date for delivery.[97]

Acceptance of an anticipatory breach involves rescission of the contract and consequently the seller is not thereafter entitled to avail himself as a defence of any circumstances which might have excused or justified non-performance, had the contract continued in force down to the due date for performance.[99]

Measure of damages—where there is no market

Where there is no available market for the goods in question, the value of the goods for the purpose of damages must be measured otherwise. Many of the cases illustrating the application of section 51 (2) have already been considered in the discussion of the first branch of *Hadley* v. *Baxendale* [1] which the subsection in substance reproduces. When there is no market by reference to which the value of the goods to the buyer at the time of breach can be calculated, the mode of estimating the value must depend to some extent on the nature of the transaction and care must be taken that due regard is had to the principles of mitigation of damages and remoteness of damage.

Circumstances peculiar to one or other of the parties or accidental as between them, such as an intermediate contract with a third party for the purchase or sale of the goods is *res inter alios acta* and cannot be taken into account in quantifying the damages.[2] "When there is no delivery . . . the defaulting seller is neither mulct in damages for the extra profit which the buyer would have got owing to a forward resale at over the market price, nor can he take benefit of the fact that the buyer has made a forward resale at under the market price." [3]

Thus the buyer's loss may be measured by the loss of profit which would normally have been made on the transaction,[4] and possibly also a sum of damages [5] or penalties [6] paid to a sub-purchaser for a consequential

96 *Payzu* v. *Saunders* [1919] 2 K.B. 581.
97 *Melachrino, supra*; *Millett, supra*.
98 *Tredegar Coal Co.* v. *Hawthorn* (1902) 18 T.L.R. 716.
99 *Melachrino* v. *Nickoll & Knight* [1920] 1 K.B. 693; *Birchgrove Steel Co.* v. *Shaw Iron Co.* (1891) 7 T.L.R. 246.
1 (1854) 9 Ex. 341; *supra*, Chap. 28.
2 *Rodocanachi* v. *Milburn* (1886) 18 Q.B.D. 67, approved in *Williams Bros.* v. *Agius* [1914] A.C. 510.
3 *Williams, supra*, at p. 522, *per* Lord Dunedin.
4 *Duff* v. *Iron Buildings Co.* (1891) 19 R. 199, esp. Lord McLaren at pp. 204–5; *Trans Trust S.P.R.L.* v. *Danubian Trading Co.* [1952] 1 All E.R. 970; *cf.* also *Govan Rope and Sail Co.* v. *Weir* (1897) 24 R. 368. See too *Horne* v. *Midland Ry.* (1872) L.R. 8 C.P. 131; *Borries* v. *Hutchinson* (1865) 18 C.B.(N.S.) 445; *Williams, supra*.
5 *Grébert-Borgnis* v. *Nugent* (1885) 15 Q.B.D. 85. See also *Dorman Long* v. *Harrower* (1899) 1 F. 1109; *Brush Electric Co.* v. *Scott, Stirling & Co.* (1907) 14 S.L.T. 751.
6 *Elbinger A/G* v. *Armstrong* (1874) L.R. 9 Q.B. 473, and see *Hydraulic Engineering Co.* v. *McHaffie* (1878) 4 Q.B.D. 670, 678.

default (if not a too remote consequence), loss of profit on resale,[7] the cost of substitute goods, as nearly as possible of the same quality,[8] or the loss of profits of use of the goods.[9] The measure of damages may also depend on whether or not the innocent party has acted reasonably in mitigating damages.[10]

Subsales—where there is a market

Where goods have been bought for subsale or have actually been resold in anticipation of delivery and the seller defaults in delivery, the buyer must purchase other goods in the market to supply his sub-purchaser [11] and recover any excess cost from the seller as damages. It is material whether the seller knew or did not know, at the time he entered into the contract, of the resale or the buyer's intention to resell. In the absence of such knowledge he cannot be held liable for any greater damages than the difference in price, on the ordinary principle of remoteness of damage.[12] If he has adequate knowledge, he will be liable for loss incurred on the subsale consequential on the breach of the main contract.[13]

Subsales—where no market

Where there is no market for the goods in question and the seller does not know that goods were being bought for resale or probably would be resold or had already been resold, the buyer may on the seller's default either obtain the best available substitute which will enable him to perform his contract with the sub-purchaser and charge the defaulting seller with the difference between the contract price and what he has to pay to obtain this substitute [14]; or he may recover from the seller the difference between the contract price and the value of the goods, *i.e.* loss of profits. What the value of the goods was may be evidenced by the price at which the unknown subsale was effected,[15] or their price at another market, together with the cost of carriage therefrom,[16] or their market price at the place of delivery at some time other than the contractual date of delivery.[17] Thus in

[7] *Leavey* v. *Hirst* [1944] K.B. 24; *Household Machines Ltd.* v. *Cosmos Exporters Ltd.* [1946] 2 All E.R. 622.

[8] *Hinde* v. *Liddell* (1875) L.R. 10 Q.B. 265. See also *Erie Gas Co.* v. *Carroll* [1911] A.C. 105, 117. *Cf. British Westinghouse* v. *Underground Rys.* [1912] A.C. 673.

[9] *Fletcher* v. *Tayleur* (1855) 17 C.B. 21; *Portman* v. *Middleton* (1858) 4 C.B.(N.S.) 322; *Cory* v. *Thames Ironworks Co.* (1868) L.R. 3 Q.B. 181; *Re Trent and Humber Co.* (1868) L.R. 6 Eq. 396; *cf. Wilson* v. *General Screw Collier Co.* (1877) 47 L.J.Q.B. 239.

[10] *Lesters Leather Co.* v. *Home and Overseas Brokers* (1948) 64 T.L.R. 569.

[11] *Grébert-Borgnis* v. *Nugent* (1885) 15 Q.B.D. 85, 89; *Hinde* v. *Liddell* (1875) L.R. 10 Q.B. 265.

[12] Chap. 28, *supra*; *e.g. Portman* v. *Middleton* (1858) 4 C.B. (N.S.) 322; *cf. Horne* v. *Midland Ry.* (1872) L.R. 8 C.P. 131.

[13] *Cf. Hydraulic Engineering Co.* v. *McHaffie* (1878) 4 Q.B.D. 670; *Elbinger A/G* v. *Armstrong* (1874) L.R. 9 Q.B. 473; *Grébert-Borgnis, supra.*

[14] *Hinde* v. *Liddell* (1875) L.R. 10 Q.B. 265.

[15] *Grébert-Borgnis* v. *Nugent* (1885) 15 Q.B.D. 85, 89; *Stroud* v. *Austin* (1883) Cab. & E. 119; *Engell* v. *Fitch* (1869) L.R. 4 Q.B. 659; *Leavey* v. *Hirst* [1944] K.B. 24; *Household Machines* v. *Cosmos Exporters Ltd.* [1946] 2 All E.R. 622.

[16] *Wertheim* v. *Chicoutimi Pulp Co.* [1911] A.C. 301.

[17] *Stroud* v. *Austin* (1883) Cab. & E. 119.

Borries v. *Hutchinson*[18] loss of profits was given but damages paid to the sub-purchaser for breach of the contract with him were refused as too remote.

If the seller fails to deliver in the knowledge when he made the contract that the goods were being bought for resale, or would probably be resold,[19] or had actually been resold,[20] then the buyer may obtain the nearest substitute goods which will satisfy the sub-contract and charge the defaulting seller with the excess over the contract price as damages[21]; or the buyer may default on the sub-contract and recover from the seller the actual or anticipated profits which he would have made on the sub-contract,[22] a reasonable indemnity against his liability to the sub-purchaser for penalty or damages for the consequential breach of the sub-contract,[23] and any expenses properly and reasonably incurred.[24]

The recovery of any or all of these heads of consequential damages is subject to the ordinary rules of remoteness,[25] and the seller will not be held liable in damages for exceptional profits on a sub-contract unless at the time of entering into the original contract the seller was properly apprised of the amount of those profits and undertook his contract having in contemplation the special responsibility attached in the event of failure.[26] He will otherwise only be liable to the extent of ordinary reasonable commercial profits.[27] Similarly in the absence of full prior knowledge of amount the seller will not be liable to the buyer for the full amount of any damages or penalty payable by the buyer to the sub-buyer in respect of default on the sub-contract, though the amount so payable is evidence of what is a reasonable indemnity, and may be accepted as such.[28]

Instalment deliveries

Apart from contrary agreement[29] a buyer cannot insist on[30] and is not bound to accept delivery by instalments.[31] The principal question of difficulty with regard to damages for breach of a contract providing for delivery by instalments is whether a breach in respect of one or more instalments entitles the buyer to treat the whole contract as repudiated

18 (1865) 18 C.B.(N.S.) 445.
19 *Hammond* v. *Bussey* (1887) 20 Q.B.D. 79.
20 *Patrick* v. *Russo-British Grain Co.* [1927] 2 K.B. 535.
21 *Hinde* v. *Liddell, supra.*
22 *Hydraulic Engineering Co.* v. *McHaffie* (1878) 4 Q.B.D. 670; *Grébert-Borgnis* v. *Nugent* (1885) 15 Q.B.D. 85; *McNeill* v. *Richards* [1899] 1 Ir.R. 79; *Patrick* v. *Russo-British Grain Co.* [1927] 2 K.B. 535; *Hall* v. *Pim* (1928) 139 L.T. 50.
23 *Elbinger* v. *Armstrong* (1874) L.R. 9 Q.B. 473; *Grébert-Borgnis, supra.*
24 *Hammond* v. *Bussey* (1887) 20 Q.B.D. 79; *Agius* v. *G.W. Colliery* [1899] 1 Q.B. 413; *British Oil & Cake Co.* v. *Burstall* (1923) 39 T.L.R. 406; *Pinnock Bros.* v. *Lewis & Peat* [1923] 1 K.B. 690; *Bennett* v. *Kreeger* (1925) 41 T.L.R. 609; *Slavonski* v. *La Pelleterie* (1927) 137 L.T. 645; *Kasler* v. *Slavonski* [1928] 1 K.B. 78; *Hall* v. *Pim, supra.*
25 Chap. 28, *supra.*
26 *British Columbia Sawmill Co.* v. *Nettleship* (1868) L.R. 3 C.P. 499.
27 *Horne* v. *Midland Ry.* (1872) L.R. 8 C.P. 131.
28 *Elbinger* v. *Armstrong, supra*; *Grébert-Borgnis* v. *Nugent, supra.*
29 See *Whitson* v. *Neilson* (1828) 6 S. 579.
30 *Kingdom* v. *Cox* (1848) 5 C.B. 522, 526; *Honck* v. *Muller* (1881) 7 Q.B.D. 92.
31 Act, s. 31 (1).

and act and claim damages on that basis or whether he must claim damages in respect only of that instalment failure but allow the contract to subsist for the future. The contract may expressly provide for this contingency,[32] but otherwise the tendency in Scottish cases has been to maintain the unity of the contract, provision for instalment delivery being held incidental thereto.[33] Yet it has been laid down that where instalment delivery is justified by the character of the goods or by the terms of the contract, the strict rule is payment for each lot as it is delivered, though in practice this is seldom insisted on.[34] Section 31 (2) provides that where there is a contract for the sale of goods to be delivered by stated instalments, which are to be separately paid for, and the seller makes defective deliveries, *i.e.* short in quantity, disconform to description, or complete non-delivery, it depends on the terms of the contract and the circumstances of the case whether the breach is a repudiation of the whole contract or a severable breach giving rise to a claim for compensation,[35] but not to a right to treat the whole contract as repudiated. These provisions do not cover cases of complete non-delivery [36] or refusal to deliver, nor cases where the price of instalments is not separately payable,[37] or the amount of instalments not stated.[38] But the section does apply even though the contract provides that each delivery is to constitute a separate contract, and in such a case one party may repudiate the whole contract on a breach by the other if he could have done so apart from the provision in the contract.[39]

Cases not covered by the provisions of section 31 (2) have to be determined on general common law principles. These principles are in general that it depends whether in the circumstances the failure amounts to an express or implied refusal to complete performance of the contract, as not every breach, but only one going to the root of the contract, gives the other party the right of rescission.[40] It is then a question of fact in the circumstances of each case what effect a partial breach has, whether it amounts to complete repudiation of the whole contract, or is merely a partial failure giving rise to a right of compensation for the loss and

[32] *e.g. Higgins* v. *Pumpherston Oil Co.* (1893) 20 R. 532, where it was provided that each instalment was to be a separate contract.

[33] *Turnbull* v. *McLean* (1874) 1 R. 730, 738, 739; *Somerville* v. *B. F. Goodrich Co.* (1904) 12 S.L.T. 188, 190. *Cf. Honck* v. *Muller* (1881) 7 Q.B.D. 92, 100; *Mersey Steel Co.* v. *Naylor* (1884) 9 App.Cas. 434, 439. See also *Claddagh S.S. Co.* v. *Stevens*, 1919 S.C.(H.L.) 132 (sale of two ships).

[34] *Hall* v. *Scott* (1860) 22 D. 413, 420, *per* L.J.C. Inglis; *Linn* v. *Shields* (1863) 2 M. 88, 93. See also *Baird's Trs.* v. *Baird* (1877) 4 R. 1005, as to adjustment of overpayment for some instalment.

[35] This covers price of an instalment as well as damages: *Workman, Clark & Co.* v. *Lloyd Brazileno* [1908] 1 K.B. 968, 979.

[36] *Coddington* v. *Paleologo* (1867) L.R. 2 Ex. 193; *Bergheim* v. *Blaenavon Iron Co.* (1875) L.R. 10 Q.B. 319.

[37] *Roper* v. *Johnson* (1873) L.R. 8 C.P. 167.

[38] *Roper, supra.*

[39] *Berk* v. *Day* (1897) 13 T.L.R. 475; *Munro* v. *Meyer* [1930] 2 K.B. 312.

[40] *Mersey Steel Co.* v. *Naylor* (1884) 9 App.Cas. 434, 442, *per* Lord Blackburn; *Rhymney Ry.* v. *Brecon Ry.* (1900) 83 L.T. 111, 114; *cf. Cornwall* v. *Henson* [1900] 2 Ch. 298, 300; *Wade* v. *Waldon*, 1909 S.C. 571. See also *Freeth* v. *Burr* (1874) L.R. 9 C.P. 208; *Forslind* v. *Bechely-Crundall*, 1922 S.C.(H.L.) 173; *Amos and Wood* v. *Kaprow* (1948) 64 T.L.R. 110.

damage caused by that failure, the contract *quoad ultra* standing unaffected.[41]

There is *in dubio* a certain presumption in favour of the view that a contract is a *unum quid* even where delivery and payment are to be made by instalments [42] and the mutuality of counter obligations in a contract has been rather strictly enforced.[43] Hence short delivery given or taken in any period does not necessarily involve waiver of any right to the balance later. The provision for delivery in stages is incidental and not essential to the contract.

Where the contract has been treated as a series of separate contracts the principle has been followed of awarding as damages the sum of the damages due on each breach.[44] Where the unity of the whole contract has been stressed damages fall to be assessed on the whole contract by reference to the date of breach.[45]

Time of performance

Whether a stipulation as to time of performance is of the essence of the contract or not depends on the terms of the contract.[46] With regard to time of performance, the task of the court is to ascertain the real intention of the parties, and where it appears from consideration of the language of the contract and the circumstances that time is of the essence of the contract, the court will hold a stipulation thereasto to be material and consequently a breach thereof will justify repudiation of the contract and a claim of damages, rather than a claim of damages *simpliciter*.[47] In ordinary commercial contracts the time of delivery is prima facie of the essence of the contract,[48] or time may be made of the essence of the con-

[41] Act, s. 31 (2).

[42] *Mersey Steel and Iron Co.* v. *Naylor* (1884) 9 App.Cas. 434, 439, *per* Lord Selborne; *Somerville* v. *B. F. Goodrich* (1904) 12 S.L.T. 188, 190; *Turnbull* v. *McLean & Co.* (1874) 1 R. 730, 738, 739.

[43] *Somerville* v. *B. F. Goodrich* (1904) 12 S.L.T. 188, *per* Lord Low, quoting *Barclay* v. *Anderston Foundry Co.* (1856) 18 D. 1190.

[44] *Brown* v. *Muller* (1872) L.R. 7 Ex. 319; *Ireland* v. *Merryton Coal Co.* (1894) 21 R. 989. *Cf.* also *Higgins* v. *Pumpherston Oil Co.* (1893) 20 R. 532; *Roper* v. *Johnson* (1873) L.R. 8 C.P. 167; *Barningham* v. *Smith* (1874) 31 L.T. 540; *Nederlandsche Cacao-Fabrik* v. *Challen* (1898) 14 T.L.R. 322.

[45] *Govan Rope and Sail Co.* v. *Weir* (1897) 24 R. 368; *Somerville, supra.* See also *Veit* v. *Ireland* (1896) 22 S.L.R. 526; *West Limerigg Colliery Co.* v. *Robertson* (1873) 10 S.L.R. 467; *Merry & Cunninghame* v. *Stevenson* (1895) 2 S.L.T. 489; *Barr* v. *Waldie* (1893) 21 R. 224; *Angus Bros.* v. *Scott*, 1916, 2 S.L.T. 181. *Cf.* also *Brandt* v. *Lawrence* (1876) 46 L.J.Q.B. 237; *Calaminas* v. *Dowlais Iron Co.* (1878) 47 L.J.Q.B. 575.

[46] If it is essential, it should be clearly expressed to be so: *Raeburn* v. *Baird* (1832) 10 S. 761, 765; *cf. Grieve* v. *Konig* (1880) 7 R. 521, 524.

[47] *Cf.* Lord Dunedin in *Wade* v. *Waldon*, 1909 S.C. 571.

[48] *Hartley* v. *Hymans* [1920] 3 K.B. 475; see also *Craig* v. *Hamilton* (1823) 2 S. 347; *Anderson* v. *Wilson* (1856) 19 D. 39; *Philips* v. *Blair & Martin* (1801) 4 Paton 256 (supervening illegality); *Bowes* v. *Shand* (1877) L.R. 2 App.Cas. 455; *Reuter* v. *Sala* (1879) 4 C.P.D. 239; *Sharp* v. *Christmas* (1892) 8 T.L.R. 687; *Woolfe* v. *Horne* (1877) 2 Q.B.D. 355 (auction); *Wimshurst* v. *Deeley* (1845) 2 C.B. 253; *Thames Sack Co.* v. *Knowles* (1919) 88 L.J.K.B. 585; *Brooke Tool Co.* v. *Hydraulic Gear Co.* (1920) 89 L.J.K.B. 263; *McDougall* v. *Aeromarine Ltd.* [1958] 3 All E.R. 431. It was also held to be of the essence of the contract in *Nannay* v. *Stothert* (1788) Mor. 14194; *Robb* v. *Cruikshank* (1840) 2 D. 988; *Colvin* v. *Short* (1857) 19 D. 890; *Kelman* v. *Barr's Tr.* (1878) 5 R. 817; *Shaw* v. *Waddell* (1900) 2 F. 1070. See also *Cowles* v. *Gale* (1871) L.R. 7 Ch. 12; *Warren* v. *Moore* (1898) 14 T.L.R. 497; *Ashmore* v. *Cox* [1899] 1 Q.B. 436.

tract by reasonable notice to the seller.[49] But it has been said that, " When a purchaser means to make it an essential condition of his bargain that certain things should be done by a given day, he must take care to express this condition in the most distinct terms, and on failure to fulfil the condition he should immediately declare his bargain to be at an end." [50] Thus, in *Paton* v. *Payne* [51] it was held that the time of delivery of a printing machine was not of the essence of the contract.[52] And in a case of a contract to make and fit up machinery [53] time was held to be of the essence of the contract, yet the court held that it would be inexpedient for both parties to permit rescission of the contract, and damages for delay only were allowed.

Where goods are sold " to arrive " any condition as to notice of the name of the ship on which the goods are expected is of the essence of the contract.[54] So is a provision that goods are " to be shipped " within a certain time or during a certain period. This has been held to amount to a warranty of description [55] and the natural interpretation of this phrase in the absence of any proved usage is that the goods shall be loaded on board ship during the specified period.[56]

A provision that a bill of lading shall bear a certain date is similarly an essential which justifies rejection of the goods if not complied with, even if the goods were in fact shipped timeously.[57]

Similar considerations apply to a stipulation that the ship carrying the goods should be " cleared," *i.e.* authorised by customs to sail, by a certain date.[58]

Measure of damages for breach as to time

In the event of a stipulation as to time being held as of the essence of the contract, the party not in breach is entitled on general principles to recover damages and to rescind the contract. If the stipulation is not essential he may only claim damages.[59] In such a case what is the measure of damages? No clear statement appears to have been made and reliance

[49] *Rickards* v. *Oppenhaim* [1950] 1 K.B. 616; as to tests of reasonableness, see *Stickney* v. *Keeble* [1915] A.C. 386.

[50] *Raeburn* v. *Baird* (1832) 10 S. 761, 765, *per* Lord Balgray; *cf. Grieve* v. *Konig* (1880) 7 R. 521, 524.

[51] (1897) 35 S.L.R. 112 (H.L.).

[52] Other instances are *Dunn* v. *McGavin* (1825) 1 W. & Sh. 4 (" goods about to be shipped ": but this decision cannot stand in view of *Bowes* v. *Shand* (1877) L.R. 2 App.Cas. 455); *Whitson* v. *Neilson* (1828) 6 S. 579; *Raeburn, supra*; *Kidston* v. *Monceau Co.* (1902) 86 L.T. 556.

[53] *Macbride* v. *Hamilton* (1875) 2 R. 755.

[54] *Reuter* v. *Sala* (1879) 4 C.P.D. 239, 246; see also *Busk* v. *Spence* (1815) 4 Camp. 329; *Graves* v. *Legg* (1854) 9 Ex. 709.

[55] *i.e.* under s. 13; *cf. McGavin* v. *Dunn* (1825) 1 W. & Sh. 4.

[56] *Bowes* v. *Shand* (1877) L.R. 2 App.Cas. 455. *Cf. Ashmore* v. *Cox* [1899] 1 Q.B. 436, and as to reshipment, *Re Carver & Co.* (1912) 17 Com.Cas. 59. See also *Aron* v. *Comptoir Wegimont* [1921] 3 K.B. 435, where date held not part of " description."

[57] *Re General Trading Co.* (1911) 16 Com.Cas. 95; *cf. Berg* v. *Landauer* (1925) 42 T.L.R. 142; *Finlay* v. *Kwik Hoo Tong* [1929] 1 K.B. 400.

[58] *Thalman* v. *Texas Star Flour Mills* (1900) 82 L.T. 833.

[59] *Wade* v. *Waldon*, 1909 S.C. 571.

must be put on the provisions of section 53 (2), which provides, in accordance with general principle, that the measure of damages is the estimated loss directly and naturally resulting from the breach. This measure should adequately compensate the party not in breach for the loss and damage he has sustained by non-performance at the due time. If appropriate, consequential damages can be recovered under section 54. If the non-performance was in respect of payment and was essential, the damages for non-payment will be interest in the usual way. But it is a consequence of section 10 that not any or every delay to make payment will justify interest, still less rescission and a claim for interest. The date of payment must first be shown to be of the essence of the contract,[60] and then that payment has been wrongfully withheld.[61]

Where breach takes place by delayed performance an award may be made in respect of trouble and inconvenience where the delay is not serious, the goods are accepted though tendered late, and no actual pecuniary damage or loss of use is shown by their not having been delivered by the due date.[62] But if the delay is such that the buyer sustains loss, as where he has to buy in elsewhere to enable him to fulfil another contract, or to default on such a contract and pay damages for his breach thereof, damages will fall to be measured by the increased cost of the buyer supplying himself from an alternative source,[63] or his loss of profit,[64] or the damages he has to pay his sub-contractor [65] as the case may be, provided always that the principles of remoteness may apply in any case to cut off certain heads of claim. If the delay in performance is in the circumstances so material as to justify rescission of the contract, damages must be quantified on the basis of non-delivery.[66]

Delay in delivery

If a seller is in default by not making delivery on the due date but the buyer nevertheless and despite the delay accepts the goods, he may recover damages for any loss occasioned him by the delay.[67] Claims on this ground are not expressly dealt with in the Sale of Goods Act 1893.

In *Macbride* v. *Hamilton* [68] the pursuer sued for the contract price of certain apparatus fitted up by him in the defenders' premises. The defenders pleaded that the completion had been delayed and that this had

[60] s. 10.
[61] *Carmichael* v. *Caledonian Ry.* (1870) 8 M.(H.L.) 131; *Edinburgh & Glasgow Union Canal Co.* v. *Carmichael* (1842) 1 Bell's App. 316.
[62] *Webster* v. *Cramond Iron Co.* (1875) 2 R. 752. In such a case the breach is probably not sufficiently material to justify rescission of the contract.
[63] *Portman* v. *Middleton* (1858) 4 C.B.(N.S.) 322.
[64] *Fletcher* v. *Tayleur* (1855) 17 C.B. 21; *Re Trent and Humber Co.* (1868) L.R. 6 Eq. 396.
[65] *Elbinger A/G* v. *Armstrong* (1874) L.R. 9 Q.B. 473; *Grébert-Borgnis* v. *Nugent* (1885) 15 Q.B.D. 85.
[66] On the different measures for delayed delivery and non-delivery see *Williams Bros.* v. *Agius* [1914] A.C. 510.
[67] *Cf. Webster* v. *Cramond Iron Co.* (1875) 2 R. 752; *Bradley* v. *Dollar* (1886) 13 R. 893; *Sutherland* v. *Montrose Shipbuilding Co.* (1860) 22 D. 665.
[68] (1875) 2 R. 775.

caused the defenders loss to a greater extent than the price, and they claimed a right to retain the price to meet that claim. The right of retention was admitted, but the observation that, where there was no time stipulated, a claim for damages on the ground that the work was not completed within a reasonable time could not be pleaded *ope exceptionis*, was overruled in *British Motor Body Co.* v. *Shaw*,[69] where a claim of damages for failure to deliver goods sold within a reasonable time was allowed as a plea in defence to a claim for the price of goods sold. Neither case discusses the measure of damages and consequently one is thrown back on the general principles applicable to damages in contract [70] for assessing these.

In *Williams* v. *Agius* [71] Lord Dunedin distinguished between cases of delay in delivery and of non-delivery altogether. In the case of non-delivery, the measure of damages is the difference between contract and market price.[72] In the case of late delivery the measure of damages to indemnify the buyer is the difference between the market price at the dates of due and actual delivery of the goods purchased [73]; and if the purchaser has resold them in the interval at a price greater than that ruling at the actual date of delivery, he must give credit for that in estimating his damages.[74] In *Wertheim* v. *Chicoutimi Pulp Co.*[74] the buyer claimed to recover the difference between the market price at the due date of delivery and the much lower market price on the date of actual delivery. He had sold the goods at a slight loss and was held entitled to the slight loss only, *i.e.* the difference between the market price at the due date and the resale price. This decision is not entirely consonant with *Rodocanachi* v. *Milburn* [75] and was doubted, *obiter*, by the Court of Appeal in *Slater* v. *Hoyle*.[76] In *Rodocanachi* [75] it was held in an action for non-delivery that, in estimating the damages, the market value at the due date of delivery must be regarded and not the lesser price at which the buyers had resold the goods. In *Slater* [76] the action was for breach of warranty of quality and it was held that the sub-contract was not to be taken into account in assessing damages.

Specific implement

Whether or not the property has passed,[77] the buyer may, apart from suing for damages under section 51, claim for specific implement or performance under section 52. The claims for damages and specific

[69] 1914 S.C. 922.
[70] *Supra*, Chaps. 27, 30.
[71] [1914] A.C. 510, 522.
[72] *Williams* v. *Agius*, *supra*; Act, s. 51.
[73] *Borries* v. *Hutchison* (1865) 18 C.B.(N.S.) 445; *Wertheim*, *infra*.
[74] *Wertheim* v. *Chicoutimi Pulp Co.*, 1911 S.C. 301, and see observations thereon in *Williams*, *supra*.
[75] (1886) 18 Q.B.D. 67, approved in *Williams*, *supra*.
[76] [1920] 2 K.B. 11.
[77] *Jones* v. *Tankerville* [1909] 2 Ch. 440.

performance may be made alternatively in one action.[78] The provisions of this section are deemed to be supplementary to, and not in derogation of, the right of specific implement in Scotland.[79]

Specific implement is a remedy open only to the buyer where the sale is of a specific article [80] or of ascertained goods, *i.e.* probably goods made specific after the contract of sale, subsequently manufactured, acquired or appropriated to the contract,[81] or such that their individuality has been found out.[82] Even though specific implement is a general remedy in Scots law [83] the buyer must show some *pretium affectionis* or reason for preferring the subject of sale to others of the same kind and to monetary compensation for not having it.[84] It is not competent where the sale is merely of a certain quantity of some particular commodity,[85] and the court has an equitable discretion to refuse the remedy.[86]

Remedies of the buyer after delivery—defective performance

Even when full performance of the contract of sale has been timeously made by the seller and the property has passed to the buyer, that performance may be found to be unsatisfactory, in respect of failure to comply with some or all of the conditions or warranties affecting the contract. These conditions or warranties may be incorporated by express stipulation of the parties, or may be implied in the contract, and the Sale of Goods Act specifies certain conditions and warranties which, unless excluded, are to be implied in contracts of sale,[87] or they may be annexed by custom of trade.

The interpretation of the term conditions and warranties involves some trouble. These conditions fall to be distinguished from conditions suspensive or resolutive affecting the existence of the contract as a whole.[88] The terms " conditions " and " warranties " are unfortuntely used in different senses in English and in Scots law.[89] A breach of condition may in English law entitle the party damnified to repudiate the contract and also recover damages, while a breach of warranty justifies the recovery of damages only.[90] It depends on the intention of the parties whether

78 *Linn* v. *Shields* (1863) 2 M. 88, 93, *per* Ld. Pres. Inglis.
79 On specific implement generally, see Chap. 13, *supra*.
80 Defined, s. 62 (1).
81 *Holroyd* v. *Marshall* (1862) 10 H.L.C. 191; *Re Wait* [1927] 1 Ch. 606; *Thames Sack Co.* v. *Knowles* (1919) 88 L.J.K.B. 585: *cf. Price and Pierce* v. *Bank of Scotland*, 1910 S.C. 1095.
82 *Thames Sack and Bag Co.* v. *Knowles* (1919) 88 L.J.K.B. 585.
83 *Stewart* v. *Kennedy* (1890) 17 R.(H.L.) 1, 5, 10; Bell, *Comm.* I, 477.
84 *Falcke* v. *Gray* (1859) 4 Drew. 657, 658 (contract for purchase of articles of unusual beauty, rarity and distinction held specifically enforceable); *Behnke* v. *Bede Shipping Co.* [1927] 1 K.B. 649 (ship).
85 *Sutherland* v. *Montrose Shipbuilding Co.* (1860) 22 D. 665, 671; *Davidson* v. *Macpherson* (1889) 30 S.L.R. 2, 6; *Union Electric Co.* v. *Holman*, 1913 S.C. 954, 958.
86 *Moore* v. *Paterson* (1881) 9 R. 337; *Aurdal* v. *Estrella*, 1916 S.C. 882; *cf. Whiteley* v. *Hilt* [1918] 2 K.B. 808; *Cohen* v. *Roche* [1927] 1 K.B. 169.
87 Act, ss. 12–15.
88 On these, see generally *Benjamin on Sale*, 8th ed., 553 *et seq.*; *Mackay* v. *Dick* (1881) 8 R.(H.L.) 37.
89 See *Gloag on Contract*, 2nd ed., 270 *et seq.*
90 s.11 (1); *Wallis* v. *Pratt* [1910] 2 K.B. 1003, 1012, affd. [1911] A.C. 394.

a particular stipulation is a condition or a warranty.[91] Both terms appear in the Sale of Goods Act, but the effective distinction is of no consequence in Scotland as a warranty is taken in the etymological sense of " guarantee " and a breach of warranty is defined [92] for Scotland as a failure to perform a material part of the contract, which entitles the buyer to reject the goods and claim damages, or to accept them and claim damages.[93] In Scotland the distinction is between breaches in a fundamental or material respect, which justify rescission of the contract and also a claim of damages, and breaches in a non-fundamental or immaterial respect, which justify a claim of damages only.[93a]

Defective performance at common law

The common law position as to defective performance was that the only remedy was to reject the goods and rescind the contract. The purchaser was not entitled to retain the goods and demand an abatement from the contract price corresponding to the disconformity of the goods to order.[94] Just as little was the purchaser entitled, while rescinding the contract, to retain the goods in security of a claim of damages for breach of contract.[95]

There was, however, an exception or non-application of these rules arising from the nature of the article of supply, such as machinery *in situ*, where latent defects could only be ascertained by continued working, or otherwise when the defect could not be discovered until it was too late to reject the goods,[96] as in the case of defective seed.[97] In such a case the purchaser had the alternative remedy of claiming damages for the defective quality of the goods without returning them.

Remedies under the Act

This alternative remedy thus allowed in exceptional cases was adopted as the general rule by the Act, which provides in section 11:

> " (2): In Scotland, failure by the seller to perform any material part of a contract of sale [98] is a breach of contract, which entitles the buyer either within a reasonable time after delivery to reject the goods and treat the contract as repudiated, or to retain the goods and treat

91 *Bentsen* v. *Taylor* [1893] 2 Q.B. 274, 281.

92 s. 62 (1).

93 s. 11 (2).

93a *Cf. Wade* v. *Waldon*, 1909 S.C. 571.

94 *McCormick* v. *Rittmeyer* (1869) 7 M. 854, 858 approved by Lord Dunedin in *Pollock* v. *Macrae*, 1922 S.C.(H.L.) 192, 200.

95 *Cf. Padgett* v. *McNair* (1852) 15 D. 76, and, since the Act, *Lupton & Co.* v. *Schulze* (1900) 2 F. 1118.

96 *Pearce Bros.* v. *Irons* (1869) 7 M. 571, 573.

97 *Pearce Bros.* v. *Irons* (1869) 7 M. 571; *Spencer & Co.* v. *Dobie* (1879) 7 R. 396; *Fleming* v. *Airdrie Iron Co.* (1882) 9 R. 473; *Dick & Stevenson* v. *Woodside Steel Co.* (1888) 16 R. 242. See also *Louttit's Trs.* v. *Highland Ry.* (1892) 19 R. 791, 800, *per* Lord McLaren.

98 By s. 62 (1) " as regards Scotland a breach of warranty shall be deemed to be a failure to perform a material part of the contract."

the failure to perform such material part as a breach which may give rise to a claim for compensation or damages.[99]

(3) Nothing in this section shall affect the case of any condition or warranty fulfilment of which is excused by law by reason of impossibility or otherwise."

Interaction of alternative remedies

The buyer, then, after delivery and even though the property in the goods has passed to him [1] has the alternatives of rejecting the goods, treating the contract as repudiated and claiming damages, and of retaining the goods subject to a claim of damages for their defect or deficiency. The right to reject will be barred if he has finally [1a] accepted the goods as in satisfaction of the contract; if he should do any act in relation to the goods which is inconsistent with the seller's right of ownership he is held to have accepted them [2]; and he is deemed to have accepted the goods when, after the lapse of a reasonable time, he retains them without intimating to the seller that he has rejected them.[2] He is not barred from rejecting goods for disconformity to order by the mere fact of having sold part of the goods before the fault is discovered, but he must restore the value, not the price, of the goods not returned.[3]

If a buyer seeks ineffectively to reject goods and treat the contract as repudiated, his election is not final against him, and he may subsequently have recourse to the alternative remedy of acceptance subject to his claim of damages.[4]

A buyer who elects to reject may not seek to retain the goods in his possession in purported exercise of a right of retention in security of his claim of damages and expenses,[5] nor refuse to allow the seller to remove them without replacement.[6] But where goods were sold and part of the price paid, but delivery was not complete, a rejecting purchaser was held entitled to retain the goods in security of repayment of the price.[7] And a buyer who intimates rejection but continues to use the goods, on the seller's refusal to take them back, cannot insist on the right to reject,[8]

[99] This does not affect the right to refer disputes to arbitration: *Sanderson* v. *Armour*, 1922 S.C.(H.L.) 117.

[1] *Morrison and Mason* v. *Clarkson* (1898) 25 R. 427, 437.

[1a] *Morrison, supra*; *Nelson* v. *Chalmers*, 1913 S.C. 441, where it was held in the case of a yacht, that property might pass as built, and yet be rejected before final acceptance.

[2] s. 35. *Hunt* v. *Barry* (1905) 13 S.L.T. 34; *Mechan* v. *Bow, McLachlan & Co.*, 1910 S.C. 758; *Strachan* v. *Marshall*, 1910, 2 S.L.T. 108; *Woodburn* v. *Motherwell*, 1917 S.C. 533; *Dick* v. *Cochrane and Fleming*, 1935 S.L.T. 432; *Hardy* v. *Hillerns* [1923] 2 K.B. 490. See also *Goddard* v. *Raahe*, 53 Ll.L.R. 208; *Johnston* v. *Dove* (1875) 3 R. 202; *Wallace and Brown* v. *Robinson, Fleming & Co.* (1885) 22 S.L.R. 830.

[3] *McCormick* v. *Rittmeyer* (1869) 7 M. 854.

[4] *Pollock* v. *Macrae*, 1922 S.C.(H.L.) 192, disapproving on this point *Electric Construction Co.* v. *Hurry and Young* (1897) 24 R. 312.

[5] *Lupton* v. *Schulze* (1900) 2 F. 1118.

[6] *Jardine* v. *Pendreigh* (1869) 6 S.L.R. 272.

[7] *Laing* v. *Westren* (1858) 20 D. 519.

[8] *Electric Construction Co.* v. *Hurry and Young* (1897) 24 R. 312; *Croom and Arthur* v. *Stewart* (1905) 7 F. 563.

but *semble* his claim to damages *quanti minoris* would stand unaffected.[9] A rejecting buyer is, failing express provision, not bound to return the goods.[10] In the case of perishable goods he is entitled, and probably bound, to resell at once,[11] and in case of difficulty the goods should be placed in neutral custody or judicial warrant obtained for resale.[12] The buyer is entitled to recover expenses reasonably incurred in keeping and reselling.[13]

Duty of examination

When goods are sold with a warranty, either express or one implied by the Act, the buyer is prima facie entitled to rely on that warranty and is not bound to subject the goods to all known tests to see if they conform to the contract specification.[14] This is particularly so where from the nature of the goods or their packing, full examination would not be possible without destruction.[15] But the buyer is bound to examine the goods within a reasonable time,[16] so far as they admit of reasonable examination, and should he fail to do so, or if a discoverable defect is not noticed,[17] any loss sustained will fall on him,[18] and his entitlement to damages thereafter would be limited to the difference between the value of the goods as they were and as they should have been, under section 53 (3), and will not extend to further loss sustained as by using, or mixing with other ingredients. Moreover if a buyer is going to reject the goods, he must do so within a reasonable time or else he may be held to have accepted them.[19] If the buyer has inspected the goods before making the purchase, he is not entitled to a second inspection afterwards to ascertain if they are of the quality desired but may inspect to ascertain if they are in fact the goods purchased, and it is a breach of contract to refuse such an inspection, on the ground that the buyer intended to utilise the opportunity for an illegitimate inspection.[20]

The buyer is probably entitled to reject the goods only if they suffer from a material defect: if the defect is not material [21] it seems probable

9 *Pollock* v. *Macrae*, 1922 S.C.(H.L.) 192.
10 Act, s. 36.
11 *Pommer* v. *Mowat* (1906) 14 S.L.T. 373.
12 *Malcolm* v. *Cross* (1898) 25 R. 1089. See also *Robson* v. *Thomson* (1864) 2 M. 593; *Sellar* v. *Gladstone* (1868) 5 S.L.R. 417; *Gardiner* v. *McLeavy* (1880) 7 R. 612; Brown's *Sale of Goods*, 302.
13 *Chesterman* v. *Lamb* (1834) 2 A. & E. 129; *Ellis* v. *Chinnock* (1835) 7 C. & P. 169; see also *Caswell* v. *Coare* (1809) 1 Taunt. 566.
14 *Bostock* v. *Nicholson* [1904] 1 K.B. 725. *Cf. Pinnock* v. *Lewis and Peat* [1923] 1 K.B. 690, 697; *Dobell* v. *Barber and Garratt* [1931] 1 K.B. 219, 231.
15 *e.g.* bottled mineral waters, as in *Donoghue, supra. Cf. Morrison and Mason* v. *Clarkson* (1898) 25 R. 427; *Aird and Coghill* v. *Pullan and Adams* (1904) 7 F. 258.
16 *Fleming* v. *Airdrie Iron Co.* (1882) 9 R. 473; *Hyslop* v. *Shirlaw* (1905) 7 F. 875.
17 *Mechan* v. *Bow, McLachlan & Co.*, 1910 S.C. 758.
18 *Blenkhorn* v. *Milnathort Spinning Co.* (1883) 20 S.L.R. 707; *Wagstaff* v. *Shorthorn Dairy* (1883) Cab. & E. 324; *Hammond* v. *Bussey* (1887) 20 Q.B.D. 79; *Vogan* v. *Oulton* (1899) 81 L.T. 435.
19 *Cf. Dick* v. *Cochran and Fleming*, 1935 S.L.T. 432.
20 *Chalmers* v. *Paterson* (1897) 24 R. 1020.
21 *Brandt* v. *Renny and Brown* (1881) 18 S.L.R. 525.

that the remedy is only a claim of damages.[22] " Material " is not defined by the Act and is therefore probably a question of fact. The opinion has also been expressed that it is for the buyer who proposes to reject to show that the defect is sufficiently material to justify taking this course.[23] But delivery of a quantity smaller than that ordered [24] or a larger quantity,[25] unless the excess is slight,[26] or of the goods ordered mixed with goods of a different description [27] are all material failures which justify rejection. It is probable that in the case of machinery rejection is not justifiable if the defect is remediable, and the remedy then consists in having the defect cured by the seller, or a claim of damages measured by the cost of the necessary repair.[28]

If in the circumstances goods are to a small extent disconform it may not be enough to entitle the buyer to reject.[29] So too, slight breakages in machinery required for work of a violent character may justify a demand for a repair, but not rejection.[30]

It is, however, established that where defects are apparently remediable and the seller makes efforts to cure the defect, then ultimate rejection by the buyer will not be barred either by lapse of time or by continued use of the goods so long as the remedial efforts are still being carried on.[31] Rejection may also be excluded by a compromise agreement.[32] Also where goods have been ordered for export or onward transmission, the buyer is bound to examine the goods before sending them on, so far as their nature admits of this, and if he does not do so, he cannot seek to reject on the ground of any defect which timeous examination would have revealed, as the seller is entitled to the opportunity of remedying such defects in the goods before they go further.[33-35]

If part of a consignment of goods is of contract quality and part is inferior, though not of different description, the buyer may not reject the part disconform to contract and keep the rest, but must reject the whole and treat the contract as repudiated.[36] If, on the other hand, the goods ordered are delivered mixed with goods of a different description, the buyer may keep the goods which conform to the contract and reject the rest, or

22 *Webster* v. *Cramond Iron Co.* (1875) 2 R. 752; *Bradley* v. *G. & W. Dollar* (1886) 13 R. 893. *Cf. Wade* v. *Waldon*, 1909 S.C. 571.

23 *Fewson* v. *Gemmell* (1903) 11 S.L.T. 153.

24 Act, s. 30 (1).

25 s. 30 (2).

26 *Shipton, Anderson* v. *Weil* (1912) 28 T.L.R. 269: no extra charge was made.

27 s. 30 (3).

28 *Morrison and Mason* v. *Clarkson* (1898) 25 R. 427, 437, *per* Lord McLaren.

29 *Brandt* v. *Renny and Brown* (1881) 18 S.L.R. 525; *Fewson* v. *Gemmell* (1904) 11 S.L.T. 153, 697.

30 *Bradley* v. *Dollar* (1886) 13 R. 893; *cf. Roberts* v. *Yule* (1896) 23 R. 855; *Sinclair* v. *McEwan* (1887) 25 S.L.R. 76; *Forbes* v. *Campbell* (1885) 12 R. 1065.

31 *Munro* v. *Bennett*, 1911 S.C. 337; *Aird and Coghill* v. *Pullan and Adams* (1904) 7 F. 258 (machinery).

32 *Bradley, supra*; *Smith Bros.* v. *Scott* (1875) 2 R. 601.

33-35 *Pini* v. *Smith* (1895) 22 R. 699; *Mags. of Glasgow* v. *Ireland* (1895) 22 R. 818; *Dick* v. *Cochrane and Fleming*, 1935 S.L.T. 432.

36 *Aitken, Campbell & Co.* v. *Boullen*, 1908 S.C. 490.

he may reject the whole,[37] and likewise if a quantity larger than that ordered is delivered.[38] If less are delivered than ordered the buyer may keep or reject them.[39] In each case he must pay for what he keeps at the contract rate.[40]

If a buyer retains the goods, he must do so as purchaser and not seek to retain them in security of a claim of damages for the breach which he claims justifies repudiation.[41] He may, however, intimate rejection and withhold redelivery of the goods until repayment of the price be made, if already paid, or redelivery of a bill, if such has been granted for the price.[42] Where more than one distinct thing is sold as one transaction, if one is unsound, the purchaser may reject both,[43] and *a fortiori* if they are a pair or a set.

The right to reject and claim damages may be excluded by an express provision in the contract, such as that any dispute should be referred to arbitration, but that notwithstanding the dispute, the buyer should take possession and pay the price.[44] The exclusion of the right to reject by a clause providing for acceptance and payment if no objection be taken by a stated time does not exclude the right to damages.[45]

Rejection is completely precluded by acceptance, which may be done [46] by intimation of acceptance to the seller, by doing any act to the goods inconsistent with the ownership of the seller,[47] or retaining the goods after the lapse of a reasonable time without intimating rejection to the seller.[48] What is a reasonable time is a question of fact.[49] Among the acts which have been held inconsistent with the sellers' ownership may be instanced using them,[50] fitting goods into a manufactured article in the belief that they had passed a requisite test,[51] breaking bulk,[52] resale,[53] or possibly even attempt to resell,[54] though probably not in the case of perishables,[55]

37 Act, s. 30 (3).
38 Act, s. 30 (2).
39 Act, s. 30 (1).
40 Act, s. 35.
41 *Padgett* v. *McNair* (1852) 15 D. 76; *Lupton* v. *Schulze* (1900) 2 F. 1118.
42 *Melville* v. *Critchley* (1856) 18 D. 643.
43 *Hamilton* v. *Hart* (1830) 8 S. 596. *Cf. Claddagh S.S. Co.* v. *Steven*, 1919 S.C. 184.
44 *Leary* v. *Briggs* (1904) 6 F. 857.
45 *Beck* v. *Szymanowski* [1924] A.C. 43.
46 Act, s. 35.
47 Including refusal to let the seller remove them: *Jardine* v. *Pendreigh* (1869) 6 S.L.R. 272.
48 *Croom and Arthur* v. *Stewart* (1905) 7 F. 563; *Heilbutt* v. *Hickson* (1872) L.R. 7 C.P. 438, 451, reviewing English cases: contrast *Caledonian Ry.* v. *Rankin* (1882) 10 R. 63. See also *Jardine* v. *Pendreigh* (1869) 2 S.L.R. 272.
49 Act, s. 56. Cases in Brown on *Sale*, 68.
50 *Ramsay* v. *McLellan* (1845) 8 D. 142; *Bailey* v. *Paterson* (1828) 4 Mur. 478; *Blenkhorn* v. *Milnathort Spinning Co.* (1883) 20 S.L.R. 707. But see *Fleming* v. *Airdrie Iron Co.* (1882) 9 R. 473.
51 *Mechan* v. *Bow, McLachlan & Co.*, 1910 S.C. 758; *Pini* v. *Smith* (1895) 22 R. 699; *Strachan* v. *Marshall*, 1910, 2 S.L.T. 108; *Woodburn* v. *Motherwell*, 1917 S.C. 533; *Hardy* v. *Hillerns* [1923] 2 K.B. 490; *Ruben* v. *Faire* [1949] 1 K.B. 254.
52 *Wallace and Brown* v. *Robinson, Fleming & Co.* (1885) 22 S.L.R. 830; *cf. Johnston* v. *Dove* (1875) 3 R. 202.
53 *Wallace and Brown* v. *Robinson, Fleming & Co.* (1885) 22 S.L.R. 830; *Hardy* v. *Hillerns and Fowler* [1923] 2 K.B. 490; *Bennoch* v. *McKail*, Jan. 27, 1820, F.C.
54 *Hunt* v. *Barry* (1905) 13 S.L.T. 34; *McFadzean* v. *Harsewell* (1802) Hume 330.
55 *Pommer & Thomsen* v. *Mowat* (1906) 14 S.L.T. 373.

nor resale of only a part.[56] But rejection is not barred by lapse of time or continued use where a remediable defect has been pointed out and the seller is still attempting to cure it,[57] and it may be possible by agreement to keep open the right to reject.[58]

In the case of goods intended for export or onward transmission the buyer must, if it is practicable, examine the goods and cannot reject if there should be a defect which timeous objection would have revealed, as the seller is entitled to an opportunity of rectifying defects,[59] and he is likewise barred from claiming damages if he exports and resells without inspection, unless the defect be latent.[60]

In the case of machinery it must be fitted up on the premises and tried and the seller allowed a reasonable opportunity to rectify defects before the question of rejection can apply.[61]

Intimation of rejection involves rescission of the contract so that the buyer is no longer entitled to retain or use the goods. If the seller has acquiesced in the rejection, further use by the buyer after intimation of rejection will not prejudice the rejection and rescission of the contract, but the buyer remains liable for unauthorised use of the sellers' property.[62] But if the seller does not accept the rejection nor admit its justification, the buyer's continued use of the goods precludes insistence on the rejection and involves an implied acceptance of the goods.[63] It does not, however, preclude the buyer's claim of damages,[64] and is not affected by the ultimate decision whether or not the rejection was justifiable. Even expense, trouble and inconvenience to the seller will not justify his continued use of the goods in the latter case.

Rejection may be barred by conventional provisions, as for arbitration [65] or an agreement to compromise [66] or guarantee provisions under which the seller should be called on to make good the defects in question,[67] or on the principle of personal bar.[68]

56 *McCormick* v. *Rittmeyer* (1869) 7 M. 854.

57 *Munro* v. *Bennet*, 1911 S.C. 337.

58 *Paton* v. *Payne* (1897) 35 S.L.R. 112 (H.L.).

59 *Pini*, *supra*; *Strachan*, *supra*; *Glasgow Magistrates* v. *Ireland* (1895) 22 R. 818; *Dick* v. *Cochrane & Fleming*, 1935 S.L.T. 432.

60 *Strachan* v. *Marshall*, 1910, 2 S.L.T. 108.

61 *Pearce* v. *Irons* (1869) 7 M. 571; *Fleming* v. *Airdrie Iron Co.* (1882) 9 R. 473; *Dick* v. *Woodside* (1888) 16 R. 242; *Smith* v. *Scott* (1875) 2 R. 601; *Beesley* v. *McEwan* (1884) 12 R. 384; *Bradley* v. *Dollar* (1886) 13 R. 893; *Roberts* v. *Yule* (1896) 23 R. 855; *Electric Construction Co.* v. *Hurry & Young* (1897) 24 R. 312; *Morrison* v. *Clarkson* (1898) 25 R. 427; *McCaw* v. *McLaren* (1893) 20 R. 437; *Paton* v. *Payne* (1897) 35 S.L.R. 112 (H.L.); *Aird & Coghill* v. *Pullan* (1904) 7 F. 258.

62 *Electric Construction Co.* v. *Hurry & Young* (1897) 24 R. 312, 322, *per* Lord McLaren.

63 *Electric Construction Co.*, *supra*; *Chapman* v. *Couston, Thomson & Co.* (1872) 10 M. (H.L.) 74; *Croom & Arthur* v. *Stewart & Co.* (1905) 7 F. 563. See also *Fleming* v. *Airdrie Iron Co.* (1882) 9 R. 473.

64 *Pollock* v. *Macrae*, 1922 S.C.(H.L.) 192.

65 *Leary* v. *Briggs* (1904) 6 F. 857.

66 *Bradley* v. *Dollar* (1886) 13 R. 893; *Smith Bros.* v. *Scott* (1875) 2 R. 601.

67 *Cowell* v. *Glasgow Motor Co.* (1904) 11 S.L.T. 500, 758.

68 *Croan* v. *Vallance* (1881) 8 R. 700; *Watt* v. *Glen* (1829) 7 S. 372.

Action if buyer rejects goods

By section 36, in the absence of agreement to the contrary, if goods are delivered to the buyer and rejected by him for some sufficient reason, he is not bound to return them to the seller but need only intimate his refusal to accept.[69] In consequence he will not be liable in damages for any deterioration in the goods after his rejection has been intimated and a reasonable opportunity has elapsed to allow the seller to collect them. If the rejection be wrongful, the buyer has no right to return the goods. But, *semble*, an action of damages based on negligence might lie if the buyer wilfully left the rejected goods in such a situation as to cause them to be damaged, or did not otherwise take reasonable care pending their removal. The fact that he will not take them does not entitle him to put them in any worse condition, as another market might be found for them.

If the seller wrongfully refuses to take back the goods the buyer may recover from him such expenses as are necessarily caused by their lying in his custody for a reasonable time until they can be resold.[70] It will depend on the circumstances of each case what is a reasonable time, and the buyer must offer the return of the article to the seller to entitle him to the claim. He may not claim that the seller shall not remove the goods till replaced by others,[71] nor may he subsequently sell or use part of the goods. If so he will be held liable for the price of the whole.[72]

Bell states that the buyer must challenge the goods instantly and goes on to say that on rejection the buyer must act as custodier for the seller on the principles of *negotiorum gestio*.[73] The older Scottish authority tended to impose on the dissatisfied buyer a duty to return the goods, but probably intimation to the seller that the goods were rejected and lay at his disposal was sufficient.[74] It has been laid down too, that, especially in sales of horses, the animals should be placed in neutral custody,[75] but otherwise neutral custody is a matter of circumstances.[76] It is essential that the right of rejection be exercised timeously and the right will be lost by delaying the offer to return until litigation has begun,[77] or by an act of acceptance within the meaning of section 35.[78] If the buyer rejects upon a wrong ground and later discovers ground on which he is entitled to

[69] s. 36. Any unequivocal act will do: *Grimoldy* v. *Wells* (1875) L.R. 10 C.P. 391, 395, *per* Brett J. See Stair I, 10, 5; Ersk. III, 3, 10; Bankt. I, 19, 2.

[70] *Caswell* v. *Coare* (1809) 1 Taunt. 566; *Chesterman* v. *Lamb* (1834) 2 A. & E. 129; *Ellis* v. *Chinnock* (1835) 7 C. & P. 169.

[71] *Jardine* v. *Pendreigh* (1869) 6 S.L.R. 272.

[72] *Robb* v. *Cruickshank* (1840) 2 D. 988; *Ransan* v. *Mitchell* (1845) 7 D. 813.

[73] *Prin.* § 99; *Comm.* I, 464.

[74] *M. P. Brown on Sale*, 309; *Webster* v. *Thomson* (1830) 8 S. 528; *Padgett* v. *McNair* (1852) 15 D. 76, 79, *per* L.J.-C. Hope; *Jowitt* v. *Stead* (1860) 22 D. 1400.

[75] *McBey* v. *Gardiner* (1858) 20 D. 1151, 1153, *per* Lord Cowan.

[76] *Caledonian Ry.* v. *Rankin* (1882) 10 R. 63, 65, *per* L.J.-C. Moncreiff. See *Robson* v. *Thomson* (1864) 2 M. 593; *Malcolm* v. *Cross* (1898) 25 R. 1089.

[77] *Couston, Thomson & Co.* v. *Chapman* (1872) 10 M.(H.L.) 74; explained in *Grimoldy* v. *Wells* (1875) L.R. 10 C.P. 391.

[78] *Hardy* v. *Hillerns* [1923] 2 K.B. 490; *cf. Morrison* v. *Clarkson* (1898) 25 R. 427.

reject, he is not entitled to reject but may claim damages as under a warranty.[79]

Reasonable time for rejection

While it is provided that the " reasonable time " within which the buyer must intimate rejection of the goods in terms of section 11 (2) is a question of fact,[80] decisions show that only a short period is usually allowed. Decisions prior to the Act required the buyer " to examine without delay," [81] " immediately to reject," [82] " to return . . . instantly," [83] especially in the case of patent defects; if, however, the breach is latent, as in the case of seeds,[84] or machinery,[85] or coloured plates,[86] rejection immediately on discovery of the defect is sufficient.[87]

Rejection has been held timeous in the following cases: *McBey* v. *Gardiner* [88] (mare, three days); *Lamb* v. *McKenzie* [89] (wheat, three days); *McCarter* v. *Stewart* [90] (rope, five days); *Wallace* v. *Robinson* [91] (logs of wood, seven days); *McCarter* v. *Stewart* [92] (rope, four weeks, but the deliveries were made without the buyer's knowledge and after he had instructed deliveries to stop); *Aird & Coghill* v. *Pullan & Adams* [93] (printing machine, sixteen months, during which time repairs had been attempted by the seller); *Johnston* v. *Lawrie* [94] (violin, sold with a warranty as a Stradivarius, but found to have been pieced together from bits of different violins, eight years); *Munro* v. *Bennet* [95] (pump, eighteen months, but delay due to seller's representations that pump conform to contract and repairable); *Burrell* v. *Harding* [96] (antique reredos, over two years, but the goods had been stored and the defect discovered only when they were taken out).

Non-timeous rejection

In the following cases rejection has been held to have been made too late: *Ralston* v. *Robb* [96a] (horse, two days); *Hunt* v. *Barry* [96b] (rags, ten

[79] *Braithwaite* v. *Foreign Hardwood Co.* [1905] 2 K.B. 543.
[80] s. 56.
[81] *Smart* v. *Begg* (1852) 14 D. 912, 915.
[82] *McCarter* v. *Stewart* (1877) 4 R. 890.
[83] *Carter* v. *Campbell* (1885) 12 R. 1075, 1079.
[84] *Wilson* v. *Carmichael* (1894) 21 R. 732; *cf. Carter, supra.*
[85] *Pearce* v. *Irons* (1869) 7 M. 571; *Fleming* v. *Airdrie Iron Co.* (1882) 9 R. 473.
[86] *McCaw* v. *McLaren* (1893) 20 R. 437.
[87] See also *Morrison & Mason* v. *Clarkson* (1898) 25 R. 427; *Aird & Coghill* v. *Pullan & Adams* (1904) 7 F. 258.
[88] (1858) 20 D. 1151.
[89] (1891) 8 Sh.Ct.R. 28.
[90] (1877) 4 R. 890.
[91] (1885) 22 S.L.R. 830.
[92] (1877) 4 R. 890.
[93] (1904) 7 F. 258.
[94] Feb. 1, 1890, not reported: (O.H.—Lord Kyllachy) referred to in 7 F. 878.
[95] 1911 S.C. 337.
[96] 1931 S.L.T. 76.
[96a] July 9, 1808, F.C. *Cf. Hendrie* v. *Stewart* (1842) 4 D. 1417 (five days); *Jardine* v. *Campbell* Jan. 15, 1806 (10 days).
[96b] (1905) 13 S.L.T. 34.

days); *Stevenson* v. *Dalrymple* [97] (kelp, three weeks); *Pini* v. *Smith* [98] (iron pipes, one month); *Couston Thomson* v. *Chapman* [99] (wine, five weeks); *Sinclair* v. *McEwan* [1] (furniture, six months); *Hyslop* v. *Shirlaw* [2] (pictures, twenty months); *Carter* v. *Campbell* [3] (oats, four months); *Malcolm* v. *Cross* [5] (horse, six weeks); *Flynn* v. *Scott* [6] (motor van, three weeks); *Paton* v. *Payne* [7] (machine, two months); *Chaplin* v. *Jardine* [8] (horse, two months); *Smart* v. *Begg* [9] (meal, two months); *Jardine* v. *Pendreigh* [10] (flour, where removal was not allowed for a fortnight and replacement was demanded); *Vickers & Co.* v. *Sheriff* [11] (linen, five weeks, and offer to accept at a discount of 20 per cent.); *Jaffray* v. *Webster* [12] (rum, three months); *Newmann, Hunt & Co.* v. *Harris* [13] (wine, nine months); *Morrison & Mason* v. *Clarkson* [14] (water pump, ten months, the price having been paid eight months earlier); *Dick* v. *Cochran & Fleming* [15] (earthenware, exported and then returned); *Pitcairn* v. *Brown* [16] (herrings, ten years).

Retention in security of claim of damages

Where a purchaser intimates rejection of goods supplied as being disconform to contract, he is not entitled at common law to retain them except as a purchaser, that is, he may not withhold them in security of a claim of damages for non-fulfilment of the order, nor until alternative goods are sent. If he intends to reject them, he must intimate accordingly and return the goods, while if he retains them he is held to have accepted and is therefore liable for the contract price. In *Padgett* v. *McNair* [18] P sued M for the price of shawls sold them by sample. On delivery M intimated rejection and demanded that other shawls be sent, or that they would claim a sum of damages for non-fulfilment of the bargain. Lord Justice-Clerk Hope described the buyer as being, if he were of the opinion that the goods were not up to standard, " not only entitled, but bound to return the goods to the seller."

In *Lupton & Co.* v. *Schulze & Co.*[19] an attempt was made to retain rejected goods in security of a claim of damages, and the Second Division

97 (1808) Mor.Appx. Sale 5.
98 (1895) 22 R. 699: contrast *Glasgow Mags.* v. *Ireland* (1895) 22 R. 818.
99 (1872) 10 M.(H.L.) 74.
1 (1887) 25 S.L.R. 76.
2 (1905) 7 F. 875; but *cf. Leaf* v. *International Galleries* [1950] 2 K.B. 86.
3 (1885) 12 R. 1075.
5 (1898) 25 R. 1089.
6 1949 S.C. 442.
7 (1897) 35 S.L.R. 112, H.L.
8 (1886) 23 S.L.R. 487.
9 (1852) 14 D. 912.
10 (1869) 6 S.L.R. 272.
11 (1803) Hume 332.
12 (1801) Hume 680.
13 (1803) Hume 335.
14 (1898) 25 R. 427.
15 1935 S.L.T. 432.
16 (1823) 2 S. 576.
18 (1852) 15 D. 76, 79. See, too, *Melville* v. *Critchley* (1856) 18 D. 643.
19 (1900) 2 F. 1118.

held that the buyer could not then withdraw his rejection and claim damages under section 11 (2), and that, having retained the goods, he was liable for the price and could not claim damages for breach of contract. Lord Trayner said that the election between the alternative remedies of rejection and *actio quanti minoris* was final, once made and intimated. But this must be read as qualified by Lord Dunedin's dictum in the House of Lords in *Pollock & Co.* v. *Macrae*,[20] and by the dissenting opinion of Lord Kinnear in *Electric Construction Co.* v. *Hurry & Young*,[1] to the effect that an ineffective rejection, or a repudiation of the contract which is held to be made too late to be effective, will not bar the alternative remedy of damages under the *actio quanti minoris*. Lord Moncreiff reserved his opinion on whether there might not perhaps be exceptional cases in which a purchaser has rejected goods as being not conform to contract, yet might be entitled to retain and use them, claiming damages in respect of defects in quality. It was held that the 1893 Act did not affect the rights of parties as laid down prior thereto in *Padgett* v. *McNair*.[2]

Particularly in the case of machinery retention of the goods in the buyer's custody for a time does not necessarily imply acceptance. In *Aird and Coghill* v. *Pullan and Adams* [3] A ordered a printing machine and P installed it. It was used for 16 months and the price paid, but frequent complaints were made and requests for repairs which P unsuccessfully tried to effect. It was held that P was in breach of contract and A had timeously rejected. The lapse of time was balanced by the constant requests for repairs which indicated that no final acceptance had been made. Payment of the price [4] or nearly all of it [5] is not conclusive evidence of acceptance; but to elide that presumption there must have been continued complaint, no abandonment of objections to the defects alleged, and no final acceptance.[5] But in *Pollock & Co.* v. *Macrae* [6] the opinion was expressed by Lord Dunedin, in which the rest of the House of Lords concurred, that the fact that the buyer has ineffectively elected to reject the goods and treat the contract as repudiated does not debar him from subsequently falling back upon the alternative remedy of damages under the *actio quanti minoris*.[7] In this case a contract for supplying a set of marine engines, while containing a clause requiring replacement of parts faulty through bad material or workmanship, excluded liablity for direct or consequential damages arising from these faults. It was held that this did not avail where there was such a breach of contract as rendered the engines practically unserviceable.

[20] 1922 S.C.(H.L.) 192, 201.
[1] (1897) 24 R. 312, 324. See also Lord Kyllachy's doubt in *Croom & Arthur* v. *Stewart & Co.* (1905) 7 F. 563, 567.
[2] (1852) 15 D. 76.
[3] (1904) 7 F. 258; *cf. Morrison & Mason* v. *Clarkson Bros.* (1898) 25 R. 427.
[4] *Morrison & Mason* v. *Clarkson Bros.* (1898) 25 R. 427.
[5] *Aird & Coghill* v. *Pullan & Adams* (1904) 7 F. 258.
[6] 1922 S.C.(H.L.) 192.
[7] Disapproving on this point, *Electric Construction Co.* v. *Hurry & Young* (1897) 24 R. 312 (except Lord Kinnear's dissenting judgment). See also *Nelson* v. *Chalmers*, 1913 S.C. 441; *Sutherland* v. *Montrose Shipbuilding Co.* (1860) 22 D. 665; *Aitken, Campbell & Co.* v. *Boullen & Gatenby*, 1908 S.C. 490.

Lord Kinnear's view in the *Electric Construction Co.* case [8] was that the condition which has been broken is to be treated as a warranty or independent agreement giving rise to a claim of damages, which might be set up against a claim for the price.

Damages where goods rejected

Where a buyer has justifiably and timeously rejected goods delivered to him in purported satisfaction of the contract he is in the same position as if goods had not been delivered at all and may accordingly claim damages on the same basis as they may be recovered under section 51 of the Act.[9] If he has sustained no loss by the defective delivery he may doubtless claim nominal damages.[10] Any money paid in advance may be recovered on the basis of *condictio causa data, causa non secuta* as paid for a consideration which has failed.[11]

Measure of damages for breach of warranty where goods kept

The measure is prescribed by the Act as follows:

" Section 53 (1): Where there is a breach of warranty by the seller, or where the buyer elects, or is compelled, to treat any breach of a condition on the part of the seller as a breach of warranty,[12] the buyer is not by reason only of such breach of warranty entitled to reject the goods [13]; but he may

(*a*) set up against the seller the breach of warranty in diminution or extinction of the price [14]; or

(*b*) maintain an action against the seller for damages for the breach of warranty.[15]

(2) The measure of damages for breach of warranty is the estimated loss directly and naturally resulting, in the ordinary course of events, from the breach of warranty.

(3) In the case of breach of warranty of quality such loss is prima facie the difference between the value of the goods at the time of delivery to the buyer and the value they would have had if they answered to the warranty.

(4) The fact that the buyer has set up the breach of warranty in diminution or extinction of the price does not prevent him from maintaining an action for the same breach of warranty if he has suffered further damage.

8 (1897) 24 R. at 325.
9 *Heilbutt* v. *Hickson* (1872) L.R. 7 C.P. 438.
10 *Taylor* v. *Bank of Athens* (1922) 91 L.J.K.B. 776.
11 *Cantiere San Rocco* v. *Clydebank Shipbuilding Co.*, 1923 S.C.(H.L.) 105.
12 These words dealing with treating a breach of condition as a breach of warranty are applicable to England only: see s. 11 (1) of the Act.
13 These words deal with English law and are subordinate to subsection (5) which maintains the right of the buyer in Scotland to reject for breach of warranty.
14 *Poulton* v. *Lattimore* (1809) 9 B. & C. 259; *Street* v. *Blay* (1831) 2 B. & Ad. 456; *cf. Kinnear* v. *Brodie* (1901) 3 F. 540; *British Motor Body Co.* v. *Shaw*, 1914 S.C. 922.
15 The buyer may pay in full and then sue: *Davis* v. *Hedges* (1871) L.R. 6 Q.B. 687.

(5) Nothing in this section shall prejudice or affect the buyer's right of rejection in Scotland as declared by this Act.[16]

Section 54. Nothing in this Act shall affect the right of the buyer or seller to recover interest or special damages in any case where by law interest or special damages may be recoverable, or to recover money paid where the consideration for the payment of it has failed."

The general rule for arriving at the quantum of damages prescribed by section 53 (2) is again founded on the first rule of *Hadley* v. *Baxendale*.[17] The operation of the second rule of *Hadley* [17] is provided for by section 54, and this provision applies to both subsections 53 (2) and (3).[18] Section 53 (3) lays down a prima facie rule for a case of breach of warranty of *quality* [18a] only, and not of description [18b] or fitness,[18c] and it is only applicable where the difference is to be calculated at the date of delivery; if some other date falls to be taken then the rule in subsection (2) is applicable.[19]

Section 53 (4) will apply where the fault in the goods is not exhausted by their being unsatisfactory themselves, but where the fault has caused further loss to the buyer, as by ruining other goods to which he unwittingly applied them.[20] In *Mondel* v. *Steel* [21] the buyer of a ship obtained an abatement from the price in respect of defects, and successfully brought another action when a voyage disclosed further defects. But this rule cannot extend to infringe the principle that damages arising from one cause of action must be recovered once and for all in one action.[22]

If the price has already been paid, the buyer may recover it by a conclusion for repetition (*condictio causa data, causa non secuta*), which may be in the same action as a conclusion for damages in respect of the seller's failure to implement the contract satisfactorily.[22a] Alternatively the buyer might sue under section 51 in respect that the seller has failed to deliver goods answering to the contract. The latter course is more appropriate where the goods are so disconform as to amount to an altogether different commodity.

The value of the goods as warranted is in terms of section 53 their intrinsic value and takes no account of any peculiar *pretium affectionis* as this might have the effect of permitting the buyer to obtain special damages without having first brought to the notice of the seller the particular circumstances which give the goods their special value. A special value may, however, be added by such circumstances as a sub-sale

16 In s. 11 (2).
17 (1854) 9 Ex. 341, 354.
18 *Bostock* v. *Nicholson* [1904] 1 K.B. 725; *Hamilton* v. *Magill* (1883) L.R. 12 Ir. 186.
18a s. 14 (2).
18b s. 13.
18c s. 14 (1).
19 *Loder* v. *Kekulé* (1858) 3 C.B.(N.S.) 128.
20 *Birnie* v. *Weir* (1800) 4 Paton 144 (bleach ruining cloth): *Pontifex* v. *Robertson* (1876) 2 Guthrie Sel.Cas. 508; *Bostock* v. *Nicholson* [1904] 1 K.B. 725, 741.
21 (1841) 8 M. & W. 858. The actual decision depends much on matters of English pleading.
22 *Stevenson* v. *Pontifex and Wood* (1887) 15 R. 125.
22a s. 54, last phrase.

known to the seller and the absence of a market. So in *Hamilton* v. *Magill* [23] where the proposed sub-sale was known the damages recovered amounted to the difference between the value of the articles supplied and the sub-sale price rather than the contract price.

Payment into court

Section 59 provides that where a buyer has elected to accept goods which he might have rejected and only to claim damages he may in an action by the seller for the price be required in the discretion of the court to consign or pay into court the price or part of it or to give other reasonable security for its due payment. This is to provide against frivolous claims of damages in diminution of the price and seems rarely to have been applied.[24]

Damages where buyer keeps goods

The damages fall to be measured by the loss sustained in consequence of the defect in the goods. In *Electric Construction Co.* v. *Hurry & Young* [29] Lord Kinnear described the measure of damages under the *actio quanti minoris*: " The damage claimable for breach of one condition would not necessarily be the same as for the breach of the entire contract. I presume that the claim should be measured by the difference between the value of the machinery actually supplied and the value which it would have had to the defenders if it had been in all respects conform to contract." The measure of damages will be prima facie the difference measured as at the time fixed for delivery between the value of the goods as they should have been and their value as they are, decreased by reason of the defect constituting the breach of warranty of quality,[30] or alternatively will be the estimated loss directly and naturally resulting in the ordinary course of events,[31] and this sum may be increased by proof of special damage,[32] subject to the usual rules of remoteness of damage. The claim may be made by substantive action for damages or as a counterclaim in diminution or extinction of the seller's claim for the price.[33] A claim of damages on one of these bases may be pleaded in diminution or extinction of the price [34] and this course of action would not prevent a subsequent action for the same breach of warranty if he has suffered further damage.[35]

In *Mondel* v. *Steel* [36] a buyer of a ship secured a reduction in price by setting up a breach of warranty in respect of difference between the ship as

23 (1883) 12 L.R.Ir. 186. *Cf. Slater & Co.* v. *Hoyle* [1920] 2 K.B. 32, where sellers had no knowledge of sub-sale.

24 *Watson* v. *Thordahl* (1898) 7 S.L.T. 7.

29 (1897) 24 R. 312, 325, approved in *Pollock* v. *Macrae*, 1922 S.C.(H.L.) 192, 201.

30 s. 53 (3): *Jones* v. *Just* (1868) L.R. 3 Q.B. 197; *cf. British Westinghouse* v. *Underground Rys.* [1912] A.C. 673.

31 s. 53 (2).

32 s. 54.

33 s. 53 (1).

34 s. 53 (1).

35 s. 53 (4).

36 (1841) 8 M. & W. 858.

she was and she should have been at the time of delivery, against the seller's action for the price of the ship, and subsequently recovered further damages in respect of subsequent repairs rendered necessary by the same breach of contract which deprived him of the use of the vessel. This case was followed in *Davis* v. *Hedges* [37] and it was further held that the buyer was not bound to plead for a reduction of the price in the seller's action but might pay the price in full and then sue on the breach of warranty, though such a course in Scotland is liable to be met by the plea of " competent and omitted " and is not advisable.

In *Kinnear* v. *Brodie* [38] the counter-claim extinguished the seller's claim for the price. A horse was sold, warranted " correct in wind and work." It proved unruly and was drowned next day when it ran away. It was held that it was disconform to warranty, that the defenders could have rejected had it not been drowned, and that as their inability to do so arose from the breach of warranty and the horse's innate vice, they were not liable for the price. In *Wright* v. *Blackwood*,[39] where a horse died after purchase by reason of a pre-existing latent disease, repetition of the price was the measure of damages. The section was not given effect to in *Robey* v. *Stein*,[40] where damages in respect of defective power were set up against a claim for the price of a steam engine, but it was held on the facts that the statement founded on was an innocent misrepresentation and not a warranty as to the subject of sale. Claims for further loss under section 53 (4) were given effect to in *Birnie* v. *Weir* [41] and *Pontifex* v. *Robertson*,[42] where the defenders' claim both extinguished the price and justified a further award of damages. Again in *Bostock* v. *Nicholson* [43] the sellers had supplied sugar, defective in that it contained sulphuric acid, to brewers who in ignorance used it in the brewing process. They were held entitled to recover the whole price paid for the goods on the basis of entire failure of consideration and also, as further damages, to the value of the goods rendered useless by being mixed with the poisonous acid.

Damages have been given under section 54 in several cases where the prima facie measure of damages under section 53 is obviously inadequate, as where an anchor is lost by reason of a defective cable [44] or a specially made carriage-pole broke and caused injury,[45] or food contains germs causing injury.[46]

[37] (1871) L.R. 6 Q.B. 687.
[38] (1901) 3 F. 540.
[39] (1833) 11 S. 722.
[40] (1900) 3 F. 278.
[41] (1800) 4 Pat.App. 144 (bleaching powder).
[42] 2 Guthrie's Sel.Sh.Ct.Cas. 508 (paste for coachbuilding).
[43] [1904] 1 K.B. 725.
[44] *Borrodaile* v. *Brunton* (1818) 8 Taunt. 535; *cf. Agincourt S.S. Co.* v. *Eastern Extension Telegraph Co.* [1907] 2 K.B. 305.
[45] *Randall* v. *Newson* (1877) 2 Q.B.D. 102.
[46] *Wallis* v. *Russell* [1902] 2 Ir.R. 585 (crabs); *Holden* v. *Bostock* (1902) 18 T.L.R. 317 (arsenic in sugar); *Frost* v. *Aylesbury Dairy Co.* [1905] 1 K.B. 608 (milk); *Square* v. *Model Farm Dairies* [1939] 2 K.B. 365 (milk); *Jackson* v. *Watson* [1909] 2 K.B. 193 (tinned salmon); *Donoghue* v. *Stevenson*, 1932 S.C.(H.L.) 31; *Lockhart* v. *Barr*, 1943 S.C.(H.L.) 1 (aerated water). See also *Heil* v. *Hedges* [1951] 1 T.L.R. 512.

The commonest measure of damages in cases falling under section 53 is that prescribed by section 53 (3), namely, the difference between the value of the goods as warranted and that as delivered, as in the case of seeds,[47] food for cattle [48] or for persons,[49] or clothing.[50]

In other cases the rule of section 53 (2) applies, as where lime was supplied disconform to warranty in consequence of which a wall was condemned; the damages allowed were the cost of pulling down and rebuilding and loss of ground rent [51]; or a defective chain broke and a man was injured, the damages being the damages and expenses paid to him in compensation.[52]

Conditions and warranties implied by Act

The Sale of Goods Act 1893 implies various conditions and warranties into contracts to which the Act applies,[53] subject to the liberty of the parties to negative any or all of these [54] by their express agreement,[55] or by the course of dealing between the parties,[56] or by usage, if the usage be such as to bind both parties to the contract.[57] An express warranty or condition does not negative a warranty or condition implied by the Act unless inconsistent therewith.[58]

Implied undertakings as to title

It seems probable that prior to the Act the warranty in the case of sale of goods was only against eviction,[60] though the statutory rule had been foreshadowed in *Eichholz* v. *Bannister*.[61]

S. 12 of the 1893 Act, as substituted by section 1 of the Supply of Goods (Implied Terms) Act, 1973, provides:

> " 12 (1) In every contract of sale, other than one to which subsection (2) of this section applies, there is:
>
> (*a*) an implied condition on the part of the seller that in the case of a sale, he has a right to sell the goods, and in the case of an agreement to sell he will have a right to sell the goods at the time when the property is to pass; and

47 *Randall* v. *Raper* (1858) E.B. & E. 84; *Wilson* v. *Carmichael* (1894) 21 R. 732.
48 *Pinnock Bros.* v. *Lewis and Peat* [1923] 1 K.B. 690; *Dobell* v. *Barber & Garratt* [1931] 1 K.B. 219.
49 Cases in note 46, *supra*.
50 *Grant* v. *Australian Knitting Mills Ltd.* [1936] A.C. 85.
51 *Smith* v. *Johnson* (1899) 15 T.L.R. 179.
52 *Mowbray* v. *Merryweather* [1895] 2 Q.B. 640; doubted in *Wood* v. *Mackay* (1906) 8 F. 625.
53 ss. 12–15.
54 s. 55.
55 *e.g. Ward* v. *Hobbs* (1878) 4 App.Cas. 13; *Pinnock Bros.* v. *Lewis & Peat* [1923] 1 K.B. 690; *Canada Atlantic Grain Export Co.* v. *Eilers* (1929) 35 Com.Cas. 90.
56 *Re Marquis of Anglesey* [1910] 2 Ch. 548.
57 *e.g. Cointat* v. *Myham* (1914) 30 T.L.R. 282; *Produce Brokers Co.* v. *Olympia Oil and Cake Co.* [1916] 1 A.C. 314.
58 s. 14 (4); *Bigge* v. *Parkinson* (1862) 7 H. & N. 955.
60 *M. P. Brown on Sale*, 231, 239; *Swan* v. *Martin* (1865) 3 M. 851. See Stair I, 14, 1. As regards heritage, *vide infra*, Chap. 46.
61 (1864) 17 C.B.(N.S.) 708.

(b) an implied warranty that the goods are free, and will remain free until the time when the property is to pass from any charge or encumbrance not disclosed or known to the buyer before the contract is made and that the buyer will enjoy quiet possession of the goods except so far as it may be disturbed by the owner or other person entitled to the benefit of any charge or encumbrance so disclosed or known.

(2) In a contract of sale, in the case of which there appears from the contract or is to be inferred from the circumstances of the contract an intention that the seller shall transfer only such title as he or she or a third person may have, there is

(a) an implied warranty that all charges or encumbrances known to the seller and not known to the buyer have been disclosed to the buyer before the contract is made and

(b) an implied warranty that neither

(i) the seller; nor

(ii) in a case where the parties to the contract intend that the seller should transfer only such title as a third person may have, that person; nor

(iii) anyone claiming through or under the seller or that third person otherwise than under a charge or encumbrance disclosed or known to the buyer before the contract is made;

will disturb the buyer's quiet possession of the goods."

By section 55, as substituted by the 1973 Act, section 4, a clause excluding the provisions of section 12 is void.

On the basis that in Scotland the word warranty is taken to be equivalent to condition, it follows that breach of any of the four implied warranties provided by this section is a breach of contract entitling the buyer to the remedies provided by section 11 (2). Where, however, *restitutio in integrum* is impossible, as, for example, where the subject of sale has been used by the buyer, rescission of the contract is precluded and the only remedy still open to the buyer is that of claiming damages measured under section 53 (2). The damages in such a case are assessed on the principle of indemnification, and may therefore include interest and expenses necessarily incurred by the buyer.[62] The measure of damages may amount to repayment of the full price where seed has been sown resulting in a complete failure of the crop,[62] or where a horse died a fortnight after purchase from an anterior defect.[63]

If the buyer knows that the seller has only a limited right to the goods he cannot insist on any implied warranty of an absolute title.[64] It has

62 *Adamson* v. *Smith* (1799) Mor. 14244.

63 *Wright* v. *Blackwood* (1833) 11 Sh. 722. See also *Bell* v. *Queensberry's Exors* (1824) 3 Sh. 416 (lease); *Stephen* v. *Lord Advocate* (1876) 6 R. 282.

64 *Leith Heritages Co.* v. *Edinburgh Glass Co.* (1876) 3 R. 789.

been held that a seller was in breach of his warranty of right to sell when he sold goods in tins bearing a label which infringed another firm's trade-mark, and which the buyer could not handle without the danger of exposing himself to an action. The remedy was to reject the entire consignment or to remove the offending labels and recover damages from the seller in respect of the reduced sale-value.[65]

Damages under this section might be claimed in the case of stolen goods sold, which subsequently have to be returned to the true owner, as in Scotland a *vitium reale* attaches to stolen goods so that the true owner can always recover them from a purchaser.[66] So, where a man bought a car and used it for some months and had then to restore it to its true owner from whom it had been stolen, he was held entitled to recover the full price from the seller.[67] A not dissimilar result was reached on the basis of breach of warranty of authority to sell in *Anderson* v. *Croall.*[68]

Quiet enjoyment—section 12 (1) (b)

Breach of warranty of quiet enjoyment is well illustrated by *Mason* v. *Burningham.*[69] There the plaintiff purchased from the defendant, both acting in good faith, a typewriter which was later found to have been stolen, and which had to be returned to the true owner. The plaintiff recovered the price of the typewriter and also a sum spent on having the typewriter overhauled after purchasing it, as damages for breach of warranty. It was held that the overhaul was the ordinary and natural thing to do and so the damages flowed " directly and naturally " from the breach of contract within the meaning of section 53 (2).

The scope of this subsection has been stated [70] as being—" that nobody shall interfere with the possession of the goods by reason of want of title of the vendor, or of any act done or committed by anyone having authority from the vendor. It is little more than a covenant of title. It is a warranty that the vendor shall not, nor shall anybody claiming under a superior title, or under his authority, interfere with the quiet enjoyment of the vendee." It also covers the case where though the seller could sell, a third party might be able to interdict the buyer from dealing with the goods, as being an infringement of a patent.[71]

The warranty of quiet possession does not, however, import any warranty against third parties making unfounded claims, and hence, if a third party makes such a claim, the expenses incurred by the buyer in

65 *Niblett* v. *Confectioners' Materials Co.* [1921] 3 K.B. 387, overruling *Montforts* v. *Marsden* (1895) 12 R.P.C. 266 (machine made under invalid patent).

66 *Todd* v. *Armour* (1882) 9 R. 901.

67 *Rowland* v. *Divall* [1923] 2 K.B. 500, applied in *Butterworth* v. *Kingsway Motors Ltd.* [1954] 2 All E.R. 694. *Cf. Warman* v. *Southern Counties Car Finance Corpn.* [1949] 2 K.B. 576.

68 (1903) 6 F. 153.

69 [1949] 2 K.B. 545.

70 *Montforts* v. *Marsden* (1895) 12 R.P.C. 266, *per* Lord Russell C.J.

71 *Niblett* v. *Confectioners' Materials Co.* [1921] 3 K.B. 387; see also Lord McLaren in *Welsh* v. *Russell* (1894) 21 R. 769, 773.

resisting such a claim are not recoverable from the seller.[72] *Contra*, if the third party makes good his title to the goods, the warranty applies.

Quiet enjoyment—section 12 (2)

The warranty arises also where the intention is that the seller transfer only a limited title.[73]

Sale by description, or sample and description

This is regulated by section 13 of the Act as amended by Supply of Goods (Implied Terms) Act, 1973, section 2:

> " 13 (1) Where there is a contract for the sale of goods by description, there is an implied condition that the goods shall correspond with the description; and if the sale be by sample, as well as by description,[73a] it is not sufficient that the bulk of the goods correspond with the sample if the goods do not also correspond with the description."
>
> (2) A sale of goods shall not be prevented from being a sale by description by reason only that, being exposed for sale or hire, they are selected by the buyer."

It is accordingly a breach of a condition of the contract if the seller fails to produce goods which answer the description by which the goods were sold, or the sample and description, as the case may be. It matters not that he tenders goods of another's manufacture.[74] The rule applies both to a specific article, or to unascertained goods. Description or sample and description are usually opposed to inspection of the goods.[75] Description must apply to all cases where the buyer has not seen the goods,[76] and may apply even if he has seen the goods if the deviation from description is not apparent.[77] Description may mean, particularly with reference to unascertained goods, kind, species, or class.[78] But with regard to specific articles it may be verbal identification and may or may not further imply a warranty that the article possesses the characteristics mentioned in the description.[78a]

The term " description " has been interpreted fairly liberally and extends to statements that the goods were part of a particular stock,[79]

[72] *Stephen* v. *Lord Advocate* (1878) 6 R. 282; *Dougall* v. *Mags. of Dunfermline*, 1908 S.C. 151. Compare the position of heritage under a clause of warrandice.

[73] See *e.g. Payne* v. *Elsden* (1900) 17 T.L.R. 161; *Niblett* v. *Confectioners' Materials Co.* [1921] 3 K.B. 387; *Rowland* v. *Divall* [1923] 2 K.B. 500.

[73a] As to sale by sample alone, see s. 15, *infra*.

[74] *West Stockton Iron Co.* v. *Nielson & Maxwell* (1880) 7 R. 1055; *Johnson & Reay* v. *Nicholl* (1881) 8 R. 437.

[75] *Varley* v. *Whipp* [1900] 1 Q.B. 513, 516.

[76] *Varley* v. *Whipp* [1900] 1 Q.B. 513, 516.

[77] *Cf. Thornton and Fehr* v. *Beers* [1919] 1 K.B. 486; *Medway Oil and Storage Co.* v. *Silica Oil Corporation* (1928) 33 Com.Cas. 195; *Beale* v. *Taylor* [1967] 3 All E.R. 253.

[78] *e.g. Heyworth* v. *Hutchinson* (1867) L.R. 2 Q.B. 447.

[78a] *e.g. Parsons* v. *Sexton* (1847) 4 C.B. 899 (specific machine described as " fourteen-horse engine ").

[79] *Thomson Bros.* v. *Thomson* (1885) 13 R. 88.

shipped in a particular month,[80] carried [81] or packed in a specified way,[82] being carried in a ship due on a stated date,[83] compounded according to an agreed formula [84] or of a certain origin [85]; so, too, the quantity of goods,[86] the size of the bags,[87] or the average weight of the parcels [88] may be part of the description. It is, however, questionable whether when there is a breach of " condition " but there is no difference in the value of the goods [89] the buyer may reject in Scotland. He may in England,[90] except in the case of a trivial failure.[91] It is somewhat doubtful if he might in Scotland having regard to the provisions of section 11 (2), and the general rule requiring materiality of breach to justify rescission.[1]

Hence a sale in which the goods are described may be a contract for the particular thing identified by the terms used without any condition that it is or can do what those words imply.[2] But if the buyer contracted for the goods as described so that the inaccuracy of the description made them substantially different though their identity was not in question, the description is a condition of the sale.[3] To come within this section of the Act, the buyer must rely on the description [4] which may be tacitly inferred from the circumstances of the sale.[5] If goods are sold as being of a particular brand, that is part of the description and they may be rejected if they do not bear that brand, even though made by the same maker.[6]

Section 13 carries no provision as to quality or fitness,[6a] but the goods supplied must not be so deficient in quality as not to answer the description by which they were sold, and if they do not answer that description it is a different article and a non-performance of the contract.[7] Thus a thing described as a " car " must be capable of self-propelled motion and have

80 *Bowes* v. *Shand* (1877) 2 App.Cas. 455.
81 *Meyer* v. *Trevara* (1930) 46 T.L.R. 553; contrast *Meyer* v. *Kivisto* (1929) 142 L.T. 480.
82 *Re Moore & Landauer* [1921] 2 K.B. 519.
83 *Macpherson Train* v. *Ross* [1955] 2 All E.R. 445.
84 *Hill* v. *Ashington Piggeries* [1969] 3 All E.R. 1496.
85 *Jones* v. *Clarke* (1858) 2 H. & N. 725.
86 *Green* v. *Arcos* (1931) 147 L.T. 336.
87 *Manbre Saccharine Co.* v. *Corn Products Co.* [1919] 1 K.B. 198; *cf. Dower* v. *Corrie Maccoll & Co.* (1925) T.L.R. 43.
88 *Ballantine* v. *Camp & Bosman* (1923) 129 L.T. 502.
89 *e.g. Hopkins* v. *Hitchcock* (1863) 14 C.B.(N.S.) 65.
90 *Moore, supra.*
91 *Shipton, Anderson & Co.* v. *Weil Bros.* [1912] 1 K.B. 574.
1 *Wade* v. *Waldon*, 1909 S.C. 571.
2 *Attwater* v. *Kinnes*, 1906 (H.L.,Sc.) not reported. See *Scotsman*, May 29, 1906; *Benjamin on Sale*, 8th ed., 616.
3 *Kennedy* v. *Panama Mail Co.* (1867) L.R. 2 Q.B. 580; *Kirkpatrick* v. *Gowan* (1875) 9 Ir.R.C.L. 521.
4 *Varley* v. *Whipp* [1900] 1 Q.B. 513.
5 *Wren* v. *Holt* [1903] 1 K.B. 610; *Morelli* v. *Fitch & Gibbons* [1928] 2 K.B. 636; *Grant* v. *Australian Knitting Mills* [1936] A.C. 85.
6 *Scaliaris* v. *Ofverberg* (1920) 37 T.L.R. 307. Contrast *Hopkins* v. *Hitchcock* (1863) 14 C.B.(N.S.) 65; *Powell* v. *Horton* (1836) 2 Bing.N.C. 668; *Parsons* v. *N.Z. Shipping Co.* [1901] 1 Q.B. 548.
6a *Grenfell* v. *Meyrowitz* [1936] 2 All E.R. 1313.
7 *Chanter* v. *Hopkins* (1838) 4 M. & W. 399, 404; *Jaffé* v. *Ritchie* (1860) 23 D. 242; *cf. Carson Warren & Co.* v. *Couston, Chapman & Co.* (1868) 5 S.L.R. 207.

a passenger-carrying body: a wreck of a lorry is not a " car." A statement of quality may be part of the description by which goods are sold,[8] but if it refers only to some state or condition of the goods, it is not part of the description and section 14 must be invoked. So, too, where goods are sold under a trade name that may be merely nominal and descriptive and does not imply any particular capacity.[9-21]

The cases on this section mostly relate to the buyers' rejection, as where a reaper was sold as " almost new," and rejected,[22] or a vehicle sold as a " new Singer car " which was not such,[23] or a gas engine sold as " in excellent order," [24] but several illustrate the recovery of damages under section 53 (2). In *Wallis* v. *Pratt*,[25] P sold seed by sample and description to W and delivered another kind, the discrepancy not being discoverable till the seed was sown. A sub-purchaser sowed it and recovered damages when it produced a wrong crop: hence W could recover from P for breach of warranty the sum paid to the sub-purchaser in damages. A similar result was arrived at in *Pinnock Bros.* v. *Lewis & Peat*,[26] where damages and expenses recovered by sub-purchasers were held recoverable from the original suppliers as the goods supplied were of a different description.

In *Taylor* v. *Bank of Athens* [27] beans were sold, to be shipped in August. It later appeared that they had been shipped in September, but as there was no difference in value, only nominal damages were recoverable. Similarly in *Finlay* v. *Kwik Hoo Tong* [28] a bill of lading failed to state the correct date of shipment. The buyer in ignorance accepted and resold the goods and on discovering the breach was held entitled to recover the difference between the market price and the contract price ot the goods. The market price had fallen and, had the bill of lading been correctly dated, the buyer could have rejected the goods and bought more cheaply in the market.

In *Wilson* v. *Dunville*,[29] distillers sold a farmer grain for feeding cattle, and it was found that the grain did not reasonably answer the description. The farmer recovered the value of cattle which had died as a result of eating the grain, and the plea was repelled that the defendants could not be liable for the consequences of such an unforeseen breach of contract as the presence of the poisonous substances in the grain. The court held that it was not necessary that the particular loss which ensued should have been within the contemplation of the parties.

In *Bostock* v. *Nicholson* [30] sulphuric acid was sold to sugar refiners, but the purpose for which it was required was not communicated. The acid

[8] *Re N.W. Rubber Co.* [1908] 2 K.B. 907; *Wimble* v. *Lillico* (1922) 38 T.L.R. 296.
[9-21] *Rowan* v. *Coats Iron Co.* (1885) 12 R. 395 (" 4 cwt. per hour size gas producers "). *Cf. Roberts* v. *Yule* (1896) 23 R. 855.
[22] *Varley* v. *Whipp* [1900] 1 Q.B. 513.
[23] *Andrew Bros. Ltd.* v. *Singer & Co. Ltd.* [1934] 1 K.B. 17.
[24] *Roberts* v. *Yule* (1896) 23 R. 855. But see *Bradley* v. *Dollar* (1886) 13 R. 893.
[25] [1911] A.C. 394. *Cf. Rutherford* v. *Miln*, 1941 S.C. 125.
[26] [1923] 1 K.B. 690. So, too, *Randall* v. *Raper* (1858) E.B. & E. 84 (seed barley).
[27] (1922) 91 L.J.K.B. 776.
[28] [1929] 1 K.B. 400.
[29] (1879) 6 L.R.Ir. 210.
[30] [1904] 1 K.B. 725. See further *Holden* v. *Bostock* (1902) 18 T.L.R. 317.

delivered contained arsenic which poisoned the eventual consumers of the beer made from the plaintiff's products, and was found not to answer the description of sulphuric acid. The damages were assessed at the price paid for the worthless acid, and the value of ingredients mixed with it in manufacture before the plaintiffs became aware of the poisonous nature of the acid. But loss of goodwill and business consequent on the supply of poisonous matter did not " directly and naturally " result from the breach, and so were too remote, as were the damages recovered from the plaintiffs by their sub-purchasers, as these contracts had not been brought to the defendants' knowledge.[31]

In *Smith* v. *Waite, Nash & Co.*[32] the pursuer purchased turnip seed from the defender by description. The terms of sale excluded all warranties. The seed turned out to be a mixture of two kinds, though indistinguishable in seed form. It was held on the failure of the crop that the notice of exclusion of warranties protected the sellers from a claim of damages made by the buyers which represented the damages which the purchasers had paid to sub-purchasers, who had recovered from them in respect of the failure of the seed retailed to them. Claims for loss by injury to business reputation and loss of custom were also made unsuccessfully. But it has been observed [33] that the Scottish courts are more lenient towards a seller in the matter of these clauses and allow him more easily to escape the consequences of a sale by description.[34]

Implied conditions as to quality and fitness

The common law was expressed in the statement that a fair price demanded a fair article and it was consequently held that if there were no provision to the contrary, the seller was bound to supply goods of reasonably good quality.

S. 14 of the 1893 Act, as substituted by the Supply of Goods (Implied Terms) Act, 1973, section 3, provides:

" 14 (1) Except as provided by this section, and section 15 of this Act and subject to the provisions of any other enactment, there is no implied condition or warranty as to the quality or fitness for any particular purpose of goods supplied under a contract of sale.

(2) Where the seller sells goods in the course of a business, there is an implied condition that the goods supplied under the contract are of merchantable quality, except that there is no such condition

(*a*) as regards defects specifically drawn to the buyer's attention before the contract is made; or

(*b*) if the buyer examines the goods before the contract is made, as regards defects which that examination ought to reveal.

31 *Cf. Pinnock Bros.* v. *Lewis & Peat* [1923] 1 K.B. 690.
32 (1888) 15 R. 533; followed, in *Rutherford* v. *Miln*, 1941 S.C. 125.
33 *Benjamin on Sale*, 8th ed., 627. *Cf. Rutherford, supra, per* Lord Mackay, 131.
34 For an unsuccessful attempt to exclude liability under s. 13, see *Nicholson and Venn* v. *Smith Marriott* (1947) 77 L.T. 189, where parties contracted under common error.

(3) Where the seller sells goods in the course of a business and the buyer, expressly or by implication, makes known to the seller any particular purpose for which the goods are being bought there is an implied condition that the goods supplied under the contract are reasonably fit for that purpose, whether or not that is a purpose for which such goods are commonly supplied, except where the circumstances show that the buyer does not rely, or that it is unreasonable for him to rely, on the seller's skill or judgment.

(4) An implied condition or warranty as to quality or fitness for a particular purpose may be annexed to a contract of sale by usage.

(5) The foregoing provisions of this section apply to a sale by a person who in the course of a business is acting as agent for another as they apply to a sale by a principal in the course of a business, except where that other is not selling in the course of a business and either the buyer knows that fact or reasonable steps are taken to bring it to the notice of the buyer before the contract is made.

(6) In the application of subsection (3) above to an agreement for the sale of goods under which the purchase price or part of it is payable by instalments any reference to the seller shall include a reference to the person by whom any antecedent negotiations are conducted; and section 58 (3) and (5) of the Hire-Purchase Act, 1965, section 54 (3) and (5) of the Hire-Purchase (Scotland) Act, 1965, and section 65 (3) and (5) of the Hire-Purchase (Northern Ireland) Act, 1966 (meaning of antecedent negotiations and related expressions) shall apply in relation to this subsection as they apply in relation to each of these Acts, but as if a reference to any such agreement were included in the references in subsection (3) of each of those sections to the agreements there mentioned."

Condition of merchantable quality—section 14 (2)

This provision is wider than section 14 (2) as originally enacted, and applies to all sales in the course of a business.[36] " Merchantable quality " is defined [37] as meaning " as fit for the purpose or purposes for which goods of that kind are commonly bought as it is reasonable to expect having regard to any description applied to them, the price (if relevant) and all the other relevant circumstances." The condition is excluded only if the defects were disclosed, or the actual examination made should have revealed the defect.[38]

Goods acquired for disclosed purpose—section 14 (3)

This provision replaces that in section 14 (1) as originally enacted. The purpose disclosed for the purchase may be the obvious one for which

[36] " Business " is defined in the 1973 Act, s. 7 (1).

[37] 1973 Act, s. 7 (2). See also *Bristol Tramways* v. *Fiat Motors Ltd.* [1910] 2 K.B. 831; *Cammell Laird* v. *Manganese Bronze Co.* [1934] A.C. 402; *Grant* v. *A.K.M. Ltd.* [1936] A.C. 85; *Bartlett* v. *Sidney Marcus Ltd.* [1965] 2 All E.R. 753; *Kendall* v. *Lillico* [1969] 2 A.C. 31; *Brown* v. *Craiks*, 1970 S.L.T. 141.

[38] *Cf. Thornett & Fehr* v. *Beer* [1919] 1 K.B. 486.

such goods are ordinarily bought,[39] or an exceptional purpose. In either case the implied condition of reasonable fitness arises, unless either exception applies.

Sales by sample

The provisions regulating sales by sample are in section 15.

"(1) A contract of sale is a contract for sale by sample where there is a term in the contract, express or implied, to that effect.

(2) In the case of a contract for sale by sample—

(*a*) There is an implied condition that the bulk shall correspond with the sample in quality [1];

(*b*) There is an implied condition that the buyer shall have a reasonable opportunity of comparing the bulk with the sample.

(*c*) There is an implied condition that the goods shall be free from any defect, rendering them unmerchantable, which would not be apparent on reasonable examination of the sample."

From these provisions it follows that on proof of failure of bulk to correspond to the sample, or if goods are found, after reasonable examination of the sample, to suffer from a defect rendering them unmerchantable, the goods may be rejected or a claim of damages made in respect of the breach of warranty.[2] The fact that a sample is open to inspection does not make the sale a sale by sample if printed conditions of sale provide that intending purchasers must satisfy themselves of the condition of the goods in bulk,[3] and sales where samples have been exhibited by the seller are not necessarily sales by sample.[4] Where a buyer asked for a guaranteed analysis, which was supplied with the sample, the seller was held to have warranted that the bulk was equal to the sample and also that the analysis was a fair analysis of the bulk.[5]

[39] *e.g.* food: *Wallis* v. *Russell* [1902] 2 L.R. 585; milk: *Frost* v. *Aylesbury Dairy Co.* [1905] 1 K.B. 608; hot-water bottle: *Priest* v. *Last* [1903] 2 K.B. 148; boots: *Thompson* v. *Sears* 1926 S.L.T. 221; coals: *Gillespie Bros. & Co.* v. *Cheney, Eggars & Co.* [1896] 2 Q.B. 59; *Crichton & Stevenson* v. *Love*, 1908 S.C. 818; *Duke* v. *Jackson*, 1921 S.C. 362; *Fitzpatrick* v. *Barr*, 1948 S.L.T. (Sh.Ct.) 5; *Wilson* v. *Rickett Cockerell & Co.* [1954] 1 Q.B. 598.

[1] "Quality" includes state or condition: s. 62 (1).

[2] *Drummond* v. *Van Ingen* (1887) 12 App.Cas. 284. See also *Aitken, Campbell & Co.* v. *Boullen & Gatenby*, 1908 S.C. 490.

[3] *White* v. *Dougherty* (1891) 18 R. 972.

[4] *Kerr* v. *McDowall* (1828) 6 S. 1029; *Muil* v. *Gibb* (1840) 2 D. 1227; *White* v. *Dougherty* (1891) 18 R. 972; *Tye* v. *Fynmore* (1813) 3 Camp. 462; *Meyer* v. *Everth* (1814) 4 Camp. 22; *Gardiner* v. *Gray* (1815) 4 Camp. 144; *Powell* v. *Horton* (1836) 2 Bing.N.C. 668; *Josling* v. *Kingsford* (1863) 13 C.B.(N.S.) 447. See also *Hills* v. *Buchanan* (1786) Mor. 14200; 3 Paton 47; *Ginner* v. *King* (1890) 7 T.L.R. 140.

Cases of sales by sample are *Watt* v. *Glen* (1829) 7 S. 372; *Padgett* v. *McNair* (1852) 15 D 76; *Jowett* v. *Stead* (1860) 22 D. 1400; *Couston, Thomson & Co.* v. *Chapman* (1872) 10 M.(H.L.) 74; *Glasgow Mags.* v. *Ireland* (1895) 22 R. 818; *Hunt* v. *Barry* (1905) 13 S.L.T. 34; *Parker* v. *Palmer* (1821) 4 B. & Ald. 387; *Lorymer* v. *Smith* (1822) 1 B. & C. 1; *Carter* v. *Crick* (1859) 4 H. & N. 412; *Russell* v. *Nicolopulo* (1860) 8 C.B.(N.S.) 362.

[5] *Towerson* v. *Agricultural Aspatria Socy.* (1872) 27 L.T. 276.

Comparison of bulk with sample

The place of delivery is prima facie the place for comparing the bulk with the sample.[5a] An improper refusal by the seller to allow the buyer to compare the bulk with the sample is a breach of warranty under section 15 (2) (*b*) which justifies rejection or damages.[6] The buyer may repudiate the contract if inspection be refused before delivery.[6] The right may be waived, but the goods may still be inspected and rejected on delivery.[7] Where an agent in Dundee obtained a sample from Glasgow and sent it to his buyer in Hamburg, and the cargo was rejected at Hamburg as disconform to sample, the opinion was expressed that the rejection was timeous as the agent had no chance of comparing the bulk and the seller knew the goods were for export.[8]

Freedom from latent defects

Sale by sample ordinarily negatives any condition that the goods are merchantable [9] but there remains the implied condition of freedom from a latent defect which would make them unmerchantable. In *Mody* v. *Gregson* [10] sellers were held liable for delivering goods containing a foreign ingredient not discoverable on inspection introduced to make the goods weigh the requisite amount but rendering them unmerchantable. In *Drummond* v. *Van Ingen* [11] an action for the price was met by a claim for breach of warranty. The goods, worsted coatings, corresponded with the samples, but both suffered from a latent defect which caused them to give way when made up and it was held that there was an implied warranty that the goods should be merchantable as worsted coatings. Hence the counterclaim succeeded. In *Godley* v. *Perry* [12] the same principle was applied to a child's catapult which broke in use and injured him.

Cases under section 15

In *Aitken, Campbell & Co.* v. *Boullen* [12a] a purchaser by sample discovered that part of the goods was disconform to sample in quality and sought to return that part of them, but the seller sent them back again to the buyer. Despite this, it was held that the buyer was not barred from claiming damages for breach of contract, the amount being agreed and

5a *Perkins* v. *Bell* [1893] 1 Q.B. 193; but see *Heilbutt* v. *Hickson* (1872) L.R. 7 C.P. 438.

6 *Lorymer* v. *Smith* (1822) 1 B. & C. 1; *cf.* s. 34 (1), specifying the buyer's right to examine on delivery. See also *Pettitt* v. *Mitchell* (1842) 4 M. & G. 819; *Chalmers* v. *Paterson* (1897) 24 R. 1020.

7 Under s. 34 (1); *Polenghi* v. *Dried Milk Co.* (1904) 10 Com.Cas. 42; *E. Clemens Horst Co.* v. *Biddell* [1912] A.C. 18.

8 *Mags. of Glasgow* v. *Ireland* (1895) 22 R. 818; *cf. Hunt* v. *Barry* (1905) 13 S.L.T. 34, where a week's delay after examination before rejection was intimated was held not to be timeous.

9 *Mody* v. *Gregson* (1868) L.R. 4 Ex. 49, 53; *Sayers* v. *London Flint Glass Co.* (1858) 27 L.J.Ex. 294.

10 *Supra.*

11 (1887) 12 App.Cas. 284.

12 [1960] 1 All E.R. 36.

12a 1908 S.C. 490.

apparently assessed at the difference between the price paid for the defective items and their value, and the loss of profit consequent on the breach. In that case the pursuer was held not to be entitled to keep some and reject some of the goods, as the discrepancy did not amount to their being goods of a different description, where that would be competent.[13] But it is otherwise if the contract be severable.[14]

In *Heilbutt* v. *Hickson*,[15] shoes were sold by sample to a firm of agents for the French Government. It was eventually found that the shoes delivered were not equal to sample and suffered from defects not discoverable by any reasonable examination. The agents sued for return of the price, expenses and their loss of profit on the whole transaction and damages were awarded on all heads.

Where a sale by sample has a provision that the goods are sold subject to " all faults and imperfections " the seller must still supply goods conform to sample though this clause may relieve him from liability for defects which are not apparent on reasonable inspection.[16] Goods are not conform to sample even though any discrepancy between the bulk and the sample could be eliminated by a simple process, no matter how simple.[17]

In *Travers* v. *Longel*[18] overboots were sold and described as " waders " but were found not to be waterproof and were resold at a loss, which sum the buyers claimed from the original sellers. It was held that the overboots had been bought as they were and that it was a sale by sample and not by description, and that as they were not defective so as to be unmerchantable under section 15 (2) there had been no breach of contract.

Express warranties

By section 14 (4) an express warranty or condition does not negative a warranty or condition implied by the Act unless inconsistent therewith.[19] But the parties may annex such warranty or condition as they think fit within the limits of possibility and legality and failure therein will normally be deemed (section 62 (1)) to be a failure to perform a material part of the contract giving rise (section 11 (2)) to a right of rejection and damages, or of damages measured by section 53 (2) and section 54 if appropriate.

Express warranties may have to be distinguished from representations made by the seller as inducements to conclude the sale but not forming part of the concluded contract. If a representation is material and untrue it justifies rescission but not damages unless it has been made fraudulently; but if the statement in question be a warranty it is part of the contract and a failure justifies rescission and damages, or damages alone, as for a breach

13 s. 30 (3).
14 *Jackson* v. *Rotax Motor Co.* [1910] 2 K.B. 937.
15 (1872) L.R. 7 C.P. 438.
16 *Champanhac Ltd.* v. *Waller Ltd.* [1948] 2 All E.R. 724.
17 *Ruben* v. *Faire* [1949] 1 K.B. 254.
18 (1948) 64 T.L.R. 150.
19 *Cf. Douglas* v. *Milne* (1895) 23 R. 163; *Cooper and Aves* v. *Clydesdale Shipping Co.* (1863) 1 M. 677.

of warranty.[20] It is a question of intention whether any statement so enters into the bargain to sell as to be a part of it and a warranty.[21] To establish an express oral warranty, the actual words must be proved, so that the court may judge if it is a warranty.[22]

In *Malcolm* v. *Cross* [23] an offer was made to buy a horse in April. There was a conflict of evidence whether there was any mention of soundness. The animal was purchased in June by a letter which said nothing about a warranty. The horse was later found to be unsound. It was held that this was not a sale with a warranty of soundness, even if the earlier offer was an offer to sell with a warranty. Similarly in *Hopkins* v. *Tanqueray* [24] an oral assurance of soundness of a horse given the day before an auction was held to be an oral representation of the seller's opinion and judgment and not a warranty for which he could be held responsible. But in *Schawel* v. *Reade* [25] a similar oral assurance of soundness was held to have been made for the purpose of a sale on which the plaintiff had acted and thus to be a warranty as designed to form part of the contract.

In *Couchman* v. *Hill* [26] a heifer was to be sold by auction. Both catalogue and conditions of sale described the sale as " with all faults, imperfections and errors of description." The plaintiff at the sale got an oral assurance from defendant and auctioneer that the heifer was unserved which, in fact, unknown to all, it was not. It died and the plaintiff was held entitled to recover on the ground that the answers were a warranty which overrode the catalogue conditions. But an oral assurance does not always imply a warranty.[27]

Even when there is a particular warranty a purchaser may be barred from objecting if his testing and handling of the goods has been exceptional or unreasonable.[28]

An oral warranty may be given in such terms as to override printed conditions of sale to the effect that no warranty was given.[29]

When a party seeks to found on an express warranty he must normally prove the exact terms of the warranty he relies on.[30]

No special words need be used to constitute an express warranty.[31] It

[20] On the different measure of damages applicable to the two cases, see p. 484, *supra*. See also *Geddes* v. *Pennington* (1817) 5 Dow. 159.

[21] *De Lassalle* v. *Guildford* [1901] 2 K.B. 221. *Cf. Cranston* v. *Mallow & Lien*, 1912 S.C. 112; *Rowan* v. *Coats Iron Co.* (1885) 12 R. 395; *Hardie* v. *Austin & McAslan* (1870) 8 M. 798; *Hardie* v. *Smith & Simons* (1870) 7 S.L.R. 492; *Rough* v. *Moir* (1875) 2 R. 529.

[22] *Robeson* v. *Waugh* (1874) 2 R. 63; *Rose* v. *Johnston* (1878) 5 R. 600.

[23] (1898) 25 R. 1089.

[24] (1854) 15 C.B. 130; but *cf. Bannerman* v. *White* (1861) 10 C.B.(N.S.) 844.

[25] [1913] 2 Ir.R. 81 (H.L.). See also *Stucley* v. *Baily* (1862) 1 H. & C. 405; *Camac* v. *Warriner* (1845) 1 C.B. 356.

[26] [1947] 1 K.B. 554. *Cf. Kyle* v. *Sim*, 1925 S.C. 425; *Harling* v. *Eddy* [1951] 2 K.B. 739.

[27] *Wilson* v. *Turnbull* (1896) 23 R. 714. See also *Campbell* v. *Henderson* (1886) 23 S.L.R. 712; *Malcolm* v. *Cross* (1898) 25 R. 1089.

[28] *Newlands* v. *Leggatt* (1885) 12 R. 820; *Wilson* v. *Turnbull* (1896) 23 R. 714. Contrast *Brown* v. *Boreland* (1848) 10 D. 1460. See also *Hill* v. *Pringle* (1827) 6 S. 229.

[29] *Harling* v. *Eddy* [1951] 2 K.B. 739.

[30] *Robeson* v. *Waugh* (1874) 2 R. 63; *Dunn* v. *East Newington Garage Co.*, 1946 S.N. 144.

[31] *Heilbut, Symons* v. *Buckleton* [1913] A.C. 30; *Harrison* v. *Knowles* [1918] 1 K.B. 608; *Scott* v. *Steel* (1857) 20 D. 253.

is a question of fact whether the intention was to create a warranty even where the warranty is in writing. This may appear from the nature of the sale and the circumstances of the particular case; one test, though not decisive, is whether the seller is asserting a fact of which the purchaser is ignorant, or is merely stating an opinion or judgment on a matter as to which the buyer may also exercise his judgment and form his opinion, and of which the seller has no special knowledge.[32] Thus the genuineness of old pictures has frequently been held to be a matter of opinion and not of warranty.[33] An express warranty may, however, be interpreted by usage of trade [34] or attendant circumstances,[35] so long as not unreasonable or contrary to the contract.[36] Regard may also be had for the purposes of interpretation to the context of the words in the case of a written warranty.[37] A warranty in an advertisement is not part of the contract unless imported into it.[38]

Express warranties limited in time

Goods may be sold with an express warranty limited in time, in which case the prima facie meaning is that the goods shall conform to the warranty for the whole of that time.[39] It may, however, depending on the construction of the contract and the usage of trade be held to import a limitation to breaches of warranty notified or enforced by action of damages within that time.[40]

Warranty and patent defect

An express warranty in general terms does not cover the buyer against defects of which he knew at the time of the contract, or which were apparent to one without special skill and the buyer had made an examination.[41] But a buyer is not bound to examine the goods and may rely on an express warranty.[42]

Statutory warranties

Warranties which fall to be implied into certain contracts under particular statutes are saved by section 14 of the Act.

[32] *Pasley* v. *Freeman* (1797) 3 T.R. 57; *Jeudwine* v. *Slade* (1797) 2 Esp. 572; *Power* v. *Barham* (1836) 4 A. & E. 473; *Stucley* v. *Baily* (1862) 1 H. & C. 405; *Heilbut, Symons, supra.*
[33] *Hyslop* v. *Shirlaw* (1905) 7 F. 875; *Jeudwine, supra*; *Power, supra.*
[34] *Powell* v. *Horton* (1836) 2 Bing.N.C. 668; *Lucas* v. *Bristow* (1858) E.B. & E. 907.
[35] *Jones* v. *Clarke* (1858) 2 H. & N. 725.
[36] *Yates* v. *Pim* (1816) 6 Taunt. 446. Contrast *Johnson* v. *Raylton* (1881) 7 Q.B.D. 438.
[37] *Richardson* v. *Brown* (1823) 1 Bing. 344; *Budd* v. *Fairmaner* (1831) 8 Bing. 38; and *Dickenson* v. *Gupp* (1821) quoted therein at p. 50; *Anthony* v. *Halstead* (1877) 37 L.T.(N.S.) 433; *Taylor* v. *Bullen* (1850) 5 Ex. 779.
[38] *Paul* v. *Glasgow Corpn.* (1900) 3 F. 119; *cf. Robey* v. *Stein* (1900) 3 F. 278.
[39] *Chapman* v. *Gwyther* (1866) L.R. 1 Q.B. 463; see also *Barre Johnston & Co.* v. *Oldham* (1895) 11 T.L.R. 401.
[40] *Chapman, supra*; see also *Bywater* v. *Richardson* (1834) 1 Ad. & El. 508; *Smart* v. *Hyde* (1841) 8 M. & W. 723; *Speak* v. *Taylor* (1894) 10 T.L.R. 224.
[41] *Margetson* v. *Wright* (1832) 8 Bing. 454; *Holliday* v. *Morgan* (1858) 1 E. & E. 1; *Cowdy* v. *Thomas* (1876) 36 L.T. 22.
[42] *Scott* v. *Foley, Aikman & Co.* (1899) 16 T.L.R. 55.

Exclusion of warranties by contract

By section 55, as substituted by the Supply of Goods (Implied Terms) Act, 1973, s. 4, any right, duty or liability arising under a contract of sale of goods or by implication of law may be negatived or varied by express agreement of parties, or by the course of dealing between them, or by usage if the usage is such as to bind both parties to the contract. An express condition or warranty does not negative a condition or warranty implied by the Act unless inconsistent therewith. A term exempting from the provisions of section 12 is void. A provision in the contract or any other contract exempting from all or any of the provisions of section 13, 14 or 15 is void in the case of a consumer sale (as defined by s. 55 (7)) and in any other case is not enforceable to the extent that it is shown that it would not be fair or reasonable to allow reliance on the term. In determining whether reliance would be fair or reasonable regard must be had to all the circumstances and in particular to matters specified in s. 55 (5).

Breach of warranty and subsales

Where goods have been subsold and suffer from breach of warranty the question arises whether damages to which the buyer is subjected in respect of his breach of the subcontract are recoverable from the seller as part of the damages for breach of warranty. In general, subcontracts are matters with which the original seller has no concern [64] but there are exceptions to this where the subsale, actual or intended, is known to the seller at the time of the sale,[65] or where the buyer being to the seller's knowledge a broker, merchant, or retailer of that class of goods, the seller must as a reasonable man have contemplated that the goods had been purchased for resale.[66] Information of intention to subsell [67] or the probability of a subsale [68] will bring it within contemplation. If the buyer's liability to his subpurchaser is the same as the seller's to the buyer, such damages are clearly recoverable.[69] Where the subcontracts can be taken into account as having been within the contemplation of the parties at the time the original contract was entered into, then the buyer can recover such loss as must have been contemplated as the natural consequence of the breach in those circumstances, such as the whole damages payable to the subpurchaser and expenses properly and reasonably incurred in connection with that claim. In *Pinnock Bros.* v. *Lewis and Peat* [70] the defendants were

64 *Re Hall & Pim, Junior & Co.'s Arbitration* (1928) 33 Com.Cas. 324; *Finlay* v. *Kwik Hoo Tong* [1929] 1 K.B. 400.

65 *Hammond* v. *Bussey* (1887) 20 Q.B.D. 79; *Agius* v. *G.W. Colliery* [1899] 1 Q.B. 413.

66 *Pinnock Bros.* v. *Lewis & Peat* [1923] 1 K.B. 690; *British Oil and Cake Co. Ltd.* v. *Burstall* (1923) 39 T.L.R. 406; *Patrick* v. *Russo-British Grain Export Co.* [1927] 2 K.B. 535; *Dobell* v. *Barber & Garrett* [1931] 1 K.B. 219. There is an increasing tendency today to hold that resales must have been contemplated. Reservation in the contract of a right of resale is enough: *Re Hall & Pim, Junior's Arbitration* (1928) 33 Com.Cas. 324.

67 *Grébert-Borgnis* v. *Nugent* (1885) 15 Q.B.D. 85; see also *Patrick, supra.*

68 *Hammond* v. *Bussey* (1887) 20 Q.B.D. 79, 89.

69 *Randall* v. *Raper* (1858) 1 E.B. & E. 84.

70 [1923] 1 K.B. 690.

held liable in damages for injury to cattle: they had put poisonous beans in copra cake which the plaintiffs purchased and resold to manufacturers of cattle food and it was held to have been in the contemplation of parties that the cake would be used as such food and nothing else, whether in manufactured form or not. The plaintiffs recovered the damages and costs they had had to pay to eventual buyers and their own costs in those cases. In *Bennett* v. *Kreeger* [71] the eventual buyer of a coat with a fur collar from which she had contracted skin disease from the dye recovered damages and costs from the plaintiffs, who in turn recovered these sums, together with their own costs of defending the action, from the defendant.

Series of subpurchasers

The same principles hold good where the goods pass through the hands of several parties between the original default and the ultimate damage or complaint of defect. But if a sum recovered for the breach of the last contract in a chain is to be taken as the measure of damages for a similar breach higher up in the chain, it is essential that the contracts along the chain should be the same in respect of the warranty,[72] or, at least, not be at all materially different.[73] If the warranty which each successive purchaser gives to his subpurchaser is not the same as that given by the original seller to the first buyer, then the damages will be too remote.[74] These principles also apply where claims are compromised at a reasonable figure rather than fought out.[75]

Damages for breach of warranty and for fraudulent misrepresentation

In view of the narrowness of the question it may be worth while comparing the measure of damages recoverable where, on the one hand, a contract has been induced by fraudulent misrepresentation and the buyer repudiates the contract and claims damages and, on the other hand, cases where a buyer has received goods which are in breach of warranty, has kept them and claimed damages in compensation for the defect and breach of warranty.[75a] It has been observed that a seller's liability for selling as good something which he knows to be bad arises not from any breach of warranty but from fraud.[76]

In the case of fraud the measure of damages is prima facie the difference between the price paid and the actual value of the goods at the time of delivery.[77] In the case of breach of warranty the measure is the difference between the value of the goods as they should have been, *i.e.* warranted

71 (1925) 41 T.L.R. 609.
72 *Dexters* v. *Hill Crest Oil Co.* [1926] 1 K.B. 348.
73 *Pinnock Bros.* v. *Lewis & Peat* [1923] 1 K.B. 690; *British Oil & Cake Co.* v. *Burstall* (1923) 39 T.L.R. 406; *Biggin* v. *Permanite Ltd.* [1951] 2 K.B. 314.
74 *Dexters*, *supra*, where the description varied at one link in the chain.
75 *Biggin*, *supra*.
75a On the distinction see also *Oscar Chess Ltd.* v. *Williams* [1957] 1 All E.R. 325.
76 *Stewart* v. *Jamieson* (1863) 1 M. 525. *Cf. Philip's Trs.* v. *Reid* (1884) 21 S.L.R. 698.
77 *Waddell* v. *Blockey* (1879) 4 Q.B.D. 678; *Peek* v. *Derry* (1887) 37 Ch.D. 541, 578; *McConnel* v. *Wright* [1903] 1 Ch. 546; *Broome* v. *Speak* [1903] 1 Ch. 586.

value, and that as they actually are, *i.e.* actual value. In the former case, the criterion is, how much has the buyer lost or overpaid by the seller's deceit? In the latter it is, How much is the difference in value short of the contractual value? In the case of breach of warranty the goods may be kept, and only the deficient balance of value recovered by way of damages, or they may be rejected entirely.[79]

[79] Sale of Goods Act 1893, s. 11 (2).

Chapter 44

CONTRACTS OF HIRE-PURCHASE, CREDIT-SALE AND CONDITIONAL SALE OF GOODS

HIRE-PURCHASE is a contract for the letting and taking of goods on hire with an option, during or on the expiry of the period of hire, to purchase the goods outright; credit sale is the sale and purchase of goods outright but with the provision that credit is to be given for the whole or part of the price for a time; conditional sale is the sale and purchase of goods subject to certain conditions, which may include conditions deferring the passing of the property and/or providing for payment of the price by instalments. If not governed by the Hire Purchase (Scotland) Act 1965 [1] claims of damages arising out of a hire-purchase contract must be determined by principles applicable to common law hiring of goods.[2] But contracts of credit-sale and conditional sale not governed by the Hire-Purchase (Scotland) Act 1965 [1] are governed by the Sale of Goods Act 1893 and claims of damages must be determined in accordance with that Act.[3]

Under the Hire-Purchase (Scotland) Act 1965 a hire-purchase contract is one " whereby goods are taken on hire by one person from another person in consideration of periodical payments to be made by the first mentioned person to the other person, with an option to the first mentioned person to become the buyer of the goods "; a credit-sale is " an agreement for the sale of goods under which the purchase price is payable by five or more instalments, not being a conditional sale agreement "; a conditional sale agreement is " an agreement for the sale of goods under which the purchase price or part of it is payable by instalments and the property in the goods is to remain in the seller (notwithstanding that the buyer is to be in possession of the goods) until such conditions as to payment of instalments or otherwise as may be specified in the agreement are fulfilled." [4]

Moreover, the 1965 Act applies,[5] as to sections 5 to 52, only to hire-purchase agreements or conditional sale agreements under which the hire-purchase price or total purchase price does not exceed £2,000,[6] and as to sections 5 to 32, to credit-sale agreements under which the total purchase price exceeds £30 but does not exceed £2,000,[6] except in cases to which section 2 (4) is expressed to apply, where the Act applies to credit-sale

[1] For cases governed by the 1965 Act see next paragraphs.
[2] Chap. 41, *supra*.
[3] Chap. 43, *supra*.
[4] Hire-Purchase (Sc.) Act 1965, s. 1.
[5] s. 2.
[6] The upper limit may be raised by Order in Council: s. 3.

agreements not exceeding £2,000.[6] The 1965 Act also does not apply to agreements made by or on behalf of a body corporate as hirer or buyer.[7]

Making and rescission of contract

Where the 1965 Act applies, it lays down detailed provisions relative to the making of agreements of one or another of the three kinds, and to their form and contents,[8] and provides for a hirer or purchaser serving a notice of cancellation in stated circumstances which is to operate as a withdrawal of offer to contract, or as a rescission of the contract.[9] If the hirer or purchaser has obtained possession of the goods he is under an obligation to redeliver the goods only at his own premises and in pursuance of a request in writing by the owner, and subject to any lien the hirer or purchaser may have under section 14 (2) or 15 (3) of the Act for the return of money paid. He is, however, under an obligation to take reasonable care of the goods for twenty-one days from the service of the notice of cancellation,[10] or until he redelivers them.[11] If he does redeliver the goods to an authorised person, he must take reasonable care to see that they are received by that person and are not damaged in transit to him but in other respects his obligation to take care of the goods ceases on his sending the goods to that person.[11] If the hirer or purchaser receives a written request to return the goods and unreasonably refuses or fails to comply with it, his obligation to take reasonable care of the goods continues until he redelivers them or sends them to an authorised person.[12]

Any such obligation is owed to the person for the time being entitled to possession of the goods and any breach of the obligation is actionable at that person's insistence as a breach of statutory duty.[13] The measure of damages for failure is not specified; it is suggested that the proper measure of damages is the diminution in the value of the goods attributable to lack of reasonable care. In the short period of time involved the goods should not normally have suffered any appreciable wear and tear or become " second hand " in other than a technical sense.

Claims by Hirer or Buyer

Breaches of contract giving rise to claims

The kinds of breaches of contract giving rise to claims of damages would seem to be total non-delivery of the goods taken on hire-purchase, credit-sale or conditional sale, delay in delivery, or delivery of goods defective in some respect.

7 s. 4.
8 ss. 5–10.
9 ss. 11–12.
10 s. 13 (4).
11 s. 13 (5).
12 s. 13 (6).
13 s. 13 (7).

Non-delivery

Total non-delivery of goods let on hire-purchase or agreed to be sold on conditional sale terms or sold on credit, would appear normally to be a fundamental breach justifying rescission of the contract and a claim of damages for any loss caused thereby. The loss may be merely inconvenience or, where the goods were required for trade or business purposes, would be, it is submitted, any extra cost of hiring goods elsewhere or obtaining goods elsewhere on hire-purchase or conditional sale terms in substitution for those not delivered under the former contract.

Delay in delivery

It would seem to be a question of circumstances and degree whether delay in delivery of goods is a sufficiently fundamental breach to justify rescission. It will always justify a claim of damages for the loss caused by the delay, measured by the inconvenience caused or the expense of obtaining alternative goods elsewhere, even temporarily.

Delivery of defective goods

Defective delivery will take the form of delivery of goods which in some respect do not measure up to the standard stipulated, expressly or implied, by the contract.

Dealer to be agent of owner or seller in respect of certain representations

Any representations, including any statement or undertaking, whether constituting a stipulation of the contract or not, with respect to the goods to which a hire-purchase, credit-sale or conditional sale agreement relates, made orally or in writing by a person other than the owner or seller in the course of any antecedent negotiations conducted by that person shall be deemed to have been made by him as agent of the owner or seller.[14]

Breach of express stipulation

Whether there is defective performance in respect of an element expressly stipulated depends on the terms of the stipulation and on the nature and extent of the defect.[15] If the defect is material the contract may be rescinded, the goods returned, and damages claimed for the loss caused by the defect; the measure of damages is the whole sum paid for the goods less an allowance for the use the hirer had of the goods.[16] If the defect is not material damages alone may be claimed. The prima facie measure of damages is the difference in value between the thing as stipulated to be and the thing as it is.[17]

[14] s. 16.
[15] *Cf. Andrews* v. *Hopkinson* [1957] 1 Q.B. 229; *Yeoman Credit Ltd.* v. *Odgers* [1962] 1 All E.R. 789.
[16] *Charterhouse Credit Co.* v. *Tolly* [1963] 2 Q.B. 683; *Farnworth Finance Facilities* v. *Attryde* [1970] 2 All E.R. 774.
[17] *Yeoman Credit, supra*, 793.

Consequential damages are recoverable if within contemplation, such as injuries which followed directly and naturally from the breach of stipulation,[18] or loss incurred under the hire-purchase agreement itself,[19] or loss of use of a defective article while it was under repair.[20]

Breach of implied terms—what terms are implied

In every hire-purchase agreement, whether within the 1965 Act or not, there is an implied stipulation on the part of the owner that he will have a right to sell the goods when the property is to pass and an implied stipulation that the goods are free, and will remain free until the time when the property is to pass, from any charge or encumbrance not disclosed or known to the hirer before the agreement was made and that the hirer will enjoy quiet possession of the goods except so far as it may be disturbed by any person entitled to the benefit of any charge or encumbrance so disclosed or known, save that, where there appears from the hire-purchase agreement or is to be inferred from the circumstances of the agreement an intention that the owner should transfer only such title as he or a third person may have, there is an implied stipulation that all charges or encumbrances known to the owner and not known to the hirer have been disclosed to the hirer before the agreement was made, and an implied stipulation that neither the owner nor, in a case where the parties to the agreement intend that any title which may be transferred shall be only such title as a third person may have, that person, nor anyone claiming through or under the owner or that third person otherwise than under a charge or encumbrance disclosed or known to the hirer before the agreement was made, will disturb the hirer's quiet possession of the goods.[21]

Where under a hire-purchase agreement goods are let by description there is an implied stipulation that the goods will correspond with the description, and if under the agreement the goods are let by reference to a sample as well as a description, it is not sufficient that the bulk of the goods corresponds with the sample if the goods do not also correspond with the description. Goods are not prevented from being let by description by reason only that, being exposed for sale or hire, they are selected by the hirer.[22]

Except as provided by sections 10 and 11 and subject to the provisions of any other enactment, there is no implied stipulation as to the quality or fitness for any particular purpose of goods let under a hire-purchase

[18] *Andrews, supra.*
[19] *Yeoman Credit, supra.*
[20] *Charterhouse, supra.*
[21] Supply of Goods (Implied Terms) Act, 1973, s. 8, superseding 1965 Act, s. 17 (1). *Cf.* Sale of Goods Act, 1893, s. 12 (1); *Karflex Ltd.* v. *Poole* [1933] 2 K.B. 351; *Mercantile Union Guarantee Corpn. Ltd.* v. *Wheatley* [1938] 1 K.B. 490; *Warman* v. *Southern Counties Car Finance Corpn. Ltd.* [1949] 2 K.B. 576.
[22] *Ibid.* s. 9, replacing 1965 Act, s. 19 (2). *Cf.* Sale of Goods Act, 1893, s. 13.

agreement.[23] Sections 10 and 11 imply certain conditions and warranties into all hire-purchase agreements, whether or not within the 1965 Act.[24]

An express condition or warranty does not negative a condition or warranty implied by the 1973 Act unless inconsistent therewith.[25] A term of a hire-purchase agreement or any other agreement exempting from all or any of the provisions of section 8 is void.[26] A term of a hire-purchase agreement or any other agreement exempting from all or any of the provisions of sections 9, 10 or 11 is void in the case of a " consumer agreement " [27] and in any other case is not enforceable to the extent that it is shown that it would not be fair or reasonable to allow reliance on the term.[28] Matters are specified [29] which have to be taken into account in determining whether or not reliance on any such term is fair or reasonable, but this does not [30] prevent the court from holding in accordance with any rule of law, that a term which purports to exclude or restrict any of the provisions of section 9, 10 or 11 is not a term of the agreement. The onus of proving that a hire purchase agreement falls to be treated for the purposes of section 12 as not being a " consumer agreement " is on the party so contending.[31]

The implied stipulations under sections 8–12 do not apply to credit sales nor to conditional sales, to which the conditions and warranties implied by sections 1–7, replacing sections 12–14 of the Sale of Goods Act, 1893, apply.

Stipulations implied at common law

There may also be stipulations implied by the courts at common law, such as that a car supplied on hire-purchase has a log book, to enable it to be licensed and used.[39]

Effect of breach of implied stipulation

Where the stipulation breached is material, by agreement or under the Act, or one held to be material, the hirer or purchaser may rescind the contract; whether or not it is material he may claim damages for loss caused him by the defective performance constituted by breach of the implied stipulation in question.

The measure of damages, it is suggested, if the contract is justifiably rescinded, is the loss naturally resulting from the non-supply of goods complying with the stipulations, which is prima facie the whole sum paid

[23] *Ibid.* s. 10, replacing 1965 Act, ss. 17, 19 (1). *Cf.* Sale of Goods Act, 1893, ss. 14, 15.
[24] *Ibid.* ss. 10, 11.
[25] *Ibid.* s. 12 (1), replacing 1965 Act, ss. 18 and 29. *Cf.* Sale of Goods Act, 1893 s. 55, as amended by 1973 Act, s. 4.
[26] *Ibid.* s. 12 (2).
[27] Defined, s. 12 (6).
[28] *Ibid.* s. 12 (3).
[29] *Ibid.* s. 12 (4).
[30] *Ibid.* s. 12 (5).
[31] *Ibid.* s. 12 (7).
[39] *Bentworth Finance Ltd.* v. *Lubert* [1967] 2 All E.R. 810. The Court of Appeal treated the supply of a log book as a suspensive condition.

less allowance for the use of the goods while the hirer had them. If the contract is not rescinded the measure should be the difference in value between goods complying with the implied stipulation and the goods actually supplied.

Termination by owner or seller

A hire-purchase or conditional sale contract may be terminated by the owner or seller by agreement with the hirer or buyer, on such terms as they may agree. In default of agreement termination is a breach of contract and the hirer or buyer is in breach of contract and the hirer or buyer would be entitled to damages for the inconvenience and loss caused him by the premature termination of the contract.

LESSOR'S OR SELLER'S CLAIMS

Breach by hirer or buyer—failure to take delivery

If the hirer or buyer fails to take delivery of the goods he is in breach, probably in material breach, and liable at least for damages for the inconvenience to the lessor or seller of having to relet or resell the goods and loss of revenue till then. Unless the contract so provides the lessor or seller is probably not entitled to remain inactive and claim instalments of rent or price as they fall due,[40] but should take reasonable steps to relet or resell the goods.

Repudiation of contract by hirer or buyer

If a hirer or buyer expressly or by conduct totally repudiates the contract the owner or seller may normally under the contract rescind it, repossess the goods, and claim under a minimum payment clause or, alternatively, at common law, for the loss caused by the premature termination of the agreement.[41] In the latter case account must be taken of the loss of future instalments, the depreciation of the goods and the trouble and inconvenience of having to relet or resell them, but credit must be given where the goods have been relet or resold.[42]

Non-payment of hire or instalment of price

At common law non-payment or delayed payment of a sum due as hire or instalment of the price justifies a claim for the sum due, with interest, and if there are circumstances suggesting that non-payment or delayed payment is likely to be repeated or that it evidences an intention

40 *Cf. National Cash Register Co.* v. *Stanley* [1921] 3 K.B. 292; *Yeoman Credit Co.* v. *Waragowski* [1961] 3 All E.R. 145; *Yeoman Credit Co.* v. *McLean* [1962] 1 W.L.R. 131; *Overstone* v. *Shipway* [1962] 1 All E.R. 52.

41 *Financings Ltd., supra.*

42 *Yeoman Credit Ltd.* v. *Waragowski* [1961] 3 All E.R. 145; *Overstone Ltd.* v. *Shipway* [1962] 1 All E.R. 52.

to repudiate the contract, it may be treated as such repudiation and the contract rescinded. It is easier to draw the inference of intention to repudiate if the non-payment or delay in payment comes early in the agreed duration of the contract, rather than later, or if it is repeated.[43]

Non-payment or delayed payment of a sum due is normally dealt with expressly by the contract, and thereunder it normally justifies rescission of the contract, a claim to repossess the goods, and a claim for the arrears of rent with interest.[44]

Default notices

The consequences of rescission of the contract and accrual of the right to recover possession do not, however, arise in cases subject to the 1965 Act unless the owner or seller serves on the hirer or buyer a default notice stating specified particulars.[45]

Care of goods while agreement running

It is submitted that, at common law, the hirer under hire-purchase or buyer under conditional sale is bound to take reasonable care of the goods during the currency of the agreement. An express obligation to do so may be included in a hire-purchase or conditional sale contract. The duty is to keep the goods in the condition they should have been if properly looked after. Thus a car should be washed, serviced and repaired when necessary.[46] Breach of this duty of care will be important only if the agreement is later terminated but before full ownership vests in the hirer or purchaser. Where a hire-purchase or conditional sale agreement is terminated by the hirer or buyer giving notice of termination under section 27, the hirer or buyer is liable, if he has failed to take reasonable care of the goods, to pay damages for the failure.[47] Where it is terminated by the owner or seller serving a notice of default in payment, expiry of the period for payment of arrears without payment thereof, and termination of the agreement for that default,[48] and possibly after a subsequent action for recovery of possession of the goods,[49] the owner or seller may also have a claim for loss caused by failure to take reasonable care of the goods, which must be brought in any action for the possession of protected goods[50] or, probably, in any action claiming under a minimum payment provision.[51] This could be important where by lack of reasonable care the goods had been deteriorated to an extent beyond that covered by the minimum payment clause.

43 *Cornwall* v. *Henson* [1900] 2 Ch. 298, 304; *Maple Flock Co.* v. *Universal Furniture Products Ltd.* [1934] 1 K.B. 148, 157.

44 *Financings Ltd.* v. *Baldock* [1963] 1 All E.R. 443; *Brady* v. *St. Margaret's Trust Ltd.* [1963] 2 All E.R. 275.

45 1965 Act, s. 25.

46 *Cf. Brady* v. *St. Margaret's Trust Ltd.* [1963] 2 All E.R. 275.

47 1965 Act, s. 28 (3).

48 *Ibid.* s. 25.

49 *Ibid.* ss. 33–40 and 45.

50 *Ibid.* ss. 41 and 45.

51 See also ss. 43–44 and 45.

Sale by hirer or buyer

If a hirer under a hire-purchase agreement or buyer under a conditional sale agreement purports to sell the goods, which are the subject of the agreement, before the property has vested in him thereunder, he commits theft [52] and acts in fundamental breach of his contract with the lessor or seller, even though in some cases he may be able to confer a good title on the purchaser from him under the Hire-Purchase Act 1964, s. 27. In this event the lessor or seller can recover as damages the full hire-purchase price less instalments paid to date.[53] If the purported sale is one under which a good title does not pass, the lessor or seller can doubtless recover possession of the goods as having passed under a void contract,[54] and also damages for loss caused by the hirer's or buyer's having acted in breach of an implied, if not express, term of the contract by purporting to sell.

Termination of contract by hirer or buyer

A hirer under hire-purchase or buyer under conditional sale may terminate the agreement by mutual agreement [55] or by giving notice of termination under the 1965 Act, s. 27. In such a case he must surrender the goods or be liable for their fair market value at the time when he should have surrendered them.

Minimum payment provision

The agreement frequently provides for payment by the hirer or buyer, in the event of its premature termination, of a sum which, together with payments made, will amount to a stated sum. The first question is whether this provision is, in the circumstances, a penalty provision or a provision for liquidate damages.[56]

In a case within the statute, if a hirer or buyer terminates the agreement by giving notice of termination under section 27, he is liable, without prejudice to any liability which has accrued before the termination,[57] to pay the amount, if any, by which one-half of the hire-purchase price or total purchase price exceeds the total of the sums paid and the sums due in respect thereof immediately before the termination, or any lesser sum specified in the agreement, or such lesser sum as the court is satisfied is equal to the loss sustained by the owner or seller in consequence of the other's termination of the agreement.[58] If the hirer or buyer wrongfully retains possession of the goods, the court, unless satisfied that having regard to the circumstances it would not be just and equitable to do so,

52 *Cf. O'Brien* v. *Strathern*, 1922 J.C. 55.
53 *Cf. Wickham Holdings* v. *Brooke House Motors* [1967] 1 All E.R. 117.
54 *Cf. Morrisson* v. *Robertson*, 1908 S.C. 332.
55 1965 Act, s. 27 (4).
56 Chap. 7, *supra*.
57 *e.g.* for unpaid instalments of hire or price.
58 1965 Act, s. 28 (1)–(2).

shall order the goods to be delivered to the owner or seller without giving the hirer or buyer an option to pay the value of the goods.[59]

Recovery of possession of goods

The owner or seller may recover possession of the goods let or sold without legal process if such is stipulated for in the contract, but in the case of goods within the 1965 Act, if they are protected goods, as defined by section 33, possession may be recovered only by action.[60]

Claim under minimum payment provision

Where a hire-purchase agreement validly provides for payment by the hirer on or after termination of the agreement of a sum to make up the payments made to a stated minimum, and a claim is made in an action for recovery of possession of protected goods, and the court makes an order for the specific delivery to the hirer of the owner's title to the remainder of the goods, the claim for the minimum payment shall be disallowed.[61] If a claim is made for a minimum payment and the court makes an order for the specific delivery of the goods to the owner and postpones the operation of the order, then the court shall not entertain the claim unless and until the postponement is revoked, and shall then deal with the claim as if the agreement had just been terminated,[62] save that if, after an action for recovery of possession of protected goods, the owner has recovered possession of all the goods, he may in the same action make or proceed with a claim for the payment of one or more instalments which had accrued due under the agreement before the action was brought, or for the payment of any minimum payment for which the agreement makes provision.[62]

59 *Ibid.* s. 28 (4).
60 *Ibid.* s. 34.
61 *Ibid.* s. 43 (1) and (2).
62 *Ibid.* ss. 43 (3) and 44.

CHAPTER 45

CONTRACTS OF CARRIAGE

THIS chapter deals with the circumstances in which claims of damages may arise out of a contract for the carriage of goods or passengers, by land, sea or air.

While modern legislation has made great changes in the control and organisation of the transport industry, the main principles of law relative to breach of a duty created by the contract of carriage were settled much earlier and the modern position must be considered in the light of the older law from which it has developed.

At common law the fundamental distinctions were that between common carriers and private carriers, and the cross-distinction between carriers of goods and carriers of passengers. Certain differences exist between carriage by road, by rail, by sea and by air. The criteria for distinguishing between common carriers and private carriers are the same in the case of goods and in the case of passengers but the duties attaching by law differ. Furthermore most claims by passengers against carriers, whether common or private carriers, are for losses caused by personal injuries or death, and to such claims, whether founded on breach of contract or on delict, the considerations applicable to damages for personal injuries or death apply,[1] not considerations applicable to damages for breach of contract.

Whether a carrier is a common carrier or not is partly a question of law, there being now in some cases statutory provisions to the effect that particular carriers are not common carriers, but subject thereto, is a question of fact.[2] A carrier who regularly receives goods on terms limiting his liability is still a common carrier unless the limitation is so extensive as to be inconsistent with the profession of common carrier.[3]

CARRIAGE BY LAND GENERALLY

Common carriers of goods

A common carrier of goods is one who makes a standing offer to anyone who may choose to employ him to carry goods of any kind which he publicly professes to carry, for hire, between the places between which he plies.[4] He is justified in refusing goods offered for carriage only if they

[1] Chaps. 53–54, *infra*.
[2] *Tamvaco* v. *Timothy & Green* (1882) Cab. & El. 1.
[3] *G.N. Ry.* v. *L.E.P. Transport* [1922] 2 K.B. 742.
[4] Bell, *Comm.* I, 491; Bell, *Prin.* § 160. One place may be beyond the seas: *Crouch* v. *L.N.W. Ry.* (1854) 14 C.B. 255.

are not of a kind which he professes to carry,[5] or he does not go to that place,[6] or the charges are not paid or offered,[7] or they are dangerous in their nature,[8] or the nature or value of the goods is not disclosed,[9] or he has no space in his vehicle,[10] or they are not delivered in sufficient time for packing and loading,[11] or are not properly packed,[12] or the country is in a disturbed condition.[13] He cannot insist on the sender agreeing to unreasonable conditions.[14] He is liable in damages for an unjustified refusal to carry.[15]

He impliedly undertakes that his vehicle will be reasonably fit and in good repair, that the crew will be reasonably competent and skilled, and that they will exercise reasonable skill and care in executing the commission to carry. The measure of damages for refusal to carry will be nominal if no actual loss has been sustained,[16] or otherwise the extra cost incurred in sending by other means,[17] or the loss suffered by having the goods left on his hands.[18]

Strict liability of common carrier for loss or damage

At common law a common carrier is strictly liable for the loss of goods in his charge. In Scotland this is based on the rule of the Praetorian Edict,[19] and in England on the custom of the realm.[20] While a private carrier is only liable for default or negligence,[21] a common carrier of goods [22] is an insurer and is liable for loss of or injury to the goods in his charge without proof of negligence,[23] subject only to the exceptions of default of the consignor, act of God or *damnum fatale*, act of the Queen's enemies, or inherent vice of the goods.[24] A common carrier by land is liable for loss by fire.[25] Theft is not an exception. If, however, in emergency, the

5 *Johnson* v. *Midland Ry.* (1849) 4 Ex. 397.
6 *Johnson, supra*; *Sutcliffe* v. *G.W. Ry.* [1910] 1 K.B. 478.
7 *Pickford* v. *Grand Junction Ry.* (1841) 8 M. & W. 372; *Wyld* v. *Pickford* (1841) 8 M. & W. 443; *Ashmole* v. *Wainwright* (1842) 2 Q.B. 837; *Crouch, supra.*
8 *McManus* v. *L. & Y. Ry.* (1859) 28 L.J.Ex. 353; *Bamfield* v. *Goole* [1910] 2 K.B. 84; *G.N. Ry.* v. *L.E.P. Transport* [1922] 2 K.B. 742.
9 *Macklin* v. *Waterhouse* (1828) 5 Bing. 212.
10 *Macklin, supra*; *Riley* v. *Horne* (1828) 5 Bing. 217; *Johnson, supra.*
11 *Lane* v. *Cotton* (1701) 1 Ld.Raym. 652.
12 *Sutcliffe* v. *G.W. Ry.* [1910] 1 K.B. 478; *L.N.W. Ry.* v. *Hudson* [1920] A.C. 324.
13 *Edwards* v. *Sherratt* (1801) 1 East 604.
14 *Garton* v. *Bristol & Exter Ry.* (1861) 1 B. & S. 112.
15 *Crouch* v. *L.N.W. Ry.* (1854) 14 C.B. 255; *Crouch* v. *G.N. Ry.* (1856) 11 Ex. 742; *Irvine* v. *Midland G.W. Ry.* (1880) 6 L.R.Ir. 55.
16 *Waller* v. *Midland G.W. Ry.* (1879) 4 L.R.Ir. 376; *Flaherty* v. *Midland G.W. Ry.* (1914) 48 I.L.T. 216.
17 *Irvine* v. *Midland G.W. Ry.* (1880) 6 L.R.Ir. 55.
18 *Crouch* v. *G.N. Ry.* (1856) 11 Ex. 742.
19 Dig. IV, 9, 1; Stair, I, 13, 3; Bell, *Comm.* I, 495; Bell, *Prin.* § 235; Mackenzie Stuart, " Liability of Common Carrier " (1926) 38 Jur.Rev. 205.
20 O. W. Holmes, *The Common Law*, 164; Beale, in *Sel. Essays in A.A.L.H.* III, 148.
21 Stair and Bell, *ut supra*: *cf. Copland* v. *Brogan*, 1916 S.C. 277.
22 As to passengers, see *infra*.
23 *Cf. Trent & Mersey Co.* v. *Wood* (1785) 3 Esp. 127.
24 *Ralston* v. *Caledonian Ry.* (1878) 5 R. 671.
25 Mercantile Law Amendment (Scotland) Act 1856, s. 17.

carrier disposes of goods to prevent their being wasted and he has been unable to communicate with the owner, he is not liable in damages for failing to deliver the goods [26]; but the carrier is so liable if he sells but fails to show the impossibility of getting in touch with the owner.[27] He is not liable for the consequences of goods being inadequately addressed.[28]

Limits to strict liability

The liability does not, in the absence of special contract, extend to delivery within any given time but only within a reasonable time [29]: he is not liable for delay, *e.g.* by a strike, even of his own employees,[30] so long as attributable to causes beyond his control, and if he has neither acted negligently nor unreasonably.[31] Nor is he bound to travel by the shortest route, but only by the route by which he usually and professedly travels,[32] though he is liable if delay is caused by unnecessary deviation from the ordinary route.[33]

Scope of exceptions

The recognised exceptions limit the liability, but not the duty, of the carrier,[34] and he must do what reasonable skill and care can effect to avoid perils, and remains liable if his negligence has caused the peril [35] or aggravated the loss resulting therefrom.[36] Nor do the exceptions apply where the carrier deviates from the usual or stipulated route,[37] or does something at variance with the contract,[38] unless he can show that the loss would have happened in any case.[39]

Damageable goods

The responsibility for packing goods is on the consignor [40] and he is barred from recovering damages if he does not pack the goods properly. If the damageable nature of the goods is not disclosed the carrier is bound only to take the same reasonable care of the packages as of others of the same type [41] and even if he knows of their nature he is not liable if he takes

26 *Springer* v. *G.W. Ry.* [1921] 1 K.B. 257 (tomatoes going bad).
27 *Springer, supra*; *Sims* v. *Midland Ry.* [1913] 1 K.B. 103.
28 *Weir* v. *Howie* (1798) Hume 304; *Caledonian Ry.* v. *Hunter* (1858) 20 D. 1097. But see *Campbell* v. *Caledonian Ry.* (1852) 14 D. 806; *Stewart* v. *Gordon* (1852) 14 D. 434.
29 *Taylor* v. *G.N. Ry.* (1866) L.R. 1 C.P. 385; *Hales* v. *L.N.W. Ry.* (1863) 4 B. & S. 66; *cf.* *Hawes* v. *S.E. Ry.* (1884) 54 L.J.Q.B. 174; *Nicholls* v. *N.E. Ry.* (1888) 59 L.T. 137.
30 *Sims* v. *Midland Ry.* [1913] 1 K.B. 103.
31 *Hicks* v. *Raymond* [1893] A.C. at 33.
32 *Myers* v. *L. & S.W. Ry.* (1869) L.R. 5 C.P. 1 at 3.
33 *Hales, supra*; *Mallet* v. *G.E. Ry.* [1899] 1 Q.B. 309.
34 *Blower* v. *G.W. Ry.* (1872) L.R. 7 C.P. 655.
35 *Gill* v. *Manchester Ry.* (1873) L.R. 8 Q.B. 186.
36 *Notara* v. *Henderson* (1872) L.R. 7 Q.B. 225.
37 *Hales* v. *L.N.W. Ry.* (1862) 4 B. & S. 66; *Mallet* v. *G.E. Ry.* [1899] 1 Q.B. 309; *L.N.W. Ry.* v. *Neilson* [1922] 2 A.C. 263.
38 *Blower, supra*; *Gill* v. *M.S. & L. Ry.* (1873) L.R. 8 Q.B. 186.
39 *Morrison* v. *Shaw, Savill* [1916] 2 K.B. 783.
40 *L.N.W. Ry.* v. *Hudson* [1920] A.C. 324.
41 *Baldwin* v. *L.C. & D. Ry.* (1882) 9 Q.B.D. 582.

reasonable care considering the nature of the goods, and even if the goods are obviously faultily packed.[42] If goods are not properly packed the carrier may repack them properly and charge for doing so.[43]

Damages for loss of or damage to goods

It is the duty of the consignor to pack the goods in a way reasonably sufficient for the journey,[44] and to address them sufficiently and correctly. Any loss or damage sustained due to the address not being full, distinct and ample, falls on the consignor,[45] and the carrier may still take this plea though he has accepted goods of an ambiguous address, as where there are two places of the same name.[45] But a carrier may be barred from such pleas if he has accepted goods obviously badly packed or addressed. If the consignor himself undertakes the stowage and packing in the vehicle, he will be responsible for any loss due to defective stowage,[46] though mere presence at the stowage without complaint at the method will not relieve the carrier from liability.[47]

Loss of goods

If the goods are entirely lost, or must be treated as such, the consignor is entitled to recover the full value.[48] The value will be the market price at the destination at the due date of delivery, less charges.[49] If there is no market price, the price at which he has agreed to sell,[50] or the price of obtaining a substitute,[51] are the best available estimates of value to the owner. A reasonable estimate of profit is allowable.[52]

The consignee is entitled to the market price as damages even though he has contracted to sell for less,[53] as the market price is the presumed cost of replacement. If there be no such market, then it will be the cost price of the goods plus the cost of carriage and an allowance for the profit normally and reasonably to be made from the transaction, in the absence of knowledge or notice inferring special liability in addition.[54] If only part of the goods be lost, the cost of replacement of that part only is a relevant charge, in the absence of fuller knowledge or notice on the carrier's part, and its value will be arrived at in the same way.[55] Where a carrier put goods on

[42] *Gould* v. *S.E. & Chatham Ry.* [1920] 2 K.B. 186.
[43] *Littleton Collieries* v. *L.N.W. Ry.* (1916) 115 L.T. 840.
[44] *L.N.W. Ry.* v. *Hudson* [1920] A.C. 324.
[45] *Caledonian Ry.* v. *Hunter & Co.* (1858) 20 D. 1097.
[46] *Rain* v. *G.S.W. Ry.* (1869) 7 M. 439.
[47] *Paxton* v. *N.B. Ry.* (1870) 9 M. 50.
[48] *Crouch* v. *L.N.W. Ry.* (1849) 2 C. & K. 789; *Riley* v. *Horne* (1828) 5 Bing. 217; *Rice* v. *Baxendale* (1861) 7 H. & N. 96.
[49] *O'Hanlan* v. *G.W. Ry.* (1865) 6 B. & S. 484; *Rice, supra.*
[50] *France* v. *Gaudet* (1871) L.R. 6 Q.B. 199.
[51] *Hinde* v. *Liddell* (1875) L.R. 10 Q.B. 265.
[52] *O'Hanlan, supra.*
[53] *Rodocanachi* v. *Milburn* (1886) 18 Q.B.D. 67.
[54] *O'Hanlan* v. *G.W. Ry.* (1865) 6 B. & S. 484; *Mitsui* v. *Watts* [1916] 2 K.B. 826.
[55] *British Columbia Sawmills Co.* v. *Nettleship* (1868) L.R. 3 C.P. 499.

board the wrong ship, which was lost, he was held liable for the price of the goods.[56]

Damage to goods

If goods are damaged in transit it is clear on principle that the measure of damages will be the diminution in value thereby caused. If the goods are irreparably damaged or only repairable at considerable expense, or otherwise constructively totally damaged, the consignee has been held entitled to reject the goods and recover the full value from the carrier [57]; but this is not necessarily a general rule. The consignee must examine the goods promptly on delivery and claim without delay. He may not claim for injury to part of a consignment and then later claim again when one proper inspection would have revealed all the damage.[58] Where part of a consignment is damaged and the rest is rendered unusable thereby, allowance should be made for the loss of use of the rest of the consignment as by interest on the price.[59] Damages have also been allowed for loss of market where that was a direct result of damage to goods while in the carrier's possession.[60]

Where one of a pair of horses died owing to the carrier's negligence, it was held that the depreciation in the value of the other as one of a pair could not be recovered.[61]

Damages for delay in delivery of goods

When delay takes place in the carriage and delivery of goods, the damages recoverable from the carrier are such as may fairly and reasonably be considered as arising naturally, in the usual and ordinary course of things, from the carrier's breach of contract, or such as may reasonably be supposed to have been in the contemplation of both parties at the time when they made the contract as the probable consequences of the delay. If, at the time of the contract, special circumstances which may result in more serious damage in the event of delay are brought to the knowledge of the carrier, damages which result as a natural consequence from the failure of the contract in those specially disclosed circumstances will also be recoverable.[62] These are just the general principles of damages for breach of contract.[63] The question has already been considered to what extent acceptance of exceptional liability may be inferred from acceptance

56 *Gilmours* v. *Clark* (1853) 15 D. 478; *Johnson* v. *L. & Y. Ry.* (1878) 3 C.P.D. 499; *cf. Bain* v. *Brown*, Dec. 4, 1824, F.C. Contrast cases of through journey: *McKenzie* v. *Howie* (1802) Hume 312; *Bain* v. *Bowie*, May 6, 1821, F.C.

57 *Dick* v. *E. Coast Rys.* (1901) 4 F. 178.

58 *Stewart* v. *N.B. Ry.* (1878) 5 R. 426.

59 *Cf. British Columbia Sawmills* v. *Nettleship* (1868) L.R. 3 C.P. 499.

60 *Keddie Gordon & Co.* v. *N.B. Ry.* (1886) 14 R. 233.

61 *Berry* v. *S.E. & C. & D. Committee* (1902) 18 T.L.R. 159. But see *Cleghorn* v. *Spittal's Trs.* (1856) 18 D. 664, where the element of breaking a set of things was considered.

62 *Hadley* v. *Baxendale* (1854) 9 Ex. 341, 354; *Horne* v. *Midland Ry.* (1873) L.R. 8 C.P. 131; *Simpson* v. *L.N.W. Ry.* (1876) 1 Q.B.D. 274; *Monte Video Gas Co.* v. *Clan Line Steamers* (1921) 37 T.L.R. 866; *Victoria Laundry* v. *Newman* [1949] 2 K.B. 528.

63 *Vide, supra*, Chaps. 27 and 28.

of the contract without making an increased charge.[64] The inference that the carrier accepted liability for exceptional loss cannot be drawn from the mere fact that he took the goods with notice of extraordinary circumstances.[65]

It is still somewhat doubtful to what extent a common carrier, to whom adequate notice is given of special circumstances, is justified in refusing the extra liability. In *Gee* v. *Lancs and Yorks Ry.*[66] it was suggested that he might refuse unless a higher freight was tendered.

It has been laid down that where goods are delivered too late, the owner should instantly sell at market price and realise his loss, the difference between that price and the price he would have obtained being the measure of damages.[67] A long delay may entitle the consignee to reject the goods, in which case damages must be assessed as for non-delivery.[68]

Damages recoverable for loss by delay in transit—depreciation

Damages will extend without special notice of circumstances peculiar to the contract to diminution in value of the goods consequent on delay, and hence the difference in value between the goods when they should have been delivered and their value at the actual time of delivery is normally recoverable,[69] measureable, where there is an available market, by the difference between the market price at the contractual place and time of delivery and that at the time of actual delivery.[70] So too where perishables were delayed and depreciated the diminution in value was given.[71] Where part of a consignment was damaged by delay so that the whole was rejected and depreciated, the plaintiff was held entitled to recover the amount of the depreciation in market value and the difference between the market price on the day when they should have been delivered originally and the day when they were sold.[72] Again where cattle were negligently delayed and were depreciated by losing condition the loss of value was recoverable.[73]

Deterioration or destruction

Where the result of delay is naturally to deteriorate [74] or completely destroy the goods, as in the case of perishables generally, then if their

64 *Supra*, Chap. 28.
65 *Gee* v. *Lancs. & Yorks. Ry.* (1860) 6 H. & N. 211; *Wilson* v. *Lancs. & Yorks. Ry.* (1861) 9 C.B.(N.S.) 632.
66 (1860) 6 H. & N. 211. See also *Horne* v. *Midland Ry.* (1873) L.R. 8 C.P. 131, 136.
67 *Simmons* v. *S.E. Ry.* (1861) 7 Jur.(N.S.) 849.
68 *Levene* v. *G.W.Ry.* (1868) 18 L.T. 295.
69 *Wilson* v. *Lancs. & Yorks. Ry.* (1861) 9 C.B.(N.S.) 632 (where loss of season allowed); *Schulze* v. *G.E. Ry.* (1887) 19 Q.B.D. 30.
70 *Cf. Crawford* v. *L.M.S. Ry.*, 1929 S.N. 66.
71 *Macdonald* v. *Highland Ry.* (1873) 11 M. 614. See also *McConnachie* v. *G.N.S. Ry.* (1875) 3 R. 79; *Fulton* v. *Caledonian Ry.* (1894) 10 Sh.Ct.R. 119.
72 *Collard* v. *S.E. Ry.* (1861) 7 H. & N. 79.
73 *Allday* v. *G.W. Ry.* (1864) 5 B. & S. 903.
74 *Cf. Waller* v. *Midland G.W. Ry. I.* (1879) 4 L.R.Ir. 376 (horse box not provided; horses sent by road to sale and condition deteriorated: only such damages awarded as resulting if horses in proper condition).

nature be known the whole value will be recoverable as the ordinary and natural consequences of the delay.[75] Where the delay would not have caused any damage but for some defect in the condition or packing of the goods, unknown to the carrier, the carrier is not liable for the consequences of delay.[76]

Diminution in value by fall in market price

If a fall in market price or value takes place between the time when the goods should have been delivered and that when they are eventually delivered, even though accidental, and in nowise arising from the nature of the article, the difference is recoverable from the carrier.[77] Where part only of a consignment was delayed so that the consignee had a claim for non-delivery but accepted the later portion, the measure of damage was taken as the fall in market price, but the subsequent delivery could be taken in mitigation of damages.[78] If there has been no fall in market price nominal damages are due.[79]

Loss of use

Where goods are not delivered so that the consignee is deprived of their use and prevented from making the profits he would have by that use, the damages will be the cost of hiring a substitute, or the profits lost by not having that article [80] or the diminished profit through being put into use later,[81] or the excess cost of doing the work by other means.[82]

Damages and expenses

Where the consequence of the delay is that the consignee necessarily becomes liable to a third party in damages for delay in delivery to him, the damages and expenses reasonably incurred will be recoverable from the defaulting carrier [83] if not too remote in the circumstances.

Loss of profits

Without special notice to the carrier loss of exceptional profits is consequential damage and not recoverable.[84] But even without special

75 *Margetson* v. *Glynn* [1892] 1 Q.B. 337; *Macdonald* v. *Highland Ry.* (1873) 11 M. 614.

76 *Baldwin* v. *L.C. & D. Ry.* (1882) 9 Q.B.D. 582 (rags rotted in delayed transit because packed wet). *Cf. Cox* v. *L.N.W. Ry.* (1862) 3 F. & F. 77; *Barbour* v. *S.E. Ry.* (1876) 34 L.T. 67.

77 *Collard* v. *S.E. Ry.* (1861) 7 H. & N. 79; *Schulze* v. *G.E. Ry.* (1887) 19 Q.B.D. 30. See also *Simmons* v. *S.E. Ry.* (1861) 7 Jur.(N.S.) 849; *Leaburn* v. *G.N.S. Ry.* (1887) 3 Sh.Ct.Rep. 169.

78 *Smith Edwards & Co.* v. *Tregarthen* (1887) 3 T.L.R. 688.

79 *Blackwell* v. *Sutton* (1887) 3 T.L.R. 630.

80 *L.N.W. Ry.* v. *Neilson* [1922] 2 A.C. 263. But not the whole loss of profits on something of which the delayed goods were only a component or a portion: *Hadley* v. *Baxendale* (1854) 9 Ex. 341; *Den of Ogil* v. *Caledonian Ry.* (1902) 5 F. 99.

81 *Fletcher* v. *Tayleur* (1855) 17 C.B. 21; *Victoria Laundry* v. *Newman* [1949] 2 K.B. 528.

82 *Henderson* v. *Mayer* (1941) 46 Com.Cas. 209; *Cory* v. *Thames Ironworks Co.* (1868) L.R. 3 Q.B. 181; *Wilson* v. *Lancs. & Yorks. Ry.* (1861) 9 C.B.(N.S.) 632.

83 *Baxendale* v. *L.C. & D. Ry.* (1874) L.R. 10 Ex. 35.

84 *Horne* v. *Midland Ry.* (1860) 6 H. & N. 211; *Den of Ogil* v. *Caledonian Ry.* (1902) 5 F. 99; *Le Peintur* v. *S.E. Ry.* (1860) 2 L.T. 170; *Wilson, supra*; *G.W. Ry.* v. *Redmayne* (1866) L.R. 1 C.P. 329; *Simmons* v. *S.E. Ry.* (1861) 7 Jur.(N.S.) 849; *cf. Heskell* v. *Continental Express* [1950] 1 All E.R. 1033.

notice in the contract, a carrier must be taken to appreciate that delay in delivery of a profit-making asset will cause the consignee to sustain some diminution in his normal profits, and damages are recoverable on this account.[85] This does not extend to loss of the whole profits of an undertaking.[86] Where there is adequate notice to the carrier before or at the time of the contract full loss of profits is recoverable.[87] Loss of profits has also been refused where the loss was speculative and uncertain.[88]

Loss of market

Damages for loss of market are in general only recoverable where the circumstances have been brought to the notice of the carrier so that the damages are within his reasonable contemplation, as loss of market is not in general an ordinary consequence of delay.[89] In one case where carriers delayed to forward they were held liable for the invoice price of the goods which had lost the market thereby.[90]

Loss of contract of sale

Similarly damages for loss of the whole contract of sale in consequence of the carrier's delay is too remote to be recoverable unless the knowledge of the carrier was such as to make the remote damages recoverable.[91] So too where samples were delayed in transit until the season when they could have been used to obtain orders was past the consignors were held entitled to recover as damages only the value of the samples at the time when they should have been delivered.[92]

Expenditure

Loss of wages paid to workmen kept idle in consequence of delay in delivery of material for them is similarly consequential damage and not recoverable without special notice.[93] Loss of wages paid to seamen whose ship could not sail owing to a carrier's delay was refused,[94] as was the cost of coal and the ship's running expenses. So, too, expenses of travellers despatched fruitlessly, being unable to execute orders by the carrier's delay to deliver material, were refused.[95]

85 *Victoria Laundry* v. *Newman* [1949] 2 K.B. 528.

86 *Hadley* v. *Baxendale* (1854) 9 Ex. 341; *G.W. Ry.* v. *Redmayne* (1866) L.R. 1 C.P. 329.

87 *Simpson* v. *L.N.W. Ry.* (1876) 1 Q.B.D. 274; *Jameson* v. *Midland Ry.* (1884) 50 L.T. 426; *Levi Bros.* v. *S.E. Ry.* (1886) 2 T.L.R. 817; *cf. Monte Video Gas Co.* v. *Clan Line Steamers* (1921) 37 T.L.R. 866.

88 *The Parana* (1877) 2 P.D. 118; but see *Dunn* v. *Bucknall Bros.* [1902] 2 K.B. 614; *Koufos* v. *Czarnikow* [1969] 1 A.C. 350.

89 *Hawes* v. *S.E. Ry.* (1884) 52 L.T. 514; *Duckham* v. *G.W. Ry.* (1899) 15 T.L.R. 328; *Horne* v. *Midland Ry.* (1873) L.R. 8 C.P. 131; *Lord* v. *Midland Ry.* (1867) L.R. 2 C.P. 339; *Hales* v. *L.N.W. Ry.* (1863) 4 B. & S. 66; see also *Dunn* v. *Bucknall Bros.* [1902] 2 K.B. 614.

90 *Bates* v. *Cameron* (1855) 18 D. 186; *cf. Finlay* v. *N.B. Ry.* (1870) 8 M. 959.

91 *Horne, supra*; *Rodocanachi* v. *Milburn* (1886) 18 Q.B.D. 67.

92 *Schulze* v. *G.E. Ry.* (1887) 19 Q.B.D. 30.

93 *Le Peintur* v. *S.E. Ry.* (1860) 2 L.T. 170; *Hadley* v. *Baxendale* (1854) 9 Ex. 341.

94 *Den of Ogil* v. *Caledonian Ry.* (1902) 5 F. 99.

95 *Wilson* v. *L. & Y. Ry.* (1861) 9 C.B.(N.S.) 632.

But reasonable expenditure incurred in searching for goods delayed in transit is allowable, though not hotel and similar expenses while waiting for them to arrive.[96]

Other consequences of delay

Other consequences of delay are generally too remote to sound in damages in accordance with the general principles of remoteness of damage.[97] Examples are loss of custom,[98] loss of place in a competition.[99] But where a comedian was travelling and his costumes were lost, having been entrusted to a railway servant who knew him and of his engagement, the company was held liable for the loss of his fee for performing.[1]

Personal bar

Where goods are lost or injured in transit through the fault of the consignor himself he is personally barred from holding the common carrier liable as an insurer.[2] So damage arising from neglect of the consignor's duty to pack properly, if not apparent to the carrier, is not damage for which he is liable.[3] Similarly, if the nature of the goods is concealed so that the carrier has no opportunity of exercising any unusual care which the nature of the goods requires, he is not liable for damage due to not using extraordinary care, but is only bound to use such ordinary care as the goods seem to require.[4] The same applies to fraudulent overloading [5]; but the onus of proving the exception rests on the carrier and if an accident remains unexplained he is still liable as an insurer.[6] So, too, he is excused if the goods are not properly addressed.[7]

Even where danger arises such as would exempt the carrier from liability as being an inevitable accident, the carrier must check the loss so far as possible. His duty is always to do what is reasonable in the circumstances, but this does not extend to taking precautions against the risk of unusual happenings unless there were good reason to fear their happening.[8] In any such emergency, however, the owner's instructions should be obtained, if there is time, and followed so far as possible.

Stoppage in transitu

An unpaid seller may exercise his right of stoppage *in transitu*, which

96 *Woodger* v. *G.W. Ry.* (1867) L.R. 2 C.P. 318; see also *Candy* v. *Midland Ry.* (1878) 38 L.T. 226; *Hales* v. *L.N.W. Ry.* (1863) 4 B. & S. 66; *Adams* v. *Midland Ry.* (1861) 31 L.J.Ex. 35; *Black* v. *Baxendale* (1847) 1 Ex. 410.

97 *Supra*, Chap. 28.

98 *Mann* v. *General S.N. Co.* (1856) 20 L.T.(o.s.) 247.

99 *Watson* v. *Ambergate Ry.* (1857) 15 Jur. 448.

1 *Fowlds* v. *Caledonian Ry.* (1907) 23 Sh.Ct.Rep. 84.

2 *Talley* v. *G.W. Ry.* (1870) L.R. 6 C.P. 44.

3 *L.N.W.R.* v. *Hudson* [1920] A.C. 324.

4 *Crouch* v. *L.N.W. Ry.* (1854) 14 C.B. 255.

5 *Gibbon* v. *Paynton* (1769) 4 Burr. 2298.

6 *Mustard* v. *Paterson*, 1923 S.C. 142.

7 *Caledonian Ry.* v. *Hunter* (1858) 20 D. 1097; *cf. Campbell* v. *Caledonian Ry.* (1852) 14 D. 806.

8 *Briddon* v. *G.N. Ry.* (1858) 28 L.J.Ex. 51.

puts an end to the carrier's obligation to deliver,[9] on the insolvency of the purchaser. The goods must still be in transit and not have reached the consignee.[10] A carrier will be liable in damages for failure to implement the instructions of the unpaid seller.[11] If he gives such notice the seller must retake the goods and give orders for their disposal and pay the freight on them.[12] Questions of difficulty may arise whether the goods have or have not reached the constructive possession of the buyer.[13] In general the carrier is not discharged so long as anything remains for him to do either by custom or by contract in his capacity as carrier.[14]

The measure of damages against a carrier who has ignored a justifiable order to stop *in transitu* in circumstances when he could have effected stoppage should, on principle, be the loss sustained in the natural course of things from the carrier's failure in duty. Again, it is submitted in principle that this figure can be arrived at by taking the difference between the price contractually payable by the consignee for the goods on delivery and the dividend on that price actually eventually received by the seller, the consignee being *ex hypothesi* bankrupt and the goods once delivered falling to be included as part of the assets in the consignee's bankruptcy. In *Mechan* [15] the pursuers recovered the full sum sued for, being the whole cost or value of the goods in question, but it was averred that the claim against the bankrupt estate was believed to be valueless and the pursuers offered to assign their claim against the estate. Where the dividend from the estate is unpaid or doubtful this seems an appropriate course to follow. It does not, however, affect the theoretical quantum of damages.

Statutory limitation of carrier's liability

While a private carrier may limit his liability by contract, a common carrier's responsibility *ex lege* is very heavy, and it became customary for carriers to post notices at their receiving offices, limiting the carrier's liability to certain causes of loss or injury or excluding it entirely. If it were proved that such had come to the knowledge of the consignor his consent was presumed and the carrier escaped liability, except for gross negligence. The courts tended to the presumption that an opportunity to read the notice was enough and frequently held such binding, so as to amount to binding bilateral agreements. Much litigation ensued raising difficult questions as to the construction of such notices and how far the consignors were bound. The Carriers Act of 1830 sought to remedy this

9 Sale of Goods Act 1893, ss. 44–48.

10 See *McLeod* v. *Harrison* (1880) 8 R. 227; *Reid* v. *Snowball Co.* (1904) 7 F. 35, and Sale of Goods Act 1893, s. 45.

11 *Verschures Creameries* v. *Hull Steamship Co.* [1921] 2 K.B. 608; *Mechan* v. *N.E. Ry.*, 1911 S.C. 1348.

12 *Booth Steamship Co.* v. *Cargo Fleet Iron Co.* [1916] 2 K.B. 570.

13 See *Ex p. Cooper, re Maclaren* (1879) 11 Ch.D. 68; *Bethell* v. *Clark* (1888) 20 Q.B.D. 615; *Lyons* v. *Hoffnung* (1890) 15 App.Cas. 391; *Kendal* v. *Marshall, Stevens & Co.* (1883) 11 Q.B.D. 356.

14 *Bishop* v. *Mersey & Clyde Navigation Co.* (1830) 8 S. 558.

15 *Supra*: see Session Papers for details of claim.

state of affairs.[16] The effect of the Act was to divide goods into valuables, which comprise certain enumerated types of property of great value in small compass, and fragile goods, and general goods. By section 4 no public notice or declaration is in any way to limit or affect the common law liability of common carriers by land for hire in respect of any goods to be conveyed by them, though they may still enter into special contracts with individual customers limiting their liability by agreement expressly made between the carrier and the other party with respect to a particular consignment of goods (s. 6), as by delivery of a ticket or notice containing conditions [17] which bind the consignor if brought home to him.[18] If a carrier accepts goods without making a special contract relative thereto, he is fully liable, as at common law,[19] as modified by section 1 of the Act. There is no requirement of writing and the existence of a special contract is a question of fact.[20] Only public notices and declarations are struck at, and an individual special contract is competent. A carrier receiving goods without making a special contract under section 6 is still protected by section 1 unless the special contract is inconsistent with his having accepted the goods as a common carrier.[21]

Special contract or notice

In cases not affected by section 4 of the Act, therefore, conditions may be incorporated into the contract by reference in the ticket or another document which contains the terms and conditions [22] or by special contract or notice given personally to the sender,[23] and it remains a question of fact whether reasonable notice of the conditions affecting liability is given to a consignor [24] and whether the goods were sent subject thereto [25]; these conditions may limit or exclude liability for loss of or injury to the goods carried,[26] and such conditions will be given effect to if clear,

[16] See the preamble to the Act for a review of the circumstances in which it was passed. So far as concerns railway carriage it was extended by the Railways Act 1921, to include a common carrier by land who is also a common carrier by water: as regards other common carriers the Act only applies to the land part of their carriage. *Le Conteur* v. *L.S.W. Ry.* (1865) L.R. 1 Q.B. 54. See also the history outlined in *Peek* v. *N. Staffordshire Ry.* (1863) 10 H.L.Cas. 473, 491–500.

[17] *Shaw* v. *Y. & N. Midland Ry.* (1849) 13 Q.B. 347; *G.N. Ry.* v. *Morville* (1852) 21 L.J.Q.B. 319; *Carr* v. *L. & Y. Ry.* (1852) 7 Ex. 707; *Walker* v. *York & N. Midland Ry.* (1853) 2 E. & B. 750.

[18] *Henderson* v. *Stevenson* (1875) 2 R.(H.L.) 71; *Shaw* v. *G.W. Ry.* [1894] 1 Q.B. 373; *Richardson* v. *Rowntree* [1894] A.C. 217; *Hood* v. *Anchor Line*, 1918 S.C.(H.L.) 143.

[19] *Cahill* v. *L.N.W. Ry.* (1863) 13 C.B.(N.S.) 818; *Wilkinson* v. *L. & Y. Ry.* [1907] 2 K.B. 222.

[20] *Walker* v. *York & N. Midland Ry.* (1853) 2 E. & B. 750.

[21] *Baxendale* v. *G.E. Ry.* (1869) L.R. 4 Q.B. 244; *G.N. Ry.* v. *L.E.P. Tpt.* [1922] 2 K.B. 742; *cf. Shaw* v. *G.W. Ry.* [1894] 1 Q.B. 373, 379.

[22] *Walker* v. *York & N. Midland Ry.* (1853) 2 E. & B. 750.

[23] *Walker, supra*; *Van Toll* v. *S.E. Ry.* (1862) 31 L.J.C.P. 241.

[24] *Hood* v. *Anchor Line Ltd.*, 1918 S.C.(H.L.) 143.

[25] *Crouch* v. *G.N. Ry.* (1854) 9 Ex. 566; *Walker, supra.*

[26] *Peek* v. *N. Staffs. Ry.* (1863) 10 H.L.C. 473; *Clarke* v. *West Ham Corporation* [1909] 2 K.B. 858; but probably not covering wilful personal wrong; *Peek, supra*; *Shaw* v. *G.W. Ry.* (1894) 1 Q.B. 373.

but construed strictly [27] and contra proferentem.[28] The special arrangements need not even be in writing,[29] but the carrier loses the benefit of them by deviation,[30] and they remain special, requiring to be entered into separately for every individual contract of carriage. The carrier remains liable as a common carrier for all risks not excepted,[31] and a special contract under section 6 will not deprive the carrier of the benefit of section 1 of the Act of 1830 unless the terms of the contract are inconsistent with the goods having been received by him as a common carrier.[32]

Provisions of Carriers Act

The Carriers Act provides by section 1 that a common carrier by land for hire is liable as an insurer of articles of certain descriptions contained in any parcel or package delivered, either for carriage for hire or as passenger's luggage in a public conveyance when the value contained therein [33] exceeds £10,[34] unless the value is expressly declared [35] when the goods are handed over [36] at the carrier's office or to his servant, and an increased charge or agreement to pay such increased charge is made and accepted by the carrier. Such increased rate must be notified by a notice conspicuously affixed in every place where such parcels are received (s. 2) which shall bind persons sending goods to which the Act applies. If no notice is affixed the carrier loses the benefit of the Act, must refund the increase, and is liable as at common law. The carrier must give a receipt for the increased charge when required or lose the benefit of the Act (s.3). A consignor who is entitled to damages is entitled to recover the increased charges in addition to compensation for loss or injury to the goods (s.7).

The carrier may plead the Act even though he does not publish in statutory form his rate of increased charges, as a notice under section 2 has been held to be merely a condition of the carrier's right to make an increased charge in excess of the usual rates, and so a carrier in whose hands goods within the Act were lost was well entitled to claim exemption from liability as declaration had been made in terms of section 1, though

27 General words of exemption only exclude liability where no misconduct: *Steinman* v. *Angier Line* [1891] 1 Q.B. 619.

28 *L.N.W. Ry.* v. *Neilson* [1922] 2 A.C. 263; *Shaw* v. *G.W. Ry.* [1894] 1 Q.B. 373; *Price* v. *Union Lighterage Co.* [1904] 1 K.B. 412.

29 Carriers Act 1830, ss. 4, 6.

30 *Polwarth* v. *N.B. Ry.*, 1908 S.C. 1275; *L.N.W. Ry.* v. *Neilson, supra*; *Hain S.S. Co.* v. *Tate & Lyle* [1936] 2 All E.R. 597.

31 *Sutton* v. *Ciceri* (1880) 17 R.(H.L.) 40.

32 *Baxendale* v. *G.E. Ry.* (1869) L.R. 4 Q.B. 244.

33 *Bernstein* v. *Baxendale* (1859) 6 C.B.(N.S.) 251; *Stoessiger* v. *S.E. Ry.* (1854) 3 E. & B. 549.

34 In the case of railways only, now £25: Railways Act 1921, Sched. VI (now repealed).

35 *Rusk* v. *N.B. Ry.*, 1920, 2 S.L.T. 139. See also *Stewart* v. *Grimshaw* (1923) 39 Sh.Ct.Rep. 8. The consignor must show that the carrier acquired knowledge by a declaration under the Act: there is no set form of declaration: *Bradbury* v. *Sutton* (1872) 19 W.R. 800; 21 W.R. 128; *Robinson* v. *L.S.W. Ry.* (1865) 19 C.B.(N.S.) 57; *Hirschel* v. *G.E. Ry.* (1906) 12 Com. Cas. 11. It is not enough that the nature of the goods was obvious: *Doey* v. *L.N.W. Ry.* [1919] 1 K.B. 623. The declaration must cover nature and value of the goods: *Bradbury* v. *Sutton* (1872) 21 W.R. 128; *Doey, supra.*

36 *Stephens* v. *L.S.W. Ry.* (1886) 18 Q.B.D. 121, 126.

there was no notice in terms of section 2.[37] If the consignor makes a declaration to bring articles within the protection of the Act, the carrier becomes subject to the common law obligations even though he makes no extra charge.[38] If no declaration is made the carrier is not liable at all, not even for the minimum amount.

Articles within the Carriers Act

The articles within the Carriers Act for which protection is given are those of great value in small compass; they are gold and silver coin,[39] gold or silver in a manufactured or unmanufactured state, precious stones, jewellery, trinkets,[40] watches, clocks, any kind of timepieces,[41] bills,[42] banknotes, orders, notes or securities for payment of money, British or foreign stamps, maps,[43] writings, title-deeds, paintings, though not coloured designs for commercial purposes,[44] engravings, prints and coloured prints,[45] pictures and frames,[46] gold or silver plate or plated articles,[40] including looking-glasses, smelling-bottles and the like,[47] glass, china, silks, manufactured or not, and whether or not wrought up with other materials,[48] furs [49] and lace (but not machine-made lace).[50] It is always a question of fact whether particular goods fall within the Act,[51] and articles merely accessory to articles within the Act are themselves within it.[52]

The carrier is protected provided the goods are in a package [53] and not loose, and also in the case where the package contains goods some of which fall outside the Act. It applies to a passenger's luggage carried along with him, so that if a mixed package be lost and no declaration has been made the value of the goods outwith the Act may be recovered, but not those within the Act.[54] So, too, in the case of a mixed package the carrier is liable for the value of the box or case, which he is not if it contained only goods within the Act but not declared thereunder.

37 *Rusk* v. *N.B. Ry.*, 1920, 2 S.L.T. 139 (O.H.).
38 *Behrens* v. *G.N. Ry.* (1862) 31 L.J.Ex. 299; see also *Hart* v. *Baxendale* (1851) 6 Ex. 769.
39 Including cupro-nickel coins: S.I. 1951, No. 1032, but not copper: *Royal Insce. Co.* v. *Atlas Express Co.*, 1916, 2 S.L.T. 192. See now Coinage Act 1971, ss. 12, 13.
40 *Bernstein* v. *Baxendale* (1859) 6 C.B.(N.S.) 251; *Levi Jones* v. *C.L.C.* (1901) 17 T.L.R. 444.
41 *Le Conteur* v. *L.S.W. Ry.* (1865) L.R. 1 Q.B. 54 (chronometer).
42 *Stoessiger* v. *S.E. Ry.* (1854) 3 E. & B. 549.
43 *Wyld* v. *Pickford* (1841) 8 M. & W. 443.
44 *Woodward* v. *L.N.W. Ry.* (1878) 3 Ex.D. 121.
45 *Boys* v. *Pink* (1838) 8 C. & P. 361. As to lithographs, see *Campbell* v. *Pickford*, 1 Guthrie Sel.Cas. 124.
46 *Henderson* v. *L.N.W. Ry.* (1870) L.R. 5 Ex. 90.
47 *Owen* v. *Burnett* (1834) 2 C. & M. 353; *Bernstein* v. *Baxendale, supra*.
48 Repealed *quoad* railways by Railways Act 1921, s. 56 and Sched. 6 (now repealed). It includes dresses: *Flowers* v. *S.E. Ry.* (1867) 16 L.T. 329; *Hart* v. *Baxendale* (1851) 6 Ex. 769; *Bernstein, supra*; *Brunt* v. *Midland Ry.* (1864) 2 H. & C. 889.
49 *Mayhew* v. *Nelson* (1833) 6 C. & P. 58.
50 Amended by Carriers Act Amdt. Act 1865; and see *Treadwin* v. *G.E. Ry.* (1868) L.R. 3 C.P. 308.
51 *Brunt* v. *Midland Ry.* (1864) 2 H. & C. 889.
52 *Treadwin, supra*; *Henderson* v. *L.N.W. Ry.* (1868) L.R. 5 Ex. 90.
53 A parcel or package may be of any size or value, or even be a wagon: *Whaite* v. *L.N. Ry.* (1874) L.R. 9 Ex. 67.
54 *Flowers* v. *S.E. Ry.* (1867) 16 L.T. 329; *Treadwin* v. *G.E. Ry.* (1868) L.R. 3 C.P. 308.

Liability for felonious acts

The carrier is not relieved by the Act from liability for loss or injury from felonious acts of his servants,[55] nor are servants absolved from personal liability (s. 8), and this extends even to sub-contractors [56] engaged in the carriage, though only to acts involving something substantially criminal and more than mere negligence: the onus of proof of this is required from the person claiming damages.[57] It is not sufficient to show that the felony was more probably committed by the carrier's servants than by strangers, though it is adequate to show that it must have been one or other of the servants, without specifying which one,[58] though it has been held sufficient to show that a considerable time was taken to open the package and none but railway servants had access to the package.[59] A carrier may contract out of section 8 of the Act.[60]

Extent of protection conferred

The protection of the Act covers negligence of the carrier even in the case of goods carried beyond their destination,[61] and probably also even wilful damage, only felonious acts being excluded.[61] So far as concerns the value of the goods, nothing more than the actual value of the articles as declared can be recovered, though that declaration is not conclusive and the loss must be proved as to value [62]; it merely serves to limit the liability. Where goods have been sent by a seller to a buyer, the value is the invoice price to the buyer, not the price the seller paid for them.[63] Nor does the Act cover every loss.

The Act protects only against claims of damages for loss or damage, but not against damages for delay.[64] But goods may be " lost " within the meaning of the Act though only temporarily lost and subsequently recovered.[65] The Act also protects the carrier where goods within the Act but undeclared have been lost during deviation, although no other defence would avail the carrier.[66] And the loss in question must be *by the carrier.*[67] Loss or injury has been held to cover theft by other than the carrier's servants.[68]

[55] In respect only of goods falling within s. 1 of the Act: *G.W. Ry.* v. *Rimell* (1856) 18 C.B. 575; *Metcalfe* v. *L.B.S.C. Ry.* (1858) 4 C.B.(N.S.) 307; *Shaw* v. *G.W. Ry.* [1894] 1 Q.B. 373, 383. On what must be proved, see *Turner* v. *G.W. Ry.* (1876) 34 L.T. 22; *Kirkstall Brewery* v. *Furness Ry.* (1874) L.R. 9 Q.B. 468.
[56] *Stephens* v. *L.S.W. Ry.* (1886) 18 Q.B.D. 121; *Machin* v. *L.S.W. Ry.* (1848) 2 Ex. 415.
[57] *Campbells* v. *N.B. Ry.* (1875) 2 R. 433; *McQueen* v. *G.W. Ry.* (1875) L.R. 10 Q.B. 569.
[58] *Vaughton* v. *L.N.W. Ry.* (1874) L.R. 9 Ex. 93; *cf. G.W. Ry.* v. *Rimell* (1856) 18 C.B. 575; *Metcalfe* v. *L.B.S.C. Ry.* (1858) 4 C.B.(N.S.) 307.
[59] *Smith* v. *Midland Ry.* (1918) 88 L.J.K.B. 868.
[60] *Shaw* v. *G.W. Ry.* [1894] 1 Q.B. 373.
[61] *Morritt* v. *N.E. Ry.* (1876) 1 Q.B.D. 302.
[62] Carriers Act 1830, s. 9.
[63] *Blankensee* v. *L.N.W. Ry.* (1882) 45 L.T. 761.
[64] *Hearn* v. *L.S.W. Ry.* (1855) 10 Ex. 793.
[65] *Millen* v. *Brasch* (1882) 10 Q.B.D. 142; *cf. Gordon* v. *G.W. Ry.* (1881) 8 Q.B.D. 44.
[66] *Morritt* v. *N.E. Ry.* (1876) 1 Q.B.D. 302.
[67] *Pianciani* v. *L.S.W. Ry.* (1856) 18 C.B. 226; *Hearn, supra.*
[68] *Covington* v. *Willan* (1819) Gow 115.

Claims by carrier against consignor—freight

The carrier's first claim is for the freight or charge for carrying the goods. Though the contract is actually with the consignor [69] the consignee may be liable, as agent for the consignor, or by accepting the goods raise an implied contract to pay.[70] The freight demanded must be a reasonable one, and a demand of an unreasonable sum is tantamount to a refusal to carry for which an action of damages lies.[71] He cannot sue for the freight until he has carried and is ready and willing to deliver,[72] though a common carrier may demand the full freight in advance.[73]

The carrier has a lien over the goods for his charges; if he relinquishes it by delivering the goods this may imply a contract by the consignee to pay the freight.[70]

Delay in loading or unloading

If unreasonable delay occurs in loading or unloading his vehicle, so that it is detained for a time exceeding any period contractually allowed, or any period reasonable in the circumstances the carrier may claim for the detention of his vehicle.[74]

Expenditure on goods being carried

A carrier must take reasonable care of the goods while in his charge and if he reasonably incurs expense in so doing he may recover it from the owner of the goods.[75] British Railways are statutorily bound to provide water and food at railway stations for animals being carried, and may recover the cost from the consignor.[76]

Damage done by dangerous goods carried

A consignor impliedly warrants that goods tendered to be carried are fit to be carried in the ordinary way and are not dangerous, unless the carrier had been given adequate notice of the nature of the goods or he had other means of knowing their nature, and will accordingly be liable for damage to the carrier, his vehicle and crew, or other goods being carried by him, by unknown danger in the goods carried.[77]

Private carriers of goods

A private carrier of goods such as a haulage contractor [78] or furniture

[69] *G.W. Ry.* v. *Bagge* (1885) 15 Q.B.D. 625.
[70] *World Transport Co.* v. *Tealing* [1936] 2 All E.R. 573.
[71] *Allday* v. *G.W. Ry.* (1864) 5 B. & S. 903.
[72] *Barnes* v. *Marshall* (1852) 18 Q.B. 785.
[73] *Wyld* v. *Pickford* (1841) 8 M. & W. 443.
[74] *Cf. Hick* v. *Rodocanachi* [1893] A.C. 22; *A/S D/S Hansa* v. *Alexander*, 1919 S.C.(H.L.) 122.
[75] *G.N. Ry.* v. *Swaffield* (1874) L.R. 9 Ex. 132 (feeding animal).
[76] Diseases of Animals Act 1950, s. 22.
[77] *Brass* v. *Maitland* (1856) 6 E. & B. 470; *Farrant* v. *Barnes* (1862) 11 C.B.(N.S.) 553; *Cramb* v. *Caledonian Ry.* (1892) 19 R. 1054; *Bamfield* v. *Goole and Sheffield Tpt. Co.* [1910] 2 K.B. 94; *G.N. Ry.* v. *L.E.P. Transport Ltd.* [1922] 2 K.B. 742; *Burley* v. *Stepney Corpn.* [1947] 1 All E.R. 507.
[78] *Belfast Ropework Co.* v. *Bushell* [1918] 1 K.B. 210.

remover [79] may accept or decline any request to carry goods, and if he accepts, the rights and liabilities of parties are determined by their contract. No action lies for mere refusal to carry. The contract may include terms limiting or excluding liability for stated kinds of losses.

If he carries gratuitously he will be liable for gross negligence [80] and must take reasonable care of goods carried.[81] If he carries for reward he will be liable for negligence and for any non-performance of the contract.[82] The onus of proof that loss occurred without negligence is on the carrier.[83] A private carrier, like a common carrier, is liable to the owner for loss arising from accidental fire while the goods were in his custody.[84]

Common carriers of passengers

A common carrier of passengers makes a standing offer to carry any passenger presenting himself at a departure point or stopping place. He is justified in refusing a passenger only if there is no room in the vehicle, or the passenger refuses, or appears to be unable, to pay the fare,[85] or is not in a fit condition to be carried, as where he is drunk or troublesome.[85]

Liability

Unlike the common carrier of goods, the common carrier of passengers is not automatically liable for delay, non-delivery, or injury to or death of a passenger, but liable only if fault be shown on his part.[86] His duty is to take due care to carry the passenger safely.[87] But he is held by law bound to take reasonable precautions to have a vehicle in sound condition and good repair,[88] to provide a crew who are reasonably skilled and competent [89] and through his servants to operate his service in a careful manner.[90] There is no liability for mere accident, unless there be proof of misconduct or negligence.[91]

79 *Electric Sy. Stores* v. *Gaywood* (1909) 100 L.T. 855; *Watkins* v. *Cottell* [1916] 1 K.B. 10; *Turner* v. *Civil Service Supply Assocn.* [1926] 1 K.B. 50; *Fagan* v. *Green & Edwards* [1926] 1 K.B. 102. *Cf. Ingate* v. *Christie* (1850) 3 C. & K. 61; *Liver Alkali Co.* v. *Johnson* (1874) L.R. 9 Ex. 338.
80 *Giblin* v. *McMullen* (1868) L.R. 2 P.C. 317; *Bullen* v. *Swan Electric Co.* (1907) 23 T.L.R. 258; *Wiehe* v. *Dennis Bros.* (1913) 29 T.L.R. 250. *Cf. Copland* v. *Brogan*, 1916 S.C. 277.
81 *Richardson* v. *N.E. Ry.* (1872) L.R. 7 C.P. 75; *Travers* v. *Cooper* [1915] 1 K.B. 73.
82 *Sutton* v. *Ciceri* (1890) 17 R.(H.L.) 40.
83 *W.L.R. Traders (London) Ltd.* v. *British & Northern Shipping Agency Ltd.* [1955] 1 Lloyd's Rep. 554.
84 Mercantile Law Amendment (Sc.) Act 1856, s. 17; *Kemp (Leslie) Ltd.* v. *Robertson*, 1967 S.L.T. 213.
85 *Clarke* v. *West Ham Corpn.* [1909] 2 K.B. 858.
86 *Anderson* v. *Pyper* (1820) 2 Mur. 261.
87 *Collett* v. *L.N.W. Ry.* (1851) 16 Q.B. 984; *Readhead* v. *Midland Ry.* (1869) L.R. 4 Q.B. 379.
88 *Speirs* v. *Drysdale* (1813) Hume 316; *Richardson* v. *G.E. Ry.* (1876) 1 C.P.D. 342; *Inglis* v. *L.M.S. Ry.*, 1941 S.C. 551; *Easson* v. *L.N.E. Ry.* [1944] K.B. 421.
89 *Allan* v. *McLeish* (1819) 2 Mur. 158; *Gunn* v. *Gardiner* (1820) 2 Mur. 196.
90 *e.g. Drummond* v. *McGregor*, Feb. 26, 1813, F.C.; *McGlashan* v. *Dundee & Perth Ry.* (1848) 10 D. 1397; *Cargill* v. *Dundee & Perth Ry.* (1848) 11 D. 216; *Mottram* v. *S. Lancs. Transport Co.* [1942] 2 All E.R. 452; *Parkinson* v. *Liverpool Corpn.* [1950] 1 All E.R. 367.
91 *Aston* v. *Heaven* (1797) 2 Esp. 533; *Christie* v. *Griggs* (1809) 2 Camp. 79; *Daniel* v. *Metropolitan Ry.* (1871) L.R. 5 H.L. 45; *Ferns* v. *N.B. Ry.* (1872) 9 S.L.R. 652; *E.I. Ry.* v. *Kalidas Mukerjee* [1901] A.C. 396; *Newberry* v. *Bristol Tramways Co.* (1912) 29 T.L.R. 177.

Limitation of liability

British Railways may limit its liability in this respect by a clause in the timetable,[92] though this will not preclude liability for the consequences of negligence.[93] Such limitations are strictly construed.[94] The " Conditions of Issue of Passenger Tickets " provide that the carrier does not undertake that the train shall start or arrive at the time specified. The Railways Board also declines responsibility for any loss, inconvenience or injury which may arise from delay or detention, unless there is proof that the loss, inconvenience, injury, delay or detention arose in consequence of wilful misconduct on the part of the railway servants. There is also reserved the right to alter the timetables without notice. The question whether any such conditions have been duly imported into the contract has already been mentioned.[95]

The contract made by the taking of a ticket is indivisible and the passenger may not break the journey [93] unless that is permitted by the contract.

So far as concerns liability *ex delicto* this is sometimes limited or excluded by conditions incorporated into the contract by reference on the ticket, in which case the passenger is bound, whether or not he has read the conditions, if reasonable steps have been taken to bring the conditions to his notice.[96]

Damages for delay

In the event of it being established that unreasonable delay occurred due to fault on the part of the carrier not covered by an exception, the passenger would be entitled to damages as compensation for loss flowing from the breach of contract, but not for inconvenience or loss consequent thereon and outwith the contemplation of the parties when they made the contract. So damages have been awarded amounting to the wages for a day's work lost,[97] for inconvenience in having to walk home,[98] but not for damage sustained by being late for engagements,[99] nor for consequential illness.[1] The extent of loss will normally be the reasonable expense of

[92] *Prevost* v. *G.E. Ry.* (1865) 13 L.T. 20; *Thompson* v. *Midland Ry.* (1875) 34 L.T. 34; *Woodgate* v. *G.W. Ry.* (1884) 51 L.T. 826; *Sutton* v. *L.C. & D. Ry.* (1896) 12 T.L.R. 425; *McCartan* v. *N.E. Ry.* (1885) 54 L.J.Q.B. 441; *Duckworth* v. *L. & Y. Ry.* (1901) 84 L.T. 774.

[93] *Ashton* v. *L. & Y. Ry.* [1904] 2 K.B. 313; *Bastable* v. *Metcalf* [1906] 2 K.B. 288; see also *L.N.W. Ry.* v. *Hinchcliffe* [1903] 2 K.B. 32; *G.N. Ry.* v. *Winder* [1892] 2 Q.B. 595; *G.N. Ry.* v. *Palmer* [1895] 1 Q.B. 862.

[94] *Buckmaster* v. *G.E. Ry.* (1870) 23 L.T. 471. See also *Le Blanche* v. *L.N.W. Ry.* (1876) 1 C.P.D. 286; *Woodgate* v. *G.W. Ry.* (1884) 51 L.T. 826; *McCartan, supra*; *Duckworth* v. *L. & Y. Ry.* (1901) 84 L.T. 774.

[95] *Supra*, Chap. 25.

[96] *Gray* v. *L.N.E. Ry.*, 1930 S.C. 989; *Thompson* v. *L.M.S. Ry.* [1930] 1 K.B. 41; *Coyle* v. *L.M.S. Ry.*, 1930 S.L.T. 349; *Highland Ry.* v. *Menzies* (1878) 5 R. 887; *Parker* v. *S.E. Ry.* (1877) 2 C.P.D. 416; and see also Chap. 25, *supra*.

[97] *Cooke* v. *Midland Ry.* (1892) 9 T.L.R. 147.

[98] *Hobbs* v. *L.S.W. Ry.* (1875) L.R. 10 Q.B. 111.

[99] *Hamlin* v. *G.N. Ry.* (1856) 1 H. & N. 408: unless in the contemplation of both parties: *Buckmaster* v. *G.E. Ry.* (1870) 23 L.T. 471.

[1] *Hobbs, supra*. But see *McMahon* v. *Field* (1881) 7 Q.B.D. 591, 596.

getting to the destination by alternative means.[2] The reasonable expenses of detention are recoverable, such as an hotel bill.[3]

A passenger who claims damages for delay must have taken reasonable steps to mitigate his damages by taking alternative transport and may recover expenditure reasonably incurred in doing so. If he does not he will fail to recover damages [4] unless possibly he can show that even all reasonable efforts would not have avoided the loss. But a passenger cannot recover exceptional expenditure, as of a special train,[5] unless it was a reasonable thing to do in the circumstances,[6] which may be determined by considering whether a prudent man would have taken a special train at his own expense if the delay had been caused by his own fault,[5] but he may finish his journey by other means and recover.[7] The Railways Board is not bound to forward a passenger by special train if he has been prevented from making a connection by delay due to exceptional causes, such as the line being impassable, or flooding.[8] Probably no more than nominal damages would be recoverable for delay which caused only inconvenience and no actual loss,[9] as when proceeding purely for pleasure.

Carriage of passenger's luggage

At common law the liability in respect of loss of or injury to luggage is the same as that of the common carrier of goods,[10] and subject to the same exceptions except that the carriers' responsibility as insurer does not extend to loss of or injury to goods which the passenger has kept under his own immediate control and is caused by the passenger's own default or want of care.[11] It is now, apart from special contract, carried at carriers' risk conditions.[12] The Carriers Act applies.[13]

The question of what is or is not luggage has frequently been judicially considered, generally by excluding some articles from the general category.[14] It is a question of fact [15] in every case, but in general it extends to the class of articles ordinarily and usually carried by passengers as their luggage and what they usually take with them for their personal use and

[2] *Clark* v. *N.B. Ry.* (1886) 2 Sh.Ct.Rep. 92.

[3] *Hamlin, supra*; *Hobbs, supra.*

[4] *Hamlin* v. *G.N. Ry.* (1856) 1 H. & N. 408 (hiring cab).

[5] *Le Blanche* v. *L.N.W. Ry.* (1876) 1 C.P.D. 286.

[6] *Buckmaster* v. *G.E. Ry.* (1870) 23 L.T. 471.

[7] *G.N. Ry.* v. *Hawcroft* (1852) 21 L.J.Q.B. 178.

[8] *Fitzgerald* v. *Midland Ry.* (1876) 34 L.T. 771; see too *G.W. Ry.* v. *Lowenfeld* (1892) 8 T.L.R. 230.

[9] *Cf. Webster* v. *Cramond Iron Co.* (1875) 2 R. 752.

[10] *Macrow* v. *G.W. Ry.* (1871) L.R. 6 Q.B. 612; *Cohen* v. *S.E. Ry.* (1867) 2 Ex.D. 253; *Stuart-Brown* v. *Caledonian Ry.* (1922) 38 Sh.Ct.Rep. 60.

[11] *G.W. Ry.* v. *Bunch* (1888) 13 App.Cas. 31, 42, 48, overruling *Bergheim* v. *G.E. Ry.* (1878) 3 C.P.D. 221; *Talley* v. *G.W. Ry.* (1871) L.R. 6 C.P. 44.

[12] Railways Act 1921, s. 44 (1); *Page* v. *L.M.S. Ry.* (1943) 168 L.T. 168.

[13] *Macrow, supra*; *Dyke* v. *S.E. Ry.* (1900) 17 T.L.R. 651; *Carswell* v. *Cheshire Lines Committee*, 76 L.J.K.B. 734.

[14] *Cf. Britten* v. *G.N. Ry.* [1899] 1 Q.B. 243; *Jenkyns* v. *Southampton S.P. Co.* [1919] 2 K.B. 135.

[15] *Jenkyns* v. *Southampton Steam Packet Co.* [1919] 2 K.B. 135.

convenience, having regard to the requirements of the class to which they belong, the immediate necessities or the ultimate purpose of the journey.[16] Luggage does not include merchandise or articles for sale,[17] articles for business purposes such as legal documents [18]; artists' sketches [19]; a professional musician's instrument [20]; a typewriter carried for business [21]; a large rocking-horse [22]; an invalid chair [23]; an actor's stage clothing [24]; a commercial traveller's effects [25]; a bicycle [26]; furniture or household goods.[27] Nor probably does it cover personal articles in the possession of the passenger, when the obligation is to take reasonable care.[28] It does include an army officer's revolver, torch, and binoculars.[29]

The Railways Board is not liable for loss of or damage to goods such as merchandise taken as private luggage,[30] but if a passenger is permitted to take as luggage what is obviously not within that category, the Board is barred from denying that it is luggage and hence is liable for its loss or damage.[31]

Extent of liability

The responsibility of the Board for luggage in the van only arises where the goods are handed over to the company's servants for transit and lasts until they have been delivered up or a reasonable time has been allowed for their removal.[32] It does not arise when they are handed over for custody [33] as when the passenger intends to leave the station for a time,[34] though not if he merely go to the booking-office,[35] or refreshment-room,[36] or leave the station temporarily, but the articles are retained in transit [37] so long as the passenger is still prosecuting his journey.[38]

It must be shown that loss occurred while the luggage was in the custody

16 *Hudston* v. *Midland Ry.* (1869) L.R. 4 Q.B. 366; *Macrow* v. *G.W. Ry.* (1871) L.R. 6 Q.B. 612.
17 *G.N. Ry.* v. *Shepherd* (1852) 8 Ex. 30; *Belfast Ry.* v. *Keys* (1861) 9 H.L.C. 556; *Cahill* v. *L.N.W. Ry.* (1863) 13 C.B.(N.S.) 818; *Hudston, supra*; *Gormally Co.* v. *Midland Ry.* (1897) 14 T.L.R. 84.
18 *Phelps* v. *L.N.W. Ry.* (1865) 19 C.B.(N.S.) 321.
19 *Mytton* v. *Midland Ry.* (1859) 4 H. & N. 615.
20 *G.W. Ry.* v. *Evans* (1921) 38 T.L.R. 166.
21 *Hastie* v. *G.E. Ry.* (1911) 46 L.J. 507.
22 *Hudston* v. *Midland Ry.* (1869) L.R. 4 Q.B. 366.
23 *Casack* v. *L.N.W. Ry.* (1891) 7 T.L.R. 452.
24 *Gilbey* v. *G.N. Ry.* (1920) 36 T.L.R. 562.
25 *Gormally* v. *Midland Ry.* (1897) 14 T.L.R. 84.
26 *Britten* v. *G.N. Ry.* [1899] 1 Q.B. 243.
27 *Macrow* v. *G.W. Ry.* (1871) L.R. 6 Q.B. 612.
28 *Smitton* v. *Orient S.N. Co.* (1907) 96 L.T. 848.
29 *Jenkyns* v. *Southampton Steam Packet Co.* [1919] 2 K.B. 135.
30 *Belfast & Ballymena Ry.* v. *Keys* (1861) 9 H.L.Cas. 556; *Cahill, supra*; *G.N. Ry.* v. *Shepherd, supra.*
31 *Cahill, supra*; *G.N. Ry.* v. *Shepherd, supra*; *Wilkinson* v. *L. & Y. Ry.* [1907] 2 K.B. 222.
32 *Patscheider* v. *G.W. Ry.* (1878) 3 Ex.D. 153; *Fitzgerald* v. *N.B. Ry.* (1920) 36 Sh.Ct.Rep. 224.
33 *G.W. Ry.* v. *Bunch* (1888) 13 App.Cas. 31.
34 *Welch* v. *L.N.W. Ry.* (1884) 34 W.R. 166; *Mackenzie* v. *Caledonian Ry.* (1923) 39 Sh.Ct. Rep. 116.
35 *Lovell* v. *L.C. & D. Ry.* (1876) 45 L.J.Q.B. 476.
36 *Soanes* v. *L.S.W. Ry.* (1919) 35 T.L.R. 267.
37 *Steers* v. *Midland Ry.* (1920) 36 T.L.R. 703.
38 *Welch* v. *L.N.W. Ry.* (1884) 34 W.R. 166; *Hodkinson* v. *L.N.W. Ry.* (1884) 14 Q.B.D. 228.

of the railway servants [39] and liability ends when the articles have been delivered up or possibly until they are put in a taxi.[40] The Board is not liable if a railway servant is asked to look after the luggage after transit has ended,[41] or if delivery is requested, unless a charge is made for this service.[42] A passenger may be allowed long enough after arrival to telephone before taking delivery of his luggage,[43] but, in general, liability ends on arrival and redelivery of the luggage.[44]

It has been held that a company issuing a through ticket is under the same liability whether the loss occurs on its own line or that of another company [45] and the same is doubtless true of the regions of British Railways. The acceptance of luggage infers liability, even though not addressed [46] and though the passenger has not yet taken his ticket,[47] and there is no onus on the passenger to inquire after it when changing trains at a junction.[48]

Compartment luggage

The liability as a carrier extends to luggage taken by the passenger into the compartment with him, except that there is no liability for loss or injury by the passenger's own default,[49] *i.e.* if the passenger fails to exercise the care of a prudent man.[50] It matters not whether the luggage is placed there by the passenger,[51] or on his behalf,[52] or by a railway servant.[53] It is not negligence on the passenger's part to leave it in a sleeping compartment to go for a meal [54] or even in certain cases to leave it quite unsupervised.[55] The Board is, however, not responsible for articles in a passenger's pocket [56] nor for articles left by him in the train, unless they come into the hands of the railway servants,[57] nor if the passenger takes entire charge of the luggage himself,[58] in which cases the liability is

39 *Midland Ry.* v. *Bromley* (1856) 17 C.B. 372; *Campbell* v. *Caledonian Ry.* (1852) 14 D. 806.
40 *Richards* v. *L.B. & S.C. Ry.* (1849) 7 C.B. 839; *Butcher* v. *L.S.W. Ry.* (1855) 16 C.B. 13.
41 *Fearnley* v. *G.N. Ry.* (1852) 16 J.P. 822; *Hodkinson, supra.*
42 *Reith* v. *L.T. & S. Ry.* (1912) 47 L.J. 649.
43 *Parker* v. *L.M.S. Ry.*, 1930 S.C. 822.
44 *Hodkinson, supra.*
45 *Buxton* v. *N.E. Ry.* (1868) L.R. 3 Q.B. 549; *Thomas* v. *Rhymney Ry.* (1871) L.R. 6 Q.B. 266; *Kent* v. *Midland Ry.* (1874) L.R. 10 Q.B. 1; *Hooper* v. *L.N.W. Ry.* (1880) 50 L.J.Q.B. 103.
46 *Campbell* v. *Caledonian Ry.* (1852) 14 D. 806; *Butler* v. *Caledonian Ry.*, 2 Guthrie Sel.Sh. Ct.Cas. 65.
47 *Lovell* v. *L.C. & D. Ry.* (1876) 34 L.T. 127; *Leach* v. *S.E. Ry.* (1876) 34 L.T. 134; *G.W. Ry.* v. *Bunch* (1888) 13 App.Cas. 31.
48 *Campbell, supra.* As to handing over case to station hotel porter, see *Demetriadi* v. *L.N.E. Ry.* (1935) 51 Sh.Ct.Rep. 5.
49 *G.W. Ry.* v. *Bunch* (1888) 13 App.Cas. 31; *Jenkyns* v. *Southampton S.P. Co.* [1919] 2 K.B. 135; *Ehinger* v. *S.E. Ry.* (1922) 38 T.L.R. 678.
50 *Talley* v. *G.W. Ry.* (1870) L.R. 6 C.P. 44.
51 *G.N. Ry.* v. *Shepherd* (1852) 8 Ex. 30; *Stuart-Brown* v. *Caledonian Ry.* (1922) 38 Sh.Ct.Rep. 60.
52 *Jenkyns, supra*; *Ehinger, supra.*
53 *Steers* v. *Midland Ry.* (1920) 36 T.L.R. 703.
54 *Steers, supra.*
55 *Vosper* v. *G.W. Ry.* [1928] 1 K.B. 340; *Carr* v. *L.M.S. Ry.* [1931] N.I. 94.
56 *Smitton* v. *Orient S.N. Co.* (1907) 12 Com.Cas. 270.
57 *Glover* v. *L.S.W. Ry.* (1867) L.R. 3 Q.B. 25.
58 *Le Conteur* v. *L.S.W. Ry.* (1865) L.R. 1 Q.B. 54.

the same as that to the passenger, namely to exercise reasonable care.[59] The Carriers Act does not apply to compartment luggage.[60]

Luggage left in cloakrooms

Luggage deposited in a cloakroom or left luggage office is taken by the Board not as common carrier but only as custodier [61]: hence at common law, it is only liable for negligence, and may make any conditions it thinks fit so long as not extravagant or irrelevant.[62] Conditions exempting the Board from liability for articles over a certain value are usually inserted, but otherwise the Board will be liable for the value of the article.[63] The only question which may arise is whether the conditions have been adequately brought to the notice of the passengers.[64]

The Board is probably bound to keep the office open and redeliver the articles on request,[65] and will be liable for damage caused by unreasonable delay in redelivering articles,[66] or for damage thereto [67] unless excepted by terms in the contract.[68] There is a lien over the luggage for the charges,[69] and no obligation to deliver anywhere.[70] It is a question of the terms of the contract whether in accepting goods for safe custody the Board is bound to put them in the cloakroom.[71] Failure to put the goods in the cloakroom may or may not disentitle the Board from founding on a condition in the ticket limiting liability for loss, depending on the terms of the contract.[72]

On ordinary principles there will be no liability for remote or consequential damages.

Where railway servants allowed a person to abstract articles from a case in a left luggage office without producing the ticket in respect of the case or having other reasonable belief that the person was entitled to do so, they were held to have committed a fundamental breach of contract, so that the conditions on the ticket did not apply and the Board was fully liable for the value of the luggage lost.[73]

Where the carrier is also an innkeeper narrow questions may arise whether liability attaches *qua* carrier, *qua* depositary, or *qua* innkeeper.[74]

59 *Smitton, supra*; *Richards* v. *L.B.S.C. Ry.* (1849) 7 C.B. 839.
60 *Bergheim* v. *G.E. Ry.* (1878) 3 C.P.D. 221; *Naish* v. *G.S.W. Ry.*, 2 Guthrie Sel.Cas. 61.
61 *Parker* v. *S.E. Ry.* (1877) 2 C.P.D. 416.
62 *Gibaud* v. *G.E. Ry.* [1921] 2 K.B. 426.
63 *Anderson* v. *N.E. Ry.* (1861) 4 L.T. 216.
64 *Gibaud, supra*; *Harris* v. *G.W. Ry.* (1876) 1 Q.B.D. 515; *Henderson* v. *Stevenson* (1875) 2 R. (H.L.) 71; *Van Toll* v. *S.E. Ry.* (1862) 12 C.B.(N.S.) 75.
65 *Stallard* v. *G.W. Ry.* (1862) 2 B. & S. 419.
66 *Stallard, supra.*
67 *Pratt* v. *S.E. Ry.* (1876) 1 Q.B.D. 718.
68 *Pepper* v. *S.E. Ry.* (1868) 17 L.T. 469; *Skipwith* v. *G.W. Ry.* (1888) 59 L.T. 520.
69 *Singer Mfg. Co.* v. *L.S.W. Ry.* [1894] 1 Q.B. 833.
70 *Dimsdale* v. *L. & B. Ry.* (1862) 3 F. & F. 167.
71 *Handon* v. *Caledonian Ry.* (1880) 7 R. 966; *Harris, supra*; *Lyons* v. *Caledonian Ry.*, 1909 S.C. 1185; *Gibaud, supra.*
72 *Handon* v. *Caledonian Ry.* (1880) 7 R. 966. See also *Harris* v. *G.W. Ry.* (1876) 1 Q.B.D. 515; *Lyons* v. *Caledonian Ry.* 1909 S.C. 1185; *Gibaud* v. *G.E. Ry.* [1921] 2 K.B. 426. See also *Lilley* v. *Doubleday* (1881) 7 Q.B.D. 510.
73 *Alexander* v. *Railway Executive* [1951] 2 K.B. 882.
74 See *e.g.* *Demetriadi* v. *L.N.E. Ry.* (1934) 51 Sh.Ct.Rep. 5.

Statutory provisions applicable to luggage

The Carriers Act 1830 applies to the case of passengers' luggage so as to modify the liability of common carrier otherwise attaching, whether or not the company has agreed to carry it free of charge.[75] The Board may enter into special contracts.[76] Apart from that the liability in respect of the classes of goods enumerated in the Carriers Act 1830 is restricted to £25 unless the nature and value of the goods has been declared at the time of delivery to the railway company and an increased charge paid, if requested. A notice of these must be posted up.

Provision is made in the standard charges for the carriage of a quantity of luggage free of charge, and for payment for excess. Special provisions may be made for excursion trains.[77] A workman travelling on a workman's ticket may take with him free of charge tools up to 60 lb. weight, but there is no liability for loss or damage.[78]

Measure of damages

In the event of the loss of passengers' luggage in circumstances in which the Board is liable, the damages recoverable will be the value of the lost items, subject to the limitation of amount under the Carriers Act. No damages are recoverable beyond the actual value of goods deposited in a left-luggage room.[79]

Damages may be recovered for unreasonable delay in forwarding a passenger's luggage.[80]

Private carriers of passengers

A private carrier of passengers, such as a taxi-owner, may accept or reject any offer to hire him, and the terms and conditions of the carriage are determined by the contract, failing which by terms implied in the contractual relationship.

He is not automatically liable for delay, non-arrival, or injury to or death of a passenger, but liable only if fault be shown on his part. A private carrier is impliedly bound to have his vehicle in sound condition and good repair, to provide a crew who are reasonably skilled and competent, and through his servants to perform the hiring in a careful manner.[81] His liabilities, save so far as stated in the contract, are accordingly the same as those of a common carrier of passengers.[82]

75 *Caswell* v. *Cheshire Lines Committee* [1907] 2 K.B. 499; *Dyke* v. *S.E. & Chatham Ry. Managing Committee* (1901) 7 T.L.R. 561.

76 *Cohen* v. *S.E. Ry.* (1877) 2 Ex.D. 253.

77 *Rumsey* v. *N.E. Ry.* (1863) 14 C.B.(N.S.) 641.

78 S.R. & O. 1927 Nos. 848–851, Part VII; S.R. & O. 1929 Nos. 1228–1231.

79 *Anderson* v. *N.E. Ry.* (1861) 4 L.T. 216. *Cf. Alexander* v. *Railway Executive* [1951] 2 K.B. 882.

80 *Hooper* v. *L.N.W. Ry.* (1880) 50 L.J.C.P. 103.

81 *Cf. White* v. *Steadman* [1913] 3 K.B. 340.

82 For this reason many cases do not decide whether the carrier was a common carrier or a private carrier.

Carriage of Goods by Road

The carriage of goods for reward by road is effected by (a) the National Freight Corporation,[83] subsidiaries of which include British Road Services Ltd., B.R.S. (Contracts) Ltd., B.R.S. Parcels Ltd., Pickfords Ltd. and other transport groups.[84] It is not a common carrier in respect of any of its activities.[85] It may also be effected by (b) the Scottish Transport Group [86] and its subsidiaries, which include Scottish Bus Group Ltd., David MacBrayne Ltd., Caledonian Steam Packet Co. Ltd., which are not common carriers in respect of any of their activities concerned with the carriage of goods.[87]

It may also be effected by (c) persons or bodies carrying on the business of local carriers, who are common carriers, and (d) persons or bodies carrying on the business of haulage contractors, who are not common carriers. Lastly it may be effected by (e) persons or bodies engaged in manufacturing or distributing, conveying goods in their own vehicles; these are not common carriers.

Goods vehicles (including those operated by a local or public authority) require to be operated under an " operator's licence " under the Transport Act 1968, Part V (ss. 59–94), but this does not apply to small goods vehicles.[88] Large goods vehicles require in addition special authorisations.[89] Vehicles with an unladen weight not exceeding 30 cwt. do not require a carrier's licence.[90]

Claims arising

The kinds of claims which may arise will commonly be for total or partial non-delivery of goods consigned, for delayed delivery, or for delivery in a damaged condition.

Common carriers

Common law principles still apply to those carriers who are common carriers.

Private carriers

In the first place regard must be had to any relevant condition of the contract to ascertain if there is any exemption from or limitation of liability. If there has been a fundamental breach of the contract it may be that the exception or exemption clauses do not apply at all,[91] but if this is

[83] Transport Act 1968, s. 1.
[84] *Ibid.* Sched. 3.
[85] *Ibid.* s. 2 (2).
[86] *Ibid.* s. 24.
[87] *Ibid.* s. 26 (2).
[88] s. 60 (2) and (4).
[89] s. 71.
[90] s. 93.
[91] *Bontex Knitting Works Ltd.* v. *St. Johns Garage* [1943] 2 All E.R. 690; affd. [1944] 1 All E.R. 381; *Suisse Atlantique Société* v. *N.V. Rotterdamsche Kolen Centrale* [1967] 1 A.C. 361.

not contended or not upheld, the main question is whether they do apply to the circumstances which took place.[92] Fundamental breach may include sub-contracting the carriage without authority in circumstances where the consignor would not have agreed to sub-contracting.[93]

In some cases the cause of loss or damage may not be known or discoverable. In that case prima facie any relevant exception or limitation clause applies, and there is no onus on the carrier to prove that there had been no fundamental breach.[94]

If there is no relevant excepting or limiting clause the next question is as to the cause of the loss or damage, and whether that is a cause for which the carrier is liable. Negligence on the part of the carrier, or his servants, infers liability. It may consist in failure to take reasonable care to supply a roadworthy vehicle, or a competent or honest driver,[95] or the driver's leaving the vehicle unattended so that goods are stolen from it.[96]

Non-contractual duty

A carrier for reward owes a contractual duty to his employer but, where he knows that the goods he is carrying belong not to the employer but to another, also owes a duty to that other to take reasonable care while the goods are in his hands for carriage and, if he does not discharge that duty, is liable for the natural consequences, such as the theft of the goods.[97]

Measure of damages

If the goods are lost in circumstances in which the carrier is liable the prima facie measure of damages is the full value of the goods.[98] If they are delivered damaged the prima facie measure is the diminution in value attributable to the damage, a guide to which may be given by the cost of repairing and making good the damage or by the lesser price obtaining on sale of the damaged goods, and if delivered late the measure will be the loss naturally resulting from the delay, which may be, or include, loss of profits,[99] loss of a sub-contract, the incurring of liability in damages to third parties or otherwise.

International carriage by road

Contracts of carriage of goods by road in vehicles for reward, where the place of taking over the goods and the place designated for delivery are situated in two different countries, of which at least one is a contracting country under the Convention on the Contract for the International

[92] *John Carter Ltd.* v. *Hanson Haulage (Leeds) Ltd.* [1965] 2 Q.B. 495.
[93] *Garnham, Harris & Elton* v. *Ellis (Transport) Ltd.* [1967] 2 All E.R. 940.
[94] *Hunt & Winterbotham Ltd.* v. *B.R.S. (Parcels) Ltd.* [1962] 1 Q.B. 617.
[95] *John Carter Ltd., supra.*
[96] *Lee Cooper* v. *C. H. Jeakins & Sons* [1967] 2 Q.B. 1.
[97] *Lee Cooper Ltd.* v. *Jeakins* [1967] 2 Q.B. 1.
[98] *Rigby* v. *Reliance Insurance Co.* [1956] 2 Q.B. 468; *Garnham, Harris & Elton, supra*; *Lee Cooper Ltd.* v. *Jeakins, supra.*
[99] *Cf. Hadley* v. *Baxendale* (1854) 9 Ex. 341.

Carriage of Goods by Road of 1965, are regulated by the Carriage of Goods by Road Act 1965, the Convention, scheduled to that Act, having the force of law in the United Kingdom. It makes detailed provision for the carrier's liability and for claims and actions. Stipulations contrary to the Convention are null and void.

CARRIAGE OF PASSENGERS BY ROAD

The carriage of passengers by road is effected by (a) lessors of taxis or private cars for hire, who are not common carriers, (b) lessors of buses for carriage by contract, who are not common carriers, (c) operators of bus services who are common carriers of passengers; these may be either local authorities, or subsidiaries of the Scottish Transport Group [1]; and (d) bodies conveying their own staff in their own vehicles; these are not common carriers.

The Transport Act 1968, Part II (ss. 9–23), made provision for the establishment in areas of a Passenger Transport Authority (the policy-directing body) and a Passenger Transport Executive (the providing body) to provide public passenger transport services in their areas. The Executive for a given area is probably a common carrier of passengers. Local authority transport undertakings may be transferred to a Passenger Transport Executive.

Passengers and common carriers

The rights and liabilities of passengers *vis-à-vis* those carriers who are common carriers of passengers is determined by common law. The contract, which in most cases is made by implication from the fact of boarding the vehicle and paying the fare, is subject to such implied terms as that the vehicle is reasonably fit for the carriage of passengers, that the driver is reasonably competent, and that the driver and any other crew will exercise reasonable skill and care in operating the vehicle.

The liability which normally is in issue is liability for personal injuries caused by the defective state of the vehicle,[3] or its negligent handling by its driver. The measure of damages applicable in such a case is that applicable to a claim of damages for delict rather than for breach of contract.

Contractual conditions excluding liability void

"A contract for the conveyance of a passenger in a public service vehicle shall, so far as it purports to negative or to restrict the liability of a person in respect of a claim which may be made against him in respect of the death of, or bodily injury to, the passenger while being carried in, entering or alighting from the vehicle, or purports to impose any condition

[1] Established by Transport Act 1968, s. 24.

[3] *e.g. Wyngrove's Exrx.* v. *Scottish Omnibuses Ltd.*, 1966 S.C.(H.L.) 47.

with respect to the enforcement of such liability, be void." [4] This has been held applicable to a " free pass " issued by a local authority to an elderly person which bore to exclude liability.[5]

Claims by passengers, whether based on breach of contract or on delict, are commonly for personal injuries or death, in which case the factors relevant to the claim of damages are those applicable to a claim for personal injuries or death.[6]

Passengers and private carriers

The rights and liabilities of passengers *vis-à-vis* carriers who are not common carriers must be determined by the terms of the contract in the particular case. There are certainly implied terms of such a contract that the vehicle is reasonably fit for the conveyance of passengers, that the driver is reasonably competent and that he will drive with reasonable skill, care and regard for the safety of his passengers. There are probably no implied terms guaranteeing arrival at any particular destination on time.

CARRIAGE OF GOODS BY RAIL

Services for the carriage of goods by rail in the United Kingdom are provided by the British Railways Board.[7] The Board is not a common carrier.[8]

The Board has settled four sets of General Conditions of Carriage for (a) Merchandise (other than dangerous goods and merchandise for which conditions are specially provided) carried at Board's risk [9]; (b) livestock (other than wild animals); (c) coal, coke and patent fuel; and (d) carriage by water. Such General Conditions will normally be imported into the contract for the carriage of any particular consignment. They replace the Standard Terms and Conditions of Carriage of Merchandise settled under the Railways Act 1921.

Under the General Conditions of Carriage [10] the Board accepts liability for

> " any loss or misdelivery [11] of or damage to merchandise occasioned during transit as defined by these Conditions unless the Board shall prove that such loss, misdelivery or damage has arisen from:—

4 Road Traffic Act 1960, s. 151.

5 *Gore* v. *Van der Lann* [1967] 1 All E.R. 360; contrast *Wilkie* v. *L.P.T.B.* [1947] 1 All E.R. 258, where free pass issued to employee of Board and not under contract. The point was not raised in *Genys* v. *Matthews* [1965] 3 All E.R. 24, where it was held that, in any event, the exclusion conditions on a free pass could not protect a negligent bus driver from liability.

6 Chaps. 53–54, *infra*.

7 Transport Act 1962, s. 3.

8 *Ibid.* s. 43 (6).

9 Further conditions are added applicable to merchandise carried at (a) owner's risk or (b) as damageable goods not properly protected by packing.

10 cl. 8.

11 Held to mean delivery to the wrong consignee, and not merely delay or detention: *Hartstoke Fruiterers Ltd.* v. *L.M.S. Ry.* [1943] 1 All E.R. 470.

(*a*) act of God;

(*b*) any consequences of war, invasion, act of foreign enemy (whether war be declared or not) civil war, rebellion, insurrection, military or usurped power or confiscation, requisition, destruction of or damage to property by or under the order of any government or public or local authority;

(*c*) seizure under legal process;

(*d*) act or omission of the trader his servants or agents;

(*e*) inherent liability to wastage in bulk or weight, latent defect or inherent defect, vice or natural deterioration of the merchandise;

(*f*) casualty (including fire or explosion).

Provided that:

(i) where loss, misdelivery or damage arises and the Board have failed to prove that they used all reasonable foresight and care in the delivery of the merchandise the Board shall not be relieved from liability for such loss, misdelivery or damage;

(ii) the Board shall not incur liability of any kind in respect of merchandise where there has been fraud on the part of the Trader.

" The Board shall not in any case be liable for loss,[12] damage or delay, proved by the Board to have been caused by or to have arisen from:—

(*a*) insufficient or improper packing; or

(*b*) riots, civil commotions, strikes, lockouts, stoppage or restraint of labour from whatever cause, whether partial or general; or

(*c*) consignee not taking or accepting delivery within a reasonable time.[13]

" The Board shall, subject to these conditions, be liable for loss proved by the trader to have been caused by delay to, or detention of, or unreasonable deviation in the carriage of merchandise unless the Board prove that such delay or detention or unreasonable deviation has arisen without negligence on the part of the Board, their servants or agents.[14]

" Subject to these Conditions the liability of the Board under the preceding Conditions in respect of any one consignment shall in any case be limited:—

(i) where the monetary loss however sustained is in respect of the whole of the consignment to a sum at the rate of £800 per ton on the gross weight of the consignment;

(ii) where the monetary loss, however sustained, is in respect

[12] Held to mean physical loss and not pecuniary loss: *Young* v. *B.T.C.* [1953] 2 All E.R. 98.
[13] General Conditions, cl. 9.
[14] General Conditions, cl. 10.

of part of a consignment to the proportion of the sum ascertained in accordance with (i) of this Condition which the actual value of that part of the consignment bears to the actual value of the whole of the consignment.

Provided that:—

(*a*) nothing in this Condition shall limit the Board's liability below the sum of £10 in respect of any one consignment; and

(*b*) the Board shall be entitled to require proof of the value of the whole of the consignment.[15]

" The Board shall not in any case be liable for indirect or consequential damages or for loss of a particular market whether held daily or at intervals." [16]

A time limit is provided for claims,[17] a power to sell undelivered or unclaimed merchandise,[18] and a general lien is claimed over merchandise delivered for moneys due for carriage and other proper charges, and for moneys due for any services rendered or accommodation provided in relation to the carriage or custody of merchandise with a power of sale to give effect thereto.[19]

Further special conditions apply to merchandise carried at (a) owner's risk, or (b) as damageable goods not properly protected by packing.

Carriage of Passengers by Rail

Services for the carriage of passengers by rail are provided by the British Railways Board.[20] The Board is probably a common carrier of passengers.[21] The contract of carriage is made when a booking clerk issues a ticket in return for a fare. The contract includes, imported by notice and by reference on tickets, conditions set out in the Board's General Regulations.

No exclusion or limitation of liability

" The Board shall not carry passengers by rail on terms or conditions which:—

(*a*) purport, whether directly or indirectly, to exclude or limit their liability in respect of the death of, or bodily injury to, any passenger other than a passenger travelling on a free pass, or

(*b*) purport, whether directly or indirectly, to prescribe the time within which or the manner in which any such liability may be enforced,

and any such terms or conditions shall be void and of no effect." [22]

15 General Conditions, cl. 13.
16 cl. 14.
17 cl. 15.
18 cl. 17.
19 cl. 18.
20 Transport Act 1962, s. 3.
21 It is uncertain whether the Transport Act, s. 43 (6), providing that the Board is not a common carrier by rail, is general or applicable to goods only. As it makes no difference to liability for injury to passengers by rail, it would be strange if the Board were other than a common carrier of passengers.
22 Transport Act 1962, s. 43 (7).

There are also implied terms of the contract of carriage that the Railways Board will take reasonable care for the safety of passengers in respect of the provision of safe rolling-stock, of competent staff, and of the maintenance of a safe system of operation of trains.[23] In many cases of accidents the principle of *res ipsa loquitur* applies.

The liability of British Railways for death of or injury to passengers and damage to or loss of articles which they have with them, by an accident occurring on the territory of a state which is a party to the Additional Convention to the International Convention concerning the Carriage of Passengers and Luggage by Rail, is determined by the Additional Convention scheduled to the Carriage by Railway Act 1972, which has thereby the force of law in the United Kingdom and has effect notwithstanding the Transport Act 1962, s. 43 (7).

So far as breach of duty causes personal injuries or death, the factors relevant to damages are the same as those relevant to other cases of such losses, however caused.[24]

Carriage of Goods by Sea

The contract of carriage of goods by sea is normally evidenced by a charter-party of a ship, or by a bill of lading of goods shipped in a general ship. Problems and disputes arising out of such contracts fall within the Admiralty jurisdiction of the courts and are considered in the context of Admiralty remedies.[25]

Carriage of Passengers by Sea

The contract of carriage of passengers by sea is governed by principles of Admiralty law which do not differ materially from the principles of common law applicable to non-maritime carriage of passengers, but which also fall within the Admiralty jurisdiction of the courts and are considered in the context of Admiralty remedies.[26]

Carriage of Goods by Air

There is no legal reason why a carrier by air should not be a common carrier of goods or passengers or both, but in practice all air carriers probably are private carriers. Nothing in the Carriage by Air Act 1961 or the Warsaw Convention scheduled thereto makes the carrier by air a common carrier.[27] A carrier by air operating in the U.K. must have an air transport licence[28] and an air operator's certificate.[29]

[23] See *e.g. Skinner* v. *L.B. & S.C. Ry.* (1850) 5 Ex. 787; *Burns* v. *N.B. Ry.*, 1914 S.C. 754; *Inglis* v. *L.M.S. Ry.*, 1941 S.C. 551; *Easson* v. *L.N.E. Ry.* [1944] 2 All E.R. 425; *O'Connor* v. *B.T.C.* [1958] 1 All E.R. 558.
[24] See Chaps. 53–54, *infra*.
[25] Chap. 63, *infra*.
[26] Chap. 63, *infra*.
[27] Carriage by Air Act 1961, Sched. I, Art. 33.
[28] Civil Aviation Act 1971, s. 21.
[29] Civil Aviation Act 1949, s. 8; Air Navigation Order 1966.

In practice most carriers by air use forms of waybills and tickets settled by the International Air Transport Association.

Carriage, both of goods and of passengers, is either international carriage or non-international carriage, both of which are regulated by international conventions, unmodified or modified, or carriage performed gratuitously by other than an air transport undertaking which is governed by common law principles.

International carriage

By the Carriage by Air Act 1961, s. 1 (1), the international convention known as the Warsaw Convention as amended at The Hague 1955, set out in the First Schedule thereto, has the force of law in the U.K. in relation to any carriage by air to which the convention applies, irrespective of the nationality of the aircraft performing that carriage. The French text is authoritative, and the courts should construe domestic legislation consistently with it as international law binding on all countries which ratified it.[30]

The convention applies to all international carriage[31] of persons, baggage or cargo performed by aircraft for reward, and to gratuitous carriage by aircraft performed by an air transport undertaking.[32]

A further convention applies to international carriage performed by a person other than the contracting carrier known as the actual carrier. Both contracting carrier and actual carrier are subject to the Warsaw Convention, the former for the whole carriage contemplated and the latter for the carriage which he performs.[33]

The carrier may require the consignor to make out an " air waybill," and every consignor may require the carrier to accept this document. The absence, irregularity or loss of this document does not affect the existence or validity of the contract of carriage, which shall, subject to Article 9, be nonetheless governed by the Convention.[34] The requisites of the air waybill are laid down.[35] If, with the consent of the carrier, cargo is loaded without an air waybill, or if it does not contain a notice required by Article 8, the carrier is not entitled to avail himself of the provisions of Article 22 (2).[36]

The consignor is responsible for the correction of the particulars and statements relating to the cargo which he inserts in the air waybill, and he must indemnify the carrier against all damage suffered by him, or by any

30 *Corocraft Ltd.* v. *Pan American Airways* [1969] 1 All E.R. 82.

31 Defined Sched., Art. 1 (2); see also *Grein* v. *Imperial Airways Ltd.* [1937] 1 K.B. 50; *Phillipson* v. *Imperial Airways Ltd.* [1939] A.C. 332.

32 Art. 1 (1).

33 Carriage by Air (Supplementary Provisions) Act 1962.

34 Sched., Art. 5.

35 Arts. 6–8. On this, see *Montagu* v. *Swiss Air Transport Ltd.* [1966] 1 All E.R. 814; *Corocraft Ltd.* v. *Pan American Airways* [1969] 1 All E.R. 82, decided on the different wording of the earlier Warsaw convention.

36 Art. 9. By Art. 34 the provisions of Arts. 3–9 do not apply in the case of carriage performed in extraordinary circumstances outside the normal scope of an air carrier's business.

other person to whom the carrier is liable, by reason of the irregularity, incorrectness or incompleteness of the particulars and statements furnished by the consignor.[37]

The air waybill is prima facie evidence of the conclusion of the contract, the receipt of the cargo and the conditions of carriage. The statements in the air waybill relating to the weight, dimensions and packing of the cargo, as well as those relating to the number of packages, are prima facie evidence of the facts stated; those relating to the quantity, volume and condition of the cargo do not constitute evidence against the carrier except so far as they both have been, and are stated in the waybill to have been, checked by him in the presence of the consignor, or relate to the apparent condition of the cargo.[38]

The further rights and liabilities of consignor and carrier are set out in Articles 12–16.[39]

The carrier is liable for damage [40] sustained in the event of the destruction or loss of, or of damage to, any registered baggage or any cargo, if the occurrence which caused the damage so sustained took place during the carriage by air, which comprises the period during which the baggage or cargo is in charge of the carrier, whether in an aerodrome or on board an aircraft, or, in the case of a landing outside an aerodrome, in any place whatsoever, but does not extend to any carriage by land, sea or river performed outside an aerodrome, but if such a carriage takes place in the performance of a contract for carriage by air, for the purpose of loading, delivery or transhipment, any damage is presumed, subject to proof to the contrary, to have been the result of an event which took place during the carriage by air.[41]

The carrier is liable for damage occasioned by delay in the carriage by air of passengers, baggage or cargo.[42]

Any action for damages, however founded, in cases covered by Articles 18 and 19, can only be brought subject to the conditions and limits set out in the Convention.[43]

The carrier is not liable if he proves that he and his servants or agents have taken all necessary measures to avoid the damage or that it was impossible for him or them to take such measures.[44]

If the carrier proves that the damage was caused by or contributed to by the negligence of the injured person the court may, in accordance with the provisions of its own law, exonerate the carrier wholly or partly from his liability.[45]

[37] Art. 10.
[38] Art. 11.
[39] Art. 12 makes provision for the right of stoppage *in transitu*.
[40] Financial damage, not physical damage.
[41] Art. 18. *Cf. Westminster Bank* v. *Imperial Airways Ltd.* [1936] 2 All E.R. 890, where goods were stolen from store before flight commenced.
[42] Art. 19.
[43] Art. 24 (1).
[44] Art. 20.
[45] Art. 21. On this, see also 1961 Act, s. 6.

In the carriage of registered baggage and of cargo, the liability of the carrier is limited to a sum of two hundred and fifty francs [46] per kilogramme, unless the passenger or consignor has made, at the time when the package was handed over to the carrier, a special declaration of interest in delivery at destination and had paid a supplementary sum if the case so requires. In that case the carrier will be liable to pay a sum not exceeding the declared sum, unless he proves that the sum is greater than the passenger's or consignor's actual interest in delivery at destination.[47]

In the case of loss, damage or delay of part of registered baggage or cargo, or of any object contained therein, the weight to be taken into consideration in determining the amount to which the carrier's liability is limited shall be only the total weight of the package or packages concerned. Nevertheless, when the loss, damage or delay of a part of the registered baggage or cargo, or of an object contained therein, affects the value of other packages covered by the same baggage check or the same air waybill, the total weight of such package or packages shall also be taken into consideration in determining the limit of liability.[48]

As regards objects of which the passenger takes charge himself the liability of the carrier is limited to 5,000 francs per passenger.[49]

The limits prescribed in Article 22 do not prevent the court from awarding, in accordance with its own law, in addition, the whole or part of the court costs and of the other expenses of the litigation incurred by the plaintiff. This provision does not apply if the amount of damages awarded, excluding court costs and other expenses of the litigation, does not exceed the sum which the carrier has offered in writing to the plaintiff within six months from the occurrence causing the damages, or before the commencement of the action, if that is later.[50]

Any provision tending to relieve the carrier of liability or to fix a lower limit than that which is laid down in the Convention is null and void, but the nullity does not involve the nullity of the whole contract, which remains subject to the Convention. This does not apply to provisions governing loss or damage resulting from the inherent defect, quality or vice of the cargo carried.[51]

The limits of liability specified in Article 22 do not apply if it is proved that the damage resulted from an act or omission of the carrier, his servants or agents, done with intent to cause damage or recklessly and with knowledge that damage would probably result; provided that, in the case of such act or omission of a servant or agent, it is also proved that he was acting within the scope of his employment.[52]

[46] Conversion rate defined in Art. 22 (5). Now £7·78 per kilo: Carriage by Air (Sterling Equivalents) Order 1973 (S.I. 1973, No. 1189).

[47] Art. 22 (2) (*a*). *Cf. Montagu* v. *Swiss Air Transport* [1966] 1 All E.R. 814. On whether a deviation deprives the carrier of the benefit of the convention see *Rotterdamsche Bank* v. *B.O.A.C.* [1953] 1 All E.R. 675.

[48] Art. 22 (2) (*b*).

[49] Art. 22 (3). Now £155·47 per kilo: Carriage by Air (Sterling Equivalents) Order, *supra*.

[50] Art. 22 (4). On the application of Art. 22, see the 1961 Act, s. 4.

[51] Art. 23.

[52] Art. 25. *Cf.* " wilful misconduct " in *Horabin* v. *B.O.A.C.* [1952] 2 All E.R. 1016.

If an action is brought against a servant or agent of the carrier arising out of damage to which the Convention relates, such servant or agent, if he proves that he acted within the scope of his employment, is entitled to avail himself of the limits of liability which the carrier himself is entitled to invoke under Article 22. The aggregate of the amounts recoverable from the carrier, his servants and agents, in that case, may not exceed those limits. These provisions do not apply if it is proved that the damage resulted from an act or omission of the servant done with intent to cause damage or recklessly and with knowledge that damage would probably result.[53]

Receipt by the person entitled to delivery of baggage or cargo without complaint is prima facie evidence that it has been delivered in good condition and in accordance with the document of carriage. In the case of damage, the person entitled to delivery must complain to the carrier forthwith after the discovery of the damage, and, at latest, within seven days from the date of receipt in the case of baggage and fourteen days in the case of cargo. In case of delay the complaint must be made at latest within twenty-one days from the date when the baggage or cargo was placed at the carrier's disposal. Every complaint must be made in writing on the document of carriage or by separate notice in writing dispatched within the times stated. Failing complaint in time, no action lies against the carrier, save in the case of fraud on his part.[54]

The right to damages is extinguished if action is not brought within two years from the date of arrival at the destination, or from the date when the aircraft ought to have arrived or from the date when the carriage stopped. The method of calculating the period of limitation is determined by the law of the court seised of the case.[55]

Any clause contained in the contract and all special agreements entered into before the damage occurred by which the parties purport to infringe the rules laid down by the Convention, whether by deciding the law to be applied, or by altering the rules of jurisdiction, are null and void, save that arbitration clauses are permitted.[56]

Non-international carriage

The provisions of the amended Convention have been applied with modifications to non-international carriage.[57]

Carriage of Passengers by Air

At common law a carrier of passengers by air, whether a common carrier or a private carrier, is bound to carry with due care, and he is liable only

[53] Art. 25A. *Cf. Adler* v. *Dickson* [1955] 1 Q.B. 158; *Midland Silicones* v. *Scruttons* [1961] 1 Q B. 106.
[54] Art. 26.
[55] Art. 29. On this, see also 1961 Act, s. 5.
[56] Art. 32.
[57] Carriage by Air Acts (Application of Provisions) Order 1967 (S.I. 1967 No. 480).

for loss caused by wilful default or recklessness or negligence.[58] This obligation has commonly been qualified by conditions contained in the contract of carriage [59] and by conditions contained in international conventions which are part of British law. In view of the grave danger to life attaching to carriage by air wilful misconduct or recklessness or negligence may include even comparatively minor breaches of safety regulations or minor lapses from accepted standards of care.[60] A crash while in the course of taking off is *res ipsa loquitur* and evidences negligence.[61]

International carriage

The Warsaw Convention, as amended at The Hague, *i.e.* First Schedule to the Carriage by Air Act 1961, applies to carriage of passengers also.

In respect of the carriage of passengers a ticket must be delivered containing (a) an indication of the places of departure and destination; (b) if there is a stopping place in the territory of a party to the Convention, other than the territory containing the places of departure and destination; (c) a notice to the effect that if the passenger's journey involves an ultimate destination or stop in a country other than the country of departure, the Convention may be applicable and that it governs and in most cases limits the liability of carriers for death or personal injury and in respect of loss of or damage to baggage. The passenger ticket is prima facie evidence of the conclusion and conditions of the contract of carriage. The absence, irregularity or loss of the passenger ticket does not affect the existence or the validity of the contract of carriage which is, nonetheless, subject to the Convention. Nevertheless, if with the consent of the carrier, the passenger embarks without a passenger ticket having been delivered, or if the ticket does not include the notice required by (c), the carrier is not entitled to avail himself of the provisions of Article 22.[62]

In respect of registered baggage, a baggage check must be delivered, containing specified particulars and having a legal effect similar to that of the passenger ticket.[63] In respect of carriers' liability for baggage, baggage is treated in the same way as cargo.[64]

The carrier is liable for damage [65] sustained in the event of the death or wounding of a passenger or any other bodily injury suffered by a passenger if the accident which caused the damage so sustained took place on board the aircraft or in the course of any of the operations of

58 *Ludditt* v. *Ginger Coote Airways* [1947] 1 All E.R. 328.

59 *Grein* v. *Imperial Airways Ltd.* [1936] 2 All ER. 1258; *McKay* v. *Scottish Airways*, 1948 S.C. 254.

60 *Horabin* v. *B.O.A.C.* [1952] 2 All E.R. 1016.

61 *Fosbroke-Hobbes* v. *Airwork Ltd.* [1937] 1 All E.R. 108.

62 Art. 3; see also *Westminster Bank* v. *Imperial Airways Ltd.* [1936] 2 All E.R. 890; *Phillipson, supra*; *Preston* v. *Hunting Air Transport Ltd.* [1956] 1 Q.B. 454.

63 Art. 4.

64 Arts. 18–30.

65 This includes compensation for more intangible damage than mere financial loss: *Preston* v. *Hunting Air Transport Ltd.* [1956] 1 Q.B. 454.

embarking or disembarking.[66] He is liable for damage occasioned by delay in the carriage by air of passengers,[67] but not if he proves that he and his servants or agents have taken all necessary measures to avoid the damage or that it was impossible for him or them to take such measures.[68] If the carrier proves that the damage was caused by or contributed to by the negligence of the injured person the court may, in accordance with its own law, exonerate the carrier wholly or partly from his liability.[69]

In the carriage of persons the liability of the carrier for each passenger is limited to 250,000 francs.[70] Where, in accordance with the law of the court seised of the case, damages may be awarded in the form of periodical payments the equivalent capital value of the payments may not exceed that sum. By special contract the carrier and the passenger may agree to a higher limit of liability.[71]

Any provision tending to relieve the carrier of liability or to fix a lower limit than that laid down in the Convention is null and void, but the nullity of the provision does not involve the nullity of the whole contract, which remains subject to the Convention.[72] The exclusion of limitations on liability (Art. 25) and the protection for servants and agents sued (Art. 25A) apply also to claims by passengers, as do the provisions as to jurisdiction (Art. 28), limitation of time for action (Art. 29) [73] and the avoidance of agreements infringing the Convention (Art. 32).[74]

Application to non-international carriage

By the 1961 Act, s. 10, the Convention contained in the First Schedule may be applied by Order in Council to carriage by air, not being carriage by air to which the Convention applies and this has been applied, with modifications.[75] The Carriage by Air (Supplementary Provisions) Act 1962 applies with modifications to non-international carriage.

Special charters

A plane can doubtless be hired on special charter, in which case the liability of its owner to passengers is determined by any terms of, or validly imported into, the charter [76] and by the general principle of taking reasonable care for the safe carriage of the passengers.[77]

[66] Art. 17. In cases governed by Art. 17, by Art. 24 (2) any action for damages, however founded, can only be brought subject to the conditions and limits set out in the Convention, without prejudice to the questions as to who are the persons who have the right to bring suit and what are their respective rights. On the application of Art. 17 in Scotland, see also 1961 Act, s. 3, as substituted by s. 11 (*b*).

[67] Art. 19.

[68] Art. 20.

[69] Art. 21. On this, see also 1961 Act, s. 6.

[70] Conversion rate defined in Art. 22 (5). Now £7773·43: Carriage by Air (Sterling Equivalents) Order 1973 (S.I. 1973 No. 1189).

[71] Art. 22 (1). On the application of Art. 22, see the 1961 Act, s. 4.

[72] Art. 23.

[73] On this, see also 1961 Act, s. 5.

[74] On these Articles, see under Carriage of Goods by Air.

[75] Carriage by Air Acts (Application of Provisions) Order 1967 (S.I. 1967 No. 480).

[76] See *e.g. Fosbroke-Hobbes* v. *Airwork Ltd.* [1937] 1 All E.R. 108.

[77] *Ludditt* v. *Ginger Coote Airways* [1947] 1 All E.R. 328.

CHAPTER 46

CONTRACTS OF FEU OR SALE OF LAND

THE contract to grant a piece of land to be held on feudal tenure may give rise to claims of various kinds.

SUPERIOR'S CLAIMS

Vassal's failure to take feu

If a person, having undertaken to accept a feu, refuses or fails without adequate justification to proceed and accept the feu, he will be liable in damages,[1] which must be measured by the loss naturally resulting from his breach of contract, including the loss of feuduty until another accepts the feu, the difference between the feuduty agreed and that at which another later takes the feu, grossed up at a number of years' purchase, and expenses fruitlessly incurred.

Non-payment of feuduty

In the event of non-payment of feuduty the superior has various remedies, proceedings for sequestration of the vassal's *invecta et illata*, to make effective the superior's hypothec for satisfaction of the last or current feuduty,[2] poinding of the ground,[3] adjudication,[4] personal action for payment,[5] and action to enforce the legal irritancy *ob non solutum canonem*, or any conventional irritancy for non-payment of feuduty inserted in the feu-charter.[6] But a vassal is entitled to withhold payment of feu-duties as long as an obligation by the superior, such as to form streets and sewers, is unfulfilled.[7]

Conditions relating to use of feu

Conditions commonly attach to a grant of a feu, requiring certain things to be done, such as buildings erected, and prohibiting other things, such as the use of the feu for certain purposes. The former may be enforced by actions for specific implement, the latter by petitions for interdict. In either case damages may be claimed alternatively, and sometimes

1 *Cf. Colquhoun* v. *Wilson's Trs.* (1860) 22 D. 1035.
2 Bell, *Prin.* § 698; Chap. 19, *supra.*
3 *Ibid.* § 699; Chap. 20, *supra.*
4 *Ibid.* § 699A; Chap. 13, *supra.*
5 *Ibid.* § 700; Chap. 15, *supra.* Unless stipulated for, interest is not due on unpaid feu-duties.
6 *Ibid.* § 701; Chap. 6, *supra.*
7 *Arnott's Trs.* v. *Forbes* (1881) 9 R. 89; contrast *Thom* v. *Chalmers* (1886) 13 R. 1026.

damages only have been given.[8] In one case [9] it was a condition that the vassal complete certain buildings; on his failure to do so the superior resumed possession of the subjects and finished the work; it was held that in the circumstances he was justified and the vassal's action of damages was rejected.

Problems have several times arisen as to the liability of the representatives or successors of the original vassal for failure to implement obligations imposed on them by the feu-contract. It depends on the terms of the contract,[10] and an obligation may be binding on both old and new vassals.[11]

In *Macrae* [11a] the damages claimed represented the capitalised value of the required annual value of the houses to be built, at twenty years' purchase, less the present value of the feu and existing buildings. In the circumstances the question of quantum was not discussed as the defender was held to be under no liability under the feu-contract. In *Rankine* v. *Logie Den Land Co.*[12] a condition (declared a real burden) bound the vassal, his heirs and assignees, to erect certain buildings of the value of £300 at least and of £1,000 and £4,000 on two other plots. The buildings not having been erected, the pursuer sought decree *ad factum praestandum* or for damages of £7,500; a proof was allowed on the question of damages. Furthermore, decree for damages against the executrix of a prior vassal was not prevented by the pursuer also obtaining decree *ad factum praestandum* against the vassal in possession.

A tenant of a vassal has no title to sue the superior for declarator of entitlement to act in contravention of the feu-contract.[13] nor doubtless can a tenant sue the superior for any contravention by him of the feu-contract. If a tenant wishes to challenge the superior with regard to any condition of the feu, he must require the vassal to lend his name and bring the necessary action; if the vassal has granted or agreed to grant the tenant the right to do what he wants to do, and refuses or fails to assist the tenant to obtain the right to do so from the superior, he will be liable in damages to the tenant.[14]

Vassal's Claims

Failure to grant feu

If a superior has undertaken to grant a feu and refuses or fails without adequate justification to do so in the terms agreed upon the primary

8 *Macnair* v. *Cathcart*, May 18, 1802, F.C.; *Sanderson* v. *Geddes* (1874) 1 R. 1198; *Jack* v. *Begg* (1895) 3 R. 35; *Grahame* v. *Kirkcaldy Mags.* (1882) 9 R.(H.L.) 91; *Wilson* v. *Pottinger*, 1908 S.C. 580.

9 *Borland & Co.'s Tr.* v. *Paterson* (1881) 19 S.L.R. 261.

10 Compare *Marshall's Tr.* v. *Macneill* (1888) 15 R. 762 with *Macrae* v. *Mackenzie's Tr.* (1891) 19 R. 138.

11 *Marshall* v. *Callander Hydropathic Co.* (1896) 23 R.(H.L.) 55; *Rankine* v. *Logie Den Land Co.* (1902) 4 F. 1074.

11a (1891) 19 R. 138.

12 (1902) 4 F. 1074.

13 *Eagle Lodge Ltd.* v. *Keir and Cawder Estates Ltd.*, 1964 S.C. 30.

14 *Eagle Lodge Ltd.*, *supra*, 47, *per* Lord Guthrie.

remedy is a claim for specific implement,[15] but there should be an alternative conclusion for damages, which would fall to be measured by the loss sustained by not obtaining the feu as contracted for. This could include any extra cost of obtaining a feu of alternative land, expenses incurred and compensation for failing to get the land contracted for and having to accept a less suitable alternative. Similarly, if the feu being granted is not in accordance with what the superior had undertaken to grant, then, assuming the contract to grant was sufficiently specific to be enforceable,[16] an action for implement or for damages would lie.

Superior's failure to implement obligations of feu-contract

The superior may be under obligations as, for example, in relation to streets and gardens. In *Moore* v. *Paterson*[17] he was bound to form a street and continue it through the ground of a third party. He assigned the obligation to one of the feuars, reserving his own right to enforce the obligation. Another feuar sought implement or damages. The action was dismissed for want of title but opinions were expressed that damages would have been appropriate. Lord Shand, obiter,[18] considered how damages might be assessed in different cases to give effect to the principle of compensating feuars for what they had lost by non-performance.

If a superior has bound himself in a feu-charter to insert conditions similar to those inserted therein in all subsequent charters granted of land within a particular area, and fails to do so, not only is the first feuar released from the restrictive obligations,[19] but the superior may be liable in damages to the first feuar for breach of contract,[20] or liable to relieve him of expenses incurred in consequence of the superior's failure.[21] The appropriate measure of damages would appear to be the loss or expense incurred in consequence of the failure, such as the part of the cost of forming a road irrecoverable from the other feuars.[20]

Damage resulting from mining

If a superior has reserved mineral rights under lands feued he is bound, unless he has clearly excluded any liability to do so,[22] to compensate for damage to the surface consequent on mining operations.[23]

SALE OF LAND

The obligations of the parties to a contract of sale of land are determined by the terms of their contract (the missives) and those terms im-

15 *e.g. Mitchell* v. *Stornoway Trs.*, 1936 S.C.(H.L.) 56.
16 *Cf. Lord Clinton* v. *Brown* (1874) 1 R. 1137.
17 (1881) 9 R. 337.
18 At p. 351.
19 *Dixon's Trs.* v. *Allan's Trs.* (1870) 8 M.(H.L.) 182; *Stevenson* v. *Steel Co. of Scotland* (1899) 1 F.(H.L.) 91.
20 *Leith School Board* v. *Rattray's Trs.*, 1918 S.C. 94.
21 *McKenzie* v. *Morrison's Trs.* (1830) 9 S. 44.
22 *Andrew* v. *Buchanan & Henderson* (1873) 11 M.(H.L.) 13.
23 *Buchanan* v. *Andrew* (1873) 11 M.(H.L.) 13; *Livingstone* v. *Rawyards Coal Co.* (1880) 7 R.(H.L.) 1.

plied therein by law or custom. The claims which are competent may be classified into seller's claims for non-implement by the buyer; buyers' claims for non-implement by the seller, or delay in implement, or defective implement.

SELLER'S CLAIMS

The purchaser's obligations are primarily to pay the purchase price, possibly with interest, and, probably, secondly to become infeft by recording his title in the Register of Sasines so as completely to divest the seller and free him of liability for the feu-duty,[24] though there is no express authority to this effect.[25]

The precise nature of the seller's claim against the purchaser for breach of his obligations depends partly on the precise terms of the contract and partly on what steps the seller has taken in the circumstances. It may be (i) an action for the price with interest,[25a] or (ii) a claim on the purchaser's default to treat the contract as repudiated, resell the property and claim damages, or claim forfeiture of any deposit or payment of any liquidate damages or penalty provided for by the contract.[26]

Action for the price

Where the seller sues for the price he must still be able and willing to convey and give a good title to the subjects sold,[27] and in all respects perform the obligations incumbent on him. The price falls to be paid on the day fixed in the contract for payment, failing which, at the date of entry, or if that be past, on the day of settlement, in exchange for the disposition. The action for the price is suitable particularly where the buyer is delaying to complete the transaction but it is not evident whether he is wholly unable or unwilling to complete and has not clearly evinced the intention no longer to be bound by the contract.

Interest on the price

The only form of damages generally competent for delay or failure to pay the price is an award of interest thereon. The purchase price carries interest *ex lege* from the due date of settlement until it is paid [28] if the purchaser is in possession and is drawing the rents, even though the delay be due to the fault of the seller.[29] It is subject to deductions for income tax.[30]

24 Conveyancing Act 1874, s. 4.
25 But *cf. McDonald* v. *City of Glasgow Bank* (1879) 6 R. 621; *Stevenson* v. *Wilson*, 1907 S.C. 445. It is the seller who intimates the change of ownership to the superior's agents.
25a *Infra.*
26 *Commercial Bank of Scotland* v. *Beal* (1890) 18 R. 80.
27 *Robertson* v. *Rutherford* (1840) 2 D. 1494; *cf. McConnell* v. *Chassels* (1903) 10 S.L.T. 790; *Bremner* v. *Dick*, 1911 S.C. 887.
28 *Stewart* v. *Earl of Cassilis*, Dec. 21, 1811, F.C.
29 *Grandison's Trs.* v. *Jardine* (1895) 22 R. 925.
30 *Bebb* v. *Bunny* (1854) 1 Kay & J. 216.

The customary rate of interest is the full legal rate but less may be taken. In the *Greenock Harbour* case [31] it was held that, when an action had been necessary to determine a difficult question whether or not the record were clear, the buyer was not bound to pay the price until the judgment of the court had become final, or at least not unless the seller found caution against the risk of that judgment being reversed in the House of Lords, even though no appeal had then been taken.

Consignation

Liability for interest continuing on an unpaid price may be avoided by consigning the price in bank so as to put it beyond the sole control of the purchaser or his agents,[32] usually by consignation on deposit receipt in the joint names of the agents for the buyer and seller. When consignation is effected at a date intermediate between entry and settlement the price carries legal interest till consignation and deposit-receipt interest thereafter until it is uplifted at settlement.[33] The effect of partial consignation is undecided: in one case interest on the consigned part of the price was restricted to 2 per cent.[34] On settlement the seller takes the deposit-receipt interest on the price. There seems to be no reported case where undue delay on either part has entitled a seller to recover full interest notwithstanding consignation.[33]

Rescission for purchaser's delay to settle

In a contract for the sale of heritage, payment of the price on the day stipulated therefor is not in general an essential condition of the contract and failure to pay on that date will not in general entitle the seller to rescind. Payment on a particular date may, however, be made an essential condition of the contract. If there is unnecessary or unjustifiable delay on the part of the purchaser in paying the price, the seller may limit the time within which payment must be made, and provided the time limit is a reasonable one in the circumstances, failure to pay within that time will be treated as breach of an essential condition entitling the seller to rescind.[35] A distinction may be taken between cases where the price will ultimately be forthcoming and cases where there is reason to doubt this, and then a time limit may be more readily resorted to.[36]

On prolonged failure to accept the title and settle, the seller may sue for the price with interest, provided he is still ready to deliver a valid title

31 *Traill* v. *Connon* (1877) 5 R. 24 (4 per cent.); *Greenock Harbour* v. *G.S.W. Ry.*, 1909 S.C.(H.L.) 49 (3½ per cent.). The point was left open in *Prestwick Cinema Co.* v. *Gardiner*, 1951 S.C. 98.

32 *Grandison's Trs.* v. *Jardine* (1895) 22 R. 925; Ersk., III, 3, 79.

33 *Prestwick Cinema Co.* v. *Gardiner*, 1951 S.C. 98; *Grandison's Trs.*, *supra*.

34 *Dickson* v. *Munro* (1855) 17 D. 524.

35 *Black* v. *Dick* (1814) Hume 699; *Burns* v. *Garscadden* (1901) 8 S.L.T. 321; *Rodgers* v. *Fawdry*, 1950 S.C. 482. *Cf. Stickney* v. *Keeble* [1915] A.C. 386.

36 *Rodgers*, *supra*, 487, *per* Lord Sorn.

in terms of his contract. An action for implement, being in effect for the implement of an obligation to pay money, is, generally speaking, incompetent, but there may be exceptional cases. Prolonged failure may indicate an intention to repudiate the contract. Time in furnishing a valid title is not impliedly of the essence of the contract and must be stipulated for if it is essential that it be tendered by a particular date.[37] In view of the latitude of time allowed to state and meet objections to title probably neither party may resile without intimation to the other,[38] and a further reasonable period of grace.[39] The buyer is probably entitled to the same consideration as to time to produce the price as in an ordinary mercantile transaction. If the seller does not allow a sufficient length of time before he rescinds, he will be liable in damages to the disappointed purchaser.[40]

In the case, however, of sales under articles of roup strict conditions are frequently imposed for punctual payment and advance deposits, and such conditions are strictly enforced as regards time, that being of the essence of the contract in view of the seller's right to hold the next highest offerer liable under the articles to implement the purchase. Furthermore, the buyer's conduct may be such as to amount to a repudiation of the contract and generally this is necessary before delay to settle will justify rescission.[41]

Rescission and damages

If, however, on a default by the purchaser taking place, the seller has accepted the repudiation of the contract, action by him for the price is necessarily precluded, whether or not the seller has resold the property, and he must claim damages, measured by the loss he has sustained on the contract,[42] as by losing a particularly good bargain or particularly good conditions of sale. He is not entitled to recover the whole price as damages.[43] In such a case the damages may be measured by the difference in price obtained at a subsequent sale.[44] In an old case [45] a purchaser who failed to implement the articles of roup was held liable for the difference between the price he had agreed to give and the price to be got at a new sale, and the difference between the interest on the price and the rents till sold, though this was not to exceed the penalty stipulated in the articles of roup. The seller may furthermore have entered into other engagements on the faith of the sale being duly completed, and claims made against him in consequence of his consequential failure therein may or may not be too remote to be recoverable, depending on the knowledge

[37] *Little's Trs.* v. *Spankie* (1830) 8 S. 418; *Kelman* v. *Barr's Tr.* (1878) 5 R. 816; *Gilfillan* v. *Cadell & Grant* (1893) 21 R. 269.

[38] *Stickney* v. *Keeble* [1915] A.C. 386.

[39] *Cf. Burns* v. *Garscadden* (1901) 8 S.L.T. 321; *Rodgers* v. *Fawdry*, 1950 S.C. 482.

[40] *Burns* v. *Garscadden* (1901) 8 S.L.T. 321; *cf. Rodgers* v. *Fawdry*, 1950 S.C. 482.

[41] *Cornwall* v. *Henson* [1900] 2 Ch. 298; *cf. Farrant* v. *Olver* (1922) 91 L.J.Ch. 758.

[42] *Laird* v. *Pim* (1841) 7 M. & W. 474; *Noble* v. *Edwardes* (1877) 5 Ch.D. 378; *Campbell* v. *McCutcheon*, 1963 S.C. 505.

[43] *Laird* v. *Pim, supra.*

[44] *Burns* v. *Garscadden, supra.*

[45] *Johnstone's Trs.* v. *Johnstone*, Jan. 19, 1819, F.C.

of the purchaser and on the circumstances of the case.[46] Expenses reasonably and necessarily incurred in connection with the sale will be recoverable, though if a subsequent sale be made at once, the whole expenses of, *e.g.*, advertisement and legal expenses, could not reasonably be attributable to the breached contract.

Special cases

There may be specialties in any particular contract of sale, such as that any deposit paid by the purchaser shall be forfeited,[47] in which case such a provision will normally be held to be in lieu of damages. Proof of actual damage is unnecessary.[48] Alternatively, there may be a provision expressly for penalty or liquidate damages, in which case it must be determined whether this provision is contractual and enforceable, or penal and consequently subject to modification,[49] in accordance with principles discussed elsewhere.[50]

Competency of resale

When a seller has justifiably rescinded a sale for the breach of an essential condition of the contract of sale he is, of course, entitled to resell and any loss on the resale may be recovered from the defaulting purchaser as damages. In order to mitigate damages he must seek to resell at as good a price as possible. If, however, the second purchaser does not take in bona fide he cannot rely on his missives or even a recorded title and the sale is liable to be set aside if the prior sale turns out to be a subsisting one. He does not take in bona fide if he has notice of the prior sale and, being then put on his inquiry, does not satisfy himself that the original sale is not being maintained.[51] It is accordingly of great materiality to determine whether a purchaser's delay to tender the price or other default is sufficiently material to entitle the seller to rescind the contract and resell to another. His unequivocal repudiation of the contract is, of course, enough to justify this course, but a less conclusive attitude, such as an objection to the title, may raise difficult questions.

If, however, a sale has been concluded and the seller justifiably rescinds in respect of a material breach by the buyer, there is no reason to doubt on principle that he is entitled to recover damages for the loss of the sale, and these will be conveniently measured by any loss sustained on a resale to a third party,[52] together with an element for extra expenses incurred by the failure of the first sale.[53] The seller can recover the difference

46 See *Mansfield* v. *Campbell* (1836) 14 S. 585.
47 *Soper* v. *Arnold* (1889) 14 App.Cas. 429.
48 *Commercial Bank* v. *Beal* (1890) 18 R. 80.
49 *Re Dagenham (Thames) Dock Co.* (1873) 8 Ch.App. 1022.
50 *Vide* Chap. 7, *supra*.
51 *Marshall* v. *Hynd* (1828) 6 S. 384; *Petrie* v. *Forsyth* (1874) 2 R. 214; *Stodart* v. *Dalziel* (1876) 4 R. 236; *Rodgers* v. *Fawdry*, 1950 S.C. 482.
52 *Ockenden* v. *Henly* (1858) E.B. & E. 485; *Watkins* v. *Watkins* (1849) 12 L.T.(o.s.) 353; *Noble* v. *Edwardes* (1877) 5 Ch.D. 378.
53 *Tanner* v. *Radford* (1834) 4 My. & Cr. 519n.; *Hawkins* v. *Bone* (1865) 4 F. & F. 311.

between the contract price and the resale price if realised within a reasonable time of the date of the breach.[54] In *Allan* v. *Gilchrist* [55] sellers sued for damages caused by the refusal of the buyer to implement the contract, and claimed in respect of having discharged employees and made arrangements for retiring from business on the faith of the contract. The action was, however, dismissed on the ground that there were inadequate averments to infer a binding contract and that a claim of damages for non-implement would not lie unless implement could have been insisted in. The question of the remoteness of these heads of claim was therefore not decided.

Seller's remedies after settlement

The remedies open to a seller after settlement of the transaction would appear to be limited to reduction of the contract of sale and disposition, subject to repayment of the price paid with an allowance in respect of expenditure effected or meliorations made on the property by the purchaser.[56] An action based on *quanti minoris* would appear to be certainly incompetent. To justify reduction of the contract it will normally be necessary to be able to make complete, or at least substantial, restitution of the seller *in integrum*. The breach must moreover be material.

In *Steuart's Trs.* v. *Hart* [56] a proprietor sold a property believing the feu-duty to be very materially greater than the purchaser in fact knew it to be. The buyer took possession and spent money on the property. The seller then sued for reduction of the disposition on the ground of essential error and for restitution and this was granted subject to payment by the seller to the dispossessed buyer of a sum in recompense for the outlays on permanent additions or improvements to the subjects.[57] The alternative course of reforming the contract was strongly disapproved as quite incompetent, and it was not suggested that the seller was entitled to recover the capitalised value of the difference between the feu-duty and what he had believed it to be, or otherwise to recover the excess price which he would have demanded had he known the true facts.

In *Anderson* v. *Lambie* [58] the pursuer sold " the farm of B . . . occupied by M ": B consisted of an area farmed by M and a smaller area leased to the National Coal Board. Three years after a disposition had been recorded the seller brought a reduction on the ground of essential error, the buyer having claimed the smaller area as well as the farm, and offered to grant a disposition of the farm only: no damages were sought. The

54 *Keck* v. *Faber* (1915) 60 S.J. 253.
55 (1875) 2 R. 587.
56 *Steuart's Trs.* v. *Hart* (1875) 3 R. 192.
57 This remedy is doubtless precluded if substantial restitution is precluded, *e.g.*, if the purchaser has demolished the premises, or made drastic alterations, *e.g. Boyd and Forrest* v. *G.S.W. Ry.*, 1915 S.C.(H.L.) 20. As to substantial restitution, see *Spence* v. *Crawford*, 1939 S.C.(H.L.) 52; whether it is possible in a given case will depend on the facts.
58 1954 S.C.(H.L.) 43.

court allowed reduction holding that the disposition could not stand in face of proof of a clerical error whereby the parties' intention was not truly expressed.

BUYER'S CLAIMS

The buyer has a claim if the seller refuses or delays unjustifiably to, or finds himself unable to, implement any of the obligations incumbent on the seller. The seller's obligations may be stated briefly as being to give (i) a good title to the subjects of sale [1]; (ii) vacant possession, unless qualified by agreement to the contrary; (iii) a search showing the records clear of incumbrances not agreed to be taken over,[2] and (iv) warrandice against eviction. A failure in any of the first three particulars will disentitle the seller from insisting in the transaction or recovering anything for breach thereof: the buyer on the other hand may resile and recover his expenses and damages for the loss of bargain. The obligation of warrandice against eviction comes into play after settlement of the transaction so as to indemnify the buyer against subsequent dispossession.

Good title to subjects sold

When the seller is unable to convey the whole of the precise subjects sold, the purchaser is not bound to take the property at all and no claim can be made against him for his refusal.[3] In *Whyte* v. *Lee* [4] missives made no mention of restrictions: it later appeared that the titles contained a reservation of minerals. The seller's action for implement accordingly failed. But this does not extend to resiling on the ground merely that the cellars were damp.[5] A seller's failure to disclose servitudes [6] or restrictions on the use to be made of the subjects entitles a buyer to resile and the seller cannot insist on damages,[7] and buyers have been held entitled to resile in several such cases.[8]

A purchaser's right to have a marketable title which will protect him from eviction and even from reasonable challenge is not affected by an offer to grant absolute warrandice [9] or by a condition in the missives that no search shall be given by the seller,[10] but it is otherwise where the seller has expressly or impliedly undertaken only to put the purchaser in his place.[11] And a seller is entitled to an opportunity to cure a defect in a

1 This is independent of warrandice: *Nairne* v. *Scrimgeour* (1676) Mor. 14169. But see *Leith Heritages* v. *Edinburgh & Leith Glass Co.* (1876) 3 R. 789.

2 Even though the contract says that no search shall be given: *Mackenzie* v. *Clark* (1895) 3 S.L.T. 128.

3 *Moray* v. *Pearson* (1842) 4 D. 1411; *Scottish Temperance Assce. Co.* v. *Law Union and Rock Insce. Co.*, 1917 S.C. 175.

4 (1879) 6 R. 699.

5 *Rutherford* v. *Edinburgh Co-op. Bldg. Socy.* (1873) 11 S.L.R. 28.

6 Bell, *Prin.* § 895; *Welsh* v. *Russell* (1894) 21 R. 769.

7 *Smith* v. *Soeder* (1895) 23 R. 60.

8 *Urquhart* v. *Halden* (1835) 13 S. 844; *Robertson* v. *Rutherford* (1841) 4 D. 141; *Louttit's Trs.* v. *Highland Ry.* (1892) 19 R. 791; *McConnel* v. *Chassels* (1903) 10 S.L.T. 790.

9 *Nairne* v. *Scrimgeour* (1676) Mor. 14169.

10 *Mackenzie* v. *Clark* (1895) 3 S.L.T. 128.

11 *Leith Heritages Co.* v. *Edinburgh & Leith Glass Co.* (1876) 3 R. 789.

title if he offers to do so, especially where entry is immediate, or is postponed under the contract.[12] The right does not, however, extend without express agreement to delivery of any titles other than the disposition in his favour,[13] though there is an implied right to exhibition of prior and common writs.[14] A purchaser cannot demand specific implement together with compensation for a defect in title.[15]

Agreement to take title as it stands

Even an agreement to accept the title as it stands and subject to all exceptions has been held not to bind a purchaser to accept a title which was not marketable and which could not be made marketable by any expenditure on his part [16]; nor does it bind a purchaser to take something quite different from what he contracted for.[17] In such a case he must retain the property or rescind the contract: there can be no *actio quanti minoris*.[18] But it does cover an immaterial discrepancy,[19] and a defect which is remediable by the purchaser at his own expense,[20] and a possible liability for a real burden.[21] The seller is bound to disclose a doubtful question arising out of the title.[21]

Claims of damages have, however, been barred in some cases as where a restrictive condition was not disclosed but the buyer had by agreeing to the articles of roup, which contained a provision that the purchaser should satisfy himself as to the sufficiency of the seller's title, bound himself to search the record or take the risk of any such error as had occurred [22]; in another case articles of roup provided that purchasers should be held to have satisfied themselves as to the extent of the subjects. This clause was held to bar a claim of damages under the warrandice clause in the disposition, as the purchaser should have satisfied himself as to the extent of the subjects.[23]

Timeous furnishing of title

The title must be furnished timeously but not necessarily by the date of entry, and purchasers have been held entitled to resile after moderate delay,[24] while in other cases they have been held bound despite greater

12 *Kinnear* v. *Young*, 1936 S.L.T. 574.
13 *Cf. Porteous* v. *Henderson* (1898) 25 R. 563.
14 Ersk. I, 52, 53; *Bald* v. *Scott* (1841) 3 D. 564; *contra* in leasehold, *Denniston, Macnayr & Co.* v. *Macfarlane*, Feb. 16, 1808, F.C.
15 *Stewart* v. *Kennedy* (1890) 17 R.(H.L.) 1.
16 *Carter* v. *Lornie* (1890) 18 R. 353; contrast *Sorley's Trs.* v. *Grahame* (1832) 10 S. 319.
17 *Hamilton* v. *Western Bank* (1861) 23 D. 1033.
18 *Waddell* v. *Pollock* (1828) 6 S. 999; *Wood* v. *Edinburgh Mags.* (1886) 13 R. 1006.
19 *Morton* v. *Smith* (1877) 5 R. 83.
20 *Smith* v. *Aiken* (1827) 5 S. 340; *Waddell* v. *Pollock* (1828) 6 S. 999; *Sorley's Trs.* v. *Grahame* (1832) 10 S. 319; *Young* v. *Grierson* (1849) 11 D. 1482.
21 *Davidson* v. *Dalziel* (1881) 8 R. 990.
22 *Wood* v. *Magistrates of Edinburgh* (1886) 13 R. 1006; *cf. Carruthers* v. *Stott* (1825) 4 S. 34.
23 *Young* v. *McKellar Ltd.*, 1909 S.C. 1340.
24 *Hunter* v. *Carswell* (1823) 1 S. 248; *Fleming* v. *Harley's Trs.* (1823) 2 S. 373 (5 years); *Hutchinson* v. *Scott* (1830) 8 S. 377 (14 months); *Kelman* v. *Barr's Trs.* (1878) 5 R. 816 (6 months).

delays.[25] Time is not prima facie, but may by stipulation be made, of the essence of the contract,[26] or this may appear from circumstances.[27] In such cases reasonable notice should be given before resiling.[28]

Where a seller's agent failed to produce a complete title timeously so that the purchaser was himself subjected to several claims of damages, he was held entitled to damages, and to relief in respect of the other claims of damages, against the seller's representatives.[29] Where the title is sound but delay arises in completing formalities connected therewith, resiling is not justified.[30] It is permissible, if one title is objected to, and the objection upheld by the court, to tender another and valid one,[31] and a purchaser is bound if a valid title is eventually produced, even though he took possession on a defective one, so long as he did so without reservation.[32]

Right to subjects sold

The purchaser is entitled to the precise property purchased [33] and not an equivalent or substitute,[34] either better or worse. He may resile if there is found to be an error in extent amounting to *error in substantialibus* [35] even though the missives seek to bind him [36] (and a statement in the missives does not amount to a warranty),[36] or if there is an error as to the ground burden.[37] But a purchaser cannot object to an ordinary amount of feu-duty even though not mentioned in the missives, though he can refuse to take a title subject to an unallocated *cumulo* feu-duty whether or not the balance is well secured.[38] If the ground burdens are substantially less than mentioned in the missives, the seller may have the sale reduced on repaying the price and paying compensation for improvements.[39] If the burdens were materially greater than provided for, the purchaser would be entitled to indemnity under the warrandice clause, but

25 *Ross* v. *Southern District Markets Co.* (1829) 7 S. 738 (20 months); *Smith* v. *Aitken* (1829) 8 S. 84 (2 years); *Dick* v. *Cuthbertson* (1831) 5 W. & Sh. 712 (11 years); *Raeburn* v. *Baird* (1832) 10 S. 761 (6 months); *Carter* v. *Lornie* (1890) 18 R. 353 (18 months).

26 *Little's Trs.* v. *Spankie* (1830) 8 S. 418; *Raeburn, supra*; *Kelman, supra*; *cf. Bernard* v. *Williams* (1928) 44 T.L.R. 437.

27 *Raeburn* v. *Baird* (1832) 10 S. 761.

28 *Raeburn, supra*; *Burns* v. *Garscadden* (1901) 8 S.L.T. 321; *cf. Dick, supra*; *McNeill* v. *Cameron* (1830) 8 S. 362; *Compton* v. *Bagley* [1892] 1 Ch. 313; *Gilfillan* v. *Cadell & Grant* (1893) 21 R. 269; *Stickney* v. *Keeble* [1915] A.C. 386; *Rodgers* v. *Fawdry*, 1950 S.C. 483.

29 *Little's Trs.* v. *Spankie* (1830) 8 S. 418.

30 *Forbes* v. *Campbell* (1885) 12 R. 1065; *Hatten* v. *Russell* (1888) 38 Ch.D. 334.

31 *Raeburn, supra*; *Carter, supra.*

32 *Carter, supra.*

33 *E. Moray* v. *Pearson* (1842) 4 D. 1411; *Hamilton* v. *Western Bank* (1861) 23 D. 1033.

34 *E. Moray* v. *Pearson* (1842) 4 D. 1411. As to precision required, see *Scottish Temperance Assce. Co.* v. *Law Union and Rock Insce. Co.*, 1917 S.C. 175. *Cf. Ayles* v. *Cox* (1852) 16 Beav. 23.

35 Bell, *Prin.* § 893. See *Hamilton, infra*; *Morton* v. *Smith* (1877) 5 R. 83; *Kelvinside Estate Co.* v. *Donaldson's Trs.* (1879) 6 R. 995; *Woods* v. *Tulloch* (1893) 20 R. 477.

36 *Hamilton* v. *Western Bank* (1861) 23 D. 1033 (essential error as to extent).

37 *Clason* v. *Steuart* (1844) 6 D. 1201; see also *Johnston* v. *Clark* (1855) 18 D. 70; *Steuart's Trs.* v. *Hart* (1875) 3 R. 192.

38 *Bremner* v. *Dick*, 1911 S.C. 887; see also *Robertson* v. *Douglas* (1886) 13 R. 1133; *Morrison* v. *Gray*, 1932 S.C. 712.

39 *Steuart's Trs.* v. *Hart* (1875) 3 R. 192.

not to reduction and repetition of the price or present value of the property.[40] The purchaser cannot be compelled to take a long leasehold or anything short of a permanent feudal title [41] unless provided for by the contract.

Again the purchaser is entitled to the exclusive and absolute property in the subjects,[42] subject only to the incidentals implied in feu-tenure, such as existence of a superiority [43] and the mutual obligations of co-terminous proprietors.[44] The purchaser is, however, bound if the discrepancy between the subjects contracted for and as actually handed over is not essential.[45]

Rescission has been held justifiable in case of an undisclosed servitude,[46] or undisclosed restrictions on building and use,[47] or reservations unknown though common in the district.[48] In other cases a purchaser has been personally barred by knowledge.[49] An ordinary lease is not an incumbrance which the seller is bound to purge [50] nor is it a breach of warrandice.[51]

Clear searches

Even an agreement to purchase without a search does not bar a purchaser from objecting to the seller's title if a clear marketable title is not disclosed.[52] A " clear search " must be literally clear and it is not sufficient if it discloses a deed or burden affecting the subjects even though its validity may be impugned.[53] The buyer may resile from the contract if a search discloses any incumbrances or diligences and if the seller does not have them removed. Even where there is a stipulation that no search is to be supplied, the buyer can call on the seller to clear the record of any incumbrances of which the latter knows or ought to know.[54]

Possession of subjects sold

A purchaser may resile if the seller does not give him natural or civil

[40] *Welsh* v. *Russell* (1894) 21 R. 769.
[41] *McConnell* v. *Chassels* (1903) 10 S.L.T. 790.
[42] Bell, *Prin.* § 938.
[43] *Bremner* v. *Dick*, 1911 S.C. 887.
[44] Bell, *Prin.* § 1086; *Smith* v. *Giuliani*, 1925 S.C.(H.L.) 45.
[45] *Rutherford* v. *Edinburgh Co-operative Building Co.* (1873) 11 S.L.R. 29. *Cf. Heys* v. *Kimball and Morton* (1890) 17 R. 381.
[46] *Urquhart* v. *Halden* (1835) 13 S. 844; see also *Gordonstoun* v. *Paton* (1682) Mor. 16606; *Corbett* v. *Robertson* (1872) 10 M. 329; *Cowan* v. *Stewart* (1872) 10 M. 735; *Welsh* v. *Russell* (1894) 21 R. 769; *Campbell's Trs.* v. *Glasgow Corpn.* (1902) 4 F. 752.
[47] *Robertson* v. *Rutherford* (1841) 4 D. 121; *Ewing* v. *Hastie* (1878) 5 R. 439; *Louttit's Trs.* v. *Highland Ry.* (1892) 19 R. 791; *Smith* v. *Soeder* (1895) 23 R. 60; *Graham* v. *Shiels* (1901) 8 S.L.T. 368; *McConnell* v. *Chassels* (1903) 10 S.L.T. 790; *Kelly* v. *Clark*, 1967 S.L.T. 141.
[48] *Crofts* v. *Stewart's Trs.*, 1927 S.C.(H.L.) 65; *Mossend Theatre* v. *Livingstone*, 1930 S.C. 90. As to minerals, see also *Todd* v. *McCarroll* (1917) 55 S.L.R. 17; *Whyte* v. *Lee* (1879) 6 R. 699; *Campbell* v. *McCutcheon*, 1963 S.L.T. 290.
[49] *Gall* v. *Gall*, 1918, 1 S.L.T. 261; *Macdonald* v. *Newall* (1898) 1 F. 68.
[50] Bell's *Conveyancing*, I, 644.
[51] *Lothian and Border Farmers* v. *McCutchion*, 1952 S.L.T. 450.
[52] *Mackenzie* v. *Clark*, 1895, 3 S.L.T. 128.
[53] *Christie* v. *Cameron* (1898) 25 R. 824. On an agent's obligations with regard to searches, see *Fea* v. *Macfarlane* (1887) 24 S.L.R. 628; *Graham* v. *Hunter's Trs.* (1831) 9 S. 543; *Campbell* v. *Clason* (1838) 1 D. 270; *Fearn* v. *Gordon and Craig* (1893) 20 R. 352.
[54] See *Horne* v. *Kay* (1824) 3 S. 81; *Moir* v. *Paul* (1830) 8 S. 823; *Ralston* v. *Farquharson* (1830) 8 S. 927; *Davidson* v. *Dalziel* (1881) 8 R. 990.

possession conform to the contract. A purchaser is not affected by personal rights of occupancy of the property valid against the seller only.[54a] The fact that a purchaser has taken possession may bar him from seeking to resile if the seller delays unduly to produce a marketable title, when he might otherwise have withdrawn.[55] But if possession of only a part be given,[56] or presumably if possession is taken subject to reservation, the right to resile will not be barred. The phrase " immediate entry " means merely such early possession as is possible and practicable in the circumstances, and entry given on the fourth day was held not to be any ground for repudiating the contract.[57] Time of implement may, however, be material and bar him from enforcing contractual rights.[58] If immediate possession is of the essence of the contract, delay in giving possession will justify rescission by the buyer.[59]

If a purchaser is forced to resile on account of delay in completing the contract on the seller's part, the damages should be such as may reasonably be said to have arisen through delay and non-delivery of possession, or as may reasonably be supposed to have been in the contemplation of the parties as likely to arise from the partial breach of contract.[60] It seems probable that in the case of a temporary delay to give vacant possession, damages might be assessed at the cost of providing suitable alternative accommodation,[61] or the cost of removing rubbish which encumbered the premises.[62]

In *Beard* v. *Porter* [63] a contract for the sale of a rent-restricted house with vacant possession was entered into: the sale was completed but the tenant did not quit and the buyer then sued for damages for breach of the undertaking to give vacant possession. He was held entitled to (i) the difference in value between the purchase price and the value of the house subject to the tenancy; (ii) legal expenses and stamp duty incurred in buying another house to live in,[64] and (iii) expenditure on lodgings for a period till he could get entry to the alternative house. No claim was made to rescind the sale and it was suggested that no claim could be made.[65]

Buyer's remedies for seller's breach of contract

If the seller of heritage is in breach of contract several remedies may be open to the purchaser, depending on the circumstances. If the seller is able to convey the property as sold but refuses or delays to do so, an action

54a *Wallace* v. *Simmers*, 1960 S.C. 255.
55 *Carter* v. *Lornie* (1890) 18 R. 353.
56 *Hunter* v. *Carsewell* (1823) 1 S. 248.
57 *Heys* v. *Kimball and Morton* (1890) 17 R. 381.
58 *Kelman* v. *Barr's Tr.* (1878) 5 R. 816.
59 *Carter, supra.*
60 *Jones* v. *Gardiner* [1902] 1 Ch. 191.
61 *Tolman* v. *Dyson* [1952] C.P.L. 745.
62 *Cumberland Mansions* v. *Ireland* [1946] 1 K.B. 164.
63 [1948] 1 K.B. 321.
64 Evershed L.J. dissented on this point, considering these elements of damage too remote even if they could be said to flow from the seller's breach of the first contract.
65 It is thought that this last point would be otherwise in Scotland.

for specific implement of the contract and alternatively for damages is appropriate.[66] The same applies if the seller so delays that it cannot be known whether or not he can give a good title to the subject of sale. It lies in the discretion of the court to say whether specific implement or damages is the proper and suitable remedy in the circumstances.[67] Damages may be given rather than specific implement where specific implement would put the defender to unreasonable expense without fault on his own part,[67] or where specific implement is impossible,[68] *e.g.* if the subjects should be wholly destroyed by the seller's negligence, or if the seller has put it outwith his power to implement, by selling and conveying to a third party in circumstances when the second sale cannot be impugned.[69] If, however, the second sale was invalid by reason of *mala fides*, it may yet be reduced even though the disposition has been recorded and implement of the earlier contract decreed.[70] Damages are also appropriate where the seller's breach is not so material as to justify resiling.[70a]

Measure of damages

The measure of damages in such cases might not include any element for loss of bargain representing the enhanced price which the pursuer would require to pay to obtain a comparable property elsewhere. There is authority in England that such are not recoverable if the seller's default is due to defect in title,[71] but not otherwise.[72] It may be doubtful whether any element could be claimed in respect of the *pretium affectionis* of the particular property concerned. This would depend to a large extent on the materiality of the loss of the particular property and the purpose for which it was required. It is thought that the loss of any peculiar advantages of the property thus lost would not necessarily be too remote a consequence of the defender's breach of contract. In *Burns* v. *Garscadden* [73] £100 damages were awarded apparently to cover all heads of claim where a property worth £3,800 had been wrongfully resold. In *Rodgers* v. *Fawdry* [74] £14,000 damages were claimed, alternatively to implement, the price of the subjects being £18,250. In *Mackay* v. *Campbell* [74a] £10,000 was claimed.

The measure of damages must be such a sum as reasonably compensates the purchaser for the loss suffered. Other heads which may require

66 *McKellar* v. *Dallas's Ltd.*, 1928 S.C. 503; *Mackay* v. *Campbell*, 1967 S.C.(H.L.) 53.
67 *Moore* v. *Paterson* (1881) 9 R. 337.
68 *Cocker* v. *Crombie* (1893) 20 R. 954. *Cf. Plato* v. *Newman*, 1950 S.L.T.(Notes) 30.
69 *Marshall* v. *Hynd* (1828) 6 S. 384; *Petrie* v. *Forsyth* (1874) 2 R. 214; *Stodart* v. *Dalziel* (1876) 4 R. 236; *Burns* v. *Garscadden* (1901) 8 S.L.T. 321.
70 *Rodger (Builders) Ltd.* v. *Fawdry*, 1950 S.C. 482.
70a *Speevack* v. *Robson*, 1949 S.L.T.(Notes) 39.
71 *Bain* v. *Fothergill* (1874) L.R. 7 H.L. 158; *Keen* v. *Mear* [1920] 2 Ch. 574.
72 *Engell* v. *Fitch* (1869) L.R. 4 Q.B. 659; *Godwin* v. *Francis* (1870) L.R. 5 C.P. 295; *Re Daniel* [1917] 2 Ch. 405; *Braybrooks* v. *Whaley* [1919] 1 K.B. 435. See *Louttit's Trs.* v. *Highland Ry.* (1892) 19 R. 791, 800.
73 (1901) 8 S.L.T. 321.
74 1950 S.C. 482.
74a 1967 S.C.(H.L.) 53.

investigation are the consideration of what the purchaser has suffered by losing this particular property, and this loss may be measured by a subsequent transaction.[75] The purchaser may further have become liable to third parties for consequential breaches of subsale [76] or other contracts, such as transactions with prospective bondholders.[77] Expenses directly arising out of the ineffective contract may also be recovered, such as those incurred in the fruitless examination of title.[78] In many cases the element of general damages must be rather arbitrary, as no exactly or reasonably comparable property may be available to enable the loss to be gauged, while the loss of a unique property cannot accurately be assessed.

Actio quanti minoris

It is still not a finally decided question whether this form of claim of damages is competent in Scotland in respect of heritage, if a title is tendered, but is not good or does not cover the whole subjects of sale. If competent, it applies only to those cases where it is discovered before settlement that the seller's title does not cover the property as sold by him or is not a fully marketable title to the subjects; in such a case the purchaser might possibly, instead of resiling from the contract and claiming damages, require the seller to convey the property for a lesser price, representing the contract price diminished by an amount which fairly and reasonably represents the discrepancy between the values of the property as contracted to be sold and as actually conveyed. But there is no clear authority for the competency of this form of claim of implement with damages in relation to heritage [79] and modern cases do not support it.[80] It might possibly be different if fraud were averred,[81] or possibly essential error.

On the other hand, after settlement of the transaction a claim of substantially similar nature founded on the seller's obligation of warrandice is competent.[82] This is considered separately later. It is also competent to retain possession of the subjects and sue for damages for the breach of a collateral obligation connected with the same property and constituted by the same agreement,[83] but this course is possibly not invariable.[84]

The incompetency of a claim of damages by the *actio quanti minoris* where there is no obstacle to rescission of the contract has been repeatedly asserted.[85] This was clearly the common law in the case of sales of cor-

[75] *Burns* v. *Garscadden* (1901) 8 S.L.T. 321.
[76] *Little's Trs.* v. *Spankie* (1830) 8 S. 418.
[77] *Cf.* the converse case of a seller, *Mansfield* v. *Campbell* (1836) 14 S. 585.
[78] *Bain* v. *Fothergill* (1874) L.R. 7 H.L. 158.
[79] *Wilson* v. *Campbell's Trs.* (1764) M. 13330; *Gordon* v. *Hughes*, June 15, 1815, F.C.
[80] Bell, *Prin.* § 890–893; *Louttit's Trs.* v. *Highland Ry.* (1892) 19 R. 791; *Brownlie* v. *Miller* (1878) 5 R. 1076, 1089; affd. (1880) 7 R.(H.L.) 66, 71, 79; *Waddell* v. *Pollock* (1828) 6 S. 999; *Wood* v. *Mags. of Edinburgh* (1886) 13 R. 1006.
[81] *Louttit's Trs., supra*; *Dobbie* v. *Duncanson* (1872) 10 M. 810.
[82] *Louttit's Trs., supra, per* Lord McLaren.
[83] *McKillop* v. *Mutual Securities Ltd.*, 1945 S.C. 166.
[84] See *Reddie* v. *Syme* (1831) 9 S. 413; affd. (1832) 6 W. & S. 188.
[85] Bell, *Prin.* § 893; *Hannay* v. *Creditors of Bargaly* (1785) Mor. 13334; *Lloyd* v. *Paterson's Heirs* (1782) Mor. 13334; *Gray* v. *Hamilton* (1802) Mor. s.v. Sale, Appx. No. 2; *Bald* v. *Scott* (1847) 10 D. 289, 294; *Louttit's Trs.* v. *Highland Ry.* (1892) 19 R. 791, 795–796, 798.

poreal movables [86] until the law was changed in 1893 and the *actio quanti minoris* allowed.[87]

If, however, the defect in the title can be removed by the seller, as by purging an undisclosed bond, he may be ordained to do so to clear the record.[88] The purchaser is not entitled to take possession and rely on the negative prescription to cure the defect in the title, he retaining the price all the while.[89] So too if there has been a collateral breach by the seller, as of a warranty that the subjects possessed certain advantages, rescission appears to be the only remedy and not damages *quanti minoris*.[90] But damages are recoverable where there was breach of a collateral contract.[90a]

Rescission of the contract

On the basis that an action of damages on the basis of *quanti minoris* is incompetent, rescission is the only remedy open to a purchaser whose seller cannot produce a valid marketable title to the whole subjects he has sold. Restitution must be made *hinc inde* by both parties as a condition of rescission so that the price, if paid, or any instalment of it, must be repaid and the property handed back.[91] Examples of such cases are the cases of examination of the title disclosing qualifications such as reservations of minerals [91] not disclosed in the contract of sale, and it appears in such cases that the distinction between material and trivial breaches of contract does not apply.[92] Rescission is competent though the value of the property is not apparently affected. The contract must be wholly rescinded as there is no authority in Scotland for the court exercising a power to reform or reconstruct the contract.[93]

Damages may in such a case be recovered for the loss of bargain consequent on the seller's default, and for any naturally consequential expenses, such as those connected with the examination of title.

In England damages for the loss of bargain are not given where the seller had no title nor means of giving a good title.[94] In other cases such damages can be recovered, measured by the loss sustained in consequence of not obtaining that particular property.[95]

Where rescission impossible

As *restitutio in integrum* is an essential prerequisite of the right to

[86] *McCormick* v. *Rittmeyer* (1869) 7 M. 854, 858.
[87] Sale of Goods Act 1893, ss. 11 (2) and 53.
[88] *Christie* v. *Cameron* (1898) 25 R. 824.
[89] *Aikman* v. *Hepburn* (1772) Mor. 14179.
[90] *Reddie* v. *Syme* (1831) 9 S. 413; affd. (1832) 6 W. & S. 188.
[90a] *McKillop* v. *Mutual Securities Ltd.*, 1945 S.C. 166.
[91] *Crofts* v. *Stewart's Trs.*, 1927 S.C.(H.L.) 65.
[92] *Gloag on Contract*, 614, citing *Robertson* v. *Rutherford* (1841) 4 D. 121; *Whyte* v. *Lee* (1879) 6 R. 699; *Crofts* v. *Stewart's Trs.*, 1927 S.C.(H.L.) 65; see also *Mossend Theatre* v. *Livingstone*, 1930 S.C. 90 (all cases of reservation of minerals where the reservation made no difference to the value of the subjects).
[93] *Steuart's Trs.* v. *Hart* (1875) 3 R. 192.
[94] *Bain* v. *Fothergill* (1874) L.R. 7 H.L. 207; *Morgan* v. *Russell* [1909] 1 K.B. 357; *Keen* v. *Mear* [1920] 2 Ch. 574.
[95] *Jaques* v. *Miller* (1877) 6 Ch.D. 153; *Jones* v. *Gardiner* [1902] 1 Ch. 191.

rescind a contract,[96] the remedy of rescission will be precluded where restitution is impracticable, as where the defect has not been discovered until a measure of *rei interventus* has taken place and alterations been done on the subjects, even though before settlement. In such a case it is conceived that a claim of damages is doubtful, but possibly competent.[97] Such a claim has been admitted in cases which seem truly to rest on warrandice, as where part of a feu was evicted and a proportionate abatement of feu-duty was allowed,[98] where an estate was sold with an assurance that it carried a qualification to vote and this was subsequently found to be bad [99]; where a third party established right to a mineral field which had by then been partly worked and restitution *in integrum* was consequently impossible,[1] and where a building restriction was discovered after the buyers were in possession and the price paid, though no action had been taken as to the ground.[2]

The observations in *Louttit's Trustees* [3] affirm the competency of a claim of damages *quanti minoris* under a clause of warrandice. They do not settle the question whether damages may be claimed without rescission and restitution where rescission is yet possible, and the better opinion seems to be that damages without rescission is incompetent in sales of heritage: if rescission and restitution *hinc inde* cannot be made, damages cannot be claimed. In *Wood* v. *Edinburgh Magistrates* [4] subjects were misdescribed in articles of roup so that a building restriction was not disclosed. After buildings had been erected the purchaser claimed damages for being debarred from making use of the subjects as intended. The action was dismissed on the ground that the purchaser had by the articles of roup undertaken the duty of satisfying himself of the sufficiency of the titles, but the Lord Ordinary observed that " the pursuer does not attempt to reduce the contract. Holding, as he does, by the contract, and the right which he has acquired under it, he can have no remedy on the principle of the *actio quanti minoris*," and Lord President Inglis and Lord Mure reserved their opinions on the competency of such an action, at least in the absence of averments of fraud or essential error. Where fraud is averred, damages may possibly be claimed without rescission of the contract.[5]

Measure of damages

The measure of damages, if any be competent, in such a case, is such proportion of the value or price paid as may be ascribed to the portion or

96 *Boyd & Forrest* v. *G.S.W. R.*, 1915 S.C.(H.L.) 20.
97 *Louttit's Trs.* v. *Highland Ry.* (1892) 19 R. 791; *contra, Wood* v. *Mags. of Edinburgh* (1886) 13 R. 1006, 1008, *per* Lord Kinnear *obiter.*
98 *Russel* v. *Harrowers* (1751) Mor. 16629.
99 *Gordon* v. *Hughes*, June 15, 1815, F.C., revd. on another ground (1819) 1 Bligh 287.
1 *Bald* v. *Scott* (1847) 10 D. 289.
2 *Louttit's Trs.* v. *Highland Ry.* (1892) 19 R. 791 (*dub.* L.P. Robertson and Lord Adam).
3 (1892) 19 R. 791.
4 (1886) 13 R. 1006.
5 *Dobbie* v. *Duncanson* (1872) 10 M. 810; *cf. Campbell* v. *Blair* (1897) 5 S.L.T. 28; see also *Bryson* v. *Bryson*, 1916, 1 S.L.T. 361.

rights from which the purchaser has been evicted.[6] The damages have never and probably could never exceed what the parties thought was a fair value of the property at the time of sale.[7] In *Louttit's Trustees* [8] the award of damages was said to represent the difference in value between the subjects as they were and as they would have been without the restriction which the title contained.

Claims after settlement—warrandice

After settlement of a transaction, a purchaser's claim is usually made under the warrandice clause. The clause of warrandice in a deed imports an obligation by the granter thereof that the deed or right thereby granted shall be good and effectual to the grantee; it expresses or implies that in case of reduction of the deed or of eviction, in whole or in part, from the subjects conveyed by it, on account of any fact or deed of the granter, or of his predecessors, or any defect in the granter's title, or it may be on any ground not attributable to the grantee, the granter shall make good the loss or damage thence arising to the grantee.[9] When not expressed, warrandice will be implied, and it can be so expressed as to exclude any claim founded on implied warrandice in the discretion of the contracting parties. Personal warrandice may be simple, from fact and deed, or absolute. Absolute warrandice is implied in dispositions for full and onerous cause, leases and other writs. The statutory clause "I grant warrandice" in dispositions in the form authorised by the Titles to Land Consolidation Act of 1868,[10] imports, unless specially qualified, absolute warrandice as regards the lands and writs thereof,[11] and warrandice from fact and deed as regards the rents.[12] In the event of eviction in consequence of defect in the right or title of the granter to convey the subjects, or by reason of a subsequent deed granted by him, the obligation of warrandice founds the grantee in an action of recourse against the granter to the extent of full indemnity for the whole damage he sustains as at the date of the eviction.[13] It has been held in the case of a lease that the claim extends to the loss or damage estimated to arise to the tenant during the whole term of the lease.[14] It has also been held that having to pay the price of teinds is sufficient eviction to ground a claim of warrandice,[15] as is liability for an undisclosed bond,[16] or discovery of a servitude over the property.[17]

[6] Interlocutor in *Bald* v. *Scott* (1847) 10 D. 289, 305.
[7] *Louttit's Trs.* v. *Highland Ry.* (1892) 19 R. 791, 800.
[8] *Ibid.* at p. 795.
[9] Bell's *Conveyancing*, I, 214.
[10] s. 5.
[11] It does not warrant the sufficiency of the titles for any specified result in law: *Brownlie* v. *Miller* (1880) 7 R.(H.L.) 66; Bell, *Prin.* § 895.
[12] s. 8. The same applies to the phrase occurring in the assignation of a registered lease: Registration of Leases Act 1857, s. 20.
[13] Stair, II, 3, 46; Erskine II, 3, 30; *Carmichael* v. *Anstruther* (1821) 1 S. 22; *Cairns* v. *Howden* (1870) 9 M. 284.
[14] *Middleton* v. *Megget* (1828) 7 S. 76.
[15] *Briggs' Trs.* v. *Dalyell* (1851) 14 D. 173.
[16] *Dewar* v. *Aitken* (1780) Mor. 16637.
[17] *Welsh* v. *Russell* (1894) 21 R. 769, 775.

There must be precise averments of the loss sustained by the eviction founded on,[18] and it has been said that the court is entitled in considering the claim for breach of warrandice to look beyond technicalities of conveyancing to the true understanding and intent of the parties,[19] but this view may be inconsistent with a later House of Lords authority.[20] The obligation involved in warrandice is to recompense in case of eviction, and not to maintain the grantee in possession of the subjects.[21] Hence circumstances which justify a claim under warrandice do not *per se* justify an attempt to rescind the contract.[21]

When claim may arise

As warrandice is a claim for indemnification, no claim arises thereunder until eviction has taken place, unless it is due to the act of the granter of the obligation of warrandice, when an action is competent without waiting for eviction.[22] Immediate recourse against the granter is also competent if he should dispute his liability to indemnify.[23] It has been held that a purchaser had still a claim on the seller and a title to sue him even after he had resold and assigned the seller's obligation of warrandice.[24]

The obligation only comes into effect on eviction so that in the absence of express contrary stipulation, no claim can be made for the expenses of defence if the grantee successfully defends his right against eviction.[25] On the other hand, if the defence is unsuccessful, the condition precedent to a claim under the warrandice is satisfied, and the grantee is entitled to recover the expenses of the unsuccessful defence as part of his claim of indemnification,[26] unless, of course, the defence was not properly undertaken and some obviously competent and relevant defence not tabled, which would have been successful. In such a case the whole claim may be barred.[27] It is probably the law that it is not incumbent on the grantee of the obligation to litigate at all in defence of his right where it is plainly bad and if he has given notice to the person liable to indemnify him.[28] A tenant who had fought an action and been partially evicted from the subjects let to him was held entitled to recover under the obligation of warrandice, not only his expenses but expenses for which he had been found liable in seeking to vindicate his right against third-party intruders.[29]

18 *Welsh* v. *Russell* (1894) 21 R. 769.
19 *Leith Heritages Co.* v. *Edinburgh and Leith Glass Co.* (1876) 3 R. 789.
20 *Lee* v. *Alexander* (1883) 10 R.(H.L.) 91.
21 *Welsh* v. *Russell* (1894) 21 R. 769.
22 *Smith* v. *Ross* (1672) Mor. 16596; *Gordon* v. *Hughes* (1819) 1 Bligh 287; Bell, *Prin.* § 895; Ersk. II, 3, 30.
23 *Lord Melville* v. *Wemyss* (1842) 4 D. 385; *Leith Heritages Co.* v. *Edinburgh and Leith Glass Co.* (1876) 3 R. 789.
24 *Christie* v. *Cameron* (1898) 25 R. 824. See further, *Duke of Bedford* v. *Earl of Galloway's Trs.* (1904) 6 F. 971.
25 Bell, *Conveyancing*, I, 218; Stair, II, 3, 46; Ersk. II, 3, 32; *Inglis* v. *Anstruther* (1771) Mor. 16633.
26 Bell, *Conveyancing*, I, 219.
27 Bell, *Prin.* § 895; *Clerk* v. *Gordon* (1681) Mor. 16605.
28 *Downie* v. *Campbell*, Jan. 31, 1815, F.C.
29 *Dougall* v. *Mags. of Dunfermline*, 1908 S.C. 151.

Evictions not covered by warrandice

There are certain evictions against which warrandice will not indemnify and in these cases the buyer has no recourse against the seller. Thus there is no claim if the property fails or disappears, as distinct from failure or defect in the title,[30] or complete eviction results from supervenient legislation [31] or presumably from a compulsory purchase order [32] or requisition,[33] nor will it indemnify against losses and burdens natural to the purchaser's right [34] or arising from the nature of ownership [35] such as feu-duties and the ordinary incidents of feudal tenure,[36] nor from the existence of leases,[37] nor probably against servitudes unless of a particularly burdensome character,[38] though where actual damage is proved the granter of absolute warrandice must indemnify,[39] and in practice the safest course is to exempt servitudes from warrandice [40]; nor does it cover the expenses of resisting an unsuccessful attempt at eviction, though it will extend to the whole expenses of an unsuccessful defence against eviction provided the seller cannot complain of its being mishandled.[41]

It has also been held that a clause of absolute warrandice does not entitle a purchaser to claim thereunder in respect of alleged want of title to a portion only of the property, when the purchaser had agreed in the contract of sale to satisfy himself on all questions, to take the title as it stood, and when he had had opportunity to examine the property and the site. The clause in the articles of roup barred him from claiming damages for breach of warrandice.[42]

Quantum of claim on warrandice

The quantum of damages to be sought in an action brought on a clause of warrandice must be measured by the full extent of loss sustained by the pursuer, that is, the value by which the property has been diminished in consequence of the breach of the obligation to maintain in possession covered by warrandice,[43] together with the expenses of an unsuccessful

30 Bell, *Prin.* § 122.
31 Bell, *Prin.* § 895; *Watson* v. *Law* (1667) Mor. 16588; *Elphingstone* v. *Lord Blantyre* (1663) Mor. 16585; *Bonar* v. *Lyon* (1683) Mor. 16600; *Muirhead* v. *Lord Colvil* (1715) 5 B.S. 125.
32 *Cf. Venables* v. *Dept. of Agriculture*, 1932 S.C. 573.
33 *Cf. Tay Salmon Fisheries* v. *Speedie*, 1929 S.C. 593; *Mackeson* v. *Boyd*, 1942 S.C. 56.
34 Bell, *Prin.* § 895; *Drummond* v. *Stewart* (1549) Mor. 16565; *Cunningham* v. *Cuthbertson* (1829) S. Teind Cas. 175; *MacRitchie's Trs.* v. *Hope* (1836) 14 S. 578.
35 *Lumsden* v. *Gordon* (1682) Mor. 16606; *Plenderleath* v. *E. Tweeddale* (1800) Mor. 16639.
36 *Brownlie* v. *Miller* (1878) 5 R. 1076; affd. (1880) 7 R.(H.L.) 66.
37 Duff, 89; Bell, *Conveyancing* I, 644; *Lothian and Border Farmers* v. *McCutchion*, 1952 S.L.T. 450.
38 Bell, *Prin.* § 895.
39 *Welsh* v. *Russell* (1894) 21 R. 769, 774.
40 *Urquhart* v. *Halden* (1835) 13 S. 844; *Gordonstoun* v. *Paton* (1682) Mor. 16606; *Sandilands* v. *E. Haddington* (1672) Mor. 16599; *Symington* v. *Cranston* (1780) Mor. 16637; *Reid* v. *Shaw* (1822) 1 S. 334; Bell, *Conveyancing*, I, 644.
41 Bell, *Conveyancing*, I, 643; *Dougall* v. *Mags. of Dunfermline*, 1908 S.C. 151.
42 *Wood* v. *Mags. of Edinburgh* (1886) 13 R. 1006; *Young* v. *McKellar*, 1909 S.C. 1340.
43 *Welsh* v. *Russell* (1894) 21 R. 769, 773, 776.

defence against eviction so long as it was not misconducted.[44] If the value of the property has risen since the purchase when the warrandice was granted, the warrandice covers this and is not limited to the price paid, but the question is unsettled where the value has fallen in the interval.[45] In the case of partial eviction it has been held that the purchaser is not entitled to tender a reconveyance of the whole property and claim repetition of the full value.[46]

As warrandice is a personal obligation it falls primarily on the seller's executors rather than heir [47] though both are liable to the purchaser, and there are exceptions to this rule, *e.g.* an heir of entail.[48]

In *Welsh* v. *Russell*,[49] Lord McLaren said that the extent of the obligation of indemnity contained in a clause of warrandice was measured by the extent of the injury which the buyer has sustained, because such obligations are designed " to indemnify the purchaser not only against the consequences of complete eviction but against the loss of the most inconsiderable fraction of the estate or its diminution in value by reason of the establishment of a burden of any kind."

Lord Kinnear indicated that in the case where there had been total eviction from the subjects covered by the warrandice, the claim is for payment of the present value of the subjects of which the purchaser has been deprived (and not, as Lord McLaren also pointed out, for repayment of the price). Where the eviction is only partial, as by failure of the title as to part of the property, or a debt affecting the property to an extent less than its full value, and the purchaser remains in possession of the subjects he is entitled to recover the diminution in value by reason of what he has lost.[50] As the action is in effect a claim of damages there must be such conclusion and averments as enable the court to estimate or give effect to such a claim. The purchaser may not tender a reconveyance of what is left in exchange for the value of the whole property.

44 Bell's *Conveyancing*, I, 643; *Dougall* v. *Mags. of Dunfermline*, 1908 S.C. 151. See also *Houston* v. *Corbet* (1717) Mor. 16619; *Hill* v. *Yeaman* (1769) Mor. 16631; *Livingston's Heir* v. *Napier* (1777) 5 B.S. 636; *Carmichael* v. *Anstruther* (1821) 1 S. 25; *Galloway* v. *Gardner* (1838) 1 D. 74; *Cairns* v. *Howden* (1870) 9 M. 284. *Cf.* also, *Pilkington* v. *Wood* [1953] 1 Ch. 770.

45 *Cairns* v. *Howden* (1870) 9 M. 284.

46 *Welsh* v. *Russell* (1894) 21 R. 769.

47 *Duchess of Montrose* v. *Stuart* (1887) 15 R.(H.L.) 19.

48 *Duke of Bedford* v. *Galloway's Tr.* (1904) 6 F. 971. *Cf. Lord Abinger's Trs.* v. *Cameron*, 1909 S.C. 1245.

49 (1894) 21 R. 769, 773.

50 *Cf. Louttit's Trs.* v. *Highland Ry.* (1892) 19 R. 791, 795.

CHAPTER 47

CONTRACTS OF LEASE

THE contract of lease is subject to the rules applicable to contracts in general, and breach of an express or implied term gives rise to a claim of damages, and sometimes to other claims as well.

Claims arising from creation of contract

Damages may be recovered in respect of fraudulent misrepresentation inducing the contract,[1] as in other cases of contract, as well as reduction of the lease,[2] though such a claim may be barred by delay.[3] It has been held that where a lease granted by trustees was reduced as being *ultra vires* after being acted on for fourteen years, the tenant was bound by the terms of the purported lease during the period of his occupancy so as to be liable to a claim of damages by the landlord.[4] It was further observed in this case that where in the case of a lease for a term of years, the landlord has a claim of damages against his tenant, he is bound without delay to intimate his claim and his intention to enforce it, otherwise he will be barred from doing so.[5] On English authority the measure of damages for loss consequent on the granter's having no title to grant a lease is the difference between the value of the lease professedly granted and the lease which the tenant actually obtains,[6] including natural consequences and expenses.[7] If the granter could, but fails in breach of contract to, grant a lease the damages will be the loss arising directly and naturally from the breach.[8]

LANDLORD'S CLAIMS

Tenant's obligation to take possession

A tenant is under an obligation to take possession of the subjects let to him [9] and an action to compel him to implement the lease is always competent in the sheriff court.[10] In the event of breach of this obligation

1 On constitution and proof of the contract, see *Rankine on Leases*, 3rd ed., 100 *et seq.*
2 *Beresford's Trs.* v. *Gardner* (1877) 4 R. 885; *McPherson* v. *Campbell's Trs.* (1869) 41 Jur. 634; *cf. Brash* v. *Munro* (1903) 5 F. 1102.
3 *Grieve* v. *Rutherford's Trs.* (1871) 9 S.L.R. 60.
4 *Elliott's Trs.* v. *Elliott* (1894) 21 R. 858.
5 *Ibid.* 866.
6 *Lock* v. *Furze* (1866) L.R. 1 C.P. 441; *Gas Light and Coke Co.* v. *Towse* (1887) 35 Ch.D. 519; *Pease* v. *Courteney* [1904] 2 Ch. 503.
7 *Grosvenor Hotel Co.* v. *Hamilton* [1894] 2 Q.B. 836.
8 *Jacques* v. *Millar* (1877) 6 Ch.D. 153; *Wesley* v. *Walker* (1878) 38 L.T. 284; *Singleton* [1899] 2 Ch. 320; *Milch* v. *Coburn* (1911) 27 T.L.R. 372.
9 Stair II, 9, 31; Bankt. II, 9, 21; Ersk. II, 6, 39; Bell, *Prin.* § 1222; *Rankine on Leases*, 233; *Lord Randifuird* v. *His Tenants* (1623) Mor. 15256.
10 *Robertson* v. *Cockburn* (1875) 3 R. 21.

the tenant is liable in damages,[11] for the deterioration of the premises and dislocation of management which readily follow on lack of occupation and maintenance. The executors of a deceased tenant are probably liable to the landlord for loss caused by the failure of the heir to take up a lease held by the deceased tenant and to implement any outstanding prestations thereof.[12] It is not a sufficient excuse that a non-essential part of the subjects let is still wanting,[13] or that the former tenant is still in actual possession.[14]

The measure of damages will be arrived at by consideration of the loss actually sustained by reason of the failure to take possession and the extra cost of putting the premises in good order after the period of non-possession. If the tenant fails completely to take possession the damages would be the difference between the contractual rent and the rent obtainable from another tenant.[15]

Obligation to retain possession

Unless there has been a lawful transfer to a subtenant or assignee, or such legal grounds exist as justify the tenant in throwing up the lease,[16] a tenant is obliged to remain in possession and not to abandon the subjects of let. The requisite possession may, in the absence of contrary stipulation, such as a clause requiring personal residence,[17] be retained vicariously.[18] The landlord's remedies on breach of the tenant's obligation as to possession may be to terminate the lease, as where the tenant received a substantial prison sentence,[19] or where the failure is merely covering a prohibited sublet or assignation,[20] or to demand resumption of possession, or to sue for damages.[21] In such a case there must be taken into account all damage and loss which arises naturally and directly from the tenant's failure to possess the subjects; so, under this head, have been considered the loss done to the custom and goodwill of an inn by its being shut to customers for a considerable period,[22] damage to a house by boys entering it while unoccupied, to the amount of necessary repairs,[23] damage by weather and deterioration and lack of maintenance of a villa, measured by the sum which would be required to renew defects over and above ordinary wear

11 *Graham* v. *Stevenson* (1792) Hume 781; *Mathieson* v. *Nicolson* (1819) 2 Mur. 141. See also *Smith* v. *Henderson* (1897) 24 R. 1102.
12 *Bethune* v. *Morgan* (1874) 2 R. 186; *Scott's Exors* v. *Bethune* (1876) 3 R. 816.
13 *Duncan* v. *McDougal* (1796) Hume 792.
14 *Lisk* v. *Rob* (1674) 1 Br.S. 715.
15 *Cf. Ex p. Llynvi Coal and Iron Co.* (1871) L.R. 7 Ch. 28.
16 A tenant who has illegally abandoned the subjects is not entitled to be reinstated: *Taylor* v. *Maxwell* (1728) Mor. 15310; *Taylor* v. *Taylor* (1826) 2 W. & Sh. 101.
17 *Rankine on Leases*, 3rd ed., p. 235, for examples.
18 *Lander* v. *Bagley's Contract* [1892] 3 Ch. 41.
19 *Blair Trust* v. *Gilbert*, 1940 S.L.T. 322, affd. 1941 S.N. 2.
20 *Durham* v. *Henderson* (1773) Mor. 15283; *E. Dalhousie* v. *Wilson* (1802) M. 15311; *Munro* v. *Miller*, Dec. 11, 1811, F.C.; *Watson* v. *Douglas*, Dec. 13, 1811, F.C.; *Young's Trs.* v. *Anderson* (1809) Hume 843.
21 *Graham* v. *Stevenson* (1792) Hume 781; *Whitelaw* v. *Fulton* (1871) 10 M. 27; *Smith* v. *Henderson* (1897) 24 R. 1102.
22 *Graham* v. *Stevenson* (1792) Hume 781.
23 *Bell* v. *Greer* (1891) 8 Sh.Ct.Rep. 215.

and tear,[24] damage to a house from exposure to damp, frost and dirt, damage caused by burst water-pipes, and broken windows consequent on the deserted appearance of the house.[25] But though it is obligatory to plenish and heat a shop, it is not obligatory to open it for business.[26]

Where personal residence is a stipulation a reasonable time is allowed a tenant to enter,[27] but he is not excused simply because of circumstances such as absence on public service,[28] fugitation or banishment,[29] imprisonment,[30] residence by a tenant and his family,[31] or possession by a manager and subtenants,[32] or occasional residence for short periods [33] even with a resident manager.[34]

In *Smith* v. *Harrison & Co.'s Trustee* [35] a tenant granted a trust-deed and his trustee abandoned the lease: the landlord agreed to take over at a valuation certain buildings which the tenant would have been entitled to remove, but the landlord was held entitled to retain the price and set off against the trustee's claim for that amount his own loss due to the premature abandonment of the lease. This loss was ascertained by reference to the diminished rents probably obtainable during what remained of the lease.

Obligation not to invert possession

Inversion of possession on a tenant's part involves a course of conduct inconsistent with the objects of his lease and to some extent contrary to them, and possibly even involving alterations in the subjects let, done without the consent of his landlord.[36] It does not extend to occasional misconduct. In the absence of qualification in the lease, a tenant is entitled to the exclusive and reasonable use of the subjects let for all purposes not contrary to or inconsistent with the general purposes of the lease. So no challenge can be made of selling a different kind of goods in a shop,[37] nor an occasional auction sale in a shop let for retail trading.[38] But a tenant cannot set up an ale-house on a subject let as a " farm," [39] use a building on his farm as a posting station,[40] establish a factory on ground let as a

24 *Wiseman* v. *Alley* (1891) 9 Sh.Ct.Rep. 254.
25 *Smith* v. *Henderson* (1897) 24 R. 1102.
26 *Whitelaw* v. *Fulton* (1871) 10 M. 27. See also *Keith* v. *Reid* (1870) 8 M.(H.L.) 110; *Gordon* v. *Crawford* (1825) 4 S. 95.
27 *Stirling* v. *Miller*, June 29, 1813, F.C.
28 *Cameron* v. *Cameron*, Dec. 18, 1810, F.C., but modern emergency legislation limits this principle.
29 *Drummond* v. *McPherson* (1799) M.Appx.Tack. 6.
30 *Blair Trust* v. *Gilbert*, 1940 S.L.T. 322; 1941 S.N. 2.
31 *Drummond, supra.*
32 *Cameron, supra.*
33 *Edmond* v. *Reid* (1871) 9 M. 782.
34 *Smart* v. *Warnocks* (1883) 20 S.L.R. 863.
35 (1893) 21 R. 330.
36 *Rankine on Leases*, 236; *Leck* v. *Merryflats Patent Brick Co.* (1868) 5 S.L.R. 619.
37 *Gordon* v. *Crawford* (1825) 4 S. 95.
38 *Keith* v. *Reid* (1870) 8 M.(H.L.) 110. See too *Walker* v. *Grant* (1838) 1 D. 38; *Morrison* v. *Forsyth*, 1909 S.C. 329.
39 *Miln* v. *Mitchell* (1787) Mor. 15254.
40 *Baillie* v. *Mackay* (1842) 4 D. 1520.

" corn-mill and mill-lands," [41] use a meal-mill as a saw-mill,[42] erect a dwelling-house on a piece of ground intended as a flower-plot,[43] use the stables and offices (with or without alterations) for the accommodation of stage-coach horses,[44] whether or not it injures the interest of the landlord in a neighbouring inn, nor is he entitled to sublet land to a railway company for use as a general traffic siding,[45] to turn a grist-mill into a flour-mill,[46] or to turn a market-garden into a place of public amusement,[47] or to convert a shop into a showroom for exhibition of waxworks,[48] nor to use rented rooms for committing suicide,[49] nor presumably to keep a brothel or other public nuisance.

It is still more serious if the change involves structural alterations on the premises,[50] such as building a chimney,[51] or a railway,[52] building a " house " and using it as a stable.[53] It is a matter of circumstances whether showcases and advertisement signs may be objected to.[54] Where the change of use constitutes a nuisance the inversion is aggravated,[55] and if the tenant's action contravenes an express stipulation in the lease the breach is also more serious. Inversion does not extend to isolated acts such as poaching [56] nor to merely altering the position of furniture and pictures.[57]

The question must in every case be one of the construction of the lease as between the parties, as to what inference must be drawn from the wording of the lease and the circumstances in which it was granted and the nature and kind of use apparently contemplated when it was entered into, subject to such alterations as may have been tacitly or expressly imported into it during its currency.

What is incompetent for the tenant to do is equally unlawful for his assignee or subtenant, and an assignation or sublease, if granted for any purpose which would be or would involve inversion of possession, is invalid to that extent.[58]

A tenant may also subject himself to liability by misuse of the premises,

41 *Ford* v. *Hillocks* (1808) Mor. " Tack." Appx. 17.
42 *Bayley* v. *Addison* (1901) 8 S.L.T. 379.
43 *Inglis* v. *Balfour* (1778) Mor. " Tack." Appx. 34. See *Armstrong* v. *Bryson* (1807) Hume 837 and *Kehoe* v. *M. Lansdowne* [1893] A.C. 451 (priest building huts for evicted tenants).
44 *D. Argyll* v. *McArthur* (1861) 23 D. 1326.
45 *Mercer* v. *Esk Valley Ry.* (1867) 5 M. 1024.
46 *Bayley* v. *Addison* (1901) 8 S.L.T. 379.
47 *Heriot's Hosp.* v. *Heriot's Gardener* (1751) Elch. *Pact. Illicit.* No. 20.
48 *Leechman* v. *Sievewright* (1826) 4 S. 683.
49 *A* v. *B's Trs.* (1906) 13 S.L.T. 830.
50 *Muir* v. *Wilson* (1822) 1 S. 406 (stove setting building on fire).
51 *Leck* v. *Fulton* (1854) 17 D. 408.
52 *Leck* v. *Merryflats Brick Co.* (1868) 5 S.L.R. 619; *Galbraith's Tr.* v. *Eglinton Iron Co.* (1868) 7 M. 167.
53 *Hood* v. *Miller* (1855) 17 D. 411.
54 *British Linen Co.* v. *Purdie* (1905) 7 F. 923; *Morrison* v. *Forsyth*, 1909 S.C. 329.
55 *Muir* v. *Wilson, supra*; *Skene* v. *Maberly* (1820) 2 Mur. 352; 1 S. 369; *Mowbray* v. *Ewbank* (1833) 11 S. 714. But see *D'Eresby's Trs.* v. *Strathearn Hydro* (1873) 1 R. 35.
56 *Rankine on Leases*, 236.
57 *Miller* v. *Stewart* (1899) 2 F. 309.
58 Bell, *Comm.* I, 76; II, 32; Bell, *Prin.*, § 1274; *Anderson* v. *Alexander*, July 10, 1811, F.C.; *Leechman* v. *Sievewright* (1826) 4 S. 683; *Gordon* v. *Crawford* (1825) 4 S. 95.

as by overloading a store or warehouse [59]: while a building must be reasonably fit for the purpose for which it is let, the tenant is bound to use it reasonably, having regard in the case of trade to the general and recognised practice.

The right of the landlord to object to inversion is readily lost by acquiescence from which his consent may clearly be inferred,[60] or by express renunciation, though non-use of powers within the scope of the subjects let will not restrict the grant or measure its scope.[61] So too a landlord may be barred by acquiescence from objecting to miscropping.[62] In such, as in other cases,[63] notice of the claim must be made timeously.

If possession be inverted the landlord is usually justified in rescinding the lease or interdicting the offending action or at least claiming damages. The measure of damages would depend largely on the nature of the inversion: in general the cost of effecting restitution of the subjects *in integrum*,[64] the loss of rent until a new tenant comes in,[65] depreciation of the property, and trouble and inconvenience are heads under which claims may be made but the topic has not yet been fully discussed in any case. The damages should in any event be such as compensate the landlord for the damage to his property.

Assignation and sublease

Assignation of a lease is impliedly prohibited,[66] save in the case of leases of urban subjects, and leases of extraordinary duration.[67] The same rules apply to subletting. Assignation and/or subletting is frequently expressly prohibited. Breach of an express or implied prohibition is frequently fenced with an irritancy clause which, as being conventional, is not purgeable [68] but provision might also be made for damages. A prohibition is strictly construed and exclusion of one category does not imply that of the other too.[69] Consent must be actually given and is not implied by the absence of prohibition.[70] Damages for unauthorised assignation have been held to be such as would compensate the landlord for the breach, and may include the loss from having an insolvent tenant and damage to the premises caused by his dangerous business.[71]

59 *Caledonian Ry.* v. *Greenock Sacking Co.* (1875) 2 R. 671; *Corrie, Mackie & Co.* v. *Stewart* (1885) 22 S.L.R. 350; *Glebe Sugar Co.* v. *Paterson* (1900) 2 F. 615.

60 *Ferguson* v. *Methven* (1857) 19 D. 794; *Moore* v. *Munro* (1896) 4 S.L.T. 172; *Skene* v. *Maberly* (1822) 1 S. 369; *Young* v. *Ramsay* (1824) 2 S. 793; affd. 1 W. & S. 560; *D. Portland* v. *Samson* (1843) 5 D. 476; contrast *Macdonald* v. *Campbell* (1889) 16 R. 540.

61 *Ewan's Trs.* v. *Muirkirk Iron Co.* (1850) 12 D. 622.

62 *Taylor* v. *Duff's Trs.* (1869) 7 M. 351; *Baird* v. *Mount* (1874) 2 R. 101; *Lamb* v. *Mitchell's Trs.* (1883) 10 R. 640.

63 *Elliott's Trs.* v. *Elliott* (1894) 21 R. 858.

64 *Cf. Henderson* v. *Thorn* [1893] 2 Q.B. 164; *Joyner* v. *Weeks* [1891] 2 Q.B. 31.

65 *Cf. Birch* v. *Clifford* (1891) 8 T.L.R. 103.

66 Bell, *Prin.* § 1214; *Mackintosh* v. *May* (1895) 22 R. 345.

67 *Robb* v. *Brearton* (1895) 22 R. 885. If the subjects are furnished, they are probably no assignable.

68 *Lyon* v. *Irvine* (1874) 1 R. 512; see *Porter* v. *Paterson* (1813) Hume 862.

69 Bell, *Comm.* I, 77.

70 *Dalrymple's Trs.* v. *Brown*, 1945 S.C. 190.

71 *Williams* v. *Earle* (1868) L.R. 3 Q.B. 739; *Lepla* v. *Rogers* [1893] 1 Q.B. 31; *Cohen* v. *Popular Restaurants Ltd.* [1917] 1 K.B. 480.

In the case of subleases the subtenant may claim damages against the principal tenant for breach of obligations in the sublease such as under the warrandice implied or expressed in the sublease for eviction, if the landlord's or principal tenant's right is reduced [72] or the landlord exercises a right of resumption reserved to him in the principal lease.[73]

No rights and obligations arise *ex contractu* as between lessor and subtenant, so that there can be no direct action by subtenant against landlord for damages for eviction if the principal lease is reduced, and even though the warrandice clause therein be expressed in favour of subtenants.[74] The subtenant can only come against the tenant, founding on the warrandice expressed or implied in the sublease, and leaving the tenant to obtain reliefs against the landlord.[75] If recourse against the tenant is impossible, the subtenant has no redress.[76-78]

Maintenance of subjects—agricultural

In an agricultural lease a tenant is bound to maintain and uphold buildings and fences,[79] which the landlord was bound to put into a tenantable state of repair [80] at the tenant's entry, and to leave them in the same tenantable condition as he received them,[81] except for natural decay and fair wear and tear.[82] The tenant's failure to do so will give rise to a claim of damages [83] which will be measured by the expense reasonably required to put the subjects into such a tenantable condition as the tenant should have maintained them in.[84] But a tenant is not bound either during a lease or at the risk to repair extraordinary damage caused by *damnum fatale* or pure accident such as fire or even by a storm of extraordinary violence,[85] nor to make good ordinary wear and tear or disrepair due to defective construction.

Where a tenant bound himself during the currency of the lease to reclaim certain waste lands and failed fully to complete this obligation, the landlord was held entitled to damages in respect of the failure, the damages being the price at which the landlord would require to get the

72 *Middleton* v. *Yorstoun* (1826) 5 S. 162; *Middleton* v. *Megget* (1828) 7 S. 76; *Dick* v. *Taylor's Trs.* (1831) 10 S. 19; *cf. Crichton* v. *Meason* (1828) 6 S. 403; and see *Laidlaw* v. *Wilson* (1830) 8 S. 440.

73 *Downie* v. *Laird* (1902) 10 S.L.T. 28.

74 *Maxwell* v. *Queensberry's Exors.* (1827) 5 S. 935; revd. 5 W. & Sh. 771.

75 *Dick* v. *Taylor's Trs.* (1831) 10 S. 19.

76-78 *Hutchison* v. *Queensberry's Exors.* (1828) 6 S. 849; *Watson's Reps.* v. *Turner* (1831) 11 S. 687.

79 As to march fences, see *Dudgeon* v. *Howden*, Nov. 23, 1813, F.C.; *Rankine on Landownership*, 610. But the landlord cannot erect additional subdivision fences during the lease so as to increase the tenant's liability: Rankine, *Leases*, 251.

80 Bankton, I, 20, 10; II, 11, 21; Ersk. II, 6, 39; Bell, *Prin.*, § 1253; *Buchanan* v. *Stark* (1776) 5 B.S. 515.

81 Bankton, *supra*; Ersk., *supra*; Bell, *Prin.*, § 1254; *Whites* v. *Houston* (1707) Mor. 15258.

82 Bell, *Prin.*, § 1254; *Mossman* v. *Brocket* (1810) Hume 850; *Napier* v. *Ferrier* (1847) 9 D. 1354; *Johnstone* v. *Hughan* (1894) 21 R. 777.

83 In the case of the tenant's bankruptcy the landlord has a preferable claim and may enforce it by retention: *Munro* v. *Fraser* (1858) 21 D. 103.

84 *Joyner* v. *Weeks* [1891] 2 Q.B. 31, 43, *per* Esher M.R.

85 *York Buildings Co.* v. *Adams* (1741) Mor. 10127; *Clerk* v. *Baird* (1741) Mor. 10128.

work done.[86] After the expiry of a lease the landlord cannot call on a tenant to execute operations on the subjects of let which he should have done from time to time during the currency of the lease, and the only remedy for a breach of such obligations is a claim of damages.[87]

The Agricultural Holdings (Scotland) Act 1949, s. 5 (2) requires a landlord to put fixed equipment, *i.e.* buildings, fences and dykes, gates, ditches, open and tile drains,[88] pens, roads, water and sewerage systems, electrical installations, etc.,[89] into a thorough state of repair and to repair and renew it as necessary. The tenant must, on the other hand, maintain the fixed equipment [89] in as good a state of repair (natural decay and fair wear and tear excepted) as it was in after being repaired by the landlord, or after being replaced or renewed.

Apart from statutory provisions a tenant is impliedly bound to stock a holding, to care for the buildings, and cultivate the land in a reasonable and careful manner.[90]

By statute [91] a landlord may recover from a tenant on the latter's quitting the holding on the termination of the tenancy compensation for any dilapidation or deterioration of, or damage to, any part of the holding or anything in or on the holding, caused by non-fulfilment by the tenant of his responsibilities to farm in accordance with the rules of good husbandry. Alternatively [92] the landlord may claim compensation in respect of these matters under a written lease on the tenant's quitting the holding on the termination of the tenancy. The amount of compensation in the former case shall be the cost, as at the date of the tenant's quitting the holding, of making good the dilapidation, deterioration or damage.[93]

Furthermore,[94] where the landlord shows that at that date the value of the holding generally has been reduced whether by reason of any such dilapidation, deterioration or damage or by non-fulfilment by the tenant of his responsibilities to farm in accordance with the rules of good husbandry, the landlord is entitled to recover compensation, so far as not already compensated therefor [95] of an amount equal to the decrease attributable thereto in the value of the holding. The quantum of this compensation will depend on the amount of expenditure required to bring the land and buildings back to proper condition and also on the loss incurred during the period when the subjects are not capable of earning the full rent.[96]

86 *Davidson* v. *Macpherson* (1889) 30 S.L.R. 2.
87 *Sinclair* v. *Caithness Flagstone Co.* (1898) 25 R. 703.
88 See *Wight* v. *Newton*, 1911 S.C. 762.
89 Defined, s. 93 (1).
90 Ersk. II, 6, 39.
91 Agricultural Holdings (Scotland) Act 1949, s. 57 (1).
92 *Ibid.* s. 57 (3).
93 *Ibid.* s. 57 (2).
94 *Ibid.* s. 58.
95 Under s. 57 (1) or (3), *supra*.
96 See also the conditions and supplementary provisions in s. 59, and also s. 63. On questions affecting claims, see *Douglas* v. *Cassillis and Culzean Estates*, 1944 S.C. 355; *Edinburgh Corpn.* v. *Gray*, 1948 S.C. 538; *Adam* v. *Smythe*, 1948 S.C. 445.

Maintenance of subjects—urban

The landlord is bound at common law to put a house into habitable or tenantable condition at entry and to maintain it in wind- and water-tight condition during the currency of the lease.[97] But the tenant is bound to take reasonable care of the premises,[98] and not to injure or damage the subjects of let by fault or negligence,[99] which may be done by failure to take and retain possession of the subjects [1]: he is liable in damages for failure to take such care.[98] But the tenant is not bound to repair against ordinary wear and tear, natural decay or *damnum fatale* though he must execute ordinary repairs to keep the premises tenantable if bound to leave them so at the expiry of the lease.[2] Even if the tenant binds himself in the lease to execute necessary repairs to a house, the landlord may be bound to execute them if they prove to be substantial and radical, or at least in such a case, the tenant will not be bound to perform them.[3] In *Turner's Trs.* v. *Steel*,[4] Lord McLaren expressed the opinion that in the event of a dispute between landlord and tenant as to the liability for particular repairs, the tenant is not entitled, at least if he holds the subjects for subletting, to leave the premises vacant and claim damages for loss of rent, but must execute the necessary repairs himself so as to minimise his claim of damages for that loss, which would be recoverable as well as the outlay on repairs.

The measure of damages exigible from a tenant in default will not necessarily be the cost of repairs necessary,[5] but the extent of deterioration in value of the general condition of the subjects due to the tenant's lack of reasonable care,[6] or as expressed in English cases, the extent to which the marketable value of the reversion is injured.[7] The real question is what damage the owner has really suffered.[8]

If the action is brought after the expiry of the lease, this measure is probably the sum required to put the premises into the reasonable state of repair in which the tenant should have left them, fair wear and tear

97 *Mechan* v. *Watson*, 1907 S.C. 25.

98 *Whitelaw* v. *Fulton* (1871) 10 M. 27; *Mickel* v. *McCoard*, 1913 S.C. 896; *Smith* v. *Henderson* (1897) 24 R. 1102; *Earl of Mansfield* v. *Caird* (1884) 21 S.L.R. 720; *Turner's Trs.* v. *Steel* (1900) 2 F. 363.

99 *Sutherland* v. *Robertson* (1736) Mor. 13979; *Hardie* v. *Black* (1768) Mor. 10133; *McLellan* v. *Ker* (1797) Mor. 10134.

1 *Supra*, p. 756.

2 *Turner's Trs.* v. *Steel* (1900) 2 F. 363; *Campbell* v. *McLachlan's Exor.* (1944) 61 Sh.Ct.Rep. 86. A stipulation that the tenant bound himself to keep the subjects in repair has been held not to bind him to repair damage by fire: *Duff* v. *Fleming* (1870) 8 M. 769.

3 *Napier* v. *Ferrier* (1847) 9 D. 1354.

4 (1900) 2 F. 363.

5 *Campbell* v. *McLachlan's Exor.* (1944) 61 Sh.Ct.Rep. 86.

6 *Cf. Whitelaw* v. *Fulton* (1871) 10 M. 27.

7 *Smith* v. *Peat* (1853) 9 Ex. 161; *Mills* v. *E. London Union* (1872) L.R. 8 C.P. 79; *Willliams* v. *Williams* (1874) L.R. 9 C.P. 659; *Joyner* v. *Weeks* [1891] 2 Q.B. 31; *Henderson* v. *Thorn* [1893] 2 Q.B. 164; *Conquest* v. *Ebbetts* [1896] A.C. 490; *Gooderham and Worts Ltd.* v. *Canadian Broadcasting Corpn.* [1947] A.C. 66, 83; *James* v. *Hutton and Cook* [1950] 1 K.B. 9; *Smiley* v. *Townshend* [1950] 2 K.B. 311; *cf. Moss* v. *Christchurch R.D.C.* [1925] 2 K.B. 750; *Hutchison* v. *Davidson*, 1945 S.C. 395; *Jeffs* v. *West London Property Corpn.* [1954] J.P.L. 114.

8 *D. Westminster* v. *Swinton* [1948] 1 K.B. 524.

excepted.[9] The cost of effecting the necessary repairs may be evidence of the extent of the damage to the landlord's interest.[10] If the premises are under requisition at the end of the lease only nominal damages are recoverable.[11] In general, damages fall to be assessed as at the end of the lease.[12]

Despite the protection afforded to tenants by the Rent Act an ejection order may be made against a tenant without proof of suitable alternative accommodation if the court considers it reasonable to do so and if, *inter alia*, owing to acts of waste by or the neglect or default of the tenant or any person residing or lodging with him, the condition of the dwelling-house has, in the opinion of the court, deteriorated and, in the case of a lodger or subtenant, the tenant has not before the date of the ejection order taken reasonable steps to remove him.[13]

The Housing (Scotland) Act 1966, s. 186 subjects to a penalty any person who wilfully or by culpable negligence damages or suffers to be damaged any house provided under that Act, or any of its fittings and appurtenances, without prejudice to any remedy for the recovery of the amount of the damage.

Management—agricultural

Agricultural leases commonly contain express provisions as to the conduct and management [14] of the farm, such as an obligation to conform to the rules of good husbandry.[15] Under the Agricultural Holdings (Scotland) Act 1949, s. 12, the tenant is free notwithstanding any custom of the country or provisions of any lease or agreement to dispose of produce other than manure in any way he chooses, and to practise any system of cropping, except in the last year, and provided the tenant returns to the holding the equivalent manurial value [16] of crops sold off or takes steps to protect the holding from deterioration. But if this right is exercised in a manner which does or is likely to injure or deteriorate the holding the landlord may interdict the tenant and recover damages for any injury to or deterioration of the holding attributable to the exercise by the tenant of these statutory rights on his quitting the holding. Claims on this ground may be barred by acquiescence.[17]

In the event of deterioration the measure of damages is the injury to the landlord's reversion occasioned by the breach, which amounts in

[9] *Woodhouse* v. *Walker* (1880) 5 Q.B.D. 404, 408; *Whitham* v. *Kershaw* (1885) 16 Q.B.D. 613, 616; *Joyner* v. *Weeks* [1891] 2 Q.B. 31.

[10] *Jones* v. *Herxheimer* [1950] 2 K.B. 106; *Espir* v. *Basil Street Hotel Ltd.* [1936] 3 All E.R. 91; *James* v. *Hutton* [1950] 1 K.B. 9; *Smiley* v. *Townshend* [1950] 2 K.B. 311.

[11] *James, supra.*

[12] *Smiley* v. *Townshend* [1950] 2 K.B. 311.

[13] Rent (Scotland) Act 1971, s. 10 (1) and Sched. 3, Part I, case 3. See *Peach* v. *Lowe* [1947] 1 All E.R. 441.

[14] See *Tweeddale* v. *Brown* (1821) 2 Mur. 563.

[15] *Maxwell* v. *McMurray* (1776) 5 B.S. 515.

[16] See *Brown* v. *Mitchell*, 1910 S.C. 369.

[17] *Murray's Trs.* v. *Gordon* (1806) Hume 823; *Fraser* v. *Maitland* (1824) 2 Shaw's App. 37; *cf. Hall* v. *McGill* (1847) 9 D. 1557; *Taylor* v. *Duff's Trs.* (1869) 7 M. 351.

practice to the diminution in rent which can be obtained on reietting, or the allowance the landlord must make to an incoming tenant by way of a reduction in rent or a period rent-free if the land is below proper condition.[18] Where the only complaint is that manure has been improperly sold or removed,[19] loss of manurial value may be a good guide in assessing the damages.

Liquidate damages

A landlord's right to higher rent or other provision in a lease for payment of liquidate damages for the breach or non-fulfilment of any of the terms or conditions in the lease, is restricted by statute to the damage actually suffered by him in consequence of the breach or non-fulfilment.[20]

The courts have not in the past attempted to adject rules of good husbandry to a lease, and parties have frequently supplied the omission themselves. In this connection it has been held that a tenant who was sued for damages for deterioration of the lands arising from non-observance of the rules of good husbandry was entitled to absolvitor on proof that he had followed the course of cultivation laid down in the lease.[21] The court will only interfere to restrain unwarrantable acts or to exact compensation therefor if committed.[22]

Management towards the ish

Obligations to ensure that the outgoing tenant does not take undue profit out of the land are strictly enforced.[23] Damages have been given against tenants for failure to leave young grass hained for a hay crop (which contravened the rotation of crops in operation on the farm) even though the tenants proposed to leave the same acreage of young grass as they had received hained at their entry.[24] The measure of damage was the value of what the landlord had been deprived of, *viz.* a hay crop, valued at so much per acre.[25]

A departing tenant customarily enjoys certain periods of grace extending beyond the actual date of termination of the lease to thresh his last crop, and damages have been given where a tenant was ejected before the expiry of his period of grace allowed by local custom.[26]

18 *Williams* v. *Lewis* [1915] 3 K.B. 493. In *Fraser* v. *Macdonald* (1834) 12 S. 684, the measure of damage by miscropping, etc., was said to be the sum required to put the farm back in the condition it should have been kept and left in. See also *Hamilton* v. *Hamilton* (1825) 4 Mur. 6; *Thomson's Reps.* v. *Oliphant* (1824) 3 S. 275.

19 On this see Agricultural Holdings (Scotland) Act 1949, s. 13.

20 Agricultural Holdings (Scotland) Act 1949, s. 16; *cf. Wilson* v. *Love* [1896] 1 Q.B. 626. For certificates of bad husbandry, see ss. 28 *et seq.*

21 *Stark* v. *Edmondstone* (1826) 5 S. 45.

22 *Meldrum* v. *Gibb* (1738) Elch. Tack. 4.

23 *Lyall* v. *Cooper* (1832) 11 S. 96.

24 *McCulloch* v. *Grierson* (1862) 1 M. 53.

25 *Ibid.*

26 *McLeod* v. *Crawford*, noted in *Anderson* v. *Tod* (1809) Hume 842.

Management—urban

Reference has already been made to the legal implications in urban leases relative to assignation and subletting, and the obligations to take, maintain and not invert possession.[27] Various other conditions are commonly expressly included in leases of urban subjects, such as prohibiting the establishment or carrying on of any business or trade, or of noxious trades or of certain specified trades.[28] Breach of such an agreement may give rise to an action of damages, though contravention is more frequently sanctioned by an irritancy clause. If the landlord persistently violates a material condition of the lease, the tenant is entitled to rescind the lease.[29] The converse proposition is also true and a less essential breach of the contract will justify a claim of damages. Interdict may also be invoked in many cases.

Among express restrictions commonly imposed on tenants are a prohibition of building on the subjects of let [30] and a prohibition of carrying on any or certain specified businesses or trades on the premises. Breach of these conditions will frequently be so essential as to demand declarator of irritancy. The measure of damages for breach of a covenant against alterations has been held in England to be, not the cost of restoring the premises, but the diminution in value of the reversion due to the breach of contract.[31]

In the converse case where premises are expressly let for a particular purpose of the kind usually prohibited, such as a public-house, the landlord may obtain interdict [32] or damages [33] against a tenant who seeks to relinquish his licence prior to the termination of the lease, on securing another elsewhere: the damages were assessed [33] on the principle of *Hadley* v. *Baxendale* [34] at the difference between the rent obtainable for a licensed and that for an unlicensed shop on a lease for five years.

Prohibition on carrying on business or trade covers cases where no payment is taken, *e.g.* a charitable home,[35] a hospital,[36] but possibly a doctor's private nursing home is not a trading place.[37] "Trade" has apparently a more restricted meaning than "business." [38] Letting lodgings is apparently a business,[39] as is altering the premises into flats,[40]

27 *Supra*, pp. 756–760.
28 See cases in Rankine, *Leases* (3rd ed.), 440 *et seq.*
29 *Davie* v. *Stark* (1876) 3 R. 1114.
30 This is an inversion at common law. Building a wall is an infringement: *Bowes* v. *Law* (1870) L.R. 9 Eq. 636.
31 *Whitham* v. *Kershaw* (1885) 16 Q.B.D. 613; *Espir* v. *Basil Street Hotel Co.* [1936] 3 All E.R. 91.
32 *Gordon* v. *Smith* (1899) 15 Sh.Ct.Rep. 261.
33 *Don* v. *Brew* (1879) 2 Guthrie Sel.Sh.Ct.Cas. 117.
34 (1854) 9 Ex. 341, 354.
35 *Rolls* v. *Miller* (1884) 27 Ch.D. 71.
36 *Bramwell* v. *Lacy* (1879) 10 Ch.D. 691; *Portman* v. *Home Hospital Lessee* (1884) 27 Ch.D. 71, 81, note; *Tod-Heatley* v. *Benham* (1889) 40 Ch.D. 80.
37 *Graham* v. *Shiels* (1901) 8 S.L.T. 368.
38 *Rolls*, *supra*, 85.
39 *Barton* v. *Keeble* [1928] Ch. 517; *cf. Thorn* v. *Madden* [1925] Ch. 847.
40 *Barton* v. *Reed* [1932] 1 Ch. 362; see also *Day* v. *Waldron* (1919) 88 L.J.K.B 937.

and letting gable-ends to billposters is to permit trade,[41] and possibly also a breach of a clause forbidding subletting.[42] So is carrying on a boys' school.[43]

Where the prohibition is an express restriction to the use of the premises as a dwelling-house a slight contravention is a breach of the stipulation though probably not sufficient to incur an irritancy.[44]

Advertisements may contravene a building prohibition [45] or a covenant against trade,[46] or possibly subletting,[47] or one of use only as a private house,[48] or one expressly against notice of trade or business,[49] but not one against injury, annoyance or inconvenience.[50]

Prohibition on noxious trade

The principal question in such a case is one of interpretation, whether the trade in question is noxious or nauseous or a nuisance within the terms of the prohibition. The construction adopted is that in favour of freedom,[51] but much depends on situation and whether the trade were carried on there at the time of the lease, in which case it could hardly fall within the clause.[52]

Prohibition of particular trades

The cases most commonly specifically forbidden are those of butcher,[53]

[41] *Tubbs* v. *Esser* (1909) 26 T.L.R. 145.

[42] *Heard* v. *Stuart* (1907) 24 T.L.R. 104.

[43] *Wanton* v. *Coppard* [1899] 1 Ch. 92.

[44] *e.g.* business sign on window-blind: *Wilkinson* v. *Rogers* (1863) 2 De G.J. & S. 62; see also *Evans* v. *Davis* (1879) 10 Ch.D. 747; building studio in garden: *Patman* v. *Harland* (1881) 17 Ch.D. 353; but not stable with bedroom: *Russell* v. *Baber* (1870) 18 W.R. 1021; *cf. Murison* v. *Wallace* (1883) 10 R. 1239; school in a large house: *Ewing* v. *Hastie* (1878) 5 R. 439; *cf. Colville* v. *Carrick* (1883) 10 R. 1241; *German* v. *Chapman* (1877) 7 Ch.D. 271; *Hobson* v. *Tulloch* [1898] 1 Ch. 424; *Wanton* v. *Coppard* [1899] 1 Ch. 92; *Reckitt* v. *Cody* [1920] 2 Ch. 453; day-school and dancing academy in a house: *Wickenden* v. *Webster* (1856) 6 E. & B. 387; see also *Johnstone* v. *Hall* (1856) 2 K. & J. 414; but a school is not a nuisance: *Harrison* v. *Good* (1871) L.R. 11 Eq. 338; and " school " does not include a school of music: *Lawrence* v. *South County Freeholds Ltd.* (1939) 55 T.L.R. 662; taking paying guests regularly: *Thorn* v. *Madden* [1925] Ch. 847; *cf. Porter* v. *Gibbons* (1904) 48 S.J. 559; hospital: *Frost* v. *K. Edward VII Welsh Assocn.* [1918] 2 Ch. 180.

[45] *Pocock* v. *Gilham* (1883) Cab. & E. 104.

[46] *Tubbs* v. *Esser* (1909) 26 T.L.R. 145.

[47] *Heard* v. *Stuart* (1907) 24 T.L.R. 104.

[48] *Wilkinson* v. *Rogers* (1863) 2 De G.J. & S. 62.

[49] *Att.-Gen.* v. *Playhouse Ltd.* (1903) 19 T.L.R. 580; *Evans* v. *Davis* (1878) 10 Ch.D. 747.

[50] *Our Boys' Clothing Co.* v. *Holborn Viaduct Land Co.* (1896) 12 T.L.R. 344.

[51] The prohibition in various terms has been held to apply to slaughter-houses: *Lauder*, June 16, 1815, F.C.; *Porteous* v. *Grieve* (1839) 1 D. 561. Prohibitory clauses have, however, not cut at cattle shows and sales: *Anderson* v. *Aberdeen Agricultural Hall Co.* (1879) 6 R. 901; *cf. Hall* v. *Ewin* (1888) 37 Ch.D. 74; a private lunatic asylum: *Doe* d. *Wetherall* v. *Bird* (1834) 6 C. & P. 195; a cholera hospital: *Mutter* v. *Fyffe* (1848) 11 D. 211, 303; *cf. Metropolitan Asylums* v. *Hill* (1881) 6 App.Cas. 193; steam-engine when not offensive: *Frame* v. *Cameron* (1864) 3 M. 290; use as a licensed grocer's shop: *Jones* v. *Thorne* (1823) 1 B. & C. 715; or as a match store: *Hickman* v. *Isaacs* (1861) 4 L.T. 285; or as a hospital: *Frost* v. *King Edward VII Welsh Assocn.* [1918] 2 Ch. 180; or for a fish-frying business: *D. Devonshire* v. *Brookshaw* (1899) 81 L.T. 83; *cf. Errington* v. *Birt* (1911) 105 L.T. 373.

[52] *Gutteridge* v. *Munyard* (1834) 7 C. & P. 129.

[53] See *Doe* d. *Gaskell* v. *Spry* (1818) 1 B. & A. 617; *Doe* d. *Davies* v. *Elsam* (1828) Moo. & M. 189.

innkeeper,[54] and publican,[55] and questions of construction again arise, but examples of other specific prohibitions are found [56] or prohibitions of all but a particular trade,[57] which are not broken by merely incidental transgressions.[58]

Interest on rent

In the absence of express stipulation it remains undecided whether interest runs *ex lege* on arrears of rent. Rent is not mentioned by any authoritative writer as bearing interest *ex lege*,[59] and analogous payments do not.[60] The general view is that rent does not carry interest.[61] In the usual lease interest is expressly provided for and in that case it will probably run from the date of citation in an action or of a charge to enforce payment rather than from the date of a formal extrajudicial demand for payment.[62] If a question arises between landlord and tenant the running of interest on the sum due can only be avoided by consigning it or paying it to account.[63] Acquiescence in a local custom of postponing actual receipt of the rent or of irregular settlement of accounts may bar a landlord's claim for interest.[64]

Pactional rent and penalty

Formal leases frequently provide for liquidate damages in the shape of pactional rent [65] for the breach of certain conditions of the lease, particularly those relating to management. Such clauses are modified by statute. The Agricultural Holdings (Scotland) Act 1949, s. 16, replacing earlier provisions, provides that, notwithstanding any provision in a lease requiring a tenant to pay a higher rent or other liquidate damages in the event of a breach or non-fulfilment of any of the terms or conditions in the lease, the landlord is not entitled to recover any sum in consequence of any breach or non-fulfilment in excess of the damage actually suffered by him in consequence of the breach or non-fulfilment. This provision supersedes

[54] See *Ewing* v. *Campbell* (1877) 5 R. 230; *Gold* v. *Holdsworth* (1870) 8 M. 1006.

[55] *Lorden* v. *Brooke-Hitching* [1927] 2 K.B. 237; *Dartford Brewery Co.* v. *Till* (1906) 95 L.T. 636; *Wells* v. *Attenborough* (1871) 24 L.T. 312; *Bp. of St. Albans* v. *Battersby* (1878) 3 Q.B.D. 359; and contrast *Holt* v. *Collyer* (1881) 16 Ch.D. 718; *London Land Co.* v. *Field* (1881) 16 Ch.D. 645. See also *Ranken* v. *Hunt* (1894) 10 The Reports, 249; *Fairclough* v. *Whitmore* (1895) 64 L.J.Ch. 386; *Seaward* v. *Paterson* (1896) 13 T.L.R. 525 (clubs); *Fitz* v. *Iles* [1893] 1 Ch. 77 (coffee-house).

[56] *e.g.* ladies' outfitter, *Smart* v. *Diplock* (1889) 43 Ch.D. 343; draper, *Wills* v. *Adams* (1908) 25 T.L.R.85.

[57] *e.g.* tailor, *Heard* v. *Stuart* (1907) 24 T.L.R. 104; hatter or hosier, *Wartski* v. *Mecker* (1914) 110 L.T. 473. As to restrictions on letting adjoining shops, see *Randall* v. *Summers*, 1919 S.C. 396; *L.S.G. Ltd.* v. *Lawrence* (1925) 42 T.L.R. 85.

[58] *Smart, supra*; *Randall, supra*; *Lewis & Co. (Westminster) Ltd.* v. *Bell Property Trust* [1940] 1 Ch. 345.

[59] Bankt. I, 21, 6; Ersk.III, 3, 77, 80, 82; Bell, *Comm.* II, 647; *Prin.* § 32.

[60] Chap. 23, *supra*.

[61] *Dawson* v. *Pringle* (1802) M. Appx. Annual rent, 5, *arguendo*; *Moncrieff* v. *Dundas* (1835) 14 S. 61; *Stirling & Dunfermline Ry.* v. *Edinburgh & Glasgow Ry.* (1857) 19 D. 598.

[62] *Cf.* cases of feuduties: *Tweeddale* v. *Aytoun* (1842) 4 D. 862.

[63] *Graham* v. *Moir* (1821) 1 S. 16.

[64] *McLeod* v. *McLeod* (1799) Hume 800.

[65] See *Baird* v. *Mount* (1874) 2 R. 101.

the common-law rule that a pactional rent clause will be modified only if it is unconscionable, extravagant or exorbitant having regard to the circumstances in which it was made,[66] while a penalty clause may be modified by the court to the extent of damage actually suffered.[67]

Such a provision in a lease does not confer on the tenant a right to infringe the lease on payment of the penalty, unless the lease should expressly allow him to do so.[68] It is " by and attour performance." The purpose of such a clause was, however, largely to avoid proof of the amount of damage where this would be complex, difficult or expensive,[69] or where it would be impossible at the time of the lease to foresee the full extent of uncertain injury which might be incurred by the breach or the difficulty and expense of proving it.[70] These difficulties the statute brings back.

Penalty

A penalty provision such as on failure to make punctual payment of rent is subject to the usual rules of modification of penalties.[71] Accordingly, if the penalty stated exceeds the amount of damage suffered, it is not exigible in full but will be equitably modified to cover the actual damage only.[72] Like pactional rent, a penalty provision does not avoid the necessity of performance but proof of actual damage suffered is avoided. Section 16 of the Agricultural Holdings (Scotland) Act 1949 does not affect penalty provisions so that equitable modification may be sought only on common-law principles,[71] the onus being on the defender to prove the need for and the extent of modification.[73]

A prohibition on a certain use of subjects fenced by a penalty does not give the tenant the option to contravene the prohibition on paying the penalty: it remains an absolute prohibition.[74]

Irritancy

The nature of this remedy is treated elsewhere.[75] Where the landlord has the remedy of irritating the lease he may not use it and also claim damages for premature termination of the lease by the tenant,[76] or at least unless he had reserved his right to do so in accepting the tenant's

66 *Forrest & Barr* v. *Henderson* (1869) 8 M. 913; Chap. 7, *supra*.
67 Stair I, 10, 14.
68 *Stration* v. *Graham* (1789) 3 Pat. 119; *McKenzie* v. *Craigie* (1815) 6 Pat. 117; *Gold* v. *Holdsworth* (1870) 8 M. 1006; *Weston* v. *Metropolitan Asylums Dist.* (1882) 9 Q.B.D. 404.
69 *Clydebank Engineering Co.* v. *Castaneda* (1904) 7 F.(H.L.) 77.
70 *Webster* v. *Bosanquet* [1912] A.C. 394, and Chap. 7, *supra*, generally. See old cases collected in Rankine, *Leases*, 462.
71 *Vide*, *supra*, Chap. 7. See *Cooper* v. *Campbell*, January 18, 1805, F.C.; *Hall* v. *Grant* (1831) 9 S. 612.
72 Bell, *Prin.*, § 34, 149, 1221; Bell, *Comm.* I, 655; Bell, *Convg.* I, 254. See the rule applied to leases in *Veitch* v. *Paterson* (1664) M. 11383.
73 *Craig* v. *McBeath* (1863) 1 M. 1020.
74 *Gold* v. *Houldsworth* (1870) 8 M. 1006.
75 *Supra*, Chap. 7.
76 *Walker's Trs.* v. *Manson* (1886) 13 R. 1198; *Bidoulac* v. *Sinclair's Tr.* (1889) 17 R. 144; *Buttercase & Geddie's Tr.* v. *Geddie* (1897) 24 R. 1128.

renunciation,[77] on the ground that the landlord has himself by exercising his option to enforce the irritancy caused the termination.[78] But there seems to be no ground for doubting that a claim of damages in respect of earlier breaches of contract or mismanagement would remain exigible unless the landlord, in accepting a tenant's renunciation of the lease in circumstances which incurred the irritancy, had done so without qualification, when he will readily be held to have passed from all his claims for damages.[77] Possibly also they are not exigible if the irritancy is being enforced in respect of the same mismanagement or deterioration as ground the claims of damages, in which case the irritancy might be held to be in lieu of damages, especially where the actual loss is small or difficult of proof. But if irritancy is incurred on one ground, *e.g.* bankruptcy, and prior claims for mismanagement are outstanding, they should be reserved and claimed separately,[79] and irritancy may be incurred, *e.g.* by bankruptcy without inferring a breach of lease sounding in damages.[80]

Violent profits

Violent profits are a form of penal damages exigible to prevent any taking or keeping possession of heritable subjects without proper and legal warrant or authority.[81] In the contract of lease anyone entitled to bring an action of removing [82] may move that the tenant be ordained to find caution for violent profits.[83] If an order for caution is made and not implemented decree of removal or ejection may be granted at once. Violent profits may be demanded in all cases where there never was a right to possess [84] or where a right which existed has terminated [85]: it applies equally to removings, summary removings and summary ejections,[86] but not to extraordinary removings [87] where *ex facie* the tenant's right subsists and the landlord must prove further facts to establish his case.[88] Similarly a tenant whose tenancy was in the discretion of the landlord and who refused to quit after intimation of the landlord's intention to remove him was liable for violent profits.[89]

77 *Walker's Trs., supra*; *Lyons* v. *Anderson* (1886) 13 R. 1020.
78 *Buttercase & Geddie's Tr., supra*, at p. 1133. *Cf. Edinburgh Mags.* v. *Horsburgh* (1834) 12 S. 593, an anomalous case.
79 *Cf. Gloag on Contract*, 2nd ed., 669, and p. 764, *supra*.
80 *Bidoulac, supra*.
81 Ersk. II, 6, 54. See also Stair II, 9, 44; IV, 29; Hunter, *Landlord and Tenant*, II, 64; *Rankine on Landownership*, 4th ed., 23.
82 Rankine, *Leases*, 513.
83 Sheriff Courts Act 1907, rr. 110, 121 (as amended by 1913 Act, Sched. II). The Sheriff has a discretion: see *Milne* v. *Darroch* (1937) 53 Sh.Ct.Rep. 3.
84 *Fife C.C.* v. *Hatten* (1950) 66 Sh.Ct.Rep. 38 (squatters); *Cheshire* v. *Irvine*, 1963 S.L.T. (Sh.Ct.) 28.
85 See *Ross* v. *Duff* (1899) 15 Sh.Ct.Rep. 227; *Burton* v. *Mackie* (1903) 21 Sh.Ct.Rep. 63 (irritancy cases). As to caution for violent profits in the case of tenancies under the Rent Acts, see *Heritable and General Assets Co.* v. *Asple* (1919) 35 Sh.Ct.Rep. 14; *Milne* v. *Darroch* (1937) 53 Sh.Ct.Rep. 3.
86 Rules 110, 121, *supra*; *Robb* v. *Menzies* (1859) 21 D. 277.
87 As to which see Dobie, *Sheriff Court Practice*, 415.
88 *Oliver* v. *Weir's Trs.* (1870) 8 M. 786.
89 *Houldsworth* v. *Brand's Trs.* (1876) 3 R. 304.

Subtenants are also liable, as for refusing to remove after the tenant had agreed to quit, and having had warnings despite the fact that the landlord did not recognise them.[90] A tenant possessing after decree of removing although warrant of ejection was not executed for a year was held liable for the period after the decree.[91]

Violent profits may be claimed and recovered as an action of damages and irrespective of whether caution has been or could have been demanded or obtained.[92] Caution for violent profits may be demanded in a summary ejection.[93]

Possession in good faith is a complete answer to a demand for violent profits, and liability therefor only exists if and from the time when good faith ceases.[94] The precise date is always a question of fact, and the change can only be effected in the course of a judicial proceeding, but exceptionally bona fide possession is held to cease at the date of citation or litiscontestation,[95] where the possessor is faced by a right requiring no extrinsic proof.[96] Normally, however, bona fides is founded on grounds which it is only reasonable to defend at law, in which case only a judgment of a competent court will terminate it,[97] from the date of the Outer House decision,[98] or, if more important, of the Inner House,[99] or even of the House of Lords.[1]

The general rules for the determination of the time when mala fides supervenes have been laid down as follows [2]:—" First, when the possession has commenced in good faith, it lies with the true owner to show when it ceased to be so before the right to demand violent profits can prevail. Secondly, where possession has been continued during a litigation regarding the title of the possessor, it is sufficient to support the possessor's plea of bona fides that he had *probabilis causa litigandi*. And thirdly, the principle is equally applicable whether the possession be challenged in respect of want of title in the possessor's author or in respect of the nature and conditions of his own right." [3] Wrongful possession ends with the date

90 *Ramage* v. *Briggs* (1831) 9 S. 281.
91 *Watt* v. *Bell* (1822) 1 S. 556.
92 *Cf. Tod* v. *Fraser* (1889) 17 R. 226.
93 *Fife County Council* v. *Hatten* (1950) 66 Sh.Ct.Rep. 38.
94 *Macdonald* v. *Macdonald* (1906) 22 Sh.Ct.Rep. 11.
95 *Seaton* v. *Seaton* (1817) Mor. 1753; *D. Atholl* v. *Dalgleish* (1822) 1 S. 511.
96 Cases in *Rankine on Landownership*, 81. See also *Hunter on Landlord and Tenant*, II, 526.
97 *Kinminity* v. *Sutherland* (1751) Mor. 1727; *Selkirk Mags.* v. *Clapperton* (1830) 9 S. 9.
98 *Smith & Beaton Prs.*, Feb. 6, 1810, F.C.; *D. Roxburghe* v. *Wauchope*, June 13, 1822, F.C.; affd. (1825) 1 W. & Sh. 41.
99 *Laurie* v. *Spalding* (1769) Mor. 1764; *Henderson*, Dec. 14, 1815, F.C.; *Gordon's Trs.* v. *Innes* (1830) 4 W. & S. 305.
1 *Carnegy* v. *Scott* (1830) 4 W. & S. 431; *Houldsworth* v. *Brand's Trs.* (1876) 3 R. 304, summing up results of earlier cases: see also *Stirling* v. *Dunn* (1831) 9 S. 276; *D. Gordon* v. *Innes* (1830) 4 W. & Sh. 305. No violent profits are due if prior to the date when bona fides is held to have terminated the lease is terminated: *Brisbane's Trs.* v. *Lead* (1828) 7 S. 65.
2 *Houldsworth* v. *Brand's Trs.* (1876) 3 R. 304, 310, *per* L.J.C. Moncreiff.
3 *Houldsworth* v. *Brand's Trs.* (1876) 3 R. 304; see also *Howard* v. *Muir* (1870) 8 S.L.R. 6; *Baird* v. *Kerr* (1894) 10 Sh.Ct.Rep. 128.

when the subjects are restored empty to the landlord, free of tenants, subtenants [4] and squatters.[5]

Even apart from violent profits a tenant who remains in possession after giving notice of intention to remove is liable in damages for continuing in possession without title. In one such case [6] half a year's rent was given as damages, the sum which the landlord was willing to take, though the view was expressed that the defender had exposed himself to an action of violent profits. The fact that misfortune had caused the defender to remain was no answer to the claim of damages.

Amount of violent profits

By ancient custom the amount exigible as violent profits is double the rent in the case of urban property within royal burghs, burghs of regality and considerable burghs of barony.[7] The amount to be taken as rent and any permissible deductions are nowhere stated. It is submitted that today the gross annual value of the property as appearing in the valuation roll is prima facie a reasonable criterion of the true rent.[8] In the case of other subjects such as lands, quarries, and minerals violent profits normally signifies " the greatest profits that the pursuer can prove he would have made." [9] In addition reparation may be claimed for " all damages which the subjects may receive at the hands of the defender." [10] No allowance falls to be made for the improvements or for interest of money spent thereon during the period of mala fide possession. A claim for violent profits prescribes in five years.[11] Such a claim may be started alternatively to a claim for damages and the latter may succeed, though the measure of damages will be less than the quantum of violent profits.[12]

The difference between violent and normal profits as the measure of damages for continued possession may be substantial. In *Houldsworth* v. *Brand's Trustees* [13] the tenants of a colliery were bound by a special agreement to give up possession if the landlord intimated that he was dissatisfied with their working: he intimated dissatisfaction, but the tenant's representatives refused to quit until litigation had determined the true construction of the contract. The court determined against them [14] and

4 *E. Argyle* v. *McNaughton* (1674) Mor. 13889.
5 Stair II, 9, 43; IV, 26, 10; Ersk. II, 6, 54; *Greenlaw* v. *Adamson* (1624) Mor. 13888; *Budge* v. *Sinclair* (1713) Mor. 13890.
6 *Tod* v. *Fraser* (1889) 17 R. 226.
7 Hope, Minor Pr. 13, 33; Stair I, 9, 27; II, 9, 44; IV, 29, 3; Mack. II, 6, 11; Bankton, I, 10, 133, 147; Ersk. II, 6, 54; *Weddell* v. *Buchan* (1611) Mor. 16460; *Milne* v. *Darroch* (1941) 53 Sh.Ct.Rep. 3.
8 *Cf. Yellowlees* v. *Alexander* (1882) 9 R. 765. In *Macdonald* v. *Macdonald* (1906) 22 Sh.Ct. Rep. 11, double the actual rent of the subjects occupied was taken.
9 Stair II, 9, 44; but see special rules in Stair I, 9, 27. The rent of a sublease is not conclusive: *Buccleuch* v. *Grierson* (1827) 5 S. 676.
10 *Gardner* v. *Beresford's Trs.* (1877) 4 R. 1091, 1092; *Morton* v. *Colquhoun* (1783) Mor. 13893.
11 Prescription and Limitation (Sc.) Act, 1973, S. 6, replacing Act 1579, c. 81, construed by Stair, *ut supra*; Ersk. III, 7, 16.
12 *Houldsworth* v. *Brand's Trs.* (1876) 3 R. 304; *cf. L.Adv.* v. *Glengarnock Iron Co.*, 1909, 1 S.L.T. 15.
13 (1875) 2 R. 683, (1876) 3 R. 304, and (1877) 4 R. 369.
14 (1875) 2 R. 683.

the landlord then claimed violent profits for the period during which they had delayed to remove or, alternatively, damages. It was held [15] that the landlord's remedy against the tenants in these circumstances was not a claim for violent profits but only for damages for breach of contract in not removing in terms of the special agreement. The basis of this decision was that the tenants were *in bona fide* and had had a *probabilis causa litigandi* in the former action [16] so were not liable for violent profits at least prior to that decision, but that thereafter, the meaning of the agreement having been declared, *viz.*, that they were bound to remove, they were in breach of contract in not doing so, and were liable to the landlord in damages for the loss he had sustained thereby.[17] The damages fell to be estimated in these circumstances on a jury basis: the pursuer was entitled to be placed as nearly as possible in the same position as if there had been no breach of contract, and regard might be had to the profits which might fairly be held to have resulted from the tenant's continued operations and the loss of increased lordship sustained by the landlord which he might have received under a new lease, but that in estimating the tenant's profits allowance had to be made for wear and tear and interest on cost but not for depreciation in the market value of their machinery.[18]

Claims by landlord on death of tenant

The obligations under a lease will transmit on the tenant's death to his executor by virtue of confirmation [18a] or, in the absence of restrictions in the lease, may be bequeathed by testamentary writing.[18b] The contract of lease, however, and the obligations thereunder remain enforceable and if the lease has not come to its natural termination at the death and the heir refuses to take up the lease, a number of obligations which had been undertaken by the deceased tenant will probably remain partly unfulfilled at his death; for the non-implement of these a claim of damages is open to the landlord. The measure of damages suggested in one case [18c] was the amount of rent due till the ish under deduction of the sum received by the landlord on reletting for the remainder of the term to another party.[18d] If there are other prestations of the lease still outstanding and unperformed, and injury has been caused thereby to the landlord's interests, such as by non-implement of

15 (1876) 3 R. 304.
16 (1875) 2 R. 683.
17 (1876) 3 R. 304. The result would have been the same if the special agreement had not existed: the tenants would then have been in breach of the implied condition in their lease that they would remove on the termination of the lease being intimated by the landlord, *e.g.*, at a term providing for a break in the lease, though such a case might have given less scope for debate on the construction of the lease.
18 (1877) 4 R. 369.
18a Succession (Sc.) Act, 1964, s. 14.
18b *Stewart* v. *Pirie* (1832) 11 S. 139; but see Agricultural Holdings (Scotland) Act 1949, ss. 20–21, as to landlord's rights to object.
18c *Bethune* v. *Morgan* (1874) 2 R. 186.
18d *Ibid.* 187, *per* Lord Gifford.

provisions as to repairs, improvements and so on, the personal representatives will be liable to compensate the landlord therefor. An offer made by the executors to take up the lease would be a sufficient answer to a claim of damages for breach of contract based on failure to continue possession and occupancy of the farm, but the landlord will not be bound to accept any such offer on the ground of *delectus personae*, and it is not an adequate defence to a claim which becomes due only at removing.[18e]

TENANT'S CLAIMS

Possession

The primary right of the tenant as against his landlord is to be put in possession of the subjects let to him [19] with the right to remove or eject the present possessors by legal forms, or with the title to call on the landlord to do so at his own expense.[20] Possession must be given timeously [21] to the whole subjects of let [22] in good order and condition.[23] The subjects transferred must reasonably correspond with the description thereof in the lease, and otherwise a claim of damages for loss resulting from misdescription will lie, as well as entitling the tenant to repudiate the lease.[25] If there is a gross discrepancy between the subjects let and the premises actually handed over, an action of reduction of the lease and for damages may be brought, provided *restitutio in integrum* is still possible,[26] or alternatively for damages in the shape of a deduction from the rent [27] in respect of past periods of possession and reduction of the lease [28]; or the tenant may claim to retain the rent for the future till a less material deficiency is remedied [29] or make a claim of damages if the sum claimed would exceed what is recoverable by abatement from or retention of rent.[30] Where the rent has been paid beforehand [31] or no possession has been given [32] or the damage is greater than any amount of rent, an action of damages is the only remedy.[30] There may also be a claim for surface

18e *Scott's Exors.* v. *Hepburn* (1876) 3 R. 816.

19 *Seaforth's Trs.* v. *Macaulay* (1844) 7 D. 180; *Tennent's Trs.* v. *Maxwell* (1880) 17 S.L.R. 463.

20 Stair I, 6, 15; Bankton, II, 9, 21; Ersk. II, 6, 28; *Winans* v. *Mackenzie* (1883) 10 R. 941, a very special case.

21 *Brown* v. *Maxwell* (1633) Mor. 3109. In *Drummond* v. *Hunter* (1869) 7 M. 347, 35 days' accidental delay freed the tenant from the lease: *cf. Glen* v. *Steele* (1895) 12 Sh.Ct.Rep. 19.

22 *Tennent's Trs.* v. *Maxwell* (1880) 17 S.L.R. 463; *Guthrie* v. *Shearer* (1873) 1 R. 181; but see *Webster* v. *Lyell* (1860) 22 D. 1423; *Walker* v. *Turnbull* (1843) 5 D. 1334.

23 *Davidson* v. *Logan*, 1908 S.C. 350; *Reid* v. *Baird* (1876) 4 R. 234.

25 *Brodie* v. *Maclachlan* (1900) 8 S.L.T. 145; see generally, *Rankine on Landownership*, 4th ed., 101 *et seq.*, on boundaries, and as to access: *Addison* v. *Brown* (1907) 15 S.L.T. 674; *Duncan* v. *Scott* (1876) 3 R.(H.L.) 69.

26 *Oliver* v. *Suttie* (1840) 2 D. 514.

27 *Cf. Duncan* v. *Brooks* (1894) 21 R. 760.

28 *Riddell* v. *Grosset* (1791) 3 Paton 203; see also *Yeaman* v. *Gilruth* (1792) Hume 783.

29 *Kilmarnock Gas Co.* v. *Smith* (1872) 11 M. 58; *Guthrie* v. *Shearer* (1873) 1 R. 181; *Gray* v. *Renton* (1840) 3 D. 203; *cf. Humphrey* v. *Mackay* (1883) 10 R. 647.

30 *Goskirk* v. *Edin. Ry. Access Co.* (1863) 2 M. 383.

31 *Critchley* v. *Campbell* (1884) 11 R. 475.

32 *Matheson* v. *Nicolson* (1819) 2 Mur. 141; *Smith* v. *Robertson* (1832) 10 S. 829.

damage consequent on the landlord's working a quarry or other reserved part of the subjects.[33]

An agreement to grant a lease is specifically enforceable and a disappointed tenant cannot be compelled to take damages in lieu thereof.[34] A tenant is entitled to compensation for any period when he is kept out of possession of the subjects leased, unless it be trivial.[35]

In *Smith* v. *Robertson* [36] a tenant was refused access to the farm, though he had been granted a tack for twelve years; the rent was £16 16s. and twelve geese, payable yearly in advance. The tenant recovered £240 damages, the items of loss relied on being the removal of furniture, cattle, carts, etc., to the vicinity of the farm (a distance of some twenty miles), preparation of manure, fuel, seed and fodder, want of accommodation for family and animals over the winter in consequence of being refused access, and the death of one of his cattle in consequence of lack of shelter.

Right to be maintained in possession—claim under warrandice

The general rule is that when possession has once been taken the landlord shall do nothing, and so far as is in his power allow nothing to be done to oust the tenant from the subjects let or any material part of them during the lease.[37] The principal remedy, though not the only one, is an action of damages founded on the clause of warrandice in the lease.[38] The warrandice which is usually expressed and is otherwise always implied in leases is absolute warrandice.[39] It is in effect a personal obligation by the lessor that the lessee will be maintained, throughout the period of the lease, in complete and undisturbed possession of the subjects let, and that in the event of his being evicted from the subjects of let in whole or in part, the lessor will indemnify him for the loss sustained through the eviction.[40] It is an obligation primarily *ad factum praestandum* and only subsidiarily for damages.[41] Such only applies to the subjects really let and a question may arise whether certain premises fall under the warrandice or not.[42] It will not extend, for example, to subjects held only by favour and not under the lease,[43] nor to a loss which both parties risked in full knowledge of the limitations on the granter's rights,[44] nor to a loss caused by a servitude enjoyed by third parties at the date of the lease, it being presumed that the tenant should have made inquiry [45] and the landlord not being bound

33 See further p. 779, *infra*.
34 *Seaforth's Trs.* v. *Macaulay* (1844) 7 D. 180.
35 *Tennent's Trs.* v. *Maxwell* (1880) 17 S.L.R. 463.
36 (1832) 10 S. 829.
37 *Rankine on Leases*, 213; *Paterson* v. *Blair* (1819) 2 Mur. 177; *Dalziell* v. *D. Queensberry's Exors.* (1826) 4 Mur. 10, 18; *Wauchope* v. *Stevens* (1826) 4 S. 766; *Murray* v. *Douglas* (1837) 15 S. 890.
38 Bell, *Prin.* § 141, 894, 1208, 1253; Bell, *Comm.* I, 644; Bell, *Convg.* I, 200.
39 *Middletons* v. *Yorstoun* (1826) 5 S. 162; *Middletons* v. *Meggar* (1828) 7 S. 76.
40 *Menzies* v. *Whyte* (1888) 15 R. 470.
41 *Cairns* v. *Howden* (1870) 9 M. 284, 290.
42 *Kinloch* v. *Fraser* (1829) 7 S. 819.
43 *Burnett* v. *Stewart* (1863) 1 M. 524.
44 *Reid* v. *Shaw* (1822) 1 S. 334.
45 *Gordon* v. *Ruxton* (1797) Hume 798; *Fraser* v. *E. & G. Union Canal* (1830) 9 S. 46.

to disclose any and every burden which the tenant should reasonably find for himself.[46]

Warrandice comes into effect only when eviction has either taken place, or is certain to take place and the fault of the landlord is the ground of the demand, or where eviction is threatened where liability is disputed,[47] or where eviction is only avoided by the expiry of the lease leaving outstanding a liability for violent profits. The eviction need only be partial, as by loss of the full use of the subjects.[48] There can be no indemnification for eviction which results from the fault or carelessness of the tenant himself.[49] When a claim for eviction is made the tenant should give notice to the landlord, in which case he is not bound to defend his right judicially.[50] His failure so to notify submits him to the risk of the omission of any relevant defence.[51] The implied warrandice against eviction extends to a sublease and gives the subtenant a claim against the landlord.[52]

The extent of the claim to indemnification is complete as to past, present and future loss.

Where claim under warrandice excluded

When the eviction is effected by supervenient legislation there is no breach of warrandice and no recourse against the landlord is competent under the warrandice clause in cases of partial[53] or total[54] eviction. There is no recourse under warrandice against *damnum fatale* or inevitable loss arising from causes independent of the title, and in such cases the tenant may neither claim damages nor terminate the lease on the ground of eviction,[55] nor does a landlord warrant, unless expressly, that he will abstain from entering into competition with the tenant.[56]

Nor is there liability under warrandice for eviction which results from the illegal act of another tenant of the same landlord, or of a third party,[57] and the tenant must take the risk of that,[58] except that there may be liability if the landlord could have prevented or stopped the third party's

46 *Symington* v. *Cranston* (1780) M. 16637; Hailes, 844. See further, *McDonald* v. *Hamilton* (1831) 9 S. 402, and *Sawers* v. *McConnell* (1874) 1 R. 392 discussed in Rankine, 215. *Cf. Dunlop* v. *Steel Co. of Scotland* (1879) 7 R. 283.

47 Balfour, 319; Ersk. II, 3, 30; Ross, Lect. 2, 493; Bell, *Comm.* II, 645; Rankine, *Leases*, 215; *Smith* v. *Ross* (1672) Mor. 16596; *Menzies* v. *D. Queensberry's Exors.* (1832) 11 S. 18; *Lyall* v. *Shepherd* (1894) 2 S.L.T. 440.

48 *Guthrie* v. *Shearer* (1873) 1 R. 181; *Stewart* v. *Wand* (1838) 16 S. 408; *Christie* v. *Wilson*, 1915 S.C. 645; *Dougall* v. *Dunfermline Mags.*, 1908 S.C. 151.

49 *Stewart* v. *Wand* (1838) 16 S. 408.

50 *Downie* v. *Campbell*, Jan. 31, 1815, F.C.; *Menzies* v. *Whyte* (1888) 15 R. 470.

51 Bell, *Comm.* I, 645.

52 *Downie* v. *Laird* (1902) 10 S.L.T. 28.

53 *Goldie* v. *Williamson* (1796) Hume, 793; *Holliday* v. *Scott* (1829) 8 S. 831; *Donald* v. *Leitch* (1886) 13 R. 790.

54 *Tay Salmon Fisheries* v. *Speedie*, 1929 S.C. 593, 601, *per* L.P. Clyde; *Mackeson* v. *Boyd*, 1942 S.C. 56, 63.

55 *Mackeson* v. *Boyd*, 1942 S.C. 56, 61.

56 *Craig* v. *Millar* (1888) 15 R. 1005.

57 *Lyons* v. *Anderson* (1886) 13 R. 1020. *Cf. Gardner* v. *Walker* (1862) 24 D. 1430; *Reid* v. *Shaw* (1822) 1 S. 334.

58 *Reid* v. *Shaw, supra*; *Piers* v. *Black* (1776) Mor. 16636.

injurious actings.[59] So too the tenant must take the risk of the loss of a licence [60] or the prohibition of his trade as a nuisance, unless the premises were warranted fit for carrying on that trade.[61] Where an heir of entail granted an *ultra vires* lease, his executor was held not to be liable under the warrandice clause to tenants evicted after the granter's death, the obligation being construed as personal to the granter.[62]

Warranty of fitness

There is also a warranty implied that the subjects are fit for the purpose for which they are let [63] but not that they will always remain so,[64] and there is no warranty implied that the landlord will not engage in or permit competition.[65]

Partial eviction

Where the eviction is partial only or temporary, the remedy is a claim for damages,[66] which is cast usually in the form of a demand for reduction of rent, at least where the eviction is of a permanent kind. Such are cases where the landlord ousts the tenant from possession, by conducting operations which he is not entitled to do,[67] or injures his property as by neglecting to erect an embankment which he had agreed to build against inundation,[68] or causes flooding on the tenant's land by negligently exercising a reserved right to lay out water-courses,[69] or even interfering with the tenant's business by carrying on operations on adjacent parts of the property,[70] or deprives the tenant of the use of one of his access roads,[71] or deprives the tenant of the use of a stream for watering cattle,[72] or, in the case of lease of power, causes loss by extraordinary stoppages beyond those contemplated by a clause covering ordinary stoppages,[73] or where a mill lade was rendered useless in consequence of a storm,[74] or where buildings were not repaired for five years.[75]

The quantum of damages will be measured by the amount of injury naturally and directly arising in consequence of the landlord's acts or

59 *Paton* v. *Hunter* (1875) 12 S.L.R. 305.
60 *Donald, supra.*
61 *Murray* v. *Buchanan* (1776) Mor. 16636.
62 *D. of Bedford* v. *E. of Galloway's Tr.* (1904) 6 F. 971.
63 *Caledonian Ry.* v. *Greenock Sacking Co.* (1875) 2 R. 671; *Glebe Sugar Co.* v. *Paterson* (1900) 2 F. 615; *Corrie Mackie & Co.* v. *Stewart* (1885) 22 S.L.R. 350.
64 *Glebe Sugar Co.* v. *Paterson* (1900) 2 F. 615; *Sandeman* v. *Duncan's Trs.* (1897) 5 S.L.T. 21.
65 *Craig* v. *Millar* (1888) 15 R. 1005.
66 *Tennent's Trs.* v. *Maxwell* (1880) 17 S.L.R. 463.
67 *Bisset* v. *Whitson* (1842) 5 D. 5 (illegally unroofing tenant's house).
68 *Scott* v. *Tait* (1826) 4 Mur. 57.
69 *Menmuir* v. *Airth* (1863) 1 M. 929.
70 *Huber* v. *Ross*, 1912 S.C. 898.
71 *Guthrie* v. *Shearer* (1873) 1 R. 181.
72 *Stewart* v. *Wand* (1838) 16 S. 408; *Christie* v. *Wilson*, 1915 S.C. 645. *Cf. Dougall* v. *Dunfermline Mags.*, 1908 S.C. 151.
73 *Wilson* v. *Norris*, March 10, 1810, F.C.; *Gordon* v. *Suttie* (1826) 4 Mur. 86; *Kilmarnock Gas Co.* v. *Smith* (1872) 11 M. 58.
74 *Sharp* v. *Thomson*, 1930 S.C. 1092.
75 *Johnstone* v. *Hughan* (1894) 21 R. 777.

omissions. They will include reimbursement of any expenses fairly and reasonably incurred by the tenant in the preservation of the property, with an element as indemnification for the loss and inconvenience entailed as the results of the landlord's operations or neglect.[76]

In *Huber* v. *Ross* [77] the proprietor of an urban tenement made extensive building operations and alterations which caused structural and other damage to the leased premises and interference with and detriment to the tenant's business. The landlord was held bound to restore the structural damage done, and was found liable in damages for injury done to the tenant's furniture and materials; for injury to his business during the landlord's operations, so far only (Lord Johnston dissenting on this point) as due to physical and tangible injury to the premises from such causes as dust and vibration, but not from immaterial and temporary injury, such as noise and occasional obstruction to the tenant's access; and for injury to his business during the work of restoration. The general principle may be expressed as being that there is an obligation on every one not to conduct operations on his land in a reckless, unskilful or negligent manner such as to injure neighbouring premises or the occupancy of them, and though a landlord is entitled to make alterations, he must ensure that reasonable care is taken to do as little damage as possible beyond the inevitable inconvenience occasioned by such operations. An obligation is incumbent on the landlord not to derogate from the grant to the tenant contained in the lease so far as causing structural or material physical tangible injury to the premises.

Partial but permanent eviction

Where the eviction from the premises is permanent though only partial the normal form of claim of damages consists in a claim for an abatement of rent in proportion to the value of the subjects from which eviction has taken place.[78]

Abatement may be allowed where there has been actual interference with the premises let which results in injury to the tenant, as where a dock was built within the area of fishings let,[79] or a right of cutting peats was lost,[80] but refused where the landlord's action was legal, and not excluded by the lease, though distinctly prejudicial to the tenant's business, in respect that the landlord himself set up a rival business in adjacent premises.[81] A right to prevent the landlord so acting may be included in

[76] *Robertson* v. *Menzies* (1828) 6 S. 452; *Perera* v. *Vandiyar* [1953] 1 W.L.R. 672.

[77] 1912 S.C. 898. Observe Lord Dunedin's warnings in this case, at p. 909, on the dangers of English authority, and the same in *Mackeson* v. *Boyd*, 1942 S.C. 56, 61. See further *Alexander* v. *Couper* (1840) 3 D. 249; *Blanc* v. *Grieg* (1856) 18 D. 1315; *Miller* v. *Renton* (1885) 13 R. 309; *Laurent* v. *Ld. Advocate* (1869) 7 M. 607.

[78] As to the case where the landlord resumes land under a power in the lease, see Agricultural Holdings (Scotland) Act 1949, s. 34.

[79] *Hall* v. *Ross* (1813) 1 Dow 201.

[80] *Duncan* v. *Brooks* (1894) 21 R. 760.

[81] *Craig* v. *Millar* (1888) 15 R. 1005, overruling *Campbell* v. *Watt* (1795) Hume, 788. See also *Smith* v. *Cameron* (1879) 15 R. 1007, note.

a lease and if carefully formulated with respect to the locality over which it is to operate will be enforceable,[82] if it is reasonable in the interests of the parties and also of the public. In one case where ground was resumed by the landlord for mineral workings in accordance with a reserved power of resumption in the lease, it was held that the provision for abatement of rent was all that could be claimed, and damages in respect of severance were not recoverable in addition.[83]

A tenant has been held entitled to deduction of rent in respect of land taken from a farm for public purposes such as a road without his consent,[84] or land resumed for housing.[85] Under the Lands Clauses Act 1845, ss. 112–115, if part of the land held on lease is acquired for compulsory purposes, the rent is to be apportioned by agreement of parties between the parts taken and the parts left, or, failing agreement, by the Sheriff, and the tenant is to be compensated for severance of the lands acquired from those not needed,[86] or otherwise. The statute also provides for the claims of yearly tenants.[87]

The Acquisition of Land (Authorisation Procedure) Act 1946, Sched. II, Part I, incorporates the Lands Clauses Act with the particular enactment under which is authorised a compulsory purchase for which the 1946 Act lays down the procedure, and consequently the foregoing provisions will apply unless expressly excluded by the particular enactment in question in a given instance of compulsory acquisition of land.

Apart from this, substantially the same result has been achieved by the rule that sequestration for rent will be refused or a charge for rent unpaid will be suspended, if it is shown that an essential part of the subject let has been withdrawn by the landlord,[88] either directly or indirectly,[89] provided that the tenant makes a distinct averment of the partial eviction founded on which is instantly verifiable.[90]

Damages or abatement of rent are not however permissible if the tenant takes the risk of the landlord's acts and their consequences.[91] A tenant will be barred from claiming abatement of rent if he has given a written promise to pay the full rent,[92] or if an adequate substitution has been made for the part of the holding of which he has been deprived,[93] or if he allows the lease to run out without complaint.[94] Again, loss caused by third parties for whom the landlord has no responsibility gives no claim for

82 *Davie* v. *Stark* (1876) 3 R. 1114.
83 *Robertson* v. *Ross* (1892) 19 R. 967; *cf.* also *Lanarkshire Middle Ward District Committee* v. *Marshall* (1896) 24 R. 139; *Edinburgh Corpn.* v. *Gray*, 1948 S.C. 538.
84 *Brown* v. *Brown* (1825) 4 S. 489.
85 *Edinburgh Corpn.* v. *Gray*, 1948 S.C. 538.
86 *N.B. Ry.* v. *Renton* (1864) 2 M. 442, 449; see also *N.B. Ry.* v. *Stevenson* (1902) 4 F. 224.
87 s. 114. *Ferguson* v. *Hood* (1882) 9 R. 168; *Caledonian Ry.* v. *Morrison* (1898) 25 R. 1001.
88 *Kilmarnock Gaslight Co.* v. *Smith* (1872) 11 M. 58; *Guthrie* v. *Shearer* (1873) 1 R. 181.
89 *Gordon* v. *Suttie* (1826) 4 Mur. 86; *Humphrey* v. *Mackay* (1883) 10 R. 647.
90 *Humphrey* v. *Mackay*, *supra*.
91 *Aitchison* v. *Glasgow Mags.* (1825) 1 W. & S. 153 (water supply); *Slowan* v. *Hawthorn* (1756) Mor. 16052; *Chalmers* v. *Wilson* (1769) M. 16060.
92 *Maxwell* v. *Montgomery* (1681) M. 15173.
93 *Butter* v. *Loch* (1830) 8 S. 408.
94 *Burns* v. *Stewart* (1830) 8 S. 61; affd. 5 W. & S. 356.

abatement,[95] unless provided for in the lease, or for damages, whether the acts be lawful or not. So too there is no remedy for such eviction from accident or public misfortune,[96] or *damnum fatale*, though the tenant can call on the landlord to share the loss by a partial abatement of rent [97] unless the loss be trivial [98] or acquiesced in.[99]

Where partial eviction has taken place the tenant will be entitled to recover any expenses reasonably incurred by him in taking legal action to resist the eviction even though it should be unsuccessful. So where a tenant unsuccessfully tried to interdict persons fishing in a stream on his land apparently without authority,[1] and intimated each step in the action to the landlords, who were the magistrates of a burgh and who had refused to interfere, he was held entitled to a diminution of rent when the public right of fishing by townspeople of the burgh was vindicated, and also to recover the expenses incurred by him and also those paid by him in the action. " If an action of eviction be properly defended, and if, notwithstanding such defence, eviction follows, the granter of the warrandice will be liable, not only for the direct loss caused by the breach of warrandice, but for all expenses properly and reasonably incurred in defending the rights which he and the granter alike had an interest to defend." [2]

In the absence of special stipulation no claim will lie against the landlord for abatement of rent [3] or for damages for acts done by third parties causing loss, in which the landlord has no hand, and that whether these acts be lawful or unlawful. If the actings are lawful both landlord and tenant equally suffer as regards their respective interests [4]; if unlawful both are equally entitled and have an interest to put a stop to the nuisance or otherwise protect their just interests.[5]

Should partial but permanent eviction result from *damnum fatale* or public calamity,[6] it is quite well settled that the tenant may secure an abatement of rent [7] so that the landlord will share the loss, unless the loss

95 *Donald* v. *Leitch* (1886) 13 R. 790; *Hart's Trs.* v. *Arrol* (1903) 6 F. 36.
96 *e.g.* war: Bankt. I, 20, 18; *Wilkie* v. *Ker* (1662) Mor. 10120; *Customs Tacksman* v. *Greenhead* (1667) Mor. 10121; *Edinburgh Bailies* v. *E. Lothian Heritors* (1663) M. 10120; *Strachan* v. *Christie* (1751) M. 10129; *Sinclair* v. *Hutchison* (1751) Mor. 10130.
97 Stair I, 15, 3; Ersk. II, 6, 41; Bell, *Prin.* § 1208; *E. Eglinton* v. *Tenants* (1742) Mor. 10128; *White* v. *Moncreiff* (1849) 11 D. 1031; *Walker* v. *Bayne*, May 30, 1811, F.C.; revd. 3 Dow, 233, 241; see also *Hamilton's Trs.* v. *Fleming* (1870) 9 M. 320; *Muir* v. *McIntyres* (1887) 14 R. 470.
98 *Piers* v. *Black* (1680) Mor. 16605; *Steedman* v. *Kennedy* (1744) Elchies, Tack No. 7; *Sharpe's Factor* v. *Monboddo* (1778) Mor. 10134.
99 *Kinnaird* v. *Mathewson* (1802) 4 Pat. 429.
1 *Dougall* v. *Lowe* (1906) 13 S.L.T. 831.
2 *Dougall* v. *Mags. of Dunfermline*, 1908 S.C. 151, 163, approving Ersk. II, 3, 32, and doubting Bell, *Prin.* § 895 (*k*). See also *Stephen* v. *Lord Advocate* (1878) 6 R. 282.
3 *Donald* v. *Leitch* (1886) 13 R. 790; *Hart's Trs.* v. *Arrol* (1903) 6 F. 36.
4 *Dunsmore* v. *Oswald* (1821) 1 S. 170.
5 Rankine, pp. 708 *et seq.*
6 Bankton, I, 20, 18; *Wilkie* v. *Ker* (1662) M. 10120; *Customs Tacksman* v. *Greenhead* (1667) M. 10121; *Edin. Bailies* v. *E. Lothian Heritors* (1663) M. 10120; *Strachan* v. *Christie* (1751) M. 10129; *Sinclair* v. *Hutchinson* (1751) M. 10130.
7 Stair I, 15, 3; Ersk. II, 6, 41; Bell, *Prin.* § 1208; *E. Eglinton* v. *His Tenants* (1742) M. 10128; *White* v. *Moncreiff* (1849) 11 D. 1031; *Walker* v. *Bayne*, May 30, 1811, F.C.; revd. 3 Dow. 233, 241. See also *D. Hamilton's Trs.* v. *Fleming* (1870) 9 M. 329; *Muir* v. *Macintyre* (1887) 14 R. 470.

be trifling [8] or the claim has been waived by acquiescence or delay.[9] The principle of *rei interitus* may bring a lease to an end where the contract is frustrated without fault on either party [10] as by requisition,[11] exercise of statutory powers [12] but not merely the loss of a liquor licence.[13]

Total and permanent eviction

A claim for damages against the landlord will lie where a lease is reduced by a third party, as in the Queensberry cases, where leases were reduced as being in contravention of powers under an entail.[14] But if there never has been a completed lease, and possession has been taken on an incomplete contract, no claim of damage may be made on either side and any loss falls where it lights.[15] But if on the other hand, a lease has been validly entered into, damages may be claimed for its breach, as the parties are bound and it is a subsisting contract, even though in the end it may be reduced as having been entered into *ultra vires*.[16]

Where total eviction takes place the value for the purposes of a claim under the warrandice clause is usually to be taken as the actual value at the date of eviction,[17] but exceptionally it has been held to be the price paid, *i.e.* the value at the commencement of possession.[17]

In cases where the eviction arises from *damnum fatale* or inevitable accident, that is, from an occurrence unprecedented and not reasonably to be anticipated,[18] or such that human foresight cannot provide against or be bound to recognise its possibility,[19] or from lesser and foreseeable calamities such as fires occurring without fault on the part of the parties, the tenant is entitled to abandon the lease or demand an abatement of rent according as the *rei interitus* is actually or constructively total or is only partial. Neither party is bound to restore the subjects to their previous state.[20]

To justify the tenant in abandoning the lease or in claiming abatement from rent (which may be done by way of defence to an action for payment of the full rent [21]) the loss must be either total or at least substantial and material. This includes cases where lands were covered with sand and rendered unproductive,[22] carried away by avulsion,[23] rendered sterile by

8 *Piers* v. *Black* (1680) M. 16605; *Steedman* v. *Kennedy*, 1744, Elch.Tack No. 7; *Sharpe's Factor* v. *L. Monboddo* (1778) M. 10134.
9 *Kinnaird* v. *Mathewson* (1802) 4 Pat. 429.
10 *Allan* v. *Markland* (1882) 10 R. 383, 389.
11 *Mackeson* v. *Boyd*, 1942 S.C. 56.
12 *Tay Salmon Fisheries* v. *Speedie*, 1929 S.C. 593.
13 *Hart's Trs.* v. *Arrol* (1903) 6 F. 36; *Donald* v. *Leitch* (1886) 13 R. 790.
14 *M. Queensberry* v. *D. of Queensberry's Exors.*, Nov. 15, 1815, F.C.; affd. 6 Paton, 557. But see *D. Bedford* v. *E. Galloway's Tr.* (1904) 6 F. 971.
15 *Dallas* v. *Fraser* (1849) 11 D. 1058; *Allan* v. *Gilchrist* (1875) 2 R. 587.
16 *Elliots' Trs.* v. *Elliot* (1894) 21 R. 858.
17 *Cairns* v. *Howden* (1870) 9 M. 284.
18 *Potter* v. *Hamilton Ry.* (1864) 3 M. 83, 87. *Cf. Davidson* v. *Macpherson* (1889) 30 S.L.R. 2.
19 *Tenant* v. *E. Glasgow* (1864) 2 M.(H.L.) 22, 27. See Rankine, *Landownership*, 4th ed., 375.
20 *Walker* v. *Bayne*, May 20, 1811, F.C.; revd. (1815) 3 Dow. 233; 6 Paton, 217; *Duff* v. *Fleming* (1870) 8 M. 769.
21 *Muir* v. *McIntyre* (1887) 14 R. 470.
22 *Lindsay* v. *Home* (1612) M. 10120.
23 *Futt* v. *Ruthven* (1671) 2 B.S. 504.

inundation, or if houses are buried and rendered uninhabitable,[24] unless of course the landlord offers to restore within a reasonable time.[25] It is a question of degree whether premises have been made unfit for occupation so as to entitle the tenant to abandon.[24] The tenant if he elects to abandon must do so without undue delay.[26]

Quantum of damages for total eviction

Where a tenant's right has been totally reduced without fault on his part, the loss sustained by the tenants and not any gain by the landlords is the material consideration but the precise loss is difficult of ascertainment. It has been held [27] that farms had been valued in three ways, (i) by stating the estimated produce, and the price at which it would have sold during the past years and at which it would probably sell during the future years, and then deducting from this the expense of cultivation, (ii) by stating the rent which a subtenant would have given, or (iii) by proving the rent paid under the new leases and putting a value on the additional conditions contained in them. The court directed in that case that if the first two were proved, either was a legitimate basis, but the second was the best and simplest way of ascertaining the value; that where the tenant remained on the farm, the difference of rent under the old and new leases was probably the best rule with an allowance for the difference of the conditions; that where the tenant was removed from the farm, whether the jury took the new rent or the estimated sub-rent, they must give what they thought a reasonable sum as tenant's profit, but this profit should not be given for the whole years of the lease, but for such time as the jury thought necessary to enable the tenant to get another farm; that if they took the estimated produce, this profit was included in it; that where the stock was sold, they must give what they thought proved as the difference between the sum for which it sold, and that for which it would probably have sold at the end of the lease; and that there must have been some disturbance of the possession during the dependence of the reduction, the claim upon which ground was of the nature of *solatium*. As was observed in the same case on appeal [28] the period for which the loss of profit is to be given is material and should be limited to a few years according to the probability of the tenant getting a farm. The damage moreover must be direct and not consequential.[29]

Under the Agricultural Holdings (Scotland) Act 1949, s. 35, a tenant is entitled in certain circumstances to claim compensation for disturbance, when he leaves a holding in consequence of a notice to quit. The minimum compensation is one year's rent; if the tenant proves

24 *Allan* v. *Markland* (1883) 10 R. 389, Ld. Shand.
25 *Duff* v. *Fleming* (1870) 8 M. 769.
26 *Drummond* v. *Hunter* (1869) 7 M. 347.
27 *Dalziel* v. *D. Queensberry's Exors.* (1825) 4 Mur. 10 and 18.
28 (1824) 4 Mur. 18, 22.
29 *Ibid.* p. 24; *Roberts* v. *Earl of Rosebery* (1825) 4 Mur. 1.

additional loss directly attributable to the removal, he may recover up to two years' rent.[30]

Repairs and maintenance—urban leases

The common law rule is that urban subjects must be put into and be maintained by the landlord in a habitable or tenantable condition,[31] which is a question of fact.[32] This means wind- and water-tight against the ordinary attacks of the elements, but not against exceptional encroachments.[33] It does not extend to decoration,[34] nor to dampness from foundations.[34a] If the landlord fails to implement this obligation he may be liable in damages to the tenant.[35] His obligation is however not a warranty [36] and he is under no obligation to repair until notice is given to him of the defect [37] and he fail to remedy it. There are exceptions in that the landlord is not liable for deterioration or destruction resulting from the negligence or default of the tenant himself [38] or of a third party [39] such as a competent contractor employed by him, where there is no absolute duty incumbent on the landlord,[40] nor for the consequences of *damnum fatale* or pure accident. Delay in making complaint may bar the right to resile.[41] The landlord is only liable in damages when injury has been caused to the health of the tenants by defects in the house, if it is shown that the defects were the result of his fault.[42] In *Fingland and Mitchell* v. *Howie* [43] the tenant on averments that the landlord had failed to maintain the house in tenantable condition was held entitled to retain the rent and to counterclaim for the damage suffered by the landlord's breach of obligation when the latter sued for the rent. This case was also held a relevant claim

30 See further *Keswick* v. *Wright*, 1924 S.C. 766; *McHarg* v. *Spiers*, 1924 S.C. 272; *Macgregor* v. *Board of Agriculture*, 1925 S.C. 613.

31 This is a question of fact and depends partly on the class of house; *Mechan* v. *Watson*, 1907 S.C. 25; *cf. Crawford* v. *Newton*, 36 W.R. 54. See also *Proudfoot* v. *Hart* (1890) 25 Q.B.D. 42; *Calthorpe* v. *McOscar* [1924] 1 K.B. 716.

32 Bank. I, 20, 15; II, 9, 20; Ersk. II, 6, 39 & 43; Bell, *Prin.* § 1253; *Dickie* v. *Amicable Prop. Investment Socy.*, 1911 S.C. 1079, 1085; *Marianski* v. *Jackson* (1872) 9 S.L.R. 480; *Whitelaw* v. *Fulton* (1871) 10 M. 27; *Mechan* v. *Watson*, 1907 S.C. 25. As to proof of standard, see *N.B. Storage Co.* v. *Steele's Trs.*, 1920 S.C. 194.

33 *Wolfson* v. *Forrester*, 1910 S.C. 675; *cf. Reid* v. *Baird* (1876) 4 R. 234.

34 *Crawford, supra.*

34a *McGonigal* v. *Pickard*, 1954 S.L.T.(Notes) 62.

35 Not, at least *ex contractu*, to third parties; *Cavalier* v. *Pope* [1906] A.C. 428; *Cameron* v. *Young*, 1908 S.C.(H.L.) 7; *Kennedy* v. *Bruce*, 1907 S.C. 845; *Mathieson's Tutor* v. *Aikman's Tr.*, 1910 S.C. 11; *Gaunt* v. *McIntyre*, 1914 S.C. 43.

36 *Wolfson, supra*; *Dickie, supra*; *Hampton* v. *Galloway* (1899) 1 F. 501; *Sandeman* v. *Duncan's Trs.* (1897) 4 S.L.T. 336; 5 S.L.T. 21.

37 See *Baikie* v. *Wordie's Trs.* (1897) 24 R. 1098; *Irvine* v. *C. Ry.* (1902) 10 S.L.T. 363.

38 *Sutherland* v. *Robertson* (1736) M. 13979; *Hardie* v. *Black* (1768) Mor. 10133; *McLellan* v. *Ker* (1797) M. 10134.

39 *Allen* v. *Robertson's Trs.* (1891) 18 R. 932.

40 *Wolfson, supra*; *Brown* v. *Keay* (1902) 9 S.L.T. 442; *Sandeman, supra*; *Rickards* v. *Lothian* [1913] A.C. 263.

41 *Whitelaw* v. *Fulton* (1871) 10 M. 27; contrast *Scottish Heritable Security Co.* v. *Granger* (1881) 8 R. 459.

42 *Irvine* v. *Caledonian Ry.* (1902) 10 S.L.T. 363; *N.B. Storage Co.* v. *Steele's Trs.*, 1920 S.C. 194.

43 1926 S.C. 319.

of damages in that although the immediate cause of the defect was fortuitous, it really arose from the defective condition of the premises at entry.

Statutory provisions

The Housing (Scotland) Act 1966, s. 6 (1),[44] implies into any contract (with certain exceptions) for the letting of a dwelling-house at a rent not exceeding £26 (£16 if lease entered into before July 31, 1923), not withstanding any stipulation to the contrary, a condition that the house is, at the commencement of the tenancy, in all respects reasonably fit for human habitation [45] and an undertaking that it will be kept so during the tenancy. This condition and undertaking are not implied where a house is let for a period of not less than three years upon the terms that it will be put by the lessee into a condition in all respects reasonably fit for human habitation, and the lease is not determinable at the option of either party before the expiration of three years. The landlord has a right of entry for inspection.[46] These provisions apply equally to a house occupied in connection with a contract of employment in agriculture.[47]

The standard of repair required is that the house must be decently fit for human beings to live in [48] and the premises cannot be regarded as fit for human habitation if injury may result from the ordinary use of the premises.[49] The tenant [50] may sue the landlord for damages for breach of this implied condition [51] but notice to the landlord of the want of repair is a pre-requisite to his liability.[52] These provisions impose no obligation on the landlord to keep a common stair in order.[53] Breaches have been constituted by defective drains resulting in scarlet fever,[54] a broken sash-cord,[55] and regular infestation with rats, though not by occasional incursions by rats,[56] and possibly by flooding.[56a]

[44] Re-enacting the Act of 1925, s. 1, and the Act of 1950, s. 3.

[45] The phrase is discussed in *Morgan* v. *Liverpool Corpn.* [1927] 2 K.B. 131.

[46] s. 6 (3).

[47] s. 7.

[48] *Jones* v. *Green* [1925] 1 K.B. 659, 668.

[49] *Summers* v. *Salford Corpn.* [1943] A.C. 283.

[50] But not strangers to the contract of lease, *e.g.* tenant's wife (*Middleton* v. *Hall* (1913) 108 L.T. 804) or daughter (*Ryall* v. *Kidwell* [1914] 3 K.B. 135), nor can they at common law: *Cavalier* v. *Pope* [1906] A.C. 428; *Cameron* v. *Young*, 1908 S.C.(H.L.) 7; *McCormick* v. *Fife Coal Co.*, 1931 S.C. 19. Persons who are third parties to the lease may, however, sue on the basis of negligence: Occupiers Liability (Scotland) Act 1960, s. 3.

[51] *Walker* v. *Hobbs* (1889) 23 Q.B.D. 458, decided under a corresponding provision of the Housing of the Working Classes Act 1885.

[52] *Morgan* v. *Liverpool Corpn.* [1927] 2 K.B. 131, approved in *McCarrick* v. *Liverpool Corpn.* [1947] A.C. 219; see also *Summers*, *supra*.

[53] *Dunster* v. *Hollis* [1918] 2 K.B. 795.

[54] *Chester* v. *Powell* (1885) 52 L.T. 722. See also *Smith* v. *Marrable* (1843) 11 M. & W. 5; *Campbell* v. *Wenlock* (1866) 4 F. & F. 716.

[55] *Summers*, *supra*; *Morgan* v. *Liverpool Corpn.* [1927] 2 K.B. 131.

[56] *Stanton* v. *Southwick* [1920] 2 K.B. 642.

[56a] *Duff* v. *Glasgow Corpn.*, 1958 S.L.T.(Sh.Ct.) 6.

Recent views are that the obligation is not a warranty [57] and that no rent is payable so long as the house is not kept reasonably fit for human habitation.[58]

The Housing (Scotland) Act 1966, ss. 8–9, implies in any lease (including a sublease) of a house granted on or after July 3, 1962, for less than seven years a provision that the lessor will keep in repair the structure and exterior of the house and keep in repair and proper working order the installations for water, gas, electricity, sanitation and for space heating or heating water. The lessor has a right of entry for inspection and repair. By section 10 exclusion or limitation of these provisions is void unless authorised by the sheriff.

If the subjects of let are or become unfit for the purpose of habitation the tenant may (i) refuse to take possession and rescind the contract [59] without being under any liability to the landlord for breach of contract if his repudiation is justified but himself being entitled to damages against the landlord for breach of an implied condition of the let. Any such action must be taken and intimated without delay as mora and acquiescence may bar the right to resile.[60] Or he may (ii) take possession and suspend it for a time,[61] claiming damages as well. Or he may (iii) abandon possession and repudiate the lease, with a claim of damages.[62] Or he may (iv) claim damages, either directly or as a counterclaim in an action for rent.[63] " When a tenant finds that his house is not in a habitable or tenantable condition he may either treat the mischief as a breach of a material condition of the lease, and claim to rescind the contract as from the date when the evil became intolerable, or he may found on the implied warranty in the contract a claim upon his landlord to put the building into a condition in which, by the agreement, it ought to have been when he took it." [64]

Refusal to enter

Where a tenant finds that the subjects let to him are uninhabitable, *e.g.* owing to bad sanitation [65] or disconformity with description [65] or infestation by vermin,[65] he may throw up the lease at once and claim damages. To do so he must act quickly [65] or he may be barred by delay

[57] *Morgan* v. *Liverpool Corpn.* [1927] 2 K.B. 131; *Euman's Trs.* v. *Warnock* (1930) 46 Sh.Ct. Rep. 164 (which see also for the relationship of the statutory provision to the common law obligations); *McKeown* v. *Anderson* (1933) 49 Sh.Ct.Rep. 140; *contra Weston* v. *Mories* (1923) 39 Sh.Ct.Rep. 86; *McGlory* v. *Playfair* (1925) 41 Sh.Ct.Rep. 223, following English authorities such as *Walker*, *Middleton* and *Ryall*, *supra*, and *Fisher* v. *Walters* [1926] 2 K.B. 315.

[58] *Euman, supra.*

[59] *Drummond* v. *Hunter* (1869) 7 M. 347; *Kippen* v. *Oppenheim* (1847) 10 D. 242; *Anderson* v. *Watson* (1894) 2 S.L.T. 293.

[60] *Cf. Drummond* v. *Hunter* (1869) 7 M. 347 (house damaged by fire before term: abandonment intimated three days after term: held timeous).

[61] See *Burns* v. *McNeil* (1898) 5 S.L.T. 289.

[62] *McKimmie's Trs.* v. *Armour* (1899) 2 F. 156, 161, *per* Lord McLaren.

[63] *Scottish Heritable Security Co.* v. *Granger* (1881) 8 R. 459.

[64] *McKimmie's Trs., supra.*

[65] *Brodie* v. *McLachlan* (1900) 8 S.L.T. 145 (three days' grace allowed in lease for two months). *Cf. Scottish Heritable Security Co.* v. *Granger* (1881) 8 R. 459.

and acquiescence. The damages in the case referred to [65] were only in respect of expenses and travelling charges, but there seems to be no reason why damages should not be recovered for the excess rent required to obtain another similar lease, and for incidental trouble and inconvenience, so long as these losses are fairly attributable to the fault of the landlord. While the tenant is not bound to wait to see if the nuisance can be cured when this cannot easily be done,[66] it may be a narrow question in cases of a remediable nuisance or ground of complaint. Acceptance of the premises as in tenantable order without seeing them had this result, and even though possession of some rooms was not given.[67]

Suspending possession after entry

A tenant may, particularly in a lease of considerable duration, suspend it for a time if the subjects are not habitable and resume possession after the necessary repairs have been effected.[68] If his action is justified he is entitled to an abatement of rent in respect of at least the period of dispossession.[69]

Right to abandon

If during a tenancy a house becomes uninhabitable it is a question of circumstances and reasonable conduct whether the tenant may or may not abandon the lease, having regard to the nature of the defects and time and measures likely to be required in abating them.[70] Delay in making complaint may bar the right to resile,[71] but where a tenant had to remove before the ish due to the house being uninhabitable he was held entitled to resile from an agreement to prolong the lease even though the defects were remedied before the ish.[72] Rescission is the appropriate remedy when a material condition of the lease has been persistently violated by the landlord.[73]

If the tenant proposes to resile, he must give immediate notice as otherwise, his repudiation of the lease being accepted, he will be held to have passed from his claim of damages.[74] Abandonment is a rescission of the contract and only competent where the stipulations violated are material or essential: the breach of minor and incidental stipulations, though it may be a ground for damages, will not justify rescission of the contract and abandonment of the lease.[75]

[66] *Kippen* v. *Oppenheim* (1847) 10 D. 242.
[67] *Webster* v. *Lyell* (1860) 22 D. 1423.
[68] *Burns* v. *McNeil* (1898) 5 S.L.T. 289.
[69] *Scottish Heritable Security Co.* v. *Granger* (1881) 8 R. 459 (abatement of half-year's rent allowed where dispossessed for two months).
[70] *Allan* v. *Markland* (1882) 10 R. 383; *McKimmie's Trs.* v. *Armour* (1899) 2 F. 156.
[71] *Whitelaw* v. *Fulton* (1871) 10 M. 27.
[72] *Scottish Heritable Security Co.* v. *Granger* (1881) 8 R. 459; *cf. Brodie* v. *MacLachlan* (1900) 8 S.L.T. 145.
[73] *Davie* v. *Stark* (1876) 3 R. 1114.
[74] *Lyons* v. *Anderson* (1886) 13 R. 1020.
[75] *Davie* v. *Stark* (1876) 3 R. 1114, 1119, *per* L.J.C. Moncreiff.

Where a landlord went bankrupt an action against his trustee in bankruptcy for damages for repairs which the landlord had undertaken to carry out and had failed to do was held irrelevant, as the trustee was not liable for the bankrupt's personal obligations.[76]

Among the circumstances which have been held to justify abandonment of the lease are dampness and intolerable smell,[77] and serious defects in drainage causing illness.[78] A tenant who continues to occupy the house in the knowledge that it is in a dangerous condition may be barred from claiming damages on the principle of *volenti non fit injuria*,[79] and abandonment of the lease which is accepted by the landlord without reservation infers an abandonment of the tenant's claim of damages.[80]

It is irrelevant to claim damages in respect of annoyance and discomfort in a case where the lease is abandoned, but, provided the specification is given, a claim for medicine, medical attendance and removal to another house necessitated by the deficiencies of the subjects of lease is relevant.[81]

The tenant's right to take the extreme step of quitting possession is dependent on having given due notice of the defects complained of to the landlord, and having thereafter allowed him a reasonable time to effect repairs and render the premises habitable.[82] A tenant who leaves without taking these steps is in breach of contract, and if he stays on after notice and a reasonable time for repairs has elapsed he may be held to have accepted the consequences,[83] unless he stays in reliance on repeated assurances of safety [84] or promises of speedy repair.[85] When the tenant could not easily obtain alternative accommodation he will not readily be held to have accepted the premises as they stand, particularly if repeated complaints be made. It is always a question of circumstances and reasonableness on both sides what remedial action must be taken, what delay is permissible, whether quitting is justifiable or not in the particular case, having regard to the state of the house.[86]

If, however, there be a defect in the original construction of the house and this is quite as obvious to the tenant as to the landlord or the latter's

76 *Harkness* v. *Rattray* (1878) 16 S.L.R. 117.
77 *McKimmie's Trs.* v. *Armour* (1899) 2 F. 156.
78 *Scottish Heritable Security Co.* v. *Granger* (1881) 8 R. 459. See also *Brodie* v. *McLachlan* (1900) 8 S.L.T. 145.
79 *Dickie* v. *Amicable Property Investment Co.*, 1911 S.C. 1079; *Mullen* v. *Dumbarton C.C.*, 1933 S.L.T. 185.
80 *Lyons* v. *Anderson* (1886) 13 R. 1020.
81 *Souter* v. *Mulhern*, 1907 S.C. 723.
82 *Webster* v. *Brown* (1892) 19 R. 765; *cf. Henderson* v. *Munn* (1888) 15 R. 859.
83 *Webster*, *supra* (outside stair); *McManus* v. *Armour* (1901) 3 F. 1078 (wash-house floor); *Baikie* v. *Wordie's Trs.* (1897) 24 R. 1098 (defective drains); *Russel* v. *Macknight* (1896) 24 R. 118 (common stair without handrail).
84 At least where the danger is not obvious; *Caldwell* v. *McCallum* (1901) 4 F. 371; *Hall* v. *Hubner* (1897) 24 R. 875, overruled on another point in *Cameron* v. *Young*, 1908 S.C.(H.L.) 7.
85 *Shields* v. *Dalziel* (1897) 24 R. 849; *McMartin* v. *Hannay* (1872) 10 M. 411; *Grant* v. *McClafferty*, 1907 S.C. 201; *McKinlay* v. *McClymont* (1905) 43 S.L.R. 9; *Cameron* v. *Young*, 1907 S.C. 475; affd. on another point, 1908 S.C.(H.L.) 7.
86 *McKimmie's Trs.* v. *Armour* (1899) 2 F. 156.

factor and this be allowed to continue without objection or protest on the tenant's part, the tenant can have no remedy on the basis of fault or negligence against the landlord, though injury be alleged to have resulted.[87]

Abandonment under principle of rei interitus

The clearest cases for the right to abandon the lease are cases where the subjects are completely or substantially destroyed without fault on either side so as not to be habitable or tenantable. In such a case the principle of *rei interitus* applies to frustrate the lease and it is avoided, no damages being recoverable.[88] If *rei interitus* results from the fault of either party, the loss will fall on the party in fault.[89]

It is a question of circumstances whether the destruction of the subjects let is so extensive as to justify abandonment.[90] The loss of the licence in licensed premises is not necessarily sufficient [91] to amount to *rei interitus*, but requisition [92] or substantial interference by a department of State have sufficed.[93]

In the event of complete destruction of the subjects the landlord is under no obligation to rebuild.[88]

If the destruction of the subjects is only partial it may be difficult to determine whether the tenant is or is not entitled to abandon under the principle of *rei interitus*. If the tenant does remain he is entitled to an abatement of rent corresponding to the extent of dispossession from the subjects which he has suffered.

Where a tenant renounced a lease on account of the land being flooded and the landlord accepted it, this was held to imply a discharge by the tenant of all claims of damages competent to him, it being observed that if any claim of damages was to have been reserved, notice should have been given by the tenant of his intention to make such a claim.[94]

Cases of damages alone

A tenant has been held entitled to recover damages where the fall of a neighbouring building damaged his house [95]; where the proprietor of an upper flat took off the roof without the landlord's consent to heighten the building and injury ensued to a lower flat tenanted by the pursuer [96]; where snow accumulated on a faulty roof and percolated and injured goods

87 *Mechan* v. *Watson*, 1907 S.C. 25; *Davidson* v. *Sprengel*, 1909 S.C. 566.

88 *Drummond* v. *Hunter* (1869) 7 M. 347; *Duff* v. *Fleming* (1870) 8 M. 769; *Devon Iron Co.* v. *E. Mansfield* (1839) 2 D. 268.

89 *Kippen* v. *Oppenheim* (1847) 10 D. 242.

90 *Allan* v. *Markland* (1882) 10 R. 383; *McKimmie's Trs.* v. *Armour* (1899) 2 F. 156.

91 *Donald* v. *Leitch* (1886) 13 R. 790; *Hart's Trs.* v. *Arrol* (1903) 6 F. 36.

92 *Mackeson* v. *Boyd*, 1942 S.C. 56; *Ben Aerated Waters* v. *Alexander* (1942) 58 Sh.Ct.Rep. 108.

93 *Tay Salmon Fisheries* v. *Speedie*, 1929 S.C. 593.

94 *Lyons* v. *Anderson* (1886) 13 R. 1020, 1025, *per* Lord McLaren.

95 *Hamilton* (1667) Mor. 10121.

96 *Deans* v. *Abercrombie* (1681) Mor. 10122; *cf. Scott* v. *Moir* (1895) 3 S.L.T. 70.

in a shop below.[97] It is a question of circumstances whether there is a duty on a landlord to keep down rats in premises let.[98] Specification of the particular faults founded on is essential and averment merely of disagreeable smells and insanitary conditions has been held irrelevant [99]: so have averments of serious defects in the construction of the house, for which the defender was alleged to be responsible.[1]

Even where the health of the tenant is injured in consequence of the defects, the landlord can only be held liable in damages where it is proved that the defects are due to his *culpa*.[2]

In serious cases a tenant may refuse to take or renew [3] possession or may suspend or even throw up the lease without himself incurring any liability in damages to the landlord. But if a tenant takes such action on inadequate grounds he is in breach of contract and liable in damages therefor to the extent of the loss sustained by the landlord. So a tenant was held not bound by the lease where a house was found infested with vermin, damp, and smelly, and when after notice the landlord had made no attempt to remedy the defects.[4] Other cases related to rats and bugs,[5] and defective drains.[3]

Where a tenant continues to occupy a house in the knowledge that it is dangerous he may be held on the principle of *volenti non fit injuria* to be barred from his claim of damages.[6] Where alternative accommodation is not reasonably available this defence is of little moment. It is a question of circumstances whether, when a tenant has paid rent without objection, he may yet be barred from claiming damages ultimately in respect of defects which existed during the period for which the rent was paid.[7] If repairs are necessary and the landlord after due notice and warning refuses or fails to execute them, the tenant may do so at his own hand and recover his disbursements by deduction from the rent or claim of damages. But the repairs should not be more than is necessary to bring the premises into habitable and tenantable condition as that is the standard which the landlord should have maintained. For the tenant's protection, a warrant from the Dean of Guild or Sheriff based on tradesmen's estimates of the cost of necessary repairs should be obtained, to be evidence both of the necessity of the repairs and their cost.

97 *Reid* v. *Baird* (1876) 4 R. 234; *Wilson, Guthrie & Co.* v. *Wright* (1891) 8 Sh.Ct.Rep. 51; *Hennon* v. *McDougall* (1896) 3 S.L.T. 265.
98 *Anderson* v. *Watson* (1894) 2 S.L.T. 293. See also *McNee* v. *Brownlie's Trs.* (1889) 26 S.L.R. 590; *Maitland* v. *Allan* (1896) 4 S.L.T. 121.
99 *Henderson* v. *Munn* (1888) 15 R. 859.
1 *Forbes* v. *Ferguson* (1899) 7 S.L.T. 293.
2 *Irvine* v. *Caledonian Ry.* (1902) 10 S.L.T. 363; *Baikie* v. *Wordie's Trs.* (1897) 24 R. 1098; *Burns* v. *McNeil* (1898) 5 S.L.T. 289.
3 *Scottish Heritable Co.* v. *Granger* (1881) 8 R. 459.
4 *Kippen* v. *Oppenheim* (1847) 10 D. 242.
5 *Anderson* v. *Watson* (1894) 2 S.L.T. 293.
6 *Dickie* v. *Amicable Property Co.*, 1911 S.C. 1079; *Mullen* v. *Dumbarton C.C.*, 1933 S.L.T. 185.
7 *Ramsay* v. *Howieson*, 1908 S.C. 697; see also *Haig* v. *Boswall Preston*, 1915 S.C. 339.

The claim is usually enforced by way of deduction from rent or counterclaim in a landlord's action for rent, or may be by separate action of damages.[8] A counterclaim may be made in a landlord's action for rent, and also a right of retention of that rent exercised.[9]

Measure of damages

The appropriate measure of damages is the loss sustained by the tenant in consequence of the landlord's fault, or the difference in value to the tenant of the house as unrepaired and as it would have been if duly repaired.[10] This will not always be the same as the cost of effecting the necessary repairs [11] but the tenant can probably recover the cost of repairs he has to do.[12] Actual personal injury,[13] and loss such as damage to furniture are additional possible heads of claim.[14] Expenditure on an alternative house has been refused in England [15] though the leased premises had not been habitable, but allowance might be made for the cost of an enforced delay in an alternative home, if reasonable and necessarily due to the landlord's delay to repair.[15] If the tenant were required to remove to allow repairs to be executed the expenses of removal would be recoverable.

It has also been held in England that it was competent where there was a continuing breach to recover damages during the currency of the lease and then again at the expiry, allowance being given for the sum already received.[16]

Repairs—agricultural leases

The landlord is under an implied obligation to put the house, offices, and fences, but not the drains,[17] on a farm into a tenantable state of repair,[18] that is, such a condition as will last to the ish, with ordinary care,[19] and to furnish such buildings as will enable the tenant to cultivate the land according to the mode contemplated in the lease.[20] In *Davidson* v. *Logan* [21] it was held that the obligation of a landlord to put buildings, fences [22] and drains, etc., in "tenantable condition and repair" at the

[8] *Scottish Heritable Co.* v. *Granger* (1881) 8 R. 459.
[9] *Fingland & Mitchell* v. *Howie*, 1926 S.C. 319.
[10] *Hewitt* v. *Rowlands* (1924) 93 L.J.K.B. 1080; *Cockburn* v. *Smith* [1924] 2 K.B. 119; *Porter* v. *Jones* (1943) 112 L.J.K.B. 173.
[11] *Ebbetts* v. *Conquest* (1900) 82 L.T. 560; *Henderson* v. *Thorn* [1893] 2 Q.B. 164.
[12] *Waters* v. *Weigall* (1795) 2 Anst. 575.
[13] *Griffin* v. *Pillett* [1926] 1 K.B. 17.
[14] *Hewitt* v. *Rowlands* (1924) 93 L.J.K.B. 1080.
[15] *Green* v. *Eales* (1841) 2 Q.B. 225.
[16] *Coward* v. *Gregory* (1866) L.R. 2 C.P. 153.
[17] *Wight* v. *Newton*, 1911 S.C. 762; *Rankine on Leases*, 3rd ed., 249. *Contra*, *Brown* v. *Simpson*, 1910, 1 S.L.T. 133.
[18] Bankton, I, 20, 10; II, 11, 21; Ersk. II, 6, 39; Bell, *Prin.* § 1253; *Buchanan* v. *Stark* (1776) 5 B.S. 515.
[19] *Mossman* v. *Brocket* (1810) Hume 850; *Davidson* v. *Logan*, 1908 S.C. 350; but see *Harrold* v. *Pollexfen* (1844) 6 D. 1103.
[20] *Barclay* v. *Neilson* (1878) 5 R. 909. See also *Burrell* v. *Gebbie* (1868) 6 S.L.R. 187.
[21] 1908 S.C. 350.
[22] See *Burrell* v. *Gebbie* (1868) 6 S.L.R. 187.

commencement of a lease is more onerous than the obligation of an outgoing tenant to leave these subjects in tenantable condition and repair. The essential distinction is that a landlord is liable at the commencement of a new lease to repair against natural decay and wear and tear, and also to make radical repairs and renewals which properly amount to extraordinary expenditure. The landlord's obligation extends to extraordinary repairs necessitated by natural decay.[23] A landlord has been held bound at common law to put an existing gravitation water supply into proper repair,[24] and liable for £10 as damages for inconvenience caused by his failure to do so. A temporary failure in water supply does not necessarily entitle a tenant to withhold payment of rent.[25]

Where a tenant proposes to make a claim against his landlord for damages for failure in an obligation of repair or maintenance, timeous intimation of the specific claim should be made in each year of the lease, so that each year's damage may be checked and evidence relative thereto be preserved, and this may be done by protest and reservation of rights when making payment of rent.[26] But payment of rent for several years without reservation does not necessarily involve a waiver of the claim,[27] where there is a history of repeated complaints or the damage is cumulative.[27]

The landlord may also be liable for damage done to the tenant during the course of the lease, as by flooding where the landlord was bound to maintain the necessary embankments.[28]

Statutory changes

The Agricultural Holdings (Scotland) Act 1949 provides [29] that in all fresh agricultural leases a record of the condition of the fixed equipment [30] on the holding shall be made and held to form part of the lease. There is to be deemed to be included in every lease of an agricultural holding a provision that the liability of the landlord [31] is to put the fixed equipment in a thorough state of repair at the commencement of the tenancy or as soon as practicable thereafter, and to provide such buildings and other fixed equipment as will enable a reasonably skilled occupier to maintain efficient production, and thereafter to replace and renew the buildings and other fixed equipment as rendered necessary by natural decay and fair wear and tear. Either party may by agreement undertake to execute at his own or wholly or partly at the other party's expense any work the other is

[23] *Johnstone* v. *Hughan* (1894) 21 R. 777; *cf. Swinton* v. *McDougall*, Jan. 16, 1810, F.C. Contrast *Walker* v. *Bayne* (1815) 6 Pat. 217.
[24] *Christie* v. *Wilson*, 1915 S.C. 645.
[25] *Russell* v. *Sime*, 1912, 2 S.L.T. 344; *cf. Wilkie* v. *Gibson* (1902) 9 S.L.T. 431; *Christie* v. *Wilson*, 1915 S.C. 645.
[26] *Hamilton* v. *Duke of Montrose* (1906) 8 F. 1026; *cf. Broadwood* v. *Hunter* (1855) 17 D. 340.
[27] *Ramsay* v. *Howison*, 1908 S.C. 697; *cf. Macdonald* v. *Johnstone* (1883) 10 R. 959. Contrast *Emslie* v. *Young's Trs.* (1894) 21 R. 710.
[28] *Scott* v. *Tait* (1826) 4 Mur. 57; *Hill* v. *Kinloch* (1856) 18 D. 722.
[29] s. 5 (1).
[30] Defined by s. 93 as including buildings, fences and dykes, ditches, drains, pens, roads, etc.
[31] For tenant's liabilities under same section, *vide supra*, p. 762.

required to execute under the lease,[32] but an agreement under a lease requiring the tenant to pay the whole or any part of the fire insurance policy over fixed equipment is to be null and void.[33]

The tenant's rights of action in case of default are the same as have been outlined in relation to urban subjects.[34] A tenant has been held to have waived all claims to damages for breach of the obligation to repair, as against the landlord's heir, when he renounced the lease and all claims thereunder, and as against his representatives by having possessed for eight years without complaint.[35]

Compensation for improvements, or disturbance, or high farming

The compensation which a tenant may in certain circumstances claim from the landlord for improvements [36] or disturbance,[37] or adoption of a special standard of farming,[38] does not partake of the nature of damages but rather of statutory compensation. Reference should be made to the standard work on the topic.[39] Similarly a landlord may have a claim for compensation for deterioration of the holding.[40]

Game damage

At common law the right to pursue and kill game is an incident of ownership [41] and game is accordingly reserved to the landlord *ex lege* in a lease.[42] He may, of course, let the shooting rights to a separate tenant. The agricultural tenant may neither take the game nor scare it away [43] and may not prevent the owner utilising his right to pursue game [44] except in the policies.[45] His remedy is damages and not interdict.[43]

The tenant may, however, kill vermin,[46] including rabbits,[47] foxes [48] and probably wood-pigeons [49]: he has no claim for damages or compensation for damage done by any bird or animal which he is entitled to destroy,

32 *Ibid.* s. 5 (3).
33 *Ibid.*s. 5 (4). All these provisions only apply to post-1948 leases.
34 *Supra*, p. 785.
35 *Waterson* v. *Stewart* (1881) 9 R. 155; see also *Johnstone* v. *Hughan* (1894) 21 R. 777; *Hamilton* v. *D. Montrose* (1906) 8 F. 1026.
36 Agricultural Holdings (Scotland) Act 1949, ss. 36–55.
37 *Ibid.* s. 35.
38 *Ibid.* s. 56.
39 Connell, *Agricultural Holdings Acts*, 6th ed., pp. 165–171.
40 *Ibid.* ss. 57–59.
41 *Pollock, Gilmour & Co.* v. *Harvey* (1828) 6 S. 913; *Birkbeck* v. *Ross* (1865) 4 M. 272. See further *Rankine on Landownership*, 145 *et seq.*
42 *Welwood* v. *Husband* (1874) 1 R. 507.
43 *Wemyss* v. *Gulland* (1847) 10 D. 204.
44 Ersk. II, 6, 6; Bell, *Prin.* §§ 953, 1224, 1226; *Ronaldson* v. *Ballantyne* (1804) Mor. 15270; *E. Hopetoun* v. *Wright*, Jan. 17, 1810, F.C.
45 *Graham* v. *McKenzie* (1810) Hume 641; see also *McDouall* v. *Caird* (1869) 6 S.L.R. 583; *Wood* v. *McRitchie* (1881) 2 Guth. 263.
46 *Brown* v. *Thompson* (1882) 9 R. 1183; *Fraser* v. *Lawson* (1882) 10 R. 396; *Crawshay* v. *Duncan*, 1915 S.C.(J.) 64.
47 *Moncrieff* v. *Arnott* (1828) 6 S. 530; see also *North* v. *Cumming* (1864) 3 M. 173; *Porter* v. *Stewart* (1858) 3 Irv. 57; *Inglis* v. *Moir's Trs.* (1871) 10 M. 204; *Jack* v. *Nairne* (1887) 1 White 350; *Crawshay* v. *Duncan*, 1915 S.C.(J.) 64. See further Rankine, *Leases*, 491; Tait on *The Game Laws*, 44.
48 *Colquhoun* v. *Buchanan* (1785) Mor. 4997.
49 *Connacher* v. *Bryson* (1875) cited in Rankine, *Leases*, 485.

unless prevented from exercising his right by the landlord.[50] Where the shootings were let to a person other than the agricultural tenant, it was held that the landlord was the person liable when he had planted trees and allowed rabbits to breed there.[51]

Under the Ground Game Acts 1880 and 1906 every occupier of land is given a right,[52] concurrently with any other person entitled, to kill hares and rabbits on the land, and therefore a tenant has no claim in respect of damage done by these unless the *status quo* is altered as regards plantations or places to which the tenant does not have access.[53]

" A tenant may have a claim of damage for the injury done by game, but in order to support such a claim it is necessary to prove not merely a certain visible damage arising from game, but a certain and visible increase of the game and a consequent alteration of the circumstances contemplated in the contract, imputable to the act of the landlord. The true ground of damage seems to be, not that the game is abundant, but that its abundance has been materially increased since the date of the lease, in consequence either of the active measures of the landlord or his failure to keep down the burden—which last circumstance must be held as equivalent to his act, as the right so to keep it down is one expressly withheld from the tenant." [54] Hence there is liability for damage caused by an artificially stimulated increase of game subsequent to [55] but not prior to [56] the lease, or by any alteration of the *status quo*,[57] and the measure of damages is the difference between what would have been done by an ordinary stock of game and that actually done.

The claim may be limited or excluded by clear stipulation in the lease [58] but these clauses are strictly construed against the landlord.[59]

The tenant may be barred by mora, as by failing to give adequate and timeous notice of his intention to make the claim, whereby the evidence is lost.[60] Thus payment of rent without deduction or notification of a claim will bar the claim,[61] and it has been held that retention of the whole rent of the holding is not justified, as the obligation is only collateral and not an

50 *Wood* v. *Paton* (1874) 1 R. 868; *cf. Gowans* v. *Spottiswoode* (1914) 31 Sh.Ct.Rep. 30; *Roddan* v. *Pollock* (1916) 32 Sh.Ct.Rep. 18.

51 *Inglis* v. *Moir's Tutors* (1871) 10 M. 204. Contrast *Drysdale* v. *Jameson* (1832) 11 S. 147.

52 As to the persons entitled to exercise the right see *Smart* v. *Murray* (1884) 5 Coup. 526; *Bruce* v. *Prosser* (1897) 2 Adam 487; *Richardson* v. *Maitland* (1897) 2 Adam 243; *Brodie* v. *Cowie* (1889) 5 Sh.Ct.Rep. 428.

53 *Cameron* v. *Drummond* (1888) 15 R. 489.

54 *Drysdale* v. *Jameson* (1832) 11 S. 147, 149, *per* Lord Fullerton. *Cf. Syme* v. *E. Moray* (1868) 5 S.L.R. 272.

55 *Wemyss* v. *Wilson* (1847) 10 D. 194; *Broadwood* v. *Hunter* (1855) 17 D. 340, 1139; see also *Morton* v. *Graham* (1867) 6 M. 71; *Kidd* v. *Byrne* (1875) 3 R. 255; *Cadzow* v. *Lockhart* (1876) 3 R. 666.

56 *Drysdale, supra.*

57 *Cameron* v. *Drummond* (1888) 15 R. 489; see *Ormston* v. *Hope* (1917) 33 Sh.Ct.Rep. 128.

58 *Roddan* v. *McCowan* (1890) 17 R. 1056.

59 *Morton* v. *Graham* (1867) 6 M. 71; *Cadzow* v. *Lockhart* (1875) 2 R. 928 and 3 R. 666.

60 *Elliott's Trs.* v. *Elliott* (1894) 21 R. 858; *Emslie* v. *Young's Trs.* (1894) 21 R. 710; *Broadwood* v. *Hunter* (1855) 17 D. 340.

61 *Elliott, Emslie, Broadwood, supra*; *Macdonald* v. *Johnstone* (1883) 10 R. 959; *Hardie* v. *D. Hamilton* (1878) 15 S.L.R. 329; *cf. Ramsay* v. *Howison*, 1908 S.C. 697.

essential of the lease.[62] Moreover the tenant must prove that the damage was in fact caused by game and not by another cause, such as miscropping.[63] The claim is restricted to loss in the year preceding the claim [60] and will be refused altogether if the claim is delayed till long after the landlord has sold the farm,[64] but a claim made each year is not barred [65] nor are repeated claims in respect of cumulative damage.[66]

The tenant's claim for damages will cover not only damage done by game but damage done to crops by the shooting tenant in the course of killing the game; the latter must take all reasonable care to avoid damage to the lands.[67] So too a person hunting on horseback, even if he be the landlord, is liable to the tenant for any damage he may do.[68]

Claims for game damage under Agricultural Holdings (Scotland) Act 1949

By section 15, where the tenant of an agricultural holding has sustained damage to his crops from game (defined [69] as deer, pheasants, partridges, grouse, and black game) the right to kill and take which is vested neither in him nor in anyone claiming under him other than the landlord, and which the tenant has not permission in writing to kill,[70] he is entitled to compensation if the damage exceeds in amount the sum of five pence per acre of the area over which it extends,[71] provided he gives notice in writing and a reasonable opportunity to the landlord to inspect the damage before the crop has begun to be reaped, raised or consumed, or if already raised or reaped, before removal from the land. The notice must be given within one month of the end of the calendar year [72] or such other period of twelve months as may be agreed.[73] Permission to kill one of the enumerated kinds of game excludes a claim for compensation for damage by that kind of game.[74]

The quantum of compensation is to be determined by arbitration, failing agreement [75] and the landlord has a claim of relief against any person in whom the right to kill and take the game is vested.[76]

The game tenant may contract out of this liability in his lease, and probably at common law the landlord has a right of indemnity against any

62 *Meikle* v. *Ramsay* (1901) 17 Sh.Ct.Rep. 138; *Todd* v. *Haggarty, ibid.* 245.
63 *Milne* v. *E. Dalhousie* (1868) 5 S.L.R. 268.
64 *Emslie, supra.*
65 *Hardie* v. *D. Hamilton* (1878) 15 S.L.R. 327.
66 *Ramsay* v. *Howison,* 1908 S.C. 697 (continued neglect of muirburn).
67 *Hilton* v. *Green* (1862) 2 F. & F. 821.
68 *Ronaldson* v. *Ballantine,* Nov. 21, 1804, F.C.
69 *Ibid.* s. 15 (4); this excludes ground game which the tenant may kill.
70 Including game coming from an adjacent estate, and even during close season: *Thomson* v. *E. Galloway,* 1919 S.C. 611.
71 Compensation is due even if the landlord shows that he took all reasonable steps to keep down the game. The difficulty is to say whether the damage is to be computed over the affected area or the whole field or holding. If it is due, it is the full sum without deduction of the five pence: that is merely to exclude trivial claims.
72 *Morton's Trs.* v. *McDougall,* 1944 S.C. 410.
73 s. 15 (1). Similarly under Small Landholders (Scotland) Act 1911, s. 10 (3).
74 *Ross* v. *Watson,* 1943 S.C. 406.
75 s. 15 (2).
76 s. 15 (3). *Cf. Kidd* v. *Byrne* (1875) 3 R. 255.

neighbouring proprietor if the game came from his lands.[77] The tenant has no direct claim against the tenant of the shootings.[78] He may claim from the landlord and the latter will be able to recover from the game tenant, if the latter is responsible as by keeping an unreasonably large stock of game on the lands.[79] If the tenant is also the tenant of the shooting rights the landlord is immune from such claims.[80]

Quantum of damages

The quantum of damages at common law, and presumably the quantum of compensation under the Act is the difference between the damage which would be done by an ordinary stock of game and the damage actually done by the increased stock. The basis of calculation is the fair stock of game understood at common law to be contemplated in any ordinary farm lease.[81]

Furnished leases

Apart from express stipulations in the lease, the let of a furnished house presents few specialties. Such leases are impliedly not assignable nor may the premises be sublet but otherwise the ordinary rights and liabilities incidental to urban leases apply.

" The landlord warrants the furniture fit for use; is discharged of his duty wholly or partially by accidental destruction of the subject; and is bound to protect the tenant in his possession and to indemnify him for loss which is not the result of pure accident or the tenant's fault. The tenant is bound to pay the rent," subject usually to an obligation to remove in the event of failure to pay it within a certain period, " to take only the contemplated use; to bestow due care, and to restore, barring accidents, the complex subject in as good repair, both as to quantity and quality, as he got it, tear and wear excepted." [82]

In the absence of contrary stipulations, the tenant may take down pictures and store them in the house, so long as no damage is done thereby. He may also shift furniture from room to room.[83]

Otherwise the ordinary obligations of the contract of location will apply [84]: the landlord must protect the tenant's possession and indemnify him for loss not accidental or the tenant's fault. The tenant must take due care of the subjects and restore them in the same order as he took them, apart from ordinary wear and tear.

77 *Cf. Farrer* v. *Nelson* (1890) 15 Q.B.D. 258.
78 *Inglis* v. *Moir's Tutors* (1871) 10 M. 204.
79 *Kidd* v. *Byrne, Byrne* v. *Johnson* (1875) 3 R. 255.
80 *Sutherland* v. *Secretary of State for Scotland* (1942) 30 L.C. 26, 30.
81 *Drysdale* v. *Jameson* (1832) 11 S. 147.
82 *Rankine on Leases*, 3rd ed., 288.
83 *Miller* v. *Stewart* (1899) 2 F. 309.
84 Bell, *Prin.* § 137; Comm. I, 452.

Lease of business premises

The lease of this kind resembles the urban lease in having an implied warranty that the premises are wind- and water-tight,[85] but this does not extend to stability under excessive loads [86] nor to fitness for the purpose of the tenant's business.[87]

Lodgings

The contract of lodging contains no specialties distinct from general principles of urban leases. It is an inversion of possession to commit suicide in the lodgings.[88]

Mineral leases

So far as concerns damages between landlord and tenant the principal grounds of claim are, on the landlord's part, claims for disrepair and dilapidation of buildings and fences and for surface damage,[89] and on the tenant's part, claims for non-possession or eviction from the subjects or for hindrance in the execution of the contemplated operations. There is no warranty implied that the subjects are reasonably fit for the purposes for which they are let.

Enforcement of tenant's claim by retention of rent

A tenant's claim against his landlord is regularly enforced by way of retaining rent.[90] In this way he may have ascertained and allowed an abatement in respect of partial eviction from the subjects of lease, as in cases of loss of water-power,[91] or access,[92] or accidental loss of certain buildings,[93] or in cases where the subjects of let have not been put into a tenantable state of repair,[94] so long as the landlord's failure is material.[95] Consignation may be ordered [96] and the claim may be elided by an offer to execute repairs,[97] or continuing payments of rent without reservation

[85] *N. B. Storage Co.* v. *Steele's Trs.*, 1920 S.C. 194.

[86] *Glebe Sugar Co.* v. *Paterson* (1900) 2 F. 615. See also *Manchester Bonded Warehouse Co.* v. *Carr* (1880) 5 C.P.D. 507.

[87] *Aitchison* v. *Glasgow Mags.* (1825) 1 W. & Sh. 153; *Hart's Trs.* v. *Arrol* (1903) 6 F. 36, 38.

[88] *A.* v. *B.'s Trs.* (1906) 13 S.L.T. 830.

[89] *Oswald* v. *Gordon* (1853) 16 D. 70. See also *Galbraith's Tr.* v. *Eglinton Iron Co.* (1868) 7 M. 167; *Russel* v. *Gillespie* (1868) 6 M. 925; 9 M(H.L.) 130; *Ogilvy* v. *Devon Iron Co.* (1845) 8 D. 241; *Daniel Stewart's Hosp.* v. *Waddell* (1890) 17 R. 1077.

[90] In *Daniel Stewart's Hospital* v. *Waddell* (1890) 17 R. 1077, the lease conferred the right.

[91] *Gordon* v. *Suttie* (1826) 4 Mur. 86.

[92] *Guthrie* v. *Shearer* (1873) 1 R. 181.

[93] *Muir* v. *Macintyres* (1887) 14 R. 470; older cases cited therein. See also *Critchley* v. *Campbell* (1884) 11 R. 475; *Dougall* v. *Dunfermline Mags.*, 1908 S.C. 157; *Kilmarnock Gas Co.* v. *Smith* (1872) 11 M. 58; *Duncan* v. *Brooks* (1894) 21 R. 760; *Drybrough* v. *Drybrough* (1874) 1 R. 909.

[94] *Graham* v. *Gordon* (1843) 5 D. 1207; *Munro* v. *McGeoghs* (1888) 16 R. 93; *Sivright* v. *Lightbourne* (1890) 17 R. 917; *E. of Galloway* v. *McConnell*, 1911 S.C. 846; *Haig* v. *Boswall-Preston*, 1915 S.C. 339. Contrast *Stewart* v. *Campbell* (1889) 16 R. 346.

[95] *Sharp's Factor* v. *Monboddo* (1778) Mor. 10134; *Davie* v. *Stark* (1876) 3 R. 1114; *Macdonald* v. *Kydd* (1901) 3 F. 923; *Christie* v. *Birrells*, 1910 S.C. 986; *Russell* v. *Sime*, 1912, 2 S.L.T. 344.

[96] *Clark* v. *Finlay* (1823) 2 S. 480; *Cumming* v. *Williamson* (1842) 4 D. 1304.

[97] *McRae* v. *Macpherson* (1843) 6 D. 302; *Dods* v. *Fortune* (1854) 16 D. 478.

or notice of claim.[98] It may be excluded by the terms of the lease [99] and cannot be exercised in conjunction with the right to retain rent under the Rent Acts.[1] It may be exercised in respect of a claim for compensation for improvements, if that claim is liquid.[2] But a claim of damages against the landlord for loss sustained in consequence of the landlord's delay to implement does not justify retention of rent after repairs have been carried out,[3] nor may a tenant retain rent in security of a claim of damages for delay or failure in the past to implement his obligations,[4] nor again in security of an anticipated loss in the future, the defect giving rise to his claim of retention having been remedied.[5] Where an illiquid claim of damages arises from a matter distinct from the lease it must be established by a substantive action.[6] There may be a claim of retention and also a counterclaim for damages.[7]

98 *Stewart* v. *Campbell* (1889) 16 R. 346.
99 *Skene* v. *Cameron*, 1942 S.C. 393.
1 *Stobbs* v. *Hislop*, 1948 S.C. 216.
2 *Duke of Argyll* (1935) 23 L.C. 58.
3 *Christie* v. *Birrells*, 1910 S.C. 986.
4 *Guthrie* v. *Shearer* (1873) 1 R. 181; *Stewart* v. *Campbell* (1889) 16 R. 346; *Christie* v. *Birrells*, 1910 S.C. 986.
5 *Christie* v. *Wilson*, 1915 S.C. 645.
6 *Sheppard* v. *McNab* (1896) 3 S.L.T. 240.
7 *Fingland & Mitchell* v. *Howie*, 1926 S.C. 319.

CHAPTER 48

CONSTITUTION OF LOANS AND RIGHTS IN SECURITY

THE contract to lend money, and to constitute security over heritage for the repayment thereof, may give rise to various claims.

Borrower's claims

If a person or body has undertaken to borrow and the lender defaults by failing or refusing unjustifiably to advance the money, the borrower is entitled to damages for the breach of contract, measured by any higher rate of interest he has to pay to another lender for the inconvenience of having to make an alternative arrangement, and for any naturally consequential losses, such as having to abandon the purchase of particular premises or incurring liability to a third party for breach of contract with him.

Lender's claims

If the borrower defaults by failing or refusing unjustifiably to take on loan money which he has undertaken to borrow, the lender is entitled to damages measured by the interest which he would have received until such time as he can, or could with reasonable diligence, find an alternative borrower, and for any direct and natural consequences of the borrower's default.

Breach in respect of security

A lender will not normally pay the sum agreed to be lent until he has obtained an *ex facie* valid deed constituting security in his favour and has had it recorded to complete his right in security. If he does pay money before the security deed is executed and recorded he may rescind the contract if there is unjustifiable delay or refusal to complete the agreed security in his favour, and claim damages.

Prejudice to security-holder's rights

The debtor, in exercising his powers of using and managing the subjects of security, may not act prejudicially to the rights of the bondholder. Thus where a lease by a debtor in possession was such that it could not be regarded as fair administration, it was held that the lease was not binding on the bondholder.[1] Bondholders have been held entitled to sue the representative of a tenant of security subjects for reduction in value of the

[1] *Reid* v. *McGill*, 1912, 2 S.L.T. 246; contrast *Neilson* v. *McNab* (1903) 11 S.L.T. 387.

subjects caused by his dilapidation thereof; the damages claimed were measured by the diminished value of the security subjects, it being averred that the creditors would be unable to recover their loan to that extent.[2]

Exercise of security-holder's rights to prejudice of debtor

A lender, in exercising any right vested in him by virtue of his right in security, must have reasonable regard for the radical right of the borrower in the security subjects. Thus where a creditor held a house under a disposition *ex facie* absolute but truly in security, and sold it, without, it was held, having due regard to the debtor's interests, he was held liable in damages to the debtor.[3] Similarly a bondholder has been held to have a duty, in carrying through a sale, to avoid prejudicing the rights of postponed security-holders.[4]

[2] *Edinburgh & Leith Gas Commrs.* v. *Smart*, 1917, 1 S.L.T. 44.
[3] *Shrubb* v. *Clark* (1897) 5 S.L.T. 125. *Cf. Baillie* v. *Drew* (1884) 12 R. 199; *Waddell* v. *Hutton*, 1911 S.C. 575.
[4] *Stewart* v. *Brown* (1882) 10 R. 192.

CHAPTER 49

ASSIGNATION OF INCORPOREAL RIGHTS

Sale and assignation of incorporeal moveables

The Sale of Goods Act 1893 does not apply to the sale or assignation of incorporeal moveable rights such as stocks and shares, life assurance policies, debts, goodwill, patents, trade marks, registered designs, copyright, or plant breeders' rights, and so far as concerns damages for breach of a contract to sell or assign, the principles of common law apply, at least in so far as the nature of the subject-matter will permit. There are, however, few reported illustrations of the application of these principles in the case of incorporeal subjects, and much remains to be determined in any particular case from the general principles of damages.

Some of the instances in question may well be more suitable for seeking decree of specific implement in view of some *pretium affectionis* or unique quality of the subject-matter of the transaction, *e.g.* the goodwill attaching to particular premises, a block of shares not readily available on the market, a particular patent, etc., but in many cases, as of shares readily available in the market, damages will be adequate compensation.

Stocks and shares

When parties contract to buy and sell shares the prima facie measure of damages in the event of the buyer refusing to accept [1] or the seller declining to deliver,[2] is the difference between the contract price of the transaction and the best market price of the shares on the day when the contract should have been performed.[3] In the former case, it has been held that the seller is under no obligation to resell at all, but any loss which is consequent on further fall in price falls on him and does not enter into damages [4]; while, conversely, a rise in market value benefits the seller and does not lessen the damages recoverable.[5] In *Dickson* v. *Henderson* [6] a seller whose broker had exceeded his instructions refused delivery of the scrip: the purchaser at the broker's request delayed to buy in against him, during which time the price rose. The broker paid the purchaser for the stock bought in and recovered from the seller the full sum, as it was found that the seller was bound to have implemented the original sale and he was liable in the full consequences of the breach.

1 *Jamal* v. *Moolla, Dawood & Co.* [1916] 1 A.C. 175.
2 *Shaw* v. *Holland* (1846) 15 M. & W. 136; *Powell* v. *Jessopp* (1856) 18 C.B. 336.
3 *Howie* v. *Anderson* (1848) 10 D. 355; *Jamal, supra.*
4 *Jamal, supra*, 176.
5 *Jamal, supra.*
6 (1849) 12 D. 306. *Cf. Tulloch* v. *Davidson* (1860) 3 Macq. 783.

In *Michael* v. *Hart*,[7] a case of anticipatory breach not accepted, damages were measured at the date when the stock should have been available for sale, the court using the analogy of cases relating to non-delivery of goods.

Where shares unissued at time of contract

If there is a transaction in respect of shares as yet unissued, the earliest date for performance must be the date of issue, so that even if the buyer purport to repudiate the contract earlier, damages can only fall to be assessed by reference to the first day on which they are issued.[8] In one case, however, it was held that as a letter of allotment, which was all that was in existence, might have been transferred, the date of repudiation was the date of breach for the purposes of computing damages,[9] subject to the observation that the innocent party was not bound to accept any such anticipatory repudiation.

Failure to replace stock

Where stock has been lent and a breach of the agreement to replace it has taken place, the measure of damages is the whole value of the stock lent, taken at a rate to indemnify the pursuer, as in such a case the borrower has the lender's valuable assets in his possession so that the lender is deprived of the use of his money. So, where the stock had risen since the due date for transfer, its value was taken as at or before the date of trial.[10] The defender may replace the stock at any time thereafter if he can take advantage of a rise in the market.[11] Where the value has fallen it has been taken as the value of the stock on the date when it should have been replaced,[12] or the date it was transferred to the borrower.[13] The possibility of speculative profits must be ignored.[14] Similar principles seem to apply in the case of the non-delivery of stock already paid for [15] where damages have been given proportioned to the price when delivery should have been made.

Life assurance policies

A life policy is a marketable commodity assignable to persons who have no interest in the life,[16] and damages might be given where an assignment was induced by the fraud of one party.[17] It is suggested that an appropriate measure of damages would be the whole consideration given if the

7 [1902] 1 K.B. 482; affd. (1904) 89 L.T. 422. *Cf. Murray* v. *Hewitt* (1886) 2 T.L.R. 872; *Samuel & Escombe* v. *Rowe* (1892) 8 T.L.R. 488.
8 *Pott* v. *Flather* (1847) 16 L.J.Q.B. 66.
9 *Tempest* v. *Kilner* (1845) 3 C. & B. 249. See too *Ellis* v. *Pond* [1898] 1 Q.B. 426.
10 *Harrison* v. *Harrison* (1824) 1 C. & P. 412; *Owen* v. *Routh* (1854) 14 C.B. 327.
11 *Shepherd* v. *Johnson* (1802) 2 East 211.
12 *Sanders* v. *Kentish* (1799) 8 T.R. 162.
13 *Forrest* v. *Elwes* (1799) 4 Vesey 492.
14 *McArthur* v. *Lord Seaforth* (1810) 2 Taunt. 257; *Mansell* v. *B. L. Co.* [1892] 3 Ch. 159.
15 *Startup* v. *Cortazzi* (1835) 2 C.M. & R. 165; *Dutch* v. *Warren* (1720) 2 Burr. 1010.
16 *Ashley* v. *Ashley* (1829) 3 Sim. 149.
17 *Barber* v. *Morris* (1831) 1 Mood. & Rob. 62.

assignment be valueless, or the difference between the consideration given and the value of the policy if the interest conveyed is different from that understood to have been purchased, or otherwise the whole loss sustained as the direct and natural consequence of the breach of contract.

Debts and bonds

An assignation of a bond if for onerous consideration, contains an implied clause of warrandice from fact and deed that *debitum subesse*, *i.e.* that there is a subsisting debt due by the debtor to the cedent in the assignation.[18] Thus, in *Reid* v. *Barclay*,[19] a bond was assigned without express warrandice for onerous consideration: it proved to be invalid *quoad* the cautioners and the debtor became bankrupt. The court held the assignee entitled to repetition of the sum in the bond, which was the consideration given for the assignation. But to give an assignee recourse against a cedent in the event of the insolvency of the debtor a special clause of warrandice to that effect is necessary, as not even absolute warrandice will have that effect by implication.[20] The implied warrandice extends to the full debt and is not limited to the price for the assignation.[21]

Damages may also probably be claimed where a person who has agreed to lend refuses to do so without justification. Any loss, such as the excess cost of obtaining the loan elsewhere, will be recoverable as the natural result of the breach.[22]

Goodwill

If goodwill is transferred in connection with particular premises, specific implement is appropriate in the event of breach of contract [23]: if there be no such connection it depends principally on circumstances whether specific implement or damages is appropriate. If the seller be entitled under the contract to receive a share of profits in the form of an annuity, the purchaser becomes impliedly bound to continue the business, and is liable in damages if he should unjustifiably fail to do so.[24]

Damages are generally recoverable for any breach of contract, such as the failure to deliver business books, to transfer the goodwill, or to implement some collateral agreement such as to refrain from competition, or implement may be sought at the discretion of the court, particularly if the transaction is connected with a sale of heritage.[25] A failure in implement on one side, as by setting up a new firm, may be pleaded in defence to an action for the price.[26]

18 *Ferrier* v. *Graham's Trs.* (1828) 6 S. 818; *Sinclair* v. *Wilson and Maclellan* (1829) 7 S. 401; *Leith Heritages Co.* v. *Edinburgh & Leith Glass Co.* (1876) 3 R. 789.

19 (1879) 6 R. 1007; *cf. Houston* v. *Corbet* (1717) Mor. 16619.

20 *Liddell* v. *Barclay* (1671) Mor. 16594; Bell, *Prin.* § 1469.

21 *Houston, supra.*

22 *Aston Properties* v. *Tunbridge Wells Friendly Socy.* [1936] 1 All E.R. 531.

23 *Darbey* v. *Whitaker*, 4 Dr. 139. As to cases where there is no dependence on premises, see *Robertson* v. *Quiddington*, 28 Beav. 529; *England* v. *Downs*, 6 Beav. 269; *Llewelyn* v. *Rutherford* (1875) L.R. 10 C.P. 456.

24 *MacIntyre* v. *Belcher* (1864) 32 L.J.C.P. 254; 14 C.B.(N.S.) 654.

25 Bell, *Prin.* § 29; *Stewart* v. *Kennedy* (1890) 17 R.(H.L.) 1, 9.

26 *McKirdy* v. *Paterson* (1854) 16 D. 1013.

A claim of damages may also be made when it turns out that the nature or value of the goodwill transferred is materially different from what it was represented to be so much so as to be essentially different, if the representations were fraudulent, or the transaction may be reducible for essential error or innocent misrepresentation. Reduction may still take place if heritage has been sold and goodwill assigned as an indivisible transaction, even though there is no misrepresentation *quoad* the heritage and title has been made up.[27]

If lapse of time and change of circumstances have taken place, it is questionable if a claim of damages *quanti minoris* may be made,[28] unless, possibly, heritage is an indivisible element in the transaction.[29] If there is fraudulent misrepresentation the deficiency would be compensated by the recovery of damages for the fraud.[28]

Trade marks

The assignation of trade marks is competent [30] and is frequently connected with the transfer of goodwill; a sale of a business carries with it the goodwill and trade marks,[31] while a sale of a business and goodwill carries the right to the trade name.[32] Damages for breach of the contract to assign must be assessed on general principles.

Patents

Specific implement is more appropriate as a rule for a case of failure to perform a contract to assign a patent [33]; but in some circumstances damages may be recoverable: where a patentee agreed to sell his patent and guaranteed it to be valid and in full force and part of the price was paid, and the assignee then pleaded in defence to an action for the balance of the price that the patent was invalid, and counterclaimed for return of the money paid or damages, he was held entitled to damages amounting to the difference between the money paid and the real value of the business acquired.[34]

Such a sale carries no implied warranty that the patent right is a *good* right, at least where each party knew what the invention was and had equal means of ascertaining its value.[35] Similarly, a contract for the sale or assignment of a patent involves no warranty that the invention is new, but merely that Her Majesty has granted to the seller the letters patent, which are the subjects of sale.[36]

[27] *Straker* v. *Campbell*, 1926 S.L.T. 262.
[28] *Bryson* v. *Bryson*, 1916, 1 S.L.T. 361.
[29] *Straker, supra*; *cf. Louttit's Trs.* v. *Highland Ry.* (1892) 19 R. 191.
[30] Trade Marks Act 1938, ss. 22, 25.
[31] *Inland Revenue* v. *Muller* [1901] A.C. 217.
[32] *Levy* v. *Walker* (1888) 10 Ch.D. 436.
[33] Assignation is dealt with in Patents Act 1949, s. 74.
[34] *Berchem* v. *Wren* (1904) 21 R.P.C. 683.
[35] *Hall* v. *Conder* (1857) 2 C.B.(N.S.) 22. *Cf. Montforts* v. *Marsden* (1895) 12 R.P.C. 266.
[36] *Smith* v. *Neale* (1857) 2 C.B.(N.S.) 67.

Registered designs

A registered design may be assigned [37] and damages may flow from a breach of the contract to assign, but there appears to be no case in which the question of damages has been discussed and, in consequence, general principles will have to be applied should a case arise.

Copyright

The assignation of copyright is regulated by section 36 of the Copyright Act 1956 and it may be effected outright, or by a licence to exercise some or all of the owner's rights on payment of a royalty. Such contracts may be breached in various ways, from which claims of damages may flow. There is little authority on the topic and recourse must be had to general principles of the law of damages for breach of contract, modified and applied to suit the circumstances of the particular case which has arisen.

It has been held that where an executor granted a full assignation of his author's copyright, he was held to have given an express warranty of title, and was held liable in damages for breach of warranty, when it was disclosed that a prior equitable assignment had been made, unknown to the executor.[38] It is suggested that an appropriate measure of damages is the estimated loss of profit by reason of the invalidity of the assignation. At least in the similar case where an author has agreed to supply a manuscript for publication, damages are recoverable for his failure to do so,[39] the sum to be awarded being any outlays made on the faith of the unexecuted contract and the estimated loss of profit,[40] so long as the work would not have been libellous or obnoxious.[41]

After assignment an author's work may not be revised by another hand and represented as the original author's work; if there is deception of the public and damage to the original author or deprivation of sales, he may recover damages.[42]

Plant breeders' rights

Plant breeders' rights [43] are capable of assignation in the same way as other incorporeal proprietary rights,[44] and the same general principles probably apply to breach of a contract to assign the rights.

Industrial " know-how "

Independently of patents and trade marks, and of business goodwill, a person possessed of the knowledge of how to achieve some industrial

[37] Registered Designs Act 1949, s. 19.
[38] *Sims* v. *Marryat* (1851) 17 Q.B. 281. *Cf. Kyle* v. *Jeffreys* (1859) 3 Macq. 611.
[39] *Gale* v. *Leckie* (1817) 2 Starkie N.P. 107.
[40] *Clarke* v. *Price* (1819) 2 Wils.C.C. 157.
[41] *Gale, supra.* On the measure of damages for failure to publish, see *Abrahams* v. *Reiach* [1922] 1 K.B. 477; *cf. Gollancz* v. *Dent* (1903) 88 L.T. 358.
[42] *Rudge* v. *English Illustrated Mag.*, Macg.Cop.Cas. (1911–17), 91.
[43] Plant Varieties and Seeds Act 1964, s. 4.
[44] *Ibid.* s. 4 (4).

result [45] may sell some or all of that knowledge. Claims of damages are doubtless competent on the one hand for failure to communicate " know-how " as undertaken, and on the other hand for misuse of the information communicated.

[45] See the discussion of the nature of " know-how " in *Moriarty* v. *Evans Medical Supplies Ltd.* [1957] 3 All E.R. 718, and *Rolls-Royce Ltd.* v. *Jeffrey* [1962] 1 All E.R. 801, 805.

CHAPTER 50

DAMAGES FOR BREACH OF OBLIGATION OF RESTITUTION

WHERE a legal obligation arises to make restitution, for the avoidance of the unjust benefit which will otherwise arise,[1] and restitution is not made, a claim of damages arises in those cases where the restitution should have been effected *in specie*, as an alternative to restitution, and the remedy appropriate where restitution cannot be made. Where the restitution required is a payment or repayment of money,[2] a claim for damages in the alternative is pointless as it in effect asks for the same thing as should have been, but has not been, paid, but interest can doubtless be asked for the wrongful withholding of the money.

Restitution of moveables

Where restitution of moveables is claimed it is appropriate to claim alternatively, failing delivery, damages, amounting to the fair market value of the goods which should have been redelivered and have not been re-delivered. The basis of this alternative claim is truly reparation for delict. Thus where one person stole moveables a claim was competently brought against him for restitution of the moveables, or alternatively, for reparation in the form of damages for the fair value of the moveables stolen.[3] A resetter is liable for the value of goods reset and not recovered.[4] Again where restitution cannot be made because the goods have been converted into another form and are not reconvertible, or have been mixed with other goods so as to have given rise to a new substance, the claim can only be for the fair value of the goods used and of the property in which the claimant has been deprived.[5]

Negotiorum gestio

A person who acts as *negotiorum gestor* on behalf of another may incur liability in damages in various circumstances.

Gestor discontinuing acting

A *gestor* who, having undertaken some function on behalf of another, discontinues his *gestio* before the task has been completed, or without

[1] For the cases where this arises see Chap. 14, *supra*.
[2] *i.e.* cases of repetition of money and of recompense.
[3] *Cf. Gorebridge Co-operative Socy.* v. *Turnbull*, 1952 S.L.T.(Sh.Ct.) 91.
[4] *Dalhanna Knitwear Ltd.* v. *Mohammed Ali*, 1967 S.L.T.(Sh.Ct.) 74.
[5] *International Banking Corpn.* v. *Ferguson, Shaw & Sons*, 1910 S.C. 182.

handing over to another who is competent to relieve him, is liable in damages for any loss caused by his premature discontinuance.[6]

Failure to take reasonable care in acting

Where a party takes it on himself to act as a *negotiorum gestor* he is bound to take reasonable care in the circumstances, and to exercise the care and diligence which a prudent man would have taken in relation to his own property and is liable in damages for loss caused by his failure to act according to that standard.[7] The measure of damages is the loss sustained by reason of the defender's failure. Thus if goods have been taken into custody and wholly lost, the full value would be the proper damages.

Gestor's claim

The *gestor's* counter-claim for reimbursement of outlays and expenses necessarily incurred is not a claim of damages, but a claim for recompense, and is measured by the amount he has expended in rendering the services in question.[8]

Inability to account

A *gestor* is liable in damages if he is unable to account for his intromissions with the owner's property.[9] Damages should probably be assessed on the basis of deeming lost and replaceable at the gestor's expense all property which he can be shown to have taken under his charge, and which he has not satisfactorily accounted for.

[6] *Cf.* Bell, *Prin.* § 541.
[7] Bell, *Prin.* § 541; *Kolbin* v. *United Shipping Co.*, 1930 S.C. 724, 746, 753, 757; 1931 S.C. (H.L.) 128, 139.
[8] Bell, *Prin.* § 541.
[9] *Cf. Kolbin, supra.*

CHAPTER 51

GENERAL PRINCIPLES OF DAMAGES FOR DELICT

General

A delict or civil wrong is constituted by the breach of a duty, fixed primarily by the general law and independently of any agreement of parties, incumbent in the circumstances on the defender and owed to, *inter alios*, the pursuer, resulting in loss, injury or damage to the pursuer and redressible by an award of unliquidate damages.[1] The remedy of an award of damages is always available for such wrongs: " Money is the universal solvent; everything can be turned into money that is either a gain or a loss; money is asked, and damages are due for reparation of every possible suffering or injury." [2] The duties for breach of which liability to pay damages arises are distinct from those arising from contract in that they are fixed by the general law and are binding on persons generally, whereas contractual duties bind only the parties to the contract. Nevertheless there are cases where the boundary between contractual and delictual obligations becomes indefinite, as where parties are brought into proximity by a contractual relationship and this furnishes the opportunity of committing a wrong which is a breach of a general, apart from a contractual, duty of care to avoid doing harm.[3]

Purpose of award

As in contract, the purpose of an award of damages in an action founded on delict is to restore the pursuer, so far as that is possible by payment of money, to the position he would have been in but for the commission of the wrong complained of.[4] While it is commonly said that the general principle governing the assessment of damages is *restitutio in integrum*,[5] it has been pointed out that this cannot be strictly applied to cases of delict. " If by somebody's fault I lose my leg and am paid damages, can anyone in his senses say I have had *restitutio in integrum*? " [6] " There is real difficulty in treating solatium as being compensation, for

1 Stair I, 9, 2–4; Ersk. III, 1, 12–3; Bell, *Prin.* §§ 544, 553.
2 *Auld* v. *Shairp* (1874) 2 R. 191, 199, *per* Lord Neaves.
3 *Donoghue* v. *Stevenson*, 1932 S.C.(H.L.) 31, 64.
4 Stair I, 9, 2; *Livingstone* v. *Rawyards Coal Co.* (1880) 7 R.(H.L.) 1, 7; *Watson, Laidlaw & Co.* v. *Pott, Cassels & Williamson*, 1914 S.C.(H.L.) 18, 29; *Clyde Nav. Trs.* v. *Bowring S.S. Co.*, 1929 S.C. 715; *Hutchison* v. *Davidson*, 1945 S.C. 395; *Cruickshank* v. *Shiels*, 1951 S.C. 741, 753; *McCallum* v. *Paterson*, 1968 S.C. 280, 285; Bell, *Prin.* § 553, speaks of " indemnity."
5 *e.g. The Kate* [1899] P. 168; *Liesbosch* v. *Edison* [1933] A.C. 449, 459; *The Argentino* (1888) 13 P.D. 200; affd. (1889) 14 App.Cas. 519; *Pomphrey* v. *Cuthbertson*, 1951 S.C. 147.
6 *Admiralty Commrs.* v. *S.S. Valeria* [1922] 2 A.C. 248, *per* Lord Dunedin. *Cf. The Edison* [1932] P. 67, *per* Scrutton L.J.; Jolowicz in *Cambridge Legal Essays*, 203 *et seq.*

no amount of money can compensate suffering." [6a] In the nature of things *restitutio in integrum* in any literal sense is frequently impossible in cases of delict and the phrase is not appropriate in such cases.[7] In delict, moreover, the measure of damages is necessarily frequently much more speculative than in contract as the loss sustained by a breach of contract may frequently be calculated with reasonable accuracy, whereas no sum of money can ever be truly compensation to an individual for serious or disabling personal injury, nor is there any possible means by which compensation for a personal wrong such as injury or defamation can ever be exactly quantified. Every man considering a case is liable to arrive at a different assessment of the damages due and, unless in extreme cases, no one such estimate is more right or wrong than another. The speculative element in delictual damages is enhanced to some extent by the fact that their estimation is commonly assigned in Scottish practice to a jury who have no experience in these matters. It remains unknown what items of claim the jury have taken account of or ignored and the relative importance and the amount of money which they have attached to each. Moreover, unless a jury errs widely in their estimation of the damages due, no modification of the award can be made.[8]

Where an award of damages is made by a judge sitting alone he may and indeed must apply what principles can be derived from past cases and the settled course of practice. A lesser margin of error is allowed in respect of this, and also because the judge's opinion should disclose his reasons for arriving at the figure awarded.[9]

Compensation the general principle

Subject to that qualification of the phrase *restitutio in integrum*, the general principle to be sought in actions *ex delicto* as much as in actions *ex contractu* is compensation to the party wronged.[10] "The common law says that the damages due either for breach of contract or for tort are damages which, so far as money can compensate, will give the injured party reparation for the wrongful act and for all the natural and direct consequences of the wrongful act," and this applies both at common law and in Admiralty.[11] This principle, however, goes no distance towards determining the proper quantum of damages in money in any given case, as the extent of loss for which compensation is due frequently cannot be estimated with any accuracy at all and is in any event truly incommensurable in money. Difficulty of assessment is, however, no reason for giving

6a *McCallum* v. *Paterson*, 1968 S.C. 280, 284, *per* Lord Walker.

7 *Admiralty Commrs.* v. *S.S. Valeria* [1922] 2 A.C. at p. 248, *per* Lord Dunedin; *Livingstone* v. *Rawyards Coal Co.* (1880) 7 R.(H.L.) 1; *cf. The Mediana* [1900] A.C. 113, 116.

8 *Infra*, Chap. 61.

9 *Purdie* v. *Allan*, 1949 S.C. 477.

10 *Gibson* v. *Anderson* (1846) 9 D. 1, 6, *per* L.P. Boyle; *Tucker* v. *Aitchison* (1846) 9 D. 21, 23; *Muckarsie* v. *Dixon* (1848) 11 D. 4, 5.

11 *Admiralty Commrs.* v. *S.S. Susquehanna* [1926] A.C. 655, 661, frequently cited and approved in Scotland, *e.g. Clyde Navigation Trs.* v. *Bowring S.S. Co.*, 1929 S.C. 715: *Hutchison* v. *Davidson*, 1945 S.C. 395; *Pomphrey* v. *Cuthbertson*, 1951 S.C. 147.

no award or only a nominal or insubstantial sum of damages.[12] It will be seen later that a course of practice has tended within broad limits to accept certain sums or methods of computation as affording appropriate compensation in different sets of circumstances. "The measure of damages, though not controlled by rigid rules, is not to be ascertained by caprice, but only by application of the proper principle which is the principle of *restitutio in integrum*." [13] More measures than one may legitimately be employed and compared to estimate the money value of the damage sought to be compensated.[14]

Necessity for legal damage

It is essential as much as in contract before a loss *ex delicto* should sound in damages that the loss should be legal damage, that is, a temporal and material loss which may be estimated in money and of which the law takes account and not merely a social loss: thus loss of the society of friends is insufficient,[15] though loss of their hospitality is sufficient damage [16] to ground a claim.

The kinds of damages in delict

It is necessary to distinguish certain categories of awards of damages which may be met with in actions of reparation. These may be taken as (i) nominal or insubstantial or contemptuous damages, (ii) ordinary or substantial damages, and (iii) exemplary, punitive or aggravated damages.

Nominal damages

In English law nominal damages signifies a small sum awarded not by way of compensation but merely in recognition of the existence of a legal right vested in the plaintiff and violated by the defendant. It does not follow because an award of damages is very small that it is nominal. Nominal damages truly represent *injuria sine damno*.[17] Consideration of nominal damages raises first the question whether Scots law recognises that all wrongs *ex delicto* automatically sound in damages. In England it is well established that at least nominal damages fall to be awarded when there has been an infringement of a plaintiff's legal right, except in certain exceptional cases when special damage, *i.e.* actual damage suffered, must be averred before the suit can be maintained at all.[18]

While this rule is somewhat stringent it is both logical in penalising any infraction of a legal right and yet illogical in that if damages are properly

[12] *Chaplin* v. *Hicks* [1911] 2 K.B. 786; *Thomson* v. *Dailly* (1897) 24 R. 1173.
[13] *Hutchison* v. *Davidson*, 1945 S.C. 395, 410.
[14] *Duke of Portland* v. *Wood's Trs.*, 1926 S.C. 640, 651; *Hutchison*, *supra*.
[15] *Lynch* v. *Knight* (1861) 9 H.L.Cas. 599.
[16] *Davies* v. *Solomon* (1871) L.R. 7 Q.B. 112.
[17] *Ashby* v. *White* (1703) 2 Ld.Raym. 938, 955. See also *The Mediana* [1900] A.C. 113; *Nicholls* v. *Ely Beet Co.* [1936] Ch. 365, 380; *Constantine* v. *Imperial Hotels Ltd.* [1944] K.B. 693. *Cf.* *Neville* v. *London Express Newspapers* [1919] A.C. 368, 392.
[18] *McGregor on Damages*, 13, 604.

intended as compensation, no compensation at all can truly be due unless the pursuer has actually sustained some discernible loss or injury which requires to be compensated.

In *Morton* v. *Barclay*,[19] an action for infringement of a patent, it was stated that where an action is brought to establish a right and concluding for damages, but no damages have been proved, a verdict should be returned for nominal damages. This, however, expressly bears to be an unprecedented case and also to proceed purely on the analogy of English jury practice. Certainly the general statement is not acceptable in modern Scots law.

It is thought that the rule in Scots law is that in those actions founded on the principle of the *actio legis Aquiliae*, concluding for damages for actual damage to person or property, no damages may be awarded unless there is evidence of actual loss or harm, if not in patrimonial or pecuniary respects, at least in the shape of pain and hurt but that in actions founded on the principle of the *actio injuriarum*, concluding for damages for affront, dishonour or hurt feelings, as for defamation, damages may be awarded if there is evidence of circumstances naturally giving rise to affront, dishonour or hurt feelings though there be no evidence of actual harm or loss. The Lord Chief Commissioner said in *Cameron* v. *Camerons*[20]: " If no damages are proved you cannot find them, but there is a claim for solatium, and you must consider what evidence there is of the injury to the mind and feelings." In *Aarons* v. *Fletcher*[21] wrongful detention of property without proof of actual loss suffered was held to justify an award of £10, but this result was arrived at partly, at least, on the basis of compensation for trouble and inconvenience caused to the pursuer. Lord Justice-Clerk Aitchison,[22] founding on *Webster* v. *Cramond Iron Co.*,[23] a case of breach of contract, and the English case of *The Mediana*,[24] thought that nominal damages were due for wrongful detention, and so did Lord Anderson.[25] Lord Hunter was doubtful, but Lord Murray laid down that *damnum* was an essential factor to any claim of damages, though he concurred in the award proposed in respect of the trouble caused.[26] This case is therefore equivocal authority.

Furthermore, any trespass is sufficient to found a claim for nominal damages in England.[27] But in Scotland it seems established that unintentional trespass on property belonging to another person will afford no remedy by action for nominal damages, nor even will a petition for interdict be granted unless it be shown that there is reasonable ground for

19 (1824) 3 Mur. 401.
20 (1820) 2 Mur. 232, 235.
21 1934 S.C. 137.
22 p. 140.
23 (1874) 2 R. 752.
24 [1900] A.C. 113.
25 p. 141.
26 *Bell* v. *Simpson* (1867) 5 M. 298, is not truly an authority for the competency of nominal damages.
27 *Ashby, supra*; *Embry* v. *Owen* (1851) 6 Ex. 353; *Gayford* v. *Chouler* [1898] 1 Q.B. 316.

apprehension of repetition of the intrusion.[28] All that a proprietor can do is to turn the trespasser away. Damages can be claimed only if actual injury to his premises can be shown, such as by breaking down fences or treading down growing crops,[29] that is, special or actual damage must be proved.[30]

So, too, in England a person who without negligence has purchased and resold stolen goods is liable for their value in respect of a wrongful conversion [31]: under Scots law his liability is dependent on the quasi-contractual obligation of restitution and not on reparation, and liability for damages is limited to the profit he may have made on the resale.[32]

Similarly it has been held that no damages are recoverable for wrongful interdict if no loss has been suffered by the pursuer, as a claim of damages will not lie merely for the pronouncement of interdict, but only for the loss incurred in being prevented from doing the forbidden act, which might otherwise have been done.[33] A pursuer claiming *solatium* for the loss of a relative is not entitled to anything at all unless he shows that grief was actually sustained: the jury is not bound to make at least a nominal award.[34]

In actions founded on negligence, no damages at all will be awarded if no loss has been sustained, as damage arising from the defender's breach of duty is of the essence of an action for negligence, and there is no presumption in such cases of loss sustained.[35] The general rule of Scots law is therefore, it is submitted, that a pursuer is not entitled to any damages unless he shows loss, or at least circumstances in which the law will infer some loss. "A breach of contract, or wrongful act, is no doubt an *injuria*, but it may be *injuria sine damno*, and *damnum* is an essential factor to any claim of damages." [36] Hence nominal damages will not in Scotland be given generally for any infraction of a right, as in England.

It is otherwise, however, in a case of an *actio injuriarum*, such as slander where the fact of uttering a defamatory statement subjects to liability for damages. "But if a slander has been uttered the pursuer is prima facie entitled to some damages or . . . an apology." [35] This is explicable on the basis that just as the law presumes malice from the uttering of a defamatory statement,[37] so it presumes some damage and injury to the pursuer's

28 *Hay's Trs.* v. *Young* (1877) 4 R. 398.

29 *Watson* v. *Earl of Errol* (1763) Mor. 4991; *Colquhoun* v. *Buchanan* (1785) Mor. 4997.

30 *Graham* v. *Duke of Hamilton* (1868) 6 M. 965; *Lord Advocate* v. *Glengarnock Co.*, 1909, 1 S.L.T. 15.

31 *Hollins* v. *Fowler* (1875) L.R. 7 H.L. 757.

32 *Scot* v. *Low* (1704) M. 9123. See further on the application to Scotland of the English law of conversion and trespass, *Leitch* v. *Leydon*, 1929 S.C.(H.L.) 1, *per* Lords Dunedin and Blanesburgh.

33 *Aird* v. *Tarbert School Board*, 1907 S.C. 305, approving *Bostock* v. *Ramsay Urban Council* [1900] 2 Q.B. 616; *Clippens Oil Co.* v. *Edinburgh Water Trs.* (1906) 8 F. 731; *Bell* v. *Simpson* (1867) 5 M. 298.

34 *Rankin* v. *Waddell*, 1949 S.C. 555. *Cf. Cameron* v. *Camerons* (1820) 2 Mur. 232, 235.

35 *Millar's Trs.* v. *Polson* (1897) 24 R. 1038.

36 *Aarons* v. *Fraser*, 1934 S.C. 137, 143, *per* Lord Murray.

37 *Cassidy* v. *Connochie*, 1907 S.C. 1112, 1116, *per* Lord Stormonth-Darling.

feelings and reputation. Hence if a slander is proved at least a small sum of damages must be awarded,[38] and in some cases the award is truly nominal.[39]

It is consequently doubtfully competent in Scotland to sue for nominal damages as a means of establishing the infringement of a pursuer's rights, even if other forms of process were not more appropriate for such a purpose.

Even if it is competent in any case to sue for only nominal damages solely in order to vindicate a right, such an action would be practically pointless in Scotland as it could only be raised in the sheriff's summary court, and the recovery in a higher court of only nominal damages where substantial damages had been claimed but not established would probably cost the pursuer his expenses at least in part.[40] The claim for nominal damages merely to assert the right alleged to have been infringed is accordingly at least inappropriate in modern practice. That result could frequently be achieved by actions of declarator or interdict or other process.

Insubstantial awards

There are, however, several instances in the reports where very small awards of damages have been made and these awards are sometimes characterised as " nominal." [41] Despite the use of the word, however, these appear properly to be cases of insubstantial damages where the loss was considered to be trivial, although real and actual, rather than of proper nominal damages given purely in recognition of the infraction of the pursuer's rights. Thus awards of £5,[42] £10,[43] £20,[44] £25,[45] £30,[46] £35,[47] £40,[48] £50,[49] are not truly nominal but insubstantial. In *Madden* v. *Glasgow Corporation* [50] the pursuer in an action of damages for personal injuries was awarded " nominal damages " of one farthing although the evidence established that she had sustained substantial injuries. This verdict was characterised as illogical and perverse on the facts as it manifestly appears to be. Inability to make a proper estimate of the loss is no reason for an award of small or nominal amount.[51]

38 *Nelson* v. *Irving* (1897) 24 R. 1054, 1058; *Shaw* v. *Morgan* (1888) 15 R. 865; *Harkness* v. *Daily Record*, 1924 S.L.T. 759.
39 *Bradley* v. *Menley & James*, 1913 S.C. 923.
40 *Stewart* v. *Caledonian Ry.* (1870) 8 M. 486; *Wilkie* v. *Alloa Ry.* (1884) 12 R. 219; *Lumsden* v. *G.N.S. Ry.* (1870) 8 M. 791; *Shearer* v. *Malcolm* (1899) 1 F. 574.
41 *e.g. Fairbairn* v. *Cockburn's Tr.* (1878) 15 S.L.R. 705.
42 *Gordon* v. *O'Hara*, 1931 S.C. 172.
43 *Gorman* v. *Hughes*, 1907 S.C. 405; *McGilp* v. *Caledonian Ry.* (1904) 7 F. 4; *Hughes* v. *Morgan*, 1910 S.C. 712.
44 *Hughes* v. *Allen*, 1909 S.C. 1210.
45 *McDaid* v. *Coltness Iron Co.* (1904) 7 F. 32; *Fraser* v. *Caledonian Ry.* (1903) 5 F. 476; *Casey* v. *Mags. of Govan* (1902) 4 F. 811.
46 *Lafferty* v. *Watson, Gow & Co.* (1903) 5 F. 885.
47 *Ridley* v. *Kimball & Morton* (1905) 7 F. 655.
48 *Shearer* v. *Malcolm* (1899) 1 F. 574; *Watt* v. *Mags. of Alva* (1903) 11 S.L.T. 118; *Adlington* v. *Inveraray Coach Co.* (1874) 1 R. 911; *Brennan* v. *Dundee & Arbroath Ry.* (1903) 5 F. 811.
49 *United Horse Shoe Co.* v. *Stewart* (1887) 14 R. 266; revd. 15 R.(H.L.) 45.
50 1923 S.C. 102. *Cf. Stewart* v. *Caledonian Ry.* (1870) 8 M. 486.
51 *Thomson* v. *Dailly* (1897) 24 R. 1173.

Contemptuous awards

So, too, a very small award is frequently contemptuous rather than nominal and is not so much a recognition of an infringed right as compensation when the loss has been one which the pursuer on his own conduct morally deserved to sustain or one which really gave him scant justification for complaint. Thus awards of one farthing for personal injuries [52] or for the seduction of a wife [53] are contemptuous rather than nominal. In actions for vindication of character, however, small awards may more easily be described as nominal: such are awards of one farthing,[54] sixpence [55] or one shilling [56] and it is rather a question of circumstances whether they should be described as nominal or contemptuous.

Ordinary or substantial damages

This is the kind of award of damages normally made, where some actual loss or damage is proved to have flowed from the infringement of the right and an award of a more or less substantial sum is made to compensate therefor, so far as money can compensate the pursuer for the loss suffered. The award may or may not be held to be adequate, or inadequate, or excessive, but it is an award intended to have some reasonable relation to the extent of loss. Such an award is subject to mitigation or aggravation by circumstances and its amount is determined by the trend of practice and by consideration of various factors more fully dealt with in subsequent chapters. If the loss proved is very slight the award may be so small as to approach being described as insubstantial or even, though erroneously, as nominal damages. On the other hand the award may be very substantial indeed but may not, in Scotland at least, go beyond attempted compensation so as to be exemplary or vindictive or punitive, because the purpose of an award is compensatory, not retributive.

While the intention in making an award of ordinary damages is to effect compensation in fair measure and to restore the pursuer, so far as money can effect this, to the position he would have been in, this does not necessarily or always mean that the cost of restoration of the pursuer's former condition, if that be practicable, is the true measure of damages. Compensation, rather than restitution, is the test and in this way also the phrase *restitutio in integrum* as applied to damages in delict is not strictly accurate nor should it be interpreted literally.

In the case of wrongs which partake of the nature of insult or outrage, substantial damages are given on the basis of an estimate of the effect of the wrong on the pursuer's feelings and reputation, rather than in respect

52 *Adlington* v. *Inveraray Coach Co.* (1874) 1 R. 911.
53 *Thain* v. *Thain*, 1948 S.L.T.(Notes) 89.
54 *Bonnar* v. *Roden* (1887) 14 R. 761; *Sproll* v. *Walker* (1899) 2 F. 73; *Craig* v. *Jex-Blake* (1871) 9 M. 973; *Graham* v. *Napier* (1874) 1 R. 391; *Dawson* v. *Giffen*, 1915, 2 S.L.T. 256; *Winn* v. *Quillan* (1899) 2 F. 322.
55 *Bradley* v. *Menley & James*, 1913 S.C. 923.
56 *Pirie* v. *Meikle* (1874) 2 R. 40; *Stewart* v. *Caledonian Ry.* (1870) 8 M. 486.

of any ascertainable loss which can be quantified in money. In such cases it is sometimes hard to say whether the damages do or do not contain an exemplary, vindictive or punitive element.

Exemplary damages

In *Black* v. *N.B. Ry.*[57] enhanced damages were claimed on the ground that damages are imposed partly *in poenam*, and this view received some sanction from the case of *Morton* (*Cooley's Factor*) v. *Edinburgh and Glasgow Ry.*,[58] where the degree of negligence was held to be a consideration relevant to increase damages. Alternatively it was contended in *Black* [57] that exemplary damages should be awarded where the degree of fault and culpability of the defenders is great. Lord President Dunedin stated that he could find no authority for any distinction between damages and exemplary damages in Scots law, and remarked that the very heading " Reparation " excluded this idea. He thought that malice was the foundation of the doctrine and it could consequently not apply to cases where the person sued was not the actual wrongdoer, but was only held liable on the ground of *respondeat superior*.[59] The Lord President accordingly came to the conclusion that it was not relevant to inquire whether the accident was caused by gross or ordinary negligence, and Lord Ardwall also thought that the degree of negligence or fault ought not to form an element in arriving at the amount of damages. Similarly in the old case of *Hyslop* v. *Staig* [60] it was said that a jury should not convert compensation for injury into punishment.[61] Exemplary damages are, however, recognised in English law, where they are a sum awarded in excess of any material loss and by way of *solatium* for any insult or other outrage to the plaintiff's feelings that is involved in the injury complained of.[62]

A distinction must be taken between exemplary and aggravated damages. Though the former are not, the latter are, recognised in Scotland and are appropriate where damages are at large but the extent of loss is made more serious by certain factors, such as the grossness or repetition of a slander,[63] or the gravity of the injury to the pursuer in the circumstances. This element is not, however, in any sense punitive but merely compensatory for more grievous wrong.

Certain older dicta in Scottish cases, however, recognise exemplary damages in cases of insult or outrage where the loss cannot be exactly

[57] 1908 S.C. 444, 453.

[58] (1845) 8 D. 288. See also *Cunningham* v. *Duncan* (1889) 16 R. 383, *per* Lords Shand (389) and Adam (391); *Hillcoat* v. *G.S.W. Ry.* (1907) 15 S.L.T. 433.

[59] *Quaere*, could it apply in cases of the defender's personal fault? There is no clear authority for this but awards in defamation and assault cases may contain an element of exemplariness.

[60] (1816) 1 Mur. 24.

[61] *Cf. Gibson* v. *Anderson* (1846) 9 D. 1, 6; *Tucker* v. *Aitchison* (1846) 9 D. 21, 23; *Muckarsie* v. *Dixon* (1848) 11 D. 4, 5.

[62] *McGregor on Damages*, 218.

[63] *Cf. Cunningham* v. *Duncan* (1889) 16 R. 383; *Stein* v. *Beaverbrook Newspapers Ltd.*, 1968 S.C. 272.

quantified. Thus Lord Justice-Clerk Boyle said in a case of breach of promise of marriage[64] that "the principles of justice authorise us to award the most exemplary damages," and in *Thomson* v. *Dailly*,[65] a case of infringement of trade name, Lord Trayner said that he thought it was a case for exemplary damages.

Modern practice seems to follow Lord Dunedin's dictum and even in cases such as defamation and adultery, where the essence of the wrong lies in the outraged feelings, the awards of damages made in Scotland do not rise so high as to be exemplary or punitive. There seems neither justification in principle, nor necessity, for recognising exemplary damages in Scots law today.

General and special damages

A distinction is regularly drawn in English practice between general and special damages and the terminology has to some extent penetrated into Scots law.[66] But in English law the terms are used to distinguish at least four pairs of contrasting kinds of damages.[67] General damages in the English law of tort are sometimes such as the law presumes to follow from the commission of the legal wrong: they need not be expressly pleaded, but are claimed generally. Special damages are such further damages as have actually been sustained in consequence of the wrong, and they must be expressly averred and proved.[68] In other cases special damage is of the essence of the action and no action will lie unless such be averred: such is the case of slander, if the words complained of be not actionable of themselves. In Scotland on the other hand this distinction is not fully maintained,[69] but the general rule is that to ground any action of reparation some special or actual damage must be shown and a lump sum is claimed to cover all heads of damages. In only a few cases such as slander will actual damage at least to feelings be presumed by law from the mere fact of the slander being uttered. In negligence on the other hand actual damage is an essential to the relevancy of the action,[70] and an action for slander of title will only lie where special damage is averred.[71]

So under English law a plaintiff who has lost the use of a ship or vehicle by collision caused by the defendant's fault, may recover general damages for loss of use during the period of repairs even though the ship or vehicle were not being used for trading or even for pleasure purposes.[72] In Scotland there would probably require to be at least an averment of loss of use and consequent inconvenience to justify an award and *semble*,

64 *Hogg* v. *Gow*, May 27, 1812, F.C.
65 (1897) 24 R. 1173.
66 *Aarons* v. *Fraser*, 1934 S.C. 137, 143; *cf. Rankin* v. *Waddell*, 1949 S.C. 555.
67 *McGregor on Damages*, 12 *et seq.*
68 *Admiralty Commrs.* v. *S.S. Susquehanna* [1926] A.C. 655, 661.
69 The terms are used in the English sense in *Pomphrey* v. *Cuthbertson*, 1951 S.C. 147.
70 *Millar's Trs.* v. *Polson* (1897) 24 R. 1038.
71 *Harpers* v. *Greenwood & Batley* (1896) 4 S.L.T. 116.
72 *Admiralty Commrs.* v. *S.S. Susquehanna* [1926] A.C. 655; *Admiralty Commrs.* v. *S.S. Chekiang* [1926] A.C. 637.

if a ship laid up were damaged, nothing would be due in respect of loss of use during the period she was laid up.[73] But the loss of the reasonable possibility of use would probably be sufficient to ground a claim,[74] and equally in Scotland and England actual proven loss of use will certainly justify an award of damages,[75] *i.e.* special damages.

The terms " general " and " special " damages are also sometimes applied to the two classes of damages better distinguished as ordinary, natural or direct damages and extraordinary, remote, indirect or consequential damages.[76]

Comparison of damages in contract and in delict generally

The principal differences in legal principle between damages in contract and damages in delict are:

(1) The basis of the obligation to compensate is different, breach of an obligation voluntarily undertaken in the one case, breach of an obligation imposed in the circumstances by law in the other.

(2) The rules for determining whether certain losses are too remote to be recoverable are different.[76a]

(3) From the nature of the legal obligations breached and the forms which loss may assume, pecuniary compensation is usually a less complete, exact and satisfactory compensation in delict than in contract.

(4) From the intangible nature of the losses in delict, awards of damages are more frequently at large, *i.e.* lump sums arrived at by taking a broad overall view of the pursuer's losses.

(5) In consequence of these differences, the guidance to be derived from the study of reported cases and dicta and the trend of practice is not so much as to what kinds of loss and heads of claim are admissible, as it is in contract, but more as to how much money is generally allowed in practice as fair and reasonable compensation for a particular kind of loss in its particular circumstances.[77]

(6) Evidence of malicious conduct is admissible in some cases of delict[78] though not in contract,[79] in aggravation of damages, or its absence in mitigation.[80]

(7) It appears probable that the practice of entrusting the quantification of damages in delict to juries does in fact, though not in law, permit legally irrelevant considerations to be taken into effect, and renders the quantification of damages still more uncertain and speculative.

73 *Cf. Robertson* v. *Connolly* (1851) 14 D. 315; *Carslogie S.S. Co.* v. *Royal Norwegian Government* [1952] A.C. 292.

74 *The Mediana* [1900] A.C. 117; *cf. The London Corporation* [1935] P. 70; *Caxton Publishing Co.* v. *Sutherland Publishing Co.* [1939] A.C. 192, 203.

75 *Vitruvia S.S. Co.* v. *Ropner Shipping Co.*, 1923 S.C. 574.

76 Chaps. 28, *supra*, and 52, *infra*.

76a Chaps. 28, *supra*, and 52, *infra*.

77 *Cf. Bird* v. *Cocking* [1951] 2 T.L.R. 1260; *Rushton* v. *N.C.B.* [1953] 1 W.L.R. 292.

78 *Sears* v. *Lyons* (1818) 2 Stark. 317; *cf. Thomson* v. *Dailly* (1897) 24 R. 1173; *Cunningham* v. *Duncan* (1889) 16 R. 383, 387; *Morrison* v. *Ritchie* (1902) 4 F. 645, 652; *Pratt* v. *B.M.A.* [1919] 1 K.B. 244, 281; *Stein* v. *Beaverbrook Newspapers Ltd.*, 1968 S.C. 272.

79 *Addis* v. *Gramophone Co.* [1909] A.C. 488; *cf. Walter* v. *Alltools Ltd.* [1944] 2 All E.R. 214.

80 *Lowe* v. *Taylor* (1844) 7 D. 117; *White* v. *Clough* (1847) 10 D. 332; *Paul* v. *Jackson* (1884) 11 R. 460, 463.

CHAPTER 52

LIMITATIONS ON CLAIMS OF DAMAGES FOR DELICT

A PERSON who complains that he has sustained loss, injury or damage at the hands of another and who seeks damages as compensation therefor on the ground that the causing of the loss or injury was a delict done to him must, first, satisfy the court that he has title and interest to sue for the alleged loss, and, secondly, satisfy the court that in the circumstances there had been incumbent on the defender a legal duty to have prevented, or not to have permitted to happen, the incident alleged to have caused the harm, that that legal duty was owed to him, or to him *inter alios*, and that in some specified way the defender was in breach of that duty to refrain from causing harm. The legal duty may have been one *e.g.* not to assault, which can only be breached by intentional conduct, or one, *e.g.* not to defame or to injure in person or property, which can be breached either deliberately or unintentionally. These issues belong entirely to matters of liability, and to the substantive law of delict, rather than to the law of remedies therefor.[1]

But before a court can attach liability to make reparation to a defender for having been in breach of legal duty to the pursuer it must further be satisfied (1) that the loss, injury or damage of which he complains was in fact caused by the defender's conduct which amounted to breach of duty—the problem of causation; (2) that the causal connection between breach of duty and loss or injury was legally proximate and not too remote—the problem of proximity or remoteness of injury; (3) as to whether any of the damage or loss consequential on the initial injury was or was not too remote—the problem of extent of liability or remoteness of damage; (4) that the loss or injury was not increased by any fault on the pursuer's own part; and (5) that the pursuer was not himself contributorily negligent and, in whole or in part, the author of his own misfortune. These factors are all limitations on claims of damages for delict in that the successful invocation of any one or more of them will limit the defender's liability or may even wholly exclude it.[2]

(1) CAUSATION

The pursuer must prove that each distinguishably distinct element of the injury or loss for which he seeks compensation was caused mainly by

[1] See further Walker, *Principles of Scottish Private Law*, Chap. 59 *et seq.*; Walker, *Delict*, *passim.*

[2] The plea of voluntary assumption of risk or *volenti non fit injuria* is either a denial of the existence of any duty by the defender to the pursuer, or the acceptance by the pursuer of the risk of harm, and consideration of it belongs to the sphere of liability or non-liability, not to that of extent of liability or measure of remedy.

happenings for which the defender was legally responsible, in that he, in breach of duty, caused or permitted them to happen. If the defender's conduct, even though in breach of duty, was not the main cause of the injury or loss, then the pursuer cannot recover in respect thereof from the defender.

The problem of causation is a difficult one [3] but the courts and jurists generally approach cases from the common sense standpoint that one person's conduct, by act or omission, can be said to have "caused" loss or damage to another if the conduct not merely preceded the loss but was so closely connected with it in space and time that it can fairly be said to have brought it about and to have made it happen.[4] It must be established that the harm was not merely *post hoc* but also *propter hoc*.

"If a man is too late to catch a train, because his car broke down on the way to the station, we should all naturally say that he lost the train because of the car breaking down. We recognise that the two things or events are causally connected. Causation is a mental concept, generally based on inference or induction from uniformity of sequence as between two events that there is a causal connection between them." [5]

Onus of proof

The onus of proof of causal connection between breach of legal duty to the pursuer and harm to the pursuer is on the pursuer.[6] If the facts are equivocal and equally consistent with causal connection and with absence of it, the pursuer fails.[7] But the court may be able to draw an inference of causal connection from the facts proved,[8] and to reach the conclusion that they suggest causal connection rather than merely congruence of time and space.

Thus in *Liesbosch (Owners)* v. *Edison (Owners)* [9] the E caused the sinking of the L, and admitted sole liability for the loss. Part of the financial loss sustained by the plaintiffs was the need to hire a replacement vessel at heavy cost, because they could not afford to buy a replacement. The House of Lords held that the loss, so far as due to impecuniosity, arose from that factor as a "separate and concurrent cause extraneous to and distinct in character from the tort." That particular loss was not caused by the defendants' fault but by another factor.

Not physical causation but responsibility being investigated

Furthermore it must be remembered that what is under investigation

[3] See generally Hart and Honoré, *Causation in the Law*.
[4] *Weld-Blundell* v. *Stephens* [1920] A.C. 956; *Yorkshire Dale S.S. Co.* v. *M.O.W.T.* [1942] A.C. 691; *A/B Karlshamns Oljefabriker* v. *Monarch S.S. Co.*, 1949 S.C.(H.L.) 1, 24; *Stapley* v. *Gypsum Mines Ltd.* [1953] A.C. 663.
[5] *A/B Karlshamns Oljefabriker* v. *Monarch S.S. Co.*, 1949 S.C.(H.L.) 1, 24, *per* Lord Wright.
[6] *Wardlaw* v. *Bonnington Castings Ltd.*, 1956 S.C.(H.L.) 26, 31, 34, 35; *McWilliams* v. *Arrol*, 1962 S.C.(H.L.) 70.
[7] *Metropolitan Ry.* v. *Jackson* (1877) 3 App.Cas. 193; *Wakelin* v. *L.S.W. Ry.* (1886) 12 App.Cas. 41.
[8] *Craig* v. *Glasgow Corpn.*, 1919 S.C.(H.L.) 1.
[9] [1933] A.C. 449.

in an action for damages for delict is not merely causation of harm in the physical sense, but causation of harm from the point of view of fixing responsibility for causing the harm. In a case of contact between a railway engine and a person standing on the line,[10] the harm (death) is always caused physically by the engine to the human and it is hardly possible for the human to cause any physical damage to the engine. What the court is considering is whether the fact that the engine was moving, had not whistled, and so on, " caused " the harm, or the fact that the human was in its path, being a trespasser on the line, and so on, " caused " the harm. It does not matter which inflicted the blow. Causation is being investigated, that is, not for the purpose of completing the column of the death certificate headed " cause of death," but for the purpose of deciding where to allocate responsibility for the contact, and legal liability or non-liability for the consequences. In such unequal contests as contact between engine or motor-vehicle and human the physical cause of harm is inevitably hard metal hurting soft flesh, but that does *not* solve the legal problem. " Unless the proper inference from the evidence here is that the *negligence* of the defenders *caused* the injury to the pursuer. . . ." [11]

In cases where the defender's negligence, or omission in breach of duty, is founded on, this is particularly important. If by reason of the employer's failure to provide a safety-belt an employee falls and is injured or killed, the cause of his death in the physical sense is multiple lesions sustained by falling heavily from a height, but the cause in the legal sense may be the failure to provide the safety-belt. " The immediate cause of the deceased's death was the fact that at the time of the fall he was not wearing a safety belt. The cause or reason why he was not wearing a safety-belt may have been the fact that one was not provided, but the failure to provide operates only through the failure to wear. The correct way of stating the appellant's case is, I think, as follows. The immediate cause of the deceased's death was that at the time of the fall he was not wearing a safety-belt; but for the fault of his employers, he would have been wearing a safety-belt: therefore the fault of his employers was an effective cause of his death." [12]

Court only interested in defender's conduct as cause

In examining causal factors of a situation in which a pursuer has sustained loss or harm, the court is not concerned to determine what the cause was, but solely to determine whether particular conduct by the defender which has been complained of can fairly be said to have been, or not to have been, the sole or at least predominant cause. If the court holds that the defender's conduct complained of was *not* the cause, it is not obliged to find or to say what in its view *was* the cause. Thus in *Wakelin's* case [13]

[10] *e.g. Wakelin, supra.*
[11] *Craig, supra,* 9, *per* Lord Finlay.
[12] *McWilliams* v. *Arrol,* 1962 S.C.(H.L.) 70, 84–85, *per* Lord Devlin. (The action failed because it was held that the deceased would *not* have been wearing a safety-belt.)
[13] *Supra.*

the court was concerned with whether or not the engine-driver's breach of duty caused the death; if it did not, the court was not interested in whether Wakelin committed suicide, or suffered a heart attack, or was made to stand in the engine's path by an enemy's hypnotic influence, or had wandered on the line by mistake and in ignorance of where he was.

Cause and consequence must be proximate

Before a person can be held legally liable for a harmful consequence which he is deemed to have caused, the cause and consequence must be reasonably proximate, and not connected too distantly or remotely. This principle is traditionally embodied in the maxim *causa proxima non remota spectatur* or in the statement that the defender is liable only if his fault is the proximate cause of the harm complained of. But the traditional maxim *causa proxima non remota spectatur* " is either meaningless or misleading until ' *remota* ' and ' *proxima* ' are defined. Thus unseaworthiness as a cause cannot from its very nature operate by itself; it needs the ' peril ' in order to evince that the vessel, or some part or quality of it, is less fit than it should have been and would have been if it had been seaworthy and hence the casualty ensues. A fitter ship would have passed through the peril unscathed. In this way unseaworthiness is a decisive cause or, as it is called, a dominant cause." [14]

In judging of proximity of cause and consequence, proximity or closeness in space and time are relevant, and the further apart alleged cause and harmful consequence are in space or time or both the easier it is to hold that the consequence was not brought about by the alleged cause. But space and time are not the main factors; the main factor is proximity in efficacy, in causative potency, and conduct may be held to be the proximate cause of harm despite the intervention of space, time, or other acts or events, if the main impulse for the happening of the harm can still be regarded as coming from the initial fault.

Causal factors classified

Further, in examining the defender's conduct, alleged to have been done in breach of legal duty and to have caused the harm, the court not infrequently distinguishes between factors not causal but merely prior or concomitant, factors which are prerequisites of or necessary conditions for the occurrence of the harm or loss, and factors which had effect in bringing about the harm or loss.

Factors not causal but merely prior or concomitant

The court may decide that a particular event or piece of conduct was not a causal factor at all but merely a fact prior to or concomitant of the harm or loss. Such a fact is clearly irrelevant to the connection of breach

14 *A/B Karlshamns Oljefabriker* v. *Monarch S.S. Co.*, 1949 S.C.(H.L.) 1, 24, *per* Lord Wright.

of duty and harm essential for liability. The injured person's presence at the locus at the material time is no doubt always a prerequisite of his being injured then and there, but his mere presence does not by itself make him the author of his own misfortune, in whole or in part. No doubt if Miss Stone had not been in the particular road at the particular time she would not have been struck by the cricket ball,[15] and similarly with Mrs. Bourhill.[16] Presence at the point of danger is normally only a prior or concomitant fact, not a causal factor at all.

Among merely prior, but not causal, factors may be included cases where there was, or at least may have been, fault on the defender's part and harm has subsequently befallen the pursuer but the connection between them has been so distant, in space or time or both, that the fault has been deemed exhausted and the harm too remotely connected with the fault for it to be fair to hold the defender liable. Thus in *Gray* v. *N.B. Ry.*[17] a collie dog, being transported by rail, escaped at Waverley Station, Edinburgh, found its way to the Botanic Gardens more than a mile away, and bit Gray. " If it could be shown that the necessary and immediate result of the escape was the injury of someone, it might be a different case, but it is impossible to conceive of anything more remote than the injury suffered by the pursuer." [18] " Even if the company had been in fault in regard to the dog's escape, they would not be responsible for all the remote consequences of that escape . . . I think [the gardeners'] conduct must be held to be the proximate cause of the injury." [19]

Causa sine qua non

A *causa sine qua non* is a factor which preceded, and was prerequisite to, and a necessary condition of, the occurrence to the pursuer of the loss or harm complained of, and without which that loss would not have been suffered, but which is nevertheless not necessarily the main factor which brought about the harm. It is an essential prerequisite of the harm, but not necessarily the real cause.

The defender's conduct, if in breach of duty, is a *causa sine qua non* of the harm complained of if it was an essential prerequisite or condition of the suffering of the harm, and if the harm would not have been suffered if the conduct had not taken place.

In *Carse* v. *N.B. Steam Packet Co.*,[20] C was fishing from a small boat moored in the path of steamers approaching Dunoon pier; a steamer ran the boat down and C was drowned. It was held that C's folly in anchoring there was merely *causa sine qua non* of his death,[21] the real cause being the

[15] *Bolton* v. *Stone* [1951] A.C. 850.
[16] *Bourhill* v. *Young*, 1942 S.C.(H.L.) 78.
[17] (1890) 18 R. 76.
[18] *Ibid.* 78, *per* L.P. Inglis.
[19] *Ibid.* 79, *per* Lord Adam.
[20] (1895) 22 R. 475 (as the law then stood it was not possible to find both parties partly to blame).
[21] Lord Kinnear (p. 486) called it " antecedent rashness " and Lord Wellwood said (p. 487): " any fault . . . was antecedent, and not truly in any proper sense the cause of the accident. . . ."

absence of look-out on the steamer; the steamer should have seen and avoided him.

The defender's conduct, even if negligent, on the other hand, is not even a *causa sine qua non* if the damage would equally have occurred without it. It does not, however, cease to be a *causa sine qua non* merely because the injury *might have* occurred independently of the defender's conduct, but only if it would certainly, or almost certainly, have occurred without it.

For a pursuer to succeed he must show that the defender's conduct was at least a *causa sine qua non*, and further, that it was an effective cause. If the defender's conduct complained of is not at least a *causa sine qua non* of the harm in issue, the action must fail and the defender escapes liability altogether.

Causa causans

The court must, accordingly, go further and consider whether the defender's conduct, alleged to have been done or permitted in contravention of a principle of law enjoining him not to do or permit that kind of thing, has been not merely a prerequisite of or necessary condition for the occurrence of the harm or loss complained of but been a powerful or effective factor in bringing it about, what has been called the *causa causans*, the dominant cause, the effective cause, the proximate cause, the direct cause. " It is tautologous to speak of ' effective ' cause or to say that damages too remote from the cause are irrecoverable, for an effective cause is simply that which causes, and in law what is ineffective or too remote is not a cause at all; still, I venture to think that direct cause is the best of expressions. Proximate cause has acquired a special connotation through its use in reference to contracts of insurance. Direct cause excludes what is indirect, conveys the essential distinction, which *causa causans* and *causa sine qua non* rather cumbrously indicate, and is consistent with the possibility of the concurrence of more direct causes than one, operating at the same time and leading to a common result as in *Burrows* v. *March Gas Co.*[22] and *Hill* v. *New River Co.*[23] " [24]

Where the conduct in issue is a positive act, the court must be satisfied that the act brought about the harm, and that if the act had not been done, the harm would not have happened.

Where the conduct in issue is an omission, the court must be satisfied that if the conduct, such as taking a safety precaution, had not been omitted, the harm would not have happened, that it was the absence of the precaution which brought about the harm.[25]

The pursuer accordingly succeeds if the defender's misconduct was a major causal factor, and fails if it was a negligible causal factor. Thus the

[22] (1872) L.R. 7 Ex. 96.
[23] (1868) 6 B. & S. 303.
[24] *Weld-Blundell* v. *Stephens* [1920] A.C. 956, 983, *per* Lord Sumner.
[25] *McWilliams* v. *Arrol*, 1962 S.C.(H.L.) 70, 77.

pursuer succeeded where he had had to work in proximity to a tool which gave off particles of dust, there was defective dust extraction plant, and he had contracted pneumoconiosis; he failed where it was proved that, though on the material day, in breach of duty, a safety-belt had not been provided, the deceased would not have worn one on the day of the accident even if one had been available.[26]

It need not be proved that the defender's misconduct was the sole and exclusive cause, if it at least materially contributed to, the harm sustained.[27] " What is a material contribution must be a question of degree. A contribution which comes within the exception *de minimis non curat lex* is not material, but I think that any contribution which does not fall within that exception must be material." [28]

" It has always been the law that a pursuer succeeds if he can show that fault of the defender caused or materially contributed to his injury. There may have been two separate causes but it is enough if one of the causes arose from fault of the defender. The pursuer does not have to prove that this cause would of itself have been enough to cause him injury. This is well illustrated by the decision of this House in *Wardlaw* v. *Bonnington Castings Ltd.*[29] " [30] The failure to take a safety or health precaution which failure materially increased the risk of harm or injury is equivalent to and indistinguishable from materially contributing to causing the harm or injury.[31]

Sole cause and multiple cause

If the defender's misconduct is shown to have been the sole cause of the pursuer's harm, the pursuer clearly succeeds. But if he only establishes that the defender's misconduct was one of two or more co-operating causal factors he still succeeds, the defender having a right of relief against any other party who, if sued, might also have been held liable for the same harm.[32] If two or more defenders are sued jointly and severally, it is clearly possible to find that both or all contributed to bringing about the harm, and that they are jointly and severally liable, the degrees of responsibility being recognised by the proportion in which each is found liable.[33] It is sufficient to prove that each of the defenders materially contributed to the harm complained of.[34] " When separate and independent acts of negligence on the part of two or more persons have directly contributed to cause injury and damage to another, the person injured may recover damages from any one of the wrongdoers, or from all of them." [35]

26 *McWilliams* v. *Arrol*, 1962 S.C.(H.L.) 70.
27 *Wardlaw* v. *Bonnington Castings Ltd.*, 1956 S.C.(H.L.) 26; *McGhee* v. *N.C.B.*, 1973 S.L.T. 14.
28 *Wardlaw, supra*, 32, *per* Lord Reid.
29 *Supra.*
30 *McGhee* v. *N.C.B.*, 1973 S.L.T. 14, *per* Lord Reid.
31 *McGhee, supra.*
32 Law Reform (Misc. Prov.) (Sc.) Act 1940, s. 3 (2).
33 *Ibid.* s. 3 (1).
34 *Duke of Buccleuch* v. *Cowan* (1866) 5 M. 214.
35 *Grant* v. *Sun Shipping Co.*, 1948 S.C.(H.L.) 73.

Indirect causation

Once it is determined that a defender's conduct has started a reaction of causal connection, he will be held responsible for the ultimate result, just as the jerks and bumps when a locomotive accelerates or applies its brakes pass on from wagon to wagon till they affect the brake van. But the defender may be held not responsible if, though he started the reaction, some other factor for which he is not responsible has then had an influence. In such circumstances it is for the court to weigh the relative efficacy of the different causal factors and decide whether the defender, having initiated the causal reaction, must bear the responsibility for the ultimate harm despite the intervention of the fresh factor, or whether the fresh factor must be deemed to have superseded and replaced the defender's initial conduct as the major causative factor, or whether both must be deemed to have had causal effect in bringing about the ultimate harm.[36] The fresh factor is usually called *novus actus interveniens* or *nova causa interveniens*, and it may take the form of conduct by a third party, the influence of a natural force, or conduct by the complaining party himself.[37] " Certain well-known formulae are invoked, such as that the chain of causation was broken and that there was a *novus actus interveniens*. These phrases, sanctified as they are by standing authority, only mean that there was not such a direct relationship between the act of negligence and the injury that the one could be treated as flowing directly from the other." [38]

> " Again, between the negligence of a defendant and the infliction of hurt or loss on a plaintiff, the action of human beings may intervene in a great variety of ways—the action of children, or other irresponsible creatures, of persons in a state of excusable ignorance acting without any intention to injure: *Elkins, Bly & Co.* v. *McKean* [39]; of persons in a state of excusable alarm produced by the wrongful acts of the defendant: *Scott* v. *Shepherd* [40]; *Jones* v. *Boyce* [41]; of persons acting in the exercise or the defence of their rights and without intention to injure others: *Clark* v. *Chambers* [42]; *The Sisters* [43]; *Halestrap* v. *Gregory* [44]; of persons acting as the defendant meant them to act or acting as the defendant must have foreseen that they would act, in consequence of things done by him for his own purposes or in a state

[36] This last decision seems open to the court only if the persons responsible for both factors are before the court.

[37] Logically, it may also take the form of further and different conduct by the defender, but as the defender is responsible for initial misconduct and supervening misconduct, it does not relieve him of liability. Thus if a doctor by careless driving knocks X down and injures him, then takes X to hospital and kills him by negligent treatment, it will not avail the doctor to prove which piece of misconduct was the major cause of the death.

[38] *Lord* v. *Pacific S.N. Co., The Oropesa* [1943] P. 32, 36, *per* Lord Wright.

[39] (1875) 79 Penn. 493.

[40] (1773) 2 Wm.Bl. 892.

[41] (1816) 1 Stark. 493.

[42] (1878) 3 Q.B.D. 327.

[43] (1876) 1 P.D. 117.

[44] [1895] 1 Q.B. 561.

of indifference as to the result to others: *Scott's Trs.* v. *Moss* [45]; *R.* v. *Moore.*[46] " [47]

" In general (apart from special contracts and relations and the maxim *respondeat superior*) even though A is in fault he is not responsible for injury to C which B, a stranger to him, deliberately chooses to do. Though A may have given the occasion for B's mischievous activity, B then becomes a new and independent cause: *e.g. Cobb* v. *G.W. Ry.*[48]; *A.G.* v. *Conduit Colliery Co.*[49] It is hard to steer clear of metaphors. Perhaps one may be forgiven for saying that B snaps the chain of causation; he is no mere conduit pipe through which consequences flow from A to C, no mere moving part in a transmission gear set in motion by A; in a word, he insulates A from C." [50]

One proposition settled in this class of case is that " human action does not *per se* sever the connected sequence of acts. The mere fact that human action intervenes does not prevent the sufferer from saying that damages for injury due to that human action, as one of the elements in the sequence, is recoverable from the original wrongdoer." [51] " ' Reasonable human conduct is part of the ordinary course of things ' (Haldane L.C. in *Baron Vernon*),[52] and that ' human action does not *per se* sever the connected sequence of acts ' (Lord Wright in *The Oropesa*).[53] It follows that human conduct, if reasonable in the sense to be defined, may be one of the reasonable and probable consequences, flowing from an act of negligence, which the ordinary reasonable man ought to foresee." [54]

Conduct of third party as novus actus interveniens

A defender responsible for having initiated a chain of consequences is not responsible for the ultimate consequence to the complainer if there supervened on his initiation some misconduct by a third party which in the view of the court superseded and replaced the defender's misconduct as the main causal force in producing the ultimate consequence. But " if the negligence, or breach of duty of one person is the cause of injury to another, the wrongdoer cannot in all circumstances escape liability by proving that, though he was to blame, yet but for the negligence of a third person the injured man would not have suffered the damage of which he complains. There is abundant authority for the proposition that the mere fact that a subsequent act of negligence has been the immediate cause of disaster does not exonerate the original offender." [55] Whether the

45 (1889) 17 R. 32.
46 (1832) 3 B. & Ad. 184.
47 *Weld-Blundell* v. *Stephens* [1920] A.C. 956, 984, *per* Lord Sumner.
48 [1893] 1 Q.B. 459.
49 [1895] 1 Q.B. 301.
50 *Weld-Blundell* v. *Stephens* [1920] A.C. 956, 986, *per* Lord Sumner.
51 *The Oropesa* [1943] P. 32, 37, *per* Lord Wright, citing *The City of Lincoln* (1890) 15 P.D. 15.
52 1928 S.C.(H.L.) 21, 25.
53 [1943] P. 32, 37.
54 *Steel* v. *Glasgow Iron and Steel Co.*, 1944 S.C. 237, 248, *per* L.J.C. Cooper.
55 *Grant* v. *Sun Shipping Co.*, 1948 S.C.(H.L.) 73, 94, *per* Lord du Parcq.

defender's original fault or the third party's supervening conduct is the effective or proximate cause of the ultimate harm is a question of fact in each case.

Among the kinds of conduct by a third party which have been held to amount to *novus actus interveniens* have been unskilled or negligent medical diagnosis or treatment which, rather than the initial injury, has been held to have caused physical incapacity.[56] " The proposition . . . seems to me to be axiomatic, that if a surgeon, by lack of skill or failure in reasonable care, causes additional injury or aggravates an existing injury and so renders himself liable in damages, the reasonable conclusion must be that his intervention is a new cause and that the additional injury or the aggravation of the existing injury should be attributed to it and not to the original accident. On the other hand an operation prudently advised and skilfully and carefully carried out should not be treated as a new cause, whatever its consequences may be." [57]

Chain not broken by natural and probable consequence

But the fact that the damage has been caused by the subsequent act of some third party does not prevent damages being recoverable if such an act was, even though wrongful, a natural and probable consequence of the defender's fault.[58] Thus the chain has been held not broken where a railway company in the execution of building work left an opening through which a thief obtained access to the pursuer's premises,[59] a lorryman left his horse-drawn lorry unattended and boys frightened the horses and caused them to run away and cause injuries,[60] a painter left a house unlocked and a thief entered and stole property,[61] or a carrier mistakenly delivered inflammable material and an employee's cigarette set off an explosion.[62]

" If what is relied upon as *novus actus interveniens* is the very kind of thing which is likely to happen if the want of care which is alleged takes place, the principle embodied in the maxim is no defence." [63]

Chain not usually broken by acts of children, animals or persons reacting involuntarily

The connection is not usually held broken if the intervention is by a child, an animal or a person not fully responsible for his actions.

56 *Humber Towing Co.* v. *Barclay* (1911) 5 B.W.C.C. 142; *Rocca* v. *Stanley Jones & Co. Ltd.* (1914) 7 B.W.C.C. 101; *Lakey* v. *Blair* (1916) 10 B.W.C.C. 58; *Rothwell* v. *Caverswall Stone Co.* [1944] 2 All E.R. 350.

57 *Hogan* v. *Bentinck West Hartley Collieries (Owners) Ltd.* [1949] 1 All E.R. 588, 596, *per* Lord Normand.

58 *R.* v. *Moore* (1832) 3 B. & Ad. 184; *Burrows* v. *March Gas Co.* (1872) L.R. 7 Ex. 96; *Clark* v. *Chambers* (1878) 3 Q.B.D. 327; *Bowen* v. *Hall* (1881) 6 Q.B.D. 333; *Scott's Trs.* v. *Moss* (1889) 17 R. 32; *Engelhart* v. *Farrant* [1897] 1 Q.B. 240; *Weld-Blundell* v. *Stephens* [1920] A.C. 956, 971, *per* Viscount Finlay, dissenting.

59 *Marshall* v. *Caledonian Ry.* (1899) 1 F. 1060.

60 *Haynes* v. *Harwood* [1935] 1 K.B. 146; *cf. Lynch* v. *Nurdin* (1841) 1 Q.B. 29.

61 *Stansbie* v. *Troman* [1948] 2 K.B. 48.

62 *Philco Radio Ltd.* v. *Spurling* [1949] 2 All E.R. 882.

63 *Haynes* v. *Harwood* [1935] 1 K.B. 146, 156, *per* Greer L.J.

" Children acting in the wantonness of infancy and adults acting on the impulse of personal peril may be and often are only links in a chain of causation extending from such initial negligence to the subsequent injury. No doubt each intervener is a *causa sine qua non*, but unless the intervention is a fresh, independent cause, the person guilty of the original negligence will still be the effective cause, if he ought reasonably to have anticipated such intervention and to have foreseen that if they occurred the result would be that his negligence would lead to mischief. Thus in many cases the intervening act of a child has been held not to relieve the original wrongdoer of liability.[64] Similarly the custodier of an animal, if initially negligent in controlling it, is not relieved if the animal causes harm, but may be if the damage is due to a spontaneous act of the animal for which the want of care gives the opportunity, but of which it is not the cause.[65]

Nor is causal connection broken if the third party's act is an uncontrolled, instinctive or involuntary reaction, as in *Scott* v. *Shepherd*[66] where a man threw a lighted squib into a market-house and three persons successively, beside whom it landed, threw it away, and it finally hit and injured the plaintiff; all that was done, subsequent to the original throwing, was a continuation of the first act.

Chain may be broken by deliberate intervention

Where the intervening act by the third party is done by deliberate choice and harm results, the court may be more likely to hold that the initial wrongdoer's fault was exhausted and that the intervener's act was the main cause of the ultimate harm. This result has been reached in case of initial injury and, subsequently, negligent medical treatment causing greater harm.[67] But an opposite view has been taken in other sets of circumstances.[68]

Conduct by complainer himself as novus actus interveniens

Similarly conduct by the complainer himself may be held to supersede the defender's misconduct and replace it as the predominant causal factor in the complainer's loss or harm. This may take the form of deliberate

[64] *e.g. Bebee* v. *Sales* (1916) 32 T.L.R. 413 (child firing gun left loaded); *Martin* v. *Stanborough* (1924) 41 T.L.R. 1 (child removing block from under wheel of car left with no brake on); *Haynes* v. *Harwood* [1935] 1 K.B. 146 (child throwing stone, frightening horses left unattended); *Shiffman* v. *Order of St. John* [1936] 1 All E.R. 557 (child pulling guy-ropes of flagpole otherwise unsupported); *Coates* v. *Rawtenstall B.C.* [1937] 3 All E.R. 602 (child putting chain across chute); *Wells* v. *Metropolitan Water Board* [1937] 4 All E.R. 639 (child meddling with stopcock cover); *Burfitt* v. *Kille* [1939] 2 K.B. 743 (child firing gun).

[65] *Aldham* v. *United Dairies* [1940] 1 K.B. 507; *cf. Manton* v. *Brocklebank* [1923] 2 K.B. 212; *Buckle* v. *Holmes* [1926] 2 K.B. 125.

[66] (1773) 2 Wm.Bl. 892.

[67] *Rothwell* v. *Caverswall Stone Co.* [1944] 2 All E.R. 350; *Hogan* v. *Bentinck West Hartley Collieries* [1949] 1 All E.R. 588.

[68] *Philco Radio* v. *Spurling* [1949] 2 All E.R. 882; *Dorset Yacht Co.* v. *Home Office* [1970] A.C. 1004.

conduct, as where a person whose store has been set on fire by the defender's fault in delivering to him naphtha instead of paraffin climbed onto the roof to try to extinguish the blaze and fell and was injured,[69] or an injured person has refused, unreasonably in the view of the court, to submit to some treatment and has been incapacitated.[70] Or it may be conduct by the complainer himself which appears to the court to be unreasonable in the circumstances, such as descending a flight of stairs without support or assistance, despite a prior injury to a leg, and then jumping down the last steps [71]: " His unreasonable conduct is *novus actus interveniens.* The chain of causation has been broken and what follows must be regarded as caused by his own conduct and not by the defender's fault or the disability caused by it. Or one may say that unreasonable conduct by the pursuer and what follows from it is not the natural and probable result of the original fault of the defender or of the ensuing liability." [72]

But the injured person's own act, even if deliberate, does not break the chain, when there is no identifiable intervention in the causal sequence, and the events followed one another naturally and directly, as where a man sustained injuries to his head, suffered from anxiety neurosis and depression, and, in consequence, took his own life: the defendants were held liable for his death [73]; or a person placed in a situation of danger by the defendant's fault, attempted to escape and was injured [74]; or the tenant of a house injured herself by moving a window which was dangerous by reason of the landlord's prior breach of duty in respect thereof.[75]

Even deliberate intervention is not deemed to break the chain of causation where the pursuer, having been placed in a difficult situation by the defender's fault, runs a risk or neglects to seek to save himself in the interest of saving another person, or property. " The law does not think so meanly of mankind as to hold it otherwise than a natural and probable consequence of a helpless person being put in danger that some able-bodied person should expose himself to the same danger to effect a rescue." [76] Thus a person who ran into the roadway to save a child endangered by the defendant's negligence was not barred (nor guilty of contributory negligence),[77] nor was a rescuer who deliberately ran a risk to save life and was himself killed [78]: " If what is relied upon as *novus actus interveniens* is the very kind of thing which is likely to happen if the want of care which is alleged takes place, the principle embodied in the

[69] *Macdonald* v. *Macbrayne Ltd.*, 1915 S.C. 716.
[70] *Steele* v. *Robert George & Co. Ltd.* [1942] A.C. 497; *secus* if the refusal had been reasonable.
[71] *McKew* v. *Holland & Hannen & Cubitts (Scotland) Ltd.*, 1970 S.L.T. 68.
[72] *McKew, supra*, 70, *per* Lord Reid.
[73] *Pigney* v. *Pointers Transport Services Ltd.* [1957] 2 All E.R. 807.
[74] *Jones* v. *Boyce* (1816) 1 Stark. 493; *Sayers* v. *Harlow U.D.C.* [1958] 2 All E.R. 342.
[75] *Summers* v. *Salford Corpn.* [1943] A.C. 283.
[76] *Pollock on Torts* (15th ed.) 370.
[77] *Morgan* v. *Aylen* [1942] 1 All E.R. 489.
[78] *Haynes* v. *Harwood* [1935] 1 K.B. 146; *Baker* v. *Hopkins* [1959] 3 All E.R. 225; see also *Woods* v. *Caledonian Ry.* (1886) 13 R. 1118; *Wilkinson* v. *Kinneil Cannel and Coking Coal Co.* (1897) 24 R. 1001; *Cutler* v. *United Dairies Ltd.* [1933] 2 K.B. 297; *D'Urso* v. *Sanson* [1939] 4 All E.R. 26.

maxim is no defence " [79]; nor was a man who in emergency tried to save his employer's property.[80]

A rescuer, moreover, may sue and is not barred by the plea of *novus actus interveniens* even though the victim could not sue the wrongdoer successfully; a duty is owed to a possible rescuer if a wrongdoer creates a situation where the intervention of a person to effect a rescue is likely and natural.[81]

But a person may be barred by the plea of *novus actus* if his intervention was deemed unwarrantable.[82]

Still less does intervention break the causal connection when the action is instinctive or involuntary, as where a wife injured herself by instinctively trying to pull her husband from a place of danger where he had been imperilled by the defendants' fault.[83]

Influence of a natural, external force as novus actus interveniens

Similarly a natural force such as weather, terrain, disease, or wild animal may be held to supersede a defender's misconduct and replace it as the predominant causal factor of the pursuer's ultimate loss or harm. To have this effect the natural force must have been, if not deliberately encountered, avoidable or something not inevitably incurred in the circumstances.

But the natural force will not have such an effect if incurring the danger thereof is a natural or, *a fortiori*, an inevitable consequence of the defender's prior fault. Where after a ship collision the master and some of the crew of one ship tried to row to the other ship to arrange for salvage assistance and the boat was capsized by a wave and men drowned, the deaths were held attributable to the collision, the heavy seas not being enough to break the chain of causation.[84] Similarly if the defender's fault causes injury which renders the injured person susceptible to infection and he becomes infected and is more seriously injured or dies, the infection does not break the causal connection.[85]

Plea distinguished from contributory negligence

The plea that the pursuer's own conduct has amounted to *novus actus interveniens* is not always readily distinguishable from the plea that the pursuer was contributorily negligent. The difference is that for the plea of *novus actus* there must first have been misconduct by the defender, but in contributory negligence the pursuer's own misconduct and lack of regard for his own safety may have been contemporaneous with, or even preceded, the defender's misconduct.

79 *Haynes*, *supra*, 156, *per* Greer L.J.
80 *Steel* v. *Glasgow Iron & Steel Co.*, 1944 S.C. 237.
81 *Videan* v. *B.T.C.* [1963] 2 Q.B. 650.
82 *Sylvester* v. *Chapman* (1935) 79 Sol.Jo. 777.
83 *Brandon* v. *Osborne, Garrett & Co.* [1924] 1 K.B. 548.
84 *The Oropesa* [1943] P. 32.
85 *Cf. Rothwell* v. *Caverswall Stone Co.* [1944] 2 All E.R. 350, 365, *per* du Parcq L.J.; *Hogan* v. *Bentinck West Hartley Collieries Ltd.* [1949] 1 All E.R. 588.

Evaluation of multiple causal factors

Where more than one possible causal factor can be pointed to, the court has to decide whether (1) both or all can be regarded as equally potent causal factors, or (2) the earlier can be regarded as merely *causa sine qua non* and the later as the effective cause, or (3) the earlier can be regarded as the effective cause and the later as a mere *novus actus interveniens* insufficient to displace the earlier as the effective cause. In cases (2) and (3) the court traditionally describes what it does as finding the proximate cause of the injury or harm. But proximity has to be determined not solely by reference to proximity in space or time, but by reference to efficacy.

In *Leyland Shipping Co.* v. *Norwich Union Fire Ins. Socy. Ltd.*[86] a ship was torpedoed but towed into port where she was berthed in the outer harbour, grounded at low tides and the tides and grounding caused further damage so that ultimately she became a total loss. It was held that the torpedoing was the proximate cause of her loss, the grounding and tides being merely subsequent. Lord Shaw observed [87]:

> " The chain of causation is a handy expression, but the figure is inadequate. Causation is not a chain, but a net. At each point, influences, forces, events, precedent and simultaneous, meet; and the radiation from each point extends infinitely. At the point where these various influences meet it is for the judgment as upon a matter of fact to declare which of the causes thus joined at the point of effect was the proximate and which was the remote cause.
>
> " What does ' proximate ' here mean. To treat proximate cause as if it was the cause which is proximate in time is, as I have said, out of the question. The cause which is truly proximate is that which is proximate in efficiency. That efficiency may have been preserved, although other causes may meantime have sprung up which have yet not destroyed it, or truly impaired it; and it may culminate in a result of which it still remains the real efficient cause to which the event can be ascribed."

(2) " Culpability " or Existence of Liability or Remoteness of Injury

Even though an unbroken chain of causal connection exists between a particular breach of duty by the defender to the pursuer and harm sustained by the pursuer, the court may decline to hold the defender liable at all therefor if, in its view, the injury, *i.e.* breach of duty, was too remote from the harm.[88] Though not quite *damnum sine injuria*, if *damnum* is not proximate to, but deemed too remote from, the *injuria* complained of, the pursuer's action fails, even if direct and uninterrupted causal connection can be established. This question is not a question of damages or remedy

[86] [1918] A.C. 250.
[87] *Ibid.* 369.
[88] On this problem, see further *Walker on Delict*, I, 238 *et seq.*

but one aspect of the problem of liability, of whether it is just that the court should hold the defender liable for any part of the harm which has befallen the pursuer, but it is discussed here because it is so frequently confused with the different question of remoteness of damage, which is a possible limitation of the extent of liability. Many of the cases can be explained, or could equally well have been decided, on the basis that the pursuer had no title to sue, or that no such duty of care as is alleged is in fact recognised, or that the pursuer was outwith the ambit of any such duty. The fact that deciding that harm is too remote to sound in damages is a technique of decision on liability, not on damages, is reinforced by the fact that a negative decision is *always* that the defender is *not liable at all,* and *never* that he is liable but *not* for *all* the damages claimed. The distinction is neatly pointed in the antithesis of " culpability " and " compensation " based on Lord Sumner's dictum in *Weld-Blundell* v. *Stephens* [89]: " What a defendant ought to have anticipated as a reasonable man is material when the question is whether or not he is guilty of negligence, that is, of want of due care according to the circumstances. This, however, goes to culpability, not to compensation." This was quoted by Bankes L.J. in *In re Polemis* [90] but, quite incomprehensibly, said by the Privy Council in *The Wagon Mound* [91] to be fundamentally false.

The test of whether breach of duty is proximate or too remotely connected with losses sustained is whether the losses are " such as naturally and directly arise out of the wrong done; and such, therefore, as may reasonably be supposed to have been in the view of the wrongdoer " [92]; or " The duty to take care is the duty to avoid doing or omitting to do anything the doing or omitting to do which may have as its reasonable and probable consequence injury to others. . . ." [93] " [The precept *alterum non laedere*] does not impose liability for every injury which our conduct may occasion; in Scotland at any rate it has never been a maxim of the law that a man acts at his peril. Legal liability is limited to those consequences of our acts which a reasonable man of ordinary intelligence and experience so acting would have in contemplation." [94] " Is the consequence fairly to be regarded as within the risk created by the negligence? If so, the negligent person is liable for it; but otherwise not." [95] " The test of proximity is whether what has flowed from the act is what would have been anticipated by a reasonable man as a natural and probable consequence of it. If it fails to pass that test, it is too remote for the law to take cognisance of it. Furthermore . . . if a court is satisfied that something which flowed from the original act is ' remote ' in the sense in which

89 [1920] A.C. 956, 983.
90 [1921] 3 K.B. 560.
91 [1961] A.C. 388.
92 *Allan* v. *Barclay* (1863) 2 M. 873, 874, *per* Lord Kinloch; decision followed in *Reavis* v. *Clan Line Steamers*, 1925 S.C. 725.
93 *Bourhill* v. *Young*, 1942 S.C.(H.L.) 78, 88, *per* Lord Macmillan.
94 *Muir* v. *Glasgow Corpn.*, 1943 S.C.(H.L.) 3, 10, *per* Lord Macmillan.
95 *Roe* v. *Minister of Health* [1954] 2 Q.B. 66, 85, *per* Denning L.J.

I have set out, a pursuer's case must be dismissed. The reason for this is that no legal ground of action exists." [96]

" I take it to be settled law that, in the chapter of law which we call 'reparation,' a man is only responsible for the reasonable and probable consequences of his failure to take care. . . . Now, in Scotland, it has been held for a century that it is not sufficient to enable an injured party to recover that he prove that the defender was negligent, and that there is a causal connection between the acts of negligence and the damage . . . legal liability is limited to the reasonable and probable consequences of the failure to take care." [97] " The case depends primarily upon the question whether the death of the engine driver was a reasonable and probable consequence of the alleged negligence upon which the action is based. . . . The question . . . is whether the damage founded on by the pursuers is too remote from the alleged negligence to create liability on the defenders. . . . A negligent person is not liable for *all* the consequences of his negligence. It is, I think, settled law, in Scotland at any rate, that he is liable only for the reasonable and probable consequences." [98]

General not particular foresight required

In this context it is not necessary that the defender should have foreseen the exact consequence which has happened, or the exact chain of events which resulted in injury.

> " It is not necessary to foresee the precise accident that happened and similarly it is not necessary, in my opinion, to postulate foreseeability of the precise chain of circumstances leading up to an accident. . . . The question is: Was what happened so remote that it could not be reasonably foreseeable? " [1] " I do not think that the law demands that employers who should have foreseen the existence of a danger and eliminated it, should also have been able to foresee the precise details of an accident before they can be said to have contributed to cause it. It is sufficient, if the accident is of the type they should have foreseen and guarded against, if at the time of its happening the injured person was a person who should have been guarded against the danger, and if the particular accident is such that it would have been avoided by the precautions which a reasonable employer would have foreseen as necessary, and would have taken." [2] " In order to establish a coherent chain of causation it is not necessary that the precise details leading up to the accident should have been

[96] *Malcolm* v. *Dickson*, 1951 S.C. 542, 547–548, *per* L.J.C. Thomson.
[97] *Blaikie* v. *British Transport Commission*, 1961 S.C. 44, 51–52, *per* Lord Patrick.
[98] *Ibid.* 52–53, *per* Lord Strachan. For other statements of the same principle in Scotland, see *Couper* v. *Macfarlane* (1879) 6 R. 690; *Woods* v. *Caledonian Ry.* (1886) 13 R. 1118, 1123; *Scott's Trs.* v. *Moss* (1889) 17 R. 32, 37; *McGarrot* v. *Addie's Collieries* (1894) 2 S.L.T. 11; *Wilkinson* v. *Kinneil Coal Co.* (1897) 24 R. 1001, 1006, 1007, 1009; *Cooper* v. *Caledonian Ry.* (1902) 4 F. 880, 882; *Macdonald* v. *Macbrayne*, 1915 S.C. 716; *Ross* v. *Glasgow Corpn.*, 1919 S.C. 174; *Ross* v. *McCallum's Trs.*, 1922 S.C. 322; *Fraser* v. *Pate*, 1923 S.C. 748.
[1] *Miller* v. *S.S.E.B.*, 1958 S.C.(H.L.) 20, 34, *per* Lord Keith.
[2] *Harvey* v. *Singer Mfg. Co.*, 1960 S.C. 155, 167–168, *per* Lord Patrick.

reasonably foreseeable; it is sufficient if the accident which occurred is of a type which should have been foreseeable by a reasonably careful person . . . the precise concatenation of circumstances need not be envisaged." [3] "When an accident is of a different type and kind from anything that a defender could have foreseen, he is not liable for it—see *The Wagon Mound.*[4] . . . The accident was but a variant of the foreseeable." [5]

The much discussed decision in *The Wagon Mound*,[6] properly understood, is a decision on remoteness of injury, not on remoteness of damage at all, and the *ratio* is that, as it was not reasonably foreseeable by the defenders when they negligently spilled oil that it could take fire and do damage by fire, they were not liable at all for the damage done by the fire which in fact started. In *Oman* v. *Macintyre*,[7] where it was held that the defender need not have foreseen the precise type of physical injury which resulted but only to have foreseen some kind of physical injury, Lord Milligan observed that "the case [*The Wagon Mound*] was, accordingly, concerned primarily with culpability rather than with compensation."

In *The Wagon Mound* (*No.* 2) [8] Lord Reid said: "It has now been established by *The Wagon Mound* (*No.* 1) [9] and by *Hughes* v. *Lord Advocate* [10] that in such cases [*i.e.* cases based purely on negligence] damages can only be recovered if the injury complained of not only was caused by the alleged negligence but also was an injury of a class or character foreseeable as a possible result of it."

Similarly in *Doughty* v. *Turner Manufacturing Co.*[11] a workman accidentally knocked the asbestos cover of a cauldron of molten liquid into it; by reason of chemical reaction it caused the molten liquid to erupt violently and injure the plaintiff. It was held that all that was reasonably foreseeable was that knocking the cover into the liquid might cause it to splash over; it was not reasonably foreseeable that immersion of the cover would cause a violent chemical reaction and virtually an explosion of the molten matter. The damage which occurred was of a kind quite different from that foreseeable, and accordingly the defendants were not liable.

In *Dynamco* v. *Holland & Hannen & Cubitts* (*Scotland*) [12] a factory occupier claimed damages when the defenders' workmen damaged the electric cable conducting power to the factory, causing loss of production and of profit. The action was held irrelevant; the loss was unforeseeable

[3] *Hughes* v. *Lord Advocate*, 1963 S.C.(H.L.) 31, 46–47, *per* Lord Guest.

[4] *Overseas Tankship* (*U.K.*) *Ltd.* v. *Morts Dock & Engineering Co.* [1961] A.C. 388.

[5] *Hughes*, *supra*, 48, *per* Lord Pearce.

[6] *Supra*, discussed fully in section (3), *infra*. It is significant that the authorities founded on in that case, such as *Bourhill* v. *Young*, 1942 S.C.(H.L.) 78; *Muir* v. *Glasgow Corpn.*, 1943 S.C.(H.L.) 3; and *Woods* v. *Duncan* [1946] A.C. 401, were cases of remoteness of injury.

[7] 1962 S.L.T. 168, 171.

[8] *Overseas Tankship* (*U.K.*) *Ltd.* v. *Miller Steamship Co. Pty.* [1967] 1 A.C. 617.

[9] *Supra.*

[10] 1963 S.C.(H.L.) 31.

[11] [1964] 1 Q.B. 518.

[12] 1971 S.L.T. 150.

and it was competent to sue for financial loss only if physical damage to property (*e.g.* collision damage to a ship) owned or possessed was the cause of the loss.

Conclusion

It seems clearly settled, accordingly, that whether a person is liable at all or not depends on whether some harm of the general kind which has happened was reasonably foreseeable by an ordinary reasonable man in the position of the defender, or was deemed a reasonable and probable consequence of the defender's failure to take care. The fact that the harm was caused by the conduct challenged does not establish liability if the particular consequence was not among the general class of happenings foreseeably likely to follow from the conduct.

If the application of this test of foresight elicits a negative answer, it means that injury and harm are too remote, and the pursuer's case fails completely and must be dismissed.[13] If it elicits a positive answer, injury is proximate and the defender may be liable, but, even assuming that the pursuer proves that the loss was in fact caused by the breach of duty, it does not follow that the pursuer is entitled to damages for all the loss he has actually suffered. There is still the problem of remoteness of damage, of how far and for what consequences the liability extends.[14]

This factor, of proximity of breach of duty and harm, is a material limitation of liability in that, even though there have been proved or admitted breach of duty and harm, and direct and uninterrupted causal connection between one and the other, the defender still escapes liability if the harm were of a kind unforeseeable and not a natural and probable consequence.

(3) " COMPENSATION " OR EXTENT OF LIABILITY OR REMOTENESS OF DAMAGE

A problem of remoteness of damage arises where a defender's conduct in breach of duty has caused or permitted to happen some event causing loss or harm to the pursuer and that loss or harm has led to further harmful consequences or set off a chain-reaction of harmful consequences. The problem is acute where the consequential harm was unforeseeable. The question accordingly arises of how far the defender's liability extends, and of whether any and, if so, on what principle a limit is to be set to the liability.[15] In generalised form the problem is: if X's conduct, in breach of duty to Y, causes Y harm A, which leads to harm B, then to harm C and so on, how far is X liable? For A only, or for all, or what?

There are very many examples in cases founded on delict of wrongful

[13] *e.g. Malcolm, supra*; *Blaikie, supra.*
[14] Section (3), *infra.*
[15] See further *Walker on Delict*, I, 248 *et seq.*

conduct causing some harm, which has led on to other harm, and to ultimate consequences much more serious than might have been expected, as where a workman suffered an injury to an eye, became almost blind, became insane, and committed suicide [16]; or negligent navigation of one ship caused a collision and damage to another, and the latter ship then sank and closed a navigable channel.[17]

Consequential and separate concurrent harms distinguished

Consequential harm must be distinguished from separate concurrent harms. If A's breach of duty causes initial harm to B which leads on to another harm the latter is consequential, but if A's breach of duty causes two distinct harms to B, such as personal injuries and damage to his vehicle, or distinct harms to B and C, such as personal injuries to each, they are separate concurrent harms. The former kind does, but the latter does not, raise a question of remoteness of damage. Thus the spillage of oil on a bay which both fouls a slipway and, taking fire, burns a wharf [18] is a case of separate concurrent harms, not a case of initial and consequential harm.

Consequential and unforeseeably serious harm distinguished

Consequential harm must also be distinguished from initial harm which is in fact much more serious than anyone would have foreseen or expected. If A's breach of duty causes harm to B and, to everyone's surprise, the harm is that B is killed in circumstances where nobody would have expected more than injuries, the death is not consequential but only surprisingly serious. It raises no question of remoteness of damage.[19]

Consequential harm must have been caused by defender's fault

To rank as consequential for the purposes of a decision on remoteness of damage the harm must have been caused by the defender's fault through the medium of, and have followed on, other harm caused thereby but more immediately. It must be established that the defender caused harm A which led to harm B which led to harm C and so on. If harm B was mainly caused by some *nova causa interveniens* it is not harm consequential but separate later harm.[20]

[16] *Malone* v. *Cayzer, Irvine & Co.*, 1908 S.C. 479 (decided under Workmen's Compensation Act). *Cf. Grime* v. *Fletcher* [1915] 1 K.B. 734; *Withers* v. *L.B. & S.C. Ry.* [1916] 2 K.B. 772; *Marriott* v. *Maltby Main Colliery Co.* (1920) 37 T.L.R. 123; *Hogan* v. *Bentinck West Hartley Collieries Ltd.* [1949] 1 All E.R. 588; *Pigney* v. *Pointers Transport Services Ltd.* [1957] 2 All E.R. 807; *Farmer* v. *Rash* [1969] 1 All E.R. 705.

[17] *S.S. Baron Vernon* v. *S.S. Metagama*, 1928 S.C.(H.L.) 21.

[18] *Overseas Tankship (U.K.) Ltd.* v. *Morts Dock & Engineering Co.* [1961] A.C. 388.

[19] *Cf. Millar* v. *Galashiels Gas Co.*, 1949 S.C.(H.L.) 31 (if any injury foreseeable would death have been foreseen?) and *Malcolm* v. *Dickson*, 1951 S.C. 542 (if any harm to persons had been foreseen, probably only shock would have been foreseen, but death took place).

[20] *Cf. McKew* v. *Holland & Hannen & Cubitts (Scotland) Ltd.*, 1970 S.L.T. 68.

No liability for all consequences

It is clear that the defender, even if admitted or proved to be liable for at least the initial harm, is not necessarily liable for all the consequences in the chain reaction set off by his original fault. "The law cannot take account of everything that follows a wrongful act; it regards some subsequent matters as outside the scope of its selection because 'it were infinite for the law to judge the cause of causes' or consequence of consequences. Thus the loss of a ship by collision, due to the other ship's sole fault, may force the shipowner into bankruptcy and that again may involve his family in suffering, loss of education and opportunities in life, but no such loss can be recovered from the wrongdoer. In the varied web of affairs, the law must abstract some consequences as relevant, not perhaps on grounds of pure logic but simply for practical reasons." [21]

The test for remoteness of damage in breach of contract and in delict

The problem of remoteness of damage is common to breach of contract and to delict. In both cases there is a breach of duty which has resulted in some harm or loss, and in both cases the question is: if the defender is liable, having been in breach of duty and having caused loss thereby, how far does his liability extend, and on what principle can the court limit his liability by saying that some losses are too remote consequences to be fairly chargeable against him in damages? The similarity ends there however. The basis of the legal duty is different; in contract it has been voluntarily assumed and on terms negotiated and agreed; in delict it has been imposed by force of law independently of the will of the parties.

Secondly, in cases of contract parties have an opportunity to consider beforehand what losses may result if a contract is not implemented in particular respects, to make express provision for that possibility, to enlarge the range of foreseeable losses by express communication of relevant circumstances, to charge more to cover the risk, and even, in most cases, in the light of the foreseeable circumstances, to decline to contract. None of these opportunities are available in cases of delict. The wrongdoer can, at most, provide against contingencies of the kinds he can foresee, but cannot provide against the chances of unusual loss in particular circumstances, because he cannot foresee who may come to have a claim against him, nor what losses may follow on breach of duty on his part.

Nevertheless the principle relevant to determining the extent of a defender's liability for remote or consequential losses arising from a breach of contract, discussed and settled in the cases of *Hadley* v. *Baxendale*,[22] *Victoria Laundry* v. *Newman* [23] and *A/B Karlshamns Oljefabriker* v. *Monarch S.S. Co.*,[24] has several times been referred to as applicable to

21 *Liesbosch* v. *Edison* [1933] A.C. 449, 460.
22 (1854) 9 Ex. 341.
23 [1949] 2 K.B. 528.
24 1949 S.C.(H.L.) 1.

tort also,[25] but such expressions of view have now been condemned as erroneous.[26]

> "The modern rule in tort is quite different and it imposes a much wider liability. The defendant will be liable for any type of damage which is reasonably foreseeable as likely to happen even in the most unusual case, unless the risk is so small that a reasonable man would in the whole circumstances feel justified in neglecting it; and there is good reason for the difference. In contract, if one party wishes to protect himself against a risk which to the other party would appear unusual, he can direct the other party's attention to it before the contract is made, and I need not stop to consider in what circumstances the other party will then be held to have accepted responsibility in that event. In tort, however, there is no opportunity for the injured party to protect himself in that way and the tortfeasor cannot reasonably complain if he has to pay for some very unusual but nevertheless foreseeable damage which results from his wrongdoing." [27]

No attempt seems to have been made in Scottish cases to equate the test for remoteness in delict to that in breach of contract, and it is submitted that the two grounds of liability should be kept entirely separate and that cases dealing with breach of contract have no relevance in cases of delict.

Remoteness of injury and remoteness of damage distinguished

A question of remoteness of damage must be carefully distinguished from a question of remoteness of injury.[28] "The distinction of proximate from remote consequences is needful firstly to ascertain whether there is any liability at all, and then, if it is established that wrong has been committed, to settle the footing on which compensation for the wrong is to be awarded." [29] A question of the former kind is not concerned with damages at all, but with whether or not there is any liability whatever on the defender for any part at all of the injury or harm which has befallen.

The distinction can be put in many ways: remoteness of injury is concerned with "culpability," remoteness of damage with "compensation," the former with liability to make reparation at all, the latter with the extent of that liability, the former with the interests protected by the law, the

[25] *The Notting Hill* (1884) 9 P.D. 104, 113; *Cobb* v. *G.W. Ry.* [1893] 1 Q.B. 459; *cf. The Argentino* (1888) 13 P.D. 191, 197, 201; *Weld-Blundell* v. *Stephens* [1920] A.C. 954, 979; *Re Hall and Pim's Arbitration* (1928) 139 L.T. 55; *The Edison* [1932] P. 52, 61; *The Arpad* [1934] P. 189, 216; *Haynes* v. *Harwood* [1935] 1 K.B. 146; *Sunley* v. *Cunard White Star* [1940] 1 K.B. 748; *The Wagon Mound* [1961] A.C. 388, 419.

[26] *The Wagon Mound* (*No.* 2) [1967] 1 A.C. 617, *per* Lord Reid; *Koufos* v. *Czarnikow* [1969] 1 A.C. 350, 385, *per* Lord Reid.

[27] *Koufos*, *supra*, 386, *per* Lord Reid, citing *Horne* v. *Midland Ry.* (1873) L.R. 7 C.P. 583, 590–591.

[28] Section (2), *supra*.

[29] *Pollock on Torts* (15th ed.) 23.

latter with valuation of the interests, the former with liability, the latter with damages.

> " The question of liability is always anterior to the question of the measure of the consequences that go with liability. If there is no tort to be redressed, there is no occasion to consider what damage might be recovered if there were a finding of tort. We may assume, without deciding, that negligence, not at large or in the abstract, but in relation to the plaintiff, would entail liability for any and all consequences, however novel or extraordinary." [30]

The practical difference in Scottish practice is that, proximity or remoteness in both senses being a question for the court and not for the jury,[31] the result of a particular injury or breach of duty being held too remote in law is that the action is irrelevant and must be dismissed, there being no liability in reparation at all, whereas the result of a particular item of loss or damage being held too remote in law is that that loss must be ignored in the quantification of damages as being irrelevant, but that *quoad ultra* the action is relevant. A question of remoteness of *injury* results in the action being held relevant or wholly irrelevant; a question of remoteness of *damage* results in certain heads of loss being taken into account, or excluded from account, in the quantification of damages.

Remoteness of damage

Remoteness of damage, accordingly, is a question which arises for consideration *only if and when liability* on the defender's part for at least some of the injury suffered by the pursuer *has been admitted or proved,* and the question is: the defender being liable, how far is he liable? For what consequences, for the immediate injuries only, or for their consequences so far as foreseeable, or for all the consequences which follow directly, or for all the consequences which can somehow be shown to be in any way connected with the defender's initial fault and injury? If on any ground of fact [32] or law,[33] including the ground that the injury was too remote from the alleged breach of duty, the defender is not liable at all, there can be no question of remoteness of damage, of the extent of liability. The justification for this is that liability should not, and cannot reasonably, be held to continue indefinitely. " The precept *alterum non laedere* . . . does not impose liability for every injury which our conduct

30 *Palsgraf* v. *Long Island Railroad Co.* (1928) 248 N.Y. 339, *per* Cardozo C.J. The first sentence was quoted, without mention of the source, by Lord Wright in *Bourhill* v. *Young,* 1942 S.C.(H.L.) 78, 92.

31 *Wilkinson* v. *Kinneil Cannel & Coking Coal Co.* (1897) 24 R. 1001; *Malcolm* v. *Dickson,* 1951 S.C. 542, 547.

32 These include the pursuer's failure to satisfy the court that the defender was in breach of duty, or that any breach proved was a substantial cause of the harm complained of.

33 These include the grounds that the pursuer had no title or interest to sue the action, that no such duty of care as is alleged is recognised in law, that any relevant duty recognised was not in the circumstances incumbent on the defender, that any such duty was not in the circumstances owed to the pursuer, or that the injury which befell was too remote, being of a kind not reasonably foreseeable by the defender.

may occasion. In Scotland at any rate, it has never been a maxim of the law that a man acts at his peril." [34]

Many cases and judicial dicta exhibit unfortunate confusion between remoteness of injury and remoteness of damage, and dicta from cases truly decided on one of these points have not infrequently been cited in later cases dealing with the other point. The distinction is really quite clear: the plea that *injury* is too remote is a defender's plea on liability or no liability, to the effect that the harm was of a kind not a natural and probable consequence of any alleged breach of duty, or of a kind not reasonably foreseeable as a consequence thereof, and accordingly too remotely connected with any breach of duty for the defender fairly to be held liable therefor at all; if this plea is sustained the pursuer's case must be dismissed as irrelevant; if it is rejected there must be inquiry to ascertain whether there was breach of duty, and whether it in fact caused the injury complained of, and as to the amount of loss suffered. The plea that *damage* is too remote is a defender's plea that, on the basis that there is *admitted or proved liability to make reparation*, some element or elements of the loss actually sustained are too remotely connected with the breach of duty to be fairly chargeable against the defender in damages. Remoteness of injury is concerned with the *existence of liability*; remoteness of damage is concerned with the *extent of that liability.*

The test for remoteness of damage

In view of the constant citation of English authorities in this branch of the law it is necessary to examine both Scottish and English cases. While variant verbal formulations are adopted in different cases they are of two classes: (1) that, if the defender is liable, he is liable only for the foreseeable consequences of his initial breach of duty, and no further; (2) that, if the defender is liable, he is liable for the direct consequences of his intial breach of duty, foreseeable or not. It is generally accepted that the second principle imposes a more extensive liability, in that direct consequences may extend beyond what was foreseeable by any reasonable man.

Views of text-writers

Bankton [35] states: "The offender is not only answerable for the immediate damage, but likewise for what further ensues from the criminal facts, and for the value of the thing as it would have been worth had not the damage happened, but not for remote consequential damage; thus one, through whose fault a house is set on fire is liable for *all the damage* that is occasioned through the progress of the flames." [36]

[34] *Muir* v. *Glasgow Corpn.*, 1943 S.C.(H.L.) 3, 10, *per* Lord Macmillan.
[35] I, 10, 7.
[36] *Cf. Smith* v. *L.S.W. Ry.* (1870) L.R. 6 C.P. 14; *Duke of Portland* v. *Wood's Trs.*, 1926 S.C. 640, 650; *Hutchison* v. *Davidson*, 1945 S.C. 395; *Gilmour* v. *Simpson*, 1958 S.C. 477.

Hume [37] laid down that shipowners in relation to their shipmaster were " liable for all damage occasioned by the want of due skill or care on the part of master or mariners."

Older Scottish cases

In *Lord Keith* v. *Keir* [38] the defender's servants began to burn brush and heath to clear land. The fire escaped and set fire to a wood 400 feet away. The court held that their master was liable " for every damage that had occurred."

In *Robertson* v. *Connolly* [39] R hired the grazing of a horse in C's field; the horse caught a disease from the defender's horse in the field and died, and infected two other horses in the pursuer's stable, which also died. It was held that the defender was liable for the value of all three horses. The case seems to have been argued and decided on the basis of delict,[40] though there must have been a contract initially. But it was not argued as a case of breach of contract. All the judges held the defender liable for the consequences of the transmission of the disease to the other two horses, as a " direct consequence of the defender's misconduct," [41] a common and natural consequence of the disease . . . a natural and probable consequence," [42] " a direct consequence of the defender's misconduct," [43] " liable for all the damage sustained from infection . . . damage sustained immediately and directly from the defender's fault." [44]

In *Allan* v. *Barclay*,[45] A sued B for having left a broken-down engine in the roadway, which caused a horse in the charge of H, an employee of A, to bolt, injuring H and damaging the horse and cart; A claimed for loss of H's services, and for damage to the horse and cart. H also, separately, sued B for his personal injuries.[46] The court dismissed A's action holding that a claim for loss of services was irrelevant and that the claim for damage to the horse and cart was incompetent in the Court of Session, being below the financial minimum of that court's competence. Lord Kinloch observed [47] that: " The grand rule on the subject of damages is that none can be claimed except such as naturally and directly arise out of the wrong done; and such, therefore, as may reasonably be supposed to have been in the view of the wrongdoer. Tried by this test, the present claim appears to fail. The personal injuries of the individual himself will be properly held to have been in the contemplation of the wrongdoer.

[37] *Lect.* III, 192.
[38] June 10, 1812, F.C.
[39] (1851) 13 D. 779; sequel, 14 D. 315; followed in *Baird* v. *Graham* (1852) 14 D. 615. *Cf. Smith* v. *Green* (1875) 1 C.P.D. 92, where the same result was arrived at on similar facts on the basis of a breach of warranty in sale.
[40] See Lord Cowan's note in *Baird* v. *Graham* (1852) 14 D. 615, 617.
[41] L.P. Boyle at p. 781.
[42] Lord Mackenzie at p. 781.
[43] Lord Fullerton at p. 782.
[44] Lord Cuninghame at p. 782.
[45] (1864) 2 M. 873.
[46] *Ibid.* 873, footnote. This action was held relevant.
[47] *Ibid.* 874.

But he cannot be held bound to have surmised the secondary injuries done to all holding relations with the individual, whether that of a master, or any other." The First Division affirmed the decision. In view of the uses to which Lord Kinloch's dictum have repeatedly been put it must be emphasised that it was made in relation to an issue of liability or of remoteness of injury, *not* an issue of remoteness of damage. He did not decide that the defender was liable for personal injuries to the carter and not liable for the consequential loss of services to the pursuer; the claim for the carter's personal injuries was a separate action,[48] and the *ratio* was that there was no liability to Allan for the loss of the carter's services because such loss could not have been contemplated by the defender. The loss of services was the basis of claim, and not a loss claimed for as consequential on any other claim.

The decision was approved and followed, as a decision on remoteness of injury, and Lord Kinloch's dictum quoted, in *Reavis* v. *Clan Line Steamers*,[49] where it was also observed [50] that the pursuer could recover "(as the direct and natural consequence of personal injury) any loss which she can prove to have arisen in consequence of her disability."

In *Scott's Trs.* v. *Moss* [51] the occupier of agricultural land claimed damages from the occupier of a recreation ground, who had advertised that a descent from a balloon would be made at a certain time. The descent took place into the pursuer's field and it was devastated by spectators. The action was held relevant, it being averred that the damage by the spectators was foreseeable and a natural and probable consequence of the advertised spectacle. This again is a decision on remoteness of injury, not remoteness of damage.

Similarly *Marshall* v. *Caledonian Ry. Co.*[52] was a decision on remoteness of injury; the defenders in constructing a railway had left an opening in the pursuer's wall, through which a person obtained access to his premises and stole property. The theft was held a natural and probable consequence, and the defenders liable for the loss occasioned thereby.

In *Clippens Oil Co.* v. *Edinburgh and District Water Trs.*,[53] a claim of damages for wrongful interdict whereby the pursuers had lost their business connection, Lord Chancellor Loreburn said [54]: "The result of [this blunder] is that they are liable in damages for whatever loss was sustained by pursuers in consequence of the interdict being in excess of what it ought to have been." And Lord Collins [55]:

> "In my opinion the wrongdoer must take his victim *talem qualem*, and if the position of the latter is aggravated because he is without

[48] *Ibid.* 873, footnote. This action was held relevant.
[49] 1925 S.C. 725, Lord Constable at p. 730, L.P. Clyde at p. 740.
[50] L.P. Clyde at p. 738.
[51] (1889) 17 R. 32.
[52] (1899) 1 F. 1060.
[53] 1907 S.C.(H.L.) 9.
[54] *Ibid.* 11.
[55] *Ibid.* 14.

the means of mitigating it, so much the worse for the wrongdoer, who has got to be answerable for the consequences flowing from his tortious act. On the other hand, the victim being in fact a poor man is not entitled to claim damages in respect of lost opportunities which he could not have utilised unless he had been rich.... If the pecuniary disability were traceable to the wrongdoer the case would of course be different.... The loss [the wrongdoer] has to pay for is that which has actually followed. . . . The defenders do not, as I understand them, dispute that if what Lord Dunedin [56] described as ' total loss ' or what [counsel] called ' bleeding to death ' were legally traceable to the wrong done by the defenders, they would be liable to pay damages measured by that standard. . . ."

In *Main* v. *Leask* [57] a steam drifter was lost in consequence of a collision. Liability was admitted for the full value of the boat, and it was further held that a claim for the estimated amount of profit lost for the remainder of the fishing season was not necessarily excluded as being remote or consequential, and a proof before answer was allowed thereon, Lord Ardwall remarking [58] that it was the " direct and immediate loss . . . directly caused. . . ."

Older English cases

In *Rigby* v. *Hewitt*,[59] followed in *Greenland* v. *Chaplin*,[60] Pollock C.B. " entertained considerable doubt whether a person who is guilty of negligence is responsible for all the consequences which may under any circumstances arise and in respect of mischief which could by no possibility have been foreseen and which no reasonable person would have anticipated," and suggested that the rule was that a man is expected to guard against all reasonable consequences. But he spoke for himself, and the majority of the court (Parke, Rolfe and Platt BB.) were evidently of a different view; but the difference of opinion was not material in the circumstances.

In *Smith* v. *L.S.W. Ry.*[61] on the other hand, a spark from an engine set fire to grass and hedge trimmings lying along the line. The fire burned through the hedge, across a stubble field, across a road and burned the plaintiff's cottage; he recovered from the railway company. Blackburn J. said [62]: " What the defendants might reasonably anticipate is . . . only material with reference to the question whether the defendants were negligent or not, and cannot alter their liability if they were guilty of negligence." An outbreak of fire was reasonably foreseeable and the

56 At (1906) 8 F. 731, 752.
57 1910 S.C. 772.
58 *Ibid.* p. 779.
59 (1850) 5 Ex. 240, 243.
60 (1850) 5 Ex. 243, 248, approved in *Cory* v. *France* [1911] 1 K.B. 114, 122.
61 (1870) L.R. 6 C.P. 14.
62 *Ibid.* 21.

defendants were liable for the consequences though the actual consequences could not have been foreseen.

In *Sharp* v. *Powell*,[63] where the defendant washed a van in the street and the water froze on the road and the plaintiff's horse fell and was injured, the defendant was held not responsible, but this seems a decision more on liability than on remoteness of damage. *Sharp* v. *Powell*[63] was approved in *Clark* v. *Chambers*[64] where a person placed an obstruction across a highway, somebody else moved it, and the plaintiff walked into it in the dark and was injured. The injured person was held entitled to recover, the injury being a natural consequence.

In *H.M.S. London*[65] it was said: " The court is not concerned in the present case with any inquiry as to the chain of causes resulting in the creation of a legal liability from which such damage as the law allows would flow. The tortious act, *i.e.* the negligence of the defendants, which imposes on them a liability in law for damages—is admitted. This gets rid at once of an element which requires consideration in a claim of causation in testing the question of legal liability—namely, the foresight or anticipation of the reasonable man . . . what the defendants might reasonably anticipate is only material with reference to the question whether the defendants were negligent or not, and cannot alter their liability if they were guilty of negligence." And in *Weld-Blundell* v. *Stephens*[66]: " What a defendant ought to have anticipated as a reasonable man is material when the question is whether or not he was guilty of negligence, that is, of want of due care according to the circumstances. This, however, goes to culpability not to compensation: *Blyth* v. *Birmingham Waterworks Co.*; *Smith* v. *L.S.W. Ry.*, *per* Blackburn J. Again, what ordinarily happens, or may reasonably be expected to happen, is material where a mere series of physical phenomena has to be investigated and the remoteness of the damage or the reverse is to be decided accordingly."

The rule in Re Polemis

In *Re Polemis and Furness Withy & Co.*[67] a ship was destroyed by fire. Arbitrators found in fact " (a) that the ship was lost by fire, (b) that the fire arose from a spark igniting petrol vapour in the hold, (c) that the spark was caused by the falling board coming in contact with some substance in the hold, (d) that the fall of the board was caused by the negligence of the [stevedores] . . . , (e) that the causing of the spark could not reasonably have been anticipated from the falling of the board, though some damage to the ship might reasonably have been anticipated. . . ." On these facts the Court of Appeal[68] held the charterers liable for the total loss of the

[63] (1872) L.R. 7 C.P. 253.
[64] (1878) 3 Q.B.D. 327.
[65] [1914] P. 72, 78, *per* Evans P.
[66] [1920] A.C. 956, 984, *per* Lord Sumner.
[67] [1921] 3 K.B. 560.
[68] Affirming Sankey J., who had affirmed the arbitrators' award.

ship. Bankes L.J. said " according to the one view,[69] the consequences which may reasonably be expected to result from a particular act are material only in reference to the question whether the act is or is not a negligent act; according to the other view,[70] those consequences are the test whether the damages resulting from the act, assuming it to be negligent, are or are not too remote to be recoverable. . . . In the present case the arbitrators have found as a fact that the falling of the plank was due to the negligence of the defendants' servants. The fire appears to me to have been directly caused by the falling of the plank. In these circumstances I consider that it is immaterial that the causing of the spark by the falling of the plank could not have been reasonably anticipated. . . . Given the breach of duty which constitutes the negligence, and given the damage as a direct result of that negligence, the anticipations of the person whose negligent act has produced the damage appears to me to be irrelevant." Similarly Warrington L.J. said, " The presence or absence of reasonable anticipation of damage determines the legal quality of the act as negligent or innocent. If it be thus determined to be negligent, then the question whether particular damages are recoverable depends only on the answer to the question whether they are the direct consequence of the act." And Scrutton L.J. said " To determine whether an act is negligent, it is relevant to determine whether any reasonable person would foresee that the act would cause damage; if he would not, the act is not negligent. But if the act would or might probably cause damage, the fact that the damage it in fact causes is not the exact kind of damage one would expect is immaterial, so long as the damage is in fact caused sufficiently directly by the negligent act, and not by the operation of independent causes having no connection with the negligent act, except that they could not avoid its results. Once the act is negligent, the fact that its exact operation was not foreseen is immaterial."

This decision settled English law in the sense that, if fault were admitted or proved, liability existed for the direct consequences of the fault, whether foreseeable or not.[71]

Later dicta in English cases were to the same effect. Thus in *Hambrook* v. *Stokes* [72] Atkin L.J. said: " Once a breach of duty to the plaintiff is established one has no longer to consider whether the consequences could reasonably be anticipated by the wrongdoer. The question is whether the consequences causing damage are the direct result of the wrongful act or

[69] *i.e.* that represented by *Smith* v. *L.S.W. Ry.* (1870) L.R. 6 C.P. 14, 21, *per* Channell B. and Blackburn J.; *H.M.S. London* [1914] P. 72, 76, *per* Evans P.; *Weld-Blundell* v. *Stephens* [1920] A.C. 956, 983, *per* Lord Sumner.

[70] *i.e.* that represented by the dictum of Pollock C.B. in *Rigby* v. *Hewitt* (1850) 5 Exch. 240, 243, and *Greenland* v. *Chaplin* (1850) 5 Exch. 243, 248.

[71] For discussion of the decision see Pollock, 38 L.Q.R. 165; Goodhart, *Essays*, 110; (1951) 4 *Current Legal Problems* 177; 68 L.Q.R. 514; McLaughlin 39 H.L.R. 149; McNair, 4 Camb.L.J. 125; Porter, 5 Camb.L.J. 176; Wright, 14 M.L.R. 393; Middleton, 48 J.R. 133; 63 J.R. 276; Holdsworth, *H.E.L.*, VIII, 462; Payne (1952) 5 *Current Legal Problems* 189. The decision accorded with the views of Beven, *Negligence*, I, 91; Bohlen, *Studies in the Law of Tort*, I, and Street, *Foundations of Legal Liability*, I, 111–116.

[72] [1925] 1 K.B. 141, 156.

omission. . . . Here, then, was a breach of duty owed to Mrs. Hambrook. No doubt the particular injury was not contemplated by the defendants, but it is plain from *In re Polemis and Furness Withy & Co.* that this is immaterial. If the act would or might probably cause damage, the fact that the damage it in fact causes is not the exact kind of damage one would expect, is immaterial, so long as the damage is in fact directly traceable to the negligent act, and not due to operation of independent causes having no connection with the negligent act: *per* Scrutton L.J."

The principle of the decision seemed to have been subsequently accepted by the House of Lords [73] and Privy Council,[74] even if not expressly approved, though in *Minister of Pensions* v. *Chennell*,[75] Denning J. doubted whether *Polemis* could survive the decisions in *Donoghue* v. *Stevenson*,[76] *Bourhill* v. *Young*,[77] *Aldham* v. *United Dairies* [78] and *Woods* v. *Duncan* [79]: "If it does, it is only in respect of neglect of duty to the plaintiff which is the immediate or precipitating cause of damage of an unforeseeable kind." It is submitted that none of the decisions cited in any way impinge on the *Polemis* principle, and in *Thurogood* v. *Van den Berghs* [80] the Court of Appeal said that the binding character of the decision was in no way shaken.

Cases subsequent to Re Polemis

In *Currie* v. *Wardrop* [81] where a young couple were struck by a vehicle and the girl sustained shock by apprehension for her own safety and shock attributable to anxiety for her friend, Lord Murray said [82]: "I am further of opinion that such liability extends to full compensation for the loss and damage consequent upon the injury sustained, provided (a) that the amount of such loss and damage is proved—a question of fact; and (b) that it is not open to objection as being too remote—a question of mixed fact and law. . . . Where, as here, the injured party is directly concerned in the accident, where negligence and breach of duty to the injured party are admitted or proved, as also that the injury suffered is the direct result of that breach of duty, I do not think that the law restricts the full compensation for the injury which would otherwise follow by any such consideration as is here suggested."

In *The Cameronia* v. *The Hauk* [83] demurrage and dock charges incurred

[73] *G.W. Ry.* v. *S.S. Mostyn* [1928] A.C. 57, 91, *per* Lord Phillimore; *S.S. Baron Vernon* v. *S.S. Metagama*, 1928 S.C.(H.L.) 21; *Liesbosch Dredger* v. *Edison* [1933] A.C. 449, 461, *per* Lord Wright; *Morrison S.S. Co.* v. *Greystoke Castle (Owners)* [1947] A.C. 265, 295, *per* Lord Porter.
[74] *Grant* v. *Australian Knitting Mills* [1936] A.C. 107.
[75] [1947] K.B. 250.
[76] 1932 S.C.(H.L.) 31.
[77] 1942 S.C.(H.L.) 78.
[78] [1940] 1 K.B. 507.
[79] [1946] A.C. 401.
[80] [1951] 2 K.B. 537.
[81] 1927 S.C. 538.
[82] pp. 554–555.
[83] 1928 S.L.T. 71, sequel to 1927 S.C. 518.

in consequence of collision were spoken of as " natural and direct consequences " and allowed.

In *S.S. Baron Vernon* v. *S.S. Metagama*,[84] the M collided with the BV in the Clyde, *the M being admittedly solely liable for the collision*. The BV was damaged and beached, then slipped off the bank and grounded on the other bank, then two days later sank in the fairway, rendering the owners liable to the Clyde Navigation Trustees [85] for the expenses of removing the sunken vessel and other outlays.

The M's owners, though admitting liability for the collision, alleged that much of the damage sustained by the pursuers was occasioned by the improper handling of the BV after the accident. It was held that the defenders were liable for the whole damage sustained, and that the M would have been entitled to a diminution of damages only if it had been proved that those in charge of the BV had, after the collision, been guilty of negligence, amounting to a *novus actus interveniens* which caused the extra damage, as opposed to mere error in judgment.

In the Court of Session [86] Lord Hunter said [87] " The whole injury in the accepted sense of the phrase is the direct consequence of the wrongdoer's act," and he cited *H.M.S. London* [88] and *De La Bere* v. *Pearson* [89] where Lord Alverstone C.J. said: ". . . The rule of law appears to me to be now well established that if the defendants' breach of contract or duty is the primary and substantial cause of the damage sustained by the plaintiff the defendants will be held responsible for the whole loss, though it may have been increased by the wrongful conduct of a third person, and although that wrongful conduct may have contributed to the loss." Then, having cited *Weld-Blundell* v. *Stephens* [90] and *In re Polemis* [91] he reached the conclusion that " the loss sustained by the pursuers in consequence of the *Baron Vernon* having to be salved . . . is the direct consequence of the *Metagama* having collided with that vessel." Lord Anderson said [92]: " The liability of the defenders is to make good all the damage done to the *Baron Vernon* which was the natural and reasonable result of the defenders' act—which, in the ordinary course of things, would flow from that act—*The Argentino*, 14 App.Cas. 519; *The City of Lincoln*, 15 P.D. 15. This would seem to make the defenders responsible for all damage which, in point of fact, the *Baron Vernon* has suffered and is claiming for, unless they can make out that any part of the damages claimed for was not an inevitable consequence of the collision, but was due to intervening negligence of the pursuers."

84 1927 S.C. 498; 1928 S.C.(H.L.) 21.
85 See *Clyde Navigation Trs.* v. *Kelvin Shipping Co. Ltd.*, 1927 S.C. 622.
86 1927 S.C. 498.
87 p. 515.
88 [1914] P. 72.
89 [1907] 1 K.B. 483.
90 [1920] A.C. 956.
91 [1921] 3 K.B. 560.
92 1927 S.C. at 518.

The judgment was affirmed in the House of Lords. Viscount Haldane said [93]: " When a collision takes place by the fault of the defending ship, the damage is recoverable, in an action for damages, if it is the natural and reasonable result of the negligent act, and it will assume this character if it can be shown to be such a consequence as in the ordinary course of things would flow from the situation which the offending ship had created. Further, what those in charge of the injured ship do to save it may be mistaken but, if they do whatever they do reasonably, although unsuccessfully, their mistaken judgment may be a natural consequence for which the offending ship is liable, just as much as any physical occurrence. Reasonable human conduct is part of the ordinary course of things which extends to the reasonable conduct of those who have sustained the damage and who are seeking to save further loss." Viscount Dunedin said [93a]: " The *Metagama*, having been in fault for the collision, is liable for the damage occasioned thereby, and, if the ship with which she collided sinks subsequently to the collision, she is, if no more is to be said, liable for that sinking." The House made no attempt to limit the liability by reference to the foreseeability of the post-collision happenings. These followed directly from the collision and there was liability to the extent of all the losses.

In *Liesbosch Dredger* v. *The Edison*,[94] the E collided with and sank the L, and admitted liability for the collision. The claimants were held entitled to the value of their ship, but not to anything for loss due to their financial inability at once to buy a replacement, this being damage not flowing from the defendant's wrong or, if it did, being too remote. Lord Wright [95] stated that the appellant's loss, so far as due to their impecuniosity arose from " a separate and concurrent cause, extraneous to and distinct in character from the tort; the impecuniosity was not traceable to the respondents' acts, and, in my view was outside the legal purview of the consequences of these acts."... " *Polemis* v. *Furness, Withy & Co.*,[96] a case in tort of negligence, was cited as illustrating the wide scope possible in damages for tort. That case, however, was concerned with the immediate physical consequences of the negligent act, and not with the co-operation of an extraneous matter such as the plaintiffs' want of means. I think, therefore, that it is not material further to consider that case here. Nor is the appellants' financial disability to be compared with the physical delicacy or weakness which may aggravate the damage in the case of personal injuries, or with the possibility that the injured man in such a case may be either a poor labourer or a highly paid professional man. The former class of circumstances goes to the extent of actual physical damage, and the latter consideration goes to interference with profit earning capacity; whereas the appellants' want of means was, as already stated,

93 1928 S.C.(H.L.) 21, 25.
93a p. 27.
94 [1933] A.C. 449.
95 p. 460; Lords Buckmaster, Warrington, Tomlin and Russell of Killowen concurring.
96 [1921] 3 K.B. 560.

extrinsic." This decision was later explained [97] as being that " the loss due to the party's impecuniosity was too remote and therefore to be neglected in the calculation of damages; it was special loss due to his financial position. A different conclusion was arrived at in *Muhammad Issa el Sheikh Ahmad* v. *Ali* [98] where damages consequent on impecuniosity were held not too remote, because, as I understand, the loss was such as might reasonably be expected to be in the contemplation of the parties as likely to flow from breach of the obligation undertaken."

Discussion in Bourhill v. Young

The question of remoteness of damage was discussed *obiter* in *Bourhill* v. *Young* [1] where it was held that a woman (pursuer) was outwith the ambit of the duty of care owed by a reckless motor-cyclist, who killed himself in an accident, and that his executor was therefore not liable at all to the woman, though she claimed that by reason of the accident she had sustained serious nervous shock and a consequent miscarriage. As the case was decided on the issue of negligence or no negligence, or of the ambit of the duty of care, and against the pursuer, the issue of remoteness of damage was irrelevant.[2] But Lord Mackay [3] said that " *Polemis*, as counsel on both sides said,[4] has never been accepted in Scotland.[5] I have myself in the Outer House followed this general Scottish outlook." Lord Jamieson [6] said *obiter* " [*Polemis*] has never been followed in Scotland and, it appears to me, is contrary to well-established principles with regard to damages here." [7] He quoted Lord Kinloch's dictum in *Allan* v. *Barclay* and went on to consider other cases of liability. Lord Justice-Clerk Aitchison, however, dissenting, held that the defender had owed a duty of care to the pursuer, had been in breach thereof, and had caused the shock and miscarriage. " Once the breach of duty is established, the consequence of negligence becomes inevitable unless the damage caused to the pursuer is in law too remote to infer negligence, or, assuming negligence, the consequence is one for which, for practical reasons, the law will not assign responsibility to the wrongdoer." [8] He held that " the causal relation between the damage and the act was direct and immediate " and that the case fell within " the principle of *Polemis*, which makes the wrongdoer answerable for the immediate physical consequences of his act. . . . There is nothing very startling in that decision. No one would have thought it startling but for the unexpected nature of the consequence and

[97] *A/B Karlshamns Oljefabriker* v. *Monarch S.S. Co.*, 1949 S.C.(H.L.) 1, 21, *per* Lord Wright.
[98] [1947] A.C. 414.
[1] 1941 S.C. 395; 1942 S.C.(H.L.) 78.
[2] Except for L.J.C. Aitchison who dissented (1941 S.C. 395, 429) and held that the defender was liable, and liable for the miscarriage, though he could not possibly have foreseen that consequence.
[3] 1941 S.C. 395, 421.
[4] Wrongly.
[5] *Quaere.*
[6] 1941 S.C. 395, 427.
[7] *Quaere.*
[8] *Ibid.* 433.

the extent of the damage. It has been aptly put by an American writer thus: ' The idea is that the man who starts something should be responsible for what he has started.' "[9]

In the House of Lords, where the pursuer's claim was again rejected on the ground that she had been outwith the ambit of the duty of care owed by the careless cyclist, Lord Thankerton[10] carefully and rightly distinguished *Polemis* as one " where the issue only related to the measure of damages." Lord Russell of Killowen[11] said that the consideration of what the defendant ought to have contemplated as a reasonable man " may play a double role. It is relevant in cases of admitted negligence (where the duty and breach are admitted) to the question of remoteness of damage, *i.e.* to the question of compensation, not to culpability, but it is also relevant in testing the existence of a duty as to the foundation of the alleged negligence, *i.e.* to the question of culpability not to compensation." Lord Macmillan[12] said that it had been argued that " once an act is properly characterized as negligent, that is to say, as a breach of a duty of care owed to a particular person, then the party at fault is liable to that person for everything that directly follows from the negligent act, whether or not it could have been foreseen as a natural and probable result of the negligent act. For this *In re Polemis and Furness, Withy & Co.* was cited. . . . As at present advised, I doubt if it is the law of Scotland, and I could cite ample authority to the contrary,[13] but, again, this is not a point which I deem it necessary to discuss now." Lord Wright[14] observed: " No doubt it has long ago been stated and often restated that, if the wrong is established, the wrongdoer must take the victim as he finds him. That, however, is only true, as the *Polemis*[15] case shows, on the condition that the wrong has been established or admitted. The question of liability is anterior to the question of the measure of the consequences which go with the liability. That was the second point, decided not for the first time, but merely reiterated in the *Polemis*[16] case. It must be understood to be limited, however, to ' direct ' consequences to the particular interest of the plaintiff which is affected. *Liesbosch Dredger* v. *Edison S.S.* (*Owners*)[17] illustrates this limitation." And Lord Porter[18] said: " I think it is essential to bear in mind the distinction drawn in *In re Polemis*,[16] a distinction which is perhaps best expressed in the words of Channell B. taken from *Smith* v. *L.S.W. Ry.*,[19] which are quoted by Warrington L.J. (at p. 574):

[9] *Ibid.* 437.
[10] 1942 S.C.(H.L.) 78, 84.
[11] *Ibid.* 85. He cites no authority for the first branch of the dictum, which, it is submitted, is unsound in Scots law.
[12] *Ibid.* 89.
[13] It is much to be regretted that his Lordship did not cite the cases he had in mind, because the author cannot find any, and denies that there are any.
[14] 1942 S.C.(H.L.) 78, 90, citing *Smith* v. *L.S.W. Ry.* (1870) L.R. 6 C.P. 14, and *Polemis, supra*.
[15] [1921] 3 K.B. 560.
[16] [1921] 3 K.B. 560.
[17] [1933] A.C. 449.
[18] 1942 S.C.(H.L.) 78, 94–95.
[19] (1870) L.R. 6 C.P. 14, 21.

'Where there is no direct evidence of negligence, the question what a reasonable man might foresee is of importance in considering the question whether there is evidence for the jury of negligence or not . . . but when it has been once determined that there is evidence of negligence, the person guilty of it is equally liable for its consequences, whether he could have foreseen them or not.' For the present I think it immaterial to consider whether the second proposition is accurate or not."

In *Thurogood* v. *Van den Berghs and Jurgens Ltd.*[20] a workman was injured when his hand was caught in the unguarded blades of a fan which had been removed for repair. Negligence was held to exist in that it was reasonably foreseeable that some damage might have befallen the workman, and some damage did happen, though it was not explained how or why, and it seemed to have arisen from mere inadvertence on the workman's part. Having pointed out that the decision in *In Re Polemis* [21] had never been overruled and was still binding on the Court of Appeal, Asquith L.J.[22] held that:

> " when one is considering whether the damage was directly caused it matters not whether the precise way in which in the event it came about is explained or unexplained, foreseeable or unforeseeable. It was unexplained why in *Re Polemis* [21] the fall of the plank caused the spark. It was unexplained in *Aldham* v. *United Dairies* (*London*) *Ltd.*[23] . . . why the unattended pony, who had never before been more than restive, came to bite the plaintiff. In *Caswell* v. *Powell Duffryn Associated Collieries Ltd.*[24] it was unexplained through what act of inadvertence, occurring how, Caswell was injured. Nonetheless these unexplained events were held to result directly from the defendants' negligence or, at all events, not to break the chain of direct causation leading from that negligence to the damages. . . . Then, again, although reasonable foresight of possible injury is the true criterion where negligence *vel non* is the issue, an employer who has created or permitted a dangerous condition to arise is reasonably expected to foresee and provide against the possibility of injury resulting therefrom even though it so results through the intermediation of an act of inadvertence by the employee and even though that act of inadvertence be of a character which cannot be precisely forecast and remains in the event ' unexplained.' It is enough if he ought reasonably to anticipate that injury or damage of some sort to a workman was likely, or damage of some sort to a workman was likely to result, and in applying his foresight to this question he cannot leave out of account the tendency of factory operatives to commit acts of inadvertence such as those which occupied so much of the time of the court in *Caswell* v. *Powell Duffryn Associated Collieries Ltd.*[25] "

[20] [1951] 2 K.B. 537.
[21] [1921] 3 K.B. 560.
[22] Cohen and Birkett L.JJ. concurring.
[23] [1940] 1 K.B. 507.
[24] [1940] A.C. 152.
[25] [1940] A.C. 152.

> Asquith L.J. further observed: "Nor do I consider that the decision in *Re Polemis & Furness, Withy & Co.*[26] has been overruled, or its binding character, so far as this court is concerned, in any degree shaken. The utmost that can be said is that certain of the Lords of Appeal in Ordinary have reserved the right to reconsider it if and when, before the House of Lords, its authoritative character should come directly in issue. Meanwhile it stands. It has been suggested that decisions such as *Donoghue* v. *Stevenson*[27] and *Hay* (*or Bourhill*) v. *Young*[28] have in some way undermined it. I respectfully dissent. The issue in both those cases was: 'Did the defendant owe a duty of care to the plaintiff?' not 'Did the damage suffered by the plaintiff result directly from the breach of such duty of care?' If in either case a duty existed on the part of the defendant, no one doubted that the indisposition of the plaintiff in *Donoghue's* case[27] was directly caused by drinking contaminated ginger beer, or the miscarriage of the plaintiff in *Bourhill's* case[28] was directly caused by the conduct on the high road of the defendant in that case. In my view, *Re Polemis & Furness, Withy & Co.*[29] has not been overruled, and this is all that it is necessary or proper to say here."

In *Taylor* v. *Scottish Boiler & General Insurance Co. Ltd.*[30] a woman sustained a broken left leg and alleged that, two months later, she fell in consequence of the weak condition of her leg and sustained further injuries. The Lord Ordinary allowed a proof, though observing that the pursuer's claim, so far as founded on the second accident, might in the end turn out to be irrelevant. This decision is not helpful.

In *Cowan* v. *N.C.B.*[31] a workman sustained an eye injury. In an action by his widow and children it was alleged that the accident to the eye was caused by the defenders' fault, that in consequence he became nervous and depressed and mentally deranged so that he ultimately committed suicide. The Lord Ordinary held that it had not been proved that the initial accident was caused by the defenders' fault, so that there was no liability and consequently his observations on the other points were *obiter*. But he expressed the view[32] that the rule in *Re Polemis*[33] was not the law of Scotland.

> "The true test of whether the death of the deceased was caused by the negligence of the defenders is whether the death naturally and directly arose out of the supposed wrong done to him[34] and was therefore such a consequence as might reasonably be supposed to

26 [1921] 3 K.B. 560.
27 1932 S.C.(H.L.) 31.
28 1942 S.C.(H.L.) 78.
29 [1921] 3 K.B. 560.
30 1951 S.L.T.(Notes) 36.
31 1958 S.L.T.(Notes) 19; on the facts compare *Marriott* v. *Maltby Main Colliery Co. Ltd.* (1920) 37 T.L.R. 123, and *Pigney* v. *Pointers Transport Services Ltd.* [1957] 2 All E.R. 807.
32 By reference to all the earlier Scottish cases on remoteness of *injury* (not remoteness of damage).
33 [1921] 3 K.B. 560.
34 *i.e.* the injury to his eye. Thus far the statement of the law is acceptable.

have been in the view of the wrongdoer. . . .[35] But no wrongdoer is bound to foresee and therefore to be liable for all the consequences of his wrongdoing in the matter of the actual injury inflicted or loss sustained. Now in the present case if it were held to be established that the deceased had received a comparatively moderate injury through the negligence of the defenders and had . . . then committed suicide . . . it does not follow that such a result could properly be described in the ordinary use of language as the natural and direct result of the initial injury so as to make the delinquent liable in damages to the dependants. . . ." [36]

The Wagon Mound decision

In *Overseas Tankship* (*U.K.*) *Ltd.* v. *Morts Dock & Engineering Co. Ltd.*,[37] M. owned a timber wharf and workmen were using welding equipment thereon. O.T. were charterers of the ship *Wagon Mound*; through the carelessness of O.T.'s servants a quantity of bunker oil was spilled on the surface of a bay and was concentrated along the foreshore near M.'s wharf. The oil under the wharf became ignited and the fire damaged the wharf. The outbreak of fire was probably due to the fact that there was floating in the oil underneath the wharf a piece of debris on which lay some cotton waste or rag which had been set on fire by molten metal falling from the wharf. But it was also found in fact that O.T.'s servants did not know, and could not reasonably be expected to have known, that furnace oil was capable of being set afire when spread on water. Apart from the damage by fire to the wharf, M. suffered some other damage from the spillage of oil in that it had got on their slipways and congealed on them and interfered with their use of the slips, but no claim for compensation was made in respect of this.

The first point about the decision is that a decision of the Privy Council in an appeal from Australia, in which Scots law was not relevant and was not argued, is not at all a binding authority for Scottish courts, and anything said about Scots law therein is entirely *obiter*.

The second point about the decision is that it seems to have been argued and decided on the basis that the fire which damaged the wharf was damage in some way consequential on the slight damage caused by the oil fouling the slipway. But this is not so. The oil fouling the slipway, and the other oil taking fire and damaging the wharf were separate concurrent harms both caused by O.T.'s carelessness in spilling oil on the surface of the bay; the one, damage by fire, was not consequential on the other, damage by fouling.

[35] This clause is an illegitimate inference. It does not follow from a consequence being " direct " that it should be foreseeable.

[36] The suicide might well have been an indirect consequence if following mainly from a state of mind not brought about by the initial injury.

[37] [1961] A.C. 388. On this case see Goodhart, 76 L.Q.R. 567; 77 L.Q.R. 175; Williams, 77 L.Q.R. 179; 25 M.L.R. 1; Dias [1962] C.L.J. 178; [1967] C.L.J. 62; Weir, 35 Tulane L.R. 619.

What should have been considered was whether there was any liability as separate concurrent harms for (a) the fouling of the slipway, and for (b) the presence of the oil which took fire and damaged the wharf. No question of consequential damage was truly raised, and no problem of remoteness of damage. The whole discussion of remoteness of damage was irrelevant, unnecessary and *obiter*. In view of the absence of claim for loss (a), no liability arose therefor. In view of the finding of fact that bunker oil was not known to be capable of being set on fire when spread on the water, there was clearly no liability for loss (b).[38] The Board's disposal of the case is therefore right, but for the wrong reasons in that it seems to have thought it was dealing with a case of remoteness of damage, whereas it was really dealing with a straightforward case of liability or no liability. It is noteworthy that in a subsequent case arising out of the same incident,[39] but decided on different proven facts, the Privy Council said that " It has now been established by *The Wagon Mound* (*No.* 1) and by *Hughes* v. *Lord Advocate* [40] that in such cases damages can only be recovered if the injury complained of not only was caused by the alleged negligence but also was an injury of a class or character foreseeable as a possible result of it." If this is a statement of the ratio of *The Wagon Mound* (*No.* 1), it is plain that the former case had nothing to do with remoteness of damage, or with the rule in *Re Polemis*, and that it decided absolutely nothing new.

The third point is that the Board was obviously determined to strike down *Re Polemis* as a matter of policy, and any arguments which might help to do this were acceptable, and no arguments which might have served to justify that decision were acceptable.

The Board criticised the judgments in *Re Polemis* [41] for not having discussed *Hadley* v. *Baxendale*,[42] because up to that date it had been " universally accepted that the law in regard to damages for breach of contract and for tort was, generally speaking, and particularly in regard to the tort of negligence, the same." This was then very questionable, and in the light of subsequent consideration of the point,[43] is wrong. Similarly, later,[44] a dictum in *Victoria Laundry* v. *Newman* [45] (a case of damages for breach of contract) was cited as *not* suggesting that Asquith L.J. regarded the measure of damage as different in tort and breach of contract, a matter not under consideration there at all and probably not

38 The point does not seem to have been taken that the setting of the floating oil on fire was a *novus actus interveniens* brought about by M's use of welding equipment on the wharf, discharging sparks and fragments of hot metal, after oil was known to be floating under the wharf.

39 *Overseas Tankship* (*U.K.*) *Ltd.* v. *Miller Steamship Co. Pty.* (*The Wagon Mound No.* 2) [1967] 1 A.C. 617.

40 1963 S.C.(H.L.) 31.

41 [1921] 3 K.B. 560.

42 (1854) 9 Ex. 341.

43 *The Wagon Mound* (*No.* 2) [1967] 1 A.C. 617; *Koufos* v. *Czarnikow, The Heron* II [1969] 1 A.C. 350.

44 p. 420.

45 [1949] 2 K.B. 534.

considered. Next the Board asserted [46] that, if the line of authority had stopped with *Polemis*,[47] their Lordships, whatever their own views as to its unreason, might have hesitated to overrule it,[48] but that, in England and many parts of the Commonwealth, the decision had from time to time been followed: " but in Scotland it has been rejected with determination." The statement is completely incorrect and wholly unsound, and unwarranted in a case in which Scots law was not before the court, nor argued, nor examined. As an instance of " deviation from the rule in *Polemis* " [47] the Board then cited *Glasgow Corpn.* v. *Muir*,[49] a case concerned only with liability or no liability and not dealing at all with the question of remoteness of damage,[50] mentioning a passage in the speech of Lord Thankerton [51] clearly concerned only with the test for liability, allegedly as being a deviation from the rule of *Polemis*,[52] and a passage from Lord Macmillan [53] which also has nothing whatever to do with remoteness of damage, and concluding, " Here there is no suggestion of one criterion for determining culpability (or liability) and another for determining compensation." There is certainly no suggestion, because in the passages cited, and in the case of *Muir* as a whole, only liability was being considered, and the courts never had occasion to consider the criterion for remoteness of damage, if indeed there had been any question of remote or consequential losses in that case at all, and there quite certainly was not.

But the Board continued [54]: " In *Hay* (*or Bourhill*) v. *Young* [55] the double criterion is more directly denied," and a passage was cited from Lord Russell of Killowen,[56] followed by the observation that the passage cited appears to be in flat contradiction to the rule in *Polemis*.[57] Here again, in *Bourhill*, culpability or liability only was in issue, and the case was decided on the basis that there was none, so that everything said about remoteness of damage was *obiter* and superfluous, and, secondly, the Board cited Lord Russell of Killowen, whose expression of views suited their argument, but not the contradictory views of Lord Wright and Lord Porter. The Board next mentioned *Woods* v. *Duncan*,[58] where again liability only was in issue,[59] and then concluded that *Polemis* should no

46 p. 420.
47 [1921] 3 K.B. 560.
48 Their Lordships, sitting as Judical Committee of the Privy Council, could not, strictly speaking, overrule a decision of the Court of Appeal.
49 Sub nom. *Muir* v. *Glasgow Corpn.*, 1943 S.C.(H.L.) 3.
50 *Polemis* does not appear ever to have been mentioned in *Muir*, either in the Court of Session or House of Lords.
51 1943 S.C.(H.L.) 3, 8.
52 [1921] 3 K.B. 560.
53 1943 S.C.(H.L.) 3, 10.
54 p. 421.
55 1942 S.C.(H.L.) 78.
56 1942 S.C.(H.L.) 78, 85, cited *supra*.
57 [1921] 3 K.B. 560.
58 [1946] A.C. 401.
59 This leads inevitably to the doubt whether counsel arguing the case, or the Board, fully understood the difference between liability, culpability or remoteness of injury and extent of liability, compensation, or remoteness of damage.

longer be regarded as good law, on the grounds that " it does not seem consonant with current ideas of justice or morality that for an act of negligence, however slight or venial, which results in some foreseeable damage, the actor should be liable for all consequences, however unforeseeable and however grave, so long as they can be said to be direct." This is a matter of opinion, and the statement is open to the answer: Why not? If X is in breach of duty to Y and causes Y damage of a foreseeable kind, and unforeseeable consequences follow directly, why should X not be fully liable? Why should the man who started things not be liable for the direct consequences, even though he did not foresee them, even though the reasonable man could not have foreseen the frightful consequences of what he had unleashed.

Finally [60] the Board addressed itself to the dictum of Lord Sumner,[61] " This, however, goes to culpability, not to compensation," and felt " bound to state their view that this proposition is fundamentally false." The Board went on: " There can be no liability until the damage has been done. . . . It may, of course, become relevant to know what duty B owed to A but the only liability that is in question is the liability for damage by fire. It is vain to isolate the liability from its context and to say that B is or is not liable, and then to ask for what damage he is liable. For his liability is in respect of that damage and no other. If, as admittedly it is, B's liability (culpability) depends on the reasonable foreseeability of the consequent damage,[62] how is that to be determined except by the foreseeability of the damage which in fact happened—the damage in suit? " . . . " We have come back to the plain common sense stated by Lord Russell of Killowen in *Hay* (*or Bourhill*) v. *Young*.[63] As Denning L.J. said in *King* v. *Phillips* [64] ' There can be no doubt since *Hay* (*or Bourhill*) v. *Young* [63] that the test of liability for shock is foreseeability of injury by shock.' " [65]

Criticism of The Wagon Mound decision

In the first place the decision does not lay down that the test for liability or culpability is the foreseeability of some harm and that the test for remoteness of damage or compensation is that liability is limited to the damage which was foreseeable.[66] The decision attempts to amalgamate,

60 p. 424.

61 In *Weld-Blundell* v. *Stephens* [1920] A.C. 956, 984. The dictum, it should be noted, was *obiter*.

62 The writer does not accept the inclusion of the words " the consequent " in this as a correct statement of law.

63 1942 S.C.(H.L.) 78.

64 [1953] 1 Q.B. 429, 441.

65 It is submitted that this is *not* the *ratio* of *Bourhill* v. *Young*, but that the *ratio* of that case is: the test of liability for shock is the foreseeability of injury, whether physical, by shock or otherwise, and the fact that shock has been caused. Even if, which is denied, the *ratio* of *Bourhill* is as stated it is apparent that *Bourhill* was concerned only with liability or not, and not with its extent.

66 It does not, that is, approve the line of authority comprising *Rigby* v. *Hewitt* (1850) 5 Exch. 240, 243 and *Greenland* v. *Chaplin* (1850) 5 Exch. 243, 248, and disapprove the line of authority comprising *Smith* v. *L.S.W. Ry.* (1871) L.R. 6 C.P. 14; *H.M.S. London* [1914] P. 72 and *Re Polemis* [1921] 3 K.B. 560.

but only succeeds in confusing, the questions of culpability and compensation.

The statement that the defender's liability " is in respect of that damage and no other " ignores the fact that in a remoteness of damage case the court is not concerned with " that damage," with single undivided damage, but with two or more distinguishable items of damage, one consequential on the other, such as, in *Re Polemis*,[67] the damage caused by dropping the plank and the consequential destruction of the ship by fire, or in the *Metagama*,[68] the collision damage and the consequential ultimate sinking, or in many of the personal injury cases, the initial injury and the ultimate death. The whole problem is to determine on what basis and at what point to draw the line and limit the liability.

The further difficulty about this principle of liability for " the damage in suit " is that, if the ultimate harm is deemed by the court unforeseeable, there is no liability, not even for any initial injury however much it may have been foreseeable. It is an " all-or-nothing " doctrine. Thus if ship A navigates carelessly and, foreseeably, collides with and damages ship B, and ship B, unforeseeably, becomes a total loss, ship A is under this principle not liable *at all.* Surely ship A should at least be liable for the initial collision damage. The principle seems quite inappropriate to the case where fault has started a chain-reaction of harmful consequences; why should the defender not be liable for some, even though not for all? Alternatively, the principle may be that the court must distinguish each identifiable head of loss, such as collision damage, total loss of ship, bankruptcy of owner, or personal injury, complications, death, and ask in respect of *each head*: is the defender liable, on the principle of reasonable foresight, for *this* particular head, an approach which ignores the causal connection between the different losses and the fact that the ultimate harm would not have happened without the initial harm?

The Board concluded by admitting that they had been concerned primarily to displace the proposition that unforeseeability is irrelevant if damage were " direct," and had insisted that the essential factor in determining liability was whether the damage was of such a kind as the reasonable man should have foreseen, and went on to point out that it would be wrong if a man should escape liability however " indirect " the damage, if he foresaw or could reasonably foresee the intervening events which led to its being done.[69]

Assessment of The Wagon Mound decision

As a decision of the Privy Council the decision is no doubt entitled to respect, but it is not binding in any Scottish court. Scottish authorities

67 [1921] 3 K.B. 560.

68 1928 S.C.(H.L.) 21.

69 In *Overseas Tankship (U.K.) Ltd.* v. *Miller Steamship Co. Pty.* (*The Wagon Mound No.* 2) [1967] 1 A.C. 617, the Privy Council held, on different evidence, that negligence was established, the damages were not too remote, and the respondents were entitled to damages for the damage to their vessels caused by the oil burning on the water.

were not fully or properly examined, and the most important ones were not mentioned. None of the counsel concerned, and of the Board only one, was competent to discuss Scots law on the matter, and everything said about Scots law was *obiter* and wholly unwarranted.

But the major criticism of the decision must be that the case did not raise a question of remoteness of damage at all, but only a question of remoteness of injury, of the foreseeability or not of the happening of an instance of the general kind of harm which in fact happened. The case was decided under a misapprehension as to what it was about. Had the claim been for the fouling of the slipway by oil the claim would have been unanswerable, because it must have been foreseeable that spillage of oil in a harbour was liable to foul a slipway. As a decision on the facts it is perfectly sound but it raised no question of remoteness of damage at all, and could have been decided in the same way without *Polemis* ever being mentioned.

In *Oman* v. *McIntyre* [70] it was held that *The Wagon Mound* was a decision on liability, not on remoteness of damage at all. This is clearly right.

English cases subsequent to The Wagon Mound

In *Smith* v. *Leech Brain & Co. Ltd.*[71] S sustained a burn on the lip, later contracted cancer, and died. It was found that the burn had promoted cancer in tissues which already had a pre-malignant condition. It was held that since the type of injury was reasonably foreseeable the defendants were liable for the death, although they could not reasonably have foreseen the ultimate consequences, *viz.* that the burn would cause cancer and death, and that *The Wagon Mound* had not altered the rule that a wrongdoer took his victim as he found him. " The Judicial Committee [in *The Wagon Mound*] were, I think, disagreeing with the decision in *Re Polemis* that a man is no longer liable for the type of damage which he could not reasonably anticipate.[72] The Judicial Committee were not, I think, saying that a man is only liable for the extent of damage which he could anticipate, always assuming the type of injury could have been anticipated. That view is really supported by the way in which cases of this sort have been dealt with in Scotland. Scotland has never,[73] as far as I know, adopted the principle laid down in *Re Polemis*, and yet I am quite satisfied that they have throughout proceeded on the basis that the tortfeasor takes the victim as he finds him."

The " unusually susceptible victim " cases really depend on a different principle from *Re Polemis* altogether, but one consistent therewith, the principle that if harm of the general kind which happened was reasonably

70 1962 S.L.T. 168.
71 [1962] 2 Q.B. 405.
72 The latter part of the sentence, from " that a man . . .", seems to be an explanation of *The Wagon Mound*, not of *Re Polemis*.
73 This is a wholly incorrect statement of Scots law.

foreseeable to an ordinary person, the fact that unusually or unforeseeably serious consequences actually resulted to the victim because of his unusual susceptibility does not in any way relieve the wrongdoer; he is liable for what happens, foreseeable or not. This principle is independent of the principle which applies where by one person's fault harm of a reasonably foreseeable kind befalls another person, and there follow consequences making the loss unusually severe.

In *Doughty* v. *Turner Mfg. Co.*[74] a man was injured by an explosion of a kind entirely unforeseeable; the defendants were held not liable. All the judges [75] thought *The Wagon Mound* should be treated as English law, whether that decision was technically binding or not. " In *The Wagon Mound* [76] case the Board held that *Re Polemis and Furness Withy & Co.*[77] should no longer be regarded as good law and that the essential factor in determining *liability* for the consequence of a tortious act of negligence is whether the damage is of such a kind as the reasonable man should have foreseen." [78] This is unexceptionable, but no question of remoteness of damage was in issue, only a question of remoteness of injury, of liability or no liability for the single harm which had happened.

In *Wieland* v. *Cyril Lord Carpets Ltd.*[79] the plaintiff suffered injury by reason of the defendants' admitted negligence. In consequence of her injuries she fell and sustained further injuries; the defendants were held liable for these also. In determining liability for consequences " it is not necessary to show that each was within the foreseeable extent or foreseeable scope of the original injury in the same way that the possibility of injury must be foreseen when determining whether or not the defendants' conduct gives a claim in negligence." [80]

In *Vacwell Engineering Co.* v. *B.D.H. Chemicals Ltd.*[81] chemicals were supplied in glass ampoules without warning that there might be a violent reaction if the chemicals came in contact with water. When a chemist was washing ampoules a violent explosion occurred, seriously damaging the plaintiffs' premises. The plaintiffs recovered damages on the basis both of breach of contract and of negligence. " Here it was a foreseeable consequence of the supply of [the chemical] without a warning . . . that in the ordinary course of industrial user, it could come into contact with water and cause a violent reaction and possibly an explosion. It would also be foreseeable that some damage to property would, or might, result. In my judgment, the explosion and the type of damage being foreseeable, it matters not in the law that the magnitude of the former and the extent of the latter were not." [82] This would appear to be consistent with *Re Polemis* rather than with *The Wagon Mound.*

[74] [1964] 1 Q.B. 518.
[75] Lord Pearce, Harman and Diplock L.JJ.
[76] [1961] A.C. 388.
[77] [1921] 3 K.B. 560.
[78] [1964] 1 Q.B. 518, 525, *per* Lord Pearce.
[79] [1969] 3 All E.R. 1006.
[80] *Ibid.* 1009–1010, *per* Eveleigh J.
[81] [1969] 3 All E.R. 1681.
[82] *Ibid.* 1698–1699, *per* Rees J.

Scottish cases subsequent to The Wagon Mound

In *Oman* v. *McIntyre* [83] it was stated *obiter* but rightly that *The Wagon Mound* was a decision on liability, not on remoteness of damage at all.

In *Hughes* v. *Lord Advocate*,[84] post office workmen opened a manhole in a street, erected a canvas shelter, and left the site unattended. Two small boys, looking down the manhole, tumbled a paraffin lamp into it, whereupon an explosion took place injuring the boys. The House of Lords held that negligence was established in that there was a foreseeable danger of fire from the lamp and that explosion was not essentially different from fire. The accident was but a variant of the foreseeable. No question was raised of the foreseeability of the particular injuries. " No doubt it was not to be expected that the injuries would be as serious as those which the appellant sustained. But a defender is liable, although the damage *may be a good deal greater in extent than was foreseeable*. He can only escape liability if the damage can be regarded as differing in kind from what was foreseeable." [85]

In *McKillen* v. *Barclay Curle & Co.*,[86] M sustained a fractured rib at work in 1961; he had previously suffered from tuberculosis; later in 1961 he was found again to be suffering from tuberculosis and claimed damages for that also, as having been reactivated by the injury at work. The First Division held that he had failed to prove that the renewed attack of tuberculosis had been caused by the fracture of the rib, but that, if it had, the defenders would have been liable. Lord President Clyde said [87]:

> " In my opinion it has never been the law of Scotland that a man guilty of negligence towards another is only liable for the damage in respect of physical injuries which a reasonable man would foresee as likely to follow from it. On the contrary it has always been the law of Scotland as I understand it that once a man is negligent and injures another by his negligence he is liable for all the damage to the injured man which naturally and directly arises out of the negligence. He must take his victim as he finds him, and if his victim has a weak heart and dies as a result of the injury the negligent man is liable in damages for his death, even though a normal man might only in the same circumstances have sustained a relatively trivial injury. The principle of Scots law was laid down as long ago as 1864 by Lord Kinloch in *Allan* v. *Barclay* (1864) 2 M. 873, at p. 874,[88] and his statement of the law has never since been controverted. The doctrine of reasonable foreseeability with all its subtle ramifications may be applied in determining questions of liability (see *Bourhill* v. *Young*, 1942 S.C. (H.L.) 78; *Muir* v. *Glasgow Corporation*, 1943 S.C.(H.L.) 3). It has

[83] 1962 S.L.T. 168.
[84] 1963 S.C.(H.L.) 31.
[85] *Ibid.* 38, *per* Lord Reid. *Cf. Tremain* v. *Pike* [1969] 3 All E.R. 1303.
[86] 1967 S.L.T. 41.
[87] p. 42.
[88] But, as previously pointed out, this was laid down in a question of liability or no liability, not in a context of remoteness of damage at all.

no relevance once liability is established and the measure of damage is being determined. Indeed any other conclusion than this would have startling results. The measure of damages would depend not upon the actual injuries naturally and directly following from the negligence, but upon the injuries reasonably to be anticipated to follow. These might be very much less or might even be larger than the unfortunate victim in fact sustained. That was never our law.

"We were referred to several English decisions which seem to disclose inconsistencies *inter se* (*In re Polemis and Furness, Withy & Co.* [1921] 3 K.B. 560 and *The Wagon Mound* case in [1961] A.C. 388). I do not find it necessary to examine these in any detail. I am content to accept the position in England now as set out by Lord Parker C.J., in *Smith* v. *Leech Brain & Co. Ltd.* [1962] 2 Q.B. 405 at p. 415, where he recognises that whatever may have been the position at one time the law in England in this matter is now precisely in conformity with the law of Scotland—namely that a tortfeasor takes the victim as he finds him. Had I considered therefore that the pursuer had established a causal connection between the injury to his ribs and the reactivation of the tuberculosis I should have held that the defenders were liable in damages in respect of both the rib injury and the reactivation."

Lord Guthrie said [89]: "The Lord Ordinary's opinion and the debate before us were largely taken up with the discussion of the Privy Council in *The Wagon Mound* [1961] A.C. 388. I do not think it is necessary to consider these cases, since the rule of Scots law is well settled. It was stated by Lord Kinloch [90] in *Allan* v. *Barclay* (1863) 2 M. 873 in terms which have since been frequently quoted with approval: 'The grand rule on the subject of damages is, that none can be claimed except such as naturally and directly arise out of the wrong done, and such, therefore, as may reasonably be supposed to have been in the view of the wrongdoer.' . . . If the accident reactivated the tuberculosis, then the reactivation arose naturally, in the ordinary course of nature, out of the defenders' negligence and was the direct cause of it. No other cause intervened. The conditions as stated by Lord Kinloch are therefore satisfied, and the pursuer is entitled to claim for this item of damage."

Lord Migdale said [91]: "It is conceded that the doctrine of reasonable foreseeability can be invoked where a pursuer is seeking to establish liability against an alleged wrongdoer (see *Bourhill* v. *Young*, 1942 S.C.(H.L.) 78 and *Muir* v. *Glasgow Corporation*, 1943 S.C.(H.L.) 3). The contention here is whether that doctrine can be invoked after liability has been established, to restrict the amount of damages.

89 p. 43.

90 Here again Lord Kinloch's dictum is transferred to a context and issue (remoteness of damage) other than the context in which he used the words.

91 p. 44.

This contention was put forward on the assumption that the tubercular infection was the direct and natural consequence of the injury. The defenders maintained that even on that basis they were not liable to pay compensation in respect of that part of the pursuer's disability because they did not know of his earlier condition and could not reasonably foresee that a fall on the step would give rise to tuberculosis. It was argued to us that the effect of the Privy Council decision in *The Wagon Mound* [1961] A.C. 388 was that a defender was not liable for damage which he could not have reasonably foreseen. I do not propose to embark on the contentious sea which has beaten upon the earlier decision of *In re Polemis* [1921] 3 K.B. 560. It concerns English law. I will content myself with saying that there is a formidable body of opinion to support the view that the rule laid down in *In re Polemis* (*supra*) was not and is not the law of Scotland.[92] I would refer to what was said by Lord Russell of Killowen and by Lord Macmillan in *Bourhill* v. *Young* (*supra*) at pp. 85 and 89 [93] and by Lord Justice-Clerk Cooper in *Steel* v. *Glasgow Iron and Steel Company*, 1944 S.C. 237 at p. 248, where he says that 'the rule of the reasonable and probable consequence is a key which opens several locks . . . may be whether the damages claimed are too remote.' [94]

"On the other hand I know of no case of personal injury where damages have been refused where they flowed directly from the injury but could not be reasonably foreseen.[95] It may be that the doctrine of reasonable foreseeability gives way in the class of personal injuries to the other rule that a wrongdoer must take his victim as he finds him.[96]

"But I prefer the view that the doctrine of reasonable foreseeability does extend to the measure of damage and can be invoked by a defender if the damages are too remote but not in a case of personal injuries.[97] In such a case the wrongdoer is liable in reparation for the loss, injury and damage which flow naturally and directly from his wrongful act, because he ought to have had in contemplation that his victim might be a sickly person whose health was such that a fall would start off complications which would not be likely to afflict a person in normal health.

"That is what Lord Kinloch said in the case of *Allan* v. *Barclay* (*supra*) at p. 874.[98] 'The grand rule. . . .' This statement of the law has stood unchallenged for over a hundred years and is still sound.

[92] Where is this body of opinion? The citations which follow do not support this sentence.
[93] Both tentative *obiter dicta* in a case concerned solely with liability or no liability.
[94] This again is a very tentative statement, in a case concerned with causation, not remoteness of damage.
[95] This sentence seems to support the *Polemis* principle and to contradict the previous two sentences.
[96] This sentence evidences confusion. There is no ground for saying that there is a special rule in personal injuries cases.
[97] There is absolutely no warrant in principle or precedent for this sentence.
[98] Here again Lord Kinloch's dictum is taken out of context and applied to a matter (remoteness of damage) in relation to which it was *not* used.

> The wrongdoer must pay for the injuries suffered by his victim provided they arise naturally and directly from the wrongful act, because he ought to have contemplated that he might be an unusually frail person or one afflicted with a latent trouble liable to be reactivated." [99]
>
> Lord Cameron said [1]: " The issue here is as to the measure of damages, not as to the ascertainment of liability, and the measure of damages in this case is relative to the physical consequences of the injury done to the pursuer's person. In such a case as this I am of opinion that the words of Lord Kinloch in *Allan* v. *Barclay* (1863) 2 M. 873, provide the proper test of the extent of a wrongdoer's liability in damages. This case has stood as an authority on the law of Scotland for over 100 years and while the dictum of Lord Kinloch was pronounced in a case which was concerned with the ascertainment of liability,[2] his *dictum* is in the broadest terms and has been applied in the ascertainment of damages in such cases as the present without challenge on countless occasions.[3] Nothing which has happened in the past century appears to me to have cast doubt on its soundness or applicability or to provide reason to qualify its terms. . . . I cannot see at what point you can draw the line and say for damage beyond this point there shall be no reparation. In my opinion once the integrity of the human frame has been invaded by the act of a wrongdoer all that physical damage which thereafter ensues in the course of nature—as that may be established in evidence—and without the intervention of a subsequent extraneous agency unassociated with the actions of a wrongdoer may properly be taken into account in assessment of reparation for the wrong which has been done."

McKillen is an important decision and lends no support to the adoption of the principle of *The Wagon Mound* in Scotland. On the contrary it reaffirms the distinction between culpability or liability and compensation or remoteness of damage and affirms that while foresight is the test of the former, natural and direct connection is the test of the latter.

Conclusions on remoteness of damage

From the foregoing examination of the case-law it seems possible to state the following conclusions as representing the law of Scotland:

(1) Whether a defender is, or is not, liable at all in damages for harmful consequences caused by his conduct depends on whether some harm, of the general kind of harm which in fact happened, occurring to such a person as the pursuer, should have been foreseen by the defender as a distinct possibility, on the basis that he is a person of ordinary reasonable

[99] This sentence seems unjustified, and extends foresight far beyond that of the reasonable man. It is the foresight of the reasonable man that the law has hitherto taken as its standard, not that of the Brahan seer.

[1] p. 46.

[2] This acknowledgment is welcome.

[3] But was it ever intended to be so quoted and applied? This is an acknowledgment of a century of judicial misuse of the dictum.

prevision.[4] It is not enough if harm of the general kind which happened was not reasonably foreseeable, or was only a remote possibility.[5] The harmful consequences must be proved to have been caused by the defender's failure to take precautions, which were reasonable and practicable in the circumstances, to prevent harm of that kind.[6]

(2) If the defender is liable under the foregoing rule he is liable for further consequences of the initial harm which were intended,[7] or were or should have been foreseen as certain or likely,[8] if he had been a man of reasonable knowledge, experience and prevision,[9] or, even if not so foreseeable, in fact followed as direct consequences of the initial and immediate harm caused by the defender's failure to take precautions,[10] but not if they in fact followed as indirect consequences, attributable mainly to other independent or intervening causal factors.[11]

It is *not* the law of Scotland that liability for consequential harm is limited to the reasonably foreseeable consequences of the fault or of the harm it has caused initially.

There is no Scottish case in which, liability for some initial loss having been admitted or proved, the extent of the defender's liability has been limited on the ground that some or all of the items of consequential loss suffered had been unforeseeable and were therefore too remote. Nor is there any warrant in any statement of principle for such a limitation.

Notwithstanding all the assertions to the contrary, the rule of *Polemis* [12] *is* the law of Scotland. *Polemis* [12] has been cited repeatedly in Scottish courts [13] and expressly followed [14] and said, at least *obiter*,[15] in the House of Lords to be the law of Scotland.

The contrary dicta all proceed on the fundamental misapprehension, the confusion between existence of liability, or culpability, or remoteness of injury, and extent of liability, or compensation, or remoteness of damage. *Polemis* [12] is not concerned with the first issue, but only with the second. *The Wagon Mound* [16] case, despite all that is said therein, is con-

[4] Section (2), *supra*; *Bourhill* v. *Young*, 1942 S.C.(H.L.) 78; *Muir* v. *Glasgow Corpn.*, 1943 S.C.(H.L.) 3; *Malcolm* v. *Dickson*, 1951 S.C. 542; *Blaikie* v. *B.T.C.*, 1961 S.C. 44; *Carmarthenshire C.C.* v. *Lewis* [1955] A.C. 549; *Miller* v. *S.S.E.B.*, 1958 S.C.(H.L.) 20; *Harvey* v. *Singer Mfg. Co.*, 1960 S.C. 155; *Hughes* v. *Lord Advocate*, 1963 S.C.(H.L.) 31.

[5] *Fardon* v. *Harcourt-Rivington* (1932) 146 L.T. 391, 392; *Bolton* v. *Stone* [1951] A.C. 850, 858.

[6] Section (1), *supra*.

[7] *Quinn* v. *Leathem* [1901] A.C. 495, 537, *per* Lord Lindley. Consequences intended include those which are the necessary and natural consequences of intentional conduct: *Scott* v. *Shepherd* (1773) 2 Wm.Bl. 892; *Emblem* v. *Myers* (1860) 6 H. & N. 54; *Scott's Trs.* v. *Moss* (1889) 17 R. 32.

[8] This seems implied in all the relevant decisions.

[9] *Wilkinson* v. *Downton* [1897] 2 Q.B. 57; *Janvier* v. *Sweeney* [1919] 2 K.B. 316.

[10] *S.S. Baron Vernon* v. *S.S. Metagama*, 1928 S.C.(H.L.) 21; *McKillen* v. *Barclay Curle & Co.*, 1967 S.L.T. 41.

[11] *McKew* v. *Holland and Hannen and Cubitts (Sc.) Ltd.*, 1970 S.L.T. 68 (H.L.); *cf. Wieland* v. *Cyril Lord Carpets Ltd.* [1969] 3 All E.R. 1006.

[12] [1921] 3 K.B. 560.

[13] *Reavis* v. *Clan Line Steamers*, 1925 S.C. 725, 738; *S.S. Baron Vernon* v. *S.S. Metagama*, 1927 S.C. 498, 516.

[14] *Bourhill* v. *Young's Exor.*, 1941 S.C. 395, 437, *per* L.J.C. Aitchison (dissenting on the facts).

[15] *Bourhill* v. *Young's Exor.*, 1942 S.C.(H.L.) 78, 90, *per* Lord Wright; *cf.* 95, *per* Lord Porter.

[16] [1961] A.C. 388.

cerned only with the first issue, and not with the second at all [17] and is not an authority on Scots law.

Approach of the courts in practice

Whatever the arguments and whatever may be said to be the attitude of the Scottish courts it is quite clear that, where there has been held to be liability for some loss attributable to the defender's fault, the uniform practice of the Scottish courts has been to award damages for all the direct consequences of the immediate harm, whether or not those consequences were, or could reasonably have been, foreseen by the defender. In *Main* v. *Leask* [18] a steam drifter was lost by collision. Liability was admitted for the full value of the boat and a proof was allowed as to profit lost for the rest of the fishing season, as being "direct and immediate loss . . . directly caused." In *Nautilus S.S. Co.* v. *D. & W. Henderson*,[19] ship-repairers caused damage to a ship by fire; the court found that the defenders were liable "for any damage caused by said fire which may be proved to have been suffered by the pursuers." There seems to be no case, whether of personal injury, property damage, or economic loss, where damages have been restricted because only lesser loss or injury was all that was reasonably foreseeable by the defender. The plea has never been sustained, if indeed ever advanced, that the extent of personal injuries actually sustained were unforeseeable and that damages should be given for only the foreseeable extent of injuries.

In cases of claims by the dependants of persons killed the same principle applies. It may be held to have been reasonably foreseeable that a person, if killed by the defender's breach of duty, would leave certain dependants, but damages have always been given however many the dependants, and heavier damages than normal in the case where a dependant would never be able to earn his or her living,[20] though that could hardly have been foreseen.

The "direct loss" principle is also illustrated by the cases of victims of unusual susceptibility to harm.

The "unusually susceptible victim" cases

Some difficulty and confusion in relation to remoteness of injury and remoteness of damage has arisen in cases where the victim has been unusually susceptible to harm, so that if injured he is more severely hurt than a normal person.

The principles applicable to such cases are that the unusual susceptibility of a person to injury by reason of bad heart, pregnancy, haemophilia, or other exceptional condition, is not relevant to liability, and that no

[17] See what the Privy Council itself says in *The Wagon Mound* (*No.* 2) [1967] 1 A.C. 617 that it decided.
[18] 1910 S.C. 722.
[19] 1919 S.C. 605, especially findings at p. 611.
[20] *Paterson* v. *L.M.S. Ry.*, 1942 S.C. 156 (mentally defective daughter).

other or greater duty is owed to such a person than that of taking reasonable precautions against harm of foreseeable kinds,[21] *except* (1) in the case where it is *actually known* by the defender that the person to whom the duty of care was owed was in some way exceptional,[22] and (2) in the case where the presence of persons of unusual susceptibility, such as blind persons, in the area of risk, should have been foreseen,[23] in both of which cases a higher duty of care is owed, the duty to take precautions reasonably sufficient to avoid dangers to persons so handicapped or prone to injury.

> " What is now being considered is the question of liability and this . . . must generally depend on a normal standard of susceptibility. . . . It is here, as elsewhere, a question of what the hypothetical reasonable man, viewing the position, I suppose, *ex post facto*, would say it was proper to foresee. What danger of particular infirmity that would include must depend on all the circumstances but generally, I think, a reasonably normal condition, if medical evidence is capable of defining it, would be the standard. The test of the plaintiff's extraordinary susceptibility, if unknown to the defendant, would in effect make him an insurer." [24]

If, however, liability is held by admission or proof to exist, the rule applies that the wrongdoer must take his victim as he finds him, and if the victim, by reason of his unusual state or susceptibility, suffers unusually serious loss or injury, the wrongdoer is liable for the loss actually suffered, and cannot limit his liability on the basis that a normal person would not have suffered such serious harm, nor on the basis that only lesser harm was reasonably foreseeable. " No doubt, it has long ago been stated and often restated that, if the wrong is established the wrongdoer must take the victim as he finds him. That, however, is only true, as the *Polemis* case shows, on the condition that the wrong has been established or admitted. The question of liability is anterior to the question of the measure of the consequences which go with the liability." [25]

(4) Minimisation of Damage

In the context of claims arising *ex delicto*, where personal injuries, physical harm, or economic loss frequently happen unexpectedly and without warning, it is sometimes an unsuitable formulation of principle to say that a pursuer must take reasonable steps to minimise the damage done him. This formulation may be appropriate to cases of property damage, such as ship or vehicle collision.[26] It is commonly more accurate to say

[21] *Bourhill* v. *Young*, 1942 S.C.(H.L.) 78, 92, *per* Lord Wright.
[22] *Paris* v. *Stepney Borough Council* [1951] A.C. 367 (one-eyed man).
[23] *Haley* v. *London Electricity Board* [1964] 3 All E.R. 185 (blind man) explaining *McKibbin* v. *Glasgow Corpn.*, 1920 S.C. 590.
[24] *Bourhill* v. *Young*, 1942 S.C.(H.L.) 78, 92–93, *per* Lord Wright.
[25] *Ibid.* 92, *per* Lord Wright.
[26] *Cf. Pomphrey* v. *Cuthbertson*, 1951 S.C. 147.

that a pursuer must not deliberately or negligently do anything which will prolong or aggravate the harm done, and an award of damages may be modified if he seriously neglects any reasonable steps which would minimise the harm, or acts unreasonably.

The course of action adopted by the pursuer will not be too harshly judged by the court. " The wrongdoer is not entitled to criticise the course honestly taken by the injured person on the advice of his experts, even though it should appear by the light of after events that another course might have saved loss. The loss he has to pay for is that which has actually followed under such circumstances upon his wrong." [27] In *Rubens* v. *Walker* [28] it was held that an injured pursuer was entitled to act on the advice of his medical advisers and recover the cost of treatment from the defender in damages, though it was held that the injury was not proved and accordingly that the treatment had been unnecessary. " In my opinion it is a reasonable and probable consequence of a wrongdoer's breach of duty that a person hurt thereby will incur expense in following the treatment prescribed by reputable experts employed by him to cure him. . . . The results might be very different if the injured person acted on the advice of a quack, or if, considering all the advice he had received, no reasonable person would have taken the course he did." [29]

In the context of personal injuries, this duty requires a pursuer to take reasonable steps to have his injuries treated.

If the person injured acts reasonably to minimise the consequences of the harm done him, but the course adopted turns out, by reason of mischance, to lead to greater loss, or if his injuries are aggravated by some supervening illness or injury, he is not to be penalised on that account, and his further loss will be recoverable as a direct consequence of the initial harm.[30] But if on the other hand the course adopted leads to greater loss by reason of the grave lack of skill or attention, or actionable negligence of those concerned therewith, that negligence may be held to be *novus actus interveniens* releasing the original wrongdoer from liability for the consequential harm, leaving liability only for the initial harm.[31]

It has several times been held that unwillingness to undergo an operation or other curative treatment was, in particular circumstances, unreasonable and accordingly that the claimant's state was not the result of the defender's breach of duty.[32] If, however, the refusal were reasonable as where the treatment proposed would be particularly unpleasant or very

[27] *Clippens Oil Co.* v. *Edinburgh Water Trs.*, 1907 S.C.(H.L.) 9, 14, *per* Lord Collins. *Cf. S.S. Baron Vernon* v. *S.S. Metagama*, 1928 S.C.(H.L.) 21, 28, *per* Lord Dunedin.

[28] 1946 S.C. 215.

[29] *Ibid.* 216, *per* Lord Patrick. *Cf. Humber Towing Co.* v. *Barclay* (1911) 5 B.W.C.C. 142, where injured person resorted to local bonesetter rather than qualified doctor and the question was said to be: " Is or is not the condition of this man due substantially to the original accident or to the mismanagement of the medical man? "

[30] *Dunham* v. *Clare* [1902] 2 K.B. 292.

[31] *Rocca* v. *Stanley Jones & Co.* (1914) 7 B.W.C.C. 101; *Lakey* v. *Blair* (1916) 10 B.W.C.C. 58; *Rothwell* v. *Caverswall Stone Co. Ltd.* [1944] 2 All E.R. 350; *Hogan* v. *Bentinck West Hartley Collieries Ltd.* [1949] 1 All E.R. 588.

[32] *e.g. Steele* v. *Robert George & Co.* [1942] A.C. 497.

questionably likely to be beneficial, the claimant is not to be penalised if he refused to undergo it. " If the injured man acts unreasonably he cannot hold the defender liable for injury caused by his own unreasonable conduct. His unreasonable conduct is *novus actus interveniens.* The chain of causation has been broken and what follows must be regarded as caused by his own conduct and not by the defender's fault or the disability caused by it. Or one may say that unreasonable conduct of the pursuer and what follows from it is not the natural and probable result of the original fault of the defender or of the ensuing disability." [33]

In the context of damage to property, on the other hand, to formulate the principle as a duty on the pursuer to act so as to minimise his loss and consequently his claim against the defender remains proper. " It is a pursuer's duty to take reasonable steps to minimise a defender's loss. When a thing is so severely damaged that to repair it and hire a substitute during the period of repair is more costly than to treat it as a total loss, a pursuer must prefer that course which is less costly to the defender." [34] " The party aggrieved must take all reasonable steps to mitigate the resulting loss. He is not entitled to adopt a method of restoring himself to a position equivalent to that which he occupied before the casualty if there is another and cheaper method of effecting such restoration." [35] Hence in ship and vehicle collision cases the owner of the damaged vessel or vehicle must weigh the alternative costs of repairing the damage, hiring a substitute during the period of repairs, of treating the thing as a constructive total loss, obtaining a replacement and claiming the pre-accident value of the thing under deduction of its scrap value, and of treating the thing as an actual total loss, and must adopt the cheapest course. If he does not do so he cannot recover any more from the defender. Where pursuers did not use the best method of extinguishing a fire caused by the defenders' negligence they were held entitled to recover the cost of the best method only.[36]

(5) Contributory Negligence

Contributory negligence is carelessness or disregard of his own interests by an injured person which has combined with conduct by a defender in breach of duty to the injured person and contributed to the injured person's ultimate loss. It does not depend on there being any legal duty of care for his own safety owed to himself, or to the negligent party, by the injured person, but only on whether the injured person's conduct was lacking in reasonable regard for his own interests.[37] " The real question is not

[33] *McKew* v. *Holland and Hannen and Cubitts (Sc.) Ltd.*, 1970 S.L.T. 68, *per* Lord Reid.
[34] *Pomphrey* v. *Cuthbertson*, 1951 S.C. 147, 152, *per* L.J.C. Thomson.
[35] *Ibid.* 162, *per* Lord Patrick.
[36] *B.R.* v. *South of Scotland Electricity Board*, 1973 S.L.T.(Notes) 9.
[37] *Davey* v. *L.S.W. Ry.* (1883) 12 Q.B.D. 70; *Ellerman Lines Ltd.* v. *Grayson* [1919] 2 K.B. 514, 535; [1920] A.C. 475–477; *Lewis* v. *Denye* [1939] 1 K.B. 540, 554; *Nance* v. *British Columbia Electric Ry.* [1951] A.C. 601, 611. *Cf. Jones* v. *Livox Quarries Ltd.* [1952] 2 Q.B. 608, 615.

whether the plaintiff was neglecting some legal duty, but whether he was acting as a responsible man and with reasonable care." [38] It is "negligence materially contributing to the injury." [39] "The test is whether the pursuer in the ordinary plain commonsense of this business . . . contributed to the accident." [40]

At common law the pursuer's contributory negligence to even the smallest degree was a complete defence and defeated his claim entirely. The question was: Whose act caused the harm?,[41] and the court had to find that the defender's act, or the pursuer's own act, caused the harm. In the latter case the pursuer's claim failed completely. Contributory negligence was a complete defence and total exclusion of liability.[42]

By the Law Reform (Contributory Negligence) Act 1945 it is provided:

> "1 (1) Where any person suffers damage [43] as the result partly of his own fault [44] and partly of the fault [44] of any other person or persons, a claim in respect of that damage [43] shall not be defeated by reason of the fault of the person suffering the damage, but the damages recoverable in respect thereof shall be reduced to such extent as the court thinks just and equitable having regard to the claimant's share in the responsibility for the damage:
>
> Provided that—
>
> (*a*) this subsection shall not operate to defeat any defence arising under a contract;
>
> (*b*) where any contract or enactment providing for the limitation of liability is applicable to the claim, the amount of damages recoverable by the claimant by virtue of this subsection shall not exceed the maximum limit so applicable.
>
> (2) Where damages are recoverable by any person by virtue of the foregoing subsection subject to such reduction as is therein mentioned, the court shall find and record the total damages which would have been recoverable if the claimant had not been at fault.
>
> (3) [45] Section three of the Law Reform (Miscellaneous Provisions) (Scotland) Act 1940 (which relates to contribution among joint wrongdoers) shall apply in any case where two or more persons are liable or would, if they had all been sued, be liable by virtue of subsection (1) of this section in respect of the damage suffered by any person.
>
> (4) [46] Where any person dies as the result partly of his own fault

[38] *Davies* v. *Swan Motor Co.* [1949] 2 K.B. 291, 324, *per* Denning L.J.
[39] *Caswell* v. *Powell Duffryn Ltd.* [1940] A.C. 152, 186, *per* Lord Porter.
[40] *Admiralty Commrs.* v. *S.S. Volute* [1922] 1 A.C. 129, 144, *per* L.C. Birkenhead.
[41] *Admiralty Commrs.* v. *S.S. Volute* [1922] 1 A.C. 129; *Swadling* v. *Cooper* [1931] A.C. 1; *Caswell* v. *Powell Duffryn Assoc. Collieries* [1940] A.C. 152; *Boy Andrew* v. *St. Rognvald,* 1947 S.C.(H.L.) 70, 76, *per* Viscount Simon, quoting Law Revision Committee report.
[42] *e.g. McNaughton* v. *Caledonian Ry.* (1858) 21 D. 160.
[43] Defined by s. 4 as including loss of life and personal injury.
[44] Defined by s. 5 (*a*) as wrongful act, breach of statutory duty or negligent act or omission which gives rise to liability in damages or would, apart from the Act, give rise to the defence of contributory negligence.
[45] As applied to Scotland by s. 5 (*b*).
[46] As substituted for Scotland by s. 5 (*c*).

and partly of the fault of any other person or persons, a claim by any dependant [47] of the first mentioned person for damages or solatium in respect of that person's death shall not be defeated by reason of his fault, but the damages or solatium recoverable shall be reduced to such extent as the court thinks just and equitable having regard to the share of the said person in the responsibility for his death.

(5) [Not applicable to Scotland].

(6) Where any case to which subsection (1) of this section applies is tried with a jury, the jury shall determine the total damages which would have been recoverable if the claimant had not been at fault and the extent to which those damages are to be reduced.[48]

(7) Article 21 of the Convention contained in the First Schedule to the Carriage by Air Act 1932 [49] (which empowers a court to exonerate wholly or partly a carrier who proves that the damage was caused by or contributed to by the negligence of the injured person), shall have effect subject to the provisions of this section."

Application of Act

The Act may apply to damage sustained by reason of breach of contract [50] and certainly applies to damage sustained by reason of delict. It applies both to delict constituted by common law fault and by breach of statutory duty [51] and to delict causing personal injuries,[52] death of a relative,[53] and property damage.[54]

Effect and interpretation of the Act

The general effect of the Act is that the pursuer's own fault is no longer a complete defence, but it is only a ground for limiting the damages which he would otherwise have received. The share in responsibility attributable to the injured claimant or a deceased for whose death a claim is being made has to be fixed by stating a fraction or percentage of the loss as being attributable to the claimant, and the gross damages being reduced by that fraction or percentage. The court or jury must determine (1) whether the defender was or was not legally negligent *vis-à-vis* the pursuer and his negligence a cause of the harm; (2) if so, whether the pursuer was contributorily negligent; (3) if so, what fraction or percentage of the total responsibility should be allocated to each?

47 Defined by s. 5 (*a*) as any person who would in the event of a person's death through the fault of a third party be entitled to sue that third party for damages or solatium.

48 The jury, that is, must find the gross damages and the degree or proportion of contributory negligence, but does not find the net damages, or the sum which the pursuer is actually to receive.

49 Now replaced by Carriage by Air Act 1961. Art. 21 of the Convention contained in Sched. I thereof replaces the provision in the 1932 Act with the same effect.

50 *Quinn* v. *Burch Bros.* [1966] 2 Q.B. 370.

51 *Grant* v. *Sun Shipping Co.*, 1948 S.C.(H.L.) 73.

52 *e.g. Smith* v. *L.M.S. Ry.*, 1948 S.C. 125.

53 1945 Act, s. 1 (4).

54 *e.g. Smith, supra.*

It appears from the words of section 1 (1) and (4) that the reduction must be made by reference to the pursuer's and defender's respective shares in *responsibility for causing* the injury or damage. It is not a question of which party mainly *caused* the injury, but of which party was mainly *responsible for causing* the injury or damage. The emphasis is on responsibility, fault or blame, not on causation. The difference may be material. If X by careless driving places Y in a dilemma, and X stops but Y cannot, and collides with X, the resultant injuries to X may be mainly or entirely caused by Y, the moving vehicle, but the responsibility would be mainly or entirely that of X, even though X had stopped.[55] Responsibility for the damage or death involves a moral judgment, the determination of fault, whereas determination of causation of the damage or death involves a judgment of fact. In *Davies* v. *Swan Motor Co.* (*Swansea*) *Ltd.*[56] Denning L.J. said:

> " While causation is the decisive factor in determining whether there should be a reduced amount payable to the plaintiff nevertheless the amount of the reduction does not depend solely on the degree of causation. The amount of the reduction is such an amount as may be found by the court to be 'just and equitable' having regard to the claimant's share in the responsibility for the damage. This involves a consideration not only of the causative potency of a particular factor, but also of its blameworthiness. The fact of standing on the steps of the dustcart is just as potent a factor in causing damage, whether the person standing there be a servant acting negligently in the course of his employment, or a boy in play or a youth doing it for a 'lark' but the degree of blameworthiness may be very different.
>
> " Speaking generally, therefore, the questions in road accidents are simply these: What faults were there which caused the damage? What are the proportions in which the damages should be apportioned having regard to the respective responsibilities of those in fault? "

In *Stapley* v. *Gypsum Mines Ltd.*[57] Lord Reid said:

> " A court must deal broadly with the problem of apportionment, and, in considering what is just and equitable, must have regard to the blameworthiness of each party, but the claimant's share in the responsibility for the damage cannot, I think, be assessed without considering the relative importance of the acts in causing the damage apart from his blameworthiness." " The investigation is concerned with fault which includes blameworthiness as well as causation; and no true apportionment can be reached unless both these factors are

[55] *Cf. Henley* v. *Cameron* [1949] L.J.R. 989, where C left his car unlit and H ran into it; H caused the injuries to himself but C was responsible for the accident.

[56] [1949] 2 K.B. 291.

[57] [1953] A.C. 663, 682.

borne in mind." [58] "Blameworthiness, which is one of the two factors which must be taken into consideration when one is apportioning blame, embraces a number of different factors . . . the age and the experience (or the alleged experience) of the injured workman . . . [It] must also have regard to the extent to which the workman has contrived to place himself in a position which endangers him because of his lack of the very experience which he had wrongly represented he possessed." [59] "There are two elements in an assessment of liability, causation and blameworthiness." [60]

Furthermore, even though an injured person was not at all to blame for the occurrence of the accident he may be held guilty of contributory negligence if an act or omission on his part contributed to the nature or extent of the injuries he sustained in consequence of the accident.[61] He was partly responsible for the *damage*, though not for the accident.

The 1945 Act appears to have altered the law in laying down that apportionment be made by reference to responsibility, as earlier cases contain many references to the causation of the accident.

Post-1945 cases also sometimes contain reference to causation as the basis of apportionment. Thus in *Thurogood* v. *Van den Berghs* [62] Asquith L.J. said that "The chain of causation would in this case have been broken or impaired if the workman's act had gone beyond inadvertence and had amounted to an act of contributory negligence—broken, if occurring before the Law Reform (Contributory Negligence) Act 1945; impaired, to the extent of compelling an apportionment of the damage, if occurring after that enactment came into force."

Onus of averment and proof of contributory negligence

The onus of averment and proof of contributory negligence is on the defender.[63] He must establish that even if he was himself in breach of duty to the pursuer, nevertheless the pursuer by his careless conduct exposed himself to certain risks of harm, that one of these risks eventuated, and that the harm sustained was attributable at least in part to the pursuer's own carelessness. It may be that the defender's breach of duty was merely *causa sine qua non* and that the pursuer's own fault is the sole cause of the harm to him.

Standard of care in contributory negligence

The standard of care demanded of a pursuer for his own safety is the

58 *The Miraflores and The Abadesa* [1967] 1 A.C. 826, *per* Lord Pearce; *Brown* v. *Thompson* [1968] 2 All E.R. 708.
59 *Kerry* v. *Carter* [1969] 3 All E.R. 723, 726, *per* Edmund Davies L.J.
60 *Baker* v. *Willoughby* [1969] 3 All E.R. 1528, 1530, *per* Lord Reid.
61 *O'Connell* v. *Jackson* [1971] 3 All E.R. 129 (moped rider not wearing crash helmet; injuries to head).
62 [1951] 2 K.B. 537.
63 *Wakelin* v. *L.S.W. Ry.* (1886) 12 App.Cas. 41, 47; *Taylor* v. *Glasgow Corpn.*, 1922 S.C. (H.L.) 1, 13; *Stimson* v. *Standard Telephone & Cables Ltd.* [1940] 1 K.B. 342; *Caswell* v. *Powell Duffryn Associated Collieries Ltd.* [1940] A.C. 152, 172.

same as that demanded of the defender for the pursuer's safety, reasonable care in all the circumstances. "Although contributory negligence does not depend on a duty of care, it does depend on foreseeability. Just as actionable negligence requires the foreseeability of harm to others, so contributory negligence requires the foreseeability of harm to oneself. A person is guilty of contributory negligence if he ought reasonably to have foreseen that, if he did not act as a reasonably prudent man, he might hurt himself; and in his reckonings he must take into account the possibility of others being careless." [64]

Conduct amounting to contributory negligence

It is clear from all the cases that a pursuer is not to be held contributorily negligent merely on account of some error of judgment, momentary indiscretion or inadvertence,[65] or failure to do what, in the light of hindsight, would have been the correct or ideal thing.[66] The conduct must have amounted to substantial carelessness, disregard of reasonable precautions or safety, though it need not have amounted to recklessness or deliberate assumption of a risk.

Danger or emergency or dilemma

In circumstances of danger or emergency a person is not to be penalised by a finding of contributory negligence merely because he has taken a risk or not adopted the best course.[67]

Taking a risk

Where a continuing risk has been created by the defender's fault the pursuer is not necessarily contributorily negligent if he takes that risk even in the full knowledge of it.[68] He may be, if assumption of the risk was imprudent and clearly foolish, but not if the risk was one which would reasonably be accepted. A driver is not contributorily negligent because he knows that the roads are busy and another driver may be negligent; that is a normal risk.

Attempt to rescue generally not contributory negligence

Where a defender's fault has placed someone in a position of danger and another person intervenes to try to save him, that intervention is not necessarily contributorily negligent. It may be, but only if it amounts to foolhardiness or wholly unreasonable disregard for the rescuer's own safety.[69]

64 *Jones* v. *Livox Quarries Ltd.* [1952] 2 Q.B. 608, 615, *per* Denning L.J.
65 *Thurogood* v. *Van den Berghs* [1951] 2 K.B. 537; *Kansara* v. *Osram (G.E.C.) Ltd.* [1967] 3 All E.R. 230.
66 *Foulder* v. *C.P.S. Ltd.* [1969] 1 All E.R. 283.
67 *Jones* v. *Boyce* (1816) 1 Starkie 493; *Wallace* v. *Bergius*, 1915 S.C. 205; *Maclenan* v. *Segar* [1917] 2 K.B. 325; *Admiralty Commrs.* v. *S.S. Volute* [1922] 1 A.C. 129; *Brandon* v. *Osborne Garrett & Co.* [1924] 1 K.B. 548; *Swadling* v. *Cooper* [1931] A.C. 1. *Cf. S.S. Baron Vernon* v. *S.S. Metagama*, 1928 S.C.(H.L.) 21.
68 *e.g. Groom* v. *G.W. Ry.* (1892) 8 T.L.R. 253; *Porter* v. *Jones* [1942] 2 All E.R. 570; *Greene* v. *Chelsea B.C.* [1954] 2 Q.B. 127; *Summers* v. *Salford Corpn.* [1943] A.C. 283.
69 *Baker* v. *Hopkins* [1959] 3 All E.R. 225, 244.

Pursuer's fault must have contributed to harm

Carelessness by the pursuer amounts to contributory negligence only if it contributed to the harm sustained in consequence of the defender's breach of duty. If the same harm would have been sustained whether he had been careful or regardless of his own safety his contributory negligence is an immaterial factor. Thus if a workman working high up a building disregards a safety-belt and the building collapses by reason of some fault on the defender's part, the belt would not have saved him, neglect to use it is not a cause of the accident, and his failure to wear it is no defence; it is not negligence contributory to the harm in question. But if he falls and a belt would have saved him it is contributory negligence not to have worn one, or alternatively the non-provision of a safety-belt was not the cause of the accident.[70] Similarly it has been held that, where a moped rider had not been wearing a crash helmet and was injured about the head, his lack of care had contributed to the extent of the injury sustained, even though he was in no way to blame for the occurrence of the accident, and his damages were reduced accordingly.[71]

Contributory negligence of children, infirm persons, etc.

In determining whether a pursuer was contributorily negligent, it is relevant to consider the age and mental and physical capacities of the pursuer. Such persons may certainly be contributorily negligent [72] but courts are more reluctant to find contributory negligence where the injured person had, or may well have had, an inadequate or limited appreciation of the risk he ran and of the precautions he should have taken, and what would be contributory negligence in an adult may not be in a child or person of subnormal mental capacity who did not fully appreciate the risk.[73] A person suffering from physical defect, as one blind or deaf, must have regard to his own disability, and may be contributorily negligent if he does what would be safe in a normal person but is unsafe for him. His disability, unless known to, or foreseeable by, the defender, does not enhance the duty of care incumbent on the defender to him,[74] but the defender is not entitled to assume that everyone will be normally capable of taking care of his own safety, and will do so; if in fact he is less than normally so capable he may be held contributorily negligent only in lesser degree than a normal person would have been, or not contributorily negligent at all. " When you come to the case of a blind or nearly blind person who is in the habit of using the streets, it is impossible, as it seems to me, to suggest a defence of contributory negligence . . . on a

[70] *McWilliams* v. *Arrol*, 1962 S.C.(H.L.) 70.

[71] *O'Connell* v. *Jackson* [1971] 3 All E.R. 129.

[72] *Cass* v. *Edinburgh Tramways*, 1909 S.C. 1068 (boy 4½); *Plantza* v. *Glasgow Corpn.*, 1910 S.C. 786 (5); *Grant* v. *Caledonian Ry.* (1870) 9 M. 258 (6); *Fraser* v. *Edinburgh Tramways* (1882) 10 R. 264 (6).

[73] *Yachuk* v. *Oliver Blais Co. Ltd.* [1949] A.C. 386.

[74] *Taylor* v. *Glasgow Corpn.*, 1922 S.C.(H.L.) 1, 15; *Bourhill* v. *Young*, 1942 S.C.(H.L.) 78, 92; *Paris* v. *Stepney B.C.* [1951] A.C. 367.

question of contributory negligence you are entitled to take into account the defective eyesight or other infirmity of a person who meets with an accident." [75]

If the injured person's disability is self-induced, as by drink, this cannot be taken into account. The reasonable man does not get incapably drunk. A man cannot plead his own drunken state as an excuse for not taking the care for himself which he could and should take when sober; if he cannot look after himself, so much the worse for him.[76]

Contributory negligence of workmen

The rules of contributory negligence apply to workmen as to other pursuers.[77] But it is recognised that familiarity with dangers encountered at work breeds contempt and workmen become careless and take risks: " In considering whether an ordinary prudent workman would have taken more care than the injured man, the tribunal of fact has to take into account all the circumstances of work in a factory and . . . it is not for every risky thing which a workman in a factory may do in his familiarity with the machinery that a plaintiff ought to be held guilty of contributory negligence." [78] " I always directed myself to be exceedingly chary of finding contributory negligence where the contributory negligence alleged was the very thing which the statutory duty of the employer was designed to prevent." [79]

Allocating responsibility

Under the 1945 Act the court or jury determines the total damages which it would have awarded on the basis that the defender was wholly responsible, which sum cannot exceed the sum sued for, and determines the extent to which the pursuer was himself responsible by fixing a fraction or percentage and then the court, or the clerk of court, in the case of a jury trial, deducts the fraction or percentage from the total award, the net award being the sum for which decree issues. This allocation can only proceed on the basis of common sense and impression of the whole circumstances of the case.

Contribution in relation to joint wrongdoers

Where a case involves questions both of contributory negligence and division of liability among joint wrongdoers held jointly and severally

[75] *McKibbin* v. *Glasgow Corpn.*, 1920 S.C. 590, 597, *per* Lord Salvesen, citing *Rennie* v. *G.N.S. Ry.* (1905) 12 S.L.T. 667.

[76] *McCormick* v. *Caledonian Ry.* (1904) 6 F. 362.

[77] *Lewis* v. *Denye* [1940] A.C. 921; *Grant* v. *Sun Shipping Co.*, 1948 S.C.(H.L.) 73; *Stapley* v. *Gypsum Mines Ltd.* [1957] A.C. 663; *N.C.B.* v. *England* [1954] A.C. 403; *Summers* v. *Frost* [1955] A.C. 740.

[78] *Flower* v. *Ebbw Vale Steel Co.* [1934] 2 K.B. 132, 139–140, *per* Lawrence J. (revd. on other grounds [1936] A.C. 206), approved in *Caswell* v. *Powell Duffryn* [1940] A.C. 152; *Lewis* v. *Denye* [1940] A.C. 921; *Summers* v. *Frost* [1955] A.C. 740.

[79] *Hutchinson* v. *L.N.E. Ry.* [1942] 1 K.B. 481, 488, *per* Goddard L.J.

liable, the proper order is to ascertain first the degree or proportion of contributory negligence and make the appropriate deduction from the gross award of damages, and then to allocate liability for the net award among the joint wrongdoers in the proportions which the court or jury thinks proper.[80]

Altering proportions of blame or appeal

An appellate court should not alter the proportions of blame fixed by a trial judge save in exceptional circumstances,[81] but may do so where there was an error in principle or a mistake of fact or the appellate court is of opinion that the apportionment itself was erroneous.[82] Where the judge of first instance found the defendants in breach of statutory duty but the Court of Appeal found them negligent at common law, it has been held that the Court of Appeal could reconsider apportionment on the new basis.[83] But it was not suggested that the different bases involved any different considerations.

EFFECT OF LIMITATIONS

These limiting factors all operate to limit the defender's liability in damages, but in different ways. The requirement of proof of causal connection [84] may exclude liability completely or may limit liability by determining that two or more causal factors operated, for only one of which a particular defender may be responsible. The principle of remoteness of injury,[85] if it operates at all, limits liability to nil, and excludes it completely. The principle of remoteness of damage [86] may limit the extent of loss for which the defender has to pay damages. The rule requiring minimisation of damage [87] may similarly limit the items of loss for which the defender has to pay damages, and the principle of contributory negligence,[88] if it applies, effects a fractional or percentage reduction of the total award of damages.

[80] Under Law Reform (Misc. Prov.) (Scotland) Act 1940, s. 3.

[81] *British Fame (Owners)* v. *Macgregor (Owners)* [1943] A.C. 197; *Boy Andrew* v. *St. Rognvald*, 1947 S.C.(H.L.) 70, 78; *Quintas* v. *National Smelting Co. Ltd.* [1961] 1 All E.R. 630, 636; *Brown* v. *Thompson* [1968] 2 All E.R. 708; *Kerry* v. *Carter* [1969] 3 All E.R. 723; *Baker* v. *Willoughby* [1969] 3 All E.R. 1528. In *Stapley* v. *Gypsum Mines* [1953] A.C. 663 the House of Lords altered apportionment on appeal.

[82] *Kerry, supra*; 80:20 altered to 33:67.

[83] *Quintas* v. *National Smelting Co.* [1961] 1 All E.R. 630.

[84] Section (1), *supra*.

[85] Section (2), *supra*.

[86] Section (3), *supra*.

[87] Section (4), *supra*.

[88] Section (5), *supra*.

CHAPTER 53

DAMAGES FOR PERSONAL INJURIES

GENERALLY

IT is well settled that every living individual has a legally recognised and protected interest in his personal integrity, in freedom from being injured or harmed, whether in body or in mind, by the conduct of another which is held to have been in breach of a legal duty, owed in the circumstances to, *inter alios*, that individual, to refrain from, or not to permit the happening of, conduct foreseeably likely to cause some kind of personal injuries, and by the breach to have caused some personal injuries. Infringement of that interest is remediable by an award of damages.

The principle of *restitutio in integrum* is the governing principle but it " affords little guidance in the assessment of damages for the pain and suffering undergone and for the impairment which results from the injuries; and in fixing such damages, the judge can do no more than endeavour to arrive at a fair estimate taking into account all the relevant considerations." [1]

If some personal injuries, in body or mind or both, have been caused damages are due to the injured person in compensation for the injury and loss sustained by reason of the defender's breach of duty. Quantification of what is a fair, proper and reasonable sum to award (in this field there can be no such thing as an award which is " right ") requires identification of the heads under which it is competent to award damages, discussion of the factors which have been held relevant or irrelevant to fixing or increasing or diminishing the sum contemplated, and finally the fixing of a sum of money which is deemed proper in the circumstances.

Onus of proof

As in other matters generally the onus of proof of loss is on the pursuer, and he must put before the court or jury evidence justifying it in finding that loss under various heads was sustained, and enabling it to make an informed assessment of the extent and degree of loss and of what is fair compensation therefor. " In the first place, it is for the pursuer [2] to prove her husband's loss, injury and damage. The burden of proof is upon her." [3] " A pursuer must always prove his damage, and if he wants to recover a large sum in respect of pain and inconvenience, he ought to tell the court about these elements." [4]

1 *British Transport Commission* v. *Gourley* [1956] A.C. 185, 197, *per* Earl Jowitt.
2 As executor, continuing an action raised by her injured and now deceased husband.
3 *Traynor's Exrx.* v. *Bairds & Scottish Steel*, 1957 S.C. 311, 313, *per* Lord Guthrie.
4 *Butler* v. *Lynn*, 1965 S.C. 137, 144, *per* Lord Migdale.

Damages to be assessed once and for all

It is a settled principle that damages for all the losses arising from one ground of action must be recovered in the one claim. It is not competent to bring a further action on such grounds as that the damages were inadequate, or that it has been later ascertained that the injuries and loss are more serious than were suspected at the time of the original claim and award.[5] The matter is *res judicata.* Nor is a second action permissible for a different head of damages which might have been claimed in the first action: that is not a separate ground of action.[6]

What is a " ground of action " for the purposes of this rule? A ground of action is an act or omission or event constituting a distinct kind of infringement of right and giving rise to an action of damages; thus personal injury caused by negligence is a ground of action, loss of or damage to property, though caused by the same negligence, a separate ground of action, the death of a relative, though caused by the same negligence, yet another ground of action, and so on. It is convenient that a pursuer should bring all his claims against a particular defender, though founded on distinct grounds of action, in one process, though with separate conclusions, averments, and pleas-in-law applicable to the different grounds, but it is competent to bring separate actions.[7] This rule does not, however, apply in the case of a continuing injury, where each fresh harm is a separate wrong and actionable as such.[8]

Nor is it competent to recover damages from one defender and subsequently to sue another defender, alleging that the latter was also partly responsible for the same loss.[9]

Regard to changes in circumstances

A semi-exception to this principle is recognised in that changes of circumstances after the date of trial and the initial assessment of damages, but before an appeal is heard,[10] may be taken into consideration by the appellate tribunal.

In England the Court of Appeal has held [11] that if the basis on which damages have been assessed proves very shortly after the trial to have been wrong and the point is promptly raised, then the Court of Appeal may give leave to call further evidence. The House of Lords [12] considered this case as very near the borderline: it was said [13]: " where damages have to be assessed on estimates as to the future, the likelihood of dismissal or further ill-health, or in the case of a widow making a claim under the

[5] *Stevenson* v. *Pontifex and Wood* (1887) 15 R. 125.
[6] *Derrick* v. *Williams* [1939] 2 All E.R. 559.
[7] *Brunsden* v. *Humphrey* (1884) 14 Q.B.D. 141.
[8] *Darley Main Colliery* v. *Mitchell* (1886) 11 App.Cas. 127.
[9] Ersk. III, 1, 15; *Steven* v. *Broady Norman & Co.*, 1928 S.C. 351; *Balfour* v. *Baird*, 1959 S.C. 64.
[10] *e.g.* where a widow had remarried: *Curwen* v. *James* [1963] 2 All E.R. 619.
[11] *Jenkins* v. *Richard Thomas & Baldwins Ltd.* [1966] 2 All E.R. 15.
[12] *Murphy* v. *Stone-Wallwork Ltd.* [1969] 2 All E.R. 949.
[13] *Ibid.* 955, *per* Lord Upjohn.

Fatal Accidents Acts the probability of her remarriage (these are, of course, only examples) then the court does in proper cases look at the facts that have happened since judgment . . . I have no doubt that your Lordships have ample power to admit further evidence in cases which seem proper to your Lordships."

In *Mulholland* v. *Mitchell*[14] damages were awarded on the basis that the plaintiff would be nursed at home. Before the appeal it had become apparent that this was unworkable and that the cost of maintenance in a nursing home would be greater. The House of Lords affirmed the Court of Appeal's grant of leave to adduce evidence of these new matters at the appeal.

In Scotland the Inner House has power[15] to order proof or additional proof in any appeal from an inferior court under the Act and though the power has been exercised,[16] it does not seem to have been exercised to the effect of obtaining further evidence relevant to damages. There appears to be no other power to hear further evidence in a case heard by way of proof or jury trial in the Outer House, save that after a proof a remit back to the Lord Ordinary is probably competent, and that after a jury trial the emergence of new evidence on loss might be a " cause essential to the justice of the case " justifying the allowance of a new trial.[17] In any event the new evidence would have to be evidence only newly obtained and not further evidence which could have been led at the original trial.

All Scottish courts have, of course, power to, and must, consider changes in relevant circumstances occurring between the date of the event giving rise to the claim and the proof or trial.[18] They must consider the circumstances as at the date of decree. This does not mean that every change between the date of injury and the date of decree, particularly if involving aggravation of the harm or loss, must be attributed to the defender. In particular a subsequent accident causing greater disability or loss may be attributable to the pursuer himself[19] or to a third party.[20] Deterioration in the pursuer's condition may be attributable not to consequences of the injury but to independent natural causes.

After the litigation has been finally determined an award cannot be altered by any means or in any circumstances. " If [the pursuer] has invited a competent court to give him full satisfaction for the loss sustained by him and if he is awarded damages on that footing that is an end of it. He has got all he is entitled to." [21]

14 [1971] A.C. 666. *Cf. McCann* v. *Sheppard* [1973] 1 W.L.R. 540.

15 Court of Session (Scotland) Act 1868, ss. 62, 72.

16 *Pirie* v. *Leask*, 1964 S.C. 103.

17 Jury Trials (Scotland) Act 1815, s. 6; *cf. Shields* v. *N.B. Ry.* (1875) 2 R. 126; *Miller* v. *MacFisheries*, 1922 S.C. 157; and see also *Maltman* v. *Tarmac Civil Engineering Ltd.*, 1967 S.C. 177.

18 *e.g. Kelly* v. *Glasgow Corpn.*, 1951 S.C.(H.L.) 15 (one parent killed; other parent died later but before proof); *Pellow* v. *Lord Advocate*, 1953 S.L.T.(Notes) 41.

19 *McKew* v. *Holland & Hannen & Cubitts (Scotland) Ltd.*, 1970 S.L.T. 68.

20 *Cf. Baker* v. *Willoughby* [1970] A.C. 467.

21 *Balfour* v. *Baird*, 1959 S.C. 64, 73, *per* L.J.C. Thomson.

Regard to principle and practice in quantifying damages

In quantifying damages for personal injury regard must be had to legal principle to determine what elements or factors are relevant for consideration, and what irrelevant, and to practice to determine about what sum of money is currently regarded as fair under particular heads. " Now, what is an appropriate award of damages is always a question of fact depending on the particular circumstances of the particular case. . . ." [22]

It cannot be too strongly emphasised that there are no binding precedents on quantum of damages; there is and can be no such thing as the " proper " award for a broken arm or the loss of a leg, nor is the fact that £x were given in a previous case at all conclusive. Every case must be considered in its own circumstances, and a sum fair in those circumstances assessed. " The ultimate test in such cases must be practice and experience, moulded when necessary by quasi-permanent changes in the value of money and in social conditions." [23]

Nevertheless reports of awards made in fairly recent cases of comparable circumstances do give courts some guidance, and it is proper to consider how an award accords with the general run of awards made in recent years in comparable cases.[24] " In the process there must be the endeavour to secure some uniformity in the general method of approach. . . . Furthermore it is eminently desirable that so far as possible comparable injuries should be compensated by comparable awards." [25]

In assessing the amount to award as solatium for injuries awards in comparable cases in England should be considered by the Scottish courts. Solatium in personal injuries cases [26] corresponds to awards of general damages for pain and suffering in English law and there is no adequate reason why awards in Scotland should be different from those in England.[27]

Need for moderation

It is obvious that in cases of serious personal injuries any award of damages will fail to be real or adequate compensation for the loss sustained, but a court or jury is not on that account justified in making an inordinately large award. " It would be most unjust if, whenever any accident occurs, juries were to visit the unfortunate cause of it with the utmost amount which they think an equivalent for this mischief done. Scarcely any sum could compensate a labouring man for the loss of limb,

[22] *Traynor's Exrx.* v. *Bairds & Scottish Steel*, 1957 S.C. 311, 313, *per* Lord Guthrie.

[23] *McGinley* v. *Pacitti*, 1950 S.C. 364, 369, *per* L.P. Cooper.

[24] *Bird* v. *Cocking* [1951] 2 T.L.R. 1260; *Rushton* v. *N.C.B.* [1953] 1 Q.B. 495; *Mulready* v. *Bell* [1953] 2 Q.B. 117; *Waldon* v. *War Office* [1956] 1 All E.R. 108.

[25] *West* v. *Shephard* [1964] A.C. 326, 346, *per* Lord Morris. For examples of awards made see Appendix I.

[26] Solatium in wrongful death cases (Chap. 54, *infra*) is different, and has no counterpart at all in English wrongful death cases. The principle of *Allan* applies only to personal injuries cases.

[27] *Allan* v. *Scott*, 1972 S.L.T. 45; *Williams* v. *Scottish Gas Board*, 1972 S.L.T. (Notes) 66.

yet you do not in such a case give him enough to maintain him for life." [28] Damages must accordingly be kept within moderation and there must be some reasonable relation between the wrong done and the solatium applied.[29] "All that judges and courts can do is to award sums which must be regarded as giving reasonable compensation. In the process there must be the endeavour to secure some uniformity in the general method of approach. By common assent awards must be reasonable and must be assessed with moderation." [30]

"The distinction that they [the judges in *Rowley* [31] and *Phillips* [32]] drew between fairness and fullness is now in danger of being lost altogether. The quest after perfect compensation results only in the piling up of massive sums which the plaintiffs themselves can probably never use, and which serve only to express the sense of pity which judges as well as juries must feel for the tragedy of broken lives." [33]

Changes in the value of money—Inflation

It is clear, both on principle and on authority, that the courts must have regard to the current value of money and, in looking to past cases for guidance, must take into account the steady decline in the value of money over the years, particularly since 1945.[34] Accordingly modern awards must be much greater in money terms than awards for similar injuries some or, *a fortiori*, many years back. Pre-1945 awards are really of practically no value for that reason.

Possibly more important and difficult is the question whether continuing inflation should be assumed, and be taken into account in computing an award for loss extending into the future? In *Cavanagh* v. *Ulster Weaving Co.*[35] Lord Tucker thought it right to advert to inflation prospects, and several other cases [36] have taken the same line but in *Mallett* v. *McMonagle* [37] Lord Diplock said that the only practicable course was to leave inflation out of account, since one could not isolate inflation from national incomes policy, tax rates and structure and interest rates, and one was no more likely to be wrong by treating the world as standing still than by trying to take account of various future uncertain factors.

In *Mitchell* v. *Mulholland* [38] it was held that economists' evidence as

[28] *Armsworth* v. *S.E. Ry.* (1847) 11 Jur. 759, *per* Parke B.; *cf. Rowley* v. *L.N.W. Ry.* (1873) L.R. 8 Ex. 221; *Johnston* v. *G.W. Ry.* [1904] 2 K.B. 250.

[29] *Greenslands* v. *Wilmshurst* [1913] 3 K.B. 507, 532, *per* Hamilton L.J.: revd. on other grounds [1916] 2 A.C. 15.

[30] *West* v. *Shephard* [1964] A.C. 326, 346, *per* Lord Morris.

[31] *Rowley* v. *L.N.W. Ry.* (1873) L.R. 8 Ex. 221.

[32] (1879) 5 Q.B.D. 78.

[33] *West* v. *Shephard* [1964] A.C. 326, 358, *per* Lord Devlin.

[34] *Sands* v. *Devan*, 1945 S.C. 380; *Kelly* v. *Glasgow Corpn.*, 1951 S.C.(H.L.) 15 (fatal accident cases).

[35] [1960] A.C. 145, 163.

[36] *Miller* v. *B.R.S. Ltd.* [1967] 1 All E.R. 1027; *Aiken* v. *P.L.A.* [1963] 1 Lloyd's Rep. 44; *Taylor* v. *O'Connor* [1971] A.C. 115.

[37] [1970] A.C. 166, 176; see also the same judge in *Fletcher* v. *Autocar and Transporters Ltd.* [1968] 2 Q.B. 322, 348.

[38] [1971] 2 All E.R. 1205.

to the impact of cost inflation on post-trial financial loss was not admissible because only in rare cases would it be helpful; it could only be so where it was sound and precise, but that evidence as to productivity inflation was admissible as relevant to assessing damages for loss of ability to earn. Also, though it was proper to increase an award of damages to take account of the reduction in the value of money at the date of the award, an award should not be increased merely because the sum awarded might have decreased in five or ten years' time. Once an award was made the plaintiff must protect himself from subsequent fall in the value of money by prudent investment, and this applied as much to an award for solatium as to an award for loss of ability to earn.

Inflation in any event can hardly be relevant to an award for solatium, even though some or all of the solatium is in respect of loss for the future because, however large in money, it is a token compensation and not an attempted equivalent for any loss quantifiable in money.

Main kinds of losses

The main kinds of losses for which compensation is due in a personal injuries case fall into two categories, non-pecuniary losses, where the pursuer has not suffered any loss in money, earnings or financial capital, as in the form of pain and damage to bodily functions, and pecuniary losses, where there is some such loss, such as loss of earnings. Obviously the former kind are not truly calculable in money at all and any award of damages is token compensation, but the latter are quantifiable in money with some pretence to reasonable estimation if not to accuracy. " Take the most familiar and ordinary case: how is anybody to measure pain and suffering in moneys counted? Nobody can suggest that you can by any arithmetical calculation establish what is the exact sum of money which would represent such a thing as the pain and suffering which a person has undergone by reason of an accident. . . . But nevertheless the law recognises that as a topic upon which damages may be given." [39] To give effect to the basic principle of effecting restitution *in integrum*, in so far as money can do so, an award of damages should under the former category give what is currently regarded as fair and reasonable compensation [40] and under the latter category should give full compensation for the financial loss sustained.

Heads of damages

" In the process of assessing damages judges endeavour to take into account all the relevant changes in a claimant's circumstances which have been caused by the tortfeasor. These are often conveniently described as 'heads of damage.' " [41]

[39] *The Mediana* [1900] A.C. 113, 116, *per* L.C. Halsbury.
[40] *Cf. West* v. *Shephard* [1964] A.C. 326, 346.
[41] *West* v. *Shephard* [1964] A.C. 326, 346, *per* Lord Morris.

The main heads of damages

In all cases of this kind damages may be due under each of three main heads, provided always that some evidence is given, and accepted, of loss within the kinds of losses sought to be compensated by the relevant head of damages.

The recognised main heads in Scots law are solatium, patrimonial loss, and outlays and expenses.

> " There are three elements to be taken into consideration in arriving at the amount of compensation which ought to be awarded in a case of this kind. In the first place it must be given for the expenses to which the pursuer has been put on account of the accident, for medical attendance and lodging; in the second place, it must be given for the physical suffering which has been thereby occasioned, whether temporary or permanent; and, in the third place, it must be given for the loss of business which has resulted, so far as that can be proved." [42] " I think it is enough for the present purpose to see generally what the elements were upon which damage should be awarded. In the first place, there was a certain amount of pecuniary loss which the jury necessarily took into account; and then, in the second place, there was the prospect of the pursuer being unable to carry on his business as he had hitherto done and to earn the amount of income, or anything like the amount of income, which he had earned when in sound health. These are items of damage which the jury might reasonably find proper matter for more or less accurate calculation in money. But then, I think, in this case, there was an element of much greater difficulty to deal with—I mean the probable effects upon the man's future life of the injury he has sustained. That is a question of some difficulty in itself, but it is also a matter upon which there can be no precise data for estimating damages. In addition to that, I think there is still a more troublesome element, and that is the damage, which the pursuer is entitled to have taken into account, for personal pain and suffering and loss of health which he has endured." [43]
>
> " With regard to the assessment of damages there is no question as to the elements which must be taken into account—medical and other expenses consequent on the injuries; solatium for suffering and inconvenience arising from physical injuries or impaired senses and bodily or mental powers; and compenation for patrimonial loss arising from similar causes." [44]

Similarly in a leading English case [45] it was said:

[42] *Young* v. *Glasgow Tramways Co.* (1882) 10 R. 242, 243, *per* Lord McLaren. See also *Black* v. *Croall* (1854) 16 D. 431.
[43] *Thoms* v. *Caledonian Ry.*, 1913 S.C. 804, 808, *per* Lord Kinnear.
[44] *Lewis* v. *Laird Line*, 1925 S.L.T. 316, 319, *per* Lord Constable.
[45] *Phillips* v. *L.S.W. Ry.* (1879) 4 Q.B.D. 406; 5 Q.B.D. 78.

> " A jury cannot be said to take a reasonable view of the case unless they consider and take into account all the heads of damage in respect of which a plaintiff complaining of a personal injury is entitled to compensation. These are the bodily injury sustained; the pain undergone; the effect on the health of the sufferer according to its degree and its probable duration as likely to be temporary or permanent; the expenses incidental to attempts to effect a cure or to lessen the amount of injury; the pecuniary loss sustained through inability to attend to a profession or business as to which again, the injury may be of a temporary character, or may be such as to incapacitate the party for the remainder of his life."

Claims and awards not differentiated

While these three main heads of damages are recognised, a pursuer does not claim separately under each head. He makes a general claim for a lump sum of damages, and a jury award, if made, is of a lump sum to cover all relevant heads of claim. It is accordingly impossible to say how much the jury had in mind for each head of loss. " The way in which I have always understood that such compensation should be estimated, and in which it has always been estimated in practice, is by the jury taking into their consideration the whole circumstances of the case, and looking at both the present suffering and permanent injury, without trying to put a money figure on each separately, to fix a sum which will do justice between the parties." [46] If an award is made by a judge or sheriff he is, in modern practice, expected to state how much he awards under each of the three main heads, but is not required to differentiate in more detail.[47] " In reference to a judicial process which must so often be undertaken such as that of the assessment of damages for personal injuries I would favour simplicity of expression and an absence to the greatest extent possible of any elaborate or complex formulae. I consider that it is sufficient to say that a money award is given by way of compensation and that it must take into account the actual consequences which have resulted from the tort." [48]

" There is only one cause of action for personal injuries, not several causes of action for the several items. The award of damages is, therefore, an award of one figure only, a composite figure, made up of several parts. Some of the parts may be capable of being estimated in terms of money, such as loss of future earnings. Others cannot truly be estimated in money at all but must proceed on a conventional basis, such as compensation for pain and suffering and loss of amenities (see *Ward* v. *James* [49]). At the end all the parts must be brought together to give fair compensation for the injuries. If a man is awarded a very large sum for loss of future

[46] *Young* v. *Glasgow Tramways Co.* (1882) 10 R. 242, 244, *per* Lord Shand.
[47] See *e.g. Butler* v. *Lynn*, 1965 S.C. 137, 140, 141.
[48] *West* v. *Shephard* [1964] A.C. 326, 349, *per* Lord Morris.
[49] [1966] 1 Q.B. 273.

earnings, it may help to compensate him for his future pain and suffering. If he has no loss of earnings, he may be more generously compensated for pain and suffering—and so forth." [50]

The rules requiring awards of interest on damages [51] are, however, increasingly requiring judges and juries to itemise their awards in order to provide bases for calculating interest.[52]

Whether the final award is a composite one or the aggregate of awards under several heads it should be arrived at by considering separately what loss the pursuer has proved under each of the heads of solatium, patrimonial loss, and outlays and expenses, and, in appropriate cases, considering under each of these heads both loss already sustained or incurred, and also loss which it is fairly established will certainly or probably be incurred in the future, and determining what is fair compensation under all relevant heads. Each head, and within each head, past loss and future loss, requires consideration to be given to different relevant factors, some of which react one on another, so that a final award is necessarily an aggregate rather than choice of one sum of money which seems fair. Moreover, patrimonial loss, past and future, and expenses, past and future, are calculable, whereas solatium is not.

Use of award irrelevant

It is of no concern to the court awarding damages how the award will be used. The use to which a particular victim puts money awarded him is a matter for him alone and an award should not be pared down or inflated because it is thought that a particular pursuer will or will not be able to use the money.[53]

Relevance of injured person's reaction to injuries

Is it relevant to consider whether the pursuer has given in to his injuries and abandoned his former life and his hopes for the future, or on the other hand set himself, so far as he can, to overcome his injuries and handicaps and, so far as possible, to do what he would have done if he had not been injured? In *Wise* v. *Kaye* [54] it was said that a brave man who makes light of his disabilities and finds other outlets to replace activities no longer open to him must not receive less compensation on that account. In *Povey* v. *Rydal School Governors* [55] it was held that an injury was not any the less nor loss of the amenities of life any the less because the plaintiff was, by courage and intelligence, in substantial measure overcoming his crippling handicaps.

50 *Watson* v. *Powles* [1968] 1 Q.B. 596, 603, *per* Lord Denning M.R. The last sentence seems questionable.

51 Interest on Damages (Scotland) Acts 1958 and 1971; Chap. 23, *supra*.

52 *Cf.* form of issue approved in *Macdonald* v. *Glasgow Corpn.*, 1973 S.L.T.(Notes) 2.

53 *West* v. *Shephard* [1964] A.C. 326, 350.

54 [1962] 1 Q.B. 638, 651, approved in *West* v. *Shephard* [1964] A.C. 326.

55 [1970] 1 All E.R. 841.

Where there is financial loss damages must be awarded irrespective of the pursuer's mental condition or the extent of his suffering.

SOLATIUM

The term solatium [56] is given to an award, or the part of an award, made as solace or compensation for intangible and non-pecuniary loss, such as pain and suffering or hurt feelings, as distinct from patrimonial or financial loss. It follows that, while evidence may be, and to justify any more than a nominal award, must be, given of pain or hurt feelings, no evidence need be, or can be, given under this head of actual financial loss. A man is not necessarily financially the poorer because he has been injured in body or mind, or hurt in his feelings, but he is nevertheless entitled to solatium.

> "Solatium in the law of Scotland probably means reparation for the pain inflicted on anyone in consequence of the commission of a delict against him. The pain may consist in physical sufferings, or it may consist in wounded feelings. But as a competent element in the assessment of damages, it is in contrast with patrimonial loss." [57]
> "Solatium is simply a Latin word for 'solace' or compensation for an injury which the deceased [58] has sustained and its consequent pain and suffering. . . . An award of solatium is simply part of the damages to which an injured person is entitled, and, therefore, the amount of such an award is always dependent on the particular facts of the particular case. Solatium is compensation for injury and for the pain caused by injury. It is, of course, an impossible task to translate injury or pain into pounds, shillings and pence, and, therefore, solatium is incapable of exact ascertainment, and whether it is awarded by a judge or a jury, the tribunal making the award must use a broad axe, and can only do its best to perform an exceedingly difficult task. There is no rule of law which lays down the limit which can be awarded as solatium. In particular, there is no rule of law to the effect that solatium for pain and suffering and injuries caused by an accident must be measured in all cases in hundreds of pounds. It would be highly regrettable if that were the law, because in these days we know that the value of the pound is changing. . . . Consequently, ladies and gentlemen, I want you, in considering solatium, to make such an award as you think is moderate and reasonable but adequate, having in view the particular circumstances of this case, because the only rule of law which applies to an award of solatium is that it is dependent upon the particular circumstances—for example, upon such matters as the gravity of the injury; upon its permanent or temporary character; upon the

[56] On the term and its derivation see Chap. 54, *infra*.
[57] *Duffy* v. *Kinneil Coal Co.*, 1930 S.C. 596, 597, *per* L.P. Clyde.
[58] The action was one being continued after the injured man's death by his executor.

amount of pain endured by the injured party and upon the duration of that pain." [59]

"It is true that in Scots law the Latin term solatium is used without distinction both to indicate a claim for compensation for the grief and suffering sustained by the death of a near relative and also for the pain and suffering occasioned to an injured party. But in my view the term solatium may connote different rights. Solatium properly so called denotes a separate right of action given only to near relatives whereas solatium for pain and suffering of an injured party—a term not known apparently to English law [60]—connotes an element in the ascertainment of damages for the injuries suffered by a plaintiff. These consist of various elements, solatium for the pain and suffering, out-of-pocket expenses, actual loss of wages and future problematical patrimonial loss due to loss of earning capacity. These elements comprise the head of damages due to an injured person by English law. It would not be correct in my view, to talk of compensation for pain and suffering as a head of damage apart from patrimonial loss. It is merely an element in the quantification of the total compensation. [Following a quotation from Lord Sorn in *Mackinnon* v. *Iberia Shipping Co.*[61]] I am inclined to agree with Lord Sorn that the claim for solatium for pain and suffering is 'comprised' in the ordinary action of damages for injuries." [62]

If a wrong to the claimant has been proved, which caused, or must have caused, some hurt or suffering, it is probable that some award, at least nominal, in name of solatium must be given.[63]

"I think there is real difficulty in treating solatium as being compensation, for no amount of money can compensate suffering. Money and suffering are not comparable or commensurate. The more usual and, I think, the proper course is to quantify solatium as being such sum of money as will reasonably mark the jury's (or the judge's) sense of the seriousness of the suffering, or as reasonable recognition of its seriousness." [64]

Full compensation impracticable

In relation to the losses for which solatium is given full compensation is impracticable because no amount of money is full compensation for serious physical or mental injuries, and there is no conceivable means of measuring the loss or of fixing awards for particular losses within this class. What must be sought is not full compensation but compensation which is fair having regard to the level of awards currently being made for generally

59 *Traynor's Exrx.* v. *Bairds & Scottish Steel Ltd.*, 1957 S.C. 311, 313, *per* Lord Guthrie.
60 The term is unknown, but the corresponding element in a claim is the claim for general damages.
61 1955 S.C. 20, 37.
62 *Boys* v. *Chaplin* [1971] A.C. 356, 382, *per* Lord Guest.
63 *Cf. Gibson* v. *Kyle*, 1933 S.C. 30 (claim for the death of a relative).
64 *McCallum* v. *Paterson*, 1968 S.C. 280, 284, *per* Lord Walker.

comparable pain and losses. " What is a fair award of solatium is consequently a matter of fact, and is therefore peculiarly a matter within the competence of a jury. What is a reasonable award must depend on the particular circumstances of the case. There can be no tariff for solatium. No limits as to permissible awards can be laid down *ab ante*. Consequently I agree with what was said in *Von Mehren's C.B.* v. *Wood* [65] and by Lord Justice-Clerk Grant in *McCallum* v. *Paterson*,[66] at p. 282, at the previous hearing of the present case that amounts held due in other cases are of little assistance in deciding whether an award of damages is reasonable or excessive." [67] " No precise rule can be laid down as a yardstick for solatium awards, which must of necessity be of a somewhat arbitrary character. Money cannot compensate for pain and suffering and it is impossible, by a monetary award under this head, to put the victim in the situation in which he would have been had the accident not occurred. The test must always be what is fair and reasonable in the circumstances and, because of that, and because of the absence of any specific rules for quantification, reasonable men may vary considerably in their assessment of what the appropriate award should be." [68]

Reference to comparable awards

While every case must be looked at individually " provided that one makes the comparison on a fairly broad basis and keeps in mind differences in regard to age, loss of expectation of life, the nature and extent of disability and so on, it is possible, having isolated the solatium element with reasonable accuracy here, to obtain some assistance from recent awards by judges in respect of pure solatium in paraplegic or analogous cases. . . . These awards can be no more than a rough guide in the present case." [69] " Guidance in very general terms can be obtained from considering judicial awards in cases which present certain similarities of outline and circumstances. I am far from saying, however, that it is possible or even desirable to lay down a tariff of damages. Circumstances of particular cases vary infinitely even where the actual injuries are similar, while the constant erosion in the value of money by inflation tends to render obsolete and inapplicable illustrative cases decided even a few years back." [70]

Reference to comparable awards includes comparable cases in England, solatium being the counterpart of general damages in English law.[71]

Solatium for past and for future

Where appropriate solatium may and should be given for the past, the

[65] 1966 S.L.T.(Notes) 28.
[66] 1968 S.C. 280.
[67] *McCallum* v. *Paterson*, 1969 S.C. 85, 90, *per* Lord Guthrie.
[68] *McCallum* v. *Paterson*, 1968 S.C. 280, 282, *per* L.J.C. Grant.
[69] *McCallum* v. *Paterson*, 1968 S.C. 280, 282, *per* L.J.C. Grant.
[70] *McCallum, supra*, 286, *per* Lord Cameron.
[71] *Allan* v. *Scott*, 1972 S.L.T. 45.

period between the date of the injury and the date of award, and for the future, the period from the date of award to the time when it is estimated that the loss will have been worked out and the pursuer have ceased to sustain a compensable loss. In some cases this may be the whole remaining duration of the pursuer's life.

Where solatium is having to be awarded for the future, it is relevant to consider the pursuer's age and how long he or she may be expected to live with the pain, disability and loss in issue. Where the injured party is older, allowance should be made for the fact that he will not have so long to suffer and has not therefore lost so much as a younger person who suffered the same injury.[72]

Solatium not relative to social class or income

An award of solatium is not relative to or affected by a pursuer's social class, sex, income or similar external factors. One man or woman is as much liable to suffer pain or hurt feelings as another, and is equally entitled to compensation therefor. " Now even if the pursuer were independent and possessed of private means I think she would be entitled to compensation for her present and prospective suffering, and for the inconvenience to which she has had to submit." [73] It has, however, been said in England [74] that possession of independent income may be relevant to damages for pain and suffering and loss of amenities of life, because a man may suffer very much more from bodily injury when he is deprived of all means of support, and is reduced to such poverty that he cannot provide for himself what will alleviate his sufferings, and is in a different position from the man who, having an independent income, meets with a similar accident. With the development of the National Health Service and the social services generally this argument is less valid now than a century ago, but is probably not wholly invalid. Yet it would be unfortunate if awards of solatium were related to class, income or wealth and modern authority is against awards being related to the injured person's income or wealth.[75]

Solatium not relative to loss of earnings

The element of award for solatium is not related in any way to the amount claimed or awarded for loss of earnings or other patrimonial loss. The losses are different and different factors are relevant to assessment of the sums due.

While it is convenient to consider separately the kinds of losses for which a pursuer may recover solatium, a court or jury in assessing damages is not required to, and in practice does not, specify precisely which of the relevant factors have weighed with it, nor attempt to state how much it awards in respect of any factor.

[72] *Nelson* v. *Clyde Nav. Trs.*, 1946 S.L.T.(Notes) 29.
[73] *Young* v. *Glasgow Tramways Co.* (1882) 10 R. 242, 243, *per* Lord McLaren.
[74] *Phillips* v. *L.S.W. Ry.* (1879) 5 C.P.D. 280, 294.
[75] *Fletcher* v. *Autocar and Transporters* [1968] 2 Q.B. 322.

Relevance of consciousness of injuries

Solatium is given as solace for pain and suffering, loss of amenities of life and similar subjective losses. If the pursuer has been for a material time, or been rendered permanently, unconscious or insane, he cannot and does not feel all or possibly any of these losses and accordingly cannot be awarded anything for these losses. In *Wise* v. *Kaye* [76] the injured person was rendered wholly unconscious with no prospect of ever regaining consciousness and nothing was awarded for pain and suffering. In *West* v. *Shephard* [77] the injured person was only partially conscious and it was said:

> "To the extent to which any of these last-mentioned matters [pain, loss of a limb, awareness of the deprivations which the loss of a limb entails] depend for their existence on an awareness in the victim it must follow that they will not exist and will not call for compensation if the victim is unconscious. An unconscious person will be spared pain and suffering and will not experience the mental anguish which may result from knowledge of what has in life been lost or from knowledge that life has been shortened. The fact of unconsciousness is therefore relevant in respect of, and will eliminate, those heads or elements of damage which can only exist by being felt or thought or experienced.[78] The fact of unconsciousness does not, however, eliminate the actuality of the deprivations of the ordinary experiences and amenities of life which may be the inevitable result of some physical injury."

While therefore awards cannot logically be made in such cases for pain and suffering, awards can be made, under the head of solatium, on other grounds, for loss of faculties, loss of the amenities of life and loss of expectation of life.

LOSSES FOR WHICH SOLATIUM RECOVERABLE

Pain and suffering undergone

Compensation is due under the head of solatium for physical pain and suffering undergone in consequence of an injury.[79] Regard must be had to its degree and intensity, and to the period for which it was suffered and, it may be, will continue to be suffered.[80] Shock suffered at the time of the accident is also relevant.[81] The court or jury must consider "the bodily injury sustained; the pain undergone; the effect on the health of the sufferer

[76] [1962] 1 Q.B. 638.
[77] [1964] A.C. 326, 349, *per* Lord Morris.
[78] *Cf. Brown* v. *Hemphill*, 1959 S.L.T.(Notes) 51.
[79] *McLaurin* v. *N.B. Ry.* (1892) 19 R. 346; *Traynor's Exrx.* v. *Bairds & Scottish Steel*, 1957 S.C. 311.
[80] *Aitken* v. *Laidlay*, 1938 S.C. 303, 309; *Lafferty* v. *N.C.B.*, 1960 S.L.T.(Notes) 35.
[81] *Traynor's Exrx.*, *supra*.

according to its degree and its probable duration as likely to be temporary or permanent. . . ." [82]

Detention while undergoing treatment

Consideration has to be given to the duration of any detention in hospital or similar place while undergoing treatment for the repair of injuries caused,[83] and to such related factors as having to lie in a constrained position,[84] having to submit to anaesthetics and operative treatment,[85] and similar unpleasant experiences.

Future pain and suffering

If pain and suffering is going to continue, or is likely to continue, permanently or for some time after the date of the trial, allowance must be made for the continuing duration of the pain.[86]

Loss of or damage to limbs or physical faculties

Loss of a limb, hand or foot, or even finger or toe, is similarly a factor to be taken into account: " the loss of a limb is a life-long disability and handicap." [87]

> " Then there is or may be a temporary or permanent loss of a limb, organ or faculty. Whether it is the limb itself that is lost or the use of it is immaterial. What is to be compensated for is the loss of use and the deprivation thereby occasioned. This deprivation may bring with it three consequences. First, it may result in loss of earnings and they can be calculated. Secondly, it may put the victim to expense in that he has to pay others for doing what he formerly did for himself; and that also can be calculated. Thirdly, it produces loss of enjoyment, loss of amenities as it is sometimes called, a diminution in the full pleasure of living. This is incalculable and at large. This deprivation with its three consequences is something that is personal to the victim. You do not, for instance, put an arbitrary value on the loss of a limb, as is commonly done in an accident insurance policy. You must ascertain the use to which the limb would have been put, so as to ascertain what it is of which the victim has actually been deprived. . . . There are two ways in which this loss of enjoyment can be considered. It can be said that from beginning to end it is really all mental suffering. . . . If this is the true view, then total unconsciousness as in *Wise* v. *Kaye* [88] relieves all mental suffering, and

[82] *Phillips* v. *L.S.W. Ry.* (1879) 4 Q.B.D. 406.
[83] *Butler* v. *Lynn*, 1965 S.C. 137, 142; *McVeigh* v. *N.C.B.*, 1969 S.C. 268, 284.
[84] *McLaurin* v. *N.B. Ry.* (1892) 19 R. 346, 348.
[85] *Aitken* v. *Laidlay*, 1938 S.C. 303, 306; *Traynor's Exrx.*, *supra*, 314.
[86] *Heaps* v. *Perrite* [1937] 2 All E.R. 60.
[87] *Aitken* v. *Laidlay*, 1938 S.C. 303, 306. *Cf. McGinley* v. *Pacitti*, 1950 S.C. 364; *Traynor's Exrx.* v. *Bairds & Scottish Steel*, 1957 S.C. 311, 314; *McVeigh* v. *N.C.B.*, 1969 S.C. 268, 284, 289.
[88] [1962] 1 Q.B. 638.

nothing can be recovered for a deprivation which is not being experienced.

"The other way to look on the deprivation of a limb is as the loss of a personal asset, something in the nature of property. A limb can be put both to profitable use and to pleasurable use. In so far as it is put to profitable use, the loss is compensated for by calculating loss of earnings and not by assessing mental pain. On the same principle, it can be said, a sum must be assessed for loss of pleasurable use irrespective of whether there is mental suffering or not. . . . English law . . . favours a compound of both. The elements to be compounded have been called the objective and the subjective. The loss of property element is objective; it requires some sort of valuation that is in no way dependent on the victim's sense of loss. The other element is subjective because it depends entirely on mental suffering actually experienced." [89]

Though a limb may not be lost it may be damaged consequentially; thus fractures of a leg may unite but leave the leg permanently shortened, leaving the victim with a limp,[90] or the range of movement of a limb may be impaired.[91]

Damage to central nervous system

Such damage resulting in total or partial paralysis is relevant.[92]

Damage to bodily functions

Damage to digestive organs and functions or to bowel or bladder functions is similarly relevant.[93] Damage to lungs and respiration is relevant.[94]

Damage to sex organs

Damage to sex and reproductive organs or their functioning is relevant.[95]

Personal disfigurement

A factor relevant to solatium is if the injured person has suffered physical disfigurement, whether temporary or permanent.[96] "Personal disfigurement is a different thing from broken bones or any other injury

[89] *West* v. *Shephard* [1964] A.C. 326, 355, *per* Lord Devlin.
[90] *Alexander* v. *Brown*, 1952 S.L.T.(Notes) 11; *Elliot* v. *N.C.B.*, 1956 S.C. 484.
[91] *Dyer* v. *Clyde Crane Co.*, 1957 S.L.T.(Notes) 43; *Kemp* v. *Sellars*, 1962 S.L.T.(Notes) 7; *McMenamin* v. *Lothian's Trs.*, 1963 S.L.T.(Notes) 28.
[92] *e.g. Williams* v. *Hemphill*, 1966 S.C.(H.L.) 31; *McCallum* v. *Paterson*, 1969 S.C. 85.
[93] *McCallum* v. *Paterson*, 1969 S.C. 85. *Cf. Paton* v. *N.C.B.*, 1963 S.L.T.(Notes) 79; *Reid* v. *Scottish Omnibuses*, 1971 S.L.T.(Notes) 22.
[94] *e.g. Balfour* v. *Beardmore*, 1956 S.L.T. 205.
[95] *Cf. Best* v. *Fox* [1952] A.C. 716; *McCorquodale* v. *Moir*, 1960 S.L.T.(Notes) 47; *Reid* v. *Scottish Omnibuses*, 1971 S.L.T.(Notes) 22.
[96] *McWhinnie* v. *Western S.M.T. Co.*, 1949 S.L.T.(Notes) 8.

which can be completely repaired. The sufferer has the prospect of going through life disfigured, a thing that will continue to be a source of pain and annoyance to himself and of distress to his friends." [97]

It has been indicated in England that if a woman lost her husband in consequence of her disfigurement this would be admissible consequential loss and not too remote.[98]

Disfigurement may also in some cases, such as cases of an actor or a model, be relevant to loss of future business and earnings.

Loss of senses

It is relevant to solatium that an injured person has, temporarily or permanently, lost the use of one or more of the senses of sight,[1] smell,[2] hearing, touch and taste. Such a loss may seriously impair a person's capacity for enjoying life, and it may indirectly affect his capacity for work or the enjoyment of leisure. " This loss of smell is not only a loss of all the pleasures connected with that sense, but of a certain safeguard against familiar dangers. It has also been shown that this loss of the sense of smell would disable him from detecting certain defects in the yarns in which he dealt, and would then directly incapacitate him to that extent for business." [2]

Mental injuries

Brain and mental injuries, sometimes resulting in the victim being rendered totally incapax, are relevant claims for solatium and are frequently relevant to patrimonial loss also.[3] Nervous shock is similarly a valid head of claim, if among the risks which the wrongdoer should have contemplated.[4] Fright [5] and anxiety neurosis [6] have also been taken into account in particular cases.

Damage to memory, concentration or mental powers

Damage to mental powers, if proved, should be taken into consideration. " When he went back to business, he was found wanting in the nerve, the energy, the power of concentration, and the activity which had before enabled him to take a successful part in the conduct of his affairs. . . .

97 *McLaurin* v. *N.B. Ry.* (1892) 19 R. 346, 350, *per* Lord McLaren.

98 *Lampert* v. *Eastern National Omnibus Co.* [1954] 2 All E.R. 719 (claim failed on evidence).

1 *e.g. McNabney* v. *Scottish Ice Rinks Assocn.*, 1949 S.L.T.(Notes) 43.

2 *McLaurin* v. *N.B. Ry.* (1892) 19 R. 346, 348, *per* L.P. Robertson. *Cf. Kearns* v. *Higgs and Hill* (1968) 4 K.I.R. 393; *Cook* v. *Kier & Co.* [1970] 2 All E.R. 513 (loss of taste and smell).

3 *e.g. Dunsmore* v. *Glasgow Corpn.*, 1956 S.L.T.(Notes) 18; *Polland's Curator* v. *Elliott*, 1959 S.L.T.(Notes) 34; *Brown* v. *Hemphill*, 1959 S.L.T.(Notes) 51; *Waddell's C.B.* v. *Lindsay*, 1960 S.L.T. 189; *Steen* v. *Macnicol*, 1968 S.L.T.(Notes) 77.

4 *Bourhill* v. *Young*, 1942 S.C.(H.L.) 78; on damages see *Currie* v. *Wardrop*, 1927 S.C. 538 (£150); *Walker* v. *Pitlochry Motor Co.*, 1930 S.C. 565 (£500 claimed); *Bourhill* v. *Young*, 1941 S.C. 395, 407; *Durward* v. *Dunoon Motor Services*, 1952 S.L.T.(Notes) 2.

5 *Stedman* v. *Henderson* (1924) 40 Sh.Ct.Rep. 8. But see *Wallace* v. *Kennedy* (1908) 16 S.L.T. 485.

6 *Griffiths* v. *Green* (1948) 81 Ll.L.R. 378; *Lucy* v. *Mariehamns Rederi* [1971] 2 Lloyd's Rep. 314.

His activity was impaired, his memory was blunted, and his general alertness perceptibly diminished." [7] Such a loss is relevant as affecting the claimant's aptitude and capacity in his business or occupation. So too amnesia and a change of personality due to brain injury have been taken into account,[8] as have consequential moodiness and depression.[9]

Loss of matrimonial or family prospects

If by reason of injuries a pursuer, particularly a young woman, would appear to have a materially diminished chance of marrying and/or of having a family and enjoying normal married life, that is relevant.[9a] In evaluating this head of claim, the age and pre-accident appearance and health of the pursuer, any declared intention or possibility of marriage, and any actual breach of engagement to marry consequent on the injury, must be considered. It is probably within judicial knowledge that the great majority of persons in Great Britain do in fact marry and that the majority of marriages are productive of pleasure and companionship.

Miscarriage

Akin to this head of claim is the case where the harm suffered consists in or includes a miscarriage,[10] or a therapeutic abortion becomes necessary. In such a case compensation is due for the loss and disappointment of not having a child.

Resultant incapacity

It is highly relevant if an injured person, apart from any specific injuries, is completely or substantially incapacitated, for a time or permanently, by his injuries,[11] if he has " to endure the hard fate to an active man of finding himself reduced from activity to decrepitude." [12]

Foreseeable and direct consequences

Account must be taken not only of immediate physical or mental injuries but of such consequences thereof as, on the medical evidence will, or probably will, result as foreseeable or direct consequences. Thus the likelihood that injuries will bring on arthritis or degenerative changes is relevant.[13] Allowance has been made for the fact that the pursuer, as a result of an accident, developed disseminated sclerosis earlier than he would otherwise have done.[14]

[7] *McLaurin* v. *N.B. Ry.* (1892) 19 R. 346, 348.
[8] *Waddell's C.B.* v. *Lindsay*, 1960 S.L.T. 189.
[9] *Ewan* v. *Alexander*, 1960 S.L.T.(Notes) 83.
[9a] *Harris* v. *Harris* [1973] 1 Lloyd's Rep. 445.
[10] *Cf. Bourhill* v. *Young*, 1941 S.C. 395, 431; affd. on other points, 1942 S.C.(H.L.) 78.
[11] *Aitken* v. *Laidlay*, 1938 S.C. 303, 309.
[12] *Thoms* v. *Caledonian Ry.*, 1913 S.C. 804, 809, *per* Lord Johnson.
[13] *McLeman* v. *Consolidated Pneumatic Tool Co.* (1950) 66 Sh.Ct.Rep. 3.
[14] *Pollock* v. *Alexander*, 1972 S.L.T.(Notes) 39.

Loss of amenities of life

In assessing damages weight may be attached to loss of the amenities of life consequential on the injury, apart from such direct losses as the loss of a limb. Impaired health and vitality is not merely a cause of pain and suffering, but the loss of a good thing in itself.[15] Thus even if there be no residual pain or loss, an injured person suffers a continuing loss if he or she is prevented from taking exercise, participating in games, recreations and pursuits, and doing the things he or she was in the habit of doing and liked doing, the things normal persons are capable of doing and the things which make life enjoyable.[16] This covers loss of sexual capacity [16a] and loss of the ability to enjoy doing a particular job or pursuing a hobby.[17]

Loss of expectation of life

A person has " a legal interest entitling him to complain if the integrity of his life is impaired by tortious acts not only in regard to pain, suffering and disability but in regard to the continuance of life for its normal expectancy. A man has a legal right that his life should not be shortened by the tortious act of another. His normal expectancy of life is a thing of temporal value, so that its impairment is something for which damages should be given." [18] Accordingly if there is evidence that an injured person's probable pre-accident expectation of life has probably been materially abridged by the injury, he is entitled to damages. In *Reid* v. *Lanarkshire Traction Co.*,[19] where a claim for damages was being continued after an injured person's death by his executor, the Lord Ordinary (Wark) said that if the deceased " had been pursuing the action he would have been entitled to put before a jury evidence to prove that the effect of the accident would inevitably be to shorten his expectancy of life, and the jury would have been entitled in assessing damages to take that evidence into account. In dealing with this element of damage, however, I think the jury would have had to weigh considerations somewhat different from those which would have faced them in a case of permanent injury. In that case they would have had to estimate the handicap on earning capacity during the rest of the pursuer's life, making of course due allowance for the ordinary risks of life. In considering the element of shortening of life they would not, in my opinion, be entitled to assess damages on the footing that the pursuer should not get less for shortening of life than for serious and permanent injury. Nor would they be entitled to give a sum based on

15 *Rose* v. *Ford* [1937] A.C. 826, 859.
16 *Cf. Manley* v. *Rugby Portland Cement Co.* (1951) C.A. No. 286 (Kemp and Kemp, *The Quantum of Damages*, vol. I (3rd ed.) 74); *Rieley* v. *Kingslaw Riding School*, 1973 S.L.T. (Notes) 72.
16a *Cook* v. *Kier & Co.* [1970] 2 All E.R. 513.
17 *Morris* v. *Johnson Matthey & Co.* (1967) 112 Sol.Jo. 32.
18 *Rose* v. *Ford* [1937] A.C. 826, 847.
19 1934 S.C. 79, 81; there had earlier been suggestions as to the competency of an award under this head in *McMaster* v. *Caledonian Ry.* (1885) 13 R. 252, and *McEnaney* (*Leigh's Exrx.*) v. *Caledonian Ry.*, 1913, 2 S.L.T. 293. In England something seems first to have been given for loss of expectation of life in *Flint* v. *Lovell* [1935] 1 K.B. 354.

the shortening of his expectation of life, with subsequent earlier cessation of earning capacity, less the anticipated diminution in the cost of maintenance during the period between the anticipated earlier date of death and the date of his expectation had the accident not taken place. What, in my view they would have been entitled to consider would have been the additional handicap on his enjoyment of life due to the anticipation of earlier death—in effect an additional award of solatium." Lord Sands thought that a jury must be left to take account of the factor of shortening of life but give only moderate weight to this, and not consider what price the man would have put upon his life.

In *Benham* v. *Gambling* [20] the House of Lords laid down that " the right conclusion is not to be reached by applying what may be called the statistical or actuarial test. Figures calculated to represent the expectation of human life at various ages are averages arrived at from a vast mass of vital statistics. The figure is not necessarily one which can be properly attributed to a given individual. In any case the thing to be valued is not the prospect of length of days, but the prospect of a predominantly happy life. The age of the individual may, in some cases, be a relevant factor. . . . It would be fallacious to assume, for this purpose, that all human life is continuously an enjoyable thing. . . . In assessing damages for shortening of life, therefore, such damages should not be calculated solely, or even mainly on the basis of the length of life which has been lost. . . . Before damages are awarded in respect of the shortened life of a given individual under this head, it is necessary for the court to be satisfied that the circumstances of the individual life were calculated to lead, on balance, to a positive measure of happiness, of which the victim has been deprived by the defendant's negligence. If the character or habits of the individual were calculated to lead him to a future of unhappiness or despondency, that would be a circumstance justifying a smaller award. . . .[21] The question is not whether the deceased had the capacity or ability to appreciate that his further life on earth would bring him happiness. The test is not subjective, and the right sum to award depends on an objective estimate of what kind of future on earth the victim might have enjoyed, whether he had justly estimated that future or not. Of course, no regard must be had to financial gains or losses during the period of which the victim has been deprived. The damages are in respect of loss of life, not of loss of future pecuniary prospects." The House went on to lay down that in the case of a young child no confident estimate of prospective happiness could be made, so that only a very moderate award could be made [22]; an individual with established character and firmer hopes and a more definite future prospect would be entitled to higher damages. Social position and prospects of wordly possessions are irrelevant.

[20] [1941] A.C. 157. See also *Yorkshire Electricity Board* v. *Naylor* [1968] A.C. 529.
[21] *Cf. Burns* v. *Edman* [1970] 2 Q.B. 541, where victim had led criminal career, which the court assumed would be unhappy.
[22] But *Naylor* v. *Yorkshire Electricity Board* [1968] A.C. 529 suggests that reduction on account of youth should not be significant.

In attempting to quantify an award under this head, it is clearly relevant to know the victim's age, his pre-accident expectation of life, and by how much that has been diminished. It is also relevant to know whether the victim was or is capable of understanding that his life had been shortened, whether his life had hitherto been happy and pleasant or miserable and painful, what the prospects of success and happiness, or the reverse, were, and whether the prospect of earlier death was in the circumstances painful or rather to be viewed as a release from misery. It has been said in England that it is no ground for reducing damages that the victim due to the accident itself is reduced to such a state of misery that he does not wish to go on living,[23] and also that an award should not be reduced because the victim's occupation was hazardous.[24]

It is probable that, in Scotland as in England,[25] an award for loss of expectation of life to a young child should be very moderate, and it is necessarily very moderate in the case of an elderly person. The permissible award probably rises to a peak in the case of the young adult. English cases where this has figured as a separate element of award suggest that about £500 is the normal award today.[26]

Impact on other heads of claim

An award for loss of expectation of life conflicts with an award of solatium for continuing pain and suffering in that the more the expectation of life has been shortened the less can be awarded for continuing pain and suffering.[27]

Relevance of shortened expectation of life to solatium generally

Apart from any element of claim for loss of expectation of life, the duration of the victim's expectation of life is relevant to the quantification of awards for solatium in every case except where the pain, suffering, disability or other loss has ceased or is taken as going to cease within a reasonable time. For in all cases of solatium for continuing loss, the probable duration of that loss is relevant. To suffer pain or be deprived of the ability to see or walk at the age of 20, with an expectation of life of 50 or so years, is far worse than the same loss at the age of 50, with an expectation of life of 20 or so years, and deserves a much larger award. " The length of the period of life during which the deprivation will continue will be a relevant factor." [28]

23 *Roach* v. *Yates* [1938] 1 K.B. 256.

24 *Bishop* v. *Cunard White Star* [1950] P. 240; contrast *The Aizkarai Mendi* [1938] P. 263.

25 *Benham* v. *Gambling, supra.*

26 See *e.g.* *Andrews* v. *Freeborough* [1967] 1 Q.B. 1; *Naylor* v. *Yorkshire Electricity Board* [1968] A.C. 529; *Cain* v. *Wilcock* [1968] 3 All E.R. 817. In *Balfour* v. *Beardmore*, 1952 S.L.T. 205, £200 was awarded under this head.

27 Thus if X aged 30, with an expectation of life of 45 years, is badly injured, and the 45 years cut to probably 15 years, solatium can be given for the loss of 30 years expectation of life, but solatium for continuing pain and suffering can be given for 15 years only.

28 *West* v. *Shephard* [1964] A.C. 326, 349; *cf.* *Bird* v. *Cocking* [1951] 2 T.L.R. 1260, 1262.

PATRIMONIAL LOSS

The pursuer can also recover for whatever actual financial or patrimonial loss he can prove he has sustained. For this head of claim evidence is necessary of the actual extent of loss, or of circumstances from which actual loss may be calculated or estimated. The loss for which compensation is due includes both loss ot income, earnings or profits by reason ot the accident between the date ot the injury and the date of the proof or trial, and estimated future losses under these heads. As these losses are calculable the proper basis of award is full compensation, rather than merely fair compensation, though admittedly the calculation is normally based on several uncertain factors. Nevertheless there are many judicial dicta to the effect that the court should try only to give fair compensation. Thus it was said in *Rowley* v. *L.N.W. Ry.*[29] that a jury " must not attempt to give damages to the full amount of a perfect compensation for the pecuniary injury, but must take a reasonable view of the case, and give what they consider, under all the circumstances, a fair compensation." Given that the calculations are based on estimates, why should an attempt not be made to give full compensation? Is anything less fair?

Loss of earnings to date

Earnings lost by reason of absence from employment or business between the date of the harm and the date of the trial ot the action, so far as caused by the accident complained of, are recoverable. All kinds of earnings, basic earnings, overtime, at least if regular and not merely occasional, tips, if normal and regular, and so on must be included. If the earnings were fluctuating because of seasonal unemployment, trade fluctuations, weather, piece-rates, or other reason, a fair average figure per week or month or year must be arrived at.[30] If earnings or profits were a mere possible contingency little or nothing can be awarded.

Payments in kind and perquisites

Account must be taken of, and a value set on, benefits to a person other than money earnings or profits, such as payments in kind, board and lodging supplied by an employer, rent-free or cheap accommodation, free or subsidised holidays, provision of a " company car " and permission to use it for private purposes, and so on. It is submitted that everything which would be valued and included by the Inland Revenue in " earned income " should be taken into account, and valued for the purposes of computing damages.

29 (1873) L.R. 8 Ex. 221, 231, *per* Brett J. (a fatal accident case) cited in *Rose* v. *Ford* [1936] 1 K.B. 90; *Owen* v. *Sykes* [1936] 1 K.B. 192; *B.T.C.* v. *Gourley* [1956] A.C. 185, 209; *West* v. *Shephard* [1964] A.C. 326, 356; *Watson* v. *Powles* [1968] 1 Q.B. 596 ,603; *Fletcher* v. *Autocar and Transporters* [1968] 2 Q.B. 322, 335.

30 *Phillips* v. *L.S.W. Ry.* (1879) 5 C.P.D. 280, 291.

Earnings of married women

The chargeable income of a married woman living with her husband is deemed for income tax purposes to be his income and tax assessable thereon must be assessed on him.[31] But if a married woman is injured and suffers loss of earnings it is submitted that the question who, as between the spouses and the Inland Revenue, is assessable and liable is irrelevant, and the real question is: what were the wife's net earnings, after taking into account the proportion of the spouses' total tax liability properly chargeable against her earnings. Furthermore, the court should not, it is submitted, concern itself with any issues between husband and wife, *e.g.* with whether the husband pays the surtax on his wife's earnings.

Reduced earnings

Where in consequence of the accident the pursuer has been transferred to lighter work, downgraded or otherwise, though not prevented from earning, prevented from earning as much as he would otherwise have earned, the basis of computation is the difference between what he was, and would probably, but for the accident, have continued to earn, and what he actually earned.[32]

Loss or damage to business

Injury to an individual may cause him loss of or in or damage to a business or professional practice conducted by him, both in the shape of causing a decline in its profits and his earnings, and in the form of causing contraction or closing of, or preventing or slowing expansion of, a developing business or practice, which is a capital asset. Injury to business consequent on personal injuries is a relevant claim, and not too remote. "There was the prospect of the pursuer being unable to carry on his business as he had hitherto done and to earn the amount of income, or anything like the amount of income, which he had earned when in sound health. These are items of damage or injury which the jury might reasonably find proper matter for more or less accurate calculation in money." [33]

Where a pursuer makes a claim for injury to business, the defender is entitled to inspect the pursuer's business books.[34]

The amount to be awarded for loss of business is a question of circumstances and of evidence; in *Phillips* v. *L.S.W. Ry.*[35] an award to an injured doctor of three years' loss of income was approved; in *Young* v. *Glasgow Tramways Co.*[36] Lord McLaren allowed three years' profits for loss of business though the other judges would not have given so much. In

31 Income and Corporation Taxes Act 1970, s. 37.
32 *Rouse* v. *P.L.A.* [1953] 2 Lloyd's Rep. 179; *Barry* v. *B.T.C.* [1954] 1 Lloyd's Rep. 372; *Robb* v. *Clyde Alloy Steel Co.*, 1956 S.L.T.(Notes) 58.
33 *Thoms* v. *Caledonian Ry.*, 1913 S.C. 804, 808. *Cf. McHarg* v. *McMillan*, 1947 S.L.T. (Notes) 13.
34 *Craig* v. *N.B. Ry.* (1888) 15 R. 808; *Johnston* v. *Caledonian Ry.* (1892) 20 R. 222.
35 (1879) 5 C.P.D. 280, 287.
36 (1882) 9 R. 242, 243; *cf.* also *Johnston* v. *Caledonian Ry.* (1892) 20 R. 222.

Thoms v. *Caledonian Ry.*[37] about three years' earnings would seem to have been given to an injured farmer.

Relevance of taxation to loss of earnings

In *British Transport Commission* v. *Gourley*[38] it was held that, in assessing damages for personal injuries, allowance must be made for the incidence of income tax and surtax on the pursuer's earnings, where the damages themselves are not taxable in the hands of the recipient. The principle is that if the victim had not been injured and had earned money, it would have been subject to income tax and surtax, and that he should be compensated for his lost net earnings, his lost " take-home pay," not for loss of gross earnings a part of which he would never have received or not been allowed to keep. In principle this is obviously right; in practice it is difficult to apply fairly. In particular courts or juries in awarding damages should not be led into a detailed examination of the pursuer's tax position. They should approach the problem in a broad, common-sense, way. Similarly, questions of how the pursuer's tax liability was computed, under what Schedules and so on, does not matter. The real questions are: what were his gross earnings? What percentage of those gross earnings had to go to the tax collector?

The House of Lords, moreover, in *Gourley* thought that it would " be unfortunate if, as a result of our decision, the fixation of damages in a running-down case were to involve an elaborate assessment of tax liability. It will, no doubt, become necessary for the tribunal assessing damages to form an estimate of what the tax would have been if the money had been earned, but such an estimate will be none the worse if it is formed on broad lines, even though it may be described as rough and ready. It is impossible to assess with mathematical accuracy what reduction should be made by reason of the tax position, just as it is impossible to assess with mathematical accuracy the amount of damages which should be awarded for the injury itself and for the pain and suffering endured." [39]

The tax factor is relevant only to those parts of an award which are in respect of money which would have been taxable, *i.e.* in respect of loss of earnings, past and future, and benefits, such as board and lodging, or the use of a car, which are equivalents of income and accountable for tax. It is not relevant to money which would not have been received but for the accident, such as all sums awarded under any head of solatium, or for outlays and expenses, but only to those parts of the total award of damages which are a surrogatum for taxable income.

The most satisfactory way of dealing with the problem is accordingly

[37] 1913 S.C. 804.

[38] [1956] A.C. 185, approving *McDaid* v. *Clyde Navigation Trs.*, 1946 S.C. 462, disapproving *Blackwood* v. *Andre*, 1947 S.C. 333 and *Billingham* v. *Hughes* [1949] 1 K.B. 643. On some of the problems raised by the decision see [English] Law Reform Committee Seventh Report 1958 (Cmnd. 501); Law Reform Committee for Scotland, Sixth Report, 1959 (Cmnd. 635). See also Chap. 26, *supra*.

[39] *Ibid.* 203, *per* Earl Jowitt.

to ascertain, and take as the basis for calculation, the pursuer's pre-accident net earnings.

National insurance contributions

Where national insurance contributions have been paid, the earnings lost are the net sum after deduction of such contributions.[40] As national insurance and national insurance (industrial injuries) contributions, where appropriate, and contributions to the National Health Service, are made by a single deduction and a stamp the principle applies to these contributions also. In substance these contributions are compulsory deductions under statute from gross earnings just like income tax and diminish the net earnings which are the basis for computing compensation. In *McCreadie* v. *Clydebank Co-operative Society* [41] the Lord Ordinary declined to follow *Cooper*,[40] and expressed the opinion that national insurance contributions were not a proper deduction from gross earnings. It is submitted that *Cooper* is preferable to *McCreadie*. The basic figure for calculating loss is the pursuer's " take-home " pay, and national insurance contributions are a deduction as inevitable as income tax. Moreover an injured person is entitled to part of the benefit of his contributions in addition to damages, so that he should not have the contributions ignored in assessing his earnings.

In *Cowan* v. *Greig* [42] the Lord Ordinary declined to make any deduction holding that averments about the deductions and their amount should be made in the pleadings if deduction is sought.

Trade union or professional organisation dues

It appears to be undecided whether sums paid by an injured person as dues to a trade union or subscription to a professional organisation should also be deducted from a pursuer's gross earnings. It is submitted that if membership of the union or organisation is by law or custom a necessary qualification for holding the job or performing the duties which the pursuer had, the sums are deductible, but not if membership were merely voluntary, still less if the body were only remotely connected or wholly unconnected with the job.

Net earnings to be considered

Accordingly the basic figure for consideration is the pursuer's net earnings, after deduction of all compulsory deductions from his gross earnings.

Subsidiary earnings

Subsidiary or " spare-time " earnings may or may not be affected by injuries. If the victim is prevented from making spare-time earnings as

[40] *Cooper* v. *Firth Brown Ltd.* [1963] 2 All E.R. 31.
[41] 1966 S.C. 71; fuller report in 1966 S.L.T.(Notes) 22.
[42] 1969 S L.T.(Notes) 34.

much as from carrying on his main money-earning occupation compensation is due as much for loss of the subsidiary as for the loss of principal income. But if the victim is not prevented from making his spare-time earnings, *e.g.* a professional footballer who in his spare-time writes thrillers and who suffers a disabling leg injury, the spare-time earnings are irrelevant. Even though irrelevant, if the subsidiary earnings are at all substantial in amount, their impact on the pursuer's tax position must be considered, both in relation to the amount of tax and to the effect of those earnings on the pursuer's effective rate of tax. Moreover consideration must be given to the question whether a victim, prevented from carrying on a principal occupation, could then devote more time to, or take up, a subsidiary occupation.

Alternative earnings

Account must be taken if an injured person, prevented from earning in one way, is thereby enabled to take up an alternative mode of earning, or to expand an alternative mode. Thus in *Billingham* v. *Hughes* [43] a doctor was rendered incapable of carrying on general medical practice but was not prevented from, and indeed would be able to devote his full time to, what had hitherto been a subsidiary appointment, as a radiologist.

Spouse's earnings

In assessing compensation for loss of earnings consequent on injuries the existence or amount of the injured person's spouse's earnings are irrelevant, save that, if those earnings are at all substantial, they will, by reason of the rule of aggregation of spouses' incomes for purposes of income tax affect the spouse's total income, total tax paid, and effective rate of tax. If, in consequence of the injuries to one spouse, the other spouse has to give up work or otherwise suffers loss of earnings, that is not a loss sustained by the injured spouse but may give the other spouse a claim for consequential loss.

Unearned or investment income

In compensating for loss of income no compensation falls to be given for " unearned income " for that, *ex hypothesi*, will not have been lost or diminished by reason of the injuries, and will continue. If substantial in amount, however, the impact of the unearned income on the pursuer's tax position must be considered, both in its amount and in its effect on his effective rate of tax.

FUTURE LOSS OF EARNINGS

Future loss of earnings

Where incapacity for returning to the pre-injury employment or business still continues at the date of the action, damages are also recoverable

[43] [1949] 1 K.B. 643.

for the estimated loss of prospective earnings and profits. The court or jury must take into account whether the incapacity will diminish, will continue, or will increase, and the duration of that incapacity, forming its view on the evidence submitted as to probable or possible recovery or deterioration. The court's function is to assess and give " the present value of prospective loss." [44]

Loss of future earnings or of earning capacity

Properly speaking, where a person, by reason of his injuries, will be prevented for a future period from earning as he had been before the accident, compensation is due not for loss of future earnings, but for loss of or diminution in future earning capacity. What he has lost, and what he should be compensated for, is damage to his capacity to go on earning. This is particularly evident in the case of injury to a young person, who may not have even started earning.[45] But that loss of capacity is most easily quantified by trying to estimate what earnings the pursuer would have made for the period of the incapacity if it had not in fact been inflicted on him.

The basic figures are the pursuer's net pre-accident earnings, any certain or probable increases during the period of incapacity, any diminution in earnings during that period by reason of the incapacity, as by having to accept a less well-paid job, and the period for which the incapacity may be expected to continue. In serious cases the period of incapacity will be the remaining duration of the pursuer's working lifetime, or of his total life, if expected to be shorter.

> " A plaintiff is not entitled to damages for loss of capacity to earn money unless it is established that he would, but for his injuries, have exercised that capacity in order to earn money. A plaintiff who at the time of his injuries has retired from any gainful occupation, has suffered no pecuniary loss from being disabled from doing what in any event he would never have done." [46]

Where expectation of life reduced

Where for any reason the pursuer has a life expectancy less than that of his normal working life he can be awarded damages for diminished earning capacity only on the basis of that reduced expectancy, not of a normal lifetime.[47] If the reduced expectancy is attributable to the defender's fault, the reduction is a separate head of claim, an element of solatium, but if not so attributable, but attributable to disease, or previous injury, it is not admissible as a separate head of claim at all. If for any reason a

[44] *B.T.C.* v. *Gourley* [1956] A.C. 185, 212.
[45] *e.g. Oliver* v. *Ashman* [1962] 2 Q.B. 210 (child of four).
[46] *Browning* v. *War Office* [1963] 1 Q.B. 750, 766, *per* Diplock L.J.
[47] *Reid* v. *Lanarkshire Traction Co.*, 1934 S.C. 79–81; *Harris* v. *Bright's Asphalt Contractors* [1953] 1 Q.B. 617; *Richards* v. *Highway Ironfounders Ltd.* [1955] 3 All E.R. 205; *Oliver* v. *Ashman* [1962] 2 Q.B. 210; not following *Phillips* v. *L.S.W. Ry.* (1879) 5 Q.B.D. 78, 80; *Pope* v. *Murphy* [1960] 2 All E.R. 873.

man's expectancy of life is in fact ten years it would seem right to give him something for loss of or diminished earning capacity for ten years, but wrong to give it to him for thirty years because in other circumstances he might have gone on earning for thirty years. As was said in relation to loss of expectation of life: " no regard must be had to financial gains or losses during the period of which the victim has been deprived. The damages are in respect of loss of life, not of loss of future pecuniary prospects." [48] The loss of the possibility of earnings after the date of accelerated death is not an admissible item of claim.

> " The prospective earnings which a person might have earned during a period when *ex hypothesi* he will already be dead strike me as far too speculative to be capable of assessment by any court of law. . . . To enquire what would have been the value to a person in the position of this plaintiff of any earnings which he might have made after the date when *ex hypothesi* he will be dead strikes me as a hopeless task. All that one can say is that he has lost the opportunity of enjoying what he would have earned during the remainder of his normal expectation of life; and this, as it seems to me, is merely one of the factors to be considered in making what I may call a *Benham* v. *Gambling* [49] award for loss of expectation of life." [50]

Damage to educational and employment prospects

A young person may by reason of injuries sustain damage to his educational prospects. " The loss of the opportunity of grammar school education and the permanent impairment of powers of concentration are significant in relation to the infant plaintiff's future opportunity of attaining the kind of job that would otherwise have been open to him . . . that loss of opportunity . . . implies some loss of future money earning capacity." [51]

Similarly injuries may affect an intended change of career as where a young man averred that the loss of a finger had not only deprived him of his hobby (boxing) but that he had intended to become a professional boxer, and had accordingly lost potential earnings.[52]

Basic calculation

The basic calculation of loss of future earnings is to ascertain the annual loss of earnings and to multiply this by a number of years, related to the duration for which the victim is expected to continue to sustain that loss. Both figures, however, that of annual loss (the multiplicand) and the number of years (the multiplier) are subject to various adjustments to make allowance for certain factors.

48 *Benham* v. *Gambling* [1941] A.C. 157, 167, *per* Viscount Simon L.C. *Cf. Rose* v. *Ford* [1937] A.C. 826, 861.
49 [1941] A.C. 157.
50 *Oliver*, *supra*, 240, *per* Willmer L.J.
51 *Jones* v. *Lawrence* [1969] 3 All E.R. 267, 271, *per* Cumming-Bruce J.
52 *Kelly* v. *Leith Cardle & Co.*, 1954 S.L.T.(Notes) 80.

Future earnings

The basic assumption must be that earnings would have continued at the rate they had done for some time before the accident.[53] But in computing future loss of earnings the court must take into account the effect of the natural development of an incapacitating condition.[54] Where the pursuer was employed his pre-accident earnings are the basic figure. Earnings include the value of remuneration for services which was not paid in money, such as board and lodging provided,[55] rent-free or low-rent accommodation, and other benefits.

Where the pursuer was self-employed, it is necessary to ascertain his net earnings from business or professional practice prior to the accident.

Where the pursuer was not earning the reason for not doing so must be ascertained. If he were retired, or living on investment income, he may be entitled to a nominal award for the loss of his earning capacity but what that is may be speculative and is in some cases negligible. He can be given nothing for loss of future earnings when there is no evidence that he would have made any. If on the other hand the pursuer was not earning because he was then unemployed the court would have to make the best estimate it could of his prospects of getting employment, and of what he might earn in such employment. If again the pursuer was not earning because he was ill an estimate would have to be made of the possibility of recovery, of the kind of work for which the pursuer would have been fit and his prospects of getting a job of that kind, and of what he might earn in such a job. In the case of persons not earning, *e.g.* children [56] and housewives,[57] but who would take up employment, an estimate must be made of what such a person might make having regard to the kind of employment the person might secure.

Future increase or diminution of income

It is relevant to consider what seem reasonable probabilities, but not merely speculative possibilities, as to increases or decreases in the pursuer's income in future. On this point the court or jury must consider the pursuer's age, health, qualifications and abilities, the possibility or certainty of promotion or retiral, whether the pursuer was on an incremental scale, or a partner likely to enjoy an increasing share of the firm profits with increasing seniority, or on the other hand a person devoting less time to his business and letting younger men take over. " It would be really monstrous that because a young man has only arrived at a certain position

[53] Where a man was injured on his first day at work, it was held relevant to aver what he had earned in his previous job: *Sweeney* v. *Colvilles*, 1962 S.L.T.(Notes) 42.

[54] *Forbes* v. *British Railways Board*, 1971 S.L.T.(Notes) 21.

[55] *Liffen* v. *Watson* [1940] 1 K.B. 556.

[56] *Cf. Jones* v. *Lawrence* [1969] 3 All E.R. 267; *S.* v. *Distillers Co.* (*Biochemicals*) [1969] 3 All E.R. 1412.

[57] *Cf. Cutts* v. *Chumley* [1967] 2 All E.R. 89; *McCallum* v. *Paterson*, 1969 S.C. 85 (" nebulous claim for loss of part-time employment in the future "); *Drummond* v. *Foulis*, 1972 S.L.T. (Notes) 11.

—though from past experience you can see with tolerable certainty that he will within a reasonable time greatly increase his income—you are to exclude this most important element from consideration . . . the very reverse should be the rule . . . when the jury came to the consideration of pecuniary loss, they have to take into account not only his present loss, but his incapacity to earn a future increased income." [58] Pure speculation, such as that he might have written a best-selling novel and made a fortune, must be ignored. "The victim being in fact a poor man is not entitled to claim damages in respect of lost opportunities which he could not have utilised unless he had been rich." [59] Thus no damages have been given for profit anticipated from a contract which plaintiff was unable to enter into by reason of his injuries: "But you cannot recover damages for loss alleged to have been sustained from a possible contingency. Supposing a lady to have been injured and disfigured in a railway accident, she could not say that she ought to recover damages because she was prevented from going to a ball, at which she might have met a rich husband." [60] In *Armstrong* v. *Paterson* [61] an N.C.O. in the R.A.F. alleged that by reason of injuries he had had to postpone a promotion examination by six months, thereby losing the opportunity of increased pay for that period: this was described as a "highly speculative ground of action." In *McCall* v. *Foulis* [62] it was held relevant to aver that by reason of the accident the pursuer had to delay for a year sitting a professional examination and lost the opportunity of earning an increase in salary, but irrelevant to aver the intention to become a professional senior football player; these prospects were too speculative to be taken into account.

Regard must be paid to the fact that in some occupations, such as professional sportsmen, such persons cannot continue in such careers all their working lives. They must retire early and turn to alternatives long before the end of their working lives. The same is true, though in lesser degree, of active careers such as in the armed forces and the police.

Subsidiary employment

If a pursuer's injuries prevent him pursuing not only his main employment but also a subsidiary employment, such as a barman or musician in the evenings, losses under both heads must be considered. If on the other hand the injuries prevent continuance of only one of those employments losses from that only must be considered. And the possibility has to be considered that restriction of, or total, inability to continue one employment may permit the pursuer to devote more time to what had previously been his subsidiary employment.

58 *Fair* v. *L.N.W. Ry.* (1869) 21 L.T. 326, *per* Cockburn C.J.; *cf. Johnston* v. *G.W. Ry.* [1904] 2 K.B. 250; *Smith* v. *Comrie's Exrx.*, 1944 S.C. 499.

59 *Clippens Oil Co.* v. *Edinburgh & District Water Trs.*, 1907 S.C.(H.L.) 9, 14, *per* Lord Collins.

60 *Priestley* v. *Maclean* (1860) 2 F. & F. 288, *per* Erle C.J.

61 1935 S.C. 464; *cf. Williamson* v. *N. of Scotland S.N. Co.*, 1915, 2 S.L.T. 165, 168; *Cowan* v. *Sevilla Whaling Co.*, 1950 S.C. 370 n.

62 1965 S.L.T.(Notes) 88.

Alternative employment

As against earnings lost for the future account must be taken of any probable alternative employment and of earnings therefrom. If a professional footballer is injured and disabled from continuing playing but can, and intended, when he gave up playing, to take up management of a public house, and does so, probable earnings therefrom must be set against future loss of earnings. Thus in *Browning* v. *War Office* [63] an Air Force technician was disabled by accident and discharged; he took up running a grocery store in his home town and it was accepted that he must give credit for the earnings therefrom.

Effect of inflation

Account must be taken of the fact that, even without any change of grade or appointment, there has been a steady upward movement of salaries and wages since 1945, that this is continuing, and that if future earnings for any length of time are being considered it is only realistic to assume periodical increases. Moreover an annual increase of 10 per cent. on previous wage rates will double wages in 7½ years.

In *Taylor* v. *O'Connor*,[64] a fatal accident case, a majority of the House of Lords was of the view that the prospect of inflation was not a valid reason for increasing the number of years used as multiplier in calculating the plaintiff's loss of support but Lord Reid thought it quite unrealistic to refuse wholly to take inflation into account. This was followed in *Mitchell* v. *Mulholland* (*No.* 2),[65] though it was recognised that there would probably be a compensating increase in the value of investments made with the damages award.

Superannuation or retired pay

If the period of disability includes a period during which the injured person would in the normal course have been retired and receiving superannuation or retired pay, no deduction should be made from damages on this account, as it would have been paid without services being rendered and the pursuer does not lose because he cannot render services; he has already earned this pay, and is entitled to it; moreover, having already worked for it, it is not a gratuitous benefit to him, and he must recover it in full. The calculation of loss of earning capacity must of course stop at the time when superannuation starts, because earning capacity becomes irrelevant, save in relation to subsidiary earnings, when a person retires.

Taxation on future earnings

It is clear that, as in the case of compensation for income and earnings

63 [1963] 1 Q.B. 750.

64 [1971] A.C. 115, 129. See also *Cavanagh* v. *Ulster Weaving Co.* [1960] A.C. 145, 163; *Aiken* v. *P.L.A.* [1963] 1 Lloyd's Rep. 44, 52; *Naylor* v. *Yorkshire Electricity Board* [1968] A.C. 529, 552.

65 [1971] 2 All E.R. 1205 (C.A.).

actually lost, so in seeking to compensate for damage to or loss of future earning capacity, regard must be had to the fact that, if the pursuer had gone on earning, those earnings would have been subjected to income tax.[66] The difficulty is that not only are future earnings difficult to predict, but the impact of taxation in future is even more unpredictable, and this may be affected by external factors, such as the existence, increase or diminution of unearned income, spouse's earnings, insurance policies and the like. The only practicable course is to ascertain the injured person's pre-accident earnings, both gross and net, after deduction of taxation, and to assume that the weight of personal taxation will be generally similar in the future, and to compute damages for future loss on the basis of the estimated net earnings lost.

The court should not, it is submitted, concern itself with speculative possibilities, such as that the pursuer would have had ten children and thereby reduced his liability to taxation, or married a woman with large earnings as a music-hall artiste, or a large investment income, and thereby increased his tax liability.

Method of computing award for future loss of earnings

Where an award must be made of a lump sum (as it must be, it being incompetent to award an annuity or periodical payment) the first step is, as indicated, to ascertain an average net annual loss for the period for which that loss may be expected to be sustained. The second step is to determine the number of years for which the loss will be sustained. This will be, at most, the whole balance of the pursuer's working life, to the age at which he would otherwise have retired. This involves ascertaining some or all of his age at the date of assessment, the estimated duration of the loss of or diminution of earnings by reason of the accident, the age at which he would normally have retired, the age at which in the normal course he would die and the extent, if at all, to which his life has been shortened by reason of the accident. Some of these facts are readily ascertainable, but some depend on the evaluation of medical evidence. Tables of life expectancies have been referred to, to assist in determining life expectancy.[67] On the basis of these facts the court must determine that the loss is to be taken as likely to be incurred for X years still to come.

Where expectation of life reduced

Where the pursuer's expectation of life has been reduced, whether by previous accident or natural causes, or by the accident giving rise to the claim, damages can be calculated only on the basis of the reduced life expectancy.[68] This may have the result of prejudicing the victim's dependants, who are left without support from him earlier than they would have

[66] *British Transport Commission* v. *Gourley* [1956] A.C. 185.
[67] *Cf. Mitchell* v. *Mulholland* (*No.* 2) [1971] 2 All E.R. 1205.
[68] *Harris* v. *Bright's Asphalt Contractors* [1953] 1 Q.B. 617; *Oliver* v. *Ashman* [1962] 2 Q.B. 210; *contra*, *Pope* v. *Murphy* [1961] 1 Q.B. 222; *McCann* v. *Sheppard* [1973] 1 W.L.R. 540.

been if the accident had not happened, but who have themselves no claim. On the other hand to give damages in compensation for earnings lost during years when the victim will, it is calculated, be dead is unreasonable, particularly if he had already been, for other reasons, a person with a sub-average life expectancy.[69] Such a case, moreover will normally justify something for loss of expectation of life under the head of solatium.

Simple multiplication incorrect

It is, however, incorrect simply to multiply the assumed annual loss by the number of years for which it is expected to be lost because this produces a figure which, if awarded as a lump sum, could and should, and, it must be assumed, will be invested and produce income, so that the pursuer would be given both a capital sum and the income produced thereby.[70] A reduction of the figure obtained by this multiplication by roughly one-third would in fact produce a sum which would, if properly invested, from annually increasing slices of capital and annually decreasing elements of income from the declining capital, taken together, produce a sum equal to the annual loss for the requisite number of years. Alternatively a reduced multiplier can be used. To put it another way the result produced by simple multiplication must be discounted substantially to take account of the assumption that the lump sum award will be invested and produce income.[71]

Liferent principle incorrect

Similarly the award should not be of such a capital sum as, properly invested, would produce an annual income, after tax, equivalent to the pursuer's estimated annual future net loss, because this would fully compensate the pursuer from income and give him the capital in addition.[72] This would be serious over-compensation.

Annuity principle appropriate

More appropriate, however, is the annuity principle. The award, that is, should be such capital sum as, properly invested, will yield annually, from combined slices of capital and of income from the unspent capital, a

[69] See further Howroyd, " Damages for Pecuniary Loss Occasioned by Shortened Expectation of Life " (1960) 77 S.A.L.J. 448; Fleming, " The Lost Years " (1962) 50 Calif.L.R.

[70] Thus if P proves an average net loss of £500 p.a. for the next 15 years, an award of £7,500, (£500 × 15) if made and invested at 5 per cent. would produce £375 p.a. gross. This income, though possibly taxable, would itself go a considerable way to compensating for the loss of £500 p.a.

[71] Accurate calculation of the proper discount depends of course on the rate of interest which, it is assumed, the money would earn and the allowance for tax deducted from the interest. Allowance for tax can be made by assuming a lower rate of interest than the award is in fact likely to earn on the basis that interest at, say, 5 per cent., is equivalent to interest at 7 per cent., less tax.

[72] Thus if P proves an average net loss of £500 p.a. for the next 15 years, an award of £12,000, if made and invested at 5 per cent. would produce £600 p.a. gross, and about £500 p.a. net, depending on the pursuer's tax position. This would fully compensate his annual loss and also give him £12,000 capital.

sum equivalent to the pursuer's estimated annual loss for the period for which, on the evidence, it probably will be lost. The sum should be such that with annually increasing slices from the capital and decreasing accretions of income from the balance it will properly compensate for the annual loss for the probable period of loss but will then be used up completely. The accurate calculation of the proper capital sum is a matter of actuarial calculation. A reasonable calculation may, however, be made by multiplying the estimated annual loss by a figure about one-third less than the number of years for which it is expected that the loss will last. This reduction is to take account of the fact that the sum awarded can, and, it must be assumed, will, be invested and earn interest. The precise reduction will depend on the rate of interest it is estimated that it will earn, being greater if a high rate is assumed and less if a lower rate is assumed. But in fixing the assumed rate of interest it must be remembered that the interest will be taxable, and a lower rate must be assumed to allow for that than the money will actually earn.

Acceptance of the annuity principle does not imply that a court should merely receive evidence of actuarial calculations or read the answer off annuity tables, but it should have regard to the answers produced by these means because these calculations or tables are based on the true principle to be followed in computing damages.

> " The present value of lost future earnings is not to be taken as the price at which the appropriate annuity can be purchased from a Life Office. There is a variety of reasons for this. For example, the assumptions on which the price of annuities are calculated are made in favour of longevity to minimise the risk that the Life Office will suffer a loss. The price must also make allowance for expenses and profit. Moreover, most Life Offices annuities are bought voluntarily by the annuitants, who thereby back themselves to live longer than the average life . . . Life Offices allow for the fact that annuitants as a class are subject to a much lighter mortality than is any other class of person." [73]

Actuarial tables have been prepared [74] showing separately for heavy mortality cases, *i.e.* unhealthy or dangerous occupations for general population, and for light mortality cases, *i.e.* non-dangerous and healthy occupations, for men and for women separately, the present capital cost of producing an annuity of £100 per annum, payable for life till normal retiring age or till death, whichever occurs first, for persons of different ages. Different calculations have been made at different rates of interest, a higher rate of interest being appropriate where the income from the damages is likely to be subject to little or no taxation, a lower rate where it is likely to be subject to the standard rate of taxation. The figures

[73] Kemp and Kemp, *Quantum of Damages*, Vol. I—*Personal Injury Claims* (3rd ed., 1967) 38–39.

[74] See Kemp and Kemp, *supra*, 35–51.

produced by use of such tables should not be further discounted because of immediate cash payment of a lump sum, or because of the possibility of prior death, these factors being taken into account in the compilation of the tables, but other contingencies, such as the fluctuating nature of the pursuer's employment, are not allowed for therein.

Similarly the [English] Law Commission published in 1970 a Working Paper [75] containing a set of actuarial tables specially prepared for use in relatively simple cases as an aid to calculating loss of future earnings, each allowing the user to read off the table the present capital value of £100 of net annual income lost after tax by the plaintiff. The tables prepared deal separately with males and with females; separate sets of tables deal with the situations (i) where the plaintiff's loss continues, at a constant rate, throughout his life; (ii) where his loss continues at a constant rate until a retiring age, assumed as 65 for males and 60 for females; (iii) his loss continues throughout his life but is assumed to increase at a uniform compound rate of 5 per cent. per annum; and (iv) where his loss continues only till the age of 65 or 60 but is assumed to increase at a uniform compound rate of 5 per cent. per annum. Sets (iii) and (iv) of the tables could be used to take account of increases in salary or earnings, probable promotion, inflation, or a combination of these factors. Sets of tables also quote discount rates between 3 per cent. and 10 per cent.

Selection of the appropriate table depends on the pursuer's sex, what assumptions are being made as to duration of his loss and increments and/or inflation, and the rate of discount. The selection of discount-rate depends on the average gross yield on equities and on whether the plaintiff is likely to pay little tax, or the standard rate of tax, on the income derived from investing the lump sum award. Thus a 5 per cent. table would be appropriate in the former case, a 3 per cent. table in the latter.

Where the loss to be compensated is a multiple of £100 the figure found from the appropriate table, which is calculated on the basis of loss of £100, must be multiplied accordingly.

The utility of such tables is considerable but their value depends on appreciating the assumptions on which they have been calculated and on the proximity of coincidence of these assumptions with the facts of a particular case.

Judicial reluctance to use annuity method

The courts have hitherto shown extreme hesitation to recognise the annuity method.

> " The pursuer's wages at the time he received the injury were 10s. a week, or £26 a year, and the actuary examined proves that to purchase an annuity of that amount at the pursuer's age would cost £520. . . . It is a most fallacious way, in estimating such damages, to

[75] No. 27: Itemisation of Pecuniary Loss and the Use of Actuarial Tables as an Aid to Assessment.

> take the price of an annuity effeiring to the amount of the pursuer's wages at the time. In addition to this there must be considered the chances of the pursuer's health failing, or his employment fluctuating or ceasing or being affected with some of the severe casualties to which all classes, and particularly those employed about machinery, are subject."[76] "The rule is well settled both in Scotland[77] and in England[78] that the damages are not the fully calculated equivalent of the pecuniary loss sustained by the person on whose behalf the action is brought. The appropriate direction to a jury was thus stated by Lord Kinnear in *Casey's* case[79]: 'A direction to a jury which had been generally approved, and which certainly has often been given in cases of this kind, is that they ought not to attempt to fix damages on the full amount of the compensation for the injury that a man has suffered, but that they should take a reasonable view of the case and give what they consider in the circumstances to be fair compensation'."[80]

It is doubtful, however, if anything less than an honest attempt to give full compensation, at least for loss of earnings or profits, can be called fair compensation.

Actuarial evidence is, however, competent and may be an aid to arriving at fair and reasonable compensation.[81]

At the same time some judges have seen the value of the annuity principle. In *Phillips* v. *L.S.W. Ry.*,[82] James L.J. said: "The proper direction to the jury, as it seems to me, would have been to tell them to calculate the value of the income as a life annuity, and then make an allowance for its being subject to the contingencies of the plaintiff retiring, failing in his practice, and so forth."

In *Roach* v. *Yates*,[83] where a man of 32 was permanently incapacitated from work, Slesser L.J. said: "I think the proper way of approaching the problem . . . is first to consider what would have been the sum which he would have been likely to have made during his normal life if he had not met with the accident." The actuarial expectation of life was held to be about another 30 years, and he continued:

> "On that hypothesis, it is said that it is wrong, nevertheless, in trying to find out what capital sum would bring in the wages he would have earned but for the accident, to have any recourse at all to the consideration of annuity tables and the like. I do not for a moment

[76] *McKechnie* v. *Henderson* (1858) 20 D. 551, 552, *per* Sheriff-depute Alison.

[77] *Casey* v. *United Collieries Ltd.*, 1907 S.C. 690.

[78] *Rapson* v. *Cubitt* (1842) C. & M. 64; *Rowley* v. *L.N.W. Ry.* (1873) L.R. 8 Ex. 221; *Phillips* v. *L.S.W. Ry.* (1879) 5 Q.B.D. 78; 5 C.P.D. 280; *Johnston* v. *G.W. Ry.* [1904] 2 K.B. 250.

[79] *Supra.*

[80] *Lewis* v. *Laird Line Ltd.*, 1925 S.L.T. 316, 319.

[81] *Watson* v. *Powles* [1968] 1 Q.B. 596; *Fletcher* v. *Autocar & Transporters Ltd.* [1968] 2 Q.B. 322, 336, 346; *S.* v. *Distillers Co. Ltd.* [1969] 3 All E.R. 1412.

[82] (1879) 5 Q.B.D. 78, 84.

[83] [1938] 1 K.B. 256.

understand [counsel] to say that, when one has arrived at an estimation of a figure based on annuity tables, one is not to make the proper discounts and deductions for contingencies of every kind; but he says that that is, at any rate, a method by which one can capitalise the sum he is now to receive at once, rather than by weekly instalments for the rest of his life, as a basis for consideration. It is not the only method which is open to the court. . . . That does not mean that you must not have regard to all the contingencies, the reasonable contingencies, of life; you are not to assume that this man would have necessarily gone on earning this money for the rest of his life. . . ."

Criticism of actuarial tables

Courts have hitherto generally demurred to using annuity tables to ascertain the pursuer's future loss.[84]

> "It has been persuasively argued in this case [85] that since the capital value of an annuity can be precisely determined by reference to appropriate tables, the judge should take advantage of this, and should begin his calculations by ascertaining the capital value of an annuity of an amount equal to his multiplicand and payable for a period equal to the estimated pre-accident working life of the plaintiff. It is recognised that the amount so ascertained will have to be discounted to allow for all the chances of the plaintiff's working life being prematurely determined for reasons unconnected with the accident giving rise to the claim, but it is said that the use of annuity tables in this way introduces certainty into at least one of the elements of calculation which otherwise depends on little more than guess work. . . . I think it is a fallacy to suppose that a more precise and accurate answer is obtained by injecting an element of certainty into one only of a number of imponderables which have to be weighed against each other and, when it is remembered that a figure taken from the annuity tables must itself be at once discounted for hazards of life not allowed for in those tables, it cannot seriously be contended that any element of certainty is being introduced at all."

But examination of various cases indicates quite clearly that, particularly in Scotland but also in England, the conventional method of multiplying the annual loss by a multiplier representing a number of years' loss and making certain adjustments has in the past produced results enormously different from the results which the tables produce, and it must be submitted that, subject to discounting for the chances of life apart from the accident, the use of tables would give a better indication

[84] See *e.g. Watson* v. *Powles* [1968] 1 Q.B. 596, 604, 605; *Fletcher* v. *Autocar and Transporters* [1968] 2 Q.B. 322, 346; *S.* v. *Distillers Co.* (*Biochemicals*) [1969] 3 All E.R. 1412. *Cf. Taylor* v. *O'Connor* [1971] A.C. 115 (fatal accident case).

[85] *Mitchell* v. *Mulholland* (*No.* 2) [1971] 2 All E.R. 1205, 1217, *per* Widgery L.J.

of the kind of sum which is proper to award than choice of a multiplier which is almost invariably too small. Certainty and accuracy are unattainable but awards should be closer to the results brought out by tables than they are.

Discounting for contingencies

The gross sum for loss of future earnings produced by calculation must, however, be further discounted where the hypothesis that the pursuer would survive for the period of years considered is more or less doubtful. Regard must be had to the possibility of his premature death from natural causes, the chance of his being killed or injured in other circumstances, the possibility of loss of employment, redundancy, and so on.[86] The possibility of premature death is in fact taken account of in annuity tables, and the contingency that the victim will confound the doctors and live far longer than expected has also to be considered.

It has been suggested [87] that a reduction for general contingencies of this kind should be within the range of 2 to 4 per cent. of the capital value of the sum for loss of earnings, the lower percentage being appropriate for a person of normal health in stable employment, the higher for a person of above-average propensity to illness, or engaged in an occupation with a bad record for strikes, redundancy, and the like, or in a dangerous trade. If the pursuer's pre-accident health had been definitely sub-standard a greater deduction is necessary for contingencies. Nevertheless the allowance for such contingencies should not be anything like as great as courts have sometimes thought proper to make.

In *Mitchell* v. *Mulholland* (*No.* 2) [88] it was said that a 2 per cent. discount for contingencies was too little. Earning a living depended not only on length of days, on skill and capacity, but on business disasters, industrial unrest, sickness, non-fatal accidents and other factors. Each case depended on its own facts. While this is all undoubtedly true deductions for contingencies should not always be substantial and in some cases should be very small.

Supervening injuries

Where an injured person subsequently, but before the date of assessment of damages, suffers further injuries by the fault of a third party,[89] the second injury does not necessarily terminate or diminish the loss sustained in consequence of the first wrongdoer's fault, and therefore does not diminish his liability in damages. If, however, it should reduce the disabilities from the initial injury, or shorten the period during which they will be suffered, as by shortening his expectation of life, the first

86 *Phillips* v. *L.S.W. Ry.* (1879) 5 Q.B.D. 78, 81, 84; (1879) 5 C.P.D. 280, 290; *cf. Whittome* v. *Coates* [1965] 3 All E.R. 268.
87 Law Commission Working Paper No. 27 Appx. B, p. 12.
88 [1971] 2 All E.R. 1205.
89 Contrast the case where he suffers further injury by his own fault: *McKew* v. *Holland & Hannen & Cubitts (Scotland) Ltd.* 1970 S.L.T. 68.

wrongdoer's liability will be diminished.[90] The second wrongdoer is, of course, separately liable, but in the assessment of damages due by him, there must be taken into account the fact, if it be relevant, that the pursuer had been previously injured.

Where on the other hand the injured person subsequently suffers further injuries by reason of an accident caused by a disability brought about by the first accident, the person liable for the first accident is liable for the further injuries so long as they can be said to be the natural and direct consequence of the first accident.[91]

Deductions from Damages

Deductions from damages

The basic principle is that any factor which goes to diminish the pursuer's financial loss consequent on his injury must be taken into account in diminution of damages. A pursuer must not be compensated for loss of earnings if, or in so far as, that loss is made up from another source. But to this principle there are various exceptions and many of the decisions are in conflict.

Where wages still paid

If despite injury and absence from work wages are still paid in whole or in part, there is no, or only partial, loss of earnings and no damages are due, or only modified damages.[92] If such a payment terminates after a period full damages are due for loss of earnings from the date of termination only.

Promised alternative employment

If a defender is willing to take the pursuer back in his former or another capacity, or to find light work for him, or otherwise to re-employ him,[93] that must be taken into account, and damages can be given only in respect of the difference between pre-accident earnings and earnings as thus re-employed.

Similarly in other cases a pursuer must, in pursuance of the duty to minimise damages, look for and take work as closely comparable to his pre-accident employment as he can, having regard to any diminished capacity for work, and is entitled to damages only in respect of the difference between pre-accident earnings and earnings in the new post.

Collateral benefits

When in consequence of injuries a pursuer becomes entitled to certain

[90] *Baker* v. *Willoughby* [1969] 3 All E.R. 1528.
[91] *e.g. Wieland* v. *Cyril Lord Carpets Ltd.* [1969] 3 All E.R. 1006.
[92] *Browning* v. *War Office* [1963] 1 Q.B. 750; *cf. Monmouthshire C.C.* v. *Smith* [1956] 2 All E.R. 800, 810; *Metropolitan Police District Receiver* v. *Croydon Corpn.* [1957] 2 Q.B. 154, 163.
[93] *e.g. Cook* v. *Grubb*, 1963 S.C. 1.

financial benefits which go to mitigate the loss of earnings or profits resulting from his injuries some of these must be, while others are not, taken into account and deducted from the element of award for loss of earnings.

Substituted earnings

Where instead of salary or wages a man who has been injured is paid sick-pay or partial wages by his employer, during incapacity or for a period, such payments go to minimise his loss and are deductible.[94] It probably does not matter whether such a payment is a matter of contract or voluntary. If, however, they are paid on the understanding that, if damages are recovered, they are to be repaid, then no deduction should be made.[95]

Similarly if he obtains earnings from another employment they go to minimise his loss, and must be deducted from his claim for damages.

Payments from charitable fund

Any benefit received from a charitable fund falls to be disregarded, because the subscribers to the fund have contributed to help the injured, not to diminish the wrongdoer's liability in damages, and also because the injured person had no legal right whatever to the benefit; it is pure windfall.[96] " It would be revolting to the ordinary man's sense of justice, and therefore contrary to public policy, that the sufferer should have his damages reduced so that he would gain nothing from the benevolence of his friends or relations or of the public at large, and that the only gainer would be the wrongdoer." This outweighs the considerations that the victim may in the end be over-compensated or be compensated more than a victim similarly injured in a case where there is no disaster fund. Similarly it has been held wrong to reduce an award for lost future earnings on the ground that the injured person will be maintained by the National Health Service and will have few living expenses.[96a]

Gifts

A gift or allowance made quite voluntarily by a relative or employer is in the same position.[97]

Post-retiral income

A defender's fault, by injuring a pursuer, may affect not only his earnings for the rest of his working life but also his post-retiral income. If

94 *Doonan* v. *S.M.T. Co.*, 1950 S.C. 136; *Parry* v. *Cleaver* [1970] A.C. 1.

95 *Dennis* v. *L.P.T.B.* [1948] 1 All E.R. 779; *Schneider* v. *Eisovitch* [1960] 2 Q.B. 430.

96 *Redpath* v. *Belfast & County Down Ry.* [1947] N.I. 167; approved in *Peacock* v. *Amusement Equipment Co. Ltd.* [1954] 2 Q.B. 347; *Browning* v. *War Office* [1963] 1 Q.B. 750; and *Parry* v. *Cleaver* [1970] A.C. 1.

96a *Daish* v. *Wauton* [1972] 1 All E.R. 25.

97 *Peacock* v. *Amusement Equipment Co. Ltd.* [1954] 2 Q.B. 347; *Cunningham* v. *Harrison* [1973] 3 W.L.R. 97.

that retirement income is dependent on having served a stated number of years it may be diminished,[98] or even totally forfeited, if the pursuer is prevented, by the injuries caused by the defender's fault, from serving the requisite number of years. If so the loss is an element requiring compensation in damages, and a calculation must be made of the present value of the loss of income during the period of retirement. If the retirement income is National Insurance retirement pension it will not be affected, unless the injuries affect the pursuer's capacity to pay contributions and thereby qualify for this pension. If so the diminution in National Insurance retirement pension by reason of the inability to pay contributions is also a loss for which damages are due.

Retirement pension

If an injured person is forced by his injuries to retire, but is entitled to a retirement pension from his employers, such is not taken into account in mitigation of damages.[1] He has earned such pension by his service and it is payable independently of his injuries and of the fact that the injuries caused retirement at that time rather than later.

If a person is forced by injuries to retire from one employment but can and does obtain another job carrying entitlement to retirement pension, account must be taken of the extent to which that pension is greater than it would have been if he had only obtained the other job after retiral in the normal course from his first job, at a later age.[2]

If by reason of injuries a person has to retire prematurely and thereby obtains only a lesser retirement pension than if he had been able to continue work to the normal date of retirement, the loss is an element in damages.[3] If he loses retirement pension but gets disability pension, the latter must be taken into account against the loss of the retirement pension.[3]

Disability pensions

If a person who has been injured becomes entitled to a disablement pension from his employer, this should not be taken into account, whether it is a contributory pension or not, because such payments are part of the wage and salary structure and of the conditions of employment, even though the receipt of the pension goes to minimise the victim's financial loss.[4] If the pension is paid wholly voluntarily it should probably be treated as a gift or benevolence and be disregarded on that account.

[98] *e.g. Parry* v. *Cleaver* [1970] A.C. 1.

[1] *Hewson* v. *Downs* [1969] 3 All E.R. 193.

[2] *Parry* v. *Cleaver* [1970] A.C. 1 (policeman would have retired at 48 and taken another job; in fact by reason of injuries retired at 36 and obtained other job).

[3] *Parry* v. *Cleaver* [1970] A.C. 1.

[4] *Parry* v. *Cleaver* [1970] A.C. 1, explaining and approving *Payne* v. *Railway Executive* [1952] 1 K.B. 26; *Monmouthshire C.C.* v. *Smith* [1957] 2 Q.B. 154; *Judd* v. *Hammersmith, etc. Hospitals* [1960] 1 All E.R. 607; *Carroll* v. *Hooper* [1964] 1 All E.R. 845; *Elstob* v. *Robinson* [1964] 1 All E.R. 848, overruling *Browning* v. *War Office* [1963] 1 Q.B. 750.

If the authority paying the pension has a discretion to reduce it or terminate it if damages are recovered, the pension should be disregarded, and if in fact it is not reduced or terminated the pursuer is to that extent fortunate.[5]

Insurance benefits

If the injured person is entitled to and recovers compensation under an accident insurance policy that is *res inter alios* in a question with the party in fault, and no deduction falls to be made from damages in respect thereof. The injured person is entitled to the contractual benefit of his insurance and also to full damages; the defender cannot be allowed to minimise his liability because the pursuer had been provident.[6] The same applies to an allowance from a friendly society [7] or similar body.

Social security benefits

A person claiming damages for personal injuries is not prevented from also claiming such social security benefits as he considers himself entitled to, nor from obtaining payment thereof. But the Law Reform (Personal Injuries) Act 1948, s. 2, provides:

> " (1) In an action for damages for personal injuries [8] (including any such action arising out of a contract), there shall in assessing those damages be taken into account, against any loss of earnings or profits which has accrued or probably will accrue to the injured person from the injuries, one-half of the value of any rights which have accrued or probably will accrue to him therefrom in respect of industrial injury benefit,[9] industrial disablement benefit,[10] invalidity benefit [11] or sickness benefit [12] for the five years beginning with the time when the cause of action accrued.
>
> This subsection shall not be taken as requiring both the gross amount of the damages before taking into account the said rights and the net amount after taking them into account to be found separately.
>
> " (2) In determining the value of the said rights there shall be disregarded any increase of an industrial disablement pension in respect of the need of constant attendance.[13]

[5] *Payne, supra,* as explained in *Parry, supra.*

[6] *Bradburn* v. *G.W. Ry.* (1874) L.R. 10 Ex. 1; *cf. Shearman* v. *Folland* [1950] 2 K.B. 43, 46; *Parry* v. *Cleaver* [1970] A.C. 1.

[7] *Forgie* v. *Henderson* (1818) 1 Mur. 413.

[8] " Personal injury " is defined by s. 3 as including " any disease and any impairment of a person's physical or mental condition."

[9] Payable under National Insurance (Industrial Injuries) Act 1965, ss. 5 (1) (*a*), 11, 17–18, 27.

[10] Payable under National Insurance (Industrial Injuries) Act 1965, ss. 5 (1) (*b*), 12, 16–18, 27. By s. 1 (6) (*c*) of the 1948 Act an industrial disablement gratuity (1965 Act, s. 12 (3)) is to be treated as benefit for the period taken into account by the assessment of the extent of the disablement in respect of which it is payable.

[11] Two words added by National Insurance Act 1971, Sched. 5, para. 1. This benefit is payable under that Act, s. 3.

[12] Payable under National Insurance Act 1965, ss. 17 (*b*), 19–22, 40–43, 48–52.

[13] Under National Insurance (Industrial Injuries) Act 1965, s. 15. By implication it would seem that other increases of industrial disablement pension, increase on account of un-

"(3) The reference in subsection (1) of this section to assessing the damages for personal injuries shall, in cases where the damages otherwise recoverable are subject to reduction under the law relating to contributory negligence or are limited by or under any Act or by contract, be taken as referring to the total damages which would have been recoverable apart from the reduction or limitation."

"Shall . . . be taken into account . . ."

It is mandatory to take account of these benefits, not discretionary. The phrase "taken into account" is, however, ambiguous and in *Stott* v. *Arrol*[14] it was held that they implied discretion, and the trial judge held that he was not obliged to deduct the full half of the value of rights which had accrued or would accrue. In *Flowers* v. *Wimpey*[15] it was held that "taken into account" required that half of the sum paid be deducted; there was no discretion, save that the court was not obliged to make an absolutely exact calculation. Incapacity attributable to injury was three or four weeks, incapacity thereafter being attributable to causes not the result of the accident, but industrial injury benefit and later sickness benefit had been paid for, in all, about ten months, and certain disablement gratuities and a disablement pension had also been paid. Loss of earnings by reason of the injuries amounted to £68 and benefits paid to £136. The judge held that the total of the sums paid had to be considered, halved, and set against the award for loss of earnings, in the result extinguishing the claim for loss of earnings. This decision also takes the view that the court is concerned with not only the period of incapacity for which damages are due but with the total period for which the social security authorities have made payments even where that period was composed of (a) a period of incapacity attributable to the defender's fault, and (b) a period of incapacity attributable to another disability and to the plaintiff's mental condition, an attack of "compensitis."

"Against any loss of earnings or profits . . ."

Deduction is competent only where there is some loss of earnings or profits, past or future, for which damages, under the head of patrimonial loss, are being awarded. If an unemployed person, or one living on private income, or otherwise having no claim for loss of earnings or profits, is injured there is nothing from which to make a deduction. Deduction is not competent from the award so far as made under the head of solatium or of outlays and expenses.

employability (1965 Act, s. 13), increase in cases of special hardship (1965 Act, s. 14), or increase of industrial disablement benefit during hospital treatment (1965 Act, s. 16), or increases in respect of children (1965 Act, s. 17) or adult dependants (1965 Act, s. 18) have to be regarded.

14 [1953] 2 Q.B. 92.

15 [1956] 1 Q.B. 73, followed in *Eley* v. *Bedford* [1971] 3 All E.R. 285; approved by C.A. in *Hultquist* v. *Universal Pattern & Precision Engineering Co. Ltd.* [1960] 2 Q.B. 467.

" One-half of the value of any rights which have accrued or probably will accrue "

It is arguable that what must be taken into account is half of the value of any *rights to* stated benefits, whether in fact benefit has been claimed, or paid, or not. If benefits are claimed, the only criterion of whether the pursuer had any right to them or any of them is whether they are in fact adjudged payable to him, a question determined not by the courts but by insurance officers, appeal tribunals and the National Insurance Commissioner. If benefits are not claimed there may still be a *right to* benefit. In *Flowers* v. *Wimpey* [16] Devlin J. accepted the submission that these rights are worth what is paid in respect of them under the statute, neither more nor less, and what is paid is determined by the insurance officer.

The rights mentioned include rights to benefit which may still be payable at the time of assessment of damages and may go on being paid for years thereafter. In *Harris* v. *Bright's Asphalt Contractors* [17] the judge found as a fact that the injured man would live only eighteen months and he accordingly deducted half of the expected benefits for that period. In other cases the court must estimate what the value of the benefits will be until five years after the date of the accident. This is difficult because rates of benefit are periodically changed, because industrial injury benefit is exhausted after six months,[18] and sickness benefit after one year.[19]

Where disablement is assessed as amounting to less than 20 per cent. it takes the form of an industrial disablement gratuity [20] which must [21] be treated as " benefit for the period taken into account by the assessment of the extent of the disablement in respect of which it is payable." In *Hultquist* v. *Universal Pattern Co. Ltd.*[22] the Court of Appeal held that the amount of a disablement gratuity which had to be taken into account was half of such proportion of the gratuity as the five-year period, or the unexpired portion thereof, bore to the injured person's expectation of life, or to any lesser period specified as the duration of the gratuity.

" Five years beginning . . . when the cause of action accrued "

A cause of action accrues when the breach of duty has taken place and has caused, or at least initiated the causation of, the harm complained of. This is not necessarily the date when the accident took place, nor when the harm becomes apparent, still less the date when action is brought. Thus if an employer in breach of duty fails to fence machinery, there is no cause of action unless and until some person is actually injured by reason of the failure to fence; only then does that person have a cause of action. But if the employer fails to provide respirators and a worker by reason thereof

16 [1956] 1 Q.B. 73.
17 [1953] 1 Q.B. 617.
18 National Insurance (Industrial Injuries) Act 1965, s. 11 (4).
19 National Insurance Act 1965, s. 21 (2).
20 National Insurance (Industrial Injuries) Act 1965, s. 12 (3).
21 1948 Act, s. 2 (6) (*c*).
22 [1960] 2 Q.B. 467.

inhales dust and contracts pneumoconiosis, a cause of action then accrues, though he may not appreciate the injury nor claim damages therefor for months or years thereafter. Just as the *terminus a quo* for the running of a limitation period may have been long before injury was apparent,[23] so the starting date for the period of national insurance benefits may have been long before injury was apparent. " A cause of action accrues as soon as a wrongful act has caused personal injury beyond what can be regarded as negligible, even when that injury is unknown to and cannot be discovered by the sufferer; and that further injury arising from the same act at a later date does not give rise to a further cause of action." [24] It has been held that benefits accruing over five years should be taken into account, not merely those accruing for the period of disability.[25]

Successive accidents

Where a workman sustained an injury, and was still in right of benefits therefor when he resumed work and sustained a second accident, received benefit in respect of this accident and recovered damages from his employer for the second accident, it was held that the benefits of which half fell to be deducted were those received during the period after the second accident, there being no evidence that he had right to benefits thereafter arising out of the second accident.[26]

Amount of benefits

The amount of benefit received should be agreed by the parties or, if they cannot agree, they should produce two sets of agreed figures corresponding to the alternative decisions on principle open to the court. It is not for the court to find out and compute the benefits received.[27]

Other social security benefits—unemployment benefit

Various social security benefits are not mentioned in the Law Reform (Personal Injuries) Act 1948, s. 2. It has been held in England [28] that unemployment benefit, to which the plaintiff was entitled by reason of unemployment caused by the defendant's wrong, had to be deducted from damages, because it mitigated the plaintiff's loss. This view does not appear to give any weight to the argument that the Law Reform (Personal Injuries) Act 1948, as amended, by providing that certain stated social security benefits shall be taken into account to a stated extent, may be thought to have provided by implication that other benefits should be

23 *Cf. Cartledge* v. *Jopling* [1963] A.C. 758 (the actual decision in that case has been modified by the Limitation Act 1963).
24 *Cartledge*, *supra*, 771, *per* Lord Reid.
25 *Bond* v. *B.R. Board*, 1970 S.L.T.(Notes) 44.
26 *Dunn* v. *Weir*, 1959 S.L.T.(Sh.Ct.) 13.
27 *Johnston* v. *Nelson Briquetting Co. Ltd.*, 1966 S.L.T.(Sh.Ct.) 49.
28 *Linstedt* v. *Wimborne Steamship Co. Ltd.* (1949) 83 Lloyd's Rep. 19; *Foxley* v. *Olton* [1964] 3 All E.R. 248; *cf. Parsons* v. *B.N.M. Laboratories Ltd.* [1964] 1 Q.B. 95 (wrongful dismissal).

ignored and be recovered in addition to damages. Also the attitude of the House of Lords in *Parry* v. *Cleaver* [29] was against deduction of collateral benefits.

In *Rigley* v. *Remington Rand Ltd.*[30] the Lord Ordinary held that if deduction in respect of payment of unemployment benefit were to be claimed, evidence of a technical or professional character should be adduced vouching such payments. In *McCreadie* v. *Clydebank Co-operative Socy. Ltd.*[31] it was conceded that unemployment benefit should be taken into account, and the Lord Ordinary (Hunter) therefore expressed no view on the matter but reserved his opinion. In *McPherson* v. *Kelsey Roofing Industries Ltd.*[32] it was held by Lord Kissen that such benefit should be deducted but in *Coull* v. *Sutherland* [33] Lord Hunter again refused to take the matter into consideration as it had not been referred to on record. In *Gallagher* v. *I.C.I. Ltd.*[34] Lord Kissen held *obiter* that unemployment benefit should be taken into account, but reserved his opinion as to supplementary allowance. In *Duffy* v. *Sportworks* [35] it was held that supplementary allowance should be deducted.

Retirement pension

In *Hewson* v. *Downs* [36] it was held that a retirement pension from the Ministry of Social Security should not be taken into account. The true justification for this is a person becomes entitled to this benefit by payment of contributions and that it is akin to a contractual benefit such as insurance.

National Assistance (now Supplementary Benefits)

It has been held in England that national assistance grants, now supplementary benefits, should not be deducted from an award of damages.[37] In *Rigley* v. *Remington Rand Ltd.*[38] the Lord Ordinary, without deciding for or against deduction, observed that if deduction were made the result would be that the taxpayer, through the Supplementary Benefits Commission, would be subsidising the loss of wages which it was the duty of the employer to satisfy. If an award of damages is made, a question of supplementary benefits could probably only arise in respect of the period prior to the assessment of damages and it is submitted that deduction should be made, even though the taxpayer has been relieving

[29] (1970) A.C. 1.
[30] 1965 S.L.T. 322.
[31] 1966 S.L.T.(Notes) 22; 1966 S.C. 71.
[32] 1967 S.L.T.(Notes) 93.
[33] 1970 S.L.T.(Notes) 2.
[34] 1970 S.L.T.(Notes) 41; see also *Hill* v. *Cunningham* [1968] N.I. 58.
[35] 1971 S.L.T.(Notes) 19.
[36] [1969] 3 All E.R. 193, following principle of *Parry* v. *Cleaver* [1970] A.C. 1.
[37] *Eldridge* v. *Videtta* (1964) 108 Sol.Jo. 137; *Foxley*, *supra*.
[38] 1965 S.L.T. 322. Lord Kissen also reserved his opinion on this point in *Gallagher* v. *I.C.I. Ltd.*, 1970 S.L.T.(Notes) 41.

the wrongdoer, unless the court makes an award without deduction but on condition that the claimant repays the Ministry of Social Security.[39]

Foreign social security payments

Payments received by way of social security from a foreign authority are not affected by the provisions of the 1948 Act, s. 2. Thus it was held in *McGinty* v. *Howard*[40] that sums received from the Irish Ministry of Social Welfare must be deducted in full.

Redundancy payment

In a case founded on breach of contract it has been held that a redundancy payment was analogous to unemployment benefit rather than to retirement pension and must be deducted in calculating damages.[41]

Outlays and Expenses

An injured person is further entitled to recover all pecuniary outlays and expenses reasonably incurred by him, or likely to be reasonably incurred by him in future, the incurring of which has been necessitated by the injuries inflicted. This similarly is divisible into expenses already incurred by the date of assessment of damages, and expenses likely to be incurred. The former can be, and must be, proved, the latter must be estimated but evidence must be given of probable costs as bases for estimation. It is not for the court to estimate or guess.

Medical attendance and treatment

Money spent on medical attendance and treatment is undoubtedly recoverable,[42] and on nursing attendance between the place of injury and the pursuer's home.[43]

The cost of an artificial limb is allowable,[44] as are the cost of a wheelchair, the cost of a specially adapted vehicle for transport, and the cost of adapting a house to a cripple.[45]

Future expenses

Future certain or probable expenses are also recoverable. These would include expenditure on nursing or other attendance and assistance if this is going to be incurred, certainly or probably,[46] or a nominal sum if such

[39] For recovery by the Ministry of sums paid in certain cases see Ministry of Social Security Act 1966, s. 26.

[40] 1969 S.L.T.(Notes) 83.

[41] *Stocks* v. *Magna Merchants* [1973] 2 All E.R. 329.

[42] *McLaurin* v. *N.B. Ry.* (1892) 19 R. 346, 347.

[43] *Schneider* v. *Eisovitch* [1960] 2 Q.B. 430, 438.

[44] *Aitken* v. *Laidlay*, 1938 S.C. 303, 305.

[45] *Povey* v. *Rydal School* [1970] 1 All E.R. 841.

[46] *Roach* v. *Yates* [1938] 1 K.B. 256.

is possibly going to be incurred,[47] the charges for being maintained in a nursing home or hospital, possibly for the whole remainder of the pursuer's expected life,[48] or alternatively the cost of extra laundry and bedding, of special clothing, holidays, and special transport, again possibly for the whole remainder of the pursuer's expected life.[49]

If a spouse, parent or other relative has to give up employment and be paid to look after the victim that is an admissible item of expense[50]; if such a person suffers financial loss by choosing to, or having to, assist the victim, that gives that person a separate claim of damages and is not an admissible element in the victim's own claim, unless there has been an undertaking or understanding that the victim will pay for such services out of damages.[51]

Other expenses which, if justifiable in the circumstances, would be allowable would be extra domestic help, extra help with the garden, moving house,[52] a different car, and so on.

Expenses diminished by other savings

Expenses necessitated by injuries may, however, be counterbalanced or diminished to some extent by savings elsewhere. If the injured pursuer is to be maintained in a nursing home or similar place, a small deduction must be made from the cost of doing so in recognition of the savings made in the cost of housekeeping at home by reason of his absence.[53] In *Shearman* v. *Folland*[54] an injured person had lived in hotels and, in consequence of her injuries, had to spend a long period in nursing homes at greater expense; the court held that the two payments were not *in pari materia* and that the nursing home expenses were recoverable without deduction, but that a deduction should be made in respect of the cost of food, which would have been incurred, wherever the plaintiff had lived. Only ordinary living expenses can be deducted and if the victim had in fact lived in a club or hotel the wrongdoer cannot deduct the whole of his previous living expenses.[55]

No deduction by reason of existence of National Health Service facilities

By the Law Reform (Personal Injuries) Act 1948, s. 2 (4) " in an action of damages for personal injuries (including any such action arising out of a contract) there shall be disregarded, in determining the reasonableness of any expenses, the possibility of avoiding those expenses or part of them by

[47] *Harris* v. *Bright's Asphalt Contractors* [1953] 1 Q.B. 617. *cf. Cunningham* v. *Harrison* [1973] 3 W.L.R. 97.
[48] *Fletcher* v. *Autocar & Transporters Ltd.* [1968] 2 Q.B. 822; *Mitchell* v. *Mulholland* [1971] 2 All E.R. 1205.
[49] *Povey* v. *Rydal School Governors* [1970] 1 All E.R. 841.
[50] *Roach* v. *Yates* [1938] 1 K.B. 256.
[51] *McCallum* v. *Paterson*, 1968 S.C. 280, 283.
[52] *Cf. McCallum* v. *Paterson*, 1969 S.C. 85, 92; *George* v. *Pinnock* [1973] 1 W.L.R. 118.
[53] *Fletcher, supra*; *Mitchell, supra*, 1216.
[54] [1950] 2 K.B. 43.
[55] *Shearman, supra*, 47, *per* Asquith L.J.

taking advantage of facilities available under the National Health Service Act 1946, or the National Health Service (Scotland) Act 1947, or of any corresponding facilities in Northern Ireland." Accordingly if an injured person in fact has had private treatment he is still entitled to recover the proved cost. But if he has in fact been cared for under the National Health Service he is not entitled to any award. In *Harris* v. *Bright's Asphalt Contractors* [56] it was said that this provision did not enact that a plaintiff should be entitled to recover expenses which in fact he would never incur, but that the court must still have regard to the possibility that some expense might be incurred for nursing attendance in the future outwith the National Health Service. Where a victim has in fact been cared for under the National Health Service it is thought that he is not entitled to damages for future expenditure on private care unless it is established that he is going to be, or likely to be, transferred to an institution where expenditure will be incurred.

Collateral benefits in relation to expenses

Though the matter has been little discussed in cases problems of the deductibility or not of certain benefits may arise in relation to expenses. It is probable that if the pursuer is entitled to recover part or all of his medical expenses from a provident fund or insurance company, no deduction should be made as he has paid for the benefit under contract.[57] If medical or other expenses are paid by a person morally, or even legally, obliged to do so, as by a parent, spouse or employer, the injured person cannot claim in respect thereof and no deduction should be made from the damages on that account, but the person paying may have an independent claim for these expenses. Nor should any deduction be made if the pursuer's expenses have been paid voluntarily by a third party; if the pursuer is morally obliged to repay full damages should be awarded with a condition of making repayment.[58]

Unreasonable expenditure on treatment

Expenditure on medical or surgical attention and treatment may be disallowed if or in so far as it is unreasonable in the circumstances. What is reasonable and what is unreasonable or unnecessary is entirely a question of fact. Treatment is not unreasonable merely because it is expensive or unusual or unsuccessful. An injured person is entitled to act on the advice of his medical and other advisers, and to recover the cost of following their advice, even though it be held in the end of the day that the treatment was unnecessary, ill-advised, or unsuccessful. It might be otherwise if the injured person acted on the advice of some quack or if, considering the advice he had had, no reasonable person would have taken the course he did.[59]

56 [1953] 1 Q.B. 617, 635.
57 *Cf. Bradburn* v. *G.W. Ry.* (1874) L.R. 10 Ex. 1; *Parry* v. *Cleaver* [1970] A.C. 1.
58 *Dennis* v. *L.P.T.B.* [1948] 1 All E.R. 779; *Parry, supra.*
59 *Rubens* v. *Walker*, 1946 S.C. 215.

Loss of or damage to property

Financial loss by reason of loss of or damage to property in the incident which caused physical injury, such as damage to clothing, or jewellery, money and clothing lost when a ship was sunk in collision,[60] is, properly speaking, a distinct ground of action and not merely a separate head of patrimonial loss for personal injuries.[61]

Awards to Relatives of Injured Persons

It is settled that one person cannot recover solatium for loss resulting from injuries suffered by another; the person directly injured alone has a right of action.[62] Nor can one recover for loss of services caused to him by reason of injury directly suffered by another.[63]

But it is not necessarily the case that one person cannot recover damages for financial loss or outlays and expenses incurred by him in consequence of the injuries to another. If a man is injured and his wife has to give up work to nurse him, can she recover her loss of earnings? If a wife is injured, she certainly can recover solatium for her own injuries and damages for her own loss of earnings, if any; but can her husband recover for the cost of employing a housekeeper during her incapacity, or for the cost of her medical treatment which he has defrayed? The question is as to the extent of the duty of care owed by the wrongdoer; he should reasonably have foreseen that his conduct, assuming it to be lacking in due care for the safety of persons within the ambit of the duty, might directly injure one person; should he not be held also to have foreseen that he might in consequence cause expenses or other financial loss to a spouse or parent of the person directly injured? Divergent answers have been given to this problem in different cases.

In *Murphy* v. *Baxter's Bus Services Ltd.*[64] a married woman, injured in a bus accident, claimed damages for her injuries and alleged further that, as she was by reason thereof unable to look after her children, her husband, instead of engaging domestic help, temporarily gave up work to look after the children and thereby incurred loss of earnings. The Lord Ordinary held these averments relevant, following *Thomson* v. *Angus County Council.*[65] *Murphy*[64] and *Thomson*[65] were, however, overruled in *Edgar* v. *Lord Advocate*[66] where the pursuer averred that, while he was off work by reason of injuries, his wife had had to discontinue full-time employment and, in lieu of engaging domestic assistance, attend to him and do only part-time work, with a consequent loss of wages. The wife was not a party to the action. The court held this claim irrelevant, as the loss alleged was

[60] *e.g. Lewis* v. *Laird Line*, 1925 S.L.T. 316, 320.
[61] Chap. 57, *infra.*
[62] *Cf. Quin* v. *Greenock Tramways*, 1926 S.C. 544; *Young* v. *Ormiston*, 1936 S.L.T. 79.
[63] *Allan* v. *Barclay* (1863) 2 M. 873; *Reavis* v. *Clan Line*, 1925 S.C. 725.
[64] 1962 S.C. 589.
[65] 1962 S.C. 590, n.
[66] 1965 S.C. 67. *Cf. Robertson* v. *Glasgow Corpn.*, 1965 S.L.T. 143.

not one sustained by the pursuer and he had no title to present his wife's claim. Procedurally this is understandable. It seems, however, anomalous that if the pursuer had himself engaged and paid for domestic assistance the cost would have been recoverable, and that if he had made up, or promised to make up, from any damages recovered, to his wife her loss of earnings, that would have been recoverable,[67] but that because he had not done so the loss, though actually incurred, was irrecoverable; moreover, to say that the wife rendered her services gratuitously when she had had to limit her employment and consequently her contribution to the household finances is hardly accurate. The only safe course in such a case is for the other spouse to make a separate claim in the same action [68] for financial loss suffered in consequence of the accident.

In *McBay* v. *Hamlett* [69] the pursuer's wife was injured by the fault of the defender and the pursuer sustained a continuing financial loss by reason of the need, in consequence of the wife's injuries, to employ domestic help. This claim was held relevant.

> " If the victim is a married woman who is thereby disabled from discharging what would be her normal domestic tasks, and as a consequence her husband is put to expense or incurs pecuniary loss, I think that the relationship between husband and wife is so close that such loss or additional expense is just something which a delinquent might reasonably be expected to have in view in the event of his causing injury to a married woman living in family with her husband. This has long been recognised in the case where it is death that has prevented the wife from performing her domestic duties. If this is the case in the event of death, why should the fact that the wife is not killed, but only totally disabled, alter the right of her husband." [70]

McBay was cited but not discussed in *Edgar*; if it was wrongly decided it is surprising that *Edgar* did not say so.

McBay v. *Hamlett* was, however, questioned by Lord Keith in *Jack* v. *McDougall* [71] where the husband was injured and his wife claimed that she had lost earnings by having to give up work for a time to nurse him and had incurred expenses in visiting him in hospital. Lord Keith's view was that the defender's breach of duty to the husband conferred no rights of action for anything on anyone else and he dismissed the wife's claim [72] but, with hesitation, allowed to go to proof the husband's claim for loss of earnings, so far as founded on loss to the family income by reason of the cessation of the wife's contributions. It is hard to see why if a defender is deemed to have foreseen that, if he kills a person, that person may leave

67 In *Dryburgh* v. *Gilbert*, 1967 S.L.T.(Notes) 28, a claim by an injured person for wages which a relative acting as housekeeper " expected " to receive was held irrelevant.

68 *McCallum* v. *Paterson*, 1968 S.L.T.(Notes) 98.

69 1963 S.C. 282. The report does not deal with the wife's claim. It must be assumed that she made a separate claim in her own name, at least for solatium.

70 *Ibid.* 286, *per* Lord Cameron.

71 1972 S.L.T.(Notes) 81. See also *McCallum* v. *Paterson*, 1968 S.L.T.(Notes) 98.

72 It is settled that in such a case the wife has no claim for solatium.

dependants with a claim for loss of support, but, if he merely injures a person, he is not deemed to have foreseen that that person's dependants may incur loss of support and expenses by having to look after the victim. If the victim has undertaken to make good to his wife loss of earnings resulting from having to look after him, he can doubtless recover the sum he will have to pay her.[73]

The same principle was applied to the parent and child relationship in *Soutar* v. *Mulhern*,[74] where the loss consisted in medical expenses incurred by the father in respect of illness contracted by the child due to the defender's fault. This is clearly justifiable by the father's duty to provide medical care for his children.

It is, of course, clear that if a spouse or parent truly renders services gratuitously, nothing can be recovered merely because those services would otherwise have cost money; no loss has been sustained and no damages are due. If a wife, who had not been earning, nurses her injured husband, nothing can be recovered merely because, if he had employed and paid for a nurse, he could have recovered the expense thereof.

To pursue a claim of this kind the person sustaining the financial loss must be a pursuer in the action, either alone [75] or along with the spouse claiming damages independently for his or her personal injuries. Further, it may be that a claim is competent not only by those relatives who naturally and as a matter of moral if not of legal obligation, incur expense but by third parties. If a Good Samaritan or *negotiorum gestor* incurs expense, should it not be recoverable?

Loss of consortium

A further related question is whether, if one spouse is injured by the fault of a third party, the other spouse can claim for loss of consortium, that is for loss to the claiming (not the injured) spouse of the affection, consolation, companionship, mutual assistance and other factors which make normal married life pleasant.[76] Such a claim is competent in England,[77] but there the action is founded largely on loss of services, is competent only to a husband and not to a wife,[78] is a relic of the husband's former quasi-proprietary interest in his wife, and may not lie for impairment of consortium but only for total, even though temporary, loss of consortium.[79] In Australia, however, the High Court has held that damages might be given for impairment of consortium as well as for total loss of consortium.[80] None of these grounds is a good basis for a claim

[73] *Cf. Doonan* v. *S.M.T. Co.*, 1950 S.C. 136.
[74] 1907 S.C. 723. *Cf.* also *Higgins* v. *Burton*, 1967 S.L.T.(Notes) 61.
[75] *Cf. McCallum* v. *Paterson*, 1968 S.C. 280, 283.
[76] *Cf.* the elements of consortium discussed in *Best* v. *Samuel Fox & Co.* [1952] A.C. 716.
[77] *Hare* v. *B.T.C.* [1956] 1 All E.R. 578; *Lawrence* v. *Biddle* [1966] 2 Q.B. 504; *Cutts* v. *Chumley* [1967] 2 All E.R. 89.
[78] The 11th Report of the English Law Commission recommended that it should be available to a wife also.
[79] *Best* v. *Samuel Fox & Co.* [1952] A.C. 716; so too *Spaight and Spaight* v. *Dondon* [1961] I.R. 201.
[80] *Toohey* v. *Hollier* [1955] A.L.R. 302.

under Scots law, but other grounds exist. A claim for loss of consortium does not appear ever to have been admitted in Scotland, and there appears to be no precedent for such a claim, but these facts are not at all conclusive if such a claim is justifiable on principle, and it is submitted that it is. In *McBay* v. *Hamlett* [81] no claim was advanced on this ground. The question is: can there be said to be any duty owed to persons closely related to the one directly injured, who may suffer in consequence of the injuries to him? It is submitted that such a claim is justifiable on the principle that, if a person acts in breach of duty, he must be taken to foresee that he may not only injure the person directly harmed by his fault, but also, albeit in a different way, injure persons so closely related that they will naturally suffer grief and hurt feelings, and/or patrimonial loss, and/or incur outlays and expenses in consequence of the injuries.[82] It is accepted that if a defender's fault causes the death of a person, grief and/or patrimonial loss and/or expenses caused to a spouse or parent or child are not unforeseeable nor too remote a consequence to justify claims of damages by them.[83] That being so, why should it be unforeseeable or too remote a consequence if the defender's fault renders the person immediately injured not dead but a helpless invalid, or insane, or otherwise incapable of continuing to consort as husband or wife in any reasonable sense of that term? Indeed in the latter case the loss sustained by the spouse of the injured person may be even worse than in a case of death, by having to contemplate the wrecked life, and by not being able to remarry and build another life as the widowed may do.[84] Is nothing recoverable by a spouse who has his or her life wrecked by injuries to the other spouse? Can a rational distinction be drawn between loss of consortium by the death of one's spouse and loss of consortium if the spouse is reduced to a helpless but living creature? A claim should certainly be competent.[85]

The courts have declined to extend the claim competent to a surviving spouse on the death of his or her partner from grief and distress to cover injury to health [86] but this is a quite distinct kind of claim.

Awards not to be confused

If competent, damages for loss of consortium must be carefully limited to compensation to the spouse or parent or child for his or her consequential loss, and kept apart from compensation to the other, directly injured, party, for his or her immediate loss. Thus on the facts of *Best* v. *Samuel*

81 1963 S.C. 282, 285.
82 The case of outlays and expenses seems to have been accepted in *McBay, supra*.
83 *Eisten* v. *N.B. Ry.* (1870) 8 M. 980; Chap. 54, *infra*.
84 If the facts amount to incurable insanity divorce would be possible.
85 Suppose the cases of A and B and their wives involved in a car accident for which the other driver is solely liable; if A's wife is killed, he can recover damages, for solatium and loss of support and outlays caused by the death; if B's wife is physically and mentally wrecked, she can recover damages for her injuries but can B recover nothing for the ruin of his marriage? Consider the position of the pursuer's husband in *McCallum* v. *Paterson*, 1969 S.C. 85.
86 *Kirkpatrick* v. *Anderson*, 1948 S.C. 251; *Nicolson* v. *Cursiter*, 1959 S.C. 350.

Fox & Co.[87] B was injured at work and, *inter alia*, rendered impotent. His wife claimed for the loss of marital relations and the opportunity of having further children. In such a case the wife would, it is submitted, be entitled under Scots law to a sum in solatium for these losses. In *Lawrence* v. *Biddle* [88] L's wife was injured, lost interest in cooking and housework and in going out with him, and L was held entitled to damages for having had extra housework and cooking to do for himself. In *Cutts* v. *Chumley* [89] C's wife was badly injured physically and mentally, and reduced to the level of a child of three to five. She would never again be able to be a wife in any sense of the term, but had an expectation of life of twenty-five years. The husband was awarded £5,200 for loss of consortium, of which £200 was for loss of society and £5,000 for loss of services.[90]

Who have title to sue?

A question also arises, assuming such a claim to be competent, of which relatives have a title to sue for loss of consortium. It may be confined to spouses, as it is questionable if the idea of consortium can be applied to the relationship of parent and child or to more remote relations, but the ruin of family life caused by serious injuries to one parent could have serious psychological consequences for children also. Should all those who have a title to sue for the death of a relative [91] not also have a title to sue for loss caused them by the ruined life of such a relative?

Amount of award

A further difficult question is whether, assuming such a claim is competent, an award should be nominal or modest or substantial. In the case where a spouse is killed, the award to the survivor for solatium is modest, an acknowledgment of pain and grief, which, however sharp at the time, diminishes with time, rather than compensation for specific loss.[92] But in the case where one spouse's life is wrecked, the other spouse will suffer continuing sorrow and grief, possibly for years, and a token or modest acknowledgment is not adequate for a loss which may cause continuing anguish for years. The sorrow and anguish and torture to feelings may be far greater than if the injured spouse had been killed. A modest acknowledgment will not suffice, though on the other hand there is admittedly no identifiable pecuniary loss to be compensated.[93] It is submitted that in serious cases the award should be on the basis of substantial acknowledgment, and should amount to several thousand pounds. In *Mitchell* v.

[87] [1952] A.C. 716.
[88] [1966] 2 Q.B. 504.
[89] [1967] 2 All E.R. 89.
[90] It is not suggested that the head of loss of services would be relevant in Scots law: see *Reavis* v. *Clan Line Steamers*, 1925 S.C. 725.
[91] Chap. 54, *infra*.
[92] Chap. 54, *infra*.
[93] The cost of *e.g.* engaging a housekeeper, would be recoverable as an expense necessitated by the injury, not under the head of loss of consortium.

Mulholland[94] a man of 32 suffered severe head injuries, intellectual deterioration and personality change. He could be expected to live till 71 but would have to be constantly maintained in hospital. In such circumstances is his wife not entitled to a substantial sum for the utter ruin of her married life? She would have been better to have been widowed.

AWARDS TO EXECUTORS

If an individual has suffered injuries by the fault of another and has subsequently died,[1] his executor may take up and continue an action for damages commenced [2] (but not if merely intimated but not commenced [3]) by the deceased before his death, or may himself initiate and pursue an action for the deceased's patrimonial loss suffered by reason of the defender's fault, even if the deceased had not himself initiated such an action,[4] but may not initiate or pursue an action for solatium to the deceased for injuries suffered by him, before his death, by reason of the defender's fault.[5] In short, if an injured person dies his claim for solatium dies with him, but his claim for patrimonial loss, being loss to the estate, survives, and if he had sued before his death, his action may be continued by his executor *quoad* both elements.

Any claim by an executor is inconsistent with a claim made by entitled surviving relatives for the loss to them caused by the death in that both claims cannot be pursued in respect of the same period of time,[6] but the executor may make or continue a claim for the period between the date of injury and the date of death and, provided the death was caused by the defender's fault, the entitled relatives may claim for the loss thereby caused to them thereafter.[7] Alternatively the executor may abandon his claim and allow the relatives to make their claim.[8]

Measure of damages recoverable by executor

In any such case the executor may recover only under such heads of damages as the deceased himself could have done,[9] and the awards made must be limited by regard to the period of survival. In effect the estate is claiming what the deceased could have recovered as at the date of death.

94 [1971] 2 All E.R. 1205.

1 The death may or may not have been a consequence of the injuries.

2 *Neilson* v. *Rodger* (1854) 16 D. 325; *Darling* v. *Gray* (1891) 19 R.(H.L.) 31; *Smith* v. *Stewart*, 1960 S.C. 329.

3 *Leigh's Exrx.* v. *Caledonian Ry.*, 1913 S.C. 838, overruled in *Smith* v. *Stewart, supra.*

4 *Smith* v. *Stewart, supra*; *Smith* v. *Stewart*, 1961 S.C. 91.

5 *Auld* v. *Shairp* (1875) 2 R. 191; *Bern's Exor.* v. *Montrose Asylum* (1893) 20 R. 859; *Boyce's Exor.* v. *McDougall* (1903) 5 F. 452; *Stewart* v. *L.M.S. Ry.*, 1943 S.C.(H.L.) 19; *Smith* v. *Stewart*, 1960 S.C. 329; *cf. Muir's Tr.* v. *Braidwood*, 1958 S.C. 169; *Parker's Exors.* v. *Esso Petroleum Co.*, 1971 S.L.T.(Sh.Ct.) 28.

6 *Darling* v. *Gray, supra*; *McCann's Exrx.* v. *Wright's Insulations Ltd.* 1965 S.L.T. (Sh.Ct) 19.

7 *McGhie* v. *B.T.C.*, 1964 S.L.T. 25; *Gray* v. *N.B. Steel Foundry Co.*, 1968 S.L.T.(Notes) 95.

8 *Bruce* v. *Stephen*, 1957 S.L.T. 78.

9 *Reid* v. *Lanarkshire Traction Co.*, 1934 S.C. 79; *Traynor's Exrx.* v. *Bairds & Scottish Steel Ltd.*, 1957 S.C. 311.

Thus solatium is due but for the period between injury and death only,[10] and any award for loss of expectation of life is similarly limited by the fact that the injured person suffered the realisation of the shortening of his own life for only a short time.[12] Under the latter head the court or jury is not " entitled to assess damages on the footing that the pursuer should not get less for shortening of life than for serious and permanent injury. Nor would they be entitled to give a sum based on the shortening of his expectation of life, with subsequent earlier cessation of earning capacity, less the anticipated diminution in the cost of maintenance during the period between the anticipated earlier date of death and the date of his expectation had the accident not taken place. What in my view they would have been entitled to consider would have been the additional handicap on his enjoyment of life due to the anticipation of earlier death—in effect an additional award of solatium." [13]

Patrimonial loss may be recovered in the shape of earnings lost between the date of injury and of death,[14] whether or not the death was due to the accident,[15] but nothing can be recovered for loss of earning capacity or future earnings since, *ex hypothesi*, the deceased could never have earned any such sums.

Expenses incurred between the date of injury and the date of death may also be recovered.[16] Damages may also be recovered by an executor for other patrimonial loss, such as damage to a vehicle. But the deceased's funeral expenses are not recoverable in an executor's claim, not being an expense which the deceased could himself have claimed.[16a]

It is irrelevant that the deceased had relatives, such as wife and child, dependent on him.[17] If dependants wish to recover for the loss to *them* in consequence of the death, the action must be by *them*,[18] and the claim not be brought into an action by the deceased's estate for loss sustained by the deceased.

Disposal of award recovered by executor

Any award of damages made to an executor belongs to the deceased's estate and not to either the executor as an individual or to any relative or relatives. The award falls into the estate, is liable in payment of debts and death duties, if applicable, and falls to be disposed of in accordance with the rules of intestate succession or the provisions of the deceased's will.

10 *Reid* v. *Lanarkshire Traction Co.*, 1934 S.C. 79.

12 *Reid, supra*; *Traynor's Exrx.* v. *Bairds & Scottish Steel Ltd.*, 1957 S.C. 311.

13 *Reid, supra*, 81–82, *per* Lord Wark. The last sentence must be read in light of the later dicta in the House of Lords in *Benham* v. *Gambling* [1941] A.C. 157.

14 *Neilson* v. *Rodger* (1854) 16 D. 325; *Reid* v. *Lanarkshire Traction Co.*, *supra*; *Smith* v. *Stewart*, 1961 S.C. 91.

15 *Russell's Exrx.* v. *British Railways Board*, 1965 S.C. 422.

16 *Neilson, supra.*

16a *McEnaney* v. *Caledonian Ry.*, 1913, 2 S.L.T. 293. Funeral expenses can be recovered by surviving dependants: *Tran* v. *Road Haulage Executive*, 1952 S.L.T. (Notes) 58, *Drummond* v. *B.R. Board*, 1965 S.L.T. (Notes) 82.

17 *Reid* v. *Lanarkshire Traction Co., supra.*

18 Chap. 54, *infra.*

INTEREST

Under the Interest on Damages (Scotland) Acts 1958 and 1971,[19] where a court decerns for payment of " a sum which consists of or includes damages or solatium in respect of personal injuries " the court must, unless it finds special reasons for refusing to do so, give interest on the damages or solatium or on such part of each as it considers appropriate.

[19] Examined in Chap. 23, *supra*.

CHAPTER 54

DAMAGES FOR DEATH OF A RELATIVE

GENERALLY

WHERE a person has, by conduct in breach of legal duty, caused the death of another, it is well-settled that certain surviving relatives of the deceased have title to sue, in their own right and not by virtue of any inheritance or transmission of a right of action from the deceased, for damages for the loss caused to each of them by the death.[1] The wrongdoer is deemed to have foreseen that, if he caused the death of the now deceased, that deceased was likely to be survived by certain relatives who would suffer grief and loss by reason of the death, and their loss is not too remote a consequence to be actionable by them.

In *Clarke* v. *Carfin Coal Co.*[2] Lord Watson said that this right of action did not rest on any definite principle but was " an arbitrary exception from the general law which excludes all such actions, founded in inveterate custom, and having no other ratio to support it." The last words seem quite incorrect, in that the right of action can well be justified on the principle of imputing to the wrongdoer foresight of the fact that, if he caused the death of a person, he would thereby cause loss to certain close relatives of the deceased, even though he did not actually know of their existence. In *Dickson* v. *N.C.B.*[2a] Lord Justice-Clerk Thomson said that " the recognition of the right (of relatives to sue) appears to rest on inveterate practice rather than on legal principle." It is nevertheless justifiable on principle, as well as by precedent and expediency.

This right of action is an independent one, not one derived from any right of action vested in the now deceased by any process of succession or transmission.[3]

When action arises

The right of action arises on the death of the person primarily injured. If he was killed outright, or, having been injured, died without having initiated any action for his injuries, no right of action was vested in him, and his executor cannot sue for any solatium he might have claimed,[4] but may sue for any patrimonial loss his estate may have suffered by reason

[1] *Eisten* v. *N.B. Ry.*(1870) 8 M. 980. Changes have been proposed; see Scottish Law Commission Report on the Law relating to Damages for injuries causing Death (Scot Law Com. No. 31, 1973).
[2] (1891) 18 R.(H.L.) 63, 65.
[2a] 1957 S.C. 157, 162.
[3] *Davidson* v. *Sprengel*, 1909 S.C. 566, 570; *Naftalin* v. *L.M.S. Ry.*, 1933 S.C. 259, 265, 273; *McKay* v. *Scottish Airways*, 1948 S.C. 254, 264.
[4] *Stewart* v. *L.M.S. Ry.*, 1943 S.C.(H.L.) 19; *Smith* v. *Stewart*, 1960 S.C. 329.

of the breach of duty to him, such as for damage to his vehicle, or loss of earnings suffered by him between the moment of injury and the time of death.[5] If he survived the injury long enough to commence an action of damages for those injuries, his executor can after his death carry on the now deceased's action to the effect of recovering for the benefit of the estate an award under such heads as the deceased could himself have claimed under, but quantified by reference to the period for which he survived only.[6] An executor can never recover anything in respect of future, *i.e.* post-mortem, loss to anyone.

Interaction of claim by deceased or his executor and claim by surviving relatives

A claim for damages for personal injury initiated by an injured person and carried on after his death by his executor is inconsistent with a claim by the surviving relatives of the deceased in that both cannot be pursued in respect of losses covering the same period.[7] But an executor's claim may be continued claiming for the benefit of the estate damages for the period down to the date of death, and a relatives' claim also made claiming for their own benefit damages for the period after the date of death without any inconsistency,[8] and an executor's claim may be abandoned so as not to prejudice a relatives' claim.[9]

Persons having title to sue in relatives' action

The class of persons having title to sue was defined in the leading case [10] as follows: " In the law of Scotland . . . a claim of this kind is sustained at the instance of a wife for the death of her husband, a husband for the death of his wife, a parent for the death of his child, and a child for the death of his parent, when the death has been caused by delict or culpa. . . . It appears to me that the true foundation of this claim is partly nearness of relationship between the deceased and the party claiming on account of the death, and partly the existence during life, as between the deceased and the claimant, of a mutual obligation of support in case of necessity." In the first place the range of persons entitled to sue has been extended both by decisions and by statute. In the second place, failing precedent, whether a pursuer is entitled to claim or not depends on whether he could, in case of necessity, have claimed aliment from the deceased. That he was in fact being alimented is unnecessary. Thus a father has been held entitled to sue averring that his son's death deprived him of a contingent right of support [11] or that he had lost support in the form of voluntary, though not absolutely necessary, support from his son.[12]

5 *Smith* v. *Stewart*, 1961 S.C. 91; *Russell's Exrx.* v. *British Railways Board*, 1965 S.C. 422.
6 *Reid* v. *Lanarkshire Traction Co.*, 1934 S.C. 79.
7 *Darling* v. *Gray* (1892) 19 R.(H.L.) 31; *McCann's Exrx.* v. *Wright's Insulation Ltd.*, 1965 S.L.T.(Sh.Ct.) 19.
8 *McGhie* v. *B.T.C.*, 1964 S.L.T. 25.
9 *Bruce* v. *Stephen*, 1957 S.L.T. 78; *Gray* v. *N.B. Steel Foundry Ltd.*, 1968 S.L.T.(Notes) 95.
10 *Eisten* v. *N.B. Ry.* (1870) 8 M. 980, 984, *per* L.P. Inglis.
11 *Sagar* v. *N.C.B.*, 1955 S.C. 424.
12 *Dickson* v. *N.C.B.*, 1957 S.C. 157.

Accordingly persons have title to sue for damages for the death of relatives only if within limited ranges of relationship with the deceased. It has been recognised that a person may sue for the death of his wife,[13] or of her husband,[14] even if separated,[15] or even if he or she has remarried since the death, or taken up cohabitation with another,[16] of his or her parent of either sex,[17] even if the relationship were adoptive [18] or illegitimate,[19] or by legitimation, of his or her legitimate grandparent of either sex, provided that no intermediate person, against whom a claim of support in case of necessity would have lain in priority to that grandparent, such as an intervening parent, survives,[20] of his or her more remote legitimate ascendant, subject to the same proviso, of his,[21] her [21] or their [21] child, whether legitimate, legitimated,[22] illegitimate,[23] or adopted,[24] even if posthumous [25] or his, her or their legitimate grandchild or more remote descendant, subject to the same proviso of there being no intermediate person against whom a claim for support would have lain in priority. No claim lies for the death of a child who is not a child of the pursuer, such as a child of the pursuer's spouse by a previous marriage, there being no legal obligation of support in case of need in such a case, but in such a case the other spouse has a claim along with the other parent, if still alive, of the child.

No claim lies at the instance of, or for the death of, a former spouse,[26] a paramour or mistress, brother,[27] sister,[28] or more remote collateral, nor for the death of any other person who could not, in case of necessity, have been sued by the pursuer for aliment.

It is noteworthy that there are not different groups of persons entitled to sue for solatium and for loss of support. Particular relatives either are or are not entitled to sue; if they are entitled to sue they may claim under

13 *Eisten* v. *N.B. Ry.* (1870) 8 M. 980, 984; *McKinlay* v. *Glasgow Corpn.*, 1951 S.C. 495.

14 *e.g. Black* v. *Cadell* (1804) Mor. 13905; *Brown* v. *Macgregor*, Feb. 26, 1813, F.C.; *Eisten, supra*; *Blaikie* v. *B.T.C.*, 1961 S.C. 44.

15 *Cf. Donnelly* v. *Donnelly*, 1959 S.C. 97; *Jack* v. *Jack*, 1961 S.C. 24; *Beveridge* v. *Beveridge*, 1963 S.L.T. 248; *Longster* v. *British Road Services*, 1967 S.L.T.(Notes) 9 (where wife had been defending action for divorce).

16 *Donnelly* v. *Glasgow Corpn.*, 1949 S.L.T. 248.

17 *e.g. Mc Rae* v. *Glasgow Corpn.*, 1915, 2 S.L.T. 94; *Mill* v. *Dundas*, 1919, 2 S.L.T. 65; *Rankin* v. *Waddell*, 1949 S.C. 555; *Kelly* v. *Glasgow Corpn.*, 1951 S.C.(H.L.) 15.

18 Law Reform (Misc. Prov.) (Sc.) Act 1940, s. 2 (1).

19 *Ibid.* s. 2 (2).

20 *Hanlin* v. *Melrose* (1899) 1 F. 1012; *Cooper* v. *Fife Coal Co.*, 1907 S.C. 564; *Ewart* v. *R. & W. Ferguson*, 1932 S.C. 277; see also *Gay's Tutrix* v. *Gay's Tr.*, 1953 S.L.T. 278.

21 *Horn* v. *N.B. Ry.* (1878) 5 R. 1055; Law Reform (Damages and Solatium) (Scotland) Act 1962, s. 1 (1); *Kelly* v. *Nuttall*, 1965 S.C. 427; *Mackenzie* v. *Macleod* 1973 S.L.T. (Notes) 64.

22 *McLean* v. *Glasgow Corpn.*, 1933 S.L.T. 396; see also *NcNeill* v. *McGregor* (1901) 4 F. 123.

23 Law Reform (Damages and Solatium) (Scotland) Act 1962, s. 2, overruling *Weir* v. *Coltness Iron Co.* (1889) 16 R. 614; *Clarke* v. *Carfin Coal Co.* (1891) 18 R.(H.L.) 63 and *Clement* v. *Bell* (1899) 1 F. 924.

24 Law Reform (Misc. Prov.) (Sc.) Act 1940, s. 2 (1).

25 *Moorcraft* v. *Alexander*, 1946 S.C. 466.

26 *Cf. Hemmens* v. *B.T.C.*, 1955 S.L.T.(Notes) 48.

27 *Greenhorn* v. *Addie* (1855) 17 D. 860; *Eisten* v. *N.B. Ry.* (1870) 8 M. 980; *Weir* v. *Coltness Iron* (1889) 16 R. 614, 617.

28 *Eisten, supra.*

both the heads of solatium and of loss of support, though under either head a nil award may be proper, and may be made; if they are not entitled to sue, they may not sue under either head.

The Carriage by Air Act 1961, s. 11 (6), makes the statutory liability thereunder include liability to such persons as are entitled, apart from the Act, to sue the carrier (whether for patrimonial damage or solatium or both) in respect of a death.

In many cases there are several or many relatives each of whom has a title to sue. In such a case each must be named as a pursuer, and there must be a conclusion for a sum of damages in respect of each. If the defenders make a tender it must be a tender to each pursuer, and not a lump sum to be apportioned.[29]

Though a person is one of those entitled to sue, evaluation of the worth of his or her claim depends on the quality of the relationship. A wife may still sue for her husband's death though in desertion or guilty of adultery or about to be divorced, but what value will be set on her claim will depend on what she may be thought to have suffered in feelings and by way of loss of support by reason of the death. Either or both of these elements may be held of negligible value.[30]

All entitled pursuers to concur in one action

It is an established rule of practice that where, as frequently happens, more than one person is entitled to sue, all must concur in one action,[31] to avoid the defender being troubled by a number of claims, to avoid the possibility of the evidence having to be elicited more than once, and to enable the court or jury, in assessing damages, to view the claims in relation to one another and, where appropriate, to consider claims, such as by a widow and her children, as related parts of a general family claim.[32] If any entitled relatives' whereabouts are unknown, the action should be intimated to them by calling them as defenders for their interest.[33] If any decline to concur in the action it may proceed, on evidence of that fact,[34] at the instance of the others, but the non-concurring relatives' claims are barred thereby for ever.[35]

Claim a family one

The persons having title to sue in an action of this kind are all members

29 *Flanagan* v. *Dempster, Moore & Co.*, 1928 S.C. 308; *McNeil* v. *N.C.B.*, 1966 S.C. 72.

30 *Cf. Longster* v. *B.R.S.*, 1967 S.L.T.(Notes) 9 (wife defending action of divorce); *Gray* v. *Barr* [1971] 2 All E.R. 949 (wife separated: damages halved); *Davies* v. *Taylor* [1972] 3 All E.R. 836 (wife about to be divorced).

31 *Darling* v. *Gray* (1892) 19 R.(H.L.) 31, 32–33; *Pollok* v. *Workman* (1900) 2 F. 354; *Slorach* v. *Kerr*, 1921 S.C. 285; *Mill* v. *Dundas*, 1919, 2 S.L.T. 65; *Thomson* v. *Donaldson*, 1922 S.L.T. 66; *McNeil* v. *N.C.B.*, 1966 S.C. 72, 83.

32 *Kelly* v. *Glasgow Corpn.*, 1951 S.C.(H.L.) 15; *Campbell* v. *West of Scotland Shipbreaking Co.*, 1953 S.C. 173; *Hewitt* v. *West's Gas Improvement Co.*, 1955 S.C. 162.

33 *Smith* v. *Wilsons & Clyde Coal Co.* (1893) 21 R. 162; *Macdonald* v. *Glasgow Corpn.*, 1915, 2 S.L.T. 249.

34 *Pollok, supra*; *Grant* v. *Wood* (1902) 10 S.L.T. 296.

35 *Kinnaird* v. *McLean*, 1942 S.C. 448.

of the same family as the deceased, and the claim is a family claim, not in the sense that a single award is made (because that is not competent) but in the senses that the loss is a single one,[36] though sustained in various degrees by different members of the family, that the losses by, and the awards to, each pursuer must be considered in relation to each other,[37] that the question of inadequacy or excess of the awards must be determined by granting or refusing a new jury trial in respect of all of the claims, not of one or two only,[38] and that when an appellate court is considering whether to interfere or not with awards made the proper comparison is between the aggregate of the sums awarded and the aggregate of the sums which should properly have been awarded.[39] Nevertheless if a tender is made by the defender it must be a tender of a sum to each pursuer, not a lump sum.[40]

Legal basis of relatives' action

The legal basis of the relatives' action is a breach of legal duty owed by the defender not to them but to the now deceased, and all defences which could competently have been adduced, if the action had been brought by the deceased, may be adduced as defences against the claims of the relatives.[41] Similarly all pleas which could have been adduced to limit a claim, if made by the now deceased, may be adduced to limit a claim by his relatives, such as that the harm was too remote from the alleged wrong to be actionable (remoteness of injury) [42] or that the harm had been caused by the deceased's voluntary assumption of the risk,[43] or by his own unwarrantable intervention,[44] or by his own contributory negligence,[45] or by his contractual exclusion of claims,[46] or, doubtless, by his acceptance between the date of injury and of consequent death, of an offer in settlement of his claim.[47] A claim may also be barred by the running of the period of limitation [48] or of prescription.

Claims of damages competent to relatives

In *Eisten* v. *N.B. Ry.*[49] Lord President Inglis said: " This claim may be maintained, although the party raising the action cannot qualify any direct pecuniary loss by the death of his relative. It appears to me that the true foundation of this claim is partly nearness of relationship between

36 *Love* v. *N.C.B.*, 1956 S.C. 459, 462.
37 *Kelly* v. *Glasgow Corpn.*, 1951 S.C.(H.L.) 15; *Campbell* v. *West of Scotland Shipbreaking Co.*, 1953 S.C. 173; *Hewitt* v. *West's Gas Improvement Co.*, 1955 S.C. 162.
38 *Campbell, supra,* not following *Leadbetter* v. *N.C.B.*, 1952 S.C. 19.
39 *Kelly, supra,* 20; *Hewitt, supra,* 166; *Love* v. *N.C.B.*, 1956 S.C. 459.
40 *Flanagan* v. *Dempster, Moore & Co.*, 1928 S.C. 308; *McNeil* v. *N.C.B.*, 1966 S.C. 72.
41 *e.g. McWilliams* v. *Arrol*, 1962 S.C.(H.L.) 70.
42 *e.g. Malcolm* v. *Dickson*, 1951 S.C. 542.
43 *e.g. McWilliams, supra*; *cf. Steel, infra.*
44 *e.g. Steel* v. *Glasgow Iron & Steel Co.*, 1944 S.C. 237.
45 *e.g. McNaughton* v. *Caledonian Ry.* (1858) 21 D. 160.
46 *McKay* v. *Scottish Airways*, 1948 S.C. 254.
47 *Cf. Read* v. *G.E. Ry.* (1868) L.R. 3 Q.B. 555.
48 Prescription and Limitation (Sc.) Act, 1973, ss. 7, 17, 19.
49 (1870) 8 M. 980, 984.

the deceased and the person claiming on account of the death and partly the existence during life, as between the deceased and the claimant, of a mutual obligation of support in case of necessity. On these two considerations in combination our law has held that a person standing in one of these relations to the deceased may sue an action like this for solatium, where he can qualify no real damage, and for pecuniary loss in addition, where such loss can be proved." From this it was deduced that "the only heads under which reparation can be recovered . . . are (1) solatium for lacerated feelings, and (2) damages for the loss of the natural support which the deceased afforded to the pursuer, or might in the future have afforded." [50]

> "The pursuer of an *actio injuriarum* . . . is entitled, on the defender's liability being proved or admitted, to an award in name of solatium for wounded feelings and also to get reparation for such patrimonial loss as may be proved to have been occasioned to the pursuer by the death which gave rise to the action." [51]
>
> "The right which our law affords to certain relatives to claim damages from the person by whose fault another person has been killed is a right which has long been recognised as containing two elements: (1) the element of solatium, and (2) the element of patrimonial loss associated with deprivation of support." [52]

The claim for solatium seems to have been taken over from the action of assythment, itself developed from the payment of money to stop a blood-feud,[53] and the claim for patrimonial loss, for loss of financial support and expenses, to be based on extension of the *actio legis Aquiliae*.

In *Naftalin* v. *L.M.S. Ry.*[54] and *McElroy* v. *McAllister* [55] it was emphasised that a claim for damages based on solatium was a substantive and independent *jus actionis* and not a mere head or item of damages.[56] This has emerged particularly in cases raising problems of international private law, which have brought out, particularly by comparison with English law, that there is nothing corresponding in English law to the Scottish claim for solatium, though to the Scottish common law claim for loss of support there correspond in English law statutory claims under the Fatal Accidents Acts 1846–1959 and the Law Reform (Misc. Prov.) Act 1934.

The practice has long been to award each pursuer damages as a lump sum, covering all relevant heads of claim.[57] But as Lord Carmont has

[50] *Quin* v. *Greenock Tramways Co.*, 1926 S.C. 544, 547. *Cf. Naftalin* v. *L.M.S. Ry.*, 1933 S.C. 259, 264, 269, 272; *McElroy* v. *McAllister*, 1949 S.C. 110; *Hewitt* v. *West's Gas Improvement Co.*, 1955 S.C. 162.

[51] *Smith* v. *Comrie's Exrx.*, 1944 S.C. 499, 500, *per* Lord Mackintosh.

[52] *Kirkpatrick* v. *Anderson*, 1948 S.C. 251, 253, *per* L.P. Cooper.

[53] *Cf.* Walker, "Solatium," 62 J.R. 144; "The Development of Reparation," 64 J.R. 101.

[54] 1933 S.C. 259.

[55] 1949 S.C. 110.

[56] *Naftalin*, *supra*, 270, 273; *McElroy*, *supra*, 117, 128, 134; See also *Kendrick* v. *Burnett* (1898) 25 R. 82; *Convery* v. *Lanarkshire Tramways Co.* (1905) 8 F. 117.

[57] *e.g. Riddell* v. *Reid*, 1941 S.C. 277, 1942 S.C.(H.L.) 51; *Paterson* v. *L.M.S. Ry.*, 1942 S.C. 156; *Smith* v. *Comrie's Exrx.*, 1944 S.C. 499.

pointed out [58] it has for a long time been accepted that a claim for solatium is based on a distinct and separate right from the claim in respect of patrimonial loss, and that claims so separately based used to go before juries with separate schedules of damages, appropriate to each claim.[59] He continued: " The practice of taking a verdict from a jury combining both these rights and the assessment of a single sum of damages to cover both claims has resulted in judges and juries coming to regard solatium as a mere element making up a general right to damages. . . . It is quite easy to see how the practice of taking an award of a single sum in name of damages from juries came about, because the two rights were most commonly existing side by side in a pursuer claiming reparation. But the proper practice is, I think, to separate the awards, and there are obvious advantages not only to one or other of the parties but also for the court."

This implies that the proper course for a sheriff or judge, even more than for a jury, is to make distinct awards for solatium and for patrimonial loss to each entitled pursuer, and the necessity, under the Interest on Damages (Scotland) Acts 1958 and 1971 [60] to have distinct bases for awarding interest emphasises this necessity.[61] Moreover to make distinct awards indicates to all concerned that the court or jury has taken each kind of claim into account and may ease the task of an appellate tribunal. On the other hand it may encourage appeals, if it appears that one claim is over- or under-valued.

Onus and need for proof

In relation to losses and damages the onus of proof is on the pursuer.[62] " A pursuer must in all reparation cases prove his damage. If he is injured, he must prove his injuries; if he has sustained patrimonial loss, he must prove the elements making up that loss. Similarly if he says that he was injured in his feelings, he must prove that he suffered grief. . . . If proof of grief is necessary, it is for the jury to consider whether sufficient proof has been brought forward to show that grief was actually sustained." [63]

In respect of patrimonial loss it is necessary to put before the court or jury information and figures enabling it or them to calculate an award proper in the circumstances.

Regard to principle and practice

As in the case of awards of damages to persons injured, suing on their own behalf, awards to the relatives of deceased persons must be arrived at having regard to legal principle determining what factors may and must be taken into account or excluded from account, and to the course of practice

58 *Hewitt* v. *West's Gas Improvement Co.*, 1955 S.C. 162, 166–167.
59 Instancing *Horn* v. *N.B. Ry.* (1878) 5 R. 1055 and *Juridical Styles*, III, 810.
60 Chap. 23, *supra*.
61 *Cf.* issue for jury settled in *Macdonald* v. *Glasgow Corpn.*, 1973 S.L.T. 107.
62 *Cruickshank* v. *Shiels*, 1951 S.C. 741, 746.
63 *Rankin* v. *Waddell*, 1949 S.C. 555, 558, *per* L.J.C. Thomson.

and the levels of awards currently regarded as fair and reasonable. In relation to solatium the only standard can be what is currently deemed fair and reasonable. In relation to loss of financial support calculation is possible though the data for the calculation cannot be fixed very exactly.

As solatium is an award peculiar to Scots law no assistance can be got from English cases, but in relation to loss of support, while a Scottish claim is founded on common law and an English claim founded on statute there is no justification for great variations between awards based on comparable financial losses, nor for adopting very different multipliers in grossing up the claimants' loss of support.

Relation of awards to value of money

Awards for loss of support and for outlays and expenses are necessarily related to the current and reasonably anticipated costs of what has been lost or expended, or will be lost or expended. In relation to solatium also account must be taken of falls in the value of money and larger awards in money must be given today than in comparable cases some years back.[64]

Court to consider post-accident developments

In making calculations a court must have regard to any development or material changes in circumstances after the accident giving rise to the claim but before the date of assessment, or after the assessment but before the appeal is decided, such as the widow's death, leaving children completely orphaned.[65]

SOLATIUM

Solatium is an award made to a person harmed or injured as solace or compensation for the intangible and immaterial losses sustained in consequence of the defender's breach of duty.

The term solatium seems to have originated in the ancient claim for assythment, where certain relations of a person killed by the defender's criminal act claimed compensation from him, and is thus derived from the even older claim for wergeld or blood-money. From assythment the term was taken over into the common-law action, miscalled an *actio injuriarum*, which in the nineteenth century [66] came to be allowed to certain relatives of a person killed by the defender's culpable act or omission, not amounting to criminal conduct.[67] The term was also applied to compensation for non-financial loss in actions by injured persons themselves.[68]

64 *Sands* v. *Devan*, 1945 S.C. 380, 381.

65 *Williamson* v. *Thornycroft & Co.* [1940] 4 All E.R. 61; *Kelly* v. *Glasgow Corpn.*, 1951 S.C. (H.L.) 15; *Pellow* v. *Lord Advocate*, 1953 S.L.T.(Notes) 41; *Voller* v. *Dairy Produce Packers Ltd.* [1962] 3 All E.R. 938; *McCann* v. *Sheppard* [1973] 2 All E.R. 881.

66 The kind of action first fully recognised in *Eisten* v. *N.B. Ry.* (1870) 8 M. 980.

67 For the development see Walker " Solatium," 62 J.R. 144; " The Development of Reparation," 64 J.R. 101.

68 Chap. 53, *supra*.

"Solatium in the law of Scotland properly means reparation for the pain inflicted on anyone in consequence of the commission of a delict against him. The pain may consist in physical suffering, or it may consist in wounded feelings. But, as a competent element in the assessment of damages, it is in contrast with patrimonial loss. Cases occur in which the element of solatium so greatly preponderates over that of patrimonial loss that it is common to speak of the whole reparation due in them as solatium. Examples are breach of promise of marriage (see *Fraser on Husband and Wife* (2nd ed.) Vol. I, pp.487–488), and defamation; yet in the first, patrimonial loss in respect of expenses laid out with a view to the marriage is also a competent element, and in the second, loss of credit or injury to business interests is often an element which counts for more in money than offended feelings. So, in the *actio injuriarum*,[69] the reparation due is described generally by Lord President Inglis in *Eisten* v. *North British Railway Co.*[70] as solatium, although the action is founded not merely on the pain of bereavement but also on the deprivation of a mutual obligation of support; yet the latter element sounds in patrimonial loss, and not at all in injury to feelings. The true contrast is clearly brought out by Lord President Dunedin in *Black* v. *North British Railway Co.*[71] In some cases of this peculiar class (the *actio injuriarum* [69]), where the patrimonial loss happens to be more or less capable of definite ascertainment, the distinction is necessarily tightly drawn—*Horn* v. *North British Railway Co.*[72]; *Wallace* v. *West Calder Co-operative Society* [73]—and in such cases the element of solatium appears in isolation in the same pure form as it did in *Elliot's* case.[74] But in most cases the element of patrimonial loss is incapable—apart from such general considerations as the position in life of the parties—of any definite standard of assessment, and it must vary according to circumstances. The death of the family breadwinner involves material patrimonial consequences out of all proportion to those which may speculatively attend the death of an infant. The element of patrimonial loss in the case of young children thus often becomes so attenuated as to be, for all practical purposes, negligible, and, when that is so, pure solatium may well be held to cover the whole field of reparation, just as it did in *Elliot's* [74] case." [75]

"Solatium is an acknowledgement of, rather than reparation for, the pursuer's wounded feelings." [76] "The element of solatium has again and again been described by learned judges as damages 'in

69 *i.e.* the action for damages for death of a close relative, mis-named an, or the, *actio injuriarum*.
70 (1870) 8 M. 980, 984.
71 1908 S.C. 444, 452–453.
72 (1878) 5 R. 1055.
73 (1888) 15 R. 307.
74 1922 S.C. 146.
75 *Duffy* v. *Kinneil Cannel and Coking Coal Co.*, 1930 S.C. 596.
76 *Smith* v. *Comrie's Exrx.*, 1944 S.C. 499, 500, *per* Lord Mackintosh.

acknowledgement of wounded feelings' or 'injured feelings' or 'pain and grief.'" [77]

Need to award solatium

Provided evidence has been given, and accepted, of grief felt at the death [78] a court or jury is perverse if it makes no award for solatium.[79] But a court or jury may competently regard the evidence of grief as so formal or nominal as not to justify any award.[80]

Factors relevant to award of solatium

The main factor relevant to an award of solatium is evidence of the existence and degree of pain and grief and sorrow felt at the premature death of the deceased. There must be evidence that grief was actually felt; accordingly where grown-up and forisfamiliated children gave no evidence of sorrow a nil award for solatium was upheld as competent and proper.[81] While it is competent, and necessary, to give general evidence of pain, grief and wounded feelings, it is not competent to put before the court as a distinct matter a specific consequential injury to the pursuer's physical or mental health, supported by medical evidence and evidence of expenses incurred. Thus evidence of shock and nervous disorder consequent on bereavement [82] and consequential injury to health [83] are inadmissible, as is evidence that a widow had lost the comfort of her husband on the death of her son a few days previous to the husband's death.[84] It is, however, competent to give evidence of how the survivor's feelings were shocked and lacerated by the contemplation of the pain and suffering to which the deceased was exposed before death actually supervened.[85] "Although solatium is in general described as compensation for injured feelings, these include not only the immediate personal grief felt, but also the subsequent continuing sense of loss arising from the deprivation, as in the present case, of a mother's care and affection (*quoad* the children) and of a wife's society and companionship (*quoad* the husband)." [86]

The award of solatium is necessarily relative to such factors as the age of the pursuer, his or her relationship to the deceased, factors which enhance or minimise the grief naturally felt such as a long and happy married life broken by the defender's fault [87] or, on the other hand, an

[77] *Kirkpatrick* v. *Anderson*, 1948 S.C. 251, 253, *per* L.P. Cooper.
[78] *McPhail* v. *Caledonian Ry.* (1903) 5 F. 306; *Rankin* v. *Waddell*, 1949 S.C. 555.
[79] *Gibson* v. *Kyle*, 1933 S.C. 30; *Wason* v. *B.T.C.*, 1960 S.C. 261, 265.
[80] *Rankin*, *supra*.
[81] *McPhail* v. *Caledonian Ry.* (1903) 5 F. 306; *Rankin* v. *Waddell*, 1949 S.C. 555.
[82] *Kirkpatrick* v. *Anderson*, 1948 S.C. 251; contrast *Schneider* v. *Eisovitch* [1960] 1 All E.R. 169, where the plaintiff recovered for her own injuries, and for shock at hearing of her husband's death.
[83] *Nicolson* v. *Cursiter*, 1959 S.C. 350.
[84] *Early* v. *Dall*, 1950 S.L.T.(Notes) 13.
[85] *Black* v. *N.B. Ry.*, 1908 S.C. 444, 453; *Smith* v. *Comrie's Exrx.*, 1944 S.C. 499, 501; *McLeish* v. *Fulton*, 1955 S.C. 46.
[86] *Kelly* v. *Glasgow Corpn.*, 1949 S.C. 496, 501, *per* Lord Russell; affd. 1951 S.C.(H.L.) 15.
[87] *McKinlay* v. *Glasgow Corpn.*, 1951 S.C. 495 (couple married 48 years).

unhappy or quarrelsome existence,[88] and to the duration of the grief and sorrow. "Some award for solatium falls to be given whatever was the age or position in life of the victim of the accident.... The amount of the award may vary according to circumstances, *e.g.* the degree of attachment which existed between the pursuer and the deceased, the pain and suffering of the deceased before death supervened...." [89] If a claimant survives the death only a short time only a restricted award can be given.[90]

The fact that the deceased was, from the financial point of view, a burden rather than a benefit to his family, is irrelevant in relation to solatium; relatives may feel just as much grief in such a case on his death.[91] The grossness of the negligence which caused the death does not affect the amount of the award.[92]

Solatium has been said to be "an element which is under any circumstances, extremely difficult to quantify and may not unfairly be said to represent no more than a mark or acknowledgement of the grief and sorrow needlessly inflicted on the surviving relative." [93] But though it is a token rather than an attempt to make compensation it is not merely a nominal award. "When there is nothing to place in the scales except the pain and grief which the accident has occasioned to a bereaved survivor, no standard for fixing the amount to be awarded as solatium is available. No parents, for example, would pass through such an experience for any sum of money. On the other hand, it is quite clear that solatium is not met by a nominal award.... The sum awarded must be a substantial acknowledgement... of the pain and grief ... which the defender's action has caused, but must be confined strictly within a moderate range." [94]

"Stating the matter so far as spouses are in question, solatium is given in respect of injury to feelings, and it is an acknowledgement of having caused grief and pain through fault. It reflects the loss of the care and affection of the spouse deceased." [95]

It follows that while, in an action of damages for personal injuries, an award of solatium in respect of pain and suffering, loss of functions, loss of amenities of life, loss of expectation of life and other relevant factors, may run to many thousands of pounds,[96] solatium in a claim for the death of a relative is an acknowledgment only and is much more limited in size.

Loss of deceased's amenities of life or expectation of life

In an action by surviving relatives nothing should be given for the deceased's loss of amenities of life or expectation of life, as the action is

[88] *Cf. Longster* v. *B.R.S.*, 1967 S.L.T.(Notes) 9, where pursuing widow had at the time of husband's death been defending an action by him for divorce.

[89] *Smith* v. *Comrie's Exrx.*, 1944 S.C. 499, 500, *per* Lord Mackintosh; *cf. Moorcraft* v. *Alexander*, 1946 S.C. 466, 467.

[90] *Cf. Kelly* v. *Glasgow Corpn.*, 1949 S.C. 496, 499, 500.

[91] *Brown* v. *Macgregor*, Feb. 26, 1813, F.C.; *Richmond* v. *Russell, Macnee & Co.* (1849) 11 D. 1035; *Elder* v. *Croall* (1849) 11 D. 1040; *Rankin* v. *Waddell*, 1949 S.C. 555.

[92] *Black* v. *N.B. Ry.*, 1908 S.C. 444; *Smith, supra*, 500.

[93] *Quin* v. *Greenock Tramways*, 1926 S.C. 544, 547, *per* L.P. Clyde

[94] *Elliot* v. *Glasgow Corpn.*, 1922 S.C. 146–148, *per* L.P. Clyde.

[95] *McLeish* v. *Fulton*, 1955 S.C. 46, 48, *per* Lord Carmont.

[96] Chap. 53, *supra*.

for compensation *to the relatives* and loss of amenities of life or of expectation of life was a loss to the deceased, not to them. Awards are made under the latter head in comparable English cases, but in these cases the plaintiffs are the executors on behalf of the estate, not the surviving relatives on their own behalf, and such cases are for this reason not valid precedents for Scotland. The deceased's expectation of life is, however, relevant to quantification of the survivor's claim for loss of support.

Awards for death of child

" The relation of money compensation to the grief and suffering of a father is necessarily vague and even arbitrary, and the very attempt to measure such suffering by money is pitifully discordant. There are many authoritative warnings in the books against excessive awards induced by sympathy." [97]

Awards to children

In making awards of solatium to children, each child has to be considered separately, and the same award to all is unjustifiable.[1] In the case of a posthumous or very young child he will be unable to feel immediate grief and pain at the parent's death [1a] but may suffer acutely in later years from the lack of companionship, guidance and assistance which might have been afforded by the deceased parent, and that lack will continue through all the years of childhood and adolescence.[2] A child mentally incapable of feeling grief and pain at the death can receive only a modest award.[3] An older child may appreciate the loss at once and feel immediate grief and pain but will lack parental companionship and guidance for a shorter period. At the other end of the age-scale only a nominal award can be given to a person who has reached maturity and whose parent is killed, particularly if the parent was of such an age that he could not have been expected in the normal course to have lived much longer.[3]

These considerations suggest that the pattern of awards of solatium should be one of small awards to very young children, rising rapidly to much larger awards for young children, then declining gradually to very moderate, or even nominal awards, in the case of grown-up children,[3] or even, if they give no adequate evidence of grief at the death, a nil award to grown-up children.[4]

Amount to be awarded for solatium

The amount to be awarded must have regard to the circumstances and the evidence; it must be a substantial acknowledgment and not, unless

[97] *Sands* v. *Devan*, 1945 S.C. 380, 381, *per* L. P. Normand.
[1] *Kelly* v. *Glasgow Corpn.*, 1951 S.C.(H.L.) 15, 19.
[1a] *Moorcraft* v. *Alexander*, 1946 S.C. 466, 468.
[2] *Kelly* v. *Glasgow Corpn.*, 1949 S.C. 496, 499.
[3] *Cf. Paterson* v. *L.M.S. Ry.*, 1942 S.C. 156; *McKinlay* v. *Glasgow Corpn.*, 1951 S.C. 495.
[4] *Rankin* v. *Waddell*, 1949 S.C. 555.

there be little evidence to support the claim, merely nominal, but yet confined within comparatively modest limits.[5]

Some guidance is provided by awards considered in reported cases, but in considering them, the considerable fall in the value of money after 1914, and even more sharply since 1945, must be remembered.[6] In 1922 Lord President Clyde said: " Stating the matter very generally I think the usual award for solatium only—both according to the verdict of juries, and according to the course of decisions in which verdicts have been upset as excessive—runs in the neighbourhood of one to two hundred pounds, according to the circumstances, whatever be the age or position in life of the victim of the accident. I am not laying down any taxative limit for all awards in respect of solatium only; for each case must depend on its own circumstances, and the award made in one case cannot be used to fix an unsurpassable limit, or to help in forming a proportional scale or standard by which the amount of a reasonable award can be artificially determined in another case. Uniformity and standardisation are alike impossible counsels of perfection in such a department as this." [7] It has been observed that between the wars an award to a surviving spouse in the region of £350 would not have been challengeable.[8] Awards of £300 were made in 1941 [9] and £250 in 1945 [10] and 1949.[11]

Fifty years after *Elliot's* case awards of seven times that amount are more the range within which courts and juries should think in normal cases. In *McKinlay* v. *Glasgow Corpn.*[8] an award of about £700 to a widower was described as very generous and substantial, but not so excessive as to require retrial. In *McLeish* v. *Fulton* [12] an award of solatium was reduced to £500. In *Wason* v. *B.T.C.*[13] in 1960 Lord Justice-Clerk Thomson said that a reasonable allowance of solatium to a widow would have been £750 and Lord Patrick mentions £500 as a quite normal award in such circumstances.

Examples of awards

Awards in past cases [14] cannot be regarded as precedents but may be of some value as examples, and as guides to the range within which awards have been made or been held proper.

Loss of Support

The basis of the claim of damages by one or more entitled surviving relatives for loss of support is that by reason of the death each pursuer has

[5] *Smith* v. *Comrie's Exrx.*, 1944 S.C. 499, 500.
[6] *Sands* v. *Devan*, 1945 S.C. 380; *Kelly* v. *Glasgow Corpn.*, 1951 S.C.(H.L.) 15.
[7] *Elliot* v. *Glasgow Corpn.*, 1922 S.C. 146, 148–149, *per* L.P. Clyde.
[8] 1951 S.C. 495.
[9] *Inglis* v. *L.M.S. Ry.*, 1941 S.C. 551.
[10] *Sands* v. *Devan*, 1945 S.C. 380.
[11] *Kelly* v. *Glasgow Corpn.*, 1949 S.C. 496; affd. 1951 S.C.(H.L.) 15.
[12] 1955 S.C. 46.
[13] 1960 S.C. 261, 264.
[14] See Appendix I.

lost financial support which he or she was actually enjoying or, at least, was legally entitled to have in case of need. The proper basis for an award for that loss is not fair compensation but full compensation.[15] " The general principle is not in doubt. [The relatives] are entitled to such a sum as will make good to them the financial loss which they have suffered and will suffer as a result of the death." [16] It is not a question whether the pursuer *needed* that support, or had or has adequate income and/or capital for his or her own support without reliance on the deceased's financial support, but whether he or she was in fact being supported financially by the deceased to any extent, and has lost financially by the cessation of that support by reason of the death.[17] If on the other hand the pursuer was in fact living on his or her own earnings and not being supported by the deceased, the claim is only for the loss of the right to support in case of need. In every case it is for the pursuer to prove the fact of, and the extent of, his or her financial dependency on the deceased's income. The rich wife whose husband is killed has a substantial claim if in fact she was supported by him and did not spend her own income, but only a nominal claim if in fact she lived on her own income.[17] In the case of aliment it is awarded on proof of need only, and a spouse who can support himself or herself has no claim for aliment.

Equally if a pursuer who, while not actually requiring support, was in fact receiving it, voluntarily paid by the deceased, he is entitled to damages for loss of support.[18]

Conversely it is no justification for making a substantial award, or indeed any award, that the pursuer needed the money if in fact he or she had not been receiving it and had accordingly not lost by reason of the death. If a waster of a husband, who spent all he earned on beer, cigarettes and gambling, and did not support his family is killed, his widow, who has had to go out to work to keep the family, is entitled to only a nominal award. What, in financial terms, has she lost by her husband's death? If she was actually getting no financial support her loss is limited to the loss of the legal right to support from him in case of need, a right of negligible value in the circumstances. In such a case the only real claim is for solatium.[19]

To justify a claim for loss of support it is necessary that a mutual obligation of support as between deceased and claimant existed by law, so that the relative could have, if need be, called on the deceased, or sued the deceased, for aliment. The obligation of support may have been one currently being honoured at the time of death, or be one merely con-

15 *Cf. Livingstone* v. *Rawyards Coal Co.* (1880) 7 R.(H.L.) 1, 7, *per* Lord Blackburn; *B.T.C.* v. *Gourley* [1956] A.C. 185, 197, *per* Earl Jowitt.

16 *Taylor* v. *O'Connor* [1970] 1 All E.R. 365, 366, *per* Lord Reid. *Cf. Mallett* v. *McMonagle* [1969] 2 All E.R. 178, 189 F, *per* Lord Diplock.

17 *Cruikshank* v. *Shiels*, 1951 S.C. 741; 1953 S.C.(H.L.) 1.

18 *Dickson* v. *N.C.B.*, 1957 S.C. 157.

19 *Brown* v. *McGregor*, Feb. 26, 1813, F.C. *Cf. Gunn* v. *McAdam* [1949] C.L.Y. 4499; 1949 S.C. 31.

tingent,[20] or potential,[21] so long as not merely speculative.[22] Loss of educational prospects by a child has been held enough to justify a claim.[23]

Loss of potential support, in the shape of the death of a relative from whom the pursuer might, if need be, have claimed support is relevant. Thus in *Kelly* [24] a mother was killed, and a year later the father died. "The claim of the children, in so far as based on potential support by their mother, rested only on a remote and conjectural estimate so long as their father who was in the prime of life was still alive. By his supervening and premature death a seemingly remote and insignificant potentiality has become immediate and real, and a conjectural factor of small consequence has been elevated into an ascertained fact of manifest importance. In my opinion this factor should have been taken into consideration by the Lord Ordinary."

Similarly if a wife was in desertion or living in adultery with another her claim on her husband's death is a claim for contingent loss of support only.[24a]

Though title to sue depends on liability in case of need to have alimented the pursuer, the measure of damages is not limited to the amount which the deceased would have been held liable to pay the pursuer in fulfilment of the obligation to aliment. Damages are measured by loss sustained, aliment by what can fairly be given and is limited to what is necessary to maintain a tolerable standard of living.[25]

It has been said [26] that the amount of damages for loss of support is essentially a jury question to be dealt with on broad lines and that mathematical calculations can never lead to a precisely accurate estimate of the loss suffered, but in practice calculations must be made and courts cannot simply fix on a sum and award that as damages. On the other hand pure arithmetic does not always lead to a just result; there are many imponderables.

Claims where multiple pursuers

Where there are several entitled pursuers claiming together attention must be directed to the point whether the deceased had in fact been supporting all of them, or had in fact not actually been supporting one or more, *e.g.* forisfamiliated children. Also where the deceased was actually supporting some or all regard must be had to the nature of the support, whether, *e.g.* the wife was separated and being paid aliment, and the children being maintained in family. Furthermore if all were being maintained in family it has to be remembered that all the support was coming

20 *Mill* v. *Dundas*, 1919, 2 S.L.T. 65; *Sagar* v. *N.C.B.*, 1955 S.C. 424.
21 *Kelly* v. *Glasgow Corpn.*, 1949 S.C. 496, 499.
22 *Barnett* v. *Cohen* [1921] 2 K.B. 461.
23 *Pym* v. *G.N. Ry.* (1862) 2 B. & S. 759; (1863) 4 B. & S. 396.
24 *Supra, per* L.P. Cooper; similarly at pp. 501–502, *per* Lord Russell.
24a *Cf. Gray* v. *Barr* [1971] 2 All E.R. 949 (parties separated); *Davies* v. *Taylor* [1972] 3 All E.R. 836 (divorce proceedings started).
25 *Dickson* v. *N.C.B.*, 1957 S.C. 157.
26 *Kassam* v. *Kampala Aerated Water Co.* [1965] 2 All E.R. 875, P.C.

from one lot of earnings. Though all entitled relatives have separate claims they must not be compensated as if each had been supported separately, but the aggregate of individual awards also must be looked at in relation to the total of support formerly afforded.[27]

Past and future loss of support

An award for loss of support must take account of the support actually lost between the date of death and the date of the assessment of damages, and also of the support likely to be lost in the future. The factors relevant for consideration in each case are the same, but loss of support down to the date of assessment is usually calculable with some certainty, whereas loss of support for the future is much more difficult to calculate and involves making allowances for various factors which can only be estimated rather than exactly calculated.

Methods of calculation of award for future loss

Various methods of calculation are possible though some must be mentioned only to be discarded. The basic data required are ascertainment of the " dependency," that is, the estimated financial loss per annum sustained by the pursuers, or the sum which the deceased contributed to and made available for their support and would have continued to do if he had not been killed. This is the multiplicand. The other necessary figure is the estimated period for which the deceased would have continued to afford that support to the pursuers or his expected working life.

Simple multiplication

It is wrong simply to multiply the annual dependency by the number of years of expected working life because this takes no account of contingencies, such as the deceased's premature death for other reasons, and particularly because this multiplication makes no allowance for the fact that it produces a lump sum payable now, which can and should be invested, and which will produce interest which itself would go some way towards meeting the pursuer's claim. This calculation accordingly would seriously over-compensate.

Liferent principle

It is similarly a wrong calculation, and effects over-compensation, to award such a sum as will, if invested, furnish the claimant with an annual income about the same as the support lost, but leaving the capital untouched.[28] An award which, invested, brings the claimant a greater sum

[27] *Love* v. *N.C.B.*, 1956 S.C. 459, 462.

[28] Thus if a widow's loss of support be £1,000 p.a. and if the expected period of lost support be assessed at 25 or more years, an award of £25,000 would be wrong as £25,000 invested at 5 per cent. would produce £1,250 p.a. gross, and about £1,000 p.a. net without her touching the capital. This seriously overcompensates. *Cf. Love* v. *N.C.B.*, 1956 S.C. 459; *Wason* v. *B.T.C.*, 1960 S.C. 261, 265, 266; *Urquhart* v. *Baxter*, 1961 S.C. 149, 151.

in interest than the amount of annual support lost is manifestly excessive.[29] A calculation of this kind, however, may be a useful check on the appropriateness of awards calculated in other ways.

Annuity principle more correct

It is more correct to work on a similar principle to that involved in the calculation of the price of an immediate annuity purchased from an insurance company for a lump sum, where the purchase price is calculated on the basis that the whole sum will be initially invested and repaid to the annuitant in annual amounts, composed of elements of interest and of returned capital, the interest element declining and the capital element increasing each year. If the annuitant predeceases the calculated time the insurance company benefits, and conversely if the annuitant outlives that time. Some guidance accordingly can be obtained from annuity tables giving figures from which to calculate the present capital cost of purchasing an immediate annuity for a person of the pursuer's age and sex for a given period of an amount equal to the gross annual loss of support.[30] But published tables and quotations from insurance companies are normally for annuities for the rest of the annuitant's life, whereas in damages cases one is concerned with an estimated period of dependency normally ending before death, such as, for example, the period between the deceased's death and the date when he would in the normal course have given up earning. Guidance can, however, be got from such tables by ascertaining (a) the capital cost of an immediate annuity for a person of the pursuer's age and sex of a sum equal to the gross [30] loss of earnings, (b) the capital cost of an immediate annuity for a person of the pursuer's sex at the age when the earnings would normally have ceased, and then deducting (b) from (a). Thus if X is widowed at 30, her late husband being 35 and the gross loss of earnings being £1,000 p.a. an annuity of £1,000 p.a. gross for a woman of 30 to death would cost, say, £22,000; the earnings, and the loss, would cease in 30 years time, and an annuity of £1,000 p.a. for a woman of 60 to death would cost, say, £11,000; the difference represents the cost of an annuity for the years 30 to 60.

> " It has often been suggested that the sum to be awarded as damages should be equal to the cost of purchasing an annuity of the relevant amount for the relevant period. This is no doubt a convenient and useful check but I think that it is not on quite the right basis, and therefore not wholly reliable. An annuity would give the [claimant] no protection against inflation.[31] She could only have a fixed lump sum per annum however much inflation there might be. As an annuity is not the article she requires, the price of it is not the correct measure of the sum she should receive." [32]

[29] *e.g. Mallett* v. *McMonagle* [1969] 2 All E.R. 178.
[30] An annuity is taxable as to the interest element just as were the deceased's earnings.
[31] An annuity allowing for annual increases of stated percentages to cater for inflation is readily calculable.
[32] *Taylor* v. *O'Connor* [1970] 1 All E.R. 365, 380, *per* Lord Pearson.

Annuity tables are, however, calculated for persons of average health, longevity and so on; but a court in assessing damages must consider both the general possibility, and any specific factors which render it likely that the pursuer would not have average longevity.

The courts have in general declined to use annuity tables in such cases. " It has been suggested that a more precise method of arriving at the extent of the loss would be to obtain actuarial figures as to what sum would be required, based on the respondent's expectancy of life, to purchase an annuity of the extent of the loss. This method has been disapproved in the past and never adopted except as a very rough guide. Its adoption would depend on current rates of interest and would not allow for inflation. If it were adopted it would have to be discounted in respect that it provides certainty and does not allow for contingencies." [33]

Annuity tables, moreover, take no account of the specialties of particular cases, such as allowances for capital inherited from the deceased, loss of the benefit of future saving by the deceased, and other special features.

In *Mallett* v. *McMonagle* [34] Lord Diplock said:

> " To assess the damages it is necessary to form a view on three matters each of which is in greater or less degree one of speculation: (i) the value of the material benefits for his dependants which the deceased would have provided out of his earnings for each year in the future during which he would have provided them had he not been killed; (ii) the value of any material benefits which the dependants will be able to obtain in each such year from sources (other than insurance) which would not have been available to them had the deceased lived but which will become available to them as a result of his death; (iii) the amount of the capital sum which with prudent management will produce annual amounts equal to the difference between (i) and (ii), (*i.e.* " the dependency ") for each of the years during which the deceased would have provided material benefits for the dependants had he not been killed."

In Scottish cases down to about 1950 the basis taken for calculation seems to have been the deceased's gross earnings.[35] In later cases the English practice of trying to ascertain the dependency has been taken, and this is the more accurate and preferable basis.

> In *Taylor* v. *O'Connor* [36] Lord Reid stated: " Damages to make good the loss of dependency over a period of years must be awarded as a lump sum, and that sum is generally calculated by applying a

[33] *Taylor* v. *O'Connor* [1970] 1 All E.R. 365, 373, *per* Lord Guest.

[34] [1969] 2 All E.R. 178, 189.

[35] *e.g. Riddell* v. *Reid*, 1941 S.C. 277; 1942 S.C.(H.L.) 51; *Paterson* v. *L.M.S. Ry.*, 1942 S.C. 156; *Smith* v. *Comrie's Exrx.*, 1944 S.C. 499; *Nash* v. *Edinburgh Corpn.*, 1945 S.L.T. 301; *Millar* v. *Galashiels Gas Co.*, 1947 S.N. 114; affd. 1949 S.C.(H.L.) 31.

[36] [1970] 1 All E.R. 365, 367.

multiplier to the amount of one year's dependency. That is a perfectly good method in the ordinary case, but it conceals the fact that there are two quite separate matters involved—the present value of the series of future payments, and the discounting of that present value to allow for the fact that, for one reason or another, the person receiving the damages might never have enjoyed the whole of the benefit of the dependency. . . . But in a case where the facts are special, I think that these matters must have separate consideration if even rough justice is to be done, and expert evidence may be valuable or even essential. . . . The prudent person receiving a lump sum to make good his loss over a period is expected to invest it and to use it up gradually. If the period is a long one the multiplier will be much smaller than the number of years even where the contingencies which are allowed for are of small account. The reason is that, while and in so far as the lump sum of damages is unspent, it will be earning interest and the damages and interest together will be adequate to last out for the period."

Factors relevant to claim for future loss of support

The first factor to be considered in any claim for future loss of support is the amount of financial support actually being afforded to the pursuer or pursuers before the death. This is not the same as the deceased's net income, but is the deceased's gross income under deduction of taxation and other compulsory deductions, and of sums retained by the deceased for his own purposes or personal spending. Nor, on the other hand, is the amount of financial support lost the same as the amounts given to the pursuer as personal allowance and housekeeping money, if the deceased himself also paid some items, such as rent or rates or electricity bills or clothing or holidays or the car, in addition to giving the weekly or monthly housekeeping money. If so, these must be added.

As Lord Wright said in *Davies* v. *Powell Duffryn Associated Collieries Ltd.*[37]:

> "It is a hard matter of pounds, shillings and pence, subject to the element of reasonable future probabilities. The starting point is the amount of wages which the deceased was earning, the ascertainment of which to some extent may depend on the regularity of his employment. Then there is an estimate of how much was required or expended for his own personal and living expenses. The balance will give a datum or basic figure which will generally be turned into a lump sum by taking a certain number of years' purchase. That sum, however, has to be taxed down by having due regard to uncertainties, for instance, that the widow might have again married [38] and thus ceased to be dependent, and other like matters of speculation and doubt."

[37] [1942] A.C. 601, 608.

[38] But see now Law Reform (Misc. Prov.) Act 1971, s. 4.

Basic figure—deceased's annual net earnings

Nevertheless the basic figure, as a start for calculations, is the deceased's pre-accident average earnings from all sources [39] (including spare time jobs,[40] casual earnings, perquisites, payments in kind,[41] board and lodging [42] and the like). From this deduction must be made in respect of the income tax and other compulsory deductions made from it to arrive at the deceased's net earnings.[43] In judging the effect of the incidence of tax any private income of the recipient of the damages must however be ignored,[44] because that is not affected by the death but may affect the effective rate of tax on the deceased's earnings.[45] In *Cooper* v. *Firth Brown Ltd.*[46] Lawton J. held national insurance contributions deductible but in *McCreadie* v. *Clydebank Co-operative Socy.*[47] Lord Hunter was of a contrary opinion. It is submitted that deduction should be made of all such legally compulsory deductions from gross income.[48]

As in the case of personal injuries regard must be had to any known certainties or probabilities as to future increase or diminution in earnings, by promotion or seniority, or by retirement or decline of the victim's business.[49] In view of experience of inflation since 1945 the chance of rises in money earnings in years to come even without promotion or change of job must be considered.[50] Where there is reasonable ground for the estimate a figure may be arrived at as the probable average earnings during the whole future period of the pursuer's dependency.[51]

Deceased's spending on himself and cost of living

Deduction must also be made from net earnings of sums kept or spent by the deceased on himself,[52] but not of sums spent by the deceased on general family benefits, such as the home or a car or holidays, still less of sums spent on benefits for particular members of the family, such as his wife's clothing or a child's education.

A further small deduction must be made in recognition of the fact that

39 *Wason* v. *B.T.C.*, 1960 S.C. 261; *Urquhart* v. *Baxter*, 1961 S.C. 149.
40 *Cf. Mallett* v. *McMonagle* [1969] 2 All E.R. 178, where the deceased sang with a dance band in the evenings.
41 *Cf. Cameron* v. *Findlay*, 1959 S.L.T.(Notes) 69, where deceased was a farmworker with a free house and certain food as well as wages.
42 *Doonan* v. *S.M.T. Co.*, 1950 S.C. 136, where housekeeper got her " keep."
43 It has to be assumed that the principle of *British Transport Commission* v. *Gourley* [1956] A.C. 185, applies to fatal accident cases as much as to injury cases where the victim survives.
44 *Taylor* v. *O'Connor* [1970] 1 All E.R. 365, 368, 376.
45 Consider the case of a widow who had £10,000 p.a. private income.
46 [1963] 2 All E.R. 31.
47 1966 S.C. 72.
48 National insurance contributions were deducted in *Howitt* v. *Heads* [1972] 1 All E.R. 491.
49 *Cf. Mallett, supra*, where there was no evidence that the deceased would have risen above the level of manual work. Conversely in *Taylor* v. *O'Connor* [1970] 1 All E.R. 365, the deceased's income was steadily increasing.
50 *Taylor, supra.*
51 *Cf. Daniels* v. *Jones* [1961] 3 All E.R. 24, where average net earnings over the next 13 years was taken as the basis.
52 *Love* v. *N.C.B.*, 1956 S.C. 459, 462; *Wason* v. *B.T.C.*, 1960 S.C. 261, 264; *Urquhart* v. *Baxter*, 1961 S.C. 149, 151.

the pursuer is relieved, by the death, of a small part of the household expenses; a widow, that is, has one fewer mouth to feed.[53] But many household expenses, such as rent or loan interest, rates, furnishings, cleaning, electricity, and so on are not diminished at all, or at least not appreciably, by the death, and it would be wrong to make more than a small token deduction in respect of diminished household expenses. Indeed any deduction on this account may be outweighed by the fact, if it be the case, that the deceased did household repairs and maintenance himself, for which services a widow may have to pay. Nor is it always reasonable to say that they could be minimised by moving to a smaller house.

Deceased's " unearned " income

In so far as the deceased's income was " unearned " income from investments, it will not be ended by his death. But the court may have to investigate whether that income had been used for the deceased's own purposes, or put into a common fund with his earned income, or devoted entirely to wife and family, or to some charity or other outside interest, and how it will fall to be dealt with in view of his will, or the rules of intestacy. It cannot, however, be assumed that the income of investments is all used by the person in whom the investments are nominally vested and in many cases unearned income is family income just as much as earned income. If the deceased's whole estate, except in so far as coming to the claimant under the doctrine of legal rights, has been given away by his will to a charity or a mistress, a widow may, by reason of the death, be losing the benefit of some of the deceased's unearned income as well as of some of his earned income.

Unearned income such as a liferent under a trust, or a payment under covenant by a relative, may be terminated by reason of the death. Here again a pursuer, such as a widow, may have lost by the premature termination of a source of income from which she benefited. If she did so, she must include this loss in her claim.

Deceased's illegal or undisclosed earnings

If the deceased's earnings were to any extent illegal, as where he lived by crime,[54] unlicensed gambling, running a brothel or the like, these earnings should be left out of account and compensation not given for loss consequent on their cessation: *ex turpi causa non oritur actio.* Earnings which were legal but not disclosed to the Inland Revenue should also probably be left out of account.

Deceased's savings from income

Income saved by the deceased and banked or invested or used in payment of life insurance policies should not be treated as if spent on the

[53] *Love* v. *N.C.B.*, 1956 S.C. 459, 462; *Wason* v. *B.T.C.*, 1960 S.C. 261, 264.
[54] *Burns* v. *Edman* [1970] 2 Q.B. 541.

deceased's own purposes, but as set aside for the family benefit, for future support or as reserve for emergencies, rather than on present support, and no deduction from his gross income should be made in respect thereof. It is settled that money payable on his death from policies of life assurance is not deductible in arriving at an award of damages, and it is submitted that money spent in paying premiums should not be deducted from his earnings either. "I do not think it is right to look only at what he actually expended by way of allowances to them. In so far as he did not spend his income, but invested it, he was, as it seems to me, equally doing so for the benefit of his wife and family. They enjoyed the benefit not only of his generous expenditure on them, but also the security of living with a man of large income and growing capital resources, the great part of which was available for their benefit even if not immediately used in expenditure on them." [55]

If money saved is deducted, and not counted as support lost, the only result is to benefit the wrongdoer and penalise the pursuing relatives. Moreover if a deceased was able to and in the habit of saving, he would probably have continued to save, so that those dependent on him have also lost the chance of inheriting a greater capital reserve, if he had lived longer.

In *Taylor* v. *O'Connor* [56] apart from spending on himself and on the support of his family the deceased would have been putting £1,500 p.a. into his business and would have had about £2,000 p.a. more available to be used as savings or to allow an increased standard of living. Damages were awarded for the present value of the capital invested in the business, which would have been repayable after the deceased had retired, and for the present value of the savings which would probably have been made. "The judge estimated that, of the husband's net spendable income, two-thirds . . . would have enured to the benefit of the [plaintiffs]. That must include both elements of the lost pecuniary benefit, namely, the maintenance element and the savings element." [57]

Money saved and invested should accordingly be included in the "dependency," [58] or be calculated separately and something awarded in addition in respect of the loss thereof.[59]

Deceased's pension

If the deceased, had he not been killed, would have retired on pension, other than National Insurance retirement pension, and if the pursuer would then have been still dependent on him, the calculation must have regard to so many years of earnings and so many years on pension.[60]

[55] *Daniels* v. *Jones* [1961] 3 All E.R. 24, 30, *per* Willmer L.J.
[56] [1970] 1 All E.R. 365.
[57] *Ibid.* 378, *per* Lord Pearson.
[58] The approach of Lords Morris, Guest and Pearson in *Taylor*.
[59] The approach of Lord Reid and Viscount Dilhorne in *Taylor*.
[60] *e.g.* *Whittome* v. *Coates* [1965] 3 All E.R. 268 (deceased 58: would have retired at 65); damages computed on basis of six years at £600 p.a. and six years (the rest of the plaintiff's expectation of life) at £450 p.a.

Inflation and future fiscal policy

Since 1945 inflation has consistently been eroding the value of money and changes in fiscal policy may falsify calculations of the proper capital sum needed to compensate a given loss. It has been said [61] that the only practicable course for courts to adopt is to leave out of account the risk of further inflation with its concomitant high interest rates and capital appreciation: money should be treated as retaining its value at the date of the judgment, and future fiscal changes must be disregarded as pure speculation. But this is not realistic in view of experience since 1945, and all experience suggests that a steady rise in money incomes and in the cost of living over future years must be expected and taken into account. In *Taylor* v. *O'Connor* [62] most of the House of Lords accepted that the prospect of future inflation had to be taken account of, by adjusting upward the figure for anticipated annual loss of support, though the adjustment made in that case was in fact small.

Where non-earning member of family killed

Where the member of the family killed was a housewife or other member who was not actually earning the loss is by way of loss of services rendered gratuitously but of pecuniary value. In so far as these services have to be replaced by the services of another who has to be paid to give them, *e.g.* a housekeeper, they are compensable under the head of outlays and expenses, but an allowance must be made for savings on the wife's maintenance. It is questionable whether the services of a wife and mother to her husband and children, valuable as they are, can be regarded as having a financial value or as being a patrimonial loss.

Where a member of the family too old or too young to be earning is the victim, the loss is a token sum, depending on an estimate of what support the victim might have later afforded in case of need.[63] In assessing this, regard must be had to such facts as that sons and daughters marry and become less able to support their parents,[64] and old persons are frequently totally unable to do so. On the other hand in the case of very young children the loss is a speculative possibility rather than a contingency.[65]

Awards to several entitled relatives

Where several entitled relatives sue together in the one action care must be taken that there is no duplication of damages, particularly under the head of loss of support. The deceased's net earnings, less the cost of

[61] *Mallet* v. *McMonagle* [1969] 2 All E.R. 178, 190; *Taylor* v. *O'Connor* [1970] 1 All E.R. 365, 374.

[62] *Supra*, especially Lord Reid at p. 368: " It would, I think, be quite unrealistic to refuse to take it into account at all."

[63] *Taff Vale Ry.* v. *Jenkins* [1913] A.C. 1; *Buckland* v. *Guildford Gas Light Co.* [1949] 1 K.B. 410; *Wathen* v. *Vernon* [1970] R.T.R. 471. *Cf. Sagar* v. *N.C.B.*, 1955 S.C. 424; *Dickson* v. *N.C.B.*, 1957 S.C. 157.

[64] *Cf. Dolbey* v. *Goodwin* [1955] 2 All E.R. 166; *Dickson, supra*, 170.

[65] *Barnett* v. *Cohen* [1921] 2 K.B. 461.

maintaining himself, was a single fund from which all entitled relatives, *e.g.* widow and several children, had to be supported. Accordingly in making the calculations it must be notionally apportioned, *e.g.* £a to the widow for keeping the house and maintaining herself, £b for the first child, £c for the second child, and so on, and £a+£b+£c+the cost of maintaining the deceased cannot exceed the deceased's net earnings.

Pursuer's own earnings

If the pursuer can establish loss of financial support to him or her by reason of the death it is irrelevant that the pursuer does, or could, earn himself or herself,[66] or could earn more, or possibly could earn more by reason of the death.

Pursuer's own loss of earnings in consequence of the death

If the pursuer and the deceased were, in fact or in law, in partnership and, as well as the deceased's contribution to their support, the pursuer sustains financial loss in consequence of the death by the break-up of the partnership, it is questionable if anything can be recovered under that head, the loss probably being consequential. In *Burgess* v. *Florence Nightingale Hospital*,[67] plaintiff and his wife were professional ballroom dancers and it was held under the [English] Fatal Accidents Act 1846, that the plaintiff could recover for loss of the wife's earning power and her contribution to the joint expenses, but no damages were recoverable for the value of the wife to him as his dancing partner, this loss not being attributable to the severance of the matrimonial relationship. On the latter point the decision depends partly on the terms of the English legislation but it is thought that a similar principle in Scottish common law would prevent a court in such a case from giving anything for the loss resulting from the break-up of the partnership, until such time as the pursuer could find another partner. The loss, in short, results from the loss of the pursuer's business partner, not of his or her spouse.

Similarly if the pursuer had employed, or had been employed by, the deceased and loses by reason of the termination of the contractual relationship, this loss cannot be taken into account because it arises not from relationship and the resultant obligation, actual or potential, to support, but from the contract. In such a case in England [68] it was said: " The plaintiff was bound to prove a benefit accruing to him from his relationship with the deceased; but he merely showed that he derived an advantage from a contract with his son." The employer has no right of action for loss resulting from injury to, or death of, the employee,[69] and conversely, and it matters not that employer or employee is also a relative.[70]

66 *Cf. Cruikshank* v. *Shiels*, 1953 S.C.(H.L.) 1.
67 [1955] 1 All E.R. 511.
68 *Sykes* v. *N.E. Ry.* (1875) 44 L.J.C.P. 191, 192.
69 *Allan* v. *Barclay* (1864) 2 M. 873; *Reavis* v. *Clan Line*, 1925 S.C. 725.
70 *Cf. Quin* v. *Greenock Tramways Co.*, 1926 S.C. 544 (son employee of father's trustees); *Malyon* v. *Plummer* [1964] 1 Q.B. 330 (widow employee of late husband).

On the other hand where a husband on his wife's death lost an old-age pension which he had enjoyed in respect of her before her death, this was held a loss of benefit derived from the relationship and recoverable.[71]

The multiplier

The customary method of reaching a figure for future loss of support is to ascertain the net annual loss of support in the way indicated and multiply it by a number of years. The number of years chosen should have regard to the number of years for which the deceased would probably, in the normal course, have continued to earn, and to live thereafter, and to the number of years, if less than that, for which each pursuer would probably have remained dependent on the deceased and for which, accordingly, each pursuer has lost support.[72]

If the deceased himself had a limited expectation of life, no greater figure can be taken as the multiplier, because that is the maximum number of years for which support would have continued to be furnished even if the deceased had not been killed. If any pursuer has an expectation of life less than that of the deceased that lesser period must be taken as the multiplier in his or her case, because that is the maximum number of years for which that pursuer could have claimed support. Thus a child with a life expectancy of fifty years can claim loss of support for only three years if the evidence is that his deceased parent would, if he had not been killed, only have lived three years, and a child with a life expectancy of five years can claim only for that period, even though the deceased would still be alive at the notional date of that child's death, because the child will lose support for that period only.

Thus in *Whittome* v. *Coates* [73] the plaintiff (widow) had an expectation of life of twelve to fifteen years only, which was probably much less than the deceased husband's expectation of life had been. Damages were awarded on the basis of the plaintiff's shorter expectation of life.

The same multiplier is accordingly not necessarily appropriate for all the pursuers. If the evidence is that a deceased had a life expectation of ten years, that his widow has an expectation of life of only three years, that there is a son of twenty, about to qualify professionally and to embark on his own career, and a daughter of twelve who is handicapped, may not live more than seven years, and will never be able to earn her living, different multipliers must be applied to each. In the simple case of several children of differing ages they will become self-supporting after different periods of time.[74]

In calculating life expectancies statistical tables are of value and in the absence of medical evidence to the contrary it may be assumed that parties

71 *Feay* v. *Barnwell* [1938] 1 All E.R. 31.
72 Assistance in ascertaining these facts may be found in the Life Tables published by the Registrar-General for Scotland.
73 [1965] 3 All E.R. 268.
74 *Cf. Kassam* v. *Kampala Aerated Water Co.* [1965] 2 All E.R. 875.

involved have average expectancy of life. In the case of claims for loss of support from children regard must also be had to the probability of the child marrying and thereby becoming less able, or unable, to contribute support to his parents.

If any one or more of the claiming relatives has himself died before the assessment of damages the award for loss of support must be limited to the period of survivance. So too if one is, *e.g.* an aged mother, who cannot be expected to survive for long, the award must be limited to the expected period of survival and accordingly of lost support.[75]

In many Scottish cases in the past the multiplier taken seems to have been far too low; in *Riddell* v. *Reid* [76] the award was in the region of four times the deceased husband's annual earnings; in *Paterson* v. *L.M.S. Ry.*[77] roughly the same measure was adopted; in *Smith* v. *Comrie's Exrx.*[78] something like the same multiplier seems again to have been used. In all cases the base figure taken was the deceased's gross earnings, not net earnings after deduction of tax and personal expenses, but these considerations would have made little difference.

The multiplication

There are two possible ways of making the calculation; the first is to base the multiplier on the deceased's normal expectation of life, allowing for the possibility of earlier death or disabling ill-health, and to discount the resultant figure, having regard to its being paid as a lump sum, and further discount it for such contingencies as the premature death of the widow [79]; the other is to fix an estimated sum for annual dependency and use an appropriate multiplier, and in choosing both to try to take into account the various contingencies and deductions which must be borne in mind in the calculation.[80] The two methods should come to much the same answer. Thus if X is killed, aged thirty, earning £1,200 p.a. net,[81] under the first method a multiplier of 35 might be taken (35 years working life), less 10 per cent. for contingencies, which results in £37,800, less 40 per cent. for being paid as a lump sum (£24,680) less a further 5 per cent. for contingencies affecting the widow, (leaving £20,596). Under the second method if the dependency was £1,200 p.a.[81] and a multiplier of 17½ (half the remaining working life) were taken, the award would be £21,000. The second method appears to be the one more commonly used in recent Scottish cases where the Inner House has been considering the adequacy or excessiveness of an award. The former seems, however, to

[75] *Cf. Kelly* v. *Glasgow Corpn.*, 1949 S.C. 496, 499.

[76] 1941 S.C. 277; 1942 S.C.(H.L.) 51.

[77] 1942 S.C. 156.

[78] 1944 S.C. 499. Similarly see *Horn* v. *N.B. Ry.* (1878) 5 R. 1055; *Wallace* v. *West Calder Co-operative Socy.* (1888) 15 R. 307; *Duffy* v. *Kinneil Coal Co.*, 1930 S.C. 596.

[79] Method used in *Nance* v. *British Columbia Electric Ry.* [1951] A.C. 601.

[80] Method used in *Taylor* v. *O'Connor* [1970] 1 All E.R. 365.

[81] *i.e.* the deceased's gross earnings, less tax and an allowance for what he spent himself and what was necessarily attributable to feeding him.

be the more accurate method and to allow better for adjustment to take account of such factors as different rates of interest on money invested.

It has to be remembered that, though in such cases the court necessarily makes arithmetical calculations, various means of reaching a correct estimate may be adopted. But such calculations are not a substitute for common sense and a calculation which suggests that a family has lost nothing by the death of a highly paid breadwinner must be rejected as repugnant to common sense.[82]

Method A

As has been indicated the first method is to ascertain the "dependency" and multiply by the deceased's normal expectation of working life, then making allowances for contingencies affecting the deceased, for the fact that the money is paid in a lump sum, and for contingencies affecting the pursuer. Normal expectations of working life can be ascertained from life expectancy tables and from knowledge of when persons in various occupations normally retire. But allowance must be made in particular cases for dangerous or unhealthy occupations, and for any specialties attaching to the particular deceased which indicate a probability of death at an age less than normal.

Allowance for contingencies affecting deceased

The product of multiplication done with reference to working life expectancies must, however, be corrected by an allowance for contingencies, such that the deceased, even if not killed as he was, might have been killed in another accident, died or been disabled by natural causes, failed in business, become redundant, unemployed, or otherwise incapable of supporting the pursuers. While these are real possibilities they have almost certainly been seriously overrated in the past. In any event contingencies vary very much with different kinds of employments and with the known health and habits of the deceased. No fixed allowance can be suggested for all cases. As with loss of future earnings by an injured person, a reduction for general contingencies of 2 per cent. to 4 per cent. of the capital value has been suggested,[83] the lower figure being appropriate for a person of normal health in stable employment, the higher for one of poorer health or in a more uncertain or risky occupation.

Discount for lump sum payment

The support lost was being received by the pursuers in weekly or monthly instalments and only by saving could any capital sums be built up and invested to yield interest. But an award of damages is paid as a lump sum and can be invested and yield interest, and some deduction must be made to allow for the factor of potential interest.[84] Otherwise a

[82] *Daniels* v. *Jones* [1961] 3 All E.R. 24.
[83] [English] Law Commission, Working Paper No. 27 (1970) para. 26.
[84] *Whittome* v. *Coates* [1965] 3 All E.R. 268.

capital sum paid now, which could produce interest, would be substantially greater than the aggregate of the weekly or monthly amounts of support lost over the estimated period of dependency.[85] The extent to which a lump sum should be discounted for this reason will depend on the average rate of interest which, if prudently invested, it could earn, but a discount of one-third would probably be a fair average deduction.[86] The proper discount in a particular case depends on the rate of interest which it is assumed the award could earn, and on what allowance is made for capital appreciation. A discount of 25 per cent. represents an assumed interest rate of under 4 per cent.; a discount of 45 per cent. a rate of about 6 per cent.; in each case no allowance is made for capital appreciation. The result will be to require the recipient to draw on the capital to an increasing extent each year to compensate his or her loss of support, and so to exhaust the capital of the award about the time when the estimated loss of support would have ceased in the normal course.

Effect of tax on income from damages

The annual loss for which damages are awarded in compensation is the loss of a net sum, after payment of income tax. The award of damages compensates, partly in the shape of annual slices of capital of the award and partly in the form of income from the investment of that capital. But the income element of each year's compensation will itself be a gross sum and taxable, in some cases at a heavy rate, and accordingly to effect proper compensation the award must be increased to make allowance for the tax to be paid on the income element of the damages. In *Taylor* v. *O'Connor* [87] where the net annual loss by the widow was taken as £3,050, Viscount Dilhorne said:

> "The £3,050 must be a sum free of tax. If it is not, then the respondent will not be receiving full compensation for her loss. The capital sum awarded to her will produce income and, if her expenditure is at the rate of £3,050 per annum throughout her life, part of that will be derived from capital and part from the income that capital produces. Presumably in the earlier years the income element will form a larger part of the £3,050 than in later years. She will be liable to tax on the income element, so, to secure that she can have the £3,050 free of tax, an addition to that sum must be made to cover the tax payable. In *British Transport Commission* v. *Gourley* [88] the net figure after deduction of tax was used for the purpose of assessing

[85] Thus an estimated net loss of support averaging £100 per month or £1,200 per annum for an estimated 20 years would aggregate £24,000. A lump sum award of £24,000, if invested at 5 per cent., would produce £1,200 p.a. gross, or about £1,000 net, interest and leave the capital intact.

[86] In the example given above an award of £16,000, invested at 5 per cent. would produce £800 p.a. gross, or about £700 p.a. net, initially. The balance of each year's support has to be made up out of capital.

[87] [1970] 1 All E.R. 365, 375–376.

[88] [1956] A.C. 185.

damages. Here the net figure should be grossed up to provide the tax which the respondent would have to pay so that she will be able to receive £3,050 net. . . . If some regard is not had to the tax liability on the income element, the result will be that such a widow will receive a capital sum less than that sufficient to compensate for the loss. I cannot estimate the amount of tax that the respondent would have to pay on the income element in the figure of £3,050, or what addition should be made to that figure so that, after paying tax, she can receive that figure net, but it would not be unreasonable to assume that it would be of the order of £500 a year and I propose to make that assumption. Were the respondent a rich woman it would not be right, in my opinion, to increase the provision for tax on account of her increased liability to tax on account of her personal income. I feel that some allowance should be made on the basis that the income element is her only income."

Allowance for the effect of taxation may be by increasing the multiplicand,[89] or the multiplier,[90] or decreasing the rate of interest which, it is assumed, the award will earn.[91] The correct allowance is a matter of great difficulty because, apart from any future changes in taxation, the rate and amount of tax will depend partly on the size of the loss and of the award, *i.e.* whether it is big enough to be taxable at all and, if so, at what rate, and partly on whether the pursuer has other income and, if so, how much, which is aggregated with the income element of the damages.[92] In a case where the whole of the income element will be taxable at the basic rate of 30 per cent., the damages must be increased to make the income element yield 144 per cent. of the net loss compensable thereby.

Deduction for contingencies affecting pursuers

A further small deduction, say 2 per cent. to 4 per cent.,[93] should be made to take account of the fact that each entitled pursuer might not survive the number of years considered in calculating the damages. The higher rate of deduction should be taken where the risk of some of the contingencies eventuating seems substantial, the lower where there are no factors suggesting any special risk that any such thing would happen. Thus in a widow's claim it was said: "(The jury) have also given no effect to the

[89] *Taylor, supra, per* Lords Reid, Morris and Viscount Dilhorne.

[90] *Taylor, supra, per* Lords Guest and Pearson.

[91] That is, to calculate on the basis that the damages would earn, say, 5 per cent., knowing that they could probably earn 7 per cent. or 8 per cent., the difference taking account of the tax on the income of the damages. At a tax rate of 30 per cent., 8 per cent. gross interest is equivalent to 5·6 per cent. net interest, and 7 per cent. gross equivalent to 4·9 per cent. net.

[92] In *Taylor, supra,* Lord Reid (368) and Viscount Dilhorne (376) said that in assessing the effect of the incidence of tax on an award of damages, any private income of the recipient should be ignored. *Sed quaere.* A question also arises whether the income from the damages is to be regarded as the first, or the last, slice of the pursuer's income.

[93] Figure proposed in [English] Law Commission Working Paper, No. 27 (1970) paras. 26–27.

possibilities that she might not survive to old age, or that she may remarry, or that her husband might not have survived until his days of earning were past." [94]

Method B

Method B, as indicated, requires ascertainment of a sum for annual dependency and the choice of an appropriate multiplier and in choosing both to try to make allowances for the various contingencies affecting the deceased and the pursuer and, particularly, for the fact that the award will be made as a lump sum and must be assumed to produce interest subject, however, to tax. The choice of multiplier is very vitally affected by the rate of interest which it is assumed the award can earn, the award being smaller the higher the rate of interest assumed.

> " There are three stages in the normal calculation, namely: (i) to estimate the lost earnings, *i.e.* the sums which the deceased would probably have earned but for the fatal accident; (ii) to estimate the lost benefit, *i.e.* the pecuniary benefit which the dependants probably would have derived from the lost earnings, and to express the lost benefit as an annual sum over the period of the lost earnings; and (iii) to choose the appropriate multiplier which when applied to the lost benefit expressed as an annual sum, gives the amount of the damages which is a lump sum." [95]
>
> " Since the essentially arithmetical character of this assessment is the calculation of the present value of an annuity it has become usual both in England and in Northern Ireland to arrive at the total award by multiplying a figure assessed as the amount of the annual ' dependency ' by a number of years' purchase. If the figure for the annual ' dependency ' remained constant . . . and if the number of years for which it would have continued were also ascertainable with certainty it would be possible . . . to calculate with certainty the number of years' purchase of the dependency which would provide a capital sum sufficient to produce an annuity equal in amount to the dependency for the number of years for which it would have continued. . . ." [96]

Because a lump sum award will earn interest while it is being used up the multiplier must always be less than the number of years for which the dependency is estimated to exist. In *Daniels* v. *Jones* [97] the trial judge estimated the dependency as £3,000 p.a. and its duration as 13 years. He used a multiplier of 9·9 being the figure for finding the present value of an annuity of £3,000 p.a. for 13 years at 4 per cent. interest.

[94] *Wason* v. *B.T.C.*, 1960 S.C. 261, 265, *per* Lord Patrick. The contingency of remarriage is now irrelevant: Law Reform (Miscellaneous Provisions) Act 1971, s. 4. The contingency of the husband's survival is a separate matter, a contingency affecting the deceased, which should be considered separately.
[95] *Taylor* v. *O'Connor* [1970] 1 All E.R. 365, 377, *per* Lord Pearson.
[96] *Mallett* v. *McMonagle* [1969] 2 All E.R. 178, 189, *per* Lord Diplock.
[97] [1961] 3 All E.R. 24, 26.

"The starting point in any estimate of the number of years that a dependency would have endured is the number of years between the date of the deceased's death and that at which he would have reached normal retiring age. That falls to be reduced to take account of the chance not only that he might not have lived till retiring age but also the chance that by illness or injury he might have been disabled from gainful occupation. The former risk can be calculated from available actuarial tables. The latter cannot. There is also the chance that the widow may die before the deceased would have reached the normal retiring age (which can be calculated from actuarial tables) or that she may remarry and thus replace her dependency from some other source which would not have been available to her had her husband lived.[98] The prospects of remarriage may be affected by the amount of the award of damages. But in so far as the chances that death or incapacitating illness or injury would bring the dependency to an end increase in later years when from the nature of the arithmetical calculation their effect on the present capital value of the annual dependency diminishes, a small allowance for them may be sufficient where the deceased and his widow were young and in good health at the date of his death. Similarly even in the case of a young widow the prospect of remarriage may be thought to be reduced by the existence of several young children to a point at which little account need be taken of this factor. In cases such as the present where the deceased was aged 25 and the appellant, his widow, about the same age, courts have not infrequently awarded 16 years' purchase of the dependency. It is seldom that this number of years' purchase is exceeded.[98a] It represents the capital value of an annuity certain for a period of 26 years at interest rates of 4 per cent., 29 years at interest rates of 4½ per cent. or 33 years at interest rates of 5 per cent. Having regard to the uncertainties to be taken into account 16 years would appear to represent a reasonable maximum number of years' purchase where the deceased died in his twenties. Even if the period were extended to 40 years, *i.e.* when the deceased would have attained the age of 65, the additional number of years' purchase at interest rates of 4 per cent. would be less than four years, at 4½ per cent. would be less than two-and-a-half years, and at 5 per cent. would be little more than one year." [99]

The cases give little further guidance on the choice of the multiplier. "Judges and counsel have a wealth of experience which is an adequate guide to the selection of the multiplier and any expert evidence is rightly discouraged. . . . If the period is a long one, the multiplier will be much smaller than the number of years even where the contingencies which are

[98] But this point is now irrelevant; see Law Reform (Misc. Prov.) Act 1971, s. 4.

[98a] In *Howitt* v. *Heads* [1972] 1 All E.R. 491, where the deceased was 21 and the widow 20 a multiplier of 18 was taken.

[99] *Mallett* v. *McMonagle* [1969] 2 All E.R. 178, 191, *per* Lord Diplock.

allowed for are of small account." [1] "In fixing a multiplier judges do the best they can to make fair allowance for all the uncertainties and possibilities. . . ." [2] "In my opinion the multiplier is intended to provide in a rough measure adequate compensation for the loss sustained. No precise method can be expected. It is well hallowed in practice, and depends in some measure on the expertise of judges accustomed to try these cases." [3]

It is submitted that in the normal case a multiplier of half of the number of years of the deceased's expectation of working life would be reasonable, but this has to be varied depending on what factors are being allowed for, the rate of interest being earned by investments, the allowance being made for inflation and the allowance being made for tax on the interest earned by the damages.

Criticism

The criticism of reported awards in the Scottish courts is difficult because many awards are made by juries, and it is impossible to know what factors the jury took into calculation, and furthermore, unless a jury award is reconsidered on appeal it may be very incorrect. Even if a jury award is considered on appeal it will not be interfered with unless seriously inadequate or excessive, and the Inner House need not disclose what award it would have considered right.

It must be said that many of the calculations overtly made in reported Scottish cases are notably unscientific. Thus in *Wason* v. *B.T.C.*[4] the judges considered the income which the award would have brought in for the pursuer's lifetime, not for a calculated period of dependency.

Furthermore in many cases the multiplier used has been too low. In *Smith* v. *Comrie's Exrx.*[5] the Lord Ordinary refers to awards of "four times the deceased husband's annual earnings" as a general guide. In *Love* v. *N.C.B.*[6] it was argued that "loss of support seemed to average between three and four years of the husband's earnings." The husband had been 36, and in such a case to take less than 12 as the multiplier is far too low.

Deductions from gross awards

Benefits to the pursuer from the death

In so far as a pursuer has his or her loss of financial support, incurred by reason of the death, compensated from another source, support is not lost. "In principle, if, as a direct result of his death, support is provided for her otherwise, it seems to me that such other means of support should

1 *Taylor* v. *O'Connor* [1970] 1 All E.R. 365, 367, *per* Lord Reid. (In that case the deceased had an expectation of life of 18 years; the House of Lords approved use of a multiplier of 12.)
2 *Taylor*, *supra*, 372, *per* Lord Morris.
3 *Taylor*, *supra*, 373, *per* Lord Guest.
4 1960 S.C. 261.
5 1944 S.C. 499, 500. (At that time the multiplicand was the deceased's gross earnings.)
6 1956 S.C. 459, 460.

be taken into account in assessing the damages due." [7] The benefit must have accrued not merely on, but as a result of, the death. This principle is not, however, invariable or without exception and some kinds of benefits are ignored.

Social security benefits

The Law Reform (Personal Injuries) (Amendment) Act 1953 provides that in section 2 of the Law Reform (Personal Injuries) Act 1948 there shall be added:

> "(5A) In an action for damages in Scotland in respect of a person's death there shall not in assessing those damages be taken into account any right to benefit [8] resulting from that person's death." [9]

The rights to benefit [8] arising on a death are:

(*d*) widow's benefit, including
(i) widow's allowance;
(ii) widowed mother's allowance;
(iii) widow's pension [10];
(*e*) guardian's allowance [11];
(*i*) death grant [12];
and
(*c*) industrial death benefit.[13]

Insurance benefits

Benefit in the shape of payment under a life insurance or personal accident policy taken out by the deceased on his own life is not taken into account because such a transaction is, in a matter between a relative and the wrongdoer, *res inter alios*, and because if such a deduction were allowed the obvious result would be that the wrongdoer would have received the full benefit of the insurance, without paying any of the premiums.[14] In fact the deceased's estate would be worse off, to the full extent of the premiums and interest upon them, than if the deceased had never insured his life at all.[15] At most, the pursuer has benefited by getting the payment

[7] *Adams* v. *Spencer*, 1951 S.C. 175, 187, *per* Lord Jamieson. *Cf. Davies* v. *Powell Duffryn Collieries* [1942] A.C. 601, 609.

[8] "Benefit" means (1948 Act, s. 2 (6) (*a*)) benefit under the National Insurance Acts 1946 (now the National Insurance Act 1965 and the National Insurance (Industrial Injuries) Act 1965) or any corresponding Act of the Parliament of Northern Ireland.

[9] In *Adams* v. *Spencer*, 1951 S.C. 175, it was held that death benefit under the National Insurance (Industrial Injuries) Act 1946 had to be taken into account, s. 2 (5) of the 1948 Act (now replaced in relation to England by Fatal Accidents Act 1959, s. 2) being inapplicable to a claim made not under either of the Acts mentioned therein but under Scottish common law.

[10] National Insurance Act 1965, ss. 17 (*d*), 26–28, 40–42.

[11] *Ibid.* s. 17 (*e*).

[12] *Ibid.* ss. 17 (*i*), 39.

[13] National Insurance (Industrial Injuries) Act 1965, ss. 5 (1) (*c*), 19–24.

[14] *Smith* v. *Comrie's Exrx.*, 1944 S.C. 499, 501; *Cruikshank* v. *Shiels*, 1951 S.C. 741, 747.

[15] *Adams* v. *Spencer*, 1951 S.C. 175, 188, *per* Lord Jamieson, quoting *Mayne on Damages* (11th ed.), 487. In English law the Fatal Accidents (Damages) Act 1908 (now Fatal Accidents Act 1959) expressly provides that voluntary insurances should not be taken into account. See *Taylor* v. *O'Connor* (1970) 1 All E.R. 365.

earlier than he or she should otherwise have done.[16] The same would doubtless apply in the case of a policy taken out by the pursuer on the deceased's life. In such a case no deduction should be made because the pursuer had been relieved of the obligation to pay further premiums.

If, however, the pursuer benefits under an insurance policy on which neither he or she nor the deceased but someone else paid the premiums, as in the case of a motor insurance policy, kept up by the driver, under which money is payable to an injured passenger or the surviving relatives of a passenger killed, it is submitted that the general rule must apply and the benefits be deducted from an award of damages.[17] Neither pursuer nor deceased paid any premiums, nor had any interest under the policy.

Friendly society, trade union or other benefits

It is submitted that no deduction should be made because a pursuer has received payment of any friendly society, trade union or other benefit, because such is contractual and has been paid for by the pursuer or the deceased by way of contributions, dues, and the like.[18]

Pension rights

Where by reason of the death the pursuer has become entitled to, or even has a reasonable prospect of, a pension, as from the Crown or an employer, some deduction must be made from damages on that account. " It would be entirely unreasonable that she should obtain a full compensation for loss of support from the wrongdoer and also a full or partial compensation for loss of support from the State." [19] This is so even though the pension is liable to be reduced or even cancelled if compensation is recovered from the wrongdoer.[20] Evidence of the practice of the pension-giving authority must be considered, to enable the court to decide the likelihood of any reduction; if cancellation or drastic reduction is certain no deduction or only a nominal deduction from the award seems appropriate; if some reduction is likely a greater deduction may be made. If the pension is payable by the employer, whose fault caused the death, it is clearer still that the pension must be taken into account.[21]

Even if the payment of pension were voluntary on the employer's part and one to which the pursuer had no enforceable right, it must be taken into account, so far as paid and as likely to continue to be paid.[22]

16 *Grand Trunk Ry. of Canada* v. *Jennings* (1888) 13 App.Cas. 800.

17 *Cf. Smith* v. *B.E.A.* [1951] 2 K.B. 893; *O'Neill* v. *S. J. Smith & Co.* [1957] 3 All E.R. 255. A contrary decision was reached in *Green* v. *Russell* [1959] 2 All E.R. 525 on the interpretation of [English] Fatal Accidents (Damages) Act 1908. See also *Bowskill* v. *Dawson* [1955] 1 Q.B. 13.

18 In English law such benefits must be disregarded under the Fatal Accidents Act 1959, s. 2 (1) and (2).

19 *Moorcraft* v. *Alexander*, 1946 S.C. 466. *Cf. Baker* v. *Dalgleish S.S. Co.* [1922] 1 K.B. 361; *Carling* v. *Lebbon* [1927] 2 K.B. 108; *Lory* v. *G.W. Ry.* [1942] 1 All E.R. 230; *Johnston* v. *Hill* [1945] 2 All E.R. 272; *Bishop* v. *Cunard White Star* [1950] P. 240.

20 *Baker, supra*; *Johnson, supra.*

21 *Leadbetter* v. *N.C.B.*, 1952 S.L.T. 179 (point not dealt with in 1952 S.C. 19).

22 *Jenner* v. *Allen West & Co. Ltd.* [1959] 2 All E.R. 115, 125, 126.

Pension or lump sum award from charitable fund

If a surviving relative is awarded a pension, or a lump sum payment, from a charitable fund, such as a pit or railway disaster fund, it must be ignored, because it is voluntary.[23] "Charity and benevolence and pure altruistic kindness are still alive and vigorous in this country. It would to my mind be quite odious if a court had to assess what benefits had accrued, or were likely to accrue, to a victim of a tragedy from such motives." [24] Moreover, persons do not contribute to charitable funds to relieve a wrongdoer, or his insurers, but to help the survivors, whether they get damages or not.

Voluntary assistance by other relatives

If other relatives assist one or more of the pursuers by gifts of money or in kind, or by taking in and looking after a child of the deceased [25] this assistance should be ignored as it has been given from motives of benevolence and compassion.

Inheritance from the deceased

It frequently happens that the pursuer has, on the death of the deceased, inherited something from him, and the question arises whether the value of the inheritance has to be, to any extent, set off against the loss of support sustained by the pursuer, as minimising the loss of support or as a positive gain to the pursuer. Early cases deal somewhat uncritically with the problem. In *Smith* v. *Comrie's Executrix* [26] it was held without much consideration that some deduction from damages fell to be made because the pursuer, a widow, had inherited capital from her late husband. In *Cruikshank* v. *Sheils* [27] it was observed that "the defender takes the point, and the pursuer does not contest, that any benefit which she takes directly from her husband's death must be set off against any loss sustained by her." This seems to proceed on an incautious concession. But more careful analysis is necessary and it is quite wrong to contend that, if a widow has lost £500 p.a. by reason of her husband's death but under his will or intestacy acquired title to his estate which yields a net £500 p.a., she has lost nothing. English judges were more hesitant. In *Roughead* v. *Railway Executive* [28] the trial judge was "not in the least satisfied" that deduction of a sum representing the acceleration of the payment to the widow of the amount left her by her husband was a universal rule and was very doubtful whether it was right.[29]

23 *Redpath* v. *Belfast & County Down Ry.* [1947] N.I. 167; *Peacock* v. *Amusement Equipment Co. Ltd.* [1954] 2 Q.B. 347; *secus, Lory* v. *G.W. Ry.* [1942] 1 All E.R. 230.
24 *Moore* v. *Babcock & Wilcox Ltd.* [1963] 3 All E.R. 882, 887, *per* Chapman J.
25 As in *Rawlinson* v. *Babcock & Wilcox* [1966] 3 All E.R. 882.
26 1944 S.C. 499, 501.
27 1951 S.C. 741, 753.
28 (1949) 65 T.L.R. 435.
29 *Cf. Muirhead* v. *Railway Executive* (1951) C.A. No. 178, (Kemp and Kemp, *The Quantum of Damages*, Vol. 2 (2nd ed.) 226).

In the first place if the deceased had earned income, such as salary, wages and other profits of work, and also so-called unearned income, such as income from investments, benefits under a trust, or the like, this death will normally cause a cessation of the earned income, but may or may not cause a cessation of all or part of the unearned income, *e.g.* where the deceased enjoyed the liferent of certain funds held by trustees, or owned income-producing investments. But, secondly, where the deceased's assets brought him within the reach of estate duty, the death may require the sale of some income-producing investments with consequent loss of capital and of income, and where the deceased enjoyed a liferent the death may, by prematurely cutting it off, materially prejudice the pursuer's standard of living quite apart from the prejudice caused by cessation of the husband's earnings.

In taking account of these factors it is important not to penalise the pursuer for the deceased's providence and thrift, in which in any event the pursuer would frequently be a collaborator, and not to place too much reliance on the question: in whose name were the assets, now inherited by the pursuer in consequence of the death? It is important to remember that in the common case of the death of a salary or wage-earning man he will have been saving to provide for his widow and family, not to relieve a wrongdoer from liability for cutting him down prematurely.

Inheritance of personal effects

In *Bishop* v. *Cunard White Star Ltd.*[30] it was said that " personal effects are not automatically to be deducted pound for pound any more than the value of the deceased's estate should be so deducted " and not if they consisted of articles of which a widow claimant would have had the use. Thus if by the death a family car owned by both spouses became transferred nominally from the ownership of the husband to that of the widow it would not be deducted as a " gain " to the widow. Still less should inheritance of her husband's watch, cuff-links and golf clubs be deemed a " gain " to her, even though they might be realised for cash.

Inheritance of house and furniture

If a claimant, such as a widow, in consequence of the death inherits a house and furnishings, and was herself living there before the death, it is submitted that she receives no benefit and that nothing should be deducted from damages. She acquires the legal title to the house but gets no more use of it than she did before.[31] At most there is an acceleration of benefit.[32] If she sells it she will have to acquire another residence, and can, at most, be deemed to have profited to the extent of any balance of proceeds of the house sold over the price of the house bought.

30 [1950] P. 240.
31 *Bishop* v. *Cunard White Star* [1950] 2 All E.R. 22, 26; *Heatley* v. *Steel Co. of Wales* [1953] 1 All E.R. 489.
32 *Voller* v. *Dairy Produce Packers Ltd.* [1962] 3 All E.R. 938, 944.

If any account is taken of house and furniture as a benefit, deduction must be made of bonds and other debts secured over the house, and an estimate of value made on the basis of probable realised price.

Inheritance of cash in hand

If a pursuer becomes entitled on the death by inheritance to sums of cash in hand or in bank hitherto vested in the deceased, it cannot be said that this is a benefit the pursuer would not have had but for the death.[33] Though technically the property of the deceased it may well have been available for the use of the pursuer quite as much as if it had belonged to her, and it is wrong to stress the legal ownership of the money; such sums may be taken into account, but must not be deducted pound for pound. If such a sum is in an account in joint names, it is probably not right to inquire how the fund was built up or replenished. It could be drawn on by, and can be treated as belonging to, the pursuer, not the deceased.

Inheritance of capital from the deceased

If a claimant has, under the deceased's will or intestacy, inherited a capital sum from him on his death, it has sometimes been said that the claimant's need for support could be partially met therefrom and that some diminution of the award for loss of the deceased's support had to be made. In *Smith* v. *Comrie's Exrx.*[34] Lord Mackintosh held that this factor had to be taken into account, saying that " on principle it seems to me that it must be taken into account, and that, where the claimant's need for support can be partially met by estate inherited from the deceased and formerly supporting relative, only a diminished award of damages for the loss of that relative's support can be given," but described the question of " the extent to which, if at all, such estate falls to be taken into account " as " still an open question in our law." He did not indicate what deduction he made on this ground but acted on the basis that " some deduction does fall to be made by reason of the fact, that the free estate left by the deceased will now fall to be made over to, or held for behoof of, the pursuer." It is not clear what argument was presented on the matter, and no authority was given for the line of action followed.

In *Bishop* v. *Cunard White Star Ltd.*,[35] Hodson J. stated, *obiter*, " where stocks and shares and comparable income-producing investments are concerned and the probable family interest is thereby accelerated, the deduction will normally be made in full. To take the extreme case where the whole family income is derived from the husband's investments, the widow who takes his whole estate on his death will have no claim." The first sentence of this is plainly wrong and grossly unjust.

The fact is that in the normal case of a widow or child the only gain is

[33] *Whittome* v. *Coates* [1965] 3 All E.R. 268, 270.
[34] 1944 S.C. 499, 501.
[35] [1950] P. 240.

the acceleration of benefit, in that the claimant has inherited the estate earlier than he or she would otherwise have done.

In *Daniels* v. *Jones* [36] the Court of Appeal took into account the fact that the widow and children inherited considerable capital sums, but refused to set off the value of the estate in full against the loss of income. " The reality of the situation is that for all practical purposes the widow (and her family) were enjoying the benefit of it almost as much before the death of the deceased as they do now. The fact that the wife, under the will of the deceased, has now become absolutely entitled to what is left of the estate is in the circumstances a change of form rather than of substance." [37] In cases where widow and deceased were on good terms this is the true situation, that investments, irrespective of whose name they stand in, are capital reserves and sources of additional income for the family. All that the widow gets by inheritance is the nominal title to the investments, and the title *now*, instead of in some years' time if the husband had lived his normal span. It may be otherwise if the nominal owner of the investments kept them strictly to himself and spent the income therefrom himself.

Similarly Lord Diplock indicated, *obiter*, in *Mallett* v. *McMonagle* [38] that damages had to be given to supply the gap between the benefits the deceased would have provided and " the value of any material benefits which the dependants will be able to obtain in each such year from sources (other than insurance) which would not have been available to them had the deceased lived but which will become available to them as a result of his death." And in *Taylor* v. *O'Connor* [39] Lord Reid said " the only deduction to be considered in valuing the dependency [of £3,000 per annum] arises from the fact that the respondent was due to receive £10,000 from the husband's estate . . . the learned trial judge deducted £250 from the annual value of the dependency but he started from a figure which is now agreed to be wrong. So I would deduct £200." In *Gray* v. *Barr* [40] where the husband left £16,500, £14,000 of that was deducted from the damages, but the marriage had already failed.

In some cases, however, such as of parents inheriting from their child, they inherit estate which they would normally probably not have inherited at all, and there may be some justification for making a deduction.

Loss of probability that deceased would have saved more

Moreover account must be taken of the counter-vailing fact that the deceased, if he had not been killed, might or even, depending on the evidence, probably would, have made further savings and investments, and something must be given in compensation for this probable loss. The

36 [1961] 3 All E.R. 24.
37 *Ibid.* 31, *per* Willmer L.J.
38 [1969] 2 All E.R. 178, 189.
39 [1970] 1 All E.R. 365, 367; other Lords estimated the dependence at £4,000 p.a. but kept the deduction at £250.
40 [1971] 2 All E.R. 949, 957.

claimants get now, say £20,000, but if the deceased had lived his normal span would have got £50,000. "There remains to be taken into account the savings which he would have made during his working life out of the free spendable income . . . it seems highly probable that he would at that stage have saved as much as possible to provide for the future . . . I think that a conservative estimate would be that he would have accumulated £20,000 capital which would ultimately have come to the respondent . . . I do not think that £5,000 would be too much to take as damages in respect of this element." [41] In *Kassam* v. *Kampala Aerated Water Co.*[42] the Privy Council held that there should be no deduction on account of the accelerated acquisition of title by the claimants, as this would be largely cancelled out by the further savings which would reasonable be expected to have been made by the deceased if he had lived.

It is submitted accordingly that in the case of a close-knit family inheritance of estate should be ignored. The pursuers admittedly acquire title *now* instead of at a later date, but were almost as much in enjoyment of the estate before the deceased's death as if they had owned it themselves, and it may suffer diminution by death duties while the pursuers have lost the probability that the inheritance would have grown as time passed.

Inheritance of business from deceased

No doubt any business, such as a farm, shop, or professional practice can be valued as at the date of the deceased's death, and has to be valued for estate duty purposes, on the basis of what it would fetch if sold, but for damages purposes it is essential to try to forecast how it would have developed over the remainder of the deceased's estimated working life, and what income it would have yielded over that time. The pursuer is entitled to compensation both for the loss of appreciation of the capital asset, if that be the evidence, and for the loss of income which it would have yielded over the period. If the business is *e.g.* a farm or shop, which can be sold as a going concern, and it is sold, that yields a capital sum which goes towards meeting the pursuer's loss of income. If on the other hand the business is a non-saleable professional practice or one which, such as that of an advocate, stops when he retires or dies, the only value of the business is in the income produced.

In *Gillan* v. *McGawn's Motors Ltd.*[43] a hard-working young farmer (32) whose farm was prospering greatly was killed. The widow was 31 and the expectation of life of both must be taken as about 40 years, and of working life 30 or 35 years. He had built up a prosperous farming business and was putting a substantial amount of the profits back into the business. The farm, stock, implements, etc. were valued at nearly £40,000 and passed under the deceased's will to his widow; the capital of the business was

[41] *Taylor, supra,* 369, *per* Lord Reid. *Cf. Nance* v. *British Columbia Electric Ry. Co.* [1951] A.C. 601, 615.

[42] [1965] 2 All E.R. 875.

[43] 1970 S.L.T. 250.

shown in balance sheets as roughly £30,000 of which more than a fifth belonged to the widow; and the net earnings of the business in the year of death were taken as £3,800. If the deceased had not been killed, the evidence was that he would probably have become a leading farmer in the county with a gross profit of about £8,500 p.a., but £4,000 had to be taken as the average of the deceased's probable annual net earnings over the next ten years. The evidence was that the widow had continued to live in the farm but could not work it as a unit, and had to let the lands for grazing but to let the buildings stand empty and the land deteriorate; the letting brought in a gross income of about £1,850 p.a. The Lord Ordinary awarded the widow only £6,500, including £1,500 for solatium and £5,000 for loss of support, and the two young children each £750 solatium and £3,500 for loss of support. The total award for loss of support was thus £12,000. He took the probable average net income of the deceased husband (£4,000 p.a.) for ten years, deducted something for money needed for the deceased's own support (£500 p.a.) and for what would probably have been expended on capital improvements (£1,000 p.a.), and using a multiplier of 10 (which had regard to the widow's remarriage prospects) [44] reached a gross figure of £25,000 for loss of support. From this £25,000 he deducted the capital value of the inherited estate, less death duties and the part of the value thereof belonging to the widow, or £19,350, and from this he deducted the capitalised value of the widow's net income from the inheritance (£850 p.a. grossed at 6½ per cent., or £13,000) leaving a balance of £12,000, apportioned £5,000 to the widow and £7,000 to the children. He found no reliable basis for a fair assessment of the estate to which the pursuers might have succeeded if the deceased had lived out his full life and rejected this head of claim as speculative.

It is submitted that this is a completely unsatisfactory and most unjust decision. The calculations are unconvincing. The multiplier used is far too low. It takes completely inadequate account of future probabilities of greatly enhanced capital value and profitability of the business. It treats as a windfall and benefit to the widow what she was in fact, if not in law, a partner in building up. All that the widow obtained by inheritance was the accelerated transfer to her of the proprietary right in a farming business in which she was participating and which, but for the accident, would probably have grown to a capital value of £100,000 or more over the next thirty or so years and which would probably have provided the widow and her children with a steadily increasing income over that period but which in fact was necessarily a sadly diminished asset, an unworkable farm, which would not have fetched much in the market by the date of trial.

The proper approach to such a case, it is submitted, is to consider separately the capital of the business and the income derived from it.[45]

[44] Now, by Law Reform (Miscellaneous Provisions) Act 1971, s. 4, irrelevant.

[45] In *Taylor* v. *O'Connor* [1970] 1 All E.R. 365, the House of Lords considered separately the working capital the deceased had in, and for the rest of his working life would have had to contribute to, his firm, and the loss of income derived from the firm.

In respect of the capital, what would have been a reasonable estimate of its value if the deceased had lived to, say, 65, and had then wanted to sell out? While estimating is difficult it is thought that it would possibly have risen to £100,000 and that this sum, discounted by half to allow for accelerated payment and for contingencies, and under deduction of the diminished realisable value of the land, stock and equipment actually transferred, would leave a loss of, say, £30,000 under the head of capital. If, as was the case in *Gillan*, some of the capital already belonged to the wife this would have to be deducted. In respect of income from the business, it would, on the evidence probably have risen steadily but might have evened out when the deceased passed middle age. At an average future loss of income of £4,000 p.a. net a fair capitalisation, even making an allowance of one-half for accelerated payment and contingencies,[46] but plus an allowance for the income tax required to be paid on the income to leave a net sum of £4,000 p.a., made up partly of slices from capital and partly from income from the award, would have been £70,000. From this an allowance has to be made for the income actually being furnished; accepting £13,000 for this it leaves a loss on the income side of £57,000. It is submitted accordingly that an award for loss of support of £87,000 would not have been ridiculous.[47]

Other capital assets passing to pursuer

Other capital assets may pass to a pursuer on a death, such as a collection of books or pictures or silver, or copyrights or patents, or horses or cars. If these are to be taken into account at all (and it is the height of injustice that a widow should have to sell off her late husband's assets to relieve the wrongdoer's liability) a fair valuation must be made, and account taken of the wasting character of some assets.

Criticism

The grounds for making any deduction for estate passing on death are unsatisfactory. Savings and investments are really in the same situation as contractual insurance provisions, which are not taken into account. Some modes of savings and investment are in fact tied to life insurance provisions. To take capital, savings or investments into account is open to the same objection as that levelled against considering insurance policies, that the wrongdoer benefits from the deceased's providence and abstinence from spending. If a man chooses to spend money on his wife during his life, or to save with a view to ensuring her comfort after his

[46] This could be done by multiplying the annual loss of £4,000 by say 33 (the deceased's probable expectation of working life) and deducting one-half for acceleration and contingencies, or taking a multiplier of 16½ (which takes account of these factors). Either calculation produces a figure of £66,000.

[47] In *Taylor* v. *O'Connor* [1970] 1 All E.R. 365, the widow and child of a man of 53 with much less capital in his business but with prospects of rapidly rising earnings were awarded £54,000.

(natural) death, that is his choice, but it should not affect the damages the wrongdoer has to pay for killing him.[48]

Moreover, to take savings and investments from savings into account may be doubly unfair in that if the savings are not counted as money spent on the wife, they diminish the support she had actually been receiving, and if the investments built up from the savings are treated as available for her support they also diminish her award for loss of support.

Moreover, can it be said that the deceased's estate " would not have been available to them had the deceased lived but which will become available to them as a result of his death "? [49] No doubt it might not have been available as of right, by virtue of legal ownership of the items in the estate, but one of the purposes of saving and accumulating capital is normally to have a family reserve which can be made available in case of need to supplement a cessation or deficiency of income. If the deceased, instead of being killed, had lost his job or had to give up work, would he not have drawn on his capital? To regard his estate accordingly as something " not available " to his wife and family but becoming available only by his death is fallacious, putting excessive emphasis on legal ownership. Their claims, if brought as claims for aliment, would be prestable against capital. In *Daniels* v. *Jones*,[50] Pearce and Willmer L.JJ. both indicated [51] that in the case before them the wife could have called on the capital, if need be, as much as if it had been in her own name. " I cannot bring myself to think that the mere change in the title to the shares which passed brought any substantial benefit to the widow." [52]

Again, if the pursuer has capital, that is held irrelevant if she had been receiving support and has lost it by reason of the death.[53] Why should capital be taken into account if it was in the deceased's name, but not if it was in the survivor's name? Furthermore, what would be the position if the estate were in joint names of the deceased and his widow?

Again, by virtue of the doctrine of legal rights in succession, a Scottish widow and children have a quasi-proprietary interest in estate vested in the husband and father during his lifetime, in that he cannot, in general, defeat their claims, which emerge and become vested rights immediately on his death, testate or intestate. A widow is only getting accordingly something to which she was, at least in part, already entitled.

Again, though capital and savings may be nominally vested in a husband, the saving and accumulation of the capital is normally possible only by the co-operation, and sometimes largely by the efforts, of the wife

48 If X earns £2,000 p.a. net and spends £200 on himself and £1,800 on his wife and home, damages to his widow must be assessed on the basis of £1,800 multiplied by a number of years. If Y earns £2,000 p.a. and spends £200 p.a. on himself, £1,500 on his wife and home, and saves £300 p.a., why should damages to his widow be assessed differently?

49 Lord Diplock in *Mallett* v. *McMonagle* [1966] 2 All E.R. 178, 189.

50 [1961] 3 All E.R. 24.

51 pp. 28E, 31B.

52 *Ibid.* p. 31, *per* Willmer L.J.; *cf.* Pearson L.J. at p. 33A.

53 *Cruikshank* v. *Shiels*, 1953 S.C.(H.L.) 1.

and to treat the capital on the husband's death as his alone, a fund to which she had contributed nothing, is quite unfair.

The decisions to make deduction also fail to take account of the fact that the most powerful incentives for a man to save and accumulate capital are to provide for retiral, for a widow, to provide for children's education and starting in life, and to build up a capital asset, such as a farm or a collection of paintings.

A further important factor is that " if the deceased had not been killed, it is reasonably certain that by wise investment of his surplus income he would have been able, as the years passed, materially to increase the value of the estate, to which the widow would have succeeded if he had still predeceased her. If it be right to set off against the loss of income such pecuniary benefit as the widow received if succeeding now to the estate of the deceased, it must also be right to take into account the fact that, owing to the premature death of the deceased, the estate is of less value now than it would have been if he had completed his normal expectation of life." [54] In short, a widow may, if her husband is killed, inherit £x now, but if he had lived out his life, she would probably have inherited £(x+y).

To take inherited estate into account requires the widow or other person left to use the capital of the inheritance as income in replacement of other income lost by the fault of the defender, and to use that from an earlier date than would otherwise have been the case. Thus if A is widowed at 40, and inherited estate is deducted, she is being expected to use the income and capital of the inherited estate from the age of 40 when in the normal course she would not have had to do this till, say, 65.

Not least, inheritance cases could easily offend against the principle that, if a person has suffered the death of a close relative and calculations suggest that he has lost nothing by the death, there is something wrong with the calculations. Thus, if A, earning £2,000 p.a. net and having £100,000 invested (yield £2,000 p.a. net) is killed, and Mrs. A's loss of support is calculated at £1,200 p.a. for fifteen years, or £18,000, it can be argued that by inheriting £100,000 (less death duties) which will yield, say, £1,200 p.a. net, she has lost absolutely nothing.

It is submitted accordingly that in the ordinary case of close-knit families inherited estate should be ignored. The only case in which a survivor gains by inheritance on the death is where the estate inherited was kept quite distinct and was not available, as to interest or capital, to the survivor, prior to the deceased's death.[54a]

Voluntary benefit from estate

Where a relative receives a part of the estate transmitted by the

[54] *Daniels* v. *Jones* [1961] 3 All E.R. 24, 31, *per* Willmer L.J.

[54a] The Scottish Law Commission has recommended that no account should be taken of what dependants receive in consequence of the death by way of succession or settlements: Report on the Law Relating to Damages for Injuries Causing Death (Scots. Law Com. No. 31, 1973).

deceased on death, not by law or by the will but by the voluntary benevolence of those taking it by law or under the will no account falls to be taken of the estate received.[55] It is not a benefit taken by reason of the death nor of the law, but by reason of donation. Thus, if on the one parent's death intestate, children relinquish their claims to legal rights in favour of the surviving spouse, he or she benefits from their benevolence, not under the law or a will, and no deduction at all should be made from damages.

Effect of pursuer's own tax position on award

If a pursuer, such as a widow, herself has income subject to tax the income produced by the investment of the capital sum received as damages may be more heavily taxed than it would be if she had no income from her own efforts, and the benefit of the damages to that extent will be reduced.

Inheritance by child or children

In the case of children living in family with the deceased it will frequently happen that they are enjoying the benefit of the deceased's capital even though it is not legally vested in them, and that in consequence by the death they may obtain no benefit at all or only the technical benefit of having the capital or parts of it transferred to their names. But in the case of forisfamiliated children, they may have been receiving no benefit from the parent's capital, and have had no interest in it save an expectancy under the doctrines of legal rights and of rights on intestacy or under his will. In such a case the acquisition of rights to parts of the estate can be held to go some way to cancel any contingent claim to support lost by reason of the death.

Acceleration of interest in capital by the death

If it be held that a claiming relative has in fact benefited by inheritance in consequence of the death the benefit consists merely in acceleration of the vesting of interests in the deceased's capital rather than in getting what he or she would otherwise have not got, and some deduction should be made from the damages in respect of the accelerated benefit.[56] On the other hand, having regard to the probability that the deceased, if he had not been killed, would have saved further and increased the capital, a court may decline to make any deduction in respect of the acceleration of inheritance.[57]

Pursuer's earnings from deceased

If the pursuer received a salary or wages from the deceased for services truly rendered, *e.g.* as his secretary, that is not a benefit lost by reason of

[55] *Peacock* v. *Amusement Equipment Co.* [1954] 2 All E.R. 689.
[56] *Voller* v. *Dairy Produce Packers Ltd.* [1962] 3 All E.R. 938, 944.
[57] *Kassam* v. *Kampala Aerated Water Co.* [1965] 2 All E.R. 875.

the deceased's death, because it could be earned from another for the same services but in so far as the salary exceeds the true value of her services, and was really paid because she was his wife that is a benefit lost and must be taken into account in assessing loss of support.[58]

Pursuer's private or independent income

If a pursuer, such as a widow, has private income or independent earnings, these earnings are wholly irrelevant to a claim for loss of support if she was in fact being supported by the deceased and has lost that support by his death.[59] If, on the other hand, the pursuer was living entirely on her own earnings and was not being supported at all, she has not lost support by the death, but only a claim to support in case of necessity. In the intermediate case where both spouses were contributing to a family purse, it is necessary to ascertain how much was being contributed by the deceased and how much, accordingly, the joint fund has lost by reason of the death. The question is not: does she need the money to keep her from penury? but: what has the pursuer lost by reason of the death? But " if the wife's private means at the time of the award are to diminish to any extent the sum she is to get for loss of support, the jury will have to take into account a factor so speculative as the limits within which her fortune may increase or diminish from time to time in the future." [60] The pursuer's private income or independent earnings may materially affect her tax liability and, if it puts her into a higher rate of tax, might require an increase in damages to compensate therefor.[61]

Pursuer's private capital

It follows further that the fact that a pursuer has capital amply sufficient to support her, whether from the income thereof or by consuming the capital is quite irrelevant, if she was in fact being supported by the deceased and has lost support by reason of the death.

Widow's actual or possible remarriage

At common law the court had to consider the fact, if it had taken place, that a widow had remarried, or was about to do so, or the possibility that she would remarry, because by doing so she acquired a new source of support in place of that provided by her late husband.[62] The Law Reform (Miscellaneous Provisions) Act 1971, s. 4 (2), however, provides that " in assessing damages payable to a widow " in respect of the death of her husband in consequence of personal injuries " there shall not be taken into

[58] *Malyon* v. *Plummer* [1963] 2 All E.R. 344.
[59] *Cruikshank* v. *Shiels*, 1953 S.C.(H.L.) 1.
[60] *Cruikshank* v. *Shiels*, 1951 S.C. 741, 746–747, *per* Lord Patrick.
[61] *Cf. Taylor* v. *O'Connor* [1970] 1 All E.R. 365, 368.
[62] *Lloyds Bank and Mellows* v. *Railway Executive* [1952] 1 T.L.R. 1207; *Mead* v. *Clarke, Chapman & Co.* [1956] 1 All E.R. 44; *Curwen* v. *James* [1963] 2 All E.R. 619; *Reincke* v. *Gray* [1964] 2 All E.R. 687; *Buckley* v. *Allan & Ford* [1967] 2 Q.B. 637; *Goodburn* v. *Cotton* [1968] 1 All E.R. 518; *Cowan* v. *Greig*, 1969 S.L.T.(Notes) 34. *Cf. Donnelly* v. *Glasgow Corpn.*, 1949 S.L.T. 362.

account the remarriage of the widow or her prospects of remarriage." This so-called reforming provision compels the court to ignore a factor very relevant to her future support and to damages, and offends against the principle that changes in circumstances after the right of action accrued which are relevant to damages must be taken into account.

Actual or possible remarriage of a widower, even with a millionairess, is not affected by the Act and must be taken into account as against *e.g.* the prospective cost of a housekeeper. Nor does the Act affect the position of a child; even if the mother remarries the child has still lost the support of its father, because a stepfather is under a moral rather than a legal obligation to support his step-child.[63]

In *Donnelly* v. *Glasgow Corporation* [64] the defenders averred that since her husband's death a widow had taken up cohabitation with another man and borne him a child. These averments were held irrelevant. This is questionable. Such a case is not affected by the 1971 Act and, while it is true that a woman has no legal right to support from a man with whom she merely cohabits, if the relationship appears to be stable and more than temporary and support is in fact being given, some deduction could justifiably be made from the widow's damages.

Widow's ability to take employment

Is it relevant to consider whether a pursuer, having regard to age, health, ability and qualifications, family commitments and other circumstances, could take up, or resume, employment? Whether a particular pursuer can be expected to do so, and how taking employment would affect loss of support and consequently damages of course depends on the facts of each case. It is submitted that if a widow was being supported by her husband, the wrongdoer is not entitled to demand that she take up employment, even if available to do so, in relief of his obligation to make reparation to her, nor to have damages reduced because she could start or restart to earn money to support herself. In England it has been held [65] that no deduction should be made because of a widow's capacity to earn, even where she had stated an intention to resume employment when family commitments permitted.

Awards for death of children

In making an award to a parent or parents, account must be taken of loss of the right of potential support, that is to claim support if at some time the parent or parents required aliment, and loss of any support which was actually being afforded. In estimating loss the court must take into account that the child may cease to contribute and will almost certainly

[63] *Mead* v. *Clarke, Chapman & Co.* [1956] 1 All E.R. 44; *Howitt* v. *Heads* [1972] 1 All E.R. 491; *Thompson* v. *Price* [1973] 2 All E.R. 846. But see also Matrimonial Proceedings (Children) Act 1958, s. 7 (1) (*b*) and (2).

[64] 1949 S.L.T. 362.

[65] *Howitt* v. *Heads* [1972] 1 All E.R. 491.

cease to do so when he becomes forisfamiliated on account of his marriage or otherwise.[66]

Awards to children

In making awards for patrimonial loss to children of a deceased, each child has to be considered separately, and the same award to all children is not proper. Regard must be had to the fact that the younger the child, the longer the period for which it will lack parental support and accordingly the larger the award must be.[67] Children of full age, particularly if forisfamiliated, are not entitled to any more than a nominal award, in respect of the loss of patrimonial support in case of necessity. On the other hand, if there are special circumstances, such as the child's ill-health or incapacity, which seem likely to prolong that child's dependency beyond the normal period, a larger award is appropriate.[68] It has also to be remembered that awards are parts of a general family claim, and if an award is being made to a parent of the children, it will normally be contemplated that that parent will maintain a family home for the children, so that the award made to each child should not take account of the cost of having to maintain a home, but only of the obligation to contribute to one's keep within the family.

These considerations suggest that in normal cases the largest awards should be made to very young children, declining gradually with age to very moderate, or even nominal, awards in the case of grown-up children.[69]

If before the assessment of damages children's other parent has died, that justifies an enhanced award of damages, the potentiality of being entirely orphaned and unsupported having become actuality.[70]

In the case where a widow has remarried, it cannot be assumed that a child's loss of support has been met by his mother's remarriage, because the financial position of the stepfather may be better or may be worse than that of the real father but the moral obligation of a stepfather to support a child is not the financial equivalent of the legal obligation of a father to aliment his own child, and there may be further children diminishing the amount of support available for the child claiming.[71] Evidence may, however, satisfy the court that in all reasonable probability the child will not suffer any lesser support in future than he would have done if the real father had not been killed.

Other pecuniary losses

The pecuniary loss for which compensation can be claimed is limited to loss of support. Hence where a son, claiming damages for the death of

66 *Duffy* v. *Kinneil Coal Co.*, 1930 S.C. 596; *Gibson* v. *Kyle*, 1933 S.C. 30; *Dickson* v. *N.C.B.*, 1957 S.C. 157, 170.
67 *Kelly* v. *Glasgow Corpn.*, 1951 S.C.(H.L.) 15.
68 *Paterson* v. *L.M.S. Ry.*, 1942 S.C. 156 (mentally defective daughter).
69 *Cf. Paterson, supra*; *Kelly, supra*; *Wason* v. *B.T.C.*, 1960 S.C. 261.
70 *Kelly, supra*; *Voller* v. *Dairy Produce Packers Ltd.* [1962] 3 All E.R. 938.
71 *Mead* v. *Clarke, Chapman & Co.* [1956] 1 All E.R. 44, distinguished in *Reincke* v. *Gray* [1964] 2 All E.R. 687, which was decided on statutes not applicable to Scotland.

his father, averred that the father had covenanted to pay him £2,000 p.a. during their joint lives, the estimated loss under the deed of covenant was held irrelevant.[72]

The final allocation

While each pursuer having title to sue makes a separate claim and is entitled to a separate award the loss of support is a single one and it is convenient to calculate the compensation therefor as a single total and then allocate it among the pursuers. To seek to calculate each pursuer's loss separately would involve great danger of double-counting.

In the allocation, where there is a widow, it is customary to award the largest sum to her, recognising that she normally has the responsibility of maintaining a family home for some of the other pursuers as well, and will bear the general overheads of that, and because her dependency is frequently likely to be more prolonged than that of the children. If, however, there are doubts as to the widow's capacity to handle money, it would be better to apportion the total among the pursuers strictly according to probable periods of dependency, to appoint one or more factors to manage children's awards and to have them contribute to their mother if and so long as she provides a home for them.

Outlays and Expenses

If any outlays or expenses are incurred by or in respect of the deceased between the date of the accident and the date of death, they are recoverable by his executor, not by a relative. By custom, and frequently by concession, outlays and expenses incurred by one or more relatives, as on a funeral, are included in an award to him or them.[73] This is illogical. In the first place funeral and related expenses are payable by the deceased's executor, and out of the assets of the deceased's estate; they are not a charge against any particular relative.[73a] The mistake is obvious in the case where the executor is not one of the surviving entitled relatives, where, for example, a son-in-law is executor. If a relative other than the executor, such as a widow, pays the funeral expenses she is, properly speaking, voluntarily defraying an expense, and the fact that an entitled relative is frequently also executor, or that there is no estate and no executor, merely confuses the issue.

Secondly, funeral and related expenses are incurred sooner or later in respect of everyone and the death by accident has merely accelerated an expense which would sooner or later have had to be faced. The death has not caused an unavoidable loss but merely brought it forward in time.[74]

72 *Daniell* v. *Aviemore Station Hotel Co.*, 1951 S.L.T.(Notes) 76.

73 *e.g. Paterson* v. *L.M.S. Ry.*, 1942 S.C. 156, 159; *Redpath* v. *L.N.E. Ry.*, 1944 S.C. 154, 170; *Smith* v. *Comrie's Exrx.*, 1944 S.C. 499, 599; *McElroy* v. *McAllister*, 1949 S.C. 110; *McKinlay* v. *Glasgow Corpn.*, 1951 S.C. 495; *Dickson* v. *N.C.B.*, 1957 S.C. 157.

73a *Cf. Rees* v. *Hughes* [1946] 2 All E.R. 47.

74 No claim for funeral expenses was competent under the corresponding English Acts, the Fatal Accidents Acts 1846–1959, but such a claim is competent under them by the Law Reform (Miscellaneous Provisions) Act 1934, if incurred by the parties for whose benefit the action is brought.

In *McEnaney* v. *Caledonian Ry.*[75] an executor was refused funeral expenses as the deceased could never have claimed them if he had claimed damages himself. This view cannot stand along with the later view [76] that an executor can recover for patrimonial loss to the estate caused by the death. But in *Murray* v. *Gourlay* [77] funeral expenses were expressly allowed in a workmen's compensation case, while in *Gibson* v. *Kyle* [78] Lord Morison indicated that he had told the jury that " they must award the pursuer, first of all, £40 in name of funeral expenses, a sum which was not challenged by the defender. . . ."

In the case of the death of a child, funeral expenses have been allowed,[79] but there the pursuer had been put to an expense, unlooked for and avoidable, but for the accident.

It is probably implied that the expenses were reasonable in the circumstances, and that an unreasonable claim may be reduced.

Questions have arisen as to the recoverability of death expenses other than the essential ones. Whether a tombstone is a reasonable expense is a question of fact in each case.[80] In *Hart* v. *Griffith-Jones* [81] it was held that the expenses of having a body embalmed were not unreasonable or extravagant. On the other hand the cost of a gravestone or monument was disallowed. Reasonable expenditure on a gravestone was allowed in *Stanton* v. *Youlden*,[82] where McNair J. said: " The legal position is that a stone over a grave may properly be considered as part of the funeral expenses if it is a reasonable expenditure for a person in the position of the deceased and of the relatives who are responsible for the actual ordering of the stone; but in so far as it is merely a memorial set up as a sign of love and affection, then it should not be included." This distinction depends on the fact that the (English) Fatal Accidents Acts 1846–1959, under which the claim was brought, specifies " funeral expenses "; in Scotland the question would be whether it was an outlay or expense reasonable incurred by reason of the death.[83]

Deduction of death grant

If a dependant has recovered a death grant in respect of funeral expenses [84] account should not be taken of this as diminishing the expenses.[84a]

[75] 1913, 2 S.L.T. 293.
[76] *Smith* v. *Stewart*, 1961 S.C. 91.
[77] 1908 S.C. 769.
[78] 1933 S.C. 30, 32.
[79] *Duffy* v. *Kinneil Cannel & Coking Coal Co.*, 1930 S.C. 596; *Gibson*, *supra*; *Sands* v. *Devan*, 1945 S.C. 380.
[80] *Goldstein* v. *Salvation Army Assce. Socy.* [1917] 2 K.B. 291.
[81] [1948] 2 All E.R. 729; see also *Bridge* v. *Brown* (1843) 2 Y. & C.Ch. 181.
[82] [1960] 1 All E.R. 429, 432.
[83] *Cf. Tran* v. *Road Haulage Executive*, 1952 S.L.T. (Notes) 58; *Drummond* v. *B.R. Board* 1965 S.L.T. (Notes) 82.
[84] National Insurance Act 1965, ss. 17 (*i*) and 39.
[84a] Law Reform (Personal Injuries) (Amdt.) Act 1953, S.I.

Other outlays

Where relatives have themselves incurred expense as in travelling to bring home the deceased's body,[85] their outlays are recoverable as a natural consequence of the wrong to them. Similarly, outlays in travelling to visit the deceased between the date of injury and the date of death seems admissible, provided the death was a consequence of the injury and not an unconnected event.

If persons other than relatives entitled to sue, such as a brother, have incurred such outlays, the best course is for the entitled relatives to repay, or undertake to repay, him or them, and then to claim the outlays.

The expenses of relatives coming to the funeral, or of answering letters of condolence, are not recoverable.[86]

Where a woman died as a result of injuries in a vehicle collision her daughter claimed damages, *inter alia*, for expenses incurred in employing a nurse-housekeeper to look after her stepfather between the date of the accident and his death, and for expenses incurred in maintaining her mother between the date of the accident and her death. Both were held irrelevant as going beyond the limits recognised for this category of action.[87]

Prospective outlays

There appears to be no Scottish authority but there seems no reason to doubt that if, *e.g.* a wife and mother is killed, the husband can recover for prospective expenditure on a housekeeper or other domestic assistance if that can be shown to be reasonably necessary, as where he has several young children,[88] and additional housekeeping expenses by reason of having to employ a housekeeper,[89] subject to allowance for savings on wife's maintenance. The same would apply if, *e.g.* the wife acted as the husband's secretary, or bookkeeper, or otherwise assisted him, and in consequence of her death he had to employ someone to do what she had done.

Claims by Relative's Executor

If an entitled relative has survived the death of the person whose death gave rise to his claim (the victim), and has himself then died the ordinary rule probably applies, that the relative's executor has no title to sue for solatium for the grief and sorrow felt,[90] but has for patrimonial loss suffered by the relative by reason of the death of the victim,[91] but only for the period

85 *Cf. Schneider* v. *Eisovitch* [1960] 1 All E.R. 169.

86 *Bedwell* v. *Goulding* (1902) 18 T.L.R. 436; *Drummond* v. *British Railways Board*, 1965 S.L.T. (Notes) 82. *Cf. Thomson* v. *Neilly*, 1973 S.L.T. (Notes) 42.

87 *Robertson* v. *Glasgow Corpn.*, 1965 S.L.T. 143.

88 *Cf. Berry* v. *Humm* [1915] 1 K.B. 627; *Morris* v. *Rigby* (1966) 110 Sol.Jo. 834.

89 *Cf. Feay* v. *Barnwell* [1938] 1 All E.R. 31.

90 *Fraser* v. *Livermore Bros.* (1900) 7 S.L.T. 450; *Smith* v. *Duncan Stewart & Co.*, 1960 S.C. 329; but see *Masson* v. *Rubislaw Granite Co.*, 1959 S.L.T.(Notes) 37.

91 *Smith* v. *Duncan Stewart & Co.*, 1961 S.C. 91.

during which the relative survived the victim,[92] and for outlays and expenses paid by the relative by reason of the victim's death during that period. If the entitled relative survived the victim's death, and brought an action for solatium and patrimonial loss sustained by him by reason thereof, and has then himself died the relative's right of action passes to his executor, who may have himself sisted as pursuer.[93] It is not certain but it would seem that in such circumstances the executor may recover under all the heads under which the relative could have recovered if he had lived, but in respect of the period of survivance only, because it was only for that limited time that the relative felt grief, and lacked financial support. The fact of the relative's death may moreover be relevant to the quantum of awards to any other entitled relatives; thus children may have to be considered as complete orphans, instead of children merely lacking one parent.[94] That the second death thereby increases the sums payable by the defender, who may well have had no responsibility at all for the second death, seems to be the defender's misfortune, just as much as it would if the victim's death had followed on, instead of preceded, the other death. The second death may require reconsideration of awards on appeal.[94]

No account can be taken of a relative's death after damages for the victim's death have been assessed and the action concluded.

A member of the family has no title, as *negotiorum gestor*, to claim solatium for a now deceased person for the death of his spouse in the same accident.[95]

Interest

Under the Interest on Damages (Scotland) Acts 1958 and 1971,[96] where a court decerns for payment of " a sum which consists of or includes damages or solatium in respect of personal injuries sustained by the pursuer or any other person " the court must, unless it finds special reasons for refusing to do so, give interest on the damages or solatium or on such part of each as it considers appropriate. The language used is wide enough to apply to fatal accident cases.[97]

Summary

In view of the numerous factors to be considered it may be useful to try to summarise them, bearing in mind that there is no single fixed method of computing damages, particularly under the head of loss of support and that every case must be considered individually.

92 *Reid* v. *Lanarkshire Traction Co.*, 1934 S.C. 79; *Nevay* v. *B.T.C.*, 1955 S.L.T.(Notes) 28. *Nevay* must now be read in the light of *Smith*, *supra*.
93 *Kelly* v. *Glasgow Corpn.*, 1951 S.C.(H.L.) 15.
94 *Kelly*, *supra*, 19.
95 *Parker's Exors.* v. *Esso Petroleum Co.*, 1971 S.L.T.(Sh.Ct.) 28.
96 Examined in Chap. 23, *supra*.
97 *Cf. Webster* v. *Simpson's Motors*, 1967 S.L.T.(Notes) 36.

(1) *Solatium*

Determine a fair sum for each pursuer, having regard to the evidence and to the factors of age, relationship, extent of grief, sorrow and loss and the time for which it will be experienced.

(2) *Loss of support*

(i) Ascertain deceased's pre-accident gross earnings; make deductions for income tax and other compulsory deductions, for sums spent by or on deceased himself.

(ii) Estimate how long he would probably have continued to earn and how his earnings would have moved over that time; fix an average figure for earnings over that period.

(iii) Fix a multiplier, having regard to the fact that contingencies affecting deceased or pursuer might affect the estimated period of dependency, and having regard particularly to the fact that the product of multiplication, awarded as a lump sum, should be invested and earn interest.

(iv) Make allowance, either by the rate of interest assumed under (iii) or by an addition to the multiplicand or separately for the fact that the interest earned by the award will be taxed.

(v) Ascertain whether any capital passes to pursuers under will or intestacy and whether pursuers had actual or potential enjoyment of this or its profits. Make a token deduction for the acceleration of the pursuer's inheritance but consider whether additional award should not be made because capital would have been increased by future savings.

(vi) Allocate the loss among the pursuers.

(3) *Outlays and expenses*

Determine what has been proved by each pursuer and what it is fair and reasonable to allow.

(4) *Interest*

Determine what interest should be awarded on each element of the award for each pursuer.

(5) *Final award*

Set out the various awards to each pursuer.

CHAPTER 55

OTHER PERSONAL WRONGS

AN *actio injuriarum* is one claiming compensation for affront, dishonour or disgrace, naturally causing hurt feelings, though not necessarily any actual patrimonial loss. The compensation due is accordingly entirely or predominantly solatium for the intangible loss suffered in the shape of hurt to feelings.

BREACH OF PROMISE OF MARRIAGE

It is arguable that breach of a promise to enter into a marriage is a breach of contract and should be considered in that context, but in truth it is not so. The agreement in question is not a commercial contract, and is never today specifically enforceable, and the main burden of the aggrieved party's complaint is of hurt feelings at being let down, or jilted. In truth, and in practice, the claim for breach of promise is akin to, and may be combined with, a claim of damages for seduction. In one case it was said that the action was " based on the hypothesis of a broken contract, yet it is attended with some of the consequences of a personal wrong." [1]

If it be established that there was a promise, express or implied,[2] to marry the pursuer, and that the defender has, without legal justification, refused to do so,[3] or so acted as to justify the inference that he will not do so,[4] or disabled himself from doing so,[5] the pursuer has a right of action.[6] Conduct may not amount to breach but yet justify the pursuer in refusing to marry.[7] The right is available equally to either party, but a court or jury might not rate highly a male pursuer's claim.

No Scottish authority discusses the elements to be considered in assessing damages, but English cases [8] give some guidance.

The claim falls under the main heads of solatium, patrimonial loss, and outlays and expenses.

Solatium

An award of solatium is due in compensation for the hurt to feelings caused by being jilted. Much depends on the manner in which the engage-

1 *Finlay* v. *Chirney* (1888) 20 Q.B.D. 494, 504, *per* Bowen L.J.
2 *Murray* v. *Napier* (1861) 23 D. 1244.
3 *Cattanach* v. *Robertson* (1864) 2 M. 839.
4 *Stoole* v. *McLeish* (1870) 8 M. 613.
5 *Murray, supra.*
6 *Graham* v. *Burn* (1685) Mor. 8472; *Hog* v. *Gow*, May 27, 1812, F.C.; Bell, *Prin.* § 1508.
7 *Stoole* v. *McLeish* (1870) 8 M. 613.
8 The right of action was abolished in England by the Law Reform (Miscellaneous Provisions) Act 1970, s. 1.

ment is terminated, and on whether there is any justification for it. A pursuer's conduct may not completely justify the defender's breach, but yet go far to explain it. If the breach, in the manner in which it was made, or the reason for it, *e.g.* that the defender was already married,[9] is particularly shocking, heartless or hurtful, a substantial award is justifiable.

Account may be taken of " loss of market," that is, of having lost an opportunity of being married, and of possibly having a diminished chance of marrying at all in the future.

If the breach of promise were connected with seduction, the latter is properly a separate ground of action and not merely an aggravating factor.

Damages must be moderated if it appears that the defender was of bad character or health or habits, and such a person as offered a poor chance of a happy and successful marriage, or if he honestly, even though mistakenly, had formed the opinion that the pursuer was unhealthy and unfit to marry.[10]

Patrimonial loss

Patrimonial loss consists in any financial loss sustained by acting in reliance on the fact that a marriage was going to take place (*lucrum cessans*), as by resigning an appointment or giving up a job,[11] or by loss of financial advantages which would certainly, or at least probably, have accrued if the marriage had taken place (*damnum emergens*). In respect of the first kind of patrimonial loss, the general principle that a pursuer must take reasonable steps to minimise loss applies, and she must have tried to obtain other comparable employment, and can be compensated only in so far as reasonably comparable alternative employment cannot be obtained. In respect of the second kind courts and juries today should place less reliance on the position and financial advantages which might have accrued from the marriage; this factor is much less important than in the eighteenth and nineteenth centuries when " a good match " was in many cases the only career open to a girl and her only chance of livelihood. A marriage with a person of high position or wealth may be less valuable today than marriage with a person of ability, sympathy and understanding. Subject to that observation the wealth and social position of the defender is relevant as indicating what the pursuer has lost by the breach of contract.[12]

A claim for patrimonial loss has been held to lie when the plaintiff accepted the defendant's promise to marry her, went through a ceremony of marriage, and cohabited with him as his wife, being unaware that he was already married; she thereby failed to enjoy the rights which she would have done, and expected to enjoy, as widow.[13]

9 *Cf. Beyers* v. *Green* [1936] 1 All E.R. 613; *Shaw* v. *Shaw* [1954] 2 All E.R. 638.
10 *Jefferson* v. *Paskell* [1916] 1 K.B. 57.
11 *e.g. Quirk* v. *Thomas* [1916] 1 K.B. 516.
12 *Berry* v. *Da Costa* (1866) L.R. 1 C.P. 331, 336; *Finlay* v. *Chirney* (1888) 20 Q.B.D. 494, 506.
13 *Shaw* v. *Shaw* [1954] 2 All E.R. 638.

Outlays and expenses

The pursuer is entitled to compensation for any outlays and expenses fruitlessly incurred in reliance on the marriage, such as the purchase of a house, furniture, clothing, or other expenditure made or commitments undertaken. The resale value of any things bought must be taken into account, and not all expenditure will necessarily be thrown away.

SEDUCTION

A claim for seduction lies at the instance of a girl who was a virgin but who has been persuaded, and whose reluctance been overcome, by the wiles and persuasion of a man, to yield to intercourse with him, and who has thereby lost her virginity. It is essential that prior to the events giving rise to the action the pursuer was a virgin [14]; the action is accordingly not competent to a widow, or divorced woman, or a girl previously unchaste.[15] The basis of the action is the loss of virginity.[16]

No action lies for consensual extra-marital relations, and the seductive arts used, " any artful practices, or false insinuations, held out to entrap a resolute chastity; any deliberate plan to corrupt the principles or inflame the passions of an inexperienced female, or even any long and persevering solicitations after repeated repulse and resistance," [17] must be averred and proved,[18] and that they were instrumental in securing her consent. If, as is common, the seductive arts consisted in promise of marriage later not implemented, the claim may be combined with one for breach of promise.[19] It is not necessary that the seduction resulted in pregnancy; if it did the damages will be substantially increased, and a separate claim for affiliation and aliment may also be brought.

The major element of the claim is for solatium, for hurt feelings and possible diminished attractiveness for later marriage. It may be aggravated if the evidence is of calculated, heartless deception and deliberate leading astray.

Evidence of the pursuer's prior unchastity not merely mitigates damages but defeats the claim completely, as it negates the basis of the claim, namely, loss of virginity.

ADULTERY

An action lies at the instance of either spouse against a third party who has interfered with the pursuer's matrimonial rights by committing

14 The decision in *Walker* v. *McIsaac* (1857) 19 D. 340 is not truly to the contrary.

15 Such persons may, if they wish, claim damages for loss by fraud.

16 *McCandy* v. *Turpy* (1826) 4 S. 520, 522.

17 *Stewart* v. *Menzies* (1837) 15 S. 1198, 1199, *per* Lord Jeffrey.

18 *McCandy*, *supra* (belief of intent to marry); *Stewart*, *supra*; *Kay* v. *Wilson's Trs.* (1850) 12 D. 845; *Walker*, *supra*; *Paton* v. *Brodie* (1857) 20 D. 258; *Forbes*, *infra*; *Gray* v. *Brown* (1878) 5 R. 971.

19 *Forbes* v. *Wilson* (1868) 6 M. 770.

adultery with his or her spouse.[20] The term " seduce " is frequently used inaccurately in this context. Only the aggrieved spouse may sue, the other spouse *ex hypothesi* being a consenting party. The adultery need not have resulted in the breakdown of the marriage, nor in divorce; if divorce has followed, the claim may be brought in the divorce action,[21] or after obtaining divorce.[22] The third party is not absolved by the pursuer's condonation of the adultery,[23] though this seems relevant to the measure of damages. To be liable the third party must normally be proved to have known that his partner in adultery was married. The wrong is the more serious if the third party deliberately persuaded the spouse to consent to adultery, but less if the erring spouse took the lead or was equally guilty with the third party, if she importuned the third party, or gave a willing consent.[24]

The claim is for solatium for the insult and hurt feelings caused to the pursuer [25] and, where this has happened, for the breakdown of his marriage and the loss of his wife. In the latter case regard must be had to her value as a social partner, as a housekeeper, as a mother, possibly as a business partner or assistant. Damages must be mitigated if relations between husband and wife had been bad or deteriorating, or if they had been living apart, or if the wife had been of bad character.[26]

The claim may, in an appropriate case, be combined with a declarator of bastardy of a child, as being the fruit of the adultery and not of the marriage.

ENTICEMENT

A person of either sex may sue a third party who, without justification, has persuaded the pursuer's spouse to desert him or her and to go off with that third party.[27] The essence of the wrong consists in the breach of matrimonial relations deliberately brought about by the third party. In Scots law the action is not based on any proprietary right a husband had in his wife, but on the idea of wrongful interference with the relations of spouses. It is not necessary to prove that the enticement was for the purpose of, nor that it resulted in, sexual relations. Thus enticement may be to enter a convent, or join an expedition to Mongolia. It may be committed by a relative of the defender but a relative, particularly a parent, will be

20 Bell, *Prin.* § 2033; *cf. Black* v. *Duncan*, 1924 S.C. 738. The right of action has been abolished in England: Law Reform (Misc. Prov.) Act 1970, s. 4.

21 *Fraser* v. *Fraser and Hibbert* (1870) 8 M. 400.

22 *Steedman* v. *Coupar* (1743) Mor. 7337; *Kirk* v. *Guthrie* (1817) 1 Mur. 271; *Baillie* v. *Bryson* (1818) 1 Mur. 317; *Glover* v. *Samson* (1856) 18 D. 609.

23 Fraser, *H. & W.*, II, 1204; *Maxwell* v. *Montgomery* (1787) Mor. 13919; *Paterson* v. *Bone* (1803) Mor. 13920; *Collins* v. *Collins* (1882) 10 R. 250, 257; *Macdonald* v. *Macdonald* (1885) 12 R. 1327.

24 Fraser, *H. & W.*, II, 1204–1205.

25 *Cf. Evans* v. *E.* [1899] P. 195.

26 *Cf. Keyse* v. *Keyse* (1886) 11 P.D. 100; *Lord* v. *Lord* [1900] P. 297; *Watson* v. *Watson* (1905) 21 T.L.R. 320; *Smith* v. *Smith* [1922] P. 1.

27 Actions for enticement of a spouse, seduction of a child, and harbouring a spouse or child have been abolished in England: Law Reform (Misc. Prov.) Act 1970, s. 5.

less hardly judged for enticing back a child who has been ill-used than will an outsider without such partial justification.[28]

But no wrong is committed by a person who merely concurs in the spouse's intention to leave the pursuer, or even advises the spouse to do so; there must have been persuasion overcoming the spouse's natural reluctance to leave the pursuer.[29] And damages must be moderated, if not indeed wholly refused, if it appears that the defender's action was motivated by honest desire to save the other spouse from misery or ill-treatment.

Similarly a parent is probably entitled to sue a third party who entices his minor or pupil child to leave the family, whether for sexual relations or for any other purpose, as being an interference with his right to control his child and his or her upbringing.[30] Again there is probably no wrong if a party merely acquiesces in a child's own determination to leave home.

Indecent Assault and Rape

Any woman may sue a man who has perpetrated on her any kind of conduct which can be deemed an indecent assault, or, *a fortiori*, has committed a rape on her.[31] The claim is for solatium for the insult, hurt to her feelings and honour, and possible damage to her reputation. Consent, if genuine, is a defence.

The husband of such a woman also has an independent right of action.[32] " His right to the exclusive possession of his wife's body has been violated, and his marriage bed has thus been defiled." [33] " His bed has been dishonoured—that there has been violation of his right to the exclusive possession of his wife. . . . The wrong done to the husband would seem to be aggravated in a case of rape." [34] The claim is for solatium for the hurt feelings, insult, disgrace and dishonour done to him, and damages should be much heavier than in a claim of damages for adultery.

Assault

A claim for solatium lies for assault, both for technical assaults without physical contact, such as putting a person in a state of fear and alarm,[35] and unauthorised medical examination,[36] and for actual assaults (sometime

28 *Adamson* v. *Gillibrand*, 1923 S.L.T. 328.
29 *Cf. Gray* v. *Gee* (1923) 39 T.L.R. 429; *Place* v. *Searle* [1932] 2 K.B. 497.
30 *Cf. Lough* v. *Ward* [1945] 2 All E.R. 338 (£500 awarded). See also *Delaney* v. *Edinburgh Children's Refuge* (1891) 19 R. 8 (£100 accepted); *Delaney* v. *Stirling* (1893) 20 R. 506 (£1,000 claimed).
31 *Hill* v. *Fletcher* (1847) 10 D. 7; *Armstrong* v. *Thomson* (1894) 2 S.L.T. 70; *A.* v. *B.* (1895) 22 R. 402; *E.T.* v. *T.B.M.* (1905) 21 Sh.Ct.Rep. 156; *A.* v. *C.* (1919) 35 Sh.Ct.Rep. 166; *McSorley* v. *Archibald*, 1922 S.C. 26. See also *Black* v. *Duncan*, 1924 S.C. 738, *obiter*.
32 *Colonel Charteris* (1723) *Hume on Crimes*, I, 309; II, 123; *Black* v. *Duncan*, 1924 S.C. 738.
33 *Black*, *supra*, 743, *per* L.J.C. Alness.
34 *Black*, *supra*, 747–748, *per* Lord Anderson.
35 *Hyslop* v. *Staig* (1816) 1 Mur. 22; *Lang* v. *Lillie* (1826) 4 Mur. 82, 86; *Tullis* v. *Glenday* (1834) 13 S. 698; *Ewing* v. *Mar* (1851) 14 D. 314; *Robson* v. *Hawick School Board* (1900) 2 F. 411; *Macdonald* v. *Robertson* (1910) 27 Sh.Ct.Rep. 103.
36 *Thomson* v. *Devon* (1899) 15 Sh.Ct.Rep. 209.

called batteries) where there is physical contact and some actual physical damage is done.[37] The damages are by way of solatium for fear, fright and shock caused and, where there is any, for any actual pain and injury caused. If any patrimonial loss, as by absence from work, be caused, damages therefor are recoverable in addition.

Provocation may mitigate damages[38] and self-defence is a good defence.[39] Damages may be increased by reason of the enormity of the affront or insult,[40] or the gravity of the harm done,[41] or the concomitant circumstances.[42]

Intentional Shock

A claim lies similarly for damages against one who intentionally causes shock or emotional disturbance to another, or does that which has as a natural and probable consequence the production of shock or upset,[43] such as carrying out an unauthorised post-mortem operation on a close relative of the pursuer.[44]

Verbal Injury

Of the three forms of verbal injury, two, convicium and defamation, are *actiones injuriarum*, whereas the third, malicious or injurious falsehood, affects a man in his proprietary rights rather than in his honour and reputation, and is accordingly a kind of *actio legis Aquiliae*.

Convicium

In an action for convicium the pursuer's claim is for solatium for the hurt to his feelings and to his public reputation by being brought into public hatred, contempt and ridicule[45] by some statement made, either truly,[46] or falsely, by the defender to one or more third parties, *animo injuriandi*. Ridicule without hatred is insufficient,[47] as is mere criticism of business methods.[48] It was formerly necessary in all cases to prove

[37] *e.g. Gordon* v. *Stewart* (1842) 5 D. 8; *Reekie* v. *Norrie* (1842) 5 D. 368; *Gillespie* v. *Hunter* (1898) 25 R. 916; *Bryce* v. *Glasgow Tramways Co.* (1898) 6 S.L.T. 49; *Wilson* v. *Bennett* (1904) 6 F. 269; *Stevenson* v. *Glasgow Corpn.*, 1922 S.L.T. 185; *Gordon* v. *O'Hara*, 1931 S.C. 172; *Houston* v. *McIndoe*, 1934 S.C. 362; *McGregor* v. *Shepherd* (1946) 62 Sh.Ct.Rep. 139; *McGeever* v. *McFarlane* (1951) 67 Sh.Ct.Rep. 48; *Marco* v. *Merrens*, 1964 S.L.T. (Sh.Ct.) 74.

[38] *Seymour* v. *McLaren* (1828) 6 S. 969; *Thom* v. *Graham* (1835) 13 S. 1129; *Ross* v. *Bryce*, 1972 S.L.T.(Sh.Ct.) 76.

[39] *Hallowell* v. *Niven* (1843) 5 D. 759.

[40] *Gordon* v. *O'Hara*, 1931 S.C. 172.

[41] *Kerr* v. *Anderson* (1837) 15 S. 928.

[42] *Thom* v. *Graham* (1835) 13 S. 1129.

[43] *Cf. Wilkinson* v. *Downton* [1897] 2 Q.B. 57 (£100 given); *Janvier* v. *Sweeney* [1919] 2 K.B. 316.

[44] *Pollok* v. *Workman* (1900) 2 F. 354; *Conway* v. *Dalziel* (1901) 3 F. 918; *Hughes* v. *Robertson*, 1913 S.C. 394.

[45] *Sheriff* v. *Wilson* (1855) 17 D. 528; *Paterson* v. *Welch* (1893) 20 R. 744; *Waddell* v. *Roxburgh* (1894) 21 R. 883; *Andrew* v. *Macara*, 1917 S.C. 247; *Lamond* v. *Daily Record*, 1923 S.L.T. 512; *Steele* v. *Scottish Daily Record*, 1970 S.L.T. 53.

[46] *Veritas convicii non excusat.*

[47] *McLaughlan* v. *Orr* (1894) 22 R. 38.

[48] *Lever* v. *Daily Record*, 1909 S.C. 1004.

special or actual damage [49] but this need not now be proved if the words founded on are calculated to cause pecuniary damage to the pursuer.[50]

Differing in this respect from defamation there is no presumption of injury to the pursuer's feelings.[51] Such loss may, however, doubtless be proved. In *Lamond* [52] it was said that the jury must consider injury to business reputation, loss to business credit, and present or probably apprehended injury to business reputation.

Defamation

In an action for defamation the pursuer complains that statements or other communications of ideas have been made to him, or to others, of and concerning him, which are untrue in fact, hurtful to him in his feelings and derogatory of his reputation, and productive of loss, injury and damage to him, at least in feelings and possibly also in business or professional standing.[53]

Hurt feelings and damage to reputation

If a slander has been uttered the pursuer is *prima facie* entitled to some damages or, at all events, to an apology.[54] Where there is a relevant averment of slander the question whether there has been damage to the pursuer cannot be decided without inquiry into the facts.[55] But to justify a verdict a pursuer need not prove real or actual damage.[56] Where the only harm proved is hurt to feelings, the award is purely by way of solatium.[57]

A claim for solatium is competent though the defamatory statement, whether written or oral, has been communicated only to the pursuer and not more widely,[58] though the width of dissemination of the slander is relevant to the measure of damages.

On the other hand a firm or company has no feelings to be hurt [59] but only a business reputation to be damaged,[60] and an award of solatium to such a body would be incompetent.[61] Individual members of a company cannot sue for defamation which tends to depreciate its business probity or practice.[62] An action for slander against the pursuer's business has

49 *Paterson, supra.*
50 Defamation Act 1952, s. 3, as applied to Scotland by s. 14.
51 *Andrew* v. *Macara*, 1917 S.C. 247; *Lamond* v. *Daily Record*, 1923 S.L.T. 512.
52 *Supra.*
53 See generally *Walker on Delict*, II, 746.
54 *Cassidy* v. *Connochie*, 1907 S.C. 1112, 1116.
55 *Ibid.* 1117.
56 *Fletcher* v. *Wilsons* (1885) 12 R. 683, 686 (£50 for imputation of theft).
57 *Ritchie* v. *Barton* (1883) 10 R. 813, 817 (awards of £40 and £25).
58 *Kennedy* v. *Baillie* (1855) 18 D. 138, 157; *Mackay* v. *McCankie* (1883) 10 R. 537; *Stuart* v. *Moss* (1886) 13 R. 299; *Ramsay* v. *Mackay* (1890) 18 R. 130.
59 *Manchester Corpn.* v. *Williams* [1891] 1 Q.B. 94.
60 *N. of S. Bank* v. *Duncan* (1857) 19 D. 881; *Ogston & Tennant Ltd.* v. *Daily Record*, 1909 S.C. 1000; *Lever Bros. Ltd.* v. *Daily Record*, 1909 S.C. 1004; *Highland Dancing Board* v. *Alloa Printing Co.*, 1971 S.L.T.(Sh.Ct.) 50.
61 *Cf. Socy. of Solicitors* v. *Robertson* (1781) Mor. 13935.
62 *Campbell* v. *Wilson*, 1934 S.L.T. 249; *cf. Browne* v. *Thompson*, 1912 S.C. 359.

been held irrelevant because, *inter alia*, there was no averment of patrimonial loss, and there could be no claim for solatium.[63]

In relation to hurt feelings the court or jury must have regard to the nature and terms of the imputation, to the hurt such a statement would naturally do to a person in the pursuer's position, and to the evidence given of hurt feelings, pain and mental anguish. Statements may affect different people differently.

In relation to reputation some classes of persons are naturally, and rightly, specially concerned with their reputations in particular respects, and particular kinds of imputations may be particularly harmful. Thus imputations of sexual immorality may be specially damaging to doctors and clergymen, of professional ignorance or negligence to solicitors or accountants, of peculation to accountants or bankers, of indulgence in alcohol to airline pilots, and so on.

Nominal awards

Nominal awards have been made where a jury has affirmed everything in the issue put before them except the averment as to loss, injury and damage.[64] Lord Justice-Clerk Macdonald once observed [65]: " The jury cannot find a verdict for the pursuer—where the claim is for damages—without finding some damages due; but there are cases in which the facts present themselves so unsatisfactorily for the pursuer, that the jury, although the pursuer is entitled to a verdict, may give a small sum of damages as was done in this case. There are also cases in which the purpose of the action, although it may take the form of an action for damages, is to establish some particular fact of importance to the pursuer, and he may often not ask any substantial damages, and in such a case the jury being required to find damages due, will award but a nominal amount." Where the pursuer in a sheriff court action said he wanted vindication and not damages, he was held entitled to nominal damages and an award of £3 made.[66]

Harm to business

If any actual loss of business can be proved, the pursuer is entitled to compensation for this also.[67] A defender has been allowed a diligence to recover the pursuer's business books to ascertain the extent of his alleged loss.[68]

[63] *Thompson* v. *Fifeshire Advertiser*, 1936 S.N. 56.
[64] *Craig* v. *Jex Blake* (1871) 9 M. 973; *Graham* v. *Napier* (1874) 1 R. 391; *Bonnar* v. *Roden* (1887) 14 R. 761; *Sproll* v. *Walker* (1899) 2 F. 73; *Winn* v. *Quillan* (1899) 2 F. 322; *Dawson* v. *Giffen*, 1915, 2 S.L.T. 256 (all one farthing); *Bradley* v. *Menley & James Ltd.*, 1913 S.C. 923 (6d. on each of three issues); *Duncan* v. *Brown* (1868) 6 S.L.R. 17 (£2,000 claimed, one shilling awarded); *Pine* v. *Meikle* (1874) 2 R. 40 (one shilling).
[65] *Bradley*, *supra*, 926.
[66] *Fraser* v. *Finlayson* (1937) 53 Sh.Ct.Rep. 97.
[67] *Ritchie* v. *Barton* (1883) 10 R. 813, 817.
[68] *Christie* v. *Craik* (1900) 2 F. 1287; *Gray* v. *Wyllie* (1904) 6 F. 448; as to income tax receipts see *Gray*, *supra*, and *Macdonald* v. *Hedderwick* (1901) 3 F. 674.

Factors taken into account

When considering damages a court or jury is entitled to have regard to the whole circumstances of the case. Elements held proper for consideration have included: the nature of the imputation,[69] the pursuer's conduct,[70] the extent of publication,[71] the absence of withdrawal or apology,[72] the defender's conduct throughout.[73]

Aggravation of damages

In aggravation of damages the pursuer may prove any facts which indicate actual malice and its degree,[74] or deliberate intention to injure,[75] or publication with reckless indifference to truth or falsity and to defamatory character or otherwise of the statement made,[76] or absence of inquiry as to the correctness of statements made by the originator of the slander,[77] and generally the whole circumstances in which the slander or libel was uttered, including the state of mind of the author or publisher.[78]

The pursuer's character is presumed to be unblemished, and it is incompetent to give evidence of the pursuer's good character in aggravation of damages, unless the plea of *veritas* has been tabled by the defender, in which case the pursuer may give evidence as to character in relation to the imputations made in the statement objected to and sought to be affirmed as fact by the plea of *veritas*.[79] Such evidence is necessarily restricted to the questions affecting character or reputation raised on record; the pursuer's general character is not in issue, unless the imputation is a general one, as of dishonesty, in which case general evidence may be given of general character but not of particular facts.[80]

Mitigation of damages

In mitigation of damages a defender may prove facts which, though not amounting to justification, modify the gravity of the wrong, and show that the offence and consequent injury to the pursuer is not so great as is represented, so as to diminish the amount of damages,[81] such as that the matter was generally reported,[82] or that an editorial article was written under such circumstances as to lead the editor to the belief that the

[69] *Simpson* v. *Robertson* (1848) 12 Q.B. 511.
[70] *Kelly* v. *Sherlock* (1866) L.R. 1 Q.B. 686; *C.* v. *M.*, 1923 S.C. 1.
[71] *Tytler* v. *Macintosh* (1818) 3 Mur. 236, 245.
[72] *Vines* v. *Serrell* (1835) 7 C. & P. 163.
[73] *Praed* v. *Graham* (1889) 24 Q.B.D. 53; *Gordon* v. *Street* (1889) 69 L.J.Q.B. 45; *Anderson* v. *Calvert* (1908) 24 T.L.R. 399.
[74] *Cunningham* v. *Duncan & Jamieson* (1889) 16 R. 383, 388.
[75] *Scotland* v. *Thomson* (1781) 2 Hailes 716; *Cunningham, supra.*
[76] *Christie* v. *Robertson* (1899) 1 F. 1155.
[77] *Cunningham, supra.*
[78] *Browne* v. *McFarlane* (1889) 16 R. 368; *Cunningham, supra*, 388, 390; *Morrison* v. *Ritchie* (1902) 4 F. 645, 652.
[79] Dickson, *Evidence*, § 6 *et seq.*
[80] *Hobbs* v. *Tinling* [1929] 2 K.B. 39.
[81] *Paul* v. *Jackson* (1884) 11 R. 460, 464.
[82] *Scott* v. *McGavin* (1821) 2 Mur. 486; *Brodie* v. *Blair* (1834) 12 S. 941; (1836) 14 S. 267; *McNeill* v. *Rorison* (1848) 10 D. 15.

statements were true,[83] or the circumstances in which the slander was written, in order to show that the writer was not acting through any malicious intention towards the pursuer,[84] or due inquiry as to the correctness of statements made by the originator of the alleged slander,[85] or if the defender discloses the name of the originator of the alleged slander and proves that he was a person whose word the defender was justified in believing,[86] or that a correction and apology has been made, or offered to be made but rejected,[87] or that the statement was provoked,[88] or may admit and regret the publication but plead having succumbed to pressure.[89]

If there is no plea of *veritas* facts cannot be proved in mitigation of damages if the evidence of those facts cannot be distinguished from evidence in support of a plea of *veritas*.[90] Evidence of truth of the imputation is a defence, not a plea in mitigation, and so is the argument that the statement was not defamatory.

It is also incompetent to prove in mitigation of damages that the pursuer was himself a wrongdoer; *compensatio injuriarum* is not a good plea in mitigation.[91]

The defender may, in mitigation of damages, on the basis that the pursuer puts his character in issue, and if it is such that it will not have suffered any damage even if the imputations are false, attack the pursuer's character, but only as to the general bad character or reputation of the pursuer, and may not seek to prove particular facts.[92] Specific instances may, if fair notice has been given in the pleadings, be put to the pursuer in cross-examination, though they may not be made the subject of direct evidence.[93]

The defender's own good character is irrelevant in mitigation of damages.[94]

By the Defamation Act 1952, s. 12, the defender may, in mitigation of damages, give evidence that the pursuer has recovered damages, or has brought actions for damages, for defamation in respect of the publication of words to the same effect as the words on which the action is founded, or has received or agreed to receive compensation in respect of any such publication.

83 *Cunningham* v. *Duncan & Jamieson* (1889) 16 R. 383, 387.
84 *Ibid.* 388.
85 *Ibid.* 390.
86 *Morrison* v. *Ritchie* (1902) 4 F. 645, 652.
87 *Ibid.* 652.
88 *Kennedy* v. *Baillie* (1855) 18 D. 138, 145; *Paul* v. *Jackson* (1884) 11 R. 460, 466.
89 *Cunningham*, *supra*, 389.
90 *Scott* v. *McGavin* (1821) 2 Mur. 486; *McNeill* v. *Rorison* (1848) 10 D. 15; *Craig* v. *Jex-Blake* (1871) 9 M. 973; *Paul* v. *Jackson* (1884) 11 R. 460.
91 *Tullis* v. *Crichton* (1850) 12 D. 867; *Bertram* v. *Pace* (1885) 12 R. 798.
92 *Hyslop* v. *Staig* (1816) 1 Mur. 15; *Scott* v. *McGavin* (1821) 2 Mur. 484; *Walker* v. *Robertson* (1821) 2 Mur. 508; *Tytler* v. *Mackintosh* (1823) 3 Mur. 236; *Kingan* v. *Watson* (1838) 4 Mur. 485; *McDonald* v. *Begg* (1862) 24 D. 685; *Bern's Exor.* v. *Montrose Asylum* (1893) 20 R. 859, 863; *C.* v. *M.*, 1923 S.C. 1. *Cf. Scott* v. *Sampson* (1882) 8 Q.B.D. 491.
93 *C.* v. *M.*, *supra*, 5.
94 *Scott* v. *McGavin*, *supra*.

Apology and tender of amends

Under the Defamation Act 1952, s. 4, a person who has published words alleged to be defamatory may, if he claims that the words were published innocently, make an offer of amends under the section. This provision is designed to meet the circumstances of such cases as *Hulton* v. *Jones*.[95] An offer of amends must be expressed to be made for the purposes of the section accompanied by a signed declaration specifying the facts relied upon to show that the words were published innocently, and no other facts are admissible in defence to an action brought if the offer is not accepted. Notice of the intention to lead such evidence must be given in the defences. If the offer is accepted and performed, no action may be brought against the person making the offer; if it is rejected, it is still a defence to show that the words were published innocently and that an offer of amends was made as soon as practicable and not withdrawn. An offer of amends under the section means (s. 4 (3)) an offer to publish a suitable correction and a sufficient apology, and to take reasonably practicable steps to notify persons to whom copies of the defamatory document have been distributed that it is defamatory. Innocent publication is defined (s. 4 (5)) as lack of intention to publish the words concerning the person, and ignorance of circumstances by virtue of which they might be understood to refer to him, or that the words were not *ex facie* defamatory, and the publisher did not know of circumstances by virtue of which they might be understood to be defamatory to the person, provided always that the publisher exercised all reasonable care in relation to the publication. Disputed questions as to the steps to be taken in fulfilment of an accepted offer are determinable by the Court of Session or the sheriff (s. 4 (4)).

Tender

A verdict for the pursuer in a defamation action not merely awards him some damages but, and more importantly, implies a finding that the statement complained of was untrue, and defamatory of the pursuer. To be at all equivalent to such a finding, a tender in a defamation action must accordingly contain a retraction of the statement complained of,[1] as well as an offer of a sum of money in settlement.[2] The retraction must admit the falsity of the statement complained of, as innuendoed by the pursuer,[3] but it need not admit that the defender made the statement,[4] nor that it bears the innuendo put on it by the pursuer.[5]

[95] [1910] A.C. 20; see also *Marshall* v. *Renwick* (1835) 13 S. 1127; *Fletcher* v. *Wilsons* (1885) 12 R. 683; *Gordon* v. *Stubbs* (1895) 3 S.L.T. 10; *Morrison* v. *Ritchie* (1902) 4 F. 645; *Harkness* v. *Daily Record*, 1924 S.L.T. 759.

[1] *Curror* v. *Martin* (1839) 11 Sc.Jur. 463; *Faulks* v. *Park* (1854) 17 D. 247; *MacFie* v. *MacWilliam* (1854) 26 Sc.Jur. 459.

[2] *Bisset* v. *Anderson* (1847) 10 D. 233.

[3] *Faulks, supra*.

[4] *Arrol* v. *King* (1855) 18 D. 98; *Mitchell* v. *Nicoll* (1890) 17 R. 795; *Malcolm* v. *Moore* (1901) 4 F. 23.

[5] *Hunter* v. *Russell* (1901) 3 F. 596.

Quantum of damages

The precise quantum of damages is entirely a matter for the jury [6] and the assessment does not depend on any legal rule.[7] The reported cases give little guidance as to what kind of sum may reasonably be claimed or awarded, though the practice seems to be to make a larger claim when the pursuer is a public figure, a person of reputation or importance, or one whose public esteem and reputation are not confined to a narrow circle of acquaintances but are matters of public concern, or where the imputation is particularly gross or serious, or liable to be particularly damaging to honour and credit.

Actual loss suffered

It is always competent to prove any actual loss or damage suffered in consequence of the defamation complained of.[8] When a pursuer avers actual consequential loss the defender is normally entitled to a diligence for the recovery of the pursuer's business books [9] and possibly also income tax receipts,[10] but access to private books of a company to which the pursuer had transferred his assets have been refused.[11] Actual loss sustained must be assessable in terms of patrimonial or monetary loss [12] and speculative or apprehended future loss is irrelevant.

Cross-actions and counterclaims

The doctrine of *compensatio injuriarum* [13] no longer applies [14] and where both parties complain of defamatory utterances by the other the proper practice is to make separate claims and to set off the damages obtained in one action against those in the other.[15] In *Dawson* v. *Giffen* [16] two parties brought cross-actions which were tried together; in each case the jury found for the pursuer and awarded £180 and one farthing respectively. Similarly a claim for defamation may be brought to counter an action of damages for assault. In *Pirie* v. *Meikle* [17] the jury found for the pursuer in the slander action and awarded 1s., and for the pursuer in the assault action and awarded £5.

6 *Davis* v. *Shepstone* (1886) 11 App.Cas. 187, 191; *Bray* v. *Ford* [1896] A.C. 44.
7 *Bray, supra.*
8 *Outram* v. *Reid* (1852) 14 D. 577; *English and Scottish Co-operative* v. *Odhams Press* [1940] 1 K.B. 440.
9 *Christie* v. *Craik* (1900) 2 F. 1287; *Gray* v. *Wyllie* (1904) 6 F. 448.
10 Granted in *Macdonald* v. *Hedderwick* (1900) 3 F. 574; refused in *Gray, supra.*
11 *Gray, supra.*
12 *Chamberlain* v. *Boyd* (1883) 11 Q.B.D. 407.
13 As to this see *Robertson* v. *Falconer* (1798) Hume 603; *Lovi* v. *Wood* (1802) Hume 613; *Forbes* v. *Young* (1805) Hume 627; *McGuffie* v. *McDonnell* (1809) Hume 638; *Allan* v. *Douglas* (1810) Hume 639.
14 *Hyslop* v. *Miller* (1816) 1 Mur. 43.
15 *Edwards* v. *Mackintosh* (1823) 3 Mur. 369, 387; *Tullis* v. *Crichton* (1850) 12 D. 867.
16 1915, 2 S.L.T. 256.
17 (1874) 2 R. 40.

Wrongful Detention

A person who is wrongfully detained in premises suffers mainly by the infringement of his liberty of movement, and to some extent from indignity and outrage.[18]

Factors relevant to damages are the whole circumstances in which, the place in which, and the time for which the pursuer was detained.

In the case of unjustified detention as a person of unsound mind damages would be heavy.

Wrongful Use of Civil Process

The use of any kind of civil process against a person is an actionable wrong only if the proceedings were instituted maliciously and without probable cause,[19] or in bad faith, if in the knowledge that the claim had been satisfied,[20] or in breach of an undertaking or contract not to sue.[21] It is not sufficient if decree were taken mistakenly or inadvertently.[22]

In such a case the damages due are for the disgrace and possible damage to reputation involved in unjustifiably taking decree. This is particularly so if the proceedings were such as reflect on the pursuer's character, reputation or credit, such as *e.g.* a claim of damages for alleged rape or adultery, or an unfounded petition for sequestration.[23] In considering damages regard must be had to any direct consequences of the wrongful taking of the decree, such as the publication of the debtor's name in a " black-list." [24]

Interdict

In respect of interdict, interim interdict is normally obtained on only an *ex parte* statement by the petitioner, so that it is generally sufficient to justify a claim for damages to prove that it was obtained unjustifiably, which is established by the fact that it was subsequently withdrawn by the court.

In the case of perpetual interdict it is granted only after consideration of the whole evidence, or at least after full opportunity to the defender to appear and contest the grant of interdict against his actings.

Interdict will not ground any action of damages as having been

18 *Mackenzie* v. *Cluny Hill Hydro Co. Ltd.*, 1908 S.C. 200. (£400 claimed for 15 minutes detention.)

19 *Hallam* v. *Gye* (1835) 14 S. 199; *Ormiston* v. *Redpath Brown & Co.* (1846) 4 M. 498; *Kennedy* v. *Fort William Police Commrs.* (1877) 5 R. 302, 307; *Harpers* v. *Greenwood* (1896) 4 S.L.T. 116; *McGregor* v. *McLaughlin* (1905) 8 F. 70, 74.

20 *Ormiston, supra*; contrast *Pollock* v. *Goodwin's Trs.* (1898) 25 R. 1051.

21 *Sturrock* v. *Welsh & Forbes* (1890) 18 R. 109; *MacRobbie* v. *MacLellan's Trs.* (1891) 18 R. 470; *Gibson* v. *Anderson* (1897) 24 R. 556. See also *Turnbull* v. *Oliver* (1891) 19 R. 154; *Mackersy* v. *Davis* (1895) 22 R. 368.

22 *Ormiston, supra.*

23 *Cf. Kinnes* v. *Adam* (1882) 9 R. 698; *Quartz Hill Gold Mining Co.* v. *Eyre* (1883) 11 Q.B.D. 674, 683, 689; *Harpers* v. *Greenwood* (1896) 4 S.L.T. 116.

24 *Gibson* v. *Anderson* (1897) 24 R. 556.

granted wrongfully until it has taken effect.[25] The pursuer must prove that the interdict has taken effect and that his operations have been stopped,[26] and that the restraint was an invasion of his rights.[27] Hence the pursuer has failed where, even though interdict had been recalled as not the proper remedy, he could only show that he had been stopped from doing something he had no right to do,[28] or had been interdicted from building on ground which he had no legal right to enter or build on,[29] or that he had been wrongfully interdicted from performing his duties, though without loss of salary, and then suspended and interdicted afresh and rightfully.[30] The pursuer has, however, succeeded where his legal rights had been invaded, as where he was interdicted from selling what he had a right to sell.[31]

It must also have been wrongful at the time it was obtained, in respect of such an element as having been obtained by a mis-statement of facts, for the truth of which the petitioner was responsible,[32] or as to whether the application was made fairly and reasonably,[33] or whether the statements were misrepresentations, suppressions or non-disclosures.[34]

In respect of wrongful interdict the general principles of damages apply, so that the party who obtained interdict wrongfully will be liable for all loss which is the natural and probable consequence of the wrongful obtaining of interdict. The ordinary rules of remoteness apply, and no claim arises in respect of remote or merely contingent damage.[35] In *Clippens Oil Co.* v. *Edinburgh & District Water Trs.*[36] the pursuers were interdicted for eleven months from working their main seam of shale. Shale could have been obtained to keep the works going at a cost which would have caused considerable loss, so that the company closed their works; in consequence the plant deteriorated, the business connection was lost and when the interdict was recalled the works could not be restarted. In these circumstances it was held that a claim for total loss was inadmissible and that the defenders should not be prejudiced by the fact that times were bad and the company was not rich.[37] The pursuers, it was held, should have got shale in the most convenient way to enable them to carry on their oil works, even though this had resulted in loss, and the true measure of damages was the loss which would have been incurred thereby

25 *Clippens Oil Co.* v. *Edinburgh Water Trs.* (1906) 8 F. 731; *Wilson* v. *Gilchrist* (1900) 2 F. 391.
26 *Welsh* v. *Stewart* (1818) 1 Mur. 397.
27 *Macdonald* v. *Lord Blythswood*, 1914 S.C. 930.
28 *Jack* v. *Begg* (1875) 3 R. 35; *cf. Mudie* v. *Miln* (1828) 6 S. 967.
29 *Macdonald, supra.*
30 *Aird* v. *Tarbert School Board*, 1907 S.C. 305.
31 *Lord Elibank* v. *Renton* (1833) 11 S. 238; *Fife* v. *Orr* (1895) 23 R. 8.
32 *Wolthekker* v. *Northern Agricultural Co.* (1862) 1 M. 211; *Fife* v. *Orr* (1895) 23 R. 8.
33 *Fife, supra.*
34 *Fife, supra.*
35 *Arnot* v. *Dowie* (1863) 2 M. 119.
36 (1906) 8 F. 731; 1907 S.C.(H.L.) 9.
37 On collateral impecuniosity *cf.* Lord Collins at p. 14 and *Liesbosch* v. *Edison* [1933] A.C. 449.

and the cost of reverting to their own workings when the interdict was recalled.

There are dicta in older cases indicating that the degree of blame attaching to the defender's conduct was relevant to enhance damages,[38] but these views are no longer authoritative, and it has been observed that to show that the defenders were trying of set purpose to cripple the pursuers had nothing to do with the interdict being wrongful.[39]

Petition for sequestration or liquidation

It is wrongful to petition unjustifiably for sequestration of a person or for the liquidation of a company. Petitioning for either is a remedy which the law gives absolutely and without qualification.[40] It is essential that the petition was refused, or recalled. If all the substantials were right and the objection to the petition is a technical one then the petitioning is actionable as wrongful only if averred and proved to have been done maliciously and without probable cause.[40]

If on the other hand, there was an averment that the debt alleged was fictitious,[41] or that the evidence of the notour bankruptcy was fictitious,[41] or that it proceeded on an inadequate period of charge [42] or that notour bankruptcy and sequestration had been obtained on a fabricated warrant [43] it would be sufficient to aver such facts and that in consequence the petitioning was wrongful.

The same principles apply to a petition for judicial winding up of a company.[44]

In any such case the main element in damages would be the damage to public reputation and business credit naturally resulting from the taking of proceedings of either of the kinds in question.

Sequestration for Rent

This process is of the nature of a diligence and warrant is granted on the landlord's *ex parte* application.[45] Hence a tenant complaining need only show that it was obtained wrongfully and need not aver malice and want of probable cause.[46] The right to sequestrate is measured by the terms of the lease and within the limits appropriate thereto. Hence

[38] *Morton* v. *Edinburgh & Glasgow Ry.* (1845) 8 D. 288; *Miller* v. *Hunter* (1865) 3 M. 740, 747; *Thomson* v. *Dailly* (1897) 24 R. 1173.
[39] *Clippens Oil Co., supra*, 8 F. at 732.
[40] *Kinnes* v. *Adam* (1882) 9 R. 698.
[41] *Kinnes, supra*, 702.
[42] *Smith* v. *Taylor* (1882) 10 R. 291.
[43] *Beaumont* v. *Watson* (1895) 2 S.L.T. 454.
[44] *Quartz Hill Gold Mining Co.* v. *Eyre* (1883) 11 Q.B.D. 674; *Aitchison* v. *McEwan* (1902) 10 S.L.T. 501; see also *Seaspray S.S. Co.* v. *Tenant* (1903) 15 S.L.T. 784.
[45] *MacLaughlan* v. *Reilly* (1892) 20 R. 41.
[46] *Wolthekker* v. *Northern Agricultural Co.* (1862) 1 M. 211; *Watson* v. *McCulloch* (1878) 5 R. 843; *Gray* v. *Weir* (1891) 19 R. 25; *Robertson* v. *Galbraith* (1857) 19 D. 1016; *Shearer* v. *Nicoll*, 1935 S.L.T. 313.

sequestration does not cover payments other than rent, due under a collateral contract,[47] or property not of the tenant,[48] though a third party whose goods have been taken has possibly no claim in respect of an innocent mistake.[49] The goods falling under the landlord's hypothec must have been on the premises during the occupancy [50] and the landlord must have given full possession to the tenant, so that sequestration for rent is bad and wrongful and infers liability in damages if the landlord did not give the tenant the full possession of the whole subjects [51] or possession for the whole term [52] or resumed possession of part of the lands without allowing an abatement from the rent.[53]

Other ways in which sequestration for rent may be sought wrongfully so as to infer liability to make reparation include overstating the amount of rent due and unpaid,[54] and starting proceedings after a cheque had been given.[55] No credit need be given for an illiquid counterclaim the tenant may have against the landlord, even though it subsequently is found to be exigible from him.[56] It is incompetent to modify the terms of a lease by parole to qualify the ordinary extent of the right.[57]

Where a landlord's sequestration was dismissed and he immediately repeated the process for the same rents, his course of action was held to be unjustifiable and, there being no real damage sustained, an award of £10 was made.[58]

Warrant to carry back

This is similarly granted *periculo petentis* and so must, if challenged, be justified by the applicant on pain of liability in damages, which follows, independently of malice and want of probable cause, if the request were improper and unjustifiable in the circumstances.[59] In *Jack* v. *Black* [60] warrant to carry back was obtained without notice and a claim for £500 damages was made on the averment that it had been obtained " wrongfully." A tender of £75 was accepted.

47 *Catterns* v. *Tennent* (1835) 1 Sh. & MacL. 694; *Clark* v. *Stewart* (1872) 10 S.L.R. 152.

48 *Bell* v. *Andrews* (1885) 12 R. 961; *Pulsometer Co.* v. *Gracie* (1887) 14 R. 316 (samples); *MacDonald* v. *Westren* (1888) 15 R. 988.

49 *Nelmes* v. *Gillies* (1883) 10 R. 890; *cf. Lippe* v. *Colville* (1894) 1 S.L.T. 616.

50 *Horn* v. *Maclean* (1830) 8 S. 454; *Thomson* v. *Barclay* (1883) 10 R. 694.

51 *MacLeod* v. *MacLeod* (1829) 7 S. 396; *Munro* v. *MacGeoghs* (1888) 16 R. 93; *Graham* v. *Gordon* (1843) 5 D. at 1211.

52 *Cumming* v. *Maxwell* (1880) 17 S.L.R. 463.

53 *Oswald* v. *Graeme* (1851) 13 D. 1229.

54 *Oswald* v. *Graeme* (1851) 13 D. 1229, 1234; *Watson* v. *McCulloch* (1878) 5 R. 843; *Pollock* v. *Goodwin's Trs.* (1898) 25 R. 1051, 1052.

55 *Gilmour* v. *Craig* (1908) 45 S.L.R. 362.

56 *MacLaughlan* v. *Reilly* (1892) 20 R. 41; *Alexander* v. *Campbell* (1903) 5 F. 634; *Craig* v. *Harkness* (1894) 2 S.L.T. 307.

57 *Riddle* v. *Mitchell* (1870) 8 S.L.R. 140; *Turnbull* v. *Oliver* (1891) 19 R. 154; *Lippe* v. *Colville* (1894) 31 S.L.R. 615. See also *Campbell* v. *Boswall* (1839) 1 D. 1023.

58 *Hunter* v. *McDougall* (1909) 25 Sh.Ct.Rep. 364.

59 *McLaughlan* v. *Reilly* (1892) 20 R. 41; *Gray* v. *Weir* (1891) 19 R. 25; *Brown* v. *Halley* (1895) 3 S.L.T. 22; *McDonald* v. *Grant* (1903) 11 S.L.T. 575.

60 1911 S.C. 691.

Wrongful Use of Diligence

The use of any form of legal diligence which is wrongful as being irregular in point of procedure,[61] or as being regular but used unjustifiably,[62] or as being regular but having been used maliciously and without probable cause,[63] gives rise to a claim of damages for the insult, outrage, possible inconvenience and damages to reputation involved in the wrong.

An action of damages is incompetent where statute precludes the review or reduction of the decree which is the foundation of the diligence.[64]

Wrongful use of diligence generally

A distinction must be drawn in the case of wrongful diligence between diligence which follows in the ordinary course of proceedings, such as arrestments on the dependence, and diligence which can be obtained only on the strength of *ex parte* applications and statements, such as interim interdict or *meditatione fugae* warrants.[65] A litigant using any legal right or remedy to which he was absolutely entitled and which he required no special warrant to enable him to use, can never be made liable for the consequences of its use, unless he was shown to have resorted to it maliciously and without probable cause.[66]

On the other hand, where a party applies to the court for some special diligence or remedy and requires to make some statement or representation to induce the court to grant the requisite authority in cases such as interdict, landlord's sequestration, and warrants against parties *in meditatione fugae*, the applicant is answerable for the truth of the statements on the faith of which he obtains that warrant. He will accordingly be liable in damages for the consequences if the statement was inconsistent with fact and unjustifiable whether made in good or in bad faith. In short, mere want of success will show that the use of the diligence was wrongful as it was employed on the basis of an *ex parte* statement and *periculo petentis*.[67] It may also be wrongful as being irregularly executed.

Even in the first case, as Lord Dunedin pointed out in *McGregor*,[65] if there is some irregularity in the steps of process, and diligence is persisted in notwithstanding, that might amount to a wrongful use giving rise to an action of damages, though a merely unsuccessful use of diligence in the ordinary course of process is not necessarily a wrong.

No action lies merely in respect of the doing of diligence provided it be

61 *e.g. Pollock* v. *Goodwin's Trs.* (1898) 25 R. 1051; *MacTaggart* v. *McKillop*, 1939 S.L.T. 65.

62 *Wolthekker* v. *Northern Agricultural Co.* (1862) 1 M. 211, 212–213; *Kinnes* v. *Adam* (1882) 9 R. 698, 702.

63 *Wolthekker, supra*; *Kinnes, supra*.

64 Justices of the Peace Small Debt (Scotland) Act 1825, ss. 14–15; Small Debt Courts (Sc.) Act 1837, ss. 30–31; see *Crombie* v. *McEwan* (1861) 23 D. 333; *Gray* v. *Smart* (1892) 19 R. 692; *Mackenzie* v. *Paul* (1895) 3 S.L.T. 71; *Pollock* v. *Goodwin's Trs.* (1898) 25 R. 1051; *Riach* v. *Wallace* (1899) 2 F. 149.

65 *McGregor* v. *McLaughlin* (1905) 8 F. 70.

66 *Wolthekker* v. *Northern Agricultural Co.* (1862) 1 M. 211; *cf. Grant* v. *Airdrie Magistrates*, 1939 S.C. 738, 758.

67 (1905) 8 F. 70, 74.

regular and proceed on grounds which cannot be assailed. It matters not that it may have been unnecessary or more injurious to the debtor than another remedy available to the creditor.[68] Nor are damages recoverable for a trifling inaccuracy which cannot cause any loss [69] and may not even invalidate the diligence.[70]

Quantum of damages for wrongful personal diligence

The pursuer in such a case is entitled to an award in respect of solatium for the inconvenience and insult suffered, which unless there is evidence of malice or hostility on the part of the defender, should be moderate.[71] He is also entitled to damages for any actual damage suffered. If he is himself partly to blame for the use of the diligence, no damages may be found due to him.[72] It is incompetent to prove the defender's character [73] but in an old case it has been held that it can be shown in aggravation of damages that the pursuer is married and one of his family is ill.[74] Formerly no damages were given in the case of a merely technical defect [75] but more recently a nominal award has been made in several cases.[76]

The sum sued for in such cases has been frequently £500 [77] but the amount properly to be awarded remains very much a matter of discretion.

In *Gordon's Exors.* v. *Dunlop*,[78] the award was £10 for imprisonment on an incompetent decree and in *Hamilton* v. *Anderson*,[79] where the wrong debtor was imprisoned, £50 was given, and in *Dunlop* v. *Buchanan*, where a protected bankrupt was arrested, £5.[80]

In *Johnstone* v. *McCraw* [81] no damages were given where there had been a misnomer in a *meditatio fugae* warrant which resulted in a brief detention and in *Inch* v. *Thomson* [82] 1s. was given for wrongous apprehension on inept diligence. In these cases the defect in the diligence was somewhat technical.

Quantum of damages for wrongful diligence against property

The quantum of damages which may be awarded when the use of diligence against property has been found to be wrongful is not fully

68 *Johnston* v. *Commercial Bank* (1858) 20 D. 790; *Henderson* v. *Rollo* (1871) 10 M. 104.
69 *Beattie* v. *MacLellan* (1844) 6 D. 1093.
70 *Gordon* v. *Sloss* (1848) 10 D. 1129; *Glen* v. *Black* (1841) 4 D. 36; *Henderson, supra*.
71 *Wilson* v. *Alexander* (1846) 9 D. 7; *Johnstone* v. *McCraw* (1833) 12 S. 560; *Inch* v. *Thomson* (1836) 14 S. 1129.
72 *Pearson* v. *Anderson* (1833) 11 S. 1008; *Scott* v. *Curle* (1840) 2 D. 348; affd. 2 Rob. 317; *Menzies* v. *Stevenson* (1839) McF. 281.
73 *Simpson* v. *Liddle* (1821) 2 Mur. 580.
74 *Beveridge* v. *Scott* (1822) 3 Mur. 108.
75 *Rankine* v. *McLaren* (1825) 3 Mur. 494.
76 *Meikle* v. *Sneddon* (1862) 24 D. 720 (£500 claimed); *Johnstone* v. *McCraw* (1833) 12 S. 560 (£500 claimed: no award); *Inch* v. *Thomson* (1836) 14 S. 1129 (£500 claimed: 1s. awarded); *Borthwick* v. *Gilkison* (1863) 2 M. 125 (1s. given).
77 *Stewart* v. *McDougall*, 1908 S.C. 315.
78 (1825) 3 Mur. 515.
79 (1830) 5 Mur. 312.
80 (1828) 5 Mur. 16.
81 (1833) 12 S. 560.
82 (1836) 14 S. 1129.

discussed in any case. The amount sued for is usually substantial [83] and where actual damage has been sustained, substantial damages will be awarded. Even where no actual damage has been sustained " it is a wrong to any one to use the diligence of the law against his estate, without legal warrant, be the consequences of that illegal act what they may." [84] " I think a party against whom arrestments have been improperly used is entitled to have that found by the verdict of a jury. The use of arrestments against a mercantile man is very injurious to his credit, and therefore he is entitled to have it vindicated." [85]

Injury sustained by the fact of publication of the fact in the press is a relevant item of damages if that is a natural and almost invariable consequence of the wrongful use of diligence.[86]

Awards

A poinding executed before the days of charge had expired give rise to a claim for £50 of damages, settled by a tender of £5 5s.[87] Where arrestment was effected of the wages of a person not the debtor but having the same name, and his wages were held up over the weekend, damages of a guinea were given.[88]

In another similar case it was observed that the pursuer would primarily be entitled at any rate to " formal damages " [89] and that the usual ground for giving more was injury to the pursuer's financial status or credit, but that solatium could well be given, there being evidence that the pursuer had suffered in his feelings and in the social estimation of his workmates. In the result £10 was given.[90]

In a case of wrongful poinding the claim was £250 and the sheriff's award £50 [91] apportioned three-quarters to the sheriff-officer and one-quarter to the creditors; an award of £70 was made where a sheriff-officer had taken decree wrongfully and charged thereon.[92]

It has been said that " it is of no consequence whether the pursuers have sustained any substantial damage. Suppose the damage to be such that one farthing is recovered, that will show that a wrong has been done by the defenders to the pursuers." [93] In that case, £500 was claimed as solatium for the loss and damage sustained by the pursuers in their feelings, character, trade and business by the arrestment without warrant of their

[83] *e.g.* £2,000: *Borthwick* v. *Gilkison* (1863) 2 M. 125 (1s. awarded, and expenses); £500: *Rhind* v. *Kemp* (1894) 21 R. 275; £250: *Broomberg* v. *Reinhold & Others*, 1943 S.L.T.(Sh.Ct.) 21; £250: *Grant* v. *Airdrie Mags.*, 1939 S.C. 738 (teacher's salary arrested); £100: *Clark* v. *Beattie*, 1909 S.C. 299 (35s. of draper's wages arrested).

[84] *Meikle* v. *Sneddon* (1862) 24 D. 720.

[85] *Borthwick* v. *Gilkison* (1863) 2 M. 125.

[86] *Gibson* v. *Anderson* (1897) 24 R. 556.

[87] *Banks* v. *Aitken & Michie* (1911) 27 Sh.Ct.Rep. 315.

[88] *Gillespie* v. *Nicolson & Co.* (1909) 26 Sh.Ct.Rep. 99.

[89] Presumably nominal damages.

[90] *Russell* v. *Munro & McCulloch* (1941) 58 Sh.Ct.Rep. 57.

[91] *Broomberg* v. *Reinhold* (1942) 60 Sh.Ct.Rep. 45.

[92] *Allan* v. *Scottish Auto Services* (1934) 50 Sh.Ct.Rep. 10.

[93] *Meikle* v. *Sneddon* (1862) 24 D. 720, 723, *per* L.J.-C. Inglis.

ship. In a case where a charge was served illegally, the sum being not yet overdue, £3 damages was awarded.[94]

Remoteness

The ordinary principles of remoteness seem to apply to wrongful diligence against property. In *Broomberg* v. *Reinhold*[95] a wrongous poinding took place, and the pursuer averred that in consequence she suffered a severe nervous and mental shock, for which she claimed £50, her total claim being £250. These averments were held irrelevant but an award of £50 was made for other heads of damage.

Persons liable

The creditor is always personally liable for any wrongful use of legal diligence, but also for the negligence or lack of skill of an agent[96] or officer[97] employed by him to execute diligence, even in the circumstances where such employment was not essential, or even for the fault of a judge or court official who issues the warrant. But an intermediary, such as a debt collector who employs a solicitor, is only liable for his own faults.[98]

Right of relief

When a creditor has been made liable in damages for a wrongful use of diligence he is entitled to relief from the agent,[99] messenger, or magistrate actually to blame for the irregular or unjustifiable diligence.

Liability of agents

Thus a creditor may recover from his solicitor if the latter fails to use reasonable skill and care: the court will probably take a stricter view of the skill and care which an agent must exhibit if the diligence used is an extraordinary remedy.[1]

An agent is only liable when he knows the facts which make regular diligence illegal,[2] as when the debt has been partially paid[3] or delay has

94 *Addison* v. *Brown* (1905) 22 Sh.Ct.Rep. 49.

95 (1942) 60 Sh.Ct.Rep. 45.

96 *Anderson* v. *Ormiston* (1750) Mor. 13949; *Gordon's Exors.* v. *Dunlop* (1825) 3 Mur. 515; *Dunlop* v. *Buchanan* (1828) 5 Mur. 16; *Pearson* v. *Anderson* (1833) 11 S. 1008; *Smith* v. *Taylor* (1882) 10 R. 291; *Taylor* v. *Rutherford* (1888) 15 R. 608; *Hutchison* v. *Innerleithen Mags.*, 1933 S.L.T. 52.

97 *Anderson, supra*; *Paterson* (1811) Hume 278; *Fraser* (1825) 3 S. 590; *Macdonell* v. *Bank of Scotland* (1835) 13 S. 701; *Brodie* v. *Smith* (1836) 14 S. 983; *Struthers* v. *Dykes* (1845) 7 D. 436, 9 D. 1437; *Beattie* v. *McLellan* (1846) 8 D. 930, 6 D. 1088; *Petersen* v. *McLean* (1868) 6 M. 218; *Le Conte* v. *Douglas* (1880) 8 R. 175; *Wright* v. *Morgan* (1897) 5 S.L.T. No. 259. *Cf. Stewart* v. *Macdonald* (1784) M. 13989.

98 *Taylor, supra*; *Rhind* v. *Kemp* (1893) 21 R. 275.

99 *Wood* v. *Fullarton* (1710) Mor. 13960; *McDonald* v. *Kelly* (1821) 1 S. 105 (102). See too *Smith* v. *Grant* (1858) 20 D. 1077; *Frame* v. *Campbell* (1836) 14 S. 914, affd. (1839) McL. & Rob. 595.

1 *Smith* v. *Grant* (1858) 20 D. 1077; *Landell* v. *Purves* (1842) 4 D. 1300, 1543; revd. 4 Bell's App. 46.

2 *Henderson* v. *Rollo* (1871) 10 M. 104; *Ritchie* v. *Dunbar* (1849) 11 D. 882.

3 *Watson* v. *Gardner* (1834) 12 S. 567.

been agreed [4] or payment tendered [5] or diligence sisted,[6] but he is liable for irregular diligence as by giving an officer a defective warrant to execute [7] or instructing a wrongful act [8] or against the wrong debtor [9]; he is probably not liable for misconduct of officers [10] but only for irregularities in the execution of their instructions.[11]

Liability of an officer or messenger

An officer employed to execute diligence is liable to the employing creditor for want of reasonable skill and care and when a creditor has failed to recover a debt, or has been subjected to a claim of damages or expenses to a debtor, he has a claim of relief against the officer.[12] The messenger or officer's liability is co-extensive with that of the creditor. So where the debtor suspended an irregular charge and sued the creditor for damages and later abandoned his action, the messenger was found liable for the expenses of the suspension and for the creditor's expenses in the action of damages.[13]

When action is raised against the creditor for an irregularity for which he holds the messenger liable, intimation should be made to him at once to give him an opportunity of proponing any competent defence,[14] but intimation to his cautioner is not necessary.[15] The messenger is liable for any damages awarded against the creditor and all his expenses, whether the action has been settled or contested.[16]

Wrongful Criminal Proceedings

Wrongful information of crime

It is the duty of everyone to report suspicious circumstances [17] and consequently to communicate to the police or procurator-fiscal information that a person is believed to have committed some crime is actionable not if the information were incorrect but only if the communication was made maliciously and without probable cause.[18] If these requisites are

4 *Cameron* v. *Mortimer* (1872) 10 M. 461, 817.
5 *Inglis* v. *McIntyre* (1861) 23 D. 1240.
6 *Ritchie* v. *Dunbar* (1849) 11 D. 882; *Hendry* v. *Brown* (1851) 13 D. 1046.
7 *Johnstone* v. *McCraw* (1833) 12 S. 560.
8 *Stewart* v. *Macdonald* (1784) Mor. 13989; *Inglis* v. *McIntyre* (1861) 23 D. 1240.
9 *Hamilton* v. *Anderson* (1830) 5 Mur. 312.
10 *Inglis, supra*; *Russell* v. *Hedderwick* (1859) 21 D. 1325.
11 *Macdonnell* v. *Bank of Scotland* (1835) 13 S. 701; *Beattie* v. *McLellan* (1846) 8 D. 930.
12 *Hamilton* v. *Emslie* (1868) 7 M. 173.
13 *Brock* v. *Kemp* (1844) 6 D. 709.
14 *Fraser* v. *Andrew* (1831) 9 S. 345; *Collier* v. *Wilson* (1836) 15 S. 195; *Struthers* v. *Dykes* (1845) 7 D. 436, 9 D. 1437.
15 *Supra*. See also *Clason* v. *Black* (1842) 4 D. 743.
16 *Struthers, supra*.
17 *Lightbody* v. *Gordon* (1882) 9 R. 934, 940; see also *Urquhart* v. *McKenzie* (1886) 14 R. 18; *Douglas* v. *Main* (1893) 20 R. 793; *Currie* v. *Weir* (1900) 2 F. 522.
18 *Arbuckle* v. *Taylor* (1815) 3 Dow 160; *Young* v. *Leven* (1822) 1 Sh.App. 179; *Sheppeard* v. *Fraser* (1849) 11 D. 496; *Dallas* v. *Mann* (1853) 15 D. 746; *Thomson* v. *Adam* (1865) 4 M. 29; *Rae* v. *Linton* (1875) 2 R. 669; *Green* v. *Chalmers* (1878) 6 R. 318; *Shaw* v. *Burns*, 1911 S.C. 537.

satisfied damages are due as solatium for the hurt to feelings, trouble and inconvenience, and damage to reputation which will result, for any loss of business which has resulted, and for any outlays and expenses incurred.

Wrongful search of the person

A constable may not search a person in quest of evidence to determine whether or not to apprehend, but may lawfully do so after justifiably apprehending him.[19] To search a person not liable to apprehension, save under warrant, is palpably illegal.[19] The search may be directed to finding things about his person, such as housebreaking implements in pockets, stolen property in pockets, or to finding physical traits, such as cuts, scars, etc. which may be relevant to identification.[20]

At common law the police have power to take an accused's finger-prints after apprehension,[21] though not after he has been released on bail,[22] nor when he is illegally under arrest, at least if the finger-prints are taken for record purposes and not as part of the process of identification.[23] The same principle applies to scrapings from finger-nails [24] and similar real evidence obtained from a suspect's body.[25]

Akin to physical search is physical testing by taking blood samples, testing reactions, etc. Such testing can in general only be effected with the consent of the person; if he refuses, he may be observed and inferences drawn from observation,[26] or the refusal may be an offence.[27]

Wrongful search of premises

Search of premises for property alleged to be stolen may generally only be made by virtue of a warrant to search granted by a sheriff or magistrate, which must be specific and not a general warrant to search for something which may implicate the occupier,[28] but in serious emergency search may be made without a warrant.[29]

It is not illegal to grant, nor to execute, a warrant to search premises for stolen goods, though the occupier of the premises has neither been apprehended nor charged with an offence,[30] though special circumstances productive of exceptional hardship may make the granting of a search warrant illegal and in such a case the absence of charge or application may be a relevant consideration.[31]

19 *Jackson* v. *Stevenson* (1897) 24 R.(J.) 38.
20 *e.g. Forrester* v. *H.M.A.*, 1952 J.C. 28; *Hay* v. *H.M.A.*, 1968 J.C. 40.
21 *Adair* v. *McGarry*, 1933 J.C. 72; *Hamilton* v. *H.M.A.*, 1934 J.C. 1; *H.M.A.* v. *Rolley*, 1945 J.C. 155.
22 *Adamson* v. *Martin*, 1916 S.C. 319.
23 *Dumbell* v. *Roberts* [1944] 1 All E.R. 326, 330.
24 *McGovern* v. *H.M.A.*, 1950 J.C. 33.
25 *Cf. Hay, supra* (impressions of tooth-marks).
26 *Reid* v. *Nixon*, 1948 J.C. 68.
27 Road Traffic Act 1972, s. 2 (3).
28 *Bell* v. *Black and Morrison* (1865) 3 M. 1026; *Nelson* v. *Black and Morrison* (1866) 4 M. 328.
29 *H.M.A.* v. *McGuigan*, 1936 J.C. 16.
30 *Stewart* v. *Roach*, 1950 S.C. 318.
31 *Stewart, supra*, 330.

Where a search has been wrongful substantial damages will normally be due for the trouble, inconvenience and disturbance caused, and for the damage to reputation necessarily incidental to such a happening.[32]

Wrongful apprehension

To be apprehended on a criminal charge wrongfully is a serious aspersion on character justifying substantial damages for hurt feelings and injury to reputation. The cases turn mostly on the question whether apprehension in particular circumstances was wrongful or not. Apprehension authorised by warrant cannot be wrongful, at least as against the officers executing it, though it might conceivably not exclude an action against the person granting the warrant, though such a person enjoys a high degree of privilege and specific averments that he was motivated by malice and had no probable cause for granting the warrant would be necessary. Apprehension without warrant may or may not be justifiable, and accordingly may or may not be wrongful [33] but to be unjustifiable must have been effected maliciously and without probable cause.[34] The fact that the complainer was subsequently charged and convicted does not prove that his apprehension was justifiable; a man could be guilty of crime, but yet it be unjustifiable to have arrested him.[35]

The relevant cases give little guidance on the factors to be considered in awarding damages.

Wrongful prosecution

Prosecution for crime is in Scotland almost entirely in the hands of public officials prosecuting in the public interest and to make a case of wrongful prosecution there must be specific averments,[36] and proof,[37] that he acted not merely incorrectly but maliciously and without probable cause.[38] The fact that the prosecution is dropped, or ends in a verdict of not proven or not guilty, does not by any means establish that the prosecution was wrongful, though it is a prerequisite of an action for damages. A conviction obtained, and standing unquashed, is conclusive that the prosecution, whether brought maliciously or not, was not brought without reasonable cause.[39]

[32] In *Stewart* v. *Roach*, *supra*, £30 was awarded but recalled on appeal.

[33] Hume on *Crimes*, II, 75; Alison, II, 116–117; *Peggie* v. *Clark* (1868) 7 M. 89; *Beaton* v. *Ivory* (1887) 14 R. 1057; *Leask* v. *Burt* (1893) 21 R. 32; *Lundie* v. *MacBrayne* (1894) 21 R. 1085; *Wood* v. *N.B. Ry*. (1899) 1 F. 562; *Somerville* v. *Sutherland* (1899) 2 F. 185, 188.

[34] *Hill* v. *Campbell* (1905) 8 F. 220.

[35] *Wood*, *supra*, distinguishing *Gilchrist* v. *Anderson* (1838) 1 D. 37; *McCrae* v. *Young* (1908) 25 Sh.Ct.Rep. 230.

[36] *Arbuckle* v. *Taylor* (1815) 3 Dow 160; *Munro* v. *Taylor* (1845) 7 D. 500; *Henderson* v. *Robertson* (1853) 15 D. 292; *Craig* v. *Peebles* (1876) 3 R. 441; *Malcolm* v. *Duncan* (1897) 24 R. 747; *Pyper* v. *Ingram* (1901) 3 F. 514; see also *Hastings* v. *Chalmers* (1890) 18 R. 244.

[37] *Young* v. *Glasgow Mags*. (1891) 18 R. 825.

[38] *Cf.* Summary Jurisdiction (Scotland) Act 1954, s. 75.

[39] *MacLellan* v. *Miller* (1832) 11 S. 187; *Gilchrist* v. *Anderson* (1838) 1 D. 37; *Kennedy* v. *Wise* (1890) 17 R. 1036; *Hill* v. *Campbell* (1905) 8 F. 220.

In the few cases in which private prosecutions are competent, the prosecutor enjoys similar privilege so long as the proceedings are taken in the interest in which they are intended to be used.[40]

The major factors in a competent claim of damages are solatium for a malicious and unjustified attack on the pursuer's character and credit,[41] and compensation for any pecuniary loss which has followed as a natural consequence from the prosecution.[42]

Wrongful imprisonment

Wrongful imprisonment may be temporary incarceration pending release on bail or further inquiries, or imprisonment (or other custodial detention) in pursuance of a sentence pronounced by a court of criminal jurisdiction. The cases all turn on issues of the competency or relevancy of the pursuer's case.[43] The wrong consists in the imprisonment rather than in any defect in the sentence imposed.[44] The order for committal must have been illegal [45] or made in excess of jurisdiction.[46] If a claim can be established it is submitted that damages would be due for the hurt to feelings, the personal discomfort, inconvenience and worry, and any attendant damage to reputation, caused by the imprisonment. The duration of the imprisonment would be highly relevant.

In such cases substantial claims have been made [47] and, in the event of success, a substantial award should be made.[48]

40 *Cook* v. *Spence* (1897) 4 S.L.T. 295.
41 *Graham* v. *Strathern*, 1924 S.C. 699, 720.
42 *Cf. Childs* v. *Lewis* (1924) 40 T.L.R. 870.
43 See *Walker on Delict*, II, 695.
44 *McCreadie* v. *Thomson*, 1907 S.C. 1176, 1184.
45 *Watt* v. *Ligertwood* (1874) 1 R.(H.L.) 21.
46 *McCreadie*, *supra*.
47 *e.g. Rae* v. *Linton* (1876) 3 R. 669 (£2,000 claimed for 20 days' imprisonment); *McCreadie* v. *Thomson*, 1907 S.C. 1176 (£1,000 for 12 days); *McPhee* v. *Macfarlane's Exor.*, 1933 S.C. 163 (£100 for 5 days' detention on charge).
48 *Gibson* v. *Anderson* (1846) 9 D. 1, 6 (£100 to a blacksmith for 15 days' imprisonment); *Wilson* v. *Alexander* (1846) 9 D. 7, 11 (£20 to a farmer for some hours' detention).

CHAPTER 56

ECONOMIC LOSSES

BY no means every economic loss justifies a claim for damages against the person responsible. The commonest kind of economic harm, capturing some of the custom or trade of a competitor, is legitimate, even where the causing of loss to him is deliberate. The law is complicated by the special rules applicable to industrial relations.

Fraud

Fraud is a machination or contrivance to deceive.[1] It involves making a false statement in the knowledge of its falsity, or without belief in its truth, or recklessly, not caring whether it be true or false, with the intention that the other party should rely on it, and the result that he does so act and sustains loss in consequence.[2] It is most commonly met with as inducing a contract on the faith of the representor's untrue representations.[3] Fraud may also, however, be purely delictual and result in damage to the pursuer quite distinct from any contract with the defender. So if A fraudulently misrepresents to B with reference to C's property or business and thereby induces B to contract with C with reference to that property or business the contract is valid as between B and C and cannot be reduced, and B's only remedy is an action *ex delicto* against A.[4] The defrauded party cannot insist on the guilty party relieving him of the contract, but may only claim from him the loss on the contract,[5] namely the loss directly or naturally resulting from his fraud.[6] Or the contract may not have been wholly induced but only on terms more onerous than would otherwise have been agreed, as where second-hand goods were sold as new.[7] Again where a man contracts to sell what he does not own and knows he could not acquire, he will be liable in damages for the fraud.[8]

Apart from cases where the detriment results from a contract undertaken in reliance on the fraud,[9] actionable damage has been held to include personal or physical injury which results from taking some action on the

[1] Bell, *Prin.* § 13; *cf. Lees* v. *Tod* (1882) 9 R. 807.

[2] *Derry* v. *Peek* (1889) 14 App.Cas. 337; *Bradford Building Socy.* v. *Borders* [1941] 1 All E.R. 205; *Heskell* v. *Continental Express* [1950] 1 All E.R. 1033.

[3] Chap. 29, *supra.*

[4] *Cf.* misrepresentations as to another person's character or credit. Gloag on *Contract*, 2nd ed., 482; *cf. Cooper* v. *Nat. Prov. Bank* [1946] 1 K.B. 1.

[5] Gloag, 482; *Brown* v. *Stewart* (1898) 1 F. 316, 323.

[6] *Thin & Sinclair* v. *Arrol* (1896) 24 R. 198, 206.

[7] *Gibson* v. *National Cash Register Co.*, 1925 S.C. 500.

[8] *Bain* v. *Fothergill* (1872) L.R. 7 H.L. 207.

[9] *e.g. Bryson & Co.* v. *Bryson*, 1916, 1 S.L.T. 361.

faith of the fraudulent representation,[10] mental distress and shock amounting to physical injury,[11] loss of wages and earning capacity,[12] medical[13] and other expenses.[14]

Measure of damages

The measure of damages should be the full extent of loss, past and future, sustained or likely to be sustained by the defrauded party in consequence of reliance on the fraudulent misrepresentation. So the pursuer is entitled to recover property which he has parted with to the defender or money paid away and irrecoverable[15] or money which the pursuer has become liable to pay.[16] The measure of damages is not confined to any difference between the value of the property acquired in reliance on the fraudulent misrepresentation and the value which it would have had if that representation had been true,[17] nor does it extend to profits which would or might have been made if the representation had been true.[18] It does, however, cover injury which is the direct and natural result of the actings on the faith of the representation.[19] Where the loss is in the form of physical injury the amount of damages will fall to be quantified in the same way as in other cases of injury.

When the pursuer's change of position has been in respect of a contract entered into with a third party the damages, as in the case of contracts with the maker of the fraudulent representation, amount to the loss sustained on the contract. Questions of difficulty may, however, arise as to how a figure should be ascertained for this. If the pursuer has received nothing of any value he is entitled as the ultimate standard of loss to the total value of everything paid or to be paid, and property transferred or to be transferred by him under the contract.[20] If he has received or will receive anything under the contract this must be deducted from his claim and if on balance he has sustained no loss he is not entitled to any damages.[21]

The value of benefits or interests received is to be taken as their real

10 *Burrows* v. *Rhodes* [1899] 1 Q.B. 816 (plaintiff induced to join Jameson Raid and injured); *Langridge* v. *Levy* (1838) 4 M. & W. 337 (gun bursting); *Longmeid* v. *Holliday* (1851) 6 Exch. 761 (lamp); *Burtsal* v. *Bianchi* (1891) 65 L.T. 678 (house with defective drains); see also *Robinson* v. *National Bank*, 1916 S.C. 46; affd. 1916 S.C.(H.L.) 154.

11 *Wilkinson* v. *Downton* [1897] 2 Q.B. 57; *Janvier* v. *Sweeney* [1919] 2 K.B. 316.

12 *Burrows*, *supra*; *Wilkinson*, *supra*.

13 *Burrows*, *supra*.

14 *Denton* v. *G.N. Ry.* (1856) 5 E. & B. 860.

15 *e.g.* railway fares, *Wilkinson* v. *Downton* [1897] 2 Q.B. 57; or money paid to third parties, *Richardson* v. *Silvester* (1873) L.R. 9 Q.B. 34.

16 *Polhill* v. *Walter* (1832) 3 B. & Ad. 114; *Smout* v. *Ilbery* (1842) 10 M. & W. 1, 9; *Randell* v. *Trimen* (1856) 18 C.B. 786; *Starkey* v. *Bank of England* [1903] A.C. 114.

17 *Twycross* v. *Grant* (1877) 2 C.P.D. 469; *Broome* v. *Speak* [1903] 1 Ch. 586; *Clark* v. *Urquhart* [1930] A.C. 28.

18 *Cassaboglou* v. *Gibb* (1883) 11 Q.B.D. 797; *cf.* *Johnston* v. *Braham & Campbell* [1917] 1 K.B. 586.

19 *Mullett* v. *Mason* (1866) L.R. 1 C.P. 559: see also *Ward* v. *Hobbs* (1877) 4 App.Cas. 13, 24, 29.

20 *Twycross* v. *Grant* (1877) 2 C.P.D. 469; *Thomson* v. *Clanmorris* [1900] 1 Ch. 718; *Goldrei* v. *Sinclair* [1918] 1 K.B. 180.

21 *McConnel* v. *Wright* [1903] 1 Ch. 546, 554.

or actual value, that is the price which the property would have fetched as between honest and reasonable parties with full knowledge of the true facts [22]; in the case of marketable securities current or market price must be disregarded as this may have been affected by the same fraudulent devices as give the cause of action. Such ascertainment of the true value usually benefits the defrauded pursuer [22] but may do the contrary.[23]

The date of ascertainment of value has been said to be the date at which the property or rights were acquired.[22] If the pursuer chooses to sell, he must make allowance in respect of the sum received but he is not bound to sell on discovery of the fraud or at any other time.[24] If, however, the pursuer elects to sell and the price declines from independent causes after he has had a reasonable time to determine on his course of conduct and study the market, the pursuer may have to give credit for the price which he could have obtained at the date the rights in question were acquired, so long as the decline in price was caused independently of the fraud, or the inherent defects of the property or article in question.[25]

The pursuer must also take reasonable steps to minimise damages but a hesitant and delayed admission of fault by the pursuer without an offer to make restitution cannot be pleaded by a defender in mitigation, and during such a delay the pursuer must still perform his obligations and add these to his claim of damages.

Negligent misrepresentation

It is now [26] recognised that an innocent but negligent misrepresentation is actionable. *Prima facie* the damages recoverable in such a case should be compensation for all loss which follows naturally and directly from reliance on the misrepresentation, such as money advanced and lost, but not such speculative loss as the profit which might have been made if the representation had been true.

Malicious or injurious falsehood

This species of verbal injury consists of doing harm to a person in his business relations by oral or written falsehoods,[27] the main forms being slander of title,[28] slander of property,[29] slander of goods [30] and slander of business.[31] The appropriate measure of damages would appear to be a

[22] *Twycross* v. *Grant* (1877) 2 C.P.D. 469; *Arkwright* v. *Newbold* (1881) 17 Ch.D. 301, 312; *Peek* v. *Derry* (1887) 37 Ch.D. 541; *Glasier* v. *Rolls* (1889) 42 Ch.D. 436, 455; *McConnel* v. *Wright* [1903] 1 Ch. 546; *Cackett* v. *Keswick* [1902] 2 Ch. 456; *Shepheard* v. *Broome* [1904] A.C. 342.

[23] *Pearson* v. *Wheeler* (1825) Ry. & M. 303.

[24] *Peek* v. *Derry* (1887) 37 Ch.D. 541, 591.

[25] *Peek* v. *Derry* (1887) 37 Ch.D. 541, 591–594; *Waddell* v. *Blockey* (1879) 4 Q.B.D. 678.

[26] *Hedley Byrne & Co.* v. *Heller & Partners Ltd.* [1964] A.C. 465.

[27] See generally Walker on *Delict*, II, 904; Defamation Act 1952, s. 14 (*b*).

[28] *Philp* v. *Morton* (1816) Hume 865; *Yeo* v. *Wallace* (1867) 5 S.L.R. 253; *Montgomerie* v. *Paterson* (1894) 11 R.P.C. 221, 633; *Harpers* v. *Greenwood & Batley* (1896) 4 S.L.T. 116.

[29] *Macrae* v. *Wicks* (1886) 13 R. 732; *Bruce* v. *Smith* (1898) 1 F. 327.

[30] *Wilts United Dairies* v. *Robinson* [1958] R.P.C. 94.

[31] *Buchan* v. *Welch* (1857) 20 D. 222; *Ratcliffe* v. *Evans* [1892] 2 Q.B. 524.

fair estimate of the loss of business or profits sustained in consequence of the publication of the malicious falsehood.

Breach of confidence

Breach of an express or implied bond of secrecy arising out of employment is a relevant ground of damages.[32] Thus disclosure by a doctor of information obtained when on confidential employment has been held actionable,[33] though this is not invariable and depends on the character of the disclosure made.[34] So, too, disclosure by an accountant to the Inland Revenue of information obtained while investigating a client's affairs,[35] and the showing by a printer of a proof to a trade rival of his client [36] have been held relevant. There must have been a relation of confidentiality raising a duty of non-disclosure before the action can be brought.[37]

Kindred cases are the publication of a manuscript without authority,[38] or of lectures,[39] and allowing a defamatory private letter to be published to the individuals defamed,[40] or communicating to an employee on his dismissal a defamatory report from his previous employers.[41]

Damages

The damages recoverable in such a case will normally be of the nature of solatium unless actual damage and loss is proved.[42] Where a clerk was bribed to disclose information relative to the pursuer's title expenses and solatium were given.[43]

Harbouring servant

An action will lie against an employer for harbouring and continuing to employ a servant in the knowledge that he is still under contract to a former employer.[44] It is not barred by a previous action against the employee for breach of contract,[45] and both may be found liable jointly and severally.[45] The basis of damages against the harbouring employer is probably the loss and inconvenience caused by lacking a servant whose

[32] *Robb* v. *Green* [1895] 2 Q.B. 315; *Wessex Dairies* v. *Smith* [1935] 2 K.B. 80; *Bent's Brewery Co.* v. *Hogan* [1945] 2 All E.R. 570; *Hivac* v. *Park Royal Scientific Instruments Ltd.* [1946] Ch. 169.
[33] *A B* v. *C D* (1851) 14 D. 177; contrast *Stevenson Jordan & Harrison* v. *Macdonald & Evans* [1952] 1 T.L.R. 101.
[34] *Watson* v. *McEwan* (1905) 7 F.(H.L.) 109.
[35] *Brown's Trs.* v. *Hay* (1898) 25 R. 1112.
[36] *Neumann* v. *Kennedy* (1905) 12 S.L.T. 763.
[37] *Fulton* v. *Stubbs* (1903) 5 F. 814; *Mushets* v. *Mackenzie* (1899) 1 F. 756.
[38] *Cadell & Davies* v. *Stewart* (1804) Mor.Appx. Literary Property, No. 4.
[39] *Caird* v. *Sime* (1887) 18 R.(H.L.) 37.
[40] *Weld-Blundell* v. *Stephens* [1920] A.C. 956.
[41] *Mushets* v. *Mackenzie* (1899) 1 F. 756.
[42] *Brown's Trs.* v. *Hay* (1898) 25 R. 1112.
[43] *Kerr* v. *Duke of Roxburgh* (1822) 3 Mur. 126.
[44] *Dickson* v. *Taylor* (1816) 1 Mur. 141; *Rose Street Foundry Co.* v. *Lewis*, 1917 S.C. 341.
[45] *Rose Street Foundry Co.*, *supra*; *Belmont Laundry Co.* v. *Aberdeen Steam Laundry Co.* (1898) 1 F. 45.

contract had not yet entitled him to go. The amount is at large and the court or jury, once financial loss be proved, may award a sum appropriate to the whole circumstances of the wrong inflicted.[46]

Intimidation

It is actionable, by threats of illegitimate pressure, to coerce a person to act to the pursuer's detriment,[47] or to the detriment of another with whom he was in contractual relations.[48] The appropriate measure of damages appears to be the loss sustained in consequence of the intimidation, such as the difference between earnings in the employment from which the pursuer was driven and those in the alternative employment secured.[49]

Conspiracy to injure

If a person does an act lawful in itself and without employing unlawful means, resulting loss to another party is not actionable, even though the motive be malicious.[50] But a combination of several persons in action wilfully injurious to another in his trade is unlawful and actionable,[51] and if the real or predominant object of the combination is to injure it is actionable if damage follows, even where the protection or furtherance of trade or other interests was a subsidiary object. But if the real or predominant object is the protection of trade interests in the honest belief that they would otherwise suffer, the knowledge that damage to another's trade will result does not prejudice the defence.[52] So, too, combination to do something rendered unlawful by the way it is done is actionable conspiracy.[53]

Actual damage to the pursuer is an essential of actionable conspiracy, but malice is not unless the parties combining had no benefit to themselves in view. A pursuer cannot sue an action based on combination in doing an unlawful act and subsequently bring an action on the alternative ground of the defenders' doing a lawful thing by unlawful means.[54]

Measure of damages

Too few cases of this kind have been successful to enable any conclusions to be drawn on the appropriate measure of damages. The loss which

[46] *Pratt* v. *B.M.A.* [1919] 1 K.B. 244, 281; *Allen* v. *Flood* [1898] A.C. 79; *Quinn* v. *Leathem* [1901] A.C. 495; *Larkin* v. *Long* [1915] A.C. 814. But see *Jones Bros. (Hunstanton)* v. *Stevens* [1955] 1 Q.B. 275.

[47] *Tarleton* v. *McGawley* (1804) Peake 270.

[48] *Rookes* v. *Barnard* [1964] A.C. 1129 (actual decision overruled by Trade Disputes Act 1965 (now Industrial Relations Act 1971, s. 132 (1))).

[49] *Morgan* v. *Fry* [1968] 1 Q.B. 521.

[50] *Bradford* v. *Pickles* [1895] A.C. 587; *Allen* v. *Flood* [1898] A.C. 1.

[51] *Sorrell* v. *Smith* [1925] A.C. 700.

[52] *Crofter Co.* v. *Veitch*, 1942 S.C.(H.L.) 1; *Mogul Co.* v. *McGregor* [1892] A.C. 25; *D. C. Thomson Ltd.* v. *Deakin* [1952] Ch. 646; *cf. S. C. W. S.* v. *Glasgow Fleshers* (1898) 5 S.L.T. 263.

[53] *Quinn* v. *Leathem* [1901] A.C. 495; *Crofter Co., supra.* See, further, *Ware and De Freville* v. *M. T. A.* [1921] 3 K.B. 40; *Thorne* v. *M. T. A.* [1937] A.C. 797.

[54] *Greenhalgh* v. *Mallard* [1947] 2 All E.R. 225; *cf. Wright* v. *Bennett* [1948] 1 K.B. 601.

would probably be sustained in such a case would be the loss of business and the ordinary profits thereof and possible consequential loss of contracts and new business. In addition claims of damages might be incurred for the delay or failure to perform current contracts.

Inducing breach of contract

Damages are recoverable where a person not a party to a lawful contract knowingly and unjustifiably [55] procures a breach thereof.[56] Malice may be presumed [57] unless in a case of lawful trade competition,[58] but there should be evidence of intention to injure,[59] and improper [60] as well as wrongful [61] motive. It may be effected by bribery [61] or solicitation [62] or persuasion [63] or concerted agreement,[64] but it is not actionable for one party to persuade another to do a lawful act the consequence of which is to prevent performance of a contract.[63]

Actual damage as the natural and probable consequence of the defender's actings is essential,[64] but there is a sufficient ground of action when an inference may reasonably be drawn that some damage must result, and it is not necessary to prove specific damage.[65] The pecuniary loss must be estimated as well as can be and the difficulties and expenses incurred in detecting and unravelling the circumstances must be considered.[66]

Inducing disclosure of secrets

An action similarly lies where one party induces an employee to disclose trade or other business secrets [67] in breach of the latter's obligation of confidentiality to his employer,[68] and even though the employment has been terminated.[69] A similar action may be brought against the employee.[70] Damages must be assessed by reference broadly to the loss suffered by the disclosure.

Loss of profits consequential on other injury

Where physical injury or property damage is done it is frequently a

[55] *e.g. Brimelow* v. *Casson* [1924] 1 Ch. 302; *Findlay* v. *Blaylock*, 1937 S.C. 21; see also *Salvadori* v. *B. M. T. A.* [1949] Ch. 556.
[56] *Rutherford* v. *Boak* (1836) 14 S. 732; *Lumley* v. *Gye* (1853) 2 E. & B. 216; *Couper* v. *Macfarlane* (1879) 6 R. 683; *Quinn* v. *Leathem* [1901] A.C. 495, 510; *Rose Street Engineering Co.* v. *Lewis*, 1917 S.C. 341; *British Motor Trade Assocn.* v. *Gray*, 1951 S.C. 586.
[57] *Lumley, supra*, 224.
[58] *Mogul* v. *McGregor* [1892] A.C. 25; *Jenkinson* v. *Mild* (1892) 8 T.L.R. 540.
[59] *Bowen* v. *Hall* (1881) 6 Q.B.D. 333; *B. M. T. A.* v. *Gray, supra.*
[60] *Glamorgan Coal Co.* v. *South Wales Miners* [1903] 1 K.B. 118.
[61] *Couper* v. *Macfarlane* (1879) 6 R. 683.
[62] *Belmont Laundry Co.* v. *Aberdeen Steam Laundry Co.* (1898) 1 F. 45.
[63] *D. C. Thomson & Co.* v. *Deakin* [1952] Ch. 646.
[64] *B. M. T. A.* v. *Gray*, 1951 S.C. 586.
[65] *Exchange Telegraph Co.* v. *Gregory* [1896] 1 Q.B. 147; *Goldsoll* v. *Goldman* [1914] 2 Ch. 603; *B. M. T. A.* v. *Gray, supra.*
[66] *B. M. T. A.* v. *Salvadori* [1949] Ch. 556; *cf. B. M. T. A.* v. *Gilbert* [1951] 2 All E.R. 641.
[67] *Kerr* v. *Duke of Roxburgh* (1822) 3 Mur. 126 (law-clerk).
[68] *Rutherford* v. *Boak* (1836) 14 S. 732; *Roxburgh* v. *McArthur* (1841) 3 D. 556.
[69] *Rutherford, supra.*
[70] *Liverpool Victoria Legal Friendly Socy.* v. *Houston* (1900) 3 F. 42.

natural and direct consequence that the person affected will sustain loss of earnings or profits as well, and such are recoverable. Thus in cases of personal injuries losses caused by resultant inability to attend to one's profession or business are recoverable. In *Kerr* v. *Earl of Orkney* [71] where a mill was damaged the miller recovered the loss of profits incurred while the mill was under repair. In *Reavis* v. *Clan Line Steamers* [72] where the pursuer lost manuscript music in a ship collision, it was held that he could recover for loss of profits made by the use of it, but not for contingent profits from copyright royalties and disposal of performing and mechanical rights in relation to the music. As Lord Hunter neatly put it [73]: " Injury to property may involve injury to business. If A's property is injured by B's negligence and as a direct result of that injury A loses profit in connection with his business, I do not doubt that that loss of profit may form a legitimate claim by him against B." In *Dynamco* v. *Holland & Hannen & Cubitts* (*Scotland*) *Ltd.*[74] it was affirmed that it was incompetent to sue for financial loss resulting from negligence unless the negligence had operated initially by way of damage to property owned or possessed.

Strikes

A strike, or concerted cessation of work by a number of employees, whether spontaneously or in response to a call from a trade union or organisation of employees, is not by itself automatically or necessarily actionable. If no due notice of intention to stop work is given cessation of work is a breach of contract by each man and actionable as such. If due notice is given, participation in a strike, unless striking is contrary to a term of the contract of employment of each or any of them, excluding or restricting the employee's right to take part in a strike,[75] is not a breach of contract for the purposes of proceedings in contract for breach of that contract, or proceedings for reparation, or for certain other purposes.

Irregular industrial action short of a strike

Irregular industrial action short of a strike is any concerted course of conduct (other than a strike) which, in contemplation or furtherance of an industrial dispute (a) is carried on by a group of workers with the intention of preventing, reducing or otherwise interfering with the production of goods or the provision of services, and (b) in the case of some or all of them, is carried on in breach of their contracts of employment or (where they are not employees) in breach of their terms and conditions of service.[76]

[71] (1857) 20 D. 298.
[72] 1926 S.C. 215.
[73] *Ibid.* 226.
[74] 1971 S.L.T. 150.
[75] Industrial Relations Act 1971, s. 147. " Due notice " is notice not shorter than the notice which the employee would be required to give to terminate his contract of employment.
[76] Industrial Relations Act 1971, s. 33 (4), modified in relation to s. 65 (7).

Acts in contemplation or furtherance of industrial disputes

An act done by a person in contemplation or furtherance of an industrial dispute is not actionable as giving rise to liability in reparation on the ground only (a) that it induces another person to break a contract to which that other person is a party or prevents another person from performing such a contract, or (b) that it consists in his threatening that a contract (whether one to which he is a party or not) will be broken or will be prevented from being performed, or that he will induce another person to break a contract to which that other person is a party or will prevent another person from performing such a contract.[77]

An act done by a person in contemplation or furtherance of an industrial dispute is not actionable as giving rise to liability in reparation on the ground only that it is an interference with the trade, business or employment of another person, or with the right of another person to dispose of his capital or his labour as he wills.[78]

An agreement or combination by two or more persons to do or procure to be done any act in contemplation or furtherance of an industrial dispute is not actionable for reparation if the act in question is one which, if done without any such agreement or combination, would not be actionable for reparation.[79]

Where in any court proceedings for reparation are brought in respect of an agreement or combination by two or more persons to do or procure to be done an act in contemplation or furtherance of an industrial dispute, and section 132 (3) does not afford a defence to the proceedings, the court shall nevertheless sist the proceedings if it is satisfied that either of the conditions specified in section 131 (2) is fulfilled in relation to the act in question.[80]

Unfair industrial practices

The Industrial Relations Act 1971 created various " unfair industrial practices." [81] These do not appear to have a single or uniform consequence. A complaint may be presented to the Industrial Court by any person that action has been taken by a person against him and that under the Act, other than sections 5 and 22,[82] it constituted an unfair industrial

77 Industrial Relations Act 1971, s. 132 (1). Branch (a) resembles the former Trade Disputes Act 1906, s. 3, on which see *Conway* v. *Wade* [1909] A.C. 506; *Bent's Brewery Co.* v. *Hogan* [1945] 2 All E.R. 570; *Huntley* v. *Thornton* [1957] 1 All E.R. 234; *Beetham* v. *Trinidad Cement Ltd.* [1960] A.C. 132; *Stratford* v. *Lindley* [1965] A.C. 269; *Torquay Hotel Co. Ltd.* v. *Cousins* [1969] 2 Ch. 106. It clearly does not exclude liability for independent wrongs such as assault or malicious damage. Branch (b) resembles the former Trade Disputes Act 1965, s. 1, overruling *Rookes* v. *Barnard* [1964] A.C. 1129.

78 *Ibid.* s. 132 (2).

79 *Ibid.* s. 132 (3). This protects persons who commit what would otherwise be " conspiracy to injure."

80 *Ibid.* s. 132 (4). Proceedings must be sisted if the case discloses an unfair industrial practice in respect of which proceedings have been or could be brought before the Industrial Court or an industrial tribunal.

81 See ss. 5, 13, 16, 22, 33, 36, 54, 55, 66, 70, 96, 97, 98.

82 As to these see s. 106; as to complaint under ss. 66 or 70, see s. 107.

practice. That court may, if it considers that it would be just and equitable to do so, grant the complainer one or more of (a) an order determining the rights of the parties in relation to the action specified [83]; (b) an award of compensation from the respondent in respect of that action [84]; and (c) an order directing the respondent to refrain from continuing to take that action, and to refrain from taking any other action of a like nature. If the complaint is against an official of a trade union or employers' association and he acted in his capacity as an official the Industrial Court may not make an award or order in pursuance of paragraph (b) or (c), but nothing prevents the grant of any remedy against the trade union or employers' association in the same or other proceedings.[85]

Amount of compensation

Where in proceedings on a complaint the Industrial Court or an industrial tribunal awards compensation, the amount is such as the court or tribunal considers just and equitable in all the circumstances, having regard to the loss sustained by the aggrieved party in consequence of the matters to which the complaint relates, in so far as that loss was attributable to action taken by or on behalf of the party in default, including any expenses reasonably incurred by him in consequence of the matters to which the complaint relates and any benefit which he might reasonably be expected to have had but for those matters, subject, however, to the common law principle of mitigation of loss. A reduction may be made if the matters of complaint were to any extent caused or contributed to by any action of the aggrieved party.[86]

Where in a complaint under section 106 relating to dismissal the court or a tribunal has made a recommendation and it has not been complied with, then if the court or tribunal finds that the reason for non-compliance was that the complainer refused an offer of re-engagement or engagement on the terms stated in the recommendation, and that he acted unreasonably in doing so, it must reduce the assessment of his loss, or if it finds that the reason for which the recommendation was not complied with was that the employer refused or failed to make such an offer, and it considers that he acted unreasonably in doing so, it must increase the assessment, in either case to such extent as in the circumstances it considers just and equitable. In determining in such a complaint how far any loss sustained by the complainant was attributable to action taken by or on behalf of the employer, no account is to be taken of any pressure which was exercised on that employer as mentioned in section 33 (1) (*a*), and that question shall be determined as if no such pressure had been exercised.[87]

[83] *Cf. Palmer* v. *Post Office* [1972] I.T.R. 239; *Crouch* v. *Post Office* [1972] I.T.R. 242; *Jones* v. *Vauxhall Motors* [1972] I.T.R. 250.

[84] *e.g. Hewitson* v. *Anderston Springs* [1972] I.T.R. 391.

[85] s. 101.

[86] s. 116 (1)–(3).

[87] *Ibid.* s. 116 (4) and (5).

Limits on compensation awarded against trade union

In proceedings before the Industrial Court on a complaint under the Act where an award of compensation is made by the court against a trade union (whether or not it is also made against any other party to the proceedings) the compensation awarded against the trade union is not to exceed the following limits:

(a) trade union membership less than 5,000, £5,000;
(b) membership 5,000 but less than 25,000, £25,000;
(c) membership 25,000 but less than 100,000, £50,000;
(d) membership of 100,000 or more, £100,000.[88]

Limits on compensation under section 103, 106 or 109

Without prejudice to section 117 the compensation which the court or a tribunal may award to a person under section 103, 106 or 109 is not to exceed 104 weeks' pay or £4,160 (*i.e.* 104 × £40) whichever is the less. Provision is made for calculating the amount of a week's pay and for amending the figures of £4,160 and £40.[89]

Contribution to compensation on complaint under section 106

Where in proceedings on a complaint under section 106 the court or a tribunal awards compensation to be paid by an employer in consequence of action taken by the employer or by a person acting on his behalf, and the employer claims (a) that the action so taken by him or on his behalf was induced by pressure exercised on him by a third party by means of action to which section 33 of the Act applies, and (b) by virtue of section 33 (3) the action taken, whereby pressure was so exercised on the employer, constituted an unfair industrial practice, the employer may require the third party to be joined as a party to the proceedings, and if in the proceedings the court or a tribunal finds that the claim of the employer is well-founded, it may, subject to subsection (4), if it considers that it would be just and equitable to do so, make an order requiring the third party to pay to the employer a contribution in respect of the compensation awarded against him. The amount of any such contribution ordered to be paid in respect of any compensation (a) is to be such amount as the court or an industrial tribunal considers to be just and equitable in the circumstances and (b) may, if the court or tribunal so determines, constitute a complete indemnity. Where the third party is a trade-union official acting in his official capacity the court or tribunal is not to order him to pay any contribution but may order a contribution to be paid by the trade union.[90]

88 *Ibid.* s. 117.
89 *Ibid.* s. 118.
90 *Ibid.* s. 119.

CHAPTER 57

DAMAGE TO INTERESTS IN PROPERTY

A PERSON is entitled to damages if another has, without legal justification or excuse, infringed a legally protected interest vested in him in property, heritable or moveable, corporeal or incorporeal, and thereby caused him some patrimonial or pecuniary loss.

HERITABLE PROPERTY

Infringement of title of ownership

The Scottish system of land rights and conveyancing, based on the Register of Sasines, is so reliable that the chance of one person accidentally or fraudulently becoming registered as entitled to ownership of any piece of land in place of another truly so entitled is very small indeed. No doubt it would be actionable to defraud another of his land. In *Stobie* v. *Smith* [1] a person who was not the nearest heir of a deceased owner had himself served as heir, completed title and sold the property to bona fide onerous disponees who granted a bond and disposition in security over the property in favour of third parties. The court at the instance of the true heir, four years later, reduced the decree of service, disposition and bond. If the challenge had been delayed so long as to allow the onerous disponees' title to be fortified by prescription it would seem that the true heir's claim would have been one of damages only, and the appropriate measure of damages would have been the value of the property of which the pursuer had been disinherited.

Infringement of interests of possession

A person entitled to lawful possession of heritable property may recover damages for loss caused by any of various infringements of his possessory interests.

Trespass

Trespass is any temporary intrusion into or being or entering upon the lands or heritages of another [2] without his permission [3] or legal justification.[4] The primary remedy is merely to request the trespasser to go, and

[1] 1921 S.C. 894; *cf. Mackie* v. *Mackie* (1896) 4 S.L.T. 3.
[2] *Rankine on Landownership* (4th ed.) 139; *Geils* v. *Thompson* (1872) 10 M. 327; *Stirling Craufurd* v. *Clyde Nav. Trs.* (1881) 8 R. 826.
[3] *McAdam* v. *Laurie* (1876) 3 R.(J.) 20, 21; *Duncan* v. *Shaw* (1945) 61 Sh.Ct.Rep. 116.
[4] Bell, *Prin.* § 957; *Morton* v. *McMillan* (1893) 1 S.L.T. 92. *Cf. Carter* v. *Thomas* [1893] 1 Q.B. 673; *Cope* v. *Sharpe* [1912] 1 K.B. 496.

if he declines, to eject him from the premises with such force as is necessary. No damages are recoverable for a bare trespass, particularly if innocent, there being no identifiable harm or loss, but if the trespass is accompanied by any actual harm, as by trampling down growing crops, damages are recoverable for the harm done,[5] measured by the estimated diminution in value of the crop by reason of the damage done by the trespass.

Interdict is competent only if there is reasonable apprehension of repetition or continuance of the same or a closely related trespass.[6]

Damages may also be claimed where it is a natural and probable consequence of something done by the defender, such as organising an entertainment, that persons will gather and trespass on the pursuer's lands.[7]

Exceptionally trespass is a criminal offence.[8]

Aircraft

No action lies in respect of trespass or of nuisance by reason only of the flight of an aircraft [9] over any property at a height above the ground, which, having regard to wind, weather and all the circumstances of the case is reasonable, or the ordinary incidents of such flight so long as stated statutory conditions are only complied with.[10]

Encroachment on heritage

Encroachment is more permanent dispossession than trespass and may be effected by unauthorised mining or quarrying within the pursuer's lands, or constructing a building, bridge, cableway or similar erection on or over the pursuer's lands without his permission or legal authority. Where such a wrong is done the pursuer's claim is for the loss of use of the land affected and the value of anything wrongfully extracted or taken from the lands.

This infringement of the right of exclusive possession and enjoyment of property is an injury sounding in damages and it is unnecessary to show present or apprehended future patrimonial loss or any actual damage.[11]

If loss has been actually sustained the basic principle of damages is the damage actually sustained and not necessarily the cost of reinstatement or restitution *in integrum*.[12] Thus, where a mine was driven under a highway

[5] *Watson* v. *E. Errol* (1763) Mor. 4991; *Colquhoun* v. *Buchanan* (1785) Mor. 4997.

[6] *Geils, supra*; *Inverurie Mags.* v. *Sorrie*, 1956 S.C. 175.

[7] *Scott's Trs.* v. *Moss* (1889) 17 R. 32 (where the action seems to have been founded on nuisance or negligence).

[8] Regulation of Railways Act 1840, s. 16; Regulation of Railways Act 1868, s. 23; Trespass (Sc.) Act 1865 (and see Civil Aviation Act 1949, s. 38).

[9] Not defined in the Act.

[10] Civil Aviation Act 1949, s. 40 (1).

[11] *Miln* v. *Mudie* (1828) 6 S. 967; *Hazle* v. *Turner* (1840) 2 D. 886; see too *Bannatyne* v. *Cranston* (1624) Mor. 12769; *Burgess* v. *Brown* (1790) Hume 504; *Hamilton* v. *Eddington* (1793) Mor. 12824; *Burling* v. *Read* (1850) 11 Q.B. 904; *Ewing* v. *Colquhoun's Trs.* (1877) 4 R.(H.L.) 116, 126; *Wilson* v. *Pottinger*, 1908 S.C. 580.

[12] *Jones* v. *Gooday* (1841) 8 M. & W. 146; *Lodge Holes Colliery Co.* v. *Wednesbury Corpn.* [1908] A.C. 323; *Rochford* v. *Essex C.C.* (1916) 85 L.J.Ch. 281.

and the surface thereof let down in consequence, the owners of the highway restored it to its former level at great cost, though an equally convenient road might have been made more cheaply. It was held that the road authority was entitled to recover from the mine owners only what it would have cost to make an equally commodious road.[13] The diminution in value may be the same as the cost of restoration, but it will normally be less.

Encroachment by mining

In the case of encroachment by mining beyond the boundary a distinction is drawn between encroachment effected inadvertently,[14] mistakenly,[15] fairly and honestly,[16] or under bona fide belief in title,[17] and that which has been effected by fraud,[18] or gross negligence,[19] wilfully,[20] or in a manner entirely unauthorised and unlawful,[21] or furtively or in bad faith.[22]

Damages recoverable

In the first category of cases the damages recoverable will be the value of the abstracted minerals under deduction of the whole expenses of severing and winning the minerals, and also of raising them,[23] but in the latter case the only permissible deductions are the expenses of raising.[24] Separate compensation may have to be assessed for injury to the soil by the mining.[25] If, in the former case, the cost of mining were allowed, the defender would be in fact paid for his own unlawful acting.[26]

13 *Lodge Holes Colliery Co., supra.*

14 *Hilton* v. *Woods* (1867) L.R. 4 Eq. 432.

15 *Re United Merthyr Collieries* (1872) L.R. 15 Eq. 46; *Livingstone* v. *Rawyards Coal Co.* (1880) 7 R.(H.L.) 1.

16 *Wood* v. *Morewood* (1841) 3 Q.B. 440n.; *Trotter* v. *Maclean* (1879) 13 Ch.D. 574; *Townend* v. *Askern Coal Co.* [1934] Ch. 463.

17 *Jegon* v. *Vivian* (1871) L.R. 6 Ch. 742; *Ashton* v. *Stock* (1877) 6 Ch.D. 719; *Whitwham* v. *Westminster Brymbo Coal Co.* [1896] 2 Ch. 538.

18 *Fothergill* v. *Phillips* (1871) L.R. 6 Ch. 770; *Ecclesiastical Commrs.* v. *N.E. Ry.* (1877) 4 Ch.D. 45, disapproved on another point in *Bulli Co.* v. *Osborne* [1899] A.C. 351; *Taylor* v. *Mostyn* (1886) 33 Ch.D. 226.

19 *Martin* v. *Porter* (1839) 5 M. & W. 352; *Morgan* v. *Powell* (1842) 3 Q.B. 278; *Wild* v. *Holt* (1842) 9 M. & W. 672; *Phillips* v. *Homfray* (1871) 6 Ch. 770; *Wood* v. *Morewood, supra.*

20 *Martin, supra*; *Llynvi Co.* v. *Brogden* (1870) L.R. 11 Eq. 188; *Taylor* v. *Mostyn* (1886) 33 Ch.D. 226.

21 *Livingstone* v. *Rawyards Co.* (1880) 7 R.(H.L.) 1; *Bulli Co., supra.*

22 *Livingstone, supra*; *Durham* v. *Hood* (1871) 9 M. 474; *Wilsons* v. *Waddell* (1876) 4 R.(H.L.) 29; *Ramsay* v. *Blair* (1876) 3 R.(H.L.) 41; *Bulli Co.* v. *Osborne* [1899] A.C. 351; *Davidson's Trs.* v. *C. Ry.* (1895) 23 R. 45. See also *D. of Portland* v. *Wood's Trs.*, 1927 S.C.(H.L.) 1.

23 *Re United Merthyr Collieries* (1872) L.R. 15 Eq. 46; *Job* v. *Potton* (1875) L.R. 20 Eq. 84; *Trotter* v. *Maclean* (1880) 13 Ch.D. 574; *Jegon, supra*; *Hilton* v. *Woods* (1867) L.R. 4 Eq. 432; *Ashton* v. *Stock* (1877) 6 Ch.D. 719; *Townend* v. *Askern Coal Co.* [1934] Ch. 463.

24 *Wood* v. *Morewood, supra*; *Martin, supra*; *Trotter* v. *Maclean* (1880) 13 Ch.D. 574, and cases there cited; *Joicey* v. *Dickinson*, 45 L.T.(N.S.) 643; *Taylor* v. *Mostyn* (1886) 33 Ch.D. 226; *Re Barrington* (1886) 33 Ch.D. 523; *Peruvian Guano Co.* v. *Dreyfus* [1892] A.C. 166, 175; *Townend* v. *Askern Coal Co.* [1934] Ch. 463.

25 *Morgan* v. *Powell* (1842) 3 Q.B. 278; *Martin* v. *Porter* (1839) 5 M. & W. 352; *Wild* v. *Holt* (1842) 9 M. & W. 672.

26 *Morgan* v. *Powell* (1842) 3 Q.B. 278.

In both classes of cases the element of claim in respect of surface damage is allowable if any such damage has been caused [27]; it has, however, been held that a claim for wayleave over the roads or waste made in working on the land which has been encroached on is not admissible.[28] The distinction has been disapproved for Scotland on the ground that it arose from the division between law and equity in England,[29] and there has been a tendency to measure the damage by the loss actually sustained in either case,[30] though there are dicta in favour of a stricter standard where there has been *mala fides*,[31] and the consideration seems quite valid.

Other ways of computing damages have been adopted in certain particular cases, as where a proprietor of a small feu, where the minerals were not reserved to the superior as they were all around, recovered damages determined proportionally by the rate paid by the mineral lessees to the superior as royalty for the surrounding coalfield.[28] This was a case of common error and bona fides, and it was held that neither the encroacher's profits less actual working costs, nor the commercial impossibility of working the coal under such a small subject were appropriate considerations to determine the measure of damages. The royalty was not taken as the measure of damages but only evidence in the special circumstances of the value for which the owner was entitled to be compensated.[32]

Again, where a railway company excavated freestone which had been reserved to the superiors, even after warning and in face of title, the superiors were awarded the market value of the freestone under deduction of the cost of working, even though the superiors could not have worked the stone themselves or let it at a profit, and it was only the abstraction by the railway company which had created the market value.[33]

In *Houldsworth* v. *Brand's Trs.*[34] a landlord was entitled on certain conditions to resume possession of a colliery, and this he did only after the tenant had defended an action of removing. The landlord then sued for £10,000 for violent profits in respect of the wrongful retention of possession, and *separatim* for damages for the wrongful retention of possession. It was held that damages fell to be awarded for breach of contract in failing to remove in terms of the lease but not for violent profits, on the ground that the tenant had resisted the removing in bona fide and was not liable as a mere intruder. It seems, however, implied in the judgments,

27 *Davidson's Trs.* v. *Caledonian Ry.* (1895) 23 R. 45 and [1903] A.C. 22.

28 *Livingstone* v. *Rawyards Co.* (1880) 7 R.(H.L.) 1.

29 *Davidson's Trs., supra*, at 47, *per* Lord Stormonth-Darling.

30 *Houldsworth* v. *Brand's Trs.* (1876) 3 R. 304; *Livingstone* v. *Rawyards Coal Co., supra*; *Davidson's Trs., supra*; *Duke of Portland* v. *Wood's Trs.*, 1927 S.C.(H.L.) 1.

31 *Houldsworth, supra*, at 308 (Lord Curriehill), 310 (L. J.-C. Moncreiff); *Livingstone, supra*, at 2, *per* Ld. Chan. Cairns; *Davidson's Trs., supra*, 45, *per* Lord Stormonth-Darling, 47, *per* Lord Trayner.

32 *Livingstone, supra*, 10, *per* Lord Blackburn; *cf. Duke of Portland* v. *Wood's Trs.*, 1927 S.C.(H.L.) 1, 4.

33 *Davidson's Trs.* v. *Caledonian Ry.* (1895) 23 R. 45.

34 (1876) 3 R. 304.

that in other circumstances, such as the complete absence of bona fides in retaining possession, a claim for violent profits would lie.

In *Duke of Portland* v. *Wood's Trs.*,[35] mineral tenants were bound to leave the workings in good condition, free of water, so as to enable the landlord to pursue the workings. The workings were left flooded and the landlord sued for the cost of putting the subjects in the condition they would have been in if the defenders had fulfilled their obligations under the lease. The defenders pleaded that the claim should be limited to the loss of royalties. The courts decided against this, laying down that the loss which had resulted from the breach was to be considered in measuring the damages, and the true value of the loss might have to be discovered by the application of more than one method.

Other elements

An element for surface damage, if incurred, is included in the claim of damages,[36] and any claim for wayleave over the roads made in working in the land encroached upon if it has caused loss or damage.[37]

Interference with support

A natural right [38] connected with the ownership of land consists in the right to have land in its natural state supported by the adjacent and subjacent land [39]; when the land is in its natural state this right is said to be unqualified.[40] In this branch of the law the rules of Scots and English law have been said to be identical.[41]

No distinction need generally be drawn between vertical and lateral support [42] and in practice support of a given spot frequently depends on both in conjunction. The right is not affected by the nature of the ground, nor by the difficulty of providing the support.[43]

Interdict is competent where there is knowledge of working in a manner detrimental to the surface,[44] and damages may be claimed on subsidence occurring unless the right of compensation for loss of support has been displaced by provision or clear implication. Each fresh subsidence is a new and separate wrong allowing of a further claim of damages, and even though no further mining or operations have taken place between the earlier and the later subsidence, and though the proximate cause of injury

35 1926 S.C. 640; affd. 1927 S.C.(H.L.) 1.

36 *Davidson's Trs.* v. *Caledonian Ry.* (1895) 23 R. 45.

37 *Livingstone* v. *Rawyards Coal Co.* (1880) 7 R.(H.L.) 1; *Morgan* v. *Powell* (1842) 3 Q.B. 278; *Jegon* v. *Vivian* (1871) L.R. 6 Ch. 742; *Llynvi Coal Co.* v. *Brogden* (1870) 11 Eq. 188; *Att.-Gen.* v. *Tomline* (1877) 5 Ch.D. 750.

38 *Humphries* v. *Brogden* (1850) 12 Q.B. 739; *White* v. *Dixon* (1883) 10 R.(H.L.) 45.

39 *Humphries, supra*; *Bonomi* v. *Backhouse* (1859) E.B. & E. 622; 9 H.L.C. 503.

40 *Dalton* v. *Angus* (1881) 6 App.Cas. 740; *Bank of Scotland* v. *Stewart* (1891) 18 R. 957.

41 *Caledonian Ry.* v. *Sprot* (1854) 2 Macq. 449, 461; *Andrew* v. *Buchanan* (1873) 11 M.(H.L.) 13, 16.

42 *Caledonian Ry., supra*; *Humphries, supra*; *Bonomi, supra*; *Dalton, supra*; *White, supra.*

43 *Humphries, supra*; *Rowbotham* v. *Wilson* (1856) 6 E. & B. 593.

44 *Andrew* v. *Buchanan* (1872) 11 M.(H.L.) 13; *Siddons* v. *Short* (1877) 2 C.P.D. 572; *Mayor of Birmingham* v. *Allen* (1877) 6 Ch.D. 284.

was the working of minerals on an adjacent estate, provided always that the subsidence is a consequence of the same operations.[45] As the ground of action is the subsidence and not the mining, this is not a true exception to the rule that damages can only be claimed once for all loss resulting from one wrong. Damages cannot be recovered for prospective injury such as depreciation of the property caused by risk of future subsidence,[46] nor in respect of the capitalised value of expenses likely to be required to keep remedial works in order.[47] It is probable that mere subsidence is sufficient damage to found an action without further damage.[48]

Support by land to land alone

The owner of ground is entitled to such support vertically and laterally as is sufficient to retain the land in its natural state as a natural adjunct of his right of property.[49] Hence damage by subsidence gives a claim of damages without reference to the nature of the strata, the difficulty of support and the comparative value of the surface and minerals or other qualifications.

The right of support is not, however, absolute, so as to admit of an action when no appreciable damage has been sustained,[50] nor does it extend to licensees from the landlord for the destruction of their gas-pipes by subsidence caused by the mineral tenants, in the absence of a contract between them. The duty is to the landlord only.[51]

A cause of action only emerges when the complainer's land has been materially changed or substantially interfered with by the withdrawal of the vertical or lateral support.[52]

Every fresh subsidence is a fresh cause of action, even though indemnity has been recovered for prior claims, and though no further action has been taken with regard to the minerals in the interval, and though the proximate cause of injury was the working of minerals on an adjacent estate.[53] Hence, damages are not recoverable for danger of future subsi-

45 *Darley Main Co.* v. *Mitchell* (1886) 11 App.Cas. 127; *D. Abercorn* v. *Merry & Cunninghame*, 1909, 1 S.L.T. 319; *Geddes* v. *Haldane* (1906) 13 S.L.T. 707. See too *Greenwell* v. *Low Beechburn Co.* [1897] 2 Q.B. 165; *Hall* v. *Duke of Norfolk* [1900] 2 Ch. 493; *West Leigh Co.* v. *Tunnicliffe* [1908] A.C. 27.

46 *West Leigh Co., supra.*

47 *Kennard* v. *Cory* [1922] 1 Ch. 265.

48 *Mitchell* v. *Darley Main Colliery* (1884) 14 Q.B.D. 125, 137; *Att.-Gen.* v. *Conduit Coal Co.* [1895] 1 Q.B. 301, 311.

49 *Humphries* v. *Brogden* (1848) 12 Q.B. 739; *White* v. *Dixon* (1883) 10 R.(H.L.) 45, 46; *Dalton* v. *Angus* (1881) 6 App.Cas. 740; *Davis* v. *Treharne* (1881) 6 App.Cas. 460; *Love* v. *Bell* (1884) 9 App.Cas. 286; *Hayles* v. *Pease* [1899] 1 Ch. 567; *Elliott* v. *N.E. Ry.* (1863) 10 H.L.C. 333; *Caledonian Ry.* v. *Sprot* (1856) 2 Macq. 449; *Bonomi* v. *Backhouse* (1861) 9 H.L.C. 503; *Pountney* v. *Clayton* (1883) 11 Q.B.D. 820; *Att.-Gen.* v. *Conduit Colliery Co.* [1895] 1 Q.B. 301; Bell, *Prin.*, § 970.

50 *Bonomi* v. *Backhouse* (1861) 9 H.L.C. 503.

51 *Mid. & E. Calder Gas Co.* v. *Oakbank Oil Co.* (1891) 28 S.L.R. 564.

52 *Bonomi* v. *Backhouse* (1861) 9 H.L.C. 503, 512; *Darley Main Co.* v. *Mitchell* (1884) 14 Q.B.D. 125, 130, 137, 140; *cf. Lamb* v. *Walker* (1878) 3 Q.B.D. 389, 402.

53 *Darley Main Co.* v. *Mitchell* (1886) 11 App.Cas. 127; *Abercorn* v. *Merry & Cunninghame*, 1909, 1 S.L.T. 319; *Geddes* v. *Haldane* (1906) 13 S.L.T. 707; see also *Greenwell* v. *Low Beechburn Co.* [1897] 2 Q.B. 165; *Hall* v. *Duke of Norfolk* [1900] 2 Ch. 493; *West Leigh Co.* v. *Tunnicliffe* [1908] A.C. 27.

dence or prospective injury.[54] The person in possession at the date of subsidence may not be liable if he did nothing to cause it and it resulted from operations by his predecessor, as he does not warrant that he will maintain support.[55]

Necessity of proving actual damage

It is doubtful to what extent it is necessary to prove actual damage suffered by the complainer to recover damages. It being admitted that the right to support for land unencumbered by buildings is a natural right of property, there seems no reason why a perceptible alteration in the surface should not give a claim of damages without proof of actual pecuniary damage. This is the case with the right to flowing water,[56] but there is authority in the case of support for the view that only actual pecuniary loss resulting from physical damage wrongfully caused to the land gives a right of action.[57] Furthermore, where buildings have been erected on the land and are damaged by subsidence, the value of the buildings may be recovered if it is shown that the erection of the buildings did not contribute to the subsidence but that it would have occurred even though no such buildings had existed.[58] In such a case loss resulting from damage to the buildings may be recovered as the consequence of the wrong done by withdrawing the natural right of support.[59]

It is, however, quite clear that while the actual physical damage to the land gives the right of action, if there has been pecuniary loss following on the physical damage, the owner may recover as and when the physical damage occurs.[60]

Compensation clauses in mineral leases

Mineral leases and dispositions of underlying strata may provide for compensation being payable for " surface damage," which term probably includes, as well as damage to crops and trees, damage to buildings erected on the land or in contemplation at the date of the agreement.[61] If a disposition is to take away the common law right of support for the land it must do so expressly or by clear implication.[62]

[54] *West Leigh Co.* v. *Tunnicliffe* [1908] A.C. 27.

[55] *Geddes's Trs.* v. *Haldane* (1907) 14 S.L.T. 328; *Dennett* v. *Atherton* (1872) L.R. 7 Q.B. 316; *Spoor* v. *Green* (1874) L.R. 9 Ex. 99; *Greenwell, supra*; *Hall, supra*. See also *Baird's Trs.* v. *Innes* (1851) 13 D. 982.

[56] *Morris* v. *Bicket* (1866) 4 M.(H.L.) 44; *Embrey* v. *Owen* (1851) 6 Ex. 353.

[57] *Darley Main Colliery* v. *Mitchell* (1886) 11 App.Cas. 127; *West Leigh Colliery Co.* v. *Tunnicliffe & Hampson* [1908] A.C. 27.

[58] *Browne* v. *Robins* (1859) 4 H. & N. 186; *Stroyan* v. *Knowles* (1861) 6 H. & N. 454; *Chapman* v. *Day* (1883) 47 L.T. 705.

[59] *Hamilton* v. *Turner* (1867) 5 M. 1086, 1099, 1100; *Browne* v. *Robins* (1859) 4 H. & N. 186; *Stroyan* v. *Knowles* (1861) 6 H. & N. 454; *Siddons* v. *Short* (1877) 2 C.P.D. 572; *Love* v. *Bell* (1884) 9 App.Cas. 386; *cf. Smith* v. *Thackerah* (1866) L.R. 1 C.P. 564.

[60] *Cf. Rankine on Landownership*, 4th ed., 494.

[61] *Neill's Trs.* v. *Dixon* (1880) 7 R. 141; *Stewart's Hosp.* v. *Waddell* (1890) 17 R. 1077. *Cf. Barr* v. *Baird* (1904) 6 F. 524; *Hallpenny* v. *Dewar* (1898) 25 R. 889; *Galbraith's Trs.* v. *Eglinton Iron Co.* (1868) 7 M. 167. As to measure of compensation under such a clause, see *Taylor* v. *Auchinlea Coal Co.*, 1912, 2 S.L.T. 10.

[62] *White* v. *Dixon* (1883) 10 R.(H.L.) 45; *Smart* v. *Morton* (1855) 5 E. & B. 30; *Butterknowle Colliery Co.* v. *Bishop Auckland Co-op. Co.* [1906] A.C. 313.

Measure of damages

The measure of damages is not necessarily the cost of reinstatement of the surface, but a reasonable indemnity for the harm done.[63] In *Baird's Trs.* v. *Innes*,[64] the surface of a deer-park was seriously and permanently damaged by subsidence, and it was averred that loss had been sustained on its sale. In the circumstances, however, the defenders were assoilzied. Had there been liability it is thought that proof or a reasonable estimate of the loss on sale would have been a reasonable measure of damages.

The damages recoverable for causing subsidence of land will include consequential damage to buildings, unless the subsidence has been caused by the additional weight and pressure of the building.[65]

Similar considerations apply to questions of lateral support between adjacent owners in such cases as digging and quarrying close to a boundary: excavation must be stopped at such a distance from the boundary as will leave adequate support for the adjacent land. The same also holds as between upper and lower mine owners.[66]

Support by land to land with buildings

There can be no natural right of support for land altered by buildings placed on it, and any right must be acquired by express or implied grant.[67] There can be no implication that a mineral owner has undertaken to support the ground and also any buildings which may subsequently be erected thereon, on pain of liability for damages for harm caused them by subsidence.[68] If, however, at the time of the severance of ownership, the surface was conveyed for the erection of buildings or it was in contemplation that buildings or other use was to be made of the land requiring increased support, there is an implied right to such support as the use requires,[69] unless the contrary be stipulated.[70] The state of affairs at the date of the separation of ownership must be looked at. If it be shown that the subsidence was not substantially caused by the buildings there is still a good claim in respect of the continuing absolute right to support for the ground.[71]

Similar questions may arise in the case of lateral support to walls at the edge of an adjoining property.[72]

The right to support and the question of compensation or damages are frequently determined by the terms of the disposition of the lands, or of

63 *Lodge Holes Co.* v. *Wednesbury Corpn.* [1908] A.C. 323.
64 (1845) 7 D. 1001; (1846) 8 D. 464; (1851) 13 D. 982.
65 *Browne* v. *Robins* (1859) 4 H. & N. 186; *Stroyan* v. *Knowles* (1861) 6 H. & N. 454.
66 *Hurlet and Campsie Alum Co.* v. *Glasgow* (1850) 12 D. 704, affd. 7 Bell's App. 100; *Mundy* v. *Duke of Rutland* (1882) 23 Ch.D. 81.
67 *Dalton* v. *Angus* (1881) 6 App.Cas. 740, 792, 830.
68 *Hamilton* v. *Turner* (1867) 5 M. 1086, 1090.
69 *Dalton, supra*; *Caledonian Ry.* v. *Sprot* (1856) 2 Macq. 449; *N.B. Ry.* v. *Turners* (1904) 6 F. 900; *Neill's Trs.* v. *Dixon* (1880) 7 R. 741, 743; *Elliott* v. *N.E. Ry.* (1863) 10 H.L.C. 333.
70 *Buchanan* v. *Andrew* (1873) 11 M.(H.L.) 13.
71 *Hamilton, supra*, 1098.
72 *Campbell's Trs.* v. *Henderson* (1884) 11 R. 520.

minerals or a clause of reservation of minerals. In such cases they fall to be determined primarily by the construction of the clause in question.[73] A surface-damage clause may extend to damage to buildings [74] but normally only extends to damage such as to crops or by smoke which affects the agricultural use of the land,[73] and not to injury occasioned by subsidence.

Occasionally, however, a clause for surface-damages has been held to extend to damage caused by underground operations though not to smoke and ashes.[75] Such a clause, too, was held to cover damage to a house erected after the disposal of the mineral strata but reasonably suitable to the ground as it was at that period, though possibly not if it came to be covered with streets.[76] In *Dryburgh* v. *Fife Coal Co.*[77] there was a large increase in feuing subsequent to the date of the mineral lease, but the pursuer was nevertheless held entitled to damages as he had not renounced his common law rights against the mineral tenant.

Exemption clauses

In many cases any liability for damage is excepted by the terms of the feu contract, or other title by which the owner of the surface holds his land. In every case it is a question of the construction of the particular deed and clause in question to determine whether there is any liability for damage to land and buildings.[78] Clauses such as of reservations of minerals may also vitally affect the question of whom it is appropriate to sue, whether superior or mineral tenant. A clause reserving minerals subject to payment of compensation may extend to compensation for damage to buildings [79]; but a reservation of minerals subject to payment of " surface damages " has been held to cover damage to buildings caused by underground workings as well as to damage affecting the agricultural use of the lands.[80] A clause relieving a mine owner from liability for damage must be clear and unequivocal.[81]

Statutory provisions

The Coal Mining (Subsidence) Act 1950 makes it the responsibility of the National Coal Board to carry out repairs and to make payment in respect of subsidence damage caused by working and getting coal, and occurring after 1946 to a private dwelling-house with a rateable value not exceeding, in Scotland, £52. The Coal Board must carry out reasonable repairs or make a payment equal to the cost reasonably incurred in doing

[73] *Galbraith's Tr.* v. *Eglinton Iron Co.* (1868) 7 M. 167, 172.
[74] *Dunlop's Trs.* v. *Corbet*, June 20, 1809, F.C.
[75] *Oswald* v. *Gordon* (1853) 16 D. 70.
[76] *Neill's Trs.* v. *Dixon* (1880) 7 R. 441.
[77] (1905) 7 F. 1083.
[78] See, *e.g. Galbraith's Tr.* v. *Eglinton Iron Co.* (1868) 7 M. 167; *Oswald* v. *Gordon* (1853) 16 D. 70; *White's Trs.* v. *Duke of Hamilton* (1887) 14 R. 597; *Stewart's Hosp.* v. *Waddell* (1890) 17 R. 1077; *Gray* v. *Burns* (1894) 2 S.L.T. 187; *Pringle* v. *Carron Co.* (1905) 7 F. 820; *Highgate* v. *Paisley Mags.* (1896) 23 R. 992.
[79] *Dunlop's Trs.* v. *Corbet*, June 20, 1809, F.C.
[80] *Hallpenny* v. *Dewar* (1898) 25 R. 889; *Neill's Trs.* v. *Dixon* (1880) 7 R. 741.
[81] *Buchanan* v. *Andrew* (1873) 11 M.(H.L.) 13.

so. In lieu thereof a payment may be made equal to the amount of the depreciation in the value of the house caused by the subsidence. There are further provisions for anticipated or continuing damage, and for making preventive works. The court may (s. 12) require the National Coal Board to carry out their obligations under the Act or award damages in respect of their failure to do so within a reasonable time. The rights under the Act are alternative to any right to damages or compensation existing independently thereof, and a claimant must elect his remedy.

The Coal-Mining (Subsidence) Act 1957 prescribes the duty of the Coal Board to remedy or to compensate for subsidence damage to property, the claim to statutory compensation being alternative to other claims to damages or compensation.

Damages recoverable

When support is wrongfully removed and damage results, compensation may be sought for the whole, past, present and future damage caused by this particular subsidence.[82] Each fresh subsidence is a fresh cause of action.[83] In *Gibson* v. *Farie* [84] glass-houses in a market garden were destroyed by subsidence. Lord Cullen awarded the cost of replacement, which was in excess of what the pursuer had paid when he bought the premises, and additional sums for loss of stock and loss of custom. In the circumstances the original cost price of the glass-houses would not have sufficed to effect restitution *in integrum*.

The contention that the proper basic measure of damages is the depreciation in the value of the buildings receives support from the statutory provisions already noted. In cases of less serious damage the amount awardable under this head may well be the same as the cost of repair or reinstatement. In *Taylor* v. *Auchinlea Coal Co.*,[85] where houses had been damaged by mineral workings, it was held that compensation was recoverable for loss of rental which was a necessary consequence of the damage, but not in respect of depreciation due to a lower class of tenant being introduced, nor for compensation paid to tenants for compulsory removal. Apart from that, damages have been given for loss of rent, cost of repairs, structural depreciation and cost of removal of the business.[86] The wrongdoer cannot be heard to impugn the injured party's every act or petty mistake in effecting repairs, so long as he acts honestly and reasonably,[87] though he may prove that the property had a limited value owing to inherent defect.[88] Damages have also been given for loss of profits and cost

[82] *Bonomi* v. *Backhouse* (1859) E.B. & E. 659; 9 H.L.C. 503.

[83] *Mitchell* v. *Darley Main Colliery Co.* (1886) 11 App.Cas. 127; *Crumbie* v. *Wallsend Local Board* [1891] 1 Q.B. 503.

[84] 1918, 1 S.L.T. 405.

[85] 1912, 2 S.L.T. 10.

[86] *Bonomi* v. *Backhouse* (1859) E.B. & E. 622, 638; *Grosvenor Hotel Co.* v. *Hamilton* [1894] 2 Q.B. 836; *West Leigh Colliery Co.* v. *Tunnicliffe* [1908] A.C. 32.

[87] *Lodge Holes Co.* v. *Wednesbury Corpn.* [1908] A.C. 323, 325.

[88] *Jones* v. *Consolidated Anthracite Collieries* [1916] 1 K.B. 123, 137.

of restoration where a profit-earning property, such as a shipyard, is damaged.[89] As each fresh subsidence is a fresh cause of action, depreciated market value owing to the risk of further subsidence is not relevant.[90]

Support of buildings by other buildings

Part of this branch of the subject falls under the common interest involved in the rights and obligations of proprietors of flatted houses,[91] part under the rights of mutual gable. Apart from that, a servitude right of support for buildings *inter se* may be acquired by express or implied grant.[92] Cases of claims of damage from loss of support in circumstances of this kind have been rare, though cases are readily conceivable.

The right of action probably only arises when appreciable damage has been caused,[93] and the proper measure of damages is probably the diminution in the value of the subjects caused thereby.

Loss of amenity

Damage to the value of buildings by such as loss of amenity does not fall properly under this head. Where by unjustifiable actings amounting to nuisance on the part of a defender the amenity of heritage is materially lessened or destroyed, it would appear that the depreciation in its value would provide the measure of damages. But depreciation must be proved and a merely speculative claim is valueless.

Loss of support causing personal injury

Loss of support does not necessarily give any right of action for personal injuries or death.[94]

Damage to Heritage

Malicious damage

Malicious damage, such as vandalism, is certainly actionable as well as criminally punishable.

The appropriate measure of damages is the diminution in value of the heritable property damaged. In the ordinary case a useful guide to the extent of diminished value is the cost of effecting necessary repairs, but in the case of derelict or seriously depreciated property a somewhat lesser measure of damages may be appropriate where repair or reinstatement would, if worth doing at all, be improving the property.

[89] *Stroyan* v. *Knowles* (1860) 6 H. & N. 454; *Doxford* v. *Wearmouth Coal Co.*, 1911, not reported.

[90] *West Leigh Colliery Co.*, *supra*; *cf. Geddes* v. *Haldane* (1905) 13 S.L.T. 707.

[91] See *Smith* v. *Giuliani*, 1925 S.C.(H.L.) 45, 56, *per* Lord Dunedin; *Duncan Smith & McLaren* v. *Heatly*, 1952 J.C. 61.

[92] *Caledonian Ry.* v. *Sprot* (1856) 2 Macq. 449; *Dalton* v. *Angus* (1881) 6 App.Cas. 740.

[93] *Cf. Smith* v. *Thackerah* (1866) L.R. 1 C.P. 564; *Hall* v. *Duke of Norfolk* [1900] 2 Ch. 493.

[94] *Angus* v. *N.C.B.*, 1955 S.C. 175.

Riot damage

At common law no action lay against the magistrates of a burgh for damages in respect of injury done to the property of an individual by a riotous assembly within the burgh.[95] The only remedy would be one against individual rioters for the damage done by them. Statutory rights against the magistrates were introduced by the Malicious Damage Act 1812; Malicious Damage (Sc.) Act 1816, s. 2; and the Riotous Assemblies (Sc.) Act 1822, s. 10, all amended by the Law Reform (Limitation of Actions, etc.) Act 1954. The measure of damages is generally indicated by the statutory provisions as the full value of the property damaged, stolen or destroyed.[96] Loss of profits has probably to be rejected as too remote.[97]

Removal of fixtures

Where fixtures have been wrongfully removed from heritage its value as a subject of sale or security is diminished thereby but the measure of damages is a matter of some difficulty. In *Edinburgh and Leith Gas Commrs.* v. *Smart* [98] it was held that the reasonable cost of replacement was proper, but the court gave consideration to the possibility of replacing some of the articles secondhand, and rejected the prices obtained at a break-up sale as no test of the value of articles *in situ*. But in such cases of wrongful severance something may depend on whether the severance was wilful or not.[99]

Negligent damage

Heritable property may be damaged negligently in many ways as by fire, flooding, or by the impact by vehicles, vessels or aircraft.

Damage by vehicles

It seems indubitable that if heritable property is damaged or destroyed by a vehicle, the owner can recover damages in respect of the diminished value from the owner of the vehicle. The topic is singularly ill-covered by authority. In *Glasgow Corporation* v. *Barclay Curle*,[1] the pursuers claimed at common law for the cost of repairing a street alleged to have been broken down by the defenders running excessively heavy traffic over it.

[95] *Campbell* v. *Banff Mags.* (1744) Mor. 2504; *Capaldi* v. *Greenock Mags.*, 1941 S.C. 310, 322. See also *Johnstone* v. *Kerr* (1837) 16 S. 104; *Scottish Plate Glass Ins. Co.* v. *Edinburgh Corpn.*, 1941 S.C. 115; *Coia* v. *Robertson*, 1942 S.C. 111; *Pompa's Trs.* v. *Edinburgh Mags.*, 1942 S.C. 119.

[96] *Coia*, *supra*, 113; *Pompa's Trs.*, *supra*, 120.

[97] *Capaldi*, *supra*, 315.

[98] 1918, 1 S.L.T. 80.

[99] *Cf.* authorities on wrongful abstraction of minerals.

[1] 1922 S.C. 413; affd. 1923 S.C.(H.L.) 78. Damages are recoverable by the road authority for the cost of repairing a road damaged in consequence of the defender's breach of statutory regulations relating to the construction and use of vehicles, even though breach thereof was fenced by a penalty: *Ross and Cromarty C.C.* v. *Munro* (1945) 62 Sh.Ct.Rep. 78. As to a bridge, see *Lord Advocate* v. *A. M. Carmichael Ltd.*, 1953 S.L.T.(Notes) 12. As to telegraph lines see *P.M.G.* v. *Lee*, 1968 S.L.T.(Sh.Ct.) 32.

The defenders were assoilzied as they had only caused unusually heavy wear and tear and not destroyed the street, and the evidence did not establish negligence on their part. Under the (English) Highways and Locomotives (Amendment) Act 1878, as amended by the Locomotives Act 1898, it has been held that the measure of damages is the difference between the sum expended in repairs during the year and the average sum expended in previous years, making allowance for other causes of increased expenditure.[2]

In cases of vehicles running into and damaging property such as walls, the diminution in value of the affected property is probably the proper measure of damages. The cost of repair is not necessarily the sole criterion as repair will, in many cases, probably effect an improvement over the previous condition.

Damage by ships

Under the Harbours, Docks and Piers Clauses Act 1847, s. 74, the owner of a vessel is liable to the harbour undertakers for any damage [3] done by such vessel or any person employed about her to the harbour, dock or pier or the quays or works connected therewith, independently of fault,[4] and the master, through whose wilful act or negligence any such damage is done, is also liable to make good the damage.[5] A claim at common law is competent but negligence must be proved.[6] But the owners were not liable where the damage was occasioned by a vessel driven on the pier due to the extraordinary violence of a storm when the master and crew had had to leave her and had consequently no control of her [7] nor for inevitable accident.[8] But where a steamship went aground and blocked the channel, it was held that the damages should be limited to the extra expense necessary to restore the channel to the condition it was in before she grounded, and should not include damages for loss of use of the harbour while the channel was blocked, the harbour board having been negligent in regard to dredging.[9]

Under the same section the harbour undertakers have a possessory lien over the vessel in respect of the damage done to the dock property. Under the Merchant Shipping (Liability of Shipowners and Others) Act 1900, the right of limiting liability for damage to vessels and goods under the Merchant Shipping Act 1894, ss. 503–504, is extended to damage caused to property of any kind whether on land or water, and whether the liability

[2] *Butt* v. *Weston-super-Mare U.D.C.* [1922] 1 A.C. 340. See also *Billericay Rural Co.* v. *Poplar Union* [1911] 2 K.B. 801; *Colchester Corpn.* v. *Gepp* (1913) 77 J.P. 181.

[3] Physical damage to the *opera manufacta* of the undertaking: *Workington Harbour Board* v. *Towerfield (Owners)* [1951] A.C. 112.

[4] *The Mostyn* [1928] A.C. 57.

[5] *Cf. Baron Vernon* v. *Metagama*, 1927 S.C. 498.

[6] *Clyde Trust* v. *Kelvin Shipping Co.*, 1927 S.C. 622.

[7] *River Wear Commissioners* v. *Adamson* (1877) 2 App.Cas. 743.

[8] *The Boucan* [1909] P. 163. But see *Dennis* v. *Tovell* (1872) L.R. 8 Q.B. 10.

[9] *Workington Harbour & Dock Board* v. *Towerfield (Owners)* [1951] A.C. 112; (counter-claims by harbour and ship for damages).

arises at common law or statute, and despite anything in the statute. This provision has been applied where a vessel crashed through dock gates.[10]

Damage by aircraft

The Civil Aviation Act 1949, s. 40 (2) provides that where material loss or damage [11] is caused to a person or property on land or water by, or a person in, or a person or article falling from an aircraft while in flight, taking off [12] or landing, then unless the damage was caused or contributed to [13] by the negligence of the person by whom it was suffered, damages in respect of the loss or damage shall be recoverable without proof of negligence or intention or other cause of action, as if the loss or damage had been caused by the wilful act, neglect, or default of the owner of the aircraft.

Measure of damages generally

The proper quantum of damages for damage to heritage by fire or water, explosion of gas, electricity, explosives, or other dangerous substance, or from collision by vehicle or ship, may be broadly stated as being equivalent to the loss to the pursuer caused by the diminution in the value of the heritable property in question directly consequent on the injury done to the property. The cost of effecting *restitutio in integrum* is a factor for consideration, but is not *per se* the measure of damages,[14] because repair, rebuilding, or replacement will normally or at least frequently put the premises in a better state than they were in before. This consideration applies particularly to premises previously dilapidated.[15] Moreover, the cost of repair may exceed the diminution in value of the property if it were left unrepaired. The fullest discussion of the topic in Scotland is *Hutchison* v. *Davidson*,[16] a case of total destruction by fire. It was laid down there that damages should be compensation for the wrong and for all the natural and direct consequences thereof. The assessment is a jury question and all relevant circumstances may properly be considered, and the cost of reinstatement and replacement is only one of these items,[17] the diminution in selling value being another. In that case Lord Normand said [18] that the dominant rule of the law of damages, the principle of *restitutio in integrum* [19]

10 *Mersey Docks and Harbour Board* v. *Hay* [1923] A.C. 345. See also *The City of Edinburgh* [1921] P. 274; *The Ruapehu* [1927] A.C. 523; [1929] P. 305; but see *Clifton Trawlers* v. *McIver*, 1953 S.L.T. 230; *The Stonedale* [1956] A.C. 1.

11 This includes loss of life and personal injury: 1949 Act, s. 63 (3).

12 *Blankley* v. *Godley* [1952] 1 All E.R. 436. See also *Dunn* v. *Campbell* (1920) 4 Ll.L.R. 36; *Cubitt & Terry* v. *Gower* (1933) 47 Ll.L.R. 65; *Piper* v. *Darling* (1940) 67 Ll.L.R. 419.

13 The Law Reform (Contributory Negligence) Act 1945 probably applies.

14 Thus where soil was removed, the damages were not the cost of replacing it, but the diminution in value of the property: *Whitham* v. *Kershaw* (1886) 16 Q.B.D. 613; *cf. Rust* v. *Victoria Graving Dock Co.* (1887) 36 Ch.D. 113; *Chifferiel* v. *Watson* (1888) 40 Ch.D. 45; *Whitwham* v. *Westminster Brymbo Coal Co.* [1896] 2 Ch. 538.

15 *Lodge Holes Coal Co.* v. *Wednesbury Corpn.* [1908] A.C. 323: value of old building only allowed, not cost of new.

16 1945 S.C. 395.

17 *Gibson* v. *Farie*, 1918, 1 S.L.T. 404.

18 1945 S.C. at 413.

19 *Liesbosch* v. *Edison* [1933] A.C. 449.

applied equally where heritable subjects were destroyed and " in general the owner of such subjects is fully compensated when he is paid the full price for which the destroyed subjects might have been sold or for which other similar subjects might have been purchased at the date of the loss. Thus, if land is destroyed by letting in the sea the damage is the value of the land lost, not the cost of the engineering operations necessary to restore it. So also, if an urban tenement is destroyed, the value of the tenement, proved by the prices obtained for other similar tenements, will generally be adequate compensation." Exceptional cases require a reasonable cost of restoration to be taken as the proper measure of damages, but if the special character of the property destroyed is to be founded on and the cost of rebuilding claimed, distinct averments and proof are essential.[20]

It was accepted in the similar case of *Moss* v. *Christchurch R.D.C.*,[21] that the measure of damages was the value of the property to the owner at the time it was destroyed, being the difference between the money value of the owner's interest before the fire, and the value thereafter. In *Hutchison* v. *Davidson*,[22] however, it was said that selling value at the date of destruction was not the sole measure in a case of negligent total destruction, nor was the cost of reinstatement or rebuilding *in situ* in all cases the sole measure, but it might on occasions be relevant as one consideration to be borne in mind. Moreover, the monetary award must be so assessed so that while it compensated the claimant for all the direct and natural consequences of the wrongful act, it would neither enrich nor impoverish him beyond the position in which he would have been if the wrongful act had not occurred.[23] In the result in that case, both selling value prior to destruction and the cost of reinstatement were held to be relevant considerations in assessing damages. In other cases reinstatement cost has been the major consideration.[24]

It was pointed out [25] in the case of houses, they are so individualised by situation, aspect, amenity, and even by local accidents, that restitution can only be made by re-erection. The same would apply *a fortiori* to factories and special buildings. In other cases, such as possibly houses in a terrace or a village street, the price might be an adequate compensation.

If the special character or situation of the property is claimed as being a necessary adjunct to the full enjoyment of the owner's estate, notice of this must be given on record and claimed as " special " damages.[26]

Failure to take all reasonable steps to mitigate damages will go in reduction of the amount awarded, as where goods are not timeously removed from an affected building.[27]

20 *Ibid.* 414.
21 [1925] 2 K.B. 750. *Cf. Hosking* v. *Phillips* (1848) 3 Ex. 168; *Jones* v. *Gooday* (1841) 8 M. & W. 146; *Nalder* v. *Ilford Corpn.* [1951] 1 K.B. 822.
22 1945 S.C. 395, 407.
23 *Cf. Duke of Portland* v. *Wood's Trs.*, 1926 S.C. 640, *per* Ld. Pres. Clyde at 651.
24 *Gilmour* v. *Simpson*, 1958 S.C. 477, 487; *Fraser* v. *J. Morton Wilson*, 1965 S.L.T.(Notes) 81.
25 1945 S.C. at 411, *per* Lord Moncrieff.
26 *Ibid.*, 414, *per* Ld. Pres. Normand.
27 *Moffat* v. *Park* (1877) 5 R. 13: *cf. McIntyre* v. *Gallacher* (1883) 11 R. 64.

It is an irrelevant consideration that the property was fully insured,[28] but prospective damage is recoverable.[29]

The quantum of damages for damage by flooding would appear to be treated as a jury question, having general regard to the whole circumstances of the loss and damage sustained.[30] Even if pursuers have been negligent in the management of their property, that is no more than an important element in mitigation of damages and not a bar to recovery.[31]

In *Moffat* v. *Park*,[32] where a pipe burst due to frost, and damaged a neighbour's premises, the defence of contributory negligence in respect of not having removed goods at once was said to be pleadable only in mitigation of damages. A proprietor is liable for the consequences of a plumber's defective work, though he had been held entitled to relief from him when the flooding was clearly shown to be due to the latter's bad workmanship.[33]

In a sheriff court case, where a house was damaged by blasting 300 yards away, damages were given for disturbance, general deterioration, and a reasonable estimate of the cost of restoration.[34]

In another case [35] where walls and ceilings in a house were cracked and damaged in consequence of blasting carried out in connection with the construction of a sewer, a householder was given damages representing the rent of a furnished flat while repairs were being done, a sum for the cost of repairs, and a sum for deterioration of the property, and outlays and inconvenience.

Railway fires

A frequent example of damage by negligent escape of fire was formerly fire caused by the escape of sparks from railway engines. In this case it was held that as railways were run under statutory authority, the defender's duty was merely to use the best possible type of spark arrester, and they were not liable for sparks which the spark arrester failed to prevent,[36] *i.e.*, negligence in the construction and use of the engine must be proved. Under the Railway Fires Acts 1905 and 1923, this was modified and the railway authority is liable for damage caused to agricultural land, defined as including market-gardens, plantations and woods, orchards and fences, but not moorland or buildings, to an amount not exceeding £200 in each case, provided written notice of the fire and of the intention to claim is given within seven days of the damage, and written particulars of the

28 *Ibid.* 404; *cf. Port-Glasgow & Newark Sailcloth Co.* v. *Caledonian Ry.* (1892) 19 R.(H.L.) 608, affd. 20 R.(H.L.) 35.

29 *Townend* v. *Askern Coal Co.* [1934] Ch. 463.

30 *Hanley* v. *Edinburgh Mags.*, 1912 S.C. 1199, 1206; O.H. affd. 1913 S.C.(H.L.) 27; *Brownlie* v. *Mags. of Barrhead*, 1923 S.C. 915, 936, 939.

31 *Brownlie*, *supra*, 935, 936.

32 *Moffat* v. *Park* (1877) 5 R. 13; *cf. Cleghorn* v. *Taylor* (1856) 18 D. 664; *McIntyre* v. *Gallacher* (1883) 11 R. 64; *Reid* v. *Baird* (1876) 4 R. 234.

33 *McIntyre*, *supra*.

34 *Turner* v. *Gibson* (1926) 42 Sh.Ct.Rep. 309.

35 *Davie* v. *Edinburgh Magistrates*, 1953 S.C. 34. See Session Papers for details.

36 *Port Glasgow Sailcloth Co.* v. *Caledonian Ry.* (1893) 20 R.(H.L.) 35; *Vaughan* v. *Taff Vale Ry.* (1860) 5 H. & N. 679; *Murdoch* v. *G.S.W. Ry.* (1870) 8 M. 768.

damage and the amount of claim within twenty-one days. A claim for common law negligence may be annexed to a claim for compensation under the Acts.[37] Inevitable accident has been held in England to be no defence to actions for fire-damage caused by sparks from engines not protected by statutory authority.[38]

Damage by straying animals

Under the Winter Herding Act 1686, c. 11, beasts which have strayed may be detained by the proprietor until payment of the statutory penalty,[39] though not expressly in security of any claim of damages. That does not, however, preclude an action of damages where damage has been done to the pursuer's fields or crops, and the penalty is additional to actual damages and expenses.[40] The Act expressly bears to be enacted to prevent beasts eating or destroying a neighbour's ground, woods, hedges or planting. It is immaterial whether the ground be under crop, in grass or wood,[41] a garden [42] or a sheep-walk.[43] Erskine [44] says that detention may be exercised not only for the penalty and expenses [45] but for indemnification for the actual damage done. Even apart from the Act a common law claim is doubtless competent if there is proof of the defender's cattle causing damage to the pursuer's property.[46] In Ireland an owner of tame deer has been held liable for trespass committed by them on neighbouring land.[47] At least where the animals were wrongfully poinded, the detaining party is liable in damages, if unable to redeliver the animals without reasonable excuse.[48]

NUISANCE

Nuisance is the use of heritable property by one person so as to occasion serious disturbance or substantial inconvenience to his neighbour or material damage to his neighbour's property.[49] The critical question is whether the defender exposed the pursuer to disturbance or inconvenience *plus quam tolerabile*, and if this is established it is no defence that the use complained of was usual, familiar and normal.[49] Nuisance can be committed in innumerable ways, but particularly by the emission of noise, fumes, smoke, polluted water, and the like. Interdict is the normal redress

37 *Att.-Gen.* v. *G.W. Ry.* [1924] 2 K.B.1.
38 *Jones* v. *Festiniog Ry.* (1868) L.R. 3 Q.B. 733 (railway engine); *Powell* v. *Fall* (1880) 5 Q.B.D. 597 (traction engine).
39 *McArthur* v. *Jones* (1878) 6 R. 41.
40 *Govan* v. *Lang* (1794) Mor. 10499; *Loch* v. *Tweedie* (1799) Mor. 10501.
41 *Govan* v. *Lang* (1794) Mor. 10499.
42 *McArthur* v. *Miller* (1873) 1 R. 248.
43 *Pringle* v. *Rae* (1829) 7 S. 352.
44 III, 6, 28.
45 See also *Sorrell* v. *Paget* [1949] 2 All E.R. 609.
46 *Robertson* v. *Wright* (1885) 2 Sh.Ct.Rep. 60, sequel to 13 R. 174. See also *Porter* v. *Taylor* (1886) 2 Sh.Ct.Rep. 444; *Duncan* v. *Shaw* (1945) 61 Sh.Ct.Rep. 116; *Lady Auckland* v. *Dowie*, 1965 S.C. 37.
47 *Brady* v. *Warren* [1900] 2 Ir.R. 632.
48 *Fraser* v. *Smith* (1899) 1 F. 487 (sheep poinded and stolen).
49 *Watt* v. *Jamieson*, 1954 S.C. 56.

against the inception or continuation of a nuisance but damages are competent where actual loss has been sustained.[50]

Where damages are claimed for material damage they must be measured by the diminution in value of the property affected, which itself may be gauged by the cost of any repairs or reinstatement necessitated, subject to fair allowance for the fact that repairs substitute new for old and to some extent improve the property repaired, or by loss of use of lands affected.[51] The quantum of damages is a jury question and must be approached as it would be by a jury.[52] Where the claim is for disturbance or inconvenience any award of damages is rather of the nature of solatium.

Damages for nuisance

Nuisances are commonly remediable by interdict against their continuance, but damages are recoverable in addition,[53] or separately where there has been actual damage. No Scottish case seems to record damages merely for the creation of a nuisance, and damages are exclusively compensatory for loss suffered.[54] In England it has been said that damages are peculiarly suitable where the injury is small, estimable in and compensable by money.[55] It is clear that the primary measure of damages is the loss and inconvenience suffered,[56] or, where there is actual damage, the consequent diminution in value of the property affected, of which the cost of repairs is some evidence.[57] The onus of showing actual damage is on the pursuer.[58] Abatement must be made if some of the damage is not attributable to the nuisance: so where flood water was held up by an embankment and damaged the plaintiff's field but, had the embankment not been constructed, the water would still, though in another way, have reached the plaintiff's land, the measure of damages recoverable was the difference only between the two amounts.[59] Liability in damages is only in respect of operations beyond those legitimately or reasonably done, and not if reasonable and proper steps were taken to obviate undue inconvenience.[60]

Compensation for natural consequences of nuisance

Where damages are recoverable for nuisance they extend to cover the

50 *e.g. Collins* v. *Hamilton* (1837) 15 S. 895 (pollution).
51 *Barrie* v. *Pollok* (1891) 7 Sh.Ct.Rep. 277 (polluted stream rendering lands unfit for grazing).
52 *Sommerville* v. *Edinburgh Water Trs.* (1905) 7 F. 1060, 1083; revd. on the facts (1906) 8 F.(H.L.) 25; *cf. Bankier Distillery Co.* v. *Young* (1892) 19 R. 1083, 1088 (£250 claimed for injury to apparatus and diminished production, £25 awarded).
53 *e.g. Ewen* v. *Turnbull's Trs.* (1857) 19 D. 513.
54 *Cf. Nicholls* v. *Ely Beet Sugar Factory* [1936] Ch. 343; *Smith* v. *Giddy* [1904] 2 K.B. 448. See also *Lemmon* v. *Webb* [1895] A.C. 1.
55 *Petley* v. *Parsons* [1914] 1 Ch. 722.
56 *Cf. Barrie* v. *Pollok* (1891) 7 Sh.Ct.Rep. 277.
57 *Cf. Shelfer* v. *City of London Electric Co.* [1895] 1 Ch. 287; *Campbell* v. *Paddington Corpn.* [1911] 1 K.B. 869.
58 *Collins* v. *Hamilton* (1837) 15 S. 895; *cf. Young* v. *Bowie* (1824) 3 S. 217; *Trotter* v. *Fairnie* (1831) 5 W. & Sh. 649.
59 *Workman* v. *G.N. Ry.* (1863) 32 L.J.Q.B. 279.
60 *Andreae* v. *Selfridge* [1938] Ch. 1; *cf. Hoare* v. *McAlpine* [1923] 1 Ch. 167. See also *McEwan* v. *Steedman and McAlister*, 1912 S.C. 156; *Polsue & Alfieri* v. *Rushmer* [1907] A.C. 121.

natural consequences of the defender's wrongful acts.[61] So where premises were damaged by vibration of machinery the plaintiff recovered damages not restricted to the value of the term he had lost, but including all loss which had happened as a natural consequence, such as the expense of removing his business to other premises.[62] So, too, in a river pollution case, P. O. Lawrence J. said: " The damages to which the plaintiff is entitled are limited to such damages as are the natural and probable consequence of the defendant's wrongful acts, and are not in any way extended beyond such limit because the acts were illegal *per se*. In calculating these damages the court has to consider what is the pecuniary sum which will make good to the plaintiff, so far as money can do so, the loss which he has suffered as the natural result of the wrong done to him." [63] But damages have been held not to include the cost of restoring the premises to their original condition,[64] nor injury to amenity by pollution of a neighbouring stream.[65] They do, however, cover the cost of obtaining a new water supply and engine where the old have been rendered unusable,[65] injury to fishing [65] and cost of watering animals.[65]

Again, where it was shown that even apart from the nuisance complained of, some of the damage would have been caused, the damages awarded were only such as were attributable to the nuisance.[66]

Prospective damages must also be claimed for in the one action,[67] in the case of a permanent nuisance, but in the case of a continuing nuisance [68] an action may be brought for the creation, and there must be subsequent actions for the damage due to continuance of the nuisance, assessing damages down to the date thereof. No damages can be recovered because of prejudice against the district from fear of recurrence of a nuisance, nor because a temporary nuisance has caused a diminution in present market value.[69] Where houses were damaged by roots of trees burrowing under the walls of houses and causing soil shrinkage, damages fell to be given for damage done thereby.[70]

Moveable Property

Infringement of rights of ownership—Deprivation of ownership

The first kind of damage which a wrongdoer may do to another in respect of the latter's moveable property is to act in a way which denies the latter's title of ownership or deprives him of the right, which flows from his ownership, of the use of the thing.

61 *Grosvenor Hotel Co.* v. *Hamilton* [1894] 2 Q.B. 836; *Collins* v. *Middle Level Commrs.* (1869) L.R. 4 C.P. 279; *Marquis of Granby* v. *Bakewell U.D.C.* (1923) 87 J.P. 105.
62 *Grosvenor Hotel Co.* v. *Hamilton* [1894] 2 Q.B. 836.
63 *Marquis of Granby* v. *Bakewell U.D.C.* (1923) 87 J.P. 105.
64 *Jones* v. *Gooday* (1841) 8 M. & W. 146.
65 *Harrington* v. *Derby Corpn.* [1905] 1 Ch. 205, 225–226.
66 *Workman* v. *G.N. Ry.* (1863) 32 L.J.Q.B. 279.
67 *Moore* v. *Hall* (1878) 3 Q.B.D. 178.
68 *Hole* v. *Chard Union* [1894] 1 Ch. 293.
69 *Rust* v. *Victoria Graving Dock Co.* (1887) 36 Ch.D. 113; *Granby* v. *Bakewell U.D.C.* (1923) 87 J.P. 105.
70 *Butler* v. *Standard Telephones* [1940] 1 K.B. 399.

Spuilzie

The action of spuilzie lay for taking away goods,[71] intermeddling with them,[72] or excluding the owner from possession of them.[73] A claim on such grounds is still competent; it lies for restitution of the goods taken away, failing which for damages, which should be measured by the replacement value of the thing taken away.[74] In on case [75] where the defender wrongfully retained possession of the pursuer's car damages were given in respect of loss of use based on the hire which the pursuer would have had to pay for a substitute.

In the case of corporeal moveables other than money the claim lies not only against the person who had wrongfully dispossessed the true owner, but against any third party who has come into possession of the goods, such as one who has bought [76] or hired the goods from the taker or got them on loan from him.

A *vitium reale* attaches to the goods by virtue of their wrongful acquisition and is not purged by any kind, or number, of transmissions. It is independent of knowledge or good faith, and a third, or subsequent, party, however innocent, must restore or pay damages.[77] If the true owner recovers goods or their value from a bona fide purchaser the latter may recover from an innocent intermediate seller the full sum paid him and not merely his profit on the basis of breach of the implied undertaking to give a good title.[78]

Money, banknotes or negotiable instruments, however, are not recoverable from a third party if he took them in good faith, for value, and without notice of any defect in the title of the party from whom he received the money or other negotiable things. Their negotiable quality prevents the attaching of any *vitium reale*, so that no third party can be liable, unless he had notice that the money had been dishonestly acquired by the party from whom he received it.[79] A claim, however, lies against the thief for restitution, failing which, for damages.[79] Such a claim may be brought against a third party if he did not take the goods in good faith, or for value, or had notice of defect in the title of the party from whom he received them. In brief, a resetter is not protected.

As against intermediate parties who had, but no longer have, possession of goods tainted by wrongful acquisition, the true owner's claim is only for any profit made by that intermediate party from his handling of the tainted goods and only if the goods cannot be recovered. Thus if A

71 *Baillie* v. *Young* (1835) 13 S. 472, 475.
72 Ersk. III, 7, 16.
73 Bankt. I, 10, 124; *Lisk* v. *Scott* (1682) Falconer, No. 27.
74 *Gorebridge Co-operative Socy.* v. *Turnbull*, 1952 S.L.T.(Sh.Ct.) 91; *F.C. Finance Ltd.* v. *Brown*, 1969 S.L.T.(Sh.Ct.) 41.
75 *McNair* v. *Don* (1932) 48 Sh.Ct.Rep. 99.
76 *Morrisson* v. *Robertson*, 1908 S.C. 322.
77 *Morrisson, supra.*
78 Sale of Goods Act 1893, s. 12 (1); *Mason* v. *Burningham* [1949] 2 K.B. 544; *Bunsen* v. *Silverdale* (1951) 67 Sh.Ct.Rep. 62.
79 *Gorebridge, supra.*

stole goods from X, sold them for £50 to B, who resold for £60 to C, who resold for £75 to D, and A and D and the goods cannot be found, X can sue B and C and recover £10 from B and £15 from C.[80]

Mistaken use

If one person by mistake takes and uses the goods of another in circumstances where the goods cannot be restored he is liable to compensate the true owner for the value of the goods used.[81] This would cover taking and using another's foodstuffs or fuel, or using another's raw materials in the manufacture of a new commodity.[81] If, however, the goods could be restored the taker is bound to make restitution and to compensate for wear and tear, and for any damage done while the goods were being used.[82]

Sale by mistake

If a person having possession of the moveable property of another, deliberately or by innocent mistake, sells that property to a third person the validity of the sale depends on whether he had actual or ostensible authority to sell. If he had, the sale is valid, though he may be liable to the owner if his ostensible authority exceeded his true authority; if he had not, and sells, even by innocent mistake, he is deemed to have warranted his authority to sell, and is liable in damages to the purchaser for the loss of the bargain when the true owner reclaims the goods.[83] The damages for lost bargain must be fixed by a fair estimate of what, if anything, the goods were worth more than the price paid,[84] or by the difference between the profit which would have been made on the abortive contract and the best terms which could be obtained in the market when the misrepresentation was discovered.[85] The price is, of course, repayable.[84]

Infringements of rights of possession—Failure to return borrowed goods

A borrower who does not, at the expiry of the period of loan, or after a reasonable time, or on request, return goods borrowed, or goods equivalent to those borrowed, is similarly liable to an action for restitution, failing which, for damages, unless he can account for the inability to re-deliver by proving one of the recognised excuses.[86] With failure to return

[80] Stair, I, 7, 11; Ersk. III, 1, 10; Bell, *Comm.* I, 299; *Prin.* § 527; *Scott* v. *Low* (1704) Mor. 9123; *Walker* v. *Spence & Carfrae* (1765) Mor. 12802; *Faulds* v. *Townshend* (1861) 23 D. 437; *Jarvis* v. *Manson* (1953) 69 Sh.Ct.Rep. 93; *cf. International Banking Corpn.* v. *Ferguson, Shaw & Sons*, 1910 S.C. 182, 191.

[81] *International Banking Corpn.* v. *Ferguson, Shaw & Sons*, 1910 S.C. 182. *Cf. McLaren* v. *Mann, Byars Ltd.* (1935) 51 Sh.Ct.Rep. 57.

[82] *Cf. Spence* v. *Union Marine Ins. Co.* (1868) L.R. 3 C.P. 437; *Harris* v. *Truman* (1881) 7 Q.B.D. 358.

[83] *Anderson* v. *Croall* (1903) 6 F. 153; *Salvesen* v. *Rederi A/B Nordstjernan* (1904) 7 F.(H.L.) 101.

[84] *Mackintosh* v. *Galbraith and Arthur* (1900) 3 F. 66; *Anderson, supra*, 156, 157; *MacIntyre* v. *Corson* (1906) 22 Sh.Ct.Rep. 331.

[85] *Simons* v. *Patchett* (1857) 7 E. & B. 568; *Hughes* v. *Graeme* (1864) 33 L.J.Q.B. 335; *Rederi A/B Nordstjernan* v. *Salvesen* (1903) 6 F. 64, 76.

[86] For the excuses see Bell, *Prin.*, § 197.

may be equated the return of a thing so damaged or deteriorated as not to be usable for its purpose.

The proper measure of damages is the pre-loan value of the goods not returned, or returned unusable,[87] or, if the damage is repairable, the cost of restoring them to their pre-loan condition, making allowance for any enhancement of condition effected thereby.

Failure to return hired goods

Where a person has hired goods and failed to return them by the date of expiry of the hire, or after a reasonable time, or on request, the owner may claim restitution of the goods, failing which, damages. The hirer may seek to rely on one of the recognised defences.[88] To failure to return must be equated return of the goods so damaged or depreciated as not to be fit for further use.

The damages must be measured by the pre-hire value of the goods.[89]

Failure to return goods deposited

Where a gratuitous depositary or onerous custodier is unable, at the end of the period of deposit, or after a reasonable time, or on request, and without lawful excuse or justification, to return goods deposited, he is liable to pay the fair value of the goods deposited.[90]

Hotel proprietor's liability

At common law hotel proprietors were innkeepers and accordingly subject to the strict liability attaching to such persons under the praetorian edict *nautae, caupones, stabularii*, for the loss of guests' property. Under this the innkeeper was liable without proof of fault or negligence, but might exculpate himself by proving that the loss was caused by inevitable accident, including accidental fire and theft by housebreaking.[91]

By the Hotel Proprietors Act 1956 [92] only an hotel within the meaning of the Act [93] is deemed to be an inn, and the duties, liabilities and rights which previously attached to an innkeeper [94] attach to an hotel proprietor and not to any other person,[95] and extend to damage to property as well as to loss thereof.[96] Liability exists only if at the time of the loss or damage

87 *Robertson* v. *Ogle*, June 23, 1809, F.C.; *Lockhart* v. *Cunninghame* (1870) 8 S.L.R. 151; *Seton* v. *Paterson* (1880) 8 R. 236. See also *Marquis* v. *Ritchie* (1823) 2 S. 342; *Campbell* v. *Kennedy* (1828) 6 S. 806; *Pyper* v. *Thomson* (1843) 5 D. 498; *Wilson* v. *Orr* (1879) 7 R. 266; *Bain* v. *Strang* (1888) 16 R. 186; *Sutherland* v. *Hutton* (1896) 23 R. 718.

88 Bell, *Prin.*, § 145. *Cf. Jacksons (Edinburgh) Ltd.* v. *Constructors John Brown*, 1965 S.L.T. 37.

89 *e.g. Seton* v. *Paterson* (1880) 8 R. 236; *McLean* v. *Warnock* (1883) 10 R. 1052.

90 *Forbes* v. *Aberdeen Motors*, 1965 S.L.T. 333; *Miller* v. *Howden*, 1968 S.L.T.(Sh.Ct.) 82; *Tognini Bros.* v. *Dick Bros.*, 1968 S.L.T.(Sh.Ct.) 87.

91 Bell, *Prin.*, §§ 236–242.

92 Replacing, with modifications, the Innkeepers' Liability Act 1863.

93 Statutory definition in s. 1 (3). This definition will cover premises designated "private hotels" and the like if they are open to the public for meals, but probably not cafés or public houses.

94 *i.e.* under the Edict.

95 1956 Act, s. 1 (1).

96 *Ibid.* s. 1 (2).

sleeping accommodation at the hotel had been reserved for the traveller, and the loss or damage occurred between the midnight preceding and the midnight following the period during which the traveller was a guest at the hotel and entitled to use the accommodation so engaged.[97] The proprietor is not as an innkeeper liable to make good to any guest any loss of, or damage to, any vehicle or any property left therein, or any horse or other live animal or its harness or other equipment.[98]

> Where the hotel proprietor is liable as an innkeeper to make good the loss of or damage to property brought to the hotel his liability to any one guest shall not exceed £50 in respect of any one article,[99] or £100 in the aggregate except where
>
> (*a*) the property was stolen, lost or damaged through the default, neglect or wilful act of the proprietor or some servant of his; or
>
> (*b*) the property was deposited by or on behalf of the guest expressly for safe custody with the proprietor or some servant of his authorised, or appearing to be authorised, for the purpose, and, if so required by the proprietor or that servant, in a container fastened or sealed by the depositor; or
>
> (*c*) at a time after the guest had arrived at the hotel, either the property in question was offered for deposit as aforesaid and the proprietor or his servant refused to receive it, or the guest or some other guest acting on his behalf wished so to offer the property in question but, through the default of the proprietor or a servant of his, was unable to do so:
>
> Provided that the proprietor shall not be entitled to the protection of this subsection unless, at the time when the property in question was brought to the hotel, a copy of the notice set out in the Schedule to the Act printed in plain type was conspicuously displayed in a place where it could conveniently be read by his guests at or near the reception office or desk or, where there is no reception office or desk, at or near the main entrance to the hotel.[1]

Where limitation inapplicable

No limitation of liability applies if the statutory notice is not displayed at all,[2] or is displayed in a place which is not conspicuous or where it cannot conveniently be read,[2] or displayed only in a place which is not seen until after the contract for accommodation has been made.[3]

It would appear that no limitation of liability applies where a booking is made by an agent, or by telephone, or by letter,[4] in all of which cases the

97 *Ibid.* s. 2 (1).

98 *Ibid.* s. 2 (2).

99 Is a full suitcase one article?

1 *Ibid.* s. 2 (3).

2 These are questions of fact.

3 *Cf. Olley* v. *Marlborough Court* [1949] 1 K.B. 532 (in bedroom).

4 Unless, possibly, there is at least a mention on a letter from the hotel offering accommodation, or accepting a booking requested, that the limitation is being invoked; if this is to be effective, the notice must be displayed as well. A mention in a letter confirming a booking already made is ineffective as the contract has been made.

limitation is not a term of the contract, unless possibly there have been previous dealings between the parties from which it must be inferred that the guest must have known of the limitation on liability as existing in respect of that hotel.[5]

In all these cases the hotel proprietor is liable for the fair value of all property lost or damaged without proof of fault on his part.

Garages' liability

The strict liability of the praetorian edict, *nautae*, *caupones*, *stabularii*, does not apply to motor garages, whether connected with hotels [6] or not.[7] If the vehicle is left for safe keeping the contract is one of deposit or, more probably, of *locatio custodiae*; if it is left for repair the contract for repair (*locatio operis faciendi*) includes an implied *locatio custodiae*.[8] In either case the garage owes a duty to the owner to take such care as a prudent man would take in the circumstances, and if the vehicle is lost or damaged he is prima facie liable for the value or the diminution thereof.[9] He may escape liability by proving that the cause of the loss or damage was something not inferring fault on his part,[10] such as inevitable accident, or rely on an exception clause which has validly been made a term of the contract.

Failure to return goods left for repair, etc.

Where goods of any kind are deposited with any appropriate kind of premises for repair, alteration or other kind of treatment, the contract implies an element of *locatio custodiae* [11] and the proprietor of the premises owes a duty to the owner to take such care of the goods as a prudent man would in the circumstances, and he is accordingly prima facie liable if the goods are destroyed or damaged or lost and cannot be returned.

Disposal of uncollected goods

Under the Disposal of Uncollected Goods Act 1952 where goods have been accepted for repair or other treatment, are ready for redelivery and the depositor fails both to pay or tender the charges due in relation to the goods and to take delivery of them or to give directions for their delivery, the depositary may, subject to any agreement between the parties and to the Act, sell the goods. The Act makes extensive provision (s. 1 (3)–(7)) for notice to the depositor before sale. When goods are sold [12] under the

[5] *Cf. McCutcheon* v. *Macbrayne*, 1964 S.C.(H.L.) 28.
[6] Hotel Proprietors Act 1956, s. 2 (2), altering rule applied in *Burns* v. *Royal Hotel (St. Andrews) Ltd.*, 1958 S.C. 354.
[7] *Central Motors (Glasgow) Ltd.* v. *Cessnock Garage Co.*, 1925 S.C. 796, 803; *Sinclair* v. *Juner*, 1952 S.C. 35, 39.
[8] *Sinclair*, *supra*, 43.
[9] *Sinclair*, *supra*, 44, 46.
[10] *Cf. Wilson* v. *Orr* (1880) 7 R. 266; *McLean* v. *Warnock* (1883) 10 R. 1052; *Mustard* v. *Paterson*, 1923 S.C. 142.
[11] *Sinclair* v. *Juner*, 1952 S.C. 35. It is doubtful if it implies a *locatio custodiae* in relation to articles left in the thing deposited for repair: *cf. Croall & Croall* v. *Sharp*, 1954 S.L.T.(Sh. Ct.) 35.
[12] Sale must be by public auction: s. 1 (3).

Act any excess of the sum realised over the charges is recoverable by the depositor and any deficiency is recoverable from him.[13]

Damage to moveable property

The other major kind of infringement of a person's interest in his moveable property is, intentionally or negligently, to damage it, to any extent varying from slight damage to total destruction. The basic measure of damages is the diminution of its pre-accident value caused by the damage done, of which the cost of repair is a useful indication, subject to the maximum liability being the total pre-accident value of the thing damaged or destroyed together with compensation for the inconvenience resulting from loss of use.

Damage to ships

The general principles of reparation apply equally to damage to ships arising from collision or other negligence, such as damage sustained while loading.[14] Thus, where, owing to the negligence of stevedores a ship in dock was burned out the owners recovered the whole value thereof.[15] Where a vessel was damaged in harbour the owners recovered the estimated profit on a voyage for which the vessel had been chartered and which she had lost, but not the loss on two other voyages actually made, nor interest on the damages.[16] In another case where a vessel was strained by grounding in a foul berth, the damages given amounted to the whole damage sustained in consequence as ascertained by survey.[17] In a similar case [18] the damages included the cost of salvage and repairs and demurrage for the period of repairs, that being considered in the circumstances a safer basis for assessment of damages than the estimates of loss of profits. It has been indicated [19] that river navigation trustees would be liable for damage done to a ship in consequence of negligent performance of their statutory duty to buoy the channel.

In *Henderson* v. *McAlister* [20] a yacht was handed over to builders for reconditioning. Through their negligence she was partially submerged and damaged. Damages were awarded in respect of the extra work necessitated by the negligence beyond what the reconditioning should have required.[21]

[13] s. 3 (1).
[14] *Ballantyne* v. *Paton & Hendry*, 1912 S.C. 246.
[15] *Re Polemis and Furness Withy* [1921] 3 K.B. 560; *cf. Nautilus S.S. Co.* v. *Henderson*, 1919 S.C. 605.
[16] *Parker* v. *N.B. Ry.* (1899) 7 S.L.T. 304.
[17] *Firth Shipping Co.* v. *Morton's Trs.*, 1938 S.C. 177; *cf. Thompson* v. *Greenock Harbour Trs.* (1876) 3 R. 1226; *Robertson* v. *Portpatrick and Wigtownshire Joint Committee*, 1919 S.C. 293; *S.S. Fulwood* v. *Dumfries Harbour Commrs.*, 1907 S.C. 456; *Mackenzie* v. *Stornoway Pier Commrs.*, 1907 S.C. 435; *Mair* v. *Aberdeen Harbour Commrs.*, 1909 S.C. 271; *Cormack* v. *Dundee Harbour Trs.*, 1930 S.C. 112.
[18] *Walker* v. *Buccleugh*, 1918, 1 S.L.T. 223.
[19] *Buchanan* v. *Clyde Lighthouses Trs.* (1884) 11 R. 531; *A/S D/S Forto* v. *Orkney Harbour Commrs.* 1915 S.C. 743. As to damage from floating ice see *Mair* v. *Aberdeen Harbour Commrs.*, 1909 S.C. 721.
[20] 1948 S.L.T.(Notes) 58.
[21] *Cf. The Vancouver* (1886) 11 App.Cas. 573; *The Acanthus* [1902] P. 17.

Hence, half the cost of slipping, and the whole cost of salving and of the extra work were allowed, without deduction for the enhanced value of the yacht as a result of the repairs. No allowance fell to be made for loss of use.

Maritime collision damage

Loss of or damage to property arising out of collisions at sea is a category of Admiralty cause and dealt with under that head.[22] In fact there is no difference between common law and maritime law as to what amounts to negligence which causes damage by collision,[23] nor as to the amount of damages.[24] Where one ship is damaged in collision with another the principle of compensation by which damages are assessed is *restitutio in integrum*.[25]

Damage to vehicles

Despite the frequency with which vehicles are damaged in collisions on land, there is singularly little authority on the question of damages. Recourse must be had to the analogy of maritime collision cases, which should be generally applicable.[26] As in the case of ships, a distinction must be taken between damage, constructive total loss and actual total loss.

In the case of damage the proper measure of damages is the difference between the market-value of the vehicle before and after the accident. In the ordinary case this is represented by the cost of repairs at a proper and reasonable rate.[27] Where repair is properly possible, no allowance will be made for depreciation, unless the vehicle is repaired and then sold at a loss, nor will a deduction be made if the repairs render the vehicle more valuable than before.[27] Regard must be had to the make, size, age, use and condition of the vehicle. But where complete repair is not possible so as to restore the vehicle completely or substantially to its former state, an allowance must be made for depreciation.[28] This element of claim would be clearly established if the vehicle after repair were sold for less than its pre-accident value.

22 Chap. 63, *infra*.

23 *Cayzer* v. *Carron Co.* (1884) 9 App.Cas. 783; *S.S. Bogota* v. *S.S. Alconda*, 1924 S.C.(H.L.) 66.

24 *The Argentino* (1888) 13 P.D. 191, 195, 200; *Anglo-Algerian S.S. Co.* v. *Houlder Line* [1908] 1 K.B. 659.

25 *The Clarence* (1850) 3 W.Rob. 283, 285; *The Clyde* (1866) Swab. 23; *The Bernina* (1886) 6 Asp.M.L.C. 65; *The Kate* [1899] P. 165; *H.M.S. London* [1914] P. 72; *Admiralty Commrs.* v. *S.S. Susquehanna* [1926] A.C. 655, 661; *Liesbosch* v. *Edison* [1933] A.C. 449. See also Roscoe's *Measure of Damages in Maritime Collisions* (3rd ed., 1929).

26 As to cars burned in garages, see *Taylor* v. *Logan* (1943) 60 Sh.Ct.Rep. 13; *Paterson* v. *Spiersbridge Garage Co.* (1941) 57 Sh.Ct.Rep. 126; *Antonelli* v. *Crawford* (1939) 55 Sh.Ct. Rep. 116.

27 *Cf. The Pactolus* (1856) Swab. 173; see also *Graham* v. *Perth Corpn.* (1941) 57 Sh.Ct.Rep. 166; *Brown & Lynn* v. *Western S.M.T.*, 1945 S.C. 31; *Alexander* v. *Dundee Corpn.*, 1950 S.C. 123; *Paterson*, *supra*.

28 *Galbraith's Stores* v. *Glasgow Corpn.*, 1958 S.L.T.(Sh.Ct.) 47. *Cf. The Anglican* (1873) 21 W.R. 280.

A reasonable sum is also recoverable in respect of loss of use during the period of repairs.[29] Prima facie this element will be the sum which would have been earned by the vehicle by normal usage during the period of repair,[30] or the cost of temporary replacement, as by hiring a substitute for that period.[31] To balance these items a deduction must be made for expenses saved by reason of the detention.[32] Loss of profits which would have accrued from some contract already made are recoverable,[33] but not a mere possibility of subsequent profits,[34] or an expectation of future profits.[35] Where a doctor's car was badly damaged in a collision it was held in the Sheriff Court that he was entitled to recover the cost of hiring another car during the period of repairs, and that this was the measure of damages though no car had actually been hired.[36] When one of four buses was damaged and put off the road, damages were awarded on the basis of the cost of repairs, standing charges against the vehicle in respect of the time it stood idle, and an element for inconvenience and disturbance, the further opinion being expressed that it would have been competent for the pursuers to have proved the loss on the basis of the hire of a substitute.[37]

Where new vehicle purchased

Difficulties may arise if a pursuer chooses to purchase a new vehicle in lieu of a damaged but not a destroyed one. In such a case it would appear that he is not entitled to recover the price of the new vehicle as his damages, because he has by his own actings obtained a better article than he had before the accident and allowance must be made for that.[38] Such a course may be justifiable in mitigation of damages if the pursuer can show (and the onus is on him to do so) that the cost of the new was in fact no greater than the cost of repairs to the damaged vehicle, plus hire of a temporary substitute and such other consequential items of loss as are not too remote to be admissible. Otherwise he can only recover the cost of repairs. In *Pomphrey* v. *Cuthbertson* [39] a car was seriously damaged in collision; the owner bought a replacement, taking the view that this would be cheaper than to repair and to hire a substitute pending the repairs. He claimed as damages the price of the new car, the cost of adapting it, and the cost of hiring till it was ready. He failed to aver the market value of

[29] *Paterson* v. *Spiersbridge Garage Co.* (1941) 57 Sh.Ct.Rep. 126; *Taylor* v. *Laird*, 1952 S.L.T. (Sh.Ct.) 74; *McLaughlin* v. *Malcolm*, 1965 S.L.T.(Sh.Ct.) 70; *Nelson* v. *Santangeli*, 1971 S.L.T.(Sh.Ct.) 8. As to specification required, see *Shields* v. *Tawse* (1933) 49 Sh.Ct.Rep. 235.

[30] *e.g.* loss of profits while a taxi is off the road; *cf. Re Trent* (1868) 4 Ch.App. 112, 117.

[31] *Cf. The Mediana* [1900] A.C. 113; *The Greta Holme* [1897] A.C. 596, 603; *Taylor* v. *Ingram*, 1947 S.L.T.(Sh.Ct.) 2.

[32] *Cf. The Gazelle*, 2 W.Rob. 279; *Davies* v. *Oswald*, 7 C. & P. 804.

[33] *Taylor* v. *Laird*, 1952 S.L.T.(Sh.Ct.) 74. *Cf. The Argentino* (1889) 14 App.Cas. 519. As to claims made by the owners of goods on the lorry when it was damaged, see *Alexander* v. *Perth County Council* (1940) 56 Sh.Ct.Rep. 20.

[34] *Cf. The Bodlewell* [1907] P. 286.

[35] *Cf. The Anselma de Larinaga* (1913) 29 T.L.R. 587.

[36] *Gibb* v. *New Arrol-Johnson Motor Co.* (1911) 27 Sh.Ct.Rep. 235.

[37] *Cunningham* v. *Glasgow Corpn.* (1942) 58 Sh.Ct.Rep. 44.

[38] *Cf. British Westinghouse* v. *Underground Ry.* [1912] A.C. 673.

[39] 1951 S.C. 147.

the old car at the date of the collision and it was held that, in the absence of this, the claim was irrelevant.

The pre-accident market value is in cases of actual or constructive total loss the basis of calculation of damages. Though it is quite possible that in a particular case damages could be minimised in one way or another they can generally only be estimated by regard to that basic measure of loss.

Constructive total loss

If the vehicle is so badly damaged as to be a constructive total loss, *i.e.*, if the cost of repair would exceed the value when repaired, a prudent owner is entitled to treat the vehicle as an actual total loss and claim damages accordingly. The proper measure of damages is then the market value of the car at the date of collision, less its scrap value, plus the cost of hiring a substitute until a replacement could be procured and adapted for use.[40] In such a case the market value of a second hand car is its value as between a willing buyer and seller, not in a forced sale.[41]

Actual total loss

If there has been an actual total loss or complete destruction of the vehicle, the proper measure of damages is the market value of the vehicle as it was before the accident, under deduction of the value of any salvage.[40] On the analogy of maritime cases it seems probable that the profit lost under a contract current at the time of the loss, less the expenses necessarily to be incurred in earning it, is also recoverable.[42] The full market value may have to be reduced if the pursuer had only a limited interest in it.[43] In assessing the value V.A.T. must be included.[44]

Personal belongings

Claims for loss of personal belongings and effects are frequently made ancillary to claims for personal injury, as, for example, in respect of clothing lost or damaged in a vehicle accident, or baggage lost in a ship collision.[45] In such cases the pre-loss value of the lost or damaged items is recoverable and not the value when new.[46] Even when certain items of claim are not lost but only damaged, damages on the basis of cost of repair may be inequitable as repair of such things as clothing is only practicable for very minor damages and equally its market value is unduly low.[46] The sum at stake is, however, seldom sufficiently large to cause serious dispute and such questions are little mentioned in reported cases.

40 *Pomphrey* v. *Cuthbertson*, 1951 S.C. 147; *cf. Dallas* v. *Ayr C.C.* (1949) 65 Sh.Ct.Rep. 122.
41 *Macmillan* v. *Calder* (1927) 43 Sh.Ct.Rep. 337.
42 *The Racine* [1906] P. 273.
43 *Brierly* v. *Kendall* (1851) 17 Q.B. 937.
44 *Martin* v. *L.C.C.* [1947] K.B. 628.
45 *e.g. Reavis* v. *Clan Line Steamers*, 1925 S.C. 725, 726, 738. As to proof of value, see *Lewis* v. *Laird Line*, 1925 S.L.T. 316, 320.
46 *Lewis, supra.*

In *Lewis* [46] Lord Constable applied the test of prime cost less an allowance for depreciation to part-worn clothing, and this is probably the fairest basis.

Questions of remoteness may, however, prove troublesome as where property is stolen from an injured person [47] or from the scene of an accident. Such losses are probably too remote, a fresh cause having intervened, or as being other than a natural consequence. So too where a pursuer who managed an orchestra had lost in the sinking after collision of a steamship on which she was travelling certain music and manuscript orchestral settings, it was held irrelevant to aver that she might have obtained profits from the publishing and performance of the music which she had the sole right to do: the damages must be limited to the cost of replacement measured by ordinary market price or, failing that, the amount of payment to composers of that class of music.[48] There were no averments that the pursuer carried on a business of publishing or dealing in music, and such a case might raise different issues. As she had never been in use to make profits from royalties, publication or sale of music, or from the performing rights, her averments of loss of purely contingent profits were irrelevant and the proper measure of damages was what she would have to pay to replace as nearly as may be what has been lost.[49]

Loss of profits of personal property

A person who has in consequence of negligence lost personal property may sometimes competently recover the natural fruits and profits of the things or the industrial fruits and profits which the owner might have had.[50] Such loss of profits is relevant and admissible as a head of damages if such as the owner used to make, but not if merely speculative or contingent profits which the owner might in some circumstances have made. Thus loss of profit which it was alleged might have been made from publication and sale and grants of performing rights of lost musical manuscripts was irrelevant.[51] But where a mill was damaged, not only was the cost of reconstruction given but also the loss of profits necessarily incurred while the mill was standing idle during the period of repair,[52] though it has been indicated [53] that a possible loss of profit, if the miller had had an exclusive kind of machinery and could have made a profit if he had chosen to market it, would have been too remote.

Loss of profits of business may similarly be recoverable. "If A's property is injured by B's negligence, and as a direct result of that injury A loses profit in connection with his business, I do not doubt that that loss of profit may form a legitimate claim against him by B." [54]

[47] *Cf. Cobb* v. *G.W. Ry.* [1894] A.C. 419.
[48] *Reavis* v. *Clan Line Steamers*, 1926 S.C. 215.
[49] *Reavis, supra*, at p. 225.
[50] Stair, I, 9, 2.
[51] *Reavis* v. *Clan Line Steamers*, 1926 S.C. 215, 224.
[52] *Kerr* v. *Earl of Orkney* (1857) 20 D. 298.
[53] *Reavis, supra*, at p. 225.
[54] *Reavis* v. *Clan Line Steamers*, 1926 S.C. 215, 226.

Other goods and moveables

The majority of cases of damage to goods fall under the heads of carriage by land, sea or air discussed earlier, or are governed by principles similar to those applicable in the case of damage to heritable property by fire and water. The possible ways in which such damage may be caused are infinite. So in *Weston* v. *Tailors of Potterow*[55] books in a bookshop were damaged by the overflow of water from the house above, and in *McIntyre* v. *Gallacher*[56] stock in a shop was similarly damaged. The measure of damages in such a case is properly the value of the goods lost or destroyed or the diminution in value of goods damaged and not the cost of effecting repairs or replacement which may well be much greater. In *Cleghorn* v. *Taylor*[57] china and glassware in a shop was damaged, and the owner was given as damages the price and value of the goods destroyed, with an additional sum for sets rendered incomplete; it was treated as settled[58] that where one of a set is destroyed, the claimant is entitled to the value of the whole set.

Cargo lost in collision at sea

The owners of cargo lost in consequence of collision at sea may sue the owners of the vessel for breach of contract, always subject to the terms of the contract of carriage, and recover damages if the carrying vessel is found to have been in fault. They have also a right to sue the owners of the other vessel to the collision and recover damages from them.[59] If the vessels are each partly in fault the cargo-owners can presumably recover from each other *pro rata*.[60] The measure of damages is the market value of the goods, if there is a market at the time and place of delivery, in the state in which they should have been delivered. Failing a market, value must be calculated by regard to cost price, cost of transit and importer's profits.[61] Loss of market due to late delivery is recoverable where the market fluctuations and date of delivery are calculable with reasonable certainty.[62] It has been held an increased value which would have arisen if the cargo had been delivered was recoverable,[63] but claims for advance freight thrown away in consequence of cargo being rendered useless and for freight paid on a substitute cargo have been refused as too remote.[64]

Animals

Damage caused by injury to or death or loss of animals arises princip-

55 (1839) 1 D. 1218: absolvitor on question of landlord's liability.
56 (1883) 11 R. 64; *cf. Cleghorn* v. *Taylor* (1856) 18 D. 664; *Campbell* v. *Kennedy* (1864) 3 M. 121; *Reid* v. *Baird* (1876) 4 R. 234; *Moffat* v. *Park* (1877) 5 R. 13.
57 (1856) 18 D. 664.
58 *Ibid.* 672.
59 *The Milan* (1861) Lush. 388; *The Umona* [1914] P. 141.
60 Maritime Conventions Act 1911, s. 1.
61 *The Notting Hill* (1884) 9 P.D. 105; see also *Rodocanachi* v. *Milburn* (1886) 18 Q.B.D. 67; *The Activ* (1901) 17 T.L.R. 351.
62 *The Parana* (1877) 2 P.D. 118; *Dunn* v. *Bucknall Bros.* [1902] 2 K.B. 614.
63 *The Thyatira* (1838) 8 P.D. 155.
64 *The Canadian Transport* (1932) 43 Ll.L.R. 409.

ally from the animals being run down by vehicles [65] or being injured by other animals. The Dogs Act 1906 makes the owner of a dog liable in damages for injury done by that dog to any cattle (defined as including horses, mules, asses, sheep, goats and swine) without proof of previous mischievous propensity in the dog, or knowledge thereof, or proof that the injury was attributable to neglect on the owner's part.

Sheepworrying by dogs

The appropriate measure of damages is the fair value of any sheep killed or which have to be destroyed.[66] Distinction must be made between the values of various kinds of sheep involved [67] and an allowance may be made for the temporary depreciation of other animals due to fright and disturbance [68] and for such additional damage as lambs born dead.[69] To aid the assessment of damages it is desirable that the defender should have an opportunity of inspecting the flock and the damage as soon as possible.[70]

Apportionment of damages

Where damage is committed at one or various times by animals acting in concert belonging to different owners the modern rule is that both or all the owners are liable jointly and severally for the whole damage.[71] Where only one of the dogs is identified his owner is thus liable for the whole damage.[72] In *McIntyre* v. *Carmichael* [73] the owners of two dogs which had together worried sheep were held liable for damage to the extent of half each, but this principle would now only apply where the dogs make entirely separate raids but such that the actual damage done by each cannot be assessed. If it be shown or indeed appear probable that the damage was due to such separate incidents and more to one than the other, liability may presumably be divided unequally.

Animals killing poultry

Measure of damages has not been discussed in the cases on this point [74] but there seems no doubt that the measure of damages is the fair value of the poultry destroyed. In an English case [75] it was held that the plaintiff had acted reasonably in mitigation of damages in retaining the birds which

[65] *Wilson* v. *Wood* (1908) 24 Sh.Ct.Rep. 225 (road); *Maxwell* v. *N.B. Ry.* (1921) 37 Sh.Ct.Rep. 280 (rail); *Barclay* v. *G.N.S. Ry.* (1882) 10 R. 144 (rail).

[66] *Smith* v. *Hurll* (1885) 1 Sh.Ct.Rep. 246.

[67] *A B* v. *C D* (1911) 27 Sh.Ct.Rep. 212; *Riach* v. *Neish* (1950) 66 Sh.Ct.Rep. 286.

[68] *A B* v. *C D, supra*; *Balfour, infra.*

[69] *Riach, supra.*

[70] *Balfour* v. *Duncan* (1950) 66 Sh.Ct.Rep. 40.

[71] *Arneil* v. *Paterson,* 1931 S.C.(H.L.) 117: so too *Smith* v. *Hurll* (1885) 1 Sh.Ct.Rep. 246; *Harrison* v. *White* (1892) 8 Sh.Ct.Rep. 318; *Murray* v. *Brown* (1881) 19 S.L.R. 253.

[72] *A B* v. *C D* (1911) 27 Sh.Ct.Rep. 212.

[73] (1870) 8 M. 570.

[74] See *Allan* v. *Reekie* (1906) 22 Sh.Ct.Rep. 57; *Peden* v. *Charleton* (1906) *ibid.* 91; *Turner* v. *Simpson* (1912) 29 Sh.Ct.Rep. 81; *Paterson* v. *Howith* (1913) 29 Sh.Ct.Rep. 216.

[75] *Ives* v. *Brewer* (1951) 95 S.J. 286.

survived the attacks and nursing them back into a condition in which they began laying again, instead of selling them at once.

Person killing animal

Again the reasonable value of the animal killed [76] is the proper measure of damages: allowance may properly be made if the animal in question is a champion, pedigreed,[77] or otherwise of high market value,[78] and consideration can possibly be given to the value a pet may have for its owner by reason of affection.[79] Value may be appreciated by particular value for breeding purposes or diminished by bad character or habits.[77] In the case of dogs killing sheep it may be justifiable to shoot the dog, in which case there is no liability to its owner,[80] but not if it is merely a nuisance.[81] The shooting must be the only way of avoiding damage in case of actual attack or there must be reason to apprehend a renewal of the attack.[82]

Other damage to animals

Damages have been recoverable in some other circumstances, as where a bull trespassed and served cows which dropped cross-bred calves in consequence: damages were claimed for loss of milk supply and for feeding the calves.[83] In this case a remit was made on the question of damages.

Where cattle strayed onto a railway line and were killed by a train, the claim made (unsuccessfully) was for their value [84]; and similarly where a horse was killed by falling into a hole in a field,[85] or where cattle died from eating yew cuttings,[86] or a homing pigeon [87] or a dog [88] was lost in transit, or a pigeon was shot [89] or vixens aborted and destroyed their cubs in consequence of blasting.[90] Stablers have been held liable for the value of horses which died while in their care [91] and a hirer for the value of a horse which died in consequence of his misconduct while he had it out.[92] Where a horse was deteriorated in value by overworking, damages were assessed

76 *Blackie* v. *Stewart* (1920) 37 Sh.Ct.Rep. 60; *Mitchell* v. *Duncan* (1953) 69 Sh.Ct.Rep. 182.

77 *Watt* v. *Logan* (1945) 61 Sh.Ct.Rep. 155.

78 *Cf. Wilson* v. *Buchanan* (1943) 59 Sh.Ct.Rep. 54; *Leven* v. *Mitchell* (1949) 65 Sh.Ct.Rep. 225.

79 *Watt* v. *Logan* (1945) 61 Sh.Ct.Rep. 155, 158; *sed secus Ross* v. *Cunningham* (1927) 43 Sh.Ct.Rep. 243 (cat).

80 *Leven* v. *Mitchell* (1949) 65 Sh.Ct.Rep. 225; *Wilson, supra*; *Farrell* v. *Marshall*, 1962 S.L.T. (Sh.Ct.) 65.

81 *Watt, supra* (£5 given).

82 *Gott* v. *Measures* [1947] 2 All E.R. 609; *Cresswell* v. *Sirl* [1947] 2 All E.R. 730; *Blackie, supra*; *Duncan* v. *Rodger* (1891) 7 Sh.Ct.Rep. 313; *Wilson, supra*; *Mitchell, supra.*

83 *Harvie* v. *Turner* (1916) 32 Sh.Ct.Rep. 267; *cf. Logan* v. *Rodger*, 1952 S.L.T.(Sh.Ct.) 99.

84 *Barclay* v. *G.N.S. Ry.* (1882) 10 R. 144; *cf. Maxwell* v. *N.B. Ry.* (1920) 37 Sh.Ct.Rep. 280.

85 *McLean* v. *Warnock* (1883) 10 R. 1052. *Cf. Logan* v. *Rodger*, 1952 S.L.T.(Sh.Ct.) 99.

86 *Sloan* v. *Thomson* (1890) 7 Sh.Ct.Rep. 60; *cf. Millar* v. *Bonar* (1921) 38 Sh.Ct.Rep. 8; and *Young* v. *Houston* (1924) 40 Sh.Ct.Rep. 118; contrast *King* v. *Lyon* (1910) 26 Sh.Ct.Rep. 75.

87 *McCrorie* v. *G.S.W. Ry.* (1890) 7 Sh.Ct.Rep. 65.

88 *Wales* v. *G.S.W. Ry.* (1890) 7 Sh.Ct.Rep. 144.

89 *Muirhead* v. *Waugh* (1912) 28 Sh.Ct.Rep. 143.

90 *Western Silver Fox Ranch* v. *Ross and Cromarty C.C.*, 1940 S.C. 601.

91 *Hay* v. *Wordsworth*, Feb. 13, 1801, F.C.; *Hagart* v. *Inglis* (1832) 10 S. 506.

92 *Seton* v. *Paterson* (1880) 8 R. 236, a decision questionable as to liability.

by the fall in the horse's value,[93] and so too with sheep deteriorated while being wintered.[94]

Incorporeal Property

Patents

Claims of damages may arise in various forms out of infringements of the rights conferred by letters patent. The first form is by slander of title.[95] In the converse case, where a patentee maliciously causes special damage [96] to another person by taking proceedings or threatening action based on an invalid patent,[97] the other person has a common law right to recover damages.[98] In the case of threats, malice need not be proved if the proceedings are by means of an action for threats.[1]

Action to restrain threats

The Patents Act 1949 makes provision for an action and for the recovery of any damage occasioned by the issue by another party of threats of proceedings for infringement of patent rights. This does not affect any right of action which the person damaged by any such threats would have had at common law. Such a common law action would be of the nature of an action of slander of title, or for malicious threats and it would be necessary to prove malice in asserting a claim of right known to be without foundation [2]; and also actual damage sustained as a result of the threats.[3] Proceedings for interdict would also be competent, but would require proof of the falsity of the allegations and the danger of repetition. Section 65 of the Patents Act [4] gives a statutory right of action, for, *inter alia*, such damages as have been sustained.

Damages

The measure of damages follows the rules ordinarily applicable in cases of delict; the damages must be due to the threats alone and are only recoverable if they are the natural and reasonable consequences of the threats.[5] There is no liability for damage caused by threats not authorised by the defenders to be made.[6] It has been held that damages suffered by

[93] *Dewar* v. *Greenock Aerated Water Co.* (1890) 7 Sh.Ct.Rep. 114.
[94] *Macfarlane* v. *Macdougall* (1931) 47 Sh.Ct.Rep. 325.
[95] *Montgomerie* v. *Paterson* (1894) 1 S.L.T. 530 (O.H.); 11 R.P.C. 221.
[96] *Farr* v. *Weatherhead and Harding* (1932) 49 R.P.C. 262.
[97] *Wren* v. *Weild* (1869) L.R. 4 Q.B. 730, 737; *cf. Halsey* v. *Brotherhood* (1881) 19 Ch.D. 386.
[98] *Harpers Ltd.* v. *Greenwood & Batley* (1896) 4 S.L.T. 116.
[1] Patents Act 1949, s. 65.
[2] *Wren* v. *Weild* (1869) L.R. 4 Q.B.D. 730.
[3] *Farr* v. *Weatherhead and Harding* (1932) 49 R.P.C. 262. See also *Speed Cranes Ltd.* v. *Thomson*, 1972 S.L.T. 226.
[4] s. 65 as applied to Scotland by s. 103; replacing s. 36 of the 1907–1928 Acts and s. 36 (1) of the 1932 Act.
[5] *Ungar* v. *Sugg* (1892) 9 R.P.C. 113, 118 (C.A.); *Horne* v. *Johnston Bros.* (1921) 38 R.P.C. 366, 372.
[6] *Ungar* v. *Sugg*, *supra*.

the loss of a contract,[7] or by the breaking off of negotiations for a contract,[8] are recoverable as reasonable and not too remote consequences. If one threat is proved the pursuer is entitled to have a proof as to the damage caused by all threats.[9]

Action for infringement

Infringement of a patent consists in doing what the patent prohibits being done,[10] and the action for infringement is the method by which the patentee can ultimately enforce his privileges. Threatened infringement as well as actual infringement will be a sufficient ground of action,[11] the proceedings in the former case being for suspension and interdict against the respondents making, using, exercising or vending the invention within the United Kingdom without leave of the complaining petitioners during the continuance of the patent.[12] Where damages are being claimed, proceedings are by an action of interdict and for damages.

Remedies

The patentee whose rights have been infringed may claim interdict and also either damages or an account of profits (but not both),[13] or one or other of damages or an account of profits alternatively. It is usually better to elect to take damages as an account of profits is difficult to make and check and the amount may, in any event, be small. If recovery of profits is sought it is on the basis that the infringer holds those profits as trustee for the patentee, and in the computation it is material to ascertain how much of the invention was appropriated so as to determine what proportion of the net profits realised by the infringer was attributable to its use.[14]

Principle of damages

The principle to be sought in awarding damages is the restoration of the pursuer by means of pecuniary compensation to the position he would have been in but for the defender's wrongful acts. The infringer's profit is of no consequence: however large his gains he is liable only for nominal damages if his illegal sales do not injure the patentee's trade; and however great his loss he cannot escape from liability to make full compensation for injury which his competition may have occasioned.[14]

Measure of damages

The measure of damages in such a case will be the loss the pursuer has

[7] *Skinner* v. *Perry* (1892) 10 R.P.C. 5; *Hoffnung* v. *Salsbury* (1898) 16 R.P.C. 375.
[8] *Solanite Signs Ltd.* v. *Wood* (1933) 50 R.P.C. 315.
[9] *Stillitz* v. *Taylor* (1941) 58 R.P.C. 136.
[10] *Walton* v. *Bateman* (1842) 1 W.P.C. 615; *Sykes* v. *Howarth* (1879) 12 Ch.D. 826.
[11] *Dowling* v. *Billington* (1890) 7 R.P.C. 201; *Frearson* v. *Loe* (1878) 9 Ch.D. 65. *Cf. Weir* v. *Glenny* (1834) 7 W. & Sh. 244.
[12] As to interdict, see *Harvie* v. *Ross* (1886) 14 R. 71.
[13] Patents Act 1949, s. 60. *Cf. Neilson* v. *Betts* (1870) L.R. 5 H.L. 1.
[14] *United Horse Shoe & Nail Co.* v. *Stewart* (1886) 15 R.(H.L.) 45, 48. As to the principles of taking an account of profits, see *Neilson* v. *Baird* (1843) 6 D. 51, 60.

sustained as the natural and direct consequence of the defender's actings in contravention of his right of monopoly. In the leading case of *United Horse Shoe and Nail Co.* v. *Stewart & Co.*[15] Lord Macnaghten laid this down and went on to reject a claim for damages for loss of profits caused by a reduction in the price of the patented goods made by the patentee consequent on the competition of the infringing goods on the market. This he did not hold to be the natural and direct result of the defender's acts as the pursuers must have been taken to have had faith in their own case, as well as to have known the identity of the infringing competitors and that on establishing their rights they would be entitled to recover their proved damages or the defender's profits. Consequently, the reduction in price and the loss of trade caused thereby were not a reasonable course to take. Loss of sales by virtue of the infringing competition was, however, a valid head of damage and it was not limited to the period during which the pursuers had a title to the patent from their predecessors in title.

It was also not to be assumed that the absence of competition would have permitted the pursuers to sell the aggregate amount of fact sold by them and their competitors. A moderate percentage to represent the increased sales due to increased activity of competition must be deducted. Lord Watson was of opinion on the facts that the pursuer's sales could not have been maintained without a reduction in price, and that consequently any loss on that head was not attributable to the infringement of the patent but to the ordinary course of trade.[16]

General considerations affecting measure of damages

As is usual in such cases the true measure of damages can only be generally indicated as representing compensation for the loss the pursuer has actually sustained as the natural and direct consequence of the defender's acts.[16] It is a jury question.[17] The pursuer is entitled to recover what he has lost by orders for the patented article going elsewhere.[18] The pursuer is further entitled to recover the profits on the whole machine though only part of it was an infringement of the patent.[19] He will not in the ordinary case be limited to what sum he would have been willing to accept as a royalty,[20] but where he has actually let out the patented articles at a royalty, the natural measure of damages will be the amount of royalty applicable to the period during which the infringer has been in possession of the offending article, whether or not he has in fact been making use of it.[21] Damages may also be recovered from purchasers in respect of their

[15] (1886) 15 R.(H.L.) 45; 5 R.P.C. 260.

[16] *United Horse Shoe & Nail Co.* v. *Stewart*, *supra*, 48–49.

[17] *Brown* v. *Hastie* (1904) 7 F. 97.

[18] *Boyd* v. *Tootal Broadhurst Lee Co.* (1894) 11 R.P.C. 181; *Brown* v. *Hastie* (1904) 7 F. 97.

[19] *United Horse Shoe & Nail Co.* v. *Stewart*, *supra*.

[20] *Neilson* v. *Baird* (1843) 6 D. 60.

[21] *Penn* v. *Jack* (1867) L.R. 5 Eq. 84; *United Telephone Co.* v. *Walker* (1887) 4 R.P.C. 63; *English & American Machinery Co.* v. *Union Boot & Shoe Machine Co.* (1896) 13 R.P.C. 64; *Pneumatic Tyre Co.* v. *Puncture Proof Pneumatic Tyre Co. Ltd.* (1899) 16 R.P.C. 209 (C.A.); *British Motor Syndicate* v. *John Taylor & Sons Ltd.* (1900) 17 R.P.C. 723 (C.A.); *B.T.H.* v. *Charlesworth Peebles & Co.*, 1923 S.C. 599; 40 R.P.C. 119, 127.

use of the infringing articles, although the pursuer has already previously recovered damages from the manufacturer, who sold the articles to them.[22] If the patent is indorsed " licences of right " and the defender gives an undertaking to obtain a licence, the damages cannot exceed double the amount the pursuer would have charged for a licence to do what the defender has done.[23]

More difficult questions of computation of damages arise where the patentee profits from his monopoly by manufacture on his own account, with or without granting licences as well, but difficulty or impossibility of assessing or stating the precise ground for awarding damages is not a sufficient reason for giving only a nominal sum.[24] The court will readily infer that the wrongful invasion of a right of monopoly causes the grantee of the patent damage but it remains for him to prove his loss. It may be necessary to take into account loss of goodwill and business connection. If the patentee is a manufacturer and does not himself grant licences difficulty may be occasioned by infringements which do not directly compete with the goods manufactured by him, as where they are of entirely different quality or price, or where it is established that in any event the order would not have been given to him. In such a case the defender is still liable to pay substantial damages on the basis of what would, at a reasonable estimate, be the royalty which the patentee could fairly have obtained under the circumstances.[25]

If damages are to be sought in respect of reduction of prices of the pursuers' goods it must be established that such a reduction was necessitated by the defender's wrongful competition and was not voluntary or resulting from the ordinary course of trade.[26] Thus where it was shown that the only reduction was compelled by the defendants and to the level of their price and the plaintiffs would have sold all they did and also all the defendants did at their own original price, damages were given for loss by reduction of price.[27] If reduction in price has taken place, regard may have to be had to any effect it has had in stimulating demand for the product.[28]

Again regard should be given to the fact that if the pursuers had obtained the business which was in fact captured by the defenders, they would have been enabled to make a larger profit than they actually did make on such articles, or than the defenders did make on the infringing articles, because of the lower overhead charges per article and other advantages and economies of large-scale production.[29]

[22] *United Telephone Co.* v. *Walker, supra.*
[23] Patents Act 1949, s. 35 (2) (*c*).
[24] *Ungar* v. *Sugg* (1891) 8 R.P.C. 385, 388; 9 R.P.C. 113, 117.
[25] *Watson, Laidlaw & Co.* v. *Pott, Cassels and Williamson*, 1914 S.C.(H.L.) 18; 31 R.P.C. 104; *British United Shoe Machinery Co.* v. *Fussell* (1910) 27 R.P.C. 205; *British Thomson-Houston Co.* v. *Charlesworth Peebles*, 1923 S.C. 599.
[26] *United Horse Shoe & Nail Co.* v. *Stewart* (1886) 15 R.(H.L.) 45; 5 R.P.C. 260; *Alexander & Co.* v. *Henry & Co.* (1893) 12 R.P.C. 360, 367.
[27] *American Braided Wire Co.* v. *Thomson* (1888) 7 R.P.C. 152; *cf. Wellman* v. *Burstinghaus* (1911) 28 R.P.C. 326.
[28] *American Braided Wire Co., supra.*
[29] *Leeds Forge Co.* v. *Deighton's Patent Flue Co.* (1918) 25 R.P.C. 209.

If the infringement is in some integral part of the whole machine, damages may be based on the lost orders for and lost profits of the whole machine [30] but conversely if the infringement is merely in respect of something accessory to the defender's article of manufacture, then damages may be recovered only in respect of that accessory.[31]

If it is an exclusive licensee who sues for damages, the damages must be such as he alone has suffered or is likely to suffer so far as his exclusive licence has been infringed since the date it was granted.[32]

Among considerations irrelevant to the measure of damages are the importance of the invention patented and infringed, the ease with which manufacture could have been effected without infringement, or the degree of wrong involved in the defender's actings.[33]

Damages are recoverable in the ordinary course from the date of publication of the complete specification.[34] If there has been infringement both before and after amendment of the patents separate sums must be distinguished in the conclusions for damages.[35]

Section 59 of the Patents Act 1949 imposes restrictions on the recovery of damages for infringement, and section 62 makes provision for relief for the infringement of a partially valid specification.

Trade marks

There are two main forms of action in which questions of damages may arise with relation to trade marks. There is the action to prevent or recover damages for the infringement of a trade mark, and the other is the complaint that the defender is using means which are calculated to pass off, or to cause to be passed off, the goods of the defender as and for those of the pursuer, and the means may or may not comprise or consist of an infringement of a trade mark to which the pursuer has a title.[36] While the two kinds of claims are frequently combined, registration of the trade mark is generally a condition precedent to actions of infringement.

Actions for infringement

Infringement is the use by the defender, for purposes of trade,[37] upon or in connection with goods of the kind for which the pursuer's right to exclusive use exists by virtue of the registration of a mark in respect thereof,[38] which are not the pursuer's goods,[39] of a mark identical with [40]

30 *Meters Ltd.* v. *Metropolitan Gas Meters Ltd.* (1910) 27 R.P.C. 721.
31 *Clement Talbot Ltd.* v. *Wilson* (1909) 26 R.P.C. 467; *cf. United Telephone Co.* v. *Walker* (1885) 4 R.P.C. 63.
32 Patents Act 1949, s. 63.
33 *United Horse Shoe & Nail Co.* v. *Stewart* (1886) 15 R.(H.L.) 45; 5 R.P.C. 260.
34 Patents Act 1949, s. 13 (4).
35 *Mica Insulator Co.* v. *Bruce Peebles & Co.* (1905) 7 F. 944.
36 *Kerly on Trade Marks*, 8th ed., 332.
37 *Levy* v. *Walker* (1879) 10 Ch.D. 436 (C.A.); *Richards* v. *Butcher* (1890) 7 R.P.C. 288. See too *Upmann* v. *Forester* (1883) 24 Ch.D. 231.
38 Trade Marks Act 1938, ss. 4–5. See also *Coca-cola Co.* v. *Struthers*, 1968 S.L.T. 353.
39 *Siegert* v. *Findlater* (1878) 7 Ch.D. 801.
40 *Welch* v. *Knott* (1857) 4 K. & J. 747.

the pursuer's mark, or comprising certain essential features of it, or colourably resembling it,[41] so as to be calculated to cause the goods in question to be accepted by ordinary purchasers [42] for the pursuer's goods.[43] The relative quality of the pursuer's goods and those of the defender may affect the amount of damages recoverable by a successful pursuer, as damages are sometimes allowed in respect of injury occasioned to the pursuer's trade reputation by the defender's infringement or fraud,[44] and if the infringing goods are of as good quality as the genuine ones of the pursuer, no damage can have been sustained on that ground.

Apart from damages the pursuer may in appropriate cases conclude for declarator, interdict,[45] or delivery of the offending goods. Damages or an account of profits may be concluded for alternatively but it is only competent to award one or other and to justify this conclusion there must be proof of deception. Because the pursuer's sales of his goods have decreased it does not follow that this is the result of the defender's actings. Actual loss must be shown to be due to the deception complained of.[46] On the other hand if deception is proved and particularly if there is an element of fraud present tending to injure the pursuer's trade substantially, substantial damages will be awarded, though it may not be possible to prove the exact figure of damage sustained,[47] but the inference is that substantial and not merely nominal damage has been sustained. Lord Trayner [48] spoke of this case as one for exemplary though not vindictive damages. In that case the contention was that the award of damages should include the expenses incurred in establishing the pursuer's case and detecting the defender's fraud. The point was not decided but the Lord Justice-Clerk's opinion was unfavourable.

It is probably unnecessary to aver any damages suffered to justify an award of nominal damages,[49] but in the usual case it is necessary to aver and prove damage suffered if a substantial sum of damages is claimed, and the onus lies on the pursuer to prove this.

It will not be presumed but must be proved that the quantities of goods sold under the infringing trade mark by the defender would in the absence of his deception have been sold by the pursuer under his own trade mark.[50] Apart from proved diminution of sales attributable to the infringement, further damage which may be done, compensation for which may be

41 *Upper Assam Tea Co.* v. *Herbert* (1889) 7 R.P.C. 186; *Singer Mfg. Co.* v. *Loog* (1882) 8 App.Cas. 18; *Cope* v. *Evans* (1874) L.R. 18 Eq. 138; *Beddow* v. *Boyd* (1887) 4 R.P.C. 310.

42 Kerly, 402.

43 Kerly, 251.

44 *Alexander* v. *Henry* (1895) 12 R.P.C. 360.

45 *Kinnell* v. *Ballantine*, 1910 S.C. 246. See also *Montgomerie* v. *Young Bros.* (1904) 11 S.L.T. 298, 600; *Bass, Ratcliffe & Gretton* v. *Laidlaw* (1908) 16 S.L.T. 660.

46 *Kinnell* v. *Ballantine, supra.*

47 *Thomson* v. *Dailly* (1897) 24 R. 1173 (£100).

48 p. 1184.

49 *Blofeld* v. *Payne* (1833) 4 B. & Ad. 410; *Daniel* v. *Whitehouse* (1898) 15 R.P.C. 134; *Rodgers* v. *Nowill* (1847) 5 C.B. 109.

50 *Leather Cloth Co.* v. *Hirschfeld* (1865) L.R. 1 Eq. 299; *Magnolia Metal Co.* v. *Atlas Metal Co.* (1896) 14 R.P.C. 389 (passing-off). *Cf. United Horse Shoe Co.* v. *Stewart* (1886) 15 R.(H.L.) 45 (patent case) and *Kinnell* v. *Ballantine*, 1910 S.C. 246.

recovered includes the case where the infringing goods are so much inferior to the genuine in quality as to injure the pursuer's trade reputation.[51] The question may be difficult where stress of competition forces the pursuer to reduce his prices to enable him to stay in the market at all but does not give him an increase of business sufficient to make up for the profit lost on each article sold. In *American Braided Wire Co.* v. *Thomson*,[52] a patent case, it was held that where the plaintiffs claimed damages in respect of reductions of price, the damages were occasioned by the wrongful acts of the defendants and the plaintiffs were consequently entitled to damages in respect of the loss of profits sustained consequent on the reduction of prices. The rule of damages was accepted as being for loss which was the " natural and direct consequence " of the infringement. This case was distinguished from the *United Horse Shoe Co.'s* case [53] on the ground that the latter was one where " the defendants were manufacturing a thing which the plaintiffs had particular machinery for making and there was the competition in the market of very similar nails to those which the plaintiffs made more cheaply by their machinery, and the defendants had been making a good many of these nails and selling them, using the machinery for which the plaintiffs had a patent. But the plaintiffs had done this: they had not merely followed the lead of the defendants in reducing their prices, but they had always gone a little before the defendants in reducing their prices and had reduced their prices below those at which the defendants were selling," [54] whereas in the present case the plaintiffs had never reduced their prices below those quoted by the defendants but had only followed their reductions and only to the same levels.

Both these cases were discussed in *Alexander* v. *Henry* [55] which unlike them was a trade mark case. The plaintiffs in that case had had a complete monopoly of the market in Mexico for thread manufactured by them down to the time when they lost it by reason of fraudulent imitations of their trade marks. These imitations resulted in the defendants being able to make sales which would otherwise have been made by the plaintiffs, in the plaintiffs being compelled to reduce their prices and in the ruin of the plaintiffs' trade to such an extent that the defendants were able to sell goods openly in competition with them. Substantial damages were awarded under each of these heads. Kekewich J. distinguished the *United Horse Shoe Co.* case as being one where the manufacturer thought fit to reduce prices as a matter of policy or for other reasons, and the *American Braided Wire Co.* case as one where the reduction in price was the result of the infringement and the loss of profit was the natural consequence of the infringement caused directly to the manufacturer by what the infringer did.

[51] *Sykes* v. *Sykes* (1824) 3 B. & Cr. 541.

[52] (1890) 7 R.P.C. 152 (C.A.).

[53] *Supra*, Note 50.

[54] *Ibid.* 159–160, *per* Cotton L.J. See also Lindley L.J. at 161.

[55] (1895) 12 R.P.C. 360. See also *British Motor Syndicate* v. *Taylor* (1900) 17 R.P.C. 189, 723; *Leeds Forge Co. Ltd.* v. *Deighton* (1908) 25 R.P.C. 209; *Wellman, Seaver & Head Ltd.* v. *Burstinghaus & Co. Ltd.* (1911) 28 R.P.C. 326.

Measure of damages

The question of measure of damages was discussed in the passing-off case of *Spalding & Bros.* v. *Gamage*,[56] and Swinfen Eady L.J. said [57]: "The defendants are liable, in my opinion, for all loss actually sustained by the plaintiffs which is the natural and direct consequence of the unlawful acts of the defendants; this will include any loss of trade actually suffered by the plaintiffs, either directly from the acts complained of, or properly attributable to injury to the plaintiffs' reputation, business, goodwill, and trade and business connections caused by the acts complained of; in other words such damages as flow directly, and in the usual course of things from the wrongful acts, and excluding any speculative and unproven damage." In that case it had been held that a case of misrepresentation calculated to produce damage had been established. It was further held that the cost of issuing advertisements to counter those of the defendants was not a proper basis for the assessment of damages, and the damages were assessed at the sum of £250 paid into court by the defendants. A claim of £5,000 for loss of profits was dismissed as extravagant.

In the Scottish case of *Ledger, Sons & Co.* v. *Munro & Co. Ltd.*,[58] which was a passing-off case, it was held by Lord Hunter, following *Thomson & Co.* v. *Dailly* [58a] that, where damages could not be exactly measured but a fair inference was that trade had been injured, the damages to be awarded fell to be estimated as a juryman would do, upon the whole circumstances of the case, making the best reasonable estimate possible.

It is now established that a claim for damages and for an account of profits are alternative [59] and inconsistent, as accepting an account of profits involves condonation of the infringement complained of.[60] It has been held in England that neither an account nor an inquiry as to damages will be granted if the evidence of sales made under the mark objected to is not sufficient to make the inquiry worth while,[61] or if it should appear that the infringing mark has only been in use a short time,[62] or if only a single instance of use is complained of.[63] It has further been held in England that an inquiry as to damages or an account of profits will only be granted against an infringing defender if the infringement has been done after he has had knowledge of the existence of the plaintiff s trade mark; though ignorance of the existence of the genuine trade mark and consequent innocent infringement would be no answer to a conclusion for interdict. In such a case the damages or profits which can be taken into consideration will be limited to those calculated with regard to sales and

[56] (1913) 30 R.P.C. 388; 31 R.P.C. 125; 32 R.P.C. 273; 34 R.P.C. 289; 35 R.P.C. 101.
[57] (1918) 35 R.P.C. 101.
[58] (1916) 33 R.P.C. 53 (O.H., Lord Hunter).
[58a] (1897) 24 R. 1173.
[59] *Lever* v. *Goodwin* (1887) 36 Ch.D. 1.
[60] *Neilson* v. *Betts* (1871) L.R. 5 H.L. 1; *De Vitre* v. *Betts* (1873) L.R. 6 H.L. 319 (both patent cases).
[61] *Sanitas Co.* v. *Condy* (1887) 4 R.P.C. 530; *Magnolia Co.* v. *Atlas Co.* (1896) 14 R.P.C. 389. See also *Crosfield* v. *Caton* (1912) 29 R.P.C. 47.
[62] *McAndrew* v. *Bassett* (1864) 10 Jur.(N.S.) 495.
[63] *Rose* v. *Loftus* (1878) 47 L.J.Ch. 576.

other infringing transactions committed after the defendant has become aware of the existence of the genuine mark.[64] It was held in *Montgomerie* v. *Young* [65] by the Second Division, reversing Lord Kyllachy, that no relief was due to a pursuer who had only proved one or two inadvertent sales by servants of the defender contrary to his instructions of goods under the pursuer's special trade name.

Passing-off action

This action may be brought to obtain redress for the wrong done by representing for purposes of trade that the defender's goods are those of the pursuer.[66] Proof of damage actually sustained is not always essential as circumstances may raise a presumption of loss: otherwise proof of actual damage is necessary. As in actions for infringement an account of profits or damages can be claimed alternatively: the same principles of assessment apply.

Registered designs

Registration of a design under the Registered Designs Act 1949,[67] gives the registered proprietor copyright in that registered design for five years, extensible to ten or fifteen years on application [68] which gives him certain exclusive rights.

For infringement [69] of the copyright in a design the remedies are suspension and interdict,[70] delivery of the infringing designs,[71] and for an account of profits or for damages (but not both). The amount of the damages will in general follow the principles of patent cases and be the profits which the pursuer has lost in consequence of the defender's actions, and which he would reasonably have made himself if he had sold the articles himself or obtained a royalty on them.[72]

By section 9, as applied to Scotland by section 45, an innocent infringer is exempt from liability for damages on certain conditions.

Action for threats

Section 26 of the Act gives a right to, *inter alia*, damages for loss sustained by groundless threats of infringement proceedings.

[64] *Edelsten* v. *Edelsten* (1863) 1 De G.J. & S. 185; *Moet* v. *Couston* (1864) 33 Beav. 578; *Ellen* v. *Slack* (1880) 24 S.J. 290; *Slazenger* v. *Spalding* [1910] 1 Ch. 257. But see *Heath* v. *Gorringe* (1924) 41 R.P.C. 457, where inquiry ordered though infringement innocent.

[65] (1904) 21 R.P.C. 285.

[66] *Haig & Co.* v. *Forth Blending Co.*, 1954 S.C. 35, surveys the whole law.

[67] ss. 17 *et seq.*

[68] s. 7.

[69] It is a question of fact to be determined by visual inspection: *Holdsworth* v. *McCrea* (1867) L.R. 2 H.L. 380, 386; *Staples* v. *Warwick* (1906) 23 R.P.C. 609.

[70] *Walker, Hunter & Co.* v. *Falkirk Iron Co.* (1887) 14 R. 1072; *Hutchison, Main & Co.* v. *St. Mungo Mfg. Co.* (1907) 24 R.P.C. 265.

[71] *Wallpaper Mfrs. Ltd.* v. *Derby Paper Staining Co.* (1924) 42 R.P.C. 449; *Dunlop Rubber Co.* v. *Booth* (1925) 43 R.P.C. 139.

[72] *United Horse-Shoe & Nail Co.* v. *Stewart* (1886) 15 R.(H.L.) 45; 5 R.P.C. 260; *Pneumatic Tyre Co.* v. *Puncture Proof Pneumatic Tyre Co.* (1897) 16 R.P.C. 209.

The measure of damages for threats is compensation for the damage caused solely by the threats made and made known to third parties, but not for threats not authorised,[73] nor for consequences which go beyond the natural and reasonable consequences thereof.[74] Damage suffered by losing a contract [75] or the ending of negotiations for a contract [76] have been held recoverable.

Copyright

Copyright subsists only under and in accordance with the Copyright Act 1956,[77] and consequently all questions relating to what is or is not an infringement of copyright depend upon the interpretation of the statute.

The quantity or proportion of matter copied is only one criterion, and more important is the quality, whether or not the original author's work is substantially appropriated by the infringement.[78] Section 6 of the Act of 1956 excepts certain publications from constituting infringement, and section 7 makes special exceptions for libraries and archives.

Remedies

The Copyright Act 1956 provides by section 17 that the owner of the copyright infringed is, except as otherwise provided by the Act, entitled to all such remedies by way of damages, injunction or interdict, accounts and otherwise, as are or may be conferred by law for the infringement of a right.

Damages under section 17

Where damages are sought the appropriate measure is the depreciation caused by the infringement to the value of the copyright.[79] Account must be taken in quantifying this of any loss which the owner of the copyright has suffered by a diminution in the sales of his work, or loss of the profits which he might otherwise have made.[80] Some allowance may be made to cover the possibility that the copyright owner would not have sold quite so many copies as the defender.[81] No account will be taken of any benefit the defender may have derived from the use of the work. If the infringing work be shown to have damaged the reputation of the original, this element may be considered in aggravation of damages.[82] It has even been held

[73] *Ungar* v. *Sugg* (1891) 9 R.P.C. 113, 118.

[74] *Horne* v. *Johnston Bros.* (1921) 38 R.P.C. 366.

[75] *Skinner* v. *Perry* (1893) 11 R.P.C. 406.

[76] *Solanite* v. *Wood* (1933) 50 R.P.C. 315.

[77] s. 46 (5). See, generally, *Copinger and Skone James on Copyright*, 11th ed.

[78] *Warne* v. *Seebohm* (1888) 39 Ch.D. 73.

[79] *Sutherland Pub. Co.* v. *Caxton Pub. Co.* [1936] Ch. 323, 336. See also *Beloff* v. *Pressdram* [1973] 1 All E.R. 241.

[80] *Birn* v. *Keen* [1918] 2 Ch. 281; *Fenning Film Service* v. *Wolverhampton Cinemas* [1914] 3 K.B. 1171.

[81] *Birn, supra.*

[82] *Hanfstaengl* v. *Smith* [1905] 1 Ch. 519; *Birn, supra.*

competent in aggravation of damages to withdraw the whole stock, the design of which had been vulgarised by the infringing copy.[83]

Damages under section 18

A claim for damages may also be brought against persons possessing or dealing with infringing copies under section 18 (1) and (4) of the Act, which provides that " The owner of any copyright shall be entitled to all such rights and remedies, in respect of the intromission by any person with an infringing copy, or with any plate used or intended to be used for making infringing copies, as he would be entitled to if he were the owner of every such copy or plate and had been the owner thereof since the time it was made." This is an adoption of the English common law action for detinue under which a plaintiff claims delivery of chattels or their value, and the Scottish equivalent is an action for delivery of the goods, failing which for their value. It has been held in England that a plaintiff was entitled as of right to an order for delivery though the alternative of damages does not appear to have been argued to the court.[84] Independently of this there is a right at common law to the delivery up of infringements, although only for their destruction or the cancellation of infringing parts.[85] Where the infringing material is mixed with original work then the order for delivery may apply only to the infringing part if physically severable,[86] but otherwise to the whole work.[87]

It has been held under the former Act that a complainer may recover damages both for infringement under section 17 and damages for conversion under section 18; the remedies are cumulative and not alternative,[88] though the damages under the two sections should not overlap. The measure of damages for conversion is the value of the article converted, *i.e.* wrongfully possessed, at the date of the conversion,[89] or the proportion borne by the value of the offending part to the value of the work as a whole.

Section 18 raises distinct difficulties of interpretation in Scotland in that the primary remedy for " intromission " is properly restitution and only failing such, damages.[90] If damages fall to be awarded under section 18 the wholesale and not the retail price is the basis of assessment.[91]

Accounting

A pursuer may also demand an account of profits incidentally to an interdict, but not an account, and also damages for infringement or con-

83 *Mansell* v. *Wesley*, Macg.Cop.Cas. (1938–1939) 288.
84 *Boosey* v. *Whight* (*No.* 2) (1899) 81 L.T. 265.
85 *Warne* v. *Seebohm* (1888) 39 Ch.D. 73; *Chappell* v. *Columbia Gramophone Co.* [1914] 2 Ch. 124, 745.
86 *Warne*, *supra*; *Boosey*, *supra*.
87 *Stevens* v. *Wildy* (1850) 19 L.J.Ch. 190.
88 *Caxton Pub. Co.* v. *Sutherland Pub. Co.* [1939] A.C. 178.
89 *Caxton*, *supra*, at p. 192; *Birn* v. *Keen* [1918] 2 Ch. 281.
90 *Cf. Leitch* v. *Leydon*, 1931 S.C.(H.L.) 1, 8.
91 *Mansell* v. *Wesley*, Macg.Cop.Cas. (1938–1939) 288.

version [92] in respect that an account condones the infringement.[93] The profits which can be recovered are the net profits,[94] and if there are obviously no profits an accounting will be refused,[95] in which case damages may be claimed.[96]

Innocent infringement

Section 18 (2) of the Act provides that the pursuer in an action for infringement is not entitled to any damages or to any other pecuniary remedy (except costs) if it is proved or admitted that, at the time of the intromission in question, (a) the defender was not aware, and had no reasonable grounds for suspecting, that copyright subsisted in the work or other subject-matter to which the action relates, or (b) where the articles intromitted with were infringing copies, the defender believed, and had reasonable grounds for believing, that they were not infringing copies, or (c) where the article converted or detained was a plate used or intended to be used for making any articles, the defender believed, and had reasonable grounds for believing, that the articles so made or intended to be made were not, or (as the case may be) would not be, infringing copies.

Section 19 deals with the case of copyright subject to exclusive licence.

These rules are not easily reconciled with the rule that good faith is no defence to infringement [97] and it does not protect against a claim under section 18.

Limitation

No special period of limitation is now prescribed. The effect of the proviso to section 18 (1) is uncertain in Scotland; it appears to be meaningless.

Trade names

At common law a trader who puts on goods he manufactures, selects or exclusively produces and sells a distinctive name or mark indicating that they are produced or made by him [98] may acquire a right to have this name or mark, if used to deceive the public [99] and injure his business, protected by interdict and by damages for its infringement or violation.[1]

[92] *De Vitre* v. *Betts* (1873) L.R. 6 H.L. 319.
[93] *Caxton Co.* v. *Sutherland Co.* [1939] A.C. 178, 198; *De Vitre* v. *Betts* (1873) L.R. 6 H.L. 319; *Colburn* v. *Simms* (1843) 2 Hare 543.
[94] *Delfe* v. *Delamotte* (1857) 3 K. & J. 587.
[95] *Colburn, supra*; *Powell* v. *Aikin* (1857) 4 K. & J. 343.
[96] *Mawman* v. *Tegg* (1826) 2 Russ. 385, 400.
[97] *Scott* v. *Stanford* (1867) L.R. 3 Eq. 718; *Mansell* v. *Valley Printing Co.* [1908] 2 Ch. 441; *Byrne* v. *Statist Co.*, [1914] 1 K.B. 622.
[98] *Cellular Clothing Co.* v. *Maxton & Murray* (1899) 1 F.(H.L.) 29; *Kinnell* v. *Ballantine*, 1910 S.C. 246; *Boord* v. *Thom & Cameron*, 1907 S.C. 1326; *Reddaway* v. *Banham* [1896] A.C. 199; *Massam* v. *Thorley's Cattle Food Co.* (1880) 14 Ch.D. 748.
[99] *Dunlop Tyre Co.* v. *Dunlop Motor Co.*, 1907 S.C.(H.L.) 15; *Williamson* v. *Meikle*, 1909 S.C. 1272; *Kinnell, supra*; *Edge* v. *Niccolls* [1911] A.C. 693.
[1] Bell, *Prin.* § 1361c.

Remedies for infringement

The remedies are interdict,[2] damages or an account of profits alternatively, possibly combined with a declarator of the exclusive right to the trade name in question, and delivery of infringing goods. For damages or profits it must be shown that there has been deception, but that inference cannot be drawn merely because the pursuer's sales have declined.[3] Though an exact figure cannot be proved, substantial damages may be awarded where deception has been proved and particularly if there has been fraud.[4] It is doubtful if the expenses of detecting the fraud and obtaining evidence thereof can be regarded as a proper element in the claim of damages.[4] But admissible heads of damage are loss of sales, injury to trade reputation, and any reduction in prices which the pursuers were compelled to make.[5]

Passing-off

It is an actionable wrong quite independently of patents and trade marks legislation to seek to mislead the public or any member thereof into believing that goods offered for sale or the nature of the business carried on is that of another person. It is frequently effected by infringing the other party's trade-name,[6] mark [7] or description.[8] The wrong is truly one to the goodwill of the pursuer's business [9] and fraudulent intent need not be proved.[9]

Damages

Apart from interdict the remedies are damages or an account of profits alternatively. Actual resulting damage need not be shown to justify at least nominal damages.[10] It may be that no more than nominal damages can be given in a case of innocent passing-off,[11] and it has been held that no damages or profits will be given in respect of use before having actual notice of the pursuer's right. It is assumed that the presence of deceptive goods on the market will injure the pursuer's business and he is entitled to damages in respect of the damage to his business, even if there is no evidence of resale by the retailer, innocent or fraudulent, to the public. In the case of a sale of deceptive goods to a middleman, the pursuer's loss of profit is not a relevant consideration in assessing damages, but the proper consideration is the damage fairly attributable to the wrong of selling

2 *Kinnell* v. *Ballantine*, 1910 S.C. 246; *Montgomerie* v. *Young* (1904) 11 S.L.T. 298, 600; *Bass* v. *Laidlaw* (1908) 16 S.L.T. 660.
3 *Kinnell, supra.*
4 *Thomson* v. *Dailly* (1897) 24 R. 1173.
5 *Alexander* v. *Henry* (1895) 12 R.P.C. 360.
6 *Wotherspoon* v. *Currie* (1872) L.R. 5 H.L. 508; *Powell* v. *Birmingham Vinegar Co.* [1896] 2 Ch. 54; *Montgomery* v. *Thompson* [1891] A.C. 217; *Havana Cigar Co.* v. *Oddenino* [1924] 1 Ch. 179.
7 Trade Marks Act 1938, s. 2. This does not affect the action for passing-off at common law.
8 *Reddaway* v. *Banham* [1896] A.C. 199.
9 *Draper* v. *Trist* [1939] 3 All E.R. 513, 526; *Haig & Co.* v. *Forth Blending Co.*, 1954 S.C. 35.
10 *Draper* v. *Trist* [1939] 3 All E.R. 513, 526.
11 *Draper, supra*, 518, 525.

deceptive goods to the retailer.[12] There is no onus on the pursuer to show that purchasers are deceived, nor on the defender to show the contrary.[13] Within these limits the actual quantification is a jury question.

Goodwill

Goodwill consists of those advantages arising from locality,[14] personality,[15] reputation and connection [16] which tend to maintain a steady and continuing business and give it an identity and permanence,[17] and it amounts to an incorporeal business asset capable of transfer and having a distinct value.

Infringement of goodwill

This is normally protected by restrictive covenants made on transfer of the business and designed to limit competition and preserve the goodwill. Such covenants are enforceable [18] primarily by proceedings for interdict though damages may form an ancillary conclusion, where infringement has taken place and already caused damage and loss. The measure of damages does not appear to have been thoroughly discussed, but the principles of patent and trade-mark cases would probably be appropriate.

An assignee has the exclusive right to carry on the business assigned, to use its name,[19] and to represent himself as doing so,[20] and hence to sue the assignor for damages if he has infringed these rights as well as to restrain an intention of doing so.[21]

In *McKirdy* v. *Paterson* [22] M retired from his partnership with P and was to receive in compensation £2,500 together with his share of capital and past profits. P refused payment on the ground that M had set up a new business and solicited and withdrawn customers in breach of the agreement. The court held that M had not forfeited his compensation and the question was raised whether P's allegations of soliciting would have sufficed to support an action for solatium and damages. The court was of opinion that the alleged breach of the agreement was not a defence but gave rise only to " an action of damages to the extent of the injury sustained and solatium for the breach of agreement." [23] " Whatever claim the defender (P) has . . . is one merely for specific damages, requiring to be

[12] *Draper, supra,* 523. See also *Spalding & Bros.* v. *Gamage Ltd.* (1918) 35 R.P.C. 101; *Alexander* v. *Henry & Co.* (1895) 12 R.P.C. 360.
[13] *Draper, supra.*
[14] *Philp's Exor.* v. *Philp's Exor.* (1894) 21 R. 482.
[15] *Drummond* v. *Leith Assessor* (1886) 13 R. 540.
[16] *Morrison* v. *Morrison* (1900) 2 F. 382; see also *Smith* v. *Macbride* (1888) 16 R. 36; *Cowan* v. *Millar* (1895) 22 R. 833.
[17] *Churton* v. *Douglas* (1859) John. 174; *Trego* v. *Hunt* [1896] A.C. 7; *cf. Wankie Coal Co.* v. *I.R.C.* [1920] A.C. 66, 69.
[18] On the general question of their enforceability in various circumstances, see *Gloag on Contract,* 2nd ed., 571 *et seq.*; *Pollock on Contract,* 13th ed., 326 *et seq.*
[19] *Thynne* v. *Shove* (1890) 45 Ch.D. 577; *Burchell* v. *Wilde* [1900] 1 Ch. 551.
[20] *Walker* v. *Mottram* (1881) 19 Ch.D. 355, 363.
[21] *Walker* v. *Mottram* (1881) 19 Ch.D. 355, 363; *Burrows* v. *Foster* (1862) 1 N.R. 156.
[22] (1854) 16 D. 1013.
[23] 16 D. at p. 1018, *per* L. J.-C. Hope. See also *Shackle* v. *Baker* (1808) 14 Ves.Jun. 468.

specifically set forth as such and to be proved. . . ." In *Randall* v. *Summers*[24] a lease contained a covenant not to let adjacent premises to a competing business. On the facts it was held that no breach had been committed, but opinions were expressed that if it had the pursuer's remedy might have been a claim for abatement of rent.

Partnership deeds frequently provide for payment of liquidate damages for breach of an agreement not to solicit former clients after retiral from the firm.

[24] 1919 S.C. 396.

CHAPTER 58

DAMAGES FOR BREACH OF TRUST

BREACH of trust is a breach of duty *sui generis* and not wholly partaking either of breach of contract or of delict.[1] The duties of a trustee appointed to hold and administer a trust estate may be summed up by saying that his duty is to take care and conserve the trust estate and to administer it with the degree of diligence which a reasonably careful and prudent man would show in his own affairs.[2] If owing to a failure in that duty of care incumbent on him a loss accrues to the trust estate under his charge, the trustee or trustees will be liable to the trust in damages for breach of trust. In all cases of breach of trust the result is simply to create a liability by the trustee to make good to the trust estate the loss which he has caused.[3]

Title to sue

Any beneficiary may sue for a breach of trust and it is not necessary that all should concur, but all other than the persons pursuing should have intimation of the action, so that they may, if so advised, sist themselves thereto.[3a]

Defenders

An action for breach of trust may be brought against one or more of the trustees, without calling them all [4] even where it is alleged that that one misled the others.[4a] They are all liable jointly and severally, but one may be sued as prime obligant. Any one found liable has a claim for rateable relief against the others.[4b]

Liability for previous trustees

The beneficiaries may call the existing trustees to account not only for their own intromissions but also for those of their predecessors in office [5] and the existing may sue the former trustees for an accounting [6] or, if

[1] *Allen* v. *McCombie's Trs.*, 1909 S.C. 710, 717, 720.

[2] *Learoyd* v. *Whiteley* (1887) 12 App.Cas. 727, 733; *Speight* v. *Gaunt* (1883) 9 App.Cas. 1, 20; *Raes* v. *Meek* (1889) 16 R.(H.L.) 31, 33; *Knox* v. *Mackinnon* (1888) 15 R.(H.L.) 83, 87; *Buchanan* v. *Eaton*, 1911 S.C.(H.L.) 40, 45; *McLaren on Wills*, ss. 2239 *et seq.*; *Mackenzie Stuart on Trusts*, 157 *et seq.*

[3] *Town and County Bank Ltd.* v. *Walker* (1904) 12 S.L.T. 411, 412, *per* Lord Kyllachy.

[3a] *Allen* v. *McCombie's Trs.*, 1909 S.C. 710.

[4] *Croskery* v. *Gilmour's Trs.* (1890) 17 R. 697; *Allen* v. *McCombie's Trs.*, 1909 S.C. 710.

[4a] *Aitkenhead* v. *Oliver*, 1933 S.N. 18.

[4b] *Pearson* v. *Houston's Trs.* (1868) 6 M. 286; *Croskery* v. *Gilmour's Trs.* (1890) 17 R. 697; *Chillingworth* v. *Chambers* [1896] 1 Ch. 685; *cf. Palmer* v. *Wick, etc. S.S. Co.* (1894) 21 R.(H.L.) 39.

[5] *Sommerville's Trs.* v. *Wemyss* (1854) 17 D. 151; *Pearson* v. *Houston's Trs.* (1868) 6 M. 286; *Town and County Bank* v. *Walker* (1904) 12 S.L.T. 411; *Lees' Trs.* v. *Dun*, 1913 S.C.(H.L.) 12; *Hastie's J. F.* v. *Morham's Executors*, 1951 S.C. 668.

[6] *Henderson* v. *Watson*, 1939 S.C. 711.

they refuse, any beneficiary with sufficient interest may do so.[7] The trustees' liability ceases if there is no continuing trust when they hand over the estate in terms of the truster's instructions.[8]

If, however, later trustees do not rectify mismanagement by earlier trustees, the latter remain liable for the breach of trust.[9]

The liability of previous trustees to account is not limited by the long negative prescription, but if a discharge has been granted in favour of a resigning trustee it must be reduced before he can be called to account.[10]

An existing trustee is not necessarily liable for a breach of trust committed by a predecessor as, in the absence of reason to believe otherwise, he may assume that the predecessor has performed his duties.[11]

Liability of trustee's firm

If a trustee is a partner in a firm and trust money comes to be in the hands of the firm, with the sanction of the partners, either express or implied, and is misapplied, the trustee and also his partners are liable.[12] Similarly if a solicitor commits a fraud on trustees for whom he acts, the firm is liable.[13] It is well settled that a firm cannot retain fees received for work done by a partner who is a trustee unless specially authorised.[14]

Joint trustees

Where several trustees have jointly committed a breach of trust, they are equally liable, irrespective of the degrees of personal fault, all jointly and severally, and any one trustee who pays has a claim of relief against the others. When one of several defaulting trustees has been compelled to replace the lost trust estate, the right of contribution from the others is not affected by the fact that damages have been exacted from one of them.[15] There may however be cases where a trustee is entitled to full indemnity against a co-trustee even though both may be liable as regards the beneficiaries. It has been held that relief may be granted against a co-trustee who has benefited from a breach of trust, or if a relationship has existed between him and the other trustees which entitled the court to treat him as solely liable for the breach of trust.[16]

Exceptionally, a trustee resident in England who relied on the advice

[7] *Watt* v. *Roger's Trs.* (1890) 17 R. 1201; *Allen* v. *McCombie's Trs.*, 1909 S.C. 710.

[8] *Masson* v. *Scott's Trs.*, 1910, 2 S.L.T. 28; *Gow's Trs.* v. *Gow*, 1912, 2 S.L.T. 256.

[9] *Duncan* v. *Newland's Exors.* (1882) 20 S.L.R. 8; *Lees' Trs., supra*; *Oswald's Trs.* v. *City of Glasgow Bank* (1879) 6 R. 461.

[10] *Hastie's J. F.* v. *Morham's Exors.*, 1951 S.C. 668.

[11] *Re Strahan* (1856) 8 De G. M. & G. 291.

[12] *Sadler* v. *Lee* (1843) 6 Beav. 324; *Blyth* v. *Fladgate* [1891] 1 Ch. 337, 352; *Moore* v. *Knight* [1891] 1 Ch. 547; *Rhodes* v. *Moules* [1895] 1 Ch. 236. See also Partnership Act 1890, ss. 5, 11, 13.

[13] *Sawyer* v. *Goodwin* (1867) 36 L.J.Ch. 578.

[14] *Henderson* v. *Watson*, 1939 S.C. 711.

[15] *Pearson* v. *Houston's Trs.* (1868) 6 M. 286; *Croskery* v. *Gilmour's Trs.* (1890) 17 R. 697; *Palmer* v. *Wick & Pulteneytown S.S. Co.* (1894) 21 R.(H.L.) 39, 46; *Chillingworth* v. *Chambers* [1896] 1 Ch. 685.

[16] *Bahin* v. *Hughes* (1886) 31 Ch.D. 390, 394.

of a co-trustee, who was law agent of the trust, the consent of another co-trustee, and of the liferenter, was held not liable for concurring in an investment which proved worthless.[17]

If a trustee guilty of a breach of trust be also a beneficiary, his breach must be repaired before he can claim his beneficial rights, even if those rights be only derivative from an original beneficiary, as on intestacy,[18] and this extends to an assignee of his beneficial interest.[19]

Basis of claim

A beneficiary is entitled to receive from the trustee the share of the trust estate to which he is entitled on the footing that the trust has been properly administered, and a trustee must therefore account to the beneficiary for that share. The beneficiary is entitled to an accounting on the basis that the trustees had done everything they should have done and any deficiency due to mismanagement or to causes for which the trustees are answerable must be made up, including anything constructively belonging to the trust estate by reason of a trustee having been *auctor in rem suam*. The claim is one for damages but may be decided by a process of count, reckoning and payment.[20]

If a trustee has been guilty of misconduct and loss ensues to the trust estate, he is not entitled to be acquitted because the loss was caused more immediately by some event entirely beyond his control, or by accident,[21] or by contributory negligence of the beneficiary.[22] On the contrary, a trustee acting within the bounds of his duty is not liable for depreciation of the funds due to external causes.

The Court of Session may be prevailed on to approve retrospectively actings in breach of trust, such as the sale of trust estate contrary to the express terms of the trust [22a] or sale contrary to the express interlocutor of the Court giving powers of sale,[22b] but such will usually be refused,[22c] though in special circumstances [22d] even in such a case the court may give retrospective confirmation.[22e] If the court does not the trustees are in breach of trust.

Other instances of breach of trust

A trustee directed to sell property who delayed to do so for an unreasonable time was held liable for the loss which ensued from the

17 *Kennedy* v. *Kennedy* (1884) 12 R. 275.
18 *Jacubs* v. *Rylance* (1874) L.R. 17 Eq. 341.
19 *Doering* v. *Doering* (1889) 42 Ch.D. 203; *Re Dacre*; *Whitaker* v. *Dacre* [1916] 1 Ch. 344.
20 *Clarke* v. *Clarke's Trs.*, 1925 S.C. 693. In such a case trustees must lodge accounts as a body: *Campbell* v. *Campbell's Trs.*, 1957 S.L.T.(Sh.Ct.) 53.
21 *Caffrey* v. *Darby* (1801) 6 Ves. 498; *Fyler* v. *Fyler* (1841) 3 Beav. 550; *Kellaway* v. *Johnson* (1842) 5 Beav. 324; *Munch* v. *Cockerell* (1839) 5 My. & C. 212; *Clough* v. *Bond* (1838) 3 My. & C. 496.
22 *Magnus* v. *Queensland National Bank* (1888) 37 Ch.D. 466.
22a *Clyne* (1894) 21 R. 849.
22b *Drummond's J. F.* (1894) 21 R. 932.
22c *East Kilbride District Nursing Association*, 1951 S.C. 64.
22d *Dow's Trs.*, 1947 S.C. 524.
22e *Campbell-Wyndham-Long's Trs.*, 1962 S.C. 132.

deterioration of the property.[23] So, too, a trustee who invested in heritable property instead of stock as directed and who failed to accumulate as directed, was ordered to purchase the proper amount of stock and to make good the sum which should have been accumulated.[24] A trustee who improperly gave up an insurance policy was held liable for the amount of the bonus thereon and for moneys received on the surrender.[25] Again trustees have been held liable for the loss incurred in consequence of failure to intimate an assignation or to record a deed.[26]

When trustees improperly invested trust funds in their partnership business, it was held that there must be taken into account, not merely the capital of the partners but also loans and other funds invested in the firm business, and the proportion which the trust fund bore to the whole determined the share of profits to be credited to the trust; periodical docquets settling the interests of partners *inter se* were of no importance.[27]

Where a trustee allowed trust funds to remain in his firm's hands for business purposes, he was held liable to account for the profits accruing to him on those trust funds, but not for profits appropriated by his co-partners, and the co-trustees are not under any liability to account for the profits which accrued to him individually if there is no case against them of neglect to call him to account.[28]

In *Hood* v. *Macdonald's Trustee* [29] a beneficiary sued a testamentary trustee for damages for failing to have given the pursuer the option, to which he was entitled under the will, of purchasing the testator's business, of which he had previously been manager. It was held that the trustee's failure to give the pursuer the opportunity to purchase was a breach of trust and that the pursuer was entitled to damages if he could prove that he had suffered damage by deprivation of his rights under the will through the trustee's action. The court declined to lay down *ab ante* any criterion for assessing the damages but it was suggested [30] that the pursuer's willingness to pay the price at which the business had been sold elsewhere and the pursuer's financial ability to have paid that price might be a starting point. But it was possible that the pursuer had sustained no damage despite the breach of trust, the loss of opportunity being insufficient by itself. Only if satisfied that the pursuer could and would have bought the business could the court assess the pursuer's loss, by reference to past and prospective profits.

Where a stockbroker bought shares for a client, had them registered in the name of a bank nominee company and later, without the client's consent, pledged them to the bank under a general letter of hypothecation

23 *Devaynes* v. *Robinson* (1857) 24 Beav. 86; *Sculthorpe* v. *Tipper* (1872) L.R. 13 Eq. 232.
24 *Pride* v. *Fooks* (1840) 2 Beav. 430.
25 *Kingdon* v. *Castleman* (1877) 46 L.J.Ch. 448.
26 *Macnamara* v. *Carey* (1867) 1 Ir.R.Eq. 9.
27 *Cochrane* v. *Black* (1857) 19 D. 1019.
28 *Laird* v. *Laird* (1858) 20 D. 972. See further, *Laird's Tr.* v. *Laird's Legatees* (1862) 24 D. 1041.
29 1949 S.C. 24.
30 *Ibid.* p. 31, *per* Lord Keith.

in security of advances made by the bank to him, it was held, as between the client and a judicial factor on the deceased stockbroker's estate, who had sold the shares, that the shares had not lost their identity as trust property and as they were still identifiable in the hands of the bankrupt the client was entitled to a preferential ranking for the value of the shares.[30a]

Following trust property

Where the trustee's failure has lain in mixing trust funds or assets with his own, the trust assets still belong to the trust if still identifiable and the court will order them to be repaid or restored.[30b] If the assets are no longer identifiable the claim is only for damages for the loss sustained, measured by the value of the assets intermixed.[30c]

Claims by creditors other than trust beneficiaries

In *Heritable Securities Investment Association* v. *Miller's Trustees*[31] the trustees paid away sums to trust debtors and beneficiaries at a time when heritable property disponed in security to the pursuers was thought to be sufficient to satisfy the pursuer's claims, though the property was found in the end to be insufficient. The trustees were held personally liable, as having acted in breach of trust, although in good faith. The rights of creditors had priority over the claims of beneficiaries, and trustees paid money away at their peril. The measure of the award was the sums paid away with interest which, as the trustees had not sought to benefit themselves, was restricted to three per cent., as being the average rate of trust interest. The trustees' duty to creditors is prior to their duty to beneficiaries.[32]

Similarly where ordinary debts were paid before a preferential debt trustees were held liable to make good the balance on the latter claim.[32] But a trustee may in safety pay away to beneficiaries after reasonable inquiry and lapse of time[33] without liability to creditors, if he does so in bona fide and in ignorance of outstanding claims against the estate.[34] Where trustees handed over a specific bequest and then ascertained that the estate was insolvent, they were held bound to account for the value of the bequest to the creditors.[35]

Quantum of damages for breach of trust

In the case of breach of trust by neglect the basic amount of damages recoverable from the trustees is the sum which suffices to replace the actual

30a *Newton's Exrx.* v. *Meiklejohn's J. F.*, 1959 S.L.T. 71.
30b Bell, *Comm.* I, 236, 295; *Macadam* v. *Martin's Tr.* (1872) 11 M. 33; *Jopp* v. *Johnston's Trs.* (1904) 6 F. 1028; *Newton's Exrx., supra.*
30c *Cf. Hofford* v. *Gowans*, 1909, 1 S.L.T. 153.
31 (1892) 20 R. 675. *Cf. Campbell* v. *Borthwick's Trs.* [1930] S.N. 156.
32 *Lamond's Trs.* v. *Croom* (1871) 9 M. 662.
33 Six months: *Stewart* v. *Evans* (1871) 9 M. 810.
34 *Stewart* v. *Evans* (1871) 9 M. 810; *Beith* v. *Mackenzie* (1875) 3 R. 185.
35 *Murray's Trs.* v. *Murray* (1905) 13 S.L.T. 274.

loss to the trust estate consequential on the breach and thereby restores it to the position it would have been in but for the trustees' conduct and if they had properly performed their duty of trust.[36] It matters not whether the trustee gained or lost by the breach of trust.[37] Examples are liability for the sum used in making an unauthorised investment,[38] the sum which would have been received by realising an investment at the proper time,[39] the sum required to replace a proper investment wrongly sold.[40] In case of an investment made *ultra vires* though in bona fide the beneficiary may take the subject of the investment or the sum of money invested with interest.[41] Where the breach is not innocent but consists in misapplication or embezzlement interest may be exacted as well as replacement of capital. In a case of negligence the precise nature of the breach of trust and the degree of fault are quite immaterial to the measure of damages, the sole question being *restitutio in integrum.*[42]

If the action of trustees, though technically a breach of trust, has caused no loss to the trust estate, no damages can be exacted as they are not exigible simply on account of the existence of a breach of trust.[43] So too no claim will lie against a trustee in default if he has replaced the loss to the trust before action is taken against him.[44] And a trustee admittedly in breach of trust can avoid any liability if he can show, the onus being on him, that the loss would have been sustained independently of his actings or omissions and that the result would have followed even if he had done all that he should have.[45]

A trustee who has incurred liability to make good the loss occasioned by a breach of trust in respect of one portion of the trust funds may not set off against this liability any gain which has accrued to another portion of the trust funds through the same or a distinct and unconnected breach of trust. Still less can he seek to offset such a loss by a normal profit of proper administration in another branch of the trust, nor even may he seek to show that the general administration of the trust has been beneficial and the aggregate value of the trust estate been maintained or substantially increased.[46] Each distinct transaction must be looked at, and if it is in breach of trust, the trustee must make good any loss thereon.[47]

A trustee is not, however, liable if he has set aside a sufficient sum to meet a legacy not yet payable, properly invested it and distributed the rest

36 *Knott* v. *Cottee* (1852) 16 Beav. 77. See also Strachan, " Compensation for Breach of Trust " (1918) 34 L.Q.R. 168.
37 *Dornford* v. *Dornford* (1806) 12 Ves. 129; *Montfort* v. *Cadogan* (1810) 17 Ves. 485.
38 *Knott, supra.*
39 *Fry* v. *Fry* (1859) 27 Beav. 144. *Cf. Sculthorpe* v. *Tipper* (1871) 13 Eq. 232.
40 *Phillipson* v. *Gatty* (1850) 7 Hare 516.
41 *Douglas* v. *Douglas' Trs.* (1864) 2 M. 1380; *Pollexfen* v. *Stewart* (1841) 3 D. 1215; 4 D. 224.
42 *Town and County Bank* v. *Walker* (1904) 12 S.L.T. 411, 412.
43 *Millar's Trs.* v. *Polson* (1897) 24 R. 1038.
44 *Buchanan* v. *Eaton*, 1911 S.C.(H.L.) 40; *McKnight's Trs.* v. *Free Church of Scotland*, 1916 S.C. 349; *Re Brogden* (1888) 38 Ch.D. 546.
45 *Carruthers* v. *Carruthers* (1896) 23 R.(H.L.) 55; *Millar's Trs., supra.*
46 *Clarke* v. *Clarke's Trs.*, 1925 S.C. 693.
47 *Vyse* v. *Foster* (1874) L.R. 7 H.L. 318; *Wills* v. *Gresham* (1854) 2 Drew. 258; 5 De G. M. & G. 770; *Dimes* v. *Scott* (1828) 4 Russ. 195; *cf. Fletcher* v. *Green* (1864) 33 Beav. 426.

of the estate, and the fund turns out to be inadequate to meet the legacy owing to a depreciation of the investment.[48]

Wilful breach of trust

Where a trustee has committed a deliberate breach of trust as by embezzling trust funds, utilising trust funds in his own business, or applying them to purposes outwith the purposes of the trust his liability may be more extensive. If he has made a profit by the employment of the trust fund the profit belongs constructively to the trust and must be accounted for to it. He may also have to take steps to rectify his failure, if that can be done. Thus where trustees under a marriage contract invested, contrary to the trust deed, in stock which appreciated, they had to credit the trust estate with the increased value, and also to realise the stock and invest in terms of their directions.[49]

A defaulting trustee will not generally be liable for more than he has actually received from the breach of trust except in cases of gross negligence and deliberate breach.[50] Examples are where a trustee took a loan of trust funds,[51] or transacted business with the trust estate,[52] or acted as a salaried manager to the trust estate.[53] Where trustees have invested trust funds in trading they are bound to impute the whole profits to the trust.[54]

Liability for interest

Where trustees have committed a breach of trust they are liable in many cases not only to repay capital but to pay interest thereon.[55] This applies particularly to cases not of breach by neglect but breach by misappropriation, or active delinquency,[56] or wrongful investment, or failure to invest.[57] Thus where a trustee mixes trust funds with private or other funds, he is held constructive trustee of the profits of those funds for the trust and, owing to difficulties of computation, the court will usually charge the trustee with interest[58] at the highest legal rate on sums improperly retained in his own hands, accumulating the interest year by year.[59] But no interest is recoverable if the funds put into the trustee's private account

48 *Robinson* v. *Fraser's Tr.* (1881) 8 R.(H.L.) 127; *Heritable Securities Investment Assocn.* v. *Miller's Trs.* (1893) 20 R. 675; *Scott's Trs.* v. *Scott* (1895) 23 R. 52.

49 *Grant* v. *Baillie* (1869) 8 M. 77.

50 *Pybus* v. *Smith* (1791) 1 Ves. 193.

51 *Ritchie* v. *Ritchie's Trustees* (1888) 15 R. 1086.

52 *Cherry's Trs.* v. *Patrick*, 1911, 2 S.L.T. 313.

53 *Mills* v. *Brown's Trustees* (1901) 3 F. 1012.

54 *Cochrane* v. *Black* (1855) 17 D. 321; *Laird* v. *Laird* (1855) 17 D. 984; *Torrie* v. *Mounsey* (1832) 10 S. 597; *Grant* v. *Baillie* (1869) 8 M. 77.

55 *Lees' Trs.* v. *Dun*, 1913 S.C.(H.L.) 12.

56 *Att.-Gen.* v. *Alford* (1855) 4 De G.M. & G. 843, 852.

57 *Bryson* v. *Bryson's Trs.* (1907) 14 S.L.T. 750 (5 per cent.).

58 *McLaren on Wills*, s. 2257.

59 *Malcolm's Exors.* v. *Malcolm* (1869) 8 M. 272, 277; *cf. Burdick* v. *Garrick* (1870) L.R. 5 Ch. 233.

would not have been earning anything and so caused no loss.[60] The full penal rate of interest is not, however, always exacted.[61]

If the breach of trust consists in leaving money in bank in an account or on deposit receipt instead of investing it, the interest chargeable will be the difference, if any, between the rate of bank interest and the rate which the trust estate might reasonably have earned if put into proper trust investments.[62]

Where the breach consists in not investing at all or investing in unauthorised investments, the trustee must account to the beneficiaries for the capital sum and the full rate of interest which the money would have earned by prudent investment. If the beneficiaries elect to adopt an *ultra vires* investment it becomes trust property; if they do not the trustee must make good the principal and interest to the trust as if no investment had been made, but if the *ultra vires* investment should have been profitable and is not adopted the profit belongs to the trustee.[63]

The rate of interest on money lost is not fixed. Five per cent. is not now taken as the standard rate,[64] this being frequently a penal rate for circumstances of culpable nature,[65] but as a rule the court will take the figure which would be a good return for the money if it were properly invested.[66] Thus 4 per cent. has been given [67] or even 3 per cent. where the default was not serious and where it was shown that the highest rate of interest could not have been obtained for the whole period.[68] Representatives of a deceased trustee who had to refund to the trust estate a sum lost by his negligence were found liable to pay interest at $3\frac{1}{2}$ per cent.[69] A trustee who in bona fide accepted a salary for managing a trust business had to repay it, but in the circumstances was not liable in interest.[70]

Trustees are also liable for interest on sums which they unreasonably delay to make over to beneficiaries. In this case, however, it is only if there is personal negligence or wrongful withholding on the part of the trustee that he will be personally liable.[71]

60 *Malcolm's Exors., supra*; *Wellwood's Trs.* v. *Boswell* (1856) 19 D. 187.

61 As where trustees paid beneficiaries in priority to creditors in the belief that the creditor's security was adequate to cover his claim: *Heritable Securities Investment Assocn. Ltd.* v. *Miller's Trs.* (1893) 20 R. 675 (3 per cent.). So, too, *Lees's Trs.* v. *Dun*, 1913 S.C.(H.L.) 12 ($3\frac{1}{2}$ per cent.); *Melville* v. *Noble's Trs.* (1896) 24 R. 243 (4 per cent.); *Ferrie's Curator* (1897) 5 S.L.T. 62 (4 per cent.); *Malcolm's Exors* v. *Malcolm* (1869) 8 M. 272 (4 per cent.); *Hardie's Trs.* v. *Graham* (1896) 3 S.L.T. 277 (4 per cent.); *Graham's Trs.* v. *Graham* (1870) 8 S.L.R. 107 (4 per cent.).

62 *Melville* v. *Noble's Trs.* (1896) 24 R. 293; *Clarke* v. *Clarke's Trs.*, 1925 S.C. 693.

63 *Henderson* v. *Henderson's Trs.* (1900) 2 F. 1295, 1311; *Head* v. *Gould* [1898] 2 Ch. 250.

64 *Ross* v. *Ross* (1896) 23 R. 802, 806; *Kearon* v. *Thomson's Trs.*, 1949 S.C. 287.

65 *Cf. Heritable Securities Investment Assocn. Ltd.* v. *Miller's Trs.* (1893) 20 R. 675; *Bryson* v. *Bryson's Trs.* (1907) 14 S.L.T. 750; *Miller's Exrx.* v. *Miller's Trs.*, 1922 S.C. 150.

66 *Paterson* v. *Dawson* (1897) 5 S.L.T. 64; *Baird's Trs.* v. *Duncanson* (1892) 19 R. 1045, 1049; *Inglis's Trs.* v. *Breen* (1891) 18 R. 487, 490.

67 *Carruthers* v. *Carruthers* (1896) 23 R.(H.L.) 55, 59; *Graham's Tr.* v. *Graham* (1870) 8 S.L.R. 107; *Malcolm's Exor.* v. *Malcolm* (1869) 8 M. 272; *Hardie's Trs.* v. *Graham* (1896) 3 S.L.T. 277; *Mustard* v. *Robertson* (1899) 7 S.L.T. 71; *Paterson, supra*; *Baird's Trs., supra*.

68 *Melville* v. *Noble's Trs.* (1896) 24 R. 243; *Pursell's Trs.* v. *Newbigging* (1871) 8 S.L.R. 710.

69 *Lees's Trs.* v. *Dun*, 1913 S.C.(H.L.) 12.

70 *Mills* v. *Brown's Trustees* (1901) 3 F. 1012.

71 See Ch. 23, *supra*.

Recovery of bequests wrongly paid

Where trustees have paid away funds to the wrong beneficiary, other beneficiaries or heirs *ab intestato* may demand repetition of the payment as made in error, as in one case on the ground that a bequest of residue, although paid, was void from uncertainty and truly belonged to the heirs *ab intestato*.[72] The taker is the person primarily liable but the trustee is bound to make good anything which cannot be recovered from the wrongly paid beneficiary. "Trustees, in distributing the trust estate, are bound to pay it away to the party in right to receive it, and are liable to that party if they pay it away to any other." [73] If, however, the taker of the property has taken it in bona fide, for value, and without notice of the trust, he is protected and the property irrecoverable, in which case the beneficiary's only remedy is against the trustee.[74] But a person who takes trust property gratuitously, with or without knowledge, or one who takes it for consideration in the knowledge of breach of trust is a constructive trustee of the property and bound to surrender it to the true beneficiary.

Statutory qualifications of liability

The Trusts (Scotland) Act 1921, provides by section 29 that where a trustee has improperly advanced trust money on a heritable security which would, at the time of investment, have been a proper investment in all respects for a less sum than was actually advanced thereon, the security shall be deemed an authorised investment for such less sum, and the trustee shall only be liable to make good the sum advanced in excess thereof with interest.[75]

Section 30 further provides that any trustee lending money on the security of any property shall not be chargeable with breach of trust by reason only of the proportion borne by the amount of the loan to the value of such property at the time when the loan was made, provided that it shall appear to the court that in making such loan the trustee was acting upon a report as to the value of the property made by a person whom the trustee reasonably believed to be an able practical valuator instructed and employed independently of any owner of the property, whether such valuator carried on business in the locality where the property is situated or elsewhere, and that the amount of the loan by itself or in combination with any other loan or loans upon the property ranking prior to or *pari passu* with the loan in question does not exceed two equal third parts of the value of the property as stated in such report, and this section shall apply to a loan, upon any property on which the trustees can lawfully lend.[76]

[72] *Armour* v. *Glasgow Royal Infirmary*, 1909 S.C. 916; *cf. Re Diplock* [1948] Ch. 465; affd. [1951] A.C. 251.
[73] *Lamond's Trs.* v. *Croom* (1871) 9 M. 662, 671.
[74] *Smith* v. *Patrick* (1901) 3 F.(H.L.) 14; *cf. Lees* v. *Dun*, 1912 S.C. 50, 66.
[75] See *Re Walker* (1890) 62 L.T. 449.
[76] See *Re Somerset* [1894] 1 Ch. 231; *cf. Boyd* v. *Greig*, 1913, 1 S.L.T. 398; *Wood* (1893) 1 S.L.T. 309. See also *Raes* v. *Meek* (1889) 16 R.(H.L.) 31; *Crabbe* v. *Whyte* (1891) 18 R. 1065; *Fry* v. *Tapson* (1884) 28 Ch.D. 268; *Re Stuart* [1897] 2 Ch. 583; *Shaw* v. *Cates* [1909] 1 Ch. 389.

Section 30 is declared to apply to transfers of existing securities as well as to new securities, and in its application to a partial transfer of an existing security the expression " the amount of the loan " shall include the amount of any other loan or loans upon the property ranking prior to or *pari passu* with the loan in question.[77]

Section 33 further provides that a trustee is not to be liable for breach of trust by reason only of his continuing to hold an investment which has ceased to be an investment authorised by the trust deed or by or under the Act.

Effect of immunity clauses

In defence to a claim of damages for breach of trust the trustee may be able to invoke an express clause of immunity in the trust deed, or seek to bring himself within the protection afforded by statute. It is very doubtful if a truster can confer complete immunity on his trustees by any express words in the trust deed. The trend of decisions is that such clauses confer no protection beyond that open as a defence at common law [78]; while they may protect trustees who have committed mere errors of judgment, such clauses are quite ineffectual to protect a trustee from the consequences of *culpa lata*, or gross negligence, or of any conduct inconsistent with bona fides,[79] or a positive breach of law,[80] or conduct inconsistent with the trustee's fundamental duty of care.[81] Even where the fault alleged against the trustee had been provided for in exact terms in the clause of immunity in the trust deed, the House of Lords have held that the trustee was liable for his default.[82] More recently it has been observed that it is hard to imagine any clause of indemnity in a trust settlement capable of being construed to the effect that the trustees might with impunity neglect to exercise their duties as trustees, or that they should be licensed to perform their duty carelessly.[83]

A clause of immunity may be framed so as to exclude liability on certain specified grounds but it would appear that, while a truster may define the duties of his trustees and exclude their liability in those respects usually incidental to their office, in which case the court will not impose on the trustees a more onerous liability,[84] any such clause is subordinate to the general principle that there is a fundamental duty on a trustee to exercise care in the execution of the trust. Hence it has been held that immunity

77 s. 30 (2).

78 McLaren, § 2281; Mackenzie Stuart, 377; see also *Seton* v. *Dawson* (1841) 4 D. 310; *Knox* v. *Mackinnon* (1888) 15 R.(H.L.) 83; *Alexander* v. *Johnstone* (1899) 1 F. 639; *Carruthers* v. *Cairns* (1890) 17 R. 769; *Wilson* v. *Guthrie Smith* (1894) 2 S.L.T. 338; *Melville* v. *Noble's Trs.* (1896) 24 R. 243; *Raes* v. *Meek* (1889) 16 R.(H.L.) 31.

79 *Knox* v. *Mackinnon* (1888) 15 R.(H.L.) 83, 86, *per* Lord Watson.

80 *Ferguson* v. *Paterson* (1900) 2 F.(H.L.) 37.

81 *Clarke* v. *Clarke's Trs.*, 1925 S.C. 693.

82 *Raes* v. *Meek* (1888) 15 R. 1033; revd. (1889) 16 R.(H.L.) 31.

83 *Clarke* v. *Clarke's Trs.*, 1925 S.C. 693, 707, *per* L.P. Clyde.

84 *Wilkins* v. *Hogg* (1861) 31 L.J.Ch. 41; *Pass* v. *Dundas* (1880) 43 L.T. 665.

from liability for "neglect of any sort" did not absolve a trustee who had neglected to ingather trust funds.[85]

An immunity clause exempting a trustee from liability except "for his actual intromissions" protected a trustee for the loss of a debt irrecoverable through his negligence.[86] But such a clause did not protect one trustee when a debt was incurred by another trustee who went bankrupt,[87] or possibly when another trustee went bankrupt thereby losing the balance of the trust estate.[88] It has been questioned how far an immunity clause was effectual to protect a trustee who had himself taken no share in the management of the trust funds, but had concurred in enabling the co-trustee to uplift the funds.[89]

Statutory clause of immunity

Section 3 (*d*) of the Trusts (Scotland) Act 1921 enacts that all trusts shall, unless the contrary be expressed, be held to include a provision that each trustee shall be liable only for his own acts and intromissions and shall not be liable for the acts and intromissions of co-trustees and shall not be liable for omissions. This extends to all trustees, gratuitous or not.[90] It does not relieve the trustee from liability to account for his intromissions with any matter in which he has participated, such as signing a disposition or receipt.[91] This provision does not appear to confer on trustees any protection which they would not enjoy without it. It certainly does not free them from the consequences of negligence or positive breaches of duty.[92]

This clause has no effect on the liability of a trustee for acts of his co-trustees. At common law he is only liable for their actings in so far as he has authorised or ratified them, expressly or by implication.[93] There are three main ways in which a trustee may become liable to answer for the acts of his co-trustees: Where the trustee receives money and transmits it to his co-trustees without taking any steps for its proper application; where the trustee permits a co-trustee to receive trust-estate and makes no due inquiry as to his disposal thereof; and where he becomes aware of a breach of trust, either in contemplation or in fact performed, and fails to take the necessary steps to obtain redress or restoration of the trust property.[94] Such cases would obviously not be covered by the immunity clause, as they truly arise from the fault of the trustee himself; though the actual loss

85 *Thomson* v. *Christie* (1852) 1 Macq. 236.
86 *Fraser's Trs.* v. *Falconer* (1830) 9 S. 178.
87 *Gordon* v. *Wishart* (1834) 12 S. 369.
88 *McNair* v. *Broomfield* (1830) 8 S. 968.
89 *McMillan* v. *Armstrong* (1848) 11 D. 191.
90 s. 2. See also McLaren, §§ 2267 *et seq.*
91 *Lees's Trs.* v. *Dun*, 1913 S.C.(H.L.) 12; *Seton* v. *Dawson* (1841) 4 D. 310; *Wyman* v. *Paterson* (1900) 2 F.(H.L.) 37.
92 *Knox* v. *Mackinnon* (1888) 15 R.(H.L.) 83, 86. See also *City of Glasgow Bank* v. *Parkhurst* (1880) 7 R. 749, 753; *Carruthers* v. *Carruthers* (1896) 23 R.(H.L.) 55; *Ferguson* v. *Paterson* (1900) 2 F.(H.L.) 37; *Alexander* v. *Johnstone* (1899) 1 F. 639; *Seton* v. *Dawson* (1841) 4 D. 310.
93 Ersk. III, 3, 36; Bell, *Prin.* § 2000; McLaren, § 217.
94 *Wilkins* v. *Hogg* (1861) 31 L.J.Ch. 41.

may be the default of the other the first trustee's negligence was a *sine qua non*. It has, however, to be inferred from this provision that trustees in office are liable for their own intromissions only and are entitled to a discharge in respect of their own acts and intromissions only, irrespective of the discharge of their predecessors in office.[94a]

Statutory relief

Section 32 of the Trusts (Scotland) Act 1921 provides that when a trustee is personally liable for breach of trust he may be relieved by the court. It provides—(1) If it appears to the court that a trustee is or may be personally liable for any breach of trust, whether the transaction alleged to be a breach of trust occurred before or after the passing of this Act, but has acted honestly and reasonably, and ought fairly to be excused for the breach of trust then the court may relieve the trustee either wholly or partly from personal liability for the same. The court in question is (subs. (2)) any court of competent jurisdiction in which a question relative to the actings, liability or removal of a trustee comes to be tried.

To entitle it to grant relief from liability under this section the court must be satisfied, the onus being on the trustee,[95] that the conduct of the trustee has been both honest and reasonable and further that he ought reasonably to be excused.[96] It is not sufficient that he has been honest, and negligence infers unreasonableness so that, despite honesty, there is want of such reasonable conduct as to bring him within the provisions of the section.[97] Honesty is more easily determined, but the question of whether a trustee's conduct has been reasonable may be one of difficulty. The court will consider whether a prudent man would have taken that course.[98] Complete reliance on a co-trustee probably excludes honesty.[99] Relief may be given where the breach of trust has been caused by a construction of a provision of the trust-deed which is not unreasonable in the circumstances, even though it may ultimately be held by the court to be incorrect.[1] But this does not extend to permitting trustees to act on their own interpretation in a case of grave doubt when they should, and must if they are to be held as acting reasonably, obtain skilled advice.[2] Trustees have been relieved where they made a proper sale of property, but had no power of sale.[3]

Nor is a trustee liable for a breach of trust if this ensues in consequence

94a *Mackenzies' Exor* v. *Thomson's Trs.*, 1965 S.C. 154.
95 *Re Stuart* [1897] 2 Ch. 583.
96 *Re Stuart* [1897] 2 Ch. 583; *Re Turner* [1897] 1 Ch. 536.
97 *Clarke* v. *Clarke's Trs.*, 1925 S.C. 693; *Re Stuart*, *Smith* v. *Stuart* [1897] 2 Ch. 583; *Chapman* v. *Brown* [1902] 1 Ch. 785; *National Trs. Co. of Australasia* v. *General Finance Co. of Australasia* [1905] A.C. 373.
98 *Re Turner*, *supra*; *cf. Re Grindey* [1898] 2 Ch. 593.
99 *Re Second East Dulwich Building Socy.* (1899) 68 L.J.Ch. 196.
1 *Re Grindey*, *Clews* v. *Grindey* [1898] 2 Ch. 593; *Re Allsop*, *Whittaker* v. *Bamford* [1914] 1 Ch. 1; *Re Claridge's Patent Asphalte Co.* [1921] 1 Ch. 543; *Re Mackay*, *Greissemann* v. *Carr* [1911] 1 Ch. 300; see also *Warren's J. F.* v. *Warren's Exrx.* (1903) 5 F. 890.
2 *Clarke* v. *Clarke's Trs.*, 1925 S.C. 693.
3 *Perrins* v. *Bellamy* [1899] 1 Ch. 797.

of being deceived by the language of a statutory provision, at least when there is no decision on the matter.[4] Similarly it has been held not to be breach of trust to follow a well-established practice, even though it may be subsequently disapproved.[5] The immunity does not cover a failure by a trustee to observe an unambiguous statutory direction such as concerning forbidden investments [6] or independent valuation of heritage over which a loan is to be granted.[7]

Furthermore, having established that his conduct has been both honest and reasonable, the trustee must still satisfy the court that he ought fairly to be excused for his breach of trust in the circumstances of the particular case. This section has been narrowly construed particularly as the granting of relief will generally be prejudicial to the interests of creditors and beneficiaries. Each case falls to be considered on its own facts.[8]

In England the corresponding section [9] has been applied to a case where trustees made a mistake in law, as by selling trust estate when there was no power of sale,[10] where there was doubt whether any liability on the ground of negligence was incumbent on the trustee,[11] where loss was caused by failure to ingather the estate when it was believed that proceedings were useless,[12] where excessive confidence in and reliance on the trust law-agent made embezzlement possible [13]; where payments were made in error, though on expert advice later held to be wrong,[14] and where money was paid to a law-agent to meet death duties allegedly due and it was misappropriated.[15]

The relief section will not however protect trustees who neglect to supervise their co-trustees. Nor does it cover the actings of non-gratuitous trustees who make payments in error,[16] nor any trustee who acts as a trustee as part of his professional business, such as an accountant acting as a liquidator.[17] The section does, however, extend to the right of creditors as well as of beneficiaries.[18] It does not protect a trustee who concurs in an improper investment in reliance on the superior knowledge of a co-trustee,[19] nor one who permits trust-moneys to be received by a solicitor-trustee and paid into his firm's account,[20] nor one who accepts the state-

[4] *Ogle* (1873) 8 Ch.App. 711, 715.
[5] *Horne* v. *Pringle* (1841) 2 Rob.App. 384. But see *Rennie* v. *Morison* (1849) 6 Bell's App. 422.
[6] *Chapman* v. *Browne* [1902] 1 Ch. 785.
[7] *Re Stuart, Smith* v. *Stuart* [1897] 2 Ch. 583.
[8] *Re Turner, Baker* v. *Ivimey* [1897] 1 Ch. 536; *Re Kay, Mosley* v. *Keyworth* [1897] 2 Ch. 518; *Re Mackay, Greissemann* v. *Carr* [1911] 1 Ch. 300.
[9] Trustee Act 1925, s. 61.
[10] *Perrins* v. *Bellamy* [1899] 1 Ch. 797.
[11] *Re Grindey, Clews* v. *Grindey* [1898] 2 Ch. 593.
[12] *Re Roberts, Knight* v. *Roberts* (1897) 76 L.T. 479.
[13] *Re Lord de Clifford, De Clifford* v. *Quilter* [1900] 2 Ch. 707.
[14] *Re Allsop, Whittaker* v. *Bamford* [1914] 1 Ch. 1; *Re Claridge's Patent Asphalte Co.* [1921] 1 Ch. 543.
[15] *Re Mackay* [1911] 1 Ch. 300.
[16] *Nat. Trs. Co. of Australasia* v. *Gen. Finance Co. of Australasia* [1905] A.C. 373.
[17] *Re Windsor Steam Coal Co.* [1929] 1 Ch. 151.
[18] *Re Kay, Mosley* v. *Keyworth* [1897] 2 Ch. 518; *Re Windsor Steam Coal Co., supra.*
[19] *Re Turner* [1897] 1 Ch. 536.
[20] *Wynne* v. *Tempest* (1897) 13 T.L.R. 360.

ments of a co-trustee without inquiry,[21] but it is not confined to executive and administrative acts and relief may in appropriate circumstances be granted where payment has been made to the wrong person.[22]

Relief against co-trustees and beneficiaries

It has been held that where a trustee, in breach of trust, makes an investment which is improper, even the express approval and knowledge by the beneficiary does not imply an obligation to relieve the trustee of his personal liability for loss incurred thereon.[23] It may at most bar that beneficiary from making any claim upon the trustee in consequence of his breach but no more.[24] According to English authority a trustee may claim to be indemnified by a beneficiary against the consequences of a breach of trust committed at the request and for the benefit of that beneficiary.[25] Under section 31 of the Trusts (Scotland) Act 1921, it is provided that "where a trustee shall have committed a breach of trust at the instigation or request or with the consent in writing [26] of a beneficiary, the court [27] may, if it shall think fit, make such order as to the court shall seem just for applying all or any part of the interest of the beneficiary in the trust estate by way of indemnity to the trustee or person claiming through him." This section does not, however, give any ground of personal action to the trustee against the beneficiary. It is necessary that the instigation, request or consent should be to do something which the beneficiary knows to be a breach of trust or reasonably should have known from facts in his possession. It must be shown that the beneficiary knew that a breach of trust was involved, if it is sought to found on the instigation or consent of a beneficiary.[28] The act involved must moreover be one which is necessarily a breach of trust and not merely one which provides an opportunity for negligence or carelessness of the trustee to make it a breach of trust, as a beneficiary is entitled to rely on the trustee, acting with due care and within his powers.[29] *Ex post facto* approval does not fall within the section.[30] The section, moreover, is only permissive, enabling the trustee to ask the court to exercise its judicial discretion in his favour. It gives the trustee no absolute right to demand relief.[31]

21 *Re Second East Dulwich, etc. Building Socy.* (1899) 68 L.J.Ch. 196.

22 *Re Allsop* [1914] 1 Ch. 1; *cf. Re Windsor, supra.*

23 *Sanders* v. *Sanders' Trustees* (1879) 7 R. 157; *City of Glasgow Bank* v. *Parkhurst* (1880) 7 R. 749.

24 *City of Glasgow Bank* v. *Parkhurst* (1880) 7 R. 749; *Raes* v. *Meek* (1889) 16 R.(H.L.) 31; *Cathcart's Trs.* v. *Cathcart* (1907) 15 S.L.T. 646; *Fletcher* v. *Collis* [1905] 2 Ch. 24.

25 *Chillingworth* v. *Chambers* [1896] 1 Ch. 685.

26 "In writing" applies to "consent" only: *Griffith* v. *Hughes* [1892] 3 Ch. 105; *Re Somerset* [1894] 1 Ch. 265; *Mara* v. *Browne* [1895] 2 Ch. 92.

27 Any court of competent jurisdiction: s. 32 (2).

28 *Henderson's Trs.* v. *Henderson* (1900) 2 F. 1295; *Cathcart's Trs.* v. *Cathcart* (1907) 15 S.L.T. 646; *Re Somerset, Somerset* v. *Earl Poulett* [1894] 1 Ch. 231; *Mara* v. *Browne* [1895] 2 Ch. 69.

29 *Cathcart's Trs., supra.*

30 *Henderson's Trs., supra.*

31 *Henderson's Trs., supra*; *Re Somerset, supra.*

As between trustees and a third party who has obtained the ultimate benefit of a breach of trust, the trustees are primarily liable to reimburse the trust estate, but the loss will eventually fall on the party who gained by the breach of trust if the trustee can follow the trust property and recover it.[32]

Trustees who have committed a breach of trust are liable jointly and severally so that any one has a claim for rateable relief against the others.[33] But in certain circumstances, though both or all trustees are equally liable in a question with the beneficiary, one may be entitled to full indemnity from the others *inter se*, if the one trustee has himself benefited from the breach of trust or if the court feels justified in treating that one as solely responsible for the breach of trust.[34]

In one case a trustee was found liable to make good to the trust a sum lost by improper investment, but his liability was limited by the House of Lords so that no benefit should arise therefrom to beneficiaries who had been also trustees and had taken part in the breach of trust.[35]

In *Johnstone* v. *Thorburn* [36] an unsuccessful attempt was made to obtain relief in respect of loss on an imprudent investment from the law agent of the trust.

In *Wilson* v. *Smith's Trustees* [37] one trustee had lent to the body of trustees money to settle an outstanding account and later sued them for repayment. He had during the currency of the loan accepted simple interest on the loan for recovery of which the trustees counterclaimed. The original loan was held to be voidable, the pursuer having been *auctor in rem suam*, but he was held not bound to repay the interest to the trust estate.

Again in *Cherry's Trs.* v. *Patrick* [38] a trustee had had business dealings with the truster and continued them afterwards with his trustees. The co-trustees sued for repayment to the trust estate of the profits therefrom and it was held that the trustee must communicate the profits he had made to the trust estate.

Acquiescence in breach of trust

The parties entitled to challenge a breach of trust may acquiesce or concur in it and even ratify it, in which case the actings of the trustees are unchallengeable. But before such a case can arise it must be shown that all parties with a vested or contingent interest in the trust estate, and in the

32 *Re Hallett's Estate* (1880) 13 Ch.D. 696; *Sinclair* v. *Brougham* [1914] A.C. 388. *Cf. Carson* v. *Sloane* (1884) 13 L.R.Ir. 139; *Price* v. *Blakemore*, 6 Beav. 507.

33 *Pearson* v. *Houston's Trs.* (1868) 6 M. 286; *Croskery* v. *Gilmour's Trs.* (1890) 17 R. 697; *Palmer* v. *Wick and Pulteneytown S.S. Co.* (1894) 21 R.(H.L.) 39; *Chillingworth* v. *Chambers* [1896] 1 Ch. 685.

34 *Bahin* v. *Hughes* (1886) 31 Ch.D. 390, 394; *Re Turner* [1897] 1 Ch. 536; *Jackson* v. *Dickinson* [1903] 1 Ch. 947; *Blyth* v. *Fladgate* [1891] 1 Ch. 337.

35 *Raes* v. *Meek* (1889) 16 R.(H.L.) 31.

36 (1901) 3 F. 497.

37 1939 S.L.T. 120; *cf. Perston* v. *Perston's Trs.* (1863) 1 M. 245.

38 1911, 2 S.L.T. 313.

full knowledge of their rights, had consented to the course of action alleged to amount to a breach of trust.[39] Thus where a solicitor trustee paid his firm for professional services to the trust without authority and all but two of the beneficiaries had consented in writing, it was held that a succeeding trustee was entitled to sue for recovery of the fees paid.[40] Parties can be held to have concurred in a breach of trust only if they had the means of knowing that the actings to which they were parties were breaches of trust.[41]

Acquiescence in a breach of trust may bar a claim against the trustee after the lapse of less than twenty years, particularly where combined with alteration of position to the trustee's detriment,[42] but while acquiescence may bar challenge of a past breach it can never give a trustee the right to perpetuate a breach of trust.[43] Nor is a beneficiary who recovers from the trustee part of the relief to which the trustee is entitled, as a means of saving something of the loss, to be held thereby to have given up his rights to full relief.[44]

Prescription

The long negative prescription will not preclude a trustee, even when retired from the trust, from being called on to account for his intromissions[45] and no lapse of time will bar a claim by a beneficiary for trust property so long as it remains extant in the hands of the trustee,[46] but a personal claim of damages against a present or former trustee may be barred by the lapse of the prescriptive period.[47] Fraud on the part of the trustee will, however, prevent the running of prescription until at least from the date when the fraudulent breach could reasonably have been discovered.[48]

39 *Taylor* v. *Hillhouse* (1901) 9 S.L.T. 31; *Henderson* v. *Watson*, 1939 S.C. 711.

40 *Henderson* v. *Watson*, 1939 S.C. 711.

41 *Re Somerset* [1894] 1 Ch. 231; *Seath* v. *Taylor* (1848) 10 D. 377; *cf. Bain* v. *Assets Co.* (1905) 7 F.(H.L.) 104, 108.

42 *Thomson* v. *Eastwood* (1877) 2 App.Cas. 215, 257; *Cullen* v. *Wemyss* (1838) 1 D. 32; *Robson* v. *Bywater* (1870) 8 M. 757; see also *Howden* v. *Howden* (1841) 3 D. 388; *Douglas* v. *Murray* (1797) 4 Paton 4, 9, 11; *York Buildings Co.* v. *Mackenzie* (1795) 3 Paton 378; *Jeffrey* v. *Aitken* (1826) 4 S. 722.

43 *Thain* v. *Thain* (1891) 18 R. 1196, 1201; *cf. Ferguson Bequest Fund Case* (1879) 6 R. 486.

44 *Re Cross* (1882) 20 Ch.D. 109, 122; *cf. Cochrane* v. *Black* (1855) 17 D. 321.

45 *Hastie's J. F.* v. *Morham's Executors*, 1951 S.C. 668.

46 *Aberdeen University* v. *Irvine* (1868) 6 M.(H.L.) 29; *Aberdeen Magistrates* v. *Aberdeen University* (1877) 4 R.(H.L.) 48; *Bertram, Gardner & Co.* v. *K. & L. T. R.*, 1920 S.C. 555; *Cooper Scott* v. *Gill Scott*, 1924 S.C. 309.

47 *Pollock* v. *Porterfield* (1778) Mor. 10702; (1779) 2 Paton 495; *Barns* v. *Barns' Trs.* (1857) 19 D. 626; *Murray* v. *Mackenzie* (1897) 34 S.L.R. 571. See also *Hastie's J. F., supra.*

48 *Thorne* v. *Heard* [1894] 1 Ch. 599, 605; affd. [1895] A.C. 495; *Bulli* v. *Osborne* [1899] A.C. 351; *Fife* v. *Duff* (1887) 15 R. 238.

CHAPTER 59

BREACH OF STATUTORY DUTY

IN many circumstances statutes, or regulations made under statutory authority and having equivalent force, impose statutory duties on individuals. Prima facie the sanction for failure to implement a statutory duty is prosecution and punishment in the criminal courts, and provision is normally made in the statute for such prosecution and punishment. Indeed a statutory duty is frequently imposed only by inference, the statute providing expressly only that a person who does this or that, or fails to do this or that, shall be liable to prosecution, and only inferentially creating a legal duty not to do this or that, or to do this or that. If no sanction is expressly provided it is implied that prosecution on indictment, as for a common law offence, is competent, as it cannot be assumed that Parliament intended merely to express a pious exhortation. But in many cases it has been argued that the breach of a statutory duty, resulting in harm or injury to the pursuer, gives him a civil remedy, by way of ordinary action of damages. And it is occasionally provided that breach of a particular statutory duty is actionable but does not give rise to criminal proceedings.[1]

Nature of action for breach of statutory duty

A civil action claiming damages for loss or injury caused by the defender's breach of a statutory duty presents an apparent parallel to an action claiming damages for loss or injury caused by the defender's breach of a common-law duty. There are, however, material differences. " The authorities [2] show clearly that a claim for damages for breach of a statutory duty intended to protect a person in the position of the particular plaintiff is a specific common law right which is not to be confused in essence with a claim for negligence. The statutory right has its origin in the statute, but the particular remedy of an action for damages is given by the common law in order to make effective, for the benefit of the injured plaintiff, his right to the performance by the defendant of the defendant's statutory duty. It is an effective sanction. It is not a claim in negligence in the strict or ordinary sense. As I said in *Caswell's* case: ' I do not think that an action for breach of a statutory duty such as that in question is completely or accurately described as an action in negligence. It is a common law action based on the purpose of the statute to protect the workman, and belongs to the category often described as that of cases of

[1] *e.g.* Restrictive Trade Practices Act 1956, s. 24 (6) and (7); Resale Prices Act 1964, s. 4.
[2] Citing *Caswell* v. *Powell Duffryn Assoc. Collieries* [1940] A.C. 152; *Lewis* v. *Denye* [1940] A.C. 921; *Sparks* v. *Edward Ash Ltd.* [1943] 1 K.B. 223.

strict or absolute liability. At the same time it resembles actions in negligence in that the claim is based on a breach of a duty to take care for the safety of the workman. But whatever the resemblances, it is essential to keep in mind the fundamental differences of the two classes of claim . . . . the same damage may be caused by action which might equally be characterised as ordinary negligence at common law or as breach of the statutory duty. On the other hand, the damage may be due either to negligence or to breach of the statutory duty. . . .' "[3]

The differences are: the source of the duty to have regard for the interest of the pursuer; most importantly, whether breach of the duty was intended to give a remedy by way of civil action for damages at all, or to be sanctioned only in some other way; frequently, the standard of duty of care imposed; and the qualifications on liability or defences available.

Interests protected by statutory duties

While a statutory duty is not uncommonly imposed to protect interests in personal safety, health and welfare, in some cases statutes have been held to have protected interests in public rights, such as the right to vote,[4] or interests in land,[5] or in moveable property, or in economic rights.[6]

An action for damages for breach of statutory duty is rarely permitted against a public authority, on the ground that the duty is one owed to the whole community, not merely to the pursuer, or the pursuer *inter alios*.[7]

Whether Act in force

Before an individual can recover damages for injury or loss to him allegedly resulting from the breach of the statutory duty, he must satisfy the court that the section of the Act, or the regulation, imposing the statutory duty he founds on is in force. If not, it does not impose any duty.

That Act imposes a duty

It must furthermore be apparent from the section of the Act, or the regulation, in question that it imposes a duty, and not merely confers a discretionary power. No action lies for loss caused by mere failure to exercise a power, unless the power can be construed as one which the defender was bound to exercise, which is the case where the object of the statutory power is to effectuate a legal right, whether it be vested in the public or a private person.[8]

[3] *L.P.T.B.* v. *Upson* [1949] A.C. 155, 168, *per* Lord Wright.

[4] *Ashby* v. *White* (1703) 2 Ld.Raym. 938; but contrast *Watt* v. *Kesteven C.C.* [1955] 1 Q.B. 408.

[5] *Ross* v. *Rugge-Price* (1876) 1 Ex.D. 269.

[6] *Balkis Consolidated Co.* v. *Tomkinson* [1893] A.C. 396; *Simmonds* v. *Newport Abercarn Coal Co.* [1921] 1 K.B. 616; *Moore* v. *Canadian Pacific S.S. Co.* [1945] 1 All E.R. 128.

[7] *Saunders* v. *Holborn District Board of Works* [1895] 1 Q.B. 64; *Watt, supra.*

[8] *Julius* v. *Bishop of Oxford* (1880) 5 App.Cas. 214, 241; *cf. Gray* v. *St. Andrews District Cttee*, 1911 S.C. 266, 278; *Degan* v. *Dundee Corpn.*, 1940 S.C. 457, 464; *Fleming & Ferguson* v. *Paisley Mags.*, 1948 S.C. 547, 553, 561.

Whether duty incumbent on defender

The court must also be satisfied that the duty is one imposed on the defender, and not on the pursuer himself,[9] or only on a third party.

If, however, the duty is imposed on the defender he cannot evade liability by saying that he had appointed reasonably competent persons to see to its implement and that the non-implement was their fault,[10] or that the fault was that of his independent contractor.[11]

To whom duty owed

If breach is to be actionable the duty must have been owed to, *inter alios*, the pursuer, and not to other persons only, nor to the general public only. A factory occupier may owe duties of care to the employee of an independent contractor [12] and to any person legitimately present on the premises [13] as well as to his own employees.[14]

Whether Act applicable

Furthermore the pursuer in any such claim must satisfy the court that the section of the Act, or the regulation, which imposes the duty, breach of which he founds on as giving him a civil remedy, was at the material time applicable to the place or kind of premises or circumstances in which the alleged contravention, resulting in loss or injury, took place. If it is not, there is no duty incumbent on the defender.[15] Similarly if the duty does not extend to the place where the happening took place, there is no breach by reason of the happening.[16]

Whether statutory provision gives civil claim

The question which has not infrequently arisen, and which is the most important, and difficult, in this category of case, is whether an alleged breach of a statutory duty, alleged to have caused loss, injury or damage to the pursuer, is a ground of civil action for damages at all, or is a ground for prosecution only, or for the grant of some special kind of remedy provided by the Act.

This raises a question of statutory interpretation, of whether Parliament intended that an injured person was to be entitled to recover damages, as to which " the only rule which in all circumstances is valid is that the answer must depend on a consideration of the whole Act and the circum-

9 *e.g. Harrison* v. *N.C.B.* [1951] A.C. 639.
10 *McMullan* v. *Lochgelly Iron Co.*, 1933 S.C.(H.L.) 64.
11 *Hosking* v. *De Havilland Aircraft Co.* [1949] 1 All E.R. 540.
12 *McWilliams* v. *Arrol*, 1962 S.C.(H.L.) 70.
13 *Ward* v. *Coltness Iron Co.*, 1944 S.C. 318.
14 *e.g. Ashwood* v. *Steel Co. of Scotland*, 1957 S.C. 17.
15 *e.g. Riddell* v. *Reid*, 1942 S.C.(H.L.) 51 (premises); *Parvin* v. *Morton Machine Co.*, 1952 S.C.(H.L.) 9 (duty to fence machinery not applicable to machinery being made or tested); *Neeson* v. *Denny & Bros. Ltd.*, 1962 S.C. 153 (precaution desiderated not necessary); *Gardiner* v. *Admiralty Commrs.*, 1964 S.C.(H.L.) 85 (premises).
16 *Kirby* v. *N.C.B.*, 1958 S.C. 514.

stances, including the pre-existing law, in which it was enacted." [17] "In every case the problem is to ascertain the intention of Parliament from the terms of the statute—whether any and, if so, what civil liability is to be implied." [18]

Indications of parliamentary intent

Various factors have in various cases been held to yield some indication of Parliament's intention.

Whether existing common law affords a remedy

A relevant factor in deciding whether or not an action lies for harm caused by breach of statutory duty is whether there exists at common law an adequate right of action for loss or harm caused in such circumstances. If so the view may more readily be reached that the statutory requirements were imposed to try to minimise the occurrence of circumstances giving rise to harm requiring remedy by common law, rather than to confer a parallel right of action. Thus statutory requirements relative to the construction and use, and management, of vehicles have generally been held not to give any right of action independent of that recognised at common law.[19] If, however, no right of action is recognised at common law for loss or harm caused in circumstances struck at by the statutory provision, it is easier to hold that the statute has created a new right of action.

No sanction prescribed

If a statutory duty is prescribed, but no sanction by way of penalty or otherwise for its breach is imposed, it can be assumed that a right of civil action accrues to the person who is damnified by the breach. For, if it were not so, the statute would be but a pious aspiration.[20]

Sanction prescribed

The general rule is that where an Act creates an obligation, and enforces the performance in a specified manner, that performance cannot be enforced in any other manner [21] than by the sanction. The sanction of criminal proceedings suggests that the statutory duty is imposed for the public benefit, and that the breach of it is a public and not a private wrong.[22]

"Where damages are claimed for breach of a statutory duty without any allegation of negligence, the pursuer must establish two things, first that the breach is intended, not only to be visited by a penalty, but also

[17] *Cutler* v. *Wandsworth Stadium* [1949] A.C. 398, 407, *per* Lord Simonds.

[18] *Grant* v. *N.C.B.*, 1956 S.C.(H.L.) 48, 57, *per* Lord Reid.

[19] *e.g. Phillips* v. *Britannia Hygienic Laundry Co.* [1923] 2 K.B. 832 (defective axle); *Clarke* v. *Brims* [1947] K.B. 497 (failure to exhibit red tail light); *Balmer* v. *Hayes*, 1950 S.C. 477 (failure to disclose liability to fits, when applying for licence).

[20] *Cutler, supra*, 407, *per* Lord Simonds; 413, *per* Lord Normand.

[21] *Doe* v. *Bridges* (1831) 1 B. & A. 847, 859, approved *Pasmore* v. *Oswaldtwistle U.D.C.* [1898] A.C. 387, 394, cited *Phillips* v. *Britannia Hygienic Laundry Co.* [1923] 2 K.B. 832.

[22] *Cutler, supra*, 408 *per* Lord Simonds.

to be the ground of civil liability to a class of persons of whom the pursuer is one, and secondly that the injury was one against which the legislation was designed to protect him." [23]

But whether this general rule is to prevail, or an exception to the general rule be admitted, must depend on the scope and language of the Act which creates the obligation and on considerations of policy and convenience.[24]

It may be that, though a specific remedy is provided by the Act, the injured person has a personal right of action in addition, as in cases where the major object of the statute is to compel the taking of safety precautions and the persons for whose benefit the precautions must be taken are the persons exposed to danger. When a duty of this kind is imposed for the benefit of particular persons, there arises at common law a correlative right in those persons who may be injured by its contravention.[25] The inference that there is a concurrent right of civil action is easily drawn where the predominant purpose is manifestly the protection of a class of workmen by imposing on their employers the duty of taking special measures to secure their safety.[26]

Whether duty to public or to a class of the public

In many cases the decision whether a civil action lies for breach of a statutory duty depends on whether, in the view of the court, the duty has been imposed for the general welfare or the general public benefit, or on the other hand in the interests of individuals or of a defined or definable class of the public on the other.[27] But the fact that the statute was passed for the protection of the public is not conclusive against the existence of a right of civil action. As Atkin L.J. expressed the principle [28]: "The question is not to be solved by considering whether or not the person aggrieved can bring himself within some special class of the community or whether he is some designated individual. The duty may be of such paramount importance that it is owed to all the public. It would be strange if a less important duty, which is owed to a section of the public, may be enforced by an action, while a more important duty owed to the public at large cannot. The right of action does not depend on whether a statutory commandment or prohibition is pronounced for the benefit of the public or for the benefit of a class. It may be conferred on anyone who can bring himself within the benefit of the Act, including one who cannot be otherwise specified than as a person using the highway."

23 *Grant* v. *N.C.B.*, 1956 S.C.(H.L.) 48, 52, *per* Viscount Simonds L.C.

24 *Atkinson* v. *Newcastle Waterworks Co.* (1877) 2 Ex.D. 441; *Cowley* v. *Newmarket Local Board* [1892] A.C. 34; *Pasmore, supra*, 397, *per* Lord Macnaghten.

25 *Kelly* v. *Glebe Sugar Refining Co.* (1893) 20 R. 833; *Groves* v. *Wimborne* [1898] 2 Q.B. 402; *Black* v. *Fife Coal Co.*, 1912 S.C.(H.L.) 33, 45; *McMullan* v. *Lochgelly Iron Co.*, 1933 S.C. (H.L.) 64, 70; *Monk* v. *Warbey* [1935] 1 K.B. 75; *Riddell* v. *Reid*, 1942 S.C.(H.L.) 51, 60.

26 *Black, supra*; *Cutler, supra, per* Lord Normand.

27 *Gorris* v. *Scott* (1874) L.R. 9 Ex. 125; *Solomons* v. *Gertzenstein* [1954] 2 All E.R. 625, 637, *per* Romer L.J.

28 *Phillips* v. *Britannia Hygienic Laundry Co.* [1923] 2 K.B. 832, 841, followed in *Monk* v. *Warbey* [1935] 1 K.B. 75; *Square* v. *Model Farm Dairies Ltd.* [1935] 2 K.B. 365; *Clarke* v. *Brims* [1947] K.B. 497.

Furthermore, if the class of persons for whose protection it is alleged that the duty was imposed is indefinite and difficult to define, this would tend to exclude the construction of the section which would give a right to damages for breach and would favour the view that Parliament intended the sanction of prosecution for a penalty as appropriate and sufficient for the obligation imposed. But where on the other hand the predominant purpose of the statute is manifestly the protection of a particular class of workmen, by imposing on their employers, for instance, the duty of taking special measures to secure their safety, then the inference is readily drawn that Parliament intended to confer on those workmen a right to sue for damages where the duty is not fulfilled.[29]

Whether injured person protected by Act

Even where a breach of statutory duty is held to give a civil claim the pursuer must be within the categories of persons whom the legislation is intended to protect. " Where damages are claimed for breach of a statutory duty without any allegation of negligence, the pursuer must establish two things, first that the breach is intended, not only to be visited by a penalty, but also to be the ground of civil liability *to a class of persons of whom the pursuer is one. . . .*" [30] Thus provisions as to the maintenance of level crossing gates are intended, it has been held, to protect road users from trains and not to protect an engine driver whose engine was struck.[31]

Examples of general rule—no civil claim competent

There have been held to fall under the general rule the following cases: the failure of a water company to keep the water in fire-plug pipes at a prescribed pressure [32]; the failure of a local authority to make such sewers as are necessary for effectually draining their district [33]; failure to comply with a Motor Vehicles (Use and Construction) Order [34]; failure to supply milk free from contamination by germs [35]; sale of a vehicle in a condition so defective that its use would be unlawful [36]; breach of the duty to exhibit a rear light on a vehicle [37]; failure of the occupier of a dog-racing track to provide bookmakers with space to carry on book-making [38]; failure, when applying for a driving licence, to disclose liability to fits [39]; failure to provide means of escape in case of fire [40]; persons

29 *Pullar* v. *Window Clean Ltd.*, 1956 S.C. 13, 21, citing *Cutler, supra*; *Black, supra*; *Bett, supra*; and *Groves, supra.*
30 *Grant* v. *N.C.B.*, 1956 S.C.(H.L.) 48, 52, *per* Viscount Simonds L.C.
31 *Knapp* v. *Railway Executive* [1949] 2 All E.R. 508.
32 *Atkinson* v. *Newcastle Waterworks Co.* (1877) 2 Ex.D. 441.
33 *Pasmore* v. *Oswaldtwistle U.D.C.* [1898] A.C. 387.
34 *Phillips* v. *Britannia Hygienic Laundry Co.* [1923] 2 K.B. 832.
35 *Square* v. *Model Farm Dairies Ltd.* [1939] 2 K.B. 365.
36 *Badham* v. *Lambs* [1946] K.B. 45.
37 *Clarke* v. *Brims* [1947] K.B. 497.
38 *Cutler* v. *Wandsworth Stadium Ltd.* [1949] A.C. 398.
39 *Balmer* v. *Hayes*, 1950 S.C. 477.
40 *Solomons* v. *Gertzenstein* [1954] 2 All E.R. 625.

owning a house the windows of which could not be cleaned from the inside [41]; and a local authority allowing unlicensed cabs to operate.[42]

Example of exception to rule—civil claim competent

There have been held to fall under the exception to the general rule the following cases: the absence from a ship of the required medicines [43]; breach of duty to take precautions for the safety of employees in mines, quarries, factories, etc.[44]; failure to label a fire-plug, which caused delay in extinguishing fire [45]; permitting a car to be used while uninsured [46]; supplying domestic water which, because of defective precautions, was impure [47]; and failure to provide safe means of access to places at which a person had to work.[48]

Scope of the duty—harm sought to be prevented

It is further essential to satisfy the court that the kind of harm alleged to have befallen the pursuer and caused him loss, injury or damage, is the kind of harm, or among the kinds of harms, which the statutory provision in question was aimed at stopping. If a statute is held to be intended to prevent X and a contravention occurs and Y happens the party in breach is not liable. The injury must be " one against which the legislation was designed to protect him." [49] " If the statute is only aimed at preventing a certain kind of injury, then it seems reasonable to hold (as in *Gorris* v. *Scott* [50]) that civil liability only results if that kind of injury is caused by a breach." [51]

Thus actions have failed where an order was made to prevent the spread of disease among animals on board ship, and the plaintiff claimed that by reason of its non-observance his animals were washed overboard [52]; where an Act required machinery to be fenced to prevent operators coming in contact with the machinery and the machinery ejected material being processed.[53]

But the action succeeded where liability under the section founded on was not limited to a class of injuries caused in some particular way.[54]

41 *Pullar* v. *Window Clean Ltd.*, 1956 S.C. 13.
42 *Reid* v. *Mini-cabs*, 1966 S.C. 137.
43 *Couch* v. *Steel* (1854) 3 E. & B. 402.
44 *Britton* v. *Great Western Cotton Co.* (1872) L.R. 7 Ex. 130; *Groves* v. *Wimborne* [1898] 2 Q.B. 402; *Britannic Merthyr Coal Co.* v. *David* [1910] A.C. 74; *Black* v. *Fife Coal Co.*, 1912 S.C.(H.L.) 33; *McMullan* v. *Lochgelly Iron Co.*, 1933 S.C.(H.L.) 64; *Riddell* v. *Reid*, 1942 S.C.(H.L.) 51; *Grant* v. *N.C.B.*, 1956 S.C.(H.L.) 48.
45 *Dawson* v. *Bingley U.D.C.* [1911] 2 K.B. 149.
46 *Monk* v. *Warbey* [1935] 1 K.B. 75; *Houston* v. *Buchanan*, 1940 S.C.(H.L.) 17.
47 *Read* v. *Croydon Corpn.* [1938] 4 All E.R. 631.
48 *Lavender* v. *Diamints Ltd.* [1949] 1 K.B. 585.
49 *Grant* v. *N.C.B.*, 1956 S.C.(H.L.) 48, 52, *per* Viscount Simonds L.C.
50 (1874) L.R. 9 Ex. 125.
51 *Grant*, *supra*, 57, *per* Lord Reid.
52 *Gorris* v. *Scott* (1874) L.R. 9 Ex. 125.
53 *Nicholls* v. *Austin (Leyton) Ltd.* [1946] A.C. 493; *Carroll* v. *Barclay*, 1948 S.C.(H.L.) 100; *Kilgollan* v. *Cooke* [1956] 2 All E.R. 294.
54 *Grant*, *supra*. *Cf. Hall* v. *Fairfield Shipbuilding Co. Ltd.*, 1964 S.C.(H.L.) 72.

Standard of the statutory duty

Whether the standard of diligence required by the statutory duty in question is the normal common law one of taking reasonable care and precautions against the occurrence of harms of kinds reasonably foreseeable, or a more stringent one, or even an absolute duty, held to have been breached if the kind of harm sought to be excluded and prevented happens at all, is a question of interpretation. " Negligence is the failure to use the requisite amount of care required by law in the case where a duty to use care exists. At common law the degree required is that expected of the 'reasonable man.' When a statutory duty is imposed, if it be absolute the degree required is the fulfilment of the statutory obligation. If it be not fulfilled, the person on whom the duty is imposed is negligent: see *McMullan* v. *Lochgelly Iron Co.*,[55] and though the negligence may not amount to criminal negligence so as to constitute an offence, it still may be, and I think must be, negligence sufficient to impose a civil liability. The duty is broken though no crime has been committed." [56]

Qualifications on liability

If there is any qualification on the defenders' liability this must be found in the words of the Act or regulation in question, and the onus is on the defender to show that he is entitled to rely on the qualification,[57] unless the qualifying words are an essential part of the definition of the breach of duty.[58] Prima facie, qualifying words which are directed to affording a defence against criminal responsibility do not affect civil liability for damages.[59]

Whether statutory duty breached

Whether there was or was not a breach of the statutory duty imposed in the particular case is a question of fact.

Causation of the loss or harm

As at common law it must be proved by the pursuer, by the ordinary standard of proof in civil actions, that the breach of statutory duty founded on was the cause of, or at least had materially contributed to, the harm complained of.[60]

Need to prove loss or damage

It may be that a breach of statutory duty is actionable without proof

55 1933 S.C.(H.L.) 64.
56 *Riddell* v. *Reid*, 1942 S.C.(H.L.) 51, 77, *per* Lord Porter.
57 *Britannic Merthyr Coal Co.* v. *David* [1910] A.C. 74; *Watkins* v. *Naval Colliery Co. Ltd.* [1912] A.C. 693, 705; *Smith* v. *Cammell Laird & Co.* [1940] A.C. 242; *Riddell* v. *Reid*, 1942 S.C.(H.L.) 51, 71.
58 *Black* v. *Fife Coal Co.*, 1912 S.C.(H.L.) 33, 44.
59 *Riddell*, *supra*, 71–72, 77.
60 *Wardlaw* v. *Bonnington Castings Ltd.*, 1956 S.C.(H.L.) 26; *McWilliams* v. *Arrol*, 1962 S.C. (H.L.) 70.

of any actual loss or damage, or that loss, injury and damage must be proved or at least circumstances be proved from which some loss may be inferred. This again depends on the particular statute in question, but the courts tend to hold actionable without proof of loss only infringements of rights so fundamental that they must be protected, loss or no loss. This has hitherto been held only in cases of public rights,[61] and not in cases of infringements of the pursuer's interest in his life or person or property.

Limitation by principle of remoteness

There seems to be no authority even suggesting that limitations on claims of damages, under the principle of remoteness of damage, apply any differently to claims for breach of statutory duty from claims for breach of common law duty. It would be very unfortunate and likely to be productive of confusion if there were a difference.

Measure of damages

In the absence of contrary indication in the statute or regulation in question, it may be assumed that damages are recoverable for given kinds of losses, under the same heads, taking account of the same factors, and in the same measure, as in claims brought for loss caused by breach of common law duties.[62] This would appear to be the case in claims for loss caused by personal injuries or death. But any indications in the relevant statute may require a special measure of damages to be applied.

[61] *e.g. Ashby* v. *White* (1703) 2 Ld.Raym. 938 (right to vote); *Ferguson* v. *Kinnoull* (1842) 9 Cl. & F. 251 (right to have minister's suitability for presentation determined).
[62] *e.g. Millar* v. *Galashiels Gas Co.*, 1948 S.C. 191; affd. 1949 S.C.(H.L.) 31.

CHAPTER 60

PRACTICE IN RELATION TO DAMAGES

Transmission of claims of damages—assignation

A claim for damages or solatium once vested in an individual is assignable by him by voluntary assignation in the usual manner and the assignee has then a title to sue in his own name.[1] The assignation may be made at any time within which the person injured might himself have raised an action. The right to sue does not, however, without express assignation, pass to the transferee of damaged property.[2] A joint and several decree may be enforced against one wrongdoer and then assigned to him to enable him to work out his relief against the co-delinquents,[3] though the terms of the Law Reform (Miscellaneous Provisions) (Scotland) Act 1940, s. 3 (2), probably render express assignation quite unnecessary now.[4]

Inheritance of claims

Where an individual has suffered damage by breach of contract the right of action passes on his death to his executors in all cases,[5] save where the claim is expressly left to a particular person.[6] Where an individual has suffered damage by delictual act or omission and then dies, it is necessary to distinguish between patrimonial and personal injury. A right of action for patrimonial loss transmits to the executors of the deceased and may be enforced by them for the benefit of the deceased's estate,[7] or be enforced by a trustee in bankruptcy.[8] If action has been commenced by the deceased before his death, his executors may, of course, be sisted in his place to pursue the action to a conclusion. Thus, claims for damage to a ship or infringement of a patent pass on the death to the executor. A widow has been held entitled as executrix to pursue an action based on slander of and illegal proceedings against her late husband.[9]

In case of personal injuries or slander to the deceased, without patri-

1 *Milne* v. *Gauld's Trs.* (1841) 3 D. 345; *Mein* v. *McCall* (1844) 6 D. 1112; *Neilson* v. *Rodger* (1853) 16 D. 325, 329; *Gardiner* v. *Main* (1895) 22 R. 100; *Traill* v. *A/S Dalbeattie* (1904) 6 F. 798; *Ryan* v. *McBurnie*, 1940 S.C. 173; *Bentley* v. *Macfarlane*, 1963 S.C. 279; *Cole-Hamilton* v. *Boyd*, 1963 S.C.(H.L.) 1.

2 *Symington* v. *Campbell* (1894) 21 R. 434. *Cf. Blumer* v. *Scott* (1874) 1 R. 379.

3 *Palmer* v. *Wick & Pulteneytown S.S. Co.* (1894) 21 R.(H.L.) 39.

4 *Central S.M.T. Co.* v. *Lanarkshire C.C.*, 1949 S.C. 450.

5 *Hinton* v. *Connell's Trs.* (1883) 10 R. 1110; *Morrison* v. *Morrison's Exrx.*, 1912 S.C. 893.

6 *Lyle* v. *Falconer* (1842) 5 D. 236.

7 *Haggart's Trs.* v. *Hope* (1824) 2 Sh.App. 125; *Milne* v. *Gauld's Trs.* (1841) 3 D. 345; *Neilson* v. *Rodger* (1853) 16 D. 325, 329; *Davidson* v. *Tulloch* (1860) 3 Macq. 783; *Gordon* v. *Davidson* (1864) 2 M. 758; *Smith* v. *Stewart*, 1960 S.C. 329.

8 *Riley* v. *Ellis*, 1910 S.C. 934; *Muir's Tr.* v. *Braidwood*, 1958 S.C. 169.

9 *Auld* v. *Shairp* (1874) 2 R. 191; see also *Wight* v. *Burns* (1883) 11 R. 217; *Bern's Exor.* v. *Montrose Asylum* (1893) 20 R. 859; and *cf. Broom* v. *Ritchie* (1904) 6 F. 942.

monial loss, and sounding in solatium only, the claim of damages is personal and only transmits to his executors if an action has been begun by the deceased prior to his death and not completed, in which case his executors may continue it,[10] but not if a claim has been merely intimated by him prior to his death.[11] If the individual has died without taking any steps to enforce his claim for injuries the only title to sue will repose in the relatives entitled to sue in their own right for solatium and patrimonial loss caused to them in consequence of his death.[12] An executor has no title as such to sue an action for damages for personal injury to his deceased predecessor,[13] nor even where he, in the capacity of *curator bonis* to a lunatic, had given instructions to raise an action prior to the death of the lunatic.[14]

Where an action has been begun by a deceased and is carried on by his executor, that excludes any second action by relatives for solatium and patrimonial loss.[15] But an executor's action may be abandoned to allow a relatives' claim,[16] and an executor may sue for patrimonial loss prior to death and relatives for solatium and patrimonial loss, all in one action.[17]

In the case of slander, if the claim is not at least intimated during the lifetime of the injured party it lapses, as relatives have no title to sue for the slander of a now deceased relative unless patrimonial loss can be qualified.[18]

Bankruptcy

A party who is or becomes bankrupt is alone entitled to pursue an action of damages for personal injuries,[19] and the ordinary rule that an undischarged bankrupt may not sue unless he finds caution for expenses, or unless his trustee sists himself as a party,[20] is somewhat modified. An action for vindication of character is sometimes allowed to be brought without finding caution, but only in exceptional circumstances at the court's discretion.[21] Hence no rules can be laid down as to when caution will be dispensed with,[22] but anything unfavourable to the good faith of the action or the prospect of success [23] or even unexplained delay,[24] will weigh against the privilege, and it has usually been ordered,[25] and only

10 *Neilson* v. *Rodger* (1853) 16 D. 325; *Borthwick* v. *Borthwick* (1896) 24 R. 211.

11 *Smith* v. *Stewart*, 1960 S.C. 329, overruling *Leigh's Exrx.* v. *Caledonian Ry.*, 1913 S.C. 838.

12 *Stewart's Exrx.*, v. *L.M.S. Ry.* 1943 S.C.(H.L.) 19.

13 *Bern's Exor.* v. *Montrose Asylum* (1893) 20 R. 859; *Stewart's Exrx.*, *supra*. See also *Riley* v. *Ellis*, 1910 S.C. 934, 944, *per* Ld. Pres. Dunedin.

14 *Boyce's Exor.* v. *MacDougall* (1903) 5 F. 452.

15 *Darling* v. *Gray* (1892) 19 R.(H.L.) 31.

16 *Bruce* v. *Stephen*, 1957 S.L.T. 78.

17 *McGhie* v. *B.T.C.*, 1964 S.L.T. 25; *Gray* v. *N.B. Steel Foundry Co.*, 1968 S.L.T.(Notes) 95.

18 *Broom* v. *Ritchie* (1904) 6 F. 942; *Auld* v. *Shairp* (1874) 2 R. 191. But see Bankton, I, 10, 29; *Walker* v. *Robertson* (1821) 2 Mur. 508.

19 *Muir's Tr.* v. *Braidwood*, 1958 S.C. 169.

20 *Horn* v. *Sanderson* (1872) 10 M. 295; *Crichton* v. *Crichton* (1902) 5 F. 178, 181.

21 *Clarke* v. *Muller* (1884) 11 R. 418.

22 *Scott* v. *Johnston* (1885) 12 R. 1022.

23 *Scott* v. *Ray* (1886) 13 R. 1173; *Powell* v. *Long* (1896) 23 R. 955.

24 *Collier* v. *Ritchie* (1884) 12 R. 47.

25 *Clarke* v. *Muller*, *supra*; *Brown* v. *Oliver* (1895) 3 S.L.T. No. 63; *Cook* v. *Kinghorn* (1904) 12 S.L.T. 186; *G.* v. *H.* (1899) 1 F. 701 (where pursuer's husband bankrupt).

occasionally dispensed with,[26] unless there is danger of hardship to the bankrupt, especially where the other party to the action is the cause of the bankruptcy or a person primarily interested in it.[27] If the trustee sists himself as a litigant he becomes liable for expenses from the beginning of the action. If caution is ordered and not found the defender may be assoilzied [28] or the action may be dismissed.

These principles extend also to actions for damages for assault and spuilzie [29] but not an illegal poinding.[30]

Where the claim of damages is for patrimonial loss rather than for injury to person or character caution will be ordered unless the trustee sists himself as a party, which he should do, as his Act and Warrant entitles him to recover any debt due to the bankrupt and to maintain actions, in the same way as the bankrupt might have done if his estate had not been sequestrated.[31] He also has a title to sue in respect of *acquirenda*. The bankrupt's own right to sue revives when he has been discharged and reinvested in his estates, and also his trustee discharged: if the latter has not been discharged he has no title to sue. In any event, any damages recovered will go to the trustee under the Bankruptcy Act, whether or not the injury was before or after the bankruptcy [32] and whether personal or patrimonial.

Subrogation

The effect of subrogation is to place insurers in the position of the insured and to succeed to all rights and remedies *ex contractu* [33] and *ex delicto* [34] competent to him in respect of the subject-matter of the insurance.[35] It only arises when insurers have paid the sum due under a valid and subsisting policy.[36] Actions are still brought in name of the assured and defences competent against him are still available [37] unless there has been actual assignation. It is no defence that the assured has been indemnified or that the insurers were not entitled to pay.

The assured must give the insurers all assistance in the action, not prejudice their recovery from a third party, and give them the benefit of any sum recovered from a third party.

Death of defender

The death of a wrongdoer does not end his liability to make reparation and his estate is still liable to pay damages. A claim of reparation trans-

26 *Scott* v. *Johnston* (1885) 12 R. 1022.
27 *Gallagher* v. *Edinburgh Mags.*, 1929 S.L.T. 356; *Neil* v. *S.E. Lancs. Insce. Co.*, 1930 S.C. 629; *Fraser* v. *McMurrich*, 1924 S.C. 93; *Rennie* v. *Campbell*, 1929 S.L.T. 27.
28 *Cunningham* v. *Skinner* (1902) 4 F. 1124, 1127, 1131.
29 *Thom* v. *Andrew* (1888) 15 R. 780; see also *Buchanan* v. *Stevenson* (1880) 8 R. 220; *Thom* v. *Bridges* (1857) 19 D. 721.
30 *Gray* v. *Ireland* (1884) 21 S.L.R. 766.
31 Bankruptcy (Scotland) Act 1913, s. 70; *Corbidge* v. *Somerville*, 1913 S.C. 858.
32 *Jackson* v. *McKechnie* (1875) 3 R. 130.
33 *Castellain*, *infra*; *Bank of Montreal* v. *Dominion Guarantee Co.* [1930] A.C. 659.
34 *King* v. *Victoria Assce. Co.* [1896] A.C. 250; *Castellain*, *infra*.
35 *Castellain* v. *Preston* (1883) 11 Q.B.D. 380; *Simpson* v. *Thomson* (1877) 3 App.Cas. 279.
36 *Edwards* v. *M. U. Insce. Co.* [1922] 2 K.B. 249; *Austin* v. *Zurich Insce. Co.* [1945] K.B. 250.
37 *West of England Fire Insce. Co.* v. *Isaacs* [1897] 1 Q.B. 226; *Austin*, *supra*.

mits against his executors [38] as being a civil debt, so far as they are *lucrati.*[39] It does not matter whether an action has been begun,[40] and claims for solatium,[41] seduction,[42] and slander [43] have all been made against representatives.

Bankruptcy of defender

A defender who is or becomes bankrupt is none the less still liable to make reparation. He is not usually required to find caution for expenses,[44] nor can the pursuer complain if the trustee does not concur in the action. Neither can be insisted on [45] even though the bankrupt defender reclaims,[46] though the trustee may sist himself.[47] A claim of damages for a wrong done prior to sequestration is a debt due at that date and the amount is ascertained by the decree.[48] If the trustee sists himself he may render himself personally liable for expenses,[49] but not for implementing the decree.[50]

Conveyance of property

Liability to make reparation is thus far personal that it does not transmit to another person by virtue of the conveyance of the property or business in connection with which the wrong complained of has been suffered. So the amalgamation of one firm with another,[51] or the sale of one business to another,[52] leave unaffected the personal liability of the original wrongdoer.

Contributory negligence

At common law a pursuer could not recover damages for loss or injury caused by a defender's negligence, if his own negligence had been either the effective cause of the damage or been so closely implicated with the defender's negligence as to make indistinguishable whose negligence was the decisive cause. The Maritime Conventions Act 1911,[53] provided that where, by the fault of two or more vessels, damage or loss was caused to one or more of them, or to their cargoes or freight or to any property on board, the liability of each to make good the damage or loss should be in propor-

[38] Ersk. III, 1, 15; Bell, *Prin.* § 546; *Calder* v. *Mackenzie's Reps.* (1776) Mor. *voce* Personal and Transmissible, App. No. 2; *Auld* v. *Shairp* (1874) 2 R. 191.
[39] *Davidson* v. *Tulloch* (1860) 3 Macq. 783, 790.
[40] *Macnaughton* v. *Robertson*, Feb. 17, 1809, F.C.; *Morrison* v. *Cameron*, May 25, 1809, F.C.
[41] *Evans* v. *Stool* (1885) 12 R. 1295; *Bourhill* v. *Young's Exor.*, 1942 S.C.(H.L.) 78.
[42] *Kay* v. *Wilson's Trs.* (1850) 12 D. 845; *cf. Evans, supra.*
[43] *Auld* v. *Shairp* (1874) 2 R. 191.
[44] *Lawrie* v. *Pearson* (1888) 16 R. 62.
[45] *Crichton* v. *Crichton* (1902) 5 F. 178, 181; *Robertson* v. *Henderson* (1833) 12 S. 70; *Taylor* v. *Fairlie's Trs.* (1833) 6 W. & S. 301.
[46] *Buchanan* v. *Stevenson* (1880) 8 R. 220.
[47] *Miller* v. *MacIntosh* (1884) 21 S.L.R. 500.
[48] *Miller* v. *MacIntosh* (1884) 21 S.L.R. 500.
[49] *Crichton, supra.*
[50] *Harkness* v. *Rattray* (1878) 16 S.L.R. 117.
[51] *Smith* v. *Edinburgh and Glasgow Ry.* (1866) 4 M. 362.
[52] *Henderson* v. *Stubbs* (1894) 22 R. 51.
[53] See Marsden, *Collisions at Sea*, 10th ed., Chap. 6. This is unaffected by the 1945 Act.

tion to the degree in which each vessel was at fault. If in the circumstances of the case, it was impossible to establish different degrees of fault, the liability was to be apportioned equally, but no vessel was to be liable for any loss or damage to which her fault had not contributed.

The Law Reform (Contributory Negligence) Act 1945 applied this principle to cases of contributory negligence in general. It provides that where a person suffers damage [54] as the result partly of his own fault and partly of the fault of any other person or persons, a claim in respect of that damage shall not be defeated by reason of the fault of the person suffering the damage, but the damages recoverable in respect thereof shall be reduced to such extent as the court thinks just and equitable [55] having regard to the claimant's share in the responsibility for the damage.[56] A defender who wishes to put joint fault before the jury must lodge a counter-issue.[57] This is not, however, to operate so as to defeat any defence arising under a contract. Where any contract or enactment [58] providing for the limitation of liability is applicable to the claim, the amount of damages recoverable by the claimant by virtue of the subsection shall not exceed the maximum limit so applicable. Damage includes [59] loss of life and personal injury: fault means [60] wrongful act, breach of statutory duty or negligent act or omission which gives rise to liability in damages.

Application of Act

The court [61] is required to find and record the total damages which would have been recoverable if the claimant had not been at fault, and if the case is tried by jury,[62] the jury shall determine the total damages which would have been recoverable if the claimant had not been at fault and the extent to which those damages are to be reduced. The court or jury therefore finds a gross award and, if the pursuer is himself in fault, the degree of that fault, usually expressed by a fraction or percentage. The net award, and the sum the pursuer will actually receive is then arrived at, by the clerk of court, by deducting the requisite fraction or percentage from the gross damages already found.[63]

It appears to be undecided whether the Act applies to actions founded on breach of contract or not.[64]

Where there is a question of joint and several liability of wrongdoers,

[54] Physical damage and not financial loss: *Drinkwater* v. *Kimber* [1952] 2 Q.B. 281.

[55] See *Daniel* v. *Rickett, Cockerell & Co.* [1938] 2 K.B. 322. This calls for the exercise of a broad judgment and any arithmetical conclusion is qualified by what is deemed to be fair and reasonable: *Palser* v. *Grinling* [1948] A.C. 291, 315; see also *Newport B.C.* v. *Monmouthshire C.C.* [1947] A.C. 520, 534; *Stapley* v. *Gypsum Mines* [1953] A.C. 663.

[56] s. 1 (1). See also *Davies* v. *Swan Motor Co.* [1949] 2 K.B. 291, 326; *Stapley, supra*, 682.

[57] *Lawrie* v. *Glasgow Corpn.*, 1952 S.C. 361.

[58] *e.g.* Merchant Shipping Act 1894, s. 503.

[59] s. 4.

[60] s. 5 (*a*).

[61] s. 1 (2).

[62] s. 1 (6).

[63] *Ghannan* v. *Glasgow Corpn.*, 1950 S.C. 23.

[64] *Sayers* v. *Harlow U.D.C.* [1958] 2 All E.R. 342, where it was held applicable in a contract case.

any deduction for contributory negligence must be made first and then the balance of liability allocated between the joint wrongdoers, though without prejudice to the pursuer's right to a joint and several decree against the defenders.[65]

Cases where Act does not apply

The 1945 Act only applies where a person suffered damage as the result partly of his own fault and partly of the fault of another, but not where a party not in fault is damnified. Thus in *Mallett* v. *Dunn* [66] a wife was injured in a vehicle accident and sued for damages, and her husband also sued for consequential losses and expenses. It was held that the husband's claim was independent and not subject to the same abatement as the wife's claim in consequence of her own partial fault. If such husband's expenses are claimed separately [67] they are not liable to be reduced, but if they were included in the wife's claim, they will abate in the same way as her claim for personal injuries if some measure of contributory negligence be established. But it is clear law that persons pursuing an action for solatium and patrimonial loss arising out of the death of a relative are liable to have their claims reduced or defeated by reason of the deceased's contributory negligence.[68]

Settlement of action

Parties, including a curator *ad litem* to a pupil,[69] but not a mandatary without special authority,[70] may compromise or settle an action of damages on such terms as they agree. Any such compromise may be proved by writings neither holograph nor tested, taken in conjunction with parole evidence.[71] It is not, however, competent to establish by parole evidence an alleged verbal agreement to vary the terms on which an action had been settled by joint minute signed by counsel.[72] The ordinary practice is to embody the terms of settlement in a joint minute signed by counsel for the parties to which the court is moved to interpone authority, but such a settlement once signed is binding without the interposition of the authority of the court,[73] and an action may effectually be settled extra-judicially as by granting a receipt for money without the interposition of authority [74] though in such a case steps must still be taken to take the case out of court,

[65] *Cf. Davies* v. *Swan Motor Co. Ltd.* [1949] 2 K.B. 291.
[66] [1949] 2 K.B. 180; *cf. Bruce* v. *Murray*, 1926 S.L.T. 236.
[67] *e.g. Bern's Exor.* v. *Montrose Asylum* (1893) 20 R. 859, 870; *Soutar* v. *Mulhern*, 1907 S.C. 723.
[68] *McNaughton* v. *Caledonian Ry.* (1858) 21 D. 160; *Wilson* v. *Merry & Cunningham* (1868) 6 M.(H.L.) 84; *cf. McKay* v. *Scottish Airways*, 1948 S.C. 254: Law Reform (Contributory Negligence) Act 1945, s. 5 (*c*).
[69] *Dewar* v. *Dewar's Trs.* (1906) 14 S.L.T. 238.
[70] *Thom* v. *Bain* (1888) 15 R. 613; as to judicial factor see *Tennent's J.F.* v. *Tennent*, 1954 S.C. 215.
[71] *Love* v. *Marshall* (1872) 10 M. 795; *cf. Thomson* v. *Fraser* (1868) 7 M. 39; *Anderson* v. *Dick* (1901) 4 F. 68.
[72] *Hamilton & Baird* v. *Lewis* (1893) 21 R. 120.
[73] *McAthey* v. *Patriotic Investment Socy.*, 1910 S.C. 584.
[74] *Gow* v. *Henry* (1899) 2 F. 48.

as by abandonment. Where a joint minute has been lodged and counsel moves for the interposition of authority, evidence must be produced of intimation of the motion to the other party if no appearance is made for him.[75]

Once agreement has been reached between the parties,[76] even by parole, neither may resile,[77] unless possibly on sufficient averments to ground a reduction, but not if the defender has gone bankrupt,[78] and the court is not bound to construe an agreement before giving effect to it as a settlement if the parties differ as to its true construction.[79] But a pursuer has been held entitled to resile from acceptance of a tender when it appeared that there was no concluded bargain, the tender being of a lump sum unallocated among the several pursuers,[80] and the court cannot interpone authority to an incompetent minute, as by a liquidator granting a preferential ranking.[81]

A settlement is not avoided by the fact that an agent does not disclose to his client that he has received a sum as his expenses from the defender, so long as the sum fixed is not excessive or unreasonable,[82] nor by the fact that the defenders have not disclosed to the pursuer the fact that they had previously tendered a larger sum to his solicitors,[83] nor by a subsequent dispute as to the construction of the agreement to settle.[84]

Tenders and settlement

A defender, or pursuer in the case of a counterclaim, may wish to make the other party a formal offer or tender so as to effect a settlement of an action. A tender in the proper sense of the term is a judicial offer—that is, an offer by a party to pay part of the sum asked by his adversary after the action is raised.[1]

Requisites of tender

A tender must be explicit and unambiguous and without conditions or qualifications.[2] But nevertheless a tender may contain an affirmation of innocence and of the desire to avoid litigation,[3] and it regularly does bear to be without admission of liability and under reservation of all rights and

75 *Ferris* v. *Glasgow Corporation*, 1914, 1 S.L.T. 99.
76 See *Macdonald* v. *Small*, 1926 S.L.T. 258.
77 *Dewar* v. *Ainslie* (1892) 20 R. 203; *Davidson, infra.*
78 *Davidson* v. *Whatmough*, 1930 S.L.T. 536.
79 *Anderson* v. *Dick* (1901) 4 F. 68; *cf. Christie* v. *Fife Coal Co.* (1899) 2 F. 192.
80 *Murphy* v. *Smith*, 1920 S.C. 104; *cf. Flanagan* v. *Dempster, Moore & Co.*, 1928 S.C. 308.
81 *McAthey* v. *Patriotic Investment Socy.*, 1910 S.C. 584.
82 *McLaughlin* v. *Pumpherston Oil Co.*, 1915 S.C. 65.
83 *Welsh* v. *Cousin* (1899) 2 F. 277; but *cf. Clarke* v. *Cumming* (1891) 28 S.L.R. 343.
84 *Christie* v. *Fife Coal Co.* (1899) 2 F. 192.
1 *Smeaton* v. *Dundee Corpn.*, 1941 S.C. 600; *Avery* v. *Cantilever Shoe Co.*, 1942 S.C. 469. It should normally be made by separate minute: *Smeaton, supra.* See also *Ramsay's Trs.* v. *Souter* (1864) 2 M. 891.
2 *Bisset* v. *Anderson* (1847) 10 D. 233; *Gunn* v. *Breadalbane* (1849) 11 D. 1046; *Low* v. *Spences* (1895) 3 S.L.T. 170; *Thomson* v. *Dailly* (1896) 4 S.L.T. 172. In *Corvi* v. *Ellis*, 1969 S.C. 312 no objection was taken to a conditional tender.
3 *Thomson, supra.*

pleas.[3] It is incompetent to tender a lump sum to several joint pursuers and differentiation must be made.[4] A tender must also always be accompanied by an offer of the expenses of process and the refusal of a tender and subsequent failure to obtain an award of damages so great as that tendered has a serious effect on the pursuer's expenses.[5] A judicial tender made by minute should not be brought to the notice of the jury or of the judge except when he is dealing with expenses, nor should an extra-judicial tender repeated on record be brought to the notice of the jury: such an extra-judicial tender being on record necessarily comes to the notice of the judge but should not be referred to in evidence, nor in debate except on the question of expenses.[6] A tender lodged in the Outer House lapses on the Lord Ordinary delivering judgment and cannot thereafter be accepted.[7]

Tender presumed to include interest

A tender, unless otherwise stated therein, is held to be in full satisfaction of any claim to interest thereunder by any person in whose favour the tender is made, and in considering in any such action whether an award is equal to or greater than an amount tendered in the action, the court shall take account of the amount of any interest awarded under the Interest on Damages (Scotland) Acts 1958 and 1971, or such part of that interest as the court considers appropriate.[7a]

Specialties in defamation actions

In actions of damages for slander a tender, before it can be effective, must contain a full retraction of the alleged slander, so as to clear the pursuer's character in the same way as a jury verdict and an award of damages would do.[8] It has been accepted as sufficient to tender with a statement that the defender was not conscious of having used the words complained of, and that he did not believe that in fact he had done so, but with a full retraction and apology if he had really done so.[9] A pursuer has been held entitled to expenses where the pursuer accepted the apology when the defender lodged a minute stating that if expressions used by him could be construed as making reflections on the pursuer, he withdrew them unreservedly and expressed his regret.[10]

Multiplicity of parties

When there are several pursuers in one action concluding (as they

[4] *Flanagan* v. *Dempster*, 1928 S.C. 308; *Wilkinson* v. *Richards*, 1967 S.L.T. 270; *cf. Wilson* v. *Rapp*, 1911 S.C. 1360.

[5] See *McLaren on Expenses*, 81 *et seq.*

[6] *Avery* v. *Cantilever Shoe Co.*, 1942 S.C. 469.

[7] *Bright* v. *Low*, 1940 S.C. 280.

[7a] Interest on Damages (Scotland) Act 1958, s. 1 (1B), added by 1971 Act, s. 1 (1).

[8] *Faulks* v. *Park* (1854) 17 D. 247.

[9] *Mitchells* v. *Nicoll* (1890) 17 R. 795; *Sproll* v. *Walker* (1899) 2 F. 73.

[10] *Hunter* v. *Russell* (1901) 3 F. 596; *Sturrock* v. *Deas*, 1913, 1 S.L.T. 60; *Davidson* v. *Panti*, 1915, 1 S.L.T. 273.

must [11]) for separate sums of damages to be awarded to each, it is incompetent to lodge a single tender of a lump sum, thereafter to be apportioned by the pursuers among themselves.[12] There must in such circumstances be separate tenders of separate sums to each pursuer,[13] and it is competent for some of these to be accepted and decree pronounced therefor, and to have the case proceed as regards the remainder.[14]

It has been held, in the case of conjoined actions as where separate actions had been raised for salvage services by two pursuers who had conflicting interests against the same defender, that if the defender wished to put in a tender in the conjoined actions, he should be required to apportion the sum tendered as between the pursuers.[15]

Tender by one of several defenders

If one of several defenders sued jointly and severally makes a tender, he thereby becomes liable in expenses to the other defender or defenders. It is usual in practice to advise the other defender that his expenses will be paid if the tender is accepted.[16] Where a pursuer accepted a tender from one defender he was held entitled to a right of relief against the defender in respect of the second defender's expenses.[16a] Acceptance of the tender does not preclude the pursuer from continuing the action against the other defender.[17]

Effective date of tender

The date from which a tender is effective is of great importance with regard to expenses. In the absence of an express date, it is a question of fact. If a tender is made by adjustment of the record the date of the tender is the date of closing the record.[18] Where the action does not get to the length of closing the record the true date of the tender must be ascertained otherwise, making allowance for a reasonable period within which it should have been refused or accepted.[19] Modern practice favours leaving the precise date to the determination of the Auditor of Court,[19] though if a remit to the Auditor is not otherwise necessary the court may determine the true date.[20]

Where a tender is made by minute, the date of its being lodged in

11 *Gray* v. *Caledonian Ry.*, 1912 S.C. 339.

12 *Flanagan* v. *Dempster*, 1928 S.C. 308; *Wilkinson* v. *Richards*, 1967 S.L.T. 270.

13 *McNeil* v. *N.C.B.*, 1966 S.C. 72. *Cf. Wilson* v. *Rapp*, 1911 S.C. 1360 (one tender lodged in two conjoined actions and accepted by both pursuers to full extent).

14 *e.g. Rankin* v. *Waddell*, 1949 S.C. 555.

15 *Boyle* v. *Olsen*; *Lindsey Steam Fishing Co.* v. *A/S Bonheur*, 1912 S.C. 1235.

16 As to expenses, see also *Williamson* v. *McPherson*, 1951 S.C. 438; *Houston* v. *B.R.S.*, 1967 S.L.T. 329.

16a *Maclinden* v. *Colvilles Ltd.*, 1967 S.L.T.(Notes) 80.

17 *McNair* v. *Dunfermline Corpn.*, 1953 S.C. 183.

18 *Bryden* v. *Devlin* (1899) 6 S.L.T. 297; *cf. Critchley* v. *Campbell* (1884) 11 R. 475; *Gunn* v. *Hunter* (1886) 13 R. 573.

19 *Smeaton* v. *Dundee Corpn.*, 1941 S.C. 600.

20 *Jack* v. *Black*, 1911 S.C. 691.

process having been duly intimated to the other party is probably its effective date.[21]

A tender has been held to be too late when it came after the Lord Ordinary had given judgment and was in terms which he had said would have been a complete answer to the action.[22]

Acceptance of tender

As with ordinary contracts the acceptance must meet the tender; a tender to a pursuer as an individual and as administratrix for pupil children is only partially accepted if accepted by the pursuer as an individual.[22a] A reasonable time has to be allowed for the pursuer to consult with his legal and other advisers whether or not to accept the sum tendered.[23] What is a reasonable time is a question of circumstances, regard being had to the pursuer's whereabouts, the need for further information, vacations, and the availability of the pursuer's advisers.[24] The expenses of considering a tender are properly allowable.[25] In cases of undue delay in accepting the pursuer may be found liable in partial expenses.[26] A pursuer's executor may competently accept a tender lodged before defences were lodged,[26a] but not one lodged with the defences.[26b]

It appears to be undecided whether a tender, if not withdrawn, remains open for acceptance until a verdict has been returned at the trial or decree granted. It seems to be suggested by *McLaughlin* v. *Glasgow Tramways* [27] that a tender should be accepted if at all in three or four days, and expenses were only allowed for three days in that case, but more probably a tender remains open for acceptance until withdrawn [28] or foreclosed by decision of the case, though the court in its discretion may only allow expenses for what is considered a reasonable time after the tender is lodged and intimated.

Withdrawal of tender

A tender may be withdrawn at any time before acceptance by a minute lodged in process and intimated to the other party.[29] Where the defenders in an action tendered and alternatively offered to refer the whole cause to arbitration, and the latter course was accepted, it was held that the first

21 *McGuiness* v. *Glasgow Corpn.*, 1914, 1 S.L.T. 99.
22 *Whitworth Bros.* v. *Shepherd* (1884) 12 R. 204.
22a *Wilkinson* v. *Richards*, 1967 S.L.T. 270.
23 *Carnegie* v. *Edin. and Granton Ry.* (1849) 11 D. 576; *Shaw* v. *Edin. and Glasgow Ry.* (1863) 2 M. 142; *Jack* v. *Black*, 1911 S.C. 691; *Smeaton* v. *Dundee Corpn.*, 1941 S.C. 600.
24 See *McLaughlin* v. *Glasgow Tramways Co.* (1897) 24 R. 992; *Murray* v. *Caledonian Ry.* (1899) 7 S.L.T. 238; *Wilson* v. *Rapp*, 1909, 2 S.L.T. 295; *Jack* v. *Black*, 1911 S.C. 691; *Smeaton* v. *Dundee Corpn.*, 1941 S.C. 600, 607.
25 *Jack* v. *Black*, 1911 S.C. 691, 700.
26 *McLaughlin*, *supra*.
26a *Stoddart* v. *McLeod*, 1963 S.L.T.(Notes) 23. *Sed quaere*.
26b *Sommerville* v. *N.C.B.*, 1963 S.C. 666, possibly overruling *Stoddart*, *supra*.
27 *Supra*.
28 *Cf. McMillan* v. *Meikleham*, 1934 S.L.T. 357, where withdrawal made but not intimated in time and acceptance held valid.
29 *McMillan* v. *Meikleham*, 1934 S.L.T. 357.

alternative was no longer open and the pursuer was not entitled to decree in terms thereof, even when nothing was done under the reference to the arbiter to which authority had been interponed by joint minute.[30] A tender falls when notes of an arbiter's intended award are issued [31] or on delivery of judgment in a court of first instance and subsequent acceptance is too late.[32] Probably the same would apply in the case of a jury verdict. A judgment of a court of first instance is such a material change as to render a previous tender inoperative so that acceptance after decree in and reclaiming from the Outer House is ineffectual [33]; such a decision operates impliedly to withdraw the tender. Similarly the death of a pursuer invalidates any prior tender.[33a] It is uncertain whether the death of the defender invalidates a tender made.[33a]

Discharges of claims of damages

A pursuer who has a claim of damages against a person may discharge that claim on such terms and conditions as the parties may agree. A full and unconditional discharge bars any further claim of damages,[34] and it is irrelevant to aver that it was granted for inadequate consideration. A minor may grant a discharge and payment may be made in safety in reliance thereon [35] although the agreement is liable to reduction on the ground of minority and lesion *intra quadriennium utile.*[36] It has been suggested that a mother could grant a valid discharge of a claim by a pupil child arising out of the father's death.[37] A discharge of a claim of damages need not be a probative writ.[38] It may be proved *prout de jure* and an improbative discharge may be set up by acknowledgment of the signature.[38] A discharge may be founded on only by the party in whose favour it was granted and not by a third party [39]: thus when an employee granted a discharge in favour of the employer he could still sue a doctor who had treated him negligently.[40]

Implied discharge

Circumstances may be such as to lead to an implication of discharge of a claim of damages. Thus where a tenant renounced his lease and, after the landlord had accepted the renunciation, sued him for damages for injury alleged to have been suffered by flooding for which the landlord was responsible, it was held despite a notice of the claim in general terms that

30 *Reid* v. *Firth & Stott* (1886) 23 S.L.R. 845.
31 *Macrae* v. *Edin. Street Tramways* (1885) 13 R. 265; *Bright* v. *Low*, 1940 S.C. 280.
32 *Bright* v. *Low*, 1940 S.C. 280.
33 *Bright* v. *Low*, 1940 S.C. 280.
33a *Sommerville* v. *N.C.B.* 1963 S.C. 666.
34 *McLean* v. *Hassard* (1903) 10 S.L.T. 593.
35 *Jack* v. *N.B. Ry.* (1886) 24 S.L.R. 211.
36 *Cf. N.B. Ry.* v. *Wood* (1891) 18 R.(H.L.) 27; *McFeetridge* v. *Stewarts & Lloyds*, 1913 S.C. 773; *Robertson* v. *Henderson* (1904) 6 F. 770.
37 *Murphy* v. *Smith*, 1920 S.C. 104, 107, *per* Ld. Pres. Strathclyde.
38 *Davies* v. *Hunter*, 1934 S.C. 10.
39 *Dillon* v. *Napier, Shanks & Bell* (1893) 30 S.L.R. 685.
40 *McAlinn* v. *Brown*, 1951 S.L.T.(Notes) 45.

acceptance of the renunciation of the lease implied a discharge of all claims competent to the tenant.[41] A *pactum de non petendo* if absolute [42] and in favour of one person [43] imports a discharge of the claim.[44]

In the case of personal injuries, acceptance of National Insurance benefits cannot imply any discharge of claims as those benefits are payable independently of any action of damages though the amount of benefit has to be taken into account in the computation of damages.

In *Wright* v. *Howard, Baker & Co.*[45] the discharge was implied by the workman's acceptance of insurance benefits from a contributory scheme run by the employers, it being proved that notices were adequately posted to the effect that acceptance of such benefits would discharge common-law claims and that the pursuer had known of these notices.

So too where a woman gave a document to her seducer binding herself to " take no action, legal or otherwise " against him, it was held that she had thereby discharged any claim against him for damages for the seduction.[46]

Discharges of co-delinquents

Where an injured party claims damages from more than one defender, the granting of a discharge to one or more but not all of the defenders may raise difficult questions as to its effect on the liability of the other defenders, and may have repercussions on the rights of the defenders *inter se*.

A distinction has been taken between a discharge of the whole claim as a ground of action [47] and a mere discharge of the liability of one or more of several defenders jointly liable for the claim.[48] So long as only the liability of a particular delinquent, liable jointly and severally, is discharged, it follows from the principle of joint and several liability that one or more delinquents may be discharged without impairing the pursuer's right to proceed against the remaining defenders [49] for the balance of the sum sued for, which should be restricted accordingly.[50] If, however, defenders were alternative and only liable severally, a discharge of one would necessarily discharge the other.

In *Campbell* v. *Morrison* [51] an injured workman sued three defenders. He failed on jurisdiction and accepted offers from two of them and granted discharges, one " in full of expenses " and the other discharging " from

41 *Lyons* v. *Anderson* (1886) 13 R. 1020; *cf. Walker* v. *McKnights* (1886) 13 R. 599; *Skinner* v. *Lord Saltoun* (1886) 13 R. 823.
42 *Thin & Sinclair* v. *Arrol* (1896) 24 R. 198.
43 *Secus* where discharging one and reserving claims against co-obligants: *Muir* v. *Crawford* (1875) 2 R.(H.L.) 148; *cf. Smith* v. *Harding* (1877) 5 R. 147.
44 Stair IV, 30, 31.
45 (1893) 21 R. 25.
46 *McLean* v. *Hassard* (1903) 10 S.L.T. 593.
47 *Delaney* v. *Stirling* (1893) 20 R. 506.
48 *Western Bank* v. *Bairds* (1862) 24 D. 859, 912; *Campbell* v. *Morrison* (1891) 19 R. 282.
49 *Western Bank* v. *Bairds* (1862) 24 D. 859, 901, 912, 921; *Delaney* v. *Stirling* (1893) 20 R. 506; *Cormie* v. *Grigor* (1862) 24 D. 985; *Robinson* v. *Reid's Trs.* (1900) 2 F. 928, 931.
50 *Douglas* v. *Hogarth* (1901) 4 F. 148; *McNair* v. *Dunfermline Corpn.*, 1953 S.C. 183.
51 (1891) 19 R. 282.

all claims of reparation." He then sued the third defender in a new action and it was held in the Outer House that he was not barred by the payments or discharges principally on the ground that the payments were only really made to get rid of unfounded claims; in the Inner House opinions were reserved on the point.[52] In *Delaney* v. *Stirling* [53] the pursuer sued the superintendent of an institution and was held barred by the terms of a discharge granted by him in settlement of a previous action on the same grounds against the directors of the institution and not naming the present defender. The terms of the discharge were very wide extending to " all claims of damage competent to me " and clearly covered the incident giving rise to the claim of damages.

In *Dillon* v. *Napier, Shanks & Bell* [54] the pursuer discharged his claim against his employers and then sued the present defenders. All the judges of the First Division were of the opinion that the discharge, from its terms and the terms of a subsequent letter did not import full satisfaction of the pursuer's claims.

In *Douglas* v. *Hogarth* [55] the defenders were sued jointly and severally, or severally, and one was granted a discharge; the pursuer was held not barred from insisting in his claim against the other. The opinion was also expressed that the discharge did not impair the defenders' right of relief *inter se*.

The only general doctrine that can be drawn from the cases is that, in the case of several defenders, what effect the particular discharge granted has is a question of construction, and for safety any discharge granted should reserve claims against other defenders or at least not be phrased any more widely and generally than necessary to discharge the liability of the grantee.

Decree does not import discharge of co-delinquent

If several defenders are liable jointly and severally and decree is obtained against one, that does not operate as a discharge of the others so as to preclude the pursuer from bringing a fresh action against the others if he cannot recover under the decree he holds, as where the defender in the first action is unable to pay.[56] It would be otherwise if the delinquents were alternative.[57] If there is any danger of the pursuer obtaining more than his due by bringing the second action, this can be obviated by assigning the first, nugatory, decree to the defender in the second action.[58] In *Steven* v. *Broady Norman & Co.*,[56] S obtained decree against the driver of a car but was unable to recover anything; then, having ascertained that the defender had at the material time been driving a company's car on company busi-

52 Lord Trayner was " inclined to agree " with the Lord Ordinary.
53 (1893) 20 R. 506.
54 (1893) 1 S.L.T. 55.
55 (1901) 4 F. 148, followed in *McNair* v. *Dunfermline Corpn.*, 1953 S.C. 183.
56 *Steven* v. *Broady Norman & Co.*, 1928 S.C. 351.
57 *e.g.* agent for an undisclosed principal, *Meier* v. *Kuchenmeister* (1881) 8 R. 642.
58 *Cf. Kohnke* v. *Karger* [1951] 2 K.B. 670.

ness,[59] he sued the company, offering to assign them the decree he held; the former decree was held to be no bar to the second action though negligence would have to be proved afresh. In *Houston* v. *Buchanan* [60] it was observed that where an unenforceable or nugatory decree is obtained and a subsequent action brought against the co-delinquent or the employer the proper measure of damages was the whole sum in the worthless decree together with the sum awarded as expenses, and these sums could only be challenged by the defender on very special averments of excess and extravagance.

Setting aside discharge

A discharge, even though granted in the widest terms may be reduced on the ground of essential error induced by misrepresentation [61] or impetration by fraud or other recognised ground of reduction, but the onus of proof is on the pursuer.[61] If a discharge has been granted and it is sought thereafter to recover damages, that discharge must be reduced before the action can be proceeded with unless it can be shown that the discharge does not in terms exclude the proposed action.

In general a discharge granted by a person capable of understanding its effect and without misrepresentation is not reducible merely because its significance was not appreciated or the consideration was inadequate,[62] nor is it reducible because granted in ignorance of a larger tender made to the pursuer's agent,[63] but reduction has been granted where the granter had not the chance to understand and did not understand the consequences of his action.[64]

Where an injured workman accepted a trivial sum " as full compensation " for his injuries and signed a discharge without consulting his law-agent, it was held that the receipt had been granted in ignorance that it was a full discharge, and on repayment of the sum paid the workman was entitled to proceed with an action for damages against the employers.[65] It was observed that it was undesirable to induce or permit a discharge by a party not negotiating on an equal footing without legal advice when he had previously consulted a solicitor.[66] In *N.B. Ry.* v. *Wood* [67] there was no legal advice, the discharge was granted nine days after the accident and there was evidence of nervous shock, yet it was held that the discharge was valid, there being no attempt to mislead and the injured pursuer being

59 The driver and the company were not in this case properly joint delinquents.
60 1937 S.C. 460, 471; affd. on another point, 1940 S.C.(H.L.) 17.
61 *Davies* v. *Hunter*, 1933 S.L.T. 158; *cf.* also cases under Workmen's Compensation Acts, *e.g. McGuire* v. *Paterson*, 1913 S.C. 400; *Ellis* v. *Lochgelly Iron Co.*, 1909 S.C. 1278; *Dornan* v. *Allan* (1900) 3 F. 112; *Park* v. *Anderson Bros.*, 1924 S.C. 1017.
62 *N.B. Ry.* v. *Wood* (1891) 18 R.(H.L.) 27, and cases, *supra.*
63 *Welsh* v. *Cousin* (1899) 2 F. 277.
64 *McDonagh* v. *MacLellan* (1886) 13 R. 1000; *Macandrew* v. *Gilhooley*, 1911 S.C. 448.
65 *McDonagh* v. *MacLellan* (1886) 13 R. 1000.
66 *Ibid.* 1002, *per* L. J.-C. Moncreiff.
67 (1891) 18 R.(H.L.) 27; followed in *Mackie* v. *Strachan, Kinmond & Co.* (1896) 23 R. 1030, and *Mathieson* v. *Hawthorns & Co.* (1899) 1 F. 468 (where the discharge was notarially executed) but there is force in Lord Young's dissent in the latter case (p. 472): see also *Stewart Bros.* v. *Kiddie* (1899) 7 S.L.T. 92.

capable of understanding the meaning of the discharge. It was pointed out that any mental reservation attached to the acceptance of the offer must be clear and known to the other side.

Factors for administration of damages

In any action of reparation in which decree is granted for payment of a sum of money as damages to (i) a pupil child, acting with the concurrence of a curator *ad litem*, or (ii) a minor acting with or without [68] the concurrence of his or her father, or of a curator *ad litem*, or (iii) a parent, acting on behalf of his or her pupil child, it is competent [69] for the court [70] granting the decree, to appoint *de plano* some responsible person as factor *loco tutoris* with certain duties and powers, if it appears that there is no person available to give a full and valid discharge for the sum of damages,[71] or if the court is satisfied that the administration of the sum in the decree for the benefit of such minor or pupil cannot otherwise be reasonably secured.[72] The party desiring a factor makes application by minute which may be incorporated in a minute of tender or joint minute.[73]

It is necessary to aver facts and circumstances which might indicate to the court that risk would be involved if the money were left with the natural guardian before an appointment will be made.[74] It is not sufficient merely to aver that the sum involved is substantial.[75] The court has a fairly wide discretion to consider *ex proprio motu* the whole known circumstances and to appoint a factor where this appears to be the only way in which administration for the benefit of the child can be secured and this discretion should not be too closely fettered.[76] In *Boylan* [77] the practice of paying the money to a trustee rather than to a judicial factor was disapproved. A recommendation by the jury is not essential provided the unfitness of the legal guardian is disclosed at the trial to the satisfaction of the presiding judge.[77]

[68] In two cases the court directed that the damages were to be paid to a named person in trust for the minor: *Sharp* v. *Pathhead Spinning Co.* (1885) 12 R. 574; *Spring* v. *Blackall* (1901) 9 S.L.T. 162. These cases are disapproved by *Boylan, infra.*

[69] Not essential, at least for a minor, see *Jack* v. *N.B. Ry.* (1886) 14 R. 263. Contrast *Anderson* v. *Muirhead* (1884) 11 R. 870.

[70] The Inner House may do so on an incidental motion: *Collins* v. *Eglinton Iron Co.* (1882) 9 R. 500; *McAvoy* v. *Young's Paraffin Co.* (1882) 19 S.L.R. 441.

[71] *Connolly* v. *Bent Colliery Co.* (1897) 24 R. 1172; *cf. Anderson* v. *Muirhead* (1884) 11 R. 870.

[72] R.C. 131. See also *Boylan* v. *Hunter*, 1922 S.C. 80.

[73] R.C. 132.

[74] *Boylan, supra.*

[75] *Fairley* v. *Allan*, 1948 S.L.T.(Notes) 81.

[76] *Falconer* v. *Robertson*, 1949 S.L.T.(Notes) 57.

[77] 1922 S.C. 80.

CHAPTER 61

REVIEW OF AWARDS OF DAMAGES

EITHER party, if dissatisfied with the award of damages made by the sheriff or judge or jury, as much as with the decision on liability to make reparation in damages, may competently appeal on that matter, as much as on any other point. An appeal on the decision of liability or no liability is inferentially an appeal on damages also, since a reversal of the judgment of first instance on liability implies a finding of some damages being due as compared with none, or none as against the sum awarded at first instance.

Damages for breach of contract

An appeal on the amount of damages awarded for breach of contract is competent.[1] In such a case the appellate court has to make its own assessment of the loss sustained and may vary to any extent the award made at first instance.

Damages for delict

An award of damages for delict is more readily a basis for appeal because of the element of subjectivity which attaches to many such awards. The judge or sheriff has little more to guide him than any available recent records of similar cases, including in cases of solatium for personal injuries, recent similar cases decided in the English courts, where the corresponding head of award is general damages for pain, suffering and loss of amenities.[2]

Damages for personal injury or death

The Inner House has long recognised that in making awards of damages as compensation for loss caused by personal injury or death there is room for legitimate difference of opinion on what is fair and reasonable compensation. Accordingly, it will not alter an award, or allow a new jury trial, merely because it thinks the award inaccurate. The figures taken as the basis of argument for the purposes of appeal or a motion for a new trial are the gross awards, not the net or actual awards after suffering any abatement required by a finding of contributory negligence. The proportion found in respect of contributory negligence may be a separate point for appeal.

Review of judicial awards

The Inner House has power when reviewing an award on a reclaiming

[1] *e.g. Spencer* v. *Macmillan's Trs.*, 1958 S.C. 300.
[2] *Allan* v. *Scott*, 1972 S.L.T. 45.

motion from the Outer House [3] or an appeal from the Sheriff Court,[4] to vary the interlocutor in such a way and to such an extent as the Inner House thinks fit. Where it reverses a Lord Ordinary who has assoilzied the defenders, the Division may itself assess the damages without remitting to the Lord Ordinary.[5]

Review of jury awards

A motion may be made in the Inner House for the allowance of a new jury trial on the grounds, *inter alia*, of excess of damages,[6] or for such other cause as is essential to the justice of the case,[7] which has been interpreted as capable of including inadequacy of damages.[8] The court also has power, of consent of both [9] parties, to reduce the sum awarded instead of ordering a new trial,[10] or to set aside the verdict and enter judgment for the defenders, if of the opinion that all obtainable relevant evidence was before the jury and that the verdict was contrary to the evidence, which disclosed no ground on which a verdict for the pursuer could be returned,[11] or to set aside the verdict and order a new trial on the grounds *inter alia* of excess or inadequacy of damages.[12] If parties do not consent to a reduction of damages the whole case must be sent for retrial, as the court has no power to refuse a new trial and itself assess damages.[13] When, on a motion for a new trial, the court is of opinion that the only ground for granting a new trial is excess or inadequacy of damages, it shall grant a new trial restricted to the quantum of damages.[14] If it allows a new trial on damages it must do so in respect of all the claims made by the whole group of pursuers and not in respect of some only.[15] A jury is not entitled to award a sum greater than that concluded for and stated in the issue.[16]

3 *Brownlie* v. *Barrhead Mags.*, 1925 S.C.(H.L.) 41.

4 *e.g. Paterson* v. *L.M.S. Ry.*, 1942 S.C. 156; *Kelly* v. *Glasgow Corpn.*, 1949 S.C. 496 (affd. 1951 S.C.(H.L.) 15); *McLeish* v. *Fulton*, 1955 S.C. 46.

5 *e.g. Purdie* v. *Allan*, 1949 S.C. 477.

6 Jury Trials (Sc.) Act 1815, s. 6.

7 *Ibid.*

8 *Black* v. *Croall* (1854) 16 D. 431; *Reid* v. *Morton* (1902) 4 F. 438; *Gibson* v. *Kyle*, 1933 S.C. 30; *Aitken* v. *Laidlay*, 1938 S.C. 303. Contrast *Madden* v. *Glasgow Corpn.*, 1923 S.C. 102.

9 *Watt* v. *Watt* [1905] A.C. 115; *Boal* v. *Scottish Catholic Printing Co.*, 1908 S.C. 667.

10 *Johnston* v. *Dilke* (1875) 2 R. 836; *Ritchie* v. *Barton* (1883) 10 R. 813; *Wallace* v. *West Calder Co-operative Socy.* (1888) 15 R. 307; *Middlemas* v. *N.B. Ry.* (1893) 1 S.L.T. 12; *McKiernan* v. *Glasgow Corpn.*, 1919 S.C. 407; *Boal, supra.*

11 Jury Trials Amendment (Sc.) Act 1910, s. 2; *Mills* v. *Kelvin & White*, 1913 S.C. 521; *Macleod* v. *Edinburgh & Dist. Tramways*, 1913 S.C. 624; *West* v. *Mackenzie*, 1917 S.C. 513; see also *Simpson* v. *Glasgow Corpn.*, 1916 S.C. 345; *Madden* v. *Glasgow Corpn.*, 1923 S.C. 102; *Collum* v. *Carmichael*, 1957 S.C. 349; *Potec* v. *Edinburgh Corpn.*, 1962 S.C.(H.L.) 1; *Brennan* v. *Edinburgh Corpn.*, 1962 S.C. 36. In *Moyes* v. *Burntisland Shipbuilding Co.*, 1952 S.C. 429, and *Kerr* v. *John Brown & Co.*, 1965 S.C. 144, an amendment of the record was allowed and the case reheard by proof before answer. Similarly in *Ewart* v. *R. & W. Ferguson*, 1932 S.C. 277 and *Milne* v. *Glasgow Corpn.*, 1951 S.C. 340, cases remitted to the Court of Session for jury trial were amended and heard by proof before answer. Only the Inner House can alter the mode of trial.

12 R.C. 126.

13 *Boal, supra.* See also *McCallum* v. *Paterson*, 1969 S.C. 85, 92.

14 A.S. (Jury Trials Amendment) 1965, amending Jury Trials (Scotland) Act 1815, s. 6.

15 *Campbell* v. *West of Scotland Shipbreaking Co.*, 1953 S.C. 173, disapproving *Leadbetter* v. *N.C.B.*, 1952 S.C. 19.

16 *Clark* v. *Thomson* (1817) 1 Mur. 188.

Lord President Dunedin has observed [17] that " the grounds for disturbing a verdict on account of an excessive award of damages ought to be much stronger than they are for disturbing a verdict as being contrary to evidence, because in the one case there is, and in the other case there is not, what may be called certainty. If a bench of trained judges comes to the conclusion that a verdict is not supported by evidence, I think you may take it that if anything human is right, that is right. In cases where a jury has given a verdict which is contrary to law, I think it only right that such a verdict should be set aside and a new trial given, so that a more reasonable jury may come to another conclusion. On a mere question of *quantum* of damages, while a judge would, by long experience, probably be a better appraiser of damages than a juryman, still at the same time there is no certainty that he would be right, for in this matter there really is no standard of right. After all is said and done, the assessment of damages for personal injuries is, as people say, a very haphazard operation, as to which there is no certainty and the law, accordingly, has taken as the standard the amount which twelve ordinary men shall think right."

Different attitudes to judge's awards and jury's awards

Furthermore the Inner House recognises that judges and sheriffs are, or should be, familiar with the relevant principles laid down in cases and also with the current practice and trends in cases and also with the current practices and trends in awards, whereas juries are unfamiliar with these guides and are having to make an award, for the first time in their careers, without any knowledge or experience in the matter and with only the necessarily somewhat vague guidance given in the judge's charge to guide them. Accordingly greater latitude is allowed to juries, and their awards must deviate further from what is deemed fair and reasonable before a new trial will be granted.[18]

" In reviewing a decision of a sheriff-substitute in a question of damages we are not at all in the same position as that in which we are placed when we are asked to consider the verdict of a jury, because there is no appeal to this court against the verdict of a jury in determining damages. We do not review their verdict and give a judgment of our own according to what we think their judgment ought to have been. We may set it aside if we see sufficient ground for holding that a reasonable jury, honestly regarding what is laid down for their guidance—which in the present case is supposed to be, that they are to give reasonable and temperate though substantial damages—could not possibly have awarded so excessive an amount as has been actually given in a particular case. We may set aside the verdict and order

[17] *Casey* v. *United Collieries Ltd.*, 1907 S.C. 690, 692.
[18] *Young* v. *Glasgow Tramways Co.* (1882) 10 R. 242, 245.

the case to be tried again, but we do not review their verdict and make up our own minds as to what is the proper amount and so decide. But in the case of an appeal from a sheriff, then we are bound to review the judgment of the sheriff, just as much on that point as on any other. We are to exercise the same functions as he exercised, and if we think him wrong, then we are to do what we think he ought to have done in the first instance; but while there is that very material distinction, I still think with your Lordships that it is not reasonable to interfere on slight grounds with the sheriff's estimate of damage, especially in a case in which no exact measure can be fixed." [19]

Similarly: " In approaching an award which is made by a sheriff one does not just follow the same course as one follows in approaching a jury's award. As far as a jury's award is concerned there are certain principles laid down and clearly understood. A judge does not receive the same latitude from an appeal court, largely, I think, because he is capable of explaining the grounds upon which he proceeded, and is expected to do so, and it is open to the court to consider what these grounds are. If a sheriff in his assessment makes an error in law, or applies a wrong principle, he can be corrected." [20] " The extent to which a court of review can interfere with the award of damages by a judge is less restricted than its right to interfere with the award of a jury, and one of the reasons for this is that, unlike a jury, a judge has to give the grounds on which he arrives at his conclusion . . . a considerable latitude must necessarily be given to the judge in fixing the amount. . . . Hence a court reviewing a judge's award will not interfere with the amount merely because it thinks the judge awarded a sum a little more or a little less than the court of review would have done. The disparity must be substantial, whether the original award is described as wholly unreasonable (Lord President Normand's test in *Inglis* v. *London, Midland and Scottish Ry. Co.*[21]) or as clearly excessive (Lord Justice Clerk Thomson in *Purdie* [22])." [23] " Four rules can be derived from the opinion of the Lord Justice Clerk [in *Purdie*].[22] First, the award of a judge does not have the same degree of ' sanctity ' as that of a jury. Second, the court of appeal will interfere with such an award if the judge has made an error in law or applied a wrong principle. Third, in reviewing the amount of an award for solatium for pain and suffering the court of appeal gives full weight to the privileged position of the judge who was at the proof, whose decision may have been influenced by this advantage and by the impressions he formed. Fourth, the court of appeal will not interfere with the discretion of the judge in the assessment of solatium unless

19 *King* v. *B.L. Co.* (1899) 1 F. 928, 935, *per* Lord Kinnear; *cf.* L.P. Robertson at p. 931, Lord Adam at p. 932, Lord McLaren at p. 933.
20 *Purdie* v. *Allan*, 1949 S.C. 477, 479, *per* L.J.C. Thomson.
21 1941 S.C. 551, 560.
22 *Purdie* v. *Allan*, 1949 S.C. 477, 479, *per* L.J.C. Thomson.
23 *Butler* v. *Adam Lynn Ltd.*, 1965 S.C. 137, 140, *per* L.P. Clyde, referring to *Purdie, supra.*

the sum awarded is out of all proportion to what the court thinks should have been awarded." [24] "Whether [the court will interfere] depends on whether it regards the award of the judge of the court of first instance as being so much above or below the normal range of such awards in comparable circumstances, as to be unreasonable and unfair to one side or the other. An award of solatium is not capable of exact calculation. It is arrived at by a combination of considerations, including the facts in the case, knowledge of other awards and judicial experience. It is important that judges should make awards which are related to the general run of awards at that time and this the judge does within the exercise of his discretion. To this discretion there is an upper and a lower limit, and if an appellate court thinks that a particular award is above or below that limit, it will recall that award and exercise its own discretion." [25]

Difference between position of sheriff-principal and sheriff

When a sheriff's award is reviewed by the Inner House, having already been reviewed by the sheriff-principal, the latter's view is not entitled to the same weight as that of the trial judge. The sheriff on appeal has not the privileged position of a trial judge, and does not have the advantage of impressions formed at the proof, though his view is in a matter not admitting of exact calculation, and not to be interfered with unless plainly wrong.[26]

Principles applicable where award by judge or sheriff

An award of solatium for personal injuries is an exercise of judicial discretion and in reviewing it "a court of appeal is not entitled simply to substitute its own ideas for those of the trial judge. It must give full weight to the privileged position in which the trial judge is and interfere only if it is satisfied that the trial judge has misused or misunderstood his privileged opportunity. Nevertheless, if a judge in the exercise of his discretion awards a sum which appears to be out of all proportion to the true sum which ought in the view of the appeal court to have been awarded, then I think we are bound to revise his estimate." [27] Similarly "the court of appeal will interfere with such an award if the judge has made an error in law or applied a wrong principle . . . the court of appeal will not interfere with the discretion of the judge in the assessment of solatium unless the sum awarded is out of all proportion to what the court thinks should have been awarded." [28]

[24] *Butler*, *supra*, 142, *per* Lord Guthrie.
[25] *Butler*, *supra*, 143, *per* Lord Migdale.
[26] *Butler* v. *Adam Lynn Ltd.*, 1965 S.C. 137, 143, *per* Lord Guthrie.
[27] *Purdie* v. *Allan*, 1949 S.C. 477, 480, *per* L.J.C. Thomson.
[28] *Butler* v. *Adam Lynn Ltd.*, 1965 S.C. 137, 142, *per* Lord Guthrie. See also *Paterson* v. *L.M.S. Ry.*, 1942 S.C. 156; *Kelly* v. *Glasgow Corpn.*, 1949 S.C. 496; affd. 1951 S.C.(H.L.) 15; *McLeish* v. *Fulton*, 1955 S.C. 46.

Similarly in a fatal accident case it was observed [29] that " it would be most unwise for the court to interfere with an award for solatium made by a sheriff or judge unless it was satisfied that the amount was wholly unreasonable."

It has been indicated, moreover, that a judge or sheriff should itemise his award and indicate how much he awarded under each of the main heads of claim.[30] This should certainly be done in a death case because the pursuing relatives are truly bringing distinct claims for solatium and for patrimonial loss.[31]

In the English courts, where awards are normally made by judges sitting alone, the same general approach is adopted, and the award of the trial judge will not be altered unless the judge acted on a wrong principle of law, or the award was so high or low as to be, in the view of the Court of Appeal, an entirely erroneous estimate of the damages to which the plaintiff was entitled.[32]

Principles applicable where award by jury

The Inner House will not allow a new trial for excess or inadequacy of damages merely because it thinks the award more or less, even substantially more or less, than it should have been [33] or than a trial judge would have awarded.[34] The court must be able to say, the damages are beyond measure unreasonable; though they cannot say exactly what damages ought to be given.[35] The verdict of a jury is not readily to be interfered with: " The law enjoins and encourages a strong judicial aversion to disturb verdicts, especially on the ground of excess of damages—damages being a matter which it is the special business of juries to estimate." [36] " Unless the damages appear to be so unreasonable that, as was said in one case, all hands are lifted up in astonishment, the court will not set aside the verdict." [37]

In another case it was said: " This is a verdict which, to use the expression of an old judge, would make people hold up their hands in astonishment." [38]

Similarly in one English case it was said that counsel " expressed the test graphically and rightly when he said that this court [Court of Appeal]

29 *Inglis* v. *L.M.S. Ry.*, 1941 S.C. 551, 560, *per* L.P. Normand.

30 *Purdie* v. *Allan*, 1949 S.C. 477.

31 See Lord Carmont's explanation in *Hewitt* v. *West's Gas Improvement Co.*, 1955 S.C. 162, 166–167.

32 *Flint* v. *Lovell* [1935] 2 K.B. 354; *Owen* v. *Sykes* [1936] 1 K.B. 192; *Grein* v. *Imperial Airways* [1937] 1 K.B. 50; *The Aizkarai Mendi* [1938] P. 263; *Roach* v. *Yates* [1938] 1 K.B. 256; *Phillips* v. *Lloyd* [1938] 1 All E.R. 226; *Rook* v. *Fairrie* [1941] 1 K.B. 507; *Davies* v. *Powell Duffryn* [1942] A.C. 601; *Greenfield* v. *L.N.E. Ry.* [1945] K.B. 89.

33 *Houlden* v. *Couper* (1871) 9 S.L.R. 169; *Casey* v. *United Collieries*, 1907 S.C. 690.

34 *Potter* v. *N.B. Ry.* (1873) 11 M. 664; *Gibson* v. *Anderson* (1897) 24 R. 556.

35 *Adam on Jury Trial*, 197.

36 *Landell* v. *Landell* (1841) 3 D. 819, 826, *per* Lord Cockburn.

37 *Landell*, *supra*, 823, *per* L.J.C. Boyle.

38 *Johnston* v. *Dilke* (1875) 2 R. 836, 841, *per* Lord Gifford (slander—damages of £1,275 reduced by court to £100).

would interfere if on seeing the figure it said to itself ' Good gracious me—as high as that? '." [39]

> In *Landell* v. *Landell* [40] the consulted judges [41] stated: "It is evidently not enough, in order to bring the damages within the description of excessive that they are more, and even a great deal more, than the amount at which the injury sustained might have been estimated, in the opinion of the individual members of the court to whom the application is made. Indeed, if that were enough, the court would just be called upon to review the verdict of the jury, in a matter peculiarly within their province, and that upon a comparatively imperfect view of the evidence. It is clear that, in order to warrant the application of the term ' excessive ' the damages must be held to exceed, not what the court might think enough, but even that latitude, which, in a question of amount so very vague, any set of reasonable men could be permitted to indulge. The excess must be such as to raise on the part of the court the moral conviction that the jury, whether from wrong intention or incapacity, or some mistake, have committed gross injustice, and have given higher damages than any jury of ordinary men fairly and without gross mistake exercising their functions, could have awarded. It must be admitted that, even in this sense, there can be no definition of the term excessive, and indeed no form of expression can be well devised that does not leave this very point somewhat vague, and does not raise a kind of secondary jury question to be decided by the court."

In *McGinley* v. *Pacitti* [42] Lord President Cooper said that in cases of damages for personal injuries, involving the appraisal and assessment of a number of elements of which some at least are capable of more or less precise quantification, the ultimate test must be " practice and experience, moulded where necessary by quasi-permanent changes in the value of money and in social conditions," and in *Campbell* v. *West of Scotland Shipbreaking Co.* [43] that " the ultimate test still is whether the damages exceed not merely what the court might think enough, but even that latitude which, in a question of amount so very vague, any set of reasonable men could be permitted to indulge; or that the excess must be such as to

39 *McCarthy* v. *Coldair* [1951] 2 T.L.R. 1226. For other expressions in English cases see *Praed* v. *Graham* (1890) 24 Q.B.D. 53, 55; *Smith* v. *Schilling* [1928] 1 K.B. 429; *Mechanical & General Inventions Co.* v. *Austin* [1935] A.C. 346, 378.

40 (1841) 3 D. 819 (a case of damages for wrongful imprisonment, but regularly cited as laying down a principle equally applicable to damages for personal injuries or death).

41 *Ibid.* 825–826, *per* Lords Fullerton, Mackenzie, Jeffrey and Murray jointly, approved in *Casey* v. *United Collieries*, 1907 S.C. 690; *Thomas* v. *Caledonian Ry.*, 1913 S.C. 804, and *McGinley* v. *Pacitti*, 1950 S.C. 364, 367, *per* L.P. Cooper, as " the foundation pronouncement on the review of the quantum of jury verdicts." See also *Adamson* v. *Whitson* (1849) 11 D. 680; *Shields* v. *N.B. Ry.* (1874) 2 R. 126; *Young* v. *Glasgow Tramways Co.* (1882) 10 R. 242, 245; *McMaster* v. *Caledonian Ry. Co.* (1885) 13 R. 252; *Wallace* v. *West Calder Co-operative Socy.* (1888) 15 R. 307.

42 1950 S.C. 364, 369.

43 1953 S.C. 173, 175, approved in *Hewitt* v. *West's Gas Improvement Co.*, 1955 S.C. 162, 166, *per* L.P. Clyde.

raise the moral conviction that the jury have committed gross injustice and a gross mistake in the exercise of their function."

In *McCallum* v. *Paterson* [44] Lord President Clyde said: " The nearest definition one can get is that an award is excessive if it is so high that no reasonable jury properly instructed could have made it."

Accordingly in many cases the Inner House has held that, while a jury award was high, it was not so grossly excessive as to require the granting of a new trial.[45]

The " double or half " principle

In *Young* v. *Glasgow Tramways Co.*,[46] a personal injuries case, Lord President Inglis observed that " unless it can be said that the verdict ought not to have been for more than one-half of the sum awarded, there is not according to our practice, any room for interference." This gave rise to a supposed rule that a jury award would be overturned if it were deemed to be more than double or less than half what would have been a fair and reasonable award, that is, giving the jury a margin of error of one hundred per cent. The dictum (for it is no more) was relied on in *McKiernan* v. *Glasgow Corpn.*[47] and applied in *Elliot* v. *Glasgow Corpn.*[48] (where it was described as a " working rule "), *Duffy* v. *Kinneil Cannel and Coking Coal Co.*,[49] and in *Inglis* v. *L.M.S. Ry.*,[50] where Lord President Normand observed that " when solatium is awarded by a jury, it is a working rule that the court will not interfere unless the award is so excessive as to be in the region of twice what a reasonable jury might award."

But in *McGinley* v. *Pacitti* [51] Lord President Cooper, having reviewed the cases, concluded that the working rule was applicable to awards for pure solatium only,[52] in which cases it was " little more than one method of stating the rule in *Landell* v. *Landell* [53] in its application to a special case." But in relation to damages for personal injuries, and to awards for loss of support, the " double or half " rule was inadequate: " justice is not visibly done when we abdicate the judicial function and, instead of making the assessment of damages a rational process, take refuge behind the inscrutable oracular pronouncements of a jury, which is deliberately allowed to

44 1969 S.C. 85, 88. Similarly Lord Guthrie at p. 91.
45 *e.g. Love* v. *N.C.B.*, 1956 S.C. 459; *Wason* v. *B.T.C.*, 1960 S.C. 261.
46 (1883) 10 R. 242, 245.
47 1919 S.C. 407.
48 1922 S.C. 146.
49 1930 S.C. 596.
50 1941 S.C. 551.
51 1950 S.C. 364, 368.
52 *i.e.* solatium to one or more persons for the death of a relative. Lord Cooper stated that, save in *Casey*, the working rule had never been applied except to awards for pure solatium, or in one case (*Duffy*) to pure solatium plus an element of patrimonial loss. In *McCallum* v. *Paterson*, 1968 S.C. 280, 284, Lord Cameron explained this as not expressly or specifically limited to cases of solatium for the death of a relative. As the dictum was originally pronounced in a personal injuries case, and as it is in personal injuries cases that the element of solatium is largest, and least capable of calculation, it may be that the dictum should be confined to these cases rather than, as Lord Cooper thought, to cases of solatium for death of a relative where the size of award is conventionally restricted within fairly narrow limits.
53 (1841) 3 D. 819.

award a claim worth £5,000 anything from £2,500 to £10,000." [54] Special considerations would doubtless continue to be applied to awards of pure solatium and cases of defamation, where there is no means of gauging awards accurately.

Even in cases where the " working rule " may still have some relevance,[55] it has been said [56] to be undesirable to encourage appeals against awards for solatium which would result only in small modifications of the awards. " It is difficult to estimate in money the main elements which go to solatium, and still more difficult to estimate in money each relevant specialty in the circumstances of the several claimants in each particular case. There must always be an element of the arbitrary in any award, and it would perhaps do more harm than good to insist upon small variations grounded on the strict application of general principles."

Aggregate awards to be considered

Where awards have been made in a single action to several entitled pursuers, each claiming for solatium and patrimonial loss resulting from the death of a relative, all the claims have to be considered as parts of a family claim, and consequently, when reviewing the reasonableness of awards, whether by judge or jury, consideration should properly be directed at the aggregate of the awards.[57] " The proper comparison is between the aggregate of the sums actually awarded and the aggregate of the sums which should properly have been awarded." [58] Lord Carmont however,[59] doubted whether aggregation was appropriate in cases of patrimonial loss, though he considered it appropriate to aggregate all claims given in name of solatium. It is submitted that aggregation of patrimonial loss claims is at least as appropriate, in that one income has been lost, though several pursuers have lost thereby, but their aggregate losses cannot exceed the one income lost.

The prevailing view is, however, that the aggregate of combined claims has to be considered. " The crucial matter is the cumulo amount awarded, and the fact that one of the individual awards may appear quite excessive is not sufficient to justify our interference." [60]

Furthermore, it is not competent to grant a new trial in respect of some only of the pursuers' claims, letting the others stand.[61] In *Wason* v. *B.T.C.*[62] the court held that the amount awarded to a widow was excessive and a new trial was allowed; no objection was made to the awards to the

[54] 1950 S.C. at 369.
[55] It was taken as the basis of his opinion by Lord Cameron in *McCallum* v. *Paterson*, 1968 S.C. 280, 284, a personal injury case.
[56] *Kelly* v. *Glasgow Corpn.*, 1951 S.C.(H.L.) 15, 20, *per* Lord Normand.
[57] *Kelly* v. *Glasgow Corpn.*, 1951 S.C.(H.L.) 15, 20.
[58] *Hewitt* v. *West's Gas Improvement Co.*, 1955 S.C. 162, 166, *per* L.P. Clyde.
[59] *Hewitt*, *supra*, 167; see also Lord Russell at pp. 169–172.
[60] *Love* v. *N.C.B.*, 1956 S.C. 459, 461, *per* L.P. Clyde.
[61] *Campbell* v. *West of Scotland Shipbreaking Co.*, 1953 S.C. 173, not following *Leadbetter* v. *N.C.B.*, 1952 S.C. 19; 1952 S.L.T. 179.
[62] 1960 S.C. 261.

three children who also sued in the action. Where a tender has been made and accepted by some pursuers and a new trial is allowed in respect of awards to the others it is inevitably a new trial on some of the awards only.

Distinguishing elements of awards

In actions by the surviving relatives of a deceased it used to be the practice for even a jury to make distinct awards in respect of the separate claims for solatium and for patrimonial loss, but in more modern practice it has been usual to claim, and award, lump sums to cover both claims. Lord Carmont, however, expressed the view [63] that the proper practice is, even for a jury, to separate the awards, and observed: " Where separate awards were made, it was quite possible to attack each award as being excessive, and it was very much easier to dispose of an extravagant amount given in name of solatium for the reason that the character of that right had been for a long time put within the limits little removed from nominal damages. It was but a step from such a limitation to recognising solatium as an award applicable in equal measure to every member of a family who cares to come forward to tell the jury that his or her feelings had been lacerated by the death on which the claim was made. Hence the appropriateness of aggregating all the sums given in name of solatium so as to test adequacy or inadequacy. Such a case of pure solatium was *Kelly*,[64] and the principle of aggregation was approved in the House of Lords. I do not think, however, that we should read what was said in that case as being applicable to cases of patrimonial loss which are not suitable for aggregation. The actual case was one covering solatium only." While this is doubtless, in theory, the proper course, two practical objections exist to the course of getting a jury to make distinct awards to each pursuer under each of the separate heads of solatium and of patrimonial loss, first, that it enhances the danger of misunderstanding by the jury, or prolonged argument in the jury room, and of mistaken or absurd awards, and, second, that it may encourage motions for a new trial, based on detailed criticism of the different awards, whether they are inadequate, reasonable or excessive, separately or in aggregate, if all the solatium awards be taken together, if all the total awards be taken together, and so on.[65] If juries are to be trusted with the awarding of damages the simpler and more inscrutable their awards the better; the more they are required to condescend on details the more the awards are open to argument.

The need for a jury to distinguish the elements in its award is, however, now greater in view of the need for the court to have a basis for awarding interest on parts of the award of damages, and it has been held that a jury should be instructed to distinguish the elements in its award.[66]

[63] *Hewitt* v. *West's Gas Improvement Co.*, 1955 S.C. 162, 167.

[64] 1951 S.C.(H.L.) 15.

[65] Consider the possible arguments which could have arisen in *Hewitt* v. *West's Gas Improvement Co.*, 1955 S.C. 162, where separate awards had to be made to a widow and seven children, if the jury had had to distinguish between awards for solatium and awards for patrimonial loss.

[66] *Macdonald* v. *Glasgow Corpn.*, 1973 S.L.T. 107.

Appeal on finding of contributory negligence

An appeal as to a finding of contributory negligence or not and as to its extent is similarly inferentially an appeal on damages because variation of the finding on this point will affect the amount of damages actually recoverable. Where contributory negligence is pleaded and a jury trial is allowed the failure of the presiding judge or sheriff to put the matter of contributory negligence before the jury and to ascertain their view on it is a ground of appeal.[67]

Appeal on allocation of fault between wrongdoers

Where an action has been brought against two or more defenders as joint wrongdoers and one has been assoilzied at first instance but the other or another has appealed, it has been held that, in view of the right of relief competent under statute,[68] the defender appealing is entitled to insist on the other defender remaining a party to the cause.[69]

Appeal on award of interest

It is competent to reclaim to the Inner House on the matter of interest, the grant or withholding thereof, the rate or rates of interest, and generally the way in which the Lord Ordinary has exercised his discretion in relation to interest on the damages.[70]

In sheriff court cases the grant or refusal of an award of interest, and the amount of interest, are also grounds of appeal.[71]

Third or subsequent trials

In a case where a new jury trial has been allowed the court is not bound to accept the verdict of a second jury, but must consider the reasonableness of the second award in the same way as previously. " But when a question of fact has been tried twice over and two separate juries have come to the same conclusion upon the facts, I think it extremely desirable that litigation should come to an end, and I do not think it would be right or expedient in the court to order a third trial except in the kind of case that was pointed out by Lord McLaren. I quite agree with Lord McLaren that if it had appeared that the verdict must have proceeded upon some direct disregard of law clearly laid down to them, it would be the duty of the court to set aside two or three verdicts in order that justice might be done." [72] " Great weight ought always to attach to the verdict of a jury on a question of fact, and if a second jury under a different judge reach the same conclusion as the first jury, it must be doubly clear that the verdict cannot be supported by the evidence before we should be justified in

[67] *Armstrong* v. *Lithgows Ltd.*, 1954 S.C. 233.
[68] Law Reform (Miscellaneous Provisions) (Scotland) Act 1940, s. 3.
[69] *Davidson* v. *North of Scotland Hydro-Electric Board*, 1954 S.C. 230.
[70] *Macrae* v. *Reed & Mallik Ltd.*, 1961 S.C. 68.
[71] Interest on Damages (Scotland) Act 1958, s. 2.
[72] *Grant* v. *William Baird & Co.* (1903) 5 F. 459, 462, *per* Lord Kinnear.

setting the second verdict aside." [73] But in the same case another judge [74] did not think that one was " bound to say that, because there has been a previous re-trial, there should not be another one " and a third judge [75] did not " see how a court of review, without stultifying itself, could affirm that an unjust verdict becomes just merely because a second jury have affirmed it. It is said that there must be finality in these matters, but finality must not be sought by the perpetuation of injustice."

The court is accordingly more reluctant to set aside a second jury verdict, if to the same effect as the first, on a question of liability, but certainly not bound to do so. There are numerous examples of a third trial being allowed [76] and of being refused,[77] all cases where the question was whether the verdict was justified by the evidence or not.

But the same considerations do not wholly apply to the allowing or refusing of a third trial on the ground of excess or inadequacy of damages. An award is not the less excessive or inadequate merely because it has been repeated, or nearly repeated, by a second jury. In *McCallum* v. *Paterson*,[78] where liability was admitted, the Second Division allowed a new trial, the damages being excessive. A second jury having awarded almost the same amount the First Division again allowed a new trial for excess of damages.[79] Lord President Clyde [80] denied that it was a matter of expediency not to order a third trial in any case. " Parliament has envisaged that, if an excessive award is made, the court, on a motion for a new trial may order a fresh one, even if this means a succession of abortive trials." " Of course, the fact that two different juries at two different times have given similar verdicts is a very strong element against allowing the present motion. On the other hand we are bound to give great weight to the fact that the other Division, on substantially the same evidence, has held that the earlier award was excessive. The decision of the Second Division is not *res judicata* in favour of the defender, and it was not contended that it was. This court must still fulfil its statutory duty of deciding whether the present award was excessive upon a consideration of the evidence led at the second trial and of the whole circumstances of the case." [81]

Appeals to House of Lords on damages

Interlocutors by a sheriff or Lord Ordinary awarding damages may be appealed, via the Inner House, to the House of Lords,[82] and an inter-

[73] *McKnight* v. *General Motor Carrying Co.*, 1936 S.C. 17, 21, *per* L.J.C. Aitchison. Lord Murray (p. 25) appears to agree.
[74] Lord Hunter, at p. 23 (dissenting).
[75] Lord Anderson, at p. 24.
[76] *Flood* v. *Caledonian Ry. Co.* (1899) 27 S.L.R. 127; *Watson* v. *N.B. Ry.* (1905) 7 F. 220; *Mitchell* v. *Caledonian Ry.*, 1910 S.C. 546.
[77] *McQuilkin* v. *Glasgow District Subway Co.* (1902) 4 F. 462; *Grant* v. *William Baird & Co.* (1903) 5 F. 459; *McKnight* v. *General Motor Carrying Co.*, 1936 S.C. 17.
[78] 1968 S.C. 280.
[79] 1969 S.C. 85.
[80] p. 88.
[81] *Ibid.* 91, *per* Lord Guthrie.
[82] *e.g. Kelly* v. *Glasgow Corpn.*, 1951 S.C.(H.L.) 15.

locutor granting or refusing a new jury trial can now be appealed there.[83] There is also a right of appeal against an interlocutor under section 2 of the Jury Trials Amendment (Scotland) Act 1910, setting aside the verdict and entering judgment for the party unsuccessful at the trial,[84] against an interlocutor on the matter of an exception to the presiding judge's direction in law,[85] and against a judgment in point of law as applicable to or arising out of the finding by the verdict of the jury.[86] The House of Lords has been said to have an unlimited discretion in the matter of awarding interest.[87]

[83] Administration of Justice (Scotland) Act 1972, s. 2, amending the Jury Trials (Sc.) Act 1815, s. 6. In such an appeal the House has the same powers as are exercisable by the Court of Session on a motion for a new trial.
[84] *Lyal* v. *Henderson*, 1916 S.C.(H.L.) 167.
[85] Jury Trials (Sc.) Act 1815, s. 7.
[86] *Ibid.* s. 9. See *Park* v. *Wilsons & Clyde Coal Co.*, 1929 S.C. 679.
[87] *Green* v. *Brown & Gracie Ltd.*, 1960 S.L.T.(Notes) 43.

PART IX

CONSISTORIAL REMEDIES

CHAPTER 62

CONSISTORIAL REMEDIES

CONSISTORIAL remedies are those granted originally by the consistorial courts of the dioceses, subsequently by the Commissary Court, and today by the Court of Session and sheriff courts in succession thereto.

Consistorial actions comprise declarators of marriage and of nullity of marriage, declarators of legitimacy and of bastardy, actions of separation *a mensa et thoro*, of adherence, of divorce and of putting to silence, and actions of aliment between husband and wife instituted in the Court of Session.[1] Of these the declarators and divorce are competent only in the Court of Session.[2] Actions of aliment, provided that as between husband and wife they are actions of separation and aliment, adherence and aliment, or interim aliment, and actions for regulating the custody of children, are competent also in the sheriff court [3] but in that context are not usually called consistorial remedies.

DECLARATORS OF MARRIAGE, NULLITY, LEGITIMACY OR BASTARDY

Though falling within the class of consistorial remedies these claims are properly declaratory in character and have been discussed under that heading.[4] Their function is to have declared judicially certain aspects of the status of individuals.[5] A declarator of marriage may be brought by a child of the marriage after the death of one spouse [6] and may be continued by the pursuer's executor after her death *pendente lite*, in view of its financial consequences.[7]

JUDICIAL SEPARATION

The remedy of judicial separation *a mensa et thoro* may be granted to either spouse on the ground of the adultery [8] or cruelty [9] (including habitual drunkenness [10]) of the other spouse. The effect of the decree is to entitle the spouse granted it to live apart from the other spouse, without

1 Conjugal Rights (Sc.) Amdt. Act 1861, s. 19.
2 Court of Session Act 1830, s. 33.
3 Sheriff Courts (Sc.) Act 1907, s. 5 (2).
4 Chap. 8, *supra*.
5 *Cf. Administrator of Austrian Property* v. *Von Lorang*, 1927 S.C.(H.L.) 80, 86.
6 *X* v. *Y*, 1921, 1 S.L.T. 69.
7 *Borthwick* v. *Borthwick* (1896) 24 R. 211; *cf. Mackie* v. *Mackie*, 1917 S.C. 276.
8 At common law. For what constitutes adultery see Walker, *Principles of Scottish Private Law*, 229, 237.
9 At common law. For what constitutes cruelty see Walker, *Principles of Scottish Private Law*, 229.
10 Habitual Drunkards Act 1879, s. 3; Licensing (Sc.) Act 1903, s. 73; *Cox* v. *Cox*, 1942 S.C. 352; *Hutchison* v. *Hutchison*, 1945 S.C. 427.

incurring any of the legal consequences of non-adherence. The husband ceases to be liable for his wife's acts and contracts, and even for necessaries supplied to her, and on her death intestate her property passes as if she were unmarried. But decree does not dissolve the marriage nor entitle either spouse to remarry.[11]

Aliment in actions for judicial separation

Despite the grant of a decree of separation the spouses are still married and the duty of a husband to aliment his wife continues and must be discharged by payment of money. A claim for separation, at least one brought by a wife, is accordingly normally conjoined with a petitory claim for payment of aliment, so long as the separation lasts,[12] and also for aliment for any children whom the pursuer has in her care and is supporting.[13] The claim for aliment is for " permanent " aliment, but this does not preclude it from being subject to review.[14] Any such award is *ad interim* and either party may apply for it to be increased or restricted in view of changed circumstances.[15]

Adherence and Aliment

When either spouse is failing to implement the duty to adhere to and cohabit with his or her spouse but is unjustifiably failing to do so the other spouse may crave that the non-adhering spouse be ordained to adhere, or alternatively to pay aliment. It has been held that a husband was not in non-adherence if he insisted on his wife living in premises provided for her separate use,[16] and either spouse may have the other ejected from his or her house and interdicted from returning,[17] so long as the husband aliments his wife.[18] The crave for adherence is in modern practice not specifically enforceable and the alternative conclusion is the important one. For such an action to be relevant the pursuer must himself be willing to adhere [19] and it is accordingly inconsistent with bringing simultaneously an action for divorce.[20]

The award of aliment in this case is always an interim one, in that if the defender chooses to adhere to the pursuer and support her at bed and board the claim for aliment will lapse. Even while it is payable, the amount is subject to review at the instance of either party having regard to changed circumstances of the parties.[21] There is no rule that, if the wife is earning

11 *Cf. Shirrefs* v. *Shirrefs* (1896) 23 R. 807.
12 *e.g. Wotherspoon* v. *Wotherspoon* (1869) 8 M. 81.
13 *e.g. Scott* v. *Scott* (1894) 21 R. 853.
14 *Donnelly* v. *Donnelly*, 1959 S.C. 97, 102.
15 *e.g. Purdom* v. *Purdom*, 1934 S.L.T. 315; *Dowswell* v. *Dowswell*, 1943 S.C. 23.
16 *Colquhoun* v. *Colquhoun* (1804) Mor.Appx. Husband and Wife, 5.
17 *MacLure* v. *MacLure*, 1911 S.C. 200; *Millar* v. *Millar*, 1940 S.C. 6.
18 *MacLure, supra.*
19 *Beveridge* v. *Beveridge*, 1963 S.C. 572.
20 *Farquharson* v. *Farquharson*, 1968 S.L.T.(Sh.Ct.) 45.
21 *Dowswell* v. *Dowswell*, 1943 S.C. 23.

money or acquires money from another source, the whole of this must be expended on her maintenance to the relief of her husband's obligation under the decree for aliment.[21]

ALIMENT BETWEEN HUSBAND AND WIFE

> " A husband is bound to support his wife so long as the marriage endures. The obligation is normally performed by supporting her while she lives with him. If, however, he puts her from him for any cause, and she is indigent, he becomes liable to aliment her until he receives her into family with him again, or until the marriage is annulled or dissolved. This is clear in the case where he puts her from him for no cause which would justify in law his non-adherence. She then may obtain her aliment through the medium of an action of adherence and aliment, although this is not her only remedy. . . . In the case where he puts her from him for a cause which justifies him in not adhering to her, for example, on account of her cruelty to him, or her adultery, he may divorce her, in which case his liability to aliment her ends with the dissolution of the marriage bond. But he may not wish to have the marriage dissolved, and may seek a decree of separation from her. In this latter case, if her offence be cruelty, he will be bound to continue to aliment her notwithstanding the decree of separation—*Nisbet* v. *Nisbet*.[22] The same result will follow, if her offence is adultery and he obtains decree of separation from her —*Milne* v. *Milne* [23]." [24]

The husband's liability for aliment, notwithstanding separation, subsists, however, only if she was willing to adhere, though guilty of adultery,[25] or is justifiably unwilling to adhere, alleging adultery by him [26] or cruelty on his part to her,[27] or such conduct by the defender as gives the pursuer just cause for living in separation from him.[28] But if she alleges no reasonable cause for her non-adherence, and is not herself willing to adhere, she is not entitled to aliment, his duty to aliment her, and her duty to adhere, being correlative.[29] There is no duty to aliment a wife who is in desertion.[30]

An action for permanent aliment is incompetent unless there is also a crave for separation or for adherence, and a claim for aliment alone is always for interim aliment only.[31]

22 (1897) 4 S.L.T. 158.
23 (1901) 8 S.L.T. 375.
24 *Donnelly* v. *Donnelly*, 1959 S.C. 97, 103, *per* Lord Patrick.
25 *Donnelly, supra.*
26 *Barbour* v. *Barbour*, 1965 S.C. 158.
27 *Beveridge* v. *Beveridge*, 1963 S.C. 572; *cf. Kelly* v. *Kelly* (1830) 9 S. 872.
28 Divorce (Scotland) Act 1964, s. 6.
29 *Beveridge* v. *Beveridge*, 1963 S.C. 572; *cf. Kelly* v. *Kelly* (1830) 9 S. 872.
30 *Jack* v. *Jack*, 1962 S.C. 24, explained in *Barbour, supra.*
31 *Jack, supra.*

Divorce

A marriage may be dissolved by the court and divorce *a vinculo matrimonii* granted if it is proved that either spouse has committed adultery,[32] or has wilfully and without reasonable cause deserted the other spouse and has persisted in such desertion for not less than three years,[33] or the defender has been for five years continuously immediately preceding the action under care and treatment as an insane person,[34] or the defender has been guilty of such cruelty towards the defender (including habitual drunkenness [35]) as would justify, according to the previously existing law and practice, the granting of a decree of separation *a mensa et thoro*,[36] or has been guilty of sodomy or bestiality.[37]

Dissolution of marriage on ground of presumed death

The court may, alternatively, dissolve a marriage if one party satisfies it that reasonable grounds exist for supposing that the other party to the marriage is dead, the fact that for a period of seven years or upward the other party has been continuously absent from the petitioner and the petitioner has no reason to believe that the other party has been living within that time being evidence of that fact unless the contrary is proved.[38]

Effect of decree

The effect of a decree of divorce or of dissolution of marriage is to change the status of the parties, releasing each from the rights and duties resulting from marriage, and entitling each to contract another marriage.

Remedies subsidiary to divorce

In an action of divorce on any ground other than incurable insanity [39] the pursuer may,[40] at any time prior to decree, apply to the court for an order for the payment to him by the defender, or the defender's executor, of a capital sum,[41] or a periodical allowance,[42] or both [43]; and either party may apply to the court for an order varying the terms of any settlement [44]

32 At common law. As to what is " adultery," see Walker, *Principles of Scottish Private Law*, 237.

33 Divorce (Sc.) Act 1938, s. 1 (1) (*a*). As to what is " desertion " see Walker, *Principles*, 241.

34 Divorce (Sc.) Act 1938, s. 1 (1) (*b*). As to " under care and treatment as an insane person " see 1938 Act, s. 6, as amended by Divorce (Insanity and Desertion) Act 1958, s. 1 and Mental Health (Scotland) Act 1960, Sch. 4.

35 *Rooney* v. *Rooney*, 1962 S.L.T. 294.

36 Divorce (Sc.) Act 1938, s. 1 (1) (*c*). As to what is " cruelty " see Divorce (Scotland) Act 1964, s. 4, and Walker, *Principles*, 249.

37 Divorce (Sc.) Act 1938, s. 1 (1) (*d*).

38 Divorce (Sc.) Act 1938, s. 5. See also *Labacianskas* v. *Labacianskas*, 1949 S.C. 280. *Cf. Lench* v. *Lench*, 1945 S.C. 295; see also *Gilchrist*, 1950 S.L.T.(Notes) 6.

39 Succession (Scotland) Act 1964, s. 26.

40 *Ibid.* s. 26 (1), (2).

41 *e.g. Murray* v. *Murray*, 1967 S.L.T.(Notes) 103.

42 *e.g. Gould* v. *Gould*, 1966 S.C. 88; *Gray* v. *Gray*, 1968 S.C. 189.

43 *e.g. Robertson* v. *Robertson*, 1967 S.L.T.(Notes) 78.

44 Including a settlement by policy of assurance under the Married Women's Policies of Assurance (Scotland) Act 1880.

made in contemplation of or during the marriage, so far as taking effect on or after the termination of the marriage. The court shall make such order as it thinks fit, having regard to the respective means of the parties to the marriage and to all the circumstances of the case, including any settlement or other arrangements made for financial provision for any children of the marriage.[45]

Where an application for a periodical allowance has been withdrawn or refused or no application made, the pursuer may apply after the divorce, if there has been a change in the circumstances of either party, and the court may make an order.[46]

An order for payment of a periodical allowance may, on application by or on behalf of either party or his or her executor on a change of circumstances, be varied or recalled by a subsequent order.[47] Any order for a periodical allowance ceases to have effect on the remarriage or death of the pursuer, except in relation to any arrears then due.[48] Such an order may be enforced throughout the United Kingdom under the Maintenance Orders Act 1950.[49]

Where an application has been made under section 26 (1) (*a*) or (3) or (4), the pursuer may, at any time before the expiry of one year from the disposal of the application apply to the Court of Session for an order (a) reducing or varying any settlement or disposition of property belonging to the defender made by him in favour of any third party at any time after the date three years before making the application, or (b) interdicting the defender from making any such settlement or disposition, or transferring out of the jurisdiction, or otherwise dealing with, any property belonging to the defender.[50]

On application for such an order the court may [51] make such an order if satisfied that the settlement or disposition was made or is about to be made, or that the property is about to be transferred or otherwise dealt with, primarily for the purpose of defeating, wholly or partly, any claim which the pursuer has made or might make under section 26.[52] But any such order does not prejudice the rights, if any, in the property of any person who has in good faith acquired it or any of it from the defender for value, or who derives title to the property or any of it from any person who has done so.

In the case of divorce for incurable insanity the court may make such order, if any, as, having regard to the respective means of either party it shall think fit, for payment by either party or by his executors, of a capital

45 A wife has been granted a periodical allowance though the husband was successful in his cross-action: *Thomson* v. *Thomson*, 1966 S.L.T.(Notes) 49.

46 *Ibid.* s. 26 (3).

47 *Ibid.* s. 26 (4).

48 *Ibid.* s. 26 (5).

49 *Ibid.* s. 26 (6).

50 *Ibid.* s. 27 (1).

51 *Ibid.* s. 27 (2).

52 *e.g. Johnstone* v. *Johnstone*, 1967 S.C. 143.

sum or an annual or periodical allowance to or for behoof of the other party or of any children of the marriage. Such an order may be varied or recalled.[53]

Putting to Silence

An action of putting to silence is competent to have a defender, who falsely asserts that he is married to the pursuer,[54] or otherwise related to the pursuer,[55] ordained to desist from such assertion and to maintain silence on the matter on pain of being in contempt of court. This remedy is of the nature of an interdict. It may be combined with a declarator of freedom,[54] *i.e.* of not being married, as the defender falsely asserts, or of bastardy.[55]

Aliment between Parent and Child

Such a claim is not a consistorial remedy, but a claim of debt. A parent is bound to aliment each and all of his children [56] so long as the child is unable to support himself. The obligation is incumbent primarily on the father,[57] whom failing on the mother.[58] Failing both parents it falls successively on the paternal grandfather,[59] paternal grandmother,[60] higher ascendants in the paternal line, maternal grandfather,[61] maternal grandmother,[62] and higher ascendants in the maternal line. No claim lies against brothers, sisters or other collaterals,[63] save where the father's estate has passed chiefly to one child of the family, in which case he takes it, so far as *lucratus* by the succession, with the liability to aliment the other children *jure representationis*, as representing his father.[64] This liability by representation may extend to the representatives of grandparents,[65] certainly where the grandparent acknowledged the obligation during his lifetime.[66]

A person is not legally liable to aliment his relatives by marriage.[67]

53 Divorce (Scotland) Act 1964, s. 7.

54 *e.g. Williams* v. *Forsythe*, 1909, 2 S.L.T. 252; *cf. A.B.* v. *C.D.* (1901) 8 S.L.T. 406.

55 *e.g. Imre* v. *Mitchell*, 1958 S.C. 439 (attempt to have man ordained to desist from asserting that pursuer's child was his).

56 Including posthumous children: *Spalding* v. *Spalding's Trs.* (1874) 2 R. 237.

57 Stair, I, 3, 3; I, 9, 1; Ersk. I, 6, 56; III, 1, 9; Bell, *Prin.* §§ 1629–1631; *Fairgrieves* v. *Hendersons* (1885) 13 R. 98.

58 Bell, *Prin.* §§ 1632–1633; Fraser, *Parent and Child*, 100; *Ewart* v. *R. & W. Ferguson*, 1932 S.C. 277.

59 *Ewart, supra*; *Gay's Tutrix* v. *Gay's Tr.*, 1953 S.L.T. 278.

60 *Muirhead* v. *Muirhead* (1849) 12 D. 356.

61 *Cooper* v. *Fife Coal Co.*, 1907 S.C. 564.

62 Fraser, *P. & Ch.*, 102.

63 *Eisten* v. *N.B. Ry. Co.* (1870) 8 M. 980.

64 *Hutchison* v. *Hutchison's Trs.*, 1951 S.C. 108; contrast *Beaton* v. *Beaton*, 1935 S.C. 187.

65 *Spalding* v. *Spalding's Trs.* (1874) 2 R. 237; *Anderson* v. *Grant* (1899) 1 F. 484; *Gay's Tutrix* v. *Gay's Tr.*, 1953 S.L.T. 278.

66 *Leslie Parish Council* v. *Gibson's Trs.* (1899) 1 F. 601.

67 *Macdonald* v. *Macdonald* (1846) 8 D. 830; *Hoseason* v. *Hoseason* (1870) 9 M. 37; *Barty's Trs.* v. *Barty* (1888) 15 R. 496; *McAllan* v. *Alexander* (1888) 15 R. 863; *Dear* v. *Duncan* (1896) 3 S.L.T. 241; *Reid* v. *Reid* (1904) 6 F. 935; *Mackay* v. *Mackay's Trs.* (1904) 6 F. 936.

Conversely a child is liable to aliment his or her parents and other ascendants.[68]

In case of choice a person's claim for aliment lies first against his descendants, and only failing them against his ascendants.[69]

Under the National Assistance Act 1948,[70] and the Ministry of Social Security Act 1966,[71] each parent is liable to maintain his or her spouse and children, and the Supplementary Benefits Commission may recover from persons liable the cost of assistance given to an indigent child.[72]

[68] Stair, I, 5, 8; Ersk. I, 6, 57; Bell, *Prin.* § 1634; *Hamilton* v. *Hamilton* (1877) 4 R. 688; *Duncan* v. *Duncan* (1882) 19 S.L.R. 696; *Foulis* v. *Fairbairn* (1887) 14 R. 1088; *Dear* v. *Duncan* (1896) 3 S.L.T. 241; *Sagar* v. *N.C.B.*, 1955 S.C. 424; *Dickson* v. *N.C.B.*, 1957 S.C. 157.

[69] *Beaton* v. *Beaton*, 1935 S.C. 187.

[70] ss. 42–43, amended Ministry of Social Security Act 1966, s. 39.

[71] s. 22.

[72] Parents' liability is joint and several: *N.A. Board* v. *Casey*, 1967 S.L.T.(Sh.Ct.) 11.

Part X

ADMIRALTY REMEDIES

CHAPTER 63

ADMIRALTY REMEDIES

IN the exercise of its jurisdiction inherited from the Scottish Court of Admiralty [1] the Court of Session may grant remedies in maritime causes, which are causes involving charterparties, freights, salvages, wrecks, bottomries, policies of marine insurance, contracts concerning the loading and unloading of ships, actions for the delivery of goods shipped or for their value, the ownership or possession of ships, actions arising from collisions, claims for wages and master's disbursements, and the like.[2]

The modern Rules of Court 1965 define Admiralty causes [3] as including causes arising out of:

(i) claims for possession of a ship, or the earnings of a ship, or the protection of the interests of one or more co-owners as against the others to enable a ship to be employed, the examination of accounts between the co-owners, or the apportionment of the earnings of a ship after such examination;

(ii) claims or disputes in regard to mortgages of ships or shares in a ship;

(iii) contracts of bottomry and respondentia;

(iv) claims under contracts of affreightment, charter-parties and bills of lading;

(v) (a) loss of life or personal injury and (b) loss of or damage to property arising out of collisions at sea;

(vi) claims by owners of cargo for damage occurring to cargo;

(vii) claims for limitation of liability;

(viii) pilotage;

(ix) civil salvage;

(x) claims for necessaries;

(xi) towage;

(xii) master's and seamen's wages and disbursements;

(xiii) general average;

(xiv) forfeiture of ships to the Crown;

(xv) marine insurance;

(xvi) maritime liens.

The sheriff court has jurisdiction in admiralty causes provided the defender is subject to the sheriff's jurisdiction on any legal ground of jurisdiction.[4]

[1] Court of Session Act 1830, ss. 21–22.
[2] Ersk. I, 3, 33; Bell, *Comm.* I, 546.
[3] R.C. 135.
[4] Sheriff Courts (Scotland) Act 1907, s. 4; *Pirie* v. *Warden* (1867) 5 M. 497; *Sheaf Steamship Co. Ltd.* v. *Compania Transmediterranea*, 1930 S.C. 660.

Under many of these heads the remedies granted are the same as granted in common law actions, and in general they proceed under the same procedural rules as common law actions.[5] But in certain matters the remedies in Admiralty or maritime causes are special and peculiar to such causes, and in certain matters the procedure is special.

The law in maritime questions is British, the law of Scotland and of England being identical,[6] and both being based on the general international custom of the sea adopted and applied by the former Admiralty courts, and in certain matters restated or modified by statute.[7]

Admiralty action in rem or in personam or both

An Admiralty action *in rem* is one directed against the owners or parties interested in a ship or cargo, with conclusions directed to recovery in respect of a lien against the ship or cargo or the proceeds thereof, as sold under order of court. An action *in personam* has conclusions directed to a decree in common form against the defender. An action *in rem* and *in personam* is directed to both of these ends.[8]

In an action *in rem* the ship or cargo must be arrested by arrestment *in rem*, effected on a warrant to arrest contained in the summons.[9] An arrestment *in rem* cannot validly be effected if the ship has been detained in port only under a prior, invalid, arrestment.[10]

Quite apart from arrestment under maritime law a ship may, like any other corporeal moveable, be arrested in security or in execution, while in the hands of a third party. If the possessor of the ship claims that the arrestment is invalid he petitions for recall of the arrestment on the ground that it is nimious and oppressive, in which case the arrestment may be recalled *simpliciter* or on caution.[11] The arrestee may also petition and is entitled to have the arrestment recalled unless the arrester can give a prima facie reason for his assertion that the property arrested belongs to his debtor. If it is plain that the property belongs to the arrestee the arrestment must be recalled.[12]

(i) Ownership and Possession of a Ship

Ownership of a ship is a question of fact and does not depend on registration of the title.[13] If his title is registered a person having right of ownership is the legal owner, but if not, he is beneficial owner.[14]

[5] R.C. 135, *ad finem.*

[6] *Currie* v. *McKnight* (1897) 24 R.(H.L.) 1; *Clydesdale Bank* v. *Walker & Bain*, 1926 S.C. 72, 82.

[7] *Boettcher* v. *Carron Co.* (1861) 23 D. 322, 330; *The Gas Float Whitton No.* 2 [1896] P. 42, 47–48; [1897] A.C. 337.

[8] R.C. 136.

[9] R.C. 137. As to execution of arrestments and intimation and advertisement of action *in rem*, see R.C. 140.

[10] *Carlberg* v. *Borjesson* (1878) 5 R.(H.L.) 217; *Azcarate* v. *Iturrizaga*, 1938 S.C. 573.

[11] *Barclay, Curle & Co.* v. *Laing*, 1908 S.C. 82, 86.

[12] *Barclay, Curle, supra.*

[13] *Union Bank of London* v. *Lenanton* (1878) 3 C.P.D. 243; *Chartered Mercantile Bank of India* v. *Netherlands India S.N. Co.* (1883) 10 Q.B.D. 521.

[14] As to " beneficial owner " see Merchant Shipping Act 1894, s. 57. In *Watson* v. *Duncan* (1879) 6 R. 1247 it was held that a bill of sale followed by possession in the shape of receipt of profits was a good title against the registered owner's trustee in bankruptcy.

Ownership is acquired by building,[15] by transfer from builder to first owner,[16] by transfer from one owner to another,[17] and by transmission of shares on death or bankruptcy.[18] The contract to sell and purchase property in a ship need not be constituted or proved in writing,[19] though the transfer of title must be effected by bill of sale.

Specific implement may be decreed of a contract to sell a ship.[20]

A dispute as to ownership may be decided in an action for declarator that the pursuer has right to a ship.[21]

In case of disputes between owners the court may order the sale of the ship, but is particularly hesitant to do so at the instance of minority owners.[22]

Set and sale

An action of set and sale is competent where one part-owner of a vessel is in disagreement with the other or others such that the continued employment of the vessel in their common interest is impracticable. By the action the pursuing part-owner seeks to have the other part-owners compelled to sell their shares to him, or to purchase his shares, at a stated price. The summons seeks declarator that the defenders should purchase the pursuer's shares at the price placed on them, or sell their shares to the pursuer at the same price, or that the ship should be sold by public auction.[23] The pursuer's offer must be to sell all his shares or to buy all the defender's shares,[24] so that it is not satisfied by acceptance by some only of the defenders.[25]

If judicial sale is necessary, an independent person will be called by the court to value the ship. The court may accept the pursuer's figure or the independent valuator's, as the upset price.[26]

The pursuer may himself bid at the sale but only with the leave of the court, as he is in a quasi-fiduciary position in relation to his co-owners.[27]

Process of sale

A process of sale is a claim whereby a ship or cargo may be brought to judicial sale where this is necessary for the enforcement of a real or personal right. It may proceed on the basis of a debt already constituted, or the debt may be constituted and sale be concluded for in the one action.[28]

[15] At common law.
[16] The Sale of Goods Act 1893 applies: *Laing* v. *Barclay, Curle & Co.*, 1908 S.C.(H.L.) 1.
[17] Merchant Shipping Act 1894, ss. 20, 24–26.
[18] *Ibid.* ss. 27–29; *Watson, supra.*
[19] *McConnachie* v. *Geddes*, 1918 S.C. 391.
[20] *Behnke* v. *Bede Shipping Co.* [1927] 1 K.B. 649.
[21] *Azcarate* v. *Iturrizaga*, 1938 S.C. 573.
[22] M.S.A. 1894, s. 29; *The Nelly Schneider* (1878) 3 P.D. 152; *The Marion* (1884) 10 P.D. 4; *The Hereward* [1895] P. 284.
[23] Juridical Styles, III, 180.
[24] *Hutton* v. *Hay* (1880) 2 Guthrie Sel.Shf.Ct.Cas. 537.
[25] *Anderson* v. *Sillars* (1894) 22 R. 105.
[26] *Elias* v. *Black* (1856) 18 D. 1225; *Morice* v. *Craig* (1901) 39 S.L.R. 609.
[27] *Elias* v. *Black* (1856) 18 D. 1225.
[28] *Taylor* v. *Williamson* (1831) 9 S. 265.

Apart from any conclusions relative to constitution of the debt, the conclusions are for declarator that the vessel should be sold judicially, for payment to the pursuer of the free proceeds of sale after payment of necessary expenses, for deposit of the balance, if any, in court, and for adjudication of the vessel to the purchaser free of all incumbrances.[29]

If the vessel is sold under authority of the court the pursuer by minute seeks approval of the sale, a finding that the vessel is now the property of the pursuer, a finding that the pursuer is entitled, in preference to other claims, to the expenses of bringing about the sale, and to the sum sued for out of the balance, or to the whole in extinction of his debt *pro tanto* if it be inadequate to satisfy his claim in full.

If there are competing claims on the sum realised the court must rank and prefer them according to their proper priorities, normally shipwright's lien, maritime liens, mortgages, and personal unsecured claims in the order in which diligence has been done.[30]

Possession

The right to possession and control of a ship rests with the majority of the owners and if the ship is in the actual possession of a minority owner the majority owners may arrest the ship and obtain from the court a decree of declarator of right to possession and for delivery, to enable them to use the ship as they wish.[31] The minority owners may conversely arrest the ship and seek an order that she be restrained from employment contrary to their wishes,[32] but it is only in a strong case that the court will interfere with the right of the majority owners to decide how the ship shall be employed.

(ii) Claims in Relation to Mortgages or Shares in a Ship

The property in a ship is divided into sixty-four shares, and a person may not be registered as owner of a fractional part of a share, though not more than five persons may be registered as joint owners of one or more shares, but this does not prevent the beneficial title of any number of persons represented by any registered owner.[33]

Where property in a ship or a share therein is transmitted to an unqualified person on death, bankruptcy, or otherwise, the appropriate court having jurisdiction may, on the application of such person, order a sale of the ship or share for his benefit.[34] It may, on the application of any interested person, make an order prohibiting for a time any dealing with a ship or share on such conditions as the justice of the case requires.[35]

29 Juridical Styles, III, 181.
30 *Cf. Inter-Islands Exporters Ltd.* v. *Berna Steamship Co. Ltd.*, 1960 S.L.T. 21.
31 *The New Draper* (1802) 4 Ch.Rob. 287; *The Valiant* (1839) 1 Wm.Rob. 64; *The Victoria* (1859) Sw. 408; *The Kent* (1862) Lush. 495; *Azcarate* v. *Iturrizaga*, 1938 S.C. 573.
32 *The Talca* (1880) 5 P.D. 169; *The England* (1886) 12 P.D. 32.
33 M.S.A. 1894, s. 5.
34 *Ibid.* s. 28.
35 *Ibid.* s. 30.

A registered ship or a share therein may be mortgaged in statutory form, recorded by the registrar of the ship's port of registry, and may be discharged similarly.[36] The registrar may grant a certificate of mortgage and sale for use at a place out of the country in which the port of registry is situated.[37]

A mortgagee is entitled to take possession of the ship, actually [38] or constructively.[39] Once in possession a mortgagee has complete control over the ship.[40]

(iii) CONTRACTS OF BOTTOMRY AND RESPONDENTIA

A bond of bottomry is a bond granted by a shipowner, or by the master of a ship in a foreign port, if he is unable to proceed with his voyage without obtaining an advance of money and it is not obtainable on the owner's personal credit.[41] Before granting the bond the master must, if it is in the circumstances practicable, communicate with the owner and only failing that may he grant the bond on his own authority.[42] The bond, for which there is no standard form, creates a conventional hypothec, a security over the ship without possession thereof. It may be granted over cargo as well,[43] but owners or master are not entitled to hypothecate the cargo without the consent of the cargo-owners, if obtainable. It must state the voyage, the risk, and the event on which it will become exigible. A bond which has not been authorised by the owner, or is wanting in any of the material particulars, is not a valid bond and not binding on the owner.[44]

The lender on a bottomry bond must show that an attempt was made to communicate with the owner, that the circumstances justified the bond, and that the ship arrived at her port of destination. In case of competition the bond latest in date is preferable, being presumed to be that which enabled the ship to arrive safely.[45] A bond is preferable to a mortgage of the ship, and to any unsecured creditor, but not to the maritime lien of master or seaman.[46] If the bond covered cargo, and the cargo-owners' consent was not obtained, the lender has no preference against the cargo.[47]

A lender on bottomry may enforce his claim by action *in rem* or *in personam*, may arrest the ship [48] and insist on judicial sale of her.

A bond of respondentia is of the same nature but covers the cargo, not

36 *Ibid.* ss. 31–38.
37 *Ibid.* ss. 39–46.
38 *Cf. The Manor* [1907] P. 339; *The Lord Strathcona* [1925] P. 143. See also *Haviland Routh & Co.* v. *Thomson* (1864) 3 M. 313; *Lanning* v. *Seater* (1889) 16 R. 828.
39 *The Benwell Tower* (1895) 8 Asp.M.L.C. 13.
40 *The Fairport* (1884) 10 P.D. 13.
41 Bell, *Prin.* § 452. *Cf. Anderston Foundry Co.* v. *Low* (1869) 7 M. 836, 844.
42 *Kleinworth, Cohen & Co.* v. *Cassa Maritima* (1877) L.R. 2 App.Cas. 156.
43 *Dymond* v. *Scott* (1877) 2 R. 196.
44 *Miller* v. *Potter, Wilson & Co.* (1875) 3 R. 105; *The Elwell* [1921] P. 351.
45 Bell, *Prin.* § 456.
46 *The Daring* (1868) L.R. 2 Adm. & Ecc. 260.
47 *Dymond* v. *Scott, supra.*
48 *Lucovitch, Petr.* (1885) 12 R. 1090.

the vessel. It is effectual if the cargo arrives at the destination, even if not by the ship by which it was consigned.[49]

Independently of questions as to the validity of a respondentia bond as between the bondholder and the shipowners the latter are liable to the cargo owners on the ground of recompense if the cargo be attached or sold by the bondholders for its value.[50]

In modern practice both bottomry and respondentia are practically obsolete.

(iv) Claims under Contracts of Affreightment, Charterparties and Bills of Lading

Such claims are normally claims for payment on the owner's or charterer's side, for freight, dead freight or demurrage, or on the shipper's side for damages for delay in carriage, non-delivery, or delivery in damaged condition.

The contract of affreightment is normally entered into by way of charterparty or bill of lading.[51]

Contracts by charterparty

Under a contract by charterparty the ship is hired by a charterer from the owner completely so as to be, during the hiring, the vessel of the charterer (charterparty by demise), or for a stated time, or for one or more voyages, the charterer merely acquiring the right to have his goods carried therein.[52] A charterparty is not normally specifically enforceable, but interdict may be granted against using the ship in a manner inconsistent with the charterparty.[53]

There are many decisions on the interpretation of common terms in charterparties.[54]

Contracts by bill of lading

Contracts evidenced by bills of lading are usual where the ship is employed as a general ship. If the charterer supplies the cargo the bill of lading is merely a receipt for the goods and the charterparty governs the rights of shipowner and charterer.[55] If the shipper of the goods is not the charterer his rights against the charterer depend only on the bill of lading unless any provisions of the charterparty are expressly incorporated therein and only in so far as the stipulations in the charterparty affect the delivery of the goods.[56] In cases to which it applies the Carriage of Goods

49 Bell, *Comm.* I, 584.

50 *Benson* v. *Duncan* (1849) 18 L.J.Ex. 169; *Anderston Foundry Co.* v. *Low* (1869) 7 M. 836.

51 Letters will suffice: *Nordstjernan* v. *Salvesen* (1903) 6 F. 64, 74; altered on other points (1905) 7 F.(H.L.) 101.

52 *Sandeman* v. *Scurr* (1867) L.R. 1 Q.B. 86; *Baumwoll* v. *Furness* [1893] A.C. 8.

53 *Cf. Sociedade Portuguesa* v. *Hvalfangerselskapet Polaris* [1952] 1 Lloyd's Rep. 407.

54 See generally *Carver on Carriage by Sea* (11th ed.) 427 *et seq.*; *Scrutton on Charterparties and Bills of Lading* (17th ed.) 71 *et seq.*

55 *Rodocanachi* v. *Milburn* (1886) 18 Q.B.D. 67.

56 As to discrepancies between the two see *Kruger* v. *Moel Tryvan Ship Co.* [1907] A.C. 272.

by Sea Act 1971 may modify a bill of lading. Apart from that and from express contrary stipulation there are implied conditions in every contract of the seaworthiness of the vessel,[57] that the vessel will not deviate or delay without justification,[58] and that the goods are not dangerous. There are many decisions on the interpretation of customary terms in bills of lading.[59]

Carrier's claims against shipper—freight

The carrier has a claim against the shipper of goods for the freight for the carriage. It is payable only when the voyage has been completed and the goods delivered, unless there is express provision for advance freight, *i.e.* for payment before completion of the voyage. Advance freight is,[60] but freight is not,[61] payable if the voyage is not completed. Freight *pro rata* may be payable if the goods have voluntarily been accepted at a point short of their destination, in such a way as to justify the inference that the further carriage was intentionally dispensed with and that a new contract should be implied to pay for the part of the voyage actually performed.[62]

Lien for freight

The shipowner has a lien over the goods carried for the freight, until he delivers the goods. It extends to all goods consigned by the same person on the same voyage under the same contract. Delivery of a portion of the goods does not defeat the lien over the remainder.

Delivery of goods and lien for freight

If the owner of goods imported from foreign parts into the United Kingdom fails to make entry thereof, or to land and take delivery of them, the shipowner may do so, and if at the time he does so the shipowner gives to the wharfinger or warehouseman notice in writing that the goods are to remain subject to a lien for freight or other charges payable to the shipowner to an amount mentioned in the notice, the goods so landed continue subject to the same lien, if any, as before the landing thereof, and the warehouseman shall retain them until the lien is discharged, failing which, he must make good to the shipowner any loss thereby occasioned to him.[63] The lien may be discharged by payment, or the owner of the goods may make a deposit of a sum equal to the amount claimed.[64] If the lien is not discharged and no deposit made, the wharfinger may sell the goods or so much thereof as may be necessary to satisfy the charges, and apply the

57 *A/B Karlshamns Oljefabriker* v. *Monarch S.S. Co.*, 1949 S.C.(H.L.) 1.
58 *Collard* v. *Carswell* (1892) 19 R. 987.
59 See Carver, 427 *et seq.*; Scrutton, 71 *et seq.*
60 *Byrne* v. *Schiller* (1871) L.R. 6 Ex. 319; *Smith* v. *Pyman* [1891] 1 Q.B. 742.
61 *Liddard* v. *Lopes* (1809) 10 East 526; *Weir* v. *Girvin* [1900] 1 Q.B. 45.
62 *St. Enoch Shipping Co.* v. *Phosphate Mining Co.* [1916] 2 K.B. 624.
63 Merchant Shipping Act 1894, s. 494.
64 *Ibid.* ss. 495–496.

proceeds of sale in payment of customs or excise duties, expenses, wharfinger's charges and shipowner's freight, the surplus if any being paid to the owner of the goods.[65]

Dead freight

If the shipper fails without lawful excuse to load a full cargo in terms of his contract, he is liable for dead freight, in effect for damages for the space not taken up in the ship,[66] measured by the difference between the freight actually earned and the freight which would have been earned if the charterer had fulfilled his obligation.[67]

Total failure to provide cargo

Damages are recoverable if the shipper fails without lawful excuse to provide the cargo stipulated for.[68] The measure of damages is the estimated amount of freight which would have been earned if the shipper had provided the cargo,[69] less the cost of earning it,[70] and less any sum earned by alternative employment of the ship.[71]

Demurrage

Demurrage is the agreed additional payment, normally stated at so much per day, for detention of the ship when loading or unloading, beyond the specified number of lay-days, or a reasonable period,[72] or the compensation by way of unliquidated damages for undue detention of the ship not provided for in the charterparty.[73] Demurrage in the strict sense is payable only where there is a stipulation to that effect in the contract. If there is no stipulation therefor, excessive detention is a breach of contract importing liability in unliquidated damages as soon as the lay-days expire. There is liability if the delay is due to the default of the owner or those for whom he is responsible.[74]

Liability ceases as soon as the shipper has fully performed his obligation of loading or unloading, and he is not liable for subsequent delay not due to his fault.

Dangerous goods

Shippers impliedly undertake not to ship on a general ship without

65 *Ibid.* ss. 497–500.
66 *McLean and Hope* v. *Fleming* (1872) 9 M.(H.L.) 38.
67 *Aitken, Lilburn & Co.* v. *Ernsthausen* [1894] 1 Q.B. 773; *Young* v. *Canning Jarrah Timber Co.* (1899) 4 Com.Cas. 96.
68 *Heugh* v. *Escombe* (1861) 4 L.T. 517; *cf. Staniforth* v. *Lyall* (1830) 7 Bing. 169.
69 *Weir* v. *Dobell* [1916] 1 K.B. 722; *Steven* v. *Bromley* [1919] 2 K.B. 722.
70 *Smith* v. *McGuire* (1858) 3 H. & N. 554.
71 *Smith, supra*; see also *Puller* v. *Staniforth* (1809) 11 East 232; *Staniforth* v. *Lyall* (1830) 7 Bing. 169.
72 *Budgett* v. *Binnington* [1891] 1 Q.B. 38; *Hick* v. *Rodocanachi* [1893] A.C. 22; *Lilly* v. *Stevenson* (1895) 22 R. 278; *A/S D/S Hansa* v. *Alexander*, 1919 S.C.(H.L.) 122.
73 *Moor Line* v. *Distillers Co.*, 1912 S.C. 514; *A/S Reidar* v. *Arcos* [1927] 1 K.B. 352; *Chandris* v. *Isbrandsten-Moller Co.* [1951] 1 K.B. 240.
74 *Cantière Navale Trièstina* v. *Russian Soviet Agency* [1925] 2 K.B. 172.

notice dangerous goods or packages or goods so dangerously packed that the shipowner and his agents and servants may not reasonably be expected to know or could not by reasonable diligence and inspection become aware of their character.[75] They are accordingly liable in damages to the carrier for any damage done to other goods on board for which the shipowner has to compensate the owners thereof,[76] and for personal injury caused to the carrier or his servants which is the natural and probable consequence of not disclosing the nature of the goods.[77] In effect then, unless the shipowner knows or ought to know, *i.e.*, has constructive notice, of the dangerous character of the goods,[78] there is an implied warranty by the shipper that the goods are not dangerous but fit for carriage in the ordinary course.[76]

Goods may be held to be dangerous within the scope of this principle if they may cause detention of the ship by reason of undisclosed legal obstacles to their carriage or discharge,[79] but if the nature of the cargo and any such legal difficulty be known to both parties, the shipper will not be liable for delay caused thereby.[80] In *Chandris* v. *Isbrandtsen-Moller Co.*[81] dangerous cargo was loaded, despite the charterparty, to the knowledge and with the consent of the master, in consequence of which the vessel had to unload in the river into barges, which took sixteen days longer than normal. It was held that the demurrage clause governed this period as despite the charterer's breach in loading dangerous cargo, the shipowners had known of it and affirmed the contract which accordingly still subsisted and regulated the damages recoverable.

Mitigation of damages

The shipowner must take reasonable steps to obtain other goods if his charterer does not load or loads incompletely.[82] The master or owner is probably not under any express duty of going in search of freight purely for the purpose of diminishing the burden of damages to fall on the defaulting shipper.[83] The conduct of the owner or master must, however, be reasonable and in ordinary cases he must do his best to obtain another cargo, but during the lay-days he is not entitled, unless the charter has been repudiated or the charterer has informed him of his inability to load

[75] But see Carriage of Goods by Sea Act 1924, Sched., Art. 4, rule 6, in cases where the Act applies, and M.S.A. 1894, ss. 446–448, whereby the shipper must declare dangerous goods and the carrier may refuse them. See also the Explosives Act 1875 relative to the carriage of certain dangerous goods by land.

[76] *Brass* v. *Maitland* (1856) 6 E. & B. 470; *Hutchison* v. *Guion* (1858) 5 C.B.(N.S.) 149; *Bamfield* v. *Goole Transport Co.* [1910] 2 K.B. 94.

[77] *Farrant* v. *Barnes* (1862) 11 C.B.(N.S.) 553.

[78] *Acatos* v. *Burns* (1878) 3 Ex.D. 282. See *Bamfield, supra*; *Greenshields* v. *Stephens* [1908] A.C. 431; *Transoceanica* v. *Shipton* [1923] 1 K.B. 31; and *Rederi A/B Transatlantic* v. *B.O.T.* (1924) 30 Com.Cas. 117.

[79] *Mitchell* v. *Steel* [1916] 2 K.B. 610.

[80] *Owners of S.S. Sebastian* v. *de Vizcaya* [1920] 1 K.B. 332; *The Domald* [1920] P. 56.

[81] [1951] 1 K.B. 240, following *Inverkip S.S. Co.* v. *Bunge* [1917] 2 K.B. 193.

[82] *The Argentino* (1888) 13 P.D. 191; 14 App.Cas. 579; *Wilson* v. *Hicks* (1857) 26 L.J.Ex. 242.

[83] *Contra*, Abbott, 5th ed., 428; doubtful, *Maclachlan*, 7th ed., 502.

a cargo, to accept any alternative offer of freight made to him.[84] Nor is he bound to accept any freight which may be offered to him if the terms are such that he could not reasonably be expected to agree to them.[85] In *Weir* v. *Dobell*[86] a sub-charterer refused to supply a cargo, and it was held that the principal charterer's duty to mitigate damages must be taken into account in estimating damages and the fact that they were entitled to cancel their own charterparty. Hence the measure of damages was the difference between the freight payable by the charterer and that payable by the sub-charterer, and not the greater difference between that payable by the sub-charterer and the market rate of freight at the time of the breach.

Collateral benefits, however, will profit the shipowner and not diminish the liability of the charterer, as where in consequence of the detention of one ship, another ship belonging to the same owner was able to earn increased freight.[87]

If a charterparty makes provision for a stipulated sum to be payable as liquidate damages in case of non-performance, the shipowner is still entitled to recover that sum on breach, without any deduction in respect of freight subsequently carried by the ship during the period of the charter.[88]

If the shipowner does obtain an alternative charter from which his earnings are actually greater than the stipulated amount of freight, he is still entitled to damages, but only to nominal damages, for the breach.[89]

Carrier's default—failure to provide ship

The shipper has a claim if the owner wholly fails to provide the ship at the agreed place and time, or if delay in doing so is so material as to justify rescission of the contract, measured by the additional cost of making alternative arrangements for the conveyance of the cargo.[90]

Measure of damages—failure to furnish ship for loading

Where a shipowner completely fails to provide a ship in terms of the charterparty, the shipper of the goods is entitled to damages. If a substitute charterparty can be entered into and an alternative ship obtained, the damages will be prima facie any excess in freight necessary to secure her,[91]

84 *Harries* v. *Edmonds* (1845) 1 C. & K. 686; *Dimech* v. *Corlett* (1858) 12 Moo.P.C. 199; *Hudson* v. *Hill* (1874) 43 L.J.C.P. 273.

85 *Aitken* v. *Ernsthausen* [1894] 1 Q.B. 773.

86 [1916] 1 K.B. 722. Contrast *Rutherford* v. *Goldthorpe* [1922] 1 K.B. 508, where charterers were refused loss of profit on a subcharter as they could not have supplied the ship in any case, not having renewed their own charter.

87 *Jebsen* v. *E. and W. India Dock Co.* (1875) L.R. 10 C.P. 300; *cf. Aitken* v. *Ernsthausen* [1894] 1 Q.B. 773; *The City of Peking* (1890) 15 App.Cas. 438; *The Mediana* [1900] A.C. 113.

88 *Bell* v. *Puller* (1810) 2 Taunt. 285; *contra Puller* v. *Staniforth* (1809) 11 East 232.

89 *Staniforth* v. *Lyall* (1830) 7 Bing. 169.

90 *Jackson* v. *Union Marine Ins. Co.* (1874) L.R. 10 C.P. 125; *Bank Line* v. *Capel* [1919] A.C. 435.

91 *Nelson* v. *Dundee East Coast S.S. Co.*, 1907 S.C. 927.

together with any expenses necessarily incurred in warehousing the goods pending shipment, and an element for any delay and inconvenience.[92] This holds even if the charterers had and exercised an option to cancel under a cancellation clause,[91] and even if they do not actually enter into the substituted contract.[93]

If the charterer cannot obtain another ship of the same size or type, he may and probably must take the best substitute reasonably available to him.[94] If it is reasonable to do so, he must take a substitute vessel offered by the shipowner, in mitigation of damages.[95] He may take a larger vessel in which case the damages will be the difference between the freight on the whole cargo of the substituted ship, and that which would have been payable for the ship first contracted for, but if any profit be made on the carriage of surplus cargo in the extra space of the larger ship, credit for that must be allowed.[96] Similarly in *Irvine* v. *Midland G.W. Ry.*[97] wagons of the particular kind ordered were not supplied and the plaintiff sold the goods at a loss. It was held that he could not recover for loss of profit and that, while the proper measure of damages was the extra cost of sending in other wagons, the plaintiff could only obtain this in respect of such of the goods as had been actually sent. Where the shipper adopts an alternative means of transport, he is entitled to the full amount of the difference of freight, unless the carrier can prove (and the onus is on him) that he had neglected a cheaper means of conveyance which was practicable and open to him.[98] If the freight payable for the substituted vessel was less than that due under the original charter, nominal damages for breach of contract would presumably be recoverable.[99]

If no alternative means of carriage is available, the measure of damages must be the cost of replacing the goods at the port of destination at the time when they should have arrived,[1] less the value of the goods at the port of loading and the amount of freight and insurance payable to have them shipped to that destination. In *Ströms Bruks Aktie Bolag* v. *Hutchison* [2] the pursuers entered into a charterparty with the defenders for the carriage of two cargoes of wood-pulp from Sweden to Cardiff in September: they failed to send a ship for the second cargo or to give the pursuers sufficient notice to enable them to secure alternative transport. The purchasers from the pursuers bought other wood-pulp at Cardiff and recovered from the pursuers the difference between the cost of doing so and the price

92 *McWilliam* v. *Fletcher* (1905) 13 S.L.T. 455. Including a rise in price of the goods to be shipped during the period of delay: *Featherston* v. *Wilkinson* (1873) L.R. 8 Ex. 122.

93 *Collard* v. *Carswell* (1892) 19 R. 987; affd. 20 R.(H.L.) 47, loss of profit was given where hire of a passenger steamer was wrongfully rescinded.

94 *Hinde* v. *Liddell* (1875) L.R. 10 Q.B. 265.

95 *Société Navale* v. *Sutherland* (1920) 36 T.L.R. 682. *Cf. Payzu* v. *Saunders* [1919] 2 K.B. 581; *Dunford & Elliot* v. *Macleod* (1902) 4 F. 912.

96 *Mitchell* v. *Kahl* (1862) 2 F. & F. 709, *per* Cockburn C.J.

97 (1880) 6 L.R.Ir. 55. *Cf. Waller* v. *M.G.W. Ry.* (1879) 4 L.R.Ir. 376.

98 *Connal, Cotton & Co.* v. *Fisher Renwick* (1883) 10 R. 824.

99 *Horne* v. *Hough* (1874) L.R. 9 C.P. 137.

1 *Watts* v. *Mitsui* [1917] A.C. 227.

2 (1905) 7 F.(H.L.) 77, reversing (1904) 6 F. 486. *Cf. Rice* v. *Baxendale* (1861) 7 H. & N. 96; *O'Hanlon* v. *G.W. Ry.* (1865) 6 B. & S. 484.

they had agreed to pay to the pursuers for the shipment. It was held that the cost of these purchases was good evidence of the cost of replacing in Cardiff at the date of the breach, the goods which the pursuers ought to have shipped and that the pursuers could recover this sum from the shipowners, less the value of the goods in Sweden and the cost of freight and insurance.[3] If the shipowner does not take the full amount of cargo contracted for, the shipper is entitled to the difference between the contract and the market rate of freight on the quantity not carried.

Remoteness of damage

Certain consequences of failure to supply a ship in terms of a charter may require to be excluded as too remote and not the direct consequence of the owner's failure, unless due notice has been given of such possible consequences. So inability to obtain a hoped-for return cargo is too remote [4] but not the necessity of obtaining alternative supplies to replace those which the ship would have brought,[5] nor increase in price of the commodity while waiting to get another ship to take the cargo.[6] But where a ship in breach of charterparty left a port of call without waiting for instructions as to discharging so that the charterers had to pay damages to their purchasers, they were held entitled to recover this sum from the shipowners as it was a natural and reasonable consequence of the shipowners' breach of charterparty in the circumstances that they should have been made liable to pay those damages.[7] And where a vessel was supplied but too late to allow her to perform the contract, it was held that sufficient disclosure had been made of the fact that her services were required for salvage purposes with consequent high rewards and that loss of profits on that basis was recoverable.[8] Again the difference in freight is not the whole measure of damages but damages must include loss fairly incurred as arising in the ordinary course of business out of the breach of contract and recompense for serious inconvenience, trouble and annoyance caused thereby.[9]

Failure to supply under time-charter

Where a vessel has been time-chartered and has not been supplied the appropriate measure of damages is the difference between the hire under the charter and the rate of hire which has to be paid for a similar vessel at the current market rate.[10] If a ship has been supplied under a time-charter and during its currency is temporarily withdrawn the charterer

[3] See also *Watts* v. *Mitsui* [1917] A.C. 227; *Nissho* v. *Livanos* (1941) 69 Ll.L.R. 125. *Cf. European Shipping Co.* v. *Anglo-Russian Co.* (1928) 30 Ll.L.R. 337.
[4] *Walton* v. *Fothergill* (1835) 7 C. & P. 394.
[5] *Walton* v. *Fothergill, supra*; *Ströms Bruks A/B* v. *Hutchison* (1905) 7 F.(H.L.) 77.
[6] *Featherston* v. *Wilkinson* (1873) L.R. 8 Ex. 122.
[7] *Proctor Garrett* v. *Oakwin S.S. Co.* [1926] 1 K.B. 44.
[8] *Mackenzie* v. *Liddell* (1883) 10 R. 705.
[9] *McWilliam* v. *Fletcher* (1905) 13 S.L.T. 455.
[10] *Goldberg* v. *Bjornstad* (1921) 8 Ll.L.R. 7.

may recover as damages the hire paid, expenses incurred and a sum for loss of profit during the time the vessel was withdrawn,[11] but damages should be mitigated by hiring a similar ship if possible,[11] in which case the measure of damages is the difference between the charter rate and the market rate of hire for a similar ship.

If the ship is delivered late the charterer may claim the difference between the market freight for the period when the ship should have been under charter and the market freight for the period she actually was under charter [12]: these periods are of equal duration.

Failure to have ship in readiness to load

The consequence of a shipowner's failure to have the ship in readiness to load at the due date may be the same as failing to provide a ship at all if the delay is so material as to frustrate the purpose of the contract. But a lesser delay may still give rise to questions of damages without requiring alternative means of transport to be arranged. In general a ship must be taken to the port of loading without unreasonable delay or deviation [13] or by the day fixed, if there be one.[14] And an owner may be liable if the ship is to sail for loading on a fixed date and does not do so.[15] So where a shipowner was not ready and delay in loading ensued, he was held liable in damages to a shipper who had incurred charges for demurrage on railway wagons, even though this consequence was the result of a special bargain between the shipper and the railway company. It was still the natural result of the breach of contract.[16] Again where a shipowner sought to perform an intermediate charter before the due date of readiness to load and was delayed so that he was a week late in commencing loading he was held liable for the expenses incurred by the charterer in consequence of the delay.[17]

Provision may be made for cancelling the charterparty if the vessel does not arrive within a stated time, and in one such case it was held that the owner was liable in damages for making it impossible for the vessel to arrive in time, and that the right to damages was not affected by the exercise of the right to cancel.[18] But excepted perils in the charterparty apply to the voyage to the loading-port [19] and may excuse the owner's breach.[20]

[11] *Sina Societa* v. *Suzuki* (1924) 29 Com.Cas. 284.
[12] *Bakkevig* v. *Harris* (1923) 14 Ll.L.R. 348.
[13] *Cf. Hudson* v. *Hill* (1874) 43 L.J.C.P. 273.
[14] *Jackson* v. *Union Marine Insurance Co.* (1874) L.R. 10 C.P. 125; *Nelson* v. *Dahl* (1879) 12 Ch.D. 568, 581.
[15] *Glaholm* v. *Hayes* (1841) 2 M. & G. 257.
[16] *Welch, Perrin & Co.* v. *Anderson* (1891) 8 T.L.R. 119. See also *Giachetti* v. *Speeding* (1899) 15 T.L.R. 401, *per* Bigham J.
[17] *Monroe* v. *Ryan* [1935] 2 K.B. 28; *cf. Donaldson Bros.* v. *Little* (1882) 10 R. 413; *Dreyfus* v. *Lauro* (1938) 60 Ll.L.R. 94.
[18] *Nelson* v. *Dundee East Coast S.S. Co.*, 1907 S.C. 927.
[19] *Hudson, supra*; *Bruce* v. *Nicolopoulo* (1856) 11 Exch. 129.
[20] *Smith* v. *Dart* (1884) 14 Q.B.D. 105.

Breach as to capacity

In the same way if the ship supplied is not of the guaranteed capacity, the shipowner will not be liable for any consequential loss of profit on the amount short, unless knowledge of any sub-contract has been brought home to the shipowner.[21] But he will be liable for damages for the cost of sending the remainder of the cargo to the destination by other means of transport or, if a lump freight is payable, for the difference between the market value of the ship hired from one of the agreed capacity [22] or, where freight is payable in proportion to capacity, for the excess of market rate of freight over the contractual rate for the amount unable to be carried.[23] If no vessel can be obtained to take the balance of the cargo the appropriate damages will be those applicable where no ship is supplied at all,[23] and where lump-sum freight was payable and the balance of the cargo could not be taken by another vessel the charterer has been held entitled to the difference in market values as above and also to damages on the basis of the replacement cost of the goods at the place and time of delivery, less their value at the place of shipment, freight and insurance.[24]

The ship must take a full cargo and is liable in damages for failure to do so,[25] which will usually amount to the extra cost of sending on the balance of the goods by another vessel, and some element for loss of profit.[26]

Master's duty for care of goods

The master on behalf of the owner must take reasonable care of the goods while in transit, subject to any excepted perils, by doing what is necessary to preserve them during the ordinary incidents of the voyage,[27] and he is liable for their safety, subject to any such exceptions.[28] He must also take necessary measures to prevent or check loss or deterioration of the goods even due to accidents for which the owner is not liable and even if requiring expenditure, and the owner will be liable in damages if he fails to take these steps.[27] The whole circumstances of the case must be considered and he need not deviate, though reasonable delay in port will be permissible.[27] The owner will only be liable if it be shown that the master has been guilty of a breach of duty in the exercise of his discretion.[27] The master is entitled and bound to sell the goods if that is necessary [29] and

21 *Scaramanga* v. *English* (1895) 1 Com.Cas. 99.

22 *Tibbermede* v. *Graham* (1921) 7 Ll.L.R. 250; *Sterns* v. *Salterns* (1922) 12 Ll.L.R. 385.

23 *Walford* v. *Czarnikow* (1924) 19 Ll.L.R. 354.

24 *Heimdal A/S* v. *Questier* (1949) 82 Ll.L.R. 452.

25 *Atkinson* v. *Ritchie* (1809) 10 East 530; *Gifford* v. *Dishington* (1871) 8 S.L.R. 665. *Cf. Brunner* v. *Webster* (1900) 5 Com.Cas. 167. So, too, if a full cargo is not taken due to unskilful loading: *Anglo-African Co.* v. *Lamzed* (1866) L.R. 1 C.P. 226; *cf. Canadian Tpt. Co.* v. *Court Line* [1940] A.C. 934.

26 *Gifford, supra.*

27 *Notara* v. *Henderson* (1872) L.R. 7 Q.B. 225; *Australian S.N. Co.* v. *Morse* (1872) L.R. 4 P.C. 222; *cf. Garriock* v. *Walker* (1873) 1 R. 100; *Adam* v. *Morris* (1890) 18 R. 153; *Hansen* v. *Dunn* (1906) 11 Com.Cas. 100. See also *The Pearlmoor* [1904] P, 286, where negligent stowage nullified an excepted peril.

28 *Gillespie* v. *Thompson* (1856) 6 E. & B. 477n.

29 *Atlantic Mutual Marine Insce. Co.* v. *Huth* (1880) 16 Ch.D. 474.

the most prudent course and if he cannot obtain the cargo owner's instructions.[30] If communication is possible it must be made, failing which the cargo owner will be entitled to damages for his loss even if the sale was reasonable.[31]

When goods have been sold in this way by the master but unjustifiably, the shipper is entitled to damages for non-delivery amounting to the value of the goods to the owner if they had not been sold.[32] If the sale was in the circumstances justified the owner of the cargo is entitled to the proceeds of the sale or, if the ship arrives at her port of destination, to the sum the cargo would have realised at the port of destination, under deduction of freight and charges. If the goods were damaged, the shipowner not being responsible, the amount of damages is what the goods would have been worth to their owners if they had not been sold, having regard also to the carrier's obligation under the contract.[33]

The shipowner is not, however, liable for damage to goods due to the dangerous qualities of other goods not known and which could not reasonably have been known to the shipowner.[34] Even where the damage is caused by an excepted peril the shipowner must take reasonable measures to minimise the loss or deterioration [35] and he is entitled to be recompensed for expenses properly incurred in preserving the cargo.[36]

The shipowner is also liable if the master neglected to sell the goods when he should have done so, having regard to the interests of the shipper, for the consequences of that failure, as by complete deterioration of goods which would have fetched something if sold earlier.[37]

Transhipment

If a voyage is delayed by an excepted peril or damage which cannot be repaired in a reasonable time or at reasonable expense [38] the shipowner may tranship the goods but he is liable to the owner of the goods for damage due to delay in electing whether to do so.[39] If the delay is not due to an excepted peril the shipowner will be liable in damages for delay [40] and is not entitled to tranship on his own account on more onerous terms but may be bound to do so on account of the owner of the cargo.

30 *Australasian S.N. Co.* v. *Morse* (1872) L.R. 4 P.C. 222; *Tronson* v. *Dent* (1853) 8 Moo.P.C. 419; *Atlantic Insce. Co.* v. *Huth* (1880) 16 Ch.D. 474.

31 *Acatos* v. *Burns* (1878) 3 Ex.D. 282; *cf. Atlantic Insce. Co., supra.* See also *Klein* v. *Lindsay*, 1910 S.C. 231.

32 *Acatos* v. *Burns* (1878) 3 Ex.D. 282; *Tronson* v. *Dent* (1853) 8 Moo.P.C. 419; *Atlantic Insce. Co.* v. *Huth* (1880) 16 Ch.D. 474; *Gemmill* v. *Somerville* (1905) 12 S.L.T. 674.

33 *Ewbank* v. *Nutting* (1849) 7 C.B. 797; *Acatos, supra.*

34 *Hutchinson* v. *Guion* (1858) 5 C.B.(N.S.) 149. See also *Brass* v. *Maitland* (1856) 6 E. & B. 471; *Mitchell, Cotts* v. *Steel* [1916] 2 K.B. 610 (illegal goods).

35 *Adam* v. *Morris* (1890) 18 R. 153.

36 *Garriock* v. *Walker* (1873) 1 R. 100.

37 *Notara* v. *Henderson* (1872) L.R. 7 Q.B. 225; *Hansen* v. *Dunn* (1906) 11 Com.Cas. 100; *cf. Garriock* v. *Walker* (1873) 1 R. 100; *Adam* v. *Morris* (1890) 18 R. 153.

38 *Assicurazioni* v. *Bessie Morris S.S. Co.* [1892] 2 Q.B. 652; *Carras* v. *London and Scottish Assce. Co.* [1936] 1 K.B. 291; *Kulukundis* v. *Norwich Union* [1937] 1 K.B. 1.

39 *Hansen* v. *Dunn* (1906) 11 Com.Cas. 100; *cf. Boase* v. *Glasgow United Spinning Co.*, 1917, 2 S.L.T. 108.

40 *Shipton* v. *Thornton* (1838) 9 A. & E. 314; *The Bernina* (1886) 12 P.D. 36. *Cf. A/B Karlshamns Oljefabriker* v. *Monarch S.S. Co.*, 1949 S.C.(H.L.) 1.

Delivery

On arrival the shipper must co-operate with the charterer to use reasonable diligence to have the goods unloaded within a reasonable time having regard to the circumstances and methods of the port.[41] Hence the carrier will be liable in damages for unreasonable delay in discharging the goods.

Moreover, having discharged, if the consignee fails timeously to take delivery of the goods the shipowner may, by arrangement or custom deposit them in a warehouse and he is then subject to the liability of a depositary only.[42] He may be liable if he delivers and does not have due regard to safeguarding the rights of the cargo owner.[43]

Where delivery is made at a port short of the proper destination, the cost of transhipment and of carriage onward to the destination is the proper measure of damages.[44]

It is a breach of contract on the charterer's part if he orders the vessel to an unsafe port to discharge and he is liable in damages for the consequences thereof, the ordinary rules of remoteness applying, so that the master's decision to accept such an order may amount to *novus actus interveniens.*[45]

Safety of goods in transit—liability at common law

At common law the strict liability for the safe carriage and delivery of goods incumbent on a common carrier [46] together with the other obligations of the common carrier [47] apply to a carrier for hire of goods by sea [48] who offers his ship as a general ship, subject to the usual exceptions of *damnum fatale*,[49] act of the Queen's enemies,[50] inherent defect of the goods [51] unless caused by the carrier [52] and goods justifiably jettisoned.[53] These exceptions do not however apply to excuse the shipowner if there has been any failure on his part to take reasonable steps to avoid or guard

41 *Cunningham* v. *Dunn* (1878) 3 C.P.D. 443; *Ford* v. *Cotesworth* (1870) L.R. 5 Q.B. 544.

42 *Re Webb* (1818) 8 Taunt. 443; *Meyerstein* v. *Barber* (1866) L.R. 2 C.P. 38. *Cf. Mitchell* v. *L. & Y. Ry.* (1875) L.R. 10 Q.B. 256; *Crouch* v. *G.W. Ry.* (1858) 2 H. & N. 491; *Heugh* v. *L.N.W. Ry.* (1870) L.R. 5 Ex. 51; *Chapman* v. *G.W. Ry.* (1880) 5 Q.B.D. 278. See also M.S.A., 1894, ss. 493 *et seq.*

43 *Kolbin* v. *Kinnear*, 1931 S.C.(H.L.) 128.

44 *A/B Karlshamns Oljefabriker* v. *Monarch S.S. Co.*, 1949 S.C.(H.L.) 1.

45 *Grace* v. *General S.N. Co.* (1949) 66 T.L.R. (Pt. 1) 147; see also *West* v. *Wright* (1935) 40 Com.Cas. 186; *The Pass of Leny* (1936) 54 Ll.L.R. 288.

46 Chap. 45, *supra.*

47 Chap. 45, *supra.*

48 *Nugent* v. *Smith* (1876) 1 C.P.D. 19, 423; *Hill* v. *Scott* [1895] 2 Q.B. 713; *Liver Alkali Co.* v. *Johnson* (1874) L.R. 9 Ex. 338; *Pandorf* v. *Hamilton* (1886) 17 Q.B.D. 683.

49 *Nugent, supra*; *The Marpesia* (1872) L.R. 4 P.C. 212; *The Merchant Prince* [1892] P. 179.

50 *Russell* v. *Niemann* (1864) 34 L.J.C.P. 10; *cf. The Teutonia* (1872) L.R. 4 P.C. 171; *Kawasaki Kisen* v. *Bantham S.S. Co.* [1939] 2 K.B. 544.

51 *Nugent, supra*; *Blower* v. *G.W. Ry.* (1872) L.R. 7 C.P. 655; *The Barcore* [1896] P. 294; *Lindsay* v. *Scholefield* (1897) 24 R. 530.

52 *Baldwin* v. *L.C. & D. Ry.* (1882) 9 Q.B.D. 582.

53 *Burton* v. *English* (1883) 12 Q.B.D. 218; *Royal Exchange S.S. Co.* v. *Dixon* (1886) 12 App. Cas. 11; *Newall* v. *Royal Exchange S.S. Co.* (1885) 1 T.L.R. 490. See also *Morrison S.S. Co.* v. *Greystoke Castle* (*Cargo Owners*) [1947] A.C. 265.

against the causes [54] or to avert their consequences.[55] Nor is the shipowner protected if loss due to one of the excepted causes has taken place in consequence of a departure from the proper prosecution of the voyage, as during deviation,[56] improper delay,[57] improper deck stowage or jettison [58] nor if the ship was not seaworthy when she commenced her voyage and the loss would not otherwise have occurred.[59] The obligation of seaworthiness is absolute at common law [60] but in contracts to which the Carriage of Goods by Sea Act 1971,[61] applies the undertaking is only that the shipowner will before, and at the beginning of, the voyage exercise due diligence to make the ship seaworthy.

In practice the importance of the contract by charterparty or bill of lading is such that the pure common law rules of carriage are rarely of importance in carriage by sea, but the statutory qualifications and the express contractual provisions are built on this foundation.

Statutory qualifications

The liability of the common carrier by sea is further qualified by statute.

The Merchant Shipping Act 1894, Part VIII, s. 502,[62] provides:

> The owner of a British seagoing ship, or any share therein, shall not be liable to make good to any extent whatever any loss or damage happening without his actual fault or privity [63] in the following cases; namely:
>
> (i) Where any goods, merchandise, or other things whatsoever taken in or put on board his ship are lost or damaged by reason of fire [64] on board the ship [65]; or
>
> (ii) Where any gold, silver, diamonds, watches, jewels, or precious stones [66] taken in or put on board his ship,[67] the true nature

54 *The Freedom* (1869) 38 L.J.Adm. 25; L.R. 3 P.C. 594.

55 *Notara* v. *Henderson* (1872) L.R. 7 Q.B. 225.

56 *Leduc* v. *Ward* (1888) 20 Q.B.D. 475; *The Dunbeth* [1897] P. 133.

57 *Lindsay* v. *Scholefield* (1897) 24 R. 530; *Glynn* v. *Margetson* [1893] A.C. 351.

58 *Royal Exchange Co.* v. *Dixon* (1886) 12 App.Cas. 11.

59 *The Europa* [1908] P. 84; *Kish* v. *Taylor* [1912] A.C. 604; *Scrutton on Charterparties*, 17th ed., s. 29; *Carver on Carriage of Goods by Sea*, 11th ed., 19.

60 *Steel* v. *State Line Co.* (1877) 4 R.(H.L.) 103; *The Glenfruin* (1885) 10 P.D. 103; Scrutton, ss. 28–29.

61 *Infra.*

62 See generally Carver, 11th ed., 174 *et seq.*

63 *The Obey* (1866) L.R. 1 A. & E. 102; *Wilson* v. *Dickson* (1818) 2 B. & Ald. 2; *The Bristol City* [1921] P. 444. See also *Smitton* v. *Orient S.N. Co.* (1907) 23 T.L.R. 359; *Lennard's Carrying Co.* v. *Asiatic Petroleum Co.* [1915] A.C. 705; *Standard Oil Co.* v. *Clan Line*, 1924 S.C.(H.L.) 1. The onus is on the shipowner pleading the section to bring himself within it; *Lennard, supra*; *Standard Oil, supra.*

64 Including damage from smoke and from water used to extinguish the fire: *The Diamond* [1906] P. 282. See also *Virginia Carolina Chemical Co.* v. *Norfolk S.S. Co.* [1912] 1 K.B. 229; *Tempus Shipping Co.* v. *Dreyfus* [1931] A.C. 726; *Ingram & Royle* v. *Services Maritimes* [1914] 1 K.B. 541.

65 Excluding fire on a lighter used in landing goods from a ship: *Morewood* v. *Pollok* (1853) 1 E. & B. 743. This does not relieve the shipowner from making general average contribution in case of fire; *Greenshields* v. *Stephens* [1908] A.C. 431.

66 Including jewellery carried as ordinary luggage: *Acton* v. *Castle Mail Packet Co.* (1895) 1 Com.Cas. 135. *Cf.* also cases interpreting the Carriers Act 1830: Chap. 45, *supra.*

67 Held not to apply to a watch in a passenger's pocket, but possibly when put in a cabin receptacle at night: *Smitton* v. *Orient S.N. Co.* (1907) 23 T.L.R. 359.

and value [68] of which have not at the time of shipment been declared by the owner or shipper thereof to the owner or master of the ship in the bills of lading or otherwise in writing, are lost or damaged by reason of any robbery, embezzlement, making away with, or secreting thereof.

The same Act further provides by section 508 that " Nothing in this part [69] of this Act shall be construed to lessen or take away any liability to which any master or seaman being also owner or part owner of the ship to which he belongs is subject in his capacity of master or seaman; or to extend to any British ship which is not recognised as a British ship within the meaning of this Act."

Shipowner's liability ex contractu

The shipowner's duty *ex contractu* is an absolute undertaking, subject to the excepted perils, to deliver the goods shipped at their destination in good condition as they were shipped.[70] The only other qualifications of his liability for non-delivery in good condition are inherent vice of the goods,[71] general average losses [72] and the statutory exemptions of the Merchant Shipping Act 1894, ss. 502–503, and other statutes, such as the Carriers Act 1830.[73] Consequently liability for loss arising from numerous specified perils was excluded by express stipulation, subject always to certain fundamental implied conditions such that if they were breached the express exceptions did not protect the shipper. These fundamental conditions could only be excluded by clear and express words free from ambiguity.[74] The fundamental liability is as in other cases of breach of contract, to pay such damages for breach as will place the charterers in the position they would have been in if the contract had been performed, but without regard to any particular contract of which the shipowners had no notice, for which no damages can be recovered unless the charter was made with it in view and in the knowledge of parties.[75]

Expressly excepted perils in contracts of affreightment

The shipowner or charterer under a charterparty or the shipowner or carrier under a bill of lading are not liable in damages for the consequences of perils excepted in the contract,[76] so long as the peril is the sole immediate

[68] Exact statement is necessary. *Williams* v. *African S.S. Co.* (1856) 1 H. & N. 300; *Gibbs* v. *Potter* (1842) 10 M. & W. 70.
[69] Part VIII, ss. 502–509.
[70] *Bradley* v. *Federal S.N. Co.* (1927) 27 Ll.L.R. 395.
[71] *The Freedom* (1869) L.R. 3 P.C. 594.
[72] *Burton* v. *English* (1883) 12 Q.B.D. 218.
[73] *Baxendale* v. *G.E. Ry.* (1869) L.R. 4 Q.B. 244.
[74] *Scrutton on Charterparties*, 17th ed., Art. 28. As to clauses excepting unseaworthiness see *Carver on Carriage by Sea*, 11th ed., pp. 104–111.
[75] *A/S D/S Heimdal* v. *Questier* (1949) 82 Ll.L.R. 452, applying *Stroms Bruks A/B* v. *Hutchison* (1905) 7 F.(H.L.) 131.
[76] *The Xantho* (1887) 12 App.Cas. 503; *Hamilton* v. *Pandorf* (1887) 12 App.Cas. 518; see also *Notara* v. *Henderson* (1872) L.R. 7 Q.B. 225; *Bulman* v. *Fenwick* [1894] 1 Q.B. 179; *The Glendarroch* [1894] P. 226; *Dunn* v. *Currie* [1902] 2 K.B. 614, 621; *Searle* v. *Lund* (1903) 20 T.L.R. 390; *D/S Danmark* v. *Poulsen*, 1913 S.C. 1043.

direct or dominant cause of the breach [77] and the peril and its consequences were not avoidable by reasonable care and diligence on the part of the shipowner or charterer or carrier and their servants. It is a question for the court whether the circumstances of a particular case fall within the terms of a particular exception,[78] the onus of proof being on the shipowner.[79] Where the Carriage of Goods by Sea Act 1971 applies,[80] it must be considered whether a particular exception in a bill of lading is permitted and whether any additional exception is introduced thereby. Fire on board is an excepted peril by statute [81] if it happens without the shipowner's actual fault or privity, but the owner may contract out of this section, and it may be waived by reliance on an inconsistent exception.[82] An exemption from liability in the contract between the shipowner and a lighterman employed by him may become imported into the contract between the shipowner and freighter.[83]

Negligence of the master and mariners may be excepted but the courts construe this and like exceptions strongly against the shipowner,[84] and it will not protect from the consequences of the shipowner's personal negligence,[85] nor unless clearly worded, will it relieve the shipowner against a breach of the implied undertaking that the ship should be seaworthy at starting,[86] but a clearly expressed exception of negligence of the shipowner's servants will receive full effect.[87] The Carriage of Goods by Sea Act 1971 impliedly distinguishes between negligence in navigation and management of the ship, which may be excepted, and other negligence which may not.[88] Exceptions normally limit the shipowner's liability during the whole time he possesses the goods as carrier and so include loading and discharge.[89] If the owner prima facie brings himself within an exception, the shipper must disprove that by showing that the real cause of loss was otherwise.[90] Exceptions in the contract do not relieve from the obliga-

[77] *The Xantho, supra*; *Hamilton, supra*; *Letricheux* v. *Dunlop* (1891) 19 R. 209; *Becker Gray* v. *London Assce. Corpn.* [1918] A.C. 101; *Leyland S.S. Co.* v. *Norwich Union* [1918] A.C. 350; *The Christel Vinnen* [1924] P. 208.

[78] For exceptions construed in the past, see *Scrutton on Charterparties*, Arts. 80–95; *Carver on Carriage by Sea*, 11th ed., pp. 130–167.

[79] *Smith* v. *Bedouin S.N. Co.* [1896] A.C. 70; see also *Moes, Moliere* v. *Leith and Amsterdam Shipping Co.* (1867) 5 M. 988.

[80] See *infra*.

[81] M.S.A., 1894, s. 502.

[82] *Virginia Co.* v. *Norfolk Co.* [1912] 1 K.B. 229.

[83] *Aberdeen Grit Co.* v. *Ellerman's Wilson Line*, 1933 S.C. 9.

[84] *The Pearlmoor* [1904] P. 286; *Price* v. *Union Lighterage Co.* [1904] 1 K.B. 412; and see Scrutton, Art. 90; Carver, pp. 111 *et seq.*

[85] *City of Lincoln* v. *Smith* [1904] A.C. 250; *cf. Chartered Mercantile Bank of India* v. *Netherlands India S.N. Co.* (1883) 10 Q.B.D. 521; *Norman* v. *Binnington* (1890) 25 Q.B.D. 475.

[86] See Scrutton, Art. 29.

[87] *Briscoe* v. *Powell* (1905) 22 T.L.R. 128; *cf. The Torbryan* [1903] P. 194; *Marriott* v. *Yeoward* [1909] 2 K.B. 987.

[88] See Schedule, Art. IV (2) (*a*).

[89] *Norman, supra*; *The Carron Park* (1890) 15 P.D. 203; *De Clermont* v. *G.S.N. Co.* (1891) 7 T.L.R. 187.

[90] *The Northumbria* [1906] P. 292; *L.N.W. Ry.* v. *Ashton* [1920] A.C. 84; *cf. Moes* v. *Leith and Amsterdam Co.* (1867) 5 M. 988; *Williams* v. *Dobbie* (1884) 11 R. 982; *Cunningham* v. *Colvils* (1888) 16 R. 295.

tion to contribute in general average contributions unless clearly expressed so to do.[91]

Liability of shipowners under statute—Carriage of Goods by Sea Act 1971

As an alternative to liability at common law as modified by statute, a shipowner may be liable under the Carriage of Goods by Sea Act 1971.[92] The Act has no application where there is no express contract, but enacts that, where the port of shipment is a port in the United Kingdom and the contract is evidenced by a bill of lading or similar document of title, *i.e.* for an " outward " voyage,[93] the responsibilities and liabilities which a shipowner undertakes and in relation to which any terms expressed in the contract must be considered shall be those set out in the rules scheduled to the Act. The Act has wide application, affecting all cases except (i) where the goods carried are outside the definition of " goods " in the Act [94]; (ii) where goods are carried in the coasting trade, otherwise than on bills of lading [95]; and, (iii) in certain exceptional circumstances.[96] In effect it introduced standard clauses defining the risks undertaken by the carriers for the duration of the voyage and their rights and immunities and provided that in any contract to which the rules apply, no absolute undertaking to provide a seaworthy ship is to be implied. The rights and immunities conferred by the Act may be surrendered in whole or in part by a clause in the bill of lading but exclusion of liability otherwise than as provided in the rules of the Schedule are null and void.[97] It fixes maxima for the liability for loss of goods unless their value has been declared.[98] Special agreements may be made as to liability for custody before loading and after unloading.[99] Article VIII preserves the operation of any statute in force relating to limitation of liability of owners. The liabilities undertaken are irreducible minima. Accordingly an action of damages will lie prima facie when failure in the liability undertaken causes loss or damage. It must be brought within one year of the due date of delivery.[1]

Total failure to deliver or delivery damaged

In such a case apart from special circumstances the shipowner must make compensation of the market value of the goods: the value is to be

[91] *Schmidt* v. *Royal Mail S.S. Co.* (1876) 45 L.J.Q.B. 646; *Crooks* v. *Allan* (1879) 5 Q.B.D. 38.
[92] Replacing a similar Act of 1924. See commentary thereon in Scrutton, Sec. XIII; Carver, p. 187. On the interpretation of the 1924 Act see *Stag Line* v. *Foscolo Mango* [1932] A.C. 328, 343, *per* Lord Atkin.
[93] *Vita Food Products* v. *Unus Shipping Co.* [1939] A.C. 277.
[94] Sched., Art. I, c.
[95] s. 4 and Sched., Art. VI. See *Harland and Wolff* v. *Burns and Laird Lines*, 1931 S.C. 722, 729; *Mack* v. *Burns and Laird Lines* (1944) 77 Ll.L.R. 377.
[96] Sched., Art. VI, *infra*.
[97] Sched., Art. V.
[98] Sched., Art. IV, 5.
[99] Sched., Art. VII.
[1] Sched., Art. III, 6.

arrived at as at the time and place where they ought to have been delivered.[2] This is applicable even where the shipper may have contracted to sell the goods at a price less than they would have realised on arrival,[3] or sells damaged goods under an existing contract at a price greater than their market value.[4] If however there is no proper market price for the goods at the time and place of arrival so that they could not have been purchased at all or only at an unreasonable price, a true measure of their value must be found by taking into account other factors, such as the cost of manufacture together with the expenses of transit and a reasonable allowance for profit.[5] Charges or freight which the shipper would have had to pay to get the goods to market must be deducted from the estimated value,[6] but not freight paid in advance, though the shipowner may have made an allowance to the shipper for insurance of the advance.[7] Where there was a partial non-delivery but the balance of the goods came later by another ship and were accepted it was held that this went in mitigation of the damages for non-delivery.[8] If goods have been sold at a port to pay for repairs the freighter can claim the proceeds or the amounts which would have been realised at the port of delivery, under deduction of freight and expenses [9] as also if the sale were wrongful, unless the goods were damaged without the fault of the shipowner, in which case the amount in question is what the goods would have been worth in their existing condition and having regard to the carrier's obligations.[10]

Delivery in damaged condition

In the case where there has been damage to the goods the damages must be ascertained as at the difference between the net amount which sound goods would have realised at the time and place of delivery and the net amount which could in fact be recovered for the goods on arrival in the condition in which they arrived.[11] But loss from a contract for resale entered into prior to the delivery and unknown to the shipowner has been refused as too remote.[12] But damage may be so substantial as to amount to actual or at least constructive loss of the whole cargo.[13]

2 *Brandt* v. *Bowlby* (1831) 2 B. & A. 932; *Gillies* v. *Smith* (1832) 10 S. 636; *Bishop* v. *Mersey & Clyde S.N. Co.* (1830) 8 S. 558; *The Thyatira* (1883) 8 P.D. 155; *Rice* v. *Baxendale* (1861) 7 H. & N. 96; *O'Hanlon* v. *G.W. Ry.* (1865) 6 B. & S. 484; *G.I.P. Ry.* v. *Turnbull* (1885) 53 L.T. 325. So too in *Smith* v. *Tregarthen* (1887) 56 L.J.Q.B. 437 and see *Watts* v. *Mitsui* [1917] A.C. 227.

3 *Rodocanachi* v. *Milburn* (1886) 18 Q.B.D. 67; *Williams* v. *Agius* [1914] A.C. 510; *Weir* v. *Dobell* [1916] 1 K.B. 722.

4 *Slater* v. *Hoyle* [1920] 2 K.B. 11.

5 *O'Hanlon* v. *G.W. Ry.* (1865) 6 B. & S. 484; *Rodocanachi, supra.*

6 *Watts, supra.*

7 *Rodocanachi, supra.*

8 *Smith* v. *Tregarthen* (1887) 56 L.J.Q.B. 437. *Cf. Sargant* v. *E. Asiatic Co.* (1915) 21 Com. Cas. 344.

9 *Hallett* v. *Wigram* (1850) 9 C.B. 580; *Hopper* v. *Burness* (1876) 1 C.P.D. 137, 141.

10 *Ewbank* v. *Nutting* (1849) 7 C.B. 797; *Acatos* v. *Burns* (1878) 3 Ex.D. 282. *Cf. Bartholomew* v. *Ruxton* (1862) 24 D. 277.

11 *Cf. Sprott* v. *Brown*, June 15, 1803, F.C.; *Jones* v. *Ross* (1830) 8 S. 495.

12 *The St. Cloud* (1863) Br. & Lush. 4.

13 *Dickson* v. *Buchanan* (1876) 13 S.L.R. 401.

Under M.S.A. 1894, s. 503,[14] the shipowner's liability is limited to an aggregate amount of 1,000 gold francs per ton of the ship's tonnage, if the loss happened without his actual fault or privity, but a charterer contracting personally by bill of lading will not have the benefit of this provision, unless he is a charterer by demise.[15] The Carriage of Goods by Sea Act 1971,[16] where it applies, limits the shipowner's liability to 1,000 francs per package or unit or 30 francs per kilo of gross weight of the goods lost or damaged, whichever is the higher, unless certain conditions are complied with.

Damages for delay in carrying

When delay takes place in carrying the goods to their destination, the shipowner will likewise be liable to the charterer in damages [17] so long as the delay was the cause of the loss.[18] If the result of the delay is to destroy the goods entirely, as in the case of perishable commodities, then, provided the nature of the commodity was known to the shipper, the whole value thereof will be recoverable, as their total loss is the natural and ordinary consequence of the delay in transit.[19] It was formerly considered that, in the case of a long sea voyage of uncertain duration no amount could be recovered in respect of the diminution in value caused by a fall in market price nor damages for the mere fact of the detention,[20] but the modern view is to the contrary. Sea voyages are commonly performed nowadays with exactitude and little or no uncertainty, consequently the state of the market at a foreseeable and anticipated date of arrival may easily have been within the contemplation of the contracting parties.[21] When that can be shown to be the case, and that some proposed and intended transaction with the goods was prejudiced by the delay, the element of fall in market price should be considered, just as in land transit.[22]

Where the delay does not ruin the goods, the ordinary measure of damages will be applicable, namely, the difference between the market price at the time and place where the goods should have been delivered in terms of the contract and that ruling at the time when they were delivered at that place.[23] The court will be slower to give damages for loss of profits in cases of delayed carriage than in cases of sale because a carrier normally knows less about the purposes for which the goods are required and the possibility of exceptional loss if delivery is withheld.[24]

14 Amended by M.S. (Liability of Shipowners and Others) Act 1958.

15 See *The Okehampton* [1913] P. 173; *The Hopper* (*No.* 66) [1908] A.C. 126; M.S.A., 1906, s. 71.

16 Sched., Art. IV, Rule 5.

17 *The Wilhelm* (1866) 2 Asp.M.L.C. 343.

18 *Associated Portland Cement Co.* v. *Houlder* (1917) 86 L.J.K.B. 1495; *A/B Karlshamns Oljefabriker* v. *Monarch S.S. Co.*, 1949 S.C.(H.L.) 1.

19 *Margetson* v. *Glynn* [1892] 1 Q.B. 337.

20 *The Parana* (1877) 2 P.D. 118; *The Notting Hill* (1884) 9 P.D. 105.

21 *e.g.*, that the goods were wanted for a particular market or season or sub-contract at which they would have an enhanced value. See *Koufos* v. *Czarnikow* [1969] 1 A.C. 350.

22 *Dunn* v. *Bucknall* [1902] 2 K.B. 614; *Sargant* v. *E. Asiatic Co.* (1915) 21 Com.Cas. 344.

23 *Collard* v. *S.E. Ry.* (1861) 7 H. & N. 79.

24 *Victoria Laundry* v. *Newman* [1949] 2 K.B. 528, 536. *Cf. British Columbia Sawmill Co.* v. *Nettleship* (1868) L.R. 3 C.P. 499.

Reasonably foreseeable consequences of delay will also sound in damages as where a delay resulted in the shippers becoming liable to a periodical increase in import duty.[25]

Loss of use of goods

Where delay takes place in the delivery of the goods intended for use damages may be claimed for the loss of the ordinary use of the goods themselves or of the price they represent, for such is a natural and necessary consequence of the delay, and so the interest on the value of the goods for the time lost has been allowed in such a case.[26] If however the use to which the goods were intended to be put was special, a question of remoteness is raised, whether the carrier had adequate notice of the special use and the special loss consequential on his failure, so as to justify the inference that he contracted on the terms of accepting liability for such loss.[27] So too a prior sub-sale at a price either higher [28] or lower [29] than the market price as at the presumed date of arrival cannot be taken into account [30] nor can stoppage of a business due to non-delivery [31] nor a fall in their price [32] unless the goods are to the knowledge of both parties required for a particular market or sub-contract or the voyage's duration can be accurately predicted.[33]

Deterioration of goods

A further natural and probable consequence of delay is a loss by reason of the physical deterioration or wasting of the goods owing to the delay, at least so far as the loss is of such a nature and extent as might ordinarily be expected to happen to goods of such a kind in their ordinary condition.[34] But where the loss is in consequence of some specially sensitive condition of the goods not brought to the notice of the carriers, the principle of remoteness will defeat the claim. In the case of perishable goods this consequence is certainly to be apprehended and in the event of complete loss of the goods, their whole value will be recoverable as damages, always provided the carrier knew that the goods were perishable.

Loss of market value by delay

A claim of damages for loss of market value differs from a claim for deterioration in that the market value moves independently of the delay

25 *The Ardennes* [1951] 1 K.B. 55.
26 *British Columbia Sawmill Co.* v. *Nettleship* (1868) L.R. 3 C.P. 499.
27 *Vide*, Chap. 28, *supra*, generally; *Wilson* v. *L. & Y. Ry.* (1861) 9 C.B.(N.S.) 632.
28 *The St. Cloud* (1863) B. & L. 4.
29 *Rodocanachi* v. *Milburn* (1886) 18 Q.B.D. 67; *Williams* v. *Agius* [1914] A.C. 510. See also *Slater* v. *Hoyle* [1920] 2 K.B. 11.
30 But a subsale is more to be expected in carriage by sea than in land carriage: *Heskell* v. *Continental Express* [1950] 1 All E.R. 1033.
31 *British Columbia Sawmill Co., supra.*
32 *The Parana* (1877) 2 P.D. 118.
33 *Dunn* v. *Bucknall Bros.* [1902] 2 K.B. 614.
34 *The Parana* (1877) 1 P.D. 452; 2 P.D. 118. *Cf. Hawes* v. *S.E. Ry.* (1884) 54 L.J.Q.B. 174; *Baldwin* v. *L.C. & D. Ry.* (1882) 9 Q.B.D. 582; *Mackenzie* v. *Pitblado* (1870) 8 S.L.R. 51, where damages for loss of market were also given; so too *The Ardennes* [1951] 1 K.B. 55.

and a fall therein is not necessarily a consequence of the delay. So long as it is not a regular periodical or recurrent fluctuation which was anticipated as a matter of general expectation, it is not among the circumstances which go to enhance the carrier's liability. In *The Parana* [35] hemp and sugar were delayed in transit owing to the defective condition of the ship's boilers. Damages were allowed for loss of weight of sugar by drainage during the delay and for loss of interest on the value of the cargo, but no damages were allowed for loss of market on the hemp, the price having fallen during the period of delay. But it was observed that damages for loss of market may be recovered if the goods are sent to be sold at a particular market and miss it by reason of the delay, or if they are sent to be sold at a particular season when prices are high, or if it is known to both parties that they will sell at a better price if they arrive at one time than if they arrive at a later time.

In *The Notting Hill* [36] case a ship was damaged in a collision and the cargo owners claimed damages from the other ship for, *inter alia*, loss of market in consequence of some of the goods having been delayed in arrival at the port of destination. It was held that this was too remote and that the measure of damages in case of delay due to collision was the same as in any other case of breach of contract. But in *Dunn* v. *Bucknall Bros.*[37] it was found that shipowners knew that the goods would sell for a much higher price if delivered at the due time than at a later. In *Koufos* v. *Czarnikow* [36] the same conclusion was reached; the shipowners should have realised that delay was liable to result in loss.

Penalty clauses

Provision is frequently made in a charterparty or bill of lading for penalties or agreed sums of damages for particular specified breaches or limiting the shipowner's liability by agreeing as to the value of the goods. Where such a clause limits liability in this way it does not affect the quantification of damages but merely provides a maximum.

The common penalty provision in charterparties " penalty for non-performance estimated amount of freight " is practically ineffective, neither permitting a claim to that amount for a partial breach,[38] nor limiting the amount of damages which may be claimed, as such clauses are well settled to be penalty clauses rather than provisions for liquidate damages,[39] though in *Wall* [40] the court rather tended to consider such a clause as a provision for liquidate damages. If a provision be one for liquidate damages it is enforceable according to its terms.

35 (1877) 2 P.D. 118 overruled in part in *Koufos* v. *Czarnikow* [1969] 1 A.C. 350. *Cf.* railway cases, *Collard* v. *S.E. Ry.* (1861) 7 H. & N. 79; *Wilson* v. *L. & Y. Ry.* (1861) 9 C.B.(N.S.) 632.

36 (1884) 9 P.D. 105. Criticised in *Koufos* v. *Czarnikow* [1969] 1 A.C. 350. *Cf. Smith* v. *Tregarthen* (1887) 56 L.J.Q.B. 437.

37 [1902] 2 K.B. 614.

38 *Rayner* v. *A/B Condor* [1895] 2 Q.B. 289; *Stroms Bruks A/B* v. *Hutchison* (1905) 7 F.(H.L.) 131.

39 On this distinction, see further Chap. 7, *supra*.

40 *Wall* v. *Rederi A/B Luggude* [1915] 3 K.B. 66; *Watts* v. *Mitsui* [1917] A.C. 227.

Carriage of passengers and luggage by sea

The general common law principles of carriage of passengers by land applies equally to their transit by sea, and the rules and provisions as to the carriage of goods by sea are not applicable. Thus shipowners have been held liable as common carriers for refusing to take a passenger.[41] Passengers' luggage is, however, of the nature of goods and the liability of the shipowner appears to be that of a common carrier of goods,[42] unless the luggage was under the passenger's own control, when his interference with the control of the goods modifies the carrier's liability to the extent of relieving him from responsibility for any loss sustained in consequence of the passenger's own want of care.[43] In the case of personal luggage in the actual personal custody of the passenger, the shipowner's liability is the same as in respect of the passenger himself and he is liable only for failure to exercise reasonable and proper care and has also contractual and statutory protection.[44]

Liability ex delicto

The responsibility of carriers of passengers by sea is to use all reasonable care, skill and foresight to carry their passengers in safety.[45] The liability *ex delicto* depends on ordinary principles of negligence which may be modified or excluded by conditions in the contract if reasonable notice be given to the passenger.[46] The standard of care is high and the shipowner must provide a ship as seaworthy as care and skill can make it.[47] Numerous statutory provisions and regulations also relate to the safety of passengers conveyed on merchant ships.

Limitation of liability may also extend to the passengers' luggage,[48] and in any event the statutory limitation under M.S.A., 1894, s. 503 (1) applies to luggage [49] so long as the loss arises on board and not after transhipment.[50] Special provisions apply to emigrant ships.[51]

41 *Bennett* v. *P. & O.S.N. Co.* (1847) 6 C.B. 775.

42 *G.W. Ry.* v. *Bunch* (1888) 13 App.Cas. 31; *Macrow* v. *G.W. Ry.* (1871) L.R. 6 Q.B. 612; *cf. Upperton* v. *Union Castle Co.* (1903) 8 Com.Cas. 96; 9 Com.Cas. 50.

43 *G.W. Ry.* v. *Bunch, supra*; *Vosper* v. *G.W. Ry.* [1928] 1 K.B. 340.

44 *Smitton* v. *Orient S.N. Co* (1907) 12 Com.Cas. 270.

45 *e.g. Lewis* v. *Laird Line*, 1925 S.L.T. 316; *Morris* v. *Clan Line*, 1925 S.L.T. 321. *Cf.* Occupiers' Liability (Scotland) Act, 1960, s. 2.

46 *Henderson* v. *Stevenson* (1875) 2 R.(H.L.) 71; *Williamson* v. *North of Scotland Navigation Co.*, 1916 S.C. 554; *Hood* v. *Anchor Line*, 1918 S.C.(H.L.) 143; *Lewis* v. *Laird Line*, 1925 S.L.T. 316; *Morris* v. *Clan Line*, 1925 S.L.T. 321. See also *Jones* v. *Oceanic S.N. Co.* [1924] 2 K.B. 730; *Haigh* v. *R.M.S.P. Co.* (1883) 5 Asp.M.L.C. 189; *Acton* v. *Castle Mail Packet Co.* (1895) 8 Asp.M.L.C. 73; *Taubman* v. *Pacific S.N. Co.* (1872) 26 L.T. 704; *Marriott* v. *Yeoward* [1909] 2 K.B. 987; *Smitton* v. *Orient S.N. Co.* (1907) 23 T.L.R. 359; *Cooke* v. *Wilson, Sons & Co.* (1915) 88 L.J.K.B. 888.

47 *Hyman* v. *Nye* (1881) 6 Q.B.D. 685; *Anderson* v. *Pyper & Co.* (1820) 2 Mur. 261; *Lyon* v. *Lamb* (1838) 16 S. 1188. See *John* v. *Bacon* (1870) L.R. 5 C.P. 437. But there is no warranty of freedom from defects likely to cause peril.

48 *Wilton* v. *Atlantic R.M. Co.* (1861) 10 C.B.(N.S.) 453; *P. & O.S.N. Co.* v. *Shand* (1865) 3 Moo.P.C.(N.S.) 272; *Taubman* v. *Pacific S.N. Co.* (1872) 1 Asp.M.L.C. 336; *Thompson* v. *R.M.S.P. Co.* (1875) 5 Asp.M.L.C. 190, note; *The Stella* [1900] P. 161, and cases in note 46, *supra*.

49 *The Stella* [1900] P. 161.

50 *The Bernina* (1886) 12 P.D. 36.

51 Merchant Shipping Act 1894, s. 320; *Ryan* v. *Oceanic S.N. Co.* [1914] 3 K.B. 731.

Failure to carry passengers, or delay

The general common law principles applicable to carriage by land apply to the carriage of passengers by sea.

(v) (a) Claims for Loss of Life or Personal Injury on Board Ship

Where loss of life or personal injury is caused to a person on board ship the shipowner's liability is governed by the Occupiers' Liability (Scotland) Act 1960, which by section 1 (3) (*a*) and (*b*) applies to persons having control of " any fixed or moveable structure, including any vessel, vehicle or aircraft, and to persons entering thereon . . . and to property thereon, including the property of persons who have not themselves entered on the premises or structure." No specialty of maritime law is involved.

Claims for loss of life or personal injury arising out of collisions at sea

Where loss of life or personal injuries are suffered by any person on board a vessel owing to the fault of that vessel and of any other vessel or vessels, liability is affected by the applicability of the International Regulations for Preventing Collisions at Sea 1948. If any damage to person or property arises from the non-observance of the collision regulations by any ship or seaplane, the damage is deemed to have been occasioned by the wilful default of the person in charge of the ship or seaplane, unless it is shown that the circumstances of the case made departure from the regulations necessary.[52] There is no presumption of fault on the part of a ship disobeying the regulations.[53] The liability of the owners of the vessels is joint and several, without prejudice to any defences otherwise competent.[54] In such a case if a proportion of the damages is recovered against the owners of one of the vessels which exceeds the proportion in which she was in fault, they may recover by way of contribution the amount of the excess from the owners of the other vessel or vessels to the extent to which those vessels were respectively in fault, but no amount shall be recovered which could not, by reason of any statutory or contractual limitation of, or exemption from, liability, or which could not for any other reason, have been recovered in the first instance as damages by the persons entitled to sue therefor.[55]

The heads of damages under which claims are competent, both in cases of loss of life and of personal injuries, are the same as in claims brought at common law.

(v) (b) Claims for Loss of or Damage to Property Arising out of Collision at Sea

So far as concerns loss of or damage to property owned by passengers or crew of a ship involved in a collision no specialty of liability or remedy

52 Merchant Shipping Act 1894, s. 419 (3); Civil Aviation Act 1949, s. 52 (1).
53 Maritime Conventions Act 1911, s. 4 (1); *cf. The Heranger* v. *The Diamond* [1939] A.C. 94.
54 Maritime Conventions Act 1911, s. 2; *Reavis* v. *Clan Line and Laird Line*, 1925 S.C. 725.
55 *Ibid.* s. 3. See *The Cedric* [1920] P. 193; *The Moliere* [1925] P. 27.

arises merely because the cause of the loss or damage was maritime collision.[56]

So far as concerns liability for loss of or damage to one ship caused by maritime collision, liability depends on proof of negligence, which may be in construction, equipping or manning of the ship, or in her navigation or handling. Impact without damage,[57] and impact causing damage but without fault,[58] give no right of action. The defender will be liable at least in part if he caused the damage, if not the collision.[59]

Maritime collision damage [60]

There is no difference between maritime law and common law as to what amounts to negligence which causes damage by collision,[61] nor as to the amount of damages.[62] Where one ship is damaged in collision with another the principle of compensation by which damages are assessed is *restitutio in integrum*.[63] The owner is entitled to be fully compensated for the loss and this extends to the immediate expenses necessitated by the collision, repairs, and the detention of the ship, subject always to there being no *novus actus interveniens*,[64] and to the ordinary rules of remoteness of damage.[62]

Repairs

This includes such necessary outlays as raising and docking,[65] the employment of a tug [66] or salvage expenses.[67] The owner is entitled to a complete repair of all the damage done by the collision,[68] even though this may result in his ship being rendered more valuable than she was before the collision,[69] and the cost thereof [70] is the cost of execution at the nearest convenient port at which repairs could have been executed.[71]

56 *Cf. Reavis* v. *Clan Line*, 1925 S.C. 725.

57 *The Margaret* (1881) 6 P.D. 76.

58 *Morgan* v. *Castlegate Steamship Co.* [1893] A.C. 38.

59 *The Margaret, supra.*

60 See further Roscoe's *Measure of Damages in Maritime Collisions*, 3rd ed., 1929.

61 *Cayzer* v. *Carron Co.* (1884) 9 App.Cas. 873; *S.S. Bogota* v. *S.S. Alconda*, 1924 S.C.(H.L.) 66.

62 *The Argentino* (1888) 13 P.D. 191, 195, 200; *Anglo-Algerian S.S. Co.* v. *Houlder Line* [1908] 1 K.B. 659.

63 *The Clarence* (1850) 3 W.Rob. 283, 285; *The Clyde* (1866) Swab. 23; *The Bernina* (1886) 6 Asp.M.L.C. 65; *The Kate* [1899] P. 165; *H.M.S. London* [1914] P. 72; *Admiralty Commrs.* v. *S.S. Susquehanna* [1926] A.C. 655, 661; *Liesbosch* v. *Edison* [1933] A.C. 449.

64 *S.S. Baron Vernon* v. *S.S. Metagama*, 1928 S.C.(H.L.) 22.

65 *The Empress Eugenie* (1860) Lush. 138; *The Annie* (1887) 12 P.D. 50.

66 *The Inflexible* (1857) Swab. 200.

67 *The Legatus* (1856) Swab. 168; *The Pensher* (1857) Swab. 211; *The Williamina* (1878) 3 P.D. 97.

68 *The Princess* (1885) 5 Asp.M.L.C. 451.

69 *The Pactolus* (1857) Swab. 173; *The Gazelle* (1844) 2 W.Rob. 279; *The Bernina, supra*; *The Star of India* (1876) 1 P.D. 466; *The Kingsway* [1918] P. 344.

70 The insurance rule of deducting one-third because new material is more valuable than old has no application in the case of repairs: *The Pactolus, supra*; *Lohre* v. *Aitchison* (1879) 4 App.Cas. 755.

71 *Admiralty* v. *Aberdeen Steam Trawling Co.*, 1910 S.C. 553; *Beucker* v. *Aberdeen Steam Trawling Co.*, 1910 S.C. 655.

Graving dock and similar dues fall under the same rule.[72] A complete replacement will not be allowed where an ordinary repair will do,[73] nor will the cost of repairs be enhanced by delay or intermediate voyages.[74] The cost is recoverable even if the repairs are not done [75] or the vessel sold for breaking up.[76] Both temporary and permanent repairs have been allowed where the latter could only have been executed with difficulty and by withdrawing the ship from earning at a time when freights were high and the cost of permanent repairs and demurrage were then calculated in advance.[77]

The expenses of docking are recoverable even though advantage is taken of the opportunity to fit bilge keels,[78] or to make a periodical overhaul,[79] or if it is reasonable though not essential to do owner's repairs simultaneously.[80] When neither collision repairs nor voyage repairs were then necessary, the cost of dry-docking has been divided.[81] Where there have been two collisions, the cost of docking is attributable to the first, if not increased by the second.[82] A surveyor's fee may be recovered.[83] An allowance has also been given for depreciation in value when collision repairs had been executed.[84]

Detention and loss of profit

Detention of the ship includes principally the claim arising out of the loss to the owner of the services of the ship and the loss of business. It is not recoverable if the vessel be wholly lost,[85] nor if damages are assessed on the basis of a total loss.[86] Indemnity for loss of time during the detention must be estimated upon the principle, as nearly as may be, of what would certainly or most probably have been obtained, if there had been no collision. As to the time for which such compensation must be made, it ought to be reckoned from the period when the vessel, in the ordinary course, would have been ready for sea if there had been no collision, up to the period when with due diligence the repairs ought to have been completed.[87]

The loss of freight by reason of the detention is allowable. The pursuer must prove that the vessel would have been earning freight, and that this

[72] *The Black Prince* (1862) 1 Lush. 568.
[73] *The J. T. Easton*, 24 U.S.Fed.Rep. 95.
[74] *The Henry M. Clark*, 22 U.S.Fed.Rep. 752.
[75] *The Endeavour* (1890) 6 Asp.M.L.C. 511.
[76] *The London Corporation* [1935] P. 70; *Porter* v. *Robb*, 1961 S.L.T.(Sh.Ct.) 14.
[77] *The Kingsway* [1918] P. 344.
[78] *Ruabon S.S. Co.* v. *London Assurance Co.* [1900] A.C. 6; *The Acanthus* [1902] P. 17.
[79] *Admiralty Commrs.* v. *S.S. Chekiang* [1926] A.C. 627.
[80] *Carslogie S.S. Co.* v. *Royal Norwegian Govt.* [1952] A.C. 292.
[81] *The Royal Fusilier*, 25 Ll.L.R. 566; *Cameronia* v. *Hauk*, 1928 S.L.T. 71.
[82] *Carslogie S.S. Co.* v. *Royal Norwegian Govt.* [1952] A.C. 292.
[83] *Beucker* v. *Aberdeen Steam Trawling Co.*, 1910 S.C. 655.
[84] *Hamilton* v. *Galloway Steam Packet Co.* (1894) 1 S.L.T. 432.
[85] *The Kingsway* [1918] P. 344.
[86] *The Columbus* (1849) 3 W.Rob. 158.
[87] *The Inflexible* (1857) Swab. 200.

was lost by the collision.[88] Moreover, compensation for time lost will only be allowed on the basis of repairs being executed as quickly and cheaply as is reasonably possible.[89]

Loss of earnings under charter, but less expenses, is recoverable,[90] but not both demurrage and loss of freight under a charter or other agreement.[91] Loss of future definite employment is also allowable.[91] If there was no charter but reasonable certainty of employment, regard may be had to the profits of previous voyages.[92]

Where a vessel was at the time of the collision running at a loss with a view to the building up of a profitable trade, nothing was allowed for loss of use during the period of repairs.[93] Even though the owners are a public authority or a foreign State, damages for loss of use are recoverable just as in the case of a private owner,[94] even in the case of warships.[95]

If, however, there was no detention during repairs nothing is recoverable under this head.[96] Deductions must be made from the gross freight the ship would have earned to cover the wear and tear and expenses incurred in earning it,[90] and a proportion for contingencies.[97] In another case [98] damages were allowed for loss of profits due to detention even though voyages for which she had been chartered were not frustrated.

Where a fishing boat was totally lost the estimated loss of profits for the rest of that fishing season was held to be not necessarily too remote,[99] though in England [1] a claim in similar circumstances for loss of possible future fishing till a new vessel could be procured was not maintainable.

When collision repairs and heavy weather repairs are done concurrently, the owners are still entitled to damages for detention at least for the period attributable to the collision repairs [2]; but where supervening heavy weather damage rendered a damaged vessel unseaworthy no damages were recoverable for detention merely because she also underwent

88 *The Clarence* (1850) 3 Rob.Adm. 283; *The Star of India* (1876) 1 P.D. 466; *The Consett* (1880) 5 P.D. 229; *The Thyatira* (1883) 8 P.D. 155; *The Argentino* (1888) 14 App.Cas. 519; *The Greta Holme* [1897] A.C. 596; *The Kate* [1899] P. 165; *Admiralty Commrs.* v. *S.S. Valeria* [1922] 2 A.C. 242; *Strathfillan* v. *Ikala* [1929] A.C. 196; *Carslogie S.S. Co.* v. *Royal Norwegian Govt.* [1952] A.C. 292.

89 *Beucker* v. *Aberdeen Steam Trawling and Fishing Co.*, 1910 S.C. 655.

90 *The Gazelle* (1844) 2 W.Rob. 279; *The Star of India* (1876) 1 P.D. 466; *The Argentino* (1889) 14 App.Cas. 519; see also *Morrison S.S. Co.* v. *Greystoke Castle* [1947] A.C. 265, 308.

91 *The Argentino* (1889) 14 App.Cas. 519; *The Racine* [1906] P. 273; *The Empress of Britain* (1913) 29 T.L.R. 423.

92 *The Hebe* (1847) 2 W.Rob. 530.

93 *The Bodlewell* [1907] P. 286.

94 *The Astrakhan* [1910] P. 172; *The Greta Holme* [1897] A.C. 596; *The Mediana* [1900] A.C. 113; *The Marpessa* [1907] A.C. 241; *Clyde Nav. Trs.* v. *Bowring S.S. Co.*, 1929 S.C. 715.

95 *Admiralty Commrs.* v. *S.S. Susquehanna* [1926] A.C. 655; but see *The West Wales* [1932] P. 165.

96 *H.M.S. Inflexible* (1857) Swab. 200; *The Glenfinlas* [1918] P. 363n.; *The York* [1929] P. 178; *S.S. Strathfillan* v. *S.S. Ikala* [1929] A.C. 196; *The Veraston* [1920] P. 12.

97 *Baron Vernon* v. *Metagama*, 1927 S.C. 498 (10 per cent.).

98 *Vitruvia S.S. Co.* v. *Ropner Shipping Co.*, 1923 S.C. 574.

99 *Main* v. *Leask*, 1910 S.C. 772; *Christie* v. *Buchan* (1935) 51 Sh.Ct.Rep. 219.

1 *The Anselma de Larrinaga* (1913) 29 T.L.R. 587.

2 *Ruabon S.S. Co.* v. *London Assurance* [1900] A.C. 6; *The Acanthus* [1902] P. 17; *Admiralty Commrs.* v. *S.S. Chekiang* [1926] A.C. 637.

collision repairs [3]; and no damages are recoverable if the vessel was unseaworthy from another cause.[4] When detention arises from two supervening collisions the loss will be attributed to the earlier in time.[5]

Wages of crew

The outlay involved in the wages and maintenance of officers and crew while the ship is detained may be recovered if, in the circumstances, it is reasonable and proper to keep them on.[6] This may depend in part on custom. But where it would be reasonable to discharge the crew during the period of detention such an outlay will not be allowed in the claim of damages.[7] If the owner has to incur expense by the repatriation of seamen, it is recoverable.[8]

Replacement vessel employed

Where a ship is put out of commission by collision, and a ship belonging to another owner carries out the services she would have done, the amount of freight lost is recoverable from the wrongdoer.[9] If she is hired by the owner to replace his damaged vessel the hire is the measure of loss.[10] If the substitute vessel, however, is another provided by the owners of the damaged ship, it has been questioned whether any damages are due. In *The City of Peking* [11] the cargo and passengers of a damaged ship were transhipped and forwarded in two vessels under the same control as the damaged ship. The expenses incurred in using both were allowed, but a claim for loss of use of the damaged ship was disallowed on the ground that all damage arising from the transhipments had been paid, and that no further loss had been sustained by the company in consequence of the dislocation of service. In *The Greta Holme*,[12] a dredger belonging to a non-profit-making body of trustees was damaged, but damages were nevertheless awarded by the House of Lords on the general ground that the wrongdoer is bound to pay damages for deprivation of the use of another's property, even though no specific pecuniary loss can be shown to have resulted. Similarly, in *The Mediana*,[13] a lightship belonging to a harbour board was damaged. It was replaced by a spare lightship kept in reserve by the board for such a contingency. Hence, no additional loss was in fact incurred by the detention of the damaged vessel, but damages were nevertheless awarded on the ground that if a reserve had not been available one would have had to be hired, and the wrongdoer was equally

[3] *Carslogie S.S. Co.* v. *Royal Norwegian Govt.* [1952] A.C. 292.
[4] *Vitruvia S.S. Co.* v. *Ropner Shipping Co.*, 1925 S.C.(H.L.) 1; *Cameronia* v. *The Hauk*, 1928 S.L.T. 71.
[5] *The Haversham Grange* [1905] P. 307.
[6] This covers naval vessels: *The Susquehanna* [1926] A.C. 655.
[7] *The Black Prince* (1862) 1 Lush. 568; *The Inflexible* (1857) Swab. 200.
[8] *The Craftsman* [1906] P. 153.
[9] *The Black Prince* (1862) 1 Lush. 568.
[10] *The Yorkshireman* (1827) 2 Hag.Adm. 30n.
[11] (1890) 15 App.Cas. 438.
[12] [1897] A.C. 596. See also *The Marpessa* [1907] A.C. 241.
[13] [1900] A.C. 113.

liable to pay in the one case as in the other, and the principle of *The Greta Holme* [14] was approved. In *The Chekiang*,[15] the principle was again approved, and it was observed that there was no absolute rule that damages for detention of a non-profit-earning ship must be calculated on the basis of a percentage of the vessel's capital value. Regard must be had to her character and duties. There a warship was damaged and sent for repairs: the Admiralty decided to carry out her annual refit at the same time. It was held that a sum calculated on the basis of 5 per cent. on the estimated capital value of the ship was rightly allowed in respect of the period of detention attributable to repair of the collision damage. In *The Susquehanna* [16] that principle was again approved and applied in the case of an Admiralty oil tanker. In *The Tugela*,[17] where a dredger was sunk and sand silted around her, damages were given for loss of use and also for the hire of another dredger, after she was raised, to clear the sand bank.

Loss following on collision

When a vessel is damaged by collision and later is further damaged or totally lost, the presumption is that the loss was caused by the original negligence,[18] and the onus is then on the defender to show that the original negligence has been exhausted.[19] This extends to subsequent loss from heavy weather,[20] or in consequence of the damage done by the collision,[21] but not if the subsequent loss were due to failure to take all reasonable measures to save the ship,[22] refusal of necessary assistance,[23] doing only inadequate repairs,[24] or unjustifiable abandonment.[25] In such cases, only the cost of repairing the damage caused by the collision is allowable, and not the cost of salvage and the value of the ship.[25] So, too, damage to cargo was refused as a head of damages when it was caused partly by the master's failure to carry it on to the port of discharge without delay.[26]

Where the damages have been increased by the weak state of the injured vessel, the ship at fault is liable for the whole loss [27] unless the pre-existing defects can be readily discriminated.[28] This does not extend to loss caused

14 [1897] A.C. 596; see also *The Marpessa* [1907] A.C. 241.
15 *Admiralty Commrs.* v. *S.S. Chekiang* [1926] A.C. 637.
16 *Admiralty Commrs.* v. *S.S. Susquehanna* [1926] A.C. 655; see also *The West Wales* [1932] P. 165.
17 (1914) 30 T.L.R. 101.
18 *The Pensher* (1857) Swab. 211; *The Mellona* (1847) 3 W.Rob. 7.
19 *S.S. Baron Vernon* v. *S.S. Metagama*, 1928 S.C.(H.L.) 22; *cf. S.S. Rowan* v. *S.S. West Camak*, 1923 S.C. 316.
20 *The Despatch* (1860) 14 Moo.P.C. 83; *The Maid of Kent* (1881) 6 P.D. 178; *The George and Richard* (1871) L.R. 3 A. & E. 466; *cf. The Oropesa* [1942] P. 140 (loss of life).
21 *The City of Lincoln* (1890) 15 P.D. 15; *Reischer* v. *Borwick* [1894] 2 Q.B. 548.
22 *The Thuringia* (1872) 1 Asp.M.L.C. 283; *The Paludina* [1927] A.C. 16; *S.S. Baron Vernon* v. *S.S. Metagama*, 1928 S.C.(H.L.) 22; *The Hansa* (1889) 6 Asp.M.L.C. 268; *The Egyptian* [1910] P. 38.
23 *The Flying Fish* (1864) Br. & Lush. 436.
24 *The Bruxellesville* [1908] P. 312.
25 *The Thuringia, supra*; *The Linda* (1857) Swab. 306. See also *The Blenheim* (1854) 1 Sp. 285.
26 *The Elina* (1880) 5 P.D. 237n.
27 *The Egyptian* (1864) 10 L.T. 910; *The Bernina* (*No.* 3) (1886) 6 Asp.M.C. 65.
28 *The Princess* (1886) 5 Asp.M.L.C. 451.

by the pursuer's financial weakness.[29] Damages may, however, be recovered for the loss of business on which the vessel was engaged at the time.[30]

Damages are not recoverable for loss after or in consequence of the collision if caused partly by the pursuer's own negligence.[31] The owner is not obliged to raise a sunken vessel, even if practicable.[32] If she is raised and found not worth repairing, the damages will be the cost of raising and docking, less scrap value. If she is repaired at a cost exceeding the value, damages are limited to the value without allowance for demurrage.[33] If the repairs are not done, the damages will be the value before the collision less the proceeds of sale, with interest.[34] A sum paid to a wreck-raising authority for salving is recoverable as damages.[35] The owners are entitled to the full sum of damages even if part of that sum has been recovered from underwriters.[36]

Interest [37]

Interest accrues on damages from the moment when the damage was suffered until the liability has been adjudged and the amount finally ascertained, even though a period has intervened when no proceedings could have been taken.[38] It has been allowed from the probable termination of the voyage till payment,[39] but in a repair case [40] it was limited to repairs done and detention already incurred, and refused on estimated repairs and estimated demurrage. In *Vitruvia S.S. Co.* v. *Ropner S.S. Co.*[41] interest was allowed on the cost of repairs from the date of payment, but on detention damages only from the date of decree, and in *Laird Line* v. *Clan Line*,[42] where a ship was so damaged that she would have required three months' repairs and then was sunk by collision, interest was held to run on the total loss damage only from three months after the loss. Where repairs have been effected and their extent and liability for them has been admitted, interest runs from the date when they were paid for.[43]

29 *Liesbosch* v. *Edison* [1933] A.C. 449.

30 *The Risoluto* (1883) 8 P.D. 109; *The Veraston* [1920] P. 12; *The Kingsway* [1918] P. 344; *The Consett* (1880) 5 P.D. 229; *The Kate* [1899] P. 165; *cf. Vitruvia S.S. Co.* v. *Ropner Shipping Co.*, 1923 S.C. 574.

31 *The Marigola* (1929) 34 Ll.L.R. 217; *The Massachusetts* (1840) 1 W.Rob. 371; *cf. The Flying Fish* (1864) Br. & Lush. 436; *Grill* v. *General Iron Screw Co.* (1868) L.R. 3 C.P. 476.

32 *The Columbus* (1849) 3 W.Rob. 158.

33 *The Empress Eugenie* (1860) Lush. 138.

34 *The South Sea* (1857) Swab. 141.

35 *The North Britain* [1894] P. 77; *The Engineer* [1898] P. 382. See also *The Crystal* [1894] A.C. 508; *Smith* v. *Wilson* [1896] A.C. 579; *The Ella* [1915] P. 111.

36 *Morison & Milne* v. *Bartolomeo & Massa* (1867) 5 M. 848.

37 Practice varies slightly from England: *Vitruvia S.S. Co.* v. *Ropner Shipping Co.*, 1923 S.C. 574, 586.

38 *The Crathie* [1897] P. 178; *The Kong Magnus* [1891] P. 223; *The Joannis Vatis* (*No.* 2) [1922] P. 213; *The Berwickshire* [1950] P. 204.

39 *The Kong Magnus* [1891] P. 223; *The Kate* [1899] P. 165; *The Racine* [1906] P. 273.

40 *The Napier Star* (1933) 49 T.L.R. 342.

41 1923 S.C. 574.

42 1924, not reported.

43 *Vitruvia, supra.*

Constructive total loss

Where a vessel is so much damaged by collision that a prudent owner would not repair her, she falls to be considered a constructive total loss, and the owner is entitled to recover on the same basis as if she had been in fact totally lost. The basic measure of damages is accordingly not the cost of repair but the pre-collision value of the vessel.[44] In addition, the owner is entitled to the cost of raising the vessel if practicable and reasonable to do so.[45] The defender is entitled to the wreck, or to have the value, if sold, deducted from the damages.[45] The owner is bound to act to minimise his loss so far as possible and realise the wreck as soon as he has determined not to repair her.

As neither estimated value nor the estimated cost of repair can be more than approximately ascertained, it will not be held unreasonable for an owner to repair his ship, though it may turn out in the end that the cost of repairs exceeds a liberal estimate of the value of the ship.[46]

Loss of freight and interest are governed by the same considerations as in the case of a total loss.[47]

Total loss

If a ship be totally lost by collision, the owner is entitled prima facie to recover the market value at the time of the collision [48] at her home port,[49] less the value of any saleable wreck. If she be of special type or construction, and with no market value, though of special value to her owners, the damages must be estimated by consideration of her value to her owners as at the time of her loss.[50] Factors for consideration are the original cost, condition, age, amount spent on upkeep, state of the market, whether under charter, whether offered to be purchased,[51] and past earnings.[52] Interest on the damages is allowed from the date of collision, if the vessel were not earning freight [53]: a deduction may, however, be made if there is unreasonable delay in commencing proceedings.[54] If the market value allowed is based on that of similar vessels whose value is inflated by the certainty of future profitable employment, no more is allowed for future trading profits than the profit on the voyage in progress at the time of loss.[55] The fact of requisition, if in time of war, is also

44 *The Minnehaha* (1920) 6 Ll.L.R. 12.
45 *The Columbus* (1849) 3 W.Rob. 158; *cf. The Empress Eugenie* (1860) Lush. 138.
46 *The Mashona* (1904) Fo. 338.
47 *Infra.*
48 *The Philadelphia* [1917] P. 101; *The Clyde* (1856) Swab. 23; *The Ironmaster* (1859) Swab. 441; *The Columbus* (1849) 3 W.Rob. 158; *The Clarence* (1850) 3 W.Rob. 283; *The Kate* [1899] P. 165; *The Racine* [1906] P. 273.
49 *The Blenheim*, 17 U.S.Fed.Rep. 608.
50 *The Harmonides* [1903] P. 1; *cf. Liesbosch* v. *Edison* [1933] A.C. 449; *Clyde Nav. Trs.* v. *Bowring*, 1929 S.C. 715.
51 *The Ironmaster* (1859) Swab. 441.
52 *Cf. La Normandie*, 58 U.S.Fed.Rep. 427; *The Ironmaster, supra.*
53 *The Ikala* [1928] P. 86; *The Crispin* (1929) 35 Ll.L.R. 197.
54 *The Ikala, supra*; *The Crispin, supra*; *The St. Charles* (1927) 17 Asp.M.L.C. 399.
55 *The Llanover* [1947] P. 80.

material.[56] Her insurance value is irrelevant,[57] and damages for detention during repair are not recoverable.[58]

Freight and interest

If the ship was earning freight, the owner is entitled to her estimated value at the time of loss, with the freight she would have earned, less the cost of completing the voyage or charter, and having regard to contingencies,[59] wear and tear, and any special terms of the charterparty.[60] Where the voyage or charter would have been completed before payment, the owner may recover interest from the probable date of completion, and if payment is made prior to that date, an allowance is made for discount. If the vessel was proceeding in ballast to load under charter, damages are recoverable in the same way.[61] If she were not a freight-earning vessel but were otherwise profitably employed, the owner may recover her value as a profit-earning vessel at the time and place of her loss.[62]

If the pursuer's loss exceeds the amount of the defender's liability under statute, interest runs from the date of collision, whether or not freight was being earned.[63] Where a vessel was proceeding to take up a cargo, the owner may recover her value and the profits she would have made under that charter, but not speculative or uncertain profits, as where no charter was in view.[64]

Non-trading and special vessels

In these cases the vessel may have no market value or earning capacity so that the basic measure of the market value is inapplicable. Regard must then be had to her value to the owner as a going concern. In *Liesbosch* v. *Edison* [65] a dredger became a total loss and the owners recovered the market price of a replacement dredger, the cost of adaptation and transport, compensation for loss and inconvenience between the time of the loss and the time when the substitute could reasonably have been made available, with interest on the whole sum since the date of loss. In *Clyde Navigation Trs.* v. *Bowring S.S. Co.*,[66] a hopper digger barge, for which there was no market value, was lost. The pursuers recovered the cost of a reasonably efficient secondhand hopper barge, the cost of adaptation to the pursuers'

[56] *Harris* v. *Shipping Controller* (1918) 23 Com.Cas. 311.

[57] *The Ironmaster, supra*; *The Philadelphia, supra.*

[58] *The Kingsway* [1918] P. 344.

[59] *S.S. Baron Vernon* v. *S.S. Metagama*, 1927 S.C. 498; *The Philadelphia* [1917] P. 101.

[60] *The Philadelphia* [1917] P. 101; *The Kate* [1899] P. 165; *The Racine* [1906] P. 273.

[61] *The Kate, supra*; *The Racine, supra.*

[62] *Liesbosch* v. *Edison* [1933] A.C. 449.

[63] *The Northumbria* (1869) L.R. 3 A. & E. 6; *The Empress of Britain* (1913) 29 T.L.R. 423.

[64] *The Philadelphia, supra*, citing earlier cases; *The Kate, supra*; *The Racine, supra*; *The Clyde* (1856) Swab. 23; *The Columbus* (1849) 3 W.Rob. 158; *cf. The Anselma de Larinaga* (1913) 29 T.L.R. 587 (expected fishing profits refused); and contrast *Main* v. *Leask*, 1910 S.C. 772; *The City of Rome* (1890) 8 Asp.M.L.C. 542n.

[65] [1933] A.C. 449; *cf. Clyde Nav. Trs.* v. *Bowring*, 1929 S.C. 715; *cf. The St. Charles* (1927) 138 L.T. 456.

[66] 1929 S.C. 715.

purposes, a sum for the loss of use during the period until the pursuers obtained a substitute, and interest.

Remoteness

In many cases certain heads of damage are rendered irrecoverable by the application of the rules of remoteness. Some examples are: probable future earnings and profits of the master as a part-owner of a vessel lost [67]; damage caused by stranding while attempting to salve the other vessel which had been alone to blame [68]; damages for incapacity caused by fright at seeing the defendants' vessel bearing down out of the fog [69]; total loss due to unreasonable attempt to make port after sustaining collision damage.[70]

Special cases

Substantial damages have been awarded for damage to vessels in the service of public bodies though not profit-earning, such as a dredger,[71] a lightship,[72] a warship,[73] a naval oil tanker [74]; in these cases the award was on the basis of interest and depreciation on prime cost. The cost of occupation and use of a naval dock and plant have been allowed.[75] Where collision caused detention of a tug, maintenance costs were held recoverable even though there had been no work for the vessel, as she was always kept available.[76]

In *Clyde Nav. Trs.* v. *Bowring S.S. Co.*,[77] a special barge was totally lost. Neither market value nor interest on total value for loss of services was awarded, but the cost of a reasonably efficient secondhand barge and the cost of specially adapting it, a sum for loss of use for a period and interest on the whole sum. There seems here to be an overlap between loss of use and interest.

Apportionment

The old Admiralty rule was that in the case of collision, the damages were equally divided between the parties when the parties were both to blame.[78] Under the Maritime Conventions Act 1911,[79] the liability to

67 *The Columbus* (1849) 3 W.Rob. 158.
68 *The San Onofre* [1922] P. 243.
69 *The Rigel* [1912] P. 99.
70 *The Glendinning* (1943) 76 Ll.L.R. 86; *cf. The Empire Squire* (1943) 76 Ll.L.R. 134.
71 *The Greta Holme* [1897] A.C. 596; *The Marpessa* [1907] A.C. 241.
72 *The Mediana* [1900] A.C. 113.
73 *The Chekiang* [1926] A.C. 637.
74 *The Susquehanna* [1926] A.C. 655.
75 *The West Wales* [1932] P. 165.
76 *Edmund Hancock* v. *Ernesto* [1952] 1 Ll.L.R. 467.
77 1929 S.C. 715.
78 *The Frankland* [1901] P. 161; *Vaux* v. *Sheffer* (1852) 8 Moo.P.C. 75; *Cayzer, Irvine* v. *Carron Co.* (1885) 13 R. 114; (1884) 9 App.Cas. 873, 881; *Marsden on Collisions at Sea*, 9th ed., 132 *et seq.* See also *The Lord Melville* (1816) 2 Shaw's App. 402; *Hay* v. *Le Neve* (1824) *ibid.* 409.
79 s. 1.

make good any loss or damage to vessels, cargo or freight, is to be proportioned to the degree in which each vessel is found to be in fault [80]: if different degrees of fault cannot be established, liability is to be apportioned equally. The provision has no effect on any liability under any contract of carriage or any contract, nor does it affect any contractual or legal limitation of liability, or other right to limit liability.

The Act applies to all courts, all waters, and all vessels,[81] and is to be construed along with the Merchant Shipping Acts; hence, it does not apply to contact with objects which are not " vessels," [82] though it does to such as sunken ships and wreck-marking ships.[83] It now applies to the Crown.[81] The Act probably does not alter the law that both ships must be guilty of negligence contributing to the loss, but there need not be a collision.[84]

Where one of two vessels collides with a third, both are liable for a proportion of the damage caused the third, and one can recover from the other her own damage and the adjudged proportion of the damages paid to the third ship.[85]

The fault to the degree of which liability is to be proportional must be fault causing or contributing to the collision.[86]

Actions of damages or loss by collision to certain property, and actions of damages for loss of life or personal injuries must be brought in two years, and there is a limitation of one year for certain actions to enforce contribution between the owners of different vessels.[87]

(vi) Claims by Cargo Owners for Damage Occurring to Cargo

A cargo owner whose cargo is damaged while on board ship has an action, founded on breach of contract, against the shipowner, subject to any conditions in the charterparty or bill of lading, for the diminution in value of the cargo thereby caused.

Where cargo in one vessel is damaged in consequence of collision between it and another vessel, the cargo owner is entitled, on the ground of breach of contract, to recover in full from the ship carrying his cargo, but subject to any qualifications in the charterparty or bill of lading. He is also entitled on the ground of delict to recover from each vessel a proportion of his loss corresponding to the degree in which that vessel was to

80 *The Rosalia* [1912] P. 109; *Cameronia* v. *The Hauk*, 1927 S.C. 518; *Boy Andrew* v. *St. Rognvald*, 1947 S.C.(H.L.) 70.
81 As to Crown vessels, ss. 1–3 and 8 apply, by Crown Proceedings Act, 1947 ss. 6, 30 (1).
82 *e.g.* piers, gas-floats (*Gas Float Whitton No.* 2 [1897] A.C. 337; *The Upcerne* [1912] P. 160), craft used for dredging (*The Blowboat* [1912] P. 217); launch on artificial lake (*Southport Corpn.* v. *Morriss* [1893] 1 Q.B. 359).
83 *The Manorbier Castle*, 129 L.T. 31.
84 *The Dunstanborough* [1892] P. 363n.; *cf. The Vectis* [1929] P. 204; *The Monte Rosa* [1893] P. 23; *The Scotia* (1890) 6 Asp.M.C. 541; *The United States* (1865) 12 L.T. 33 (launch).
85 *The Cairnbahn* [1914] P. 25; *The Frankland* [1901] P. 161. But see *The Socrates and The Champion* [1923] P. 76, 162; *The Englishman and The Australia* [1894] P. 239, a case of tug and tow; *The Morgengry and The Blackcock* [1900] P. 1.
86 *The Peter Benoit* (1915) 84 L.J.P. 87.
87 Act, s. 8. The time may be extended by the court: see *The Cambric* (1912) 29 T.L.R. 69.

blame for the collision.[88] The loss will be measured by the market value of the goods at the time and place, and in the condition in which, they should have been delivered to the consignee.[89] If there is no market price the loss must be ascertained by reference to the selling price, the cost of transport and insurance, and the purchaser's profit.[90]

(vii) Claims for Limitation of Liability

In certain circumstances, an owner, charterer, person interested in or operator of a ship may invoke statutory provisions limiting his liability.[91]

The owners of a British or foreign ship, and other persons covered by the statutory provision, are not liable in damages beyond statutorily fixed amounts where, without their actual fault or privity [92] (a) any loss of life or personal injury is caused to any person being carried in the ship [93]; (b) any damage or loss is caused to any goods, merchandise or other things whatsoever on board the ship [94]; (c) any loss of life or personal injury is caused to any person not carried in the ship through the act or omission of any person (whether on board the ship or not) in the navigation or management of the ship or in the loading, carriage or discharge of its cargo or in embarkation, carriage or disembarkation of its passengers, or through any other act or omission of any person on board the ship; (d) where any loss or damage is caused to any property (other than any property mentioned in paragraph (b) of this subsection) or any rights are infringed through the act or omission of any person (whether on board the ship or not) in the navigation or management of the ship, or in the loading,

88 Maritime Conventions Act 1911, s. 1; *The Umona* [1914] P. 141.

89 *Koufos* v. *Czarnikow, The Heron II* [1969] 1 A.C. 350.

90 *The Notting Hill* (1884) 9 P.D. 105; *Rodocanachi* v. *Milburn* (1886) 18 Q.B.D. 67; *The Activ* (1901) 17 T.L.R. 351.

91 Merchant Shipping Act 1894, s. 503 (1), amended by M.S. (Liability of Shipowners and Others) Act 1958, s. 2.

92 " Actual fault or privity " implies something personal and blameworthy as distinct from technical liability for servants or agents: *Lennard's Carrying Co. Ltd.* v. *Asiatic Petroleum Co.* [1915] A.C. 705. In the case of a corporate owner there must be absence of fault on the part of the directing persons of the corporation. Though a breach of a duty incumbent on the shipowner by statute or common law is personal to him and not discharged by delegation, this does not prevent him limiting his liability if the actual fault is that of a person employed by him to which he is not privy: *The Admiralty* v. *Divina* (*Owners*) [1952] P. 1; *Beauchamp* v. *Turrell* [1952] 2 Q.B. 207. The fault or privity of one owner does not prevent co-owners from limiting their liability: *The Spirit of the Ocean* (1865) Brown. & Lush. 336; *The Obey* (1866) L.R. 1 Ad. & Ecc. 102; *The Cricket, The Endeavour* (1882) 5 Asp.M.L.C. 53.

Instances of " actual fault or privity " include failure to supply a ship with sufficient ground tackle: *The British City* [1921] P. 444; failure to inform the master of need for special care as to stability: *Standard Oil Co. Ltd.* v. *Clan Line Steamers*, 1924 S.C.(H.L.) 1; allowing a barge to be used with her hull defective: *The Thames* [1940] P. 143; failure to give the master adequate instructions: *The Teal* (1949) 82 Ll.L.Rep. 414; *Everard* v. *London and Thames Haven Oil Wharves Ltd.* [1961] 2 Lloyd's Rep. 117; *The Lady Gwendolen* [1965] P. 294; allowing a ship to sail with wrong navigation lights: *The Admiralty* v. *Divina* (*Owners*) [1952] P. 1; failure to warn the master of navigational dangers: *The Norman* [1960] 1 Lloyd's Rep. 1.

93 Including a member of the crew: *Innes* v. *Ross*, 1956 S.C. 468; and a member of the crew injured while boarding the ship: *Moore* v. *Metcalf Motor Cruises* [1958] 2 Lloyd's Rep. 179.

94 Including passengers' baggage lost or damaged aboard: *The Stella* [1900] P. 161.

carriage or discharge of its cargo or in the embarkation, carriage or disembarkation of its passengers, or through any other act or omission of any person on board the ship.[95] The onus of proof that the occurrence happened without his actual fault or privity is on the person seeking to limit liability,[96] and the fault or privity must have been in some respect which caused or contributed to the incident giving rise to the damage.[97]

The right to limit liability is not excluded by reason only that the occurrence giving rise to liability was not due to the negligence of any person.[98]

The amounts

The amounts to which liability is limited are [1]: (i) in respect of loss of life or personal injury, either alone or together with such loss, damage or infringement as is mentioned in (*b*) and (*d*) of the subsection, an aggregate amount not exceeding 3,100 gold francs [2] for each ton of their ship's tonnage [3]; and (ii) in respect of such loss, damage or infringement as is mentioned in (*b*) and (*d*) of the subsection, whether there be in addition loss for life or personal injury or not, an aggregate amount not exceeding 1,000 gold francs [2] for each ton of their ship's tonnage.[3] The Board of Trade may by order specify the sterling equivalents of the amounts stated.[6]

Incidents to which limitation applies

The limited amount of liability applies to the total of the liabilities incurred on any one occasion, the test of which is whether both or all liabilities are the result of the same act of negligence,[7] and in respect of each distinct occasion independently of liability incurred on another occasion.[8]

Pleading limitation provisions

A party seeking to avail himself of the limitation provisions should have the limit fixed by the court in proceedings for that purpose,[9] which

95 Heads (c) and (d) are substituted by 1958 Act, s. 2 (1).
96 *Standard Oil Co.* v. *Clan Line*, 1924 S.C.(H.L.) 1; *The Norman* [1960] 1 Lloyd's Rep. 1.
97 *The Empire Jamaica* [1957] A.C. 386; *The Elna II and the Mission San Francisco* [1961] 1 Lloyd's Rep. 322.
98 1958 Act, s. 2 (3).
1 Merchant Shipping Act 1894, s. 503 (1), amended by Merchant Shipping (Liability of Shipowners and Others) Act 1958, s. 1 (1) and 2 (1).
2 Gold franc defined: 1958 Act, s. 1 (2).
3 Method of calculating tonnage defined: 1894 Act, s. 503 (2); M.S.A. 1906, s. 69; M.S.A. 1948, ss. 4 (3), 10; where the tonnage concerned is less than 300 the multiplier for the purposes of sub-para. (i) is to be 300: 1958 Act, s. 1 (1). As to Crown ships, see Crown Proceedings Act 1947, s. 5 (5). As to tonnage of tug and tow, see *The Bramley Moore* [1964] 1 All E.R. 105.
6 1958 Act, s. 1 (3). They are now £85.6826 and £27.6396 respectively (S.I. 1972, No. 734). The conversion rate applicable is that provided by the order in force when the sterling equivalent has to be ascertained, unless consignation has been made: *Furness Houlder* v. *Miraflores (Owners)* [1968] P. 656; *United Arab Maritime Co.* v. *Blue Star Line Ltd.* [1968] P. 665.
7 *The Creadon* (1886) 5 Asp.M.L.C. 585; *The Schwan* [1892] P. 419; *The Rajah* (1872) L.R. 3 Ad. & Ecc. 539; *Lucullite* v. *R. Mackay*, 1929 S.C. 401.
8 1894 Act, s. 503 (3); 1958 Act, s. 8 (2).
9 *e.g. Lucullite* v. *R. Mackay*, 1929 S.C. 401.

will be defended by any party alleging that there was actual fault or privity on the owner's part and whose claim might exceed the limited sum. It may be possible to plead the right to limit as a defence.[10]

Where there has been a collision between two ships which results in a liability by one ship to the other, under deduction of its own claim, the liability for the balance payable is the liability which may be limited.[11] Where a party has limited his liability he is entitled to have claims settled out of court or enforced by action elsewhere taken into account in the distribution of the limited fund.[12]

Other parties entitled to limit liability

Dock and canal owners and harbour and conservancy authorities[13] entitled to limitation of liability are not liable in damages beyond an amount equivalent to 1,000 gold francs per ton of the largest British ship which, at the time of the occurrence giving rise to their liability is, or within the period of five years previous thereto has been, within the area over which they perform any duty or exercise any power.[14]

(viii) PILOTAGE

Pilotage orders under the Pilotage Act 1913 may provide for the establishment of pilotage authorities for particular waters, and may provide that pilotage shall be compulsory in particular areas, though certain classes of ships are exempted from that requirement. The fact that a ship is under compulsory pilotage does not relieve the owner or master of any liability for loss or damage caused by her wrongful navigation,[15] though the defence of compulsory pilotage may be raised in respect of places to which the Pilotage Act 1913 does not apply, and where, by common law, the owner or the master is not liable for the negligence of a pilot taken on board under legal compulsion.[16]

An authority which fails to maintain an adequate pilotage service may incur liability to the owner of a ship which, by reason of the absence of a pilot, has incurred damage.[17]

A pilotage authority is not, where without their actual fault or privity any loss or damage is caused to any vessel or vessels or to any goods, merchandise or other things whatsoever on board any vessel or vessels or to

10 *Cf. Beauchamp* v. *Turrell* [1952] 2 Q.B. 207; *Hook* v. *Consolidated Fisheries Ltd.* [1955] 2 Lloyd's Rep. 647.

11 *Stoomvart Maatschappy Nederland* v. *P. & O. S.N. Co.* (1882) 7 App.Cas. 795.

12 *Rankine* v. *Raschen* (1877) 4 R. 225; *The Foscolino* (1885) 5 Asp.M.L.C. 420; *The Coaster* (1922) 15 Asp.M.L.C. 560; *The Crathie* [1897] P. 178.

13 All as defined in Merchant Shipping (Liability of Shipowners and Others) Act 1900, s. 2. As to the Crown in such capacities see Crown Proceedings Act 1947, s. 7.

14 Merchant Shipping (Liability of Shipowners and Others) Acts 1900, s. 2, and 1958, s. 1; *The Ruapehu* (*No.* 2) [1929] P. 305.

15 Pilotage Act 1913, s. 15; *The Chyebassa* [1919] P. 201.

16 *The Arum* [1921] P. 12; *The Waziristan* [1953] 2 All E.R. 1213.

17 *Anchor Line* v. *Dundee Harbour Trs.*, 1922 S.C.(H.L.) 79.

any other property or rights of any kind, whether on land or on water or whether fixed or moveable, be liable in damages beyond the amount of £100 multiplied by the number of pilots holding licences from the pilotage authority for the district at the date when the loss or damage occurs.[18] This limitation relates to the whole of any losses and damages which may arise upon any one distinct occasion although sustained by more than one person, and whether the liability arises at common law or under statute and notwithstanding anything in the statute.[19] If there are several claims the authority may apply to the Court of Session, which may determine the liability of the authority and distribute that amount rateably among the claimants, and otherwise do as it thinks just.[20] This Act does not affect pilotage authorities as owners of ships.[21]

Where a licensed pilot has given a bond for the purpose of the statutory provisions limiting liability, he is not liable for neglect or want of skill beyond the penalty provided in the bond, together with the amount payable to him as pilotage for that voyage.[22] The court has powers in a claim against a pilot to determine his liability, distribute the amount rateably among the claimants, and to exercise various other powers as the court thinks just.[23]

(ix) Civil Salvage

Salvage is a reward or recompense given to those by means of whose labour, intrepidity or perseverance, goods,[24] or the lives of persons from a British ship or a foreign ship within British territorial waters or a ship of a foreign country outwith British territorial waters if that country's government has assented to the exercise of jurisdiction by the British courts,[25] have been preserved from loss by shipwreck, fire or capture.[26] Services rendered in assisting, or saving life from, or saving the cargo or apparel of an aircraft in or over the sea or tidal waters are deemed to be salvage services if they would have been salvage services if rendered in relation to a ship, and justify similar reward.[27] A claim for salvage is competent only for the rescue of a ship or aircraft, her equipment, cargo, or the lives of persons on board, and not for any analogous services unconnected with sea or air transport,[28] though such cases might justify a claim based on recompense.

The claim is based not on contract but on the equitable obligation

[18] Pilotage Authorities (Limitation of Liability) Act 1936, s. 1.
[19] *Ibid.* s. 2.
[20] *Ibid.* s. 3.
[21] *Ibid.* s. 4.
[22] Pilotage Act 1913, s. 35 (1).
[23] *Ibid.* s. 35 (3), modifying *Deering* v. *Targett* [1913] 1 K.B. 129.
[24] By the general maritime law.
[25] Merchant Shipping Act 1894, ss. 544–545.
[26] Bell, *Comm.* I, 638; *Prin.* § 443; *Kennedy on Civil Salvage, passim.* The term " salvage " is also applied to the salvor's services, and to the salved property.
[27] Civil Aviation Act 1949, s. 51 (1).
[28] *Falcke* v. *Scottish Imperial Assce. Co.* (1886) 34 Ch.D. 234.

incumbent on persons benefited to remunerate a salvor,[29] though the services and their reward may in fact be made a matter of express contract,[30] and arises where property of the specified kinds is so placed that a prudent owner of the property would accept services offered, and services are offered.[31]

No claim arises if services are clearly declined, but acquiescence in a vessel standing by is sufficient to amount to acceptance of salvage services.

Conditions of claim

A claim is competent only where the subjects allegedly salved were in some real and appreciable danger, as by reason of the position of the salved vessel, from her condition,[32] from the master's lack of skill or ignorance of his position or ignorance of local conditions,[33] or from the deficiency or sickness or incompetence of her crew.[34]

In case of doubt the salvors must prove the existence, nature and degree of danger to the salved vessel [35]; it may be evidenced by the salved vessel's putting up distress signals or sending out radio calls for help or accepting assistance offered.[36]

Success requisite

Success is an essential of a salvage claim; if nothing is saving, no reward is due, however much time, effort and money has been expended and however much skill has been shown in the attempt.[37] The reward is for benefits conferred, not for services sought to be given.[38] Failure includes removing a ship from danger but only to another place of equal danger.[39] It suffices, however, to show that the salvor contributed materially to the ultimate safety, and the salvor need not prove that his services alone would have secured the safety of the vessel.[40] *In dubio* the court will take the view that services have contributed to saving.[41]

29 *Five Steel Barges* (1890) 15 P.D. 142, 146; *Cargo ex Port Victor* [1901] P. 243; *The Hestia* [1895] P. 193.

30 See *infra*.

31 *The Vandyck* (1881) 7 P.D. 42; (1882) 5 Asp.M.L.C. 17; *The Liffey* (1887) 6 Asp.M.L.C. 255; *The Auguste Legembre* [1902] P. 123; *The Emilie Galline* [1903] P. 106; *The Port Caledonia and the Anna* [1903] P. 184; *The Kangaroo* [1918] P. 327.

32 *The Ella Constance* (1864) 33 L.J.P.M. & A. 189; *The Troilus* [1951] A.C. 820 (dropped propeller); *cf. A/B Karlshamns Oljefabriker* v. *Monarch S.S. Co.* (defective boilers).

33 *The Eugenie* (1844) 3 Notes of Cases 430; *The Lomonosoff* [1921] P. 97; *The Tower Bridge* [1936] P. 30; *The Tres* (1936) 55 Ll.L.R. 16.

34 *The Aglaia* (1888) 13 P.D. 160.

35 *The Wilhelmine* (1842) 1 Notes of Cases 376.

36 *The Bomarsund* (1860) Lush. 77.

37 *Cargo ex Sarpedon* (1877) 3 P.D. 28; *The Renpor* (1883) 8 P.D. 115; *The Elton* [1891] P. 265; *Cargo ex Port Victor* [1901] P. 243.

38 *The Zephyrus* (1842) 1 Wm.Rob. 329; *The E.U.* (1853) 1 Ecc. & Ad. 63; *The Killeena* (1881) 6 P.D. 193; *The Camellia* (1884) 9 P.D. 27; *The City of Chester* (1884) 9 P.D. 182; *The Dart* (1899) 8 Asp.M.L.C. 481; *Melanie* v. *San Onofre* [1925] A.C. 246.

39 *The Cheerful* (1885) 11 P.D. 3; *The Benlarig* (1888) 14 P.D. 3; *The Lepanto* [1892] P. 122; *The Dart, supra*; *The Tarbert* [1921] P. 372; *Melanie* v. *San Onofre* [1925] A.C. 246.

40 *The Jonge Bastiann* (1804) 5 Ch.Rob. 322; *The Atlas* (1862) Lush. 518; *The Camellia, supra*; *The Hestia* [1895] P. 193; *The August Korff* [1903] P. 166; *The Kangaroo* [1918] P. 327.

41 *The E.U., supra*; *The Santipore* (1854) 1 Ecc. & Ad. 231.

An exception exists where services have been rendered at the request of the master of the salved vessel in circumstances implying a contract to pay for the services, in which case salvage reward is due although the service did not contribute to the ultimate safety.[42] Also if the master of the vessel in danger discontinues such service after it has been begun and while those giving it are able and willing to continue to give it, the service is rewardable though no material benefit has resulted from it.[43]

Persons entitled to claim salvage

The persons entitled to claim salvage are persons, not legally obliged to save the property in danger, including in particular the owners, masters and crew of all the ships which have rendered material assistance, and all who render personal service in the performance of salvage services.

The owners, master and crew of the ship in danger are already obliged, in the case of the master and crew by their contracts of employment, to do all that they reasonably can to avert the danger to or minimise the harmful consequences.[44] Passengers are obliged to assist in their own rescue and have no claim, save in the case where they could have left the ship but elected not to do so and remained on board voluntarily and assisted in saving her.[45] A pilot is in the same position.[46]

Parties liable to pay salvage

The parties liable are those having different interests in the vessel salved, namely the owners of the ship, the persons entitled to the freight, and the owners of the cargo.

Amount of salvage award

The amount of an award is in the discretion of the court [47] subject to two general principles, namely, that an award should be generous, to encourage and reward salvage efforts, and, secondly, that regard must be had to the danger the salved vessel was in and to the value of the ship itself, cargo and freight which have been salved, and to the skill, seamanship, effort, expenditure of time and money, risk to themselves and their vessel encountered, in effecting the salvage.

The award is limited to the value of the property, or interest in the property, salved,[48] and in general where the owners appear in the process,

[42] *The Undaunted* (1860) Lush. 90; *The Helvetia* (1894) 8 Asp.M.L.C. 264n.; *The Cambrian* (1897) 8 Asp.M.L.C. 263; *The Dart, supra*; *The Stiklestad* [1926] P. 205; *The Tarbert, supra*; *The Loch Tulla* (1950) 84 Ll.L.R. 62; *The Alenquer, The Rene* [1955] 1 Lloyd's Rep. 101.

[43] *The Mande* (1876) 3 Asp.M.L.C. 338; *The Maasdam* (1893) 7 Asp.M.L.C. 400.

[44] Bell, *Prin.* § 444.

[45] *Newman* v. *Walters* (1804) 3 B. & P. 612.

[46] *Akerblom* v. *Price* (1881) 7 Q.B.D. 129.

[47] *The Ewell Grove* (1835) 3 Hag.Adm. 209; *The Cuba* (1860) Lush. 14; *The City of Chester* (1884) 9 P.D. 182.

[48] *Cargo ex Schiller* (1877) 2 P.D. 145.

the court will not normally award more than half of the value of the salved property,[49] whether derelict [50] or not.[51]

Salvage award for saving life is payable in priority to all other claims for salvage award,[52] and the danger to life arising from the position of the vessel endangered or from the difficulty of the salvage service is the first consideration.[53]

In respect of salvage awards for property the major considerations are the value of the salved property [54]; the more valuable the property is, the smaller the proportion thereof usually awarded as salvage,[55] but where the value is large a liberal award is frequently given to encourage the practice of salvage,[56] though this should not increase the award to an amount disproportionate to the services rendered [57]; secondly, the degree of danger from which the property has been preserved; the danger is greatest to derelict property,[58] but apart from that depends on the whole circumstances of the case; thirdly, the degree of skill, seamanship, knowledge and care shown by the salvors [59]; fourthly, the duration of the services [60]; fifthly, the value of the property employed in the salvage services and thereby risked [61]; and, lastly, any expenses or losses incurred by the salvor in performing his services.[62]

The salvage award is liable to be diminished if the salvors fail to show the standard of skill and care reasonably to be expected in the circumstances,[63] and if the salved vessel suffers loss in consequence.[64] But in considering this issue regard must be had to any sudden emergency or other mitigating circumstances, and to the fact that the damage arose from rendering assistance asked for by the vessel in danger.[65] Actual misconduct by the salvors, whether or not it causes actual damage,[66] will, if proved by

49 For examples of awards see Kennedy, *Civil Salvage* (4th ed.) 161.
50 As to awards in derelict cases see *The Rasche* (1873) L.R. 4 A. & E. 127; *The Boiler ex Elephant* (1891) 64 L.T. 543; *The Louisa* [1906] P. 145.
51 *The Erato* (1888) 13 P.D. 163; *The Mercator* (1910) 26 T.L.R. 450.
52 M.S.A. 1894, s. 544 (2).
53 *The Suevic* [1908] P. 154.
54 *The Amerique* (1874) L.R. 6 P.C. 468; *The City of Chester* (1884) 9 P.D. 182.
55 *The Amerique, supra*; *The City of Chester, supra.*
56 *The Earl of Eglinton* (1855) Sw. 7.
57 *The Amerique* (1874) L.R. 6 P.C. 468; *The Glengyle* [1898] P. 97; *The Queen Elizabeth* (1949) 82 Ll.L.R. 803.
58 *The True Blue* (1866) L.R. 1 P.C. 250; *The Anna Helena* (1883) 5 Asp.M.L.C. 142; *The Janet Court* [1897] P. 59.
59 *Anglo Saxon Petroleum Co.* v. *Damant* [1947] K.B. 794.
60 *The Strathgarry* [1895] P. 264.
61 *The City of Chester* (1884) 9 P.D. 182; *The Werra* (1886) 12 P.D. 52; *The Rambler* v. *The Kotka* [1917] 2 I.R. 406.
62 *The James Armstrong* (1875) 3 Asp.M.L.C. 46; *The Silesia* (1880) 5 P.D. 177; *The Sunniside* (1883) 8 P.D. 137; *The De Bay* (1883) 8 App.Cas. 559; *The Edenmore* [1893] P. 79; *The Bremen* (1906) 10 Asp.M.L.C. 229; *The Cato* (1930) 37 Ll.L.R. 33; *The St. Melante* (1947) 80 Ll.L.R. 588; *The Tresco* (1944) 77 Ll.L.R. 514; *The Perfective* (1949) 82 Ll.L.Rep. 873; *The Ebor Jewel* (1949) 83 Ll.L.R. 64.
63 *Anglo-Saxon Petroleum Co.* v. *Damant* [1947] K.B. 794.
64 *The Rosalie* (1853) 1 Ecc. & Ad. 188; *The Perla* (1857) Sw. 230; *The Magdalen* (1861) 31 L.J.P.M. & A. 22; *The Dwina* [1892] P. 58; *The Clan Sutherland* [1918] P. 332; *The Alenquer, The René* [1955] 1 Lloyd's Rep. 101.
65 *The C. S. Butler, The Baltic* (1874) 2 Asp.M.L.C. 237.
66 *The Glory* (1849) 13 Jur. 991; *The Marie* (1882) 7 P.D. 203.

the salved ship,[67] diminish, or may even be held to extinguish, the claim for salvage.[68]

Salvage agreements

An express agreement relative to salvage may be made by or on behalf of the salving and salved vessels. It need not be in writing or in any particular form,[69] but must be clearly proved,[70] and fix the services to be rendered and the reward for them.[71]

Normally it does not infringe the requisites for a salvage award, in particular that some part at least of the property in danger be saved,[72] but by express provision salvage reward may be agreed to be paid irrespective of the ultimate safety of the property endangered.[73]

It may be rescinded by consent, by agreement to that effect, or by conduct clearly evidencing departure from the agreement.[74]

An agreement may be rescinded if induced by fraud,[75] misrepresentation or concealment of a material fact,[76] relevant to the danger to the property, or the duration, difficulty or risk of the salvage services.[77] It may be held not binding, if, without the fault of either party, circumstances prevent performance of the agreed services, or if in the circumstances the services actually rendered turn out to be wholly different from those agreed.[78]

It may also be challenged and be set aside by the court as being inequitable, as where the reward agreed is exorbitant,[79] in which case an important factor is whether the circumstances virtually compelled the master to make the agreement,[80] or wholly inadequate,[81] but the court will not set aside an agreement merely because it would itself have given more or less, nor because the services turned out in the event to be more or less difficult or

[67] *The Atlas* (1862) Lush. 518.

[68] *The Magdalen, supra*; *The Atlas, supra*; *The Yan-Yean* (1883) 8 P.D. 147; *The Capella* [1892] P. 70; *The Clan Sutherland, supra.*

[69] *The Graces* (1844) 2 Wm.Rob. 294; *The Arthur* (1862) 6 L.T. 556; *The Cumbrian* (1887) 6 Asp.M.L.C. 151.

[70] *The Graces, supra.*

[71] *The William Lushington* (1850) 7 Notes of Cases 361.

[72] *The Hestia* [1895] P. 193.

[73] *The Alfred* (1884) 5 Asp.M.L.C. 214; *The Prinz Heinrich* (1888) 13 P.D. 31; *The Edenmore* [1893] P. 79; *The Strathgarry* [1895] P. 264.

[74] *The Repulse* (1845) 2 Wm.Rob. 396; *The Africa* (1854) 1 Ecc. & Ad. 299; *The Samuel* (1851) 15 Jur. 407.

[75] *The Henry* (1851) 15 Jur. 183; *The Helen and George* (1858) Sw. 368; *The Crus V.* (1862) Lush. 583; *The Generous* (1868) L.R. 2 A. & E. 57; *The Kolpino* (1904) 73 L.J.P. 29.

[76] Even innocent misrepresentation will suffice: *The Kingalock* (1854) 1 Ecc. & Ad. 263; *The Canova* (1866) L.R. 1 A. & E. 54. See also *The Henry* (1851) 15 Jur. 183; *The Jonge Andries* (1857) Sw. 226, 303.

[77] *The Kingalock, supra.*

[78] *The Westbourne* (1889) 14 P.D. 132; *The Hestia* [1895] P. 193.

[79] *The Henry* (1851) 15 Jur. 183; *The Theodore* (1858) Sw. 351; *Cargo ex Woosung* (1876) 1 P.D. 260; *Akerblom* v. *Price* (1881) 7 Q.B.D. 129; *The Strathgarry* [1895] P. 264.

[80] *The True Blue* (1843) 2 Wm.Rob. 176; *The Medina* (1876) 2 P.D. 5; *The Mark Lane* (1890) 15 P.D. 135; *The Rialto* [1891] P. 175; *The Altair* [1897] P. 105; *The Port Caledonia and The Anna* [1903] P. 184.

[81] *The Phantom* (1866) L.R. 1 A. & E. 58.

dangerous or lengthy than anticipated,[82] nor because the salved value turns out less than the agreed reward.[83]

An agreement, or settlement of a claim, after the salvage services have been rendered, is binding unless it was unauthorised,[84] or the reward is quite inadequate and the salvor could not properly appreciate the value of his services,[85] or the circumstances attending the agreement are not satisfactorily explained.[86]

(x) Claims for Necessaries

A shipmaster has implied authority to contract, as agent for the shipowner, for such things as are necessary for the use of the ship and for these necessaries a claim lies against the shipowner.[87] The onus of proof is on the supplier who seeks to establish the shipowner's liability,[88] and it must be established that obtaining goods or borrowing money was reasonably necessary according to the ordinary course of prudent conduct and that it was reasonably necessary that the master obtain them on the owner's credit.[89] Necessaries include the obtaining of anchors and cables,[90] fuel,[91] provisions and clothing for the crew,[1] a propeller,[2] and necessary repairs, such as are fit and proper for the voyage and such as a prudent owner would himself have ordered.[3] The principle extends to the obtaining of an advance of money to pay for necessaries,[4] to pay off a shipwright's lien for necessary repairs,[5] to pay towage and dock dues,[6] or to make such other payments as a prudent owner would have authorised the master to order if he had been present.[7] The money must be expressed to have been advanced for necessary purposes,[8] and the lender can recover from the shipowner only the amount actually necessary for the purposes of the ship.[9]

82 *The True Blue, supra*; *The Cato* (1866) 35 L.J.Adm. 116; *The Waverley* (1871) L.R. 3 A. & E. 369; *The Strathgarry* [1895] P. 264.
83 *The Inna* [1938] P. 149.
84 *The Hermione* [1922] P. 162.
85 *Silver Bullion* (1854) 2 Ecc. & Ad. 70.
86 *The Macgregor Laird* [1867] W.N. 308.
87 *Grant* v. *Norway* (1851) 10 C.B. 665; *The Pontida* (1884) 9 P.D. 177.
88 *The Alexander* (1842) 1 Wm.Rob. 346; *The Sophie* (1842) 1 Wm.Rob. 368; *Mackintosh* v. *Mitcheson* (1849) 4 Exch. 175.
89 *Gunn* v. *Roberts* (1874) L.R. 9 C.P. 331.
90 *The Alexander, supra*; *The Sophie, supra.*
91 *The West Friesland* (1859) Swab. 454; *The Comtesse de Fregeville* (1861) Lush. 329; *The Mecca* [1895] P. 95.
1 *The N. R. Gosfabrick* (1858) Swab. 344; *The William E. Safford* (1860) Lush. 329; *The Mecca* [1895] P. 95.
2 *The Flecha* (1854) 1 Ecc. & Adm. 438, 441.
3 *Webster* v. *Seekamp* (1821) 4 B. & Ald. 352.
4 *Arthur* v. *Barton* (1840) 6 M. & W. 138, 144; *The Sophie* (1842) 1 Wm.Rob. 368; *The Onni* (1860) Lush. 154; *The Albert Crosby* (1870) L.R. 3 A. & E. 37; *The Anna* (1876) 1 P.D. 253.
5 *The Albert Crosby, supra.*
6 *The St. Lawrence* (1880) 5 P.D. 250.
7 *Webster, supra*; *The Riga* (1872) L.R. 3 A. & E. 516.
8 *Thacker* v. *Moates* (1831) 1 Mood. & R. 79.
9 *Mackintosh* v. *Mitcheson* (1849) 4 Exch. 175; *The Pontida* (1884) 9 P.D. 177.

(xi) Towage

The contract of towage is one whereby one vessel undertakes to tow another.

The owner of the tug impliedly warrants that at the outset the crew, tackle and equipment are equal to the work to be undertaken in circumstances reasonably to be expected,[10] and impliedly undertakes that thereafter competent skill and the best endeavours shall be used in doing the work.[11] There is no warranty that the tug shall be able to accomplish the work in all circumstances and the contract may be discharged by impossibility.[12] Unforeseen difficulties may justify a claim for salvage reward rather than for towage remuneration.[13] But the tug may not recover for salvage where it has failed to implement its obligations and in consequence circumstances arise necessitating salvage.[14]

Normally the tug is under the direction and control of the tow, and if without justification the tug disobeys directions and the tow is damaged, the tug is liable therefor and forfeits towage remuneration.[15]

Special conditions in the contract may relieve the tug from any of the obligations ordinarily incidental to the contract of towage,[16] but the tugowner may not rely on an exception clause if himself in fundamental breach of contract.[17]

(xii) Master's and Seamen's Wages and Disbursements

A seaman or apprentice, or a person authorised on his behalf, may, as soon as any wages due to him, not exceeding £50, become payable,[18] sue for them before a court of summary jurisdiction in or near the place at which his service has terminated, or at which he has been discharged, or at which any person on whom the claim is made is or resides, and the order made by the court in the matter shall be final.[19] Only exceptionally may proceedings be taken in a superior court.[20] In certain cases wages are not recoverable abroad.[21] The master has the same rights, liens and remedies for the recovery of his wages as a seamen has, and the master, or any person acting as the master, has the same rights for the recovery of disbursement or liabilities properly made or incurred by him, as for the recovery of his wages.[22]

10 *The Maréchal Suchet* [1911] P. 1.
11 *The West Cock* [1911] P. 208; see also *The Refrigerant* [1925] P. 130.
12 *The Salvador* (1909) 26 T.L.R. 149.
13 *The Minnehaha* (1861) Lush. 335.
14 *The Minnehaha, supra*; *The Robert Dixon* (1879) 5 P.D. 54; *The Maréchal Suchet, supra.*
15 *The Christina* (1848) 6 Moo.P.C. 371; *Spaight* v. *Tedcastle* (1881) 6 App.Cas. 217.
16 *The United Service* (1883) 9 P.D. 3; *The Tasmania* (1888) 13 P.D. 110; *The Richmond* (1902) 19 T.L.R. 29; *The Luna* [1920] P. 22.
17 *The Albion* [1953] 2 All E.R. 679.
18 As to payment of wages to seamen see generally Merchant Shipping Act 1894, ss. 131–163. As to recovery of wages of seamen lost with their ship, *ibid.* s. 174.
19 Merchant Shipping Act 1894, s. 164.
20 *Ibid.* s. 165.
21 *Ibid.* s. 166.
22 *Ibid.* s. 167.

(xiii) General Average

A general average claim arises where one of the main interests involved in sea transport, the ship, the cargo, or the freight, is voluntarily sacrificed, in whole or in part, in time of peril for the common safety for the purpose of preserving from peril the property involved in a maritime adventure,[23] and is for a proportionate contribution to the loss from the other interests involved. It differs from particular average, which is any loss not due to a voluntary act, or not due to a recognised general average act, and which must be borne solely by the person whose interest is damaged thereby.

This claim of the owners of sacrificed property rests on the same equitable foundation as claims for recompense.[24] The general maritime law of Europe has adopted the principle from the civil law which itself embodied the *Lex Rhodia de jactu.*[25]

General average acts

To amount to a general average act the act must be intentional and deliberate, and voluntarily incurred,[26] and not be damage or loss directly caused by heavy weather, sea or wind, though it may have been necessitated by such forces. Thus jettison of cargo to lighten a ship is a general average act, but if cargo is swept overboard or damaged, this is not.

It must be an extraordinary sacrifice or expenditure, and not such as is incurred in the normal course, such as the burning of fuel or the consumption of stores. But it extends to damage to engines to get a ship off a bank,[27] or the use of sails to stop a leak,[28] and to salvage expenditure [29] so long as concerned with saving all the interests concerned.

Losses which are the natural consequence of general average acts are themselves general average losses. Thus if water is poured on burning cargo to extinguish the fire and other goods are damaged, the latter loss is a general average one.[30]

Conditions of claim for contribution

Contribution is recoverable where one or more of the interests involved in a maritime adventure has been injured by a general average act. By custom contribution is not recoverable in respect of the jettison of cargo carried on deck,[31] unless loading on deck is in accordance with the

[23] Marine Insurance Act 1906, s. 66 (2); *cf.* York-Antwerp Rules on General Average 1950, Rule A.
[24] Bell, *Prin.* § 538; see generally *Lowndes and Rudolf on General Average and the York-Antwerp Rules.*
[25] Dig. XIV, 2, 1.
[26] *The Seapool* [1934] P. 53; *Athel Line* v. *Liverpool and London War Risks Association Ltd.* [1944] K.B. 87.
[27] *The Bona* [1895] P. 125.
[28] *Robinson* v. *Price* (1877) 2 Q.B.D. 91, 295.
[29] *Job* v. *Langton* (1856) 6 E. & B. 779.
[30] *Whitecross Wire Co.* v. *Savill* (1882) 8 Q.B.D. 653; *The Birkhall* (1896) 1 Com.Cas. 448; *Austin Friars S.S. Co. Ltd.* v. *Spillers and Bakers Ltd.* [1915] 3 K.B. 586.
[31] *Wright* v. *Marwood* (1881) 7 Q.B.D. 62; *Burton* v. *English* (1883) 12 Q.B.D. 218.

common usage of trade on the voyage on which the goods are shipped.[32] Also it is not recoverable if the peril which gave rise to the general average act was occasioned by the fault of the claimant or his servant; thus a shipowner's claim is barred if it be established that the loss was caused by the ship's unseaworthiness.[33]

Adjustment of average loss

Adjustment of general average loss should be made at the ship's port of destination or discharge, or at an intermediate port, by consent of parties or if the voyage is there necessarily broken.

York-Antwerp Rules

Rules formulated at international conferences, known as the York-Antwerp Rules 1890 (now 1950) are commonly incorporated in charterparties and marine insurance policies, and, where they apply, give guidance on the adjustment of general average claims.[34] The rules are not a complete code and may have to be supplemented by the provisions of the general law applicable to the contract.[35]

Amount of claim

The principle underlying any claim is that the person in right of the interest which has been sacrificed must determine his true loss, plus the cost of raising funds for general average, and claim proportionately from the ship, cargo, freight and property sacrificed. In case of sacrifice of cargo, the loss is the market value of the goods jettisoned or otherwise sacrificed, or their lesser value if they had been already damaged. If freight is sacrificed the basic loss is the freight under the original bill of lading. If the ship is sacrificed in part, the loss is prima facie measurable by the cost of repairing the damage done, less deduction for improvements effected incidentally thereby, this deduction being in general fixed at one-third.

As regards the interests bound to contribute to making good the loss, the ship's value is taken as its market value before the general average act, the value of the cargo as its actual or assumed market value at the time and place of adjustment, less freight, landing and warehousing charges, duty and brokerage, and the value of the freight as the freight earned by the voyage less the expenses of earning it which would not have been incurred if the ship had been lost. The owner of the property sacrificed must also contribute on the basis of the amount falling to be made good in general average added to its value, if any, at the termination of the adventure, as otherwise his loss would be made good in full by the other interests involved.

32 *Strang* v. *Scott* (1889) 14 App.Cas. 601, 609.
33 *Schloss* v. *Heriot* (1863) 14 C.B.(N.S.) 59; but see *Dreyfus* v. *Tempus Shipping Co.* [1931] A.C. 726.
34 For the rules see Lowndes and Rudolf's *General Average and the York-Antwerp Rules.*
35 *Goulandris Bros.* v. *Goldman* [1957] 3 All E.R. 100.

Enforcement of claim

At common law a shipowner has a lien on the cargo while in his possession for the cargo's share of general average, which can be used to require the giving of satisfactory security, such as an average bond or cash deposit, before delivery of the goods. By statute [36] the shipowner may, when goods are landed, give notice in writing to any wharf or warehouse owner in whose custody the goods are placed, requiring him to retain the goods subject to the claim for freight or other charges. The owner of the goods can obtain delivery only by depositing the sum claimed with the warehouse owner.[37]

If a shipowner fails to exercise a right of lien for the benefit of the owner of goods sacrificed he will be liable in damages to the owner of the jettisoned cargo.[38]

Shipowner and cargo-owner may each sue to recover contributions from other contributing interests.[39]

(xiv) Forfeiture of Ships to the Crown

A ship or share therein becomes subject to forfeiture if a person attempts to use a certificate not legally granted,[40] or no application is made for the sale of a ship transmitted to a foreigner,[41] or he wilfully makes a false declaration touching the qualification of himself or of any other person or corporation to own a British ship or any share therein,[42] or if a person uses the British flag and assumes the British national character for the purpose of making a ship appear to be a British ship,[43] or tries to conceal the British character of the ship or assume a foreign character,[44] or an unqualified person acquires as owner any interest, legal or beneficial, in a British ship,[45] or a ship has been engaged in piracy,[46] illegal trade or smuggling, and in certain other cases.[47]

Where a ship has become liable to forfeiture persons statutorily authorised may seize and detain the ship and bring her for adjudication before the Court of Session and the court may thereupon adjudge the ship to be forfeited to the Crown, and make such order in the case as to the court seems just, and may award to the officer bringing in the ship for adjudication such portion of the proceeds of the sale of the ship, or any share therein, as the court thinks fit.[48]

36 Merchant Shipping Act 1894, ss. 492–501.
37 See further *Smailes* v. *Hans Dessen* (1905) 11 Com.Cas. 74; (1906) 12 Com.Cas. 117.
38 *Crooks* v. *Allan* (1879) 5 Q.B.D. 38; *Strang* v. *Scott* (1889) 14 App.Cas. 601.
39 *Hain S.S. Co.* v. *Tate & Lyle* (1936) 41 Com.Cas. 350; *Morrison S.S. Co.* v. *Greystoke Castle* [1947] A.C. 265.
40 M.S.A. 1894, s. 16.
41 *Ibid.* s. 28.
42 *Ibid.* s. 67.
43 *Ibid.* s. 69; *The Annandale* (1877) 2 P.D. 218.
44 *Ibid.* s. 70.
45 *Ibid.* s. 71; see also s. 72.
46 *R.* v. *McCleverty* (1871) L.R. 3 P.C. 673.
47 M.S.A. 1894, s. 319; M.S.A. 1906, s. 51.
48 *Ibid.* s. 76.

(xv) Marine Insurance

Marine insurance is a contract of indemnity against losses incidental to a marine adventure occurring to a ship, cargo, freight or other subject-matter of the policy during an agreed time or an agreed voyage or voyages. The law is mainly contained in the Marine Insurance Act 1906.

The claims which may arise relate mainly to liability or non-liability on the policy, to the question whether a loss sustained was proximately caused by a peril insured against or not,[49] and the extent of loss sustained.

(xvi) Maritime Liens

A maritime lien is truly a hypothec, in that where it exists a creditor has security over a vessel for payments due to him without possession thereof. A maritime lien confers a right preferable to the holder of a mortgage over the ship, as well as to that of any personal creditor.[50] If there is doubt whether a claimant has a maritime lien or not he may bring a declarator of that fact.[51]

Maritime lien exists in the cases of the master of a ship, for his wages,[52] of seamen, for their wages,[53] of salvors, for any sum due for salvage,[54] of owners, for damages for collision damage, provided that the other ship was itself the direct cause of the damage, but not where the master of the other ship had, without actual impact, caused injury to the claiming ship.[55]

The master also has a maritime lien for disbursements made or liabilities incurred by him in that capacity and as one entitled to pledge the owner's credit,[56] if necessary for the protection of the owner's interest [57] in circumstances where he could not communicate with the owner.[58]

Maritime lien does not attach for repairs executed while a ship is in a home port,[59] nor for services rendered to a ship in a home port,[60] nor for necessaries supplied to a ship in a home port.[61]

49 See *e.g. France, Fenwick & Co.* v. *North of England Association* [1917] 2 K.B. 522; *Becker, Gray & Co.* v. *London Assurance Corpn.* [1918] A.C. 101; *Leyland Shipping Co.* v. *Norwich Union Fire Ins. Co.* [1918] A.C. 350.

50 *Harmer* v. *Bell* (*The Bold Buccleugh*) (1851) 7 Moo.P.C. 267.

51 *e.g. Metal Industries* (*Salvage*) *Ltd.* v. *Owners of Harle*, 1962 S.L.T. 114.

52 Merchant Shipping Act 1894, s. 167.

53 *Ibid.* s. 156. A person who pays seamen's wages is entitled to the preference enjoyed by them by virtue of their maritime lien, without assignation, unless he made payment in reliance on the owner's credit: *Clark* v. *Bowring*, 1908 S.C. 1168, doubted in *Clydesdale Bank* v. *Walker & Bain*, 1926 S.C. 72. But ship's riggers are not seamen: *Inter-Islands Exporters Ltd.* v. *Berna S.S. Co. Ltd.*, 1960 S.L.T. 21.

54 *Harmer*, *supra.*

55 *Currie* v. *McKnight* (1896) 24 R.(H.L.) 1.

56 Merchant Shipping Act 1894, s. 167; *The Ripon City* [1897] P. 226.

57 *The Castlegate* [1893] A.C. 38; *The Orienta* [1895] P. 49.

58 *The Orienta*, *supra.*

59 *Wood* v. *Hamilton* (1788) Mor. 6269; affd. 3 Paton 148, overruling *Watson* v. *Arbuckle* (1711) Mor. 6262.

60 *Northcote* v. *Owners of Henrich Bjorn* (1886) 11 App.Cas. 270.

61 *Clydesdale Bank* v. *Walker & Bain*, 1926 S.C. 72.

Part XI

STATUTORY REMEDIES

CHAPTER 64

STATUTORY REMEDIES

STATUTORY remedies are those remedies the right to obtain which depends solely on some statutory provision and which could not have been demanded by common law. Examples are the right to recover compensation for damage caused by rioting from the inhabitants of the locality, and compensation for land compulsorily purchased. The statute conferring the right to the remedy frequently also prescribes special procedure, or resort to a special tribunal, for the enforcement and determination of the remedy. In some cases it may be a narrow question whether the circumstances justify a claim at common law or a claim to a statutory remedy.

Claims for social security benefits are not within the category of statutory civil remedies because they are claims of right, not for remedies to redress the failure of duty of another person.[1]

Statutory remedies are not the same as remedies for breach of statutory duties. The latter may be redressed in some cases by action of damages at common law, and in some cases give no right of action to an aggrieved individual but are sanctioned only by criminal prosecution.[2]

Where applicable, statutory remedies exclusive

The general rule is that where a special statutory remedy is provided and the circumstances for invoking it apply that remedy alone may be invoked and in such circumstances it is not open to the aggrieved individual to utilise a common law remedy instead.[3]

Reference is frequently made [4] to the statement of Willes J. in *Wolverhampton New Waterworks Co.* v. *Hawkesford* [5]: " There are three classes of cases in which a liability may be established founded upon a statute. One is, where there was a liability existing at common law, and that liability is affirmed by a statute which gives a special and peculiar form of remedy different from the remedy which existed at common law. There unless the statute contains words which, expressly or by necessary implication, exclude the common law remedy, the party suing has his election to

[1] An outline of the claims for social security benefits competent is in Appx. 3.
[2] See Chap. 58, *supra*.
[3] *Doe* v. *Bridges* (1831) 1 B. & A. 847, 859; *Marshall* v. *Nicholls* (1852) 18 Q.B. 882, 888; *L. Blantyre* v. *Clyde Nav. Trs.* (1867) 5 M. 508, 523, 525; *Denny Bros.* v. *Board of Trade* (1880) 7 R. 1019; *Murray* v. *G.S.W. Ry.* (1883) 11 R. 205, approved in *Denaby Main Colliery Co.* v. *M.S. & L. Ry. Co.* (1885) 11 App.Cas. 97 and explained in *B.O.C.* v. *S.W. Scotland Electricity Board*, 1958 S.C. 53, 71; *R.* v. *Essex County Court Judge* (1887) 18 Q.B.D. 704, 707; *Clegg, Parkinson & Co.* v. *Earby Gas Co.* [1896] 1 Q.B. 592, 595; *Dante* v. *Ayr Assessor*, 1922 S.C. 109; *Stornoway Mags.* v. *Macdonald*, 1971 S.L.T. 154.
[4] *e.g. Davie* v. *Edinburgh Mags.*, 1951 S.C. 720, 733, 740; *Secy. of State for Scotland* v. *Fife C.C.*, 1953 S.C. 257.
[5] (1859) 6 C.B.(N.S.) 336, 356.

pursue either that or the statutory remedy.[6] The second class of cases is, where the statute gives the right to sue merely, but provides no particular form of remedy. There the party can only proceed by action at common law.[7] But there is a third class, viz., where a liability not existing at common law is created by a statute, which at the same time gives a special and particular remedy for enforcing it. There the remedy provided by the statute must be followed, and it is not competent to the party to pursue the course applicable to cases of the second class.[8] The form given by the statute must be adopted and adhered to."

As a matter of pleading it is a general rule that a person who invokes a statutory remedy must give his opponent fair notice of the remedy on which he founds, normally by specifying in his pleadings the statute which provides the remedy.[9]

Whether statutory remedy applicable

Whether a statutory remedy is applicable in particular circumstances is a question of the interpretation of the relevant provision in the particular circumstances. Thus a railway company, statutorily bound to compensate the owners of land injuriously affected by the construction of the railway, was held not bound to compensate for damage to lands caused by the construction of sewers which had to be reconstructed in consequence of the construction of the railway. The claim to statutory compensation applied only to harm arising directly from the construction of the railway.[10]

The fact that a statutory remedy is applicable in particular circumstances does not exclude the possibility of invoking ordinary common law remedies to resolve subsequently claims *inter se* by parties who may have been affected by an initial default.[11]

Procedure

If a statute gives a remedy but makes no particular provision as to the mode of enforcing it, enforcement by one of the ordinary forms of process is competent.[12] If, on the other hand, a special procedure or special machinery is prescribed this must, unless it is clearly permissive or optional only, be used, and any other procedure is incompetent.[13] Similarly, the questions of who is entitled to sue,[14] and who is the proper defender,[15]

[6] *e.g. Blackpool Corpn.* v. *Starr* [1922] 1 A.C. 27.

[7] *e.g. Ross* v. *Rugge Price* (1876) 1 Ex.D. 269; *Dormont* v. *Furness Ry.* (1883) 11 Q.B.D. 496; *Denaby Main Colliery Co., supra*; *Davie, supra*. This category covers cases where a breach of statutory duty is held, by implication, to confer a right of action as well.

[8] *e.g. Barraclough* v. *Brown* [1897] A.C. 615; *Pasmore* v. *Oswaldtwistle U.D.C.* [1898] A.C. 387.

[9] *Coia* v. *Robertson*, 1942 S.C. 111, 117, 118.

[10] *Caledonian Ry.* v. *McBride* (1891) 19 R. 255.

[11] *Secretary of State for Scotland* v. *Fife C.C.*, 1953 S.C. 257.

[12] *Davie* v. *Edinburgh Mags.*, 1951 S.C. 720; *Alexander* v. *N. of S. Hydro Electric Board*, 1952 S.C. 367.

[13] *Murray, supra*; *Capaldi* v. *Greenock Mags.*, 1941 S.C. 310; explained in *Coia* v. *Robertson*, 1942 S.C. 111 and *Pompa's Trs.* v. *Edinburgh Mags.*, 1942 S.C. 119.

[14] *Scottish Plate Glass Ins. Co.* v. *Edinburgh Corpn.*, 1941 S.C. 115.

[15] *Capaldi, supra*; *Pompa's Trs.* v. *Edinburgh Mags.*, 1942 S.C. 119.

must be determined by the statute. Thus claims for redundancy payments [16] must be pursued before industrial tribunals and may come before the Court of Session only by appeal on a point of law.[17] But where any statutory remedy is inapplicable to the particular case which has arisen, an appropriate common law process may be adopted.[18]

Particular cases

It is impossible to list all the circumstances in which some statute or other confers a special remedy different from, or wholly unknown to, the categories of remedies recognised at common law. Nor is there a list in the *Index to the Statutes in Force*. The only course is to search that work under the heading of the branch of law in question in a particular case to see if any statute appears to confer a special remedy, and to search the books purporting to state the substantive rights of parties to the kind of relationship in question.

[16] Redundancy Payments Act 1955.
[17] *Carron Co.* v. *Robertson*, 1967 S.C. 273.
[18] *Fraser* v. *McNeill*, 1948 S.C. 517.

Part XII

MISCELLANEOUS REMEDIES

CHAPTER 65

APPLICATIONS TO THE NOBILE OFFICIUM

IN some cases a person unable to invoke any other remedy may obtain a remedy by having the Court of Session exercise its *nobile officium* in his favour.

The *nobile officium* is an extraordinary equitable power vested only in the Court of Session [1] as Supreme Court entitling it to exercise jurisdiction in certain circumstances and to certain effects not warranted save by the necessity of intervening in the interest of justice. Stair [2] derives it from the powers of the praetor in Roman law and, following the terminology appropriate thereto, distinguishes *officium ordinarium*, which all courts have by the rules giving them jurisdiction and powers, and *officium nobile*, which is extraordinary and which only the Court of Session possesses. As examples of the cases in which the Court of Session exercises its *nobile officium* he instances [3] modification of exorbitant penalties in bonds, strict judging of legal execution, attention to material justice in considering reduction of the court's own decrees, granting a remedy to creditors where the apparent heir of the debtor has renounced, supplying defects in conveyances by adjudication in implement, examining witnesses *ad rimandam veritatem*, and allowing of proof before answer as to the relevancy of the case.

> "The Session is a court of equity, as well as of law; and as such may and ought to proceed by the rules of conscience, in abating the rigour of the law, and in giving aid, in the actions brought before them, to those who can have no remedy in a court of law. This power, which is called the *nobile officium* of the judges, is inherent in the supreme judicatory of every state, unless where separate courts are established for law and for equity, as in England. . . ." [4]
>
> "Owing to its peculiar history, the law of Scotland has never known either distinction or conflict between common law and the principles of equity. It is often said, and truly said, that in the law of Scotland law is equity and equity law; and when a Scots lawyer uses the expression common law, he uses it in contradistinction to laws made by Parliament.
>
> "From this it at once appears that considerable reserve must be used in accepting too literally some of the descriptions of the *nobile*

[1] Including the judges of the Court of Session sitting as Teind Court: *Minister of Cumbernauld* v. *Heritors of Dunbartonshire*, 1920 S.C. 625.
[2] IV, 3, 1.
[3] IV, 3, 2.
[4] Ersk. I, 3, 22.

officium in the text-books, which might be read as suggesting that the *nobile officium* is only another name for our general jurisdiction, in as much as our whole jurisdiction is nothing unless equitable. It may not be easy to trace historically the connection between what the commentators called the *nobile officium* of the praetor (Vulteius, *De Judiciis*, II, iv, 31; Bartolus, *Ad Digestum*, II, 1, 12, *De jurisdictione omnium judicium*), and what we know as the *nobile officium* of the Court of Session." [5]

" The limits of the *nobile officium* are hard to define. No judicial definition of these limits has, so far as I know, ever been attempted. I do not essay that task now. But I bear in mind that Stair said long ago, in dealing with the topic, that ' in new cases, there is necessity of new cures, which must be supplied by the Lords, who are authorised for that effect by the Institution of the College of Justice '—IV, iii, 1. Again, More in his Notes on Stair, after quoting the passage to which I have referred, and attributing to Lord Stair the view that ' in many instances the strict rules of law should be relieved by the equitable interpretation of the judge,' adds: ' Amid much that is uncertain as to the exercise of the *nobile officium*, this may be laid down as a fixed principle—that it will never be exercised except in cases of necessity, or very strong expediency, and where the ordinary procedure would provide no remedy ' (Quoted in footnote to Erskine, I, iii, 22). Erskine, in the paragraph which I have cited, states that the Court, as a Court of Equity, ' may and ought to proceed by the rules of conscience in abating the rigour of the law, and in giving aid in the actions brought before them to those who can have no remedy in a court of law.' " [6]

" It is idle to attempt to define precisely all that is included in the term *nobile officium*. Erskine states (I, iii, 22) that it ' is inherent in the supreme judicatory of every state, unless where separate courts are established for law and for equity, as in England '; and again in the same paragraph, that the Session as a Court of equity ' may and ought to proceed by the rules of conscience in abating the rigour of the law, and in giving aid, in the actions brought before them, to those who can have no remedy in a court of law.' There can be little doubt that the *nobile officium* embraces powers of a very wide description although in practice it is only exercised in cases of ' necessity or very strong expediency '; and never where it is possible for the petitioner to obtain by the ordinary procedure of the Court the power which he desires." [7]

" [The *nobile officium*] is an inherent equitable jurisdiction whereby, in exceptional cases, the Court intervenes for the purpose of redressing a wrong or vindicating a right. It is difficult, if not

[5] *Gibson's Trs.*, 1933 S.C. 190, 198–199, *per* L.P. Clyde.
[6] *Gibson's Trs.*, *supra*, 205, *per* L.J.C. Alness.
[7] *Gibson's Trs.*, *supra*, 216, *per* Lord Blackburn.

impossible, to give a positive definition of the ambit of this jurisdiction. It may, however, be stated negatively that the Court will not exercise the jurisdiction where it is against the provisions of a statutory enactment to do so, where a remedy is provided by statute or the common law, or where the circumstances do not make judicial intervention necessary." [8]

Jurisdiction

Exercise of the *nobile officium* is competent only to the Court of Session and is exercised by a division of the Inner House only,[9] save where a power originally and in nature belonging to the *nobile officium* has been conferred on judges of the Outer House. In vacation the Lord Ordinary officiating may in urgent cases exercise the *nobile officium.*[10] When a petition was presented partly under statute and partly to the *nobile officium* it was held that it might competently proceed before the Inner House.[11]

Conflict with ordinary jurisdiction

There is no scope for application to the *nobile officium* where the matter can be dealt with under statutory or common law powers. These must be invoked first and resort made to the *nobile officium* only if there be no statutory or common law power or it be inapplicable or inadequate.[12] Appeal may be made to both statutory or common law jurisdiction and to extraordinary, or *nobile officium*, jurisdiction in one petition.[13]

Furthermore the *nobile officium* cannot be appealed to in order to override the express provisions of a statute,[14] nor to extend the application of a statute to cover a person or class of persons other than those to whom it was made applicable.[15] It cannot be invoked to permit an appeal from an inferior court where appeal is not competent, even though there are allegations of irregularities in procedure.[16]

Limits of nobile officium

"To a certain extent the powers of the Court (if, within the Court, in the exercise of the *nobile officium*, be included the Court of last resort) resemble the powers of Parliament. There is no authority which can declare an Act of Parliament beyond the power of Parlia-

8 *B's Exor.* v. *Keeper of the Registers and Records of Scotland*, 1935 S.C. 745, 752, *per* Lord Anderson.

9 R.C. 190; see also *Brown*, 1936 S.C. 689; *Smith's Trs.*, 1939 S.C. 489. Similarly the *nobile officium* of the High Court of Justiciary may not be exercised by a single Lord Commissioner of Justiciary: *H.M.A.* v. *Lowson* (1909) 6 Adam 118.

10 *Viscountess Hawarden* v. *Dunlop* (1861) 23 D. 923; *Naismith, Petrs.* (1910) 47 S.L.R. 625; *Buchanan, Petrs.*, 1910 S.C. 685. Contrast *Steuart* v. *Chalmers* (1864) 2 M. 1216; *Greigs, Petrs.* (1866) 4 M. 1103; *Aberdeen University Court, Petrs.* (1901) 4 F. 122.

11 *Prime Gilt Box Society*, 1920 S.C. 534; *Anderson's Trs.*, 1921 S.C. 315.

12 *Edinburgh Tailors* v. *Muir's Tr.*, 1912 S.C. 608.

13 *Prime Gilt Box Society*, 1920 S.C. 534.

14 *MacGown* v. *Cramb* (1897) 24 R. 481; *Adair* v. *Colvilles*, 1922 S.C. 672.

15 *Crichton-Stuart's Tutrix*, 1921 S.C. 840.

16 *Adair, supra.*

ment, so there is no constitutional authority that can declare an exercise of the *nobile officium* invalid as beyond the lawful authority of the Court. But this immunity from external control, so far from encouraging laxity, prescribes extreme caution, in the exercise of powers so uncircumscribed. The circumstance that there is no external authority to prevent Parliament, in violation of the Treaty of Union, transferring this Court to London, is suggestive not of licence but of restraint on the part of Parliament in entertaining any such suggestion.

"The *nobile officium* is hedged in its legitimate exercise by the limitation that it shall only be used when it is necessary to do so. But this raises the question—necessary for what purpose?" [17]

"Immense changes, however, have taken place in the last hundred years in countless ways. Is it unreasonable to suggest that this may be allowed to react upon the *nobile officium* and to sanction a somewhat freer exercise of it? Or must we say: 'This is not within the *nobile officium* as contemplated by Kames and Hailes, and by this consideration we are bound.'" [18]

"The jurisdiction associated with the *nobile officium* in this court gives us a right to come to the assistance of petitioners where no other remedy is available." [19]

The *nobile officium* does not allow the court to order or permit anything forbidden by statute or common law, such as to authorise the Keeper of the Registers to exclude passages from a will being registered in the Books of Council and Session.[20] "I never heard of the *nobile officium* being appealed to in order to override the express provisions of a statute, and I think it is quite incompetent for the Court to exercise the *nobile officium* to do so." [21]

Exercise now limited to cases for which precedent exists

The clear modern tendency, however, is to limit the exercise of the *nobile officium* to circumstances for which there is precedent or analogy and there is great judicial hesitation to extend it or apply it to cases for which there is neither precedent nor analogy. "It is an extraordinary equitable jurisdiction, the exercise of which has always been scrupulously guarded and rarely carried beyond precedent. There is but one instance in the books of such a power having been granted. That was done . . . in the case of . . . I . . . have come to the conclusion that it was an exceptional case, which does not make, and was not intended to make a precedent which can be appealed to in any other case not precisely the same in its circumstances." [22]

[17] *Gibson's Trs., supra*, 211, *per* Lord Sands.
[18] *Ibid.* 215, *per* Lord Sands.
[19] *Glasgow Magdalene Institution*, 1964 S.C. 227, 229, *per* L.P. Clyde.
[20] *B's Exor.* v. *Keeper of the Registers and Records*, 1935 S.C. 745.
[21] *Adair* v. *Colville & Sons*, 1922 S.C. 672, 677, *per* L.J.C. Scott Dickson.
[22] *Hall's Trs.* v. *McArthur*, 1918 S.C. 646, 650, *per* Lord Johnston.

" It is an unprecedented application . . . [Counsel] was unable to produce any authority for a petition in the terms we have before us." [23]

" We are not in use to expand the *nobile officium* beyond its accepted limits." [24]

" It may, I think, be said that before we interfere in any case in the exercise of our *nobile officium*, we must be satisfied of two things, *viz.* (1) that there is a necessity which requires the remedy of an evil, and (2) that there is a cure direct and palpable for the evil experienced." [25] " I do not wish to put strict limits on the *nobile officium*, where its exercise would be reasonable and beneficial, but it should only be exercised when the circumstances and the conduct of the parties clearly call for it." [26] Hence where there is not necessity the court will not intervene.[27]

Application to nobile officium appropriate only where no other remedy

" The *nobile officium* can be called into play only if matters are inextricable." [28] Accordingly, a petition to declare a sequestration void *ab initio* for non-compliance with statutory requirements was rejected as incompetent or at least premature since the petitioners had failed to show that they could not obtain their remedy by an action of reduction.[29] It was there observed [30] that " I do not think that it is legitimate to ask the court to exercise its *nobile officium* unless it is made clear that there is no other remedy open to the petitioners. . . . It is the duty of the petitioners to try these remedies before asking an extraordinary remedy from us." " But the ordinary law does provide a remedy to them; and that being so, there is no sufficient ground for invoking the *nobile officium*." [31]

The *nobile officium*, furthermore, cannot be invoked simply to get out of a difficulty,[32] or to correct a blunder,[33] nor to substitute different provisions for those in a statute, nor to dispense with statutory powers.[34]

Nor can it be utilised to extend a statutory right to persons or classes of persons other than those for whom the statutory right exists,[35] nor to alter the provisions of a statute as to allow something to be done which was prohibited or rendered ineffective by the statute,[36] nor to extend the operation of a statute beyond what Parliament intended,[37] nor to permit an appeal in circumstances where it is incompetent.[38]

[23] *Central Motor Engineering Co.* v. *Gibbs*, 1917 S.C. 490, 493, *per* Lord Mackenzie.
[24] *Horne's Trs.*, 1952 S.C. 70, 72, *per* L.P. Cooper.
[25] *Tod* v. *Anderson* (1869) 7 M. 412, 413, *per* L.J.C. Patton.
[26] *Tod, supra*, 415, *per* Lord Neaves.
[27] *Tod, supra.*
[28] *Lord Macdonald's Curator*, 1924 S.C. 163, 166, *per* Lord Sands.
[29] *Central Motor Engineering Co.* v. *Gibbs*, 1917 S.C. 490; *Craig & Co.*, 1946 S.C. 19, 22.
[30] *Central Motor Co., supra*, 493, *per* Lord Skerrington.
[31] *Forth Shipbreaking Co.*, 1924 S.C. 489, 493, *per* L.P. Clyde.
[32] *Cf. Cruickshank* v. *Gowans* (1899) 1 F. 692.
[33] *Tod* v. *Anderson* (1869) 7 M. 412, 415.
[34] *Ibid.* 413.
[35] *Crichton-Stuart's Tutrix*, 1921 S.C. 840.
[36] *McLaughlin*, 1965 S.C. 243, 245; *cf. Robertson* v. *Tough's Tr.*, 1925 S.C. 234.
[37] *Smart* v. *Registrar-General*, 1954 S.C. 81; *West Highland Woodlands Ltd.*, 1963 S.C. 494, 496.
[38] *Adair* v. *Colville & Sons* 1922 S.C. 672.

An application for the exercise of the *nobile officium* is never granted as a matter of course; it is always necessary to show cause.[39]

Applications of Nobile Officium

In relation to private trusts

Trusts are an important field for the exercise of the *nobile officium*, but resort is " practically confined to cases where something administrative or executive is wanting in the constituting document to enable the trust purposes to be effectually carried out, and such cases are now largely met by the provisions of the modern Trusts Acts. But, where no such executive or administrative provisions are wanting in the trust deeds, the court will not interfere, for the court in Scotland does not undertake, as does the Court of Chancery in England, the administration of trusts." [40]

Thus the court, under the *nobile officium*, has appointed an additional trustee where the two trustees could not agree,[41] and authorised trustees to borrow money and purchase heritage to give effect to the main purpose of the trust.[42] Where trustees might be assumed with the consent of spouses and one spouse became insane, the court authorised dispensing with her consent.[43]

In relation to trustees' powers

The need for applications to the *nobile officium* to confer particular powers on trustees has been greatly reduced by the width of the powers conferred by statute on trustees,[44] where such acts are not at variance with the terms or purposes of the trust. Trustees do not need authority to do ordinary acts of trust administration.[45] But in cases not covered by powers contained in the trust deed or conferred by statute, the court may still grant a power requested, if satisfied that its exercise is necessary, or at least highly expedient, for the careful and diligent administration of the trust.[46] Thus powers have been granted to make advances out of trust funds to a beneficiary who had not a vested but only a contingent right; such advances will be authorised only where there has arisen a *casus improvisus*, not in the contemplation of the truster, and where an advance is

[39] *Gibson's Trs.*, 1933 S.C. 190, 210.
[40] *Hall's Trs.* v. *McArthur*, 1918 S.C. 646, 650, *per* Lord Johnston.
[41] *Dick* (1899) 2 F. 316; *Taylor*, 1932 S.C. 1.
[42] *Anderson's Trs.*, 1921 S.C. 315, 321.
[43] *Adamson's Trs.*, 1917 S.C. 440.
[44] Trusts (Sc.) Acts 1921, s. 4, and 1961, s. 4.
[45] *Noble's Trs.*, 1912 S.C. 1230; *Dunbar's Trs.*, 1915 S.C. 860.
[46] *e.g. Colt* v. *Colt* (1801) Mor. Tutor, Appx. 1 (sale); *Vere* v. *Dale* (1804) Mor. 16389; *E. Buchan* (1835) 1 D. 637 (borrowing); *Crawford* (1839) 1 D. 1183 (borrowing); *Mackenzie* (1855) 17 D. 314 (sale); *Kincaid* (1856) 18 D. 1208 (leasing); *Lord Clinton* (1875) 3 R. 62 (feuing); *Campbell* (1880) 7 R. 1032; *Logan* (1898) 25 R. 51 (sale); *Shearer's Tutor*, 1924 S.C. 445 (power to sell heritage); *Ferrier's Tutrix*, 1925 S.C. 571 (power to sell heritage); *Anderson's Trs.*, 1921 S.C. 315 (power to borrow and purchase heritage); *Fletcher's Trs.*, 1949 S.C. 330 (power to purchase heritage).

necessary for the maintenance or education of the beneficiary.[47] But only occasionally has an advance been authorised in favour of a beneficiary who was major [48] or to one outside the family circle.[49] Similarly power has been granted to apply the income of a capital fund to revenue purposes [50]; and to supplement a widow's annuity out of capital.[51]

> " There is no dispute that some considerable power of inroad on the literal meaning of a will delaying enjoyment is now established in this court. That group of cases has cumulated rapidly since the earlier views (*Mundell's Trs.*[52] and *Robertson's Trs.*) [53] leading as these undoubtedly did towards the opinion that such a discretion to overrule the literal words of a testator as to vesting should be negatived or used with great caution. And now *Macfarlane's Trs.*[54] (at p. 100), *Sinclair's Trs.*,[55] *Christie's Trs.*,[56] *Anderson's Trs.*[57] (negative), *Frew's Trs.*,[58] *Gibson's Trs.*,[59] *Craig's Trs.*,[60] *Glasgow Young Men's Christian Association* [61] all illustrate carefully guarded invasions by way of anticipation, where necessitous circumstances and clear intention that benefit shall not be missed go hand in hand. Lord President Clyde took off the severity of his dictum expressed in *Anderson's Trs.*,[57] by his reasoning in *Frew's Trs.*[58]; and a useful passage as to the ' equitable ' principles of relaxation will be discovered in Lord Morison in *Gibson's Trs.*[59] at p. 220. In *Robertson's Trs.*[53] the court refused to authorise an advance in the case of one child and granted an advance in the case of the other." [62] " The power of the court, in the exercise of its *nobile officium*, to authorise advances out of trust funds to a beneficiary whose right has not vested but is merely contingent is one which should be exercised with caution. The result of the cases, I think, is to show that such advances will only be authorised where there has arisen a *casus improvisus*, not in the contemplation of the truster, and where an advance is necessary for the maintenance or education of the beneficiary." [63]

47 *Stewart* v. *Brown's Trs.*, 1941 S.C. 300, 308. For examples see *Mundell's Trs.* (1862) 24 D. 327; *Robertson's Trs.*, 1909 S.C. 236; *Milne's Trs.* (1919) 57 S.L.R. 112; *Sinclair's Trs.*, 1921 S.C. 484; *Macfarlane's Trs.*, 1931 S.C. 95; *Christie's Trs.*, 1932 S.C. 189; *Anderson's Trs.*, 1932 S.C. 226; *Frew's Trs.*, 1932 S.C. 501; *Gibson's Trs.*, 1933 S.C. 190; *Craig's Trs.*, 1934 S.C. 34. On procedure see *Smith's Trs.*, 1939 S.C. 489.

48 *Frew's Trs.*, *supra*; *Stewart* v. *Brown's Trs.*, *supra*.

49 *Stewart*, *supra*.

50 *Glasgow Y.M.C.A.*, 1934 S.C. 452.

51 *Bett's Trs.*, 1922 S.C. 21.

52 (1862) 24 D. 327.

53 1909 S.C. 236.

54 1931 S.C. 95.

55 1921 S.C. 484.

56 1932 S.C. 189.

57 1932 S.C. 226.

58 1932 S.C. 501.

59 1933 S.C. 190.

60 1934 S.C. 34.

61 1934 S.C. 452.

62 *Stewart* v. *Brown's Trs.*, 1941 S.C. 300, 307, *per* Lord Mackay.

63 *Ibid.* 308, *per* Lord Jamieson.

The court has authorised trustees to sell part of the trust estate, expressly with the condition that one trustee might purchase some of the items.[64]

But the court has declined to authorise trustees to expend the capital of a bequest in purchasing an annuity for the beneficiary entitled thereto, as this would be altering the bequest merely to ensure a larger income to the beneficiary [65]; and refused to allow a liferentrix to appoint the fee to herself even though the liferentrix averred that she was beyond child-bearing age and that accordingly there could be no fiar [66]; and refused to authorise trustees to sell property with permission to some trustees to bid therefor.[67]

In a case where it was doubtful whether a mother, as tutrix, had power to sell heritage, the court granted power to sell.[68]

The court has refused to sanction a proposed assignation by a married woman of a proportion of her alimentary income under a marriage-contract in return for an immediate capital payment, on the grounds that it could not be affirmed that the sum proposed to be assigned would never be required for alimentary purposes, and that the assignees could not be given an absolute right to the sum assigned in preference to any future creditors of the lady.[69]

Auxiliary jurisdiction

Where a trust was a non-Scottish one but owned Scottish heritage, the court may grant power of sale, as an auxiliary jurisdiction to facilitate the carrying out of the order of the foreign court.[70] Similarly, it may authorise new trustees appointed by a foreign court to have Scottish investments transferred into their names from that of the trustee removed.[71] It has authorised a non-Scottish administrator of the affairs of a pupil child to sell heritage in Scotland.[72]

On the other hand, though the court has power to give retrospective sanction to *ultra vires* acts of administration by trustees,[73] this will be done only exceptionally and for compelling reasons and it has repeatedly refused to ratify *ex post facto* an unauthorised or *ultra vires* sale or purchase of land by trustees,[74] both Scottish and foreign.[75]

64 *Coats's Trs.*, 1914 S.C. 723.
65 *Anderson's Trs.*, 1932 S.C. 226.
66 *Snodgrass*, 1922 S.C. 491.
67 *Hall's Trs.* v. *McArthur*, 1918 S.C. 646.
68 *Ferrier's Tutrix*, 1925 S.C. 571.
69 *Coles*, 1951 S.C. 608.
70 *Allan's Trs.* (1897) 24 R. 718; *Pender's Trs.* (1903) 5 F. 504; *Harris's Trs.*, 1919 S.C. 432; *Campbell, Petr.*, 1958 S.C. 275; *Campbell-Wyndham-Long's Trs.*, 1951 S.C. 685; 1962 S.C. 132.
71 *Evans-Freke's Trs.*, 1945 S.C. 382.
72 *McFadzean*, 1917 S.C. 142.
73 *Christie's Trs.*, 1932 S.C. 189; *Dow's Trs.*, *infra*.
74 *Clyne* (1894) 21 R. 849; *Drummond's J.F.* (1894) 21 R. 932; *Dow's Trs.*, 1947 S.C. 524; *Prudential Assurance Co. Ltd.*, 1951 S.C. 70.
75 *Horne's Trs.*, 1951 S.C. 70.

In relation to public trusts

The court has wide powers under the *nobile officium* in relation to public trusts, provided the intervention sought can be shown to be necessary, or at least strongly expedient.[76] " If the trustees of a charitable trust can satisfy the court that the circumstances of the trust are such that the carrying out of the trust will be seriously hampered unless the powers craved are granted, then it is within the power of the court to intervene. In other words, to save a charitable trust from wreckage it is not necessary for the court to hesitate until the trust is actually upon the rocks." [77]

Thus if a truster has clearly manifested an intention to establish some specific kind of charitable institution, but has failed to provide his trustees with the powers and machinery to establish and work it, the endowment will not only not be allowed to fail, but the court will take it upon itself to carry out the establishment of the specific institution by creating the powers and machinery, and placing them in the hands of the trustees.[78]

But the equitable powers of the court over charitable trusts have never been held to extend beyond what may be necessary (a) to put the testator's general charitable intention in a practicable shape at the beginning (including in that case the setting up of a body of managers or trustees), or (b) to adapt the testator's trust directions with regard to the particular mode of administering his bequest to circumstances which have altered in course of time; and does not include jurisdiction to vary the ordinary trust clauses (such as those regarding investments) as these have been framed by the testator himself.[79] " Broadly speaking, this court will not, in the exercise of the *nobile officium* (1) set up a new body to administer a charitable trust unless the trustees appointed by the testator are unable, or are not a suitable body, to do so; nor (2) approve changes in the methods of executing such a trust unless the methods prescribed by the testator cannot reasonably be carried out, and unless the new proposals sufficiently approximate to the original charitable purpose." [80]

Thus the court has, in the exercise of its equitable jurisdiction, appointed new trustees where the *ex officio* trustees' posts had been abolished by statute,[81] reduced the number of *ex officio* trustees,[82] authorised trustees to transfer trust property to the local authority,[83] authorised trustees to use the income of a capital fund in their hands to meet current expenditure,[84] authorised them to sell heritage as an essential part of a *cy près* scheme,[85] authorised them to sell heritage and to apply to general purposes

[76] *Scott's Hospital Trs.*, 1913 S.C. 289.
[77] *Glasgow Y.M.C.A.*, 1934 S.C. 452, 458, *per* Lord Blackburn.
[78] *Dundee Mags.* v. *Morris* (1858) 3 Macq. 134; *Gibson's Trs.*, 1933 S.C. 190, 199.
[79] *Thomson's Trs.*, 1930 S.C. 767, 769–770.
[80] *Lipton's Trs.*, 1943 S.C. 521, 525, *per* L.J.C. Cooper.
[81] *Thomson's Trs.*, 1930 S.C. 767; *Mackay*, 1955 S.C. 361. In a proper public trust the sole right to appoint new trustees is in the court, by way of exercise of the *nobile officium*: *Glentanar* v. *Scottish Industrial Musical Assocn.*, 1925 S.C. 226.
[82] *Gibson's Trs.*, 1933 S.C. 190, 196.
[83] *Earl of Rosebery* (1892) 29 S.L.R. 865.
[84] *Glasgow Y.M.C.A.*, 1934 S.C. 452.
[85] *Chalmers Hospital (Banff) Trs.*, 1923 S.C. 220; *Stranraer Original Secession Congregation*, 1923 S.C. 722.

a fund bequeathed for a special purpose, no longer required if the sale were carried through,[86] authorised the disposal of surplus funds,[87] given trustees power to borrow,[88] extended a bursary fund to benefit female students,[89] enlarged trustees' powers of investment.[90]

In relation to cy près applications

Where property is held by trustees for public purposes, whether eleemosynary, educational or religious, and these purposes have failed completely, or the trust requires to be reconstituted owing to a change of circumstances, the Court of Session has frequently sanctioned a scheme for the application of its property to a purpose different from but *ejusdem generis* with, the purpose for which the property was previously held.[91] " It is a general principle of charity law and administration that where it is not possible to carry out the intention of a testator in the precise manner directed by him, either from a failure in the objects of a charity, or from an increase in the trust funds beyond the sum required for the prescribed purpose, it is within the power of the court to direct that the funds shall be applied to other purposes as near as possible to those prescribed by the testator. There are traces of the application of this principle in some of the older cases, but in recent times it has been applied unequivocally in more than one important case . . . [The Trinity Hospital case [92]] . . . was a strong assertion of the principle of *cy près* administration, and as we may term it, the principle of approximation." [93] The principle is not confined to trusts which are charitable in the narrow sense of relieving poverty, but extends to trusts for purposes beneficial to the community or large sections of the public, though the court might not extend the concept of " public " to everything deemed " charitable " by the Chancery Division in England.

The principle of *cy près* or approximation " properly applies only to cases in which the object of a charitable foundation can—owing to changed circumstances—no longer be carried into practical effect in the particular form or by the particular means prescribed by the founder. In such cases the court has power to vary the means and to substitute for a particular form of charity another form approximating as closely as may be to the old one." [94] " In a case of this class it is a prerequisite of the exercise of

86 *Prime Gilt Box Society*, 1920 S.C. 534.
87 *Gibson* (1900) 2 F. 1195.
88 *Glasgow and West of Scotland Technical College* (1902) 4 F. 982.
89 *Clark Bursary Fund (Mile-end) Trs.* (1903) 5 F. 433; contrast *Grigor Medical Bursary Fund Trs.* (1903) 5 F. 1143.
90 *McCrie's Trs.*, 1927 S.C. 556.
91 *Anderson's Trs.* v. *Scott*, 1914 S.C. 942; *Gibson's Trs.*, 1933 S.C. 190, 199; *Clephane* v. *Edinburgh Mags.* (1868) 7 M.(H.L.) 7 (eleemosynary); *University of Aberdeen* v. *Irvine* (1869) 7 M. 1089 (educational); *Grant* v. *McQueen* (1877) 4 R. 734; *Glasgow Royal Infirmary* (1888) 15 R. 264; *Prestonpans Kirk Session* v. *Prestonpans School Board* (1891) 19 R. 193; *Old Monkland School Board* v. *Bargeddie Kirk Session* (1893) 21 R. 122 (educational and religious); *Gibson* (1900) 2 F. 1195; *Clutterbuck*, 1961 S.L.T. 427.
92 *Clephane* v. *Edinburgh Mags.* (1860) 22 D. 1222; (1863) 2 M.(H.L.) 7; (1866) 5 M. 115; (1868) 7 M.(H.L.) 7; *Edinburgh Mags.* v. *McLaren* (1881) 8 R.(H.L.) 140.
93 *Carnegie Park Orphanage Trs.* (1892) 19 R. 605.
94 *Glasgow Domestic Training School*, 1923 S.C. 892, 895, *per* L.P. Clyde.

the *nobile officium* that it should be shown (i) that the intentions of the truster cannot be carried into effect by obedience to his explicit instructions, and (ii) that it is possible to find in the settlement an overriding charitable purpose of which the truster's explicit instructions are only the machinery." [95]

It is not a legitimate ground for the application of the *cy près* principle that the administration of a charity has become increasingly arduous and discouraging in its results.[96] Nor is it necessary for trustees to come to the court where the truster's directions are adequate and sufficient and there is no lack of machinery prescribed by him.[97]

Need for general charitable intention

It is a prerequisite of the exercise of the *nobile officium* in cases of this kind that it be shown that the truster's intentions cannot be carried into effect by obedience to his explicit instructions, and also that it is possible to find in the trust settlement an overriding charitable purpose of which the truster's explicit instructions are only the machinery.[98] If the petitioners cannot satisfy the court on both points the court will not exercise its power to settle a scheme.

No overriding charitable intent

On the second point, if the charitable intent is intended to benefit specific and particular objects only the settlement of a scheme to benefit other objects, albeit *ejusdem generis*, is clearly inconsistent with the truster's intention, and cannot be done, even though the result may be a total failure of the intended benevolence.

Exceptionally, the court has held that, where the machinery provided for a charitable bequest was substantially unworkable, it was not necessary to try to make it work and fail, but that an application might be made at once for settlement of a scheme of administration on modified lines.[1]

Once a *cy près* scheme has been approved the court may entertain applications to vary or extend the powers under an existing scheme, including authorising an extended power of investment,[2] but not extending to authorising investment in ways not authorised by the Trusts Acts and the Trustee Investments Act 1961.[3]

It is not usual for the court to exercise its *cy près* jurisdiction in the case of a body incorporated by royal charter, particularly where the Crown itself has reserved right to vary or modify the terms of the charter, but if the Crown does not propose to do so, and the necessity of some such

95 *The Pringle Trust*, 1946 S.C. 353, 364, *per* L.J.C. Cooper.
96 *Glasgow Domestic Training School*, 1923 S.C. 892, 895.
97 *Robertson's Trs.*, 1948 S.C. 1.
98 *The Pringle Trust*, 1946 S.C. 353, 364.
1 *Robertson's Trs.*, 1948 S.C. 1.
2 *McCrie's Trs.*, 1927 S.C. 556, 560; *Gibson's Trs.*, 1933 S.C. 190, 204, 213.
3 *Mitchell Bequest Trs.*, 1959 S.C. 395.

change as is proposed is established, the court may exercise its *nobile officium*.[4]

The court will not normally approve retrospectively action taken before application is made for a scheme.[5]

Auxiliary jurisdiction

Where a charitable public trust has been set up in another jurisdiction and subject to its courts, the Court of Session may be approached to assist in making effective the order of the foreign court. The proper course is to have a scheme settled and approved by the court having primary jurisdiction over the trust, and then submitted to the Court of Session for final approval.[6]

The jurisdiction of the court is invoked by petition setting out the terms of the trust, the state of the trust funds and other assets, the reason for the failure of the trust and the alteration of the trust purposes proposed.

In relation to judicial factors

The court has several times granted additional or exceptional powers to judicial factors, such as to exhume the truster's body, re-inter it, and erect a mausoleum,[7] to make charitable donations,[8] and to have his ward retire from a firm.[8] In some cases the court has ratified *ultra vires* actings by a factor,[9] but in other cases has refused.[10]

In relation to incorporations

The court has refused to sanction a scheme of payment to members of an incorporation and their widows when the effect would have been to encroach on the incorporation's capital funds.[11]

In relation to casus improvisi vel omissi in statutes

> " The *nobile officium* of this court involves a power in the Supreme Court in Scotland to enable justice to be done where, *per incuriam*, some formal step has been omitted and quite unnecessary delay and expense would be involved if the procedure had to be gone through all over again. It is often invoked in connection with the omission of some procedural, technical step in bankruptcy or in the liquidation of companies. But it would, in my view, be invoked in vain if it were to be used as a mere cloak for incompetence on the part of the applicant's

4 *Glasgow Magdalene Institution*, 1964 S.C. 227.
5 *East Kilbride District Nursing Assocn.*, 1951 S.C. 64.
6 *Marr Trust* [1936] 1 Ch. 671, further explained in *Lipton's Trs.*, 1943 S.C. 521, 527.
7 *Kilpatrick* (1881) 8 R. 592.
8 *M's C.B.* (1904) 12 S.L.T. 30. *Cf. Laidlaw* (1882) 10 R. 130.
9 *e.g. Robertson's Curator* (1876) 3 R. 619; *Blair's C.B.*, 1921, 1 S.L.T. 248.
10 *Campbell* v. *Grant* (1869) 8 M. 227; *Semple* v. *Tennent* (1888) 15 R. 810; *Drummond's J.F.* (1894) 21 R. 932; *Clyne* (1894) 21 R. 849.
11 *Muir* v. *Rodger* (1881) 9 R. 149. See also *Tailors of Edinburgh* v. *Muir's Tr.*, 1912 S.C. 603.

representatives, and it cannot be invoked to extend the application of an Act of Parliament so as, for instance, to give a remedy to someone other than the parties to whom Parliament has chosen to give a remedy, still less can it be invoked, even by agreement of all parties interested, to enable the court to supplement the statutory procedure by what would, in effect, be an amendment of a statute."[12] "The *nobile officium* of the court can be invoked to meet a *casus improvisus* in the statutory code or to cure some procedural technicality where *per incuriam* some formal step in procedure has been omitted."[13]

If there is no *casus improvisus*, there is no warrant for invoking the *nobile officium*.[14]

It is incompetent under the *nobile officium* to alter the provisions of a statute or to enable anything to be done which has been expressly rendered ineffective by statute,[15] or to extend the operation of a statute beyond what Parliament has enacted,[16] or to supply a gap in a statute on a matter on which there was no common law.[17]

In relation to procedural slips in bankruptcy

> "It is necessary when we are asked to interpone in the exercise of our *nobile officium* to set right proceedings in a sequestration which have been misconducted or by accident have got out of shape to be satisfied, in the first place, that a *dignus nodus* has been made out—a sufficient reason for interfering in the exercise of our *nobile officium*; and, in the second place, that we have parties before us who are justified in presenting the application."[18]

The court has frequently intervened where procedure in bankruptcy has not been correctly followed, there being no other means of having the proper procedure readopted. Examples include: granting warrant to insert a fresh *Gazette* notice,[19] holding an incorrect notice sufficient,[20] allowing notices to be reinserted in statutory form,[21] ordering fresh intimation where the *Gazette* notice was erroneous,[22] allowing an abbreviate to be recorded late,[23] fixing a fresh meeting when that fixed had been too early,[24] appointing a meeting when there was doubt whether the first one

12 *Maitland*, 1961 S.C. 291, 293, *per* L.P. Clyde.
13 *McLaughlan*, 1965 S.C. 243, 245, *per* L.P. Clyde.
14 *Smart* v. *Registrar General*, 1954 S.C. 81.
15 *McLaughlin*, 1965 S.C. 243, 245. *Cf. Robertson* v. *Tough's Tr.*, 1925 S.C. 234.
16 *Smart* v. *Registrar-General*, 1954 S.C. 81; *West Highland Woodlands Ltd.*, 1963 S.C. 494, 496.
17 *Borthwick Parochial Board* v. *Temple Parochial Board* (1891) 18 R. 1190; *West Highland Ry.* v. *Inverness C.C.* (1904) 6 F. 1052.
18 *Steuart* v. *Chalmers* (1864) 2 M. 1216, 1218, *per* L.J.C. Inglis, quoted in *Aitken* v. *Robson*, 1914 S.C. 224, 226, *per* Lord Dundas.
19 *Morrison* (1874) 1 R. 392; *Von Rotberg* (1876) 4 R. 263; *Somerville & Co.* (1905) 7 F. 651; *Murray* (1906) 8 F. 957; *Robertson*, 1909 S.C. 444; *Car Mart Ltd.*, 1924 S.C. 269. *Cf. Robertson* v. *Wilson* (1885) 12 R. 1361.
20 *Taylor* (1900) 2 F. 1139; *Naismith* (1910) 47 S.L.R. 625.
21 *Morgan*, 1922 S.C. 589.
22 *Foubister* (1869) 8 M. 31; *McCosh* (1898) 25 R. 1019.
23 *Stark & Hogg* (1886) 23 S.L.R. 507; *Kippen's Tr.*, 1966 S.L.T.(Notes) 2.
24 *Watt, Philp & Co.* (1877) 4 R. 641.

had been properly intimated,[25] authorising a fresh notice as to a dividend,[26] where there was a clerical error in the copy of the petition for sequestration,[27] where an abbreviate of sequestration had not been recorded timeously.[28]

Similarly resort has been had to the *nobile officium* where no other machinery existed for resolving a deadlock. Instances include: where creditors met, but elected no trustee, and resolved not to proceed further with sequestration [29]; where sequestration was awarded but the debtor discharged by agreement, and the sequestration not recalled [30]; where the bankrupt was unable to obtain a report from the trustee as a prerequisite to discharge [31]; where the process had been lost [32]; where no creditors attended a meeting [33]; where there had been no proceedings in the sequestration for over seventy years [34]; where the trustee was found to be disqualified and a new one had to be elected [35]; where a new trustee had been appointed but the papers had been lost [36]; where three trustees had acted over 40 years and most of the documents had been lost [37]; where trustee and bankrupt had been discharged but fresh assets had emerged [38]; where recall of sequestration was desired but was out of time [39]; where a trustee had been elected but not confirmed and no further procedure had followed and discharge could not be obtained [40]; where no trustee had been appointed so that the bankrupt could not obtain his discharge.[41]

The court has refused to allow a creditor relief where she had known for two years that the ground of her claim was missing.[42]

In relation to companies

The court has in some cases exercised the *nobile officium*, as by granting warrant to officers of court to search for and seize books and papers of the company [43]; appointing a committee of inspection where a creditor had failed timeously to do so [44]; authorising belated insertion of notices

25 *Union Bank of Scotland* (1891) 29 S.L.R. 102.
26 *Lipman & Co.'s Tr.* (1893) 20 R. 818.
27 *Lochrie* v. *McGregor*, 1911 S.C. 21.
28 *Munro* v. *Fraser's Tr.* (1851) 13 D. 1209; *A.B.* (1858) 21 D. 24; *Allan* (1861) 23 D. 972; *Stark and Hogg* (1886) 23 S.L.R. 507; *Train & McIntyre*, 1923 S.C. 291; *White Cross Insurance Assocn. Ltd.*, 1924 S.C. 372; *Kippen*, 1966 S.C. 3.
29 *Steuart* v. *Chalmers* (1864) 2 M. 1216.
30 *Anderson* (1866) 4 M. 577.
31 *White* (1893) 20 R. 600.
32 *Foulds* (1872) 9 S.L.R. 631; *Wilson* (1883) 20 S.L.R. 777; *Wilson's Tr.* v. *Wilson* (1899) 1 F. 694. See also *Anderson* (1884) 11 R. 405.
33 *Robb & Co.*, 1925 S.N. 31; *Sinclair*, 1932 S.N. 53.
34 *Cheyne's Trs.*, 1933 S.L.T. 184.
35 *Philip Woolfson Ltd.*, 1962 S.L.T. 252.
36 *Skirving's Tr.* (1883) 11 R. 17.
37 *Coull's Tr.*, 1934 S.C. 415.
38 *Cockburn's Trs.*, 1941 S.C. 187.
39 *Craig & Co.*, 1946 S.C. 19.
40 *Aitken* v. *Robson*, 1914 S.C. 224; *Laings*, 1962 S.C. 168.
41 *Black*, 1964 S.C. 276; *Fraser* v. *Glasgow Corpn.*, 1967 S.C. 120.
42 *Robertson* v. *Tough's Tr.*, 1925 S.C. 234.
43 *Ker* v. *Hughes*, 1907 S.C. 380. *Cf. Glasgow Investments Co. Liqdr.* (1885) 22 S.L.R. 739.
44 *Robertson*, 1909 S.C. 444; *Marlow*, 1912 S.C. 625; *Clyde Marine Ins. Co. Liqdr.*, 1921 S.C. 472.

in the *Gazette* [45]; authorising a director to inspect the minutes of directors' meetings [46] and books of account.

But the court has refused to declare the dissolution of a company void after more than two years,[47] and refused to ratify a repayment of preference shares made before a reduction of capital had been confirmed by the court.[48]

Casus improvisi: in relation to municipal elections

The court has several times, there being *casus improvisus* in the statutory provisions, made provision for a returning officer in municipal elections [49]; and in other cases remedied difficulties in local government.[50]

In relation to public records

The Court of Session has a general supervisory function over the public registers and records and has sometimes authorised steps for the maintenance and correction of such registers. Accordingly, the court has several times granted authority to a new holder of office to complete the registration of deeds in the burgh register of sasines, left incomplete by his predecessor,[51] and authorised the completion of parish registers destroyed by fire.[52]

But it has declined to authorise the Registrar-General to rectify the Register of Marriages by noting the fact that the petitioner had been divorced by decree of a foreign court.[53]

The court has allowed access to deeds for correction of clerical errors in the testing clause [54] or to have the witnesses' signatures added.[55]

The court will not, however, necessarily ordain the Keeper of the General Register of Sasines to record a deed. The Keeper has a discretion to reject deeds, particularly those inappropriate for the Register, or those defective in description, and in case of controversy the matter should be referred to the Deputy Clerk Register and further, if need be, to the Court of Session for direction and guidance.[56]

The court has also, where a deed recorded in the Books of Council and Session was sought to be reduced as being forged, allowed chemical

[45] *Nairn Public Hall Co. Liqdr.*, 1946 S.C. 395.
[46] *McCusker* v. *McRae*, 1966 S.C. 253.
[47] *Lord Macdonald's Curator*, 1924 S.C. 163; *Forth Shipbreaking Co.*, 1924 S.C. 489. Contrast *Collins Bros. & Co.*, 1916 S.C. 620; *McCall & Stephens' Liqdr.*, 1920, 2 S.L.T. 26.
[48] *Alex. Henderson Ltd.*, 1967 S.L.T.(Notes) 17.
[49] *Dunfermline Mags.* (1877) 5 R. 47; *Herron* (1880) 7 R. 497; *Musselburgh Mags.* (1881) 9 R. 78; *Peebles Mags.* (1881) 9 R. 80; *Pollokshaws Mags.* (1882) 20 S.L.R. 19; *Kirriemuir Police Commrs.* (1884) 12 R. 103; *Muirhead* (1886) 14 R. 18; *Stromness Mags.* (1891) 19 R. 207; *Renfrew Mags.* (1897) 25 R. 18.
[50] *Brander* (1890) 17 R. 1254; *McCallum* v. *Lochhead* (1896) 24 R. 26. Contrast *Tod* v. *Anderson* (1869) 7 M. 412.
[51] *Cowper* (1885) 12 R. 415; *Elgin Mags.* (1885) 12 R. 1136; *Hepburn* (1905) 7 F. 484.
[52] *Dundas* (1875) 3 R. 273; *Stair Agnew* (1890) 28 S.L.R. 164; *Registrar-General for Scotland*, 1949 S.L.T. 385.
[53] *Smart* v. *Registrar-General*, 1954 S.C. 81; contrast *Arnott* v. *L.A.*, 1932 S.L.T. 46.
[54] *Caldwell* (1871) 10 M. 99; contrast *Thoms* (1870) 8 M. 857.
[55] *Murray* (1904) 6 F. 840; *sed quaere*; see *Walker's Trs.* v. *Whitwell*, 1916 S.C.(H.L.) 20.
[56] *Macdonald* v. *Keeper of the General Register of Sasines*, 1914 S.C. 854.

examination of the recorded deed,[57] but has declined to allow a deed to be recorded in those Books otherwise than in full, even when containing defamatory matter.[58]

It has similarly authorised the transmission of deeds within Scotland for exhibition in judicial proceedings.[59]

It has sometimes authorised the Keeper of the Registers to take a recorded deed furth of Scotland when it has been needed for legal proceedings elsewhere, subject to his not surrendering custody thereof,[60] and has sometimes declined, when not satisfied that production of the original was indispensable,[61] or authorised exhibition on caution for return of the deed.[62]

It has similarly allowed documents and models lodged in process to be borrowed for use in an action in England,[63] and authorised a certified copy of the proceedings in the Court of Session to be made for production in the Irish courts.[64]

In relation to notaries public

The Court of Session has statutory power to admit solicitors to the roll of notaries public,[65] and power *ex nobili officio* to strike notaries off such roll.[66]

Lapsed boards and bodies

The court has sometimes authorised the reconstitution of a board which has lapsed.[67]

Interim appointments

The court has frequently, in the exercise of the *nobile officium*, made interim appointments to public offices, such as of a person to be Interim Keeper of the Great Seal,[68] or of the Privy Seal,[69] or Lyon King-at-Arms,[70] or Interim Keeper of the Signet,[71] or Keeper of the Register of Sasines,[72]

57 *Irvine* v. *Powrie's Trs.*, 1915 S.C. 1006.
58 *B.'s Exor.* v. *Keeper of the Registers and Records of Scotland*, 1935 S.C. 745.
59 *Jamieson's Trs.* v. *Jamieson* (1899) 2 F. 96; *Chevenix-Trench*, 1917 S.C. 168. *Cf. Gordon* (1871) 8 S.L.R. 445. See also *Chalmers* v. *Thomson*, 1922 S.L.T. 364.
60 *Leigh-Bennett* (1893) 20 R. 787; *Campbell's Trs.*, 1934 S.C. 8. See also *Macdonald* (1877) 5 R. 44; *Inglis* (1882) 9 R. 761; *King's Remembrancer* (1902) 4 F. 559; *Pheysey* (1906) 8 F. 801.
61 *Western Bank Liqdrs.* (1868) 6 M. 656. *Cf. Kennedy* (1880) 7 R. 1129.
62 *Garrett* (1883) 20 S.L.R. 756.
63 *United Telephone Co.* v. *Maclean* (1882) 9 R. 710.
64 *Walker* (1889) 16 R. 926.
65 Solicitors (Sc.) Act 1933, s. 17.
66 *Incorporated Society of Law Agents in Scotland* v. *Laing* (1893) 21 R. 267. On the consequences, see Solicitors (Sc.) Act 1933, s. 30 (2).
67 *Campbells, Petrs.* (1883) 10 R. 819; *Brodie, Petrs.* (1884) 21 S.L.R. 309; *Sandeman's Trs.*, 1947 S.C. 304; *West Highland Woodlands Ltd.*, 1963 S.C. 494. See also *Duke of Argyll* (1896) 23 R. 991.
68 *Lord Advocate* (1885) 12 R. 925.
69 *Dundas* (1874) 1 R. 1198.
70 *Lord Advocate* (1866) Mackay's *Practice*, I, 210.
71 *Hope* (1878) 5 R. 762; *Logan* (1890) 17 R. 757.
72 *Lord Advocate* (1860) 22 D. 555.

or Director of Chancery,[73] or Auditor of the Court of Session,[74] or Sheriff-clerk,[75] or town-clerk,[76] or clerk of the peace.[77] It has appointed a retiring magistrate to act as returning officer at a municipal election.[78]

In relation to change of name

A change of name may be made without the authority of the court,[79] but in special circumstances, where it is necessary, as where evidence of change was necessary for ordination in the Church of England,[80] or in the case of notaries public,[81] the court may grant authority and order the petition and its deliverance thereon to be recorded in the Books of Sederunt.

Execution of deeds

The court has several times authorised and ordained the Clerk of Court to execute a disposition of heritage where a defender has sold heritage but refused to grant the necessary disposition,[82] or has gone abroad and cannot be reached.[83]

In relation to process and diligence

The court has allowed the Keeper of the Signet to signet printed copies of a summons, but not a summons signed by the pursuer alone,[84] granted warrant to arrest a ship *ad interim*,[85] allowed correction of a clerical error in a note to the court and on the extract decree thereon,[86] dealt with the loss of a complete process,[87] allowed evidence to be retaken where the shorthand writer's notes were lost,[88] dispensed with induciae,[89] allowed evidence to be taken on commission and to be held *in retentis*, where an important witness was about to go abroad.[90]

It has refused *in hoc statu* a motion to take the evidence on commission of a witness to be held *in retentis* pending the hearing of an appeal.[91]

[73] *Dundas* (1837) 15 S. 398.
[74] *Baxter* (1894) 2 S.L.T. 133.
[75] *Lord Advocate* (1880) 8 R. 13; *Lord Advocate* (1882) 10 R. 53.
[76] *Rothesay Mags.* v. *Carse* (1902) 4 F. 641.
[77] *Lord Advocate* (1890) 17 R. 293.
[78] *Pollokshaws Mags.* (1882) 20 S.L.R. 19.
[79] *Forlong* (1880) 7 R. 910; *Robertson* (1899) 2 F. 127; *Silverstone*, 1935 S.C. 223.
[80] *Johnston* (1899) 2 F. 75.
[81] *Johnston, supra*, 76; *cf. Silverstone, supra.*
[82] *Whyte* v. *Whyte*, 1913, 2 S.L.T. 85; *Pennell's Trs.*, 1928 S.C. 605; *Wallace's C.B.* v. *Wallace*, 1924 S.C. 212; *Lennox*, 1950 S.C. 546; *Mackay* v. *Campbell*, 1966 S.C. 237.
[83] *Boag*, 1967 S.C. 322.
[84] *Hoey* (1885) 13 R. 207.
[85] *Lucovich* (1885) 12 R. 1090.
[86] *Benhar Coal Co. Liqdrs.* (1891) 19 R. 108; *cf.* also *Clark & Macdonald* v. *Bain* (1895) 23 R. 102.
[87] *Scottish Heritable Security Co. Liqdr.* (1894) 21 R. 1082.
[88] *Yates* v. *Robertson* (1891) 18 R. 1206.
[89] *McKidd* (1890) 17 R. 547.
[90] *Galloway Water Power Co.* v. *Carmichael*, 1937 S.C. 135.
[91] *McLachlan* v. *Lewis*, 1925 S.C. 597.

In relation to execution of process and diligence

The court has several times authorised sheriff-officers to execute Court of Session process,[92] and authorised the Extractor to extract a decree of a statutory tribunal as if it were a decree of court.[93]

Grants of exceptional powers

In circumstances where there is clear necessity the court may grant exceptional powers, such as to search for and seize books and papers,[94] to sell burgh lands,[95] to make advances from trust funds to a beneficiary not having a vested interest,[96] to sell trust assets by public roup on the terms that one trustee might as an individual bid for them.[97]

Miscellaneous cases

In addition to all the foregoing cases there are other examples of the use of the *nobile officium* which cannot conveniently be classified.

In one case [98] the court declined to order one of two arbiters to proceed, holding that an order under a summary petition was inappropriate in the circumstances though not incompetent. It also declined to order a department of a local authority to divulge information for use in a pending action.[99]

The court has granted warrant to search for and seize books and papers of a company in liquidation,[1] has authorised road trustees to make a list of bridges which, *per incuriam*, they had failed to do,[2] authorised a change of *ex officio* trustees holding property of a dissenting church,[3] and, where fiars prices had not been struck for the county, allowed them to be done by reference to the adjoining county.[4] It has authorised petitioners to do acts perpetually interdicted many years earlier,[5] ordered an electoral registration officer to restore a name to the register,[6] appointed a special meeting of a licensing court to finalise a grant,[7] and allowed church trustees to remove and re-erect gravestones.[8]

In *B.'s Exor.* v. *Keeper of the Registers and Records* [9] it was observed that there might be an exceptional case where the court might declare that certain passages in a deed were extraneous thereto so that the deed might be recorded omitting such passages.

92 *Muir* (1868) 5 S.L.R. 154; *Schweitzer* (1868) 7 M. 24; *North of Scotland Bank* (1891) 18 R. 460; *Robertson* (1893) 20 R. 712; *Whyte, Ridsdale & Co.*, 1912 S.C. 1095; see also *Buchanan* v. *British Natural Premium Provident Assocn.* (1903) 11 S.L.T. 465; *Riach* v. *Smith*, 1923 S.L.T. 314.

93 *L.M.S. Ry.*, 1937 S.C. 643.

94 *Ker* v. *Hughes*, 1907 S.C. 380.

95 *Linlithgow Police Commrs.* (1887) 14 R. 444.

96 *Stewart* v. *Brown's Trs.*, 1941 S.C. 300.

97 *Coats's Trs.*, 1914 S.C. 723.

98 *Watson* v. *Robertson* (1895) 22 R. 362.

99 *Jennings* v. *Glasgow Corpn.*, 1937 S.C. 180.

1 *Ker* v. *Hughes*, 1907 S.C. 380.

2 *Banffshire Road Trustees* (1881) 9 R. 20.

3 *Harrison* (1893) 20 R. 827.

4 *Minister of Cumbernauld* v. *Dunbartonshire Heritors*, 1920 S.C. 625.

5 *Bowie*, 1967 S.C. 36.

6 *Ferguson*, 1965 S.C. 16.

7 *Maitland*, 1961 S.C. 291.

8 *Christie*, 1926 S.C. 750.

9 1935 S.C. 745.

Chapter 66

APPLICATION FOR LAWBURROWS

Lawburrows is a very ancient remedy, signifying finding caution to keep the law.[1] The word is derived from *borrow* or *borgh*, an old word for caution. It is founded on the Lawburrows Acts 1429, 1581 and 1597 and the now repealed Scots Acts of 1449, c. 12, 1491, c. 27, 1597, c. 77, and 1593, c. 170. The procedure was substantially altered by, and is now regulated by, the Civil Imprisonment Act 1882, s. 6, but, save as modified thereby, the older principles still apply.[2] It may still be a useful remedy, as to protect a workman against violence threatened by fellow-workmen holding different opinions.

Parties

A person may apply for lawburrows against anyone, even his wife [3] or child,[4] but not against a pupil child.[5] In the case of near relations some evidence of the cause of fear is necessary.[6] A corporation or community might, and doubtless still may, serve or be served with letters of lawburrows,[7] but in the case of a community the complaint must specify some conduct on the part of the corporation or community as such which he fears, and which would be contravention of lawburrows.

Application

Formerly application was made to the Court of Session, High Court of Justiciary, or the sheriff or any justice of the county in which the defender resided. The modern procedure is that application is made to a sheriff-principal or sheriff or justice of the peace, who must immediately order the petition to be served on the person complained against, and grant warrant to both parties to cite witnesses. The application is to be disposed of summarily after proof, without written pleadings or evidence being recorded, and the court may grant the petition on the sworn testimony of one credible witness, who may be a party. If the court is satisfied, it may order caution to be found, the amount to be in its discretion.[8]

1 Stair, IV, 48, 2; Bankt. I, 10, 157; Ersk. IV, 1, 16.
2 1882 Act, s. 6, proviso.
3 *Thomson* v. *Thomson*, Mar. 7, 1815, F.C.; *Calder* (1841) 3 D. 615.
4 *Taylor* v. *Taylor* (1829) 7 S. 794.
5 *Seytoun* v. *Ballingall* (1532) Mor. 8023.
6 *Taylor, supra.*
7 *Reid* v. *Sheriffdom of Ayr* (1541) Mor. 8023; *Old Town of Aberdeen* v. *New Town* (1549) Mor. 8026.
8 1882 Act, s. 6 (1)–(5).

Grounds for grant

The applicant must satisfy the court as to the fact of, and the cause of, his fear,[9] such as the receipt of threatening letters.[10] There must be some reasonable cause for apprehension to justify the grant of the remedy.[11] The application may be granted even though the defender is at that time prevented from executing the threat, as where he is in prison or in hospital.[12] At first the remedy extended only to threats to the complainer's life, but later it was extended to threats of any unjustifiable harm to the complainer's person, property, relatives, tenants and servants. The harm apprehended may be of any kind, physical injury, damage to property, defamation or otherwise.

If satisfied the court orders the defender to find caution for a specified sum, such as it thinks right, not to molest the pursuer, on pain of imprisonment. An applicant may be liable in damages for wrongfully applying for lawburrows if it can be shown that he did so maliciously and without probable cause.[13]

The amount of caution

The amount is now in the discretion of the court.[14]

The order to grant a bond of caution

The court may order the party complained against to grant his own bond without caution for duly implementing the terms of the order, under pain of imprisonment.

Duration of caution

No period is prescribed, and an order to find caution may be without limitation of time.

Failure to find caution

The court which orders caution to be found may further order that the party complained against shall, failing his finding caution, be imprisoned for a period not exceeding six months, if the order be made by a sheriff-principal or sheriff, and not exceeding fourteen days, if made by a justice of the peace.[15] If imprisoned the defender is treated in the same way as one imprisoned for contempt of court.[16]

9 Ersk. IV, 1, 16; *Sellars* v. *Anderson* (1778) Mor. 8042.
10 As in *Brock* v. *Rankine* (1874) 1 R. 991.
11 *Brock, supra*, 1002.
12 *Brock, supra*.
13 *Brock* v. *Rankine* (1874) 1 R. 991: see also *Smith* v. *Baird* (1799) Mor. 8043.
14 Civil Imprisonment (Scotland) Act 1882, s. 6 (5).
15 *Ibid.* s. 6 (6).
16 *Ibid.* s. 6 (8).

Appeal

The justification for granting or refusing an application may be challenged only by stated case under the Summary Jurisdiction (Scotland) Act 1954.[17]

Contravention of lawburrows

If the person complained of, though he has found caution, commits the kind of conduct which he had found caution not to commit, the court may, on the complainer's application, order the caution money to be forfeited and payment recovered from the person bound or from his cautioner. Contravention has been held not to be constituted by mere words or threats of violence [18] or chasing a man without striking [19] or mere threats and knocking off his hat [20] or pasturing cattle without herding them,[21] but was held constituted by pursuit with a weapon,[22] injurious words and spitting in his face,[23] stopping a passage,[24] violent entry into possession of land,[25] and ploughing up a sown field.[26]

Only the person in right of the lawburrows may sue on the bond and only for loss to himself arising from the contravention.[27] If the acts of contravention be slight the penalty has sometimes been reduced to a lesser sum, and at other times no more has been decreed against the contravener than the real damage sustained by the pursuer.[28] The penalty is not incurred on every damage, but *ex damno injuria dato*, when the damage is done wittingly and wilfully.[29]

The contravener is liable not only for his own acts but for harm done by others with his knowledge or authority.[30]

The penalty was at first divided equally between the Crown and the complainer.[31] The action is probably still penal, for exaction of a penalty, rather than compensatory.

The action is excluded by the complainer's forgiveness of the wrong [32] or subsequent permission.[33]

17 *Mackenzie* v. *Maclennan*, 1916 S.C. 617.
18 Ersk. IV, 1, 16.
19 *Wallace* v. *Laird of Hayning* (1604) Mor. 8027.
20 *Constable of Dundee* v. *Flescheour* (1605) Mor. 8028.
21 *McKie* v. *McKie* (1607) Mor. 8029; *cf. Bruce* v. *Clackmanan* (1609) Mor. 8030.
22 *Shaw* v. *Wilkieson* (1604) Mor. 8027.
23 *A.* v. *B.* (1629) Mor. 8033.
24 *Strange* v. *Sandilands* (1591) Mor. 8024.
25 *Laird of Whittingham* v. *The Lady* (1631) Mor. 8034.
26 *Muirhead* v. *Laird of Barsinok* (1616) Mor. 8031.
27 Stair, IV, 48, 10.
28 Ersk. IV, 1, 16, citing *Anderson* v. *Blackwood* (1629) Mor. 8033.
29 Stair, IV, 48, 7, referring to *Shaw, supra.*
30 Stair, IV, 48, 11.
31 Acts 1491, c. 27, and 1581, c. 22; Ersk. IV, 1, 16.
32 *Somerville* v. —— (1613) Mor. 8028; *Sheriff of Forrest* v. *Turnbull* (1613) Mor. 7898.
33 *King's Advocate* v. *Lindsay* (1633) Mor. 8038.

Concurrent remedies

Contravention may concur with other penal actions, such as spuilzie, but the court has not been in the habit of allowing both remedies but only the one chosen by the injured party.[34] It does not exclude any criminal prosecution, such as for assault.[35]

[34] Stair, IV, 48, 9.
[35] *King* v. *Crichton* (1517) Mor. 8023.

CHAPTER 67

RECTIFICATION OF REGISTERS

UNDER many statutes registers of various kinds are required to be kept and an individual may be aggrieved to discover that his name is included in, or excluded from, the register. In many circumstances his remedy is to make application for rectification of the register. These registers are, broadly, registers of persons who alone are entitled to practise certain professions, and registers of particular kinds of rights and claims, showing who are entitled to these rights. In some other cases registration is required in the interests of public health or the maintenance of proper standards in the conduct of some kinds of businesses.

Adopted children

The Registrar-General for Scotland maintains an Adopted Children Register and all adoptions made in Scotland are recorded therein.[1] An adoption order may be amended and the register rectified.[2] If a person has been adopted and is subsequently legitimated the adoption order may be revoked and the Register rectified.[3]

Adoption societies

An adoption society refused registration, or the registration of which is proposed to be cancelled, may appeal to the sheriff within whose jurisdiction the society's administrative centre is situated within 21 days.[4]

Animal trainers

A person who exhibits or trains performing animals, must be registered with the local authority, and on conviction of stated offences, his registration may be cancelled, or he may be disqualified from being registered under the Act, in addition to or in lieu of any other penalty.[5] Appeal presumably lies as in other summary convictions.

Architects

A person practising as an architect must be registered.[6] If the Architects Registration Council decides not to register an applicant he may appeal to a Tribunal of Appeal.[7]

1 Adoption Act 1958, ss. 22–23.
2 *Ibid.* s. 24.
3 *Ibid.* ss. 26–27.
4 Adoption Act 1958, s. 31.
5 Performing Animals (Regulation) Act 1925, ss. 2, 4 (2) and 6.
6 Architects Registration Act 1931, ss. 2, 3.
7 Architects Registration Act 1938, s. 2.

Births, deaths and marriages

Births and still-births, both legitimate and illegitimate, deaths, and marriages must be registered with the registrar of the registration district in which the event occurred within statutorily specified periods.[8] Provision is made for a Register of Corrections to record changes of surname,[9] and decrees of court altering status.[10]

Business names

Persons and firms carrying on business under business names must have them registered, subject to penalty and to disabilities affecting unregistered persons. A person aggrieved by the registrar's refusal to register a business name containing the word " British " or a similar word may appeal to the Department of Trade and Industry.[11]

Clubs

Clubs must be registered under the Licensing (Scotland) Acts 1959 and 1961 before they can sell excisable liquor. A certificate of registration may be refused, or its renewal refused, or it be cancelled by the sheriff. No appeal lies.[12]

Common lodging-houses

Common lodging-houses must be registered with the local authority, which may refuse registration, or petition the sheriff to remove a house from the register. If a lodging-house is removed from the register for inadequate water-supply or toilet accommodation, any person interested may appeal to the sheriff against the resolution of the local authority removing it; in a landward area appeal to the sheriff arises only after the county council has disposed of any appeal brought before them.[13]

Companies—Register of members

Under the Companies Act 1948, s. 116, if the name of any person is, without sufficient cause, entered in or omitted from the register of members of a company, or default is made or unnecessary delay takes place in entering on the register the fact of any person having ceased to be a member, the person aggrieved, or any member of the company, or the company, may apply to the court for rectification of the register. Petition for rectification may be presented by the company[14] and the jurisdiction may be exercised before or after winding-up.[15] It has been exercised in

[8] Registration of Births, Deaths and Marriages (Scotland) Act 1965.
[9] 1965 Act, ss. 43–44.
[10] 1965 Act, s. 48.
[11] Registration of Business Names Act 1916, s. 14.
[12] 1959 Act, ss. 168, 173, 175.
[13] Public Health (Scotland) Act 1897, ss. 89, 90, 94.
[14] *Re Indo-China S.N. Co.* [1917] 2 Ch. 100.
[15] *Stocker* v. *Coustonholm Paper Mill Co. Liqdrs.* (1891) 19 R. 17; *Re Sussex Brick Co.* [1904] 1 Ch. 598.

such cases as where the applicant was induced by misrepresentation to take shares,[16] where the company improperly neglected to register a transfer [17]; where shares had been issued without complying with the Act [18]; where the company had removed the applicant's name, acting in reliance on a forged transfer [19]; where there was a dispute between buyer and seller of shares [20]; where shares had been irregularly allotted to the applicant [21]; where the signatory of an under-writing letter had been placed on that register [22]; where a shareholder who had made an *ultra vires* surrender of his shares to the company claimed to be reinstated [23]; and where a trustee shareholder had instructed his resignation from the office of trustee.[24]

Such a petition is not incompetent merely because a decree for calls against the petitioner has been allowed to become final.[25] It is questionable if the company can rectify the register at its own hand.[26] The opinion has been expressed that rectification by way of reduction *ope exceptionis* is not competent.[27]

The statutory provision is not exhaustive and does not prevent the court from altering the register in other cases.[28]

Companies—Register of charges

A company registered in England must register charges of certain kinds created by the company.[29] If the court is satisfied that the omission to register a charge or that a mistake therein was accidental, it may order that the time for registration be extended or that the omission or misstatement be rectified.[30] The company must also maintain a register of charges.[31]

A company registered in Scotland must within 21 days register charges of stated kinds created by the company.[32] If the court is satisfied that an omission to register a charge within the time required by the Act, or that a

16 *Stewart's Case* (1866) L.R. 1 Ch.App. 574; *Anderson's Case* (1881) 17 Ch.D. 373; *Chambers* v. *Edinburgh and Glasgow Aerated Bread Co.* (1891) 18 R. 1039; *Blakiston* v. *London and Scottish Banking Corpn.* (1894) 21 R. 417; *Mair* v. *Rio Grande Rubber Estates*, 1913 S.C. (H.L.) 74. But see *Sleigh* v. *Glasgow and Transvaal Options* (1904) 6 F. 420.
17 *Re Stranton Iron & Steel Co.* (1873) L.R. 16 Eq. 559.
18 *New Zealand Kapanga Co.* (1874) L.R. 18 Eq. 17; *Blaikie* v. *Coats* (1893) 21 R. 150.
19 *Bahia and San Francisco Ry.* (1868) L.R. 3 Q.B. 584.
20 *Re Denton Colliery Co., ex parte Shaw* (1866) 2 Q.B.D. 463.
21 *Homer District Consolidated Gold Mines* (1887) 39 Ch.D. 546; *Portuguese Consolidated Copper Mines* (1889) 42 Ch.D. 160.
22 *Re Consort Gold Mines* [1897] 1 Ch. 575.
23 *Bellerby* v. *Rowland and Marwood's Steamship Co.* [1902] 2 Ch. 14.
24 *Dalgleish* v. *Land Feuing Co.* (1885) 13 R. 223.
25 *Jackson* v. *Star Fire and Burglary Ins. Co. Liqdr.* (1902) 10 S.L.T. 279.
26 *Anglo-American Land Mortgage and Agency Co.* v. *Scottish Investment Trust Co.* (1896) 4 S.L.T. 37.
27 *National Bank Glasgow Nominees Ltd.* v. *Adamson*, 1932 S.L.T. 492.
28 *e.g. Burns* v. *Siemens Bros. Dynamo Works* [1919] 1 Ch. 225.
29 1948 Act, ss. 95–100.
30 *Ibid.* s. 101. See also *Re Jackson* [1899] 1 Ch. 348.
31 *Ibid.* s. 104.
32 *Ibid.* s. 106A, added by Companies (Floating Charges and Receivers) (Scotland) Act 1972, Sch.

mistake therein was accidental, it may order that the time for registration be extended or that the omission or misstatement be rectified.[33] The company also must maintain a register of charges.[34]

Dairies

To carry on the trade of dairyman a person must have a certificate of registration by the local authority in respect of his premises. A certificate may be granted, granted only provisionally, refused, or revoked, in which case any person aggrieved may appeal in summary manner to the sheriff and to the sheriff-principal.[35]

Dentists

Dentists must be registered, and a registered dentist's name may be erased from the register for crime or infamous conduct, but he may appeal to the Queen in Council, and his name may subsequently be restored.[36]

Electors

Certain persons are entitled to be registered as electors at parliamentary and local government elections [37] and appeal lies to the sheriff (a) from any decision of the registration officer on any claim for registration or objection to a person's registration made to and considered by him: (b) from any decision of the registration officer disallowing a person's application to be treated as an absent voter or to vote by post or proxy, in any case where the application is not made for a particular election only; (c) from any decision of the registration officer to place or not to place against any name in the register a mark indicating that the person registered is, or is not, registered as a service voter or as a non-resident or is, or is not, entitled to vote for a particular local government area: Provided that an appeal shall not lie where the person desiring to appeal has not availed himself of the prescribed right to be heard by or make representations to the registration officer on the matter which is the subject of the appeal, or has not given the prescribed notice of appeal within the prescribed time.[38]

An appeal lies on a point of law from the sheriff to a court of three judges of the Court of Session appointed by Act of Sederunt and drawn, one from each Division of the Inner House and one from the Outer House.[39]

These provisions apply also to decisions on claims and objections with respect to any corrupt and illegal practices list.[40]

33 *Ibid.* s. 106G.
34 *Ibid.* s. 106B.
35 Milks and Dairies (Scotland) Act 1914, s. 7; Milk and Dairies (Amendment) Act 1922, ss. 2, 14.
36 Dentists Act 1957, ss. 25, 29.
37 Representation of the People Act 1949, ss. 1–5, amended Electoral Registers Acts 1949, s. 2, and 1953.
38 *Ibid.* s. 45 (1).
39 *Ibid.* s. 45 (8)–(10).
40 *Ibid.* s. 45 (7).

Firearms certificate holders

Users of firearms or shotguns must obtain certificates from the police, and the conditions attached to the certificate may be varied; a person aggrieved by the refusal to grant or review or vary a certificate or its revocation may appeal to the sheriff.[41]

Firearms dealers

A firearms dealer must be registered with the police and obtain an annual certificate. The chief officer of police may in certain circumstances refuse registration, in which case the person aggrieved may appeal against the refusal to the sheriff.[42] Conditions may be imposed on registration and appeal may similarly be taken against the imposition or variation of, or refusal to vary or revoke, any conditions.[43] A dealer may have a new place of business registered and may similarly appeal against refusal.[44] A person aggrieved by the removal of his name or a place of business from the register, may similarly appeal.[45]

Friendly societies

Societies of the kinds which may be registered [46] under the Friendly Societies Act 1896 may apply for registration and if the application is refused appeal lies from the assistant registrar of friendly societies for Scotland to the Chief Registrar of Friendly Societies and, if he refuses, to the Court of Session in Scotland.[47]

Industrial and Provident Societies

Societies which may be registered under the Industrial and Provident Societies Act 1965 may register thereunder. Registration may be cancelled,[48] or suspended,[49] but notice of intended cancellation or suspension must be given and a society may appeal against refusal to register or cancellation or suspension of registration to the Chief Registrar of Friendly Societies and from there to the Court of Session.[50]

Medical practitioners

A person holding stated qualifications is entitled to be registered as a registered medical practitioner,[51] and a person holding recognised qualifications granted in a Commonwealth or foreign country is entitled to be

[41] Firearms Act 1968, ss. 26, 29, 30 and 44.
[42] Firearms Act 1968, ss. 33–34 and 44.
[43] *Ibid.* ss. 36 and 44.
[44] *Ibid.* ss. 37 and 44.
[45] *Ibid.* ss. 38 and 44.
[46] 1896 Act, s. 8.
[47] *Ibid.* s. 12; see also s. 20.
[48] 1965 Act, s. 16.
[49] *Ibid.* s. 17.
[50] *Ibid.* s. 18.
[51] Medical Act 1956, s. 7.

registered on certain conditions.[52] A person in the latter category seeking registration, if refused on any ground other than that the qualification held by him is not recognised for the purposes of the Act, or that he does not satisfy the requirements of the Act as to experience, or a person in the latter category refused provisional registration on stated grounds, may appeal to the Privy Council which may dismiss the appeal or direct the General Medical Council that the appellant is to be treated as having proved the matters in question.[53]

Midwives

The Central Midwives Board for Scotland must maintain a roll of certified midwives [54]; a woman aggrieved by the removal of her name from the roll or a prohibition on her attending women in childbirth may appeal to the Court of Session, whose decision is final.[55]

Moneylenders

Moneylenders must obtain certificates granted by the local licensing court, and moneylenders' excise licences; appeal against a refusal to grant a certificate lies to the licensing court of appeal.[56] A moneylender convicted of an offence against stated relevant Acts may have his certificate suspended or forfeited, in which case he may appeal against that decision in the same way as an appeal against conviction.[57]

Notaries public

An enrolled solicitor may be admitted a notary public on petition to the Court of Session. His name and other particulars are registered by the Keeper of the Roll of Notaries.[58]

A person struck off the roll of solicitors for disciplinary reasons or having his name removed at his own request shall, if he is also a notary public, be struck off the roll of notaries public, and if restored thereto shall be restored to the roll of notaries public.[59]

Nurses

The General Nursing Council for Scotland must maintain a register of nurses, and a roll of assistant nurses,[60] and a person aggrieved by the removal of her name from the register or roll may appeal to the Court of Session, whose decision is final.[61]

52 *Ibid.* s. 18.
53 *Ibid.* s. 24.
54 Midwives (Scotland) Act 1951, s. 2.
55 *Ibid.* s. 4 (5).
56 Moneylenders Act 1927, ss. 1, 2 and 18.
57 *Ibid.* s. 3.
58 Solicitors (Scotland) Act 1933, s. 17.
59 Solicitors (Scotland) Act 1958, s. 11.
60 Nurses (Scotland) Act 1951, ss. 2, 3.
61 *Ibid.* s. 10.

Nursing homes

Nursing homes must be registered with the local authority in whose area the home is situated.[62] The local authority may refuse to register on certain grounds, or may cancel the registration.[63] A person aggrieved by an order refusing an application for registration or cancelling any registration may, within 14 days, appeal against it to the sheriff, whose decision shall be final and shall be given effect to by the local authority.[64]

Partnerships (Limited)

A limited partnership under the Limited Partnerships Act 1907 must be registered as such with the Registrar of Joint Stock Companies, and change in the particulars must be notified.[65] No express provision is made for rectification of the register but an aggrieved individual could probably proceed by declarator.

Patents

There is maintained at the Patent Office a register of patents, containing particulars of patents in force, assignments and transmission of patents and of licences under patents, and persons becoming entitled to a patent or a share therein by assignment, transmission or operation of law may apply for the registration of their titles therein.[66] The court may, on the application of any person aggrieved, order the register of patents to be rectified by the making of any entry therein or the variation or deletion of any entry therein, and may determine any question which it may be necessary or expedient to decide in connection with the rectification of the register.[67] The comptroller may correct any clerical error in any patent, application for a patent or error in the register of patents.[68]

Pharmaceutical chemists

Pharmaceutical chemists must be registered with the Pharmaceutical Society of Great Britain. A person rendered unfit, in the opinion of the Statutory Committee, to be on the register, may be refused registration, or removed from the register, or not restored thereto. A person aggrieved by a direction of the Statutory Committee may appeal to the Court of Session against the direction or refusal.[69]

Plant breeders' rights

The Controller of the Plant Variety Rights Office may grant an appli-

[62] Nursing Homes Registration (Sc.) Act 1938, s. 1.
[63] *Ibid.* ss. 1–2.
[64] *Ibid.* s. 3.
[65] 1907 Act, ss. 5, 8–9.
[66] Patents Act 1949, ss. 73–74.
[67] *Ibid.* s. 75.
[68] *Ibid.* s. 76.
[69] Pharmacy Act 1954, ss. 2, 8, 10, 24 (2).

cant plant breeders' rights.[70] An appeal lies to the Plant Variety Rights Tribunal [71] against the decision of the Controller to allow or refuse an application for the grant of plant breeders' rights.[72] The periods for which plant breeders' rights are granted may be extended, and appeal lies to the Tribunal against the Controller's decision to allow or refuse an application,[73] or application may be made to surrender the rights,[74] or the rights may be revoked,[75] in each case subject to the same appeal. The Controller may also grant or refuse a compulsory licence, subject to appeal to the Tribunal.[76]

The Minister of Agriculture and the Secretary of State for Scotland may prepare an index of names of plant varieties, and shall not refuse an application for inclusion of a plant variety in the appropriate section of the index save on the ground that it is not a distinct plant variety; an appeal lies to the Tribunal against a refusal.[77]

Professions supplementary to medicine

By the Professions Supplementary to Medicine Act 1960, Boards are established for the professions of chiropodists, dietitians, medical laboratory technicians, occupational therapists, physiotherapists, radiographers, and remedial gymnasts, each of which maintains a register of all persons entitled to be registered. A person's name may be removed from the register if convicted of a criminal offence which in the opinion of the disciplinary committee of the relevant Board renders him unfit to be registered, or he is judged by that committee to be guilty of infamous conduct in any professional respect, or the committee is satisfied that the person's name was fraudulently entered on the register.[78]

Registered designs

There is maintained at the Patent Office a register of designs containing the names of proprietors of registered designs, notices of assignments and of transmissions of registered designs and of such other matters as may be prescribed or as the registrar may think fit.[79] The court may, on the application of any person aggrieved, order the register of designs to be rectified by the making of any entry therein or the variation or deletion of any entry therein, and in proceedings for rectification, the court may determine any question which it may be necessary or expedient to decide in connection with the rectification of the register.[80] The registrar may also correct any

[70] Plant Varieties and Seeds Act 1964, s. 1; the nature of the rights are dealt with in s. 4.
[71] Established under 1964 Act, s. 10.
[72] *Ibid.* s. 1 (4).
[73] *Ibid.* s. 3 (5).
[74] *Ibid.* s. 3 (6).
[75] *Ibid.* ss. 3 (7)–(9), 6 (4) and (5).
[76] *Ibid.* s. 7.
[77] *Ibid.* s. 21.
[78] 1960 Act, s. 9.
[79] Registered Designs Act 1949, ss. 17–19.
[80] *Ibid.* s. 20.

error in an application for the registration or the representation of a design, or any error in the register of designs.[81]

Solicitors

A roll of solicitors in Scotland is kept by the Law Society of Scotland, and a person enrolled may be struck off on the application of the solicitor himself.[82]

The Discipline Committee may order a solicitor to be suspended from practice or struck off the roll of solicitors or censure and/or fine him.[83] A person struck off may in certain circumstances be restored to the roll.[84] A person aggrieved by a decision of the Discipline Committee may appeal against the decision to the court, which may give such direction as they think fit, which shall be final.[85]

Teachers

The General Teaching Council for Scotland must maintain a register of persons entitled to be registered and who apply to be so registered.[86] The Disciplinary Committee may under certain conditions direct that a person's name shall be removed from the register, or that a person's application for registration should be refused.[87] A person whose name has been removed, or whose application for registration has been refused, or whose application for restoration has been refused, or whose application for registration, his certificate having been previously withdrawn or suspended and not restored, has been refused, may appeal to the Court of Session, whose decision is final.[88]

Trade marks

There is maintained at the Patent Office a register of trade marks containing all registered trade marks with the names of their proprietors, notifications of assignments and transmissions, names of registered users and such other matters relating to registered trade marks as may be prescribed. It is divided into two parts, A and B.[89] Registration may be opposed.[90] Any person aggrieved by the non-insertion in or omission from the register of any entry, or by any entry made in the register without sufficient cause, or by any entry wrongly remaining on the register, or by any error or defect in any entry in the register, may apply to the Court of Session, or at the option of the appellant and subject to section 54 of the

[81] *Ibid.* s. 21.
[82] Solicitors (Scotland) Act 1933, s. 18, amended by Legal Aid and Solicitors (Scotland) Act 1949, s. 18 (3), and Solicitors (Scotland) Act 1958, Sched. 3.
[83] Solicitors (Scotland) Act 1958, s. 5.
[84] *Ibid.* s. 6.
[85] *Ibid.* s. 7.
[86] Teaching Council (Scotland) Act 1965, ss. 1, 6.
[87] *Ibid.* ss. 10–11.
[88] *Ibid.* s. 12.
[89] Trade Marks Act 1938, s. 1.
[90] *Ibid.* s. 18.

Act, to the Registrar, and the tribunal (Court of Session or registrar) may make such order for making, expunging or varying the entry as the tribunal may think fit, and may in any proceeding under the section decide any question that it may be necessary or expedient to decide in connection with the rectification of the register.[91] It may also make an order for expunging or varying the registration of a trade mark on the ground of any contravention of, or failure to observe, a condition entered on the register in relation thereto.[92] The Registrar may also correct any error in the name of a registered proprietor, enter a change of name or description, cancel the entry of a trade mark on the register, strike out any class of goods from those in respect of which a trade mark is registered, or enter a disclaimer or memorandum relating to a trade mark which does not in any way extend the rights given by the existing registration of the trade mark, or correct or enter a change in the name or description of a registered user. Any decision by the Registrar under this section shall be subject to appeal to the Department of Trade and Industry or to the Court of Session.[93]

A registered proprietor may apply for leave to add to or alter the trade mark in any manner not substantially affecting the identity thereof; any decision by the Registrar under this section shall be subject to appeal to the Department or to the court.[94]

Trade unions

Under the Industrial Relations Act 1971 any organisation of workers [1] may apply to the Assistant Registrar of Trade Unions and Employers' Associations for Scotland for registration as a trade union under the Act.[2] Any organisation of employers [3] may apply to the same officer for registration as an employers' association under the Act.[4] The Registrar must examine the rules of the organisation and may give notice requiring defects in the rules to be remedied.[5] The Assistant Registrar may apply to the National Industrial Relations Court for an order directing the cancellation of the registration of an organisation on stated grounds, and an organisation which has submitted its rules may apply to the same court for an order allowing it a further period to alter its rules, or directing the Registrar to approve the rules already submitted.[6] The Registrar may apply to the court for cancellation of registration on other grounds.[7] Registration may be cancelled on request or where the organisation ceases to exist.[8]

91 *Ibid.* s. 32.
92 *Ibid.* s. 33.
93 *Ibid.* s. 34.
94 *Ibid.* s. 35. On appeals generally see also ss. 48–54.
1 Defined, s. 61. As to eligibility for registration, see s. 67.
2 *Ibid.* s. 68.
3 Defined, s. 62. As to eligibility for registration, see s. 71.
4 *Ibid.* s. 72. As to certificates of and legal consequences of registration see ss. 73–74.
5 *Ibid.* s. 75.
6 *Ibid.* s. 76.
7 *Ibid.* s. 77.
8 *Ibid.* s. 92.

The Registrar was required to institute a provisional register including every organisation previously registered as a trade union under the previous Trade Union Acts, and to maintain it until organisations registered thereon are transferred to the permanent register or " deregister." [9]

There is also a special register for certain anomalous kinds of organisations.[10]

Veterinary surgeons

The Council of the Royal College of Veterinary Surgeons maintains a register of veterinary surgeons.[11] The name of a person may be removed for crime or disgraceful conduct,[12] appeal lying to the Privy Council,[13] or it may be restored thereto.[14]

[9] *Ibid.* ss. 78–80. As to the registrar's powers of investigation see ss. 81–83, and as to his powers to appoint an inspector and to apply for a winding up order see s. 90.
[10] *Ibid.* ss. 84–86.
[11] Veterinary Surgeons Act 1966, ss. 1–2, 9.
[12] *Ibid.* s. 16.
[13] *Ibid.* s. 17.
[14] *Ibid.* s. 18.

CHAPTER 68

JUDICIAL POWERS TO RESOLVE PARTNERSHIP AND COMPANY DISPUTES

WHERE parties are linked by partnership agreement or the agreement implied in membership of a company a remedy may sometimes be found in an application to the court.

Partnership

Apart from dissolution of partnership by expiry of time or by notice, the court may,[1] on the application of a partner, decree a dissolution of the partnership

(*a*) when a partner is found lunatic by cognition, or is shown to the satisfaction of the court to be of permanently unsound mind, in either of which cases the application may be made as well on behalf of that partner by his *curator bonis* or person having title to intervene as by any other partner [2];

(*b*) when a partner, other than the partner suing, becomes in any other way permanently incapable of performing his part of the partnership contract;

(*c*) when a partner, other than the partner suing, has been guilty of such conduct as, in the opinion of the court, regard being had to the nature of the business, is calculated to prejudicially affect the carrying on of the business;

(*d*) when a partner, other than the partner suing, wilfully or persistently commits a breach of the partnership agreement, or otherwise so conducts himself in matters relating to the partnership business that it is not reasonably practicable for the other partner or partners to carry on the business in partnership with him;

(*e*) when the business of the partnership can only be carried on at a loss [3];

(*f*) whenever in any case circumstances have arisen, which, in the opinion of the court, render it just and equitable that the partnership be dissolved.

If dissolution be decreed each partner is entitled to have the partnership property applied in payment of the firm's debts and liabilities, and the

[1] Partnership Act 1890, s. 35.
[2] *Cf. Jones* v. *Lloyd* (1874) L.R. 18 Eq. 265.
[3] Not temporary or special circumstances but factors rendering trading at a profit practically impossible: *Handyside* v. *Campbell* (1901) 17 T.L.R. 623.

surplus assets applied in payment of what may be due to the partners respectively, and for that purpose any partner or his representatives may apply to the court to wind up the business and affairs of the firm.[4] This right has been said to be a kind of floating lien enforceable, failing contrary agreement, by a sale of the whole of the assets.[5]

Companies—winding up

A company may be wound up by the Court of Session or, if the share capital paid up or credited as paid up does not exceed £10,000, by the sheriff court of the sheriffdom in which the registered office is situated,[6] on the ground, *inter alia*, that " the court is of opinion that it is just and equitable that the company should be wound up." [7]

It is impossible to imagine all the kinds of circumstances in which the court might hold it just and equitable to appoint a liquidator or provisional liquidator. " Just and equitable " is not limited to cases of the same kind as those listed in earlier sub-heads of section 222.[8] Among the reported instances are: where no meetings of shareholders had been held, no accounts submitted, no ascertainment of profits, no appointment of directors or auditors, and there had been other irregularities [9]; where the preponderant shareholder of a private company treated it as his own [10]; where the substratum of the company had gone and the petitioner was apprehensive that the proceeds of the sale of its business were being depleted in its hands to his prejudice as a deferred shareholder.[11]

Companies—the remedy for oppression

Under the Companies Act 1948, s. 210, if a member of a company complains that the affairs of the company are being conducted in a manner oppressive to some part of the members, including himself, he may apply to the court, which, if satisfied that the company's affairs are being conducted oppressively and that to wind up the company would unfairly prejudice that part of the members but otherwise the facts would justify a winding-up order on the ground that it was just and equitable that the company should be wound up, may make such order as it thinks fit, whether for regulating the conduct of the company's affairs in future, or for the purchase of the shares of any members of the company by other members of the company or by the company, and, in the case of a purchase by the company, for the reduction accordingly of the company's capital.

For this remedy to be invoked successfully it must be shown that

4 1890 Act, s. 39.
5 *Wild* v. *Milne* (1859) 26 Beav. 504; see also *Re Bourne* [1906] 2 Ch. 427.
6 Companies Act 1948, s. 220.
7 *Ibid.* s. 222(*f*).
8 *Symington* v. *Symington's Quarries Ltd.* (1905) 8 F. 211; *Re Yenidje Tobacco Co.* [1916] 2 Ch. 426, 432.
9 *Baird* v. *Lees*, 1924 S.C. 83; see also *Loch* v. *Blackwood* [1924] A.C. 783.
10 *Thomson* v. *Drysdale*, 1925 S.C. 311.
11 *Levy* v. *Napier*, 1962 S.C. 468; see also *Levy, Petr.*, 1963 S.C. 46.

there has been oppression of the minority shareholders and also that the affairs of the company have been conducted in an oppressive manner.[12] "Oppressive" means "burdensome, harsh and wrongful."[13] It is not sufficient that the petitioners were dealt with oppressively as directors or employees of the company, if not oppressed as members of the company.[14] Mismanagement is not oppression; and the petitioner must make clear what he wants, not merely ask the court to do what it thinks just, or regulate the company's affairs.[15] This kind of relief is not confined to discrimination between classes of shareholders, nor to such conduct as was designed to obtain pecuniary advantage as distinct from such as expressed an overweening desire for power.[16]

[12] *Meyer* v. *S.C.W.S.*, 1958 S.C.(H.L.) 40, 45.
[13] *Ibid., per* Viscount Simonds,; *Re H. R. Harmer Ltd.* [1958] 3 All E.R. 589.
[14] *Elder* v. *Elder & Watson*, 1952 S.C. 49.
[15] *Re Antigen Laboratories Ltd.* [1951] 1 All E.R. 110.
[16] *Re H. R. Harmer Ltd., supra.*

CHAPTER 69

SEQUESTRATION

WHEREVER property appears to be ownerless, or there is danger that property in which parties other than the actual possessor thereof are interested may be dissipated, damaged, sold, removed from the jurisdiction, or otherwise be rendered unavailable for satisfying claims against it, or against the actual possessor, the court may sequestrate that property and take it into the notional custody of the court.[1]

Two important applications of this principle are the sequestration for rent or feuduty of the tenant's or vassal's *invecta et illata*, over which the landlord or superior has a right of hypothec,[2] and mercantile sequestration of the assets of a person who is notour bankrupt.[3] But the principle is not confined to such cases. Thus the court has sequestrated a trust-estate where one trustee refused to co-operate in the administration of the trust, and appointed a judicial factor thereon,[4] or sequestrated a partnership estate and appointed a judicial factor.[5]

1 *Cf.* Bell, *Comm.* II, 244.
2 Chap. 19, *supra*.
3 Chap. 18, *supra*.
4 *McAlley's J.F.* (1900) 2 F. 1198; *cf. Courage* v. *Ballantine*, 1946 S.C. 351.
5 *Carabine* v. *Carabine*, 1949 S.C. 521.

CHAPTER 70

RANKING AND SALE

THE action of judicial ranking and sale is one whereby any creditor who holds a real security over an insolvent estate is empowered to bring it to public sale and have the price divided.[1] Though now less commonly resorted to than procedure under the Bankruptcy (Scotland) Act 1913,[2] it is still competent.[3] The action may be at the instance of a creditor, in which case it narrates the ground of debt, the real security held by or diligence done by the pursuer, the debtor's notour bankruptcy, and the fact that the creditor is in possession. The conclusions are for judicial sale of the whole lands and heritable rights of the debtor, and for division of the proceeds among the creditors according to their rights and interests.[4] Or the action may be brought by the debtor's apparent heir, in which case the ancestor need not be notour bankrupt.[5] The estate is sequestrated during the dependence of the action so that it may be properly managed in the meantime for the common advantage.[6]

In either case a common agent is appointed by the creditors to superintend for the common interest all the proceedings in the action, to conduct the sale, to call the factor, if there be a sequestration, to account, to prevent any of the creditors from gaining an advantage to the prejudice of the general interest, to prevent undue delays, and to discuss all questions in which the creditors or the funds are concerned.[7]

The action must establish the value of the lands. The lands are then exposed to sale by public roup, in one or more lots as may appear appropriate. On sale being effected the court adjudges the lands to the purchaser and extinguishes all the real security rights over the lands.[8]

Sale having converted the debtor's estate into a distributable fund the common agent must ascertain the claims of creditors and make up a state of the debts and a scheme of division. This, if approved by the court, is approved by decree, which authorises payment to those entitled.

[1] Bell, *Comm.* II, 233.
[2] ss. 92, 110.
[3] *Cannon's Trs.* v. *Lake* (1883) 21 S.L.R. 101. But in view of the absence of modern use of this process the procedure is rather uncertain.
[4] Bell, *Comm.* II, 237–238, 240.
[5] *Ibid.* 238, 240.
[6] *Ibid.* 244.
[7] *Ibid.* 249.
[8] *Ibid.* 258.

CHAPTER 71

DIVISION OR DIVISION AND SALE OF PROPERTY: DIVISION OF COMMONTY: MARCH FENCES

WHERE several persons are owners in common [1] of heritable property, no one can be compelled to remain such owner in common and any one may at any time bring an action for division of the common property,[2] or where division is impracticable or would be inequitable to some of the parties,[3] for sale of the joint property and division of the price,[4] on the basis of the maxim *nemo in communione invitus detineri potest*. One *pro indiviso* proprietor in common may by contract bar himself from resorting to an action of division, or division and sale.[5] But it is probably incompetent for a testator to gift heritage to legatees in common but to seek to exclude the right of any one of them to bring an action of division, or of division and sale.[6]

This right does not exist in the case of joint owners [1] because they, as a group, have a single title to the lands and no one of them has any individual title to any share thereof.

Jurisdiction

Both the Court of Session and the sheriff court of the district wherein is situated the property in dispute have jurisdiction. If the value of the subject exceeds £50 per annum, or £1,000 in all, either party, if the action is brought in the sheriff court, may, at the closing of the record or within six days thereafter, require the cause to be remitted to the Court of Session.[7]

Title to sue

Any owner in common may raise the action, and cannot be required to show cause for doing so.[8] He may do so whether his right is beneficial or in trust and, in the latter case, whether or not he has power to sell, the sale in this case not being a sale but the exercise of an administrative power.[9] Trustees holding heritage cannot bring an action along with some

1 For the difference between joint owners and owners in common see *Banff Mags.* v. *Ruthin Castle*, 1944 S.C. 36, 68; Walker, *Principles of Scottish Private Law*, II, 1260.
2 *Morrison* v. *Kirk*, 1912 S.C. 44.
3 *Thom* v. *Macbeth* (1875) 3 R. 161; *Morrison, supra*, 48.
4 Stair, I, 16, 4; IV, 3, 12; Ersk. III, 3, 56; III, 8, 13; Bell, *Prin.* § 1079; *Rankine on Land-ownership*, 591; Bell, *Conveyancing* II, 831; *Milligan* v. *Barnhill* (1782) Mor. 2486; *Bryden* v. *Gibson* (1837) 15 S. 486; *Brock* v. *Hamilton* (1852) 19 D. 701; *Grant* v. *Heriot's Trust* (1906) 8 F. 647.
5 *Morrison, supra*, 47.
6 *Grant, supra*, 658.
7 Sheriff Courts (Scotland) Act 1907, s. 5.
8 *Frizell* v. *Thomson* (1860) 22 D. 1176.
9 *Craig* v. *Fleming* (1863) 1 M. 612.

of the beneficiaries against the other beneficiaries unless the trust has failed and the trustees are entitled to be quit of it, their remedy being an application under the Trusts Acts for power to sell.[10]

Defenders

All the other owners in common must be called as defenders.[11]

Procedure

It is usual to remit to a man of skill to recommend a scheme of division, which may be effected by disposition or under the Conveyancing Act 1874, s. 35. Where sale is expedient or necessary, it is common to appoint the sale to proceed at the sight of the Clerk of Court on articles of roup to be adjusted at his sight. Power to the owners in common to bid at the sale may be reserved.[12] In the articles of roup the proprietors in common should be taken bound to execute dispositions necessary to give effect to the sale, and it is possible to include a conclusion for adjudication of the subjects to the purchaser, thereby ensuring him a good title.[13] Sale by private bargain is permissible subject to a minimum price being fixed by an independent valuator.[14]

The price, under deduction of expenses, is consigned in bank in name of the Clerk of Court, and the sale reported to the court. On the report being approved the pursuer is found entitled to his expenses and decree granted dividing the balance among the parties and authorising payment to them. The Clerk of Court is ordained to deliver the disposition to the purchaser. If any party refuses to execute the necessary disposition the court may authorise the Clerk of Court to do so in his stead.[15]

In such an action a claim for rent by non-possessing co-owners may be a good set-off against a claim for outlays made by a co-owner who has been in possession.[16]

Absent persons

Where one of two or more *pro indiviso* proprietors of heritable estate has disappeared and not been heard of for seven years or upwards, and the other proprietor or proprietors desire to sell the estate, he or they may petition the court which may authorise him or them to sell the estate by public roup or private bargain, and the title granted by him or them under such authority shall be as good and valid to the purchaser as if the absent person had been a party to the sale and conveyance, and the share of the

[10] *Kennedy and Tullis* v. *Maltmen of Glasgow* (1885) 12 R. 1026.
[11] *Campbell* (1893) 1 S.L.T. 157.
[12] *Thom* v. *Macbeth* (1875) 3 R. 161.
[13] *Campbell* (1893) 1 S.L.T. 157. As to irregularities in the conduct of the roup, see *Goudie* v. *Goudie* (1903) 11 S.L.T. 27.
[14] *Campbells* v. *Murray*, 1972 S.L.T. 249.
[15] *Whyte* v. *Whyte*, 1913, 2 S.L.T. 85; *Lennox*, 1950 S.C. 546. As to expenses see *Reidford* v. *Liston*, 1931 S.L.T. 418.
[16] *Miller* v. *Crichton* (1893) 1 S.L.T. 262.

price belonging to the absent person is to be paid into bank for behoof of such absent person and be deemed to be heritable estate of his and subject to the Act.[17]

In cases of absence not falling within that Act, a factor *loco absentis* may be appointed to the absentee and called as defender in an action of division and sale. In this case the sale has the effect of converting the succession from heritable to moveable.[18]

Moveable property and incorporeal property

Such kinds of property, if held in common, may be divided, or divided and sold, at the instance of any of the proprietors in common.[19]

Division of Commonty

Under the Division of Commonties Act 1695 all commonties [20] excepting the commonties belonging to the king in property or to royal burghs in burgage may be divided at the instance of any having interest by summons raised against all parties concerned before the Court of Session, which is empowered to determine the rights and interests of all parties concerned and to value and divide them according to the value of the rights and interests of the several parties concerned, to divide mosses or to keep them common with free ish and entry thereto. The interest of heritors having right in commonties is to be estimated according to the valuation of their respective lands or properties, and divisions are appointed to be made of that part of the commonty that is next adjacent to each heritor's property.

Jurisdiction

Jurisdiction is conferred by the Act on the Court of Session. It is extended to the sheriff court by the Sheriff Courts (Scotland) Act 1907 s. 5 (3).

Title to sue: defenders

Any one having a right in the commonty may sue for its division. All others having interest must be called as defenders.

Procedure

Investigation of the feasibility [21] and, if so, the mode of division, is normally entrusted by the court to a person of suitable skill. As between commoners the statutory basis for division is the valuation of their

17 Presumption of Life Limitation (Scotland) Act 1891, s. 4.
18 *Macfarlane* v. *Greig* (1895) 22 R. 405.
19 Stair, I, 16, 4; Ersk. III, 3, 56.
20 On commonties generally see *Rankine on Landownership*, 598–608, and older authorities there cited. A common grazing has been held not to be a commonty within the Act: *Macandrew* v. *Crerar*, 1929 S.C. 699.
21 *Cf. Macandrew, supra*, where allocation in terms of the Act was impossible.

respective private lands, and this must apply notwithstanding contrary practice.[22] But in the case of mosses the practice has been to divide according to frontage.[23]

On report being made to the court and approved, decree is granted in terms thereof and may be given effect to by any necessary mutual dispositions, or the decree may be utilised to make up titles to the divided lots under the Conveyancing (Scotland) Act 1874, s. 35.[24] The court will not interfere with the decision of the man of skill in matters of practical detail.[25]

March Fences

The March Dykes Act 1661 enacts that where enclosures fall on the border of any person's inheritance the next adjacent heritor [26] shall be at equal pains and charges in building, ditching and planting that dyke which parteth their inheritance.[27] This Act was intended to apply to landward estates only. It justifies a claim for repayment of half the expense of a march-fence, provided the other heritor had concurred, or at least had been called upon to concur in the expenditure,[28] and applies only where advantage, though not necessarily equal, will accrue to both estates.[29] Failing agreement the court may remit to a man of skill to recommend the mode of fencing and its placing.[30] Under the Act a court has jurisdiction to order a fence to be rebuilt, as well as to be repaired, and in the reconstruction to approve an alteration in the style of the fence which experience has recommended.[31] Where one proprietor has converted his property to a different use requiring a different fence, as from sheep farm to deer forest, the other is still liable for his share of maintenance of the common fence.[32] Though a dyke is a march fence one proprietor may put pipes through it to carry away surface water.[33]

The March Dykes Act 1669 enacts that where the marches are crooked and unequal, whenever any person intends to enclose by a dyke or ditch on the march between his and the contiguous heritor's lands, he may require the sheriff to visit the marches and adjudge parts of each heritor's ground to the other so as may be least to the prejudice of either party,

22 *D. Douglas* v. *Baillie* (1740) Mor. 2474; *Sharp* v. *Carlile* (1748) Mor. 2478.
23 *Campbell* v. *Lord Douglas* (1804) Mor. Commonty, Appx. 4.
24 As to title with right of commonty as a basis for prescription, see *Walker* v. *Miln* (1871) 9 M. 823; see also *Edmonstone* v. *Jeffray* (1886) 13 R. 1038.
25 *Bruce* v. *Bain* (1883) 11 R. 192.
26 The Act cannot be invoked by a crofter, as he is a tenant: *Macdonald* v. *Dalgleish* (1894) 21 R. 900. As between landlord and landholder liability for erecting a march fence falls on the landlord: *Ross* v. *Secretary of State for Scotland* (1953) 41 L.C. 39.
27 See generally Stair II, 3, 75; IV, 27, 2; Ersk. II, 6, 4; IV, 4, 39.
28 *Ord* v. *Ewing* (1738) Mor. 10479; *Secker* v. *Cameron*, 1914 S.C. 354.
29 *E. Peterborough* v. *Garioch* (1784) Mor. 10497; *Pollock* v. *Ewing* (1869) 7 M. 815; *E. Airlie* v. *Farquharson* (1887) 24 S.L.R. 761; *Blackburn* v. *Head* (1904) 11 S.L.T. 521; *Scott* v. *D. Argyll* (1907) 14 S.L.T. 829.
30 *Steel* v. *Steel* (1898) 25 R. 715; *Graham* v. *Irving* (1899) 2 F. 29. As to jurisdiction of Land Court, see *Fraser* v. *Seafield Trs.* (1937) 26 L.C. 34.
31 *Paterson* v. *Macdonald* (1880) 7 R. 958.
32 *Blackburn* v. *Head* (1903) 11 S.L.T. 521.
33 *Aitken* v. *Quarrier's Trs.* (1900) 8 S.L.T. 175.

and to adjust compensation to whichever of them is prejudiced thereby.[34] The visit by the sheriff is obligatory.[35] As under the earlier Act, the objections of lack of common benefit and of expense disproportionate to benefit are relevant.[36] The adjustment of ground involved may be substantial.[37]

[34] *Cf.* Ersk. I, 4, 3; II, 6, 4; Bell, *Prin.* § 958.
[35] *Lord Advocate* v. *Sinclair* (1872) 11 M. 137.
[36] *Cf. E. Cassilis* v. *Paterson*, Feb. 28, 1809, F.C.; *Lord Advocate, supra.*
[37] *Pew* v. *Miller* (1754) Mor. 10484; *E. Kintore* v. *E. Kintore's Trs.* (1886) 13 R. 997.

CHAPTER 72

COMPETING CLAIMS

WHERE two or more parties have claims on a fund or property held by another party, the holder is entitled to obtain judicial authority for paying to one rather than another, or to certain claimants in certain proportions, and to be exonered and discharged of his liability for holding the fund or property, by an action of multiplepoinding. In origin the action was competent only where there was double distress, where two or more arrestments of the fund had been lodged in the hands of the holder, but this has gradually been extended and this form of action is competent wherever there is a double claim to one fund on separate and hostile grounds.[1] " It is not necessary that there should be double diligence to constitute double distress if there are competing claims." [2] The court is more liberal towards the competency of an action raised by a holder of a fund than by a claimant. " We allow an action of multiplepoinding to be brought by a competing party in name of the neutral person, but that is never allowed except where there is double distress in the strict and proper sense of the term. . . . The practice of our courts, however, warrants a much greater latitude in the case of the holder of a fund than in the case of the competitors, and for the reason that the holder of the fund can never raise a direct action, and is not bound to remain a depositary till the day of his death, or till the disputing parties agree to settle their claims. He is entitled to be relieved by means of an action of multiplepoinding after a reasonable time, and accordingly it is a sufficient justification of the institution of the action, and is the criterion of its competency, that the claims intimated make it impossible for the depositary to pay to one of the parties without running the risk of an action at the instance of the other." [3] " There are two competing claimants to funds in the hands of a third party, and that, I think, is enough to make the action competent." [4] " There must, at least, be a fund in neutral custody, a dispute as to the persons entitled to the fund and competing claims made to it, and in general a demand on the holder by one or more of the disputants. But as to the degree of strictness with which these requisites have to be complied with that depends, as the decisions show, on the nature of the fund and the circumstances of the case, and the decision on one question of competency is not of

[1] Bell, *Comm.* II, 276; *Russell* v. *Johnston* (1859) 21 D. 886.

[2] *Winchester* v. *Blakey* (1890) 17 R. 1046, 1048, *per* L.P. Inglis.

[3] *Winchester* v. *Blakey* (1890) 17 R. 1046, 1050, *per* Lord McLaren.

[4] *Commercial Bank* v. *Muir* (1897) 25 R. 219, 231, *per* Lord Adam; *cf.* 223, *per* Lord Kinnear; *Colonial Mutual Life Assce. Socy.* v. *Brown* (1911) 48 S.L.R. 427.

very much value in determining other questions arising in different circumstances." [5]

Actions have frequently been dismissed on the ground that there was no double distress, and that another form of action was the proper one,[6] and even actions by holders seeking exoneration have sometimes been dismissed as incompetent on this ground.[7] A holder has, however, frequently been held entitled to bring a multiplepoinding even where a claim was obviously bad, as otherwise he would be liable to have to defend an unfounded action by that claimant.[8]

The requirement of conflicting claims is not insisted on in the case of trustees, who may raise an action of multiplepoinding, even where there are no claimants at all, to enable them to obtain a judicial discharge, as where they are unable to obtain a discharge from the beneficiaries or where there is doubt as to the identity of all parties entitled in a succession.[9] It has, however, been held incompetent for trustees to bring a multiplepoinding where they sought guidance on the administration of the trust estate but not exoneration and discharge.[10]

It is incompetent for a judicial factor to raise a multiplepoinding merely for his own exoneration and discharge.[11]

A multiplepoinding is also competent as to any part of a fund not disputed or not claimed by others.[12]

Jurisdiction

Jurisdiction is created by the existence of the fund or property in

[5] *Commercial Bank*, *supra*, 221, *per* Lord McLaren.

[6] *e.g. Stewart* v. *Stewart* (1828) 7 S. 145; *Crichton* v. *Irvine* (1836) 14 S. 628; *Crokat* v. *Lord Panmure* (1853) 15 D. 737; *Mitchell* v. *Strachan* (1869) 8 M. 154; *Clark* v. *Campbell* (1873) 1 R. 281; *Campbell* v. *Grant* (1870) 8 M. 988; *Bank of Scotland* v. *Comrie* (1871) 8 S.L.R. 419; *Kydd* v. *Waterson* (1880) 7 R. 884; *Robb's Trs.* v. *Robb* (1880) 7 R. 1049; *Gordon* v. *Gordon* (1894) 32 S.L.R. 355; *Mackenzie's Trs.* v. *Sutherland* (1895) 22 R. 233; *Milne* v. *Louttit's Tr.* (1898) 5 S.L.T. 297; *Glass* v. *Robertson* (1899) 1 F. 391; *Royal Bank* v. *Ellis* (1902) 10 S.L.T. 167; *Richardson* v. *Wilson* (1905) 12 S.L.T. 775; *Johnston* v. *Richardson* (1905) 13 S.L.T. 537; *Commercial Union Assce. Co.* v. *Globe Ins. Co.*, 1916, 1 S.L.T. 343; *French* v. *Hohbach*, 1921, 2 S.L.T. 53.

[7] *Moncrieff* v. *Bethune* (1844) 6 D. 1100; *Dennistoun* v. *Stewart* (1853) 16 D. 154; *Logan* v. *Wilkie* (1855) 17 D. 485; *G.N.S. Ry.* v. *Gauld* (1863) 1 M. 1053; *Mitchell* v. *Strachan* (1869) 8 M. 154; *Connell's Tr.* v. *Chalk* (1878) 5 R. 735; *Mackenzie's Trs.* v. *Sutherland* (1895) 22 R. 233; *Glen's Trs.* v. *Miller*, 1911 S.C. 1178.

[8] *Pollard* v. *Galloway & Nivison* (1881) 9 R. 21; *Dill, Wilson & Muirhead* v. *Ricardo's Tr.* (1885) 12 R. 404; *Royal Bank* v. *Price* (1893) 20 R. 290; *Fraser's Exrx.* v. *Wallace's Trs.* (1893) 20 R. 374; *Commercial Bank* v. *Muir* (1897) 25 R. 219; *Agnew* v. *White* (1899) 1 F. 1026; *Ross* v. *Plano Co.* (1902) 10 S.L.T. 314; *McDowall and Neilson's Tr.* v. *Hagart* (1905) 8 F. 235; *Greenshield's Trs.* v. *Greenshields*, 1915, 2 S.L.T. 189.

[9] *McDougal's Trs.* v. *McDougal* (1830) 8 S. 1036; *Taylor* v. *Noble* (1836) 14 S. 817; *Blair's Trs.* v. *Blair* (1863) 2 M. 284; *Dunbar* v. *Sinclair* (1850) 13 D. 54; *Tait's J.F.* v. *Meikle* (1890) 17 R. 1182; *Davidson* v. *Ewen* (1895) 3 S.L.T. 162; *Paterson's Trs.* v. *Paterson* (1899) 7 S.L.T. 134; *McClement's Trs.* v. *Lord Advocate*, 1949 S.L.T.(Notes) 60; but contrast *Mackenzie's Trs.* v. *Sutherland* (1895) 22 R. 233; *Glen's Trs.* v. *Miller*, 1911 S.C. 1178. *Cf. Connell's Tr.* v. *Chalk* (1878) 5 R. 735.

[10] *Paterson's Trs.* v. *Paterson* (1899) 7 S.L.T. 134.

[11] *Campbell* v. *Grant* (1870) 8 M. 988; contrast *Tait's J.F.* v. *Meikle* (1890) 17 R. 1182.

[12] *Dunn's Trs.* v. *Barstow* (1870) 9 M. 281; *Macnab* v. *Waddell* (1894) 21 R. 827; *Commercial Bank* v. *Muir* (1897) 25 R. 219; *MacGillivray's Trs.* v. *Dallas* (1905) 7 F. 733.

dispute in Scotland,[13] and persons may be parties to a multiplepoinding though not otherwise subject to the jurisdiction of the Scottish courts. Arrestment *ad fundandam jurisdictionem* is unnecessary.[14] The plea of *forum non conveniens* is competent.[15]

Title to sue and to defend

Title to sue is vested in either the holder of the fund, or in any claimant on the fund. The holder is always pursuer in the action and may raise it himself, in which case he is pursuer and real raiser, or it may be raised by a claimant, in which case the holder is designated pursuer and nominal raiser and the claimant is designated defender and real raiser. All who have, or may have, claims on the fund or property are entitled to be called as defenders. Intimation may be ordered to any person thought to have interest, or, more generally, by advertisement.

Necessity for fund in medio

There must be a fund *in medio* [16] and an action is incompetent if there is no debt which the holder is obliged to pay to someone. Thus there can be no multiplepoinding in respect of a right to future rents,[17] or a fund only in expectation,[18] or not yet received.[19]

The amount or value of the fund need not, however, be definitely ascertained, so long as there is a fund. Thus an action has been held competent as to a sum due under contract, though the amount had not been certified by an engineer responsible for granting certificates for work done.[20]

What assets may be fund in medio

The action is appropriate both in the case of funds, such as an intestate estate,[21] moveable property, such as a vehicle,[22] and incorporeal rights, such as the right to an office.[23] Land or other heritable property has been said to be not a proper subject, and competing claims to land might be decided in some other kind of process, though title to land has been decided in such an action [24] and the right to title deeds has been decided

13 *Mansfield, Ramsay & Co.* v. *Smith, Wright & Gray* (1795) Mor. 2594; *Cameron* v. *Chapman* (1838) 16 S. 907; *Bell* v. *Stewart* (1852) 14 D. 837; *Crockart* v. *Dundee & Arbroath Ry.* (1852) 15 D. 202.
14 *Miller* v. *Ure* (1838) 16 S. 1204.
15 *Okell* v. *Foden* (1884) 11 R. 906; *French* v. *Hohbach*, 1921, 2 S.L.T. 53.
16 *Nimmo* v. *Murray* (1863) 1 M. 791; *Richardson* v. *Wilson* (1905) 12 S.L.T. 775.
17 *Pentland* v. *Royal Exchange Assce. Co.* (1830) 9 S. 164.
18 *Provan* v. *Provan* (1840) 2 D. 298; *cf. Allardice* v. *Lautour* (1845) 7 D. 362; *Nimmo* v. *Murray* (1863) 1 M. 791.
19 *Anderson* v. *Cameron's Trs.* (1844) 17 Sc.Jur. 42.
20 *Highland Ry.* v. *British Linen Co.* (1901) 38 S.L.R. 584.
21 *Taylor* v. *Noble* (1836) 14 S. 817; *Blair's Trs.* v. *Blair* (1863) 2 M. 284.
22 *e.g. MacLeod* v. *Kerr*, 1965 S.C. 253.
23 *Cattanach* v. *Hamilton Gordon* (1744) Mor. 12253.
24 *Logan* v. *Byres* (1895) 2 S.L.T. 455; *Edinburgh Merchant Maiden Hospital* v. *Greig's Exors.* (1902) 10 S.L.T. 317; *Boyd's Trs.* v. *Boyd* (1906) 13 S.L.T. 878; see also *Dunn's Trs.* v. *Barstow* (1870) 9 M. 281.

in a multiplepoinding,[25] and the right to demand a conveyance of property, heritable or moveable, may be determined in a multiplepoinding.[26] In another case [27] the fund *in medio* consisted of heritage but the Lord Ordinary found that it was to be regarded and dealt with as moveable succession.

Only the part of the land which is in dispute may be made the fund *in medio* in the action; it is incompetent to bring the whole fund into court.[28] A claimant has been allowed to lodge objections to the holder's condescendence of the fund *in medio*.[29]

What may be decided in multiplepoinding

In the course of a multiplepoinding there may be discussed and decided all questions necessary for the decision of the main issue, to whom the fund *in medio* truly belongs. Deeds may be construed and upheld as valid,[30] or reduced,[31] and a decree in absence set aside *ope exceptionis* [32]; it may be decided whether deeds sealed up should be opened and put on record,[33] to whom a bond should be delivered,[34] whether and when an absentee had died,[35] and which party was entitled to the possession of some timber.[37] The question may be raised of the construction of a decree in the circumstances in which it was obtained,[38] or of the priority of decrees against the holder.[39]

A multiplepoinding has been preferred to an action of count, reckoning and payment as a means of determining a question of vesting between trustees and beneficiaries.

The claims

No claim can be lodged until an order for claims is made.[40] A mere random claim on a fund does not entitle a party to bring an action of multiplepoinding, but on the other hand a claim need not be for a determinate sum; it may be, for example, for a determinate part of an estate. Claims must be " real and intelligible claims upon a fund *in medio* set forth upon grounds which may or may not be well founded in law, but which are at least stated with sufficient precision to show that there is in

25 *Baillie* v. *Baillie* (1830) 8 S. 318.
26 *Campbell* v. *E. Craufurd* (1783) Mor. 3973.
27 *Cowan's Trs.* v. *Cowan* (1888) 16 R. 7.
28 *Macnab* v. *Waddell* (1894) 21 R. 827; *MacGillivray's Trs.* v. *Dallas* (1905) 7 F. 733.
29 *Donaldson's Tr.* v. *Beattie*, 1914, 1 S.L.T. 170.
30 *Ogilvy's Trs.* v. *Chevallier* (1874) 1 R. 693; but see *French* v. *Hohbach*, 1921, 2 S.L.T. 53.
31 More's Notes to Stair, 378; *Logan* v. *Byres* (1895) 2 S.L.T. 455; *Macfarlane* v. *Macfarlane*, 1947 S.L.T.(Notes) 34.
32 *Jarvie's Trs.* v. *Bannatyne*, 1927 S.C. 34.
33 *Logan* v. *Logan* (1823) 2 S. 253.
34 *Ramsay* v. *Maule* (1828) 6 S. 343.
35 *Tait's J.F.* v. *Meikle* (1890) 17 R. 1182; *Davidson* v. *Ewen* (1895) 3 S.L.T. 162; but contrast *Clark's Exor.* v. *Clark*, 1953 S.L.T.(Notes) 59.
37 *McDowall & Neilson's Tr.* v. *Hagart* (1905) 8 F. 235.
38 *Commercial Bank* v. *Muir* (1897) 25 R. 219, 222.
39 *Girvan and Portpatrick Ry.* v. *Lamond* (1886) 13 R. 931.
40 *Connell* v. *Ferguson* (1861) 23 D. 683.

truth a double claim upon one fund maintained by persons having hostile interests." [41]

The practice has been said to be [42] that where a claim is illiquid it must be constituted, and the claimant may put in a decree of constitution as the basis of his claim.

A contingent claim may be sufficient to make a multiplepoinding competent; thus the mother of an illegitimate child gave money by donation *mortis causa* to another who brought a multiplepoinding to determine who was entitled to the money; multiplepoinding was held competent in that the child would have a claim on the sum for aliment in the event of his mother's executry funds being exhausted.[43]

A party who has not been cited nor received notice of the dependence of the action has sometimes been allowed to lodge a claim even after final judgment, provided the funds are still *in manibus curiae*, on payment of expenses.[44]

An unsuccessful claimant has on occasion been allowed to tender a fresh claim on the fund on a new ground even after judgment in the Inner House, but only on payment of expenses.[45] Once an interlocutor ranking and preferring one or more particular claimants has become final a fresh claim cannot be admitted.[46]

Ranking and preference

After hearing parties the court ranks and prefers certain claimants in terms of their claims, or to a specified extent, and orders payment or delivery to the person or persons preferred. Decerniture for payment or delivery secures the holder of the fund, after payment or delivery, against any further claims at the instance of parties called in the action.[47] Once a decree preferring particular claimants has become final, the only remedy open to a person cited as a defender [48] is to bring a reduction of the decree, and where payment had been made, the only remedy is an action against the party who has received payment, the holder of the fund being no longer liable.[49]

The court may rank and prefer a claimant or claimants " for aught yet seen " where another claim may yet be substantiated, and may also rank a claimant subject to a declaration that in the event of the other possible

[41] *Commercial Bank* v. *Muir* (1897) 25 R. 219, 222, *per* Lord Kinnear.

[42] *Ibid.* 222, *per* Lord McLaren.

[43] *Royal Bank* v. *Livie* (1903) 11 S.L.T. 549.

[44] *Morgan* v. *Morris* (1856) 18 D. 797; 3 Macq. 347.

[45] *Ferguson's Trs.* v. *Hamilton* (1862) 4 Macq. 397; *Dymond* v. *Scott* (1877) 5 R. 196; *Binnie's Trs.* v. *Henry's Trs.* (1883) 10 R. 1075; but contrast *Morgan, supra*; *Wilson's Trs.* v. *Clydesdale Bank* (1900) 8 S.L.T. 68; *Landale* v. *Wilson* (1900) 2 F. 1047; *Terrell* v. *Kerr* (1900) 2 F. 1055; *National Bank* v. *Campbell* (1901) 4 F. 17; *Ramsay's J.F.* v. *B.L. Bank*, 1911 S.C. 832.

[46] *Landale, supra*; *Ramsay's J.F., supra.*

[47] Stair IV, 6, 3; Ersk. IV, 3, 25.

[48] *Morgan* v. *Morris* (1856) 18 D. 797; (1858) 3 Macq. 347; *Stodart* v. *Bell* (1860) 22 D. 1092.

[49] *Geikie* v. *Morris* (1858) 3 Macq. 353.

claim being established he should be bound to repay.[50] An order for payment will not be pronounced if the claims could be defeated by a claim by an absent person.[51] Thus in one case [52] claimants whose existence had been unknown were discovered four years later and a fresh record was made up. An interlocutor "for aught yet seen" is conclusive against claimants called in the action, but not against others who may be reponed against it, sometimes without payment of expenses.[53]

No decree for exoneration and discharge of any judicial factor appointed to manage a trust estate may issue until there is lodged a certificate by the proper officer of the Inland Revenue that all duty payable to the Inland Revenue has been paid.[54] This rule must be strictly observed.[55]

Reduction of decrees of preference

A decree preferring a particular claimant and ordering payment to him is reducible. A person not called in the action may reduce the decree if he adduces a preferable claim. By the Decrees in Absence Act 1584 (c. 10) a person expressly called in a multiplepoinding may bring a reduction of the decree if he can show reasonable cause for his absence from the original competition. A party may also reduce the decree if at that time he was a minor without curator.[56]

Riding claim

A riding claim is a claim lodged which is dependent on another claim made by another party, who is debtor to the party making the riding claim.[57] A riding claim must be lodged before the original claimant has obtained and extracted a decree for payment,[58] but may be lodged after judgment in the Inner House.[59] It must be constituted and liquid.[60]

A claim validly constituted by decree is not enforceable against a trustee in sequestration by way of riding claim to the effect of giving the holder a preference not otherwise competent to him.[61]

A pursuer and real raiser may, in a condescendence of the fund *in medio* lodged after claimants had been ranked by final interlocutor, state any claim of retention or compensation which he has against a claimant who has been ranked and preferred.[62]

50 *Union Bank* v. *Gracie* (1887) 25 S.L.R. 61.
51 *Kerr's Tr.* (1894) 2 S.L.T. 10.
52 *Ganden's Tr.* v. *Jamieson* (1902) 10 S.L.T. 326.
53 *Johnston* v. *Elder* (1832) 10 S. 195; *Morgan* v. *Morris* (1856) 18 D. 797; *Geikie* v. *Morris* (1858) 3 Macq. 347, 358.
54 R.C. 36.
55 *Simpson's Trs.* v. *Fox*, 1954 S.L.T.(Notes) 12.
56 *Stodart* v. *Bell* (1860) 22 D. 1092.
57 *Gill's Trs.* v. *Patrick* (1889) 16 R. 403.
58 *Anglo-Foreign Banking Co.* (1879) 16 S.L.R. 731; *Scottish Life Assurance Co.* v. *Donald* (1902) 9 S.L.T. 348.
59 *Scottish Life Assce. Co., supra*; *Ramsay's J.F., supra.*
60 *Home's Trs.* v. *Ralston's Trs.* (1834) 12 S. 727; *Royal Bank* v. *Stevenson* (1849) 12 D. 250; *Wilson* v. *Young* (1851) 13 D. 1366.
61 *Thomson* v. *Friese-Greene's Tr.*, 1944 S.C. 336.
62 *Ramsay's J.F.* v. *B.L. Bank*, 1912 S.C. 206.

Effect of action on diligence

The object of a multiplepoinding is to resolve conflicts of diligence, and no person who has claimed or appeared in an action, once raised, may use personal diligence against the holder of the fund.[63] Diligence by a person who has not appeared in the action may be suspended. The fund itself in the hands of the holder becomes litigious by the raising of the action, so that the holder may not grant any voluntary conveyance of it to anyone else.[64] But diligence against the fund is not precluded, nor rendered unnecessary, by the raising of a multiplepoinding.[64] " A multiplepoinding does not stop the race of diligence. . . ." [65] A claim in a multiplepoinding has by itself no effect as diligence. A person not a party to the action may proceed with every diligence that can operate against the fund, and even a party to the action may do diligence to acquire a preference.[66] A poinding creditor may proceed to a sale of the poinded effects notwithstanding another creditor's arrestments and a multiplepoinding raised by the debtor.[67]

63 *White* v. *Brown* (1772) Mor. 9133.
64 Bell, *Comm.* II, 278; *Smith's Trs.* v. *Grant* (1862) 24 D. 1142, 1168.
65 *Smith's Trs., supra,* 1173, *per* Lord Deas.
66 Bell, *Comm.* II, 279.
67 *Ferguson* v. *Bothwell* (1882) 9 R. 687.

CHAPTER 73

INDEMNITY PROVISIONS AND RELIEF

Indemnity provisions

It is competent to provide in a contract that if, arising out of the performance thereof, one party incurs legal liability of a stated kind, or on stated legal grounds, to a third party the other party will indemnify the party held primarily liable. Thus it is common to take a contractor bound to indemnify his employer against claims brought against the employer arising out of accidents to the contractor's workmen or third parties, occurring during the execution of the contractor's work.

Whether an indemnity clause applies to a particular claim is a question of interpretation.[1] Such a clause should normally be interpreted in a way which gives it business efficacy.[2] It may require indemnification against expenses of process incurred in defending claims,[3] against breaches of common law duty, or breaches of statutory duty, or both, by the employer.

Apart from express contractual provision for indemnity a party who has to pay damages, or even to defend an action for damages brought against him, may be able to make a claim against another party who is, he contends, the real cause of his having been sued or held liable, either by way of action of relief or of action for damages for breach of contract.

Indemnity by action of relief

In an action of relief a party seeks to be relieved of or indemnified against certain payments which he has had to make to a third party. The classic case is of the cautioner who has to pay the creditor and now seeks relief against the principal debtor.[4] To assist him in working out his relief he is entitled, if he makes payment in full, to an assignation of the debt from the creditor.[5] Similarly one cautioner who has to pay is entitled to relief against a co-cautioner.[6]

The principle has been extended to cases where one person, such as an employer, has been held liable to injured persons in damages for fault which, though his by rule of law, was in truth and in fact that of another, such as another employee, or an independent contractor employed by him. The original claim, and the claim of relief, must be at least substantially

[1] See *e.g. Hansens Rederi A/S* v. *Donside Paper Co.*, 1927 S.N. 120; *Hamilton* v. *Anderson*, 1953 S.C. 129; *North of Scotland Hydro-Electric Board* v. *Taylor*, 1956 S.C. 1; *McGill* v. *Pirie & Co. (Paisley) Ltd.*, 1967 S.L.T. 152; *McKay* v. *Balfour, Beatty & Co.*, 1967 S.L.T. (Notes) 15.

[2] *Hamilton, supra*; *McGill, supra*; *McKay, supra.*

[3] *e.g. McGill, supra.*

[4] Bell, *Prin.* § 255.

[5] *Cf. Ewart* v. *Latta* (1865) 3 M.(H.L.) 36.

[6] *Marshall* v. *Pennycook*, 1908 S.C. 276.

commensurate and founded on the same kind of liability.[7] The person paying has no claim to relief if he has compromised the claims or otherwise settled them ultroneously and not had them constituted by decree against him.[8] It is logically inconsistent to settle a pursuer's claim and simultaneously to contend that a third party was solely liable for it. But a party sued may in consideration of a sum of money obtain an assignation of the pursuer's claim against him and make that the basis of a claim against the third party whom he alleges to be solely responsible.[9] If the assignation is taken by one co-delinquent to enable him to sue another the amount paid for the assignation becomes important, and whether it was the price paid for the assignation or was a sum paid by way of damages or compensation.[10] If the latter, the sum paid must be taken into account in any claim by the injured person against any delinquent still defending the action.

An action of relief has been dismissed as premature where the pursuer averred only that he was being sued and not that he was liable, or had been held liable, to the third party.[11]

Indemnity by action of damages for breach of contract

Where one party has supplied to another goods which are defective and in breach of contract and, by reason of the defect, a third party suffers loss or injury the second party is entitled to recover from the first the damages paid by him (second party) to the third party, and judicial expenses incurred in defending the claim, as being losses arising naturally and directly, and not too remotely, from the first party's breach of contract.[12] Thus in *Buchanan & Carswell* v. *Eugene Ltd.*,[13] E supplied to B a hair-drying machine which was defective and caused P to receive an electric shock. P recovered damages from B, who then sued E for damages for breach of the Sale of Goods Act 1893, s. 14 (1). B was held to have a relevant claim for recovering the damages paid to P, interest thereon, judicial expenses awarded to P, and judicial expenses incurred in defending P's claim. In any such claim it is essential to establish that the defect be one for which the first party was liable and not one arising, *e.g.* from misuse or faulty maintenance of a thing which, as supplied, was sound. Thus a driver, held liable in damages to a pedestrian injured by his vehicle, may have a claim of relief if the accident were caused by defect in the vehicle, but not if caused by bad driving or lack of maintenance.

Relief against joint delinquents—common law

At common law joint delinquents were jointly and severally liable and

7 *Colt* v. *Caledonian Ry.* (1859) 21 D. 1108; *Weems* v. *Mathieson* (1861) 4 Macq. 215.

8 *Ovington* v. *McVicar* (1864) 2 M. 1066; *Gardiner* v. *Main* (1894) 22 R. 100; *cf. N.C.B.* v. *Thomson*, 1959 S.C. 353; see also *Duncan's Trs.* v. *Steven* (1897) 24 R. 880; *Henry* v. *Gladstone*, 1934 S.C.(H.L.) 43, 47.

9 *Gardiner*, *supra*, 104.

10 *Cole-Hamilton* v. *Boyd*, 1963 S.C.(H.L.) 1, 14, 18.

11 *Duncan's Trs.* v. *Steven* (1897) 24 R. 880.

12 See *e.g. Wood* v. *Mackay* (1906) 8 F. 625; *Baxter* v. *Boswell* (1899) 6 S.L.T. 278.

13 1936 S.C. 160. See also *Scouller* v. *Robertson* (1829) 7 S. 344; *Mansfield* v. *Campbell* (1836) 14 S. 585; *Houldsworth* v. *B.L. Co.* (1850) 13 D. 376; *Brand* v. *Bell's Trs.* (1872) 11 M. 42.

any wrongdoer who was sued and paid the pursuer's claim had a right of relief against the co-delinquents *pro rata, i.e.* for an equal share, where the claim was founded on negligence but not where it was founded on any kind of fraud or moral delinquency.[14] If action was not brought against all co-delinquents the one held liable might claim relief *pro rata* by establishing that another was or others were also in part responsible for the harm to the pursuer.

Relief against joint delinquent under statute

Where in an action of damages for loss arising from delict two or more parties are held jointly and severally liable in damages or expenses, they are liable *inter se* to contribute to such damages or expenses in such proportions as the jury or the court, as the case may be, may deem just.[15] Nothing in this provision is to affect the right of the pursuer to obtain a joint and several decree against the defenders found liable.[15] The jury or court may fix the respective liabilities of the defenders in such percentages or proportions as they think fit.[16] Accordingly the pursuer may recover all of his award from any one defender and leave that one to recover the due proportion from the other or others. No action to recover a contribution by virtue of this right may be brought after two years from the date on which the right to recover contribution accrued[17]; this will normally be the date when the joint and several decree, with allocation of responsibility, passes against the defenders.

Where two or more defenders are sued one defender may insist on the other defenders, though assoilzied at first instance, remaining parties to the cause at the stage of appeal to keep open the possibility of apportioning liability.[18]

Relief against other party who might have been sued

Where any person has paid any damages or expenses in which he has been found liable in any action of damages for delict, he is entitled to recover from any other person who, if sued, might also have been held liable in respect of the loss or damage on which the action was founded, such contribution, if any, as the court may deem just.[19] In this case also a claim for contribution must now be brought within two years.[20]

This subsection deals with the case where only one of several possible joint wrongdoers is sued, so that no question of a joint and several decree arises. But the defender, if held liable, contends that another party should

14 *Palmer* v. *Wick and Pulteneytown S.S. Co. Ltd.* (1894) 21 R.(H.L.) 39.
15 Law Reform (Miscellaneous Provisions) (Scotland) Act 1940, s. 3 (1). For an exceptional case on expenses see *Williamson* v. *McPherson*, 1951 S.C. 438.
16 On the basis of apportionment see *The Miraflores and the Abadesa* [1967] 1 A.C. 826.
17 Prescription and Limitation (Scotland) Act 1973, s. 20. See further *Central S.M.T. Co.* v. *Lanarkshire C.C.*, 1949 S.C. 450.
18 *Davidson* v. *North of Scotland Hydro-Electric Board*, 1954 S.C. 230, explaining *McDermott* v. *Western S.M.T. Co.*, 1937 S.C. 239 as superseded by the 1940 Act.
19 Law Reform (Miscellaneous Provisions) (Scotland) Act 1940, s. 3 (2).
20 Prescription and Limitation (Scotland) Act, 1973, s. 20.

have been sued and, if sued, might also have been held liable, and should therefore bear part of the weight of the award.[21] In such a claim it is essential that the claimant's liability to the injured person was constituted by decree and not arrived at by compromise or agreement.[22]

This kind of case is now less likely to arise since it is now competent [23] for a defender sued to serve a " third-party notice " on, and thus bring in, as second defender, any other party who, he contends, should also have been sued and might have been held liable jointly and severally. It is competent to impute sole fault to the third party, or joint fault of the defender and the third party.[24] Third-party procedure does not entitle the pursuer to a decree against a defender against whom he has directed no conclusion.[25] If a pursuer has sued two defenders jointly and severally and has abandoned the action against one, who is accordingly assoilzied, it is incompetent for the other defender to serve a third party notice and seek to bring that defender back into the process so as to recover a contribution from him under section 3 (2).[26]

It has been held that, *quoad* the third party, such an action is an action of relief by the defender first called and not affected by the limitation of time for suing introduced by the Law Reform (Limitation of Actions, etc.) Act 1954, s. 6 (now Prescription and Limitation (Scotland) Act, 1973, s. 17).[27]

Relief against other party on other grounds

The rights of relief under the Law Reform (Miscellaneous Provisions) (Scotland) Act 1940, s. 3, do not (3) affect any contractual or other right of relief or indemnity or render enforceable any agreement for indemnity which could not have been enforced if section 3 had not been enacted. Opinions have been expressed to the effect that " other right of relief " does [28] and does not [29] include the common law right of relief declared in *Palmer* v. *Wick and Pulteneytown S.S. Co. Ltd.*[30]

The provisions of the 1940 Act are applicable in actions involving the Crown.[31]

21 *Glasgow Corpn.* v. *Turnbull*, 1932 S.L.T. 457.
22 *N.C.B.* v. *Thomson*, 1959 S.C. 353.
23 R.C. 85. Formerly only a pursuer could, by amendment, bring in another party as second defender.
24 *Beedie* v. *Norrie*, 1966 S.C. 207.
25 *Aitken* v. *Norrie*, 1966 S.C. 168.
26 *Travers* v. *Neilson*, 1967 S.C. 155.
27 *Findlay* v. *N.C.B.*, 1965 S.L.T. 328; *Aitken* v. *Norrie*, 1966 S.C. 168; *Travers, supra.*
28 *N.C.B.* v. *Thomson*, 386, *per* Lord Strachan.
29 *N.C.B., supra*, 372, *per* Lord Patrick.
30 (1894) 21 R.(H.L.) 39.
31 Crown Proceedings Act 1947, ss. 4 (2), 43 (*b*).

Chapter 74

REMEDIES ANCILLARY TO PROCEDURE

Erskine [1] lists as " accessory actions which do not subsist by themselves, but merely prepare the way for, or are subservient to, other actions " those of exhibition of writings, of transumpts, of proving the tenor, of transference, and of wakening. Of these, transference and wakening are now effected by minute and action is unnecessary.

Exhibition

An action of exhibition, based on a right of property in deeds libelled, may be insisted on by the proprietor against everyone who holds the deeds in his custody, to have them delivered to him, to be used as his own property.[2] Such is the action of exhibition *ad deliberandum*, to enable an heir to decide whether or not to make up title, which is a substantive or principal action rather than one ancillary to procedure. Where in such an action the court is satisfied that the titles called for should be produced, the proper course is to ordain them to be exhibited in the hands of the clerk of court.[3] The exhibition of deeds held by a third party, incidentally to an action, can be obtained by commission and diligence granted in the action, and action is unnecessary unless the court hearing the action has no power to order production of documents.[4]

Transumpt

An action of transumpt is competent to any person who has a partial interest in a writing, or immediate use for it to support his titles or defences in other actions, against him in whose custody the writing lies, to exhibit it, so that a transumpt thereof may be judicially made out and delivered to the pursuer. The transumpts or copies are, by the court's decree, declared to bear as full faith and credit as an extract from the record of the court.[5] The action is probably still competent, but will not be allowed where the same result can be obtained in any other way.[6]

Proving the tenor

An action of proving of the tenor may be brought by itself, or as accessory to and for the purposes of another action. It is the action by

1 IV, 1, 52.
2 Stair, I, 7, 14; Ersk. IV, 1, 52.
3 *Clark* v. *Melville* (1880) 8 R. 81.
4 *Campbell* v. *Campbell* (1869) 7 M. 759, 762.
5 Stair, IV, 31, 5; Ersk. IV, 1, 53.
6 *Selkirk* v. *Service* (1880) 8 R. 29, 30.

which the tenor or substance of a writing which is lost or destroyed is sought to be established.[7] It is competent only in the Court of Session.[8] It is incompetent to set up incidentally in the course of an action the tenor of a document founded on as the basis of the action,[9] though a pursuer has been allowed to establish incidentally the contents of a less important document.[10] The writings may be private or judicial, such as a decree,[11] or public documents,[12] or deeds in public.[13]

Proving the tenor has been said to be inappropriate where a deed has been found in the repositories of a deceased person in a cancelled state, since the question whether the cancellation has destroyed the deed or whether the deed can be restored to full effect against the cancellation is unsuitable for such a process.[14] Proving the tenor is, however, appropriate where the deed was extant in the state in which it was executed and has subsequently been obliterated or cancelled.[15]

The pursuer must libel the *casus amissionis* or accident whereby the deed came to be lost or destroyed. In deeds which are normally in the custody of the grantee, or require renunciations or discharges to extinguish them, a general *casus amissionis* is sufficient, and it may suffice to allege that the deed was lost by accident or mischance.[16] But where the deed embodied an obligation extinguishable by the debtor's destruction or cancellation of it, a special *casus amissionis* must be proved, showing exactly how the deed was lost.[17] The sufficiency of the *casus amissionis* varies according to the nature and purpose of the writ.[18]

In *Winchester* v. *Smith* [19] it was laid down that it was incumbent on the pursuer not only to prove that such a writing as is libelled existed and that it was expressed in the terms alleged, but that it had been lost or destroyed in some way which did not affect its validity, and that if it be such a writing as is usually cancelled or destroyed when it has served its purpose, such as a bill, promissory note or personal bond, and it has been destroyed or lost, the presumption is that the right which it evidenced no longer subsists,

7 Ersk. IV, 1, 54.

8 *Walker* v. *Nisbet*, 1915 S.C. 639; *Dunbar* v. *Scottish County Investment Co. Ltd.*, 1920 S.C. 210.

9 *Gordon* v. *Robertson* (1873) 11 S.L.R. 35; *Shaw* v. *Shaw's Trs.* (1876) 3 R. 813; *Gilchrist* v. *Morrison* (1891) 18 R. 599; *Steele* v. *Law* (1895) 3 S.L.T. 190; *Walker, supra.*

10 *Maxwell* v. *Reid* (1863) 1 M. 932; *Young* v. *Thomson*, 1909 S.C. 529; see also *Wilson* v. *Leckie* (1870) 7 S.L.R. 563; *Mackinnon's Tr.* v. *Bank of Scotland*, 1915 S.C. 411; *Elliott* v. *Galpern*, 1927 S.C. 29; *Simpson's Trs.* v. *Simpson*, 1933 S.N. 22.

11 *D. Argyle* v. *McLean* (1781) Mor. 15828.

12 *Sanquhar Mags.* v. *Officers of State* (1864) 2 M. 499.

13 *Richmond* v. *Officers of State* (1869) 7 M. 956; *Browne* v. *Orr* (1872) 10 M. 397; *D. Argyll* v. *Campbell* (1873) 11 M. 611.

14 *Winchester* v. *Smith* (1863) 1 M. 685, 697, 699. See also *Anderson* v. *Boyd* (1827) 5 S. 927; *Dow* v. *Dow* (1848) 10 D. 1465.

15 *Falconer* v. *Stephen* (1849) 11 D. 1338.

16 Stair, IV, 32, 4; Ersk., *supra*; *cf. Brodie* v. *Brodie* (1901) 4 F. 132 (bond of annuity); *Cullen's Exor.* v. *Elphinstone*, 1948 S.C. 662 (will).

17 Stair, IV, 32, 3; Ersk., *supra*; *Carson* v. *McMicken*, May 14, 1811, F.C. (bill of exchange); *McFarlane* v. *McNee* (1826) 4 S. 509 (bill of exchange); *Smith* v. *Ferguson* (1882) 9 R. 866 (marriage-contract).

18 *Clyde* v. *Clyde*, 1958 S.C. 343.

19 (1863) 1 M. 685 (mutual will—signatures cancelled).

and very clear evidence is necessary to overcome the presumption.[20] It has several times been held that if a will in the testator's own custody is missing it must be presumed destroyed *animo revocandi.*[21]

The whole contents of the deed must be libelled,[22] with all limitations, provisos and qualifications, otherwise a right might be created of a quite different nature or extent from that which is lost.

The tenor or substance of the lost writing may be proved by the oath of the granter, or by writing, or by parole evidence. In the last case, the pursuer should, normally, produce some adminicle in writing, such as a draft or copy or acknowledgement.[23] In personal obligations, where a special *casus amissionis* is proved, such as theft or fire, adminicles in writing are dispensed with. Where the nature of the deed is such that no adminicle is to be expected the court will allow proof without averment of adminicles,[24] though their absence must be accounted for.[25]

By the Hornings Act 1579 the tenor of letters of horning and their executions, if lost and never judicially produced, cannot be proved by witnesses, but this does not seem to exclude proof by written adminicles.[26] Apart from this the tenor may be proved of any writing.

The effect of decree is to revive the lost deed with the same force and effect as the original, and subject to the same challenges as the original.[27]

20 *Cf. Mackinnon's Tr., supra.*

21 *Bonthrone* v. *Ireland* (1883) 10 R. 779; *Clyde* v. *Clyde*, 1958 S.C. 343; contrast *Young* v. *Anderson* (1904) 7 F. 128.

22 *Cf. Rannie* v. *Ogg* (1891) 18 R. 903, where the pursuer failed to prove the tenor of the testing clause.

23 *e.g. Cunningham* v. *Mouat's Trs.* (1851) 13 D. 1376; *McLeod* v. *Leslie* (1865) 3 M. 840; *Richmond* v. *Officers of State* (1869) 7 M. 956. In *Symington's J.F.* v. *Symington*, 1947 S.L.T.(Notes) 40 a photostat copy was produced. In *Borland* v. *Andrew's J.F.* (1901) 4 F. 129 parole evidence without written adminicles was in the circumstances accepted.

24 *Winton* v. *Thomson* (1862) 24 D. 1094. *Cf.* Stair, IV, 32, 7; Ersk. IV, 1, 55.

25 *Graham* v. *Graham* (1847) 10 D. 45; *Ross* v. *Mellis* (1871) 10 M. 197; *Thomson* v. *Dunlop* (1884) 11 R. 453.

26 Ersk. IV, 1, 58.

27 Ersk. IV, 1, 59.

CHAPTER 75

EXCLUSION, LIMITATION AND PRESCRIPTION OF CLAIMS FOR REMEDIES

A REMEDY prima facie competent may be precluded for various reasons, particularly by statutory provision excluding it in certain circumstances or allowing it only subject to certain conditions, or limiting the time within which the claim may be brought, or excluding it entirely by reason of lapse of time.

EXCLUSION PROVISIONS

Under the Vexatious Actions (Scotland) Act 1898 the court has power to make an order prohibiting the initiation without the leave of a Lord Ordinary of any actions by a pursuer if they are believed to be frivolous, vexatious or ill-founded.[1]

The Department of Health for Scotland and local authorities are not liable in damages for any irregularity committed by their officers in the execution of the Act, or for anything done by themselves in the bona fide execution of this Act; and every officer acting in the bona fide execution of the Act is to be indemnified by the local authority for costs, liabilities and charges to which he may be subjected.[1a]

The above provision applies also in relation to National Health Service authorities and Health boards.[2] The limitation of time for suing in each case has been repealed.

An officer of a local authority is not personally liable in respect of any act done by him in the execution or purported execution of the Food and Drugs Act 1938, if he did that act in the honest belief that his duty under the Act required or entitled him to do it. This does not relieve the authority.[3]

By the Summary Jurisdiction (Scotland) Act 1954, s. 75,

1 *L.A.* v. *Arnold,* 1951 S.C. 256; *cf. Att. Gen.* v. *Chaffers* (1897) 76 L.T. 351; *Re Jones* (1902) 18 T.L.R. 476; *Re Boaler* [1915] 1 K.B. 21.

1a Public Health (Scotland) Act 1897, s. 166. See *Gillilan* v. *Lanarkshire C.C.* (1902) 9 S.L.T. 432; *Duncan* v. *Hamilton Mags.* (1902) 5 F. 160; *Baker* v. *Glasgow Corpn.*, 1916 S.C. 199; *Brash* v. *Peebles Mags.*, 1926 S.C. 995; *Davis's Tutor* v. *Glasgow Victoria Hospitals,* 1950 S.C. 382; *Morris* v. *Caithness Hospitals Board,* 1950 S.C. 390; *Callaghan* v. *Greenock Hospitals,* 1950 S.L.T.(Notes) 68; *McGinty* v. *Glasgow Victoria Hospitals,* 1951 S.C. 200; *Walker* v. *Greenock Hospital Board,* 1951 S.C. 464; *Bennett* v. *Renfrewshire Mental Hospitals,* 1952 S.C. 20; *McQueen* v. *Glasgow Victoria Hospitals,* 1956 S.C. 535. See also *Glasgow Corpn.* v. *Smithfield Meat Co.*, 1912 S.C. 364; *Edwards* v. *Parochial Board of Kinloss* (1891) 18 R. 867; *Mitchell* v. *Aberdeen Mags.* (1893) 20 R. 253; *Sutherland* v. *Aberdeen Mags.* (1894) 22 R. 95.

2 National Health Service (Sc.) Act 1947, s. 70, amended by National Health Service (Scotland) Act, 1972, Sch. 6.

3 Food and Drugs Act 1938, s. 94.

(1) No judge,[4] clerk of court, or prosecutor in the public interest shall be found liable by any court in damages for or in respect of any proceedings taken, act done, or judgment, decree or sentence pronounced under the Act, unless (a) the person suing has suffered imprisonment in consequence thereof; and (b) such proceeding, act, judgment, decree or sentence has been quashed, and (c) the person suing shall specifically aver and prove that such proceeding, act, judgment, decree or sentence was taken, done or pronounced maliciously and without probable cause.[5]

(2) No such liability as aforesaid shall be incurred or found where such judge, clerk of court, or prosecutor shall establish that the person suing was guilty of the offence in respect whereof he had been apprehended or had otherwise suffered, and that he had undergone no greater punishment than was assigned by law to such offence.

(3) No action to enforce such liability as aforesaid shall lie unless it is commenced within two months after the proceeding, act, judgment, decree or sentence founded on, or in the case where the Act under which the action is brought fixes a shorter period, within that shorter period.

The protection of the section is confined to proceedings under the Act. It does not protect a person acting outwith his jurisdiction[6] or without a warrant or with a warrant from a person not qualified to grant it,[7] or prosecuting on a charge not setting forth any known crime.[8]

No person is liable to any civil or criminal proceedings to which he would have been liable otherwise in respect of any act purporting to be done in pursuance of the Mental Health (Scotland) Act 1960 or any regulations thereunder, unless the act was done in bad faith or without reasonable care.[9]

An officer of a local authority is not personally liable for any act done by him in the execution of any enactment relating to a function of the authority and within the scope of his employment if he acted reasonably and in the honest belief that his duty required or entitled him to do it, without prejudice to the liability of the authority and his

[4] By s. 75 (4) "judge" does not include "sheriff" and the provisions of the section are without prejudice to the privileges and immunities possessed by sheriffs. By s. 77 "judge" includes any justice of the peace, and any magistrate or other judge of a court of summary jurisdiction. Sheriffs are immune from action at common law: *Harvey* v. *Dyce* (1876) 4 R. 265.

[5] *Cf. Ferguson* v. *MacNab* (1885) 12 R. 1083; *Beaton* v. *Ivory* (1887) 14 R. 1057; *McPherson* v. *McLennan* (1887) 14 R. 1063; *Hastings* v. *Henderson* (1890) 17 R. 1130; *Lundie* v. *MacBrayne* (1894) 21 R. 1085; *Rae* v. *Strathern*, 1924 S.C. 147; *Graham* v. *Strathern*, 1924 S.C. 699.

[6] *McCrone* v. *Sawers* (1835) 13 S. 443.

[7] *Bell* v. *Black and Morrison* (1865) 3 M. 1026; *Hester* v. *Macdonald*, 1961 S.C. 370, 381; *cf. Robertson* v. *Keith*, 1936 S.C. 29.

[8] *Ferguson* v. *McNab* (1885) 12 R. 1083, 1089.

[9] 1960 Act, s. 107.

liability to be surcharged. Even where he is not entitled to indemnity the authority may indemnify him.[10]

LIMITATION PROVISIONS

Many statutes fix particular periods of time after the expiry of which the seeking of a particular remedy is barred.[11] These are:

Fourteen days

Claims against a candidate or his election agent in respect of his election expenses.[12]

Two months

(1) Actions of damages against judges, clerks of court or public prosecutors in respect of proceedings taken under the Summary Jurisdiction Act 1954.[13]

(2) Proceedings against sheriffs and other officials on account of anything done in execution of the Licensing (Scotland) Acts.[14]

Three months

(1) A claim for damages under the Seditious Meetings Act 1817.[15]

(2) An action by a broker or dealer to recover possession of goods or articles delivered to the owner by a magistrate's order.[16]

Six months

(1) An action of damages for trespass on land.[17]

(2) Actions for any act in pursuance or execution of the Foreign Jurisdiction Act.[18]

(3) Actions to recover payments to, or deductions from wages made by, an employer contrary to the Truck Act 1896.[18a]

Twelve months or one year

(1) An action for damages for wrongous imprisonment.[19]

10 Local Government (Scotland) Act 1947, s. 103.

11 The following list includes limitation provisions relevant to civil remedies only, and not all limitation provisions. See further Walker, *Law of Prescription and Limitation in Scotland.*

12 Representation of the People Act 1949, s. 66 (1).

13 Summary Jurisdiction (Sc.) Act 1954, s. 75. This in effect supersedes older unrepealed provisions, *viz.*: Justices Protection Act 1802; Circuit Courts (Scotland) Act 1828, s. 26; Criminal Law (Scotland) Act 1830, s. 13.

14 Licensing (Sc.) Act 1959, s. 195, amended by Licensing (Sc.) Act 1962, s. 26. *Cf. Boyd* v. *Hislop* (1902) 9 S.L.T. 466.

15 1817 Act, ss. 30 and 38; *Capaldi* v. *Greenock Mags.*, 1941 S.C. 110; *Coia* v. *Robertson*, 1942 S.C. 111; *Pompa's Trs.* v. *Edinburgh Mags.*, 1942 S.C. 119.

16 Burgh Police (Sc.) Act 1892, s. 413.

17 Game (Sc.) Act 1832 (Day Trespass Act), s. 17. One month's notice must be given of the action. See also *Russell* v. *Lang* (1845) 7 D. 919.

18 Foreign Jurisdiction Act 1890, s. 13.

18a s. 5.

19 Criminal Procedure Act 1701.

(2) An action for continuing damage caused by anything done in pursuance of any public local and personal, or local and personal Act.[20]

(3) An action to enforce contribution in respect of an overpaid proportion of damages resulting from maritime collision.[21]

(4) An action for loss of or damage to goods carried by sea.[22]

(5) An action by a moneylender for any money lent or interest, or enforcement of any agreement made or security taken in respect of a loan.[23]

(6) An action arising out of carriage under the Convention on Carriage of Goods by Road.[24]

(7) An action against the Post Office in respect of loss of, or damage to, a registered inland packet.[25]

Two years

(1) An action for anything done in pursuance of a public local and personal, or local and personal Act.[26]

(2) An action for anything done in execution of the Habitual Drunkards Act 1879.[27]

(3) A claim of debt by a creditor of a deceased seaman against his property.[28]

(4) An action to enforce a claim or lien against a ship or her owners for damage to another vessel, or to cargo, freight, property, life or injuries, or for salvage services.[29]

(5) An action of damages for death or injury or delay in the carriage of passengers, luggage or goods,[30] or an arbitration to recover from a carrier a contribution in respect of damages.[31]

(6) Proceedings to recover any amount due under the Superannuation (Miscellaneous Provisions) Act 1967.[32]

Three years

(1) A claim of damages for wrongful imprisonment on a criminal charge.[33]

[20] Limitation of Actions and Costs Act 1842, s. 5.

[21] Maritime Conventions Act 1911, s. 8. The period may be extended by the court.

[22] Carriage of Goods by Sea Act 1971, Sch., Art. III, 6.

[23] Moneylenders Act 1927, s. 13.

[24] Carriage of Goods by Road Act 1965, Sch., Art. 32.

[25] Post Office Act 1969, s. 30.

[26] Limitation of Actions and Costs Act 1842, s. 5. If the conduct causes continuing damage the limitation period is one year from the termination of the damage.

[27] Habitual Drunkards Act 1879, s. 31. One month's notice of action must be given.

[28] Merchant Shipping Act 1894, s. 178. The debt must have accrued not more than three years before death.

[29] Maritime Conventions Act 1911, s. 8, amended by Crown Proceedings Act 1947, s. 30 and Law Reform (Limitation of Actions) Act 1954, s. 5. The period may be extended by the court. See *Birkdale S.S. Co.*, 1922 S.L.T. 575; *Reresby* v. *Cobetas*, 1923 S.L.T. 492, 719; *Dorie S.S. Co.*, 1923 S.C. 593; *Essien* v. *Clan Line Steamers*, 1925 S.N. 75; *The Heselmoor and The Sergeant* [1951] 1 Ll.L.Rep. 146; *Brown* v. *Devanha Fishing Co.*, 1968 S.L.T.(Notes) 4.

[30] Carriage by Air Act 1961, Sch. I, Art. 29.

[31] Limitation Act 1963, s. 10 (3)–(6).

[32] Superannuation (Miscellaneous Provisions) Act 1967, s. 8.

[33] Criminal Procedure Act 1701.

(2) Certain claims of damages for personal injuries or death: by the Prescription and Limitation (Scotland) Act 1973, s. 17, replacing the Law Reform (Limitation of Actions, etc.) Act 1954, s. 6.

> " 17.—(1) No action of damages where the damages claimed consist of or include damages or solatium in respect of personal injuries [34] to any person shall be brought against any person unless it is commenced [35]—
>
> (*a*) In the case of an action brought by or on behalf of a person in respect of injuries sustained by him as a result of any act, neglect or default,[36] before the expiration of three years from the date when the injuries were sustained or, where such act, neglect or default was a continuing one, from that date or the date on which the act, neglect or default ceased,[37] whichever is the later;
>
> (*b*) In the case of an action brought by or on behalf of a person to whom a right of action has accrued on the death of another person in consequence of injuries sustained by that other person,[38] before the expiration of three years from the date of that death:
>
> Provided that for the purposes of paragraph (*b*) of this subsection a right of action shall be deemed not to have accrued to a person on the death of another person by whom injuries have been sustained if that other person or someone on his behalf was not, immediately before his death, himself entitled to bring or continue an action in respect of the injuries.[39]
>
> (2) If on the date when any right of action accrued for which a

[34] Defined in s. 22 (1) as including " any disease and any impairment of a person's physical or mental condition." The ground of action (contract, delict, or other) is irrelevant so long as the claim includes an element for personal injuries or death.

[35] An action is " commenced " when the defender is cited: *McGraddie* v. *Clark*, 1966 S.L.T. (Sh.Ct.) 36. If an action has been commenced in time, the court may allow it to be amended outwith the three-year period so long as the amendments do not amount to making it in substance a new action: *Coyle* v. *N.C.B.*, 1959 S.L.T. 114; *McCluskie* v. *N.C.B.*, 1961 S.C. 87; *Mackenzie* v. *Fairfields*, 1964 S.C. 90; *O'Hare's Exrx.* v. *Western Heritable Investment Co.*, 1965 S.C. 97; *Mowatt* v. *Shore Porters Society*, 1965 S.L.T. (Notes) 10; but will not allow radical amendment such as introducing additional defenders: *Miller* v. *N.C.B.*, 1960 S.C. 376, or substituting new grounds of fault: *Dryburgh* v. *N.C.B.*, 1962 S.C. 485; or bringing in a third-party defender: *Aitken* v. *Norrie*, 1966 S.C. 168.

[36] An act, neglect or default does not give rise to an action until all the requisites for action are complete, including loss and injury resulting from the act, neglect or default: *Watson* v. *Fram Reinforced Concrete Co.*, 1960 S.C.(H.L.) 92. See also *Brown* v. *N.B. Steel Foundry Co.*, 1968 S.C. 51; *Ellis* v. *Brand*, 1969 S.L.T. 132.

[37] See *Brownlie* v. *Barrhead Magistrates*, 1925 S.C.(H.L.) 41; *Rawlins* v. *Gillingham Corpn.* (1932) 146 L.T. 486; *Freeborn* v. *Leeming* [1926] 1 K.B. 160; *Venn* v. *Tedesco* [1926] 2 K.B. 227. Continuance of damage alone will not prevent time running if the default is no longer continuing: *Rawlins, supra*; *Huyton & Roby Gas Co.* v. *Liverpool Corpn.* [1926] 1 K.B. 146; *Strawhorn* v. *Kilmarnock Magistrates*, 1952 S.L.T.(Notes) 83. See also *Darley Main Colliery* v. *Mitchell* (1886) 11 App.Cas. 127; *Boynton* v. *Aucholme Drainage Commrs.* [1921] 1 K.B. 213. Time may run though there is no present evidence to support a claim: *Ellis* v. *Brand*, 1969 S.L.T. 132.

[38] This covers the case of an executor continuing a claim brought by an injured person before his death, and the case of a relative, within the group of those entitled to one for solatium and patrimonial loss, bringing a claim for his or her own interest: *Gray* v. *N.B. Steel Foundry Co. Ltd.*, 1969 S.C. 231, disapproving *Emslie* v. *Tognarelli's Exors.*, 1969 S.L.T. 20.

[39] If the deceased had by contract excluded his right of action, that excludes the claim by an executor or entitled relative also: *cf. McKay* v. *Scottish Airways*, 1948 S.C. 254.

period of limitation is prescribed by the foregoing subsection the person to whom it accrued was under legal disability by reason of nonage, or if on that date the said person was or became under legal disability by reason of unsoundness of mind, and in either case that person was not in the custody of a parent, the action may be brought at any time before the expiration of three years from the date when the person ceased to be under disability, notwithstanding that the period of limitation has expired.

For the purposes of this subsection ' parent ' includes a step-parent and a grand-parent and in deducing any relationship an illegitimate person and a person adopted in pursuance of any enactment shall be treated as the legitimate child of his mother or, as the case may be, of his adoptor."

Where the cause of action arose before the 1954 Act came into force the pursuer's claim is not barred thereby.[40]

By the 1973 Act, s. 18, s. 17 is not to afford a defence if it is proved that the material facts [41] relating to the right of action were or included facts of a decisive character [42] which were at all times outside the knowledge (actual or constructive) of the pursuer [43] until a date which was not earlier than three years before the date on which the action was brought. The section does not affect any other defence or any other rule permitting action outwith three years.[44]

By the 1973 Act, s. 19, relating to actions in respect of the death of a person, section 17 of the 1973 Act is not to afford a defence if it is proved that the material facts relating to the right of action were or included facts of a decisive character which were outside the knowledge (actual or constructive) of the deceased at all times until his death or until a date less than three years before his death or a date not earlier than three years before he brought any action which at the time of his death he was pursuing, and either the action was brought not later than three years after the deceased's death, or the said facts of a decisive character were at all times outside the knowledge (actual or constructive) of each " relevant person " until a date which was not earlier than three years before the date on which the action was brought.[46] A " relevant person " [47] is an executor, or any person by whom or on whose behalf the action is brought, as the case may be. In actions within this section the death of the deceased is not, but any circumstances which would have constituted a right of action in relation to an action brought by the deceased before his death in respect of the personal injuries which caused his death is, to be regarded as constituting

[40] 1954 Act, s. 7; *Clark* v. *Tennent*, 1962 S.C. 578; *Davie* v. *Scottish Enamelling Co.*, 1962 S.C. 582.
[41] Defined by 1973 Act, s. 22
[42] Explained: *Avinou* v. *Scottish Insulation Co.*, 1970 S.L.T. 146.
[43] On this see *Brown* v. *N.B. Steel Foundry Co.*, 1968 S.C. 51, 60.
[44] s. 18 (4).
[46] s. 19 (1)–(3).
[47] Defined by s. 19 (4).

a right of action.[48] The section does not affect any other defence or any other rule permitting action outwith three years.[49]

No action to recover from another person a contribution in respect of any damages or expenses under the Law Reform (Miscellaneous Provisions) (Scotland) Act 1940, s. 3, may be brought after two years from the date on which the right accrued to the person claiming.[53]

Where the operation of section 17 (1) of the 1973 Act is precluded by section 18 (1) or 19 (1) of that Act, an action is not to be tried by jury.[54]

The three-year period does not apply to actions of damages which do not include claims for damages or solatium for personal injuries or death, such as claims for property damage or economic loss only, nor to a claim of damages for professional negligence in allowing a claim for damages for personal injuries to be cut off by the 1954 Act,[55] nor to the defender bringing in a second defender by third-party notice for the purpose of establishing a right to relief against him.[56] It is not, however, competent to introduce a new claim by way of assignation outwith the three-year period by way of adjustment of or amendment to a claim brought within that period.[57]

(3) Actions for liability incurred by the escape or discharge of oil from a ship.[57a]

(4) Actions of damages brought under the Convention scheduled to the Carriage by Railway Act 1972 must be brought,[58] in the case of a passenger who has sustained an accident, three years from the day after the accident, and in the case of other claimants, three years from the day after the death of the passenger, or five years from the day after the accident, whichever is the earlier.[59]

Six years

Proceedings by the owner of a disused tip to recover compensation for damage or disturbance.[60]

Ten years

Claims for compensation in respect of deterioration of trees taking place after the refusal of a felling licence for the trees.[61]

48 s. 19 (5)–(6).
49 s. 19 (7).
53 Prescription and Limitation (Sc.) Act 1973, s. 20 (1).
54 *Ibid.* s. 22 (6).
55 *Robertson* v. *Bannigan*, 1965 S.C. 20.
56 *Travers* v. *Neilson*, 1967 S.C. 155. *Cf. Findlay* v. *N.C.B.*, 1965 S.L.T. 328 and contrast *Aitken* v. *Norrie*, 1966 S.C. 168.
57 *N.C.B.* v. *Thomson*, 1959 S.C. 353, 379–380.
57a Merchant Shipping (Oil Pollution) Act 1971, s. 9.
58 1972 Act, Sch., Art. 17 (not yet in force).
59 Notice of the accident must be given (Art. 13) within three months of the claimant becoming aware of the damage, subject to certain exceptions.
60 Mines and Quarries (Tips) Act 1969, s. 20 and Sch. 3, para. 6.
61 Forestry Act 1967, s. 11 (3).

Thirteen years

A demand for recovery by a person who had disappeared of any estate obtained by another under the Presumption of Life Limitation (Scotland) Act 1891.[62]

Twenty years

Claims in respect of injury or damage caused by an occurrence involving nuclear matter stolen from or lost by a person whose breach of duty gave rise to the claim.[63]

PRESCRIPTION

By various statutes of prescription the lapse of stated periods of time wholly extinguishes certain rights and consequently any remedy for infringement of the right.[64] The prescriptions falling within this category are:

Three years

Actions of spuilzie prescribe in three years from the commission of the fact on which the action is founded; but actions for simple restitution of goods taken continue for forty (now twenty) years.[65]

Actions of ejection competent to a lawful possessor of heritage against a person who has turned him out are also limited to three years.[65]

All suits grounded on acts of violence or wrong committed by the defender where the pursuer is entitled to a proof of damages by his own oath *in litem*, such as the old action of intrusion, are similarly limited.[65]

Six years

Bills of exchange (but not bank-notes) are ineffectual to justify action or diligence after six years from the term of payment.[66] Thereafter, though the bill cannot be founded on, the debt, if proved by writ or oath to be still due and resting-owing, may be sued for,[67] until that in turn is cut off by the long negative prescription.[68]

Seven years

The septennial prescription of cautionary obligations[69] extinguishes

[62] 1891 Act, s. 7.

[63] Nuclear Installations Act 1965, s. 15.

[64] This category falls to be distinguished from the triennial and quinquennial prescriptions and the sexennial prescription of bills of exchange, which alter the mode and onus of proof but do not extinguish the right. See generally Walker, *Law of Prescription and Limitation of Actions in Scotland.*

[65] Prescription (Ejections) Act 1579 repealed as from 25th July 1976 by Prescription and Limitation (Scotland) Act, 1973, Sch. 5. Ersk, III, 7, 16; *Baillie* v. *Young* (1835) 13 S. 472.

[66] Bills of Exchange (Scotland) Act 1772, ss. 37, 39, repealed from 1976, *ut supra.*

[67] *Darnley* v. *Kirkwood* (1845) 7 D. 595.

[68] *Drummond* v. *Lees* (1880) 7 R. 452. See also *Storeys* v. *Paxton* (1878) 6 R. 293; *Milne's Trs.* v. *Ormiston's Trs.* (1893) 20 R. 523.

[69] Cautioners Act 1695; repealed from 1976, *ut supra.*

the liability of a cautioner, if bound as co-principal, or if bound as express cautioner or as co-principal if he has a clause of relief in the bond or a separate bond of relief intimated to the creditor at the time of his receiving the principal obligation. It does not apply to bonds of corroboration, nor where the condition is not purified, nor where the term of payment is beyond seven years, nor to judicial cautioners, cautioners for the discharge of an office, cautioners *ad factum praestandum*, nor to relief between co-cautioners.[70]

Ten years

Action of count and reckoning competent to pupils and minors against their tutors and curators prescribe ten years after the majority of the said pupils and minors. The contrary action at the instance of tutors and curators against their pupils and minors prescribes in the same way.[71]

Twenty years

Claims in respect of injury or damage caused by an occurrence involving nuclear matter stolen from or lost, jettisoned or abandoned by the person whose breach of the Act gave rise to the claim.[72]

Vicennial prescription

Holograph missive letters and holograph bonds and subscriptions in account books without witnesses prescribe in twenty years if not pursued for, unless the pursuer proves their verity by the defender's oath.[73] The prescription is excluded by the raising of an action on the writing within twenty years.[74]

Long negative prescription, until 1976

The long negative prescription, of forty years [75] reduced by statute to twenty years,[76] except in relation to the period of disuse necessary to extinguish servitudes, public rights of way or other public rights, effects the forfeiture of rights, and consequently of claims to remedies for enforcing them. If a person has delayed for more than that time to seek to enforce his right he is presumed to have relinquished it. The period runs from the date of the occurrence of the wrong, unless the wrongful quality of the act is not known till later, in which case it runs from the later date.[77]

[70] Ersk. III, 7, 23.
[71] Prescription Act 1696; repealed from 1976, *ut supra*. *Gowans* v. *Oswald* (1831) 105, 144.
[72] Nuclear Installations Act 1965, s. 15. For certain claims under ss. 7–11 the period for action is thirty years.
[73] Ersk. III, 7, 26; Bell, *Prin.* § 580; *Mowat* v. *Banks* (1856) 18 D. 1093, also repealed from 1976, *ut supra*.
[74] *Simpson* v. *Brown* (1791) Bell's Oct.Cas. 380.
[75] Prescription Acts, 1469, 1474 and 1617. See generally Ersk. III, 7, 8–13; Bell, *Prin.* §§ 605–627; Walker, *Law of Prescription and Limitation of Actions in Scotland*.
[76] Conveyancing (Scotland) Act 1924, s. 17; Conveyancing Amendment (Scotland) Act 1938, s. 4. See also *Sutherland C.C.* v. *Macdonald*, 1935 S.C. 915.
[77] *Harvie* v. *Robertson* (1903) 5 F. 338.

Thus where a defect was discovered in the execution of letters of inhibition eight years after their date and an action of damages was raised against the solicitor who had instructed the execution, it was said that prescription ran only from the date of the discovery of the defect.[78]

It applies to exclude the right of setting aside any deed upon extrinsic objections which do not appear *ex facie* of the writing,[79] but not objections arising from intrinsic nullities, such as absence of subscribing witnesses,[79] nor property rights,[80] nor *res merae facultatis*,[81] nor the right to challenge a deed on the ground of falsehood or forgery[82]; to a claim to interdict a nuisance[83]; to a claim for repayment of money lodged with a bank[84]; to a claim for payment of legal rights,[85] a claim by a legatee against an executor,[86] a claim that persons divest themselves of trust funds,[87] claims against trustees generally,[88] claims of damage for personal injuries,[89] slander,[90] and other harms.

It does not extinguish the liability of trustees to account for their intromissions,[91] nor does the running of the prescriptive period preclude challenge on the ground of fraud.[92]

Prescription, from 1976

From 25th July 1976, when Part I of the Prescription and Limitation (Scotland) Act 1973 comes into force, any obligation arising from liability to make reparation is extinguished after five years, unless within that time a relevant claim has been made in relation thereto or the subsistence of the obligation has been relevantly acknowledged.[92a]

Any obligation, not being an imprescriptible one,[92b] is extinguished after twenty years, unless there has been relevant claim or acknowledgment within that period[92c] and any right relating to property, not being imprescriptible or falling under section 6 or 7 is similarly extinguished after twenty years.[92d]

78 *Cooke* v. *Falconer* (1850) 13 D. 157, 171.

79 Ersk. III, 7, 9; *Paul* v. *Reid*, Feb. 8, 1814, F.C.; *E. Dundonald* v. *Dykes* (1836) 14 S. 737; *Cubbison* v. *Hyslop* (1837) 16 S. 112; *Pettigrew* v. *Harton*, 1956 S.C. 67.

80 *Pettigrew, supra.*

81 Ersk. III, 7, 10.

82 Ersk. III, 7, 12.

83 *Harvie* v. *Robertson* (1905) 5 F. 338.

84 *Macdonald* v. *North of Scotland Bank*, 1942 S.C. 369.

85 *Earl of Fife* v. *Duff* (1888) 15 R. 238; *Sanderson* v. *Lockhart-Mure*, 1946 S.C. 298; *Campbell's Trs.* v. *Campbell's Trs.*, 1950 S.C. 48; *Mill's Trs.* v. *Mill's Trs.*, 1964 S.C. 384.

86 *Jamieson* v. *Clark* (1872) 10 M. 399; contrast *Briggs* v. *Swan's Exors.* (1854) 16 D. 385.

87 *Baird* v. *Dundee Mags.* (1863) 1 M.(H.L.) 6.

88 *Pollock* v. *Porterfield* (1779) 2 Pat. 495.

89 *Brown* v. *N.B. Steel Foundry Co.*, 1968 S.C. 51, 67.

90 *Young* v. *Young* (1903) 5 F. 330, 331.

91 *Hastie's J.F.* v. *Morham's Exors.*, 1951 S.C. 668; Prescription and Limitation (Sc.) Act 1973, Sch. 3.

92 *Irvine* v. *Kirkpatrick* (1850) 7 Bell's App. 186, 217; *Napier on Prescription*, 607.

92a Prescription and Limitation (Sc.) Act 1973, s. 6 and Sch. 1, para. 1 (d); see also s. 11.

92b Defined, *ibid.*, Sch. 3.

92c *Ibid.*, s. 7.

92d *Ibid.*, s. 8.

Non valentia agere

The prescriptive period does not run against one who was *non valens agere cum effectu*, or subject to legal impediment preventing him making his claim effectual during the whole of the prescriptive period.[93] It is not constituted by physical incapacity or by any failure on the part of the claimant to investigate or press his claim.[94]

Minority and legal disability

In reckoning the prescriptive period under the Act of 1617, as amended by the Act of 1924, no deduction is made on account of the years of minority of those against whom the prescription is used or of any period during which any person against whom the prescription is used was under legal disability.[95]

Interruption

The prescription operates only if the period of twenty years is uninterrupted. If interrupted the period starts to run afresh and any earlier period is cancelled.

Interruption may be effected judicially by citation in an action which, unless renewed, is itself extinguished after seven years,[96] or by an action brought into court, or by doing diligence or extra-judicially, by any conduct amounting on the one hand to an acknowledgment that the debt still existed, or on the other to an attempt to make a claim.[97]

Limitation (Enemies and War Prisoners)

The period of limitation under any of the listed statutes is deemed not to have run if during any period of less than ten years prescribed thereby any person who would have been a necessary party was an enemy or detained in enemy territory, and is in no case to expire before the end of twelve months from the date when he ceased to be an enemy or to be so detained.[98]

Mora

Delay short of any relevant limitation or prescriptive period does not bar an action but is not irrelevant. A reduction of a discharge was dismissed when it appeared that nearly twenty years had elapsed since facts

[93] *Graham* v. *Watt* (1843) 5 D. 1368; *Harvie* v. *Robertson* (1903) 5 F. 338. See also *Campbell's Trs.* v. *Campbell's Trs.*, 1950 S.C. 48. See also 1973 Act, s. 14 (1).

[94] *Earl of Fife* v. *Duff* (1887) 15 R. 238; *Pettigrew* v. *Harton*, 1956 S.C. 57.

[95] Conveyancing (Sc.) Act 1924, s. 17, amended by Conveyancing (Sc.) Amendment Act 1938, s. 4. See also 1973 Act, s. 14 (1).

[96] *Briggs* v. *Swan's Exors.* (1854) 16 D. 385; *Kermack* v. *Kermack* (1874) 2 R. 156; *Marr's Exrx.* v. *Marr's Trs.*, 1936 S.C. 56.

[97] Prescription Act 1669. See also 1973 Act, ss. 6–10.

[98] Limitation (Enemies and War Prisoners) Act 1945, s. 4, amended by Limitation Act 1963, s. 11 and Prescription and Limitation (Sc.) Act 1973, Sch. 4.

had taken place relevant to the reduction which might have been investigated at the time but had not been and the matters could not now be disentangled.[1] In an action for personal injuries [2] it was held that *mora* was constituted not merely by delay but delay which led the other party to believe that the claim had been abandoned, which yielded an inference of acquiescence. The proper plea is accordingly that the action is barred by mora, taciturnity and acquiescence. This plea is a plea to the merits and not a preliminary plea.[3] Where the claim was one which required constitution, such as one of damages, wherever such lapse of time has occurred as places the other party at a disadvantage and makes him think that the claim has been satisfied, the claim is cut off.

Delay may also be held to be a ground for refusing jury trial, if evidence has been lost by the delay,[4] or for refusing to allow an action or defence to be amended.[5]

1 *Bain* v. *Assets Co.* (1904) 6 F. 676, 684, 692; (1905) 7 F.(H.L.) 105.

2 *Cook* v. *N.B. Ry.* (1872) 10 M. 513 (25 years' delay). See also *Fraser* v. *Laing* (1878) 5 R. 596; *N.B. Ry.* v. *Moon* (1879) 16 S.L.R. 265; *Murdoch* v. *Wallace* (1881) 8 R. 855; *Barclay* v. *G.N.S. Ry.* (1882) 10 R. 144; *MacNeill* v. *Forbes* (1883) 10 R. 867; *Maloy* v. *Macadam* (1885) 22 S.L.R. 790; *Colvin* v. *Johnstone* (1890) 18 R. 115; *Cunningham* v. *Skinner* (1902) 4 F. 1124; *Cassidy* v. *Connachie*, 1907 S.C. 1112, 1115.

3 *Halley* v. *Watt*, 1956 S.C. 370.

4 *Woods* v. *A.C.S. Motors*, 1930 S.C. 1035; *Ewart* v. *Ferguson*, 1932 S.C. 277; *McLellan* v. *Western S.M.T. Co.*, 1950 S.C. 112; *Milne* v. *Glasgow Corporation*, 1951 S.C. 340; *McLeish* v. *Howden*, 1952 S.L.T.(Notes) 73; *Lynch* v. *Arnott Young*, 1952 S.L.T.(Notes) 79; *Porter* v. *Gordon*, 1952 S.L.T.(Notes) 80; *Devine* v. *Beardmore*, 1955 S.C. 311; *Hally* v. *Watt*, 1956 S.C. 370; *Hunter* v. *John Brown & Co.*, 1961 S.C. 231.

5 *Strachan* v. *Caledonian Fish-Selling Co.*, 1963 S.C. 157.

APPENDIX I

EXAMPLES OF DAMAGES AWARDS

IN considering the following awards, it must be remembered that

(i) reported awards are not precedents to be followed, but specimens or examples of what has been awarded;

(ii) there has been a steady upward trend in awards since 1945 as the value of money has declined;

(iii) it is not always possible to isolate the amount of award for a particular injury from that for other injuries, or for injuries from the amount of award for loss of earnings; so far as discoverable the awards listed under the head of Personal Injuries are for solatium only;

(iv) since 1971 there has been said to be no ground for awarding less in Scotland than for comparable injuries in England: for awards in England, see Kemp and Kemp, *Quantum of Damages, Vol. I—Personal Injury Claims* (3rd ed., 1967), *Vol. II—Fatal Accident Claims* (2nd ed., 1962), and *Current Law*;

(v) inclusion in the lists does not at all imply that the award is in any way right or reasonable.

PERSONAL INJURIES

General disablement and injuries

Serious injuries: incapable of future employment		*Erskine* v. *G.C.*, 1964 S.L.T.(Notes) 8.
Child (3) limited physical disability and some disfigurement	£750	*McWhinnie* v. *Western S.M.T.*, 1949 S.L.T. (Notes) 8.
Paralysis below waist	£12,000 less 66%	*Warburton* v. *Smith & Sanders* [1955] C.L.Y. 3090.
Child (3) paralysed from waist down and expectation of life impaired	£4,000 generous	*Fisher* v. *Mitchell*, 1952 S.L.T.(Notes) 58.
Back injuries	£300	*Bruce* v. *L.A.* [1955] C.L.Y. 3090.
General bruising and strain	£200 less 50%	*Quinn* v. *C.N. Trs.* [1955] C.L.Y. 3090.
Wrenched back	£900	*McDermott* v. *Railway Executive* [1955] C.L.Y. 3090.
Man crushed and made unfit for work	£2,000	*Ward* v. *A. M. Carmichael Ltd.* [1955] C.L.Y. 3090.
Injuries to head, chest and arm; stammering; insomnia	£2,500	*Bannerman* v. *McCartney* [1956] C.L.Y. 10295.

Injuries to neck, shoulders and back	£2,065	*Whittet* v. *Stoddart* [1956] C.L.Y. 10295.
Crushing injuries to back	£2,000 less 25%	*McKinnon* v. *Iberia* [1956] C.L.Y. 10295.
One kidney removed	£1,000 less 67%	*McLean* v. *Harland & Wolff* [1956] C.L.Y. 10295.
Spinal injuries	£3,000	*Bell* v. *Edinburgh Dairy*, 1958 S.L.T.(Notes) 51.
Paralysis below waist	£20,000 not excessive	*McCorquodale* v. *Moir*, 1960 S.L.T.(Notes) 47.
Rendered helpless and hopeless invalid	£4,000	*Polland's Curator* v. *Elliot*, 1959 S.L.T. (Notes) 34.
Fracture of arm, both wrists and foot; dislocated pelvis	£1,200	*Kemp* v. *Sellars*, 1962 S.L.T.(Notes) 7.
Rendered paraplegic	£5,000	*Wright* v. *B.T.C.*, 1962 S.L.T.(Notes) 45.
Loss of both legs, bowel and bladder injuries	£27,000	*Paton* v. *N.C.B.*, 1963 S.L.T.(Notes) 79.
Rendered paraplegic	£7,000 plus loss of earnings	*Smith* v. *Colvilles*, 1964 S.L.T. (Notes) 91.
Youth rendered paraplegic	£24,000	*Williams* v. *Hemphill*, 1966 S.C.(H.L.) 31.
Brain damage, paralysis and incontinence	£30,000 excessive	*Von Mehren's C.B.* v. *Wood*, 1966 S.L.T. (Notes) 28.
Paraplegic; loss of expectation of life	£20,000 excessive £19,000 excessive	*McCallum* v. *Paterson* (1) 1968 S.C. 280; 1968 S.L.T. 381; (2) 1969 S.C. 85; 1969 S.L.T. 177.
Paraplegic	£9,000 plus loss of earnings	*Pullar* v. *N.C.B.*, 1969 S.L.T.(Notes) 62.
Paraplegic (16)	£20,000	*Allan* v. *Scott*, 1972 S.L.T. 45.
Disseminated sclerosis accelerated	£2,500	*Pollock* v. *Alexander*, 1972 S.L.T.(Notes) 39.
Spastic quadriplegia	£21,500	*Sellar's C.B.* v. *Glasgow Victoria Hospitals*, 1973 S.L.T.(Notes) 3.

Mental injuries

Nervous condition after traffic accident	£1,100 considered high	*Durward* v. *Dunoon Motor Services Ltd.*, 1952 S.L.T.(Notes) 2.
Mental capacity impaired by blow	£3,500	*Dickson* v. *N.C.B.* [1955] C.L.Y. 3090.
Severe injuries and shock to nervous system	£2,000	*Gordon* v. *Clutha Stevedoring Co.* [1955] C.L.Y. 3090.

Severe brain injuries	£17,500 considered high	*Brown* v. *Hemphill*, 1959 S.L.T.(Notes) 51.
Nervous shock, memory impaired; palpitation and tremors	£2,000	*Burke* v. *Brown* [1956] C.L.Y. 10295.
Head noises; dizzy spells; pain	£3,000	*Kelly* v. *G. Corpn.* [1956] C.L.Y. 10295.
Shock to nervous system	£300	*Donnelly* v. *Barclay Curle* [1956] C.L.Y. 10295.
Brain injury, amnesia and personality change	£8,000, including £1,900 lost wages	*Waddell's C.B.* v. *Lindsay*, 1960 S.L.T. 189.
Brain damage and unsoundness of mind	£7,500	*Patton's C.B.* v. *Western S.M.T.*, 1966 S.L.T. (Notes) 30.
Brain damage, paralysis and incontinence	£30,000 excessive	*Von Mehren's C.B.* v. *Wood*, 1966 S.L.T. (Notes) 28.
Serious brain damage	£8,000 plus loss of earnings	*Smith's C.B.* v. *Sc. Gas Board*, 1966 S.L.T. (Notes) 71.
Boy (9) permanently mentally impaired	£17,000	*Steen* v. *McNicol*, 1968 S.L.T.(Notes) 77.
Boy (14) serious brain damage	£19,625	*Dickson* v. *Edinburgh Corpn.*, 1970 S.L.T. (Notes) 56.
Child (5) permanently incapable of normal life	£10,000	*McKinnell* v. *White*, 1971 S.L.T.(Notes) 61.

Head

Minor injuries: woman (18)	£300	*Macfadyen* v. *S.M.T. Co.*, 1946 S.L.T.(Notes) 17.
Dock labourer	£850	*Nelson* v. *C.N. Trs.*, 1946 S.L.T.(Notes) 29.
Face crushed and scalp wounds	£1,400	*Mallon* v. *Christie* [1955] C.L.Y. 3090.
Paralysis of palate; damage to speech	£850	*Henderson* v. *Henderson* [1955] C.L.Y. 3090.
Fractured skull and brain injury (child)	£1,000	*Plank* v. *Stirling Mags.*, 1955 S.L.T.(Notes) 44.
Speech defect aggravated	£900	*Hevern* v. *Thaw & Campbell* [1956] C.L.Y. 10295.
Injuries to neck: moodiness and depression	£2,500	*Ewan* v. *Alexander*, 1960 S.L.T.(Notes) 83.
Headaches, dizziness and fainting fits	£1,000	*Reid* v. *Spencer*, 1966 S.L.T.(Notes) 65.

Neck injury and anxiety state	£1,500	*McClymont* v. *Glasgow Corpn.*, 1971 S.L.T. (Notes) 45.

Eyesight

Eye lost: ice-hockey player	£300 solatium	*McNabney* v. *Scottish Ice Rinks Assocn.*, 1950 S.L.T.(Notes) 6.
Injuries to, *inter alia*, eye: mechanic (30)	£5,500 in all	*Shannon* v. *Waddell*, 1951 S.L.T.(Notes) 58.
Eye lost: apprentice (17)	£625	*Wells* v. *Speedwell Wire Co.* [1955] C.L.Y. 3090.
Labourer blinded	£1,500 less 25%	*Taylor* v. *Falkirk Iron Co.* [1955] C.L.Y. 3090.
Loss of eyes, *inter alia*	£10,000 less 25%	*Fraser* v. *Wimpey* [1955] C.L.Y. 3090.
Eye lost: apprentice (17)	£1,000 solatium	*Summers* v. *N.C.B.*, 1959 S.L.T.(Notes) 14.
Loss of sight: electromechanic (35)	£1,000 solatium	*Gillies* v. *Union Fireclay Products Ltd.*, 1960 S.L.T.(Notes) 90.
Loss of eye	£1,000	*McHugh* v. *Leslie*, 1961 S.L.T.(Notes) 65.
Total blindness	£8,000 plus loss of earnings	*McGilvray* v. *B.I.C.C.*, 1965 S.L.T.(Notes) 61.
One-eyed man losing other eye	£2,000	*Porteous* v. *N.C.B.*, 1967 S.L.T. 117.
One eye damaged, other defective	£1,250	*McFarlane* v. *Williamson*, 1971 S.L.T.(Notes) 72.
Loss of 80% vision in one eye, loss of toe and neck injury	£2,000	*Williams* v. *Whatlings*, 1972 S.L.T.(Notes) 10.
Loss of eye	£2,250	*Kent* v. *Scottish Omnibuses*, 1972 S.L.T. (Notes) 62.
Loss of eye	£3,250	*Williams* v. *Scottish Gas Board*, 1972 S.L.T. (Notes) 66.

Injury to arms and hands

Hand crushed	£300	*McLeman* v. *Consolidated Pneumatic Tool Co.* (1950) 66 Sh.Ct.Rep. 3.
Loss of arm near shoulder	£4,000	*McCormack* v. *N.C.B.*, 1955 S.L.T.(Notes) 2.
Injury, *inter alia*, to finger	£5,500	*Shannon* v. *Waddell*, 1951 S.L.T.(Notes) 58.
Minor injuries to hand	£200	*Neil* v. *Muir*, 1954 S.L.T. (Notes) 50.

Loss of fingers and injuries to both hands: boy (9)	£2,250	*McLeod* v. *L.A.*, 1951 S.L.T.(Notes) 52.
Thumb wrenched	£300 less 50%	*Stacey* v. *Reed & Mallik* [1955] C.L.Y. 3090.
Loss of finger and damage to grip	£300	*Greenhorn* v. *Philips, Hamilton Works Ltd.* [1955] C.L.Y. 3090.
Dislocated collarbone and fractures	£400 less 60%	*Love* v. *Bastow* [1955] C.L.Y. 3090.
Thumb torn out; arm fractured	£1,000	*Erskine* v. *Hall* [1956] C.L.Y. 10295.
Collarbone and two ribs broken	£400	*Kelly* v. *B.T.C.* [1956] C.L.Y. 10295.
Restricted arm movement	£1,500 less 25%	*McDonald* v. *Butler* [1956] C.L.Y. 10295.
Hand rendered useless	£2,000	*Walls* v. *Drummond*, 1962 S.L.T.(Notes) 79.
Fractured rib; inability to lift arm	£500	*McMenamin* v. *Lothian's Trs.*, 1963 S.L.T.(Notes) 28.
Loss of two fingers	£1,500	*Miller* v. *Aberdeen*, 1964 S.L.T.(Notes) 28.
Fractured arm and thigh	£750	*Butler* v. *Lynn*, 1965 S.L.T. 197.
Loss of index finger and part of thumb	£1,200	*McVeigh* v. *N.C.B.*, 1968 S.L.T.(Notes) 93, but see 1970 S.L.T. 3.
Injury to arm	£1,750	*Dailly* v. *Cameron*, 1970 S.L.T.(Notes) 74.
Two fingers of left hand	£250	*Miller* v. *Mackenzie & Moncur*, 1971 S.L.T. (Notes) 56.
Loss of last joint of ring finger	£700	*Smith* v. *Woolworth*, 1972 S.L.T.(Notes) 22.
Fractured wrist	£750	*Corrigan* v. *B.R.*, 1972 S.L.T.(Notes) 74.

Injury to legs and feet

Loss of leg	£2,500	*Smith* v. *India Tyre Co.*, 1947 S.L.T.(Notes) 65.
Loss of leg	£8,000, including loss of earnings—excessive	*McGinley* v. *Pacitti*, 1950 S.C. 364.
Loss of leg	£7,500—excessive	*Cowan* v. *Sevilla Whaling Co.*, 1950 S.C. 364n.
Loss of leg	£1,750	*Kilgower* v. *N.C.B.*, 1958 S.L.T.(Notes) 48.

Inter alia, severe injuries to leg	£5,500	*Shannon* v. *Waddell*, 1951 S.L.T.(Notes) 58.
Severe injuries to one leg and foot, permanent limp	£3,000, including loss of earnings	*Alexander* v. *Brown*, 1952 S.L.T.(Notes) 11.
Broken leg: two operations	£70, said to be very modest	*McWhinnie* v. *Colville's Constructional Co.*, 1953 S.L.T.(Notes) 58.
Achilles tendon injured	£240	*Watson* v. *City Lines Ltd.*, 1956 S.L.T.(Notes) 57.
Fracture of leg	£800	*Gordon* v. *Clutha Stevedoring Co.* [1955] C.L.Y. 3090.
Fractured femur, restriction of knee movement and shock	£110	*Dyer* v. *Clyde Crane Co.*, 1957 S.L.T.(Notes) 43.
Serious fracture	£2,000, despite death shortly thereafter	*Lafferty* v *N.C.B.*, 1960 S.L.T.(Notes) 12.
Fracture and shortening of leg, burns and shock	£800	*Reid* v. *Fairfield Shipbuilding Co.*, 1960 S.L.T. (Notes) 59.
Loss of leg (child, 12)	£5,500 less 60%	*Thornburn* v. *Scottish Omnibuses* [1955] C.L.Y. 3090.
Loss of leg, *inter alia*	£10,000 less 25%	*Fraser* v. *Wimpey* [1955] C.L.Y. 3090.
Injuries to foot	£2,000	*Forbes* v. *A. M. Carmichael Ltd.* [1955] C.L.Y. 3090.
Ankle broken	£570 less 40%	*Campbell* v. *Arnott Young* [1955] C.L.Y. 3090.
Leg badly injured	£3,000 less 20%	*Halas* v. *N.C.B.* [1955] C.L.Y. 3090.
Injuries to leg (girl, 15)	£3,000 less 40%	*Quinn* v. *S.C.W.S.* [1955] C.L.Y. 3090.
Loss of leg	£4,000 less 33%	*Muir* v. *N.C.B.* [1956] C.L.Y. 10295.
Broken thigh, ankle and shock	£5,500	*Andrew* v. *N.C.B.* [1956] C.L.Y. 10295.
Bruising and laceration of stump of leg previously removed	£1,000	*Brown* v. *G.C.* [1956] C.L.Y. 10295.
Loss of three-and-a-half toes	£1,250	*Bryson* v. *B.T.C.* [1956] C.L.Y. 10295.
Broken thigh; shortened leg	*c.* £750	*Elliot* v. *N.C.B.*, 1956 S.C. 484.
Badly fractured leg: later died	£2,000	*Lafferty* v. *N.C.B.*, 1960 S.L.T.(Notes) 35.

Fractured ankle	£400	*Rafferty* v. *N.C.B.*, 1961 S.L.T.(Notes) 41.
Loss of leg	£2,500	*Togher* v. *McClung*, 1962 S.L.T.(Notes) 31.
Loss of leg	£1,000	*Shaw* v. *Young*, 1962 S.L.T.(Notes) 85.
Broken ankle	£300	*Lyon* v. *G.C.*, 1963 S.L.T. (Notes) 20.
Fractured arm and thigh	£750—rather low	*Butler* v. *Lynn*, 1965 S.L.T. 197.
Severe leg injuries	£3,750	*McGeechan* v. *Russell*, 1970 S.L.T.(Notes) 76.
Torn cartilage in knee	£450	*Hutchison* v. *B.M.C. (Scotland)*, 1971 S.L.T. (Notes) 52.
Fractures	£850	*Sweeney* v. *Smith*, 1971 S.L.T.(Notes) 78.
Serious fracture	£1,750	*Wilson* v. *Anderson McGregor*, 1971 S.L.T. (Notes) 85.
Fracture of toe	£300	*Cassidy* v. *Howden*, 1971 S.L.T.(Notes) 84.
Fracture of ankle	£650	*Wilson* v. *Carmichael*, 1971 S.L.T.(Notes) 82.
Loss of big toe	£850	*Bourke* v. *Mitchell Construction Co.*, 1972 S.L.T.(Notes) 3.
Fractured leg: fit for light work only	£2,500	*Ward* v. *Tarmac*, 1972 S.L.T.(Notes) 52.

Respiratory system—pneumoconiosis, etc.

Pneumoconiosis, but bad heart	£400	*Robb* v. *Clyde Alloy Steel Co.*, 1956 S.L.T.(Notes) 58.
Pneumoconiosis: survived only short time	£450	*Bennett's Exor.* v. *Beardmore* [1956] C.L.Y. 10295.
Contracting tuberculosis	£2,000	*Sorman* v. *Royal Sc. Nat. Inst.*, 1960 S.L.T. (Notes) 32.
Pneumoconiosis	£1,000	*Davie* v. *Scottish Enamelling Co.*, 1961 S.L.T. (Notes) 74.
Pneumoconiosis	£400	*Macdonald* v. *N.B. Steel Foundry Co.*, 1963 S.L.T. (Notes) 49.
Pneumoconiosis	£1,750, including loss of earnings	*Watt* v. *Clyde Alloy Co.*, 1966 S.L.T.(Notes) 64.

Burns

Severe burns	£6,000—excessive	*Rae* v. *N.C.B.*, 1951 S.L.T.(Notes) 72.
Severe burns, shock and shortening of leg	£800	*Reid* v. *Fairfield Co.*, 1960 S.L.T.(Notes) 59.
Burning injuries	£600	*Heron* v. *Scottish Spade and Shovel Works*, 1960 S.L.T.(Notes) 37.
Severe burns to leg	£450	*McColl* v. *McAulay & Noble*, 1961 S.L.T. (Notes) 46.
Severe burns	£450	*Larry* v. *Yale & Town Inc.*, 1971 S.L.T.(Notes) 21.

Dermatitis

Dermatitis	£1,250 less 50%	*Foster* v. *Braby* [1955] C.L.Y. 3090.

Warts

Warts	£800	*Bell* v. *N.B. Aluminium Co.*, 1960 S.L.T.(Notes) 16.

Bowel and bladder function

Damage thereto	£4,000	*Reid* v. *Scottish Omnibuses*, 1971 S.L.T. (Notes) 22.

Loss of expectation of life

Child (3) paralysed from waist	£4,000	*Fisher* v. *Mitchell*, 1952 S.L.T.(Notes) 58.
Foundry worker—pneumoconiosis	£200	*Balfour* v. *Beardmore*, 1956 S.L.T. 205.
Steel dresser—pneumoconiosis	£200	*Bennett's Exor.* v. *Beardmore* [1956] C.L.Y. 10295.
Woman (46) expectation of life reduced by 10–15 years and paralysed	£20,000—excessive	*McCallum* v. *Paterson*, 1968 S.C. 280; 1968 S.L.T. 381.
	£19,000—excessive	*McCallum* v. *Paterson*, 1969 S.C. 85; 1969 S.L.T. 177.

Fatal Accidents

It has not always been possible to isolate the amount of awards for solatium from those for loss of support; so far as discoverable the awards quoted are for solatium only. Where an award is for solatium and loss of support it would be pure guesswork to say how much is attributable to each.

Inclusion in the lists does not at all imply that the award is in any way right or reasonable.

(*a*) *Awards to widow for death of husband*

£2,500, including patrimonial loss	*Fryers* v. *Short Bros. & Harland*, 1949 S.L.T.(Notes) 19.
£600, where family life unhappy	*Gunn* v. *McAdam* [1949] C.L.Y. 4499.
£3,000, including patrimonial loss—said to be excessive	*Leadbetter* v. *N.C.B.*, 1952 S.L.T. 179.
£500 for solatium	*McLeish* v. *Fulton*, 1955 S.C. 46.
£2,500, including patrimonial loss	*Campbell* v. *West of Scotland Shipbreaking Co.*, 1953 S.C. 173.
£4,850, including patrimonial loss	*Hewitt* v. *West's Gas Improvement Co.*, 1955 S.C. 162.
£4,500, including patrimonial loss	*Love* v. *N.C.B.*, 1956 S.C. 459.
£5,500, including patrimonial loss—held excessive	*Wason* v. *B.T.C.*, 1960 S.C. 261.
£500, including patrimonial loss, inadequate; altered to £1,000 less 50%	*Gill* v. *N.C.B.*, 1954 S.L.T. (Notes) 41; [1955] C.L.Y. 3090.
£3,000, including patrimonial loss	*Mackintosh* v. *Central General Services Ltd.* [1955] C.L.Y. 3090.
£2,000, including loss of support	*Nicholson* v. *Atlas Steel Foundry Co.*, 1955 S.L.T. (Notes) 42.
£1,000, including loss of support	*Anderson* v. *Railway Executive*, 1955 S.L.T.(Notes) 48.
£2,750, including loss of support	*Blues* v. *Edinburgh Corpn.* [1955] C.L.Y. 3090.
£4,400, including loss of support	*Macdonald* v. *Glasgow Western Hospitals Bd.*, 1955 S.L.T. (Notes) 82.
£1,500, including loss of support	*Preston* v. *Dept. of Agriculture* [1956] C.L.Y. 10295.
£2,700, including loss of support	*Guthrie* v. *A. M. Carmichael* [1956] C.L.Y. 10295.
£4,050, including loss of support	*McFadden* v. *N.C.B.* [1956] C.L.Y. 10295.
£3,500, including loss of support	*Fitzpatrick* v. *Scottish Omnibuses* [1956] C.L.Y. 10295.
£500, plus £750 for loss of support	*Masson* v. *Rubislaw Granite Co.*, 1959 S.L.T.(Notes) 37.

£750, plus £1,500 for loss of support	*McMillan* v. *B.P.*, 1960 S.L.T. (Notes) 67.
£5,500, including loss of support—excessive (£500–£1,000 suggested for solatium)	*Wason* v. *B.T.C.*, 1960 S.C. 261.
£5,800, including loss of support—excessive	*Urquhart* v. *Baxter*, 1961 S.C. 149.
£1,500, plus loss of support	*Hastie* v. *Risborough*, 1962 S.L.T.(Notes) 15.
£750, plus loss of support	*Robertson* v. *Mitchell*, 1962 S.L.T.(Notes) 80.
£4,250, including loss of support	*Owen* v. *Brown*, 1963 S.L.T. (Notes) 5.
£3,000, including loss of support	*Murdoch* v. *McKendrick*, 1963 S.L.T.(Notes) 25.
£4,750, including loss of support	*McLaughlin* v. *Elliot*, 1964 S.L.T.(Notes) 33.
£3,558, including loss of support	*Sweeney* v. *Whatlings*, 1964 S.L.T.(Notes) 44.
£1,000, plus loss of support	*Milne* v. *Lindsay*, 1965 S.L.T. (Notes) 89.
£4,250, including loss of support	*McNeil* v. *N.C.B.*, 1966 S.L.T. (Notes) 4.
£6,000, including loss of support—excessive	*Graham* v. *A.E.I.*, 1966 S.L.T. (Notes) 27.
£4,000, including loss of support	*O'Donnell* v. *D. & R. Ferrying*, 1966 S.L.T.(Notes) 71.
£10,500, including loss of support	*Davies* v. *A.C.D. Bridge Co.*, 1967 S.L.T.(Notes) 38.
£7,500, including loss of support	*Orr* v. *A.C.D. Bridge Co.*, 1967 S.L.T.(Notes) 38.
£15,250, including loss of support	*Webster* v. *Simpson's Motors*, 1967 S.L.T.(Notes) 36.
£5,500, including loss of support	*McCusker* v. *Davidson & Pickering*, 1968 S.L.T.(Notes) 41.
£2,350, including loss of support	*Rae* v. *Stewart*, 1968 S.L.T. (Notes) 62.
£1,000, plus loss of support	*Cowan* v. *Greig*, 1969 S.L.T. (Notes) 34.
£4,000, including loss of support	*Henderson* v. *S. Wales Switchgear*, 1969 S.L.T.(Notes) 52.
£1,250, plus loss of support	*O'Connor* v. *Holst*, 1969 S.L.T. (Notes) 66.
£1,250, plus loss of support	*Gray* v. *Allied Ironfounders*, 1969 S.L.T.(Notes) 95.
£1,500, plus loss of support	*Gillan* v. *McGawn's Motors*, 1970 S.L.T. 250.
£2,750, including loss of support	*Curran* v. *Sc. Gas Board*, 1970 S.L.T.(Notes) 33.

£6,750, including loss of support	*Riddell* v. *Longmuir*, 1971 S.L.T.(Notes) 33.
£1,500, plus loss of support	*Smith* v. *Middleton*, 1971 S.L.T.(Notes) 65.
£8,000, including loss of support	*McKinnon* v. *B.R.*, 1972 S.L.T. (Notes) 2.
£11,331, including loss of support	*McCuaig* v. *Redpath Dorman Long*, 1972 S.L.T.(Notes) 42.

(b) Awards to widower for death of wife

£250	*Kelly* v. *G.C.*, 1951 S.C.(H.L.) 15	Husband survived wife only a year.
£750	*McKinlay* v. *G.C.*, 1951 S.C. 495	Said to be larger than appropriate.

(c) Awards to child for death of parent

Age of child	*Award*	*Case*
23	£75	*Robertson* v. *Mitchell*, 1962 S.L.T.(Notes) 80.
22	nil	*Hewitt* v. *West's Gas Improvement Co.*, 1955 S.C. 162.
	£150	*Milne* v. *Lindsay*, 1965 S.L.T.(Notes) 89.
21	—	—
20	nil	*Hewitt, supra.*
19	—	—
18	£500	*Hewitt, supra.*
	nil	*Wason* v. *B.T.C.*, 1960 S.C. 261.
	£250	*Milne* v. *Lindsay, supra.*
17	nil	*Wason, supra.*
	£150	*Blues* v. *Edinburgh Corpn.* [1955] C.L.Y. 3090.
	£750	*Owen* v. *Brown*, 1963 S.L.T.(Notes) 5.
	£750	*Milne* v. *Lindsay, supra.*
16	£500	*Hewitt, supra.*
	£500	*Macdonald* v. *Glasgow Western Hospitals Bd.*, 1955 S.L.T.(Notes) 82.
	£350	*Guthrie* v. *A. M. Carmichael* [1956] C.L.Y. 10295.
	£700	*McCuaig* v. *Redpath Dorman Long*, 1972 S.L.T.(Notes) 42.
15	£550	*Hewitt, supra.*
	£250	*Blues, supra.*
	£1,000	*McNeil* v. *N.C.B.*, 1966 S.L.T.(Notes) 4.
	£800	*McCuaig, supra.*
	£1,350	*Webster* v. *Simpson*, 1967 S.L.T.(Notes) 36.
	£600	*Gray* v. *Allied Ironfounders*, 1969 S.L.T.(Notes) 95.
	£750	*Riddell* v. *Longmuir*, 1971 S.L.T.(Notes) 33.

Age of child	*Award*	*Case*
14	£875	*Webster, supra.*
	£1,250	*McCusker* v. *Davidson & Pickering*, 1968 S.L.T.(Notes) 41.
	£850	*McKinnon* v. *B.R.*, 1972 S.L.T.(Notes) 2.
13	£150	*Kelly* v. *G.C.*, 1951 S.C.(H.L.) 15.
	£450	*Nicholson* v. *Atlas*, 1955 S.L.T.(Notes) 42.
	£350	*Blues, supra.*
	£750	*Macdonald, supra.*
	£500	*McMillan* v. *B.P.*, 1960 S.L.T.(Notes) 67.
	£1,000	*Owen* v. *Brown, supra.*
	£500	*Murdoch* v. *McKendrick*, 1963 S.L.T.(Notes) 25.
	£600	*Gray* v. *Allied Ironfounders*, 1969 S.L.T.(Notes) 95.
	£750	*Riddell, supra.*
	£700	*Smith* v. *Middleton*, 1971 S.L.T.(Notes) 65.
12	£700	*Hewitt, supra.*
	£425	*Guthrie, supra.*
	£400	*Cameron* v. *Findlay*, 1959 S.L.T.(Notes) 59.
	£500	*McMillan, supra.*
11	£800	*Love* v. *N.C.B.*, 1956 S.C. 459.
	£550	*McLaughlin* v. *Elliot*, 1965 S.L.T.(Notes) 33.
	£700	*Smith, supra.*
10	£850	*Love, supra.*
	£750	*Nicholson* v. *Atlas*, 1955 S.L.T.(Notes) 42.
	£500	*Guthrie, supra.*
	£2,250 including loss of support	*Forsyth* v. *N.C.B.*, 1963 S.L.T.(Notes) 12.
	£650	*Milne* v. *Lindsay*, 1965 S.L.T.(Notes) 89.
	£1,150	*McKinnon* v. *B.R.*, 1972 S.L.T.(Notes) 2.
9	£200	*Kelly, supra.*
	£850	*Love, supra.*
	£1,500	*McFadden* v. *N.C.B.*, 1956 C.L.Y. 10295.
	£750	*Murdoch, supra.*
	£750	*Gillan* v. *McGawn's Motors*, 1970 S.L.T. 250.
8	£250	*Kelly, supra.*
	£500	*Blues, supra.*
	£600	*Guthrie, supra.*
	£850	*Milne, supra.*
	£500	*Riddell, supra.*
7	£300	*Kelly, supra.*

Age of child	*Award*	*Case*
7	£1,250	*Love, supra.*
	£2,500 including loss of support	*Forsyth, supra.*
	£850	*Murdoch, supra.*
	£1,650	*Rae* v. *Stewart*, 1968 S.L.T.(Notes) 62.
	£750	*Gillan, supra.*
6	£1,000	*Hewitt, supra.*
	£1,500	*Wason, supra.*
	£2,000	*McCusker, supra.*
	£500	*Riddell, supra.*
5	£350	*Kelly, supra.*
	£700	*Guthrie, supra.*
	£1,700 including loss of support	*Urquhart* v. *Baxter*, 1961 S.C. 149.
	£850	*McLaughlin, supra.*
	£2,000 including patrimonial loss	*Pellow* v. *L.A.*, 1953 S.L.T.(Notes) 14.
4	£3,375	*Webster, supra.*
	£1,700	*Rae, supra.*
3	£800	*Leadbetter* v. *N.C.B.*, 1952 S.L.T. 179.
	£800	*Guthrie, supra.*
2½	£250 inadequate	*Gill* v. *N.C.B.*, 1954 S.L.T.(Notes) 41.
2	£750	*Cameron, supra.*
1½	£1,700	*Urquhart, supra.*
16 months	£2,100 including loss of support	*Urquhart* v. *Baxter*, 1961 S.C. 149.
8 months	£1,250	*Love, supra.*
5 months	£2,250	*Pellow, supra.*
5 months	£250 inadequate	*Gill, supra.*
infant	£250	*Cowan* v. *Greig*, 1969 S.L.T.(Notes) 34.
Posthumous	£1,000	*Leadbetter, supra.*
Posthumous	£250	*Riddell* v. *Longmuir*, 1971 S.L.T.(Notes) 33.

(*d*) *Awards to parent for death of child*

Youth (16) killed	£750	*Sagar* v. *N.C.B.* [1956] C.L.Y. 10295.

APPENDIX II

CRIMINAL INJURIES COMPENSATION

A PERSON who is a victim of a crime of violence, except a motoring offence save where the motor-vehicle is used as a weapon, or is injured while assisting the police, may apply in writing to the Criminal Injuries Compensation Board for *ex gratia* payment of compensation.[1] The Board comprises a Chairman and five members, legally qualified, appointed by the Home Secretary and the Secretary of State for Scotland. The Board considers applications where the applicant or, in the case of an application by a spouse or dependant, the deceased, suffered personal injury directly attributable either to a crime of violence (including fire-raising and poisoning) or to an arrest or attempted arrest of an offender or suspected offender or to the prevention or attempted prevention of an offence or to the giving of help to any constable who was engaged in arresting or attempting to arrest an offender or suspected offender or preventing or attempting to prevent an offence. Hearings are informal and the Board does not consider itself bound by the rules of evidence. The injury must be one for which compensation of not less than £50 would be awarded. The circumstances of the injury must have been reported to the police without delay or have been the subject of criminal proceedings. The applicant must be prepared to submit to medical examination and must give all reasonable assistance to the Board. Offences committed against a member of the offender's family living with him or against a person cohabiting with him at the time are excluded.

Compensation is assessed on the basis of common law damages. Where the victim is alive compensation is limited by taking into account loss of earnings at a rate which does not exceed twice the average of industrial earnings at the time the accident was sustained.[2] Where the victim has died no compensation will be payable for the benefit of his estate but compensation will be payable to his spouse and entitled dependants, as at common law. Payment is by way of a lump-sum payment, but more than one payment may sometimes be made.[3] The Board may make arrangements for the administration of any sum paid to a minor or pupil.

If, by reason of provocation or otherwise, the victim of the crime bears any share of responsibility the Board may reduce the award of compensation or reject the claim altogether.

Compensation must be repaid from any damages or settlement the applicant may obtain by a common law action, and will be reduced by the amount of any payments from public funds as a result of the injury or

[1] The Board operates a scheme set out in a White Paper (Cmnd. 2323) announced in Parliament on June 24, 1964, and later amended.

[2] Average weekly earnings are published in the *Ministry of Labour Gazette*.

[3] Examples of awards made are reported each month in *Current Law*.

death.[4] The Board may require an applicant to claim any payments recoverable from public funds before making an award.

Any award is made *ex gratia* and without admission of any legal liability to make it. A decision of the Board is not subject to appeal, or ministerial review but it is subject to the review jurisdiction of the courts, in England by certiorari [4] and, in Scotland, presumably by reduction for error of law or injustice in procedure.

[4] *R.* v. *Criminal Injuries Board* [1967] 2 Q.B. 864.

APPENDIX III

CLAIMS FOR SOCIAL SECURITY BENEFITS

CLAIMS for social security benefits are not claims for civil remedies within the scope of this book, but in view of their interaction with, and possible overlap on, civil remedies, a brief account of them is given here.[1]

National insurance benefits

Under the National Insurance Acts 1965–72, replacing earlier legislation, persons in Great Britain may, subject to the conditions imposed by the relevant legislation, have claims to one or more of the following benefits [2]:

(a) unemployment benefit;
(b) sickness benefit;
(bb) invalidity benefit, consisting of
  (i) invalidity pension;
  (ii) invalidity allowance;
(bbb) attendance allowance;
(c) maternity benefit, including—
  (i) maternity grant;
  (ii) maternity allowance;
(d) widow's benefit, including—
  (i) widow's allowance;
  (ii) widowed mother's allowance;
  (iii) widow's pension;
(e) guardian's allowance;
(f) retirement pension;
(ff) age addition;
(g) graduated retirement benefit;
(h) child's special allowance;
(i) death grant.

Claims are made to the local social security office.

Certain questions, if disputed, fall to be determined by the Secretary of State for Social Services, subject in some cases to reference to the Court of Session.[3] Questions as the right to benefit, or of disqualification for receiving unemployment benefit or sickness benefit, are determined by insurance officers, local tribunals, and the National Insurance Commissioners.[4]

Industrial injuries benefits

All persons employed in insurable employment are insured under the

[1] For full accounts, see Halsbury's *Laws of England*, tit. National Insurance, and Supplements thereto.
[2] 1965 Act, s. 17, amended by 1971 Act, s. 14.
[3] 1965 Act, ss. 64–66.
[4] 1965 Act, ss. 67–82.

National Insurance (Industrial Injuries) Acts 1965–72 against personal injury caused after July 4, 1948, by accident arising out of and in the course of such employment.[5] An accident arising in the course of an insured person's employment is deemed, in the absence of evidence to the contrary, also to have arisen out of that employment.[6] A claimant may claim

(a) industrial injury benefit;
(b) industrial disablement benefit;
(c) industrial death benefit.[7]

Insurance extends to any prescribed disease and against any prescribed personal injury not caused by accident, being a disease or injury due to the nature of that employment and developed after July 4, 1948.[8]

Certain questions fall to be determined by the Secretary of State for Social Services, subject, in certain cases, to reference to the Court of Session,[9] certain other questions in accordance with Part IV of the National Insurance Act,[10] disablement questions by medical boards or medical appeal tribunals,[11] and claims for benefit by insurance officers, local appeal tribunals and the National Insurance Commissioners.[12]

Family allowances

Under the Family Allowances Act 1965 there is payable for every family which includes two or more children an allowance in respect of each child in the family other than the elder or eldest.[13] Claims and determination of questions are made under Part IV of the National Insurance Act 1965.

Family income supplement

Under the Family Income Supplements Act 1970 family income supplement is payable for any family in Great Britain if the weekly amount of its resources falls short of the prescribed amount.[14]

Questions as to the right to, or the amount of, a family income supplement are determined by the Supplementary Benefits Commission, subject to appeal to the Appeal Tribunal.[15]

Supplementary benefits

Under the Ministry of Social Security Act 1966 every person in Great Britain of or over the age of 16 whose resources are insufficient to meet his requirements is entitled to a supplementary allowance or, if he has attained

[5] 1965 Act, s. 1.
[6] 1965 Act, s. 6; see also ss. 7–10.
[7] 1965 Act, ss. 5, 11–24.
[8] 1965 Act, ss. 56–58.
[9] 1965 Act, s. 35.
[10] 1965 Act, s. 36.
[11] 1965 Act, ss. 37–42.
[12] 1965 Act, ss. 43–49.
[13] 1965 Act, s. 1. " Child " and " family " are defined in ss. 2–3. See also s. 11 and Schedule.
[14] 1970 Act, s. 1. " Family " is there defined.
[15] 1970 Act, ss. 6–7.

pension age, to a supplementary pension.[16] Certain requirements have to be taken into account for the purposes of the Act.[17]

The questions of entitlement to, and the amount of, any benefit, are determined by the Supplementary Benefits Commission.[18] Determinations may be reviewed by appeal to the Appeal Tribunal.[19]

[16] 1966 Act, s. 4. This scheme supersedes that under the National Assistance Act 1948.
[17] 1966 Act, s. 6.
[18] 1966 Act, ss. 5–16.
[19] 1966 Act, s. 18.

INDEX